THE GREAT BOOK OF
FIGHTERS

THE GREAT BOOK OF
FIGHTERS

An illustrated encyclopedia of every fighter aircraft built and flown

William Green • Gordon Swanborough

MBI Publishing Company

A Salamander Book

This edition first published in 2001 by MBI Publishing Company,
729 Prospect Avenue, PO Box 1,
Osceola, WI 54020-0001 USA

© (Contents) Greenborough Associates Ltd., 1994
© (Presentation) Books Limited 2001

A member of the Chrysalis Group plc

MBI Publishing Company books are also available at discounts in
bulk quantity for industrial or sales-promotional use. For details
write to Special Sales Manager at Motorbooks International
Wholesalers & Distributors,
729 Prospect Avenue, PO Box 1, Osceola, WI 54020-0001 USA.

Library of Congress Cataloging-in-Publication Data Available

ISBN 0-7603-1194-3

CREDITS

Project Manager:
Ray Bonds
Editor:
Philip de Ste. Croix
Designers:
Richard Hawke and Interprep Ltd
Colour artwork:
John Weal © Greenborough Associates Ltd.
Three-view drawings:
Dennis Punnett © Greenborough Associates Ltd.
Produced by Toppan (Hong Kong) Ltd.
Printed and bound in China

THE AUTHORS

William Green entered aviation journalism early in World War II
with the *Air Training Corps Gazette* (now *Air Pictorial*) and has
gained an international reputation for his many works of aviation
reference, covering both aeronautical history and the current aviation scene. Following RAF service, he was European correspondent to American, Canadian and South African aeronautical jour-
nals and British correspondent to several European publications.
He was Technical Director to the RAF *Flying Review*, then
Editorial Director when it became *Flying Review International*. In
1971 he and Gordon Swanborough jointly created the monthly *Air
International*, of which he remained Managing Editor until late
1990. They produced a number of books under joint authorship,
including the Salamander titles *The Illustrated Encyclopedia of
the World's Commercial Aircraft*, *An Illustrated Anatomy of the
World's Fighters* and *Flying Colours*.

Gordon Swanborough spent his working life as an aviation jour-
nalist and author, with the exception of a year-long appointment
in 1964 as a Sales Publicity Officer with the British Aircraft
Corporation. From 1943 until 1963 he was on the editorial staff of
the weekly magazine *The Aeroplane*, specializing for much of that
time in air transport affairs. In 1965 he became Editor of *Flying
Review International*, and in 1971 he joined forces with William Green
to create *Air International* and *Air Enthusiast*, remaining Editor of
those two publications until the end of 1990. As well as jointly
editing the annual RAF Yearbook from 1975 to 1987, he was
responsible for a series of authoritative works on both current aircraft and aspects of aeronautical history.

Mike Spick is a leading commentator on military aviation, with
more than 28 books to his credit. His works, which have included
the internationally acclaimed *Modern Air Combat* (with Bill
Gunston), *Designed for the Kill*, and *Luftwaffe Fighter Aces*, have
been published in several languages. He maintains close ties with
former and current serving fighter pilots and aircraft design personnel, and several distinguished test pilots. For many years a
consultant to the Swiss-based helicopter programme Project Atlas,
he has also been Consultant Editor to *AirForces Monthly* journal,
and contributor to *Air International*, *Air Enthusiast*, and the
Malaysian-based *Asia Pacific Defense Review*.

PREFACE

At the start of the 20th century, reconnaissance was the almost exclusive preserve of the light cavalry, which exploited gaps and open flanks. This ended in the final months of 1914, when the Western Front hardened into fixed lines of trenches, extending from the Belgian coast to the Swiss border. With no open flanks to exploit, the reconnaissance mission inevitably passed to the aeroplane, with its ability to overfly the lines and reconnoitre the rear areas. These were the scouts.

The other function of light cavalry had been to deny reconnaissance to the enemy, and this burden also fell to the airmen. This was easier said than done; aircraft performance in 1914 was barely adequate. The extra weight of weapons often made this marginal, and decisive combats were few and far between. Gradually, more suitable aircraft were developed. Thus was born, of necessity, the fighting scout, or fighter.

Actually, the need had been foreseen by a few visionaries in the British Admiralty, which placed a contract with Vickers for an experimental fighting biplane as early as 19 November 1912. This resulted in the disappointing EFB.1, which crashed on its first, very brief flight, in Spring 1913. However, the concept was developed, emerging as the FB.5 Gunbus, which first flew on 17 July 1914. Unfortunately, the idea had far outstripped the available technology, and the performance of the Gunbus, which reached the Western Front in February 1915, was inadequate for the task. But this notwithstanding, it was the first purpose-designed fighter to go to war.

In 1914, the best ways of using fighters had yet to be developed. In a process of trial and error, mainly the latter, proper tactics were evolved, and these largely drove fighter design. After experiments with a variety of weapons such as carbines, grapnels with small bombs on them, and even the blunderbuss, the fixed, forward-firing machine gun, aimed by pointing the whole aeroplane, emerged as the preferred weapon.

Initially the pusher configuration, with the engine behind the pilot and a clear field of fire ahead, was widely used. The more aerodynamically efficient tractor configuration, with the engine ahead of the pilot, came into its own once the problems of firing through, or outside the propeller disc without hitting it had been solved, although the pusher concept was still extant in the 1940s.

Basic combat tactics evolved according to circumstance. The main scenario was that of the day fighter, able to intercept reconnaissance aircraft, artillery spotters and bombers, and also to drive off enemy day fighters. Then, as now, fighter design was a compromise between conflicting requirements. Two schools of thought quickly emerged.

The first was the performance fighter, with outstanding speed, acceleration, rate of climb, and ceiling. These could gain a position of superiority before launching an attack, force battle on an inferior opponent, and could disengage at will. Classic examples were the British SE 5a, the French SPAD series, and the German Albatros D V.

The second was the manoeuvrability fighter, with rapid rates of pitch and roll, essential for changing direction quickly, and the ability to turn on a dime, sixpence, franc or pfennig! While unable to force battle on, or disengage from, a performance opponent, the manoeuvrability fighter was a formidable opponent in the dogfight. It was also perfectly adequate against reconnaissance aircraft or artillery spotters. Classic examples were the British Sopwith Camel, the French Nieuport series, and the German Fokker Dr 1 triplane.

Other, more specialised fighters, were designed during the Great War. Of these, the Zeppelin interceptor was possibly the most interesting. The requirements were a long loiter time, waiting for their huge opponents to arrive, and heavy armament to destroy it in short order. In practice, virtually all giant airships downed by aircraft fell to standard fighters with minimal modifications for night operations. This also applied to fighters which opposed night bombers.

The fighter-bomber also appeared during the Great War. When circumstances either permitted or demanded, standard fighters were loaded with bombs and sent off to "have at" the unfortunate surface forces. Just a few types were purpose-made for this task, with a secondary air-to-air capability.

The 1930s saw tremendous technical advances in aerodynamics, construction, and powerplants. Initially this resulted in fast bombers, and the need to intercept them put the accent firmly on the performance fighter at the expense of manoeuvrability, coupled with great fire power. As in any other field of human endeavour, fashion played its part. The 1930s saw the development of long range escort fighters, notably the German Bf 110, the Dutch Fokker G.1, and the American P-38 Lightning, all of which were twin-engined. Little credence was given to the fact that they could be outfought by contemporary single-engined fighters.

The Second World War saw three major innovations. The first was the use of cannon rather than machine guns, by all major combatants except the USA. The second was the radar-equipped night fighter, able to stalk its prey in the hours of darkness. The third was the advent of the jet engine. Reciprocating engines had become close to the limits of the possible; jets opened up a whole new performance regime.

The 1950s was an exciting decade for the fighter world. Maximum speeds more than doubled, rates of climb increased by a factor of three, and ceilings were higher than ever. The extra power available enabled night fighters, with a two-man crew and radar, to match the performance of single-seaters, to become truly all-weather fighters. Homing missiles greatly increased attack ranges, and made (so many thought) the gun superfluous.

The next two decades of fighter development were largely the domain of the superpowers – the USSR and the USA. The former chose numerical strength; the latter technological superiority. The USA produced the F-14 and F-15 which, for the want of a better term, were superfighters. They were also unaffordable in sufficient numbers, which forced the decision to supplement them with austere but very manoeuvrable dogfighters, notably the F-16, in what was known as a hi-lo mix – a combination of performance and manoeuvrability.

This process continues today, with the F-22 Raptor, backed by the eventual winner of the Joint Strike Fighter (JSF) competition. Performance and manoeuvrability now have equal importance in the fighter world, coupled with stealth. All three date from the Great War; the first stealth fighter flew in 1916, although it was not a success.

Over nearly nine decades, designers have vied with each other to produce an outstanding fighter. Very few have succeeded, and many lines of development have proved to be dead ends. All of these aircraft, some well known but others totally unrecorded hitherto, are catalogued in this volume, which, unique in being the first comprehensive encyclopaedia of the fighter genus, is the product of many years' research. It attempts to describe concisely the development of every fighter type flown up to the beginning of 2001, anywhere in the world. Unrivalled in scope among published references, it endeavours to correct many errors of fact, some perpetrated long since, and today widely accepted owing to constant repetition. It defines "FIGHTER" in its broadest sense, embracing attack, strike, torpedo and reconnaissance fighters which are designed to fulfill the air combat rôle as a secondary task, although not as a mere self-defence capability.

The criterion for inclusion is that it should have flown, however briefly. Consequently, fighters that were built but not flown are excluded. Other omissions are fighters used as engine test beds, which had no intended operational usage. Also omitted are aircraft such as the F-117A, which although having a fighter designation, are not true fighters.

The entries are arranged strictly in alphabetical order of manufacturer's (or originator's) appellation and chronologically by first flight date when there is more than one entry under the heading. Indexing references to the entries also appear at the head of each page to facilitate the location of manufacturer's names or designations. The index provides a cross-reference for aircraft names and designations if the maker/designer is not known. Also included in the index are all Allied reporting names allocated to Japanese fighters in the Second World War, and the NATO reporting names used for Russian (including Soviet) and Chinese fighters.

Mike Spick, 2001

INDEX

The entries in this volume are arranged strictly in alphabetical order of manufacturer's (or originator's) appellation and chronologically by first flight date when there is more than one entry for a single manufacturer. Indexing references to the entries also appear at the head of each page to facilitate location of manufacturers' names or designations. The index on these pages provides a cross-reference for aircraft names and designations if the maker/designer is not known. Also included here (in italics) are all Allied reporting names allocated to Japanese fighters during World War II, and the NATO Co-ordinating Committee reporting names used for Soviet (and some Chinese) fighters – names that have not been quoted in the relevant aircraft descriptions since they were not part of the original factory or service nomenclature for those types.

A

A-1, AIDC Ching-Kuo, 11
A1N, Nakajima, 422
A2N, Nakajima, 422
A4N, Nakajima, 423
A5M, Mitsubishi, 408
A6M, Mitsubishi, 409
A6M2-N, Nakajima, 423
A7M, Mitsubishi, 412
A8V, Seversky, 524
A.10, Saunders, 519
Abdul, Nakajima Ki-27, 425
AC-1, Comte, 116
A.D.C.1, Martinsyde, 364
A.E.3 Ram, R.A.F., 509
AFAMF (Cho) X-PO, 113
A.F.G.1, Memel, 16
Airabonita, Bell, 57
Airacobra, Bell, 55
Airacomet, Bell, 58
Airacuda, Bell, 55
Airguard, Chengdu, 113
Ajeet, HAL, 272
Alfaro 8, 300
Ambrosini, S.A.I., 517-8
Anadis, Anatra, 18
ANT-5, Tupolev, 571
ANT-13, Tupolev, 571
ANT-21, Tupolev, 571
ANT-23, Tupolev, 572
ANT-31, Tupolev, 572
ANT-46, Tupolev, 573
ANT-63P, Tupolev, 573
A.P.1, Caproni Bergamasca, 108
AP-2, Seversky, 525
AP-4, Seversky, 525
AP-7, Seversky, 525
AP-9, Republic, 492
Apache, Wright, 598
Aquilon, Sud-Est, 546
Ara, Armstrong Whitworth, 26
Ariete, Aerfer, 9
Ariete, Reggiane, 489
Armadillo, Armstrong Whitworth, 25
Arrow, Avro Canada, 48
Attacker, Supermarine, 564
AV-8B Harrier II Plus, McDonnell Douglas, 374
Avenger, Avro 47
Avocet, Avro, 47
Avon-Sabre, Commonwealth, 115

B

B 34 to B 634, Avia, 36-8
B 35 to B 135, Avia, 39
Ba 439, Bachem, 52
Baby, Sopwith, 533
Badger, Bristol, 94
Bagshot, Bristol, 95

Banshee, McDonnell, 365
Bantam, B.A.T., 52
Baroudeur, Sud-Est, 546
Barrón, Hispano, 300
Basilisk, B.A.T., 53
B.E.2, R.A.F., 506
B.E.12, R.A.F., 506
Bearcat, Grumman, 265
Beaufighter, Bristol, 100
Berg (Aviatik), 41-4
Bernard 10 to 15, 531
Bf 109, Messerschmitt, 375
Bf 110, Messerschmitt, 378
BF2C, Curtiss, 131
BH 3 to BH 33L, Avia, 33-6
Bittern, Boulton & Paul, 81
Black Widow, Northrop, 455
BLC, Breguet, 87
Blenheim, Bristol, 99
Bloodhound, Bristol, 95
B.N.1, Nieuport, 443
Bobolink, Boulton & Paul, 81
Boomerang, Commonwealth, 113
BP 20, Bachem, 52
Brunet 3C2, 421
Brunet 4C2, 421
BUC, Breguet, 87
Buffalo, Brewster, 90
Bulldog, Bristol, 96
Bulldog, Sopwith, 538
Bullet, Cantilever Aero, 106
Bullfinch, Bristol, 94
Bullpup, Bristol, 98
Buzzard, Martinsyde, 364
Byakko, Yokosuka, 608

C

C.200 to C.205, Macchi, 358-61
CA-15, Commonwealth, 114
Camel, Sopwith, 535
CB, Curtiss, 121
CC, Brandenburg, 83
CCF FDB-1, 256
Centauro, Fiat, 210
CF-100, Avro Canada, 47
CF-105, Avro Canada, 48
CH-1, Caproni, 108
Cheetah, Atlas, 32
Ching-Kuo, AIDC, 11
Christmas Bullet, 106
Chu (AFAMF) X-PO, 113
CJ 14, Caspar, 110
Claude, Mitsubishi A5M, 408
Comanche, Eberhart, 192
Comet, Whitehead, 595
Corsair, Vought, 586
Cougar, Grumman, 269
Crusader, Vought, 588
CR.1 to CR.42, Fiat, 204-7
CS 14, Caspar, 110

CSO-A, Waco, 590
CTO-A, Waco, 590
Cutlass, Vought, 588
CV-11, IAR, 303
CW-21, Curtiss-Wright, 144
Cyclone, Caudron-Renault, 111

D

D-3800, 419
D-3801, 419
D-3802, Doflug, 184
D-3803, Doflug, 185
Danecock, Hawker, 281
Dardo, S.A.I. Ambrosini, 518
Defiant, Boulton Paul, 82
Delta Dagger, Convair, 119
Delta Dart Convair, 120
Demon, Hawker, 284
Demon, McDonnell, 366
D.H.2 to D.H.5, Airco, 12
D.H.77, de Havilland, 163
DH.110, de Havilland, 173
DI-1, Polikarpov, 471
DI-2, Polikarpov, 472
DI-3, Grigorovich, 257
DI-4, Laville, 325
DI-6, Kocherigin, 322
DI-8, Tupolev, 573
Dick, Seversky A8V, 524
Dinah, Mitsubishi Ki-46-III KAI, 412
DIS, Mikoyan-Gurevich, 386
Dolphin, Sopwith, 536
Dragon, Sopwith, 539
Draken, Saab 35, 513
Durandal, Sud-Est, 547

E

E.1/44, Gloster, 251
Eagle, Fisher, 212
Eagle, McDonnell Douglas, 371
Eastchurch Kitten, Port Victoria, 480
E.F.B.1 to 3, Vickers, 574
Elephant, Martinsyde, 363
EM, Elias, 192
English Electric Lightning, 49
EP-1, Republic, 491
Epervier, Renard, 490
E.S.1, Vickers, 575
Espadon, Sud-Ouest, 547
Etendard, Dassault, 150
Eurofighter Typhoon, 196
Express-Marin, Mureaux, 421
Ezüstnyil, WM-23, 591

F

F1, Mitsubishi, 413
F-1, North American, 452
F2, Bristol, 92-4
F2, Fairey, 196
F2A, Brewster, 90
F2B, Boeing, 74
F2G, Goodyear, 252
F2H, McDonnell, 365
F2Y, Convair, 117
F-2, Mitsubishi, 413
F-3, McDonnell, 366
F3B, Boeing, 74
F3D, Douglas, 189
F3F, Grumman, 260
F3H, McDonnell, 366
F-4, McDonnell Douglas, 367-71
F4B, Boeing, 75
F4C, Curtiss, 123
F4D, Douglas, 189
F4F, Grumman, 261
F-5, Northrop, 458
F5/34, Gloster, 248
F5D, Douglas, 191
F-6, Douglas, 189

F6C, Curtiss, 123
F6F, Grumman, 264
F6U, Vought, 587
F.7/30, Supermarine, 557
F.7/30, Westland, 593
F7C, Curtiss, 125
F7F, Grumman, 265
F-7M Airguard, Chengdu, 113
F7U, Vought, 588
F8C, Curtiss, 125
F8F, Grumman, 265
F8U, Vought, 588
F-9, Grumman, 269
F9/37, Gloster, 248
F9C, Curtiss, 129
F9F, Grumman, 266
F-10, Douglas, 189
F-11, Grumman, 269
F11C, Curtiss, 130
F11F, Grumman, 268
F-14, Grumman, 269
F-15, McDonnell Douglas, 371
F-16, General Dynamics, 237
F-18, McDonnell Douglas, 371-374
F-20, Northrop, 460
F20/27, Hawker, 282
F20/27, Westland, 592
F-22, Lockheed, 350
F29/27, Westland, 593
F-82, North American, 448
F-84, Republic, 496
F-84F, Republic, 498
F-86, North American, 449
F-89, Northrop, 457
F-94, Lockheed, 345
F-100, North American, 454
F-101, McDonnell, 367
F-102, Convair, 119
F-104, Lockheed, 348
F-105, Republic, 500
F-106, Convair, 120
F-107, North American, 454
F-110, McDonnell Douglas, 369
F-111, General Dynamics, 237
F/A-18, McDonnell Douglas, 371
Faceplate, Ye-2, 396
Fagot, MiG-15, 390
Faithless, MiG-23PD, 400
Falco, Fiat CR.42, 207
Falke, Dornier H, 185
Fang, La-11, 329
Fantail, La-15, 330
Fantôme, Fairey, 200
Fargo, MiG-9, 389
Farmer, MiG-19, 394
FB, Boeing, 73
F.B.5 to F.B.26, Vickers, 575-8
FDB-1, Gregor, 256
F.E.3, R.A.F., 504
F.E.6, R.A.F., 504
F.E.8, R.A.F., 507
F.E.9, R.A.F., 508
Feather, Yak-15, 604
Féroce, Fairey, 200
FF-1, Grumman, 259
FH-1, McDonnell, 365
Fiddler, Tupolev, 573
Fighting Falcon, General Dynamics, 237
Fin, La-7, 327
Finback, SAC J-8, 526
Firebail, Ryan, 511
Firebar, Yak-28, 606
Firebrand, Blackburn, 64
Firefly, Fairey, 197
Firefly (II), Fairey, 201
Fishbed, MiG-21, 396
Fishpot, Su-9 & Su-11, 551-3
Fitter-A-B, Su-7, 552

Fitter-C-K, Su-17, 555
FJ-1, North American, 449
F.K.6 to F.K.10, Armstrong Whitworth, 25
F.K.22 to F.K.25, B.A.T., 52-3
F.K.31, NVI, 461
F.K.52 to F.K.58, Koolhoven, 323-4
Flagon, Su-15, 553
Flanker, Su-27, 556
Flashlight, Yak-25, 606
Fleetwing, Fairey, 199
Flipper, Ye-152, 399
Flogger, MiG-23, 401
Floh, DFW T 28, 183
Flora, Yak-23, 604
Flycatcher, Fairey, 197
FM, General Motors, 263
FM-1, Airacuda, Bell, 55
F.M.4, Armstrong Whitworth, 25
Folgore, Macchi, 360
Forger, Yak-38, 607
Fox VIC, Fairey, 199
Foxbat, MiG-25, 400
Foxhound, MiG-31, 401
FR-1 Fireball, Ryan, 511
Frank, Nakajima Ki-84, 428
Frank, Yak-9, 601
Freccia, Fiat G.50, 209
Fred, Bell P-63, 57
Freestyle, Yak-141, 607
Frances, Yokosuka P1Y, 608
Fresco, MiG-17, 392
Fritz, La-9, 328
FU-1, Vought, 584
Fulcrum, MiG-29, 402
Fulmar, Fairey, 200
Fury, Hawker, 282
Fury (II), Hawker, 289
Fury, North American, 451
FVL-8, Engineering Div, 193

G

G-23, Grumman, 260
G.50, Fiat, 209
G.55, Fiat, 210
G.56, Fiat, 210
G.59, Fiat, 211
G.91, Fiat, 211
Gambet, Gloster, 245
Gamecock, Gloster, 243
Gamma, Pomilio, 478
Gauntlet, Gloster, 245
Gekko, Nakajima, 426
Gelber Hund, Euler, 194
George, Kawanishi NIK, 314
Gladiator, Gloster, 246
Gnat, Folland, 234
Gnatsnapper, Gloster, 245
Goblin, CCF, 260
Goblin, McDonnell, 366
Goldfinch, Gloster, 244
Gorcock, Gloster, 244
Goshawk, Curtiss, 130
Grain Kitten, Port Victoria, 480
Grebe, Gloster, 243
Greyhound, Austin, 33
Gripen, Saab 39, 515
GS, Curtiss, 121
Guan, Gloster, 244
Gun Bus, Sopwith, 532
Gunbus, Vickers, 575
Gurnard, Short, 526

H

H 22, Junkers, 312
HA, Curtiss, 121
Hamble Baby, Fairey, 196
Hamp, Mitsubishi A6M, 409
Hap, Mitsubishi A6M, 409
Haukka, I.V.L., 310
Havoc, Douglas, 187
Hawk I, Curtiss, 126
Hawk II, Curtiss, 130
Hawk III, Curtiss, 132

Hawk IV, Curtiss, 132
Hawk 75, Curtiss, 135-7
Hawk 81, Curtiss, 138
Hawk 87, Curtiss, 139
Hawk 200, British Aerospace, 103
Hawfinch, Hawker, 282
Hayabusa, Mitsubishi, 407
Hayabusa, Nakajima, 426
Hayate, Nakajima, 428
HD 23 to HD 43, Heinkel, 292-4
Héjja II, MAVAG, 365
Hellcat, Grumman, 264
Helldiver, Curtiss, 125
Heron, Hawker, 281
Hien, Kawasaki, 318
Hippo, Sopwith, 538
Hoopoe, Hawker, 282
Hornbill, Hawker, 281
Hornet, de Havilland, 169
Hornet, McDonnell Douglas, 371
Hotspur, Hawker, 287
HPS-1, Handley Page, 275
HT-2, Burgess, 103
HT-B, Burgess, 103
Humu, VL, 583
Hunter, Hawker, 291
Hurricane, Hawker, 284

I

I-1, Grigorovich, 256
I-1M-5, Polikarpov, 471
I-2bis, Grigorovich, 257
I-3, Polikarpov, 472
I-4, Tupolev, 571
I-5, Polikarpov, 472
I-6, Polikarpov, 472
I-8, Tupolev, 571
I-12, Tupolev, 572
I-14, Tupolev, 572
I-15, Polikarpov, 473
I-16, Polikarpov, 473
I-16, VEF, 574
I-17, Polikarpov, 476
I-21, Ilyushin, 307
I-21, Pashinin, 464
I-26, Yakovlev, 599
I-28, Yakovlev, 600
I-28, Yatsenko, 608
I-29, Yakovlev, 599
I-30, Yakovlev, 600
I-75, Mikoyan-Gurevich, 399
I-152, Polikarpov, 476
I-153, Polikarpov, 476
I-180, Polikarpov, 477
I-185, Polikarpov, 477
I-190, Polikarpov, 477
I-207, Borovkov-Florov, 81
I-210, Mikoyan-Gurevich, 386
I-211, Alekseev, 17
I-211, Mikoyan-Gurevich, 387
I-215, Alekseev, 17
I-220, Mikoyan-Gurevich, 387
I-221 to I-225, Mikoyan-Gurevich, 388
I-230 & I-231, Mikoyan-Gurevich, 387
I-250, Mikoyan-Gurevich, 389
I-270, Mikoyan-Gurevich, 390
I-300, Mikoyan-Gurevich, 389
I-310 to I-370, Mikoyan-Gurevich, 396
I.Aé.27, FMA, 212
I.Aé.30, FMA, 212
I.Aé.33, FMA, 213
IK-3, Rogožarski, 502
IL-400, Polikarpov, 471
IP-1, Grigorovich, 257
IP-4, Grigorovich, 259

Irving, Nakajima J1N, 427
IS, Silvanskii, 531
IS-1, Nikitin-Shevchenko, 443
IS-2, Nikitin-Shevchenko, 444
I.S.V.A., Ansaldo, 20
ITP, Polikarpov, 478
I-Z, Grigorovich, 257

J
J1N, Nakajima, 427
J2M, Mitsubishi, 410
J5N, Nakajima, 428
J 6B, ASJA, 32
J-7, Chengdu, 113
J7W, Kyushu, 324
J-8, Shenyang, 526
J8M, Mitsubishi, 413
J-10, Chengdu, 113
J 21, Saab, 512
J 22, FFVS, 204
J-22, SOKO, 532
J 23, FVM, 235
J 24B, FVM, 235
J 29, Saab, 513
J 32B, Saab, 513
J 35, Saab, 513
J 37, Saab, 515
Jack, Mitsubishi J2M, 410
Jaguar, Grumman, 269
Jaktfalk, ASJA, 32
Jaktfalk, Svenska Aero, 566
JAS 39, Saab, 515
Jastrzab, P.Z.L., 488
Javelin, Gloster, 251
Jerry, Heinkel He 112B, 297
JH-7, XAC, 599
Jim, Nakajima Ki-43, 426
Jockey, Vickers, 580

K
K 47, Junkers, 312
K 53, Junkers, 312
Ka-14, Mitsubishi, 407
Kauz, Dornier Do 17Z 185-6
KD, Brandenburg, 83
KDA-3, Kawasaki, 315
KDA-5, Kawasaki, 315
KDW, Brandenburg, 83
Kestrel, Hawker Siddeley, 292
KF, Brandenburg, 82
Kfir, IAI, 302
Ki-5, Kawasaki, 316
Ki-8, Nakajima, 423
Ki-10, Kawasaki, 316
Ki-11, Nakajima, 424
Ki-12, Nakajima, 424
Ki-18, Mitsubishi, 408
Ki-27, Nakajima, 425
Ki-28, Kawasaki, 316
Ki-33, Mitsubishi, 408
Ki-43, Nakajima, 426
Ki-44, Nakajima, 427
Ki-45, Kawasaki, 316
Ki-46-III KAI, Mitsubishi, 412
Ki-60, Kawasaki, 317
Ki-61, Kawasaki, 318
Ki-64, Kawasaki, 319
Ki-83, Mitsubishi, 412
Ki-84, Nakajima, 428
Ki-93, Rikugun, 501
Ki-96, Kawasaki, 320
Ki-100, Kawasaki, 320
Ki-102, Kawasaki, 320
Ki-106, Tachikawa, 567
Ki-108, Kawasaki, 321
Ki-109, Mitsubishi, 412
Kingcobra, Bell, 57
Kittyhawk, Curtiss, 139
Koshiki-2, Tokorozawa, 570
Kwangsi Type 3, Liuchow, 340
Kyofu, Kawanishi, 314
Kyokko, Yokosuka, 608

L
L 6 to L 14, Daimler, 145-6
L 14, Brandenburg, 84
L 16, Brandenburg, 84
L 65, Albatros, 16
L 77v, Albatros, 16
L 84, Albatros, 17
Lancer, Republic, 492
Lansen, Saab, 513
Lavi, IAI, 303
LCA, HAL, 273
LE, Breguet, 88
LGL-32, Loire-Gourdou-Leseurre, 254
Lightning, BAC, 49
Lightning, Lockheed, 341
Lincock, Blackburn, 64
L.R.T.Tr., Sopwith, 535
LUSAC-11, Packard, 462

M
M.1C, Bristol, 92
M-8, Loening, 351
Mars, Gloster, 241
Martlet, Grumman, 263
Marut, HAL, 272
Master Fighter, Miles, 405
MB-1 to MB-9, Thomas-Morse, 569
MD.450 Ouragan, Dassault, 146
Memel A.F.G.1, 16, 374
Meteor, Armstrong Whitworth, 29
Meteor, Gloster, 250
MI-3, Tupolev, 571
Microplano, TNCA, 570
Midge, Folland, 234
Mikoyan 1.42/1.44, 405
Milan, Dassault, 159
Mirage, Dassault, 150-162
Mistral, Sud-Est, 546
Mohawk, Curtiss, 135
Mörkö, Morane-Saulnier, 420
Mosquito, de Havilland, 164
Mustang, North American, 445
Myrsky, VL, 583
Mystère, Dassault, 148

N
N.1B, Westland, 591
N1K, Kawanishi, 314
Ñamcú, FMA, 212
Nammer, IAI, 303
Narval, Sud-Ouest, 548
Nate, Nakajima Ki-27, 425
Natter, Bachem, 52
Nautilus, Blackburn, 63
NC 600, Centre, 112
NC 1080, Aérocentre, 11
Nesher, IAI, 302
NF-1, Seversky, 524
Nick, Kawasaki Ki-45, 316
Nighthawk, Gloster, 241
Nimbus, Martinsyde, 364
Nimrod, Hawker, 283

O
OKO-6, Tairov, 567
Orao, SOKO, 532
Orione, Macchi, 361
Oscar, Nakajima Ki-43, 426
Osprey, Hawker, 283
Ouragan, Dassault, 146

P
P-1, Curtiss, 123
P-1, Sukhoi, 552
P1Y, Yokosuka, 608
P-2, Curtiss, 125
P-3A, Curtiss, 125
P-5, Curtiss, 126
P-6, Curtiss, 126
P-12, Boeing, 76
P-16, Berliner-Joyce, 59

P-16, FFA, 202
P-26, Boeing, 77
P-30, Consolidated, 116
P-35, Seversky, 522
P-35A, Republic, 491
P-36, Curtiss, 134
P-37, Curtiss, 137
P-38, Lockheed, 341
P-39, Bell, 59
P-40, Curtiss, 138
P-43, Republic, 492
P-47, Republic, 492
P-51, North American, 445
P-59, Bell, 58
P-61, Northrop, 455
P-63, Bell, 57
P-64, North American, 444
P-66, Vultee, 590
P-70, Douglas, 188
P-75A, Fisher, 212
P-80, Lockheed, 344
P.1040, Hawker, 290
P.1081, Hawker, 291
PA-1, Loening, 351
Pantera, ENAER, 192
Panther, Grumman, 266
PB-1, Berliner-Joyce, 59
PB-2, Consolidated, 116
Perry, Kawasaki Ki-10, 316
PG-1, Aeromarine, 11
Phantom, McDonnell FH-1, 365
Phantom II, McDonnell Douglas F-4, 367
Pike, Avro, 46
Pintail, Fairey, 197
Pipit, Parnall, 463
Pirate, Vought, 587
P.L.5, Levasseur, 335
P.L.6, Levasseur, 335
PN-1, Curtiss, 123
Plover, Parnall, 463
PS-1, Dayton-Wright, 163
Pulqui, FMA, 212
Pup, Sopwith, 533
P.V.3, Hawker, 284
P.V.2 to P.V.9, Port Victoria, 479-80
PW-1, Engineering Div, 193
PW-2, Loening, 351
PW-5, Fokker F VI, 228
PW-6, Fokker D IX, 228
PW-7, Fokker D XI, 228
PW-8, Curtiss, 123
PW-9, Boeing, 72
PWS A, 36
Pyörremyrsky, VL, 584

R
Rafale, Dassault, 162
Raiden, Mitsubishi, 410
Ram, R.A.F., 509
Randy, Kawasaki Ki-102, 320
Reppu, Mitsubishi, 412
Rex, Kawanishi N1K, 314
Ro 41 to Ro 58, I.M.AM, 308-9
Rob, Kawasaki Ki-64, 319
Roc, Blackburn, 64
Rofix, Rohrbach, 502
Roland, D I to D XVII, LFG, 337-40
Rufe, Nakajima A6M, 427
Rybka, Korvin, 324

S
S.2A, Bristol, 91
S-3, Curtiss, 121
Š 3 to Š 431, Letov, 333-5
S-6, Curtiss, 121
S-37 Berkut, Sukhoi, 557
S-49, Ikarus (VTI), 306
S 92 Turbina, Avia, 40
S 199, Avia, 40
Sabre, Canadair, 106
Sabre, Commonwealth, 115

Sabre, North American, 449
Saetta, Macchi, 358
Sagittario, Reggiane, 490
Salamander, Sopwith, 538
Sam, Mitsubishi A7M, 412
SAM-7, Moskalev, 420
SAM-13, Moskalev, 420
Sandy, Mitsubishi A5M, 408
Schneider, Sopwith, 532
Scimitar, Armstrong Whitworth, 28
Scimitar, Supermarine, 566
Scorpion, Northrop, 457
Scout, Bristol, 91
Scout F, Bristol, 94
SD I to SD III, Arado, 21-22
S.E.2, R.A.F., 504
S.E.4, R.A.F., 506
S.E.5, R.A.F., 507
Sea Dart, Convair, 117
Seafang, Supermarine, 564
Seafire, Supermarine, 560
Sea Fury, Hawker, 290
Sea Harrier, British Aerospace, 102
Seahawk, Curtiss, 125
Sea Hawk, Hawker, 290
Sea Hornet, de Havilland, 169
Sea Venom, de Havilland, 172
Sea Vixen, de Havilland, 174
Shiden, Kawanishi, 314
Shinden, Kyushu, 324
Shoki, Nakajima, 427
Shooting Star, Lockheed, 344
Shusui, Mitsubishi, 413
Sikorsky S-XVI, 488
Sikorsky S-XX, 488
Simoun, Wibault, 596
Sirocco, Wibault, 596
Siskin, Armstrong Whitworth, 26
Siskin, Siddeley, 528
SK-2, Bisnovat, 63
Skyknight, Douglas, 189
Skylancer, Douglas, 191
Skyray, Douglas, 189
SM-12, Mikoyan-Gurevich, 398
SN, Mikoyan-Gurevich, 394
Snail, Sopwith, 538
Snapper, Sopwith, 539
Snark, Sopwith, 539
Snipe, Sopwith, 536
Sparrow, A.D., 8
Sparrowhawk, Curtiss, 129
Sparrowhawk, Gloster, 241
Speed Scout, Berkmans, 59
Spider, Avro 46
Spiteful, Supermarine, 564
Spitfire, Supermarine, 557-63
SSD 1, Arado, 22
STA-Special, Ryan, 511
Starfighter, Lockheed, 348
Starfire, Lockheed, 345
Starling, Armstrong Whitworth, 27
Super Etendard, Dassault, 158
Super Mystère, Dassault, 149
Super Sabre, North American, 454
Swallow, Sopwith, 539
Swift, Curtiss, 131
Swift, Supermarine, 565
S.V.A., Ansaldo, 19-20

T
T-3, Sukhoi, 551
T-28 Floh, DFW, 183
T 34, DFW, 183

Ta 152, Focke-Wulf, 217
Ta 154, Focke-Wulf, 218
Taka, Mitsubishi, 406
Taon, Breguet, 89
Tempest, Hawker, 288
Tenrai, Nakajima, 428
TF, N.A.F., 429
Thunderbolt, Republic, 492
Thunderchief, Republic, 500
Thunderjet, Republic, 498
Thunderstreak, Republic, 498
Tiger, Grumman, 268
Tiger II, Northrop, 459
Tigercat, Grumman, 265
Tigershark, Northrop, 460
TIS, Polikarpov, 478
Tojo, Nakajima Ki-44, 427
Tololoche, TNCA, 570
Tomahawk, Curtiss, 138
Tomcat, Grumman, 269
Tony, Kawasaki Ki-61, 318
Tornado, Wibault, 597
Tornado, Hawker, 287
Tornado, Panavia, 461
TP-1, Engineering Div, 193
Trident, Sud-Ouest, 549
Triplane, Sopwith, 534
Trombe, Wibault, 597
TS-1, N.A.F., 429
TsAGI (Bisnovat) SK-2, 63
T.T.A., Bristol, 92
Turbina, Avia, 40
Turcock, Blackburn, 63
Twin Mustang, North American, 448
Typhoon, Hawker, 2,38

U
Umbra T.18, 33

V
Vampire, de Havilland, 166
Vampire, Vickers, 578
Vanguard, Vultee, 590
Vautour, Sud-Ouest, 548
VB-10, Arsenal, 31
VCP-1, Engineering Div, 193
VE-7, Lewis & Vought, 336
VE-8, Lewis & Vought, 336
VE-9, Lewis & Vought, 337
Veltro, Macchi, 360
Venom, de Havilland, 170
Venom, Vickers, 581
VG 30 to VG 39, Arsenal, 30
VG 90, Arsenal, 31
VI-100, Petlyakov, 465
Viggen, Saab, 515
Viper, Thomas-Morse, 569
Vireo, Vickers, 579
Voodoo, McDonnell, 367
VT-11, Polikarpov, 473

W
Wagtail, Westland, 591
Warhawk, Curtiss, 139
W.B.II to W.B.V, Beardmore, 53
W.R.26, Beardmore, 54
Weasel, Westland, 591
Welkin, Westland, 593
Westbury, Westland, 592
Whirlwind, Westland, 593
Wibault Scout, Vickers, 579
Wildcat, Grumman, 261
Wilk, P.Z.L., 487
Wizard, Westland, 592
Woodcock, Hawker, 280
WP-1, Dornier Do H, 185
Wyvern, Westland, 594

X
X-32 JSF, Boeing, 80
X-35 JSF, Lockheed, 350
XA-26A, Douglas, 189
XF2J, Berliner-Joyce, 60
XF2U, Vought, 585

XF3J, Berliner-Joyce, 60
XF3U, Vought, 585
XF3W, Wright, 598
XF4F, Grumman, 261
XF5B, Boeing, 77
XF5F, Grumman, 263
XF6B, Boeing, 79
XF7B, Boeing, 79
XF8B, Boeing, 80
XF10F, Grumman, 269
XF12C, Curtiss, 133
XF13C, Curtiss, 134
XF14C, Curtiss, 143
XF15C, Curtiss, 143
XF-85, McDonnell, 366
XF-87, Curtiss, 144
XF-88, McDonnell, 366
XF-90, Lockheed, 347
XF-91, Republic, 499
XFA, General Aviation, 236
XFD, Douglas, 187
XFG, Eberhart, 192
XFH, Hall, 275
XFJ, Berliner-Joyce, 60
XFL, Bell, 57
XFN, Seversky, 524
XFV, Lockheed, 346
XFY, Convair, 118
XP-4, Boeing, 74
XP-7, Boeing, 74
XP-8, Boeing, 74
XP-9, Boeing, 77
XP-10, Curtiss, 127
XP-13, Thomas-Morse, 569
XP-15, Boeing, 77
XP-17, Curtiss, 127
XP-21, Curtiss, 129
XP-22, Curtiss, 129
XP-23, Curtiss, 130
XP-31, Curtiss, 131
XP-41, Seversky, 525
XP-49, Lockheed, 344
XP-50, Grumman, 264
XP-54, Consolidated Vultee, 117
XP-55, Curtiss, 142
XP-56, Northrop, 455
XP-58, Lockheed, 344
XP-60, Curtiss, 141
XP-62, Curtiss, 142
XP-67, McDonnell, 365
XP-72, Republic, 496
XP-77, Bell, 58
XP-79B, Northrop, 456
XP-81, Consolidated Vultee, 117
XP-83, Bell, 58
X-PO, Chu, 113
XV-6, Hawker Siddeley, 292

Y
Y1P-25, Consolidated, 116
Ye-2, Mikoyan-Gurevich, 396
Ye-8, Mikoyan-Gurevich, 400
Ye-50, Mikoyan-Gurevich, 398
Ye-152, Mikoyan-Gurevich, 399
YF-12A, Lockheed, 350
YF-17, Northrop, 460
YF-23, Northrop/McDonnell Douglas, 461
YP-20, Curtiss, 129
YP-24, Lockheed, 341
YP-29, Boeing, 80

Z
Zeebrugge C.2, 8
Zeke, Mitsubishi A6M, 409

A

A.C.A.Z. C.2   Belgium

Flown early in 1926 and evaluated by the Belgian *Aéronautique Militaire*, the C.2 tandem two-seat fighter-reconnaissance biplane was built by the Ateliers de Construction Aéronautique de Zeebrugge (A.C.A.Z.). Of all-metal construction, the C.2 was powered by a 450 hp Hispano-Suiza 12Ha 12-cylinder liquid-cooled engine, and an interesting feature was the interchangeability of all four main wing panels. The pilot and observer/gunner were seated in tandem and armament comprised a single fixed forward-firing synchronised 7,7-mm Vickers machine gun and twin Lewis guns of similar calibre on a flexible mount. No production order for the C.2 was placed by the *Aéronautique Militaire*, and, on 9 March 1928, the sole prototype was employed for an attempt to fly to the Belgian Congo, this ending in a forced landing in France. The aircraft was written off on 25 January 1933. *Max speed, 155 mph (250 km/h). Time to 19,685 ft (6 000 m), 35 min. Endurance (full power), 3.5 hrs. Empty weight, 2,778 lb (1 260 kg). Loaded weight, 4,563 lb (2 070 kg). Span 41 ft 0⅛ in (12,50 m). Length, 27 ft 0⅘ in (8,25 m). Height 11 ft 1⅞ in (3,40 m). Wing area, 436.58 sq ft (40,56 m²).*

The A.C.A.Z. C.2 (above and below) evaluated by Belgium's *Aéronautique Militaire* during 1926.

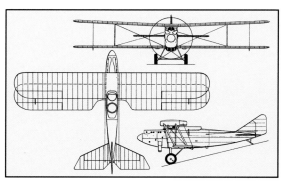

A.D. SCOUT (SPARROW)   UK

Designed by Harris Booth of the Air Department of the Admiralty as a single-seat anti-airship fighter, the A.D. Scout – later to become known unofficially as the "Sparrow" – was an extraordinary single-bay staggered biplane intended to carry a Davis two-pounder recoilless gun. The rudders and outsize tailplane were carried by four parallel tailbooms, and the unusual appearance of the A.D. Scout resulted primarily from the fact that the large mainplane gap was below rather than above the nacelle accommodating the pilot. The gun was intended to be mounted in the bottom of the nacelle, to the tail of which was attached a 100 hp nine-cylinder Gnome Monosoupape rotary engine driving a pusher propeller. Construction was of wood with fabric covering, and four prototypes were ordered and built (two by Hewlett & Blondeau and two by Blackburn) in 1915. Delivered to the RNAS, the A.D. Scouts proved seriously overweight and difficult to handle in the air. In consequence, all four aircraft were scrapped. *Max speed, 84 mph (135 km/h). Endurance, 2.5 hrs. Span, 33 ft 5 in (10,18 m). Length, 22 ft 9 in (6,93 m). Height, 10 ft 3 in (3,12 m).*

An anti-airship fighter, the A.D. Scout (above and below) proved overweight and handled badly.

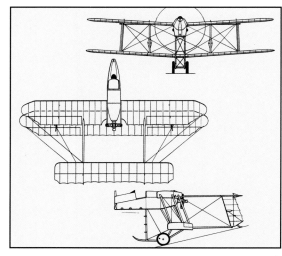

ADAMOLI-CATTANI   Italy

In 1918, *Signori* Adamoli and Cattani designed the smallest practicable single-seat fighter around the then most powerful rotary engine extant, the 200 hp Le Rhône. The fighter, which was of wooden construction with fabric skinning, was an unequal-span unstaggered biplane with Warren-truss type interplane bracing, unusual features consisting of the supplanting of orthodox ailerons with hinged and interlinked wing

(Below) The diminutive Adamoli-Cattani fighter.

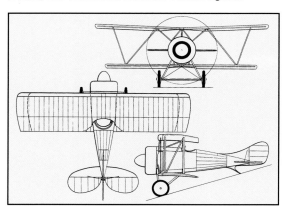

leading edges, and the use of rigid tubes rather than cables for actuation of the movable tail surfaces. The prototype was begun at the Farina works in Turin, but transferred to the Officine Moncenisio in Condove for completion. Armament comprised two 7,7-mm machine guns. When flight testing was initiated it was discovered that the Le Rhône engine developed only 160 hp and the fighter was thus seriously underpowered, development being abandoned after limited trials. The following estimated performance data were based on the use of a fully rated engine. *Max speed, 186 mph (300 km/h). Endurance, 2.25 hrs. Empty weight, 1,036 lb (470 kg). Loaded weight, 1,488 lb (675 kg). Span, 28 ft 2½ in (8,60 m). Length 20 ft 0⅛ in (6,10 m).*

A.E.G. D I   Germany

The first fighter produced by A.E.G. (Allgemeine Elektrizitäts Gesellschaft), the D I single-bay biplane was primarily of steel tube construction with single-spar wings and fabric skinning, power being provided by a 160 hp Daimler D IIIa six-cylinder water-cooled engine and armament comprising twin 7,92-mm LMG 08/15 synchronised guns. The first of three prototypes appeared in May 1917, type testing being conducted during August-September after the fuselage was lengthened by 15¾ in (40 cm), the second and third pro-

(Below) The second prototype of the A.E.G. D I.

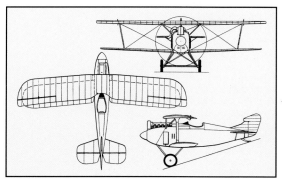

totypes differing in having cheek-type radiators. Difficult to fly, one prototype crashing during type testing, the D I was nevertheless ordered as a pre-series of 20

The first A.E.G. D I which appeared in May 1917.

The Adamoli-Cattani fighter prior to flight test.

for frontline evaluation. This contract was cancelled, however, after a second prototype crashed on 5 September 1917. *Max speed, 127 mph (205 km/h). Time to 3,280 ft (1 000 m), 2.2 min. Empty weight, 1,510 lb (685 kg). Loaded weight, 2,072 lb (940 kg). Span, 27 ft 10⅝ in (8,50 m). Length, 20 ft 0⅛ in (6,10 m). Height, 8 ft 8⅓ in (2,65 m). Wing area, 173.73 sq ft (16,14 m²).*

A.E.G. Dr I   Germany

Essentially a *Dreidecker*, or triplane, derivative of the D I, the Dr I was inspired by a circular of 27 July 1917 inviting inspection of a Sopwith Triplane that had been captured intact and proposals for fighters possessing at least comparable characteristics. A.E.G.'s contribution to the programme appeared in October 1917, this mating a triple-wing cellule with the fuselage, tail surfaces, 160 hp Daimler D IIIa engine and twin-gun armament of the D I. The Dr I revealed poor performance and unpleasant handling characteristics, development being quickly abandoned. *Max speed, 106 mph (170 km/h). Empty weight, 1,565 lb (710 kg). Loaded weight, 2,138 lb (970 kg). Span, 30 ft 10 in (9,40 m). Length 20 ft 0⅛ in (6,10 m).*

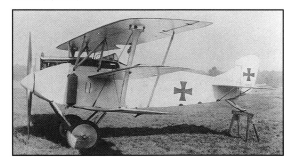

The sole prototype of the A.E.G. Dr I triplane.

A.E.G. PE   Germany

The PE (*Panzer-Einsitzer*) was a single-seat armoured ground attack fighter and proved to be unique among aircraft designed for this task in being of triplane configuration. Featuring an armoured light alloy-covered fuselage and fabric-covered dural wings, the PE was powered by a 195 hp Benz Bz IIIb eight-cylinder water-cooled engine and was first flown in March 1918. Armament consisted of two synchronised 7,92-mm LMG 08/15 machine guns supplemented by racks for small bombs. The PE proved easy to fly but was found to have poor stability and was considered by the *Idflieg* (*Inspektion der Fliegertruppe*) to possess inadequate

A.E.G.'s first *Panzer-Einsitzer* armoured fighter.

performance for fighter-versus-fighter combat, a *dedicated* ground attack aircraft being considered unacceptable. Nonetheless, A.E.G. was to persist with the concept with the DJ. *Max speed, 103 mph (166 km/h). Time to 3,280 ft (1 000 m), 5.8 min. Empty weight, 2,606 lb (1 182 kg). Loaded weight, 3,113 lb (1 412 kg). Span, 36 ft 8⅞ in (11,20 m). Length, 21 ft 7⅞ in (6,60 m).*

A.E.G. DJ I   Germany

Pursuing the concept of the single-seat armoured ground attack fighter, A.E.G. had begun the development of an aerodynamically advanced biplane as a

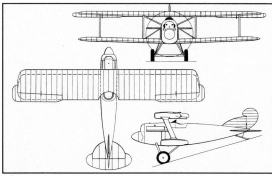

(Above) The A.E.G. DJ I armoured attack fighter.

Panzer-Einsitzer before the initiation of flight testing of the PE triplane, and this, the DJ I, was to be flown in July 1918. Two prototypes of the DJ I were completed with the 195 hp Benz Bz IIIb engine and a third prototype with the 240 hp Maybach Mb IVa engine, armament standardising on twin synchronised 7,92-mm LMG 08/15 guns with provision for anti-personnel bombs. An equi-span two-bay biplane, the DJ I wing cellule dispensed with flying wires, interplane bracing

The DJ I (above) entered flight test in July 1918.

being provided by I-section struts. The wings were of dural construction with fabric covering, and the fuselage, which embodied some armour protection for the engine, fuel tank and pilot, had sheet aluminium skinning. Hostilities terminated while flight testing of the DJ I was still in progress. The following data relate to the Benz-engined version. *Max speed, 112 mph (180 km/h). Empty weight, 2,606 lb (1 182 kg). Loaded weight, 3,031 lb (1 375 kg). Span, 32 ft 9¾ in (10,00 m). Length, 21 ft 11⅓ in (6,69 m). Height, 9 ft 10⅛ in (3,00 m).*

AERFER SAGITTARIO 2   Italy

Designed by Ing Sergio Stefanutti and built by Industrie Meccaniche Aeronautiche Meridionali AERFER, the Sagittario (Archer) 2 was an all-metal light fighter intended for clear-weather intercept and tactical support rôles. Powered by a 3,600 lb st (1 633 kgp) Rolls-Royce Derwent 9, the sole prototype flew on 19 May 1956 and

The sole prototype of the lightweight Sagittario 2.

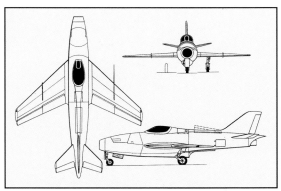

(Above) The Ariete fighter with booster turbojet to improve climb and combat performance.

attained Mach=1.1 in a dive on 4 December 1956. Armament comprised two 30-mm Hispano-Suiza HDD-825 cannon. *Max speed, 646 mph (1 040 km/h) at sea level, 634 mph (1 020 km/h) at 27,230 ft (8 300 m). Time to 39,370 ft (12 000 m), 10 min. Normal range, 475 mls (765 km). Empty weight, 5,070 lb (2 300 kg). Loaded weight, 7,275 lb (3 300 kg). Span, 24 ft 7¼ in (7,50 m). Length, 31 ft 2 in (9,50 m). Wing area, 156.08 sq ft (14,50 m²).*

AERFER ARIETE   Italy

Evolved from the Sagittario 2, the Ariete (Ram) retained the wing of the earlier fighter, marrying this to a redesigned fuselage in which the 3,600 lb st (1 633 kgp) Derwent 9 was supplemented by a 1,810 lb st (820 kgp) Rolls-Royce Soar RSr 2 auxiliary turbojet. To boost take-off, climb and combat performance, this engine drew air through a retractable dorsal intake. The Ariete flew on 27 March 1958, and possessed an armament of two 30-mm HDD-825 cannon. Only one prototype was completed, and a progressive development, the mixed-power Leone (Lion), was abandoned. *Max speed, 671 mph (1 080 km/h). Time to 39,370 ft (12 000 m), 4.33 min. Empty weight, 5,291 lb (2 400 kg). Loaded weight, 7,793 lb (3 535 kg). Span, 24 ft 7¼ in (7,50 m). Length, 31 ft 5⅞ in (9,60 m). Wing area, 156.08 sq ft (14,50 m²).*

Ariete with auxiliary dorsal air intake dotted open.

AERO Ae 02   Czechoslovakia

The first single-seat fighter of original Czechoslovak design, the Ae 02 designed by Antonín Vlasák and Antonín Husník was built by the Aero Továrna Letadel. A single-bay biplane with I-type interplane struts and ailerons on the upper wing only, the Ae 02 was of mixed construction with fabric-covered wooden wings

The first Czech indigenous fighter, the Aero Ae 02.

and a dural-frame fuselage. Powered by an Hispano-Suiza HS 8Ba eight-cylinder vee-type engine rated at 220 hp with all fuel accommodated by a tank between the undercarriage mainwheels and carrying an armament of two 7,92-mm Vickers machine guns, the Ae 02 was flown for the first time in 1920. Piloted by Josef Novak, the Ae 02 was adjudged winner of the 1st International Flying Meeting held in Czechoslovakia in 1921, but only one prototype was completed, further development continuing with the Ae 04. *Max speed, 140 mph (225 km/h). Cruise, 118 mph (190 km/h). Time to 16,405 ft (5 000 m), 18.8 min. Empty weight, 1,488 lb (675 kg). Loaded weight, 2,083 lb (945 kg). Span, 25 ft 3⅛ in (7,70 m). Length, 17 ft 10½ in (5,45 m). Wing area, 179.76 sq ft (16,70 m²).*

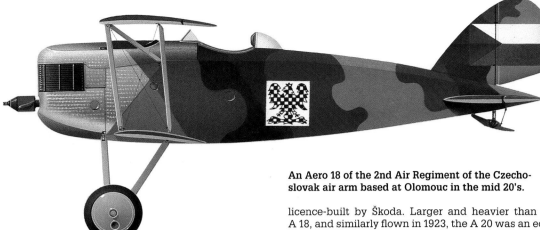

(Below) The mixed-construction Aero Ae 02 fighter.

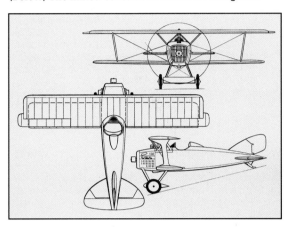

AERO Aᴇ 04   Czechoslovakia

Successful testing of the Ae 02 led Vlasák and Husník to revise the basic design in accordance with the requirements of the air component of the Czechoslovakian Army and to accept the BMW IIIa six-cylinder water-cooled engine rated at 185 hp and for which a manufacturing licence had been acquired by Walter. Flown as the Ae 04 in 1921, the new prototype established a national altitude record of 20,869 ft (6 361 m) and was then displayed at the 2nd International Aircraft Exhibition in Prague. Retaining the structure and armament of the Ae 02, the Ae 04 transferred fuel tankage to the fuselage and initially flew with an automobile-style frontal radiator, this giving place to a chin-type radiator during flight development. Only one prototype of the Ae 04 was built, further development resulting in the A 18. *Max speed, 140 mph (225 km/h). Cruise, 115 mph (185 km/h). Time to 16,405 ft (5 000 m), 14.0 min. Endurance, 1.0 hr. Empty weight, 1,477 lb (670 kg). Loaded weight, 1,984 lb (900 kg). Span, 25 ft 3⅛ in (7,70 m). Length, 18 ft 4½ in (5,60 m). Wing area, 157.15 sq ft (14,60 m²).*

Ae 04 with initial (above) and final engine cowls.

AERO A 18   Czechoslovakia

Evolved from the Ae 04, the A 18 was designed by Antonín Vlasák and Antonín Husník to a Czechoslovak Army specification. Retaining the Walter-built 185 hp BMW IIIa engine and armament of twin synchronised 7,92-mm Vickers guns, the A 18 also retained

(Above and below) The Aero A 18 was the only one of the company's fighters to achieve production status.

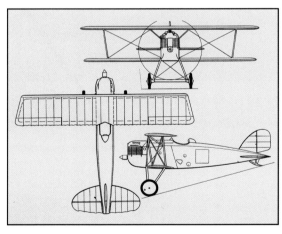

the mixed construction of the preceding fighter prototypes, but dispensed with the overhung upper wing ailerons in favour of ailerons inset flush with the wingtips, and also adopted tandem interplane struts. The A 18 prototype was flown in March 1923, and a production series of 20 aircraft was ordered. The standard A 18 was to establish three national altitude records, and the A 18B and A 18C were one-off high-speed examples which participated in the 1923 and 1924 national air races respectively. *Max speed, 142 mph (229 km/h) at 8,200 ft (2 500 m). Time to 16,405 ft (5 000 m), 8.5 min. Range, 249 mls (400 km). Empty weight, 1,404 lb (637 kg). Loaded weight, 1,900 lb (862 kg). Span, 24 ft 11¼ in (7,60 m). Length, 19 ft 4⅓ in (5,90 m). Wing area, 171.15 sq ft (15,90 m²).*

AERO A 20   Czechoslovakia

Developed in parallel with the A 18 to an MNO (*Ministerstvo národní obrany*, or Ministry of Defence) contract, the A 20 single-seat fighter was designed around the 310 hp Hispano-Suiza 8Fb engine which was being

An Aero 18 of the 2nd Air Regiment of the Czechoslovak air arm based at Olomouc in the mid 20's.

licence-built by Škoda. Larger and heavier than the A 18, and similarly flown in 1923, the A 20 was an equispan, single-bay staggered biplane of mixed construction carrying the standard armament of twin 7,92-mm machine guns. Despite its appreciably more powerful engine, the A 20 proved to possess an inferior performance to that of the A 18, and no further development was undertaken beyond the single prototype. *Max speed, 140 mph (225 km/h). Time to 16,405 ft (5 000 m),*

The A 20 (below) evolved in parallel with the A 18.

14.2 min. Range, 249 mls (400 km). Empty weight, 1,728 lb (784 kg). Loaded weight, 2,381 lb (1 080 kg). Span, 31 ft 9⅞ in (9,70 m). Length, 21 ft 7¾ in (6,60 m). Wing area, 250.8 sq ft (23,30 m²).

AERO A 102   Czechoslovakia

Denoting a major departure from previous Aero fighter design practice, the A 102 was ordered by the MNO in 1933 and was intended to reflect the latest state of the art. The A 102 was to be designed around the Walter-built Gnome-Rhône Mistral Major 14Kfs 14-cylinder radial air-cooled engine of 800 hp, be of all-metal construction and carry an armament of four 7,7-mm machine guns. Initially, the A 102 was an elegant single-bay biplane with the upper wing gulled into the fuselage decking. This proposal gave place to a semi-cantilever low wing monoplane (A 102D), and, in turn, to a gull wing monoplane, this configuration having become fashionable in Europe in the mid 'thirties. The first of two prototypes of the A 102 was flown in July 1934, the armament of four Model 30 guns being installed in the wing to fire outboard of the propeller arc. Climb rate and manoeuvrability proved good, and plans were prepared to install a 930 hp Mistral Major Krsd engine in one of the prototypes, but landing

The Aero A 102, of which two prototypes were built.

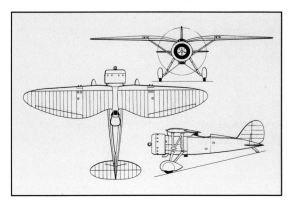

The Aero A 102 featured a gulled wing, a configuration that was fashionable in mid 'thirties Europe.

characteristics were poor, and, lacking flaps and having a wing loading of 22.5 lb/sq ft (110 kg/m²), the A 102's touch down speed was 68 mph (110 km/h), which was viewed as excessive by the MNO. A forced landing resulted from an engine failure shortly after the commencement of flight trials, and a further accident occurred in 1936, but the aircraft was repaired and exhibited at the 1937 National Aircraft Exhibition. By this time, the MNO considered the B 35 monoplane being proposed by Avia to possess more promise and further development of the A 102 was discontinued. *Max speed, 269 mph (434 km/h). Time to 16,405 ft (5 000 m), 5.8min. Range, 416 mls (670km). Empty weight, 3,258 lb (1 478 kg). Loaded weight, 4,488 lb (2 036 kg). Span, 37 ft³/₄ in (11,50 m). Length, 23 ft 11³/₈ in (7,30 m). Wing area, 199.13 sq ft (18,50 m²).*

AÉROCENTRE NC 1080   France

Designed under the direction of *Ingeńieur* Pillon and built by the SNCA du Centre (Aérocentre), the NC 1080 was developed as part of a single-seat shipboard fighter programme (competing designs being the Arsenal VG 90 and Nord 2200). The NC 1080 was powered by a 5,000 lb st (2 268 kgp) Rolls-Royce Nene turbojet, featured 22 deg 30 min wing sweepback at

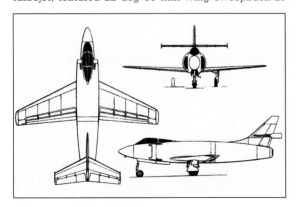

The NC 1080 (above and below) was a contender in a late 'forties shipboard fighter contest.

quarter-chord and was intended to mount an armament of three 30-mm cannon. The prototype was flown on 29 July 1949, and modifications were immediately found necessary to the spoilers and tail surfaces. The Aérocentre had meanwhile been dispersed, but testing of the NC 1080 continued at Brétigny and Villaroche, servo controls being fitted in February-March 1950, the aircraft being destroyed in an accident (the cause of which was never ascertained) on 10 April. No further development was undertaken. *Max speed, 608 mph (978 km/h) at 16,405 ft (5 000 m). Max initial climb, 4,920 ft/min (25 m/sec). Time to 29,530 ft (9 000 m), 12.2 min. Max range, 963 mls (1550 km). Empty weight, 11,334 lb (5 141 kg). Loaded weight, 16,975 lb (7 700 kg). Span, 39ft 4¹/₂ in (12,00 m). Length, 42 ft 2⁵/₈ in (12,87 m). Height, 15ft 5 in (4,70 m). Wing area, 305.7 sq ft (28,40 m²).*

centre section being cut away ahead of the single-seat cockpit which had quarter-inch (6,30-mm) armour protection. A particularly innovative feature of the PG-1 was the installation of a 37-mm Baldwin cannon firing through the propeller hub, plus a single 0.5-in (12,7mm) machine gun. The intended power plant was a 330 hp Wright K-2 eight-cylinder water-cooled engine, and a contract for the construction of three prototypes was let to the Aeromarine Plane and Motor Company of Keyport, NJ, in May 1921. The first of these was flown on 22 August 1922 with a Packard 1A-1116 engine of 346 hp, the K-2 having still to be cleared for flight testing. A second example was completed and both were flight tested for the Army Air Service at McCook Field, but performance proved disappointing and the aircraft was unpopular with its pilots owing to poor visibility from the cockpit and high vibration levels. The PG-1 was tested with the Packard 1A-1116 and 1A-1237 engines, and the Wright K-2, but was soon abandoned.

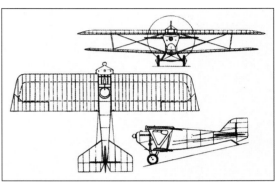

(Above and below) The PG-1 was a dual-rôle aircraft intended to fulfil both pursuit and attack tasks.

AEROMARINE PG-1   USA

The sole example of the PG (Pursuit and Ground Attack) category aircraft to be developed for the US Army, the PG-1 was designed by the Service's Engineering Division for the dual role of destroying armoured attack aircraft and ground strafing. Created by a team headed by Isaac: M Laddon, the PG-1 was a single-bay biplane with ailerons in the upper wing only, V-type interplane struts and a narrow-chord lower wing. There was only a nominal gap between the upper wing and the forward fuselage decking, the

Max speed, 130 mph (209 km/h). Time to 6,500 ft (1 980 m), 9.5 min. Range, 195 mls (314 km) at max speed. Empty weight, 3,030 lb (1 374 kg). Loaded weight, 3,918 lb (1 777 kg). Span, 40 ft 0 in (12,19 m). Length, 24 ft 6 in (7,47 m). Height, 8 ft 0 in (2,44 m). Wing area, 389 sq ft (36,13 m²).

AICHI TYPE H   Japan

The designation Type H Carrier Fighter was applied to two examples of the Heinkel HD 23 single-seat shipboard fighter biplane designed and built by the Ernst Heinkel Flugzeugwerke at the request of the Aichi Tokei Denki KK. These were delivered to Japan in 1927 and modified by Tetsuo Miki of Aichi to provide them with some flotation capability. Two further examples were built by the Japanese company, but no series production ensued (see Heinkel HD 23).

AIDC A-1 CHING-KUO   Taiwan

In 1979, pressure from the People's Republic of China caused the USA to halt aircraft deliveries to the Republic of China (Taiwan) Air Force from 1981. Needing a modern fighter to supplement, then to replace, its ageing fleet of F-5Es and F-104s, the Taiwanese commenced the development of an Indigenous Defence Fighter (IDF) in 1982, with technical assistance from General Dynamics. This finally emerged as the Ching-Kuo, which predictably showed a distinct family resemblance to the F-16. Ideally, Ching-Kuo should have been single-engined, but a suitable powerplant was unavailable. To overcome this, two ITEC TFE1042-70 afterburning turbofans were used, developed from the Garrett/Allied Signaal TFE731. Each gave a maximum thrust of 9,500 lb (4 309 kgp), and a military thrust of 6,060 lb (2 749 kgp), fed by fixed geometry intakes under the LERX. The wing was high-mounted to clear the intake ducts, and differs from that of the F-16 in having a pronounced forward sweep on the trailing edge. Triple digital FBW was used for the control system. First flight of the single-seater pre-production aircraft took place on 28 May 1989, and it achieved initial operational capability in 1995. Avionics were developed in the West; the radar is the Golden Dragon 53, based on the Westinghouse APG-67(V). Armament consists of a 20-mm M61 Vulcan cannon; four heat homing Sky Sword I, and two SARH Sky Sword II missiles, the latter carried in tandem on the centreline. Initially, 350 Ching-Kuos were planned, 50 of them two-seater conversion trainers. When production ceased in 2000, only 102 single-seaters and 28 two-seaters had been built, although sources vary. *Max speed hi, Mach 1.65; max speed lo, Mach 1.04. Operational ceiling, c55,000 ft (16 763 m). Initial climb rate, c50,000 ft/min (254 m/sec). Empty weight, 14,300 lb (6 486 kg). Max take-off weight, 21,000 lb (9 526 kg). Span, 30 ft 10¼ in (9,42 m). Length, 46 ft 7¾ in (15,98 m). Height, 15 ft 6 in (4,72 m). Wing area, 260 sq ft (24,20 m²).*

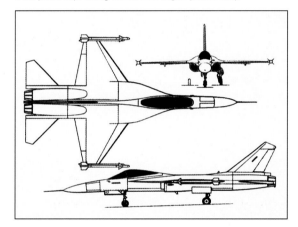

The Ching-Kuo (above and below) air defence fighter was named after a former president of Taiwan.

AIRCO D.H.2   UK

Designed by Geoffrey de Havilland of the Aircraft Manufacturing Company (Airco), the D.H.2 single-seat fighter was an unstaggered two-bay biplane of fabric-covered wooden construction with tubular steel booms carrying the tail surfaces. The prototype was first flown on 1 June 1915, but, having been sent to France for evaluation under operational conditions, fell into German hands substantially intact on 15 August. A few series D.H.2s were to be fitted with the 100 hp Le Rhône nine-cylinder rotary, but the standard engine was the 100 hp Gnome Monosoupape rotary mounted as a pusher. Armament comprised a free-mounted 0.303-in (7,7-mm) Lewis machine gun, and the D.H.2 proved an extremely sturdy aircraft and fully aerobatic with delightful handling qualities. A total of 266 served with the British Expeditionary Force in France from 400 delivered. The following data relate to the Gnome-engined version. *Max speed, 93 mph (150 km/h) at sea level, 77 mph (124 km/h) at 10,000 ft (3 050 m). Time to 5,000 ft (1 525 m), 8.45 min. Empty weight, 943 lb (428 kg). Loaded weight, 1,441 lb (654 kg). Span, 28 ft 3 in (8,61 m). Length, 25 ft 2½ in (7,68 m). Height, 9 ft 6½ in (2,91 m). Wing area, 249 sq ft (23,13 m²).*

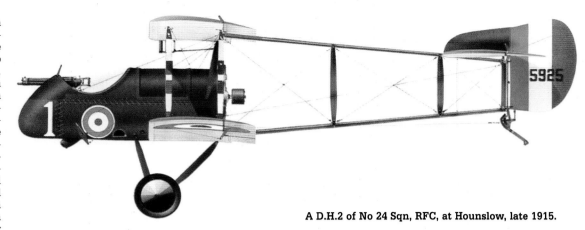

(Below) A D.H.2 of the first Airco production batch.

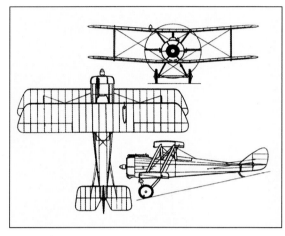

AIRCO D.H.5   UK

Characterised by the pronounced negative stagger of its mainplanes, which resulted from an attempt on the part of Geoffrey de Havilland to combine the performance of the tractor biplane with the cockpit visibility of pusher aircraft, the D.H.5 was flown late in 1916, and entered service in May 1917. Immensely strong and possessing docile handling qualities, but easily outflown by contemporary fighters at altitudes above 10,000 ft (3 050 m), the D.H.5 was of wooden construction with plywood and fabric skinning. Power was provided by a 100 hp Le Rhône 9J nine-cylinder rotary and armament consisted of a single 0.303-in (7,7-mm) Vickers gun. Some 550 were built by the parent company; Darracq Motor Engineering; March, Jones and Cribb, and British Caudron, but the D.H.5 was deemed to be of limited success and had been withdrawn from operations by the end of January 1918. *Max speed, 102 mph (164 km/h) at 10,000 ft (3 050 m), 89 mph (143 km/h) at 15,000 ft (4 570 m). Initial climb, 1,200 ft/min (6,1 m/sec). Endurance, 2.75 hrs. Empty weight, 1,101 lb (458 kg). Loaded weight, 1,492 lb (677 kg). Span, 25 ft 8 in (7,82 m). Length, 22 ft 0 in (6,71 m). Height, 9ft 1½ in (2,78 m). Wing area, 212.1 sq ft (19,70m²).*

A D.H.5 of the batch of 200 fighters of this type built in 1917 by the Darracq Motor Engineering Co.

A D.H.2 of No 24 Sqn, RFC, at Hounslow, late 1915.

Negative stagger characterised the D.H.5 (below).

ALBATROS D I   Germany

Designed by *Herren* Thelen, Schubert and Gnädig in a successful endeavour to wrest from the Allies the aerial superiority gained over the Fokker monoplanes by the Nieuport 11 *Bébé* and the Airco D.H.2, D I was the first fighter to be developed by the Albatros-Werke. Introduced in August 1916 were 12 pre-series aircraft ordered in the previous June after April *Typen-Prüfung* by the *Idflieg*. Aerodynamically clean for its time, the D I had a semi-monocoque wooden fuselage which differed radically from the fabric-skinned, braced box-girder type fuselages then in almost universal use. The wings were conventional fabric-covered wooden structures, the power plant was either the 150 hp Benz Bz III or 160 hp Mercedes D III six-cylinder inline water-cooled engine, and armament consisted of paired 7,92-mm LMG 08/15 synchronised machine guns. Fifty series D Is were ordered in July 1916, and these were delivered to the Front (where 50 pre-series and series

D Is were in service in November), but no further production of this fighter was undertaken as the D I had been overtaken by the D II which, in fact, arrived at the Front at the same time as the earlier type. *Max speed, 109 mph (175 km/h). Time to 3,280 ft (1 000 m), 6.0 min. Endurance, 1.5 hrs. Empty weight, 1,422 lb (645 kg). Loaded weight, 1,809 lb (898 kg). Span, 27 ft 10⅔ in (8,50 m). Length, 24 ft 3⅓ in (7,40 m). Height, 9 ft 6⅜ in (2,95 m). Wing area, 246.50 sq ft (22,90 m²).*

(Above) The Albatros D I prototype with vertical exhaust pipe and unbalanced elevator, and (below) the series D I which appeared at the Front in autumn 1916.

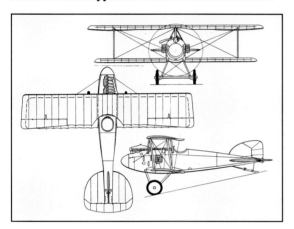

ALBATROS D II   Germany

(Above) A D II licence-built by LVG. The modestly staggered wing cellule is well shown by this photo.

One of the most serious design faults of the D I was the poor forward and upward fields of vision provided for the pilot, and to rectify this deficiency the upper wing was lowered and the wing cellule was staggered, reducing overall height by 14 in (36 cm). With this and other more minor changes, the fighter was redesignated D II, and an initial production batch of 100 was ordered in August 1916, arrangements being made for the D II to be licence-built by LVG (Luft-Verkehrs-Gesellschaft). It was also to be built by Oeffag (Oesterreichische Flugzeugfabrik) for the Austro-Hungarian *K.u.K. Luftfahrttruppen* with a 185 hp Austro-Daimler engine. The standard D II had the 160 hp Daimler D III and armament remained a pair of LMG 08/15 guns. Twenty-eight D IIs were at the Front in November 1916, and the strength of this type peaked in January 1917, when 214 were recorded at the Front. *Max speed, 109 mph (175 km/h). Time to 3,280 ft (1 000 m), 5.5 min. Endurance, 1.5 hrs. Empty weight, 1,404 lb (637 kg). Loaded weight, 1,958 lb (888 kg). Span, 27 ft 10⅔ in (8,50 m). Length, 24 ft 3⅓ in (7,40 m). Height, 8 ft 6 in (2,59 m). Wing area, 263.72 sq ft (24,50 m²).*

ALBATROS W 4   Germany

Ordered as a prototype in June 1916 and tested at Warnemünde in the following September, the W 4 single-seat fighter floatplane mated a D II fuselage with new wings and tail surfaces, the 160 hp Daimler D III engine being retained. The twin floats had to be redesigned and reinforced, and the transparent *Cellon* wing centre section panel featured by early production W 4s be-

(Above) A W 4 of the fourth production batch.

came brittle and tore in flight, necessitating replacement by fabric. From June 1917, the side radiators – which tended to boil over in hot weather – were replaced, and, with the sixth production batch commencing with the 68th series aircraft, ailerons were introduced also in the lower wing. With an armament of either one or two 7,92-mm guns, the W 4 operated over both the North Sea and the Baltic, and 128 (including the prototype) were built, the last of eight batches being ordered in August 1917 with deliveries being completed in the following December. As late as June 1918, 65 W 4s were still listed as active (24 more being with various seaplane stations as practice machines). *Max speed, 99 mph (160 km/h). Time to 3,280 ft (1 000 m), 6.5 min. Empty weight, 1,742 lb (790 kg). Loaded weight, 2,359 lb (1 070 kg). Span, 31 ft 2 in (9,50 m). Length, 27 ft 1¼ in (8,26 m). Height, 11 ft 11¾ in (3,65 m). Wing area, 340.15 sq ft (31,60 m²).*

A late production W 4 with wing-mounted radiator.

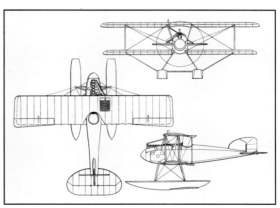

ALBATROS D III   Germany

Dipl-Ing Robert Thelen and Dipl-Ing Schubert, at the behest of the *Idflieg*, endeavoured to adapt the sesquiplane wing cellule utilised by Nieuport fighters to the

semi-monocoque fuselage and tail surfaces of the D II to produce the D III. Featuring the single-spar lower wing and Vee-strutted cellule *à la* Nieuport, the D III was powered by the 180 hp Mercedes D IIIa six-cylinder inline water-cooled engine and had twin synchronised LMG 08/15 7,92-mm guns. The prototype flown in August 1916, was, in fact, one of a batch of 12 D IIIs ordered during the previous June, 400 more being ordered by *Idflieg* from Albatros during October. The D III was issued to the *Jastas* from December 1916, and began to suffer recurrent wing failures, these resulting from the torsional flexibility of the lower wing (although this was not appreciated at the time). Albatros' OAW (Ostdeutsche Albatros-Werke) at Schneidemühl received orders for 840 D IIIs during April-August 1917, these featuring reinforced wings. The D III was also licence-built by Oeffag and fitted progressively with Austro-Daimler engines of 185, 200 and 225 hp, the first production examples with the highest-powered of these engines being accepted in May 1918, and some 220 being delivered to the Austro-Hungarian *K.u.K.Luftfahrttruppen* to the end of October 1918. After World War I, Poland procured 60 of the 200 hp Oeffag-

The D III with Vee-strutted wing cellule.

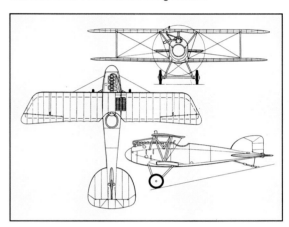

built D IIIs, some being flown with 7.*Eskadra Kosciuszkowska* between August 1920 and May 1921 by US volunteer pilots. The following data relate to the standard D III with the D IIIa engine boosted to 180 hp by means of an increase in compression ratio. *Max speed, 103 mph (165 km/h). Time to 3,280 ft (1 000 m), 3.75 min. Empty weight, 1,457 lb (661 kg). Loaded weight, 1,953 lb (886 kg). Span, 29 ft 8 in (9,04 m). Length, 24 ft 0⅝ in (7,33 m). Height, 9 ft 9¼ in (2,98 m). Wing area, 220.66 sq ft (20,50 m²).*

ALBATROS D IV   Germany

The D IV was developed essentially to test the geared version of the 160 hp Mercedes engine (this having reduced the 1,400 rpm of the engine crankshaft to 900 rpm at the propeller). It was based on the D II cellule, but substantially enlarged, and three D IVs were ordered in November 1916. It is believed that only one of these was completed and flown. It was tested with

An early ex-works Albatros D III (below) with the original centrally-located radiator.

The D IV featured a close-cowled, geared engine.

two-, three- and four-bladed propellers until April 1918, but excessive vibration led to the discontinuation of the programme. *Max speed, 103 mph (165 km/h). Endurance, 2.2 hrs. Span, 29 ft 8 in (9,04 m). Length, 24 ft 0⅝ in (7,33 m). Wing area, 220.66 sq ft (20,50 m²).*

ALBATROS D V   Germany

At the same time as the OAW received its first contract for the D III in April 1917, Albatros received an order from *Idflieg* for 200 D Vs, referred to as "lightened D IIIs". The D V retained the wings of the D III (although the aileron cables were led through the upper wing), was powered by the high-compression Mercedes D IIIa with oversize cylinders and offering 180 hp, and mounted twin 7,92-mm synchronised LMG 08/15 machine guns. The D V experienced a recurrence of the wing failures (previously suffered by the D III) as early as May 1917. Four hundred more D Vs were ordered, nevertheless, in May 1917 and 300 in July, after which the *Idflieg* terminated production in favour of the D Va which reverted to the D III-type aileron control cable arrangement and was reinforced throughout. The last Albatros fighter to see operational use in World War I, the D Va arrived at the Front in October 1917, by which time 1,612 fighters of this ver-

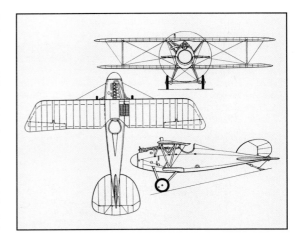

The D V (above) reached the Front in September 1917.

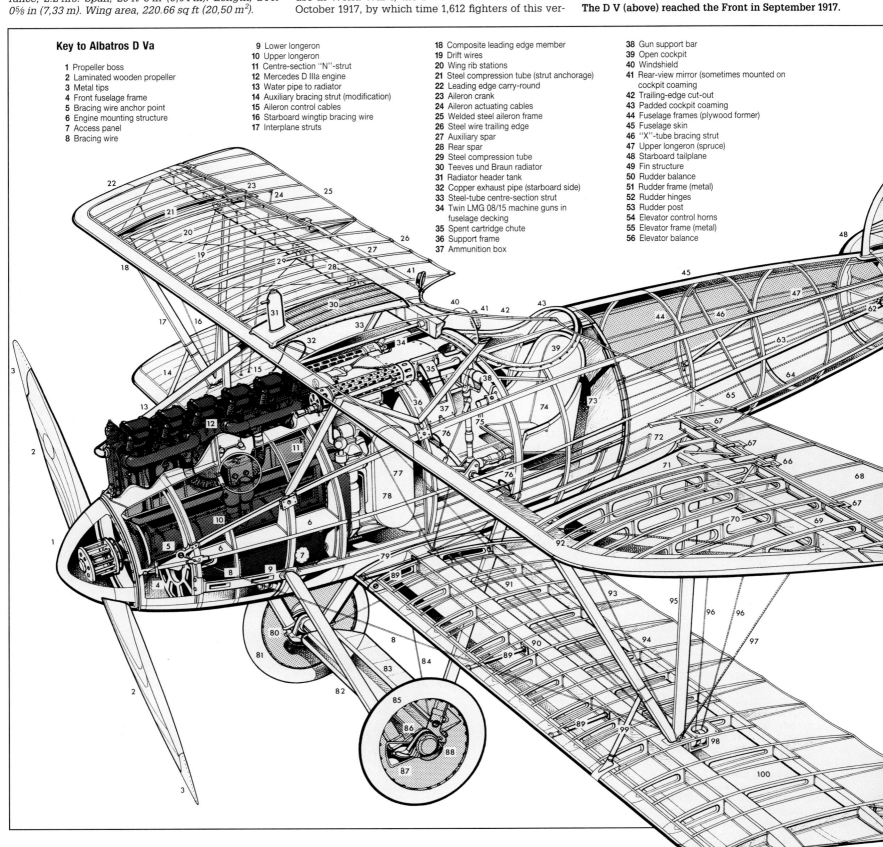

Key to Albatros D Va

1 Propeller boss
2 Laminated wooden propeller
3 Metal tips
4 Front fuselage frame
5 Bracing wire anchor point
6 Engine mounting structure
7 Access panel
8 Bracing wire
9 Lower longeron
10 Upper longeron
11 Centre-section "N"-strut
12 Mercedes D IIIa engine
13 Water pipe to radiator
14 Auxiliary bracing strut (modification)
15 Aileron control cables
16 Starboard wingtip bracing wire
17 Interplane struts
18 Composite leading edge member
19 Drift wires
20 Wing rib stations
21 Steel compression tube (strut anchorage)
22 Leading edge carry-round
23 Aileron crank
24 Aileron actuating cables
25 Welded steel aileron frame
26 Steel wire trailing edge
27 Auxiliary spar
28 Rear spar
29 Steel compression tube
30 Teeves und Braun radiator
31 Radiator header tank
32 Copper exhaust pipe (starboard side)
33 Steel-tube centre-section strut
34 Twin LMG 08/15 machine guns in fuselage decking
35 Spent cartridge chute
36 Support frame
37 Ammunition box
38 Gun support bar
39 Open cockpit
40 Windshield
41 Rear-view mirror (sometimes mounted on cockpit coaming)
42 Trailing-edge cut-out
43 Padded cockpit coaming
44 Fuselage frames (plywood former)
45 Fuselage skin
46 "X"-tube bracing strut
47 Upper longeron (spruce)
48 Starboard tailplane
49 Fin structure
50 Rudder balance
51 Rudder frame (metal)
52 Rudder hinges
53 Rudder post
54 Elevator control horns
55 Elevator frame (metal)
56 Elevator balance

The Albatros Dr I triplane (above) utilised a D V fuselage and was tested in the summer of 1917.

ALBATROS D VII Germany

Flown in August 1917, the D VII was powered by a 195 hp Benz Bz IIIb eight-cylinder water-cooled Vee

(Below) The Albatros D VII was tested with a Benz Bz IIIb eight-cylinder engine in the summer of 1917.

The Albatros D V above was flown by Vzfw Barth of Jasta 10 in the late autumn of 1917.

sion had been ordered. Service of the D Va peaked in May 1918 when there were 928 (plus 131 D Vs) in operational use. *Max speed, 115 mph (185 km/h). Time to 3,280 ft (1 000 m), 4.35 min. Endurance, 2.0 hrs. Empty weight, 1,515 lb (687 kg). Loaded weight, 2,066 lb (937 kg). Span, 29 ft 8 in (9,04 m). Length, 24 ft 0⅝ in (7,33 m). Height, 8 ft 10¼ in (2,70 m). Wing area, 228.19 sq ft (21,20 m²).*

ALBATROS D VI Germany

The D VI twin-boom single-seat pusher biplane powered by a 180 hp Daimler D IIIa engine was built during 1917, and was flown for the first time in February 1918. The undercarriage was damaged during the initial landing and had still to be repaired in May when further work on the D VI was suspended due to higher priority allocated to other projects. The engine was then removed for another application. Armament comprised a fixed forward-firing 20-mm Becker cannon and a 7,92-mm LMG 08/15 machine gun. *Empty weight, 1,406 lb (638 kg). Loaded weight, 1,940 lb (880 kg). Span, 32 ft 1⅞ in (9,80 m). Length, 25 ft 5⅛ in (7,75 m).*

ALBATROS Dr I Germany

The Dr I was essentially a D V fuselage, tail surfaces and undercarriage married to three pairs of wings, and flown in the summer of 1917 for comparison trials with the standard biplane. Powered by a Daimler D IIIa engine, the Dr I proved to offer no advantage over the D V, and progressed no further than prototype evaluation. Armament consisted of the usual pair of 7,92-mm machine guns. *Span, 28 ft 6½ in (8,70 m). Length, 24 ft 0⅝ in (7,33 m).*

engine. Strut-linked ailerons were carried by all wings and armament comprised two 7,92-mm machine guns. The characteristics of the D VII offered an insufficient advance to warrant development beyond prototype status. *Max speed, 127 mph (204 km/h). Time to 6,560 ft (2 000 m), 7 min. Endurance, 2 hrs. Empty weight, 1,389 lb (630kg). Loaded weight, 1,951 lb (885 kg). Span, 30 ft 6⅞ in (9,32 m). Length, 21 ft 8¼ in (6,61 m).*

ALBATROS D IX Germany

The D IX (above) introduced a slab-sided fuselage.

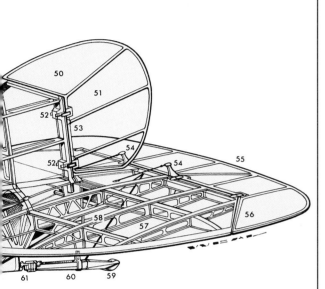

57 Tailplane structure (wooden framed)
58 Under-fin
59 Steel shoe
60 Ash tail-skid
61 Elastic cord shock-absorber
62 Tailplane stub attachment
63 Control cables (rudder)
64 Lower longeron (spruce)
65 Control cables (elevator)
66 Aileron crank
67 Wooden hinge blocks
68 Welded steel aileron frame
69 Rear spar
70 Plywood wing ribs
71 Strut anchorage
72 Entry step
73 Plywood bulkhead
74 Pilot's seat
75 Control column
76 Rudder pedals
77 Interplane bracing wires
78 Fuel tank
79 Wing stub
80 Starboard wheel
81 700 mm×100 mm tyre
82 Axle
83 Compression strut
84 Undercarriage bracing
85 Port tyre
86 Metal retaining strap
87 Access panel
88 Elastic cord shock-absorber
89 Forward section compression struts (3)
90 Wing spar
91 Aileron cables
92 Upper mainplane front spar
93 Interplane bracing wire
94 False rear spar (not anchored)
95 Interplane struts
96 Aileron control cables
97 Port wingtip bracing wire
98 Aileron control pulley housing
99 Auxiliary bracing strut (modification)
100 Lower wing structure

(Above, top) An Albatros D V of Jasta 5 with a Bavarian Lion motif, and (immediately above) a D V of Jasta 5's Jastaführer, Lt Wilhelm Lehmann.

Unlike previous Albatros fighters, the D IX featured a slab-sided, flat-bottomed fuselage. The wings were similar to those of the D VII, as were also the tail surfaces, power was provided by a 180 hp Daimler D IIIa engine, and armament consisted of the usual twin synchronised 7,92-mm LMG 08/15 machine guns. The sole prototype appeared early in 1918, but performance proved disappointing and development was discontinued. *Max speed, 96 mph (155 km/h). Time to 3,280 ft (1 000 m), 4 min. Endurance, 1.5 hrs. Empty weight, 1,492 lb (677 kg). Loaded weight, 1,977 lb (897 kg). Span 34 ft 1½ in (10,40 m). Length, 21 ft 9⅞in (6,65 m).*

ALBATROS D X   Germany

Developed in parallel with the D IX and possessing a similar slab-sided fuselage, the D X was powered by a 195 hp Benz Bz IIIbo eight-cylinder water-cooled engine, and participated in the second D-type Contest held at Adlershof in June 1918. Armament comprised the usual pair of machine guns. Development progressed no further than prototype trials. *Max speed, 106 mph (170 km/h). Endurance, 1.5 hrs. Empty weight, 1,468 lb (666 kg). Loaded weight, 1,995 lb (905 kg). Span, 32 ft 3⅓ in (9,84 m). Length, 20 ft 3⅓ in (6,18 m).*

A parallel development to the D IX, the D X (above) participated in the 2nd D-type Contest of June 1918.

ALBATROS Dr II   Germany

Built for comparison with the Albatros D X, the sole prototype of the Dr II is illustrated above.

The Dr II was, in effect, a triplane variant of the D X biplane with a similar 195 hp Benz Bz IIIbo engine. Ailerons were fitted to all wings, and these, of parallel chord and heavily staggered, were braced by broad I-struts. Armament consisted of two 7,92-mm machine guns, and the sole prototype of the Dr II was flown in the spring of 1918. *Empty weight, 1,490 lb (676 kg). Loaded weight, 2,017 lb (915 kg). Span, 32 ft 9⅔ in (10,00 m). Length, 20 ft 3⅓ in (6,18 m). Wing area, 286.32 sq ft (26,6 m²).*

ALBATROS D XI   Germany

Flown for the first time in February 1918, the D XI departed from the traditional Albatros formula in certain respects. Like its predecessors, it was of wooden

Seen here is the second prototype D XI, this fighter departing from the traditional Albatros formula.

construction with fabric-covered wings and plywood-covered fuselage, but the unequal-span staggered wings had inclined aerofoil-section I-struts braced from their bases by pairs of diagonal struts which eliminated the need for wire bracing. For the first time in an Albatros fighter a rotary engine was employed, this being a 160 hp Siemens-Halske Sh III, and the unusually large propeller necessitated an exceptionally tall undercarriage. Armament comprised the usual twin 7,92-mm machine guns, and two prototypes were built, the first having a four-blade propeller and balanced parallel-chord ailerons, and the second having a two-blade propeller and unbalanced ailerons of inverse taper. *Max speed, 118 mph (190 km/h). Time to 6,560 ft (2 000 m), 4.65 min. Endurance, 1.5 hrs. Empty weight, 1,089 lb (494 kg). Loaded weight, 1,519-1,594 lb (689-723 kg). Span, 26 ft 3 in (8,00 m). Length, 18 ft 3½ in (5,58 m). Wing area, 199.13 sq ft (18,5 m²).*

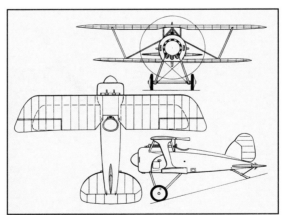

First rotary-engined Albatros, the D XI (above).

ALBATROS D XII   Germany

The last Albatros fighter of World War I actually completed and flown, the D XII featured the slab-sided plywood-covered fuselage introduced by the D X, and the first of two prototypes was flown in March 1918 with a

The D XII, the last World War I Albatros fighter.

180 hp Daimler D IIIa engine. The second prototype, fitted with a Bohme undercarriage embodying compressed-air shock absorbers, and unbalanced ailerons of inverse taper in place of the balanced parallel-chord ailerons of the first prototype, followed in April 1918, and was later fitted with a 185 hp BMW IIIa engine for participation in the third D-type contest of October. *Max speed (D IIIa), 112 mph (180 km/h). Endurance, 1 hr. Empty weight, 1,279 lb (580 kg). Loaded weight, 1,675lb (760 kg). Span, 26 ft 10¾ in (8,20 m). Length, 18 ft 11½ in (5,78 m). Wing area, 213.55 sq ft (19,84 m²).*

ALBATROS L 65 (MEMEL A.F.G.1) (Lithuania) Germany

In order to evade the restrictions on the development of military aircraft in Germany imposed by the Allied Control Commission, the Albatros Flugzeugwerke of Berlin–Johannisthal established a Lithuanian subsidiary in 1925 as the Allgemeine Flug-Gesellschaft (A.F.G.) Memel. Its first production was a two-seat reconnaissance fighter referred to as the A.F.G.1, but, in fact, an Albatros design, the L 65. A single-bay staggered biplane with aerofoil-section broad I-type interplane struts, the L 65 alias A.F.G.1 was of wooden construction with plywood skinning, the first prototype

The Albatros L 65 alias A.F.G.1 (above) was built in Lithuania to evade restrictions on Germany.

being powered by a 450 hp Napier Lion 12-cylinder "broad arrow" water-cooled engine. A second prototype, the L 65-II flown in 1926, was powered by a 565 hp Lion and was evaluated by the *Reichswehr*, but no series production was undertaken. *Max speed, 155 mph (250 km/h) at sea level. Ceiling, 26,245 ft (8 000 m). Span, 33 ft 9½ in (10,30m). Length, 20 ft 2⅛ in (6,15 m). Height, 9 ft 2¼ in (2,80 m).*

ALBATROS L 77v   Germany

In late 1928, the Albatros Flugzeugwerke at Johannisthal accepted from the Ernst Heinkel Flugzeugwerke four L 77v tandem two-seat fighter and reconnaissance aircraft that had been built by the latter under Albatros licence. Developed to a *Reichswehr* contract, the L 77v was a derivative of the L 76 Aeolus trainer and reconnaissance two-seater of 1926 which saw extensive use at the clandestine German flying training school at Lipezk in the Soviet Union. Possessing an airframe essentially similar to that of the L 76, with two-spar wooden wings primarily plywood covered, N-type interplane struts and a fabric-covered, welded steel-tube fuselage, the L 77v was powered by a 600 hp BMW VI 5,5 water-cooled 12-cylinder Vee-type engine. Armament comprised two fixed forward-firing 7,9-mm machine guns and a similar weapon on a ring mounting in the rear cockpit. One of the L 77v aircraft was destroyed while under test in March 1929, the remaining three being assigned to Lipezk for armament trials, one being tested with a free-mounted 20-mm cannon. From December 1929, these aircraft were flown from the *Erprobungsstelle*, or Test Centre, at Staaken, and were retired in October 1931. *Max speed, 137 mph (220 km/h) at 4,920 ft (1 500 m). Endurance, 2.2 hrs. Empty weight, 3,796 lb (1 722 kg). Loaded weight, 5,688 lb (2 580 kg). Span, 41 ft 10⅓ in (12,76 m).*

The L 77v (above and below) was developed for the *Reichswehr* and saw some limited service at Lipezk.

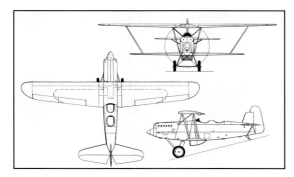

ALBATROS L 84   Germany

When, in 1931, economic circumstances dictated amalgamation of the Albatros Flugzeugwerke with the Focke-Wulf Flugzeugbau, flight testing had just commenced of a new tandem two-seat fighter, the L 84 powered by a 660 hp BMW VIu 7,3Z water-cooled 12-cylinder Vee-type engine. A single-bay biplane with V-type interplane struts, the L 84 had plywood-covered wooden wings and a welded steel-tube fuselage primarily fabric covered. Armament consisted of two fixed forward-firing 7,9-mm machine guns and a similar weapon on an aft ring mounting. The first prototype was destroyed during flight testing, but a second prototype was completed by Focke-Wulf and flown in February 1933, this being referred to as the L 84C and featuring a revised cooling system. Twelve L 84 fighters were ordered from Focke-Wulf by the *Reichswehr*, but, in the event, only three were completed, the remainder being cancelled. One was used under the designation L 84E to evaluate the Rolls-Royce Kestrel IIIS engine, and another, fitted with a fuel-injection version

(Below) The first prototype of the L 84 two-seat fighter in its initial form.

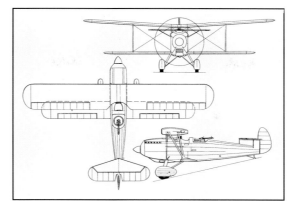

The L 84, only three series aircraft being built.

sion of the BMW VIu engine, was known as the L 84F. At least one L 84 was supplied to China. No specification for the L 84 is available apart from a normal loaded weight of 4,740 lb (2 150 kg).

ALCOCK A.1   UK

Evolved at the RNAS base at Mudros, in the Aegean, by Lt John Alcock during the summer of 1917, the A.1 employed modified components of the Sopwith Triplane (forward fuselage and lower wings), Sopwith Pup (upper wings), and Sopwith Camel (tailplane and elevators) which were married to a rear fuselage and vertical tail surfaces of original design. Powered by a 110 hp Clerget 9Z nine-cylinder rotary engine and carrying a 0.303-in (7,7-mm) Vickers machine gun, the A.1 (which was also referred to by its designers as the "Sopwith Mouse" in recognition of its part parentage) flew at Mudros in October 1917, but was written off after crashing early in 1918. *Approx span, 24 ft 3 in (7,39 m). Approx length, 19 ft 1 in (5,82 m). Approx height, 7 ft 9 in (2,36 m).*

The Alcock A.1 (above) was largely a melange of Sopwith Triplane, Pup and Camel components.

ALEKSEEV I-211   USSR

Having worked during World War II in the S A Lavochkin OKB, Semyon M Alekseev established his own OKB in September 1946, and initiated the design of a single-seat fighter powered by two 3,010 lb st (1 365 kgp) Lyulka TR-1 axial-flow turbojets. Designated I-211, the first prototype made its initial flight in the autumn of

(Below) The Alekseev I-211 was a Soviet first-generation jet fighter prototype.

1947, but the TR-1 turbojets were developing only 70 per cent power. An initial series of six flights revealed that the fighter handled satisfactorily, but was seriously underpowered. The proposed armament comprised three 37-mm or two 57-mm cannon, but these were not installed pending the availability of TR-1A turbojets, which, to be fitted to the second prototype, theoretically offered 3,318 lb st (1 505 kgp) each. The TR-1A had not been cleared for flight testing by the time Alekseev's OKB was assigned a pair of Rolls-Royce Derwent centrifugal-flow turbojets imported from the UK. The second prototype I-211 was duly modified to take the Derwent engines as the I-215 (which see). Discontinuation of the TR-1A turbojet led to abandonment of the I-211 in favour of the I-215. The following data are OKB estimates based on fully-rated TR-1 engines. *Max speed, 581 mph (935 km/h) at sea level, 565 mph (910 km/h) at 13,125 ft (4 000 m). Time to 16,405 ft (5 000 m), 3.0 min. Range, 963 mls (1 550 km). Empty weight, 9,612 lb (4 360 kg). Loaded weight, 16,424 lb (7 450 kg). Span, 40 ft 2¼ in (12,25 m). Length, 37 ft 10⅓ in (11,54 m). Height, 12 ft 0⅞ in (3,68 m). Wing area, 269.1 sq ft (25,00 m²).*

The I-211 (above) proved seriously underpowered.

ALEKSEEV I-215   USSR

Semyon Alekseev's OKB encountered little difficulty in adapting the basic I-211 to take a Rolls-Royce Derwent centrifugal-flow engine in place of the axial-flow Lyulka TR-1. Owing to the centrally-mounted wing nacelles of the fighter, it proved possible to mount the larger-diameter compressor of the British engine forward of the wing leading edge. Thus, apart from some structural redesign associated with and adjacent to the wing nacelles, the I-215, as the Derwent-engined aircraft was designated, was virtually identical with the I-211, and the first flight took place on 31 December

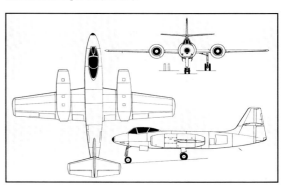

The Derwent-powered I-215 (above) began life as the second prototype of the Alekseev I-211 fighter.

1947. The Derwent turbojets were rated at 3,504 lb st (1 590 kgp) each, rectifying the power inadequacy of the earlier fighter, but the wing centre section structure began to display fatigue cracking early in the test programme. Strengthening of the centre section dictated transfer of the twin-wheel main undercarriage units from wing wells to the fuselage, a second prototype, the I-215D (the suffix indicating *dubler*), being completed with a bicycle arrangement of larger-diameter paired wheels retracting into the fuselage fore and aft of the main fuel tanks, with small outriggers retracting into fairings beneath the engine nacelles. The I-215D was flown in the spring of 1948. Tests resulted in a recommendation by the Ministry of the Aviation Industry that series production be undertaken. A tandem two-seat night fighter version of the same basic design, the I-212 powered by two 5,004 lb st (2 270 kgp) Rolls-Royce Nene turbojets and having a larger wing, was being readied for flight testing at this time. However, Aleksandr Yakovlev's comment during a Kremlin meeting to the effect that the I-212 was "another copy of the Me 262" may be presumed to have influenced Yosif Stalin in his decision to disband the Alekseev OKB without flight testing the I-212, and, as a consequence, terminating the I-215. The following data relate to the first prototype I-215. *Max speed, 603 mph (970 km/h) at sea level, 596 mph (960 km/h) at 19,685 ft (6 000 m). Time to 16,405 ft (5 000 m), 2.8 min. Normal range, 1,056 mls (1 700 km). Empty weight, 8,840 lb (4 010 kg). Loaded weight, 15,190 lb (6 890 kg). Dimensions as for I-211.*

ALTER A.1 — Germany

Conceptually adhering closely to the Nie 11 *Bébé* if not an outright copy of the French design, the A.1 single-seat fighter, designed by Kallweit and Ketterer and built by the Ludwig Alter-Werke of Darmstadt, was first flown in February 1917 by Georg Sell. A single-bay sesquiplane with I-type interplane struts, the A.1 was of wooden construction with fabric and plywood covering. Armament consisted of two synchronised 7,92-mm LMG 08/15 machine guns and power was provided by a 110 hp Goebel Goe II seven-cylinder rotary engine. The A.1 was demonstrated to the *Idflieg* (*Inspektion der Fliegertruppe*), but the type was rejected, performance being considered inadequate and the structure being

The Alter A.1 followed closely the design of the Nieuport Bébé, but offered inadequate performance.

viewed as insufficiently robust, further development being discontinued. *Max speed, 110 mph (177 km/h). Time to 9,840 ft (3 000 m), 12.8 min. Loaded weight, 1,124 lb (510 kg).*

AMIOT-S.E.C.M. 110 — France

Flown for the first time in June 1928, the Type 110 was designed by M Dutartre as a contender in the so-called "Jockey" lightweight interceptor contest in which it competed against nine other types. Two prototypes were built, these being of all-metal construction and powered by the 500 hp Hispano-Suiza 12Mb 12-cylinder liquid-cooled engine, the first prototype having fabric and the second metal wing skinning. Basically a parasol monoplane, the Type 110 was fitted with a jettisonable aerofoil-section fuel tank inserted in the fuselage aft of the main undercarriage members in the form of stub wings. Armament comprised two Vickers guns. On 1 July 1929, the first prototype was destroyed in an accident and no further development was undertaken.

The Amiot-S.E.C.M. 110 (above and below) was one of 10 contenders in the so-called "Jockey" lightweight fighter contest of the late 'twenties.

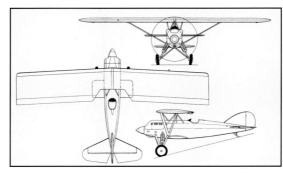

Max speed, 184 mph (296 km/h). Range, 310 mls (500 km). Time to 13,125 ft (4 000 m), 6 min. Empty weight, 2,469 lb (1 120 kg). Loaded weight, 3,307 lb (1 500 kg). Span, 34 ft 5⅓ in (10,50 m). Length, 21 ft 4 in (6,50 m). Height, 9 ft 2¼ in (2,83 m). Wing area, 226.05 sq ft (21,00 m²).

ANATRA ANADIS — Russia

In the spring of 1916, the chief engineer of the Anatra company of Odessa, a French designer named Elisée Alfred Descamps, was ordered to build a single-seat fighter based on the Anasal (also known as the Anatra DS) two-seat reconnaissance biplane. Retaining the Anasal's two-bay configuration and fabric-covered wooden construction, the fighter, dubbed the Anadis, differed only in having the rear cockpit deleted, provision made for forward-firing armament and the unusual 150 hp Salmson 9U (Canton-Unné) *water*-cooled radial replaced by a similarly-rated Hispano-Suiza Vee-eight water-cooled engine. The prototype Anadis was flown on 23 October 1916 by the factory test pilot, another Frenchman, Jean Robinet. He and Descamps then planned to modify the Anadis as a two-seater and fit it with extra tankage for their use in escaping Russia in the event that the threatened revolution took place. This plan was discovered and exposed by one Lt Kononenko, an Imperial Army acceptance pilot attached to Anatra, flight testing consequently continuing as a single-seater. Trials continued until 11 November, the official report to the Imperial Army stating that it was ". . . not inferior to any German aircraft of the same type (*sic*) and with greater power." Nevertheless, no further examples were ordered and the prototype languished at the Odessa factory until 14 October 1917, when, piloted by Staff Capt N A Makarov, it took-off for a flight Odessa-Salonika-Rome-Marseilles-Paris and back to Russia. Unfortunately, the Anadis suffered engine failure near Iasi, Romania, and was written-off as a result of the ensuing forced landing. No photograph of the Anadis is known to have survived. *Max speed, 95 mph (153 km/h). Time to 3,280 ft (1 000 m), 7.5 min. Empty weight, 1,466 lb (665 kg). Loaded weight, 2,568 lb (1 165 kg). Span, 37 ft 4⅘ in (11,40 m). Length, 25 ft 5¹⁄₁₀ in (7,75 m). Wing area, 398.27 sq ft (37,00 m²).*

ANF-MUREAUX 114 — France

In 1930, the Ateliers des Mureaux amalgamated with the Ateliers de Construction du Nord de la France (ANF), and the first aircraft to appear after the amalgamation were the Mureaux 110 and 111 designed by André Brunet to participate in the two-seat reconnaissance aircraft programme initiated in 1928. The first of these all-metal parasol monoplanes was flown in April 1931, the initial production derivative being the Mureaux 113. Two early production airframes were completed during the summer of 1933 as two-seat night fighters under the designation Mureaux 114, these differing from the Mureaux 113 primarily in being equipped with searchlights. Powered by a 650 hp Hispano-Suiza 12 Ybrs 12-cylinder liquid-cooled engine, the Mureaux 114 carried an armament of two fixed forward-firing 7,7-mm MAC machine guns in the fuselage and two Lewis guns on a flexible mounting in the rear cockpit. *Max speed, 194 mph (312 km/h) at 16,405 ft (5 000 m). Climb to 16,405 ft (5 000 m), 8.9 min. Range, 572 mls (920 km). Empty weight, 3,704 lb (1 680 kg). Loaded weight, 5,644 lb (2 560 kg). Span, 50 ft 6⅓ in (15,40 m). Length, 32 ft 11⅔ in (10,05 m). Height, 12 ft 6 in (3,81 m). Wing area, 375.67 sq ft (34,90 m²).*

The Mureaux 114 two-seat night fighter was fundamentally similar to the reconnaissance Type 113.

ANF-MUREAUX 170 — France

Designed to meet the requirements of the 1930 single-seat fighter programme which specified the use of a supercharged engine and a maximum speed of at least 217 mph (350 km/h), the Mureaux 170 was powered by a 690 hp Hispano-Suiza 12 Xbrs 12-cylinder liquid-

The Mureaux 170 offered a poor view for landing.

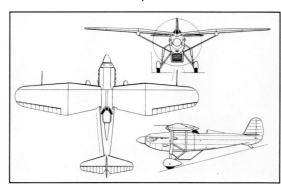

(Above) The first of two prototypes of the Mureaux 170 which competed in the 1930 fighter programme.

The Mureaux 190 (above) conformed with the French mid 'thirties vogue for lightweight fighters.

cooled engine and carried an armament of two 7,7-mm MAC (Vickers) machine guns in the wings. Of all-metal construction, the Mureaux 170 was first flown in November 1932, a second prototype, built as a private venture, flying in March 1934. Several changes were made to the size and positioning of the radiator bath, and the fighter was rejected primarily because of the poor visibility from the cockpit for landing. *Max speed, 236 mph (380 km/h) at 14,765 ft (4 500 m). Climb to 32,810 ft (10 000 m), 23.4 min. Empty weight, 2,643 lb (1 199 kg). Loaded weight, 3,682 lb (1 670 kg). Span, 37 ft 4 in (11,38 m). Length, 25 ft 11 in (7,90 m). Height, 9 ft 10⅛ in (3,00 m). Wing area, 210.54 sq ft (19,56 m².)*

ANF-MUREAUX 180   France

Essentially a two-seat derivative of the Mureaux 170, the Mureaux 180 employed a similar all-metal structure, but a frontal radiator was provided for the 690 hp Hispano-Suiza 12 Xbrs engine. The sole prototype was first flown on 10 February 1935, but in April the original single fin-and-rudder assembly was replaced by twin fins and rudders, and an HS 12 Xcrs engine with provision for a 20-mm Hispano-Suiza cannon firing through the propeller shaft was installed, engine output being unchanged. Proposed armament comprised one 20-mm engine-mounted cannon, two wing-mounted 7,7-mm MAC machine guns and one 7,7-mm gun on a flexible mounting in the rear cockpit. The following figures relate to the Mureaux 180 in its final form. *Max speed, 235 mph (379 km/h) at 16,405 ft (5 000 m). Climb to 21,325 ft (6 500 m), 7.5 min. Range, 466 mls (750 km). Empty weight, 2,791 lb (1 266 kg). Loaded weight,*

The Mureaux 180 is illustrated (below) in the form in which it originally flew and (above) with the later twin-fin-and-rudder tail assembly.

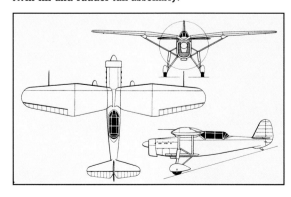

4,306 lb (1 953 kg). Span, 37 ft 4¾ in (11,40 m). Length, 25 ft 8¼ in (7,83 m). Height, 10 ft 8⅜ in (3,26 m). Wing area, 210.54 sq ft (19,56 m²).

ANF-MUREAUX 190   France

Designed by André Brunet, the Mureaux 190 lightweight single-seat fighter was of all-metal construction

and powered by a Salmson 12 Vars 12-cylinder inverted-Vee air-cooled engine of 450 hp. Proposed armament comprised an engine-mounted 20-mm cannon and two wing-mounted 7,7-mm machine guns. The prototype Mureaux 190 was flown for the first time in July 1936, but tests were abandoned in 1937 because of the poor reliability of the Salmson engine, and a projected development with a retractable undercarriage, the Mureaux 191, was dropped. *Max speed, 311 mph (500 km/h) at 13,125 ft (4 000 m), 267 mph (430 km/h) at sea level. Endurance, 2.5 hrs. Empty weight, 1,874 lb (850 kg). Loaded weight, 2,844 lb (1 290 kg). Span, 27 ft 6 in (8,38 m). Length, 23 ft 7½ in (7,20 m). Height, 9 ft 10⅛ in (3,00 m). Wing area, 107.64 sq ft (10,00 m²).*

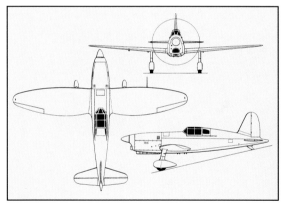

The Mureaux 190 suffered poor engine reliability.

ANSALDO S.V.A.   Italy

In the summer of 1916, *Ingegneri* Umberto Savoia and Rodolfo Verduzio of the *Direzione Tecnica dell' Aeronautica Militare* (Technical Directorate of Military Aviation), together with *Ingegner* Celestino Rosatelli, began designing a single-seat fighter around the 205 hp SPA 6A six-cylinder water-cooled engine. The task of supervising the development and production of the fighter was assigned to the *Società Ansaldo*, and thus the prototype, first flown on 19 March 1917, was

(Below) The original S.V.A. fighter prototype which entered flight test in March 1917.

designated S.V.A. (Savoia-Verduzio-Ansaldo). The S.V.A. was a conventional biplane of wooden construction with interplane bracing of the Warren truss type and an armament of two synchronised 7,7-mm Vickers machine guns. It displayed exceptional speed but, inherently stable, was considered to lack the manoeuvrability demanded for fighter-versus-fighter combat. However, its excellent range rendered it suitable for the reconnaissance fighter rôle, and the *Aviazione Militare* decided to adopt the S.V.A. for this task. Deliveries of the initial production version, the S.V.A.2, had meanwhile commenced in the autumn of 1917, 65 being built by the year's end and this model being assigned to training. *Max speed, 137 mph (220 km/h). Time to 9,840 ft (3 000 m), 11.35 min. Endurance, 3 hrs. Empty weight, 1,477 lb (670 kg). Loaded weight, 2,100 lb (952 kg). Span, 29 ft 10¼ in (9,10 m). Length, 26 ft 6⅞ in (8,10 m). Height, 8 ft 8⅓ in (2,65 m). Wing area, 260.49 sq ft (24,2 m²).*

ANSALDO S.V.A.3   Italy

Built under licence by the AER concern at Orbassano, the S.V.A.3 was a reconnaissance fighter production

(Above and below) The S.V.A.3 is illustrated here in its *ridotto* (reduced) span version which was used primarily for airship interception in 1918.

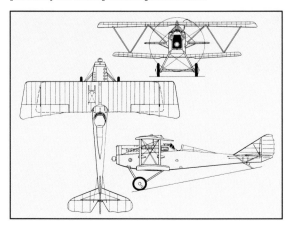

derivative of the S.V.A. fighter, and essentially similar to the S.V.A.4 built in parallel by the Ansaldo factories at Borzoli and Bolzaneto. In the spring of 1918 a special interceptor version was produced, this having wings of reduced span and area. Known as the S.V.A.3 *ridotto* (reduced), this model was used primarily for airship interception, and although standard armament remained two synchronised 7,7-mm Vickers guns, some examples were fitted with an additional weapon firing upwards at an oblique angle. Power was provided by an SPA 6A engine of 220 hp. *Max speed, 149 mph (240 km/h). Time to 13,125 ft (4 000 m), 13 min. Endurance, 3 hrs. Empty weight, 1,470 lb (667 kg). Loaded weight, 1,965 lb (891 kg). Span, 25 ft 5⅛ in (7,75 m). Length, 26 ft 6⅞ in (8.10 m). Height, 8 ft 8⅓ in (2,65 m). Wing area, 236.8 sq ft (22,0 m²),*

ANSALDO S.V.A.4   Italy

The S.V.A.4 was the first reconnaissance fighter development of the S.V.A. to be built in substantial quantities. It did not demand an escort in performing reconnaissance missions as it could accept combat with fighters on reasonably equal terms, and break off combat at will by utilising its high speed. It was powered by

Evolved as a reconnaissance fighter, the S.V.A.4 (above) entered service early in 1918.

a 205 hp SPA 6A six-cylinder water-cooled engine, and normally carried two synchronised 7,7-mm Vickers guns, although the starboard gun was sometimes removed when a reconnaissance camera was carried. The S.V.A.4 entered service with the *Aviazione Militare* early in 1918. *Max speed, 134 mph (216 km/h). Time to 9,840 ft (3 000m), 12 min. Max endurance, 3.6 hrs. Empty weight, 1,545 lb (701 kg). Loaded weight, 2,150 lb (975 kg). Span, 29 ft 10¼ in (9,10 m). Length, 26 ft 6⅞ in (8,10 m). Height, 8 ft 8⅓ in (2,65 m). Wing area, 260.49 sq ft (24,20 m²).*

ANSALDO S.V.A.5   Italy

Built in larger numbers than any other single-seat derivative of the S.V.A., the S.V.A.5 was a reconnaissance-fighter-bomber armed with two 7,7-mm synchronised Vickers machine guns and carrying two reconnaissance cameras or light bombs slung on the fuselage sides on special clips. Initial production examples were powered by the 205 hp SPA 6A engine, but later examples had the higher compression version of that engine rated at 230hp. Some S.V.A.5s were fitted with the 250 hp Isotta-Fraschini V6 engine with which a maximum speed of 149 mph (240 km/h) was attainable. The majority of the 1,248 S.V.A. aircraft built during 1917-18 were S.V.A.5s. *Max speed,· 143 mph (230 km/h). Time to 9,840 ft (3 000 m), 10 min. Normal endurance, 3 hrs. Empty weight, 1,500 lb (680 kg). Loaded weight, 2,315 lb (1 050 kg). Span, 29 ft 10¼ in*

The S.V.A.5 (below) was a multi-rôle aircraft.

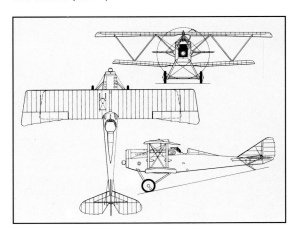

The S.V.A.5 (above) was built in larger numbers than any other Savoia-Verduzio-Ansaldo fighter.

(9,10 m). Length, 26ft 6⅞ in (8,10 m). Height, 8 ft 8⅓ in (2,65 m). Wing area, 260.49 sq ft (24,20 m²).

ANSALDO I.S.V.A.   Italy

A single-seat float fighter version of the S.V.A., the I.S.V.A. (the ''I'' prefix indicating *Idro* or water) was built at La Spezia in 1918. Power was provided by a 205 hp SPA 6A engine and armament consisted of two synchronised 7,7-mm Vickers machine guns. A total of 50 I.S.V.A. fighters was manufactured and these aircraft were used both for the defence of naval bases and coastal reconnaissance. *Max speed, 121 mph (195 km/h) at sea level, 112 mph (180 km/h) at 6,560 ft (2 000 m). Endurance, 3 hrs. Empty weight, 1,936 lb (878 kg). Loaded weight, 2,425 lb (1 100 kg). Span, 29 ft 10¼ in (9,10 m). Length, 30 ft 6⅛ in (9,30 m). Height, 12 ft 1⅔ in (3,70 m). Wing area, 263.72 sq ft (24,5 m²).*

The I.S.V.A. float fighter (above) was used for the defence of naval bases and coastal reconnaissance.

ANSALDO A.1 BALILLA   Italy

Owing much to the S.V.A., the A.1 Balilla (Hunter) single-seat fighter was flown for the first time in the autumn of 1917, but, lacking the agility of its contemporaries, it was manufactured in only limited quantiies, a total of 166 Balillas being built in 1918. These

The Ansaldo A.1 Balilla (below) was built in limited numbers and confined largely to home defence.

were confined to home defence tasks, and 75 were supplied to Poland in 1920-1, a further 50 being licence-built by Plage & Laśkiewicz. The Balilla was of wooden construction and carried an armament of two synchronised 7,7-mm Vickers guns. The power plant was either the 205 hp SPA 6A or the 220 hp higher compression version of that engine, while the A.1*bis* was fitted with the 250 hp Isotta-Fraschini V6. The following details apply to the 220 hp A.1. *Max speed, 137 mph (220 km/h) at sea level. Time to 9,840 ft (3 000 m), 8.5 min. Endurance, 2.5 hrs. Empty weight, 1,411 lb (640 kg). Loaded weight, 1,951 lb (885 kg). Span, 25 ft 2⅓ in (7,68 m). Length, 21 ft 3⅞ in (6,50 m). Height, 9 ft 4¼ in (2,85 m). Wing area, 226.05 sq ft (21,00 m²).*

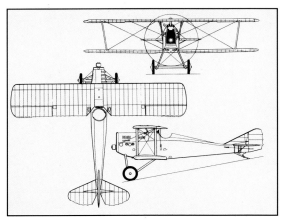

The A.1 Balilla (above) was licence-built in Poland.

ANSALDO A.C.2   Italy

In 1924, Aeronautica Ansaldo SA acquired manufacturing rights in the Dewoitine D.1 single-seat fighter, assembling one example as the A.C.1. This served as a basis for a modified version of the fighter with marginally smaller overall dimensions which entered production as the A.C.2 in 1925. Powered by a 300 hp Hispano-Suiza HS 42-8 eight-cylinder water-cooled engine and carrying an armament of two synchronised 7,7-mm Vickers guns, the A.C.2 was of metal construction and

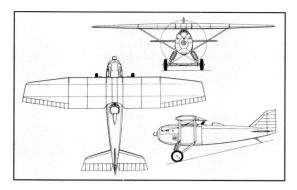

The A.C.2 (above) was a modified Dewoitine D.1.

112 examples were delivered to the *Regia Aeronautica* during 1925. *Max speed, 150 mph (242 km/h) at sea level. Time to 3,280 ft (1 000 m), 2.15 min, to 9,840 ft (3 000 m) 8.15 min. Endurance, 2.6 hrs. Empty weight, 1,828 lb (829 kg). Loaded weight, 2,522 lb (1 144 kg). Span, 35 ft 8⅓ in (10,88 m). Length, 24 ft 2½ in (7,38 m). Height, 9 ft 1⅞ in (2,79 m). Wing area, 215.28 sq ft (20,00 m²).*

Evolved from the Dewoitine D.1, the A.C.2 (above) for the *Regia Aeronautica* was dimensionally smaller.

ANSALDO A.C.3   Italy

Based on the Dewoitine D.9, the A.C.3 differed primarily in having slightly increased wing span and area, and a marginally reduced overall length. Powered by a 420 hp Gnome-Rhône Jupiter IV nine-cylinder radial, the prototype was flown early in 1926, and a total of 150 A.C.3s was delivered between September 1926 and April 1927. Armament normally comprised two fuselage-mounted and two wing-mounted 7,62-mm Darne machine guns, but the latter were sometimes replaced by a single gun above the wing centre section mounted to fire upward at an oblique angle. During the 'thirties, the A.C.3s were employed in the assault rôle and were finally phased out in the summer of 1938. *Max speed, 153 mph (247 km/h) at sea level. Time to 3,280 ft (1 000 m), 1.7 min, to 9,840 ft (3,000 m), 6.2 min. Endurance, 2.83 hrs. Empty weight, 2,114 lb (959 kg). Loaded weight, 2,981 lb (1 352 kg). Span, 41 ft 11⅞ in (12,80 m). Length, 23 ft 10⅔ in (7,28 m). Height, 9 ft 7⅓ in (2,93 m). Wing area, 269.1 sq ft (25,00 m²).*

During the 'thirties, the A.C.3 fighter (below) was given the assault rôle until phased out in 1938.

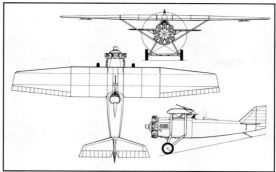

The A.C.3 (above) was based on the Dewoitine D.9.

ANSALDO A.C.4   Italy

The A.C.4 was a direct development of the A.C.2 from which it differed primarily in having a 410 hp Fiat A.20 engine. Possessing a similar armament to the earlier fighter, the A.C.4 was flown in 1927, but only one prototype was built. *Max speed, 157 mph (253 km/h) at sea*

The A.C.4 (above) was derived from the A.C.2, but failed to progress further than prototype stage.

level. Time to 3,280 ft (1 000 m), 2.2 min, to 9,840 ft (3 000 m), 7.65 min. Endurance, 2.33 hrs. Empty weight, 2,227 lb (1 010 kg). Loaded weight, 2,879 lb (1 306 kg). Span, 35 ft 8⅓ in (10,88 m). Length, 24 ft 2½ in (7,38 m). Height, 9 ft 1⅞ in (2,79 m). Wing area, 215.28 sq ft (20,00 m²).

ARADO SD I   Germany

Of relatively advanced concept and the first fighter to be built by the Arado Handelsgesellschaft of Warnemünde, the SD I was designed by Ing Walter Rethel and owed much to experience gained with Fokker. Of comparatively small overall dimensions, the SD I was a single-seat sesquiplane of mixed construction. The fuselage was of welded steel tubing with light alloy skinning to the cockpit firewall and fabric aft. The wings were wooden with plywood skinning, featuring ailerons in the upper wing only, the cellule having V-type interplane struts and lacking conventional flying wires. The SD I was powered by a 425 hp nine-cylinder Gnome-Rhône Jupiter air-cooled radial and armament comprised two synchronised 7,9-mm 08/15 machine guns. The first fighter design to be the subject

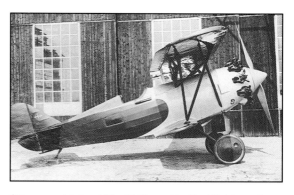

(Above and below) The SD I was the first fighter to be built by Arado and owed much to the experience gained by its designer while working with Fokker.

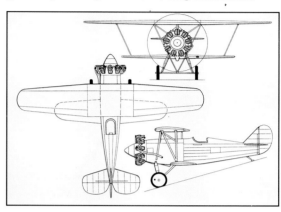

of a contract from the *Reichswehrministerium*, the SD I was built clandestinely, the first of two prototypes flying on 11 October 1927. Evaluation revealed poor low-speed handling characteristics, and, as it was considered to be structurally unsound by the RWM, its development was discontinued in favour of an entirely new design, the SD II. *Max speed, 171 mph (275 km/h) at 16,405 ft (5 000 m), 152 mph (245 km/h) at sea level. Empty weight, 1,874 lb (850 kg). Loaded weight, 2,712 lb (1 230 kg). Span, 27 ft 6¾ in (8,40 m). Length, 22 ft 1¾ in (6,75 m).*

ARADO SD II   Germany

Larger and substantially heavier than the preceding SD I, and utilising a more conventional unequal-span biplane wing cellule with N-type interplane struts and flying wires, the SD II was designed by Ing Walter Rethel and a sole prototype was completed in 1929 as a competitor for the HD 37, a second airframe becoming the SD III. Of mixed construction, with fabric-covered wooden wings and a welded steel-tube fuselage, the

The SD II (above) initiated the line of fighter development that was to lead, in 1930, to the Ar 64.

SD II was powered by a geared Siemens und Halske-built Jupiter VI nine-cylinder radial, which, with a maximum rating of 530 hp, drove a large-diameter, slow-running three-bladed propeller requiring a high angle of attack on the ground. Armament remained two 7,9-mm synchronised 08/15 machine guns. The SD II demonstrated rather difficult flying characteristics, but, together with the SD III, provided a basis for the series-production Ar 64. *Max speed, 146 mph (235 km/h) at 16,405 ft (5 000 m), 138 mph (222 km/h) at* sea level. *Empty weight, 3,186 lb (1 445 kg). Loaded weight, 3,902 lb (1 770 kg). Span, 32 ft 5¾ in (9,90 m). Length, 24 ft 4⅓ in (7,40 m). Wing area, 247.58 sq ft (23,00 m²).*

ARADO SD III   Germany

Built in parallel with the SD II, the SD III employed a basically similar airframe, but replaced the geared engine with a direct-drive Siemens und Halske-built Jupiter VI with a maximum output of 510 hp and a smaller-diameter two-bladed propeller. The contours of the forward fuselage were revised and a shorter undercarriage with increased rake was fitted. Armament was identical to that of the SD II, and the SD III similarly served as a development aircraft for the Ar 64 fighter. *Max speed, 140 mph (225 km/h) at 13,125 ft (4 000 m), 132 mph (212 km/h) at sea level. Span, 32 ft 5¾ in (9,90 m). Length, 25 ft 5⅛ in (7,75 m). Wing area, 247.58 sq ft (23,00 m²).*

(Above and below) The SD III was to lead directly to the first production fighter of Arado design, the Ar 64, and was basically similar to the SD II.

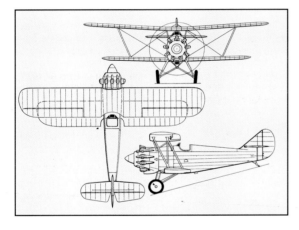

ARADO SSD I   Germany

Built in 1930 as a catapultable single-seat float fighter, the SSD I possessed no commonality with other Arado fighters of the period. A single-bay equi-span biplane with plywood-covered wooden wings with N-type interplane struts, and, unlike preceding fighter aircraft from the Warnemünde-based company, ailerons in both upper and lower wings, the SSD I was powered by a 640 hp BMW VI 6,3 12-cylinder Vee-type water-cooled engine. The upper wing was gulled into the top decking of the welded steel-tube fuselage ahead of the cockpit and the lower wing was suspended below the fuselage, the gap being occupied by the tunnel-type radiator. Initial water trials were conducted at Trave-

The SSD I (below) bore no relationship to the parallel Ar 64 and was intended for catapult launch.

The SSD I is seen above with the somewhat rudimentary undercarriage with which it was tested at Lipezk, and, below, as tested at Travemünde in 1930.

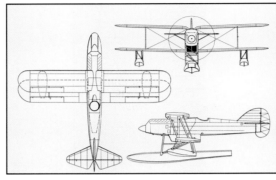

münde with a central main float and twin outrigger stabilising floats. The SSD I was subsequently fitted with a somewhat rudimentary wheel undercarriage to permit trials at Lipezk, the clandestine German flying school in the Soviet Union, where the armament of twin 7,9-mm guns was fitted. The Heinkel HD 38 was selected in preference to the SSD I, the sole prototype of which was assigned in April 1932 to the Luftdienst GmbH, and, a year later, to the *Deutsche Verkehrsfliegerschule* (DVS), the German commercial pilots' school. The following data relate to the SSD I with wheel undercarriage. *Max speed, 174 mph (280 km/h). Empty weight, 3,587 lb (1 627 kg). Loaded weight, 4,475 lb (2 030 kg). Span, 32 ft 9⅝ in (10,00 m). Length, 27 ft 10⅔ in (8,50 m). Wing area, 333.69 sq ft (31,00 m²).*

ARADO AR 64   Germany

Essentially a derivative of the SD II and III, the Ar 64 single-seat fighter was produced by the Arado Handelsgesellschaft as a result of an invitation received in 1929 from the *Reichswehrministerium* to develop a successor for the Fokker D XIII fighters then in use at Lipezk. The first prototype, the Ar 64a which entered flight test in the spring of 1930, was powered by a 530 hp Siemens und Halske-built direct-drive Jupiter VI nine-cylinder radial. Like preceding Arado fighters, the Ar 64a was of mixed construction, and it was joined by two examples of the Ar 64b powered by the 640 hp

The Ar 64d (below) was built in parallel with the Ar 64e which differed in having a direct-drive engine.

BMW VI 6,3 12-cylinder Vee-type water-cooled engine. These were evaluated at Lipezk during 1931. The Ar 64c was similarly powered to the first prototype, but embodied some minor structural changes. Production was initiated simultaneously of the Ar 64d and Ar 64e which were the first fighters to be built in quantity in Germany since the termination of World War I. The Ar 64d, which introduced redesigned, enlarged vertical tail surfaces and a revised undercarriage, was basically similar to the Ar 64e, but had a geared Jupiter VI driving a four-bladed propeller whereas the latter had a direct-drive version of the engine and a two-bladed propeller. A contract for 20 aircraft was placed by the *Reichswehrministerium*, deliveries commencing in the summer of 1932, and 19 of these were assigned to the *Jagdfliegerschule* at Schleissheim and subsequently to the *Jagdstaffeln* of the *Fliegergruppe* Döberitz and *Fliegergruppe* Damm, together with Ar 65s. *Max speed, 155 mph (250 km/h) at 16,405 ft (5 000 m). Empty weight, 2,745 lb (1 245 kg). Loaded weight, 3,682 lb (1 670 kg). Span, 32 ft 5¾ in (9,90 m). Length, 25 ft 7⅞ in (7,82 m).*

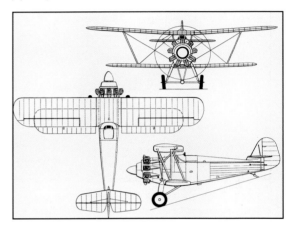

The first Arado production fighter, the Ar 64d.

ARADO AR 65   Germany

Intended as a successor to the Ar 64, the Ar 65 appeared in 1931 with a 750 hp BMW VI 7,3 12-cylinder water-cooled engine and an armament of two 7,9-mm synchronised machine guns. Three prototypes, the Ar 65a, 65b and 65c, which embodied equipment changes and differed in minor structural details, were followed by the initial production model, the Ar 65d, in 1933. Minor changes resulted in the Ar 65e and 65f production models, which had the vertical fuselage magazine for six 22-lb (10-kg) bombs deleted. The Ar 65 was operated, alongside the Ar 64, by both the *Fliegergruppe* Döberitz and *Fliegergruppe* Damm, and, in 1935, relegated to the tuitional role. Twelve aircraft were presented to the Royal Bulgarian Air Force in 1937. Production of the Ar 65 terminated early in 1936, a total of 85 Ar 65e and Ar 65f aircraft having been delivered. The following data relate to the Ar 65e. *Max speed, 186 mph (300 km/h) at 5,415 ft (1 650 m). Time to*

3,280 ft (1 000 m), 1.5 min. Empty weight, 3,329 lb (1 510 kg). Loaded weight, 4,255 lb (1 930 kg). Span, 36 ft 9 in (11,20 m). Length, 27 ft 6¾ in (8,40 m). Height, 11 ft 2¾ in (3,42 m). Wing area, 322.92 sq ft (30,00 m²).

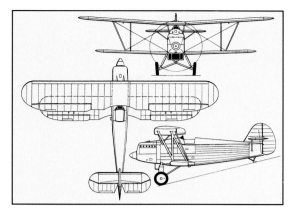

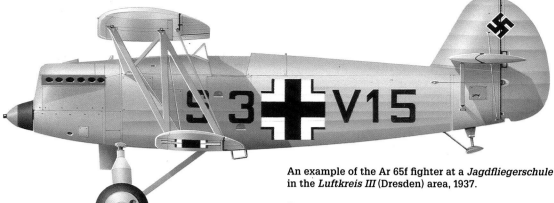

An example of the Ar 65f fighter at a *Jagdfliegerschule* in the *Luftkreis III* (Dresden) area, 1937.

The Ar 65f is illustrated above and is seen below in service with the Royal Bulgarian Air Force.

ing a welded steel-tube fuselage, wooden wings and fabric and plywood skinning, the Ar 67 was to have carried an armament of two 7,9-mm MG 17 machine guns, but development was abandoned in favour of the Ar 68, only one prototype being completed. *Max speed, 211 mph (340 km/h) at 12,370 ft (3 770 m). Initial climb, 1,575 ft/min (8,0 m/sec). Empty weight, 2,800 lb (1 270 kg). Loaded weight, 3,660 lb (1 660 kg). Span, 31 ft 9 in (9,68 m). Length, 25 ft 11 in (7,90 m). Height, 10 ft 2 in (3,10 m). Wing area, 269.74 sq ft (25,06 m²).*

Shortages of the Jumo engine delayed planned quantity manufacture of the Ar 68E-1, an interim production version, the Ar 68F-1 with the BMW VI 7,3Z engine, being produced during the spring and summer of 1936. This was followed by the Ar 68E-1 with the Jumo 210Da engine later in the year, this engine later giving place to the similarly rated Jumo 210Ea. Two Ar 68Es underwent operational trials in Spain during 1938, and during the early weeks of World War II this type was operated as a night fighter by the *Luftwaffe*. The Ar 68H, which

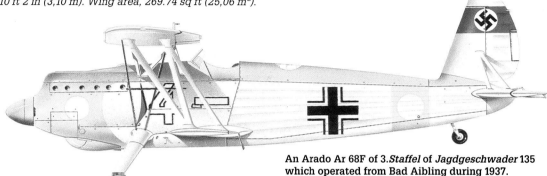

An Arado Ar 68F of 3.*Staffel* of *Jagdgeschwader* 135 which operated from Bad Aibling during 1937.

ARADO Ar 67   Germany

Appreciably smaller and lighter than the Ar 65, the Ar 67a, powered by a Rolls-Royce Kestrel VI 12-cylinder liquid-cooled engine rated at 640 hp at 14,000 ft (4 267 m), was flown in the late autumn of 1933. Featur-

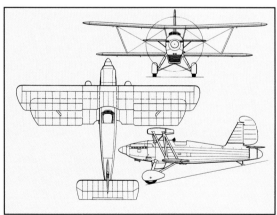

ARADO Ar 68   Germany

Developed in parallel with the Ar 67, the Ar 68 was first flown in the summer of 1934, the initial prototype, the Ar 68a, having a BMW VId engine rated at 750 hp for one minute at sea level. The second and third prototypes, the Ar 68b and 68c, differed primarily in having the later Junkers Jumo 210A 12-cylinder inverted-Vee liquid-cooled engine rated at 680 hp for take-off, the latter carrying an armament of two 7,9-mm MG 17 machine guns with 500 rpg. The fourth and fifth prototypes, the Ar 68d and 68e respectively powered by the BMW VI and Jumo 210Da, were production prototypes.

(Immediately left and below) The Rolls-Royce Kestrel-engined Ar 67a which was developed in parallel with the Ar 68 which proved superior under test.

appeared as a single prototype in the spring of 1937, featured an 850 hp supercharged BMW 132Da nine-cylinder air-cooled radial and an enclosed cockpit. The following data are for the Ar 68E-1. *Max speed, 190 mph (306 km/h) at sea level, 208 mph (335 km/h) at 8,695 ft (2 650 m). Initial climb, 2,480 ft/min (12,6 m/sec). Range, 310 mls (500 km). Empty weight, 3,527 lb*

(Above) The fifth prototype, the Ar 68 V5, served as a production prototype for the Jumo 210Da-engined Ar 68E-1 (below) which served into World War II.

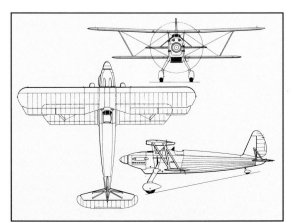

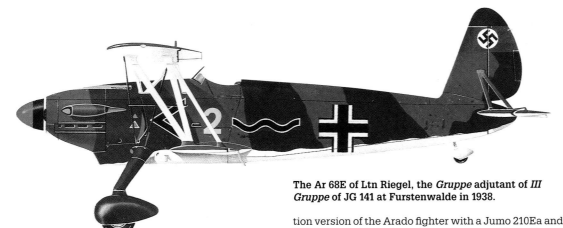

The Ar 68E of Ltn Riegel, the *Gruppe* adjutant of *III Gruppe* of JG 141 at Furstenwalde in 1938.

(1 600 kg). Loaded weight, 4,453 lb (2 020 kg). Span, 36 ft 1 in (11,00 m). Length, 31 ft 2 in (9,50 m). Height, 10 ft 10 in (3,30 m). Wing area, 293.85 sq ft (27,3 m²).

tion version of the Arado fighter with a Jumo 210Ea and fully-retractable main undercarriage was discontinued upon selection of the Messerschmitt Bf 109 to fulfil the requirement. The following data relate to the Ar 80 V3. *Max speed, 264 mph (425 km/h) at 13,125 ft (4 000 m).*

powered by a Daimler-Benz DB 600 12-cylinder liquid-cooled engine rated at 910 hp at 13,125 ft (4 000 m) and was not navalised. The Ar 197 V2 differed primarily in having a BMW 132J nine-cylinder radial rated at 815 hp for take-off, an arrester hook and catapult spools. The Ar 197 V3, which was considered as the production prototype, had a BMW 132Dc rated at 880 hp for take-off, provision for a drop tank, and an armament of two 20-mm MG FF cannon and two 7,9-mm MG 17 machine guns. Provision was made for four 110-lb (50-kg) SC 50 bombs. No further development was undertaken. The following data relate to the Ar 197 V3. *Max speed, 248 mph (400 km/h) at 8,200 ft (2 500 m). Cruising speed, 220 mph (354 km/h) at 4,920 ft (1 500 m). Time to 13,125 ft (4 000 m), 5.3 min. Normal range, 432 mls (695 km). Empty weight, 4,056 lb (1 840 kg). Loaded weight, 5,456 lb (2 475 kg). Span, 36 ft 1 in (11,00 m). Length, 30 ft 2¼ in (9,20 m). Height, 11 ft 9¾ in (3,60 m). Wing area, 299.25 sq ft (27,8 m²).*

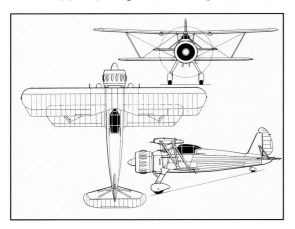

(Above and below) The Ar 68H was built as a single prototype, this upgraded, BMW 132-powered version of the basic fighter appearing in spring of 1937.

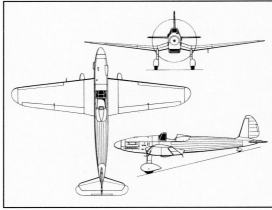

The Ar 80 V2 (above and below) was initially flown with a Rolls-Royce Kestrel V, but was re-engined with a Jumo 210Ca as illustrated here.

The Ar 197 V3 (above and below) was considered as a production prototype, and, at one time, was expected to be built for service aboard the *Graf Zeppelin*.

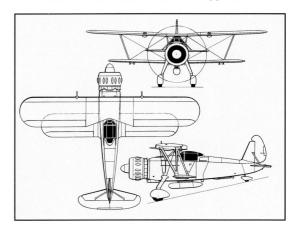

ARADO Ar 80   Germany

Designed by Dipl-Ing Walter Rethel, the Ar 80 was one of four contenders in a single-seat fighter monoplane contest and for which the company was awarded a development contract in February 1934. Of all-metal construction with a reverse-gulled cantilever low wing and fixed, spatted undercarriage, the first prototype, the Ar 80 V1, was powered by a Rolls-Royce Kestrel V engine with a continuous rating of 695 hp and 812 hp available for take-off. This aircraft was destroyed in a landing accident. Initially, the second prototype, the Ar 80 V2, was similarly powered, but it was subsequently re-engined with a Junkers Jumo 210Ca affording 695 hp for take-off. Also powered by the Jumo 210Ca, the Ar 80 V3 was the first prototype fitted with armament, comprising one engine-mounted 20-mm cannon and two 7,9-mm machine guns in the engine cowling. The Ar 80 V4 was fitted with a fuel-injection Jumo 210Ga engine and featured an enclosed cockpit, both this and the Ar 80 V5 undergoing extensive testing at Rechlin for the evaluation of new instrumentation and subsequently at the Tarnewitz armament test centre, finally being returned to Arado for the defence of the company's airfield at Warnemünde. The Ar 80 V3 was fitted with a revised wing eliminating the inverted gull arrangement and was modified as a two-seater. A proposed produc-

(Right) The fourth Ar 80 prototype, the V4, featured an enclosed cockpit and a fuel-injection engine.

Time to 13,125 ft (4 000 m), 5.8 min. Normal range, 373 mls (600 km). Empty weight, 3,626 lb (1 645 kg). Loaded weight, 4,630 lb (2 100 kg). Span, 38 ft 8½ in (11,80 m). Length, 33 ft 1⅔ in (10,10 m). Height, 9 ft 8⅛ in (2,95 m). Wing area, 226.05 sq ft (21,00 m²).

ARADO Ar 197   Germany

Designed to meet a requirement for a shipboard fighter for use from the carrier *Graf Zeppelin*, the all-metal Ar 197 appeared early in 1937. The Ar 197 V1 was

ARADO Ar 240C-2   Germany

Several fighter derivatives of the Ar 240 multi-purpose aircraft were projected, but only the Ar 240C-2 night fighter progressed further than the drawing board, one prototype, the Ar 240 V10 (alias Ar 240C-02), being flown. The Ar 240 V10, which flew in the early summer of 1943, was powered by two Daimler-Benz DB 603A-2 12-cylinder liquid-cooled engines each rated at 1,750 hp for take-off and 1,850 hp at 6,900 ft (2 100 m). Forward-firing armament comprised four 20-mm MG 151 cannon,

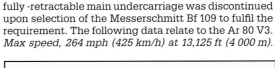

and remotely-controlled dorsal and ventral gun barbettes each mounted two 13-mm MG 131s. An FuG 202 *Lichtenstein* radar array was carried. No further prototypes of the night fighter model were flown, development being abandoned. *Max speed, 419 mph (675 km/h) at 19,685 ft (6 000 m). Normal range, 1,162 mls (1 870 km). Empty weight, 20,400 lb (9 253 kg). Loaded weight, 28,300 lb (12 837 kg). Span, 54 ft 5⅛ in (16,60 m). Length, 43 ft 9½ in (13,35 m). Height, 12 ft 11½ in (3.95 m). Wing area, 376.75 sq ft (35,00 m²).*

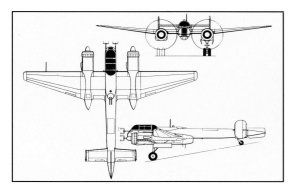

(Above) The Ar 240 V10 (alias Ar 240C-2) fighter.

ARMSTRONG WHITWORTH F.K.6 UK

In 1915, Frederick Koolhoven, the chief designer of Sir W G Armstrong Whitworth & Co Ltd, initiated work on a highly unorthodox three-seat triplane powered by a 250 hp Rolls-Royce 12-cylinder water-cooled engine. It was intended to accommodate two gunners each with a 0.303-in (7,7-mm) machine gun in shallow nacelles mounted above the centre wing on each side of the fuselage, the gunners being seated ahead of the propeller plane of the tractor engine. Although a prototype was completed and allegedly designated F.K.5, this was never flown, being extensively damaged as a re-

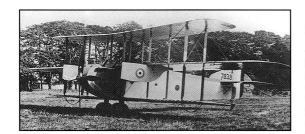

Believed to have been designated F.K.6, only one prototype (above and below) was built.

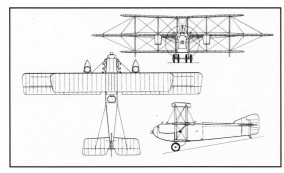

sult of a ground loop during its first take-off attempt. The design was extensively revised early in 1916 to meet an RFC requirement for an airship interceptor and long-range escort fighter. The revised design is believed to have been designated F.K.6 (and certainly not F.K.12 as has sometimes been stated) and four examples were ordered, two of these being intended for the RNAS. In the event, only one F.K.6 was built. The gunners' nacelles were underslung on the central mainplane, armament remained two 0.303-in (7,7-mm) Lewis guns and the 250 hp Rolls-Royce engine was retained. It is believed that relatively limited flight testing was undertaken. *Span, 62 ft 0 in (18,89 m). Length, 37 ft 0¾ in (11,29 m). Height, 17 ft 0 in (5,18 m).*

ARMSTRONG WHITWORTH F.K.9 UK

The F.K.9 two-seat fighter-reconnaissance quadruplane was built by Sir W G Armstrong Whitworth & Co Ltd as a private venture, and was initially flown in the summer of 1916. Initial trials dictated a number of modifications, including new wings with enlarged ailerons, an enlarged fin, a redesigned engine cowling and increased undercarriage track. In this form, powered by a 110 hp Clerget 9Z rotary engine, and with a designated armament of one fixed 0.303-in (7,7-mm) Vickers gun and one free 0.303-in (7,7-mm) Lewis gun, the F.K.9 was officially tested in November-December 1916 at the Central Flying School. A production contract for 50 examples of an improved version, the F.K.10, was awarded. *Max speed, 94 mph (151 km/h) at 6,500 ft (1 980 m), 87 mph (140 km/h) at 10,000 ft (3 050 m). Time to 6,500 ft (1 980 m), 14.33 min. Endurance, 3 hrs. Empty weight, 1,226 lb (556 kg). Loaded weight, 2,038 lb (924 kg). No dimensions available.*

ARMSTRONG WHITWORTH F.K.10 UK

Derived from the F.K.9, but embodying considerable redesign, the F.K.10 two-seat fighter-reconnaissance quadruplane retained virtually no more than the basic wing structure of its immediate predecessor. A production contract for 50 F.K.10s was given to Angus Sanderson & Company of Newcastle-on-Tyne on 30 December 1916 on behalf of the RFC, but only five aircraft were destined to be completed before the contract was cancelled. Three were ordered for the RNAS, two of these from the Phoenix Dynamo Manufacturing Company and one from Armstrong Whitworth, these eventually being completed and tested. The F.K.10 was normally powered by a 130 hp Clerget 9B rotary, but at least one was flown with a 110 hp Le Rhône, and armament comprised one fixed 0.303-in (7,7-mm) Vickers gun and one free 0.303-in (7,7-mm) Lewis. *Max speed, 84 mph (135 km/h) at 6,500 ft (1 980 m), 74 mph*

(Below) The F.K.10 fighter-recce quadruplane.

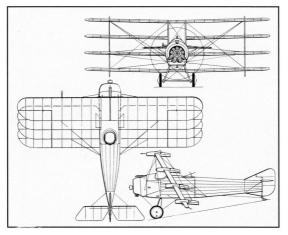

Built as a private venture, the F.K.9 quadruplane (above) entered flight test in the summer of 1916.

(119 km/h) at 10,000 ft (3 050 m). Time to 6,500 ft (1 980 m), 15.85 min. Endurance, 2.5 hrs. Empty weight, 1,236 lb (560 kg). Loaded weight, 2,019 lb (916 kg). Span, 27 ft 10 in (8,48 m). Length, 22 ft 3 in (6,78 m). Height, 11 ft 6 in (3,50 m). Wing area, 390.4 sq ft (36,27 m²).

Derived from the F.K.9, the F.K.10 (below) was ordered into production, but only eight were built owing to contract cancellations.

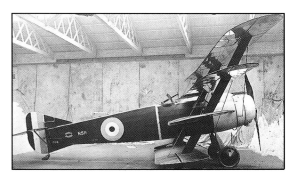

ARMSTRONG WHITWORTH F.M.4 ARMADILLO UK

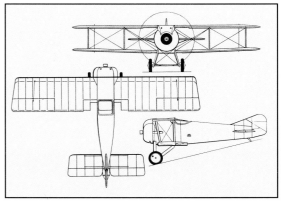

The Armadillo (above and below) was found to possess unsatisfactory flying characteristics and a second prototype was completed but never flown.

The Armadillo, designed by F Murphy, who had succeeded F Koolhoven as chief designer to Armstrong Whitworth, was initiated late in 1917, and the construction of two prototypes began early in 1918 as a private venture, the first of these being flown in April of that year. Powered by a 230 hp Bentley B.R.2 nine-cylinder rotary, the Armadillo had provision for an armament of two synchronised 0.303-in (7,7-mm) Vickers machine guns, but flying characteristics were declared to be most unsatisfactory and flight testing was terminated in June 1918, the second prototype never being flown. *Max speed, 125 mph (201 km/h) at sea level, 113 mph (182 km/h) at 10,000 ft (3 050 m). Time to 10,000 ft (3 050 m), 6.5 min. Endurance, 2.75 hrs. Empty weight, 1,250 lb (567 kg). Loaded weight, 1,860 lb (844 kg). Span, 27 ft 9 in (8,46 m). Length, 18 ft 10 in (5,74 m). Height, 7 ft 10 in (2,38 m). Wing area, 232 sq ft (21,55 m²).*

ARMSTRONG WHITWORTH ARA
UK

The Ara was designed in 1918 to use the extremely promising ABC Dragonfly nine-cylinder air-cooled radial of 320 hp and three prototypes were ordered. However, delays in delivery of the Dragonfly engine led, in October 1918, to the decision to abandon all plans to produce a Dragonfly-powered fighter in quantity, and those companies with such warplanes under development were each allocated one Dragonfly engine in December 1918 in order to enable them to complete and test one prototype of each of their designs. In the event, the ABC engine proved extremely unreliable when the Ara commenced trials early in 1919. Nevertheless, a second prototype was completed and flown before, late in 1919, Sir W G Armstrong Whitworth & Co Ltd closed its aircraft department. The planned armament of the Ara comprised two 0.303-in (7,7-mm) Vickers guns. *Max speed, 150 mph (241 km/h) at sea level, 145 mph (233 km/h) at 10,000 ft (3 050 m). Time to 10,000 ft (3 050 m), 4.5 min. Endurance, 3.25 hrs. Empty weight, 1,320 lb (599 kg). Loaded weight, 1,930 lb (875 kg). Span, 27 ft 5 in (8,35 m). Length, 20 ft 3 in (6,17 m). Height, 7 ft 10 in (2,39 m). Wing area, 257 sq ft (23,87 m²).*

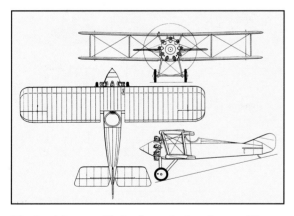

The Ara (above and below) was designed around the unsuccessful ABC Dragonfly engine, but two prototypes were completed and flown during 1919.

ARMSTRONG WHITWORTH SISKIN II
UK

Derived from the Siddeley S.R.2 Siskin, a single-seat fighter of 1919 built by the Siddeley Deasy Car Co Ltd, the Siskin II was evolved after the latter concern acquired in 1921 the name and goodwill of Sir W G Arm-

The Siskin II (above and below) was a progressive development of the Siddeley S.R.2 Siskin of 1919.

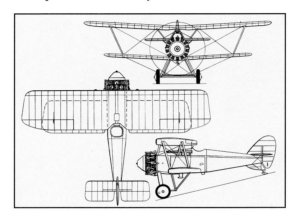

strong Whitworth & Co Ltd, which had closed down its aviation department. Retaining the basic features of its predecessor, the Siskin II was completely redesigned structurally, and embodied fuselage and wing spars of high-tensile steel tubing and strip. Powered by a 325 hp Armstrong Siddeley Jaguar I 14-cylinder two-row radial, the Siskin II appeared in August 1922 as a two-seater, a second prototype which followed in October 1923 being completed as a single-seat fighter. The first prototype was later modified as a single-seater, but the Siskin II failed to attract orders, and the second prototype was eventually sold to the Swedish Air Force. *Max speed, 148 mph (238 km/h) at sea level, 140 mph (225 km/h) at 10,000 ft (3 050 m). Initial climb, 1,250 ft/min (6,35 m/sec). Time to 10,000 ft (3 050 m), 8 min. Loaded weight, 2,250 lb (1 021 kg). Span, 28 ft 4 in (8,63 m). Length, 21 ft 6 in (6,55 m). Height, 9 ft 6 in (2,89 m). Wing area, 253 sq ft (23,50 m²).*

ARMSTRONG WHITWORTH SISKIN III
UK

Embodying considerable redesign by comparison with the Siskin II, the Siskin III featured an enlarged upper

wing, a lower wing of reduced chord and Vee-type instead of parallel interplane struts. The Siskin III was powered by the 350 hp Armstrong Siddeley Jaguar III engine, and was ordered for the RAF to Specification 15/22. The prototype was tested in 1923, the first production example flying on 24 March 1924. Armament comprised two 0.303-in (7,7-mm) Vickers machine

The first series version of the Siskin for the RAF, the second production Mk III is seen above.

guns, and 50 single-seat examples were built for the RAF, one of these later being passed to the RCAF. Twelve two-seat trainer models were also built. *Max speed, 134 mph (216 km/h) at 6,500 ft (1 980 m), 128 mph (206 km/h) at 15,000 ft (4 572 m). Time to 10,000 ft (3 050 m), 8.5 min. Empty weight, 1,830 lb (830 kg). Loaded weight, 2,735 lb (1 241 kg). Span, 33 ft 1 in (10,08 m). Length, 22 ft 6 in (6,85 m). Height, 9 ft 9 in (2,97 m). Wing area, 296 sq ft (27,50 m²).*

ARMSTRONG WHITWORTH SISKIN IIIA
UK

By comparison with the Siskin III, the Siskin IIIA introduced a number of major design changes, including a lengthened fuselage with raised aft decking, greater gap and less upper wing dihedral, and redesigned vertical tail surfaces lacking the ventral fin. Retaining the twin 0.303-in (7,7-mm) Vickers gun armament, the Siskin IIIA was powered by the 425 hp Jaguar IV or super-

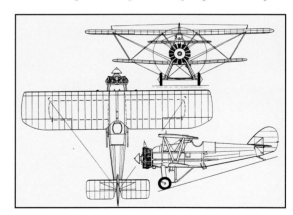

(Above) The Siskin IIIA entered RAF service in 1927.

charged Jaguar IVS engine, and the slab-sided fuselage gave place to a fuselage with rounded sides. The Siskin IIIA, to Specification 19/23, first flew on 20 October 1925, and was ordered for the RAF in June 1926, 412 being built, including 47 dual-control trainers,

A Royal Canadian Air Force Siskin IIIA (below) seen fitted with skis while serving at Camp Borden.

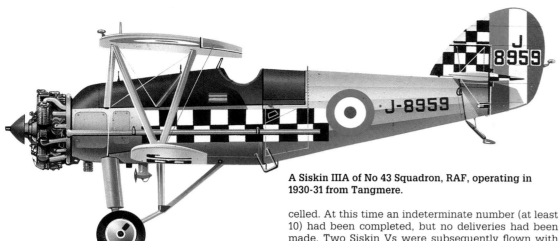

A Siskin IIIA of No 43 Squadron, RAF, operating in 1930-31 from Tangmere.

17 of the single-seaters being supplied to the RCAF. Of the total production, the parent company built 159 (Blackburn building 42, Bristol 85, Gloster 74 and Vickers 52). At least one was completed as the experimental Siskin IIIB with an uprated engine enclosed by a Townend ring. *Max speed, 156 mph (251 km/h) at sea level, 142 mph (228 km/h) at 15,000 ft (4 570 m). Time to 5,000 ft (1 525 m), 3.5 min, to 15,000 ft (4 570 m), 10.5 min. Empty weight, 2,061 lb (935 kg). Loaded weight, 3,012 lb (1 366 kg). Span, 33 ft 2 in (10,10 m). Length, 25 ft 4 in (7,72 m). Height, 10 ft 2 in (3,10 m). Wing area, 293 sq ft (27,22 m²).*

The Siskin IIIB (above) was criticised on the score of handling and endurance, and was not ordered.

ARMSTRONG WHITWORTH SISKIN V   UK

The Siskin V actually preceded the Siskin IIIA and was essentially a progressive development of the Siskin II, retaining the shorter span upper wing, broader chord lower wing and parallel struts of the original model, coupling these features with redesigned vertical tail surfaces, a forward fuselage with rounded sides, and a 385 hp Armstrong Siddeley Jaguar III. Armament comprised two 7,7-mm machine guns, and the Siskin V was the recipient of an order for 70 examples from the Romanian government. Production was initiated early in 1925, but in March of that year one of the Romanian Siskin Vs was destroyed in a crash while being flown in the UK by a Romanian test pilot, and the order was can-

The Siskin V (right and below) was ordered by the Romanian government, which cancelled the contract after one example was destroyed while under test.

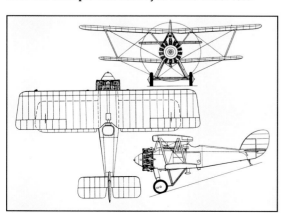

celled. At this time an indeterminate number (at least 10) had been completed, but no deliveries had been made. Two Siskin Vs were subsequently flown with civil registrations. The Siskin IV, the sole example of which was built for the 1925 King's Cup Race, was similar. *Max speed, 155 mph (249 km/h) at sea level. Initial climb, 1,650 ft/min (8,38m/sec). Loaded weight, 2,460 lb (1 116 kg). Span, 28 ft 4 in (8,63 m). Length, 21 ft 6 in (6,55 m). Height, 9 ft 6 in (2,89 m). Wing area, 253 sq ft (23,50 m²).*

ARMSTRONG WHITWORTH A.W.14 STARLING   UK

Designed by J Lloyd to meet the requirements of Air Ministry specification F.9/26, the A.W.14 Starling was a staggered biplane with wings of unequal span and

(Below) The original Starling flown in May 1927.

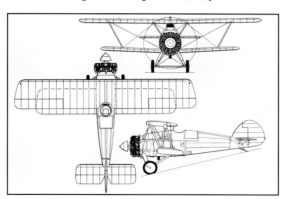

chord. It featured a fabric-covered rectangular-section steel-tube fuselage, and wings of mixed construction consisting of steel spars, wooden ribs and fabric skinning. Two prototypes were ordered, the first of these flying on 19 May 1927 with an uncowled 385 hp Arm-

strong Siddeley Jaguar VII two-row 14-cylinder radial, this later being replaced by a supercharged Jaguar IV rated at 410 hp at 9,000 ft (2 745 m) and enclosed by a Townend ring cowling. Armament comprised two 0.303-in (7,7-mm) Vickers Mk II machine guns. The characteristics of the Starling proved disappointing, and the second prototype was abandoned in favour of an entirely new design known as the Starling II. *Max speed, 173 mph (278 km/h) at 10,000 ft (3 050 m), 177.5 mph (286 km/h) at 15,000 ft (4 570 m). Time to 10,000 ft (3 050 m), 7 min, to 15,000 ft (4 570 m), 11.5 min. Empty weight, 2,060 lb (934 kg). Loaded weight, 3,095 lb (1 404 kg). Span, 31 ft 4 in (9,55 m). Length, 25 ft 2 in (7,67 m). Height, 10 ft 6 in (3,20 m). Wing area, 246.4 sq ft (22,89 m²).*

Only one prototype of the original Starling (below) was completed, development being abandoned.

ARMSTRONG WHITWORTH A.W.14 STARLING II   UK

The A.W.14 Starling II bore no relationship to the original Starling apart from a common design origin and similar construction. It was powered by an Armstrong Siddeley Panther IIIA 14-cylinder two-row radial rated at 540 hp and carried two Vickers Mk II machine guns. Three prototypes were completed and flown in 1930, one being a shore-based fighter to the require-

The Starling II (below) bore no relationship to the original Starling apart from its design origin.

ments of F.9/26 and the other two being private venture tenders to the N.21/26 fleet fighter specification. The land-based prototype had an uncowled engine and the shipboard prototypes featured Townend ring engine cowlings. No production orders were received. *Max speed, 183.5 mph (295 km/h) at 5,000 ft (1 525 m), 179 mph (288 km/h) at 10,000 ft (3 050 m). Time to 10,000 ft (3 050 m), 6.5 min. Loaded weight, 3,225 lb (1 463 kg). Span, 34 ft 3 in (10,44 m). Length, 24 ft 8½ in (7,53 m).*

(Below) The private-venture shipboard Starling II.

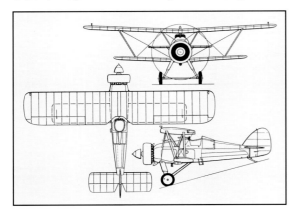

ARMSTRONG WHITWORTH
A.W.16   UK

Developed as a private venture to meet the requirements of both N.21/26 and F.9/26, the A.W.16 appeared in 1931. Two prototypes were flown, the first conforming to the former specification and the second to the latter, both being initially powered by the geared and supercharged Panther IIIA of 540 hp. The second prototype was re-engined with a 565 hp Panther VII during the course of protracted trials at the A & AEE in 1933. Eighteen production examples of the A.W.16 were produced late in 1931, 17 of these for delivery to the Chinese Kwangsi Air Force and one being used as an engine test bed before being passed to the Alan Cobham circus. Armament comprised two 0.303-in (7,7-mm) Vickers machine guns. *Max speed, 200 mph (322 km/h) at 15,000 ft (4 570 m), 195 mph (314 km/h) at 20,000 ft (6 100 m). Time to 10,000 ft (3 050 m), 6 min. Endurance, 2 hrs. Loaded weight, 3,520 lb (1 597 kg). Span, 33 ft 0 in (10,06 m). Length, 25 ft 0 in (7,62 m). Height, 11 ft 6 in (3,50 m). Wing area, 261 sq ft (24,24 m²).*

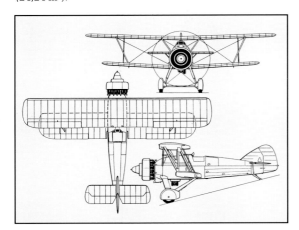

(Above and below) The A.W.16 was intended for both shipboard and shore-based use, the first (naval) prototype being illustrated by the photograph.

ARMSTRONG WHITWORTH
A.W.35 SCIMITAR   UK

A refined development of the A.W.16, the A.W.35 Scimitar was powered by a Panther VII engine enclosed by a long-chord cowling and rated at 565 hp at 12,000 ft (3 660 m), but having a maximum output of 605 hp at

One of the four production examples of the Scimitar that were delivered to the Norwegian Army Air Force.

13,500 ft (4 115 m). Armament comprised two 0.303-in (7,7-mm) Vickers Type E machine guns and provision was made for four 20-lb (9,07-kg) bombs to be carried beneath the lower mainplane. Two prototypes of the

The Scimitar was the last A.W. fighter biplane.

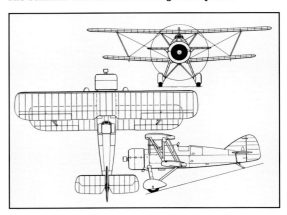

Key to Armstrong Whitworth (Gloster) Meteor NF Mk 12

1 Radome
2 Radar antenna dish
3 Waveguide
4 Antenna tracking mechanism
5 Radar power unit
6 Radome latches
7 Radar equipment mounting bulkhead
8 Nosewheel leg door
9 Landing/taxiing lamps
10 Nose undercarriage shock absorber
11 Nosewheel forks
12 Nosewheel
13 Mudguard
14 Nose undercarriage pivot mounting
15 Equipment access door
16 Radar modulator
17 Nose electronic equipment bay
18 Ballast weights
19 Nose undercarriage hydraulic retraction jack
20 Nosewheel mounting sub-frame
21 Venturi
22 Nosewheel doors
23 Front pressure bulkhead
24 Rudder pedals
25 Ballast weight
26 Control column
27 Instrument panel
28 Instrument panel access door
29 Retractable gyro gunsight
30 Windscreen panel
31 Starboard engine air intake
32 Direct vision opening side window panel
33 Throttle levers
34 Gyro sight dimmer and selector switch
35 Chart case
36 Cabin pressure control valve
37 Cockpit floor level
38 Ground power socket
39 Lower IFF aerial
40 Ground/flight switch access panel
41 Fuselage lower longeron
42 "Kick-in" step
43 Trim control handwheels
44 Fuel cocks
45 Cockpit section fuselage framing
46 Pilot's seat
47 Cockpit canopy cover, hinged to starboard
48 Canopy framing
49 Starboard engine intake duct framing
50 First aid kit
51 Radar equipment racks

52 Gee navigation system equipment
53 Rectifier
54 "Kick-in" steps
55 Navigator/radar operator's footrests
56 Oxygen bottles (three)
57 Ventral fuel tank, capacity 175 Imp gal (796 l)
58 Pull-out boarding steps
59 Cockpit rear pressure bulkhead
60 Radar visor stowage
61 Navigator/radar operator's seat
62 Cockpit pressure seal
63 Whip aerial
64 Starboard engine bay
65 Engine mounting ring frame
66 Main engine mounting
67 Starboard wing cannon bay
68 Jettisonable external fuel tank, capacity 100 Imp gal (455 l)
69 Cannon muzzles
70 Aileron operating rod
71 Ammunition tanks
72 Starboard outer wing panel
73 Starboard navigation light
74 Wing tip fairing
75 Starboard aileron
76 Aileron hinge control
77 Balance tab
78 Trim tab

79 Fixed portion of trailing-edge
80 Rear spar ring frame
81 Starboard airbrake, open
82 Canopy aft fairing
83 Hydraulic equipment access panel
84 Hydraulic equipment bay
85 Hydraulic accumulator
86 Fuel tank bay frame construction
87 Fuselage upper longeron
88 Main fuel tank, capacity 325 Imp gal (1477 l)
89 Fuel filler cap
90 Starboard engine exhaust nozzle
91 VHF aerial
92 Fire extinguisher bottle
93 Radio and electronics equipment bay
94 Electrical system inverters

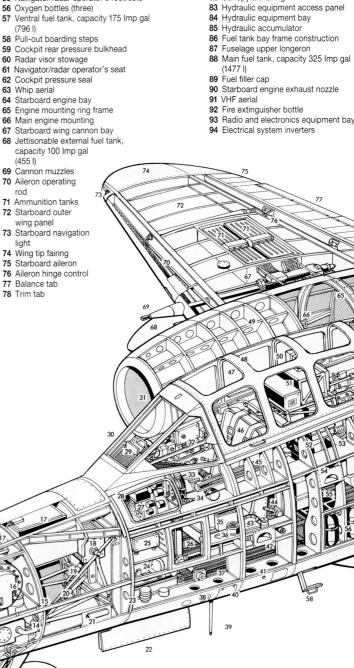

Scimitar were flown in 1933, and these were followed by four production examples for the Norwegian Army Air Force which were delivered at the beginning of 1936. These were powered by the Panther XIA with a maximum rating of 730 hp. The following data relate to the Panther XIA-engined version. *Max speed, 213 mph (343 km/h) at 14,000 ft (4 270 m). Time to 6,560 ft (2 000 m), 3.8 min. Empty weight, 2,814 lb (1 276 kg). Loaded weight, 4,100 lb (1 860 kg). Span, 33 ft 0 in (10,06 m). Length, 25 ft 0 in (7,62 m). Height, 11 ft 7 in (3,53 m). Wing area, 261.35 sq ft (24,28 m²).*

ARMSTRONG WHITWORTH METEOR NF Mᴋs 11 ᴛᴏ 14   UK

The Meteor NF Mk 11 was a tandem two-seat night fighter developed by Armstrong Whitworth from the Gloster Meteor single-seat day fighter, with a lengthened nose to accommodate radar and an additional seat for the radar navigator. The first complete NF Mk 11 prototype was flown on 31 May 1950, and the first of 307 production fighters of this type followed on 13

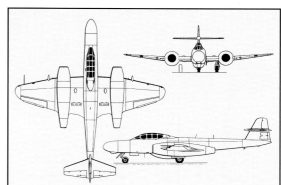

(Above) The definitive night fighting version of the Meteor, the NF Mk 14 which had a new canopy.

November 1950. The NF Mk 11 was powered by two 3,600 lb (1 633 kg) thrust Rolls-Royce Derwent 8 turbojets, and armament comprised four 20-mm Hispano cannon. A tropicalised version, the NF Mk 13, flew on 23 December 1952, and was externally similar apart from enlarged engine air intakes which permitted an increase in engine thrust to 3,700 lb st (1 678 kgp). Forty NF Mk 13s were built. The NF Mk 12 differed from the NF Mk 11 in having Derwent 9s of 3,800 lb st (1 724 kgp) and different radar increasing nose length by 17 in (43 cm). The first NF Mk 12 flew on 21 April

(Below) The Meteor NF Mk 11 two-seat night fighter.

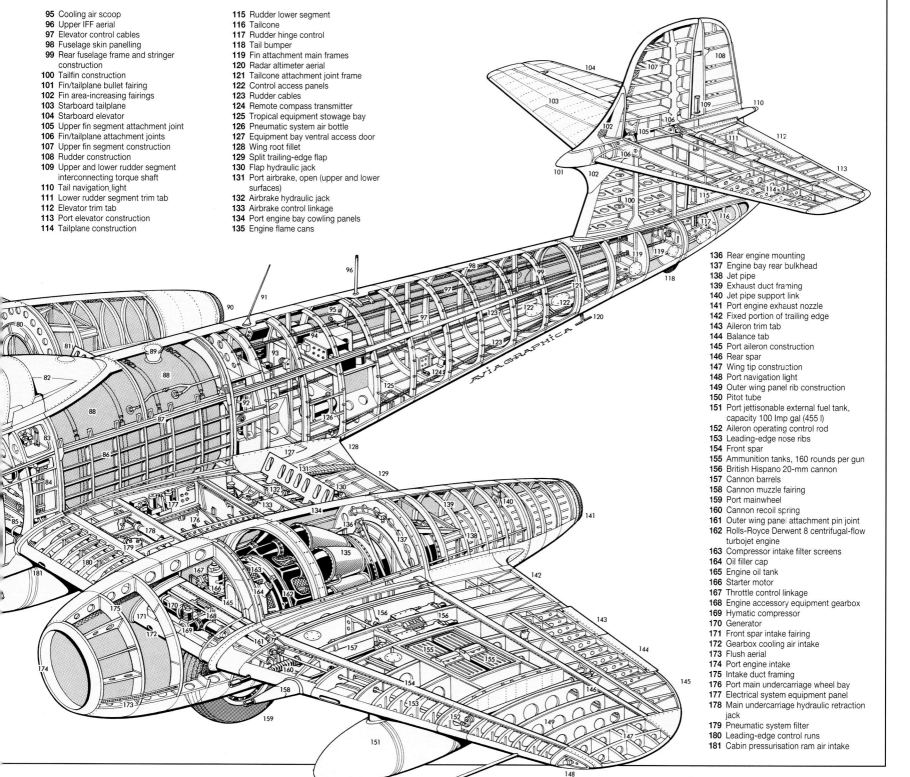

95 Cooling air scoop
96 Upper IFF aerial
97 Elevator control cables
98 Fuselage skin panelling
99 Rear fuselage frame and stringer construction
100 Tailfin construction
101 Fin/tailplane bullet fairing
102 Fin area-increasing fairings
103 Starboard tailplane
104 Starboard elevator
105 Upper fin segment attachment joint
106 Fin/tailplane attachment joints
107 Upper fin segment construction
108 Rudder construction
109 Upper and lower rudder segment interconnecting torque shaft
110 Tail navigation light
111 Lower rudder segment trim tab
112 Elevator trim tab
113 Port elevator construction
114 Tailplane construction
115 Rudder lower segment
116 Tailcone
117 Rudder hinge control
118 Tail bumper
119 Fin attachment main frames
120 Radar altimeter aerial
121 Tailcone attachment joint frame
122 Control access panels
123 Rudder cables
124 Remote compass transmitter
125 Tropical equipment stowage bay
126 Pneumatic system air bottle
127 Equipment bay ventral access door
128 Wing root fillet
129 Split trailing-edge flap
130 Flap hydraulic jack
131 Port airbrake, open (upper and lower surfaces)
132 Airbrake hydraulic jack
133 Airbrake control linkage
134 Port engine bay cowling panels
135 Engine flame cans
136 Rear engine mounting
137 Engine bay rear bulkhead
138 Jet pipe
139 Exhaust duct framing
140 Jet pipe support link
141 Port engine exhaust nozzle
142 Fixed portion of trailing edge
143 Aileron trim tab
144 Balance tab
145 Port aileron construction
146 Rear spar
147 Wing tip construction
148 Port navigation light
149 Outer wing panel rib construction
150 Pitot tube
151 Port jettisonable external fuel tank, capacity 100 Imp gal (455 l)
152 Aileron operating control rod
153 Leading-edge nose ribs
154 Front spar
155 Ammunition tanks, 160 rounds per gun
156 British Hispano 20-mm cannon
157 Cannon barrels
158 Cannon muzzle fairing
159 Port mainwheel
160 Cannon recoil spring
161 Outer wing panel attachment pin joint
162 Rolls-Royce Derwent 8 centrifugal-flow turbojet engine
163 Compressor intake filter screens
164 Oil filler cap
165 Engine oil tank
166 Starter motor
167 Throttle control linkage
168 Engine accessory equipment gearbox
169 Hymatic compressor
170 Generator
171 Front spar intake fairing
172 Gearbox cooling air intake
173 Flush aerial
174 Port engine intake
175 Intake duct framing
176 Port main undercarriage wheel bay
177 Electrical system equipment panel
178 Main undercarriage hydraulic retraction jack
179 Pneumatic system filter
180 Leading-edge control runs
181 Cabin pressurisation ram air intake

(Above top) A Meteor NF Mk 11 of No 68 Sqn, RAF Germany, at Wahn, 1952-53, (immediately above) a Meteor NF Mk 14 of No 85 Sqn, West Malling, 1954-57, and (below) a Meteor NF Mk 11 of No 256 Sqn.

1953, and 100 were built. The final model, the NF Mk 14, was similar to the NF Mk 12 but featured a clear-vision cockpit canopy. It was first flown on 23 October 1953, and 100 were delivered to bring total Meteor night fighter production by Armstrong Whitworth to 547. The performances of all versions were generally similar and the following data relate specifically to the NF Mk 11. *Max speed, 505 mph (813 km/h) at sea level, 541 mph (871 km/h) at 30,000 ft (9 150 m). Initial climb, 5,800 ft/ min (29,46 m/sec). Max range, 950 mls (1 529 km). Basic operational weight, 13,909 lb (6 309 kg). Max loaded weight, 19,790 lb (8 976 kg). Span, 43 ft 0 in (13,11 m). Length, 48 ft 6 in (14,78 m). Height, 13 ft 11 in (4,24 m). Wing area, 374 sq ft (34,74 m²).*

ARSENAL VG 30   France

The VG 30 single-seat fighter built by the Arsenal de l'Aéronautique and designed by *Ingénieur-Général* Vernisse and Jean Galtier was evolved to compete with the Caudron C.713 and meet a lightweight interceptor requirement. The VG 30 was of wooden stressed-skin construction and was intended to be powered by a Potez 12 Dc ''flat-twelve'' air-cooled engine rated at 610 hp at 3,280 ft (1 000 m) and mounting a 20-mm Hispano motor cannon. A full-scale mock-up of the VG 30 was exhibited at the *Exposition Internationale* held in Paris in the summer of 1936, but development was delayed by the non-availability of the Potez 12 Dc engine, and the prototype was eventually flown at Villacoublay on 1 October 1938 with a 690 hp Hispano-Suiza 12 Xcrs 12-cylinder liquid-cooled engine. The VG 30 proved faster than the Morane-Saulnier 406 and, in July 1939, allegedly attained 500 mph (805 km/h) in a dive between 13,125 ft (4 000 m) and 6,560 ft (2 000 m).

The mock-up of the VG 30 (below), progenitor of the Vernisse-Galtier fighters, exhibited at the *Exposition Internationale* in Paris in summer 1936.

Proposed armament comprised one 20-mm Hispano-Suiza 404 cannon and four 7,5-mm MAC machine guns. Development was abandoned in favour of the VG 33. *Span, 35 ft 5¼ in (10,80 m). Length, 27 ft 6¾ in (8,40 m). Height (tail up), 10 ft 10⅓ in (3,31 m). Wing area, 150.70 sq ft (14,00 m²).*

ARSENAL VG 33   France

The initial derivative of the VG 30, the VG 31, differed from its predecessor in having the radiator bath moved aft for CG reasons, and in having a smaller wing of 129.17 sq ft (12,00 m²). It was proposed to power this development with an 860 hp Hispano-Suiza 12Y31 12-cylinder liquid-cooled engine, but the prototype was never assembled. The VG 32 reverted to the original wing and was powered by a 1,040 hp Allison V-1710-C15 engine, but the prototype was captured by German forces at Villacoublay two weeks before its scheduled maiden flight in 1940. The first development of the basic design to fly was thus the VG 33, which commenced its test programme on 24 May 1939. A production contract for 220 examples was placed in September 1939, this contract eventually being increased to 1,000 machines, but only 19 had been completed by the Chantiers Aéro-Maritimes de la Seine by the time France collapsed. The VG 33 carried an armament of one 20-mm Hispano-Suiza 404 cannon and four 7,5-mm MAC 1934 M 39 machine guns, and was powered by an

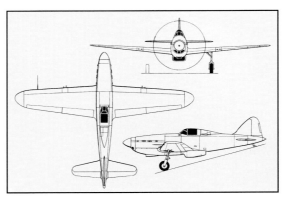

The VG 33 (above and below) was in production at the Chantiers Aéro-Maritimes de la Seine by the time France collapsed, but only 19 were completed.

860 hp Hispano-Suiza 12Y31 engine. *Max speed, 347 mph (558 km/h) at 17,060 ft (5 200 m). Normal range, 746 mls (1 200 km). Endurance, 2.85 hrs. Empty weight, 4,519 lb (2 050 kg). Normal loaded weight, 5,855 lb (2 656 kg). Span, 35 ft 5¼ in (10,80 m). Length, 28 ft 0⅔ in (8,55 m). Height (tail up), 10 ft 10⅓ in (3,31 m). Wing area, 150.70 sq ft (14,00 m²).*

ARSENAL VG 34 TO VG 36   France

Progressive developments of the VG 33 under test in 1940 included the VG 34, flown on 20 January 1940 with a 910 hp Hispano-Suiza 12Y45 engine, and the VG 35 with a 1,000 hp Hispano-Suiza 12Y51 which flew on 25 February 1940. The former attained a maximum speed of 357 mph (575 km/h) at 20,340 ft (6 200 m) during tests, and the airframes and armament of both the VG 34 and VG 35 were identical to those of the VG 33. A third development, the VG 36 flown on 14 May 1940, had a similar 1,000 hp HS 12Y51 to that of the VG 35, but embodied some redesign of the rear fuselage into

The VG 36 (above) entered flight test four days after commencement of the assault on France.

which a shallower, wider radiator bath was faired. Armament of the VG 36 comprised one 20-mm HS 404 cannon and four 7,5-mm MAC 1934 M 39 machine guns, and the following data apply to this type. *Max speed, 367 mph (590 km/h) at 22,966 ft (7 000 m). Normal range, 684 mls (1 100 km). Span, 35 ft 5¼ in (10,80 m). Length, 26ft 6⅞ in (8,10 m). Height (tail up), 10 ft 10⅓ in (3,31 m). Wing area, 150.70 sq ft (14,00 m²).*

ARSENAL VG 39   France

The final development in the VG 30 series of fighters to be flown, the VG 39 commenced its flight test programme on 3 May 1940, and the prototype differed from

The VG 39 (immediately above) was the most powerful of the Vernisse-Galtier piston-engined fighters.

the VG 33 primarily in having a 1,200 hp Hispano-Suiza Type 89ter 12-cylinder liquid-cooled engine with an elongated propeller shaft, a revised wing structure which retained the profile and contours of the earlier wing, and a wing-mounted armament of six 7,5-mm MAC 1934 M 39 machine guns. During flight testing the prototype VG 39 attained a maximum speed of 388 mph (625 km/h) at an altitude of 18,865 ft (5 750 m). The planned production model, the VG 39bis, was to have embodied a fuselage similar to that of the VG 36 and to have supplemented the wing armament with a 20-mm engine-mounted cannon, the definitive model having a 1,600 hp Hispano-Suiza 12Z engine. *Max speed, 388 mph (625 km/h) at 18,865 ft (5 750 m). Span, 35 ft 5¼ in (10,80 m). Length, 28 ft 8½ in (8,75 m). Wing area, 150.70 sq ft (14,00 m^2).*

Final development of the VG 30 series, the VG 39.

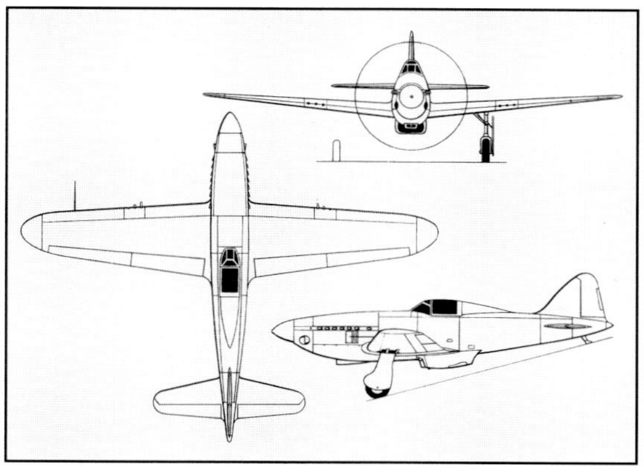

ARSENAL VB 10 France

Evolved by *Ingénieur-Général* Vernisse and M Badie, the VB 10 was an all-metal single-seat fighter powered by engines mounted in tandem fore and aft of the pilot's cockpit and driving contra-rotating co-axial propellers. Thirty VG 10s were ordered off the drawing board in May 1940, and work continued under the Vichy government. The first prototype with two 860 hp Hispano-Suiza 12Y31 12-cylinder liquid-cooled engines was

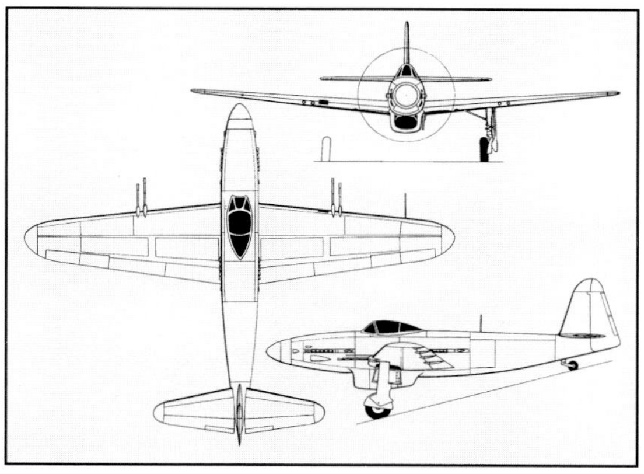

(Above and below) The tandem-engined VB 10 which entered production immediately after World War II, the first series aircraft being seen in the photo.

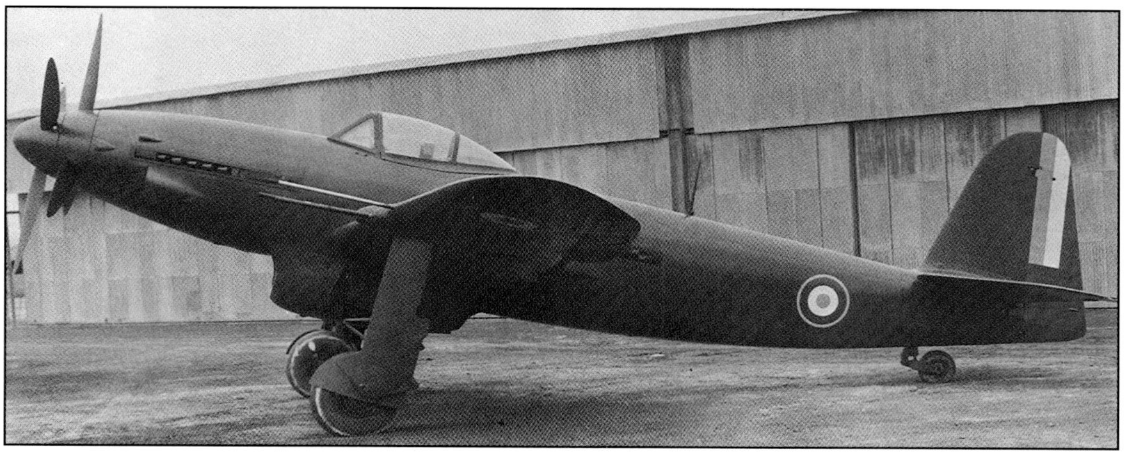

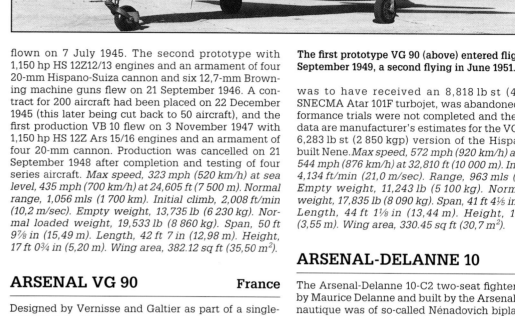

flown on 7 July 1945. The second prototype with 1,150 hp HS 12Z12/13 engines and an armament of four 20-mm Hispano-Suiza cannon and six 12,7-mm Browning machine guns flew on 21 September 1946. A contract for 200 aircraft had been placed on 22 December 1945 (this later being cut back to 50 aircraft), and the first production VB 10 flew on 3 November 1947 with 1,150 hp HS 12Z Ars 15/16 engines and an armament of four 20-mm cannon. Production was cancelled on 21 September 1948 after completion and testing of four series aircraft. *Max speed, 323 mph (520 km/h) at sea level, 435 mph (700 km/h) at 24,605 ft (7 500 m). Normal range, 1,056 mls (1 700 km). Initial climb, 2,008 ft/min (10,2 m/sec). Empty weight, 13,735 lb (6 230 kg). Normal loaded weight, 19,533 lb (8 860 kg). Span, 50 ft 9⅞ in (15,49 m). Length, 42 ft 7 in (12,98 m). Height, 17 ft 0¾ in (5,20 m). Wing area, 382.12 sq ft (35,50 m^2).*

ARSENAL VG 90 France

Designed by Vernisse and Galtier as part of a single-seat shipboard interceptor and strike fighter development programme, the VG 90 was evolved in competition with the Aérocentre NC 1080 and the Nord 2200. Powered by a 5,000 lb st (2 268 kgp) Rolls-Royce Nene turbojet, the VG 90 had an all-metal fuselage, and the

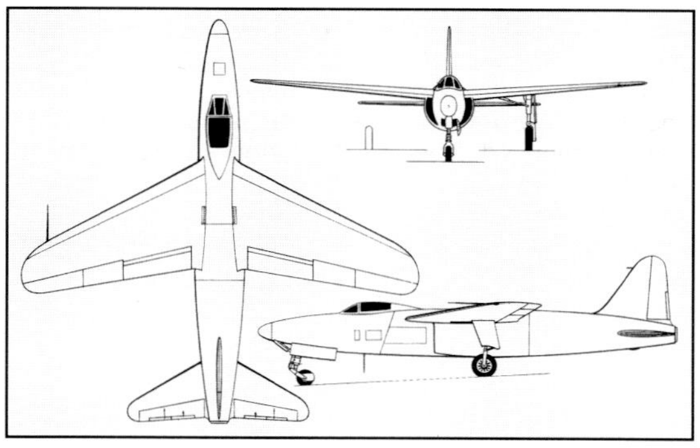

(Above) The VG 90 experimental shipboard fighter.

wing and tail surfaces were metal structures with plywood skinning. Two prototypes were built, the first being flown on 27 September 1949 and the second following in June 1951. Planned armament comprised three 30-mm Hispano-Suiza cannon and provision was made for underwing ordnance loads, such as two 1,102-lb (500-kg) bombs. The second prototype had provision for two 20-mm cannon, two 7,7-mm machine guns and 36 RAC 50 rockets internally, plus 16 T10 or 80 RAC 50 rockets on wing racks. A third prototype, which

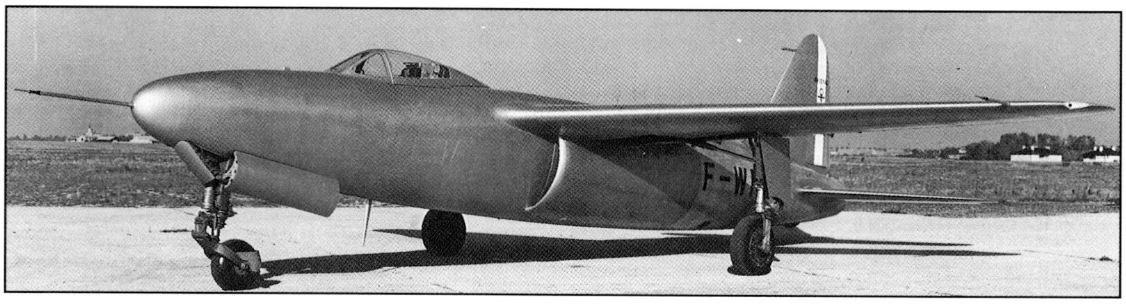

The first prototype VG 90 (above) entered flight test in September 1949, a second flying in June 1951.

was to have received an 8,818 lb st (4 000 kgp) SNECMA Atar 101F turbojet, was abandoned. Full performance trials were not completed and the following data are manufacturer's estimates for the VG 90 with a 6,283 lb st (2 850 kgp) version of the Hispano-Suiza-built Nene. *Max speed, 572 mph (920 km/h) at sea level, 544 mph (876 km/h) at 32,810 ft (10 000 m). Initial climb, 4,134 ft/min (21,0 m/sec). Range, 963 mls (1 550 km). Empty weight, 11,243 lb (5 100 kg). Normal loaded weight, 17,835 lb (8 090 kg). Span, 41 ft 4⅙ in (12,60 m). Length, 44 ft 1⅛ in (13,44 m). Height, 11 ft 7¾ in (3,55 m). Wing area, 330.45 sq ft (30,7 m^2).*

ARSENAL-DELANNE 10 France

The Arsenal-Delanne 10-C2 two-seat fighter designed by Maurice Delanne and built by the Arsenal de l'Aéronautique was of so-called Nénadovich biplane configuration, the tandem-mounted wings providing a continuous slot effect and offering exceptional CG travel. Of metal stressed-skin construction and powered by an 860 hp Hispano-Suiza 12Ycrs 12-cylinder liquid-cooled engine, the Arsenal-Delanne 10-C2 prototype was virtually complete at Villacoublay when German forces occupied the factory in June 1940, work on the aircraft continuing in a desultory fashion and the first flight test being made in October 1941. After completion of the initial test programme, the aircraft was ferried to Germany for further trials. The intended armament comprised an engine-mounted 20-mm Hispano-Suiza cannon, two wing-mounted 7,5-mm MAC 1934 machine guns and two further 7,5-mm weapons on a flexible mounting. *Max speed, 342 mph (550 km/h) at 14,764 ft (4 500 m). Time to 16,405 ft (5 000 m), 6.5 min. Endurance, 1.5 hrs. Loaded weight, 6,349 lb (2 880 kg). Span, 33 ft 2 in (10,11 m). Length, 24 ft 0½ in (7,33 m). Height 10 ft 0½ in (3,06 m). Wing area, 242.19 sq ft (22,5 m^2).*

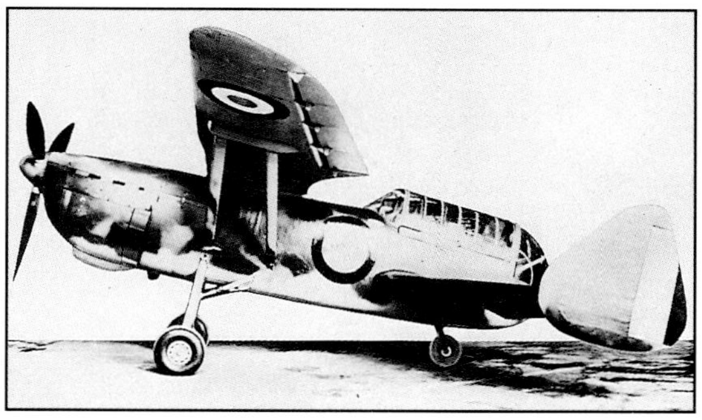

The Arsenal-Delanne 10-C2 was innovative in being of tandem-wing or Nénadovich biplane configuration.

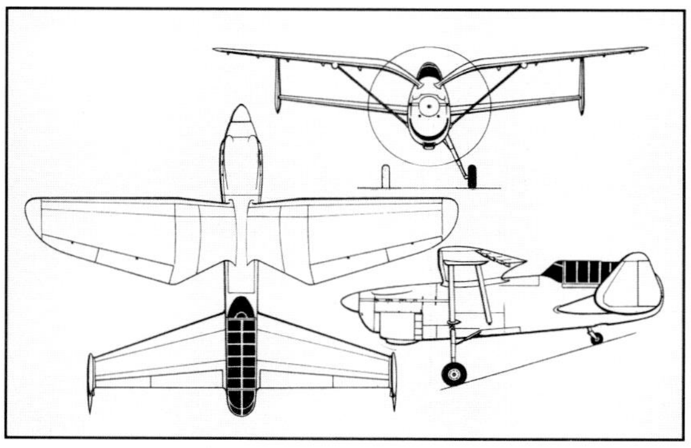

ASJA

ASJA JAKTFALK II — Sweden

When, on 1 January 1933, the newly-established aviation department of the Linköping-based railway wagon and carriage manufacturer, the AB Svenska Järnvägsverkstäderna (ASJA) acquired the assets of Svenska Aero AB of Lidingö, it took over the continued development of the latter company's S.A. 14 Jaktfalk (Gerfalcon) single-seat fighter. An improved version of the J 6A was evolved by ASJA as the J 6B Jaktfalk II, this being offered with Armstrong Siddeley Jaguar or Panther engines, or the Bristol Jupiter. The Jaktfalk II retained the revised wing structure and lengthened fuselage of the J 6A, to which were added redesigned horizontal tail surfaces from which the bracing struts were eliminated. Seven were ordered by *Flygvapnet* with the supercharged nine-cylinder Bristol Jupiter VIIF radial rated at 520 hp at 10,000 ft (3 050 m), armament comprising the standard paired 8-mm synchronised machine guns. The contract was placed with ASJA on 1 May 1933, and the seven aircraft were

(Above and below) The J 6B Jaktfalk II, the photo depicting one of the two donated to Finland in 1939.

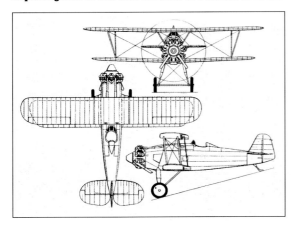

delivered during the following October-November, serving, like the Svenska Aero-built J 6s and J 6As, with *Flygflottilj* 1 at Västerås. Two of the J 6B Jaktfalkar (together with a single Svenska Aero-built J 6A) were donated to Finland in December 1939, subsequently serving in the fighter training rôle. *Max speed, 193 mph (310 km/h) at 14,765 ft (4 500 m). Cruising speed, 161 mph (260 km/h). Time to 3,280 ft (1000 m), 4.0 min. Empty weight, 2,085 lb (946 kg). Loaded weight, 3,240 lb (1 470 kg). Span, 28 ft 10¹/₂ in (8,80 m). Length, 24 ft 7¹/₄ in (7,50 m). Height, 11 ft 4¹/₄ in (3,46 m). Wing area, 234.66 sq ft (21,80 m²).*

ATLAS CHEETAH — South Africa

Studies to upgrade the elderly Mirage IIIZs of the South African Air Force were begun in the early 1980s, with Israeli assistance it is believed. The heavily modified aircraft, renamed Cheetah, was unveiled on 16 July 1986, entering service in the following year. In many ways it resembled the Israeli Kfir. The obvious external differences were fixed canards on the intake cheeks, and a lengthened and drooped nose with a small strake on each side. The wings were modified with a drooped fixed leading edge, and a vortex-inducing dogtooth discontinuity outboard. This feature gave a measurable increase in manoeuvrability. The engine was a single licence-built SNECMA Atar 9K50, rated at 15,846 lb (7 188 kgp) max and 11,060 lb (5 017 kgp) military thrust. A bolt-on refuelling probe could also be fitted. The cockpit was extensively remodelled, with an Elta Hud and "glass" multi-function displays. Elta also provide the

(Above) A Cheetah EZ upgrade of the Mirage IIIEZ produced by Atlas for the South African Air Force.

multi-mode radar, either an EL/M-2001 or -2035, and an electronic warfare system. Armament consists of two 30-mm DEFA cannon, and two or four R.550 Magic or V3 Kukri heat homing AAMs. *Max speed hi, Mach 1.8. Cruising speed, 540 kt (1 007 km/h). Landing speed 160 kt (296 km/h). No other performance data available. Empty weight, 16,182 lb (7 340 kg). Max weight, 29,983 lb (13 600 kg). Span, 26ft 11³/₄in (8,22 m). Length 52ft 9¹/₂in (16,09 m). Height, 13 ft 11 in (4,25 m). Wing area, c380 sq ft (35,30 m²).*

AUSTIN A.F.B.1 — UK

Frequently referred to as the "Austin Ball Scout" because the Austin Motor Company incorporated some of the ideas of Capt Albert Ball, VC, DSO, MC, in this fighter's design, the A.F.B.1 was designed by C H Brooks and was flown for the first time in July 1917. It was of wooden construction with fabric covering, and was powered by a 200 hp Hispano-Suiza eight-cylinder liquid-cooled engine. Armament comprised a single 0.303-in (7,7-mm) Lewis machine gun firing through the hollow propeller shaft, and a similar weapon on a Foster mounting above the upper wing centre section. As originally built, the sole prototype of the A.F.B.1 had slightly sweptback wing surfaces and conventional single-bay bracing, but during the course of

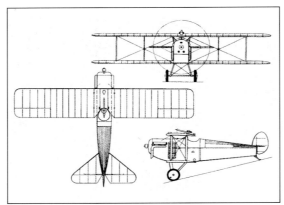

(Above and below) The Austin A.F.B.1 in its revised and definitive configuration as flown autumn 1917.

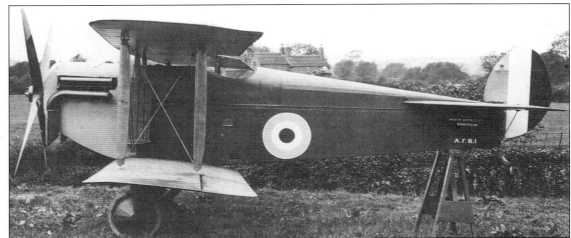

development new unswept surfaces accompanied by revised interplane bracing of two-bay form were introduced. The aircraft flew for the first time after these modifications on 17 September 1917. The following data relate to the A.F.B.1 in its original form. *Max speed, 138 mph (222 km/h) at sea level, 120 mph (193 km/h) at 15, 000 ft (4 570 m). Time to 10,000 ft (3 050 m), 8.9 min. Endurance, 2.25 hrs. Empty weight, 1,525 lb (692 kg). Loaded weight, 2,077 lb (942 kg). Span, 30ft 0 in (9,14 m). Length, 21 ft 6 in (6,55 m). Height, 9 ft 3 in (2,82 m). Wing area, 290 sq ft (26,94 m²).*

AUSTIN A.F.T.3 OSPREY — UK

A private venture intended to compete with the Sopwith Snipe, the Osprey was of wooden construction with fabric skinning and was powered by a 230 hp Bentley B.R.2 nine-cylinder rotary engine. Armament comprised two fixed and synchronised (7,7-mm) Vickers machine guns and one semi-free Lewis gun of similar calibre on the rear spanwise member of the middle-wing centre section. The Osprey was flown for the first time in February 1918, but performance proved to be inferior to that of the Snipe, and construction of second and third prototypes was abandoned. *Max speed, 118mph (190 km/h) at 10,000ft (3 050 m), 110 mph (177 km/h) at 15,000 ft (4 570 m). Time to*

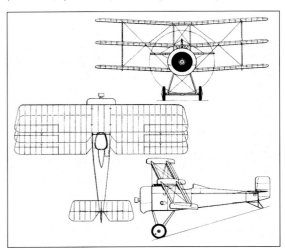

The A.F.T.3 Osprey (above and below) was intended to compete with the Snipe, but proved inferior.

10,000 ft (3 050 m), 10.35 min. Endurance, 3 hrs. Empty weight, 1,106 lb (502 kg). Loaded weight, 1,888 lb (856 kg). Span, 23 ft 0 in (7,01 m). Length, 17 ft 7 in (5,36 m). Height, 10 ft 8 in (3,25 m). Wing area, 233 sq ft (21,64 m²).

AUSTIN GREYHOUND　　　　　UK

The Greyhound tandem two-seat fighter-reconnaissance aircraft was designed by J Kenworthy as a potential successor to the Bristol Fighter, but the first prototype was not completed until after the Armistice of 1918 owing to difficulties with its 320 hp ABC Dragonfly I nine-cylinder radial engine. Flight testing eventually commenced in May 1919, and three prototypes were built and flown, but no further development was undertaken. Armament comprised two fixed synchronised 0.303-in (7,7-mm) Vickers guns and a single 0.303-in (7,7-mm). Lewis gun on a Scarff ring in the rear cockpit. Max speed, 129 mph (207 km/h) at 6,500 ft (1 980 m), 126 mph (203 km/h) at 10,000 ft (3 050 m). Time to 10,000 ft (3 050 m), 10.83 min. Endurance, 3 hrs. Empty weight, 1,838 lb (834 kg). Loaded weight, 3,032 lb (1 375 kg). Span, 39 ft 0 in (11,89 m). Length, 26 ft 8½ in (8,14 m). Height, 10 ft 4 in (3,15 m). Wing area, 400 sq ft (36,16 m²).

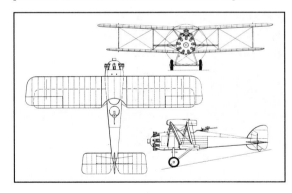

The Greyhound (above and below) was envisaged as a potential successor to the two-seat Bristol Fighter.

A.U.T.18　　　　　Italy

The A.U.T.18 – the designation signifying Aeronautica Umbra S.A., the manufacturer, Ing Felice Trojani, the designer, and the originally-planned wing area of 18 m² – was an all-metal stressed-skin single-seat fighter, one example of which was ordered in 1936 for evaluation by the Regia Aeronautica. Unusual among contemporary Italian single-seat fighters in having its armament of

(Below) The A.U.T.18 with definitive engine cowling.

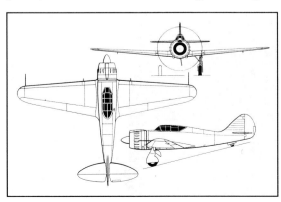

Unusual among contemporary Italian fighters in having wing-mounted armament was the A.U.T.18 (above).

twin 12,7-mm guns mounted in the wings, the A.U.T.18 was powered by a Fiat A.80 R.C.41 18-cylinder radial engine rated at 1,030 hp for take-off, and flew for the first time on 22 April 1939. Initial trials were performed with an NACA-type engine cowling, but this was supplanted from April 1940 by a close-fitting cowling with the rocker arms partly enclosed by fairings. Evaluation of the sole prototype was completed on 5 November 1940, when the aircraft was delivered to the Regia Aeronautica, but the Ministero dell'Aeronautica did not consider that the Trojani fighter offered any advantages over the Macchi C.200 and Fiat G.50, both of which were in production, and further development of the A.U.T.18 was discontinued. Max speed, 298 mph (480 km/h). Time to 19,685 ft (6 000 m), 8.2 min. Range, 497 mls (800 km). Empty weight, 5,115 lb (2 320 kg). Loaded weight, 6,559 lb (2 975 kg). Span, 37 ft 8¾ in (11,50 m). Length, 28 ft 0⅞ in (8,56 m). Height, 9 ft 5⅓ in (2,88 m). Wing area, 201.29 sq ft (18,70 m²).

AVIA BH-3　　　　　Czechoslovakia

The first fighter produced by the Avia concern, the BH-3 designed by Paul Beneš and Miroslav Hajn was a logical development of the BH-1 and BH-2 sporting monoplanes. The prototype, flown in 1921, was powered by a 185 hp BMW IIIa six-cylinder water-cooled engine, and the excellent climb rate and manoeuvrability revealed by the BH-3 prompted the Air Force Directorate of the Ministry of Defence to order a series of 10 production aircraft, the first five powered by the BMW IIIa and the remaining five by the 220 hp Walter-built BMW IV six-cylinder water-cooled engine. Armament comprised two 7,7-mm Vickers machine

The BH-3 (below) was both the first Avia-designed fighter and the first to be built in series.

guns. The following details relate to the BMW IV-powered BH-3. Max speed, 140 mph (225 km/h). Cruise, 118 mph (190 km/h). Time to 16,405 ft (5 000 m), 10.5 min. Range, 280 mls (450 km). Empty weight, 1,753 lb (795 kg). Loaded weight, 2,308 lb (1 047 kg). Span, 33 ft 7⅛ in (10,24 m). Length, 22 ft 11¼ in (6,99 m). Height, 9 ft 2 in (2,79 m). Wing area, 169.64 sq ft (15,76 m²).

The BH-3 (below) first entered flight test in 1921.

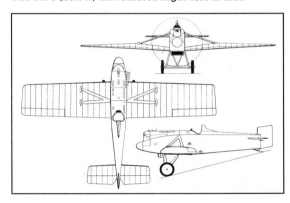

AVIA BH-4　　　　　Czechoslovakia

Some redesign and minor strengthening of the BH-3 forward fuselage was undertaken in 1922 to permit installation of the 220 hp Hispano-Suiza 8ba eight-cylinder water-cooled Vee engine in place of the six-cylinder upright BMW engine. Apart from the forward fuselage, a taller turnover pylon aft of the cockpit and a modified undercarriage with larger mainwheels, the HS-powered aircraft, initially designated B-HS-3 and subsequently BH-4, was essentially similar to the BH-3, and intended armament comprised two 7,7-mm Vickers guns. Performance of the BH-4 proved to be marginally inferior to that of the earlier fighter and development was confined to a single prototype. *Max speed, 138 mph (222 km/h). Cruise, 118 mph (190 km/h). Time to 16,405 ft (5 000 m), 20 min. Range, 317 mls (510 km). Empty weight, 1,596 lb (724 kg). Loaded weight, 2,238 lb (1 015 kg). Span, 33 ft 7⅛ in (10,24 m). Length, 21 ft 2¾ in (6,47 m). Height, 9 ft 9 in (2,97 m). Wing area, 169.64 sq ft (15,76 m²).*

Fundamentally a re-engined version of the BH-3, the BH-4 (below) was found inferior to its predecessor.

AVIA BH-6   Czechoslovakia

In the spring of 1923, Avia completed prototypes of two single-seat fighters evolved to a Ministry of Defence specification stipulating the use of a Škoda-built Hispano-Suiza 8Fb eight-cylinder water-cooled Vee engine rated at 310 hp for take-off, and employing essentially similar fuselages and undercarriages. The designers of the fighters, Beneš and Hajn, paid close attention to aerodynamic cleanliness, and whereas the first of these fighters, the BH-6, was completed as a single-bay biplane, the parallel BH-7A was a parasol monoplane. The BH-6 was of wooden construction, carried an armament of two 7,7-mm Vickers machine guns and had coolant radiators attached to the undercarriage legs. The lower wing had a greater span than that of the upper wing, the interplane struts were of inward-splayed "I" type, and the upper wing was carried above the fuselage by a pyramid fairing. The sole BH-6 was destroyed in an accident shortly after commencing flight trials. *Max speed, 137 mph (220 km/h). Cruise, 124 mph (200 km/h). Empty weight, 1,936 lb (878 kg). Loaded weight, 2,601 lb (1 180 kg). Span, 32 ft 8⅞ in (9,98 m). Length, 21 ft 2¾ in (6,47 m). Height, 9 ft 5⅓ in (2,88 m). Wing area, 243.26 sq ft (22,60 m²).*

The BH-6 (below) was unusual among biplane fighters in having a shorter span upper plane.

AVIA BH-7A   Czechoslovakia

The BH-7A parasol monoplane fighter, which, like the BH-6 biplane, commenced its flight test programme in the spring of 1923, enjoyed little better fortune than did its contemporary, being abandoned after involvement in two accidents. With similar power plant and armament to the BH-6, and basically the same fuselage and undercarriage, the BH-7A featured splayed N-type bracing struts and an unusually small gap between fuselage and wing. A further development of the basic

Built in parallel with the BH-6, the parasol BH-7A (below) had essentially the same fuselage.

design intended for high-speed competition flying, the BH-7B, had the wing lowered to fair directly into the upper fuselage, and a supercharged version of the HS 8Fb engine. *Max speed, 149 mph (240 km/h). Cruise, 127 mph (205 km/h). Time to 16,405 ft (5 000 m), 12.5 min. Empty weight, 1,885 lb (855 kg). Loaded weight, 2,538 lb (1 151 kg). Span, 34 ft 1⅜ in (10,4 m). Length, 22 ft 5¼ in (6,84 m). Height, 9 ft 3⅜ in (2,83 m). Wing area, 195.37 sq ft (18,15 m²).*

AVIA BH-8   Czechoslovakia

Although the BH-8 single-seat fighter biplane owed much to experience gained by Beneš and Hajn with the BH-6 and BH-7A, and had commenced its flight test programme before the end of 1923, it was essentially a new design. Power was provided by a Škoda-built HS 8Fb engine, and, as on the BH-6, its lower wing had a greater span than the upper wing, with inward-inclined I-type interplane struts and a faired pyramid structure carrying the upper wing above the fuselage. Development was abandoned in favour of the BH-17. *Max speed, 138 mph (222 km/h). Time to 16,405 ft (5 000 m), 14.66 min. Empty weight, 1,858 lb (843 kg). Loaded weight, 2,520 lb (1 143 kg). Span, 31 ft 1¼ in (9,48 m). Length, 21 ft 3½ in (6.49 m). Height, 9 ft 1 in (2,77 m). Wing area, 237.99 sq ft (22,11 m²).*

(Right) The BH-19 proved unsatisfactory, leading to a Ministerial request to discontinue monoplanes.

The BH-8 (below) owed much to experience gained with BH-6 and -7A, but was dropped in favour of BH-17.

AVIA BH-17   Czechoslovakia

Progressive refinement of the BH-8 resulted in the BH-17 which, somewhat lighter and featuring wings of reduced span and area, was placed in production in 1924, a batch of 24 being built for the Czechoslovak air arm with which the fighter served as the B 17. Powered by the Škoda-built HS 8Fb engine and armed with two synchronised 7,7-mm Vickers machine guns, the BH-17 displayed better flying characteristics than its predecessors, but proved unreliable in service and was soon relegated to the reserve park. *Max speed, 146 mph (235 km/h). Cruise, 128 mph (206 km/h). Time to 16,405 ft (5 000 m), 14 min. Empty weight, 1,680 lb (762 kg). Loaded weight, 2,363 lb (1 072 kg). Span, 29 ft 0⅞ in (8,86 m). Length, 22 ft 6 in (6,86 m). Wing area, 229.27 sq ft (21,30 m²).*

Built in small series for the Czechoslovak air arm, the BH-17 (below) proved unreliable in service.

AVIA BH-19   Czechoslovakia

Anxious to break the supremacy in the fighter field enjoyed by the biplane configuration, and to emulate the success they had enjoyed with the first fighter monoplane, the BH-3, Beneš and Hajn initiated work on a new monoplane, the BH-19, in 1924. Powered by the Škoda-built HS 8Fb engine, the BH-19 demonstrated a high speed, but control response left much to be desired, and the prototype was prone to aileron flutter. The Ministry of Defence signified its willingness to place an order for the BH-19 if Avia could rectify its control shortcomings, but during speed trials over a course between Poćernice and Nehvizd the aircraft crashed and was destroyed. A second prototype was completed and flown, but the Ministry considered the results unsatisfactory and requested that Avia discontinue the further development of fighters of monoplane configuration. *Max speed, 152 mph (245 km/h). Cruise, 133 mph (215 km/h). Time to 16,405 ft (5 000 m), 15 min. Empty weight, 1,746 lb (792 kg). Loaded weight, 2,546 lb (1 155 kg). Span, 35 ft 5¼ in (10,80 m). Length, 24 ft 2⅛ in (7,37 m). Wing area, 196.98 sq ft (18,30 m²).*

AVIA BH-21   Czechoslovakia

The first Avia fighter to be built in substantial quantities, the BH-21 was a progressive development of the BH-17. It retained the Škoda-built HS 8Fb water-cooled engine, but the radiator was transferred from the undercarriage to the underside of the fuselage, and the faired pyramid between the fuselage and upper wing which obstructed forward view was discarded. Prototype trials began in February 1925, and production was

The BH-21 (below) entered series production in 1925.

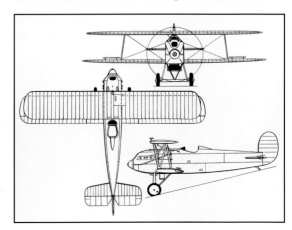

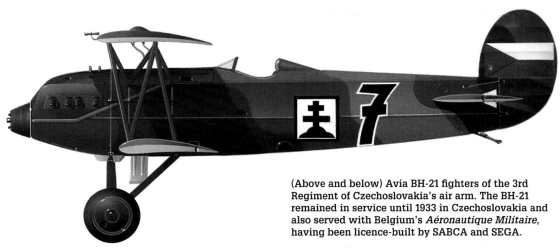

(Above and below) Avia BH-21 fighters of the 3rd Regiment of Czechoslovakia's air arm. The BH-21 remained in service until 1933 in Czechoslovakia and also served with Belgium's *Aéronautique Militaire*, having been licence-built by SABCA and SEGA.

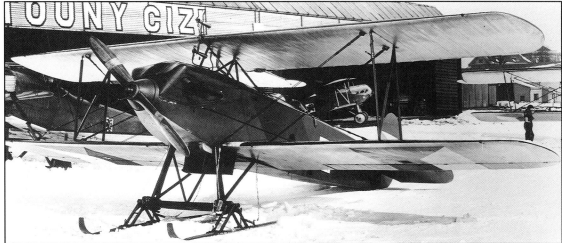

ordered for the Czechoslovak air arm as the B 21, a total of 139 subsequently being built. Following successful participation in a Belgian *Aéronautique Militaire* contest held in June 1925, one BH-21 was procured from Avia and a further 44 were licence-built in Belgium, 39 by SABCA (Société Anonyme Belge de Constructions Aéronautiques) and five by SEGA (Société d'Etudes Générales d'Aviation), these being delivered to the *Aéronautique Militaire* between September 1927 and November 1928. The BH-21 carried an armament of two synchronised 7,7-mm machine guns. *Max speed, 152 mph (245 km/h) at 9,840 ft (3 000 m). Range, 342 mls (550 km). Time to 16,405 ft (5 000 m), 13 min. Empty weight, 1,587 lb (720 kg). Loaded weight, 2,390 lb (1 084 kg). Span, 29 ft 2⅛ in (8,90 m). Length, 22 ft 6½ in (6,87 m). Height, 8 ft 11¾ in (2,74 m). Wing area, 236.38 sq ft (21,96 m²).*

AVIA BH-23   Czechoslovakia

In parallel with production of the BH-21 fighter, Avia manufactured a lighter, lower-powered aerobatic advanced training version without armament, 30 examples being built as the BH-22. By a reverse process, a single-seat light night fighter was evolved by introducing armament on the BH-22 trainer in 1925, two prototypes being completed and evaluated as the BH-23 (also known as the BH-22N). The BH-23 was powered by a Škoda-built HS 8Aa eight-cylinder water-cooled Vee engine rated at 180 hp, and armament comprised two 7,7-mm machine guns. No production of the

The BH-23 (below) was a lightweight fighter based broadly on the BH-22 advanced aerobatic trainer.

BH-23 was undertaken. *Max speed, 130 mph (210 km/h). Cruise, 118 mph (190 km/h). Empty weight, 1,554 lb (705 kg). Loaded weight, 1,938 lb (879 kg). Span, 29 ft 2⅛ in (8,90 m). Length, 22 ft 6½ in (6,87 m). Height, 8 ft 11¾ in (2,74 m). Wing area, 236.38 sq ft (21,96 m²).*

AVIA BH-26   Czechoslovakia

The BH-26 (above) represented Avia's first attempt to produce a two-seat fighter, this flying in 1927.

Flown for the first time in 1927, the BH-26 represented Avia's first attempt to produce a two-seat fighter. Employing a basically similar wooden structure to that of earlier Avia fighter biplanes, and retaining the un-equal-span single-bay configuration, the BH-26 was powered by a Walter-built Jupiter IV nine-cylinder radial with an international rating of 450 hp. Armament

comprised two synchronised 7,7-mm Vickers guns firing through the propeller and twin Lewis guns on a Škoda flexible mounting in the rear cockpit. Whereas the prototype had no fixed vertical tail fin, this feature was introduced on the production model which entered service with the Czechoslovak air arm as the B 26. *Max speed, 150 mph (242 km/h). Cruise, 137 mph (220 km/h). Time to 16,405 ft (5 000 m), 13.33 min. Range, 373 mls (600 km). Empty weight, 2,381 lb (1 080 kg). Loaded weight, 3,800 lb (1 760 kg). Span, 35 ft 5⅛ in (10,80 m). Length, 29 ft 0⅜ in (8,85 m). Height, 10 ft 11⅞ in (3,35 m). Wing area, 333.69 sq ft (31,00 m²).*

(Below) The BH-26 Jupiter-engined two-seat fighter.

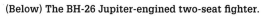

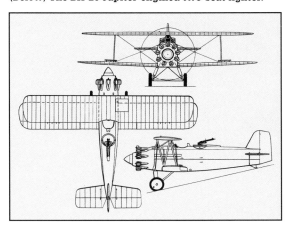

AVIA BH-33   Czechoslovakia

During the course of 1926, Avia tested the Gnome-Rhône version of the Bristol Jupiter nine-cylinder radial air-cooled engine in a BH-21 airframe, and elected to

(Below) The BH-33 which entered flight test in 1927.

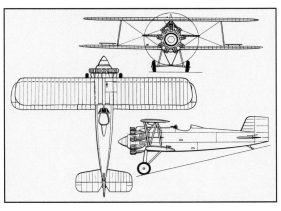

employ this power plant for a new fighter, the BH-33. This, the last fighter design to be produced by Beneš and Hajn for the Avia concern, was the first Avia fighter to feature a fixed tail fin from the outset, and commenced flight trials in 1927. It was ordered into production for the Czechoslovak air arm with a Walter-built Jupiter VI rated at 543 hp for take-off, armament comprising two 7,7-mm machine guns. A manufacturing

A BH-26 tandem two-seat fighter serving with the Central Flying School at Prostejov in 1932 for advanced tactical instruction.

licence for the BH-33 was acquired by Poland in 1928, PZL building 10 pre-production fighters of this type and PWS building some 50 production examples for the Polish Air Force as the PWS A from 1930. Three BH-33s were supplied to Belgium in 1929. *Max speed, 177 mph (285 km/h). Cruise, 148 mph (238 km/h). Initial climb, 2,067 ft/min (10,5 m/sec). Empty weight, 1,830 lb (830 kg). Loaded weight, 2,762 lb (1 253 kg). Span, 29 ft 2⅛ in (8,90 m). Length, 23 ft 1⅛ in (7,04 m). Wing area, 238.96 sq ft (22,20 m².).*

AVIA BH-33E   Czechoslovakia

The BH-33E, which appeared in 1929, differed from the BH-33 built for the Czechoslovak and Polish air arms in a number of major respects. The slab-sided wooden fuselage gave place to a welded steel-tube structure, an elliptical cross section being obtained with the aid of light formers, and a split-axle Vee-type undercarriage was introduced in place of the cross-axle undercarriage. Although the BH-33E was not ordered by the Czechoslovak Ministry of Defence in quantity, having been overtaken by the BH-33L, it enjoyed some export success, three evaluation examples being purchased by the Soviet Union and 20 being procured by Yugoslavia, which also obtained a manufacturing licence. Series production for the Yugoslav air arm subsequently took place at the Ikarus plant at Zemun. The BH-33E was offered with both the Jupiter VI and the supercharged Jupiter VII, but the former was installed in most aircraft, and armament comprised two 7,7-mm machine guns. One BH-33E airframe was fitted with a 525 hp BMW Hornet engine experimentally as the B-133. *Max speed, 177 mph (285 km/h). Cruise, 155 mph (250 km/h). Time to 9,845 ft (3 000 m), 4.3 min, to 16,405 ft (5 000 m), 8.12 min. Empty weight, 1,874 lb (850 kg). Loaded weight, 2,800 lb (1 270 kg). Span, 29 ft 2⅛ in (8,90 m). Length, 23 ft 1⅛ in (7,04 m). Height, 9 ft 1⅞ in (2,79 m). Wing area, 238.96 sq ft (22,20 m².).*

(Above) A BH-33E with a non-standard engine cowling, and (below) the sole example of the BH-33E fitted with a BMW Hornet engine (as the B-133).

AVIA BH-33L   Czechoslovakia

The third and definitive stage in the development of the basic BH-33 fighter was represented by the BH-33L which was to be used by all fighter units of the Czechoslovak air arm as the Ba 33. Flown in prototype form in 1929, the BH-33L had essentially similar fuselage and undercarriage to those of the BH-33E, but introduced longer-span wings of greater area and employed the Škoda L three-bank 12-cylinder water-cooled engine offering 580 hp for take-off and having a normal maximum rating of 500 hp. Two Mk 28 (modified Vickers) machine guns were mounted between the cylinder

(Right) The BH-33L, designated BA-33 in Czechoslovak service, was the definitive version of the fighter.

A BH-33 licence was obtained by Poland in 1928 and the fighter built as the P.W.S. A as seen above.

banks. The BH-33L served as the standard Czechoslovak fighter throughout the early 'thirties. *Max speed, 184 mph (297 km/h). Cruise, 155 mph (250 km/h). Initial climb, 2,165 ft/min (11,0 m/sec). Range, 280 mls (450 km). Empty weight, 2,469 lb (1 120 kg). Loaded weight, 3,589 lb (1 628 kg). Span, 31 ft 2 in (9,50 m). Length, 23 ft 8⅓ in (7,22 m). Height, 10 ft 3¼ in (3,13 m). Wing area, 274.06 sq ft (25,46 m².).*

(Below) The BH-33L which entered service in 1930.

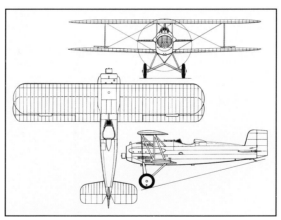

AVIA B 34   Czechoslovakia

The B 34, designed by Ing František Novotný, owed nothing to previous Avia single-seat fighters, and was an all-metal fabric-covered single-bay biplane powered

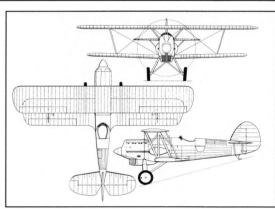

(Above) Forerunner of the renowned B 534, the B 34.

by a 740 hp Hispano-Suiza 12Nbr 12-cylinder liquid-cooled engine. Flown for the first time in 1932 by Vaclav Koči, the B 34 initially proved disappointing and the prototype was promptly returned to the factory for modifications, re-emerging as the B 34/1 with a new propeller, a redesigned engine cowling in which the face of the underslung radiator bath was cut back, and redesigned vertical tail surfaces. With these changes flight testing was resumed, and a production batch of 12 B 34 fighters was ordered for the Czechoslovak air arm. The production B 34 embodied further redesign of the vertical tail surfaces, which were enlarged, and other changes by comparison with the prototype, including narrower-chord interplane bracing struts and the discarding of the streamlined mainwheel fairings. Power was provided by an Avia (Škoda) Vr 30 (licence-built HS 12Nbr) rated at 760 hp for take-off, and armament comprised two 7,7-mm fuselage-mounted Mk 28 machine guns. *Max speed, 196 mph (315 km/h) at sea*

level. Cruise, 174 mph (280 km/h). Initial climb, 2,362 ft/min (12 m/sec). Range, 373 mls (600 km/h). Empty weight, 2,877 lb (1 305 kg). Loaded weight, 3,814 lb (1 730 kg). Span, 30 ft 10 in (9,40 m). Length, 23 ft 9⅓ in (7,25 m). Wing area, 257.26 sq ft (23,9 m²).

The B 34 prototype is seen below after modifications as the B 34/1 in which form it was ordered.

AVIA B 534.I & II   Czechoslovakia

In developing the B 34, Ing František Novotný had considered installation of several alternative engines, versions offered being the B 134 with the 800 hp Walter-built Mistral 14Kbs, the B 234 with the 600 hp Avia Rr 29 nine-cylinder radial, the B 334 with the 650 hp AS Panther and the B 434 with the 690 hp HS 12Xbrs. A second prototype, the B 34/2, was completed, this having larger, less angular vertical tail surfaces and armament transferred to wing fairings. It was to have had the Rr 29 engine, but the failure of this power plant resulted in the B 34/2 being re-engined with an HS 12Ybrs rated at 860 hp at 13,123 ft (4 000 m). The twin-gun armament was reinstated in the fuselage and, with a redesigned rudder, the B 34/2 was flown in August 1933, being subsequently referred to as the B 534/1 after successfully completing official trials. A further prototype was then built as the B 534/2, this introducing mainwheel fairings, a forward-extended radiator bath, redesigned vertical tail surfaces, raised aft fuselage decking, a cockpit canopy, and the fuselage-mounted guns moved farther aft for CG reasons. On 17 July 1933, an order was placed for 146 production examples of the B 534. The production B 534 omitted the refinements of wheel spats and cockpit canopy, but was otherwise similar to the B 534/2 prototype. The Avia-built HS 12Ydrs engine of 830 hp for take-off was installed and armament comprised four 7,7-mm Model 28 or 30 guns, two in the fuselage and two in lower-wing fairings, aircraft so armed being referred to as the B 534 Series I (or B 534.I). With the 48th aircraft, all four guns were mounted in the fuselage, this being the first B 534.II and the arrangement being standardised for all subsequent machines. A further 54 had meanwhile been ordered with an alternative armament as the Bk 534. Similar in other respects to the B 534.II, the Bk 534 was to have had an engine-mounted 20-mm Oerlikon FFS cannon, machine gun armament being reduced to two Model 30 weapons. Difficulties with the cannon shell feed arrangement eventually led to the Oerlikon being discarded in favour of a third 7,7-mm weapon. The specifications of Series I and II B 534s were similar. Max speed, 241 mph (388 km/h) at 14,765 ft (4 500 m). Cruising speed, 211 mph (340 km/h). Initial climb, 2,913 ft/min (14,8 m/sec). Range, 360 mls (580 km). Empty weight, 3,053 lb (1 385 kg). Loaded weight, 4,217 lb (1 913 kg). Span, 30 ft 10 in (9,40 m). Length, 26 ft 10⅞ in (8,20 m). Wing area, 253.6 sq ft (23,56 m²).

The B 534.II (below) was the second production model.

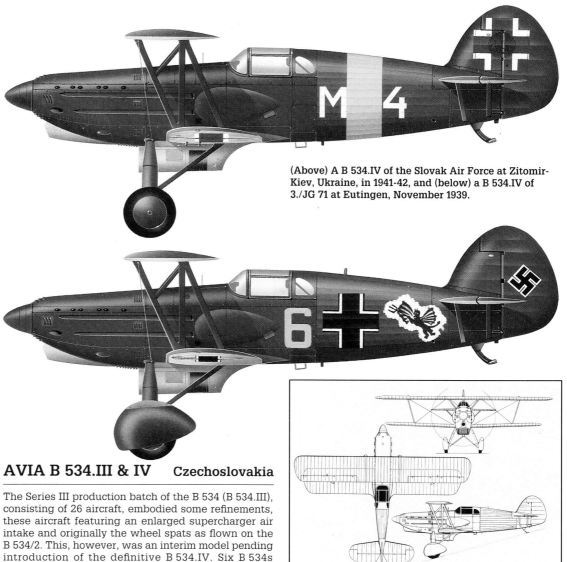

(Above) A B 534.IV of the Slovak Air Force at Zitomir-Kiev, Ukraine, in 1941-42, and (below) a B 534.IV of 3./JG 71 at Eutingen, November 1939.

AVIA B 534.III & IV   Czechoslovakia

The Series III production batch of the B 534 (B 534.III), consisting of 26 aircraft, embodied some refinements, these aircraft featuring an enlarged supercharger air intake and originally the wheel spats as flown on the B 534/2. This, however, was an interim model pending introduction of the definitive B 534.IV. Six B 534s essentially similar to the Series III were exported to Greece and 14 to Yugoslavia. The Series IV was similar to its immediate predecessor apart from having a metal rather than wooden propeller and in adopting an aft-sliding cockpit canopy with raised fuselage rear decking. A total of 272 B 534.IV fighters was built, these being powered by the Avia-built HS 12Ydrs engine and mounting four 7,7-mm guns. Of some 450 B 534s and Bk 534s in the inventory of the Czechoslovak air arm on 15 March 1939, a number was absorbed by the newly-created Slovak Air Force, 78 were sold to Bulgaria and the remainder were taken into the inventory of the Luftwaffe. (B 534.IV) Max speed, 252 mph (405 km/h) at

(Above) The definitive B 534, the Series IV.

14,435 ft (4 400 m). Cruising speed, 214 mph (345 km/h). Initial climb, 2,953 ft/min (15,0 m/sec). Range, 360 mls (580 km). Empty weight, 3,219 lb (1 460 kg). Loaded weight, 4,376 lb (1 985 kg). Span, 30 ft 10 in (9,40 m). Length, 26 ft 10⅞ in (8,20 m). Wing area, 253.6 sq ft (23,56 m²).

A ski-equipped B 534.IV (below) of the Slovak Air Force at Nitra in the winter of 1941.

AVIA B 634   Czechoslovakia

The B 634 represented the ultimate in the aerodynamic development of the basic B 34 single-seat fighter biplane design, and was to be numbered among the cleanest aircraft in its category ever flown. Tested in 1936, the B 634 was powered by an Avia-built HS 12Ycrs engine mounting a 20-mm Oerlikon FFS cannon, two 7,7-mm Model 30 machine guns being installed in the upper fuselage decking. There was virtually no commonality of components between the B 634 and the B 534.I from which it was derived. By comparison with the earlier fighter, the upper wing of the B 634 featured increased chord while the lower wing had reduced chord, the wingtips were redesigned, the ailerons were broader, the gap was reduced (increasing the splay of the interplane struts), the stagger was greatly increased, and cut-outs were introduced on the lower wing roots. The curvature of the engine cowling and cockpit sill was refined, cantilever undercarriage legs were adopted and the radiator bath was faired cleanly

between the leg roots. Despite a substantial reduction in drag, performance offered an insufficient improvement over that of the B 534 to warrant series production, the disappointing results provided by the B 634 being due primarily to a substantial increase in structural weight. *Max speed, 258 mph (415 km/h). Initial climb, 3,150 ft/min (16,0 m/sec). Range, 310 mls (500 km). Empty weight, 3,770 lb (1 710 kg). Span, 30 ft 10 in (9,40 m). Length, 27 ft 4¾ in (8,35 m).*

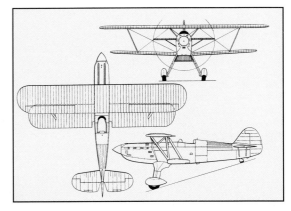

(Above and left) The B 634 was considered the ultimate development of the B 34 of 1932, but was conceptually dated when it appeared in 1936, and its performance was disappointing.

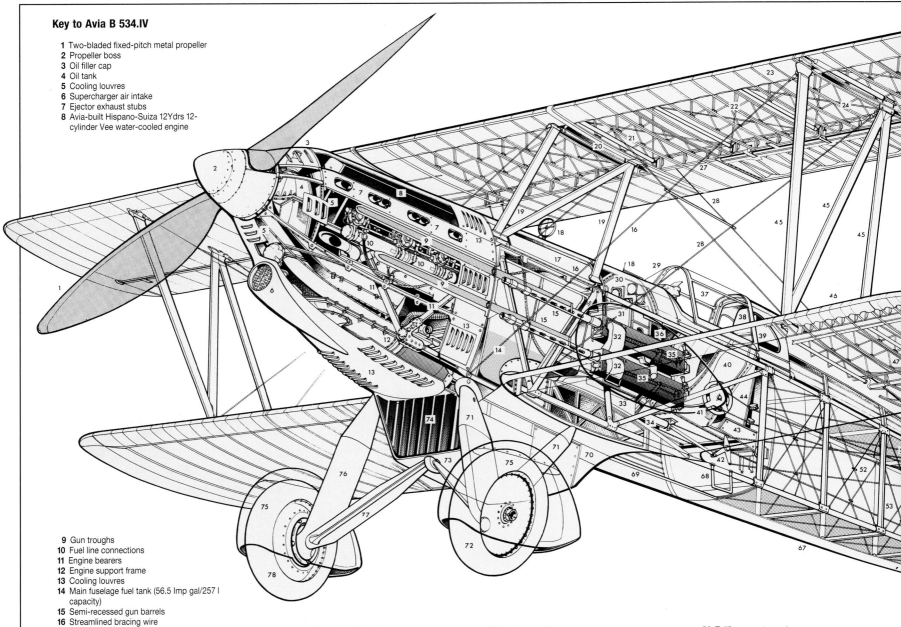

Key to Avia B 534.IV

1 Two-bladed fixed-pitch metal propeller
2 Propeller boss
3 Oil filler cap
4 Oil tank
5 Cooling louvres
6 Supercharger air intake
7 Ejector exhaust stubs
8 Avia-built Hispano-Suiza 12Ydrs 12-cylinder Vee water-cooled engine
9 Gun troughs
10 Fuel line connections
11 Engine bearers
12 Engine support frame
13 Cooling louvres
14 Main fuselage fuel tank (56.5 Imp gal/257 l capacity)
15 Semi-recessed gun barrels
16 Streamlined bracing wire
17 Gravity fuel tank (19.8 Imp gal/90 l capacity)
18 Ring-and-bead sight
19 Centre-section steel-tube N-struts
20 Strut support tube
21 Strengthened wing frame
22 Wing rib construction (riveted steel)
23 Fabric skinning
24 Wing rib/spar cross bracing
25 Aileron control hinge
26 Port (balanced) aileron
27 Rear spar
28 Bracing wires
29 One-piece curved windscreen
30 Instrument panel
31 Ammunition tank (300 rpg)
32 Cartridge chutes
33 Collector box
34 Gun support frame
35 Two 7,92-mm Model 30 synchronised machine guns
36 Control column
37 Three-position sliding canopy (4-mm Plexiglass)
38 Pilot's headrest
39 Rear-vision side glazing
40 Pilot's adjustable seat (provision for back-type parachute)
41 Tailplane incidence adjustment wheel
42 Elevator controls
43 Seat support frame
44 Control runs
45 Main interplane steel-tube N-type struts
46 Fabric-covered lower wing
47 Wing rib construction
48 Rear spar
49 Metal trailing-edge framework
50 Dorsal decking
51 Elevator control runs
52 Fuselage cross-bracing
53 Fuselage rectangular steel-tube framework (tubes riveted and bolted together and wire braced)
54 Rudder controls
55 Tailskid shock damper
56 Tailfin support member
57 Tailfin construction (fin adjustable on ground)
58 Rudder balance
59 Rudder construction
60 Tailplane construction (riveted steel strip)
61 Elevator balance
62 Elevator construction
63 Steel-tube tailplane struts
64 Rudder post
65 Rudder lower hinge
66 Tailwheel (interchangeable with tailwheel and oleo-pneumatic shock-absorber strut)
67 Fabric fuselage skinning

AVIA B 35   Czechoslovakia

To provide a potential successor to the B 534 in service with the Czechoslovak air arm, the Ministry of National Defence prepared an outline requirement for a single-seat fighter monoplane in late 1935. To meet this requirement, Ing František Novotný designed the B 35 for which a two-prototype contract was awarded in 1936. The B 35 was of mixed construction, with wooden wings covered by plywood bonded to an outer duralumin skin – a stressed skinning similar to *Plymax* that was being used for the Morane-Saulnier MS 405 – and a welded steel-tube fuselage with duralumin panelling forward and fabric skinning aft. With an HS 12Ydrs rated at 860 hp at 13,125 ft (4 000 m), the first prototype, the B 35.1, flew on 28 September 1938. It was re-engined with an HS 12Ycrs which, similarly rated to the Ydrs, made provision for a 20-mm cannon in the Vee of the cylinders, but it crashed on 21 November, being replaced in the test programme on 30 December 1938 by the second prototype, the B 35.2. This featured some

The second prototype of the B 35 (above) and the third prototype (immediately below). Initially designated B 35.3, the latter became the Av 135.1.

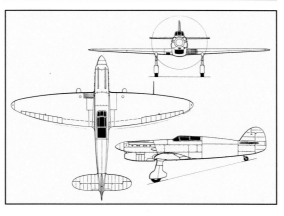

(Immediately above) The B 35.1 fighter prototype.

increase in fuselage cross section, smaller ailerons and extended flaps. Work continued after the German annexation of Bohemia and Moravia, a third prototype, the B 35.3, flying on 26 June 1939. This had a retractable undercarriage, a non-elliptical wing leading edge and an armament of one 20-mm cannon and two 7,92-mm machine guns. Prior to the commencement of flight test, the B 35.3 was exhibited at the *Salon de l'Aéronautique* in Brussels as the Avia 135. The following data relate to the B 35.1. *Max speed, 307 mph (495 km/h) at 13,125 ft (4 000 m). Initial climb, 2,559 ft/min (13,0 m/sec). Range, 310 mls (500 km). Empty weight, 3,726 lb (1 690 kg). Loaded weight, 4,850 lb (2 200 kg). Span, 33 ft 7½ in (10,25 m). Length, 27 ft 10⅔ in (8,50 m). Height, 8 ft 6⅓ in (2,60 m). Wing area, 185.47 sq ft (17,23 m²).*

AVIA B 135   Czechoslovakia

Bulgarian evaluation pilots had flown the B 35.2 in November 1939, and, in June 1940, flew the B 35.3 alias Av 135.1. With the agreement of the RLM in Berlin, the development programme of the Avia fighter was permitted to continue in what by now was the so-called "Protectorate" of Bohemia-Moravia specifically for the Bulgarian Ministry of War. A contract was placed with Avia for 12 Av 135 fighters for final assembly at Lovech,

The series Av 135 (above) with redesigned wing.

(Above) One of the 12 series Av 135 fighters delivered in 1942 to the Royal Bulgarian Air Force.

Although delivered to a fighter pilot school, the Av 135 (below) saw operational use in 1944.

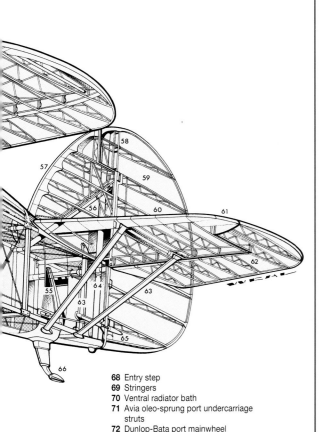

68 Entry step
69 Stringers
70 Ventral radiator bath
71 Avia oleo-sprung port undercarriage struts
72 Dunlop-Bata port mainwheel
73 Axle-strut attachment point (hinged beneath radiator bath)
74 Temperature control shutters for ventral radiator
75 Wheel spats (usually removed for operation from grass fields)
76 Starboard undercarriage strut
77 Half-axle
78 Starboard mainwheel

AVIA

in Central Bulgaria, where a further 50 were to be licence-built for the Royal Bulgarian Air Force as the DAR-11 Ljastuvka (Swallow). The dozen Avia-built Av 135 fighters were delivered in the summer of 1942, but only 35 of the 62 HS 12Ycrs engines intended for the licence-built aircraft reached Bulgaria and the licence construction programme was cancelled. The Av 135s were consigned to a Fighter Pilot School, but did see some operational use in 1944. The Av 135 was of similar construction to the B 35, was powered by an Avia-built Hispano-Suiza 12Ycrs engine rated at 860 hp at 13,125 ft (4 000 m) and 800 hp at sea level, and carried an armament of one 20-mm and two 7,92-mm guns. It differed from the B 35.3 essentially in having shorter-span ailerons and enlarged flaps. *Max speed, 332 mph (535 km/h) at 13,125 ft (4 000 m). Max initial climb, 2,638 ft/min (13,4 m/sec). Max range, 584 mls (940 km). Empty equipped weight, 4,548 lb (2 063 kg). Max loaded weight, 5,615 lb (2 547 kg). Span, 35 ft 7⅛ in (10,85 m). Length, 27 ft 10⅔ in (8,50 m). Height, 8 ft 6⅓ in (2,60 m). Wing area, 182.99 sq ft (17,00 m²).*

AVIA S 199   Czechoslovakia

During the latter part of World War II, the Avia factory at Prague-Čakovice was assigned the task of assembling Messerschmitt Bf 109G-6 and G-14 single-seat fighters, and G-12 two-seat conversion trainers. With the end of hostilities large stocks of component parts remained intact at the factory and a small series of Bf 109Gs was completed under the designation S 99, 20 of these being assigned to the National Air Guard. Lack of Daimler-Benz DB 605 engines led to adaptation of the basic Bf 109G airframe to take the Junkers Jumo 211F engine, of which large stocks were available. Rated at 1,350 hp for take-off and 1,060 hp at 17,390 ft (5 300 m), this engine drove a paddle-bladed VS 11 propeller and, as the S 199, the first example was flown on 25 March 1947. Although the S 199 possessed poor handling characteristics, production was undertaken for the Air Force which received the first aircraft in February 1948,

a total of 551 being produced (including a small number of two-seat CS 199s). Of these, 129 were assembled at the Letov factory at Letňany, production ceasing in 1951. Twenty-five S 199s were exported to Israel in 1948. Standard armament comprised two 20-mm cannon beneath the wings and two fuselage-mounted 13-mm machine guns. *Max speed, 328 mph (528 km/h) at sea level, 371 mph (598 km/h) at 19,685 ft (6 000 m). Max initial climb, 2,697 ft/min (13,7 m/sec). Max range, 534 mls (860 km). Empty weight, 6,305 lb (2 860 kg). Max loaded weight, 8,236 lb (3 736 kg). Span, 32 ft 6½ in (9,92 m). Length, 29 ft 4 in (8,94 m). Height, 8 ft 6 in (2,59 m). Wing area, 177.61 sq ft (16,50 m²).*

AVIA S 92 TURBÍNA   Czechoslovakia

All jigs, tools and components for the Messerschmitt Me 262 jet fighter in Czechoslovakia at the time of the German surrender were seized by the Soviet forces and then handed over to the newly restored Czechoslovak

(Above) The S 92.1, the first Me 262 to be built by Avia from components recovered after World War II.

government by Marshal Ivan Konev. Forward fuselages and other components of the Me 262 had been manufactured at Letňany, some components had been produced in converted railway tunnels, and the CKD and Walter works had built the Junkers Jumo 004 turbojet, assembly of the fighters having been undertaken at Cheb, near the German border. Sufficient components were recovered for Avia to build 17 single- and two-seat Me 262s, the first single-seater flying as the S 92.1 on 27 August 1946. On 5 September, this aircraft was lost in an accident, a second, S 92.2, flying on 24 October, and what was referred to as the first *series* aircraft, a two-seater (CS 92.3), following on 10 December. Dubbed the *Turbína* (Turbine), the S 92 was demonstrated to a Yugoslav delegation which placed an order with Avia for two examples although, in the event, these were not delivered. The seventh aircraft, CS 92.7, was experimentally fitted with BMW 003 turbojets, the thrust of which had been boosted to 2,094 lb st (950 kgp), but flight testing was not entirely successful and the aircraft was re-engined to take the standard Jumo 004 turbojets. The eleventh and twelfth aircraft, S 92.11 and S 92.12 were completed during 1949, and during the summer of 1950, the 5th Fighter Sqn was formed on the *Turbinas*, but a year later this unit was disbanded, most S 92s and CS 92s being scrapped. The specification of the S 92 Turbina was the same as that of the Me 262A.

AVIATIK D II   Germany

The Automobil und Aviatik AG of Leipzig-Heiterblick licence-built the Halberstadt D II as the Aviatik D I – later known as the Halberstadt D II(Av) – before, in late 1916, developing and building an original single-seat fighter as the D II. Powered by the 160 hp Daimler D III six-cylinder water-cooled engine and carrying an armament of two synchronised 7,92-mm LMG 08/15 machine guns, the D II was a staggered single-bay biplane with wooden, fabric-covered wings and a steel-tube (forward) and wood (aft) fuselage largely ply covered. The Aviatik fighter did not find favour with the *Idflieg* as a result of the *Typen-Prüfung* and further de-

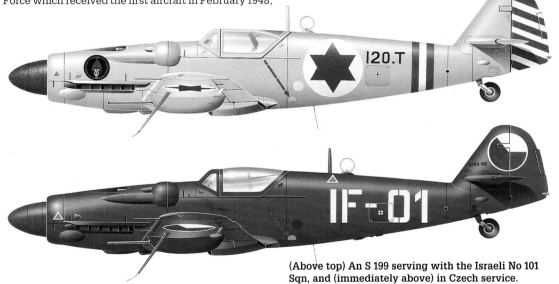

(Above top) An S 199 serving with the Israeli No 101 Sqn, and (immediately above) in Czech service.

(Below and right) The S 199 was a Czechoslovak development of the Bf 109G powered by the decidedly unsuitable but readily available Junkers Jumo 211F.

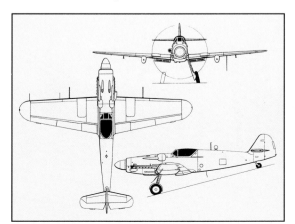

40

velopment was discontinued, only the one prototype being built. *Max speed, 93 mph (150 km/h). Time to 3,280 ft (1 000 m), 7.2 min. Span, 29 ft 0 in (8,84 m). Length, 22 ft 4½ in (6,82 m). Height, 9 ft 5 in (2,87 m).*

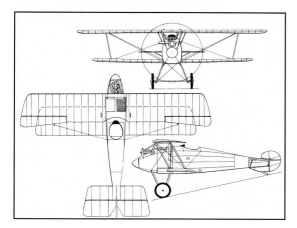

(Above and below) The D II was the first original fighter from the Automobil und Aviatik AG.

AVIATIK D III   Germany

Flown for the first time in November 1917, the first prototype D III was powered by an ungeared Benz Bz IIIbo eight-cylinder Vee engine rated at 195 hp, was of mixed construction with a steel-tube forward fuselage, plywood fuselage skinning and fabric wing skinning, and carried an armament of twin synchronised 7,92-mm LMG 08/15 machine guns. A distinguishing feature was provided by a small, keel-like extension beneath the fuselage which served to increase the wing gap. Initial *Typen-Prüfung* was performed at Adlershof during 9-12 February 1918, and after modifications by Aviatik, the D III was returned to Adlershof in April for resumption of type testing, together with a second prototype powered by a geared Bz IIIbm engine. By this time a small series of Bz IIIbo-powered D IIIs was under construction for service test and evaluation. Performance of the D III was considered to be superior to that of the Albatros D V although no details have apparently survived other than those relating to climb tests conducted in March 1918 with the Bz IIIbo-powered first prototype. *Time to 3,280 ft (1 000 m), 2.5 min, to 6,560 ft (2 000 m), 5.7 min, to 9,840 ft (3 000 m), 11 min, to 13,125 ft (4 000 m), 17 min. Loaded weight, 1,905 lb (864 kg). Span, 29 ft 6⅜ in ((9,0 m). Wing area, 226.05 sq ft (21,0 m²).*

The D III (below) was type tested in February 1918.

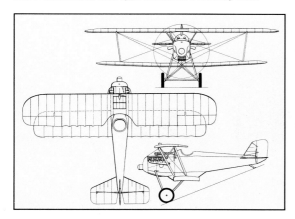

The Aviatik D III (above) was allegedly considered superior in performance to the Albatros D V.

AVIATIK D VI   Germany

During 1918, Aviatik was working on prototypes of several single-seat fighter biplanes simultaneously, two of these, the D IV and the D V, being powered by the Benz Bz IIIbv geared engine which was a larger-volume version of the Bz IIIbm. Apart from its power plant and a redesigned and enlarged rudder, the D IV was essentially similar to the D III, while the D V was a new fighter design which discarded flying wires. Prototypes of both types were built, but protracted engine teething troubles delayed the programmes, and there is no evidence that either was flown. The D VI, the sole prototype of which was flown in August 1918, bore little relationship to earlier Aviatik single-seat fighters, and was a two-bay biplane of wooden construction with ply-covered fuselage and fabric-covered wings and tail surfaces. Armament comprised two synchronised 7,92-mm LMG 08/15 machine guns and power was provided by a geared Benz Bz IIIbm. The D VI was intended to participate in the second D-type Contest held at Adlershof in June 1918. Owing to problems provided by the reduction gear of the Bz IIIbm, it was too late to

The Aviatik D VI (above) was too late to join the D-type Contest of June 1918 due to engine problems.

participate in this contest, and by the time type-testing had revealed excellent flight characteristics, the D VI had already been overtaken by the D VII. *Max speed, 117 mph (188 km/h). Time to 16,405 ft (5 000 m), 17.8 min. Empty weight, 1,653 lb (750 kg). Loaded weight, 2,072 lb (940 kg). Span, 31 ft 8⅓ in (9,66 m). Length, 20 ft 0⅛ in (6,10 m). Height, 8 ft 2½ in (2,50 m).*

AVIATIK D VII   Germany

The D VII, which was intended to participate in the third D-type Contest of October 1918, was essentially similar to the D VI apart from having completely redesigned vertical and horizontal tail surfaces. Like its pre-

decessor, it was powered by a geared Benz Bz IIIbm eight-cylinder Vee engine driving a four-bladed propeller. Armament comprised the standard twin 7,92-mm synchronised machine guns, and only one prototype was completed. *Max speed,119 mph (192 km/h). Time to 19,685 ft (6 000 m), 24 min. Empty weight, 1,642 lb (745 kg). Loaded weight, 2,083 lb (945 kg). Span, 31 ft 8⅓ in (9,66 m). Length, 20 ft 0⅛ in (6,10 m). Height, 8 ft 2½ in (2,50 m).*

The D VII (below) was the last Aviatik fighter.

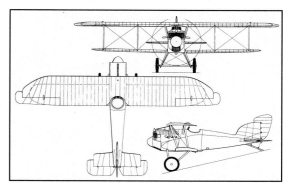

AVIATIK (BERG) 30.14   Austria-Hungary

The first single-seat fighter to be built by the Österreichisch-Ungarische Flugzeugfabrik Aviatik to the designs of Dipl Ing Julius von Berg, the Aviatik 30.14 (the designation indicating the 14th experimental aircraft produced by Ö-UF Aviatik) was powered by a 185 hp Austro-Daimler six-cylinder inline water-cooled engine. Armament consisted of a single 8-mm

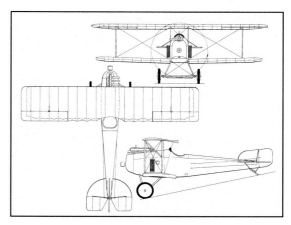

Julius von Berg's first fighter (above), the 30.14.

Schwarzlose synchronised machine gun. Of wooden construction with ply and fabric skinning, the Aviatik 30.14 crashed at Aspern on its first flight on 16 October 1916, the test pilot, Ferdinand Konschel, losing his life. However, the programme had revealed sufficient promise to warrant further development of the basic design. The wing gap was drastically reduced, wing stagger was introduced, the vertical tail surfaces were

The Aviatik D VII (below) was fundamentally similar to the D VI apart from its tail surfaces.

enlarged and, with more minor changes, three further prototypes were built, the 30.19, 30.20 and 30.21, which led to the D I. *Max speed, 109 mph (175 km/h). Span, 26 ft 3 in (8,00 m). Length, 22 ft 6 in (6,86 m).*

The Aviatik 30.14 (below) was the forerunner of a line of fighters from Dipl Ing Julius von Berg.

AVIATIK (BERG) D I Austria-Hungary

Designed by Dipl Ing Julius von Berg and frequently referred to as the Berg Scout, the D I was the first single-seat fighter of indigenous design to be manufactured in quantity by the Österreichisch-Ungarische Flugzeug-fabrik Aviatik of Vienna. The prototypes of the D I were the Av 30.19, 30.20 and 30.21, and the first of these was flown on 24 January 1917, differing from the subsequent production model primarily in lacking armament. Of wooden construction with ply fuselage skinning and fabric wing skinning, the D I entered service with the Austro-Hungarian *Luftfahrttruppe* in the autumn of 1917, by which time armament had standardised on two synchronised 8-mm Schwarzlose machine guns. Initial D Is had the 185 hp Austro-Daimler six-cylinder inline engine, some 140 were built with the 160 hp Austro-Daimler, and 200 and 225 hp Austro-Daimlers were progressively introduced. Some 700 fighters of this Berg type were manufactured by the parent concern and under licence by Lohner, Lloyd, Thöne und Fiala,

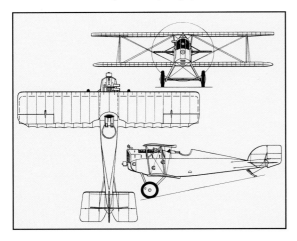

(Above) The Aviatik (Berg) D I in standard form, and (below) a D I fitted with a 200 hp Austro-Daimler engine, this being an aircraft of the first series.

MAG and WKF. The following specification relates to the model powered by the 200 hp Austro-Daimler engine. *Max speed, 115 mph (185 km/h). Time to 3,280 ft (1 000 m), 2.23 min, to 6,560 ft (2 000 m), 7.63 min. Endurance, 2.5 hrs. Empty weight, 1,345 lb (610 kg). Loaded weight, 1,878 lb (852 kg). Span, 26 ft 3 in (8,00 m). Length, 22 ft 6 in (6,86 m). Height, 8 ft 2 in (2,48 m). Wing area, 234.66 sq ft (21,80 m²).*

AVIATIK (BERG) 30.24 Austria-Hungary

The Aviatik 30.24 (this designation indicating that it was the 24th experimental aircraft produced by Ö-UF Aviatik) single-seat fighter triplane designed by von Berg appeared in May 1917. Employing a similar structure to that of the D I and a basically similar fuselage, the Aviatik 30.24 was powered by a 200 hp Austro-

(Above and below) The Aviatik (Berg) 30.24 was a triplane derivative of the D I with a 200 hp Austro-Daimler. Only one triplane prototype was completed.

(Above top) A D I Series 138 forced down at Treviso on 23 June 1918, and (immediately above) a D I Series 115 (Löhner-built) operated by Flik 60J in 1918.

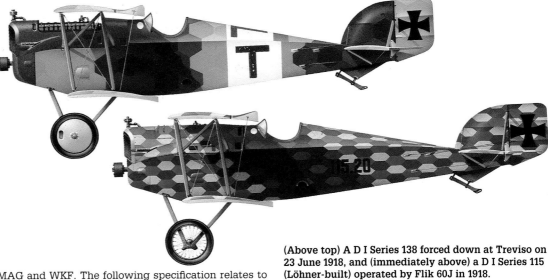

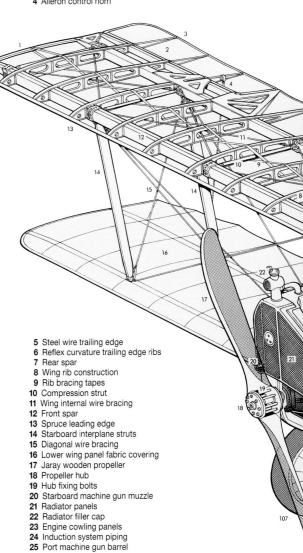

Key to Aviatik (Berg) D I

1 Wing-tip edge member
2 Starboard aileron
3 Aileron trailing edge wash-out
4 Aileron control horn
5 Steel wire trailing edge
6 Reflex curvature trailing edge ribs
7 Rear spar
8 Wing rib construction
9 Rib bracing tapes
10 Compression strut
11 Wing internal wire bracing
12 Front spar
13 Spruce leading edge
14 Starboard interplane struts
15 Diagonal wire bracing
16 Lower wing panel fabric covering
17 Jaray wooden propeller
18 Propeller hub
19 Hub fixing bolts
20 Starboard machine gun muzzle
21 Radiator panels
22 Radiator filler cap
23 Engine cowling panels
24 Induction system piping
25 Port machine gun barrel
26 Austro-Daimler six-cylinder inline engine
27 Engine mountings
28 Bottom cowlings
29 Engine bay bulkheads
30 Engine bearer
31 Ammunition box, 300 rounds per gun
32 Access panel
33 Ammunition feed chute

(Right) The Aviatik (Berg) 30.25 was essentially a single-seat version of the C I recce two-seater.

Daimler engine and carried an armament of two synchronised 8-mm Schwarzlose 07/12 machine guns. Performance was marginally inferior to that of the similarly-powered D I, and only one prototype of the triplane was therefore completed. *Max speed, 108 mph (174 km/h). Time to 3,280 ft (1 000 m), 2.66 min, to 6,560 ft (2 000 m), 4.15 min. Empty weight, 1,367 lb (620 kg). Loaded weight, 1,900 lb (862 kg). Span, 23 ft 8¼ in (7,22 m). Length, 22 ft 6 in (6,86 m). Height, 9 ft 0 in (2,75 m). Wing area, 242.19 sq ft (22,50 m²).*

AVIATIK (BERG) 30.25   Austria-Hungary

The requirement of the Austro-Hungarian Army Command for a long-range single-seat reconnaissance fighter led Dipl Ing Julius von Berg to develop the Aviatik 30.25. Completed in March 1918, this was basically a single-seat version of the two-seat Aviatik (Berg) C I reconnaissance aircraft, with similar fuel tankage, and provision for the installation of an automatic camera and two synchronised 8-mm Schwarzlose 07/12 machine guns. It was also proposed to install radio equipment. Power was provided by a 200 hp Austro-Daimler six-cylinder engine, and speed performance was comparable with that of the Aviatik 30.30 fighter then under test, but no production was undertaken.

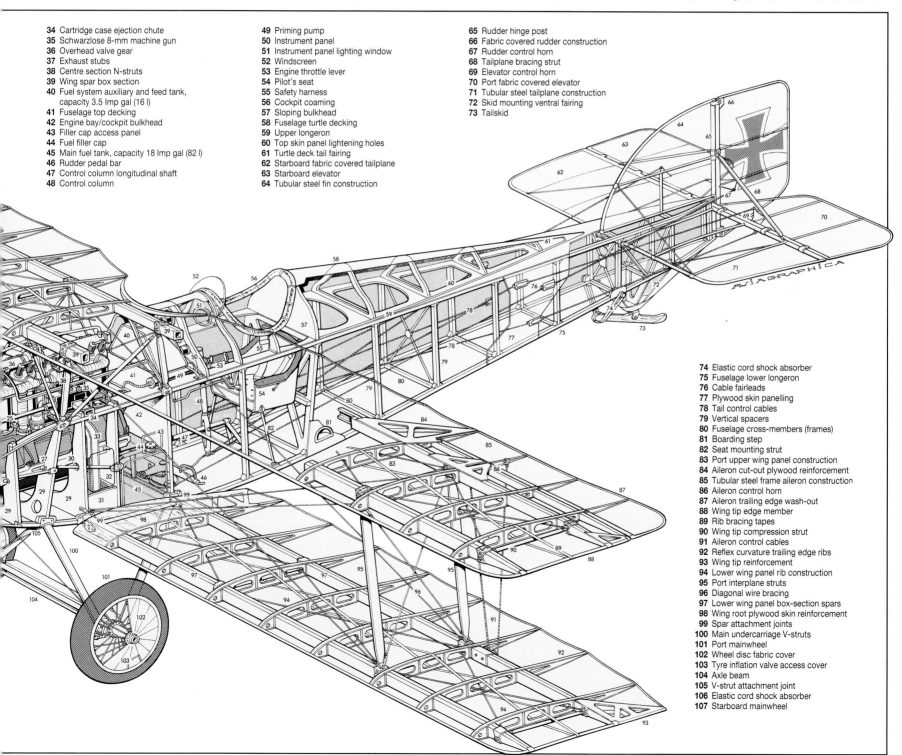

34 Cartridge case ejection chute
35 Schwarzlose 8-mm machine gun
36 Overhead valve gear
37 Exhaust stubs
38 Centre section N-struts
39 Wing spar box section
40 Fuel system auxiliary and feed tank, capacity 3.5 Imp gal (16 l)
41 Fuselage top decking
42 Engine bay/cockpit bulkhead
43 Filler cap access panel
44 Fuel filler cap
45 Main fuel tank, capacity 18 Imp gal (82 l)
46 Rudder pedal bar
47 Control column longitudinal shaft
48 Control column
49 Priming pump
50 Instrument panel
51 Instrument panel lighting window
52 Windscreen
53 Engine throttle lever
54 Pilot's seat
55 Safety harness
56 Cockpit coaming
57 Sloping bulkhead
58 Fuselage turtle decking
59 Upper longeron
60 Top skin panel lightening holes
61 Turtle deck tail fairing
62 Starboard fabric covered tailplane
63 Starboard elevator
64 Tubular steel fin construction
65 Rudder hinge post
66 Fabric covered rudder construction
67 Rudder control horn
68 Tailplane bracing strut
69 Elevator control horn
70 Port fabric covered elevator
71 Tubular steel tailplane construction
72 Skid mounting ventral fairing
73 Tailskid
74 Elastic cord shock absorber
75 Fuselage lower longeron
76 Cable fairleads
77 Plywood skin panelling
78 Tail control cables
79 Vertical spacers
80 Fuselage cross-members (frames)
81 Boarding step
82 Seat mounting strut
83 Port upper wing panel construction
84 Aileron cut-out plywood reinforcement
85 Tubular steel frame aileron construction
86 Aileron control horn
87 Aileron trailing edge wash-out
88 Wing tip edge member
89 Rib bracing tapes
90 Wing tip compression strut
91 Aileron control cables
92 Reflex curvature trailing edge ribs
93 Wing tip reinforcement
94 Lower wing panel rib construction
95 Port interplane struts
96 Diagonal wire bracing
97 Lower wing panel box-section spars
98 Wing root plywood skin reinforcement
99 Spar attachment joints
100 Main undercarriage V-struts
101 Port mainwheel
102 Wheel disc fabric cover
103 Tyre inflation valve access cover
104 Axle beam
105 V-strut attachment joint
106 Elastic cord shock absorber
107 Starboard mainwheel

AVIATIK (BERG)
30.27 & 29   Austria-Hungary

Whereas all previous single-seat fighters designed by von Berg had utilised Austro-Daimler inline engines, the Aviatik 30.27 and the similar 30.29, which appeared early in 1918, were powered by the 160 hp Steyr Le Rhône 11-cylinder rotary. Of wooden construction with plywood fuselage skinning, apart from the forward section which was covered by light metal panels, and fabric-covered wings, the Aviatik 30.27 and 30.29 each carried the standard twin-Schwarzlose gun armament, and were initially flown with two-bladed propellers. Subsequently, the original engine cowling (which left the lowest three cylinders exposed) was replaced by a full ring cowling, and the four-bladed Jaray propeller was adopted. Both participated in the July 1918 D-Contest, 30.29 crashing when the upper wing leading-edge collapsed as its pilot initiated a loop. The following details apply to the 30.27 in its final form. *Max speed, 115 mph (185 km/h) at 2,625 ft (800 m). Time to 3,280 ft (1 000 m), 1.42 min, to 6,560 ft (2 000 m), 3.75 min. Empty weight, 851 lb (386 kg). Loaded weight, 1,336 lb (606 kg). Span, 22 ft 4½ in (6,82 m). Length, 16 ft 4¾ in (5,00 m). Height, 8 ft 6¾ in (2,61 m).*

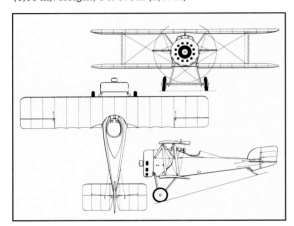

(Above and below) The Aviatik (Berg) 30.27 appeared early in 1918 with a Steyr Le Rhône rotary engine.

AVIATIK (BERG)
D II   Austria-Hungary

Featuring a fuselage virtually identical to that of the D I, the D II was flown as a prototype in the summer of 1917, this, the Aviatik 30.22, actually employing much of the structure of the 30.21 (see D I). The D II was characterised by a short-span cantilever lower wing, and a series of 19 aircraft was built for frontline evaluation, these being powered by either the 200 hp (Series 39) or 225 hp (Series 339) Austro-Daimler engine. A four-bladed Jaray propeller was fitted, and armament con-

The first prototype of the D II, the Aviatik (Berg) 30.22 (below) entered flight test in summer 1917.

sisted of the usual paired Schwarzlose 8-mm guns. The first three series aircraft were tested in November 1917, and seven were evaluated at the front, but the decision that Ö-UF Aviatik should licence-manufacture the Fokker D VII terminated any plans to build the D II in quantity. One D II airframe was experimentally fitted with a 200 hp Hiero engine as the Aviatik 30.38, and participated in the July 1918 D-Contest. With the 225 hp Austro-Daimler engine the D II attained 137 mph (220 km/h). The following details relate to the 200 hp version. *Max speed, 130 mph (210 km/h). Time to 3,280 ft (1 000 m), 2.6 min, to 6,560 ft (2 000 m), 6.6 min. Empty weight, 1,294 lb (587 kg). Loaded weight, 1,786 lb (810 kg). Span, 24 ft 7¼ in (7.50 m). Length, 22 ft 10¾ in (6,98 m).*

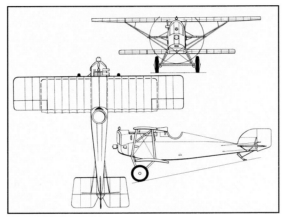

The D II (above and below) series aircraft was tested in November 1917, but plans for large-scale production ended with the choice of the Fokker D VII.

AVIATIK (BERG)
30.30   Austria-Hungary

Developed specifically for high altitude combat over the Italian front, the Aviatik 30.30 (which has sometimes been referred to as the D III although no evidence exists to support the application of this designation) had wings similar to those of the D I, married to a new fuselage, redesigned vertical tail surfaces and a 230 hp Hiero six-cylinder inline engine, the radiator for which was mounted above the upper wing centre section.

The Aviatik (Berg) 30.30 (above) was developed for high altitude combat over the Italian front.

Time to 3,280 ft (1 000 m), 2.17 min, to 6,560 ft (2 000 m), 5.1 min, to 9,840 ft (3 000 m), 9.1 min. Empty weight, 1,506 lb (683 kg). Loaded weight, 2,079 lb (943 kg).

AVIATIK (BERG)
30.40   Austria-Hungary

A parasol monoplane derivative of the Aviatik 30.27, the Aviatik 30.40 was powered by a similar 160 hp Steyr Le Rhône 11-cylinder rotary engine, and only one prototype was built and flown during the summer of 1918. The Aviatik 30.40 was of wooden construction. The forward fuselage was covered by light metal panels and the remainder of the fuselage was ply covered. The wing had fabric skinning, and steel-tube bracing struts were employed. *Max speed, 119 mph (192 km/h). Time to 3,280 ft (1 000 m), 1.5 min, to 6,560 ft (2 000 m), 2.83 min., to 9,840 ft (3 000 m), 6.83 min. Empty weight, 807 lb (366 kg). Loaded weight, 1,292 lb (586 kg).*

AVIMÉTA 88   France

Designed by Capt Georges Lepère, who, while on loan to the US government, had been primarily responsible

(Below) The Aviméta 88 was Schneider-Creusot-built.

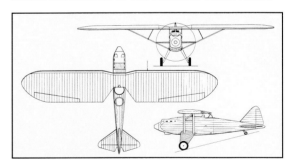

During the summer of 1918, Ö-UF Aviatik flew the 30.40 (below), a monoplane derivative of the 30.30.

for the Packard-Lepère LUSAC-11 and -21 two-seat fighters, the Av'méta 88 two-seat parasol monoplane fighter was built by the aviation department of the

The Aviméta 88 (above) was discontinued when the official requirement for its class was dropped.

Schneider-Creusot industrial group, and appeared in 1926. Constructed entirely of a metal alloy known as alférium, the Aviméta 88 had corrugated alférium skinning and was powered by a 500 hp Hispano-Suiza 12Hb 12-cylinder liquid-cooled engine. Armament comprised two synchronised 7,7-mm MAC (Vickers) machine guns and two Lewis guns on a flexible mounting in the rear cockpit. Only one prototype of the Aviméta 88 was built, development being abandoned when the official requirement for a new two-seat fighter and reconnaissance aircraft was discarded. *Max speed, 149 mph (240 km/h) at sea level, 137 mph (220 km/h) at 16,405 ft (5 000 m). Ceiling, 24,605 ft (7 500 m). Empty weight, 3,417 lb (1 550 kg). Loaded weight, 5,291 lb (2 400 kg). Span, 55 ft 9¼ in (17,00 m). Length, 32 ft 0 in (9,76 m). Wing area, 430.57 sq ft (40,00 m²).*

AVIS I   Hungary

During the course of 1931, the Central Repair Workshops at Székesfehérvár-Sóstó began construction of the AVIS (Anderlik-Varga-Iskola-Sport) aircraft, osten-

The AVIS I (above) was completed and flown in 1933, but proved to be seriously underpowered with its Jupiter engine and was relegated to training use.

sibly a single-seat trainer and sports aircraft, but, in fact, a fighter intended for use by the *Légüyi Hivatal* (Aviation Department), the clandestine Hungarian air arm. An all-metal, single-bay, staggered biplane designed by Prof Elöd Abody-Anderlik, László Varga, István Liszt and Deszö Fridrik, the first aircraft, the AVIS I, was completed and flown in 1933. Powered by a 420 hp Manfréd Weiss-built Jupiter VI nine-cylinder radial, intended armament being twin synchronised 7,62-mm Gebauer machine guns, the AVIS I proved seriously underpowered, prompting major redesign as the AVIS II. The sole example of the AVIS I was eventually delivered to the flying school at Szombathely where it was to serve until 1936. *Max speed, 174 mph (280 km/h). Max range, 310 mls (500 km). Service ceiling, 19,685 ft (6 000 m). Empty weight, 2,668 lb (1 210 kg). Loaded weight, 3,263 lb (1 480 kg). Span, 29 ft 6⅓ in (9,00 m). Length, 24 ft 7¼ in (7,50 m). Height, 9 ft 6⅛ in (2,90 m). Wing area, 228.19 sq ft (21,20 m²).*

AVIS II   Hungary

The poor results achieved with the AVIS I fighter prompted Prof Abody-Anderlik and his team to redesign the aircraft despite the decision of the *Légüyi Hivatal* to acquire 21 Fiat CR.20bis fighters from Italy. While retaining the Jupiter VI engine, the redesigned fighter, the AVIS II, featured a slimmer, slab-sided fuselage, redesigned vertical tail surfaces, narrower interplane bracing struts and increased gap. Empty weight

was reduced by 220 lb (100 kg) and, after initial trials, the engine was enclosed by a Townend ring. The AVIS II commenced flight test early in 1935, but still proved

The AVIS II (above) represented a major redesign of its predecessor, but was heavy and lacked agility.

overweight and lacking in the agility demonstrated by contemporary foreign fighters. The planned armament of twin 7,62-mm Gebauer guns was never fitted. Development was abandoned in favour of the higher-powered AVIS III. *Max speed, 186 mph (300 km/h). Service ceiling, 20,015 ft (6 100 m). Max range, 310 mls (500 km). Empty weight, 2,447 lb (1 110 kg). Loaded weight, 2,910 lb (1 320 kg). Span, 29 ft 6⅓ in (9,00 m). Length, 25 ft 7 in (7,80 m). Height, 9 ft 6⅛ in (2,90 m). Wing area, 228.19 sq ft (21,20 m²).*

AVIS III   Hungary

Developed in parallel with the AVIS II and entering flight test shortly afterwards in 1935, the AVIS III was powered by a 550 hp Manfréd Weiss-built Gnome-Rhône 9Krsd Mistral nine-cylinder radial engine driving a three-bladed adjustable-pitch Hamilton Standard propeller. Unlike the preceding AVIS fighters which were of all-metal construction, the AVIS III had wooden wings with a combination of plywood and fabric skinning, and four prototypes were laid down. The AVIS III demonstrated improved characteristics, but lacking the agility of the Fiat CR.32, which was meanwhile evaluated by the *Légüyi Hivatal* and adopted for service, it was not ordered into production. The armament of the AVIS III was two 7.62-mm Gebauer machine guns, and one of the four prototypes was completed with minor modifications as the AVIS IV. *Max speed, 193 mph (310 km/h). Service ceiling, 21,325 ft (6 500 m). Max range, 248 mls (400 km). Empty weight, 2,668 lb*

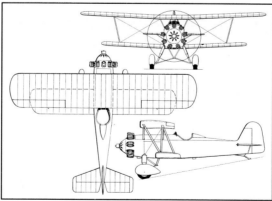

(Above and below) The AVIS III proved inferior to the Fiat CR.32 when evaluated in competition with the Italian fighter and was therefore dropped.

(1 210 kg). Loaded weight, 3,042 lb (1 380 kg). Span, 31 ft 2 in (9,50 m). Length, 25 ft 7 in (7,80 m). Height, 10 ft 6 in (3,20 m).

AVRO 504   UK

Although the Avro 504 saw most widespread use as a two-seater for reconnaissance, bombing and training, it also saw some service as a single-seat fighter, initially with the Royal Naval Air Service for airship interception. The first variant intended specifically for this rôle was the Avro 504C which, powered by the 80 hp Gnome seven-cylinder rotary, was essentially similar to the two-seat Avro 504B apart from having a fuel tank occupying the space normally taken up by the forward cockpit, and a gap in the top centre section through which a 0.303-in (7,7-mm) Lewis gun could be fired upward at an angle of 45 deg. Eighty Avro 504Cs were ordered for the RNAS, 50 of these being built by Brush Electrical Engineering, and these were operated on home defence duties from various RNAS stations.

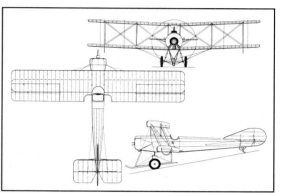

The Avro 504C (above and below) was the first variant of the basic design to be intended specifically for the interception of airships.

One was modified in 1916 to take a 75 hp Rolls-Royce Hawk inline engine, and 30 were ordered for the RNAS as the Avro 504F, but, in the event, these were completed with the standard Gnome rotary. The Royal Flying Corps equivalent of the Avro 504C was the Avro 504D, but only six were produced, these being delivered in August 1915. Early in 1918, a number of single-seat fighter conversions of the 110 hp Le Rhône 9J nine-cylinder rotary-powered Avro 504K was produced for issue to Home Defence squadrons, these having a single Lewis gun on a Foster mounting above the upper wing centre section. Several of these were later fitted with a V-type undercarriage similar to that of the Avro 521. The following data relate to the Avro 504C. *Max speed, 83 mph (134 km/h) at sea level. Time to 3,500 ft (1 065 m), 7.2 min. Endurance, 8 hrs. Empty weight, 930 lb (422 kg). Loaded weight, 1,592 lb (722 kg). Span, 36 ft 0 in (10,97 m). Length, 29 ft 5 in (8,96 m). Height, 10 ft 5 in (3,17 m). Wing area, 330 sq ft (30,66 m²).*

AVRO 521   UK

The Avro 521 two-seat fighter, which was flown late in 1915, was something of a hybrid in that it embodied a number of Avro 504 components. Powered by a 110 hp Clerget 9Z nine-cylinder rotary, the prototype had provision for a free-mounted 0.303-in (7,7-mm) Lewis gun fired from the rear cockpit. The prototype underwent official trials early in 1916, and 25 aircraft were ordered for the RFC, but this contract was subsequently cancelled, and there is no evidence that any Avro 521 other than the prototype (which crashed at Upavon on 21 September 1916) was built. *Max speed, 90 mph (145 km/h) at sea level. Time to 6,000 ft (1 830 m), 14 min. Endu-*

(Above) The Avro 521 was a hybrid embodying Avro 504 components; only one prototype was completed.

rance, 4.5 hrs. Empty weight, 1,150 lb (522 kg). Loaded weight, 1,995 lb (905 kg). Span, 30 ft 0 in (9,14 m). Length, 28 ft 2 in (8,58 m). Wing area, 266 sq ft (24,71 m²).

AVRO 523 PIKE — UK

Flown for the first time in May 1916, the Pike three-seat twin-engined biplane was designed primarily to meet an Admiralty requirement for a long-range escort and anti-airship fighter. The pilot was seated just ahead of the mainplanes with gunners' cockpits, each with a free-mounted 0.303-in (7,7-mm) Lewis, fore and aft. Of wooden construction with fabric skinning, the first prototype Pike had two 150 hp Sunbeam eight-cylinder liquid-cooled engines mounted as pushers driving two-

The Pike (above) was intended to meet a requirement for a long-range escort and anti-airship fighter.

bladed propellers via extension shafts. A second Pike, the Avro 523A, differed primarily in having two 150 hp Green six-cylinder liquid-cooled engines driving tractor propellers and a Scarff-type ring mounting for the forward Lewis gun. No production of the Pike was ordered following completion of official trials. The following data relate to the Avro 523. Max speed, 97 mph (156 km/h) at sea level, 88 mph (142 km/h) at 10,000 ft (3 050 m). Time to 5,000 ft (1 525 m), 9.5 min, to 10,000 ft (3 050 m), 27 min. Endurance, 7 hrs. Empty weight, 4,000 lb (1 814 kg). Loaded weight, 6,064 lb (2 751 kg). Span, 60 ft 0 in (18,29 m). Length, 39 ft 1 in (11,91 m). Height, 11 ft 8 in (3,55 m). Wing area, 815 sq ft (75,71 m²).

AVRO 527 — UK

The final two-seat fighter derivative of the basic Avro 504 design, the Avro 527 was built for the RFC and flown for the first time early in 1916 with a 150 hp Sunbeam Nubian eight-cylinder water-cooled engine. The mainplanes, undercarriage and tail assembly were basically similar to those of the Avro 504, but the fuselage differed markedly from that of the earlier aircraft. Proposed armament consisted of a single free-mounted 0.303-in (7,7-mm) Lewis gun in the rear cockpit. The Avro 527 displayed a poor climb rate and the pilot's forward view was seriously impaired by the twin exhaust stacks of the Nubian engine. Only one prototype was completed, and development was discontinued during the course of 1916, a version with a longer-span wing,

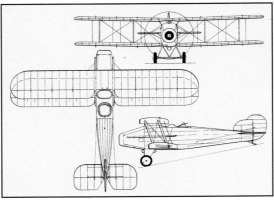

The final two-seat fighter derivative of the basic Avro 504 was the Avro 527 (above).

the 527A, being discarded at the same time. Max speed, 103 mph (166 km/h) at sea level. Span, 36 ft 0 in (10,97 m).

AVRO 530 — UK

The Avro 530 (above and below) was designed in 1916 as a competitor for the Bristol F.2A, but, when flown, did not afford a sufficient advance.

Of relatively clean aerodynamic design by contemporary standards and featuring a ducted propeller spinner, the Avro 530 two-seat fighter was designed in 1916 to compete with the Bristol F.2A, but the first prototype was not flown until July 1917. Powered by a 200 hp Hispano-Suiza 8Bd eight-cylinder water-cooled engine, the Avro 530 was of wooden construction with fabric skinning, and mounted an armament of a single fixed and synchronised 0.303-in (7,7-mm) Vickers gun, a Lewis gun of similar calibre being mounted on a Scarff ring in the rear cockpit. Although performance of the Avro 530 proved to be good, it did not improve sufficiently on that of the Bristol F.2A to warrant production orders. Furthermore, priority in the supply of the Hispano-Suiza engine was being given to the S.E.5a. During 1918, one of the two Avro 530 prototypes was flown with a 200 hp Sunbeam Arab engine, revised undercarriage, an extended tail fin and flapless wings of new section with long-span ailerons, but development was subsequently abandoned. Max speed, 114 mph (183 km/h) at sea level, 102 mph (164 km/h) at 10,000 ft (3 050 m). Time to 10,000 ft (3 050 m), 15 min. Endurance, 4 hrs. Empty weight, 1,695 lb (769 kg). Loaded weight, 2,680 lb (1 216 kg). Span, 36 ft 0 in (10,97 m). Length, 28 ft 6 in (8,69 m). Height, 9 ft 7 in (2,92 m). Wing area, 325.5 sq ft (30,23 m²).

AVRO 531 SPIDER — UK

An unsponsored private-venture single-seat fighter designed by Roy Chadwick and flown for the first time in April 1918, the Spider made use of a number of Avro 504 components and had a fabric-covered wooden structure with a system of Warren-girder steel-tube interplane struts. The upper wing was mounted close to the fuselage and directly above the cockpit. In its original form, the Spider was powered by a 110 hp Le Rhône 9J nine-cylinder rotary engine, and proved to possess ex-

The Spider (above) was an unsponsored private-venture fighter which proved extremely manoeuvrable.

ceptional manoeuvrability, but overall performance was not sufficiently in advance of the contemporary Sopwith Camel to warrant quantity production. Armament comprised one fixed synchronised 0.303-in (7,7-mm) Vickers machine gun, and a 130 hp Clerget 9B rotary was later fitted, the following details relating to the Spider fitted with this power plant. Max speed, 120 mph (193 km/h) at sea level, 110 mph (177 km/h) at 10,000 ft (3 050 m). Time to 10,000 ft (3 050 m), 9.5 min.

Empty weight, 963 lb (437 kg). Loaded weight, 1,517 lb (688 kg). Span, 28 ft 6 in (8,68 m). Length, 20 ft 6 in (6,25 m). Height, 7 ft 10 in (2,38 m). Wing area, 189 sq ft (17,55 m²).

(Below) The Spider sesquiplane fighter of 1918.

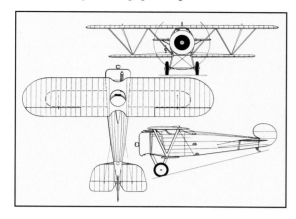

AVRO 566 AVENGER   UK

Aerodynamically one of the cleanest fighter biplanes of its era, the Avenger, designed as a private venture by Roy Chadwick, was first flown on 26 June 1926. Of wooden construction with fabric skinning, the Avenger was initially flown with a 525 hp Napier Lion VIII engine, but no order was obtained, and, in May 1928, the aircraft was modified for racing purposes. It was fitted with equi-span wings of 28 ft 0 in (8,53 m), streamlined I-type interplane struts, ailerons on both upper and lower wings, and a 553 hp Lion IX engine. In this form it was redesignated Avro 567 Avenger II. Various progressive developments were proposed, but none saw fruition, and the Avenger was dismantled for use as an instructional airframe in 1931. The following data relate to the Avro 566. *Max speed, 180 mph (290 km/h).*

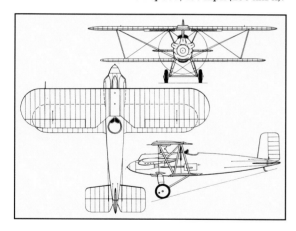

The Avenger (above and below) placed emphasis on aerodynamic cleanliness and was first flown as a private venture in June 1926.

Cruise, 130 mph (209 km/h). Initial climb, 2,100 ft/min (10,67 m/sec). Empty weight, 2,368 lb (1 074 kg). Loaded weight, 3,220 lb (1 460 kg). Span, 32 ft 0 in (9,75 m). Length, 25 ft 6 in (7,77 m). Height, 10 ft 3 in (3,12 m).

AVRO 584 AVOCET   UK

The Avocet was designed to the requirements of Specification 17/25, which, issued in June 1926, called for an all-metal stressed-skin shipboard fighter with inter-

changeable wheel and float undercarriages and powered by a 180 hp Armstrong Siddeley Lynx IV nine-cylinder air-cooled radial engine. Two prototypes were ordered, these being identical apart from the vertical tail surfaces, but for manufacturer's trials the first prototype was completed as a landplane and the second

An all-metal shipboard fighter, the Avocet (above and below) was flown with both wheels and floats.

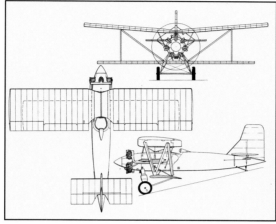

prototype as a twin-float seaplane, these flying respectively in December 1927 and April 1928. The second prototype was also fitted with a land undercarriage in June 1928. Armament comprised two 0.303-in (7,7-mm) Vickers machine guns synchronised to fire through the propeller disc. Performance of the Avocet during evaluation at Martlesham proved unspectacular and no production order was placed. *Max speed, 133 mph (214 km/h). Empty weight, 1,621 lb (735 kg). Loaded weight, 2,495 lb (1 132 kg). Span, 29 ft 0 in (8,84 m). Length, 24 ft 6 in (7,46 m). Height, 11 ft 8¼ in (3,56 m). Wing area, 308 sq ft (28,61 m²).*

AVRO CANADA CF-100
Mᴋs 1 ᴛᴏ 3   Canada

Design of the CF-100 tandem two-seat all-weather interceptor was initiated in October 1946 to meet an RCAF requirement, and the first of two prototypes

The CF-100 Mk 3 (below) was the initial series model, deliveries to the RCAF commencing in 1952.

(CF-100 Mk 1) powered by 6,500 lb st (2 948 kgp) Rolls-Royce·Avon RA 3 turbojets was flown on 19 January 1950. Ten unarmed pre-production aircraft (CF-100 Mk 2) followed, the first of these flying on 20 June 1951 with 6,000 lb st (2 722 kgp) Orenda 2 engines, and the initial production model (CF-100 Mk 3) differed in having Orenda 8 engines of similar rating, nose-mounted APG-33 radar and eight 0.5-in (12,7-mm) Colt-Browning machine guns in a ventral pack. The first CF-100 Mk 3 was delivered in September 1952, and 70 were built of which 50 were eventually converted to dual-control Mk 3CT and 3D trainers. *Max speed, 635 mph (1 022 km/h) at 10,000 ft (3 050 m), 566 mph (911 km/h) at 40,000 ft (12 200 m). Initial climb, 9,200 ft/min (46,7 m/sec). Loaded weight, 34,000 lb (15 422 kg). Max overload 39,750 lb (18 030 kg). Span, 52 ft 0 in (15,85 m). Length, 52 ft 3¾ in (15,94 m). Height, 15 ft 6½ in (4,73 m). Wing area, 540 sq ft (50,17 m²).*

AVRO CANADA CF-100
Mᴋs 4 & 5   Canada

Embodying major structural redesign, APG-40 radar and 6,500 lb st (2 948 kgp) Orenda 9 engines, the CF-100 Mk 4A was flown on 24 October 1953, being preceded by a prototype (Mk 4) on 11 October 1952, this having been originally the tenth and last Mk 2. Armament comprised 48 2.75-in (70-cm) unguided missiles in a ventral pack and 29 similar missiles in each of two wingtip pods which increased wing span to 53 ft 7 in

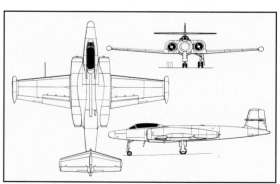

The CF-100 Mk 4B is illustrated above (with No 445 Sqn) and below (with wingtip missile pods).

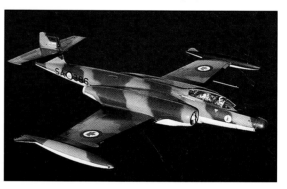

(16,33 m). The ventral pack was interchangeable with one containing eight 0.5-in (12.7-mm) guns. An improved model, the CF-100 Mk 4B, differed primarily in having 7,275 lb st (3 300 kgp) thrust Orenda 11s. Totals of 137 Mk 4A and 144 Mk 4B CF-100s were built, 50 later being modified to Mk 5 standards. The CF-100 Mk 5, powered by either the Orenda 11 or similarly-rated Orenda 14, embodied some economies in structural weight, a 6 ft (1,83 m) increase in wing span, and an extended tailplane. The prototype Mk 5 (a converted Mk 4B) flew in September 1954, and the first production example on 12 October 1955, 329 being built from the outset to Mk 5 standards, 53 of these being supplied to

the *Force Aérienne Belge*. The ventral gun or missile tray was deleted, armament being confined to the wing tip missile pods with which overall span was increased to 60 ft 10 in (18,54 m). Two Mk 5s were adapted as Mk 5Ms for Sparrow AAM trials and others converted to Mk 5Ds for ECM duties. Following details relate to CF-100 Mk 5. *Max speed, 650 mph (1 046 km/h) at 10,000 ft (3 050 m), 587 mph (945 km/h) at 40,000 ft (12 200 m). Initial climb, 8,500 ft/min (43,18 m/sec). Empty weight, 23,100 lb (10 478 kg). Max loaded weight, 37,000 lb (16 783 kg). Span, 58 ft 0 in (17,68 m). Length, 54 ft 1 in (16,48 m). Height, 15 ft 6½ in (4,73 m). Wing area, 591 sq ft (54,90 m²).*

AVRO CANADA CF-105 ARROW　　　Canada

Originating from a 1952 Royal Canadian Air Force requirement, the CF-105 was a tandem two-seat all-weather interceptor fighter, 37 development and pre-series examples being ordered. Of these, the first five, referred to as Arrow Mk 1s, were each powered by twin Pratt & Whitney J75-P-3 or -5 turbojets each rated at 12,500 lb st (5 670 kgp) and 18,500 lb st (8 392 kgp) with maximum afterburning. The sixth and subsequent aircraft were Arrow Mk 2s with paired Orenda PS-13 Iroquois turbojets each rated at 19,250 lb st (8 732 kgp)

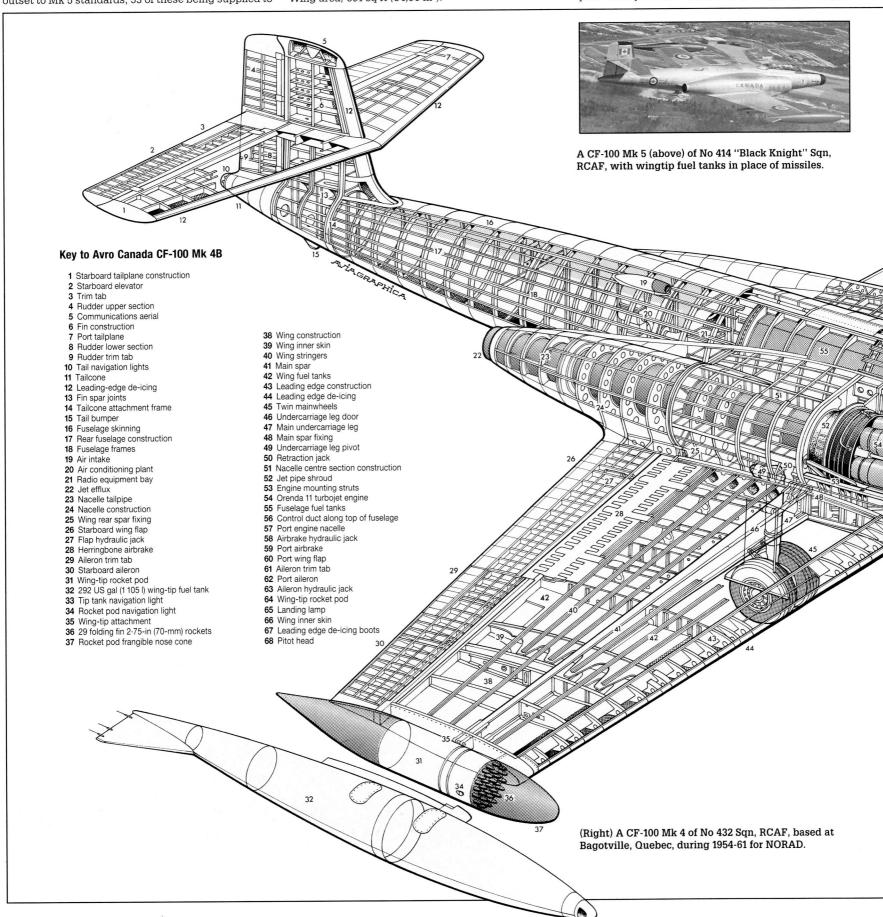

A CF-100 Mk 5 (above) of No 414 "Black Knight" Sqn, RCAF, with wingtip fuel tanks in place of missiles.

Key to Avro Canada CF-100 Mk 4B

1 Starboard tailplane construction
2 Starboard elevator
3 Trim tab
4 Rudder upper section
5 Communications aerial
6 Fin construction
7 Port tailplane
8 Rudder lower section
9 Rudder trim tab
10 Tail navigation lights
11 Tailcone
12 Leading-edge de-icing
13 Fin spar joints
14 Tailcone attachment frame
15 Tail bumper
16 Fuselage skinning
17 Rear fuselage construction
18 Fuselage frames
19 Air intake
20 Air conditioning plant
21 Radio equipment bay
22 Jet efflux
23 Nacelle tailpipe
24 Nacelle construction
25 Wing rear spar fixing
26 Starboard wing flap
27 Flap hydraulic jack
28 Herringbone airbrake
29 Aileron trim tab
30 Starboard aileron
31 Wing-tip rocket pod
32 292 US gal (1 105 l) wing-tip fuel tank
33 Tip tank navigation light
34 Rocket pod navigation light
35 Wing-tip attachment
36 29 folding fin 2·75-in (70-mm) rockets
37 Rocket pod frangible nose cone
38 Wing construction
39 Wing inner skin
40 Wing stringers
41 Main spar
42 Wing fuel tanks
43 Leading edge construction
44 Leading edge de-icing
45 Twin mainwheels
46 Undercarriage leg door
47 Main undercarriage leg
48 Main spar fixing
49 Undercarriage leg pivot
50 Retraction jack
51 Nacelle centre section construction
52 Jet pipe shroud
53 Engine mounting struts
54 Orenda 11 turbojet engine
55 Fuselage fuel tanks
56 Control duct along top of fuselage
57 Port engine nacelle
58 Airbrake hydraulic jack
59 Port airbrake
60 Port wing flap
61 Aileron trim tab
62 Port aileron
63 Aileron hydraulic jack
64 Wing-tip rocket pod
65 Landing lamp
66 Wing inner skin
67 Leading edge de-icing boots
68 Pitot head

(Right) A CF-100 Mk 4 of No 432 Sqn, RCAF, based at Bagotville, Quebec, during 1954-61 for NORAD.

(Left) The second of the five CF-105 Arrow Mk 1s that had flown before the programme was cancelled.

and 26,000 lb st (11 794 kgp) with afterburning. Armament of the Mk 2 was to have comprised six Falcon or eight Sparrow AAMs internally. The first Arrow Mk 1 was flown on 25 March 1958, the remaining four following on 1 August, 22 September and 27 October 1958, and 11 January 1959. Mach=1.5 was attained at 50,000 ft (15 240 m) during the third flight, and Mach=1.98 had been achieved when, on 20 February 1959, the entire Arrow programme was cancelled. At this time the first Iroquois-powered Mk 2 was on the point of joining the test programme and a further four Mk 2s were virtually complete. The following data relate to the Mk 1. *Max speed, 1,307 mph (2 104 km/h) at 50,000 ft (15 240 m). Max cruise 607 mph (977 km/h) at 36,000 ft (10 975 m). Max combat radius, 410 mls (660 km). Empty weight, 49,040 lb (22 244 kg). Max loaded weight, 68,602 lb (31 118 kg). Span, 50 ft 0 in (15,24 m). Length, 83 ft 0 in (25,30 m). Height, 20 ft 6 in (6,25 m). Wing area, 1,225 sq ft (113,80 m²).*

(Below) The CF-105 Arrow Mk 1 all-weather fighter.

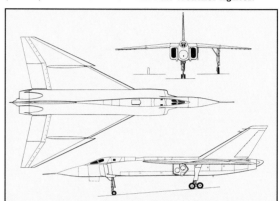

69 Port wing fuel tanks
70 Port engine cowlings
71 Sliding canopy cover
72 Canopy rails
73 Air intake
74 Engine mounting frame
75 Firewall
76 Engine driven gearbox
77 Engine bay construction
78 Nacelle lower fairing
79 Ventral gun pack
80 Ammunition boxes
81 Spent cartridge deflector plates
82 Eight 0·5-in (12,7-mm) Browning machine guns
83 Gun muzzle fairings
84 Gun port
85 Starboard engine intake guard
86 Engine air intake
87 Intake anti-ice spray
88 Ammunition bay
89 Navigator's ejector seat
90 Radar display
91 ADF loop aerial
92 Port engine intake
93 Pilot's ejector seat
94 Nosewheel bay
95 Nosewheel door
96 Pressurised cockpit structure
97 Control column
98 Engine throttles
99 Windscreen frame
100 Gun sight
101 Nose electronics compartment
102 Rudder pedals
103 Nose undercarriage pivot
104 Nosewheel leg
105 Twin nosewheels
106 Nosewheel leg door
107 Nose radar bay construction
108 Hughes APG-40 radar
109 Fire control and interrogation radar
110 Radar scanner
111 Radome

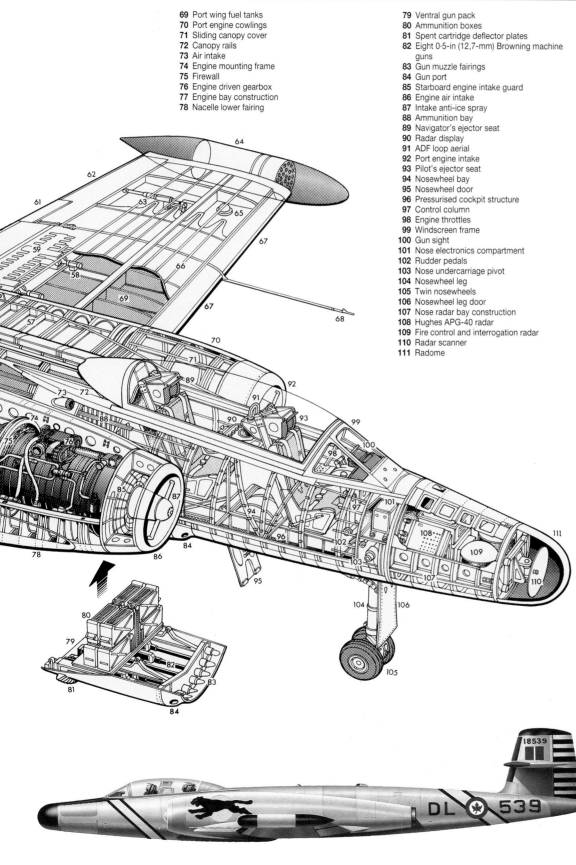

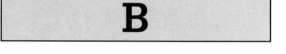

B

BAC (ENGLISH ELECTRIC) LIGHTNING F Mᴋs 1 & 2   UK

(Above) A BAC Lightning F Mk 1 of No 74 Sqn, RAF, at Coltishall, this unit equipping from June 1960.

Developed by the English Electric Company, which, on 12 January 1960, became an operating subsidiary of the newly formed British Aircraft Corporation (BAC), the Lightning was conceived as a pursuit-type weapons system, the first of three prototypes having flown as the P.1B on 4 April 1957. Twenty development aircraft had been ordered in February 1954, the first of these flying on 3 April 1958. The initial production version was the Lightning F Mk 1, the first example of which was flown on 29 October 1959. Nineteen F Mk 1s were followed by 28 F Mk 1As, the latter featuring a retractable refuelling probe. These were powered by paired and superimposed Rolls-Royce Avon 201 turbojets each rated at 11,250 lb st (5 103 kgp) boosted to 14,430 lb st (6 545 kgp) with afterburning, and carried two 30-mm cannon plus two Firestreak AAMs or 48 rockets of 2-in (5-cm) calibre. The F Mk 2, flown on 11 July 1961, differed in having Avon 210s with the same ratings as the 201s but featuring fully variable (rather than four-stage) afterburning. Armament remained unchanged. Forty-two F Mk 2s were delivered of which 31 were modified to F Mk 2As with some features of the later F Mk 6 (ie, enlarged ventral fuel tank, extended and cambered wings, and enlarged, square-tipped fin). Five ex-RAF F Mk 2s were supplied to Saudi Arabia as F Mk 52s. The following data relate to the F Mk 2. *Max speed, 777 mph (1 250 km/h) at sea level, or Mach=1.02, 1,270 mph (2 044 km/h) above 36,000 ft (10 975 m), or Mach=2.05. Max initial climb, 47,000 ft/min (239 m/sec). Endurance, 1.1 hrs. Empty weight, 27,650 lb (12 542 kg). Normal loaded weight, 38,700 lb (17 554 kg). Span, 34 ft 10 in (10,61 m). Length (including probe), 55 ft 3 in (16,84 m). Height, 19 ft 7 in (5,97m). Wing area, 458.52 sq ft (42,60 m^2).*

(Right) A BAC Lightning F Mk 3 of No 74 (Tiger) Sqn, carrying Firestreak AAMs on fuselage sides.

Key to BAC Lightning F.Mk 6

1 Pitot head boom
2 Intake bullet fairing
3 Ferranti Airpass radar antenna/scanner
4 Engine air intake lip
5 Hot-air de-icing
6 Bullet lower spacer
7 G 90 camera
8 Radar pack
9 Bullet upper spacer (electrical leads)
10 Forward equipment bay
11 Forward fuse box
12 Capacitor box
13 Lox container
14 Light fighter sight control unit
15 De-icing/de-mister air
16 Radar ground cooling air coupling
17 Nosewheel door mechanism torque shaft and operating rods
18 Nosewheel bay
19 Nosewheel doors
20 Nosewheel strut
21 Roller guide bracket
22 Forward-retracting nosewheel
23 Caster auto-disconnect
24 Shimmy damper and centering unit
25 Aft door (linked to leg)
26 Flight refuelling probe (detachable)
27 Nosewheel strut pivot pin
28 Heat exchanger
29 Nosewheel hydraulic jack
30 Intake ducting
31 Cockpit canted floor
32 Engine power control panel
33 Control column
34 Instrument panel shroud
35 Rudder pedal assembly
36 Canopy forward frames
37 Rain dispersal duct
38 Windscreen (electro-thermal)
39 CRT display unit (starboard)
40 Airpass(light fighter) attack sight
41 Standby magnetic compass
42 Canopy top panel de-misting ducts
43 Magnesium-forged canopy top frame
44 IFF aerial
45 Chemical air driers
46 Starboard (armaments) console
47 Ejection seat face-blind/firing-handle
48 Air-conditioning duct
49 Rear pressure bulkhead
50 Martin-Baker ejection seat
51 Port instrument panels
52 Cockpit ladder attachment
53 Cockpit emergency ram-air intake
54 Lower (No 1) engine intake duct frames
55 Firestreak weapons pack
56 Launch sequence units
57 Control units
58 Port missile pylon
59 Firestreak missile
60 Fuse "windows"
61 Armament safety break panel
62 Aileron accumulator pressure gauges
63 Accumulator group bay
64 Plessey LTSA starter in lower (No 1) engine nose cone
65 Lower (No 1) engine intake
66 Wingroot inboard fairing
67 Main equipment bay
68 Selector address unit
69 Electronic unit
70 Air data computer
71 Converter signal unit (data link)
72 Communications T/R (two)
73 Canopy hinge
74 Dorsal spine bays

75 AC fuse and relay box (cold-air unit and water boiler to starboard)
76 28-volt battery
77 Upper (No 2) engine intake duct
78 Fuselage frames
79 Water heater tank and extractor
80 Wing/fuselage main attachment point
81 Aileron idler lever
82 Aileron control push-pull tubes
83 Tube attachment brackets
84 Fuselage multi-bolt forward/centre section join
85 Aden gun muzzle
86 Leading-edge integral fuel
87 Muzzle blast tube
88 Aileron tube triple-roller guides
89 Access
90 Fuel lines
91 Non-return valve
92 Detachable leading-edge sections
93 Shuttle valve
94 Undercarriage strut fixed fairing
95 Shock-absorber strut
96 Port mainwheel
97 Brake unit
98 Tubeless tyre
99 Torque links
100 Red Top missile
101 Aft firing flap
102 Undercarriage pivot
103 Radius rod (inward-breaking)
104 Undercarriage retraction jack
105 Door jack sequence valve
106 Door master locking mechanism
107 Collector tank and booster pumps (two)
108 Aerodynamic leading-edge slot
109 Tank pressurizing intake/vent (in slot)
110 Mainwheel door
111 Undercarriage jack sequence valve
112 Door latch linkage
113 Port mainwheel well
114 Aileron control push-pull tubes
115 Aileron movement restrictor
116 Aileron autostabilizer actuator
117 Aileron control linkage
118 Aileron hydraulic runs
119 Cambered leading-edge extension
120 Localiser aerial
121 Port navigation light
122 Port wingtip
123 Port aileron
124 Aileron powered flying-control units
125 Control linkage
126 Wing outer structure
127 Aileron mass balance
128 Wing outer fixed section
129 Flap outer actuator jack
130 Flap sections
131 Flap integral tank
132 Angled aft spar
133 Undercarriage attachment
134 Refuelling/defuelling valve
135 Flap inner actuator jack
136 Three-way cock (manual)
137 DC transfer pump
138 Gate valves

139 Wing/fuselage rear main attachment point
140 Lower (No1) engine intermediate jet pipe forward face
141 Wing inboard structure
142 Wing integral fuel
143 Intermediate spar booms (T-section)
144 Port Aden 30-mm cannon (forward ventral pack)
145 Wing rib stations
146 Fuel vent pipe
147 Multi-bolt wing attachment plate
148 Access panels
149 Upper (No 2) engine duct frames
150 Fuselage break frame
151 Voltage regulators
152 Start tank
153 Engine pump units
154 Solenoid valves
155 Communications antenna
156 Starter control unit
157 HF igniter units
158 Fuselage frame
159 Main wing box upper skin
160 Forged centre rib (multi bolt attachment)
161 Starter exhaust
162 Upper (No 2) engine nose cone
163 Generator cooling ram-air intake
164 Stand-by generator
165 Anti-icing bleed air
166 Upper (No 2) Avon 301 turbojet engine and reheat units
167 Airpass recorder unit
168 Engine front mounting point
169 Engine accessories
170 No 2 engine bleed-air turbopump (reheat fuel)
171 Engine bay firewalls
172 Integral pumps (two)
173 HE ignition units
174 Voltage regulator
175 Current sensing unit
176 Rudder spring feel mechanism
177 Auxiliary intake
178 Main mounting trunnion
179 Aft (port) equipment bays
180 Electronic unit
181 IFF coder
182 Tailplane controls
183 Tailplane trim actuator and feel unit
184 Ventral fuel tank (aft section)
185 Fin
186 Reheat cooling lower intake
187 Tailplane autostabilizer actuator
188 Gearbox oil filler
189 AC generator

190 Glide-path receiver
191 IFF T/R unit
192 Outlet
193 No 2 engine intermediate jet pipe
194 Refrasil heat shrouds
195 Stress-bearing upper (No 2) engine hatch
196 Port airbrake
197 Airbrake hydraulic actuator jack
198 DC generator
199 Main accessory-drive unit
200 Airbrake lower frame
201 Turbine exhaust (from 199)
202 Tailplane accumulator and nitrogen bottle
203 Reheat "hotshot" igniter box

204 Tailplane drive triangular unit
205 Tailplane powered flying-control unit
206 Tailplane spigot
207 Pivot spar
208 All-moving tailplane
209 Light-alloy honeycomb structure
210 Braking parachute box internally-retracting doors
211 Cable operating assembly
212 Fuselage aft frame
213 Lower (No 1) engine reheat jet pipe
214 Trunnion access panel
215 AMCU air pipes
216 Reheat cooling upper intake
217 Rudder feel unit
218 Rudder trim actuator
219 Rudder autostabilizer actuator
220 Rudder linkage

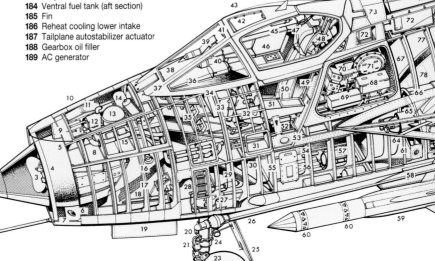

BAC (ENGLISH ELECTRIC) LIGHTNING F Mks 3 & 6   UK

Effectively a second generation development of the basic Lightning single-seat interceptor fighter, the F Mk 3, first flown on 16 June 1962, introduced Avon 301 turbojets rated at 13,220 lb st (6 000 kgp) and boosted to 16,300 lb st (7 394 kgp) with maximum afterburning. Its AI Mk 23B (rather than Mk 23) radar included a collision-course intercept mode, cannon armament was deleted and the vertical tail was enlarged by 15 per cent to compensate for the destabilising effect of paired Red Top AAMs. Seventy-two F Mk 3s were followed by the definitive Lightning version, the F Mk 6 (initially F Mk 3A), the first production example of which flew 16 June 1965, by which time English Electric had been renamed British Aircraft Corporation (Preston Division). The F

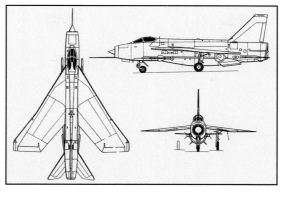

The final version of the BAC Lightning, the F Mk 6.

Mk 6 introduced a modified wing with cambered and extended outboard leading edges, and strengthening to cater for overwing ferry tanks. An enlarged ventral fuel tank was also adopted and Avon 301 turbojets were retained. From late 1970, two 30-mm cannon were mounted in the ventral tank fairing. Fifty-five newbuild F Mk 6s were delivered together with nine converted from F Mk 3s. A multi-role export derivative, the F Mk 53, was supplied to Saudi Arabia (34) and, as the F Mk 53K, to Kuwait (12). With Avon 302-C turbojets, the F Mk 53 had interchangeable packs for paired Firestreak AAMs or 44 rockets of 2-in (5-cm) calibre, plus two 30-mm cannon. The following data relate to the F Mk 6. *Max speed, 808 mph (1 300 km/h) at sea level, or Mach=1.06, 1,410 mph (2 270 km/h) above 36,000 ft (10 975 m), or Mach=2.14. Empty weight, 31,000 lb (14 062 kg). Normal loaded weight, 39,940 lb*

221 Fin spar/fuselage bolts
222 Fuselage frame formers
223 Rudder powered flying-control unit
224 Reheat jet pipe mounting rail
225 Upper (No 2) engine reheat jet pipe
226 Rear rollers
227 Air-driven nozzle actuator
228 Jet pipe trunnion access panel
229 Variable propelling nozzles
230 Streamer cable around rear lip (spring-clipped)
231 Parachute streaming anchor and jettison unit
232 Rudder light-alloy honeycomb structure
233 Flutter damper
234 Communications antenna
235 Dielectric tip
236 Compass unit
237 Angled aft spars
238 Main fin structure
239 Fin leading-edge panels
240 Accessory drive cooling air
241 Starboard aileron
242 Aileron powered flying-control units
243 Control linkage
244 Starboard flap outer actuator jack
245 Starboard flap
246 Wing panels
247 Wing skinning
248 Wing integral fuel
249 Aileron control push-pull tubes
250 Aileron movement restrictor
251 Aileron autostabilizer actuator
252 Starboard navigation light
253 Glide-slope aerial
254 Underside view showing gun ports and Red Top missiles

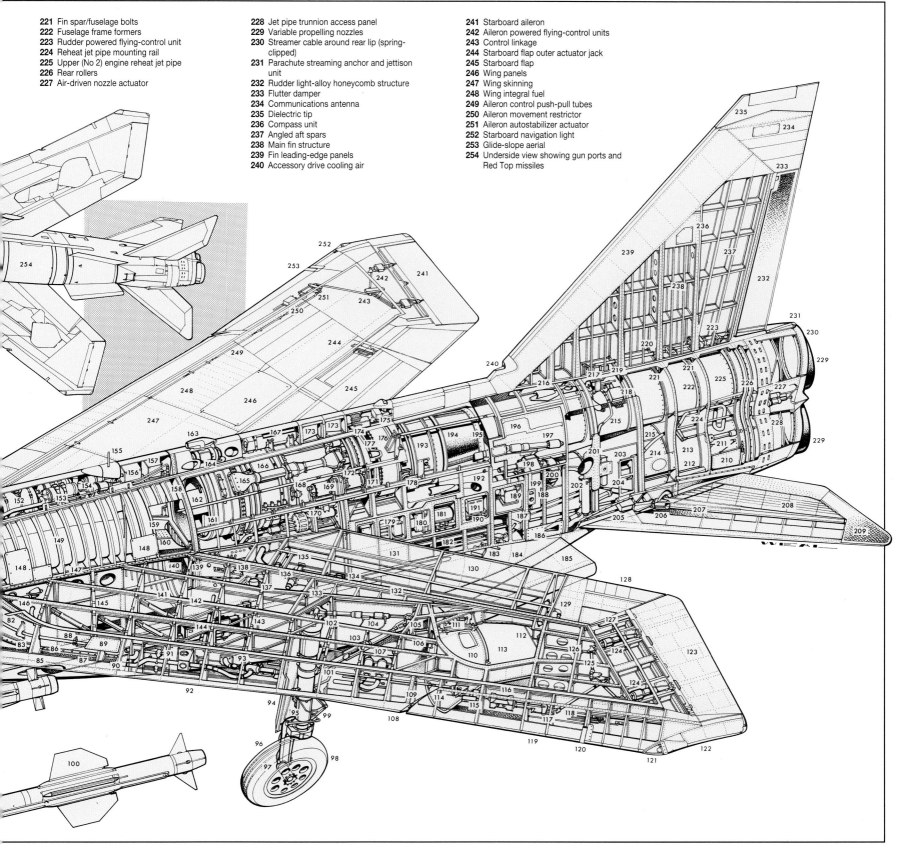

(Immediately below) A BAC Lightning F Mk 2A of No 92 Sqn, serving in RAF Germany, 1974, and (bottom) a Lightning F Mk 6 of No 11 Sqn with overwing tanks.

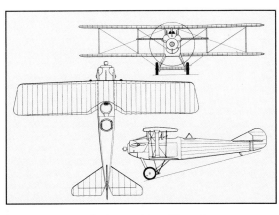

(Above and below) The BAJ Type IV tandem two-seat fighter, of which two prototypes were built in 1918.

(18 117 kg). Span, 34 ft 10 in (10,61 m). Length (including probe), 55 ft 3 in (16,84 m). Height, 19 ft 7 in (5,97 m). Wing area, 474.5 sq ft (44,08 m²).

BACHEM BA 349 (BP 20)   Germany

A semi-expendable and conceptually simple ramp-launched rocket-propelled interceptor, the Ba 349 (BP 20), conceived by Dipl-Ing Erich Bachem and unofficially known as the *Natter* (Adder), was of wooden construction. Powered by a 3,748 lb (1 700 kg) thrust Walter HWK 509A-2 bi-fuel rocket motor with two or

(Above) The Bachem BP 20A M3, with fixed undercarriage for gliding trials. (Below) The definitive Ba 349A.

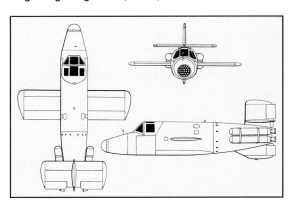

four 2,645 lb (1 200 kg) thrust Schmidding solid-fuel booster rockets providing 10 seconds supplementary power for vertical ramp launch, the Ba 349A (BP 20A) *Musterflugzeug*, or pre-series aircraft, was intended to have an armament of either (24) 73-mm Hs 217 Föhn or (33) 55-mm R4M rockets accommodated in a "honeycomb" of launch tubes in the nose. After attacking their target, the *Nattern* were intended to be abandoned by their pilots, their primary rocket motors being lowered

to the ground by parachute for re-use. The third of 50 *Musterflugzeugen*, the BP 20 M3, was first tested in towed flight on 14 December 1944; the first successful pilotless ramp launch (BP 20 M17) followed on 22 December, and the first piloted launch (BP 20 M23) took place on 1 March 1945. Two hundred of the initial series Ba 349A (BP 20A) were ordered (50 for the *Luftwaffe* and 150 for the SS), only one of these being completed, in addition to 34 of the *Musterflugzeugen*. The Ba 349B (BP 20B), referred to as an *Umbau* (literally "rebuilt") version, was larger overall, wing area being increased from 38.75 sq ft (3,60 m²) to 50.59 sq ft (4,70 m²), fuel capacity being increased and armament comprising

A Bachem BP 20A *Musterflugzeug* showing the battery of 24 Föhn unguided rockets in the nose.

two 30-mm cannon and 24 Föhn rockets. Three Ba 349Bs were completed. The definitive planned production model, the Ba 349C (BP 20C) was to have featured an improved wing and a further increase in fuel capacity. The following data are applicable to the Ba 349B. *Max speed, 621 mph (1 000 km/h) at 16,405 ft (5 000 m). Max climb, 42,520 ft/min (216 m/sec). Range, 36 mls (58 km) at 9,840 ft (3 000 m), 24 mls (39 km) at 32,810 ft (10 000 m). Empty weight, 2,414 lb (1 095 kg). Loaded weight, 5,004 lb (2 270 kg). Span, 13 ft 1½ in (4,00 m). Length, 19 ft 9 in (6,02 m). Height (fin base to fin tip), 7 ft 4½ in (2,25 m). Wing area, 50.59 sq ft (4,70 m²).*

BAJ TYPE IV   France

Designed by Charles Audenis and built by the Boncourt-Audenis-Jacob concern at Bron, the BAJ Type IV was a tandem two-seat fighter powered by a 300 hp Hispano-Suiza 8Fb eight-cylinder water-cooled engine

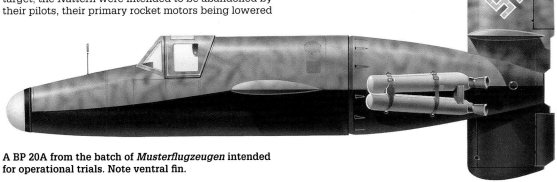

A BP 20A from the batch of *Musterflugzeugen* intended for operational trials. Note ventral fin.

and mounting an armament of one synchronised 7,7-mm Vickers machine gun and a pair of 7,7-mm Lewis guns on a T.O.3 ring mounting in the rear cockpit. Of relatively clean design, with aerofoil-section single interplane struts and a close-cowled engine, the Type IV was officially ordered on 1 May 1918 by the *Aviation Militaire*. The first prototype was delivered to Villacoublay for official trials late in November 1918, but these were apparently delayed by the need for modifications which were undertaken by the Hanriot concern and completed on 28 January 1919. The first prototype was returned to the Boncourt-Audenis-Jacob concern for repairs in the summer of 1919, official trials being continued with a second prototype. No production order for the Type IV was placed and no specification for this type has apparently survived.

B.A.T. F.K.22 (BANTAM II)   UK

The first design by Frederick (Frits) Koolhoven after joining the British Aerial Transport Company (B.A.T.), the private-venture F.K.22 single-seat fighter flown in September 1917 was of wooden construction with a monocoque fuselage. Powered by a 120 hp A.B.C. Mosquito six-cylinder radial engine, it displayed sufficient promise to win an official contract for a batch of six development aircraft. The first and third of these were powered by the 170 hp A.B.C. Wasp seven-cylinder radial (F.K.22/1) and the second by a 100 hp Gnome Monosoupape nine-cylinder rotary (F.K.22/2), the remaining three eventually being completed as prototypes for the F.K.23. The F.K.22/2, retroactively named Bantam II, was the first to fly, commencing its trials in December 1917 and being delivered to Martlesham for official trials on 19 January 1918. Armament comprised two synchronised 0.303-in (7,7-mm) Vickers guns, and this prototype, later re-engined with a 110 hp Le Rhône

The Koolhoven-designed BAT F.K.22/2 Bantam II.

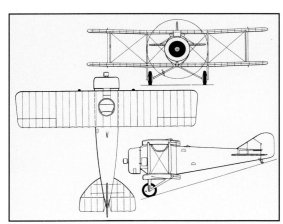

9J nine-cylinder rotary, was eventually assigned to the Central Flying School at Upavon. The fate of the two F.K.22/1s is unknown and the following details relate to the F.K.22/2 in Monosoupape-engined form. *Max speed, 100 mph (161 km/h) at 10,000 ft (3 050 m). Time to 10,000 ft (3 050 m), 16.8 min. Service ceiling, 14,500 ft (4 420 m). Empty weight, 866 lb (393 kg). Loaded weight, 1,260 lb (571 kg). Span, 24 ft 8 in (7,52 m). Length, 20 ft 8 in (6,30 m). Height, 7 ft 5 in (2.26 m). Wing area, 230 sq ft (21,37 m²).*

(Above) The original BAT F.K.22 with A.B.C. Mosquito engine, in late 1917, compared with (below) one of the F.K.22/2s with cowled Gnome Monosoupape.

B.A.T. F.K.23 (BANTAM I)   UK

The first prototype F.K.23 was originally ordered as the fourth of a batch of six development F.K.22s, and while retaining the wooden structure with monocoque fuselage, it embodied extensive redesign. Overall span and wing area were reduced to 20 ft (6,09 m) and 160 sq ft (14,86 m²) respectively, and the tail surfaces were redesigned. Armament comprised two synchronised 0.303-in (7,7-mm) Vickers guns and power was provided by a 170 hp A.B.C. Wasp I, flight testing being initiated in May 1918. Two further prototypes (originally ordered as the fifth and sixth F.K.22s) were similarly powered, but dimensionally larger, and after further redesign resulting from initial flight trials, a batch of 12 F.K.23 Bantam Is was ordered, the first of these being delivered to the RAE at Farnborough on 26 July 1918. At least nine Bantam Is were completed, one of these being sent to France and evaluated at Villacoublay in the late summer of 1918. One example was sent to the USA for evaluation at Wright Field, but this fighter's principal shortcoming was the poor reliability of its Wasp I engine. *Max speed, 128 mph (206 km/h) at 6,500 ft (1 980 m). Time to 10,000 ft (3 050 m), 9.0 min.*

(Below) The F.K.23 Bantam in its final form with A.B.C. Wasp engine, photographed on 31 August 1918.

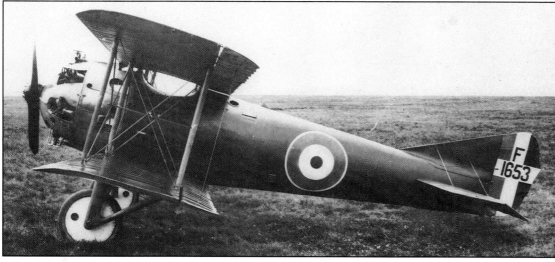

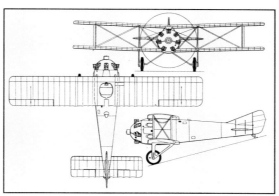

(Below) The A.B.C. Wasp-engined B.A.T. F.K.23 Bantam I. (Above) The fifth aircraft from the production batch of Bantam Is built in 1918, in racing trim.

Endurance, 2.25 hrs. Empty weight, 833 lb (378 kg). Loaded weight, 1,321 lb (599 kg). Span, 25 ft 0 in (7,62 m). Length, 18 ft 5 in (5,61 m). Height, 6 ft 9 in (2,06 m). Wing area, 185 sq ft (17,18 m²).

B.A.T. F.K.25 BASILISK   UK

The last single-seat fighter of Koolhoven design built by the British Aerial Transport Company, the F.K.25 Basilisk was designed around the 350 hp A.B.C.

(Above) First of the three F.K.25 Basilisk fighters built by B.A.T. in 1918/1919 to Koolhoven design.

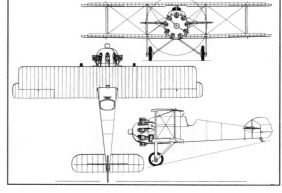

The Basilisk (above) was the last of the B.A.T. fighters.

Dragonfly I nine-cylinder radial engine and carried the usual armament of twin synchronised 0.303-in (7,7-mm) Vickers guns. Of wooden construction with a monocoque fuselage, the Basilisk featured a hood-like fairing, ahead of the cockpit, which enclosed the guns and shielded the pilot. Three prototypes were ordered, the first of these flying during the summer of 1918. The second prototype, completed in 1919, differed from its predecessor primarily in having a deeper fairing ahead of the cockpit. Further work on the Basilisk was abandoned at the end of 1919. *Max speed, 142 mph (228 km/h) at 6,500 ft (1 980 m). Time to 10,000 ft (3 050 m), 8.4 min. Endurance, 3.25 hrs. Empty weight, 1,454 lb (659 kg). Loaded weight, 2,182 lb (990 kg). Span, 25 ft 4 in (7,72 m). Length, 20 ft 5 in (6,22 m). Height, 8 ft 2 in (2,49 m). Wing area, 212 sq ft (19,69 m²).*

BEARDMORE W.B.II   UK

A two-seat fighter built as a private venture and based on the design of the B.E.2c by G Tilghman-Richards of William Beardmore & Co, the W.B.II was powered by a 200 hp Hispano-Suiza 8Bd eight-cylinder water-cooled engine. It carried an armament of two fixed synchronised 0.303-in (7,7-mm) Vickers guns and a single 0.303-in (7,7-mm) Lewis gun on a swivelling Beardmore-Richards mounting. The W.B.II was first flown on 30 August 1917, and performance proved good, but the Hispano-Suiza engine was in short supply and was required for the S.E.5a single-seater. No production of the W.B.II was therefore undertaken, although two civil examples were built in 1920 as the W.B.IIB. *Max speed,*

Built as a private venture by William Beardmore & Co Ltd in 1917, the W.B.II two-seat fighter is shown at Martlesham Heath in December that year.

120 mph (193 km/h) at sea level, 111 mph (179 km/h) at 10,000 ft (3 050 m). Time to 5,000 ft (1 524 m), 10 min. Endurance, 2.8 hrs. Empty weight, 1,765 lb (800 kg). Loaded weight, 2,650 lb (1 202 kg). Span, 34 ft 10 in (10,62 m). Length, 26 ft 10 in (8,18 m). Height, 10 ft 0 in (3,05 m). Wing area, 354 sq ft (32,88 m²).

BEARDMORE W.B.III UK

The W.B.III single-seat shipboard fighter was an extensively modified variant of the Sopwith Pup with manually-folding mainplanes and folding main undercarriage members. The prototype (a modified Pup) was officially accepted on 7 February 1917, and 100 production W.B.IIIs were ordered under the official designation S.B.3. Armament comprised a single 0.303-in (7,7-mm) Lewis gun which fired upwards through a cut-out in the upper wing centre section, and the W.B.III could be fitted with either the seven-cylinder Clerget or nine-cylinder Le Rhône 9C rotary, both of 80 hp. The first 13 production W.B.IIIs had folding undercarriages similar to the prototype and were known as S.B.3Fs, but subsequent W.B.IIIs had jettisonable undercarriages (S.B.3D) and flotation equipment. The S.B.3D version saw some service aboard British carriers, one was used in an unsuccessful attempt to fly from the forecastle of the battle cruiser HMS *Renown* and several were supplied to Japan. *Max speed, 103 mph (166 km/h) at sea level, 98 mph (158 km/h) at 6,500 ft (1 980 m). Time to 6,500 ft (1 980 m), 12.15 min. Endurance, 2.75 hrs. Empty weight, 890 lb (404 kg). Loaded weight, 1,289 lb (585 kg). Span, 25 ft 0 in (7,62 m). Length, 20 ft 2½ in (6,16 m). Height, 8 ft 1¼ in (2,46 m). Wing area, 243 sq ft (22,57 m²).*

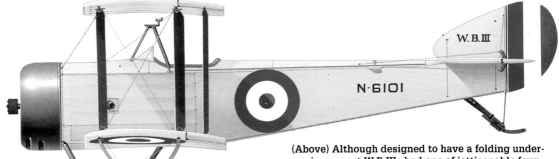

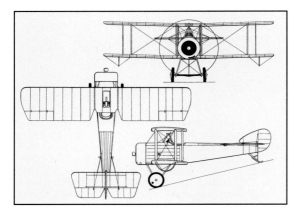

(Above) The second production Beardmore W.B.III with jettisonable undercarriage, as adopted for the subsequent S.B.3D version (below) for naval use.

BEARDMORE W.B.IV UK

The W.B.IV single-seat shipboard fighter was the first entirely original fighter to be developed by William

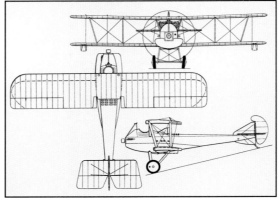

The Beardmore W.B.IV was designed for shipboard use.

Beardmore & Company and embodied several interesting features. To provide the best possible view for the pilot, the 200 hp Hispano-Suiza eight-cylinder water-cooled engine was mounted aft of the cockpit and drove the propeller via an extension shaft which passed between the pilot's legs. The cockpit was water-tight, a large flotation chamber was provided in the forward fuselage, wingtip floats were incorporated to stabilise the aircraft in the event of it alighting on the water in an emergency, and the undercarriage was jettisonable. The mainplanes could be folded, and armament comprised a single synchronised 0.303-in (7,7-mm) Vickers gun and a Lewis gun of similar calibre mounted on a tripod ahead of the cockpit. Three prototypes of the W.B.IV were ordered, the first of these flying on 12 December 1917. Performance proved creditable, but the other prototypes were not completed. *Max speed, 110 mph (177 km/h) at sea level, 102 mph (164 km/h) at 10,000 ft (3 050 m). Time to 5,000 ft (1 525 m), 7.0 min. Endurance, 2.5 hrs. Empty weight, 2,055 lb (932 kg). Loaded weight, 2,595 lb (1 177 kg). Span, 35 ft 10 in (10,92 m). Length, 26 ft 6 in (8,08 m). Height, 9 ft 10½ in (3,00 m). Wing area, 350 sq ft (32,52 m²).*

(Below) Tested at Martlesham Heath, the Beardmore W.B.IV had the original underwing tip floats removed.

(Above) Although designed to have a folding undercarriage, most W.B.IIIs had one of jettisonable form.

BEARDMORE W.B.V UK

Developed in parallel with the W.B.IV, but of more conventional design, the W.B.V single-seat shipboard fighter was intended to carry a 37-mm Puteaux cannon between the cylinder blocks of its 200 hp Hispano-Suiza eight-cylinder water-cooled engine. It featured folding wings, a jettisonable undercarriage and inflatable flotation bags beneath the underside of the leading edge of the lower wing. Three prototypes of the W.B.V were ordered, the first of these flying on 3 December 1917, but the engine-mounted cannon was quickly removed and a more conventional armament mounted, this comprising a synchronised 0.303-in (7,7-mm) Vickers gun and a 0.303-in (7,7-mm) Lewis gun on a tripod ahead of the cockpit. The second prototype W.B.V was completed and flown in 1918, but further development was abandoned before the end of World War I. *Max speed, 112 mph (180 km/h) at sea level, 103 mph (166 km/h) at 10,000 ft (3 050 m). Time to 5,000 ft (1 525 m), 6.0 min. Endurance, 2.5 hrs. Empty weight, 1,860 lb (844 kg). Loaded weight, 2,500 lb (1 134 kg). Span, 35 ft 10 in (10,92 m). Length, 26 ft 7 in (8,10 m). Height, 11 ft 10 in (3,61 m). Wing area, 394 sq ft (36,60 m²).*

(Below) Built in parallel with the W.B.IV, the Beardmore W.B.V was at first armed with a 37-mm Puteaux gun.

BEARDMORE W.B.26 UK

In the early 'twenties, William Beardmore & Company initiated work on a tandem two-seat fighter under Latvian contract. Of mixed construction with plywood skinning and designated W.B.26, the fighter was designed by W.S. Shackleton and, powered by a 360 hp Rolls-Royce Eagle IX liquid-cooled engine, was flown for the first time in 1925. Featuring aerofoil-section interplane bracing struts and angularly-clean lines, the W.B.26 had two Constantinesco-synchronised Beardmore-Farquhar machine guns and a similar weapon on a Scarff mounting in the rear cockpit. The slab-sided

The Beardmore W.B.26 two-seat fighter as built in 1925.

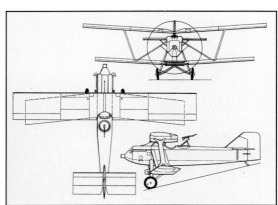

Designed by W S Shackleton under a Latvian contract, the Beardmore W.B.26 did not reach production.

fuselage was suspended between the wings, the lower wing being faired into the fuselage by a Lamblin radiator block. Despite a creditable performance only the single prototype of the W.B.26 was built. *Max speed, 145 mph (233 km/h). Time to 15,000 ft (4 572 m), 20 min. Empty weight, 2,555 lb (1 159 kg). Loaded weight, 3,980 lb (1 805 kg). Span, 37 ft 0 in (11,28 m). Wing area, 356 sq ft (33,07 m²).*

BELL FM-1 AIRACUDA   USA

Embodying many innovatory features and designed by Robert J Woods, the FM-1 Airacuda was a five-seat long-range bomber destroyer. Powered by two engines mounted as pushers, the Airacuda accommodated two gunners in forward extensions of the engine nacelles, these crew members being provided with wing crawl-ways enabling them to gain the fuselage in the event that it proved necessary to evacuate the nacelle gun positions. The prototype, the XFM-1 powered by two 1,150 hp Allison V-1710-13 12-cylinder liquid-cooled engines driving three-blade propellers via 64-in (1,62-m) extension shafts, was flown on 1 September 1937. Twelve evaluation models were subsequently ordered, nine as YFM-1s and three as YFM-1As which differed in having tricycle undercarriages. Power was provided by 1,150 hp Allison V-1710-23s, but three YFM-1s were completed with V-1710-41s of 1,090 hp as YFM-1Bs. The 12 YFMs were delivered to the USAAC between February and October 1940, and their armament comprised one 37-mm T-9 cannon with 110 rounds in each engine nacelle, one 0.3-in (7,62-mm) M-2 machine gun with 500 rounds in each of the retractable dorsal turret and ventral tunnel positions, and one 0.5-in (12,7-mm) M-2 gun firing from each of the port and starboard beam positions. Twenty 30-lb (13,6-kg) bombs could be accommodated internally. The following details relate to the YFM-1B. *Max speed, 268 mph*

(Above) The Bell Airacuda carried a crew of five as a bomber-destroyer, achieving service test status in the form of the YFM-1 (above and below).

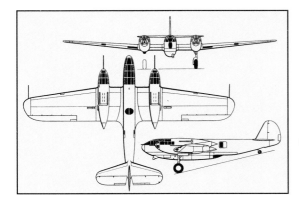

One of the most radical fighter concepts of the 'thirties, the Bell Airacuda is seen as the XFM-1 (above) and YFM-1A (below).

(431 km/h) at 12,600 ft (3 840 m). Range, 1,670 mls (2 687 km). Initial climb, 1,520 ft/min (7,72 m/sec). Empty equipped weight, 13,674 lb (6 203 kg). Loaded weight, 19,000 lb (8 618 kg). Span, 70 ft 0 in (21,33 m). Length, 45 ft 11⅜ in (14,00 m). Height, 12 ft 5 in (3,78 m). Wing area, 600 sq ft (55,74 m²).

BELL P-39 AIRACOBRA   USA

The P-39 was unusual (though not unique) at the time of its début in having an aft-mounted engine driving a tractor propeller via an extension shaft. The prototype, the XP-39, was flown on 6 April 1938 with a 1,150 hp Allison V-1710-17 12-cylinder liquid-cooled engine, this being followed by 13 YP-39s for service evaluation. The YP-39 had an engine-mounted 37-mm cannon, two fuselage-mounted 0.5-in (12,7-mm) guns and two wing-mounted 0.3-in (7,62-mm) guns. The initial production model, the P-39C, was essentially similar to the YP-39. With the completion of 20 Airacobras of this model, self-sealing fuel tanks and two additional 0.3-in (7,62-mm) wing guns were introduced, resulting in the P-39D which entered USAAC service in February 1941. The P-39D-1 replaced the 37-mm M4 cannon with a 20-mm M1, and the P-39D-2 replaced the 1,150 hp V-1710-35 with a 1,325 hp V-1710-63. Three examples with laminar-flow wings were designated XP-39E, and the next production model, the P-39F, differed from the P-39D in detail only. Twenty-five Airacobras were completed with 1,100 hp V-1710-59 engines as P-39Js; the P-39K was similar to the P-39D-2 apart from its propeller, while the P-39L differed only in having a modified nose-

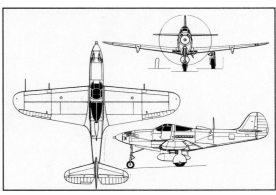

(Below) One of the service test Bell YP-39 Airacobras, with nose armament installed and (above) the Bell P-39Q, the final production version of the fighter.

wheel. The P-39M, which began to appear in November 1942, switched to a 1,200 hp V-1710-83 engine, while the P-39N with a similarly-rated V-1710-85 engine was the first Airacobra model to be manufactured in really large numbers, 2,095 being built. The final sub-type, the P-39Q, built in larger numbers than any other variant, had the wing-mounted 0.3-in (7,62-mm) guns deleted and a 0.5-in (12,7-mm) gun mounted beneath each mainplane. A total of 9,558 Airacobras of all types

(Below) P-39L of the 93rd Sqn, North Africa, 1943.
(Bottom) A P-400 Airacobra – RAF contract aircraft absorbed by AAF – of 35th FG, New Caledonia, 1942.

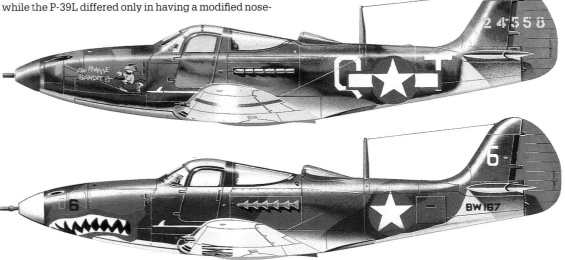

was produced, of which 4,905 were P-39Qs. The following details apply to the P-39D. *Max speed, 335 mph (539 km/h) at 5,000 ft (1 524 m), 360 mph (579 km/h) at 15,000 ft (4 572 m). Range (internal fuel), 450 mls (724 km) at 300 mph (483 km/h) at 25,000 ft (7 620 m). Empty weight, 5,462 lb (2 477 kg). Max loaded weight, 8,850 lb (4 014 kg). Span, 34 ft 0 in (10,36 m). Length, 30 ft 2 in (9,19 m). Height, 11 ft 10 in (3,60 m). Wing area, 213 sq ft (19,79 m²).*

(Right) The Bell P-39Q, which was built in larger numbers than any other Airacobra variant, introduced a 0.5-in (12,7-mm) gun pod beneath each wing.

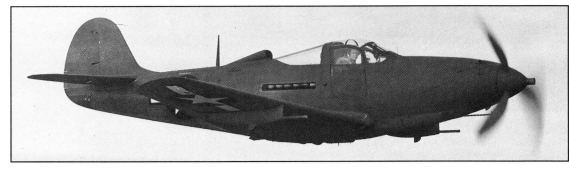

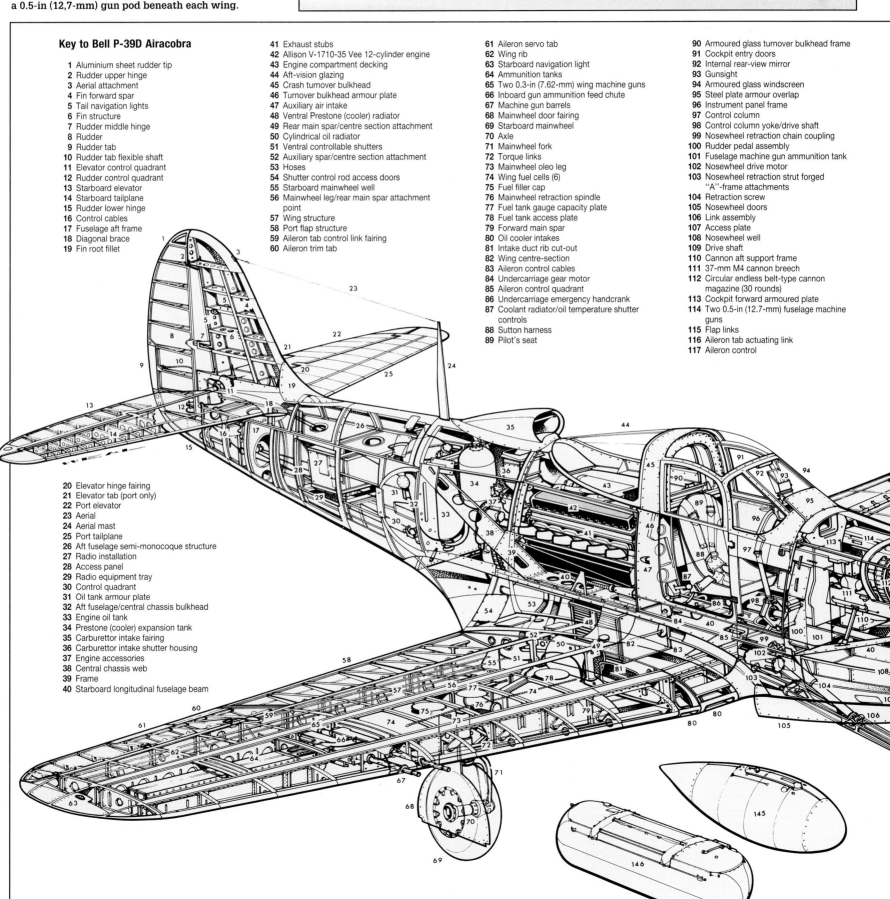

Key to Bell P-39D Airacobra

1 Aluminium sheet rudder tip
2 Rudder upper hinge
3 Aerial attachment
4 Fin forward spar
5 Tail navigation lights
6 Fin structure
7 Rudder middle hinge
8 Rudder
9 Rudder tab
10 Rudder tab flexible shaft
11 Elevator control quadrant
12 Rudder control quadrant
13 Starboard elevator
14 Starboard tailplane
15 Rudder lower hinge
16 Control cables
17 Fuselage aft frame
18 Diagonal brace
19 Fin root fillet

20 Elevator hinge fairing
21 Elevator tab (port only)
22 Port elevator
23 Aerial
24 Aerial mast
25 Port tailplane
26 Aft fuselage semi-monocoque structure
27 Radio installation
28 Access panel
29 Radio equipment tray
30 Control quadrant
31 Oil tank armour plate
32 Aft fuselage/central chassis bulkhead
33 Engine oil tank
34 Prestone (cooler) expansion tank
35 Carburettor intake fairing
36 Carburettor intake shutter housing
37 Engine accessories
38 Central chassis web
39 Frame
40 Starboard longitudinal fuselage beam

41 Exhaust stubs
42 Allison V-1710-35 Vee 12-cylinder engine
43 Engine compartment decking
44 Aft-vision glazing
45 Crash turnover bulkhead
46 Turnover bulkhead armour plate
47 Auxiliary air intake
48 Ventral Prestone (cooler) radiator
49 Rear main spar/centre section attachment
50 Cylindrical oil radiator
51 Ventral controllable shutters
52 Auxiliary spar/centre section attachment
53 Hoses
54 Shutter control rod access doors
55 Starboard mainwheel well
56 Mainwheel leg/rear main spar attachment point
57 Wing structure
58 Port flap structure
59 Aileron tab control link fairing
60 Aileron trim tab

61 Aileron servo tab
62 Wing rib
63 Starboard navigation light
64 Ammunition tanks
65 Two 0.3-in (7.62-mm) wing machine guns
66 Inboard gun ammunition feed chute
67 Machine gun barrels
68 Mainwheel door fairing
69 Starboard mainwheel
70 Axle
71 Mainwheel fork
72 Torque links
73 Mainwheel oleo leg
74 Wing fuel cells (6)
75 Fuel filler cap
76 Mainwheel retraction spindle
77 Fuel tank gauge capacity plate
78 Fuel tank access plate
79 Forward main spar
80 Oil cooler intakes
81 Intake duct rib cut-out
82 Wing centre-section
83 Aileron control cables
84 Undercarriage gear motor
85 Aileron control quadrant
86 Undercarriage emergency handcrank
87 Coolant radiator/oil temperature shutter controls
88 Sutton harness
89 Pilot's seat

90 Armoured glass turnover bulkhead frame
91 Cockpit entry doors
92 Internal rear-view mirror
93 Gunsight
94 Armoured glass windscreen
95 Steel plate armour overlap
96 Instrument panel frame
97 Control column
98 Control column yoke/drive shaft
99 Nosewheel retraction chain coupling
100 Rudder pedal assembly
101 Fuselage machine gun ammunition tank
102 Nosewheel drive motor
103 Nosewheel retraction strut forged "A"-frame attachments
104 Retraction screw
105 Nosewheel doors
106 Link assembly
107 Access plate
108 Nosewheel well
109 Drive shaft
110 Cannon aft support frame
111 37-mm M4 cannon breech
112 Circular endless belt-type cannon magazine (30 rounds)
113 Cockpit forward armoured plate
114 Two 0.5-in (12.7-mm) fuselage machine guns
115 Flap links
116 Aileron tab actuating link
117 Aileron control

This Bell P-39D carried special markings as part of "Red Force" for USAAC manoeuvres in 1941.

118 Aileron trim tab
119 Aileron servo tab
120 Wing skinning
121 Port navigation light
122 Pitot tube
123 Ammunition feed chute access
124 Gun charge cable access
125 Wing gun service access
126 Machine gun barrels
127 Aileron and tab control pulleys
128 Fuel tank filler cap
129 Reduction gear oil tank
130 Machine gun blast tubes
131 Machine gun ports
132 Reduction gearbox frontal armour
133 Three-blade Curtiss Electric constant-speed propeller
134 Spinner
135 Cannon muzzle
136 Blast tube access
137 Reduction gear casing
138 Nosewheel link
139 Nosewheel door forward fairing
140 Nosewheel oleo
141 Link assembly
142 Torque links
143 Axle fork
144 Rearward-retracting nosewheel
145 Ventral stores, options including auxiliary fuel-tank, or:
146 Two-man life raft

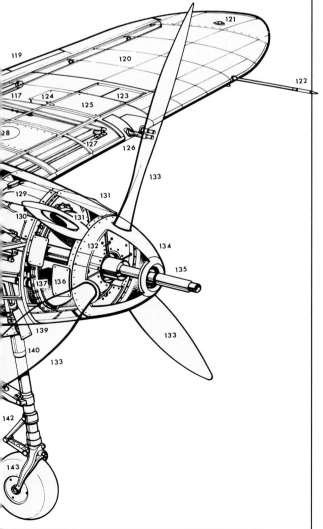

BELL XFL-1 AIRABONITA　　　USA

The XFL-1 experimental shipboard fighter was developed in parallel with the XP-39 Airacobra, and was flown for the first time on 13 May 1940. Powered by a 1,150 hp Allison XV-1710-6 12-cylinder liquid-cooled engine, the XFL-1 differed from its land-based counterpart primarily in having a tailwheel undercarriage and underwing radiators. The airframe was re-stressed for shipboard operation, and proposed armament comprised a single 0.5-in (12,7-mm) machine gun or a 37-mm cannon firing through the propeller hub and a pair of fuselage-mounted 0.3-in (7,62-mm) guns, although, in the event, no armament was installed. The XFL-1 failed its carrier qualification trials and further development was abandoned at the beginning of 1942. *Max speed, 307 mph (494 km/h) at sea level, 336 mph (541 km/h) at 10,000 ft (3 050 m). Max range, 1,072 mls (1 725 km). Initial climb, 2,630 ft/min (13,36 m/sec). Empty weight, 5,161 lb (2 341 kg). Max loaded weight, 7,212 lb (3 271 kg). Span, 35 ft 0 in (10,67 m). Length, 29 ft 9⅛ in (9,09 m). Height, 12 ft 9⅔ in (3,90 m). Wing area, 232 sq ft (21,55 m²).*

(Above and below) The Bell XFL-1 Airabonita was an unsuccessful attempt to adapt the basic P-39 design for use by the US Navy as a shipboard fighter.

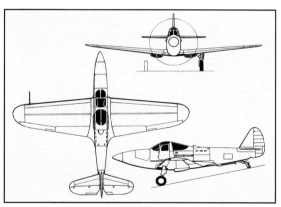

BELL P-63 KINGCOBRA　　　USA

Of similar concept to the P-39 Airacobra, but larger and more powerful, the Kingcobra was a single-seat close-support fighter and fighter-bomber. The first of two XP-63 prototypes was flown on 7 December 1942 with a

(Below) A single example of the P-63D version of the Kingcobra tested a rearward-sliding bubble canopy.

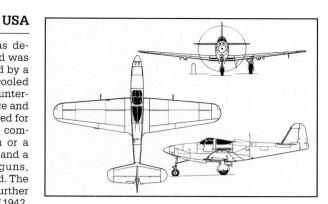

(Above) The Kingcobra in its original P-63A version and (below) a P-63C-5 as supplied to the *Armée de l'Air*.

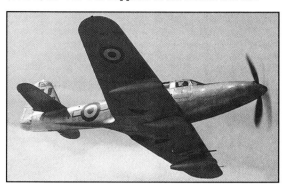

1,325 hp Allison V-1710-47 engine, a third prototype, the XP-63A, flying on 26 April 1943 with a V-1710-93 having a war emergency rating of 1,500 hp. Deliveries of the similarly-powered production P-63A-1 began in October 1943, armament comprising an engine-mounted 37-mm M4 cannon and two wing- and two fuselage-mounted 0.5-in (12,7-mm) guns. Three bombs of up to 500 lb (226,8 kg) each could be carried. Various modifications were introduced on succeeding A-series production batches, the final sub-type, the P-63A-10, giving place to the P-63C which was similar to the A-10 apart from having a V-1710-117 engine which, with water injection, offered a war emergency rating of 1,800 hp. A total of 1,725 P-63As was followed by 1,227 P-63Cs, most of these being supplied to the Soviet Union. One example of the P-63D was produced, this having a larger wing, a "bubble" cockpit canopy and a

(Above) P-63 Kingcobras ready for delivery to the Soviet Union, which was the major user of this type.

V-1710-109 engine, the final model being the P-63E, which had a similar wing and power plant to the P-63D, but reverted to the standard cockpit hood. Only 13 P-63Es were completed, together with one P-63F with redesigned vertical tail surfaces and a V-1710-135 engine. The following details apply to the P-63A-10. *Max speed, 361 mph (581 km/h) at 5,000 ft (1 524 m), 410 mph (660 km/h) at 25,000 ft (7 620 m). Max range (with max external fuel), 2,200 mls (3 540 km) at 177 mph (285 km/h) at 10,000 ft (3 048 m). Empty weight, 6,375 lb (2 892 kg). Max loaded weight, 10,500 lb (4 763 kg). Span, 38 ft 4 in (11,68 m). Length, 32 ft 8 in (9,96 m). Height, 12 ft 7 in (3,83 m). Wing area, 248 sq ft (23,04 m²).*

BELL P-59 AIRACOMET   USA

The initial turbojet-driven fighter built in the USA, the Airacomet was flown for the first time on 1 October 1942. The first XP-59A prototype was powered by two 1,250 lb st (567 kgp) General Electric Type 1-A turbojets, and was followed by second of three prototypes on 15 February 1943. Thirteen YP-59As were produced for test and evaluation, most of these receiving 1,650 lb st (748 kgp) General Electric I-16 (later J31) turbojets. Fifty production Airacomets were subsequently built with I-16 engines, 20 being completed as P-59A-1s and 30 as P-59B-1s with additional fuel capacity. The Airacomet carried an armament of one 37-mm M4 cannon and three 0.5-in (12,7-mm) machine guns, but proved an unsatisfactory gun platform and possessed an inadequate performance. *Max speed, 376 mph (605 km/h) at 5,000 ft (1 525 m), 409 mph (658 km/h) at 35,000 ft (10 670 m). Range (P-59A), 240 mls (386 km) at 298 mph (480 km/h) at 20,000 ft (6 095 m). Empty weight, 7,950 lb (3 606 kg). Loaded weight, 10,822 lb (4 909 kg). Span 45 ft 6 in (13,87 m). Length, 38 ft 1½ in (11,62 m). Height, 12 ft 0 in (3,66 m). Wing area, 385.8 sq ft (35,84 m²).*

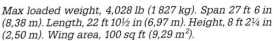

(Above) First of the production Airacomets, a P-59A-1, compared with (below) the first XP-59A, which made its maiden flight on 1 October 1942.

(Immediately below) The third and last XP-59A as tested in summer 1943. (Bottom) Eighth YP-59A after transfer to US Navy for testing in late 1943.

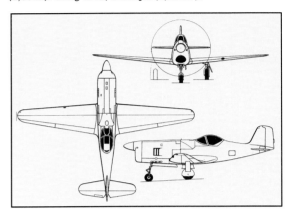

Max loaded weight, 4,028 lb (1 827 kg). Span 27 ft 6 in (8,38 m). Length, 22 ft 10½ in (6,97 m). Height, 8 ft 2¼ in (2,50 m). Wing area, 100 sq ft (9,29 m²).

(Above) The Bell XP-77 (second prototype below) achieved little success and was quickly abandoned.

BELL XP-83   USA

The XP-83 was intended as a long-range single-seat fighter, and the first of two prototypes was flown on 25 February 1945 powered by two 4,000 lb st (1 814 kgp) General Electric J33-GE-5 turbojets. Proposed armament comprised six 0.5-in (12,7-mm) machine guns in the nose, and provision was made for two 2,000-lb (907-

(Below) Bell's last fighter of original design, the XP-83.

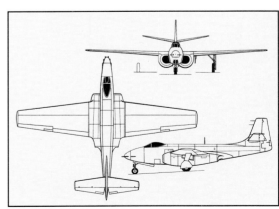

BELL XP-77   USA

Conceived as a simplified lightweight single-seat fighter employing ''non-strategic'' materials, the XP-77 was of wooden construction and was powered by a 670 hp Ranger XV-770-7 12-cylinder inverted-Vee air-cooled engine. Armament comprised two fuselage-mounted 0.5-in (12,7-mm) M2 machine guns and a single bomb of up to 300 lb (136 kg) weight, or a 325-lb (147-kg) depth charge. The first of two XP-77s was flown on 1 April 1944, but in the following December the development contract was cancelled. *Max speed, 330 mph (531 km/h) at 4,000 ft (1 220 m), 328 mph (528 km/h) at 12,600 ft (3 840 m). Range, 550 mls (885 km) at 274 mph (441 km/h). Initial climb, 3,600 ft/min (18,29 m/sec). Empty weight, 2,855 lb (1 295 kg).*

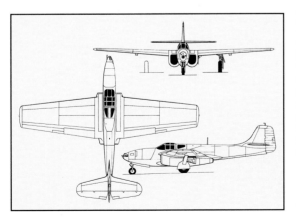

(Above) The Bell P-59B Airacomet was the final variant of the first USAF jet fighter, the original XP-59A prototype of which is seen (below) in flight.

(Below) First of the two Bell XP-77 lightweight fighters, built in 1944 using non-strategic materials.

Bell's XP-83 long-range single-seat fighter which was tested in 1945 but not further developed.

kg) bombs to be carried externally. Performance did not warrant the continuation of development and the project was abandoned. *Max speed, 522 mph (840 km/h) at 15,660 ft (4 773 m). Range (internal fuel), 1,730 mls (2 784 km) at 30,000 ft (9 144 m). Time to 30,000 ft (9 144 m), 11.5 min. Empty weight, 14,105 lb (6 398 kg). Max loaded weight, 27,500 lb (12 474 kg). Span, 53 ft 0 in (16,15 m). Length, 44 ft 10 in (13,66 m). Height, 15 ft 3 in (4,65 m). Wing area, 431 sq ft (40,04 m²).*

BEREZNYAK-ISAEV BI   USSR

Claiming the distinction of being the world's first rocket-propelled interceptor fighter, the BI, designed by Alexsandr Ya Bereznyak and Aleksei M Isaev, working under Prof Viktor F Bolkhovitinov, was of wooden construction with moulded plywood skinning. The BI was powered by a single RNII D-1A-1100 bi-fuel rocket motor of 2,425 lb (1 100 kg) thrust, and armament comprised two 20-mm cannon. The first of seven prototypes, the BI-1, was flown as a glider on 10 September 1941, and despite delays resulting from the evacuation of the factory, the first powered flight was undertaken by BI-2 on 15 May 1942. On 27 March 1943, by which time all seven prototypes had been completed, BI-3 was destroyed during the seventh powered flight as a result of an uncontrollable nose-down pitch at high speed. No obvious means of overcoming the phenomenon presented themselves and work on an initial production series of 50 BI interceptors was abandoned in

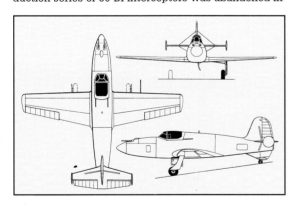

(Above) The Bereznyak-Isaev BI was the world's first rocket-powered interceptor fighter. (Immediately below) the BI-3 and (bottom) the BI-1 as a glider.

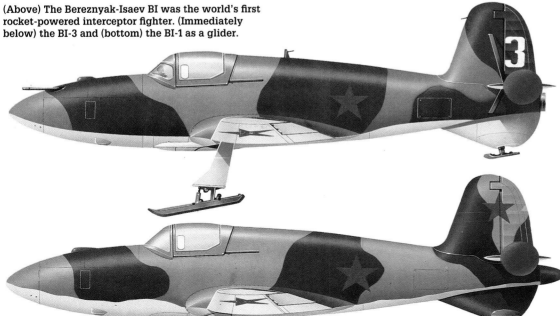

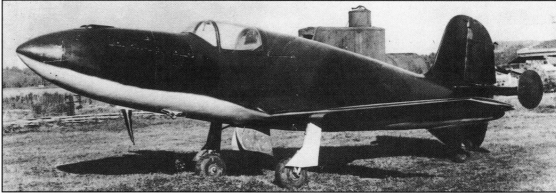

(Above) The Bereznyak-Isaev BI as first tested, in glider form. (Below) The ski-equipped third BI which was destroyed during its seventh flight.

consequence. Some flight testing was continued with the BI until 1945. *Max speed (estimated), 559 mph (900 km/h). Max initial climb, 16,142 ft/min (82 m/sec). Powered endurance, 15 min. Empty weight, 1,742 lb (790 kg). Loaded weight, 3,710 lb (1 683 kg). Span, 21 ft 3⅛ in (6,48 m). Length, 20 ft 11⅞ in (6,40 m). Height, 6 ft 9 in (2,06 m). Wing area, 75.35 sq ft (7,00 m²).*

BERKMANS SPEED SCOUT   USA

In 1916, the brothers Maurice and Emile Berkmans began design of a single-seat fighter known as the Speed Scout. Powered by a 100 hp Gnome Monosoupape nine-cylinder rotary engine, the Speed Scout was of conventional wooden construction but featured a circular-section laminated monocoque fuselage. Like the contemporary Curtiss S-2, the Speed Scout employed a rigidly-anchored cross-axle undercarriage to which a measure of shock-absorbency was imparted by the use of Ackermann spring wheels, these featuring curved spring-steel spokes which served as shock absorbers. Proposed armament comprised two synchronised 0.3-in (7,62-mm) machine guns. The fighter commenced its test programme in the spring of 1918, and demonstrated a high standard of manoeuvrability and excellent climb performance, attaining an altitude of 22,000 ft (6 706 m) on one occasion, but ground handling proved poor. The Speed Scout was demonstrated for the Army Aviation Section, which, having no need

for a new single-seat fighter with World War I virtually at an end, procured the prototype for stress analysis of the monocoque construction. *Max speed, 115 mph (185 km/h). Initial climb, 1,100 ft/min (5,59 m/sec). Endurance, 2.5 hrs. Empty weight, 820 lb (372 kg). Loaded weight, 1,190 lb (540 kg). Span, 26 ft 0 in (7,92 m). Length, 18 ft 8 in (5,69 m). Height, 7 ft 10 in (2,39 m).*

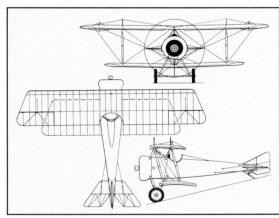

(Above and below) Berkmans Speed Scout, a private venture prototype tested by the US Army in 1918.

BERLINER-JOYCE P-16 (PB-1)   USA

The first military aircraft designed and built by the Berliner-Joyce Corporation, the P-16 (later redesignated PB-1) was a tandem two-seat fighter designed to the requirements of a USAAC contest held in April 1929. The prototype XP-16, powered by a supercharged Curtiss V-1570A Conqueror 12-cylinder liquid-cooled engine rated at 600 hp, appeared in October 1929, and

Berliner-Joyce PB-1 two-seat fighter for the USAAC.

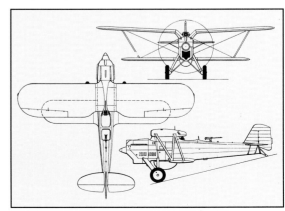

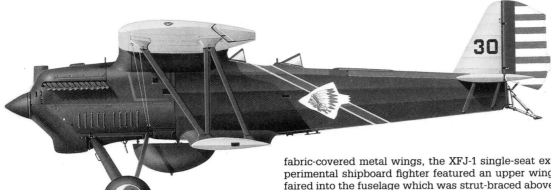

Berliner-Joyce P-16 (later redesignated PB-1) of the USAAC's 94th Pursuit Squadron, serving until 1934.

was of fabric-covered metal construction with an upper wing of gull configuration. Armament comprised two fixed forward-firing 0.3-in (7,62-mm) machine guns and a third weapon of similar calibre on a flexible mounting in the rear cockpit. Five 25-lb (11.3-kg) or two 122-lb (55.3-kg) bombs could be carried. Two contracts were issued for a total of 25 service test aircraft as Y1P-16s, these being essentially similar to the prototype apart from having the unsupercharged V-1570-25 Conqueror which was also rated at 600 hp. The Y1P-16s were delivered in 1932 and were later redesignated as PB-1s (pursuit-biplace). These proved to possess insufficient manoeuvrability to oppose single-seat fighters, offered extremely poor visibility for landing and displayed a tendency to nose over. As a consequence they were withdrawn from USAAC service on 31 January 1934. *Max speed, 175 mph (282 km/h) at sea level,172 mph (277 km/h) at 5,000 ft (1 524 m). Cruising speed, 151 mph (243 km/h). Range, 650 mls (1 046 km). Initial climb, 1,970 ft/min (10,0 m/sec). Empty weight, 2,803 lb (1 271 kg). Loaded weight, 3,996 lb (1 812 kg). Span, 34 ft 0 in (10,36 m). Length, 28 ft 2 in (8,58 m). Height, 9 ft 0 in (2,74 m). Wing area, 279 sq ft (25,92 m²).*

A Berliner-Joyce PB-1 two-seat fighter in multi-toned camouflage for War Games.

BERLINER-JOYCE XFJ-1　　USA

Having a semi-monocoque stressed-skin fuselage with

fabric-covered metal wings, the XFJ-1 single-seat experimental shipboard fighter featured an upper wing faired into the fuselage which was strut-braced above the lower wing. Proposed armament comprised two 0.3-in (7,62-mm) synchronised machine guns and power was provided by a 450 hp Pratt & Whitney R-1340C Wasp nine-cylinder radial air-cooled engine. The XFJ-1 was ordered on 16 May 1929, and flown for

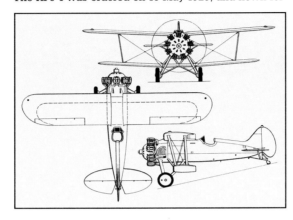

The Berliner-Joyce XFJ-1 as originally flown.

the first time in May 1930, but evinced extremely poor landing characteristics and was damaged in a landing accident at Anacostia early in its flight programme. It was returned to the Berliner-Joyce Corporation in November 1930 for reconstruction and modification, reappearing as the XFJ-2. *Max speed, 172 mph (277 km/h) at sea level. Max range, 716 mls (1 152 km). Time to 5,000 ft (1 524 m), 3.9 min. Empty weight, 2,046 lb (928 kg). Loaded weight, 2,797 lb (1 269 kg). Span, 28 ft 0 in (8.53 m). Length, 20 ft 7 in (6,27 m). Height, 9 ft 10 in (2,99 m). Wing area, 179 sq ft (16,63 m²).*

BERLINER-JOYCE XFJ-2　　USA

After the return of the XFJ-1 to Berliner-Joyce for reconstruction in November 1930, the dihedral was eliminated from the upper wing, which was given gull con-

(Below) The XFJ-1 displayed poor landing characteristics necessitating major modification.

figuration, the vertical tail surfaces were enlarged and a 500 hp R-1340D Wasp engine was installed, this being enclosed by a Townend ring and fitted with a spinner. In this form, the fighter was redesignated XFJ-2, resuming its flight test programme at Anacosta on 22 May 1931. The XFJ-2 displayed no improvement in landing characteristics by comparison with the XFJ-1 and proved unstable, and after testing by the US Navy was discarded as unsatisfactory. *Max speed, 177 mph (285 km/h) at sea level. Range, 520 mls (837 km). Time to 14,300 ft (4 359 m), 10.0 min. Empty weight, 2,102 lb (953 kg). Loaded weight, 2,847 lb (1 291 kg). Span, 28 ft 6 in (8,69 m). Length, 20 ft 7¼ in (6,28 m). Height, 9 ft 10 in (2,99 m). Wing area, 178.6 sq ft (16,59 m²).*

Modified from the XFJ-1, the Berliner-Joyce XFJ-2 featured a "gulled" upper wing and a Townend ring.

BERLINER-JOYCE XF2J-1　　USA

Essentially a navalised P-16, the XF2J-1 two-seat shipboard fighter prototype was ordered by the US Navy on 30 June 1931, but did not fly until two years later. Originally designed for a single-row Pratt & Whitney R-1690C Hornet radial, the XF2J-1 was completed with the experimental two-row 14-cylinder Wright R-1510-92 rated at 625 hp at 6,000 ft (1 830 m). As initially flown, the XF2J-1 had tandem open cockpits, but at an early stage in the test programme sliding canopies were fitted. Inadequate visibility for deck landing and inability to compete with the Grumman XFF-1 motivated against the further development of this type. *Max speed, 196 mph (315 km/h) at 6,000 ft (1 830 m). Normal range, 522 mls (840 km). Time to 5,000 ft (1 524 m), 3.1 min. Empty weight, 3,211 lb (1 456 kg). Loaded weight, 4,539 lb (2 059 kg). Span, 36 ft 0 in (10,97 m). Length, 28 ft 10 in (8,78 m). Wing area, 303.5 sq ft (28,19 m²).*

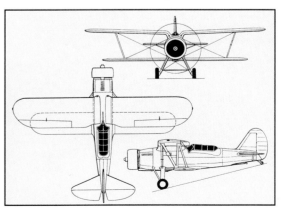

(Above and below) The XF2J-1 two-seat fighter in definitive form with covered cockpits.

BERLINER-JOYCE XF3J-1　　USA

Designed by the US Navy Bureau of Aeronautics, turned over to the Berliner-Joyce Corporation for development and construction and ordered on 30 June 1932, the XF3J-1 experimental single-seat shipboard fighter was completed in January 1934. Of all-metal construction with a semi-monocoque fuselage and

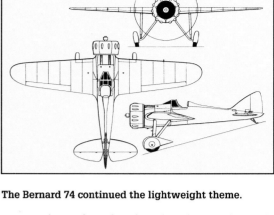

The Bernard 74 continued the lightweight theme.

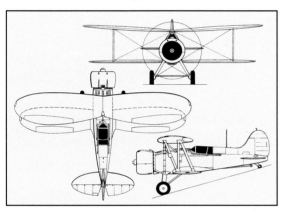

(Above and below) Last of the Berliner-Joyce fighters, the XF3J-1 was designed at the US Navy Bureau of Aeronautics in 1932 for shipboard use.

fabric-covered wings, the XF3J-1 was powered by a 625 hp Wright XR-1510-26 radial and carried an armament of two 0.3-in (7,62-mm) synchronised machine guns. Provision was made for two 116-lb (52,6-kg) bombs beneath the wings. Although offering a good performance, the XF3J-1 was surpassed by the Grumman XF2F-1, and no further development was undertaken. *Max speed, 290 mph (336 km/h) at 6,000 ft (1 830 m). Range, 719 mls (1 157 km). Time to 5,000 ft (1 524 m), 2.7 min. Empty weight, 2,717 lb (1 233 kg). Max loaded weight, 4,409 lb (2 000 kg). Span, 29 ft 0 in (8,84 m). Length, 22 ft 11 in (6,98 m). Height, 10 ft 9 in (3,28 m). Wing area, 239.6 sq ft (22,26 m²).*

BERNARD 20   France

Following the termination of the activities of S.I.M.B., a new company, the Société des Avions Bernard, was established in 1927, and immediately initiated work on a single-seat lightweight fighter of wooden construction and designed by Louis Béchereau. Intended to meet the requirements of an official specification, referred to unofficially as the *Jockey* programme, the Bernard 20 was of wooden construction and of exceptionally clean aerodynamic form. An unusual feature of

Built in 1928, the Bernard 20 was designed for the abortive *Jockey* light fighter programme.

the design was the construction of the fuselage between firewall and cockpit and the one-piece wing as a single structure. Power was provided by a 400 hp Hispano-Suiza 12Jb 12-cylinder water-cooled Vee engine and armament comprised two 7,7-mm Vickers machine guns. The Bernard 20 was flown for the first time in the spring of 1929, but, in the event, the *Jockey* programme was cancelled and none of the competing designs was ordered into production. *Max speed, 199 mph (320 km/h) at 13,125 ft (4 000 m). Service ceiling, 19,685 ft (6 000 m). Empty weight, 2,255 lb (1 023 kg). Loaded weight, 3,020 lb (1 370 kg). Span, 35 ft 5⅛ in (10,80 m). Length, 24 ft 5⅓ in (7,45 m). Height, 8 ft 2⅓ in (2,50 m). Wing area, 179.76 sq ft (16,70 m²).*

The Bernard 20 was of excellent aerodynamic form.

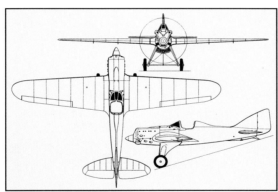

BERNARD 74   France

A lightweight fighter derivative of the Bernard 72 and 73 single-seat racing monoplanes, which, in turn, had been evolved from the Bernard 70 lightweight fighter project, the Bernard 74 was of wooden stressed-skin

(Below) In the lightweight fighter category, the Bernard 74 evolved from a series of racers.

construction and employed structural principles similar to those of the earlier Bernard 20. Armament comprised two synchronised 7,7-mm Vickers machine guns and power was provided by a 280 hp Gnome-Rhône 7Kbs seven-cylinder radial engine. The first of two prototypes was flown in February 1931, being joined by the second prototype on 21 October 1931, the latter having a 360 hp Gnome-Rhône 7Kd which increased its maximum speed to 217 mph (350 km/h) at 13,125 ft (4 000 m), loaded weight being raised to 2,734 lb (1 240 kg). The proposed production version, designated Bernard 75, was similar to the second prototype. The following details relate to the G-R 7Kbs-powered first prototype. *Max speed, 193 mph (310 km/h). Service ceiling, 26,250 ft (8 000 m). Empty weight, 1,819 lb (825 kg). Loaded weight, 2,438 lb (1 106 kg). Span, 30 ft 2¼ in (9,20 m). Length, 22 ft 11⅝ in (7,00 m). Height, 8 ft 2⅓ in (2,50 m). Wing area, 144.78 sq ft (13,45 m²).*

BERNARD 260   France

The Bernard 260 was designed to meet the requirements of a 1931 competitive specification for a single-seat fighter in the 3,748-3,968 lb (1 700-1 800 kg) weight category with a max speed ranging from 186 mph (300 km/h) at sea level to 217 mph (350 km/h) at 16,405 ft (5 000 m). It was the only one of nine competing aircraft to feature high-lift devices in the form of leading-edge slats and trailing-edge flaps. Of all-metal construction with an armament of two 7,7-mm Vickers

(Below) Bernard 260 in its short-span wing form.

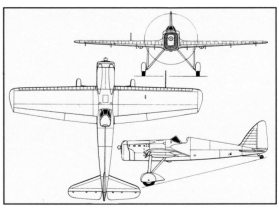

The Bernard 260 was fitted, during its test programme, with the leading-edge slats seen here.

guns beneath the wings and powered by a 690 hp Hispano-Suiza 12Xbrs 12-cylinder water-cooled engine, the Bernard 260 was flown for the first time in September 1932. Initially tested with a fixed radiator bath beneath the nose and subsequently with twin radiators attached to the undercarriage legs, and finally with a Chausson frontal radiator, the Bernard 260 underwent numerous modifications during its test programme. However, no production was undertaken, the Dewoitine 500 being selected as winning contender. *Max speed, 196 mph (315 km/h) at sea level, 224 mph (360 km/h) at 16,405 ft (5 000 m). Time to 32,810 ft (10 000 m), 30 min. Empty weight, 2,992 lb (1 357 kg). Loaded weight, 3,968 lb (1 800 kg). Span, 37 ft 0⁷⁄₈ in (11,30 m). Length, 25 ft 7 in (7,80 m). Wing area, 195.91 sq ft (18,2 m²).*

BERNARD H.52   France

During its initial trials, the Bernard H.52 fighter floatplane is seen here on the Seine, June 1933.

The H.52 (the prefix indicating *Hydravion*) resulted from a proposal to the *Marine Nationale* late in 1932 that a single-seat float fighter be built which could utilise the wing, rear fuselage and tail surfaces of the Bernard 260. Of all-metal construction, the H.52 was a mid-wing cantilever monoplane powered by a 500 hp Gnome-Rhône 9Kdrs nine-cylinder radial engine and armed with two 7,5-mm Darne machine guns mounted beneath the wings. Construction followed the practice adopted by previous Bechereau-designed Bernard fighters in that the centre fuselage between firewall and cockpit was built integral with the wing, and Handley Page slots occupied most of the wing leading edge. The first prototype was flown on 16 June 1933, and was tested with two-, three- and four-bladed propellers. A second prototype joined the test programme in 1934, but no production order was placed. *Max speed, 177 mph (285 km/h) at sea level, 204 mph (328 km/h) at 13,125 ft (4 000 m). Time to 13,125 ft (4 000 m), 9 min. Normal range, 373 mls (600 km). Empty weight, 3,263 lb (1 480 kg). Loaded weight, 4,163 lb (1 888 kg). Span, 37 ft 8³⁄₄ in (11,50 m). Length, 30 ft 6¹⁄₈ in (9,30 m). Height, 14 ft 0 in (4,27 m). Wing area, 195.91 sq ft (18,2 m²).*

BERNARD H.110   France

In the autumn of 1934, after abandoning further work on the H.52, Avions Bernard initiated development of a new single-seat float fighter, the H.110, which was to be evaluated in competition with the Loire 210 and the Romano 90. Powered by a 710 hp Hispano-Suiza 9Vbs nine-cylinder radial (licence-built derivative of the Wright Cyclone), the H.110 bore a close resemblance to the earlier H.52, and employed generally similar structure and armament, but featured fabric-covered rather than metal stressed-skin wings. With the liquidation of the Bernard concern, work on the prototype H.110 was taken over by the Société Schreck, flight trials being initiated in June 1935. In the event, the Loire 210 was selected for production to meet the float fighter requirement and development of the H.110 was abandoned. *Max speed, 205 mph (330 km/h) at 8,200 ft (2 500 m). Loaded weight, 4,189 lb (1 900 kg). Span, 38 ft 0²⁄₃ in (11,60 m). Length, 30 ft 6¹⁄₈ in (9,30 m). Wing area, 204.52 sq ft (19,00 m²).*

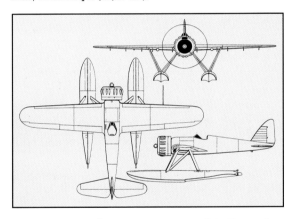

(Above and below) The sole prototype of the Bernard H 110 fighter was built by Société Schreck.

BFW Cʟ I (Tʏᴘᴇ 17)   Germany

In late 1917, the Bayerische Flugzeugwerke (BFW) of Munich, which had been organised around the former Otto Werke in the previous year, was awarded a contract to build two prototypes of the Cl I two-seat reconnaissance fighter of original design. At the time, BFW was negotiating a contract to build 100 Halberstadt Cl II reconnaissance fighters and the company's Cl I was specifically designed to require 20 per cent less manufacturing manhours than the Halberstadt aircraft. The first prototype, known by BFW as the Type 17, was completed in April 1918 with a 160 hp Mercedes D III engine. A single-bay unequal span biplane with intended armament of one fixed LMG 08/15 machine gun and an LMG 14 on a ring mounting, the Cl I was sent to the Adlershof test centre for *Typprüfung* in July 1918, but the *Idflieg* reported that it was "in no way equal" to the Hannover Cl V, requesting that improvements be made and the aircraft resubmitted for further evaluation. Accordingly, a lighter fuselage was fitted and, as

the Cl Ia, the aircraft underwent static load testing between 30 August and 14 September 1918. Results were unsatisfactory and BFW agreed to redesign the Cl Ia in accordance with "new design principles" (see Cl III). *Time to 3,280 ft (1 000 m), 2.0 min, to 13,125 ft (4 000 m), 6.5 min. Empty weight (Cl Ia), 1,587 lb (720 kg). Loaded weight (Cl Ia), 2,337 lb (1 060 kg). Span, 34 ft 10¹⁄₈ in (10,62 m). Length, 25 ft 7¹⁄₂ in (7,81 m).*

(Below) Built in 1918, the Cl I (Type 17) recce-fighter was the first military aircraft by BFW.

BFW Cʟ II (Tʏᴘᴇ 18)   Germany

The second prototype of the Cl I two-seat reconnaissance fighter was completed with a 175 hp MAN (Maschinenfabrik Augsburg-Nurnberg) Mana III six-cylinder in-line engine as the Cl II, or Type 18, in May 1918. In all other respects the Cl II was similar to the Cl I, but no details of its testing are available. *Time to 13,125 ft (4 000 m), 5.0 min. Dimensions as for Cl I.*

The second prototype of the BFW Cl I became the Cl II (above and below) with a MAN III engine.

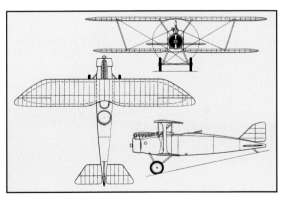

BFW Cʟ III   Germany

Redesign of the Cl Ia by BFW in accordance with the "new design principles" as requested by *Idflieg* resulted in the Cl III, a single prototype of which was completed at the close of hostilities but was not apparently

The BFW Cl III was too late for wartime service.

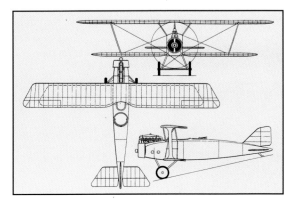

Evolved from the Cl I, the BFW Cl III (above) featured longer-span wings and a Benz Bz IV engine.

subjected to *Idflieg* testing. Adhering closely to the concept of the Cl Ia, the Cl III was powered by a 200 hp Benz Bz IV engine and featured longer-span, more angular wings. A further development, the Cl IV, remained on the BFW drawing boards. No performance data or weights are recorded. *Span, 37 ft 10⅓ in (11,54 m). Length, 25 ft 7½ in (7,81 m).*

BISNOVAT (TsAGI) SK-2   USSR

A direct result of high-speed wing research conducted at the TsAGI (Central Aerodynamics and Hydrodynamics Institute) by a team headed by Matus Bisnovat, the SK-2 single-seat fighter was evolved from the SK (*skorostnoye krylo*, or high-speed wing) aircraft tested during the winter of 1939-40. The SK was, effectively, the smallest possible airframe capable of accepting a 12-cylinder Vee-type engine, every effort being made to reduce drag (eg, a flush-fitting cockpit canopy which could be raised, together with the pilot's seat, for take-off or landing). The SK-2, flown in October 1940, had a similar small-area wing and 1,050 hp Klimov M-105 12-cylinder liquid-cooled Vee-type engine, but an orthodox cockpit, conventional carburettor and oil cooler air intakes, revised vertical tail surfaces and an armament of one 7,62-mm and two 12,7-mm machine guns. The SK-2 was of all-metal construction with dural pressed sheet stressed wing skinning and a semi-monocoque fuselage. Flight test results were allegedly promising, but not sufficiently so to warrant displacing established fighter types in production. *Max speed, 401 mph*

(Above and below) The Bisnovat SK-2 evolved from TsAGI research into high-speed wing design.

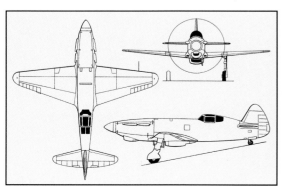

(645 km/h) at 8,860 ft (2 700 m), 410 mph (660 km/h) at 16,075 ft (4 900 m). Time to 16,405 ft (5 000 m), 4.3 min. Endurance, 0.75 hrs. Empty weight, 4,078 lb (1 850 kg). Loaded weight, 5,070 lb (2 300 kg). Span, 23 ft 11½ in (7,30 m). Length, 27 ft 2 in (8,28 m). Height, 8 ft 6⅓ in (2,60 m). Wing area, 103 sq ft (9,57 m²).

BLACKBURN TRIPLANE   UK

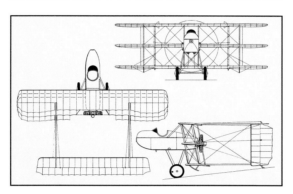

Blackburn's extraordinary Triplane fighter of 1917.

Designed by Harris Booth, who was also responsible for the A.D. Scout, the Blackburn single-seat fighter triplane was intended to carry a single Davis two-pounder quick-fire recoilless gun firing from the nose of the nacelle and was conceived for the anti-Zeppelin rôle. Possessing a fabric-covered airframe, the triplane was initially flown early in 1917 with a 100 hp Clerget 9Z nine-cylinder rotary engine driving a four-bladed propeller. The Clerget was soon replaced by a Gnome Monosoupape nine-cylinder rotary of 100 hp driving a two-blade propeller and the triplane was accepted by the Admiralty on 20 February 1917, but was struck off charge as unsatisfactory four weeks later, on 19 March. *Approx max speed, 90 mph (145 km/h). Endurance, 3 hrs. Empty weight, 1,011 lb (458,5 kg). Loaded weight, 1,500 lb (680 kg). Span, 24 ft 0 in (7,31 m). Length, 21 ft 5¼ in (6,53 m). Height, 8 ft 6 in (2,59 m). Wing area, 221 sq ft (20,53 m²).*

Designed by Harris Booth, the Blackburn Triplane (above) carried a Davis two-pounder recoilless gun.

BLACKBURN F.1 TURCOCK   UK

A clean single-seat biplane designed by F A Bumpus and B A Duncan as a private venture to meet the requirements of Specifications F.9/26 and N.21/26, the F.1 could accept a variety of air-cooled and water-cooled engines in the 450-600 hp range. The base aircraft was assigned the name Blackcock but it was intended to allocate individual names to variants as and when built. The F.1 was of all-metal construction and primarily fabric covered, and armament was intended to comprise two 0,303-in (7,7-mm) Vickers guns in the fuselage. The prototype, powered by a 446 hp Armstrong Siddeley Jaguar VI 14-cylinder two-row radial, carried no armament and was flown for the first time on 14 November 1927. Built to a Turkish government contract, the prototype was allocated the name Turcock but was destroyed in an accident on 23 January 1928, no further development being undertaken. *Max speed, 176 mph (283 km/h) at 15,000 ft (4 572 m). Time to 10,000 ft (3 050 m), 8 min. Endurance, 1.75 hrs. Empty weight, 2,282 lb (1 035 kg). Loaded weight, 2,726 lb (1 236 kg). Span, 31 ft 0 in (9,45 m). Length, 24 ft 4 in (7,41 m). Height, 8 ft 11 in (2,72 m).*

(Below) Blackburn's only Turcock was built for Turkey, but crashed before delivery in 1928.

BLACKBURN 2F.1 NAUTILUS   UK

A two-seat shipboard fighter-reconnaissance aircraft designed by F A Bumpus to Specification O.22/26, the

(Below) A single prototype of the Blackburn Nautilus shipboard fighter was built in 1929.

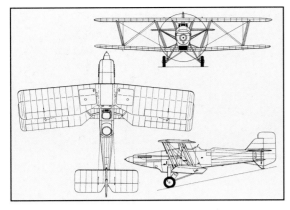

The Blackburn Nautilus naval fighter to O.22/26.

Nautilus was of all-metal construction with duralumin and fabric skinning, and was flown for the first time in May 1929 with a 525 hp Rolls-Royce F.XIIMS 12-cylinder liquid-cooled engine. Armament comprised one forward-firing 0.303-in (7,7-mm) Vickers gun and a Lewis gun of similar calibre on a ring mounting in the rear cockpit. Other contenders for the contract were the Short Gurnard, the Fairey Fleetwing and a navalized version of the Hawker Hart. After competitive trials during the autumn of 1929, the last mentioned type was selected for production as the Osprey. Only one Nautilus prototype was completed. *Max speed, 154 mph (248 km/h) at 5,000 ft (1 524 m). Initial climb, 1,260 ft/min (6,4 m/sec). Range, 375 mls (603 km). Empty weight, 3,223 lb (1 462 kg). Loaded weight, 4,750 lb (2 155 kg). Span, 37 ft 0 in (11,28 m). Length, 31 ft 8 in (9,65 m). Height, 10 ft 10 in (3,30 m). Wing area, 458 sq ft (42,55 m²).*

BLACKBURN F.2D LINCOCK III   UK

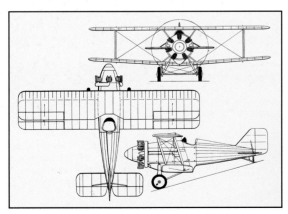

(Above and below) Five examples were built of the Blackburn Lincock III lightweight fighter.

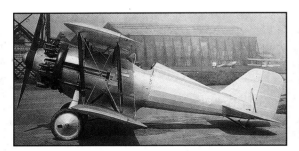

In 1927, the Blackburn company became interested in the lightweight fighter concept, building, as a private enterprise, a wooden single-seat aerodynamic prototype to the designs of F A Bumpus and G E Petty. Designated F.2 and subsequently to be known as the Lincock I, this aircraft was powered by a 250 hp Armstrong Siddeley Lynx IVc seven-cylinder radial and was flown in the spring of 1928. The Lincock I attracted the attention of the RCAF, which evinced interest in an all-metal version built as the F.2A Lincock II with a geared 255 hp Lynx IV. Flown in the autumn of 1929, the Lincock II, like its predecessor, possessed no military equipment, the first genuine fighter being the F.2D Lin-

cock III with a 270 hp Lynx Major and two 0.303-in (7,7-mm) Vickers guns in the fuselage. The Lincock III flew initially on 6 June 1930, five examples being built of which two were supplied to Japan and two to China. *Max speed, 164 mph (264 km/h) at sea level, 159 mph (256 km/h) at 10,000 ft (3 050 m). Initial climb. 1,660 ft/min (8,43 m/sec). Range, 380 mls (611 km). Empty weight, 1,326 lb (601 kg). Loaded weight, 2,082 lb (944 kg). Span 22 ft 6 in (6,86 m). Length, 19 ft 6 in (5,94·m). Height, 7 ft 4 in (2,23 m). Wing area, 170 sq ft (15,79 m²).*

BLACKBURN B-25 ROC   UK

The B-25 Roc was a two-seat shipboard fighter-bomber derivative of the B-24 Skua dive bomber designed by G E Petty. Of all-metal construction and structurally similar to the Skua, with the same 830 hp Bristol Perseus XIII nine-cylinder radial, the Roc embodied a wider aft fuselage to accommodate a Boulton Paul Type A Mk II power-driven turret with four 0.303-in (7,7-mm) Brown-

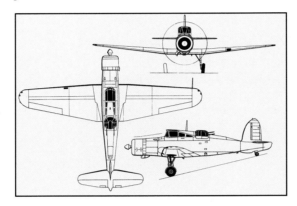

(Above) Blackburn Roc turret fighter in standard configuration and (below) in floatplane form.

ing guns. A contract for 136 Rocs to Specification O.15/37 was placed on 28 April 1937. No prototype was built and the first production aircraft flew on 23 December 1938. Performance was found to be lower than that predicted owing to the greater than anticipated effect of turret and wing drag. After brief operational service

(Below) Blackburn Roc I two-seat shipboard fighters of No 759 Sqn, Eastleigh, 1940, showing turret-decking both raised and retracted.

the Roc was relegated to second-line FAA squadrons, none being operated from carriers. All production Rocs incorporated float undercarriage attachment points as standard, and the first, third and fourth production Rocs were tested with adapted Shark floats, the first of these (the third production aircraft) being flown in November 1939. Max speed with floats was only 178 mph (286 km/h) at 6,000 ft (1 830 m) and development of the Roc floatplane was abandoned. *Max speed 223 mph (359 km/h) at 10,000 ft (3 050 m). Normal range, 610 mls (982 km). Initial climb, 1,130 ft/min (5,74 m/sec). Empty weight, 6,124 lb (2 778 kg). Loaded weight, 7,950 lb (3 606 kg). Span, 46 ft 0 in (14,02 m). Length, 35 ft 7 in (10,84 m). Height, 12 ft 1 in (3,68 m). Wing area, 310 sq ft (28,80 m²).*

BLACKBURN B-37 FIREBRAND   UK

Conceived in 1940 as a short-range shipboard interceptor, the Firebrand suffered a succession of changes which radically prolonged its gestatory period. Designed to Specification N.11/40, the first B-37 prototype flew on 27 February 1942 with a 2,305 hp Napier Sabre III 24-cylinder horizontal-H liquid-cooled engine, this being followed by a fully-armed (four wing-mounted 20-mm cannon) second prototype in July. A third prototype and nine production Firebrand Is were subsequently produced, but the decision had been taken meantime to switch mission emphasis from intercept to that of torpedo-strike fighter. This resulted in the Firebrand II with an 18-in (46-cm) widening of the wing centre section to permit an 18-in (46-cm) torpedo to be carried between the wheel wells. The second prototype Mk I was rebuilt as the prototype Mk II, flying in this form on 31 March 1943. The Firebrand II retained the wing cannon armament and had the distinction of being the first single-seat torpedo-carrying monoplane. Twelve production Firebrand IIs were completed and issued to a shore-based squadron. The following data relate to the Firebrand II. *Max speed, 355 mph (571 km/h) at 18,000 ft (5 486 m). Max range, 767 mls (1 234 km). Initial climb, 2,300 ft/min (11,68 m/sec). Normal loaded weight, 15,049 lb (6 826 kg). Span, 51 ft 3½ in (15,63 m). Length, 38 ft 2 in (11,63 m). Height, 13 ft 4 in (4,06 m). Wing area, 381.5 sq ft (35,44 m²).*

Blackburn Firebrand I shipboard interceptor.

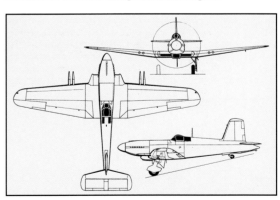

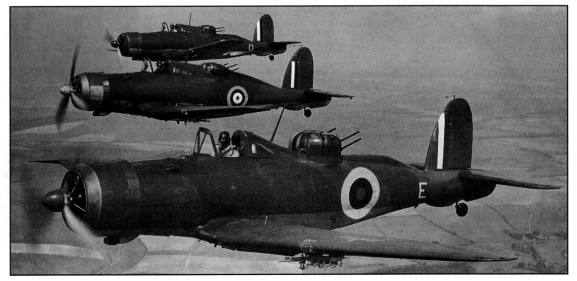

The third of the Firebrand I prototypes, built to a naval fighter specification N.11/40 in 1942.

BLACKBURN B-46 FIREBRAND   UK

Owing to limitations in Sabre engine supply, the decision was taken, in 1942, to re-engine the Firebrand with the Bristol Centaurus 18-cylinder radial engine, in accordance with Specification S.18/43. Two airframes – originally to have been the 10th and 11th Firebrand Is – were modified as prototypes for the B-45 Firebrand III, the first of these Centaurus-powered aircraft flying on 21 December 1943. By comparison with the B-37, the B-45 embodied extensive redesign, although few major changes were incorporated in the fuselage structure.

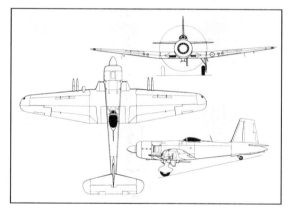

The Centaurus-engined Blackburn Firebrand III.

Twenty-seven production Firebrand III torpedo-strike fighters were built, the first of these flying in November 1944 with a 2,400 hp Centaurus VII, and the 11th and subsequent aircraft having the 2,520 hp Centaurus IX. Armament comprised four wing-mounted 20-mm Hispano cannon and a 1,850-lb (839-kg) torpedo, two 1,000-lb (453,6-kg) or 2,000-lb (907-kg) bombs, or 16 60-lb (27,2-kg) rockets. Further development resulted in the B-46 Firebrand IV, the first version to be built in substantial numbers. This differed from the Mk III primarily in having enlarged vertical tail surfaces and retractable wing spoilers. The first Firebrand IV flew on 17 May 1945, and production totalled 102 aircraft, 40 of these later being converted to Firebrand TF Mk 5s

Cannon-armed, the definitive Firebrand TF Mk 5 (below) also carried a torpedo for the strike rôle.

which featured detail improvements. Sixty-eight Mk 5s and 5As (the latter having hydraulically-boosted ailerons) had been built from scratch when Firebrand production terminated at the end of 1947. The following data relate to the Firebrand IV. *Max speed, 320 mph (515 km/h) at sea level, 350 mph (563 km/h) at 13,000 ft (3 962 m). Max range, 745 mls (1 199 km). Initial climb, 2,440 ft/min (12,39 m/sec). Empty weight, 11,689 lb (5 302 kg). Normal loaded weight, 15,671 lb (7 108 kg). Span, 51 ft 3½ in (15,63 m). Length, 39 ft 1 in (11,91 m). Height, 15 ft 2 in (4,63 m). Wing area, 381.5 sq ft (35,44 m²).*

(Below) The first production Firebrand III torpedo-fighter of 1944.

BLÉRIOT SPAD 41   France

The SPAD (Société pour l'Aviation et ses Dérives) concern, although headed by Louis Blériot, operated as a separate organisation from the Société Blériot-Aéronautique until 1921, when SPAD was absorbed and the subsequent progeny of its design team became officially known by the title of Blériot SPAD. The first fighter in the SPAD line to receive the Blériot SPAD appellation was the Blériot SPAD 41, designed by André Herbemont and essentially a single-seat derivative of the SPAD S.XX two-seater of 1918. Powered by a 300 hp Hispano-Suiza HS 8Fb eight-cylinder water-cooled engine with two individual Lamblin radiators in place of the familiar circular frontal radiator, the Blériot SPAD 41 was a staggered single-bay biplane with a sweptback upper wing and unswept lower wing. It featured a wooden monocoque fuselage. The prototype was flown for the first time at Buc on 17 July 1922, but official evaluation revealed an inadequate service ceiling and no production was ordered, the aircraft subsequently being modified for racing. *Max speed, 148 mph (238 km/h). Empty weight, 1,955 lb (887 kg). Loaded weight, 2,881 lb (1 307 kg). Span, 28 ft 5¾ in (8,68 m). Length, 21 ft 9¾ in (6,65 m). Height, 9 ft 0⅔ in (2,76 m). Wing area, 284.17 sq ft (26,40 m²).*

(Above and below) The Blériot SPAD 41 of 1922 progressed no further than a single prototype.

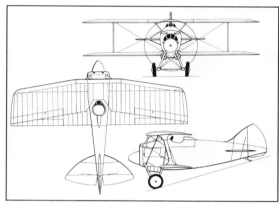

BLÉRIOT SPAD 51   France

Designed by André Herbemont and of generally similar configuration to the Type 41, the Blériot SPAD 51 had fabric-covered metal wings and a wooden monocoque fuselage, power being provided by a 420 hp Gnome-Rhône Jupiter nine-cylinder radial. The first prototype, the Type 51-1, was flown on 16 June 1924, a second modified prototype, the Type 51-2, following on 18 March 1925. Powered by a Jupiter IV and carrying an armament of two 7,7-mm MAC (Vickers) guns in the upper wing, the Blériot SPAD 51-2 was ordered for the Polish air arm, the *Lotnictwo Wojskowe*, 50 being delivered during 1925-26. A further prototype, the Type 51-3, with an improved propeller, flew on 7 September 1926, this offering a 7.5 mph (12 km/h) speed superiority and improved ceiling over the 51-2. On 30 August 1928, the final derivative of the basic model flew, this being the Type 51-4 with a special 600 hp version of the Jupiter. Ten production Type 51-4s were completed, one being sold to Turkey and another to the Soviet Union, these having provision for two fuselage-mounted Vickers and two wing-mounted Darne machine guns, and a 420 hp Jupiter 9Ab. The following

(Above) The prototype Blériot SPAD 51-1, flown in June 1924, and (below) its production derivative, the Type 51-2, which was purchased by Poland.

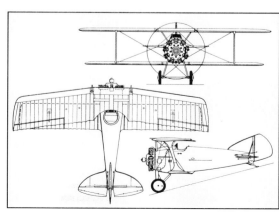

Blériot SPAD developed the Type 71 specifically for the Spanish *Concurso de aviones* in 1923.

gered single-bay biplane with a sweptback upper wing and unswept lower wing, the Blériot SPAD 71 was powered by a 300 hp Hispano-Suiza HS 8Fb eight-cylinder water-cooled engine, carried an armament of twin 7,7-mm MAC (Vickers) machine guns and was flown to Spain for evaluation in January 1923. In the fighter contest it was bested by the Nieuport 29 and no further development was undertaken. *Max speed, 147 mph (237 km/h). Empty weight, 1,911 lb (867 kg). Loaded weight, 2,879 lb (1 306 kg). Span, 31 ft 10⅔ in (9,72 m). Length, 23 ft 11⅜ in (7,30 m). Height, 9 ft 2⅛ in (2,80 m). Wing area, 322.92 sq ft (30,0 m²).*

(Above) The solitary example of the Blériot SPAD 51-4 exported to Turkey for Army evaluation.

structure of the original Type 61-1 (the production Type 61-2 having a wooden wing), and had four 7,7-mm Darne machine guns and increased fuel tankage. First flown on 9 May 1925, it was intended to participate in the 1925 fighter trials. Re-engined with a 480 hp Lorraine-Dietrich LO 12Ee, it flew on 6 June 1925 as the Type 61-4. Three examples of the Type 61-5 were built, powered by the 450 hp Hispano-Suiza HS 12Gb engine.

data relate to the Type 51-2. *Max speed, 143 mph (230 km/h). Time to 13,125 ft (4 000 m), 9.2 min. Ceiling, 29,530 ft (9 000 m). Empty weight, 2,182 lb (990 kg). Loaded weight, 2,998 lb (1 360 kg). Span, 31 ft 0⅞ in (8,47 m). Length, 21 ft 1⅞ in (6,45 m). Height, 10 ft 2 in (3,10 m). Wing area, 261.25 sq ft (24,27 m²).*

BLÉRIOT SPAD 61 France

Developed in parallel with the Type 51, the Blériot SPAD 61 was actually flown before the earlier-numbered model, the prototype being tested first on 6 November 1923. A single-bay staggered biplane with fabric-covered metal wings and a wooden monocoque fuselage, it was powered by a 12-cylinder W-type Lorraine-Dietrich LO 12Ew engine of 450 hp. Production orders were placed on behalf of both Poland (250) and Romania (100), for the Type 61-2, which appeared in 1925 carrying an armament of two synchronised 7,7-mm MAC (Vickers) machine guns. A further 30 Blériot SPAD 61-2s were built under licence in Poland from 1927 by CWL (Centralne Warszaty Lotnicze) and its successor PZL (Państwowe Zaklady Lotnicze). Variants that progressed no further than the prototype stage included the Type 61-3 which reverted to the metal wing

BLÉRIOT SPAD 81 France

The Blériot SPAD 81 paradoxically preceded the Types 51 and 61, the first prototype having flown at Buc on 13 March 1923. A single-bay staggered biplane of mixed construction with fabric-covered metal wings and a wooden monocoque fuselage, the Type 81 was powered by a 300 hp Hispano-Suiza HS 8Fb water-cooled engine and an armament of two 7,7-mm MAC (Vickers) machine guns. A production batch of 80 was ordered for France's *Aviation Militaire* on 28 March 1924. The Types 81-2 and 81-3, built in prototype form only and flown on 20 May and 18 August 1924 respectively, differed primarily in the types of radiator fitted, and a further prototype, the Type 81-4 flown on 11 September 1924, differed in having wings of wooden construction. *Max speed, 149 mph (240 km/h) at 1,640 ft (600 m), 128 mph (206 km/h) at 19,685 ft (6 000 m). Range, 310 mls (500 km). Time to 16,405 ft (5 000 m), 14 min. Empty weight, 1,865 lb (846 kg). Loaded weight, 2,791 lb (1 266 kg). Span, 31 ft 6⅓ in (9,61 m). Length, 20 ft 11⅞ in (6,40 m). Height, 9 ft 6¼ in (2,90 m). Wing area, 322.92 sq ft (30,00 m²).*

Blériot SPAD 81 for France's *Aviation Militaire*.

Developed in parallel with the Blériot SPAD 51, the Type 61-1 (above) was the first of them to fly.

The first of these was flown on 13 May 1925, and one was supplied to Turkey. The second Type 61-5 flew on 9 September 1927 as the Type 61-8 after being re-engined with a 500 hp HS 12Hb engine, and the final fighter derivative was the Type 61SES built for Polish evaluation. This differed from earlier models in being a sesquiplane with a swept upper wing. The Type 61SES was flown on 1 May 1926, but proved to have inferior characteristics to those of the standard Type 61-2. The following data relate to the Type 61-2. *Max speed, 141 mph (227 km/h). Time to 13,125 ft (4 000 m), 9.65 min. Empty weight, 2,326 lb (1 055 kg). Loaded weight, 3,450 lb (1 565 kg). Span, 31 ft 4¾ in (9,57 m). Length, 22 ft 10⅞ in (6,98 m). Height, 9 ft 6⅛ in (2,90 m). Wing area, 315.39 sq ft (29,30 m²).*

BLÉRIOT SPAD 71 France

The Type 71 was, like the Type 41, a single-seat derivative of the 1918 SPAD S.XX two-seater, but was intended specifically to participate in the Spanish *Concurso de aviones* which was to result in the selection of combat aircraft for the *Aeronáutica Militar Española* from competing indigenous and foreign types. A stag-

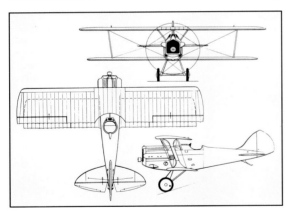

(Above and below) The Blériot SPAD 61-2 was produced for Romania and Poland, and licence-built in the latter country by CWL and PZL.

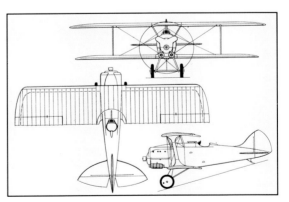

BLÉRIOT SPAD 60 France

On 24 December 1925, the Société Blériot-Aéronautique received a French government order for three prototypes of a two-seat fighter powered by a 420 hp Gnome-Rhône Jupiter 9Ab nine-cylinder radial engine. Designated Blériot SPAD 60, the fighter was a single-bay biplane of mixed construction with sweptback upper wing and unswept lower wing, armament comprising two fixed forward-firing 7,7-mm machine guns in the upper wing and two weapons of similar calibre on a ring mounting in the rear cockpit. The first prototype was flown on 26 June 1926, but as a result of stability problems development was abandoned in favour of the Blériot SPAD 70. *Max speed, 130 mph*

(Above) The Blériot SPAD 81-2, built only as a prototype, had an experimental flush radiator.

(Below) After application of smaller wings, the original Blériot SPAD 81-01 became the 81bis seen here.

radial. Early in 1931 it received a 480 hp Gnome-Rhône Jupiter 9Ae as the Type 91-5, but was destroyed on 10 May after six hours flying in the latter form. The original Type 91 *Léger* had meanwhile been fitted with a 500 hp HS 12Mb engine and, with various minor modifications, became the Type 91-4, which first flew on 4 July 1930. Rounded wingtips were then applied, the fuselage was lengthened and the tailplane was lowered to the base of the fuselage, flight testing being resumed on 10

(Above) The Blériot SPAD 91-4, rebuilt from the Type 91 prototype, shown (below) in its original form.

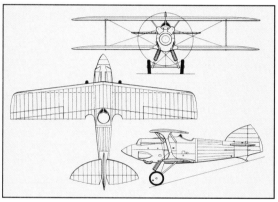

November 1931 as the Type 91-6. The tailplane was later restored to its original position, but both the 1926 and subsequent lightweight, or "Jockey", fighter programmes had meanwhile been abandoned and none of the competing designs had been ordered into production. The following data relate to the Type 91-1. *Max speed, 173 mph (278 km/h) at 13,125 ft (4 000 m). Empty weight, 2,559 lb (1 161 kg). Loaded weight, 3,230 lb (1 465 kg). Span, 28 ft 4½ in (8,65 m). Length, 21 ft 4⅔ in (6,52 m). Height, 9 ft 7¾ in (2,94 m). Wing area, 215.28 sq ft (20,00 m²).*

(209 km/h). Empty weight, 2,698 lb (1 224 kg). Loaded weight, 3,975 lb (1 803 kg). Span, 37 ft 0⅞ in (11,30 m). Length, 22 ft 6⅞ in (6,88 m). Height, 10 ft 6⅓ in (3,21 m). Wing area, 393.97 sq ft (36,60 m²).

(Below) Built in 1926, the Blériot SPAD 60 two-seat fighter prototype proved unsuccessful.

BLÉRIOT SPAD 70   France

As a result of difficulties experienced during the initial flight testing of the first prototype Blériot SPAD 60 two-seat fighter, the three-prototype order was modified to cover the conversion of the second and third prototypes as Blériot SPAD 70s. The Type 70 two-seat fighter differed from its predecessor primarily in having a 450 hp 12-cylinder W-type Lorraine-Dietrich engine with a Rateau turbo-compressor and redesigned horizontal tail surfaces. The first Type 70 was completed on 14 April 1927, and flew a week later at Buc. Its performance was little better than that of the Type 60 and no series production was ordered. *Max speed, 130 mph (210 km/h). Empty weight, 2,934 lb (1 331 kg). Loaded weight, 4,173 lb (1 893 kg). Span, 37 ft 0⅞ in (11,30 m). Length, 24 ft 7¼ in (7,50 m). Height, 10 ft 6⅓ in (3,21 m). Wing area, 393.97 sq ft (36,60 m²).*

Designed to meet the requirements of the 1926 *Jockey* lightweight fighter programme, the Blériot SPAD 91-01 (right) flew in the form shown here in 1927, later being rebuilt as the Type 91-4.

BLÉRIOT SPAD 91-1 TO -6   France

The Blériot SPAD 91 was originally designed to the requirements of the 1926 lightweight fighter specification which called for an armament of two machine guns and a range of 248 miles (400 km). An all-metal fabric-covered single-seat single-bay biplane with wings of equal span and chord, the first prototype, referred to as the Type 91 *Léger* (Light), was powered by a 500 hp Hispano-Suiza HS 12Hb 12-cylinder water-cooled engine with radiators mounted on the main undercarriage legs. Flown for the first time on 23 August 1927, the Type 91 *Léger* was followed by a second prototype, the Type 91-1, which differed primarily in having a frontal radiator in place of the twin leg-mounted radiators. This second prototype was subsequently fitted with a 500 hp HS 12Gb 12-cylinder engine of W configuration as the Type 91-2, flying in this form on 31 August 1928. After demonstrations in Romania and Greece, it was again re-engined as the Type 91-3 with a 420 hp Gnome-Rhône Jupiter 9As nine-cylinder air-cooled

BLÉRIOT SPAD 91-7 TO -9   France

Despite the "Jockey" being abandoned, André Herbemont persisted with the development of the Type 91 series fighters and, in October 1930, designed a new version. This, while retaining a fuselage similar to that of the Type 91-4, employed an entirely new wing arrangement of inverted sesquiplane configuration. Ailerons were fitted to the lower wing only, this having a span of 28 ft 4½ in (8,65 m) compared with the 22 ft 11⅝ in (7,00 m) of the upper wing. Designated Blériot

SPAD 91-7 and powered by a 500 hp Hispano-Suiza 12Mc 12-cylinder Vee water-cooled engine, the new model was flown for the first time on 23 December 1931. On 2 June 1932, it established a 500-km (311-mile) closed-circuit record of 191.87 mph (308,78 km/h). It was subsequently fitted with a supercharged Hispano-Suiza 12Xbrs engine as the Type 91-8, a variable-pitch Ratier propeller being adopted and a max speed of 224 mph (360 km/h) being reportedly achieved. The prototype was first flown in its Type 91-8 form on 20 August 1932, and in the following December was leased to Hispano-Suiza as a test-bed for the company's engine-mounted 20-mm cannon, which was duly fitted, together with a large-diameter Levasseur fixed-pitch propeller, the designation then being changed to Type 91-9. Details of the Type 91-7 follow: *Max speed, 183 mph (295 km/h) at sea level, 199 mph (320 km/h) at 13,125 ft (4 000 m). Range 311 mls (500 km). Time to 19,685 ft (6 000 m), 9.2 min. Empty weight, 2,410 lb (1 093 kg). Loaded weight, 3,214 lb (1 458 kg). Span, 28 ft 4½ in (8,65 m). Length, 20 ft 8⅛ in (6,30 m). Height, 9 ft 5 in (2,87 m). Wing area, 191.6 sq ft (17,80 m²).*

Blériot SPAD 510 C1 in service with ERC 4/561, *Armée de l'Air*, at Havre-Octeville, October 1939.

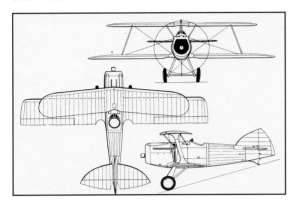

(Above and below) An unusual inverted sesquiplane layout was adopted for the Blériot SPAD 91-7, which established a closed-circuit record.

BLÉRIOT SPAD 510   France

To meet the requirements of the French 1930 fighter programme, André Herbemont evolved the Blériot SPAD 510. The Type 510, which was ordered as a single prototype to participate in the programme, was of all-metal construction with a duralumin monocoque rear fuselage, and fabric-covered wings and tail assembly. Powered by an Hispano-Suiza 12Xbrs 12-cylinder Vee

The Blériot SPAD 510 single-seat fighter of 1933.

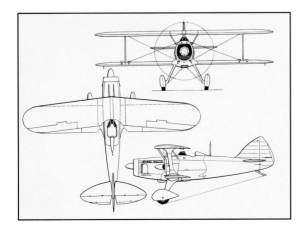

liquid-cooled engine rated at 690 hp at 13,120 ft (4 000 m), the Blériot SPAD 510 was flown for the first time on 6 January 1933. After protracted evaluation, during which the centre fuselage was lengthened by 1 ft 3¾ in (40 cm) to rectify a shortcoming in longitudinal stability and the vertical tail surfaces were enlarged to improve yaw characteristics, the type was ordered into production in August 1935. The first of 60 production examples were delivered early in the following year, the final two aircraft being accepted with the HS 12Xcrs engine and a 20-mm Hispano-Suiza motor cannon. The standard armament comprised four wing-mounted MAC 1934 7,5-mm guns. The Type 510 proved to be the last fighter biplane to be ordered for the *Armée de l'Air. Max speed, 201 mph (324 km/h) at 3,280 ft (1 000 m), 230 mph (370 km/h) at 16,405 ft (5 000 m). Range, 543 mls (875 km). Time to 9,840 ft (3 000 m), 3.37 min. Empty weight, 2,756 lb (1 250 kg). Normal loaded weight, 3,638 lb (1 650 kg). Maximum loaded weight, 4,034 lb (1 830 kg). Span, 29 ft 0 in (8,84 m). Length, 24 ft 5¾ in (7,46 m). Height, 12 ft 2½ in (3,72 m). Wing area, 236.81 sq ft (22,0 m²).*

(Below) The SPAD 510 was the last fighting biplane ordered into production for the *Armée de l'Air*.

BLÉRIOT SPAD 710   France

The last fighter design of André Herbemont to bear the SPAD appellation, and intended to participate in the

The Blériot SPAD 710 featured a Vee-type tail unit.

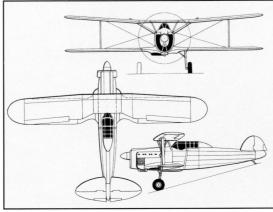

1934 fighter competition, the Blériot SPAD 710 was a single-seat, single-bay biplane embodying a number of interesting features. Of all-metal construction with a duralumin monocoque fuselage and an 860 hp Hispano-Suiza 12Ycrs 12-cylinder Vee liquid-cooled engine, it had a proposed armament of one engine-mounted 20-mm cannon, four wing-mounted 7,5-mm machine guns and one aft-firing 7,5-mm gun in the rear fuselage. Furthermore, the Blériot SPAD 710 embodied inward-retracting main undercarriage members, a completely enclosed cockpit with aft-sliding canopy and a V-type or "butterfly" tail assembly. The initial flight took place in April 1937, and, on 8 June, 186 mph (300 km/h) was exceeded in level flight with the undercarriage extended. A week later, on 15 June, tail flutter developed at an altitude of only 656 ft (200 m) and the aircraft crashed, killing the pilot, Louis Massotte. Further development was then abandoned. *Estimated max speed, 292 mph (470 km/h). Span, 29 ft 0 in (8,84 m). Length, 21 ft 4 in (6,50 m). Height, 10 ft 6 in (3,20 m). Wing area, 236.81 sq ft (22,0 m²).*

(Above) Built in 1936/37, the two-seat SPAD 710 was the last fighter to bear the SPAD appellation.

BLOCH 150   France

Designed by Maurice Roussel of Avions Marcel Bloch as a contender in the 1934 fighter programme, the Bloch 150-01 was a single-seat all-metal cantilever monoplane initially powered by a 14-cylinder radial Gnome-

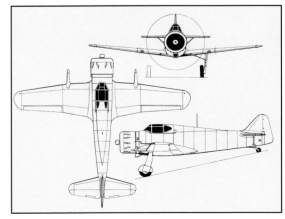

(Above and below) The Bloch 150, designed by M Roussel, flew originally in the form shown here.

Rhône 14Kfs engine rated at 930 hp at 14,270 ft (4 350 m). Unsuccessful attempts to fly the aircraft on 7 July 1936 resulted in application of an entirely new wing of increased area, and a longer-stroke undercarriage, the maiden flight eventually being performed on 4 May 1937. The Bloch 150-01 was successively fitted with a direct-drive GR 14N-07 offering 970 hp at 14,928 ft (4 550 m) and accompanied by an extended propeller shaft to allow for a longer-chord engine cowling; a geared GR 14N-01 accompanied by a larger propeller and extended wingtips which increased span from 32 ft 10½ in (10,02 m) to 33 ft 2¾ in (10,13 m), and, finally, a GR 14N-21 rated at 1,030 hp. Although 25 pre-series Bloch 150s were ordered, a complete structural redesign proved necessary for series production, this being coupled with numerous aerodynamic refinements and other changes which were to result in redesignation as the Bloch 151. Proposed armament of the Bloch 150 consisted of two 20-mm HS 404 cannon and two 7,5-mm MAC 1934 machine guns. The following data relate to the Bloch 150-01 with the GR 14N-07 engine. *Max speed, 270 mph (434 km/h) at 8,530 ft (2 600 m). Empty weight, 3,748 lb (1 700 kg). Loaded weight, 5,071 lb (2 300 kg). Span, 32 ft 10½ in (10,02 m). Length, 30 ft 10 in (9,40 m). Height, 10 ft 5½ in (3,19 m). Wing area, 165.77 sq ft (15,40 m²).*

BLOCH 151 France

Production derivative of the Bloch 150, the Bloch 151 originally flew with this close-fitting cowling.

The Bloch 151 was a re-structured, aerodynamically-refined development of the Bloch 150, flown for the first time on 18 August 1938. Armament comprised two 20-mm HS 404 cannon and two 7,5-mm MAC 1934 machine guns (although many production aircraft were subsequently to be delivered with a quartet of 7,5-mm machine guns and no cannon). Initially powered by a Gnome-Rhône 14N-11 engine rated at 920 hp at 12,140 ft (3 700 m), the Bloch 151 standardised on the GR 14N-35 offering the same power, and 144 fighters of this type were ordered, the first being taken on charge by the *Armée de l'Air* on 7 March 1939. Performance proved disappointing, the type being considered unsuited for first-line duties but, in the event, the Bloch 151 was used in combat by both the *Armée de l'Air* and the *Aéronavale*. Nine were supplied to Greece. *Max speed, 289 mph (465 km/h) at 16,405 ft (5 000 m). Range, 398 mls (640 km). Time to 3,280 ft (1 000 m), 1.95 min. Empty weight, 4,570 lb (2 073 kg). Max loaded weight, 6,173 lb (2 800 kg). Span, 34 ft 7 in (10,54 m). Length, 29 ft 10¼ in (9,10 m). Height, 9 ft 11⅓ in (3,03 m). Wing area, 186.43 sq ft (17,32 m²).*

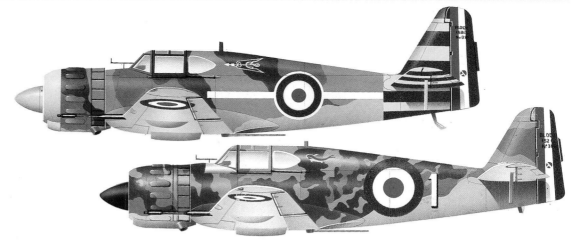

Bloch 152s of the *Armée de l'Air de l'Armistice*, with (top) GC I/8 in 1942 and (above) GC II/8 early 1943.

BLOCH 152 France

Manufactured in parallel with the Bloch 151 and flown in prototype form on 15 December 1938, the Bloch 152 differed primarily in the sub-types of the Gnome-Rhône 14N engine specified, and in armament provisions. The definitive orders for the Bloch 152 called for 200 with the GR 14N-25 and 288 with the GR 14N-49, both engines being rated at 1,000 hp at 11,810 ft (3 600 m), and armament could comprise either two 20-mm HS 404 cannon and two 7,5-mm machine guns or four 7,5-mm guns, the smaller weapons being of the MAC 1934 M39 type which, unlike the machine guns of the Bloch 151, were belt fed. The first examples of the Bloch 152 were delivered to the *Armée de l'Air* in April 1939, and a total of 482 was eventually taken on charge, 20 of these later being supplied by the Vichy government to Romania. *Max speed, 316 mph (509 km/h) at 14,765 ft (4 500 m): Range, 335 mls (540 km). Time to 6,560 ft (2 000 m), 3.4 min. Empty weight, 4,758 lb (2 158 kg). Max loaded weight, 6,173 lb (2 800 kg). Span, 34 ft 7 in (10,54 m). Length, 29 ft 10¼ in (9,10 m). Height, 9 ft 11⅓ in (3,03 m). Wing area, 186.43 sq ft (17,32 m²).*

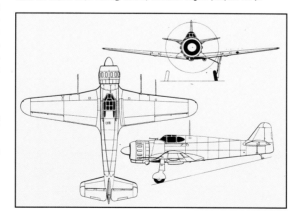

An offset engine mounting was employed by the Bloch 152 (above and below) to counter torque.

BLOCH 153 France

Two fighters basically similar to the Bloch 152 apart from engine were the Bloch 153 with a Pratt & Whitney R-1830-SC3-G Twin Wasp rated at 1,050 hp for take-off and the Bloch 154 with a Wright GR-1820-G205A Cyclone 9 rated at 1,200 hp for take-off. The first of these, the Bloch 153-01, was flown for the first time on 8 April 1939, but no series production of the Twin Wasp-powered fighter was ordered and the prototype was eventually taken on charge by the *Armée de l'Air* on 28

The sole example of the Bloch 153, flown in April 1939, was distinguished by a Twin Wasp engine.

May 1940. The Cyclone-powered Bloch 154 failed to attain flight test status owing to the late delivery of the engine, development being overtaken by that of the Bloch 155 when a Cyclone 9 finally became available. The specification of the Bloch 153 was generally similar to that of the Bloch 152.

BLOCH 155 France

The more obvious shortcomings of the Bloch 152 resulted in development of the Bloch 155, flown for the first time on 3 December 1939. This embodied a measure of redesign undertaken by an SNCASO team led by M Fandeux. By comparison with the Bloch 152, the Bloch 155 featured a larger fuselage fuel tank, CG and space considerations dictating the repositioning of the cockpit farther aft in consequence. Major structural redesign took place of the forward and centre fuselage. The tail bracing struts were eliminated but in other respects the airframe was similar to that of the Bloch 152. An order was placed for 400 Bloch 155s powered by the Gnome-Rhône 14N-49 and armed with two 20-mm HS 404 cannon and two 7,5-mm MAC 1934 M39 machine guns, and the first production aircraft flew on 3 April 1940. Ten had been completed prior to the Franco-German Armistice and a further 19 were completed subsequently for the Vichy-controlled *Armée de l'Air de l'Armistice*. *Max speed, 323 mph (520 km/h) at*

Developed from the Bloch 152, the Bloch 155 was test-flown by the *Luftwaffe* after the Armistice.

14,765 ft (4 500 m). Range, 652 mls (1 050 km). Time to 13,125 ft (4 000 m), 6.92 min. Empty weight, 4,718 lb (2 140 kg). Max loaded weight, 6,393 lb (2 900 kg). Span, 34 ft 7 in (10,54 m). Length, 29 ft 8⅓ in (9,05 m). Height, 10 ft 6 in (3,21 m). Wing area, 186.43 sq ft (17,32 m²).

(Near right) This Bloch 155 was flown by the CO of GC II/8, *Armée de l'Air de l'Armistice*, at Marignane, July 1940. (Far right) A Bloch 155 in *Luftwaffe* service as a fighter-trainer during 1942.

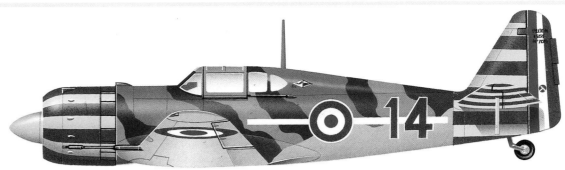

Key to Bloch 152 C1

1 Chauvière 371 constant-speed variable-pitch metal propeller
2 Spinner
3 Cowling lip
4 Cable-attached removable rocker arm cover
5 Front cowling cooling intake
6 Propeller reduction gearbox
7 Detachable engine cowlings
8 Gnome-Rhône 14N25 radial engine
9 Carburettor intake
10 Engine accessories cooling air intake
11 Rocker arm blister fairing
12 Exhaust pipe collector
13 Exhaust flame dampers
14 Engine bay bulkhead and firewall
15 Engine mount
16 Ring-and-bead auxiliary sight
17 Starboard gun bay
18 Cannon ammunition drum (60 rounds)
19 Machine gun ammunition drum (300 rounds)
20 MAC 1934 machine gun (7.5-mm calibre)
21 Pitot tube
22 Wing skin stiffeners
23 Starboard navigation light
24 Ground adjustable trim tab
25 Starboard aileron
26 Aileron control linkage
27 Machine gun mounting strut
28 Windscreen
29 Baille-Lemaire GH 38 reflector sight
30 Instrument panel
31 Control column
32 Throttle
33 Rudder pedal
34 Port wheel bay
35 Fuel tank (94 Imp gal/427 l capacity)
36 Elevator trim tab wheel
37 Pilot's seat
38 Safety harness
39 Generator/accumulator control panel
40 Oxygen bottle
41 Aft-sliding canopy
42 Electrical circuit switch box
43 Head armour
44 Cockpit aft glazing
45 Access to rear fuselage
46 Forward fuselage frame construction
47 Hand hold
48 Audio frequency amplifier
49 Antenna
50 Access panel
51 Sliding canopy track
52 Rear fuselage attachment frame
53 Radio transmitter
54 Convertor
55 Ventral antenna retraction jack
56 Fuselage top decking construction
57 Rudder control rod
58 Elevator control rod
59 Fuselage frame construction
60 Aft fairing
61 Tailplane attachment frame
62 Tailplane centre joint
63 Fin attachment joint
64 Starboard tailplane
65 Starboard elevator
66 Fin construction
67 Rudder balance horn
68 Rudder construction
69 Fixed rudder tab
70 Elevator tab (controllable)
71 Port elevator
72 Elevator horn balance
73 Tailplane construction
74 Tailplane bracing strut
75 Fixed tailskid
76 Fuselage stringer construction
77 Aft fuselage centreline joint
78 Wing root fillet
79 Rear spar attachment joint
80 Flap housing construction
81 Port flap
82 Aileron linkage connecting rod
83 Port aileron
84 Wing tip construction
85 Port navigation light
86 Rear spar
87 Lower skin panel stiffeners
88 Outer wing ribs
89 Forward spar
90 Leading edge construction
91 Landing light
92 Spent cartridge case chute
93 Machine gun mounting strut

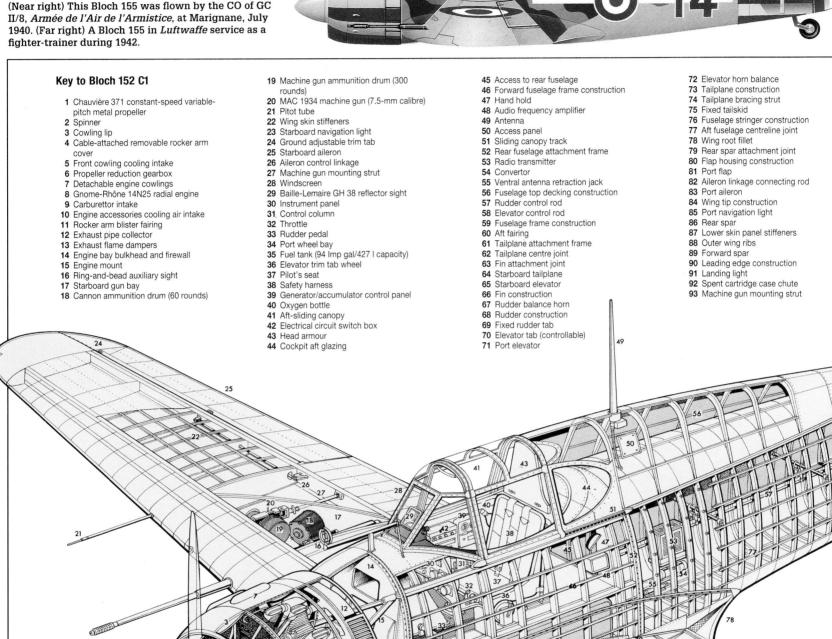

airframe of the Bloch 152 to take this power plant, the combination receiving the designation Bloch 156. However, when it was realised that such an adaptation could not take full advantage of the output offered by the GR 14R, this project was abandoned and an entirely new fighter developed around the engine by a team led by Lucien Servanty. This, the Bloch 157, was flown for the first time in March 1942 with a Gnome-Rhône 14R-4 14-cylinder radial rated at 1,580 hp for take-off and 1,480 hp at 26,250 ft (8 000 m). The proposed armament (which was never fitted) comprised two 20-mm HS 404 cannon and two 7,5-mm MAC 1934 M39 machine guns. Early in 1943, the sole prototype was delivered to the *Luftwaffe*, the engine being removed for bench testing and no further flight testing being undertaken. *Max speed, 441 mph (710 km/h) at 25,755 ft (7 850 m). Range, 683 mls (1 100 km). Time to 26,250 ft (8 000 m), 11 min. Empty weight, 5,265 lb (2 388 kg). Normal loaded weight, 7,165 lb (3 250 kg). Span, 35 ft 1¼ in (10,70 m). Length, 30ft 0¼ in (9,15 m). Height, 14 ft 1¼ in (4,30 m). Wing area, 208.82 sq ft (19,40 m²).*

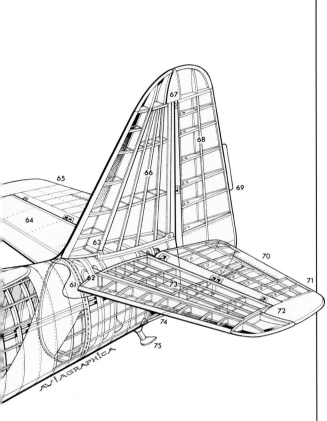

94 Machine gun ammunition drum (300 rounds)
95 Adjustable front gun mounting
96 MAC 1934 machine gun port
97 Camera (for training only -not installed for operational flights)
98 Cannon ammunition drum (60 rounds)
99 Hispano HS 404 (20-mm calibre) cannon
100 Diagonal wing ribs
101 Cannon shell case chute
102 Ventral antenna
103 Oil cooler
104 Front spar attachment
105 Oil cooler intake
106 Main leg retraction jack
107 Undercarriage leg pivot
108 Cannon muzzle
109 Muzzle brake
110 Main undercarriage leg
111 Mainwheel leg door
112 Torque scissors
113 Wheel hub brake
114 Port mainwheel

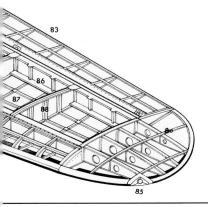

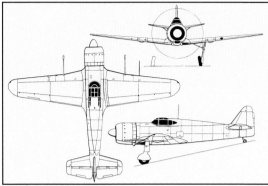

The Bloch 155 which entered production late 1939.

BLOCH 157   France

The availability of the new supercharged Gnome-Rhône 14R engine resulted in a proposal to adapt the

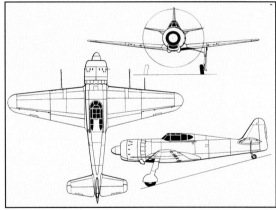

The Bloch 157 (above) was the final development in the line of Bloch fighters originated in the mid '30s.

BLOCH 700   France

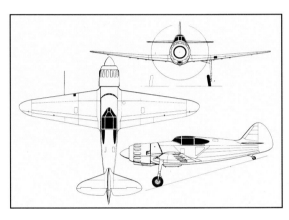

(Above) The Bloch 700 lightweight fighter of 1939.

In 1936, the *Ministère de l'Air* established a requirement for a lightweight fighter of wooden construction which resulted in the development of the Arsenal VG 30, the Caudron C 713 and the Bloch 700. The last-mentioned type, designed by André Herbemont, who had been responsible for the Blériot SPAD fighter series, was built at the former Blériot-Aéronautique plant at Suresnes which had been incorporated in the Société Nationale de Construction Aéronautiques du Sud-Ouest (SNCASO) on 1 January 1937, under the directorship of Marcel Bloch. Of stressed-skin construc-

(Above and below) The sole prototype of the Bloch 157 was delivered to the *Luftwaffe* early in 1943.

Designed by André Herbemont in 1937, the light-weight Bloch 700 was built by the SNCASO and the sole prototype was captured by the *Wehrmacht*.

tion, the Bloch 700 was powered by a Gnome-Rhône 14 M6 14-cylinder radial engine offering 700 hp for take-off and had provision for two 20-mm Hispano-Suiza 404 cannon and two 7,5-mm MAC 1934 M39 machine guns. The sole prototype was destroyed at Buc after capture by German forces. *Max speed, 342 mph (550 km/h). Max endurance, 2 hrs. Loaded weight (excluding arma-ment), 4,078 lb (1 850 kg). Span, 29 ft 2⅓ in (8,90 m). Length, 24 ft 1 in (7,34 m). Height, 11 ft 1¾ in (3,40 m). Wing area, 133.47 sq ft (12,40 m²).*

BLOHM UND VOSS BV 40   Germany

The BV 40 was unique in being a fighter *glider*; an ex-tremely small, heavily armed and armoured aircraft in-tended specifically for bomber interception after being towed to attack altitude by an orthodox fighter. De-signed by Dr Richard Vogt, the BV 40 was of mixed con-struction, the entire cockpit being constructed of welded sheet metal, the pilot occupying a prone posi-tion on a padded bench and armament comprising two 30-mm MK 108 cannon beneath the wing roots with 35 rpg. The BV 40 took-off on a jettisonable twin-wheel bogie, and, after release by the tow-plane, was in-tended to attack an intruding enemy bomber in a 20 deg angle dive. Nineteen prototypes and 200 produc-tion examples of the BV 40 were ordered, the first proto-type, the BV 40 V1, making its first flight test in May

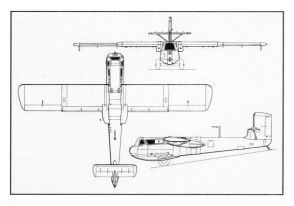

(Above and below) Uniquely for a fighter, the BV 40 was a glider, designed to attack bomber formations in a dive after being towed to height.

1944. Seven prototypes had been completed when the BV 40 programme was abandoned in the autumn of 1944. *Max speed (estimated attainable in a dive), 560 mph (900 km/h), (under Bf 109G tow), 344 mph (553 km/h) at 19,000 ft (5 790 m). Empty weight, 1,821 lb (826 kg). Loaded weight, 2,094 lb (950 kg). Span, 25 ft 11 in (7,90 m). Length, 18 ft 8½ in (5,70 m). Height, 5 ft 4 in (1,63 m). Wing area, 93.65 sq ft (8,70 m²).*

BLOHM UND VOSS BV 155   Germany

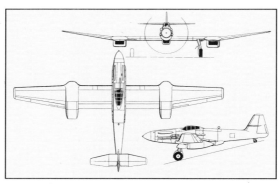

The BV 155, the V2 being illustrated above and below, featured an inordinately long-span wing.

Based on an original Messerschmitt design (Me 155B) for a single-seat high-altitude fighter, development of which was transferred to Blohm und Voss in August 1943, the BV 155 featured an inordinate wing span. The first prototype, the BV 155 V1, was flown on 1 Septem-ber 1944, and was powered by a Daimler-Benz DB 603A engine fitted with a TKL 15 turbo-supercharger and rated at 1,610hp for take-off and at 32,810 ft (10 000 m). The pilot was accommodated in a pressurised cockpit and various armament combinations were proposed, such as one engine-mounted 30-mm MK 108 and two

20-mm MG 151 cannon. The second prototype, the BV 155 V2, was flown on 8 February 1945, this embodying considerable redesign and a revised radiator arrange-ment. A third prototype, the BV 155 V3, was incomplete when hostilities terminated, this differing from the V2 in having a DB 603U engine providing 1,660 hp for take-off and 1,750 hp at 5,575 ft (1 700 m). The following data relate to the proposed production version, the BV 155B. *Max speed, 404 mph (650 km/h) at 39,370 ft (12 000 m), 429 mph (690 km/h) at 52,490 ft (16 000 m). Initial climb, 2,260 ft/min (11,48 m/sec). Range, 838 mls (1 350 km) at 32,810 ft (10 000 m). Empty weight, 10,736 lb (4 870 kg). Max loaded weight, 13,263 lb (6 016 kg). Span, 67 ft 3 in (20,50 m). Length, 39 ft 4½ in (12,00 m). Height, 9 ft 9½ in (3,00 m). Wing area, 419.8 sq ft (39,00 m²).*

BOEING PW-9   USA

The first fighter of original design to be built by Boeing was the private-venture Model 15, first flown on 29 April 1923 and powered by a 435 hp Curtiss D-12 water-cooled engine. After competitive testing against the Fokker XPW-7 and Curtiss XPW-8A, the Model 15 was purchased by the USAAC. Two additional examples were ordered and the designation XPW-9 was assigned. The third example discarded the cross-axle undercarriage in favour of a divided-axle arrangement that was to be adopted for the production model. Orders were placed for 30 production examples under the designation PW-9 (the last of these being com-pleted as the XP-4). The PW-9 had a steel-tube fuse-

Boeing's first fighter of original design was the XPW-9 (Model 15), adopted by USAAC in 1924.

lage, wooden wings and fabric skinning, and arma-ment comprised two 0.3-in (7,62-mm) machine guns. Twenty-five additional aircraft were ordered in October 1925 as PW-9As (Model 15As) with the im-proved but similarly-rated D-12C (V-1150-1) engine and duplicated flying and landing wires, the last of these being completed to PW-9B standard with a D-12D (V-1150-3) engine. Fifteen PW-9Bs were ordered but were delivered under the designation PW-9C with re-arranged flying and landing wire fittings. A further 25 PW-9Cs were purchased, the last of these being con-verted to the prototype PW-9D with redesigned radiator, a larger aerodynamically-balanced rudder and other improvements. Delivery of 16 production PW-9Ds was completed in May 1928. The following data relate to the PW-9D. *Max speed, 155 mph (249 km/h) at sea level, 152 mph (245 km/h) at 5,000 ft (1 524 m). Cruising speed, 124 mph (199 km/h). Time to 5,000 ft (1 524 m), 4 min. Endurance, 2.87 hrs. Empty weight, 2,328 lb (1 056 kg). Loaded weight, 3,234 lb (1 467 kg). Span, 32 ft 0 in (9,75 m). Length, 24 ft 2 in (7,36 m). Height, 8 ft 8 in (2,64 m). Wing area, 241 sq ft (22,39 m²).*

The PW-9C (below) was of near-sesquiplane layout.

(Above) The sole FB-4, a modification of the 14th FB-1, was distinguished by Wright engine and floats.

Features of the PW-9C, compared with earlier PW-9s, were rearranged flying and landing wire fittings.

BOEING FB-1 TO FB-3   USA

Fourteen Model 15 fighters were ordered by the US Navy under the designation FB-1 in 1925, and the first

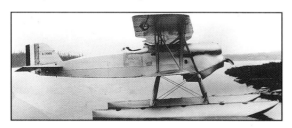

(Above) The shore-based FB-1 for the USMC closely resembled the USAAC's PW-9. The sole FB-3 floatplane (below) was fundamentally similar to the FB-2.

10 of these were essentially similar to the USAAC's PW-9 apart from minor details, no equipment for carrier operation being fitted. The FB-1, which was operated by the US Marine Corps, was powered by the 435 hp Curtiss D-12 water-cooled engine and could be fitted with either two 0.3-in (7,62-mm) machine guns or one 0.3-in and one 0.5-in (12,7 mm) weapon. The 11th and 12th aircraft ordered as FB-1s were structurally modified to accommodate arrester gear for shipboard operation, featured cross-axle rather than split-axle undercarriages, and were assigned the designation FB-2 (Model 53). The D-12 engine gave place to a 510 hp Packard 1A-1500 water-cooled engine and both FB-2s were delivered to the US Navy in December 1925. The 13th and 14th aircraft were respectively assigned the designations FB-3 and FB-4. The former (Model 55) was identical to the FB-2 but fitted with twin wooden floats and was destroyed during trials in December 1925. Two additional FB-3s were ordered with wheel undercarriages, these having a similar Packard engine to that of the FB-2, but split-axle undercarriages similar to that of the FB-1. Delivered in April 1926, these were later fitted with enlarged balanced rudders. The following data relate to the definitive FB-3. *Max speed, 170 mph (274 km/h). Time to 5,000 ft (1 524 m), 3 min. Range, 460 mls (740 km). Empty weight, 2,387 lb (1 083 kg). Loaded weight, 3,204 lb (1 453 kg). Span, 32 ft 0 in (9,75 m). Length, 22 ft 11 in (6,98 m). Height, 8 ft 9 in (2,67 m). Wing area, 241.5 sq ft (22,44 m²).*

BOEING FB-4   USA

The sole example of the FB-4 (Model 54) single-seat fighter delivered to the US Navy in January 1926 was originally ordered as the 14th FB-1, the change in designation resulting from the fitting of a 450 hp Wright P-1 radial air-cooled engine. Flight testing, initially conducted with twin wooden floats, indicated the unsuit-

(Above) After being tested as a floatplane, the FB-4 was modified to FB-6 landplane form with a Pratt & Whitney R-1340 Wasp radial.

ability of the Wright engine for fighter use and this power plant was replaced by a 400 hp Pratt & Whitney R-1340 Wasp, a wheel undercarriage being fitted in place of the floats, and in this form the aircraft was redesignated FB-6. The following data apply to the FB-4 with wheel undercarriage. *Max speed, 160 mph (257 km/h). Time to 5,000 ft (1 524 m), 3.18 min. Range, 428 mls (689 km). Empty weight, 2,000 lb (907 kg). Loaded weight, 2,817 lb (1 278 kg). Span, 32 ft 0 in (9,75 m). Length, 22 ft 10 in (6,95 m). Height, 8 ft 9 in (2,67 m). Wing area, 241.5 sq ft (22,44 m²).*

BOEING FB-5   USA

Derived from the FB-3 and powered by the 520 hp Packard 2A-1500 water-cooled engine, the FB-5 (Model 67) featured rearranged wings with increased stagger, the upper wing being moved forward and the lower wing aft by comparison with the earlier fighter. This change was coupled with various refinements and a completely new undercarriage. The first of 27 FB-5s was flown on 7 October 1926, but the type was retired after only some two years' service because of a US Navy decision to standardise on radial air-cooled engines for shipboard aircraft. Like earlier fighters in the FB series, the FB-5 was of mixed construction with a steel-tube fuselage, wooden wings and fabric skinning, armament comprising two 0.3-in (7,62-mm) Browning machine guns. The first FB-5 was initially tested as a twin-float seaplane and was redesignated XFB-5 in 1927. *Max speed, 176 mph (283 km/h) at sea level. Cruising speed, 150 mph (241 km/h). Initial climb,*

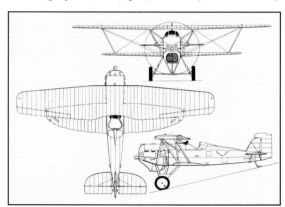

(Above) The FB-5 – the example below from VF-3B aboard *Lexington*, 1928-30 – served for only two years until US Navy standardised on radial engines.

2,100 ft/min (10,67 m/sec). Range, 420 mls (676 km). Empty weight, 2,458 lb (1 115 kg). Loaded weight, 3,249 lb (1 473 kg). Span, 32 ft 0 in (9.75 m). Length, 23 ft 9 in (7,24 m). Height, 9 ft 5 in (2,87 m). Wing area, 241 sq ft (22,39 m²).

BOEING XP-4   USA

The last aircraft built by Boeing against an order for 30 PW-9 single-seat fighters was retained by the company at the request of the USAAC for trials with a turbo-supercharged version of the 510 hp Packard 1A-1500 water-cooled engine (utilised by the FB-2). The USAAC also requested an increase in wing area, because of the higher weights involved, and while the standard PW-9 upper wing was retained, an enlarged lower wing was introduced, resulting in an equi-span biplane with vertical N-type interplane struts. The standard PW-9 armament of two 0.3-in (7,62-mm) synchronised machine guns was augmented by a pair of similar-calibre weapons mounted beneath the lower wing outside the propeller arc. With these changes the aircraft was designated XP-4 (Model 58), and delivered on 27 July 1926, but the 68 sq ft (6,32 m²) increase in gross wing area by comparison with the PW-9 failed to compensate for the 815 lb (370 kg) increase in loaded weight. The XP-4 proved to possess extremely unsatisfactory handling characteristics and after a few hours flying the test programme was abandoned. Max speed, 161 mph (259 km/h). Initial climb, 2,055 ft/min (10,44 m/sec). Range, 375 mls (603 km). Empty weight, 2,783 lb (1 262 kg). Loaded weight, 3,650 lb (1 656 kg). Span, 32 ft 0 in (9,75 m). Length, 23 ft 11 in (7,29 m). Height, 8 ft 10 in (2,69 m). Wing area, 309 sq ft (28,71 m²).

(Below) The XP-4, powered by a turbo-supercharged Packard engine, had been ordered as the last PW-9.

BOEING F2B-1   USA

The first Boeing fighter designed from the outset specifically for shipboard operation, the XF2B-1 (Model 69) utilised the engine installation developed with the FB-6 (re-engined FB-4), having a 425 hp Pratt & Whitney R-1340 Wasp air-cooled radial. Employing a steel-tube fuselage, wooden wings and fabric skinning, the XF2B-1 was first flown on 3 November 1926, and 32 production examples were ordered as F2B-1s. These differed from the prototype in discarding the propeller

Boeing's first shipboard fighter, the F2B-1 is seen below with VB-2B's "Three Sea Hawks" aerobatic team, 1928.

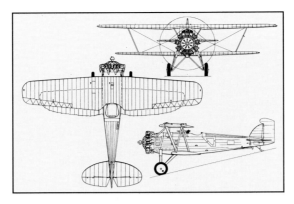

The Wasp-engined Boeing F2B-1 for the US Navy.

spinner and in having a balanced rudder. Deliveries to the US Navy began on 30 January 1928, and two additional examples were built under the company designation Model 69-B for export (one to Japan and the other to Brazil). Armament comprised either two 0.3-in (7,62-mm) machine guns or one 0.3-in (7,62-mm) and one 0.5-in (12,7-mm) weapon. Max speed, 158 mph (254 km/h). Initial climb, 1,890 ft/min (9,60 m/sec). Range, 317 mls (510 km). Empty weight, 1,989 lb (902 kg). Loaded weight, 2,805 lb (1 272 kg). Span, 30 ft 1 in (9,16 m). Length, 22 ft 11 in (6,98 m). Height, 9 ft 2¾ in (2,79 m). Wing area, 243 sq ft (22,58 m²).

BOEING XP-8   USA

The XP-8 (Model 66) actually preceded the XP-7, being delivered in July 1927, having been launched as a private venture late in the previous year. Powered by a 600 hp Packard 2A-1500 water-cooled engine, the XP-8 utilised an airframe essentially similar to that of the US Navy XF2B-1, but performance failed to meet the requirements of the 1925 USAAC specification which it had been designed to meet, and the aircraft was finally scrapped in June 1929. Armament comprised one 0.3-in (7,62-mm) and one 0.5-in (12,7-mm) machine gun. Max speed, 173 mph (278 km/h) at sea level, 166 mph (267 km/h) at 5,000 ft (1 524 m). Initial climb, 2,138 ft/ min (10,86 m/sec), Empty weight, 2,309 lb (1 084 kg). Loaded weight, 3,421 lb (1 552 kg). Span, 30 ft 1 in (9,16 m). Length, 22 ft 10 in (6,95 m). Height, 10 ft 9 in (3,27 m). Wing area, 243 sq ft (22.57 m²).

The XP-8 (above) was an unsuccessful attempt to use a Packard engine in the airframe of the XF2B-1.

BOEING XP-7   USA

The final production PW-9D (the 16th) was retained by Boeing for the experimental installation of a 600 hp water-cooled Curtiss Conqueror V-1570 engine and, as the XP-7 (Model 93), was eventually delivered to the USAAC on 4 September 1928. Distinguished from the PW-9D by a shorter, deeper nose with a larger radiator, the XP-7 enjoyed some success during trials, proving the suitability of the Conqueror for fighter installation, but proposals to build four service evaluation P-7s were

As the XP-7 (above), the last production PW-9 was used to test the Conqueror engine for fighter use.

abandoned when it was concluded that the basic PW-9 airframe had reached the limit of its development. The XP-7, the last Boeing fighter biplane to employ a liquid-cooled engine, was reconverted to PW-9D standards. Max speed, 167 mph (269 km/h) at sea level, 163 mph (262 km/h) at 5,000 ft (1 524 m). Initial climb, 1,867 ft/ min (9,48 m/sec). Empty weight, 2,323 lb (1 053 kg). Loaded weight, 3,260 lb (1 479 kg). Span, 32 ft 0 in (9,75 m). Length, 24 ft 0 in (7,31 m). Height, 9 ft 0 in (2,74 m). Wing area, 241 sq ft (22,39 m²).

BOEING F3B-1   USA

The XF3B-1 (Model 74) was built by Boeing as a private venture and externally resembled closely the F2B-1, but had provision for a single central float with outboard stabilising floats. Powered by a 425 hp Pratt & Whitney R-1340 Wasp, it was flown for the first time on 2 March 1927 as a float seaplane. Showing no significant advance over the F2B-1, the XF3B-1 was returned to Boeing by the US Navy and completely rebuilt (as the Model 77), a redesigned undercarriage, wing and tail being introduced. In this new form the fighter proved successful and was the basis of an order from the US Navy for 73 production examples as F3B-1s. The F3B-1 was of mixed construction with wooden wings, a steel-tube fuselage and fabric skinning, but the ailerons and tail surfaces were of semi-monocoque all-metal construction with corrugated covering. Armament comprised two synchronised 0.3-in (7,62-mm) machine guns and provision was made for five 25-lb (11,3-kg) bombs to be carried. The first flight of the rebuilt XF3B-1 took place on 3 February 1928, and the first production F3B-1, powered by an R-1340-B Wasp, was delivered to the US Navy on 23 November 1928. Max speed, 157 mph (253 km/h) at sea level. Initial climb, 2,020 ft/min (10,26 m/sec). Range, 340 mls (547 km). Empty weight, 2,179 lb (988 kg). Loaded weight, 2,945 lb (1 336 kg). Span, 33 ft 0 in (10,06 m). Length, 24 ft 10 in (7,56 m). Height, 9 ft 2 in (2,79 m). Wing area, 275 sq ft (25,55 m²).

The F3B-1 introduced sweepback on the upper wing.

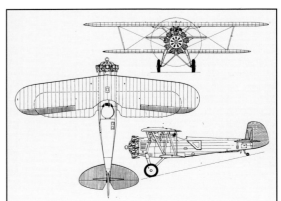

A Boeing F3B-1 (above) of the US Navy's Fighting Squadron Three flying from the *Lexington*.

(Below) Fairings first fitted behind the cylinders have been removed from this F4B-1 of VF-5B.

BOEING F4B-1 USA

Early in 1928, two fighter prototypes, the Models 83 and 89, were built as company-funded ventures, these flying on 25 June and 7 August 1928 respectively. Whereas the Model 83 had a spreader-bar undercarriage and arrester gear, the Model 89 had a split-axle undercarriage and a rack for a 500-lb (227-kg) bomb. These prototypes were eventually purchased by the US Navy (and sometimes referred to as XF4B-1s), and 27 production examples were ordered as F4B-1s (Model 99). The first of these flew on 6 May 1929, and delivery was completed by the following 22 August. Powered by the Pratt & Whitney R-1340-8 rated at 500 hp at 6,000 ft (1 830 m), the F4B-1 initially featured individual fairings behind the cylinders of the uncowled engine, but these were later removed and a ring cowling was added. The vertical tail surfaces of the F4B-4 design were fitted re-

troactively. Armament comprised two 0.3-in (7,62-mm) guns, and 10 24-lb (10,9-kg) bombs could be carried beneath the wings and a 500-lb (227-kg) bomb beneath the fuselage. *Max speed, 176 mph (284 km/h) at 6,000 ft (1 830 m). Climb to 5,000 ft (1 524 m), 2.9 min. Range, 371 mls (597 km). Empty weight, 1,950 lb (884 kg). Loaded weight, 2,750 lb (1 247 kg). Span, 30 ft 0 in (9,14 m). Length, 20 ft 1 in (6,12 m). Height, 9 ft 4 in (2,84 m). Wing area, 227.5 sq ft (21,13 m[2]).*

(Below) The F4B-2, seen here serving with VF-6, was essentially a shipboard equivalent of the AAC's P-12C.

The F4B-1 (below) initially had an uncowled engine.

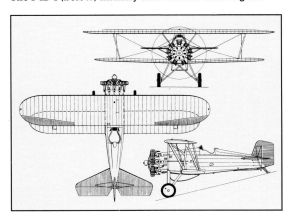

BOEING F4B-2 USA

Essentially a shipboard equivalent of the USAAC's P-12C, the F4B-2 (Model 223) differed outwardly from the F4B-1 in having Frise-type ailerons, a spreader-bar undercarriage, a tailwheel and a ring cowling from the outset, the 500 hp R-1340-8 engine being retained. A total of 46 F4B-2s was purchased by the US Navy, the first of these being delivered on 2 January 1931, and all were eventually fitted with F4B-4 vertical tail surfaces. *Max speed, 186 mph (299 km/h) at 6,000 ft (1 830 m), 170 mph (273 km/h) at sea level. Climb to 5,000 ft (1 524 m), 2.5 min. Range, 403 mls (649 km). Empty weight, 2,067 lb (938 kg). Loaded weight, 2,799 lb (1 270 kg). Span, 30 ft 0 in (9,14 m). Length, 20 ft 1 in (6,12 m). Height, 9 ft 1 in (2,77 m). Wing area, 227.5 sq ft (21,13 m[2]).*

The Boeing F4B-2 (below) had Frise-type ailerons.

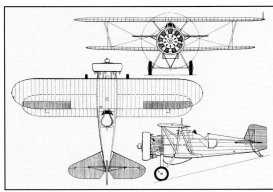

BOEING F4B-3 & F4B-4 USA

The F4B-3 was the US Navy production equivalent of the P-12E with the semi-monocoque metal fuselage, and 21 were ordered on 23 April 1931, together with 92 F4B-4s, the latter differing only in having enlarged vertical tail surfaces (and life raft stowage in an enlarged streamlined headrest on the last 45 examples). Both

The last Boeing production fighter biplane, the F4B-4 is seen here in 1937 with VB-5 on *Yorktown*.

examples were ordered, the first of these flying on 12 May 1930. The initial P-12B was tested with a turbo-supercharged Y1SR-1340G/H engine enclosed by a ring cowling and driving a three-bladed propeller, flying in this form in 1932 as the XP-12G and eventually reverting to P-12B configuration. *Max speed, 166 mph (267 km/h) at 5,000 ft (1 524 m), 157 mph (252 km/h) at sea level. Initial climb, 2,040 ft/min (10,36 m/sec). Range, 540 mls (869 km). Empty weight, 1,945 lb (882 kg). Loaded weight, 2,638 lb (1 196 kg). Span, 30 ft 0 in (9,14 m). Length, 20 ft 3 in (6,17 m). Height, 8 ft 10 in (2,69 m). Wing area, 227.5 sq ft (21,13 m²).*

(Above) This F4B-3 has been beautifully preserved in the colours of US Navy squadron VF-1. (Below) Enlarged tail surfaces characterised the F4B-4.

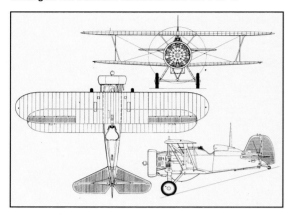

were designated Model 235 by their manufacturer. The first F4B-3 was delivered on 24 December 1931, but delivery of the F4B-4s did not commence until 21 July 1932 as the US Navy agreed to the first 14 airframes being diverted after modification to Brazil (under the designation Model 256). Nine essentially similar fighters (using F4B-3 fuselages, tails and undercarriages married to P-12E wings) were subsequently delivered to Brazil as Model 267s. Armed with two 0.3-in (7,62-mm) machine guns and having provision for two 116-lb (52,6-kg) bombs on underwing racks, the F4B-4 was powered by a 550 hp Pratt & Whitney R-1340-16 engine and remained first-line equipment until 1938. *Max speed, 188 mph (302 km/h) at 6,000 ft (1 830 m). Climb to 5,000 ft (1 524 m), 2.7 min. Range, 371 mls (597 km). Empty weight, 2,354 lb (1 068 kg). Loaded weight, 3,128 lb (1 419 kg). Span, 30 ft 0 in (9,14 m). Length, 20 ft 5 in (6,22 m). Height, 9 ft 9 in (2,97 m). Wing area, 227.5 sq ft (21,13 m²).*

BOEING P-12   USA

As a result of evaluation of the Model 89, the USAAC placed an order for 10 aircraft (essentially similar to the Navy's F4B-1) as the P-12 (Model 102) powered by the Pratt & Whitney R-1340-7 engine rated at 450 hp at 5,000 ft (1 524 m) with, initially, individual fairings aft of the cylinders. The first P-12 was flown on 11 April 1929, and armament, like that of the F4B-1, was two 0.3-in (7,62-mm) guns. Structurally, the P-12 comprised fabric covered wooden wings and a square-section bolted aluminium-tube fuselage. The tenth P-12 embodied a number of modifications and, flown on 11 April 1929, received the designation XP-12A (Model 101). The XP-12A featured a 525 hp R-1340-9 engine enclosed by a long-

One of five civil Boeing Model 100s, N872H was restored in 1978 as a P-12 of the 95th Pursuit Sqn.

(Above) The third P-12 from a production batch of ten ordered for the USAAC in 1929.

chord NACA cowling, Frise-type balanced ailerons in place of the tapered ailerons of the P-12, a shorter undercarriage and a castoring tail skid. The XP-12A was lost in a mid-air collision after four hours' flying. *Max speed, 171 mph (275 km/h) at 5,000 ft (1 524 km), 158 mph (254 km/h) at sea level. Cruising speed, 135 mph (217 km/h). Initial climb, 2,080 ft/min (10,56 m/sec). Empty weight, 1,758 lb (797 kg). Loaded weight, 2,536 lb (1 150 kg). Span, 30 ft 0 in (9,14 m). Length, 20 ft 1 in (6,12 m). Height, 9 ft 7 in (2,92 m). Wing area, 227.5 sq ft (21,13 m²).*

BOEING P-12B   USA

The first of the P-12 series to be built in substantial numbers, the P-12B (Model 102B) embodied a number of refinements, including the Frise-type ailerons tested by the XP-12A. No fairings were fitted aft of the cylinders of the R-1340-7 engine and a ring cowling was introduced after the aircraft entered service. Structure and armament were similar to those of the P-12, and 90

(Above) This P-12B had an uncowled engine, as originally delivered. (Below) The original P-12B after its modification to XP-12G configuration.

BOEING P-12C & P-12D   USA

In June 1930, the USAAC placed an order for 131 examples of an improved version of the P-12B under the designation P-12C (Model 222), this having the R-1340-9 engine which had been flown in the XP-12A. The P-12C also featured a ring cowling and a spreader-bar undercarriage, and the first example was flown on 30 January 1931. The last 35 aircraft ordered as P-12Cs were delivered with the 525 hp R-1340-17 engine as

The P-12D (above) was externally indistinguishable from the P-12C, differing only in mark of engine.

P-12Ds (Model 227s), the first of these flying on 2 March 1931, and both P-12C and P-12D were later fitted with P-12E-type vertical tail surfaces. The 33rd example of the P-12D was delivered with a geared version of the Wasp engine (XGRS-1340-E) as the XP-12H, eventually being reconverted to P-12D standards. The data relate to the P-12D. *Max speed, 188 mph (302 km/h) at 7,000 ft (2 134 m). Cruising speed, 163 mph (262 km/h). Range, 475 mls (764 km). Empty weight, 1,956 lb (887 kg). Loaded weight, 2,648 lb (1 201 kg). Span, 30 ft 0 in (9,14 m). Length, 20 ft 3 in (6,17 m). Height, 8 ft 8 in (2,64 m). Wing area, 227.5 sq ft (21,13 m²).*

BOEING P-12E & P-12F   USA

On 29 September 1930, Boeing flew the private-venture Model 218 which was basically a P-12B with a semi-monocoque metal fuselage. Allocated the designation XP-925 during USAAC trials, the Model 218 was eventually sold to China, having served as a basis for the P-12E which employed a similar fuselage and tail

One of seven YP-12Ks in AAC service, the example below has a combination wheel-ski undercarriage.

The last example of the P-12F (above) was fitted experimentally with a sliding cockpit canopy.

surfaces. A contract for 135 P-12Es was placed on 3 March 1931, the first example flying on 15 October 1931, by which time it had been redesignated XP-12E. One P-12E was fitted with an SR-1340H engine rated at 575 hp at 2,500 ft (762 m) in place of the standard 525 hp R-1340-17, being redesignated P-12J. Together with the XP-12E and five standard P-12Es, this aeroplane eventually became a YP-12K as a result of the installation of the fuel-injection SR-1340E engine, all seven YP-12Ks subsequently reverting to P-12E standards. One YP-12K (ex-XP-12E) was fitted with an F-7 turbo-supercharger as the XP-12L. The last 25 aeroplanes on the original P-12E order were completed as P-12Fs (Model 234s) with R-1340-19 engines affording 600 hp for take-off and 500 hp at 11,000 ft (3 353 m). This resulted in a marginal enhancement of max speed (194 mph/312 km/h at 10,000 ft/3 048 m) and marked improvements in climb rate and service ceiling. Deliveries of P-12Fs to the USAAC began on 6 March 1932, the last example built having an experimental sliding cockpit canopy. The following data relate to the P-12E. *Max speed, 189 mph (304 km/h) at 7,000 ft (2 134 m). Cruising speed, 160 mph (257 km/h). Climb to 10,000 ft (3 050 m), 5.8 min. Empty weight, 1,999 lb (907 kg). Loaded weight, 2,690 lb (1 220 kg). Span, 30 ft 0 in (9,14 m). Length, 20 ft 3 in (6,17 m). Height, 9 ft 0 in (2,74 m). Wing area, 227.5 sq ft (21,13 m²).*

BOEING XP-15 (XF5B-1)   USA

During the course of 1929, work began as a private venture on two prototypes of a single-seat parasol fighter monoplane, one of these prototypes (Model 202) being intended for offer to the USAAC and the other (Model 205) having arrester gear for US Navy evaluation. The Models 202 and 205 featured a semi-monocoque metal fuselage and metal wings, with smooth, non-stressed metal skinning. Provision was made for the standard twin 0.3-in (7,62-mm) gun armament and the Model 205 could carry a single 500-lb (227-kg) bomb or five 30-lb

The XP-15 (above and below) was Boeing's first attempt to produce a monoplane fighter.

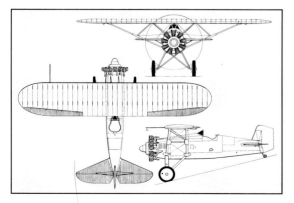

(13,6-kg) bombs. The Model 202 had a Pratt & Whitney SR-1340D Wasp rated at 450 hp at 8,000 ft (2 438 m) and the Model 205 had an SR-1340C rated at 480 hp at sea level. The Model 202 was flown in January 1930, and was unofficially assigned the designation XP-15 when evaluated by the USAAC. During evaluation it was fitted with a ring cowling and revised vertical tail surfaces, but was rejected by the USAAC and eventually crashed on 7 February 1931. The similar Model 205 was assigned the designation XF5B-1, and underwent modifications identical to those applied to the Model 202. Flown in February 1930, the XF5B-1 was used for experimental purposes for three years, no production being undertaken. The following data relate to the Model 202 (XP-15). *Max speed, 185 mph (298 km/h) at 8,000 ft (2 438 m), 163 mph (262 km/h) at sea level. Initial climb, 1,860 ft/min (9,44 m/sec). Empty weight, 2,052 lb (931 kg). Loaded weight, 2,746 lb (1 245 kg). Span, 30 ft 6 in (9,29 m). Length, 21 ft 0 in (6,40 m). Height, 9 ft 4 in (2,84 m). Wing area, 157.3 sq ft (14,61 m²).*

BOEING XP-9   USA

The XP-9 was originally flown with small vertical tail surfaces as seen above.

In May 1928, the USAAC issued a single-seat fighter specification to which Boeing responded with a shoulder-wing all-metal monoplane, the Model 96, which was assigned the official designation XP-9. Low development priority and production problems delayed the planned delivery date of the XP-9 from April 1929 until September 1930, the aircraft eventually flying for the first time on 18 November of that year. Powered by a Curtiss V-1570-15 liquid-cooled engine rated at 600 hp,

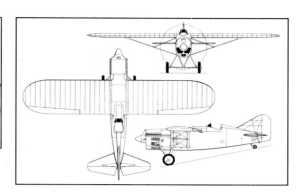

In its final form as seen here (above and below), the XP-9 had enlarged vertical tail surfaces.

but actually delivering 583 hp, the XP-9 featured a semi-monocoque fuselage of sheet Dural over metal formers. Performance proved disappointing, the poor vision from the rear-positioned cockpit and the unpleasant handling characteristics resulting in the test pilot referring to the XP-9 as "a menace". After initial tests, the original vertical tail surfaces were replaced by larger P-12 surfaces, but little improvement resulted and the USAAC did not exercise its option on five Y1P-9s. *Max speed, 213 mph (343 km/h) at 12,000 ft (3 658 m). Initial climb, 2,430 ft/min (12,34 m/sec). Empty weight, 2,669 lb (1 210 kg). Loaded weight, 3,623 lb (1 643 kg). Span, 36 ft 6 in (11,13 m). Length, 25 ft 1¾ in (7,66 m). Height, 7 ft 9 in (2,36 m). Wing area, 210 sq ft (19,51 m²).*

BOEING P-26   USA

Begun as a private venture in September 1931, the Model 248 single-seat fighter monoplane was of all-metal construction with a semi-monocoque fuselage and a two-spar wing with light alloy skinning. The first of three prototypes was flown on 20 March 1932 under the designation XP-936, being redesignated XP-26 when purchased by the USAAC and subsequently Y1P-26. A production contract was placed for an improved version, the Model 266 or P-26A. This contract called for 111 aircraft (later increased to 136), and the first P-26A was flown on 10 January 1934. The P-26A was powered by a 600 hp Pratt & Whitney R-1340-27 Wasp and carried two fuselage-mounted 0.3-in (7,62-mm) Browning M-2 machine guns. All 111 aircraft called for by the original contract were completed as P-26As,

(Below) This Boeing P-26A of the 19th Pursuit Sqn was photographed over Oahu, Hawaii, in March 1939.

Key to Boeing P-26A

1 Starter dog
2 Propeller hub sleeve
3 Sleeve attachment
4 Two-blade propeller
5 Engine face plate
6 Cooling inlets
7 Engine cowling ring
8 Pratt & Whitney Wasp engine
9 Cylinder heads
10 Gun barrel blast tube extension
11 Exhaust pipes
12 Engine bearer ring
13 Louvred exhaust stacks
14 Carburettor cold air intake
15 Engine bearer upper support struts
16 Starter primer access
17 Cowling panel fasteners
18 Hot air intake
19 Cockpit heater
20 Exhaust stub
21 Gun blast tube
22 Oil cooler
23 Lower panel access
24 Wingroot stub
25 Port gun barrel
26 Bulkhead, lower longeron attachment
27 Fuselage forward frame
28 Air intake/starter controls
29 Support strut attachment
30 Cooling louvres
31 Oil tank, capacity 8 US gal (30 l)

32 Upper louvres
33 Oil filler access
34 Gunsight tube supports
35 Tubular gunsight
36 Starboard wing fuel tank
37 Starboard landing wires support strut and brace
38 Fuel filler cap
39 Landing wires outboard attachment
40 Front spar
41 Pitot tube
42 Wing panelling
43 Aerial spring brace attachment
44 Starboard navigation lights (upper and lower surfaces)
45 Aerial lead-in
46 Electrical leads
47 Wing main rib stations
48 Starboard aileron
49 Aileron hinge points
50 Transmitter aerial mast
51 Aerials
52 Aileron tab
53 Aileron control linkage
54 Control rods
55 Rear landing wire
56 Windscreen panel
57 Main instrument panel
58 Landing wires/fuselage attachment points
59 Fuselage upper longeron
60 Lower instrument panel (fuel cocks and light switches)
61 Rudder pedal assembly

62 Ammunition loading access (magazines in cockpit floor)
63 Transmitter
64 Landing wires spacer
65 Ammunition feed
66 Port 0.3-in (7.62-mm) machine gun
67 Underseat control linkage
68 Seat support frame
69 Pilot's seat
70 Throttle quadrant
71 Maps and document holder
72 Hinged entry flap
73 Equipment pouch
74 Cockpit coaming
75 Pilot's headrest
76 Headrest fairing
77 Receiver aerial brace
78 Turnover structure
79 Wireless receiver
80 Bulkhead hatch (rear fuselage access)
81 Fuselage main frame
82 Access panel
83 Liquid oxygen vaporizer
84 Holding tray
85 Tail surface control cables
86 Receiver lead-in insulator
87 Abbreviated upper longeron
88 Fuselage frames
89 Rudder control cables
90 Elevator control cables
91 Elevator tab controls
92 Abbreviated lower longeron
93 Tailwheel control cables

94 Turnbuckles
95 Rear fuselage structure
96 Tailwheel control linkage
97 Elevator control runners
98 Fuselage aft main frame/tailplane support
99 Fin root fillet
100 Starboard elevator linkage
101 Starboard tailplane
102 Tailplane spar
103 Elevator outer hinge
104 Starboard elevator
105 Fin front spar
106 Tail identification light
107 Fin structure
108 Rudder upper hinge
109 Receiver aerial mast
110 Rudder inner frame
111 Rudder hinge
112 Elevator torque tube
113 Rudder post
114 Rudder control horns
115 Elevator tab
116 Port elevator
117 Elevator hinge
118 Tailplane structure
119 Elevator tab control linkage
120 Tailplane front spar/fuselage attachment
121 Tailwheel leg fairing
122 Tailwheel
123 Tailwheel leg
124 Tailwheel control runs
125 Fuselage skinning
126 Wingroot fillet

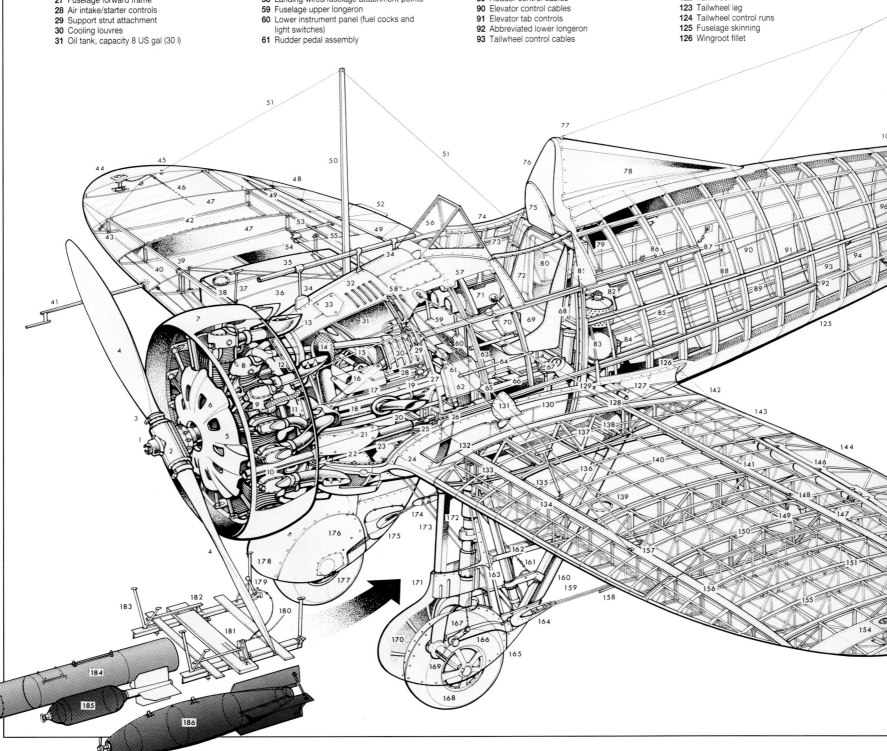

127 Aileron control rod assembly
128 Rear spar/stub wing attachment
129 Fuselage angled main frame attachment
130 Fuselage main fuel tank
131 Fuel filler access
132 Front spar/stub wing attachment
133 Mainwheel leg attachment
134 Front spar
135 Landing wires support strut and brace
136 Undercarriage "V"-strut rear member
137 Stub wing structure
138 "V"-strut/rear spar attachment
139 Fuel filler cap
140 Port wing fuel tank
141 Rear spar
142 Transmitter aerial
143 Trailing edge ribs
144 Port aileron
145 Aileron tab
146 Aileron hinges

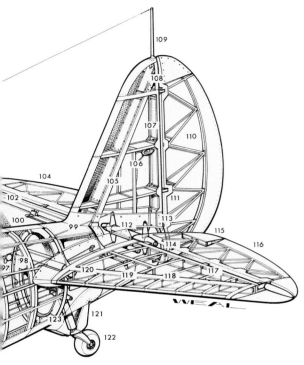

147 Aileron control linkage
148 Rear landing wire anchor point
149 Aileron control rods
150 Wing main rib stations
151 Outboard rib stations
152 Transmitter aerial lead-in
153 Port wingtip
154 Port navigation lights (upper and lower surfaces)
155 Wing structure
156 Front spar section
157 Landing wires anchor points
158 Flying wires brace
159 Outboard flying wires
160 Undercarriage trouser fairing
161 Brake cable assembly
162 Cross-brace member
163 "V"-strut front member
164 Flying wires attachment fairing
165 Wheel spat
166 Treadle
167 Brake arm
168 Port mainwheel
169 Axle
170 Spat inner frame
171 Spat/leg join
172 Mainwheel oleo leg
173 Inboard flying wires
174 Centre-line spacer
175 Starboard wheel fairing attachment
176 Spat panel
177 Starboard mainwheel
178 Under-fuselage bomb-rack installation, inc (items 179-183):
179 Arming handle
180 Bomb release wire (to cockpit)
181 Bomb-rack main member
182 Support frame
183 Forward sway braces
184 Possible loads inc (items 184-186): flare container:
185 30-lb (13.6-kg) practice bombs (five) or
186 100-lb (45-kg) bombs (two)

the last being delivered on 30 June 1934. The first two aircraft built against the supplementary order for 25 were completed as P-26Bs with fuel-injection SR-1340-33 engines and the remainder were delivered as P-26Cs, these being similarly-powered to the P-26A but having provision for one 0.5-in (12,7-mm) and one 0.3-in (7,62-min) gun. The P-26Cs were later fitted with fuel injection engines as P26Bs. Twelve examples of an export version, the Model 281, were built, 11 of these being purchased on behalf of China and one being sent to Spain for evaluation. The following data relate to the P-26A. *Max speed, 211 mph (339 km/h) at sea level, 234 mph (376 km/h) at 7,500 ft (2 286 m). Initial climb, 2,360 ft/min (11,99 m/sec). Range, 570 mls (917 km). Empty weight, 2,194 lb (995 kg). Loaded weight, 2,935 lb (1 331 kg). Span, 27 ft 11⁵/₈ in (8,52 m). Length, 23 ft 7¹/₄ in (7,19 m). Height, 10 ft 5 in (3,17 m). Wing area, 149.5 sq ft (13,89 m²).*

The P-26A (above and below) was the first monoplane fighter in service with the US Army Air Corps, the P-26B and P-26C being externally similar.

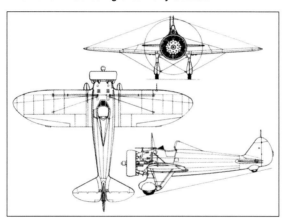

BOEING XF6B-1   USA

The last Boeing fighter of biplane configuration, the Model 236 single-seat shipboard fighter was designed around the 14-cylinder two-row Pratt & Whitney R-1535 Twin Wasp Junior engine rated at 625 hp at 5,500 ft (1 676 m). Of all-metal construction with fabric-covered wings, the Model 236 was assigned the designation XF6B-1 by the US Navy and flew on 1 February 1933. Armament comprised two 0.3-in (7,62-mm) guns and provision was made for a single 500-lb (227-kg) bomb or two 115-lb (52-kg) bombs, and on 21 March 1934, the prototype was assigned the new "bomber-fighter" designation of XBFB-1. The engine

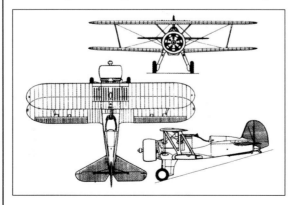

(Above) The Boeing XFB-1 (later the Xl3FB-1) with its later undercarriage leg fairings and (top right) with its original "open" leg struts.

installation and undercarriage were refined during the test and evaluation programme, but no production was undertaken. *Max speed, 200 mph (322 km/h) at 6,000 ft (1 830 m). Time to 5,000 ft (1 524 m), 4.2 min. Range, 525 mls (845 km). Empty weight, 2,288 lb (1 038 kg). Loaded weight, 3,704 lb (1 680 kg). Span, 28 ft 6 in (8,69 m). Length, 22 ft 1¹/₂ in (6,74m). Height, 10 ft 7 in (3,22m). Wing area, 252 sq ft (23,41 m²).*

BOEING XF7B-1   USA

Designed to meet the requirements of a US Navy specification issued on 6 December 1932, the XF7B-1 (Model 273) was the first all-metal cantilever low-wing monoplane single-seat fighter with a retractable undercarriage to be evaluated by that service. Powered by a Pratt & Whitney SR-1340-30 engine rated at 550 hp at 10,000 ft (3 050 m), the XF7B-1 featured a fully-enclosed cockpit and was flown for the first time on 14 September 1933. Armament comprised two 0.3-in (7,62-mm) machine guns. After initial evaluation, the XF7B-1 was returned to its manufacturer to have split flaps and a longer-chord engine cowling fitted. Subsequently the enclosed cockpit gave place to an open cockpit. The US Navy considered that the XF7B-1 offered inadequate view and too high a landing speed for shipboard operation, and the sole prototype was scrapped after, in March 1935, the fighter was inadvertently stressed to 12.1 g (although the designed load factor was only 9.0) when the pilot pulled out of a 415 mph (668 km/h) dive too abruptly following collapse of the windscreen. *Max speed, 233 mph (375 km/h) at 10,000 ft (3 050 m). Time to 5,000 ft (1 524 m), 3.4 min. Range, 750 mls (1 207 km). Empty weight, 2,782 lb (1 262 kg). Loaded weight, 3,651 lb (1 656 kg). Span, 31 ft 11 in (9,73 m). Length, 27 ft 7 in (8,41 m). Height, 7 ft 5 in (2,26 m). Wing area, 213 sq ft (19,79 m²).*

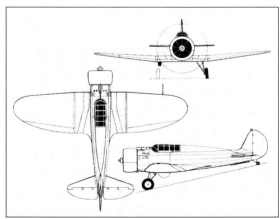

(Above) The XF713-1 with original short-chord cowling, and (below) with the longer-chord cowling as later fitted. The cockpit canopy was to be discarded.

BOEING YP-29 USA

A more advanced design than the Model 248 and preceding the Model 266 production derivative of that fighter, the Model 264 was an all-metal cantilever low-wing single-seat fighter monoplane with semi-retractable main undercarriage members and an aft-sliding cockpit canopy. Assigned the designation XP-940 by the USAAC, the first of three Model 264 prototypes to fly initiated its test programme on 20 January 1934, and was similar to, but smaller than, the XF7B-1 flown four months earlier. Powered by a Pratt & Whitney R-1340-35 Wasp rated at 570 hp at 7,500 ft (2 286 m) and carrying an armament of one 0.3-in (7,62-mm) and one 0.5-in (12,7-mm) gun, the XP-940 was returned to Boeing during March 1934 for conversion to open cockpit configuration as the YP-29A. The second Model 264 to fly was completed with a large "glasshouse" type cockpit canopy owing to USAAC dissatisfaction with the small sliding canopy initially fitted to the first prototype. With an R-1340-31 Wasp offering 550 hp at 10,000 ft (3 048 m) it was designated YP-29. The third prototype differed from the YP-29A in having one degree more wing dihedral and a one-piece centre-section trailing-edge flap, the latter also being fitted to the YP-29. The three YP-29s were extensively tested by the USAAC, but as the type was considered to offer an insufficient advance over the P-26A it was not ordered into production. The following data relate to the YP-29A. *Max speed, 242 mph (389 km/h) at 7,500 ft (2 286 m). Initial climb, 1,840 ft/min (9,34 m/sec). Empty weight, 2,502 lb (1 135 kg). Loaded weight, 3,270 lb (1 483 kg). Span, 29 ft 4¹/₂ in (8,95 m). Length, 24 ft 11³/₄ in (7,61 m). Height, 7ft 8 in (2,33 m). Wing area 176.6 sq ft (16,41 m²).*

A long "glasshouse" canopy distinguished the YP-29 (above and below) which was the second of a trio of Model 264 prototypes built by Boeing.

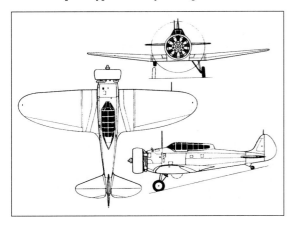

Third of the Model 264s, the YP-29B had an open cockpit and a one-piece centre-section flap.

BOEING XF8B-1 USA

A single-seat shipboard long-range interceptor and

Destined to be Boeing's last fighter the XF8B-1 (above and below) featured a contra-prop.

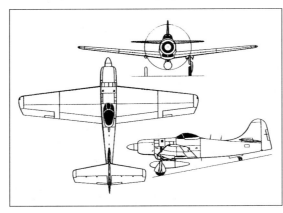

escort fighter, fighter-bomber and torpedo-fighter, the XF8B-1 (Model 400) was designed to meet the requirements of a 1943 US Navy specification, a contract for three prototypes being awarded on 4 May of that year. The first prototype was flown on 27 November 1944 with a 3,000 hp Pratt & Whitney XR-4360-10 28-cylinder four-row radial driving a six-bladed contra-rotating propeller. This had provision for a wing-mounted armament of six 0.5-in (12,7-mm) machine guns or six 20-mm cannon. The XF8B-1 was capable of carrying a 6,400-lb (2 903-kg) bomb load, including two 1,600-lb (726-kg) bombs internally, but was too late to receive a production contract, the second and third prototype flying after the end of World War II. *Max speed, 340 mph (547 km/h) at sea level, 432 mph (695 km/h) at 26,900 ft (8 200 m). Normal range, 1,305 mls (2 100 km). Initial climb, 3,660 ft/min (18,59 m/sec). Empty weight, 14,190 lb (6 436 kg). Normal loaded weight, 20,508 lb (9 302 kg). Span, 54 ft 0 in (16,46 m). Length, 43 ft 3 in (13, 18 m). Height, 16 ft 3 in (4,95 m). Wing area, 489 sq ft (45,43 m²).*

BOEING X-32 JSF USA

The Joint Strike Fighter competition, commenced in 1986, has become a medley of conflicting requirements. The USMC and RN wanted an affordable, stealthy, supersonic replacement for the Sea Harrier/AV-8B. Later, the USAF wanted replacements for the F-15E, F-16, F-111 and F-117, while the USN needed to replace the F-14 and F/A-18. Combining all these requirements gave a potentially huge production order, which went some way towards solving the affordability equation.

(Below) The first of three multi-rôle Boeing XF8B-1 fighters built to a 1943 specification.

The problem was then how to produce an all-singing, all-dancing aeroplane which could satisfy all four services. In November 1996, contracts were awarded to Boeing and Lockheed Martin to produce two concept demonstrators each, one CTOL, the other STOVL. The Boeing offerings were the CTOL X-32A and the STOVL X-32B. The X-32A first flew on 18 September 2000, piloted by Fred Knox of X-31 fame. While overall dimensions were similar to those of the Harrier, the appearance was very different. The fuselage was exceptionally deep, fronted by a massive chin inlet. A thick, shoulder-mounted delta wing with forward-swept trailing edges over most of the span, added to the impression of "huge". These were prompted by the needs of stealth, to house both weapons and 19,000 lb (8 618 kg) of fuel internally. Astern, it had steeply outward canted fins. Meanwhile, the goalposts had been moved. To meet the added requirements, the X-32 was redesigned with a more conventional swept wing and horizontal tails, but too late to feature on the X-32, which has to soldier on for the evaluation "as is". Meanwhile the X-32B has received its JSF119 engine, and was expected to fly in the late Spring of 2001. For lift-borne flight, the chin inlet hinges down to increase the mass flow to the engine. Rated at 40,000 lb (18 144 kgp) thrust, this has rotating nozzles for direct lift – two more or less under the centre of gravity, the other astern, which is also used for conventional flight. Like the Harrier, lateral control in lift-borne flight is supplied by two "puffers". It is expected that an internal gun, the 27-mm Mauser BK, will be fitted internally on CTOL models, while the STOVL variant may well have strap-on gun pods. Weapons would also include four internal AIM-120 Amraam. *Performance, not released but supersonic. Empty weight, A and B c22,000 lb (10 000 kg); C (carrier variant) c24,000 lb (10 900 kg). Span, B 30 ft (9,14 m), A and C 36 ft 1 in (11 m). Length, A and C 47 ft 3¹/₂ in (14,42 m), B 46 ft 3¹/₂ in (14,03 m). Height, A and B 13 ft 2¹/₂ in (4,02 m), C 13 ft 3¹/₂ in (4,05 m).*

Boeing artist's impression of X-32 JSF.

BOREL-BOCCACCIO
TYPE 3000 France

Designed by Paul Boccacio for the Gabriel Borel concern, the Type 3000 two-seat fighter was tested in 1919 under the official designation Borel C2. Although trials at Villacoublay revealed a good performance, the aircraft had appeared too late to warrant further development under post-World War I circumstances. A two-bay biplane powered by a 300 hp Hispano-Suiza 8Fb eight-cylinder water-cooled engine, the Type 3000 carried an armament of one fixed and synchronised 0.303-in (7,7-mm) Vickers machine gun and two 0.303-in (7,7-mm) Lewis guns on a Scarff-type mounting in the rear cockpit. Provision was made for a third Lewis gun which, fitted in the fuselage floor, was intended to fire aft and downward. Various modifications were made to the undercarriage, the tailplane bracing, the radiators and the exhaust manifolds during the course of trials, but only the one prototype was completed. *Max speed, 161 mph (260 km/h) at 3,280 ft (1 000 m). Time to 6,560 ft (2 000 m), 5.65 min. Endurance, 3 hrs. Empty weight, 1,779 lb (807 kg). Loaded weight, 2,954 lb (1 340 kg). Span, 37 ft 4¾ in (11,40 m). Length, 23 ft 5½ in (7,15 m). Wing area, 349.84 sq ft (32,5 m²).*

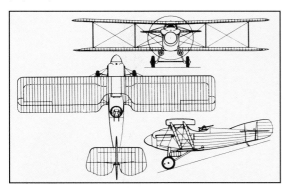

In its definitive form (above and below), the Boccaccio-designed Borel-built Type 3000 fighter underwent various modifications during 1919 trials.

BOROVKOV-FLOROV I-207 USSR

In 1937, Aleksei A Borovkov and Ilya F Florov established an experimental design bureau as OKB-7 with the object of creating the smallest possible practical single-seat fighter. The first prototype was completed before the end of 1937, and was of heavily-staggered cantilever biplane configuration with duralumin-skinned light alloy wings, a fuselage of mixed construction (the forward portion being a duralumin-skinned welded steel-tube structure and the aft portion, which included the cockpit, being a wooden monocoque with plywood skinning) and wooden tail surfaces. Power was provided by an 850 hp Mikulin M-85 14-cylinder radial. Favourable test results led to two further refined prototypes being built as I-207s,

The first prototype of the Borovkov-Florov I-207, showing the fluted cowl for its M-85 engine.

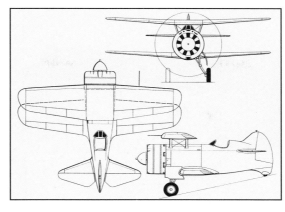

(Above) The pre-series I-207 had a retractable undercarriage, but was in most respects similar to the second prototype (below) with shuttered cowling.

these having Shvetsov M-62 and M-63 engines respectively and each carrying an armament of four 7,62-mm ShKAS machine guns. A pre-production series of four I-207s was ordered in 1938, one being powered by the 1,100 hp M-63 nine-cylinder radial, two having the 1,000 hp M-62 nine-cylinder radial and the fourth having a geared M-63R engine and a side-hingeing cockpit canopy, all having retractable main undercarriages. The I-207/M-63 attained a speed of 298 mph (480 km/h) at 14,765 ft (4 500 m) during State Trials in the summer of 1939, but the appearance of more advanced fighters resulted in the I-207 being discarded, although both I-207/M62s were allegedly employed operationally against the Finns during 1939-40. The following data relate to the I-207/M-62. *Max speed, 235 mph (378 km/h) at sea level, 290 mph (467 km/h) at 15,000 ft (4 600 m). Time to 16,405 ft (5 000 m), 4.1 min. Loaded weight, 4,387 lb (1 990 kg). Span, 22 ft 10¾ in (6,98 m). Length, 19 ft 3½ in (5,88 m). Wing area, 193.75 sq ft (18,00 m²).*

BOULTON & PAUL P.3
BOBOLINK UK

Designed by J D North, the P.3 Bobolink single-seat fighter was the first original aircraft to bear the Boulton & Paul appellation. Intended as a successor for the Sopwith Camel, the Bobolink was a two-bay biplane of wooden construction powered by a 230 hp Bentley B.R.2 nine-cylinder rotary engine and carrying an armament of two synchronised 0.303-in (7,7-mm) Vickers machine guns. The sole example of the Bobolink completed was flown for the first time in January 1918, initially with ailerons on the upper wing only, ailerons being added to the lower wing by the time official trials began at Martlesham Heath in February. Official evaluation pronounced the Bobolink as having insufficient manoeuvrability, and although tests were continued

Boulton & Paul's first fighter, the Bobolink, in its final form with a horn-balanced rudder.

by the manufacturer no further development was undertaken. *Max speed, 125 mph (201 km/h) at 10,000 ft (3 050 m). Time to 10,000 ft (3 050 m), 9.33 min. Endurance, 3.25 hrs. Empty weight, 1,226 lb (556 kg). Loaded weight, 1,992 lb (904 kg). Span, 29 ft 0 in (8,84 m). Length, 20 ft 0 in (6,10 m). Height, 8 ft 4 in (2,54 m). Wing area, 266 sq ft (24,71 m²).*

BOULTON & PAUL P.31
BITTERN UK

The second prototype of the B & P Bittern (above and below) featured a longer-span wing than the first, and underhung engines with Townend cowling rings.

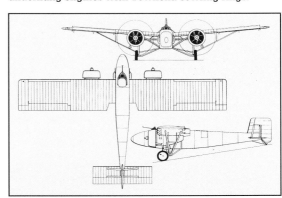

A remarkable and radical aeroplane in its day, the Bittern, designed to meet the requirements of Specification 27/24 for a night fighter, was one of the earliest single-seat twin-engined fighter monoplanes and was intended as a bomber formation interceptor. Powered by two 230 hp Armstrong Siddeley Lynx seven-cylinder radials, the first of two Bittern prototypes was flown in 1927, this having shoulder-mounted wings carrying mid-set uncowled engines. Armament comprised two fixed forward-firing 0.303-in (7,7-mm) Vickers guns in the sides of the forward fuselage. The second prototype differed in having a redesigned wing of constant chord and thickness, overall span being increased by approximately 5 ft (1,52 m) and the leading edge carrying Handley Page slots. Six pairs of V-type struts braced

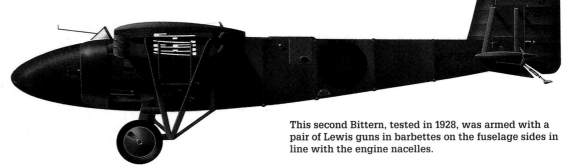

This second Bittern, tested in 1928, was armed with a pair of Lewis guns in barbettes on the fuselage sides in line with the engine nacelles.

The first prototype Bittern, with fixed Vickers guns and uncowled, centrally-mounted engines.

the outer wings to the engine nacelles and fuselage. Townend cowling rings were fitted to the engines which were lowered on the wings. In place of the fixed Vickers, two Lewis guns of similar calibre were mounted in barbettes on the fuselage sides forward and below the wing leading edge. These enabled the weapons to be elevated between 0 deg and 45 deg. Interconnected with a ring sight attached to an elevating hoop pivoted at the cockpit sides, the guns had no traverse, but their arrangement enabled bombers to be attacked from below. Although advanced in concept, the Bittern was seriously underpowered, with inadequate performance and its development was abandoned. The following details relate to the first prototype. *Max speed, 145 mph (233 km/h). Loaded weight, 4,500 lb (2 041 kg). Span, 41 ft 0 in (12,50 m). Length (approx), 32 ft 0 in (9,75 m).*

BOULTON & PAUL P.33 PARTRIDGE UK

Evolved to meet the requirements of Specification F.9/26, eventually satisfied by the Bristol Bulldog, the Partridge, designed by J D North, was of all-metal construction and its structure, surprisingly, was made up in part of components already standardised for the P.29 Sidestrand bomber. Flown for the first time in 1928 with a 440 hp Bristol Jupiter VII nine-cylinder radial (which it was intended to replace with the Mercury II in the unrealised Partridge III), it carried the standard armament of two 0.303-in (7,7-mm) Vickers machine guns in lateral fuselage bulges. The Partridge was initially flown with ailerons on the top wing only, but similar control surfaces were later introduced on the lower wing also. Only one prototype was built. *Max speed, 167 mph (269 km/h) at 10,000 ft (3 050 m). Time to 10,000 ft (3 050 m), 6.5 min. Empty weight, 2,021 lb (917 kg). Loaded weight, 3,097 lb (1 405 kg). Span, 35 ft 0 in (10,67 m). Length, 23 ft 1 in (7,03 m). Wing area, 311 sq ft (28,89 m²).*

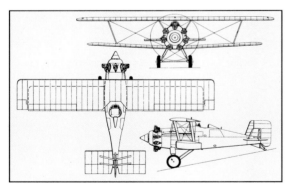

First flown in 1928, the Partridge (above and below) used components of the Sidestrand bomber.

BOULTON PAUL P.82 DEFIANT UK

Boulton Paul Aircraft (which had been formed to take over the aviation interests of Boulton & Paul on 30 June 1934) produced the P.82 Defiant to meet Specification F.9/35, which called for a two-seat turret-equipped fighter. The first prototype was flown (without turret) on 11 August 1937, a second prototype following on 18 May 1939. The production model, the Defiant I, was powered by a Rolls-Royce Merlin III rated at 1,030 hp at 16,250 ft (4 953 m) and carried four 0.303-in (7,7-mm) Brownings in a Boulton Paul A Mk IID hydraulically-operated dorsal turret, the first example flying on 30 July 1939. Progressive contracts brought total orders to 930 machines, some being delivered from the autumn of 1941 with AI Mk IV radar as Defiant IAs. The final contract for Mk Is was amended to call for 210 Defiant IIs with Merlin XX engines rated at 1,280 hp for take-off and 1,260 hp at 12,250 ft (3 734 m). The philosophy of the single-engined fighter with all armament concentrated in a power-operated turret was proven tactically incorrect on operations, and all Defiants had been withdrawn from operational rôles by the end of 1942. The following data relate to the Defiant I. *Max speed,*

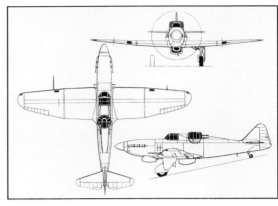

(Above) The turret-equipped Boulton Paul Defiant I.

250 mph (402 km/h) at sea level, 304 mph (489 km/h) at 17,000 ft (5 182 m). Initial climb, 1,900 ft/min (9,65 m/sec). Range, 465 mls (748 km). Empty weight, 6,078 lb (2 757 kg). Loaded weight, 8,318 lb (3 773 kg). Span, 39 ft 4 in (11,99 m). Length, 35 ft 4 in (10,77 m). Height, 11 ft 4 in (3,45 m). Wing area, 250 sq ft (23,22 m²).

BRANDENBURG KF Germany

The first fighter to be designed by Ernst Heinkel as chief designer for the Hansa- und Brandenburgische Flugzeug-Werke, the KF two-seater appeared early in 1916, and was a two-bay, twin-boom biplane powered by a 150 hp Benz Bz III six-cylinder water-cooled engine installed as a pusher and driving a two-bladed pro-

(Above top) This Defiant I was flown by Sqn Ldr P A Hunter of No 264 Sqn, mid-1940. (Immediately above) Defiant II used by No 151 Sqn as a night fighter.

Although unsuccessful as a turret-equipped day fighter, the Defiant went on to give useful service as a radar-equipped night fighter, as seen below.

The two-seat Brandenburg KF (above) was intended to fulfil both fighting and reconnaissance rôles.

peller between the tailbooms. The KF was of wooden construction with plywood-covered fuselage nacelle and tailbooms and armament was intended to consist of a single 7,92-mm Parabellum machine gun on a flexible mounting in the forward cockpit. Work on the KF was discontinued as it offered no advance in performance over the similarly-configured Ago C I which served in the reconnaissance rôle. *Max speed, 87 mph (140 km/h) at 3,280 ft (1 000 m). Empty weight, 1,675 lb (760 kg). Loaded weight, 2,844 lb (1 290 kg). Span, 38 ft 0⅔ in (11,60 m). Length, 27 ft 7¾ in (8,48 m). Wing area, 414.50 sq ft (38,6 m²).*

BRANDENBURG KD (D I)   Germany

Designed by Ernst Heinkel specifically for the Austro-Hungarian *K.u.k. Luftfahrttruppen* in 1916, the KD (*Kampf Doppeldecker*) single-seat fighter featured a novel system of wing interplane bracing in the form of four Vee struts joined in the centre of the wing bay by their apices to result in a "star" arrangement, which led to the KD being dubbed a "star strutter". Flown as a prototype with the 160 hp Mercedes D III six-cylinder water-cooled engine, the KD was manufactured in series as the D I with the 150 hp and 160 hp Austro-Daimler engines by the Hansa- und Brandenburgische Flugzeug-Werke, and with the 185 hp Austro-Daimler by the Phönix Flugzeugwerke of Vienna. Of wooden construction with fabric wing skinning, plywood fuse-

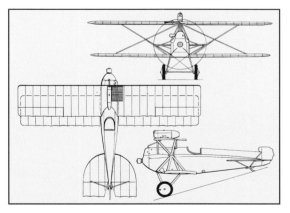

The KD "star strutter" in its 160 hp Austro-Daimler-engined D I production form (above), and (below) without the overwing gun fairing.

lage skinning and having steel-tube interplane strutting, the D I was armed with a single unsynchronised 8-mm Schwarzlose machine gun which was enclosed by a fairing on top of the cabane and fired over the propeller. The D I was reputedly difficult to fly, suffered inadequate directional stability owing to the rudder being blanketed by the deep fuselage, and had poor spin recovery characteristics. A number of Phönix-built Brandenburg D Is survived World War I to serve briefly with the *Deutschösterreichische Fliegertruppe. Max speed, 116 mph (187 km/h) at sea level. Time to 3,280 ft (1 000 m), 3.0 min. Empty weight, 1,481 lb (672 kg). Loaded weight, 2,028 lb (920 kg). Span, 27 ft 10⅔ in (8,50 m). Length, 20 ft 10 in (6,35 m). Wing area, 257.80 sq ft (23,95 m²).*

BRANDENBURG KDW   Germany

The KDW (above and below) was essentially a float-equipped conversion of the KD "star strutter".

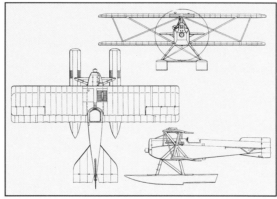

The KDW twin-float single-seat fighter seaplane was essentially a conversion of the land-based KD (D I) to provide an interim aircraft for floatplane station defence. The only major change introduced on the prototype apart from provision of a twin-float chassis was some slight extension of the wings, but the fin area was later increased to compensate for the increased keel area resulting from the addition of the floats. The prototypes were fitted with the 150 hp Benz Bz III six-cylinder water-cooled engine, but apart from a pre-production batch of 10 similarly-powered aircraft, all subsequent examples of the KDW had the 160 hp Maybach Mb III six-cylinder water-cooled engine. The first

production series was armed with a single synchronised 7,92-mm LMG 08/15 machine gun mounted on the starboard side of the nose, but the final batch of 20 delivered between October 1917 and February 1918 had a gun mounted on each side of the cockpit and additional Vee-type interplane bracing struts. A total of 58 KDW float fighters was delivered. *Max speed, 106 mph (170 km/h). Time to 3,280 ft (1 000 m), 5.9 min, to 6,560 ft (2 000 m), 14 min. Range, 310 mls (500 km). Empty weight, 1,673 lb (759 kg). Loaded weight, 2,290 lb (1 039 kg). Span, 30 ft 6⅛ in (9,30 m). Length, 25 ft 9½ in (7,86 m). Height, 10 ft 11⅞ in (3,35 m). Wing area, 313.77 sq ft (29,15 m²).*

BRANDENBURG CC   Germany

Intended primarily for use by the Austro-Hungarian Navy, the CC single-seat fighter flying boat (the de-

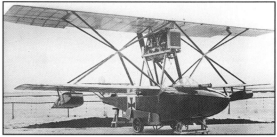

(Above) A Brandenburg CC fighter flying-boat in initial service form with plain "star" strutting.

signation was derived from the initials of Camillo Castiglioni, the financier of the Hansa- und Brandenburgische Flugzeug-Werke) was a single-bay biplane of wooden construction which appeared in prototype form in mid-1916. Retaining the "star" interplane bracing strut arrangement introduced by the KD (D I), the CC was supplied to the Austro-Hungarian Navy with both the 160 hp Austro-Daimler and 180 hp Hiero six-cylinder water-cooled engines, armament consisting of a single 8-mm Schwarzlose machine gun projecting through the windscreen. A total of 37 fighter flying boats of this type was delivered to the service. The CC was also adopted by the German Navy, which received a total of 36, with deliveries commencing in February 1917. These were powered by the 150 hp Benz Bz III, the engines of some examples being semi-cowled. The CC initially carried an armament of one 7,92-mm LMG 08/15 machine gun, but late production examples had two such weapons fixed to fire forward in the upper decking of the hull nose, and the hull was lengthened to

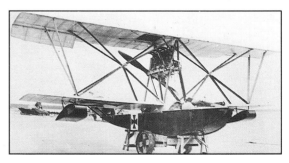

The CC (above) displays post-July 1917 additional interplane struts, and (below) as originally built.

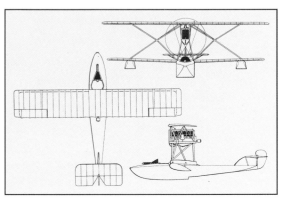

improve flying characteristics. In July 1917, the German Navy grounded the CC until all aircraft were provided with extra (Vee-type) interplane bracing struts to dampen severe wing vibration. The CC was employed extensively and with considerable success over the Adriatic by the Austro-Hungarian Navy. One example was completed experimentally as a triplane, the extra wing being placed at the intersection of the "star-struts". It was delivered to the Austro-Hungarian Navy for evaluation on 11 May 1917, but was written-off in a landing accident on the following 19 September. One CC was modified and tested in the summer of 1918 as the W 22, with broad sponsons replacing the outrigger stabilising floats. This experimental model, which crashed during testing, was intended solely to evaluate the sponson concept as part of the Staaken Rs IV development programme. *Max speed, 109 mph (175 km/h). Time to 3,280 ft (1 000 m), 4.8 min. Range, 310 mls (500 km). Empty weight, 1,764 lb (800 kg). Loaded weight, 2,381 lb (1 080 kg). Span, 30 ft 6⅛ in (9,30 m). Length, 25 ft 2¾ in (7,69 m). Height, 11 ft 8½ in (3,57 m). Wing area, 285.46 sq ft (26,52 m².)*

One CC airframe was completed in triplane configuration (below) with extra, short-span wing.

BRANDENBURG W 11   Germany

A heavier and more powerful derivative of the KDW, the W 11 single-seat twin-float fighter biplane was powered by a 220 hp Benz Bz IVa water-cooled engine and retained the "star" interplane bracing arrangement of its predecessor. Armament consisted of two synchronised LMG 08/15 machine guns, and two prototypes were completed during February-March 1917. No series production was undertaken. *Max speed, 109 mph (176 km/h). Time to 3,280 ft (1 000 m), 4.0 min. Range, 217 mls (350 km). Empty weight, 2,061 lb (935 kg). Loaded weight, 2,718 lb (1 233 kg). Span, 33 ft 1⅔ in (10,10 m). Length, 26 ft 6⅞ in (8,10 m). Height, 10 ft 10¾ in (3,32 m). Wing area, 338.2 sq ft (31,42 m²).*

BRANDENBURG W 12   Germany

A single-bay twin-float two-seat fighter biplane, the W 12 was flown for the first time in January 1917 with a 160 hp Mercedes D III six-cylinder water-cooled engine. Of wooden construction with plywood fuselage skinning, the W 12 was produced for the German Navy with both the 160 hp Mercedes D IIIa engine and the 150 hp Benz Bz III, and proved outstandingly manoeuvrable. Its first operations were conducted from the seaplane station at Zeebrugge, from where it quickly distinguished itself in service. Standard armament comprised one forward-firing synchronised 7,92-mm LMG 08/15 machine gun and a Parabellum of similar calibre

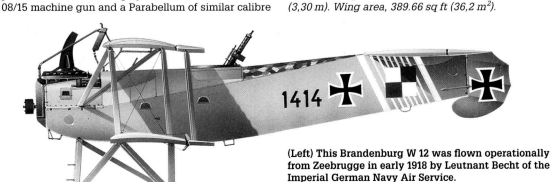

(Left) This Brandenburg W 12 was flown operationally from Zeebrugge in early 1918 by Leutnant Becht of the Imperial German Navy Air Service.

(Right) Evaluated by the Austro-Hungarian air arm in 1917, the L 16 triplane lacked promise.

The W 11 derivative of the KDW (above) was tested in 1917, but only prototypes were completed.

(Above and below) Designed by Ernst Heinkel, the W 12 float fighter proved exceptionally successful.

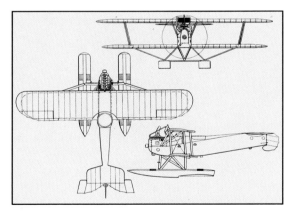

on a flexible mount in the rear cockpit, but of the 146 W 12s that had been built when production terminated in June 1918, one batch of 30 Benz-engined fighters had been delivered with a forward-firing armament of two LMGs. *Max speed, 99 mph (160 km/h). Time to 3,280 ft (1 000 m), 7.0 min, to 6,560 ft (2 000 m), 18.9 min. Endurance, 3.5 hrs. Empty weight, 2,198 lb (997 kg). Loaded weight, 3,205 lb (1 454 kg). Span, 36 ft 8⅞ in (11,2 m). Length, 31 ft 6 in (9,60 m). Height, 10 ft 10 in (3,30 m). Wing area, 389.66 sq ft (36,2 m²).*

BRANDENBURG L 14   Germany

A derivative of the KD (D I) with larger overall dimensions, simplified interplane bracing and a 200 hp Hiero six-cylinder water-cooled engine, the L 14 single-seat fighter was evaluated by the Austro-Hungarian air arm in 1917, but was not accepted for series production. Two prototypes were built and flown, these differing primarily in the arrangement of the interplane bracing struts employed, and intended armament was twin 8-mm Schwarzlose synchronised machine guns. *Max speed, 112 mph (180 km/h). Time to 3,280 ft (1 000 m), 4.0 min. Empty weight, 1,631 lb (740 kg). Loaded weight, 2,072 lb (940 kg). Span, 33 ft 5½ in (10,20 m). Length, 23 ft 1½ in (7,05 m). Wing area, 272.12 sq ft (25,28 m²).*

Tested in 1917, the L 14 (below) was a derivative of the KD (D I), only two prototypes being built.

BRANDENBURG L 16   Germany

A single-seat equi-span fighter triplane, developed for the Austro-Hungarian *K.u.k. Luftfahrttruppen*, with aerofoil-section I-type interplane bracing struts, the L 16 was powered by a 185 hp Austro-Daimler six-cylinder water-cooled engine and was intended to carry an armament of two synchronised machine guns. Various coolant radiator arrangements were evaluated on the single prototype built, but the fighter offered insufficient promise to warrant series production and development was abandoned. *Max speed, 118 mph (190 km/h). Empty weight, 1,631 lb (740 kg). Loaded weight, 2,061 lb (935 kg). Span, 29 ft 6⅓ in (9,00 m). Length, 23 ft 7⅞ in (7,21 m). Height, 12 ft 1⅔ in (3,70 m). Wing area, 360.59 sq ft (33,5 m²).*

The W 16 (above) was designed by Heinkel to succeed the KDW, but only three prototypes were built.

BRANDENBURG W 16   Germany

Intended primarily as a successor to the KDW in the station defence fighter rôle, but also to investigate the potentialities of the application of rotary engines to seaplanes, the W 16 was designed by Ernst Heinkel in 1916, and was a conventional twin-float single-seat fighter floatplane of wood and fabric construction with ply-skinned fuselage and floats. Like Heinkel's earlier "star strutter" fighters, the W 16 lacked bracing wires, these being rendered unnecessary by single struts extending from the base of the inclined Vee-type interplane struts to the top of the forward fuselage mainframe. Power was provided by a 160 hp Oberursel U III rotary engine and armament comprised two synchronised LMG 08/15 machine guns. Three prototypes were ordered, the first of these being tested in February 1917, and the third example was sent to Adlershof for static tests. No further development was undertaken as the German Navy had lost interest in single-seat fighter floatplanes. *Max speed, 106 mph (170 km/h). Time to 3,280 ft (1 000 m), 5.0 min, to 9,840 ft (3 000 m), 27 min. Approx endurance, 2.0 hrs. Empty weight, 1,402 lb (636 kg). Loaded weight, 1,975 lb (896 kg). Span, 30 ft 4⅛ in (9,25 m). Length, 24 ft 1⅓ in (7,35 m). Height, 9 ft 7 in (2,92 m). Wing area, 229.81 sq ft (21,35 m².)*

BRANDENBURG W 17 (A 49)   Germany

A single-seat fighter flying boat developed for the Austro-Hungarian Navy, the prototype of the W 17 (also designated A 49/I) was a biplane with a cantilever lower wing and was tested at Pola in July 1917. *K.u.k. Linienschiffsleutnant* Gottfried Banfield, responsible for the evaluation of the W 17, felt that the cantilever lower wing was unsuited for marine use and that the flying boat possessed inadequate manoeuvrability. Armament of the W 17 comprised two 8-mm Schwarzlose machine guns and the initial aircraft was allegedly lost when the upper wing broke away in flight. A

Few details have survived of the Brandenburg W 17, the first (biplane) prototype being illustrated.

second aircraft (the A 49/II) was completed as an equi-span triplane with interplane bracing struts. This is believed to have been submitted to the Austro-Hungarian Navy for evaluation in July 1917, but no details of these tests, or aircraft data, appear to have survived.

BRANDENBURG W 18   Germany

The W 18 single-seat fighter flying boat was, like the CC that it supplanted, intended primarily for the Austro-Hungarian Navy. The prototype was flown early in 1917 with a 150 hp Benz Bz III six-cylinder water-cooled engine, and production with a 200 hp Hiero engine was undertaken on behalf of the Austro-Hungarian Navy, a

Produced in quantity for the Austro-Hungarian Navy, the Brandenburg W 18 followed the CC into service.

total of 47 being delivered between September 1917 and May 1918. Armament normally comprised two fixed forward-firing 8-mm Schwarzlose machine guns, and the W 18 was employed for both station defence and fighter patrol tasks. One Benz-engined example was delivered to the German Navy in December 1917. *Max speed, 106 mph (170 km/h). Time to 3,280 ft (1 000 m), 5.0 min, to 9,840 ft (3 000 m), 23.0 min. Empty weight, 1,929 lb (875 kg). Loaded weight, 2,524 lb (1 145 kg). Span, 35 ft 1¼ in (10,70 m). Length, 26 ft 8⅞ in (8,15 m). Height, 11 ft 3⅞ in (3,45 m). Wing area, 370.07 sq ft (34,38 m²).*

The W 18 in production form with Hiero engine.

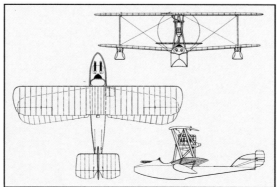

BRANDENBURG W 19   Germany

An enlarged W 12 developed to meet a demand for a two-seat fighter seaplane with greater endurance, the W 19 was first committed to operations in January 1918. Appreciably larger than the W 12, the W 19 was of similar construction with fabric-covered wings and plywood-covered fuselage and floats, and was powered by a 260 hp Maybach Mb IVa six-cylinder water-cooled engine. The substantial increase in span necessitated the adoption of a two-bay arrangement, and, apart from the three prototypes, all W 19s carried an armament of two 7,92-mm LMG 08/15 synchronised machine guns and a single Parabellum of similar calibre on a flexible mount in the rear cockpit. One W 19 was experimentally fitted with a 20-mm Becker cannon for trials. A total of 53 production W 19s was completed (one being retained for static tests). *Max speed, 93 mph (150 km/h). Time to 3,280 ft (1 000 m), 6.4 min, to 6,560 ft (2 000 m), 18.9 min. Empty weight, 3,164 lb (1 435 kg). Loaded weight, 4,420 lb (2 005 kg). Span, 45 ft 3⅓ in (13,80 m). Length, 34 ft 11¼ in (10,65 m). Height, 13 ft 5⅜ in (4,10 m). Wing area, 622.17 sq ft (57,8 m²).*

The W 19 (above and below) was a scaled-up W 12, and joined operations early in 1918.

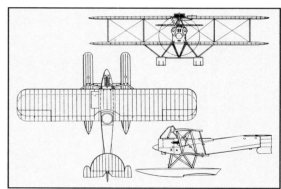

BRANDENBURG W 23   Germany

Employing single-bay biplane wings similar to those of the W 18 coupled with a lengthened, aero- and hydro-dynamically refined hull, the W 23 single-seat fighter flying boat was designed to mount a single fixed forward-firing 20-mm Becker cannon. This was mounted in the starboard side of the upper decking of the hull nose with a 7,92-mm LMG 08/15 machine gun mounted to port. Power was provided by a 160 hp Mercedes six-cylinder water-cooled engine driving a two-bladed pusher propeller. The structure was wooden with fabric and plywood skinning. Three prototypes were ordered in June 1917, these being delivered for eval-

The single prototype of the Brandenburg W 23.

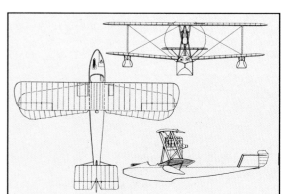

uation in January 1918. The W 23 proved to possess such poor flight characteristics that no further development was undertaken. *Max speed, 102 mph (165 km/h). Empty weight, 2,024 lb (918 kg). Loaded weight, 2,780 lb (1 261 kg). Span, 35 ft 1¼ in (10,70 m). Length, 29 ft 11⅞ in (9,14 m). Height, 10 ft 11⅞ in (3,35 m). Wing area, 373.52 sq ft (34,7 m²).*

BRANDENBURG W 25   Germany

The last of the Heinkel-designed single-seat fighter float seaplanes built by the Hansa- und Brandenburgische Flugzeug-Werke, the W 25, produced as a single prototype late in 1917, was the final development of the KDW. Reverting to the 150 hp Benz Bz III engine used

Conventional strut bracing was used for the W 25 in place of the previously-favoured "star" strutting.

by the prototype and pre-production KDWs, the W 25 possessed an essentially similar fuselage, but discarded the "star" interplane strut arrangement in favour of normal strut bracing. Initially the prototype flew with ailerons on the upper wing only, but these were subsequently added to the lower wing, each pair being joined at the wingtip by link struts. Armament comprised two synchronised 7,92-mm LMG 08/15 machine guns. Having by this time lost interest in single-seat fighter floatplanes, the German Navy did not foster further development of the W 25. *Max speed, 99 mph (160 km/h). Time to 3,280 ft (1 000 m), 6.5 min. Empty weight, 2,024 lb (918 kg). Loaded weight, 2,606 lb (1 182 kg). Span, 34 ft 1½ in (10,40 m). Length, 28 ft 10½ in (8,80 m). Height, 11 ft 3⅞ in (3,45 m). Wing area, 393.22 sq ft (36,53 m²).*

BRANDENBURG W 27 & W 32   Germany

Early in 1918, it was suggested to Ernst Heinkel that a successor to the W 12 two-seat fighter would soon be required if the German Navy was to maintain its superiority over Allied types being encountered over the North Sea. To conserve valuable time, Heinkel installed the new 195 hp Benz Bz IIIbo eight-cylinder Vee engine in a modified W 12 airframe and a 160 hp Mercedes D IIIa in a second W 12. Wing span and gap were reduced,

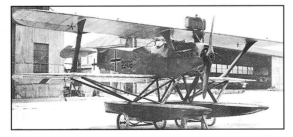

(Above) The W 27 and (below) W 32 were both derived from the W 12, with new Benz and Mercedes engine installations respectively.

stagger was increased to improve visibility, and aerofoil-section I-type interplane struts were adopted. Armament comprised two synchronised 7,92-mm LMG 08/15 machine guns and one 7,92-mm Parabellum on a flexible mount in the rear cockpit. The Benz-engined prototype received the designation W 27 while that powered by the Mercedes engine became the W 32, but both were found inferior to the W 29 monoplane and no further development was undertaken. The following data relate to the W 27. *Max speed, 106 mph (170 km/h). Empty weight, 2,445 lb (1 109 kg). Loaded weight, 3,569 lb (1 619 kg). Span, 36 ft 8⅞ in (11,20 m). Length, 30 ft 3⅓ in (9,23 m). Height, 10 ft 0½ in (3,06 m). Wing area, 388.16 sq ft (36,06 m²).*

BRANDENBURG W 29   Germany

Essentially a monoplane derivative of the W 12 biplane, the W 29 (above and below) was produced in time to serve with the German Navy from 1918.

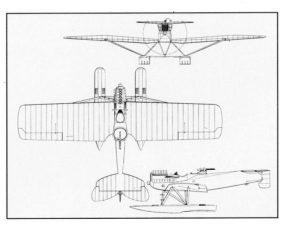

Evolved from the W 12 two-seat patrol fighter biplane in parallel with the W 27, the W 29 was essentially a monoplane derivative of the former powered, in prototype form, by the 195 hp Benz Bz IIIbo eight-cylinder Vee engine. The span and chord of the monoplane wing approximated in area to the biplane wings of the W 12, and the wing itself was a two-spar wooden structure with fabric skinning. The 150 hp Benz Bz III six-cylinder inline water-cooled engine was standardised for the production model of the W 29, which began operations with the German Navy in April 1918. Over 150 W 29s are known to have been delivered to that service in two basic versions, one equipped with radio and fitted with a single synchronised 7,92-mm LMG 08/15 machine gun plus a Parabellum on a flexible mount in the rear cockpit, and the other having two forward-firing LMGs and lacking radio equipment. The W 29, operating from Zeebrugge, Borkum and Norderney, achieved considerable operational success during the closing stages of World War I. In 1921, licence production of the W 29 was initiated by the Danish naval dockyard, 15 being built and these continuing in Danish Navy service until

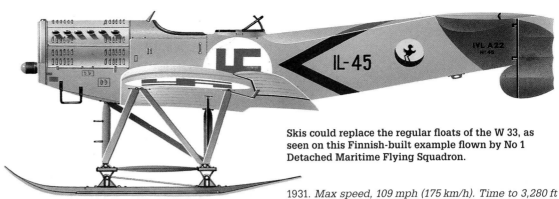

Skis could replace the regular floats of the W 33, as seen on this Finnish-built example flown by No 1 Detached Maritime Flying Squadron.

1931. *Max speed, 109 mph (175 km/h). Time to 3,280 ft (1 000 m), 6.0 min, to 6,560 ft (2 000 m), 13.0 min. Endurance, 4 hrs. Empty weight, 2,205 lb (1 000 kg). Loaded weight, 3,294 lb (1 494 kg). Span, 44 ft 3½ in (13,50 m). Length, 30 ft 8½ in (9,36 m). Height, 9 ft 10⅛ in (3,00 m). Wing area, 346.6 sq ft (32,2 m²).*

BRANDENBURG W 33   Germany

Ordered in April 1918, the W 33 was basically a larger and more powerful development of the W 29 and, augmenting the smaller fighter seaplane, saw service from North Sea air stations during the closing months of World War I. The W 33 was powered by a 260 hp Mb IVa six-cylinder inline water-cooled engine and armament normally comprised two forward-firing 7,62-mm LMG 08/15 machine guns and one Parabellum in the rear cockpit. One aircraft was experimentally fitted with a 20-mm Becker cannon in the rear cockpit, and several

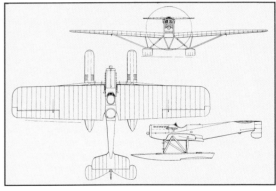

Developed from the smaller W 29, the W 33 (above and below) was built in Norway and Finland after production in Germany was halted by the Armistice.

aircraft were fitted with radio and had one of the LMGs removed. Only a handful of W 33s had been taken into the German Navy's inventory when hostilities terminated, but the Norwegian Naval Flying Boat Factory built 30 under licence and the Norwegian Army Aircraft Factory built a further 11. The Finnish Aviation Force's Aircraft Factory assembled two W 33s as pattern aircraft in 1922, and licence-manufactured a further 120 during 1923-26. *Max speed, 107 mph (173 km/h). Climb to 3,280 ft (1 000 m), 5.4 min. Empty weight, 3,130 lb (1 420 kg). Loaded weight, 4,519 lb (2 050 kg). Span, 52 ft 0 in (15,85 m). Length, 36 ft 5 in (11,10 m). Height, 11 ft 0⅔ in (3,37 m). Wing area, 473.63 sq ft (44,0 m²).*

BRANDENBURG W 34   Germany

Continuing the line of two-seat patrol fighter monoplanes initiated with the W 29, the W 34 was the final WW I development of the series of float seaplanes designed for the Hansa- und Brandenburgische Flugzeug-Werke by Ernst Heinkel and Hans Klemm. Essentially a scaled-up W 33 intended for the 300 hp Basse und Selve BuS IVa six-cylinder water-cooled engine, only one prototype of the W 34 had been completed by the end of the War. Additional examples powered by the 300 hp Fiat A 12bis engine were built after the termination of hostilities. *Max speed, 109 mph (175 km/h). Empty weight, 3,382 lb (1 534 kg). Loaded weight, 5,004 lb (2 270 kg). Span, 55 ft 5½ in (16,60 m). Length, 36 ft 5 in (11,10 m). Wing area, 527.45 sq ft (49.0 m²).*

The sole wartime prototype of the Brandenburg W 34 was essentially a scaled-up W 33 fighter seaplane.

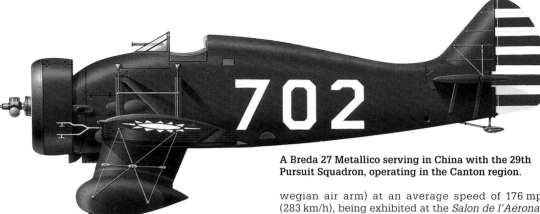

BREDA 27   Italy

Owing much to the Travel Air Model R high-speed single-seat monoplane, the fifth example of which was purchased by Italy's *Ministero dell'Aeronautica*, the Breda 27 single-seat fighter was designed by Cesare Pallavicino and was of mixed construction. The fuselage was of welded steel tube with corrugated light alloy skinning and the wing was of wood, power being provided by an Alfa Romeo-built Bristol Mercury (Mer-

(Above and below) The first of two prototypes of the Breda 27, characterized by an open cockpit, cowled engine and heavily spatted main wheels.

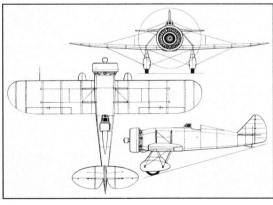

curius) IVA nine-cylinder radial rated at 540 hp. Proposed armament comprised two 12,7-mm synchronised machine guns. Two prototypes were built, flight testing commencing early 1933, and the second prototype flying from Milan to Rome-Montecelio on 10 July of that year in 90 min at an average speed of 207 mph (334 km/h). The second prototype differed from the first in several respects, additional bracing struts being introduced between the wing and fuselage, and struts added to increase the rigidity of the tailplane. The characteristics of the Breda 75 were generally unsatisfactory, the poor view from the cockpit being the subject of particular criticism, and, Ing Pallavicino having meanwhile left Breda, a total redesign of the fighter was undertaken by engineers Parano and Panzeri as the Breda 27 *Metallico*. The following data relate to the second prototype. *Max speed, 239 mph (385 km/h) at 16,405 ft (5 000 m), 196 mph (315 km/h) at sea level. Time to 16,405 ft (5 000 m), 10 min. Loaded weight, 4,195 lb (1 903 kg). Span, 35 ft 0½ in (10,68 m). Length, 25 ft 5⅛ in (7,75 m). Height, 11 ft 1⅞ in (3,40 m). Wing area, 210.98 sq ft (19,60 m²).*

BREDA 27 Metallico   Italy

The unsatisfactory characteristics of the Breda 27 prototypes led, in late 1933, to the complete redesign of the fighter by engineers Parano and Panzeri, and the construction of a further prototype. Unlike preceding Breda 27s, the new prototype was entirely of metal construction, the wing being of steel and duralumin with duralumin skinning, and the corrugated skinning of the fuselage gave place to a smooth duralumin covering. Criticism of forward view for take-off and landing was answered by moving the cockpit bodily forward and raising it by deepening the fuselage. The 540 hp Alfa Romeo-built Mercury IVA engine was retained, but the two-bladed wooden propeller gave place to a three-bladed metal propeller. The new prototype was flown in June 1934, and in September of that year it was ferried from Milan to Oslo (for demonstration to the Nor-

(Below) One of the small batch of Breda 27 Metallico fighters produced in 1936 for sale to China.

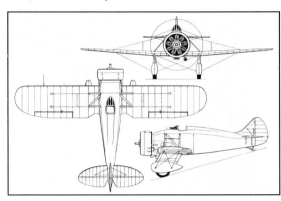

A Breda 27 Metallico serving in China with the 29th Pursuit Squadron, operating in the Canton region.

wegian air arm) at an average speed of 176 mph (283 km/h), being exhibited at the *Salon de l'Aéronautique* in Paris in November. The revised Breda 27, which now bore a marked resemblance to the Boeing P-26, was ordered by the Chinese Central Government.

The Breda 27 Metallico in its production form.

Similar to the redesigned third prototype, the series version was designated Breda 27 *Metallico* (signifying that it was of all-metal construction) and 18 were ordered by China. In the event only 11 were delivered (in 1936), these being assigned to the 29th Pursuit Sqn at Canton. An armament of two 12,7-mm machine guns was carried. The prototype was obtained by the *Regia Aeronautica*, serving with the 86ª *Squadriglia*, 5° *Stormo Assalto*, until December 1937. *Max speed, 236 mph (380 km/h) at 16,405 ft (5 000 m). Time to 16,405 ft (5 000 m), 7.5 min. Range, 466 mls (750 km). Empty weight, 2,910 lb (1 320 kg). Loaded weight, 4,078 lb (1 850 kg). Span, 35 ft 5¼ in (10,80 m). Length, 25 ft 2 in (7,67 m). Height, 11 ft 1⅞ in (3,40 m). Wing area, 202.9 sq ft (18,85 m²).*

BREGUET BUC & BLC   France

Evolved indirectly from the BU3 two-seat twin-boom pusher biplane of late 1914 as a smaller and lighter development of its bomber derivative, the BUM (B=Breguet, U=Salmson engine and M=Michelin-built), the

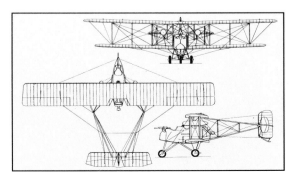

The standard production Breguet BLC (above and below) was powered by the Renault 12Fb engine.

The *Breguet de Chasse* used by the RNAS, differed from the BUC/BLC in having a Sunbeam Mohawk engine.

BUC (the letter "C" signifying *Chasse*) was intended primarily as a bomber escort. It had a similar 200 hp Salmson (Canton-Unné) 14-cylinder radial engine and carried a 37-mm Hotchkiss cannon on a flexible mounting in the forward cockpit of the fuselage nacelle. Modest production of the BUC was undertaken for the *Aviation Militaire*, and, with the installation of a 220 hp Renault 12Fb 12-cylinder water-cooled engine in place of the Salmson, prototype trials were performed in June 1915, a few additional aircraft being built under the designation BLC. The performance of both the BUC and BLC versions of the *Breguet de Chasse* was unspectacular and, with fewer than 20 delivered, they were declared obsolete by the *Aviation Militaire* before the end of 1916. During that year, a further 17 essentially similar aircraft were supplied to the Royal Naval Air Service, these differing from the BUC/BLC primarily in having the 225 hp Sunbeam Mohawk 12-cylinder engine, armament being a single 0.303-in (7,7-mm) Lewis machine gun (which was an alternative weapon to the Hotchkiss on French machines). The RNAS was disappointed with the performance of the *Breguet de Chasse*, which proved unsuitable for employment in the fighting rôle, and the service withdrew the type from its first-line inventory in June 1916. The following specification relates to the BLC. *Max speed, 86 mph (138 km/h) at sea level, 83 mph (133 km/h) at 6,560 ft (2 000 m). Time to 3,280 ft (1 000 m), 6.5 min. Endurance, 3 hrs. Empty weight, 2,557 lb (1 160 kg). Loaded weight, 3,384 lb (1 535 kg). Span, 53 ft 9½ in (16,40 m). Length, 31 ft 2 in (9,50 m). Height, 12 ft 1½ in (3,70 m). Wing area, 581.27 sq ft (54,0 m²).*

BREGUET TYPE 5   France

The Type 5, derived from the Type 4 bomber late in 1915, was regarded by the *Aviation Militaire* as a two-seat escort fighter or reconnaissance-fighter, and possessed a configuration similar to that of the earlier BUC/BLC. Powered by a 220 hp Renault 12Fb 12-cylinder water-cooled engine, the Type 5 fighter, or Bre 5 Ca2, never equipped a complete *escadrille*, a few aircraft of this type being issued to each of the units operating the Bre 5 B2 bomber version, for which it was expected to act as escort. Armament comprised a 37-mm Hotchkiss cannon on a flexible mounting in the forward cockpit and a rear-firing 7,7-mm Lewis gun on an elevated mounting over the leading edge of the upper wing. Eleven Type 5 fighters were operational with the

A 37-mm Hotchkiss cannon was mounted in the forward cockpit of the Breguet Type 5 fighter (below).

Aviation Militaire by 1 February 1916, but the type was generally unpopular. *Max speed, 83 mph (133 km/h) at 6,560 ft (2 000 m). Time to 6,560 ft (2 000 m), 22 min. Endurance, 3.5 hrs. Empty weight, 2,976 lb (1 350 kg). Loaded weight, 4,167 lb (1 890 kg). Span, 57 ft 5 in (17,50 m). Length, 32 ft 5¾ in (9,90 m). Height, 12 ft 9½ in (3,90 m). Wing area, 621.1 sq ft (57,70 m²).*

(Below) The Breguet Type 5 (Bre 5 Ca 2) fighter.

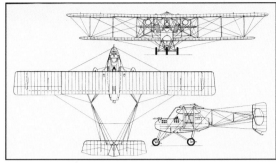

BREGUET TYPE 6   France

The Type 6 (Bre 6 Ca2) two-seat escort fighter was a 225 hp Salmson A9 water-cooled nine-cylinder radial-engined counterpart of the Renault-powered Type 5, and resulted from a fear that Renault engine production would prove inadequate to meet demands. The Type 5 airframe was modified to take the Salmson engine mounted immediately above the rear undercarriage legs and driving the propeller by means of an extension shaft, the power plant being entirely enclosed. Armament of the Type 6 fighter normally consisted of a short-barrel 37-mm Hotchkiss cannon in the forward fuselage. Performance, weights and dimensions were essentially similar to those of the Type 5.

A Salmson A9 engine installation distinguished the Type 6 (below) from the Renault-engined Type 5.

BREGUET TYPE 12   France

The Type 12 (Bre 12 Ca2) was a two-seat night fighter derivative of the basic Type 5 design which, introduced during the course of 1916, was allocated to various units defending Paris, and remained in service well into the summer of 1917. Powered by either the 220 hp Renault 12Fb or 250 hp Renault 12Fbx engine, the Type 12 featured a revised forward undercarriage unit with twin wheels and a modified fuselage nacelle. The 37-mm Hotchkiss cannon in the nose position was coupled with a Sautter-Harlé searchlight which, oper-

With searchlight attached to its Hotchkiss nose-mounted cannon, the Type 12 was a night fighter.

ated by a wind-driven generator mounted under the front of the nacelle, was aligned with and moved with the gun. An aft-firing 7,7-mm Lewis machine gun was usually fitted on an elevated mount over the upper wing leading edge, and four landing lamps were mounted beneath each lower wing. Performance, weights and dimensions were essentially similar to those of the Type 5.

BREGUET LE   France

The Breguet LE (*Laboratoire Eiffel*) single-seat fighter monoplane was aerodynamically an exceptionally advanced design for its time, emphasis being placed on minimising drag in order to achieve high performance. The basis of the design was produced by the Director of the *Laboratoire Eiffel* in collaboration with the Breguet design staff, the Breguet company having overall responsibility for translating the basic concept into a prototype. The first prototype LE was fitted with a 180 hp Hispano-Suiza 8Ab eight-cylinder water-cooled engine. Proposed armament consisted of a single 7,7-mm Vickers machine gun totally enclosed within the fuselage, although, in the event, this was never fitted. The LE made a short initial flight at Villacoublay in mid-March 1918, but the undercarriage failed on landing. After repairs, a further flight was made on 28 March, this terminating when the aircraft dived into the ground at full throttle, the pilot, Jean Sauclière, losing his life. Developments of the LE with a 220 hp Lorraine-Dietrich and a 300 hp Hispano-Suiza 8Fb were proposed, and construction of an airframe to take the latter power plant was nearing completion at the time of the loss of the first prototype, when further work was suspended. The following performance data are contemporary estimates for the LE. *Max speed, 137 mph (220 km/h) at 13,125 ft (4 000 m). Time to 13,125 ft (4 000 m), 10 min. Empty weight, 1,091 lb (495 kg). Loaded weight, 1,543 lb (700 kg). Span, 32 ft 1½ in (9,78 m). Length, 20 ft 10 in (6,35 m). Height, 6 ft 6¾ in (2,00 m). Wing area, 215.28 sq ft (20,0 m²).*

Despite its very advanced aerodynamic concept, apparent here, the sole prototype of the Breguet LE (above and below) of 1918 was flown only twice.

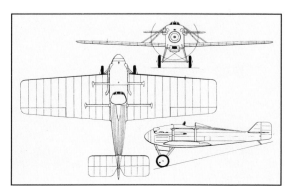

BREGUET TYPE 17 — France

The Type 17 two-seat fighter was developed from the classic Type 14 bomber, and resembled the latter in both structure and appearance, but was both more powerful and more compact. Powered by a 420 hp Renault 12K 12-cylinder water-cooled engine, the Type 17 was a two-bay biplane and a prototype appeared in the summer of 1918. Armament comprised two fixed forward-firing 7,7-mm Vickers guns and twin Lewis guns of the same calibre on a T.O.3 mount for the observer. Provision for an additional Lewis gun was made, this to fire downwards and rearwards through a trap in the fuselage floor. Official trials resulted in a request for modifications, new wings and a 450 hp Renault 12K1 engine being fitted. Limited production was undertaken as the Bre 17 C2, this having increased span wings with horn-balanced ailerons of reduced chord. Armament was unchanged and the Type 17 remained in service until the mid 'twenties. *Max speed, 135 mph (218 km/h) at 6,560 ft (2 000 m), 132 mph (213 km/h) at 9,840 ft (3 000 m). Time to 6,560 ft (2 000 m), 5.75 min. Loaded weight, 4,056 lb (1 840 kg). Span, 46 ft 10 in (14,28 m). Length, 26 ft 7 in (8,10 m). Height, 11 ft 2½ in (3,42 m). Wing area, 487.6 sq ft (45,30 m²).*

With a Renault 12K engine, the Breguet Type 17 (above and below) had an unusual wing planform with massive horn-balanced upper-wing ailerons.

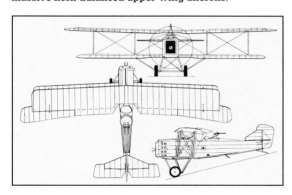

BREGUET 690 — France

In October 1934, the *Service Technique de l'Aéronautique* issued a specification calling for a C3 (*Triplace de Chasse* or Three-seat Fighter) with a fixed forward-firing cannon armament and suitable for intercept, escort and fighter director rôles. Designs to this specification that reached prototype status were the Potez 630, the Romano 110 and the Breguet 690. The last-mentioned type, designed by a team headed by Georges Ricard, was an exceptionally sturdy all-metal mid-wing cantilever monoplane powered by two Hispano-Suiza 14AB 02/03 14-cylinder radials each rated at 680 hp at 11,480 ft (3 500 m). It carried an armament of two nose-mounted 20-mm Hispano-Suiza cannon plus a single 7,5-mm MAC 1934 machine gun on a flexible mounting in the rear cockpit. The prototype Bre 690 was flown for the first time on 23 March 1938, by which time the Potez 630 had been selected to fulfil the C3 requirement, and preliminary studies had already been undertaken by the Breguet team to adapt the fighter as an AB2 (*Assaut Bombardement – Deux-place*). It was for the assault rôle that the Breguet design was ordered into production on 14 June 1938, and further development of the three-seat fighter was abandoned although a two-seat fighter derivative, the Bre 700 C2 powered by 1,070 hp Gnome-Rhône 14N 48/49 engines, attained the mock-up stage. *Max speed, 248 mph (400 km/h) at sea level, 304 mph (490 km/h) at 13,125 ft (4 000 m). Time to 13,125 ft (4 000 m), 6 min. Range, 683 mls (1 100 km). Empty weight, 6,746 lb*

(3 060 kg). Loaded weight, 9,921 lb (4 500 kg). Span, 50 ft 4¾ in (15,36 m). Length, 33 ft 7⅛ in (10,24 m). Height, 10 ft 5¾ in (3,20 m). Wing area, 310.01 sq ft (28,80 m²).

(Above and below) The sole Breguet 690 prototype in its original three-seat fighter configuration. The design was subsequently adapted for assault.

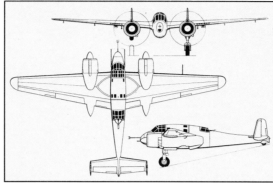

BREGUET 1001 TAON — France

Evolved to meet the requirements of a specification for a single-seat lightweight strike fighter issued by NATO, the Br 1001 Taon (Horsefly) – the name being an anagram of NATO – was designed around a 4,850 lb st (2 200 kgp) Bristol Orpheus BOr 3 turbojet and carried an armament of four 12,7-mm Colt-Browning machine guns. The first of two prototypes was flown on 25 July 1957. On the 25 April 1958, after the application of fuel-housing aerodynamic bulges at the wing roots to improve area rule distribution (being only partially area ruled in its initial form), the Taon established an international 1 000-km closed-circuit speed record of 650.37 mph (1 046,65 km/h) at 25,000 ft (7 620 m). This was equivalent to a continuous M=0.948. This record was raised once more by the Taon on 23 July 1957 to 667.9 mph (1 075 km/h). The second prototype, flown on 18 January 1958, featured a 1 ft 5¼ in (43,80-cm) in-

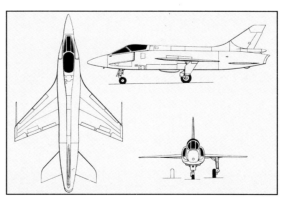

The second prototype of the Breguet 1001 (above) lacked the enlarged wing-root fairings of the first aircraft (below) which were used to carry fuel.

crease in fuselage length and minor aerodynamic changes. The Br 1003 was the projected production version of the Taon with a fully area-ruled fuselage, a 6,810 lb st (3 089 kgp) Orpheus BOr 12 boosted to 8,170 lb st (3 706 kgp) with afterburning and a wing based broadly on that of the Br 1100. The following details relate to the Br 1001-02. *Max speed, 742 mph (1 194 km/h) at sea level, or Mach=0.95, 671 mph (1 080 km/h) at 25,000 ft (7 620 m), or Mach=0.987. Empty equipped weight, 7,550 lb (3 425 kg). Loaded weight, 12,257 lb (5 560 kg). Span, 22 ft 3¾ in (6,80 m). Length, 38 ft 3⅞ in (11,68 m). Height, 12 ft 1¾ in (3,70 m). Wing area, 156.08 sq ft (14,50 m²)*

BREGUET 1100 — France

Although based broadly on the design of the Br 1001 Taon, the Br 1100 single-seat ground attack and tactical light fighter preceded the former into the air. The Taon having been delayed in order to incorporate in part the then newly discovered area rule formula, the Br 1100 first flew on 31 March 1957, not featuring area rule. Designed to meet the requirements of a *Ministère de l'Air* specification which dictated the use of paired light-weight turbojets (SNECMA R.105 Vestas, Hispano-Suiza R.800s or Turboméca Gabizos), the Br 1100 was intended to feature an internal rocket pack of 15 68-mm Brandt SNEB Type 22 rockets or two 30-mm DEFA cannon. The Gabizo turbojet was selected for installation, this offering 2,668 lb st (1 210 kgp) dry and 3,307 lb st (1 500 kgp) with afterburning. Three prototypes were ordered, the third of which was to have been navalised, but only one was flown, the second (when 80 per cent complete) and third being cancelled for budgetary reasons. *Max speed, 701 mph (1 128 km/h) at sea level, or Mach=0.92, 700 mph (1 126 km/h) at 36,000 ft (10 975 m), or Mach=1.06. Empty equipped weight, 8,362 lb (3 793 kg). Max loaded weight, 14,429 lb (6 545 kg). Span, 25 ft 8¼ in (7,83 m). Length, 41 ft 0⅞ in (12.52 m). Height, 14 ft 3¼ in (4,35 m). Wing area, 210.12 sq ft (19,52 m²).*

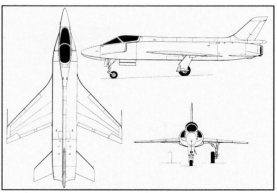

The lightweight Breguet 1100 (above and below), flown before the Taon, lacked the latter's area-ruled fuselage, but was similar in configuration.

(Above top) F2A-2 of VF-2 "Flying Chiefs", aboard USS *Lexington*, March 1941. (Immediately above) B-239 of LeLv 24 at Tiiksjärvi, Finland, 1942.

BREWSTER B-239 (F2A-1)   USA

In 1936, Dayton T Brown and R D MacCart of the Brewster Aeronautical Corporation began the design of an all-metal single-seat shipboard fighter monoplane with a retractable undercarriage (originally designed for the Boeing 278A fighter project of 1934). A prototype was ordered by the US Navy on 22 June 1936, and flew 18 months later, in December 1937, as the B-139 (XF2A-1) with a Wright XR-1820-22 Cyclone engine rated at 950 hp for take-off. On 11 June 1938, an order was placed by the US Navy for 54 examples of a developed version powered by an R-1820-34 offering 940 hp for take-off and carrying an armament of twin 0.5-in (12,7-mm) Colt machine guns in the wings and one 0.5-in

Built to US Navy contract as F2A-1s, 43 B-239s were released for export to Finland in 1940.

(12,7-mm) and one 0.3-in (7,62-mm) gun in the fuselage. Deliveries of this model, the B-239 (F2A-1), to the US Navy began in June 1939, only 11 entering service (as the US Navy's first fighter monoplanes), the remaining 43 being declared surplus to requirements and released for export to Finland. In Finnish *Ilmavoimien* service, the B-239 fighters eventually had the single 0.3-in weapon replaced by a fourth 0.5-in gun, and remained in the first-line inventory for more than eight years, the last flight of a Finnish B-239 taking place on 14 September 1948. *Max speed, 301 mph (484 km/h) at 17,000 ft (5 182 m). Normal range, 1,095 mls (1 762 km). Initial climb, 3,060 ft/min (15,54 m/sec). Empty weight, 3,785 lb (1 717 kg). Loaded weight, 5,055 lb (2 293 kg). Span, 35 ft 0 in (10,67 m). Length, 26 ft 0 in (7,92 m). Height, 11 ft 8 in (3,56 m). Wing area, 208.9 sq ft (19,41 m²).*

BREWSTER F2A-2   USA

On 22 March 1939, the US Navy ordered the installation of a Wright R-1820-40 engine in the XF2A-1, this offering 1,200 hp for take-off and 900 hp at 14,000 ft (4 267 m). An electric propeller supplanted the original hydraulic propeller, the fuel tank was redesigned for a high pressure carburettor system, and various other changes were introduced, the prototype being redesignated XF2A-2. Trials with the XF2A-2 began in July

1939, and 43 examples of the improved version were ordered as F2A-2s in lieu of the same number of F2A-1s released for export to Finland. US Navy acceptances of the F2A-2 began in September 1940, armament initially being similar to that of the F2A-1, but the 30th F2A-2 standardised on a quartet of 0.5-in (12,7-mm) Colt machine guns, introducing at the same time some armour and a protected fuel tank. *Max speed, 285 mph (459 km/h) at sea level, 323 mph (520 km/h) at 16,500 ft (5 030 m). Cruise, 157 mph (253 km/h). Initial climb, 2,500 ft/min (12,7 m/sec). Normal range, 1,015 mls (1 633 km). Empty weight, 4,576 lb (2 076 kg). Loaded weight, 5,942 lb (2 695 kg). Span, 35 ft 0 in (10,67 m). Length, 25 ft 7 in (7,80 m). Height, 11 ft 8 in (3,56 m). Wing area, 208.9 sq ft (19,41 m²).*

BREWSTER B-339 (BUFFALO)   USA

In 1939, the Brewster Aeronautical Corporation obtained its first orders for a land-based derivative of the B-239 shipboard fighter which was assigned the company designation B-339. Forty were ordered by a Belgian Purchasing Mission and a further 170 (B-339E) by a British Mission. During 1940, 72 were also ordered for the Air Division of the Royal Netherlands Indies Army (B-339D). In the event, deliveries of the B-339 were too late to reach Belgium, and 28 Belgian-contract machines were taken over by Britain. Deliveries of the B-339E to the UK began in July 1940, the name Buffalo being allocated to the type in RAF, RAAF and RNZAF service, and deliveries of the B-339D to the NEI commenced in March 1941. The B-339 differed from the B-239 in having a larger, redesigned fuel tank and a Wright GR-1820-G105A engine rated at 1,100 hp for take-off. RAF-specified armour and other equipment resulted in increased weight, with a consequent marked decrease in manoeuvrability. In an attempt to improve performance, the four 0.5-in (12,7-mm) Colt machine guns were replaced by four 0.303-in (7,7-mm)

(Below) Belgian markings appeared on B-339s only for test flights in the USA, before delivery to UK.

Browning guns, ammunition was reduced and fuel was restricted to 84 Imp gal (382 l). A supplementary NEI order called for 20 examples powered by the GR-1820-G205A engine rated at 1,200 hp for take-off, but these fighters (designated B-439) were taken on charge by the USAAF after the occupation of the NEI, 17 of them being passed to the RAAF for home defence duties during the summer of 1942. *Max speed, 313 mph (504 km/h) at 13,500 ft (4 115 m), 292 mph (470 km/h) at 20,000 ft (6 095 m). Max range, 840 mls (1 352 km). Initial climb, 2,600 ft/min (13,2 m/sec). Empty weight, 4,479 lb (2 032 kg). Max loaded weight, 6,782 lb (3 076 kg). Span, 35 ft 0 in (10,67 m). Length, 25 ft 11 in (7,90 m). Height, 12 ft 1 in (3,68 m). Wing area, 208.9 sq ft (19,41 m²).*

Propeller and fuel systems were principal features distinguishing the F2A-2 (above) from the F2A-1.

(Above) The B-339, ordered by Belgium but diverted to Britain, lacked shipboard features of earlier variants, as did (below) the B-439 intended for Dutch service.

BREWSTER F2A-3   USA

On 21 January 1941, the US Navy placed an order for 108 fighters under the designation F2A-3 which were to follow on completion of the final export B-339s, the purpose of the order being primarily that of keeping the Brewster assembly line occupied. Using an airframe essentially similar to that of the export models, with increased fuel tankage, lengthened forward fuselage and an R-1820-40 engine similar to that of the F2A-2, but set forward 9 in (22,86 cm) for CG reasons, the F2A-3 em-

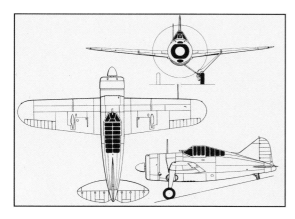

(Above) The Brewster B-239 (US Navy F2A-1) and (right) an F2A-3 featuring more fuel, lengthened forward fuselage but retaining a four-gun armament.

bodied some armour and retained the quartet of 0.5-in (12,7-mm) Colt guns. The F2A-3s were delivered to the US Navy between July and December 1941, but the higher loaded weight by comparison with earlier US Navy models adversely affected the performance and the type saw relatively brief service with the USN and the USMC, production of the Brewster fighter terminating in March 1942 with the last of the 20 NEI-contract B-439s. *Max speed, 284 mph (457 km/h) at sea level, 321 mph (516 km/h) at 16,500 ft (5 030 m). Max range, 965 mls (1 553 km). Initial climb, 2,290 ft/min (11,63 m/sec). Empty weight, 4,732 lb (2 146 kg). Loaded weight, 6,321 lb (2 867 kg). Max weight, 7,159 lb (3 247 kg). Span, 35 ft 0 in (10,67 m). Length, 26 ft 4 in (8,02 m). Height, 12 ft 1 in (3,68 m). Wing area, 208.9 sq ft (19,41 m²).*

BRISTOL SCOUT D   UK

Derived from a single-seat sports biplane designed by Frank Barnwell, first flown in February 1914 and retrospectively known as the Scout A, the Scout D was a revised design which, completed in November 1915, had provision for a fixed synchronised 0.303-in (7,7-mm) Vickers gun. The Scout D had been preceded by two Scout Bs, which, intended for reconnaissance, were officially unarmed, but one of which was fitted with a rifle on each side of the fuselage and angled outward to avoid hitting the propeller when fired. These had been followed by 161 Scout Cs (74 for the RN and 87 for the RFC) which, again, were officially unarmed, although much ingenuity was displayed in the field in fitting pistols, rifles and carbines, while some RN Scouts carried 24-round canisters of Ranken darts which it was intended to use against Zeppelins. The Scout D was thus the first model for which armament was officially intended, though relatively few of these had the synchronised Vickers gun and the armament of others varied considerably, some having a 0.303-in (7,7-mm) fixed Lewis gun firing straight ahead without synchronising equipment and others having a movable Lewis

The Scout D (right) was the first fully armed version of the Bristol biplane, but many flew unarmed such as that above in Australia in 1919.

above the upper wing. Of the 210 examples built, 80 went to the RN, of which 50 had 100 hp Gnome Monosoupape engines and the remainder the 80 hp Gnome. Most of those delivered to the RFC ultimately had the 80 hp Le Rhône engines and the following data relate to the Scout D with this engine. *Max speed, 100 mph (161 km/h) at sea level, 86 mph (138 km/h) at 10,000 ft (3 050 m). Time to 10,000 ft (3 050 m), 18.5 min. Endurance, 2.5 hrs. Empty weight, 760 lb (345 kg). Loaded weight, 1,250 lb (567 kg). Span, 24 ft 7 in (7,49 m). Length, 20 ft 8 in (6,30 m). Height, 8 ft 6 in (2,59 m). Wing area, 198 sq ft (18,39 m²).*

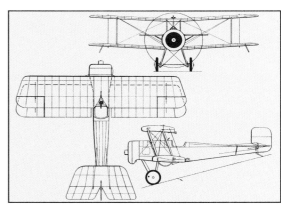

BRISTOL S.2A   UK

A derivative of the Scout D intended to meet an Admiralty specification for a two-seat fighter, the S.2A had side-by-side seating and was intended to be armed with a single 0.303-in (7,7-mm) Lewis gun. In the event, it was rejected by the Admiralty in favour of the Sop-

Bristol's S.2A (below) featured unusual side-by-side seating, but only a single Lewis gun armament.

(Above top) A Scout D from the first production batch, 55 Sqn RFC, Yatesbury, 1917. (Above) An Admiralty Scout C at RNAS Eastchurch, Isle of Sheppey, 1915.

with 1½ Strutter, but work continued on the two prototypes at the behest of the War Office which envisaged the type primarily as a potential advanced trainer for the RFC. The two prototypes were completed in May and June 1916 respectively, being powered by the 110 hp Clerget engine (although one was later re-engined with a 100 hp Gnome Monosoupape), and were delivered to the Central Flying School at Upavon. They were found to be manoeuvrable and quite fast, but no further development was undertaken. *Max speed, 95 mph (153 km/h). Endurance, 3.0 hrs. Loaded weight, 1,400 lb (635 kg). Span, 28 ft 2 in (8,58 m). Length, 21 ft 3 in (6,48 m). Height, 10 ft 0 in (3.05 m).*

BRISTOL T.T.A.   UK

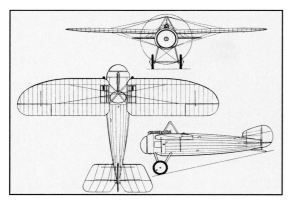

The Bristol T.T.A. (above) provided a clear field of fire for a pair of Lewis guns in the front cockpit.

Designed by Frank Barnwell assisted by Leslie G Frise, the T.T.A. (Twin Tractor Model A) was intended to meet a requirement for a two-seat twin-engined local defence fighter, the gunner in the nose having an un-obstructed field of fire for two free-mounted 0.303-in (7,7-mm) Lewis guns. Dual controls were fitted and the intended power plant comprised two 150 hp R.A.F.4a engines. In the event, non-availability of these engines resulted in the installation of two 120 hp six-cylinder Beardmore water-cooled engines in the two prototypes ordered. The first T.T.A. was flown in April 1916, but displayed poor lateral control and was adversely criti-cised on the grounds of poor pilot view. As by this time synchronising mechanisms for guns were becoming available, no further development of this category of aircraft was pursued. *Max speed, 87 mph (140 km/h) at sea level. Time to 6,000 ft (1 830 m), 21 min. Empty weight, 3,820 lb (1 733 kg). Loaded weight, 5,100 lb (2 313 kg). Span, 53 ft 6 in (16,30 m). Length, 39 ft 2 in (11,94 m). Height, 12 ft 6 in (3,81 m). Wing area, 817 sq ft (75,90 m²).*

BRISTOL M.1C   UK

The M.1C was the production derivative of the private-venture M.1A which, designed by Frank Barnwell, had flown for the first time on 14 July 1916. It was of in-novatory design in being a shoulder-wing monoplane

(Above) The Bristol M.1C, the tenth of the M.1C production batch built for the RFC being illustrated below. These were used principally in the Middle East.

with a fully faired fuselage of good streamline form and a drag-reducing hemispherical spinner. Four similar aircraft were ordered by the War Office, these each having a single 0.303-in (7,7-mm) Vickers gun mounted on the port wing root and a clear-view cut-out panel in the starboard wing root to afford the pilot a measure of downward visibility. This version received the desig-nation M.1B and a production order for 125 aircraft was placed on 3 August 1917 as M.1Cs. Powered by a 110 hp Le Rhône 9J nine-cylinder rotary engine, the M.1C had a centrally-mounted Vickers gun, but its subsequent operational career was largely confined to the Middle East where 33 M.1Cs were sent during 1917-18. No air-craft of this type were issued to RFC squadrons based in France, most being used by UK-based training units, the 49 mph (97 km/h) landing speed being considered too high for small Western Front airfields. *Max speed, 130 mph (209 km/h) at sea level, 127 mph (204 km/h) at 5,000 ft (1 525 m). Time to 10,000 ft (3 050 m), 10.45 min. Endurance, 1.75hrs. Empty weight, 896 lb (406 kg). Loaded weight, 1,348 lb (611 kg). Span, 30 ft 9 in (9,37 m). Length, 20 ft 5½ in (6,23 m). Height, 7 ft 9½ in (2,37 m). Wing area, 145 sq ft (13,47 m²).*

BRISTOL F.2A (FIGHTER)   UK

Known by the appellation of "Fighter" almost from its birth, the F.2 series of two-seat fighter-reconnaissance aircraft designed by Frank Barnwell was to join the ranks of the true immortals of World War I. Designed around the new 190 hp Rolls-Royce 12-cylinder water-cooled engine, but with provision for the alternative in-stallation of the 150 hp eight-cylinder Hispano-Suiza, the F.2A had a single forward-firing synchronised 0.303-in (7,7-mm) Vickers gun and a Lewis gun of the same calibre on a Scarff ring in the rear cockpit. The first of two prototypes was flown on 9 September 1916, a production contract for 50 aircraft having been placed 12 days earlier, on 28 August. Deliveries began early in 1917, but initial operational experience in April 1917 was disappointing, thanks to the use of incorrect com-bat techniques. Confidence in the type was restored when newly-evolved methods were proved successful. Meanwhile, the improved F.2B had been evolved, the 51st and subsequent production aircraft being of this standard, and delivery of the F.2B resulting in the with-drawal from frontline use of the F.2A. *Max speed, 110 mph (177 km/h) at sea level, 106 mph (171 km/h) at 5,000 ft (1 525 m). Time to 5,000 ft (1 525 m), 5.45 min. Endurance, 3 hrs. Empty weight, 1,727 lb (783 kg). Loaded weight, 2,667 lb (1 210 kg). Span, 39 ft 3 in (11,96 m). Length, 25 ft 10 in (7,87 m). Height, 9 ft 6 in (2,89 m). Wing area, 389 sq ft (36,14 m²).*

Second prototype of the Bristol F.2A which was powered by a 150 hp Hispano Suiza engine, only 50 aircraft of this type being built.

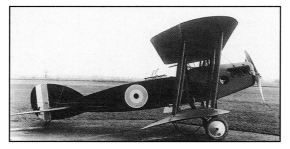

BRISTOL F.2B (FIGHTER)   UK

The F.2B two-seat fighter-reconnaissance aircraft dif-fered from the F.2A in having a revised centre fuselage to provide improved pilot view, an enlarged fuel tank, increased ammunition capacity for the synchronised Vickers gun and a modified lower wing affording a small increase in gross area. New horizontal tail sur-faces of greater span and increased aspect ratio were introduced, and after the first 150 F.2Bs had been de-livered with the 190 hp Rolls-Royce engine – by this time designated Falcon I – the 220 hp Falcon II was adopted, this being succeeded in turn by the 275 hp Falcon III which powered the majority of the F.2Bs built. F.2B deliveries began on 13 April 1917, and the

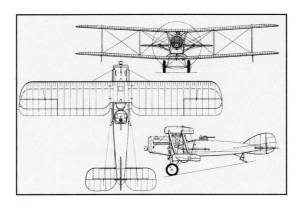

Bristol F.2B with Rolls-Royce Falcon engine.

Key to Bristol F.2B Fighter

1 Wing-tip edge member
2 Starboard upper aileron
3 Aileron control horn
4 Fixed trailing-edge ribs
5 Compression ribs
6 Wing panel internal wire bracing
7 Leading-edge stiffeners
8 Outboard interplane struts
9 Diagonal wire bracing
10 Lower wing panel fabric covering
11 Aileron operating cable
12 Inboard interplane struts
13 Upper engine cowling panels
14 Machine gun barrel
15 Blast tube vent
16 Machine gun muzzle blast tube

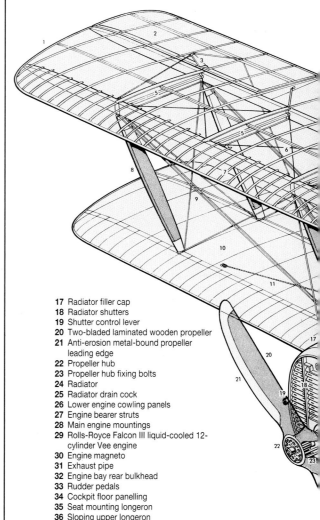

17 Radiator filler cap
18 Radiator shutters
19 Shutter control lever
20 Two-bladed laminated wooden propeller
21 Anti-erosion metal-bound propeller leading edge
22 Propeller hub
23 Propeller hub fixing bolts
24 Radiator
25 Radiator drain cock
26 Lower engine cowling panels
27 Engine bearer struts
28 Main engine mountings
29 Rolls-Royce Falcon III liquid-cooled 12-cylinder Vee engine
30 Engine magneto
31 Exhaust pipe
32 Engine bay rear bulkhead
33 Rudder pedals
34 Cockpit floor panelling
35 Seat mounting longeron
36 Sloping upper longeron
37 Control column
38 Cartridge case ejector chute
39 Upper (main) fuel tank; total fuel capacity 44 Imp gal (200 l)
40 Centre section front strut
41 Gunsight ring
42 Upper wing panel centre section
43 Compass
44 Windscreen panel
45 Aldis gunsight

success of this type led to the decision to re-equip all RFC fighter-reconnaissance squadrons with F.2Bs. Production continued, in the event, until September 1919, by which time a total number of 4,747 had been completed, 3,126 of these by the parent company. Of the final batch, 153 were delivered with the 200 hp Sunbeam Arab engine and 18 with the 230 hp Siddeley Puma. When the RAF was re-established on a peacetime footing, the F.2B was adopted as standard for the army co-operation rôle and reinstated in production for this task as the Mk II, others being refurbished to similar standards. Fifty structurally revised aircraft delivered in 1926 were designated as Mk IIIs, all surviving aircraft of this mark being converted in 1928 as Mk IVs. The following data relate to the Falcon III-powered F.2B of 1918. *Max speed, 123 mph (198 km/h) at 5,000 ft (1 525 m), 113 mph (182 km/h) at 10,000 ft (3 050 m).*

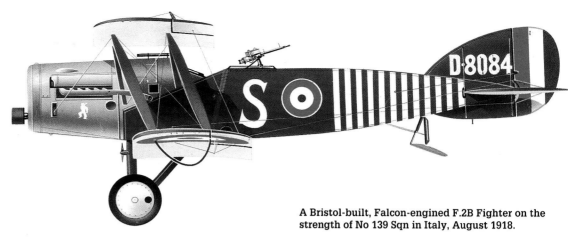

A Bristol-built, Falcon-engined F.2B Fighter on the strength of No 139 Sqn in Italy, August 1918.

46 Wing spar/centre section attachment joint
47 0.303-in (7.7-mm) Vickers machine gun
48 Machine gun mounting struts
49 Instrument panel
50 Engine throttle and mixture control levers (post-war port-side positon)
51 Lower fuel tank
52 Observer's cockpit floor panelling
53 Observer's emergency control column (offset to starboard)
54 Pilot's seat
55 Centre section rear strut
56 Cockpit coaming
57 Scarff-ring machine gun mounting
58 Gun elevating mechanism
59 Ammunition drum
60 0.303-in (7.7-mm) Lewis machine gun
61 Swivelling gun mounting
62 Spare ammunition drums
63 Observer's sliding seat
64 Seat mounting rail
65 Diagonal fuselage braces
66 Upper longeron
67 Fuselage internal wire bracing
68 Fabric top decking
69 Starboard tailplane

70 Starboard elevator
71 Fin construction
72 Sternpost
73 Rudder construction
74 Tailplane bracing cables
75 Rudder construction
76 Port elevator construction
77 Elevator control horn
78 Tailplane construction
79 Elevator control cables
80 Ventral fin segment
81 Trimming tailplane incidence control linkage
82 Rear fuselage bulkhead
83 Rudder control cables
84 Tailskid steering linkage
85 Fuselage lower longeron
86 Tailskid mounting struts
87 Steerable tailskid
88 Elastic cord shock absorber
89 Vertical spacers
90 Fuselage fabric covering
91 Fabric lacing
92 Horizontal spacers
93 Wing trailing-edge ribs
94 Rear spar

95 Compression ribs
96 Front spar
97 Wing panel internal wire bracing
98 Rib support stringers
99 Aileron balance cable
100 Aileron control horn
101 Port upper aileron
102 Wing-tip edge member
103 Aileron interconnecting cable
104 Port lower aileron
105 Ventral wing-tip skid
106 Aileron operating cable
107 Outboard interplane struts
108 Pitot tube
109 Lower wing panel rib construction
110 Leading-edge stiffeners
111 Inboard interplane struts
112 Boarding steps
113 Lower wing panel centre section attachment struts

114 Ventral bomb racks (six)
115 Wing spar/centre section attachment joint
116 Wind driven fuel pump
117 Main undercarriage Vee-struts
118 Diagonal wire bracing
119 Axle beam
120 Starboard mainwheel
121 Elastic cord shock absorbers
122 Wheel spokes
123 Tyre inflation valve
124 Wheel disc fabric cover
125 Port mainwheel
126 25-lb (11-kg) Cooper bomb (12)

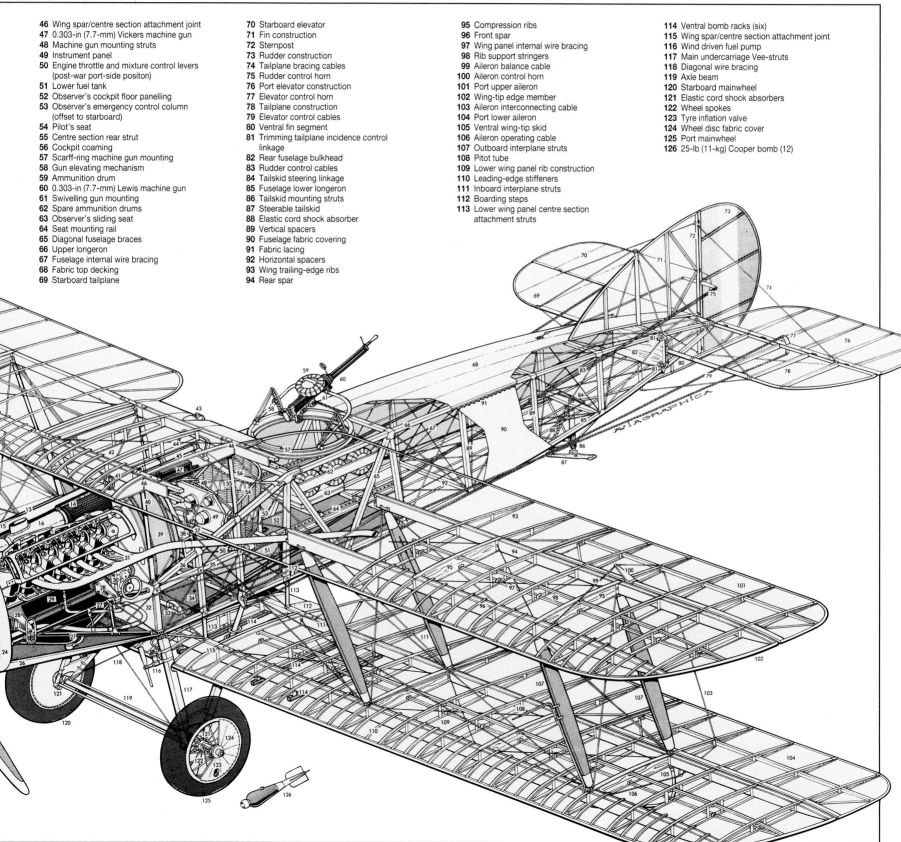

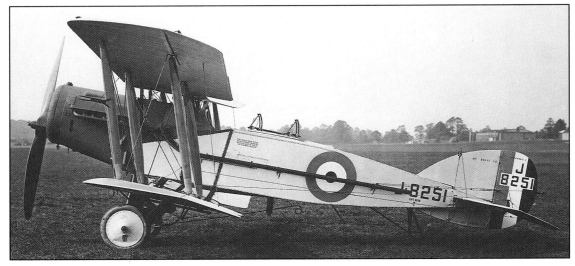

An example of the Fighter Mk III from the 1926 production batch, with structural revisions.

Time to 10,000 ft (3 050 m), 11.85 min. Empty weight, 1,930 lb (875 kg). Loaded weight, 2,848 lb (1 292 kg). Span, 39 ft 3 in (11,96 m). Length, 25 ft 10 in (7,87 m). Height, 9 ft 9 in (2,97 m). Wing area, 405.6 sq ft (37,68 m²).

BRISTOL SCOUT F   UK

Originally intended for a 200 hp Hispano-Suiza engine, the Scout F was initiated by Frank Barnwell in June 1917, subsequently being redesigned to take a 200 hp Sunbeam Arab II eight-cylinder water-cooled engine. This power plant had been ordered into large-scale production in January 1917, before adequate testing had been undertaken. Six prototypes of the Scout F were ordered, the first of these flying in March 1918, by which time it had been decided to complete only the first two aircraft with Arab engines. The Scout F possessed excellent flying qualities, but its Arab engine proved totally unreliable. Nevertheless, the second prototype was completed and flown, flight testing continuing into 1919. Armament comprised two synchronised 0.303-in (7,7-mm) Vickers guns. *Max speed, 138 mph (222 km/h) at sea level, 128 mph (206 km/h) at 10,000 ft (3 050 m). Time to 10,000 ft (3 050 m), 9.35 min. Empty weight, 1,436 lb (651 kg). Loaded weight, 2,210 lb (1 002 kg). Span, 29 ft 7½ in (9,03 m). Length, 20 ft 10 in (6,35 m). Height, 8 ft 4 in (2,54 m). Wing area, 260 sq ft (24,15 m²).*

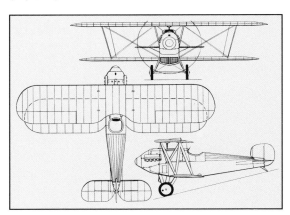

(Above) The Bristol Scout F of 1918 was powered by the unreliable Sunbeam Arab and only two prototypes were built, the first being illustrated below.

BRISTOL SCOUT F.1   UK

The shortcomings of the Arab engine led, at an early stage in the development of the Scout F, to an investigation of possible alternative power plants, and it was decided to adapt the third prototype airframe to take a new 14-cylinder two-row Brazil-Straker (later Cosmos Engineering) Mercury radial of 347 hp. Designated Scout F.1, the aircraft was first flown on 6 September 1918, and proved to possess an excellent performance, establishing new unofficial climb records in April 1919.

The sole Scout F.1, with Mercury engine in place of the Arab used in the original Scout F.

By that time, further development of the Mercury engine had been abandoned and no more work on the Scout F.1 was undertaken. *Max speed, 145 mph (233 km/h) at sea level. Time to 10,000 ft (3 050 m), 5.45 min. Loaded weight, 2,260 lb (1 025 kg). Span, 29 ft 7½ in (9,03 m). Length, 20 ft 0 in (6,09 m). Height, 8 ft 4 in (2,54 m). Wing area, 260 sq ft (24,15 m²).*

BRISTOL F.2C BADGER   UK

Intended as a successor to the F.2B two-seat fighter-reconnaissance aircraft, the F.2C Badger was designed

(Below) The original F.2C Badger as rebuilt after suffering a crash landing on its first flight.

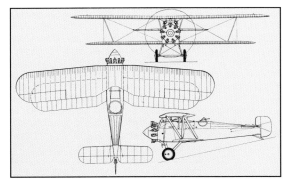

First Bristol F.2C Badger in its definitive form.

for the 320 hp ABC Dragonfly I nine-cylinder radial, three prototypes being ordered. Armament comprised two fixed 0.303-in (7,7-mm) Vickers machine guns and a 0.303-in (7,7-mm) Lewis gun mounted on a Scarff ring in the rear cockpit. The first prototype suffered a crash landing as a result of an engine failure during its first take-off on 4 February 1919, but was subsequently rebuilt and flown. The second prototype was completed with a nine-cylinder Cosmos Jupiter of 450 hp and flew on 24 May 1919, but later had a Dragonfly substituted for the Jupiter. A third aircraft was completed as the Badger II with a Cosmos Jupiter engine and redesigned wings, this being re-engined in 1921 with a 385 hp Jupiter II (this power plant having meanwhile been taken over by Bristol) and subsequently being used primarily for engine development purposes. The following data relate to the Dragonfly-engined Badger. *Max speed, 135 mph (217 km/h) at sea level, 129 mph (207 km/h) at 10,000 ft (3 050 m). Time to 10,000 ft (3 050 m), 11 min. Empty weight, 1,948 lb (884 kg). Loaded weight, 3,152 lb (1 430 kg). Span, 36 ft 9 in (11,20 m). Length, 23 ft 8 in (7,21 m). Height, 9 ft 1 in (2,76 m). Wing area, 357.2 sq ft (33,18 m²).*

BRISTOL BULLFINCH I   UK

In July 1920, Capt Frank Barnwell and his team began design work on an all-metal parasol fighter monoplane intended to be built in both single- and two-seat form, and three prototypes were ordered. In the event, wood was used for the wing construction of the prototypes, the fuselages being of steel tube. By March 1922, when

(Above) The second prototype of the Bullfinch I in the original single-seat monoplane configuration.

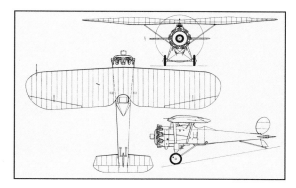

The parasol Bristol Bullfinch I single-seat fighter.

the name Bullfinch was officially adopted, the decision had been taken to complete two of the prototypes as single-seaters, these being delivered in April 1923. Armed with two 0.303-in (7,7-mm) Vickers machine guns, the Bullfinch single-seaters were flown experimentally by the RAF and were found to offer a relatively good performance on the 425 hp of a Bristol Jupiter III radial, but no production order was forthcoming. The third prototype was completed as the two-seat Bullfinch II. *Max speed,135 mph (217 km/h) at 15,000 ft (4 570 m). Endurance, 4 hrs. Empty weight, 2,175 lb (986 kg). Loaded weight, 3,205 lb (1 454 kg). Span, 38 ft 5 in (11,71 m). Length, 24 ft 5 in (7,44 m). Height, 10 ft 9 in (3,27 m). Wing area, 267 sq ft (24,8 m²).*

BRISTOL BULLFINCH II UK

During construction of the Bullfinch prototypes, it was decided to complete the third aeroplane as a two-seat fighter biplane, and this, the Bullfinch II, was first flown on 15 February 1924. The Bullfinch II differed from the single-seat model primarily in having a 3-ft (91,4-cm) section housing a self-contained gunner's cockpit inserted in the fuselage immediately aft of the pilot's cockpit and beneath which was attached a cantilever lower wing, the resultant shift of the centre of pressure compensating for the change in the CG. The only other change consisted of the repositioning of the main undercarriage members farther aft. The rear cockpit was fitted with a Scarff-mounted 0.303-in (7,7-mm) Lewis gun, and structural weight was increased by 320 lb (145 kg). The 425 hp Jupiter III engine was insufficiently powerful to cater for the additional 883 lb (400 kg) of the two-seater in fully loaded condition and the performance of the Bullfinch II suffered in consequence. *Max speed, 120 mph (193 km/h) at 15,000 ft (4 570 m). Endurance, 4 hrs. Empty weight, 2,495 lb (1 132 kg). Loaded weight, 4,088 lb (1 854 kg). Span, 38 ft 5 in (11,71 m). Length, 27 ft 6 in (8,38 m). Height, 10 ft 9 in (3,28 m). Wing area, 391 sq ft (36,32 m²).*

The third Bullfinch in its Mk II configuration as a two-seat biplane with a lengthened fuselage.

BRISTOL BLOODHOUND UK

Designed by Wilfrid T Reid to meet Air Ministry Specification 3/22 issued in June 1922 for a two-seat fighter, the Bloodhound was flown for the first time at the end of May 1923. Featuring a welded steel-tube fuselage and wooden wings, and powered by a 425 hp Bristol Jupiter IV engine, the Bloodhound carried an armament of two synchronised 0.303-in (7,7-mm) Vickers machine guns and a Lewis gun of similar calibre on a Scarff mounting on the rear cockpit. Three additional Bloodhounds were built to the order of the Air Ministry, the first of these being of all-metal construction and the others having wooden wings and tail. All three were powered by the Jupiter IV, but the engine of the third

aircraft was fitted with an RAE supercharger. The three aircraft were delivered to Martlesham and Farnborough between March and September 1925, but no production was undertaken. The original prototype was successively fitted with the Jupiter V and VI, and served primarily as an engine test bed. *Max speed, 130 mph (209 km/h). Time to 10,000 ft (3 050 m), 14.35 min. Endurance, 3 hrs. Empty weight, 2,515 lb (1 141 kg). Loaded weight, 4,236 lb (1 921 kg). Span, 40 ft 2 in (12,24 m). Length, 26 ft 6 in (8,08 m). Height, 10 ft 8 in (3,25 m). Wing area, 494 sq ft (45,89 m²).*

The original Bloodhound, (above), used as a company demonstrator, compared with (below) the third aircraft for Air Ministry trials, with an RAE supercharger.

BRISTOL JUPITER FIGHTER UK

The Jupiter Fighter was essentially an adaptation of the F.2B airframe to take a 425 hp Bristol Jupiter IV engine and an oleo-type undercarriage. Three conversions were completed, the first of these flying in June 1923. One of the three Jupiter Fighters was purchased by the Swedish government and entered service with *Flygkompaniet* in May 1924. The first Jupiter Fighter had crashed on 23 November 1923 as a result of an engine seizure at high altitude, and, in September 1924, the third example was converted as a dual-control trainer. *Max speed, 134 mph (216 km/h). Time to 10,000 ft (3 050 m), 8.25 min. Empty weight, 2,190 lb (993 kg). Loaded weight, 3,080 lb (1 397 kg). Span, 39 ft 3 in (11,96 m). Length, 25 ft 0 in (7,62 m). Height, 9 ft 6 in (2,89 m). Wing area, 405 sq ft (37,62 m²).*

BRISTOL TYPE 95 BAGSHOT UK

Specification 4/24 issued in 1924 called for a multi-seat twin-engined fighter capable of carrying two of the 37-mm Coventry Ordnance Works (COW) cannon. To

The first Bristol Jupiter Fighter, combining a Jupiter engine with the original F.2B airframe.

meet this requirement Frank Barnwell designed the radical Bagshot, the sole prototype of which was first flown on 15 July 1927. Powered by two 450 hp Bristol Jupiter VI engines, the Bagshot had an unorthodox triangular-section, steel-tube, fabric-covered fuselage and a two-spar, shoulder-mounted wing with a steel primary structure. One 37-mm COW gun was carried in an open nose turret and a similar weapon in a dorsal position, a Scarff-mounted 0.303-in (7,7-mm) Lewis being carried aft of the latter gun. The crew comprised pilot and two gunners. During flight trials it was discovered that aileron reversal resulting from wing torsional flexibility produced ineffective lateral control, and as it was concluded that the shortcomings of the aircraft could be eradicated only by virtually complete redesign, further flight trials with the Bagshot were abandoned. *Estimated max speed, 125 mph (201 km/h). Empty weight, 5,100 lb (2 313 kg). Loaded weight, 8,195 lb (3 717 kg). Span, 70 ft 0 in (21,34 m). Length, 44 ft 11 in (13,69 m). Height, 9 ft 6 in (2,89 m). Wing area, 840 sq ft (78,04 m²).*

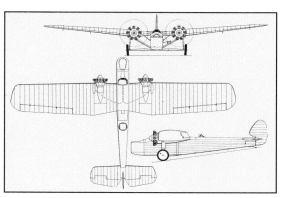

The Bristol Bagshot (above and below) which was tested only at Filton and proved unsuccessful in its designed rôle of COW gun-armed night fighter.

BRISTOL TYPE 101 UK

Designed as a private venture, the Type 101 two-seat fighter powered by a 450 hp Bristol Jupiter VI nine-cylinder radial was of mixed construction, the fuselage being a ply-covered spruce structure and the wings being of steel with fabric skinning. Armament comprised two synchronised 0.303-in (7,7-mm) Vickers guns and a Scarff-mounted Lewis gun. Cleaner and more compact than most contemporary aircraft in its category, the Type 101, which was first flown on 27 July 1927, offered a relatively high performance, but was rejected by the Air Ministry because of its use of wood. As no other customers presented themselves, the prototype served in the test bed rôle. *Max speed, 160 mph*

(257 km/h). Time to 10,000 ft (3 050 m), 9.5 min. Empty weight, 2,100 lb (953 kg). Loaded weight, 3,540 lb (1 606 kg). Span, 33 ft 7 in (10,23 m). Length, 27 ft 4 in (8,33 m). Height, 9 ft 6 in (2,89 m). Wing area, 360 sq ft (33,44 m²).

The Bristol 101 two-seat fighter prototype, fully-armed for display at Copenhagen in August 1927.

BRISTOL Type 105 BULLDOG I   UK

Designed by Frank S Barnwell and built as a private venture, the Bulldog was flown for the first time on 17 May 1927 with a 440 hp Bristol Jupiter VII engine. Of high-tensile steel strip construction, the Bulldog carried an armament of two synchronised 0.303-in (7,7-mm) Vickers guns, and although not an official contender for the F.9/26 Specification, it was evaluated at Martlesham within a month of its initial flight and displayed a superiority over all but one of the official contenders, the Hawker Hawfinch. Trials at Martlesham resulted in an Air Ministry order for one example of the modified Type 105A Bulldog II for extended competition with the Hawfinch. Meanwhile, Bristol offered an export version of the Bulldog I and built a prototype which was exhibited in Paris in June 1928, but was never flown. *Max speed, 173 mph (278 km/h). Service ceiling, 27,000 ft (8 230 m). Empty weight, 1,987 lb*

The Bulldog I prototype was built in 1927 as a PV, making use of high-tensile steel strip construction.

(901 kg). Loaded weight, 3,250 lb (1 474 kg). Span, 34 ft 0 in (10,36 m). Length, 23 ft 0 in (7,01 m). Height, 8 ft 9 in (2,66 m). Wing area, 307 sq ft (28,52 m²).

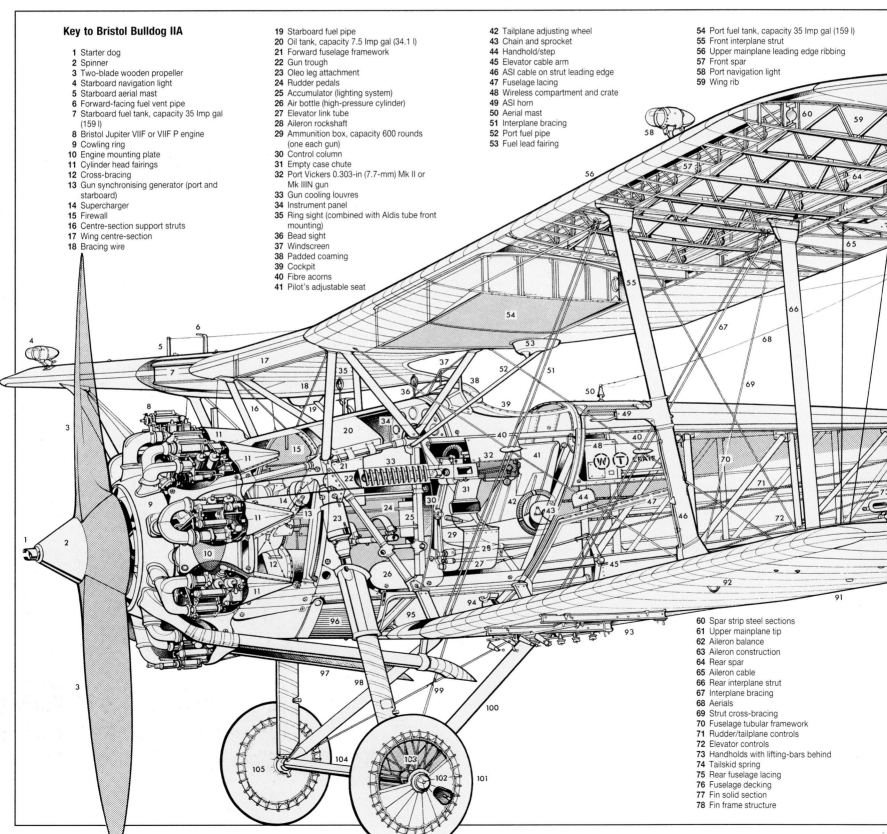

Key to Bristol Bulldog IIA

1 Starter dog
2 Spinner
3 Two-blade wooden propeller
4 Starboard navigation light
5 Starboard aerial mast
6 Forward-facing fuel vent pipe
7 Starboard fuel tank, capacity 35 Imp gal (159 l)
8 Bristol Jupiter VIIF or VIIF P engine
9 Cowling ring
10 Engine mounting plate
11 Cylinder head fairings
12 Cross-bracing
13 Gun synchronising generator (port and starboard)
14 Supercharger
15 Firewall
16 Centre-section support struts
17 Wing centre-section
18 Bracing wire

19 Starboard fuel pipe
20 Oil tank, capacity 7.5 Imp gal (34.1 l)
21 Forward fuselage framework
22 Gun trough
23 Oleo leg attachment
24 Rudder pedals
25 Accumulator (lighting system)
26 Air bottle (high-pressure cylinder)
27 Elevator link tube
28 Aileron rockshaft
29 Ammunition box, capacity 600 rounds (one each gun)
30 Control column
31 Empty case chute
32 Port Vickers 0.303-in (7.7-mm) Mk II or Mk IIIN gun
33 Gun cooling louvres
34 Instrument panel
35 Ring sight (combined with Aldis tube front mounting)
36 Bead sight
37 Windscreen
38 Padded coaming
39 Cockpit
40 Fibre acorns
41 Pilot's adjustable seat

42 Tailplane adjusting wheel
43 Chain and sprocket
44 Handhold/step
45 Elevator cable arm
46 ASI cable on strut leading edge
47 Fuselage lacing
48 Wireless compartment and crate
49 ASI horn
50 Aerial mast
51 Interplane bracing
52 Port fuel pipe
53 Fuel lead fairing

54 Port fuel tank, capacity 35 Imp gal (159 l)
55 Front interplane strut
56 Upper mainplane leading edge ribbing
57 Front spar
58 Port navigation light
59 Wing rib

60 Spar strip steel sections
61 Upper mainplane tip
62 Aileron balance
63 Aileron construction
64 Rear spar
65 Aileron cable
66 Rear interplane strut
67 Interplane bracing
68 Aerials
69 Strut cross-bracing
70 Fuselage tubular framework
71 Rudder/tailplane controls
72 Elevator controls
73 Handholds with lifting-bars behind
74 Tailskid spring
75 Rear fuselage lacing
76 Fuselage decking
77 Fin solid section
78 Fin frame structure

BRISTOL TYPE 105A BULLDOG II UK

First flown on 21 January 1928, the Bulldog II differed most noticeably from the Bulldog I in having a longer rear fuselage. It was selected as the winner in the F.9/26 contest, the RAF's most hotly-contested programme of the inter-war years (the runner-up being the Hawker Hawfinch). An initial contract for 25 Bulldog IIs was placed in August 1928, these being powered by the 440 hp Bristol Jupiter VII engine and carrying an armament of two 0.303-in (7,7-mm) Browning machine guns. Construction was of high tensile steel strip with fabric skinning. A second contract called for a further 23 aircraft, RAF deliveries commencing on 8 May 1929. Twelve Bulldog IIs with Gnome-Rhône Jupiter VI engines and Oerlikon machine guns were supplied to Latvia and 12 similar aircraft were sold to Estonia, 11 of the Estonian aircraft eventually being resold to Spain.

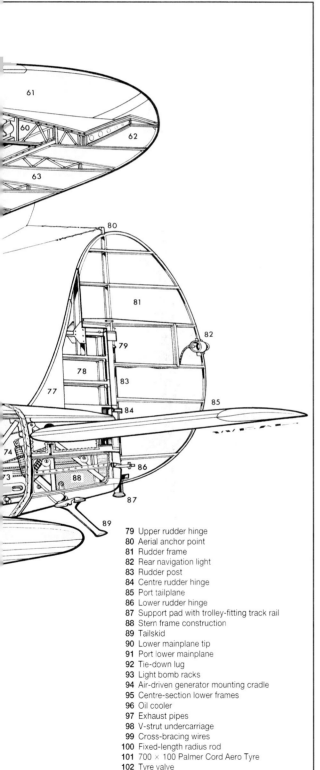

79 Upper rudder hinge
80 Aerial anchor point
81 Rudder frame
82 Rear navigation light
83 Rudder post
84 Centre rudder hinge
85 Port tailplane
86 Lower rudder hinge
87 Support pad with trolley-fitting track rail
88 Stern frame construction
89 Tailskid
90 Lower mainplane tip
91 Port lower mainplane
92 Tie-down lug
93 Light bomb racks
94 Air-driven generator mounting cradle
95 Centre-section lower frames
96 Oil cooler
97 Exhaust pipes
98 V-strut undercarriage
99 Cross-bracing wires
100 Fixed-length radius rod
101 700 × 100 Palmer Cord Aero Tyre
102 Tyre valve
103 Wheel spokes
104 Axle strut
105 Wheel cover

(Above and below) The Bulldog IIA, which was the definitive version of the fighter for RAF service and for export, powered by the Jupiter VIIF engine.

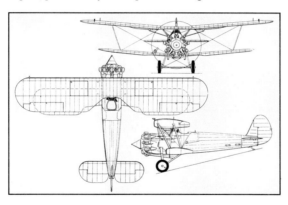

Other Bulldog IIs were sold to the US Navy (2), Siam (2), Sweden (3) and Australia (8). The Bulldog IIA, which embodied a Jupiter VIIF engine and minor structural revisions, was the subject of a contract for 92 aircraft for the RAF to Specification F.11/29, these being delivered between October 1930 and May 1931. Sweden purchased eight Bulldog IIAs, and four special Bulldog IIAs (Type 105D) were supplied to Denmark with unsupercharged Jupiter VIF.H engines and 0.3-in (7,62-mm) Madsen guns. Follow-on RAF contracts brought total

Mk IIA production to 268 aircraft, these having been preceded by 92 Mk IIs (including the prototype). The following data relate to the Mk IIA. *Max speed, 178 mph (286 km/h) at 10,000 ft (3 050 m). Range, 350 mls (563 km). Empty weight, 2,412 lb (1 094 kg). Loaded weight, 3,530 lb (1 601 kg). Span, 33 ft 10 in (10,31 m). Length, 25 ft 0 in (7,62 m). Height, 9 ft 10 in (2,99 m). Wing area, 306.5 sq ft (28,47 m²).*

BRISTOL TYPE 105 BULLDOG IIIA UK

The result of progressive experiments with Mercury engine installations and a series of wind tunnel tests, the Bulldog IIIA was built as a private venture during 1931, being flown for the first time on 17 September of that year. By comparison with the standard Mk IIA, the Bulldog IIIA had deeper, biconvex wing sections, permitting the fuel tanks to be accommodated completely within the wing profile; reduced lower wing chord to improve the pilot's view; single in place of double lift wires; a deeper rear fuselage of increased stiffness; a short-chord Townend ring for the Bristol Mercury IVS.2 engine of 560 hp, and undercarriage wheel spats. The first Bulldog IIIA crashed on 30 March 1933, after demonstrating a 33 mph (53 km/h) speed superiority over the Mk IIA at 15,000 ft (4 572 m). A second prototype was built, also as a private venture, and flown on 13 April 1933, but a year later this was converted as the

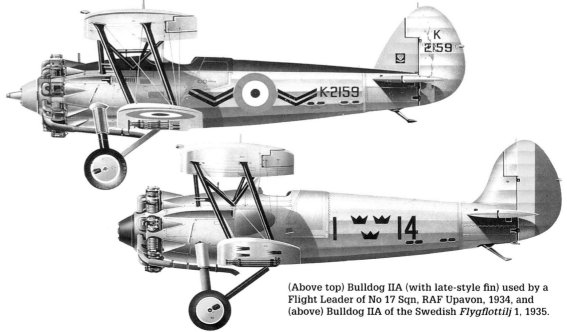

(Above top) Bulldog IIA (with late-style fin) used by a Flight Leader of No 17 Sqn, RAF Upavon, 1934, and (above) Bulldog IIA of the Swedish *Flygflottilj* 1, 1935.

The original Bulldog IIIA, fitted with a Mercury IVS.2 for extended trials at Martlesham Heath.

four-gun Bulldog IV prototype. *Max speed, 208 mph (335 km/h) at 15,000 ft (4 572 m). Empty weight, 2,800 lb (1 270 kg). Loaded weight, 4,000 lb (1 814 kg). Span, 33 ft 8 in (10,26 m). Length, 25 ft 4 in (7,72 m). Height, 9 ft 1 in (2,77 m). Wing area, 294 sq ft (27,31 m²).*

BRISTOL TYPE 105 BULLDOG IVA UK

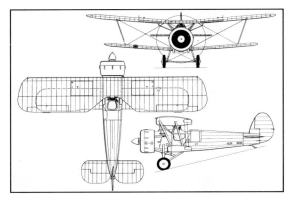

The Bulldog IVA (above) was an export variant of the Bristol fighter biplane, derived from (below) the second Bulldog IIIA built in 1932/33.

Intended to meet the requirements of Specification F.7/30 calling for a four-gun day-and-night fighter, the Bulldog IV prototype was, in fact, the second Bulldog IIIA converted. Flown in its new guise in the spring of 1934, it competed with the Gloster S.S.37 (prototype of the Gladiator) which was eventually selected to fulfil the requirement. However, in April 1934, the Finnish

The first Bulldog IVA for Finland (below), seen in October 1934, still survives in a Finnish museum.

Operating on skis, the Bulldog IVA above in Finnish service in Spring 1942 with TLeLv 35, passed to the Air Fighting School in the following summer.

government signed a contract for 17 Bulldog IVAs powered by the Mercury VIS.2 engine rated at 620 hp for take-off and 654 hp at 15,500 ft (4 724 m), enclosed by a long-chord cowling. Delivered early in 1935, the Finnish Bulldog IVAs carried an armament of two 0.303-in (7,7-mm) Vickers Mk II machine guns and remained in first-line service until the spring of 1940. *Max speed, 175 mph (282 km/h) at sea level and 225 mph (362 km/h) at 16,000 ft (4 877 m). Time to 10,000 ft (3 050 m), 4.68 min. Empty weight, 2,690 lb (1 220 kg). Max loaded weight, 4,100 lb (1 860 kg). Span, 33 ft 8 in (10,26 m). Length, 25 ft 2½ in (7,68 m). Height, 9ft 10¾ in (3,02 m). Wing area, 293.6 sq ft (27,27 m²).*

BRISTOL TYPE 107 BULLPUP UK

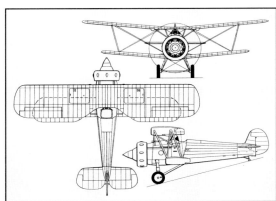

Bristol Type 107 Bullpup with Mercury IIA engine.

Of similar construction to the parallel Type 105 Bulldog, the Bullpup was ordered in prototype form to participate in the F.20/27 interceptor contest. It was first flown on 28 April 1928 with a Jupiter VI engine in place of the 480 hp Bristol Mercury IIA for which it was intended. With the latter engine it was evaluated at Martlesham in the spring of 1929. Smaller and faster than the Bulldog, and possessing superior handling characteristics to those of its stablemate, it was nevertheless

deemed to afford an insufficient advance to warrant production, and the sole prototype was utilised as an engine test-bed until 1935 when it was scrapped. *Max speed, 190 mph (306 km/h). Empty weight, 1,910 lb (866 kg). Loaded weight, 2,850 lb (1 293 kg). Span, 30 ft 0 in (9,14 m). Length, 23 ft 6 in (7,16 m). Height, 9 ft 5 in (2,87 m). Wing area, 230 sq ft (21,37 m²).*

(Below) The Bullpup with original uncowled Jupiter engine and larger rudder fitted after first flight.

BRISTOL TYPE 123 UK

The Type 123 was built as a private venture to meet the requirements of Specification F.7/30, a 695 hp Rolls-Royce Goshawk III steam-cooled engine being provided by the Air Ministry. Of high-tensile steel construction with fabric-covered wings, rear fuselage and tail assembly, the Type 123 carried an armament of four fuselage-mounted 0.303-in (7,7-mm) Vickers machine guns, and was first flown on 12 June 1934, having been delayed by difficulties with the engine cooling system. Subsequently the Type 123 was found to suffer from lateral instability at high speed and further development was abandoned. *Max (design) speed, 235 mph (378 km/h) at 14,000 ft (4 267 m). Empty weight, 3,300 lb (1 497 kg). Loaded weight, 4,737 lb (2 149 kg). Span, 29 ft 7 in (9,02 m). Length, 25 ft 2 in (7,67 m). Height, 9 ft 6 in (2,89 m). Wing area, 248 sq ft (23,04 m²).*

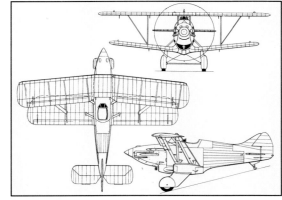

(Above and below) The Bristol Type 123 private-venture fighter prototype, which encountered lateral instability at high speed and was abandoned.

BRISTOL Type 133   UK

A further private venture design for the F.7/30 competition, the Type 133 single-seat fighter featured a forward fuselage of girder-type construction, a monocoque rear fuselage and Alclad stressed skinning. Powered by a Bristol Mercury VIS.2 rated at 620 hp for take-off and carrying an armament of two synchronised 0.303-in (7,7-mm) Vickers guns in the fuselage and a Lewis gun of similar calibre mounted above each mainwheel housing, the Type 133 flew for the first time on 8 June 1934. After completing a considerable amount of flying, on 8 March 1935 the prototype got into a flat spin and the engine stopped, the pilot baling out and the aircraft being destroyed. No further development was undertaken. *Max speed, 260 mph (418 km/h). Empty weight, 2,322 lb (1 053 kg). Loaded weight, 4,738 lb (2 149 kg). Span, 39 ft 0 in (11,89 m). Length, 28 ft 0 in (8,53 m). Height, 9 ft 9 in (2,97 m). Wing area, 247 sq ft (22,95 m²).*

(Above and below) Destroyed after nine months of flight testing, the private-venture Type 133 was Bristol's first low wing monoplane fighter.

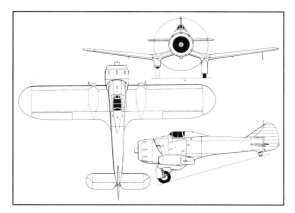

BRISTOL Type 146   UK

Embodying the lessons learned from the Type 133, the Type 146 was a single-seat eight-gun all-metal fighter of monocoque construction with stressed duralumin skinning. Intended to meet the requirements of Specification F.5/34, the Type 146 was designed for a fully-supercharged Bristol Perseus radial of 835 hp, but the sole prototype completed was fitted with an 840 hp Mercury IX owing to the non-availability of the intended power plant. Armament comprised four 0.303-in (7,7-mm) Browning machine guns in each wing. Delayed in completion through its low development priority, the Type 146 was finally flown on 11 February 1938, but was already out-dated by the Merlin-engined Hurricane and Spitfire. After trials at Martlesham Heath, it was returned to the manufacturer to participate in a local RAF display, where it collided with a display set-piece while landing and was scrapped

(Below) The Bristol Type 146, built under Air Ministry contract, introduced eight-gun armament.

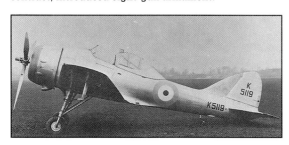

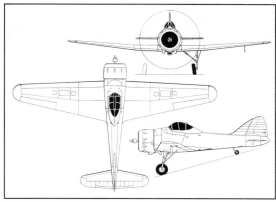

The Bristol Type 146 fighter with Mercury engine.

forthwith. *Max speed, 287 mph (462 km/h) at 15,000 ft (4 572 m). Time to 10,000 ft (3 050 m), 3.67 min. Empty weight, 3,283 lb (1 489 kg). Loaded weight, 4,600 lb (2 086 kg). Span, 39 ft 0 in (11,89 m). Length, 27 ft 0 in (8,23 m). Height, 10 ft 4 in (3,15 m). Wing area, 220 sq ft (20,44 m²).*

BRISTOL Type 142M
BLENHEIM IF   UK

The Blenheim IF three-seat long-range day and night fighter was an adaptation of the standard Blenheim I bomber. Initiated in 1938, this comprised simply the provision of some light armour protection for the pilot and a reflector sight for a quartet of 0.303-in (7,7-mm) Browning machine guns mounted in a ventral pack. These supplemented the normal armament of a single wing-mounted Browning plus a Vickers "K" gun of similar calibre installed in a semi-retractable BI Mk III

(Immediately below) Blenheim IF in day fighter finish, with No 25 Sqn at North Weald in 1940/41 and (bottom) a Blenheim IF of No 54 OTU in all-black night fighter finish.

(Above and below) For operation as a night fighter in 1940-41, the Blenheim IF was fitted with early AI Mk III radar with aerials on the port wing.

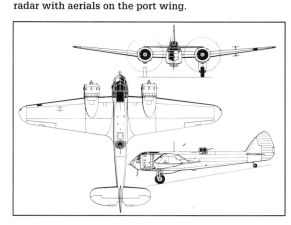

hydraulically-operated dorsal turret. The first RAF squadrons converted to the Blenheim IF late in 1938, and seven squadrons were operating this type when WW II began. Daylight operation in areas where enemy single-seat fighters were active proved suicidal and the type was eventually confined to night fighting, being virtually withdrawn from operations by mid-1941. Powered by two Bristol Mercury VIII radials rated at 840 hp at 14,000 ft (4 267 m), the Blenheim IF provided the bulk of the nocturnal fighter defence of the UK during the winter of 1940-41, equipped with early AI radar. *Max speed, 263 mph (423 km/h) at 10,000 ft (3 050 m), 278 mph (447 km/h) at 15,000 ft (4 572 m). Time to 5,000 ft (1 524 m), 3.9 min. Max range 1,050 mls (1 690 km). Empty equipped weight, 8,840 lb (4 010 kg). Normal loaded weight, 12,200 lb (5 534 kg). Span, 56 ft 4 in (17,17 m). Length, 39 ft 9 in (12,12 m). Height, 9 ft 10 in (3,00 m). Wing area, 469 sq ft (43,57 m²).*

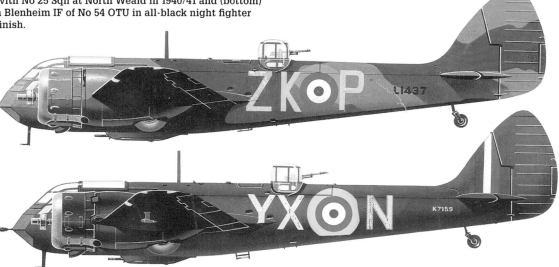

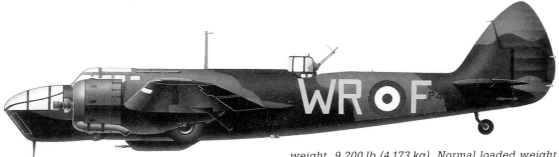

(Above) This Blenheim IVF was flying long-range shipping protection patrols with No 248 Sqn in 1940.

BRISTOL Type 149
BLENHEIM IVF   UK

The Blenheim IVF carried four Brownings in the ventral pack, for service with Coastal Command.

To provide RAF Coastal Command with a long-range anti-shipping strike fighter, the four-gun ventral pack evolved for the Blenheim IF was applied in 1939 to the long-nose Blenheim IVL bomber. This, with reflector gun sight, armour plate, self-sealing tanks and additional radio (including IFF), became the Blenheim IVF, eight Coastal Command squadrons eventually operating the type. Two RAF squadrons (Nos 25 and 600) also operated flights of AI Mk III radar-equipped Blenheim IVFs on nocturnal patrols over the North Sea and the Thames Estuary. Powered by two Bristol Mercury XV radials rated at 995 hp at 9,250 ft (2 820 m), the Blenheim IVF carried the same armament as the Blenheim IF, and had virtually disappeared from first-line service by 1943. *Max speed, 260 mph (418 km/h) at 12,000 ft (3 658 m), 253 mph (407 km/h) at 15,000 ft (4 572 m). Time to 5,000 ft (1 524 m), 4.1 min. Empty equipped weight, 9,200 lb (4 173 kg). Normal loaded weight, 13,800 lb (6 260 kg). Span, 56 ft 4 in (17,17 m). Length, 42 ft 7 in (12,98 m). Height, 9 ft 10 in (3,00 m). Wing area, 469 sq ft (43,57 m²).*

BRISTOL Type 156
BEAUFIGHTER IF   UK

Designed by L G Frise, the Type 156 Beaufighter was virtually a fighter variant of the Type 152 Beaufort reconnaissance and torpedo-bomber, the first of four prototypes flying on 17 July 1939, two weeks after an initial production contract had been placed to Specification F.17/39, calling for 300 aircraft (including the prototypes). As the Beaufighter IF, the first production version was cleared for RAF service on 26 July 1940, being powered by two 1,400 hp Bristol Hercules III engines, supplanted later in the production run by 1,500 hp Hercules XIs. Armament comprised four fuselage-mounted 20-mm Hispano cannon, supplemented, after the first 50 aircraft, by six wing-mounted 0.303-in (7,7-mm) Browning machine guns. AI Mk IV radar was fitted to the Beaufighter IF for the nocturnal rôle from September 1940, and the 100th aircraft was completed on 7 December of that year, with the 200th being rolled out five months later, on 10 May 1941. A variant evolved specifically for RAF Coastal Command for shipping strikes and the protection of coastal shipping was the Beaufighter IC. The following data relate to the Hercules XI-powered Beaufighter IF. *Max speed, 306 mph (492 km/h) at sea level, 323 mph (520 km/h) at 15,000 ft (4 572 m). Time to 10,000 ft (3 050 m), 5.8 min. Normal range, 1,170 mls (1 883 km). Empty equipped weight, 14,069 lb (6 382 kg). Max loaded weight, 21,100 lb (9 571 kg). Span, 57 ft 10 in (17,63 m). Length, 41 ft 4 in (12,60 m). Height, 15 ft 10 in (4,82 m). Wing area, 503 sq ft (46,73 m²).*

(Above top) Beaufighter IF day fighter of No 25 Sqn and (immediately above) a Mk IC of No 252 Sqn.

(Below) Carrying "arrow head" aerials of AI Mk IV, this Beaufighter IF night fighter served with No 604 Sqn.

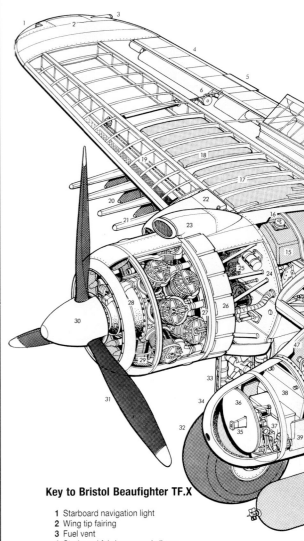

Key to Bristol Beaufighter TF.X

1 Starboard navigation light
2 Wing tip fairing
3 Fuel vent
4 Starboard fabric-covered aileron
5 Aileron tab
6 Aileron hinge control
7 Pneumatic split trailing-edge airbrake (open)
8 Airbrake air ducting
9 Flap hydraulic jack
10 Starboard split trailing-edge flap
11 Nacelle tail fairing
12 Starboard inboard fuel cell
13 Fuel jettison pipe
14 Pneumatic airbrake intake duct
15 Engine oil tank, capacity 18 Imp gal (82 l)
16 Oil filler cap
17 Outboard main fuel cell
18 Outboard long-range fuel tank (replaces machine gun armament bay)
19 Aileron control cable runs
20 90-lb (41-kg) air-to-surface rockets
21 Rocket launch rails
22 Oil cooler air duct
23 Engine air intake duct
24 Fireproof bulkhead
25 Engine accessory equipment bay
26 Cooling air flaps
27 Bristol Hercules XVIII fourteen-cylinder two-row radial engine
28 Propeller reduction gearbox
29 Exhaust collector ring
30 Propeller spinner
31 De Havilland hydromatic three-bladed propeller
32 Starboard mainwheel
33 Starboard main undercarriage leg struts
34 Radome
35 AI Mk VII "centrimetric" radar aerial
36 Radar reflector dish
37 Tilt and azimuth electric motors
38 Armoured cockpit bulkhead
39 Radar equipment access panel
40 Cannon muzzle blast tubes
41 18-in (46-cm) torpedo
42 Torpedo braces
43 Cockpit floor level
44 Rudder pedals
45 Control column
46 Instrument panel

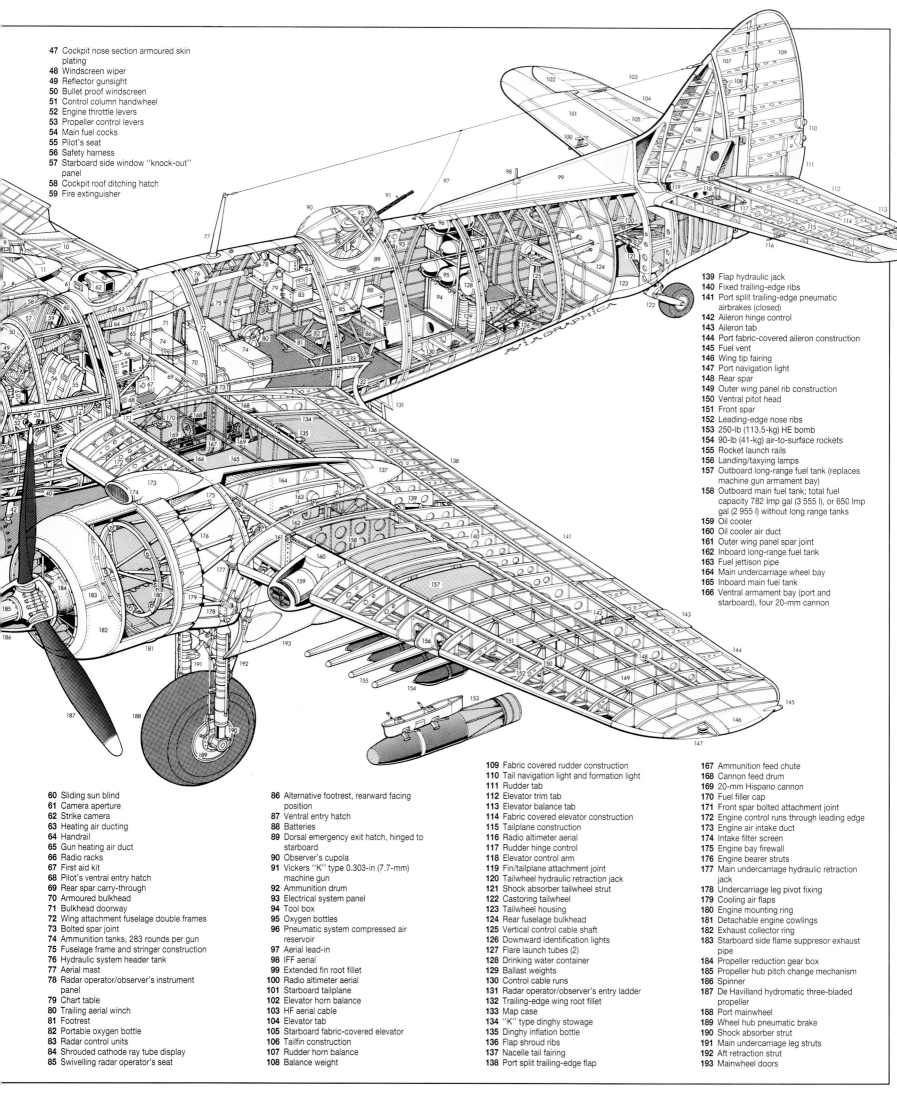

47 Cockpit nose section armoured skin plating
48 Windscreen wiper
49 Reflector gunsight
50 Bullet proof windscreen
51 Control column handwheel
52 Engine throttle levers
53 Propeller control levers
54 Main fuel cocks
55 Pilot's seat
56 Safety harness
57 Starboard side window "knock-out" panel
58 Cockpit roof ditching hatch
59 Fire extinguisher

139 Flap hydraulic jack
140 Fixed trailing-edge ribs
141 Port split trailing-edge pneumatic airbrakes (closed)
142 Aileron hinge control
143 Aileron tab
144 Port fabric-covered aileron construction
145 Fuel vent
146 Wing tip fairing
147 Port navigation light
148 Rear spar
149 Outer wing panel rib construction
150 Ventral pitot head
151 Front spar
152 Leading-edge nose ribs
153 250-lb (113.5-kg) HE bomb
154 90-lb (41-kg) air-to-surface rockets
155 Rocket launch rails
156 Landing/taxying lamps
157 Outboard long-range fuel tank (replaces machine gun armament bay)
158 Outboard main fuel tank; total fuel capacity 782 Imp gal (3 555 l), or 650 Imp gal (2 955 l) without long range tanks
159 Oil cooler
160 Oil cooler air duct
161 Outer wing panel spar joint
162 Inboard long-range fuel tank
163 Fuel jettison pipe
164 Main undercarriage wheel bay
165 Inboard main fuel tank
166 Ventral armament bay (port and starboard), four 20-mm cannon

60 Sliding sun blind
61 Camera aperture
62 Strike camera
63 Heating air ducting
64 Handrail
65 Gun heating air duct
66 Radio racks
67 First aid kit
68 Pilot's ventral entry hatch
69 Rear spar carry-through
70 Armoured bulkhead
71 Bulkhead doorway
72 Wing attachment fuselage double frames
73 Bolted spar joint
74 Ammunition tanks, 283 rounds per gun
75 Fuselage frame and stringer construction
76 Hydraulic system header tank
77 Aerial mast
78 Radar operator/observer's instrument panel
79 Chart table
80 Trailing aerial winch
81 Footrest
82 Portable oxygen bottle
83 Radar control units
84 Shrouded cathode ray tube display
85 Swivelling radar operator's seat

86 Alternative footrest, rearward facing position
87 Ventral entry hatch
88 Batteries
89 Dorsal emergency exit hatch, hinged to starboard
90 Observer's cupola
91 Vickers "K" type 0.303-in (7.7-mm) machine gun
92 Ammunition drum
93 Electrical system panel
94 Tool box
95 Oxygen bottles
96 Pneumatic system compressed air reservoir
97 Aerial lead-in
98 IFF aerial
99 Extended fin root fillet
100 Radio altimeter aerial
101 Starboard tailplane
102 Elevator horn balance
103 HF aerial cable
104 Elevator tab
105 Starboard fabric-covered elevator
106 Tailfin construction
107 Rudder horn balance
108 Balance weight

109 Fabric covered rudder construction
110 Tail navigation light and formation light
111 Rudder tab
112 Elevator trim tab
113 Elevator balance tab
114 Fabric covered elevator construction
115 Tailplane construction
116 Radio altimeter aerial
117 Rudder hinge control
118 Elevator control arm
119 Fin/tailplane attachment joint
120 Tailwheel hydraulic retraction jack
121 Shock absorber tailwheel strut
122 Castoring tailwheel
123 Tailwheel housing
124 Rear fuselage bulkhead
125 Vertical control cable shaft
126 Downward identification lights
127 Flare launch tubes (2)
128 Drinking water container
129 Ballast weights
130 Control cable runs
131 Radar operator/observer's entry ladder
132 Trailing-edge wing root fillet
133 Map case
134 "K" type dinghy stowage
135 Dinghy inflation bottle
136 Flap shroud ribs
137 Nacelle tail fairing
138 Port split trailing-edge flap

167 Ammunition feed chute
168 Cannon feed drum
169 20-mm Hispano cannon
170 Fuel filler cap
171 Front spar bolted attachment joint
172 Engine control runs through leading edge
173 Engine air intake duct
174 Intake filter screen
175 Engine bay firewall
176 Engine bearer struts
177 Main undercarriage hydraulic retraction jack
178 Undercarriage leg pivot fixing
179 Cooling air flaps
180 Engine mounting ring
181 Detachable engine cowlings
182 Exhaust collector ring
183 Starboard side flame suppresor exhaust pipe
184 Propeller reduction gear box
185 Propeller hub pitch change mechanism
186 Spinner
187 De Havilland hydromatic three-bladed propeller
188 Port mainwheel
189 Wheel hub pneumatic brake
190 Shock absorber strut
191 Main undercarriage leg struts
192 Aft retraction strut
193 Mainwheel doors

BRISTOL Type 156 BEAUFIGHTER IIF — UK

At an early stage in the Beaufighter's production life, an alternative Merlin-engined version, the Beaufighter II, was ordered to counter limitations in Hercules engine availability. Three of the first production Beaufighters had been allocated to Rolls-Royce in 1939, and these subsequently served as prototypes for the Beaufighter II, the first flying in July 1940. Powered by 1,260 hp Merlin XX engines, the first production Beaufighter IIF flew on 22 March 1941, but the performance of this model proved disappointing and particularly so when fitted with AI Mk IV radar and sporting the standard soot-black night finish. Only 450 Beaufighter IIs were therefore built, compared with 914 Beaufighter Is. Two Mk IIs were converted as prototype Beaufighter Vs which differed from the standard Merlin-engined variant in having the inboard pair of Hispano cannon and the wing-mounted machine guns supplanted by a Boulton Paul BPA I turret with four 0.303-in (7,7-mm) machine guns located just aft of the pilot's cockpit. Development of the Mk V was subsequently abandoned. Armament of the standard Mk IIF was the same as that of the Mk IF. *Max speed, 283 mph (455 km/h) at 15,000 ft (4 572 m), 321 mph (516 km/h) at 20,200 ft (6 157 m). Normal range, 1,040 mls (1 674 km). Empty equipped weight, 13,600 lb (6 169 kg). Normal loaded weight, 20,290 lb (9 203 kg). Span, 57 ft 10 in (17,63 m). Length, 42 ft 9 in (13,03 m). Height, 15 ft 10 in (4,82 m). Wing area, 503 sq ft (46,73 m²).*

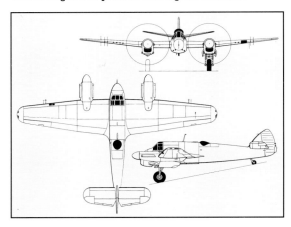

The Beaufighter IIF (above and below), with AI Mk IV radar for night fighting, was distinguished by having Merlin engines in place of the original Hercules.

BRISTOL Type 156 BEAUFIGHTER VIF — UK

Early in 1941, the Bristol Hercules VI engine rated at 1,635 hp at 6,000 ft (1 829 m) became available for Beaufighter installation. Designated Beaufighter VI with the more powerful engines, this model supplanted the interim Hercules XI-powered Mk I and began to enter service with both Fighter Command and Coastal Command at the beginning of 1942. For the nocturnal intercept rôle, the Beaufighter VIF was fitted with centimetric AI Mk VII radar in the "thimble" nose. In March 1942, work began on the adaptation of Coastal Command's Beaufighter VIC for the torpedo-fighter rôle with a single 22.5-in (57,15-cm) US or 18-in (45,7-cm) British torpedo. The introduction of the torpedo-carrying Beaufighter VIC revolutionised air-sea warfare. From May 1943, Beaufighter VICs carrying eight rocket projectiles in lieu of wing guns were also introduced. Total production of the Mks VIC and VIF amounted to 1,852 aircraft. *Max speed, 333 mph (536 km/h) at 15,600 ft (4 755 m), 325 mph (523 km/h) at 8,500 ft (2 590 m). Normal range, 1,540 mls (2 478 km) at 190 mph (306 km/h). Empty equipped weight, 14,600 lb*

As a night fighter, the Beaufighter VIF introduced the improved AI Mk VII radar in a "thimble" nose fairing.

(6 622 kg). Max loaded weight, 21,600 lb (9 798 kg). Span, 57 ft 10 in (17,63 m). Length, 41 ft 8 in (12,70 m). Height, 15 ft 10 in (4,82 m). Wing area, 503 sq ft (46,73 m²).

BRISTOL Type 156 BEAUFIGHTER TF X — UK

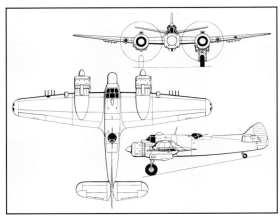

The Bristol Beaufighter TF Mk X in final configuration.

The Beaufighter TF X anti-shipping strike fighter differed from the Mk VIC in having Hercules XVII engines better suited for the low altitudes at which Coastal Command operated its Beaufighters. Apart from early production examples, it standardised on AI Mk VIII radar (which had been found suitable for the air-to-surface mode) in a "thimble" nose. A Vickers 0.303-in (7,7-mm) "K" gun was introduced for use by the observer, and two 250-lb (113,4-kg) and two 500-lb (226,8-kg) bombs or eight rockets could be carried as alterna-

tive offensive loads to the torpedo. To rectify some deterioration of handling owing to increased weights, a large dorsal fin and elevators of increased area were introduced. The TF Mk X was usually operated as a two-seater, but provision was made for a third crew member. Production of the TF Mk X totalled 2,205, and a further 163 of an essentially similar variant, the Beaufighter XIC, were produced, these differing only in that they lacked torpedo gear. Production of a version basically similar to the TF Mk X was undertaken in Australia as the Beaufighter Mk 21. Four 0-5-in (12,7-mm) guns replaced the six 0.303-in (7,7-mm) weapons in the wings and Hercules XVIII engines were installed. The first Mk 21 flew on 26 May 1944, and a total of 364 was built. The following data relate to the TF Mk X. *Max speed, 303 mph (488 km/h) at 1,300 ft (396 m); 318 mph (512 km/h) at 10,000 ft (3 050 m). Normal range, 1,470 mls (2 366 km) at 205 mph (330 km/h). Empty equipped weight, 15,592 lb (7 072 kg). Max loaded weight, 25,400 lb (11 521 kg). Span, 57 ft 10 in (17,63 m). Length, 41 ft 8 in (12,70 m). Height, 15 ft 10 in (4,82 m). Wing area, 503 sq ft (46,73 m²).*

BRITISH AEROSPACE SEA HARRIER — UK

A single-seat shipboard V/STOL multi-role fighter derived from the Hawker Siddeley Kestrel via the Harrier close air support and tactical reconnaissance aircraft, the Sea Harrier stemmed from initial project design studies completed early in 1972 by Hawker

The British Aerospace Sea Harrier FRS Mk 1.

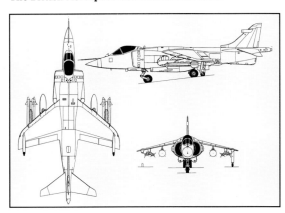

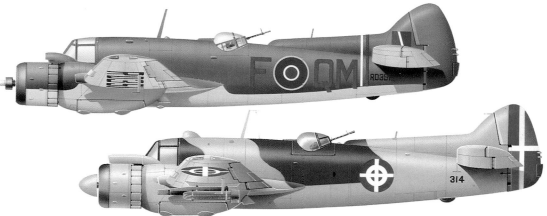

(Above top) Beaufighter TF Mk X of No 254 Sqn in 1944/45 and (above) a Dominican TF Mk X in 1948.

(Below) A late production Beaufighter TF Mk X with extended dorsal fin and underwing rocket projectiles.

(Above) A pair of Sea Harrier FRS Mk 1s, displaying the chequerboard rudders of 801 NAS, HMS *Invincible*.

The Sea Harrier FRS Mk 2 (below) introduced Blue Vixen pulse-Doppler radar and AIM-120A missiles.

Siddeley. A decision to proceed with full development was announced on 15 May 1975, the first Sea Harrier flew on 20 August 1978, and 57 of the initial production version, the FRS Mk 1, were supplied to the Royal Navy, plus 23 essentially similar Mk 51s to the Indian Navy. Powered by a 21,500 lb st (9 750 kgp) Rolls-Royce Pegasus 104 vectored-thrust turbofan, the Sea Harrier FRS Mk 1 had provision for four wing pylon-mounted AIM-9 Sidewinder (Matra Magic on Mk 51) AAMs, plus two ASMs of Sea Eagle or Harpoon type. Two 30-mm cannon pods could be attached beneath the fuselage. A mid-life upgrade of the FRS Mk 1 included provision of Blue Vixen pulse-Doppler radar providing "look-down/shoot-down" capability, the ability to carry four AIM-120 AAMs, a lengthened rear fuselage resulting from insertion of a 13.75-in (35-cm) plug aft of wing trailing edge, a redesigned cockpit, improved systems and a Pegasus 106 with the same rating as the 104. With these changes the fighter became the Sea Harrier FRS Mk 2, the first of two development aircraft flying on 19 September 1988. Now redesignated FA2, 29 Sea Harriers remain in service; about half new-build; the others upgraded FRS1s, the last of which was delivered in 2000. The following data relate to the FRS Mk 2. *Max speed, 720 mph (1 159 km/h) at 1,000 ft (305 m), or Mach=0.95, 607 mph (977 km/h) at 36,000 ft (10 975 m), or Mach=0. 92. Combat radius (high-altitude intercept), 480 mls (772 km). Empty weight (operational), 14,500 lb (6 577 kg). Max loaded weight, 26,500 lb (12 020 kg). Span, 27ft 3 in (8,31 m). Length, 46 ft 3 in (14,10 m). Height, 12 ft 2 in (3,71 m). Wing area, 201.1 sq ft (18,68 m²).*

BRITISH AEROSPACE HAWK 200 UK

The Hawk 200 is a single-seat dedicated multi-rôle lightweight fighter derivative of the two-seat Hawk basic/advanced trainer and light tactical aircraft. It shares with the Hawk 100 tandem two-seat advanced systems trainer and light attack aircraft much of the avionic equipment and the Rolls-Royce Turboméca Adour 871 turbofan of 5,845 lb st (2 650 kgp), 80 per cent structural commonality with the two-seater being retained aft of the cockpit. Armament could comprise either one or two internally-mounted 25-mm or 27-mm cannon, the maximum ordnance load (including the cannon) being 7,700 lb (3 500 kg). The first prototype Hawk 200 was flown on 19 May 1986, with the first pre-production aircraft following on 24 April 1987. A further demonstrator, fitted with APG-66H radar, flew on 13 February 1992. Customers included Indonesia (16 Mk 209), Oman (12 Mk 203) and Malaysia (18 Mk 208). *Max speed, 645 mph (1 038 km/h) at 8,000 ft (2 440 m), or Mach=0.87. Range (internal fuel), 554 mls (892 km). Empty weight, 9,100 lb (4 128 kg). Max loaded weight, 20,065*

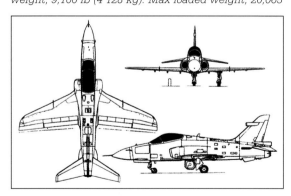

(Above) The single-seat BAe Hawk 200, in its production form and (below) carrying a full external load of seven 1,100-1b (500-kg) bombs.

lb (9 101 kg). Span, 30 ft 9³/₄ in (9,39 m). Length, 37 ft 4 in (11,38 m). Height, 13 ft 8 in (4,16 m). Wing area, 179.64 sq ft (16,69 m²).

BURGESS (HT-B) HT-2 USA

In the late autumn of 1916, the US Navy framed a requirement which, issued on 17 November, called for a float-equipped single-seat fighting scout with a max speed of at least 95 mph (153 km/h) and an endurance of 2.5 hrs. It was envisaged that a 165 hp Gnome Mono-soupape 9N rotary engine would be used. To meet this requirement, W Starling Burgess of the Burgess Company of Marblehead, Mass, a division of the Curtiss Aeroplane and Motor Corporation, produced the HT-B which was demonstrated to the Navy Department on 19 May 1917. A fabric-covered wooden sesquiplane in which close attention had been paid to aerodynamic cleanliness, the HT-B had fabric-covered K-type interplane struts, the short floats embodying shock absorbers. The intended armament comprised a single 0.3-in (7,62-mm) machine gun, but the rotary engine being unavailable, the HT-B was fitted with a water-cooled Curtiss OXX-2 of 100 hp. With this it was underpowered, max attainable speed being 85 mph (137 km/h). Nevertheless, the Navy considered the HT-B to possess excellent aerodynamic and hydrodynamic qualities, placing a contract for six examples (later amended to include two additional aircraft). Known unofficially as the Speed Scout, the first HT-B was delivered to Squantum on 11 September 1917, and the second to Pensacola in the following month, neither carrying armament. These were followed by six more of a slightly modified version known as the HT-2, all being delivered by the end of 1917. No details of the subsequent career in US Navy service of the HT-B are available, but this is understood to have been brief and did not long survive the demise of the Burgess Company in November 1918. *Max speed, 85 mph (137 km/h) at 1,000 ft (305 m). Endurance, 2.0 hrs. Span, 34 ft 4 in (10,46 m). Length, 22 ft 3 in (6,87 m). Height, 10 ft 9 in (3,28 m).*

(Above) Also known as the Speed Scout, the Burgess HT-B sesquiplane was the prototype for the slightly modified H-2 (below) of which six were built in 1917.

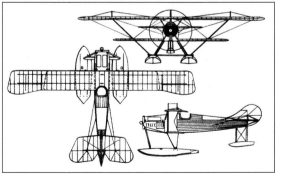

BUSCAYLET-BECHEREAU 2 France

A derivative of the Letord-Béchereau 2 embodying some redesign and built by Buscaylet Père et Fils-Bobin, the BB2 single-seat fighter was tendered to meet the requirements of the 1923 C1 programme and the sole prototype was flown in 1924. Powered by a 500 hp Salmson 18Cm 18-cylinder water-cooled engine driving the propeller via an extension shaft, the BB2 was of essentially similar configuration to that of the earlier LB2, but replaced the inclined aerofoil surfaces between the undercarriage structure and mid span with very substantial struts. Armament comprised the standard pair of 7,7-mm machine guns. Prototype trials proved disappointing and the aircraft was discarded from the official short list of contenders. However, further development as a *two*-seat fighter was later undertaken by its designer, Louis Béchereau, after his appointment as chief of the airframe design staff of the Salmson company. *Max speed, 155 mph (250 km/h) at 9,840 ft (3 000 m). Empty weight, 2,976 lb (1 350 kg). Loaded weight, 3,876 lb (1 758 kg). Span, 45 ft 11⅓ in (14,00 m). Length, 32 ft 9⁷⁄₁₀ in (10,00 m). Height, 9 ft 10 in (3,00 m). Wing area, 419.81 sq ft (39,00 m²).*

(Above and below) The Buscaylet-Béchereau 2 was offered for the 1923 C1 programme, but testing in 1924 proved this sole prototype to be unsatisfactory.

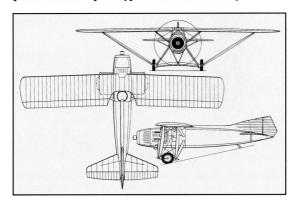

BUSCAYLET-DE MONGE 5/2 France

During 1922, Buscaylet Père et Fils-Bobin produced an exceptionally clean single-seat parasol fighter monoplane designed by Louis de Monge. Known as the Buscaylet-de Monge 5/2, the fighter was of metal construction with metal fuselage skinning and wooden wing skinning. Provision was made to fit auxiliary stub wings (serving to increase the wing area from 258.34 sq ft/24,0 m² to 344.46 sq ft/32,0 m²) to convert the aircraft to sesquiplane configuration for the high altitude rôle. Powered by a 300 hp Hispano-Suiza 8Fb

The Buscaylet-de Monge 5/2 parasol fighter.

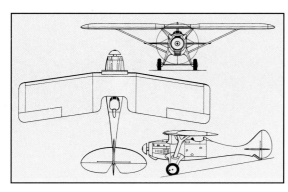

Key to British Aerospace Sea Harrier FRS.Mk 1

1 Pitot tube
2 Radome
3 Flat plate radar scanner
4 Scanner tracking mechanism
5 Ferranti Blue Fox radar equipment module
6 Radome hinge
7 Nose pitch reaction control valve
8 Pitch feel and trim mechanism
9 Starboard side oblique camera
10 Inertial platform
11 Pressurisation spill valve
12 IFF aerial
13 Cockpit ram air intake
14 Yaw vane
15 Cockpit front pressure bulkhead
16 Rudder pedals
17 Cockpit floor level
18 TACAN aerial
19 Ventral Doppler navigation aerial
20 Canopy external latch
21 Control column
22 Windscreen de-misting air duct
23 Instrument panel
24 Instrument panel shroud
25 Birdproof windscreen panels
26 Windscreen wiper
27 Head-up display
28 Starboard side console panel
29 Nozzle angle control lever
30 Engine throttle lever
31 Underfloor control linkages
32 Lower UHF aerial
33 Radome, open position
34 Detachable in-flight refuelling probe
35 Pre-closing nosewheel doors
36 Ejection seat rocket pack
37 Radar hand controller
38 Fuel cock
39 Cockpit rear pressure bulkhead
40 Cabin air discharge valve
41 Canopy handle
42 Pilot's Martin-Baker Type 10 zero-zero ejection seat
43 Sliding canopy rail
44 Miniature detonating cord (MDC) canopy breaker
45 Starboard engine-air intake
46 Cockpit canopy cover
47 Ejection seat headrest
48 Drogue parachute container
49 Parachute release mechanism
50 Boundary layer spill duct
51 Cockpit air conditioning plant
52 Intake centre-body fairing
53 Ram air discharge to engine intake
54 Hydraulic accumulator
55 Nose undercarriage hydraulic jack
56 Boundary layer bleed air duct
57 Nose undercarrige wheel bay
58 Port engine-air intake
59 Landing/taxiing lamp
60 Nosewheel forks
61 Pivoted axle beam
62 Nosewheel, forward retracting
63 Supplementary air intake doors (fully floating)
64 Intake duct framing
65 Air refuelling probe mounting and fuel connector
66 Engine intake compressor face
67 Air conditioning system ram air intakes
68 Boundary layer air spill duct canopy cut-out
69 UHF homing aerials
70 Engine bay access doors
71 Rolls-Royce Pegasus Mk 104 vectored thrust turbofan engine
72 Hydraulic filters
73 Engine oil tank
74 Forward fuselage integral fuel tank, port and starboard
75 Engine bay venting air scoop
76 Hydraulic system ground connections
77 Cushion augmentation strake, port and starboard, fitted in place of gun pack
78 Engine monitoring and recording equipment
79 Forward nozzle fairing
80 Fan air (cold stream) swivelling nozzle
81 Nozzle bearing
82 In-flight refuelling floodlight
83 Venting air intake
84 Alternator cooling air duct
85 Hydraulic pumps
86 Engine accessory equipment gearbox
87 Single alternator on starboard side
88 GTS/APU exhaust
89 Gas turbine starter/Auxiliary Power Unit (GTS/APU)
90 Aileron control rod
91 Wing front spar carry through
92 Nozzle bearing cooling air duct
93 Engine turbine section
94 Wing panel centreline joint rib
95 Wing centre section fairing panels
96 GTS/APU air intake
97 Alternator cooling air exhaust
98 190-Imp gal (864-l) jettisonable external fuel tank
99 Starboard inner stores pylon
100 Leading-edge dog-tooth
101 Reaction control air ducting
102 Aileron control rod
103 Starboard wing integral fuel tank; total internal fuel capacity 630 Imp gal (2 865 l)
104 Fuel system piping
105 Inboard pylon attachment hardpoint
106 Starboard twin Sidewinder installation
107 Starboard outer stores pylon
108 Wing fences
109 Vortex generators
110 Outer pylon hardpoint
111 Aileron hydraulic power control unit
112 Roll control reaction air valve
113 Starboard navigation light
114 Wing tip fairing
115 Starboard outrigger fairing
116 Outrigger wheel, retracted position
117 Sea Harrier FRS Mk 2 ventral view
118 Blue Vixen radar
119 AIM-120 advanced medium range air-to-air missiles (AMRAAM), four
120 Fuel-tank-mounted missile pylon
121 Rear fuselage stretched avionics equipment bay
122 Ventral gun packs
123 Starboard aileron
124 Fuel jettison pipe
125 Starboard plain flap
126 Trailing-edge root fairing
127 Water-methanol filler cap
128 Wing slinging point
129 Anti-collision light
130 Water-methanol injection system tank
131 Engine fire extinguisher bottle
132 Flap operating rod
133 Flap hydraulic jack
134 Fuel contents transmitters
135 Rear fuselage integral fuel tank
136 Ram air turbine housing
137 Turbine doors
138 Emergency ram air turbine (extended position)
139 Rear fuselage frames
140 Ram air turbine jack
141 Cooling system ram air intake
142 Air system heat exchanger
143 HF tuner
144 HF notch aerial
145 Rudder control linkage
146 Starboard all-moving tailplane
147 Temperature sensor
148 Tailfin construction
149 Forward radar warning receiver
150 VHF aerial
151 Fin tip aerial fairing
152 Rudder
153 Rudder top hinge

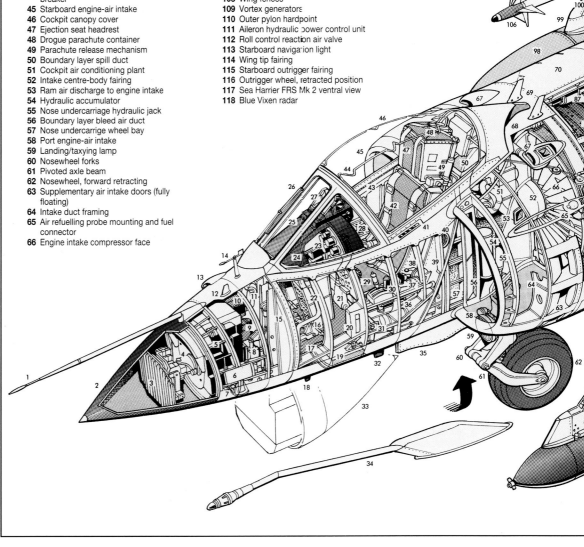

154 Honeycomb core construction
155 Rudder trim jack
156 Rudder tab
157 Tail reaction control air ducting
158 Yaw control port
159 Aft radar warning receiver
160 Rear position light
161 Pitch reaction control air valve
162 Tailplane honeycomb trailing-edge
163 Extended tailplane tip
164 Tailplane construction

165 Tail bumper
166 IFF notch aerial
167 Tailplane sealing plate
168 Fin spar attachment
169 Tailplane centre-section carry-through
170 All-moving tailplane control jack
171 Radar altimeter aerials
172 UHF standby aerial
173 Ram air exhaust
174 Equipment air conditioning plant
175 Ground power supply socket

176 Twin batteries
177 Chaff and flare dispensers
178 Dispenser electronic control units
179 Avionics equipment racks
180 Avionics bay access door
181 Ventral airbrake
182 Airbrake hydraulic jack
183 Liquid oxygen converter
184 Nitrogen pressurising bottle for hydraulic system
185 Flap drive torque shaft

186 Rear spar/fuselage attachment point
187 Nozzle blast shield
188 Rear (hot stream) swivelling exhaust nozzle
189 Wing rear spar
190 Port flap honeycomb core construction
191 Fuel jettison valve
192 Fuel jettison pipe
193 Aileron honeycomb core construction
194 Outrigger wheel fairing
195 Wing tip fairing

196 Hydraulic retraction jack
197 Shock absorber leg strut
198 Port outrigger wheel
199 Torque scissor links
200 Outrigger wheel leg fairings
201 Port navigation light
202 Roll control reaction air valve
203 Wing rib construction
204 Outer pylon hardpoint
205 Machined wing skin/stringer panel
206 Aileron power control unit
207 Front spar
208 Leading-edge nose ribs
209 Reaction control air ducting
210 Port outer stores pylon
211 Twin missile adaptor
212 Missile launch rails
213 AIM-9L Sidewinder air-to-air missiles
214 Leading-edge fences
215 Inboard stores pylon
216 Inboard pylon hardpoint
217 Fuel and air connections to pylon
218 Port wing fuel tank end rib
219 Pressure refuelling connection
220 Wing bottom skin panel/fuselage attachment point
221 No 1 hydraulic system reservoir (No 2 system to starboard)
222 Centre fuselage integral fuel tank, port and starboard
223 Nozzle fairing construction
224 Leading-edge dog-tooth
225 Twin mainwheels, aft retracting
226 190-Imp gal (864-l) external fuel tank
227 Fuselage centreline pylon
228 1,000-lb (454-kg) HE bomb
229 Ventral cannon pack
230 Frangible nose cap
231 Blast suppression ports
232 Cannon barrel
233 Aden 30-mm revolver type cannon
234 Link ejection chute
235 Ammunition feed chute
236 Ammunition tank, 100 rounds
237 BAe Dynamics Sea Eagle air-to-surface (anti-shipping) missile
238 RN 2-in (5.1-cm) rocket pack
239 Matra M.550 "Magic" air-to-air missile (Indian Navy aircraft only)

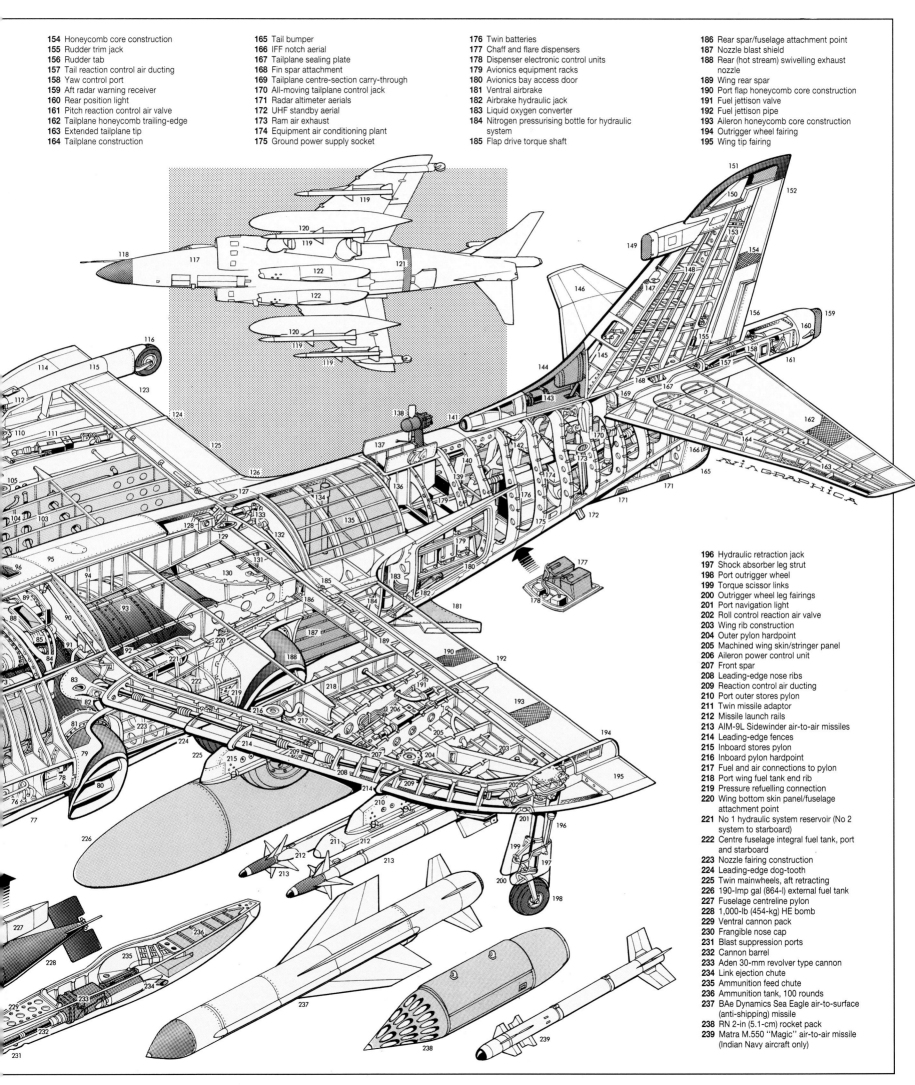

Designed to be readily adaptable as a sesquiplane, the Buscaylet-de Monge 5/2 flew only as a monoplane.

water-cooled engine and carrying an armament of two 7,7-mm synchronised machine guns, the Buscaylet-de Monge 5/2 was flown for the first time in 1923 at Villa-coublay, but was declared *trop moderne* for service use, further development being abandoned. *Max speed, 168 mph (270 km/h) at sea level, 162 mph (260 km/h) at 6,560 ft (2 000 m). Loaded weight, 2,976 lb (1 350 kg). Span, 35 ft 9⅛ in (10,90 m). Length, 23 ft 5½ in (7,15 m). Height, 8 ft 10¼ in (2,70 m). Wing area, 258.34 sq ft (24,0 m²).*

C

CAMS 31   France

The only fighter among the long line of flying boats produced in the 'twenties and 'thirties by the Chantiers Aéro-Maritimes de la Seine, the CAMS 31 single-seat two-bay equi-span unstaggered biplane was flown for the first time in November 1922. Of wooden construction and carrying an armament of two fixed forward-firing 7,7-mm Vickers machine guns, the CAMS 31 was powered by a 300 hp Hispano-Suiza 8Fb water-cooled engine driving a two-bladed pusher propeller. A second prototype was built and flown in 1923, this having a shorter-span (34 ft 11¾ in/10,66 m), broader-chord wing possessing the same gross area, the two prototypes being respectively known as the Types 22 and 23 (indicating the year in which each aircraft first flew). No production was undertaken. The CAMS 31, like other CAMS 'boats, was designed by the CGCA (Compagnie Générale de Constructions Aéronautiques) to which the rights reverted in 1925, whereupon this fighter was restyled Météore 31. The following data relate specifically to the CAMS 31 Type 22. *Max speed, 124 mph (200 km/h) at sea level. Time to 3,280 ft (1 000 m), 3 min. Range, 248 mls (400 km). Empty weight, 2,304 lb (1 045 kg). Loaded weight, 3,320 lb (1 506 kg). Span, 36 ft 8⅞ in (11,20 m). Length, 28 ft 10½ in (8,80 m). Height, 10 ft 0½ in (3,06 m). Wing area, 355.22 sq ft (33,00 m²).*

The CAMS 31 flying boat (below) did not proceed beyond the construction of two prototypes.

CANADAIR CL-13 SABRE   Canada

With the selection in 1948 by the RCAF of the North American F-86A Sabre as its next-generation fighter it was envisaged from the outset that the indigenous Orenda engine would replace the J47. In the event, this intention was to be frustrated by delays in power plant availability, and it was not until 30 July 1953 that a pre-series aircraft was flown with the Canadian engine as the CL-13A Sabre 5. Almost three years prior to this

Built under North American licence, the CL-13A Sabre 5 (above) used the Orenda 10 engine.

event, North American had re-engined an F-86A-5 with an Orenda 3 as the F-86A/O, this having flown in October 1950. The 100th licence-built F-86E airframe completed by Canadair had been similarly powered as the CL-13 Sabre 3 (alias F-86J) and flown on 4 June 1952.

The Canadair-built Sabre 6 (above) featured full-span slats and the more powerful Orenda 14 turbojet.

Fitted with a 6,355 lb st (2 883 kgp) Avro Orenda 10 turbojet, the Sabre 5 retained the armament of six 0.5-in (12,7-mm) machine guns and had the slatless extended wing leading edge introduced on the F-86F. A total of 370 Sabre 5s was built, of which 75 were presented to the Federal German *Luftwaffe*, before production deliveries commenced of what was to prove the definitive Canadair-built model, the CL-13B Sabre 6, first flown on 2 November 1954. This differed essentially from the Sabre 5 in having the two-stage Orenda 14 of 7,275 lb st (3 300 kgp), and initial aircraft had a wing similar to that of the Sabre 5, but later Sabre 6s reinstated wing slats. Of the 655 Sabre 6s built, six were supplied to Colombia, 34 to South Africa and 225 to Federal Germany. The CL-13C was a Sabre 5 with an area-ruled fuselage and the CL-13E was a Sabre 6 fitted with an afterburner. The following data relate to the Sabre 6. *Max speed, 710 mph (1 143 km/h) at sea level, 620 mph (998 km/h) at 36,000 ft (10 975 m). Initial climb, 11,800 ft/min (60 m/sec). Empty weight, 10,618 lb (4 816 kg). Loaded weight (clean), 14,613 lb (6 628 kg). Span, 37 ft 1½ in (11,31 m). Length, 37 ft 6 in (11,43 m). Height, 14 ft 9 in (4,50 m). Wing area, 313.37 sq ft (29,11 m²).*

CANT 25   Italy

Developed by the Cantieri Riuniti dell'Adriatico, the CANT 25 was a single-seat shipboard fighter flying boat of wooden construction mounting a fixed forward-firing armament of two 7,7-mm Vickers machine guns. The initial version, the CANT 25M which appeared in 1931 and was used for catapult trials aboard Italian war-

ships, had Warren truss-type interplane bracing and was powered by a 410 hp Fiat A.20 12-cylinder water-cooled engine driving a two-bladed pusher propeller. This type was succeeded by the CANT 25 AR (*Ali Ripiegabili*, or Folding Wings) powered by a 440 hp version of the A.20 engine, and featuring vertical interplane bracing struts, strengthened tailplane bracing and aft-folding outer wing panels. The following specification relates to the CANT 25 AR. *Max speed, 152 mph (245 km/h) at sea level. Time to 16,405 ft (5 000 m), 26.5 min. Range, 559 mls (900 km) at 74.5 mph (120 km/h). Empty weight, 2,813 lb (1 276 kg). Loaded weight, 3,761 lb (1 706 kg). Span, 34 ft 1½ in (10,40 m). Length, 28 ft 8½ in (8,75 m). Height, 10 ft 2⅘ in (3,12 m). Wing area, 332.6 sq ft (30,90 m²).*

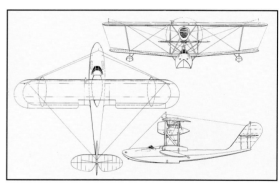

The CANT 25AR fighter flying boat (above) had folding wings, the original CANT 25M (below) having Warren-truss interplane bracing.

CANTILEVER AERO BULLET   USA

The first of two single-seat cantilever sesquiplanes designed by Dr William W Christmas of the Cantilever Aero Company with the assistance of Vincent J Burnelli, and built by the Continental Aircraft Company, was flown for the first time in mid-January 1919. It crashed and was totally destroyed shortly after its first take-off. Initially known as the Scout and subsequently as the Bullet (or Christmas Bullet), it was powered by a 185 hp Liberty 6 six-cylinder water-cooled engine and was primarily of wooden construction. Unusual features included the use of internal rotating torque tubes to operate the ailerons (although conventional cables were fitted at one stage) and a warping tailplane. The second prototype was powered by a Hall-Scott L-6 six-cylinder water-cooled engine and this also crashed on its first flight in the summer of 1919, development subsequently being abandoned. The following performance data were claimed but are believed exaggerated. *Max speed, 175 mph (282 km/h). Ceiling, 14,700 ft (4 480 m). Range, 550 mls (885 km). Empty weight, 1,820 lb (825 kg). Loaded weight, 2,100 lb (952,5 kg). Span, 28 ft 0 in (8,53 m). Length 21 ft 0 in (6,40 m). Wing area, 170 sq ft (15,79 m²).*

(Above and below) The first of the two Christmas Bullets, both of which crashed on their first flights.

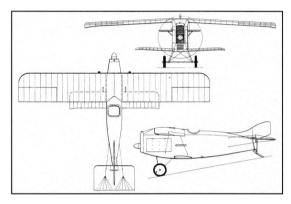

CAO 200 France

Built by the Société National de Constructions Aéronautiques de l'Ouest (SNCAO) at the former Nieuport plant as a progressive development of the Loire-Nieuport 161, the CAO 200 single-seat fighter was designed by M Marie and was intended to take the 1,100 hp Hispano-Suiza 12Y-51 12-cylinder liquid-cooled engine.

The sole CAO 200 (above and below), flown early-1939 as a prospective competitor for the D.520, was developed from the Loire-Nieuport 161.

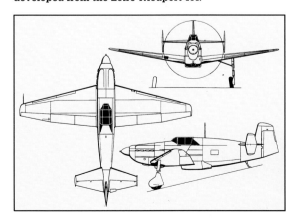

However, the sole prototype, which first flew on 31 January 1939, was fitted with an 860 hp HS 12Y-31 and proved somewhat underpowered. Of all-metal construction and making extensive use of electric welding,

the CAO 200 carried an armament of one engine-mounted 20-mm Hispano-Suiza 404 cannon and two wing-mounted 7,5-mm MAC 1934 machine guns. Development of the CAO 200 was abandoned as the competitive Dewoitine D.520 had already been selected for quantity production for the *Armée de l'Air*, and reports that work was initiated on a pre-production batch of CAO 200s and that the sole prototype participated in the defence of Chateauroux had no foundation in fact. *Max speed, 277 mph (446 km/h) at sea level, 342 mph (550 km/h) at 19,685 ft (6 000 m). Time to 6,560 ft (2 000 m), 2.45 min. Endurance, 2.0 hrs. Normal loaded weight, 5,511 lb (2 500 kg). Span, 31 ft 2 in (9,50 m). Length, 29 ft 2⅓ in (8,90 m). Height, 11 ft 5½ in (3,50 m). Wing area, 143.16 sq ft (13,30 m²).*

CAPRONI Ca 70 Italy

Claiming the distinction of having been the only Italian warplane designed from the outset as a dedicated night fighter, the Ca 70 was an unequal-span biplane in which emphasis was placed on good visibility from the two cockpits, unobstructed by structure, and low-speed handling. Powered by a 420 hp Bristol Jupiter nine-cylinder radial, the Ca 70 was of unusual configuration for a land-based aircraft. Its unconventional features included an ingenious oleo-pneumatic undercarriage shock absorber permitting the wheels to travel forward on their linkage during taxying. Armament comprised two fixed 7,7-mm Vickers machine guns and a Lewis gun of similar calibre on a Scarff-type mounting in the rear cockpit. Flown for the first time in 1925, the Ca 70 underwent official tests in the following year at Montecelio. Although it demonstrated good handling and performance characteristics, the Ca 70 aroused little official interest. *Max speed, 127 mph (205 km/h). Time to 13,125 ft (4 000 m), 14 min. Endurance, 2.0 hrs. Empty weight, 2,712 lb (1 230 kg). Loaded weight, 3,704 lb (1 680 kg). Span, 49 ft 2½ in (15,00 m). Length, 31 ft 4 in (9,55 m). Height, 12 ft 4¾ in (3,78 m). Wing area, 592 sq ft (55,00 m²).*

(Below) The Jupiter-engined Ca 70 night fighter.

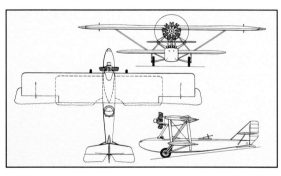

CAPRONI Ca 71 (Ca 70L) Italy

Despite the strictly limited official interest in an optimised two-seat night fighter that had been aroused by the Ca 70, Caproni persisted with the design, and, in

(Below) The Ca 70 of 1925 was designed for night fighting, with emphasis on good visibility.

At first known as the Ca 70L, the Ca 71 differed from the Ca 70 design in having a pusher engine.

1927, submitted a derivative for evaluation. This, initially known as the Ca 70L and subsequently as the Ca 71, differed from the original Ca 70 essentially in engine installation. Whereas the engine of the Ca 70 had been mounted as a tractor, that of the Ca 71 was installed as a pusher, and provision was made for various engine types to be fitted, ranging from 400 to 500 hp. The sole prototype was powered by a 400 hp Lorraine-Dietrich 12-cylinder Vee-type engine, but was, in other respects, identical to the Ca 70 and enjoyed no greater success. *Max speed, 124 mph (200 km/h). Time to 13,125 ft (4 000 m), 17 min. Empty weight, 2,888 lb (1 310 kg). Loaded weight, 3,880 lb (1 760 kg). Dimensions as for Ca 70.*

CAPRONI Ca 114 Italy

Designed in 1933 to participate in a contest intended to provide the *Regia Aeronautica* with a new single-seat fighter, the Ca 114 single-bay equi-span staggered biplane was of mixed construction with a fabric-

The Caproni Ca 114 (above and below) was rejected by the *Regia Aeronautica*, but saw combat in 1941 during a conflict between Peru and Ecuador.

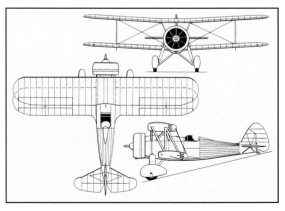

covered two-spar wooden wing and a steel-tube fuselage covered by detachable metal panels forward and fabric aft. Powered by a geared and supercharged Bristol Mercury IV radial rated at 530 hp at 13,125 ft (4 000 m) and driving a three-blade adjustable-pitch propeller, the Ca 114 carried an armament of two fixed forward-firing 7,7-mm machine guns. Rejected by the *Regia Aeronautica* in favour of the Fiat CR.32, the Ca 114 was nevertheless exported to the *Cuerpo de Aeronautica del Perú*, a total of 36 reportedly having been supplied in three batches, the last of these being delivered in January 1935. It saw some operational service as late as 1941 during a conflict between Peru and Ecuador. *Max speed, 220 mph (354 km/h) at 16,405 ft (5 000 m). Time to 3,280 ft (1 000 m), 1.17 min. Range, 373 mls (600 km). Empty weight, 2,888 lb (1 310 kg). Loaded weight, 3,651 lb (1 656 kg). Span, 34 ft 5⅓ in (10,50 m). Length, 25 ft 2⅓ in (7,68 m). Height, 8 ft 4 in (2,54 m). Wing area, 276.42 sq ft (25,68 m²).*

CAPRONI CH.1   Italy

Designed by Antonio Chiodi, the CH.1 single-seat fighter was an equi-span single-bay biplane of all-metal construction with fabric skinning and was intended to be powered by a 14-cylinder Gnome-Rhône 14Kfs Mistral Major radial rated at 780 hp at 15,585 ft (4 750 m). In the event, however, it was fitted with a nine-cylinder Piaggio P.IX R.C.40 rated at 560 hp at 13,125 ft (4 000 m). Initiated in 1934 as a private venture, the CH.1 was aerodynamically extremely clean. The cockpit was enclosed by an aft-sliding canopy, a three-blade variable-pitch propeller was fitted and the proposed armament comprised two 7,7-mm SAFAT synchronised machine guns. The CH.1 was flown for the first time in May 1935 by its designer. Trials were carried out at Guidonia during July-August, but the CH.1 turned over on its back during a landing and was written off. It had displayed exceptional climb performance, but failed to attract a production order. *Max speed, 203 mph (327 km/h) at sea level, 234 mph (377 km/h) at*

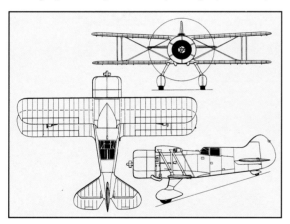

(Above and below) The attractive CH.1, built as a private venture in 1935, demonstrated good all-round performance, but gained no production order.

16,405 ft (5 000 m). Time to 13,125 ft (4 000 m), 7.26 min. Range, 621 mls (1 000 km). Empty weight, 3,086 lb (1 400 kg). Loaded weight, 4,409 lb (2 000 kg). Span, 28 ft 2½ in (8,60 m). Length, 23 ft 7 in (7,19 m). Height, 9 ft 6 in (2,90 m). Wing area, 204.52 sq ft (19,00 m²).*

CAPRONI Ca 165   Italy

The ventral radiator under the fuselage of the Ca 165 (above and below) was at first semi-retractable and is shown dotted in the drawing in extended position.

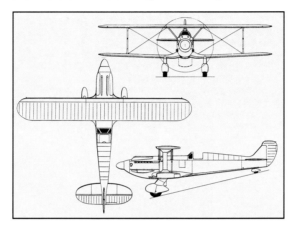

A further private-venture single-seat fighter, the Ca 165 was designed by Ing Raffaele Conflenti and first flew on 16 February 1938. Of mixed construction, with wooden wings and a chrome-molybdenum welded steel-tube fuselage with fabric skinning, the Ca 165 was powered by an Isotta Fraschini L 121 RC 40 12-cylinder liquid-cooled engine rated at 900 hp at 13,125 ft (4 000 m) and driving a three-bladed variable-pitch propeller. A semi-retractable radiator bath was initially fitted, but after individual tests this was fixed in the extended position to overcome a tendency on the part of the engine to overheat. Armament comprised two 12,7-mm SAFAT machine guns. Although extremely good characteristics were recorded at Guidonia during official trials in August 1939, an intent to order 12 pre-production examples of the Ca 165 on behalf of the *Regia Aeronautica* was not pursued owing to cost, and further development was abandoned. *Max speed, 288 mph (464 km/h) at 17,550 ft (5 350 m). Time to 13,125 ft (4 000 m), 3.8 min, to 19,685 ft (6 000 m), 6.63 min. Normal range, 417 mls (672 km) at 273 mph (440 km/h). Empty weight, 4,089 lb (1 855 kg). Loaded weight,*

5,346 lb (2 425 kg). Span, 30 ft 6 in (9,30 m). Length, 26 ft 7 in (8,10 m). Height, 9 ft 2 in (2,80 m). Wing area, 230.35 sq ft (21,40 m²).*

CAPRONI Ca 331 C.N.   Italy

The Ca 331 was originally developed by Ing Cesare Pallavicino to the requirements of a *Ministero dell'Aeronautica* specification for a tactical reconnaissance aircraft with combat capability. In May 1942, the *Ministero* ordered conversion of the second prototype for the night fighting rôle. Flown in this form in the summer of 1942 as the Ca 331 C.N. (*Caccia Notturna*), the aircraft was of all-metal stressed-skin construction, powered by two 800 hp Isotta-Fraschini Delta IV 12-cylinder air-cooled engines, and carried a fixed forward-firing armament of four 20-mm Mauser MG 151 cannon and two 12,7-mm SAFAT machine guns. Two additional 12,7-mm weapons were mounted in a dorsal turret and a ventral position (this armament actually being installed in the spring of 1943, by which time 850 hp Delta IV engines with two-stage superchargers had been fitted). Various production plans for the Ca 331 C.N. were formulated, but failed to see fruition, and a second night fighter prototype (with a nose-mounted armament of two 20-mm Ikaria cannon and four 12,7-mm SAFAT machine guns) was not flown. The following data relate to the proposed Delta IV-powered production version: *Max speed, 314 mph (505 km/h) at 17,390 ft (5 300 m). Time to 13,125 ft (4 000 m), 9.6 min. Range, 1,128 mls (1 815 km) at 199 mph (320 km/h). Empty weight, 10,141 lb (4 600 kg). Loaded weight, 14,991 lb (6 800 kg). Span, 53 ft 9⅔ in (16,40 m). Length, 38 ft 6⅛ in (11,74 m). Height, 11 ft 5 in (3,48 m). Wing area, 413,35 sq ft (38,40 m²).*

Ordered as the second prototype of the Ca 331 reconnaissance aircraft, the Ca 331 C.N. (above and below) was equipped as a dedicated night fighter.

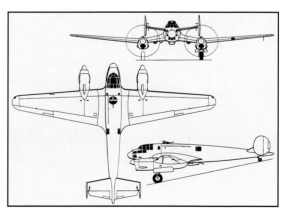

CAPRONI BERGAMASCA (C.A.B.) A.P.1 (Ca 301)   Italy

Built by Caproni Aeronautica Bergamasca to the designs of Ing Cesare Pallavicino, the A.P.1 was conceived as a dual-rôle aircraft, being intended to fulfil the tasks of both air combat fighter and assault. Also assigned the factory designation Ca 301, the A.P.1 was of mixed construction, with one-piece wooden wing with fabric and plywood skinning, and a similarly-covered welded steel tube fuselage. Powered by a 610 hp Piaggio P.IX R.C.40 nine-cylinder radial, the A.P 1 carried an armament of two unsynchronised 7,7-mm Scotti machine guns mounted in the main undercarriage fairings. Flown on 27 April 1934, the A.P.1 prototype was damaged in a heavy landing, flight testing being resumed, after modifications, on 18 May. Performance obtained during trials was not considered to warrant retention of the fighter rôle, continued development concentrating on a dedicated attack two-seater subsequently to be built both for the *Regia Aeronautica* and for export. The following data relate to the original single-seat prototype. *Max speed, 215 mph (346 km/h) at 16,400 ft (5 000 m). Time to 13,125 ft (4 000 m), 10.4 min. Empty weight, 3,704 lb (1 680 kg). Loaded weight, 5,137 lb (2 330 kg). Span, 39 ft 4½ in (12,00 m). Length, 29 ft 4¾ in (8,96 m). Height, 9 ft 3 in (2,82 m). Wing area, 258.34 sq ft (24,00 m²).*

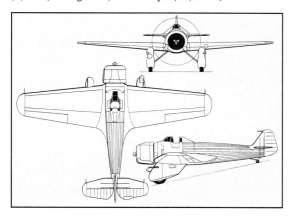

The Caproni Bergamasca Ca 301 (above and below) fighter and assault aircraft prototype provided the basis for the series A.P.1 two-seat attack aircraft.

CAPRONI REGGIANE   Italy

The aircraft produced by the Reggio Emilia-based Officine Meccaniche Italiane "Reggiane" have been frequently referred to incorrectly under the appellation of "Caproni Reggiane". The company was never, in fact, a subsidiary of the Caproni organisation as was often alleged. Accordingly, the aircraft designed at Reggio Emilia by Roberto G Longhi are to be found described under the Reggiane heading.

CAPRONI VIZZOLA F.4   Italy

Late in 1937, a design team led by F Fabrizi at the Caproni Vizzola SA of Vizzola Ticino, Varese, initiated work on a single-seat fighter of mixed construction, the wooden wing having stressed plywood skinning and the welded steel-tube fuselage having flush-riveted duralumin covering. Two versions of the fighter were proposed, the F.4 (or Fabrizi 4) with a 12-cylinder liquid-cooled Isotta-Fraschini Asso 121 R.C.40 rated at 960 hp at 13,125 ft (4 000 m), and the F.5 with a two-row 14-cylinder Fiat A.74 R.C.38 radial. As the Asso was not favoured by the *Ministero dell'Aeronautica* as a fighter power plant, the F.4 was shelved in favour of the F.5, but resurrected in the summer of 1939 when the first Daimler-Benz DB 601A engine reached Italy. Employ-

The Caproni Vizzola F.4 (below) with DB 601A engine.

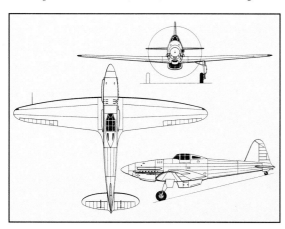

Built in parallel with the F.5, the Caproni Vizzola F.4 (above) differed in having a Daimler-Benz engine.

ing the airframe of the last pre-production F.5 fighter, the F.4 prototype was flown in July 1940. Armament comprised two 12,7-mm SAFAT machine guns. It was proposed to manufacture the fighter with the Alfa-Romeo-built DB 601A engine as the F.5bis, but the type had already been overtaken by the DB 605-powered F.6M, and the sole prototype of the F.4 was assigned to the 303ª *Squadriglia* which operated the type experimentally during 1942. *Max speed, 342 mph (550 km/h) at 12,305 ft (3 750 m). Max range, 435 mls (700 km) at 270 mph (435 km/h). Empty weight, 5,428 lb (2 462 kg). Loaded weight, 6,614 lb (3 000 kg). Span, 37 ft 0½ in (11,29 m). Length, 29 ft 2⅓ in (8,90 m). Height, 9 ft 6⅛ in (2,90 m). Wing area, 189.45 sq ft (17,60 m²).*

CAPRONI VIZZOLA F.5   Italy

Designed in parallel with the F.4, the F.5 utilised the same airframe married to a Fiat A.74 R.C.38 14-cylinder radial rated at 870 hp for take-off, and flew for the first time on 19 February 1939. The F.5 offered a very high standard of manoeuvrability, and the success that attended official evaluation resulted in an order for a second prototype and a pre-production batch of 12 aircraft. In the event, the last pre-production airframe was to be adapted as the prototype F.4. Carrying an armament of two 12,7-mm SAFAT machine guns, the pre-production F.5s were delivered to the 300ª *Squadriglia*. In 1942, the F.5s served in the night fighting rôle with the 167° *Gruppo*, but no additional aircraft were ordered. *Max speed, 308 mph (496 km/h) at 15,585 ft*

The first prototype of the Caproni Vizzola F.5 (below) which entered flight test in February 1939.

(Below) One of the small batch of F.5 fighters that was delivered to the 300ª *Squadriglia* and later served as night fighters with 167° *Gruppo*.

(4 750 m). Range, 478 mls (770 km) at 283 mph (455 km/h). Empty weight, 4,008 lb (1 818 kg). Loaded weight, 4,934 lb (2 238 kg). Span, 37 ft 0⅞ in (11,30 m). Length, 25 ft 11 in (7,90 m). Height, 9 ft 10⅛ in (3,00 m). Wing area, 189.45 sq ft (17,60 m²).

The Fabrizi-designed F.5 (above and below) demonstrated excellent manoeuvrability, but failed to progress further than a pre-series quantity.

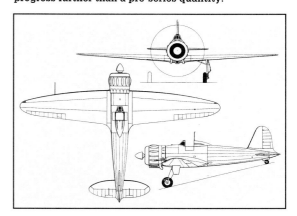

CAPRONI VIZZOLA F.6M   Italy

Adaptation of the F.5 airframe to take a 1,475 hp Daimler-Benz DB 605A engine and redesign of the wing structure for all-metal construction resulted in the F.6M (*Metallico*), the prototype of which was flown in September 1941. Armament comprised two fuselage-mounted 12,7-mm SAFAT machine guns with provision for two similar guns in the wings. As initially flown, the F.6M had a deep radiator bath beneath the nose, but drag considerations resulted in this being replaced by a ventral radiator bath. The sole prototype was damaged in a collision on Bresso airfield and further development was abandoned in favour of the aerodynamically refined F.7, which was destined never to be completed.

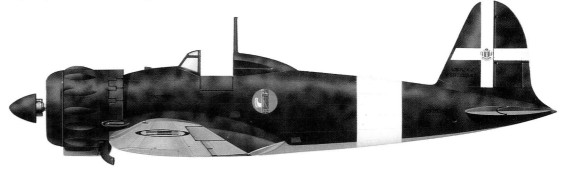

Max speed, 353 mph (569 km/h) at 16,405 ft (5 000 m). Range, 590 mls (950 km) at 296 mph (477 km/h). Empty weight, 4,993 lb (2 265 kg). Loaded weight, 6,360 lb (2 885 kg). Span, 37 ft 2⅓ in (11,35 m). Length, 30 ft 0¼ in (9,15 m). Height, 9 ft 10⅞ in (3,02 m). Wing area, 202.47 sq ft (18,81 m²).

The F.6M (above) as originally flown with a deep radiator bath and (below) in definitive form with revised engine cowling and ventral radiator bath.

CAPRONI VIZZOLA F.6Z   Italy

Shortly after work commenced on the F.6M, Caproni Vizzola received an order for a second airframe to be powered by an X-type 24-cylinder engine, the Isotta-Fraschini R.C.25/60 Zeta, which it was anticipated would offer 1,500 hp at 13,780 ft (4 200 m). Designated F.6Z (Zeta), the prototype suffered protracted delays owing to development difficulties with the engine, but was finally flown in August 1943 with a Zeta engine rated at only 1,200 hp at 19,685 ft (6 000 m), the Armistice terminating the test programme. The F.6Z was to have carried an armament of one fuselage-mounted and two wing-mounted 12,7-mm SAFAT machine guns.

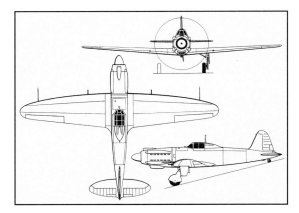

The F.6Z (above and below) was the only fighter flown with the Isotta-Fraschini Zeta engine.

The following performance data are estimates based on the use of a fully-rated engine. *Max speed, 391 mph (630 km/h) at 16,405 ft (5 000 m). Max range, 850 mls (1 370 km) at 310 mph (500 km/h). Empty weight, 7,381 lb (3 348 kg). Loaded weight, 9,021 lb (4 092 kg). Span, 38 ft 9⅓ in (11,82 m). Length, 29 ft 6¾ in (9,01 m). Height, 9 ft 10⅞ in (3,02 m). Wing area, 202.47 sq ft (18,81 m²).*

CASPAR CJ 14   Germany

Developed by the Caspar-Werke AG of Lübeck-Trave-münde to the designs of Dipl-Ing E von Lössl in 1924, the CJ 14 was built in Denmark by Dansk Aero of Copenhagen to evade the ban on the design and development of combat aircraft in Germany. The CJ 14 single-seat fighter was of wooden construction and was powered by a 325 hp Armstrong Siddeley Jaguar III 14-cylinder radial air-cooled engine, an optional power plant being the 300 hp Hispano-Suiza 8F. Featuring highly-tapered wings with an exceptionally large gap, the CJ 14 was a single-bay biplane with aerofoil-section I-type interplane struts and sloping N-type centre section struts. The intended armament was two 7,62-mm machine guns. Only a single prototype was built. *Max speed, 168 mph (270 km/h). Range, 373 mls (600 km). Empty weight, 1,764 lb (800 kg). Loaded weight, 2,645 lb (1 200 kg). Span, 29 ft 6⅓ in (9,00 m). Length, 17 ft 8½ in (5,40 m).*

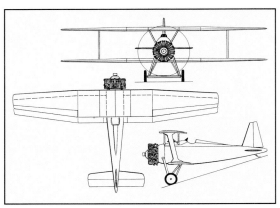

(Above) The Caspar CJ 14 was of German design, but the sole example was built in Denmark. The unique photo of the CJ 14 (below) has suffered some distortion.

CASPAR CS 14   Germany

Evolved from the CJ 14 and, like its predecessor, built by Dansk Aero to the designs of Dipl-Ing von Lössl, the CS 14 single-seat fighter biplane retained most of the features of the earlier experimental warplane. It was powered by a 450 hp Napier Lion IV 12-cylinder water-cooled engine and featured longer-span wings with N-type interplane bracing. Later adapted as a two-seater and proposed for the reconnaissance rôle, the CS 14 failed to attract orders and development was abandoned in 1926, only one prototype having been built. *Max speed, 155 mph (250 km/h). Endurance, 3.5 hrs. Empty weight, 2,491 lb (1 130 kg). Loaded weight, 3,924 lb (1 780 kg). Span, 32 ft 9¾ in (10,00 m). Length, 21 ft 7 in (6,58 m).*

Later flown as a two-seater, the CS 14 (above and below) is shown here in its original single-seat form.

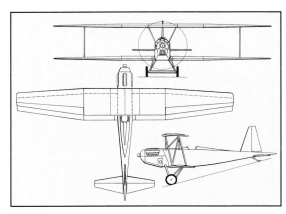

CAUDRON R XI & R XII   France

Evolved by Paul Deville from the R IV reconnaissance bomber designed by René Caudron, the R XI three-seat biplane was originally intended as a *Corps d'Armée* aircraft, but was destined to find its *forté* as a three-seat escort fighter. Powered by two 215 hp Hispano-Suiza 8Bda eight-cylinder water-cooled engines, the R XI appeared in March 1917, and entered service in February 1918. Armament comprised five 7,7-mm Lewis guns on flexible mounts – two in the nose cockpit, two in the dorsal cockpit and one firing downwards and rearwards beneath the front gunner's cockpit – and while initial models retained the HS 8Bda engines, later versions were fitted with the 235 hp HS 8Beb. The R XI enjoyed considerable success as an escort for the Breguet 14 during the closing months of WWI and during the summer of 1918. It also served in the fighter-reconnaissance rôle. At the time of the Armistice, the R XI equipped six 15-aircraft *escadrilles* of France's *Aviation Militaire*. A more powerful version, the R XII with

(Below) The Caudron R XI three-seat escort fighter.

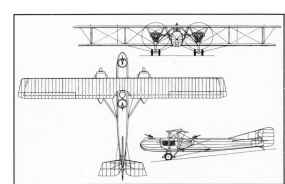

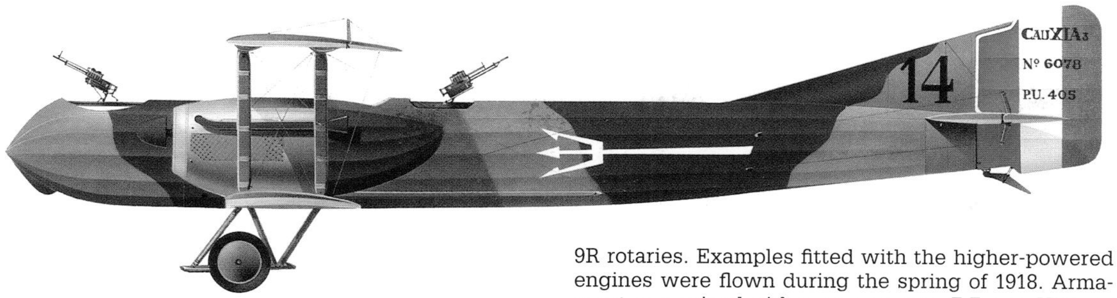

(Above) A Caudron R XI used by *Escadrille* C46 in 1918, providing escort protection for the bombers of 13^e *Escadre*. (Below) A Caudron R XI serving with the 96th Aero Squadron, US Air Service.

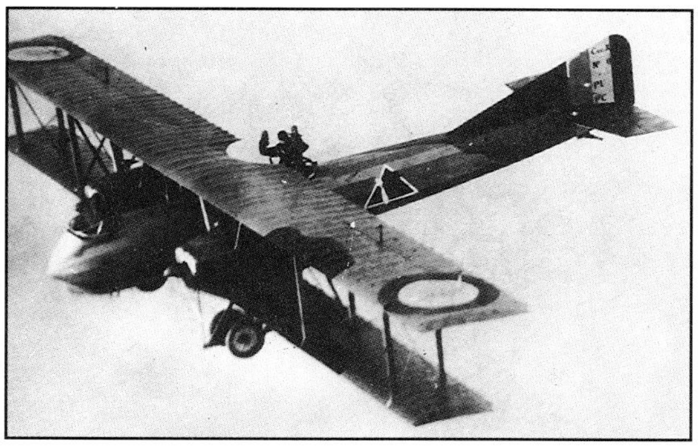

300 hp HS 8Fb engines, was tested during the summer of 1918, but apparently failed to display significantly better results than those obtained with the R XI. Prototype trials with the R XII were completed in the autumn of 1919, but no further development was undertaken. The following data relate to the HS 8Bda-engined R XI. *Max speed, 114 mph (183 km/h) at 6,560 ft (2 000 m), 108 mph (173 km/h) at 13,125 ft (4 000 m). Time to 6,560 ft (2 000 m), 8.17 min. Endurance, 3 hrs. Empty weight, 3,135 lb (1 422 kg). Loaded weight, 4,777 lb (2 167 kg). Span, 58 ft 9½ in (17,92 m). Length, 36 ft 9¾ in (11,22 m). Height, 9 ft 2¼ in (2,80 m). Wing area, 583.96 sq ft (54,25 m²).*

CAUDRON R XIV — France

Possessing a strong family resemblance to the R XI but having an increased wing span and area resulting from the introduction of an additional bracing bay on each side, an enlarged rudder and 300 hp Hispano-Suiza 8Fb eight-cylinder water-cooled engines, the R XIV was also a three-seat escort fighter. It had an armament of one 37-mm Hotchkiss cannon on a rotating mounting in the forward gunner's cockpit and paired Lewis guns in the dorsal gunner's cockpit. The fuselage was essentially similar to that of the R XI, and one example of the R XIV was completed in August 1918. No details of the subsequent testing of this aircraft have survived and the only data available are as follows: *Empty weight, 3,851 lb (1 747 kg). Wing area, 678.15 sq ft (63,00 m²).*

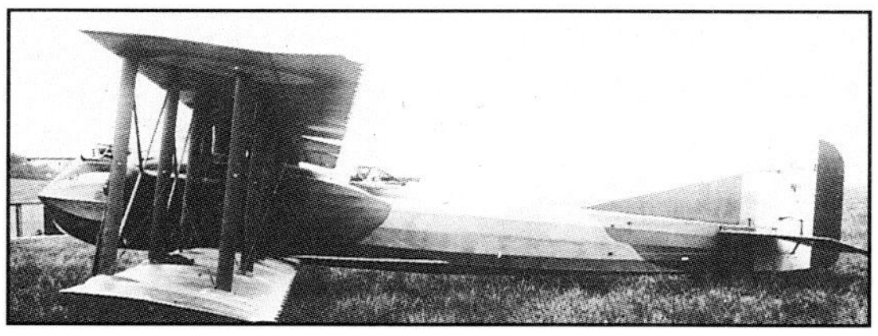

A 37-mm Hotchkiss cannon was carried in the front cockpit of the sole Caudron R XIV (above).

CAUDRON TYPE O — France

An unequal-span single-bay single-seat biplane designed by Paul Deville in 1917 for the high-altitude fighter rôle, the Caudron Type O (all Caudron types were initially assigned letter-type designations in sequence) was originally flown with a 120 hp Le Rhône nine-cylinder air-cooled rotary although designed for the 150 hp Gnome Monosoupape 9N or 170 hp Le Rhône 9R rotaries. Examples fitted with the higher-powered engines were flown during the spring of 1918. Armament comprised either one or two 7,7-mm Vickers machine guns and the aerofoil employed for the wings was of special flat section and was expected to enable the fighter to reach altitudes of the order of 29,530 ft (9 000 m). Only prototypes were completed and the following data relate to the version powered by the 170 hp Le Rhône 9R rotary. *Max speed, 130 mph (210 km/h) at 13,125 ft (4 000 m). Time to 13,125 ft (4 000 m), 10 min. Empty weight, 882 lb (400 kg). Loaded weight, 1,433 lb (650 kg). Wing area, 182.99 sq ft (17,00 m²).*

Designed for the high-altitude fighter rôle, the Caudron Type O (below) only achieved prototype status.

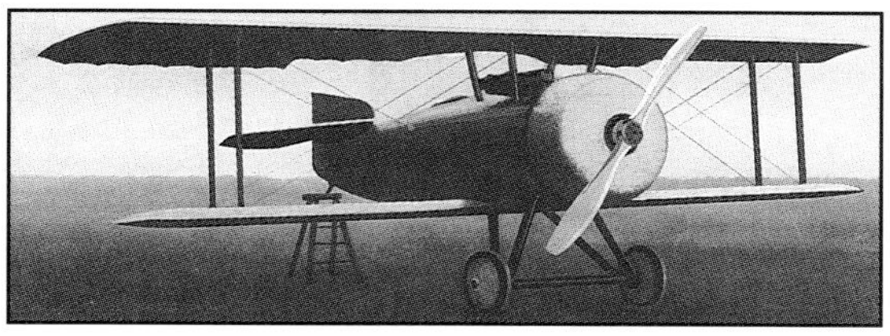

CAUDRON-RENAULT C 710 CYCLONE — France

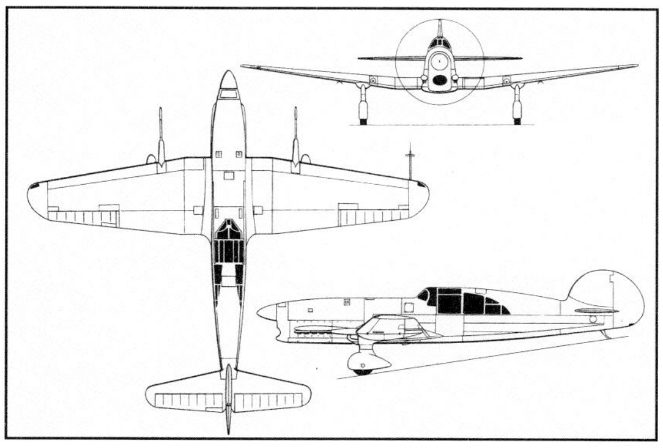

The first example of the C 710 Cyclone (above and below) flown in July 1936 and derived from the Caudron *Coupe Deutsch* racing monoplanes.

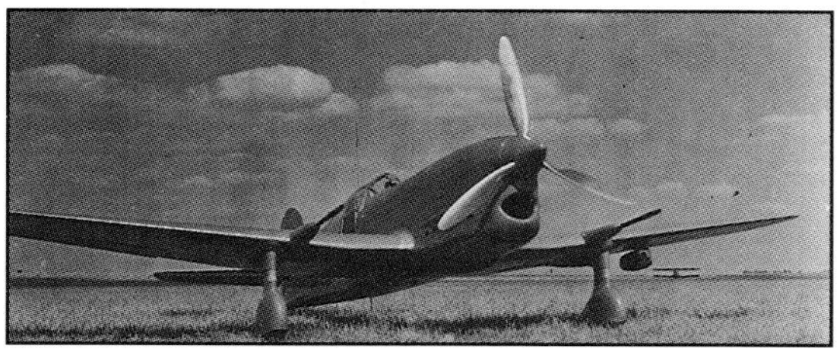

Competing with the ANF-Mureaux 190 to meet a *Service Technique de l'Aéronautique* specification for a lightweight fighter, the C 710 Cyclone, designed by Marcel Riffard, was derived from the *Coupe Deutsch de la Meurthe* racing monoplanes. It was of wooden stressed-skin construction with a Renault 12R 01 12-cylinder inverted-Vee air-cooled engine producing 500 hp for take-off. First flown on 18 July 1936, the C 710-01 was subsequently fitted with two drum-fed 20-mm HS-9 cannon in the wings, and was tested at Guyancourt and Villacoublay throughout 1937. On 1 February 1938 it crashed in the Verrières forest. Two additional airframes had meanwhile been built, the second of these being completed as the C 710-02 which differed from the first prototype in having redesigned vertical tail surfaces, these being taller and more angular. Further development of the basic design concentrated on derivatives embodying retractable undercarriages (eg, C 713, C 714). *Max speed, 283 mph (455 km/h) at 13,125 ft (4 000 m). Range, 513 mls (825 km) at 224 mph (360 km/h). Empty weight, 2,740 lb (1 243 kg). Loaded weight, 3,627 lb (1 645 kg). Span, 29 ft 5⅛ in (8,97 m). Length, 27 ft 11⅘ in (8,53 m). Height, 8 ft 1¼ in (2,47 m). Wing area, 134.55 sq ft (12,50 m²).*

CAUDRON-RENAULT C 713 CYCLONE — France

Essentially a version of the C 710 with the fixed and faired main undercarriage members supplanted by inward-retracting units, the C 713 was originally to have been the second C 710. It was initially flown on 15 December 1937 with ovoid vertical tail surfaces similar to those of the C 710-01 and with twin 20-mm HS-9 cannon armament. The cannon were subsequently removed and new vertical tail surfaces were applied, these being similar to those introduced on the C 710-02.

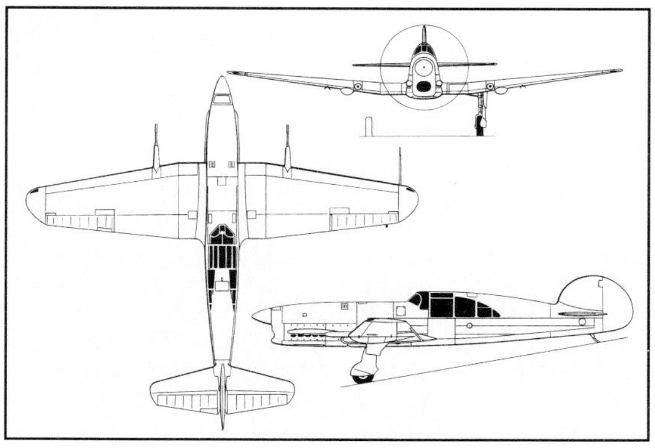

The C 713 retractable-gear derivative of the C 710.

Powered by the Renault 12R 01 air-cooled engine, as was the preceding fighter, the C 713 was productionised as the C 714. *Max speed, 292 mph (470 km/h) at 13,125 ft (4 000 m). Time to 13,125 ft (4 000 m), 9.42 min. Empty weight, 2,866 lb (1 300 kg). Loaded weight, 3,671 lb (1 665 kg). Span, 29 ft 5⅛ in (8,97 m). Length, 27 ft 11⅘ in (8,53 m). Height, 8 ft 6⅓ in (2,60 m). Wing area, 134.55 sq ft (12,50 m²).*

CAUDRON-RENAULT C 714 CYCLONE — France

The C 714, flown for the first time on 6 July 1938, was basically similar to the definitive C 713 (which had been lost in February 1938 when the tail broke up during a terminal velocity dive). Its wing-mounted cannon were supplanted by four 7,5-mm MAC machine guns mounted in flush-fitting underwing trays, this armament actually being installed in November 1938. On 5 November 1938, an order was placed for 20 C 714s and an option taken on a further 180, the first series aircraft being completed by Caudron-Renault on 10 June 1939.

The production derivative of the C 713, the C 714 Cyclone (below), was flown operationally in 1940 by the *Groupe de Chasse Polonaise* (GC I/145) at Lyon-Bron.

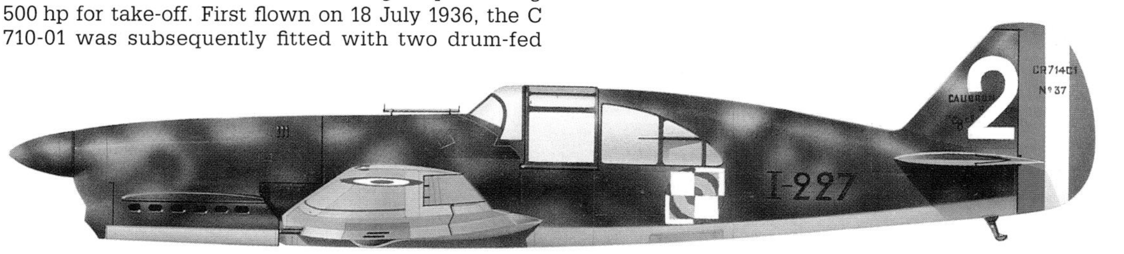

In its C 714 production form (above and below), the Cyclone differed from prototypes in having a new wing structure, revised armament and modified tail.

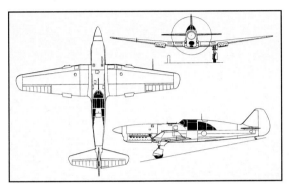

This differed from the prototype in having a new wing structure with an aerofoil of reduced camber, narrower-chord landing flaps, longer-stroke shock absorbers and a Renault 12R 03 engine (differing from the 12R 01 in having a carburettor permitting negative-g manoeuvres). The *Armée de l'Air* considered the C 714 unsuited for operational deployment, but the French government planned to donate 80 to Finland, of which only six reached their destination. Although assigned to LLv 30, the C 714s saw no operational service in Finland. A number were assigned to two Polish fighter training squadrons at Lyon-Bron, these eventually flying the C 714 operationally. A total of 63 C 714s had been completed at the time of the Armistice, when production was terminated. *Max speed, 283 mph (455 km/h) at 13,125 ft (4 000 m), 286 mph (460 km/h) at 16,405 ft (5 000 m). Time to 13,125 ft (4 000 m), 9.66 min. Range, 559 mls (900 km) at 199 mph (320 km/h). Empty weight, 3,075 lb (1 395 kg). Loaded weight, 4,145 lb (1 880 kg). Span, 29 ft 5⅛ in (8,97 m). Length, 28 ft 3⅞ in (8,63 m). Height, 9 ft 5 in (2,87 m). Wing area, 134.55 sq ft (12,50 m²).*

CAUDRON-RENAULT
CR 760 France

In August 1938, Caudron-Renault submitted to the *Service Technique de l'Aéronautique* project studies for three new lightweight fighters to meet the requirements of a specification for such a warplane framed in May 1937, these being the CR 760, CR 770 and CR 780. The first of these, design development of which had been initiated by Marcel Riffard during 1937 as the C 715, had originally been intended to have a new 16-cylinder air-cooled engine then under development by Renault. As there was prospect of obtaining earlier deliveries of an air-cooled inline engine of comparable power from Isotta-Fraschini, it was decided to substitute this for the Renault engine in the CR 760, utilising the latter power plant in a further development, the CR 770. The CR 760 had a dural-covered welded steel-tube fuselage and a two-spar wooden wing with stressed plywood skinning, the entire airframe being divided into pre-assembled elements which could be sub-contracted to non-specialised manufacturers. The 12-cylinder inverted-Vee Isotta-Fraschini Delta R.C.40 engine offered 730 hp at 13,125 ft (4 000 m) and armament comprised six 7,5-mm MAC 1934 M 39 machine

guns in underwing trays. The prototype CR 760 flew for the first time at the beginning of May 1940, but was destroyed at Orléans-Bricy on 11 June 1940 to prevent it falling into German hands. *Max speed, 345 mph (555 km/h) at 16,075 ft (4 900 m). Time to 13,125 ft (4 000 m), 5.4 min. Max range, 746 mls (1 200 km). Empty weight, 3,413 lb (1 548 kg). Loaded weight, 4,409 lb (2 000 kg). Span, 29 ft 5⅛ in (8,97 m). Length, 29 ft 2 in (8,89 m). Height, 9 ft 6⅛ in (2,90 m). Wing area, 134.55 sq ft (12,50 m²).*

The last of the Caudron lightweight fighters to fly, the CR 760 (above and below) retained the Cyclone configuration but used an Italian Delta engine.

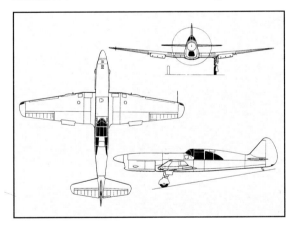

(Below) Built in parallel with the CR 760 and flown only once, the CR 770 was powered by a Renault 626 16-cylinder inverted-Vee air-cooled engine.

CAUDRON-RENAULT
CR 770 France

Flown for the first time in November 1939, paradoxically some six months prior to the CR 760, the CR 770 employed an essentially similar airframe and armament, but was powered by a Renault 626 16-cylinder inverted-Vee air-cooled engine rated at 800 hp at 13,125 ft (4 000 m). Ten minutes after taking off for the first time, the CR 770 suffered a broken crankshaft, and, before a replacement power plant could be delivered to Guyancourt where the test programme was being conducted, the prototype had to be destroyed to avoid capture by the *Wehrmacht*. The ultimate development of Marcel Riffard's series of lightweight fighters, the CR 780, was to have had a 500 hp Renault 468 12-cylinder engine driving contra-rotating three-bladed propellers and an armament of two 20-mm HS 404 cannon and two 7,5-mm MAC 1934 M 39 machine guns, but this progressed no further than the design study stage. The following performance data for the CR 770 are estimated. *Max speed, 367 mph (590 km/h) at 14,765 ft (4 500 m). Time to 13,125 ft (4 000 m), 4.67 min. Range, 932 mls (1 500 km). Empty weight, 3,836 lb (1 740 kg). Loaded weight, 4,955 lb (2 248 kg). Span, 28 ft 5¾ in (8,68 m). Length, 32 ft 5¾ in (9,90 m). Height, 9 ft 7 in (2,92 m). Wing area, 134.55 sq ft (12,50 m²).*

CENTRE NC 600 France

With the creation of the Société Nationale de Constructions Aéronautiques du Centre by the fusion of the Hanriot and Farman concerns under the Law for the Nationalisation of Military Industries, major redesign

Displayed in Brussels as the NC 600, the aircraft below was, in fact, its Hanriot H.220-2 progenitor.

was initiated of the Hanriot H.220 twin-engined three-seat fighter (which see). The first result of this redesign was the H.220-2, which was displayed statically as the NC 600 in July 1939 at the *Salon de l'Aéronautique* held in Brussels. This aircraft was not, however, the genuine NC 600, which differed from the H.220-2 in having, among other changes, a revised wing. Whereas the wing of the H.220 had a leading edge perpendicular to the fuselage, both spars featuring several degrees of forward sweep, that of the NC 600 had some three degrees of leading edge taper and perpendicular spars (span and area remaining unchanged), thus removing the last commonality with the original H.220. Although the H.220-2 had not overcome the airflow turbulence generated by the wing centre section bracing struts which produced serious tail buffet under certain conditions, the SNCA du Centre persisted in retaining this

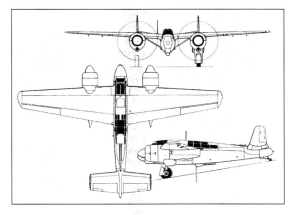

The NC 600 three-seat fighter as flown May 1940.

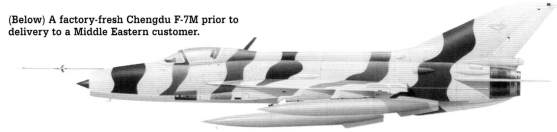

(Below) A factory-fresh Chengdu F-7M prior to delivery to a Middle Eastern customer.

feature for the NC 600, which flew for the first time on 15 May 1940. This aircraft, which introduced raised aft fuselage decking, redesigned endplate fins and rudders, and a raised tail assembly, was powered by two Gnome-Rhône 14M0/01 Mars radials each rated at 710 hp for take-off. Armament consisted of two 20-mm HS 404 cannon plus two 7,5-mm MAC 1934 machine guns firing forward and a 20-mm weapon on a flexible mounting firing aft, this partially retracting into a slot in the fuselage decking. The NC 600 was proposed as a *two*-seat fighter, and although there is no record of an official order for this type, six were under construction when the *Wehrmacht* occupied Bourges. *Max speed, 337 mph (542 km/h) at 16,400 ft (5 000 m). Time to 26,250 ft (8 000 m), 14 min. Range, 534 mls (860 km) at 302 mph (486 km/h). Empty weight, 6,499 lb (2 948 kg). Loaded weight, 8,818 lb (4 000 kg). Span, 41 ft 11⁹/₁₀ in (12,80 m). Length, 28 ft 10³/₈ in (8,80 m). Height, 11 ft 1³/₄ in (3,40 m). Wing area, 227.77 sq ft (21,16 m²).*

CHENGDU F-7M and F-7MG   China

Licence production of the MiG-21F-13 began in China in 1964 as the J-7 I/F-7A, the F prefix denoting an export version. Since that time it has spawned a whole family of derivatives, which have been exported to eleven countries. The J-7 II/F-7B, first flown on 30 December 1978, differed from the original in having an aft-hinged cockpit canopy; a continuously variable shock cone; two 30-mm cannon; provision for a centreline drop tank; and the more powerful WP-7B turbojet. It was followed by the J-7 III/ F-7M, which first flew on 26 April 1984. The F-7M Airguard was powered by the WP-13 turbojet and featured a side-hinged canopy, with provision for two AAMs. A variant specifically for Pakistan was the F-7P Skybolt, which carried four AAMs. Since then there have been several attempts at upgrading with a "solid" nose and side inlets, such as the Super-7, and more recently the FC-1. The latter is reported to have flown in 1997, powered by a Klimov RD-93 turbofan, but this has not been confirmed. Currently in production is the F-7MG, which retains the original pitot inlet. Powered by a Liyang WP-13F augmented turbofan rated at 14,550 lb (6 600 kgp) max and 9,920 lb (4 500 kgp) military thrust, the wing has been radically redesigned. Span and area

The F-7P (below) for Pakistan carried four AAMs.

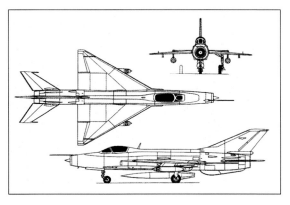

(Above and below) The F-7M Airguard, a descendant of the MiG-21, achieved some export success for China.

are both larger; the leading edge is cranked, while the outboard sections of the trailing edge show a slight reverse sweep. Weaponry consists of two 30-mm cannon with 126 rounds per gun, and four heat homing AAMs (AIM-9P, R550, or PL-7). In June 1998, yet another variant made its first flight. This was the F-7FS, with an ogival radar nose and a chin intake with an obvious splitter plate. Whether this is a technology demonstrator or a genuine fighter prototype, time alone will tell. The following data relate to the F-7MG. *Max speed hi, Mach 2; max speed lo, Mach 0.98. Operational ceiling, 57,417 ft (17 500 m). Rate of climb, 38,388 ft/min (195 m/sec). Empty weight, 11,667 lb (5 292 kg). Takeoff weight, 16,623 lb (7 540 kg). Span, 27 ft 2¹/₂ in (8,32 m). Length, 48 ft 10 in (14,885 m). Height, 13 ft 5¹/₂ in (4,103 m). Wing area, 268 sq ft (24,88 m²).*

CHENGDU J-10   China

First flown in March 1998, the J-10 has hitherto been very much of a mystery in the West. Primarily an air defence fighter, it has been developed with Israeli assistance, and has long been rumoured to be very similar to the long-defunct Lavi (which see). The only known picture appeared briefly on the internet (before being wiped by the Chinese web censor) in

January 2001, and this seems to confirm that it is a Lavi look-alike. Four or five prototypes are believed to have flown, and one has crashed. It is powered by a single Klimov RD-33 afterburning turbofan, which may at a later stage feature thrust vectoring. The radar and systems may be either Russian or Israeli in origin, but an indigenous supplier cannot be ruled out. If successful, the J-10 may well see the demise of the FC-1. *Data probably similar to those for Lavi.*

CHU (AFAMF) X-PO   China

Early in 1941, when China's fortunes in the war against Japan were at their lowest ebb, Maj Gen Chu Chia-Gen, Chief of the Air Force Technical Bureau, initiated design at the Air Force Aircraft Manufacturing Factory (AFAMF) No 1 of a single-seat fighter monoplane powered by a 1,200 hp Pratt & Whitney R-1830-S1C3-G Twin Wasp radial engine as the X-PO (Yen Chui Ling How). The design of the X-PO was based broadly on that of the Curtiss Hawk 75A and was intended to utilise indigenous materials insofar as was practicable. Of mixed construction, with wooden three-spar wings, welded steel tube fuselage, and the whole covered by plywood skinning, the X-PO was intended to carry two or four 20-mm cannon in underwing fairings, and a centreline bomb rack was to have enabled the fighter to fulfil a secondary rôle of dive bomber. It was anticipated that the X-PO would be manufactured in series at the AFAMF No 1 at Kunming, and the sole prototype was flown for the first time in 1943 at Yangling, northeast of Kunming. After circuiting the field, the aircraft landed too fast, ground-looped and was written off. In the meantime, the US entry into World War II and the consequent release of supplies of fighters to China had removed the need for indigenous fighter manufacture, and further development of the X-PO was discontinued. No data have apparently survived.

The single prototype of the X-PO fighter (above and below) which was written-off when landing from its initial flight at Yangling in 1943.

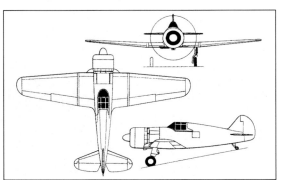

COMMONWEALTH BOOMERANG   Australia

Flown only 16 weeks and three days after the commencement of detail design, the Boomerang was developed by the Commonwealth Aircraft Corporation

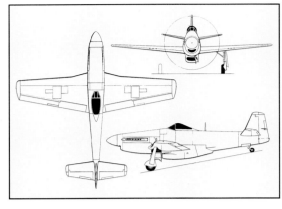

(Above) The Griffon-engined Commonwealth CA-15.

Royce Griffon 61 liquid-cooled engine with which the prototype was finally flown on 4 March 1946. The intended armament comprised six 0.5-in (12,7-mm) Browning guns. A limited and somewhat desultory flight test programme was continued until early 1950, but its results were largely of academic interest owing

The CAC Boomerang (below) was built in three batches each having minor differences, that above being from the 95-aircraft CA-13 batch.

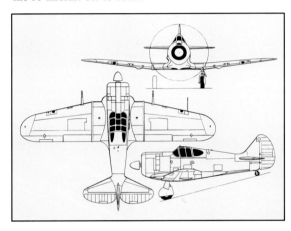

(CA-19) covered 49 aircraft, the last 39 of which were each fitted with a vertical camera for tactical reconnaissance. *Max speed, 302 mph (486 km/h) at 7,400 ft (2 255 m), 305 mph (491 km/h) at 15,500 ft (4 724 m). Normal range, 930 mls (1 497 km) at 190 mph (306 km/h). Empty weight, 5,373 lb (2 437 kg). Loaded weight, 7,699 lb (3 492 kg). Span, 36 ft 0 in (10,97 m). Length, 25 ft 6 in (7,77 m). Height, 9 ft 7 in (2,92 m). Wing area, 225 sq ft (20,90 m²).*

COMMONWEALTH CA-15 Australia

Flown in 1946, the CA-15 (above) was the most advanced fighter of Australian design to be built.

Never officially named or designated and referred to only by the contract number under which it was evolved, CA-15, this all-metal stressed-skin monoplane fighter was initiated in 1943. It was designed around the Pratt & Whitney R-2800-10W Double Wasp turbo-supercharged radial engine, but non-availability of this power plant after prototype construction began led to the aircraft being reworked to take a 2,305 hp Rolls-

Key to CA-13 Boomerang

1 Rudder frame
2 Tail navigation light
3 Forward fin spar
4 Rudder post
5 Tab control linkage
6 Rudder tab
7 Starboard elevator tab
8 Starboard elevator
9 Tailplane structure
10 Lower rudder hinge

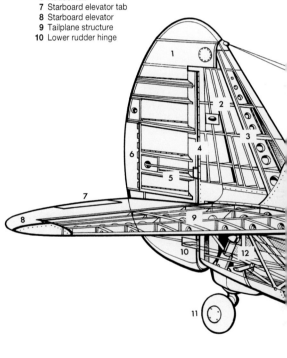

(CAC) as an emergency fighter. It employed what was essentially a Wirraway (licence-built North American NA-33) trainer airframe mated to a 1,200 hp Pratt & Whitney R-1830-S3C4-G Twin Wasp radial and an armament of four 0.303-in (7,7-mm) Browning guns and two 20-mm Hispano cannon. There was no prototype, and the first example of the Boomerang – built against contract CA-12 calling for 105 aeroplanes – flew on 29 May 1942. A follow-on contract CA-13 for 95 aircraft called for the introduction of minor modifications resulting from initial operational experience. Under contract CA-14, one aircraft was fitted with a turbo-supercharger and embodied various aerodynamic refinements, but this version of the Boomerang remained experimental. The final production contract

Both the CAC Boomerangs depicted below came from the CA-13 contract, A46-117 serving with No 4 Sqn in New Guinea and A46-126 with No 5 Sqn.

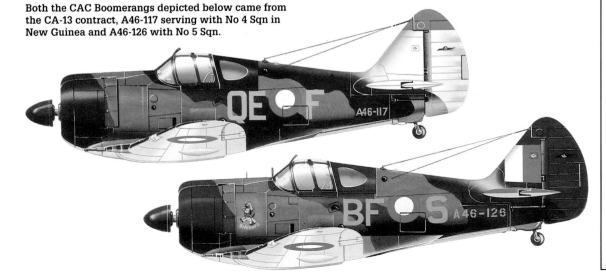

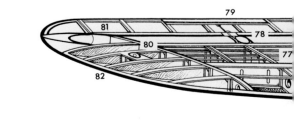

to the advent of the jet fighter. *Max speed, 368 mph (592 km/h) at sea level, 448 mph (721 km/h) at 26,400 ft (8 047 m). Max climb rate, 4,900 ft/min (24,9 m/sec). Normal range, 1,150 mls (1 850 km). Empty equipped weight, 7,540 lb (3 420 kg). Normal loaded weight, 10,764 lb (4 882 kg). Span, 36 ft 0 in (10,97 m). Length, 36 ft 2½ in (11,03 m). Height, 14 ft 2¾ in (4,34 m). Wing area, 253 sq ft (23,50 m²).*

COMMONWEALTH AVON-SABRE   Australia

Based on the North American F-86F Sabre, the Avon-Sabre evolved by the Commonwealth Aircraft Corporation to contract CA-26 embodied considerable redesign to accommodate a Rolls-Royce Avon engine in place of the General Electric J47, and twin 30-mm Aden cannon instead of a sextet of 0.5-in (12,7-mm) guns. As the Avon demanded substantially larger intake area than the US engine and weighed rather less, the fuselage of the fighter was radically modified, the forward section

being lengthened, the aft section being shortened and the whole being deepened, only 40 per cent of the original structure being retained. The prototype Avon-Sabre was flown on 3 August 1953, and 111 production examples were built against contract CA-27, the first 22 being Mk 30s with slatted wings and imported Avon RA 7 engines. The next 20 were Mk 31s having CAC-built Avon 20s and non-slatted wings with extended

leading edges, and the remaining 69 were of the definitive Mk 32 version with the 7,500 lb st (3 402 kgp) CAC-built Avon 26 and two additional wing strongpoints. All the Mk 30s became Sabre 31s when retrofitted with the "6-3" wing. Armament comprised two 30-mm Aden cannon and a pair of AIM-9 AAMs, two 500-lb (226,8-kg) bombs, or clusters of four 5-in (12,7-cm) or six 3-in (7,62-cm) rockets. Withdrawn from

11 Non-retractable tailwheel
12 Tailwheel lock
13 Fin/fuselage fairing
14 Monocoque lower fuselage structure
15 Elevator/rudder control linkage
16 Oxygen bottles
17 Main fuselage tubular structure
18 Wooden upper fuselage fairing
19 Aerials
20 Dorsal navigational light
21 Aerial lead-in
22 Tubular truss turnover pylon
23 Fuselage fuel tank filler cap (portside)
24 Generator

25 ATR5 radio pack
26 Canopy track
27 Fuselage fuel tank of 70 Imp gal (318 l) capacity
28 Pilot's back armour
29 Headrest
30 Undercarriage warning horn
31 Canopy jettison lever
32 Engine controls
33 Laminated-wood pilot's seat
34 Map case beneath seat
35 Main electrical control panel
36 Rudder/elevator tab controls
37 Reflector sight
38 Rearward-sliding canopy
39 External rear-view mirror
40 Optically-flat armourglass windscreen
41 Circular gunsight sun visor
42 Instrument panel
43 Engine firewall
44 Flame damper exhaust
45 Upper and lower engine bearers

46 Oil tank of 14 Imp gal (63,6 l) capacity
47 Cooling gills
48 Detachable engine access
49 Pratt & Whitney R-1830-S3C4-G Twin Wasp single-stage two-speed 14-cylinder two-row air-cooled radial engine
50 Carburettor air intake
51 Port aileron
52 Port navigation light
53 G45 camera gun installation
54 Port landing light
55 Hamilton Standard constant-speed propeller of 11 ft 0 in (3.35 m) diameter
56 Propeller boss
57 Oil cooler intake
58 Port mainwheel with 27-in (68,58-cm) diameter tyre
59 Undercarriage fairing
60 Wheelwell
61 Plywood ventral drop tank of 70 Imp gal (318 l) capacity
62 Muzzle of 20-mm Hispano cannon

63 Mainwheel oleo leg
64 Starboard mainwheel
65 Mainwheel doors
66 Cannon fairing
67 Starboard 45 Imp gal (204,6 l) capacity self-sealing fuel tank
68 Wing root fairing
69 Centre section/outer wing panel joint
70 Cannon shell magazine (60 rounds)
71 Machine gun ports
72 Starboard pair of 0.303-in (7,7-mm) Browning machine guns
73 Starboard flap
74 Forward mainspar
75 Starboard landing light
76 Pitot head
77 Wing structure
78 Aileron control linkage
79 Starboard aileron tab
80 Starboard navigation light
81 Aluminium-skinned aileron structure
82 Wooden wingtip

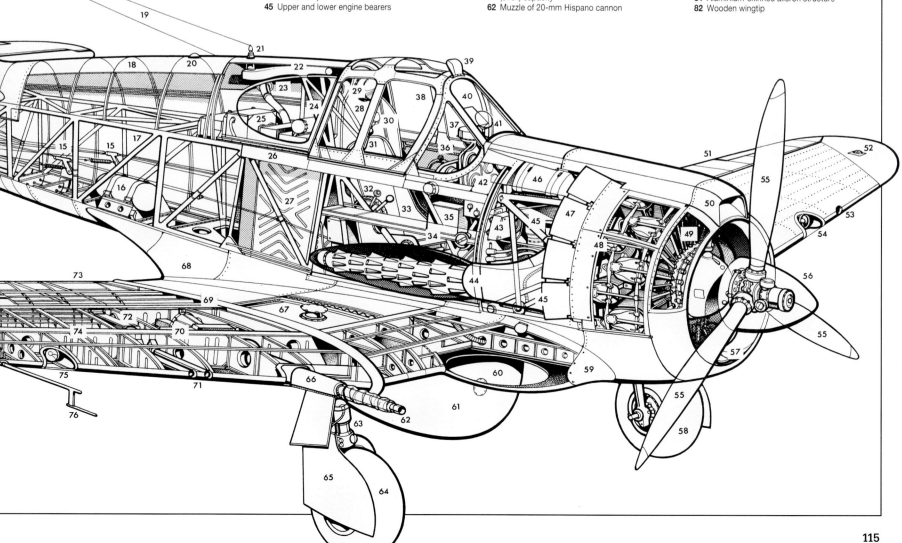

Serving with "The Black Panther" aerobatic team of No 76 Sqn, RAAF, at Williamtown in the 'fifties, A94-901 (above) was the first CA-27 contract Avon-Sabre built.

RAAF service in 1971, 18 Mk 32s were transferred to Malaysia in 1969/1971 and 18 to Indonesia in 1973 plus five transferred from Malaysia in 1976. *Max speed, 672 mph (1 081 km/h) at 10,000 ft (3 050 m), 607 mph (977 km/h) at 38,000 ft (11 580 m). Initial climb, 12,000 ft/min (61 m/sec). Empty weight, 12,120 lb (5 498 kg). Loaded weight, 15,990 lb (7 253 kg). Span, 37 ft 1¼ in (11,31 m). Length, 37 ft 6 in (11,43 m). Height, 14 ft 4¾ in (4,39 m). Wing area, 302.26 sq ft (28,08 m²).*

COMTE AC-1   Switzerland

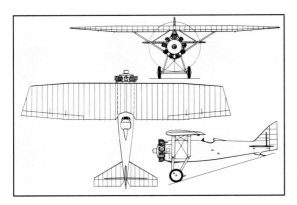

The sole AC-1 prototype in its original form (above and below) before being fitted with a D 9 wing.

Designed as a private venture by Alfred Comte to meet a Swiss *Fliegertruppe* requirement for a new single-seat fighter, the AC-1 was of metal construction with a dural-covered fuselage and fabric-skinned wing and tail surfaces. It was powered by a 420 hp Gnome-Rhône Jupiter IX. Proposed armament comprised two synchronised, fuselage-mounted machine guns. The prototype AC-1 was flown for the first time on 2 April 1927 and was subsequently evaluated by the *Fliegertruppe*, which purchased the aircraft but elected to adopt the Dewoitine D 27 to meet its fighter requirement. The sole AC-1 was acquired in the summer of 1928 by the Military Technical Service, and was then fitted with a

Dewoitine D 9 wing by the K+W at Thun. On 19 November 1928, the modified AC-1 established a new Swiss altitude record of 34,120 ft (10 400 m). *Max speed, 162 mph (260 km/h). Time to 3,280 ft (1 000 m), 1.8 min, to 9,840 ft (3 000 m), 5.0 min. Range, 280 mls (450 km). Empty weight, 2,028 lb (920 kg). Loaded weight, 2,910 lb (1 320 kg). Span, 39 ft 4½ in (12,00 m). Length, 23 ft 4¾ in (7,13 m). Height, 10 ft 2⅘ in (3,12 m). Wing area, 258.34 sq ft (24,00 m²).*

CONSOLIDATED Y1P-25   USA

The single Y1P-25 (above), tested in 1932, was a derivative of the Lockheed YP-24 by the same designer.

Designed by Robert Wood as a development of the Lockheed YP-24 (XP-900), the Y1P-25 was a tandem two-seat all-metal fighter powered by a turbo-super-charged Curtiss V-1570-27 Conqueror 12-cylinder liquid-cooled engine rated at 600 hp. It carried an armament of two fixed forward-firing 0.3-in (7,62-mm) machine guns and one flexibly-mounted weapon of similar calibre in the rear cockpit. One example of the Y1P-25 was ordered for evaluation by the Army Air Corps and this was flown late in 1932, but crashed on 13 January 1933. However, the AAC was sufficiently impressed to recommend the purchase of an improved Y1P-25 which became the P-30 (PB-2). *Max speed, 205 mph (330 km/h) at sea level, 247 mph (397 km/h) at 15,000 ft (4 572 m). Time to 10,000 ft (3 050 m), 6.7 min. Empty weight, 3,887 lb (1 763 kg). Loaded weight, 5,110 lb (2 318 kg). Span, 43 ft 10 in (13,36 m). Length, 29 ft 4 in (8,94 m). Height, 8 ft 7 in (2,62 m). Wing area, 296 sq ft (27,49 m²).*

CONSOLIDATED P-30 (PB-2)   USA

Four service test versions of the Y1P-25 embodying minor improvements were ordered in January 1933. Similar all-metal two-seaters, but having the 675 hp V-1710-57 Conqueror supercharged engine, simplified undercarriages and modified cockpit canopies, these aircraft were assigned the designation P-30 and delivered for Army Air Corps testing in the summer of 1934.

On 6 December 1934, an order was placed for 50 P-30As, these having the 700 hp V-1710-61 Conqueror engine and retaining the General Electric F-3 turbo-super-charger, but with a controllable-pitch propeller replacing the fixed-pitch unit of the P-30. Armament comprised two fixed and one flexible 0.3-in (7,62-mm) machine guns, and, shortly after the delivery of the P-30As in 1935, these aircraft were redesignated as PB-2As, the P-30s becoming PB-2s. The Consolidated aircraft was the only single-engined two-seat fighter monoplane to attain operational status with the AAC. The following data relate to the P-30A alias PB-2A. *Max speed, 255 mph (410 km/h) at 15,000 ft (4 570 m), 274 mph (441 km/h) at 25,000 ft (7 620 m). Time to 15,000 ft (4 570 m), 7.78 min. Range, 508 mls (817 km). Empty weight, 4,306 lb (1 953 kg). Loaded weight, 5,643 lb (2 560 kg). Span, 43 ft 11 in (13,38 m). Length, 30 ft 0 in (9,14 m). Height, 8 ft 3 in (2,51 m). Wing area, 297 sq ft (27,59 m²).*

(Above) One of the four service-test versions of the Y1P-25 that were built as P-30s (PB-2s later).

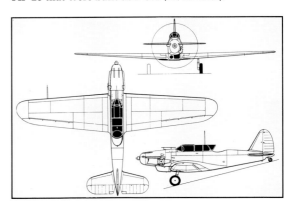

(Above) The P-30A (later PB-2A), the only single-engined two-seat fighter used by the USAAC. (Below) A PB-2A in service with the 35th Pursuit Squadron.

CONSOLIDATED PB-2A SPECIAL   USA

In May 1935, the Matériel Division of the Army Air Corps called for proposals for a single-seat fighter to succeed the Boeing P-26. Among the contenders in the third competition, held in April 1936, was a single-seat modification of Consolidated's two-seat PB-2A. Known simply as the "Special", this aircraft was, in fact, a conversion of the seventh PB-2A and, retaining the 700 hp V-1710-61 Conqueror, was the only aircraft with a liquid-cooled inline engine in the contest. The PB-2A "Special" had the aft cockpit faired over but was otherwise essentially similar to the two-seater. It was not

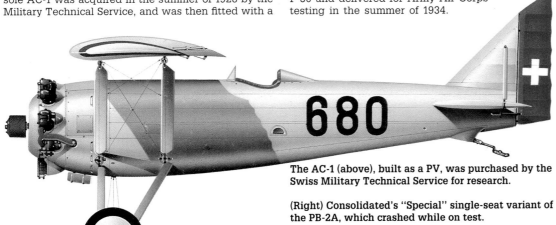

The AC-1 (above), built as a PV, was purchased by the Swiss Military Technical Service for research.

(Right) Consolidated's "Special" single-seat variant of the PB-2A, which crashed while on test.

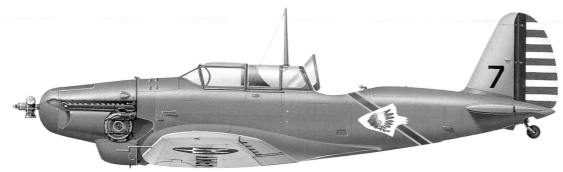

A Consolidated PB-2A – first USAAC fighter with retractable u/c – serving in 1935 with the 94th Pursuit Squadron, 1st PG, at Selfridge Field, Michigan.

favoured by the AAC as it was larger, heavier and more expensive than the competing types. During the contest this aircraft crashed and was totally destroyed. *Max speed, 275 mph (442 km/h) at 25,000 ft (7 620 m). Time to 10,000 ft (3 050 m), 5.0 min. Max range, 1,012 mls (1 629 km). Empty weight, 4,315 lb (1 957 kg). Loaded weight 5,602 lb (2 541 kg). Span, 43 ft 11 in (13,38 m). Length, 30 ft 0 in (9,14 m). Height, 8 ft 3 in (2,51 m). Wing area, 297 sq ft (27,59 m²).*

CONSOLIDATED-VULTEE
XP-54   USA

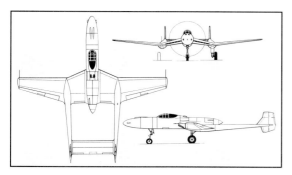

The Consolidated-Vultee XP-54, as tested in 1943.

An outgrowth of the Vultee Model 78 project and built by the Vultee Field Division of the Consolidated-Vultee Aircraft Company, the Model 84 was one of three designs awarded development contracts as a result of an informal design contest initiated by the Army Air Corps on 18 December 1939. Two prototypes were eventually ordered under the designation XP-54, these flying on 15 January 1943 and 24 May 1944 respectively. Powered by a turbo-supercharged Lycoming XH-2470-1 24-cylinder liquid-cooled engine rated at 2,300 hp for take-off, the XP-54 embodied a number of novel features, including a "ducted wing section" embodying the oil and coolant radiators and intercoolers. An electrically-operated pilot's seat also served as a lift to provide cockpit access and egress, and a pivoting (ie +3° to −6°) nose

(Above) The first of the two XP-54s, completed at the beginning of 1943 in contemporary OD finish.

Photographed in May 1944, the second of the two XP-54s is seen below during its single test flight.

section contained two 37-mm T-9 cannon mounted rigidly and two 0.5-in (12,7-mm) machine guns on movable mountings, different elevations being adopted to compensate for the differing trajectories of the two types of weapon. The XP-54 was also one of the first single-seat fighters designed from the outset for cabin pressurization. Performance of the XP-54 fell appreciably below specification and, in consequence, further development was discontinued. *Max speed, 290 mph (467 km/h) at sea level, 381 mph (613 km/h) at 28,500 ft (8 685 m). Time to 26,000 ft (7 925 m), 17.3 min. Endurance, 1.0 hr. Empty weight, 15,262 lb (6 923 kg). Normal loaded weight, 18,233 lb (8 271 kg). Span, 53 ft 10 in (16,41 m). Length, 54 ft 8¾ in (16,68 m). Height, 14 ft 6 in (4,42 m). Wing area, 455.5 sq ft (42,32 m²).*

CONSOLIDATED-VULTEE
XP-81   USA

Conceived as a long-range escort fighter combining turboprop with turbojet power, the XP-81 (Model 102) was begun on 5 January 1944, and was intended to carry an armament of either six 0.5-in (12,7-mm) machine guns or six 20-mm cannon. A single-seater, the XP-81 was designed for a single 2,300 bhp General Electric TG-100 (later redesignated XT31-GE-1) turboprop and a 3,750 lb st (1 700 kgp) Allison J33-GE-5 turbojet, the former being employed for cruise and the power of the turbojet being added for high-speed flight. Two XP-81s were ordered, the first of these flying on 7

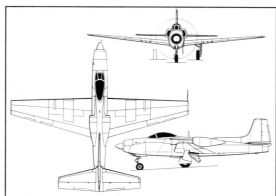

(Above) The XP-81 mixed-power plant fighter.

(Above) The one and only XP-81 as first flown with a V-1650-7 piston engine in the nose and (below) after being re-engined with the TG-100 turboprop.

February 1945 with a V-1650-7 Merlin piston engine in place of the TG-100, which was experiencing teething troubles. The XP-81 evinced very good handling characteristics and 13 YP-81 pre-production aircraft were ordered (the intention being to power these with the lighter and more powerful TG-110 turboprop). Flight tests with the TG-100 installed did not commence until 21 December 1945, by which time the pre-production YP-81s had been cancelled. The turboprop proved to be capable of producing barely more than 1,400 bhp, the performance of the XP-81 failing to meet specification and further development being abandoned. The following performance data are estimated on the basis of the anticipated engine power. *Max speed, 478 mph (769 km/h) at sea level, 507 mph (816 km/h) at 30,000 ft (9 144 m). Range 2,500 mls (4 023 km) at 275 mph (443 km/h). Empty weight, 12,755 lb (5 785 kg). Normal loaded weight, 19,500 lb (8 845 kg). Span, 50 ft 6 in (15,39 m). Length, 44 ft 10 in (13,66 m). Height, 14 ft 0 in (4,27 m). Wing area, 425 sq ft (39,48 m²).*

CONVAIR F2Y-1 (SEA DART)   USA

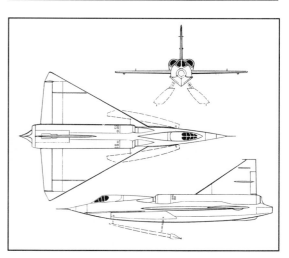

Convair F2Y-1 with the retractable hydro-skis dotted.

One of the most innovative single-seat fighters of the 'fifties, combining the then latest developments in aerodynamics and hydrodynamics, the Model 2 Sea Dart was designed to meet a requirement for a seaplane fighter capable of M=0.95, but was expected to achieve M=1.5. Utilising a blended hull and hydro-skis, the Sea Dart was ordered in prototype form on 19 January 1951, the designation XF2Y-1 being assigned. Twelve production examples were ordered on 28 August 1952 as F2Y-1s, contracts later being amended to add four YF2Y-1s. The Sea Dart was intended to be powered by two Westinghouse XJ46-WE-2 turbojets

The XF2Y-1 above was the first of five Sea Darts built to test the advanced hydrodynamics of this fighter.

each offering 6,100 lb st (2 767 kgp) with afterburning, but the first XF2Y-1, which flew on 9 April 1953, had two 3,400 lb st (1 542 kgp) Westinghouse J34-WE-32s. Severe vibration of the hydro-skis while taxying and poor high-speed performance led to the cancellation of one XF2Y-1 and all F2Y-1s. The power output forecast for the XJ46-WE-2 intended for the Sea Dart failed to measure up to expectations and indicated that a max speed no higher than M=0.99 was likely to be attained. The second XF2Y-1 was completed as one of the four YF2Y-1s, initially flying with J34s and later being retrofitted with J46-WE-2s which also powered all three remaining YF2Y-1s. Limited trials were continued until 1956, when the entire programme was abandoned, leaving two of the YF2Y-1s unflown. The full performance envelope was not explored and the following data are estimates for the YF2Y-1 with fully-rated engines. *Max speed, 695 mph (1 118 km/h) at 8,000 ft (2 440 m), 825 mph (1 328 km/h) at 36,000 ft (10 975 m), or Mach=1.25. Time to 35,000 ft (10 670 m), 1.7 min. Empty weight, 12,652 lb (5 739 kg). Loaded weight, 16,527 lb (7 497 kg). Span, 33 ft 8 in (10,26 m). Length, 52 ft 7 in (16,03 m). Height (skis down), 20 ft 9 in (6,32 m). Wing area, 563 sq ft (52,30 m²).*

CONVAIR XFY-1   USA

The XFY-1 (Model 5) was a radical experimental single-seat fighter evolved as part of a programme to examine the feasibility of operating tail-sitting, vertical-take-off-and-landing aircraft from small platforms on ships, three prototypes being ordered in March 1951. Featuring wings of modified delta planform and immense vertical tail surfaces (the ventral surfaces being jettisonable to permit an emergency landing to be made in the conventional wing-supported mode), the XFY-1 rested

The single XFY-1 "tail-sitter" (above and below) which was tested with little success in 1954, the whole programme being abandoned after a few months.

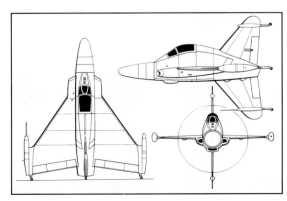

on small castoring wheels at the tips of the horizontal and vertical surfaces. The pilot's ejector seat was mounted on gimbals which permitted it to tilt 45 deg when the aircraft assumed the vertical attitude. Power was provided by a 5,850 ehp Allison YT40-A-6 (pending availability of the planned 6,955 ehp XT40-A-16) driving contra-rotating propellers, and proposed armament comprised four 20-mm cannon in wingtip pods or 48 2.75-in (70-mm) rockets. The XFY-1 effected its first vertical take-off and landing on 1 August 1954, and its first transition on 2 November 1954, but, although it was flown for some 40 hours, severe piloting difficulties led to the abandonment of the programme with only one prototype completed. The full performance envelope was not explored and the following data are applicable to the planned definitive XT40-A-16-powered aircraft. *Max speed, 610 mph (982 km/h) at 15,000 ft (4 570 m), 592 mph (953 km/h) at 35,000 ft (10 670 m). Time to 20,000 ft (6 100 m), 2.7 min, to 30,000 ft (9 150 m), 4.6 min. Empty weight, 11,742 lb (5 327 kg). Loaded weight, 16,250 lb (7 371 kg). Span, 27 ft 7¾ in (8,43 m). Length, 34 ft 11¾ in (10,66 m). Vertical span, 22 ft 11 in (6,98 m). Wing area, 355 sq ft (32,98 m²).*

Key to Convair F-102A Delta Dagger

1 Pitot head
2 Radome
3 Radar scanner
4 Scanner tracking mechanism
5 ILS glideslope aerial
6 Radar mounting bulkhead
7 Radar pulse generator and modulator units
8 Nose compartment access doors
9 Static port
10 Lower IFF aerial
11 Angle of attack transmitter
12 TACAN aerial
13 MG-10 fire control system electronics
14 Nose compartment longeron
15 Infra-red detector
16 Electronic cooling air duct
17 Windscreen panels
18 Central vision splitter
19 Instrument panel shroud
20 Rudder pedals and linkages
21 Cockpit front pressure bulkhead
22 Air conditioning system ram air intake
23 Boundary layer splitter plate
24 Electrical system equipment
25 Port air intake
26 Nosewheel door
27 Taxying lamp
28 Nosewheel, forward retracting
29 Nose undercarriage leg strut
30 Torque scissor links
31 Intake duct framing
32 Nose undercarriage pivot mounting
33 Cockpit pressure floor
34 Port side console panel
35 Engine throttle lever
36 Two-handed control grip, radar and flight controls
37 Pilot's ejection seat
38 Canopy handle
39 Starboard side console panel
40 Radar display
41 Optical sight
42 Cockpit canopy cover, upward hinged
43 Ejection seat headrest
44 Boundary layer spill duct
45 Sloping cockpit rear pressure bulkhead
46 Air conditioning plant
47 Canopy external release
48 Canopy jack
49 Air exit louvres
50 Equipment bay access hatches, port and starboard
51 Canopy hinge
52 Radio and electronics equipment bay
53 Forward position light
54 Intake trunking
55 Missile bay cooling air duct
56 Missile bay door pneumatic jacks
57 Canopy emergency release
58 Liquid oxygen converter
59 Electrical system equipment bay
60 Fuselage upper longeron
61 Upper IFF aerial
62 Wing front spar attachment bulkhead
63 Pneumatic system air bottles
64 Bifurcated intake duct
65 Close-pitched fuselage frame construction
66 Engine bleed air duct
67 Anti-collision light
68 Starboard wing forward main fuel tank. Total internal fuel capacity 1,085 US gal (4 107 l)
69 Inboard wing fence
70 Fuel system piping
71 Centre section wing dry bay
72 Wing pylon mountings and connectors
73 Starboard main undercarriage pivot mounting
74 Dorsal spine fairing
75 Intake duct mixing chamber
76 Engine intake centre-body fairing
77 Wing main spar attachment bulkheads
78 Intake compressor face
79 Forward engine mounting
80 Pratt & Whitney J57-P-23A afterburning turbojet
81 Engine oil tank, capacity 5.5 US gal (20 l)
82 Oil filler cap
83 Starboard wing aft main fuel tanks
84 Fuel feed and vent piping
85 Ventral actuator fairing
86 Outboard wing fence
87 Cambered leading edge
88 Wing tip camber wash-out
89 Starboard navigation light
90 Fixed portion of trailing edge
91 Starboard outer elevon
92 Elevon hydraulic actuator
93 Trailing-edge dry bay
94 Fin leading-edge rib construction
95 Aerial tuning units
96 Fin attachment joints
97 Tailfin construction
98 Artificial feel system pitot intakes
99 Sloping front spar
100 Upper fin multi-spar construction
101 Fin tip aerial fairing
102 UHF aerials
103 VOR localiser aerial
104 Rudder
105 Honeycomb core rudder construction
106 Split airbrake panels
107 Airbrake pneumatic jacks
108 Airbrake, open position
109 Variable area afterburner exhaust nozzle
110 Aft fuselage aerodynamic (area-rule) fairing
111 Exhaust nozzle control jacks (8)
112 Tailcone attachment joint frame (engine removal)
113 Rear position lights
114 Afterburner duct
115 Engine bay internal heat shield
116 Brake parachute housing
117 Rudder hydraulic actuator
118 Rudder trim and feel force control units
119 Afterburner fuel manifold
120 Rear engine mounting
121 Inboard elevon hydraulic actuator
122 Engine turbine section
123 Bleed air connections
124 Bleed air blow-off valve
125 Engine accessory equipment gearbox
126 Wing spar/fuselage frame pin joints
127 Wing root rib
128 Port wing aft integral fuel tanks
129 Fuel tank dividing rib
130 Rear spar
131 Trailing edge ribs
132 Runway emergency arrestor hook, lowered
133 Elevon spar
134 Inboard elevon
135 Elevon rig construction
136 Outboard elevon
137 Trailing edge honeycomb panel
138 Wingtip fairing construction
139 Port navigation light
140 Cambered leading edge rib construction
141 Outboard wing fence
142 Wing rib construction
143 Main undercarriage mounting rib
144 Twin main spars
145 Main undercarriage side strut
146 Hydraulic retraction jack
147 Main undercarriage leg pivot mounting
148 Drag strut and pneumatic brake reservoir
149 Landing lamp
150 Port wing dry bay
151 Wing pylon mountings and connectors

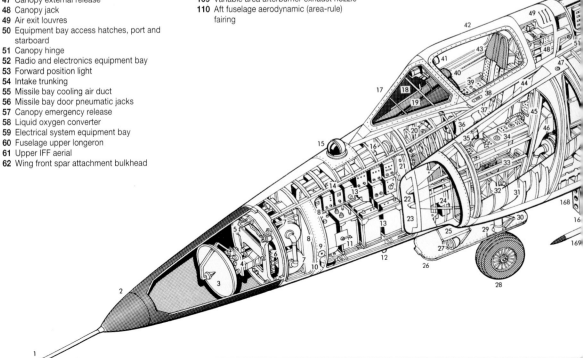

CONVAIR F-102 DELTA DAGGER USA

The first fighter of delta wing configuration to fly, the Delta Dagger was also the first fighter to dispense with gun armament completely in favour of missiles. The first of two YF-102 prototypes flew on 24 October 1953. From the outset serious deficiencies in performance were apparent, this leading to major redesign and resulting in the YF-102A conforming to the area rule formula. The first of four YF-102As was flown on 20 December 1954 (a further eight YF-102s having mean-

A Convair F-102A serving with 509th Fighter Interceptor Squadron at Clark AB in the Philippines.

while been completed for various test purposes) and the production F-102A entered service with the USAF Air Defense Command from mid-1956. Production of the Delta Dagger terminated in April 1958 with the 875th aircraft. Powered by a Pratt & Whitney J57-P-23 turbojet rated at 11,700 lb st (5 307 kgp) dry and 17,200 lb st (7 802 kgp) with afterburning, the F-102A's armament comprised three AIM-4C, D, E or F Falcon and one AIM-26A or -26B Super Falcon air-to-air missiles. Ex-USAF F-102As were supplied to the Greek (20) and Turkish (40) air forces. *Max speed, 825 mph (1 328 km/h) at 40,000 ft (12 190 m) or Mach=1.25.*

152 Main undercarriage leg door
153 Port mainwheel
154 Torque scissor links
155 Port wing forward integral fuel tank
156 Inboard wing fence
157 Mainwheel door
158 Hydraulic reservoirs
159 Position of ram air turbine on starboard side
160 Missile bay aft section doors
161 Retractable over-run barrier probe
162 Wing front spar
163 Port missile bay doors
164 Pantographic action missile displacement gear
165 Displacement gear hydraulic jack
166 Missile launch rail
167 Missile bay door integral rocket launch tubes
168 Centre missile bay door
169 2.75-in (7-cm) FFAR folding fin rockets (24)
170 AIM-4D Falcon air-to-air missile (6)
171 Port wing fuel tank pylon
172 External fuel tank, capacity 215 US gal (813 l)

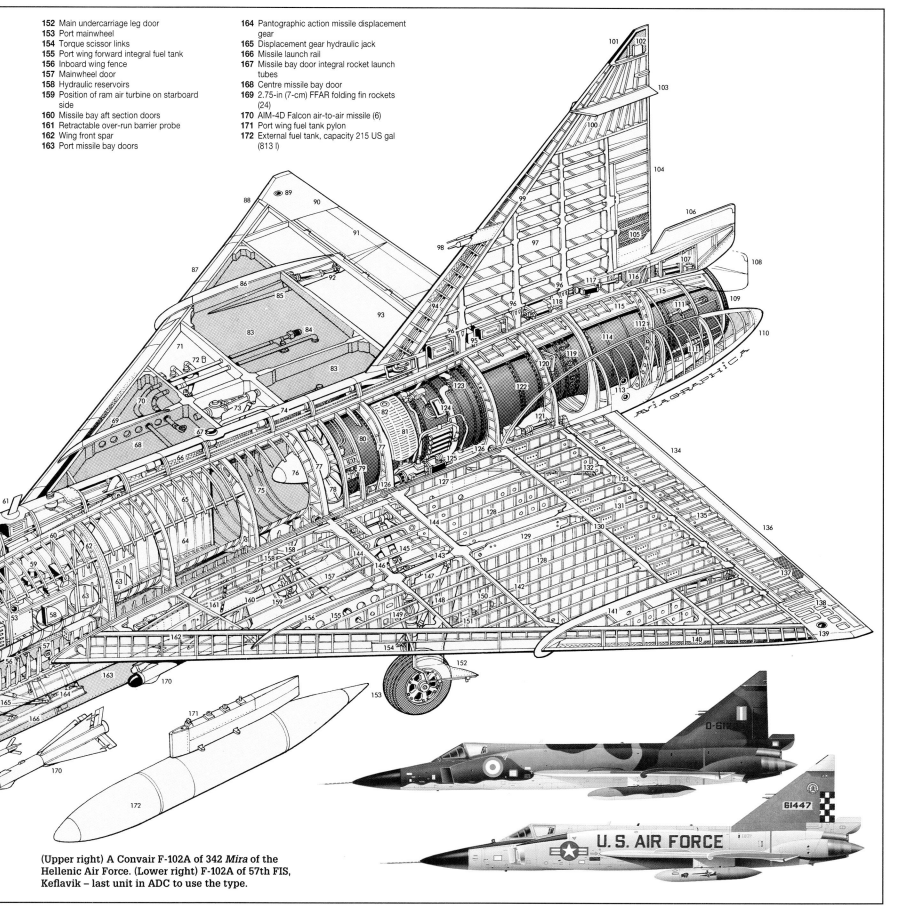

(Upper right) A Convair F-102A of 342 *Mira* of the Hellenic Air Force. (Lower right) F-102A of 57th FIS, Keflavik – last unit in ADC to use the type.

the lower mainplanes and elevated or depressed through a limited range of movement. The leading edge of the tailplane was also hinged. Intended for the 200 hp Clerget 11E eleven-cylinder rotary or, failing that, the 160 hp Gnome Monosoupape 9Nc nine-cylinder rotary, the C.S.L.1 was in fact fitted with the 140 hp Clerget 9Bf nine-cylinder rotary. A second proto-type was to have been fitted with the 200 hp unit, but it is doubtful if this was completed. The following data are estimated for the C.S.L.1 with the 200 hp engine. *Max speed, 149 mph (240 km/h) at sea level. Time to 13,125 ft (4 000 m), 14 min. Endurance, 2.5 hrs. Empty weight, 1,080 lb (490 kg). Loaded weight, 1,720 lb (780 kg). Span, 25 ft 7 in (7,80 m). Wing area 204.5 sq ft (19,0 m².)*

(Below) The Convair F-102A and (above) one of the 20 examples of the Delta Dagger that served with the 114 *Pterix Mahis* of the Hellenic Air Force at Tanagra.

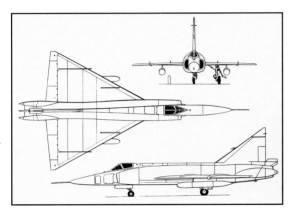

National Guard until August 1988. *Max speed, 1,328 mph (2 137 km/h) at 35,000 ft (10 670 m), or Mach=2.01. Combat radius (without external fuel), 575 mls (925 km). Empty weight, 24,315 lb (11 029 kg). Maximum loaded weight, 39,195 lb (17 779 kg). Span, 38 ft 3½ in (11,67 m). Length (over nose probe), 70 ft 8¾ in (21,55 m). Height, 20 ft 3⅓ in (6,18 m). Wing area, 697.8 sq ft (64,83 m²).*

(Below) A Convair F-106A flown by the 194th Fighter Interceptor Squadron, California ANG.

Leading-edge flaps on the lower mainplane were a feature of the C.S.L.1 (above and below), only one example of which was built and flown in 1918.

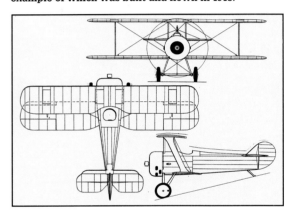

Initial climb, 13,000 ft/min (66,0 m/sec). Max range, 1,350 mls (2 173 km). Max loaded weight, 31,500 lb (14 288 kg). Span, 38 ft 1½ in (11,60 m). Length (over nose probe), 68 ft 4⅔ in (20,83 m). Height, 21 ft 2½ in (6,45 m). Wing area, 695 sq ft (64,57 m²).

CONVAIR F-106 DELTA DART USA

Essentially a derivative of the Delta Dagger initiated as the F-102B, the F-106A Delta Dart entered service with the USAF Air Defense Command in July 1959, the first trials aircraft having flown on 26 December 1956. Powered by a Pratt & Whitney J75-P-17 turbojet rated at 17,200 lb st (7 802 kgp) dry and 24,500 lb st (11 113 kgp) with afterburning, the F-106A featured an internal weapons bay for two AIR-2A or -2B Genie unguided nuclear-tipped missiles and four AIM-4F or -4G Falcon AAMs supplemented (from 1973) by a 20-mm M-61 multi-barrel rotary cannon. The F-106B was a two-seat combat training version retaining full operational capa-bility, and Delta Dart production, which was completed in July 1961, comprised 277 F-106As and 63 F-106Bs. The Delta Dart remained in service with the Air

(Below) The production Convair F-106A Delta Dart.

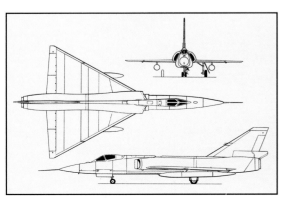

COURTOIS-SUFFIT-LESCOP
C.S.L.1   France

Designed by Roger Courtois-Suffit in collaboration with *Capitaine* Lescop, the C.S.L.1 single-seat fighter was flown for the first time in January 1918, having been constructed by the SAIB (Société Anonyme d'Applica-tions Industrielles du Bois) concern. The C.S.L.1 was, significantly, one of the first (if not *the* first) aircraft to feature leading-edge wing flaps, these being fitted to

(Above top) An F-106A of the 460th FIS, and (immediately above) US Bicentennial markings on an F-106A serving with the 125th FIG, Florida ANG.

(Below) F-106As of the 5th FIS (foreground) and 87th FIS, two of 13 Air Defense Command squadrons that were equipped with the Delta Dart.

CURTISS S-3   USA

Essentially a triplane derivative of the S-2 "Wireless" (signifying lack of wing bracing wires) unarmed biplane "scout", the S-3, or "Triplane Speed Scout", possessed a similar fuselage and 100 hp Curtiss OXX-3 engine, and initially retained the ducted propeller spinner featured by the biplane. Interplane bracing employed "K"-type struts and, on its second flight during the summer of 1917, the S-3 attained an altitude of 16,500 ft (5 030 m), which was a record at the time. For initial trials, the centre wing was attached to the fuselage at low shoulder position, but the gap between all three wings was subsequently increased and the centre wing was raised above the fuselage. After redesign of the rudder and the discarding of the ducted spinner, the S-3 successfully completed evaluation trials and four were ordered during the course of 1917 for the US Army Signal Corps. It was proposed to arm the S-3 with two unsynchronised Lewis guns which were to fire over the propeller arc, but the S-3s were, in the event, delivered to the Signal Corps without armament. *Max speed, 115 mph (185 km/h). Time to 9,000 ft (2 745 m), 10 min. Empty weight, 970 lb (440 kg). Loaded weight, 1,320 lb (599 kg). Span, 25 ft 0 in (7,62 m). Length, 19 ft 6 in (5,94 m). Height, 8 ft 7 in (2,62 m). Wing area, 142.6 sq ft (13,25 m².)*

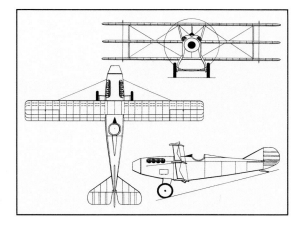

The first Curtiss S-3 seen above in August 1917 after the ducted propeller spinner had been discarded, and, below, in the form in which it was originally flown.

CURTISS S-6   USA

A refined version of the S-3 with revised strutting carrying the centre section of the upper wing and the root attachments of the centre wing, a modified undercarriage and other changes, the S-6 triplane of 1917 was the first US "scout" to be fitted with twin forward-firing

(Below) A development of the S-3, the sole Curtiss S-6 was flown in 1917 with an unusual installation of twin Lewis guns above the cockpit.

machine guns, these being gas-operated Lewis guns which were mounted side-by-side on inverted and inclined "V" struts immediately beneath the centre section of the upper wing and firing outside the propeller disc. Only a single example of the S-6 was built and tested. *Max speed, 110 mph (177 km/h). Loaded weight, 1,377 lb (625 kg). Span, 25 ft 0 in (7,62 m). Length, 19 ft 6 in (5,94 m). Height, 8 ft 7 in (2,62 m). Wing area, 142.6 sq ft (13,25 m²).*

CURTISS GS   USA

During 1917, the US Navy issued the Curtiss company with a contract for five single-seat fighting scout float seaplanes powered by a US-built version of the 100 hp Gnome nine-cylinder rotary, the GS designation indicating "Gnome Scout". These were completed under the designation GS-2 when a supplementary contract was issued for a sixth aeroplane which was assigned the designation GS-1. The GS-1 was a single-seat triplane with a single central float and outrigger stabilizing floats which drew heavily on Curtiss S-3 experience. An unusual feature was the introduction of shock absorbers in the struts between the fuselage and

The GS-1 "Gnome Scout" triplane (below) was similar in most respects to five GS-2 biplanes that preceded it.

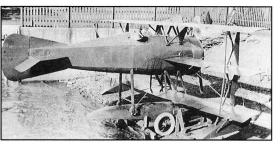

the central float. These resulted in the float angle being subject to change at high speed on the water and producing an undesirable porpoising. Delivered to the US Navy early in 1918, the GS-1 was flown several times by US Navy acceptance pilots, but was eventually damaged beyond repair as a result of a heavy landing. The five similarly-powered GS-2s differed from the GS-1 primarily in being of biplane configuration, but little is recorded of these aircraft apart from the fact that they suffered from tail heaviness. No data are available for either GS-1 or GS-2.

CURTISS CB   USA

The CB (Curtiss Battleplane), unofficially known as the "Liberty Battler", was an experimental two-seat fighter developed and flown early in 1918 as a result of difficulties being experienced with the Liberty-engined version of the Bristol F2B. Powered by a 425 hp 12-cylinder Liberty 12 water-cooled engine, the CB two-bay biplane was an early example of "Curtiss ply" construction – two layers of 2-in (5,08-cm) wide wood veneer being cross-laminated over a form to build up a

(Above and below) The sole Curtiss Battleplane (CB) of 1918, also known as the "Liberty Battler".

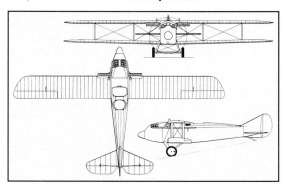

monocoque fuselage shell. In an effort to maintain fuselage streamlining, the radiators were slung under the upper wing centre section, where they were found to have a seriously detrimental effect on the airflow. The fairing of the upper wing into the top fuselage contour resulted in a very narrow wing gap, with consequent aerodynamic penalties. While it provided the rear gunner with an excellent field of fire, it impaired the forward and downward view of the pilot, necessitating the provision of small windows in the fuselage sides. Flown in May 1918, the sole prototype CB proved to have extremely poor handling characteristics and crashed early in its test programme. *Empty weight, 3,575 lb (1 622 kg). Span, 39 ft 4 in (11,98 m). Length, 27 ft 1 in (8,25 m).*

CURTISS HA   USA

Designed by Capt B L Smith of the US Marine Corps as a two-seat patrol fighter floatplane for use in the Dunkirk-Calais area, the HA – known unofficially as the "Dunkirk Fighter" – was intended to combat the Brandenburg float fighters and was built at the experimental plant of the Curtiss Engineering Corporation. Of conventional wooden construction with fabric skinning, the HA was powered by a 425 hp Liberty 12 engine and featured an unusually rotund fuselage. Proposed armament comprised two synchronized 0.3-in (7,62-mm) Marlin machine guns and two Lewis guns of the same calibre on a Scarff mounting in the rear cockpit. The HA was flown for the first time on 21 March 1918, but was found to be unstable longitudinally and seriously tail heavy. The initial test terminated in a crash. Curtiss was then awarded a contract for two further prototypes, the first of which, the HA-1, utilized salvaged

(Below) Prototype Curtiss HA, also known as the "Dunkirk Fighter", intended to serve in Europe.

components from the original HA and featured revised vertical tail surfaces, an annular-type radiator and relocated wings. The HA-1 demonstrated appreciably improved handling qualities, but was written off after a fire in the air. The third HA prototype, the HA-2, differed appreciably from the HA-1 (see following entry). The following data apply to the HA-1 float fighter. *Max speed, 126 mph (203 km/h). Time to 9,000 ft (2 743 m), 10 min. Empty weight, 2,449 lb (1 111 kg). Loaded weight, 3,602 lb (1 634 kg). Span, 36 ft 0 in (10,97 m). Length, 30 ft 9 in (9,37 m). Height, 10 ft 7 in (3,23 m). Wing area, 387 sq ft (35,95 m²).*

CURTISS HA-2   USA

The third HA float fighter prototype embodied considerable redesign as the HA-2. Powered by a 12-cylinder Liberty 12 water-cooled engine, like the preceding prototypes, the HA-2 had longer-span wings of marginally increased chord and gap, the upper wing being raised clear of the fuselage, the decking of which was lowered. The radiator was redesigned, but cooling problems were encountered and although the HA-2 proved more docile than the lighter HA-1, it possessed insufficient promise to warrant further development. *Max speed, 118 mph (190 km/h). Time to 7,900 ft (2 408 m), 10 min. Empty weight, 2,946 lb (1 336 kg). Loaded weight, 3,907 lb (1 772 kg). Span, 42 ft 0 in (12,80 m). Length, 30 ft 9 in (9,37 m). Height, 11 ft 5 in (3,48 m). Wing area, 490 sq ft (45,52 m²).*

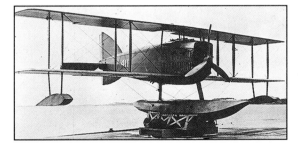

The Curtiss HA-2 (above and below), of which only a single prototype was built, differed from the HA in respect of wing and engine cowling detail.

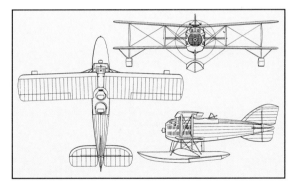

CURTISS 18-T   USA

Designed by Charles B Kirkham, the Curtiss 18-T two-seat fighter triplane was ordered by the US Navy on 30 March 1918 when a contract was placed for two prototypes. The first of these was flown on 7 May 1918. Designed around the Curtiss-Kirkham K-12 water-cooled 12-cylinder engine of 400 hp, the 18-T was of extremely clean aerodynamic design by contemporary standards and featured a monocoque three-ply fuselage and side radiators positioned between the lower wings. The proposed armament comprised two forward-firing synchronized 0.3-in (7,62-mm) Marlin machine guns and two 0.3-in (7,62-mm) Lewis guns on a Scarff mounting in the rear cockpit. Known unofficially as the "Wasp" (an allusion to the sound emitted by the K-12 engine during landing approach), the 18-T initially suffered some tail heaviness which was corrected by applying five degrees of sweepback to the wings for further trials. A max speed of 163 mph (262 km/h) was achieved with full military load in August 1918, the 18-T being acclaimed as the world's fastest aeroplane as a result. The US Navy promptly ordered two examples,

To correct tail-heaviness, the Curtiss 18-T (above and below) was given five degrees of wing sweepback soon after first flight, as illustrated here.

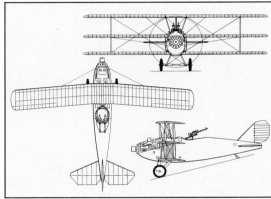

the first of which was delivered in February 1919. In the summer of 1919, the first prototype was fitted with longer-span two-bay wings, these having a span and area of 40 ft 7½ in (12,38 m) and 400 sq ft (37,16 m²) respectively, and in this form the aircraft became the 18T-2, the short-span version becoming the 18T-1. The 18T-2 established a world altitude record of 34,910 ft (10 640 m) on 18 September 1919, and a second 18T-2 was built by Curtiss for export to Bolivia, where it arrived in 1920. The following data relate to the 18T-1. *Max speed, 165 mph (265 km/h). Time to 12,500 ft (3 810 m), 10 min. Endurance, 5.9 hrs. Empty weight, 1,980 lb (898 kg). Loaded weight, 3,050 lb (1 383 kg). Span, 31 ft 10 in (9,70 m). Length, 23 ft 4 in (7,11 m). Height, 9 ft 10¾ in (3,02 m). Wing area, 288 sq ft (26,76 m²).*

Modified with long-span, two-bay wings, the second Curtiss 18T (below) was redesignated as the 18T-2.

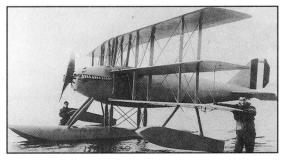

CURTISS 18-B   USA

US Army interest in the 18-T prompted Curtiss to offer the same basic design in two-bay biplane configuration, and an order was placed by the US Army for two

Apart from its biplane configuration, the Curtiss 18-B (below) was identical with the 18-T triplane.

examples in August 1918. Known unofficially as the "Hornet", the 18-B two-seat fighter employed an identical fuselage to that of the 18-T and a similar Curtiss-Kirkham K-12 engine. The proposed armament comprised two forward-firing Marlin guns and two Lewis guns on a flexible mount. The two prototypes were delivered to the US Army during the summer of 1919, one being confined to static testing and the other crashing shortly after the commencement of flight trials, and further development was then abandoned. *Max speed, 160 mph (257 km/h). Empty weight, 1,690 lb (767 kg). Loaded weight, 2,867 lb (1 300 kg). Span, 37 ft 5¾ in (11,41 m). Length, 23 ft 4 in (7,11 m). Wing area, 306 sq ft (28,43 m²).*

CURTISS-ORENCO D   USA

The first single-seat fighter of indigenous US design to achieve production status, the Model D was conceived around the 300 hp Hispano-Suiza H eight-cylinder water-cooled engine. The first of four prototypes built by the Ordnance Engineering Corporation (Orenco) was completed in January 1919. Curtiss was assigned a production contract for 50 aircraft and undertook some redesign. This included the introduction of dihedral and overhanging, balanced ailerons, and revision of the engine installation. Of wooden construction with ply-covered fuselage and fabric-covered wings, the Curtiss-built Model D utilised a 330 hp Wright-built derivative of the French engine and carried an armament of two 0.3-in (7,62-mm) machine guns, deliveries commencing in August 1921. One Model D was experimentally fitted with French Lamblin radiators attached to the fuselage sides, and another was fitted with a turbo-supercharger for high altitude trials. *Max speed, 139 mph (224 km/h) at sea level, 136 mph (219 km/h) at 6,500 ft (1 980 m). Climb, 1,140 ft/min (5.8 m/sec). Endurance, 2.5 hrs. Empty weight, 1,908 lb (865 kg). Loaded weight, 2,820 lb (1 279 kg). Span, 32 ft 11⅝ in (10,05 m). Length, 21 ft 5½ in (6,54 m). Height, 8 ft 4 in (2,54 m). Wing area, 273 sq ft (25,36 m²).*

(Above and below) For early post-war service with the Army Air Corps, Curtiss built 50 Orenco Ds after modifying designs of the Ordnance Engineering Corp.

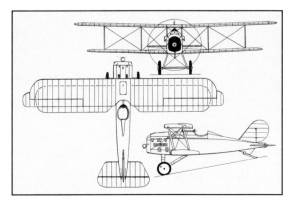

One Curtiss-Orenco D was experimentally fitted with Lamblin "pineapple" radiators as seen below.

CURTISS PN-1 USA

Designed by the US Army Engineering Division as a specialised single-seat night fighter, two prototypes of the PN-1 were built by Curtiss, powered by the 220 hp Liberty L-825 six-cylinder water-cooled engine. Optimised for docile handling characteristics at the lower end of the speed range in order to ease operation from small blacked-out fields, the PN-1 was completed without interplane struts, but steel-tube N-type struts were introduced to improve torsional stiffness before any attempt to fly the first prototype. In the event, only this one PN-1 was completed, and the results of any flight testing are not on record. It is known, however, that the sole prototype was used for static tests at McCook Field during 1921. *Max speed, 108 mph (174 km/h). Time to 6,500 ft (1 980 m), 5.5 min. Range, 255 mls (410 km). Empty weight, 1,631 lb (740 kg). Loaded weight, 2,311 lb (1 048 kg). Span, 30 ft 10 in (9,40 m). Length, 23 ft 6 in (7,16 m). Height, 10 ft 3 in (3,12 m). Wing area, 300 sq ft (27,87 m²).*

The sole PN-1 (below) was designed with cantilever wings, but interplane struts were added before flight.

CURTISS PW-8 USA

Progenitor of the famous Hawk series of fighters, the PW-8 (the "PW" prefix indicating "Pursuit Watercooled") was a single-seat two-bay fighter biplane of mixed construction – plywood-covered wooden wings and fabric-skinned welded steel tube fuselage – powered by a 440 hp Curtiss D-12 water-cooled 12-cylinder Vee engine. Three prototypes were ordered on 27 April 1923, and the first of these, flown in the previous January, was retroactively designated XPW-8 on 14 May 1924. The second prototype, flown in March 1924, embodied some aerodynamic refinement and provided the basis for the production PW-8, 25 examples being ordered on 25 September 1923 and delivered between June and August 1924. The PW-8 featured wing surface radiators and armament normally comprised two 0.3-in (7,62-mm) machine guns. A turbo-supercharger was experimentally fitted to the second production aircraft, and the third prototype (XPW-8A), delivered in February 1924, featured 30-ft (9,14-m) span single-bay wings and a revised radiator arrangement. It was subsequently fitted with a tunnel-type radiator (as the XPW-8A) and, in December 1924, with 31 ft 6 in (9,60 m) span wings of tapered planform and Clark Y

Wings of tapered planform and a Clark Y aerofoil were distinctive features of the Curtiss XPW-8B (below).

A Curtiss PW-8 of the 17th Pursuit Sqn, 1st PG, as flown in the 1924 Mitchell Trophy Race.

aerofoil section as the XPW-8B. It thus became, in effect, the prototype P-1 Hawk. *Max speed, 168 mph (270 km/h) at sea level. Cruising speed, 160 mph (257 km/h) at 10,000 ft (3 050 m). Time to 10,000 ft (3 050 m), 9.0 min. Range, 440 mls (708 km). Empty weight, 2,191 lb (994 kg). Loaded weight, 3,151 lb (1 429 kg). Span, 32 ft 0 in (9,75 m). Length, 22 ft 6 in (6,86 m). Height, 8 ft 10 in (2,69 m). Wing area, 287 sq ft (26,66 m²).*

(Above) The original PW-8 (later known as XPW-8), progenitor of the famed Curtiss Hawk series, and (below) the PW-8 in its series production form.

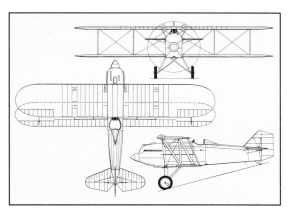

CURTISS F4C-1 USA

The first Curtiss fighter built under the US Navy designating system combining type, sequence of design and manufacturer, the F4C-1 (F2C and F3C being "paper" designations assigned to the R2C and R3C

racing aircraft respectively) was designed by Charles W Hall. It was essentially an all-metal version of the wooden Naval Aircraft Factory TS-1, which had been designed by the US Navy Bureau of Aeronautics and production of which had been assigned to Curtiss. The F4C-1, two examples of which were built in 1924 and the first flown on 4 September, embodied some aerodynamic redesign. Its wings featured tubular spars and stamped dural ribs, and the fuselage was built up of dural tubing in a Warren truss form, the whole being fabric covered. By comparison with the TS-1, the lower wing was raised to the base of the fuselage. Armament comprised two 0.3-in (7,62-mm) machine guns and

(Above and below) The Curtiss F4C-1 – the first of two being illustrated by this photograph – was a metal-framed version of the Naval Aircraft Factory TS-1.

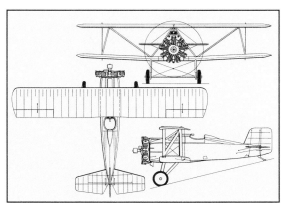

power was provided by a nine-cylinder Wright J-3 radial rated at 200 hp. *Max speed, 126 mph (203 km/h). Time to 5,000 ft (1 525 m), 3.9 min. Range, 525 mls (845 km). Empty weight, 1,027 lb (466 kg). Loaded weight, 1,707 lb (774 kg). Span 25 ft 0 in (7,62 m). Length, 18 ft 4 in (5,59 m). Height, 8 ft 9 in (2,67 m). Wing area, 185 sq ft (17,19 m²).*

CURTISS P-1 (HAWK) USA

On 7 March 1925, Curtiss was awarded a contract for 15 production examples of the XPW-8B as the P-1, this being the first fighter to which the company assigned

(Below) A Curtiss P-1, one of the 10 aircraft of this type built for the USAAC as the first Hawks.

The F6C-3 (above) for the US Navy introduced the same airframe changes as did the Army Air Corps' P-1A.

Empty weight, 2,105 lb (955 kg). Loaded weight, 2,932 lb (1 330 kg). Span, 31 ft 7 in (9,63 m). Length, 22 ft 8 in (6,91 m). Height, 8 ft 11 in (2,72 m). Wing area, 250 sq ft (23,23 m²).

The P-1B (below) closely resembled the P-1A, with changes in radiator, engine type and wheel size.

CURTISS F6C-4 (HAWK)   USA

The US Navy had decided, by 1927, to standardise on air-cooled radial engines, which were more easily maintained at sea than liquid-cooled inline engines. Accordingly, after trials with a Pratt & Whitney R-1340-engined F6C-3, a production contract was placed for 31 fighters powered by this 410 hp radial as F6C-4s. The first of these aircraft, which was retained for test purposes, was assigned the designation XF6C-4 and deliveries commenced in February 1927. Possessing the same twin-gun armament as its predecessors, the F6C-4 proved more manoeuvrable than the V-1150-powered models, but was becoming obsolescent by the

Delivered in early 1927, this P-1B (above) was flown by the 27th Pursuit Sqn, Selfridge Field.

the name Hawk. Externally similar to the XPW-8B, the P-1 was of mixed construction with wooden wings and steel-tube fuselage with fabric skinning, and was powered by a 435 hp Curtiss V-1150-1 12-cylinder water-cooled engine. The final five aircraft were completed as P-2s, three of these later being converted to P-1A standards. Follow-on contracts were placed on 9 September 1925 for 25 P-1As (which had a 3-in/7,62-cm longer fuselage); on 17 August 1926 for 25 P-1Bs (with V-1150-3 engine, larger wheels and modified radiator), and on 3 October 1928 for 33 P-1Cs (with wheel brakes). All these sub-types carried an armament of two 0.3-in (7,62-mm) guns. In the meantime, the USAAC had ordered advanced trainers utilising the same airframe, these comprising 35 AT-4s (180 hp Wright V-720), five AT-5s and 31 AT-5As (220 hp Wright R-790), and, in 1929, these were re-engined with the V-1150-3, all 35 AT-4s becoming P-1Ds and four AT-5s and 24 AT-5As becoming P-1Es and P-1Fs respectively. These conversions were essentially similar to the P-1B apart from having only one gun. Four P-1s were supplied to Bolivia, one P-1A went to Japan, and eight P-1As and eight P-1Bs were supplied to Chile. The following data relate to the P-1B. *Max speed, 160 mph (257 km/h) at sea level, 157 mph (253 km/h) at 5,000 ft (1 525 m). Initial climb, 1,540 ft/min (7,8 m/sec). Range, 600 mls (966 km).*

CURTISS F6C (HAWK)   USA

In March 1925, the US Navy ordered nine P-1s with provision for float operation as F6Cs (the F5C designation was not assigned, to avoid confusion with the F-5 flying boat), five of these being delivered as F6C-1s and four (with arrester hooks) as F6C-2s. These had similar power plant and armament to the USAAC's P-1. Two of the F6C-1s were later converted to -2 standard. In 1927, 35 additional aircraft were ordered, these using the P-1A airframe and being designated F6C-3. Two F6C-1s were converted to -3 standard and one F6C-3 was fitted with a Pratt & Whitney R-1340 radial as the XF6C-3. The following data relate to the F6C-3. *Max speed, 154 mph (248 km/h) at sea level. Time to 5,000 ft (1 525 m), 3.5 min. Max range, 655 mls (1 054 km). Empty weight, 2,161 lb (980 kg). Loaded weight, 2,963 lb (1 344 kg). Span, 31 ft 6 in (9,60 m). Length, 22 ft 10 in (6,96 m). Height, 10 ft 8 in (3,25 m). Wing area, 252 sq ft (23,41 m²).*

(Below) Curtiss F4C-4 in operational guise with engine ring cowling and (above) serving in 1930 in the training rôle with VN-4D8 at NAS Pensacola.

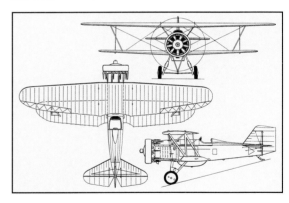

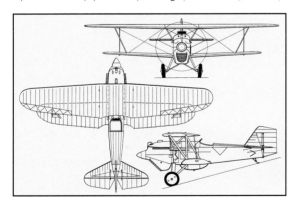

The P-1C (above), which introduced wheel brakes and (below) one of the 35 P-1Ds – re-engined AT-4 advanced trainers reclassified as pursuits.

Despite its fighter rôle, the F6C-3 (below) served for a time with the US Navy's Bombing Squadron One (VB-1).

time that it was delivered. It remained first-line equipment only until the beginning of 1930. Experimental F6C models were the XF6C-5 (first F6C-1 fitted with a 525 hp Pratt & Whitney R-1690 Hornet), XF6C-6 (an F6C-3 converted to parasol monoplane configuration for the 1930 Thompson Trophy race), F6C-6 (an F6C-3 modified for 1929 air races and returned to -3 standard), and the XF6C-7 (an F6C-4 with an inverted air-cooled Ranger SGV-770 engine). *Max speed, 155 mph (249 km/h) at sea level. Time to 5,000 ft (1 525 m), 2.5 min. Normal range, 361 mls (581 km). Empty weight,*

After conversion to F6C-4 standard, the first F6C-1 became the XF6C-5 (below) with R-1690 Hornet engine.

1,980 lb (898 kg). Loaded weight, 2,785 lb (1 263 kg). Span, 31 ft 6 in (9,60 m). Length, 22 ft 6 in (6,86 m). Height, 10 ft 11 in (3,33 m). Wing area, 252 sq ft (23,41 m²).

CURTISS P-2 (HAWK) — USA

The final five aircraft built against the initial P-1 contract were fitted with the 510 hp Curtiss V-1400 (D-12) engine and delivered early in 1926 as P-2s. The first of these, initially flown in December 1925, was experimentally fitted with a side-mounted turbo-super-charger which increased the P-2's absolute ceiling from 22,980 ft (7 005 m) to 32,790 ft (9 995 m). Three P-2s were subsequently converted to P-1A standard for squadron service. A fourth was fitted with the Curtiss V-1570 Conqueror engine of 600 hp as the XP-6 to participate in the 1927 National Air Races, in which it achieved 189 mph (304 km/h). *Max speed, 172 mph (276 km/h) at sea level, 151 mph (243 km/h) at 15,000 ft (4 575 m). Initial climb, 2,170 ft/min (11 m/sec). Time to 6,500 ft (1 980 m), 3.5 min. Empty weight, 2,081 lb (944 kg). Loaded weight, 2,869 lb (1 301 kg). Span, 31 ft 7 in (9,63 m). Length, 22 ft 10 in (6,96 m). Height, 8 ft 7 in (2,62 m). Wing area, 250 sq ft (23,23 m²).*

CURTISS P-3A (HAWK) — USA

The Pratt & Whitney Wasp engine was used in five P-3As (above), the ring cowling being added later.

The first radial-engined Hawk resulted from the mating of a P-1A airframe with a 390 hp Curtiss R-1454 engine as the XP-3 in October 1926. The failure of the Curtiss engine led to its substitution by a 410 hp Pratt & Whitney R-1340-9, with which it was tested in April 1928 as the XP-3A. Five production examples had been ordered in December 1927 as P-3As, deliveries commencing in September 1928. The P-3A was powered by the R-1340-3 version of the Wasp, also rated at 410 hp, and the first production example was flown with various experimental cowlings as the second XP-3A. Both this and the original XP-3A were eventually to become XP-21s, the second XP-3A undergoing further conversion (after testing as an XP-21) to P-1F standards. Armament of the P-3A comprised two 0.3-in (7,62-mm) machine guns and this type was fitted with a Townend ring after service entry. *Max speed, 153 mph (246 km/h) at sea level, 148 mph (238 km/h) at 10,000 ft (3 050 m). Cruise, 122 mph (196 km/h). Initial climb, 1,742 ft/min (8,8 m/sec). Empty weight, 1,956 lb (887 kg). Loaded weight, 2,788 lb (1 265 kg). Span, 31 ft 7 in (9,63 m). Length, 22 ft 5 in (6,83 m). Height, 8 ft 9 in (2,67 m). Wing area, 252 sq ft (23,41 m²).*

CURTISS F7C-1 (SEAHAWK) — USA

The first Curtiss fighter designed from the outset for shipboard use as opposed to being an adaptation of a land-based fighter, the XF7C-1 single-seat fighter was characterised by sweptback upper wing outer panels and flew for the first time on 28 February 1927. Powered by a 450 hp Pratt & Whitney R-1340-B Wasp radial, the XF7C-1 was flown both with and without a propeller spinner, and was also tested with a single central float and outrigger stabilising floats. Seventeen F7C-1s were ordered for US Navy service and delivered during December 1928 and January 1929. These differed from the prototype primarily in having tripod main undercarriage members in place of the cross axle. The propeller spinner was discarded and armament comprised two 0.3-in (7,62-mm) synchronised machine guns. In

The F7C-1 (above) was operated only by US Marine Corps, serving with VF-5M (later VF-9M) until 1933.

the event, all F7C-1s were operated by the US Marine Corps (VF-5M) at Quantico. *Max speed, 151 mph (243 km/h) at sea level. Time to 5,000 ft (1 525 m), 2.6 min. Normal range, 330 mls (531 km). Empty weight, 2,038 lb (924 kg). Loaded weight, 2,782 lb (1 262 kg). Span, 32 ft 8 in (9,96 m). Length, 22 ft 1⅞ in (6,75 m). Height, 10 ft 4 in (3,15 m). Wing area, 276 sq ft (25,64 m²).*

The F7C-1 (below) designed for shipboard use.

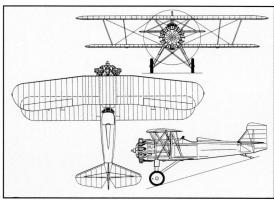

CURTISS F8C-1 & -3 — USA

To meet a US Marine Corps requirement for a two-seat fighter with bombing and observation capability, Curtiss adapted the airframe of the USAAC's O-1 Falcon. With a Pratt & Whitney R-1340 Wasp engine in place of the water-cooled Conqueror six examples were delivered, two as XF8C-1s and four as F8C-1s, in January 1928. Armament comprised two fixed forward-firing 0.3-in (7,62-mm) guns and a weapon of similar calibre on a Scarff ring in the rear cockpit, and power was provided by a 432 hp R-1340B Wasp. Twenty-one additional machines (one XF8C-3 and 20 F8C-3s) were delivered later in 1928, these being essentially similar

Seen below serving with VO-8M of the USMC in 1928, the F8C-1 was designed as a multi-rôle aircraft.

to the F8C-1s which were redesignated as OC-1s shortly after entering service, the F8C-3s becoming OC-2s. *Max speed, 144 mph (232 km/h) at sea level. Initial climb, 1,010 ft/min (5,1 m/sec). Range, 650 mls (1 046 km). Empty weight, 2,515 lb (1 141 kg). Loaded weight, 4,191 lb (1 901 kg). Span, 38 ft 0 in (11,58 m). Length, 27 ft 11 in (8,51 m). Height, 11 ft 8 in (3,55 m). Wing area, 350 sq ft (32,52 m²).*

CURTISS F8C-4 & -5 (HELLDIVER) — USA

The prototype XF8C-4 of 1929 (above) closely resembled the XF8C-2, first of the Helldivers. (Below) An F8C-4 in service with Navy Reserve unit VMS-2R.

Although designated in the F8C series, the XF8C-2 and XF8C-4 differed extensively from the F8C-1 and -3, and were dual-rôle aircraft intended for use both as two-seat fighters and as dive bombers, dive bombing techniques at that time being under development by the US Marine Corps. Possessing smaller overall dimensions than previous F8C series aircraft, featuring some structural revision and powered by a 450 hp R-1340-80 Wasp, the XF8C-2 prototype appeared early in 1929 and was equipped to carry either two 116-lb (53-kg) bombs or one 500-lb (227-kg) bomb. A second prototype, the XF8C-4, was flown in August 1929, by which time orders had been placed for 27 F8C-4s and nine F8C-5s. The XF8C-4 differed from the XF8C-2 primarily in having an R-1340-88 Wasp enclosed by a Townend ring. The latter was not initially applied to the production F8C-4s which were delivered from May 1930, a further 43 being ordered for 1931 delivery, these being

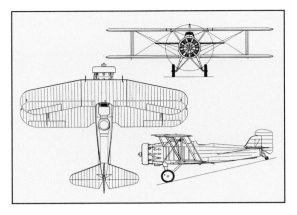

(Above) The F8C-4 Helldiver fighter and dive-bomber.

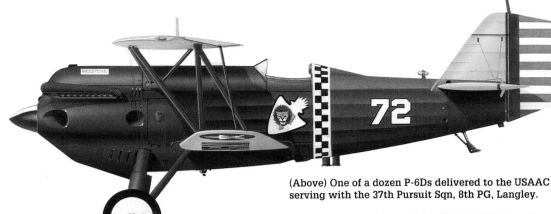

(Above) One of a dozen P-6Ds delivered to the USAAC serving with the 37th Pursuit Sqn, 8th PG, Langley.

redesignated O2C-1s. Two F8C-5s temporarily fitted with wing flaps and leading-edge slots were designated XF8C-6s, one VIP transport version with a 575 hp Wright R-1820-64 Cyclone was designated XF8C-7 (XO2C-2) and two similarly powered examples were XF8C-8s. The designation XF10C-1 was assigned to one aircraft initially powered by a Curtiss R-1510 and subsequently re-engined with a Cyclone. The following data are applicable to the F8C-4. *Max speed, 147 mph (237 km/h). Initial climb, 1,030 ft/min (5,23 m/sec). Normal range, 455 mls (732 km). Empty weight, 2,513 lb (1 140 kg). Normal loaded weight, 3,783 lb (1 716 kg). Span, 32 ft 0 in (9,75 m). Length, 25 ft 7⅞ in (7,82 m). Height, 10 ft 3 in (3,12 m). Wing area, 308 sq ft (28,61 m²).*

CURTISS P-5 (SUPERHAWK) USA

A USAAC contract placed on 14 May 1927 called for five aircraft with airframes essentially similar to that of the P-1, but powered by a turbo-supercharged Curtiss V-1150-4 12-cylinder water-cooled engine. The first of these was delivered in January 1928 as the XP-5, with the remaining four following as P-5s by June 1928.

A side-mounted turbo-supercharger on the D-12F engine was a distinctive feature of the P-5 (above).

Dubbed Superhawk by the manufacturer, the P-5 had a side-mounted exhaust-driven turbo-supercharger with which it attained a service ceiling of 31,000 ft (9 450 m). Warm air was ducted from the exhaust manifold to the cockpit, the heat being contained by a ''cape'' which snapped around the cockpit rim and fitted closely about the pilot. Two of the P-5s were lost in accidents shortly after delivery, but the remaining two served with the 94th Pursuit Squadron until April 1932. The V-1150-4 (D-12F) engine was rated at 435 hp and armament comprised two 0.3-in (7,62-mm) machine guns. *Max speed, 146 mph (235 km/h) at sea level, 173 mph (278 km/h) at 25,000 ft (7 620 m). Time to 10,000 ft (3 050 m), 8.4 min. Endurance, 1.31 hrs. Empty weight, 2,520 lb (1 143 kg). Loaded weight, 3,349 lb (1 519 kg). Span, 31 ft 6 in (9,60 m). Length, 23 ft 8 in (7,21 m). Height, 9 ft 3 in (2,82 m). Wing area, 252 sq ft (23,41 m²).*

CURTISS P-6 TO P-6D (HAWK I) USA

Installation of the new 600 hp Curtiss V-1570-1 Conqueror engine in a P-2 airframe for participation in the September 1927 air races at Spokane led to the application of the designation XP-6. A similarly-powered aircraft utilising a P-1A fuselage, XPW-8A wings and surface radiators became the XP-6A. A third Conqueror-powered conversion of a P-1C airframe for a New York-Alaska flight, in July 1929, was assigned the

designation XP-6B. Although these aircraft were intended purely to prove the Conqueror engine, the success of this power plant prompted a USAAC order for 18 P-6s on 3 October 1928, these being powered by the 600 hp water-cooled V-1570-17. Although generally similar to the P-1 in construction, they embodied extensively revised fuselage contours. Deliveries commenced in October 1929, but with the 11th aircraft Prestone (ethylene glycol) cooling was introduced, the

The P-6A (above and below) built for Service trials, featured Prestone (ethylene glycol) coolant for its V-1570-23 engine.

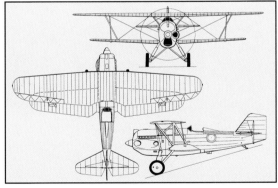

(Below) With a turbo-supercharger on its V-1570-23, this P-6D was one of 15 converted P-6/P-6As.

designation changing to P-6A. The V-1570-23 engine in the P-6A had a similar rating to that of the -17 that it supplanted; armament remained unchanged at two 0.3-in (7,62-mm) guns. In service, eight of the Army Air Corps P-6s were brought up to P-6A standards. Eight additional P-6s were delivered to the Netherlands East Indies and one to Japan under the export designation Hawk I. Subsequent to being converted as a P-6A, the first production P-6 was fitted with a side-mounted turbo-supercharger on its V-1570-23 engine as the XP-6D, and, in 1932, 10 P-6As were fitted with F-2F superchargers as P-6Ds. In addition, two aircraft originally ordered as P-11s (P-6 airframes with the unsatisfactory 600 hp Curtiss H-1640 Chieftain engine) were completed as P-6Ds. The P-6D was 269 lb (122 kg) heavier than the P-6A and featured a three-bladed propeller, and its performance included max speeds of 190 mph (306 km/h) at 10,000 ft (3 050 m) and 197 mph (317 km/h) at 13,000 ft (3 960 m), service ceiling being 32,000 ft (9 755 m). The following data relate to the P-6A. *Max speed, 178 mph (286 km/h) at sea level, 173 mph (278 km/h) at 10,000 ft (3 050 m). Time to 10,000 ft (3 050m), 5.8 min. Empty weight, 2,389 lb (1 083 kg). Loaded weight, 3,172 lb (1 439 kg). Span, 31 ft 6 in (9,60 m). Length, 23 ft 7 in (7,19 m). Height, 8 ft 7 in (2,62 m). Wing area, 252 sq ft (23,41 m²).*

CURTISS P-6E USA

When the V-1570-23 engine of the XP-22, complete with cowling and three-bladed propeller, plus its cantilever main undercarriage members, were grafted on to the YP-20 airframe in the autumn of 1931, the result of this marriage was assigned the designation XP-6E. The 45 Y1P-22s ordered during the previous July and which were briefly to be referred to as P-6Cs, were designated as P-6Es by the time deliveries began on 2 December 1931. Powered by the same 600 hp Curtiss V-1570-23 Conqueror engine, the P-6E carried an armament of two 0.3-in (7,62-mm) Browning machine guns, and 17 surviving examples were eventually assigned to ground schools during the summer of 1939. In the spring of 1932, the XP-6E was returned to Curtiss for installation of a turbo-supercharged V-1570-55 engine of 675 hp, a fully-enclosed cockpit with aft-sliding canopy being fitted at the same time and the designation being

(Above) A P-6E of the 33rd Pursuit Sqn, 8th PG, in 1934, and (below) a P-6E of the 9th Pursuit Sqn, 1st PG, this being the last of its type delivered.

changed to XP-6F. This attained 225 mph (362 km/h) at 18,000 ft (5 485 m) during tests. One P-6E was temporarily assigned the designation XP-6G while being used as a test-bed for the V-1570-51 (F-series) engine, while the first production P-6E was also fitted with this

engine and experimental wing armament as the XP-6H. This wing armament comprised two 0.3-in (7,62-mm) guns in both the upper and lower wings, these firing outside the propeller disc and augmenting the twin synchronised fuselage guns. The following data relate to the P-6E. *Max speed, 193 mph (311 km/h) at sea level, 180 mph (290 km/h) at 15,000 ft (4 575 m). Initial climb, 2,460 ft/min (12,5 m/sec). Normal range, 285 mls (459 km). Empty weight, 2,699 lb (1 224 kg). Loaded weight, 3,436 lb (1 558 kg). Span 31 ft 6 in (9,60 m). Length, 25 ft 2 in (7,67 m). Height, 8 ft 10 in (2,69 m). Wing area, 252 sq ft (23,41 m²).*

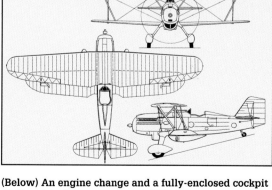

Last of the US Army Hawks, the P-6E (below), and (above) a P-6E of the 17th Pursuit Sqn, 1st PG.

(Below) An engine change and a fully-enclosed cockpit distinguished the experimental XP-6F.

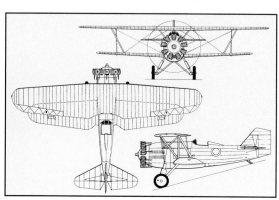

The XP-6H (above) was the first production P-6E fitted with a V-1570-51 engine and wing armament.

CURTISS P-6S (CUBAN HAWK) USA

During 1939, Curtiss offered for export a version of the basic P-6 fighter powered by a 450 hp Pratt & Whitney Wasp nine-cylinder radial air-cooled engine. The Cuban government placed a contract for three fighters of this type, which were referred to both as the P-6S and as the Cuban Hawk and should not be confused with the more powerful Hawk II, four examples of which were to be delivered to Cuba some three years later. *Max speed, 157 mph (253 km/h) at sea level. Initial*

(Below) The Curtiss P-6S (Cuban Hawk)

climb, 1,820 ft/min (9,2 m/sec). Max range, 420 mls (676 km). Loaded weight 2,910 lb (1 320 kg). Span 31 ft 6 in (9,60 m). Length, 22 ft 10 in (6,96 m). Height, 8 ft 6 in (2,59 m). Wing area, 252 sq ft (23,41 m²).

CURTISS XP-10 USA

On 18 June 1928, the USAAC placed a contract with Curtiss for one prototype of the XP-10 single-seat fighter powered by a 600 hp V-1570-17 Conqueror engine. Of mixed construction with fabric-covered steel-tube fuselage and plywood-covered wooden wings, the XP-10 placed emphasis on aerodynamic cleanliness and utilised surface evaporation wing radiators and a gulled upper wing. Delivered in August 1928, the XP-10 was tested until October 1930, but continuous problems with the cooling system prevented further development. *Max speed, 191 mph (307 km/h)*

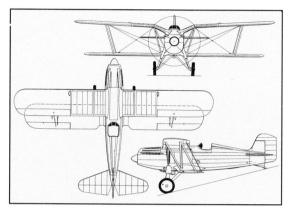

Built in 1928, the sole XP-10 (above and below) was not related to any contemporary Curtiss fighters, featuring a gulled upper wing and surface evaporation cooling.

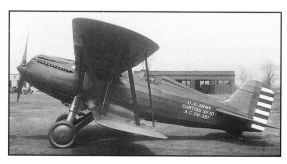

at sea level, 215 mph (346 km/h) at 12,000 ft (3 660 m). Range, 461 mls (742 km). Empty weight, 3,040 lb (1 379 kg). Loaded weight, 3,975 lb (1 803 kg). Span, 33 ft 0 in (10,06 m). Length, 24 ft 6 in (7,47 m). Height, 8 ft 8 in (2,64 m). Wing area, 270 sq ft (25,08 m²).

CURTISS XP-17 USA

With a Wright V-1460-3 Tornado, the XP-17 (above) was a modified P-1 airframe for use primarily as a test-bed.

The XP-17 comprised the airframe of the first P-1 mated to the new 480 hp Wright V-1460-3 Tornado inverted in-line air-cooled engine, and was intended primarily to test the power plant rather than extend the service life of the P-1 design. The conversion was undertaken by the US Army and flight testing was initiated in June 1930. *Max speed, 165 mph (265 km/h) at sea level, 161 mph (259 km/h) at 5,000 ft (1 525 m). Time to*

Key to Curtiss P-6E Hawk

1 Starter dog
2 Propeller hub
3 Three-blade Hamilton Standard metal propeller
4 Oil cooler chin intake
5 Nose cowling front panel line
6 Gear housing
7 Front curved panel
8 Carburettor air intake
9 Intake trunk
10 Curtiss V-1570-C Conqueror engine
11 Exhaust stubs (2 per cylinder)
12 Stainless steel trough surround
13 Gun trough
14 Machine gun muzzle
15 Cowling access panel line
16 Diagonal brace
17 Struts
18 Main engine support bearer
19 Filter
20 Lower panel lines
21 Oil cooler assembly
22 Telescopic access/servicing step
23 Radiator attachment mounts
24 Prestone radiator
25 Radiator fairing
26 Intake
27 Starboard mainwheel spat
28 Starboard undercarriage strut
29 Axle
30 Starboard low-pressure mainwheel tyre
31 Anchor point
32 Inboard access panel (brake servicing)
33 Port mainwheel spat
34 Flathead screw panel line
35 Port axle assembly
36 Port low-pressure mainwheel tyre
37 Hub assembly forging
38 Angled undercarriage strut
39 Removable spat half-section
40 Undercarriage leg fairing
41 Strut/fairing attachment
42 Strut support forged frame member
43 Strut pivot
44 Hinged cover plate
45 Front wires fuselage attachment
46 Engine accessories
47 Fuselage forward frame
48 Port ammunition magazine (600 rpg)
49 Deflector panel
50 Cartridge chute
51 Gun support strut
52 Ammunition feed fairing
53 Oleo shock strut/rebound spring
54 Upper pivot point
55 Cabane forward attachment
56 Oil access point
57 Bulkhead panel
58 Starboard wires
59 Aluminium leading-edge panels
60 Upper wing centre-section
61 Cabane struts
62 Cabane wires
63 Cabane upper wing attachment points
64 Reinforced strut
65 Starboard lower wing plan
66 Front spar
67 Interplane "N"-struts
68 Upper wing ribs
69 Internal bracing wires
70 Interplane strut upper attachment points
71 Reinforced rib
72 Outer rib assemblies
73 Starboard navigation light
74 Aerial mast
75 Aileron/rear spar join
76 Welded Steel aileron (fabric-covered)
77 Aileron hinge link
78 Metal plate
79 Aileron interplane actuating link
80 Aileron profile
81 Rear spar
82 Trailing-edge rib assembly
83 Centre-section cut-out
84 Handhold
85 Telescopic gunsight
86 Gunsight supports
87 Hinged fuel access panel
88 Filler neck
89 Fuselage main fuel tank, capacity 50 US gal (189 l)
90 Engine controls
91 Port 0.30-in (7,62-mm) Browning machine gun
92 Lower longeron
93 Fuel tank bearer
94 Lower wing front spar attachment
95 Wingroot walkway
96 Diagonal strut frame
97 Lower wing rear spar attachment
98 Aileron control linkage
99 Hanging rudder pedal assembly
100 Control column
101 Fuselage frame
102 Cabane rear attachment
103 Instrument centre panel
104 Main instrument panel
105 Windscreen
106 Control grip
107 Side switch panel
108 Engine control quadrant
109 Throttle lever
110 Upper wing trailing-edge
111 Padded forward coaming
112 Cockpit cut-out
113 Headrest/turnover frame
114 Bad-weather cover (snap-on rubber tarpaulin)
115 Oxygen access panel (starboard)
116 Pilot's seat
117 Seat support frame
118 Inspection "Vee" panel
119 Cockpit floor
120 Fuselage diagonal side frames
121 Oxygen cylinder (starboard)
122 Metal door flap
123 Parachute flare stowage (port)
124 Baggage compartment hinged side door
125 Hasp and lock
126 Baggage compartment hinged upper panel
127 Snap fasteners
128 Fuselage top frames
129 All-metal dorsal decking
130 Diagonal brace wires
131 Elevator control cables
132 Rudder control cables
133 Fuselage structure
134 Pulleys
135 Cross member

136 Dorsal cross-section transition (round/
    point)
137 Tailplane front beam attachment
138 Bearer frame
139 Tailfin front beam attachment
140 Tailfin leading-edge
141 Starboard tailplane
142 Aerials
143 Tailfin structure
144 Tailplane brace wires
145 Rudder balance
146 Aerial post
147 Tail navigation light recess
148 Rudder upper hinge
149 Rudder frame
150 Spacers
151 Rudder post
152 Elevator control horns
153 Tailfin rear beam attachment
154 Elevator control cable
155 Rudder control horns
156 Port elevator frame
157 Brace wire attachment

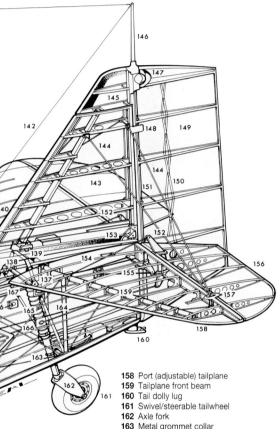

158 Port (adjustable) tailplane
159 Tailplane front beam
160 Tail dolly lug
161 Swivel/steerable tailwheel
162 Axle fork
163 Metal grommet collar
164 Fuselage strut
165 Tailwheel shock-strut leg
166 Leather grommets (elevator control
    cables)
167 Tailwheel leg upper attachment
168 Access "Vee" panel
169 Diagonal brace wires
170 Lower longeron
171 Ventral skinning
172 Port aileron
173 Aerial mast
174 Lower wingroot cut-out
175 Ventral tank aft fairing
176 Rear spar
177 Interplane "N"-struts
178 Upper wing leading-edge
179 Drop tank filler cap
180 Ventral drop tank, capacity 50 US gal
    (189 l)
181 Vent
182 Lower wing aluminium leading-edge
    panels
183 Nose ribs
184 Wire turnbuckle clamp
185 "N"-strut lower attachments
186 Port navigation light
187 Reinforced rib
188 Aileron actuating linkage
189 Lower wing trailing-edge
190 Rear spar
191 Outer rib assemblies
192 Front spar
193 Wingtip structure
194 Handling point

10,000 ft (3 050 m), 8.0 min. Empty weight, 2,204 lb (1 000 kg). Loaded weight, 2,994 lb (1 358 kg). Span, 31 ft 7 in (9,63 m). Length, 22 ft 10 in (6,96 m). Height, 8 ft 7 in (2,62 m). Wing area, 252 sq ft (23,41 m²).

CURTISS YP-20   USA

During 1928, the 600 hp Curtiss H-1640 Chieftain 12-cylinder air-cooled radial appeared to show promise as a fighter power plant, and Curtiss was assigned the task of mating this engine to the P-6 airframe. A USAAC contract was placed for three aircraft which were designated P-11s. In the event, the Chieftain proved unsatisfactory and the P-11 was abandoned (together with the projected Curtiss XP-14 that had been designed around this engine). Two of the airframes that had been ordered in January 1929 were completed as P-6Ds and the third, which was fitted with a 575 hp Wright R-1820-9 Cyclone, was assigned the designation YP-20 on delivery in October 1930. It was later fitted with the V-1570 engine of the XP-22, complete with cowling, the cantilever main undercarriage members and three-blade propeller of this aircraft to become the XP-6E. *Max speed, 187 mph (301 km/h) at sea level, 184 mph (296 km/h) at 5,000 ft (1 525 m). Initial climb, 2,400 ft/min (12,2 m/sec). Empty weight, 2,477 lb (1 124 kg). Loaded weight, 3,233 lb (1 466 kg). Span, 31 ft 6 in (9,60 m). Length, 23 ft 9 in (7,24 m). Height, 9 ft 2 in (2,79 m). Wing area, 252 sq ft (23,41 m²).*

The single YP-20 (below) was essentially a P-6 airframe fitted with a Wright Cyclone engine.

CURTISS XP-21   USA

After being flown in the National Air Races of 1929, the XP-3A was re-engined with a Pratt & Whitney R-985-1 Wasp Junior with which it was somewhat misleadingly redesignated XP-21. It later underwent further conversion to P-1F standards. The original XP-3A (converted from a P-1A airframe) was similarly re-engined as the XP-21A in December 1930, but trials with these aircraft were not associated with the further development of the basic fighter design, despite the allocation of an "Experimental Pursuit" designation.

Among the smallest of contemporary shipboard fighters, the XF9C-1 (below) was a wholly new design in 1930, but was not adopted for production.

CURTISS XP-22   USA

The sole XP-22 (above) was a cleaned-up P-6A, used to develop the engine installation for the P-6E.

In 1931, the third production P-6 (which had been converted to P-6A standard) was withdrawn from service and returned to Curtiss for extensive modification as the XP-22. Retaining the V-1570-23 engine, the XP-22 was cleaned up aerodynamically and featured cantilever main undercarriage legs and wheel spats, plus a redesigned engine cowling with, initially, an annular radiator. The radiator was subsequently returned to a position beneath the rear of the engine. On 30 June 1931, the XP-22 demonstrated a level speed of 202.4 mph (326 km/h) and on 10 July a USAAC contract was placed for 45 Y1P-22s. These were subsequently redesignated as P-6Cs, but prior to the start of production deliveries the designation was changed once more to P-6E. By this time, the engine of the XP-22, complete with cowling and three-blade propeller, plus the main undercarriage members, had been grafted on to the YP-20, which had thus become the XP-6E, while the XP-22 was returned to P-6A configuration. *Max speed, 202 mph (325 km/h) at sea level, 195 mph (314 km/h) at 10,000 ft (3 050 m). Initial climb, 2,400 ft/min (12,2 m/sec). Empty weight, 2,597 lb (1 178 kg). Loaded weight, 3,354 lb (1 521 kg). Span, 31 ft 6 in (9,60 m). Length, 23 ft 7 in (7,19 m). Height, 8 ft 10 in (2,69 m). Wing area, 252 sq ft (23,41 m²).*

CURTISS F9C (SPARROWHAWK)   USA

Designed to meet a lightweight shipboard fighter requirement – other contenders being the Berliner Joyce XFJ-1 and General Aviation XFA-1 – the XF9C-1 was flown on 12 February 1931. It failed to gain acceptance as a carrier-based aircraft, but its small dimensions commended it for use from the dirigibles *Akron* and *Macon* which had been designed with internal hangar bays. The XF9C-1 was subsequently fitted with the so-called "skyhook" which engaged the retractable trapeze carried by the dirigibles. Some directional instability resulting from the hook dictated the enlarging of the vertical tail surfaces. A second prototype, the XF9C-2 with single-strut main undercarriage members, was built at Curtiss' expense prior to the placing of a US Navy contract for six F9C-2s which featured a similar tripod undercarriage strut arrangement to that

The F9C-2 Sparrowhawk (above and below) was notable for its use as a "hook-on" defensive fighter to be carried by the airships *Akron* and *Macon*.

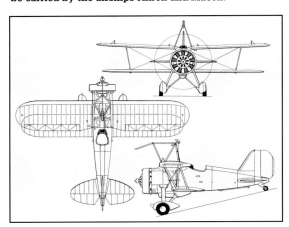

of the XF9C-1. The XF9C-2 was later purchased by the US Navy and modified to F9C-2 standard. The F9C-2 was powered by a 438 hp Wright R-975-E3 radial engine and carried an armament of two 0.3-in (7,62-mm) Browning machine guns. Originally intended to provide fighter protection for the dirigibles, the F9C-2s were used primarily to extend the reconnaissance capabilities of the parent craft. The *Macon* was lost on 12 February 1935, together with four of the F9C-2s. *Max speed, 176 mph (284 km/h) at 4,000 ft (1 220 m). Initial climb, 1,700 ft/min (8,63 m/sec). Range, 350 mls (563 km). Empty weight, 2,089 lb (947 kg). Loaded weight, 2,770 lb (1 256 kg). Span, 25 ft 5 in (7,75 m). Length, 20 ft 6⅞ in (6,27 m). Height, 10 ft 11½ in (3,34 m). Wing area, 173 sq ft (16,07 m²).*

CURTISS XP-23 USA

The last fighter biplane to be developed by Curtiss for the USAAC, the XP-23 was considered to be the ultimate refinement in this category. Ordered in July 1931, the XP-23 introduced fabric-covered metal wings of standard P-6 planform mated to an all-metal monocoque fuselage of very clean aerodynamic form, and a turbo-supercharged, geared GIV-1570C Conqueror engine. Delivered to the USAAC on 16 April 1932, the XP-23 offered too insignificant an advance in performance over the P-6E to warrant further development. The troublesome turbo-supercharger was removed, the three-bladed propeller was replaced by a two-blader and the aircraft was returned to the USAAC in April 1932 as the YP-23. It was then returned to Curtiss

and its wings used for the XF11C-1. The following data relate to the XP-23. *Max speed, 223 mph (359 km/h) at 15,000 ft (4 572 m). Initial climb, 1,370 ft/min (6,96 m/sec). Range, 435 mls (700 km). Empty weight, 3,274 lb (1 485 kg). Loaded weight, 4,124 lb (1 870 kg). Span, 31 ft 6 in (9,60 m). Length, 23 ft 10 in (7,26 m). Height, 9 ft 6 in (2,89 m). Wing area, 252 sq ft (23,41 m²).*

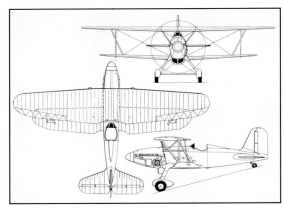

The XP-23 (above and below), the final fighter biplane developed by Curtiss for the USAAC, featured all-metal construction and a turbo-supercharger.

CURTISS F11C (GOSHAWK) USA

On 16 April 1932, the US Navy ordered two prototypes of a new shipboard fighter under the designations XF11C-1 and XF11C-2, the former with a 600 hp Wright R-1510-98 two-row radial and the latter with a 700 hp Wright R-1820-78 single-row radial. The latter was, in fact, a company demonstrator which had been flying for some time and was of mixed construction (fabric-covered wooden wings and fabric-covered metal fuselage and tail surfaces), whereas the XF11C-1, which utilised the wings of the YP-23, was of fabric-covered

The Curtiss XF11C-1 (above) with a long-chord cowling, and (below) the BFC-2 (previously F11C-2).

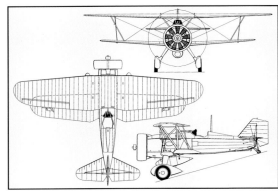

all-metal construction and was delivered in September 1932. The R-1820-78 Cyclone and mixed structure of the XF11C-2 found favour with the US Navy, and, on 18 October 1932, a production order was placed for 28 F11C-2s, deliveries of which began in February 1933 and were completed in the following May. The fourth aircraft on the contract was completed with a manually-retractable undercarriage as the XF11C-3, subsequently being redesignated XBF2C-1 with adoption of the "bomber-fighter" category in March 1934.

(Above) A Curtiss BFC-2 in service with Navy squadron VB-2B, the "High Hats", which became VB-3 in 1937.

Simultaneously, the F11C-2s were redesignated as BFC-2s. Armament comprised two 0.3-in (7,62-mm) Browning machine guns and a single bomb of up to 500 lb (227 kg) or four 112-lb (51-kg) bombs could be carried. The BFC-2 remained in US Navy service until 1938. *Max speed, 205 mph (330 km/h). Time to 5,000 ft (1 525 m), 2.6 min. Normal range, 560 mls (901 km). Empty weight, 3,037 lb (1 378 kg). Normal loaded weight, 4,120 lb (1 869 kg). Span, 31 ft 6 in (9,60 m). Length, 25 ft 0 in (7,62 m). Height, 10 ft 7¼ in (3,23 m). Wing area, 262 sq ft (24,34 m²).*

CURTISS HAWK II USA

The Hawk II was essentially an export version of the XF11C-2 with a Wright R-1820F-3 Cyclone rated at 710 hp at 5,500 ft (1 676 m) and 94 US gal (356 l) of fuel, the Hawk I differing in having only 50 US gal (189 l) of internal fuel. Only the Hawk II was exported in quantity, this having a mixed construction similar to that of the F11C-2 and normally carrying an armament of twin 0.3-in (7,62-mm) machine guns. The first customer for the Hawk II was Turkey, which began to take delivery of 19 on 30 August 1932, Colombia following suit from the end of October 1932 with an initial batch of four twin-float-equipped Hawk IIs. A total of 26 float

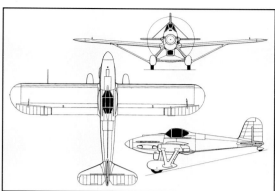

(335 km/h) at sea level, 202 mph (325 km/h) at 5,000 ft (1 525 m). Initial climb, 2,130 ft/min (10,8 m/sec). Range, 370 mls (595 km). Empty weight, 3,334 lb (1 512 kg). Loaded weight, 4,143 lb (1 879 kg). Span, 36 ft 0 in (10,97 m). Length, 26 ft 3 in (8,00 m). Height, 7 ft 9 in (2,36 m). Wing area, 203 sq ft (18,86 m²).

(Above) One of the nine Hawk IIs that were flown by the *Escuadron Punta de Alas* of the Bolivian *Cuerpo de Aviación*, in the 'thirties.

(Above and below) The Curtiss XP-934, as tested by the US Army Air Corps in 1933 after it had been re-engined with a Prestone-cooled Conqueror engine.

Preceding the US Navy's F11C-2, the Hawk II was in effect an export version of the same design. Users included (right) Turkey, which bought 19 in 1932 and (below) Germany, which evaluated two.

CURTISS BF2C-1 (F11C-3)   USA

The fourth production F11C-2 (Goshawk) was completed with manually-operated retractable main undercarriage members accommodated by a deepened forward fuselage. It was powered by an R-1820-80 Cyclone rated at 700 hp at 8,000 ft (2 440 m), and was delivered to the US Navy on 27 May 1933 as the XF11C-3. Twenty-seven production models were ordered as F11C-3s with raised aft turtle decks, partial canopies and the metal wings that had proved satisfactory on the XF11C-1. Prior to the commencement of deliveries on 7 October 1934, the designation was changed to BF2C-1. The BF2C-1 carried an armament of two 0.3-in (7,62-mm) Brownings and made provision for a single 474-lb (215-kg) bomb or up to four 116-lb (53-kg) bombs. An R-1820-04 Cyclone rated at 770 hp for take-off was fitted. In the event, at cruising rpm the Cyclone

fighters of this type was delivered to Colombia by the end of July 1934. Nine were supplied to Bolivia, of which three had interchangeable wheel/float undercarriages; four were delivered to Chile, 52 to China, four to Cuba, two to Germany, one to Norway and 12 to Thailand. The following data should be considered as typical. *Max speed, 187 mph (301 km/h) at sea level, 208 mph (335 km/h) at 6,900 ft (2 100 m). Normal range, 414 mls (666 km). Empty weight, 2,903 lb (1 317 kg). Loaded weight, 3,876 lb (1 758 kg). Span, 31 ft 6 in (9,60 m). Length, 26 ft 6 in (8,08 m). Height, 9 ft 9 in (2,97 m). Wing area, 262 sq ft (24,34 m²).*

formance proved disappointing and the prototype was therefore re-engined with a Prestone-cooled Curtiss GIV-1570-F Conqueror geared engine of 600 hp . With this it was accepted for test by the USAAC on 1 March 1933 as the XP-31. By this time, however, the Air Corps had already placed a production contract for the Boeing competitor as the P-26A. The following data relate to the Conqueror-powered XP-31. *Max speed, 208 mph*

Initially designated F11C-3, the BF2C-1 (below) served briefly with VB-5B on the USS *Ranger* in 1935.

CURTISS XP-31 (XP-934)   USA

Owing much to the design of the XA-8 attack aircraft of 1931, the XP-934 "Swift" low-wing braced fighter monoplane with enclosed cockpit and 700 hp Wright T-1820 Cyclone air-cooled radial was flown for the first time in July 1932. Featuring retractable full-span leading-edge slats and trailing-edge flaps, the XP-934 was intended to compete with the Boeing XP-936, but per-

With the company name Swift, the XP-934 (below) was the first monoplane fighter built by Curtiss.

haust collector ring for the SR-1820F-56 Cyclone, which delivered its maximum 745 hp at 12,500 ft (3 810 m). The Hawk IV attained 248 mph (399 km/h) at 12,500 ft (3 810 m) and 242 mph (390 km/h) at 16,400 ft (5 000 m). The following data relate to the standard Hawk III. *Max speed, 202 mph (325 km/h) at sea level, 240 mph (386 km/h) at 11,500 ft (3 505 m). Initial climb, 2,200 ft/min (11,2 m/sec). Normal range, 575 mls (925 km).*

The last biplane Hawk model (below), this Hawk IV demonstrator was eventually sold to Argentina in 1936.

US Navy "Bombing Five" squadron was formed in 1934 to fly the BF2C-1 (above) from the USS *Ranger*.

set up a sympathetic vibration with the metal wing structure, the aircraft shaking dramatically in this regime, and, the problem never being satisfactorily resolved, the BF2C-1s were withdrawn within a few months. *Max speed, 225 mph (362 km/h) at 8,000 ft (2 440 m). Initial climb, 2,150 ft/min (10,9 m/sec). Normal range, 570 mls (917 km). Empty weight, 3,370 lb (1 529 kg). Loaded weight, 4,555 lb (2 066 kg). Span, 31 ft 6 in (9,60 m). Length, 23 ft 0 in (7,01 m). Height, 10 ft 10 in (3,30 m). Wing area, 262 sq ft (24,34 m²).*

following from August 1935. In March 1936, the first of a total of 102 Hawk IIIs was delivered to China, 90 of these being assembled by the Central Aircraft Manufacturing Company (CAMCO) at Hangchow. One other purchaser of the Hawk III was Argentina, which took delivery of 10 from May 1936. The last-mentioned country also purchased the sole example of the Hawk IV in July 1936, this using a Hawk III airframe with a full sliding cockpit canopy, carburettor heating and an ex-

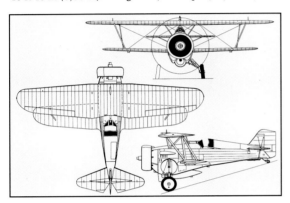

(Above) The series production Curtiss BF2C-1 (ex-F11C-3) and (below) the XF11C-3, which was a re-engined F11C-2 with a retractable undercarriage.

Key to Curtiss Hawk III

1 Starboard navigation light
2 Duralumin-framed aileron
3 Aileron push-pull actuating rod
4 Space for emergency flotation bag (optional)
5 Interplane strut attachment points
6 Built-up wood-truss wing ribs
7 Hollow-box section rear spar
8 Hollow-box section forward spar
9 Carry-over strut attachment points
10 Strengthened wing centre section
11 Aluminium alloy wire and strut attachments
12 Port interplane strut
13 Three-bladed Hamilton Standard controllable-pitch propeller
14 Gun ports
15 Wright SR-1820-F53 Cyclone nine-cylinder radial air-cooled engine
16 Machine gun barrel shroud
17 Exhaust stubs
18 Engine bearer ring
19 Welded tubular engine mounting frame
20 Forward fuselage frame
21 Cooling louvres
22 Cylindrical oil tank (7.5 Imp gal/34 l capacity)
23 Undercarriage retraction screw
24 Starboard synchronised 7,62-mm Colt-Browning machine gun
25 Forward lower fuel tank (46 Imp gal/209 l capacity)
26 Aft upper fuel tank (46 Imp gal/209 l capacity)
27 Undercarriage counter-balance
28 Fuel filler cap
29 Centre-section bracing struts
30 Telescopic sight
31 Flat windscreen
32 Shock-protected instrument panel
33 Starboard gun charger
34 Central console (static, radio battery and aircraft battery gauges)
35 Radio dial
36 Undercarriage retraction chain
37 Bracing-wire anchor points
38 Lower mainplane/fuselage attachment bolt
39 Rudder pedal
40 Auxiliary tank release lever
41 Bomb release lever
42 Fire extinguisher
43 Pilot's seat and safety straps
44 Undercarriage retraction crank
45 Wire brace
46 Leather-padded headrest
47 Interplane bracing struts
48 Corrugated aluminium sheet turtledeck
49 Canopy track (canopy optional)
50 "U" cross-section members
51 Seat brace
52 Rudder control chain
53 Elevator truss tube
54 Welded tubular fuselage framework
55 Warning beacon
56 Tailfin bracing wire
57 Interplane "N" struts

CURTISS HAWK III & IV   USA

The export version of the BF2C-1, the Hawk III, differed from the US Navy fighter-bomber in reverting to the wooden wing structure of the F11C-2 (spruce beams with plywood webs and spruce ribs) and in having a Wright SR-1820F-53 Cyclone offering 785 hp for take-off and 745 hp at 9,600 ft (2 925 m). Gun armament comprised two synchronised 0.3-in (7,62-mm) weapons. The first export of the Hawk III was a single example to Turkey delivered in April 1935, supply of 24 to Thailand

One of the total of 102 Hawk IIIs supplied to China, the majority for assembly at Hangchow.

58 Aileron push-rod
59 Metal-frame tailfin structure
60 Metal rudder post
61 Rudder construction (metal framed)
62 Flettner trim tab
63 Metal-framed tailplane
64 Elevator control
65 Metal-framed elevator
66 Lower wingtip hand-holds
67 Tailwheel steel-spring shock-absorbers
68 Bell-crank fairing
69 Fully-swivelling solid-rubber tailwheel
70 Underwing bomb shackles
71 M3 100-lb (45,3-kg) demolition bombs
72 Auxiliary fuel tank connection
73 Inspection covers
74 Auxiliary tank (41.6 Imp gal/189 l capacity) not carried with bombs

75 Mainwheel rail
76 Undercarriage retraction leg
77 Mainwheel shock-absorber strut
78 Removable wheel cover
79 Low-pressure mainwheel tyre
80 Undercarriage flap
81 Retracting "Y"-member
82 Undercarriage-extension fairing frame
83 Ventral tunnel (bomb/tank attachment point)
84 Port undercarriage door
85 Auxiliary tank wind cowl
86 Brake cord
87 Brake arm
88 Port mainwheel
89 Mainwheel/leg pivot
90 Oil cooler intake

(Immediately right) A Thai Hawk III of the 1st Wing, Watana Nakorn, early 1942. (Below right) A Chinese Hawk III of the 25th Pursuit Sqn, late 1937.

Empty weight, 3,213 lb (1 457 kg). Loaded weight, 4,317 lb (1 958 kg). Span, 31 ft 6 in (9,60 m). Length, 23 ft 5 in (7,14 m). Height, 9 ft 9½ in (2,98 m). Wing area, 262 sq ft (24,34 m²).

CURTISS XF12C-1　　　USA

Based on a US Navy Bureau of Aeronautics design for a two-seat fighter, the XF12C-1 all-metal parasol monoplane, ordered on 30 June 1932, featured aft-folding wings with leading-edge slats and trailing-edge flaps, and manually-operated retractable main undercarriage members. Flown in July 1933, the XF12C-1 was initially powered by a Wright R-1510-92 two-row radial rated at 625 hp at 6,000 ft (1 830 m). By the time the XF12C-1 was tested by the US Navy in October 1933, the Twin Whirlwind engine had been replaced by a Wright SR-1820-80 Cyclone single-row radial. With the discarding of the two-seat fighter category it was redesignated

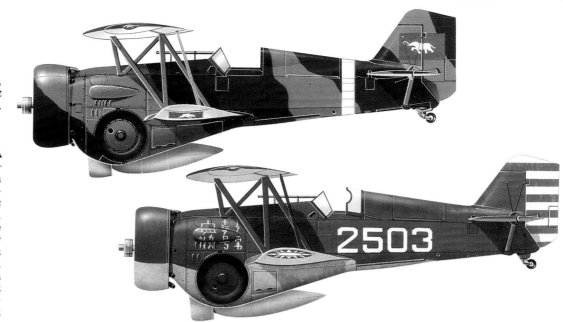

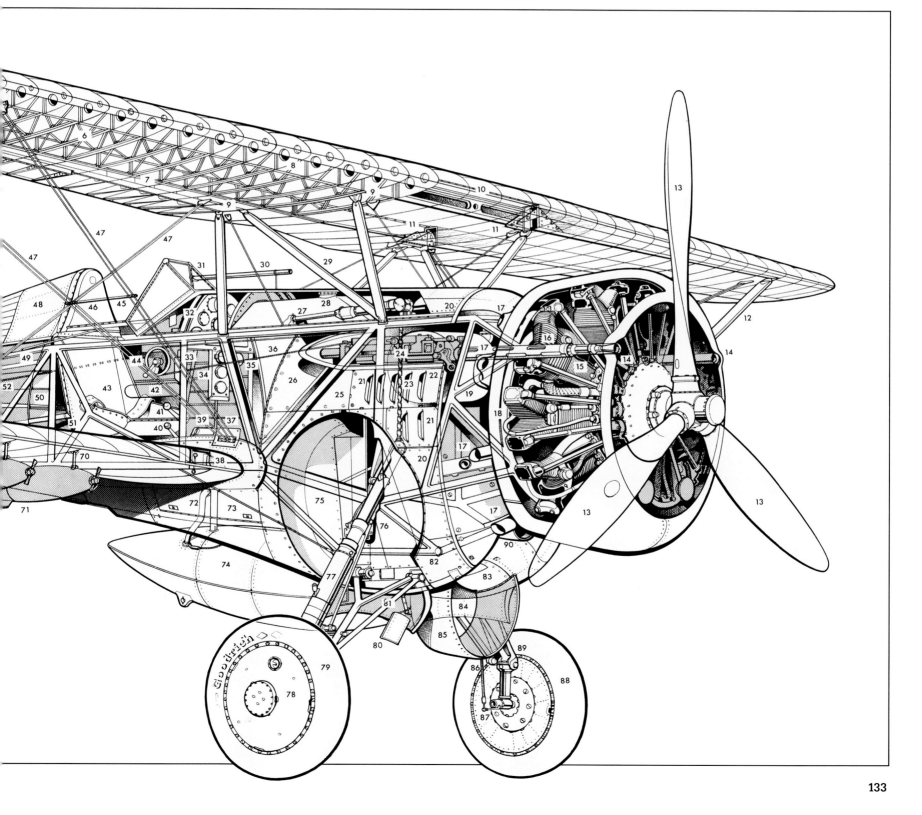

The XF12C-1 (above and below) with the single-row Cyclone engine and definitive engine cowling.

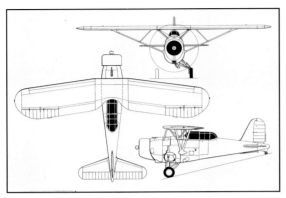

XS4C-1 in December 1933 and the XSBC-1 in January 1934 as a scout-bomber. It crashed during a preliminary demonstration on 14 June 1934, subsequently being replaced by the XSBC-2 biplane. The following data relate to the XF12C-1 with the R-1510-92 engine. *Max speed, 217 mph (349 km/h) at 6,000 ft (1 830 m). Normal range, 738 mls (1 188 km). Empty weight, 3,884 lb (1 762 kg). Normal loaded weight, 5,461 lb (2 477 kg). Span, 41 ft 6 in (12,65 m). Length, 29 ft 1 in (8,86 m). Height, 12 ft 11 in (3,94 m). Wing area, 272 sq ft (25,27 m²).*

CURTISS XF13C USA

Perhaps the most unusual single-seat fighter developed by Curtiss was the Model 70, which was designed from the outset to be flown either as a monoplane or as a biplane with the minimum of structural change. A metal semi-monocoque aircraft with fabric-covered wings, it was ordered on 23 November 1932 as the XF13C powered by a Wright SGR-1510-2 two-row radial rated at 600 hp at 10,000 ft (3 050 m). The designation XF13C-1 was assigned to it for test in monoplane form and XF13C-2 in biplane (or more strictly, sesquiplane) form. It was initially flown in December 1933 as a biplane, flying in monoplane form on 7 January 1934, and being delivered to the US Navy as the XF13C-1 on

The XF13C-1 (above and below) in monoplane configuration, in which it spent most of its flying life, eventually as the XF13C-3 with modified tail.

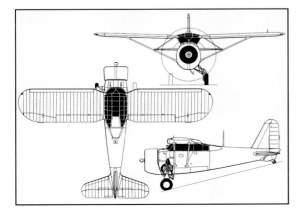

The XF13C-2 was the paper designation applied to the Model 70 sesquiplane form as seen above.

the following 10 February. Featuring a manually-operated retractable undercarriage, an enclosed cockpit, retractable upper wing leading-edge slats and trailing-edge flaps, the XF13C-1 did not revert to biplane standard, but, in February 1935, was returned to Curtiss for various modifications, including installation of an XR-1510-12 engine affording 700 hp at 7,000 ft (2 135 m). With these changes it was redesignated XF13C-3. In biplane configuration, the XF13C was 19 mph (30 km/h) slower than as a monoplane, but possessed a shorter take-off run and better low-speed characteristics. Trials were terminated in October 1935, primarily owing to lack of engine spares. The following data relate to the fighter in XF13C-3 configuration. *Max speed, 232 mph (373 km/h) at 7,000 ft (2 135 m). Time to 5,000 ft (1 525 m), 2.5 min. Endurance, 5.2 hrs. Loaded weight, 4,721 lb (2 142 kg). Span, 35 ft 0 in (10,67 m). Length, 25 ft 9½ in (7,86 m). Height, 12 ft 9 in (3,88 m). Wing area, 205 sq ft (19,04 m²).*

CURTISS MODEL 75 USA

Designed by Donovan R Berlin to participate in a USAAC fighter contest scheduled to take place on 27 May 1935, the Model 75 (the retroactive assignment of Model numbers to earlier designs was attempted at this time and the new fighter became the first design to receive a Curtiss Model designation from the outset) all-metal single-seat fighter was initiated in October 1934, flying on 15 May 1935. Featuring a monocoque fuselage and a multi-spar wing, the Model 75 was powered by a 900 hp Wright XR-1670-5 14-cylinder two-row radial. The unsatisfactory behaviour of the Wright engine resulted in its replacement by a 700 hp Pratt & Whitney R-1535

Twin Wasp Junior. This, too, proved troublesome and was succeeded by a 950 hp Wright XR-1820-39 (G5) Cyclone nine-cylinder radial with which the prototype became the Model 75B. During USAAC trials, the Model 75B took second place to the Seversky SEV-1XP, which was to enter production as the P-35. The following data relate to the Model 75B. *Max speed, 285 mph (459 km/h) at 10,000 ft (3 050 m). Time to 10,000 ft (3 050 m), 3.87 min. Range, 730 mls (1 175 km). Empty weight, 4,049 lb (1 837 kg). Loaded weight, 5,075 lb (2 302 kg). Span, 37 ft 3½ in (11,37 m). Length, 28 ft 1 in (8,56 m). Height, 9 ft 0 in (2,74 m). Wing area, 232 sq ft (21,55 m²).*

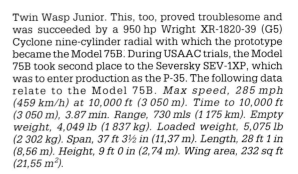

The Curtiss Model 75 in its initial guise (above) with XR-1670-5 engine and (below) as the Model 75B with XR-1820-39 for USAAC evaluation in 1936.

CURTISS P-36 USA

Despite USAAC choice of the SEV-1XP in favour of the Model 75B, the Curtiss fighter was considered to possess sufficient merit to warrant an order being placed on 7 August 1936 for three evaluation examples. These were to be powered by the Pratt & Whitney R-1830-13 Twin Wasp 14-cylinder radial rated at 900 hp at 12,000 ft (3 660 m), and were assigned the designation

(Below) Wright Field insignia on the fuselage of this early series P-36A indicated its test status.

(Top) A P-36A of the 7th Pursuit Sqn, 20th PG in 1939, and (immediately above) P-36C of training unit, 1942.

(Above) The first Model 75-H demonstrator after its sale to China, the Chinese-assembled Hawk 75-M being similar. (Below) The Hawk 75-O for Argentina.

(Above) A USAF Museum P-36A painted to represent a 27th Pursuit example in the 1939 Carolina War Games at Fort Bragg. (Below) The standard production P-36A.

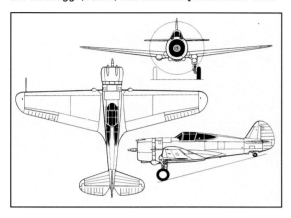

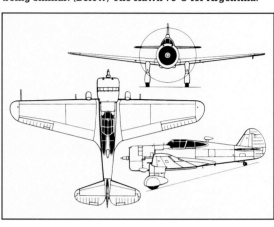

Y1P-36 (later changed to P-36), the first being completed in February 1937. Successful trials resulted, on 7 July 1937, in a contract for 210 essentially similar P-36As, the first being delivered on 20 April 1938. Armament comprised one 0.5-in (12,7-mm) and one 0.3-in (7,62-mm) gun, and the 15th and subsequent aircraft standardised on the R-1830-17 engine in place of the -13. The 20th aircraft was temporarily fitted with a

fuselage-mounted 0.5-in (12,7-mm) weapons were combined with two underwing 23-mm Danish Madsen cannon. During 1942-43, the USAAF purchased 30 survivors of 36 Hawk 75A-8s (Wright GR-1820-G205A Cyclone 9) originally ordered by the Norwegian government and subsequently used by the Norwegian flying training centre in Canada. These were assigned the designation P-36G and 28 were transferred to Peru under Lend-Lease. The following data relate to the P-36C, but are typical of all models. *Max speed, 311 mph (500 km/h) at 10,000 ft (3 050 m). Time to 15,000 ft (4 570 m), 4.9 min. Range, 820 mls (1 320 km) at 200 mph (322 km/h). Empty weight, 4,620 lb (2 096 kg). Normal loaded weight, 5,800 lb (2 631 kg). Span, 37 ft 3½ in (11,37 m). Length, 28 ft 6 in (8,69 m). Height, 12 ft 2 in (3,71 m). Wing area, 236 sq ft (21,92 m²).*

CURTISS HAWK 75   USA

Soon after receiving an order from the USAAC for an evaluation quantity of its Model 75 fighter, Curtiss began to consider the export potential of the basic de-

sign as a successor to the Hawk III biplane. A simplified version with a fixed cantilever undercarriage was evolved for which the export appellation "Hawk" was retained and to which the model number "75" was appended. Two demonstration examples of the Hawk 75 were built in parallel with the three Y1P-36s ordered by the USAAC, these being powered by the 875 hp Wright Cyclone GR-1820-G3 Cyclone nine-cylinder

(Above) The Curtiss P-36C, which featured an extra gun in each wing and (below) the single XP-36F with underwing pods carrying Madsen cannon.

1,100 hp R-1830-25 as the P-36B (later reverting to P-36A standards). The fourth and tenth airframes were converted as the XP-42 and XP-40 respectively, the 85th made provision for an additional 0.3-in (7,62-mm) gun in each wing, and the last 30 aircraft built against the original contract were then completed to a similar standard as P-36Cs. The 174th airframe was fitted in 1939 with four belt-fed, wing-mounted 0.3-in (7,62-mm) guns and two fuselage-mounted 0.5-in (12,7-mm) weapons as the XP-36D. The 147th airframe was modified to take eight wing-mounted 0.3-in (7,62-mm) guns, and the 172nd airframe became the XP-36F when twin

(Below) A Curtiss Hawk 75A-1 of the 1ᵉ *Escadrille "Lafayette"*, GC II/5, *Armée de l'Air*, winter 1939-40.

(Below) One of 20 Hawk 75-Os manufactured at Cordoba for Argentina's *Servicio de Aviación Militar*.

(Above) A Hawk 75A-7 of the 1. *Vliegtuigafdeling* in the Netherlands East Indies, December 1941.

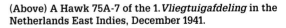

radial. One mounted an armament of one 0.5-in (12,7-mm) and one 0.3-in (7,62-mm) gun in the nose, and the other having this armament supplemented with a pair of wing-mounted 0.3-in (7,62-mm) weapons. The two demonstration aircraft were assigned the designation Hawk 75-H (Curtiss having adopted the practice of allocating suffix letters to each version of the basic design, the Y1P-36, for example, being the 75-E, the XP-37 being the 75-I, etc), the two-gun example being lost and the four-gun aircraft being sold to China. The latter country was the first quantity purchaser of the fixed-undercarriage Hawk 75, a total of 30 being delivered under the designation Hawk 75-M between May and August 1938. A further 82 were to have been assembled by CAMCO (Central Aircraft Manufacturing Company) at Loi-wing, but these were cancelled in favour of assembly of the more advanced Hawk 75A-5. The delivery followed from November 1938 of 29 aircraft to Argentina under the designation Hawk 75-O, these having an armament of four 7,62-mm guns, and a further 20 examples were licence-built by the FMA. Delivered simultaneously to Thailand were 12 Hawk 75-Ns, these having two fuselage-mounted 7,62-mm guns and two underwing 23-mm Madsen cannon. The characteristics of all versions of the fixed-undercarriage Hawk 75 were essentially similar, the following data relating specifically to the Hawk 75-O. *Max speed, 280 mph (451 km/h) at 10,700 ft (3 260 m). Initial climb, 2,340 ft/min (11,9 m/sec). Normal range, 547 mls (880 km). Empty weight, 3,975 lb (1 803 kg). Loaded weight, 5,172 lb (2 346 kg). Span, 37 ft 4 in (11,38 m). Length, 28 ft 7 in (8,71 m). Height, 9 ft 4 in (2,84 m). Wing area, 236 sq ft (21,92 m²).*

Key to Curtiss Hawk 75A-3 (Mohawk III)

1 Starboard navigation light
2 Starboard aileron
3 Aileron tab
4 Aileron ball and socket control linkage
5 Access plate
6 Wing skinning
7 Fuselage machine gun blast tubes
8 Machine gun muzzle fairings
9 Three-blade Curtiss propeller
10 Spinner hub
11 Casing
12 Pratt & Whitney R-1830-S1C3G Twin Wasp radial engine
13 Air-cooler duct
14 Starboard mainwheel
15 Exhaust outlet fairing
16 Exhaust
17 Cooling gills
18 Exhaust collector ring
19 Engine bearers
20 Engine accessories
21 Engine bearer/firewall bulkhead upper attachment
22 Machine gun barrels
23 Oil tank
24 Forward head sight
25 Ring sight
26 Two 7,5-mm FN-Browning machine guns
27 Breech fairing
28 Cooling louvres
29 Ammunition feed
30 Ammunition tank
31 Ejection chute
32 Rudder pedal assembly
33 Control column linkage
34 Control column
35 Canopy track stop
36 Gunsight mounting
37 Windscreen
38 Aft-sliding canopy
39 Pilot's headrest/back armour
40 Sutton harness
41 Pilot's seat
42 Elevator control
43 Seat support frame
44 Angled fuselage frame
45 Fuselage fuel tank, capacity 47.8 Imp gal (217 l)
46 Entry handhold
47 Canopy track
48 Fuel filler cap/neck
49 Expansion tank
50 Rear-view glazing/cut-out
51 Aerial lead-ins
52 Fuselage frame
53 Hydraulic reservoir
54 Hydraulic pump
55 Radio equipment
56 Access/service panel
57 Rudder control cable
58 Fuselage longeron
59 Lifting tube
60 Elevator control cables
61 Tailwheel retraction mechanism upper attachment
62 Fuselage skinning
63 Starboard tailplane
64 Starboard elevator
65 Aerials
66 Fin structure
67 Rear navigation lights
68 Rudder balance
69 Rudder upper (external) hinge
70 Access plate
71 Rudder
72 Rudder post
73 Tailplane attachment points
74 Elevator torque tube
75 Rudder tab
76 Elevator tab
77 Elevator structure
78 Elevator external hinge
79 Port tailplane
80 Rudder control quadrant
81 Access panels
82 Tailwheel oleo
83 Tailwheel fairing doors
84 Retractable tailwheel
85 Fuel vent/dump
86 Wingroot fairing
87 Former
88 Flap rod control link
89 Aileron control link

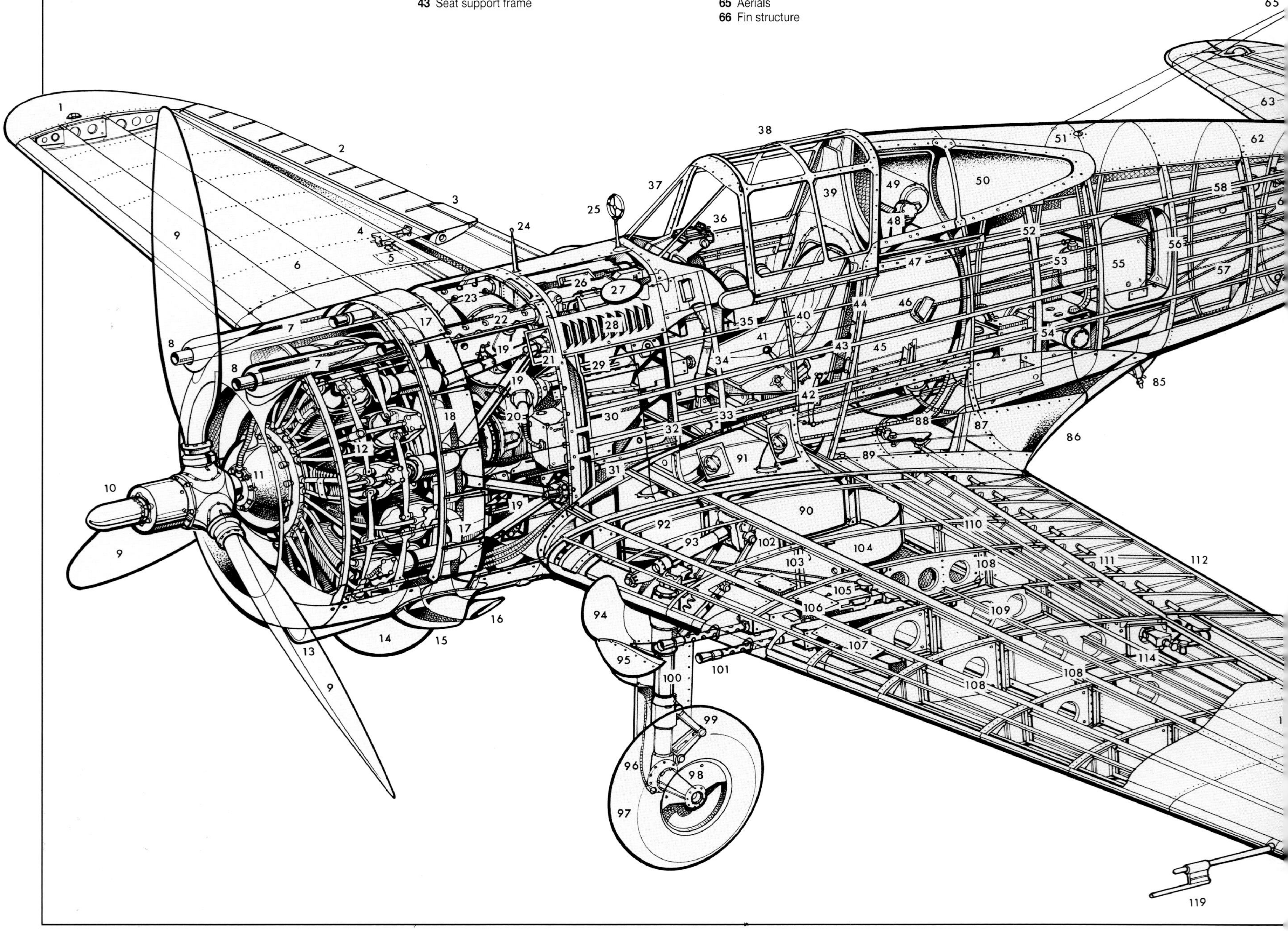

CURTISS P-37 USA

In the mid '30s, the USAAC held to its belief that liquid-cooled engines offered definite advantages over air-cooled engines for fighter aircraft. Having funded development of the 12-cylinder liquid-cooled Allison V-1710, the service placed an order with Curtiss on 16 February 1937 for an adaptation of the P-36 airframe with a V-1710-C7 engine as the XP-37 (Hawk 75-I). Although the basic airframe of the P-36 was retained, the cockpit was moved aft for CG reasons and the air-

90 Wing aft fuel tank, capacity 52.5 Imp gal
    (239 l)
91 Wing centre section fuel filler caps
92 Wing forward fuel tank, capacity 34.7 Imp
    gal (158 l)
93 Mainwheel retraction cylincer
94 Mainwheel leg fairing
95 Mainwheel leg fairing door
96 Hydraulic brake line
97 Port mainwheel
98 Axle
99 Torque links
100 Mainwheel oleo

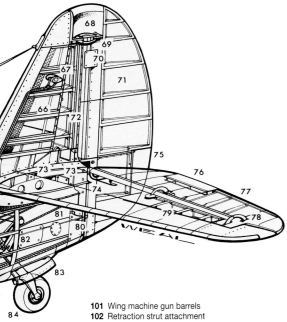

101 Wing machine gun barrels
102 Retraction strut attachment
103 Gun charging cables
104 Port mainwheel well
105 Two 0.303-in (7,7-mm) Browning machine
    guns
106 Access panels
107 Ammunition bays (inboard/outboard)
108 Wing spars
109 Wing ribs
110 Aileron control rod
111 Flap control push-rod rollers
112 Port flap structure
113 Aileron tab
114 Aileron control ball and socket joint
115 Wing skinning
116 Port aileron
117 Wingtip structure
118 Port navigation light
119 Pitot tube

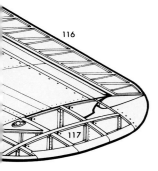

(Above) One of the 13 YP-37s acquired by the USAAC in 1939 for Service trials, which were unsuccessful.

craft was powered by a V-1710-11 (C8) engine with a General Electric turbo-supercharger and affording 1,150 hp for take-off and 1,000 hp at 20,000 ft (6 100 m). Armament remained one 0.5-in (12,7-mm) and one 0.3-in (7,62-mm) gun. Flown on 20 April 1937, the XP-37 succeeded in achieving 340 mph (547 km/h) at 20,000 ft (6 100 m), but suffered frequent turbo-supercharger malfunction. An order for 13 service test examples was placed on 11 December 1937. Powered by the V-1710-21 with an improved supercharger and rated at 1,000 hp for take-off and 880 hp at 25,000 ft (7 620 m), the service test model was designated YP-37. It featured a 1 ft 10 in (56 cm) longer fuselage and 451-lb (204,5-kg) and 539-lb (244-kg) increases in empty and normal gross weights respectively. Delivered to the USAAC between 29 April 1939 and 5 December 1939, the YP-37s were dogged by mechanical problems, and further development was discontinued. The following data relate to the YP-37. *Max speed, 331 mph (533 km/h) at 20,000 ft (6 100 m). Initial climb, 2,920 ft/min (14,8 m/sec). Normal range, 570 mls (917 km). Empty weight, 5,723 lb (2 596 kg). Loaded weight, 6,889 lb (3 125 kg). Span, 37 ft 4 in (11,38 m). Length, 32 ft 10 in (10,01 m). Height, 9 ft 6 in (2,89 m). Wing area, 236 sq ft (21,92 m²).*

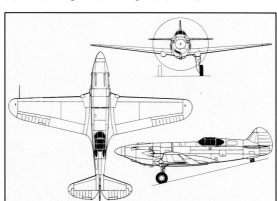

(Above) The YP-37, which had a slightly longer rear fuselage than (below) the prototype XP-37.

CURTISS HAWK 75-R USA

Completed late in 1938 as a company-owned demonstrator, the Hawk 75-R was essentially similar to the USAAC's P-36A. Its Pratt & Whitney R-1830-19 (SC2-G) Twin Wasp was, however, fitted with a turbo-supercharger mounted beneath the nose, just aft of the engine cowling, with a ventrally-mounted intercooler.

Extensively tested by the USAAC, the Hawk 75-R was eventually returned to Curtiss as the turbo-supercharger proved unreliable and the manual monitoring of the unit was considered impracticable in combat. The turbo-supercharger was subsequently removed and the aircraft re-engined with a Cyclone. *Max speed, 330 mph (531 km/h) at 15,000 ft (4 570 m). Time to 15,000 ft (4 570 m), 4.75 min. Range, 600 mls (966 km). Empty weight, 5,074 lb (2 302 kg). Loaded weight, 6,163 lb (2 795 kg). Span, 37 ft 3½ in (11,37 m). Length, 28 ft 6 in (8,69 m). Height, 12 ft 2 in (3,71 m). Wing area, 236 sq ft (21,92 m²).*

The Hawk 75-R (below) was the original Model 75A demonstrator with a turbo-supercharger.

CURTISS HAWK 75A USA

In February 1938, the French government began negotiations for the purchase of what was essentially an export version of the USAAC's P-36 and, in May, signed a contract for an initial batch of 100 aircraft. At this point, a new system of designating variants was adopted by Curtiss, the suffix letter "A" being assigned to all export models with the retractable undercarriage, numbers being appended in sequence to cover each successive contract. Thus, the aircraft covered by the initial French contract were designated Hawk 75A-1. This model was powered by a 950 hp Pratt & Whitney R-1830-SC-G Twin Wasp and carried two wing-mounted and two fuselage-mounted 7,5-mm FN-Browning guns. The 100 Hawk 75A-1s were delivered between December 1938 and April 1939. A second con-

A Hawk 75A-3 in use with the 2ᵉ *Escadrille* of GC I/5, as part of the Vichy Air Force in 1942.

tract called for 100 Hawk 75A-2s, the 41st and subsequent aircraft of this batch having two additional 7.5-mm wing guns and the 48th *et seq* having the 1,050 hp R-1830-SC3-G, these being delivered May-July 1939. In February 1940, deliveries began against a contract for 135 Hawk 75A-3s with the 1,200 hp R-1830-S1C3-G, but deliveries of 285 Hawk 75A-4s powered by the Wright GR-1820-G205A (R-1820-87) Cyclone had only just commenced to France at the time of the Armis-

(Above) Hawk 75A-7s of 1. *Vliegtuigafdeling*, KNIL *Luchtvaartafdeling*, from Madioen, late 1941.

tice. A total of 227 Hawk 75As then found their way into the RAF inventory, mostly Hawk 75A-4s delivered directly from the USA and assigned the appellation Mohawk IV. Small quantities of earlier models became Mohawk I (Hawk 75A-1), II (Hawk 75A-2) and III (Hawk 75A-3). Seventy-two Mohawk IVs were transferred to South Africa and 12 to Portugal. The Hawk 75A-5 (GR-1820-G205A) was assembled by CAMCO (30-40) at Loi-wing after the supply of one pattern aircraft, a further five being assembled by HAL in India after a transfer by CAMCO of jigs, tools, assemblies and components. The Hawk 75A-6 was similar to the 75A-2, but with four 7,9-mm guns, 24 being ordered by Norway of which 12 were delivered (the remaining 12 being taken on charge by the RAF as Mohawk IIs). Hawk 75A-7 was the designation applied to 20 GR-1820-G205A-powered aircraft supplied to the Royal Netherlands Indies Army; the Hawk 75A-8 was a version for Norway (see P-36G) and the Hawk 75A-9 was a Cyclone-powered version for Iran, 10 being ordered, sequestered by the Allies and issued to the RAF as Mohawk IVs. The following data relate to the Hawk 75A-4. *Max speed, 323 mph (520 km/h) at 15,100 ft (4 600 m). Max range, 1,003 mls (1 614 km). Empty weight, 4,541 lb (2 060 kg). Normal loaded, 5,750 lb (2 608 kg). Span, 37 ft 4 in (11,38 m). Length, 28 ft 10 in (8,79 m). Height, 9 ft 6 in (2,89 m). Wing area, 236 sq ft (21,92 m²).*

CURTISS P-40 TO P-40C (HAWK 81A) USA

Ordered in July 1937 as a rework of the 10th production P-36A with an Allison V-1710-19 (C-13) liquid-cooled engine, the XP-40 was flown on 14 October 1938. An order for 524 production examples designated P-40 was placed on 27 April 1939. The first P-40 flew a year later, on 4 April 1940, with a V-1710-33 (C-15) engine rated at 1,040 hp for take-off and with two fuselage-mounted 0.5-in (12,7-mm) M-2 machine guns. A total of 199 P-40s

Unarmed, the 20th P-40 (right) was assigned to Wright Field for testing by USAAC Matériel Division, as indicated by "MD" tail code.

Curtiss P-40C (below) showing the four wing guns.

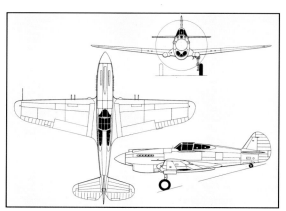

The XP-40 (above), a converted P-36A airframe, showing the original ventral radiator. (Below) A P-40 of the 35th Pursuit Group in 1941.

(Above) A Tomahawk IIB flown by Canadian-manned No 414 Sqn with the RAF, 1941.

was delivered, the remainder of the contract being made up with 131 P-40Bs with pilot armour, self-sealing tanks and armament augmented by two 0.3-in (7,62-mm) wing guns, 193 P-40Cs with an additional 0.3-in (7,62-mm) gun in each wing and provision for a ventral drop tank, and one P-40G. The last-mentioned sub-type was a P-40 fitted with Hawk 81A-2 wings, an additional 44 P-40s subsequently being converted to a similar standard. Hawk 81A was the export designation of the basic fighter, the Hawk 81A-1 being similar to the P-40, but having provision for four 7,5-mm wing guns and 230 being ordered by France. The first 140 completed against the French contract were transferred to the UK as Tomahawk Is, the remaining 90 (Hawk 81A-2s) having pilot armour and fuel tank protection, and being delivered as Tomahawk IIAs. British contracts called for 950 similar aircraft comprising 20 Tomahawk IIAs and the remainder as Tomahawk IIBs; of these 100 were released to the Chinese National Government, 195 were transferred to the Soviet Union and others to Canada, Egypt and Turkey. The final 300 had increased ammunition capacity and a revised fuel system, and were referred to by the manufacturer as Hawk 81A-3s. The following data relate to the P-40C. *Max speed, 345 mph (555 km/h) at 15,000 ft (4 575 m). Initial climb, 2,690 ft/min (13,7 m/sec). Range (clean), 800 mls (1 287 km). Empty weight, 5,812 lb (2 636 kg). Loaded weight, 7,549 lb (3 424 kg). Span, 37 ft 3½ in (11,37 m). Length, 31 ft 8½ in (9,66 m). Height, 10ft 7 in (3,22 m). Wing area, 236 sq ft (21,92 m²).*

(Immediately below) A Hawk 81A-2 flown by Charles Older, 3rd Sqn of the AVG, China, 1942. (Bottom) A Tomahawk IIB of No 112 Sqn, Sidi Haneish, Oct 1941.

CURTISS XP-42   USA

Evolved in parallel with the XP-40 and delivered to the AAC on 5 March 1939, the XP-42 was effectively an exercise in drag reduction – an attempt to reduce the drag evoked by an air-cooled radial to approximately that of a liquid-cooled inline engine. Utilising the fourth production P-36A airframe, the XP-42 had a 1,050 hp Pratt & Whitney R-1830-31 Twin Wasp with an 18-in (45,7-cm) extension shaft and with the engine enclosed by a close-fitting cowling. This cowling was, in effect, a streamlined prolongation of the propeller spinner. Inadequate cooling, carburettor ducting problems and extension shaft vibration proved troublesome, and much of the potential gain in performance from the improved streamlining was absorbed by the weight of the extension shaft and compensatory tail ballast. Both long and short, high- and low-inlet-velocity cowlings coupled with propeller cuffs and a cooling fan were evaluated, the maximum level speed attained being 344 mph (554 km/h) at 14,500 ft (4 420 m). This was achieved with both long-nose, high-inlet-velocity cowling with propeller cuffs and spinner, and with the short-nose, low-inlet-velocity cowling with spinner only. Before trials were discontinued in 1942, the XP-42 was fitted with a slab-type all-moving tailplane. The following data relate to the definitive long-cowl XP-42. *Max speed, 344 mph (554 km/h) at 14,500 ft (4 420 m). Normal range, 730 mls (1 175 km). Empty weight, 4,818 lb (2 185 kg). Loaded weight, 6,100 lb (2 767 kg). Span, 37 ft 4 in (11,38 m). Length, 30 ft 3⅛ in (9,22 m). Height, 9 ft 9 in (2,97 m). Wing area, 236 sq ft (21,92 m²).*

The sole XP-42 (below), this being the fourth P-36A with R-1830 engine and lengthened propeller shaft.

CURTISS XP-46   USA

In 1939, Donovan R Berlin attempted to combine what he considered to be some of the best features of the latest European fighters in a potential successor for the P-40, two prototypes being ordered on 29 September 1939 as the XP-46. Designed around the newly-developed Allison V-1710-39 (F3R) rated at 1,150 hp, the XP-46 was more compact that the earlier fighter. It featured automatic wing leading-edge slats, an armament of twin fuselage-mounted 0.5-in (12,7-mm) guns and eight wing-mounted 0.3-in (7,62-mm) guns, and 65 lb (29,5 kg) of pilot armour. The second prototype, which was the first to fly (as the XP-46A) on 15 February 1941, was delivered without armour, armament, radio and self-sealing fuel tanks. In this stripped form it met the specification speed of 410 mph (660 km/h), but when the fully-equipped first prototype was delivered on 22 September 1941, maximum speed was found to be 55 mph (88,5 km/h) down. Lacking supercharging, the XP-46 held no promise as a fighter at altitude, and as a similarly-powered development of the P-40 had meanwhile been programmed (ie, P-40D), further development of the experimental fighter was abandoned. *Max speed, 355 mph (571 km/h) at 12,200 ft (3 720 m). Time to 12,300 ft (3 750 m), 5.0 min. Empty weight, 5,625 lb (2 551 kg). Max loaded weight, 7,665 lb (3 477 kg). Span, 34 ft 4 in (10,46 m). Length, 30 ft 2 in (9,19 m). Height, 13 ft 0 in (3,96 m). Wing area, 208 sq ft (19,32 m²).*

The XP-46A (above) as delivered in February 1941, without armament and other items of equipment, and (below) the fully-equipped and armed XP-46.

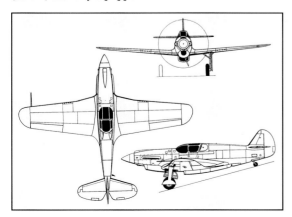

CURTISS P-40D, E, K & M (HAWK 87A) WARHAWK   USA

The availability of the Allison V-1710-39 with an external spur reduction gear and a rating of 1,150 hp for take-off which was maintained at 11,700 ft (3 566 m) prompted redesign of the basic Hawk 81A as the Hawk 87A. This was to be the recipient of a British contract for 560 aircraft in May 1940, the first example (Hawk 87A-1) flying on 22 May 1941, and being assigned the name Kittyhawk I by the RAF. After delivery of the first 20 Kittyhawk Is, armament was increased from four to six wing-mounted 0.5-in (12,7-mm) machine guns (Hawk 87A-2). A similar change was introduced on the parallel P-40D for the USAAF after completion of 22 aircraft, this change resulting in the assignment of the designation P-40E to the more heavily armed model. Orders were placed for 2,320 E-model fighters comprising 820 P-40Es (Hawk 87A-3) and 1,500 P-40E-1s (Hawk 87A-4), the latter being purchased from Lend-Lease funds for the RAF and other Commonwealth air arms as Kittyhawk IAs. The next Allison-engine production model was the P-40K with the V-1710-73 (F4R)

(Above) Built under British contract, this P-40E wears RAF camouflage although repossessed by USAAF.

(Above) A P-40E displaying the USAAF "star-and-bar" insignia introduced July 1943. (Below) A repossessed British Kittyhawk II in USAAF service, 1942.

engine rated at 1,325 hp for take-off and 1,150 hp at 11,800 ft (3 595 m), but otherwise similar to the P-40E-1. Of 1,300 built, the bulk were supplied to the Soviet Union and to the USAAF in Asia and the Pacific. The P-40K-10 production batch introduced a 1 ft 7½ in (49,53 cm) increase in fuselage length. The P-40M differed from the P-40K in having a V-1710-81 engine offering 1,200 hp for take-off, and 600 were built of which 595 were supplied to Commonwealth air forces as Kittyhawk IIIs. Performances of E, K and M models were generally similar and the following data relate to the P-40E-1. *Max speed, 362 mph (582 km/h) at 15,000 ft (4 575 m). Time to 5,000 ft (1 525 m), 2.4 min. Max range (with drop tank), 850 mls (1 368 km) at 207 mph (333 km/h). Empty weight, 6,900 lb (3 130 kg). Loaded weight, 8,400 lb (3 810 kg). Span, 37 ft 4 in (11,38 m). Length, 31 ft 9 in (9,68 m). Height, 12 ft 4 in (3,76 m). Wing area, 236 sq ft (21,92 m²).*

A P-40K-1, showing the extra fin area used on the early short-fuselage version of this improved P-40E.

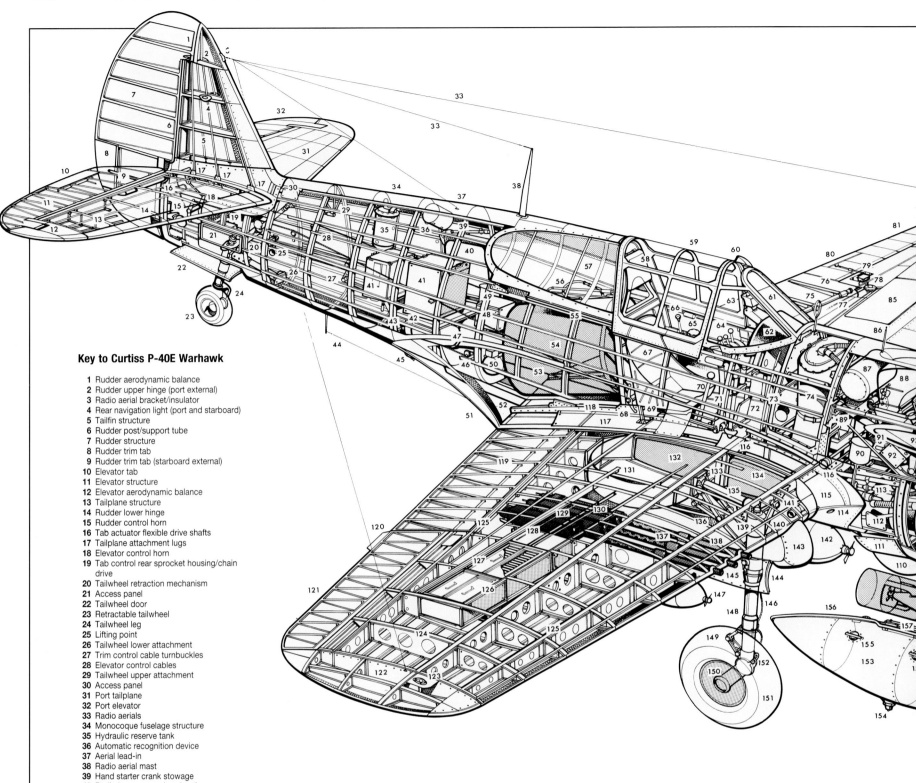

Key to Curtiss P-40E Warhawk

1 Rudder aerodynamic balance
2 Rudder upper hinge (port external)
3 Radio aerial bracket/insulator
4 Rear navigation light (port and starboard)
5 Tailfin structure
6 Rudder post/support tube
7 Rudder structure
8 Rudder trim tab
9 Rudder trim tab (starboard external)
10 Elevator tab
11 Elevator structure
12 Elevator aerodynamic balance
13 Tailplane structure
14 Rudder lower hinge
15 Rudder control horn
16 Tab actuator flexible drive shafts
17 Tailplane attachment lugs
18 Elevator control horn
19 Tab control rear sprocket housing/chain drive
20 Tailwheel retraction mechanism
21 Access panel
22 Tailwheel door
23 Retractable tailwheel
24 Tailwheel leg
25 Lifting point
26 Tailwheel lower attachment
27 Trim control cable turnbuckles
28 Elevator control cables
29 Tailwheel upper attachment
30 Access panel
31 Port tailplane
32 Port elevator
33 Radio aerials
34 Monocoque fuselage structure
35 Hydraulic reserve tank
36 Automatic recognition device
37 Aerial lead-in
38 Radio aerial mast
39 Hand starter crank stowage
40 Radio bay access door (port)
41 Radio receiver/transmitter
42 Support frame
43 Battery stowage
44 Ventral aerial (optional)
45 Hydraulic system vent and drain
46 Rudder control cable turnbuckle
47 Oxygen bottles
48 Radio equipment installation (optional)
49 Hydraulic tank
50 Hydraulic pump
51 Wingroot fillet
52 Streamlined ventral cowl
53 Wing centreline splice
54 Fuselage fuel tank, capacity 51.5 Imp gal (234 l)
55 Canopy track
56 Fuel lines
57 Rear-vision panels
58 Pilot's headrest
59 Rearward-sliding cockpit canopy
60 Rear-view mirror (external)
61 Bullet-proof windshield
62 Instrument panel coaming
63 Electric gunsight
64 Throttle control quadrant
65 Trim tab control wheels

66 Flap control lever
67 Pilot's seat
68 Elevator control cable horn
69 Seat support (wing upper surface)
70 Hydraulic pump handle
71 Control column
72 Rudder pedal/brake cylinder assembly
73 Bulkhead
74 Oil tank, capacity 10.8 Imp gal (49 l)
75 Ring sight
76 Flap control push-rod rollers
77 Aileron control cables
78 Aileron cable drum
79 Aileron trim tab drive motor
80 Aileron trim tab
81 Port aileron
82 Port navigation light
83 Pitot head
84 Wing skinning
85 Ammunition loading panels
86 Bead sight
87 Coolant expansion tank, capacity 2.9 Imp gal (13 l)
88 Carburettor intake
89 Engine bearer support attachment
90 Air vapour eliminator

91 Hydraulic emergency reserve tank
92 Junction box
93 Engine support tubes
94 Engine mounting vibration absorbers
95 Exhaust stacks
96 Cowling panel lines
97 Allison V-1710-39 engine
98 Carburettor intake fairing
99 Propeller reduction gear casing
100 Coolant thermometer
101 Propeller hub shaft
102 Spinner
103 Curtiss Electric propeller
104 Radiator (divided) intakes
105 Intake trunking
106 Oil cooler radiator (centreline)
107 Glycol radiators (port and starboard)
108 Radiator mounting brackets
109 Glycol radiator intake pipe
110 Port mainwheel
111 Controllable cooling gills
112 Access panel (oil drain)
113 Engine bearer support truss
114 Fresh air intake
115 Wingroot fairing
116 Fuselage frame/wing attachment

117 Walkway
118 Wing/fuselage splice plate
119 Split flap structure
120 Aileron fixed tab
121 Starboard aileron
122 Starboard wingtip construction
123 Starboard navigation light
124 Wing rib
125 Multi (7)-spar wing structure
126 Inboard gun ammunition box (235 rounds)
127 Centre gun ammunition box (235 rounds)
128 Outboard gun ammunition box (235 rounds)
129 Three 0.50-in (12,7-mm) M-2 Browning machine guns
130 Ammunition feed chute
131 Starboard wheel well
132 Wing centre-section main fuel tank, capacity 42.1 Imp gal (191 l)
133 Wing centre-section reserve fuel tank, capacity 29.2 Imp gal (133 l)
134 Undercarriage attachment
135 Retraction cylinder
136 Retraction arm/links
137 Machine gun barrel forward support collars

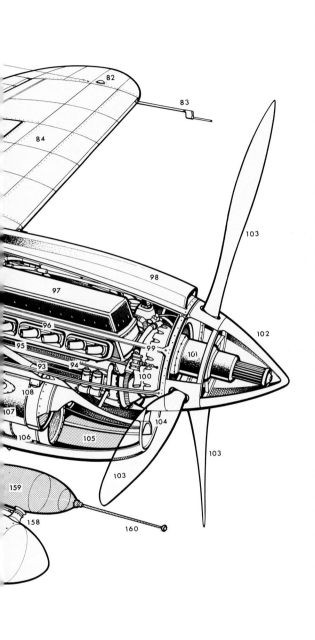

CURTISS P-40F & L WARHAWK   USA

The altitude capability of the P-40 was strictly limited by its Allison engine and in an attempt to overcome this the second P-40D airframe was fitted with a Rolls-Royce Merlin 28 and flown on 30 June 1941 as the XP-40F. Orders were subsequently placed for 1,311 P-40Fs powered by the Packard-built V-1650-1 Merlin rated at 1,300 hp for take-off. The same armament as that of the Allison-engined models (six 0.50-in/12,7-mm wing guns) was fitted. The third production airframe was provided with a deep, aft-positioned ventral radiator bath as the YP-40F, and the P-40F-5 and subsequent production batches featured a lengthened fuselage similar to that introduced on the P-40K-10. A total of 330 was allocated to the Commonwealth as Kittyhawk IIs, but, in the event, only 117 served with the RAF, RAAF and SAAF, and of the remainder, 100 were supplied to the Soviet Union. The final Merlin-engined model, the P-40L, was initially identical to the final production P-40F-20, but with the P-40L-5 production batch, two of the wing guns were removed, together with some fuel capacity, as weight-saving measures. These, in fact, produced only a 4 mph (6,43 km/h) increase in max speed at rated altitude. A total of 700 L-model Warhawks was built. Three hundred P-40Fs and P-40Ls were re-engined in 1944 with the Allison V-1710-81 as P-40R-1s and -2s because of Merlin spares shortages. The following data relate to the P-40F-5 but are typical of Merlin-powered models. *Max speed, 364 mph (586 km/h) at 20,000 ft (6 100 m). Time to 5,000 ft (1 525 m), 2.4 min. Max range (with drop tank), 1,500 mls (2 414 km) at 208 mph (335 km/h). Empty weight, 7,000 lb (3 175 kg). Loaded weight, 8,500 lb (3 855 kg). Span, 37 ft 4 in (11,38 m). Length, 33 ft 4 in (10,16 m). Height, 12 ft 4 in (3,76 m). Wing area, 236 sq ft (21,92 m²).*

The long-fuselage, Merlin-engined, P-40L-5 Warhawk.

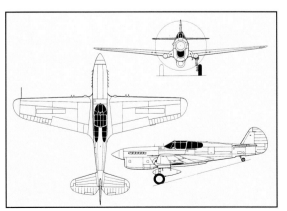

CURTISS XP-60 & XP-60D   USA

Among proposals submitted to the AAC in the summer of 1940 for a successor to the P-40 was a development of the basic P-40 design using a laminar-flow aerofoil and powered by a Continental XIV-1430-3 engine, expected to produce 1,600 hp at 15,000 ft (4 575 m). This was accepted by the AAC and two prototypes were ordered under the designation XP-53 on 1 October 1940. Subsequently, the decision was taken to complete the

(Above, top) A P-40E serving with the 11th Sqn, 343rd FG, in the Aleutians, 1942. (Immediately above) A P-40L-5 of HQ Flight, 325th FG, Tunisia, 1943.

second XP-53 with a Merlin engine as the XP-60, the first XP-53 eventually becoming a static test airframe. A new inward-retracting undercarriage was introduced, together with enlarged vertical tail surfaces, and the XP-60 flew on 18 September 1941 with a British-built Merlin 28 engine. This aircraft was later fitted with six 0.5-in (12,7-mm) wing guns and self-sealing fuel tanks.

The original Merlin-engined XP-60 (below) after it had been fitted with enlarged fin and rudder.

Trials of the XP-60 proved that performance did not comply with the manufacturer's guarantees as a result of insufficient wing smoothness and lower engine output than anticipated. As the Merlin had meanwhile been selected for installation in other fighters and there was a likelihood of delays in deliveries of the Packard licence-built version, further P-60 development was concentrated on models powered by alternative engines. The XP-60 was returned to Curtiss-Wright for the installation of a Merlin 61 engine and in this form it was designated XP-60D. The following data relate to the XP-60. *Max speed, 380 mph (611 km/h) at 20,000 ft (6 100 m). Time to 20,000 ft (6 100 m), 7.3 min. Range, 995 mls (1 601 km). Empty weight, 7,008 lb (3 179 kg). Loaded weight, 9,700 lb (4 400 kg). Span, 41 ft 5 in (12,62 m). Length, 33 ft 4 in (10,16 m). Height, 14 ft 4 in (4,37 m). Wing area, 275 sq ft (25,55 m²).*

CURTISS XP-60A   USA

On 31 October 1941, orders were placed for a total of 1,950 P-60A fighters in which the Merlin of the XP-60 was to be supplanted by an Allison V-1710-75 with General Electric B-14 turbo-supercharger and offering 1,425 hp at 25,000 ft (7 620 m). Shortly afterwards, on 17 November, it was realised that the Allison-engined P-60A would be underpowered, further work on this fighter consequently being terminated and more powerful engines suitable for P-60 installation being sought. On 2 January 1942, it was decided that one XP-60A should be built (together with one XP-60B and

A new fuselage was mated with the XP-60 laminar-flow wing to produce the XP-60A (below).

138 Blast tubes
139 Bevel gear
140 Undercarriage side support strut
141 Gun warm air
142 500-lb (227-kg) bomb (ventral stores)
143 Undercarriage oleo leg fairing
144 Undercarriage fairing door
145 Machine gun ports
146 Hydraulic brake line
147 One (or two) underwing 40-lb (18-kg) bomb(s)
148 Oleo leg
149 Torque links
150 Axle
151 30-in (76,2-mm) diameter smooth-contour mainwheel tyre
152 Tow ring/jack point
153 Ventral auxiliary tank, capacity 43.5 Imp gal (197 l)
154 Vent line
155 Sway brace pads
156 External fuel line
157 Shackle asembly
158 Filler neck
159 Alternative ventral 250-lb (113,5-kg) bomb with:
160 Extended percussion fuse

one XP-60C) for development purposes with the turbo-supercharged Allison. Having little in common with the XP-60 other than the wing and undercarriage, the XP-60A first flew on 1 November 1942, without the turbo-supercharger, which had been removed as a result of a fire in the previous month during ground trials. Armament of the XP-60A was to have comprised six 0.5-in (12,7-mm) wing-mounted guns, but without the turbo-supercharger installed, flight testing was confined to the investigation of control forces. The wings, undercarriage and other items from the XP-60A were subsequently applied to the XP-60E after the latter suffered damage in a forced landing. The following performance data are estimated for the XP-60A *with* turbo-supercharger. *Max speed, 420 mph (676 km/h) at 29,000 ft (8 840 m). Time to 10,000 ft (3 050 m), 4.20 min. Empty weight, 7,806 lb (3 541 kg). Loaded weight, 9,616 lb (4 362 kg). Span, 41 ft 4 in (12,60 m). Length, 33 ft 8 in (10,26 m). Height, 12 ft 4 in (3,76 m). Wing area, 275 sq ft (25,55 m²).*

(Below) The XP-60A with Allison V-1710-75 engine.

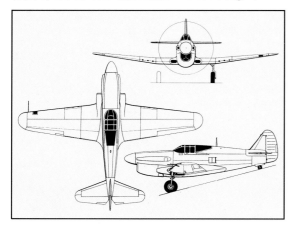

CURTISS XP-60C & XP-60E   USA

Ordered simultaneously with the XP-60A, the XP-60C was intended to have a Chrysler XIV-2220 16-cylinder engine of 2,300 hp. Studies revealed, however, that several hundred pounds of lead would have to be installed in the tail as ballast in order to avoid total fuselage redesign, and as the status of the XIV-2220 engine was questionable, in August 1942 it was proposed that a Pratt & Whitney R-2800 18-cylinder air-cooled radial be substituted. The potential performance with this engine was such that, in November 1942, a letter contract was prepared covering 500 R-2800-powered P-60A-1 fighters. The XP-60C was flown on 27 January 1943 with a 2,000 hp R-2800-53 driving contra-rotating propellers. As it appeared that the contraprops and necessary gearing would be unavailable for production aircraft, the XP-60B (originally intended for an Allison V-1710-75 engine with a Wright SU-504-2 turbo-supercharger) was modified before completion to take an R-2800-10 engine of similar power driving a four-bladed propeller. It thus provided a direct comparison with the XP-60C installation, the former XP-60B being redesignated XP-60E. Owing to the lighter propeller installation of the XP-60E, it was found necessary to move the engine 10 in (25,40 cm) forward by comparison with that of the XP-60C. The XP-60E flew on 26 May 1943,

The XP-60C, a contemporary of the XP-60A, was distinguished by an R-2800-53 turning contra-props.

but three months later, on 14 August, just prior to scheduled release to the AAF for official trials, the prototype was damaged in a forced landing. Curtiss was then asked to remove the -53 engine and contraprops from the XP-60C and install a -10 engine with four-bladed propeller. The XP-60C thus became the XP-60E, while repair of the original XP-60E with the wings, undercarriage and other items from the XP-60A, and the installation of a -53 engine and contraprops, turned this into an XP-60C. The following data relate to the XP-60C. *Max speed, 414 mph (666 km/h) at 20,350 ft (6 205 m). Initial climb, 3,890 ft/min (19,76 m/sec). Empty weight, 8,600 lb (3 901 kg). Loaded weight, 10,525 lb (4 774 kg). Span, 41 ft 4 in (12,60 m). Length, 33 ft 11 in (10,34 m). Height, 12 ft 6 in (3,81 m). Wing area, 275 sq ft (25,55 m²).*

CURTISS P-40N WARHAWK   USA

Built in substantially larger numbers than any other version of the Warhawk, the P-40N introduced a new lightweight structure and was successively fitted with the Allison V-1710-81, (P-40N-20) V-1710-99 and (P-40N-40) V-1710-115. The first 400 (P-40N-1) had four 0.5-in (12,7-mm) wing guns, subsequent aircraft having a six-gun armament, and the P-40N-5 introduced a frameless canopy and full-depth rear-vision panels. A total of 536 P-40Ns was allocated to the Commonwealth as Kittyhawk IVs, and production comprised 5,216 aircraft, a further 784 being cancelled. The last production example – the 13,738th P-40 built – was completed in December 1944. The following data relate to the P-40N-20. *Max speed, 350 mph (563 km/h) at 16,400 ft (5 000 m). Max range (internal fuel), 600 mls (966 km). Time to 5,000 ft (1 525 m), 2.4 min. Empty weight, 6,700 lb (3 039 kg). Loaded weight, 8,400 lb (3 810 kg). Span, 37 ft 4 in (11,38 m). Length, 33 ft 4 in (10,16 m). Height, 12 ft 4 in (3,76 m). Wing area, 236 sq ft (21,92 m²).*

(Above) A P-40N-1 Warhawk in 1944, and (below) a preserved example of the P-40N with the shark's mouth marking popular with many user-squadrons.

CURTISS XP-55   USA

One of three designs awarded development contracts as a result of an informal design contest for fighters of unconventional configuration – the others being the Consolidated-Vultee XP-54 and the Northrop XP-56 – the XP-55 was of radical canard configuration, albeit not a *true* canard in that it had no *fixed* forward control surfaces. Although Curtiss originally intended to fit the experimental Pratt & Whitney X-1800-A3G (H-2600) liquid-cooled engine, the 1,275 hp Allison V-1710-95 (F23R) engine was eventually installed in the three prototypes ordered on 10 July 1942. The first XP-55 was flown on 19 July 1943, but was lost during stall trials four months later, on 15 November. The second XP-55 flew on 9 January 1944, followed by the third on 25 April, the latter embodying extended wingtips with so-called "trailerons", and increased elevator travel limits. The second prototype was later modified to the same standard. Armament comprised four 0.5-in (12,7-mm) nose-mounted guns. The XP-55 revealed a tendency to over-control at low speeds, stall behaviour was both unconventional and undesirable, and engine cooling was critical. It was concluded, in consequence, that the unorthodox configuration did not justify further development. *Max speed, 390 mph (628 km/h) at 19,300 ft (5 885 m). Time to 20,000 ft (6 100 m), 7.1 min. Normal range, 635 mls (1 022 km) at 296 mph (476 km/h). Empty weight, 6,354 lb (2 882 kg). Normal loaded weight, 7,330 lb (3 325 kg). Span, 44 ft 0½ in (13,42 m). Length, 29 ft 7 in (9,02 m). Height, 10 ft 0¾ in (3,07 m). Wing area, 235 sq ft (21,83 m²).*

(Above) The second prototype of the XP-55 after the addition of the wing-tip "trailerons", also depicted (below) in the three-view drawing.

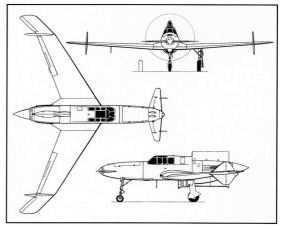

CURTISS XP-62   USA

At the beginning of 1941, design work was initiated on a heavily-armed, high-performance fighter featuring a pressure cabin and powered by the 18-cylinder two-row Wright R-3350 radial engine with an exhaust-driven turbo-supercharger and driving a six-bladed contraprop. Continuous revision of the specification seriously delayed the programme, and a letter contract for 100 P-62s, approved on 25 May 1942, was terminated two months later. The first flight test of the XP-62 did not take place until 21 July 1943, being delayed by non-availability of the pressure cabin, one of the first such installations in an interceptor fighter. Initial trials were conducted, in the event, without the pressure cabin. Although a decision to install this was taken in February 1944, the XP-62 was assigned low priority and the sole prototype was scrapped in the autumn of 1944, before pressure cabin installation was completed. The proposed armament comprised four or eight 20-mm cannon, but no guns were installed and flight testing was insufficient to secure full performance details, the following data being based on manufacturer's estimates. *Max speed, 448 mph (721 km/h) at 27,000 ft (8 230 m), 358 mph (576 km/h) at 5,000 ft (1 525 m). Time to 15,000 ft (4 575 m), 6.9 min. Normal range, 900 mls (1 448 km). Empty weight, 11,773 lb (5 340 kg). Normal loaded weight, 14,660 lb (6 650 kg). Span, 53 ft 7¾ in (16,35 m). Length, 39 ft 6 in (12,04 m). Height, 16 ft 3 in (4,95 m). Wing area, 420 sq ft (39,02 m²).*

A single prototype of the XP-62 heavily-armed high-performance fighter (above and below), flown by Curtiss with little success in 1943.

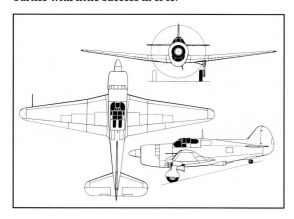

CURTISS P-40Q WARHAWK USA

Prior to the final termination of P-40 development, some effort was expended in combining aerodynamic refinement with increased power to produce a higher-performance model. A P-40K airframe was fitted with an Allison V-1710-121 engine rated at 1,425 hp for take-off and 1,100 hp at 25,000 ft (7 620 m). Semi-flush low-drag radiators were incorporated in the wing centre section and a four-bladed propeller was fitted, the designation XP-40Q being assigned. A second, similarly re-engined P-40K for the P-40Q programme reintroduced the nose radiator scoop, but featured an all-round vision bubble-type canopy (previously tested on a P-40N). The definitive XP-40Q (converted from a P-40N-25 airframe) had clipped wing tips, the cut-down aft fuselage with bubble canopy and coolant radiators faired into the wing leading edges. Four 0.5-in (12,7-mm) guns were carried but proposed production models were to have carried, either six 0.5-in (12,7-mm) or four 20-mm weapons. No production was undertaken. The following data relate

(Below) The second XP-40Q in its definitive form.

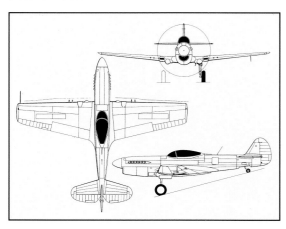

A cut-down rear fuselage for all-round vision and clipped wings distinguished the second XP-40Q.

to the definitive prototype. *Max speed, 422 mph (679 km/h) at 20,500 ft (6 250 m). Time to 20,000 ft (6 100 m), 4.8 min. Span, 35 ft 3 in (10,75 m). Length, 33 ft 4 in (10,16 m).*

CURTISS XF14C-2 USA

On 30 June 1941, Curtiss received a prototype development contract for the XF14C-1 single-seat shipboard fighter designed around the 2,200 hp Lycoming XH-2470-4 liquid-cooled engine. At a relatively early stage in the programme, the unsatisfactory state of development of the Lycoming engine led to the redesign of the fighter to accept an 18-cylinder two-row Wright R-3350 as the XF14C-2, this engine driving a six-blade contraprop. Powered by an XR-3350-16 rated at 2,300 hp, and carrying an armament of four 20-mm cannon, the XF14C-2 was flown for the first time in September 1943, but not delivered to the US Navy until July 1944. Performance proved to be substantially below that specified and the prototype suffered excessive vibration. In consequence, further development of the XF14C-2 was abandoned. *Max speed, 380 mph (611 km/h) at 20,000 ft (6 100 m), 392 mph (630 km/h) at 32,000 ft (9 755 m). Time to 20,000 ft (6 100 m), 7.9 min. Range, 1,355 mls (2 180 km) at 162 mph (261 km/h). Empty weight, 10,582 lb (4 800 kg). Normal loaded weight, 13,405 lb (6 081 kg). Span, 46 ft 0 in (14,02 m). Length, 37 ft 9 in (11,51 m). Height, 12 ft 4 in (3,76 m). Wing area, 375 sq ft (34,84 m²).*

(Above and below) The last Curtiss fighter built with a piston engine as its sole power plant, the XF14C-2 failed to meet Navy requirements.

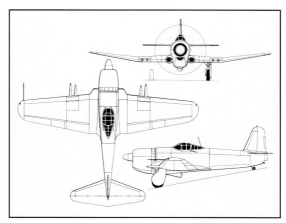

CURTISS YP-60E USA

In May 1944, Curtiss indicated to the AAF that it wished to abandon further work on the P-60 series fighters because of the disappointing results achieved with the XP-60C and XP-60E. Earlier, the P-60 had been eliminated from the production schedules, the number of aircraft on contract having been reduced to two. However, the AAF insisted on completion of one of the two aircraft still on order. These, originally ordered as YP-60As, had been redesignated as YP-60Es because the design modifications incorporated were most directly descended from the XP-60E. The YP-60E differed principally in having a 2,100 hp R-2800-18 engine, a deeper cowling incorporating the ventral cooler intake, a cut-down rear fuselage and a bubble-type cockpit canopy. The sole YP-60E completed was flown on 13 July 1944, but only one further flight was made before the aircraft was transferred to Wright Field where it was eventually disposed of without further testing. Armament comprised six wing-mounted 0.5-in (12,7-mm) machine guns. *Max speed, 405 mph (652 km/h) at 24,500 ft (7 465 m). Initial climb, 4,200 ft/min (21,3 m/sec). Empty weight, 8,285 lb (3 758 kg). Loaded weight, 10,270 lb (4 658 kg). Span, 41 ft 4 in (12,60 m). Length, 33 ft 11 in (10,34 m). Height, 12 ft 6 in (3,81 m). Wing area, 275 sq ft (22,55 m²).*

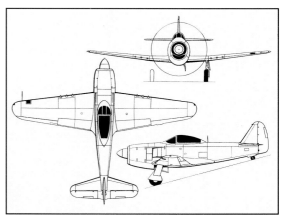

The YP-60E (above and below) existed only as a single prototype and, overtaken by the advent of jet-propelled fighters, was only flown twice.

CURTISS XF15C-1 USA

US Navy interest in the mixed-power concept for shipboard fighters – aircraft employing a piston engine for cruise and an auxiliary turbojet to provide supplemen-

(Above) The first prototype of the Curtiss XF15C-1, flying on 7 May 1945, the day before it crashed. (Below) The XF15C-1 in its definitive form.

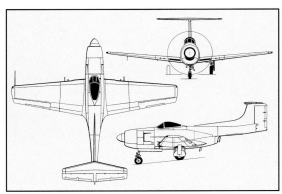

tary power for take-off, climb and maximum speed – which had resulted in orders for three prototypes of the Ryan XFR-1 and 100 production FR-1s, was taken a stage further on 7 April 1944 with the placing with Curtiss of a contract for three prototypes of the appreciably more powerful XF15C-1. This was to be powered by a 2,100 hp Pratt & Whitney R-2800-34W 18-cylinder two-row radial and a 2,700 lb st (1 226 kgp) Allis-Chalmers J36 (Halford H-1B) turbojet. Armament was to comprise four wing-mounted 20-mm cannon. The first XF15C-1 was flown on 27 February 1945, without the turbojet installed, this being fitted by April, but the aircraft was lost on 8 May when it crashed during a landing approach. The second XF15C-1 flew on 9 July 1945, and was joined soon after by the third, both subsequently having their low-set horizontal tail surfaces replaced by a T-tail arrangement. The flight test programme continued until October 1946, by which time the US Navy had lost interest in the mixed power arrangement and cancelled further development. *Max speed, 432 mph (695 km/h) at sea level, 469 mph (755 km/h) at 25,000 ft (7 620 m). Initial climb, 5,020 ft/min (25,5 m/sec). Range, 1,385 mls (2 228 km). Empty weight, 12,648 lb (5 737 kg). Normal loaded weight, 16,630 lb (7 543 kg). Span, 48 ft 0 in (14,63 m). Length, 44 ft 0 in (13,41 m). Height, 15 ft 3 in (4,65 m). Wing area, 400 sq ft (37,16 m²).*

CURTISS XF-87　　　USA

Designed to meet the requirements of a specification issued shortly after the end of World War II that called for a turbojet-powered two-seat all-weather interceptor, the XF-87, known unofficially as the "Blackhawk", was flown on 5 March 1948. It was powered by four 3,000 lb st (1 361 kgp) Westinghouse XJ34-WE-7 turbojets paired in nacelles mounted beneath the wing. Pilot and radar operator were seated side-by-side and intended armament comprised four 20-mm cannon. On 10

The last product of the Curtiss Aeroplane Division was the single XF-87 all-weather fighter (right).

June 1948, a contract was placed for 88 production F-87A fighters which, together with a second prototype, the YF-87A, were each to be powered by two 5,200 lb st (2 360 kgp) General Electric J47-GE-15 turbojets. Shortly afterwards, however, the Northrop XF-89, built to meet the same requirement, was flown and the greater potential that this displayed resulted, on 10 October 1948, in cancellation of the Curtiss fighter programme to free funds for the Northrop contender. Full performance trials with the XF-87 were not completed and the following data are extracted from company estimates. *Max speed, 580 mph (933 km/h) at sea level. Time to 35,000 ft (10 670 m), 13.8 min. Normal range, 1,000 mls (1 610 km). Empty weight, 25,930 lb (11 762 kg). Normal loaded weight, 37,350 lb (16 942 kg). Span, 60 ft 0 in (18,29 m). Length, 61 ft 10 in (18,85 m). Height, 20 ft 0 in (6,09 m). Wing area, 600 sq ft (55,74 m²).*

(Below) The XF-87 with paired XJ34 turbojets.

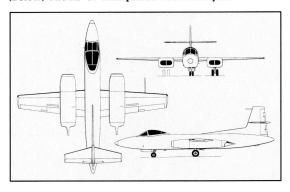

CURTISS-WRIGHT CW-21　　　USA

In 1938, chief engineer Willis Wells of the St Louis Airplane Division of the Curtiss-Wright Corporation began the development of a single-seat fighter based on the A-19R tandem two-seat military basic trainer. Designated CW-21, the fighter had a Wright R-1820-G5 Cyclone nine-cylinder radial engine rated at 1,000 hp

for take-off and 850 hp at 6,000 ft (1 830 m), and an all-metal stressed-skin structure with a semi-monocoque fuselage. Mainwheels retracted into clamshell-type underwing fairings and armament consisted of two synchronised 0.5-in (12,7-mm) machine guns. The prototype CW-21 was flown on 22 September 1938, and subsequently shipped to China for demonstration. The prototype was purchased by the Chinese government and a contract placed for three production aircraft and 27 sets of components for assembly by CAMCO. The first production CW-21 was flown on 20 March 1940, and provision was made to supplement the armament with a pair of 0.3-in (7,62-mm) weapons. All three CW-21s built by the parent company were lost as a result of engine failures (undoubtedly dirty fuel) after taking-off from Lashio while being ferried to Kunming. Assembly of CW-21s by CAMCO at Loi-wing had reached an advanced stage when it was decided to evacuate and, on 1 May 1942, burn the factory to avoid its capture by Japanese forces, the partly-assembled Curtiss-Wright fighters also being destroyed. *Max speed, 296 mph (476 km/h) at 7,500 ft (2 285 m), 315 mph (507 km/h) at 17,000 ft (5 180 m). Initial climb, 4,800 ft/min (24,4 m/sec). Range, 530 mls (853 km). Empty weight, 3,148 lb (1 428 kg). Loaded weight, 4,180 lb (1 896 kg). Span, 35 ft 0 in (10,67 m). Length, 26 ft 4 in (8,03 m). Height, 8 ft 8 in (2,64 m). Wing area, 174.3 sq ft (16,20 m²).*

(Above) The second of the four CW-21 Demons built by Curtiss-Wright at its St Louis factory and (below) the CW-21 in its production configuration.

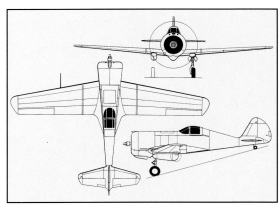

CURTISS-WRIGHT CW-21B　　　USA

In April 1939, Curtiss-Wright's St Louis Airplane Division flew the prototype of the CW-23 basic combat trainer which was essentially a tandem two-seat, lower-powered derivative of the CW-21 single-seat fighter. It introduced inward-retracting, fully-enclosed main undercarriage members and hydraulically-

actuated rather than manually-operated flaps, and these features were adopted for a new version of the single-seat fighter, the CW-21B. On 17 April 1940, the Dutch government signed a contract for 24 CW-21B fighters (of which there was no prototype) and the first of these was flown the following mid-September. The CW-21B retained the R-1820-G5 Cyclone of the earlier CW-21 and armament comprised two 0.3-in (7,62-mm) Colt machine guns mounted in the forward fuselage.

One of the CW-21Bs sold to the Netherlands East Indies in 1941, showing the inwards-retracting u/c.

The CW-21B fighters were shipped to Java during October-December 1940, entering service with the ML-KNIL, but their light structure and lack of fuel tank protection was to render them particularly vulnerable when committed to operations against Japanese forces in the early months of 1942, the last combat mission being flown by a CW-21B on 5 March. *Max speed, 314 mph (505 km/h) at 5,600 ft (1 705 m), 333 mph (536 km/h) at 18,000 ft (5 485 m). Initial climb, 4,500 ft/min (22,9 m/sec). Range, 630 mls (1 014 km). Empty weight, 3,382 lb (1 534 kg). Loaded weight, 4,500 lb (2 041 kg). Dimensions as for CW-21 apart from length of 27 ft 2 in (8,28 m).*

D

DAIMLER L 6 (D I)   Germany

During the summer of 1915, the Daimler Motoren-Gesellschaft established an aircraft division at the request of the *Inspektion der Fliegertruppen (Idflieg)*. In 1917, this *Flugzeug Abteilung* initiated work on an original single-seat fighter to the design of *Ing* Karl Schopper and powered by the company's new D IIIb eight-cylinder water-cooled engine. Flight testing of this, the L 6 (or D I) equi-span single-bay biplane, was delayed until late November 1917 by engine bearing problems. Tail heaviness was rectified by modification of the wing cellule arrangement, flight testing was completed in March 1918, and the L 6 was sent to Adlershof for *Typprüfung* in July, concurrently participating in the second D-Type Competition. Performance suffered owing to the fact that the D IIIb engine, which was rated at 185 hp, lost power at altitude, but a con-

Daimler's first fighter design, the L 6 (below) of 1917.

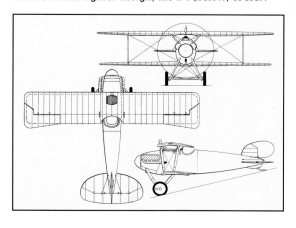

The Daimler L 6 (above) was designed to make use of the company's own D IIIb water-cooled engine.

tract for 20 examples of the Daimler fighter was awarded on 23 July 1918. These aircraft, which were armed with synchronised 7,92-mm LMG 08/15 machine guns, were delivered during December 1918. *Max speed, 114 mph (183 km/h). Time to 19,685 ft (6 000 m), 30 min. Endurance, 2 hrs. Empty weight, 1,653 lb (750 kg). Loaded weight, 2,039 lb (925 kg). Span, 32 ft 5¾ in (9,90 m). Length, 23 ft 11⅖ in (7,30 m). Height, 9 ft 0⅔ in (2,76 m). Wing area, 243.27 sq ft (22,60 m²).*

DAIMLER L 8 (Cʟ I)   Germany

Only a single prototype of the Daimler L 8 two-seat escort fighter (above and below) was completed.

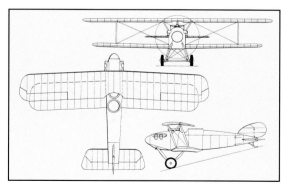

A tandem two-seat single-bay staggered biplane, the Daimler L 8 (Cl I) was intended primarily as a light escort fighter, a single prototype being built late in 1917. Powered by a 185 hp Daimler D IIIb eight-cylinder water-cooled engine, the L 8 carried an armament of one forward-firing synchronised LMG 08/15 7,92-mm machine gun and a Parabellum machine gun in the rear cockpit. No further prototypes were completed, and although, in July 1919, Daimler offered to build the L 8 for the Chilean government, no contract was signed. The following specification relates to the L 8 as offered to Chile. *Max speed, 93 mph (150 km/h) at 4,920 ft (1 500 m). Time to 16,405 ft (5 000m), 33.5 min. Endurance, 4 hrs. Empty weight, 1,808 lb (820 kg). Loaded weight, 2,711 lb (1 230 kg). Span, 38 ft 9⅓ in (11,82 m). Length, 24 ft 5⅓ in (7,45 m). Height, 9 ft 8⅛ in (2,95 m). Wing area, 339.07 sq ft (31,50 m²).*

DAIMLER L 9 (D II)   Germany

Essentially a refined development of the L 6, dispensing with interplane bracing wires and having staggered wings and new vertical tail surfaces, the L 9 single-seat fighter employed a similar 186 hp Daimler D IIIb engine. It was intended to carry an armament of twin synchronised 7,92-mm LMG 08/15 machine guns. Flown initially with fully cantilevered wings in July 1918, the L 9 was modified during August by the addition of aerofoil-section I-type interplane bracing struts. Hanns Klemm had joined Daimler's *Flugzeug Abteilung* as chief designer on 1 April 1918, and the L 9 apparently embodied some of his ideas. Only one prototype was completed and no production contract was awarded. Daimler offered the L 9 in modified form for use on postal services in 1920, but failed to obtain a purchaser. *Max speed, 118 mph (190 km/h). Initial climb, 905 ft/min (4,60 m/sec). Range, 273 mls (440 km). Empty weight, 1,636 lb (742 kg). Loaded weight, 2,182 lb (990 kg). Span, 29 ft 6⅓ in (9,00 m). Length, 23 ft 7½ in (7,20 m). Height, 8 ft 6⅓ in (2,60 m). Wing area, 240.25 sq ft (22,32 m²).*

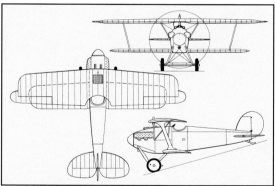

First flown with cantilever wings, the L 9 was later fitted with interplane struts (above and below).

DAIMLER L 11   Germany

The L 11 single-seat parasol monoplane fighter was the first aircraft built from the outset by Daimler's *Flugzeug Abteilung* to the designs of Hanns Klemm. Of exceptionally clean aerodynamic form, powered by a 185 hp D IIIb eight-cylinder water-cooled engine, and featuring swivelling wingtips which served as servos and balanced the ailerons, the L 11 was flown for the first time on 8 November 1918. During trials in the following

The sole Daimler L 11 (above and below) which was the first aircraft wholly designed by Hanns Klemm.

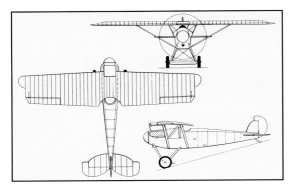

February, it attained an altitude of 19,685 ft (6 000 m) in 17 min and achieved an absolute ceiling of 27,560 ft (8 400 m). Only one prototype of the L 11 fighter was completed. *Max speed, 124 mph (200 km/h). Time to 3,280 ft (1 000 m), 3.2 min. Span, 39 ft 4½ in (12,00 m). Length, 26 ft 8⁹⁄₁₀ in (8.15 m). Wing area, 310 sq ft (28,80 m²).*

DAIMLER L 14   Germany

Owing much to Hanns Klemm's single-seat L 11, but embodying further aerodynamic refinement and featuring an exceptionally clean oval-section semi-monocoque fuselage, the L 14 tandem two-seat parasol monoplane fighter retained the 185 hp Daimler D IIIb eight-cylinder water-cooled engine and swivelling wingtips of the preceding fighter. Intended armament comprised a single forward-firing 7,92-mm LMG 08/15 machine gun and one Parabellum of similar calibre in the rear cockpit. The sole prototype of the L 14 was completed in the autumn of 1919, and, together with the L 8, was offered for sale to the Chilean government, a mail-carrying version being proposed as the L 14V. In the event, no further example was completed. *Max speed, 128 mph (206 km/h). Range, 435 mls (700 km). Time to 3,280 ft (1 000 m), 3.1 min. Empty weight, 1,918 lb (870 kg). Loaded weight, 2,800 lb (1 270 kg). Span, 40 ft 4⅕ in (12,30 m). Wing area, 322.93 sq ft (30,00 m²).*

Last of the fighters to bear the Daimler name, the L 14 (below) was a single prototype completed in 1919.

DASSAULT MD.450 OURAGAN   France

The first fighter developed by Avions Marcel Dassault and the first jet fighter of French design to attain series production, the MD.450 Ouragan (Hurricane) was designed by engineers Deplant, Cabriére and Rouault. Powered by a 5,000 lb st (2 267 kgp) Rolls-Royce Nene Mk 102, the first of three prototypes flew on 28 February 1949, the second and third following on 20 July and 2 June respectively. Twelve (later increased to 14) pre-series aircraft were followed by 350 production Oura-

Key to Dassault MD.450 Ouragan

1. Engine air intake
2. Pitot tube
3. Camera port
4. Facine CMF 7250 gun camera
5. Electrical relay panel
6. Oxygen bottle
7. Battery
8. Nosewheel bay
9. Bifurcated intake ducting
10. Nosewheel doors
11. Door operating linkage
12. VHF transmitter
13. Nose equipment compartment access panels
14. Whip aerial
15. Rudder pedals
16. Footboards
17. Nose undercarriage hydraulic retraction jack
18. Nosewheel leg pivot fixing
19. Landing/taxying lamp
20. Shock absorber strut
21. Nosewheel forks
22. Nosewheel
23. Torque scissor links
24. Cannon port
25. Underfloor radio equipment bay
26. Cockpit floor level
27. Control column
28. Rudder control rod
29. Instrument panel
30. Instrument panel shroud
31. Windscreen panels
32. Mk IVE gyro gunsight
33. Canopy framing
34. Engine throttle lever
35. Ejection seat footrests
36. VHF receiver
37. Cannon barrels
38. Radio and gun equipment access panel
39. Cannon recoil springs
40. IFF transceiver
41. Cockpit pressurization valve
42. Hydraulic accumulator
43. Cockpit rear pressure bulkhead
44. Safety harness
45. Pilot's SNCASO type E.86 (Martin-Baker) ejection seat
46. Ejection seat launch rails
47. Headrest
48. Sliding canopy rail
49. Cockpit canopy cover
50. Ejection seat (face blind type) firing handle
51. Starboard wing fuel tanks; total internal fuel capacity 330 Imp gal (1 500 l)
52. Fuel filler cap
53. Aileron control rod
54. Fuel feed pipes from tip tank
55. Jettisonable wing tip fuel tank, capacity 137 Imp gal (625 l)

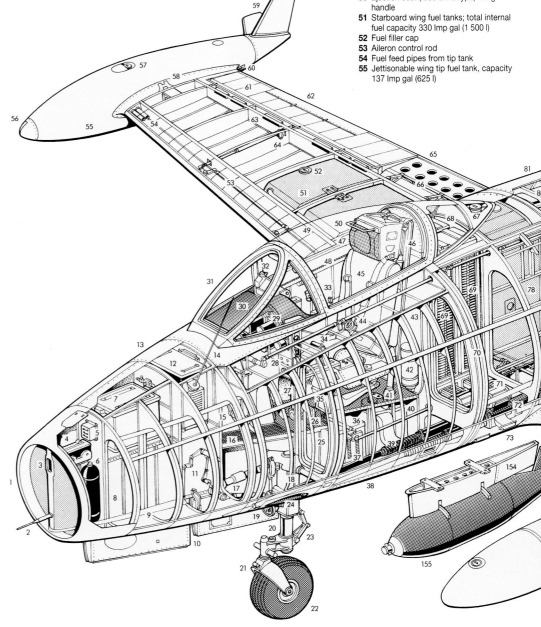

gans. Of the latter, the first 50 were completed to an interim standard as MD.450As, subsequent aircraft embodying modifications and equipment changes as MD.450Bs. Changes included replacement of the Nene 102 by the lighter Nene 104B of 5,070 lb st (2 300 kgp). Armament comprised four 20-mm cannon which could be augmented by 16 Matra T-10 rockets externally. An Indian Air Force order for 71 MD.450Bs was placed on 25 July 1953, these having the Nene 105A of 5,180 lb st (2 350 kgp) and British Mk V versions of the French 20-mm Hispano-Suiza cannon. Dubbed Toofani in Indian service (the Hindi equivalent of Ouragan), the Dassault fighter remained in first-line use until 1967, a further 33 having been procured from the *Armée de l'Air* (including 20 unused machines from storage) in March 1957. Twenty-four MD.450Bs were ordered by Israel in January 1955, these being supplied from

(Below) The Nene-engined Dassault MD.450B Ouragan.

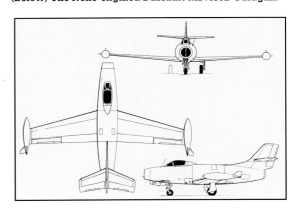

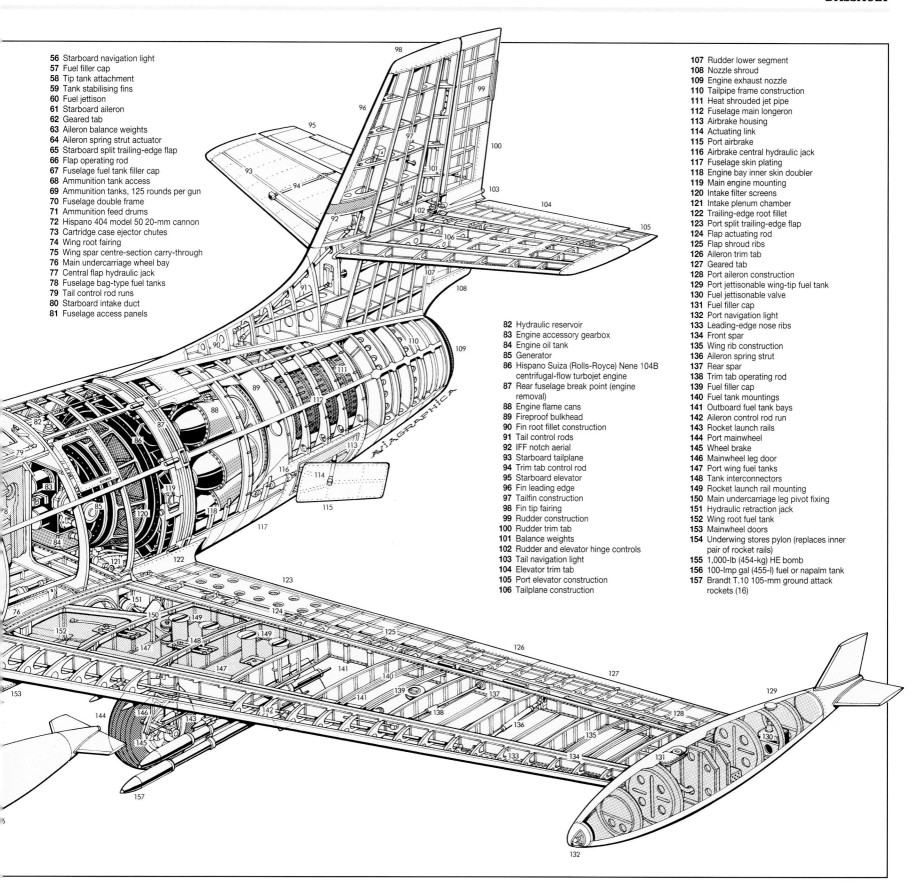

56 Starboard navigation light
57 Fuel filler cap
58 Tip tank attachment
59 Tank stabilising fins
60 Fuel jettison
61 Starboard aileron
62 Geared tab
63 Aileron balance weights
64 Aileron spring strut actuator
65 Starboard split trailing-edge flap
66 Flap operating rod
67 Fuselage fuel tank filler cap
68 Ammunition tank access
69 Ammunition tanks, 125 rounds per gun
70 Fuselage double frame
71 Ammunition feed drums
72 Hispano 404 model 50 20-mm cannon
73 Cartridge case ejector chutes
74 Wing root fairing
75 Wing spar centre-section carry-through
76 Main undercarriage wheel bay
77 Central flap hydraulic jack
78 Fuselage bag-type fuel tanks
79 Tail control rod runs
80 Starboard intake duct
81 Fuselage access panels

82 Hydraulic reservoir
83 Engine accessory gearbox
84 Engine oil tank
85 Generator
86 Hispano Suiza (Rolls-Royce) Nene 104B centrifugal-flow turbojet engine
87 Rear fuselage break point (engine removal)
88 Engine flame cans
89 Fireproof bulkhead
90 Fin root fillet construction
91 Tail control rods
92 IFF notch aerial
93 Starboard tailplane
94 Trim tab control rod
95 Starboard elevator
96 Fin leading edge
97 Tailfin construction
98 Fin tip fairing
99 Rudder construction
100 Rudder trim tab
101 Balance weights
102 Rudder and elevator hinge controls
103 Tail navigation light
104 Elevator trim tab
105 Port elevator construction
106 Tailplane construction

107 Rudder lower segment
108 Nozzle shroud
109 Engine exhaust nozzle
110 Tailpipe frame construction
111 Heat shrouded jet pipe
112 Fuselage main longeron
113 Airbrake housing
114 Actuating link
115 Port airbrake
116 Airbrake central hydraulic jack
117 Fuselage skin plating
118 Engine bay inner skin doubler
119 Main engine mounting
120 Intake filter screens
121 Intake plenum chamber
122 Trailing-edge root fillet
123 Port split trailing-edge flap
124 Flap actuating rod
125 Flap shroud ribs
126 Aileron trim tab
127 Geared tab
128 Port aileron construction
129 Port jettisonable wing-tip fuel tank
130 Fuel jettisonable valve
131 Fuel filler cap
132 Port navigation light
133 Leading-edge nose ribs
134 Front spar
135 Wing rib construction
136 Aileron spring strut
137 Rear spar
138 Trim tab operating rod
139 Fuel filler cap
140 Fuel tank mountings
141 Outboard fuel tank bays
142 Aileron control rod run
143 Rocket launch rails
144 Port mainwheel
145 Wheel brake
146 Mainwheel leg door
147 Port wing fuel tanks
148 Tank interconnectors
149 Rocket launch rail mounting
150 Main undercarriage leg pivot fixing
151 Hydraulic retraction jack
152 Wing root fuel tank
153 Mainwheel doors
154 Underwing stores pylon (replaces inner pair of rocket rails)
155 1,000-lb (454-kg) HE bomb
156 100-Imp gal (455-l) fuel or napalm tank
157 Brandt T.10 105-mm ground attack rockets (16)

Armée de l'Air stocks in the following October-November and a further 46 (including one MD.450A) being delivered subsequently. Eighteen ex-Israeli Ouragans were delivered to El Salvador in 1975, remaining in service into the late 'eighties. *Max speed, 578 mph*

(Right) An *Heyl Ha'Avir* MD.450B photographed at the time of the "Six-Day War" in 1967. **(Below)** The MD.450-30L with lateral intakes as projected for the MD.451.

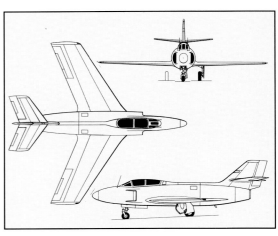

MD.453 Mystère IIIN (above and below) introduced side intakes and provision for nose-mounted radar.

(Above, top) An MD.450B of No 29 "Black Scorpions" Sqn, IAF, at Gauhati, and (immediately above) MD.450B of the Israeli No 113 Sqn, Suez campaign, 1956.

(930 km/h) at sea level, 503 mph (810 km/h) at 39,370 ft (12 000 m). Time to 9,840 ft (3 000 m), 3.15 min. Range, 520 mls (836 km) with tip tanks. Empty equipped weight,10,582 lb (4 800 kg). Normal loaded weight, 15,322 lb (6 950 kg). Span, 39 ft 3⅜ in (11,98 m). Length, 35 ft 2⅘ in (10,74 m). Height, 13 ft 7 in (4,17 m). Wing area, 251.9 sq ft (23,40 m²).

DASSAULT MD.452 MYSTÈRE II   France

The MD.452 Mystère was a progressive development of the basic MD.450 Ouragan, the first prototype, the Mystère I, flying on 23 February 1951. It retained the fuselage, Nene engine and armament of the MD.450, mating these elements with a new, sweptback (30 deg) wing and redesigned tail surfaces. Three further prototypes followed, these differing from their predecessor primarily in power plant, two having the 6,283 lb st (2 850 kgp) Hispano-Suiza Tay 250 and the third having a 5,511 lb st (2 500 kgp) Atar 101C. Eleven (later reduced to 10) pre-series Mystère IIs had been ordered in September 1951, and, of these, the first three and fifth were completed to the Tay-engined IIB standard, the third with twin 30-mm cannon. The sixth and subsequent received a similar armament, SNECMA Atar 101C-1, -3, and later D-1 or -2 engine with revised intake trunking and rearranged fuel tanks as Mystère IICs. First six of initial order for 40 added to pre-series, the final two of these receiving the afterburning Atar 101F-2 of 8,378 lb st (3 800 kgp). Production of a further 90 Mys-

tère IIC fighters ordered for the Armée de l'Air, the last flying in January 1957. The series model featured increased tail sweepback, twin 30-mm cannon and 6,173 lb st (2 800 kgp) Atar 101D-2 or D-3 turbojet. Max speed, 640 mph (1 030 km/h) at sea level, 594 mph (956 km/h) at 29,530 ft (9 000 m). Initial climb, 4,528 ft/ min (23 m/sec). Empty equipped weight, 12,632 lb (5 730 kg). Normal loaded weight, 16,446 lb (7 460 kg). Span, 37 ft 2 in (11,33 m). Length, 40 ft 1¾ in (12,24 m). Height, 14 ft 9⅛ in (4,50 m). Wing area, 325.94 sq ft (30,28 m²).

The first pre-series Mystère II (above) was also the first of five of the Tay-engined IIB version. (Below) The series production Mystère IIC.

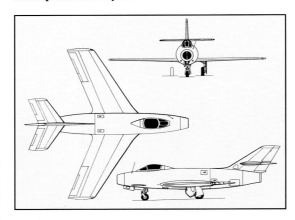

DASSAULT MD.453 MYSTÈRE IIIN   France

The development of a night fighter based on the MD.450 Ouragan day fighter was begun early in the evolution of the latter as the tandem two-seat MD.451 Aladin. It was proposed to install AI Mk 17 or APG 33 intercept radar in the extreme nose, leading to the adoption of lateral intakes. The 11th pre-series Ouragan was completed with the lateral air intakes plus twin 30-mm cannon in place of the standard quartet of

The sole Dassault Mystère I (above), in essence an Ouragan with sweptback wings. (Below) A Mystère IIC serving with EC 1/10 Parisis at Creil.

20-mm weapons, and flown on 24 January 1952 as the MD.450-30-L (signifying 30-mm cannon and lateral intakes). Development of the MD.451 was discontinued in favour of an essentially similar two-seat night fighter derivative of the Mystère II designated MD.453 Mystère IIIN, or Mystère de nuit. With lateral air intakes and a 6,283 lb st (2 850 kgp) Hispano-Suiza Tay 250 engine, the first of three prototypes ordered was flown on 18 July 1952. No radar was installed and the second and third prototypes were cancelled. The sole Mystère IIIN prototype flown had completed 146 flight tests by December 1953, when the programme terminated, the aircraft subsequently being used to test ejection seats. Max speed, 671 mph (1 080 km/h) at sea level, or Mach=0.86, 600 mph (965 km/h) at 39,370 ft (12 000 m), or Mach=0.91. Initial climb, 6,790 ft/min (34,50 m/sec). Empty equipped weight (without radar), 13,040 lb (5 915 kg). Normal loaded weight, 16,171 lb (7 335 kg). Span, 38 ft 1½ in (11,62 m). Length, 42 ft 2⅓ in (12,86 m). Height, 14 ft 8 in (4,47 m). Wing area, 343.38 sq ft (31,90 m²).

DASSAULT MYSTÈRE IVA   France

Possessing little more than a conceptual similarity to the Mystère II, the Mystère IVA featured a more robust, oval-section fuselage, a wing of increased sweepback and reduced thickness/chord ratio, and new tail surfaces. The prototype was flown on 28 September 1952 with a similar Tay 250A turbojet to that used in the Mystère IIA and IIB, and, in the following April, an off-shore procurement contract (as part of US support for NATO nations) was placed for 225 Mystère IVAs. This was subsequently supplemented with a contract from the French government for a further 100 aircraft. The first series Mystère IVA was flown on 29 May 1954, the initial batch of 50 retaining the Tay 250A engine of the prototype, all subsequent aircraft having the 7,716 lb st (3 500 kgp) Hispano-Suiza Verdon 350 (licence-built Tay). Basic armament comprised two 30-mm cannon.

The fourth production Mystère IVA (below) with EC 3/12 Cornouailles of the 12e Escadre at Cambrai, and to which it was delivered in late 1954.

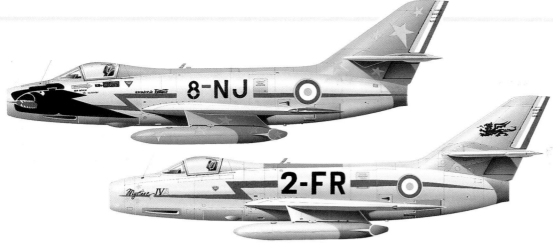

(Top) Mystère IVA decorated for farewell ceremonies for CO of EC 2/8 *Nice*, Cazaux, July 1981. (Immediately above) Mystère IVA of 1e *Esc*, EC 2/2 *Côte d'Or* at Dijon.

(Below) This Mystère IVA survived the retirement of the type from *Armée de l'Air* service and was maintained in flying trim at Dijon.

DASSAULT MYSTÈRE IVN   France

Developed in parallel with the Mystère IVB as a tandem two-seat night and all-weather interceptor, the Mystère IVN differed from the single-seat fighter in several respects. A 4 ft 7-in (1,40-m) section was added to the forward fuselage to accommodate a second crew member; internal fuel capacity was substantially increased and provision was made for an APG 33 intercept radar with the scanner above the engine air intake. Powered by a Rolls-Royce Avon RA 7R rated at 9,546 lb st (4 330 kgp) with maximum afterburning, the Mystère IVN had provision for an armament of two 30-mm cannon and a retractable rocket pack for 52 unguided air-air rockets of 68-mm calibre. The sole prototype was flown on 19 July 1954, by which time it had been decided to discontinue the development programme owing to France's inability to finance the simultaneous development of *two* night fighters (the other being the Vautour), the insufficient endurance of the Mystère IVN, and the unsuitability of the proposed APG 33 radar. *Max speed, 640 mph (1 030 km/h) at sea level, 572 mph (920 km/h) at 39,370 ft (12 000 m). Initial climb, 18,700 ft/min (95 m/sec). Empty weight, 15,741 lb (7 140 kg). Normal loaded weight, 22,751 lb (10,320 kg). Span, 36 ft 5¾ in (11,12 m). Length, 48 ft 11⅓ in (14,92 m). Height, 15 ft 1 in (4,60 m). Wing area, 344.46 sq ft (32,00 m²).*

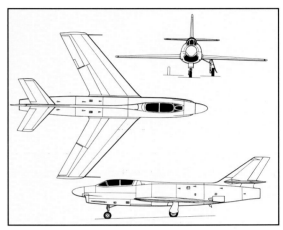

Only one prototype Mystère IVN two-seat radar-equipped night fighter (above and below) was built.

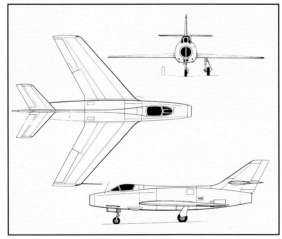

(Above) The series production Mystère IVA.

Of the 275 Verdon-powered Mystère IVAs produced, 60 were supplied to Israel, with deliveries commencing April 1956, and a further contract for 110 was placed by India with deliveries commencing in 1957. The following data relate to the Verdon-powered Mystère IVA. *Max speed, 690 mph (1 110 km/h) at sea level, 662 mph (1 065 km/h) at 20,000 ft (6 100 m). Max range (with external fuel), 1,417 mls (2 280 km) at 40,000 ft (12 200 m). Initial climb, 7,874 ft/min (40 m/sec). Empty equipped weight, 12,919 lb (5 860 kg). Normal loaded weight, 18,100 lb (8 210 kg). Span, 36 ft 5¾ in (11,12 m). Length, 42 ft 3½ in (12,89 m). Height, 15 ft 1 in (4,60 m). Wing area, 345.1 sq ft (32,06 m²).*

DASSAULT MYSTÈRE IVB   France

A process of aerodynamic refinement of the Mystère IVA led to the Mystère IVB, which, in fact, shared only wings, horizontal tail surfaces and main undercarriage members with the earlier model. The Mystère IVB was intended for an afterburning SNECMA Atar 101G axial-flow engine in place of the non-afterburning centrifugal-flow Tay or Verdon. It featured an entirely redesigned fuselage of increased fineness ratio, an upper engine air intake lip for the radar ranging aerial in place of the splitter-plate conical body and a lower-mounted horizontal tail. The first prototype was flown on 16 December 1953 with a Rolls-Royce Avon RA 7R engine

developing a maximum afterburning thrust of 9,546 lb (4 330 kg). Two additional prototypes followed, the first of these, powered by the Avon RA 7R, flying on 18 June 1954, and the second, with an Atar 101F-12, flying on 31 March 1955. Of seven pre-series Mystère IVBs completed, the first two each had a SEPR 66 bi-fuel rocket motor to augment the thrust of the Atar 101F engine, and the final two had the Atar 101G-2 engine developing an afterburning thrust of 9,920 lb (4 500 kg). The series Mystère IVB was to have been powered by an Atar 101G-31 rated at 10,360 lb st (4 700 kgp) with maximum afterburning, but the programme was cancelled owing to the superior performance potential of the Super-Mystère B2. The following data are manufacturer's estimates for the series Mystère IVB. *Max speed, 733 mph (1 180 km/h) at sea level, 677 mph (1 090 km/h) at 30,000 ft (9 150 m). Time to 20,000 ft (6 100 m), 2.25 min. Empty equipped weight, 13,602 lb (6 170 kg). Normal loaded weight, 18,298 lb (8 300 kg). Span, 36 ft 5¾ in (11,12 m). Length, 45 ft 1⅓ in (13,75 m). Height, 14 ft 10 in (4,55 m). Wing area, 344.46 sq ft (32,00 m²).*

(Above) Third prototype of the Mystère IVB, first to fly with Atar 101. (Below) The series Mystère IVB.

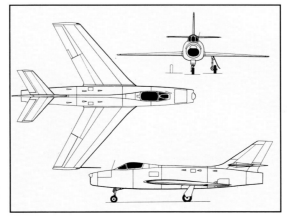

DASSAULT SUPER-MYSTÈRE   France

The first West European aircraft capable of exceeding M=1.0 in level flight to attain quantity production status, the Super-Mystère shared only a common design origin with the Mystère fighter series, being an entirely new type. The first prototype, designated Super-Mystère B1 and powered by a Rolls-Royce Avon RA 7R

Super Mystère B2s (below) serving with EC 2/10 *Seine* of the 10e *Escadre* at Creil, early 'sixties.

(Below) The Super Mystère B2 and (above) a B2 of *Escadron 1/12 Cambrésis*, painted in 1972 to take part in the annual "Tiger Meet" of NATO squadrons.

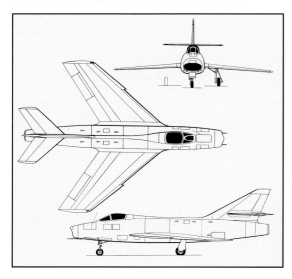

with an afterburning thrust of 9,546 lb (4 330 kg), was flown on 2 March 1955, and the first of five SNECMA Atar-powered pre-production Super-Mystère B2s followed on 15 May 1956. Production was ordered for the *Armeé de l'Air*, the first series Super-Mystère B2 flying on 26 February 1957, and a total of 180 being built of which 36 were procured by Israel in 1958. The Super-Mystère B2 was powered by an Atar 101G-2 or -3 of 7,400 lb (3 375 kg) dry thrust and 9,833 lb (4 460 kg) with maximum afterburning. Armament consisted of two 30-mm cannon and 35 internally-housed 68-mm rockets (the latter being discarded at an early service stage), external loads including two Sidewinder AAMs, two 882-1,102 lb (400-500 kg) bombs or rocket pods. Two examples were completed as Super Mystère B4s in 1958, these having Atar 9B engines rated at 13,227 lb st (6 000 kgp) with afterburning. During Israeli service, the Super-Mystère B2s were re-engined with a non-afterburning Pratt & Whitney J52-P-8A turbojet of 9,300 lb st (4 218 kgp). In 1977, 18 of these aircraft were sold by Israel to Honduras where the last surviving examples were withdrawn from service in 1989. *Max speed, 645 mph (1 038 km/h) at sea level, 739 mph (1 189 km/h) at 39,370 ft (12 000 m), or*

(Immediately below) A Super Mystère B2 serving at Cambrai with EC II/12 *Cornouailles* and (bottom) a Super Mystère B2 of EC 1/12 *Cambrésis* in 1971.

Mach=1.12. Initial climb, 10,827 ft/min (55 m/sec). Range (max external fuel), 1,112 mls (1 790 km). Empty equipped weight, 15,282 lb (6 932 kg). Normal loaded weight, 20,558 lb (9 325 kg). Span, 34 ft 5¾ in (10,51 m). Length, 45 ft 9 in (13,95 m). Height, 14 ft 11¼ in (4,55 m). Wing area, 378.36 sq ft (35,15 m²).

DASSAULT MD 550 MIRAGE I — France

Initially known as the Mystère-Delta, the MD 550 was designed to meet the requirements of a 1954 specification, calling for a small all-weather interceptor fighter capable of attaining an altitude of 59,055 ft (18 000 m) within six minutes and sustaining a speed in excess of M=1.0 in level flight. Competing with the Mystère-Delta were the SE 212 Durandal and the SO

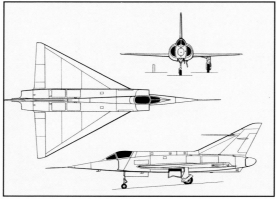

(Above and below) Dassault's first delta-wing fighter, the sole MD 550 Mystère-Delta was flown in 1955 and later adopted the name Mirage I.

9000 Trident. Powered by two MD 30R (Armstrong Siddeley) Viper turbojets each rated at 2,160 lb st (980 kgp) with afterburning supplemented by a 3,307 lb (1 500 kg) thrust SEPR 66 bi-fuel rocket motor, the Mystère-Delta flew for the first time (without afterburning and auxiliary rocket motor) on 25 June 1955. With the original delta vertical tail replaced by swept back surfaces and the SEPR 66 rocket installed, the MD 550 was renamed Mirage I, and, on 17 December 1956, attained M=1.3 in level flight without rocket power and M=1.6 with the rocket lit. Intended armament comprised a single Matra or Nord AAM carried externally. However, it was concluded that the Mirage I was too small to carry an effective military load, and a slightly enlarged version, the Mirage II with a pair of Turboméca Gabizo turbojets, was proposed. This proposal was eventually discarded in favour of the more ambitious Mirage III.

The original MD 550 after being fitted with a sweptback fin and rudder as the Mirage I in 1956.

Max speed, 1,056 mph (1 700 km/h) at 36,090 ft (11 000 m), or Mach=1.6. Empty weight, 7,341 lb (3 330 kg). Loaded weight, 11,177 lb (5 070 kg). Span, 23 ft 11⅖ in (7,30 m). Length, 36 ft 5 in (11,10 m). Wing area, 291.71 sq ft (27,10 m²).

DASSAULT ETENDARD II — France

In the mid 'fifties, the NATO (North Atlantic Treaty Organisation) issued a specification for a lightweight strike fighter powered by a single Orpheus turbojet. In France, the *Ministère de l'Air* drew up a parallel specification for an aircraft which differed essentially from that called for by NATO in having paired lightweight turbojets. Dassault prepared a basic design to meet both requirements, and, being of the opinion that the officially-backed specifications would result in underpowered aircraft, evolved a third version of the design as a private venture. The three versions of the aircraft were designated Etendard (Standard) II, IV and VI, and the first to commence its flight test programme was the Etendard II. Three prototypes had been ordered by the French government and the first of these flew on 23 July 1956. Competing with the Breguet 1100, the Etendard II was powered by two 2,072 lb st (940 kgp) Turboméca Gabizo turbojets and proposed armament

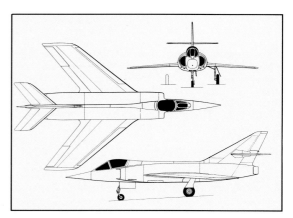

First to fly of the Etendard prototypes was the lightweight Etendard II (above and below).

included two 30-mm cannon which were to be installed as a pack interchangeable with one containing 32 Matra 105 68-mm rockets. It was intended to fit the Gabizo engines with afterburners, but as these were producing 353 lb (160 kg) less dry thrust than promised and aircraft performance was, in general, disappointing, the programme was discontinued in November 1956, the second and third prototypes being cancelled. The second prototype was to have had 2,645 lb st (1 200 kgp) SNECMA R-105 engines. *Max speed, 655 mph (1 054 km/h) at sea level, or Mach=0.86, 624 mph (1 004 km/h) at 36,090 ft (11 000 m), or Mach=0.945. Time to 32,810 ft (10 000 m), 13.0 min. Empty equipped weight, 9,281 lb (4 210 kg). Loaded weight, 12,456 lb (5 650 kg). Span,28 ft 8 in (8,74 m). Length, 42 ft 3½ in (12,89 m). Height,12 ft 5⅔ in (3,80 m). Wing area, 260.49 sq ft (24,2 m².)*

DASSAULT ETENDARD IV   France

Developed in parallel with the Etendard II and VI as a private venture, the Etendard IV light tactical fighter powered by a 7,496 lb st (3 400 kgp) SNECMA Atar 101E-4 was first flown on 24 July 1956. Apart from having substantially more power than the other versions of the basic design, the Etendard IV featured larger overall dimensions, including 15 sq ft (1,4 m²) more wing area, cabin pressurisation and longer-stroke main undercarriage members with larger wheelbase and track. Furthermore, there was provision for increased internal fuel capacity. From the outset of design, several variants of the Etendard IV were foreseen, including a tandem two-seat conversion trainer, a tactical reconnaissance model and a shipboard multi-rôle fighter version. It was for the last-mentioned mission that the aircraft attracted *Aéronavale* attention, Dassault receiving a contract for the further development of the fighter to meet the service's requirements as the Etendard IVM (which see). The armament of the sole prototype Etendard IV comprised two 30-mm DEFA cannon. *Max speed, 683 mph (1 100 km/h) at sea level, or Mach=0.895. Max climb, 8,268 ft/min (42 m/sec). Time to 29,530 ft (9 000 m), 3.9 min. Empty weight, 11,155 lb (5 060 kg). Max loaded weight, 17,306 lb (7 850 kg). Span, 29 ft 8 in (9,04 m). Length, 43 ft 11½ in (13,40 m). Height, 14 ft 1¼ in (4,30 m). Wing area, 275.6 sq ft (25,60 m²).*

The Etendard IV prototype (below) which provided the basis for the shipboard Etendard IVM.

DASSAULT ETENDARD VI   France

Intended to meet the NATO requirement for a light tactical fighter, the Etendard VI was flown for the first time on 15 March 1957, three prototypes having been ordered in July 1955. Initially, the first prototype was powered by a 3,748 lb st (1 700 kgp) Bristol Siddeley Orpheus BOr 1 turbojet, but this was later to be replaced by a BOr 3 of 4,850 lb st (2 200 kgp). Armament consisted of four 12,7-mm machine guns and up to 1,190 lb (540 kg) of ordnance could be carried on wing pylons. The second prototype, powered by the BOr 3 from the outset, had enlarged air intakes and an in-

(Below) The first of two Etendard VIs built to a NATO light fighter requirement.

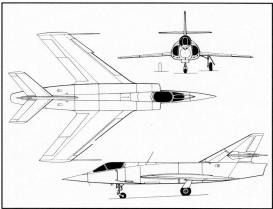

(Above) The Etendard VI light tactical fighter.

ternal armament of two 30-mm cannon, and was first flown on 14 September 1957. Both Etendard VIs participated in the NATO Concours at Brétigny-Chateauroux, from which the Fiat G.91 emerged as the winning contender. Construction of the third prototype, which was to have had a 5,952 lb st (2 700 kgp) BOr 12 engine with provision for afterburning and a fully area-ruled fuselage, had been terminated in June 1957. Both prototypes subsequently participated in the Etendard IVM development programme. The following data relate to the Etendard VI second prototype. *Max speed, 693 mph (1 116 km/h) at sea level, or Mach=0.91, 636 mph (1 024 km/h) at 32,810 ft (10 000 m), or Mach=0.95. Empty equipped weight, 8,201 lb (3 720 kg). Max loaded weight, 12,919 lb (5 860 kg). Span, 26 ft 9¼ in (8,16 m). Length, 40 ft 8⅛ in (12,40 m). Wing area, 226.04 sq ft (21.00 m²).*

DASSAULT ETENDARD IVM   France

The private venture Etendard IV, which had shared little more than a conceptual commonality with the Etendard II and VI lightweight strike fighters, attracted France's *Aéronavale* as a basis for a multi-rôle shipboard fighter. An order was placed in December 1956 for a semi-navalised prototype, this being followed on 31 May 1957 by a contract for five fully-navalised pre-

(Below) Etendard IVM as produced for *Aéronavale*.

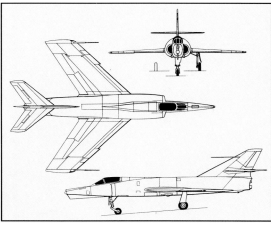

The second pre-series Etendard IVM (above) lacking the fin area under the nose later adopted.

production examples under the designation Etendard IVM. The prototype flew on 21 May 1958, being followed by the first pre-production example on 21 December, both being powered by the 9,700 lb st (4 400 kgp) SNECMA Atar 08B. The pre-series Etendard IVM featured folding wingtips, a strengthened, long-stroke undercarriage, an extendible nosewheel leg, catapult spools and an arrester hook. By comparison with the original Etendard IV, the IVM had 15.5 per cent more wing area and a larger rudder. The second pre-production aircraft was completed with an 11,200 lb st (5 080 kgp) Rolls-Royce Avon 51 engine and flap blowing as the Etendard IVB, and one additional pre-production aircraft ordered in September 1959 was completed with a camera nose as an Etendard IVP. Sixty-nine IVMs (plus 21 IVP tactical reconnaissance aircraft) were delivered between 1961 and 1965, fulfilling both intercept and tactical strike rôles from French carriers. Armament consisted of two 30-mm cannon and a variety of underwing ordnance. The Etendard IVM remained in *Aéronavale* service until 1991, being succeeded by the Super Etendard. *Max speed, 858 mph (1 380 km/h) at 36,090 ft (11 000 m), or Mach=1.3. Max climb, 19,685 ft/min (100 m/sec). Time to 32,810 ft (10 000 m), 6.0 min. Range (with max external fuel), 2,050 mls (3 300 km). Empty weight, 13,000 lb (5 897 kg). Max loaded weight, 22,486 lb (10 200 kg). Span, 31 ft 6 in (9,60 m). Length, 47 ft 1 in (14,35 m). Height, 12 ft 11½ in (3,90 m). Wing area, 305.7 sq ft (28,40 m²).*

A production Etendard IVM (below) in service with *Flottille* 11F in the late 'sixties.

DASSAULT MIRAGE IIIA AND IIIC   France

Essentially an extrapolation of the Mirage I and retaining the five per cent thickness/chord ratio 60-deg delta wing, the Mirage III was substantially larger and some 30 per cent heavier. It was powered by a SNECMA Atar 101G-1 turbojet with an afterburning thrust of 9,700 lb (4 400 kg) and had provision for a 3,307 lb (1 500 kg) SEPR 66 rocket. First flown on 17 November 1956, the prototype attained Mach=1.52 at 38,060 ft (11 600 m) during its sixth flight on 30 January

1957. After the installation of the SEPR rocket motor and introduction of manually-operated half-cones in the air intakes, the speed of Mach=1.8 was reached on 19 September 1957. A pre-series of 10 Mirage IIIAs was ordered, these having a 17.3 per cent increase in wing area, a reduction in root thickness/chord ratio to 4.5 per cent and an Atar 09B engine with an afterburning thrust of 13,230 lb (6 000 kg). Equipped with a 3,307 lb (1 500 kg) thrust SEPR 84 rocket (which could provide 3,704 lb/1 680 kg at extreme altitude), the first Mirage IIIA flew on 12 May 1958, this model eventually attaining Mach=2.2, and the tenth and last joined the test programme on 15 December 1959. One pre-series Mirage IIIA was fitted with a 16,000 lb st (7 258 kgp) Rolls-Royce Avon 67 as the prototype Mirage IIIO for Australian evaluation and first flew on 13 February 1961, but

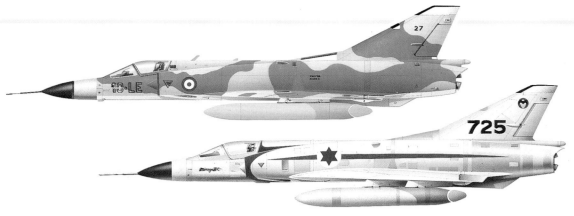

(Above, top) A Mirage IIIC of *Escadron de Chasse* 3/10 *"Vexin"* serving at BA 188 Djibouti in 1980.

(Immediately above) Mirage IIIC in service with the Israeli *Heyl Ha'Avir* in mid-1964.

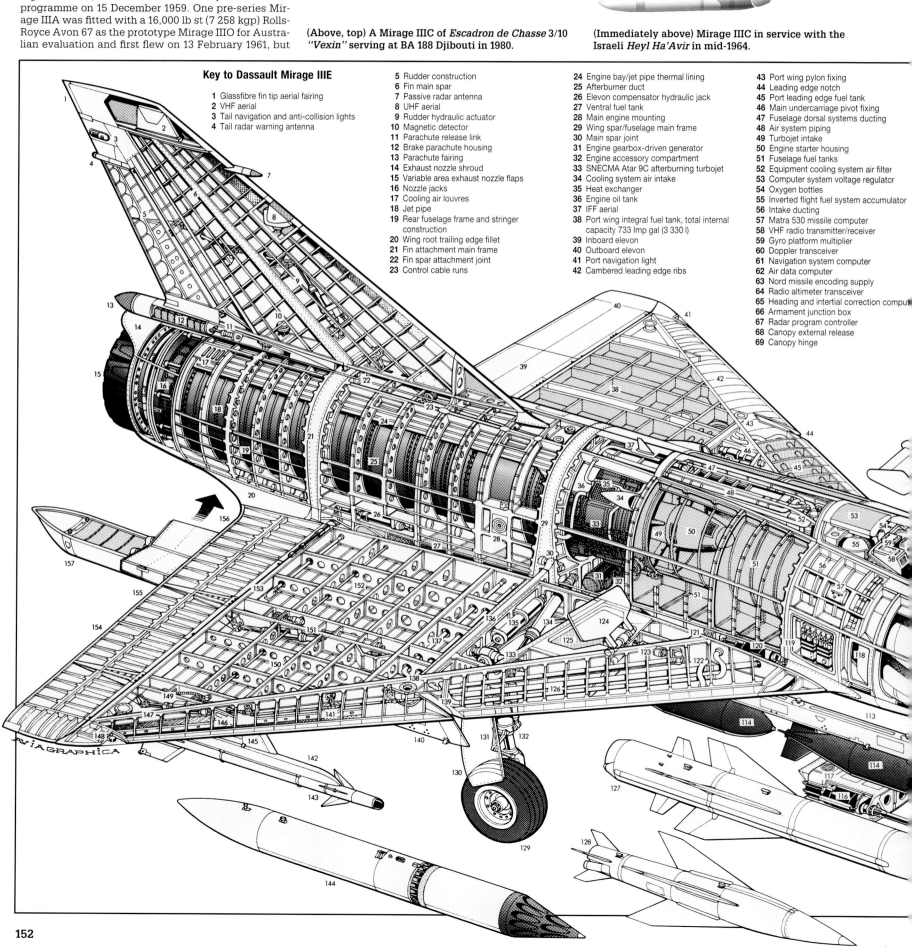

Key to Dassault Mirage IIIE

1 Glassfibre fin tip aerial fairing
2 VHF aerial
3 Tail navigation and anti-collision lights
4 Tail radar warning antenna
5 Rudder construction
6 Fin main spar
7 Passive radar antenna
8 UHF aerial
9 Rudder hydraulic actuator
10 Magnetic detector
11 Parachute release link
12 Brake parachute housing
13 Parachute fairing
14 Exhaust nozzle shroud
15 Variable area exhaust nozzle flaps
16 Nozzle jacks
17 Cooling air louvres
18 Jet pipe
19 Rear fuselage frame and stringer construction
20 Wing root trailing edge fillet
21 Fin attachment main frame
22 Fin spar attachment joint
23 Control cable runs
24 Engine bay/jet pipe thermal lining
25 Afterburner duct
26 Elevon compensator hydraulic jack
27 Ventral fuel tank
28 Main engine mounting
29 Wing spar/fuselage main frame
30 Main spar joint
31 Engine gearbox-driven generator
32 Engine accessory compartment
33 SNECMA Atar 9C afterburning turbojet
34 Cooling system air intake
35 Heat exchanger
36 Engine oil tank
37 IFF aerial
38 Port wing integral fuel tank, total internal capacity 733 Imp gal (3 330 l)
39 Inboard elevon
40 Outboard elevon
41 Port navigation light
42 Cambered leading edge ribs
43 Port wing pylon fixing
44 Leading edge notch
45 Port leading edge fuel tank
46 Main undercarriage pivot fixing
47 Fuselage dorsal systems ducting
48 Air system piping
49 Turbojet intake
50 Engine starter housing
51 Fuselage fuel tanks
52 Equipment cooling system air filter
53 Computer system voltage regulator
54 Oxygen bottles
55 Inverted flight fuel system accumulator
56 Intake ducting
57 Matra 530 missile computer
58 VHF radio transmitter/receiver
59 Gyro platform multiplier
60 Doppler transceiver
61 Navigation system computer
62 Air data computer
63 Nord missile encoding supply
64 Radio altimeter transceiver
65 Heading and intertial correction comput
66 Armament junction box
67 Radar program controller
68 Canopy external release
69 Canopy hinge

The third in a batch of 12 Mirage IIIEAs (left) delivered in 1972 for Argentina's I *Grupo de Caza*.

the Avon installation was not productionised. The Mirage IIIB and IIIC were respectively two-seat trainer and single-seat interceptor fighter production derivatives, the first example of the latter flying on 9 October 1960. The Mirage IIIC was powered by an Atar 09B-3 and a SEPR 841 rocket, and carried an armament of two 30-mm cannon, which, for a typical intercept mission, was augmented by a single Matra R 511 and two AIM-9 Sidewinder AAMs. Ninety-five Mirage IIICs were delivered to the *Armée de l'Air*, one (IIICS) to Switzerland, 72 (IIICJ) to Israel and 16 (IIICZ) to South Africa. In December 1982, 19 Mirage IIICJs, all re-engined with Atar 9C turbojets, were transferred from Israel to Argentina where some remained in service in the early 'nineties as the last of the IIIC sub-type of the Mirage. *Max speed, 1,386 mph (2 230 km/h) at 36,090 ft (11 000 m), or Mach=2.1. Tactical radius (internal fuel), 180 mls (290 km). Time to 59,055 ft (18 000 m), 6.16 min (with rocket). Empty weight, 13,055 lb (5 922 kg). Max loaded weight, 21,444 lb (9 727 kg). Span, 26 ft 11½ in (8,22 m). Length, 48 ft 3⅞ in (14,73 m). Height, 13 ft 11½ in (4,25 m). Wing area, 375.13 sq ft (34,85 m²).*

(Above) Mirage IIIA-07, one of 10 pre-series Mirage IIIs flown by Dassault in 1958-59.

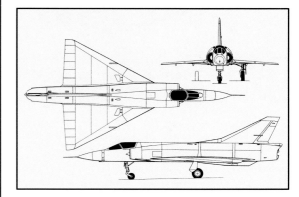

(Above) The Mirage IIIC with ventral rocket pack, and, (below), the eighth production IIIC.

70	Radio and electronics bay access fairing	
71	Fuel tank stabilising fins	
72	286-Imp gal (1 300-l) auxiliary fuel tank (374-Imp gal/1 700-l alternative)	
73	132-Imp gal (600-l) drop tank	
74	Cockpit canopy cover	
75	Canopy hydraulic jack	
76	Ejection seat headrest	
77	Face blind firing handle	
78	Martin-Baker (Hispano licence) RM.4 ejection seat	
79	Port side console panel	
80	Canopy framing	
81	Pilot's head-up display	
82	Windscreen panels	
83	Instrument panel shroud	
84	Instrument pressure sensors	
85	Thomson CSF Cyrano II fire control radar	
86	Radar scannerr dish	
87	Glassfibre radome	
88	Pitot tube	
89	Matra 530 air-to-air missile	
90	Doppler radar fairing	
91	Thomson CSF doppler navigation radar antenna	
92	Cockpit front pressure bulkhead	
93	Rudder pedals	
94	Radar scope (head-down display)	
95	Control column	

96	Cockpit floor level
97	Starboard side console panel
98	Nosewheel leg doors
99	Nose undercarriage leg strut
100	Landing/taxying lamps
101	Levered suspension axle unit
102	Nosewheel
103	Shimmy damper
104	Hydraulic retraction strut
105	Cockpit rear pressure bulkhead
106	Air conditioning ram air intake
107	Moveable intake half-cone centre-body
108	Starboard air intake
109	Nosewheel well door (open position)
110	Intake centre-body screw jack
111	Air conditioning plant
112	Boundary layer bleed air duct
113	Centre fuselage bomb rack
114	882-lb (400-kg) HE bombs
115	Cannon barrels
116	30-mm DEFA cannon (two) 250 rounds per gun
117	Ventral gun pack
118	Auxiliary air intake door
119	Electrical system servicing panel
120	Starboard 30-mm DEFA cannon
121	Front spar attachment joint
122	Fuel system piping
123	Airbrake hydraulic jack
124	Starboard airbrake, upper and lower surfaces (open position)

125	Airbrake housing
126	Starboard leading edge fuel tank
127	AS 37 Martel, radar guided air-to-ground missile
128	Nord AS 30 air-to-air missile
129	Starboard mainwheel
130	Mainwheel leg door
131	Torque scissor links
132	Shock absorber leg strut
133	Starboard main undercarriage pivot fixing
134	Hydraulic retraction jack
135	Main undercarriage hydraulic accumulator
136	Wing main spar
137	Fuel system piping
138	Inboard pylon fixing
139	Leading edge notch
140	Starboard inner stores pylon
141	Control rod runs
142	Missile launch rail
143	AIM-9 Sidewinder air-to-air missile
144	JL-100 fuel and rocket pack, 55 Imp gal (250 l) of fuel plus 18×68-mm unguided rockets
145	Outboard wing pylon
146	Outboard pylon fixing
147	Front spar
148	Starboard navigation light
149	Outboard elevon hydraulic jack
150	Starboard wing integral fuel tank
151	Inboard elevon hydraulic actuator
152	Wing multi-spar and rib construction
153	Rear spar
154	Outboard elevon construction
155	Inboard elevon construction
156	Elevon compensator
157	110-Imp gal (500-l) auxiliary ventral fuel tank

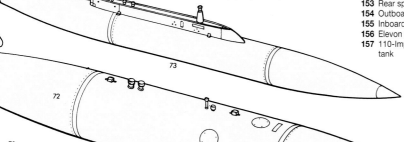

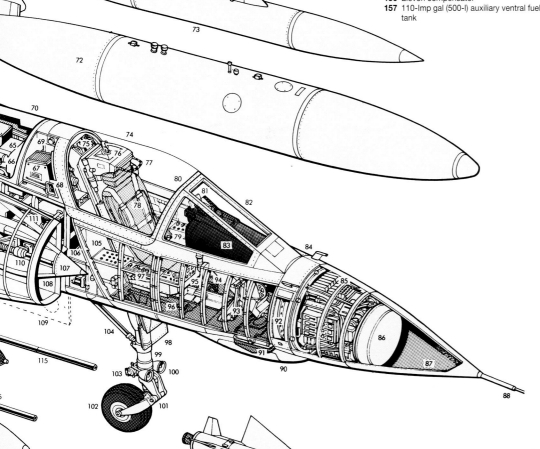

DASSAULT MIRAGE IIIE   France

At an early stage in the development of the Mirage, consideration was given to a multi-rôle version placing emphasis on strike capability, this eventually materialising as the Mirage IIIE, of which the first of three prototypes flew on 5 April 1961. The airframe differed essentially from that of the Mirage IIIC in having an 11.8-in (30-cm) extension of the forward fuselage to permit enlargement of the avionics bay behind the cockpit. Dual-rôle radar was introduced and the Atar 09C-3 engine was adopted, this providing an afterburning thrust of 13,668 lb (6 200 kg) and being augmented by the 3,307 lb (1 500 kg) thrust of a SEPR 841 rocket motor. The first production Mirage IIIE was delivered on 14 January 1964, and a total of 192 was subsequently delivered to France's *Armée de l'Air*. Built-in armament comprised two 30-mm cannon and maximum external ordnance load (distributed between five hardpoints)

(Above, top) Australian Mirage IIIO(A) with No 75 Sqn in Malaysia, 1978, and (immediately above) a Mirage III of EC 2/4 *La Fayette* at Luxeuil, 1977.

(Above) A 75 Sqn Mirage IIIO(A) in late-'eighties colours of RAAF and (below) an upgraded Brazilian Mirage IIIE showing added canard surfaces.

was 8,818 lb (4 400 kg). Versions were licence-built in Australia and Switzerland as the Mirage IIIO and IIIS respectively. Differences between the IIIE and IIIO were largely confined to avionics, and two versions were delivered to the RAAF, the IIIO(F) primarily for the intercept rôle, and the IIIO(A) for the attack task. Dassault supplied two pattern IIIO(F) aircraft, the first of which flew on 14 March 1963, and 48 IIIO(F) and 50 IIIO(A) Mirages were built for the RAAF by the Government Aircraft Factory and Commonwealth Aircraft. All IIIO(F) aircraft were converted to IIIO(A) configuration 1967-79 and the latter were finally withdrawn from service in 1988, the 50 surviving examples being procured by Pakistan in 1990. After acquiring a single Mirage IIIC for trials, Switzerland built 36 Mirage IIIS interceptors (plus 18 IIIRS reconnaissance aircraft), these entering service in 1966 with the *Flugwaffe*, and, in the early 'nineties, the 30 surviving IIIS fighters were being rotated through an upgrade programme (including the provision of canards) at Emmen. Exports by the parent company were as follows: Argentina (17 IIIEAs), Brazil (20 IIIEBRs), Lebanon (10 IIIELs), Pakistan (18 IIIEPs), South Africa (17 IIIEZs), Spain (24 IIIEEs) and Venezuela (10 IIIEVs). The Brazilian IIIEBRs, ordered in 1970, were upgraded with canards, pressure refuelling, etc,

The Mirage IIIEX (below), offered in 1989, featured longer nose, canard surfaces and AAR probe.

from 1989, and the total quoted includes four ex-*Armée de l'Air* delivered in 1988 in the upgraded configuration. The South African IIIEZs were rebuilt to Cheetah EZ standard by Atlas Aircraft (which see). In 1989, Dassault Aviation offered an upgrade of ex-*Armée de l'Air* aircraft as the Mirage IIIEX, this having canards, flight refuelling capability and a lengthened nose. *Max speed, 1,460 mph (2 350 km/h) at 39,370 ft (12 000 m), or Mach=2.2, 863 mph (1 390 km/h) at sea level, or Mach=1.13. Time to 36,090 ft (11 000 m), 3.0 min. Combat radius (with external fuel), 745 mls (1 200 km). Empty weight, 15,542 lb (7 050 kg). Max loaded weight, 30,203 lb (13 700 kg). Span, 26 ft 11½ in (8,22 m). Length, 49 ft 3½ in (15,03 m). Height, 13 ft 11½ in (4,25 m). Wing area, 375.13 sq ft (34,85 m²).*

DASSAULT MIRAGE IIIV   France

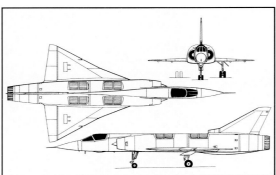

(Above) The VTOL-capable Mirage IIIV-01 and (below) the slightly-modified IIIV-02 in hovering flight.

Mating Mirage III aerodynamics with the then latest developments in vertical take-off and landing (VTOL) technology, the Mirage IIIV was evolved to meet the requirements of NBMR (NATO Basic Military Requirement) 3, and the first of two prototypes effected its first hovering trial on 12 February 1965. Possessing a substantially larger fuselage than that of the non-VTOL Mirage III, the first IIIV was powered by a SNECMA-modified Pratt & Whitney JTF10 turbofan redesignated TF-104B and providing cruise thrust, vertical thrust

being provided by a battery of eight 3,525 lb st (1 600 kgp) Rolls-Royce RB162-1 engines mounted in pairs in the centre fuselage. Wing root chord was increased by comparison with that of the non-VTOL Mirage, resulting in compound sweep. Following replacement of the 13,888 lb st (6 300 kgp) TF-104 by the TF-106A3 offering 16,755 lb st (7 600 kgp), the IIIV effected its first transition to horizontal flight on 24 March 1966 and later attained speeds up to M=1.35. The second prototype was flown on 22 June 1966. This was powered by an 18,520 lb st (8 400 kgp) TF-30 propulsion turbofan, and side-hinged doors rather than aft-hinged grills covered the lift engines. On 12 September 1966, this second aircraft attained M=2.04 in level flight, but 11 weeks later, on 28 November, it was destroyed in a crash. The production Mirage IIIV was intended to combine a 19,840 lb st (9 000 kgp) TF-306 propulsion engine (built by SNECMA) with eight 4,850 lb st (2 200 kgp) RB162-31 lift engines, and was to be optimised for the tactical strike rôle, with a low-level M=0.92 attack mode and a 290-mile (467-km) combat radius with a 2,000-lb (907-kg) nuclear payload. The development programme was suspended after the loss of the second aircraft and finally abandoned. *Approx empty weight, 22,046 lb (10 000 kg). Max loaded weight, 29,630 lb (13 440 kg). Span, 28 ft 7¼ in (8,72 m). Length, 59 ft 0½ in (18,00 m). Height, 18 ft 2⅜ in (5,55 m).*

DASSAULT MIRAGE F2   France

Early in 1964, Dassault was awarded a contract to develop a successor to the Mirage III with emphasis on the low-altitude penetration rôle, and an order followed for a single prototype of a tandem two-seat aircraft which it was intended to power with the SNECMA (Pratt & Whitney) TF-306 turbofan. Despite minimal resemblance and relationship to the delta-winged series of aircraft, the new fighter, which featured a high-mounted swept wing with horizontal tail surfaces, was assigned the designation Mirage F2 and was flown on 12 June 1966. Initial flight trials were conducted with a Pratt & Whitney TF30 turbofan rated at 18,520 lb st (8 400 kgp) with afterburning. After being re-engined with a TF-306 of 19,840 lb st (9 000 kgp), it attained M=2.0 on its second flight, on 29 December 1966. Work had begun on a single-seat version, the Mirage F3 with a 22,817 lb st (10 350 kgp) TF-306E engine, but changes in *Armée de l'Air* requirements saw interest transferred to a scaled-down and simpler version of the basic design, the Mirage F1, development of which had been pursued in parallel by Dassault, and further development of the Mirage F2 was discontinued. *Max speed, 1,460 mph (2 350 km/h), or M=2.2. Low-altitude tactical radius, 345 mls (555 km). Time to 50,000 ft (15 240 m), 4.8 min. Max endurance, 5.25 hrs. Empty weight, 20,944 lb (9 500 kg). Max loaded weight, 39,683 lb*

The Mirage F2 (above and below) emphasized low-altitude penetration, but was superseded by the F1.

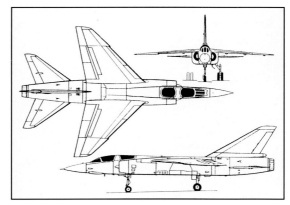

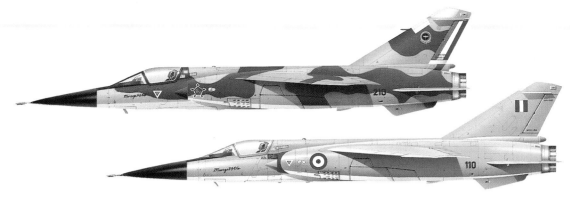

(Above, top) Mirage F1CZ of No 3 Sqn, SAAF, and (immediately above) F1CG of Greek 114ª *Pterighe*.

(Below) Carrying a Matra Super 530 and two Magic AAMs, a Mirage F1C serving with EC 2/12 *Cornouaille*.

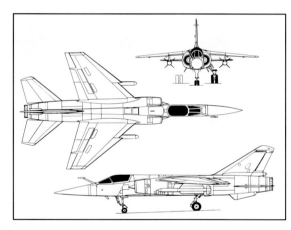

powered Mirage F1C, the Mirage F1.M53 – referred to for a brief period as the "F1E", the suffix letter signifying *Exportation* and the designation subsequently being reassigned – was powered by the SNECMA M53 turbofan rated at 12,235 lb st (5 550 kgp) dry and 18,740 lb st (8 500 kgp) with maximum afterburning. M53 installation involved significant fuselage structural redesign, and to provide suitability for ground attack and long-range interdiction tasks in addition to that of interception, provision was made for multi-rôle avionics. By comparison with the F1C, the F1.M53 had increased fuel capacity, enlarged engine air intakes and strengthened undercarriage. The nose profile was revised to provide for the introduction of a rectractable flight refuelling probe. The installed armament remained two 30-mm cannon and it was proposed to distribute up to 8,820 lb (4 000 kg) of ordnance between seven external stations. The other contenders for the multi-national fighter contract were the Saab 37 Viggen and the General Dynamics F-16. With choice of the latter as winner of the competition, plans to produce a second prototype F1.M53 for testing and integration of systems were discarded. *Max speed, 952 mph (1 532 km/h) at sea level, or Mach=1.25, 1,451 mph (2 335 km/h) at 39,370 ft (12,000 m), or Mach=2.2. Max climb, 58,460 ft/min (297 m/sec). Range (HI-LO-HI mission profile with four 1,000-lb/454-kg bombs), 745 mls (1 200 km). Empty weight, 17,689 lb (8 024 kg). Max loaded weight, 33,510 lb (15 200 kg). Span (without missiles), 27 ft 8½ in (8,45 m). Length, 50 ft 11½ in (15,53 m). Height, 14 ft 11½ in (4,56 m). Wing area, 269.1 sq ft (25,00 m²).*

(18 000 kg). Span, 34 ft 5½ in (10,50 m). Length, 57 ft 9 in (17,60 m). Height, 19 ft 0½ in (5,80 m). Wing area, 387.5 sq ft (36,00 m²).

DASSAULT MIRAGE F1 — France

Mirage F1C-200 showing the added AAR probe.

Evolved in parallel with the Mirage F2 as a scaled-down, multi-rôle single-seat fighter employing a SNECMA Atar turbojet, the Mirage F1 was conceived as a successor to the Mirage IIIC and was the subject of a government contract awarded in 1964. Possessing, like the F2, a conventional sweptback wing generously equipped with high-lift devices, and conventional swept tail surfaces, the private venture prototype F1 flew on 23 December 1966. Three pre-series aircraft were ordered in September 1967, the first of these flying on 20 March 1969. The initial production model for France's *Armée de l'Air* was designated F1C, placed emphasis on the intercept mission, was powered by an Atar 9K-50 turbojet affording 15,873 lb st (7 200 kgp) with afterburning, and had an armament of two 30-mm cannon, two Matra 550 Magic and two Matra R 530 or Super 530 AAMs. An initial order for the F1C for the *Armée de l'Air* was placed in 1969, 162 being procured by that service (plus 64 recce F1CRs and 20 two-seat F1B trainers), initial operational capability being achieved in 1974. Many of the *Armée de l'Air* aircraft were delivered in, or retroactively modified to, F1C-200 standard with a 3.15-in (8-cm) fuselage plug to accommodate a removable flight refuelling probe. Variants of the basic aircraft offered for export, in addition to the F1C, were the F1A with simplified avionics for operation under VFR conditions and the F1E multi-rôle air superiority/ground attack/reconnaissance version. Ex-

port customers were Ecuador (16 F1AJs), Greece (40 F1CGs), Iraq (113 F1EQs), Jordan (17 F1CJs and 17 F1EJs), Kuwait (27 F1CKs), Libya (16 F1ADs and 16 F1EDs), Morocco (30 F1CHs and 20 F1EHs), Qatar (12 F1EDAs), South Africa (32 F1AZs and 16 F1CZs) and Spain (45 F1CEs and 22 F1EEs). Production of the Mirage F1 was completed in 1990 with 731 built (including F1B and F1D two-seat trainers and F1CR reconnaissance aircraft). In 1991, work began on the adaptation of 30 F1C-200s as F1CT ground attack fighters. The following data relate to the F1C. *Max speed, 914 mph (1 470 km/h) at sea level, or Mach=1.2, 1,450 mph (2 335 km/h) at 39,370 ft (12 000 m), or Mach=2.2. Max climb, 41,930 ft/min (213 m/sec). Combat air patrol endurance (two Super 530 AAMs and ventral tank), 2.25 hrs. Empty weight, 16,314 lb (7 400 kg). Max loaded weight, 35,714 lb (16 200 kg). Span (without missiles), 27 ft 6¾ in (8,40 m). Length, 50 ft 2½ in (15,30 m). Height, 14 ft 9 in (4,50 m). Wing area, 269.1 sq ft (25,00 m²).*

DASSAULT MIRAGE F1.M53 — France

With an M53 turbojet replacing the Atar 9K-50, the Mirage F1.M53 (above) bid for large European orders.

First flown on 22 December 1974, and built as an engine test bed under official contract, the Mirage F1.M53 was also envisaged as the basis for a contender in the contest to find a successor for the Lockheed F-104G in service with Belgium, Denmark, the Netherlands and Norway. Evolved from the basic Atar 9K-50 turbojet-

DASSAULT MIRAGE 5 — France

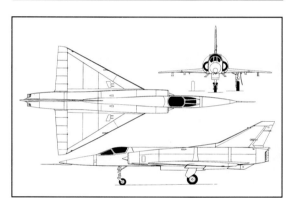

(Above) The basic Mirage 5 multi-rôle tactical fighter.

Conceived as a ground attack fighter for operation under VFR conditions and using the same airframe and power plant as the Mirage IIIE, the Mirage 5 was first flown on 19 May 1967. Possessing a redesigned nose which could accommodate an Aïda ranging radar, increased fuel capacity and two additional stores hardpoints, the Mirage 5 carried basic armament including two 30-mm cannon in an 8,818-lb (4 000-kg) weapon capability. The Mirage 5 was evolved initially to meet an Israeli requirement, but 50 aircraft originally ordered for Israel's Defence Force/Air Force were, in the event, absorbed by France's *Armée de l'Air* (as Mirage 5Fs). Although essentially a clear-weather ground attack fighter with secondary intercept capability, the Mirage 5 was delivered to some export customers with

A Mirage 5G (below) as delivered to the *Forces Aériennes Gabonaises* for service at M'vengué.

Key to Dassault Mirage F1E

1 Pitot head
2 Glassfibre radome
3 Scanner housing
4 Flat plate radar scanner
5 Scanner tracking mechanism
6 Detachable in-flight refuelling probe
7 Refuelling probe mast (offset to starboard)
8 Thomson-CSF Cyrano IV radar equipment module
9 Radome latches
10 Temperature probe
11 Incidence probe
12 Total pressure head
13 Front pressure bulkhead
14 TACAN aerial
15 Retractable landing lamp
16 Cockpit pressure floor
17 Rudder pedals
18 Instrument panel shroud
19 Windscreen panels
20 Pilot's CRT head-up display
21 Instrument panel
22 Control column
23 Engine throttle lever
24 Ejection seat rocket pack
25 Nose undercarriage leg doors
26 Hydraulic retraction jack
27 Twin nosewheel, aft retracting
28 Torque scissor links
29 Hydraulic steering actuator
30 Nose undercarriage leg strut
31 Sloping rear pressure bulkhead
32 Aileron control spring strut
33 Port side console panel
34 SEM/Martin-Baker F10M "zero-zero" ejection seat
35 Starboard side console panel
36 Ejection seat headrest
37 Canopy breaker struts
38 Upward hinged cockpit canopy cover
39 Canopy open position
40 Pilot's rear view mirrors
41 Canopy jack
42 Canopy hinge point
43 Emergency rescue handle
44 Battery
45 Nav/attack computer
46 Intake half-cone central electric drive motor
47 Air conditioning system heat exchanger ram air intake
48 Movable half-cone intake centre-body
49 Cannon muzzle blast trough
50 Port engine-air intake
51 Intake suction relief door (open)
52 Taxying lamp
53 Cannon barrel
54 Movable half-cone guide rails
55 Half-cone screw jack
56 Central air conditioning plant
57 Boundary layer spill duct
58 Oxygen bottles (2)
59 Avionics equipment racks
60 Central power amplifier
61 Avionics equipment bay access cover
62 Anti-collision light
63 Starboard air intake duct
64 External fuel tank, capacity 248 Imp gal (1 130 l)
65 Forward fuselage integral fuel tank
66 Fuel system inverted flight accumulator
67 Cable ducting
68 Fuel tank bay frame construction
69 Wing root leading-edge fillet
70 Ventral DEFA 553 30-mm cannon (two)
71 Pressure refuelling point
72 Fuel pump
73 Ammunition feed chute
74 Ammunition magazine (135 rounds per gun)
75 Port main undercarriage wheel bay
76 Inboard leading-edge flap segment
77 Mainwheel bay pre-closing doors
78 Leading-edge flap hydraulic jack
79 Front spar attachment joint
80 Engine starter housing
81 Fuel system filters
82 Electrical system equipment
83 IFF aerial
84 Forged steel wing root attachment fitting
85 Fuel system piping
86 Sealed sheath control system conduits
87 Starboard wing integral fuel tank; total internal fuel capacity, 946 Imp gal (4 300 l)
88 Pylon attachment hard points
89 Leading-edge flap operating linkages
90 Leading-edge dog-tooth
91 Starboard leading-edge flap segments (lowered)
92 F1B/D trainer variants nose profile
93 Raised instructor's seat
94 Student pilot's seat
95 F1CR reconnaissance variant nose profile
96 Ventral camera housing
97 Matra 550 Magic air-to-air missile
98 Wing tip missile launch rail
99 Starboard navigation light
100 Starboard aileron
101 Carbon fibre aileron skin panelling
102 Aileron hydraulic actuator
103 Aileron/spoiler interconnecting spring strut
104 Spoiler hydraulic actuator
105 Starboard spoiler panels (open)
106 Outboard asymmetric double-slotted flap segment
107 Flap vane
108 Inboard asymmetric double-slotted flap segment
109 Flap hydraulic jack
110 Centre fuselage integral fuel tank
111 Air conditioning system bleed air pre-cooler
112 Wing attachment double main frame
113 Attachment fitting pin joints
114 Port forged steel wing root fitting
115 Ventral engine accessory equipment gearbox
116 SNECMA Atar 9K-50 afterburning engine
117 Wing root rib
118 Rear spar attachment main frame
119 Engine oil tank
120 Central control and cable ducting
121 Access panel
122 Rear fuselage integral fuel tanks, port and starboard
123 Optional fin root HF aerial
124 Fuel system piping
125 Port wing flap jack
126 Inboard flap track
127 Wing root trailing-edge fillet
128 Hydraulic reservoir
129 Engine turbine section
130 Fuel tank contents probe
131 Afterburner ducting
132 Engine bay thermal lining
133 Sealed sheath hydraulic line conduit
134 Fin spar attachment joint
135 Rudder control cable quadrant
136 Rudder trim actuator
137 Rudder hydraulic actuator
138 Fin main spar
139 Tailfin construction
140 Starboard all-moving tailplane
141 Forward radar warning antenna
142 UHF aerial
143 VOR aerial
144 Combined IFF/VHF 1 aerial
145 Tail navigation and strobe light
146 Rear radar warning antenna
147 Rudder rib construction
148 Remote compass transmitter
149 Rudder actuator hinge point
150 VHF 2 aerial
151 Parachute release linkage
152 Brake parachute housing
153 Conic fairing parachute door
154 Cooling air scoop
155 Variable area afterburner nozzle flaps
156 Nozzle flap control jacks
157 Tailpipe support link
158 Port all-moving tailplane
159 Bonded honeycomb trailing-edge panel
160 Tailplane multi-spar construction
161 Tailplane pivot fixing
162 Pivot attachment double main frame
163 Tailplane hydraulic actuator
164 Fin spar attachment main frame
165 Autopilot actuator
166 Ventral fin, port and starboard
167 Fuel vent
168 Port two-segment asymmetric double-slotted flaps
169 Spoiler housings
170 Spoiler actuating linkage
171 Central flap track
172 Flap construction
173 Bonded honeycomb trailing-edge panel
174 Outboard flap track
175 Aileron actuator hinge point
176 Port aileron rib construction
177 Wing-tip missile interface unit
178 Port Matra 550 Magic air-to-air missile

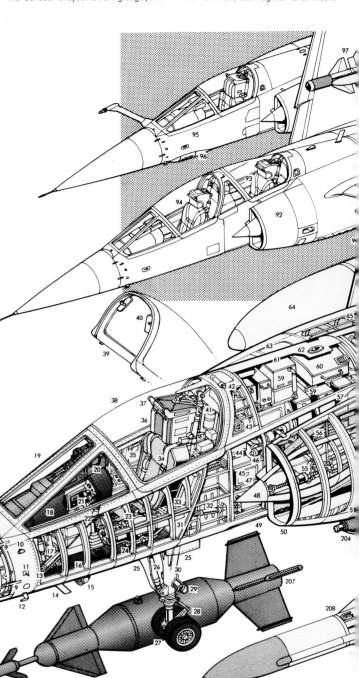

varying degrees of IFR/all-weather operational ability, and tactical reconnaissance and two-seat training versions were produced as the Mirage 5R and 5D. Customers for the single-seat fighter version of the Mirage 5 were as follows: Abu Dhabi (12 5ADs and 14 5EADs), Belgium (63 5BAs), Colombia (14 5COAs), Egypt (51 5SDEs and 16 5E2s), Gabon (three 5Gs and four 5G2s), Libya (53 5Ds and 32 5DEs), Pakistan (28 5PAs and 30 5PA2s and 5PA3s), Peru (32 5Ps and 5P3s), Venezuela (four 5Vs) and Zaire (14 5Ms). The equipment fit of the Mirage 5s varied widely, according to customer requirements, the Mirage 5E, (eg, 5DE and 5SDE), for example, having a similar equipment standard to that of the Mirage IIIE. Ten Mirage 5Ps were transferred to Argentina from Peru in June 1982, and production of an essentially similar aircraft was undertaken during 1970-72 in Israel as the IAI Nesher (which see). Total production of the Mirage 5 (including tactical reconnaissance and two-seat training versions) amounted to 531 aircraft. *Max speed, 1,451 mph (2 335 km/h) at 39,370 ft (12 000 m), or Mach=2.2. Max climb, 36,610 ft/min (186 m/sec). Combat radius (max external fuel and 1,764 lb/800 kg of bombs), 777 mls (1 250km). Empty equipped weight, 15,763 lb (7 150 kg). Max loaded weight, 30,200 lb (13 700 kg). Span, 26 ft 11½ in (8,22 m). Length, 51 ft 0½ in (15,56 m). Height, 13 ft 11½ in (4,25 m). Wing area, 375.13 sq ft (34,85 m²).*

(Immediately below) A Mirage 5PA of the Operations Group South, PAF, at Masroor and (bottom) a Mirage 5M of 21 Wing, Zaire Air Force, at Kamina.

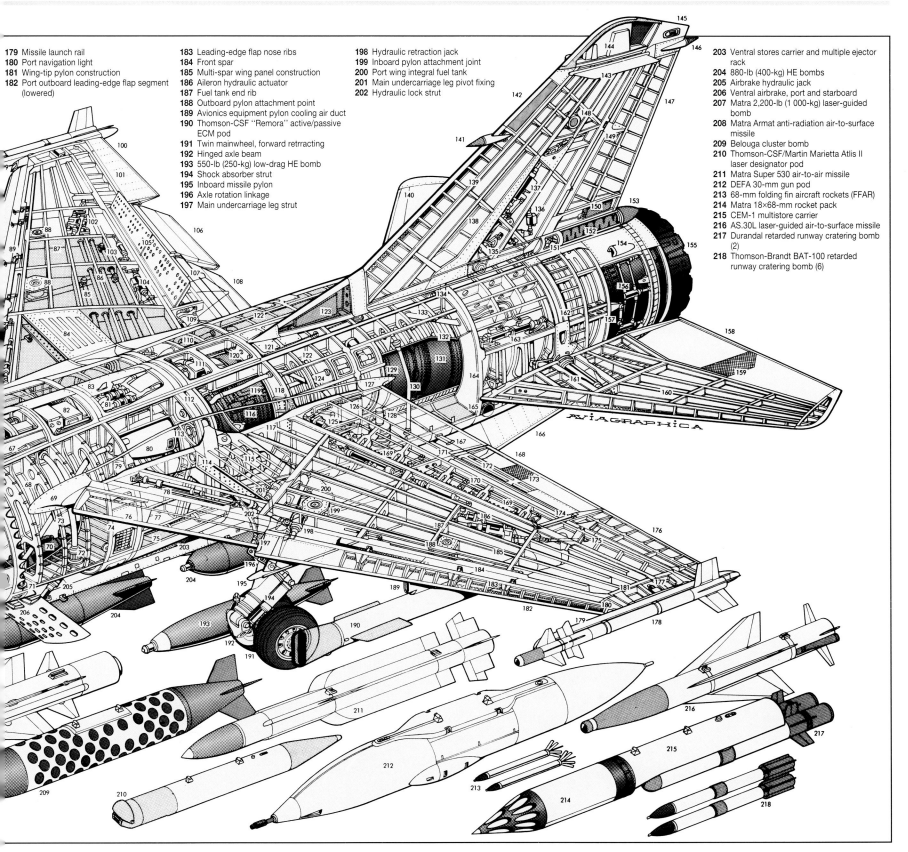

179 Missile launch rail
180 Port navigation light
181 Wing-tip pylon construction
182 Port outboard leading-edge flap segment (lowered)

183 Leading-edge flap nose ribs
184 Front spar
185 Multi-spar wing panel construction
186 Aileron hydraulic actuator
187 Fuel tank end rib
188 Outboard pylon attachment point
189 Avionics equipment pylon cooling air duct
190 Thomson-CSF ''Remora'' active/passive ECM pod
191 Twin mainwheel, forward retrracting
192 Hinged axle beam
193 550-lb (250-kg) low-drag HE bomb
194 Shock absorber strut
195 Inboard missile pylon
196 Axle rotation linkage
197 Main undercarriage leg strut

198 Hydraulic retraction jack
199 Inboard pylon attachment joint
200 Port wing integral fuel tank
201 Main undercarriage leg pivot fixing
202 Hydraulic lock strut

203 Ventral stores carrier and multiple ejector rack
204 880-lb (400-kg) HE bombs
205 Airbrake hydraulic jack
206 Ventral airbrake, port and starboard
207 Matra 2,200-lb (1 000-kg) laser-guided bomb
208 Matra Armat anti-radiation air-to-surface missile
209 Belouga cluster bomb
210 Thomson-CSF/Martin Marietta Atlis II laser designator pod
211 Matra Super 530 air-to-air missile
212 DEFA 30-mm gun pod
213 68-mm folding fin aircraft rockets (FFAR)
214 Matra 18×68-mm rocket pack
215 CEM-1 multistore carrier
216 AS.30L laser-guided air-to-surface missile
217 Durandal retarded runway cratering bomb (2)
218 Thomson-Brandt BAT-100 retarded runway cratering bomb (6)

DASSAULT MIRAGE G   France

On 13 October 1965, Avions Marcel Dassault received a contract to design and build one prototype of a two-seat variable-geometry fighter, the Mirage G. Powered by a single SNECMA (Pratt & Whitney) TF-306E turbofan rated at 20,500 lb st (9 300 kgp) with afterburning and owing much to the design of the Mirage F2, the Mirage G was first flown on 18 November 1967. Wing sweepback could be varied between 23 deg and 70 deg, maximum sweep being achieved in flight within a week of the commencement of trials and a speed of M=2.1 being attained within two months. Trials were to continue until 13 January 1971, when the Mirage G was lost in an accident, 400 hours of flying having been accumulated in 316 flights. In the meantime, late in 1968, two further prototypes had been ordered, these each being powered by two 15,873 lb st (7 200 kgp) SNECMA Atar 9K-50 turbojets. After a succession of

(Right and below) The Mirage G8-01, the first two-seat variable-geometry fighter prototype which entered flight test in May 1971.

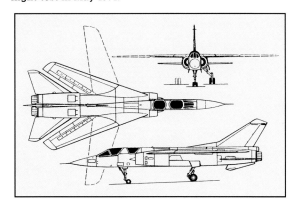

designation changes, these emerged as Mirage G8s, the two-seat first prototype flying on 8 May 1971, and the single-seat second prototype following on 13 July 1972. The Mirage G8 was envisaged as a multi-rôle fighter, capable of fulfilling intercept, patrol, attack and long-range reconnaissance missions, and was fitted with Cyrano IV multi-purpose radar, a low-altitude nav/attack system, a laser rangefinder, Doppler radar and a bombing computer. The proposed production version

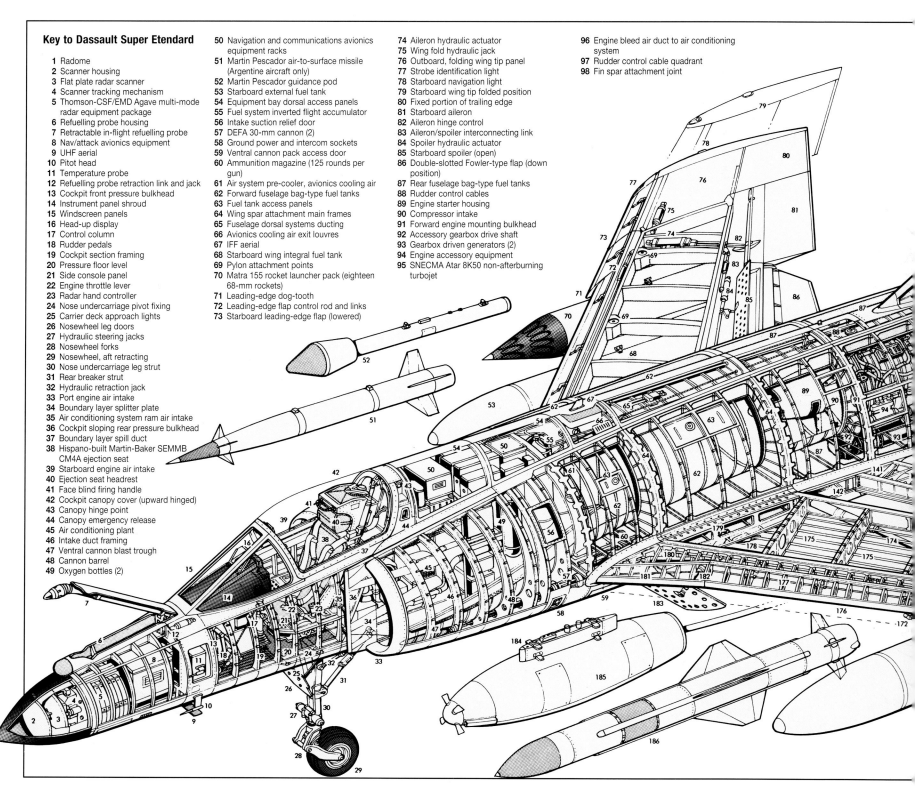

Key to Dassault Super Etendard

1. Radome
2. Scanner housing
3. Flat plate radar scanner
4. Scanner tracking mechanism
5. Thomson-CSF/EMD Agave multi-mode radar equipment package
6. Refuelling probe housing
7. Retractable in-flight refuelling probe
8. Nav/attack avionics equipment
9. UHF aerial
10. Pitot head
11. Temperature probe
12. Refuelling probe retraction link and jack
13. Cockpit front pressure bulkhead
14. Instrument panel shroud
15. Windscreen panels
16. Head-up display
17. Control column
18. Rudder pedals
19. Cockpit section framing
20. Pressure floor level
21. Side console panel
22. Engine throttle lever
23. Radar hand controller
24. Nose undercarriage pivot fixing
25. Carrier deck approach lights
26. Nosewheel leg doors
27. Hydraulic steering jacks
28. Nosewheel forks
29. Nosewheel, aft retracting
30. Nose undercarriage leg strut
31. Rear breaker strut
32. Hydraulic retraction jack
33. Port engine air intake
34. Boundary layer splitter plate
35. Air conditioning system ram air intake
36. Cockpit sloping rear pressure bulkhead
37. Boundary layer spill duct
38. Hispano-built Martin-Baker SEMMB CM4A ejection seat
39. Starboard engine air intake
40. Ejection seat headrest
41. Face blind firing handle
42. Cockpit canopy cover (upward hinged)
43. Canopy hinge point
44. Canopy emergency release
45. Air conditioning plant
46. Intake duct framing
47. Ventral cannon blast trough
48. Cannon barrel
49. Oxygen bottles (2)

50. Navigation and communications avionics equipment racks
51. Martin Pescador air-to-surface missile (Argentine aircraft only)
52. Martin Pescador guidance pod
53. Starboard external fuel tank
54. Equipment bay dorsal access panels
55. Fuel system inverted flight accumulator
56. Intake suction relief door
57. DEFA 30-mm cannon (2)
58. Ground power and intercom sockets
59. Ventral cannon pack access door
60. Ammunition magazine (125 rounds per gun)
61. Air system pre-cooler, avionics cooling air
62. Forward fuselage bag-type fuel tanks
63. Fuel tank access panels
64. Wing spar attachment main frames
65. Fuselage dorsal systems ducting
66. Avionics cooling air exit louvres
67. IFF aerial
68. Starboard wing integral fuel tank
69. Pylon attachment points
70. Matra 155 rocket launcher pack (eighteen 68-mm rockets)
71. Leading-edge dog-tooth
72. Leading-edge flap control rod and links
73. Starboard leading-edge flap (lowered)

74. Aileron hydraulic actuator
75. Wing fold hydraulic jack
76. Outboard, folding wing tip panel
77. Strobe identification light
78. Starboard navigation light
79. Starboard wing tip folded position
80. Fixed portion of trailing edge
81. Starboard aileron
82. Aileron hinge control
83. Aileron/spoiler interconnecting link
84. Spoiler hydraulic actuator
85. Starboard spoiler (open)
86. Double-slotted Fowler-type flap (down position)
87. Rear fuselage bag-type fuel tanks
88. Rudder control cables
89. Engine starter housing
90. Compressor intake
91. Forward engine mounting bulkhead
92. Accessory gearbox drive shaft
93. Gearbox driven generators (2)
94. Engine accessory equipment
95. SNECMA Atar 8K50 non-afterburning turbojet

96. Engine bleed air duct to air conditioning system
97. Rudder control cable quadrant
98. Fin spar attachment joint

was to have been powered by two SNECMA M53 turbofans. In the event, the *Armée de l'Air* concluded that the disadvantages of variable-geometry outweighed its advantages, and after study of a fixed-geometry version with 55 deg of sweepback (Mirage F8), further development was discontinued. The following data relate to the Mirage G8. *Max speed, 1,550 mph (2 495 km/h), or Mach=2.35. Max climb, 45,925 ft/min (233.3 m/sec). Max loaded weight, 52,470 lb (23 800 kg). Span, 42 ft 7¾ in (13,00 m). Length, 55 ft 1⅜ in (16,80 m). Height, 17 ft 6½ in (5,35 m). Wing area, 398.28 sq ft (37,00 m²).*

Seen (below) with wings fully-swept, the Mirage G8-02 was a two-seat derivative of the G8-01.

DASSAULT
SUPER ETENDARD   France

The Super Etendard transonic shipboard strike fighter was a progressive development of the Etendard IVM and was, in fact, 90 per cent new, having a more powerful turbojet, enhanced-capability equipment, improved aerodynamic features and revised structure. The first of three development aircraft (converted from Etendard IVM airframes) flew on 28 October 1974, and the first series Super Etendard for the *Aéronavale* flew on 24 November 1977, deliveries commencing on 28 June 1978. Powered by an 11,025 lb st (5 000 kgp) SNECMA Atar 8K-50 turbojet, the Super Etendard had a built-in armament of two 30-mm cannon and various external ordnance loads on five stores stations, such as four 551-lb (250-kg) or 882-lb (400-kg) bombs and two Matra Magic AAMs, or four pods of 18 68-mm rockets, or two AM 39 Exocet anti-shipping missiles. Fourteen were ordered by Argentina and the Super Etendard was employed operationally from shore bases in May 1982 during the Falklands conflict. Seventy-one Super Etendards were supplied to the *Aéronavale*, production ter-

minating in 1983. The prototype of an upgraded version of the Super Etendard was flown on 5 October 1990, when it was proposed that a further 54 would be upgraded to similar standards (two by Dassault and 52 by *Aéronavale*'s Cuers workshops) at a rate of 15 annually

(Below) Super Etendard shipboard strike fighter.

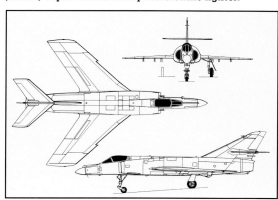

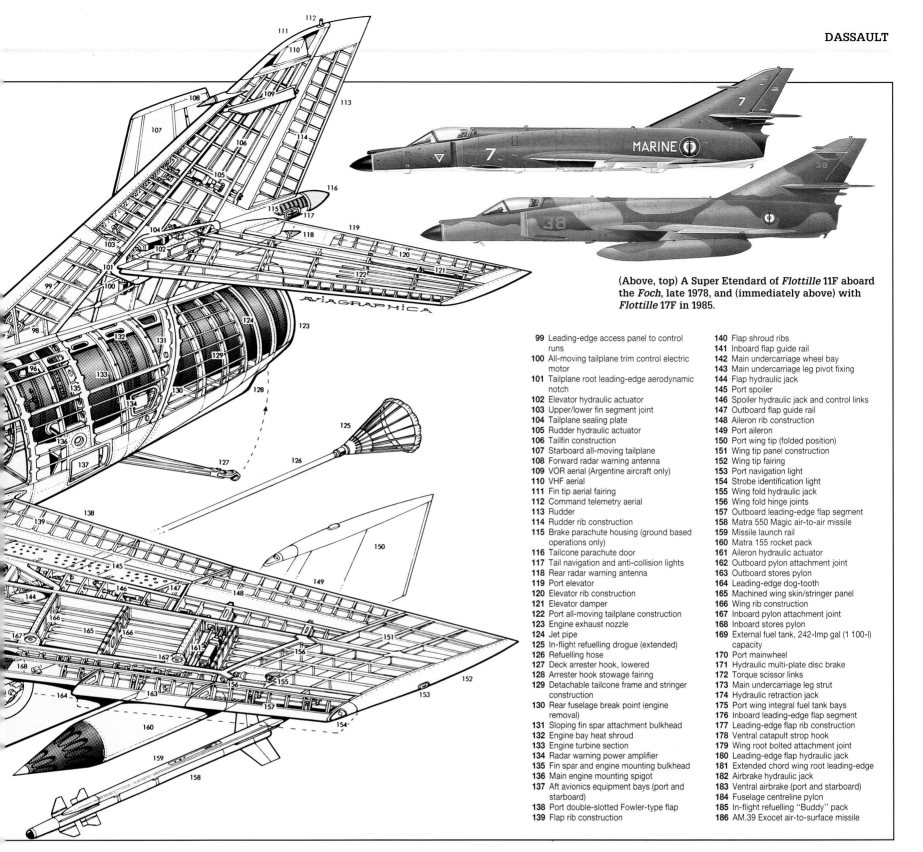

99 Leading-edge access panel to control runs	140 Flap shroud ribs
100 All-moving tailplane trim control electric motor	141 Inboard flap guide rail
101 Tailplane root leading-edge aerodynamic notch	142 Main undercarriage wheel bay
102 Elevator hydraulic actuator	143 Main undercarriage leg pivot fixing
103 Upper/lower fin segment joint	144 Flap hydraulic jack
104 Tailplane sealing plate	145 Port spoiler
105 Rudder hydraulic actuator	146 Spoiler hydraulic jack and control links
106 Tailfin construction	147 Outboard flap guide rail
107 Starboard all-moving tailplane	148 Aileron rib construction
108 Forward radar warning antenna	149 Port aileron
109 VOR aerial (Argentine aircraft only)	150 Port wing tip (folded position)
110 VHF aerial	151 Wing tip panel construction
111 Fin tip aerial fairing	152 Wing tip fairing
112 Command telemetry aerial	153 Port navigation light
113 Rudder	154 Strobe identification light
114 Rudder rib construction	155 Wing fold hydraulic jack
115 Brake parachute housing (ground based operations only)	156 Wing fold hinge joints
116 Tailcone parachute door	157 Outboard leading-edge flap segment
117 Tail navigation and anti-collision lights	158 Matra 550 Magic air-to-air missile
118 Rear radar warning antenna	159 Missile launch rail
119 Port elevator	160 Matra 155 rocket pack
120 Elevator rib construction	161 Aileron hydraulic actuator
121 Elevator damper	162 Outboard pylon attachment joint
122 Port all-moving tailplane construction	163 Outboard stores pylon
123 Engine exhaust nozzle	164 Leading-edge dog-tooth
124 Jet pipe	165 Machined wing skin/stringer panel
125 In-flight refuelling drogue (extended)	166 Wing rib construction
126 Refuelling hose	167 Inboard pylon attachment joint
127 Deck arrester hook, lowered	168 Inboard stores pylon
128 Arrester hook stowage fairing	169 External fuel tank, 242-Imp gal (1 100-l) capacity
129 Detachable tailcone frame and stringer construction	170 Port mainwheel
130 Rear fuselage break point (engine removal)	171 Hydraulic multi-plate disc brake
131 Sloping fin spar attachment bulkhead	172 Torque scissor links
132 Engine bay heat shroud	173 Main undercarriage leg strut
133 Engine turbine section	174 Hydraulic retraction jack
134 Radar warning power amplifier	175 Port wing integral fuel tank bays
135 Fin spar and engine mounting bulkhead	176 Inboard leading-edge flap segment
136 Main engine mounting spigot	177 Leading-edge flap rib construction
137 Aft avionics equipment bays (port and starboard)	178 Ventral catapult strop hook
138 Port double-slotted Fowler-type flap	179 Wing root bolted attachment joint
139 Flap rib construction	180 Leading-edge flap hydraulic jack
	181 Extended chord wing root leading-edge
	182 Airbrake hydraulic jack
	183 Ventral airbrake (port and starboard)
	184 Fuselage centreline pylon
	185 In-flight refuelling "Buddy" pack
	186 AM.39 Exocet air-to-surface missile

from 1992, to extend the service life of the Super Etendard to the year 2008. The upgrade programme included both airframe modifications and avionics updating. *Max speed, 733 mph (1 180 km/h) at 985 ft*

Seen (below) in 'nineties camouflage, the Super Etendard served with three *Aéronavale* squadrons.

(300 m), or Mach=0.96, 858 mph (1 380 km/h) at 39,370 ft (12 000 m), or Mach=1.3. Combat radius (AM 39 missile and two external tanks), 530 mls (850 km). Empty weight, 14,330 lb (6 450 kg). Max loaded weight, 26,455 lb (12 000 kg). Span, 31 ft 6 in (9,60 m). Length, 46 ft 11½ in (14,31 m). Height, 12 ft 8 in (3,85 m). Wing area 306.78 sq ft (28,50 m²).

DASSAULT MILAN   France

Developed as a private venture, the Milan (Kite) was a progressive development of the basic delta-winged Mirage and was intended primarily as a single-seat strike fighter. The distinguishing feature of the Milan was provided by two small retractable foreplanes which were referred to colloquially as "*moustaches*". These were developed by Dassault in collaboration with the Swiss aircraft industry and were intended to improve low-speed control and take-off performance, to increase the suitability of the basic design for the low-level rôle. Work on a prototype Milan, modified from a Mirage IIIE, began mid-1968, and the initial test phase, with non-retractable foreplanes, was completed in March 1969. A fully-equipped pre-series prototype, the Milan S-01, first flew on 29 May 1970. Representative of the proposed series Milan S, this was powered by a SNECMA Atar 9K-50 providing an afterburning thrust of 15,873 lb (7 200 kg). The series Milan S, which was offered for delivery from early 1972, was intended to be fitted with a nav/attack system similar to that of the Jaguar strike aircraft, and internal armament was

Key to Dassault Mirage 2000C

1 Pitot tube
2 Glass-fibre radome
3 Flat-plate radar scanner
4 Thomson-CSF RDM multi-rôle radar unit (initial production aircraft)
5 Cassegrain monopulse planar antenna
6 Thomson-CSF RDI pulse doppler radar unit (later production aircraft)
7 Radar altimeter aerial
8 Angle of attack probe
9 Front pressure bulkhead
10 Instrument pitot heads
11 Temperature probe
12 Fixed in-flight refuelling probe
13 Frameless windscreen panel
14 Instrument panel shroud
15 Static ports
16 Rudder pedals
17 Low voltage formation light strip
18 VHF aerial
19 Nosewheel jack door
20 Hydraulic retraction jack
21 Nose undercarriage leg strut
22 Twin nosewheel
23 Towing bracket
24 Torque scissor links
25 Landing/taxiing lamps
26 Nosewheel steering jacks
27 Nose undercarriage leg doors
28 Cockpit flooring
29 Centre instrument console
30 Control column
31 Pilot's head-up display (HUD)
32 Canopy arch
33 Cockpit canopy cover
34 Starboard air intake
35 Ejection seat headrest
36 Safety harness
37 Martin-Baker Mk 10 zero-zero ejection seat
38 Engine throttle control and airbrake switch
39 Port side console panel
40 Nosewheel bay
41 Cannon blast trough
42 Electrical equipment bay
43 Port air intake
44 Intake half-cone centre body
45 Air conditioning system ram air intake
46 Cockpit rear pressure bulkhead
47 Canopy emergency release handle
48 Hydraulic canopy jack
49 Canopy hinge point
50 Starboard intake strake
51 IFF aerial
52 Radio and electronics bay
53 Boundary layer bleed air duct
54 Air conditioning plant
55 Intake centre-body screw jack
56 Cannon muzzle
57 Pressure refuelling connection
58 Port intake strake

59 Intake suction relief doors (above and below)
60 DEFA 554 30-mm cannon
61 Cannon ammunition box
62 Forward fuselage integral fuel tanks
63 Radio and electronics equipment
64 Fuel system equipment
65 Anti-collision light
66 Air system pre-cooler
67 Air exit louvres
68 Starboard wing integral fuel tank (total internal fuel capacity 836 Imp gal/3 800 l)
69 Wing pylon attachment hardpoints
70 Leading-edge slat hydraulic drive motor and control shaft
71 Slat screw jacks
72 Slat guide rails
73 Starboard wing automatic leading-edge slats
74 Matra 550 Magic "dogfight" AAM
75 Missile launch rail
76 Outboard wing pylon
77 Radar warning antenna
78 Starboard navigation light
79 Outboard elevon
80 Elevon ventral hinge fairings
81 Flight control system access panels
82 Elevon hydraulic jacks
83 Engine intake by-pass air spill duct
84 Engine compressor face
85 Hydraulic accumulator
86 Microturbo auxiliary power unit
87 Main undercarriage wheel bay
88 Hydraulic pump
89 Alternator, port and starboard
90 Accessory gearbox
91 Engine transmission unit and drive shaft
92 Machined fuselage main frames
93 SNECMA M53-5 afterburning turbofan
94 Engine igniter unit
95 Electronic engine control unit
96 Bleed air ducting
97 Engine bleed air blow-off valve spill duct
98 Fin root fillet construction
99 Leading edge ribs
100 Boron/epoxy/carbon honeycomb sandwich fin skin panels
101 Tail low voltage formation light strip
102 ECM aerial fairing
103 VOR aerial
104 Di-electric fin tip fairing
105 VHF aerial

106 Tail navigation light
107 Tail radar warning antenna
108 Honeycomb rudder construction
109 Rudder hinge
110 Fin spar attachment joints
111 Rudder hydraulic jack
112 Engine bay thermal lining
113 ECM equipment housing
114 Variable area afterburning exhaust nozzle
115 Tailpipe sealing flaps
116 Fuel/hydraulic nozzle control jacks
117 Afterburner tailpipe
118 Engine withdrawal rail
119 Wing root extended trailing edge fillet
120 Ventral brake parachute housing
121 Rear engine mounting main frame
122 Runway emergency arrester hook
123 Port inboard elevon
124 Elevon honeycomb construction
125 Carbon fibre skin panels
126 Elevon hydraulic control jacks
127 Fly-by-wire electronic system command units
128 Outboard elevon
129 Elevon tip construction
130 Port navigation light
131 Radar warning antenna

132 Outboard automatic leading edge slat
133 Outboard wing pylon attachment hardpoints
134 Machined upper and lower wing skin/stringer panels
135 Port wing integral fuel tank
136 Wing rib construction
137 Rear fuselage/wing root fairing integral fuel tank
138 Wing spar attachment joints
139 Main spars
140 Undercarriage hydraulic retraction jack
141 Main undercarriage leg pivot fixing
142 Inboard pylon attachment hardpoints
143 Port airbrakes (open) above and beneath wing
144 Airbrake hydraulic jack

145 Main undercarriage leg strut
146 Leading-edge slat hydraulic drive motor
147 Mainwheel leg door
148 Port mainwheel
149 Slat guide rails
150 Screw jacks
151 Auxiliary spar
152 Wing front spar
153 Front spar attachment joint
154 Inboard automatic leading-edge slat rib construction
155 374 Imp gal (1 700-l) auxiliary fuel tank (fuselage centreline or wing inboard stations)
156 Matra Super 530 medium-range AAM
157 Missile launch rail
158 Inboard wing pylon

---

to have comprised two 30-mm cannon, with external ordnance loads up to 8,818 lb (4 000 kg) distributed between seven hardpoints. In the event, no orders were placed for the Milan, and further development was discontinued in 1972, the prototype being adapted as that of the Mirage 50. The following data are based on the manufacturer's estimates for the series version. *Max speed, 870 mph (1 400 km/h) at sea level, or Mach=1.14, 1,452 mph (2 337 km/h) at 39,370 ft (12 000 m), or Mach=2.2. Max climb, 40,157 ft/min (204 m/sec). Empty equipped weight, 15,432 lb (7 000 kg). Max loaded weight, 30,864 lb (14 000 kg). Dimensions as for Mirage IIIE except length of 52 ft 2 in (15,90 m).*

(Below) The Milan with its "moustaches" extended and a full load of ordnance underwing.

DASSAULT MIRAGE 50   France

Deriving its designation from its SNECMA Atar 9K-50 engine, the Mirage 50 retained the basic airframe of the Mirage III and 5, and the prototype – previously that of the Milan – was flown on 15 April 1975. Apart from the engine, providing an afterburning thrust of 15,873 lb (7 200 kg), the Mirage 50 introduced revised air intakes to cater for this engine's greater mass flow and some equipment repositioning to allow for the 353-lb (160-kg) engine weight penalty. By comparison with earlier first-generation Mirage deltas, the Mirage 50 offered a 15 per cent decrease in take-off distance, a 35 per cent

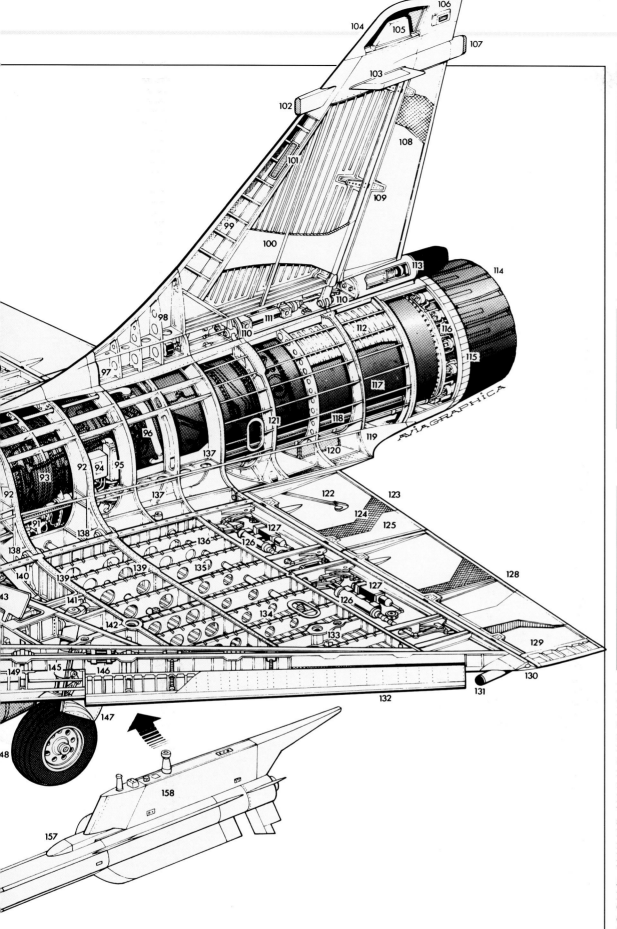

Last of the Mirage 111/5/50 series, this 50EV (above) was delivered to Venezuela for *Esc* **33 during 1991.**

Mach=0.87 HI-LO-HI*), 775 mls (1 250 km). Empty weight, 15,763 lb (7 150 kg), Max loaded weight, 30,203 lb (13 700 kg). Dimensions as for Mirage IIIE except length of 51 ft 0¹/₂ in (15,56 m).*

DASSAULT MIRAGE 2000   France

(Above) A Mirage 2000P of Peruvian *Escuadrón Caza-(Bombardeo)* **412 at La Joya, and (below) the standard series Mirage 2000C.**

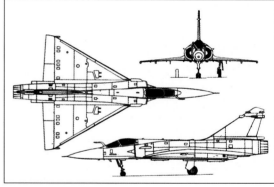

In the early 1970s, *l'Armée de l'Air* wanted an *avion de combat futur* (ACF), widely known as the Super Mirage. This was to be twin-engined, very agile, with a top speed of Mach 3, and a combat ceiling exceeding 59,000 ft (18 000 m), and with a large and capable multi-mode radar. Inevitably this proved unaffordable, and was cancelled in December 1975. Dassault foresaw this, and commenced studies for a smaller fighter in 1972. They reverted to the tail-less delta planform, as this was simple and light, gave a low wing loading, a low thickness/chord ratio for supersonic flight, and plenty of space for fuel. The drawbacks of the tail-less delta were largely overcome by moving the centre of gravity aft to give relaxed stability, using fly-by-wire, and a variable camber wing. With the cancellation of the Super Mirage, *l'Armée de l'Air* wrote their new specification around the new proposal! Progress was swift. The first prototype flew on 10 March 1978, and a two-seater conversion trainer on 11 October 1980. The first production Mirage 2000C flew on 20 November 1982, powered by a SNECMA M53-5 afterburning turbofan rated at 19,840 lb (9 000 kgp) max thrust. The M53 was a single spool turbofan, or more correctly, a continuous bleed turbojet, optimised for high speed at high altitude. Later production aircraft were fitted with the M53-P2, giving 21,363 lb (9 690 kgp) max and 14,360 lb (6 514 kgp) military thrust. Armament consisted of two 30-mm DEFA 554 cannon with 125 rounds per gun, two Matra Super 530D SARH and two Matra R550 heat homing missiles. This has since been increased to six or eight MICA active radar or heat missiles. Deliveries of the Mirage 2000C began in 1983, and initial operational capability was first attained on 2 July 1984. Two-seater conversion trainers were designated Mirage 2000D. A two-seater

improvement in initial climb, an improved ceiling and enhanced manoeuvrability. With a built-in armament of two 30-mm cannon, it was suited for air superiority missions with dogfight missiles, air patrol and supersonic interception, and ground attack combined with self-defence capability. It was offered with Agave or Cyrano IVM multi-function radar and it could carry the full range of operational stores developed for the Mirage III and 5. The first customer for the Mirage 50 was Chile which ordered 14 (plus two two-seat trainers). The first eight supplied in 1980 as Mirage 50FGs were, in fact, refurbished and re-engined ex-*Armée de l'Air* Mirage 5Fs. The remaining six single-

seaters which followed in 1982-83 were new-build Mirage 50CHs, these and the earlier 50FCs being upgraded as ENAER Panteras (which see) in the early 'nineties. During 1990, Dassault initiated the upgrading of Venezuela's surviving 10 Mirage IIIEVs and 5Vs to Mirage 50EV standard, six new-build 50EVs (plus one two-seat 50DV) for Venezuela bringing production of the first-generation Mirage delta to an end in 1991 with 1,422 aircraft delivered. *Max speed, 914 mph (1 470 km/h) at sea level, or Mach=1.2, 1,452 mph (2 337 km/h) at 39,370 ft (12 000 m), or Mach=2.2. Max climb, 36,610 ft/min (186 m/sec). Combat radius (max external fuel and two 882-lb/400-kg bombs at*

A Mirage 200OC-RDI (above) from EC 2/5 *Ile de France* carrying Matra 550 and Super 530D AAMs.

variant optimised for nuclear strike was the Mirage 2000N. The Mirage 2000E was a multi-role export variant, currently used by Abu Dhabi, Egypt, Greece, India, and Peru. In 1991 a glass cockpit was introduced, with five multi-function displays; also HOTAS. Later the Thomson-CSF RDI radar was supplanted by the more advanced RDY multi-mode radar, to give the Mirage 2000-5, now operated by France, Qatar and Taiwan. *Max speed hi, Mach 2.20; max speed lo, Mach 1.20. Operational ceiling, 59,058 ft (18 000 m). Rate of climb, 58,000 ft/min (295 m/sec). Empty weight, 16,535 lb (7 500 kg). Takeoff weight, c25,353 lb (11 500 kg). Span, 29 ft 11 in (9,13m). Length, 48 ft 1 in (14,65 m). Height, 17 ft 1 in (5,20 m). Wing area, 441 sq ft (41 m²).*

DASSAULT MIRAGE 4000   France

Developed as a private venture, the Mirage 4000 was designed to fulfil both interception and low-altitude penetration rôles, and was fundamentally a scale-up of the Mirage 2000. The prototype, originally known as the Super Mirage 4000, was flown on 9 March 1979, achieving Mach=1.6 during its first flight and Mach= 2.2 five weeks later, on 11 April, during its sixth flight. Powered initially by two SNECMA M53-2 turbofans with afterburning thrust of 18,740 lb (8 500 kg), the Mirage 4000 introduced a number of advanced features, including the extensive use of boron and carbonfibre composites for structures, and computer-derived aerodynamics and a fly-by-wire active control system making possible a rearward CG. Built-in armament consisted of two 30-mm cannon and external ordnance loads in excess of 17,637 lb (8 000 kg) could be distributed between 11 external stations. The single prototype was re-engined with M53-5

The Mirage 4000 (above and below) was basically a multi-rôle scaled-up Mirage 2000.

turbofans with afterburning thrust of 19,378 lb (8 790 kg) during the course of its flight test programme. No production contract was placed for the Mirage 4000, but in 1986, the prototype was re-engined with M53-P2 engines and participated in the Rafale programme. *Max speed (short endurance dash), 1,520 mph (2 445 km/h) at 39,370 ft (12 000 m), or Mach=2.3, (sustained), 1,320 mph (2 125 km/h), or Mach=2.2. Max climb, 60, 000 ft/min (305 m/sec). Time to 49,200 ft (15 000 m) and Mach=2.0, 3.0 min. Max radius of action, 1,245+ mls (2 000+ km). Approx empty weight, 28,660 lb (13 000 kg). Loaded weight (combat), 35,494 lb (16,100 kg). Span, 39 ft 4¹/₂ in (12,00 m). Length, 61 ft 4¹/₄ in (18,70 m). Wing area, 785.8 sq ft (73,00 m²).*

DASSAULT MIRAGE 3 NG   France

Featuring fixed foreplanes, an Atar 9K-50 engine and advanced avionics, the Mirage IIING (above and below) did not proceed beyond the prototype.

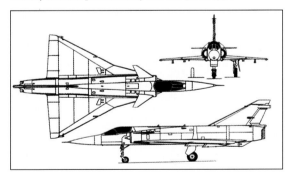

Utilising the proven airframe of the Mirage IIIE, Dassault undertook a thoroughgoing modernisation of equipment and systems to produce the Mirage 3 NG which flew as a prototype on 21 December 1982. Introducing features intended to endow it with much improved air combat performance and survivability in air-ground operations, the Mirage 3 NG (the suffix signifying Nouvelle Generation) had non-retractable swept-back foreplanes, or canards, and highly-swept wing root leading edge extensions. It possessed a fly-by-wire control system derived from that of the Mirage 2000, provision for in-flight refuelling, a SNECMA Atar 9K-50 turbojet affording a full afterburning thrust of 15,873 lb (7 200 kg), an advanced nav/attack system and optional forward-looking sensors, such as a modernised Cyrano IV radar, a laser rangefinder or Agave dual-rôle radar. Maximum take-off weight was increased by comparison with the Mirage IIIE or 5, four lateral stores stations were introduced on the fuselage, and performance improvements included (by comparison with the IIIE) a 20-25 per cent gain in take-off distance, 40 per cent in time to altitude, a 10,000-ft (3 050-m) increase in supersonic ceiling, a three-minute improvement in intercept time and comparably impressive gains in acceleration, instantaneous turn rate and combat air patrol time. No production order

was placed for the Mirage 3 NG and only one prototype was tested. Max speed, 1,320 mph (2 125 km/h) at 39,370 ft (12 000 m), or Mach=2.2. Time to 57,000 ft (17 375 m), 6.6 min. Max loaded weight, 32,407 lb (14 700 kg). Span, 26 ft 11¹/₂ in (8,22 m). Length, 51 ft 4¹/₈ in (15,65 m). Height, 14 ft 9¹/₈ in (4,50 m). Wing area, 376.75 sq ft (35,00 m²).

DASSAULT RAFALE   France

By 1983, five European nations, Britain, France, Germany, Italy and Spain, had combined to produce an agile multi-role fighter that could out-match the next generation of Soviet combat air-craft. France, foiled in her attempts to gain design leadership and a major share of production, autho-rised two *Avions de Combat Experimentale* (ACX) technology demonstrators. In 1985 France left the consortium to go it alone. The ACX demonstrator (only one was built) duly emerged as Rafale A on 4 July 1986. Powered by two F404-GE-400 turbofans, it was flown by Guy Miteaux-Maurouard to Mach 1.3 at the tropopause and put through 5g turns. This was a marked departure from normal prac-tice, which is to explore the envelope in easy stages. Rafale was originally conceived as a twin-engined single-seater with a canard delta configu-ration. It had to replace several different aircraft; the Mirage F1 and Jaguar with *l'Armée de l'Air*, while supplementing the Mirage 2000 in the air superiority role, and the Super Etendard and Crusader with *l'Aeronavale*, for which it had to be carrier-compatible. This was a tall order. The SNECMA M88-2 two spool augmented turbofan was developed specifically for Rafale, although in service this is the -3, rated at 19,558 lb (8 871 kgp) max and 10,950 lb (4 967 kgp) military thrust. The first M88 powered Rafale, C.01, flew on 19 May 1991, and was followed by the navalised M.01 in December of that year. Meanwhile the threat changed with the dissolution of the Warsaw Pact, while the Gulf War had been won. Experience in the latter showed that the workload of an attack pilot was unacceptably high. The result was that the vast majority of Rafales became two-seaters, with a back-seater to share the work. This equally

The Rafale M 01 naval prototype (above) completed seven weeks of testing in the US during 1992. (Below) The single-seat Rafale C for the *Armée de l'Air*.

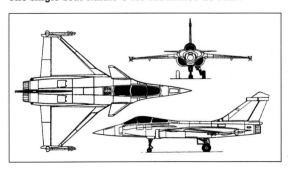

applied to *l'Aeronavale* aircraft. The two-seat con-figuration is achieved at the expense of a small increase in weight, and a small decrease in internal fuel. Like the Mirage 2000, Rafale has a "glass cock-pit" and HOTAS, and unlike it, a sidestick controller. Voice control is also used for non-critical functions; believe it or not, the language is English! Radar is the multi-mode RBE 2 phased array, with the ability to use several modes simultaneously. Armament con-

The Rafale C 01 (above), as first flown in May 1991.

sists of a 30-mm GIAT (formerly DEFA) 791, with four selectable firing rates. A typical AAM load is six MICA and two Magic R550s, although in future the latter will probably be replaced by heat-homing MICAs. A recent change is in designations. The carrier-borne Rafale M is now the F.1, and the first escadrille will be formed in 2001. *L'Armée de l'Air* Rafale C is now the F.2, which is scheduled to enter service in 2004. These will be followed by the F.3 and F.4, which should enter service in 2006 and 2008, respectively. These should have improved combat capabilities. Ironically, one of the reasons why France left the original consortium was that she wanted a smaller (i.e. cheaper) aircraft with an eye to the export market. While Rafale is smaller and cheaper, no export sales have been achieved. The following data relate to Rafale F.2. *Max speed hi, Mach 1.8. Max speed lo, Mach 1.14. Operational ceiling 54,957 ft (16 750 m). Rate of climb, 60,000 ft/min (305 m/sec). Empty weight, 19,973 lb (9 060 kg). Max takeoff 47,399 lb (21 500 kg). Span, 35ft 9¼in (10,90 m). Length 50 ft 2½in (15,30 m). Height, 17ft 6¼in (5,34 m). Wing area 495 sq ft (46 m²).*

DAYTON-WRIGHT PS-1   USA

Of extremely advanced concept in being a parasol monoplane with a retractable undercarriage, the Dayton-Wright PS-1 was conceived as a special "Alert" interceptor and three prototypes were ordered by the Army Air Service, the first of these being employed for static tests. Of mixed construction, with wooden wings and horizontal tail surfaces and steel-tube, fabric-covered fuselage and vertical tail, the PS-1 was powered by a 200 hp Lawrance J-1 air-cooled radial and featured hand-operated chain-and-sprocket main undercarriage members, which were originally

Flown in 1923, the PS-1 (above and below) was, noteworthy for its early use of a retractable undercarriage, but proved unsuccessful.

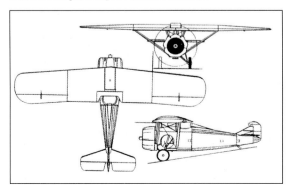

developed by Dayton-Wright for its entry in the 1920 Gordon Bennett Air Race and could be raised in 10 seconds and lowered in six seconds. Flown in 1923, the PS-1 proved to possess unsatisfactory characteristics and neither of the flight test prototypes was officially accepted. *Max speed, 146 mph (235 km/h) at 15,000 ft (4 570 m). Loaded weight, 1,715 lb (778 kg). Span, 30 ft 0 in (9,14 m). Length, 19 ft 2 in (5,84 m). Wing area, 143 sq ft (13,28 m²).*

DE BRUYÈRE C1   France

One of the most unorthodox single-seat fighters built and flown during World War I was an extraordinary

(Above and below) The bizarre de Bruyére completed in 1917, and which crashed on its first flight attempt.

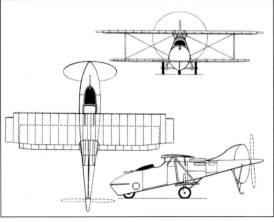

pusher biplane fighter of canard configuration and attributed to a French engineer named de Bruyére. A single-bay biplane with inverted N-type interplane struts, rotary-tip ailerons on the upper wings, a fixed canard surface, and dorsal and ventral vertical surfaces at the rear, the de Bruyére C1 was apparently powered by a 150 hp Hispano-Suiza 8Aa water-cooled engine. This was installed in the centre fuselage, immediately aft of the wings, driving a stern-mounted propeller via a long extension shaft in a fashion reminiscent of that of the Tatin-Paulhan Torpille of 1911. The fuselage was a light metal shell and a nosewheel undercarriage was used. No record has survived to indicate the reason for the highly unusual arrangement adopted by de Bruyére for his fighter, but it could have been dictated by the desire to carry a 37-mm shell-firing Hotchkiss gun. The first flight test was attempted at Etampes in April 1917, the aircraft becoming airborne, but rolling over and crashing on its back. It is not believed that any attempt was made to repair it and continue the flight test programme, and no further details have been found.

DE HAVILLAND D.H.77   UK

Conceived to meet the requirements of Specification F.20/27 which called for a short-range, fast-climbing, lightly-loaded single-seat interceptor fighter, the D.H.77 was designed by W G Carter in close collaboration with Maj F B Halford. The latter evolved specifically for the fighter a novel supercharged air-cooled engine of low frontal area which was built by D Napier, as the Napier H type and later known as the Rapier I, offering 301 hp. Of mixed construction, the wing having two steel spars and wooden ribs with fabric skinning, and the fuselage, also fabric-covered, being a box girder of steel tube with wooden formers, the D.H.77 carried an armament of two 0.303-in (7,7-mm) Vickers guns and flew early in December 1929. The sole prototype was purchased by the Air Ministry and after the completion of official trials was used primarily for

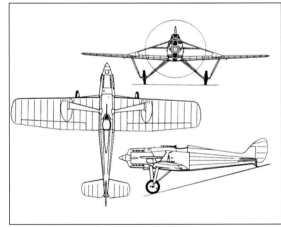

(Above and below) The single example of the de Havilland D.H.77 lightweight fighter flown in 1929.

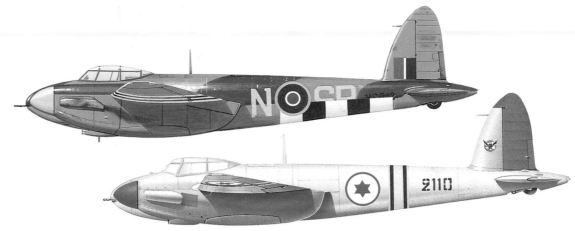

Rapier engine development. It was fitted, in December 1932, with a 295 hp Rapier II, the Hawker Hornet biplane (renamed Fury) having meanwhile been selected for production as the RAF's first standard interceptor. *Max speed, 203 mph (327 km/h) at 10,000 ft (3 050 m). Initial climb, 1,885 ft/min (9,57 m/sec). Empty weight, 1,655 lb (751 kg). Loaded weight, 2,279 lb (1 034 kg). Span, 32 ft 2 in (9,80 m). Length, 24 ft 4¾ in (7,44 m). Height, 8 ft 0 in (2,44 m). Wing area, 163 sq ft (15,14 m²).*

DE HAVILLAND MOSQUITO II   UK

The prototype Mosquito II (above) in night fighter guise, as also shown (below) with early AI radar.

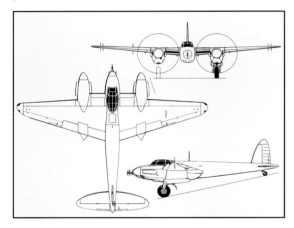

Designed under the direction of R E Bishop between 1938 and 1940, the D.H.98 Mosquito evolved in a number of distinct but related families of bomber, photo-recce and fighter variants. The first production batch of 50 ordered for the RAF on 1 March 1940 included one Mk II two-seat fighter prototype to Specification F.21/40, powered by two 1,300 hp Rolls-Royce Merlin 21s and having an armament of four 0.303-in (7,7-mm) machine guns in the nose and four 20-mm cannon in the under fuselage. The first flight of this aircraft was made on 15 May 1941, and production contracts were placed to add to 28 Mk IIs completed in the first production batch. This batch also included two fighters temporarily fitted

with four-gun Bristol power turrets behind their cockpits, and four "dual-control fighters" (which later became T Mk IIIs). Production of the Mosquito Mk II totalled 589, with Merlin 21 or 23 engines, and most were fitted with AI Mk IV or Mk V radar (with arrow head aerials) and given overall black finish to serve in the night fighter rôle. Deliveries began in March 1942, initially for service with No 157 Squadron. For No 23 Squadron, 25 Mk II Special Intruders had extra fuel and no radar. One unarmed Mk II was fitted with a Helmore Turbinlite by Alan Muntz company and tested by Nos 151, 532 and 85 Squadrons early in 1943. One standard Mk II was supplied to the RAAF in November 1942 as a pattern aircraft for Australian production. *Max speed, 370 mph (595 km/h) at 22,000 ft (6 700 m). Initial climb rate, 3,000 ft/min (15,2 m/sec). Max range, 1,705 mls (2 744 km). Empty weight, 13,431 lb (6 093 kg). Loaded weight, 18,547 lb (8 413 kg). Span, 54 ft 2 in (16,51 m). Length 40 ft 6 in (12,34 m). Height, 15 ft 3 in (4,65 m). Wing area, 450 sq ft (41,81 m²).*

DE HAVILLAND MOSQUITO
FB Mks VI, 21, 24, 26, 40 & 42   UK

The success of the Mosquito II as a day and night fighter led to the evolution, during 1942, of a fighter-bomber or intruder version to make offensive sweeps across the Channel and over enemy-occupied Europe. Designated FB Mk VI, this was basically a Mk II without radar and with provision to carry two short-finned bombs behind the cannon in the fuselage and one bomb under each wing. Series 1 aircraft carried 250-lb (113-kg) bombs and Series 2 aircraft carried 500-lb (227-kg) bombs; alternative underwing loads included SCI, mines, depth charges, 60-lb (27-kg) rockets or drop tanks of 50- or 100-Imp gal (227- or 454-l) capacity. The prototype FB Mk VI flew on 1 June 1942, and production totalled 2,305 aircraft with Merlin 21, 23 or 25 engines. First deliveries were to No 418 Squadron in May 1943. The RAAF received 38 from British production and de Havilland's Australian factory built 178 similar FB Mk

Rocket-equipped Mosquito FB Mk VI (below) of No 143 Sqn for anti-shipping patrols over North Sea, 1944.

(Above, top) Mosquito FB Mk VI of the RAAF-manned No 464 Sqn. (Immediately above) a Mk VI acquired from France for service in Israel.

40s (plus 34 in PR or trainer configuration) with Packard-built Merlin 31 or 33 engines, the first of which flew on 23 July 1943. One FB Mk 40 fitted with Merlin 69s was redesignated FB Mk 42. In Canada, de Havilland built three similar FB Mk 21s with Packard Merlin 31s or 33s, one FB Mk 24 with Merlin 301s and 337 FB Mk 26s with Packard Merlin 225s. Delivered from October 1944 onwards, 197 Mosquito 26s went to the RCAF and the balance to the RAF for use principally in the Middle East. The following data for the FB Mk VI are typical for all the fighter-bomber versions. *Max speed (with external loads), 278 mph (447 km/h). at sea level, 329 mph (529 km/h) at 20,700 ft (6 310 m), (clean), 378 mph (608 km/h) at 13,200 ft (4 025 m). Initial climb, 1,870 ft/ min (9,50 m/sec). Range, 1,120 mls (1 803 km) at 250 mph (402 km/h). Empty weight, 13,727 lb (6 227 kg). Max weight, 21,700 lb (9 843 kg). Span, 54 ft 2 in (16,51 m). Length, 40 ft 6 in (12,34 m). Height, 15 ft 3 in (4,65 m). Wing area, 450 sq ft (41,81 m²).*

Underwing bomb racks distinguished the Mosquito FB Mk VI (above) from the Mk II. The FB Mk 40 (below) was the third Mosquito built in Australia.

DE HAVILLAND MOSQUITO
NF Mks XII, XIII, XVII & XIX   UK

To take advantage of the improved centimetric radar that became available as AI Mk VIII during 1942, the Mosquito II was adapted to have the necessary radar dish in a "thimble" radome that took the place of the four machine guns in the nose. The prototype conversion was tested in the late summer of 1942, after which a second prototype was modified at Hatfield and 97 new production Mk IIs from the Leavesden production line were modified by Marshalls at Cambridge before delivery to the RAF as Mosquito NF Mk XIIs. Deliveries to No 85 Squadron began in February 1943. These were followed by 99 NF Mk XVIIs, which were Mk IIs similarly modified by Marshalls to have US-built SCR 720 (AI Mk X) in an almost identical installation. While these conversion programmes were in hand, the NF Mk XIII was evolved to use AI Mk VIII in the FB Mk VI airframe, with Merlin 21 or 23 engines, and a total of 270 was delivered from February 1944 onwards. These were followed by 280 NF Mk XIXs which had larger "universal" nose radomes able to accommodate either AI Mk VIII or the American SCR 720 (AI Mk X). First flown in April 1944, the Mk XIX also had Merlin 25s with a higher

(Above) Mosquito NF Mk XIX in intruder service with No 157 Sqn, Swannington, Norfolk, late in 1944.

(Below) Mosquito FB Mk VI of No 344 Sqn, RNorAF, over the Tyin area of Norway in June 1949.

A Mosquito NF Mk XII (above) which introduced centimetric AI Mk VIII radar, and (below) the NF Mk XVII fitted with American SCR 720 (AI Mk X).

boost for better low-medium altitude performance. The following data relate specifically to the Mosquito XIII and are generally applicable to the other night fighters. *Max speed, 356 mph (573 km/h) at 9,000 ft (2 745 m), 370 mph (595 km/h) at 14,000 ft (4 270 m). Time to 15,000 ft (4 570 m), 6.75 min. Range, 1,520 mls (2 446 km) clean, 1,860 mls (2 993 km) with 50-Imp gal (227-l) drop tanks at 255 mph (410 km/h) at 15,000 ft (4 570 m). Empty weight, 14,300 lb (6 489 kg). Max weight, 20,000 lb (9 072 kg). Span, 54 ft 2 in (16,51 m). Length, 40 ft 10¾ in (12,47 m). Height, 15 ft 3 in (4,65 m). Wing area, 450 sq ft (41,81 m²).*

DE HAVILLAND MOSQUITO NF Mᴋ XV UK

To combat high-flying *Luftwaffe* bombers, during 1942 de Havilland was asked to produce, at extremely short notice, a version of the Mosquito fighter to operate at very high altitudes. An unarmed and undesignated prototype Mosquito with a pressure cabin had first flown on 8 August 1942, powered by 1,680 hp Merlin 72/73 engines with two-speed, two-stage superchargers. Within seven days, in September, this aircraft was fitted with a Mk II fighter nose mounting four

0.303-in (7,7-mm) guns, being flown in this guise on 14 September 1942 as a single-seater, and proving capable of attaining 45,000 ft (13 715 m). The cabin was pressurised to a differential of 2 lb/sq in (0,14 kg/cm²), and extended wing tips were fitted. During November, this Mosquito was further converted for night fighting, with AI Mk VIII in the nose and the machine guns relocated in a fairing under the fuselage, resuming flight trials as a two-seater. Four Mk IIs were then converted to the same standard as Mosquito NF Mk XVs, one with Merlin 61s and the others with Merlin 77s, to serve with No 85 Squadron in the first half of 1943. *Max speed, 360+ mph (579+ km/h). Service ceiling, 44,600 ft (13 595 m). Max weight, 17,400 lb (7 892 kg). Span, 59 ft 0 in (17,98 m).*

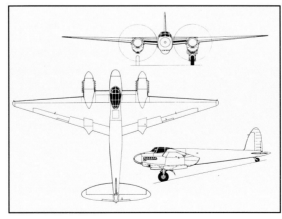

The long-span Mosquito NF Mk XV (above), and (below) one of the five NF Mk XV conversions showing the ventral four-gun pack.

DE HAVILLAND MOSQUITO FB Mᴋ XVIII UK

Experience with Mosquito FB Mk VIs serving in the convoy escort rôle with squadrons of RAF Coastal Command led to a proposal to fit a six-pounder gun in a special anti-shipping version. The Molins gun of 57-mm calibre was fitted in the fuselage of a Mosquito VI in April 1943, taking the place of the 20-mm cannon battery, and first flight of this prototype was made on 8 June. Additional fuel tanks were fitted in the fuselage to extend the range over the Bay of Biscay, and extra armour protection was fitted round the cockpit and engines to provide protection during attacks on heavily armed U-boats. With Merlin 25 engines, 25 rounds for the Molins gun, four nose-mounted 0.303-in (7,7-mm) Brownings and provision for underwing drop tanks, eight 60-lb (27-kg) RPs or two 500-lb (227-kg) bombs, 27 Mosquito FB Mk XVIIIs were converted from Mk VI airframes and served primarily with Nos 248 and 254 Squadrons, from November 1943 onwards. The operational characteristics, weights and dimensions were similar to those for the FB Mk VI.

A Mosquito FB Mk XVIII (below) of No 254 Sqn, in the North Coates Strike Wing during 1944.

DE HAVILLAND MOSQUITO NF Mᴋs 30, 36 & 38 UK

The availability of two-stage, two-speed, supercharged versions of the Merlin led to the introduction of numerous new Mosquito bomber and PR versions. Apart from their use in the high-altitude NF Mk XVs, these engines were not introduced in a fighter variant until the spring of 1944, when the Mosquito NF Mk 30 appeared. This night fighter had the same "universal" radome as the NF Mk XIX, together with 1,680 hp Merlin 72 engines (in the first 70 production examples) or 1,710 hp Merlin 76s (in the other 460 built). The first Mk 30 flew in March 1944, and operational service began in June 1944 with No 219 Sq, RAF, for home defence. Other squadrons used this type for long-range escort of RAF Bomber Command formations attacking Germany in 1944-45. The Mosquito NF Mk 36 was similar, but had

(Above and below) The Mosquito NF Mk 30, one of the late wartime night fighter versions with two-stage Merlins and SCR 720 (AI Mk X) radar.

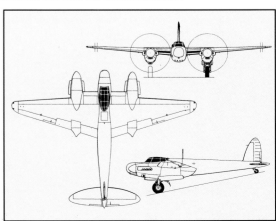

The Mosquito NF Mk 38 (above), the last production fighter version, was too late for wartime service.

(Above) The prototype of the DH Vampire fighter, as first flown with tall fins and rudders.

1,690 hp Merlin 113s. The first example flew in May 1945, and 163 were delivered up to March 1947. The *Force Aérienne Belge* acquired sufficient ex-RAF to equip two squadrons, these remaining in service until the mid 'fifties. The final fighter version of the Mosquito was the NF Mk 38, differing from the Mk 36 in having British AI Mk XI radar in place of American AI Mk X, and Merlin 113/114 engines. Of 101 built, 54 were supplied to the Yugoslav Air Force in 1950 and the others were scrapped. The following data refer to the Mosquito NF Mk 30. *Max speed, 338 mph (544 km/h) at sea level, 424 mph (682 km/h) at 26,500 ft (8 075 m). Initial climb, 2,250 ft/min (11,4 m/sec). Range, 1,180 mls (1 900 km). Empty weight, 15,156 lb (6 875 kg). Loaded weight, 21,600 lb (9 798 kg). Span, 54 ft 2 in (16,51 m). Length, 41 ft 6 in (12,64 m). Height, 15 ft 3 in (4,65 m). Wing area, 450 sq ft (41,81 m²).*

DE HAVILLAND VAMPIRE
F Mᴋs I & III   UK

The D.H.100 Vampire was the second jet fighter designed for service with the Royal Air Force, originating to Specification E.6/41 and built around a Halford-designed de Havilland H-1 Goblin turbojet of 2,700 lb st (1 225 kgp). An unarmed prototype was flown on 20 September 1943, and two more prototypes followed. One of these had the definitive armament of four 20-mm cannon in the front fuselage which, like the Mosquito, was of plywood and balsa construction, the remainder of the aircraft being metal. Production of the Vampire F Mk I, with the 3,100 lb st (1 407 kgp) Goblin II, was undertaken by English Electric (EEC), which built a total of 174 for the RAF and 70 for Sweden, and delivered from 1946. Switzerland acquired four Vampire Is for evaluation in 1946, 30 ex-RAF were supplied to France's *Armée de l'Air* for tuitional tasks between December 1948 and January 1950, and Dominica was to obtain 25 from Sweden in 1952. One was supplied to the

RCAF. The Vampire Mk III (subsequently F Mk 3) was similar to the Mk I, but carried 100-Imp gal (454-l) drop tanks and had a revised tail unit with lower tailplane, rounded rudders and tailplane/fin acorn fairings. Production by the English Electric Company totalled 117 for the RAF and 85 for the RCAF. Norway evaluated four Mk IIIs and Mexico acquired 15 from the RCAF in 1961. The following data relate to the Mk III. *Max speed, 531 mph (854 km/h) at sea level and 505 mph (813 km/h) at 30,000 ft (9 150 m). Range, 1,145 mls (1 842 km). Initial climb, 4,375 ft/min (22,2 m/sec). Empty weight, 7,134 lb (3 236 kg). Normal loaded weight, 12,170 lb (5 520 kg). Span, 40 ft 0 in (12,20 m). Length, 30 ft 9 in (9,37 m). Height, 6 ft 3 in (1,91 m). Wing area, 266 sq ft (24,71 m²).*

(Above) One of 25 Vampire Is acquired from Sweden by the *Fuerza Aérea Dominicana* and (below) Vampire F Mk 3 with drop tanks and revised tail unit.

DE HAVILLAND VAMPIRE
Mᴋ II   UK

Three Vampire Mk I airframes (from four allocated) were fitted with the 4,500 lb st (2 041 kgp) Rolls-Royce Nene 1 engine to Specification F.11/45 and designated

A Nene-engined Vampire II (above) which introduced "elephant ear" intakes for the new engine.

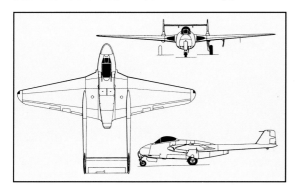

(Above) The Vampire F Mk I with definitive cockpit canopy, and (below) the fifth production example of the F Mk I with original canopy in 1946.

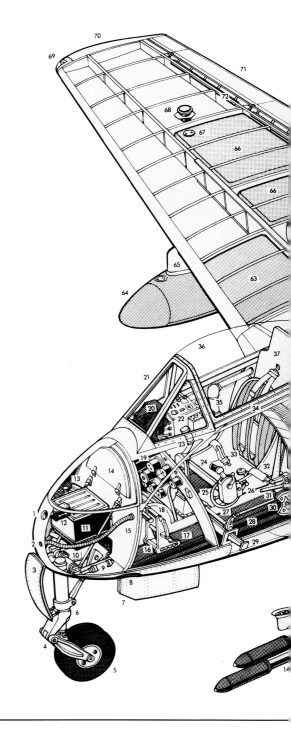

as Vampire Mk IIs. The first of these was flown on 6 March 1946, subsequently being fitted with paired supplementary "elephant ear"-type dorsal intakes to cater for the Nene's double-sided impellers. The Mk IIs were used for performance and engine trials, and the designation Vampire Mk IV was allotted to a proposed combination of the Mk III airframe with the Nene, this eventually being developed in Australia as the Mk 30 (which see), the third Mk II being shipped to Australia to serve as a prototype.

DE HAVILLAND VAMPIRE
FB Mks 5, 6 & 9   UK

To adapt the Vampire for ground attack duties, de Havilland introduced a strengthened and clipped wing (first flown on a Mk I airframe on 29 June 1948) to produce the FB Mk 5. With the basic airframe of the F Mk 3 and a 3,100 lb st (1 406 kgp) Goblin 2 or 4,400 lb st (1 996 kgp) Goblin 2/2 turbojet, the Vampire FB Mk 5 had a longer-stroke undercarriage, and, in addition to

A Vampire FB Mk 5 (above) as delivered in 1949 for service with No 247 Sqn of the RAF.

18 Nosewheel housing
19 Instrument panel
20 Reflector gunsight
21 Windscreen panels
22 Side console switch panel
23 Control column
24 Engine throttle
25 Tailplane trim handwheel
26 Undercarriage and flap selector levers
27 Control linkages
28 Cannon barrels beneath cockpit floor
29 Pull-out boarding step
30 Control system cable compensator
31 Emergency hydraulic handpump
32 Pilot's seat
33 Safety harness
34 Sliding canopy rails
35 Cockpit heater
36 Cockpit canopy cover
37 Pilot's head and back armour
38 Hydraulic system reservoir
39 Radio equipment bay
40 Ammunition tanks (150 rounds per gun)
41 Plywood/balsa/plywood fuselage skinning
42 Boundary layer splitter
43 Port engine air intake
44 Ventral gun bay (4×20-mm Hispano cannon)

45 Spent cartridge case and link ejector chute
46 Cannon bay access panel
47 Cockpit heating and pressurizing intake
48 Intake ducting
49 Fuselage/front spar attachment joint
50 Fuselage/main spar attachment joint
51 Engine bay firewall
52 Fuselage fuel tank (total internal system capacity 400 Imp gal/1 818 l)
53 Fuel filler cap
54 Wooden skin section fabric covering
55 Cockpit air heat exchanger
56 Engine bearer struts
57 De Havilland Goblin DGn 2 centrifugal-flow turbojet
58 Cabin blower
59 Engine accessories
60 Engine bay access panels
61 Starboard wing root fuel tank
62 Starboard main undercarriage retracted position
63 Leading edge fuel tank
64 Starboard drop tank (112 Imp gal/509 l)
65 Drop tank pylon
66 Starboard wing fuel tanks
67 Fuel filler cap
68 Gyrosyn compass remote transmitter
69 Starboard navigation light
70 Wing tip fairing
71 Starboard aileron

72 Aileron mass balance weights
73 Trim tab
74 Aileron hinge control
75 Starboard trailing edge airbrake segment (open)
76 Airbrake hydraulic jack
77 Starboard outer split trailing edge flap
78 Inboard split trailing edge flap
79 Engine flame tubes
80 Jet pipe heat shroud
81 Gun heater duct
82 Tailcone framing
83 Jet exhaust nozzle
84 Starboard tailboom
85 Control cable access panels
86 Tailplane bullet fairing
87 Tailplane construction
88 Starboard fin

89 Rudder mass balance
90 Starboard rudder
91 Rudder trim tab
92 Elevator construction
93 Ventral elevator mass balance weights
94 Elevator tab
95 Pitot tube
96 Port fin construction
97 Port rudder
98 Rudder trim tab
99 Tail navigation light
100 Rudder and elevator hinge controls
101 Tail bumper
102 Fin/tailplane attachment joint
103 Pilot's head
104 Control cable runs
105 Tailboom frame and stringer construction

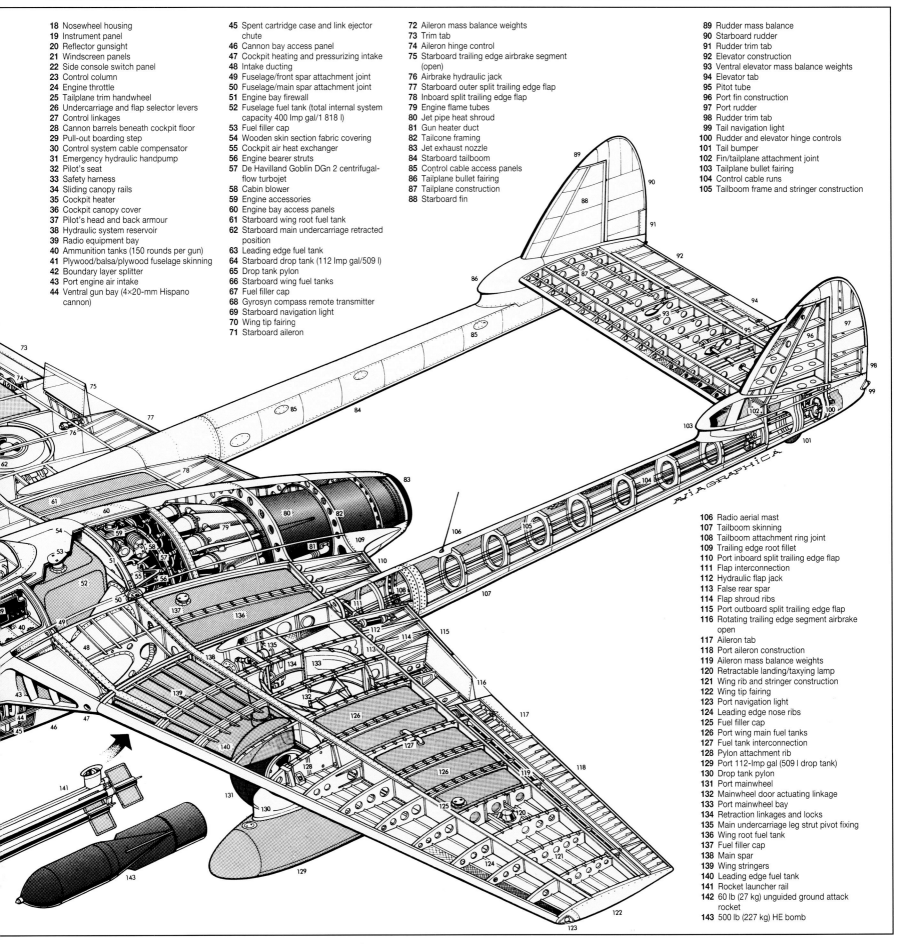

106 Radio aerial mast
107 Tailboom skinning
108 Tailboom attachment ring joint
109 Trailing edge root fillet
110 Port inboard split trailing edge flap
111 Flap interconnection
112 Hydraulic flap jack
113 False rear spar
114 Flap shroud ribs
115 Port outboard split trailing edge flap
116 Rotating trailing edge segment airbrake open
117 Aileron tab
118 Port aileron construction
119 Aileron mass balance weights
120 Retractable landing/taxiing lamp
121 Wing rib and stringer construction
122 Wing tip fairing
123 Port navigation light
124 Leading edge nose ribs
125 Fuel filler cap
126 Port wing main fuel tanks
127 Fuel tank interconnection
128 Pylon attachment rib
129 Port 112-Imp gal (509 l) drop tank
130 Drop tank pylon
131 Port mainwheel
132 Mainwheel door actuating linkage
133 Port mainwheel bay
134 Retraction linkages and locks
135 Main undercarriage leg strut pivot fixing
136 Wing root fuel tank
137 Fuel filler cap
138 Main spar
139 Wing stringers
140 Leading edge fuel tank
141 Rocket launcher rail
142 60 lb (27 kg) unguided ground attack rocket
143 500 lb (227 kg) HE bomb

DE HAVILLAND VAMPIRE
Mks 30-32   UK

In 1946, the Australian government announced its decision to order the Vampire single-seat fighter from the Australian de Havilland Aircraft Pty Ltd. The RAAF elected to procure a version, proposed as the Vampire Mk IV, that mated a Mk III airframe with a Rolls-Royce Nene engine. To serve as a prototype, the third Vampire Mk II was dispatched to Australia in August 1948. The paired "elephant ear" dorsal intakes of the Mk II, intended to improve airflow to the Nene's rear compressor stage, were retained by the Australian-built fighter, which was designated Vampire Mk 30 and embodied a number of changes to meet Australian conditions. First flying on 29 June 1949, this was powered by the Australian-assembled Nene 2-VH of 5,000 lb st (2 270 kgp), armament comprising four 20-mm cannon. Fifty-seven Mk 30s were built at Bankstown to replace Mustangs in both RAAF and Citizen Air Force (CAF) squadrons, these being followed by 23 Mk 31s with strengthened, clipped wings (à la Mk 5) for external loads, such as two 2,000-lb (907-kg) bombs, 28 of the

(Above, top) A Vampire Mk 6 built in Switzerland by F+W at Emmen and (immediately above) Mk 5 serving in the *Armée de l'Air*, early 'fifties. (Below) Vampire FB Mk 9s of the Royal Rhodesian AF in 1963.

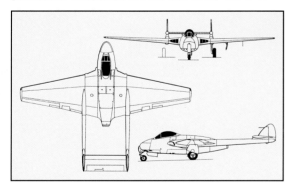

the four 20-mm British Hispano cannon, could carry, on wing strong points inboard and outboard of the booms, eight 60-lb (27-kg) RPs and two 500-lb (227-kg) or two 1,000-lb (454-kg) bombs, or two 200 Imp gal (909 l) drop tanks. The first of 888 FB Mk 5s for the RAF flew on 23 June 1948; some of these were diverted either new or secondhand to the RNZAF, the SAAF, the *Armée de l'Air*, the *Aeronautica Militare Italiana* and the Lebanon Air Force. Specific export versions similar to the FB Mk 5 had the 3,350 lb st (1 520 kgp) Goblin 3 and improved performance. These included the FB Mk 50 for Sweden and the FB Mk 52 built for Egypt, Finland, Iraq, India, New Zealand, Norway and Venezuela. Foreign licence production comprised 100 FB Mk 6s by the FFA in

Switzerland; 80 FB Mk 52As by Macchi and Fiat in Italy; 120 (plus 67 assembled from imported components) by SNCASE in France as FB Mk 51s and 281 by HAL in India, these last including 34 assembled from imported components. Production of single-seat Vampires for the RAF ended with 381 FB Mk 9s with cockpit air conditioning for Far East service. Seventeen ex-Swedish FB Mk 50s were transferred to Dominica in 1956, and ex-RAF Mk 9s went to Rhodesia, Jordan and Ceylon. The following data are for the FB Mk 5. *Max speed, 530 mph (853 km/h) at sea level and 482 mph (775 km/h) at 40,000 ft (12 200 m). Range, 1,145 mls (1 842 km). Empty weight, 7,253 lb (3 290 kg). Max loaded weight, 12,360 lb (5 606 kg). Span, 38 ft 0 in (11,58 m). Length, 30 ft 9 in (9,37 m). Height, 6 ft 3 in (1,91 m). Wing area, 262 sq ft (24,34 m²).*

DE HAVILLAND SEA VAMPIRE   UK

Deck-landing trials with the second prototype Vampire fighter began aboard HMS *Ocean* as early as 3 December 1945, these being the first-ever carrier operations by a pure jet aircraft. Successful trials with two fully-navalised Vampire I conversions led to an order for 30

A Sea Vampire F Mk 20 (below) showing V-frame hook at tail of fuselage "pod".

Sea Vampire F Mk 20s, the first of which flew in October 1948. Armed with four 20-mm cannon and using the basic airframe of the Vampire FB Mk 5, they served primarily in a training rôle to give Fleet Air Arm pilots jet experience. Six RAF Vampire F Mk 3s were converted to Sea Vampire 21s, with reinforced undersides and armament removed, for use in flexible deck landing trials at RAE Farnborough and on HMS *Warrior* in 1947-55. *Max speed, 526 mph (846 km/h). Time to 25,000 ft (7 620 m), 10 min. Range, 1,145 mls (1 842 km). Empty weight, 7,623 lb (3 458 kg). Loaded weight, 12,660 lb (5 743 kg). Dimensions as Vampire FB Mk 5.*

An Australian-built Vampire 32 with air intakes in the ventral position (originally they were dorsal).

Mk 30s being retrospectively modified to the same standard. In 1951, two Mk 30s were fitted with cockpit air conditioning as Mk 32s, and during their service lives the Mks 30 and 31 had their dorsal air intakes transferred to a ventral position in order to overcome airflow interference from the cockpit canopy. They were also fitted with ejection seats. The Vampires remained in RAAF service until replaced by Sabres in 1955, and with four CAF squadrons until 1957. The following data relate to the Mk 30. *Max speed, 548 mph (882 km/h) at sea level, 559 mph (900 km/h) at 20,000 ft (6 100 m). Initial climb, 4,800 ft/min (24,38 m/sec). Empty equipped weight, 7,680 lb (3 484 kg). Normal loaded weight, 11,160 lb (5 062 kg). Span, 38 ft 0 in (11,58 m). Length, 30 ft 9 in (9,37 m). Height, 8 ft 10 in (2,69 m). Wing area, 262 sq ft (24,34 m²).*

DE HAVILLAND VAMPIRE
NF Mk 10   UK

A side-by-side two-seat version of the Vampire Mk 5, the D.H.113, was produced in 1949 as a company-funded private venture night fighter using basically the same cockpit as those of the Mosquito NF Mks 30 and 36 and intended primarily for export. The prototype flew on 28 August 1949, Egypt placing an order for 15. In the event, the export of these aircraft was embargoed in 1951 when deliveries were ready to begin and the aircraft were transferred to the RAF as interim equipment pending availability of more sophisticated night fighters. In fact, 78 examples of the Vampire NF Mk 10,

(Below) The two-seat Vampire NF Mk 10 night fighter.

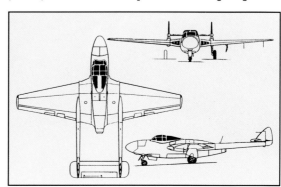

(Above) The Vampire FB Mk 5 and (below) a pair of FB Mk 6s, built in Switzerland by FFA and flying in the mid 'eighties with modified nose cones.

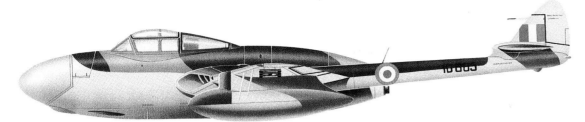

as the D.H.113 was designated by the RAF, were delivered. Of these, 29 were subsequently refurbished and sold to the Indian Air Force and 14 were delivered to the *Aeronautica Militare Italiana*, the exported aircraft being designated as Vampire NF Mk 54s. Armament remained four 20-mm cannon and power was provided by a 3,350 lb st (1 520 kgp) de Havilland Goblin 3 turbojet. *Max speed, 538 mph (866 km/h) at sea level. Initial climb, 4,500 ft/min (22,86 m/sec). Range, 1,220 mls (1 963 km). Empty weight, 6,984 lb (3 168 kg). Loaded weight, 13,100 lb (5 942 kg). Span, 38 ft 0 in (11,58 m). Length, 34 ft 7 in (10,54 m). Height, 6 ft 7 in (2,01 m). Wing area, 262 sq ft (24,34 m²).*

Like those for India, the 14 Vampire NF Mk 54s exported to Italy (below) were ex-RAF service, these serving at Amendola with the *Scuola Avanzato*.

DE HAVILLAND HORNET
Mks 1-4   UK

Design of a long-range single-seat fighter was begun by de Havilland at Hatfield in 1942 as a private venture, using experience gained with the Mosquito. Features of this D.H.103 project were its wooden fuselage and mixed wood-and-metal wing construction with Redux bonding; Rolls-Royce Merlin 130/131 engines of 2,070 hp each, "handed" to eliminate torque on take-off and installed in low-drag cowlings with wing leading-edge radiators, and an armament of four 20-mm cannon in the nose. Specification F.12/43 was issued to cover construction of two prototypes, the first of which flew on 28 July 1944, and 60 similar Hornet F Mk 1s were built for RAF service, deliveries beginning in 1946. The Hornet F Mk 3 (120 built) appeared in 1946 and featured a dorsal fin, increased internal fuel capacity and wing hard-points for two 1,000-lb (454-kg) bombs, eight 60-lb (27-kg) rockets or two 200 Imp gal (909 l) drop tanks. Production ended with the Hornet F Mk 4 (12 built) carrying a vertically-mounted F52 camera in the fuselage for fighter-reconnaissance duties. Data are for the Hornet F Mk 3. *Max speed, 393 mph (632 km/h) at sea level and 472 mph (759 km/h) at 22,000 ft (6 705 m).*

(Above) An early production Hornet F Mk 1 lacking dorsal fin, and (below), a rocket-armed Hornet F Mk 1 serving with No 33 Sqn, RAF, during the Malayan campaign in the early 'fifties.

One of the 29 Vampire NF Mk 54s supplied to India (ex-RAF) for use by Nos 10 and 73 Sqns, IAF.

Initial climb, 4,650 ft/min (23,6 m/sec). Operational ceiling, 37,500 ft (11 430 m). Range, 2,600 mls (4 184 km). Empty weight, 12,880 lb (5 842 kg). Loaded weight, 21,060 lb (9 553 kg). Span, 45 ft 0 in (13,72 m). Length, 36 ft 8 in (11,17 m). Height, 14 ft 2 in (4,32 m). Wing area, 361 sq ft (33,54 m²).

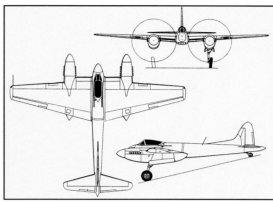

(Above) The Hornet F Mk 3 and (below) an example from the Conversion Flight, RAF Linton-on-Ouse.

DE HAVILLAND SEA HORNET
Mk 20   UK

The Sea Hornet was developed to Specification N.5/44 as a carrier-based version of the RAF's Hornet F Mk 3. Two Hornet Is were converted to have high-drag flaps, V-frame arrester hooks, tail-down catapult pick-up points, naval radar and equipment and modified landing gear. The first of these flew on 19 April 1945, and a third conversion followed with folding wings, being initially tested on HMS *Ocean* in August 1945. The first of 80 production Sea Hornet F Mk 20s flew on 13 August 1946, and the type entered service with the Royal Navy in June 1947, serving primarily in the evaluation, training and other secondary rôles. Armament and power plant were as for the Hornet F Mk 3, as were the overall dimensions, but the Sea Hornet F Mk 20 also had provision for an oblique camera in the rear fuselage with port and starboard windows. *Max speed, 371 mph*

(Above) A Sea Hornet F Mk 20 from 801 NAS based at RNAS Ford in late 1947, and (below) as used by 806 NAS for display flying in the US in 1948.

(597 km/h) at 6,000 ft (1 830 m), 400 mph (644 km/h) at 18,750 ft (5 715 m). Service ceiling, 36,700 ft (11 185 m). Range (with two 100-Imp gal/455-l drop tanks), 1,680 mls (2 703 km). Empty weight, 11,700 lb (5 307 kg). Max loaded weight, 17,782 lb (8 066 kg).

DE HAVILLAND SEA HORNET
Mk 21   UK

An urgent need on the part of the Fleet Air Arm for a carrier-based night-fighter led to development of a two-seat radar-equipped version of the Sea Hornet, to Specification N.21/45. Two prototypes were converted from Hornet F Mk 1s, with the same naval features as the Sea Hornet 20 plus ASH radar in a "thimble" nose and an observer/radar operator's position in the centre fuselage. The first, fixed-wing, prototype flew on 9 July 1946. The second prototype had folding wings, as did 78 production Sea Hornet NF Mk 21s, the first of which flew on 24 March 1948. Operational service began in January 1949, but was restricted by difficulties encountered during deployments at sea. The Sea Hornet NF Mk 21 had 2,030 hp Merlin 133/134 "handed" engines and the same armament as the Hornet F Mk 3, including provision for underwing loads. *Max speed, 365 mph (587 km/h) at sea level, 430 mph (692 km/h) at 22,000 ft (6 705 m). Initial climb, 4,400 ft/min (22,4 m/sec). Operational ceiling, 36,500 ft (11 125 m). Range, 1,500 mls (2 414 km). Empty weight, 14,230 lb (6 455 kg). Loaded weight, 19,530 lb (8 856 kg). Span, 45 ft 0 in (13,72 m). Length, 37 ft 0 in (11,28 m). Height, 14 ft 2 in (4,31 m). Wing area, 361 sq ft (33,54 m²).*

(Above) A Sea Hornet NF Mk 21 from 809 NAS at Culdrose in 1949. (Below) The two-seat radar-equipped Sea Hornet NF Mk 21 shipboard fighter.

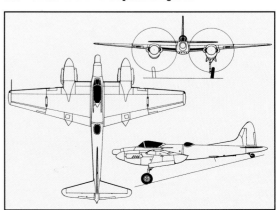

DE HAVILLAND VENOM FB
Mks 1 & 4   UK

Development of an improved version of the D.H.100 Vampire with a thinner wing and uprated engine, began in 1948 under the designation Vampire 8 and proceeded to Specification F.15/49 as the D.H.112, subsequently named Venom. With the same configuration as the Vampire, the Venom was powered by the 4,850 lb st (2 200 kgp) de Havilland Ghost 103, had slight quarter-chord sweepback on the wing and carried extra fuel in wing-tip tanks. The armament, as in the Vampire, comprised four 20-mm cannon, with strong points for up to 2,000 lb (907 kg) of bombs or rockets. The prototype D.H.112 first flew on 2 September 1949, and the first of 375 Venom FB Mk 1s for the RAF flew in June 1951. Service use began in August 1952, and later production aircraft were fitted with Martin-Baker ejection seats. The Venom FB Mk 4 was similar but had revised, flat-topped, fin-and-rudder design,

The Venom FB Mk 1 (above) was essentially similar to the Venom FB Mk 4 (below), which introduced a revised tail unit and an uprated engine.

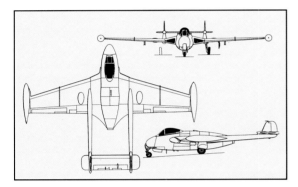

powered ailerons, the 5,150 lb st (2 336 kgp) Ghost 105 engine and provision for underwing drop tanks. The prototype (converted Mk 1) flew on 29 December 1953, and delivery of 150 for the RAF began in May 1954. Venezuela purchased 22 Venom FB Mk 4s in 1955-56, and a similar export version was designated FB Mk 50, two being supplied to Italy and 15 to Iraq. In Switzerland, the EFW consortium built 100 Venom FB Mk 1s and 150 FB Mk 4s for the Swiss Air Force. Data are for the Venom FB Mk 4: *Max speed, 597 mph (961 km/h) at sea level and 557 mph (896 km/h) at 30,000 ft (9 150 m). Initial climb, 7,230 ft/min (36,7 m/sec). Service ceiling, 48,000 ft (14 630 m). Range, 1,075 mls (1 730 km). Loaded weight, 15,310 lb (6 945 kg). Span, 41 ft 8 in (12,70 m). Length, 33 ft 0 in (10,06 m). Height, 6 ft 8 in (2,03 m). Wing area, 279.75 sq ft (25,99 m²).*

(Immediately below) A Venom FB Mk 4 of No 8 Sqn, RAF, at Khormaksar, 1960, and (bottom) export Mk 50 as used by Iraq's No 5 Sqn in the 'fifties.

Key to de Havilland Sea Hornet F Mk 20

1 Starboard navigation light
2 Wing tip fairing
3 Fuel vent pipe
4 Starboard slotted aileron
5 Starboard wing folded position
6 Wing plywood sandwich skin panelling
7 Inter-skin spruce stringers
8 Aileron tab
9 Outer split trailing edge flap segment
10 Wing fold latching mechanism
11 Hydraulic wing-fold jack
12 Engine air intake duct

13 Wing leading edge aluminium skin panelling
14 60-lb (27-kg) HVAR ground attack rockets
15 Starboard 4-bladed de Havilland Hydromatic propeller
16 Propeller spinner
17 Detachable engine cowlings
18 Exhaust stubs
19 Starboard Rolls-Royce Merlin 131 (left-hand rotation) engine nacelle
20 Nose cone
21 Camera port
22 De-icing fluid tank
23 Cockpit fresh air intake
24 Starboard mainwheel

25 Torque scissor links
26 Main undercarriage leg strut
27 Oxygen bottles
28 Gun camera
29 Armoured front bulkhead
30 Hinged access panel to instruments
31 Rudder pedals
32 Foot boards
33 Cannon muzzle
34 Control column
35 Propeller control levers
36 Instrument panel
37 Gyro gunsight
38 Starboard combined oil and intercooler radiators

39 Bullet-proof windscreen panels
40 Starboard engine oil tank
41 Canopy winding handle
42 Cockpit canopy cover
43 Headrest
44 Back armour
45 Pilot's seat
46 Safety harness

DE HAVILLAND VENOM NF
Mks 2 & 3   UK

A two-seat night fighting version of the single-seat Venom fighter was evolved in the same way that the Vampire night fighter had been derived from the original Vampire, and a company-funded prototype was first flown on 23 August 1950. The front fuselage was lengthened and widened to accommodate AI Mk 10 radar and crew of two side-by-side, the remainder of the airframe being essentially similar to that of the Venom 1 and the engine being the 4,850 lb st (2 200 kgp) Ghost 104. Ninety similar Venom NF Mk 2s (first flight 4 March 1952) were delivered to the RAF from 1953 onwards, many later being modified to NF

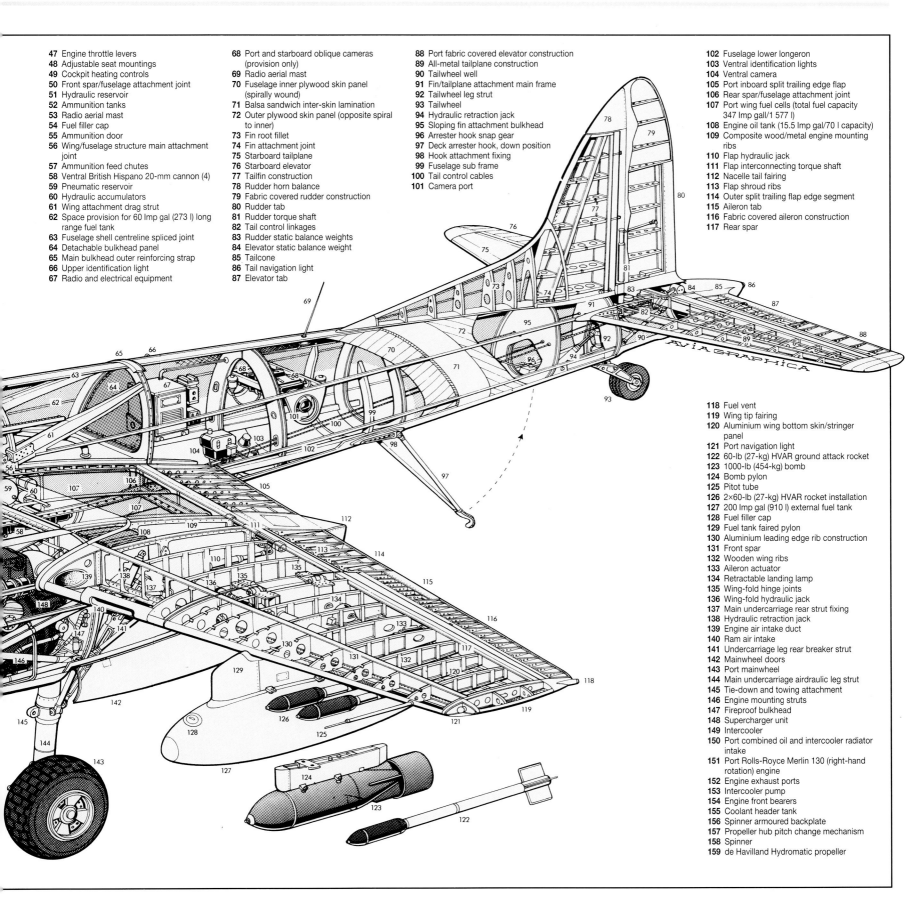

47 Engine throttle levers
48 Adjustable seat mountings
49 Cockpit heating controls
50 Front spar/fuselage attachment joint
51 Hydraulic reservoir
52 Ammunition tanks
53 Radio aerial mast
54 Fuel filler cap
55 Ammunition door
56 Wing/fuselage structure main attachment joint
57 Ammunition feed chutes
58 Ventral British Hispano 20-mm cannon (4)
59 Pneumatic reservoir
60 Hydraulic accumulators
61 Wing attachment drag strut
62 Space provision for 60 Imp gal (273 l) long range fuel tank
63 Fuselage shell centreline spliced joint
64 Detachable bulkhead panel
65 Main bulkhead outer reinforcing strap
66 Upper identification light
67 Radio and electrical equipment

68 Port and starboard oblique cameras (provision only)
69 Radio aerial mast
70 Fuselage inner plywood skin panel (spirally wound)
71 Balsa sandwich inter-skin lamination
72 Outer plywood skin panel (opposite spiral to inner)
73 Fin root fillet
74 Fin attachment joint
75 Starboard tailplane
76 Starboard elevator
77 Tailfin construction
78 Rudder horn balance
79 Fabric covered rudder construction
80 Rudder tab
81 Rudder torque shaft
82 Tail control linkages
83 Rudder static balance weights
84 Elevator static balance weight
85 Tailcone
86 Tail navigation light
87 Elevator tab

88 Port fabric covered elevator construction
89 All-metal tailplane construction
90 Tailwheel well
91 Fin/tailplane attachment main frame
92 Tailwheel leg strut
93 Tailwheel
94 Hydraulic retraction jack
95 Sloping fin attachment bulkhead
96 Arrester hook snap gear
97 Deck arrester hook, down position
98 Hook attachment fixing
99 Fuselage sub frame
100 Tail control cables
101 Camera port

102 Fuselage lower longeron
103 Ventral identification lights
104 Ventral camera
105 Port inboard split trailing edge flap
106 Rear spar/fuselage attachment joint
107 Port wing fuel cells (total fuel capacity 347 Imp gall/1 577 l)
108 Engine oil tank (15.5 Imp gal/70 l capacity)
109 Composite wood/metal engine mounting ribs
110 Flap hydraulic jack
111 Flap interconnecting torque shaft
112 Nacelle tail fairing
113 Flap shroud ribs
114 Outer split trailing flap edge segment
115 Aileron tab
116 Fabric covered aileron construction
117 Rear spar

118 Fuel vent
119 Wing tip fairing
120 Aluminium wing bottom skin/stringer panel
121 Port navigation light
122 60-lb (27-kg) HVAR ground attack rocket
123 1000-lb (454-kg) bomb
124 Bomb pylon
125 Pitot tube
126 2×60-lb (27-kg) HVAR rocket installation
127 200 Imp gal (910 l) external fuel tank
128 Fuel filler cap
129 Fuel tank faired pylon
130 Aluminium leading edge rib construction
131 Front spar
132 Wooden wing ribs
133 Aileron actuator
134 Retractable landing lamp
135 Wing-fold hinge joints
136 Wing-fold hydraulic jack
137 Main undercarriage rear strut fixing
138 Hydraulic retraction jack
139 Engine air intake duct
140 Ram air intake
141 Undercarriage leg rear breaker strut
142 Mainwheel doors
143 Port mainwheel
144 Main undercarriage airdraulic leg strut
145 Tie-down and towing attachment
146 Engine mounting struts
147 Fireproof bulkhead
148 Supercharger unit
149 Intercooler
150 Port combined oil and intercooler radiator intake
151 Port Rolls-Royce Merlin 130 (right-hand rotation) engine
152 Engine exhaust ports
153 Intercooler pump
154 Engine front bearers
155 Coolant header tank
156 Spinner armoured backplate
157 Propeller hub pitch change mechanism
158 Spinner
159 de Havilland Hydromatic propeller

Mk 2A standard with revised tail units, including dorsal fins and acorn fairings, and clear-view canopies. Further tail unit changes distinguished the Venom NF Mk 3, first flown on 22 February 1953. One hundred and twenty-nine were built for the RAF with AI Mk 21 radar, powered ailerons, 5,150 lb st (2 336 kgp) Ghost 105 engine and other changes. Sweden's *Flygvapen* bought 62 Venom NF Mk 51s, similar to the NF Mk 2s and powered by Swedish-built Ghost RM 2A engines. These served from 1953 to 1960. The following data refer to the Venom NF Mk 3. *Max speed, 576 mph (927 km/h) at sea level, 555 mph (893 km/h) at 30,000 ft (9 150 m), 529 mph (851 km/h) above 40,000 ft (12 200 m). Initial climb rate, 6,280 ft/min (31,9 m/sec). Loaded weight, 14,400 lb (6 532 kg). Span, 42 ft 10 in*

(13,06 m). Length, 36 ft 8 in (11,17 m). Height, 6 ft 6 in (1,98 m). Wing area, 279.75 sq ft (25,99 m²).

(Below) Venom NF Mk 2A flown by the CO of No 253 Sqn, RAF Waterbeach, Cambs, 1956.

(Below) The Venom NF Mk 2 and (above) an NF Mk 51, in service with Sweden's *Flygvapen*, which acquired 62 of this night fighter variant.

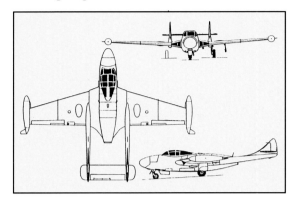

DE HAVILLAND SEA VENOM   UK

(Below) The Sea Venom FAW Mk 21, and (above), an FAW Mk 22 which had a later engine variant.

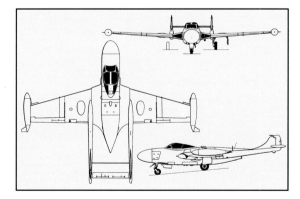

After tests with the Venom NF prototype, the Royal Navy ordered three prototypes of a navalised night fighter to Specification N.107. The first of these flew on 19 April 1951 as the Sea Venom NF (later FAW, for Fighter, All-Weather) Mk 20. Principal naval features were a V-type arrester hook, strengthened, longer-stroke undercarriage, catapult pick-up points and (from the third prototype onwards) folding wings with tip tanks of revised design. Fifty Sea Venom FAW Mk 20s with Ghost 103 engines were followed by 167 FAW Mk 21s with Ghost 104s, AI Mk 21 and powered ailerons, and 39 FAW Mk 22s with Ghost 105s. Ejection seats were introduced during Mk 21 production and applied retrospectively. Sea Venoms served with FAA squadrons from 1954 to 1960, and were operational during the Suez action. The RAAF bought 39 Sea Venom FAW Mk 53s, similar to the Mk 21 but with AI Mk 17, which served from 1955 to 1967. The designation Sea Venom NF Mk 52 referred to a version licensed for production by SNCASE for service with *Aéronavale* as the Aquilon (which see). Data that follow refer to the Sea Venom

Key to de Havilland Sea Venom FAW Mk 22

1 Radome
2 ARI 5860 (AI Mk 4) radar scanner
3 Radome hinge
4 Radar tracking mechanism
5 Nosewheel leg door
6 Approach light
7 Nosewheel forks
8 Anti-shimmy nosewheel
9 Shock absorber leg strut
10 Radar equipment access door
11 Frequency modulator unit
12 Forward electronics equipment bay
13 Laminated (plywood/balsa/plywood sandwich) forward fuselage skinning
14 IFF aerial
15 Front pressure bulkhead
16 Pilot's instrument panel
17 Nosewheel housing
18 Control column
19 Rudder pedals
20 Cockpit floor level
21 Cannon muzzle blast trough
22 Nosewheel door
23 "Pull-out" step
24 Control system linkages
25 Engine throttle lever
26 Emergency hydraulic handpump
27 Direct vision side window panels
28 Reflector gunsight
29 Navigator/radar operator's instrument console
30 Windscreen wiper
31 Armoured windscreen panel
32 Cockpit canopy cover
33 Ejection seat headrests
34 Face blind firing handle
35 Navigator/radar operator's ejection seat (behind and below level of pilot's seat)
36 Cockpit coaming

37 Pilot's Martin-Baker Mk 4 ejection seat
38 Radio and electronics equipment bay
39 Port side console panel
40 Underfloor cannon barrels
41 Spent cartridge case ejector chutes
42 Cannon bay
43 20-mm cannon (four)
44 Ammunition feed chute
45 Boundary layer splitter plate
46 Port engine air intake
47 Ammunition tanks, 150 rounds per gun
48 Cockpit rear pressure bulkhead
49 Equipment bay access panel
50 Electrical system equipment
51 External canopy handle
52 Canopy aft glazing
53 Hydraulic system header tank
54 Fuel filler access
55 Fuselage fuel tank; total system capacity including fixed tip tanks, 464 Imp gal (2 109 l)
56 Front spar attachment joint

57 Intake trunking
58 Cooling air intake
59 Air system pre-cooler
60 Wing main spar
61 Main spar/fuselage main frame attachment joint
62 Fireproof bulkhead
63 Engine equipment bay access door
64 Engine mounting struts
65 De Havilland Ghost 105 centrifugal-flow turbojet
66 Engine accessory equipment bay
67 Flame cans
68 Engine bay access panels
69 Alternator cooling air scoop

70 Wing root fuel tank
71 Starboard mainwheel (retracted position)
72 Starboard wing fuel tanks
73 Fuel filler cap
74 Wing fold links
75 Wing fold hydraulic jack
76 Starboard wing fence
77 Remote compass transmitter
78 Tip tank fuel piping
79 Fixed leading edge slat
80 Extended wingtip strake
81 Starboard navigation light
82 Fixed tip tank
83 Fuel filler caps
84 Tip tank stabilising fin

FAW Mk 22. *Max speed, 576 mph (927 km/h) at sea level, 555 mph (893 km/h) at 30,000 ft (9 150 m). Initial climb rate, 5,750 ft/min (29,2 m/sec). Loaded weight, 15,400 lb (6 985 kg). Span 42 ft 10 in (13,06 m). Length, 36 ft 8 in (11,17 m). Height, 8 ft 6¼ in (2,62 m). Wing area, 279.75 sq ft (25.99 m²).*

Flown by 839 NAS from HMS *Eagle*, the Sea Venom FAW Mk 21 (below) was operational at Suez in 1956, this type remaining with the RN until 1960.

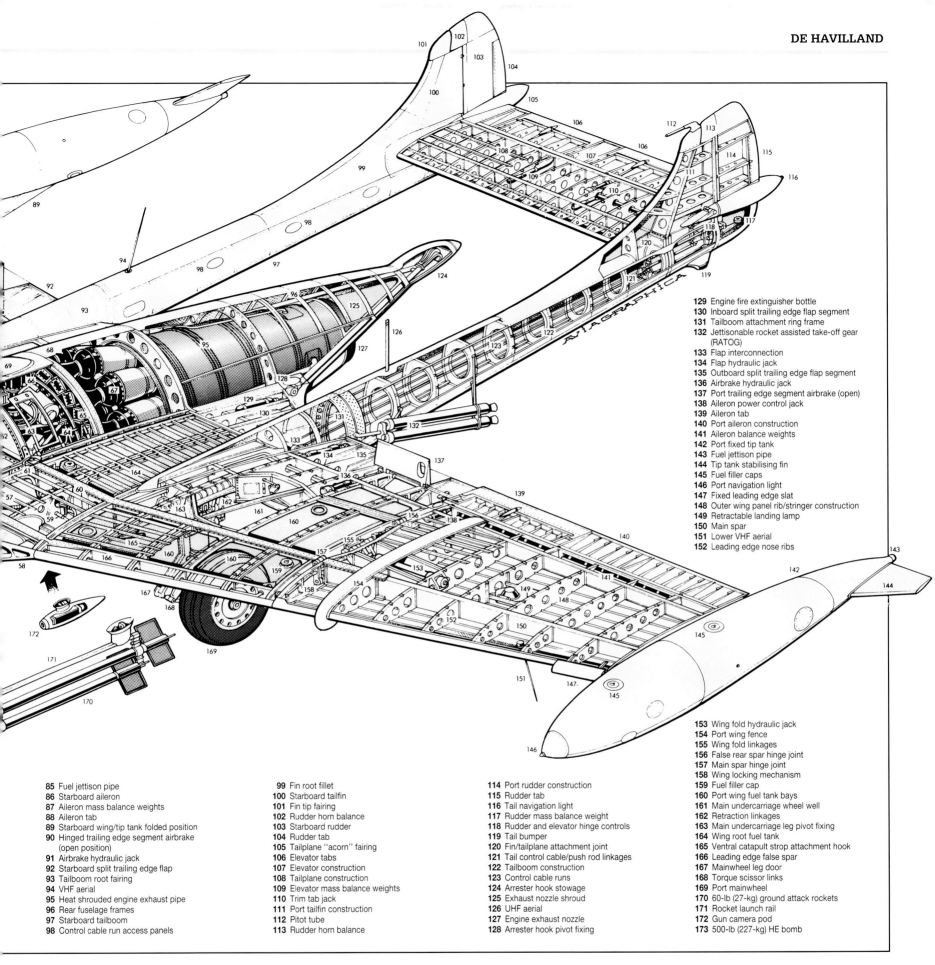

129 Engine fire extinguisher bottle
130 Inboard split trailing edge flap segment
131 Tailboom attachment ring frame
132 Jettisonable rocket assisted take-off gear (RATOG)
133 Flap interconnection
134 Flap hydraulic jack
135 Outboard split trailing edge flap segment
136 Airbrake hydraulic jack
137 Port trailing edge segment airbrake (open)
138 Aileron power control jack
139 Aileron tab
140 Port aileron construction
141 Aileron balance weights
142 Port fixed tip tank
143 Fuel jettison pipe
144 Tip tank stabilising fin
145 Fuel filler caps
146 Port navigation light
147 Fixed leading edge slat
148 Outer wing panel rib/stringer construction
149 Retractable landing lamp
150 Main spar
151 Lower VHF aerial
152 Leading edge nose ribs

85 Fuel jettison pipe
86 Starboard aileron
87 Aileron mass balance weights
88 Aileron tab
89 Starboard wing/tip tank folded position
90 Hinged trailing edge segment airbrake (open position)
91 Airbrake hydraulic jack
92 Starboard split trailing edge flap
93 Tailboom root fairing
94 VHF aerial
95 Heat shrouded engine exhaust pipe
96 Rear fuselage frames
97 Starboard tailboom
98 Control cable run access panels

99 Fin root fillet
100 Starboard tailfin
101 Fin tip fairing
102 Rudder horn balance
103 Starboard rudder
104 Rudder tab
105 Tailplane "acorn" fairing
106 Elevator tabs
107 Elevator construction
108 Tailplane construction
109 Elevator mass balance weights
110 Trim tab jack
111 Port tailfin construction
112 Pitot tube
113 Rudder horn balance

114 Port rudder construction
115 Rudder tab
116 Tail navigation light
117 Rudder mass balance weight
118 Rudder and elevator hinge controls
119 Tail bumper
120 Fin/tailplane attachment joint
121 Tail control cable/push rod linkages
122 Tailboom construction
123 Control cable runs
124 Arrester hook stowage
125 Exhaust nozzle shroud
126 UHF aerial
127 Engine exhaust nozzle
128 Arrester hook pivot fixing

153 Wing fold hydraulic jack
154 Port wing fence
155 Wing fold linkages
156 False rear spar hinge joint
157 Main spar hinge joint
158 Wing locking mechanism
159 Fuel filler cap
160 Port wing fuel tank bays
161 Main undercarriage wheel well
162 Retraction linkages
163 Main undercarriage leg pivot fixing
164 Wing root fuel tank
165 Ventral catapult strop attachment hook
166 Leading edge false spar
167 Mainwheel leg door
168 Torque scissor links
169 Port mainwheel
170 60-lb (27-kg) ground attack rockets
171 Rocket launch rail
172 Gun camera pod
173 500-lb (227-kg) HE bomb

DE HAVILLAND D.H.110   UK

The D.H.110 was designed during 1946 to meet the requirements of the Royal Navy for an advanced carrier-based all-weather fighter (Specification N.40/46) and of the RAF for a night fighter (F.44/46). In 1949, orders were placed for seven night fighters and two long-range fighter prototypes for the RAF, and two night fighter and two strike fighter prototypes for the RN. The Naval version was later cancelled and the RAF order reduced to two (to Specification F.4/48) for economy reasons. The prototypes first flew on 26 September 1951 and 25 July 1952 respectively, powered by 7,500 lb st (3 402 kgp) Rolls-Royce Avon RA7 turbojets. The

The first of two prototypes of the D.H.110 night fighter in the configuration in which it first flew.

pilot occupied a single cockpit offset to port, with the observer alongside in the fuselage nacelle. Provision was made for radar in the nose and four 30-mm Aden cannon in the fuselage. After the loss of the first prototype and selection of the Gloster Javelin to meet the F.4/48 requirement, the second D.H.110 was modified to have an all-flying "slab" tailplane, variable gearing in the aileron and tailplane primary control circuits, reduced ventral fin area and cambered leading edge extensions outboard of the wing fences. *Max speed, 657 mph (1 057 km/h) at 10,000 ft (3 050 m). Loaded weight, approx 35,000 lb (15 876 kg). Span 51 ft 0 in (15,54 m). Length, 52 ft 1½ in (15,88 m). Height, 11 ft 0 in (3,35 m). Wing area, 648 sq ft (60,19 m²).*

DE HAVILLAND SEA VIXEN   UK

Royal Navy interest in the D.H.110 revived in 1952, and while the second prototype was used for preliminary deck landing trials, a new semi-navalised prototype was built as the Mk 20X, making its first flight on 20 June 1955. It was followed by the fully-navalised Sea Vixen FAW Mk 1 which had folding wings, revised tail unit, longer stroke undercarriage, new GEC radar, nosewheel steering, ejection seats, 11,230 lb st (5 094 kgp) Avon 208s, and armament of 28 × 2-in (5,08-cm) rockets in retractable packs in the nose, plus four Firestreak infra-red-homing air-to-air missiles, or rocket pods, or two 1,000-lb (454-kg) bombs on wing hard points. The first of 114 Sea Vixen FAW Mk 1s flew on 20 March 1957, and operational use began in July 1959. The Sea Vixen FAW Mk 2 differed in having extra fuel in forward extensions of the tailbooms and provision for Red Top AAMs in place of Firestreaks. Prototypes flew on 1 June and 17 August 1962, and were followed in 1963-66 by 29 new-production Mk 2s and 67 converted Mk 1s. Service use continued until 1972, after which a small number of Sea Vixens were converted to D Mk 3 pilotless drones for use as targets at the Aberforth range. *Data for Sea Vixen FAW Mk 2: Max speed, 690 mph (1 110 km/h) at sea level. Endurance, 3.2 hrs. Climb to 10,000 ft (3 050 m), 1.5 min, to 40,000 ft (12 200 m), 8.5 min. Service ceiling, 48,000 ft (14 630 m). Empty weight, 27,952 lb (12 679 kg). Normal loaded weight, 41,575 lb (18 858 kg). Span, 51 ft 0 in (15,54 m). Length, 55 ft 7 in (16,94 m). Height, 10 ft 9 in (3,28 m). Wing area, 648 sq ft (60,19 m²).*

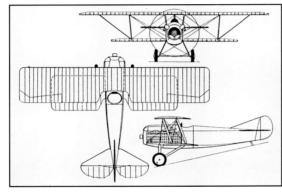

(Above) A Sea Vixen FAW Mk 1, with AAR probe fitted, and (below) the Sea Vixen FAW Mk 2, which had extra fuel capacity in the forward boom extensions.

A Sea Vixen FAW Mk 1 all-weather fighter in service with 890 NAS aboard HMS *Ark Royal* in 1964 (above).

DE MARÇAY 2   France

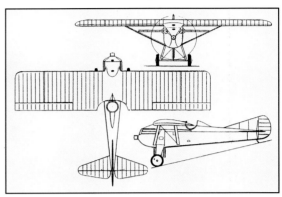

(Above and below) Powered by a 300 hp H-S 8Fb engine, the prototype de Marçay 2 flew in 1919.

During World War I, the SAECA Edmond de Marçay built substantial numbers of SPAD fighters under licence, and it was hardly surprising, therefore, that the first original de Marçay fighter should bear some resemblance to the SPAD S.XIII, although, in fact, there was no commonality between the aircraft. The initial design was based on the use of an eight-cylinder Liberty engine, but the difficulties experienced with this power plant led to revision of the design to take a 300 hp Hispano-Suiza 8Fb eight-cylinder water-cooled engine as the de Marçay 2 C1. An unequal-span staggered single-seat biplane with horn-balanced ailerons on the upper wing only and an armament of two synchronised 7,7-mm Vickers machine guns, the de Marçay 2 C1 was completed early in 1919. Although it was the fastest fighter participating in the 1919 *Service Aéronautique* contest held at Villacoublay, no production order was placed for the de Marçay 2 C1 and only one prototype was completed. *Max speed, 156 mph (252 km/h) at sea level, 144 mph (232 km/h) at 9,840 ft (3 000 m). Time to 16,405 ft (5 000 m), 16.27 min. Span, 30 ft 4⅛ in (9,25 m). Length 21 ft 8⅜ in (6,62 m). Wing area, 269.1 sq ft (25,00 m²).*

A Sea Vixen FAW Mk 2 (below) from NAS 766, the RN All-Weather Fighter Training unit at Yeovilton.

DE MARÇAY 4   France

The second fighter developed by the SAECA Edmond de Marçay was a single-seat shoulder-wing monoplane designed by engineers Botali and Lebeau to participate in the 1921 C1 programme. This, the de Marçay 4 C1, was of wooden construction with a thick wing of rectangular planform braced at three-fifths span by parallel struts and powered by a 300 hp Hispano-Suiza 8Fb eight-cylinder water-cooled engine with the radiator mounted *parallel* with the airflow, between the mainwheel legs. Armament comprised two synchronised

A single example of the de Marçay 4 (above and below) was built for the 1921 fighter contest in France, but was rejected on the score of pilot visibility.

7,7-mm Vickers machine guns. Built in five months and flown for the first time in 1923, the de Marçay 4 C1 was rejected primarily owing to the poor forward and downward visibility offered by the cockpit. *Max speed, 173 mph (279 km/h) at sea level. Empty weight, 1,786 lb (810 kg). Loaded weight, 2,535 lb (1 150 kg). Span, 32 ft 9⁷⁄₁₀ in (10,00 m). Length, 21 ft 11¾ in (6,70 m). Wing area, 215.28 sq ft (20,00 m²).*

DE MONGE M.101   France

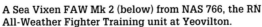

Louis de Monge's M.101 (above) was a derivative of the Koolhoven-designed NVI F.K.31.

The M.101 C2 two-seat fighter monoplane was a derivative of the NVI F.K.31 reconnaissance-fighter (which see) licence-built by Etablissements Louis de Monge and evaluated by the French *Service Technique* between October 1925 and January 1926 as part of the 1925 C2 (*biplace de chasse*) programme. Powered by a 420 hp Gnome-Rhône 9Ac Jupiter radial air-cooled engine, the M.101 C2 differed from the F.K.31 in several respects. The principal change was the adoption of a shorter-span wing, although proposed reconnaissance and bomber versions retained the F.K.31 span of 45 ft 1⅓ in (13,75 m). Proposed armament comprised two synchronised 7,5-mm Vickers guns in the engine cow-

ling, two Darne machine guns of the same calibre in the wing, and a Lewis gun on a flexible mounting in the rear cockpit. In the event, only the wing guns were installed. The STAé test report stressed the good manoeuvrability of the M.101 C2 for a two-seater – in direct contrast with the F.K.31 – and commended the handling qualities of the fighter, but criticised the lateral view offered the pilot in combat. No production orders were placed and Louis de Monge relinquished the manufacturing licence. *Max speed, 123 mph (198 km/h) at sea level, 122 mph (196 km/h) at 6,560 ft (2 000 m). Time to 6,560 ft (2 000 m), 8.1 min. Loaded weight, 4,048 lb (1 836 kg). Span, 37 ft 0¾ in (11,30 m). Length, 25 ft 7 in (7,80 m). Height, 11 ft 1⅞ in (3,40 m).*

DESCAMPS 27 — France

Formerly the chief engineer of the Anatra factory at Odessa in South Russia, Elisée Alfred Descamps returned to France after the Russian revolution and designed a single-seat fighter, the Descamps 27, which was flown for the first time in the spring of 1919. Powered by a 300 hp Hispano-Suiza 8Fb eight-cylinder water-cooled engine and carrying an armament of two synchronised 7,7-mm Vickers guns, the Descamps 27 was a two-bay biplane, but its configuration was unusual in that the lower wing featured pronounced forward sweep to improve the forward and downward view of the pilot. Twin box-like radiators flanked the cockpit. Although the fighter was found to have a good performance during official trials, choice fell on the similarly-powered Nieuport 29 and further development of the Descamps 27 was abandoned. *Max speed, 143 mph (230 km/h) at sea level, 107 mph (172 km/h) at 22,965 ft (7 000 m). Time to 6,560 ft (2 000 m), 4.76 min. Endurance, 2 hrs. Empty weight, 1,614 lb (732 kg). Loaded weight, 2,361 lb (1 071 kg). Span, 32 ft 3⅘ in (9,85 m). Length, 22 ft 9⅝ in (6,95 m). Height, 8 ft 5¼ in (2,57 m). Wing area, 248.65 sq ft (23,10 m²).*

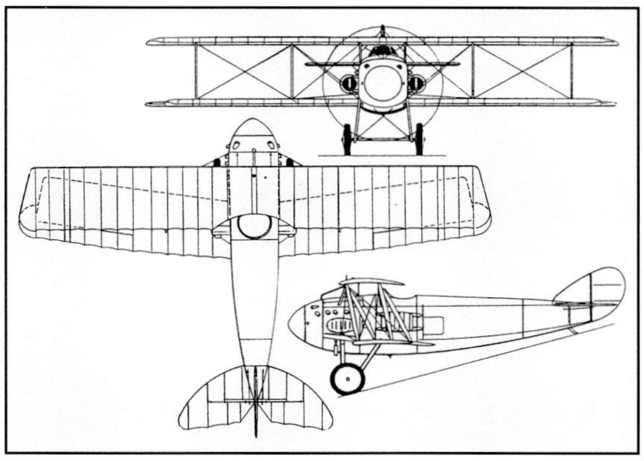

Featuring lower-wing forward sweep and built in 1919, the Descamps 27 (above and below) was bested by the Nieuport 29 in the official trials.

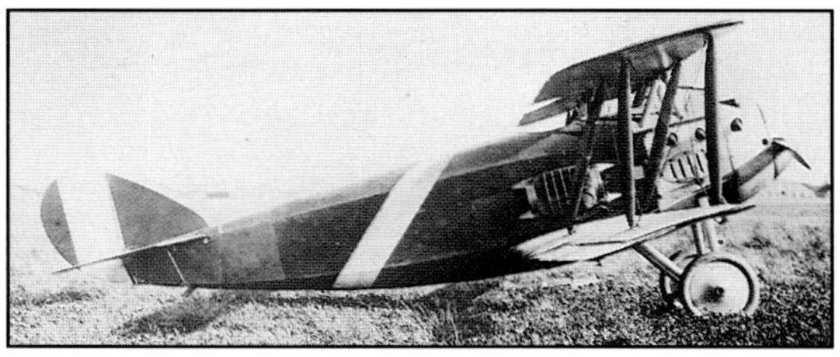

DEWOITINE D 1 — France

Conceived by Émile Dewoitine to participate in the 1921 C1 (single-seat fighter) programme, the D 1 high-wing monoplane was of advanced structural concept. It mated fabric-covered metal wings with an oval-section metal fuselage covered by duralumin sheet. Armament consisted of two 7,7-mm synchronised Vickers guns and power was provided by a 300 hp Hispano-Suiza 8Fb (HS 42) eight-cylinder water-cooled engine. The prototype was flown on 18 November 1922, the principal criticism being the poor forward visibility for the pilot. A 4.75-in (120-mm) pylon was therefore inserted between wing and fuselage, the fighter, now referred to as the D 1bis, thus becoming a parasol monoplane. This modification was effected in August 1923, by which time the first three (of 10) pre-series aircraft had been supplied for official evaluation in the initial configuration. Two of these were lost in accidents and the third was modified to D 1bis parasol form. The next five pre-series aircraft (the fourth, fifth and sixth having been ordered by Czechoslovakia, Japan and Italy respectively, and the seventh and eighth by Switzerland) were all completed to D 1bis standard, but continuing criticism of forward view led to replacement of the shallow pylon between wing and fuselage by a cabane of inverted-vee struts on the prototype which thus became the D 1ter. The two pre-series aircraft for Switzerland were modified to this standard prior to delivery,

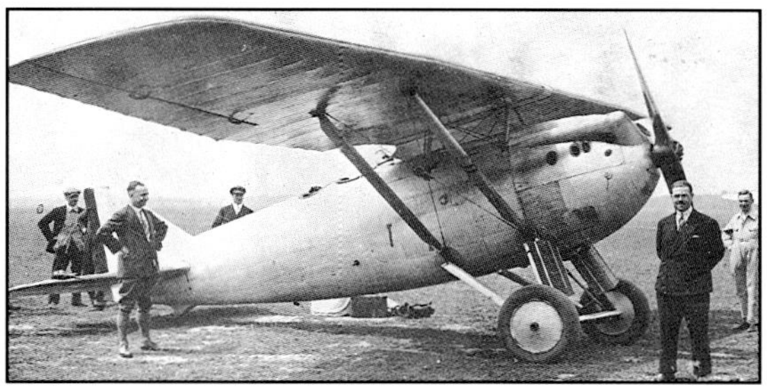

(Below) The Dewoitine D 1 in its production form and (above) a D 1ter adapted as a two-seater.

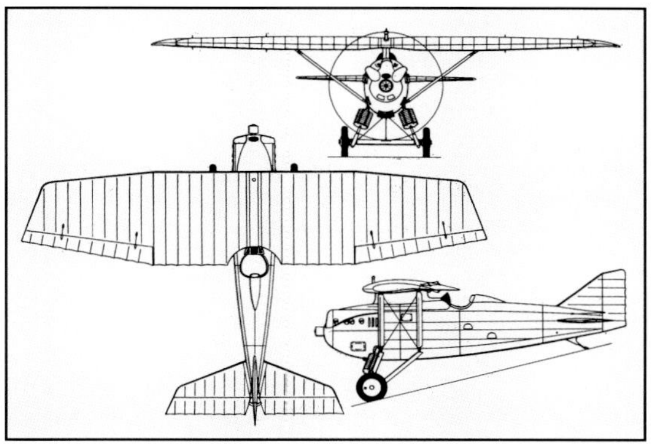

and the last two pre-series aircraft (replacements for the two lost during official trials) were completed as D 1ter fighters, the cabane struts being standardised for production D 1s. A contract had been placed in November 1923 on behalf of the *Aéronautique Navale* for 44 D 1s, with the government providing guarantees for 150 aircraft. The production contract was placed with the SECM (Société d'Emboutissage et de Constructions Mécaniques) which flew its first series D 1 on 18 January 1925. Sixty (later reduced to 44) were ordered by Yugoslavia, and after the D 1 was selected by Italy in preference to the Dornier Do H Falke, licence manufacture (with modifications) was undertaken by the Ansaldo A.C.2 (which see). The *Aéronautique Navale* took delivery of its D 1s from early 1925, and in the previous year an order for 20 had been placed on behalf of the *Forces Aériennes Terrestres*, although these were never to equip a service unit. *Max speed, 153 mph (247 km/h) at sea level, 155 mph (250 km/h) at 6,560 ft (2 000 m). Max climb, 1,476 ft/min (7,5 m/sec). Range, 248 mls (400 km). Empty weight, 1,808 lb (820 kg).*

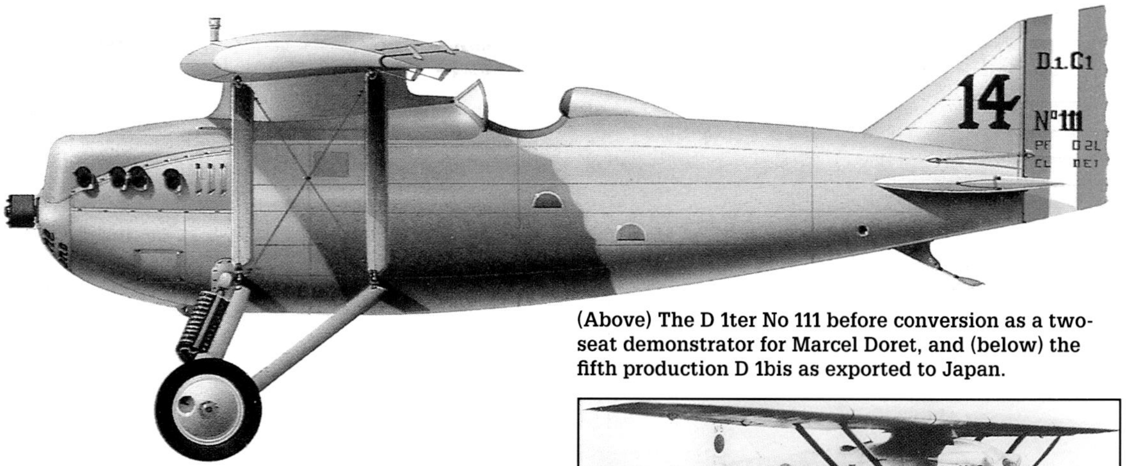

(Above) The D 1ter No 111 before conversion as a two-seat demonstrator for Marcel Doret, and (below) the fifth production D 1bis as exported to Japan.

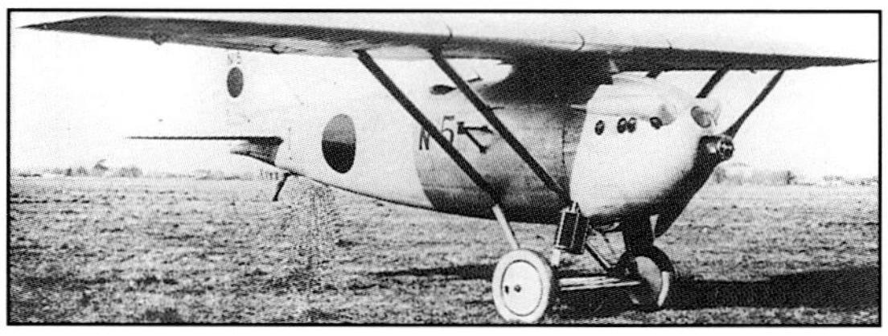

Loaded weight, 2,734 lb (1 240 kg). Span, 37 ft 8¾ in (11,50 m). Length, 24 ft 7¼ in (7,50 m). Height, 9 ft 0 in (2,75 m). Wing area, 215.28 sq ft (20,00 m²).

DEWOITINE D 8 — France

In the autumn of 1922, Dewoitine submitted to the CEDANA (Commission d'Examen des Appareils Nouveaux pour l'Aéronautique) a high-altitude version of the D 1 (which had then still to fly) designated D 8. One category of fighter in the 1921 C1 programme called for a speed of 149 mph (240 km/h) at 22,965 ft (7 000 m) and a practical ceiling of at least 27,885 ft (8 500 m). After discarding the proposal to equip the D 8 with a Rateau turbo-compressor, Dewoitine adopted a higher compression Hispano-Suiza engine, the 8Fe with a nominal rating of 360 hp. A larger wing of wooden rather than metal construction was introduced and the prototype was rolled out in the late summer of 1923. At Francazal the D 8 attained an altitude of 6,560 ft (2 000 m) in 4.25 min, 9,840 ft (3 000 m) in 6.83 min, 13,125 ft (4 000 m) in 10.5 min and 16,405 ft (5 000 m) in 15.1 min. For publicity purposes this performance was erroneously attributed contemporaneously to the D 1 fighter. The C1 requirement for a high-altitude fighter had meanwhile been abandoned, and, in June 1924, the D 8 was modified for an attempt on the world air speed record, being fitted with a lightened version of the D 1 wing. On 23 December 1924, the D 8 established 100-, 200- and 500-km closed-circuit records while being flown by Marcel Doret, and, on 12 December, set a 1 000-km (621-mile) closed-circuit record of 137.8 mph (221,775 km/h). The following data relate to the D 8 in its original form. *Max speed, 152 mph (245 km/h) at 6,560 ft (2 000 m). Time to 6,560 ft (2 000 m), 4.25 min. Empty weight, 1,720 lb (780 kg). Loaded weight, 2,425 lb (1 100 kg). Span, 41 ft 11⅞ in (12,80 m). Length, 24 ft 7¼ in (7,50 m). Height, 9 ft 0 in (2,75 m). Wing area, 269.11 sq ft (25,00 m²).*

The D 8 (below) was a high-altitude version of the D 1, with larger wing and high compression engine.

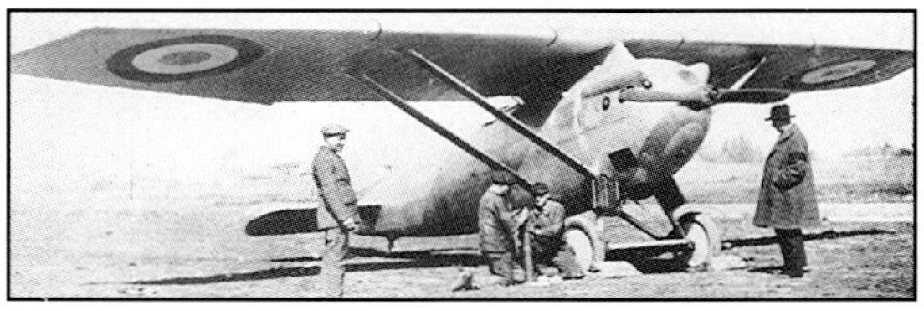

DEWOITINE D 9 — France

Flown in June 1924, the D 9 was derived from the D 1 for participation in the 1923 C1 programme and was powered by a 420 hp Gnome-Rhône 9Ab (Jupiter IV) nine-cylinder radial engine. Early in the flight test programme, the standard D 1 wing was supplanted by a new wing of 26.9 sq ft (2,5 m²) greater area, and a six-month delay in the commencement of evaluation of the contenders in the 1923 C1 programme provided Dewoi-

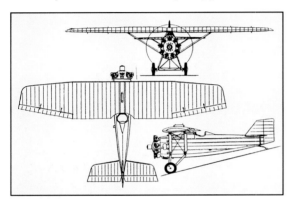

(Below) The Dewoitine D 9 derivative of the D 1 with enlarged wing and (above) one of three D 9s assembled in 1928 by EKW for the Swiss *Fliegertruppe*.

tine with the opportunity to increase wing area by yet a further 26.9 sq ft (2,5 m²). Armament consisted of two fuselage-mounted 7,7-mm Vickers guns and two Darne *modèle* 19 guns of 7,5-mm calibre mounted on the wing centre section. The D 9, placed sixth among the contenders, was destroyed on 15 October 1925. Nonetheless, it emulated the export success of the D 1. Licence-built in Italy by Ansaldo as the A.C.3 (which see), the D 9 was supplied to Yugoslavia (six) and Belgium (one) in 1925, and the components of three others were delivered in 1927 to the EKW (Eidg. Konstruktions-Werkstätte) in Switzerland for assembly, with delivery to the *Fliegertruppe* in 1928. *Max speed, 152 mph (244 km/h) at sea level, 142 mph (229 km/h) at 16,405 ft (5 000 m). Max climb, 1,713 ft/min (8,7 m/sec). Range, 248 mls (400 km). Empty weight, 2,083 lb (945 kg). Loaded weight, 2,939 lb (1 333 kg). Span, 41 ft 11⅞ in (12,80 m). Length, 23 ft 10⅔ in (7,30 m). Height, 9 ft 7⅓ in (2,93 m). Wing area, 269.1 sq ft (25,00 m²).*

DEWOITINE D 12   France

Evolved in parallel with the D 9 as a contender in the 1923 C1 programme, in which it was eventually to take third place after the Nieuport-Delage 42 and the Gourdou-Leseurre 32, the D 12 differed essentially in engine type. Possessing a basically similar fuselage to that of the D 1, the D 12 was powered by a 450 hp Lorraine-Dietrich 12EW 12-cylinder W-type water-cooled engine. First flown, like the D 9, in June 1924, the D 12 had an armament of two 7,7-mm Vickers guns, and, in Septem-

(Below) Second of two prototypes of the D 12 with a Lorraine-Dietrich 12E W-type engine.

ber, was fitted with a higher compression ratio 12Eb engine and a pair of 7,5-mm Darne *modèle* 19 guns on the wing centre section. The paired Lamblin radiators on the undercarriage legs gave place to a frontal radiator and a wing similar to that finally adopted on the D 9 was fitted. On 5 February 1926, the D 12 was written off in an accident at Cazaux. A second prototype had meanwhile entered flight test, having flown at the end of 1925, this having a W-type Hispano-Suiza 12Gb engine, but further development was discontinued. *Max speed, 148 mph (239 km/h) at 3,280 ft (1 000 m), 145 mph (233 km/h) at 16,405 ft (5 000 m). Time to 16,405 ft (5 000 m), 14.2 min. Empty weight, 2,359 lb (1 070 kg). Loaded weight, 3,607 lb (1 636 kg). Span, 41 ft 11⅞ in (12,80 m). Length, 24 ft 11¼ in (7,60 m). Height, 9 ft 10⅛ in (3,00 m). Wing area, 269.1 sq ft (25,00 m²).*

DEWOITINE D 15   France

The sole single-seat fighter of biplane configuration to be built by Émile Dewoitine, the D 15 was proposed as a simpler and more economic (from the structural viewpoint) fighter than the contemporary D 9, D 12 and D 19 monoplanes. Powered by a 450 hp Hispano-Suiza 12Ha (HS 51) 12-cylinder liquid-cooled Vee engine, the D 15 had fabric-covered metal wings with ailerons on the upper wing only, the metal fuselage being of steel longeron and duralumin tube cross-member construction with fabric-covered sides and light metal upper and lower decking. Armament comprised two fuselage-mounted 7,7-mm Vickers guns and two 7,5-mm Darne guns mounted on the upper wing centre section. Flown on 13 August 1924, the D 15 displayed inadequate longitudinal and lateral stability, and, after modification, proved to possess a markedly inferior per-

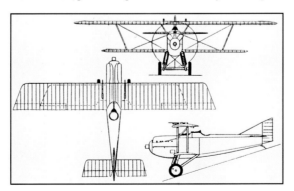

(Above and below) Dewoitine's only biplane fighter, the D 15 progressed no further than a prototype.

formance to the lower-powered D 19 monoplane during CEPA (*Commission des Essais Pratiques de l'Aviation*) testing at Villacoublay during the autumn of 1924. In consequence, it was not submitted for STAé evaluation of 1923 C1 programme contenders held in 1925-26. *Empty weight, 2,293 lb (1 040 kg). Loaded weight, 3,384 lb (1 535 kg). Span, 39 ft 4½ in (12,00 m). Length, 24 ft 3⅓ in (7,40 m). Height, 11 ft 7⅓ in (3,54 m). Wing area, 322.92 sq ft (30,00 m²).*

DEWOITINE D 19   France

Another variant of the D 1 developed in response to the C1 programme of 1923, the D 19 appeared in the summer of 1925 with a 400 hp Hispano-Suiza 12Jb 12-cylinder water-cooled Vee-type engine. By comparison with the D 1, the D 19 had longer span, narrower chord ailerons and a wing spanning 41 ft 0 in (12,50 m) with an area of 258.34 sq ft (24,00 m²). Demonstrated in Switzerland in August 1925, the D 19 received a new wing of 269.1 sq ft (25,00 m²) similar to that of the D 9 and D 12 before CEPA testing, in which performance proved mediocre owing to mismatching of the propeller. Three examples of a modified version of the D 19 were ordered by the Swiss government. Specified armament comprised two fuselage-mounted 7,7-mm guns, the paired Lamblin radiators mounted on the undercarriage legs gave place to a Chausson frontal radiator and a wing similar to that of the D 1 was

The first of three Swiss D 19s (above) showing the frontal radiator of this version.

adopted. A second D 19 prototype was completed with these modifications, this being sold in 1928 to Belgium, and the first Swiss aircraft was ferried to the EKW (Eidg. Konstruktions-Werkstätte) in March 1926. The two other Swiss aircraft were transported to Switzerland in February 1927 for assembly by the EKW, subsequently entering service with the *Fliegertruppe*. The three D 19s participated in the 1927 Zurich-Dübendorf international aviation meeting, one being winner of the closed-circuit race for fighters with a speed of 155 mph (250 km/h). Used primarily for combat training by the *Fliegertruppe*, one D 19 was lost in 1930, and the remaining two continued in service until 1940. The following data relate to the Swiss D 19. *Max speed, 166 mph (268 km/h) at sea level, 163 mph (262 km/h) at 6,560 ft (2 000 m). Max climb, 2,047 ft/min (10,4 m/sec). Range, 248 mls (400 km). Empty weight, 2,160 lb (980 kg). Loaded weight, 3,064 lb (1 390 kg). Span, 35 ft 5¼ in (10,80 m). Length, 25 ft 9¾ in (7,87 m). Height, 11 ft 5¾ in (3,50 m). Wing area, 215.28 sq ft (20,00 m²).*

DEWOITINE D 21   France

At the end of 1925, the second prototype D 12 single-seat fighter was re-engined with a 500 hp Hispano-Suiza 12Gb (HS 50) 12-cylinder W-type water-cooled engine and redesignated D 21. Intended essentially for export, the D 21 was first demonstrated in January 1926 at Bruxelles-Evère. The first export contract came from Turkey, this calling for two D 21s for evaluation. Czechoslovakia ordered three and Argentina procured 18, plus the prototype. Of these, the three Czech aircraft and seven of the Argentine aircraft were assembled by the EKW in Switzerland. A manufacturing licence was obtained by Czechoslovakia, Škoda building 26 D 21s during 1928-29 (as Škoda D 1s) with Škoda L engines (derived from the HS 12G) of 562 hp. Argentina also procured a manufacturing licence and the *Fabrica Militar de Aviones* (FMA) built 40 examples during 1930-31, but with Madsen machine guns and the licence-built Lorraine-Dietrich 12Eb W-type engine. They thus be-

came effectively D 12s, although the designation D 21 was retained. In the autumn of 1927, Turkey placed a follow-on order for 10 D 21s, these being delivered during 1928-29. *Max speed, 168 mph (270 km/h) at sea level, 163 mph (262 km/h) at 6,560 ft (2 000 m). Max climb, 1,968 ft/min (10,0 m/sec). Empty weight, 2,403 lb (1 090 kg). Loaded weight, 3,483 lb (1 580 kg). Span, 40 ft 11⅞ in (12,80 m). Length, 25 ft 0¾ in (7,64 m). Height, 9 ft 10⅛ in (3,00 m). Wing area, 266.95 sq ft (24,80 m²).*

The FMA-built D 21 (below) was to all intents equivalent to the earlier Dewoitine D 12.

DEWOITINE D 25   France

The ultimate development of the fighter formula initiated by the Dewoitine D 1 was the D 25 tandem two-seat day and night fighter also suitable for diurnal reconnaissance tasks. Developed in response to the 1925 C2 (two-seat fighter) programme, the D 25 was based on the single-seat D 21 with local reinforcement of the aft fuselage to permit installation of an open turret for a gunner. Powered by a 450 hp Lorraine-Dietrich 12Eb water-cooled W-type engine, the D 25 entered flight test in 1926, but the C2 programme for which it was intended was abandoned and the type was offered for export. Four were ordered by Argentina in 1928, and these, fitted with an armament of two 7,9-mm synchronised Madsen guns and two similar weapons on a ring mount in the rear cockpit, were built under subcontract by the Hanriot company (which also built the last 10 D 21 single-seaters for Turkey). *Max speed, 138 mph (222 km/h) at 3,280 ft (1 000 m). Endurance, 2.0 hrs. Empty weight, 2,606 lb (1 182 kg). Loaded weight, 3,858 lb (1 750 kg). Span, 40 ft 11⅞ in (12,80 m). Length, 25 ft 0¾ in (7,64 m). Height, 9 ft 10⅛ in (3,00 m). Wing area, 266.95 sq ft (24,80 m²).*

One of the four two-seat D 25s purchased in 1928 for use by Argentina's *Servicio de Aviación Militar*.

DEWOITINE D 27 (Switzerland) France

The design that took Émile Dewoitine's parasol fighter formula to the apex of its development was the D 27, which was evolved to meet the requirements of the STAé 1926 C1 *léger* programme for lightweight

fighters. Adhering closely to the structural concept of preceding fighters, but embodying much aerodynamic refinement and a split-axle (with independently articulated wheels) rather than cross-axle undercarriage, the D 27 was powered by the 500 hp Hispano-Suiza 12Mb (HS 57) 12-cylinder Vee engine and had an armament of two synchronised 7,7-mm guns. The liquidation of the Construction Aéronautique E Dewoitine in January 1927 resulted in the transfer of development of the D 27 to the EKW in Switzerland, where a prototype flew on 3 June 1928. By the end of the year, three had been ordered by Romania, one by Argentina and three by Yugoslavia (of which two were to be delivered as assemblies for completion by Zmaj at Zemun), and the prototype was undergoing evaluation by the Swiss *Fliegertruppe* in competition with Alfred Comte's AC-1. In the autumn of 1928, the EKW initiated a pre-series of 12 D 27 fighters, these adopting a redesigned tail and a revised wing of 4.84 sq ft (0.45 m²) less area, modifications first tested in the Laboratoire Eiffel wind tunnel. Meanwhile, in March 1928, Émile Dewoitine had re-established himself in France, forming the Société Aéronautique Française-Avions Dewoitine. The second and third pre-series D 27s were delivered to France in April 1929, the former being re-engined with the 400 hp HS 12Jb as the D 272 for aerobatic demonstrations, and the latter undergoing STAé evaluation at Villacoublay from 28 May equipped with two 7,7-mm Darne guns. On 29 November 1929, a contract was issued by France's DGT (*Direction Générale Technique*) of the *Ministère de l'Air* for the second and third pre-series aircraft plus three (later increased to four) additional fighters to be assembled by Lioré-et-Olivier.

(Above) A D 27 III in service with *Fliegerkompagnie* 19 of the Swiss *Fliegertruppe* at Dübendorf, 1939.

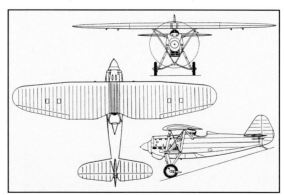

(Above) The series Dewoitine D 27. (Below) One of the final batch of D 27 IIIs built in Switzerland in 1932.

The D 27 was offered to the *Forces Aériennes Terrestres* as the D 271 with the 500 hp HS 12Hb engine and as the D 273 with a Gnome-Rhône Jupiter VII with a compressor enabling 425 hp to be delivered at 13,125 ft (4 000 m), but neither model was adopted. At the end of 1929, however, the decision was taken in principle to re-equip the fighter element of the Swiss *Fliegertruppe* with the D 27, a pre-series of five being ordered from the EKW as D 27 IIIs, with deliveries commencing in 1931. A pre-production batch of 15 followed, additional contracts being placed for 45 D 27 IIIs to bring deliveries to the *Fliegertruppe* to 66 (including the prototype). These remained first-line fighter equipment until 1940, when they were relegated to tuitional tasks, being finally scrapped in 1944. The following data relate to the Swiss D 27 III. *Max speed, 185 mph (298 km/h) at sea level, 174 mph (280 km/h) at 16,405 ft (5 000 m). Max climb, 1,968 ft/min (10 m/sec). Range, 264 mls (425 km). Empty weight, 2,288 lb (1 038 kg). Loaded weight, 3,120 lb (1 415 kg). Span, 33 ft 9½ in (10,30 m). Length, 21 ft 6¼ in (6,56 m). Height, 9 ft 1½ in (2,78 m). Wing area, 188.91 sq ft (17,55 m²).*

DEWOITINE D 53   France

The fifth D 53 (above) was fitted with an HS 12Mb engine to become one of the three D 531s.

Following the loss, at the end of July 1930, of the first pre-series D 27 as a result of a wing structural failure, a substantially reinforced wing structure was designed to meet new requirements imposed by France's *Service Technique*. Émile Dewoitine had, at this time, been assured by the *Ministère de l'Air* of an order for 90 D 27 fighters with reinforced wings, although this was not, in the event, to be confirmed. The structural changes were accompanied by a change in designation from D 27 to D 53, the first reinforced wing being completed on 27 February 1931, and this being applied by Lioré-et-Olivier to D 27 No 14 to produce the D 530 which flew at the end of the following month. The D 530 was powered by an Hispano-Suiza 12Md, a lightened version of the HS 12Mb (HS 57) engine of 500 hp. The HS 12Md was not acceptable to the STAé, the second, third and fifth D 53 series fighters therefore being fitted with the standard HS 12Mb as D 531s for official evaluation. Weighing 3,130 lb (1 420 kg), these recorded maximum

Fourth in the D 53 series, the D 532 (above) was powered by a R-R Kestrel, whereas the D 535 (below) was fitted with an Hispano-Suiza 12Xbrs.

speeds of 167 mph (269 km/h) at sea level and 160 mph (258 km/h) at 16,405 ft (5 000 m) during trials at Villacoublay. In August 1931, the Turkish government expressed interest in the D 53 and was offered versions with either the compressor-equipped Škoda Lr engine of 580 hp or the Curtiss V-1570 Conqueror of 600 hp. The fourth D 53 series fighter prototype flown in the autumn of 1931 was the D 532 with a compressor-equipped Rolls-Royce Kestrel engine. This attained 194 mph (313 km/h) at 13,125 ft (4 000 m), climbing to that altitude in 6.9 min, but excessive oscillation of the tail led to discontinuation of flight testing and re-engining with an HS 12Mb engine as the D 534 LP. Flown in April 1932, the D 535 was equipped with a 500 hp HS 12Xbrs engine, this becoming the D 536 when fitted with a Farman compressor which raised the output of the HS 12Xbrs engine to 570 hp at 19,030 ft (5 800 m). In July 1933, a twin-float fighter version of the D 535 was offered to Peru, which, in the event, procured Nieuport-Delage 123s. Only seven D 53 series aircraft were flown of which two D 531s allegedly found their way to Republican Spain during the Civil War, becoming known as *Dewoitinillos* or *Dewoitine pequeños* (little Dewoitines) to distinguish them from D 371s (which see). The dimensions of the D 53 series were similar to those of the D 27.

DEWOITINE D 370   France

Transferred by the SAF-Avions Dewoitine to the Lioré-et-Olivier (LeO) concern owing to the workload imposed on the parent company by the D 50bis (future D 500), the D 37 (later D 370) was a private venture contender in the 1930 C1 programme. The prototype, flown on 1 October 1931, was powered by a 700 hp Gnome-Rhône 14Kbrs Mistral Major 14-cylinder two-row radial. It was subsequently subjected to an extensive series of modifications: a G-R 14Kbs engine gave place, in turn, to a G-R 14Kds affording 800 hp for take-off and 740 hp at 14,765 ft (4 500 m); the engine cowling was changed; the undercarriage was redesigned, and the wing introduced dihedral and reduced chord. Yet more

The Dewoitine D 371 with Gnome-Rhône 14Kds engine.

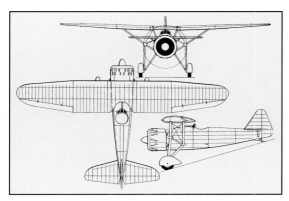

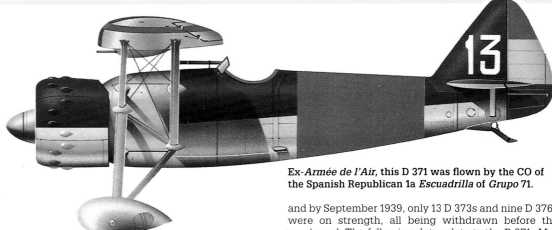

redesign was embodied by a second prototype, the D 371, which appeared late February 1934. Twenty-eight D 371s were ordered for the *Armée de l'Air* with the G-R 14Kfs engine of 930 hp for take-off and 880 hp at 10,665 ft (3 250 m), and an armament of four underwing 7,5-mm MAC 34 machine guns. Fourteen were ordered by Lithuania, and these, having two synchronised 7,7-mm Browning guns in the fuselage and two Darne guns of similar calibre in the wings, were designated D 372s. Twenty were ordered for the *Aéronautique Navale* as D 373s, these having flotation gear, an 11.8-in (30-cm) reduction in wing span and an armament of four Darne guns *within* the wing. A further 25 ordered for this service with aft-folding wings were designated as D 376s. The last D 371 left the factory at the end of December 1935, the *Armée de l'Air* fighters following the Navy's D 373s. The Lithuanian government meanwhile relinquished its D 372s in favour of D 501s, the former being sold to the Spanish Republican government and ferried to Spain during August 1936, where they were later joined by 10 of the 28 *Armée de l'Air* D 371s. The remaining D 371s equipped an *escadrille* at Bizerte, Tunis, until 1939, but were little flown owing to constant problems with their engines. The D 373s and D 376s of the *Aéronautique Navale* suffered similarly,

As first flown, the D 37 (above) bore little resemblance to the D 371, an example of which (below) is seen in Spanish Republican service in November 1937.

Ex-*Armée de l'Air*, this D 371 was flown by the CO of the Spanish Republican 1a *Escuadrilla* of *Grupo* 71.

and by September 1939, only 13 D 373s and nine D 376s were on strength, all being withdrawn before the year's end. The following data relate to the D 371. *Max speed, 236 mph (380 km/h) at 14,435 ft (4 400 m). Time to 3,280 ft (1 000 m), 1.4 min. Max range, 559 mls (900 km). Empty equipped weight, 2,910 lb (1 320 kg). Loaded weight, 4,153 lb (1 884 kg). Span, 36 ft 9¾ in (11,22 m). Length, 24 ft 3⅞ in (7,44 m). Height, 11 ft 1¾ in (3,40 m). Wing area, 187.83 sq ft (17,45 m²).*

Ex-Lithuanian D 372 (below) with the Spanish Republicans, probably at Manises, Valencia, in 1937.

DEWOITINE D 500   France

The first Dewoitine fighter monoplane to relinquish the parasol configuration in favour of a low-wing layout, the D 500 flew on 18 June 1932. Intended to meet the demands of the 1930 C1 programme and eventually selected as winning contender, the D 500 was powered by a 12-cylinder Vee Hispano-Suiza 12Xbrs (HS 72) engine rated at 660 hp for take-off and 690 hp at 13,125 ft (4 000 m). Armament comprised two 7,7-mm Vickers guns in the fuselage, these later being supplanted by 7,5-mm Darne guns with provision for two similar wing-mounted weapons. At the end of November 1933, orders were placed for 60 D 500s of which 45 were to be built by Lioré-et-Olivier and 15 by SAF-Avions Dewoitine. Of the former, 40 were to be powered by the HS 12Xbrs engine and the remaining five by the HS 12Xcrs (HS 76) with provision for a 20-mm Hispano-Suiza S7 (Oerlikon) cannon mounted between the cylinder banks. With this installation and twin wing-mounted machine guns the fighter was desig-

(Above) The first production D 500 (N° 47) actually built by the parent SAF-Avions Dewoitine, and (below), D 501 N° 250 serving with *Escadrille* 3C3.

nated D 501. The SAF-Avions Dewoitine order was eventually to comprise eight D 500s, five D 501s and two D 510s (which see). The first production D 500 was flown on 29 November 1934, contracts having meanwhile been placed for a further 50 D 500s and 80 D 501s to be built by Lioré-et-Olivier and 60 D 501s by Ateliers et Chantiers de la Loire, deliveries to the *Armée de l'Air* commencing May-June 1935. Three D 500s were ordered by Venezuela at the beginning of 1934 and delivered in July 1935, and in the following year 14 D 501s were supplied to Lithuania. The *Armée de l'Air* received 100 D 500s and 133 D 501s, 30 of the latter type also being supplied to shore-based elements of France's *Aéronautique Navale*. Small numbers of D 500s and D 501s equipped *Escadrilles Régionale de Chasse* in the early months of World War II, but had been relegated to tuitional tasks by 1940. The following data relate to the D 501. *Max speed, 196 mph (315 km/h) at sea level, 288 mph (367 km/h) at 16,405 ft (5 000 m). Time to 3,280 ft (1 000 m), 1.35 min. Range, 540 mls (870 km). Empty weight, 2,837 lb (1 287 kg). Normal loaded weight, 3,940 lb (1 787 kg). Span, 39 ft 8 in (12,09 m). Length, 24 ft 9⅝ in (7,56 m). Height, 8 ft 10⅓ in (2,70 m). Wing area, 177.6 sq ft (16,50 m²).*

The D 500 N° 75 (above) serving in a *Centre d'Instruction à la Chasse* at Toulouse in 1940.

DEWOITINE D 560   France

Aware of some prejudice against the low-wing monoplane configuration for single-seat fighters, Émile Dewoitine evolved almost simultaneously with the low-wing D 500 a fighter of shoulder-mounted gull wing configuration. This employed the same HS 12Xbrs engine of 660 hp for take-off, the same fuselage and essentially similar tail surfaces. Designated D 560, this fighter flew for the first time on 5 October 1932, proving to be somewhat slower at rated altitude than the equivalent low-wing monoplane when flown at the

Centre d'Essais at Villacoublay during the following month. The ventral radiator bath was extended forward in similar fashion to that of the D 500, and to rectify a stability problem the vertical tail was enlarged. The manoeuvrability of the D 560 proved outstanding, but evaluation pilots participating in the 1930 C1 programme universally condemned the gulled wing (which was also featured by other contenders – the Loire 43, the Gourdou-Leseurre 482 and the Mureaux 170). As a consequence, the D 560 was rebuilt as a classic parasol monoplane, the designation being changed to D 570 (which see). *Max speed, 183 mph (295 km/h) at sea level, 233 mph (375 km/h) at 14,765 ft (4 500 m). Time to 35,105 ft (10 700 m), 29.25 min. Empty weight, 2,800 lb (1 270 kg). Loaded weight, 3,743 lb (1 698 kg). Span, 40 ft 11 in (12,47 m). Length, 27 ft 10 in (8,48 m). Height, 11 ft 3 in (3,42 m). Wing area, 186.22 sq ft (17,30 m²).*

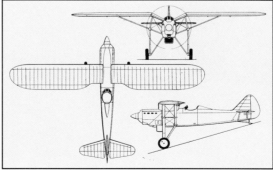

The gull-winged D 560 (above and below) was a contemporary of Dewoitine's low-wing D 500.

DEWOITINE D 570   France

At the end of March 1933, criticism of the gulled wing of the D 560 led Émile Dewoitine to replace this with a wing of classic parasol form and of marginally reduced span and area. Re-designated D 570, the modified prototype entered flight test on 27 November 1933, transferring from Francazal to the *Centre d'Essais* at Villacoublay early in December. It flew back to Francazal for minor modifications, and, on 21 December, while returning to Villacoublay, suffered an aileron failure and was destroyed. *Max speed, 182 mph (293 km/h) at sea level, 210 mph (338 km/h) at 14,765 ft (4 500 m). Empty weight, 2,831 lb (1 284 kg). Loaded weight, 3,768 lb (1 709 kg). Span, 37 ft 11⁹⁄₁₀ in (11,58 m). Length, 28 ft 0 in (8,53 m). Height, 11 ft 3 in (3,42 m). Wing area, 182.99 sq ft (17,00 m²).*

Rebuilt as a parasol monoplane (below), the D 560 was eventually redesignated as the D 570.

DEWOITINE D 510   France

Two of the 15 D 500 series aircraft (the second and tenth) comprising the initial production contract for the new low-wing fighter monoplane placed with SAF-Avions Dewoitine were fitted with the Hispano-Suiza 12Ycrs (HS 77) engine as prototypes for the D 510. Heavier and longer than the HS 12Xcrs (HS 76) of the standard D 501 fighter, the HS 12Ycrs similarly catered for a 20-mm cannon between its cylinder banks, and was rated at 775 hp at sea level and 860 hp at 13,125 ft (4 000 m). The first of the D 510 prototypes flew (without the cannon fitted) on 14 August 1934, the second (with cannon) following on 10 December. Apart from engine, the D 510 was fundamentally similar to the D 501, the cannon being complemented by a pair of 7,5-mm wing guns. In May 1935, the *Ministère de l'Air* placed an initial contract for 35 (later reduced to 25) D 510s, these being delivered from 9 October 1936. Seven more D 510s were then built for the *Armée de l'Air* as agreed replacements for a similar number of D 501s taken from the service's deliveries as part of the Lithuanian order. Follow-on contracts then called for a total of 80 more aircraft from which a contract for 24 D 510s from the Chinese Central Government was to be fulfilled. Other export D 510s were single examples to the UK and the Soviet Union, and two to Japan for evaluation purposes, and two, unofficially, to Republican Spain. These last had been the first two of a cancelled contract for Turkey and were ostensibly sold to the Hedjaz (Saudi Arabia). When it was revealed that the two D 510s had arrived in Spain, the French government insisted that their engines be returned to France. Eventually, both aircraft were fitted with M-100 (licence-built HS 12Ybrs) engines from a Tupolev SB bomber and allegedly saw some combat. Three

D 510 N° 317 (below) with the *Escadrille Régionale de Protection* at Caen-Carpiquet, March 1940.

DEWOITINE

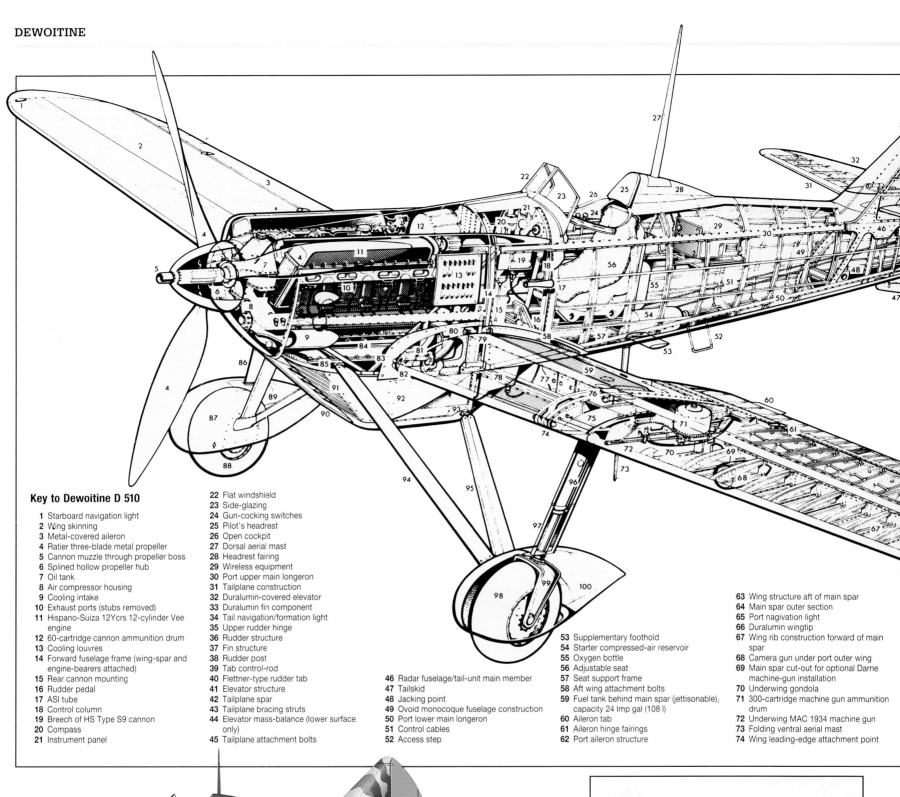

Key to Dewoitine D 510

1 Starboard navigation light
2 Wing skinning
3 Metal-covered aileron
4 Ratier three-blade metal propeller
5 Cannon muzzle through propeller boss
6 Splined hollow propeller hub
7 Oil tank
8 Air compressor housing
9 Cooling intake
10 Exhaust ports (stubs removed)
11 Hispano-Suiza 12Ycrs 12-cylinder Vee engine
12 60-cartridge cannon ammunition drum
13 Cooling louvres
14 Forward fuselage frame (wing-spar and engine-bearers attached)
15 Rear cannon mounting
16 Rudder pedal
17 ASI tube
18 Control column
19 Breech of HS Type S9 cannon
20 Compass
21 Instrument panel

22 Flat windshield
23 Side-glazing
24 Gun-cocking switches
25 Pilot's headrest
26 Open cockpit
27 Dorsal aerial mast
28 Headrest fairing
29 Wireless equipment
30 Port upper main longeron
31 Tailplane construction
32 Duralumin-covered elevator
33 Duralumin fin component
34 Tail navigation/formation light
35 Upper rudder hinge
36 Rudder structure
37 Fin structure
38 Rudder post
39 Tab control-rod
40 Flettner-type rudder tab
41 Elevator structure
42 Tailplane spar
43 Tailplane bracing struts
44 Elevator mass-balance (lower surface only)
45 Tailplane attachment bolts

46 Radar fuselage/tail-unit main member
47 Tailskid
48 Jacking point
49 Ovoid monocoque fuselage construction
50 Port lower main longeron
51 Control cables
52 Access step
53 Supplementary foothold
54 Starter compressed-air reservoir
55 Oxygen bottle
56 Adjustable seat
57 Seat support frame
58 Aft wing attachment bolts
59 Fuel tank behind main spar (jettisonable), capacity 24 Imp gal (108 l)
60 Aileron tab
61 Aileron hinge fairings
62 Port aileron structure

63 Wing structure aft of main spar
64 Main spar outer section
65 Port nagivation light
66 Duralumin wingtip
67 Wing rib construction forward of main spar
68 Camera gun under port outer wing
69 Main spar cut-out for optional Darne machine-gun installation
70 Underwing gondola
71 300-cartridge machine gun ammunition drum
72 Underwing MAC 1934 machine gun
73 Folding ventral aerial mast
74 Wing leading-edge attachment point

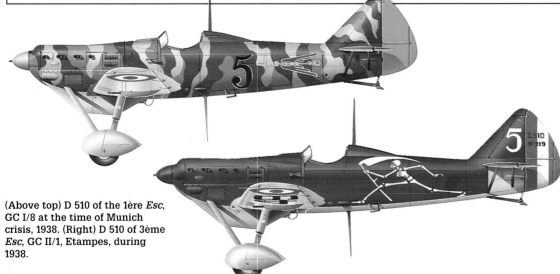

(Above top) D 510 of the 1ère *Esc*, GC I/8 at the time of Munich crisis, 1938. (Right) D 510 of 3ème *Esc*, GC II/1, Etampes, during 1938.

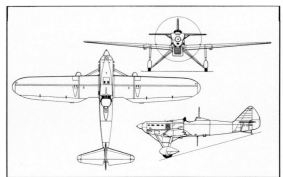

The sole D 510A (above) supplied for UK evaluation. (Below) The standard production Dewoitine D 510.

Groupes de Chasse were still flying with the D 510 at the beginning of World War II, but re-equipped during the first months of the conflict. Two *Escadrilles Régionale de Chasse* in North Africa converted to D 510s in September-October 1939, flying them until mid-1940, and two *escadrilles* of the *Aéronautique Navale* formed on D 510s in December 1939 and May 1940. *Max speed,* 250 mph (402 km/h) at 16,405 ft (5 000 m), 205 mph (330 km/h) at sea level. Time to 3,280 ft (1 000m), 1.32 min. Range, 435 mls (700 km). Empty weight, 3,298 lb (1 496 kg). Loaded weight, 4,253 lb (1 929 kg). Span, 39 ft 8 in (12,09 m). Length, 26 ft 0½ in (7,94 m). Height, 7 ft 11¼ in (2,42 m). Wing area, 177.61 sq ft (16,50 m²).

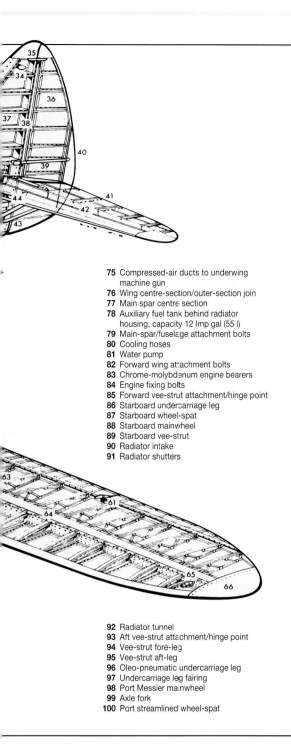

75 Compressed-air ducts to underwing machine gun
76 Wing centre-section/outer-section join
77 Main spar centre section
78 Auxiliary fuel tank behind radiator housing, capacity 12 Imp gal (55 l)
79 Main-spar/fuselage attachment bolts
80 Cooling hoses
81 Water pump
82 Forward wing attachment bolts
83 Chrome-molybdenum engine bearers
84 Engine fixing bolts
85 Forward vee-strut attachment/hinge point
86 Starboard undercarriage leg
87 Starboard wheel-spat
88 Starboard mainwheel
89 Starboard vee-strut
90 Radiator intake
91 Radiator shutters

92 Radiator tunnel
93 Aft vee-strut attachment/hinge point
94 Vee-strut fore-leg
95 Vee-strut aft-leg
96 Oleo-pneumatic undercarriage leg
97 Undercarriage leg fairing
98 Port Messier mainwheel
99 Axle fork
100 Port streamlined wheel-spat

DEWOITINE D 503 France

The D 503 (above) was a derivative of the D 500 with a smaller wing and frontal radiator.

First flown on 15 April 1935, the D 503 was, in fact, a modification of the D 511 prototype, which, although exhibited in the *Salon de l'Aéronautique* in Paris in November 1934, was not flown. The D 511 had consisted of the fuselage and tail assembly of the D 500 mated to a wing of marginally smaller span and area, cantilever main undercarriage members and an Hispano-Suiza 12Ycrs engine. Calculations indicated that the D 511 would not offer a sufficient advance in performance (despite the fact that the first production order for the D 510 was not to be placed until May 1935) and it was therefore re-engined with a 690 hp HS 12Xcrs engine with a circular frontal radiator, armament comprising a 20-mm engine-mounted cannon and two wing-

The D 503 (above) was the re-engined prototype of the D 511 which had not been flown.

mounted 7,5-mm Darne machine guns. Flight testing revealed a climb rate inferior to that of the standard D 500 and, after serving as the personal aircraft of Col Rene Fonck in the *escadrille ministérielle*, the prototype was assigned to the flying school at Etampes. *Max speed, 195 mph (314 km/h) at sea level, 233 mph (375 km/h) at 16,405 ft (5 000 m). Time to 16,405 ft (5 000 m), 7.45 min. Range, 522 mls (840 km). Empty weight, 3,038 lb (1 378 kg). Loaded weight, 4,019 lb (1 823 kg). Span, 37 ft 8 in (11,48 m). Length, 24 ft 9⅝ in (7,56 m). Height, 8 ft 10½ in (2,70 m). Wing area, 161.46 sq ft (15,00 m²).*

DEWOITINE D 513 France

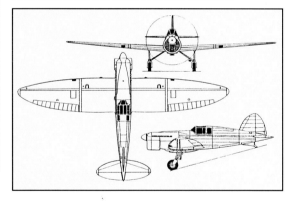

The D 513 (above and below) as first flown, with circular radiator and semi-elliptical tailplane.

Two prototypes of a new fighter, the D 513, were ordered in 1935 as part of the 1934 C1 programme, the first of these being flown on 6 January 1936. Featuring semi-elliptical horizontal and vertical surfaces, with a wing of relatively high aspect ratio, an Hispano-Suiza 12Ycrs1 engine with a frontal radiator similar to that of the D 503, and inward-retracting main undercarriage members, the D 513 proved disappointing during initial trials. It suffered serious instability and attained a maximum speed of only 264 mph (425 km/h) at 15,090 ft (4 600 m). Radical redesign followed, the wing and tailplane being mated to an entirely new fuselage, vertical tail surfaces, elevators and undercarriage, the frontal radiator giving place to a deep radiator bath beneath the nose. In this definitive form, the D 513 still proved

The D 513 (below) after radical redesign and subsequent reconstruction.

In this much-modified definitive form (above and below) the D 513 still proved unsatisfactory.

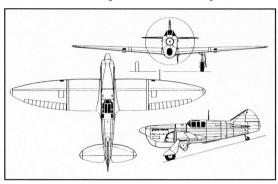

incapable of meeting specified performance, a shortcoming which, compounded by continuing instability and difficulties with both engine cooling and undercarriage retraction, led to the discontinuation of development. The second prototype was fitted with an HS 12Ydrs2 engine rated at 930 hp at 3,250 ft (990 m), and undercarriage and radiator *à la* D 503, and was employed for high-speed parachute launching trials as the D 514 LP. The following data relate to the D 513 in its definitive form. *Max speed, 234 mph (376 km/h) at sea level, 276 mph (445 km/h) at 16,730 ft (5 100 m). Time to 6,560 ft (2 000 m), 2.55 min. Loaded weight, 5,393 lb (2 446 kg). Span, 39 ft 6⅖ in (12,06 m). Length, 24 ft 5½ in (7,45 m). Wing area, 197.20 sq ft (18,32 m²).*

DEWOITINE D 520 France

Designed by Dewoitine in collaboration with Robert Castello and Jacques Henrat, the D 520 was intended to meet a requirement originally framed in June 1936, two prototypes being ordered on 3 April 1938. Of all-metal stressed-skin construction with a monocoque fuselage and monospar wing, the prototypes were flown on 2 October 1938 and 28 January 1939 respectively. These were joined by a third prototype on 5 May 1939, an initial production order for 200 D 520s having been placed on 14 March 1939. A further 510 D 520s had been ordered by 11 July 1939, by which time the decision had been taken to standardise on the Hispano-Suiza 12Y 45 engine with a Szydlowski supercharger rated at 935 hp for take-off and an armament of one engine-mounted 20-mm HS 404 cannon and four wing-mounted 7,5-mm MAC 34 M39 machine guns. Between 23 November

(Below) A D 520 for the Vichy *Armée de l'Air de l'Armistice* after production resumption in 1941.

D 520 No 465 (above) modified with an HS 12Z engine, new radiator and new undercarriage doors.

and 17 December 1939, the prototype D520-01 made a series of test flights fitted with a R-R Merlin III engine, before the latter was transferred to the D521-01 (see following entry). The first production aircraft flew on 31 October 1939, and 437 had been completed at the time of the 1940 Armistice, of which 403 had been taken on charge by the *Armée de l'Air*. Production of the D 520 was resumed, with German authorisation, in Vichy France, the first "new" fighter being flown on 26 July

This beautifully restored D 520 (above) carries the 1940 insignia of GC I/3 (*Escadrille* SPA 88).

1941, and a further 478 D 520s were built prior to and subsequent to the German occupation of Vichy France. Those built after May 1942 had the HS 12Y 49 engine which differed only in having a supercharger with a higher altitude rating. The *Wehrmacht* captured 246 Dewoitine D 520s in Vichy France, to which were

added a further 192 subsequently completed. Of these, 150 were delivered to Romania and 96 to Bulgaria, others being utilised by the *Luftwaffe* as fighter trainers. A further 72 D 520s were acquired by Italy's *Regia Aeronautica*, of which 30 were transferred to Germany in exchange for captured LeO 451 bombers. *Max speed, 264 mph (425 km/h) at sea level, 332 mph (534 km/h) at 18,045 ft (5 500 m). Time to 13,125 ft (4 000 m), 5.8 min. Max range, 1,013 mls (1 630 km) at 230 mph (370 km/h). Empty weight, 4,489 lb (2 036 kg). Loaded weight, 5,902 lb (2 677 kg). Span, 33 ft 5½ in (10,20 m). Length, 28 ft 2⅗ in (8,60 m). Height, 8 ft 5⅛ in (2,57 m). Wing area, 171.9 sq ft (15,97 m²).*

Key to Dewoitine D 520

1 Cannon port
2 Spinner
3 Three-blade Ratier Electric propeller
4 Cannon barrel blast tube
5 Coolant water tank
6 Safety vent
7 Cowling forward frame
8 Auxiliary intake
9 Chin intake
10 Coolant piping
11 Oil cooler intake
12 Intake duct
13 Oil radiator
14 Engine bearer frames
15 Engine accessories
16 Exhaust stubs
17 Hispano-Suiza 12Y 45 engine
18 Cowling rear frame
19 Cannon ammunition drum (60 rounds)
20 Oil tank
21 Starboard wing fuel tank
22 Wing skinning

23 Starboard navigation light
24 Starboard aileron
25 Aileron hinge
26 Emergency ring and bead gunsight
27 Fuselage main fuel tank
28 Fuselage main frame upper member
29 Engine bearer upper attachment
30 Bulkhead
31 20-mm HS 404 cannon breech
32 Compressor outlet
33 Extinguisher
34 Szydlowski compressor
35 Engine bearer support frame
36 Wingroot fairing
37 Starboard mainwheel
38 Port mainwheel well
39 Ventral radiator bath intake
40 Undercarriage retraction mechanism
41 Mainwheel leg pivot
42 Wing machine gun blast tubes
43 Machine gun ports
44 Mainwheel leg
45 Port mainwheel
46 Mainwheel cover

47 Mainwheel leg door
48 Port wing fuel tank
49 Wing nose ribs
50 Pitot head
51 Port navigation light
52 Wingtip
53 Port aileron frame
54 Aileron hinge
55 Wing rear false spar
56 Wing skinning
57 Wing ribs
58 Two 7,5-mm MAC 1934 machine guns
59 Ammunition feed
60 Wing main spar
61 Ammunition boxes (500 rpg)
62 Gun hot air
63 Radiator bath
64 Wing flap inboard profile
65 Radiator outlet flap
66 Port wing flap
67 Hinged receiver antenna (extended)
68 Wingroot fairing
69 Fuselage main frame lower member
70 Wing flap control linkage

71 Rudder pedal bar
72 Instrument panel
73 Command radio receiver
74 Control column grip
75 HF receiver
76 Windscreen
77 OPL RX 39 gunsight
78 Canopy track
79 Pilot's seat
80 Seat adjustment lever
81 Seat mounting frame
82 Tailplane incidence adjustment handwheel
83 Ventral antenna actuation jack
84 Oxygen cylinder
85 Fuselage frame
86 Tailplane incidence cable
87 Oleo reservoirs (2)

88 Sliding canopy (open)
89 Radio equipment (Radio-Industrie 537)
90 Aft canopy fixed glazing
91 Radio relay/lead-in
92 Transmitter antenna (fixed)
93 Dorsal decking
94 Fuselage frames
95 Stringers

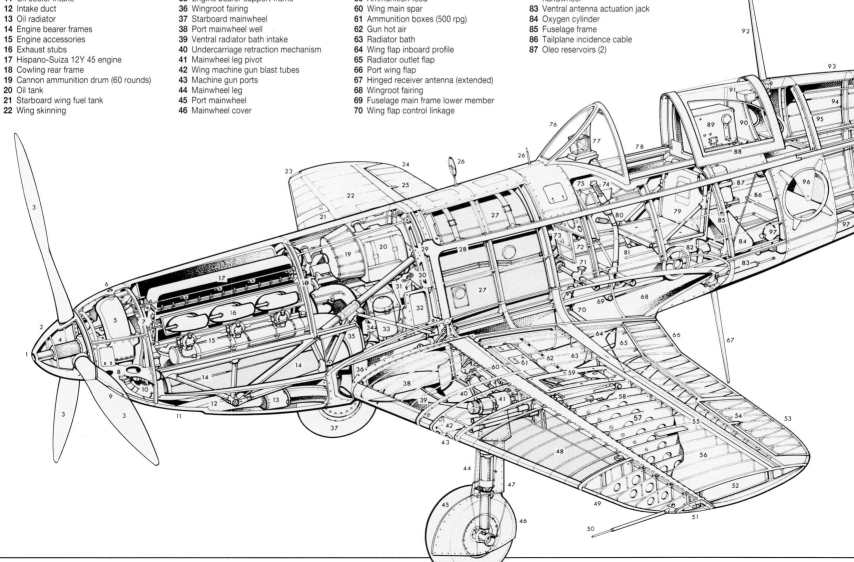

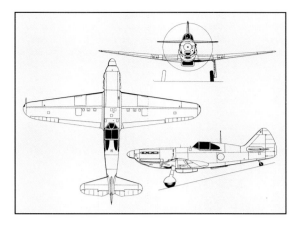

The series Dewoitine D 520 with HS 12Y engine.

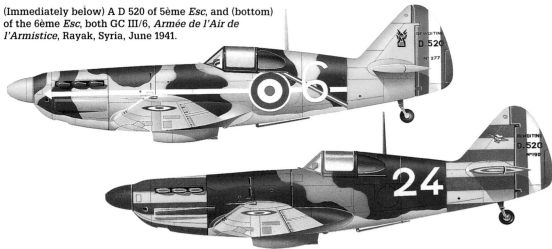

(Immediately below) A D 520 of 5ème *Esc*, and (bottom) of the 6ème *Esc*, both GC III/6, *Armée de l'Air de l'Armistice*, Rayak, Syria, June 1941.

DEWOITINE D 521   France

Owing to an envisaged shortfall in production of the Hispano-Suiza 12Y 45 engine and the demands on supplies of this power plant for combat aircraft other than the D 520, plans were formulated for its replacement by the 1,030 hp Rolls-Royce Merlin III in the 251st and sub-

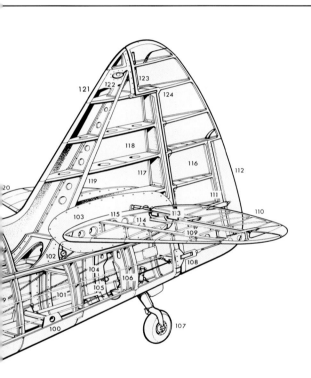

96 Equipment/baggage compartment door
97 Compressed air cylinders
98 Elevator control linkage
99 Elevator cables
100 Lift point
101 Rudder cables
102 Fuselage main frame/tailfin spar attachment
103 Tailplane root fairing
104 Fuselage frame
105 Rudder linkage
106 Tailwheel shock absorber
107 Fixed tailwheel
108 Rudder lower hinge
109 Tailplane structure
110 Port elevator frame
111 Rudder tab hinge fairing
112 Rudder tab
113 Elevator control horn
114 Elevator torque tube
115 Tailplane attachment
116 Rudder frame
117 Rudder post
118 Tailfin structure
119 Tailfin front spar
120 Starboard tailplane
121 Tailfin leading-edge
122 Tail navigation light
123 Rudder internal balance
124 Rudder upper hinge

sequent aircraft, the Merlin-engined variant being designated D 521. Although these plans were cancelled, work on a prototype D 521 continued and this, employing the airframe of the 41st production D 521, was flown on 9 February 1940. The proposed armament of the D 521 comprised two 20-mm HS 404 cannon and two 7,5-mm MAC 34 M39 machine guns, all mounted in the wings. Installation of the heavier Merlin engine resulted in CG difficulties, and stability at low speeds proved poor. After six further test flights, the D 521 was grounded for re-engining with the 1,200 hp HS 12Z as the prototype D 524, development of which was abandoned with the Armistice. *Max speed, 348-354 mph (560-570 km/h). Empty weight, 4,753 lb (2 156 kg). Loaded weight, 6,250 lb (2 835 kg). Dimensions as for D 520.*

DFW T 28 FLOH   Germany

Designed in late 1915 by *Dipl Ing* Hermann Dorner, newly appointed as chief engineer of the Deutsche Flugzeugwerke GmbH (DFW) of Leipzig-Lindenthal, the T 28 *Floh* (Flea) was, in appearance, one of the most extraordinary single-seat biplane fighter prototypes tested during World War I. Built under the supervision of Ing Theo Rockenfeller at DFW's Lübeck-Travemünde subsidiary, the T 28 featured an inordinately deep fuselage in which the 100 hp Mercedes D I six-cylinder water-cooled engine was completely buried. Of wooden construction with fabric-covered wings and wood veneer skinning for the fuselage, the T 28 carried

Despite extraordinary appearance, the T 28 Floh (above and below) achieved a respectable performance.

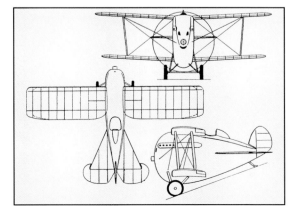

a single machine gun in the forward fuselage above the engine. During the maiden flight a speed of 112 mph (180 km/h) was attained – a noteworthy accomplishment at the time – but minor damage resulted during the landing. Some modifications were made, including the introduction of aerodynamically-balanced elevators, but the authorities evinced no interest in the aircraft and further development of the T 28 was abandoned in consequence. *Max speed, (approx) 112 mph (180 km/h). Empty weight, 926 lb (420 kg). Loaded weight, 1,433 lb (650 kg). Span, 20 ft 4 in (6,20 m). Length 14 ft 9 in (4,50 m). Height, 7 ft 6½ in (2,30 m). Wing area, 161.46 sq ft (15,00 m²).*

DFW T 34-I   Germany

A conventional single-bay biplane of wooden construction powered by a 160 hp Mercedes D III engine and mounting twin synchronised 7,92-mm machine guns, the T 34-I (frequently referred to erroneously as the D I) was developed in mid-1917, first appearing in official *Idflieg* progress reports in October of that year when the cooling system was being modified and the control surfaces enlarged. In November, new wings with a more efficient rib profile were under construction and, in January 1918, the T 34-I attained an altitude of 16,405 ft (5 000 m) in 22 min, a climb capability possessed by the Pfalz D IIIa already in operational service. By this time, the ailerons had been removed from the lower wing and the vertical tail surfaces had undergone further redesign, and in this form the T34-I was entered in the first D-type contest at Adlershof in February 1918. It was rejected on the score of poor cockpit visibility prior to the flight evaluation and thus did not appear in the official statistical tabulations. No data on the T 34-I are available.

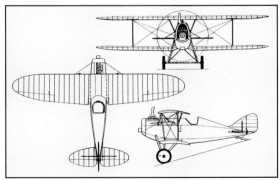

Contrasting with the T 28, the DFW T 34-I (above and below) was a conventional single-bay biplane.

The T 34-II (above and below) was essentially a triplane version of the T 34-I biplane evolved in parallel, and was tested with little success in 1918.

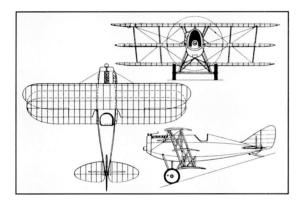

DFW T 34-II — Germany

Evolved in parallel with the T 34-I biplane, the T 34-II (sometimes referred to erroneously as the Dr I) single-seat triplane employed a similar fuselage, power plant (Mercedes D III), armament (twin synchronised LMG 08/15s) and undercarriage to those of the biplane fighter. Both top and bottom wings were one-piece units mounted well clear of the fuselage and sufficiently staggered to obviate the need for a pilot-vision cut-out. The central wing carried generous ailerons and possessed broad tips, and the tail surfaces were similar to those of the definitive T 34-I, but incorporating a somewhat larger rudder. Together with the T 34-I, the T 34-II triplane was submitted for evaluation in the first D-type contest, but was excluded from the competition flight testing for reasons of poor pilot visibility and "unsuitable design". No data on the T 34-II are available.

DFW D I — Germany

The DFW D I (which was subsequently to be referred to on occasions erroneously as the D II and by the unconfirmed and almost certainly incorrect designation of F 34) was a single-bay biplane powered by a 160 hp Mercedes D IIIa engine and mounting the usual pair of syn-

(Below) The DFW D I with Mercedes D IIIa engine.

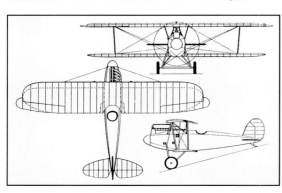

chronised 7,92-mm LMG 08/15 machine guns. Entered in the second D-type contest held in May-June 1918, the DFW D I was rejected out of hand "for any frontline utilisation" and did not participate in the subsequent flight evaluation. During July 1918, however, the D I was rebuilt and flight test results were considered sufficiently promising for full static load tests to be conducted at Adlershof during late July and early August. However, these tests revealed that the fuselage and tail demanded strengthening, and the type was not approved for service use in consequence. *Max speed, 110 mph (177 km/h). Time to 13,125 ft (4 000 m), 10 min. Empty weight, 1,409 lb (639 kg). Loaded weight, 1,806 lb (819 kg). Span, 29 ft 9½ in (9,08 m). Length, 18 ft 0½ in (5,50 m). Wing area, 247.58 sq ft (23,00 m²).*

The single D I (below) competed, with poor results, in the second D-type fighter contest in 1918.

DÍAZ TYPE C — Spain

Designed to participate in the *Concurso de Aviones* held at Cuatro Vientos in March-April 1919, the single-seat fighter built by Amalio Díaz of Getafe, Madrid, was

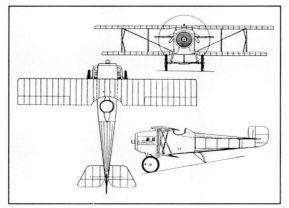

(Above and below) The Díaz Type C was a participant in Spain's 1919 *Concurso de Aviones*.

apparently based on a 1917 design of Julio Adaro, the construction of which was never completed. The Díaz Type C (*Caccia*) was a two-bay equi-span biplane with an abbreviated cabane and powered by a 180 hp Hispano-Suiza 8Ab engine. It failed to qualify in the *Concurso* as it did not fully meet the requirements of the specification that had been prepared by the *Aviación Militar*, the fighter contest being won by the Hispano-Barrón. Nevertheless, the Díaz Type C received a consolation prize of half the second prize which had not been awarded. No data for the Díaz fighter are available.

DOFLUG D-3802 — Switzerland

During 1942, the Dornier-Werke AG (Doflug) of Altenrhein received a contract to design a single-seat multi-rôle fighter to follow on production of the D-3801 (a

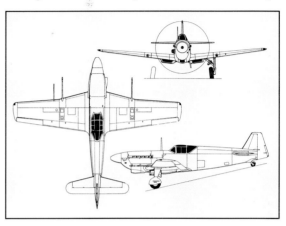

(Above) The pre-series D-3802A and (below) the prototype D-3802 which had a greater wing span.

licence-built version of the Morane-Saulnier MS 412). Powered by a 1,250 hp Saurer (Hispano-Suiza) YS-2 12-cylinder liquid-cooled engine, the D-3802 was of all-metal monocoque stressed-skin construction and carried an armament of one engine-mounted 20-mm cannon and four wing-mounted machine guns. It flew for the first time on 29 September 1944. A pre-series of 11 aircraft was ordered, these having modified outer wing panels of reduced span, but similar area, and the wing-mounted machine guns replaced by a pair of 20-mm cannon. As the D-3802A, the first of these flew on 18 May 1946. The pre-series aircraft served with *Fliegerstaffel* 17 until 1956. *Max speed, 391 mph (629 km/h) at 21,325 ft (6 500 m). Initial climb, 2,795 ft/min (14,2 m/sec). Range, 404 mls (650 km). Empty weight, 5,500 lb (2 495 kg). Max loaded weight, 8,607 lb (3 904 kg). Span, 32 ft 10½ in (10,02 m). Length, 30 ft 6⅜ in (9,31 m). Height, 10 ft 11½ in (3,34 m). Wing area, 188.37 sq ft (17,50 m²).*

(Below) Second of the pre-series D-3802As built by Doflug at Altenrhein during 1946.

184

D-3802As of the pre-series batch (above) serving with Switzerland's *Fliegerstaffel 17* in the 'fifties.

DOFLUG D-3803   Switzerland

Built concurrently with the pre-series D-3802A fighters, the D-3803 employed the same wing, tail surfaces and undercarriage, but featured a fuselage with shallower aft decking and an all-round vision canopy, and was powered by a 1,430 hp Saurer (Hispano-Suiza) YS-3 engine. Retaining the three-cannon armament of the D-3802A, the prototype D-3803 was flown for the first time in May 1947, but the flight test and evaluation programme was delayed by engine teething troubles, and before this programme could be completed, the decision was taken to acquire surplus P-51D Mustangs from the USA. The D-3803 prototype joined the pre-series D-3802As in service with *Fliegerstaffel 17*. *Max speed, 422 mph (680 km/h) at 22,965 ft (7 000 m). Initial climb, 3,012 ft/min (15,3 m/sec). Range, 404 mls (650 km). Empty weight, 6,493 lb (2 945 kg). Max loaded weight, 8,598 lb (3 900 kg). Span, 32 ft 10½ in (10,02 m). Length, 30 ft 7⅓ in (9,33 m). Height, 12 ft 4 in (3,76 m). Wing area, 188.37 sq ft (17,50 m²).*

The D-3803 (below) was the final extrapolation by Dornier from original Morane-Saulnier designs.

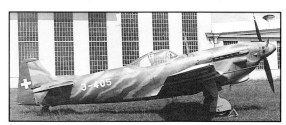

DORNIER Do H FALKE   Germany

The combination of cantilever monoplane configuration and all-metal construction in a single-seat fighter was considered singularly audacious in the early 'twenties, and thus the Do H Falke (Falcon) parasol monoplane, incorporating these features and flown for the first time on 1 November 1922, was viewed as a rather radical development. Designed by the Dornier Metallbauten GmbH (which that year had changed its title from Zeppelin-Werke Lindau GmbH), the Do H Falke could be fitted with the 275 hp Rolls-Royce Falcon III, the 300 hp Hispano-Suiza 8Fb or the 320 hp BMW IV engine, and the wheel undercarriage could be replaced by twin metal floats with which the fighter was known as the Seefalke. Five Falke fighters were built, two in Switzerland and three in Italy. One example was exported to Chile and, in 1923, the Wright Aeronautical Company imported a Falke into the USA. Fitted with a 320 hp Wright H-3 engine (a licence-built version of the Hispano-Suiza), the latter was entered in the 1923 US

Navy pursuit contest as the WP-1. Another example, powered by the BMW IV engine, was imported into Japan by Kawasaki under a licence agreement covering a range of Dornier types concluded on 6 February 1924. This was flown with both wheel and float undercarriages, and served as a basis for the Kawasaki KDA-3 experimental metal parasol fighter. The following data relate to the Wright H-3-powered Falke. *Max speed, 162 mph (261 km/h). Time to 10,000 ft (3 050 m), 6.75 min. Range, 217 mls (349 km). Empty weight, 1,819 lb (825 kg). Loaded weight, 2,674 lb (1 213 kg). Span, 32 ft 9⁷⁄₁₀ in (10,00 m). Length, 24 ft 4½ in (7,43 m). Height, 8 ft 8¾ in (2,66 m). Wing area, 215.28 sq ft (20,0 m²).*

This Falke (above) was evaluated by the USN as the Wright WP-1. (Below) BMW-engined Falke.

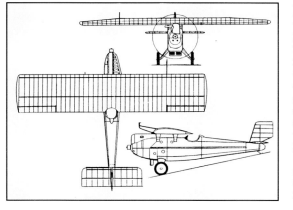

DORNIER Do 10 (C4)   Germany

The Do C was conceived as a multi-rôle aircraft capable of accepting a variety of inline liquid-cooled engines of 500-750 hp and suitable for both wheel and float undercarriages. A tandem two-seat parasol monoplane of all-metal construction with fabric skinning, the Do C was tested in several versions, including the C2 and C2a light bomber, the C3 and C3a reconnaissance seaplanes and the C4 fighter landplane, all of which were powered by various Hispano-Suiza 12-cylinder Vee-engines. The Do C4, which was to be redesignated retrospectively Do 10, was flown for the first time on 24 July 1931 with a 650 hp Hispano-Suiza 12Ybre engine, but was also proposed with the 550 hp Rolls-Royce Kestrel and the 650 hp BMW VI. Unsuccessful as a two-seat fighter, the sole prototype Do C4 alias Do 10 was used for trials of a tilting engine mount by means of which the thrust line could be raised 15 deg from the horizontal to shorten the take-off run. *Max speed, 193 mph (310 km/h). Time to 3,280 ft (1 000 m), 1.98 min. Empty weight, 4,850 lb (2 200 kg). Normal loaded weight, 5,820 lb (2 640 kg). Span, 49 ft 2½ in (15,00 m). Length, 34 ft 9⅓ in (10,60 m). Height, 14 ft 1¼ in (4,30 m). Wing area, 353.61 sq ft (32,85 m²).*

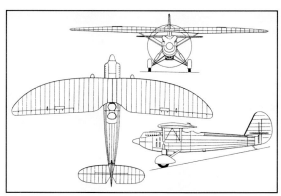

(Above and below) The Do C4 (later Do 10) two-seat fighter in the form in which it was first flown.

DORNIER Do 17Z KAUZ   Germany

In 1940, the Dornier-Werke was instructed to adapt the Do 17Z-3 reconnaissance-bomber as an interim long-range night fighter and intruder. Dubbed *Kauz* (Screech Owl) and assigned the designation Do 17Z-7, the initial conversion consisted simply of the removal of the glazed bomb-aiming nose and the mating of a suitably adapted Ju 88C-2 nose cone, complete with 11-mm armour bulkhead and fixed forward-firing armament of three 7,9-mm MG 17s with 1,000 rpg and one 20-mm MG FF (later MG 151) cannon offset to starboard. The

(Immediately below) Do 17Z-10 *Kauz* of Stab I/NJG 2, Gilze-Rijen, 1940. (Bottom) Do 215B-2 *Kauz* 3 of Stab II/NJG 2, Leeuwarden, summer 1942.

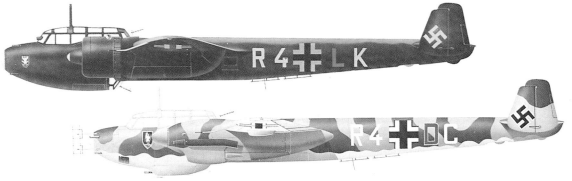

crew was reduced to three members, the upper and lower aft-firing 7,9-mm MG 15 machine guns were retained, as was also the aft bomb-bay which could accommodate 10 SD 50 or two SD 250 bombs, and power was provided by two BMW-Bramo 323P radials each rated at 1,000 hp for take-off. One of the two Do 17Z-7 conversions completed was fitted with an infra-red sensor of the so-called *Spanner-Anlage* type, and the two aircraft were employed operationally by I and II/NJG 1. A further nine aircraft (converted from the last nine production Do 17Z-3s) were completed under the designation Do 17Z-10 *Kauz 2*, these having redesigned nose cones housing four 7,9-mm MG 17s in the upper section and two 20-mm MG FF cannon below, and being equipped with the *Spanner-Anlage* (later replaced by FuG 202 *Lichtenstein* BC radar). The Do 17Z-10s served with II/NJG 1, I, II and Erg/NJG 2 and NJG 101 from 1940 until 1943. The following data relate to the Do 17Z-10. *Max speed, 261 mph (420 km/h) at 19,360 ft (5 900 m). Range, 1,243 mls (2 000 km). Service ceiling, 26,245 ft (8 000 m). Length, 54 ft 7⁹⁄₁₀in (16,66 m). Height, 15 ft 1 in (4,60 m). Wing area, 592.01 sq ft (55,0 m²).*

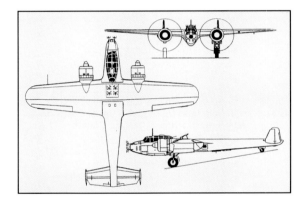

A Do 17Z-7 *Kauz* (above) with *Spanner-Anlage* and (below) the radar-equipped Do 17Z-10 *Kauz 2*.

DORNIER Do 215B-5 KAUZ 3   Germany

The successful conversion of the Do 17Z-3 for the night fighting rôle as the Do 17Z-10 *Kauz 2* prompted, in the late autumn of 1940, a similar conversion of the Do 215B-4 bomber as the Do 215B-5 *Kauz 3*. The Do 215B-5 possessed a nose cone similar to that of the Do 17Z-10, mounting the *Spanner-Anlage*, a quartet of MG 17 machine guns and a single 20-mm MG FF cannon. Powered by two 1,100 hp Daimler-Benz DB 601Aa engines, the Do 215B-5 entered service with 4./NJG 1 from early 1941, and, in the following year, the 20 or so night fighters of this type completed were modified to carry FuG 202 *Lichtenstein* BC radar, by which time armament had been supplemented by two additional cannon in a ventral tray beneath the forward fuselage

(Below) The Do 215B-5 *Kauz 3* with FuG 202 radar.

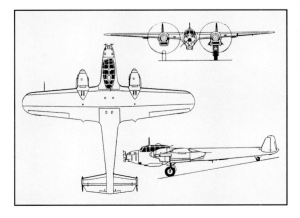

A Do 215B-5 of II/NJG 2 in 1942, displaying the aerials of the FuG 202 *Lichtenstein* BC radar.

gondola. The Do 215B-5 served with I and IV/NJG 1 and II/NJG 2 until May 1944. *Max speed, 289 mph (465 km/h) at 15,750 ft (4 800 m). Range, 1,118 mls (1 800 km). Service ceiling, 29,530 ft (9 000 m). Span, 59 ft 0²⁄₃ in (18,00 m). Length, 54 ft 7⁹⁄₁₀in (16,66 m). Height,15 ft 1 in (4,60 m). Wing area, 592.01 sq ft (55,0 m²).*

DORNIER Do 217J   Germany

Early in 1941, Dornier tendered proposals for an improvised night fighter based on the Do 217E-2 bomber airframe. The initial model, the Do 217J-1, was intended specifically for the intruder rôle, retaining the aft bomb-bay which could accommodate up to eight SC 50X bombs, the forward bay having provision for an auxiliary fuel tank. The nose cone was redesigned to accommodate four 7,9-mm MG 17 machine guns and the forward portion of the gondola was revised to accommodate four 20-mm MG FF-M cannon in vertically staggered pairs. The dorsal turret with a single 13-mm MG 131 and the aft-firing MG 131 in the ventral step were retained. As a result of an edict forbidding further nocturnal intrusion missions, the primarily offensive rôle of the Do 217J was changed to the defensive rôle of night interception. FuG 202 *Lichtenstein* BC radar was fitted as available in the Do 217J-2 version, the bomb bays being deleted and the MG FF-M cannon being replaced by MG 151s of similar calibre. Powered by two 1,580 hp BMW 801ML radials, the Do 217J served alongside the Do 217N (which see) with *Gruppen* of NJG 1, 2, 3, 4, 5, 100, 101 and 102, but had virtually disappeared from service by 1944. Six Do 217J-1s and six J-2s were supplied to the *Regia Aeronautica*. The following data relate to the Do 217J-2. *Max speed, 304 mph (489 km/h) at 18,045 ft (5 500 m). Range, 1,305 mls (2 100 km). Time to 3,280 ft (1 000 m), 3.5 min.*

Do 217J-2 night-fighters (above and below) undergoing manufacturer's trials prior to delivery to the *Nachtjagdflieger.*

Empty weight, 20,613 lb (9 350 kg). Loaded weight, 29,056 lb (13 180 kg). Span, 62 ft 4 in (19,00 m). Length, 59 ft 0²⁄₃ in (18,00 m). Height, 16 ft 3²⁄₃ in (4,97 m). Wing area, 613.56 sq ft (57,0 m²).

DORNIER Do 217N   Germany

Proposed in parallel with the Do 217J as a night-fighting derivative of the Do 217M bomber, the Do 217N flew as a prototype on 31 July 1942, and apart from the reinstatement of the aft bomb-bay and the use of 1,750 hp Daimler-Benz DB 603A engines, was similar to the Do 217J-2. Mounting FuG 202 *Lichtenstein* BC radar, the Do 217N-1 entered service during the last quarter of 1942.

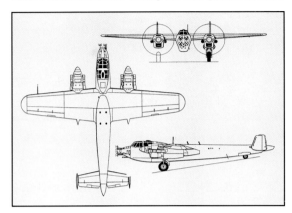

(Above) The Do 217N-2 and (below) the Do 217N-1 which differed in having a gun turret located immediately aft of the cockpit.

At an early stage, the upper turret and the free-mounted weapon in the ventral step were removed and faired over. Thus modified, the fighter variant was redesignated Do 217N-1/U-1, and with these changes introduced on the production line the designation became Do 217N-2. Some aircraft were fitted with four 20-mm MG 151 cannon firing forward and upward at an angle of 70 deg from the horizontal as the Do 217N-2/R22. Production was phased out late in 1943, deliveries of the Do 217J and Do 217N together totalling 364 aircraft. *Max speed, 320 mph (515 km/h) at 19,685 ft (6 000 m). Max cruise, 292 mph (470 km/h) at 17,715 ft (5 400 m). Normal range, 1,090 mls (1 755 km). Empty weight, 22,641 lb (10 270 kg). Loaded weight, 29,101 lb (13 200 kg). Dimensions as for Do 217J-2.*

DORNIER Do 335   Germany

Unique in conception in that it coupled a conventional tractor propeller with a pusher propeller mounted aft of a cruciform tail, the Do 335 multi-rôle fighter was projected in both single- and two-seat forms, the first single-seat prototype, the Do 335 V1, flying on 26 October 1943. The initial production model was the Do 335A-1, a single-seat fighter-bomber powered by two DB 603E-1 engines each rated at 1,800 hp for take-off and mounting an armament of one 30-mm MK 103 and two 15-mm MG 151 cannon. Of the 14 prototype (or *Versuchs*) aircraft, the V9 was completed to full pre-production standards, the V10 was the first prototype of the radar-equipped two-seat Do 335A-6, the V11 and V12 were respectively the prototypes of the Do 335A-10 and A-12 dual-control conversion trainers, and the V13 and V14 were prototypes of the Do 335B-1 and B-2, these having the internal weapons bay deleted and a heavier gun armament fitted, with 20-mm cannon supplanting the 15-mm weapons in the B-1 and two 30-mm MK 103 cannon being added to the armament of the B-2.

The Do 335 V1 (above), first prototype of the radical *Pfeil*, and (below) the pre-series Do 335A-0.

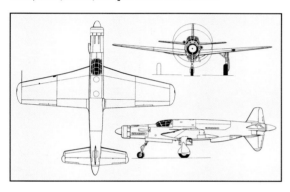

Ten pre-production Do 335A-0 aircraft were built for service evaluation, but only 11 production Do 335A-1s and two Do 335A-12 two-seaters had been completed when the Oberpfaffenhofen production facility was overrun by Allied forces in 1945. The following data relate to the Do 335A-0. *Max speed, 455 mph (732 km/h) at 23,295 ft (7 100 m). Range, 1,336 mls (2 150 km) at 286 mph (460 km/h) at 19,685 ft (6 000 m). Empty weight, 14,396 lb (6 530 kg). Loaded weight, 20,966 lb (9 510 kg). Span, 45 ft 3⅓ in (13,80 m). Length, 45 ft 5¼ in (13,85 m). Height, 16 ft 4⅞ in (5,00 m). Wing area, 414.42 sq ft (38,50 m²).*

The seventh of 10 Do 335A-0s (below) was captured in 1945 by US troops at Oberpfaffenhofen.

The Do 335 V3, third prototype of the tandem-engined fighter which entered flight test early 1944.

DOUGLAS XFD-1   USA

The first fighter to be built by the Douglas Aircraft Company, the two-seat XFD-1 was developed from the Bureau of Aeronautics Design No 113, and was an all-metal, single-bay biplane with fabric skinning and powered by a Pratt & Whitney R-1535-64 Wasp rated at 700 hp at 8,900 ft (2 710 m). Delivered to the US Navy on 18 June 1933, and carrying an armament of twin 0.3-in (7,62-mm) machine guns in the forward fuselage and a similar weapon on a flexible mounting in the rear cockpit, the XFD-1 was considered obsolescent in conception and, like the Vought XF3U-1 and Curtiss XF12C-1 ordered simultaneously (on 30 June 1932), was to be one of the last two-seat shipboard fighters of the period developed for the US Navy, this class of aircraft being supplanted by the new scout-bomber category (both the Vought and Curtiss contenders being developed for

The first fighter built by the Douglas company, the XFD-1 biplane (above and below) was virtually obsolescent by the time it was flown in 1933.

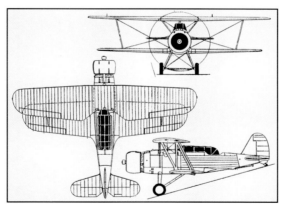

the new rôle but development of the XFD-1 being abandoned). *Max speed, 204 mph (328 km/h) at 9,000 ft (2,745 m). Initial climb, 1,600 ft/min (8,1 m/sec). Range, 576 mls (927 km). Empty weight, 3,227 lb (1 464 kg). Loaded weight, 4,745 lb (2 152 kg). Span, 31 ft 6 in (9,60 m). Length, 25 ft 4 in (7,72 m). Height, 11 ft 1 in (3,38 m). Wing area, 295 sq ft (27,40 m²).*

DOUGLAS DB-7 HAVOC   USA (UK)

A lack of aircraft combining adequate performance with the ability to carry cumbersome early AI radar for nocturnal intercept and intruder missions led the RAF, during 1940, to adapt the DB-7 light bomber for these rôles. At least 100 ex-French contract DB-7s powered by 1,200 hp Pratt & Whitney R-1830-S3C4G engines underwent conversion, approximately half as Havoc I night fighters and half as Havoc I (Intruder) aircraft.

A Havoc II night fighter (above) conversion with Martin-Baker-designed gun nose and AI Mk IV radar.

Whereas the former featured a battery of eight 0.303-in (7,7-mm) Browning guns in a "solid" nose and AI Mk IV or V radar, the latter, initially known as the Havoc IV, retained the bomb-aiming glazed nose and combined a 2,400-lb (1 090-kg) internal bomb load with four fixed forward-firing 0.303-in (7,7-mm) guns in the nose. Both versions possessed a dorsal 0.303-in (7,7-mm) Vickers "K" gun. Twenty Havoc Is were modified to carry the so-called Long Aerial Mine, these initially being known as Havoc IIIs and, later, as Havoc I(LAM)s. This device – an explosive charge attached to a cable trailed in the path of hostile bombers – proved unsuccessful. Another 31 were modified to Havoc I (Turbinlite) configuration, entailing the installation of a 2,700 million candlepower Helmore/GEC searchlight in the nose. This was accompanied by AI Mk V radar but no armament was fitted, the Havoc I (Turbinlite) operating in concert with a Hurricane or Defiant. The Havoc I conversions were followed by 99 Havoc II night fighter conversions, these being based on the DB-7A powered by 1,600 hp Wright R-2600-A5B Cyclones. About 80 of the Havoc IIs were fitted with a lengthened Martin-Baker-developed nose fairing housing 12 0.303-in (7,7-mm) machine guns, the dorsal Vickers "K" gun being discarded. Thirty-nine of these were further modified subsequently to a configuration similar to the Havoc I (Turbinlite). The following data relate to the Havoc I night fighter. *Max speed, 295 mph (475 km/h) at 13,000 ft*

(Above) Twelve guns and AI Mk IV radar were fitted in the Havoc II. (Below) A Havoc I (Turbinlite) with AI Mk V radar and nose-mounted searchlight.

(3 960 m). Range, 996 mls (1 603 km). Service ceiling, 25,800 ft (7 865 m). Empty weight, 11,400 lb (5 171 kg). Loaded weight, 19,040 lb (8 636 kg). Span, 61 ft 4 in (18,69 m). Length, 46 ft 11¾ in (14,32 m). Height, 15 ft 10 in (4,83 m). Wing area, 464.8 sq ft (43,18 m²).

DOUGLAS P-70   USA

Evolved as an interim night fighter pending availability of the Northrop P-61 Black Widow, the P-70 was an adaptation of the A-20, the US Army's equivalent of the RAF's DB-7B light bomber. The first A-20 was re-engined with non-turbo-supercharged Wright R-2600-11 Double Cyclones, each rated at 1,600 hp for take-off, and fitted with AI Mk IV radar in a "solid" nose, four 20-mm cannon being mounted in a ventral tray and the designation XP-70 being adopted. A further 59 A-20s on order were completed to a similar standard and delivered as P-70s between April and September 1942, these being followed by 39 P-70A-1s (modified A-20Cs) which had six 0.5-in (12,7-mm) guns in the ventral tray. Used operationally by four USAAF

The P-70B-1 (above) with centimetric radar in the nose and six blister guns on the front fuselage.

squadrons in the Pacific area, many P-70s carried two 0.5-in (12,7-mm) weapons in the nose for aiming purposes. Sixty-five A-20Gs were then converted as night

fighters under the designation P-70A-2, retaining the standard (A-20G) nose-mounted armament of six 0.5-in (12,7-mm) guns, and one A-20G-10 was fitted with SCR-720 centimetric radar in the nose and, with three 0.5-in (12,7-mm) guns in packs on each side of the forward fuselage, became the sole P-70B-1. An additional

---

Key to Dornier Do 335B-2

1 Upper rudder trim tab
2 Upper rudder
3 Upper tailfin (jettisonable by means of explosive bolts)
4 VDM propeller of 10 ft 10 in (3.30 m) diameter
5 Propeller spinner
6 Propeller pitch mechanism
7 Starboard elevator
8 Elevator tab
9 Metal stressed-skin tailplane structure
10 Ventral rudder
11 Tail bumper
12 Tail bumper oleo shock-absorber
13 Ventral tailfin (jettisonable for belly landing)
14 Coolant outlet
15 Rear navigation light
16 Explosive bolt seatings
17 Rudder and elevator tab controls
18 Hollow propeller extension shaft
19 Rear propeller lubricant feeds
20 Aft bulkhead
21 Coolant trunking
22 Oil cooler radiator
23 Coolant radiator
24 Fire extinguisher
25 Ventral air intake
26 FuG 25a IFF
27 FuG 125a blind landing receiver
28 Rear engine access cover latches
29 Exhaust stubs
30 Supercharger intake
31 Coolant tank
32 Engine bearer
33 Aft Daimler-Benz DB 603E-1 12-cylinder inverted-Vee liquid-cooled engine
34 Supercharger
35 Aft firewall
36 FuG 25a ring antenna
37 Fuel filler cap
38 Main fuel tank (270 Imp gal/1 230 l capacity)
39 Secondary ventral fuel tank
40 Two (9.9 Imp gal/45 l capacity) lubricant tanks (port for forward engine and starboard for rear engine)
41 Pilot's back armour

42 Rearview mirror in glazed teardrop
43 Headrest
44 Pilot's armoured ejector seat
45 Clear-vision panel
46 Jettisonable canopy (hinged to starboard)
47 Protected hydraulic fluid tank (9.9 Imp gal/45 l capacity)
48 Undercarriage hydraulics cylinder
49 Oxygen bottles
50 Port flaps
51 Aileron tab
52 Port wing fuel tank
53 Port aileron
54 Master compass
55 Pitot head
56 Twin landing lights
57 Cannon muzzle of 30-mm Rheinmetall Borsig MK 103
58 Cannon fairing
59 Ammunition tray
60 Windscreen
61 Port control console (trim settings)
62 Control column

63 Twin 20-mm Mauser MG 151/20 cannon
64 Ammunition box
65 Forward firewall
66 Breech of nose-mounted MK 103 cannon
67 Engine bearer
68 Forward DB 603E-1 engine
69 MG 151 cannon blast tubes
70 Gun trough
71 Hydraulically-operated cooling gills
72 Coolant radiator (upper segment)
73 Oil cooler radiator (lower segment)
74 VDM propeller of 11 ft 5¾ in (3,50 m) diameter
75 Propeller spinner
76 MK 103 cannon port
77 Armoured radiator ring
78 Coolant tank (3.3 Imp gal/15 l capacity)
79 Exhaust stubs
80 Nosewheel oleo leg
81 Nosewheel scissors

82 Damper
83 Nosewheel
84 Mudguard
85 Retraction strut
86 Nosewheel door
87 MK 103 cannon ammunition tray
88 Collector tray
89 Accumulator
90 Electric systems panel
91 Ejector seat compressed air bottles
92 Rudder pedals
93 Ammunition tray
94 Armour
95 Cannon fairing
96 MK 103 barrel
97 Muzzle brake
98 Ammunition feed chute
99 Starboard MK 103 wing cannon
100 Mainwheel retraction strut
101 Oleo leg

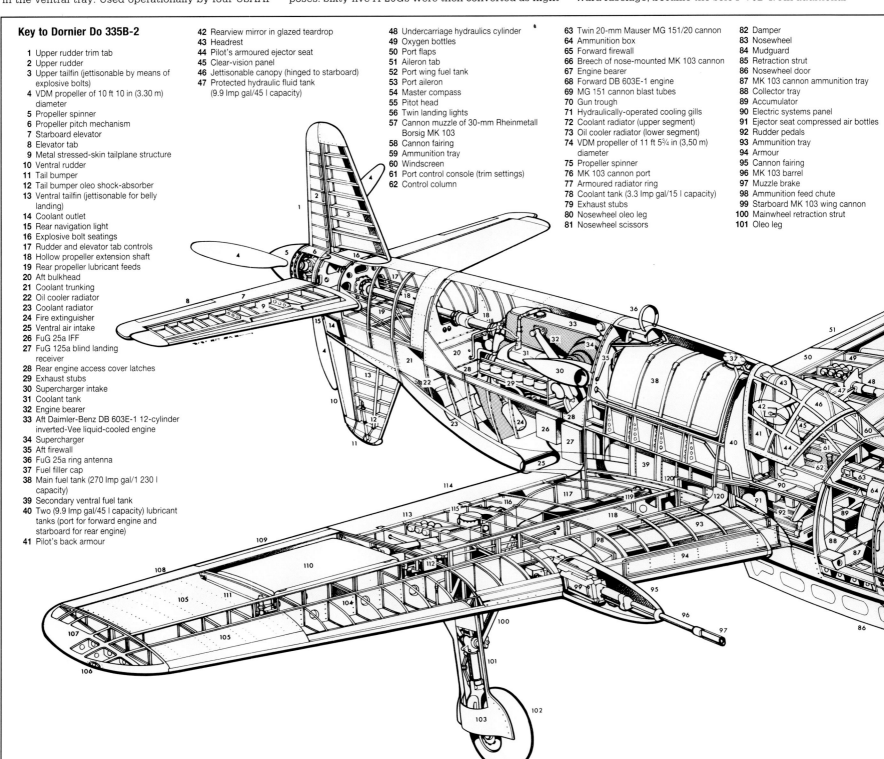

(Above) Third P-70 night fighter conversion from an A-20 with radar and ventral gun tray.

105 A-20G and A-20J airframes were fitted with SCR-720 or SCR-729 centimetric radar as night fighter trainers. Designated P-70B-2 (and TP-70B-2), these aircraft had provision for detachable lateral gun packs (similar to those of the B-1) containing a total of six 0.5-in (12,7-mm) guns. The following data relate to the P-70. *Max speed, 329 mph (529 km/h) at 14,000 ft (4 270 m). Cruising speed, 270 mph (434 km/h). Time to 12,000 ft (3 660 m), 8 min. Range, 1,060 mls (1 076 km).*

102 Starboard mainwheel
103 Mainwheel door
104 Forward face of box spar
105 Stressed wing skinning
106 Starboard navigation light
107 Wingtip structure
108 Starboard aileron
109 Aileron trim tab
110 Starboard wing fuel tank
111 Aileron control rod
112 Trim tab linkage
113 Oxygen bottles
114 Starboard flaps
115 Starter fuel tank
116 Flap hydraulic motor
117 Starboard mainwheel wel
118 Boxspar
119 Compressed air bottles (emergency undercarriage actuation)
120 Mainspar/fuselage attachment points

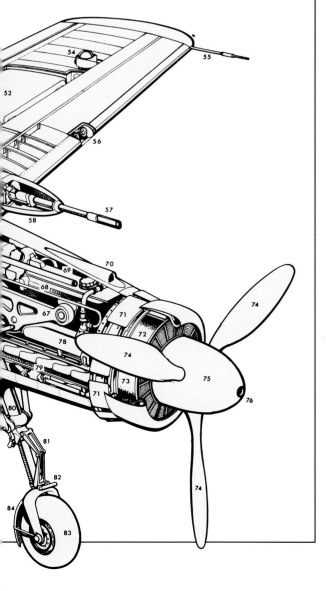

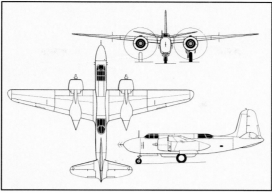

(Above) Douglas P-70 radar-equipped night fighter.

Empty weight, 16,031 lb (7 272 kg). Loaded weight, 21,264 lb (9 645 kg). Span, 61 ft 4 in (18,69 m). Length, 47 ft 7 in (14,50 m). Height, 17 ft 7 in (5,36 m). Wing area, 464.8 sq ft (43,18 m²).

DOUGLAS XA-26A   USA

Although conceived primarily as an attack bomber, the A-26, designed under the leadership of Edward Heinemann and Robert Donovan, was also foreseen as a two-seat night fighter, and the second of three prototypes, the XA-26A, was completed in nocturnal interceptor configuration. Powered by two 2,000 hp Pratt & Whitney R-2800-27 radials, the XA-26A did not appear until July 1943, and differed from the XA-26 attack bomber prototype that had preceded it in having provision for centimetric AI radar in a marginally lengthened "solid" nose, and a ventral tray housing four 20-mm cannon beneath the forward weapons bay. The crew comprised pilot and radar-operator/gunner, and it was proposed to mount a remotely-controlled dorsal turret housing four 0.5-in (12,7-mm) machine guns. The performance of the XA-26A was found to be no better than that of the Northrop P-61A Black Widow, which was already in production, and the USAAF therefore instructed Douglas to concentrate on the attack versions of the A-26, development of the night fighting variant being discontinued. *Max speed, 366 mph (589 km/h) at 17,000 ft (5 180 m). Time to 20,000 ft (6 100 m), 10.5 min. Empty weight, 22,180 lb (10 061 kg). Max loaded weight, 31,000 lb (14 062 kg). Span, 70 ft 0 in (21,34 m). Length, 52 ft 6 in (16,00 m). Height, 18 ft 6 in (5,64 m). Wing area, 540 sq ft (50,16 m²).*

The sole XA-26A (below) configured as a night fighter with centimetric radar in the nose.

DOUGLAS F3D (F-10) SKYKNIGHT   USA

A contract for three prototypes of the XF3D-1 side-by-side two-seat shipboard all-weather fighter was issued on 3 April 1946, the first of these flying on 23 March 1948. The first of 28 production F3D-1s (F-10As), powered by two 3,250 lb st (1 474 kgp) Westinghouse J34-WE-34 turbojets and carrying an armament of four 20-mm cannon, flew on 13 February 1950. Twelve were later to be modified as F3D-1M missile carriers with four Sparrow AAMs underwing. Production continued with the F3D-2 (F-10B) which, first flown on 14 February 1951, differed primarily in having 3,400 lb st (1 542 kgp) J34-WE-36 engines, 237 being built for the US Marine Corps. Some were later converted for special rôles, including 16 as F3D-2M (MF-10B) missile carriers and 30 as F3D-2Q (EF-10B) electronic reconnaissance and countermeasures aircraft. The following data relate to

the F3D-2 (F-10B). *Max speed, 490 mph (788 km/h) at 15,000 ft (4 570 m). Initial climb, 2,970 ft/min (15 m/sec). Range (clean), 1,146 mls (1 844 km) at 455 mph (732 km/h). Empty weight, 14,989 lb (6 799 kg). Max loaded weight, 26,731 lb (12 125 kg). Span, 50 ft 9 in (15,24 m). Length, 45 ft 5 in (13,84 m). Height, 16 ft 1 in (4,90 m). Wing area, 400 sq ft (37,16 m²).*

An early F3D-1 in service with Marine squadron VMF-542 and (below) an F-10B transferred to the US Army for use as an equipment test-bed.

(Below) Douglas F3D-1 Skyknight all-weather fighter.

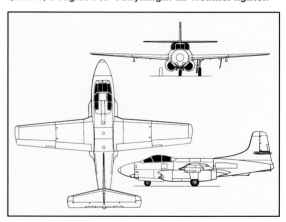

DOUGLAS F4D (F-6) SKYRAY   USA

A single-seat shipboard all-weather general-purpose fighter featuring a sweptback wing of unusually low aspect ratio and having no horizontal tail surfaces – flight control being provided by power-operated elevons performing the functions of conventional elevators and ailerons – the Skyray was designed by a team led by Edward Heinemann in 1947-48. Two prototypes were ordered under the designation XF4D-1 on 16

(Below) Douglas F4D-1 Skyray all-weather fighter.

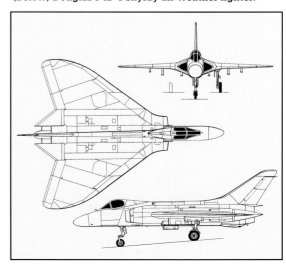

Key to Douglas F4D-1 (F-6A) Skyray

1 Radome nose
2 Radar antenna
3 Radar reflector dish
4 APQ-50A radar package
5 Weapons control package (Aero 13F system)
6 Detachable nose cone
7 Pressure head
8 Windscreen demister pipe
9 Pilot's instrument display
10 Armour-glass windscreen
11 Instrument panel shroud
12 Pilot's radar display
13 Flying control linkage
14 Forward cockpit pressure bulkhead
15 Nosewheel well and pre-closure door
16 Forward-retracting nosewheel
17 Nosewheel steering actuators
18 Nosewheel retraction strut
19 Nose gear rear door
20 Nose gear oleo leg
21 Aft cockpit pressure bulkhead
22 Engine controls on port console

23 Ejection seat base
24 Pilot's seat harness
25 Rear-view mirrors
26 Pressurized cockpit
27 Clamshell canopy
28 Seat ejection handle
29 Pilot's headrest
30 Navigation light
31 Air-conditioning vents
32 Armoured panel
33 Ejection seat rails
34 Conditioned air feed pipes
35 Canopy hinge point
36 Air-conditioning and pressurization plant
37 Hydraulic reservoirs
38 Port main air intake
39 Radio and electrical equipment bay
40 Intake boundary layer splitter plate

41 Compass
42 Inspection panel
43 Auxiliary air intakes
44 Generator
45 NAVPAC store containing ARN-14E omni-range receiver and ARN-12 marker beacon receiver
46 Catapult hook
47 Main air intake trunking

48 Autopilot equipment bay
49 Auxiliary air trunk
50 Junction of bifurcated trunk at engine face
51 Junction of mainspar with fuselage mainframe
52 Louvred air vent
53 Main fuselage longitudinal member
54 Foremost of three fuel filling points

55 "Catcher" for use during emergency barrier engagements aboard carriers
56 Inner wing pylon carrying rocket pod (19×2.75-in/70-mm missiles)
57 Elevon manual control run
58 Mainwheel well
59 Port fuel cells (320 US gal/1 211 litres each side)
60 Engine oil tank and filling point

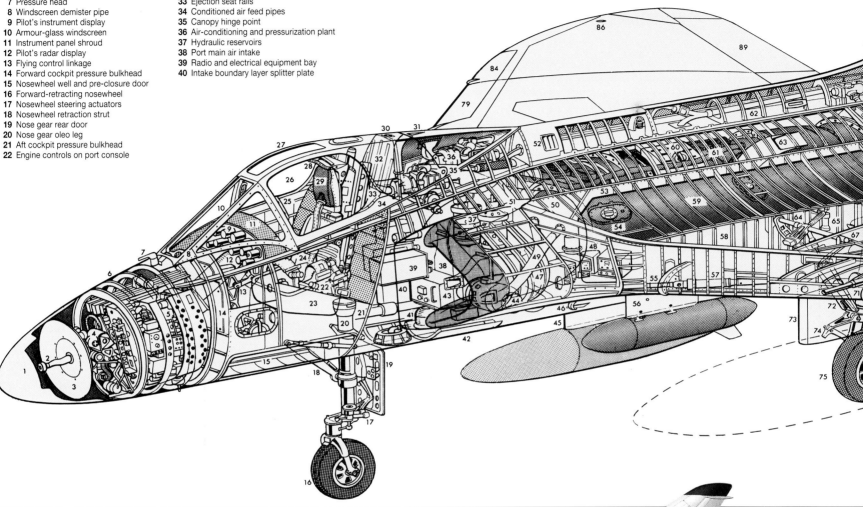

December 1948. The Skyray was designed around the Westinghouse J40 engine, but both XF4D-1s were initially flown with the 5,000 lb st (2 268 kgp) Allison J35-A-17, the first flight taking place on 23 January 1951. Both prototypes subsequently flew with the 7,000 lb st (3 175 kgp) XJ40-WE-6 and, eventually, the XJ40-WE-8 affording 11,600 lb st (5 262 kgp) with afterburning. The failure of the J40 engine led, in March 1953, to the decision to switch to the Pratt & Whitney J57, this necessitating the re-engineering of some 80 per cent of the structures, systems and installations. On 5 June 1954, the first production F4D-1 flew with a J57-P-2 engine, and deliveries to the US Navy began on 16 April 1956, a total of 420 having been built when production terminated in December 1958. Most F4D-1s (redesignated F-6As in September 1962) were powered by the J57-P-8 or -8B rated at 10,200 lb st (4 627 kgp) dry

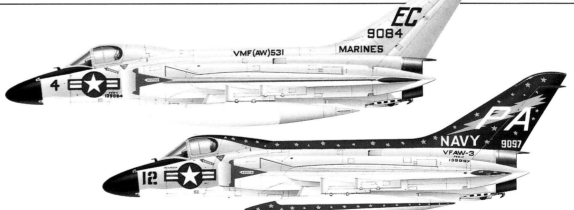

(Above, top) An F4D-1 of VMF(AW)-531 at Cherry Point, early 1958., (Immediately above) An F4D-1 of VFAW-3, serving in NORAD 1958-63. (Left) An F4D-1 with Marine Corps squadron VMF-115.

and 16,000 lb st (7 258 kgp) with afterburning, armament comprising four 20-mm cannon, or four external packs each containing seven or 19 2.75-in (6,98-cm) rockets, or four AAM-N-7 Sidewinder missiles. *Max speed (clean), 652 mph (1 049 km/h) or Mach=0.98 at 35,000 ft (10 670 m), 722 mph (1 162 km/h) or Mach=0.95 at sea level. Initial climb, 18,300 ft/min (92,96 m/sec). Empty weight, 16,024 lb (7 268 kg). Max loaded weight, 28,000 lb (12 701 kg). Span 33 ft 6 in (10,21 m). Length, 45 ft 4⅘ in (13,84 m). Height, 13 ft 0 in (3,96 m). Wing area, 557 sq ft (51,75 m²).*

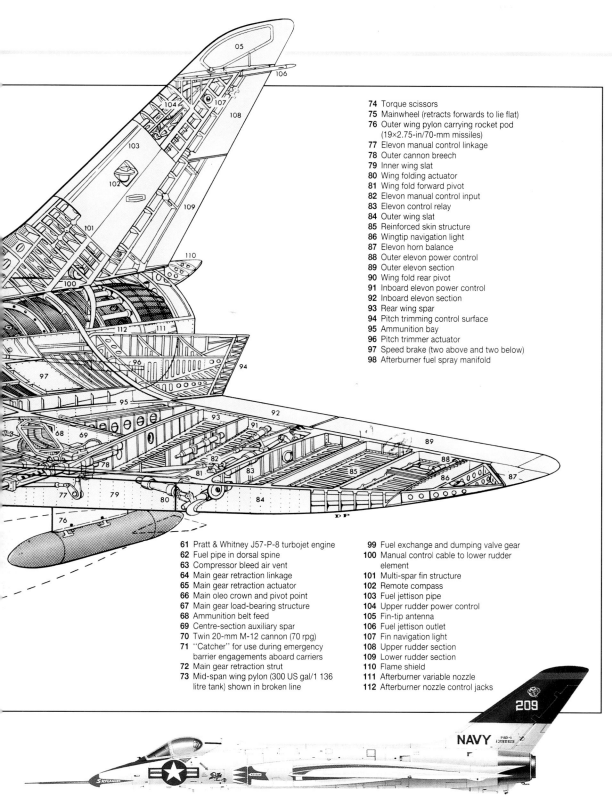

74 Torque scissors
75 Mainwheel (retracts forwards to lie flat)
76 Outer wing pylon carrying rocket pod
(19×2.75-in/70-mm missiles)
77 Elevon manual control linkage
78 Outer cannon breech
79 Inner wing slat
80 Wing folding actuator
81 Wing fold forward pivot
82 Elevon manual control input
83 Elevon control relay
84 Outer wing slat
85 Reinforced skin structure
86 Wingtip navigation light
87 Elevon horn balance
88 Outer elevon power control
89 Outer elevon section
90 Wing fold rear pivot
91 Inboard elevon power control
92 Inboard elevon section
93 Rear wing spar
94 Pitch trimming control surface
95 Ammunition bay
96 Pitch trimmer actuator
97 Speed brake (two above and two below)
98 Afterburner fuel spray manifold

61 Pratt & Whitney J57-P-8 turbojet engine
62 Fuel pipe in dorsal spine
63 Compressor bleed air vent
64 Main gear retraction linkage
65 Main gear retraction actuator
66 Main oleo crown and pivot point
67 Main gear load-bearing structure
68 Ammunition belt feed
69 Centre-section auxiliary spar
70 Twin 20-mm M-12 cannon (70 rpg)
71 "Catcher" for use during emergency
barrier engagements aboard carriers
72 Main gear retraction strut
73 Mid-span wing pylon (300 US gal/1 136
litre tank) shown in broken line
99 Fuel exchange and dumping valve gear
100 Manual control cable to lower rudder
element
101 Multi-spar fin structure
102 Remote compass
103 Fuel jettison pipe
104 Upper rudder power control
105 Fin-tip antenna
106 Fuel jettison outlet
107 Fin navigation light
108 Upper rudder section
109 Lower rudder section
110 Flame shield
111 Afterburner variable nozzle
112 Afterburner nozzle control jacks

1956. All four of these were powered by the Pratt & Whitney J57-P-8 rated at 10,200 lb st (4 627 kgp) dry and 16,000 lb st (7 258 kgp) with afterburning, the first of these flying on 21 April 1956. The proposed armament comprised four retractable rocket launchers accommodating a total of 72 2-in (5-cm) rockets or four 20-mm cannon, with two Sparrow II AAMs on underwing pylons. *Max speed, 749 mph (1 205 km/h), or Mach=0.986 at sea level, 953 mph (1 534 km/h), or Mach=1.44 at 35,000 ft (10 670 m). Initial climb, 20,790 ft/min (105,61 m/sec). Range (clean), 1,335 mls (2 148 km) at 601 mph (968 km/h) at 37,500 ft (11 430 m). Empty weight, 17,444 lb (7 912 kg). Max loaded weight, 29,122 lb (13 210 kg). Span, 33 ft 6 in (10,21 m). Length, 53 ft 9⅗ in (16,40 m). Height, 14 ft 9⅗ in (4,51 m). Wing area, 557 sq ft (51,75 m²).*

DUCROT SLD   Italy

During World War I, a number of Italian industrial concerns were invited to convert their facilities to cater for aircraft manufacture, one such being the Palermo-based firm of Vittoria Ducrot, which, in February 1916, initiated licence manufacture of flying boats. Anxious to progress from licensee to prime contractor, Ducrot established its own design office under *Ing* Manlio Stiavelli, who, with Guido Luzzatti, designed a high-performance single-seat fighter, the SLD (Stiavelli-Luzzatti-Ducrot). Powered by a 200 hp Hispano-Suiza 35 engine, the SLD placed emphasis on aerodynamic cleanliness, featuring an oval-section plywood monocoque fuselage which was carried above the lower wing by struts which also carried the undercarriage.

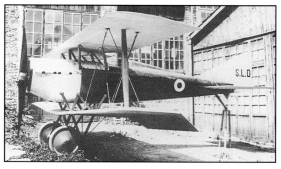

(Above) Aerodynamic cleanliness was an obvious feature of the single example of the Ducrot SLD.

(Left) Second of the four Skylancers that, originally ordered as F4D-2Ns, underwent flight testing during 1956-57.

(Below) The Ducrot SLD single-seat fighter.

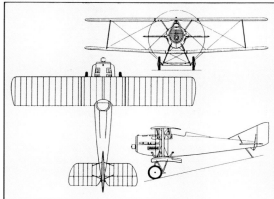

DOUGLAS F5D SKYLANCER   USA

Although possessing a similar general configuration to that of the F4D-1 and initially being known as the F4D-2, the F5D-1 retained only the planform of the low

(Below) Douglas F5D-1 Skylancer shipboard fighter.

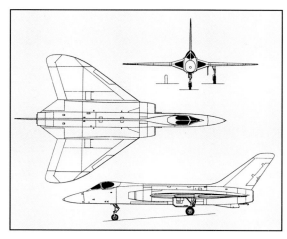

aspect ratio swept wing of its predecessor. The wing was of appreciably thinner section, the fuselage was slimmer and longer, and the vertical tail surfaces were substantially enlarged. Internal fuel capacity was increased by some 35 per cent and it was proposed that the definitive production F5D be powered by the General Electric J79 turbojet. Nineteen F5D-1s were ordered for US Navy evaluation in the all-weather shipboard fighter rôle, but only four of these had been completed when the Skylancer programme was curtailed in

(Below) The first of four F5D-1 prototypes seen soon after commencement of 1956 flight test programme.

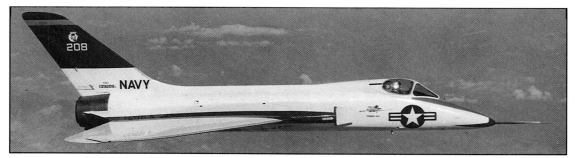

Trials commenced in October 1918, but no details of the results of these survive. *Max speed, 186 mph (300 km/h). Time to 16,405 ft (5 000 m), 10.0 min. Empty weight, 1,345 lb (610 kg). Loaded weight, 1,786 lb (810 kg). Wing area, 236.8 sq ft (22,00 m²).*

DUFAUX — France

In the early spring of 1916, Armand Dufaux completed the prototype of an original two-seat fighter biplane in which a 110 hp Le Rhône 9J air-cooled rotary engine was buried in the forward fuselage to drive a two-bladed propeller amidships, the union between the forward and rear fuselage sections being provided by a substantial tubular member which passed through the propeller hub, this support being augmented by tie rods between the undercarriage V-struts and the tail-skid support. The pilot and gunner sat in side-by-side staggered seats immediately ahead of the engine, the latter (to starboard) having a single 7,7-mm Lewis gun. Built by the Société pour la Construction et l'Entretien d'Avions (CEA), the Dufaux fighter commenced official tests at Chateaufort in April 1916, but the problems of engine cooling, structural rigidity, etc, apparently militated against further development. *Max speed, 87 mph (140 km/h) at sea level. Time to 6,560 ft (2 000 m), 13.15 min. Endurance, 2.0 hrs. Empty weight, 1,168 lb (530 kg). Loaded weight, 1,631 lb (740 kg). Span, 26 ft 1⅖ in (7,96 m). Length, 20 ft 0 in (6,10 m). Height, 9 ft 1¼ in (2,80 m).*

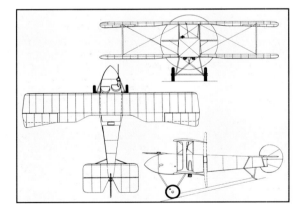

The extraordinary Dufaux fighter (above and below) in which the engine drove a propeller amidships.

DUFAUX AVION-CANON — France

Armand Dufaux's *avion-canon* was one of the most original fighters of World War I in that it was designed around a fixed forward-firing 37-mm Hotchkiss cannon. The aircraft itself was of conventional layout, being a single-bay single-seat biplane with a two-bladed tractor propeller. In order to cater for the centrally-mounted cannon firing through a hollow propeller shaft, two

nine-cylinder air-cooled rotary engines were mounted athwartships. The cannon passed between the engines and the hollow propeller shaft was driven by bevel gearing. Built in the workshops of the CEA, Dufaux's *avion-canon* was tested in 1917, and allegedly achieved speeds in excess of 124 mph (200 km/h). It was demonstrated before the Minister of Aviation of the day, but further development was not pursued and neither illustrations nor data relating to this extraordinary fighter appear to have survived.

E

EBERHART XFG-1 (COMANCHE) — USA

The Eberhart XFG-1 (above and below) in its definitive form with extended-span upper wing.

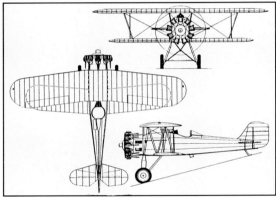

The Eberhart Aeroplane and Motor Company (formerly Eberhart Steel Products Company) produced its first original aircraft in 1927. This, the XFG-1 single-seat shipboard fighter for the US Navy, appeared in June of that year. Assigned the company name "Comanche", the XFG-1 was of welded steel-tube and dural construction with fabric skinning, and was powered by a 425 hp Pratt & Whitney R-1340-C Wasp nine-cylinder air-cooled radial. An unusual feature of the XFG-1 design was the application of sweepback to the upper mainplane and forward sweep to the lower. At an early test stage the span of the upper wing was increased from 28 ft 9 in (8,76 m) to 32 ft 0 in (9,75 m). The sole prototype was tested by the US Navy during November-December 1927, and then returned to the manufacturer for reconstruction as the XF2G-1 (which see). *Max speed, 155 mph (249 km/h). Time to 5,000 ft (1 525 m), 3.7 min. Empty weight, 2,145 lb (973 kg). Loaded weight, 2,938 lb (1 333 kg). Span, 32 ft 0 in (9,75 m).*

Length, 27 ft 3 in (8,30 m). Height, 9 ft 10 in (3,0 m). Wing area, 241 sq ft (22,38 m²).

EBERHART XF2G-1 — USA

(Above) The Eberhart XF2G-1 float-equipped fighter evaluated at Anacostia during January-March 1928.

After US Navy trials with the XFG-1, the prototype was returned to Eberhart to be reworked as a single-seat float fighter under the designation XF2G-1. Re-engined with a Pratt & Whitney R-1340-D Wasp of 400 hp, retaining the longer span wings, and equipped with a central main float and outrigger stabilising floats, the fighter was returned to Anacostia in January 1928. US Navy trials continued until March of that year, when the prototype was destroyed and further development abandoned. *Max speed, 157 mph (253 km/h). Loaded weight, 3,142 lb (1 425 kg). Span, 32 ft 0 in (9,75 m). Length, 26 ft 3¾ in (8,02 m). Height, 9 ft 9¾ in (2,99 m). Wing area, 241.26 sq ft (22,41 m²).*

ELIAS EM — USA

To meet a US Marine Corps requirement for a two-seat multi-rôle aircraft suitable for use as a fighter, light bomber or observation aircraft on wheel undercarriage or floats under conditions of minimum servicing facilities, G Elias & Brothers designed and built the EM-1. This appeared in 1922 with a 300 hp Wright-Hispano-

One of the Elias EM-2 fighters (above) fitted with central main float and outrigger stabilising floats.

Suiza "H" engine and wheel undercarriage. The EM-1 was initially flown as an unequal-span biplane, but early flight testing dictated the extension of the lower wing to match the span of the upper wing. A further six aircraft had meanwhile been ordered, but, as the initial aircraft had proved underpowered, these were fitted with the 400 hp Liberty and designated EM-2. The first EM-2 was delivered to the USMC and the remaining five to the US Navy (one as an observation aircraft under the designation EO-1), and these were flown with wheel undercarriages and both with twin floats and with single main float and outrigger stabilising floats. The USMC multi-rôle (EM=Marine Expeditionary) requirement proved short-lived, but provided a basis for the further development of true two-seat naval fighters. The following data relate to the Liberty-engined EM-2 with wheel undercarriage. *Max speed, 111 mph (178 km/h). Loaded weight, 3,916 lb (1 776 kg). Span, 39 ft 8 in (12,09 m). Length, 28 ft 6 in (8,68 m). Height, 10 ft 9 in (3,28 m).*

ENAER PANTERA (MIRAGE 50CN) — (France) Chile

Like the Atlas Cheetah (which see), the Pantera (Panther) was an extensive modification and upgrade

(Left) The prototype Pantera upgrade of the Mirage 50CH performed in Chile with the aid of IAI kits.

of the Dassault Mirage, but, in this case, by ENAER (Empresa Nacional de Aéronautica) with the aid of kits provided by IAI (Israel Aircraft Industries). The Pantera had non-moving foreplanes, or canards, an IAI Kfir C7-type extended nose, and IAI pulse-Doppler radar and generally upgraded avionics and weapons systems. Flight testing of the foreplanes and more minor aerodynamic modifications began early 1986 with one of the six Mirage 50CHs of the *Fuerza Aérea de Chile*. This same aircraft was subsequently upgraded to the initially-proposed avionics standard and rolled out by ENAER on 14 October 1988 as the Pantera (Mirage 50CN). Changes in the avionics specification delayed the upgrade programme, and trials of the definitive system began with a two-seat Mirage 50DC early 1991. Upgrade of the Mirage fleet to Pantera standard then began at a rate of four aircraft annually, with completion scheduled for late 1994. The Pantera retained the SNECMA Atar 9K with an afterburning thrust of 15,873 lb (7 200 kg) and paired 30-mm cannon. Data are essentially similar to those of the Mirage 50.

ENGELS MI — Russia

In 1916, several single-seat fighter flying boats were developed to meet a requirement formulated by the Directorate of Naval Aviation for what was referred to as a "counter-fighter"; a water-borne fighter intended specifically to oppose the Albatros W 4 that had appeared in the Baltic. The most novel of the contenders was the MI (*Morskoi istrebitel*) designed by Ye R Engels. Flown at the beginning of December 1916, this was a parasol cantilever monoplane flying boat with a V-section hull, downswept wingtips incorporating flotation chambers providing the necessary stability on the water. Control was by wing warping, power was provided by a pusher Gnome-Monosoupape rotary of 100 hp and provision was made for a single fixed forward-firing 7,62-mm Maxim gun. During its initial flight at the beginning of December 1916, the Engels MI achieved 106 mph (170 km/h), and although it suffered an accident during its third flight (the starboard rear spar breaking and the wing warping cable fouling the propeller), an order was placed with the Mel'tser factory on 27 April 1917 for 60 examples powered by the 120 hp Le Rhône. The first was completed on 24 August 1917, and the second two weeks later, on 9 September, one being transferred to the Navy on 10 October, but work at the factory subsequently came to a standstill. The second example was eventually delivered to the Naval Aviation School at Nizhny Novgorod (Gorky) in March 1920, and tested with skis, but no others were completed. *Empty weight, 849 lb (385 kg). Loaded weight, 1,224 lb (555 kg). Span, 29 ft 6⅓ in (9,00 m). Length, 24 ft 7¼ in (7,50 m). Wing area, 152.85 sq ft (14,20 m²).*

The Engels-designed MI water-borne fighter (below).

ENGINEERING DIVISION (POMILIO) FVL-8 — USA

At the request of the US Army's Engineering Division at McCook Field, Ottorino Pomilio of the Turin-based company of Pomilio Brothers undertook the design of a single-seat fighter around the then-new 280 hp Liberty eight-cylinder water-cooled engine. Designated FVL-8, the Pomilio-designed fighter was of wooden construction with plywood fuselage skinning and carried an armament of twin synchronised 0.3-in (7,7-mm) Vickers machine guns. Six prototypes of the FVL-8 were built in Indianapolis, the first of these being delivered in February 1919, but no series production was undertaken. *Max speed, 133 mph (214 km/h). Empty weight, 1,726 lb (783 kg). Loaded weight, 2,284 lb (1 036 kg). Span, 26 ft 8 in (8,13 m). Length, 21 ft 8 in (6,60 m).*

(Above and below) The Pomilio-designed FVL-8 conceived for the US Army's Engineering Division and of which six were built in Indianapolis.

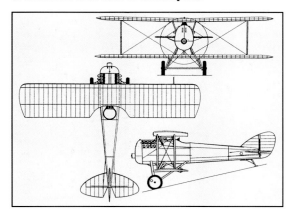

Height, 8 ft 2 in (2,49 m). Wing area, 284 sq ft (26,38 m²).

ENGINEERING DIVISION VCP-1 — USA

Designed in 1918 by Alfred Verville and Capt V E Clark, the VCP-1 (the designation indicating Verville-Clark-Pursuit) single-seat single-bay fighter biplane was built at McCook Field and powered by a 300 hp Wright-Hispano "H" engine. Advanced features for its time included a laminated wood veneer fuselage and I-type interplane struts, and the first of the two VCP-1 prototypes was completed and flown in August 1919, initially

The sole example of the VCP-1 completed (above and below) with the original annular radiator.

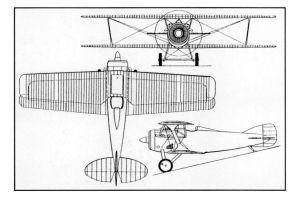

with an annular radiator and large spinner. A more conventional radiator and spinner combination was subsequently adopted, and the sole VCP-1 completed was eventually fitted with a 660 hp Packard 1A-2025 12-cylinder Vee engine to participate in the 1920 Pulitzer Prize Race as the VCP-R. Further modifications were incorporated for the 1922 Pulitzer Prize Race and the designation changed to R-1. *Max speed, 154 mph (248 km/h) at sea level, 152 mph (245 km/h) at 6,500 ft (1 980 m). Initial climb, 1,690 ft/min (8,58 m/sec). Range, 298 mls (479 km). Empty weight, 2,014 lb (913 kg). Loaded weight, 2,669 lb (1 211 kg). Span, 32 ft 0 in (9,75 m). Length, 22 ft 4 in (6,81 m). Height, 8 ft 4 in (2,54 m). Wing area, 269 sq ft (24,99 m²).*

ENGINEERING DIVISION PW-1 — USA

The PW-1 (above) with the original tapered wings, later replaced by thicker, straight-chord wings.

Another Verville-Clark design, initially to be known as the VCP-2, the PW-1 was essentially a derivative of the VCP-1 with a rectangular-section steel-tube fuselage with fabric skinning and a 350 hp Packard 1A-1237 engine. One static test and one flying model were ordered, the latter being flown for the first time in November 1921. The tapered wings of the PW-1 were later replaced by new straight-chord wings with a thicker-section Fokker aerofoil and with which the prototype fighter was redesignated PW-1A. The upper wing had a shorter span than that of the lower wing (an arrangement also adopted by the designers for the TP-1). The performance of the PW-1A proved markedly inferior to that of the PW-1. Plans were formulated to produce the PW-1 with the Curtiss D-12 engine, but these failed to materialise and development was confined to the single flying prototype. *Max speed, 146 mph (235 km/h) at sea level, 144 mph (232 km/h) at 6,500 ft (1 980 m). Endurance, 2.5 hrs at 131 mph (211 km/h). Empty weight, 2,069 lb (938 kg). Loaded weight, 3,005 lb (1 363 kg). Span, 32 ft 0 in (9,75 m). Length, 22 ft 6 in (6,86 m). Height, 8 ft 4 in (2,54 m). Wing area, 269 sq ft (24,99 m²).*

ENGINEERING DIVISION TP-1 — USA

The last fighter to be built by the US Army itself, the TP-1 two-seat fighter was designed by Verville and Clark, and built at McCook Field. Powered by a 423 hp Liberty 12 water-cooled engine, only one TP-1 was completed (a second being adapted while still under construction as an observation aircraft under the designation CO-5) and performance was considered inadequate for the fighter rôle. This aircraft was subsequently fitted experimentally with a turbo-supercharger with which it attained 150 mph (241 km/h) at

The TP-1 two-seater (above) was the last fighter actually to be built by the US Army itself.

20,300 ft (6 190 m). An unusual design feature of the TP-1 was the fact that the upper wing had a smaller span and narrower chord than the lower wing. Armament comprised two fixed forward-firing 0.3-in (7,7-mm) Browning guns, twin Lewis guns of the same calibre on a ring mounting in the rear cockpit and another Lewis firing downward through a floor hatch. On 27 March 1924, the sole TP-1 (meanwhile redesignated XTP-1) established a record by lifting a 551-lb (250 kg) load to 29,462 ft (8 980 m) and, two months later, on 21 May, a 1,102-lb (500-kg) load to 28,143 ft (8 578 m). *Max speed, 129 mph (207 km/h) at sea level, 123 mph (198 km/h) at 6,500 ft (1 980 m). Initial climb, 495 ft/min (2,5 m/sec). Endurance, 3.6 hrs. Empty weight, 2,748 lb (1 246 kg). Loaded weight, 4,363 lb (1 979 kg). Span, 36 ft 0 in (10,97 m). Length, 25 ft 1 in (7,64 m). Height, 10 ft 0 in (3,05 m). Wing area, 375 sq ft (38,84 m²).*

EULER "GELBER HUND" Germany

August Euler, proprietor of the Euler-Werke, near Frankfurt am Main, obtained a patent in 1912 for a fixed forward-firing machine gun aimed by steering the aircraft on which it was mounted in the direction of the target. This development was demonstrated to the German military authorities on 10 May 1912, the gun being mounted on a two-seat pusher biplane named "*Gelber Hund*" (Yellow Dog). In 1915, the Euler-Werke produced a single-seat fighter, which, also known as the "*Gelber Hund*", mounted a single fixed forward-firing 7,92-mm Maxim MG 08/15 machine gun in the nose of a short fuselage nacelle, power being provided by a 120 hp Mercedes D III engine mounted at the rear of the nacelle. The propeller rotated between twin wire-braced steel-frame booms carrying the tail assembly. The "*Gelber Hund*" failed to attract a production order and no specification has apparently survived.

Known as the "Gelber Hund", this single-seat pusher (below) was the first Euler-Werke fighting scout.

EULER (VERSUCHSZWEISITZER) Germany

In parallel with the single-seat "*Gelber Hund*", the Euler-Werke built, as a private venture, a two-seat fighter of generally similar configuration referred to simply as a *versuchszweisitzer* (experimental two-sea-

ter). Intended primarily for anti-airship and escort tasks, and powered by a 160 hp Mercedes D III engine, the *versuchszweisitzer* appeared in the late autumn of 1915, and, in its initial form, featured a rotating turret for a gunner in the extreme nose of the fuselage nacelle, the pilot being accommodated aft. The turret was provided with a single Bergmann MG 15n/A machine gun.

Euler's original two-seat fighter (above) in its original form with nose turret and (below) in its final form with faired, pulpit-like gun position.

After initial trials, the fuselage nacelle was rebuilt, the pilot being moved forward in the nose and provided with a fixed forward-firing Bergmann gun, and the gunner being accommodated in a pulpit-like open-frame turret providing a 360-deg field of fire and mounting a single Parabellum MG 14 machine gun. In an attempt to reduce drag, the frame supporting the turret ring-mounting was subsequently faired in and the forward decking of the fuselage nacelle was raised to partially enclose the fixed gun, but further development was

abandoned shortly afterwards. *Time to 9,840 ft (3 000 m), 44 min. Endurance, 4 hrs. Span, 48 ft 6¾ in (14,80 m). Length, 30 ft 6⅛ in (9,30 m). Height, 10 ft 6 in (3,20 m). Wing area, 566.20 sq ft (52,60 m²).*

EULER D I Germany

The Euler D I (above) adhered closely in design to that of the highly-successful French Nieuport 11.

The success at the front of the Nieuport 11 prompted the German authorities to request several manufacturers to design aircraft based on the French fighter, that produced by the Euler-Werke as the company's D I probably adhering most closely to the original. Powered by an 80 hp Oberursel U O seven-cylinder rotary and mounting a single 7,92-mm machine gun, the D I prototype was flown in the autumn of 1916, and an initial series of 50 was ordered in October of that year, despite the fact that type testing at Adlershof was not to be completed until January 1917. Two Euler D Is (presumably prototypes) were recorded as being at the front at the end of October 1916, but the production aircraft was to be employed primarily as a fighter trainer. A further 50 were ordered with the completion of the Adlershof trials, but part of this order was later transferred to the D II (which see). *Max speed, 87 mph (140 km/h). Time to 6,560 ft (2 000 m), 12.5 min. Empty weight, 838 lb (380 kg). Loaded weight, 1,323 lb (600 kg). Span, 26 ft 6⅞ in (8,10 m). Length, 19 ft 0¼ in (5,80 m). Height, 8 ft 8¾ in (2,66 m). Wing area, 139.93 sq ft (13,00 m²).*

EULER D II Germany

The Euler D II was essentially a re-engined D I, the airframe being virtually unchanged and the power plant being a 100 hp Oberursel U I seven-cylinder rotary. A batch of 30 D II fighters was ordered in March 1917, but owing to tardiness on the part of the Euler-Werke in producing these, deliveries did not commence until the following December and, in consequence, the D II was relegated to the *Jagdstaffelschulen* with which it served until the end of hostilities. *Max speed 90 mph (145 km/h). Time to 6,560 ft (2 000 m), 9.5 min. Endurance, 1.5 hrs. Empty weight, 838 lb (380 kg). Loaded weight, 1,356 lb (615 kg). Span, 24 ft 6 in (7,47 m). Length, 19 ft 5⅞ in (5,94 m). Height, 9 ft 0 in (2,75 m).*

The Euler-Werke was tardy in producing the D II (below) and it was thus relegated to training.

EULER DREIDECKER
(TYPE 2)   Germany

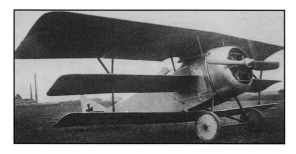

(Above) The first triplane fighter produced as a co-operative effort by Euler and Hromadnik in 1917.

In 1917, the Austro-Hungarian engineer Julius Hromadnik joined forces with August Euler, the result of this partnership being a series of private venture biplane, triplane and quadruplane fighters comprising approximately half of the 22 experimental aircraft produced by the Euler-Werke during World War I. The first-known Euler experimental fighter triplane developed in collaboration with Hromadnik was first reported in July 1917, this being Euler's second wartime triplane as, in August of the previous year, the company had flown a side-by-side two-seat training triplane powered by a 220 hp eight-cylinder Mercedes D IV engine. The fighter triplane was powered by a 14-cylinder two-row Oberursel U III engine of 160 hp and featured I-type struts between the centre and lower wing, and V-type struts between the centre and upper wing. Disappointing performance led to the modification of this experimental fighter to biplane configuration and in this form it was still under test in April 1918. No specification is available.

EULER DREIDECKER
(TYPE 3)   Germany

An entirely new single-seat fighter triplane produced by the Euler-Werke with the assistance of Julius Hromadnik was flown for the first time in November 1917. Built, like its predecessor, as a private venture, it had parallel-chord equi-span wings with I-type interplane

(Above) The private-venture Type 3 triplane was the second Euler-Werke fighter of this configuration.

struts and a 160 hp Mercedes D III engine. This type evidently fell short of requirements as, like the earlier fighter triplane, it was rebuilt in biplane form (see *Doppeldecker* Type 1) for further trials. No specification is available.

(Below) The Euler-Werke triplane fighter (Type 3).

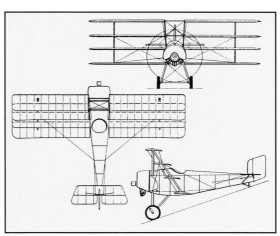

EULER VIERDECKER   Germany

Referred to as a quadruplane, the Euler fighter (above and below) was technically of triplane form.

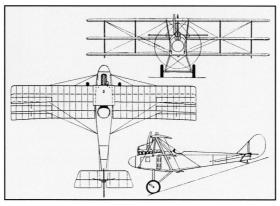

Confused erroneously with the D II, the Euler Type 2 biplane (below) appeared in April 1918.

Although referred to as a *vierdecker* (quadruplane), this Euler fighter powered by a 100 hp Oberursel U I seven-cylinder rotary, which commenced its flight test programme in December 1917, was technically a triplane in that the top surfaces were, in fact, full-span ailerons acting as a controllable fourth wing surface. The poor performance demonstrated during evaluation at Adlershof, which was continuing in May 1918, precluded further military interest in the design, although a second prototype was completed with a 110 hp Goebel Goe II seven-cylinder rotary. Both prototypes were transported out of the Allied zone of occupation in December 1918. *Empty weight, 1,948 lb (883,5 kg). Loaded weight, 3,054 lb (1 385,5 kg). Wing area, 497 sq ft (46,17 m²).*

EULER DREIDECKER
(TYPE 4)   Germany

The most successful of the Euler-Hromadnik fighter triplanes was powered by the newly-perfected Goebel Goe III nine-cylinder rotary engine of 180 hp. By virtue of having achieved an altitude of 16,405 ft (5 000 m) in 13.5 min, the Goe III-powered triplane was demonstrated during the second D-type contest at Adlershof in May 1918. However, service pilots were unimpressed by the fighter, the tailplane of which was severely damaged during taxying, and the aircraft was returned to the Euler-Werke in consequence, remaining there until removed from the factory in December 1918. No specification is available.

The most successful of the Euler-Hromadnik triplanes was the extremely neat Type 4 illustrated above.

EULER DOPPELDECKER
(TYPE 1)   Germany

In April 1918, the *Inspektion der Fliegertruppen (Idflieg)* reported that the Mercedes D III-powered triplane fighter (Type 3) had been rebuilt as a biplane and that altitude test flying was imminent. Official evaluation continued throughout May, during the course of which the I-type interplane struts were replaced by V-type struts and the inverted V-type struts of the cabane gave place to paired individual struts on each side. Testing appears to have been inconclusive, the prototype eventually being returned to the Euler-Werke. No specification is available.

Seen below in its initial form, the Type 1 Euler biplane was, in fact, the Type 3 triplane rebuilt.

EULER DOPPELDECKER
(TYPE 2)   Germany

An extremely compact fighter biplane powered by the 160 hp Siemens und Halske Sh III counter-rotating engine driving a four-bladed propeller was flown for the first time in April 1918 by the Euler-Werke. This air-

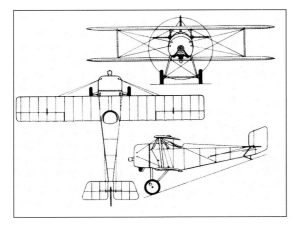

(Above) The compact Type 2 Euler fighting biplane.

craft (which has been confused with the Euler D II) was a parallel-chord equi-span single-bay biplane and was reputed to possess an exceptional performance. It was scheduled to participate in the second D-type contest in May, but did not appear, and its subsequent testing was reportedly restricted. No specification is available.

EULER DREIDECKER (TYPE 5)　　　　　　Germany

Some doubts concerning the efficacy of the full-span ailerons acting as a controllable wing, as utilised by the Euler-*Vierdecker* (which see), resulted in the development of a more orthodox triplane version of the same basic design with normal ailerons fitted. Initially powered by a similar 100 hp Oberursel U I seven-cylinder rotary, it was reportedly later re-engined with the more efficient 110 hp nine-cylinder Siemens und Halske Sh I counter-rotating power plant. At the same time, equal wing gap replaced the unequal gap with which initial flight testing was conducted, the centre wing being raised on the fuselage and the cabane struts being lengthened. No specification is available.

The final Euler fighting triplane (Type 5) is seen above in its original form and below after the application of increased gap and deeper cabane.

EUROFIGHTER TYPHOON　　　　International

By 1983, five European nations, Britain, France, Germany, Italy, and Spain, had combined to develop an agile multi-role fighter to counter the next generation of Soviet combat aircraft. In 1985 France left the consortium to develop Rafale (which see), but the remaining four continued. The first step was to produce a technology demonstrator, the European Aircraft Programme (EAP). BAe and Aeritalia, by a superhuman effort, got it into the air in August 1986, where it proved invaluable in proving such items as the quadruplex FBW system and automated wing camber. Progress was slow and it was not until 27

The second of the development-batch Eurofighters (above) was completed by BAe in the UK during 1994. The prototype EFA configuration is depicted (below).

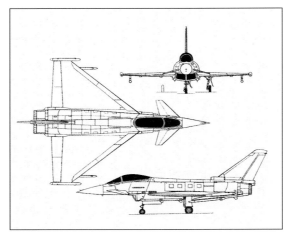

March 1994 that EF 2000, named Typhoon in 1998, first flew. A twin-engined canard delta, it differed from Rafale and Sweden's Gripen in having the canards set well forward, giving a long moment arm. The first two prototypes were powered by the RB199 turbofan. Not until 6 June 1995 did a Typhoon fly with the definitive EJ200, a two-spool turbofan designed for the aircraft by a European consortium, rated at 20,250 lb (9 185 kgp) max and 13,500 lb (6 124 kgp) military thrust. In future, this will almost certainly be fitted with thrust vectoring to improve agility. The ECR 90 multi-mode radar is also a quadrilateral production, and is supplemented by a "two-colour" Infra-Red Search and Track (IRST) system. Naturally it has a "glass cockpit" and HOTAS, and the Defensive Aids SubSystem (DASS), which provides threat warnings and automatic countermeasures, including towed decoys. Most systems are automated to reduce pilot workload. Weaponry consists of a 27-mm Mauser cannon with 150 rounds, although this has been deleted from RAF aircraft. Four AIM-120 Amraam and six Asraam will be routinely carried, although in the future Amraam will probably be replaced by Meteor. Typhoon is scheduled to enter service with all four nations from 2003, with Greece the first export customer. *Max speed hi, Mach 2 plus. Ceiling, c60,000 ft (18 287 m). Rate of climb, c60,000 ft/min (305 m/sec). Empty weight, 24,240 lb (10 995 kg). Max takeoff weight, 50,706 lb (23,000 kg). Span, 35ft 11in (10.95 m). Length, 52 ft 4 in (15,96 m). Height, 17 ft 4 in (5,28m). Wing area, 538 sq ft (50 m²).*

FAIREY HAMBLE BABY　　　　UK

The Hamble Baby represented an attempt on the part of the Fairey Aviation Company to improve the performance of the Sopwith Baby single-seat fighter float sea-plane, but, in the event, emerged as virtually a new type. The Hamble Baby used, for the first time, the Fairey Patent Camber Gear, a form of trailing-edge

flap attached to each mainplane of the redesigned wing to act as ailerons in normal flight, but capable of being deflected as lift-increasing devices for take-off and landing. The tail assembly was redesigned and Fairey designed floats were fitted. Armament consisted of a single synchronised 0.303-in (7,7-mm) machine gun with provision for two 65-lb (29,5-kg) bombs. The first 50 aircraft were powered by the 110 hp Clerget nine-cylinder rotary engine and the remaining 130 (built by Parnall and Sons) had the 130 hp Clerget. The last 74 Babies built by Parnall were fitted with wheel-and-skid undercarriages and known as Hamble Baby Converts. The Hamble Babies were operated by the RNAS in the UK, the Mediterranean and the Aegean, entering service in the summer of 1917. The data relate to the 110 hp Baby. *Max speed, 90 mph (145 km/h) at 2,000 ft (610 m). Time to 2,000 ft (610 m), 5.5 min. Endurance, 2.0 hrs. Empty weight, 1,386 lb (629 kg). Loaded weight, 1,946 lb (883 kg). Span, 27ft 9¹/₄in (8,46 m). Length, 23 ft 4 in (7,11 m). Height, 9 ft 6 in (2,89 m). Wing area, 246 sq ft (22,85 m²).*

(Above) A Fairey-built Hamble Baby fighter floatplane derived from the Sopwith Baby, and (below) a Parnall-built Hamble Baby Convert.

FAIREY F.2　　　　UK

The first aircraft to be designed entirely by Fairey Aviation, the F.2 was a massive twin-engined, three-seat, long-range fighter ordered by the Admiralty. Powered by two 190 hp Rolls-Royce Falcon 12-cylinder water-cooled engines, the F.2 was a three-bay biplane with a four-wheel "bedstead" main undercarriage, the wings folding aft from a point outboard of the engines.

The massive Fairey F.2 (below) multi-engined multi-seat fighter that entered flight test in May 1917.

Armament consisted of a 0.303-in (7,7-mm) Lewis machine gun on a Scarff ring in the extreme nose and a similar installation immediately aft of the wings. The sole prototype made its official first flight on 17 May 1917, but Admiralty interest in the F.2 had waned by then, and no further development was undertaken as no use had been found for the large, relatively slow, multi-engined, multi-seat fighter. *Max speed, 93 mph (150 km/h) at sea level. Time to 5,000 ft (1 525 m), 6.0 min. Endurance, 3.5 hrs. Loaded weight, 4,880 lb (2 213 kg). Span, 77 ft 0 in (23,47 m). Length, 40 ft 6 in (12,34 m). Height, 13 ft 6 in (4,11 m). Wing area, 814 sq ft (75,62 m²).*

FAIREY PINTAIL UK

Designed to meet the requirements of the RAF Type XXI specification calling for a two-seat amphibious fighter-reconnaissance aircraft, the Pintail flew on 7 July 1920 powered by a 475 hp Napier Lion 12-cylinder broad-arrow water-cooled engine. Initially flown with an orthodox twin-float undercarriage, it was later fitted with wheels retracting into float housings. The armament comprised a fixed forward-firing 0.303-in (7,7-mm) Vickers machine gun and a Scarff ring-mounted Lewis gun of similar calibre for the second crew member. The second prototype, the Pintail II, which flew on 25 May 1921, featured a lengthened fuselage and the third prototype, the Pintail III flown on 8 November 1921, had fixed wheels within the floats, and the camber of the wing trailing edges of all three prototypes could be varied. Three Pintails were ordered by the Imperial Japanese Navy in August 1923, the first of these, referred to as the Pintail IV, being flown on 20 August 1924. The Pintail IV differed from the III in having a 9-in (22,86 cm) increase in the wing/fuselage gap. *Max speed, 125 mph (201 km/h). Time to 5,000 ft (1 525 m), 5.13 min. Loaded weight, 4,750 lb (2 155 kg). Span, 40 ft 0 in (12,19 m). Length, 32 ft 3 in (9,80 m). Height, 11 ft 0 in (3,35 m). Wing area, 400 sq ft (37,16 m²).*

(Below) The Pintail IV amphibious fighter of which three examples were supplied to the Japanese Navy.

FAIREY FLYCATCHER UK

The Flycatcher was designed to Specification 6/22 for a single-seat shipboard fighter capable of being fitted with floats or an amphibious undercarriage. Primarily of wooden construction with fabric skinning and powered by a 400 hp 14-cylinder Armstrong Siddeley Jaguar II radial, the first prototype Flycatcher flew on 28 November 1922. It was later re-engined with a Bristol Jupiter IV nine-cylinder radial of similar power. The second prototype, flown on 5 May 1923, was completed as a twin-float seaplane with a Jaguar II engine, and the third prototype was fitted with an amphibious

The last of the second production batch of Fairey Flycatchers (below) delivered to the FAA early 1924.

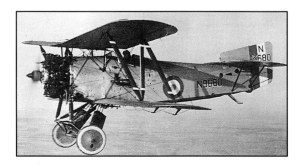

(Above) Full-scale Flycatcher replica, flown on 23 July 1979, and (below) general arrangement drawing.

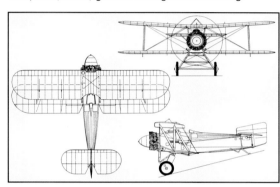

undercarriage. A further 203 Flycatchers were subsequently built, the last being completed and flown on 20 June 1930, and the type remained the standard (and only) fighter of the Fleet Air Arm until the Nimrod began to enter service in 1932. The production model was powered by the Jaguar III or IV and carried an armament of two 0.303-in (7,7-mm) Vickers machine guns. The data relate to the landplane version with the Jaguar IV. *Max speed, 134 mph (216 km/h) at sea level, 131 mph (211 km/h) at 10,000 ft (3 050 m). Time to 5,000 ft (1 525 m), 3.7 min. Empty weight, 2,038 lb (924 kg). Loaded weight, 3,028 lb (1 375 kg). Span 29 ft 0 in (8,84 m). Length, 23 ft 0 in (7,01 m). Height, 12 ft 0 in (3,66 m). Wing area, 288 sq ft (26,76 m²).*

FAIREY FLYCATCHER II UK

The sole prototype of the Flycatcher II (above) flown with both wheel and float undercarriages.

Despite its appellation, the Flycatcher II bore no relationship to the original Flycatcher other than design origin and was designed to Specification N.21/26 which called for a potential replacement for the original type. Possessing an all-metal fuselage and (as initially flown) wooden wings, the Flycatcher II flew with an Armstrong Siddeley Jaguar engine on 4 October 1926, the 540 hp supercharged Mk VIII version of this engine being substituted prior to deck-landing trials in July 1927. It was subsequently fitted with floats, with which it flew on 16 August 1927, and in the following year was again re-engined with a 480 hp Bristol Mercury IIA,

being simultaneously fitted with metal wings. Armament comprised two 0.303-in (7,7-mm) synchronised Vickers Mk II machine guns and the sole prototype was written-off in a take-off accident on 8 May 1929. The following data relate to the prototype in its definitive form. *Max speed, 153 mph (246 km/h). Loaded weight, 3,266 lb (1 481 kg). Span, 35 ft 0 in (10,67 m). Length, 24 ft 9 in (7,55 m). Height, 10 ft 9 in (3,28 m).*

FAIREY FIREFLY I UK

A private-venture single-seat fighter designed by Marcel Lobelle around the 430 hp Curtiss D.12C direct-drive unsupercharged 12-cylinder liquid-cooled engine, the Firefly I was flown for the first time on 9 November 1925. Of mixed, mainly wooden, construction, the Firefly I had a small retractable radiator interconnected with wing radiators, and armament comprised two 0.303-in (7,7-mm) Vickers machine guns firing through troughs in the fuselage sides. The Firefly 1 did not find favour with the Air Ministry, primarily because of its American engine, but it served to provide experience for a further private-venture design, the Firefly II. *Max speed,185 mph (298 km/h). Time to 5,000 ft (1 525 m), 2.4 min. Loaded weight, 2,724 lb (1 236 kg). Span, 31 ft 6 in (9,60 m). Length, 24 ft 10 in (7,57 m). Height, 9 ft 1 in (2,76 m). Wing area, 236.8 sq ft (22,0 m²).*

(Above) The Curtiss D.12C-engined Firefly I which entered flight test in November 1925.

FAIREY FIREFLY IIM UK (Belgium)

Possessing virtually no commonality in either structure or overall design with the preceding fighter of the same name, the Firefly II was a further private-venture design of Marcel Lobelle and was intended to meet the requirements of Specification F.20/27 for a single-seat interceptor. Of mixed construction, the Firefly II was powered by a 480 hp Rolls-Royce F.XIS (Kestrel IIS) 12-cylinder liquid-cooled engine and was flown on 5 February 1929, participating in the Air Ministry's fighter competition in that year (wherein the ultimate victor was the Hawker Fury). Subsequently, the prototype was rebuilt with an all-metal structure, a fixed radiator bath (replacing a retractable radiator interconnected with a surface cooling system), redesigned vertical tail surfaces and designation changed to Firefly IIM. A contract was placed in 1930 for 25 aircraft for the

FAIREY

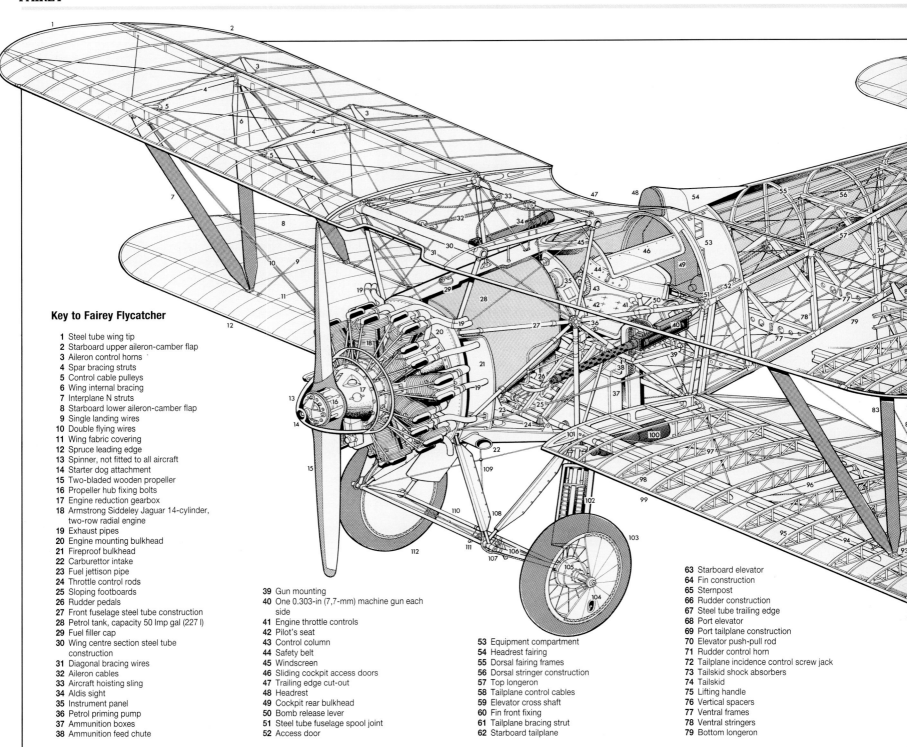

Key to Fairey Flycatcher

1 Steel tube wing tip
2 Starboard upper aileron-camber flap
3 Aileron control horns
4 Spar bracing struts
5 Control cable pulleys
6 Wing internal bracing
7 Interplane N struts
8 Starboard lower aileron-camber flap
9 Single landing wires
10 Double flying wires
11 Wing fabric covering
12 Spruce leading edge
13 Spinner, not fitted to all aircraft
14 Starter dog attachment
15 Two-bladed wooden propeller
16 Propeller hub fixing bolts
17 Engine reduction gearbox
18 Armstrong Siddeley Jaguar 14-cylinder, two-row radial engine
19 Exhaust pipes
20 Engine mounting bulkhead
21 Fireproof bulkhead
22 Carburettor intake
23 Fuel jettison pipe
24 Throttle control rods
25 Sloping footboards
26 Rudder pedals
27 Front fuselage steel tube construction
28 Petrol tank, capacity 50 Imp gal (227 l)
29 Fuel filler cap
30 Wing centre section steel tube construction
31 Diagonal bracing wires
32 Aileron cables
33 Aircraft hoisting sling
34 Aldis sight
35 Instrument panel
36 Petrol priming pump
37 Ammunition boxes
38 Ammunition feed chute

39 Gun mounting
40 One 0.303-in (7,7-mm) machine gun each side
41 Engine throttle controls
42 Pilot's seat
43 Control column
44 Safety belt
45 Windscreen
46 Sliding cockpit access doors
47 Trailing edge cut-out
48 Headrest
49 Cockpit rear bulkhead
50 Bomb release lever
51 Steel tube fuselage spool joint
52 Access door

53 Equipment compartment
54 Headrest fairing
55 Dorsal fairing frames
56 Dorsal stringer construction
57 Top longeron
58 Tailplane control cables
59 Elevator cross shaft
60 Fin front fixing
61 Tailplane bracing strut
62 Starboard tailplane

63 Starboard elevator
64 Fin construction
65 Sternpost
66 Rudder construction
67 Steel tube trailing edge
68 Port elevator
69 Port tailplane construction
70 Elevator push-pull rod
71 Rudder control horn
72 Tailplane incidence control screw jack
73 Tailskid shock absorbers
74 Tailskid
75 Lifting handle
76 Vertical spacers
77 Ventral frames
78 Ventral stringers
79 Bottom longeron

Belgian *Aéronautique Militaire* (the "M" suffix indicating all-metal construction then being discarded). A further 62 were built by Avions Fairey at Gosselies for the Belgian service, plus one for the Soviet Union, and two were later modified as Firefly IVs. The Firefly IV differed in having a 785 hp Hispano-Suiza 12Xbrs engine, but offered insufficient performance improvement to warrant further development, the Kestrel IIS being restored in one and the other being transferred to the parent company in the UK for trials. *Max speed,* *175 mph (282 km/h) at sea level, 223 mph (359 km/h) at 13,125 ft (4 000 m). Time to 19,685 ft (6 000 m), 10.9 min. Empty weight, 2,387 lb (1 083 kg). Loaded weight, 3,285 lb (1 490 kg). Span, 31 ft 6 in (9,60 m). Length, 24 ft 8 in (7,52 m). Height, 9 ft 4 in (2,85 m). Wing area, 236.8 sq ft (22,0 m²).*

(Left) The prototype Firefly IIM seen in July 1930 with civil registration, and (below) three-view drawing of the series Firefly II.

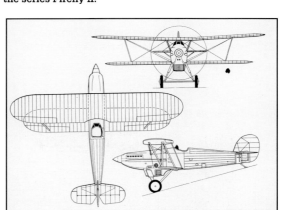

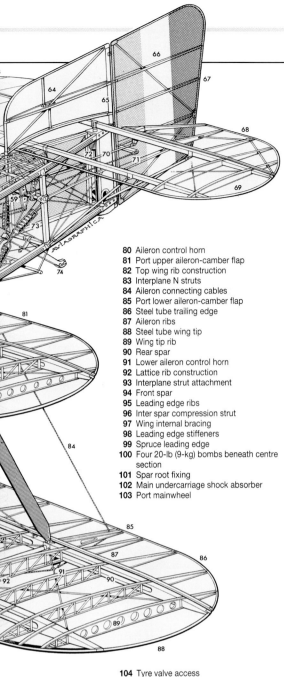

80 Aileron control horn
81 Port upper aileron-camber flap
82 Top wing rib construction
83 Interplane N struts
84 Aileron connecting cables
85 Port lower aileron-camber flap
86 Steel tube trailing edge
87 Aileron ribs
88 Steel tube wing tip
89 Wing tip rib
90 Rear spar
91 Lower aileron control horn
92 Lattice rib construction
93 Interplane strut attachment
94 Front spar
95 Leading edge ribs
96 Inter spar compression strut
97 Wing internal bracing
98 Leading edge stiffeners
99 Spruce leading edge
100 Four 20-lb (9-kg) bombs beneath centre section
101 Spar root fixing
102 Main undercarriage shock absorber
103 Port mainwheel

104 Tyre valve access
105 Brake drum
106 Pivoted axle
107 Hydraulic brake pipe
108 Undercarriage V struts
109 Diagonal bracing wires
110 Axle spreader bar
111 Arresting wire hooks, early aircraft only
112 Starboard mainwheel

The Firefly II prototype (above) in original form, and (below) Firefly II of Belgian 3e Esc, II *Groupe*.

FAIREY FIREFLY IIIM   UK

A shipboard derivation of the Firefly II was evolved by the parent company to meet Specification N.21/26 (amended) and flown for the first time on 17 May 1929 as the Firefly III. Powered by a Rolls-Royce F.XIMS engine (later replaced by an F.XIS), the Firefly III featured larger-area wings than the Mk II. During the summer of 1929, it was largely rebuilt as the Firefly IIIM with an all-metal structure and strengthened for catapulting, re-appearing in December 1929. Armament comprised two 0.303-in (7,7-mm) Vickers machine guns and provision was made for four 20-lb (9-kg) bombs. Beaten in the competition for a shipboard fighter replacement by the Hawker Nimrod, the Firefly IIIM was fitted with two floats and was subsequently used as a trainer and practice aircraft by the RAF Schneider Trophy Team. The following data relate to the Firefly IIIM with wheel undercarriage. *Max speed, 188 mph (302 km/h) at sea level. Time to 5,000 ft (1 525 m), 2.8 min. Max loaded weight, 3,816 lb (1 731 kg). Span, 33 ft 6 in (10,21 m). Length, 25 ft 4 in (7,72 m). Height, 9 ft 4 in (2,85 m).*

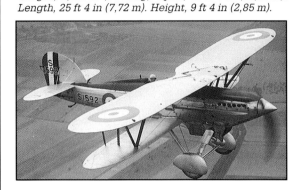

The Firefly IIIM (above) flying in July 1932 in its definitive form, and (below) at Calshot with floats with which it completed more than 80 test hours.

FAIREY FLEETWING   UK

A two-seat fleet fighter-reconnaissance aircraft, the Fleetwing was designed by Marcel Lobelle to fulfil Specification O.22/26 and was, in the form in which it flew on 16 May 1929, of mixed construction and powered by a 480 hp Rolls-Royce F.XI (Kestrel I) engine. After completing deck trials in June 1929, the Fleetwing prototype was fitted with metal wings and a moderately supercharged Kestrel IIMS engine. In this form it performed its final service trials in the following October. Armament comprised a single fixed synchronised 0.303-in (7,7-mm) Vickers machine gun and a Lewis gun on a flexible mount in the rear cockpit. In the event, the Fleetwing was pronounced runner-up to the Hawker Osprey and further development was discontinued. *Max speed, 169 mph (272 km/h). Time to*

5,000 ft (1 525 m), 4.2 min. Loaded weight, 4,737 lb (2 149 kg). Span, 37 ft 0 in (11,28 m). Length, 29 ft 4 in (8,94 m). Height, 11 ft 5 in (3,48 m). Wing area, 363 sq ft (33,73 m²).

The Fleetwing in November 1929 (above) after being fitted with metal wings, and (below) a year later at Felixstowe with a twin-float undercarriage.

FAIREY FOX VIC   Belgium

Progressive development of the Kestrel-engined Fox light reconnaissance-bomber by the Belgian Avions Fairey began with the experimental re-engining of a Kestrel-powered Mk II with a 650 hp Hispano-Suiza 12Ybrs 12-cylinder liquid-cooled engine. Flown on 31 January 1934 and designated Fox IV, this aircraft, after being loaned to the parent company in the UK (where, after modifications, it was referred to as the Fox V two-seat long-range fighter), was once again re-engined by Avions Fairey, this time with an 860 hp HS 12Ydrs as the prototype Fox VI. During the course of 1935, it was decided to equip two new squadrons of the Belgian *Aéronautique Militaire* with a two-seat day and night fighter version of the HS 12Ydrs-engined model, this variant being designated Fox VIC (the suffix letter indicating *Combat*), 50 being delivered with an armament of two fixed forward-firing 7,62-mm FN-Browning machine guns and a Lewis (later replaced by an FN-Browning) in the rear cockpit. At the time of the German invasion, Fox VIC fighters still equipped the 2ème *Régiment (Chasse)*, being flown as single-seaters for

(Below) One of two Fox VIs produced for evaluation in 1935 by the Swiss *Fliegertruppe*.

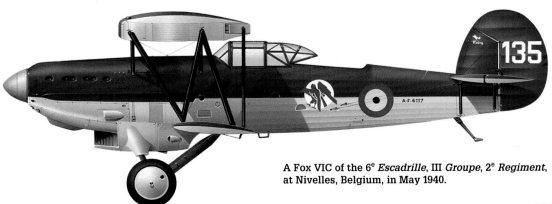

A Fox VIC of the 6e *Escadrille*, III *Groupe*, 2e *Regiment*, at Nivelles, Belgium, in May 1940.

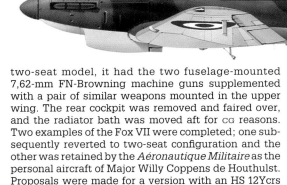

intercept missions. *Max speed, 189 mph (304 km/h) at sea level, 224 mph (360 km/h) at 6,560 ft (2 000 m). Time to 13,125 ft (4 000 m). 3.0 min. Endurance, 2.75 hrs. Loaded weight, 4,950 lb (2 245 kg). Span, 38 ft 0 in (11,85 m). Length, 30 ft 1 in (9,17 m). Height, 11 ft 0 in (3,35 m).*

(Below) General arrangement drawing of the Fox VIC.

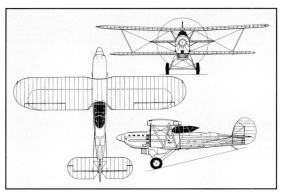

FAIREY FOX VII (MONO-FOX)   Belgium

A single-seat fighter derived from the Fox VIC two-seater was built at Gosselies and flown for the first time on 14 December 1935 as the Fox VII or Mono-Fox. Retaining the 860 hp Hispano-Suiza 12Ydrs engine of the

The Fox VII, or Mono-Fox, (above and below) was an experimental single-seat derivative of the Fox VIC.

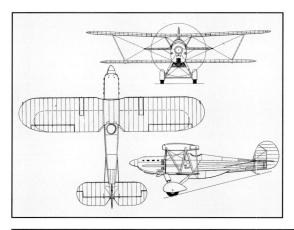

two-seat model, it had the two fuselage-mounted 7,62-mm FN-Browning machine guns supplemented with a pair of similar weapons mounted in the upper wing. The rear cockpit was removed and faired over, and the radiator bath was moved aft for CG reasons. Two examples of the Fox VII were completed; one subsequently reverted to two-seat configuration and the other was retained by the *Aéronautique Militaire* as the personal aircraft of Major Willy Coppens de Houthulst. Proposals were made for a version with an HS 12Ycrs engine and hub-mounted 20-mm cannon, but these were not pursued. *Max speed, 208 mph (335 km/h) at sea level, 233 mph (375 km/h) at 14,100 ft (4 300 m). Time to 16,405 ft (5 000 m), 7.0 min. Loaded weight, 4,744 lb (2 152 kg). Dimensions as for Fox VIC.*

FAIREY FANTÔME (FÉROCE)   UK

Considered by many to be aesthetically the most attractive fighting biplane ever built, the Fantôme was designed in 1934 by Marcel Lobelle to meet a specification drawn up on behalf of the Belgian *Aéronautique Militaire*, and was flown for the first time on 6 June 1935. Of all-metal construction with fabric skinning and powered by a 925 hp Hispano-Suiza 12Ycrs, the Fantôme had provision for an armament of one 20-mm engine-mounted cannon and two 7,62-mm Browning machine guns in the lower wing, these being augmented by two more Browning guns in the upper fuselage if the cannon was omitted. The first Fantôme crashed at Evère on 17 July 1935, but the parent company had manufactured parts and assemblies for three further aircraft which, in the following year, were shipped to Gosselies and completed there in 1936 under the name Féroce. Two of these had been ordered in Decem-

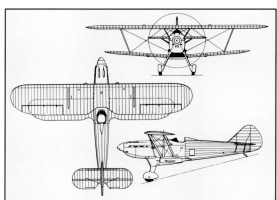

(Above) A general arrangement drawing of the Fantôme/Féroce, and (below) the first Fantôme photographed in June 1935. It later crashed at Evère.

A Fulmar I serving in 1941 in the Western Desert with the Royal Navy's Fulmar Flight.

ber 1935 by the Soviet government and were duly shipped to Moscow in February of the following year, to be evaluated by the NII V-VS (Scientific Research Institute of the Air Forces). It was to be alleged that these were subsequently delivered to the Spanish Republican air arm, but there was no truth in this allegation. The fourth aircraft was purchased by the British Air Ministry, subsequently being flown at the A&AEE and the RAE, but no further development was undertaken. *Max speed, 224 mph (360 km/h) at sea level, 270 mph (435 km/h) at 13,125 ft (4 000 m). Time to 13,125 ft (4 000 m), 5.67 min. Endurance, 2 hrs. Empty weight, 2,500 lb (1 134 kg). Loaded weight, 4,120 lb (1 869 kg). Span, 34 ft 6 in (10,52 m). Length, 27 ft 7 in (8,40 m). Height, 11 ft 4 in (3,45 m). Wing area, 273 sq ft (25,36 m²).*

FAIREY FULMAR   UK

The Fulmar II (above and below) appeared in January 1941, and, together with the Mk I, equipped a score of Royal Navy squadrons serving aboard 13 carriers.

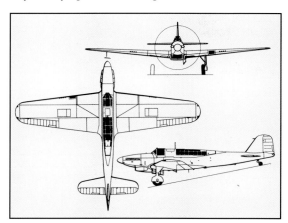

The Fulmar two-seat shipboard fleet fighter evolved to Specification O.8/38 was a derivative of the light day bomber designed by Marcel Lobelle to Specification P.4/34, and there was no prototype as such, the first example flying on 4 January 1940. Of flush-riveted, all-metal, stressed-skin construction, the initial production model, the Fulmar I, was powered by a Rolls-Royce Merlin VIII rated at 1,080 hp for take-off. It carried an armament of eight 0.303-in (7,7-mm) Browning guns in the wings plus (some aircraft) a Vickers "K" gun of similar calibre in the rear cockpit. A total of 250 Mk Is was built, a further 350 following as Fulmar IIs with a 1,300 hp Merlin 30 engine, deliveries to the FAA being completed in February 1943. The following data relate to the Mk I. *Max speed, 246 mph (396 km/h) at sea level, 256 mph (412 km/h) at 2,400 ft (730 m). Initial climb, 1,105 ft/min (5,6 m/sec). Max range, 830 mls (1 336 km) at 10,000 ft (3 050 m). Empty weight, 6,915 lb (3 137 kg). Normal loaded weight, 9,672 lb (4 387 kg). Span, 46 ft 4½ in (14,14 m). Length, 40 ft 3 in (12,27 m). Height, 10 ft 8 in (3,25 m). Wing area, 342 sq ft (31,77 m²).*

FAIREY FIREFLY Mks I & II   UK

The Firefly F Mk I shipboard day fighter (above and below) entered Royal Navy service in the summer of 1943, eight squadrons being equipped at end of WWII.

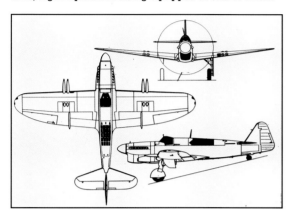

Thirty-seven Firefly NF Mk IIs (below) were produced, but subsequently converted to F Mk I standard.

Designed by a team headed by H E Chaplin as a two-seat multi-rôle shipboard fighter to the requirements of Specification N.5/40, the monoplane for which the name Firefly was resurrected flew for the first time on 22 December 1941. There was no prototype as such, but what was considered to be the first genuine production example was not flown until January 1943. The initial version, the F Mk I, was a day fighter powered by a 1,735 hp Rolls-Royce Griffon IIB engine and carrying a fixed forward-firing armament of four 20-mm Hispano cannon. Production totalled 459, later examples having the 1,990 hp Griffon XII. The F Mk I was followed by the FR Mk I fighter-reconnaissance model with an ASH surface- and underwater-vessel detecting radar pod beneath the nose (F Mk Is converted to FR Mk I standards becoming F Mk IAs), and by the NF Mk I night fighter with AI radar beneath the nose in place of the ASH. The NF Mk I was an adaptation of the FR Mk I and, of 376 examples of the latter produced, 140 were so modified. The NF Mk I was, in fact, preceded by the NF Mk II, which, for CG reasons, was lengthened 18 in (45,7 cm) aft of the engine and had wing-mounted AI Mk X radomes. Thirty-seven NF Mk IIs were completed but subsequently converted to Mk I standard. Exports of the F Mk I included 30 for the Netherlands Navy, and eight and 10 for the Ethiopian and Thai air forces respectively. The following data relate to the F Mk I. *Max speed, 284 mph (457 km/h) at sea level, 319 mph (513 km/h) at 17,000 ft (5 180 m). Max range, 1,364 mls (2 195 km) at 204 mph (328 km/h). Time to 5,000 ft (1 525 m), 2.5 min. Empty weight, 8,925 lb (4 048 kg). Max loaded weight, 14,288 lb (6 481 kg). Span, 44 ft 6 in (13,56 m). Length, 37 ft 7 in (11,46 m). Height, 13 ft 7 in (4,14 m). Wing area, 328 sq ft (30,47 m²).*

FAIREY FIREFLY Mks III to 5   UK

A second generation of Firefly monoplanes resulted from the application of the Griffon 61 engine with a two-speed two-stage supercharger which was first installed in the sixth F Mk I airframe as the prototype Mk III. Fitted with a cumbersome beard-type radiator, the prototype Firefly III flew in the spring of 1943, but proved longitudinally unstable, and, with the abandonment of trials, an order for 100 of this version of the Firefly was cancelled. The prototype, together with three other ex-Mk Is, was subsequently fitted with a Griffon 72 and wing leading-edge radiators, eventually becoming a prototype Mk IV, with four-bladed propeller, clipped wings and a dorsal fin extension. Powered by a Griffon 74 rated at 2,100 hp at sea level and 2,190 hp at 9,500 ft (2 895 m), and carrying an armament of four 20-mm Hispano cannon, the Firefly IV was ordered into production in two versions, the FR Mk IV fighter-reconnaissance aircraft, the first example of which flew on 25 May 1945, and the NF Mk IV night fighter. In the event, only 160 Mk IVs were completed,

(Above and below) The Firefly FR Mk IV featured clipped wings and was the first production model of the fighter to have a two-stage Griffon engine.

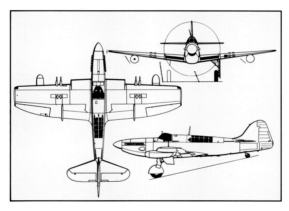

most examples of the NF Mk IV version being cancelled. Meanwhile, a "universal" airframe was evolved, which, externally virtually indistinguishable from the Mk IV and designated Firefly Mk 5, could serve in the fighter-reconnaissance, night fighting and anti-submarine rôles according to the cockpit equipment installed. The first production Mk 5 flew on 12 December

This Firefly AS Mk 6 (below) was restored to airworthy condition by the Canadian Warplane Heritage in 1972.

1947, and 352 had been built when the last was delivered on 19 May 1950. The three variants were the FR Mk 5, the NF Mk 5 and the AS Mk 5, the FR and NF versions being the only Firefly *fighters* to be built. Forty Mk IVs and 15 Mk 5s were supplied to the Netherlands Navy, and 22 Mk IVs (with seven AS Mk 5s) went to the Canadian Navy. The following data relate to the FR Mk IV. *Max speed, 316 mph (509 km/h) at sea level, 345 mph (555 km/h) at 12,500 ft (3 810 m). Max range, 1,070 mls (1 722 km). Time to 5,000 ft (1 525 m), 3.6 min. Empty weight, 9,859 lb (4 472 kg). Max loaded weight, 15,600 lb (7 076 kg). Span, 41 ft 0 in (12,49 m). Length, 38 ft 0 in (11,58 m). Height, 13 ft 11 in (4,24 m). Wing area, 330 sq ft (30,66 m²).*

FARMAN F 30   France

The F 30 (not to be confused with the earlier Farman Type 30 two-seat pusher) was developed by the Société Henry et Maurice Farman to meet a requirement for a two-seat fighter. Powered by a 260 hp Salmson 9Za water-cooled nine-cylinder radial and carrying an armament of one fixed 7,7-mm Vickers gun and one flexible 7,7-mm Lewis gun, the F 30 C2 was an unequal-span, single-bay biplane with plywood-covered fuselage and was tested in the spring of 1917 with inauspicious results. The aircraft, subsequently referred to as the F 30A, was therefore extensively revised as the F 30B (although still referred to officially as the F 30 C2) with equal-span wings and two-bay bracing, fabric skinning replacing the plywood covering of the fuselage. Testing of the F 30B was conducted at Villacoublay during the summer of 1917, but the aircraft suffered fore and aft instability, and, as its CG problems remained insoluble, was finally abandoned early in 1918. The following data relate to the F 30B. *Max speed, 129 mph (208 km/h) at 6,560 ft (2 000 m), 122 mph (196 km/h) at 13,125 ft (4 000 m). Time to 9,840 ft (3 000 m), 11 min. Endurance, 2.5 hrs. Empty weight, 1,499 lb (680 kg). Loaded weight, 2,425 lb (1 100 kg). Span, 36 ft 1½ in (11,01 m). Length, 23 ft 11¼ in (7,29 m). Height, 9 ft 8½ in (2,96 m). Wing area, 373.62 sq ft (34,71 m²).*

The Farman F 30 in its definitive form (below) as the F 30B with equi-span wings and two-bay bracing.

FARMAN F 31   France

Designed around the 400 hp Liberty 12 12-cylinder water-cooled engine, the F 31 two-seat fighter was an exceptionally angular equi-span, two-bay biplane with the fuselage mounted in mid-gap. Armament comprised two fixed forward-firing 7,7-mm Vickers guns and a single 7,7-mm Lewis gun on a flexible mounting in the rear cockpit. The sole prototype of the F 31 was completed in the summer of 1918, and was still under

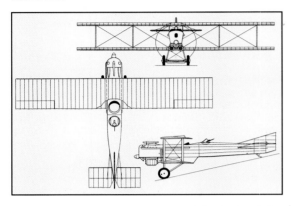

The Farman F 31 (above and below) was not completed in prototype form until summer 1918, and was abandoned with the Armistice.

test at Villacoublay in November 1918, the Armistice precluding any further development of the type. *Max speed, 134 mph (215 km/h) at 6,560 ft (2 000 m). Time to 6,560 ft (2 000 m), 5.85 min. Empty weight, 1,916 lb (869 kg). Loaded weight, 3,239 lb (1 469 kg). Span, 38 ft 6⅞ in (11,76 m). Length, 24 ft 1¼ in (7,35 m). Height, 8 ft 5½ in (2,58 m).*

FBA AVION CANON   France

Something of an oddity, the cannon-armed FBA land-based fighter (above) was derived from a flying boat.

Although the Franco-British Aviation Company (FBA) specialised in the design and development of flying boats, the company's designer, Louis Schreck, evolved a side-by-side, two-seat cannon-armed land-based fighter which was tested in 1916. Usually referred to as the FBA *Avion canon*, although also known as the FBA 1 Ca2, the aircraft mated an aerodynamically clean wooden monocoque fuselage with the wings of an FBA Type H flying boat and carried a short-barrel 37-mm Hotchkiss cannon in the extreme fuselage nose. The 150 hp water-cooled eight-cylinder Hispano-Suiza 8A engine was mounted as a pusher and this power plant was apparently replaced by a 175 hp HS 8Aa engine during the course of 1917 when the aircraft was still under development. However, performance was unsatisfactory and further development of the aircraft was not pursued. The following data relate to the *Avion canon* with the lower-powered engine. *Max speed,*

83 mph (133 km/h) at sea level, 76 mph (123 km/h) at 6,560 ft (2 000 m). Time to 3,280 ft (1 000 m), 8.55 min. Endurance, 3.0 hrs. Empty weight, 1,678 lb (761 kg). Loaded weight, 2,571 lb (1 166 kg). Span, 47 ft 6¾ in (14,50 m). Length, 33 ft 2¾ in (10,13 m). Height, 10 ft 11¾ in (3,35 m). Wing area, 441.33 sq ft (41,00 m²).

FFA P-16   Switzerland

A single-seat, transonic, attack fighter, the P-16 was developed by the Flug- und Fahrzeugwerke AG (FFA) to meet a specific Swiss requirement. The multi-spar low aspect ratio wing carried extensive high-lift devices to suit the aircraft for operation from short runways situated in high-altitude valleys. The first P-16.04 prototype powered by the 7,900 lb st (3 583 kgp) Armstrong Siddeley Sapphire ASSa 6 turbojet flew on 28 April 1955, and the second on 16 June 1956. The first of four pre-series aircraft ordered, the P-16 Mk II with an 11,000 lb st (4 990 kgp) ASSa 7, flew on 15 April 1957, but an order for 100 P-16 Mk IIIs approved by the Swiss Parliament in March 1958 was subsequently cancelled. Nevertheless, two of the remaining three pre-series aircraft were completed to P-16 Mk III standards, being flown on 8 July 1959 and 24 March 1960 respectively. This version carried an armament of two 30-mm Hispano-Suiza 825 cannon and a Matra 1000 launcher for

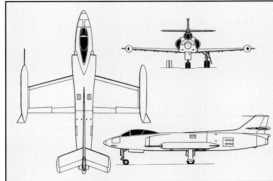

A general arrangement drawing (above) of the P-16 Mk III and (below) the fifth and final P-16, the second pre-series aircraft flown in March 1960.

(Below) The fifth P-16 was representative of the planned production series P-16 Mk III attack fighter.

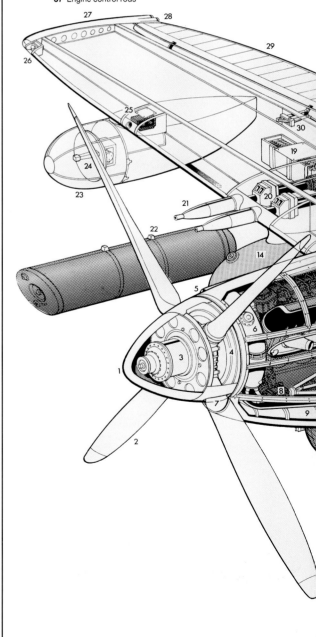

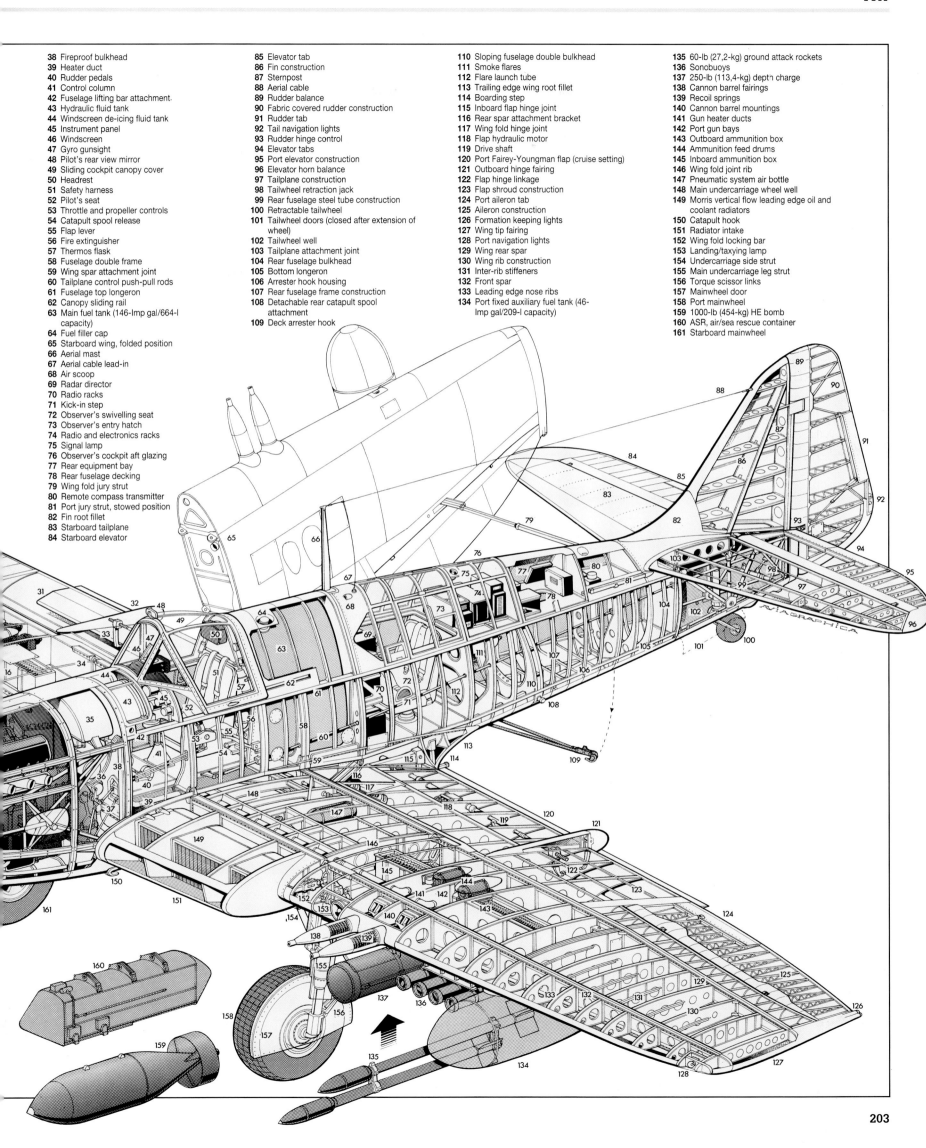

38 Fireproof bulkhead
39 Heater duct
40 Rudder pedals
41 Control column
42 Fuselage lifting bar attachment
43 Hydraulic fluid tank
44 Windscreen de-icing fluid tank
45 Instrument panel
46 Windscreen
47 Gyro gunsight
48 Pilot's rear view mirror
49 Sliding cockpit canopy cover
50 Headrest
51 Safety harness
52 Pilot's seat
53 Throttle and propeller controls
54 Catapult spool release
55 Flap lever
56 Fire extinguisher
57 Thermos flask
58 Fuselage double frame
59 Wing spar attachment joint
60 Tailplane control push-pull rods
61 Fuselage top longeron
62 Canopy sliding rail
63 Main fuel tank (146-Imp gal/664-l capacity)
64 Fuel filler cap
65 Starboard wing, folded position
66 Aerial mast
67 Aerial cable lead-in
68 Air scoop
69 Radar director
70 Radio racks
71 Kick-in step
72 Observer's swivelling seat
73 Observer's entry hatch
74 Radio and electronics racks
75 Signal lamp
76 Observer's cockpit aft glazing
77 Rear equipment bay
78 Rear fuselage decking
79 Wing fold jury strut
80 Remote compass transmitter
81 Port jury strut, stowed position
82 Fin root fillet
83 Starboard tailplane
84 Starboard elevator

85 Elevator tab
86 Fin construction
87 Sternpost
88 Aerial cable
89 Rudder balance
90 Fabric covered rudder construction
91 Rudder tab
92 Tail navigation lights
93 Rudder hinge control
94 Elevator tabs
95 Port elevator construction
96 Elevator horn balance
97 Tailplane construction
98 Tailwheel retraction jack
99 Rear fuselage steel tube construction
100 Retractable tailwheel
101 Tailwheel doors (closed after extension of wheel)
102 Tailwheel well
103 Tailplane attachment joint
104 Rear fuselage bulkhead
105 Bottom longeron
106 Arrester hook housing
107 Rear fuselage frame construction
108 Detachable rear catapult spool attachment
109 Deck arrester hook

110 Sloping fuselage double bulkhead
111 Smoke flares
112 Flare launch tube
113 Trailing edge wing root fillet
114 Boarding step
115 Inboard flap hinge joint
116 Rear spar attachment bracket
117 Wing fold hinge joint
118 Flap hydraulic motor
119 Drive shaft
120 Port Fairey-Youngman flap (cruise setting)
121 Outboard hinge fairing
122 Flap hinge linkage
123 Flap shroud construction
124 Port aileron tab
125 Aileron construction
126 Formation keeping lights
127 Wing tip fairing
128 Port navigation lights
129 Wing rear spar
130 Wing rib construction
131 Inter-rib stiffeners
132 Front spar
133 Leading edge nose ribs
134 Port fixed auxiliary fuel tank (46-Imp gal/209-l capacity)

135 60-lb (27,2-kg) ground attack rockets
136 Sonobuoys
137 250-lb (113,4-kg) depth charge
138 Cannon barrel fairings
139 Recoil springs
140 Cannon barrel mountings
141 Gun heater ducts
142 Port gun bays
143 Outboard ammunition box
144 Ammunition feed drums
145 Inboard ammunition box
146 Wing fold joint rib
147 Pneumatic system air bottle
148 Main undercarriage wheel well
149 Morris vertical flow leading edge oil and coolant radiators
150 Catapult hook
151 Radiator intake
152 Wing fold locking bar
153 Landing/taxiing lamp
154 Undercarriage side strut
155 Main undercarriage leg strut
156 Torque scissor links
157 Mainwheel door
158 Port mainwheel
159 1000-lb (454-kg) HE bomb
160 ASR, air/sea rescue container
161 Starboard mainwheel

44 68-mm rockets. External ordnance loads of up to 4,940 lb (2 240 kg) could be carried. The following data relate to the Mk III. *Max speed, 620 mph (998 km/h) at 26,245 ft (8 000 m), or M=0.92. Initial climb, 12,795 ft/ min (65 m/sec). Range (internal fuel), 920 mls (1 480 km) at 36,100 ft (11 000 m). Empty weight, 15,520 lb (7 040 kg). Max weight, 25,838 lb (11 720 kg). Span, 36 ft 7 in (11,14 m). Length, 46 ft 11 in (14,30 m). Height, 13 ft 11⅓ in (4,25 m). Wing area, 322.93 sq ft (30,00 m²).*

FFVS J 22   Sweden

Designed by Bo Lunberg and built by the Air Board Workshop, or *Flygförvaltningens Verkstad* (FFVS), created specifically for the task, the J 22 single-seat fighter was first flown on 21 September 1942. An initial batch of 60 had been ordered "off the drawing board" on the previous 21 March, production deliveries commencing on 23 November 1943. Component production was subcontracted to some 500 factories, final assembly being undertaken by the FFVS. Two prototypes were followed by 198 production aircraft, the last being delivered on 6 April 1946. The J 22 was powered by an SFA STWC3-G (a copy of the Pratt & Whitney Twin Wasp SC3-G) 14-cylinder radial of 1,065 hp and was of steel-tube and wood construction. Two versions were built, one having an armament of two 7,9-mm M/22F and two 13,2-mm M/39A guns, and the other being armed with four of the larger-calibre weapons. *Max speed, 358 mph (576 km/h) at 11,485 ft (3 500 m). Max range, 789 mls (1 270 km) at 269 mph (433 km/h).*

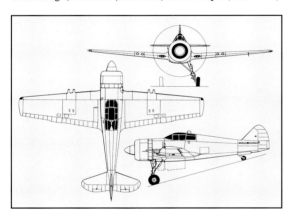

(Above) The J 22 with four 13,2-mm guns, and (immediately below) a J 22 of the 1st Division of F 9 at Gothenburg with two 13,2-mm and two 7,9-mm guns.

(Below) A preserved J 22 in the markings of the 1st Division of F 3, which flew this type until 1952.

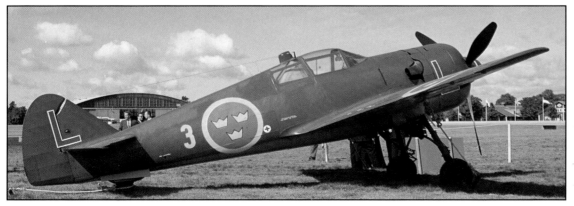

Empty weight (four M/39As), 4,453 lb (2 020 kg). Loaded weight, 6,250 lb (2 835 kg). Span, 32 ft 9½ in (10,00 m). Length, 25 ft 7 in (7,80 m). Height, 9 ft 2 in (2,80 m). Wing area, 172.23 sq ft (16,00 m²).

FIAT CR.1   Italy

In 1923, Fiat Aviazione completed two prototypes of a single-seat fighter designed by Ing Celestino Rosatelli and from which was to stem a line of fighters that was to continue for 18 years. Designated CR (Caccia Rosatelli) and powered by a 300 hp Hispano-Suiza 42-8 water-cooled engine, the fighter was an inverted sesquiplane with Warren-truss rigid wing bracing and employing mixed construction with fabric skinning.

(Above) The progenitor of the Rosatelli line of fighters, the CR, and (below) the CR.1, the first Rosatelli fighter to be manufactured in series.

Carrying an armament of two synchronised 7,7-mm guns, the CR was pronounced winner of a contest organised by the *Regia Aeronautica* and was ordered into production as the CR.1. By comparison with the prototypes, the CR.1 introduced a small reduction (5.38 sq ft/0,50 m²) in wing area and a redesigned engine cowling with a revised frontal radiator above the propeller hub. The first 100 CR.1 fighters were produced by Fiat's aircraft division, Aeronautica d'Italia, during 1924-25, 100 more were built by SIAI in 1925, and

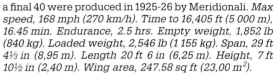

A CR.1 of the XVII *Gruppo* of the newly-established *Regia Aeronautica* at Campoformido 1925-26.

a final 40 were produced in 1925-26 by Meridionali. *Max speed, 168 mph (270 km/h). Time to 16,405 ft (5 000 m), 16.45 min. Endurance, 2.5 hrs. Empty weight, 1,852 lb (840 kg). Loaded weight, 2,546 lb (1 155 kg). Span, 29 ft 4⅓ in (8,95 m). Length 20 ft 6 in (6,25 m). Height, 7 ft 10½ in (2,40 m). Wing area, 247.58 sq ft (23,00 m²).*

(Above) The Alfa Romeo-built Jupiter-powered CR.5 prototype derived from the CR.1 (below) from which it differed primarily in type of power plant.

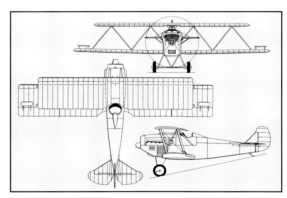

FIAT CR.5   Italy

Flown as prototypes in 1925, the two CR.5s were essentially adaptations of the CR.1 airframe, one to take a 480 hp Alfa Romeo-built Jupiter nine-cylinder radial engine and the other for the newly-developed Fiat A 20 12-cylinder water-cooled Vee engine rated at 410 hp. Apart from some local strengthening, the structure of the CR.5 was similar to that of the CR.1, but the A 20-engined prototype had Lamblin-type radiators mounted on the forward struts of the main undercarriage members. The A 20 engine resulted in noteworthy increases in level speed and climb by comparison with the CR.1, but the CR.5 was discarded in favour of the more advanced all-metal CR.20 fighter then in initial design. The following data relate to the A 20-powered CR.5. *Max speed, 186 mph (300 km/h). Time to 16,405 ft (5 000 m), 14.25 min. Endurance, 2.25 hrs. Empty weight, 1,918 lb (870 kg). Loaded weight, 2,612 lb (1 185 kg). Dimensions as for the CR.1.*

The second CR.5 (below) was fitted with the newly-developed Fiat A 20 engine with Lamblin radiators.

FIAT CR.20   Italy

The first Rosatelli-designed fighter of all-metal construction, the CR.20 reversed the wing arrangement employed by earlier fighters in the series in that the upper plane featured greater span than the lower. Two prototype CR.20s were flown in 1926, these having the 420 hp Fiat A 20 engine. Armament consisted of two synchronised fuselage-mounted 7,7-mm machine guns with provision for an additional pair of guns of similar calibre in the fuselage sides. The CR.20 was highly manoeuvrable and was ordered into production for the *Regia Aeronautica*, 88 of the initial model being built by Aeronautica d'Italia during 1927-29, and 19 being built by CMASA. Fifteen CR.20s were exported to Lithuania.

The first all-metal Rosatelli fighter, the CR.20 (above and below) is illustrated in its initial production form in which it achieved much success.

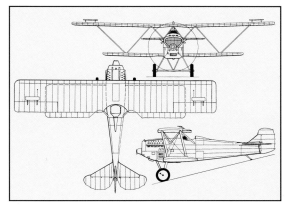

A tandem two-seat tuitional version, the CR.20B, was evolved in 1927, and a modernised version of the fighter, the CR.20bis, appeared in 1929. This had a slightly reduced wing area (by 1.61 sq ft/0,15 m²) and a split-type axle in place of the cross axle. Simultaneously, a version of the CR.20bis was produced with a 425 hp Fiat A 20AQ engine as the CR.20AQ, this offering an improved service ceiling, but reduced endurance. Aeronautica d'Italia built 211 CR.20bis and CR.20AQ fighters during 1930-32. Five CR.20bis fighters were exported to Paraguay, Austria received 30 CR.20bis fighters (two others crashing during de-

(Immediately below) A CR. 20bis of the Paraguayan *Escuadrón de Caza "Los Indios"*, 1933, and (bottom) a CR.20 of Hungarian 1st "Meteorological Grp", 1936.

livery) and four CR.20B two-seaters, and 12 CR.20bis fighters and four CR.20Bs were delivered to Hungary. The ultimate version of the basic fighter was the so-called CR."Asso", a CR.20bis airframe fitted with a 450 hp Isotta-Fraschini-420 Caccia engine. The CR."Asso" appeared in 1932, production comprising 104 from Aeronautica Macchi and 100 from CMASA during 1932-33. Overall production of the CR.20 series for the *Regia Aeronautica* totalled 541 aircraft. The following data relate to the initial production model. *Max speed, 168 mph (270 km/h). Time to 16,405 ft (5 000 m), 13.62 min. Endurance, 3.0 hrs. Empty weight, 2,160 lb (980 kg). Loaded weight, 3,086 lb (1 400 kg). Span, 32 ft 1¾ in (9,80 m). Length, 21 ft 11¾ in (6,70 m). Height, 9 ft 0 in (2,75 m). Wing area, 276.1 sq ft (25,65 m²).*

FIAT CR.20 IDRO   Italy

A float fighter version of the CR.20 for the *Squadriglie da Caccia Marittima* of the *Regia Aeronautica* was evolved in 1928 as the CR. 20 Idro (sometimes known as the ICR.20). The single prototype was followed by 16 series aircraft that were built by Aeronautica Macchi. The CR.20 Idro was essentially similar to the initial production land-based model with a 410 hp Fiat A 20 engine and was fitted with light metal floats. Armament remained two 7,7-mm machine guns. *Max speed, 158 mph (254 km/h). Time to 16,405 ft (5 000 m), 19.6 min. Endurance, 2.75 hrs. Empty weight, 2,425 lb (1 100 kg). Loaded weight, 3,351 lb (1 520 kg). Span, 32 ft 1¾ in (9,80 m). Length, 23 ft 2 in (7,06 m). Height, 10 ft 1½ in (3,09 m). Wing area, 276.1 sq ft (25,65 m²).*

The CR.20 Idro (below) float fighter was built in small numbers by Aeronautica Macchi in the late '20s.

FIAT CR.30   Italy

The CR.30 was designed around the 590 hp Fiat A 30 RA 12-cylinder Vee-type water-cooled engine, and the first of three prototypes was flown in March 1932, two of the prototypes winning the Dal Molin Cup at Zürich during the following July. A fabric-covered, all-metal biplane with an armament of two 12,7-mm machine guns which were sometimes replaced by 7,7-mm weapons, the CR.30 was manufactured by Aeronautica d'Italia during 1933-34, production of the single-seat model totalling 121 aircraft of which three were delivered to Austria. The third prototype was converted as a CR.30B two-seat trainer, and three more examples were converted from single-seaters for supply to Aus-

The CR.30 (above) was built in series for the *Regia Aeronautica* by Aeronautica d'Italia during 1933-34.

tria. Two CR.30s were converted by CMASA as ICR.30 floatplanes, flight testing being undertaken in 1934 and development subsequently being abandoned. *Max speed, 200 mph (322 km/h) at sea level, 218 mph (351 km/h) at 9,840 ft (3 000 m). Time to 9,840 ft (3 000 m), 5.67 min. Endurance, 2.75 hrs. Empty weight, 2,965 lb (1 345 kg). Loaded weight, 4,178 lb (1 895 kg). Span, 34 ft 5⅓ in (10,50 m). Length, 25 ft 10¼ in (7,88 m). Height, 9 ft 1½ in (2,78 m). Wing area, 291.17 sq ft (27,05 m²).*

FIAT CR.32   Italy

One of the most outstanding single-seat fighters of the early 'thirties, the CR.32 was essentially a scaled-down derivative of the CR.30, possessing a similar fabric-covered light alloy and steel structure and Fiat A 30 RA engine. First flown on 28 April 1933, the CR.32 carried an armament of two 7,7-mm or 12,7-mm machine guns, and the initial production series of 24 aircraft was ordered by China, although, in the event, only nine were delivered (in the spring of 1935). Between March 1934 and February 1936, 282 CR.32s were delivered to the *Regia Aeronautica*, and this fighter first saw active service in the Spanish Civil War with the *Aviacion del Tercio* in August 1936. Production of 283 examples of the CR.32bis followed for the *Regia Aeronautica*, this having the improved 600 hp A 30 RAbis engine, an armament of two 12,7-mm and two 7,7-mm guns, and more minor changes. Forty-five similar fighters were supplied to Austria and 52 to Hungary (the latter eventually receiving 38 of those originally purchased by the former). The CR.32ter, of which 150 were produced for the *Regia Aeronautica* in July-December 1937, reverted to the twin 12,7-mm gun armament, and featured improved gunsight and instrumentation. The definitive model for the Italian air arm was the similarly-armed CR.32quater, of which 337 were delivered

(Above) CR.32s of the *XXIII Gruppo "Asso di Bastoni"* of the Italian *Aviazione Legionaria* over Spain in 1938, and (below) three-view drawing of the CR.32ter.

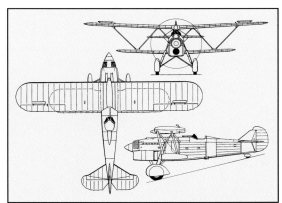

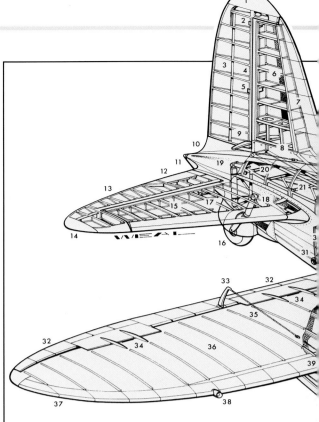

to the *Regia Aeronautica*, similar aircraft being purchased by Paraguay and Venezuela, which received five and nine respectively. A total of 377 CR.32s fought with Italian and Spanish units over Spain, and 100 CR.32quater fighters were licence-built in Spain by Hispano-Suiza during 1940-43, 40 of these subsequently being converted as two-seaters. Production of the CR.32 totalled 1,211 aircraft. The following data relate to the CR.32ter. *Max speed, 205 mph (330 km/h) at sea level, 220 mph (354 km/h) at 9,840 ft (3 000 m). Time to 3,280 ft (1 000 m), 1.58 min. Range, 485 mls (780 km) at 196 mph (315 km/h). Empty weight, 3,205 lb (1 454 kg). Loaded weight, 4,220 lb (1 914 kg). Span, 31 ft 2 in (9,50 m). Length, 24 ft 5¼ in (7,45 m). Height, 8 ft 7½ in (2,63 m). Wing area, 237.89 sq ft (22,10 m²).*

A CR.32*quater* (below), the definitive production version of this Fiat fighter for *Regia Aeronautica*.

FIAT CR.33   Italy

A derivative of the CR.32 designed to take the 690 hp A 33 RC 35 supercharged engine, the CR.33 differed little externally from its predecessor, but had marginally larger overall dimensions and was fitted with a ground-adjustable three-bladed propeller. Armament comprised two fuselage-mounted 12,7-mm guns and two wing-mounted 7,7-mm weapons, and an internal bay could accommodate either 12 4.4-lb (2-kg) anti-personnel bombs or camera equipment. Although the Fiat A 33 RC 35 engine was completed in 1935, difficulties with this engine delayed prototype trials of the CR.33 until 1937, by which time the air-cooled radial engine was officially favoured for fighter installation. The development programme was restricted to three prototypes. *Max speed, 262 mph (422 km/h). Max range, 435 mls (700 km). Empty weight, 2,998 lb*

The CR.33 (below) was marginally larger than the CR.32 and had a troublesome A 33 RC 35 engine.

(Above, top) A CR.32bis of *Jagdgeschwader* II of the Austrian *Luftstreitkräfte*, Aspern, 1937, and (immediately above) a Hungarian CR.32, late 1939.

(1 360 kg). Loaded weight, 4,211 lb (1 910 kg). Span, 32 ft 1⅘ in (9,80 m). Length, 24 ft 9⅗ in (7,56 m). Height, 8 ft 6 in (2,60 m). Wing area, 241.11 sq ft (22,40 m²).

FIAT CR.40   Italy

Evolved in parallel with the CR.33, but completed and flown appreciably earlier, thanks to engine availability, the CR.40 denoted a departure in Rosatelli fighter design. It employed a radial air-cooled engine rather than a liquid-cooled inline engine such as had been utilised by all preceding single-seat fighters from this stable. The prototype CR.40 was flown in March 1934 with a 550 hp Alfa Romeo-built Bristol Mercury IV engine. Provision was made for an armament of two synchronised 12,7-mm machine guns, and the structure was of steel and light alloy with fabric skinning. By comparison with previous Rosatelli fighters, the gap between the mainplanes was reduced, the centre section of the upper mainplane being gulled into the fuselage. The CR.40 attained a max speed of 234 mph (377 km/h) and reached an altitude of 9,840 ft (3 000 m) in 6.83 min, but climbing performance and stability proved to be inferior to those of the CR.32. A second prototype, the CR.40bis, also tested in 1934, differed only in having a Fiat A 59 R (licence-built Pratt & Whitney Hornet) engine rated at 690 hp at 6,560 ft (2 000 m) and driving a flight-variable (rather than ground-adjustable) two-pitch propeller. The CR.40 and CR.40bis prototypes and the analogous CR.41 indirectly led to the production CR.42. The following data relate to the CR.40bis. *Max*

The CR.40 (above and below) followed closely on the CR.32, but proved to possess inferior stability and climbing qualities to those of the earlier fighter.

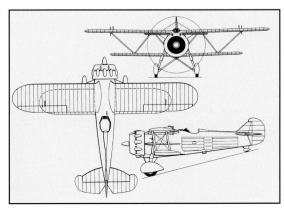

Key to Fiat CR.42 Falco

1 Rudder balance
2 Rudder upper hinge
3 Rudder frame
4 Rudder post
5 Rudder hinge
6 Tailfin structure
7 Tailfin front spar
8 Tailfin frame support
9 Rudder actuating hinge
10 Tailcone
11 Tail navigation light
12 Elevator tab
13 Starboard elevator
14 Elevator balance
15 Tailplane structure
16 Fixed tailwheel
17 Hinged tailwheel spat
18 Tailwheel leg assembly
19 Tailwheel shock absorber
20 Fuselage end post frame
21 Fuselage/tailfin frames
22 Tailfin leading edge
23 Port elevator
24 Elevator balance
25 Port tailplane
26 Rudder cable turnbuckles
27 Fuselage dorsal decking formers
28 Elevator tab control cables
29 Fuselage upper frame
30 Fuselage fabric stringers
31 Lifting point
32 Starboard aileron
33 Aileron hinge
34 Aileron leading edge balances
35 Aileron control cable
36 Wing fabric covering

37 Starboard upper wingtip
38 Starboard navigation light
39 Aileron control cable turnbuckle
40 Aileron control cable run
41 Wing ribs
42 Wing rear spar
43 Fuselage framework
44 Elevator control rod linkage
45 Rudder cables
46 Fuselage cross-frame members
47 Pilot's headrest fairing
48 Pilot's headrest
49 Cockpit coaming
50 Oxygen cylinder
51 Fire extinguisher
52 Pilot's seat
53 Compressed air cylinder
54 Air cleansing filter
55 Compressor
56 Pilot's seat support frame
57 Rudder bar assembly
58 Control column
59 Instrument panel
60 Gunsight
61 Windscreen
62 Windshield frame

speed, 241 mph (388 km/h) at 6,560 ft (2 000 m). Endurance, 1.83 hrs. Empty weight, 2,645 lb (1 200 kg). Loaded weight, 3,748 lb (1 700 kg). Span, 30 ft 6⅛ in (9,30 m). Length, 22 ft 9⁹⁄₁₀ in (6,96 m). Height, 8 ft 6 in (2,60 m). Wing area, 224.97 sq ft (20,90 m²).

FIAT CR.41   Italy

Bearing a close similarity to the CR.40 and CR.40bis, and retaining the gulled upper mainplane centre section of these prototypes, but possessing larger overall dimensions, a heavier armament and a more powerful engine, the CR.41 was first flown on 30 March 1935. It was powered by a 730 hp Gnome-Rhône 14Kfs Mistral Major 14-cylinder air-cooled radial. Armament comprised two fuselage-mounted 12,7-mm and two wing-mounted 7,7-mm guns. Various two- and three-bladed variable-pitch propellers were tested on the sole prototype during a protracted flight test programme. In the

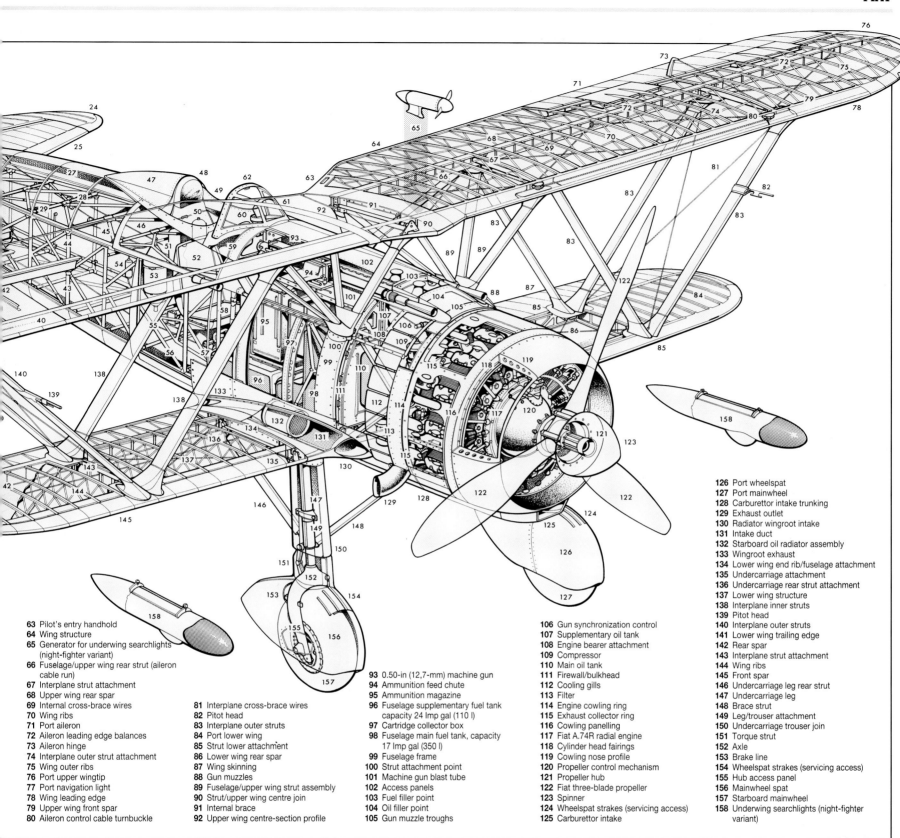

63 Pilot's entry handhold
64 Wing structure
65 Generator for underwing searchlights (night-fighter variant)
66 Fuselage/upper wing rear strut (aileron cable run)
67 Interplane strut attachment
68 Upper wing rear spar
69 Internal cross-brace wires
70 Wing ribs
71 Port aileron
72 Aileron leading edge balances
73 Aileron hinge
74 Interplane outer strut attachment
75 Wing outer ribs
76 Port upper wingtip
77 Port navigation light
78 Wing leading edge
79 Upper wing front spar
80 Aileron control cable turnbuckle

81 Interplane cross-brace wires
82 Pitot head
83 Interplane outer struts
84 Port lower wing
85 Strut lower attachment
86 Lower wing rear spar
87 Wing skinning
88 Gun muzzles
89 Fuselage/upper wing strut assembly
90 Strut/upper wing centre join
91 Internal brace
92 Upper wing centre-section profile

93 0.50-in (12,7-mm) machine gun
94 Ammunition feed chute
95 Ammunition magazine
96 Fuselage supplementary fuel tank capacity 24 Imp gal (110 l)
97 Cartridge collector box
98 Fuselage main fuel tank, capacity 17 Imp gal (350 l)
99 Fuselage frame
100 Strut attachment point
101 Machine gun blast tube
102 Access panels
103 Fuel filler point
104 Oil filler point
105 Gun muzzle troughs

106 Gun synchronization control
107 Supplementary oil tank
108 Engine bearer attachment
109 Compressor
110 Main oil tank
111 Firewall/bulkhead
112 Cooling gills
113 Filter
114 Engine cowling ring
115 Exhaust collector ring
116 Cowling panelling
117 Fiat A.74R radial engine
118 Cylinder head fairings
119 Cowling nose profile
120 Propeller control mechanism
121 Propeller hub
122 Fiat three-blade propeller
123 Spinner
124 Wheelspat strakes (servicing access)
125 Carburettor intake

126 Port wheelspat
127 Port mainwheel
128 Carburettor intake trunking
129 Exhaust outlet
130 Radiator wingroot intake
131 Intake duct
132 Starboard oil radiator assembly
133 Wingroot exhaust
134 Lower wing end rib/fuselage attachment
135 Undercarriage attachment
136 Undercarriage rear strut attachment
137 Lower wing structure
138 Interplane inner struts
139 Pitot head
140 Interplane outer struts
141 Lower wing trailing edge
142 Rear spar
143 Interplane strut attachment
144 Wing ribs
145 Front spar
146 Undercarriage leg rear strut
147 Undercarriage leg
148 Brace strut
149 Leg/trouser attachment
150 Undercarriage trouser join
151 Torque strut
152 Axle
153 Brake line
154 Wheelspat strakes (servicing access)
155 Hub access panel
156 Mainwheel spat
157 Starboard mainwheel
158 Underwing searchlights (night-fighter variant)

course of this, alternative armament installations were evaluated, including one comprising two 20-mm cannon and another consisting of four 12,7-mm machine guns. Further development was discontinued in favour of the CR.42. *Max speed, 252 mph (405 km/h). Endurance, 1.75 hrs. Empty weight, 2,888 lb (1 310 kg). Loaded weight, 4,156 lb (1 885 kg). Span, 31 ft 7⁹⁄₁₀ in (9,65 m). Length, 24 ft 4¼ in (7,42 m). Height, 8 ft 7⁹⁄₁₀ in (2,64 m). Wing area, 243.59 sq ft (22,63 m²).*

The CR.41 (below) closely resembled the CR.40, but was a larger and more powerful fighter.

FIAT CR.42 FALCO — Italy

The CR.42 Falco (Falcon), with which the line of Rosatelli single-seat fighters terminated, had the distinction of being the last single-seat fighter of biplane configuration to be manufactured by any of World War II's combatants. Flown as a prototype on 23 May 1938, and retaining the traditional structure of the Rosatelli fighters, but embodying a higher proportion of high-value materials, the CR.42 was powered by a Fiat A 74R 1C 38 14-cylinder radial rated at 840 hp at 12,465 ft (3 800 m) and carried an armament of two 12,7-mm SAFAT machine guns. Deliveries to the *Regia Aeronautica* commenced in April 1939, and the fighter was exported to several countries: Belgium ordered 34

(Above) A CR.42 of the 1st Division of F 9 flying from Säve, Gothenburg, Sweden, during 1942.

(although, in the event, received only 25), 52 were purchased by Hungary, and 72 were delivered to Sweden from total production of 1,781 aircraft. The CR.42 AS (*Africa Settentionale*) and CN (*Caccia Notturna*) were respectively fighter-bomber (with carburettor dust filter and provision for two 220-lb/100-kg bombs) and

FIAT

An early-1942 production CR.42 AS close air support fighter (above) intended for North African use.

(Above, top) A CR.42 of 83° *Squadriglia*, 18° *Gruppo*, serving in Libya, early 1941. (Immediately above) CR.42 CN of 377° *Squadriglia Autonoma*, Palermo, 1942.

night fighting (with exhaust flame dampers) variants. After the Italian Armistice, 200 examples of the slightly modified CR.42 LW were ordered from Aeronautica d'Italia (in North Italy) for the *Luftwaffe*. Intended for the nocturnal attack mission, the CR.42 LW served with the *Nachtschlachtgruppen*, the *Luftwaffe* receiving 112 of some 150 completed. Experimental versions in-

Key to Fiat G.50bis Freccia

1 Pitot static head
2 Starboard navigation light
3 Wing tip fairing
4 Aileron mass balance weights
5 Starboard fabric-covered aileron
6 Hinge control linkage
7 Aileron tab
8 Control rod linkages
9 Starboard outer wing panel
10 Hamilton-Fiat three-bladed variable-pitch propeller
11 Spinner
12 Propeller hub pitch-change mechanism
13 Engine cooling air intake
14 Cowling nose ring
15 Propeller reduction gearbox
16 Propeller governor
17 Machine gun muzzle blast trough
18 Fiat A.74 R.C.38 fourteen-cylinder two-row radial engine
19 Detachable engine cowling panels
20 Carburettor air intake
21 Starboard mainwheel
22 Wheel hub hydraulic brake
23 Exhaust stub
24 Exhaust collector ring
25 Engine accessory equipment compartment
26 Adjustable cowling air flaps
27 Welded tubular steel engine mounting frame
28 Oil tank
29 Machine gun muzzle flash guards
30 Oil filler cap
31 Machine gun barrels
32 Engine bay fireproof bulkhead
33 Outboard flap control linkage
34 Flap fabric covering
35 Starboard outer slotted flap segment
36 Machine gun blister fairings
37 Ammunition feed chute
38 Interrupter gear mechanism
39 Fuel filler caps
40 Forward fuselage fuel tank (total fuel capacity 112 Imp gal/509 l including auxiliary tank)
41 Main undercarriage wheel bay
42 Diagonal frame members
43 Centre section fuel tank
44 Fuselage access panel
45 Ammunition tank (150 rounds per gun)
46 Cartridge case collector box
47 Cartridge case ejector chute
48 Adjustable gun mounting
49 Breda-SAFAT 12,7-mm machine guns
50 Armament bay hinged access cover
51 Instrument panel access door
52 Fuselage upper longeron
53 Starboard side hydraulic accumulator
54 Rudder pedal bar
55 Footboards
56 Central flap hydraulic jack
57 Underfloor auxiliary fuel tank
58 Trim control handwheel
59 Control column
60 Engine throttle and propeller control levers
61 Instrument panel
62 Lighting control panel
63 Reflector sight
64 Armoured windscreen panel
65 Canopy arch
66 Side transparency panels
67 Hinged cockpit access doors (port and starboard)
68 Door latches
69 Pilot's seat
70 Safety harness
71 Port side console panel
72 Cockpit floor level
73 Adjustable seat mounting
74 ARC 1 radio receiver
75 Starboard side hydraulic pressure accumulator
76 Cockpit rear bulkhead
77 Headrest
78 Turn-over crash pylon
79 Aerial mast
80 Fuselage skin panelling
81 Dorsal section framing
82 Rear fuselage upper longeron
83 Rudder cable linkages
84 Sloping rear fuselage bulkhead
85 Fin spar attachment joints
86 Starboard tailplane
87 Starboard fabric covered elevator
88 Fin leading edge
89 Tailfin construction
90 Aerial cable
91 Rudder horn balance
92 Fabric covered rudder
93 Rudder rib construction
94 Tailcone
95 Tail navigation light
96 Port elevator rib construction
97 Tailplane mainspar
98 Tailplane rib construction
99 Elevator hinge control
100 Tailplane spar attachment joint
101 Welded tubular steel fin and tailplane support structure
102 Fixed castoring tailwheel
103 Tailwheel shock absorber strut
104 Rear fuselage frame and stringer construction
105 Fuselage lower longeron
106 Elevator push-pull control rod
107 Fire extinguisher bottle
108 Access panels

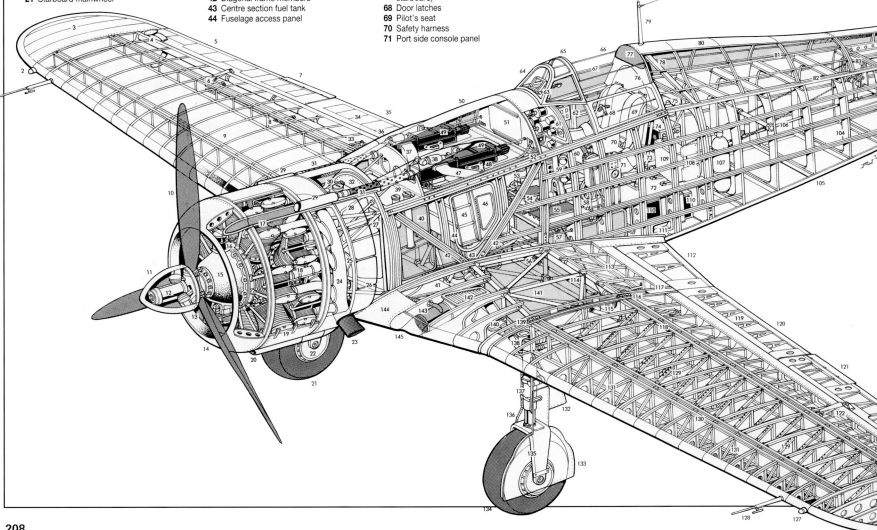

The sole example of the CR.42 DB (above), which reached speeds of the order of 323 mph (520 km/h).

cluded the CR.42 DB which was tested in prototype form with a Daimler-Benz DB 601A engine and the ICR.42 (alias CR.42 Idro) twin-float fighter evolved by CMASA (Costruzioni Meccaniche Aeronautiche SA). *Max speed, 267 mph (430 km/h) at 17,485 ft (5 330 m). Time to 19,685 ft (6 000 m), 9.11 min. Normal range, 482 mls (775 km). Empty weight, 3,765 lb (1 708 kg).*

109 Starter motor pneumatic reservoir
110 Batteries (2)
111 Boarding step
112 Inboard slotted flap segment
113 Trailing edge rib construction
114 Tubular steel wing spar centre section construction

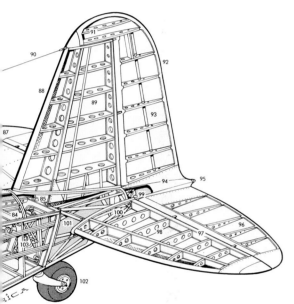

115 Aileron control cable quadrant
116 Outer wing panel spar joint
117 Wing panel joint cover strip
118 Double boom rear spar
119 Flap rib construction
120 Outboard slotted flap segment
121 Aileron tab
122 Aileron hinge control
123 Port aileron rib construction
124 Aileron mass balance weights
125 Wing tip ribs
126 Wing tip edge member
127 Port navigation light
128 Pitot static head
129 Outer wing panel lattice rib construction
130 Double boom front spar
131 Leading edge nose ribs
132 Mainwheel leg door
133 Mainwheel door
134 Port mainwheel
135 Mainwheel forks
136 Hydraulic brake pipe
137 Main undercarriage shock absorber leg strut
138 Mainwheel leg pivot fixing
139 Outer wing panel front spar attachment joint
140 Hydraulic retraction jack
141 Port wing fuel tank
142 Oil cooler air exhaust louvres
143 Oil cooler (port and starboard)
144 Extended chord inner wing panel
145 Leading edge oil cooler ram air intake

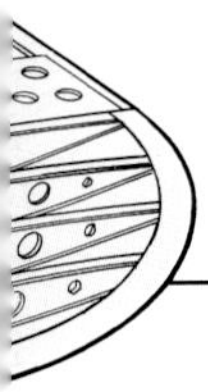

(Above) A preserved CR.42 in the markings of the Swedish *Flygflottilj* 9, and (below) a general arrangement drawing of the standard series CR.42.

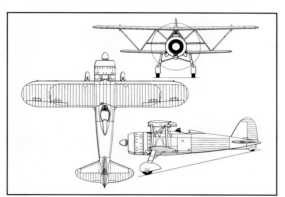

Loaded weight, 5,033 lb (2 283 kg). Span, 31 ft 9⅞ in (9,70 m). Length, 27 ft 1⅗ in (8,27 m). Height, 11 ft 9⅓ in (3,59 m). Wing area, 241.12 sq ft (22,40 m²).

FIAT CR.25　　　　　　Italy

Designed to meet an official requirement for a multi-seat, twin-engined, escort fighter, with secondary fighter-bomber and reconnaissance capabilities, the

The CR.25bis long-range escort fighter (above and below) also served in the reconnaissance rôle and saw limited Mediterranean operational service.

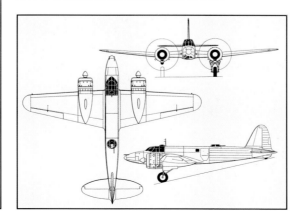

CR.25 was first flown on 22 July 1937. Of all-metal construction with light alloy and fabric skinning, the CR.25 was powered by two Fiat A 74 RC 38 radials each rated at 840 hp at 12,465 ft (3 800 m) and carried three crew members. The proposed armament comprised four fixed forward-firing 7,7-mm machine guns and one 12,7-mm gun in a dorsal turret. Two prototypes were built, the second being representative of the CR.25bis and having a fixed forward-firing armament of two 12,7-mm guns and some equipment revisions. A series of 10 aircraft was ordered, one of these being completed as a CR.25D light transport for the personal use of the Italian air attaché in Berlin. The remainder, together with the second prototype, were assigned to a strategic reconnaissance squadron (173ª) in July 1941. In the event, the CR.25bis aircraft served primarily as convoy escort fighters until withdrawn in January 1943. *Max speed, 286 mph (460 km/h) at 18,045 ft (5 500 m). Time to 19,685 ft (6 000 m), 16.65 min. Range, 1,305 mls (2 100 km). Empty weight, 9,645 lb (4 375 kg). Loaded weight, 14,385 lb (6 525 kg). Span, 52 ft 5⁹⁄₁₀ in (16,00 m). Length, 44 ft 5⅘ in (13,56 m). Height, 11 ft 1⅘ in (3,40 m). Wing area, 421.96 sq ft (39,20 m²).*

FIAT G.50 FRECCIA　　　　Italy

Designed by Giuseppe Gabrielli, the G.50 Freccia (Arrow) was the first all-metal single-seat fighter mono-plane with a retractable undercarriage produced in Italy. The first of two prototypes built by Fiat's CMASA subsidiary was flown on 26 February 1937, and CMASA built an initial series of 45 between October 1938 and July 1939, 12 of these being sent to Spain for operational evaluation by the *Gruppo Sperimentale da Caccia*. All but the first few of a further 191 G.50s produced by CMASA differed from pre-series aircraft in having the sliding canopy eliminated, and, later, a revised vertical tail, and 35 of these were purchased by Finland. The G.50 was powered by a Fiat A 74 RC 38 radial rated at 870 hp for take-off and 840 hp at 12,465 ft (3 800 m), and carried two 12,7-mm Breda-SAFAT machine guns. On 9 September 1940, a modified version, the G.50bis, was flown, this having increased internal fuel, a new under-carriage and extended tailcone. A total of 349 G.50bis fighters was subsequently built by Fiat, plus a further 97 by CMASA, the latter also building 100 examples of

(Below) The first production G.50 rolled off the Marina di Pisa assembly line late autumn of 1938.

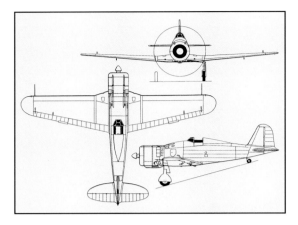

(Above) The standard production G.50bis fighter.

the tandem two-seat G.50B trainer. Single examples were produced of the G.50V, which flew on 25 August 1942 with a 1,175 hp DB 601A engine, and the G.50bis/A two-seat shipboard fighter-bomber, which, with an extended wing, flew on 3 October 1942. *Max speed, 294 mph (473 km/h) at 19,685 ft (6 000 m). Time to 9,840 ft (3 000 m), 3.17 min. Range, 620 mls (1 000 km). Empty weight, 4,579 lb (2 077 kg). Loaded weight, 5,963 lb (2 705 kg). Span, 36 ft 0¼ in (10,98 m). Length, 25 ft 7 in (7,80 m). Height, 9 ft 8½ in (2,96 m). Wing area, 196.45 sq ft (18,25 m²).*

(Below) The shipboard G.50bis/A fighter-bomber.

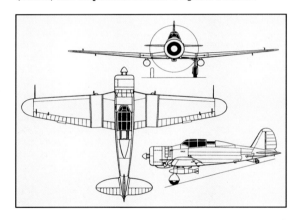

FIAT G.55 CENTAURO   Italy

The first of three prototypes of the G.55 Centauro (Centaur) flew on 30 April 1942, powered by a Daimler-Benz DB 605A engine rated at 1,475 hp for take-off. The third prototype was the first to carry armament and this comprised one engine-mounted 20-mm cannon and four fuselage-mounted synchronised 12,7-mm machine guns, the similarly-armed pre-series model being the G.55/0. Of the 34 pre-series aircraft laid down, three were fitted experimentally with the DB 603 engine at the behest of the RLM (*Reichsluftfahrtministerium*) and nine were completed to G.55/I production

(Below) A G.55/I of the 5ª *Squadriglia "Diavoli Rossi"* of the *Aviazione della RSI*, spring 1944.

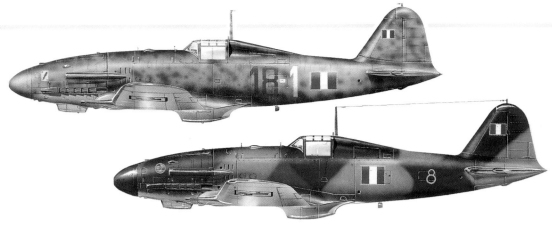

G.55/Is of the 1ª *"Asso di Bastoni"* (above, top) and 4ª *"Gigi 3 Osei"* (immediately above) *squadriglie* of the 1° and 2° *Gruppi CT, Aviazioni della RSI*, 1944.

standard. The latter had two of the fuselage-mounted 12,7-mm weapons deleted and two 20-mm cannon installed in the wings. Sixteen G.55/0 and 15 G.55/I Centauros had been delivered to the *Regia Aeronautica* prior to the Armistice of 8 September 1943, and production continued for the *Aviazione Nazionale Repubblicana* (ANR). A further 164 G.55/I Centauros (of which 148 were for the ANR) had been completed by 25 April 1944, when the factory was heavily bombed, 15 of the fighters being destroyed. One hundred and ten more Centauros had been completed and a further 37 were at an advanced stage of construction when wartime production terminated, the majority being powered by the licence-built DB 605A, the Fiat RA 1050 RC 58 Tifone (Typhoon). One G.55/I was modified to carry a 2,050-lb (930-kg) torpedo as the G.55S. *Max speed, 391 mph (630 km/h) at 26,245 ft (8 000 m). Time to 19,685 ft (6 000 m), 7.2 min. Range (internal fuel), 746 mls (1 200 km) at 254 mph (409 km/h). Empty weight, 5,798 lb (2 630 kg). Max loaded weight, 8,197 lb (3 718 kg). Span, 38 ft 10½ in (11,85 m). Length, 30 ft 8⅞ in (9,37 m). Height, 10 ft 3¼ in (3,13 m). Wing area, 227.23 sq ft (21.11 m²).*

(Below) The standard Fiat G.55/I Centauro fighter.

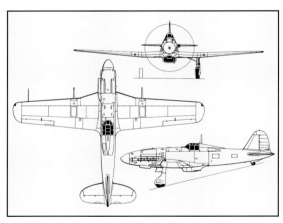

FIAT G.56   Italy

The G.56 was a progressive development of the basic G.55 Centauro to take the Daimler-Benz DB 603A engine rated at 1,750 hp at sea level and 1,850 hp at

6,890 ft (2 100 m). The first of two prototypes flew on 28 March 1944, and differed from the three G.55/0 Centauros adapted for the DB 603A in the previous year only in having some minor structural changes specifically to cater for the larger engine, minimally increased fuel tankage, and the deletion of the fuselage-mounted 12,7-mm weapons for CG reasons, armament being restricted to three 20-mm MG 151 cannon. Preparations for series production were forbidden by the RUK (the German Armaments and War Production Staff), but the first prototype G.56 survived the conflict to serve with Fiat as an engine, propeller and armament test-bed, trials including the testing of paired 20-mm Hispano cannon in wing trays. *Max speed, 426 mph (685 km/h) at 22,965 ft (7 000 m). Time to 13,125 ft (4 000 m), 3.55 min. Range, 795 mls (1 280 km). Empty weight, 6,393 lb (2 900 kg). Max loaded weight, 8,497 lb (3 854 kg). Span, 38 ft 10½ in (11,85 m). Length, 31 ft 4⅓ in (9,56 m). Height, 10 ft 3¼ in (3,13 m). Wing area, 227.23 sq ft (21,11 m²).*

(Below) The first of two prototypes of the G.56, a DB 603-engined development of the G.55 Centauro.

FIAT G.55A   Italy

A substantial number of completed and partly-completed G.55/I Centauro airframes and sizeable stocks of components survived World War II. Therefore, in 1947, Aeronautica d'Italia reinstated the G.55 assembly line, utilising wartime-manufactured assemblies and components to meet the requirements of both national and export markets. Two postwar versions of the Centauro had meanwhile been tested, the G.55A single-seat fighter and advanced armament trainer, and the G.55B tandem two-seat advanced trainer, prototypes of these models having flown on 5 September and 12 February 1946 respectively. The G.55A differed from the G.55/I Centauro only in instrumentation and radio equipment, retaining the Fiat RA 1050 RC 58 Tifone (DB 605A) engine. It was offered with an armament of four (two wing and two fuselage) 12,7-mm Breda-SAFAT or Colt-Browning machine guns, or two 20-mm Hispano-Suiza wing-mounted cannon and two fuselage-mounted machine guns. During 1947, 13 G.55s were rebuilt (seven as single-seat G.55As and six as two-seat G.55Bs) for use as advanced trainers with Italy's *Aeronautica Militare*, these being followed by a further 16 aircraft (12 G.55As and four G.55Bs) produced from

(Below) The prototype G.55A, which, produced from wartime-manufactured assemblies, flew autumn 1946.

existing Centauro assemblies and components, as were also 30 G.55As and 15 G.55Bs supplied to the *Fuerza Aérea Argentina* in 1948. The 19 G.55As delivered to the *Aeronautica Militare* possessed no armament, but, in 1948, the 17 surviving aircraft of this type were returned to Fiat, overhauled and fitted with an armament of four 12,7-mm SAFAT machine guns. Together with two G.55Bs, these were supplied to the Royal Egyptian Air Force. *Max speed, 385 mph (620 km/h) at 22,965 ft (7 000 m). Time to 19,685 ft (6 000 m). 5.33 min. Range (internal fuel), 764 mls (1 230 km). Empty weight, 5,600 lb (2 540 kg). Loaded weight, 6,878 lb (3 120 kg). Dimensions as for G.55 Centauro.*

(Above, top) A G.91R.4 of the Portuguese *Esquadra* 121 *Tigres*, BA 12 Bissalanca, 1967, and (immediately above) G.91R.3 of LeKG 43 at Oldenburg in 1971.

One of the 30 G.55As (below) supplied in 1948 to the *Fuerza Aérea Argentina*, together with 15 G.55Bs.

FIAT G.59 Italy

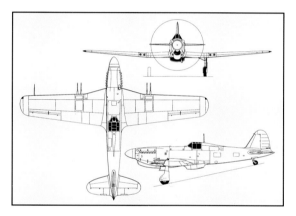

The G.59-2A (above and below) was supplied primarily to the Syrian Air Force, which received a total of 26, as well as four G.59-2Bs.

The dwindling stock of DB 605A spares led Fiat, in 1947, to adapt the basic G.55 airframe to take a Rolls-Royce Merlin T.24-2 engine rated at 1,610 hp for take-off. A prototype conversion of a G.55B flew early in 1948 as the G.55BM. An Egyptian option on 18 G.55AM fighters and two G.55BM two-seat trainers was not taken up when hostilities with Israel ceased in January 1949, but 12 existing G.55 airframes were rebuilt to G.55AM standards as fighter-trainers for the *Aeronautica Militare*. The designation was changed to G.59-1A for Italian service, and a further 16 G.59-1As and two-seat G.59-1Bs followed for Italian service in 1950. One G.59-1A was fitted with full fighter armament (four wing-mounted 20-mm Hispano cannon) and production continued with the basically similar G.59-2, of which 40 were built (30 G.59-2As and 10 G.59-2Bs). Of these, 26 G.59-2As with the four-cannon armament and four G.59-2Bs with twin 12,7-mm guns were delivered to Syria. One G.59-2A was also supplied to Argentina for evaluation. The G.59-3A was a prototype navigational trainer, and production was completed with 20 G.59-4As and 10 G.59-4B trainers for the *Aeronautica Militare*, the former having a cut-down rear fuselage and both models having bubble canopies. The following data relate to the G.59-2A. *Max speed, 368 mph*

(593 km/h) at 18,700 ft (5 700 m). Time to 19,685 ft (6 000 m), 8.4 min. Range (with internal fuel), 882 mls (1 420 km). Empty weight, 6,041 lb (2 740 kg). Loaded weight, 7,496 lb (3 400 kg). Span, 38 ft 10½ in (11,85 m). Length, 31 ft 0¾ in (9,47 m). Height, 12 ft 4 in (3,76 m). Wing area, 227.23 sq ft (21,11 m²).

FIAT G.91R Italy

Winning contender in a lightweight tactical fighter competition as part of a NATO Mutual Weapons Programme, the G.91 was designed by Giuseppe Gabrielli and flown on 9 August 1956 with a 4,050 lb st (1 837 kgp) Orpheus BOr 1 turbojet. This gave place to a 4,850 lb st (2 200 kgp) Orpheus BOr 3 in the second and third prototypes. The prototypes were followed by 27 pre-series aircraft, of which 23 were delivered to the *Aeronautica Militare* as G.91R.1s, the "R" suffix indicating *ricognizione* (reconnaissance) capability with nose-mounted Vinten cameras, armament comprising four 12,7-mm Colt-Browning machine guns. Production for the *Aeronautica Militare* continued with 25 G.91R.1As and 50 G.91R.1Bs powered by the 5,000 lb st (2 268 kgp) Fiat-built Orpheus 803. Further production by the parent company comprised 50 G.91R.3s for the *Luftwaffe*, these differing essentially in having an armament of two 30-mm DEFA cannon, and 50 G.91R.4s, which, with similar armament to the R.1, were intended

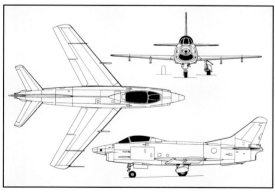

(Above) A general arrangement drawing of the G.91R.4, and (below) one of the G.91R.4s built for Hellenic Air Force use, but re-assigned to the *Luftwaffe*.

for Greece and Turkey. In the event, the latter were also supplied to the *Luftwaffe*, a further 295 G.91R.3s being built in Federal Germany (1961-66) by a consortium headed by Dornier and the type finally being retired in February 1982. Forty of the G.91R.4s were transferred by Federal Germany to Portugal in 1965, followed in 1976 by 14 G.91R.3s to make up attrition and 20 more in 1981 (36 more R.3s later being supplied for cannibalisation). *Max speed, 675 mph (1 086 km/h) at 4,920 ft (1 500 m). Initial climb, 5,990 ft/min (30,43 m/sec). Tactical radius, 196 mls (315 km). Empty weight, 7,207 lb (3 269 kg). Max loaded weight, 12,500 lb (5 670 kg). Span, 28 ft 1 in (8,56 m). Length, 33 ft 9¼ in (10,29 m). Height, 13 ft 1¼ in (4,00 m). Wing area, 176.7 sq ft (16,42 m²).*

(Below) Pre-series G.91Rs of the 103° *Gruppo* of the *Aeronautica Militare*, Practica di Mare, August 1958.

FIAT G.91Y Italy

Although evolved as a twin-engined development of the G.91R based on the airframe of the two-seat G.91T trainer, the G.91Y had virtually no commonality with its predecessor. The first of two G.91Y prototypes was flown on 27 December 1966 with two 2,720 lb st (1 234 kgp) dry and 4,080 lb st (1 850 kgp) with afterburning General Electric J85-GE-13A turbojets. Twenty pre-series aircraft were delivered to the *Aero-*

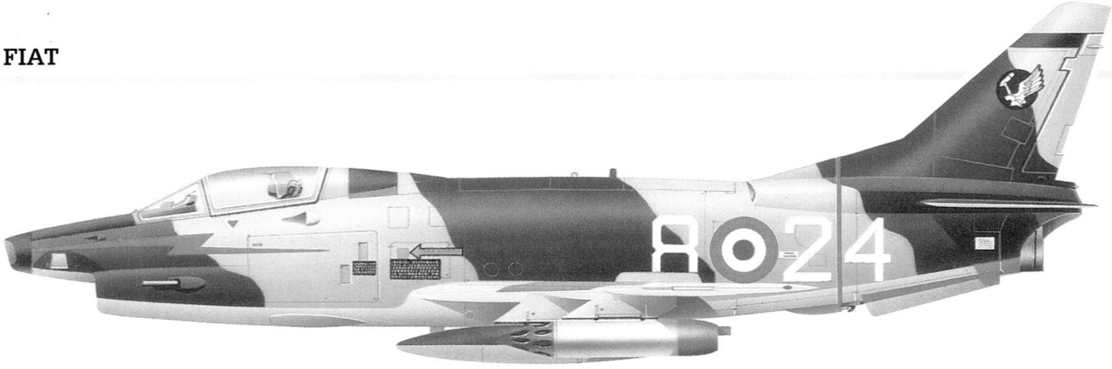

(Above) A G.91Y of the 101° *Gruppo*, 8° *Stormo*, of the *Aeronautica Militare* at San Giorgio di Cervia, 1978.

nautica Militare from 1968, these entering service in May 1970, and 45 production examples followed during 1971-76, entering service from August 1973. The G.91Y tactical fighter had an armament of two 30-mm Aden cannon and carried up to 4,000 lb (1 814 kg) of ordnance on underwing pylons and fulfilled both tactical strike and reconnaissance rôles, nose-mounted cameras being standard. *Max speed, 690 mph (1 110 km/h) at sea level. Initial climb, 17,000 ft/min (86,36 m/sec). Typical combat radius, 373 mls (600 km). Empty weight, 8,598 lb (3 900 kg). Max loaded weight, 19,180 lb (8 700 kg). Span, 29 ft 6½ in (9,01 m). Length, 38 ft 3½ in (11,67 m). Height, 14 ft 6½ in (4,43 m). Wing area, 195.16 sq ft (18,13 m^2).*

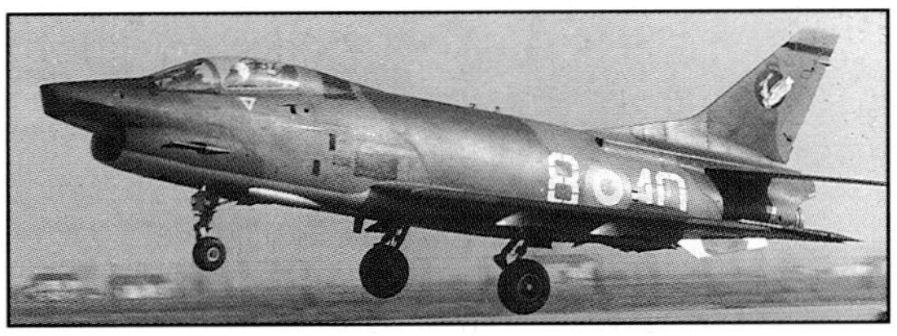

The G.91Y (above and below) was built in only small numbers, equipping two *gruppi* of the Italian *Aeronautica Militare* from 1973.

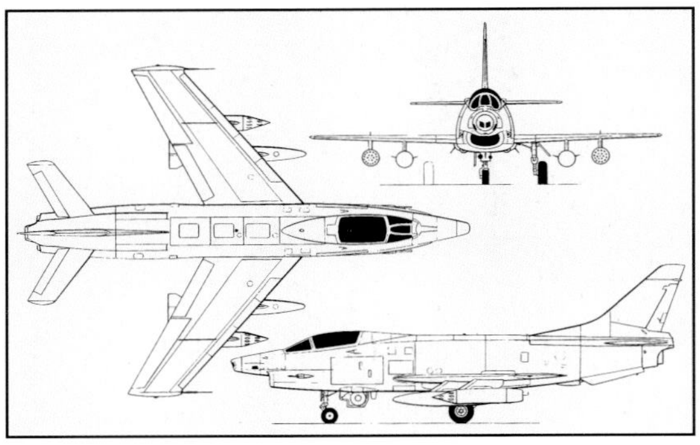

FISHER P-75A EAGLE — USA

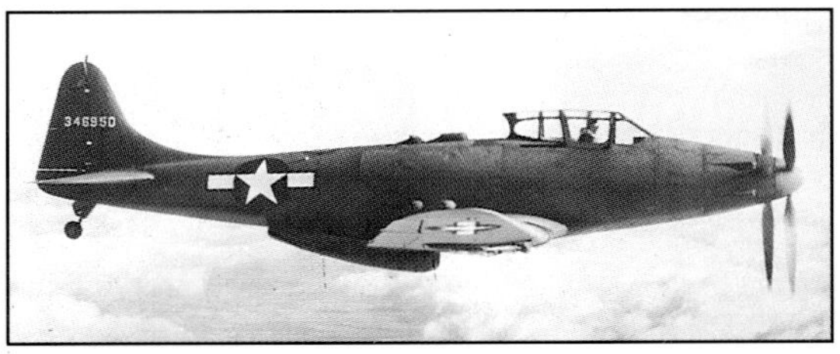

The first XP-75 (above) used assemblies from several existing aircraft and first flew in November 1943.

Radical in concept, the Eagle was designed and built by the Fisher Body Division of the General Motors Corp under the supervision of Don Berlin to meet an urgent USAAF need for a fast-climbing interceptor fighter. It was intended to mate major assemblies (eg, wing panels, tail unit and undercarriage) from existing aircraft with the most powerful liquid-cooled engine available, the 24-cylinder Allison V-3420-19 rated at 2,600 hp (2,885 hp war emergency). This was mounted aft of the cockpit and arranged to drive contraprops via an extension shaft. The first of eight XP-75 prototypes was flown in 17 November 1943, and the remaining seven were all under test by the spring of 1944, at which time 2,500 production P-75A Eagle fighters were on order. On 6 October 1944, the production contract was substantially terminated, however, and only five P-75As were completed. These differed appreciably from the XP-75s and carried an armament of four synchronised and six unsynchronised 0.5-in (12,7-mm) machine guns. The following data relate to the series P-75A. *Max speed, 400 mph (644 km/h) at 20,000 ft (6 100 m). Time to 20,000 ft (6 100 m), 5.8 min. Normal range, 2,150 mls (3 460 km). Empty weight, 11,255 lb (5 105 kg). Max loaded weight, 19,420 lb (8 809 kg). Span, 49 ft 4 in (15,03 m). Length, 41 ft 4 in (12,59 m). Height, 16 ft 6 in (5,03 m). Wing area, 347 sq ft (32,23 m^2).*

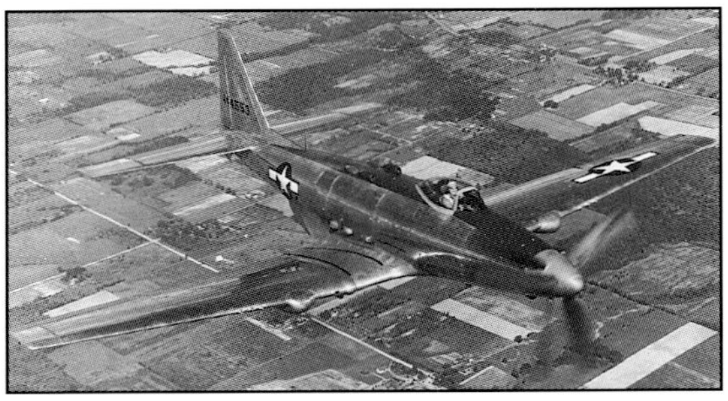

The P-75A (above and below) was ordered in large numbers in 1944, but, in the event, the contract was cancelled and only five examples were completed.

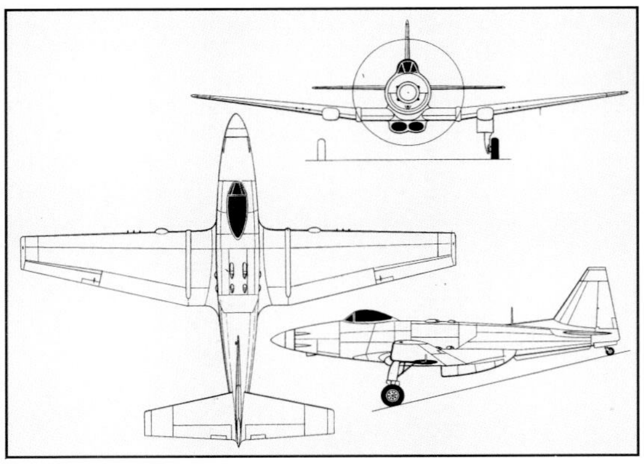

FMA I.Aé.27 PULQUI — Argentina

The first turbojet-powered aircraft to be built in Argentina, the I.Aé.27 Pulqui (Arrow) was designed (as the D 700) by Emile Dewoitine assisted by Humberto Ricciardi at the Fabrica Militar de Aviones. It was intended as a single-seat interceptor capable of operation from relatively short, poor-surfaced runways. Of all-metal construction and powered by a 3,600 lb st (1 633 kgp) Rolls-Royce Derwent 5, the Pulqui was intended to carry an armament of four 20-mm cannon. The sole prototype was flown for the first time on 9 August 1947, but performance proved disappointing, and further development was discontinued. *Max speed, 447 mph (720 km/h). Initial climb rate, 4,921 ft/min (25 m/sec). Range, 559 mls (900 km). Empty weight, 5,198 lb (2 358 kg). Loaded weight, 7,937 lb (3 600 kg). Span, 36 ft 11 in (11,25 m). Length, 31 ft 9½ in (9,69 m). Height, 11 ft 1½ in (3,39 m). Wing area, 212.05 sq ft (19,70 m^2).*

The Dewoitine-designed I.Aé.27 Pulqui (below) which entered flight test in Argentina in August 1947.

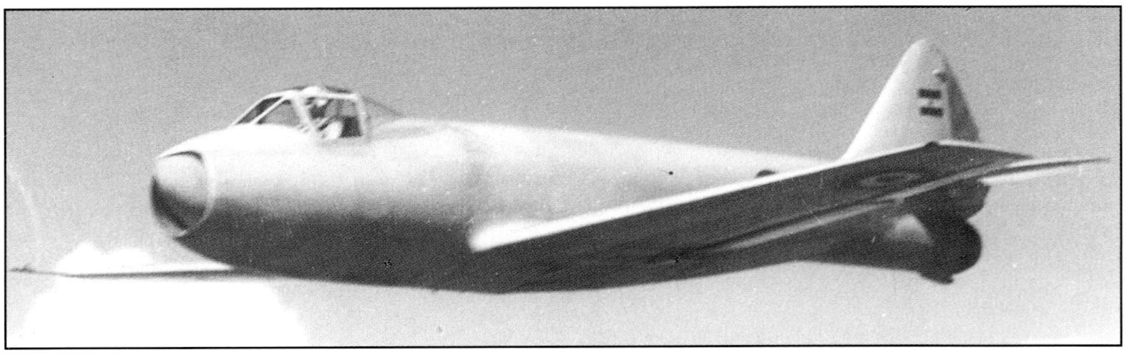

(Below) The Argentine-built I.Aé.27 Pulqui fighter.

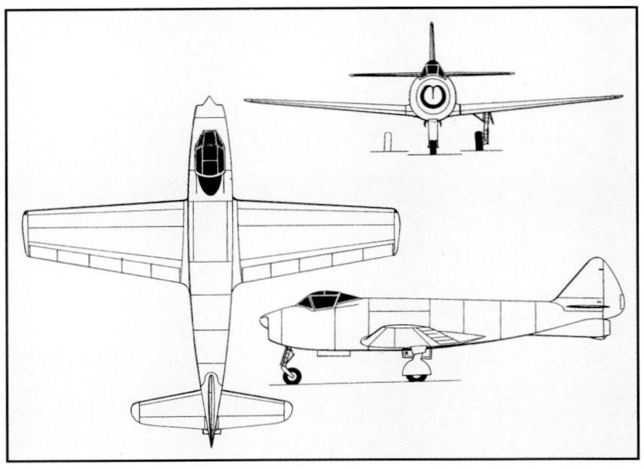

FMA I.Aé.30 ÑAMCÚ — Argentina

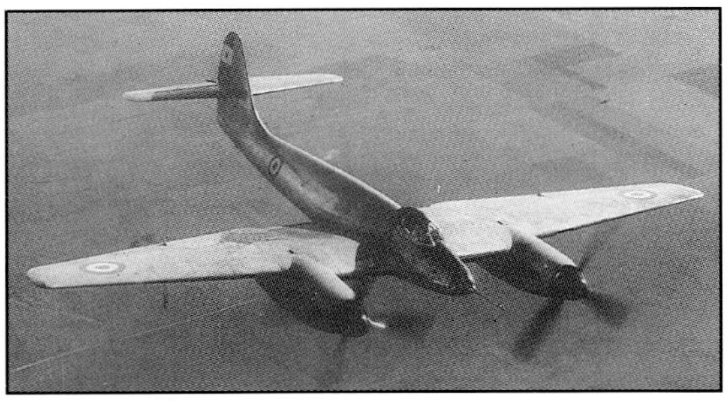

The I.Aé.30 Ñamcú (above and below) possessed an exceptional performance, but financial constraints resulted in cancellation of production contracts.

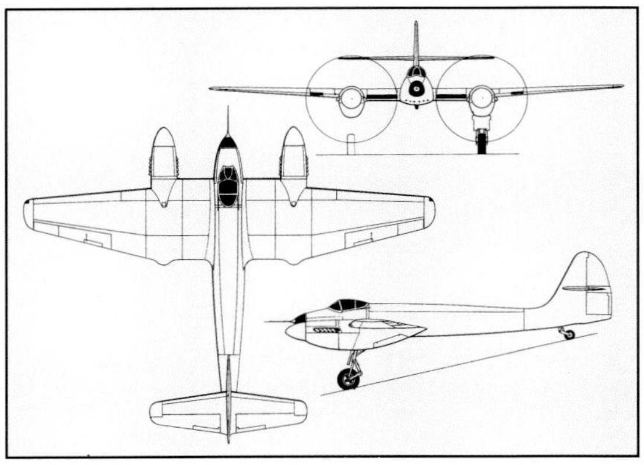

The I.Aé.30 Ñamcú twin-engined single-seat escort fighter was designed by Ing Cesare Pallavicino and was flown for the first time on 18 July 1948. The Ñamcú (Eaglet) was of all-metal construction with a triangular-section semi-monocoque fuselage and two 2,035 hp

Rolls-Royce Merlin 134/135 liquid-cooled engines. The proposed armament comprised six 20-mm Hispano-Suiza 804 cannon, with provision for a 550-lb (250-kg) bomb beneath the fuselage and 10 5-in (12,7-cm) rockets beneath the wings. The prototype Ñamcú was flown from Cordoba to Buenos Aires at an average speed of 404 mph (650 km/h) on 8 August 1948, using only 60 per cent of the available power. Production of 210 aircraft was ordered for the *Fuerza Aérea Argentina*, but, in April 1949, financial constraints dictated cancellation of production and further work on the Ñamcú was discontinued. *Max speed, 460 mph (740 km/h) at 21,000 ft (6 400 m). Time to 16,405 ft (5 000 m), 5.0 min. Max range, 1,678 mls (2 700 km). Empty weight, 12,313 lb (5 585 kg). Loaded weight, 19,301 lb (8 755 kg). Span, 49 ft 2½ in (15,00 m). Length, 37 ft 9⅓ in (11,52 m). Height (tail up), 16 ft 11 in (5,16 m). Wing area, 380.19 sq ft (35,32 m²).*

FMA. I.Aé.33 PULQUI II   Argentina

(Above) The first and (below) fourth prototypes of the I.Aé.33 Pulqui II designed in Argentina by a German team led by Dr Kurt Tank.

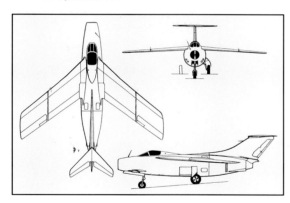

Designed by Dr Kurt Tank and embodying much of his experience in advanced design gained during World War II, the I.Aé.33 Pulqui II featured a 40-deg swept-back shoulder-mounted wing and was powered by a 4,998 lb st (2 267 kgp) Rolls-Royce Nene 2 turbojet. Armament comprised four 20-mm Hispano-Suiza cannon and the Pulqui II was envisaged as a successor to the Meteor in service with the *Fuerza Aérea Argentina*. Five prototypes were ordered, the first of these being a static test specimen and the second being the first flying prototype, the initial flight taking place on 27 June 1950. Various difficulties were encountered and this crashed near Cordoba, the development programme being protracted and the last of the prototypes not making its initial flight until 18 September 1959. Although the various problems that had delayed the development programme had by that time been overcome, Dr Tank and his team had meanwhile left Argentina, and this fact, together with the high cost of initiating series production, militated against further development. *Max speed, 652 mph (1 050 km/h) at 16,405 ft (5 000 m). Initial climb, 5,866 ft/min (29,8 m/ sec). Endurance, 2.2 hrs. Empty weight, 7,937 lb (3 600 kg). Loaded weight, 12,236 lb (5 550 kg). Span, 34 ft 9⅓ in (10,60 m). Length, 38 ft 3¾ in (11,68 m). Height, 11 ft 5¾ in (3,50 m). Wing area, 270.18 sq ft (25,10 m²).*

(Above) The sole prototype of the I.Aé.27 Pulqui, the first jet fighter to be designed in Latin America.

FOCKE-WULF FW 57   Germany

The FW 57 was designed to the *Kampfzerstörer* concept: a heavy fighter capable of clearing a path for bomber formations through defensive fighter screens.

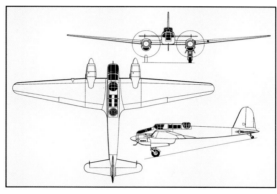

(Above and below) The FW 57, the first prototype of which is illustrated by the photograph, competed with the Messerschmitt Bf 110 for production orders.

A three-seater, conceived by Kurt Tank but primarily the responsibility of Dipl-Ing Bansemir, the FW 57 competed with the Henschel Hs 124 and Messerschmitt Bf 110, three prototypes of each of the contenders for *Luftwaffe* contracts being ordered. Of all-metal construction and powered by two 960 hp Daimler-Benz DB 600 12-cylinder liquid-cooled engines, the FW 57 was intended to be equipped with a pair of 20-mm MG FF cannon on semi-flexible mounts in the extreme nose and a similar weapon in an electrically-operated Mauser dorsal turret. The first prototype, the FW 57 V1, was flown in the late spring of 1936, by which time the *Kampfzerstörer* specification had been superseded. Structurally overweight, the FW 57 proved seriously underpowered, despite the fact that the heavy cannon armament was never fitted, and although all three prototypes were flown, the test programme had been

abandoned by the late autumn of 1936. *Max speed, 251 mph (404 km/h) at 9,840 ft (3 000 m), 227 mph (365 km/h) at sea level. Empty weight, 14,991 lb (6 800 kg). Loaded weight, 18,298 lb (8 300 kg). Span, 82 ft 0 in (25,00 m). Length, 54 ft 4⅓ in (16,57 m). Height, 13 ft 5⅓ in (4,10 m). Wing area, 791.17 sq ft (73.50 m²).*

FOCKE-WULF FW 159   Germany

One of the singularly few single-seat fighter monoplanes of parasol configuration to feature a retractable undercarriage, the FW 159 designed by Kurt Tank was of all-metal construction with a monocoque fuselage. The first of three prototypes, the FW 159 V1, flew in the spring of 1935 with a Junkers Jumo 210A engine rated at 610 hp for take-off, and was written off during the initial landing when the undercarriage failed. The second prototype, the FW 159 V2, initially differed only in having a reinforced oleo-hydraulic undercarriage actuating mechanism, but was subsequently fitted with two synchronised 7,9-mm MG 17 machine guns and a Jumo 210Da engine providing 680 hp for take-off.

The FW 159 – the V2 being illustrated above and the V3 below – was a rarity among fighters in being a parasol monoplane with a retractable undercarriage.

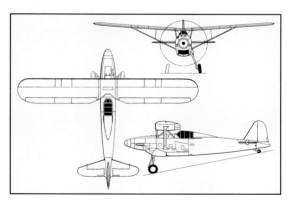

The FW 159 V3 initially flew with a Jumo 210B rated at 600 hp for take-off and 640 hp at 8,860 ft (2 700 m), but this prototype was eventually fitted with a fuel-injection Jumo 210G of 700 hp for take-off and 730 hp at 3,280 ft (1 000 m), carrying the twin-MG 17 armament and having provision for an engine-mounted 20-mm MG FF cannon. The FW 159 offered inferior performance to the competitive Heinkel He 112 and Messer-

Testing of the FW 159, the third prototype of which is illustrated below, continued into 1938.

schmitt Bf 109, and development was discontinued. The following data relate to the FW 159 V2 when fitted with the Jumo 210Da. *Max speed, 239 mph (384 km/h) at 13,125 ft (4 000 m). Time to 19,685 ft (6 000 m), 12.5 min. Range, 405 mls (652 km). Empty weight, 4,134 lb (1 875 kg). Loaded weight, 4,960 lb (2 250 kg). Span, 40 ft 8 in (12,40 m). Length, 32 ft 9½ in (10,00 m). Height, 12 ft 3⅔ in (3,75 m). Wing area, 217.44 sq ft (20,20 m²).*

FOCKE-WULF FW 187   Germany

One of the three pre-series FW 187A-0 fighters that were completed during the summer of 1939 (above).

Created as a twin-engined single-seat fighter, the FW 187 was flown for the first time in the spring of 1937. The first prototype, the FW 187 V1, was powered by two Junkers Jumo 210Da engines each rated at 680 hp for take-off and had provision for two 7,9-mm MG 17 machine guns flanking the cockpit. The FW 187 V2 was essentially similar, apart from having Jumo 210G engines and fixed (as opposed to semi-retractable) radiators. In the meantime, Focke-Wulf had been instructed to adapt the design as a two-seater, and the FW 187 V3, flown in the early spring of 1938, had provision for a second seat in tandem. It also provided for installation of a pair of 20-mm MG FF cannon in the lower fuselage. The V4 and V5 were similar to the V3, but the V6, flown early in 1939, had two Daimler-Benz DB 600A engines each rated at 1,000 hp for take-off. In October 1939, this prototype attained 394.6 mph (635 km/h) in level flight. Three pre-production FW 187A-0 fighters were completed during the summer of 1939, these

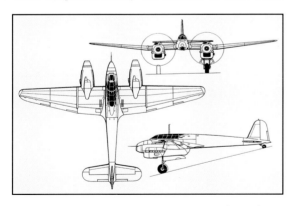

The tandem two-seat pre-series FW 187A-0 (above) and the single-seat second prototype, the FW 187 V2, (below), both of which were evaluated at Rechlin.

having Jumo 210Ga engines rated at 700 hp for take-off and 730 hp at 3,280 ft (1 000 m). Armament comprised two 20-mm MG FF cannon and four 7,9-mm MG 17 machine guns. After official trials at Rechlin, the three FW 187As were returned to Focke-Wulf and equipped a factory defence flight manned by test pilots. No further development was undertaken. The following data relate to the FW 187A-0. *Max speed, 329 mph (529 km/h) at 13,780 ft (4 200 m). Initial climb, 3,445 ft/min (17,5 m/sec). Time to 19,685 ft (6 000 m), 5.8 min. Empty weight, 8,157 lb (3 700 kg). Loaded weight, 11,023 lb (5 000 kg). Span, 50 ft 2⅓ in (15,30 m). Length, 36 ft 6 in (11,12 m). Height, 12 ft 7⅔ in (3,90 m). Wing area, 327.23 sq ft (30,40 m²).*

FOCKE-WULF FW 190A   Germany

Powered by a 1,550 hp BMW 139 two-row radial and featuring a ducted spinner, the first prototype FW 190 fighter, the V1, was flown on 1 June 1939, followed by the second, the V2, on 1 December 1939. The ducted spinner was supplanted by an orthodox NACA cowling at an early stage, the third and fourth prototypes being discontinued owing to BMW 139 difficulties. With adoption instead of the BMW 801, the wing was rede-

The first prototype of the FW 190, the V1 (above), and (below) the ultimate radial-engined production development of the fighter, the FW 190A-8.

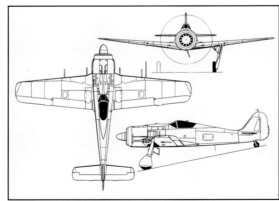

An FW 187A-0 which equipped an "*Industrie-Shutzstaffel*" for factory protection, winter 1940-41.

Key to Focke-Wulf FW 190A-3

1 Rudder fixed tab
2 Tail navigation light
3 Leads
4 Rudder hinge/attachment
5 Tailwheel extension spring
6 Tailwheel shock-absorber leg retraction guide
7 Tailfin spar
8 Rudder post assembly
9 Rudder frame
10 Rudder upper hinge
11 Aerial attachment
12 Tailfin structure
13 Canted rib progression
14 Port elevator fixed tab
15 Port elevator

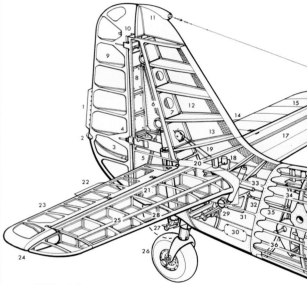

16 Mass balance
17 Port tailplane
18 Tailplane incidence motor unit
19 Tailwheel retraction pulley cables
20 Tailplane attachment
21 Starboard tailplane structure
22 Elevator fixed tab
23 Starboard elevator frame
24 Mass balance
25 Tailplane front spar
26 Semi-retracting tailwheel
27 Drag yoke
28 Tailwheel recess
29 Tailwheel locking linkage
30 Access panel
31 Actuating link
32 Push-pull rod
33 Rudder cables
34 Rudder control differential linkage
35 Fuselage/tail unit join
36 Elevator control differential
37 Fuselage lift tube
38 Elevator control cables
39 Bulkhead (No 12) fabric panel (rear fuselage equipment dust protection)
40 Leather grommets
41 Rudder push-pull rods
42 Fuselage frame
43 Master compass
44 Flat-bottomed (equipment bay floor support) frames
45 First-aid kit
46 Optional camera (2×Rb 12) installation (A-3/U4)
47 Control runs
48 Access hatch (port side)
49 Electrical leads
50 Distribution panel
51 Canopy channel slide cut-outs

signed and the airframe restressed, and these changes were embodied in a fifth prototype, the V5. The FW 190 V5 was tested with both short- (V5k) and long-span (V5g) wings, the latter being standardised with the 10th pre-series FW 190A-0. Series production commenced with the FW 190A-1 with the 1,600 hp BMW 801C-1 and an armament of four 7,9-mm MG 17 machine guns and two 20-mm MG FF cannon. It continued with the essentially similar FW 190A-2 (BMW 801C-2), 426 of

this sub-type following 102 of the initial version. The FW 190A-3 (509 built) standardised on the 1,700 hp BMW 801D-2 used by all subsequent A-series models, and two 20-mm MG 151 cannon replaced the wing root MG 17s. Seventy-two were delivered to Turkey (as FW 190Aa-3s) in 1942-43. The FW 190A-4 (894 built) differed from the A-3 in radio equipment and the A-5 (723 built) was similar, but had a lengthened engine mounting to restore the CG to the position occupied prior to

the introduction of additional equipment. The A-6 (569 built) introduced a revised wing structure and replaced the outboard MG FF cannon with MG 151s of similar calibre, and the A-7 (80 built) was similar apart from a new gunsight and fuselage-mounted 13-mm MG 131s in place of the previously-standard MG 17s. The final production A-series sub-type, the A-8 (1,334 built), had new radio, a repositioned fuselage bomb rack and provision for an internal auxiliary fuel tank. A wide variety

52 Canopy solid aft fairing
53 Aerial
54 Head armour support bracket
55 Aerial attachment/take-up pulley
56 Equipment/effects stowage
57 FuG 7a/FuG 25a radio equipment bay
58 Battery
59 Cockpit aft bulkhead
60 Control runs
61 Cockpit floor/centre-section main structure
62 Wingroot fillet
63 Underfloor aft fuel tank (64 Imp gal/291 l)
64 Underfloor forward fuel tank (51 Imp gal/232 l)
65 Cockpit sidewall control runs
66 Seat support brackets
67 Armoured bulkhead
68 Pilot's seat
69 Canopy operating handwheel
70 14-mm armoured backplate
71 Pilot's headrest
72 Canopy
73 Windscreen frame assembly
74 Armoured-glass windscreen
75 Revi gunsight

76 Instrument panel shroud
77 Throttle
78 Port control console (trim switches/buttons)
79 Control column
80 Seat pan
81 Starboard control console (circuit breakers)
82 Underfloor linkage
83 Electrical junction box
84 Rudder pedal assembly
85 Instrument panel sections
86 Screen support frame
87 Two 7,9-mm MG 17 machine guns
88 Ammunition feed chute
89 Panel release catches
90 Fuselage armament ammunition boxes
91 Forward bulkhead
92 Inboard wing cannon ammunition boxes
93 Engine mounting lower attachment point
94 Cooling air exit louvres
95 Engine mounting upper attachment point
96 Oil pump assembly
97 Engine mounting ring
98 Fuselage MG 17 ammunition cooling pipes
99 Machine gun front mounting brackets
100 Machine gun breech blister fairings
101 Port split flap section
102 Flap actuating electric motor
103 Port outer 20-mm MG FF cannon
104 Aileron control linkage
105 Aileron fixed tab

106 Port aileron
107 Aileron hinge points
108 Port detachable wingtip
109 Port navigation light
110 Front spar
111 Wing lower shell
112 MG FF muzzle
113 Port mainwheel leg fairing
114 Aileron link assembly
115 Fuselage MG 17 muzzles
116 Muzzle troughs
117 Upper cowling panel
118 Fuselage MG 17 electrical synchronizing unit
119 Exhaust pipes
120 Cowling panel ring
121 BMW 801D-2 radial engine
122 Former ring
123 Upper panel release catches
124 Forward cowling support ring
125 Oil tank armour
126 Oil tank (10 Imp gal/45,5 l)
127 Annular oil cooler assembly
128 Cooler armoured ring
129 Engine 12-bladed cooling fan
130 Three-bladed propeller
131 Propeller boss
132 Oil cooler airflow track
133 Airflow duct fairing (to rear cylinders)
134 Lower panel release catches
135 Cowling lower panel section
136 Wingroot fairing
137 Centre-section wheel covers

138 Inboard 20-mm cannon muzzle
139 Wheel cover operating cable
140 Starboard wheel well
141 Mainwheel leg rib cut-out
142 Undercarriage retraction jack
143 Locking unit assembly
144 Inboard 20-mm cannon spent cartridge chute
145 Front spar inboard assembly
146 Ammunition feed chute
147 Fuselage/front spar attachment
148 Ammunition box bay
149 Starboard inboard 20-mm MG 151 cannon
150 Breech blister fairing
151 Fuselage/rear spar attachment
152 Rear spar
153 Starboard flap assembly
154 Inboard solid ribs
155 Rotating drive undercarriage retraction unit
156 Radius rod hinge
157 Outboard 20-mm cannon muzzle
158 Mainwheel leg strut mounting assembly
159 Undercarriage actuation drive motor
160 Starboard outboard 20-mm MG FF cannon
161 Front spar assembly
162 Ammunition drum

163 Rib cut-out
164 Aileron control linkage
165 Aileron fixed tab
166 Starboard aileron frame
167 Aileron hinge points
168 Rear spar
169 Wing lower shell outer "floating ribs"
170 Wing undersurface inner skinning
171 Starboard detachable wingtip
172 Starboard navigation light
173 Leading-edge assembly
174 Nose rib attachment lips
175 Mainwheel leg fairing
176 Mainwheel leg
177 Brake lines
178 Fairing
179 Torque links
180 Axle hub assembly
181 Mainwheel fairing
182 Starboard mainwheel
183 Pitot head
184 Ventral bomb-rack aluminium aft fairing
185 Ventral bomb-rack carrier unit
186 ETC 500 ventral bomb-rack (A-3/U1)
187 SC 500 optional bomb load

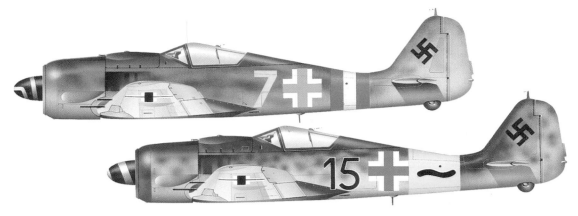

(Above top) FW 190A-8 of I/JG 6, Delmenhorst 1944-5, and (immediately above) of III/JG 11, Gross-Ostheim.

(Below) An early production FW 190A-3 undergoing factory flight testing in the spring of 1942.

The FW 190 V13 (above) was effectively the first FW 190C prototype, the general arrangement drawing (below) depicting the FW 190C in definitive form.

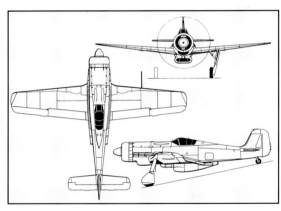

reminiscent of a kangaroo's pouch). More prototypes had meanwhile been put in hand, these being intended to lead to the production of the FW 190C-1 (without pressure cabin) and C-2 (with pressure cabin). These were overtaken by the decision to suspend the DB 603 variant in favour of the Jumo-engined FW 190D, although five more prototypes from the second batch of development airframes (V29 to V33) were completed to a standard similar to that of the V18/U1. In production form, the FW 190C was to have had two 13-mm MG 131 guns in the fuselage, four 20-mm MG 151s in the wings and a fifth MG 151 mounted between the engine cylinder banks. Continual difficulties with both turbo-supercharger and pressure cabin led to all effort being switched to the FW 190D. The following data relate to the definitive C-series prototypes with turbo-supercharged DB 603A engine and armament restricted to twin MG 151 cannon. *Max speed, 404 mph (650 km/h) at 32,810 ft (10 000 m). Time to 39,370 ft (12 000 m), 20 min. Empty weight, 7,903 lb (3 585 kg). Loaded weight, 9,369 lb (4 250 kg). Span, 40 ft 4⅛ in (12,30 m). Length, 31 ft 2 in (9,50 m), Height (over propeller), 11 ft 5¾ in (3,50 m). Wing area, 218.51 sq ft (20,30 m²).*

The FW 190 V18/U1 (below) was the first of the so-called "*Kanguruh*" prototypes of the FW 190C.

FOCKE-WULF FW 190D   Germany

While Focke-Wulf was struggling with the pressurisation and supercharging problems of the FW 190B and C, a parallel programme was being conducted with a version powered by the Junkers Jumo 213 12-cylinder inverted-Vee liquid-cooled engine, the FW 190D. Development aircraft for the D-series were the V17, V22 and V23, all of which were fitted with pressure cabins and powered by the Jumo 213A-1 rated at 1,600 hp at 18,000 ft (5 485 m). An annular radiator was adopted, similar to that used by the FW 190C's DB 603, the nose being lengthened by 2 ft (60 cm). To compensate, an extra untapered fuselage section was introduced immediately ahead of the tailplane, adding 1 ft 7½ in (50 cm) to the overall length. Six additional development aircraft (V19-21 and V25-27), originally laid down as C-series prototypes, were meanwhile completed with major wing redesign as the first genuine D-series prototypes. In the event, however, the initial production model of what was to be known as the *Langnasen-Dora* was to be essentially a marriage of the FW 190A-8 airframe with the Jumo 213A-1 engine installation, this being designated FW 190D-9. Deliveries to the *Luftwaffe* commenced in August 1944. The FW 190D-9 had

An FW 190D-9 (below) captured at Marienburg and used by the Soviet Red Banner Baltic Fleet.

of *Umrüst-Bausätze* (factory conversion sets) – their application indicated by the suffix letter "U" – and *Rüstsätze* (field conversion sets) was applicable to most sub-types to optimise them for more specific rôles. The FW 190A-9, which progressed no further than prototype trials, was intended as a *Rammjäger*, with heavily armoured wing leading edges and a turbo-supercharged BMW 801TS or TU engine. Sixty-four FW 190A-5s and A-8s were built in France by the SNCA du Centre in 1945-46, some serving briefly with the *Armée de l'Air* under the designation NC 900. The following data relate to the FW 190A-8. *Max speed, 355 mph (571 km/h) at sea level, 402 mph (647 km/h) at 18,045 ft (5 500 m). Initial climb, 3,450 ft/min (17,5 m/sec). Range (clean), 643 mls (1 035 km). Empty weight, 7,650 lb (3 470 kg). Normal loaded weight, 9,656 lb (4 380 kg). Span, 34 ft 5½ in (10,51 m). Length, 29 ft 4¼ in (8,95 m). Height (over propeller), 12 ft 11½ in (3,95 m). Wing area, 196.98 sq ft (18,30 m²).*

FOCKE-WULF FW 190B   Germany

During the course of 1942, Focke-Wulf was engaged in investigating means of improving the performance of the FW 190 at altitudes above 20,000 ft (6 100 m), one proposal being the FW 190B with a turbo-supercharged BMW 801 engine, a pressure cabin and a longer span wing. During the later months of 1942, plans were completed for the production of this sub-type. A rudimentary pressure cabin was installed in an FW 190A-0 airframe, which then became the V12 and first B-series prototype, but turbo-supercharging was not applied to the BMW 801 engine and the standard wing was retained. However, GM 1 (nitrous oxide) boost was provided to help maintain power at high altitudes. The first four of an additional batch of development airframes (ordered to follow the original batch of FW 190A-0s) were then assigned to the FW 190B programme. These were generally similar to the V12, although the first of the additional aircraft had a longer-span wing affording 21.53 sq ft (2,0 m²) added area, this wing being regarded as the future standard for the series FW 190B. Recurring difficulties with the GM 1 boost system and the pressure cabin slowed the progress of the test programme and the strictures on armament imposed by the weight of these items resulted in a waning of interest on the part of the *Luftwaffe*, although up to six FW 190B-1s are believed to have been completed. No data available.

FOCKE-WULF FW 190C   Germany

Evolved in parallel with the FW 190B, the FW 190C was developed around the Daimler-Benz DB 603 12-cylinder inverted-Vee liquid-cooled engine. The first prototype for the FW 190C was the V13. The DB 603A-0 engine was installed within an annular cowling, overall air-

craft length being increased by 2 ft 2½ in (66 cm), but in other respects the V13 was similar to the FW 190A-0. The second and third C-series prototypes, the V15 and V16, were, to all intents and purposes, similar, and were powered by the DB 603A engine rated at 1,750 hp for take-off and 1,850 hp at 6,900 ft (2,100 m). The V16 was eventually equipped with a supercharged DB 603E engine rated at 1,800 hp at sea level. With this a speed of 450 mph (724 km/h) was attained at 22,310 ft (6 800 m), and an initial climb of 4,330 ft/min (22,0 m/sec) was demonstrated before the end of 1942. The next FW 190C prototype, the V18/U1, was fitted with a DVL TK 11 exhaust-driven turbo-supercharger (which increased the output of its DB 603A engine to 1,600 hp at 35,100 ft/10 700 m) and a pressure cabin. This was the first of the so-called *Kanguruh* prototypes (the large ventral fairing housing the turbo-supercharger being

(Above) An FW 190D-9 of 10./JG 54 which crash-landed at Wemmel, Belgium, on 1 January 1945.

(Below) An FW 190D-9 of II/JG 26 "*Schlageter*" at Nordhorn, near Osnabrück, in January 1945.

FW 190G-3s (above), believed to belong to III/SG 10, photographed over Romania, early in 1943.

an armament of two 13-mm MG 131 machine guns and two 20-mm MG 151 cannon, various *Rüstsätze* being applied in service. The D-10 was to have featured a 30-mm MK 108 *Motorkannon*, but none was, in fact, delivered. Another armament change distinguished the D-11 which had two MK 108s in the outer wing bays, but only prototypes were completed. The FW 190D-12 replaced the D-9 in production in February 1945, this having a Jumo 213F-1 engine with a 30-mm MK 108 *Motorkannon* and twin wing-mounted 20-mm MG 151s. Production of D-series fighters totalled a little short of 700 aircraft. The following data relate to the FW 190D-9. *Max speed, 357 mph (574 km/h) at sea level, 426 mph (686 km/h) at 21,650 ft (6 600 m). Time to 19,685 ft (6 000 m), 7.1 min. Range (clean), 520 mls (837 km). Empty weight, 7,694 lb (3 490 kg). Normal loaded weight, 9,480 lb (4 300 kg). Span, 34 ft 5½ in (10,51 m). Length, 33 ft 5¼ in (10,19 m). Height (over propeller), 11 ft 0¼ in (3,36 m). Wing area, 196.98 sq ft (18,30 m²).*

The FW 190F-8 (above), which, based on the A-8 airframe, was the last F-series built in quantity.

The FW 190D-9 with (above) early-type cockpit canopy, and (below) in standard production configuration.

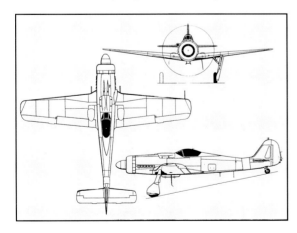

FOCKE-WULF FW 190F Germany

The FW 190F single-seat ground attack fighter was essentially a production version of the FW 190A-5/U3, the *Umrüst-Bausatz* (factory conversion set) – signified by the "U3" appended to the standard production fighter designation – being standardised on the assembly line, and a new series letter being applied for convenience. The first 25-30 F-series fighters were, in fact, based on the A-4 airframe and designated FW 190F-1. These carried an armament of two fuselage-mounted 7,9-mm MG 17s and two 20-mm MG 151s in the wing roots and had provision for a 551-lb (250-kg)

bomb beneath each wing and a 1,102-lb (500-kg) bomb beneath the fuselage. Additional protective armour was provided for the engine, oil tank and pilot. Similarly powered by the 1,700 hp BMW 801D-2, the FW 190F-2 differed in being based on the A-5 airframe and in having a new one-piece blown cockpit canopy. The FW 190F-3 was based on the A-6 airframe, some 20 of this sub-series having a 30-mm MK 103 cannon under each wing in place of bomb racks. The FW 190F-8 was based on the A-8 airframe and the final production version, the FW 190F-9, differed in having a 2,000 hp turbo-supercharged BMW 801TS engine. The following data relate specifically to the FW 190F-3. *Max speed (clean), 342 mph (550 km/h) at sea level, 394 mph (634 km/h) at 18,045 ft (5 500 m). Initial climb, 2,110 ft/min (10,7 m/sec). Max range, 466 mls (750 km). Empty weight, 7,330 lb (3 325 kg). Normal loaded weight, 9,700 lb (4 400 kg). Span, 34 ft 5½ in (10,51 m). Length, 29 ft 4¼ in (8,95 m). Height (over propeller), 12 ft 11½ in (3,95 m). Wing area, 196.98 sq ft (18,30 m²).*

FOCKE-WULF FW 190G Germany

Evolved in parallel with the FW 190F, the FW 190G was a dedicated extended-range fighter-bomber consolidating on the production line the *Umrüst-Bausätze* 8 and 13 applied retrospectively to the FW 190A. Retaining the BMW 801D-2 engine, the FW 190G had a fixed armament of only two wing root-mounted 20-mm MG 151 cannon, external bomb load being similar to that of the FW 190F. Fifty FW 190G-1s were built, these

being based on the A-4 airframe and followed by the FW 190G-2 utilising the A-5 series airframe. These were succeeded in October 1943 by the FW 190G-3 with a PKS 11 autopilot and wing leading-edge balloon-cable cutters. The final production series was the FW 190G-8, built from September 1943 to February 1944, and having the same airframe as the A-8, provision for an internal auxiliary fuel tank, and revised and repositioned equipment. The following data relate specifically to the FW 190G-3. *Max speed, 340 mph (547 km/h) at sea level, 388 mph (624 km/h) at 16,405 ft (5 000 m). Normal range, 497 mls (800 km). Empty weight, 7,959 lb (3 610 kg). Max loaded weight, 11,045 lb (5 010 kg). Dimensions as for FW 190F-3.*

FOCKE-WULF TA 152C Germany

During 1942, various new features were proposed for progressive developments of the basic FW 190 fighter, one feature common to all being a new lengthened fuselage with the cockpit relocated 16 in (40 cm) farther aft in relation to the wing. Versions of both the Jumo 213 and DB 603 12-cylinder inverted-Vee liquid-cooled engines were projected for installation, the vertical tail surfaces were enlarged and both the basic FW 190 wing and a new longer span wing were considered. When development of a new series of fighters embodying various of these features was officially sanctioned in 1943, the designation Ta 152 was assigned in recognition of the work of Kurt Tank. The Ta 152A and Ta 152B, powered by the Jumo 213A and Jumo 213C respectively, and featuring a new wing centre section mated

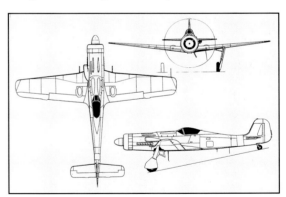

The general arrangement drawing above depicts the Ta 152C-0, and the Ta 152C V7 below was one of only three prototypes of the Ta 152C-1 to be completed.

with standard FW 190A-8 outer wings, were overtaken by the Ta 152C. This, with a similar airframe, was to be powered by the Daimler-Benz DB 603LA rated at 2,100 hp (2,300 hp with MW 50 boost) for take-off. The FW 190 V21/U1 (rebuilt V21) was completed on 3 November 1944 with a DB 603E engine (enclosed by a DB 603L cowling) as the first C-series prototype, and it was anticipated that the first Ta 152C-1s would leave the assembly lines in April 1945. In the event, only three FW 190C-1 prototypes, the V6, V7 and V8, and two Ta 152C-3 prototypes, V16 and V17, were completed, as production precedence was allocated to the Ta 152H. The Ta 152C-1 carried an armament of one engine-mounted 30-mm MK 108 cannon and four (two fuselage and two wing) 20-mm MG 151 cannon. The Ta 152C-3 differed in having a 30-mm MK 103 in place of the MK 108, and the C-2 and C-4 were proposed variants of the two initial models with FuG 15 instead of FuG 16Z-Y radio. The following data relate to the Ta 152C-1. *Max speed, 463 mph (745 km/h) at 34,450 ft (10 500 m). Initial climb, 3,050 ft/min (15,50 m/sec). Normal range, 684 mls (1 100 km). Empty weight, 8,849 lb (4 014 kg). Loaded weight, 11,684 lb (5 300 kg). Span, 36 ft 1 in (11,00 m). Length, 35 ft 6 in (10,82 m). Height, 11 ft 1 in (3,38 m). Wing area, 209.90 sq ft (19,50 m^2).*

FOCKE-WULF Ta 152H — Germany

Intended primarily as a *Hohenjäger* (altitude fighter), but also to fulfil the rôle of *Begleitjäger* (escort fighter), the Ta 152H was a parallel development of the Ta 152C. It differed in being powered by the Junkers Jumo 213E-1 engine rated at 1,750 hp for take-off (2,050 hp with MW 50) and in embodying a long-span wing of entirely new structural design. Four FW 190C prototypes, V29, V30, V32 and V33, were rebuilt to participate in the Ta 152H development programme. The genuine prototypes of the H-series fighter were the Ta 152 V3, V4 and V5, the first of these being completed mid-1944, and being the first of a batch of 26 pre-series Ta 152H-0 aircraft built at Sorau. A further batch of 20 pre-series Ta 152H-0s was built at Cottbus, where production continued with the Ta 152H-1. The Ta 152H-2 was a version with FuG 15 in place of FuG 16Z-Y that was cancelled in December 1944. The Ta 152H-1 carried an armament of one 30-mm MK 108 *Motorkannon* and two wing-mounted 20-mm MG 151 cannon. A small number of the 150 plus fighters of this type completed at Cottbus before the factory was overrun by Soviet forces saw operational use from January 1945. *Max speed, 462 mph (744 km/h) at 31,170 ft (9 500 m). Initial climb, 3,445 ft/min (17,50 m/sec). Normal range, 944 mls (1 520 km). Empty weight, 8,887 lb (4 031 kg). Loaded weight, 11,501 lb (5 217 kg). Span, 47 ft 4½ in (14,44 m). Length, 35 ft 1⅔ in (10,71 m). Height, 11 ft 1 in (3,38 m). Wing area, 250.81 sq ft (23,30 m^2).*

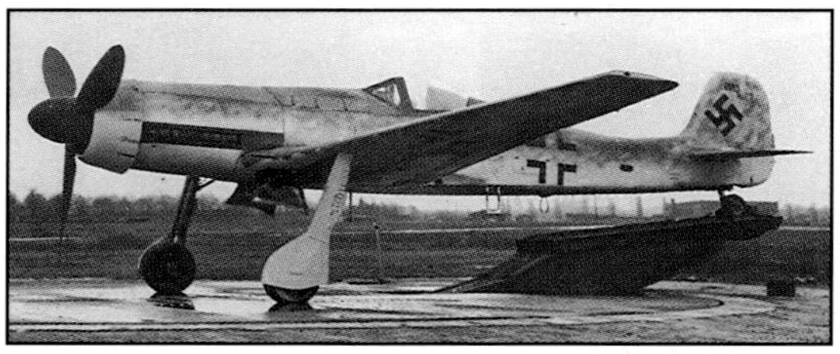

(Above) The fifth Ta 152H-0 and (below) a general arrangement drawing of this pre-series version of the fighter built at both Sorau and Cottbus.

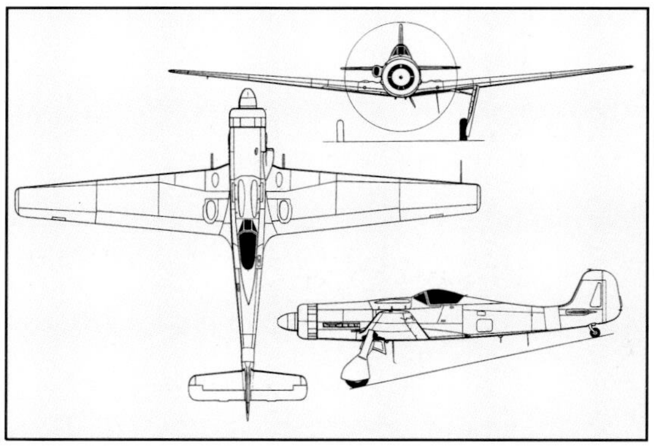

FOCKE-WULF Ta 154 — Germany

Emulating the de Havilland Mosquito in being primarily of wooden construction, the Ta 154 two-seat night and bad weather fighter was initiated in September 1942. The first prototype, the Ta 154 V1, was flown on 1 July 1943, and was powered by two Junkers Jumo 211F 12-cylinder Vee-type engines rated at 1,340 hp for take-off and 1,480 hp at 9,850 ft (3 000 m). The Ta 154 V2, which was equipped with FuG 212 *Lichtenstein C-1* radar, was initially similarly powered, but was later to be re-engined with the Jumo 211N of 1,460 hp for take-off and 1,520 hp at 4,250 ft (1 295 m). The V3, flown on 24 November 1943 for 15 minutes and then demonstrated to Adolf Hitler, had Jumo 211Fs (later 211Ns) and an armament of four 20-mm cannon. These prototypes were also considered as pre-series aircraft, of which 15 had been ordered, later supplemented by a further six.

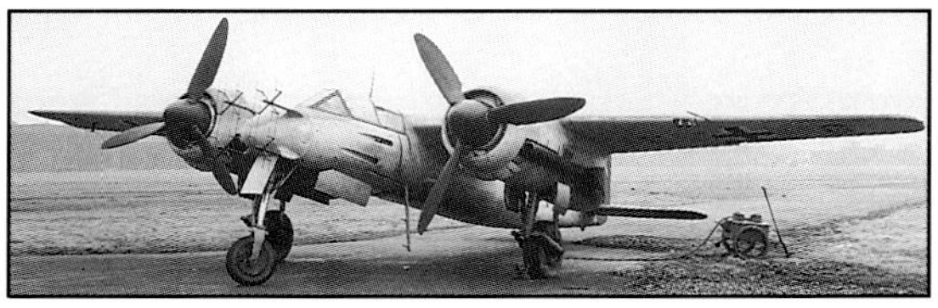

The Ta 154 V3 (above) with *Matratzen* aerial array and a quartet of 20-mm cannon, and (below) a general arrangement drawing of the series Ta 154A-1 fighter.

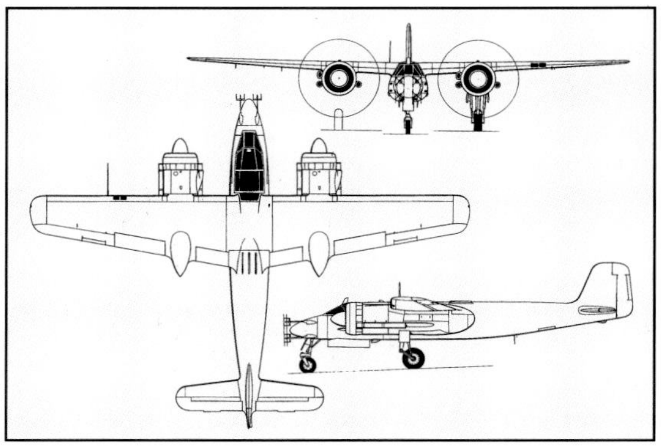

The Ta 154 V4 was the first prototype fitted with a pair each of 20-mm and 30-mm cannon (the larger calibre weapons later being removed), and the V8, initially flown with Jumo 211s on 11 August 1944, became the first of four prototypes (the others being the V10, V22 and V23) to be fitted with Jumo 213As rated at 1,776 hp for take-off. The Ta 154 V9 was the first aircraft completed at Poznan, Poland, and was intended as a pattern aircraft for series production there. The V15 was one of the first prototypes to have the *Hirschgeweih* (Stag's Antlers) radar array. An initial production contract for 250 Ta 154A-1s had been issued within weeks of the start of flight test, and a pre-series of 22 Jumo 211E-engined Ta 154A-0s for service evaluation was built at Erfurt, the first of these being completed in March 1944. The first series aircraft were Ta 154A-1s and A-4s, the former with FuG 212 radar and the latter with either FuG 220 or FuG 218 *Neptun*. The Ta 154A-2 was to have been a single-seat version and the Ta 154A-3 was a proposed two-seat conversion trainer. The problems posed by wooden aircraft construction and bonding agents led to the decision to terminate production (promulgated on 14 August 1944), but somewhat more than 50 Ta 154A-1s and A-4s were completed, most of these being issued to *Nachtjagdgruppen* with which they saw some operational use. The following data relate to the Ta 154A-4 with Jumo 211N engines and four-cannon armament. *Max speed, 382 mph (615 km/h) at 19,000 ft (5 790 m). Time to 26,245 ft (8 000 m), 16 min. Range, 851 mls (1 370 km) at 22,965 ft (7 000 m). Empty weight (less armament and radar), 13,933 lb (6 320 kg). Max loaded weight, 18,188 lb (8 250 kg). Span, 52 ft 5⅞ in (16,00 m). Length (excluding antennae), 40 ft 10⅛ in (12,45 m). Height, 11 ft 1½ in (3,40 m). Wing area, 348.76 sq ft (32,40 m^2).*

The Ta 154 V15 (below) was one of the first of the prototypes with a *Hirschgeweih* antennae for FuG 220.

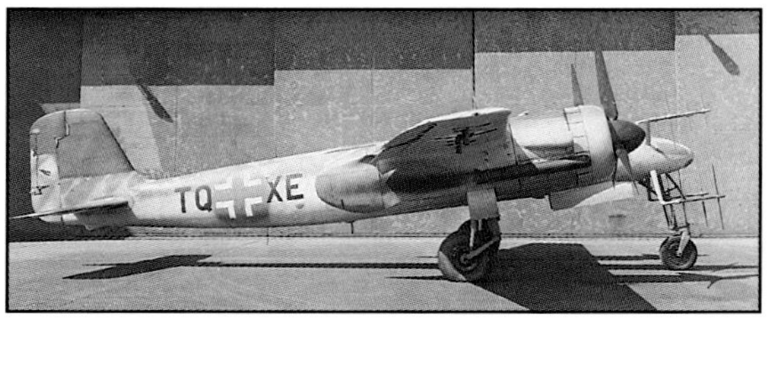

FOKKER E I (M 5K/MG) — Germany

Flown in the late spring of 1914, the M 5 (the prefix letter signifying *Militär*) was a single-seat monoplane of mixed construction, with a welded steel-tube fuselage, wooden wings and fabric skinning. It was built in two versions, the M 5L (assigned the military designation A II) with long-(*lang*) and the M 5K (A III) with short-(*kurz*) span wings. Several were supplied privately to Prussian officers and two (A IIs) to the Austro-Hungarian *Luftfahrttruppen*. One M 5K was fitted with a DWM Parabellum MG 14 with Fokker's so-called *Stangensteuerung* (push-rod control) synchronising the weapon with the propeller. This was successfully demonstrated to the *Idflieg* (Inspectorate of Flying Troops) as the M 5K/MG and was ordered in series by the *Heeresverwaltung* as the E I. The more reliable air-cooled version of the Maxim LMG 08/15 gun was standardised and the E I was powered by an 80 hp Oberursel U O (Gnome copy) seven-cylinder rotary engine.

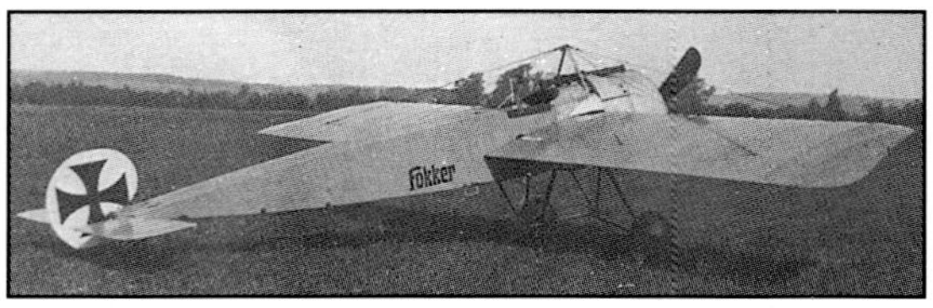

(Above) The original M 5K/MG during demonstration to *Feldfliegerabteilung* 62 near Douay, and (below) a general arrangement drawing of the production E I.

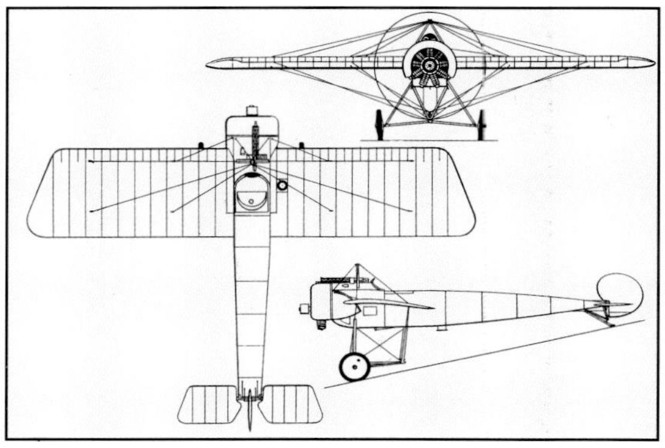

Production deliveries commenced in June 1915, a total of 54 aircraft being built, of which the majority were assigned to the *Kampf-Einsitzer-Kommando* (Single-seat Battle Command). Some E Is went to various *Feldflieger-Abteilungen*, six were ordered by the *Marine-Landflieger* and nine were assigned to the Austro-Hungarian *Luftfahrttruppen*. Deliveries of the E I were completed in June 1916. *Max speed, 81 mph (130 km/h).*

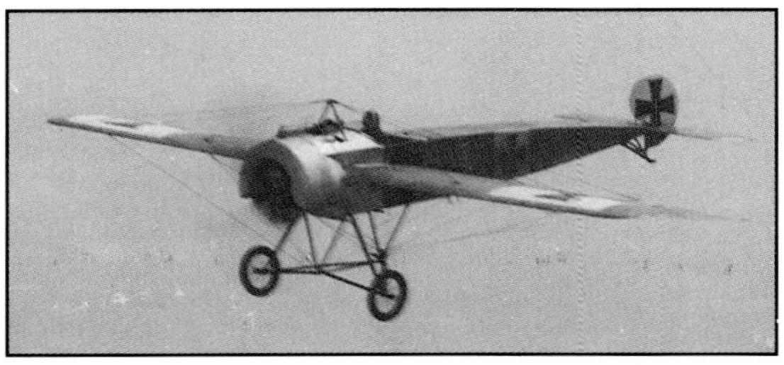

A Fokker E I (above) of the *Kampf-Einsitzer-Kommando* over the Western Front late summer 1915.

Range, 124 mls (200 km) at 68 mph (110 km/h). Service ceiling, 9,840 ft (3 000 m). Empty weight, 789 lb (358 kg). Loaded weight, 1,241 lb (563 kg). Span, 29 ft 4⅓ in (8,95 m). Length, 22 ft 1¾ in (6,75 m). Height, 7 ft 10½ in (2,40 m). Wing area, 155 sq ft (14,40 m^2).

FOKKER K I (M 9)   Germany

Original in concept in having a push-pull engine configuration and twin fuselage booms, the M 9 was developed without official encouragement as an offensive fighter, the sole prototype being completed in April 1915. Also known by the designation K I (the "K" prefix indicating *Kampfflugzeug*, or "Battle Aircraft"), the M 9 utilised two fuselages, complete with tail assemblies from conventional M 7 two-seat sesquiplanes. These were married by means of a biplane structure to a central nacelle which carried single 80 hp seven-cylinder rotary Oberursel U O engines fore and aft, with the pilot seated between. The nose of each M 7 fuselage accommodated a cockpit for a gunner. No rigid structure connected the two fuselages aft of the nacelle and, in consequence, the booms tended to twist when the wings warped. The M 9 was perfunctorily flight tested by Anthony Fokker. He complained of the flexing of the tailbooms and the marked tail heaviness which rendered control difficult. As Fokker was by then preoccupied with testing the M 5K/MG (E I) monoplane, further development of the M 9 was abandoned. No data relating to this short-lived experimental fighter have apparently survived.

Highly original in concept, the M 9 alias K I (above and below) utilised twin fuselages and two engines mounted on the fuselage centreline.

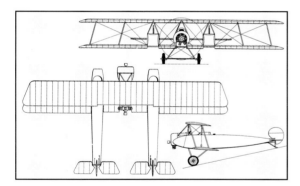

FOKKER E II & III (M 14)   Germany

Derived from the M 5K fighting scout, the M 14 was, in its initial form at least, an unarmed tuitional aircraft with 10.76 sq ft (1,00 m²) more wing area and a marginally longer fuselage. Some local structural reinforcement and minor changes were introduced in the forward fuselage decking, the upper wing bracing pylon

The E III (below) was essentially similar to the E II apart from its engine, most E IIs being converted.

The E II (above) was marginally larger than the E I and introduced some local structural reinforcement.

and the undercarriage, and the 80 hp Oberursel engine of the E I was retained. Twelve were ordered by the *Heeresverwaltung* under the designation E II. In the event, 47 additional E IIs were also to be built, with a similar armament to that of the E I, the first three of these being delivered in July 1915 and 13 more following in August *before* the first unarmed examples (six delivered in each of September and October) were taken into the inventory. The armed E IIs were re-engined with the 100 hp Oberursel U I nine-cylinder rotary during repair or overhaul, reappearing in Fokker's delivery lists as E IIIs when redelivered to the *Fliegertruppen*. The designation E III was, in fact, that applied to new-build M 14 airframes fitted with the U I rotary from the outset, improved synchronising gear being provided for the LMG 08/15 gun. Of 258 aircraft built from the outset as E IIIs, 221 were delivered to the *Fliegertruppen*, 19 were supplied to *Marine-Land-flieger*, 12 were received by the Austro-Hungarian *Luftfahrttruppen* and the remaining six went to the Austro-Hungarian Navy. The following data relate to the E III. *Max speed, 87 mph (140 km/h). Range, 149 mls (240 km) at 74 mph (120 km/h). Service ceiling, 11,810 ft (3 600 m). Empty weight, 880 lb (399 kg). Loaded weight, 1,345 lb (610 kg). Span, 31 ft 2⅘ in (9,52 m). Length, 23 ft 7½ in (7,20 m). Height, 7 ft 10½ in (2,40 m). Wing area, 165.77 sq ft (15,40 m²).*

FOKKER E IV (M 15)   Germany

Several of the most successful Fokker *Eindecker* pilots, including Max Immelmann and Oswald Boelcke, asked Anthony Fokker to develop a more powerful and more heavily armed version of his fighting scout. As a consequence, the M 15 was evolved, the first example of which was delivered in September 1915 as the E IV. Embodying modest increases in overall dimensions, the E IV was powered by the 160 hp Oberursel U III two-row 14-cylinder rotary engine, and, in standard form, was fitted with paired synchronised LMG 08/15 machine guns. At least one example of the E IV was completed (for Immelmann) with the then unprecedented fixed-gun armament of three LMG 08/15s. The success of the E IV at the Front was limited and production was restricted to 49 examples, of which the last was delivered in July 1916. *Max speed, 99 mph (160 km/h). Range, 149 mls (240 km) at 81 mph (130 km/h). Service ceiling,*

14,765 ft (4 500 m). Empty weight, 1,014 lb (460 kg). Loaded weight, 1,596 lb (724 kg). Span, 32 ft 9½ in (10,00 m). Length, 24 ft 7¼ in (7,50 m). Height, 9 ft 1 in (2,77 m). Wing area, 175.46 sq ft (16,30 m²).

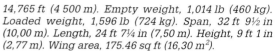

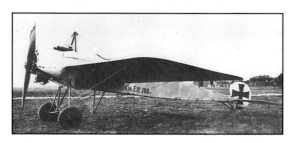

(Above and below) The E IV was more powerful and more heavily armed than preceding fighting scouts, but its success at the Front was limited.

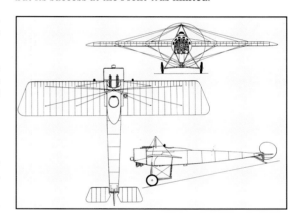

FOKKER M 16   Germany

A tandem two-seat fighter designed by Martin Kreutzer primarily for the Austro-Hungarian *Luftfahrttruppen*, the M 16 was an angular two-bay equi-span unstaggered biplane with a welded steel-tube fuselage, wooden wings and fabric skinning. It was initially powered by a 160 hp Mercedes D III six-cylinder water-cooled engine and utilised wing warping for lateral control. It was subsequently fitted with a 200 hp Austro-Daimler six-cylinder water-cooled engine, the means of lateral control being changed from wing warping to large ailerons with overhanging horn balances on the upper wing. The M 16 was shipped to the *Luftfahrttruppen* for evaluation in April 1916, and was fitted with a single synchronised Schwarzlose machine gun offset to port and another Schwarzlose machine gun on a flexible mount in the rear cockpit. Although an order for 26 aircraft was placed by the Austro-Hungarian service, no production of the M 16 was undertaken. The designations "M 16E", "M 16Z"

(Below) The M 16 in its original form with wing warping and a 160 hp Mercedes D III engine.

and "M 16ZK" were subsequently ascribed to this aircraft to signify *Einstielig* (single-strutted or single-bay), *Zweistielig* (two-bay) and *Klappenverwindung* (flap control – ailerons as opposed to wing warping) but were *not* assigned contemporaneously, being of post-World War I origin. No specification for the M 16 two-seat fighter has apparently survived.

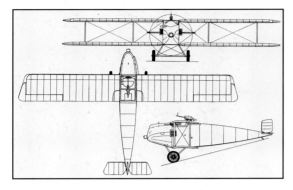

(Above and below) The M 16 in the definitive form in which it was evaluated by the *Luftfahrttruppen* of Austria-Hungary in the spring of 1916.

FOKKER D II (M 17)   Germany

Evolved in parallel with the M 16 by Kreutzer, the M 17 single-seat fighter was, in its original form, an unstaggered single-bay equi-span biplane with an inordinately deep fuselage affording extremely limited view from the cockpit. The fuselage decking was subsequently cut down to improve all-round vision from the cockpit and stagger was applied to the wings. The M 17 was flown with both the 80 hp seven-cylinder Oberursel U 0 and 100 hp nine-cylinder Oberursel I rotaries, and in both *Einstielig* (single-bay) and *Zweistielig* (two-bay) configurations. Twenty of the 80 hp single-bay M 17s were supplied to the Austro-Hungarian *Luftfahrttruppen* and assigned the designation B II, a

The single-bay first prototype of the Kreutzer-designed M 17 (above) progenitor of the D II, and (below) the standard two-bay production D II.

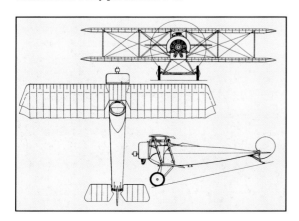

The two-bay D II (above) of the *Fliegertruppen* that arrived at the Front during the late summer of 1916.

further 42 being built by the MAG (Mágyar Altálanos Gépgyár). Some of these were fitted with a single unsynchronised Schwarzlose machine gun above the upper wing, but most were unarmed and assigned to the training rôle. Austro-Hungarian acceptances commenced in April 1916. The two-bay M 17 with the higher-powered U I engine was adopted by Germany's *Fliegertruppen* as the D II, this type having a single synchronised Maxim LMG 08/15 machine gun. It began arriving at the Front in July-August 1916, 181 being delivered. One example was supplied for evaluation to the *Marine-Landflieger*. The designations "M 17Z" and "M 17E" were purely post-World War I attributions. The following data relate to the D II. *Max speed, 93 mph (150 km/h). Time to 3,280 ft (1 000 m), 4.0 min. Range, 124 mls (200 km). Empty weight, 846 lb (384 kg). Loaded weight, 1,268 lb (575 kg). Span, 28 ft 8½ in (8,75 m). Length, 20 ft 11⅞ in (6,40 m). Height, 8 ft 4⅓ in (2,55 m). Wing area, 193.76 sq ft (18,00 m²).*

(Above) The revised single-bay M 17 prototype that was supplied to the Austro-Hungarians as the B II, and (below) the 80 hp single-bay production D II.

FOKKER D I (M 18)   Germany

A development of the M 17, the M 18 single-seat fighter was, in initial prototype form, frequently referred to erroneously by works of reference as the "M 16E". It was a similar unstaggered single-bay equi-span biplane with the upper fuselage contour parallel with

The first prototype of the M 18 (below), known unofficially as the "*Karausche*" (Crucian Carp).

An early production D I (above), and (below) a general arrangement drawing of the standard production two-bay D I issued to the *Fliegertruppen*.

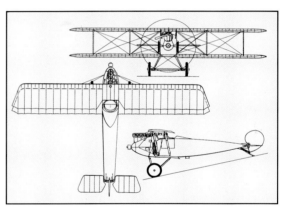

the upper wing, but differing essentially in having a 100 hp Mercedes D I six-cylinder water-cooled engine. Unofficially dubbed the *Karausche* (Crucian Carp), the M 18 prototype underwent modifications similar to those applied to the M 17 (ie, cut-down fuselage decking and wing stagger), and was also flown in twin-bay configuration. It was ordered into production in twin-bay form as the D I with a 120 hp Mercedes D II engine and an armament of a single synchronised LMG 08/15 machine gun. Like the D II, the D I began to arrive at the Front in July-August 1916, 90 being built for the German *Fliegertruppen*, six for the *Marine-Landflieger* and 16 for the Austro-Hungarian *Luftfahrttruppen* by which the fighter was designated B III. In addition, MAG (Mágyar Altálanos Gépgyár) in Hungary built eight. One of those supplied to the Austro-Hungarians was experimentally fitted with a 160 hp Mercedes D III engine and had ailerons in place of wing warping for lateral control. Another experimental model had sweptback long-span wings. *Max speed, 93 mph (105 km/h). Time to 3,280 ft (1 000 m), 5.0 min. Endurance, 1.5 hrs. Empty weight, 1,020 lb (463 kg). Loaded weight, 1,477 lb (670 kg). Span 29 ft 8¼ in (9,05 m). Length, 20 ft 7⁹⁄₁₀ in (6,30 m). Height, 8 ft 4⅓ in (2,55 m). Wing area, 215.28 sq ft (20,00 m²).*

FOKKER D III (M 19)   Germany

The capabilities of the D I and D II were by consensus indifferent, and, in an attempt to provide a single-seat fighter of higher performance and heavier firepower, Martin Kreutzer adapted the M 18 to take the 160 hp 14-

cylinder two-row rotary Oberursel U III engine and an armament of two synchronised LMG 08/15 machine guns. The new fighter was assigned the Fokker designation M 19 and when ordered by the *Idflieg* (*Inspektion der Fliegertruppen*) became the D III. A total of 210 was delivered to the German *Fliegertruppen*, late production examples supplanting wing warping with ailerons for lateral control, and 10 aileron-equipped D IIIs (including the prototype) were supplied to the Netherlands where they arrived in October 1917. The D III reached the Front in August 1916, but primarily as a result of the unreliability of its U III engine was rapidly relegated to home defence duties. One experimental example was fitted with a 110 hp Siemens-Halske Sh II engine enclosed by a full cowling, the propeller being fitted with a large spinner. *Max speed, 99 mph (160 km/h). Time to 3,280 ft (1 000 m), 3.0 min. Range, 137 mls (220 km) at 87 mph (140 km/h). Empty weight, 948 lb (430 kg). Loaded weight, 1,565 lb (710 kg). Span, 29 ft 8¼ in (9,05 m). Length, 20 ft 7⁹∕₁₀ in (6,30 m). Height, 8 ft 4⅓ in (2,55 m). Wing area, 215.28 sq ft (20,00 m²).*

A standard production D III (above), seen here with warping control, reached the Front in August 1916.

weight, 1,336 lb (606 kg). Loaded weight, 1,852 lb (840 kg). Span, 31 ft 9¹∕₁₀ in (9,70 m). Length, 20 ft 7⁹∕₁₀ in (6,30 m). Height, 9 ft 0¼ in (2,75 m). Wing area, 226.05 sq ft (21,00 m²).

(Below) The D IV in standard production form.

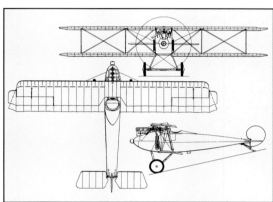

FOKKER D V (M 22)   Germany

The last single-seat fighter to be initiated by Martin Kreutzer before his death on 27 June 1916, but productionised by his successor, Reinhold Platz, the M 22 was, from several aspects, more refined than its predecessors. The most noteworthy departure from previous practice was the pronounced sweepback and increased forward stagger applied to the upper wing. Wing warping was finally discarded for lateral control, large, overhung, balanced ailerons being fitted to the upper wing, and a single-bay configuration was standardised. Illustrations purporting to depict two-

The D V (below) was ordered as an advanced trainer, but was issued to some home-based defence units.

bay versions with unswept upper wing as the "M 22ZF" – a designation of purely post-WWI origin – in fact show an M 17 with fully-cowled engine and spinner, and an M 19 with an Sh II experimental installation. The 110 hp Oberursel U I nine-cylinder rotary engine of the M 22 was fully cowled, a large propeller spinner was fitted and standard armament comprised a single

(Below) The D V, which made its début in autumn 1916.

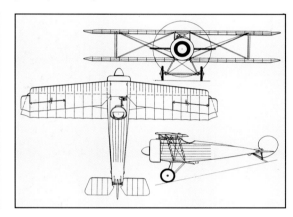

synchronised LMG 08/15 machine gun offset to starboard. The M 22 was assigned the official designation D V, the production model making its début in September 1916. The D V was, in fact, ordered as a trainer, but was, fortuitously, to be issued to some home-based defence squadrons of both *Fliegertruppen* and the *Marine-Landflieger* as an interceptor. Although it appeared at the Front in February 1917, and offered good flying qualities, its performance was eclipsed by more powerful contemporaries, and most of the 300 D Vs built were utilised for their originally intended training rôle. *Max speed, 106 mph (170 km/h). Time to 9,840 ft (3 000 m), 19 min. Range, 149 mls (240 km). Empty weight, 800 lb (363 kg). Loaded weight, 1,248 lb (566 kg). Span, 28 ft 8½ in (8,75 m). Length, 19 ft 10 in (6,05 m). Height, 7 ft 6 in (2,30 m). Wing area, 166.85 sq ft (15,50 m²).*

(Above and below) The D III in its definitive production form in which ailerons replaced wing warping for lateral control.

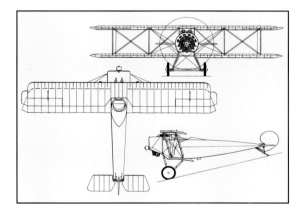

FOKKER D IV (M 21)   Germany

A contemporary of the M 19 and the last of the Fokker fighters to be ascribed solely to Martin Kreutzer, the M 21 was, to all intents and purposes, the D I (M 18) with twin-gun armament and the 160 hp Mercedes D III six-cylinder water-cooled engine. The M 21 was assigned the service designation D IV and two were at the Front on 31 August 1916, but saw no combat service. The performance of the D IV proved disappointing by comparison with contemporary types and the *Idflieg* considered that supplies of the 160 hp Mercedes should be assigned to other types. Production was, in consequence, restricted to 40 aircraft for the *Fliegertruppen*, one being experimentally fitted with a refined engine cowling and large propeller spinner. In addition, four D IVs were built for Sweden where they arrived in March 1918. *Max speed, 99 mph (160 km/h). Time to 3,280 ft (1 000 m), 3.0 min. Range, 137 mls (220 km). Empty*

The M 21 prototype (below) was the last Fokker fighter design ascribed solely to Martin Kreutzer.

FOKKER V 1   Germany

The V 1 (above and below) was a radical cantilever sesquiplane, designed by Reinhold Platz, which began its flight test programme in December 1916.

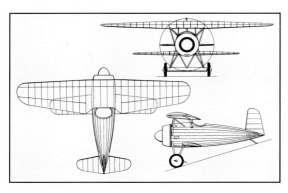

The first Fokker fighter design to be ascribed solely to Reinhold Platz was a radical single-seat cantilever sesquiplane powered by a 110 hp Le Rhône nine-cylinder rotary engine. It was also the first of the Schwerin-built *Versuchsmaschinen* (experimental machines) to be assigned a V-series designation as the V 1. Flown in December 1916, and known unofficially as the *Floh* (Flea), the V 1 possessed wings of unusually thick aerofoil section, and consisting of wooden boxspars and ribs with plywood skinning. The incidence of the upper wing could be changed in flight and conventional trailing-edge ailerons gave place to rotatable wing tips. The vertical and horizontal tail surfaces were of what were later to become known as "all-moving" type and were aerodynamically balanced. The steel-tube fuselage was faired to circular section by means of wooden hoops and stringers. Provision was made for the installation of two synchronised LMG 08/15 machine guns. Quite extensively flown, this highly innovatory fighter prototype, referred to as of *Verspannungslos* (literally "without bracing", or cantilever) type, was inspected by the *Idflieg*, but considered too radical. *Max speed, 111 mph (178 km/h). Span, 25 ft 9⅞ in (7,87 m). Length, 16 ft 4½ in (4,99 m). Height, 9 ft 0 in (2,74 m). Wing area, 161.46 sq ft (15,00 m²).*

FOKKER V 2   Germany

Developed in parallel with the V 1, the V 2 – which was also referred to contemporaneously as the D IV by Fokker despite *Idflieg* application of this designation to Kreutzer's M 21 – differed essentially in having a 160 hp Mercedes D III six-cylinder water-cooled engine. The

Evolved in parallel with the V 1, the V 2 (below) had a water-cooled engine and wing sweepback.

shift in CG resulting from introduction of the D III engine led Reinhold Platz to adopt modest sweepback on the outer upper wing panels attached to an abbreviated, unswept centre section. The vertical tail was modified to compensate for the increased side area forward provided by the D III engine, the fixed portion being increased in depth and faired into the aft fuselage. There was virtually no cabane between the engine cowling and the wing centre section, which was supported by splayed steel-tube tripods attached to the front spar. Like the V 1, the V 2 had a variable-incidence upper wing and rotatable wing tips. Although the V 2 allegedly proved "fast and sensitive" during flight test, there is no record of the V 2 having been inspected by the *Idflieg. Max speed, 118 mph (190 km/h) at 1,640 ft (500 m). Time to 3,280 ft (1 000 m), 2.8 min. Span, 25 ft 6½ in (7,82 m). Length, 17 ft 0¾ in (5,21 m). Height, 8 ft 4¾ in (2,56 m). Wing area, 165.77 sq ft (15,40 m²).*

FOKKER V 3   Germany

Difficulties experienced with the V 1 and V 2 led to the construction of yet a third fighter prototype of *Verspannungslos* configuration. This, the V 3, retained the 160 hp Mercedes D III engine, but both wings were increased in area by a total of 38.75 sq ft (3,60 m²), a deeper, more orthodox cabane was introduced to improve view from the cockpit and orthodox vertical tail surfaces were provided. The manually-variable wing incidence was discarded in favour of fixed incidence and a radiator for the D III was let into the leading edge of the wing centre section. The V 3 allegedly offered a rate of climb superior to that of the V 2, but handling characteristics were considered "too difficult" for the frontline pilot and this line of development was discarded. No data for the V 3 appear to have survived.

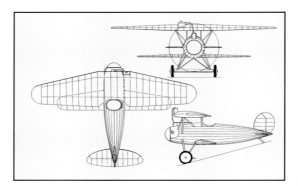

Utilising experience gained with the V 1 and V 2, the V 3 (above and below) allegedly possessed handling characteristics "too difficult" for frontline pilots.

FOKKER V 4   Germany

The V 4, also referred to contemporaneously as the D VI – although possessing no relationship other than a common design origin to the fighter subsequently to be *officially* assigned that designation – was originally designed as a single-seat fighter biplane ordered on 13 May 1917 for the Austro-Hungarian *Luftfahrttruppe*. As a result of the service début of the Sopwith Triplane, however, this aircraft was completed by Reinhold Platz – at the behest of Anthony Fokker – as a *triplane*. The V 4 (a prototype frequently to be erroneously referred to as the V 3) was an extremely compact aircraft powered by a 120 hp Le Rhône nine-cylinder rotary engine, having a slab-sided, rectangular-section, fabric-covered fuselage and three staggered cantilever wings. All three wings were of the same chord and sec-

The V 4 (above) was the original progenitor of the Dr I and entered flight test early summer 1917.

tion, but the top wing was of greater span than the equi-span middle and bottom wings. The V 4 was flown at Schwerin for the first time in May 1917, and, unlike preceding Platz fighter designs, had orthodox unbalanced ailerons on the top wing and unbalanced elevators. Aerodynamically balanced ailerons and elevators were introduced after initial flight testing, together with I-type interplane struts to reduce wing flexing. Two synchronised LMG 08/15 machine guns were fitted, and, in late August 1917, the V 4 was shipped to Austria-Hungary. Prior to this, on 5 July, a second and similar V 4 (alias D VI) had been ordered, and, six days later, a contract had been placed for two more as V 5s to be powered by the 110 hp Le Rhône, a copy of which, the Oberursel Ur II, was to power the series Dr I fighter. Performance, weights and dimensions of the V 5s were generally similar to those of the Dr I (which see).

FOKKER V 6   Germany

Developed in parallel with the V 5 (the *true* prototype of the series Dr I) the V 6, ordered on 7 July 1917, represented an attempt by Platz to mate the 160 hp Mercedes D III six-cylinder water-cooled engine with a triplane airframe. In order to achieve a wing loading similar to that of the rotary-engined V 5 despite the substantially heavier D III engine, the wing span and area were increased, overall span being extended by 35.4 in (90 cm) and mainplane chord being increased, this last

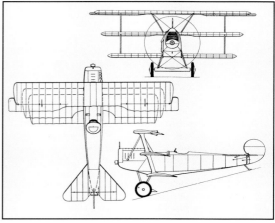

Developed in parallel with the V 5, the V 6 (above and below) had a larger wing span and area, and a water-cooled Mercedes D III engine.

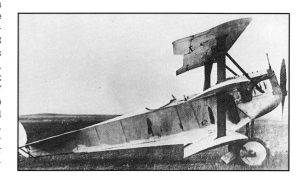

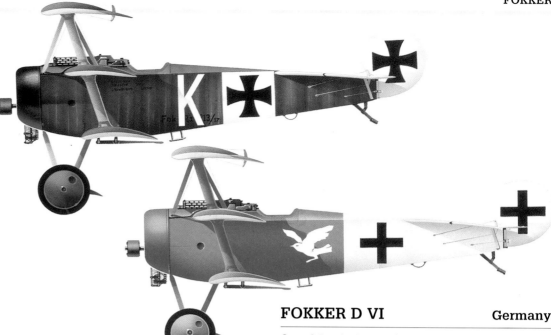

change dictating increased interplane gap. The lower position of the bottom wing led to deepening of the forward fuselage and cg considerations necessitated positioning of the cockpit well aft. The V 6, also referred to as the D VII, lacked the manoeuvrability demonstrated by the parallel V 5 (see Dr I) and development was discontinued. No data are available for this prototype.

FOKKER V 8   Germany

A decidedly bizarre single-seat fighter, the V 8 could be described both as a quintuplane and a tandem-wing aircraft. Powered by a 160 hp Mercedes D III engine, the V 8 had an unstaggered equi-span triplane wing arrangement mounted at the extreme nose and a biplane wing arrangement immediately aft of the pilot's cockpit and approximately two-and-a-half times the wing chord behind the triplane structure. The top plane of each set of wings incorporated balanced ailerons, and a conventional tail assembly was provided at the end of an inordinately long fuselage, the cg being located between the two wing systems. Anthony Fokker made an abbreviated flight – barely more than a hop – in the V 8 in October 1917, some modifications subsequently being made before a further brief flight was made two weeks later, development then being abandoned. No data for this type were recorded.

One of the oddest fighter prototypes tested during World War I was the tandem-wing V 8 (below).

FOKKER Dr I (V 5)   Germany

The series version of the V 5, which, with a 110 hp Le Rhône, differed from the V 4 (which see) primarily in having an intermediate-span centre wing, the Dr I single-seat fighter triplane began to reach the Front in October 1917. In fact the second and third series aircraft had been evaluated from the latter part of August from Courtrai by Manfred von Richthofen's Jasta. Armed with two synchronised 7,92-mm LMG 08/15 machine guns, the Dr I was powered by the 110 hp Oberursel Ur II copy of the nine-cylinder Le Rhône rotary. The Dr I enjoyed some success in combat, being extraordinarily manoeuvrable, but deliveries to the Fliegertruppen were inhibited by engine shortages and the need to replace the wings of all early production aircraft, manufacturing standards of which were considered unacceptable by the Idflieg. The original V 5 was brought up to production standards and delivered as a Dr I, and

The Dr I, illustrated by the general arrangement drawing below, enjoyed notoriety out of all proportion to its success in combat.

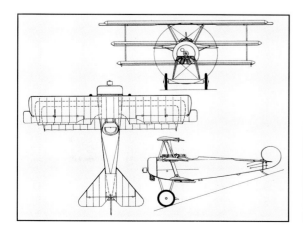

(Above, top) A Dr I flown by Ltn Fritz Kempf of Jasta Boelcke, and (immediately above) a Dr I originally operated by Jasta 18 and subsequently acquired by the French.

320 series Dr Is were delivered to the Fliegertruppen. One was supplied to the Austro-Hungarian MAG concern. Four prototypes with more powerful engines were completed as V 7s. One of these, with an 11-cylinder Oberursel Ur III rotary of 145 hp, participated in the first D-type contest at Adlershof, attaining an altitude of 16,405 ft (5 000 m) in 15.5 min. Two V 7s were delivered to Austria-Hungary, one with a 160 hp Siemens-Halske Sh III rotary and the other with a 145 hp Steyr-built Le Rhône, and the fourth was fitted with a 170 hp Goebel Goe III rotary. *Max speed, 115 mph (185 km/h) at sea level, 102 mph (165 km/h) at 13,125 ft (4 000 m). Time to 3,280 ft (1 000 m), 2.9 min. Range, 186 mls (300 km). Empty weight, 895 lb (406 kg). Loaded weight, 1,292 lb (586 kg). Span, 23 ft 7 in (7,19 m). Length, 18 ft 11 in (5,77 m). Height, 9 ft 8 in (2,95 m). Wing area, 200.9 sq ft (18,66 m²).*

(Above) Ltn Werner Voss' Dr I, and (below) a US-built Gnome-engined Dr I replica.

FOKKER D VI   Germany

One of the single-seat fighter types evolved by Fokker for participation in the first D-type competition (the so-called *D-Flugzeug-Wettbewerbe*) that was to be held at Adlershof in January 1918 was the V 9 ordered on 24 August 1917 with a 110 hp Oberursel Ur II rotary. An unequal-span, single-bay, staggered biplane with fuselage, engine installation, undercarriage and tail assembly virtually identical with those of the Dr I, the V 9 was followed by five further prototypes, these being the similarly-powered V 12 and V 16, the 160 hp Steyr-built Le Rhône-engined V 14, and two 160 hp Siemens-Halske Sh III-engined V 13s. The V 13s participated in the D-type competition, and, despite the fact that the Sh III engine was unavailable, this type was ordered into production by the Idflieg as the D VI. It was necessary to install the 100 hp Ur II engine in the series model, which, although manoeuvrable and offering a relatively good performance for the power available, was eclipsed in every respect by the parallel D VII.

The D VI (above) was confined to home defence as a result of non-availabilty of its intended engine.

Orders were, in fact, placed for 270 D VIs, but these were cut back to 60 of which seven, plus the V 12, were delivered to the Austro-Hungarian *Luftfahrttruppe*. The armament of the D VI consisted of paired synchronised 7,92-mm LMG 08/15 guns and the type was confined by the Fliegertruppen to home defence tasks. *Max speed, 122 mph (196 km/h). Time to 3,280 ft*

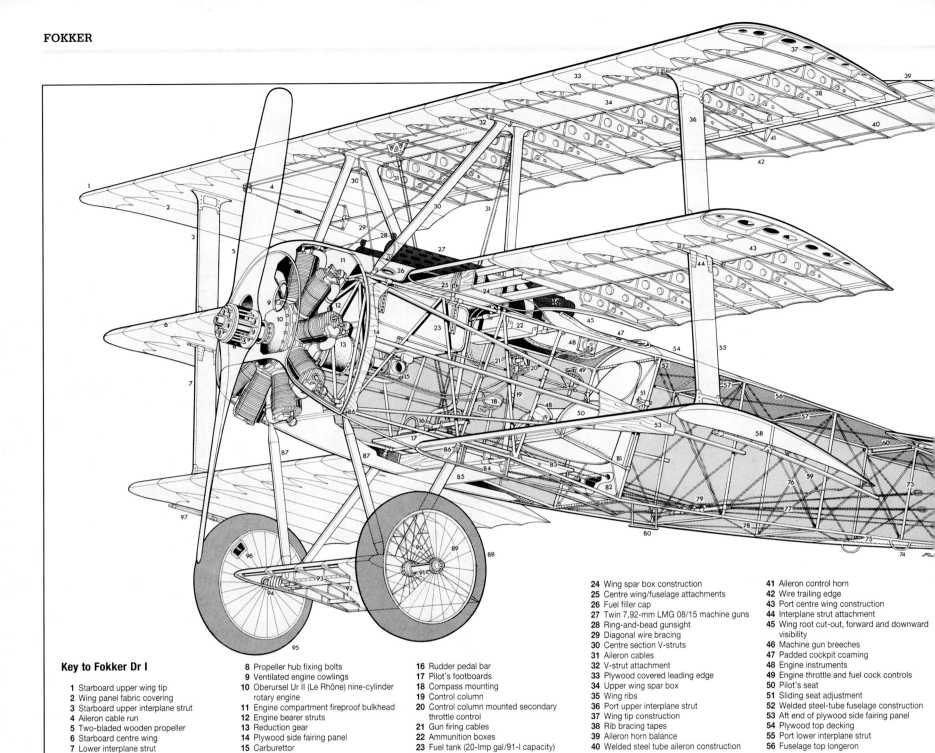

Key to Fokker Dr I

1 Starboard upper wing tip
2 Wing panel fabric covering
3 Starboard upper interplane strut
4 Aileron cable run
5 Two-bladed wooden propeller
6 Starboard centre wing
7 Lower interplane strut

8 Propeller hub fixing bolts
9 Ventilated engine cowlings
10 Oberursel Ur II (Le Rhône) nine-cylinder rotary engine
11 Engine compartment fireproof bulkhead
12 Engine bearer struts
13 Reduction gear
14 Plywood side fairing panel
15 Carburettor

16 Rudder pedal bar
17 Pilot's footboards
18 Compass mounting
19 Control column
20 Control column mounted secondary throttle control
21 Gun firing cables
22 Ammunition boxes
23 Fuel tank (20-Imp gal/91-l capacity)

24 Wing spar box construction
25 Centre wing/fuselage attachments
26 Fuel filler cap
27 Twin 7,92-mm LMG 08/15 machine guns
28 Ring-and-bead gunsight
29 Diagonal wire bracing
30 Centre section V-struts
31 Aileron cables
32 V-strut attachment
33 Plywood covered leading edge
34 Upper wing spar box
35 Wing ribs
36 Port upper interplane strut
37 Wing tip construction
38 Rib bracing tapes
39 Aileron horn balance
40 Welded steel tube aileron construction

41 Aileron control horn
42 Wire trailing edge
43 Port centre wing construction
44 Interplane strut attachment
45 Wing root cut-out, forward and downward visibility
46 Machine gun breeches
47 Padded cockpit coaming
48 Engine instruments
49 Engine throttle and fuel cock controls
50 Pilot's seat
51 Sliding seat adjustment
52 Welded steel-tube fuselage construction
53 Aft end of plywood side fairing panel
54 Plywood top decking
55 Port lower interplane strut
56 Fuselage top longeron

(1 000 m), 2.5 min. Range 186 mls (300 km). Empty weight, 866 lb (393 kg). Loaded weight, 1,290 lb (585 kg). Span, 25 ft 1 in (7,65 m). Length, 20 ft 5¼ in (6,23 m). Height, 8 ft 4⅓ in (2,55 m). Wing area, 190.53 sq ft (17,70 m²).

ceding Fokker fighters, the V 11 flew in December 1917, but revealed some directional instability and other shortcomings. These were rectified by lengthening the fuselage, reducing the wing gap and stagger, etc, and the V 11 competed at Adlershof, together with the essentially similar V 18, in the January 1918 D-type con-

test. Pronounced winning contenders by the *Idflieg*, these prototypes provided the basis for a fighter to which the designation D VII was assigned, contracts being placed with Fokker at Schwerin and the Albatros factories at Johannisthal and Schneidemühl (OAW). Other prototypes comprised V 21, the 200 hp Austro-

FOKKER D VII   Germany

Ordered on 20 September 1917 as a parallel development to the rotary-engined V 9 (from which was to be derived the D VI), the V 11, powered by a 160 hp Mercedes D III six-cylinder water-cooled engine, was the progenitor of the D VII, the most famous of all German World War I fighters. Of mixed construction like pre-

(Below) A D VII of *Fliegerkompagnie* **10 of the Swiss** *Fliegertruppe* **in the mid 'twenties.**

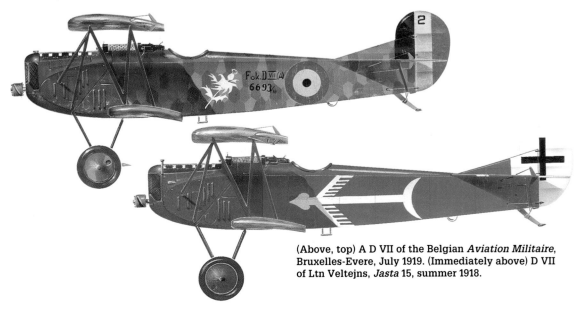

(Above, top) A D VII of the Belgian *Aviation Militaire*, Bruxelles-Evere, July 1919. (Immediately above) D VII of Ltn Veltejns, *Jasta* 15, summer 1918.

57 Horizontal spacers
58 Port lower wing tip
59 Wing tip skid
60 Tailplane centre section mounting
61 Welded steel tube tailplane construction
62 Rudder horn balance
63 Steel tube leading edge
64 Elevator horn balance
65 Steel tube elevator construction
66 Rudder fabric covering
67 Sternpost
68 Rudder control horn
69 Elevator control horn
70 Tailskid hinge mounting
71 Steel-shod tailskid
72 Elastic cord shock absorbers
73 Fuselage vertical spacers
74 Lifting handles
75 Fuselage fabric covering
76 Diagonal wire bracing (double wires)
77 Tailplane control cables
78 Fuselage bottom longeron
79 Control cable guides
80 Mounting step

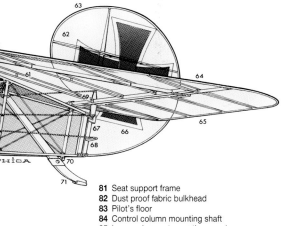

81 Seat support frame
82 Dust proof fabric bulkhead
83 Pilot's floor
84 Control column mounting shaft
85 Lower wing centre section spar box
86 Undercarriage strut attachments
87 Main undercarriage V-struts
88 Port mainwheel
89 Wheel disc fabric covering
90 Wheel spokes
91 Pivoted half-axle
92 Axle fairing construction
93 Axle spar box
94 Elastic cord shock absorbers
95 Starboard mainwheel
96 Tyre valve access
97 Starboard lower wing tip skid

Daimler-engined V 22 – which was to be evaluated at Aspern in July 1918 – and the 185 hp BMW IIIa-engined V 24. This last served as the prototype of the similarly-powered D VIIF. Armed with two 7,92-mm LMG 08/15 guns, the D III-powered D VII began to reach the Front in April 1918, followed closely by the BMW IIIa-powered D VIIF, and licence production of the D VII with the Austro-Daimler engine was undertaken by MAG (Mágyar Általános Gépgyár) in Hungary. In the event, MAG completed only 12 D VIIs, and these post-war. Fokker produced 877 series D VIIs (of which six were supplied to MAG as pattern aircraft together with the V 22), and 923 and 826 were built respectively by the Johannisthal and Schneidemühl facilities of Albatros. Ninety-eight D VIIs were smuggled from Germany to the Netherlands after the Armistice, of which 22 went to the LVA (Luchtvaartafdeling), 20 to the MLD (Marine Luchtvaartdienst), six to the KNIL (Koninklijk Nederlands Indisch Leger) and the remaining 50 were sold to the Soviet Union. Eight D VIIs and two D VIIFs were acquired from the Allied Control Commission by the Swiss Fliegertruppe – one of these later being fitted with an Hispano-Suiza 8Fb engine as the D VIIS – which obtained a further six overhauled D VIIs in 1925 from the Swiss Alfred Comte concern, which went on to build eight D VIIs during 1928-29. A total of 142 D VIIs was shipped to the USA in 1919 for evaluation and use by the US Army's Air Service, at least a dozen of these being used at McCook Field for experimental work with

(Above) A restored Albatros-built D VII in early Luchtvaartafdeling markings and originally one of 142 shipped to the USA in 1919. (Below) The D VII.

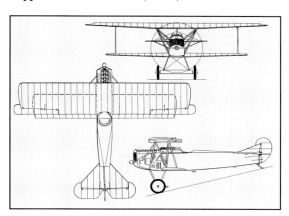

various engines, including the 230 and 290 hp Liberty, 200 hp Hall-Scott L-6 and 375 hp Packard 1A-1237. Several more D VIIs were purchased in 1920 for the Air Service from Fokker, and other countries to adopt the D VII post-World War I included Belgium, which received 75 from March 1919. Of these, 35 were delivered to the Army's Aviation Militaire, remaining in service until 1931. The following data relate to the standard D III-powered D VII. Max speed, 115 mph (185 km/h) at sea level, 116 mph (187 km/h) at 3,280 ft (1 000 m). Time to 3,280 ft (1 000 m), 5.8 min. Empty weight, 1,508 lb (684 kg). Loaded weight, 2,006 lb (910 kg). Span, 29 ft 2⅓ in (8,90 m). Length, 22 ft 9¾ in (6,95 m). Height, 9 ft 0 in (2,75 m). Wing area, 217.44 sq ft (20,20 m²).

FOKKER V 17   Germany

The first single-seat fighter monoplane to be designed by Reinhold Platz, the V 17 was ordered on 28 December 1917, and was demonstrated during the following month at Adlershof in the first D-type competition. Powered by a 110 hp Oberursel Ur II nine-cylinder rotary engine and armed with two synchronised 7,92-mm LMG 08/15 machine guns, the V 17 employed plywood skinning for both wings and fuselage. The wing, mounted in high-mid position, was manufactured in one piece and built up on two wooden box spars, and the rectangular-section fuselage was of welded steel-tube construction. Demonstrated at Adlershof by Anthony Fokker, the V 17 failed to attract

The V 17 (below) was the first single-seat fighter monoplane to the designs of Reinhold Platz.

the interest of the Idflieg. Time to 3,280 ft (1 000 m), 3.25 min. Empty weight, 840 lb (381 kg). Loaded weight, 1,237 lb (461 kg). Length, 18 ft 11⅛ in (5,77 m).

FOKKER V 20   Germany

The V 20 single-seat fighter monoplane was claimed to have been designed and built within the course of six-and-a-half days. Its development was prompted by the demonstration of the V 17 at Adlershof during the first D-type competition, Anthony Fokker believing that a more powerful aircraft of essentially similar design stood a good chance of attracting a production contract. Accordingly, Reinhold Platz designed the V 20 around the 160 hp Mercedes D III six-cylinder water-cooled engine. Although of similar configuration to the V 17 and of the same structural concept, apart from utilising fabric skinning aft of the rear spar, the V 20 had no design commonality with the earlier monoplane prototype. It reach Adlershof before conclusion of the D-type competition, but evidently did not achieve the success for which Fokker had hoped as no further development was undertaken.

The V 20 fighter monoplane (below) was allegedly designed and built within six-and-a-half days.

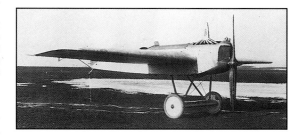

FOKKER V 23   Germany

Despite the lack of success attending the V 17 and V 20 single-seat fighter monoplanes during the first D-type competition, Reinhold Platz – who, by this time, had established quite extraordinary design prolificity – was

(Below) The Fokker V 23 fighter monoplane.

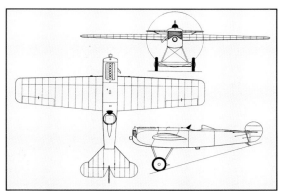

reluctant to relinquish the cantilever monoplane concept. Considering this to be aerodynamically ideal, he created further prototypes of this configuration for participation in the second D-type competition held in May-June 1918. The first of these was the V 23 powered by the 160 hp Mercedes D III engine and featuring a mid-mounted, plywood-covered, tapered two-spar wooden wing with inset ailerons which were also ply skinned. The fuselage was a rectangular welded steel-tube structure and the standard armament of paired and synchronised LMG 08/15 guns was intended. The

The V 23 (above) was demonstrated at Adlershof, but criticised for the poor view from its cockpit.

V 23 was demonstrated at Adlershof during the contest, but was criticised for the view that was offered from the cockpit which was considered inadequate for combat. It was consequently rejected by the *Idflieg* without type testing, Fokker discontinuing development. *Max speed, 124 mph (200 km/h) at 6,560 ft (2 000 m). Time to 3,280 ft (1 000 m), 3.0 min. Empty weight, 1,484 lb (673 kg). Loaded weight, 1,880 lb (853 kg). Span, 28 ft 8 in (8,73 m). Length, 19 ft 0⅓ in (5,80 m). Height, 8 ft 8 in (2,65 m). Wing area, 119.7 sq ft (11,12 m²).*

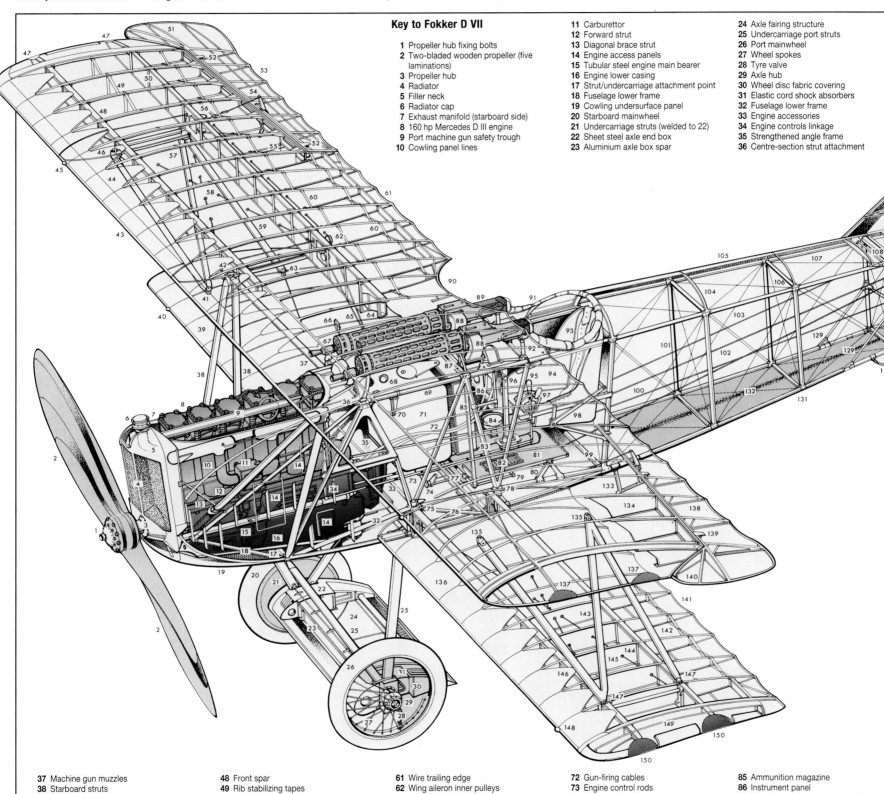

Key to Fokker D VII

1 Propeller hub fixing bolts
2 Two-bladed wooden propeller (five laminations)
3 Propeller hub
4 Radiator
5 Filler neck
6 Radiator cap
7 Exhaust manifold (starboard side)
8 160 hp Mercedes D III engine
9 Port machine gun safety trough
10 Cowling panel lines

11 Carburettor
12 Forward strut
13 Diagonal brace strut
14 Engine access panels
15 Tubular steel engine main bearer
16 Engine lower casing
17 Strut/undercarriage attachment point
18 Fuselage lower frame
19 Cowling undersurface panel
20 Starboard mainwheel
21 Undercarriage struts (welded to 22)
22 Sheet steel axle end box
23 Aluminium axle box spar

24 Axle fairing structure
25 Undercarriage port struts
26 Port mainwheel
27 Wheel spokes
28 Tyre valve
29 Axle hub
30 Wheel disc fabric covering
31 Elastic cord shock absorbers
32 Fuselage lower frame
33 Engine accessories
34 Engine controls linkage
35 Strengthened angle frame
36 Centre-section strut attachment

37 Machine gun muzzles
38 Starboard struts
39 Starboard lower mainplane
40 Leading-edge bumper
41 Interplane strut lower mainplane attachment
42 Forward strut/mainplane spar attachment
43 Plywood leading edge
44 Interplane strut upper mainplane attachment
45 Leading-edge bumper
46 Reinforced rib
47 Wing handling points

48 Front spar
49 Rib stabilizing tapes
50 Rear spar
51 Aileron horn balance
52 Aileron hinge points
53 Starboard aileron
54 Aileron control horn
55 Torque tube
56 Aileron outer pulleys
57 Interplane centre strut
58 Internal diagonal bracing
59 Interplane aft strut
60 Rib stabilizing tapes

61 Wire trailing edge
62 Wing aileron inner pulleys
63 Interplane strut lower mainplane attachment
64 Box spar structure
65 Aileron control cables
66 Ring-and-bead gunsight
67 Twin 7,92-mm Spandau LMG 08/15 machine guns
68 Fuel filler point
69 Fuselage upper longeron
70 Tank support welded bracket
71 Fuel (and oil) tank

72 Gun-firing cables
73 Engine control rods
74 Aileron control linkage
75 Lower front spar/fuselage attachment
76 Diagonal strut
77 Rudder pedal bar
78 Lower rear spar/fuselage attachment
79 Lower frame member
80 Cockpit floor support bracket
81 Cockpit floor
82 Pilot's heelboards
83 Control column mounting
84 Compass bracket

85 Ammunition magazine
86 Instrument panel
87 Machine gun centre support frame
88 Ammunition feeds
89 Machine gun breeches
90 Upper mainplane centre-section cut-out
91 Cockpit padded coaming
92 Machine gun rear support frame
93 Pilot's harness
94 Pilot's seat
95 Throttle lever
96 Control column/trigger mounting
97 Fuel control lever

FOKKER V 25   Germany

Built in parallel with the V 23 for participation in the second D-type competition, the V 25 employed a similar structure but was of low- rather than mid-wing configuration, and was powered by a 110 hp Oberursel Ur II nine-cylinder rotary engine. Appreciably smaller and lighter than the mid-wing monoplane prototype, the V 25 offered superior manoeuvrability and better initial climb, but owing to its low-powered engine had little chance of success and its development, like that of the

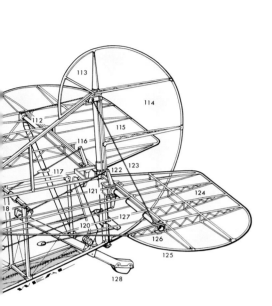

98 Seat support frame
99 Fuselage cross brace
100 Elevator control cables
101 Fuselage frame
102 Rudder control cables
103 Wire bracing
104 Dorsal formers
105 Dorsal decking
106 Horizontal spacers
107 Upper longeron
108 Tailplane centre-section mounting
109 Tailfin (adjustable) mounting bracket
110 Starboard tailplane
111 Elevator horn balance
112 Elevator torque tube
113 Rudder horn balance
114 Rudder frame
115 Starboard elevator frame
116 Elevator control horn
117 Starboard tailplane support strut
118 Tailskid upper attachment
119 Control cable leather grommets
120 Tailskid snubbing springs
121 Rudder post
122 Elevator control horn
123 Tailplane bracing wire
124 Elevator frame
125 Elevator horn balance
126 Elevator torque tube
127 Rudder control horns
128 Tailskid metal shoe
129 Aft fuselage strengthening brace
130 Handhold/lifting point (port and starboard)
131 Lower longeron
132 Fuselage ventral centre-line lacing
133 Fixed entry step
134 Solid ribs
135 Interplane strut upper attachments
136 Plywood leading edge
137 Upper mainplane wing handling points
138 Port aileron frame
139 Aileron hinge
140 Aileron horn balance
141 Wire trailing edge
142 Rib stabilizing tapes
143 Interplane struts
144 Lower mainplane rear spar
145 Internal diagonal bracing
146 Lower mainplane front spar
147 Interplane strut lower attachments
148 Leading edge bumper
149 End rib/"U"-channel tip
150 Lower mainplane wing handling points

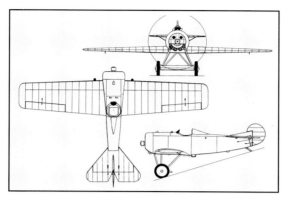

(Above and below) The V 25 participated in the 2nd D-type competition at Adlershof in May-June 1918.

V 23, was abandoned after the competition. *Max speed, 124 mph (200 km/h) at sea level. Time to 3,280 ft (1 000 m), 1.7 min. Empty weight, 847 lb (384 kg). Loaded weight, 1,243 lb (564 kg). Span, 28 ft 7¾ in (8,73 m). Length, 19 ft 5½ in (5,93 m). Height, 8 ft 7½ in (2,63 m). Wing area, 119.7 sq ft (11,12 m²).*

FOKKER D VIII (E V)   Germany

Apart from his extraordinary prolificity, Reinhold Platz also demonstrated outstanding versatility: virtually simultaneously with his series of mid- and low-wing fighter monoplane prototypes, he was engaged in developing a parasol monoplane fighter. Contrary to popular belief, this fighter was ordered into production by the *Idflieg* prior to the second D-type competition, the first production examples being accepted some two weeks before the contest ended! This fighter, initially officially designated E V by the *Idflieg* in the *Eindecker* (monoplane) series, was the production development of the V 28. This, initially flown with a 110 hp Oberursel Ur II, was also tested with the 145 hp Ur III and 160 hp Goebel Goe III 11-cylinder rotaries. Similar airframes with different engines were the 110 hp Le Rhône-powered V 26, the V 27 and V 30 with the 195 hp Benz Bz IIIb and IIIa six-cylinder water-cooled engines respectively, and the V 29 with the 160 hp Mercedes D III. The E V was manufactured with the Ur II rotary pending availability of the more powerful Ur III and Goe III, and armament consisted of the standard pair of synchronised LMG 08/15 guns. Initial contracts called for 210 aircraft, with deliveries to the *Fliegertruppe* commencing in July 1918, in which month 59 were accepted (including one for evaluation by the Austro-Hungarian *Luftfahrttruppe*). Eighty E Vs were accepted during the following month, the last of these on 23 August when further acceptances terminated owing to wing failures.

When acceptances were resumed on 8 October, a new wing was fitted, and, for some inexplicable reason, the designation was changed to D VIII (although externally it was impossible to distinguish between the E V and the D VIII). Eighty E Vs were listed at the Front on 31 August 1918 and 85 D VIIIs on 31 October. Of contracts for 335 E V/D VIII fighters placed with Fokker, a total of 289 was delivered (139 E Vs and 150 D VIIIs), 53 of the D VIIIs being delivered after 28 November 1918 without engines. All were powered by the Ur II engine, apart from 26 that received the Ur III. Operational usage of the E V/D VIII was strictly limited because of poor engine serviceability and the need to replace the wings of the E V. *Max speed, 115 mph (185 km/h) at sea level, 107 mph (173 km/h) at 14,765 ft (4 500 m). Time to 6,560 ft (2 000 m), 5.08 min. Range, 186 mls (300 km). Empty weight, 847 lb (384 kg). Loaded weight, 1,265 lb (574 kg). Span, 27 ft 4⅓ in (8,34 m). Length, 19 ft 5 in (5,92 m). Height, 8 ft 6⅓ in (2,60 m). Wing area, 115.18 sq ft (10,70 m²).*

An early production E V (above) and a general arrangement drawing (below) of the definitive production D VIII parasol monoplane.

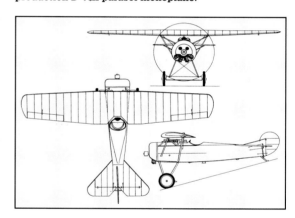

(Below) A Warner-powered full-scale D VIII replica built in the USA and first flown in September 1968.

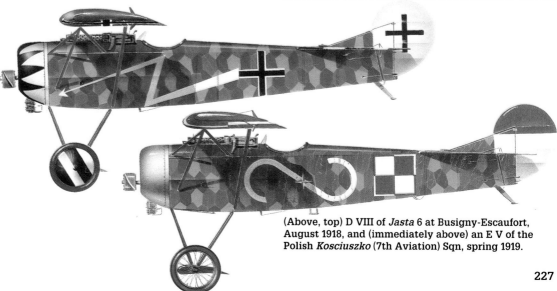

(Above, top) D VIII of *Jasta* 6 at Busigny-Escaufort, August 1918, and (immediately above) an E V of the Polish *Kosciuszko* (7th Aviation) Sqn, spring 1919.

FOKKER V 33   Germany

The V 33 was the ultimate development of the line of rotary-engined fighter biplanes stemming from the V 9. Smaller and lighter than preceding fighters in the series, the V 33 was apparently intended as a contender in the final D-type competition, although, in the event, it did not compete. It was initially flown with a 110 hp Oberursel Ur II nine-cylinder rotary, this eventually being replaced by a 145 hp Ur III 11-cylinder rotary.

The V 33 (above) was the last wartime Fokker fighter to employ a rotary engine.

The single example of the V 33 was taken to the Netherlands after the Armistice and used by Anthony Fokker as his personal aircraft until 1922. The following data are applicable to the V 33 after application of the Ur III engine. *Time to 9,840 ft (3 000 m), 7.4 min. Empty weight, 875 lb (397 kg). Loaded weight, 1,358 lb (616 kg). Span, 23 ft 9 in (7,24 m). Length, 17 ft 10⅖ in (5,46 m). Height, 7 ft 7 in (2,31 m). Wing area, 147.47 sq ft (13,70 m²).*

FOKKER V 34 & V 36   Germany

The V 34 and V 36 single-seat fighters were the final developments of the basic D VII undertaken during World War I, and differed essentially in their vertical tail surfaces. Both were powered by the 185 hp BMW IIIa six-cylinder water-cooled engine, both featured an oval frontal radiator and both were sent to Adlershof on 10 October 1918 to participate in the third D-type competition. Apart from the vertical tail (which was essentially similar to that of the D VII), the V 36 differed from

The V 34 (above) was essentially similar to the V 36 and one of the last developments of the basic D VII.

the V 34 in having one major innovation: the main fuel tank was transferred from the fuselage to the undercarriage axle fairing. Further development of these D VII derivatives terminated with the end of World War I. The following data are specifically applicable to the V 36 armed with two synchronised LMG 08/15 machine guns. *Time to 3,280 ft (1 000 m), 1.75 min. Empty weight, 1,404 lb (637 kg). Loaded weight, 1,920 lb (871 kg). Span, 29 ft 3⅜ in (8,93 m). Length, 21 ft 2¾ in (6,46 m). Height, 9 ft 11⁹⁄₁₀ in (3,04 m). Wing area, 189.45 sq ft (17,60 m²).*

FOKKER F VI (PW-5)   Netherlands

Evolved from design work undertaken in Germany during the closing stages of World War I, the F VI single-seat parasol fighter monoplane powered by a 300 hp Wright (Hispano-Suiza) H-2 water-cooled engine was of mixed construction, with a one-piece plywood-covered wooden wing and a welded steel-

The F VI (above and below) was Fokker's first post-World War I fighter, two examples being supplied to the US Army Air Service as PW-5s in 1921.

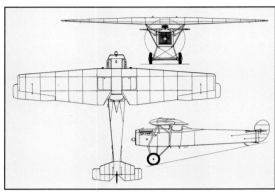

tube fuselage. Two examples were ordered for evaluation by the US Army Air Service and were delivered in 1921, being assigned the designation PW-5. Although the first of these crashed on 13 March 1922 as a result of a wing failure, a further 10 PW-5s were supplied to the USAAS that year. Armament comprised either two 0.3-in (7,62-mm) guns or one 0.5-in (12,7-mm) and one 0.3-in (7,62-mm) gun, and provision was made for small bombs to be carried on a rack beneath the fuselage. *Max speed, 144 mph (232 km/h) at sea level, 141 mph (227 km/h) at 10,000 ft (3 050 m). Initial climb, 1,585 ft/min (8,05 m/sec). Endurance, 2.0 hrs. Empty weight, 1,935 lb (878 kg). Loaded weight, 2,686 lb (1 218 kg). Span, 39 ft 5 in (12,02 m). Length, 26 ft 1 in (7,94 m). Height, 9 ft 0 in (2,74 m). Wing area, 247 sq ft (22,95 m²).*

FOKKER D IX (PW-6)   Netherlands

The ultimate development of the basic D VII single-seat fighter biplane, the D IX was flown for the first time in 1921 powered by a 300 hp Hispano-Suiza 8Fb eight-cylinder water-cooled engine. Of typical Fokker construction in employing a welded steel-tube fuselage and wooden wings each having two box spars, the D IX featured an aerofoil-shaped fuel tank between the mainwheels as first tested by the V 36. The sole prototype of the D IX was purchased for evaluation by the US Army Air Service and shipped to the USA in 1922, being assigned the designation PW-6. As evaluated by the USAAS, the aerofoil-section fuel tank was deleted, but the PW-6 was not considered to offer a sufficient advance over the D VII to warrant further development.

The ultimate D VII development, the D IX (below) went to the US Army Air Service as the PW-6.

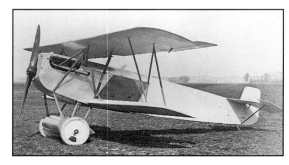

Max speed, 138 mph (223 km/h) at sea level, 129 mph (207 km/h) at 10,000 ft (3 050 m). Cruise, 117 mph (188 km/h). Time to 6,500 ft (1 980 m), 6.3 min. Range, 293 mls (471 km). Empty weight, 1,926 lb (874 kg). Loaded weight, 2,763 lb (1 253 kg). Span, 29 ft 6 in (8,99 m). Length, 23 ft 3 in (7,09 m). Height, 9 ft 0 in (2,74 m). Wing area, 238 sq ft (22,11 m²).

FOKKER D X   Netherlands

A cantilever parasol monoplane with a plywood-skinned wooden wing and a steel-tube fuselage, the D X single-seat fighter had begun life in Germany as the V 41. The partly-completed prototype was taken to the Netherlands, where, in 1921, it was completed with a 300 hp Hispano-Suiza water-cooled engine in place of the 185 hp BMW IIIa six-cylinder engine for which it had been originally intended. The prototype crashed as a result of wing flutter during a demonstration in Spain in 1922. Nevertheless, an order for 10 D X fighters was placed on behalf of the *Aeronáutica Militar Española*, these being supplied during the course of 1923. In the same year, one example of the D X was supplied to Finland. Armament comprised two 7,92-mm machine guns. *Max speed, 140 mph (225 km/h). Time to 16,405 ft (5 000 m), 16.0 min. Empty weight, 1,896 lb (860 kg). Loaded weight, 2,747 lb (1 246 kg). Span, 45 ft 1⅓ in (13,75 m). Length, 26 ft 3⅜ in (8,00 m). Height, 9 ft 9½ in (3,00 m).*

The D X (above and below) was built in small numbers for the Spanish *Aeronáutica Militar* in 1923.

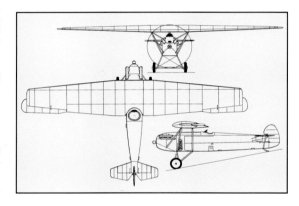

FOKKER D XI (PW-7)   Netherlands

Flown as a prototype on 5 May 1923, the D XI single-seat fighter was of sesquiplane configuration. Powered by a 300 hp Hispano-Suiza 8Fb eight-cylinder water-cooled engine and carrying an armament of two synchronised 7,92-mm LMG 08/15 machine guns, the D XI had a fabric-covered steel-tube fuselage and plywood covered wooden wings. One hundred and twenty-five were ordered by the Soviet government, and a further 50 were ordered on behalf of Germany's *Reichswehr* by the financier Hugo Stinnes for the clandestine German air training centre, which, in 1924, was being established at Lipetsk, north of Voronezh, in the Soviet Union. In the event, the German order was cancelled and, in 1925, these 50 D XIs were sold to Romania. Two others were supplied to Switzerland in 1925 for evaluation by that country's *Fliegertruppe*, and earlier, at the beginning of 1924, three had been delivered to McCook Field for evaluation by the US Army Air Service

(Below) One of the PW-7s – Curtiss D-12-engined D XIs – supplied to the US Army Air Service in 1924.

(Above) One of two D XIs supplied in 1925 to the Swiss *Fliegertruppe*, by which they were known as the *Wildsau* (Wild Boar), and (below) the standard D XI.

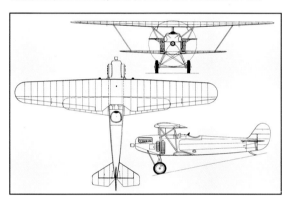

as PW-7s. The three D XIs supplied to the USAAS were non-standard in having the 440 hp V-1150 (Curtiss D-12) water-cooled engine. The first of these had standard plywood-covered wings with V-type interplane struts, and the second and third had fabric wing skinning and N-type strutting. *Max speed, 140 mph (225 km/h). Initial climb, 1,595 ft/min (8,10 m/sec). Endurance, 2.5 hrs. Range, 273 mls (440 km). Empty weight, 1,907 lb (865 kg). Loaded weight, 2,756 lb (1 250 kg). Span, 38 ft 3½ in (11,67 m). Length, 24 ft 7¼ in (7,50 m). Height, 10 ft 6 in (3,20 m). Wing area, 234.66 sq ft (21,80 m².)*

FOKKER D XII   Netherlands

The evaluation of three modified D XI fighters by the US Army Air Service prompted the design of the D XII tailored specifically to the USAAS specification. Designed from the outset for the 440 hp V-1150 (Curtiss D-12) water-cooled engine, it was flown for the first time on 21 August 1924 with an example of this power plant loaned by the US service to the manufacturer. The D XII had no design commonality with the preceding D XI, but was of similar mixed construction and, initially, retained the sesquiplane configuration of its predecessor, the upper wing having some degree of leading-

The D XII (below) in the form in which it was first flown with wing taper and short-span lower wing.

edge sweepback and overhung ailerons. Unsatisfactory characteristics displayed during initial trials necessitated major re-design, the sweepback being eliminated from the upper wing and a longer-span lower wing being introduced. Greater torsional rigidity was achieved by replacing the splayed V-type interplane struts with N-type struts and attaching these by single large-section struts to the top of the cabane strut system. At the same time, the small fixed tailfin was eliminated. Despite these extensive modifications, the D XII still proved unacceptable to the USAAS and

(Above and below) The D XII as it appeared in its definitive form with longer-span lower wing and untapered upper wing.

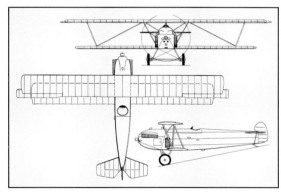

further development was abandoned. *Max speed, 155 mph (250 km/h). Cruise, 137 mph (220 km/h). Range, 684 mls (1 100 km). Empty weight, 2,200 lb (998 kg). Loaded weight, 3,086 lb (1 400 kg). Span, 36 ft 1 in (11,00 m). Length, 22 ft 1⅓ in (6,74 m). Height, 9 ft 1¼ in (2,77 m). Wing area, 235 sq ft (21,83 m².)*

FOKKER D XIII   Netherlands

The D XIII was essentially a re-engined and more powerful variant of the D XI developed at the behest of the German *Reichswehr* and powered by a 570 hp Napier Lion XI 12-cylinder water-cooled engine. Retaining the twin 7,92-mm LMG 08/15 gun armament of the D XI, the D XIII was first flown on 12 September 1924, at which time it was claimed to be the fastest fighter in the world. On 16 July 1925, the production model was used to establish a series of world records for speed and load. Production was, in the event, restricted to 50 aircraft ordered by Hugo Stinnes for the clandestine *Reichswehr* air training centre at Lipetsk, where they arrived in the summer of 1925. The D XIIIs continued in use at Lipetsk until 1933, when the centre was closed and the 30 surviving fighters of this type (which included two replacements) were handed to the Soviet government. *Max speed, 168 mph (270 km/h). Cruise, 137 mph (220 km/h). Time to 3,280 ft (1 000 m), 1.7 min. Range, 373 mls (600 km). Empty weight, 2,690 lb (1 220 kg). Loaded weight, 3,637 lb (1 650 kg). Span, 36 ft 1 in (11,00 m). Length, 25 ft 11 in (7,90 m). Height, 9 ft 6 in (2,90 m). Wing area, 231.11 sq ft (21.47 m²).*

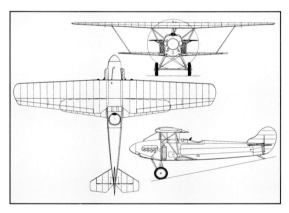

(Above and below) The D XIII was built for use by the clandestine air arm organised by the *Reichswehr*.

(Below) A D XIII on skis at the clandestine German air training centre at Lipetsk in the Soviet Union.

FOKKER D XIV   Netherlands

A semi-cantilever low-wing single-seat fighter mono-plane originally intended for the 400 hp Bristol Jupiter radial, the D XIV flew for the first time on 28 March 1925 with a 345 hp Hispano-Suiza 8Fb eight-cylinder water-cooled engine. The wooden wing was braced by lift struts to the ends of the rigid undercarriage axle, and featured marked sweepback commencing immediately aft of the frontal radiator, the D XIV thus having an unusually abbreviated fuselage nose. Subsequent to initial flight trials, a 590 hp HS 12Hb 12-cylinder engine was installed, this resulting in a somewhat more ortho-dox appearance. At the same time, the rear fuselage was lengthened for CG reasons and a smaller rudder fit-ted (the fighter had no fixed vertical surfaces). Arma-ment consisted of two synchronised 7,92-mm machine guns and the detachable engine mounting was so de-signed that various alternative power plants to the His-pano-Suiza could be fitted. The D XIV proved both fast and manoeuvrable, and test pilots of the German *Reichswehr* who evaluated the prototype commented favourably on its performance and stability as a gun platform. In the event, however, the prototype spun in, killing its pilot, and further development was discon-tinued. *Max speed, 170 mph (274 km/h). Empty weight, 2,095 lb (950 kg). Loaded weight, 2,976 lb (1 350 kg). Span, 35 ft 3⅜ in (10,76 m). Length (initial form), 25 ft 11 in (7,90 m). Height (over propeller, tail up), 10 ft 8 in (3,25 m).*

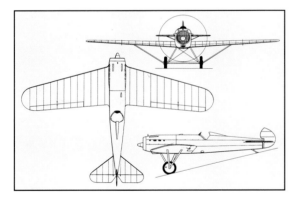

The prototype D XIV (above and below) in its final form with lengthened rear fuselage and new rudder.

FOKKER D XVI   Netherlands

Designed to meet a Netherlands LVA *(Luchtvaartaf-deling)* requirement for a successor to the World War I-vintage D VII, the D XVI single-seat unequal-span biplane was powered by a 460 hp Armstrong Siddeley Jaguar 14-cylinder air-cooled radial and flew for the first time in 1929. Possessing a fabric-covered, welded, steel-tube fuselage and ply-and-fabric-covered wooden wings, it was armed with two synchronised 7,92-mm machine guns. The D XVI was ordered by the

(Below) A Jaguar-engined D XVI in service with the Dutch *Luchtvaartafdeling* at Soesterberg in 1932.

(Above) The solitary Conqueror-powered D XVI, and (below) general arrangement drawing of series D XVI.

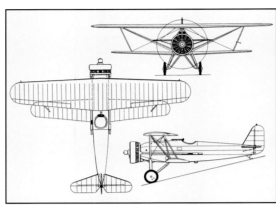

LVA, 14 aircraft being delivered to that service, these having split-axle undercarriages rather than the cross-axle type of the prototype. One D XVI was subse-quently re-engined with a Bristol Mercury radial for aerobatic display purposes. A single example was sup-plied to China, and four powered by the Gnome-Rhône Jupiter were delivered to Hungary. A further D XVI was built with a Curtiss V-1570 Conqueror 12-cylinder water-cooled engine to meet a KNIL *(Koninklijk Neder-lands Indisch Leger)* requirement, although no produc-tion order was placed for this version. *Max speed, 205 mph (330 km/h) at 14,765 ft (4 500 m). Cruising speed, 168 mph (270 km/h). Range, 398 mls (640 km). Empty weight, 2,182 lb (990 kg). Loaded weight, 3,086 lb (1 400 kg). Span, 30 ft 10 in (9,40 m). Length, 23 ft 7½ in (7,20 m). Height, 8 ft 10¼ in (2,70 m). Wing area, 199.14 sq ft (18,50 m²).*

FOKKER D XVII   Netherlands

Essentially a progressive development of the D XVI with a Curtiss V-1570 Conqueror engine, the D XVII em-bodied a number of aerodynamic refinements while re-taining the basic structure of the earlier fighter and its

(Above and below) The Kestrel-engined D XVII was delivered from October 1932, and a few saw some operational use during the assault on Holland.

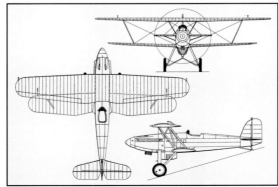

armament of two 7,92-mm M.36 machine guns. Ten production examples were ordered by the LVA, the 590 hp Rolls-Royce Kestrel IIS 12-cylinder liquid-cooled engine being selected as the standard power plant and deliveries commencing in October 1932. The ninth and tenth aircraft were respectively and temporarily powered by the 800 hp Lorraine-Dietrich Petrel 12Hfrs and the 760 hp Hispano-Suiza 12Xbrs, both eventually reverting to standard Kestrel-engined configuration. The Conqueror-engined prototype was shipped to the Netherlands East Indies for KNIL evaluation, being shipped back to Holland in 1936 after a crash, and then being rebuilt and delivered to the LVA. Relegated to the fighter training rôle prior to World War II, the seven surviving D XVII fighters saw some limited operational use during the *Wehrmacht* invasion of the Netherlands. *Max speed, 221 mph (356 km/h) at 13,125 ft (4 000 m). Max cruise, 186 mph (300 km/h). Range, 373 mls (600 km). Empty weight, 2,359 lb (1 070 kg). Loaded*

Key to Fokker D XXI

1 Starboard navigation light
2 Starboard wingtip
3 Wing skinning (bakelite plywood)
4 Starboard aileron (steel tube structure with fabric skinning)
5 Aileron tab
6 Gun and ammunition bay access panels
7 Starboard landing light
8 Machine gun barrels
9 Three-bladed two-pitch propeller
10 Propeller hub
11 Pitch change mechanism
12 Reduction gear housing
13 Cowling ring
14 Exhaust gas collector ring profile
15 Bristol Mercury VIII nine-cylinder radial air-cooled engine

16 Oil cooler air intake tubes
17 Engine cowling clips
18 Engine mounting ring
19 Starboard wheel spat
20 Starboard mainwheel
21 Carburettor air intake
22 Lower engine bearer
23 Carburettor
24 Oil cooler
25 Oil cooler air outlet
26 Engine control linkage
27 Oxygen bottles (two)
28 Upper engine bearers
29 Accessories
30 Rod-mounted half-ring and bead sight
31 Fuel filler point

FOKKER D XXI   Netherlands

Designed by a team led by Dr-Ir Erich Schatzki and retaining traditional Fokker-type mixed construction, the D XXI was conceived in answer to a specification formulated by the KNIL (*Koninklijk Nederlands Indisch Leger*), the aviation element of the Royal Netherlands Indies Army, and was flown as a prototype on 27 February 1936. In the event, the initial production order was placed by the Finnish government, which acquired a manufacturing licence, a contract subsequently being issued in the Netherlands on behalf of the home-based LVA (*Luchtvaartafdeling*). The latter purchased 36 D XXIs powered by the 825 hp Bristol Mercury VIII nine-cylinder radial engine and armed with four wing-mounted 7,9-mm FN-Browning M.36 guns. Seven were acquired from the parent company by Finland, with delivery flights commencing 27 August 1937, and a further 35 were licence-built by VL (Valtion Lentokone-

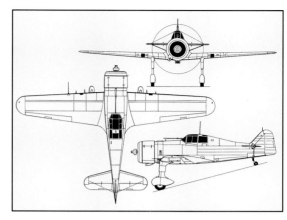

(Above) The Mercury-engined Fokker D XXI fighter.

The ninth D XVII (above) was temporarily fitted with a Lorraine-Dietrich Petrel engine.

weight, 3,373 lb (1 530 kg) Span, 31 ft 6 in (9,60 m). Length, 23 ft 9½ in (7,25 m). Height, 10 ft 2 in (3,10 m). Wing area, 215.28 sq ft (20,00 m²).

32 Fuel tank, 77-Imp gal (350-l) capacity
33 Forward fuselage longeron brace
34 Front spar/fuselage attachment point
35 Oil tank
36 Rear spar/fuselage attachment point
37 Cockpit floor step
38 Rudder pedals
39 Instrument panel
40 Engine control levers
41 Control column
42 Windscreen
43 Fixed canopy section
44 Centreline canopy hinge
45 Hinged canopy and side flap
46 Vertically-adjustable pilot's seat
47 Elevator trim wheel
48 Flap setting lever
49 Recessed foothold
50 First aid kit stowage
51 Equipment bay

52 Steel roll-over pylon
53 Radio mast
54 Cockpit aft glazing
55 Radio transmitter/receiver
56 Battery
57 Elevator control cable
58 Radio compartment hinged access cover
59 Handhold
60 Detachable dural dorsal panels
61 Welded chrome-molybdenum fuselage frame
62 Dorsal hoop formers
63 Fuselage stringers (fabric covered)

64 Signal lamp
65 Starboard tailplane
66 Elevator mass balance
67 Fin/tailplane bracing wire
68 Radio aerial
69 Starboard elevator
70 Elevator tab
71 Control pulley
72 Elevator control linkage
73 Fabric-covered fin
74 Fin structure
75 Tail navigation light
76 Aerial stub mast

77 Rudder upper hinge
78 Fin/tailplane bracing wire
79 Rudder tab
80 Rudder (metal framed and fabric covered)
81 Port elevator (metal framed and fabric covered)
82 Tailplane structure
83 Tailplane lower bracing strut
84 Elevator mass balance
85 Tailplane/fuselage attachment
86 Tailwheel strut housing
87 Control pulley

88 Compressed rubber shock absorber
89 Steerable tailwheel
90 Rudder control cables
91 Ventral formers
92 Recessed foothold
93 Control pulley
94 Wing root fairing
95 Flap profile
96 Rear spar
97 Front spar
98 Wing leading-edge construction
99 Undercarriage/front spar anchorage

100 Mainwheel leg fairing
101 Oleopneumatic strut
102 Fairing overlap
103 Ground-servicing footrest
104 Axle fork
105 Port mainwheel
106 Port wheel spat
107 Pitot head
108 Machine gun barrels
109 Port landing light
110 FN/Browning M-36 machine guns (7,9-mm calibre)
111 Ammunition boxes
112 Flap construction
113 Aileron construction
114 Aileron tab
115 Wing rib structure
116 Port navigation light
117 Reinforcement for ground handling

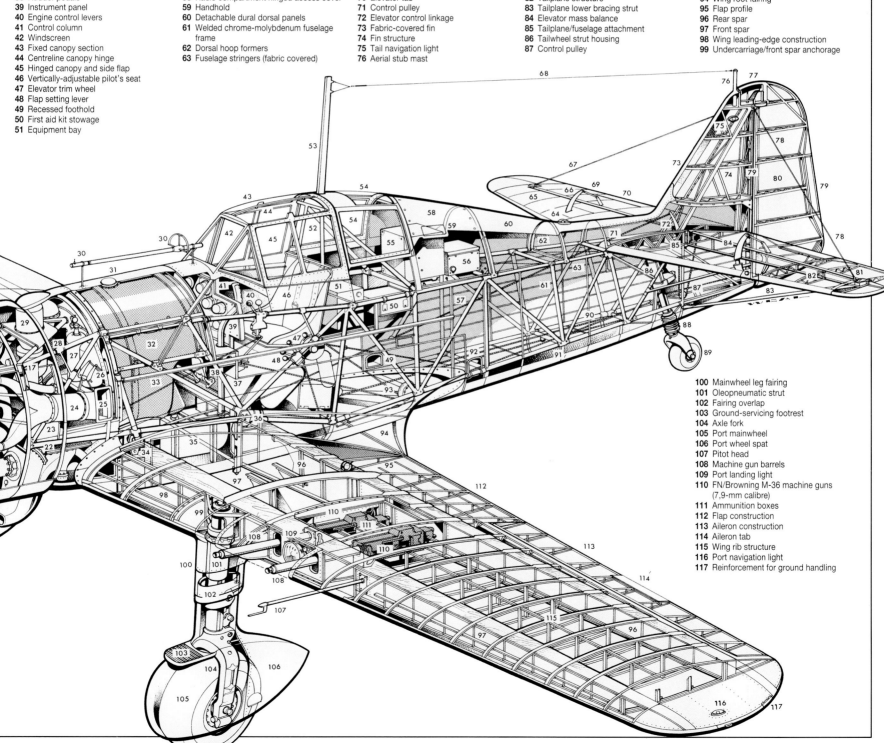

tehdas), these being armed with four 7,7-mm Brownings, two being fuselage mounted, and having PZL- or Tampella-built Mercury VII engines of 840 hp. Two D XXIs were purchased by Denmark which subsequently licence-built a further 10, these mounting a pair of 20-mm Madsen cannon and two 7,9-mm machine guns, and licence manufacture was also initiated in Spain by Hispano Aviación, assembly being undertaken at the SAF-15 factory at La Rabasa, Alicante. At least one D XXI was completed and flown in Spain with a Soviet M-25 engine taken from an I-16 before the production facility was overrun by Nationalist forces. At that time, 50 sets of wings, 25 fuselages and 25 undercarriages for D XXIs were discovered. The D XXI was offered by Fokker with various engines, including the Pratt & Whitney Twin Wasp Junior, and the basic D XXI was further developed with this engine in Finland by VL (which see). The last Finnish-built Mercury-engined D XXI was fitted with a Finnish-designed retractable undercarriage after suffering a landing accident. It was test flown on 19 June 1941, the fixed gear being restored after another landing accident a month later. The following data relate to the standard Fokker-built D XXI. *Max speed, 286 mph (460 km/h) at 16,730 ft (5 100 m). Time to 3,280 ft (1 000 m), 1.45 min. Range, 578 mls (930 km). Empty weight, 3,197 lb (1 450 kg). Loaded*

(Left) D XXIs of the 1e *Jachtvliegtuigafdeling* (JaVA) flying from De Kooy in April 1940.

Key to Fokker G I

1. Starboard navigation light
2. Forward spruce-and-ply mainspar
3. Plywood former ribs
4. Fabric-covered welded steel-tube aileron (statically and dynamically balanced)
5. Hydraulically-operated duralumin landing flap
6. Starboard aerial mast
7. Rear mainspar
8. Control runs
9. Starboard landing light
10. Three-bladed Hamilton Standard two-position propeller
11. Cowling ring
12. Nacelle panel quick-release catches
13. Duralumin boom skinning
14. Starboard fuel tank (125-Imp gal/570-l capacity)
15. Centre-hinged canopy roof
16. Pilot's headrest
17. Pilot's adjustable seat
18. Circular vision port
19. Welded chrome-molybdenum steel tube forward fuselage structure
20. Throttle controls
21. Control column
22. Instrument panel
23. Forward bulkhead
24. Ammunition tank (4,000 rounds)
25. Battery of eight 7,9-mm FN-Browning M-36 machine guns
26. Gun ports
27. Carburettor air intake
28. Gun support frame
29. Case collector box
30. Starboard mainwheel
31. Propeller pitch-control mechanism
32. Exhaust collector ring
33. Exhaust pipe
34. Carburettor air intake
35. Bristol Mercury VIII air-cooled radial engine
36. Engine bearers
37. Controllable cooling gills
38. Engine controls
39. Mainspar inboard section (integral with fuselage nacelle)
40. Port fuel tank (125-Imp gal/570-l capacity)
41. Fuel filler cap
42. Rear spar carry-through
43. Aft bulkhead
44. Centre fuselage (accommodating radio equipment)
45. Plywood monocoque fuselage nacelle centre section
46. Starboard tailboom
47. Hinged entry hatch
48. Duralumin rear fuselage construction
49. Rear gunner's couch
50. Gimbal-suspended 7,9-mm FN-Browning M-36 machine gun
51. Ammunition racks
52. Hinged entry hatch
53. Handholds
54. Gun support bar
55. Inward-hinged tailcone section
56. Perspex tailcone
57. All-metal monocoque tailboom structure
58. Tailboom/fin fairing fillet
59. Integral duralumin tailfin structure
60. Aerials
61. Welded chrome molybdenum steel-tube fabric-covered rudder

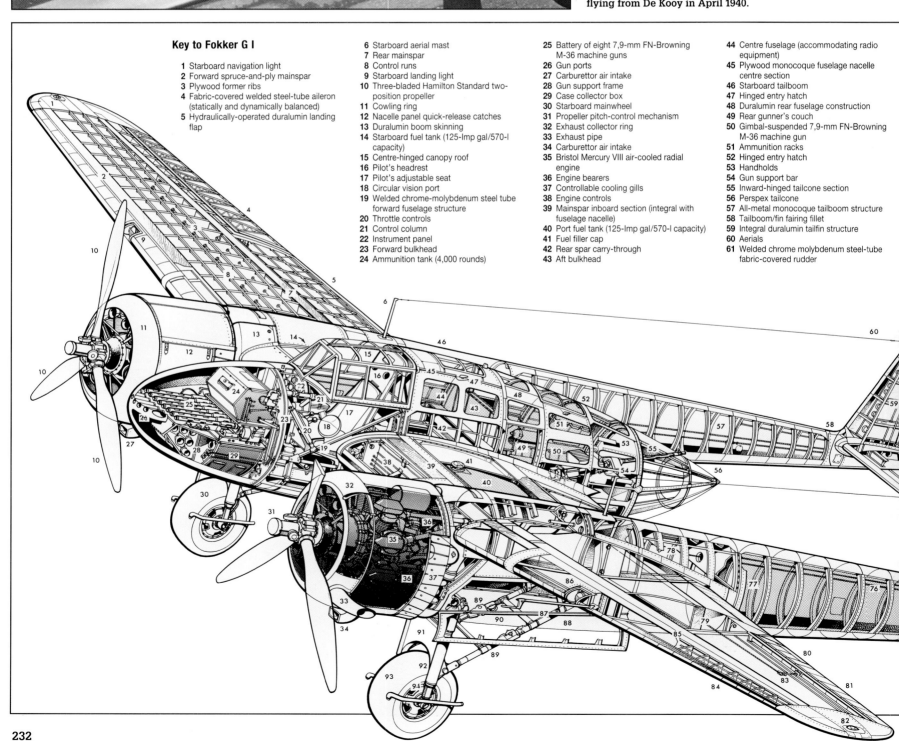

weight, *4,519 lb (2 050 kg). Span, 36 ft 1 in (11,00 m). Length, 26 ft 10¾ in (8,20 m). Height, 9 ft 8 in (2,95 m). Wing area, 174.38 sq ft (16,20 m²).*

(Above) A Danish-built D XXI, the underwing Madsen cannon having still to be fitted, and (below) a Finnish D XXI with 2./LeLv 12, Nurmoila, 1942.

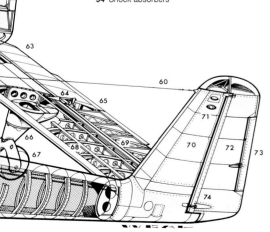

62 Rudder tab
63 Fabric-covered steel-tube elevator
64 Elevator hinge fairing
65 Elevator tab
66 Tailwheel leg fairing
67 Swivelling tailwheel
68 Dural tailplane structure (Duraplat sheet skinning)
69 Steel-tube elevator structure (fabric skinning)
70 Duraplat tailfin skinning
71 Tail navigation light
72 Port rudder
73 Rudder tab
74 Rudder hinge fairing
75 Metal monocoque tailboom construction
76 Control runs
77 Bolted joint between wooden (integral with wing centre section) and duralumin monocoque tailboom portions
78 Wooden tailboom structure
79 Wing rearspar
80 Aileron tab (port side only)
81 Port aileron (fabric-covered welded steel-tube)
82 Port navigation light
83 Aileron control linkage
84 Leading edge construction
85 Forward spruce-and-ply mainspar
86 Port landing light
87 Pitot tube
88 Mainwheel doors
89 Mainwheel retraction members
90 Mainwheel well
91 Mainwheel leg cover plate
92 Mainwheel leg
93 Port mainwheel
94 Shock absorbers

(Above, top) The second D XXI delivered to the *Luchtvaartafdeling* (LVA), and (above right) a D XXI with the 1e JaVA at De Kooy, 1940.

FOKKER G I (WASP)   Netherlands

A multi-seat, multi-rôle heavy fighter, or *jachtkruiser*, designed by Dr-Ir Erich Schatzki, the G I was radical in featuring a central fuselage nacelle with twin tail-booms. Of mixed construction, the prototype was a two-seater powered by two 680 hp Hispano-Suiza 14Ab 14-cylinder radials and was first flown on 16 March 1937. The first production order (for 25 aircraft) was placed on behalf of the Spanish Republican government, which specified Pratt & Whitney R-1535-SB4-G Twin Wasp Junior 14-cylinder radials of 825 hp, the prototype accordingly being re-engined. It first flew with these engines on 3 September 1938. The Dutch government, meanwhile, had ordered an enlarged, re-engined three-seat derivative (which see) of the G I prototype,

G I (Wasp) fighters (above) at Schiphol, May 1940, prior to assignment to the 4e JaVA.

and this was assigned production priority over the R-1535-powered model. After the imposition of a Dutch ban on the supply of war materials to the warring factions in Spain, the R-1535-engined G Is were re-ordered in January 1938 by Estonia, and six had been completed by 9 October 1939 when an embargo was placed on their export. The aircraft that were being built for the (by then defunct) Spanish Republican government were transferred to the Dutch government, but only 10 had, in fact, been accepted by the LVA at the time of the assault on the Netherlands by the *Wehrmacht*. These were without armament, apart from three that were fitted with an improvised nose-mounted battery of four 7,9-mm FN-Browning M.36 guns. About a dozen R-1535-engined G Is were subsequently utilised by the *Luftwaffe*, together with at least five Mercury-engined

G Is, as advanced trainers. *Max speed, 275 mph (443 km/h) at 10,990 ft (3 350 m). Cruising speed, 226 mph (364 km/h). Max range, 870 mls (1 400 km). Empty weight, 6,944 lb (3 150 kg). Loaded weight, 10,582 lb (4 800 kg). Span, 54 ft 1⅗ in (16,50 m). Length, 34 ft 0⅜ in (10,38 m). Height, 10 ft 11⁹⁄₁₀ in (3,35 m). Wing area, 384.28 sq ft (35,70 m²).*

FOKKER G I (MERCURY) Netherlands

To meet the specific requirements of the LVA, Fokker evolved a scaled-up, more versatile three-seat version of the G I design powered by 830 hp Bristol Mercury VIII nine-cylinder radials, 36 aircraft of this type being ordered on 21 October 1937. The Mercury- and Twin Wasp Junior-powered aircraft were to be referred to retrospectively as the G IA and G IB, these designations not being used contemporaneously, however, and being entirely unofficial. The Mercury-engined G I for the LVA standardised on an armament of eight 7,9-mm FN-Browning M.36 guns in the nose and one M.36 flexibly mounted in the fuselage nacelle tail cone. Only the first four aircraft were delivered as three-seaters, the remainder being delivered as two-seaters. On 30 March 1940, the Swedish government ordered 18 G Is similar to those acquired by the Netherlands Army and took an option on a further 77 (including 12 reconnaissance models with a ventral gondola for a camera and operator), but none was, in the event, delivered. A

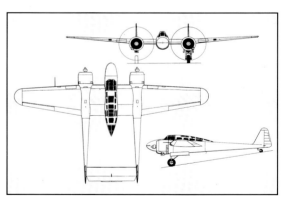

(Above) A general arrangement drawing of the G I (Mercury) and (below) the first G I (Mercury) to fly, eventually being issued to the 3e JaVA.

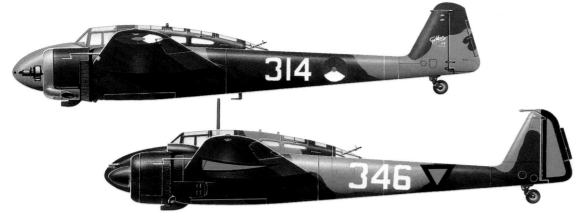

In the summer of 1916, the German Navy ordered a variety of waterborne single-seat fighters for evaluation, one of these being the FF 43 twin-float single-bay biplane from the Manzell factory of the Flugzeugbau Friedrichshafen on 8 June 1916. Powered by a 160 hp Mercedes D III engine and armed with one synchronised 7,92-mm machine gun, the FF 43 was completed on 29 August 1916, and delivered to the *Seeflugzeug Versuchs Kommando* (Seaplane Testing Command) at Warnemünde for acceptance testing on 8 September. Sent to the Zeebrügge naval air station on 6 October for evaluation under operational conditions in the North Sea, the FF 43 was not accepted for production, being officially struck-off on 13 April 1917. *Max speed, 101 mph (163 km/h). Time to 3,280 ft (1 000 m), 6.0 min, to 6,560 ft (2 000 m), 12.0 min. Empty weight, 1,759 lb (798 kg). Loaded weight, 2,377 lb (1 078 kg). Span, 32 ft 6½ in (9,92 m). Length, 28 ft 0⅗ in (8,55 m). Height, 10 ft 11⁹⁄₁₀ in (3,35 m). Wing area, 333.69 sq ft (31,00 m²).*

(Above, top) A G I (Mercury) with 4e JaVA at Bergen, 1939, and (immediately above) a G I (Wasp) assigned to 4e JaVA at Schiphol in May 1940.

licence for the manufacture of 12 G Is at Kløvermarken for the air component of the Danish Army was finalised in January 1939, and during the course of that year a licence was also acquired by the Hungarian Manfrèd Weiss concern, but no aircraft was built against either Danish or Hungarian licence. *Max speed, 295 mph (475 km/h) at 13,450 ft (4 100 m). Cruising speed, 238 mph (383 km/h) at 13,990 ft (4 265 m). Initial climb, 2,736 ft/min (13,9 m/sec). Range, 932 mls (1 500 km). Empty weight, 7,341 lb (3 330 kg). Loaded, 11,023 lb (5 000 kg). Span, 56 ft 3⅗ in (17,16 m). Length, 35 ft 7⁹⁄₁₀ in (10,87 m) Height, 12 ft 5⅗ in (3,80 m). Wing area, 412.27 sq ft (38,30 m²).*

FOKKER D XXIII Netherlands

The D XXIII single-seat fighter was unusual in employing a fore-and-aft tandem engine arrangement, the prototype being powered by two 528 hp Walter Sagitta I-SR engines and flying for the first time on 30 May 1939.

The sole prototype of the D XXIII tandem-engined fighter flown in May 1939 (above and below).

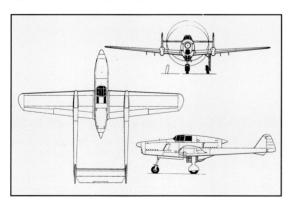

Versions of the D XXIII were also proposed with Hispano-Suiza 12Xcrs, Junkers Jumo 210G and Rolls-Royce Kestrel XV engines, and although all-metal construction was intended, the prototype was fitted with a wooden wing of greater thickness/chord ratio in order to expedite the test programme. Owing to various problems, including rear engine cooling, only four hours of flight testing had been completed when the invasion of the Netherlands brought the D XXIII development programme to a halt. The proposed armament comprised two 7,9-mm and two 13,2-mm FN-Browning machine guns. The following data are based on the use of the proposed metal wing. *Max speed, 326 mph (525 km/h) at 12,500 ft (3 810 m). Cruising speed, 242 mph (390 km/h) at 13,450 ft (4 100 m). Empty weight, 4,806 lb (2 180 kg). Loaded weight, 6,503 lb (2 950 kg).*

Span, 37 ft 8¾ in (11,50 m). Length, 33 ft 5½ in (10,20 m). Height, 12 ft 5⅔ in (3,80 m). Wing area, 199.13 sq ft (18,50 m²).

FOLLAND FO 145 GNAT UK

W E W Petter commenced design of a lightweight fighter in 1951, initially envisaging the use of a 3,800 lb st (1 724 kgp) Bristol BE 22 Saturn turbojet. Discontinuation of the Saturn led to adoption of the BE 26 Orpheus, a low-powered prototype (with a 1,640 lb st/744 kgp Viper 101) being built as the Fo 139 Midge to prove airframe aerodynamics and systems, and the first true Gnat prototype flying on 18 July 1955. A development batch of six was ordered by the Ministry of Supply for evaluation by the RAF, with two others added later. Yugoslavia acquired two and Finland 12 (plus one of the MoS aircraft). Two other ex-MoS Gnat 1s were supplied to India, which also received 23 UK-built Gnats and 20 sets of components for assembly by Hindustan Aircraft (later, Aeronautics) Ltd at Bangalore. Licence production was subsequently undertaken by HAL which built a further 195 (the last two becoming prototypes of the HAL Ajeet – which see) with deliveries completed January 1974. Powered by a 4,705 lb st (2 134 kgp) Rolls-Royce (Bristol) Orpheus 701-01 turbojet, the Gnat had an armament of two 30-mm Aden Mk 4 cannon and could carry two 500-lb (227-kg) bombs or 18 3-in (7,62-cm) rockets. *Max speed, 695 mph (1 118 km/h) at 20,000 ft (6 100 m). Tactical radius (max external fuel), 500 mls (805 km). Max climb, 20,000 ft/min (101,60 m/sec). Empty weight, 4,800 lb (2 177 kg). Max loaded, 9,040 lb (4 100 kg). Span, 22 ft 1 in (6,73 m). Length, 28 ft 8 in (8,74 m). Height, 8 ft 1 in (2,46 m). Wing area, 136.6 sq ft (12,69 m²).*

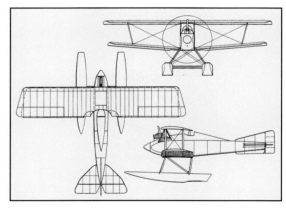

The FF 43 float fighter (above and below) evaluated under operational conditions in the North Sea from October 1916 by the *Seeflugzeug Versuchs Kommando.*

FRIEDRICHSHAFEN FF 46 (D I) Germany

In September 1916, the Flugzeugbau Friedrichshafen presented the *Idflieg (Inspektion der Fliegertruppen –* Inspectorate of Flying Troops) with a proposal for a single-seat, land-based fighter based on the FF 43 floatplane. This, the FF 46, received an order for three prototypes, which, like the FF 43, were to be powered by the 160 hp Mercedes D III, but were to be armed with twin synchronised 7,92-mm MG 08/15 machine guns. The FF 46, or D I, was a single-bay staggered biplane, the first prototype having vertical cabane strutting, but the second having splayed struts to improve forward vision. The *Idflieg* testing of the FF 46 was not com-

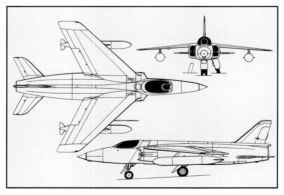

General arrangement drawing of the Fo 145 Gnat, and (below) one of those supplied to Finland in the '70s.

(Above and below) The FF 46 was based broadly on the FF 43, but, in fact, had no commonality with the float fighter other than design origin.

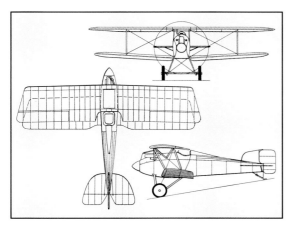

pleted until 28 April 1917, when it was concluded that the type was not acceptable for series production as its flight characteristics and performance were inferior to those of its contemporaries. There is no record of the third prototype being completed. *Empty weight, 1,512 lb (686 kg). Loaded weight, 1,986 lb (901 kg). Span, 29 ft 6⅓ in (9,00 m). Length, 23 ft 3½ in (7,10 m). Height, 8 ft 10⅓ in (2,70 m). Wing area, 277.72 sq ft (25,80 m²).*

FRIEDRICHSHAFEN FF 54 Germany

The Flugzeugbau Friedrichshafen specialised in the design of robust seaplanes and sturdy bombers, proving unsuccessful in attempting to produce lightweight structures needed for small single-seat fighters. The FF 54, designed by Dipl-Ing van Gries, proved no more suc-

The FF 54 (above) in its original quadruplane form as tested late 1917, and (below) after somewhat crude adaptation as a triplane, flown in May 1918.

cessful than preceding warplanes of this type from the Manzell factory, albeit less conventional in design approach. The FF 54 was conceived as a single-seat quadruplane powered by a 160 hp Mercedes D IIIa water-cooled engine and armed with two synchronised 7,92-mm MG 08/15 machine guns. The two narrow-chord middle wings were mounted on the centreline and baseline of the fuselage with little gap, interconnected between themselves and the bottom wing by broad, aerofoil-section interplane struts. On 31 October 1917, the FF 54 was in final assembly with flight testing anticipated within 3-4 weeks. When this began, however, the quadruplane arrangement proved unsuccessful and, in April 1918, the prototype was rebuilt as a triplane, changes being restricted to removal of the lower middle wing and redesign of the vertical tail surfaces. Flight testing of the FF 54 in its revised form began in May 1918, and continued until the following September, when a crash resulted in abandonment of further work on the aircraft. No data are available for the FF 54 in either quadruplane or triplane form.

FVM J 23 Sweden

The J 23 (above and below) parasol fighter monoplane suffered structural and aerodynamic shortcomings and was soon withdrawn from service and scrapped.

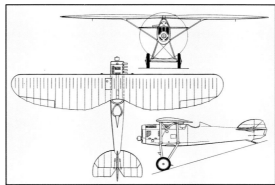

Designed by Henry Kjellson and Ivar Malmer at the Flygkompaniets Verkstäder at Malmen (FVM), the J 23 single-seat fighter was of parasol monoplane configuration and powered by a 185 hp BMW IIIa six-cylinder water-cooled engine. The J 23 was of wooden construction and carried an armament of two 8-mm m/22 machine guns synchronised to fire through the propeller disc. Work on the J 23 was initiated in 1922, five examples being built and all participating in the 1923 International Air Exhibition (ILUG) held in Gothenburg. During advanced flight testing on 15 March 1924, the wing of one J 23 failed and the pilot, Axel Norberg, was killed. By consensus, the structure of the J 23 was judged to be too weak, and although various modifications were introduced on the surviving aircraft, such as enlarged tail surfaces, the aircraft were soon withdrawn and scrapped. *Max speed, 122 mph (197 km/h). Time to 9,840 ft (3 000 m), 9.3 min. Empty weight, 1,700 lb (771 kg). Loaded weight, 2,172 lb (985 kg). Span, 36 ft 10½ in (11,24 m). Length, 22 ft 7⅔ in (6,90 m). Height, 8 ft 4⅓ in (2,55 m). Wing area, 193.76 sq ft (18,00 m²).*

FVM J 24B Sweden

Reluctance on the part of the Swedish Army to accept the parasol monoplane configuration for fighter aircraft resulted in the J 24 – essentially a more powerful version of the J 23 with a 300 hp Hispano-Suiza eight-cylinder water-cooled engine – being rebuilt in 1924 as a biplane under the designation J 24B. The J 24B was

Essentially a more powerful biplane derivative of the J 23 monoplane, the J 24B (above and below) did not offer an acceptable performance.

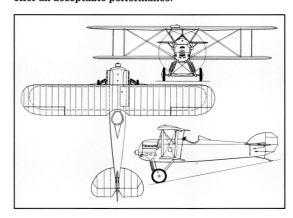

test flown during 1925, but being overweight was found to possess an unacceptable performance, the single example soon being written off and the Nieuport 29C being selected by the Swedish Army. *Max speed, 145 mph (233 km/h). Time to 19,685 ft (6 000 m), 25.5 min. Empty weight, 1,947 lb (883 kg). Loaded weight, 2,681 lb (1 216 kg). Span, 29 ft 6⅓ in (9,00 m). Length, 23 ft 9⅖ in (7,25 m). Height, 9 ft 11¼ in (3,03 m). Wing area, 258.34 sq ft (24,00 m²).*

G

GABARDINI G.8 Italy

The Società Anonima Garbardini per l'Incremento dell' Aviazione of Cameri, Novara, was established in 1914, primarily as a flying training organisation with associated workshops producing training aircraft of original design for use by the school. Whereas the Gabardini trainers were of monoplane configuration, the organisation initiated development, at the beginning of the

(Above) The G.8bis discarded the frontal radiator of the G.8 (below) in favour of side-mounted radiators and adopted a longer-span lower wing.

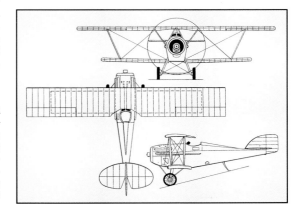

GABARDINI

The single-seat G.8 (above), produced in 1923, was offered in both fighter and training versions.

'twenties, of a series of single- and two-seat fabric-covered metal biplanes. The majority of these aircraft were also intended for instructional purposes, including the single-seat G.4bis and two-seat G.6 powered by the 120 hp Le Rhône rotary, but, in 1923, Gabardini produced the single-seat G.8 in both advanced training and fighting versions. These versions differed primarily in engine power, the eight-cylinder Vee-type Hispano-Suiza of the trainer affording 140 hp and that of the fighter being rated at 200 hp. The G.8 was an un-equal-span single-bay biplane with ailerons on the upper wing only, the fighter version having an armament of two synchronised 7,7-mm Vickers guns. A development of the basic type, with a 180 hp HS 34 engine, the G.8bis featured a longer span lower wing and discarded the frontal radiator in favour of radiators attached to the fuselage sides, over the wing leading edges. Neither G.8 nor G.8bis was adopted by the *Regia Aeronautica*, the examples built being utilised for advanced training at the Cameri school. The following data relate to the 200 hp G.8. *Max speed, 128 mph (206 km/h). Time to 3,280 ft (1 000 m), 3.2 min. Empty weight, 1,279 lb (580 kg). Loaded weight, 1,719 lb (780 kg). Span, 27 ft 4⅓ in (8,34 m). Length, 18 ft 2½ in (5,55 m). Height, 9 ft 2¼ in (2,80 m). Wing area, 237.46 sq ft (22,06 m²).*

GABARDINI G.9 — Italy

Evolved in parallel with the G.8 and possessing an essentially similar wing cellule, but with a shorter span upper wing and reduced cabane bracing, the G.9 was initially flown with a 220 hp water-cooled six-cylinder SPA 6a engine. It was subsequently re-engined with an eight-cylinder Vee-type HS 42 engine of 300 hp as the G.9bis, the cockpit being raised and the undercarriage

The SPA 6a engine in the G.9 (above) was replaced by the more powerful HS 42 (below) in the G.9bis.

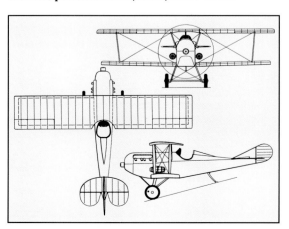

The G.9bis (below) differed from the G.9 in having increased gap, taller undercarriage and raised cockpit.

lengthened. *Ing.* Filippo Zappata, who joined Gabardini in 1923, undertook some redesign of the G.9bis, introducing, among other changes, an aerodynamically cleaner engine cowling and a large propeller spinner. During a royal visit to Cameri airfield in October 1923, the G.9bis, flown by Lodovico Zanibelli, demonstrated a maximum speed of 155 mph (250 km/h). No series production of either the G.9 or G.9bis was undertaken, the following data applying to the former. *Max speed, 146 mph (235 km/h). Time to 16,405 ft (5 000 m), 15 min. Span, 22 ft 11⅔ in (7,00 m). Length, 19 ft 8¼ in (6,00 m). Wing area, 193.76 sq ft (18,00 m²).*

GALVIN HC — France

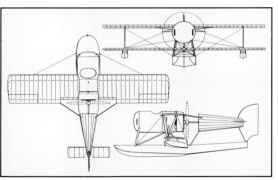

The Galvin HC, with definitive outrigger floats (above) and initial floats (below), failed to live up to expectations and was quickly abandoned.

Of extraordinarily unorthodox configuration, the Galvin *Hydravion de Chasse* reportedly underwent flight testing from the Rhône in the summer of 1919. Of wooden construction with fabric skinning and a light alloy nose cone, the Galvin single-seat float fighter was an equi-span staggered single-bay biplane. Its fuselage consisted of two entirely separate elements with a gap between in which the propeller of a 160 hp Gnome nine-cylinder rotary engine rotated. Both forward and rear

fuselage were individually supported by a remarkably long and broad central float, the former by paired N-struts and wire bracing, and the latter by I-struts fore and aft – the rearmost providing an attachment point for an inordinately large rudder – with wire bracing to the wings. Small stabilising floats were attached to the lower wing immediately beneath the V-type interplane struts. The intended armament of the Galvin fighter was allegedly three machine guns, but no records of the testing of this unique aircraft have survived. *Max speed, 124 mph (200 km/h) at sea level. Endurance, 2.0 hrs. Empty weight, 1,146 lb (520 kg). Loaded weight, 1,764 lb (800 kg). Span, 26 ft 3 in (8,00 m). Length, 23 ft 7½ in (7,20 m). Height, 7 ft 6½ in (2,30 m). Wing area, 199.14 sq ft (18,59 m²).*

GEEST — Germany

In 1916, Dr Waldemar Geest designed a single-seat fighter which, built by Automobil und Aviatik AG of Leipzig-Heiterblick, utilised his patented *Möwe* (Seagull) type wing. The *Möwe* wing featured varying incidence angle and dihedral over its planform to compensate for forward and lateral gusts, and the excellent stability that it offered had been demonstrated by six *Möwe* monoplanes built prior to World War I. The *Möwe* wing concept was adapted by Dr Geest for a fighter of staggered single-bay biplane configuration powered by a 160 hp Mercedes D III six-cylinder water-cooled engine. During military trials, performed in 1917, the Geest fighter attained an altitude of 11,485 ft (3 500 m) in 17.5 min and a maximum speed of 99 mph (160 km/h), but development was discontinued and no further aircraft employed the *Möwe* wing.

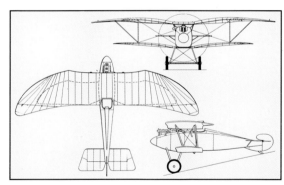

The Geest fighter (above and below) was built in 1919 to demonstrate the capabilities of the *Möwe* wing.

GENERAL AVIATION XFA-1 — USA

Designed to meet a lightweight shipboard fighter requirement in competition with the Berliner-Joyce XFJ-1 and Curtiss XF9C-1, the XFA-1 was built by the General Aviation Corporation, the successor to the US Fokker

The XFA-1 (below) with gulled upper wing proved unsuccessful when tested by the US Navy in 1932.

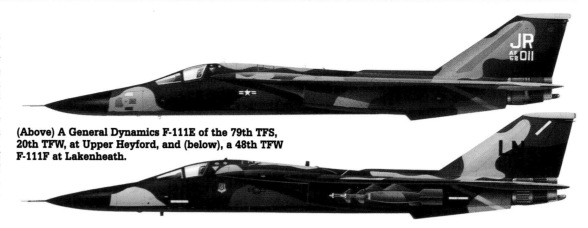

(Above) A General Dynamics F-111E of the 79th TFS, 20th TFW, at Upper Heyford, and (below), a 48th TFW F-111F at Lakenheath.

Aircraft Corporation, and was tested by the US Navy in March 1932. Powered by a 400 hp Pratt & Whitney R-985A Wasp Junior engine, the XFA-1 was a single-bay staggered biplane with the upper wing gulled into the fuselage. It employed all-metal construction with fabric skinning for wing and tail surfaces, proposed armament being two fuselage-mounted 0.3-in (7,62-mm) machine guns. The XFA-1 was not notably successful during Navy trials and further development was discontinued. *Max speed, 170 mph (273 km/h). Time to 5,000 ft (1 525 m), 3.4 min. Normal range, 375 mls (603 km). Empty weight, 1,837 lb (833 kg). Loaded weight, 2,508 lb (1 138 kg). Span, 25 ft 6 in (7,77 m). Length, 22 ft 2 in (6,75 m). Height, 9 ft 3 in (2,82 m). Wing area, 175 sq ft (16,26 m²).*

(Below) A 400 hp Wasp Junior powered the XFA-1.

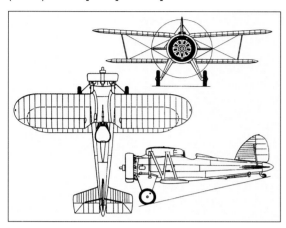

GENERAL DYNAMICS F-111   USA

The first variable-geometry combat aircraft to enter service, the F-111 two-seat fighter-bomber's principal missions were interdiction and counterair. The first of 18 F-111A development aircraft was flown on 21 December 1964, and the first development aircraft of a parallel shipboard version, the F-111B, followed on 18 May 1965. Only seven examples of the latter were built before the naval version was abandoned. The production F-111A (141 built) was powered by two 18,500 lb st (8 392 kgp) Pratt & Whitney TF30-P-3 afterburning turbofans and armed with one 20-mm M61A1 rotary cannon. An internal bay and eight external wing stations were provided for ordnance. The F-111C (24 built) for the RAAF was essentially similar to the F-111A, but possessed the longer-span wing as applied to the FB-111A strategic bomber. The F-111E (94 built) was a second fighter-bomber version for the USAF Tactical Air Command, differing from the F-111A only in having refined air intakes, but the F-111D (96 built) featured 20,840 lb st (9 453 kgp) TF30-P-9 turbofans, later-generation avionics and increased weights. Final production fighter-bomber version was the F-111F (82 built) incorporating all airframe changes

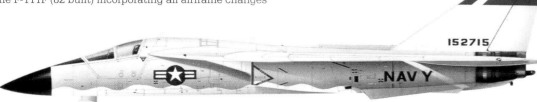

(Above) The last of seven F-111Bs (second of the production batch) completed by Grumman for the USN.

progressively introduced by preceding models, simpler yet more advanced avionics and 25,100 lb st (11 385 kgp) TF30-P-100 turbofans. In 1990-91, 59 surviving FB-111As were redesignated F-111Gs to serve as fighter-bombers in the USAF Tactical Air Command. As well as longer wings, the F-111G had higher operating weights and 20,350 lb st (9 230 kgp) TF30-P-7 turbofans. F-111s were phased out of USAF service in the late 1990s, and as at 2001 only a handful soldier on with the Royal Australian Air Force, probably to be replaced before 2010. The following data relate specifically to the F-111F *Max speed, 1,453 mph (2 338 km/h) at 52,700 ft (16 060 m), or Mach=1.38, 914 mph (1 471 km/h) at sea level, or*

(Above) An F-111A – later to be converted to EF-111A – with the 474th TFW, first to use the type. (Below) A general arrangement drawing of the F-111E.

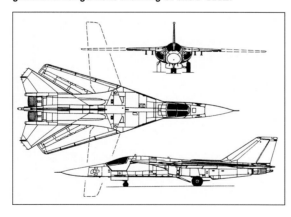

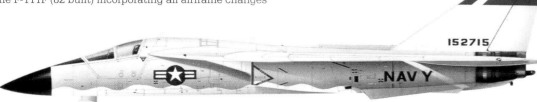

Two squadrons of the RAAF's No 82 Wing at Amberley equipped with the F-111C (below).

Mach=1.2. Combat climb, 43,050 ft/min (218,7 m/sec). Combat radius (HI-LO-HI), 1,242 mls (2 000 km). Empty weight, 47,481 lb (21 537 kg). Max loaded weight, 100,000 lb (45 360 kg). Span (swept) 31 ft 11³/₄ in (9,75 m), (extended), 63 ft 0 in (19,20 m). Length, 75 ft 6¹/₂ in (23,02 m). Height, 17 ft 0¹/₂ in (5,19 m). Wing area, 525 sq ft (48,77 m²).

An F-111E (above) and F-111B (below), both configured for subsonic flight with their wings located in the fully-forward position.

GENERAL DYNAMICS F-16A/B FIGHTING FALCON   USA

The F-16 had its origins in the USAF's lightweight fighter prototype programme of 1972, the first of two YF-6s flying on 20 January 1974. The YF-16 was selected a year later for full-scale engineering development, with the first of eight pre-series aircraft (six single-seat F16As and two two-seat F-16Bs) flying on 8 December 1976. Previously, on 7 June 1975, the F-16 had been selected as winning contender in a contest (with the Mirage Fl.M53 and Saab 37 Viggen) to provide a successor for the Lockheed F-104G in service with Belgium, Denmark, the Netherlands and Norway, production being established on a multi-national basis with final assembly lines in the USA, Belgium and the Netherlands. A Turkish assembly line was set up in 1987 after that nation had also selected the F-16. The initial production model, the F-16A, flew on 7 August 1978 with a Pratt & Whitney F100-PW-200 turbofan rated at 14,590 lb st (6 620 kgp) dry and 23,770 lb st (10 780 kgp) with maximum afterburning. Armament comprised a 20-mm M61A1 rotary cannon and (for the intercept mission) two wingtip-mounted AIM-9 Side-winder AAMs. Production of the F-16A (and its two-seat conversion trainer F-16B equivalent) was pursued in Blocks, the principal of these being Block 15, 1,222 of which (preceded by 329 of earlier Blocks) were scheduled to have been delivered by mid-1992. A total of 785 F-16As and Bs was supplied to the USAF, other recipients of these models being Belgium (160), Denmark (70), Egypt (41), Indonesia (12), Israel (75), Netherlands (213), Norway (78), Pakistan (111), Portugal (20), Singapore (8), South Korea (39), Taiwan (150), Thailand (18) and Venezuela (24). Some of these were transfers from USAF stocks. A lower-cost alternative to the F-16A was proposed with the General Electric J79-GE-119 turbojet. One of the pre-series F-16Bs was fitted with an 18,370 lb st (8 333 kgp) J79-GE-17X to serve as a proto-

Key to General Dynamics F-16C (Block 40) Fighting Falcon

1 Pitot head/air data probe
2 Glassfibre radome
3 Lightning conducting strips
4 Planar radar scanner
5 Radome hinge point, open to starboard
6 Scanner tracking mechanism
7 ILS glideslope aerial
8 Radar mounting bulkhead
9 Incidence vane, port and starboard
10 IFF aerial
11 GBU-15 laser-guided glide bomb
12 AN/APG-68 digital pulse-doppler multi-mode radar electronics equipment bay
13 Radar warning antennae (port and starboard)
14 Front pressure bulkhead
15 Static ports
16 Fuselage forebody strake fairing
17 Forward avionics equipment bay
18 Canopy jettison charge
19 Instrument panel shroud
20 Instrument panel, multifunction CRT head-down-displays
21 Side-stick controller (fly-by-wire control system)
22 Video recorder
23 GEC wide-angle head-up-display
24 Penguin air-to-surface anti-shipping missile (Norwegian aircraft)
25 LAU-3A 19-round rocket launcher
26 2,75-in (68-mm) FFAR
27 ATLIS II laser designating and ranging pod
28 Intake flank (No 5R) stores pylon adapter
29 LANTIRN (FLIR) targetting pod
30 Frameless bubble canopy
31 Ejection seat headrest
32 McDonnell-Douglas ACES II zero-zero ejection seat
33 Side console panel
34 Canopy frame fairing
35 Canopy external emergency release
36 Engine throttle lever incorporating HOTAS (hands-on-throttle-and-stick) radar controls
37 Canopy jettison handle
38 Cockpit section frame construction
39 Boundary layer splitter plate
40 Fixed geometry air intake
41 Nosewheel (aft retracting)
42 LANTIRN (FLIR/TFR) navigation pod
43 Port intake flank (No 5L) stores pylon adapter
44 Forward position light
45 Rapport III threat warning antenna fairing (Belgian and Israeli aircraft)
46 Intake duct framing
47 Gun gas suppression muzzle aperture
48 Aft avionics equipment bay
49 Cockpit rear pressure bulkhead
50 Canopy hinge point
51 Ejection seat rails
52 Canopy rotary actuator
53 Conditioned air outlet duct
54 Canopy sealing frame
55 Canopy aft glazing
56 600-US gal (500-Imp gal/2 271-l) long range fuel tank
57 Garrett turbine emergency power unit (EPU)
58 EPU hydrazine fuel tank
59 Fuel tank bay access panel
60 Forward fuselage bag-type fuel tank. Total internal capacity 6,972 lb (3 162 kg)
61 Fuselage upper longeron
62 Conditioned air ducting
63 Cannon barrels
64 Forebody frame construction
65 Air system ground connection
66 Ventral air conditioning system equipment bay
67 Centreline 300-US gal (250-Imp gal/1 136-l)
68 Mainwheel door hydraulic actuator
69 Mainwheel door
70 Hydraulic system ground connectors
71 Gun bay ventral gas vent
72 GE M61A1 20-mm rotary cannon
73 Ammunition feed chute
74 Hydraulic gun drive motor
75 Port hydraulic reservoir
76 Centre fuselage integral fuel tank
77 Leading-edge flap drive hydraulic motor
78 Ammunition drum, 511-rounds
79 Upper position light/refuelling floodlight
80 TACAN aerial

81 Hydraulic accumulator
82 Starboard hydraulic reservoir
83 Leading-edge flap drive shaft
84 Inboard, No 6 stores station (4,500-lb/2 041-kg capacity)
85 Pylon attachment hardpoint
86 Leading-edge flap drive shaft and rotary actuators
87 No 7 stores hardpoint (3,500-lb/1 588-kg capacity)
88 Radar warning antenna
89 Missile launch rails
90 AMRAAM air-to-air missiles
91 Loading pod (carriage of essential ground equipment and personal effects for off-base deployment)
92 Starboard leading-edge manoeuvre flap (down position)
93 Outboard No 8 stores station hardpoint (700-lb/318-kg capacity)
94 Wing tip No 9 stores station (425-lb/193-kg capacity)
95 Wing-tip AMRAAM missile
96 Starboard navigation light
97 Fixed portion of trailing edge
98 Static dischargers
99 Starboard flaperon
100 Starboard wing integral fuel tank
101 Fuel system piping
102 Fuel pump
103 Starboard wing root attachment fishplates
104 Fuel tank access panels
105 Universal air refuelling receptacle (UARSSI), open
106 Engine compressor intake centrebody fairing
107 Airframe-mounted accessory equipment gearbox
108 Jet fuel starter
109 Machined wing attachment bulkheads
110 Engine fuel management equipment
111 Pressure refuelling receptacle, ventral adaptor
112 Pratt & Whitney F100-PW-220 afterburning turbofan engine
113 VHF/IFF aerial
114 Starboard flaperon hydraulic actuator
115 Fuel tank tail fins
116 Sidebody fairing integral fuel tank
117 Position light
118 Cooling air ram air intake
119 Fin root fairing
120 Forward engine support link
121 Rear fuselage integral fuel tank
122 Thermally insulated tank inner skin
123 Tank access panels
124 Radar warning system power amplifier
125 Fin root attachment fittings
126 Flight control system hydraulic accumulators

127 Multi-spar fin construction
128 Starboard all-moving tailplane (tailplane panels interchangeable)
129 General Electric F110-GE-100 alternative powerplant
130 Fin leading-edge honeycomb construction
131 Dynamic pressure sensor
132 Carbon-fibre fin skin panelling
133 VHF communications aerial (AM/FM)
134 Fin tip antenna fairing
135 Anti-collision light
136 Threat warning antennae
137 Static dischargers
138 Rudder honeycomb construction
139 Rudder hydraulic actuator
140 ECM antenna fairing
141 Tail navigation light
142 Extended tailcone fairing, brake parachute housing (Norwegian aircraft) or Rapport III or Itek 69 ECM systems (Belgian or Israeli aircraft)
143 Variable area afterburner nozzle flaps
144 Nozzle sealing fairing
145 Afterburner nozzle actuators (5)
146 Port split trailing-edge airbrake, open, upper and lower surfaces
147 Airbrake actuating linkage
148 Port all-moving tailplane
149 Static dischargers
150 Graphite-epoxy tailplane skin panels
151 Leading-edge honeycomb construction
152 Corrugated aluminium sub-structure
153 Hinge pivot fixing
154 Tailplane hydraulic actuator
155 Fuel jettison chamber (port and starboard)
156 Afterburner ducting

157 Rear fuselage machined bulkheads
158 Port position light
159 AN/ALE-40 (VO-4) chaff/flare dispenser, port and starboard
160 Main engine thrust mounting, port and starboard
161 Sidebody fairing frame construction
162 Runway arrester hook
163 Composite construction ventral fin, port and starboard
164 Port flaperon hydraulic actuator
165 Flaperon hinges
166 Port flaperon, lowered
167 External fuel tank tail fairing
168 Flaperon honeycomb construction
169 Fixed portion of trailing edge
170 Static dischargers
171 Port navigation light
172 Wing tip No 1 stores station (425-lb/143-kg capacity)
173 AIM-9L Sidewinder air-to-air missiles
174 AIM-7 Sparrow air-to-air missile
175 Mk 84 low drag 2,000-lb/907 kg HE bomb

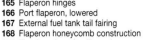

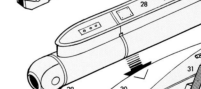

176 Mk 83 Snakeye retarded bomb
177 Missile launch rails
178 No 2 stores station (700-lb/318-kg capacity)
179 No 3 stores station (3,500-lb/1 588-kg capacity)
180 Port radar warning antenna
181 Mk 82 500-lb (227-kg) HE bombs
182 Triple ejector rack
183 Wing stores pylon
184 Leading-edge manoeuvre flap honeycomb construction
185 Flap drive shaft and rotary actuators
186 Multi-spar wing panel construction
187 Port wing integral tankage
188 No 4 stores station hardpoint (4,500-lb/2 041-kg capacity)

189 Wing root attachment fishplates
190 Undercarriage leg-mounted landing lamp
191 Retraction/breaker strut
192 Main undercarriage leg strut
193 Shock absorber strut
194 Port leading-edge manoeuvre flap, down position
195 Inboard wing pylon
196 Port mainwheel, forward retracting
197 Fuel filler caps
198 370-US gal (308-Imp gal/1 400-l) underwing fuel tank
199 Centreline No 5 stores pylon (2,200-lb/998-kg capacity)
200 AN/ALQ-131 ECM pod
201 AGM-65 Maverick air-to-surface missile
202 Triple missile carrier/launcher

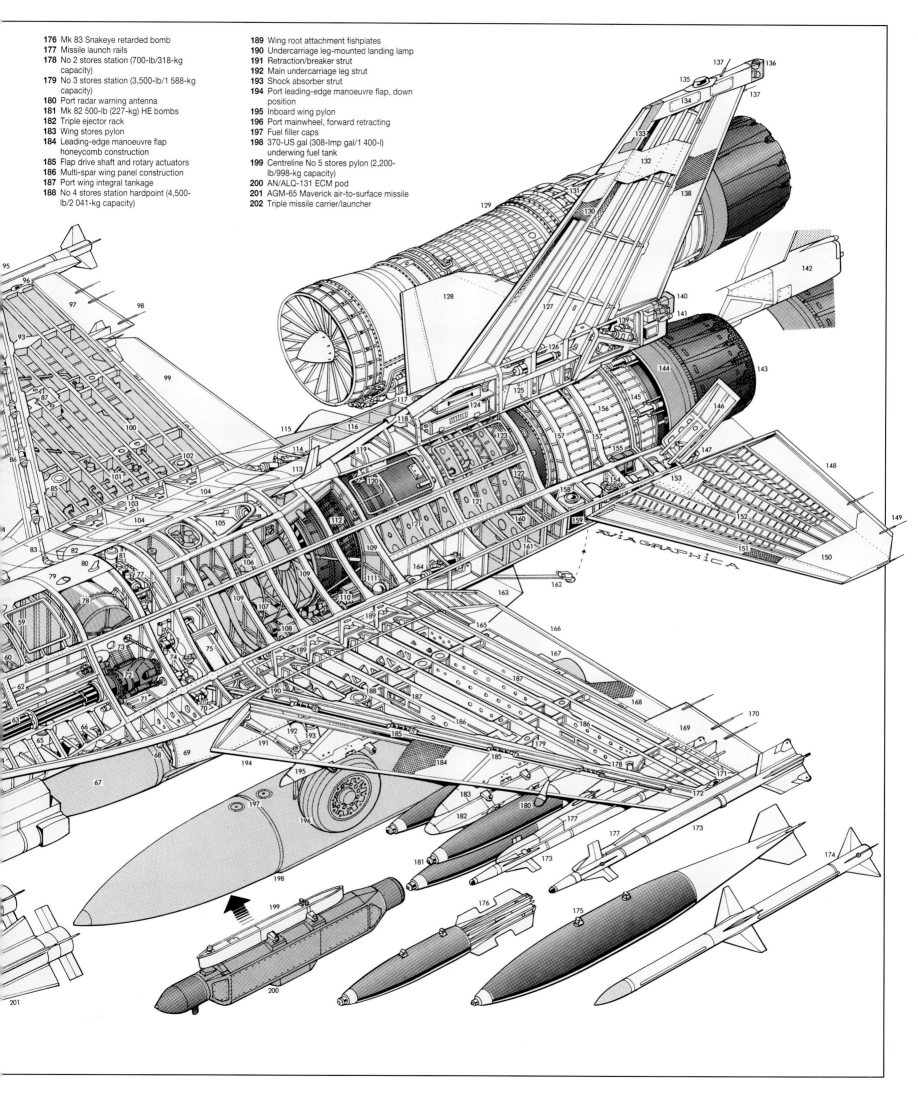

(Above, top) An F-16A of the 35th TFW ("Wolf Pack"), Pusan, Korea, in 1981. (Immediately above) F-16A of 306th Sqn, Dutch KLu, Leeuwarden.

(Below) An F-16A from the 6512th Test Squadron at Edwards AFB carrying AIM-7 Sparrows in 1989.

type, flying as the F-16/79 on 29 October 1980. Two hundred and seventy Block 15 F-16As and Bs were modified 1989-91 as air defence fighters (ADF) for use by the US Air National Guard. The F-16(ADF) had upgraded avionics and provision to carry two AIM-7 Sparrow AAMs or up to six AIM-9 or AIM-120 AAMs. The first phase of the multinational staged improvement programme (MSIP I), introduced with the Block 15 F-16A and B, involved substantial upgrading, further changes being incorporated in Block 15 aircraft with the phase-in of the OCU (Operational Capability Upgrade) modification standard, including expanded computer capacity, the F100-PW-220 engine and structural strengthening for increased take-off weight. More significant changes in production standard came with the introduction of the MSIP II as the F-16C and D (which see). The following data relate to the basic Block 15 F-16A. *Max speed (at 24,459 lb/11 094 kg), 1,333 mph (2 145 km/h) short-endurance dash at 40,000 ft (12 200 m), or Mach=2.02, and 1,247 mph (2 007 km/h) sustained, or Mach=1,89. Tactical radius (HI-LO-HI interdiction with 3,000 lb/1 360 kg of bombs), 360 mls (580 km). Empty weight, 16,234 lb (7 364 kg). Normal loaded weight (air-to-air), 24,459 lb (11 094 kg). Span (over missile launchers), 31 ft 0 in (9,45 m). Length, 47 ft 7³/₄ in (14,52 m). Height, 16 ft 5¹/₄ in (5,01 m). Wing area, 300 sq ft (27,87 m²).*

GENERAL DYNAMICS F-16C/D FIGHTING FALCON   USA

The multi-national staged improvement programme (MSIP) was introduced as a means of progressively expanding the capability of the basic F-16 by introducing systems for ground attack and beyond visual range (BVR) air combat missions. Stage I of the MSIP was applied to Block 15 aircraft delivered from November 1981, and Stage II was introduced with the first Block 25 F-16C/Ds. The first F-16C was delivered to the USAF on 19 July 1984. It differed from the F-16A only in having a slightly lengthened tail fin root fairing. The Westinghouse APG-66 multi-mode radar was replaced by the APG-68, and the cockpit instrumentation was revised to provide compatibility with advanced weaponry. The core computers were upgraded, and the structure was tweaked to cover weight increases. 212 Block 25 aircraft were followed by 498 Block 30/32 F-16s. Block 30 F-16s were powered by the F100-PW 220, while Block 32 aircraft were fitted with the F110-GE-100, rated at 28,984 lb (13 147 kgp) max thrust. The GE engine

needed a larger intake to accommodate the increased mass flow. The inevitable weight increases were largely offset by greater thrust, but wing loading, and consequently manoeuvrability, suffered. At this point, GD offered the Agile Falcon, with increased span and wing area, but there were no takers. Blocks 40/42 featured avionics and other system upgrades, while Blocks 50/52, delivered from October 1991, used the much more powerful F100-PW-229 and F110-GE-129 turbofans, both in the 29,000 lb (13 154 kgp) thrust class. Air-to-air weaponry typically consisted of the 20-mm M61A1 cannon with 511 rounds, four AIM-120 Amraam and two AIM-9 Sidewinders, or six Sidewinders, R550 Magics or Pythons. The most recent variant is the Block 60, which carries conformal fuel tanks along the fuselage above the wings. To date, Block 60 aircraft have been ordered by Bahrain and Israel, as the F-16I, a two-seater. Other F-16C/D users are Egypt, Greece, Israel, Singapore, South Korea, Turkey, UAE and the USAF. The USN used the F-16N briefly for dissimilar air combat training. Italy is expected to rent the type as an interim fighter pending the delivery of Typhoon. Total F-16 production currently exceeds 4,000. *Data basically similar to those of the F-16A except: Empty weight, 18,600 lb (8 437 kg). Loaded weight air-to-air, c27,500 lb (12 474 kg). Length, 49 ft 3¹/₂ in (15,02 m). Height, 16 ft 8¹/₂ in (5.09 m²).*

GENERAL DYNAMICS F-16XL   USA

Evolved as an advanced dual-rôle (air-air and air-ground) development of the F-16 Fighting Falcon incorporating new aerodynamic and systems technologies, the F-16XL featured a so-called "cranked arrow" wing with leading-edge compound sweepback of 50 and 70 degrees. This wing was mated to an F-16 fuselage which was lengthened by 4 ft 8 in (1,42 m) by means of two plugs. The first (single-seat) prototype of the F-16XL (adapted from the first pre-series or full-scale development F-16A) flew on 3 July 1982, followed by a second (two-seat) prototype (which combined another pre-series F-16A and a new F-16B forward fuselage) on 29 October 1982. These were respectively powered by the F100-PW-102 and the F101DFE turbo-fan. Despite its area of more than twice that of the F-16A, the "cranked arrow" wing of the F-16XL had less drag at optimum cruise, and permitted an 83 per cent increase in fuel capacity. The long chord of the wing permitted tandem semi-conformal weapons carriage,

A "cranked-arrow" wing distinguished the F-16XL, flown in both single-seat (below) and two-seat form.

A 50th TFW (313th Sqn) F-16C (above) from Hahn, Germany. (Below) Three-view drawing of the F-16C.

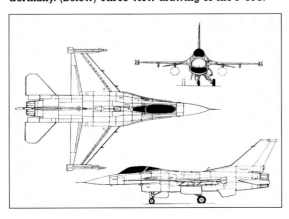

four AIM-120 AAMs being semi-submerged under the wing at the fuselage intersection and an AIM-9 Sidewinder AAM being carried at each wingtip. On 24 February 1984, the US Department of Defense announced its choice of the McDonnell Douglas F-15E to fulfil the USAF's dual-rôle fighter requirement rather than the productionised F-16XL (F-16E). The two prototypes were subsequently leased by the National Air and Space Administration after being held in flyable storage for four years, flight testing resuming in March 1989 to evaluate concepts for sustained high-speed flight. *Max speed, 1,386 mph (2 230 km/h) at 40,000 ft (12 200 m), or Mach=2.1. Maximum range, 2,875+ mls (4 630+ km). Mission weight, 43,000 lb (19 504 kg). Max loaded weight, 48,000 lb (21 772 kg). Span, 34 ft 2⅖ in (10,43 m). Length, 54 ft 1⅞ in (16,50 m). Height, 17 ft 7 in (5,36 m). Wing area, 663 sq ft (61,59 m²).*

(Below) Three-view drawing of single-seat F-16XL.

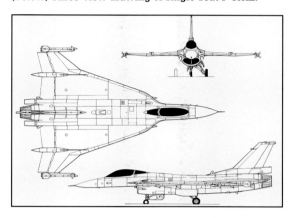

GERMANIA DB　　　Germany

Built by the Germania-Flugzeugwerke GmbH of Leipzig, the DB two-seat fighter utilised the efficient *Walfisch* (Whale) fuselage configuration which endowed the gunner, seated ahead of the pilot, with a broad forward field of fire. A two-bay biplane, the DB was powered by a 180 hp Argus As III water-cooled engine, carried a single machine gun on a ring mounting in the forward cockpit and was undergoing trials in September 1915. No production of the fighter was undertaken and no data relating to this type are available.

The Germania DB (below) two-seater carried a gunner ahead of the pilot, firing above the upper wing.

GERMANIA JM　　　Germany

The Germania JM (*Jagdmaschine*) experimental single-seat fighter was based on the promising results of wind tunnel testing with the *Walfisch* (Whale) fuselage configuration at Göttingen. Designed by J Egwin Leiber, the JM was a single-bay biplane powered by a 100 hp Argus As I water-cooled engine and made its

The *Walfisch* (whale) fuselage of the Germania JM (below) failed to gain official acceptance for the fighter.

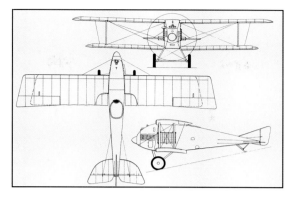

(Above) A general arrangement drawing of the JM.

début in the summer of 1916. While under test on 16 August 1916, the JM attained altitudes of 3,280 ft (1 000 m) in 4 min, 6,560 ft (2 000 m) in 11 min, 9,840 ft (3 000 m) in 19 min and 10,825 ft (3 300 m) in 20 min. No further development was undertaken and no data are available.

GLOSTER SPARROWHAWK I (MARS II)　　　UK

First of the Sparrowhawk Is (above) supplied to Japan for use as land-based single-seat fighters.

When, in 1920, the Nieuport & General Aircraft Company was closed down, the Gloucestershire Aircraft Company, which had previously manufactured the Nieuport Nighthawk (which see) under Air Ministry contract, acquired the design rights to this fighter and the services of its designer, H P Folland, for its further development. In 1921, Gloucestershire Aircraft received a contract from the Imperial Japanese Navy for 50 Nighthawks modified for naval use, plus a further 40 in component form for assembly in Japan by the Yokosuka Naval Air Arsenal. Produced from Nighthawk component stocks acquired as part of the 1919 settlement of the company's claim against the government's cancelled contract for this type, the Japanese order was fulfilled within six months. Of the 50 complete aircraft, 30, initially known as Mars IIs but subsequently as Sparrowhawk Is, were supplied as single-seat shore-based fighters, 10 as Sparrowhawk II (Mars III) two-seat dual control trainers and the remaining 10 as Sparrowhawk III (Mars IV) single-seat shipboard fighters. These last had flotation equipment, undercar-

riage arrester hooks and hydrovanes. The Sparrowhawk, which remained in Japanese service until 1928, was powered by a 230 hp Bentley B.R.2 nine-cylinder rotary engine. The armament of the single-seat models comprised two synchronised 0.303-in (7,7-mm) Vickers guns. The following data relate to the Sparrowhawk III. *Max speed, 125 mph (201 km/h) at sea level, 105 mph (169 km/h) at 15,000 ft (4 575 m). Range, 300 mls (483 km). Time to 15,000 ft (4 575 m), 25.5 min. Empty weight, 1,850 lb (839 kg). Loaded weight, 2,165 lb (982 kg). Span, 27 ft 11 in (8,51 m). Length, 19 ft 8 in (5,99 m). Height, 10 ft 6 in (3,20 m). Wing area, 270 sq ft (25,08 m²).*

A hydrovane attachment in front of the wheels gave the Sparrowhawk II (above and below) a degree of safety in the event of alighting on water.

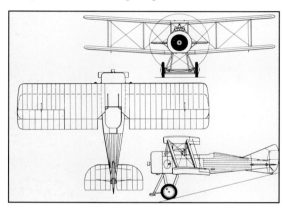

GLOSTER MARS VI NIGHTHAWK　　　UK

The Mars VI Nighthawk was a Gloucestershire Aircraft modification of the basic Nieuport Nighthawk produced to Air Ministry Specification 35/22 and fitted with either the 398 hp Bristol Jupiter IV nine-cylinder radial or 325 hp Armstrong Siddeley Jaguar II 14-cylinder radial. The first Jaguar-powered Mars VI conversion of a Nieuport-built airframe was delivered to the AEE at Martlesham Heath on 21 May 1921. Official tests with a second Jaguar-engined example were conducted at the RAE Farnborough in July 1922, the first Jupiter-powered Mars VI arriving at the RAE in Sep-

Supplied in 1923, the Mars VI Nighthawk (below) remained in Greek Army Air Force use until late '20s.

With a Jaguar engine, the Nighthawk (above and right) was extensively tested by the RAF in the early 'twenties, in the Middle East as well as at home, but it never reached squadron status.

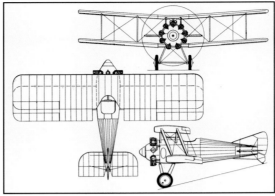

tember 1922. These embodied some metal fuselage components. In so far as can be ascertained, 29 Nighthawk airframes were rebuilt to Mars VI standard for the RAF, these being armed with two synchronised 0.303-in (7,7-mm) Vickers guns, and a further 25 powered by the Jaguar engine were purchased by the Greek government. The Greek machines were delivered early in 1923, and remained in first-line service until 1937-38. The following data relate to the Jaguar-engined Mars VI Nighthawk. *Max speed, 150 mph (241 km/h) at sea level, 142 mph (229 km/h) at 10,000 ft (3 050 m). Time to 20,000 ft (6 100 m), 24 min. Empty weight, 1,816 lb (824 kg). Loaded weight, 2,217 lb (1 006 kg). Span, 28 ft 0 in (8,53 m). Length, 18 ft 0 in (5,49 m). Height, 9 ft 0 in (2,74 m). Wing area, 270 sq ft (25,08 m²).*

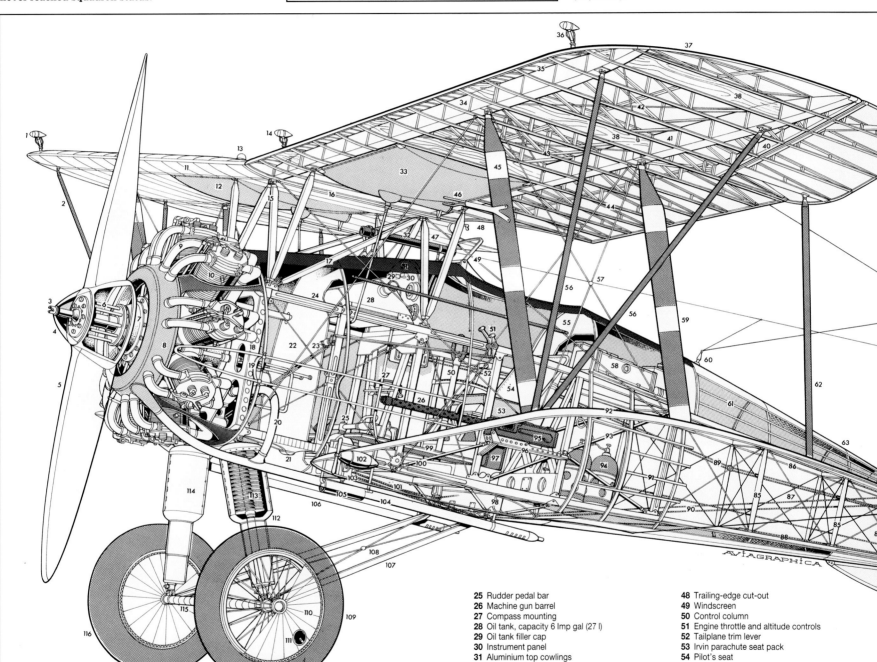

Key to Gloster Gamecock

1 Starboard navigation light
2 Outboard Vee strut
3 Starter dog attachment
4 Spinner
5 Two-bladed wooden propeller
6 Propeller hub fixing bolts
7 Engine reduction gearbox
8 Exhaust collector ring
9 Individual cylinder exhaust pipes
10 Bristol Jupiter VI nine-cylinder radial engine
11 Starboard upper wing panel, fabric covered

12 Starboard wing fuel tank, capacity 30 Imp gal (136 l)
13 Upward identification light
14 Forward navigation light
15 Centre section mounting struts
16 Centre wing joint rib
17 Diagonal centre section struts
18 Engine mounting steel bulkhead
19 Gun blast trough
20 Carburettor heating duct
21 Bottom longeron jacking pad
22 Aluminium and asbestos fireproof bulkhead
23 Engine throttle control rods
24 Upper longeron

25 Rudder pedal bar
26 Machine gun barrel
27 Compass mounting
28 Oil tank, capacity 6 Imp gal (27 l)
29 Oil tank filler cap
30 Instrument panel
31 Aluminium top cowlings
32 Aldis gunsight
33 Port wing fuel tank, capacity 30 Imp gal (136 l)
34 Laminated spruce front spar
35 Leading-edge stiffeners
36 Port navigation light
37 Wing-tip leading-edge strip
38 Compressed ribs
39 Port upper aileron construction
40 Aileron hinge spar
41 Laminated spruce rear spar
42 Wing internal wire bracing
43 Lattice rib construction
44 Fixed trailing-edge construction
45 Forward interplane strut
46 Pitot static tubes
47 Rear centre-section struts

48 Trailing-edge cut-out
49 Windscreen
50 Control column
51 Engine throttle and altitude controls
52 Tailplane trim lever
53 Irvin parachute seat pack
54 Pilot's seat
55 Cockpit rear bulkhead
56 Centre Vee struts
57 Inter-wing wire bracing
58 Radio compartment
59 Rear interplane strut
60 Aerial mast
61 Rear fuselage dorsal stringers
62 Aileron interconnecting rod
63 Rear fuselage fabric covering
64 Tailfin front fixing
65 Tailfin sliding bracing cable attachment
66 Tailfin construction
67 Stern post
68 Rudder horn balance
69 Aerial cables
70 Rudder construction
71 Steel tube trailing edge
72 Tail navigation light

GLOSTER MARS X NIGHTJAR   UK

Last of the derivatives of the Nighthawk, the Mars X Nightjar was developed as a single-seat shipboard fighter. It featured a 230 hp Bentley B.R.2 nine-cylinder rotary engine, a special wide-track undercarriage incorporating arrester gear and an armament of two 0.303-in (7,7-mm) synchronised Vickers guns. Although intended for naval use, the 22 Mars X Nightjar fighters resulting from the conversion of Nighthawk airframes by Gloucestershire Aircraft were supplied to the RAF, the first being delivered to the AEE Martlesham Heath on 8 May 1922. The Nightjar entered service in July 1922, but was withdrawn within two years. *Max speed, 120 mph (193 km/h) at sea level, 110 mph (177 km/h) at 10,000 ft (3 050 m). Time to 15,000 ft*

73 Rudder control horn
74 Port elevator
75 Rudder lower section
76 Lower tailplane bracing cable
77 Tailskid shock absorber
78 Steel tailskid shoe
79 Tailskid hinge post
80 Ventral fin plywood construction
81 Elevator hinge control
82 Tailplane spar pivot mounting
83 Port tailplane
84 Tailplane incidence screw-jack
85 Vertical spacers
86 Top longeron
87 Fuselage diagonal wire bracing
88 Bottom longeron
89 Tailplane trim control cables
90 Rudder and elevator cables
91 Rear fuselage stringer construction
92 Port bottom wing leading-edge
93 Fuselage diagonal steel struts
94 Oxygen bottles
95 Vickers 0.303-in (7,7mm) machine gun
96 Machine gun mounting
97 Ammunition magazine, 600 rounds per gun
98 Bottom wing rear spar mounting
99 Pilot's footboards
100 Gun recoil tube
101 Tailplane control cables
102 Wind driven wireless generator; lighting generator to starboard

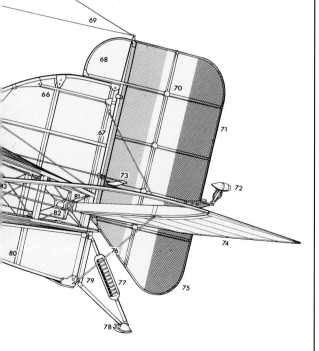

103 Bottom wing front spar fixing
104 Port exhaust pipe
105 Oil cooler
106 Starboard exhaust pipe
107 Undercarriage rear struts
108 Diagonal wire bracing
109 Port mainwheel
110 Wheel disc fabric covering
111 Tyre valve access
112 Port main undercarriage strut
113 Rubber block shock absorber
114 Starboard shock absorber strut
115 Axle beam
116 Starboard mainwheel

The Mars X Nightjar (above), seen here at the RAE in 1922, served briefly in No 203 Sqn, RAF.

(4 575 m), 23 min. Empty weight, 1,765 lb (801 kg). Loaded weight, 2,165 lb (982 kg). Span, 28 ft 0 in (8,53 m). Length, 18 ft 4 in (5,59 m). Height, 9 ft 0 in (2,74 m). Wing area, 270 sq ft (25,08 m²).

GLOSTER GREBE   UK

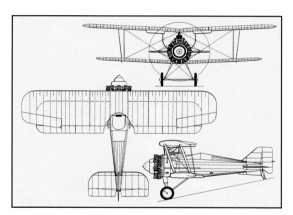

(Above) Three-view drawing of the Gloster Grebe II.

Essentially a single-seat fighter version of the lower-powered tandem two-seat Grouse trainer, the Grebe was flown in the summer of 1923 with a 350 hp Armstrong Siddeley Jaguar III, three prototypes being built. The production model, known as the Grebe II, was re-engined with a 400 hp Jaguar IV and, carrying an armament of two synchronised 0.303-in (7,7-mm) Vickers

The Grebe II (below) was the first Gloster fighter produced in substantial quantities for the RAF.

guns, entered RAF service in October 1923. Of wooden construction with fabric skinning, the Grebe II supplanted the Sopwith Snipe, 129 production examples being built during 1923-27. A small number of these was completed as tandem two-seat trainers and the type remained in first-line RAF service until replaced by the Siskin mid-1928. One two-seat and two single-seat Grebe IIs built against RAF contracts were supplied to the New Zealand government in 1928. *Max speed, 162 mph (261 km/h) at sea level. Time to 20,000 ft (6 100 m), 24 min. Endurance, 3 hrs. Empty weight, 1,695 lb (769 kg). Loaded weight, 2,538 lb (1 151 kg). Span, 29 ft 4 in (8,94 m). Length, 20 ft 3 in (6,17 m). Height, 9 ft 3 in (2,82 m). Wing area, 254 sq ft (23,60 m²).*

GLOSTER GAMECOCK   UK

In July 1924, Gloucestershire Aircraft began work on an improved Grebe single-seat fighter to Specification 37/23 and intended to be powered by the 398 hp Bristol Jupiter IV nine-cylinder radial engine. Of wooden construction with fabric skinning and retaining the then-

A Gloster Grebe II (above) serving with No 25 Squadron, RAF, in 1926.

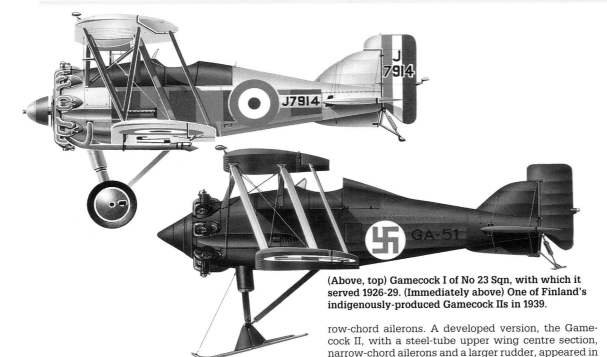

(Above, top) Gamecock I of No 23 Sqn, with which it served 1926-29. (Immediately above) One of Finland's indigenously-produced Gamecock IIs in 1939.

standard armament of two synchronised 0.303-in (7,7-mm) Vickers guns, and to receive the appellation of Gamecock, the prototype was delivered to Martlesham Heath on 20 February 1925. In the following September, an initial order was placed on behalf of the RAF for 30 Gamecock Is powered by the 425 hp Jupiter VI. In the event, a further 60 Gamecock Is were built for the RAF (1925-27), one of these (unofficially known as the Gamecock III) at one time flying with a lengthened fuselage, new and enlarged fin-and-rudder assembly and narrow-chord ailerons. A developed version, the Gamecock II, with a steel-tube upper wing centre section, narrow-chord ailerons and a larger rudder, appeared in 1928. This was adopted by Finland, two pattern aircraft and a manufacturing licence being acquired. Fifteen Gamecock IIs were built for the Finnish air arm 1929-30 by the State Aircraft Factory (Valtion Lentokonetehdas), these having the lengthened fuselage tested earlier in the UK by the so-called Gamecock III and being powered initially by the 420 hp Gnome-Rhône Jupiter (IV) 9Ab or 9Ak and later by the 480 hp Jupiter (IV) 9Ag. The last Gamecock Is were withdrawn from first-line RAF service mid-1931, Gamecock IIs remaining first-line Finnish equipment until 1935. The following data relate to the Gamecock I. *Max speed, 145 mph (233 km/h) at 10,000 ft (3 050 m). Time to 10,000 ft (3 050 m), 7.6 min. Endurance, 2.5 hrs. Empty weight, 1,930 lb (875 kg). Loaded weight, 2,742 lb (1 244 kg). Span, 29 ft 9½ in (9,08 m). Length, 19 ft 8 in (5,99 m). Height, 9 ft 8 in (2,94 m). Wing area, 264 sq ft (24,52 m²).*

(Above) A Gamecock I in service with No 43 Squadron, RAF, in 1927.

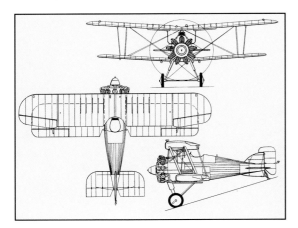

(Above) A Gamecock II of Finland's Air Fighting School in 1941. (Below) Three-view of Gamecock I.

GLOSTER GORCOCK   UK

Gloucestershire Aircraft's first military aircraft of all-metal construction was the third prototype Gorcock single-seat fighter resulting from a May 1924 Air Ministry contract for three prototypes powered by the Napier Lion 12-cylinder water-cooled engine. The first two combined a steel fuselage with wooden wings and the third had an all-steel structure. The first mixed-construction Gorcock was powered by a 450 hp geared Lion IV and was flown mid-1925, the second Gorcock having a 525-hp direct-drive Lion VIII. Engine difficulties prevented their delivery until 1927, together with the all-metal third Gorcock which had a Lion IV. All three aircraft carried the standard armament of twin synchronised 0.303-in (7,7-mm) Vickers guns and were used for research and development flying, no production being ordered. Although 158 lb (72 kg) heavier than the mixed-construction prototypes, the all-metal prototype, to which the following data refer, was 10 mph (16 km/h) faster. *Max speed, 174 mph (280 km/h) at 5,000 ft (1 525 m). Time to 15,000 ft (4 575 m), 10.5 min. Endurance, 1.8 hrs. Empty weight, 2,422 lb (1 099 kg). Loaded weight, 3,337 lb (1 514 kg). Span, 28 ft 6 in (8,69 m). Length, 26 ft 1 in (7,94 m). Height, 10 ft 2 in (3,10 m). Wing area, 250 sq ft (23,22 m²).*

The second of three Gorcocks (below) was of mixed construction and powered by a direct-drive Lion VIII.

GLOSTER GUAN   UK

The Guan single-seat high-altitude fighter was intended primarily to test the application of turbo-supercharged engines to fighters, and three prototypes were ordered at the beginning of 1925. Of mixed construction, with metal fuselage, wooden wings and fabric skinning, and provision for the standard twin synchronised 0.303-in (7,7-mm) Vickers gun armament, the Guan bore a close family resemblance to the Gorcock. The first prototype was completed in June 1926, having a geared 450 hp Napier Lion IV with an exhaust-driven turbo-supercharger below the propeller shaft. The second prototype followed early in 1927 with a direct-drive 525 hp Lion VI and turbo-supercharger mounted above the propeller shaft. Difficulties with the turbo-superchargers led to cancellation of the third prototype and abandonment of the development programme. The following data relate to the second Guan. *Max speed, 175 mph (282 km/h) at 15,000 ft (4 575 m). Time to 20,000 ft (6 100 m), 12.5 min. Empty weight, 2,972 lb (1 348 kg). Loaded weight, 3,803 lb (1 725 kg). Span, 31 ft 10 in (9,70 m). Length, 22 ft 0 in (6,70 m). Height, 10 ft 2 in (3,10 m). Wing area, 298 sq ft (27,68 m²).*

(Above and below) The second of the experimental Guans, flown with an exhaust-driven turbo-supercharger.

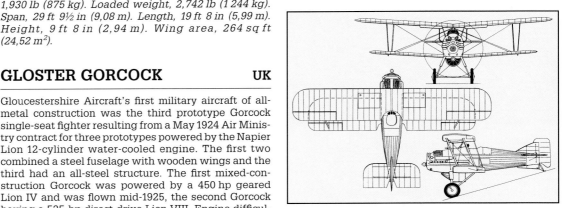

GLOSTER GOLDFINCH   UK

The second all-metal fighter designed by H P Folland, the Goldfinch was ordered in January 1926 as an all-metal version of the Gamecock, but, as initially completed, the prototype embodied a proportion of wood in its fuselage structure. After initial trials, the prototype was reworked, a lengthened, all-metal fuselage and re-

(Below) The Goldfinch in its definitive form.

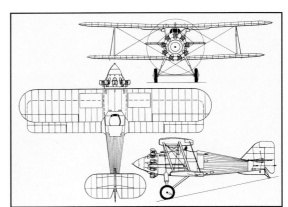

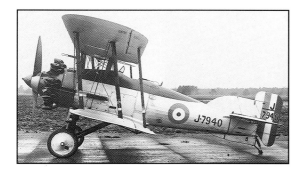

As first flown, the sole Goldfinch prototype (above) was of mixed wood and metal construction.

vised tail unit being applied. In its new form, the prototype Goldfinch was delivered to Martlesham Heath late 1927. Powered by a supercharged 450 hp Bristol Jupiter VIIF nine-cylinder radial, and having two 0.303-in (7,7-mm) Vickers Mk I synchronised machine guns, the Goldfinch offered an extremely good performance, but in competing for a production contract to Specification F.9/26 it was bested by the Bristol Bulldog. *Max speed, 172 mph (277 km/h) at 10,000 ft (3 050 m). Time to 20,000 ft (6 100 m), 16 min. Empty weight, 2,058 lb (933 kg). Loaded weight, 3,236 lb (1 468 kg). Span, 30 ft 3 in (9,14 m). Length, 22 ft 3 in (6,78 m). Height, 10 ft 6 in (3,20 m). Wing area, 274.3 sq ft (25,48 m²).*

GLOSTER GAMBET — UK

During 1926, in which year Gloucestershire Aircraft changed its name to Gloster Aircraft (on 11 November), the company was approached by the Japanese Nakajima concern, which (together with Aichi and Mitsubishi) had been asked to submit a design for a new shipboard fighter for the Imperial Japanese Navy. At this time, H P Folland was designing a shipboard fighter as a company venture. Named Gambet, the prototype was of wooden construction and powered by a 420 hp Bristol Jupiter VI nine-cylinder radial, armament consisting of two 0.303-in (7,7-mm) Vickers guns mounted in troughs in the fuselage sides. This prototype was acquired by Nakajima in July 1927, together with manufacturing rights. After modification by a team led by Takao Yoshida and installation of a 520 hp Nakajima-built Jupiter VI engine, the Gambet competed against prototypes of indigenous design and was ordered into production in April 1929 as the Navy Type 3 Carrier Fighter (A1N1). *Max speed, 152 mph (245 km/h) at 5,000 ft (1 525 m). Time to 10,000 ft*

The Gambet prototype (above and below) was built by Gloster to meet a requirement drawn up by the Imperial Japanese Navy in 1926.

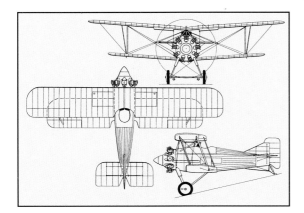

(3 050 m), 7.0 min. Endurance, 3.75 hrs. Empty weight, 2,010 lb (912 kg). Loaded weight, 3,075 lb (1 395 kg). Span, 31 ft 10 in (9,69 m). Length, 21 ft 3½ in (6,47 m). Height, 10 ft 8 in (3,24 m). Wing area, 284 sq ft (26,38 m²).

GLOSTER GNATSNAPPER — UK

As flown in 1928, the first Gnatsnapper (above) had a Jupiter VII engine and plain ailerons.

The Gnatsnapper was designed to the requirements of Specification N.21/26 calling for a single-seat shipboard fighter of all-metal construction and powered by a Bristol Mercury IIA nine-cylinder air-cooled radial. The first of two prototypes, temporarily powered by a Jupiter VII engine, flew in February 1928. The Mercury IIA was subsequently installed, but as this did not measure up to anticipated performance or reliability,

As the Mk II (above), the first Gnatsnapper had a Jaguar VIII in a revised forward fuselage.

the Jupiter VII was reinstated for official trials. The second prototype was not completed until March 1930, initially with a Mercury IIA, but the designated power plant was again discarded shortly thereafter. The first prototype was re-engined with a 540 hp Armstrong Siddeley Jaguar VIII 14-cylinder radial as the Gnatsnapper II, but suffered damage during official trials. In 1931, it was re-engined once more, with a steam-cooled 525 hp Rolls-Royce Kestrel IIS, as the Gnatsnapper III, subsequently serving as a Rolls-Royce test-bed and hack aircraft. The following data relate to the Jupiter-engined model. *Max speed, 165 mph (265 km/h) at 10,000 ft (3 050 m). Time to 15,000 ft (4 575 m), 12.2 min. Endurance, 5 hrs. Empty weight, 2,970 lb (1 347 kg). Loaded weight, 3,625 lb (1 644 kg). Span, 33 ft 6 in (10,21 m). Length, 24 ft 7 in (7,48 m). Height, 10 ft 11 in (3,32 m). Wing area, 360 sq ft (33,44 m²).*

GLOSTER GAUNTLET — UK

Competing against the Boulton Paul Partridge, the Armstrong Whitworth A.W.16 Starling II and the Hawker Hawfinch to meet the requirements of Specification F.20/27 for a single-seat fighter built principally of steel or duralumin, the Gauntlet began life as the

(Immediately below) Gauntlet II of No 17 Sqn, RAF Kenley, late 1938, with "post-Munich" codes. (Bottom) Gauntlet II as a trainer with T/LeLv 35 in 1942.

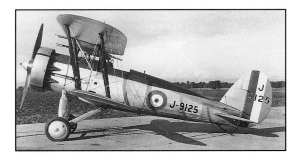

(Above) With six guns and a cowled Jupiter VIIF engine, S.S.19 became prototype of the Gauntlet.

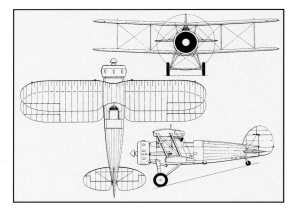

General arrangement (above) of the Gauntlet II for the RAF and export, and (below), an example of the latter on skis in Finnish service in 1940.

SS.18. It was designed to the contemporary F.10/27 specification and flew as such in January 1929, initially with a Mercury IIA engine. This power plant was subsequently replaced by a 480 hp Jupiter VIIF (as the SS.18A) and then by a 560 hp Panther III (SS.18B), the Jupiter later being reinstated (as the SS.19). In its last-mentioned form, it was tested with four wing-mounted 0.303-in (7,7-mm) Lewis guns and two fuselage-mounted Vickers guns of the same calibre. The wing-mounted guns were later removed (as the SS.19A), and with the 536 hp Mercury VIS engine (as the SS.19B), this was ordered into production in February 1934 with a twin Vickers Mk V-gun armament and a 640 hp Mercury VIS2 as the Gauntlet. The first production aircraft was completed in the following December. Twenty-four Gauntlet Is built by the parent company were followed by 204 Gauntlet IIs with revised (Hawker-type) structure. Seventeen were licence-built in Denmark by the Army Aviation Troops' Workshops (after procurement of one pattern aircraft), and ex-RAF Gauntlet IIs disposed of abroad comprised three to Rhodesia, four to South Africa and 25 to Finland. Six were later assigned to the RAAF in the Middle East. The following data relate to the Gauntlet II. *Max speed, 230 mph (370 km/h) at 15,800 ft (4 815 m). Time to 20,000 ft (6 100 m), 9 min. Empty weight, 2,770 lb (1 256 kg). Loaded weight, 3,970 lb (1 801 kg). Span, 32 ft 10 in (9,99 m). Length, 26 ft 5 in (8,00 m). Height, 10 ft 3 in (3,10 m). Wing area, 315 sq ft (29,26 m²).*

GLOSTER GLADIATOR   UK

A private venture to Specification F.7/30, the Gladiator was a derivative of the Gauntlet and flew in prototype form (as the SS.37) on 12 September 1934 with a 530 hp Mercury IV engine. Series production to Specification

Key to Gloster Gladiator I

1 Rear navigation light
2 Rudder
3 Rudder balance
4 Aerial mast
5 Tailfin
6 Tailplane bracing wires
7 Rudder post
8 Rudder hinge cables
9 Starboard elevator
10 Tailplane tubular spar
11 Tailplane adjustment screw jack
12 Sternpost
13 Tailwheel
14 Elevator control cable
15 Rudder control cable
16 Fuselage decking
17 Fuselage cross-bracing
18 Light-metal fuselage formers and stringers
19 Tubular fuselage framework (longerons and struts)
20 Formation light
21 Dorsal fairing
22 Aerials
23 Rear cockpit glazing
24 Canopy track
25 Radio (R/T) compartment
26 Compressed air bottle (brakes)
27 High-pressure oxygen cylinder
28 Oxygen regulating valve
29 Pilot's seat
30 Sutton harness
31 Hinged cockpit flap
32 Turn-over crash-bar
33 Rear-sliding cockpit canopy (Plastilume-moulded Perspex)
34 Wireless tuning control
35 Padded compass
36 Strengthened windshield frame
37 Gun button on control yoke
38 Control column
39 Centre strut
40 Fuselage fuel tank, capacity 84 Imp gal (382 l)
41 Forward fuselage framework (square-section)
42 Centre strut
43 Forward bead sight
44 Oil cooler "mat"
45 Aft ring sight
46 Port centre-section struts
47 Handhold
48 Port upper split flap (hydraulic hand-pump operation: shown lowered)
49 Port aileron
50 High tensile steel strip rear spar ("Dumb-bell" cross-section)
51 Wingtip skinning
52 Port navigation light
53 Steel and duralumin strip drag rib wing construction
54 High-tensile steel strip forward spar ("Dumb-bell" cross-section)
55 Duralumin strip drag rib leading-edge stiffeners
56 Pitot head
57 Port forward interplane strut
58 Port lower mainplane
59 Cross-bracing separator
60 Rigging fine-adjustment turnbuckle
61 Oil tank
62 Electric generator
63 Fireproof engine bulkhead
64 Engine bearers
65 Engine mounting frame
66 Bristol Mercury IX engine
67 Cowling
68 Townend exhaust collector ring
69 Two-blade propeller
70 Propeller spinner
71 Engine exhaust ports
72 Carburettor air intake
73 Port mainwheel
74 Brake cable
75 Dowty internally-sprung mainwheel
76 Wheel covering
77 Mainwheel leg fairing
78 Double-tapered cantilevered mainwheel strut
79 Exhaust pipe
80 Mainwheel strut/fuselage attachment point
81 Oil cooler/cockpit heater
82 Gun trough
83 Starboard fuselage Browning 0.303-in (7,7-mm) machine gun
84 Ammunition box (500 rpg)
85 Cartridge collector case
86 Fuselage/lower forward spar attachment point
87 Rigging turnbuckles
88 Ammunition box access door
89 Starboard front interplane strut
90 Corrugated rubber step
91 High-tensile steel strip rear spar ("Dumb-bell" cross-section)
92 Starboard underwing Browning 0.303-in (7,7-mm) machine gun
93 Gun muzzle
94 Underwing gun fairing
95 High-tensile steel strip forward spar ("Dumb-bell" cross-section)
96 Lower mainplane steel/duralumin construction
97 Starboard lower split flap (shown lowered)
98 Interplane strut cross-bracing
99 Starboard rear interplane strut
100 Aileron control cables

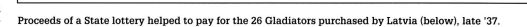

Proceeds of a State lottery helped to pay for the 26 Gladiators purchased by Latvia (below), late '37.

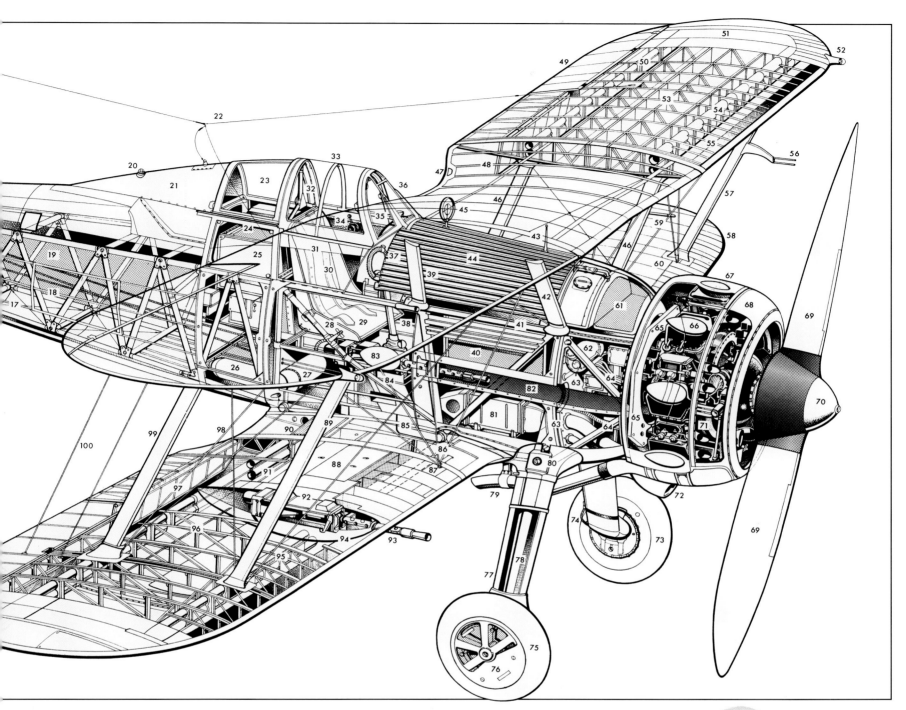

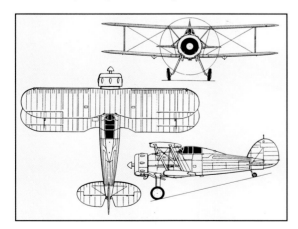

Gladiator II (below) in standard production form.

(Above, top) One of the four Sea Gladiators used to equip the RAF's Malta Fighter Flight in April 1940. (Immediately above) Gladiator I of Belgian 1e *Escadrille "La Comete"* at Diest Schaffen, 1940.

F.14/35 was initiated in the summer of 1935, and the first Gladiator Is were flown in January 1937. The Gladiator I was powered by an 830 hp Mercury IX engine and (eventually) standardised on an armament of two fuselage-mounted and two wing-mounted 0.303-in (7,7-mm) Browning guns. A total of 378 was built, followed by 270 Gladiator IIs with the similarly-rated Mercury VIIIA or VIIIAS, plus 38 completed as Sea Gladiator (Interim) shipboard fighters and a further 60 built from the outset as Sea Gladiators. Production included 26

Mk Is for Latvia, 14 Mk Is for Lithuania, six Mk Is and six Mk IIs for Norway, 37 Mk Is and 18 Mk IIs for Sweden, 22 Mk IIs for Belgium, 36 Mk Is for China, four Mk Is for Eire, two Mk Is for Greece and 15 Mk IIs for Portugal. Ex-RAF aircraft transferred to other air arms comprised 30 Mk

IIs for Finland, 17 Mk IIs for Greece, 45 Mk Is (brought up to Mk II standard) and Mk IIs for Egypt, 14 Mk Is and Mk IIs for Iraq, and one Mk I and 11 Mk IIs for South Africa. The following data relate to the Mk II. *Max speed, 257 mph (414 km/h) at 14,600 ft (4 450 m). Time*

A preserved Swedish Gladiator (above) as flown by a volunteer force operating in Finland in 1940.

to 10,000 ft (3 050 m), 4.5 min. Range, 444 mls (714 km). Empty weight, 3,444 lb (1 562 kg). Loaded weight, 4,864 lb (2 206 kg). Span, 32 ft 3 in (9,83 m). Length, 27 ft 5 in (8,36 m). Height, 10 ft 7 in (3,22 m). Wing area, 323 sq ft (30,00 m²).

GLOSTER F.5/34   UK

The last of the Gloster fighter designs created by H P Folland, the single-seat all-metal cantilever monoplane evolved to Specification F.5/34 (which ultimately produced the Hurricane and the Spitfire) was powered by an 840 hp Mercury IX nine-cylinder radial engine and carried an armament of eight 0.303-in (7,7-mm) Browning guns. This aircraft, to which no designation was assigned other than that of the specification that it was intended to meet, suffered somewhat protracted development owing to the company's preoccupation with the Gladiator. The first of two prototypes did not commence flight trials until December 1937, with the second following in March 1938. By the time that the Gloster fighter made its début, the Hurricane had entered service and the Spitfire had reached production, and further development of the Mercury-engined monoplane was not pursued. *Max speed, 316 mph (508 km/h) at 16,000 ft (4 875 m). Time to 20,000 ft (6 100 m), 11 min. Empty weight, 4,190 lb (1 900 kg). Loaded weight, 5,400 lb (2 449 kg). Span, 38 ft 2 in (11,63 m). Length, 32 ft 0 in (9,76 m). Height, 10 ft 2 in (3,09 m). Wing area, 230 sq ft (21,36 m²).*

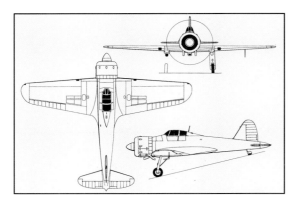

(Above) A general arrangement drawing of the F.5/34, the first of the two prototypes of which is seen (below) during flight testing in 1938.

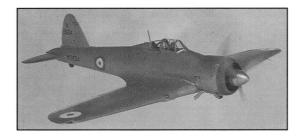

GLOSTER F.9/37   UK

Designed by W G Carter to meet the demands of Specification F.9/37 calling for a twin-engined single-seater, this Gloster fighter was of all-metal stressed skin construction. It was intended to carry a fuselage-mounted armament of two 20-mm Hispano cannon and four 0.303-in (7,7-mm) Browning machine guns. Two prototypes were ordered, the first of these, powered by two

Key to Gloster Meteor F Mk III

1 Starboard detachable wingtip
2 Starboard navigation light
3 Starboard recognition light
4 Starboard aileron
5 Aileron balance tab
6 Aileron mass balance weights
7 Aileron control coupling
8 Aileron torque shaft
9 Chain sprocket
10 Cross-over control runs
11 Front spar
12 Rear spar
13 Aileron (inboard) mass balance
14 Nacelle detachable tail section
15 Jet pipe exhaust
16 Internal stabilising struts
17 Rear spar "spectacle" frame
18 Fire extinguisher spray ring
19 Main engine mounting frame
20 Engine access panel(s)
21 Nacelle nose structure
22 Intake internal leading-edge shroud
23 Starboard engine intake
24 Windscreen de-icing spray pipe
25 Reflector gunsight
26 Cellular glass bullet-proof windscreen
27 Aft-sliding cockpit canopy
28 Demolition incendiary (cockpit starboard wall)
29 RPM indicators (left and right of gunsight)
30 Pilot's seat
31 Forward fuselage top deflector skin
32 Gun wobble button
33 Control column grip
34 Main instrument panel
35 Nosewheel armoured bulkhead
36 Nose release catches (10)
37 Nosewheel jack bulkhead housing/attachment
38 Nose ballast weight location
39 Nosewheel mounting frames
40 Radius rod (link and jack omitted)
41 Nosewheel pivot bearings
42 Shimmy-damper/self-centering strut
43 Gun camera
44 Camera access
45 Aperture
46 Nose cone
47 Cabin cold-air intake
48 Nosewheel leg door
49 Picketing rings
50 Tension shock absorber
51 Pivot bracket
52 Mudguard
53 Torque strut
54 Door hoop
55 Wheel fork
56 Retractable nosewheel
57 Nosewheel doors
58 Port cannon trough fairings
59 Nosewheel cover
60 Intermediate diaphragm
61 Blast tubes
62 Gun front mounting rails
63 Pilot's seat pan
64 Emergency crowbar
65 Canopy de-misting silica gel cylinder
66 Bullet-proof glass rear-view cut-outs
67 Canopy track
68 Seat bulkhead
69 Entry step
70 Link ejection chutes
71 Case ejection chutes
72 20-mm Hispano Mk III cannon
73 Belt fed mechanism
74 Ammunition feed necks
75 Ammunition tanks
76 Aft glazing (magazine bay top door)
77 Loading ramp
78 Front spar bulkhead
79 Oxygen bottles (2)
80 Front spar carry-through
81 Tank bearer frames
82 Rear spar carry-through
83 Self-sealing (twin compartment) main fuel tank, capacity 165 Imp gall (750l) in each half
84 Fuel connector pipe
85 Return pipe
86 Drain pipes
87 Fuel filler caps
88 Tank doors (2)
89 T.R. 1143 aerial mast
90 Rear spar bulkhead (plywood face)
91 Aerial support frame
92 R.3121 (or B.C. 966A) IFF installation
93 Tab control cables
94 Amplifier
95 Fire extinguisher bottles (2)
96 Elevator torque shaft
97 T.R. 1143 transmitter/receiver radio installation
98 Pneumatic system filter
99 Pneumatic system (compressed) air cylinders
100 Tab cable fairlead
101 Elevator control cable
102 Top longeron
103 Fuselage frame
104 IFF aerial
105 DR compass master unit
106 Rudder cables
107 Starboard lower longeron
108 Cable access panels (port and starboard)
109 Tail section joint
110 Rudder linkage
111 Tail ballast weight location
112 Fin spar/fuselage frame
113 Rudder tab control
114 Fin structure
115 Torpedo fairing
116 Tailplane spar/upper fin attachment plates
117 Upper fin section
118 Starboard tailplane
119 Elevator horn and mass balance
120 Starboard elevator
121 Rudder horn and mass balance
122 Rudder upper hinge
123 Rudder frame
124 Fixed tab
125 Rear fairing
126 Tail navigation light
127 Elevator torque shaft
128 Elevator trim tab
129 Elevator frame
130 Elevator horn and mass balance
131 Tailplane structure
132 Rudder combined balance/trim tab
133 Rudder lower section
134 Elevator push-rod linkage
135 Rudder internal lower mass balance weight
136 Emergency landing tailskid
137 Tail section riveted joint
138 Port lower longeron
139 Fuselage stressed skin
140 Wingroot fairing
141 Inboard split flap
142 Airbrake (upper and lower surfaces)
143 Flap indicator transmitter
144 Rear spar
145 Inter-coupler cables (airbrake/airbrake and flap/flap)
146 Port mainwheel well
147 Root rib station
148 Front diaphragm
149 Undercarriage beam
150 Undercarriage retraction jack
151 Undercarriage sidestay/downlock
152 Front spar
153 Nose ribs

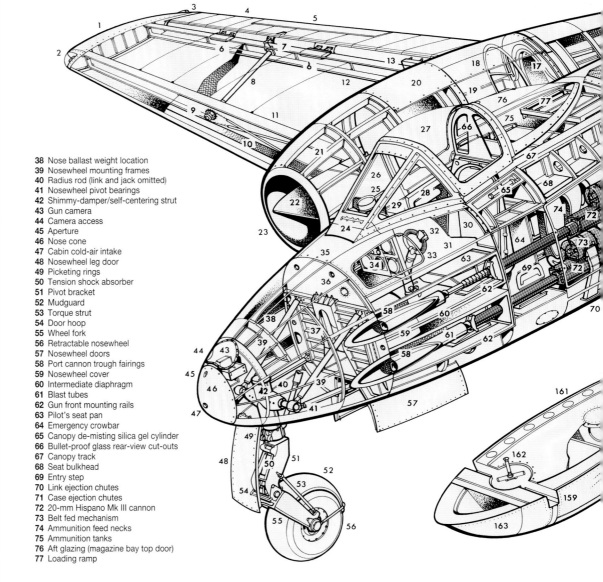

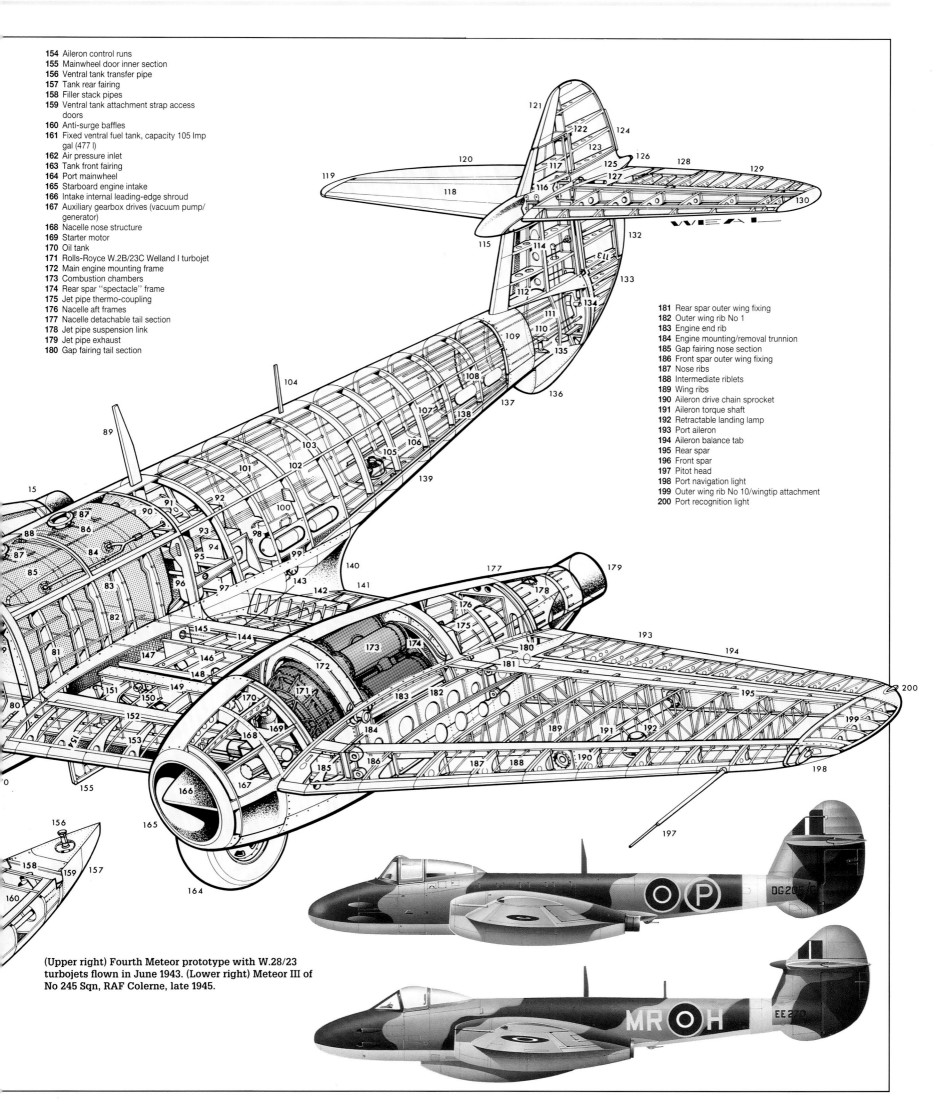

154 Aileron control runs
155 Mainwheel door inner section
156 Ventral tank transfer pipe
157 Tank rear fairing
158 Filler stack pipes
159 Ventral tank attachment strap access doors
160 Anti-surge baffles
161 Fixed ventral fuel tank, capacity 105 Imp gal (477 l)
162 Air pressure inlet
163 Tank front fairing
164 Port mainwheel
165 Starboard engine intake
166 Intake internal leading-edge shroud
167 Auxiliary gearbox drives (vacuum pump/generator)
168 Nacelle nose structure
169 Starter motor
170 Oil tank
171 Rolls-Royce W.2B/23C Welland I turbojet
172 Main engine mounting frame
173 Combustion chambers
174 Rear spar "spectacle" frame
175 Jet pipe thermo-coupling
176 Nacelle aft frames
177 Nacelle detachable tail section
178 Jet pipe suspension link
179 Jet pipe exhaust
180 Gap fairing tail section

181 Rear spar outer wing fixing
182 Outer wing rib No 1
183 Engine end rib
184 Engine mounting/removal trunnion
185 Gap fairing nose section
186 Front spar outer wing fixing
187 Nose ribs
188 Intermediate riblets
189 Wing ribs
190 Aileron drive chain sprocket
191 Aileron torque shaft
192 Retractable landing lamp
193 Port aileron
194 Aileron balance tab
195 Rear spar
196 Front spar
197 Pitot head
198 Port navigation light
199 Outer wing rib No 10/wingtip attachment
200 Port recognition light

(Upper right) Fourth Meteor prototype with W.28/23 turbojets flown in June 1943. (Lower right) Meteor III of No 245 Sqn, RAF Colerne, late 1945.

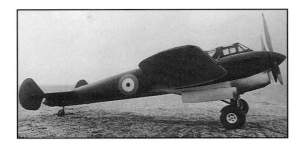

Rolls-Royce Peregrine liquid-cooled engines distinguished the second prototype F.9/37 (above).

1,050 hp Bristol Taurus T-S(a) 14-cylinder radials, being flown on 3 April 1939. The aircraft attained a maximum speed of 360 mph (579 km/h) at 15,000 ft (4 575 m), but was badly damaged in a landing accident early in its flight test programme. When testing was resumed in April 1940, it had been re-engined with 900 hp Taurus T-S(a) IIIs with the result that performance suffered, maximum attainable speed in level flight being reduced to 332 mph (534 km/h) at 15,200 ft (4 630 m). The second prototype, meanwhile, had been completed with 885 hp Rolls-Royce Peregrine liquid-cooled engines, flying for the first time on 22 February 1940, and attaining a maximum speed of 330 mph (531 km/h) during subsequent flight testing. Although the handling characteristics of Gloster's F.9/37 contender were considered highly satisfactory and performance with the original engines had proved spectacular, no production was ordered. The following data relate to the Taurus T-S(a)-powered prototype. *Max speed, 360 mph (579 km/h) at 15,000 ft (4 575 m). Climb, 2,460 ft/min (12,5 m/sec) at 12,000 ft (3 660 m). Empty weight, 8,828 lb (4 004 kg). Loaded weight, 11,615 lb (5 269 kg). Span, 50 ft 0½ in (15,24 m). Length, 37 ft 0½ in (11,27 m). Height, 11 ft 7 in (3,53 m). Wing area, 386 sq ft (35,85 m²).*

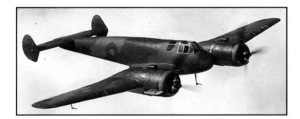

The first of two Gloster F.9/37 single-seat twin-engined fighters (above and below) emerged in 1939 with Bristol Taurus air-cooled radials.

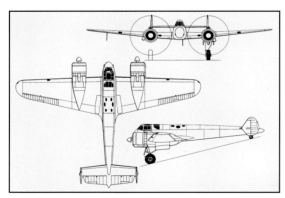

GLOSTER METEOR F Mᴋ I & F Mᴋ III   UK

Developed in accordance with the requirements of Specification F.9/40 as Britain's first jet-powered fighter, the first prototype Meteor to fly (actually the fifth prototype airframe) took to the air on 5 March 1943. It was powered by de Havilland H.1 turbojets rather than the Whittle W.2Bs intended, the first airframe flying with Rover-built W.2B/23 engines on 24 July 1943. These were two of a total of eight prototypes. A pre-series of 20 aircraft powered by Rolls-Royce Welland (W.2B/23C) turbojets of 1,700 lb (771 kg) thrust were delivered as Meteor Is, the first of these flying on 12 January 1944. One RAF squadron was fully equipped

The first series Meteor I in the US (above) after exchange for a Bell XP-59. (Below) The Meteor III.

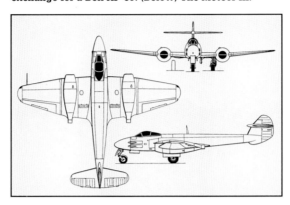

with this type by the end of the following August. The Meteor II was a proposed version with de Havilland H.1 Goblin engines which was not proceeded with, and the Meteor III was the first major production model. This had a strengthened airframe, increased internal fuel capacity and a sliding instead of hinged cockpit canopy. The Meteor III was intended to have 2,000 lb st (907 kgp) Rolls-Royce W.2B/37 Derwent I engines, but the first 15 of 210 of this version built retained the Wellands, the first of these flying in September 1944. The Meteor III had empty and loaded weights of 10,519 lb (4 771 kg) and 13,920 lb (6 314 kg), but performance and dimensions were similar to those of the Meteor I to which the following data refer. Both marks carried an armament of four 20-mm British Hispano cannon. *Max speed, 385 mph (619 km/h) at sea level, 415 mph (668 km/h) at 10,000 ft (3 050 m). Initial climb, 2,155 ft/min (10,9 m/sec). Empty weight, 8,140 lb (3 692 kg). Loaded weight, 13,795 lb (6 258 kg). Span, 43 ft 0 in (13,10 m). Length, 41 ft 3 in (12,57 m). Height, 13 ft 0 in (3,96 m). Wing area, 374 sq ft (34,74 m²).*

(Below) Short nacelles for the Welland turbojets were retained by the first 15 Meteor IIIs.

GLOSTER METEOR F Mᴋ 4   UK

On 17 May 1945, a Meteor III flew with enlarged engine nacelles housing 3,000 lb st (1 361 kgp) Rolls-Royce Derwent 5 turbojets, to serve as a prototype for the extensively modified Meteor F Mk 4. This featured further airframe strengthening and a pressurised cockpit, the wing area later being reduced six per cent by clipping the wingtips. Fully rated Derwent 5 engines of 3,500 lb st (1 588 kgp) were standardised for the series production model, which carried the standard armament of four 20-mm British Hispano cannon. A total of 535 was built for the RAF (including 46 by Armstrong Whitworth), export deliveries comprising 100 for Argentina, 38 for the Netherlands, 12 for Egypt, 48 for Belgium and 20 for Denmark. The Netherlands subsequently purchased 27 ex-RAF F Mk 4s, and two were supplied to France for development work. Deliveries were completed in 1950. One example of a fighter reconnaissance version, the Meteor FR Mk 5, was flown on 15 June 1949, but crashed during this first flight. *Max speed, 580 mph (933 km/h) at 10,000 ft (3 050 m). Initial climb, 7,500 ft/min (38,1 m/sec). Range (internal fuel),*

(Above) Meteor F Mk 4 of 323 Sqn, KLu, based at Leeuwarden, in Nato Operation "Foil", 1949.

(Below) Uprated Derwent engines in long nacelles gave the Meteor F Mk 4 improved performance.

The Meteor F Mk 4 (above) flew with five air forces as well as the RAF, which used over 500 of this mark.

610 mls (982 km) at 30,000 ft (9 150 m). Empty weight, 11,217 lb (5 088 kg). Loaded weight, 14,545 lb (6 598 kg). Span, 37 ft 2 in (11,32 m). Length, 41 ft 0 in (12,50 m). Height, 13 ft 0 in (3,96 m). Wing area, 350 sq ft (32,51 m²).

GLOSTER METEOR F MK 8   UK

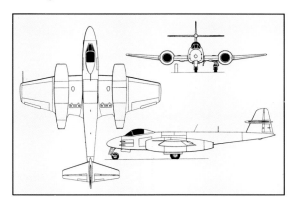

(Above) A Meteor F Mk 8 of No 1 Sqn, with a target-towing lug on the belly tank and (below) a three-view drawing of the Meteor F Mk 8.

Development of an improved Meteor, the F Mk 8, began in 1947, and the first prototype (a modified F Mk 4) flew on 12 October 1948. The F Mk 8 introduced Derwent 8 engines, which had the same 3,500 lb st (1 588 kgp) rating as the Derwent 5s that they succeeded, a 30-in (76-cm) increase in fuselage length, entirely new tail surfaces, an ejection seat, new cockpit canopy and some structural strengthening. Deliveries to the RAF commenced at the end of 1949, and a total of 1,183 was built for the service and for export. Export deliveries comprised 12 ex-RAF aircraft to Egypt, 23 ex-RAF aircraft to Belgium, 20 aircraft to Denmark, 12 aircraft (plus seven ex-RAF) to Syria, five ex-RAF to the Netherlands, 60 aircraft to Brazil and 11 aircraft to Israel. The RAAF received 93 ex-RAF Meteor F Mk 8s to operate in Korea in 1951-3, losing 52 aircraft during hostilities and taking 41 back to Australia at their end. Fokker licence-built 155 for the Dutch and 150 for the Belgian air forces, and Avions Fairey assembled a further 30 from components supplied by Fokker and 37 from sets supplied by the parent company. Fighter-reconnaissance and pure re-

(Below) No 85 Sqn markings distinguish this Meteor F Mk 8 display aircraft from RAF Binbrook in 1969.

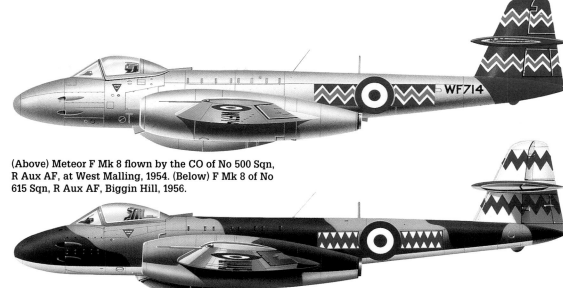

(Above) Meteor F Mk 8 flown by the CO of No 500 Sqn, R Aux AF, at West Malling, 1954. (Below) F Mk 8 of No 615 Sqn, R Aux AF, Biggin Hill, 1956.

connaissance versions were evolved as the FR Mk 9 and PR Mk 10. One hundred and twenty-six of the former were built for the RAF, of which 12 were subsequently supplied to Ecuador, seven to Israel and two to Syria, and the RAF also received 59 of the latter. *Max speed, 598 mph (962 km/h) at 10,000 ft (3 050 m). Range, 600 mls (965 km). Initial climb, 7,000 ft/min (35,6 m/sec). Empty weight, 10,684 lb (4 846 kg). Loaded weight, 15,700 lb (7 122 kg). Span, 37 ft 2 in (11,32 m). Length, 44 ft 7 in (13,59 m). Height, 13 ft 0 in (3,96 m). Wing area, 350 sq ft (32,51 m²).*

GLOSTER E.1/44   UK

Late in 1944, Gloster began construction of an all-metal single-seat fighter designed around the RB.41 centrifugal-flow turbojet being developed by Rolls-Royce and to emerge as the Nene. To the requirements of Specification E.1/44, the first prototype was completed in

The third E.1/44 (above) had the definitive high tailplane to improve handling whereas the second illustrated by the drawing (below) had a low tail.

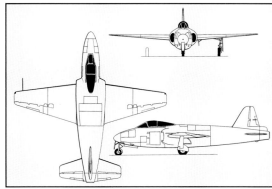

July 1947, but suffered irreparable damage when the vehicle transporting it to the A&AEE was involved in an accident. A second prototype was completed and flown on 9 March 1948, this being powered by a 5,000 lb st (2 268 kgp) Nene 2 turbojet and having provision for four 20-mm Hispano cannon. After initial flight testing the tail assembly was redesigned to improve handling. A third prototype was flown in 1949, and a fourth was nearing completion when it was decided that the single-engined fighter lacked the development potential of the twin-engined Meteor, further work being discontinued. *Max speed, 620 mph (998 km/h) at sea level. Endurance, 1 hr. Time to 40,000 ft (12 200 m), 12.5 min. Empty weight, 8,260 lb (3 747 kg). Loaded weight, 11,470 lb (5 203 kg). Span, 36 ft 0 in (10,97 m). Length, 38 ft 0 in (11,58 m). Height, 11 ft 8 in (3,55 m). Wing area, 254 sq ft (23,60 m²).*

GLOSTER JAVELIN   UK

Designed to meet the requirements of Specification F.4/48 for a two-seat twin-engined all-weather interceptor fighter, the Javelin was of tailed-delta configuration and the first of seven prototypes was flown on 26 November 1951. The initial production model, the Javelin F(AW) Mk 1, flown on 22 July 1954, was powered by two 8,000 lb st (3 629 kgp) Armstrong Siddeley Sapphire ASSa 6 turbojets and carried an armament of four 30-mm Aden cannon. Forty F(AW) Mk 1s for the RAF were followed by 30 F(AW) Mk 2s which differed essentially in having American (APQ 43) in place of British (AI 17) radar, the first example of this version flying on 31 October 1955. The next fighter version (paralleling production of 22 T Mk 3 trainers) was

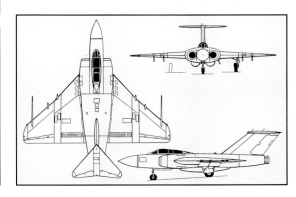

The Javelin F(AW) Mk 4 – that illustrated above being from No 11 Sqn at RAF Geilenkirchen – lacked the afterburners and missiles of the F(AW) Mk 9 (below).

(Above) A Firestreak-armed Javelin F(AW) Mk 9 of No 64 Sqn at Tengah, Singapore, from 1965 to 1967.

No 23 Sqn was second in the RAF to fly the F(AW) Mk 9 version of the Javelin (below) commencing 1960.

the F(AW) Mk 4. This, flown on 19 September 1955, differed in having a fully-powered all-moving tailplane, 50 being built. The F(AW) Mk 5 was similar apart from carrying additional fuel in the wings and having provision for four de Havilland Firestreak AAMs. Sixty-four were built, together with 33 F(AW) Mk 6s which, like the F(AW) Mk 2s, were equipped with US radar. The F(AW) Mk 7 introduced 11,000 lb st (4 990 kgp) Sapphire ASSa 7 engines, a modified flying control system, an extended rear fuselage with raised topline and other changes. Armament comprised two 30-mm Aden cannon and four Firestreak AAMs, and 142 were built. The final production version of the Javelin was the F(AW) Mk 8 with Sapphire ASSa 7R engines with limited afterburning boosting output to 12,300 lb st (5 579 kgp) above 20,000 ft (6 100 m), and US radar. Forty-seven were built during 1957-59, and 76 of the earlier F(AW) Mk 7s were brought up to similar standard as F(AW) Mk 9s during 1960-61. The Javelin was finally withdrawn from RAF service in 1967. The following data relate to the definitive F(AW) Mk 8. *Max speed, 701 mph (1 128 km/h) at sea level, 614 mph (988 km/h) at 35,000 ft (10 670 m). Time to 50,000 ft (15 250 m), 9.25 min. Loaded weight, 37,410 lb (16 969 kg). Span, 52 ft 0 in (15,85 m). Length, 56 ft 3 in (17,14 m). Height, 16 ft 0 in (4,88 m). Wing area, 927 sq ft (86,12 m²).*

GOODYEAR F2G   USA

Essentially a higher-powered, low-altitude interceptor derivative of the Vought F4U Corsair, which was being built by the Goodyear Aircraft Corporation as the FG-1, the F2G embodied extensive redesign. This took maximum advantage of the 50 per cent increase in take-off power offered by a 28-cylinder Pratt & Whitney R-4360-4 Wasp Major single-stage engine rated at 3,000 hp. Two FG-1 airframes were rebuilt as XF2G-1s, the first of these flying in May 1944, prior to which, in March 1944, Goodyear had been awarded contracts for 418 shore-based F2G-1s and 10 shipboard F2G-2s. An all-round vision "bubble"-type cockpit canopy was adopted, the tail surfaces were enlarged, internal fuel capacity was increased and provision was made for either four or six wing-mounted 0.5-in (12,7-mm) guns.

One of eight Goodyear XF2G-1s (below) that were modified from FG-1 versions of the Corsair.

A total of eight prototypes was completed, but as a result of the contractual cut-backs accompanying the end of hostilities in the Pacific, only five F2G-1s and five F2G-2s were delivered. The following data relate to the F2G-2. *Max speed, 399 mph (642 km/h) at sea level, 431 mph (694 km/h) at 16,405 ft (5 000 m). Initial climb, 4,400 ft/min (22,35 m/sec). Range (internal fuel), 1,190 mls (1 915 km). Empty weight, 10,249 lb (4 649 kg). Loaded weight (normal), 13,346 lb (6 054 kg). Span, 41 ft 0 in (12,50 m). Length, 33 ft 9 in (10,29 m). Height, 16 ft 1 in (4,90 m). Wing area, 314 sq ft (29,17 m²).*

(Above and below) The Goodyear F2G-2 was a fully-equipped shipboard derivative of the F2G-1, which was itself evolved from the F4U Corsair.

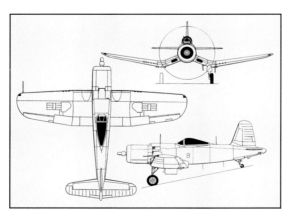

GORBUNOV 105   USSR

Early operational use of the LaGG-3 single-seat fighter revealed it to be overweight and a difficult aircraft to fly for any but experienced pilots. One of the three principal members of the design team responsible for creating that fighter, Vladimir P Gorbunov, was assigned the task of redesigning the aircraft to overcome its major shortcomings, this being referred to both as the *samolet* (aircraft) 105 and as the LaGG-3 *oblegchennyi* (lightened). The Klimov M-105PF-1 12-cylinder liquid-cooled engine rated at 1,260 hp at 2,625 ft (800 m) was retained, but the rear fuselage was cut down aft of the cabin. The leading-edge wing slats and aileron mass balances were removed, and armament was revised.

This comprised a lightweight hub-mounted B-20 (MP-20) 20-mm cannon and a single 12,7-mm UB machine gun. By comparison with the LaGG-3, empty equipped weight was reduced by 660 lb (300 kg). Flight trials with the *samolet* 105 were undertaken in 1942, but development had by then been overtaken by that of the La-5 and only prototypes were completed. *Max speed, 354 mph (570 km/h) at sea level, 387 mph (623 km/h) at 13,125 ft (4 000 m). Time to 16,405 ft (5 000 m), 6.0 min. Loaded weight, 6,316 lb (2 865 kg). Span, 32 ft 1⅞ in (9,80 m). Length, 28 ft 11 in (8,81 m). Height, 14 ft 5¼ in (4,40 m). Wing area, 188.37 sq ft (17,50 m²).*

(Below) The Gorbunov 105 derivative of the LaGG-3.

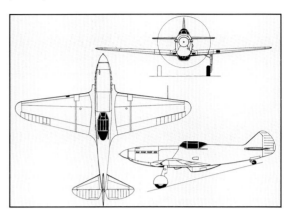

GOTHA Go 229   Germany

The Gothaer Waggonfabrik was responsible for the productionisation of the Horten H IX fighter which was assigned the official designation 8-229. Most sources have referred erroneously to the series version of the H IX (which see) as the Gotha Go 229, whereas, had this fighter attained series production, it would have been designated Horten Ho 229.

GOURDOU-LESEURRE GL-1 (Type A)   France

The first aircraft to be designed by Charles E P Gourdou and Jean A Leseurre, the GL-1 (also known as the Type A) was a single-seat parasol monoplane fighter powered by a 180 hp Hispano-Suiza 8Ab eight-cylinder water-cooled engine. Of mixed construction, with an all-metal fuselage primarily of steel tube with plywood covering and a fabric-covered wing with steel spars and wooden ribs, the GL-1 was officially evaluated at Villacoublay on 10 May 1918. Structurally overweight, the prototype was tested with one of its two 7,7-mm Vickers guns removed and with reduced fuel. It demonstrated in this configuration level speeds higher than contempory fighters powered by a 300 hp Hispano-Suiza engine. Although the design team believed that the structural weight problem could be resolved, offi-

(Above and below) Progenitor of a long line of fighting monoplanes, the GL-1 was the first aircraft designed by MM Gourdou and Leseurre.

cial testing indicated that the wing had insufficient strength, and redesign was therefore undertaken to result in the GL-2 alias Type B. *Max speed, 150 mph (242 km/h) at 3,280 ft (1 000 m). Time to 3,280 ft (1 000 m), 2.41 min. Endurance, 1.5 hrs. Empty weight, 1,323 lb (600 kg). Loaded weight, 1,733 lb (786 kg). Span, 29 ft 6⅓ in (9,00 m). Length, 21 ft 7⅘ in (6,60 m). Height, 7 ft 6½ in (2,30 m). Wing area, 179.22 sq ft (16,65 m²).*

GOURDOU-LESEURRE GL-2 (Type B) France

By comparison with its progenitor, the GL-1, the GL-2 (Type B) had an entirely new and heavily reinforced wing, new horizontal tail surfaces mounted higher on the rear fuselage, and revised rudder and undercarriage. The 180 hp Hispano-Suiza 8Ab engine was retained and armament comprised two synchronised 7,7-mm Vickers guns. The number of pairs of inclined wing bracing struts was increased from two to four, one pair attaching to the wing at half-span and another at three-quarter-span, the cantilevered portion thus being only one-quarter of the half-span. This resulted in an extremely rigid structure, the wing load factor being 10.4 compared with 3.5 for the GL-1. Twenty GL-2s were ordered for the *Aéronautique Militaire* and built by Mayen et Zodiac. The first was delivered to Villacoublay in late November 1918. Subsequent aircraft were fitted with a taller rudder and enlarged fin to rectify a directional control deficiency, but with the termination of hostilities, *Aéronautique Militaire* interest in the GL-2 waned and development was cancelled. *Max speed, 152 mph (245 km/h) at sea level. Time to 16,405 ft (5 000 m), 17.5 min. Empty weight, 1,257 lb (570 kg). Loaded weight, 1,874 lb (850 kg). Span, 30 ft 10 in (9,40 m). Length, 21 ft 1⅛ in (6,43 m). Wing area, 202.37 sq ft (18,80 m²).*

First of the Gourdou-Leseurre fighters to enter production, the GL-2 (above and below) was just too late to serve in World War I.

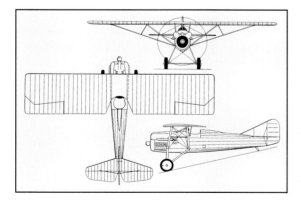

GOURDOU-LESEURRE GL-21 (Type B2) France

With the end of World War I, Charles Gourdou and Jean Leseurre established their own company at St Maur les Fossés, continuing development of the GL-2 fighter monoplane as the GL-21 (Type B2), the prototype of which was exhibited at the Paris *Salon de l'Aéronautique* of 1920. The GL-21, like its predecessors, was powered by the 180 hp HS 8Ab water-cooled engine, but the broad chord ailerons with their horn-balance areas lying within the wing planform were replaced by longer-span and narrower constant-chord ailerons. The rudder was enlarged and the series model introduced additional undercarriage bracing struts. Armament comprised two 7,7-mm Vickers machine guns in the fuselage. One GL-21 was purchased by Finland in 1923,

(Above) One of the 20 GL-21s acquired by Finland for service from 1923 to 1931. (Below) The GL-21 introduced long-span, constant-chord ailerons.

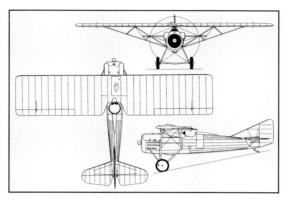

followed by a further 18 in 1924, an additional aircraft later being assembled in Finland from spares, and these remained in Finnish service until 1931. A total of 30 single-seat fighters of this type was built. *Max speed, 149 mph (240 km/h) at 3,280 ft (1 000 m). Range, 280 mls (450 km). Empty weight, 1,455 lb (660 kg). Loaded weight, 2,116 lb (960 kg). Dimensions as for GL-2.*

GOURDOU-LESEURRE GL-22 (Type B3) France

Evolved from the GL-2 in parallel with the GL-21, the GL-22 (Type B3) also made its début in 1920. It differed from the GL-21 primarily in having a new wing profile, steel-tube in place of light alloy wing bracing struts, a modified frontal radiator and a revised cockpit interior. The HS 8Ab engine and twin Vickers gun armament were retained, but some structural revision reduced empty weight by 154 lb (70 kg). The prototype, like that of the GL-21, was initially flown with twin undercarriage struts on each side, but a triple-strut arrangement was adopted for the series model. With gun armament the aircraft was designated GL-22 C1 (C = *Chasse*), but without armament it was designated GL-22 ET1 (ET = *Entrainement de Transition*) and was intended for the advanced training rôle. The first order for the GL-22 was placed with Gourdou-Leseurre on 13 December 1920, 20 examples of the single-seat fighter subsequently being built for export to Estonia, Latvia and Czechoslovakia, and 30 of the training version being supplied to France's *Aviation Marine*. In addition, a

Fifteen GL-22s acquired by the Estonian Air Force (below) in 1925 were flown by the 3rd Division.

manufacturing licence was acquired by the newly-established Zmaj concern in Yugoslavia. *Max speed, 153 mph (247 km/h) at sea level, 137 mph (220 km/h) at 16,405 ft (5 000 m). Endurance, 2.5 hrs. Time to 16,405 ft (5 000 m), 17.5 min. Empty weight, 1,301 lb (590 kg). Loaded weight, 1,940 lb (880 kg). Dimensions as for GL-2.*

GOURDOU-LESEURRE GL-23 (Type B4) France

The GL-23 single-seat fighter of 1925 was a further development of the basic GL-2 design. The HS 8Ab engine and standard GL-22 C1 fuselage and armament were mated with the longer span wing and enlarged rudder first applied to the experimental tandem two-seat GL-22 ET2 (Type B5) trainer of 1922. A total of nine GL-23 C1 aircraft was built at St Maur, two of these having different wing profiles for comparison purposes. One example had its fuselage elongated by 25.6 in (65 cm) to provide for accommodation of a single casualty stretcher aft of the pilot. This was presented at Le Bourget on 24 April 1925 as the GL-23 TS, one other example being completed (as the LGL 23 TS) in the following year. *Max speed, 130 mph (210 km/h) at 3,280 ft (1 000 m). Range, 373 mls (600 km). Empty weight, 1,455 lb (660 kg). Loaded weight, 2,116 lb (960 kg). Span, 36 ft 1 in (11,00 m). Length, 21 ft 3⁹⁄₁₀ in (6,50 m). Height, 7 ft 9⅓ in (2,37 m). Wing area, 251.88 sq ft (23,40 m²).*

(Below) GL-23 was a long-span derivative of GL-22.

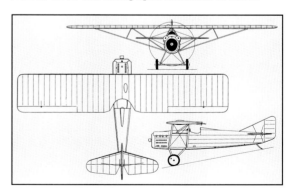

GOURDOU-LESEURRE GL-31 (Type I3) France

Although retaining the basic parasol monoplane configuration of preceding Gourdou-Leseurre fighters and similar construction (ie, all-metal structure apart from

A wholly new design by Gourdou and Leseurre, the GL-31 (above) was soon found unsatisfactory.

wooden wing ribs and fabric skinning), the GL-31 single-seat fighter was an entirely new design. Its predecessors had all been extrapolations of the original GL-2. Designed to the requirements of the 1921 C1 programme, the GL-31 C1 was powered by a 420 hp Gnome-Rhône 9A Jupiter air-cooled radial and had provision for two fuselage-mounted 7,7-mm Vickers guns and two unsynchronised Darne guns of similar calibre in the wings. The rectangular wing planform characteristic of all earlier Gourdou-Leseurre fighters gave place to a trapezoid with marked leading-edge taper, and the profusion of wing bracing struts was supplanted by one pair of struts on each side. In the event, the 1921 C1 programme was overtaken by that of 1923, and the GL-31 by the Gourdou-Leseurre contender for the later programme, the GL-32. The sole prototype of the GL-31 did not fly until 1926, development being discontinued thereafter. *Max speed, 161 mph (260 km/h). Range, 373 mls (600 km). Empty weight, 1,929 lb (875 kg). Loaded weight, 2,976 lb (1 350 kg). Span, 34 ft 5⅓ in (10,50 m). Length, 23 ft 7½ in (7,20 m). Height, 8 ft 10⅓ in (2,70 m). Wing area, 226.05 sq ft (21,00 m²).*

GOURDOU-LESEURRE GL-40
(TYPE G) France

Designed for high-altitude operation, the GL-40 (above and below) flew in 1922, but did not progress beyond the single prototype illustrated here.

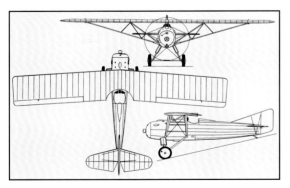

The GL-40 single-seat high-altitude fighter actually preceded the GL-31, flying for the first time in 1922. Also a contender in the 1921 C1 programme, the GL-40 was powered by a 300 hp Hispano-Suiza 8Fb water-cooled engine fitted with a Rateau turbo-supercharger. The constant-chord wing, which featured slight sweepback, was braced by a similar four-pair strut arrangement to that of the GL-2 and its derivatives, and Lamblin radiators were attached to the undercarriage legs. The GL-40 was capable of altitudes in excess of 26,245 ft (8 000 m) and, in fact, was claimed to have attained 39,587 ft (12 066 m) on 10 October 1924 with Jean Callizo at the controls. However, this claim was subsequently alleged to have been fraudulent. Only one prototype of the GL-40 was built. *Max speed, 161 mph (260 km/h) at 22,965 ft (7 000 m). Range, 497 mls (800 km). Empty weight, 2,392 lb (1 085 kg). Loaded weight, 3,329 lb (1 510 kg). Span, 47 ft 6⁹⁄₁₀ in (14,50 m). Length, 31ft 2⅔ in (9,51 m). Height, 9 ft 7 in (2,92 m). Wing area, 376.75 sq ft (35,00 m²).*

GOURDOU-LESEURRE GL-50
(TYPE F) France

Intended as a two-seat multi-rôle fighter, the GL-50 (above and below) accorded with the short-lived *Chasse, Armée, Nuit* (CAN) category.

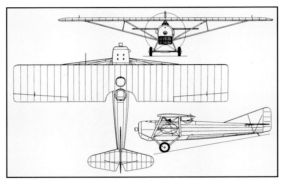

In April 1919, *Général* Duval, France's *Directeur de l'Aéronautique*, formulated a programme for the replacement of the principal categories of combat aircraft serving with the *Aéronautique Militaire*. Two of these categories were CAP2 (*Chasse, Armée, Protection, biplace*) and CAN2 (*Chasse, Armée, Nuit, biplace*) two-seaters. Although this programme was overtaken in the following year (the CAP category being discarded), Gourdou-Leseurre designed and built prototypes to meet both requirements, the GL-50 CAP2 (Type F) and the GL-51 CAN2 (Type H), which embodied considerable commonality. The GL-50 was powered by a 300 hp Hispano-Suiza 8Fb water-cooled engine and was intended to have a Rateau turbo-supercharger, although, in the event, this was not fitted. Armament comprised two fixed forward-firing 7,7-mm Darne machine guns and two guns of similar calibre on a swivelling mount in the rear cockpit. A long-span, untapered wing was fitted and the arrangement of the bracing struts was similar to that of contemporary Gourdou-Leseurre single-seaters. The GL-51 CAN2 was essentially similar apart from having a 380 hp Gnome-Rhône 9Ab Jupiter radial engine, a reduced loaded weight (3,968 lb/1 800 kg) and a marginally higher maximum speed (140 mph/225 km/h). Both prototypes were flown in

The GL-50 (above) was intended to use a Rateau turbo-supercharger, but this, in the event, was never to be fitted.

1922, but no production followed. The following data relate to the GL-50. *Max speed, 131 mph (210 km/h). Loaded weight, 4,431 lb (2 010 kg). Span, 47 ft 10⅘ in (14,60 m). Length, 30 ft 8⅛ in (9,35 m). Height, 9 ft 4⅕ in (2.85 m). Wing area, 430.57 sq ft (40,00 m²).*

(LOIRE-) GOURDOU-LESEURRE
LGL-32 France

From late 1925 (until 1928) Gourdou-Leseurre operated as a subsidiary of the shipbuilding concern Ateliers et Chantiers de la Loire. During the three years of this association, aircraft designed and built by Gourdou-Leseurre received the prefix LGL. The first so designated was the LGL-32 single-seat fighter, which proved to be the only aircraft of Gourdou-Leseurre design to be built in really substantial quantities. Designed to participate in the 1923 C1 programme, the LGL-32 was powered by a 420 hp Gnome-Rhône 9Ac Jupiter (the similarly-rated 9Ady being standardised after the five pre-series aircraft) and carried two synchronised 7,7-mm guns. Flown in 1925 and adjudged runner-up to the Nieuport-Delage NiD 42, the LGL-32 received an initial production contract (for 16 aircraft) on 16 September of that year and entered service late 1927. About 380 were eventually delivered to the *Aéronautique Militaire*, and a further 15 to the *Aviation Maritime*, remaining first-line equipment until 1934. In addition, 63 examples were exported of which 50 were delivered to Romania (in 1928) and 12 to Turkey. Totals of 415 were recorded as built at St Nazaire and 60 at St Maur from 1927 onwards. Extraordinarily, the LGL-32 was reinstated in production at the beginning of 1937,

(Above) Production of almost 500 made the LGL-32 the most numerous of all the Gourdou-Leseurre fighters.

The single example of the LGL-321 (above) was a re-engined, more powerful, pre-series LGL-32, the standard version of which is depicted below.

An LGL-32 C1, *circa* 1930, serving with the 2e *Escadrille*, 3e *Regiment d'Aviation de Chasse*.

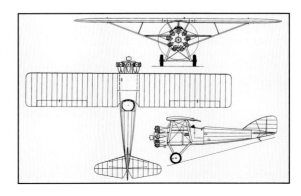

by which time it was thoroughly obsolete. In November 1936, the Basque government, which was fighting the Spanish Nationalists, obtained four ex-*Armée de l'Air* LGL-32s which were relinquished by a flying school. Despite the obsolescence of these aircraft, the Basques placed a contract with Gourdou-Leseurre for 16 new-build LGL-32s and also acquired the company-owned LGL-32 (the fifth production example) that had been used for aerobatic demonstrations by Marcel Bapt. The new LGL-32s had split- rather than the original cross-axle undercarriages, thus permitting a centreline rack for a single 220-lb (100-kg) bomb. These were delivered to Spain between March and June 1937, one being retained by Gourdou-Leseurre for conversion as a GL-633 dive bomber. This was later to be delivered to Spain together with five similar aircraft. At the end of 1927, the first pre-series LGL-32 was re-engined with a 600 hp Jupiter as the LGL-321. *Max speed, 155 mph (250 km/h) at sea level. Range, 310 mls (500 km). Time to 16,405 ft (5 000 m), 12 min. Empty weight, 2,123 lb (963 kg). Loaded weight, 3,032 lb (1 376 kg). Span, 40 ft 0¼ in (12,20 m). Length, 24 ft 9⅛ in (7,55 m). Height, 9 ft 8¼ in (2,95 m). Wing area, 268.03 sq ft (24,90 m²).*

(LOIRE-) GOURDOU-LESEURRE LGL-32HY
France

The LGL-32Hy (above) was the original LGL-32 prototype converted to floatplane configuration.

In 1927, after completing 150 hours flying, the prototype LGL-32 was fitted with twin wooden floats and, retaining its 420 hp Gnome-Rhône 9Ac engine but with much of its fuselage re-covered with light alloy, was flown as the LGL-32Hy single-seat fighter seaplane. On 28 March 1927, the LGL-32Hy attained an altitude of 30,479 ft (9 290 m) after taking-off from the Seine, but no production order was placed by the *Aviation Maritime* and development was discontinued. *Max speed, 140 mph (225 km/h). Range, 311 mls (500 km). Empty weight, 1,845 lb (837 kg). Loaded weight, 2,756 lb (1 250 kg). Span, 40 ft 0¼ in (12,20 m). Length, 27 ft 6⅜ in (8,40 m). Height, 10 ft 9⅞ in (3,30 m). Wing area, 268.03 sq ft (24,90 m²).*

(LOIRE-) GOURDOU-LESEURRE LGL-33
France

Employing essentially the same airframe as the LGL-32, the LGL-33 flown in April 1925 differed primarily in having a 450 hp Lorraine-Dietrich 12Eb 12-cylinder W-type water-cooled engine. The greater engine weight – by comparison with the Jupiter of the LGL-32 – dictated modification of the bracing struts in order to shift the wing farther aft to cater for the changed CG, and the rudder was enlarged. The LGL-33 offered better low-altitude speed than the Jupiter-engined fighter, but had a lower climb rate, and the sole prototype crashed as a result of a structural failure while being flown by André Christiany in 1927. No further development was undertaken. *Max speed,*

A Lorraine-Dietrich engine was the distinguishing feature of the LGL-33 (below) derivative of the -32.

The first of the two LGL-341 prototypes (above) had a frontal radiator for its HS 12Hb engine.

161 mph (260 km/h) at sea level. Time to 6,560 ft (2 000 m), 3.5 min. Empty weight, 2,511 lb (1 139 kg). Loaded weight, 3,492 lb (1 584 kg). Span, 40 ft 0¼ in (12,20 m). Length, 26 ft 4⅛ in (8,03 m). Height, 9 ft 8¼ in (2,95 m). Wing area, 268.03 sq ft (24,90 m²).

(LOIRE-) GOURDOU-LESEURRE LGL-34
France

Seeking enhanced performance with minimal changes to the basic LGL-32 airframe, Loire-Gourdou-Leseurre produced, in 1927, prototypes of the LGL-34 and LGL-341 single-seat fighters. These differed primarily in the type of power plant installed, the LGL-34 having a 450 hp Hispano-Suiza 12Ga 12-cylinder W-type water-cooled engine and the LGL-341 having a 500 hp Hispano-Suiza 12Hb 12-cylinder Vee-type water-cooled engine. Although the wing employed by these fighters was of similar span to that of the LGL-32, the gross area was increased by 28 sq ft (2,60 m²), the ailerons were inset and the rear cabane struts were moved forward. The LGL-34 was marginally lighter than the more powerful LGL-341, and the performances of the two aircraft were closely comparable. In May 1928, the second LGL-341 prototype was flown, this discarding the frontal radiator (featured by the LGL-34 and first LGL-341) in favour of Lamblin-type radiators attached to the forward undercarriage legs. Although the HS-engined fighters offered improved level speed and climb rates by comparison with the LGL-32, these were considered insufficient to warrant production orders. The following data relate to the second LGL-341. *Max speed, 168 mph (270 km/h) at sea level, 158 mph (255 km/h) at 16,405 ft (5 000 m). Range, 373 mls (600 km). Empty weight, 2,628 lb (1 192 kg). Loaded weight, 3,666 lb (1 663 kg). Span, 40 ft 0¼ in (12,20 m). Length, 24 ft 11⅛ in (7,60 m). Height, 9 ft 8¼ in (2,95 m). Wing area, 296.02 sq ft (27,50 m²).*

The second LGL-341 (below) had Lamblin-style radiators attached to the forward undercarriage legs.

(LOIRE-) GOURDOU-LESEURRE LGL-351
France

In 1926, the STAé (*Service Technique de l'Aéronautique*) conceived a lightweight fighter programme aimed at arresting the upward spiral of fighter costs. Known unofficially as the "Jockey" programme, this envisaged an armament restricted to two 7,7-mm Vickers guns, a range of 248 mls (400 km) and a maximum speed of at least 168 mph (270 km/h) at 16,405 ft (5 000 m). Among the many contenders for this requirement was the LGL-351 C1. Exhibited at the 1926 *Salon de l'Aéronautique* in Paris as the "LGL-33 Renault", the LGL-351 was powered by a 450 hp Renault 12Ja 12-cylinder liquid-cooled Vee engine and employed the

same wing as the LGL-33. The LGL-351 was flown in 1927 and was joined in the same year by a second example, the LGL-354, which was envisaged as an export version with greater fuel capacity and provision for an armament of four 7,7-mm guns. The "Jockey" programme proved unsuccessful, development of the LGL-351 being discontinued, and despite outstanding success at an exhibition held in Copenhagen in August 1927, the LGL-354 found no purchaser, being redesignated LGL-35 in 1929. The following data relate to the LGL-351. *Max speed, 155 mph (250 km/h) at 3,280 ft (1 000 m). Range, 280 mls (450 km). Empty weight, 2,330 lb (1 057 kg). Loaded weight, 3,155 lb (1 431 kg). Span, 40 ft 0¼ in (12,20 m). Length, 26 ft 4⅛ in (8,03 m). Height, 9 ft 10 in (3,00 m). Wing area, 268.03 sq ft (24,90 m²).*

GOURDOU-LESEURRE GL-410 & GL-450
France

With the establishment by the Ateliers et Chantiers de la Loire of its own design department at St Nazaire, the Etablissement Gourdou-Leseurre became a separate entity once more, producing the GL-410 and GL-450 to meet the requirements of the 1928 C1 programme. Both were based on the LGL-32. Whereas the GL-410 was powered by a supercharged Gnome-Rhône Jupiter 9Asb engine and had a revised wing of trapezoidal form, the GL-450 had an unsupercharged Jupiter 9Ae and retained the LGL-32 wing. Both engines were rated at 480 hp and both fighters employed independently articulated wheels in place of the old-style cross-axle that had characterised all preceding Gourdou-Leseurre fighters. Two examples of the GL-410 and one example of the GL-450 were built, both being evaluated at Villacoublay during 1932, but in the meantime, the 1928 C1 programme had been overtaken by the 1930 programme and neither Gourdou-Leseurre fighter could meet the more exacting requirements. The following data relate to the GL-450 (figures for the GL-410 being essentially similar). *Max speed, 199 mph*

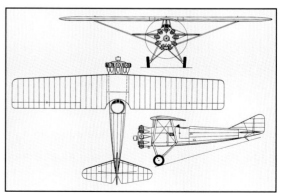

The supercharged GL-410 (above) and unsupercharged GL-450 (below) were both based on the LGL-32, and had slightly different wing planforms.

(320 km/h) at 16,405 ft (5 000 m). Range, 373 mls (600 km). Empty weight, 2,138 lb (970 kg). Loaded weight, 3,042 lb (1 380 kg). Span, 40 ft 0¼ in (12,20 m). Length, 24 ft 9⅛ in (7,55 m). Height, 9 ft 8¼ in (2,95 m). Wing area, 268.03 sq ft (24,90 m²).

GOURDOU-LESEURRE GL-482 — France

The last Gourdou-Leseurre fighter to be built and the first to diverge from the parasol monoplane configuration utilised by all the company's preceding fighters, the GL-482 was designed to participate in the 1930 C1 programme and was one of no fewer than *five* gull-winged fighters entered for that contest. Powered by a 690 hp Hispano-Suiza 12Xbrs supercharged 12-cylinder liquid-cooled engine and carrying an armament of two synchronised 7,7-mm Chatellerault-Vickers machine guns, the GL-482 was of metal construction with steel wing spars and a dural tube fuselage structure. Flown for the first time in February 1933, the prototype was found to suffer excessive drag, performance being unacceptably low as a result. It was discarded at an early stage in the evaluation programme, the Dewoitine D 500 being the winning contender. *Max speed, 186 mph (300 km/h) at 13,125 ft (4 000 m). Loaded weight, 3,483 lb (1 580 kg). Span, 32 ft 4 in (9,86 m). Length, 23 ft 10½ in (7,28 m). Height, 9 ft 2¼ in (2,80 m). Wing area, 191.06 sq ft (17,75 m²).*

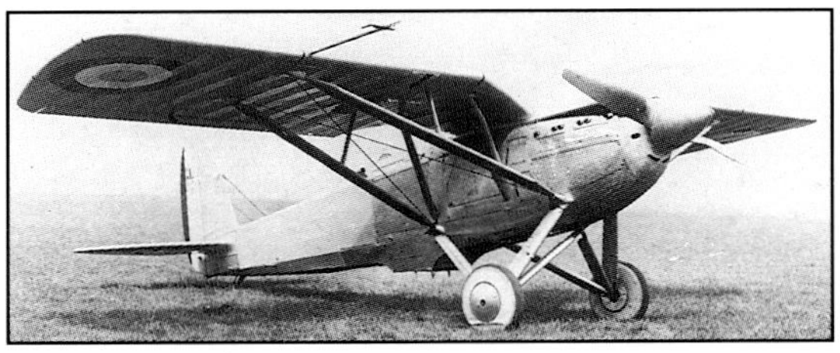

An unsatisfactory performance ended development of the GL-482 (above and below), which proved to be the last of the Gourdou-Leseurre fighters.

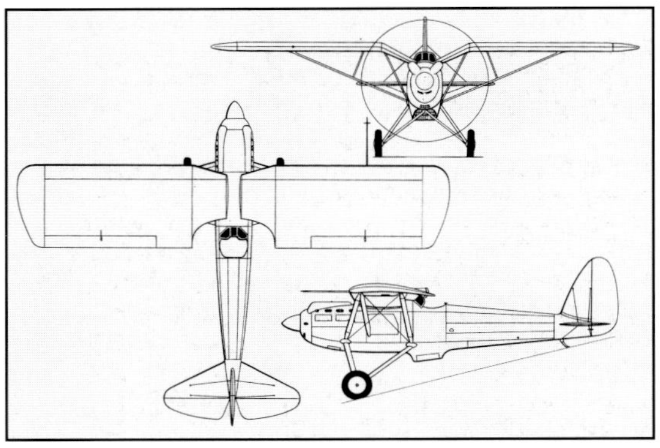

GREGOR (CCF) FDB-1 — Canada

Aerodynamically probably the cleanest and aesthetically possibly the most elegant fighter biplane ever created, the FDB-1 single-seat fighter was designed by Michael Gregor and built by Canadian Car & Foundry

The FDB-1 (below), one of the last biplane fighters.

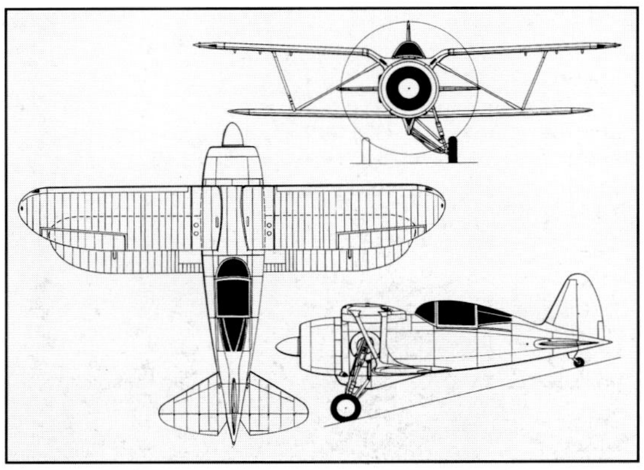

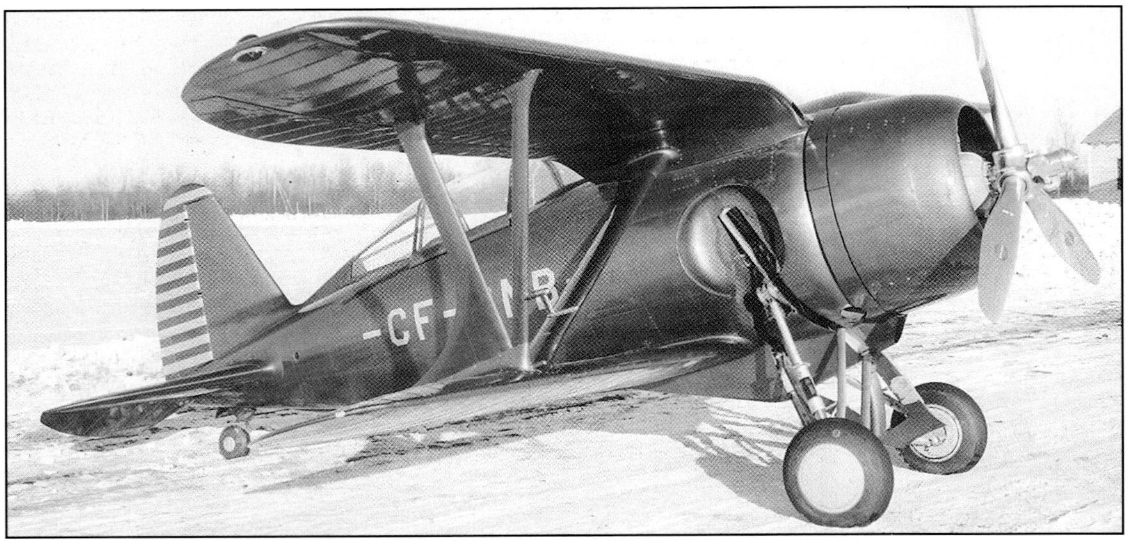

Tested by the RCAF during 1939, the elegant FDB-1 (above) was overtaken by monoplane designs.

(CCF). It was an all-metal single-bay staggered biplane with a semi-monocoque fuselage, flush-riveted and metal stressed skinning, an hydraulically-retractable undercarriage and sliding cockpit canopy. Powered by a 750 hp Pratt & Whitney R-1535-SB4-G Twin Wasp Junior 14-cylinder air-cooled radial, and carrying an armament of two 0.5-in (12,7-mm) Browning machine guns, the FDB-1 flew for the first time on 17 December 1938. It was evaluated by the RCAF during the following year, but by this time the monoplane configuration had been universally accepted as the standard formula for the single-seat fighter and no production was undertaken. *Max speed, 261 mph (420 km/h) at 13,100 ft (3 990 m). Initial climb, 2,800 ft/min (14,20 m/sec). Range, 530 mls (853 km). Empty weight, 2,880 lb (1 306 kg). Loaded weight, 4,100 lb (1 860 kg). Span, 28 ft 0 in (8,53 m). Length, 21 ft 8 in (6,60 m). Height, 9 ft 4½ in (2,86 m). Wing area, 194 sq ft (18,02 m²).*

GRIGOROVICH M-11 — Russia

In the summer of 1916, Dmitri P Grigorovich designed and built a small single-bay biplane fighter flying boat to meet a requirement of the Imperial Russian Navy. Designated M-11 (and also known as the Shch-I, indicating Shchetinin, in whose Petrograd factory it was built, and *istrebitel'*, or fighter), it was initially tested as a tandem two-seater powered by a 100 hp Gnome Monosoupape engine mounted as a pusher, this later being replaced by a 100 hp Le Rhône. Several examples of the two-seat M-11 were built, but inadequate performance resulted in their relegation to the rôle of trainers for M-5 and M-9 reconnaissance flying boat pilots.

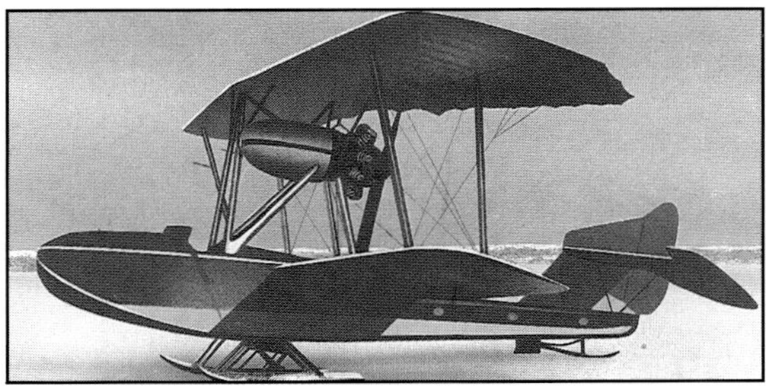

Optional skis allowed the M-11 flying boat (above) to operate from frozen lakes and compacted snow.

Development concentrated on a single-seat version, which, at the time, was claimed to be the fastest flying boat in the world. The single-seat M-11 carried one fixed forward-firing 7,62-mm gun and armour protection was provided for the pilot, a semi-circular armoured shield replacing the normal windscreen. Forward view and gun sighting were provided by a small aperture in this shield – one example being fitted with a sighting periscope. The hydrodynamic qualities of the M-11 were poor but, on 6 April 1917, series production began against a contract for 100 single-seaters with the Le Rhône engine. The M-11 was employed in the Black Sea primarily as an escort for M-9 flying boats, but was not entirely successful and only 60 were completed. *Max speed, 92 mph (148 km/h) at sea level. Time to 3,280 ft (1 000 m), 11 min. Endurance, 2.7 hrs. Empty weight, 1,490 lb (676 kg). Loaded weight, 2,041 lb (926 kg). Span, 28 ft 8⅖ in (8,75 m). Length, 24 ft 11¼ in (7,60 m). Wing area, 279.87 sq ft (26,00 m²).*

GRIGOROVICH M-12 — Russia

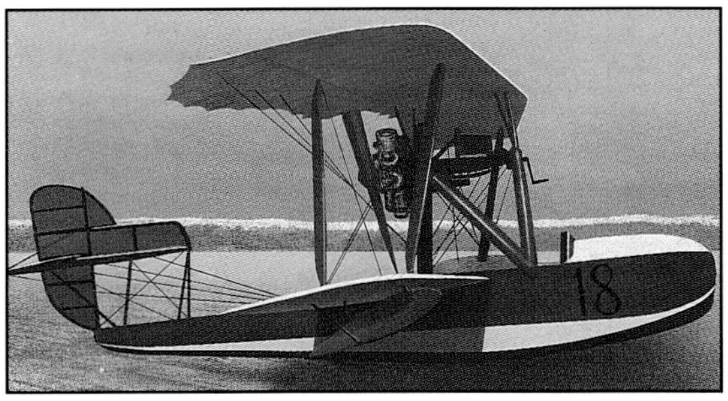

A few examples of the M-12 (above) saw service with the Imperial Russian Navy during the Revolution.

A progressive development of the M-11, the M-12 single-seat fighter flying boat retained the 110 hp Le Rhône pusher engine and fixed 7,62-mm Maxim machine gun of its predecessor. The hull nose was redesigned, however, in an attempt to obtain improved hydrodynamic characteristics, the vertical tail surfaces were revised to improve stability and some attempt was made to reduce structural weight. Climb rate and ceiling were greatly improved, but only a small number of M-12s was built, and these, together with the M-11s, were used until the end of the civil war, sometimes being fitted with skis for shore-based operations. *Max speed, 87 mph (140 km/h) at sea level. Time to 3,280 ft (1 000 m), 6 min. Endurance, 2.7 hrs. Empty weight, 1,367 lb (620 kg). Loaded weight, 1,918 lb (870 kg). Dimensions as for M-11.*

GRIGOROVICH I-1 — USSR

The first land-based fighter to be designed by D P Grigorovich, who had previously specialised in water-borne aircraft, the I-1 single-seat fighter was built at Factory No 1 at Khodinka, Moscow, and completed late in January 1924. Powered by a 400 hp Liberty water-cooled engine, the I-1 was a single-bay biplane of wooden construction, the forward portion of the slab-sided fuselage being plywood covered and the remainder of the aircraft having fabric skinning. Armament comprised two 7,7-mm Vickers machine guns. Difficulties were experienced with engine cooling and various arrangements were tested, radiators initially being attached to the undercarriage legs, but a single radiator suspended beneath the engine being finally adopted. During evaluation in the spring of 1924, the I-1 was found to offer adequate speed, but was unstable and possessed an insufficient climb rate. Grigorovich was therefore instructed to redesign the aircraft. *Max speed, 143 mph (230 km/h) at sea level, Range, 373 mls (600 km). Ceiling, 19,685 ft (6 000 m). Span, 35 ft 5⅕ in (10,80 m). Length, 24 ft 0 in (7,32 m). Wing area, 288.48 sq ft (26,80 m²).*

The I-1 (below) was one of the first Soviet fighters.

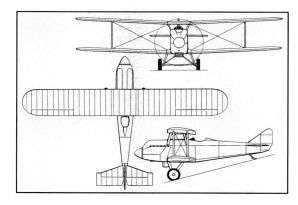

GRIGOROVICH I-2ʙɪꜱ   USSR

As a progressive development of the I-1, D P Grigorovich designed the I-2 in competition with the Polikarpov-designed IL-400 monoplane. Of wooden construction like its predecessor and similarly powered by a 400 hp Liberty engine, the I-2 was aerodynamically more refined, with an oval-section monocoque fuselage and I-type aerofoil-section interplane struts. Armament comprised two synchronised 7,62-mm PV-1 (Maxim) guns and flight testing was initiated in the autumn of 1924, the I-2 being pronounced suitable for series production. Subsequently, it was concluded that the cockpit was too cramped and offered insufficient visibility, and access to the armament was inadequate. The cockpit was therefore enlarged and the pilot's seat raised, necessitating redesign of the centre fuselage and major structural revision, including introduction of a welded steel-tube frame which also carried the engine bearers. As the I-2bis and powered by a 420 hp M-5 engine – the Soviet-built version of the water-cooled 12-cylinder Liberty – the fighter entered production at Factories Nos 1 and 23, the former building 164 and the latter 47 during 1926-29. Engine cooling problems resulted in some examples being fitted with Lamblin-type radiators, these being known as the I-2prim version. The I-2bis was the first Soviet fighter of indigenous design to serve in quantity with the V-VS. *Max speed,*

(Above) With the I-2, Grigorovich successfully competed against Polikarpov for a production contract, gained for the I-2bis version (below).

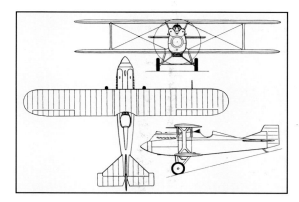

In 1926, the I-2bis (above) became the first Soviet fighter of indigenous design to attain service.

146 mph (235 km/h) at sea level. Time to 3,280 ft (1 000 m), 2.4 min. Range, 373 mls (600 km). Empty weight, 2,540 lb (1 152 kg). Loaded weight, 3,472 lb (1 575 kg). Span, 35 ft 5⅕ in (10,80 m). Length, 24 ft 0 in (7,32 m). Height, 9 ft 10 in (3,00 m). Wing area, 252.53 sq ft (23,46 m²).

GRIGOROVICH DI-3   USSR

The DI-3 (above and below) met a Soviet requirement for a two-seat escort fighter, but its development stopped short of production.

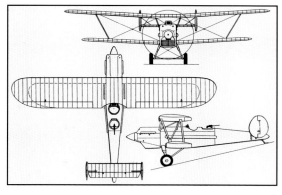

To meet a requirement formulated in 1930 for a new two-seat escort fighter, D P Grigorovich designed a single-bay biplane of mixed construction. This was powered by a 730 hp BMW VI 7,3 water-cooled 12-cylinder engine and armed with two fixed synchronised 7,62-mm PV-1 machine guns with a third gun of similar calibre on a flexible mounting in the rear cockpit. Completed in August 1931, and assigned the designation DI-3, the fighter featured a fabric-covered welded steel-tube fuselage and fabric-covered wooden wings, and was unusual for its time in having twin fins and rudders to provide a better field of fire for the gunner. State flight trials revealed that the DI-3 had a performance closely comparable with that of the single-seat I-3, but manoeuvrability was considered inadequate and further development was discontinued. *Max speed, 169 mph (272 km/h) at sea level, 176 mph (284 km/h) at 9,840 ft (3 000 m). Time to 9,840 ft (3 000 m), 7.4 min. Empty weight, 2,782 lb (1 262 kg). Loaded weight, 4,028 lb (1 827 kg). Span, 38 ft 0⅗ in (11,60 m). Length, 26 ft 3 in (8,00 m). Wing area, 330.46 sq ft (30,70 m²).*

GRIGOROVICH I-Z   USSR

Shortly after completing work on the I-5 single-seat fighter biplane, in the design of which he assisted Nikolai N Polikarpov while under detention, Dmitri P Grigorovich was assigned the task of designing a single-seat fighter specifically to carry the recoilless cannon developed by Leonid V Kurchevsky. Work was initiated in the summer of 1930 under Programme "Z" (or Zet), the

fighter evolved to this programme being designated accordingly I-Z. In order to accelerate development, the forward fuselage, together with the complete engine installation, was identical to that of the second prototype I-5, the remainder of the fuselage being a dural monocoque. The low wing was of metal construction with fabric skinning and was braced to the undercarriage at mid-span by steel-tube Vee-struts. The horizontal tail surfaces were mounted high on the fin to clear the exhaust gases of the two 76,2-mm DRP (*Dynamo-reaktivnaya pushka*) single-shot weapons slung beneath the wings inboard of the bracing strut attachment points. For aiming purposes, a single 7,62-mm PV-1 gun was mounted in the fuselage. Powered by a 525 hp Gnome-Rhône Jupiter VI nine-cylinder radial, the I-Z prototype was flown in the late summer of 1931. A second prototype, the I-Zbis, was completed early in 1932, and a pre-production series of 21 I-Z fighters followed in 1933. These were powered by the Soviet version of the Jupiter, the M-22 of 480 hp, enclosed by a Townend ring, which replaced the close-fitting helmeted cowling of the first prototype. They had wings of wooden construction. Production was transferred from Moscow to Kharkov, where a further 50 I-Zs were built, but the fighter revealed a number of defects – spin recovery presented a major problem – and most were relegated to the development rôle, notably concerning recoilless cannon and one being employed in parasite fighter trials. *Max speed, 186 mph (300 km/h) at sea level, 199 mph (320 km/h) at 8,200 ft (2 500 m). Loaded weight, 3,417 lb (1 550 kg). Span, 36 ft 1¹⁄₁₀ in (11,00 m). Length, 25 ft 11 in (7,90 m).*

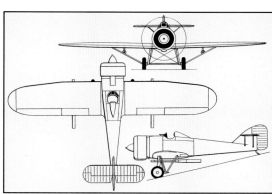

The prototype I-Z (or TsKB-7) (below) had a metal wing and lacked the Townend cowling ring of the wooden-winged series version (above).

GRIGOROVICH IP-1 (DG-52)   USSR

In 1934, the design collective led by Dmitri Grigorovich began development of a more advanced *istrebitel' pushechny* (cannon fighter). A single-seat cantilever

The IP-1 (below) in definitive service form.

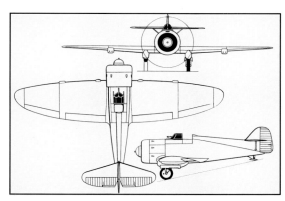

low-wing monoplane of all-metal construction, with hydraulically-operated semi-retractable main undercarriage members and a 640 hp Wright Cyclone nine-cylinder radial, this had two 76-mm Kurchevsky APK-4 recoilless cannon mounted at the extremities of the broad (55 per cent of the span) wing centre section. Designated IP-1, this fighter was placed in series production for the V-VS, armament initially comprising the two APK-4 guns, each of which was provided with five shells, and two 7,62-mm machine guns. The poor

(Left) As originally delivered, the series IP-1 was fitted underwing with a pair of recoilless cannon.

Key to Grumman FF-1

1 Hamilton Standard two-bladed propeller
2 Ground adjustable propeller hub
3 Engine cowling ring
4 Wright R-1820-78 Cyclone nine-cylinder radial engine
5 Exhaust stubs
6 Carburettor air intake
7 Engine accessories
8 Landing/taxying lamp
9 Starboard mainwheel
10 Air louvres
11 Main undercarriage wheel housing
12 Fuel pump
13 Engine control rods
14 Engine bearer struts
15 Oil tank (8.5 US gal/32 l capacity)
16 Gun muzzle blast trough
17 Oil filler cap
18 Fireproof bulkhead
19 Centre section cabane struts
20 Diagonal wire bracing
21 Fabric-covered wing panel
22 Aileron hinge controls
23 Aluminium leading-edge skins
24 Aileron push-pull rod
25 Emergency flotation bag (inflated)
26 Interplane "N" struts
27 Starboard upper wing panel
28 Aerial mast
29 Starboard navigation light
30 Spar bracing strut
31 Aerial cable
32 Starboard aileron
33 Aileron mass balance tab
34 Interplane strut mounting rib
35 Aluminium aileron skins
36 Flotation bag housing
37 Wing internal wire bracing
38 Fixed portion of trailing edge
39 Flotation bag pneumatic inflation bottle
40 Flotation bag release handle
41 Handhold
42 Gun camera
43 Upper wing panel centreline joint rib
44 Spar joint flanges
45 Telescopic gunsight
46 Twin Browning M-2 0.3-in (7,62-mm) machine guns
47 Ammunition feed chutes
48 Cartridge case ejector chute
49 Ammunition tanks
50 Rudder pedal bar
51 Reserve fuel tank (38 US gal/144 l capacity)
52 Reserve tank filler cap
53 Aileron control connector
54 Fire extinguisher
55 Control column
56 Instrument panel
57 Windscreen panels
58 Pilot's handhold
59 Sliding cockpit canopy cover
60 Pilot's seat
61 Safety harness
62 Engine throttle control box
63 Main fuel tank filler cap
64 Main fuel tank (82 US gal/310 l capacity)
65 Pilot's seat height adjustment
66 Radio transmitter and receiver
67 Chart board
68 Fuselage upper longeron
69 Sliding canopy rail
70 Fixed portion of canopy
71 Observer/gunner's canopy (open position)
72 Gunner's pivotal seat
73 Seat suspension arms
74 Seat tilting track
75 Gunner's footrests
76 Swivelling gun mount
77 Ammunition box
78 Browning M-2 0.3-in (7,62-mm) machine gun
79 Life raft stowage pack
80 Upper identification light
81 Fuselage skin plating
82 Control cable guide pulleys
83 Fin root fillet
84 Starboard tailplane
85 Identification light
86 Starboard elevator
87 Fin leading-edge skin panel joint
88 Tailfin construction
89 Sternpost
90 Rudder mass balance
91 Aerial cables
92 Aerial mast
93 Rudder construction

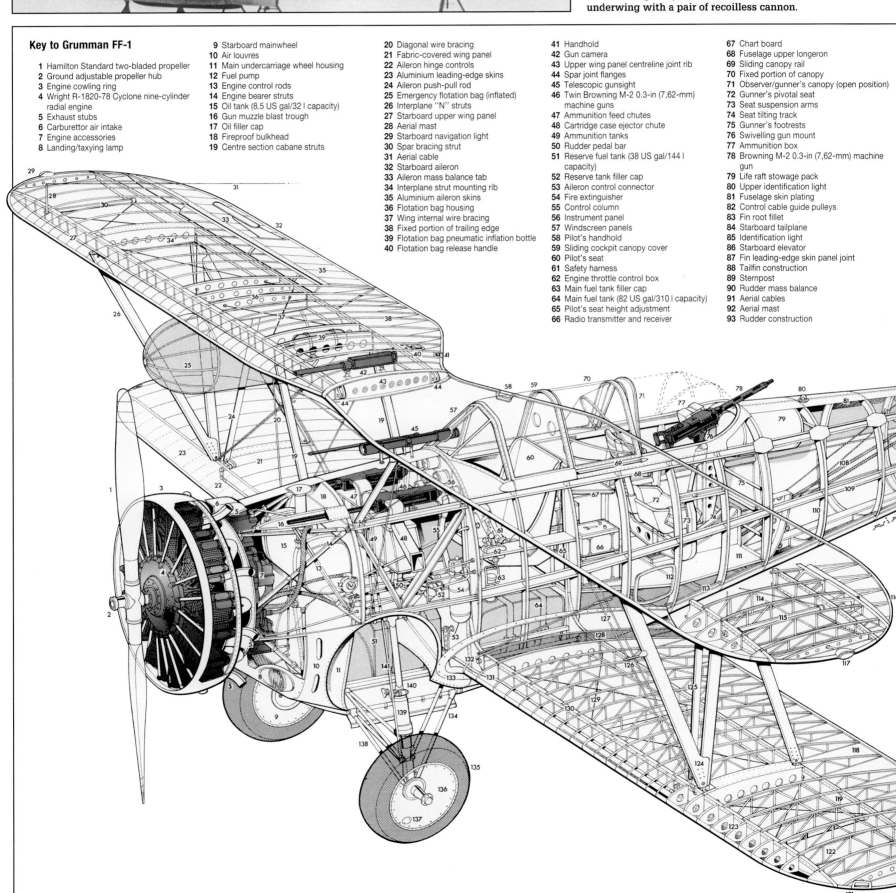

characteristics of the recoilless cannon led to the discarding of this weapon, the production IP-1 standardising on a pair of 20-mm ShVAK cannon in the wing roots and six 7,62-mm ShKAS machine guns divided between two shallow trays at the extremities of the wing centre section. With the revised armament, the CG of the fighter was found to be too far aft, resulting in poor spin recovery characteristics, which were rectified by the introduction of a large dorsal fin, extending to and incorporating the cockpit headrest. A total of 90 IP-1s was built during 1936-37, power being provided by the 635 hp M-25, the Soviet-built version of the Cyclone 9. *Max speed, 229 mph (368 km/h) at sea level, 255 mph*

94 Tailplane bracing strut
95 Tail navigation light
96 Tailcone
97 Aileron hinge control
98 Tailwheel shock absorber strut
99 All-aluminium elevator construction
100 Port identification light
101 Tailplane construction
102 Leading-edge skin joints
103 Tailwheel
104 Tailplane spar attachment joint
105 Tailplane trim mechanism

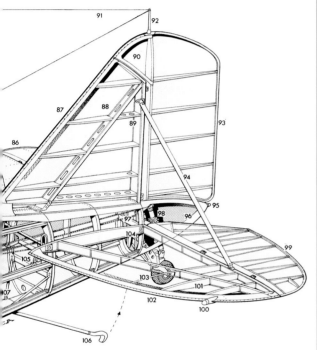

106 Arresting hook (extended)
107 Arresting hook keel support structure
108 Tailplane control cables
109 Channel section fuselage longerons
110 Fuselage frame construction
111 Observer/gunner's floor level
112 Control access panel
113 Fuselage bottom longeron
114 Upper wing panel rib construction
115 Spar bracing strut
116 Port aileron
117 Port navigation light
118 Lower wing panel trailing-edge ribs
119 Rear spar
120 Tubular steel wingtip
121 Ground handling handhold
122 Girder rib construction
123 Leading-edge nose ribs
124 Port interplane "N" struts
125 Aileron push-pull rod
126 Pitot tube
127 Diagonal wire bracing
128 Lower wing walkway
129 Wing panel internal wire bracing
130 Front spar
131 Aileron control rod
132 Spar root attachment joint
133 Wing root fillet
134 Main undercarriage radius arms
135 Port mainwheel
136 Wheel hub disc cover
137 Tyre valve access plate
138 Forward radius arms
139 Undercarriage leg shock absorber strut
140 Wing strut knee joint
141 Elastic cord locking cable

A large dorsal fin and conventional armament distinguished the service form (above) of the IP-1.

(410 km/h) at 9,840 ft (3 000 m). Time to 3,280 ft (1 000 m), 1.4 min. Max range, 621 mls (1 000 km). Loaded weight, 4,145 lb (1 880 kg). Span, 35 ft 11⁹/₁₀ in (10,97 m). Length, 23 ft 8³/₅ in (7,23 m). Wing area, 215.07 sq ft (19,98 m²).

GRIGOROVICH IP-4 (DG-53)   USSR

A scaled-down derivative of the IP-1 completed late in 1934, the IP-4 single seat fighter was structurally similar to its predecessor and powered by a 640 hp Wright Cyclone 9. Armament comprised four 45-mm APK-11 recoilless cannon and two 7,62-mm ShKAS machine guns. Only one prototype was flight tested, a second, modified prototype – which differed in that the recoilless cannon were replaced by a pair of 20-mm ShVAK cannon – being cancelled before completion. No further development was undertaken. *Max speed, 237 mph (382 km/h) at sea level, 270 mph (435 km/h) at 9,840 ft (3 000 m). Time to 3,280 ft (1 000 m). 1.1 min. Max range, 516 mls (830 km). Loaded weight, 3,415 lb (1 549 kg). Span, 31 ft 6 in (9,60 m). Length, 23 ft 2¾ in (7,08 m). Wing area, 176.1 sq ft (16,36 m²).*

Essentially a scaled-down IP-1, only a single example of the IP-4 (below) was completed.

GRUMMAN (G-5) FF-1   USA

Combining fully-enclosed cockpits with a retractable undercarriage, the XFF-1 (G-5) two-seat fighter was novel among shipboard aircraft at the time of its début.

Flown for the first time on 29 December 1931, the XFF-1 was faster than contempory single-seat carrier-based aircraft, and 27 production examples were ordered as FF-1s on 19 December 1932, the first of these being delivered on 24 April 1933. The FF-1 was powered by a 750 hp Wright R-1820-78 Cyclone radial and carried an armament of two synchronised 0.3-in (7,62-mm) Browning M-2 machine guns and a similar weapon on a flexible mount in the rear cockpit. A scout (armed reconnaissance) equivalent, the XSF-1 (G-6), was delivered 30 August 1932, and 34 production SF-1s were ordered. These had a single synchronised gun and a longer-chord engine cowling with full ring exhaust collector. Only one US Navy squadron received a full complement of FF-1s, serving from the summer of 1933 until early 1936. Of these, 22 were subsequently fitted with dual controls as FF-2s. *Max speed, 207 mph (333 km/h) at 5,300 ft (1 615 m). Range, 647 mls (1 041 km). Initial climb, 1,600 ft/min (8,1 m/sec). Empty weight, 3,076 lb (1 395 kg). Max loaded weight, 4,655 lb (2 111 kg). Span, 34 ft 6 in (10,51 m). Length, 24 ft 6 in (7,47 m). Height (tail up), 11 ft 1 in (3,38 m). Wing area, 310 sq ft (28,80 m²).*

(Above) An SF-1 from a US Naval Reserve unit in 1936, this being the scout equivalent of (below) the FF-1 which featured a retractable undercarriage.

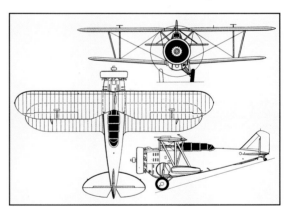

(Immediately below) A G-23 of the Spanish Republican 1a *Escuadrilla, Grupo* 28. (Bottom) The FF-1 flown by Section Leader VF-5B on USS *Lexington*, 1934-35.

GRUMMAN G-23 (CCF GOBLIN)   USA (Canada)

Spanish Republican interest in acquisition of Grumman two-seat fighters resulted in the development of the G-23 for which a manufacturing licence was granted Canadian Car & Foundry. Embodying features of both the FF-1 and SF-1, and powered by an R-1820-F52 Cyclone affording 890 hp for take-off, the G-23 was initially referred to as the "Canadian Grumman Fighter". Forty G-23s were ordered by the Spanish Republican government, Grumman manufacturing the fuselages, Brewster producing the wing and tail surfaces, and CCF undertaking assembly, but only 34 were delivered to Spain for the assault-fighter rôle. One other was supplied to Nicaragua and one to Japan, and the six undelivered Spanish aircraft, plus 10 built against a follow-on contract from Spain (less one sent to Mexico as a demonstrator), were eventually taken on charge by the RCAF in 1940, and assigned the name Goblin. These were issued to one fighter squadron, armament comprising one synchronised 0.3-in (7,62-mm) Browning machine gun and two similar weapons in the rear cockpit. The Goblin was finally replaced completely in the fighter rôle in the RCAF in May 1942 but a few survived in Spain, where they were known as Delfins, until 1955. *Max speed, 216 mph (348 km/h) at 6,890 ft (2 100 m). Range, 621 mls (1 000 km). Initial climb, 1,614 ft/min (8,2 m/sec). Empty weight, 3,276 lb (1 486 kg). Loaded weight, 4,800 lb (2 177 kg). Dimensions as for FF-1.*

GRUMMAN (G-8) F2F-1   USA

(Above) A Grumman F2F-1 of US Navy squadron VF-2 assigned to USS *Lexington* in 1937. (Below) General arrangement drawing of the F2F-1.

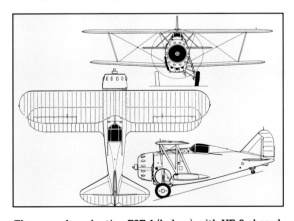

The second production F2F-1 (below) with VF-2 aboard the USS *Lexington* from 1935 until 1940.

Operated by the RCAF's No 118(F) Sqn (above), the Goblin was assembled in Canada by CCF.

As the XF2F-1, the first Grumman single-seat fighter was flown on 18 October 1933, a production series of 54 being ordered as F2F-1s on 17 May 1934 (plus one replacement in 1935). Powered by a 650 hp Pratt & Whitney R-1535-72 Twin Wasp radial and armed with two synchronised 0.3-in (7,62-mm) Browning machine guns, the first F2F-1 was delivered on 28 January 1935. Featuring all-metal construction, a retractable undercarriage and an enclosed cockpit, the F2F-1 was comparatively advanced for its time and was to remain in service with the US Navy as a shipboard fighter until 1940. *Max speed, 203 mph (327 km/h) at sea level, 231 mph (372 km/h) at 7,500 ft (2 285 m). Max range, 985 mls (1 585 km). Initial climb, 2,050 ft/min (10,4 m/ sec). Empty weight, 2,691 lb (1 221 kg). Loaded weight, 3,847 lb (1 745 kg). Span, 28 ft 6 in (8,69 m). Length, 21 ft 5 in (6,53 m). Height, 9 ft 1 in (2,77 m). Wing area, 230 sq ft (21,37 m²).*

GRUMMAN (G-11) F3F-1   USA

A major redesign of the G-8, with increased overall dimensions and some aerodynamic refinement, the G-11 was intended to combine superior directional stability and manoeuvrability with higher performance. One prototype was ordered as the XF3F-1 on 15 October 1934. This flew on 20 March 1935, but was lost as a result of a structural failure two days later. A second XF3F-1 flew on 9 May 1935, this too being lost when it failed to recover from a spin on 13 May. A third was therefore built, and, on 24 August 1935, a contract was placed for 54 F3F-1s. Powered by the 700 hp Pratt

(Below) Displaying "neutrality star" marking in April 1940, an F3F-1 in service with VF-7, USS *Wasp.*

& Whitney R-1535-84 Twin Wasp Junior and armed with one 0.5-in (12,7-mm) and one 0.3-in (7,62-mm) gun, these were delivered from 29 January to 21 September 1936, the last being relinquished by a US Navy squadron (VF-72) on 10 February 1941. *Max speed, 215 mph (346 km/h) at sea level, 256 mph (412 km/h) at 7,500 ft (2 285 m). Initial climb, 1,900 ft/min (9,65 m/sec). Max range, 998 mls (1 606 km). Empty weight, 2,952 lb (1 339 kg). Max loaded weight, 4,403 lb (1 997 kg). Span, 32 ft 0 in (9,75 m). Length, 23 ft 3⅛ in (7,09 m). Height, 9 ft 1 in (2,77 m). Wing area, 260.6 sq ft (24,21 m²).*

GRUMMAN (G-19) F3F-2 & -3   USA

On 3 June 1936, Grumman proposed the installation of a two-stage G-series Wright Cyclone engine in the final production F3F-1 as the G-19, approval being given on 28 July, when this aircraft was assigned the designation XF3F-2. Flight testing began in January 1937, and as a result of the noteworthy improvement in all-round performance, an order was placed on 23 March for 81 production F3F-2s. Fleet deliveries commenced on 1

Various improvements distinguished the F3F-1 (below).

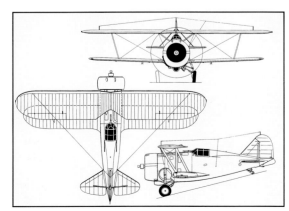

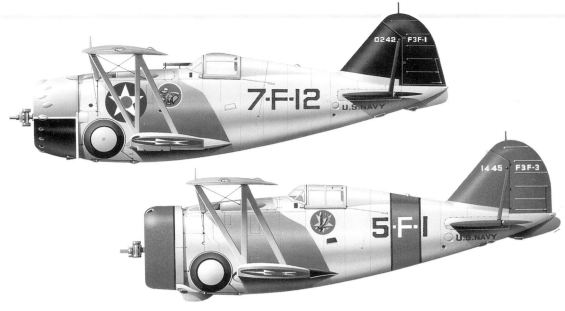

The original XF4F-2 was modified to the XF4F-3 configuration (above) with enlarged wing.

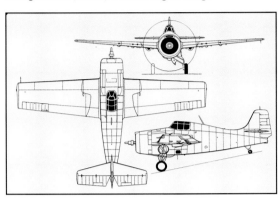

(Above, top) An F3F-1 of VF-7 aboard the USS *Wasp* in 1940. (Immediately above) F3F-3 of VF-5 aboard the USS *Yorktown*, May 1939 to mid-1941.

December 1937 and were completed on 11 May 1938, the F3F-2 having a 950 hp R-1820-22 Cyclone engine, increased fuel capacity and the same armament as that of the F3F-1. The need for an additional squadron of fighters led to one F3F-2 being subjected to an "improvement program" and becoming the XF3F-3. This embodied various aerodynamic improvements and flew on 13 October 1938. This event was preceded by a contract for 27 production F3F-3s, deliveries of which commenced 16 December 1938. The F3F-3 achieved a maximum speed of 264 mph (425 km/h) at 15,200 ft (4 635 m), but performance was generally similar to that of the F3F-2 in other respects. The F3F-2 and -3 were removed from the active squadrons in 1941, and the following data relate specifically to the former. *Max speed, 234 mph (376 km/h) at sea level, 256 mph (412 km/h) at 17,250 ft (5 260 m). Initial climb, 2,800 ft/ min (14,2 m/sec). Max range, 1,130 mls (1 818 km). Empty weight, 3,254 lb (1 476 kg). Max loaded weight, 4,750 lb (2 155 kg). Span, 32 ft 0 in (9,75 m). Length, 23 ft 0 in (7,01 m). Height, 9 ft 4 in (2,84 m). Wing area, 260.6 sq ft (24,21 m²).*

An F3F-2 (below) operated by VF-6, from 1938 to May 1941, aboard the USS *Enterprise*.

GRUMMAN (G-18) XF4F-2   USA

Grumman designed its first single-seat shipboard fighter monoplane, the G-18, around the twin-row, 14-cylinder Pratt & Whitney Twin Wasp engine. Bearing a close family resemblance to the biplane fighters that had preceded it, the G-18 possessed a similar manually-retractable undercarriage and was of all-metal construction with a flush-riveted monocoque fuselage.

First Grumman monoplane, the XF4F-2 (below) was built after the XF4F-1 biplane project was dropped.

Awarded a prototype contract as the XF4F-2 on 28 July 1936, it flew for the first time on 2 September of the following year with a 1,050 hp R-1830-66 engine. Marginally faster than the competitive Brewster XF2A-1, the XF4F-2 proved generally inferior in most other respects and suffered a number of teething troubles, mostly associated with the power plant. A production contract was awarded the Brewster contender and thereafter the Grumman fighter was subjected to major redesign as the XF4F-3. *Max speed, 288 mph (463 km/h) at 10,000 ft (3 050 m). Range, 740 mls (1 190 km). Empty weight, 4,036 lb (1 831 kg). Max loaded weight, 5,535 lb (2 511 kg). Span, 34 ft 0 in (10,37 m). Length, 26 ft 5 in (8,05 m). Wing area, 232 sq ft (21,56 m²).*

The XF4F-2 (below) was progenitor of the Wildcat.

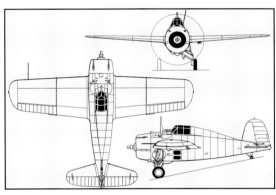

GRUMMAN (G-36) F4F-3 & -4 WILDCAT   USA

From October 1939, the XF4F-2 was subjected to a thoroughgoing rework which was to result in the extensively changed XF4F-3. The most important change was the installation of an XR-1830-76 Twin Wasp with a two-speed two-stage supercharger which delivered 1,200 hp for take-off. The increased weight resulting from supercharger, its intercooler and associated duct-

The first production Wildcat, the F4F-3 (below) lacked the folding wings needed for shipboard operation, as introduced on the F4F-4 (above).

ing dictated substantial increases in wing span and area. In addition, the tail surfaces were redesigned and numerous other changes introduced. As the XF4F-3 (G-36), flight testing was resumed on 12 February 1939, and an initial contract for 54 F4F-3s for the US Navy followed in August. The first production fighter flew in February 1940, and the last of the batch was fitted with wing folding as the XF4F-4. Follow-on contracts included 95 F4F-3As (30 of which were to be assigned to Greece) in which the two-stage R-1830-76 gave place to the single-stage R-1830-90, as first flown on 11 October 1940 in the single XF4F-6. A total of 285 F4F-3s was built with -76 or essentially similar -86 engines, the principal version of the fighter built by the parent company being the F4F-4 powered by the latter. The F4F-4 differed from its predecessor principally in having manually-folded wings and armament increased from

(Immediately below) An F4F-4 flying with VF-41 from USS *Ranger* early 1942, and (bottom) an F4F-4 of VGF-29, USS *Saratoga*, for Operation "Torch", 1942.

four to six wing-mounted 0.5-in (12,7-mm) guns. A total of 1,168 was procured for the US Navy, with the last being delivered on 31 December 1942. Twenty-one additional Wildcats were completed as F4F-7 (G-52) unarmed long-range reconnaissance aircraft, whilst a number of F4F-3Ps and F4F-4Ps carried cameras *and* guns. Two F4F-3s became XF4F-5s when fitted in mid-1940 with R-1820-40 (and, later, -54 or -48) Cyclone engines. Two XF4F-8s in 1942 were fitted with XR-1820-56 engines, four-gun armament and slotted instead of split flaps. The following data relate to the F4F-4. *Max speed, 274 mph (441 km/h) at sea level, 320 mph (515 km/h) at 18,800 ft (5 730 m). Time to*

(Left) Flying from USS *Ranger*, an F4F-4 of VF-41 displays pre-May 1942 red-and-white rudder stripes.

Key to Grumman F4F-4 Wildcat

1 Starboard navigation light
2 Wingtip
3 Starboard formation light
4 Rear spar
5 Aileron construction
6 Fixed aileron tab
7 All riveted wing construction
8 Lateral stiffeners
9 Forward canted main spar
10 "Crimped" leading-edge ribs
11 Solid web forward ribs
12 Starboard outer gun blast tube
13 Carburettor air duct
14 Intake
15 Curtiss three-blade constant-speed propeller
16 Propeller cuffs
17 Propeller hub
18 Engine front face
19 Pressure baffle
20 Forward cowling ring
21 Cooler intake
22 Cooler air duct
23 Pratt & Whitney R-1830-86 radial engine
24 Rear cowling ring/flap support
25 Controllable cowling flaps
26 Downdraft ram air duct
27 Engine mounting ring
28 Anti-detonant regulator unit
29 Cartridge starter
30 Generator

31 Intercooler
32 Engine accessories
33 Bearer assembly welded cluster joint
34 Main beam
35 Lower cowl flap
36 Exhaust stub
37 Starboard mainwheel
38 Undercarriage fairing
39 Lower drag link
40 Hydraulic brake
41 Port mainwheel
42 Detachable hub cover
43 Low-pressure tyre
44 Axle forging
45 Upper drag link
46 Oleo shock strut
47 Ventral fairing
48 Wheel well
49 Pivot point
50 Landing light
51 Main forging
52 Compression link
53 Gun camera port
54 Counter balance
55 Anti-detonant tank
56 Retraction sprocket
57 Gear box
58 Stainless steel firewall
59 Engine bearers
60 Actuation chain (undercarriage)
61 Engine oil tank
62 Oil filter
63 Hoisting sling installation

64 Bullet resistant windscreen
65 Reflector gunsight
66 Panoramic rear-view mirror
67 Wing fold position
68 Adjustable headrest
69 Shoulder harness
70 Canopy track sill
71 Pilot's adjustable seat
72 Instrument panel shroud
73 Undercarriage manual crank
74 Control column
75 Rudder pedals
76 Fuselage/front spar attachment
77 Main fuel filler cap
78 Seat harness attachment
79 Back armour
80 Oxygen cylinder
81 Reserve fuel filler cap
82 Alternative transmitter/receiver (ABA or IFF) installation
83 Battery
84 IFF and ABA dynamotor units
85 Wing flap vacuum tank
86 Handhold
87 Turnover bar
88 Rearward-sliding Plexiglas canopy

89 Streamlined aerial mast
90 Mast support
91 One-man Mk 1A life-raft stowage
92 Upper longeron
93 Toolkit
94 Aerial lead-in
95 Elevator and rudder control runs
96 'L'-section fuselage frames
97 IFF aerial
98 Dorsal lights
99 Whip aerial
100 Wing-fold jury strut
101 Fin fairing
102 Access panel
103 Tailwheel strut extension arm
104 Rudder trim tab control flexible shaft
105 Tailplane rib profile
106 Starboard tailplane
107 Static balance
108 Elevator hinge (self-aligning)
109 Fin construction
110 Rudder upper hinge
111 Aerial
112 Insulator

113 Aerial mast
114 Rudder post
115 Rudder construction
116 Aluminium alloy leading-edge
117 Rudder trim tab
118 Elevator torque tube
119 Port elevator
120 Elevator trim tab
121 Elevator hinge (self-aligning)
122 Arresting hook (extended)
123 Tailplane spar
124 Rear navigation light
125 Towing lug
126 Rudder torque tube support
127 Elevator control linkage
128 Rudder control cable
129 Arresting hook spring
130 Tailwheel shock strut
131 Rear fuselage frame/bulkhead
132 Forged castor fairing
133 Tailwheel

10,000 ft (3 050 m), 5.6 min. Max range (clean), 830 mls (1 335 km). Empty weight, 5,895 lb (2 674 kg). Max loaded weight, 8,762 lb (3 974 kg). Span, 38 ft 0 in (11,58 m). Length, 29 ft 0 in (8,84 m). Height, 11 ft 4 in (3,45 m). Wing area, 260 sq ft (24,15 m²).

GRUMMAN G-36A & B (MARTLET)   USA

In 1939, Grumman offered as the G-36A an export version of the F4F-3 ordered by the US Navy, a contract for 91 aircraft being placed on behalf of France's *Marine Nationale*. Seven were in various stages of assembly when France fell in June 1940, and the entire batch was transferred to Britain, which had also placed a contract

134 Tailwheel centering springs
135 Alclad flush-riveted stressed skin
136 Lifting tube
137 Remote compass transmitter
138 Tailwheel lock cable
139 Arresting hook cable
140 "Z"-section fuselage stringers
141 ZB relay box
142 Transmitter
143 Elevator and rudder tab controls
144 Antenna relay unit
145 Radio junction box
146 Receiver unit and adapter
147 Inertia switch

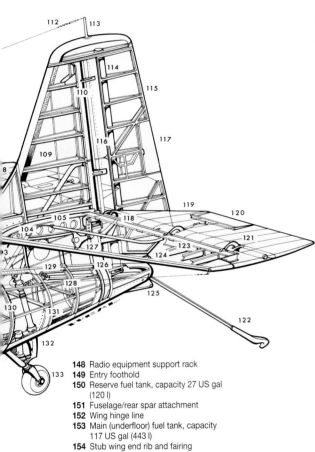

148 Radio equipment support rack
149 Entry foothold
150 Reserve fuel tank, capacity 27 US gal (120 l)
151 Fuselage/rear spar attachment
152 Wing hinge line
153 Main (underfloor) fuel tank, capacity 117 US gal (443 l)
154 Stub wing end rib and fairing
155 Inboard gun blast tubes
156 Plexiglas observation panel
157 Ventral antenna
158 Outboard gun port
159 ZB antenna
160 Fixed D/F loop
161 Two 0.50-in (12,7-mm) Browning M-2 machine guns
162 Outboard gun access/loading panels
163 ABA antenna
164 Flap profile
165 Outboard 0.50-in (12,7-mm) Browning M-2 machine gun
166 Aileron control linkage
167 Aileron trim tab
168 Port aileron
169 Aileron hinges (self-aligning)
170 Port formation light
171 Port navigation light
172 Wing skinning
173 Bomb rack (optional)
174 Fragmentation bomb
175 Pitot head

The G-36B Martlet (above) for Royal Navy had folding wings and was generally similar to the Martlet IV (below) supplied under Lend-Lease.

for 100 G-36As on its own account. Whereas the French contract aircraft were powered by the 1,200 hp Wright R-1820-G205A Cyclone, Britain selected the Pratt & Whitney S3C4-G Twin Wasp of similar power. The first (French contract) G-36A flew on 10 May 1940, and entered British service as the Martlet I. A contractual change resulted in the British order being switched to the G-36B with folding wings, this entering service as the Martlet II (although the first 10 were accepted with fixed wings). The 30 F4F-3As that had been assigned to Greece were also taken into the Royal Navy inventory as Martlet IIIs. With the passage of the Lend-Lease Act, 220 aircraft essentially similar to the F4F-4 but with the single-stage R-1820-40B engine were assigned to the Royal Navy as Martlet IVs (F4F-4Bs). These became Wildcat IVs when British and US names were standardised in March 1944. The following data relate to the Martlet II. *Max speed, 293 mph (471 km/h) at 13,000 ft (3 965 m). Initial climb, 3,050 ft/min (15,49 m/sec). Max range (clean), 890 mls (1 432 km). Empty weight, 5,425 lb (2 461 kg). Normal loaded weight, 7,580 lb (3 438 kg). Dimensions as for F4F-4.*

GRUMMAN (G-36) F4F-3S   USA

The appearance of the A6M2-N floatplane fighter in the Aleutians prompted US Navy interest in a float-equipped version of the F4F-3 shipboard fighter. One example was therefore fitted with Edo-designed and manufactured single-step metal floats, and, with auxiliary rudders mounted near the tips of the tailplane, flew on 28 February 1943. The need for additional keel area aft was revealed by initial trials, and a large ventral fin

The F4F-3S floatplane version (above and below) of the Wildcat did not have a good enough performance to justify its adoption for service use.

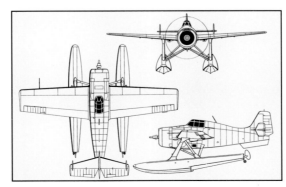

was added to improve yaw stability. The floats and their bracing struts raised the fighter's weight by only some 500 lb (227 kg), and from calm water at normal loaded weight the F4F-3S could take-off within 34 seconds. However, the dramatic effect of float drag on speed performance led to cancellation of an earlier contract to complete 100 F4F-3 Wildcats as float fighters. *Max speed, 266 mph (428 km/h) at 20,300 ft (6 185 m). Initial climb, 2,460 ft/min (12,5 m/sec). Max range, 600 mls (965 km). Empty weight, 5,804 lb (2 633 kg). Loaded weight, 7,506 lb (3 405 kg). Span, 38 ft 0 in (11,59 m). Length, 39 ft 1 in (11,91 m). Height, 18 ft 1¾ in (5,53 m). Wing area, 260 sq ft (24,15 m²).*

GRUMMAN (GENERAL MOTORS) FM WILDCAT   USA

With the transfer of production of the Wildcat from the parent company to the Eastern Aircraft Division of General Motors, manufacture of the F4F-4 continued in slightly modified form as the FM-1. The R-1830-86 Twin Wasp engine was retained, but wing armament was reduced from six to four 0.5-in (12,7-mm) guns and ammunition capacity was raised. The first FM-1 was flown on 31 August 1942, a total of 1,060 subsequently being built of which 312 were assigned to Britain as Martlet (later Wildcat) Vs. The version of the Wildcat built in largest numbers by General Motors, however, was the

Built by General Motors, the FM-2 (above) was the definitive production version of the Wildcat. (Below) Wildcat V with No 882 Sqn on HMS *Searcher* in 1944.

FM-2, the first version of the fighter produced for the US Navy to standardise on the Cyclone engine. The FM-2 was the production version of the XF4F-8, two prototypes of which were built by Grumman with the first flying on 8 November 1942. The FM-2 retained the four 0.5-in (12,7-mm) gun armament, but had a 1,350 hp Wright R-1820-56 Cyclone and redesigned, taller vertical tail surfaces. A total of 4,777 FM-2 Wildcats was built of which 370 were assigned to Britain as Wildcat VIs. The following data relate to the standard FM-2. *Max speed, 289 mph (465 km/h) at sea level, 319 mph (513 km/h) at 19,600 ft (5 980 m). Time to 10,000 ft (3 050 m), 4.5 min. Max range (clean), 780 mls (1 255 km). Empty weight, 5,542 lb (2 514 kg). Max loaded weight, 8,221 lb (3 729 kg). Span, 38 ft 0 in (11,59 m). Length, 28 ft 9 in (8,76 m). Height, 11 ft 5 in (3,48 m). Wing area, 260 sq ft (24,15 m²).*

GRUMMAN (G-34) XF5F-1   USA

Ordered as a prototype on 30 June 1938 by the US Navy Bureau of Aeronautics, the XF5F-1 was of radical concept. It was intended as a *twin*-engined shipboard fighter, and this at a time when the first *single*-engined shipboard fighter monoplanes were only just commencing flight test. Conceived as the G-34 Skyrocket, the XF5F-1 was flown on 1 April 1940, and, in its initial form, had a singular appearance resulting from an abbreviated forward fuselage, the wing leading edge extending ahead of the fighter's nose. Powered by two 1,200 hp Wright XR-1820-40/42 radials and having provision for two 23-mm Madsen cannon, the XF5F-1 underwent some redesign as a result of testing, the

GRUMMAN (G-50) F6F HELLCAT   USA

Designed as a successor to the F4F, the G-50 was ordered as the XF6F on 30 June 1941. The first prototype, powered by a 1,700 hp Wright XR-2600-10 Cyclone, flew on 26 June 1942 as the XF6F-1. A second prototype, with a 2,000 hp Pratt & Whitney R-2800-10 Double Wasp, followed on 30 July 1942 as the XF6F-3.

(Above) For night fighting, the F6F-3N carried radar on the starboard wing. (Below) F6F-5 Hellcat in post-war service with USNR at NAS Floyd Bennett, NY.

As first flown, the XF5F-1 (above) had a singularly abbreviated fuselage nose.

engine nacelles being lengthened, the fuselage nose being extended, etc. Flight testing of the XF5F-1 provided information utilised in the development of the more advanced XF7F-1 (G-51). *Max speed, 383 mph (616 km/h) at sea level, 380 mph (611 km/h) at 16,500 ft (5 030 m). Max climb, 4,000 ft/min (20,32 m/sec). Range, 1,200 mls (1 930 km) at 210 mph (338 km/h). Empty weight, 8,107 lb (3 677 kg). Loaded weight, 10,138 lb (4 599 kg). Span, 42 ft 0 in (12,80 m). Length, 28 ft 8½ in (8,75 m). Height, 11 ft 4 in (3,45 m). Wing area, 303.5 sq ft (28,19 m²).*

(Above) The XF5F-1 was eventually modified with a more conventional nose and lengthened engine nacelles, compared with (below) the initial form.

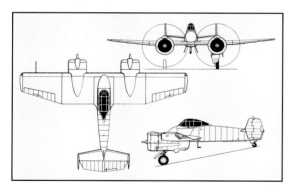

GRUMMAN (G-45) XP-50   USA

A land-based version of the shipboard XF5F-1 was offered to the US Army Air Corps as the G-45 while the prototype naval fighter was still under construction.

(Below) Only a few flights were made by the sole XP-50 before its development was abandoned.

This was ordered as the XP-50 on 25 November 1939. The XP-50 was essentially similar to its shipboard counterpart, apart from having a lengthened nose to accommodate the nosewheel member of a tricycle undercarriage. Powered by two turbo-supercharged Wright R-1820-67/69 engines, it was intended to carry an armament of two 20-mm cannon and two 0.5-in (12,7-mm) machine guns. The XP-50 flew for the first time on 14 May 1941, but the aircraft was destroyed after 20 hours of flight testing as a result of a turbo-supercharger explosion. Further development was abandoned in favour of the more advanced XP-65 (G-51), which, in the event, was also to be discontinued. The following performance data are based on manufacturer's estimates. *Max speed, 424 mph (682 km/h) at 25,000 ft (7 620 m). Range, 585 mls (941 km) at 317 mph (510 km/h) at 10,000 ft (3 050 m). Time to 20,000 ft (6 100 m), 5.0 min. Empty weight, 8,307 lb (3 768 kg). Max loaded weight, 13,060 lb (5 924 kg). Span, 42 ft 0 in (12,80 m). Length, 31 ft 11 in (9,73 m). Height, 12 ft 0 in (3,66 m). Wing area, 304 sq ft (28,24 m²).*

The XP-50 (below) was virtually a land-based XF5F.

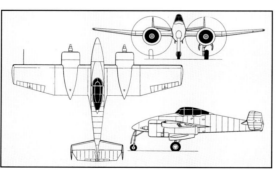

The latter version had been ordered into production on the previous 23 May, the first F6F-3 flying on 3 October 1942, and 15 squadrons being equipped within nine months. Armament comprised six 0.5-in (12,7-mm) guns, and, during 1944, the R-2800-10W (with water injection boosting emergency rating to 2,200 hp) was standardised. A total of 4,403 F6F-3s had been built when production switched to the F6F-5 on 21 April 1944. This total included 168 F6F-3E and -3N night fighters, and a number of -3P photo-recce aircraft, the Royal Navy receiving 252 F6F-3s as Hellcat Is under Lend-Lease. The F6F-5, flown on 4 April 1944, standardised progressive improvements made to the -3, retaining the -10W engine and six-gun armament. Production continued until November 1945, by which time 7,870 F6F-5s had been built. Of these, 930 had been supplied to the Royal Navy as Hellcat IIs and 1,434 of the total had been completed as F6F-5N night fighters. Experimental versions included the XF6F-4 with a two-speed R-2800-27 engine, flown on 3 October 1942, the

A Grumman F6F-3 of VF-4 (below) flying from NAS Alameda, California, mid-1943.

(Above) A Hellcat I, as flown by No 800 Sqn from HMS *Emperor* in 1943. The later F6F-5 (below) served in the FAA as the Hellcat II.

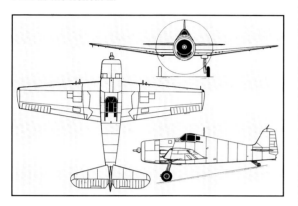

XF6F-2 with a turbo-supercharged R-2800-16 engine tested in January 1944, and two XF6F-6s with R-2800-18W engines, first flown on 6 July 1944. The following data relate to the F6F-3. *Max speed, 324 mph (521 km/h) at sea level, 376 mph (605 km/h) at 22,800 ft (6 950 m). Initial climb, 3,650 ft/min (18,5 m/sec). Range (max internal fuel), 1,085 mls (1 746 km). Empty weight, 9,042 lb (4 101 kg). Loaded, 12,186 lb (5 528 kg). Span, 42 ft 10 in (13,05 m). Length, 33 ft 4 in (10,16 m). Height, 14 ft 5 in (4,40 m). Wing area, 334 sq ft (31,03 m²).*

GRUMMAN (G-51) F7F
TIGERCAT USA

Owing much to previous experience gained in the design of the G-34 (XF5F-1), the G-51 was similarly conceived as a single-seat twin-engined shipboard fighter,

The F7F-3 (above) was a post-war fighter-bomber version of the Tigercat, the F7F-2N radar-equipped night fighter being shown by the drawing (below).

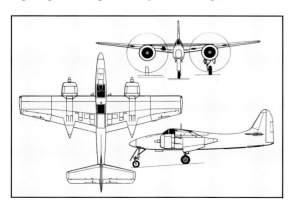

two prototypes being ordered on 30 June 1941 as XF7F-1s. The first XF7F-1 was flown on 3 November 1943, by which time 500 production examples had been ordered. The first production F7F-1 was completed in April 1944, this being powered by two 2,100 hp Pratt & Whitney R-2800-22W engines and carrying an armament of four 20-mm cannon and four 0.5-in (12,7-mm) machine guns in addition to nose-mounted AN/APS-6 radar. Meanwhile, the US Navy had decided to confine the F7F to shore-based operations with the US Marine Corps. Production of the F7F-1 was restricted to 34 aircraft and was followed by the two-seat F7F-2N with a radar operator behind the pilot. Sixty-five F7F-2Ns were built between October 1944 and August 1945. The F7F-3 was a post-World War II single-seat fighter-bomber version with R-2800-34W engines similarly rated at 2,100 hp for take-off and retaining the original -1 armament. Two hundred and fifty F7F-3s were built, of which more than 100 were completed or converted to two-seat F7F-3N night fighters and some 60 were fitted with cameras as F7F-3Ps. One was modified as an F7F-4N, embodying structural strengthening for shipboard operation. Twelve F7F-4Ns were built, production terminating in November 1946. Both F7F-3s and -3Ns were operated by USMC squadrons during the Korean conflict, being finally withdrawn in 1952.

A lengthened nose radome was one feature of the F7F-3N (below) two-seat night fighter variant.

The following data relate to the F7F-3. *Max speed, 435 mph (700 km/h) at 22,200 ft (6 765 m), 367 mph (591 km/h) at sea level. Initial climb, 4,530 ft/min (23,0 m/sec). Normal range, 1,200 mls (1 931 km). Empty weight, 16,270 lb (7 380 kg). Max loaded weight, 25,720 lb (11,667 kg). Span, 51 ft 6 in (15,70 m). Length, 45 ft 5 in (13,85 m). Height, 16 ft 7 in (5,05 m). Wing area, 455 sq ft (42,27 m²).*

GRUMMAN (G-58) F8F
BEARCAT USA

Designed to meet the requirements of the US Navy for a shipboard air superiority fighter, which, to a considerable extent, could sacrifice range to speed and manoeuvrability, the G-58 was ordered as the XF8F-1 on 31 November 1943. The first of two prototypes flew on 31 August 1944, powered by an R-2800-22W engine. Contracts were placed with the parent company for 2,023 F8F-1s – to be supplemented on 5 February 1945,

(Below) F7F-3N flown from K-3 airfield in Korea, 1953, by US Marine Corps FMAW HEDRON unit.

(Above) F8F-1 of 2nd FB Wing, R Thai AF. (Below) F8F-1B of GC I/22 *Saintonge, Armée de l'Air*, serving at Tan Son Nhut, Indochina, in 1954.

(Below) F8F-1 Bearcat was too late for WWII service.

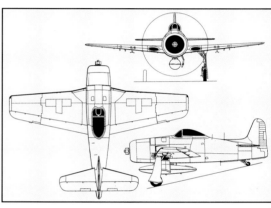

when General Motors was brought into the programme, with a contract for a further 1,876 to be designated F3M-1s. The first of 23 trials aircraft was flown on 6 January 1945, the production model standardising on the R-2800-34W engine. This, with the same 2,100 hp take-off rating as the -22W, offered combat ratings ranging from 2,750 hp at sea level to 2,450 hp at 9,600 ft (2 925 m). World War II ended before the F8F-1 achieved full operational status and contracts were immediately cut back. A total of 654 F8F-1s was delivered, these having an armament of four 0.5-in (12,7-mm) machine guns. The F8F-1 was followed by 226 F8F-1Bs with a four 20-mm cannon armament, 12 F8F-1Ns with night fighting equipment and 365 F8F-2 series models. The F8F-2 had the -1B armament, an R-2800-30W engine, taller vertical tail surfaces and some local restressing. Twelve of those built were completed for the nocturnal rôle as F8F-2Ns and 60 as F8F-2P recce fighters. Production was completed in May 1949. With fuel systems modified, about 140 F8F-1s and -1Bs were supplied to the *Armée de l'Air*, and 100 F8F-1s and 29 -1Bs (including many ex-French aircraft) to the Royal Thai Air Force. Twenty-eight *Armée de l'Air* Bearcats

(Top) F8F-1 of VF-72, USS *Leyte*, 1949-50. (Immediately above) F8F-1B of 514th Fighter Sqn, RVNAF, 1956.

Taller tail of the F8F-2 (below) is prominent on this example preserved by the Confederate Air Force.

passed to the (South) Vietnamese Air Force. The following data relate to the F8F-1. *Max speed, 423 mph (681 km/h) at 15,000 ft (4 575 m), 428 mph (689 km/h) at 18,800 ft (5 730 m). Initial climb, 3,230 ft/min (16,4 m/sec). Max range, 1,105 mls (1 778 km) at 250 mph (402 km/h). Empty weight, 7,323 lb (3 322 kg). Max loaded weight, 12,740 lb (5 779 kg). Span, 35 ft 6 in (10,82 m). Length, 27 ft 8 in (8,43 m). Height, 13 ft 8 in (4,16 m). Wing area, 144 sq ft (22,67 m².)*

GRUMMAN (G-79) F9F PANTHER   USA

Development of the G-79 single-engined, single-seat shipboard fighter was initiated as a replacement for the discontinued four-engined, two-seat G-75 shipboard night fighter, a contract for which had been placed as the XF9F-1 on 11 April 1946. The contract was transferred to the G-79 as the XF9F-2, the first of two examples of which flew on 21 November 1947 with a 5,000 lb st (2 268 kgp) Rolls-Royce Nene. The second XF9F-2 had a Pratt & Whitney J42-P-8 (licence-built

Nene), and a third prototype, the XF9F-3 flown on 16 August 1948, had a 4,600 lb st (2 086 kgp) Allison J33-A-8. Initial contracts called for 47 F9F-2s and 54 F9F-3s, but the latter were subsequently converted to -2 standard, and further contracts brought total US Navy procurement of the F9F-2 to 621 aircraft. The F9F-2 carried a built-in armament of four 20-mm cannon and this was retained by developed versions, the F9F-4 and F9F-5. The F9F-4 was powered by an Allison J33-A-16 providing 6,950 lb st (3 152 kgp) with water injection. At least one USMC squadron flew the F9F-4 in Korea, but unsatisfactory engine characteristics led to many of the 109 -4 Panthers built being later modified to -5s. The F9F-5 was engined with a J48-P-6 rated at 6,250 lb st (2 835 kgp) dry and 7,000 lb st (3 175 kgp) wet, featured a 2-ft (61-cm) fuselage extension and a taller vertical tail. A total of 616 F9F-5s was built, including a number of camera-equipped F9F-5Ps. The following data relate to the F9F-5. *Max speed, 604 mph (972 km/h) at sea level. Initial climb, 6,000 ft/min (30,48 m/sec). Range,*

Navy squadron VF-191 operated this F9F-2 (below) from USS *Princeton* during Korean conflict in 1951.

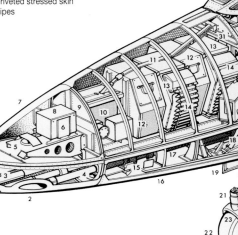

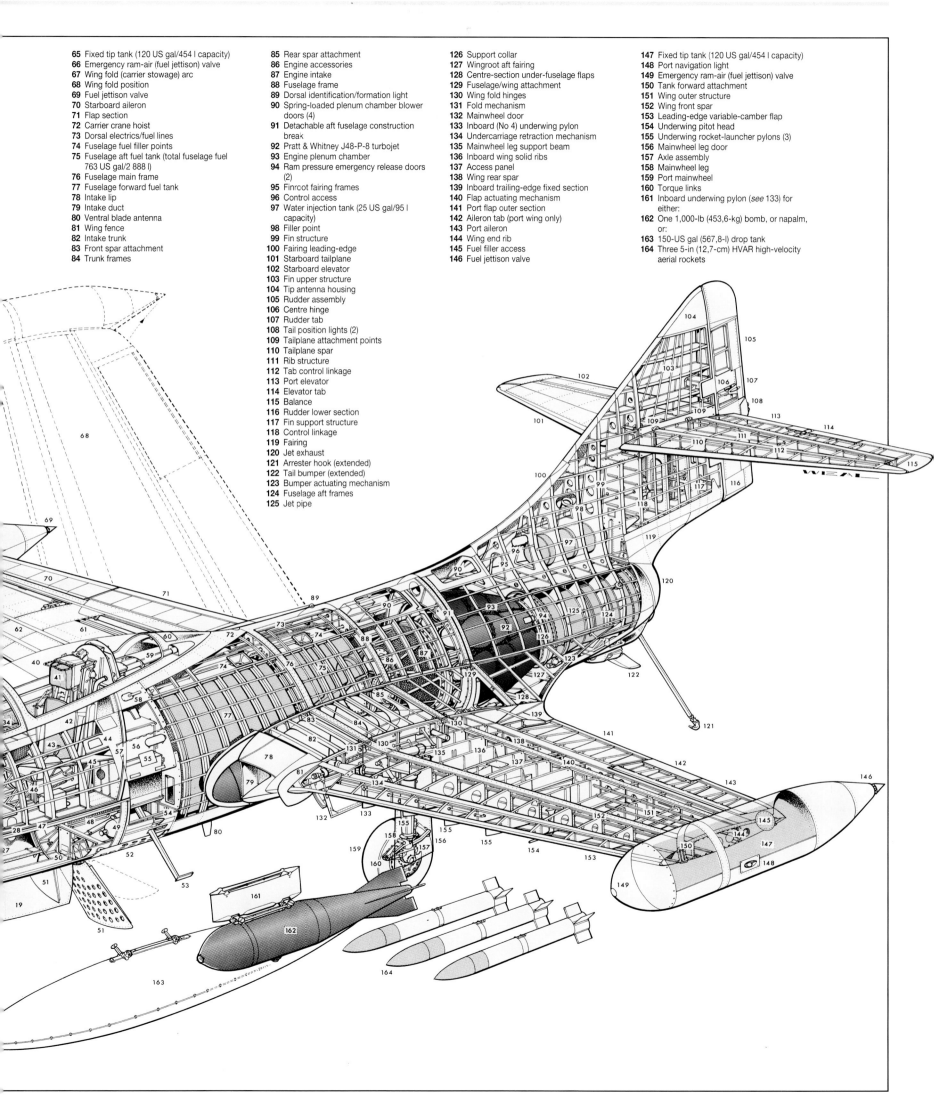

65 Fixed tip tank (120 US gal/454 l capacity)
66 Emergency ram-air (fuel jettison) valve
67 Wing fold (carrier stowage) arc
68 Wing fold position
69 Fuel jettison valve
70 Starboard aileron
71 Flap section
72 Carrier crane hoist
73 Dorsal electrics/fuel lines
74 Fuselage fuel filler points
75 Fuselage aft fuel tank (total fuselage fuel 763 US gal/2 888 l)
76 Fuselage main frame
77 Fuselage forward fuel tank
78 Intake lip
79 Intake duct
80 Ventral blade antenna
81 Wing fence
82 Intake trunk
83 Front spar attachment
84 Trunk frames

85 Rear spar attachment
86 Engine accessories
87 Engine intake
88 Fuselage frame
89 Dorsal identification/formation light
90 Spring-loaded plenum chamber blower doors (4)
91 Detachable aft fuselage construction break
92 Pratt & Whitney J48-P-8 turbojet
93 Engine plenum chamber
94 Ram pressure emergency release doors (2)
95 Fincot fairing frames
96 Control access
97 Water injection tank (25 US gal/95 l capacity)
98 Filler point
99 Fin structure
100 Fairing leading-edge
101 Starboard tailplane
102 Starboard elevator
103 Fin upper structure
104 Tip antenna housing
105 Rudder assembly
106 Centre hinge
107 Rudder tab
108 Tail position lights (2)
109 Tailplane attachment points
110 Tailplane spar
111 Rib structure
112 Tab control linkage
113 Port elevator
114 Elevator tab
115 Balance
116 Rudder lower section
117 Fin support structure
118 Control linkage
119 Fairing
120 Jet exhaust
121 Arrester hook (extended)
122 Tail bumper (extended)
123 Bumper actuating mechanism
124 Fuselage aft frames
125 Jet pipe

126 Support collar
127 Wingroot aft fairing
128 Centre-section under-fuselage flaps
129 Fuselage/wing attachment
130 Wing fold hinges
131 Fold mechanism
132 Mainwheel door
133 Inboard (No 4) underwing pylon
134 Undercarriage retraction mechanism
135 Mainwheel leg support beam
136 Inboard wing solid ribs
137 Access panel
138 Wing rear spar
139 Inboard trailing-edge fixed section
140 Flap actuating mechanism
141 Port flap outer section
142 Aileron tab (port wing only)
143 Port aileron
144 Wing end rib
145 Fuel filler access
146 Fuel jettison valve

147 Fixed tip tank (120 US gal/454 l capacity)
148 Port navigation light
149 Emergency ram-air (fuel jettison) valve
150 Tank forward attachment
151 Wing outer structure
152 Wing front spar
153 Leading-edge variable-camber flap
154 Underwing pitot head
155 Underwing rocket-launcher pylons (3)
156 Mainwheel leg door
157 Axle assembly
158 Mainwheel leg
159 Port mainwheel
160 Torque links
161 Inboard underwing pylon (see 133) for either:
162 One 1,000-lb (453,6-kg) bomb, or napalm, or:
163 150-US gal (567,8-l) drop tank
164 Three 5-in (12,7-cm) HVAR high-velocity aerial rockets

F9F-2B from VF-781, first Navy Reserve squadron to volunteer for active duty in Korea, May 1951.

1,300 mls (2 092 km) at 45,000 ft (13 715 m). Empty weight, 10,147 lb (4 603 kg). Max loaded weight, 20,600 lb (9 344 kg). Span, 38 ft 0 in (11,58 m). Length, 38 ft 10 in (11,83 m). Height, 12 ft 3 in (3,73 m). Wing area, 250 sq ft (23,22 m²).

Miami-based Marine Corps squadron VMA-334 flew the F9F-4 (above), which was slightly longer than the F9F-2 (below) version of the Panther.

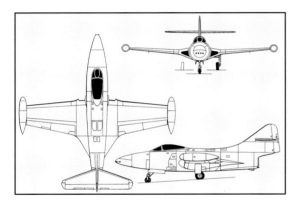

GRUMMAN (G-93) F9F COUGAR   USA

Retaining the fuselage and tail assembly of the Panther, and possessing similar built-in armament and engine, the XF9F-6 Cougar flew on 20 September 1951 with a thinner wing embodying 35 deg of sweepback and leading-edge slots. The initial production model,

F9F-7 (above) was virtually identical with the F9F-6, first of the swept-wing Cougar versions. The F9F-8 (below) had a marginally longer fuselage.

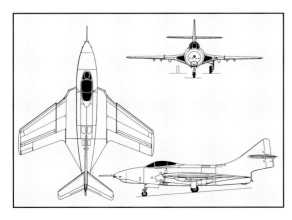

the F9F-6, entered US Navy service late in 1952, a total of 706 being built (including 60 camera-equipped F9F-6Ps) with the 6,250 lb st (2 835 kgp) J48-P-6A engine, together with 168 virtually identical F9F-7s with the similarly rated Allison J33-A-16 engine. An upgraded version with a J48-P-8A engine affording 7,250 lb st (3 289 kgp), a marginally lengthened fuselage, enlarged wing area and increased internal fuel, flew on 18 January 1954 as the F9F-8. A total of 712 was subsequently built, including 110 camera-equipped F9F-8Ps. The F9F-8 (which bore the Grumman design designation G-99) was later redesignated F-9J, some remaining with Reserve units into the early 'seventies.

Four Sidewinder AAMs could be carried by the F9F-8 (below) in addition to a pair of drop tanks.

The following data relate to the F9F-8. *Max speed, 647 mph (1 041 km/h) at sea level; range, 1,050 mls (1 690 km). Empty weight, 11,866 lb (5 382 kg). Max loaded weight, 24,763 lb (11 232 kg). Span, 34 ft 6 in (10,52 m). Length, 41 ft 9 in (12,73 m). Height, 12 ft 3 in (3,73 m). Wing area, 337 sq ft (31,31 m²).*

GRUMMAN (G-83) XF10F-1 JAGUAR   USA

The world's first variable-sweep combat aircraft, the XF10F-1 was designed as a transonic single-seat shipboard fighter with an internal armament of four 20-mm cannon and provision for an external bomb load of up to 4,000 lb (1 814 kg). The sweepback angle of the wings could be varied hydraulically between 13.5 and 42.5 deg, and high-lift devices consisted of full-span slats and an 80 per cent Fowler flap. The Jaguar was intended to be powered by a Westinghouse XJ40-WE-8 turbojet rated at 7,400 lb (3 357 kg) military thrust and 10,900 lb st (4 944 kgp) with afterburning, but when flight trials were initiated on 19 May 1952, a J40-WE-6 rated at 6,800 lb st (3 084 kgp) was fitted. Numerous problems arose during the test programme, and as some of these could not be resolved, trials terminated with the 32nd flight on 25 April 1953. Orders had been placed for 141 production F10F-1s, but these were cancelled on 1 April 1953. The following data are based on the projected characteristics with the fully-rated J40-

(Above) An F9F-7 with VF-21 aboard the USS *Midway* for operations over Korea, 1951. (Below) F9F-8 of VF-61 on USS *Intrepid*, July 1956.

Only one example was built of the XF10F-1 (above and below), which, in May 1952, became the world's first variable-sweep combat aircraft to fly.

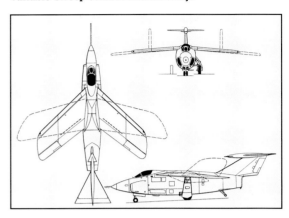

WE-8 engine and the performance figures were not attained under test. *Max speed, 710 mph (1 143 km/h) at sea level. Initial climb, 13,350 ft/min (67,8 m/sec). Combat range, 1,670 mls (2 687 km). Empty weight, 20,426 lb (9 265 kg). Max loaded weight, 35,450 lb (16 080 kg). Span (min sweep), 50 ft 7 in (15,42 m), (max sweep), 36 ft 8 in (11,17 m). Length, 54 ft 5 in (16,59 m). Height, 16 ft 3 in (4,95 m). Wing area (min sweep), 467 sq ft (43,38 m²), (max sweep), 450 sq ft (41,81 m²).*

Up to April 1953, the XF10F-1 (below) had made 32 flights, the programme then being dropped.

GRUMMAN (G-98) F11F-1 TIGER (F-11A)   USA

As the US Navy's first transonic shipboard warplane, the G-98 was ordered on 27 April 1953 as a revised and improved F9F-6. In the event, there was no commonality with the earlier fighter, but nevertheless, when the first example was flown on 30 July 1954, it was designated F9F-9. This was changed to F11F-1 in April 1955. Difficulties with the intended afterburning Wright J65-W-6 engine dictated installation of the de-rated J65-W-18 in the production F11F-1, with a maxi-

The F-14B – formerly F-14A(Plus) – (above) introduced F110-GE-400 engines in place of TF30-P-412As used to power the standard F-14A (below).

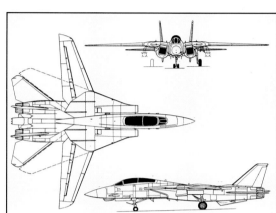

VF-21 was one of the six US Navy squadrons that flew the F11F-1 (above) on an operational basis.

mum military rating of 7,450 lb st (3 379 kgp) and 10,500 lb st (4 763 kgp) with full afterburning. In consequence, the F11F-1 failed to meet contractual performance guarantees and production was limited to 201 aeroplanes, with deliveries completed in December 1958. The last two Tigers of the initial production batch were fitted with the General Electric YJ79-GE-3 turbojet rated at 9,600 lb (4 355 kg) military thrust and 15,000 lb st (6 804 kgp) with afterburning as F11F-1Fs. The F11F-1 had an armament of four 20-mm cannon and initial deliveries to the US Navy were made in March 1957, fleet service use ending in April 1961. *Max speed, 753 mph (1 212 km/h) at sea level. Initial climb, 16,300 ft/min (82,8 m/sec). Range, 1,108 mls (1 783 km). Empty weight, 13,307 lb (6 036 kg). Max loaded weight, 23,459 lb (10 641 kg). Span, 31 ft 8 in (9,65 m). Length, 44 ft 10¾ in (13,68 m). Height, 13 ft 2¾ in (4,03 m). Wing area, 250 sq ft (23,22 m²).*

(Below) Definitive "long-nose" F11F-1 configuration.

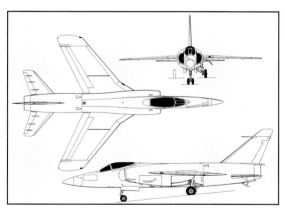

GRUMMAN (G-303) F-14 TOMCAT   USA

The first variable-geometry shipboard aircraft to achieve service, the F-14 two-seat multi-rôle fighter was announced winning contender in a US Navy design competition on 15 January 1969. Two prototypes were flown on 21 December 1970 and 24 May 1971. Twelve pre-series F-14As were also included in the total of 557 aircraft for the US Navy, initial deployment commencing in October 1972. In addition, 79 (of 80 ordered) F-14As were delivered to the (formerly Imperial) Iranian Air Force during 1976-78. The F-14A was initially powered by paired Pratt & Whitney TF-30-P-412A turbofans each having a thrust of 20,900 lb (9 480 kg) with max afterburning, these being supplanted in the final 102 aircraft by the similarly-rated -414A. Armament comprised one 20-mm M61A-1 rotary cannon with four fuselage-mounted Sparrow or Phoenix AAMs, two wing glove-mounted pylons permitting two additional Sparrow or Phoenix AAMs plus two Sidewinder AAMs to be carried. F-14A production was completed in April 1987, by which time production of the F-14A(Plus) had begun. An interim upgraded version of the basic Tomcat, the F-14A(Plus) retained the

systems of the F-14A, but switched to General Electric F110-GE-400 turbofans each rated at 14,000 lb st (6 350 kgp) dry and 23,100 lb st (10 478 kgp) with max afterburning. The first of two F-14A(Plus) prototypes was flown on 29 September 1986, and the first of 38 new-build Tomcats of this type followed on 14 November 1987. In addition, 32 F-14As were rebuilt to F-14A(Plus) standard. The first F-14A(Plus) prototype was originally the sole F-14B (the seventh pre-series aircraft) powered by Pratt & Whitney F401-PW-400 engines with which it flew on 12 September 1973. In 1991, the F-14B designation was re-adopted for the F-14A (Plus). Similarly powered to the F-14A(Plus), the definitive Tomcat upgrade, the F-14D, was flown in March 1990, featuring some 60 per cent new avionics. Contracts were placed for 37 examples with the last delivered July 1992. In addition, 18 F-14As were upgraded to similar standards as F-14D(R) Tomcats, a programme for the remanufacture of additional F-14As being curtailed in

F-14A (below) of VF-41 "Black Aces", one of two that intercepted Libyan Su-22s in August 1981.

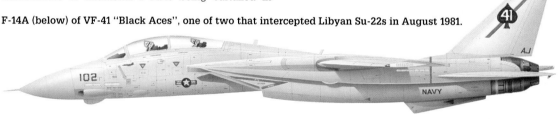

(Above) Original F-14B was the seventh pre-series Tomcat fitted with F401-PW-400 turbofans in 1973.

(Below) An early-production F-14A of VF-124 demonstrates the fully-swept, 68-deg, wing angle.

February 1991. The following data relate to the F-14A. *Max speed (with four semi-recessed Sparrow AAMs), 1,544 mph (2 485 km/h) at 40,000 ft (12 200 m), or Mach=2.34, 912 mph (1 468 km/h) at sea level, or Mach=1.2. Tactical radius, 510 mls (820 km) at Mach=1.3. Empty weight, 40,104 lb (18 191 kg). Max loaded weight, 74,349 lb (33 724 kg). Span (20 deg sweep), 64 ft 1½ in (19,55 m), (68 deg sweep), 38 ft 2½ in (11,65 m). Length, 62 ft 8 in (19,10 m). Height, 16 ft 0 in (4,88 m). Wing area, 565 sq ft (52,49 m²).*

GUDKOV GU-82   USSR

Installation of an M-82 radial engine in a LaGG-3 airframe produced the sole GU-82 (above).

Mikhail I Gudkov, who, together with Semyon A Lavochkin and Vladimir P Gorbunov, had been responsible for the wooden LaGG-3 single-seat fighter, was entrusted, in 1941, with the adaptation of the basic LaGG-3 airframe to take a 1,540 hp Shvetsov M-82 14-cylinder radial engine in place of the liquid-cooled 12-cylinder Klimov M-105PF. The M-82 installation was that of the Sukhoi Su-4 *shturmovik*, complete with bearers, cowling and propeller. Known as the Gu-82, the fighter was not, in the event, flight tested until the summer of 1942, two prototypes having been ordered, but only one of these having been completed when, in October 1941, the factory had been hurriedly evacuated. By the time testing of Gudkov's fighter began, a similarly-powered derivative of the LaGG-3 developed by S M Alekseyev, the La-5, had been ordered into production, and work on the Gu-82 was accordingly discontinued. *Endurance, 1.8 hrs. Span, 32 ft 1⅞ in (9,80 m). Length, 28 ft 6⁹⁄₁₀ in (8,71 m). Wing area, 188.37 sq ft (17,50 m²).*

(Below) GU-82 used entire power plant from an Su-4.

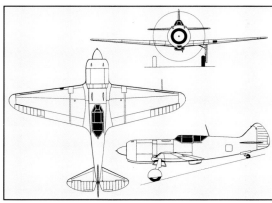

GUDKOV GU-1   USSR

The Gu-1 single-seat fighter designed by Mikhail Gudkov was almost certainly inspired by the Bell P-39 Airacobra, being of essentially similar concept, with a liquid-cooled engine installed aft of the pilot's cockpit, close to the CG, and driving the propeller via an extension shaft and reduction gear. Design of the Gu-1 began in 1940, and the fighter was of mixed construction, with welded steel-tube forward and centre fuselage covered by duralumin skinning and metal wing mainspars, the remainder of the airframe being of wood. Power was provided by a Mikulin AM-41 12-cylinder liquid-cooled engine, the main coolant radiators for which were buried in the wings. The Mikulin bureau experienced difficulties with the extension shaft and reduction gear, which were not ready for testing until 1942. Armament

Key to Grumman F-14A Tomcat

1 Pitot tube
2 Radar target horn
3 Glass-fibre radome
4 IFF aerial array
5 Hughes AWG-9 flat plate radar scanner
6 Scanner tracking mechanism
7 Ventral ALQ-100 antenna
8 Gun muzzle blast trough
9 Radar electronics equipment bay
10 AN/ASN-92 inertial navigation unit
11 Radome hinge
12 In-flight refuelling probe (extended)
13 ADF aerial
14 Windscreen rain removal air duct
15 Temperature probe
16 Cockpit front pressure bulkhead
17 Angle of attack transmitter
18 Formation lighting strip
19 Cannon barrels
20 Nosewheel doors
21 Gun gas vents
22 Rudder pedals
23 Cockpit pressurization valve
24 Navigation radar display
25 Control column
26 Instrument panel shroud
27 Kaiser AN/ANG-12 head-up display
28 Windscreen panels
29 Cockpit canopy cover
30 Face blind seat firing handle
31 Ejection seat headrest
32 Pilot's Martin-Baker GRU-7A ejection seat
33 Starboard side console panel
34 Engine throttle levers
35 Port side console panel
36 Pitot static head
37 Canopy emergency release handle
38 Foot out step
39 M-61-A1 Vulcan 20-mm six-barrel rotary cannon
40 Nose undercarriage leg strut
41 Catapult strop link
42 Catapult strop, launch position
43 Twin nosewheels
44 Folding boarding ladder
45 Hughes AIM-54A Phoenix air-to-air missile (6)
46 Fuselage missile pallet
47 Cannon ammunition drum (675 rounds)
48 Rear boarding step
49 Ammunition feed chute
50 Armament control panels
51 Kick-in step
52 Tactical information display hand controller
53 Naval Flight Officer's instrument console
54 NFO's ejection seat
55 Starboard intake lip
56 Ejection seat launch rails
57 Cockpit aft decking
58 Electrical system controller
59 Rear radio and electronics equipment bay
60 Boundary layer bleed air duct
61 Port engine intake lip
62 Electrical system relay controls
63 Glove vane pivot
64 Port air intake
65 Glove vane housing
66 Navigation light
67 Variable area intake ramp doors
68 Cooling system boundary layer duct ram air intake
69 Intake ramp door hydraulic jacks
70 Air system piping
71 Air data computer
72 Heat exchanger
73 Heat exchanger exhaust duct
74 Forward fuselage fuel tanks
75 Canopy hinge point
76 Electrical and control system ducting
77 Control rod runs
78 UHF/TACAN aerial
79 Glove vane hydraulic jack
80 Starboard glove vane, extended
81 Honeycomb panel construction
82 Navigation light
83 Main undercarriage wheel bay
84 Starboard intake duct spill door
85 Wing slat/flap flexible drive shaft
86 Dorsal spine fairing
87 Fuselage top longeron
88 Central flaps/slat drive motor
89 Emergency hydraulic generator
90 Bypass door hydraulic jack
91 Intake bypass door
92 Port intake ducting
93 Wing glove sealing horn
94 Flap/slat telescopic drive shaft
95 Port wing pivot bearing
96 Wing pivot carry through (electron beam welded titanium box construction)
97 Wing pivot box integral fuel tank
98 Fuselage longeron/pivot box attachment joint
99 UHF data link/IFF aerial
100 Honeycomb skin panelling
101 Wing glove stiffeners/dorsal fences
102 Starboard wing pivot bearing
103 Slat/flap drive shaft gearbox
104 Starboard wing integral fuel tank (total internal fuel capacity 1,969 Imp gal/8 951 l)
105 Leading-edge slat drive shaft
106 Slat guide rails
107 Starboard leading-edge slat segments (open)
108 Starboard navigation light
109 Low-voltage formation lighting
110 Wing tip fairing
111 Outboard manoeuvre flap segments (down position)
112 Port roll control spoilers
113 Spoiler hydraulic jacks
114 Inboard, high lift flap (down position)
115 Inboard flap hydraulic jack
116 Manoeuvre flap drive shaft
117 Variable wing sweep screw jack
118 Starboard undercarriage pivot fixing
119 Starboard engine compressor face
120 Wing glove sealing plates
121 Pratt & Whitney TF30-P-412A afterburning turbofan
122 Rear fuselage fuel tanks
123 Fuselage longeron joint
124 Control system artificial feel units
125 Tailplane control rods
126 Starboard engine bay
127 Wing glove pneumatic seal
128 Fin root fairing
129 Fin spar attachment joints
130 Starboard fin leading edge
131 Starboard all-moving tailplane
132 Starboard wing (fully swept position)
133 AN-ALR-45 tail warning radar antenna
134 Fin aluminium honeycomb skin panel construction
135 Fin-tip aerial fairing
136 Tail navigation light
137 Electronic countermeasures antenna (ECM)
138 Rudder honeycomb construction
139 Rudder hydraulic jack
140 Afterburning ducting
141 Variable area nozzle control jack
142 Airbrake (upper and lower surfaces)
143 Airbrake hydraulic jack
144 Starboard engine exhaust nozzle
145 Anti-collision light
146 Tail formation light
147 ECM aerial
148 Port rudder

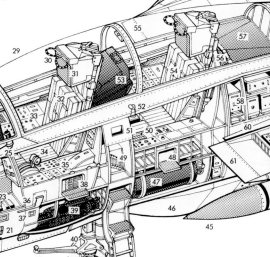

An F-14A (below) of VF-32 from USS *John F Kennedy* in original gull gray and white finish.

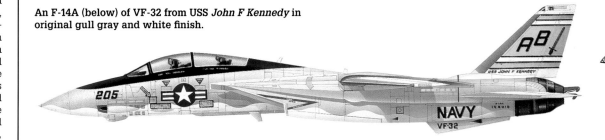

149 Beaver tail fairing
150 Fuel jettison pipe
151 ECM antenna
152 Deck arrester hook (stowed position)
153 AN/ALE-29A chaff and flare dispensers
154 Nozzle shroud sealing flaps
155 Port convergent/divergent afterburner
exhaust nozzle
156 Tailplane honeycomb construction
157 AN/ALR-45(V) tail warning radar antenna
158 Tailplane boron fibre skin panels
159 Port wing (fully swept position)
160 All-moving tailplane construction
161 Tailplane pivot fixing
162 Jet pipe mounting
163 Fin/tailplane attachment mainframe

164 Cooling air louvres
165 Tailplane hydraulic jack
166 Hydraulic system equipment pack
167 Formation lighting strip
168 Oil cooler air intake
169 Port ventral fin
170 Engine accessory compartment
171 Ventral engine access doors
172 Hydraulic reservoir
173 Bleed air ducting
174 Port engine bay
175 Intake compressor face
176 Wing variable sweep screw jack
177 Main undercarriage leg strut
178 Hydraulic retraction jack
179 Wing skin panel

180 Fuel system piping
181 Rear spar
182 Flap hinge brackets
183 Port roll control spoilers
184 Flap leading-edge eyebrow seal fairing
185 Port manoeuvre flap honeycomb
construction
186 Wing tip fairing construction
187 Low-voltage formation lighting
188 Port navigation light
189 Wing rib construction
190 Port wing integral fuel tank
191 Front spar
192 Leading-edge rib construction
193 Slat guide rails
194 Port leading-edge slat segments, open

195 Slat honeycomb construction
196 Port mainwheel
197 Torque scissor links
198 Main undercarriage front bracing strut
199 Mainwheel door
200 Ventral pylon attachment
201 External fuel tank (222 Imp gal/1 009 l
capacity)
202 Sparrow missile launch adaptor
203 AIM-7F Sparrow air-to-air missile
204 Wing glove pylon attachment
205 Cranked wing glove pylon
206 Sidewinder missile launch rail
207 AIM-9C Sidewinder air-to-air missile
208 Phoenix launch pallet
209 AIM-54A Phoenix air-to-air missile

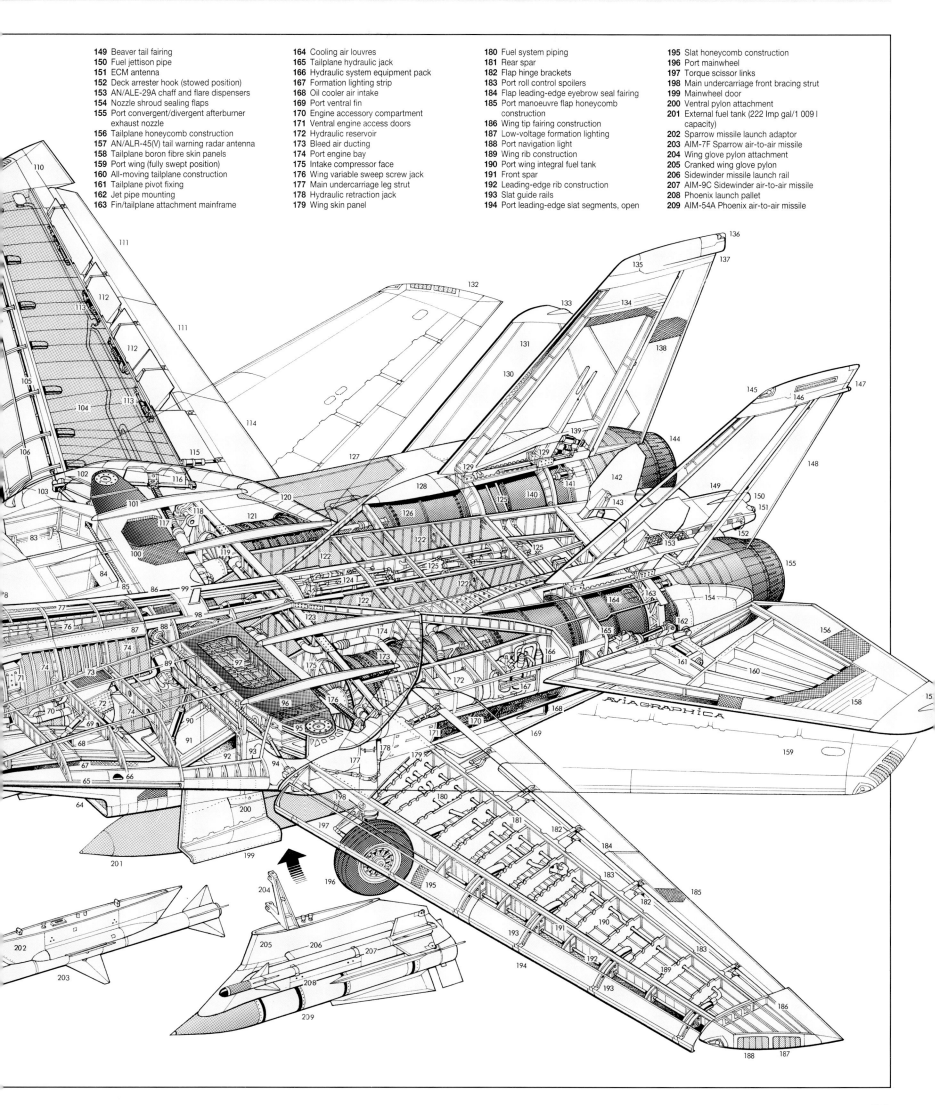

comprised a single 37-mm Taubin cannon firing through the propeller shaft. In the event, the Gu-1 proved to be seriously overweight. The initial flight test was performed by A I Nikashin on 12 July 1943, but after reaching some 650 ft (200 m), the fighter dived into the ground, killing the pilot, and further development of the Gu-1 was abandoned. No illustrations of the Gu-1 appear to have survived and the only available data are the weights. *Empty weight, 8,249 lb (3 742 kg). Loaded weight, 10,163 lb (4 610 kg).*

H

HÄFELI DHA (M IV)   Switzerland

Designed by August Häfeli and owing much to experience gained with the DH-3 (M III) series of two-seat reconnaissance aircraft, the DH-4 (M IV) single-seat fighter was powered by a 150 hp Hispano-Suiza HS-41 eight-cylinder water-cooled engine. The prototype, built by the K + W (Konstruktions-Werkstätte) at Thun, was flown early in 1918. Of wooden construction with fabric covering and carrying an armament of one synchronised machine gun, the DH-4 was found to possess a disappointing performance and poor handling characteristics. Tests by the Swiss *Fliegertruppe* were initiated in May 1918, but terminated in August, when the sole prototype was returned to the K + W for structural load testing, no further flight trials being undertaken. *Max speed, 92 mph (148 km/h). Initial climb, 886 ft/min (4,5 m/sec). Range, 186 mls (300 km). Empty weight, 1,410 lb (640 kg). Loaded weight, 1,951 lb (885 kg). Span, 32 ft 6¹/₄ in (9,80 m). Length, 19 ft 8¹/₄ in (6, 00 m). Height, 8 ft 6¹/₃ in (2,60 m). Wing area, 236.8 sq ft (22, 00 m²).*

Built for the *Schweizerische Fliegertruppe*, the DHA (above and below) failed to meet specifications.

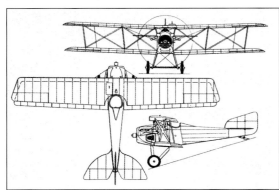

HÄFELI MA-7   Switzerland

The MA-7 (*Militär-Apparat*-7) was designed by August Häfeli to meet a 1924 Federal Military Department requirement for a single-seat fighter. Built by the K + W at Thun and owing much to the Fokker D VII, the MA-7 was powered by a 300 hp Hispano-Suiza HS-42 eight-cylinder water-cooled engine and was of wooden construction with fabric skinning. Proposed armament comprised two synchronised rifle-calibre machine guns in the fuselage ahead of the cockpit. Completed in 1925, the MA-7 was tested by the *Fliegertruppe* between 6 February and 28 April 1926, but both flight characteristics and performance failed to meet specified requirements. It was returned to the K + W

for installation of a prototype of a new engine, the LWF-12 of 400 hp, that had been developed by the Swiss Locomotive and Machine Works. In the event, the dimensions and weight of the LWF-12 engine were such that major redesign of the airframe was called for and the MA-7 project was abandoned in consequence. *Max speed, 146 mph (235 km/h). Initial climb, 1,811 ft/min (9,2 m/sec). Range, 186 mls (300 km). Empty weight, 1,858 lb (843 kg). Loaded weight, 2,674 lb (1 213 kg). Span, 32 ft 6¹/₈ in (9,91 m). Length, 21 ft 8¹/₄ in (6,61 m). Height, 9 ft 1⁷/₈ in (2,79 m). Wing area, 255.65 sq ft (23,75 m²).*

Owing much to the Fokker D VII, the MA-7 (above and below) proved no more successful than the Häfeli DH-4 when tested by the *Fliegertruppe*.

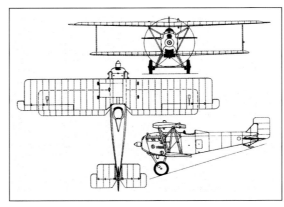

HF-24 MARUT   India

Designed under the leadership of Dr Kurt Tank, the Marut (Wind Spirit) was India's first indigenous combat aircraft. The first of two prototypes was flown on 17 June 1961. The first of 18 pre-production Marut Mk 1 single-seat ground attack fighters followed in April 1963. One of these became the Mk 1BX test flown with the Egyptian EI-300 turbojet, another was converted as the Mk 1E and two became Mk 1Rs with an experimental reheat system. One hundred and twelve production Marut Mk 1s were built, of which the first was flown on 15 November 1967, production terminating with 12 two-seat Marut Mk 1T trainers (preceded by two two-seat prototypes). The production

(Below) A formation of three HF-24 Maruts.

Marut was powered by two 4,850 lb st (2 200 kgp) HAL-built Orpheus 703 turbojets and built-in armament comprised four 30-mm Aden Mk 2 cannon plus a retractable Matra Type 103 pack containing 50 68-mm. rockets. Four 1,000-1b (454-kg) bombs or other ordnance could be carried externally. The Marut equipped three squadrons and was finally phased out of service in 1985. *Max speed, 705 mph (1 134 km/h) at sea level, 673 mph (1 083 km/h) at 40,000 ft (12 200 m). Initial climb, 8,500 ft/min (43 m/sec). Normal range, 480 mls (772 km). Empty weight (equipped), 13,658 lb (6 195 kg). Max loaded weight, 24,048 lb (10 908 kg). Span, 29 ft 6¹/₃ in (9,00 m). Length, 52 ft 0³/₄ in (15,87 m). Height, 11 ft 9³/₄ in (3,60 m). Wing area, 306. 8 sq ft (28,50m²).*

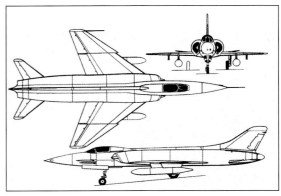

(Above) An HF-24 Marut I as used by Nos 10, 220 and 31 Squadrons of the Indian Air Force until 1985.

HAL AJEET   India

A derivative of the licence-built Folland Gnat (which see), the Ajeet (Invincible) single-seat lightweight interceptor and ground attack fighter had less than 60 per cent commonality with its progenitor. It differed from the Gnat principally in having integral wing fuel tankage, four underwing ordnance stations, a new ejection seat, improved control systems and new avionics. The final two production Gnats were completed as Ajeet prototypes, the first of these flying on 5 March 1975, and the first production Ajeet was flown on 30 September 1976. The Ajeet was powered

(Below) The Ajeet derivative of the Gnat.

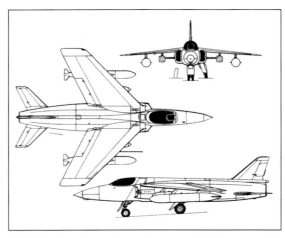

The HAL Ajeet was retained in service by No 2 Sqn of the 1AF (below) until March 1991.

by a 4,500 lb st (2 041 kgp) Orpheus 701-01 turbojet and had a built-in armament of two 30-mm Aden cannon. Production of a total of 79 was completed in February 1982, with final phase-out from Indian service taking place on 25 March 1991. Apart from the new-build Ajeets, 10 Gnats were converted to a similar standard. *Max speed, 634 mph (1 020 km/h) at 39,375 ft (12 000 m), 685 mph (1 102 km/h) at sea level. Time to 39,375 ft (12 000 m), 6.05 min. Empty weight, 5,086 lb (2 307 kg). Max loaded weight, 9,195 lb (4 171 kg). Span, 22 ft 1 in (6,73 m). Length, 29 ft 8 in (9,04 m). Height, 8 ft 1 in (2,46 m). Wing area, 157.7 sq ft (14,65 m²).*

HAL LIGHT COMBAT AIRCRAFT   India

Development of the Light Combat Aircraft (LCA) was begun in 1984 by Hindustan Aeronautics. It was rolled out in November 1995, but made its maiden flight only on 4 January 2001, piloted by Rajiv Kothiyal. This must be a record for protracted gestation. It has been projected in three variants: a fighter, a naval fighter, and a two-seater conversion trainer. LCA is a small tail-less delta with compound sweep on the leading edge. Unusually, the sweep angle is steeper inboard, rather like the Swedish Viggen. The first prototype was powered by a GE F404, but the intended powerplant is indigenous: the Kaveri, rated at 18,100 lb (8 210 kgp) max thrust. This however is not expected to become available before 2004, although SNECMA has offered to help. The radar is also indigenous, as is the quadruplex FBW system, which was originally started with assistance from GD, although this was cancelled following US sanctions imposed after India's nuclear tests in May 1998. Armament consists of a single 23-mm GSh-23 cannon, two medium range and two dogfight AAMs. *Max speed, supersonic at all altitudes; no other performance details available. Span, 26 ft 10¹/₂ in (8,20 m). Length, 43 ft 3¹/₂ in (13,20 m). Height, 14 ft 5 in (4,40m). Empty weight, c12,125 lb (5 500 kg). Clean takeoff weight, 12,125 lb (8 500 kg).*

Hindustan Aeronautics Light Combat Aircraft (LCA).

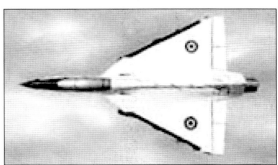

HALBERSTADT DI   Germany

First of the Halberstadt fighters, the D I (above) remained a single prototype, but led to the D II.

In the late autumn of 1915, the Halberstädter Flugzeugwerke initiated flight testing of a single-seat fighter evolved by Dipl-Ing Karl Theis from the Halberstadt B II trainer. Apart from some structural reinforcement and the mounting of a single synchronised LMG 08/15 machine gun, the Halberstadt fighter differed from its progenitor primarily in having shorter-span, staggered wings. Two prototypes were built, one powered by a 120 hp Argus

As II and the other by a 100 hp Mercedes D I. Both featured a neat, car-type frontal radiator which, it transpired, was to prove ineffectual in summer temperatures and was not to be perfected until 1918. These prototypes were at Adlershof in February 1916, the Mercedes-engined prototype undergoing static load testing, and, at this time, they were designated Halberstadt D I. An order for an initial batch of 12 D I fighters "powered by a 120 hp engine" was placed on 21 March 1916. In the event, the production model of the D I embodied a number of design refinements, and, with a 120 hp Mercedes D II engine, became the Halberstadt D II (which see). The following data relate to the 100 hp Mercedes-engined D I prototype. *Time to 3,280 ft (1 000 m), 4.5 min. Empty weight, 1,215 lb (551 kg). Loaded weight, 1,630 lb (739 kg). Wing area, 258.34 sq ft (24, 00 m²).*

HALBERSTADT D II & D III   Germany

Derived from the D I, the D II (above) was built in small numbers by three companies in 1916.

The production derivative of the D I, which entered service with the *Fliegertruppe* from June 1916 as the D II, differed from its progenitor in a number of respects apart from its 120 hp Mercedes D II six-cylinder water-cooled engine. The car-type radiator was discarded in favour of an exposed cylinder block and wing-mounted radiator, with an inordinately massive exhaust stack to starboard, and the pilot's cockpit was raised and faired by means of a turtle deck. Early production D IIs retained the balanced ailerons of the D I, but later examples adopted wide-chord, unbalanced ailerons. The armament of one LMG 08/15 machine gun on the starboard side of the forward fuselage was retained, and the D II, which possessed an exceptionally robust structure, was licence-built by the Automobil und Aviatik AG and the Hannoversche Waggonfabrik AG. Each produced 30, which, somewhat confusingly, were initially designated Aviatik D I and Hannover D I respectively. After completing an initial batch of 12 D IIs, the parent company continued with a batch of 24 D

The D III with an Argus As II (above) was otherwise similar to the Mercedes-powered D II (below).

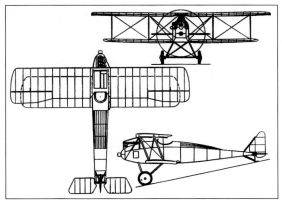

IIs and D IIIs, there being no fundamental difference between the two models apart from engine, the latter having a 120 hp Argus As II. During manufacture of a follow-on batch of 30 D IIIs by the Halberstädter Flugzeugwerke production was switched to the improved D V, and - apart from licence manufacture of the D II – total production of the D II and D III was 50 aircraft. *Max speed, 93 mph (150 km/h) at sea level. Time to 3,280 ft (1 000 m), 3.5 min. Range, 155 mls (250 km). Empty weight 1,147 lb (520 kg). Loaded weight, 1,610 lb (730 kg). Span 28 ft 103/8 in (8,80 m). Length, 23 ft 11³/₈ in (7,30 m). Wing area, 254 sqft (23,60 m²).*

HALBERSTADT D IV   Germany

On 9 March 1916, the Halberstäldter Flugzeugwerke was awarded a contract to develop a twin-gun fighter powered by a 150-160 hp engine. Designated D IV and powered by a 150 hp Benz Bz III engine, the new fighter was an elegant single-bay biplane with a neatly-cowled power plant. Three prototypes were ordered, of which one was for static load testing. Submitted at Adlershof in October 1916, the D IV was rejected by the *Idflieg* because of "unsatisfactory cabane design", but served as a basis for the highly successful Cl II two-seat fighter. The following data relate to the D II. *Max Loaded weight, 1,819 lb (825 kg). Span, 27 ft 6³/₄ in (8,40m). Wing area, 258.34 sq ft (24,00 m²).*

Two prototypes of the D IV (below) were tested in October 1916, but were found wanting by *Idflieg*.

HALBERSTADT D V   Germany

The D V, which reverted to the two-bay formula, was based on the earlier D III and was similarly powered with a 120 hp Argus As II engine. It differed in featuring aerodynamically-balanced inset ailerons and a redesigned centre section, which, with a simplified cabane structure and a large semi-circular cut-out in the upper wing, offered an improved field of view for the pilot. A single LMG 08/15 machine gun was mounted on the port side of the forward fuselage, but the last D Vs produced were armed with twin synchronised guns. The D V appeared at the Front in the autumn of 1916, some 50-55 being produced by the Halberstädter Flugzeugwerke during the course of that year. A further 37 were manufactured in 1917, these being mostly for use by Turkey where the first D Vs arrived in March 1917. Operating in high temperatures, the D Vs were fitted with additional radiators on their fuselage sides, resulting in some loss of performance. On the Western Front, the D Vs were replaced in the operational rôle in the summer of 1917, but others remained in first-line

(Below) The Halberstadt D V with Argus As II engine.

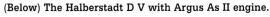

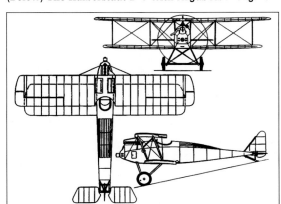

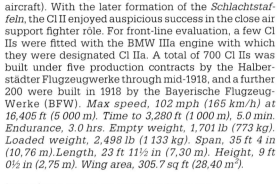

(Above) A Halberstadt D V of the Turkish Army Aviation force, as used in 1917-18.

service in Palestine well into 1918. *Max speed, 99 mph (160 km/h). Time to 3,280 ft (1 000 m), 4.0 min. Range, 124 mls (200 km). Empty weight, 1,323 lb (600 kg). Loaded weight, 1,790 lb (812 kg). Span, 28 ft 6½ in (8,70 m). Length, 23 ft 11⅜ in (7,30 m). Wing area, 258.34 sq ft (24,00 m²).*

Last of the Halberstadt single-seaters, the D V (below) remained in service well into 1918.

HALBERSTADT Cʟ II   Germany

In the autumn of 1916, the German Air Staff conceived a requirement for a two-seat "defensive patrol and pursuit aircraft"; an amalgam of features of the two-seat C-type and single-seat D-type. Accordingly, in November 1916, the Halberstädter Flugzeugwerke, among other companies, received a three-prototype contract for an aircraft fulfilling a specification prepared by the *Idflieg*. Designed by Dipl-Ing Karl Theis and based on his unsuccessful D IV single-seat fighter, this aircraft, initially designated C II but redesignated Cl II in the summer of 1917, was powered by a 160 hp Mercedes D III water-cooled engine. It was armed with a fixed LMG 08/15 machine gun for the pilot and a flexible LMG 14 on a raised ring mounting for the gunner. Within days of passing its official type test, on 7 May 1917, the first Cl II production order was placed. This two-seater reached the Front in August 1917, achieving immediate acclaim. Its excellent manoeuvrability, good climb rate and the wide field of view provided for the rear gunner enabled it to engage enemy single-seaters on equal terms. The Cl II rapidly became the mainstay of the *Schutzstaffeln*

The two-seat Cl II (below) became the maintstay of the *Schutzstaffeln* for escort duties in 1917.

(units formed to provide protection for reconnaissance aircraft). With the later formation of the *Schlachtstaffeln*, the Cl II enjoyed auspicious success in the close air support fighter rôle. For front-line evaluation, a few Cl IIs were fitted with the BMW IIIa engine with which they were designated Cl IIa. A total of 700 Cl IIs was built under five production contracts by the Halberstädter Flugzeugwerke through mid-1918, and a further 200 were built in 1918 by the Bayerische Flugzeug-Werke (BFW). *Max speed, 102 mph (165 km/h) at 16,405 ft (5 000 m). Time to 3,280 ft (1 000 m), 5.0 min. Endurance, 3.0 hrs. Empty weight, 1,701 lb (773 kg). Loaded weight, 2,498 lb (1 133 kg). Span, 35 ft 4 in (10,76 m). Length, 23 ft 11½ in (7,30 m). Height, 9 ft 0½ in (2,75 m). Wing area, 305.7 sq ft (28,40 m²).*

(Below) The Cl II in standard configuration.

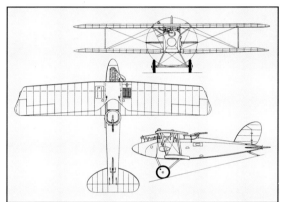

HALBERSTADT Cʟ IV   Germany

(Above) The Cl IV derivative of the Cl II offered greater manoeuvrability and better performance.

Early in 1918, the Halberstädter Flugzeugwerke began work on a higher-performance and more manoeuvrable derivative of the Cl II. By February the prototype of this Cl IV had arrived at Adlershof for its official type test. Lighter than its predecessor as a result of some structural refinement, the Cl IV possessed a similar armament and a 160 hp Mercedes D IIIa engine. It passed its type test during March-April 1918, the official report referring to its "very favourable climb rate and superlative handling qualities". Commencing in May 1918, a total of 450 Cl IVs was ordered from Halberstadt and a further 250 were ordered from the Luftfahrzeug Gesellschaft (Roland). The Cl IV supplemented the Cl II in the *Schlachtstaffeln*, and a total of 136 was recorded at the Front on 31 August 1918, deliveries still being under way when hostilities terminated. *Max speed, 104 mph (168 km/h) at 16,405 ft (5 000 m). Time to 16,405 ft (5 000 m), 32 min. Endurance, 325 hrs. Empty weight, 1,605 lb (728 kg). Loaded weight, 2,354 lb (1 068 kg). Span, 35 ft 2¾ in (10,74 m). Length, 21 ft 5½ in (6,54 m). Height, 8 ft 9 in (2,67 m). Wing area, 311.7 sq ft (28,96 m²).*

The Cl IV (above and below) was built by Luftfahrzeug Gesellschaft (Roland) as well as Halberstadt.

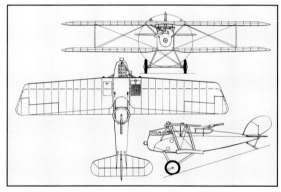

HALBERSTADT Cʟꜱ I   Germany

A requirement was formulated in September 1918 for a two-seat fighter optimised for the close air support rôle. Climb rate was considered of secondary importance, emphasis being placed on speed, manoeuvrability and dive capability. The Halberstädter Flugzeugwerke responded with a design based on the C VIII reconnaissance biplane, but having reduced wing span and a 160 hp Mercedes D IIIa engine, and designated Cls I. The requirement resulting in the Cls I had specified an increase in useful load (by comparison with the Cl IV) from 750 lb (340 kg) to 926 lb (420 kg), apparently to cater for a twin fixed-gun armament and a larger load of anti-personnel bombs, but the provision of a 20-mm Becker cannon for the gunner was also proposed. The

Based on the C VIII reconnaissance biplane, the two-seat Cls I (below) did not enter production.

Cls I was type tested in October 1918, but when the static testing of components terminated on 6 December, some strengthening of the tail surfaces was called for. Only three or four prototype Cls I close air support fighters were completed. *Max speed, 115 mph (185 km/h). Empty weight, 1,504 lb (682 kg). Loaded weight, 2,430 lb (1 102 kg). Span, 31 ft 9⅞ in (9,70 m). Length, 22 ft 9⅝ in (6,95 m). Height, 10 ft 0 in (3,05 m). Wing area, 284.18 sq ft (26,40 m²).*

HALL XFH-1   USA

Designed by Charles W Hall of the Hall Aluminum Company, the XFH-1 featured a light alloy airframe with fabric-covered wing and tail surfaces and a dural-skinned fuselage. This last was watertight in order that the fighter would stay afloat in the event of alighting on water, the main undercarriage members being jettisonable to prevent nosing over. Insofar as it featured a stressed-skin, semi-monocoque fuselage, the XFH-1 was ahead of its time when delivered to Anacostia for trials on 18 June 1929. It displayed poor control response during testing, was found to be tail heavy and suffered a structural failure in the upper wing during an early flight. It was subsequently repaired and flight trials were resumed, but US Navy interest was centred primarily on the novel structure and no production order was placed. The XFH-1 was powered by a 450 hp Pratt & Whitney R-1340B Wasp and intended armament comprised two 0.30-in (7,62-mm) machine guns. *Max speed, 153 mph (246 km/h) at sea level. Time to 5,000 ft (1 525 m), 2.8 min. Range, 275 mls (442 km). Empty weight, 1,773 lb (804 kg). Loaded weight, 2,514 lb (1 140 kg). Span, 32 ft 0 in (9,75 m). Length, 22 ft 6 in (6,86 m). Height, 11 ft 0 in (3,35 m). Wing area, 255 sq ft (23,69 m²).*

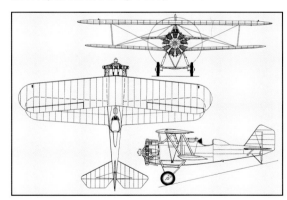

Tested in 1929, the Hall XFH-1 (above and below) was an essay in the use of light alloy structures.

HANDLEY PAGE HPS-1 (Type S)   UK

The Type S single-seat shipboard fighter (retrospectively designated H.P.21) was designed by S T A Richards to meet a US Navy requirement and was intended to operate with either wheels or floats. Employing a relatively thick Göttingen wing profile and featuring full-span leading-edge slats and full-span slotted ailerons, the Type S was of wooden construction. Both fuselage and wings were plywood covered. Power was provided by a 232 hp Gwynne-built Bentley B.R.2 rotary engine and provision was made for the installation of paired synchronised 0.30-in (7,62-mm) Marlin machine guns. The US Navy placed a contract for three prototypes (the US Navy designation being HPS-1), and the first flight of the initial Type S took place on 7 September 1923. The Type S proved dangerously deficient

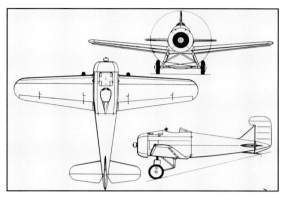

The only fighter by Handley Page, the HPS-1 (above and below) failed to meet US Navy requirements.

in directional stability, various palliatives being applied with little effect. The wings of the first prototype, with six degrees of dihedral, were then fitted to the fuselage of the second prototype, flight testing being resumed in February 1924. This mélange was wrecked soon afterwards when the undercarriage collapsed during landing (300 lb/136 kg of ballast having been clamped to the chassis radius rods to simulate the specified military load). The US Navy cancelled the contract, no further development being undertaken. *Max speed, 145 mph (233 km/h) at sea level. Initial climb, 1,800 ft/min (9,14 m/sec). Endurance, 3 hrs. Empty weight, 1,320 lb (599 kg). Max loaded weight, 2,030 lb (921 kg). Span, 29 ft 3 in (8,91 m). Length, 21 ft 5½ in (6,55 m). Height, 9 ft 7 in (2,92 m). Wing area, 114.5 sq ft (10,64 m²).*

HANNOVER Cʟ II   Germany

The concept of the comparatively light and manoeuvrable two-seat "defensive patrol and pursuit" aircraft realised by the German Air Staff in the autumn of 1916 led to the issue of three-prototype contracts to several manufacturers, including the Hannoversche Waggonfabrik AG. Initially designated C II, but redesignated Cl II in the summer of 1917, the company's contender, designed by Dipl-Ing Hermann Dorner, successfully completed its *Typenprüfung* on 21 July 1917. Powered by a 180 hp Argus As III water-cooled engine, the Hannover Cl II was armed with a single fixed LMG 08/15 machine gun and an LMG 14 machine gun on a flexible mounting. Within two months of the type test, the *Idflieg* placed orders for 500 Cl IIs and these were introduced into service from October 1917. The Cl II proved exceptionally versatile, and, in addition to its fighter rôles,

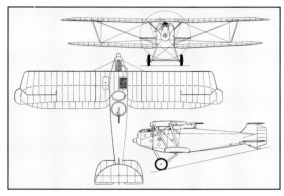

The two-seat Hannover Cl II (above and below) proved highly manoeuvrable and versatile.

it was utilised for low-altitude tactical reconnaissance. Its manoeuvrability was such that its crews were able to engage enemy single-seat fighters with confidence. The maximum frontline complement of 295 aircraft was attained in February 1918, after which the Cl II was progressively phased out in favour of the Cl III and IIIa. The Hannoversche Waggonfabrik built 439 Cl IIs, the remainder of the contract being completed as Cl IIIa's, and Roland licence-built 200 Cl II(Rol) aircraft in 1918 for use as advanced trainers. *Max speed, 102 mph (165 km/h). Climb to 3,280 ft (1 000 m), 6.1 min. Empty weight, 1,653 lb (750 kg). Loaded weight, 2,447 lb (1 110 kg). Span, 39 ft 2½ in (11,95 m). Length, 25 ft 7 in (7,80 m). Height, 9 ft 0¼ in (2,75 m). Wing area, 363.8 sq ft (33,8 m²).*

HANNOVER Cʟ III   Germany

A progressive development of the Cl II designed by Hermann Dorner, the Cl III was intended to offer improved altitude capability with the 160 hp Mercedes D

With an engine change and small improvements, the Cl III (above) evolved from the Cl II, and a further engine change led to the Cl IIIa (below).

III water-cooled engine. Despite some airframe strengthening, the Cl III had a slightly reduced structural weight and marginally smaller overall dimensions. The *Typenprüfung* was successfully passed on 23 February 1918, and an order placed for 200 aircraft with deliveries to commence in the following month. In the event, as a result of shortages of the Mercedes engine, only 80 Cl IIIs were delivered, the remainder of the order being completed with the 180 hp Argus As III(O) licence-built by Opel as the Cl IIIa. This version was to remain in production until the end of hostilities, 573 being delivered. The designation Cl IIIb was allocated to the version that was to have been powered by the 185 hp NAG C III engine, and the Cl IIIc was a twin-bay version built specifically as a test-bed for the NAG engine. The Cl III and IIIa entered service in April 1918, serving primarily with the *Schlachtstaffeln* operating in the ground attack fighter rôle. Oddly, the Hannoversche Waggonfabrik completed a further 100 Cl IIIs and 38 Cl IIIa's *after* the Armistice. The following data relate to the Cl IIIa. *Max speed, 103 mph (165 km/h) at 16,405 ft (5 000 m). Time to 3,280 ft (1 000 m), 5.3 min. Endurance, 3 hrs. Empty weight, 1,653 lb (750 kg). Loaded weight, 2,447 lb (1 110 kg). Span, 38 ft 4½ in (11,70 m). Length, 24 ft 10¼ in (7,58 m). Height, 9 ft 2¼ in (2,80 m). Wing area,351.97 sq ft (32,70 m²).*

HANNOVER Cl V   Germany

Last of the Hannover fighters, the Cl V (above and below) was too late for service in World War I.

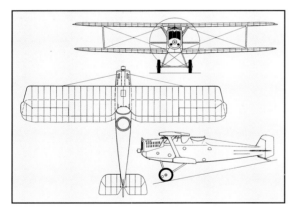

In mid-1918, the *Idflieg* prepared a specification calling for a *Jagdzweisitzer* – a two-seat fighter intended to engage the newer Allied single-seaters on even terms. It was to emphasise high speed, diving capability and manoeuvrability, and carry a fixed forward-firing armament of twin synchronised machine guns plus a third gun in the rear cockpit. To meet this requirement, which called for the aircraft to be tested to single-seat fighter load requirements, Hermann Dorner produced an extremely rugged and compact airframe. Designated Cl V, the prototype was powered by a 186 hp BMW IIIa engine. Tested against a similarly-powered Fokker D VII, it demonstrated comparable speed and climb. With the original biplane tail replaced by one of monoplane configuration, the Cl V was ordered into production, a contract for 100 aircraft being placed in September 1918, although it is doubtful if any of the 46 completed before the end of hostilities reached the Front. A further 62 were completed after the Armistice. A stripped down example of the Cl V was used to establish a world altitude record of 27,362 ft (8 340 m) on 22 November 1919. During 1923-24, the Kjeller Flyvemaskinsfabrik at Halden, Norway, built 14 Cl Vs under licence for the Norwegian Army as the F.F.7 Hauk

(Above) One of the 16 ex-Italian HD.1s used until 1930 by Switzerland's *Jagdflieger-Abteilung* III.

(Hawk), these remaining in service until 1929. *Max speed, 109 mph (175 km/h) at 6,560 ft (2 000 m). Time to 9,840 ft (3 000 m), 12 min. Range, 211 mls (340 km). Empty weight, 1,587 lb (720 kg). Loaded weight, 2,381 lb (1 080 kg). Span, 34 ft 5 in (10,49 m). Length, 22 ft 11½ in (7,00 m). Height, 9 ft 3¼ in (2,84 m). Wing area, 306.78 sq ft (28,50 m²).*

(Below) A licence-built version of the Cl V, the F.F.7 remained in service in Norway until 1929.

HANRIOT HD.1   France

The first fighter to be produced by the Société anonyme des Appareils d'Aviation Hanriot, the HD.1 was designed by Emile Dupont and was built in the summer of 1916. Powered by a 100 hp Le Rhône rotary engine and carrying an armament of one synchronised 7,7-mm Vickers machine gun (although a few aircraft were later to be fitted with two Vickers guns), the HD.1 was an extremely compact and agile single-seat fighter. Appearing later than the SPAD S.VII which was already in pro-

Of French design, the HD.1 (above and below) served principally in Italy, Belgium and Switzerland.

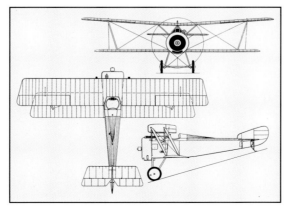

(Above) Production of the HD.1 was undertaken by Hanriot only to meet orders from Belgium.

duction, it was not ordered by France's *Aviation militaire*. It was adopted by Italy, however, and licence manufacture was undertaken by the Societá Nieuport Macchi which delivered 125 to the *Aeronautica del Regio Esercito* in 1917, 706 in 1918, and a further 70 after the Armistice. The HD.1 was also adopted by Belgium, to which country Hanriot supplied 79 fighters of this type from August 1917. The HD.1 continued in service in both Italy and Belgium into the mid-'twenties. In 1921, Switzerland purchased 16 from Italian war surplus stocks and retained these in service until 1930. The following data relate to the HD-1 powered by the 120 hp Le Rhône 9Jb. *Max speed, 115 mph (184 km/h) at sea level, 111 mph (178 km/h) at 6,560 ft (2 000 m). Time to 3,280 ft (1 000 m). 2.97 min. Ceiling, 19,685 ft (6 000 m). Range, 224 mls (360 km). Empty weight, 983 lb (446 kg). Loaded weight, 1,437 lb (652 kg). Span, 28 ft 6½ in (8,70 m). Length, 19 ft 2¼ in (5,85 m). Height, 9 ft 7½ in (2,94 m). Wing area, 195.9 sq ft (18,20 m²).*

HANRIOT HD.2   France

At the end of 1917, a derivative of the HD.1 intended for use by France's *Aviation maritime* as a single-seat fighter floatplane was tested as the HD.2. Possessing an airframe essentially similar to that of the HD.1, the HD.2 was powered by a 130 hp Clerget 9B rotary engine and carried an armament of twin synchronised Vickers machine guns. Two prototypes were tested with float undercarriages of differing lengths, and several HD.2s with wheel undercarriages were delivered to the *Aviation maritime* at Dunkirk for trials purposes. These included operations from a 40-ft (12-m) platform mounted above a turret of the battleship *Paris* in the harbour at Toulon. Later, in August and September 1918, similar trials were conducted at Saint-Raphaël with one of the HD.2 prototypes converted to landplane form and re-engined with a 120 hp Le Rhône. Ten HD.2

One of the prototype HD.2s (below) which were essentially float seaplane versions of the HD.1.

A US Navy HD.2 (above) taking off from the USS *Mississippi* after conversion from the standard floatplane form (below) as first supplied.

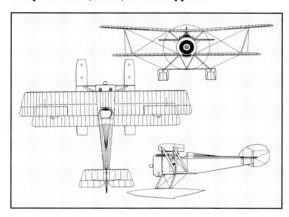

float fighters were purchased on behalf of the US Navy, these subsequently being converted to landplanes by the Naval Aircraft Factory. They were used for training at Langley Field and one was employed in August 1919 for trials from a platform mounted on the battleship USS *Mississippi*. The following data relate to the float-equipped HD.2. *Max speed, 114 mph (183 km/h). Service ceiling, 15,750 ft (4 800 m). Range, 186 mls (300 km). Empty weight, 1,091 lb (495 kg). Loaded weight, 1,594 lb (723 kg). Span, 28 ft 6½ in (8,70 m). Length, 22 ft 11½ in (7,00 m). Height, 10 ft 2 in (3,10 m). Wing area, 195.9 sq ft (18,20 m²).*

HANRIOT HD.3 France

The two-seat HD.3 (above) was the first Hanriot fighter to serve with the French military services.

Design development of a compact, well-proportioned two-seat fighter was initiated as the HD.3 in the autumn of 1917, and a prototype flew before the end of the year. Powered by the excellent new 260 hp Salmson (Canton-Unné) 9Za radial, the HD.3 had an armament of two fixed synchronised 7,7-mm Vickers guns and two 7,7-mm Lewis guns on a flexible mounting for the aft-facing gunner. A preliminary order was placed on behalf of the *Aviation militaire* for 120 HD.3s in April 1918, the total subsequently being raised to 300 when it was also ordered for the *Aviation maritime*. Few HD.3s had been delivered, in fact, by the time of the Armistice,

but at least 75 were completed for the *Aviation militaire* and a rather smaller quantity for the naval service. One example of the HD.3 was fitted with twin floats as the prototype of the HD.4, series production of which was frustrated by the Armistice, and a night fighter version was tested as the HD.3bis. This latter had mainplanes of thicker section, enlarged ailerons and a revised rudder. *Max speed, 119 mph (192 km/h) at 6,560 ft (2 000 m), 116 mph (187 km/h) at 9,840 ft (3 000 m). Time to 3,280 ft (1 000 m), 3.35 min. Service ceiling, 18,700 ft (5 700 m). Endurance, 2.0 hrs. Empty weight, 1,675 lb (760 kg). Loaded weight, 2,601 lb (1 180 kg). Span, 29 ft 6¼ in (9,00 m). Length, 22 ft 9½ in (6,95 m). Height, 9 ft 10 in (3,00 m). Wing area, 274.49 sq ft (25,50 m²).*

Wing changes distinguished the HD.3bis (above) from the standard production HD.3 (below).

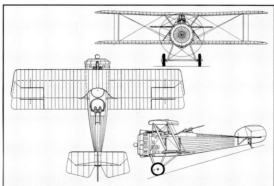

HANRIOT HD.5 France

Encouraged by the success that attended the HD.3, Emile Dupont designed another two-seat fighter around the excellent Hispano-Suiza 8Fb water-cooled engine of 300 hp. Unlike preceding Dupont designs, the HD.5 was an unstaggered two-bay biplane with an extremely small wing gap. The forward portion of the upper wing centre section was cut out to accommodate the pilot's head, the aft portion also being cut away to improve the field of fire of the gunner. Armament comprised two synchronised 7,7-mm Vickers machine guns and either one or two 7,7-mm Lewis guns on a flexible mount in the rear cockpit. Only one prototype of the HD.5 was built, flight testing commencing in the late

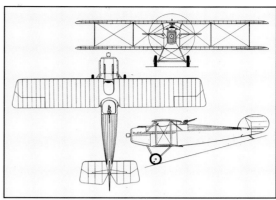

The HD-5 (above) only achieved prototype status.

spring of 1918, but further development was not pursued. *Max speed,132 mph (213 km/h) at sea level. Range, 304 mls (490 km). Empty weight, 1,764 lb (800 kg). Loaded weight, 2,756 lb (1 250 kg). Span, 34 ft 10½ in (10,63 m). Length, 24 ft 0⅞ in (7,34 m). Height, 8 ft 4 in (2,54 m). Wing area, 327.23 sq ft (30,40 m²).*

HANRIOT HD.6 France

Evolved in parallel with the HD.5 and of generally similar configuration, but larger and more powerful, the HD.6 two-seat fighter was powered by a 530 hp Salmson 18Z two-row radial water-cooled engine. This was essentially two Salmson 9Z engines on a common crankcase and flight testing was delayed by difficulties with this experimental power plant, eventually commencing in the spring of 1919. Armament consisted of two synchronised 7,7-mm Vickers guns for the pilot and three 7,7-mm Lewis guns for the gunner, two on a rotating TO.3 mount and one firing through a trap in the fuselage floor. The pilot, seated beneath a cut-out in the upper wing, was offered a singularly poor field of vision. Performance did not show a significant improvement over that of the more compact and simpler HD.3, and development was discontinued by the late summer of 1919. *Max speed, 140 mph (225 km/h). Time to 3,280 ft (1 000 m), 2.78 min. Range, 373 mls (600 km). Empty weight, 1,786 lb (810 kg). Loaded weight, 2,756 lb (1 250 kg). Span, 44 ft 7⅜ in (13,60 m). Length, 29 ft 0⅓ in (8,85 m). Height, 9 ft 6 in (2,90 m). Wing area, 511.3 sq ft (47,50 m²).*

The heavy two-seat HD.6 (above and below) was powered by the unusual Salmson water-cooled radial.

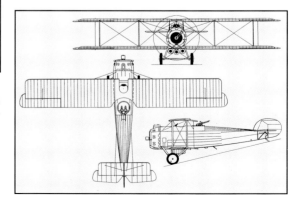

HANRIOT HD.7 France

Designed as a potential successor for the SPAD S.XIII, the HD.7 single-seat fighter employed wings and tail surfaces essentially similar to those of the two-seat

HD.3. Flown for the first time in the summer of 1918, the HD.7 was powered by a water-cooled Hispano-Suiza 8Fb eight-cylinder engine of 300 hp and mounted an armament of two 7,7-mm synchronised Vickers machine guns. The performance of the HD.7 proved good, but marginally inferior to that of its principal competitor for production orders, the Nieuport 29. With selection of the latter for series manufacture, further development of the HD.7 was discontinued. *Max speed, 135 mph (218 km/h). Time to 16,405 ft (5 000 m), 19.3 min. Range, 559 mls (900 km). Empty weight, 2,712 lb (1 230 kg). Loaded weight, 4,189 lb (1 900 kg). Span, 32 ft 1⅝ in (9,80 m). Length, 23 ft 7½ in (7,20 m). Height, 9 ft 10 in (3,00 m). Wing area, 301.39 sq ft (28,00 m²).*

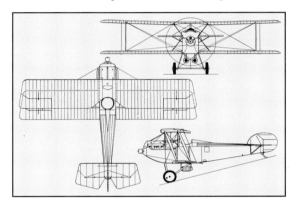

Flown in 1918, the HD.7 (above and below) was unsuccessful in competition with the Nieuport 29.

HANRIOT HD.8   France

The HD.8 single-seat fighter was designed for the experimental Le Rhône 9R nine-cylinder air-cooled rotary engine and commenced flight testing in March-April 1918. Apparently, the HD.8 was plagued by various problems, mostly stemming from its power plant, and, as a result, was never submitted by its manufacturer for official testing. No illustrations of the HD.8 seem to have survived. The following data are based on manufacturer's estimates. *Max speed, 124 mph (200 km/h) at 13,125 ft (4 000 m). Endurance, 2 hrs. Empty weight, 1,058 lb (480 kg). Loaded weight, 1,521 lb (690 kg). Span, 31 ft 5⅞ in (9,60 m). Length, 20 ft 2⅛ in (6,15 m). Wing area, 269.1 sq ft (25,00 m²).*

Derived from the HD.3, the HD.9 (below) was overtaken by the Armistice and only one was built.

HANRIOT HD.9   France

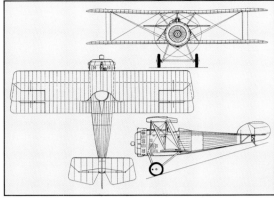

(Above) The Salmson 9Z-engined HD.9 of late 1918.

A single-seat reconnaissance fighter derived from the two-seat HD.3, the HD.9 was placed in the broad category of *Avions de Corps d'Armée* (thus being the HD.9 Ap1) and its armament consisted of a single synchronised 7,7-mm Vickers machine gun. The airframe was basically that of the HD.3 and the installation of the 260 hp Salmson 9Z radial engine was identical, but fuel capacity was considerably increased. The first example of the HD.9 was completed in November 1918 as the initial aircraft built against an order for 10 machines. However, its career was cut short by the Armistice and there is no evidence that all nine remaining aircraft were completed. *Max speed, 137 mph (220 km/h) at sea level. Range, 497 mls (800 km). Empty weight, 1,565 lb (710 kg). Span, 29 ft 6¼ in (9,00 m). Length, 22 ft 9½ in (6,95 m). Wing area, 274.49 sq ft (25,50 m²).*

HANRIOT HD.12   France

Tested in 1921, the single HD.12 (above) was quickly found to have little to offer.

What might be considered as the final variation on the original HD.1 concept was the HD.12 single-seat fighter that commenced its flight test programme in 1921. A single-bay staggered biplane, the HD.12 was powered by the 170 hp Le Rhône 9R nine-cylinder rotary air-cooled engine, and its intended armament was the standard pair of synchronised 7,7-mm Vickers machine

guns. The HD.12 was considered to be somewhat *passé* by the time it commenced flight testing, and, having a comparatively poor performance, it was quickly discarded. *Max speed, 118 mph (190 km/h) at sea level. Span, 28 ft 6½ in (8,70 m). Length, 19 ft 5⅞ in (5,94 m). Height, 8 ft 6 in (2,50 m). Wing area, 204.52 sq ft (19,00 m²).*

HANRIOT HD.15   France

A Rateau turbo-supercharger was featured on the HS 8Fb engine of the HD.15 (above and below).

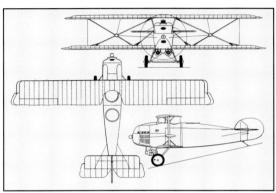

Under the technical development programme formulated in April 1919 by *Général* Duval, the newly-appointed *Directeur de l'Aéronautique*, two categories of turbo-supercharged fighter were called for, one single-seat and the other two-seat. The two-seater came within the CAP, or fighter-reconnaissance, category, and Hanriot's contribution to this programme was the HD.15, which, designed by Emile Dupont, was flown for the first time at Orly in April 1922. This competed with the Gourdou-Leseurre GL-50. The HD.15 was a rather corpulent, tandem two-seat, unstaggered biplane employing unusual rigid-X type interplane bracing. It was powered by a 300 hp Hispano-Suiza HS 8Fb eight-cylinder water-cooled engine equipped with a Rateau turbo-supercharger which was intended to maintain sea level engine power to 18,045 ft (5 500 m) altitude. Armament comprised two fixed forward-firing 7,7-mm Darne machine guns and two weapons of the same calibre on a swivelling mounting in the rear cockpit. In the event, the CAP category had been discarded before the flight testing of the HD.15 commenced and the entire turbo-supercharger fighter programme became something of a fiasco as a result of unavailability of the Rateau unit in quantity. However, the Japanese Army had begun to show interest in the potentiality of turbo-supercharged engines, and purchased the prototype HD.15, which was delivered in 1926. An order was placed for three identical examples of the HD.15 but, in the event, the vessel delivering the aircraft was struck by a tidal wave and the HD.15s never reached Japan. *Max speed, 112 mph (180 km/h). Range, 497 mls (800 km). Ceiling, 33,630 ft (10 250 m). Empty weight, 2,315 lb (1 050 kg). Loaded weight, 3,858 lb (1 750 kg). Span, 37 ft 4¾ in (11,40 m). Length, 24 ft 11⅛ in (7,60 m). Height, 8 ft 5⅛ in (2,57 m). Wing area, 349.62 sq ft (32,48 m²).*

HANRIOT HD.20   France

Completed in 1923 to the designs of *Ingénieur* Najac, the HD.20 was a single-seat shipboard fighter powered by a 300 hp Hispano-Suiza HS 8Fb eight-cylinder water-cooled engine. A staggered biplane with overhung ailerons on the upper wing only, the HD.20 was of metal construction, the intended armament comprising two fixed forward-firing 7,7-mm machine guns. It was equipped with a large Busteed inflatable flotation bag

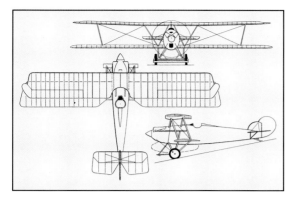

The HD.20 (above) remained a single prototype.

for emergency alighting on water. During flight testing, the prototype achieved an altitude of 16,405 ft (5 000 m) in 12 min and demonstrated a ceiling of 32,150 ft (9 800 m), but development was abandoned. *Max speed, 127 mph (205 km/h). Loaded weight, 2,998 lb (1 360 kg). Span, 41 ft 0 in (12,50 m). Length, 26 ft 6¾ in (8,10 m). Wing area, 430.57 sq ft (40,00 m²).*

HANRIOT H.26   France

Designed to compete in the 1921 C1 (single-seat fighter) programme, the H.26 was the only participant powered by the 260 hp Salmson 9Z nine-cylinder radial engine.

First of the Hanriot fighters to omit the "D" (for Dupont) from its designation, the H.26 (above and below) offered inadequate handling qualities.

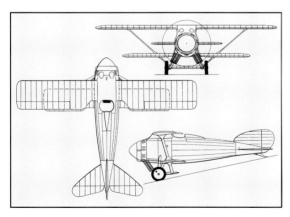

Most other contenders were intended for the water-cooled inline HS 8F. The H.26 design attempted to compensate for lower installed power by means of aerodynamic cleanliness. It was a sesquiplane of all-metal construction with metal skinning on the wing leading edges and forward fuselage, the remainder being fabric covered. The H.26 employed thick aerofoil sec-

Aerodynamic refinement was emphasised, albeit with little success, in the design of the H.26 (below).

tions, the upper wing being faired into the oval-section fuselage, and it had a close-cowled engine with a large propeller spinner. First flown at Orly in 1923, the H.26 utilised a Botali radiator arranged in a semi-circle behind the engine. As this was found to provide insufficient cooling, two Chausson radiators were attached to the undercarriage strutting. The H.26 displayed poor handling qualities, which, coupled with continued engine overheating and an inadequate view offered the pilot, led to the abandonment of further development after several test flights. The following data are manufacturer's estimates. *Max speed, 162 mph (260 km/h) at sea level. Ceiling, 27,890 ft (8 500 m). Range, 466 mls (750 km). Empty weight, 1,808 lb (820 kg). Loaded weight, 2,535 lb (1 150 kg). Span, 29 ft 8¼ in (9,05 m). Length, 24 ft 1⅓ in (7,35 m). Height, 8 ft 2⅓ in (2,50 m). Wing area, 193.76 sq ft (18,00 m²).*

HANRIOT HD.27   France

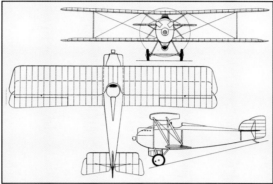

(Above) The HD.27 lightweight fighter.

Developed and built to the 1921 C1 programme like the HD.26, but of more traditional configuration, the HD.27 single-bay staggered-biplane single-seat fighter was of lightweight concept. It was also intended for shipboard operation, thus placing emphasis on short take-off and landing characteristics. Powered by a 180 hp Hispano-Suiza HS 8Ac eight-cylinder water-cooled engine, the HD.27 demonstrated the ability to take-off with a run of only 26 ft (8 m) and land within 49 ft (15 m). Flight testing commenced in 1922, but there was no requirement for the HD.27's STOL capabilities at the time. The HD.27 was therefore converted as a single-seat trainer, wing area being reduced by 53.8 sq ft (5,00 m²) and the Lamblin radiator hung beneath the fuselage being replaced by a Chausson frontal radiator. In this form, the sole example was utilised for some years as a company liaison aircraft. *Max speed, 121 mph (195 km/h). Ceiling, 22,965 ft (7 000 m). Range, 186 mls (300 km). Empty weight, 1,221 lb (554 kg). Loaded weight, 1,684 lb (764 kg). Span, 31 ft 5⅞ in (9,60 m). Length, 20 ft 2⅛ in (6,15 m). Height, 8 ft 2⅓ in (2,50 m). Wing area, 269.1 sq ft (25,00 m²).*

HANRIOT H.31   France

The H.31 was a participant in the 1923 competitive C1 programme, which, calling for single-seat fighters in the 400-500 hp category, was most noteworthy for its large number of contending designs. The H.31 was an unstaggered single-bay biplane powered by a Salmson 18Cm 18-cylinder radial engine of 500 hp and was of all-metal construction apart from the wing ribs, armament comprising four 7,7-mm synchronised machine guns. The fuselage was raised above the lower wing and the centre section of the upper wing incorporated a full-chord cut-out to improve pilot visibility. The engine was close cowled, and to provide adequate cooling for the rear cylinder row, the space between the lower wing centre section and the fuselage was occupied by a large radiator. The prototype H.31 was displayed at the 1924 *Salon de l'Aéronautique*, but did not commence its flight test programme until the following year. Submitted to the STAé for official evaluation, the H.31 was one of the heaviest of the 12 contending prototypes and proved inferior to all other competing types in both level speed and climb rate, the winning contender

being the Nieuport-Delage NiD 42 and the H.32 being abandoned. *Max speed, 161 mph (260 km/h) at sea level, 129 mph (207 km/h) at 16,405 ft (5 000 m). Time to 16,405 ft (5 000 m), 16.7 min. Empty weight, 2,837 lb (1 287 kg). Loaded weight, 3,994 lb (1 789 kg). Span, 39 ft 4½ in (12,00 m). Length, 24 ft 10½ in (7,58 m). Height, 11 ft 10½ in (3,62 m). Wing area, 365.98 sq ft (34,00 m²).*

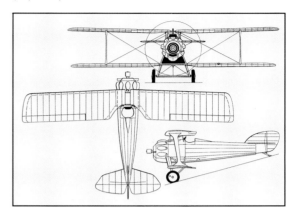

The H.31 (above and below) was displayed, before its first flight, at the 1924 Paris Air Show.

HANRIOT H.33   France

Designed to meet the requirements of the 1925 C2 programme for two-seat fighters, the H.33 suffered a rather protracted development and was, in consequence, outclassed by the time it entered flight test. Powered by a 500 hp Salmson 18Ab radial engine, the H.33 was exceptionally heavily armed: two 7,7-mm Vickers guns were synchronised to fire through the propeller, two Darne machine guns were affixed to the wing and two Lewis guns on a swivelling mounting were provided for the rear cockpit. Only limited flight testing was undertaken before further development was discontinued. *Max speed, 146 mph (235 km/h). Range, 360 mls (580 km). Ceiling, 26,245 ft (8 000 m). Empty weight, 2,473 lb (1 122 kg). Loaded weight, 4,173 lb (1 893 kg). Span 41 ft 3¼ in (12,58 m). Length, 24 ft 9½ in (7,56 m). Height, 11 ft 5¾ in (3,50 m). Wing area, 414.42 sq ft (38,50 m²).*

HANRIOT H.110   France

Viewed as something of an aberration from the mainstream of fighter development at the time of its début in April 1933, the H.110 was designed by Jean Biche. It was a contender in the C1 competition promoted initially by the *Service Technique de l'Aéronautique* in 1930 and upgraded in January 1931 by a supplement to the specification. The H.110 was a single-seat fighter in which the pilot and engine occupied a central nacelle, and twin parallel booms attached to the extremities of the wing centre section carried the tail assembly. Of all-metal construction, the H.110 was powered by a 500 hp Hispano-Suiza 12Xbrs geared and supercharged liquid-

Flown in 1933, the H.110 (above and below) was of unorthodox twin-boom pusher configuration.

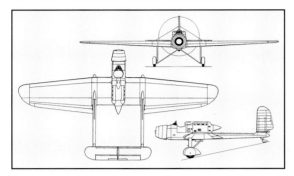

cooled engine driving a three-bladed pusher propeller. A ring-type radiator was mounted in the nose of the nacelle and embodied an adjustable cone to regulate the airflow. Largest and heaviest of the contending fighters, the H.110, which carried an armament of two fixed 7,5-mm MAC machine guns, proved slower and less manoeuvrable than most of its competitors. In March 1934, it was returned to the Bourges factory for modifications, re-emerging as the H.115. *Max speed, 220 mph (355 km/h). Time to 16,405 ft (5 000 m), 7.78 min. Range, 373 mls (600 km). Empty weight, 2,778 lb (1 260 kg). Loaded weight, 3,858 lb (1 750 kg). Span, 44 ft 3½ in (13,50 m). Length, 26 ft 1⅓ in (7,96 m). Height, 8 ft 10¼ in (2,70 m). Wing area, 258.34 sq ft (24,00 m²).*

HANRIOT H.115   France

After its return to Hanriot's Bourges factory, the H.110 was fitted with a redesigned fuselage nacelle and an uprated Hispano-Suiza 12Xbrs engine offering 690 hp. A 33-mm APX cannon was mounted in a bulged housing beneath the central nacelle and a four-bladed propeller supplanted the three-blader. With these modifications, the fighter re-emerged as the H.115 and was flown for the first time in April 1934. Further modifications were undertaken by the factory from November 1934, and, in June 1935, the H.115 was submitted to Villacoublay for official evaluation. Flight testing ended on 16 August. At this time it was concluded that, in view of its radical configuration, the H.115 was of no more than academic interest. *Max speed, 242 mph (390 km/h). Empty weight, 3,148 lb (1 428 kg). Loaded weight, 3,937 lb (1 786 kg). Span, 44 ft 3½ in (13,50 m). Length, 24 ft 11¼ in (7,60 m). Height, 8 ft 9⅞ in (2,69 m). Wing area, 258.34 sq ft (24,00 m²).*

The H.115 (below) was the original H.110 with redesigned fuselage nacelle and cannon armament.

HANRIOT H.220   France

Included among exhibits at the *Salon de l'Aéronautique* held in Paris in November 1936 was a striking all-metal twin-engined three-seat fighter. It had a somewhat abbreviated oval-section monocoque fuselage, a shoulder-mounted semi-cantilever wing carrying split trailing-edge flaps over its entire span and two 450 hp Renault 12Roi 12-cylinder inline air-cooled engines projecting ahead of the fuselage nose. This, the H.220, had been designed to a C3 requirement prepared by the *Service Technique de l'Aéronautique* and issued in October 1934. Other contenders were the Breguet 690,

the Potez 630, the Loire-Nieuport 20 and the Romano 110. As it became evident that the H.220 would be underpowered, the Renault engines were discarded in favour of 680 hp Gnome-Rhône 14M 14-cylinder radials, and, with these installed, the first flight test was made at Avord on 21 September 1937. The intended armament of the H.220 comprised two forward-firing 20-mm cannon and two aft-firing 7,5-mm MAC 1934 machine guns on a flexible mounting, but, in the event, no armament was fitted. On 17 February 1938, the prototype made a forced landing at Avord after losing the starboard propeller following a failure in the reduction gearbox. The poor stability evinced during flight testing of the H.220 (which had resulted in progressive changes in the contours and size of the vertical surfaces), coupled with inadequate internal capacity and some lack of sturdiness revealed by the forced landing (as a result of which the fuselage was irreparable), dictated major redesign, resulting in the H.220-2 (which see). *Max speed, 323 mph (520 km/h) at 19,685 ft (6 000 m). Time to 26,245 ft (8 000 m), 13.6 min. Range, 528 mls (850 km). Empty weight, 5,893 lb (2 673 kg). Loaded weight, 8,157 lb (3 700 kg). Span, 41 ft 11⁹⁄₁₀ in (12,80 m). Length, 25 ft 9⁷⁄₈ in (7,87 m). Height, 11 ft 1¾ in (3,40 m). Wing area, 227.77 sq ft (21,16 m²).*

Prior to the start of flight testing, the H.220 (above) was seen at the 1936 *Salon de l'Aéronautique*.

(Below) The H.220 as first flown and (broken line and photo above) with definitive tail unit.

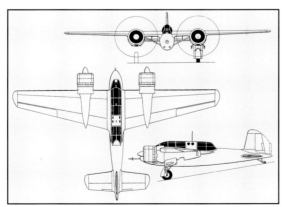

HANRIOT H.220-2   France

After the partial destruction of the H.220, major redesign was initiated by the Société Nationale de Constructions Aéronautiques du Centre, or SNCA du Centre, which had absorbed the Hanriot facility at Bourges on 1 February 1937. The oval-section monocoque fuselage of the original H.220 was discarded in favour of a fuselage built as two half shells mated by a central keel. An entirely new tail assembly with twin endplate vertical surfaces was fitted and the Gnome-

Rhône 14M radial engines were enclosed by low-drag nacelles. These features were mated with the wing of the original H.220 to result in the H.220-2, which was first flown (as the H.220 No 02) on 17 March 1939. Four months later, in July 1939, this prototype was to be displayed statically as the NC 600 No 01 multi-seat fighter at the *Salon de l'Aéronautique*. In fact, the *genuine* NC 600 was to differ from the H.220-2 in several major respects (see Centre NC 600). *Max speed, 330 mph (532 km/h) at 16,405 ft (5 000 m). Time to 22,965 ft (7 000 m), 11.5 min. Range, 478 mls (770 km) at 304 mph (490 km/h). Empty weight, 6,217 lb (2 820 kg). Loaded weight, 8,488 lb (3 850 kg). Dimensions as for H.220.*

Incorporating the wing of the original H.220, the H.220-2, or H.220 No 02, (below) flew in 1939.

HAWKER WOODCOCK   UK

The first fighter to be produced by Hawker Engineering (the successor to Sopwith Aviation), the Woodcock was designed by Capt B Thomson to meet Specification 25/22 calling for a single-seat night interceptor fighter. Of wooden construction with fabric skinning, the Woodcock was a two-bay biplane with variable-camber flaps and a 358 hp Armstrong Siddeley Jaguar II 14-cylinder radial. Mounting an armament of two 0.303-in (7,7-mm) Vickers guns, the Woodcock was flown in 1923, but its qualities proved disappointing. Lacking manoeuvrability, it suffered serious wing flutter and an ineffectual rudder. Several revisions of the vertical tail were undertaken, and the Jaguar engine was replaced by a Bristol Jupiter, but the Woodcock failed to find favour during Martlesham Heath evaluation. Further development was discarded in favour of a thoroughgoing redesign that led to the Woodcock II (which see). The following data apply to the Woodcock in its initial form. *Max speed, 143 mph (230 km/h) at sea level. Cruising speed, 105 mph (169 km/h). Time to 10,000 ft (3 050 m), 8.4 min. Empty weight, 2,083 lb (945 kg). Loaded weight, 3,023 lb (1 371 kg). Span, 34 ft 8 in (10,57 m). Length, 25 ft 7 in (7,80 m). Height, 9 ft 0 in (2,74 m). Wing area, 356 sq ft (33,07 m²).*

The first Woodcock I prototype (below) was fitted and flown with a Jaguar engine.

HAWKER WOODCOCK II   UK

The task of redesigning the Woodcock was undertaken by W G Carter, who, in fact, retained little of the original design apart from the fundamental fuselage structure. A new single-bay wing cellule was adopted, with marginally increased incidence and chord, and reduced sweepback. The fuselage decking was recontoured, tail surfaces were redesigned and the armament was repositioned. Powered by a 380 hp Bristol Jupiter IV nine-cylinder radial like that eventually installed in the original Woodcock, but featuring individual cylinder helmets, a new prototype designated Woodcock II was flown early in 1924. The redesigned fighter overcame most of the shortcomings of its progenitor, and a contract was placed on behalf of the RAF before the end of 1924. Similarly armed to the original fighter prototype,

In series form, the Jupiter-engined Woodcock II (above and below) equipped two RAF squadrons.

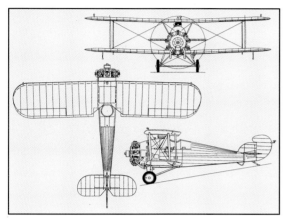

(Above) One of the 15 Danecocks (locally, Dankoks) used by No 2 Squadron of *Marine Flyvevæsenets*.

(169 km/h). Time to 10,000 ft (3 050 m), 8.25 min. Empty weight, 2,128 lb (965 kg). Loaded weight, 3,045 lb (1 381 kg). Span, 32 ft 7 in (9,92 m). Length, 26 ft 1¼ in (7,96 m). Wing area, 340 sq ft (31,59 m²).

HAWKER HERON UK

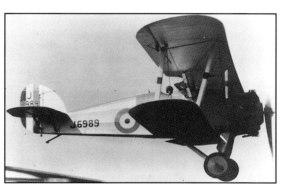

Only one Heron was built (above and below), this being primarily of metal construction.

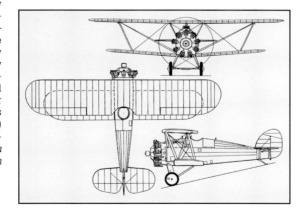

the Woodcock II was awarded successive contracts, a total of 62 being built, with deliveries being completed in 1927. The type served with two RAF squadrons until 1928, some late production examples being fitted with the Jupiter IV uprated to 416 hp. *Max speed, 141 mph (227 km/h) at sea level. Cruising speed, 103 mph (166 km/h). Time to 10,000 ft (3 050 m), 8.3 min. Empty weight, 2,014 lb (913 kg). Loaded weight, 2,979 lb (1 351 kg). Span, 32 ft 6 in (9,91 m). Length, 26 ft 2 in (7,97 m). Height, 9 ft 11 in (3,02 m). Wing area, 346 sq ft (32,14 m²).*

HAWKER DANECOCK UK

Based on the Woodcock II and designed by Sydney Camm, the Danecock was developed to meet a requirement of the Danish Naval Air Service, or *Marine Flyvevaesenets*. By comparison with the Woodcock II, the Danecock (*Dankok*) had unequal span wings, a slightly lengthened fuselage, a 385 hp Armstrong Siddeley Jaguar IV engine and an armament of two 7,7-mm Madsen machine guns. The first of three Danecocks ordered from the parent company was flown on 15 December 1925, and the licence manufacture of a further 12 was undertaken by the naval dockyard (*Orlogsvaerftet*) during 1927-28. These served until replaced by Nimrods in the mid-'thirties. *Max speed, 145 mph (233 km/h) at sea level. Cruising speed, 105 mph*

Based on the Woodcock, the Danecock (below) was built in Denmark by *Orlogsværftet* in 1927-28.

Built as a private venture, the Heron single-seat fighter was noteworthy in that it was the first of the Hawker company's fighters to have a predominantly metal structure. A single-bay biplane with provision for two 0.303-in (7,7-mm) synchronised Vickers guns, the Heron was built up of round steel and aluminium tubing bolted together (rather than welded) and braced by high-tensile wires. The result was a light and easily reparable structure, but it was perhaps the novelty of its construction rather than any shortcomings in capability that militated against service adoption. This was despite the fact that the prototype, initially flown early in 1925, was highly praised during official trials at Martlesham Heath in 1926. The prototype was subsequently returned to the manufacturer by which it was flown until mid-1928. *Max speed, 156 mph (251 km/h) at 9,800 ft (2 985 m). Time to 10,000 ft (3 050 m), 5.5 min. Empty weight, 2,120 lb (962 kg). Loaded weight, 3,126 lb (1 418 kg). Span, 31 ft 10 in (9,70 m). Length, 22 ft 3 in (6,78 m). Height, 9 ft 9 in (2,97 m). Wing area, 291 sq ft (27,03 m²).*

HAWKER HORNBILL UK

Representing an attempt to design the smallest and lightest practical airframe around the most powerful available engine suitable for fighter installation, the Hornbill was built to Specification 7/24 and flown in late summer 1925. Of mixed construction, with a duralumin-skinned steel tube forward fuselage and fabric-covered rear fuselage, wings and tail surfaces, the Hornbill was at first powered by an 826 hp Rolls-Royce Condor III eight-cylinder water-cooled inline engine with twin radiators under the lower wing. In May 1926, it flew with a 698 hp Condor IV and a single ventral radiator. It possessed an armament of one 0.303-in (7,7-mm) Vickers Mk 2 machine gun. The Hornbill was the fastest armed aircraft to have been tested by the RAF when it commenced service evaluation at Martlesham Heath in late 1925, but rate of climb and service ceiling were poor and some handling aspects unsatisfactory. In consequence no production order materialised. *Max speed, 187 mph (301 km/h) at sea level. Cruising speed, 137 mph (220 km/h). Time to 10,000 ft (3 050 m), 6.5 min. Service ceiling, 22,700 ft (6 920 m). Empty weight, 2,975 lb (1 349 kg). Loaded weight, 3,820 lb*

The Hornbill, after initial testing, was fitted (above and below) with a ventral radiator.

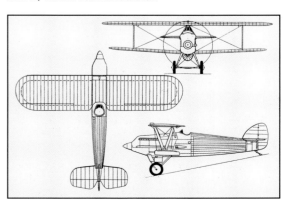

As first tested at Martlesham Heath, the Hornbill had a Condor III water-cooled inline engine and radiators under each wing.

(1 732 kg). Span, 31 ft 0 in (9,45 m). Length, 26 ft 7¼ in (8,11 m). Height, 9 ft 8 in (2,95 m). Wing area, 317.4 sq ft (29,49 m²).

HAWKER HAWFINCH   UK

Designed by Sydney Camm as a potential successor to the RAF's ageing Siskin fighter, the Hawfinch was built to Specification F.9/26, being one of nine contenders for RAF orders. Flown for the the first time in March 1927, the Hawfinch was of fabric-skinned metal construction, with an armament of twin synchronised 0.303-in (7,7-mm) Vickers guns and powered by a supercharged nine-cylinder Bristol Jupiter VII radial of 450 hp (which replaced a Jupiter VI shortly after the commencement of flight testing). Declared a close runner-up to the Bristol Bulldog, which was selected for RAF service in 1928, the Hawfinch prototype subsequently participated in various experimental programmes, during one of which the original two-bay wing cellules gave place to single-bay cellules, other tests being conducted with a twin-float undercarriage. *Max speed, 171 mph (275 km/h) at 9,840 ft (3 000 m). Time to 10,000 ft (3 050 m), 7.66 min. Empty weight, 1,925 lb (873 kg). Loaded weight, 2,910 lb (1 320 kg). Span, 33 ft 6 in (10,21 m). Length, 23 ft 8 in (7,21 m). Height, 9 ft 4 in (2,84 m). Wing area, 294 sq ft (27,31 m²).*

Flown in 1927, the Hawfinch (above and below) was a close competitor of the Bulldog for RAF orders.

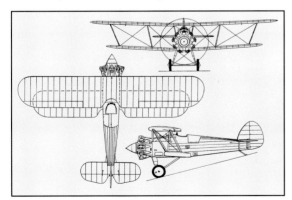

HAWKER F.20/27   UK

Precursor of the Hornet and Fury, this experimental single-seat interceptor fighter designed by Sydney Camm to meet the requirements of Specification F.20/27 was flown in August 1928 with a 450 hp Bristol Jupiter VII radial. Of metal construction with sharply staggered single-bay wings and a twin-Vickers gun armament, the prototype was re-engined with a 520 hp Mercury VI in May 1930. It demonstrated what was, for a fighter fitted with an uncowled radial engine, a very creditable maximum level speed of 202 mph

(325 km/h). By this time, however, the F.20/27 specification had prompted Hawker to initiate development of a more advanced fighter as a private venture, and this, owing much to its predecessor, was to emerge as the Hornet in 1929. The following data relate to the prototype in Mercury-engined form. *Max speed, 202 mph (325 km/h) at 10,000 ft (3 050 m). Time to 10,000 ft (3 050 m), 5.1 min. Empty weight, 2,155 lb (977 kg). Loaded weight, 3,150 lb (1 429 kg). Span, 30 ft 0 in (9,14 m). Length, 23 ft 6½ in (7,17 m). Height, 9 ft 5 in (2,87 m). Wing area, 228 sq ft (21,18 m²).*

Providing the foundation for development of the Fury, the single F.20/27 (below) flew in 1928.

HAWKER HOOPOE   UK

H G Hawker Engineering's first essay into the realm of the single-seat shipboard fighter, the Hoopoe, was built as a private venture and was flown for the first time in 1928. Intended for operation with either wheels or floats, the Hoopoe was a two-bay staggered all-metal biplane powered by a 450 hp Bristol Mercury II nine-cylinder radial. Found to be seriously underpowered when first tested as a float fighter in 1929, the Hoopoe

The Hoopoe flew with three different engine types, the last being the Panther III (below).

prototype was re-engined with a 520 hp Mercury VI. Subsequently returned to the manufacturer after official handling trials at Felixstowe, the Hoopoe was fitted with a new single-bay wing cellule, a 400 hp 14-cylinder two-row Armstrong Siddeley Jaguar V engine, and reverted to a wheel undercarriage for a further service assessment at Martlesham Heath. Various structural refinements were introduced and the Hoopoe was

once again re-engined, this time with a 560 hp Armstrong Siddeley Panther III. The prototype of the Nimrod fleet fighter had meanwhile commenced flight test, however, and thus interest in the Hoopoe had become no more than academic by mid-1930. The following data relate to the Hoopoe in its final form with Panther III engine. *Max speed, 196 mph (315 km/h) at 12,500 ft (3 810 m). Time to 10,000 ft (3 050 m), 6.66 min. Empty weight, 2,798 lb (1 270 kg). Loaded weight, 3,882 lb (1 761 kg). Span, 33 ft 2 in (10,11 m). Length, 24 ft 6 in (7,47 m). Wing area, 288.5 sq ft (26,80 m²).*

HAWKER FURY   UK

Built to Specification F.20/27, the Hornet (above) was in effect the prototype for the Fury I (below).

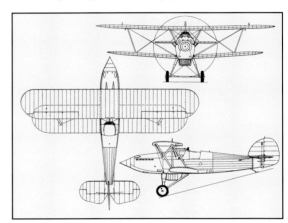

Achieving the distinction of being the first production warplane to carry level flight performance beyond the 200 mph (322 km/h) mark, the Fury established a level of design elegance entirely new to combat aircraft and fresh standards in handling qualities. The private-venture first prototype was flown in March 1929 as the Hornet. Powered by a 480 hp Rolls-Royce F.XI 12-cylinder liquid-cooled engine (later to be named Kestrel), the prototype was purchased in September 1929 by the Air Ministry and renamed Fury. A contract was placed on behalf of the RAF in August 1930 for 21 aircraft powered

(Below) A series Fury I flown by the CO of No 1 Squadron, RAF, from Tangmere in the 'thirties.

The last surviving Spanish Fury in Republican hands at La Rabasa in 1937 (above) and one of the Panther-engined Norwegian Furies (below).

by the Kestrel II.S rated at 575 hp at 13,000 ft (3 965 m) and carrying twin 0.303-in (7,7-mm) Vickers machine guns. Production of the initial model (retrospectively designated Fury I upon the début of the Fury II) for the RAF totalled 118 aircraft. A further 112 aircraft powered by the 640 hp Kestrel VI and featuring augmented fuel tankage were procured for the Service as Fury IIs. The first production Fury II for the RAF (produced under sub-contract by General Aircraft) was delivered in July 1936, seven being supplied to South Africa in the following September. Other Fury exports comprised three to Portugal and six to Yugoslavia (essentially similar to the Mk I); 24 (with Pratt & Whitney Hornet S2B1-G or Bristol Mercury VI.S2) to Iran; one (Armstrong Siddeley Panther IIA) to Norway; three (Hispano-Suiza 12Xbr) with cantilever undercarriages to Spain and 10 (Kestrel XVI) with similar undercarriages to Yugoslavia. In the last-mentioned country Ikarus and Zmaj built a further 40 under licence in 1937-38. Twenty-four ex-RAF Fury IIs were transferred to South Africa at the beginning of

World War II. The following data relate to the Fury I. *Max speed, 192 mph (309 km/h) at 5,000 ft (1 525 m), 207 mph (333 km/h) at 14,000 ft (4 270 m). Range, 305 mls (492 km) at 160 mph (257 km/h). Initial climb, 2,380 ft/min (12,09 m/sec). Empty weight, 2,623 lb (1 190 kg). Loaded weight, 3,490 lb (1 583 kg). Span, 30 ft 0 in (9,15 m). Length, 26 ft 3¾ in (8,00 m). Height, 9 ft 6 in (2,89 m). Wing area, 251.8 sq ft (23,40 m²).*

HAWKER OSPREY   UK

The issue in 1926 of Specification O.22/26 was to result in a new category of shipboard warplanes, the fast two-seat fighter-reconnaissance aircraft. Hawker submitted, initially as a private venture, an adaptation of the original Hawker Hart day bomber prototype. Modifications included aft-folding wings, jury struts and, eventually, a twin-float undercarriage. Selected in preference to the other contenders (Blackburn Nautilus, Fairey Fleetwing and Short Gurnard), two prototypes were ordered to Specification 19/30 as the Osprey, these undergoing trials during 1931-32, the first with a wheel undercarriage and the second with twin floats. The initial series version, the Osprey I, of which 37 were built for the Fleet Air Arm in two batches, was powered by a 630 hp Rolls-Royce Kestrel IIMS driving a wooden propeller. The Osprey II differed in the type of Short floats fitted, 14 being built, these later being modified to Mk III standard. The Osprey III, which appeared towards the end of 1933, was equipped with a dinghy, an engine-driven generator and a metal propeller, and 49 were delivered, plus three of stainless steel rather than conventional steel tube and aluminium. From late 1932, Osprey Is entered service in succession to Flycatchers aboard the carriers HMS *Eagle* and *Courageous*, and in the following year began to operate in mixed squadrons with single-seat Nimrods, in floatplane form, replacing Fairey IIIFs on the cata-

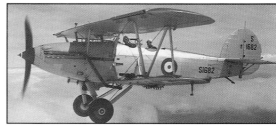

The Osprey (above) was in effect a navalised derivative of the Hart for fighter-reconnaissance.

pults ofcruisers and larger vessels. The last 26 built for the Royal Navy were fitted with the 640 hp Kestrel V engine, deliveries being completed in October 1935. Four Ospreys with Swedish-built Bristol Mercury engines were supplied to Sweden in 1934-35, two Kestrel IIMS-powered examples were delivered to Portugal in 1935, and one procured by Spain was fitted with an Hispano-Suiza 12Xbrs engine with which it first flew on 24 February 1936. Withdrawn from first line operations in 1938, the Osprey was declared obsolete in 1940. The armament of the Osprey comprised one fixed forward-firing 0.303-in (7,7-mm) gun with a weapon of the same calibre on a rear cockpit mount. The following data are applicable to the Osprey III with wheel undercarriage. *Max speed, 168 mph (270 km/h) at 5,000 ft (1 525 m). Time to 10,000 ft (3 050 m), 7.66 min. Endurance, 2.25 hrs. Empty weight, 3,405 lb (1 544 kg). Loaded weight, 4,950 lb (2 245 kg). Span, 37 ft 0 in (11,28 m). Length, 29 ft 4 in (8,94 m). Height, 10 ft 5 in (3,17 m). Wing area, 339 sq ft (31,49 m²).*

HAWKER NIMROD   UK

A Nimrod I (above) photographed prior to its delivery to No 800 Sqn and (below) the Nimrod II.

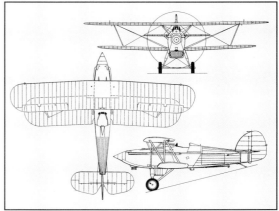

Despite its close family resemblance to the Fury, the Nimrod single-seat shipboard fighter was not a variant of the land-based warplane, the lineal development of the two aircraft having been entirely separate. Owing much to the Hoopoe, the Nimrod was of similar fabric-covered all-metal construction to the Fury. It was powered by a 477 hp Kestrel II MS engine, the prototype flying early in 1930 after Specification 16/30 had been drafted around the Hawker proposal. The first Nimrod built against an initial production order for 35 aircraft for the Fleet Air Arm was flown on 14 October 1931. All Nimrods had provision for interchangeable wheel and float undercarriages, and the second production aircraft was fitted with twin floats for Felixstowe trials. A total of 57 Nimrod Is was followed by 28

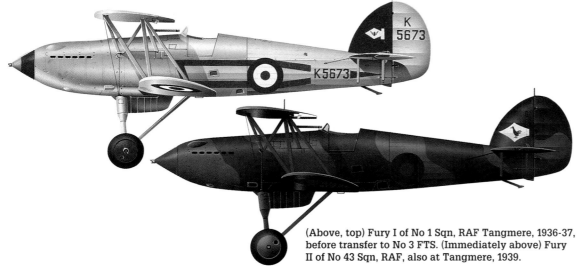

(Above, top) Fury I of No 1 Sqn, RAF Tangmere, 1936-37, before transfer to No 3 FTS. (Immediately above) Fury II of No 43 Sqn, RAF, also at Tangmere, 1939.

(Above) A Danish-built Nimrod II of 2 *Luftflotille*, serving in Denmark up to the Occupation in 1940.

Nimrod IIs, these standardising on the 608 hp Kestrel V engine, three degrees of wing sweepback and enlarged tailplanes. Three had stainless rather than conventional steel structures. A single evaluation example of the Nimrod II was supplied to each of Japan and Portugal, and two Nimrod IIs were exported to Denmark. In this last country a further 10 were licence-built by the *Orlogsvaerftet* (naval dockyard). The Nimrod remained in Royal Navy service until May 1939, and with the Danish Navy until the service's disbandment on 29 August 1943 (although these aircraft were not flown subsequent to the occupation of Denmark by the *Wehrmacht*). The following data relate to the Nimrod I. *Max speed, 196 mph (315 km/h) at 12,000 ft (3 660 m). Time to 10,000 ft (3 050 m), 6.13 min. Empty weight, 3,115 lb (1 413 kg). Loaded weight, 4,059 lb (1 841 kg). Span, 33 ft 6¾ in (10,23 m). Length, 26 ft 6½ in (8,09 m). Height, 9 ft 10 in (3,00 m). Wing area, 301 sq ft (27,96 m²).*

A ski-equipped Nimrod II (below) of the Danish *Marine Flyvevæsen*, one of 10 built in Denmark.

HAWKER DEMON   UK

The first two-seat fighter to be introduced by the RAF since World War I, the Demon was essentially a version of the Hart day bomber to Specification 15/30. It differed from its precursor in having a fully-supercharged Kestrel II.S engine of 485 hp, twin forward-firing 0.303-in (7,7-mm) Vickers machine guns and a canted rear cockpit coaming to improve the field of fire of the ring-mounted Lewis gun. Later production aircraft were powered by the 584 hp Kestrel VDR, and contracts were placed on behalf of the RAF for 108 aircraft, a further 64 being ordered for the RAAF. Before the end of 1934, one example had been fitted with the prototype of an hydraulically-operated Frazer-Nash gun turret in-

(Below) The Demon I in its series production form.

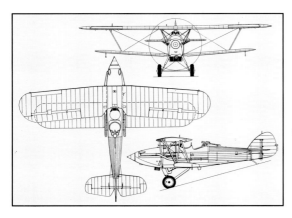

corporating a segmented folding shield ("lobster back") and accommodating the Lewis gun. From mid-1936, all new Demons were fitted with this turret and many others were retrospectively modified. The Demon was finally withdrawn from first-line RAF service during 1939. The following data relate to the definitive Kestrel VDR-engined turreted fighter. *Max speed, 182 mph (293 km/h) at 16,000 ft (4 875 m). Time to 10,000 ft (3 050 m), 7.92 min. Empty weight, 3,336 lb (1 513 kg). Loaded weight, 4,668 lb (2 117 kg). Span, 37 ft 2 in (11,33 m). Length, 29 ft 7 in (9,02 m). Height, 10 ft 5 in (3,17 m). Wing area, 347 sq ft (32,24 m²).*

A production Demon I (above) ready for delivery to No 74 Squadron, RAF. A dorsal turret was fitted later.

HAWKER P.V.3   UK

Designed to meet the requirements of Specification F.7/30 calling for a single-seat, four-gun day and night fighter, the P.V.3 was flown on 15 June 1934 with a 695 hp Rolls-Royce Goshawk III steam-cooled engine.

Inspired by Specification F.7/30, the P.V.3 (below) was the last of the Hawker fighter biplanes.

This was later to be replaced successively by B.41 and B.43 Goshawks. The P.V.3 was structurally similar to the Fury, and two of its four 0.303-in (7,7-mm) machine guns were paired over the engine and the others mounted one each side of the nose. Officially evaluated at Martlesham Heath with the 700 hp B.43 Goshawk, the P.V.3 featured a weighty and vulnerable evapora-

tive cooling system, and further development was not pursued. This was partly as a result of the unsatisfactory cooling system but primarily owing to the re-thinking of fighter requirements for the RAF that had meanwhile taken place and the imminent appearance of the Hurricane in consequence. *Max speed, 224 mph (360 km/h) at 14,000 ft (4 265 m). Time to 10,000 ft (3 050 m), 4.33 min. Empty weight, 3,530 lb (1 601 kg). Loaded weight, 4,670 lb (2 118 kg). Span, 34 ft 0 in (10,36 m). Length, 28 ft 2 in (8,58 m). Height, 10 ft 5 in (3,17 m). Wing area, 290.5 sq ft (26,99 m²).*

HAWKER HURRICANE I   UK

(Above) A Hurricane I serving with No 85 Sqn in early 1940 and (below) the series Hurricane I.

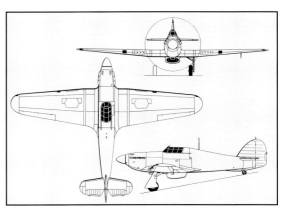

The first fighter of monoplane configuration to enter service with the RAF, the Hurricane, designed by Sydney Camm, was initiated as a private venture. Around the detail design of this fighter Specification F.36/34 was eventually written. Utilising Hawker's well-established structural principles, the fighter was of rigidly-braced steel and light alloy tubing construction with fabric skinning, a prototype being flown on 6 November 1935. A contract for 600 Hurricanes was placed on 20 July 1936, the first production example flying on 12 October 1937 with a Rolls-Royce Merlin II engine rated at 1,030 hp at 16,250 ft (4 955 m). This drove a fixed-pitch two-bladed propeller with which a max speed of 318 mph (512 km/h) was attained at 17,400 ft (5 305 m). Flight testing with the similarly-rated Merlin III and a constant-speed three-bladed propeller began on 24 January 1939, this combination eventually being standardised for the Hurricane I which carried an armament of eight 0.303-in (7,7-mm) wing-mounted Browning machine guns. Metal stressed-skin was adopted in place of fabric for the wings, aircraft embodying this change being delivered to the RAF from 29 September 1939. Deliveries of Mk Is, other than to the RAF itself, included 15 to Turkey, 12 to Romania, one to Poland and 12 to Finland during

(Above) Hawker Demon I of No 23(F) Squadron serving at RAF Biggin Hill in 1935-36.

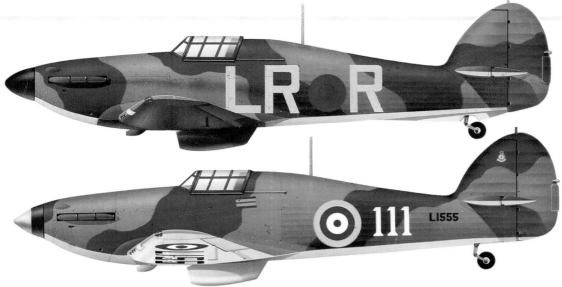

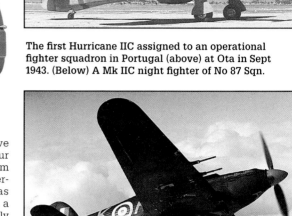

The first Hurricane IIC assigned to an operational fighter squadron in Portugal (above) at Ota in Sept 1943. (Below) A Mk IIC night fighter of No 87 Sqn.

(Above, top) Hurricane I of No 56 Sqn, North Weald, 1939, and (immediately above) a Mk I of the first Hurricane squadron, No 111, Northolt, 1937.

1939-40. Production of the Hurricane I totalled 1,924 by Hawker and 1,850 by Gloster, and manufacture was also undertaken by Canadian Car and Foundry (CCF) which flew the first of 60 Hurricane Is on 10 January 1940. Official Canadian records show that a further 1,391 Hurricanes (and Sea Hurricanes) were built in Canada in several versions. These included Mk Is with Merlin IIIs, Mk Xs with Packard-built Merlin 28s, Mk XIs with Canadian equipment and Mk XIIs with Merlin 29s and 12-gun or (Mk XIIA) eight-gun armament.

Skis were developed in Canada to allow the Hurricane (a Mk XII above) to operate from snow.

Twenty-four Hurricane Is were delivered to Yugoslavia 1938-40, and a further 100 were to have been built by Zmaj (60) and Rogozarski (40), although, in the event, only 20 were completed (by the former company). Belgium also acquired a manufacturing licence for the Hurricane I in addition to purchasing 20 (of which 15 were delivered) from the UK. Eighty were ordered from the Belgian Avions Fairey of which only three were completed. *Max speed, 316 mph (508 km/h) at 17,750 ft (5 410 m). Time to 15,000 ft (4 575 m), 6.3 min. Max range, 600 mls (965 km) at 175 mph (282 km/h). Empty weight, 5,085 lb (2 307 kg). Max loaded weight, 6,661 lb (3 021 kg). Span, 40 ft 0 in (12,19 m). Length, 31 ft 5 in (9,58 m). Height, 12 ft 11½ in (3,95 m). Wing area, 258 sq ft (23,97 m²).*

HAWKER HURRICANE II TO V   UK

On 11 June 1940, a Hurricane I airframe was flown with a two-stage supercharged Merlin XX rated at 1,300 hp at sea level and 1,460 hp at 6,250 ft (1 905 m). With the adoption of this engine, the fighter was designated Hurricane II, deliveries commencing in September 1940. The initial model, the Hurricane IIA Srs 1, retained the wings of the Mk I, the Srs 2 which followed embodying fuselage strengthening to cater for later wings featuring universal attachment points for external stores. Apart from early examples, the Srs 2 also introduced an extra fuselage bay, increasing overall length by 7 in (18 cm). Srs 2 aircraft were followed from late 1940 by the Hurricane IIB. This was armed with 12 0.303-in (7,7-mm) wing guns, and, during the course of 1941, was followed in turn by the Hurricane IIC with four 20-mm Hispano cannon. All Hurricane IIs had provision for drop tanks, bombs or other underwing stores. During 1942, the Hurricane was superseded in the air rôle in UK-based squadrons, but continued to serve as a ground attack fighter, and a dedicated anti-armour version, the Hurricane IID mounting two 40-mm cannon and two 0.303-in (7,7-mm) guns, entered service mid-1942. The designation Hurricane III was assigned to a proposed British-built version with a Packard Merlin engine, and the Hurricane IV (initially known as the Mk IIE with 270 aircraft being delivered before the designation change) featured a "low attack" or universal armament wing which was wired to permit 40-mm cannon, rockets or bombs to be carried. The prototype of this version was flown on 14 March 1943, production aircraft having either the Merlin 24 or 27, both being rated at 1,620 hp. Two Mk IV airframes were flown with 1,700 hp Merlin 32 engines driving four-bladed propellers and in this guise were designated Hurricane Vs. Production of the Hurricane II totalled 8,406 aircraft – of which almost 3,000 were supplied to the Soviet Union – and 794 Hurricane IVs were built. The following data relate to the Mk IIC. *Max speed,* 327 mph (526 km/h) at 18,000 ft (5 485 m). Initial climb, 2,750 ft/min (13,9 m/sec). Range (internal fuel), 460 mls (740 km) at 178 mph (286 km/h). Empty weight, 5,658 lb (2 566 kg). Max loaded weight, 8,044 lb (3 648 kg). Span, 40 ft 0 in (12,19 m). Length, 32 ft 3 in (9,83 m). Height, 13 ft 3 in (4,04 m). Wing area, 258 sq ft (23,97 m²).*

(Immediately below) A Hurricane IIA of No 73 Sqn in the Western Desert, 1942. (Bottom) Hurricane IIC of No 1 Sqn at RAF Acklington, summer 1942.

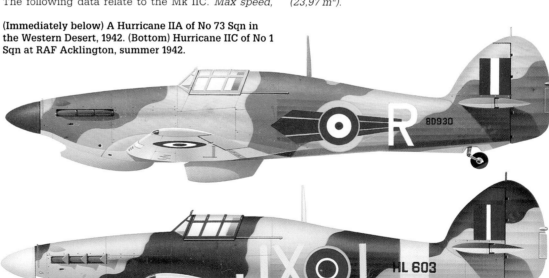

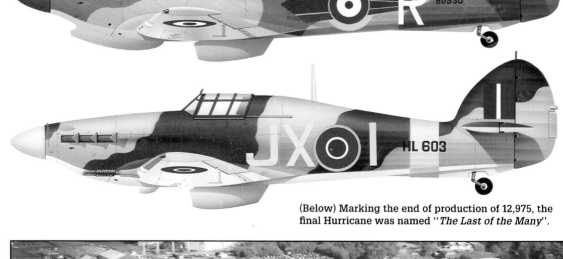

(Below) Marking the end of production of 12,975, the final Hurricane was named "*The Last of the Many*".

HAWKER SEA HURRICANE   UK

Adaptation of the shore-based Hurricane fighter for naval use was initiated early in 1941 by the fitting of V-frame arrester hook and catapult spools for trials purposes. Some 300 Hurricane Is were assigned for adaptation as Sea Hurricanes, the first 50 for catapult launching from CAM (Catapult Aircraft Merchantman) ships being known as Sea Hurricane IAs and lacking arrester hooks. Subsequent aircraft fitted with hooks for conventional shipboard operation became Sea Hurricane IBs. FAA squadrons began reforming on the Sea Hurricane IB from early 1941, this model being joined by the Mk IC from early 1942. This was essentially the mating of the Hurricane IIC outer wing panels mounting four 20-mm cannon with the navalised airframe and Merlin III engine of the late-series Hurricane I. From late 1942, the Sea Hurricane IIC appeared, this being a conversion of the Hurricane IIC with the Merlin XX engine. One other version of the naval fighter was the Canadian-built Sea Hurricane XIIA, which was

Flying in 1991, The Fighter Collection's Sea Hurricane XII (right) bore the markings of No 71 "Eagle" Sqn.

Key to Hawker Hurricane Mk IIC

1 Starboard navigation light
2 Starboard wingtip
3 Aluminium alloy aileron
4 Self-aligning ball-bearing aileron hinge
5 Aft wing spar
6 Aluminium alloy wing skinning
7 Forward wing spar
8 Starboard landing light
9 Rotol three-blade constant-speed propeller
10 Spinner
11 Propeller hub
12 Pitch-control mechanism
13 Spinner back plate
14 Cowling fairings
15 Coolant pipes
16 Rolls-Royce Merlin XX engine
17 Cowling panel fasteners
18 "Fishtail" exhaust pipes
19 Electric generator
20 Engine forward mounting feet
21 Engine upper bearer tube
22 Engine forward mount
23 Engine lower bearer tubes
24 Starboard mainwheel fairing
25 Starboard mainwheel
26 Low pressure tyre
27 Brake drum (pneumatic brakes)
28 Manual-type inertia starter
29 Hydraulic system
30 Bearer joint
31 Auxiliary intake
32 Carburettor air intake
33 Wing root fillet
34 Engine oil drain collector/breather
35 Fuel pump drain
36 Engine aft bearers
37 Magneto
38 Two-stage supercharger
39 Cowling panel attachments
40 Engine RPM indicator drive
41 External bead sight
42 Removable aluminium alloy cowling panels
43 Engine coolant header tank
44 Engine firewall (armour-plated backing)
45 Fuselage (reserve) fuel-tank (28 Imp gal/127 l)
46 Exhaust glare shield
47 Control column
48 Engine bearer attachment
49 Rudder pedals
50 Control linkage
51 Centre-section fuel tank
52 Oil system piping
53 Pneumatic system air cylinder
54 Wing centre-section/front spar girder construction
55 Engine bearer support strut
56 Oil tank (port wing root leading-edge)
57 Dowty undercarriage ram
58 Port undercarriage well
59 Wing centre-section girder frame
60 Pilot's oxygen cylinder
61 Elevator trim tab control wheel
62 Radiator flap control lever
63 Entry footstep
64 Fuselage tubular framework
65 Landing lamp control lever
66 Oxygen supply cock
67 Throttle lever
68 Safety harness
69 Pilot's seat
70 Pilot's break-out exit panel
71 Map case
72 Instrument panel
73 Cockpit ventilation inlet
74 Reflector gunsight
75 Bullet-proof windscreen
76 Rear-view mirror
77 Rearward-sliding canopy
78 Canopy frames

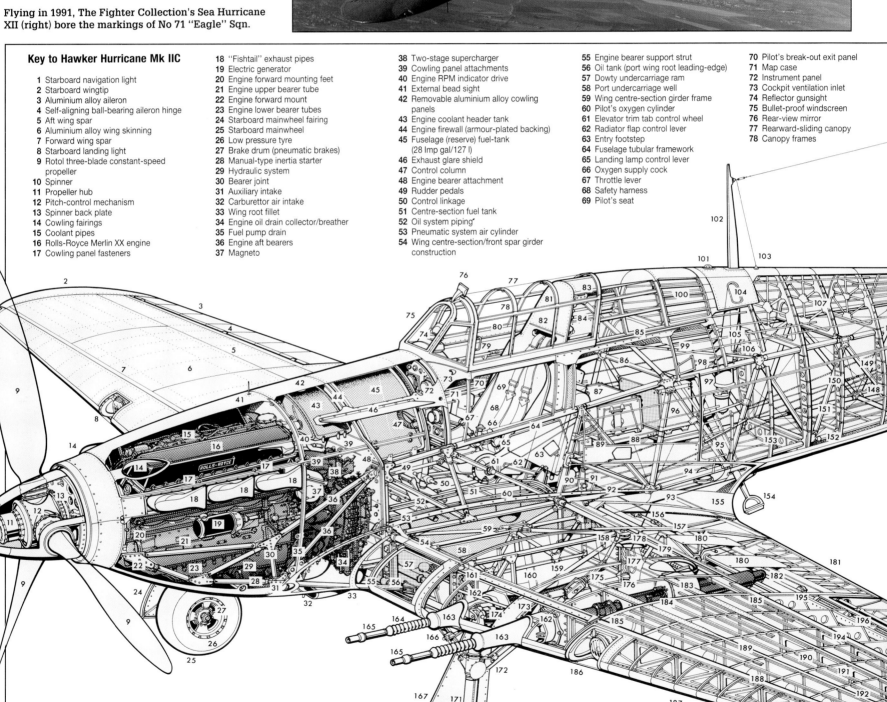

powered by the Packard-built Merlin 29 engine and reverted to the armament of eight wing-mounted 0.303-in (7,7-mm) guns. By the end of 1943, the Sea Hurricane had been superseded in most squadrons, but it was not until April 1944 that the last FAA unit equipped with this fighter was to be disembarked. No precise records survive of the number of Sea Hurricanes supplied to the FAA, but it is known that contracts for at least 800 aircraft (some built as Sea Hurricanes, as well as conversions, the latter including Canadian production conversions) were issued, and almost 600 were included in the Royal Navy inventory by mid-1942. The following data relate to the Sea Hurricane IIC. *Max speed, 342 mph (550 km/h) at 22,000 ft (6 705 m). Time to 22,000 ft (6 705 m), 9.1 min. Range (internal fuel), 460 mls (740 km) at 212 mph (341 km/h) at 20,000 ft (6 100 m). Empty weight, 5,800 lb (2 631 kg). Max loaded weight, 7,800 lb (3 538 kg). Dimensions as for Hurricane IIC.*

With arrester hook extended, a Sea Hurricane IB (below) picks up the wires on HMS Argus in 1943.

HAWKER HOTSPUR   UK

When, in 1935, Specification F.9/35 was issued for a two-seat interceptor fighter to replace the Demon, both Hawker and Boulton Paul tendered proposals for aircraft fitted with the Boulton Paul turret mounting four 0.303-in (7,7-mm) machine guns. Hawker's submission was based on redesign of the Henley light bomber, prototype construction of which had just commenced. Like the Henley, it utilised standard Hurricane outer wing panels. Dubbed Hotspur, the prototype of the two-seat fighter was not flown until 14 June 1938, and then with only a wooden mock-up of the turret and with ballast

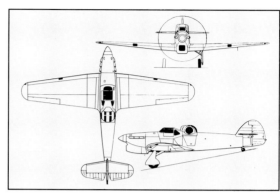

Concentration on the Hurricane precluded development of the Hotspur (above and below).

equivalent to the weight of armament. Powered by a 1,030 hp Rolls-Royce Merlin II, the Hotspur proved faster than the competitive Boulton Paul Defiant, but as Hawker and its parent Group were fully committed to production of the Hurricane, no effort was made to bring the prototype Hotspur up to representative Service standard and development was discontinued, the aircraft subsequently being utilised for flap and dive brake development. The following data relate to the aircraft as flown with mock-up turret. *Max speed, 316 mph (509 km/h) at 15,800 ft (4 815 m). Time to 15,000 ft (4 575 m), 10.85 min. Empty weight, 5,800 lb (2 631 kg). Loaded weight, 7,650 lb (3 470 kg). Span, 47 ft 10¼ in (14,59 m). Length, 36 ft 1½ in (11,01 m). Height, 14 ft 4 in (4,37 m). Wing area, 342 sq ft (31,77 m²).*

HAWKER TORNADO   UK

Sydney Camm and his team responded to Specification F.18/37 which called for a single-seat interceptor, with two tenders. One was referred to as the "R-type" and the other as the "N-type". These were to use fundamentally similar airframes and differ essentially in the type of engine installed. The former, which was to be named Tornado, initially appeared the most promising and was powered by a 24-cylinder X-type Rolls-Royce Vulture – basically two 12-cylinder Peregrine V engines driving a common crankshaft. The first of two prototypes was flown on 6 October 1939 with a 1,760 hp Vulture II, provision being made for an armament of 12

The first Tornado prototype (above) with initial ventral radiator bath and (below) the definitive chin-type radiator on the second prototype.

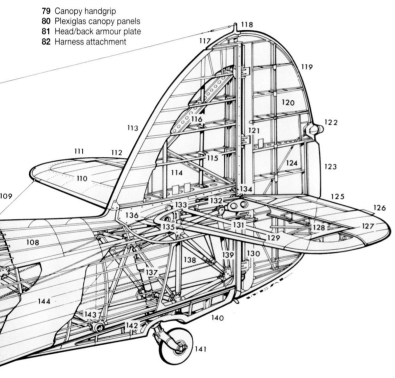

79 Canopy handgrip
80 Plexiglas canopy panels
81 Head/back armour plate
82 Harness attachment

83 Aluminium alloy decking
84 Turnover reinforcement
85 Canopy track
86 Fuselage framework cross-bracing
87 Radio equipment (TR9D/TR133)
88 Support tray
89 Removable access panel
90 Aileron cable drum
91 Elevator control lever
92 Cable adjusters
93 Aluminium alloy wing/fuselage fillet
94 Ventral identification and formation-keeping lights
95 Footstep retraction guide and support rail
96 Radio equipment (R3002)
97 Upward-firing recognition apparatus
98 Handhold
99 Diagonal support
100 Fuselage fairing
101 Dorsal identification light
102 Aerial mast
103 Aerial lead-in
104 Recognition apparatus cover panel
105 Mast support
106 Wire-braced upper truss
107 Wooden fuselage fairing formers
108 Fabric covering
109 Radio antenna
110 All-metal tailplane structure
111 Static and dynamic elevator balance
112 Starboard elevator
113 Tailfin metal leading-edge
114 Fabric covering
115 Tailfin structure
116 Diagonal bracing struts
117 Built-in static balance
118 Aerial stub
119 Fabric-covered rudder
120 Rudder structure
121 Rudder post
122 Rear navigation light
123 Balanced rudder trim tab
124 Wiring
125 Elevator trim tab
126 Fixed balance tab
127 Fabric-covered elevator
128 Tailplane rear spar
129 Tailplane front spar
130 Rudder lower hinge
131 Rudder operating lever
132 Connecting rod
133 Control pulleys
134 Elevator operating lever
135 Tailplane spar attachments

136 Aluminium alloy tailplane/fuselage fairing
137 Tailwheel shock-strut
138 Angled frame rear structure
139 Sternpost
140 Ventral fin
141 Dowty oleo-pneumatic fixed self-centering tailwheel
142 Fin framework
143 Handling-bar socket
144 Fabric covering
145 Swaged tube and steel gusset fitting and through bolts
146 Upper tube/longeron
147 Rudder cables
148 Wooden stringers
149 Elevator cables
150 Aluminium alloy formers
151 Diagonal brace wires
152 Lower tube/longeron
153 Aluminium alloy former bottom section
154 Retractable entry footstep
155 Wingroot fillet
156 Flap rod universal joint
157 Aileron cables
158 Fuselage/wing rear spar girder attachment
159 Main wing fuel tank (port and starboard: 33 lmp gal/150 l each)
160 Ventral Glycol radiator and oil cooler
161 Front spar wing fixings
162 Cannon forward mounting bracket
163 Cannon fairing
164 Recoil spring
165 Cannon barrels
166 Undercarriage retraction jack
167 Undercarriage fairing
168 Low pressure tyre
169 Port mainwheel
170 Mainwheel shock-strut
171 Oleo-pneumatic cylinder
172 Landing gear drag strut
173 Leading-edge armament access doors
174 Landing gear pivot point
175 Undercarriage sliding joint
176 Upper wing surface armament access plates
177 Rear spar wing fixing
178 Magazine blister fairings
179 Gun heating manifold
180 Breech-block access plates
181 Metal flaps
182 Cannon breech-blocks
183 Ammunition magazine drum
184 Port outer 20-mm Hispano cannon
185 Spar section change
186 Port landing light
187 Leading-edge structure
188 Front main spar
189 Forward intermediate spar
190 Stringers
191 Rib formers
192 Aluminium alloy wing skinning
193 Rear intermediate spar
194 Rear spar
195 Aileron control pulley
196 Aileron inboard hinge
197 Aluminium alloy aileron
198 Aileron control gear main pulley
199 Self-aligning ball-bearing hinge
200 Aileron outboard hinge
201 Detachable wingtip

0.303-in (7,7-mm) machine guns. The similarly-powered second prototype, flown on 5 December 1940, had provision for a four 20-mm cannon armament. A Tornado assembly line was laid down by Avro, the production model being intended to receive the Vulture V of 1,980 hp, with which both prototypes were re-engined. The Vulture, meanwhile, was suffering various problems, such as connecting rod bolt failures, and as the Merlin possessed absolute priority, Rolls-Royce was forced to abandon the production of this X-type engine. This led to cancellation of the initial production batch of 201 Tornados, only one production example being completed and flown on 29 August 1941. Approval was also given for completion of a third Tornado prototype with a 2,210 hp Bristol Centaurus CE.4S 18-cylinder air-cooled radial engine, this flying on 23 October 1941. The following data relate to the Vulture V-powered aircraft. *Max speed, 398 mph (640 km/h) at 23,000 ft (7 010 m). Time to 20,000 ft (6 100 m), 7.2 min. Empty weight, 8,377 lb (3 800 kg). Loaded weight, 10,668 lb (4 839 kg). Span, 41 ft 11 in (12,77 m). Length, 32 ft 10 in (10,00 m). Height, 14 ft 8 in (4,47 m). Wing area, 283 sq ft (26,29 m²).*

HAWKER TYPHOON   UK

The fighter design to F.18/37 tendered by Hawker as the "N-type" (see previous entry) differed primarily in having a 24-cylinder H-type Napier Sabre engine.

The Typhoon IB was used by No 257 Sqn (above) to fly bomber-intercept patrols from Exeter in 1942.

Named Typhoon, the first of two prototypes ordered on 30 August 1938 was flown on 24 February 1940, Gloster Aircraft being allocated production responsibility. Like the Tornado, the Typhoon could be fitted with either 12 0.303-in (7,7-mm) machine guns (Mk IA) or four 20-mm cannon (Mk IB). The first production aircraft flew on 27 May 1941 with the 2,100 hp Sabre I engine and machine gun armament: about 105 aircraft were to be completed with this armament owing to a shortage of cannon feed mechanisms, but the 2,180 hp Sabre IIA and cannon armament were soon standardised. The 2,200 hp Sabre IIB and 2,260 hp IIC progressively supplanted the IIA in the Typhoon, which began to enter squadron service in September 1941. Its disappointing climb rate and extremely poor altitude performance restricted the Typhoon to the low-altitude rôle, its potential being

The early framed cabin on the Typhoon IB (below) gave way later to a one-piece sliding canopy.

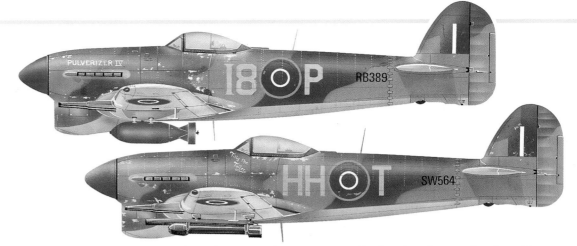

(Above, top) Typhoon IB of No 440 (RCAF) Sqn at Goch (Laarbruch) for close-support bombing, 1945. (Immediately above) Mk IB, No 175 Sqn, Celle, 1945.

fully exploited as a ground attack fighter with external ordnance. An original pair of 250-lb (113-kg) bombs was eventually increased to two 1,000-lb (454-kg) bombs or eight 60-lb (27-kg) rockets. A total of 3,315 production Typhoons was delivered, the last reaching the RAF as late as November 1945. By this time this Hawker fighter had already been largely replaced by the more efficacious Tempest. Some 60 aircraft were fitted with oblique and vertical cameras as Typhoon FR Mk IBs, one was tested as a night fighter with AI Mk IV radar, and another was tested with an annular radiator. The following data relate to the Mk IB. *Max speed, 405 mph (652 km/h) at 18,000 ft (5 485 m), 374 mph (602 km/h) at 5,500 ft (1 675 m). Range (clean on internal fuel), 610 mls (982 km). Empty weight, 9,800 lb (4 445 kg). Max loaded weight, 13,980 lb (6 341 kg). Span, 41 ft 7 in (12,67 m). Length, 31 ft 11 in (9,73 m). Height, 15 ft 3½ in (4,66 m). Wing area, 249 sq ft (23,13 m²).*

(Below) Hawker Typhoon IB with definitive canopy.

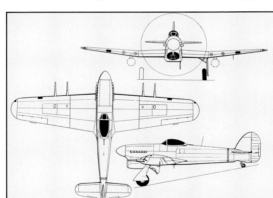

HAWKER TEMPEST I   UK

Tendered to Specification F.10/41 and originally known as the Typhoon II, the Tempest was an evolution of the Typhoon. As a result of a process of incremental design, it became progressively more different, both externally

and internally. Based on the use of a wing with a new, thinner aerofoil section and of semi-elliptical planform, it featured a 21-in (53-cm) lengthening of the forward fuselage (to permit introduction of more fuselage fuel tankage to compensate for that lost in the wing), a 2,340 hp Sabre IV and wing leading-edge radiators. Two prototypes were ordered initially, but a further four were subsequently added to the programme to investigate the possibilities of alternative engines. Two of the additional prototypes were to be fitted with the Centaurus V (as Mk IIs) and the others with the Griffon IIB (Mk III) or self-contained Griffon 61 (Mk IV). In the event, the Griffon-engined prototypes were not completed as Tempests, and because of difficulties with the

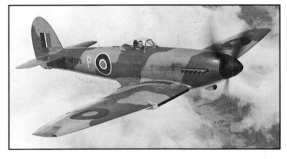

Remaining in prototype status, the Mk I (above) was the fastest of the Tempest series of fighters.

Sabre IV, one of the two Tempest I prototypes was completed with a Sabre II engine with chin-type radiator bath as the prototype Tempest V, this being the first prototype to fly. A production contract had been placed in August 1942 for 400 Tempest Is, but the delays with the Sabre IV led to this contract being transferred to the Tempest V. The Tempest I prototype was eventually flown on 24 February 1943, and proved to be the fastest of the Tempest series of fighters, but development was abandoned when Napier failed to persist with the Sabre IV engine. *Max speed, 466 mph (750 km/h) at 24,500 ft (7 470 m). Time to 15,000 ft (4 755 m), 4.25 min. Range, 770 mls (1 240 km). Loaded weight, 11,050 lb (5 012 kg). Span, 41 ft 0 in (12,49 m). Length, 33 ft 7 in (10,24 m). Height, 16 ft 0 in (4,88 m). Wing area, 310 sq ft (28,80 m²).*

HAWKER TEMPEST II   UK

Destined to become the RAF's last single-seat, single-piston-engined fighter to enter production, the Tempest II was actually preceded into service by the Tempest V, deliveries of the former not commencing until October 1944. The first of two Tempest II prototypes was flown on 28 June 1943 with a Centaurus IV 18-cylinder radial engine. The production model had the 2,520 hp Centaurus V or VI and an armament of four 20-mm cannon. The Tempest II was intended primarily for use by *Tiger Force* in operations against the Japanese, but these plans came to naught and this version of the fighter was only to see post-war service, 452 examples being built of which the last 300 or so were delivered after World War II. These equipped eight RAF squadrons; 89 ex-RAF aircraft were supplied to the Indian Air Force from 1947, and a further 24 to the Pakistan Air Force. *Max speed, 440 mph (708 km/h) at 15,900 ft (4 845 m), 417 mph (671 km/h) at 5,000 ft (1 525 m). Initial climb, 4,520 ft/min (22,96 m/sec). Range (internal fuel), 775 mls (1 247 km) at 210 mph*

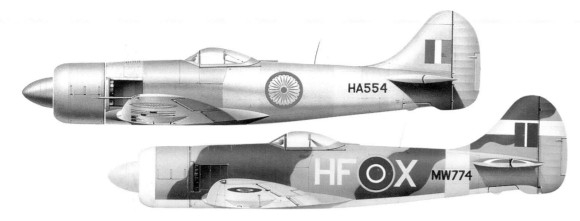

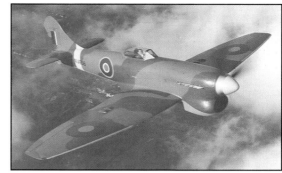

(Above, top) Tempest II, No 3 Sqn, Indian Air Force, at Kolar, early 'fifties. (Immediately above) Tempest II, No 54 Sqn, RAF Chilbolton, 1946.

(338 km/h). Empty weight, 9,300 lb (4 218 kg). Max loaded weight, 13,900 lb (6 305 kg). Span, 41 ft 0 in (12,49 m). Length, 34 ft 5 in (10,49 m). Height, 15 ft 6 in (4,72 m). Wing area, 303.7 sq ft (28,21 m²).

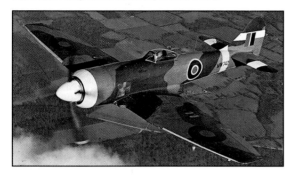

Intended for service with *Tiger Force*, the Tempest II (above and below) was too late for combat.

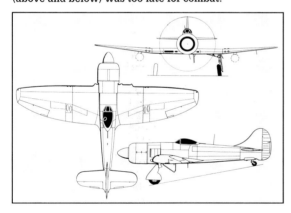

Despite its earlier mark number, the Tempest II (below) actually followed the Mk V into service.

(Right upper) Tempest V Srs 1 of No 486 (RNZAF) Sqn at Newchurch for anti-V1 patrols in 1944. (Right lower) Tempest VI, No 213 Sqn, Nicosia, Cyprus, 1947.

HAWKER TEMPEST V & VI   UK

Because of the urgency attached to the delivery of Tempests to the RAF, it was decided to proceed with production of a version using a Typhoon-type Sabre IIA installation as the Tempest V. A production contract was awarded in February 1942, more than six months before the initial flight of the Tempest V prototype on 2 September 1942. The 2,180 hp Sabre IIA-powered first pro-

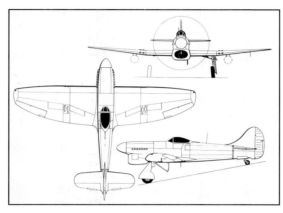

Short-barrel cannon were a distinguishing feature of the Tempest V Srs 2 (above) flown by No 501 (County of Gloucester) Sqn, RAuxAF (below).

duction example followed on 21 June 1943, and the Tempest V entered service in April 1944. Armament comprised four 20-mm cannon, the 2,200 hp Sabre IIB and the 2,260 hp Sabre IIC being progressively installed in production batches. Total orders were placed for 1,149 Sabre-engined Tempests of which the final 300 were to have been to Mk VI standard. In the event, only 142 of the latter were completed. The Tempest VI, which flew as a prototype on 9 May 1944, differed from the Mk V in having a 2,340 hp Sabre VA engine, but was too late to see operational service. Nine RAF squadrons received the Tempest VI post-war, the last of these being withdrawn in 1949. The following data relate to the Mk V. *Max speed, 435 mph (700 km/h) at 17,000 ft (5 180 m), 392 mph (631 km/h) at sea level. Initial climb, 4,700 ft/min (23,9 m/sec). Range (internal fuel), 740 mls (1 191 km). Empty weight, 9,250 lb (4 196 kg). Max loaded weight, 13,640 lb (6 187 kg). Span, 41 ft 0 in (12,49 m). Length, 33 ft 8 in (10,26 m). Height, 16 ft 1 in (4,90 m). Wing area, 302 sq ft (28,05 m²).*

The Tempest V Srs 2 (above) was the only version to see combat in WWII. (Below) A Griffon engine installation was featured by the second Fury to fly.

HAWKER FURY   UK

Heavily influenced by examination of the Focke-Wulf Fw 190A, Hawker evolved a smaller, lighter version of the Tempest, the fundamental change being elimination of the existing wing centre section. Early in 1943, Specification F.2/43 was drawn up around this project, the requirement subsequently being pooled with N.7/43 calling for a shipboard interceptor. Hawker took responsibility for development of the land-based fighter and Boulton Paul adapted the aircraft for carrier operation. Apart from smaller overall dimensions, the new fighter, which was to be named Fury, differed from preceding Hawker fighters in having a fuselage of monocoque construction throughout. Various alternative engines were considered, the first Fury prototype flying on 1 September 1944 with a Centaurus XII and a second on 27 November 1944 with a Griffon 85, the latter subsequently being re-engined with a Centaurus XV. The third prototype to fly was also fitted with the last-mentioned engine and flew on 25 July 1945. The second prototype had again been re-engined meanwhile, flying with a Napier Sabre VII rated at 3,055 hp at 2,250 ft (685 m) with which it attained a speed of 483 mph (777 km/h) at 18,500 ft (5 640 m). Although production contracts were prepared for 200 Furies for

(Above) The second Fury prototype (third to fly) was fitted with the definitive Centaurus engine.

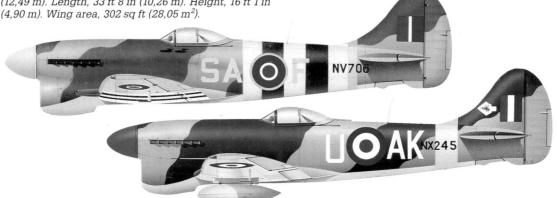

(Above) A Fury FB Mk 60 of Pakistan Air Force's No 9 Sqn, first in the service to equip on this type. (Below) A Sea Fury Mk 50 serving with No 860 Sqn of the Dutch MLD, 1951.

the RAF, these were cancelled at the end of World War II. The following data relate to the Fury powered by the 2,400 hp Bristol Centaurus XV radial. *Max speed, 455 mph (732 km/h) at 24,000 ft (7 315 m). Initial climb, 4,300 ft/min (21,8 m/sec). Empty weight, 8,615 lb (3 908 kg). Loaded weight, 11,675 lb (5 296 kg). Span, 38 ft 4¾ in (11,69 m). Length, 34 ft 7 in (10,54 m). Height, 14 ft 7½ in (4,46 m). Wing area, 284.5 sq ft (26,43 m²).*

A Napier Sabre VII engine was fitted as a trial installation in the third Fury prototype (below).

HAWKER SEA FURY   UK

Evolved in parallel with the shore-based Fury, the first semi-navalised prototype of the Sea Fury (lacking wing folding facilities) was flown on 21 February 1945. A (fully-navalised) second prototype flew eight months later, on 12 October, powered by a Bristol Centaurus 18 radial rated at 2,550 hp at 4,000 ft (1 220 m). The first example of the initial production version, the Sea Fury F Mk 10, was flown on 7 September 1946. The F Mk 10 entered Royal Navy service in the spring of the following year, 50 being built before being succeeded by the FB Mk 11 which supplemented the four 20-mm cannon armament with external ordnance. A total of 615 FB Mk 11s had been built when production terminated in November 1950, a number of these being supplied to the Australian and Canadian navies. Reconditioned aircraft were later sold to Burma (18) and Cuba (15). Export contracts comprised 22 (as F Mk 50s and FB Mk 51s) and 25 licence-built by Fokker for the Netherlands, 55 of a shore-based version for Iraq and 87 similar aircraft (plus the second Fury prototype and five Sea Fury con-

The Fury FB Mk 60 (above) flew with the Pakistan Air Force. (Below) The standard Sea Fury FB Mk 11.

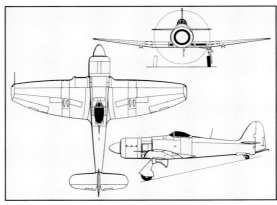

versions) for Pakistan. The following data relate to the FB Mk 11. *Max speed, 460 mph (740 km/h) at 18,000 ft (5 485 m). Initial climb, 4,320 ft/min (21,9 m/sec). Range (internal fuel), 700 mls (1 126 km). Empty weight, 9,240 lb (4 191 kg). Max loaded weight, 14,650 lb (6 645 kg). Span, 38 ft 4¾ in (11,69 m). Length, 34 ft 8 in (10,56 m). Height, 15 ft 10½ in (4,84 m). Wing area, 280 sq ft (26,01 m²).*

Twenty-two Sea Furies (below) for Nos 3 and 860 Sqns MLD, were supplemented by 25 more built by Fokker.

HAWKER SEA HAWK   UK

Conceived as the P.1040 land-based interceptor, in which form it was first flown on 2 September 1947, the Sea Hawk was a navalised adaptation of the basic design, a prototype of the shipboard fighter flying on 3 September 1948. The first production model, the Sea Hawk F Mk 1 (95 built), flew on 14 November 1951, this being followed by the F Mk 2 (40 built) with fully powered aileron controls. The Mks 1 and 2 were powered by the 5,000 lb st (2 268 kgp) Rolls-Royce Nene 101 turbojet and carried an armament of four 20-mm cannon. The similarly-powered FB Mk 3 (116 built) and FGA Mk 4 (97 built) featured a strengthened wing permitting external loads to be carried for the fighter-bomber and close air support rôles respectively. The re-engining of FB Mk 3 and FGA Mk 4 airframes with the 5,200 lb st (2 359 kgp) Nene 103 produced the FB Mk 5 and FGA Mk 6, and 86 of the latter were built from scratch. Deliveries of the FGA Mk 6 were completed early in 1956, followed by 22 similar FGA Mk 50s for the Netherlands and 66 (Mks 100 and 101) for Germany. Nine ex-RN Sea Hawk FB Mk 3s refurbished to FGA Mk 6 standards by Armstrong Whitworth were accepted by the Indian Navy in 1960. Production terminated in 1961 with a batch of 14 FGA Mk 6s for India.

Hawker's first jet fighter, the P.1040 prototype (below) led to the navalised Sea Hawk.

These were later supplemented in Indian service by 22 refurbished ex-RN Sea Hawk FGA Mk 6s and 28 ex-German *Marineflieger* Sea Hawk Mks 100 and 101, the latter with Ekco 38B search radar. The service of the Sea Hawk with the Indian Navy terminated in May 1983. The following data relate to the FGA Mk 6. *Max speed, 599 mph (964 km/h) at sea level. Initial climb, 5,700 ft/min (28,95 m/sec). Range (internal fuel), 480 mls (772 km). Empty weight, 9,278 lb (4 208 kg). Max loaded weight, 16,153 lb (7 327 kg). Span, 39 ft 0 in (11,89 m). Length, 39 ft 8 in (12,09 m). Height, 8 ft 8 in (2,64 m). Wing area, 278 sq ft (25,83 m²).*

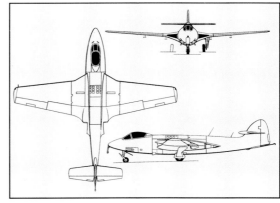

(Above) The Sea Hawk FGA Mk 6 and (below) a Mk 100 as supplied to the German *Marineflieger*, showing the taller fin of the latter mark.

(Above) Sea Hawk FB Mk 3 of No 802 Sqn aboard HMS *Albion* for the Suez campaign in 1956.

(Below) Sea Hawk FGA Mk 4 preserved by the RN Historic Flight, in the 1960 markings of No 806 Sqn.

(Above) Hunter F Mk 6 in 1974 from 229 OCU (234 Sqn), RAF Chivenor, and (below) the Hunter FGA Mk 9.

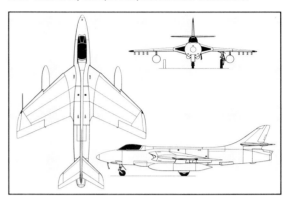

HAWKER P.1081   UK

Developed as a result of Australian interest in an operational fighter version of the P.1052 swept-wing research aircraft, the P.1081 was a rebuild of the second P.1052 incorporating a straight-through (as opposed to bifurcated) jet pipe and a new all-swept tail. Non-availability of the Rolls-Royce Tay turbojet proposed for installation resulted in retention of the original 5,000 lb st (2 268 kg) Nene R.N.2. With this power plant, the P.1081 was flown on 19 June 1950. Consideration was given to building a second, fully representative prototype with a four 20-mm cannon armament and an afterburning Tay engine, but, on 14 November 1950, further work on the Australian project was cancelled. The sole P.1081 was subsequently transferred to the RAE, but was destroyed in an accident on 3 April 1951. *Max speed, 695 mph (1 119 km/h) at sea level. Time to 35,000 ft (10 670 m), 9.2 min. Empty weight, 11,200 lb (5 080 kg). Loaded weight, 14,480 lb (6 568 kg). Span, 31 ft 6 in (9,60 m). Length, 37 ft 4 in (11,38 m). Height, 13 ft 3 in (4,04 m). Wing area, 258 sq ft (23,97 m²).*

Aimed at an Australian requirement, the P.1081 (above and below) was a rebuild of the P.1052.

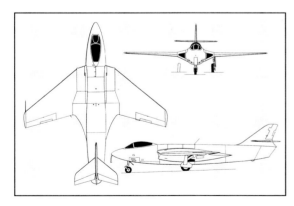

HAWKER HUNTER   UK

The first genuinely transonic British service aircraft, the Hunter first flew on 21 July 1951. Both first and second prototypes were powered by the Rolls-Royce Avon, a third prototype, flown on 30 November 1952, having an Armstrong Siddeley Sapphire. The first production model, the F Mk 1 (139 built) flew on 16 May

(Right) A Hunter F Mk 56 in service with the final IAF squadron on the type, No 20 at Kalaikunda, 1990.

1953 with an armament of four 30-mm Aden cannon and a 7,500 lb st (3 402 kgp) Avon 107. The first F Mk 2 (45 built) with an 8,000 lb st (3 629 kgp) Sapphire 101 followed on 14 October 1953. These versions briefly equipped four and two RAF squadrons respectively.

Serving in the rôle of a target tug, a Fokker-built Hunter F Mk 4 (above) of No 323 Sqn, KLu.

The next production models, the F Mk 4 (365 built) and F Mk 5 (105 built), with Avon and Sapphire, introduced internal wing fuel and provision for drop tanks. Export contracts for aircraft similar to the F Mk 4 comprised 120 Mk 50s for Sweden and 30 Mk 51s for Denmark. Sixteen converted from ex-RAF F Mk 4s were supplied to Peru as Mk 52s. The F Mk 6 (383 built) introduced the 10,150 lb st (4 605 kgp) Avon 207. Export contracts for aircraft basically similar to the F Mk 6 comprised 144 Mk 56s (plus 16 converted ex-RAF F Mk 6s) for India and 100 Mk 58s for Switzerland. Licence manufacture of 96 Mk 4s and 93 Mk 6s was undertaken in the Netherlands, and 111 Mk 4s and 144 Mk 6s in Belgium. Production of the Hunter continued into 1959, with a total of 1,972 (including training variants) being completed. Of these, almost one-third were later to be refurbished and converted for a variety of rôles for the RAF and a dozen overseas customers. Some 126 F Mk 6s were modified for the RAF for the fighter ground attack rôle as FGA Mk 9s and 34 for the reconnaissance mission as FR Mk 10s. The following data relate to the F Mk 6. *Max speed, 623 mph (1 002 km/h) at 36,000 ft (10 975 m), 715 mph (1 150 km/h) at sea level. Initial climb, 17,200 ft/min*

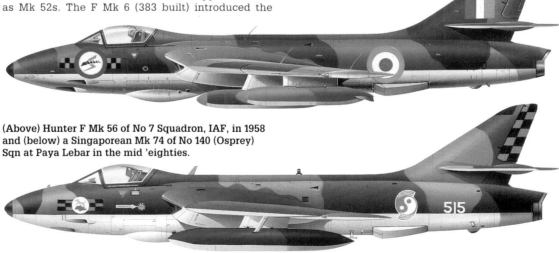

(Above) Hunter F Mk 56 of No 7 Squadron, IAF, in 1958 and (below) a Singaporean Mk 74 of No 140 (Osprey) Sqn at Paya Lebar in the mid 'eighties.

(87,37 m/sec). Ferry range (max external fuel), 1,900 mls (3 058 km). Empty equipped weight, 14,122 lb (6 406 kg). Loaded weight (clean), 17,750 lb (8 051 kg). Span, 33 ft 8 in (10,25 m). Length, 45 ft 10½ in (13,98 m). Height, 13 ft 2 in (4,02 m). Wing area, 349 sq ft (32,42 m²).

HAWKER SIDDELEY KESTREL UK

The Kestrel FGA Mk 1 ground attack fighter was an operational evaluation derivative of the P.1127 V/STOL (vertical and short take-off and landing) aircraft, development of which was initiated as a private venture in 1957. Six prototypes of the P.1127 were built, the first of these rising vertically on the vectored thrust of an 11,300 lb st (5 126 kgp) Pegasus 2 engine on 21 October 1960, followed by its first conventional flight on 13 March 1961. Nine evaluation aircraft were ordered for Tripartite (British-US-German) evaluation trials as Kestrel FGA Mk 1s, these introducing a fully-swept wing, a taller vertical tail, a bulged and slightly lengthened fuselage and a 15,000 lb st (6 804 kgp) Pegasus 5

First of the Kestrel FGA Mk 1s (above) built for the Tripartite Squadron at RAF West Raynham in 1964.

engine. The first of these flew on 7 March 1964. A Tripartite Trials Squadron existed from 15 October 1964 until 30 November 1965, after which six of the Kestrels were transferred to the USA where they were designated XV-6As. The Kestrel featured two wing hardpoints each capable of lifting gun pods or stores of up to 1,000 lb (454 kg). The Kestrel was to provide the basis for the British Aerospace Harrier (and McDonnell Douglas AV-8B) close support and tactical reconnaissance aircraft. *Max speed, 663 mph (1 067 km/h) at sea level. Endurance (VTOL operation), 35 min at sea level. Empty weight, 9,800 lb (4 445 kg). Loaded weight (VTOL), 12,400 lb (5 625 kg), (STOL), 15,500 lb (7 031 kg). Span, 22 ft 10 in (6,96 m). Length, 42 ft 6 in (12,95 m). Height, 10 ft 9 in (3,28 m). Wing area, 186 sq ft (17,28 m²).*

Here with a two-seat Hunter T Mk 7, the first Kestrel FGA Mk 1 (below) later went to the USA.

HEINKEL HD 23 Germany

The first single-seat fighter to be designed by the Ernst Heinkel Flugzeugwerke, which had been established at Warnemünde on 1 December 1922, the HD 23 was developed under Japanese contract. A shipboard aeroplane suitable for catapult launch, the HD 23 was a single-bay equi-span staggered biplane of mixed construction, the two prototypes being respectively powered by a 12-cylinder water-cooled BMW VIa engine rated at 660 hp and an Hispano-Suiza 12Ha of

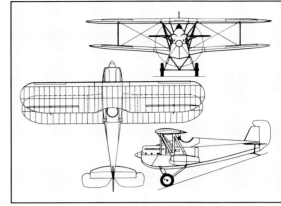

The first Heinkel single-seat fighter was the HD 23 (right), which was also known as the Aichi Type H (above) in Japan, which bought two.

Key to Hawker Hunter FGA Mk 9

1 Radome
2 Radar scanner dish
3 Ram air intake
4 Camera port
5 Radar ranging equipment
6 Camera access panel
7 Gun camera
8 Ground pressurization connection
9 Nosewheel door
10 Oxygen bottles
11 IFF aerial
12 Electronics equipment
13 Nosewheel bay
14 De-icing fluid tank
15 Pressurization control valves
16 Cockpit front bulkhead
17 Nose undercarriage leg
18 Nosewheel forks
19 Forward retracting nosewheel
20 Nosewheel leg door
21 Cannon muzzle port
22 Gun blast cascade deflectors
23 Rudder pedals
24 Bullet proof windscreen
25 Cockpit canopy framing
26 Reflector gunsight
27 Instrument panel shroud
28 Control column
29 Cockpit section fuselage frames
30 Rearward sliding cockpit canopy cover
31 Pilot's starboard side console
32 Martin-Baker Mk 3H ejection seat
33 Throttle control
34 Pilot's port side console
35 Cannon barrel tubes
36 Pneumatic system air bottles
37 Cockpit canopy emergency release
38 Cockpit rear pressure bulkhead
39 Air conditioning valve
40 Ejection seat headrest
41 Firing handle
42 Air louvres
43 Ammunition tanks
44 Ammunition link collector box
45 Cartridge case ejectors
46 Batteries
47 Port air intake
48 Boundary layer splitter plate
49 Intake lip construction

50 Radio and electronics equipment bay
51 Sliding canopy rail
52 Air conditioning supply pipes
53 Control rod linkages
54 Communications aerial
55 Fuselage double frame bulkhead
56 Boundary layer air outlet
57 Secondary air intake door, spring loaded
58 Intake duct construction
59 Forward fuselage fuel tank
60 Starboard intake duct
61 Starboard wing fuel tank
62 230-Imp gal (1 046-l) drop tank
63 Inboard pylon mounting
64 Leading-edge dog-tooth
65 100-Imp gal (455-l) drop tank
66 Outboard pylon mounting
67 Wing fence
68 Leading-edge extension
69 Starboard navigation light
70 Starboard wing tip
71 Whip aerial
72 Fairey hydraulic aileron booster jack
73 Starboard aileron
74 Aileron control rod linkage
75 Flap cut-out section for drop tank clearance
76 Starboard flap construction
77 Flap hydraulic jack
78 Flap synchronising jack
79 Starboard main undercarriage mounting
80 Retraction jack

81 Starboard undercarriage bay
82 Dorsal spine fairing
83 Main wing attachment frames
84 Main spar attachment joint
85 Engine starter fuel tank
86 Air conditioning system
87 Engine intake compressor face
88 Air conditioning pre-cooler
89 Cooling air outlet louvres
90 Rear spar attachment frames
91 Aileron control rods

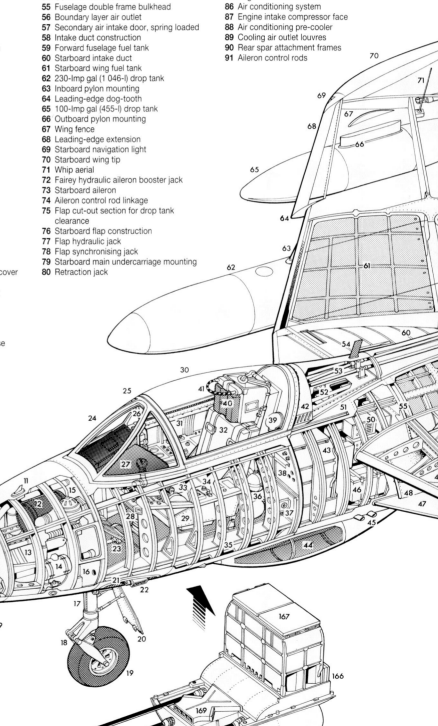

450 hp. Armament comprised two synchronised 7,7-mm machine guns and an unusual feature of the design was the lower portion of the fuselage, which, built on the lines of a boat hull, was watertight and incorporated flotation bags for emergency alighting on the water. The first of two prototypes built by the parent company was flown in 1925, both being shipped to Japan in 1927 for evaluation by the Imperial Navy. Two further examples were built by Aichi in 1927 as the Type H, these featuring a jettisonable undercarriage and movable wing slats. Although all four aircraft were extensively evaluated, the HD 23 was overweight, possessed poor manoeuvrability and was unstable at low speeds. *Max speed, 155 mph (249 km/h) at sea level. Time to 3,280 ft (1 000 m), 2.2 min, to 6,560 ft (2 000 m), 4.63 min. Empty weight, 3,241 lb (1 470 kg). Loaded weight, 4,563 lb (2 070 kg). Span, 35 ft 5⅛ in (10,80 m).*

Length, 24 ft 9¼ in (7,55 m). Height, 11 ft 1⅞ in (3,40 m). Wing area, 380.19 sq ft (35,32 m²).

HEINKEL HD 26   Germany

A single-seat, twin-float, fighter-reconnaissance aircraft developed in parallel with the HD 23 and similarly built against a Japanese contract, the HD 26 was intended for launch from a gun turret on the battleship *Nagato*. Of wooden construction and carrying an armament of one 7,7-mm synchronised machine gun, the HD 26 was powered by a 300 hp Hispano-Suiza HS 8 eight-cylinder water-cooled engine. The sole prototype built by the parent company underwent flight testing and catapult launching trials at Warnemünde in the summer of 1925 before being shipped to Japan. A second

The sole HD 26 (above) was developed for Japan as a shipboard fighter-reconnaissance aircraft.

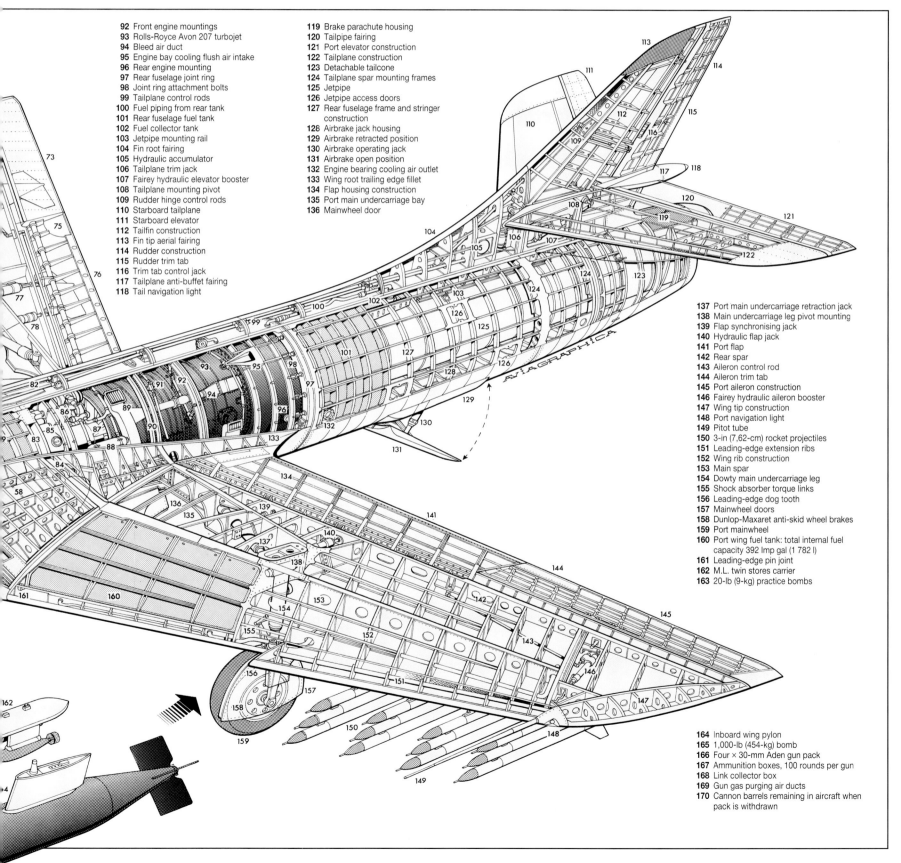

92 Front engine mountings
93 Rolls-Royce Avon 207 turbojet
94 Bleed air duct
95 Engine bay cooling flush air intake
96 Rear engine mounting
97 Rear fuselage joint ring
98 Joint ring attachment bolts
99 Tailplane control rods
100 Fuel piping from rear tank
101 Rear fuselage fuel tank
102 Fuel collector tank
103 Jetpipe mounting rail
104 Fin root fairing
105 Hydraulic accumulator
106 Tailplane trim jack
107 Fairey hydraulic elevator booster
108 Tailplane mounting pivot
109 Rudder hinge control rods
110 Starboard tailplane
111 Starboard elevator
112 Tailfin construction
113 Fin tip aerial fairing
114 Rudder construction
115 Rudder trim tab
116 Trim tab control jack
117 Tailplane anti-buffet fairing
118 Tail navigation light

119 Brake parachute housing
120 Tailpipe fairing
121 Port elevator construction
122 Tailplane construction
123 Detachable tailcone
124 Tailplane spar mounting frames
125 Jetpipe
126 Jetpipe access doors
127 Rear fuselage frame and stringer construction
128 Airbrake jack housing
129 Airbrake retracted position
130 Airbrake operating jack
131 Airbrake open position
132 Engine bearing cooling air outlet
133 Wing root trailing edge fillet
134 Flap housing construction
135 Port main undercarriage bay
136 Mainwheel door

137 Port main undercarriage retraction jack
138 Main undercarriage leg pivot mounting
139 Flap synchronising jack
140 Hydraulic flap jack
141 Port flap
142 Rear spar
143 Aileron control rod
144 Aileron trim tab
145 Port aileron construction
146 Fairey hydraulic aileron booster
147 Wing tip construction
148 Port navigation light
149 Pitot tube
150 3-in (7,62-cm) rocket projectiles
151 Leading-edge extension ribs
152 Wing rib construction
153 Main spar
154 Dowty main undercarriage leg
155 Shock absorber torque links
156 Leading-edge dog tooth
157 Mainwheel doors
158 Dunlop-Maxaret anti-skid wheel brakes
159 Port mainwheel
160 Port wing fuel tank: total internal fuel capacity 392 Imp gal (1 782 l)
161 Leading-edge pin joint
162 M.L. twin stores carrier
163 20-lb (9-kg) practice bombs

164 Inboard wing pylon
165 1,000-lb (454-kg) bomb
166 Four × 30-mm Aden gun pack
167 Ammunition boxes, 100 rounds per gun
168 Link collector box
169 Gun gas purging air ducts
170 Cannon barrels remaining in aircraft when pack is withdrawn

example was built in Japan by Aichi, this having a 420 hp British Jupiter VI nine-cylinder radial, and the two aircraft were operated from the turrets of the *Nagato* and the cruiser *Furutaka*, but the advent of catapult launching rendered the HD 26 obsolete. The following data relate to the HS-8 powered prototype. *Max speed, 115 mph (185 km/h) at sea level. Time to 9,840 ft (3 000 m), 7.5 min. Empty weight, 2,535 lb (1 150 kg). Loaded weight, 3,697 lb (1 677 kg). Span, 38 ft 8½ in (11,80 m). Length, 27 ft 8¼ in (8,44 m). Height, 11 ft 9⅓ in (3,59 m). Wing area, 407.3 sq ft (37,84 m²).*

HEINKEL HD 37   Germany

Heinkel built a small batch of its HD 37c fighters (above and below) for export to the Soviet Union.

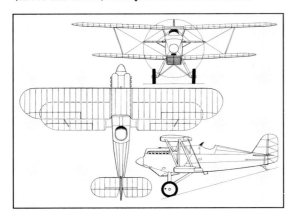

Supplementing the HD 37c fighter purchased from Germany, the Soviet Union built 134 during 1932-1934 under licence with the designation I-7 (below).

Developed with the encouragement of the *Fliegerstab* of the *Reichswehrministerium*, the HD 37 single-seat fighter was a single-bay staggered biplane powered by a 750 hp BMW VI 7,3Z water-cooled engine and armed with twin 7,7-mm machine guns. The first prototype, the HD 37a, was flown in 1928 and was of mixed construction with fabric- and plywood-covered wooden wings and a fabric-covered, steel-tube fuselage. Although the HD 37 failed to find favour with the clandestine *Reichswehr* air arm, a small number was purchased by the Soviet Union, together with a manufacturing licence, 134 being built during 1932-34 under the designation I-7 as interim equipment for Soviet fighter squadrons pending the availability of more advanced fighters of indigenous design. The HD 37c as built in the Soviet Union was powered by a licence-built version of the BMW VI engine designated M-17, and service phase-out commenced early in 1935. The following data relate to the Soviet-built HD 37c. *Max speed, 180 mph (290 km/h) at sea level, 172 mph (277 km/h) at*

16,405 ft (5 000 m). Range, 435 mls (700 km). Climb to 3,280 ft (1 000 m), 2.0 min, to 9,840 ft (3 000 m) in 6.6 min. Empty weight, 2,857 lb (1 296 kg). Loaded weight, 3,812 lb (1 729 kg). Span, 32 ft 9⅔ in (10,00 m). Length, 22 ft 9⅔ in (6,95 m). Wing area, 287.5 sq ft (26,71 m²).*

HEINKEL HD 38   Germany

Closely related to the HD 37, the HD 38a (below) was also built in HD 38aw seaplane form (above).

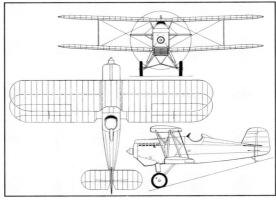

Following closely on the heels of the HD 37, and similarly powered by a 750 hp BMW VI 7,3Z engine, but aerodynamically more refined than its predecessor, the HD 38 flew in prototype form in 1929. Structurally similar to the earlier fighter, but of equi-span, single-bay configuration, the HD 38 was designed with interchangeable wheel and twin float undercarriages, and was offered as both a shipboard (HD 38a) and land-based (HD 38b) fighter. The former was stressed for catapult launch as a floatplane (HD 38aW) and the latter was offered with floats and a 310 hp Junkers L-5 engine (HD 38bW) as a fighter training seaplane. On 7 May 1929, the prototype, in HD 38aW form, established a class speed record at Warnemünde, flying a 100-km (62-mile) closed circuit with a 500-kg (1,102-lb payload) at an average speed of 259,9 km/h (161.5 mph). The HD 38a was evaluated in October 1931 at the clandestine *Reichswehr* air training centre at Lipetsk in the Soviet Union, and a batch of 12 was ordered to equip a naval fighter squadron. These were introduced into service in

1934, but within the year had been transferred to the flying training school at Schleissheim. *Max speed, 177 mph (285 km/h) at sea level. Time to 3,280 ft (1 000 m), 1.8 min, to 9,840 ft (3 000 m), 6.4 min. Empty weight, 3,119 lb (1 415 kg). Loaded weight, 4,056 lb (1 840 kg). Span, 32 ft 9⅔ in (10,00 m). Length, 23 ft 7½ in (7,20 m). Height, 11 ft 11¾ in (3,65 m). Wing area, 324.54 sq ft (30,15 m²).*

HEINKEL HD 43   Germany

By the beginning of the 'thirties, the Ernst Heinkel Flugzeugwerke was heavily committed to the design and development of aircraft for the *Reichswehrministerium*. To meet a clandestinely-formulated single-seat fighter requirement, the company produced the HD 43 which was flown in prototype form in 1931. An unequal-span staggered biplane, the HD 43 followed the constructional methods of preceding Heinkel fighters, with wings built up on spruce boxspars and a welded steel-tube fuselage, the whole fabric covered, and power was provided by a 750 hp BMW VI 7,3Z engine. The HD 43 was evaluated against the Arado Ar 65, the latter being selected for production for use by the so-called *Reklamefliegerabteilung* (Publicity Flying Department). A licence was sold to the Soviet Union, but, in the event, was not utilised, no series production of this Heinkel fighter being undertaken. *Max speed, 200 mph (322 km/h). Time to 9,840 ft (3 000 m), 4.9 min. Empty weight, 2,822 lb (1 280 kg). Loaded weight, 3,748 lb (1 700 kg). Span, 32 ft 9⅔ in (10,00 m). Length, 23 ft 3⅓ in (7,10 m). Height, 10 ft 9⅞ in (3,30 m). Wing area, 285.9 sq ft (26,56 m²).*

The HD 43 (below) remained a single prototype.

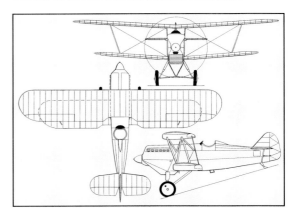

HEINKEL HE 49   Germany

The addition of the Günter brothers, Walter and Siegfried, to the Heinkel design staff was to result in a series of aircraft possessing an elegance of line that would

The sole HD 43 (below) was designed to satisfy a clandestine fighter requirement in Germany.

First Günter-designed fighter, the He 49a (above), and (below) the second prototype in He 49bw form.

Heinkel He 51Bs were flown in Spain by (above) 1./JG 88 as part of the *Legion Condor* in 1937.

An He 51B-2 fighter floatplane (below) serving with *Küstenjagdgruppe* 136 (later I/JG 136).

provide the indelible hallmark of the company's aircraft of the mid and late 'thirties. The first Heinkel design for which the Günter brothers were primarily responsible was the He 49 single-bay single-seat fighter biplane powered by a 690 hp BMW VI 6,0 12-cylinder water-cooled engine. Featuring an aerodynamically clean, low-drag fuselage and a semi-retractable radiator, the He 49 was of mixed construction with an armament of two 7,9-mm machine guns. The first prototype, the He 49a, was flown in November 1932, and a second proto-type, the He 49b with a 15.7-in (40-cm) rear fuselage lengthening, followed in February 1933. The second prototype was later fitted with a twin-float undercarriage as the He 49bW, and a third prototype, the He 49c, differed from the preceding aircraft in having a glycol-cooled BMW VI 6,0 ZU engine. Numerous changes were embodied in a refined fourth prototype which emerged as the He 51 (which see). The following data relate to the He 49b with wheel undercarriage. *Max speed, 202 mph (325 km/h) at sea level, 188 mph (302 km/h) at 11,485 ft (3 500 m). Time to 3,280 ft (1 000 m), 1.65 min. Loaded weight, 4,299 lb (1 950 kg). Span, 36 ft 1 in (11,00 m). Length, 27 ft 0⅓ in (8,24 m). Wing area, 292.79 sq ft (27,20 m²).*

HEINKEL HE 51   Germany

Essentially a refinement of the He 49c, the He 51a single-seat fighter designed by the Günter brothers flew for the first time in the summer of 1933. Overall dimensions and basic structure remained virtually un-changed, but in detail the new fighter differed mark-edly from its progenitor. A single He 51a prototype was followed by nine pre-series He 51A-0 fighters for ser-vice evaluation, and the initial production model, the He 51A-1, began to leave the assembly line in April 1935. This was powered by a 750 hp BMW VI 7,2Z liquid-cooled engine and was armed with two 7,9-mm machine guns. Production continued with the mini-mally modified He 51B-1 which had provision for a drop tank, and after 150 He 51As built by Heinkel and Arado, a further 150 He 51Bs were built by Arado and 200 by

A Heinkel He 51A-1 from the initial production batch in service with 1./JG 132 at Döberitz.

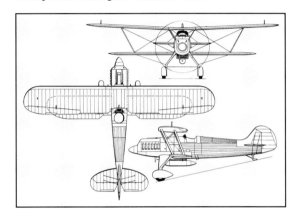

(Above) The He 51C close air support fighter.

Erla. An additional 200 were ordered from Fieseler of which the last 100 were completed as He 51Cs. The latter were intended primarily for close air support units operating in Spain and had racks of six 22-lb (10-kg) bombs. A total of 135 He 51s was shipped to Spain for use by the *Legion Condor* and the Spanish National-ists. Forty-six of the He 51Bs were completed as twin-float fighters (He 51B-2s). This type was withdrawn from first-line use and relegated to the *Jagdfliegerschu-len* in 1938. The following data relate to the He 51B-1. *Max speed, 205 mph (330 km/h) at sea level, 193 mph (310 km/h) at 13,125 ft (4 000 m). Range, 435 mls (700 km) at 137 mph (220 km/h) at 19,685 ft (6 000 m). Time to 3,280 ft (1 000 m), 1.4 min. Empty weight, 3,247 lb (1 473 kg). Normal loaded weight, 4,189 lb*

(1 900 kg). Span, 36 ft 1 in (11,00 m). Length, 27 ft 6¾ in (8,40 m). Height, 10 ft 6 in (3,20 m). Wing area, 292.79 sq ft (27,20 m²).

HEINKEL HE 112A   Germany

The first low-wing cantilever monoplane fighter de-signed by the Günter brothers, the He 112 was to undergo an extraordinary process of incremental rede-sign that would result in a totally different warplane, in its definitive production form, from that flown as a pro-totype in June 1935. The first prototype, the He 112 V1, was powered by a 695 hp Rolls-Royce Kestrel V, had a wing span of 41 ft 4 in (12,60 m) and a wing area of 249.73 sq ft (23,20 m²). The second and third proto-types, the He 112 V2 and V3, by which it was joined in November 1935 and January 1936 respectively, were powered by the 640 hp Junkers Jumo 210C and were initially otherwise similar until, in the spring of 1936,

(Above, top) He 51A-1 of 3.*Staffel, Jagdgeschwader* 233, Wien-Aspern, 1938, and (immediately above) He 51C-1, 4.*Staffel, Jagdgruppe* 88, Spain, 1937.

span and wing area were reduced to 37 ft 8¾ in (11,50 m) and 232.5 sq ft (21,60 m²). The fourth prototype, the He 112 V4, was, in fact, the first pre-series He 112A fighter with a 680 hp Jumo 210Da engine, a new wing of semi-elliptical planform and new horizontal tail surfaces. This aircraft was sent to Spain in December 1936 for operational evaluation with the *Legion Condor*. Three further A-series aircraft were meanwhile completed, these being the He 112 V5, which was essentially similar to the V4; the V6 with radiator bath and vertical tail changes, and the V8, which, completed after the radically revised B-series, served as a Daimler-Benz engine test bed, being fitted with a 1,000 hp DB 600Aa. The V8 was later re-engined with the Jumo 210Da, and, in February

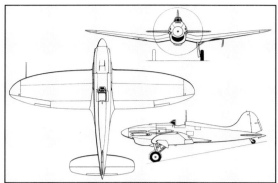

Powered by a Rolls-Royce Kestrel, the He 112 V1 (above) differed notably from the He 112A (right).

1937, assigned to the rocket propulsion development programme. The V3, V4, V5 and V6 were all fitted with twin 7,9-mm machine guns. The V5 was subsequently

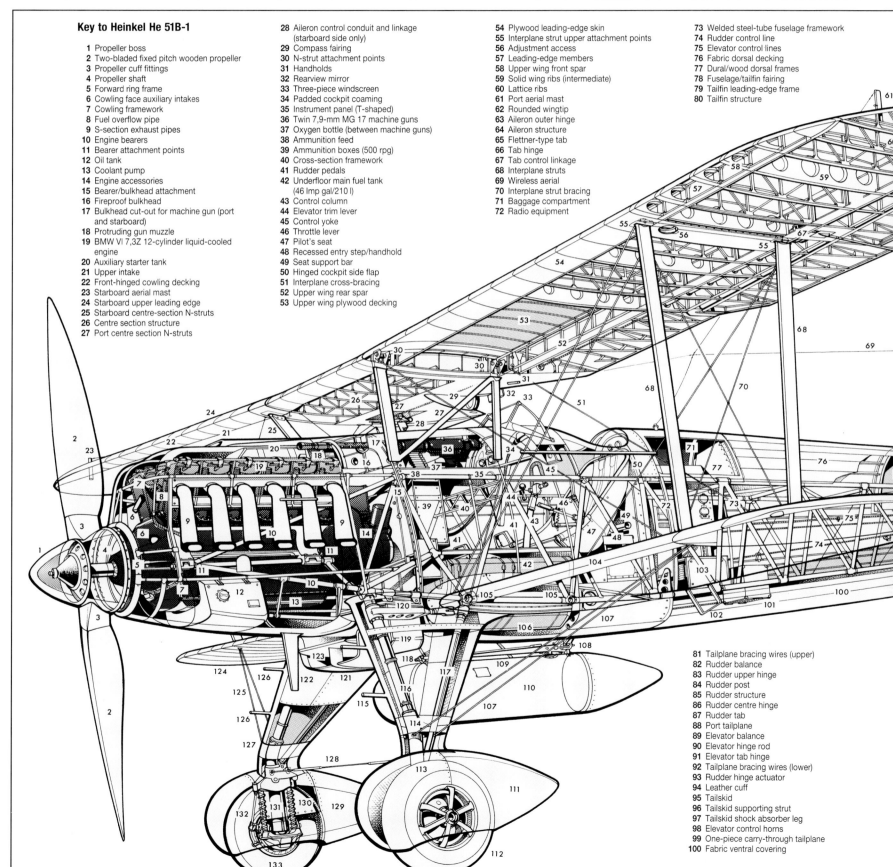

Key to Heinkel He 51B-1

1 Propeller boss
2 Two-bladed fixed pitch wooden propeller
3 Propeller cuff fittings
4 Propeller shaft
5 Forward ring frame
6 Cowling face auxiliary intakes
7 Cowling framework
8 Fuel overflow pipe
9 S-section exhaust pipes
10 Engine bearers
11 Bearer attachment points
12 Oil tank
13 Coolant pump
14 Engine accessories
15 Bearer/bulkhead attachment
16 Fireproof bulkhead
17 Bulkhead cut-out for machine gun (port and starboard)
18 Protruding gun muzzle
19 BMW VI 7,3Z 12-cylinder liquid-cooled engine
20 Auxiliary starter tank
21 Upper intake
22 Front-hinged cowling decking
23 Starboard aerial mast
24 Starboard upper leading edge
25 Starboard centre-section N-struts
26 Centre section structure
27 Port centre section N-struts

28 Aileron control conduit and linkage (starboard side only)
29 Compass fairing
30 N-strut attachment points
31 Handholds
32 Rearview mirror
33 Three-piece windscreen
34 Padded cockpit coaming
35 Instrument panel (T-shaped)
36 Twin 7,9-mm MG 17 machine guns
37 Oxygen bottle (between machine guns)
38 Ammunition feed
39 Ammunition boxes (500 rpg)
40 Cross-section framework
41 Rudder pedals
42 Underfloor main fuel tank (46 Imp gal/210 l)
43 Control column
44 Elevator trim lever
45 Control yoke
46 Throttle lever
47 Pilot's seat
48 Recessed entry step/handhold
49 Seat support bar
50 Hinged cockpit side flap
51 Interplane cross-bracing
52 Upper wing rear spar
53 Upper wing plywood decking

54 Plywood leading-edge skin
55 Interplane strut upper attachment points
56 Adjustment access
57 Leading-edge members
58 Upper wing front spar
59 Solid wing ribs (intermediate)
60 Lattice ribs
61 Port aerial mast
62 Rounded wingtip
63 Aileron outer hinge
64 Aileron structure
65 Flettner-type tab
66 Tab hinge
67 Tab control linkage
68 Interplane struts
69 Wireless aerial
70 Interplane strut bracing
71 Baggage compartment
72 Radio equipment

73 Welded steel-tube fuselage framework
74 Rudder control line
75 Elevator control lines
76 Fabric dorsal decking
77 Dural/wood dorsal frames
78 Fuselage/tailfin fairing
79 Tailfin leading-edge frame
80 Tailfin structure

81 Tailplane bracing wires (upper)
82 Rudder balance
83 Rudder upper hinge
84 Rudder post
85 Rudder structure
86 Rudder centre hinge
87 Rudder tab
88 Port tailplane
89 Elevator balance
90 Elevator hinge rod
91 Elevator tab hinge
92 Tailplane bracing wires (lower)
93 Rudder hinge actuator
94 Leather cuff
95 Tailskid
96 Tailskid supporting strut
97 Tailskid shock absorber leg
98 Elevator control horns
99 One-piece carry-through tailplane
100 Fabric ventral covering

Serving as a test-bed for an engine-mounted cannon, the He 112 V5 (above) went to Spain in late 1936.

modified to take an engine-mounted 20-mm cannon with which it was shipped to Spain. Dubbed the *Kanon-*

101 Battery
102 Entry step
103 Radio equipment
104 Port lower wing leading edge
105 Lower wing/fuselage attachment points

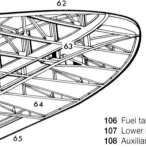

106 Fuel tank access cover plate (removed)
107 Lower bracing wires
108 Auxiliary tank rear shackles
109 Fuel line
110 Jettisonable auxiliary tank (37.4-Imp gal/170-l capacity)
111 Port mainwheel fairing
112 Port mainwheel
113 Vertical leg section
114 Chrome-molybdenum cranked "knee" section

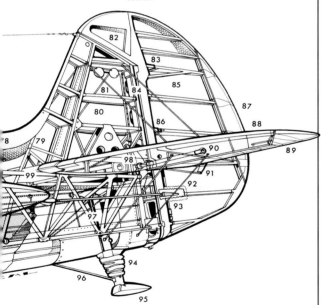

115 Inspection/maintenance footholds
116 Mainwheel leg
117 Leg support strut
118 Auxiliary tank forward shackles
119 Radiator
120 Undercarriage fairing/fuselage attachment plate
121 Ventral radiator bath
122 Airflow vane
123 Controllable shutter
124 Starboard lower wing skinning
125 Lower bracing wires
126 Inspection/maintenance footholds
127 Faired undercarriage legs
128 Twin-wire undercarriage bracing
129 Starboard mainwheel fairing
130 Springs
131 Hydraulic shock absorber dampers
132 Lubricant lead
133 Starboard mainwheel

vögel ("Canon-Bird"), it saw operational use with the *Legion Condor*. The following data relate to the He 112 V4 as representative of the A-series. *Max speed, 303 mph (488 km/h) at 11,485 ft (3 500 m). Time to 3,280 ft (1 000 m), 1.57 min. Service ceiling, 26,245 ft (8 000 m). Empty weight, 3,704 lb (1 680 kg). Loaded weight, 4,916 lb (2 230 kg). Span, 37 ft 8¾ in (11,50 m). Length, 29 ft 6⅓ in (9,00 m). Height, 12 ft 1⅔ in (3,70 m). Wing area, 249.72 sq ft (23,20 m²).*

HEINKEL HE 112B   Germany

Fundamentally a new design evolved under the supervision of Dipl-Ing Heinrich Hertel, the He 112B possessed no commonality with the preceding He 112A. Employing a lighter structure, a smaller, more highly loaded, truly elliptical single-spar wing with an aspect ratio of only 4.86:1.0, and an aerodynamically refined fuselage with an enclosed cockpit, the definitive B-series prototype, the He 112 V9, flew in July 1937, with a 680 hp Jumo 210Ea engine. In fact, the first B-series airframe had been utilised for the He 112 V7, which had been completed as a DB 600 engine test bed.

Built for Japan, these He 112B-0 fighters (above) served briefly with IV/JG 132 before going to Spain.

The Japanese Imperial Navy placed an order for 30 He 112B fighters essentially similar to the V9, the first 12 being shipped as He 112B-0s in the late spring of 1938 and entering service as A7He 1 Type He Air Defence Fighters. The second batch of 12 was requisitioned by the *Luftwaffe* immediately prior to the Sudeten *coup*, and by the time these were restored to Heinkel, Japan had cancelled the remaining 18 fighters on the contract.

Heinkel He 112B-0 of *Grupo* 27 at Melilla in Spanish Morocco (above) in 1944. (Below) The He 112B-1.

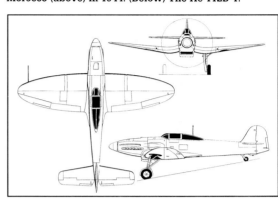

One of these was retained by Heinkel (to become the He 112 V11) and the remaining 17 were sold to the Spanish Nationalists. A second batch of 30 had meanwhile been laid down against an order from Romania placed at the beginning of 1939, the first 13 as He 112B-0s with the Jumo 210Ea engine and the remainder as He 112B-1s with the fuel-injection Jumo 210G. Three He 112B-1s were supplied to Hungary for evaluation, that country also purchasing the He 112 V9. Two further prototypes were built, the He 112 V10 with the 1,175 hp DB 601Aa engine and the V12 with the 1,000 hp DB 600Aa, the latter eventually being sold to Japan. All production examples had an armament of two 7,9-mm and two 20-mm guns. The following data relate to the He 112B-0. *Max speed, 267 mph (430 km/h) at sea level,*

(Immediately below) He 112B-0 with IV/JG 132 at Oshatz, Saxony, during Sudeten Crisis, 1938. (Bottom) He 112B-0 of *Grupo* 27 at Melilla in 1942.

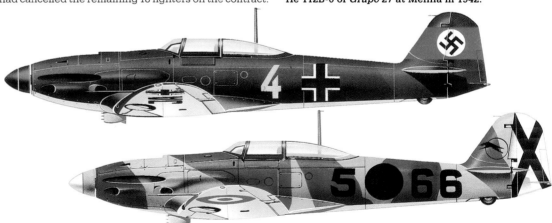

(Below) He 112B-1s served with the Romanian FARR's *Escadrile* 51 and 52 at Bucharest until early 1944.

317 mph (510 km/h) at 15,420 ft (4 700 m). Time to 6,560 ft (2 000 m), 2.6 min. Max range, 683 mls (1 100 km). Empty weight, 3,571 lb (1 620 kg). Loaded weight, 4,960 lb (2 250 kg). Span, 29 ft 10¼ in (9,10 m). Length, 30 ft 6 in (9,30 m). Height, 12 ft 7½ in (3,85 m). Wing area, 182.99 sq ft (17,00 m²).

HEINKEL HE 100   Germany

Assigned a non-sequential RLM type designation at the personal request of Ernst Heinkel, the He 100 was designed by Siegfried Günter under the overall supervision of Dipl-Ing Heinrich Hertel and was intended to employ a surface evaporation cooling system. Powered by a 1,175 hp DB 601A engine, the first prototype, the He 100 V1, was flown on 22 January 1938. A second prototype, the V2, had wing skinning of increased gauge to rectify buckling, and an enlarged vertical tail. Re-engined with a specially boosted, short-endurance DB 601 Re II engine affording 1,660 hp, the V2 established a 100-km (62-mile) closed-circuit record of 394.42 mph (634,73 km/h) on 5 June 1938. The V3 was intended to attack the absolute speed record and was fitted with a DB 601 Re V race-tuned engine providing 2,770 hp for five minutes. This aircraft was lost during the course of the attempt. The next prototype, the He 100 V4, was the first B-series airframe, which, embodying some structural refinement, was also the first built against an official contract for 10 pre-series aircraft. The V6 and V7 were C-series aircraft powered by the improved DB 601Aa engine and flown in April and May 1939 respectively. The V8, with a DB 601 Re V engine, short span wings and various aerodynamic refinements, preceded the V6 and V7, and, on 30 March 1939, established a speed record of 463.97 mph (746,666 km/h).

The He 100D-1 (above and below) was used in 1940 for an elaborate propaganda hoax as the "He 113".

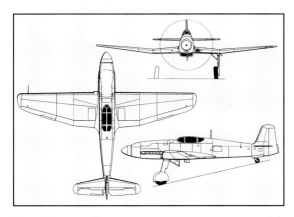

The V9 was the first prototype to mount armament, this comprising an engine-mounted 20-mm MG FF cannon and two 7,9-mm MG 17 machine guns. The last three pre-series aircraft built against the original order were completed to proposed production standards as He 100D-0s, the first of these flying in September 1939. A production batch of 12 He 100D-1s followed. Six prototypes (V1, V2, V4, V5, V6 and V7) were brought up to He 100D-1 standards and sold to the Soviet Union, and Japan acquired the three pre-production He 100D-0s, these being delivered to the Imperial Navy under the designation AXHei. A manufacturing licence was obtained by Japan, but Heinkel failed to provide pattern

jigs and tools, and planned production by Hitachi was abandoned. The He 100D-1s were the subject of numerous propaganda photographs in 1940 as part of an elaborate disinformation exercise. The following data relate to the He 100D-1. *Max speed, 358 mph (576 km/h) at sea level, 416 mph (670 km/h) at 16,405 ft (5 000 m). Time to 6,560 ft (2 000 m), 2.2 min. Max range, 628 mls (1 010 km). Empty weight, 3,990 lb (1 810 kg). Loaded weight, 5,511 lb (2 500 kg). Span, 30 ft 10 in (9,40 m). Length, 26 ft 10⅘ in (8,20 m). Height (tail up), 11 ft 9¾ in (3,60 m). Wing area, 157.16 sq ft (14,60 m²).*

HEINKEL HE 280   Germany

The He 280 V3 (above and below) flew in July 1942 as the second prototype fitted with HeS 8A engines.

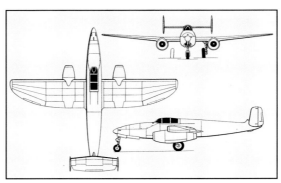

Enjoying the distinction of having been the world's first turbojet-powered fighter and the first fighter conceived from the outset with a pilot ejection seat, the He 280 was designed under the leadership of Dipl-Ing Heinrich Hertel, the chief designer being Karl Schwärzler. Of stressed-skin all-metal construction, the first prototype, the He 280 V1, was completed as a glider and was towed into the air for the first time on 22 September 1940. The second prototype, the V2, was fitted with two 1,100 lb st (500 kgp) Heinkel-Hirth HeS 8A (109-001A) turbojets and flew with these for the first time on 30 March 1941. The next prototype, the V3, was not flown until 5 June 1942, and then with HeS 8A turbojets with output boosted to 1,323 lb st (600 kgp). Five further airframes had meanwhile been built (V4 to V8 inclusive) of which the He 280 V5 had been designated the pre-series prototype for the He 280A, this being the first airframe to receive armament, comprising three 20-mm MG 151 cannon. The decision to discontinue development of the HeS 8 engine led Heinkel to investigate the use of the Junkers Jumo 004B (109-004) and BMW 003 (109-003) turbojets. The V2 was re-engined with the Jumo 004B, with which it flew on 16 March 1943, and it was planned to power the V4, V5 and V6 with the BMW 003. It was proposed to manufacture the fighter as the He 280B, initially with the Jumo 004 and subsequently with the BMW 003, and contractual negotiations were begun for 300 fighters of this type, but on 27 March 1943, Heinkel was instructed to abandon all further work on the He 280. The He 280 V1 was fitted with four Argus As 014 (109-014) pulse jets, but crashed on 13 January 1943 after being towed to altitude and before

The He 280 V3 (below) was the most extensively flown prototype of the world's first turbojet fighter.

The He 280 V3 (above) is seen here during its first flight from Marienehe on 5 July 1942.

the As 014s were lit. The V4, V5 and V6 were never completed, but the V7 and V8 were assigned to the *Deutsche Forschungsinstitut für Segelflug* (German Research Institute for Gliding) for aerodynamic research, both eventually being fitted with V-type, or "butterfly", empennages, and the V8 being fitted with Jumo 004Bs with which it first flew on 19 July 1943. The following data are manufacturer's estimates for the He 280A based on the use of two 1,653 lb st (750 kgp) HeS 8A turbojets. *Max speed, 540 mph (870 km/h) at sea level, 559 mph (900 km/h) at 19,685 ft (6 000 m). Range, 603 mls (970 km) at 32,810 ft (10 000 m). Max initial climb, 3,760 ft/min (19,1 m/sec). Empty weight, 6,735 lb (3 055 kg). Max loaded weight, 9,480 lb (4 300 kg). Span, 40 ft 0⅓ in (12,20 m). Length, 34 ft 1⅜ in (10,40 m). Height, 10 ft 0⅓ in (3,06 m). Wing area, 231.43 sq ft (21,50 m²).*

HEINKEL HE 219   Germany

Arguably the most effective night fighter of World War II, the He 219 was derived from the 1940 project for a multi-rôle aircraft in the *Kampfzerstörer* category, the first prototype, the He 219 V1, flying on 15 November 1942. Four further prototypes followed with varying

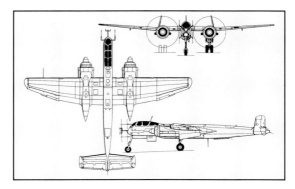

Flown in March 1943, the He 219 V3 (above) had a redesigned rear fuselage. (Below) The He 219A-5/R1.

armament, one of these (the V4) flying in March 1943 with FuG 212 *Lichtenstein C-1* intercept radar, before deliveries commenced of the pre-series He 219A-0. This

(Immediately below) He 219A-2 of 2./NJG 1 at Münster-Handorf, Sept 1944, with both *Lichtenstein* C-1 and SN-2 radars, as seen (above) on an He 219A-5/R1.

(Below right) An He 219A-5/R1 at Westerland, Sylt, in spring 1945 for night ground attack sorties flown by 1./NJG 1 against advancing Allies.

Four flights were made in England by this He 162A-2 (above) before it crashed in 1945.

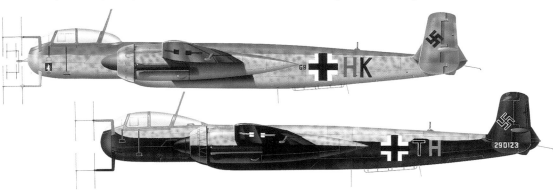

model was used operationally, but most of those built fulfilled trials purposes and were assigned *Versuchs* numbers. Eleven pre-series He 219s were delivered during 1943, and a further 257 pre-series and production aircraft were built, plus six assembled from spares at maintenance units. The initial production model was the He 219A-2 with DB 603A engines rated at 1,850 hp at 6,900 ft (2 105 m). Armament comprised two 20-mm and two 30-mm cannon firing forward, and two additional 30-mm weapons firing obliquely forward and upward. Forty of the A-2 sub-type were followed by the He 219A-5, which, initially fitted with the DB 603A, was later equipped with the DB 603G affording 1,900 hp for take-off. A stripped version intended for the "anti-Mosquito" rôle was designated He 219A-6, this having two-stage supercharged DB 603L engines with both water-methanol and nitrous oxide injection to provide 2,100 hp for take-off and 1,750 hp at 29,600 ft (9 020 m). The final production model was the He 219A-7 with DB 603G engines, FuG 220 *Lichtenstein SN-2* and FuG 218 *Neptun* radar, and the same armament as the A-2. The He 219B was a proposed version with Jumo 222 engines, three crew members and a long-span wing, and the projected He 219C mated the long-span wing with an entirely new fuselage. One further version was the He 419 with DB 603G engines and an extended redesigned wing. Six He 419B-1 fighters were built, utilising He 219A-5 fuselages. The following data relate to the He 219A-7 but are typical of all sub-types. *Max speed, 416 mph (670 km/h) at 22,965 ft (7 000 m). Initial climb, 1,810 ft/min (9,2 m/sec). Range, 1,243 mls (2 000 km) at 335 mph (540 km/h). Empty weight, 24,692 lb (11 200 kg). Loaded weight, 33,730 lb (15 300 kg). Span, 60 ft 8⅓ in (18,50 m). Length, 50 ft 11¾ in (15,54 m). Height, 13 ft 5½ in (4,10 m). Wing area, 479.01 sq ft (44,50 m²).*

HEINKEL HE 162   Germany

The He 162 was conceived to meet a so-called *Volksjäger*, or "People's Fighter", requirement and was designed by Siegfried Günter and Karl Schwärzler. A small and unsophisticated warplane, the He 162 had a light metal monocoque fuselage and a single-piece wing primarily of wood with plywood skinning. A 1,764 lb st (800 kgp) BMW 003E turbojet was attached to the top of the fuselage, aft of the cockpit, and armament comprised two 20-mm cannon. The first prototype, the He 162 V1, was flown on 6 December 1944, by which time numerous other aircraft had reached an advanced stage of construction. Prototypes, pre-production series aircraft and quantity production lines had all been launched almost simultaneously under the

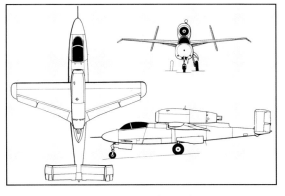

The unsophisticated He 162 V1 (below) was designed and built in 90 days to provide the so-called "*Volksjäger*". (Above) The production He 162A-2.

(Immediately below) An He 162A-2 as flown by 3./JG 1 and (bottom) an example captured at Leck in 1945 and later shipped to the USA.

code name *Salamander*. Although issued with *Versuchs* numbers, most of the prototypes were also considered as pre-series aircraft, several of these being armed with two 30-mm cannon, with which, in production form, the fighter was designated He 162A-1. However, owing to cannon vibration problems, this sub-type was overtaken almost at the beginning of the programme by the He 162A-2 with 20-mm cannon armament. Numerous other sub-types were proposed with various engine and armament changes, but none of these flew other than in prototype form. The total number of He 162s completed is unrecorded; some 150 were *officially* accepted by the *Luftwaffe* and at least 50 more were collected from the factories without any official formalities. When hostilities ended as many as 100 more were awaiting flight testing, with another 800 in advanced stages of assembly. The following data relate to the He 162A-2, the max speed being that attainable using short-period (ie, 30-sec) thrust of 2,028 lb (920 kg). *Max speed, 553 mph (890 km/h) at sea level, 562 mph (905 km/h) at 19,685 ft (6 000 m). Initial climb, 4,615 ft/min (23,45 m/sec). Range, 606 mls (975 km) at 36,090 ft (11 000 m). Empty weight, 3,666 lb (1 663 kg). Loaded weight, 6,184 lb (2 805 kg). Span, 23 ft 7½ in (7,20 m). Length, 29 ft 8⅓ in (9,05 m). Height, 8 ft 6⅓ in (2,60 m). Wing area, 120.56 sq ft (11,20 m²).*

HEINRICH PURSUIT   USA

During the 19 months in which the USA participated in World War I, several attempts were made to develop competent single-seat fighters of original design. Among these was the Heinrich Pursuit designed by Albert S Heinrich and built by the Victor Aircraft Corp. The Heinrich Pursuit was an aerodynamically clean, single-bay, unequal-span biplane powered by a 100 hp Gnome nine-cylinder rotary engine. Two examples were ordered by the US Army Signal Corps and built in 1917, the first of these being delivered in November of that year. Some testing was undertaken at McCook Field, Dayton, Ohio, but official US policy at this time was to forego fighters of national design in favour of tested foreign types. Nevertheless, the Heinrich Pursuit was considered to have potential as a fighter trainer, and two additional aircraft were ordered. These employed the more reliable Le Rhône rotary of 80 hp, had a strengthened cabane and paired rather than single struts and a lighter structure, gross weight being reduced by 170 lb (77 kg). These aircraft were

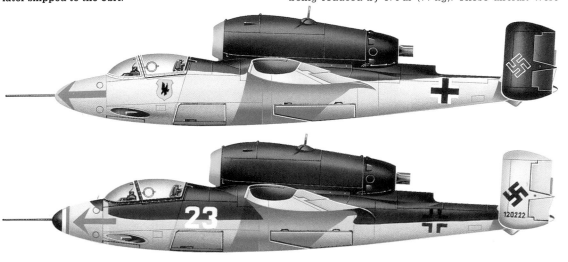

built in 1918, but no further development was undertaken. The following data relate to the Gnome-engined version. *Max speed, 115 mph (185 km/h). Loaded weight, 1,235 lb (560 kg). Span, 26 ft 0 in (7,92 m). Wing area, 162.5 sq ft (15,09 m²).*

Aerodynamically attractive, the Heinrich Pursuit (above and below) was tested at McCook Field in 1918.

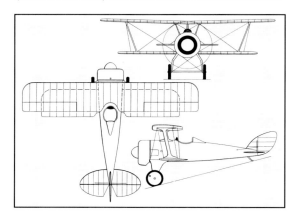

HELWAN (EGAO) HA-300   Egypt

Originally conceived to meet a Spanish *Ejército del Aire* requirement for a small M=1.5 interceptor and the design responsibility of a Germano-Spanish team supervised by Prof Willy Messerschmitt, the HA-300 programme was transferred to Egypt. Here development and construction was undertaken in Factory No 36 at Helwan, this being controlled by the Egyptian General Aero Organisation (EGAO). Originally designed for the proposed afterburning Orpheus BOr 12 turbojet, the HA-300 was modified for the Brandner-designed E-300 with a calculated afterburning rating of 10,582 lb st

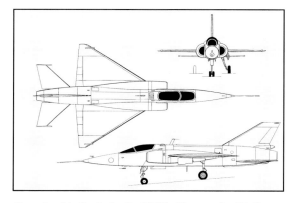

Conceived in Spain by Prof Willy Messerschmitt, the HA-300 (above and below) was built in Egypt.

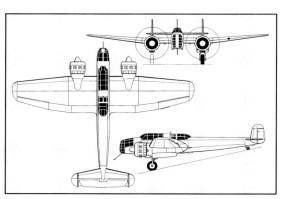

(4 800 kgp). The first prototype, powered by a 4,850 lb st (2 200 kgp) Orpheus 703-S-10, was flown on 7 March 1964, a similarly-powered second prototype flying on 22 July 1965. The definitive third prototype with the E-300 engine commenced taxi trials in November 1969, but the HA-300 programme was then terminated without flight testing of this prototype being undertaken. It was anticipated that the E-300-powered HA-300 would be capable of attaining 39,370 ft (12 000 m) and M=2.0 within 2.5 min of take-off. The Orpheus-powered prototypes achieved approx M=1.13 during flight test. The following data relate to the definitive model. *Loaded weight, 9,899 lb (4 490 kg). Span, 19 ft 2 in (5,84 m). Length, 40 ft 8 in (12,40 m). Height, 10 ft 4 in (3,15 m). Wing area (approx), 180 sq ft (16,70 m²).*

HENSCHEL Hs 124   Germany

Like the Focke-Wulf Fw 57 and Messerschmitt Bf 110, the Hs 124 was designed to fulfil the *Kampfzerstörer* requirement that had been formulated in 1933-34 by the *Führungsstab* of the still clandestine *Luftwaffe*. A twin-engined, mid-wing cantilever monoplane, the Hs 124 was proposed in two basic versions: a three-seat heavy fighter-bomber (*Kampfzerstörer*) and a two-seat dedicated heavy fighter (*Zerstörer*). Of all-metal construction with an oval-section monocoque fuselage and a three-spar stressed-skin wing, the Hs 124 was designed by a team led by Dipl-Ing Nicolaus, three prototypes being ordered. The first of these, the Hs 124 V1, was

A mock-up nose turret was fitted (above) in the Jumo-engined Hs 124 V1. (Below) The Hs 124 V2.

powered by two Junkers Jumo 210C 12-cylinder inverted-Vee liquid-cooled engines each rated at 640 hp at 8,850 ft (2 700 m) and featured an electrically-operated nose turret mounting a 20-mm belt-fed Rheinmetall Borsig cannon. Representing the initial *Kampfzerstörer* configuration, the V1 was flown with a mock-up nose turret in the spring of 1936, the V2 differing in having nine-cylinder BMW 132Dc (licence-built Pratt & Whitney Hornet) radial engines, each affording 850 hp for take-off, and in dispensing with the nose tur-

With a redesigned nose, the Hs 124 V2 (above) was to use gimbal-mounted cannon in place of a turret.

ret (development of which had been delayed). An extensively glazed, redesigned nose embodied a broad vertical slot through which two gimbal-mounted 20-mm cannon were intended to protrude. The third prototype, the Hs 124 V3, was completed as a two-seat *Zerstörer* with a fixed forward-firing armament of two 20-mm cannon and two 7,9-mm machine guns. It was intended that this would be powered by Daimler-Benz DB 601A engines, but their non-availability dictated retention of BMW 132Dc radials. The Hs 124 displayed exceptional agility for an aircraft of its configuration and size, but the *Kampfzerstörer* concept had been abandoned before the Henschel fighter entered flight test and the Bf 110 was selected to fulfil the *Zerstörer* requirement, Hs 124 development being abandoned in consequence. The following data relate to the Hs 124 V2. *Max speed, 255 mph (410 km/h) at 9,840 ft (3 000 m). Time to 6,560 ft (2 000 m), 4.4 min. Max range (standard fuel), 1,522 mls (2 450 km). Empty weight, 9,369 lb (4 250 kg). Loaded weight, 15,939 lb (7 230 kg). Span, 59 ft 8½ in (18,20 m). Length, 47 ft 6⅞ in (14,50 m). Height, 12 ft 3⅔ in (3,75 m). Wing area, 587.72 sq ft (54,60 m²).*

HERETER T.H.(ALFARO 8)   Spain

Designed for the *Concurso de Aviones* of 1919, which had been conceived to encourage the growth of an independent aircraft industry by means of competitive design of combat aircraft for the *Aviación Militar*, the Hereter T.H. (also known as the Alfaro 8) was designed by Heraclio Alfaro and built by the Talleres Hereter of Barcelona. A single-seat single-bay equi-span biplane powered by a 180 hp Hispano-Suiza 8Ab engine, the T.H. fighter had still to commence flight testing in March 1919, when the contest took place. It was flown for the first time in the following month by Domingo Rosillo, but broke its undercarriage during landing. No further development was undertaken and no data are available.

The Hereter T.H. (below) was completed too late for the fighter competition for which it was designed.

HISPANO BARRÓN   Spain

In 1919, the newly-established Hispano (later Hispano-Suiza) concern at Guadalajara built a prototype single-seat fighter to participate in the *Concurso de Aviones* to be held that year. The Hispano contender was designed by Eduardo Barrón, who, in 1917, had supervised construction of a copy of the SPAD S.VII at the Talleres Hereter SA in Barcelona, 12 being built for the *Aeronáutica Militar Española* as the *España*. The fighter designed by Barrón for Hispano was a single-bay, unstaggered biplane of wooden construction with fabric skinning and powered by a 180 hp Hispano-Suiza 8Aa eight-cylinder water-cooled engine. Armament comprised a single 7,7-mm Vickers machine gun mounted above the upper wing. Flown by a Chilean pilot, Luis O'Page, the Hispano Barrón was intended to compete with two indigenous fighters at Cuatro Vientos, the Hereter T.H. (Alfaro 8) and the Diaz Type C, and was declared the winning contender. The availability of proven single-seat fighters from abroad at low prices motivated against a production order, however, and only the one prototype was completed, this later being

Flown in 1919, the Barrón-designed fighter (above and below) was winner in the *Concurso de Aviones*.

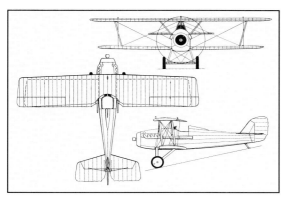

tested with a 200 hp Hispano-Suiza engine. *Max speed, 118 mph (190 km/h). Loaded weight, 1,852 lb (840 kg). No further details available.*

HISPANO HA-1112-K   Spain

In 1942, Spain acquired a manufacturing licence for the Messerschmitt Bf 109G-2, but, in the event, only incomplete manufacturing drawings and 25 airframes lacking tail assemblies, engines and armament were supplied to Hispano Aviación. The airframes were eventually completed and fitted with 1,300 hp Hispano Suiza 12Z 89 Vee engines in place of the intended inverted-Vee DB 605, a prototype conversion flying on 2 March 1945 as the HA-1109-J1L. The remaining aircraft were converted during 1947-48, but saw limited flying. Meanwhile, preparations proceeded for the manufacture of 200 HA-1109 fighters. However, the unsuitability of the Spanish-built HS 12Z 89 engine led to adoption of the French-manufactured HS 12Z 17 of similar rating. The 10th HA-1109-J1L flew with this engine in May 1951 as the prototype HA-1109-K1L, production deliveries commencing in the following year. Although one aircraft was experimentally fitted with a pair of underwing 12,7-mm machine guns, most were delivered without armament. The first production example was eventually fitted with twin 12,7-mm weapons over the

A Spanish-built HS 12Z engine installation distinguished the HA-1109-J1L (above) from the HA-1109-K1L (below), which used a French HS 12Z

engine and underwing rocket launchers as the HA-1109-K2L, and the sixth was flown with rocket launchers only as the HA-1109-K3L. Meanwhile, a re-engined HA-1109-J1L had been modified to take two wing-mounted 20-mm cannon and, with rocket launchers, became the prototype HA-1112-K1L. With standardisation of this armament, the remaining HS-engined aircraft that had reached an advanced stage in assembly were completed as HA-1112-K1Ls. A total of 69 HS-engined aircraft was completed in Spain, including the HA-1109-Js utilising partly German-built airframes. The following data relate to the HA-1112-K1L. *Max speed, 382 mph (615 km/h) at 13,780 ft (4 200 m). Time to 6,560 ft (2 000 m), 1.57 min. Endurance, 1.95 hrs. Empty weight, 5,556 lb (2 520 kg). Loaded weight, 6,834 lb (3 100 kg). Span, 32 ft 6½ in (9,92 m). Length, 29 ft 6 in (8,99 m). Height, 8 ft 6½ in (2,60 m). Wing area, 173.30 sq ft (16,10 m²).*

Underwing rockets and wing-mounted cannon armament were combined in the HA-1112-K1L (above).

HISPANO HA-1112-M   Spain

The eleventh HA-1109-J1L was fitted with a Rolls-Royce Merlin 500-45 12-cylinder Vee engine of 1,610 hp for take-off and flown as the HA-1109-M1L in 1954. The fourth, seventh and eighth Spanish-built airframes were subsequently converted as HA-1112-M1L, HA-1109-M2L and HA-1109-M3L respectively. Production standardised on the HA-1112-M1L, which was the first Spanish-built derivative of the Messerschmitt Bf 109G to see service in any numbers. With an armament of two wing-mounted 20-mm cannon and provision for eight 80-mm rockets, the HA-1112-M1L entered service

(Below) HA-1112-M1Ls of *Ala 7 de Cazabombardeo* in the early '60s, that at bottom belonging to this unit's 71 *Escuadron*.

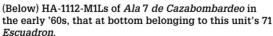

Rolls-Royce engine and Messerschmitt airframe were combined in the HA-1112-M1L (above).

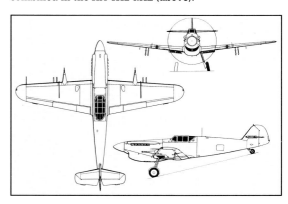

The HA-1112-M1L (above), dubbed *Buchón* in Spain, was flown primarily by the 71 (below) and 72 *Escuadrones* of the *Ala 7 de Cazabombardeo*.

in 1956, production finally phasing out in 1958 after 170 Merlin-engined fighters had been completed. The HA-1112-M1L remained in Spanish service until 1967. *Max speed, 419 mph (674 km/h) at 13,125 ft (4 000 m). Initial climb, 5,807 ft/min (29,5 m/sec). Max range, 476 mls (766 km). Empty weight, 5,855 lb (2 656 kg). Loaded weight, 7,011 lb (3 180 kg). Span, 32 ft 6½ in (9,92 m). Length, 29 ft 10 in (9,10 m). Height, 8 ft 6½ in (2,60 m). Wing area, 173.30 sq ft (16,10 m²).*

HORTEN H IX   Germany

Among the most unorthodox fighters evolved during World War II was the turbojet-driven pure flying wing conceived by Reimar and Walter Horten, the H IX. The first prototype, the H IX V1, was completed as a glider

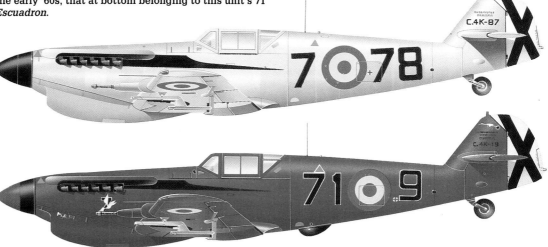

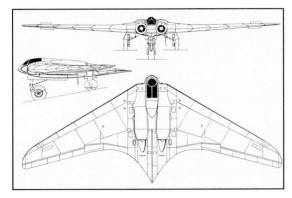

The H IX V2 (above) immediately prior to first test flight, and (below) three-view drawing of H IX V3.

and flown for the first time on 1 March 1944. The second prototype, the V2, was delayed by non-availability of the intended BMW 003 turbojets, and eventually flew shortly before Christmas 1944 with two 1,962 lb st (890 kgp) Junkers Jumo 004B turbojets. The H IX was of mixed construction, the centre section being of welded steel tube and the remainder being of wood, with ply-wood skinning overall. The RLM contracted with the Gothaer Waggonfabrik to ''productionise'' the H IX and initiate series manufacture under the official designa-tion 8-229 – had the fighter attained series production it would have been designated Ho 229. The Klemm Flug-zeugbau was to have manufactured the wooden wings and an initial contract was placed by the RLM for 40 air-craft. The H IX V2 crashed on 18 February 1945 after accumulating only two hours flying, but the 8-229 pro-gramme continued unchanged, this including con-struction of further prototypes and a pre-series of 20 aircraft. The air intake geometry was substantially re-vised and the engines were moved forward to alleviate a CG problem, with the accessory gearbox protruding above the upper surface of the wing centre section as a consequence. The V3 was intended as prototype for the initial series single-seat fighter, whilst the V6, embody-ing almost total redesign within the airframe envelope, was intended as a prototype for the definitive single-seat production series. The V4 and V5 identified Horten projects for two-seat night fighting variants. As late as 12 March 1945, the inclusion of the Horten fighter in the *Jägernot-programm* was confirmed, but within two

months the Friedrichsroda factory in which the Ho 229 was being produced was occupied by US forces. There, the V3, which was to have carried an armament of two 30-mm cannon, was found to be in final assembly. The following data are manufacturer's estimates for the initial series Ho 229A fighter. *Max speed, 590 mph (950 km/h) at sea level, or Mach=0.77, 607 mph (977 km/h) at 39,370 ft (12 000 m), or Mach=0.92. Max initial climb, 4,330 ft/min (22 m/sec). Max range, 1,180 mls (1 900 km). Empty equipped weight, 10,141 lb (4 600 kg). Max loaded weight, 17,857 lb (8 100 kg). Span, 54 ft 11¾ in (16,76 m). Length, 24 ft 6 in (7,47 m). Height, 9 ft 2¼ in (2,81 m). Wing area, 540.37 sq ft (50,20 m²).*

IAI NESHER   Israel

(Above) The IAI-built Nesher, a version of Dassault's Mirage produced without benefit of a licence.

The Nesher (Eagle) was essentially the Dassault Mir-age 5 multi-rôle fighter (which see) built by Israel Air-craft Industries without benefit of a manufacturing licence. Powered by an IAI Bedek Aviation Division-built SNECMA Atar 09C turbojet with an afterburning thrust of 13,670 lb (6 200 kg), the Nesher differed from the Mirage 5 only in having some Israeli-developed avionics, a Martin-Baker JM 6 zero-zero ejection seat and provision for either Rafael Shafrir (Dragonfly) or AIM-9 Sidewinder AAMs, or such ASMs as the Rafael Luz. The prototype Nesher, based on a French-built air-frame but incorporating IAI-manufactured compo-nents, was flown in September 1969, production de-liveries to the *Heyl Ha'Avir* following in 1971. Fifty-one (plus 10 two-seat trainers) were built before the Nesher was supplanted in production by the Kfir. Offered for export as the Dagger (effectively a refurbished ex-*Heyl Ha'Avir* Nesher), this IAI-built Mirage 5 was supplied

(Below) An IAI Dagger A (Nesher) of *II Escuadrón* of Argentina's *VI Brigada Aérea* at Tandil, 1989.

to Argentina in 1978-79 and 1981-82, the *Fuerza Aérea Argentina* receiving 35 single-seat Dagger As and four two-seat Dagger Bs. Data are similar to those for the Mirage 5.

IAI KFIR   Israel

The Kfir (Lion Cub) employed the basic airframe of the IAI-built Mirage 5 alias Nesher, the main changes being a shorter, but larger-diameter, rear fuselage to accommodate an IAI Bedek Division-built J79-IAI-J1E turbojet with a dry rating of 11,110 lb st (5 040 kgp) and an afterburning rating of 18,750 lb st (8 505 kgp). A French-built Mirage IIIC airframe was modified to take a J79 turbojet as a prototype and was flown on 19 October 1970, a more definitive prototype flying on 4 June 1973 as the Raam (Thunderbolt). Production de-liveries began in April 1975 as the Kfir-C1. Only 27 Kfir-C1s were built before this model was succeeded by the Kfir-C2. Similarly powered to the C1, the C2 had the same built-in armament of two IAI-built 30-mm DEFA 552 cannon and provision for up to 9,468 lb (4 295 kg) of ordnance on seven external hardpoints. It differed, however, in being fitted with canard surfaces, nose

The Kfir-C1 (above) lacked the canards, ''dog-tooth'' outer wing and nose strakes of the Kfir-C2 (below).

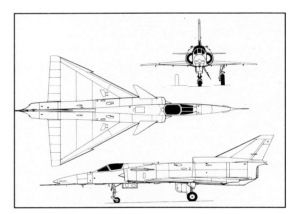

strakes and extended outer wing (''dog-tooth'') leading edges to improve dogfighting manoeuvrability at the lower end of the speed range and to enhance field per-formance. One hundred and eighty-five Kfir-C2s were built (including some TC2 two-seaters), all but two of the Kfir-C1s being retrofitted to near-C2 configuration. From 1983, remaining Kfir-C2s in *Heyl Ha'Avir* service were upgraded to Kfir-C7 standard with additional ex-ternal hardpoints and new avionics. Ten Kfir-C2s (and two two-seat Kfir-TC2s) were supplied to Ecuador in 1983, these being refurbished ex-*Heyl Ha'Avir* aircraft, as were also 13 Kfir-C7s (and two two-seat Kfir-TC7s) delivered to Colombia in 1989. In 1991, the *Heyl Ha'Avir* agreed to sell 34 Kfir-C7s and six -TC7s to Taiwan, but this order was cancelled. Twenty-five of the original Kfir-C1s (upgraded to near-C2 standard) were supplied to the USA for use as ''aggressor'' trainers by the US Navy (12 leased 1985-88) and US Marine Corps (13 leased 1987-89) under the designation F-21A. The fol-lowing data relate to the Kfir-C7. *Max speed, 863 mph (1 389 km/h) at sea level, or Mach=1.13, 1,516 mph (2 440 km/h) above 36,000 ft (10 975 m), or Mach=2.3. Max initial climb, 45,866 ft/min (233 m/sec). Combat radius (max external fuel for combat air patrol mission with two Shafrir AAMs and 60-min loiter), 548 mls (882 km). Approx empty weight, 16,072 lb (7 290 kg). Max loaded weight, 36,376 lb (16 500 kg). Span, 26 ft 11½ in (8,22 m). Length (including probe), 51 ft 4¼ in (15,65 m). Height, 14 ft 11¼ in (4,55 m). Wing area, 374.6 sq ft (34,80 m²).*

(Left) An early Kfir-C2 taking-off, this particular aircraft originally having been built as a Kfir-C1.

(Above) A Kfir-C2 in the air superiority finish adopted by *Heyl Ha'Avir* in 1978, and (below) a Kfir-C1 with No 101 Sqn, *Heyl Ha'Avir*, 1975-76.

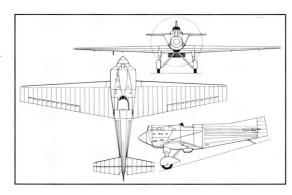

An F-21A Kfir (above) of VMFT-401, and (below) the definitive Kfir, the C7, in *Heyl Ha'Avir* service.

The CV-11 (above and below) was destroyed during an attempt on the 500-km closed-circuit speed record.

IAI NAMMER   Israel

Effectively a stretched Kfir airframe – the nose being lengthened and a plug inserted aft of the cockpit – with a configured engine bay for alternative power plant, the Nammer (Tiger) was evolved by Israel Aircraft Industries as a potential export tactical fighter. Mating the thoroughly-proven canarded-delta configuration of the earlier fighter with state-of-the-art avionics, including multi-function cockpit displays, and HOTAS (Hands on Throttle and Stick) controls, the Nammer was being offered to potential customers at the beginning of the 'nineties with either the SNECMA Atar 9K-50 turbojet rated at 11,055 lb st (5 015 kgp) and 15,870 lb st (7 200 kgp) with afterburning, or the General Electric/Volvo Flygmotor F404/RM 12 turbofan affording 12,500 lb st (5 670 kgp) and 18,140 lb st (8 228 kgp) with afterburning. A prototype Nammer with the former engine was flown early in 1991, this having a pulse-Doppler multi-mode fire control radar with an advanced interfaced weapon-delivery system. Armament consisted of two 30-mm DEFA 552 cannon, and nine external stores stations – five beneath the fuselage and two beneath each wing – could lift up to 13,800 lb (6 260 kg). Provision was made for in-flight refuelling. IAI needed international partners or minimum orders for 80 aircraft, but with no export orders, the Nammer never entered production. The following data are manufacturer's estimates for the Atar 9K-50-powered Nammer. *Max speed, 1,452 mph (2 337 km/h) above 36,000 ft (10 975 m), or Mach=2.2, 863 mph (1 389 km/h) at sea level, or Mach=1.13. Ceiling, 58,000 ft (17 680 m). Max loaded weight, 34,060 lb (15 450 kg). Span, 26 ft 11¹/₂ in (8,22 m). Length, 52 ft 6 in (16,00 m). Height, 14 ft 6 in (4,42 m). Wing area, 374.6 sq ft (34,80 m²).*

IAI LAVI   Israel

The Lavi (Young Lion) was conceived as a multi-rôle fighter with close air support and interdiction as primary missions and air defence as a secondary mission. Full-scale development began in October 1982, the Lavi featuring close-coupled delta main wings (with 54 deg of sweepback on the leading edges) and canard surfaces. Approximately 22 per cent of the structure (by weight) was built of composite materials and power was provided by a Pratt & Whitney PW1120

turbojet with an afterburning thrust of 20,620 lb (9 353 kg). Armament included an internally-mounted 30-mm cannon, and up to 16,000 lb (7 257 kg) of external stores could be distributed between seven underfuselage and four underwing stations. Both single-seat and fully combat-capable two-seat versions were developed in parallel and five prototypes were planned, the first and second of these being two-seaters and the remaining three being single-seaters. The Israeli requirement was for 300 aircraft. The first prototype flew on 31 December 1986, being followed by the second on 30 March 1987, but the Lavi programme was terminated on 30 August 1987 as a result of severe budgetary constraints. Although the first two aircraft were then scrapped, the third prototype was completed as a two-seat technology demonstrator, flying on 25 September 1989. *Max speed, 1,188 mph (1 912 km/h) at 36,000 ft (10 975 m), or Mach=1.8. Combat radius (air patrol mission), 1,151 mls (1 853 km). Operational empty weight, 15,305 lb (6 942 kg). Max loaded weight, 42,500 lb (19 278 kg). Span, 28 ft 9²/₃ in (8,78 m). Length, 47 ft 9²/₃ in (14,57 m). Height, 15 ft 8¹/₄ in (4,78 m). Wing area, 355.75 sq ft (33.05 m²).*

(Below) The Lavi single-seat multi-rôle fighter.

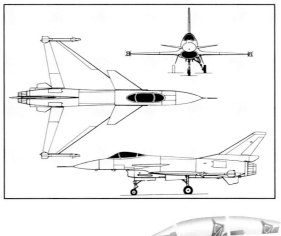

The first original aircraft design produced by the Industria Aeronautica Română (I.A.R), established in 1925, was the CV-11 single-seat fighter completed and flown in 1930. Designed by Elie Carafoli and a French engineer, M Virmoux, the CV-11 was of mixed construction and powered by a 600 hp 12-cylinder W-type Lorraine 12Fa Courlis engine, armament comprising two 7,7-mm Vickers machine guns. After completion of the initial flight test programme, the Lorraine engine was replaced by a 500 hp Hispano-Suiza 12Mc 12-cylinder Vee-type engine with which it was tested at Istres during the first quarter of 1931. It then returned to Romania, where, on 9 December 1931, the CV-11 made an attempt on the 500-km (310.7-mile) closed-circuit speed record. However, an engine failure necessitated a forced landing in which the pilot, Capt Romeo Popescu, was killed. Further development of the basic design by Carafoli led to the I.A.R.12. The following data relate to the HS-engined CV-11. *Max speed, 204 mph (329 km/h) at 985 ft (300 m), 188 mph (302 km/h) at 16,405 ft (5 000 m). Time to 16,405 ft (5 000 m), 8.25 min. Empty weight, 2,425 lb (1 100 kg). Loaded weight, 3,329 lb (1 510 kg). Span, 37 ft 8³/₄ in (11,50 m). Length, 22ft 10⁷/₈ in (6,98 m). Height, 8ft 0¹/₄ in (2,46 m). Wing area, 195.9 sq ft (18,20 m²).*

(Below) The second two-seat prototype of the Lavi taking-off on its first flight on 30 March 1987.

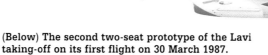

(Above) The first prototype of the Lavi, which, in two-seat form, had full combat capability.

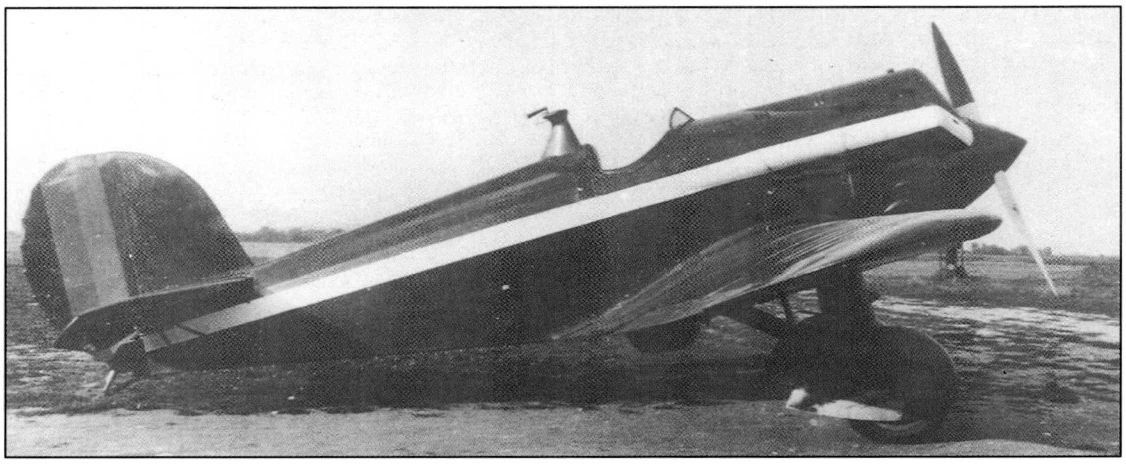

The I.A.R.12 (above) was successful, but was overtaken by the appreciably improved I.A.R.13.

I.A.R.12 — Romania

Owing much to experience gained with the CV-11, being of similar configuration and mixed construction, the I.A.R.12, designed by Elie Carafoli, was aerodynamically more advanced than its predecessor. It was heavier and had a lower-powered engine, however. Flown for the first time in 1932, the I.A.R.12 had a mixed structure of duralumin and Romanian pine. The fuselage was covered by light alloy panels forward and fabric aft of the cockpit, the wings being fabric skinned. The engine was a 450 hp Lorraine 12Eb of W type, and armament consisted of two 7,7-mm Vickers machine guns. Only one prototype of the I.A.R.12 was built, development continuing with an improved model, the I.A.R.13. *Max speed, 183 mph (294 km/h) at sea level, 163 mph (263 km/h) at 16,405 ft (5 000 m). Time to 16,405 ft (5 000 m), 10.48 min. Empty weight, 2,535 lb (1 150 kg). Loaded weight, 3,395 lb (1 540 kg). Span, 38 ft 4⅔ in (11,70 m). Length, 23 ft 7⅔ in (7,20 m). Height, 11 ft 5¾ in (3,50 m). Wing area, 213.13 sq ft (19,80 m²).*

(Below) The W-engined I.A.R.12 single-seat fighter.

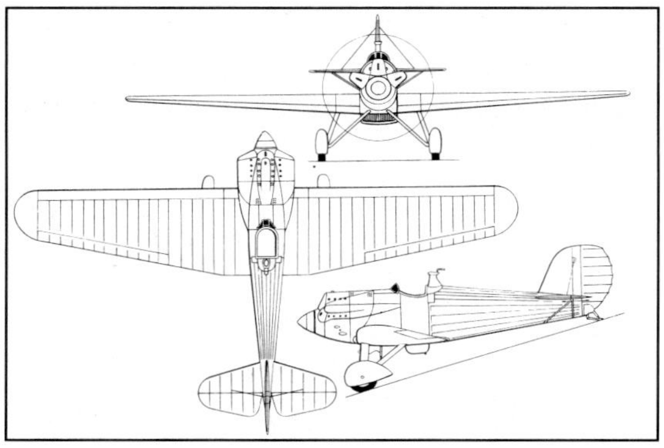

I.A.R.13 — Romania

Retaining the wings and horizontal tail surfaces of the I.A.R.12, the I.A.R.13, which made its début in 1933, achieved an aerodynamically cleaner fuselage by replacing the W-configuration Lorraine engine of the earlier prototype with a Vee-twelve type Hispano-Suiza 12Mc of 500 hp. The I.A.R.13 was of similar construction to preceding Carafoli-designed fighters, with a wooden fuselage and wing of mixed construction, and proved under test to have a very good performance. However, the Romanian *Aeronautica Militara* preferred the gulled shoulder-wing arrangement of the P.Z.L. P.11 fighter to the low-wing configuration of the I.A.R. fighters. In 1934, the Polish aircraft was selected for the re-equipment of its fighter element, with licence manufacture to be undertaken by I.A.R. Nevertheless, the Romanian company was to persist with its own line of fighter development. *Max speed, 205 mph (330 km/h) at sea level, 190 mph (306 km/h) at 16,405 ft (5 000 m). Time to 16,405 ft (5 000 m), 8.0 min. Ceiling, 30,510 ft (9 300 m). Loaded weight, 3,373 lb (1 530 kg). Span, 38 ft 4⅔ in (11,70 m). Length, 24 ft 0⅘ in (7,34 m). Height, 11 ft 5¾ in (3,50 m). Wing area, 213.13 sq ft (19,80 m²).*

The I.A.R.13 (below) was unsuccessful in competition with the P.Z.L. P.11 for *Aeronautica Militara* orders.

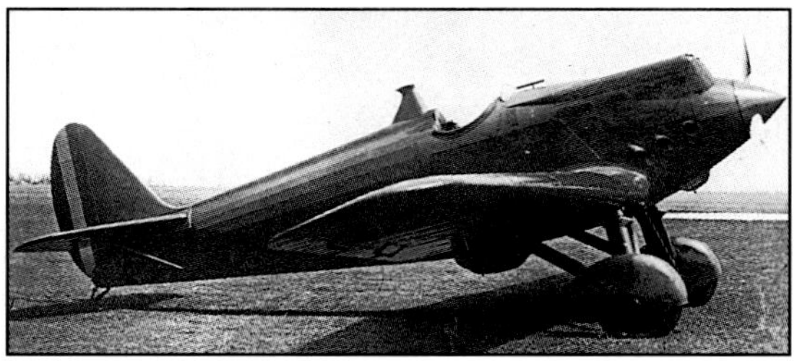

(Below) The HS 12-engined I.A.R.13 built in 1933.

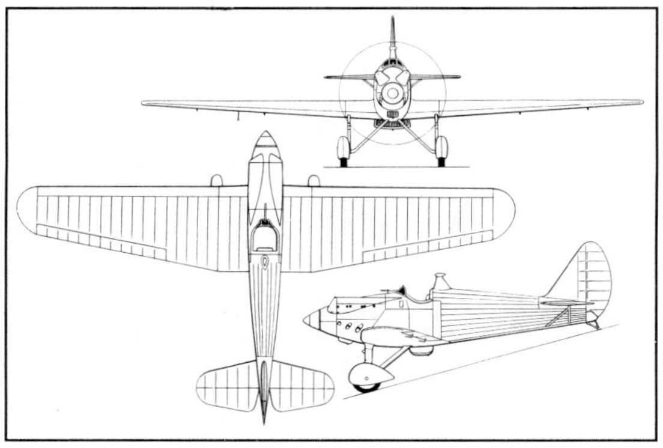

I.A.R.14 — Romania

Although the *Aeronautica Militara* in 1934 selected the P.Z.L. P.11 for the re-equipment of its fighter element, a small series of I.A.R.14s was also ordered that year for evaluation purposes. Flown in 1933, the I.A.R.14 was essentially similar to the I.A.R.13, but reverted to the Lorraine 12Eb engine, which, while inferior to the HS 12Mc for fighter installation, had the advantage of being licence-built by I.A.R. Apart from the engine change, the fuselage of the I.A.R.14 was redesigned. The turnover pylon was incorporated in a fairing aft of the cockpit, shorter-span, broad-chord ailerons were introduced, the vertical tail was redesigned and the span of the horizontal surfaces was increased, their inverted-Vee type bracing struts giving place to parallel struts. Armament remained the standard pair of 7,7-mm Vickers guns. Twenty I.A.R.14s delivered to the *Aeronautica Militara* in 1934 were utilised, after service evaluation, in the fighter training rôle. *Max speed, 183 mph (294 km/h) at sea level, 163 mph (263 km/h) at 16,405 ft (5 000 m). Time to 16,405 ft (5 000 m), 10.45 min. Endurance, 2.16 hrs. Empty weight, 2,535 lb (1 150 kg). Loaded weight, 3,395 lb (1 540 kg). Span, 38 ft 4⅔ in (11,70 m). Length, 24 ft 0⅙ in (7,32 m). Height, 8 ft 2½ in (2,50 m). Wing area, 213.13 sq ft (19,80 m²).*

(Below) The I.A.R.14 reverted to the W-type engine.

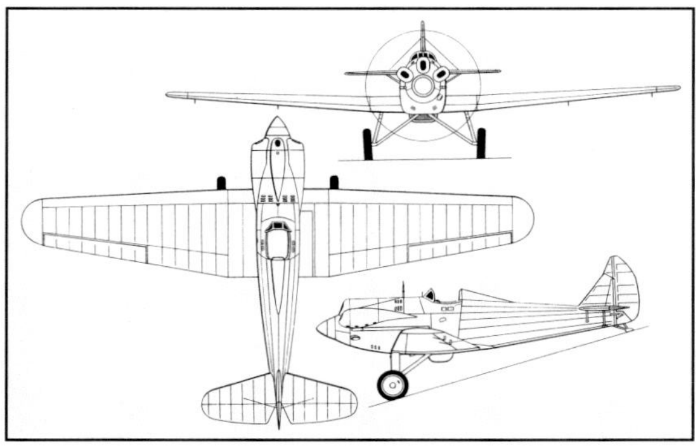

The first I.A.R. fighter to achieve production status was the I.A.R.14 (below).

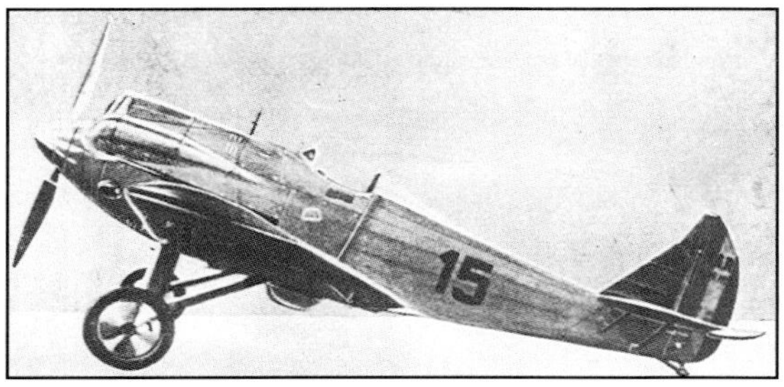

I.A.R.15 — Romania

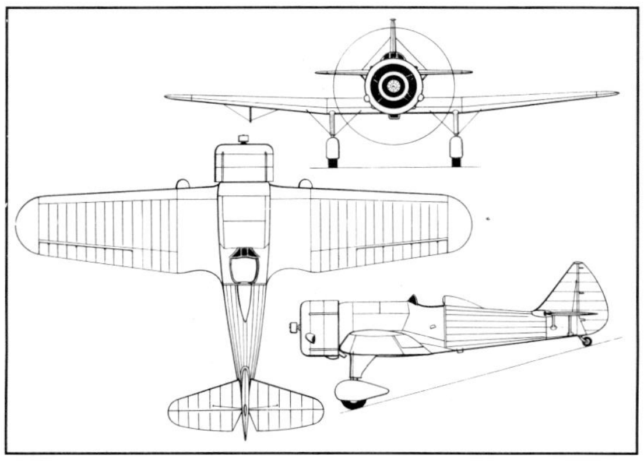

The I.A.R.15 (above) was built in small series.

Possessing little more than a configurational similarity to preceding single-seat fighters of Carafoli design, the I.A.R.15 flew for the first time late in 1933. It was powered by a 600 hp Gnome-Rhône 9Krse nine-cylinder radial and carried an armament of two 7,7-mm Vickers machine guns. The structural design followed that of the I.A.R.14. It had a welded steel-tube fuselage covered by duralumin sheet forward and fabric aft, this being mated with a three-piece wing with two duralumin spars, pine and plywood ribs and duralumin sheet skinning for the centre section with fabric covering for the outer panels. A series of five I.A.R.15s was ordered for the *Aeronautica Militara*, these differing from the prototype primarily in having three-bladed metal propellers in place of the two-bladed wooden unit. The speed capability of the I.A.R.15 was adjudged excellent and it established a national altitude record of 38,160 ft (11 631 m) in 1935. It was considered inferior to the P.Z.L. P.11, however, on the score of manoeuvrability,

Although considered favourably, the I.A.R.15 was, like the I.A.R.13, bested by the P.11 for contracts.

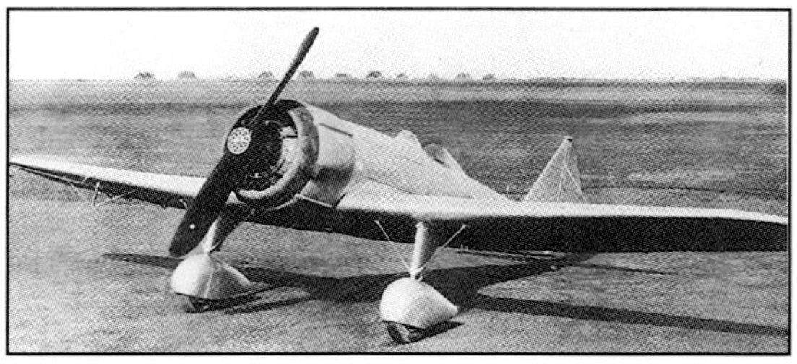

and no further examples were ordered. Max speed, 233 mph (375 km/h) at 13,125 ft (4 000 m), 230 mph (370 km/h) at 16,405 ft (5 000 m). Climb to 16,405 ft (5 000 m), 8.0 min. Range, 373 mls (600 km). Empty weight, 2,678 lb (1 215 kg). Loaded weight, 3,637 lb (1 650 kg). Span, 36 ft 1 in (11,00 m). Length, 25 ft 5½ in (7,76 m). Height, 8 ft 10¼ in (2,70 m). Wing area, 204.52 sq ft (19,00 m²).

(Above) An I.A.R.80A of *Grupul* 8 *Vinâtoare* operating under *Luftflotte* 4 command from Birlad in July 1941.

I.A.R.16   Romania

The I.A.R.16 (above and below) proved to be the last I.A.R. fighter design for half a decade.

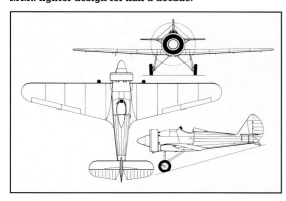

Although evolved in parallel with the I.A.R.15, the I.A.R.16, which flew for the first time in 1934, was the first of Carafoli's fighters to feature an all-metal structure, this having plywood, fabric and duralumin skinning. It was powered by a 560 hp Bristol Mercury IVS.2 nine-cylinder radial enclosed by a Townend ring and carried an armament of two 7,7-mm Vickers guns. The I.A.R.16 was not developed further than a single prototype, bringing to an end Romanian fighter design for several years. *Max speed, 212 mph (342 km/h) at 16,405 ft (5 000 m). Time to 16,405 ft (5 000 m), 6.5 min. Empty weight, 2,698 lb (1 224 kg). Loaded weight, 3,637 lb (1 650 kg). Span, 38 ft 4⅔ in (11,70 m). Length, 24 ft 2⅛ in (7,37 m). Height, 9 ft 2¼ in (2,80 m). Wing area, 218.5 sq ft (20,30 m²).*

I.A.R.80   Romania

(Below) The first production I.A.R.80 (foreground) flying in formation with a late production I.A.R.80B.

Designed as a successor to the licence-built P.Z.L. P.24E by a team comprising Ion Grosu, Ion Cosereanu, Gheorghe Zotta and Gheorghe Vallner, the I.A.R.80 single-seat fighter was flown in April 1939. The prototype was powered by a 900 hp I.A.R.-K 14-II C32 14-cylinder air-cooled radial based on the Gnome-Rhône 14K Mistral-Major and its armament consisted of two wing-mounted 7,92-mm FN-Browning guns. The series-production I.A.R.80 appeared in the spring of 1940, and featured a 20½-in (52-cm) increase in wing span, a 29-in (74-cm) increase in fuselage length, greater fuel capacity, an aft-sliding cockpit canopy, an armament of four 7,92-mm guns and a 930 hp I.A.R.-K 14-III C36 engine. The series model also discarded the tailplane bracing struts featured by the prototype. The I.A.R.80 achieved operational capability on 14 January 1941 with *Flotilla* 2 *Vinâtoare* of the Royal Air Forces of Romania (*Fortelor Aeriene Regal ale România*), or FARR. The 50th and last of the initial series was fitted with an extra pair of guns, this six-gun armament being standardised for subsequent aircraft, which were de-

(Above) The general arrangement drawing depicts the standard production I.A.R.80, the photo (immediately below) illustrating the prototype flown April 1939.

(Above) A formation of I.A.R.80s (nearest to and farthest from the camera) and I.A.R.80Bs in 1942.

(Above) An *Eskadrilă* of I.A.R.80Bs preparing to take-off from a Romanian base *circa* 1943.

(Above) An I.A.R.80C serving with one of the Romanian home defence *Eskadrile* early in 1943.

signated I.A.R.80As, these also having racks for two 110-lb (50-kg) bombs and being powered by the 1,025 hp I.A.R.-K 14-1000A engine. Ninety I.A.R.80As were followed by 50 I.A.R.80Bs, with an armament of four 7,92-mm and two 13,2-mm guns, the 21st and subsequent aircraft of this batch having a further increase in wing span of 19 in (48 cm) and provision for underwing drop tanks. Manufacture of the pure fighter version of the basic design was completed with 50 I.A.R.80Cs – originally laid down as I.A.R.81Bs, which see – with 20-mm Ikaria cannon replacing the 13,2-mm weapons and reintroducing the tailplane bracing struts. A small number of I.A.R.80s remained in Romanian service until late 1949, after which survivors with the lowest hours were rebuilt as I.A.R.80DC tandem-seat dual-control advanced trainers. The following data relate to the I.A.R.80C. *Max speed, 342 mph (550 km/h) at 22,965 ft (7 000 m), 314 mph (505 km/h) at 14,765 ft (4 500 m). Time to 16,405 ft (5 000 m), 6.55 min. Range (internal fuel), 454 mls (730 km). Empty equipped weight, 4,850 lb (2 200 kg). Max loaded weight, 6,570 lb (2 980 kg). Span, 36 ft 1 in (11,00 m). Length, 29 ft 5⅛ in (8,97 m). Height, 11 ft 6⅔ in (3,52 m). Wing area, 177.61 sq ft (16,50 m²).*

I.A.R.81   Romania

Expansion of the operational versatility of the basic I.A.R.80 design to embrace the fighter-bomber and dive bomber tasks resulted in the I.A.R.81, which was to fly its first operational sorties in the Ukraine on 15 October

1941. The 25th production I.A.R.80A was taken from the line to serve as a prototype, fitted with two wing racks for 110-lb (50-kg) bombs and a ventral crutch for a 496-lb (225-kg) bomb. Introduction of the crutch dictated modifications to the main undercarriage members and an automatic flap actuating device was introduced. The dual fighter-bomber and dive bomber version became known as the *BoPi*, an acronym for *Bombardier in Picaj*, or dive bomber. The I.A.R.81 retained the sextet of 7,92-mm FN-Browning guns and could carry three 220-lb (100-kg) bombs, or one 496-lb (225-kg) and two 110-lb (50-kg) bombs. Fifty I.A.R.81s were followed by a batch of 10 I.A.R.81As, which, like the final 10 I.A.R.81s, had an armament of two 13,2-mm and four 7,92-mm guns, and these proved to be the last of the *BoPi* aircraft. The next production version, the I.A.R.81C, was a pure fighter and was to be built in larger numbers than any I.A.R.80 variant. Essentially similar to the I.A.R.80C apart from having the Ikaria cannon replaced by the superior Mauser MG 151 and retaining only two 7,92-mm guns, the I.A.R.81C was, like other versions of the I.A.R.81, powered by the I.A.R.-K 14-1000A engine.

An I.A.R.81C (above) during the winter of 1943-44 with an *Escadrilă* engaged in oilfield defence.

A total of 161 I.A.R.81Cs was built by late 1943 when licence manufacture of the Bf 109G-6 took over. The following data relate to the initial series version of the I.A.R.81. *Max speed, 337 mph (542 km/h) at 22,965 ft (7 000 m), 310 mph (500 km/h) at 14,765 ft (4 500 m). Time to 16,405 ft (5 000 m), 6.45 min. Range (with external fuel), 640 mls (1 030 km). Empty weight, 4,685 ft (2 125 kg). Max loaded weight, 6,768 lb (3 070 kg). Span, 34 ft 6⅛ in (10,52 m). Length, 29 ft 5⅛ in (8,97 m). Height, 11 ft 9¾ in (3,60 m). Wing area, 172.23 sq ft (16,00 m²).*

I.A.R.93   Romania

In 1970, teams from Romania's Aeronautical research institute, the *Institutul de Aviatie – INCREST*, and Yugoslavia's Air Force Technical Institute, the *Vazduhoplovno Technicki Institut*, combined to design a robust single-seat transonic battlefield support fighter with secondary air defence capability under the YuRom (an acronym for Yugoslavia-Romania) programme. The aircraft was designated I.A.R.93 and J-22 Orao (Eagle) in Romania and Yugoslavia respectively, manufacturing responsibility being assigned to CNIAR in the former country and SOKO in the latter. The Romanian Turbomecanica concern was made responsible for licence-manufacture of Rolls-Royce Viper turbojets for both national assembly lines. On 31 October 1974, single-seat prototypes were flown simultaneously in each of the participating countries, two-seat prototypes following in each country on 29 January 1977. The I.A.R.93/J-22 was intended for afterburning engines from the outset, but 15 pre-series aircraft with non-afterburning Viper 633 engines were built both in Romania and in Yugoslavia, the first of these flying in 1978. Delays in development of the afterburner led to 20

The I.A.R.93A (below) was the initial, small-scale production model with non-afterburning engines.

The first single-seat prototype of the I.A.R.93 (above) which entered flight test in October 1974.

more aircraft with non-afterburning engines being produced in each country as I.A.R.93As and Orao 1s. Continuing delays with afterburner development led to service deliveries of the definitive I.A.R.93B and J-22(M) Orao 2 being postponed until 1986. Powered by two Viper 633-41 turbojets each rated at 4,000 lb st (1 814 kgp) dry and 5,000 lb st (2 268 kgp) with afterburning, the I.A.R.93B and Orao 2 had a built-in armament of two 23-mm GSh-23L twin-barrel cannon, and up to 6,173 lb (2 800 kg) of stores distributed between one centreline and four wing stations. For the intercept mission, up to eight R-73 close-range AAMs could be carried on twin launch rails at the four underwing stations. The following data are applicable to the I.A.R.93B and are essentially similar to those for the J-22(M) Orao 2. *Max speed, 721 mph (1 160 km/h) at sea level, or Mach=0.95. Max initial climb, 14,765 ft/min (75 m/sec). Combat radius (air patrol mission with max external fuel), 249 mls (400 km). Empty weight, 12,566 lb (5 700 kg). Max loaded weight, 24,692 lb (11 200 kg). Span, 31 ft 6¾ in (9,62 m). Length, 45 ft 9⅝ in (13,96 m). Height, 14 ft 9¼ in (4,50 m). Wing area, 279.87 sq ft (26,00 m²).*

IKARUS IK-2   Yugoslavia

The IK-L1 (above) is illustrated here in its earliest form, with streamlined wheel spats.

Design of a single-seat fighter monoplane with a braced, shoulder-mounted wing was initiated in 1932 by Ljubomir Ilić and Kosta Sivčev. A private venture design, it was ordered as a prototype in 1934 from the Ikarus AD at Novi Sad. Designated IK-L1 (the "IK" curiously indicating the surname of one designer and the first name of the other, and the "L1" signifying *Lovački* [Fighter] One), the prototype was first flown on 22 April 1935. It was of all-metal construction with fabric-skinned wings, rear fuselage and tail surfaces, and was powered by an Hispano Suiza 12Ycrs engine rated at 860 hp at 13,125 ft (4 000 m). Intended armament comprised one HS 404 hub-mounted 20-mm

An S-49A (below) in service with a Yugoslav Air Force fighter regiment, *circa* 1953.

The series IK-2 (above and below), that illustrated by the photograph being seen prior to the installation of the hub-mounted 20-mm cannon.

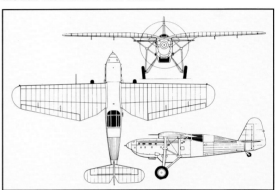

cannon and two 7,92-mm machine guns. The IK-L1 was lost as a result of an accident on 24 April 1935, a second prototype, the IK-02, flying on 24 August 1936. This embodied a revised radiator bath and metal wing skinning. It dispensed with the wheel spats of the first aircraft and carried full armament. An initial batch of 12 fighters, essentially similar to the IK-02 and designated IK-2, was ordered, and these were delivered early in 1939, but no further aircraft were built. Ilić and Sivčev, together with Slobodan Zrnić, were subsequently responsible for the IK-3 alias IK-Z built by Rogožarski AD (which see). *Max speed, 270 mph (435 km/h) at 13,125 ft (4 000 m), 224 mph (360 km/h) at sea level. Time to 16,405 ft (5 000 m), 5.4 min. Endurance, 2.35 hr. Empty weight, 3,311 lb (1 502 kg). Loaded weight, 4,094 lb (1 857 kg). Span, 37 ft 4⅞ in (11,40 m). Length, 25 ft 10¼ in (7,88 m). Height, 12 ft 7⅛ in (3,84 m). Wing area, 193.76 sq ft (18,00 m²).*

IKARUS (VTI) S-49A   Yugoslavia

In 1949, the Ikarus factory, which had been absorbed in 1946 by the then newly-created State Aircraft Industry, was assigned the task of series manufacture of the S-49 single-seat fighter. Based on the pre-World War II

An S-49A (above) photographed in 1951 during factory trials prior to delivery to the Air Force.

Rogožarski IK-3, the S-49 had been designed at the VTI (*Vazduhoplovno Technicki Institut*, or Air Force Technical Institute) by Ljubomir Ilić, Kosta Sivčev, Slobodan Zrnić and Svetozar Popović. Of mixed construction, with a plywood-skinned wooden wing and a welded steel-tube fuselage with light metal panelling forward and fabric covering aft, the S-49 was powered by a Klimov VK-105PF-2 12-cylinder liquid-cooled engine rated at 1,300 hp at 2,625 ft (800 m). Armament comprised a hub-mounted 20-mm cannon and twin fuselage-mounted 12,7-mm machine guns. A prototype flew in 1949, series production commencing in that same year as the S-49A. Deliveries began in 1951, and 45 were built before production switched to the more advanced S-49C. *Max speed, 358 mph (576 km/h) at 16,405 ft (5 000 m). Ceiling, 31,170 ft (9 500 m). Loaded weight, 6,614 lb (3 000 kg). Span, 33 ft 9½ in (10,30 m). Length, 27 ft 6¾ in (8,40 m). Height, 10 ft 6 in (3,20 m). Wing area, 179.12 sq ft (16,64 m²).*

IKARUS (VTI) S-49C　　Yugoslavia

An extensively revised and modernised version of the S-49A, the S-49C was flown as a prototype in 1952. Powered by a 1,500 hp Hispano-Suiza 12Z-17 12-cylinder liquid-cooled Vee-type engine procured from France, the S-49C retained the armament of the earlier S-49A, but was of metal construction throughout, with light metal stressed skinning. It also introduced a redesigned cockpit canopy, a new undercarriage and provision for various underwing ordnance loads (eg, four 82-mm or 127-mm rockets, or four 55-lb/25-kg or 110-lb/50-kg bombs). Like the S-49A, the S-49C was built primarily by the Ikarus factory, but the newly-established SOKO concern at Mostar contributed the wings and tail surfaces of the 112 fighters of this type produced. The S-49C remained in service until 1961. *Max speed, 390 mph (628 km/h) at 5,000 ft (1 525 m). Range,*

(Below) The S-49C, a structurally redesigned, all-metal, modernised derivative of the S-49A.

429 mls (690 km). Max loaded weight, 7,646 lb (3 468 kg). Span, 33 ft 9½ in (10,30 m). Length, 29 ft 8¾ in (9,06 m). Height, 9 ft 6 in (2,90 m). Wing area, 179.12 sq ft (16,64 m²).

(Below) The VTI-designed S-49C single-seat fighter.

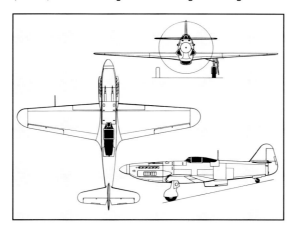

ILYUSHIN I-21 (TsKB-32)　　USSR

Shortly after joining the TsKB (Central Design Bureau), in which he assumed leadership of the No 3 Design Brigade, Sergei V Ilyushin initiated the design of an advanced single-seat fighter. Designated TsKB-32, it was also known as the I-21 (not to be confused with the M M Pashinin-designed I-21 of several years later). A low-wing cantilever monoplane of all-metal construction, the I-21 used a specially modified M-34RNF 12-cylinder liquid-cooled engine in which maximum revs were boosted from 1,800 to 2,400 rpm to produce 1,257 hp and a wing surface evaporation cooling system was employed. Two prototypes were completed late in 1936, and work began on a pre-series of 20 aircraft before the start of factory flight testing. The first prototype I-21 was flown three times by V K Kokkinaki, whereafter the entire programme was cancelled. The fighter was considerably overweight, re-

sulting in an excessive take-off run, and although the I-21 succeeded in reaching a speed of 342 mph (550 km/h) during its brief test programme, the cooling system proved ineffectual and the engine seized, the gliding angle then proving unacceptably steep. *Max speed, 342 mph (550 km/h). Estimated range, 472 mls (760 km). Time to 16,405 ft (5 000 m), 4.6 min. Empty weight, 3,783 lb (1 716 kg). Loaded weight, 4,685 lb (2 125 kg). Span, 30 ft 2⅛ in (9,20 m). Length, 22 ft 11½ in (7,00 m). Wing area, 152.53 sq ft (14,17 m²).*

(Below) The advanced Ilyushin-designed TsKB-32.

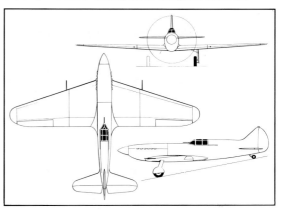

ILYUSHIN Il-1　　USSR

To meet the demands of a specification for a single-seat close air support fighter framed by the National Defence Committee, Sergei V Ilyushin's bureau designed the Il-1 in competition with the Su-7 of Pavel O Sukhoi's bureau. An all-metal low-wing cantilever monoplane powered by a Mikulin AM-42 12-cylinder liquid-cooled engine rated at 1,973 hp for take-off and carrying an armament of two 23-mm VYa cannon, the Il-1 was flown for the first time on 19 June 1944. In the event, the progress of the war rendered further development of this category of fighter unnecessary, and after completion and flight test of one Il-1 prototype, further work on this type was discontinued. *Max speed, 360 mph (580 km/h) at 8,200 ft (2 500 m). Time to 16,405 ft (5 000 m), 8.3 min. Range, 621 mls (1 000 km). Empty weight, 9,447 lb (4 285 kg). Loaded weight, 11,728 lb (5 320 kg). Span, 43 ft 11½ in (13,40 m). Length, 36 ft 5¾ in (11,12 m). Wing area, 322.93 sq ft (30,00 m²).*

The Il-1 (above and below) single-seat close air support fighter developed by Ilyushin's OKB in 1944.

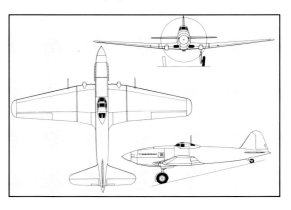

ILYUSHIN Il-2I　　USSR

During 1943, the Ilyushin bureau tested the Il-2I, a derivative of the Il-2 *tip* 3 two-seat *shturmovik* and referred to as an *istrebitel' bombardirovschikov* (literally

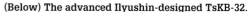

"destroyer of bombers" and hence the "I" suffix in the designation). Like the Il-2 *tip* 3, the Il-2I was powered by a 1,696 hp Mikulin AM-38F engine, and differed from its progenitor in having the gunner's station faired over, some armour removed and armament restricted to a pair of 23-mm VYa cannon. The Il-2I was intended for the dual rôle of bomber and transport interceptor, and pinpoint attacks on such targets as anti-aircraft batteries, assault guns and field-type fortifications. Flight testing revealed that, despite some 1,675 lb (760 kg) reduction in weight by comparison with the standard *shturmovik*, level speed performance was inferior to that of the two-seater. Development was therefore discontinued after the completion of trials with the sole prototype. *Max speed, 244 mph (393 km/h) at sea level and 253 mph (407 km/h) at 4,920 ft (1 500 m). Service ceiling, 21,325 ft (6 500 m). Range, 404 mls (650 km). Loaded weight, 11,867 lb (5 383 kg). Span, 47 ft 10¾ in (14,60 m). Length, 38 ft 2½ in (11,65 m). Wing area, 414.42 sq ft (38,50 m²).*

The Il-2I (below) intended to "destroy bombers" was an adaptation of the Il-2 *shturmovik*.

I.M.A.M. Ro 41   ITALY

A single-seat lightweight fighter, the Ro 41 was conceived by the SA Industrie Aeronautiche Romeo, which, when reorganised as a member of the Breda group, became the I.M.A.M. (Industrie Meccaniche e Aeronautiche Meridionali) in 1936. Designed by Giovanni Galasso, the Ro 41 was flown as a prototype late 1935, and was a small biplane of mixed construction,

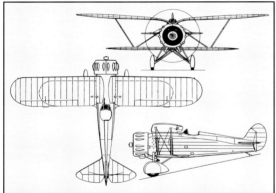

The Ro 41 (above) and a pair of this type (below) in service with 98° *Squadriglia*, 7° *Gruppo*, in 1938.

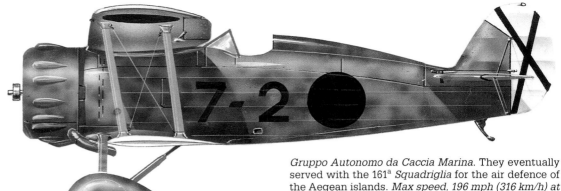

An Ro 41 (above) of an independent flight of the 3° *Stormo Caccia* of the *Aviazione Legionaria*, 1937.

with Warren truss-type interplane bracing. Armament consisted of a pair of 7,7-mm Breda Safat machine guns and power was provided by a seven-cylinder Piaggio P VII C.45 radial engine rated at 444 hp at 4,920 ft (1 500 m). Licence-manufacture of the Ro 41 was undertaken by Agusta both for the *Regia Aeronautica* and for export, 25 being delivered to the Nationalist Spanish air arm in two batches in February and November 1938 to equip the *Escuela de Caza* at Villanubla. Previously, in the spring of 1937, three Ro 41s had been sent to Seville, forming an independent flight within the III° *Stormo Caccia* of the *Aviazione Legionaria*. Shortly afterwards they were passed to the Spanish Nationalists to equip a city defence patrol at Granada. In the *Regia Aeronautica*, the Ro 41 was assigned to the advanced flying training schools (in both single- and two-seat form), but, during 1940-41, some aircraft of this type reverted to the fighter rôle, being assigned to the protection of airfields and other strategic targets. Curiously, the last example of the Ro 41 was completed by Agusta in 1952. *Max speed, 200 mph (322 km/h) at 13,125 ft (4 000 m). Time to 3,280 ft (1 000 m), 1.55 min. Range, 376 mls (606 km) at 165 mph (265 km/h) at 16,405 ft (5 000 m). Empty weight, 1,940 lb (880 kg). Loaded weight, 2,491 lb (1 130 kg). Span, 28 ft 10⅘ in (8,81 m). Length, 21 ft 6¼ in (6,56 m). Height, 8 ft 8⅓ in (2,65 m). Wing area, 133.48 sq ft (12,40 m²).*

I.M.A.M. Ro 44   Italy

Flown for the first time in October 1936, the Ro 44 single-seat fighter float seaplane was a derivative of the Ro 43 two-seat reconnaissance floatplane. It differed from the Ro 43 essentially in having the rear cockpit deleted and in mounting an armament of two 12,7-mm synchronised Breda Safat machine guns. The Ro 44 was powered by a nine-cylinder Piaggio P XR radial rated at 690 hp at 3,280 ft (1 000 m), and was of all-metal construction covered primarily by fabric. Thirty-five Ro 44s were ordered for the *Regia Marina* in February 1937, these initially being assigned to the 88°

Gruppo Autonomo da Caccia Marina. They eventually served with the 161ª *Squadriglia* for the air defence of the Aegean islands. *Max speed, 196 mph (316 km/h) at 8,200 ft (2 500 m). Time to 13,125 ft (4 000 m), 8.66 min. Max range, 746 mls (1 200 km). Empty weight, 3,902 lb (1 770 kg). Max loaded weight, 4,894 lb (2 220 kg). Span, 37 ft 11½ in (11,57 m). Length, 31 ft 10¼ in (9,71 m). Height, 11 ft 7¾ in (3,55 m). Wing area, 359.09 sq ft (33,36 m²).*

(Above and below) The Ro 44, the photograph depicting the 13th production example at Naples.

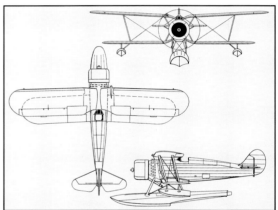

I.M.A.M. Ro 51   Italy

The first fighter monoplane designed by Giovanni Galasso, the Ro 51 was developed to the same requirement as the Fiat G.50 and Macchi C.200, the first prototype flying late in 1937. The Ro 51 was of mixed construction, with a metal fuselage and wooden wings, and was powered by a Fiat A 74 R.C.38 radial rated at 828 hp at 12,465 ft (3 800 m). Armament comprised two 12,7-mm machine guns and the first prototype was initially flown with a fixed, spatted undercarriage. After preliminary trials at the *Centro Sperimentale*, this aircraft was fitted with a fully-retractable tailwheel and semi-retractable main undercarriage members. The latter folded aft into underwing fairings *à la* Seversky, leaving the wheels semi-exposed. The second prototype was, meanwhile, completed as a float fighter, with a single central main float, small outrigger stabilising

The first prototype Ro 51 (below) with the fixed, spatted undercarriage as originally fitted.

floats and revised wing, the taper of the trailing edge being reduced to increase area. In landplane form, the Ro 51 proved unacceptable during definitive evaluation at the *Centro Sperimentale*, and the second prototype suffered an accident on the Bracciano Lake during initial testing, further development being abandoned. The following data relate to the first prototype in definitive form, with semi-retractable undercarriage and enlarged vertical tail. *Max speed, 304 mph (489 km/h). Time to 19,685 ft (6 000 m), 7.0 min. Max range, 746 mls (1 200 km). Empty weight, 3,666 lb (1 663 kg). Loaded weight, 4,612 lb (2 092 kg). Span, 32 ft 1 in (9,78 m). Length, 24 ft 5¾ in (7,46 m). Height, 8 ft 10⅞ in (2,71 m).*

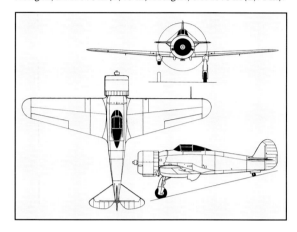

The first prototype Ro 51 (above) in definitive form, and (below) the second Ro 51 prototype.

I.M.A.M. Ro 57   Italy

Intended for use as an interceptor, the Ro 57 twin-engined single-seat fighter, designed by Giovanni Galasso assisted by Pietro Callerio and Manlio Fiore, flew in prototype form early in 1939. It was shown publicly in May of that year on the occasion of the *I Congresso Internazionale dei Giornalisti Aeronautici.* Powered by two 828 hp Fiat A 74 R.C.38 engines and carrying an armament of two 12,7-mm machine guns, the Ro 57 was of mixed construction with a metal-

(Above and below) The Ro 57bis fighter-bomber, which was built in strictly limited numbers.

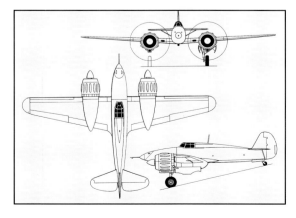

The Ro 57bis (above) enjoyed only limited success, serving with the 97° *Gruppo Autonomo Intercettori.*

skinned metal fuselage and plywood-covered wooden wings. It was concluded that the Ro 57 would be at a disadvantage when confronted by single-engined fighters, and series production was not ordered until 1942, and then in modified Ro 57bis form as a fighter-bomber. Contracts were placed for 200 aircraft, but were reduced subsequently to 90 aircraft. The Ro 57bis had provision for one 1,102-lb (500-kg) bomb beneath the fuselage and two 551-lb (250-kg) bombs beneath the wings, and entered service in February 1943 with the 97° *Gruppo.* In the event, only some 50-60 aircraft of this type were completed. *Max speed, 311 mph (500 km/h) at 16,405 ft (5 000 m). Time to 19,685 ft (6 000 m), 9.5 min. Range, 746 mls (1 200 kg). Empty weight, 7,694 lb (3 490 kg). Loaded weight, 11,000 lb (4 990 kg). Span, 41 ft 0 in (12,50 m). Length, 28 ft 10½ in (8,80 m). Height, 9 ft 6⅛ in (2,90 m). Wing area, 247.58 sq ft (23,00 m²).*

I.M.A.M. Ro 58   Italy

Intended for the rôles of long-range escort fighter, day and night bomber destroyer and close support fighter, the Ro 58 was flown in May 1942. It was of all-metal construction and carried a crew of two and an armament of five 20-mm MG 151 cannon (three in the nose and two in the ventral pack) and one flexibly-mounted aft-firing 12,7-mm machine gun. It was powered by two 1,159 hp Daimler-Benz DB 601A-1 liquid-cooled engines. Official

Despite its undoubted qualities, the Ro 58 (above and below) failed to attain production status.

flight trials revealed exceptional handling characteristics for an aircraft of its size, and the Ro 58 was pronounced superior to the Me 410 in virtually all respects. However, no decision concerning series production had been taken prior to the Italian Armistice, after which development was terminated, only the one pro-

totype being completed. *Max speed, 376 mph (605 km/h) at 16,800 ft (5 120 m). Time to 19,685 ft (6 000 m), 6.0 min. Range, 932 mls (1 500 km). Empty weight, 9,590 lb (4 350 kg). Loaded weight, 13,448 lb (6 100 kg). Span, 43 ft 11½ in (13,40 m). Length, 32 ft 5⅓ in (9,89 m). Height, 10 ft 9½ in (3,29 m). Wing area, 282.02 sq ft (26,20 m²).*

I.V.L. C.24   Finland

The C.24 (above) had the distinction of being the first Finnish-designed combat aircraft to be built

The first military aircraft to be conceived and built in Finland, the C.24 single-seat fighter was designed by Ing K W Berger and built at Sveaborg, Helsingfors, by the Ilmailuvoimien Lentokonetehdas (Aviation Forces Aircraft Factory), or I.V.L., the "C" indicating monoplane fighter and the "24" the year of construction (ie. 1924). Flown for the first time on 16 April 1924, the C.24 was a parasol monoplane of wooden construction with fabric skinning and a 160 hp Siemens-Halske Sh 3A 11-cylinder radial engine. Flight testing conducted during the summer of 1924 confirmed a comparatively good speed and climb performance. Visibility from the cockpit proved poor, however, and the prototype was plagued with engine difficulties, the C.24 being grounded after comparatively limited flying. During its brief flying career, the C.24 was modified by the introduction of a few degrees of sweepback on the mainplane, presumably to rectify a cg problem. *Max speed, 148 mph (238 km/h). Empty weight, 1,453 lb (659 kg). Loaded weight, 1,918 lb (870 kg). Span, 31 ft 2 in (9,50 m). Length, 23 ft 5⅛ in (7,14 m). Height, 9 ft 7⅓ in (2,93 m). Wing area, 204.52 sq ft (19,00 m²).*

I.V.L. C.25   Finland

Derived from the C.24, from which it differed primarily in having a narrower-chord wing with N-struts replacing the V-struts of the earlier fighter, the C.25 was of similar construction and flew for the first time on 11

Flown for six months, the C.25 (below) proved no more successful than its predecessor, the C.24.

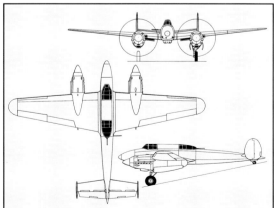

June 1925. The troublesome Siemens-Halske Sh 3A engine was surprisingly retained, this creating problems similar to those encountered during testing of the C.24, and the aircraft was found to be nose heavy. The C.25 crashed on 17 December 1925, by which time it had logged 21 hours flying, and no further development was undertaken. *Max speed, 130 mph (210 km/h). Empty weight, 1,444 lb (655 kg). Loaded weight, 1,858 lb (843 kg). Span, 31 ft 2 in (9,50 m). Length, 22 ft 7²⁄₃ in (6,90 m). Height, 9 ft 7¹⁄₃ in (2,93 m). Wing area, 175.45 sq ft (16,30 m²).*

(Below) The I.V.L.-built C.25 parasol fighter.

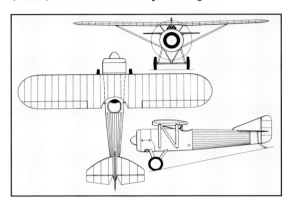

I.V.L. D.26 HAUKKA   Finland

The Haukka (Hawk) single-seat fighter biplane was designed by Ing K W Berger and built at the I.V.L. at Suomenlinna, one example having been ordered on 14 September 1926. A single-bay, unequal-span staggered biplane with the upper wing faired into the forward fuselage decking, a 414 hp Gnome-Rhône Jupiter IV 9AC nine-cylinder radial and an interchangeable wheel/ski undercarriage, the Haukka was first flown on 17 March 1927. It was handed over for official trials at the Utti air base, but, on 7 October, went into a flat spin at 1,970 ft (600 m) from which the evaluation pilot barely succeeded in recovering. The Haukka was officially pronounced to be unsuited for use as a fighter because of structural faults, inadequate visibility from the cockpit and a tendency to enter a flat spin from which recovery was difficult. The prototype was placed in storage at Utti until 21 January 1931, subsequently being stored at the I.V.L. *Max speed, 155 mph (249 km/h). Service ceiling, 25,920 ft (7 900 m). Empty weight, 2,072 lb (940 kg). Loaded weight, 2,844 lb (1 290 kg). Span, 31 ft 5⁷⁄₈ in (9,60 m). Length, 21 ft 7⁷⁄₈ in (6,60 m). Height, 8 ft 6¹⁄₃ in (2,60 m). Wing area, 258.34 sq ft (24,00 m²).*

The original D.26 Haukka (above and below), seen in the photograph with optional ski undercarriage.

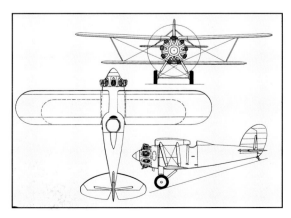

I.V.L. D.27 HAUKKA II   Finland

The Haukka II represented an attempt to rectify one of the principal shortcomings of the original Haukka, inadequate cockpit vision. It differed from its predecessor in having a cabane structure raising the upper wing and increasing the gap. The structure of the Haukka II was similar to that of the preceding fighter, the front fuselage being a plywood monocoque mated to a steel-tube rear fuselage and the wings being of wooden construction with plywood skinning. Two examples of the Haukka II were ordered on 22 September 1927, one powered by a Gnome-Rhône Jupiter 9Ac and the other by a Jupiter 9Ag, both rated at 473 hp, and both armed with two Vickers machine guns. The two aircraft were delivered in June and August 1928 respectively, and both were extensively test flown. They suffered several minor accidents and a number of forced landings resulting from engine, oil feed or propeller malfunctions.

The Haukka II, the first and second prototypes of which are seen above and below respectively, was rejected in favour of the Gloster Gamecock.

The Haukka II was considered to compare favourably with the Kukko (licence-built Gloster Gamecock) in speed and climb, but was inferior in pilot visibility and gun installation. In December 1931, both aircraft were placed in storage, being decommissioned officially on 1 July 1933, when it was pronounced that they "suffered from structural weaknesses, their tail construction was unsatisfactory and repairs would be too expensive and not necessarily successful". *Max speed, 149 mph (240 km/h) at sea level. Service ceiling, 25,920 ft (7,900 m). Endurance, 1.9 hrs. Empty weight, 2,235 lb (1 014 kg). Loaded weight, 3,078 lb (1 396 kg). Span, 31 ft 5⁷⁄₈ in (9,60 m). Length, 21 ft 11³⁄₄ in (6,70 m). Height, 9 ft 0¹⁄₄ in (2,75 m). Wing area, 258.34 sq ft (24,00 m²).*

J

JUNKERS J 2   Germany

Following the successful demonstration in December 1915 of the Junkers J 1 all-steel two-seat experimental aircraft, Junkers und Compagnie of Dessau was awarded a contract by the *Inspektion der Fliegertruppen (Idflieg)* on 31 January 1916 for six examples of a single-seat fighter derivative, the J 2. The first example, powered by a 120 hp Mercedes D II water-cooled engine and carrying an armament of one LMG 08/15 machine gun, was flown at Döberitz on 11 July 1916. As a result of flight trials, a number of changes were introduced on the subsequent five aircraft which were powered by the 160 hp Mercedes D III engine. Overall

The first all-metal fighter monoplane, the J 2 (above and below) began flight test in July 1916.

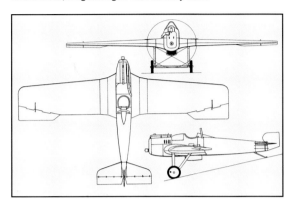

length was increased marginally, wing span was extended by 27½ in (70 cm), wing area reduced by 9 sq ft (84 cm²), long-span, shorter-chord ailerons were fitted and the forward fuselage contours revised. In its definitive form, the J 2 was 9 mph (15 km/h) faster than the best contemporary fighter and its handling characteristics were good, but because of the weight of its all-steel construction, climb rate was below the then current combat requirements. View from the cockpit was considered inadequate, and *Idflieg* coolness towards the fighter increased still further when a J 2 crashed on 23 September 1916, killing test pilot Max Schade. No further examples were ordered in consequence. The following data relate to the definitive model. *Max speed, 124 mph (200 km/h). Time to 9,840 ft (3 000 m), 21 min. Empty weight, 2,244 lb (1 018 kg). Loaded weight, 2,568 lb (1 165 kg). Span, 38 ft 4²⁄₃ in (11,70 m). Length, 24 ft 4½ in (7,43 m). Height, 10 ft 3¼ in (3,13 m). Wing area, 204.52 sq ft (19,00 m²).*

JUNKERS J 7   Germany

During the summer of 1916, Junkers switched attention from all-steel to dural construction in an effort to reduce aircraft weight. The J 3 all-duralumin single-seat fighter was discarded when partially built, because of the disinterest of the *Idflieg*. Nevertheless, Junkers proceeded, as a private venture, with the J 7 single-seat fighter, using the corrugated sheet skinning and duralumin tube construction techniques developed for the J I armoured ground attack biplane. Designed by Dipl-Ing Otto Reuter and powered by a 160 hp Mercedes D III engine, the J 7 flew for the first time on 17 September 1917. Rotating wingtip ailerons were initially fitted, these being replaced by conventional ailerons at an early stage. During the test programme a frontal radiator was introduced, together with a new wing embodying longer-span ailerons. Although not

(Below) The Junkers J 7 in its definitive form.

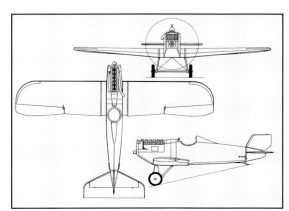

The J 7 with definitive wing (above) proved faster than all other contenders in the first D-type contest.

formally permitted to compete in the first D-type contest held at Adlershof in February 1918 because of its monoplane configuration, the J 7 proved faster than all official contenders, and, in February 1918, was finally accepted for testing by the *Idflieg*. Discussions were held concerning procurement of a small operational evaluation series of J 7s, but this fighter had meanwhile been overtaken by the J 9. *Max speed, 127 mph (205 km/h). Time to 16,405 ft (5 000 m), 24 min. Empty weight, 1,446 lb (656 kg). Loaded weight, 1,775 lb (805 kg). Span, 30 ft 2¼ in (9,20 m). Length, 21 ft 11¾ in (6,70 m). Height, 8 ft 6⅓ in (2,60 m). Wing area, 125.94 sq ft (11,70 m²).*

JUNKERS J 8   Germany

One of the three prototypes of the J 8 (above), this being the precursor of the production J 10.

On 26 December 1916, Junkers received an *Idflieg* contract to build three prototypes of the J 8 all-metal two-seat monoplane in the Cl-type category – a "defensive patrol and pursuit aircraft". Thanks to the priority accorded production of the J I ground attack biplane, however, the J 8 was not completed until 4 December 1917, being flown for the first time a few days later. Of dural construction and powered by a 160 hp Mercedes D III engine, the J 8 was demonstrated during the first D-type contest in February 1918, and in the following month the Junkers-Fokker Werke AG (established on 20 October 1917) received a contract for a pre-series of a modified version, the J 10. *Max speed, 100 mph (161 km/h). Endurance, 1.5 hrs. Empty weight, 1,565 lb (710 kg). Loaded weight, 2,315 lb (1 050 kg). Span, 39 ft 6 in (12,04 m). Length, 25 ft 11 in (7,90 m). Height, 8 ft 8¾ in (2,66 m). Wing area, 251.88 sq ft (23,40 m²).*

JUNKERS D I (J 9)   Germany

Hard on the heels of the J 7, construction of the improved J 9 single-seat fighter was begun by Junkers. Powered by a similar 160 hp Mercedes D III engine, the J 9 flew for the first time in late April 1918. Concurrently, the *Idflieg* awarded Junkers und Compagnie and the Junkers-Fokker Werke AG each a contract for 10 pre-series J 9s as D Is. The first D I prototype was entered in the 2nd D-type contest held at Adlershof in May-June 1918, but combat pilots adjudged it totally unsuited for fighter tactics then current. It was suggested that, in view of the comparative invulnerability of its metal

(Right) The short-fuselage version of the J 9 (D I) photographed fully armed on 8 July 1918.

structure, it should be produced as a specialised "balloon attack" aircraft. Accordingly, further contracts were issued for the D I for this rôle between May and November 1918, bringing the total ordered to 60 machines. Of these, Junkers delivered about 27 and Junkers-Fokker delivered 13 through February 1919. There is no record of the D I having been used in combat during World War I, but a few were active with the *Geschwader* Sachsenberg in Kurland against Bolshevik insurgents. One D I was test flown with a 185 hp Benz Bz IIIb eight-cylinder Vee engine, and another, powered by a 185 hp BMW IIIa engine, participated in the 3rd D-type contest in October 1918. *Max speed, 140 mph (225 km/h). Time to 16,405 ft (5 000 m), 24 min.*

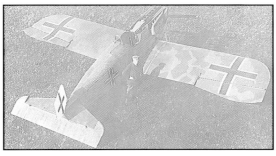

(Above and below) The early-production short-fuselage J 9, found unsuited for contemporary fighter tactics.

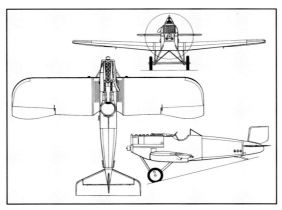

Endurance, 1.5 hrs. Empty weight, 1,442 lb (654 kg). Loaded weight, 1,839 lb (834 kg). Span, 29 ft 6⅓ in (9,00 m). Length, 23 ft 9⅜ in (7,25 m). Height, 8 ft 6⅓ in (2,60 m). Wing area, 159.31 sq ft (14,80 m²).

JUNKERS Cʟ I (J 10)   Germany

The Cl I (J 10) was an improved derivative of the J 8 intended for offensive patrol and close air support rôles. Powered by a Mercedes D III engine of 160 hp and armed with two fixed LMG 08/15 machine guns and a Parabellum in the rear cockpit, the Cl I was the subject of an order placed with the Junkers-Fokker Werke AG in March 1918 for 10 pre-series aircraft. Subsequent contracts raised the total ordered to 63 machines, of which 44 were delivered through March 1919. Together with the D I, the Cl I was used by the *Geschwader* Sachsenberg during the post-World War I fighting against Bolshevik forces in the Baltic. *Max speed, 118 mph (190 km/h). Time to 3,280 ft (1 000 m), 3.9 min. Endurance, 2.0 hrs. Empty weight, 1,620 lb (735 kg). Loaded weight, 2,546 lb (1 155 kg). Span, 40 ft 0¼ in (12,20 m). Length, 25 ft 11 in (7,90 m). Height, 10 ft 2 in (3,10 m).*

The Cl I (above and below) was the ultimate wartime development of the line of Junkers monoplanes.

The Cl I (below) served post-World War I in the Baltic with the *Geschwader* Sachsenberg.

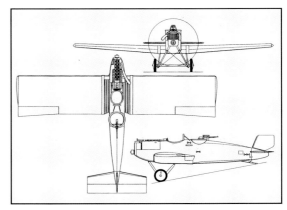

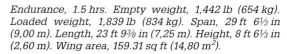

JUNKERS H 22   Germany

On 29 January 1923, Junkers obtained a concession from the Soviet government to initiate the manufacture of all-metal aircraft in the former Russo-Baltic Works at Fili, near Moscow. In the following year, Junkers commenced the assembly of the R 02 two-seat reconnaissance aircraft, essentially similar to the A 20 cantilever low-wing postal monoplane, and the H 21 two-seat parasol reconnaissance monoplane. Of typical Junkers metal construction with corrugated dural skinning, the H 21 was built in substantial numbers at Fili, and a single-seat fighter version, the H 22, was tested in 1926. Powered by the same 185 hp BMW IIIa water-cooled engine that powered the H 21, the H 22 differed from its predecessor essentially in having a lower-set wing, a redesigned vertical tail, the forward cockpit deleted and an armament of two fixed forward-firing machine guns. The performance of the H 22 proved unacceptable and no series production of this fighter was undertaken. *Max speed, 146 mph (235 km/h). Cruising speed, 113 mph (182 km/h). Time to 3,280 ft (1 000 m), 4.2 min. Loaded weight, 1,874 lb (850 kg). Span, 35 ft 4 in (10,77 m). Length, 21 ft 11¾ in (6,70 m). Height, 8 ft 2½ in (2,50 m).*

The H 22 (above and below) was offered to the Soviet Union, but proved unacceptable.

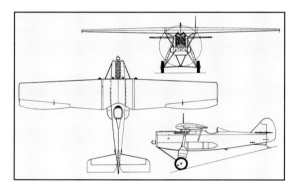

JUNKERS R 53 (K 53)   Germany

In 1926, the Junkers Flugzeugwerke AG developed a new all-metal tandem two-seat low-wing cantilever monoplane. This, like most of the company's products, was dimorphic in that both commercial and military versions were evolved in parallel. The commercial version, designated A 35 and built at Dessau, was intended ostensibly as a high-speed postal aircraft, and

The K 53 (below) was built in civilian guise at Dessau and converted as a fighter at Limhamn-Malmö.

(Above and below) The K 53 fighter, the photograph depicting one of six shipped to China early in 1929.

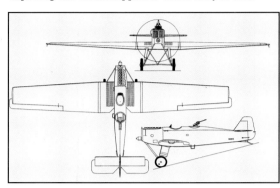

its military equivalent, initially known as the R 53 and subsequently as the K 53, was a two-seat fighter and was developed by Junkers' Swedish subsidiary, AB Flygindustri at Limhamn-Malmö. Designed by Dipl-Ing Karl Plauth, the R 53 corresponded to the commercial A 36B in having a 310 hp Junkers L 5 engine. The prototype was flown in the spring of 1926, and destroyed later that year during a demonstration in the Netherlands. The R 53 carried an armament of two fixed forward-firing Vickers machine guns and a pair of Lewis guns on a Scarff ring in the rear cockpit. The standard wheel undercarriage was interchangeable with skis and floats. More than 20 R 53s – their designation being changed to K 53 during 1927 – were built by the AB Flygindustri during 1926-29 for export, principally to Manchuria and China. *Max speed, 127 mph (205 km/h). Cruising speed, 106 mph (170 km/h). Endurance, 4.5 hrs. Empty weight, 2,370 lb (1 075 kg). Loaded weight, 3,483 lb (1 580 kg). Span, 52 ft 3½ in (15,94 m). Length, 26 ft 11⅔ in (8,22 m). Height, 11 ft 5¾ in (3,50 m). Wing area, 320.34 sq ft (29,76 m²).*

JUNKERS K 47   Germany

Designed by Dipl-Ing Karl Plauth and Hermann Pohlmann as a two-seat fighter, the K 47 was built in Sweden by the Junkers subsidiary, AB Flygindustri. The first prototype, powered by a 420 hp Siemens Jupiter VII, commenced flight trials at Bulltofta airfield in January 1929. Both this and a similarly-powered second prototype were subsequently evaluated at the clandestine German air training centre at Lipetsk, north of Voronezh. From there they were sent to Germany, the former (as the A 48dy) for evaluation at the DVL with a 540 hp Siemens Sh 20 engine, and the latter (as the A 48b) for use as a Junkers company demonstrator, eventually being fitted with a 580 hp BMW Hornet

A-2 (as the A 48ba). The AB Flygindustri initiated production of a batch of 12 K 47s which were offered with various engines and with a revised wing and modified bracing. With the Hornet A-2 engine and an armament of two fixed forward-firing 7,9-mm Madsen machine guns and a similar weapon on a Knauth mounting in the rear cockpit, six K 47s were supplied to the Chinese Central Government in June 1931. Four others were supplied to the Soviet Union and the remaining two went to Germany. These last-mentioned were both powered by the Siemens Jupiter VI, the first (as the A 48fi) having a redesigned rear fuselage with a single fin-and-rudder assembly and the second (as an A 48b) retaining the standard tail unit for comparative trials at Travemünde. *Max speed, 150 mph (242 km/h) at sea level, 180 mph (290 km/h) at 9,840 ft (3 000 m). Time to 9,840 ft (3 000 m), 6.3 min. Range, 419 mls (675 km). Empty weight, 2,535 lb (1 150 kg). Loaded weight, 3,604 lb (1 635 kg). Span, 40 ft 8¼ in (12,40 m). Length, 28 ft 10½ in (8,80 m). Height, 9 ft 6⅛ in (2,90 m). Wing area, 252.96 sq ft (23,50 m²).*

(Above) The Jupiter-engined first prototype, and (below) the Hornet-powered version of the K 47.

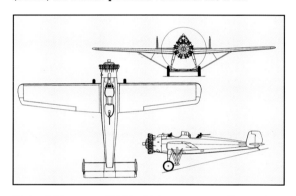

(Below) The second K 47 which was eventually used as a Junkers demonstrator designated A 48b.

JUNKERS Ju 88C & Ju 88R   Germany

Although the Ju 88 was conceived solely as a *Schnellbomber* – a high-speed bomber uncompromised in design by the needs of alternative rôles – its potential as a heavy fighter, or *Zerstörer*, was under investigation before the aircraft attained service in bomber form. A somewhat rudimentary fighter prototype was produced by adaptation of the Ju 88 V7, a fixed forward-firing armament being installed and the crew complement being reduced to three. Trials began late in 1939, and a small number of Ju 88A-1 bomber airframes was adapted on the assembly line as Ju 88C-2 fighters. The Ju 88C-2 was powered by two 1,200 hp Junkers Jumo 211B-1 engines (the Ju 88C-1 having been a proposed version with BMW 801MAs), introduced an armoured bulkhead in the nose and carried a fixed forward-firing armament of two 20-mm and two 7,9-mm weapons. It commenced diurnal operations in the spring of 1940, initiating nocturnal intrusion sorties in the following autumn. The first version to be built from the outset for the fighter rôle was the Ju 88C-4, based on the Ju 88A-4

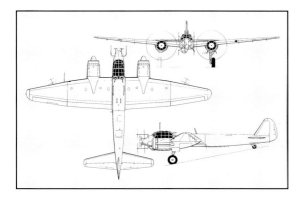

(Above) The Ju 88C-6c with *Lichtenstein SN*-2 radar, and (below) a Ju 88C-6b with *Lichtenstein BC*.

(Above) A Ju 88G-1 of 7./NJG 2 after landing in error at Woodbridge, Essex, on 13 July 1944.

bomber airframe and carrying two additional 20-mm cannon in the offset gondola. The Ju 88C-3 and C-5 were BMW 801-engined variants, the former limited to a single prototype and the latter to a pre-series of 10 for test and development tasks. Fewer than 100 Ju 88C-4s had been completed when, early in 1942, this variant was replaced by the Ju 88C-6 powered by 1,340 hp Jumo 211J engines and featuring additional armour. This version was delivered both with and without the paired 20-mm gondola-mounted cannon, and was the first Ju 88 fighter model to be built in really substantial numbers. The radar-equipped night fighter version which appeared late in 1942 was designated Ju 88C-6b. The Ju 88C-6c, which began to enter service early 1944, differed from the C-6b in having FuG 220 *Lichtenstein* SN-2 radar in place of the earlier FuG 202 *Lichtenstein* BC or FuG 212 *Lichtenstein* C-1. Early in 1943, the Ju 88C-6b was joined by the Ju 88R-1 with BMW 801MA engines but otherwise similar in all respects. The Ju 88C-7a was a diurnal attack fighter with the asymmetrical gondola replaced by a so-called *Waffentropfen* (weapon pack) which protruded from the bomb bay and, like the gondola, accommodated a pair of 20-mm cannon. The Ju 88C-7b was similar apart from provision for four external bomb racks, and the Ju 88C-7c was an experimental BMW 801MA-powered model. Some 3,200 C-series fighters were delivered to the *Luftwaffe*, the following data relating to the Ju 88C-6c. *Max speed, 307 mph (494 km/h) at 17,390 ft (5 300 m). Initial climb, 1,770 ft/min (9,0 m/sec). Normal range, 645 mls (1 038 km). Empty weight, 19,973 lb (9 060 kg). Loaded weight, 27,225 lb (12 350 kg). Span, 65 ft 10½ in (20,08 m). Length, 47 ft 1⅓ in (14,36 m). Height, 16 ft 7½ in (5,07 m). Wing area, 586.6 sq ft (54,50 m²).*

JUNKERS Ju 88G   Germany

The constant demand for the installation of additional equipment in the Ju 88C night fighter and the resultant weight escalation with consequential performance reduction led, in the spring of 1943, to the appearance of the Ju 88 V58 as the prototype for the improved Ju 88G series of night fighters. Converted from a Ju 88R, the V58 retained the BMW 801 radial engines, but the more angular vertical and horizontal tail surfaces of the Ju 188 bomber were adopted to improve stability, and

The Ju 88G-7a (below), one variant of the final production series night fighter with FuG 220 radar.

armament was re-arranged. Two vertically staggered 20-mm cannon were mounted in the starboard side of the nose and four similar weapons were installed in a weapon pack mounted asymmetrically beneath the port side of the fuselage. A single 13-mm machine gun provided rear defence. The Ju 88G-1, which appeared early in 1944, was similar but lacked the nose-mounted cannon and was fitted instead with *Lichtenstein* SN-2 radar and FuG 227 *Flensburg*. This variant, like the Ju 88G-4 which followed it on the assembly line, was powered by BMW 801D engines of 1,700 hp, the latter model differing only in that it standardised on avionics introduced progressively by the Ju 88G-1. Some Ju 88G-4s were fitted with a *schräge Musik* installation of two upward-firing 20-mm cannon, a similar installation being provided in the Ju 88G-6a manufactured in parallel and differing only in having BMW 801G engines. The

(Above) A Ju 88G-7b with *Lichtenstein SN*-3 radar, and (below) the BMW 801G-powered Ju 88G-6b.

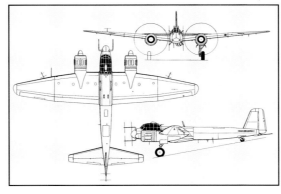

Ju 88G-6b added an FuG 350 *Naxos Z* receiver to its equipment, but this BMW 801G-powered model quickly gave place to the Ju 88G-6c with 1,750 hp Jumo 213A liquid-cooled engines. The final night fighting version

(Above) A Ju 88G-6b of *I Gruppe* of NJG 101 at Ingolstadt, late 1944, and (below) a Ju 88G-7a of *IV Gruppe* of NJG 6 at Schwäbisch Hall, 1944-45.

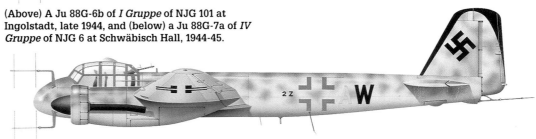

to reach production was the Ju 88G-7, the -7a version having FuG 220 *Lichtenstein* SN-2, the -7b having FuG 228 *Lichtenstein* SN-3, and the -7c having FuG 240 *Berlin* N-1a. Only 10 of the last-mentioned sub-type were completed, but a total of between 700 and 800 G-series night fighters was built. The following data relate to the Ju 88G-7b. *Max speed, 363 mph (584 km/h) at 33,465 ft (10 200 m) or (with MW 50 boost) 389 mph (626 km/h) at 29,855 ft (9 100 m). Initial climb, 1,655 ft/min (8,4 m/sec). Normal endurance, 3.72 hrs. Normal loaded weight, 28,902 lb (13 110 kg). Span, 65 ft 10½ in (20,08 m). Length, 51 ft 0¼ in (15,55 m). Height, 15 ft 11 in (4,85 m). Wing area, 586.6 sq ft (54,50 m²).*

JUNKERS Ju 388J   Germany

Under the code name *Störtebeker* (a legendary German pirate), a four-seat night and all-weather fighter, the Ju 388J, was evolved in parallel with high-altitude bomber (Ju 388K) and photo-reconnaissance (Ju 388L) versions of the same basic design. Prototypes of all three models were ordered and these utilised for the most part standard Ju 188 bomber components. The fighter prototypes, the Ju 388 V2, V4 and V5, were powered by BMW 801TJ radials rated at 1,800 hp for take-off. The first of these carried FuG 220 *Lichtenstein* SN-2 radar and a forward-firing armament of two 20-mm and two 30-mm cannon, rear defence being provided by a remotely-controlled tail barbette housing a twin 13-mm MG 131Z machine gun. The Ju 388 V2

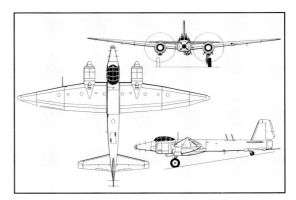

The Ju 388 V4 (above) represented the Ju 388J-1.

The Ju 388 V2 (above) was the first of the Ju 388J fighter prototypes and flew in January 1944.

entered flight test in January 1944, the V4 and V5 which followed lacking the tail barbette and featuring FuG 218 *Neptun* radar enclosed by a pointed wooden nose cone. A pressure cabin was provided for the four crew members, and the initial production version was to have been the Ju 388J-1 which would have been fundamentally similar to the V4 and V5. Production deliveries were scheduled to commence in January 1945, but, in the event, none left the assembly line before the war situation brought the programme to an end. The following data relate to the Ju 388J-1. *Max speed, 362 mph (582 km/h) at 40,300 ft (12 285 m). Initial climb, 1,240 ft/ min (6,30 m/sec). Max endurance, 4.45 hrs. Empty weight, 22,928 lb (10 400 kg). Max loaded weight, 32,350 lb (14 674 kg). Span, 72 ft 2 in (22,00 m). Length, 58 ft 1 in (17,70 m). Height, 14 ft 3 in (4,34 m). Wing area, 602.79 sq ft (56,00 m²).*

JUNKERS Ju 248   Germany

In the late summer of 1944, the Junkers-Werke was requested to develop a successor to the Messerschmitt Me 163B rocket-propelled target-defence interceptor, this being assigned the designation Ju 248. Despite the fact that the Junkers aircraft was fundamentally a new design with only limited relationship to the aircraft that it was intended to succeed, in December 1944 the project was redesignated Me 263 (which see).

KAWANISHI K-11   Japan

In April 1926, the Japanese Imperial Navy solicited proposals from Aichi, Mitsubishi and Nakajima for a new single-seat shipboard fighter. Although the Kawanishi Kokuki KK had not been invited to participate in the contest, the company elected to enter a private-venture design, the K-11 designed by Eiji Sekiguchi. A staggered equi-span single-bay biplane with a fabric-covered metal fuselage and wooden wings – the upper having fabric skinning and the lower plywood – the K-11 was powered by a water-cooled BMW VI engine affording 630 hp for take-off. It carried an armament of two synchronised 7,7-mm machine guns. Retractable radiators were mounted in the fuselage sides and the undercarriage was jettisonable. The first of two prototypes was completed in July 1927, and evaluated by the

The first prototype K-11 (below) completed in July 1927 to meet a shipboard fighter requirement.

Imperial Navy at Kagamigahara (now Gifu). The second prototype embodied a number of improvements resulting from the testing of the first example, notably to the fuselage structure and tailplane, but the contest was won by the Nakajima-submitted Gloster Gambet, which entered production as the A1N1 Navy Type 3 Carrier Fighter. Development of the K-11 was accordingly discontinued, the two prototypes being used experimentally for mail carrying by Nippon Koku KK. *Max speed, 161 mph (259 km/h). Time to 9,840 ft (3 000 m), 5.5 min. Endurance, 3.5 hrs. Empty weight, 2,579 lb (1 170 kg). Loaded weight, 3,858 lb (1 750 kg). Span, 35 ft 5¼ in (10,80 m). Length, 25 ft 10¼ in (7,88 m). Height, 10 ft 9⅛ in (3,28 m). Wing area, 363.83 sq ft (33,80 m²).*

(Below) The K-11 fighter in its definitive form.

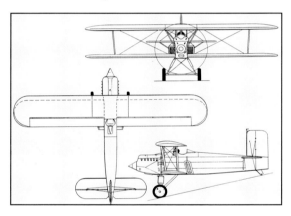

KAWANISHI N1K1 KYOFU   Japan

A specification for what was intended to be the world's most powerful and advanced single-seat float fighter was issued to Kawanishi in September 1940. Assigned the company designation K-20, the new fighter had a mid-mounted laminar-flow wing, a single central float and outrigger stabilising floats. The first prototype was fitted with a Mitsubishi MK4D Kasei 14 14-cylinder radial driving two-bladed contra-rotating propellers. The initial flight test was made on 6 May 1942, but difficulties with the contra-prop gearing led to the installation of an MK4C Kasei 13 in seven subsequent prototypes, this engine driving a conventional three-bladed propeller and having a similar 1,460 hp output for take-

An N1K1 Kyofu (below) of the Sasebo Kokutai, 1944, which attempted to intercept China-based B-29s.

off. In this form, the K-20 was adopted as the N1K1 Navy Fighter Seaplane Kyofu (Mighty Wind) Model 11 in December 1942. Armament comprised two 7,7-mm machine guns and two 20-mm cannon. Production deliveries commenced in July 1943, but only 89 were completed owing to the changing war situation and the higher priority allocated to its land-based counterpart, the N1K1-J Shiden. Late production examples of the Kyofu were fitted with the MK4E Kasei 15 rated at 1,530 hp for take-off. The following data relate to the MK4C-powered model. *Max speed, 302 mph (486 km/h) at 18,700 ft (5 700 m). Time to 16,400 ft (5 000 m), 5.52 min. Max range, 1,036 mls (1 667 km). Empty weight, 6,063 lb (2 750 kg). Max loaded weight, 8,183 lb (3 712 kg). Span, 39 ft 4½ in (12,00 m). Length, 34 ft 8¾ in (10,59 m). Height, 15 ft 7 in (4,75 m). Wing area, 252.96 sq ft (23,50 m²).*

(Above and below) The N1K1 Kyofu appeared in 1943 but relatively small numbers entered service.

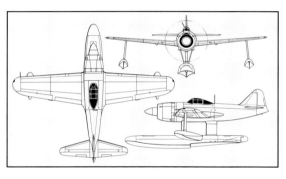

KAWANISHI N1K1-J SHIDEN   Japan

Reversing the normal process in which a float fighter was created from a land-based fighter, Kawanishi initiated in November 1942, as a private venture, the development of a derivative of the N1K1 Kyofu with retractable wheel undercarriage. The airframe was fundamentally unchanged, but the Kasei engine was replaced by a Nakajima NK9B Homare 11 eighteen-cylinder radial rated at 1,820 hp for take-off. As the X-1, the first prototype was flown on 27 December 1942, armament being similar to that of the Kyofu but the wing cannon being mounted in gondolas. The aircraft was officially adopted as the N1K1-J Navy Fighter Shiden (Violet Lightning) Model 11. A total of nine prototypes was produced, the 1,990 hp NK9H Homare 21 being adopted for the production model. Armament was augmented by two additional 20-mm cannon. Production deliveries began in July 1943, the N1K1-Ja having the machine guns deleted, the N1K1-Jb having

(Above and below) The N1K1-J was unique among service land-based fighters in having been derived from an original floatplane design.

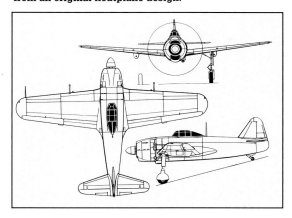

An N1K2-J Shiden-KAI (above) included in the inventory of the US Air Force Museum, Dayton, Ohio.

all four cannon mounted within the wing and the N1K1-Jc being a dedicated fighter-bomber version with four underwing bomb racks. A total of 998 production Shiden fighters was delivered. *Max speed, 362 mph (582 km/h) at 17,715 ft (5 400 m). Time to 19,685 ft (6 000 m), 7.85 min. Normal range, 888 mls (1 430 km). Empty weight, 6,387 lb (2 897 kg). Max loaded weight, 9,526 lb (4 321 kg). Span, 39 ft 4½ in (12,00 m). Length, 29 ft 1¾ in (8,88 m). Height, 13 ft 3¾ in (4,06 m). Wing area, 252.96 sq ft (23,50 m²).*

KAWANISHI N1K2-J SHIDEN-KAI   Japan

Major redesign of the N1K1-J Shiden was undertaken by Kawanishi in mid-1943. A primary objective was to shorten the excessively long main undercarriage legs which, from an early stage in the test programme, had created serious problems. In order to achieve this, the wings were moved to the lower fuselage, this change being accompanied by extensive redesign of the fuselage and tail surfaces. The result was essentially a new fighter retaining no more than the wings and four-cannon armament of the N1K1-Jb. Designated N1K2-J Shiden-KAI, the prototype was flown on 31 December 1943, seven additional prototypes being built and pro-

duction deliveries commencing in July 1944 as the Navy Fighter Shiden-KAI Model 21. The Shiden-KAI retained the NK9H Homare 21 of the Shiden, a fighter-bomber variant being designated N1K2-Ja. A small number was completed as tandem two-seat advanced trainers designated N1K2-K Shiden-Rensen. One of the principal shortcomings of the Shiden-KAI was location of the CG too far aft, and to remedy this defect the Homare 21 engine was moved forward 6 in (15 cm). This change provided sufficient additional space to permit installation of two 13,2-mm machine guns in the fuselage. Two airframes were modified to this standard under the designation N1K3-J in the spring of 1945. Two others were adapted as prototypes of the N1K4-J and a third as its shipboard equivalent, the N1K4-A. These last-mentioned models were powered by the 2,000 hp NK9H-S Homare 23 radial, but were too late to achieve production status. Series production of the N1K2-J Shiden-KAI totalled 415 aircraft. *Max speed, 369 mph (594 km/h) at 18,370 ft (5 600 m). Time to 19,685 ft (6 000 m), 7.36 min. Normal range, 1,066 mls (1 715 km). Empty weight, 5,858 lb (2 657 kg). Normal loaded weight, 8,818 lb (4 000 kg). Span, 39 ft 4½ in (12,00 m). Length, 30 ft 8 in (9,34 m). Height, 13 ft 0 in (3,96 m). Wing area, 252.96 sq ft (23,50 m²).*

KAWASAKI KDA-3   Japan

Seeking a successor to the Ko-4 (Nieuport-Delage NiD 29), the Imperial Army issued, in March 1927, a request for proposals to Kawasaki, Mitsubishi and Nakajima.

Kawasaki responded with a design by Dr-Ing Richard Vogt for a single-seat parasol monoplane, the KDA-3. Powered by a water-cooled 12-cylinder BMW VI 6,3 engine affording 630 hp for take-off, the KDA-3 had a fabric-covered wing of mixed construction and a metal-skinned all-metal fuselage based on that of the Dornier Do H Falke. Armament comprised two synchronised 7,7-mm machine guns. The first of three prototypes was completed in March 1928, but was lost in a landing accident at Kagamigahara on 1 April. The second and third prototypes, these being powered by 450 hp Hispano-Suiza engines, had been completed by May for competitive evaluation with the Mitsubishi and Nakajima contenders at Tokorozawa. In the event, the evaluation was suspended when the Mitsubishi Type Hayabusa (Peregrine Falcon) disintegrated during diving trials. An investigation revealed that none of the contenders fully met Army strength requirements, and both Kawasaki and Mitsubishi withdrew from the contest. The two surviving KDA-3 prototypes were subsequently utilised by Kawasaki for flight research. The following data relate to the first prototype. *Max speed, 177 mph (285 km/h). Time to 16,405 ft (5 000 m), 12 min. Empty weight, 2,976 lb (1 350 kg). Loaded weight, 4,299 lb (1 950 kg). Span, 41 ft 4 in (12,60 m). Length, 29 ft 0⅜ in (8,85 m). Height, 9 ft 10⅛ in (3,00 m). Wing area, 269.1 sq ft (25,00 m²).*

KAWASAKI (KDA-5) TYPE 92 FIGHTER   Japan

In June 1929, Kawasaki initiated development of a new single-seat fighter as a company-funded programme. Designed by Dr-Ing Richard Vogt, assisted by Takeo Doi, it was designated KDA-5. The new fighter embodied the latest western structural techniques and was an equi-span biplane with fabric-covered metal wings, a metal-skinned metal fuselage and a 630 hp BMW VI 6,3 engine. The first of three KDA-5 prototypes was completed in July 1930, attaining a speed of 199 mph (320 km/h) and an altitude of 32,810 ft (10 000 m) under test, both figures representing new records in Japan. The second and third prototypes were completed in January and March 1931, and, after evaluation by the Imperial Army, series production was ordered as the Type 92 Fighter. Two additional prototypes were built, and various engine cowling and radiator designs were tested before the definitive production arrangement was reached. With the designation Type 92-I, a total of 180 fighters was completed between January and December 1932, production subsequently switching to the Type 92-II, of which 200 were built. The Type 92-II had the Kawasaki-built BMW VI engine replaced with an improved version of the power plant designated by Kawasaki as the BMW VII (although unrelated to the BMW VII developed by the German engine manufacturer) and rated at 750 hp for take-off. Both -I and -II models carried an armament of two synchronised 7,7-mm guns, and the Type 92 was deployed primarily in Manchuria and Northern China from 1932 until 1935. The following data relate to the Type 92-I. *Max speed, 199 mph (320 km/h) at sea level. Time to 9,840 ft (3 000 m), 4 min. Range, 528 mls*

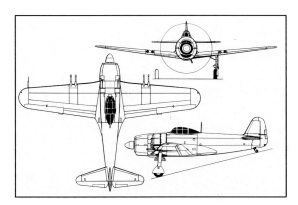

The N1K2-J (above and below) differed fundamentally from the N1K1-J in having a low-wing configuration.

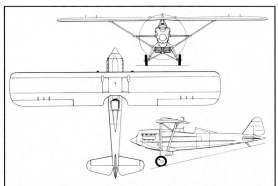

The KDA-3 (above and below) employed a fuselage based broadly on that of the Dornier H Falke.

(850 km). Empty weight, 2,822 lb (1 280 kg). Loaded weight, 3,748 lb (1 700 kg). Span, 31 ft 4 in (9,55 m). Length, 23 ft 1½ in (7,05 m). Height, 10 ft 2 in (3,10 m). Wing area, 258.34 sq ft (24,00 m²).

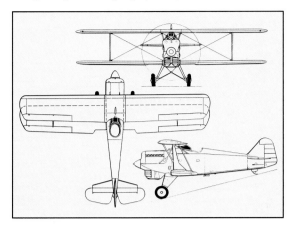

(Above and below) The first production Kawasaki fighter, the Type 92-I, which was built in series in 1932, and deployed operationally in China.

KAWASAKI Kɪ-5   Japan

As its first essay in the field of low-wing cantilever monoplane fighters, Kawasaki evolved the Ki-5 to meet requirements of the Imperial Army circulated in June 1933, which called for the development of a successor to the Type 92 biplane. Designed by Takeo Doi under the overall supervision of Dr-Ing Richard Vogt, the Ki-5 was of all-metal construction with a Kawasaki-developed BMW IX (Ha-9-I) 12-cylinder water-cooled Vee engine rated at 850 hp for take-off. The wing was of inverted gull configuration to improve view from the cockpit and to restrict the length of the undercarriage legs. Four prototypes were built, these embodying differing wing anhedral and dihedral angles, pilot seat positioning, radiator designs and undercarriages. The first was completed in February 1934, by which time Dr-Ing Vogt had returned to Germany. Poor low-speed stability, inadequate manoeuvrability, and engine cooling and vibration problems resulted in the Army discontinuing evaluation of the Ki-5 by September 1934, and all four prototypes were scrapped. *Max speed, 224 mph (360 km/h). Time to 16,405 ft (5 000 m), 8 min. Range, 620 mls (1 000 km). Empty weight, 3,307 lb (1 500 kg). Loaded weight, 4,123 lb (1 870 kg). Span, 34 ft 9⅓ in (10,60 m). Length, 25 ft 6⅓ in (7,78 m). Height, 8 ft 6⅜ in (2,60 m). Wing area, 193.76 sq ft (18,00 m²).*

(Below) The Ki-5 was confined to four prototypes.

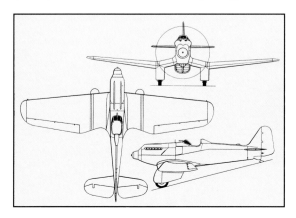

KAWASAKI (Kɪ-10) Tʏᴘᴇ 95
Fɪɢʜᴛᴇʀ   Japan

Following the failure of the Ki-5, the Imperial Army in September 1934 instructed both Kawasaki and Nakajima to initiate development of new single-seat fighters. Army demands for light construction and maximum possible manoeuvrability, combined with the company's lack of success with the monoplane formula, prompted Kawasaki to revert to the biplane configuration. Takeo Doi, assisted by Isamu Imachi, designed an all-metal single-bay aircraft with fabric-covered wings and a Kawasaki Ha-9-II-Ko water-cooled 12-cylinder engine rated at 850 hp for take-off. Designated Ki-10, the first of four prototypes was completed in March 1935, and, in the following September, the Ki-10 was selected in favour of the Nakajima Ki-11 and ordered into production as the Type 95 Fighter. Production commenced in December, but almost immediately the Army demanded improved manoeuvrability. Thus, while production of the Type 95 proceeded, work continued in parallel on a developed version, the Ki-10-II. The wings were lengthened, increasing overall span and area from 31 ft 4 in (9,55 m) and 215.28 sq ft (20,00 m²) to 32 ft 10½ in (10,02 m) and 247.58 sq ft (23,00 m²), and fuselage length was increased from 23 ft 7½ in (7,20 m) to 24 ft 9¼ in (7,55 m). After completion of 300 Type 95s in October 1937, production switched to the modified version as the Type 95-II, and 280 of this variant had been completed when production terminated in December 1938. Both models were fitted with an armament of two 7,7-mm machine guns, and these remained the mainstay of the Army fighter element until 1940. An additional four prototypes were built to participate in programmes aimed at further improving the capabilities of the basic Type 95 fighter. One of these, the 200th Type 95 fighter, with a new wing section and a close-cowled undercarriage, attained a maximum speed of 264 mph (425 km/h). Two others, completed in November 1937, featured an Ha-9-II-Otsu engine, an enclosed cockpit and single-strut main undercarriage members. These attained a speed of 276 mph (445 km/h), but Army interest had meanwhile transferred to fighters of monoplane configuration and further development of the Type 95 was not pursued. The following data relate to the Type 95-II. *Max speed, 248 mph (400 km/h) at 9,840 ft (3 000 m). Time to 16,405 ft (5 000 m), 5 min. Range, 684 mls (1 100 km). Empty weight, 2,998 lb (1 360 kg). Loaded weight, 3,836 lb (1 740 kg). Span, 32 ft 10½ in (10,02 m). Length, 24 ft 9¼ in (7,55 m). Height, 9 ft 10⅛ in (3,00 m). Wing area, 247.58 sq ft (23,00 m²).*

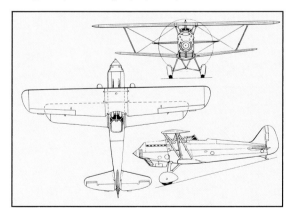

The Ki-10-I (below) and -II (above) equipped most of the Imperial Army's fighter element 1936-40.

KAWASAKI Kɪ-28   Japan

In parallel with the start of series production of the Type 95 biplane, the Imperial Army proposed unoffi-

cially to Kawasaki, Mitsubishi and Nakajima that they should commence studies for new fighters of monoplane configuration. An official requirement for such an aircraft was issued in April 1936, and whereas Mitsubishi and Nakajima opted for radial air-cooled engines, Kawasaki elected to retain a water-cooled inline engine, as used by the company's earlier fighters. Assigned the *Kitai* designation Ki-28 and designed by Takeo Doi, the new fighter was a cantilever low-wing monoplane with split flaps and an aft-sliding semi-canopy for the cockpit. Power was provided by an 850 hp Kawasaki Ha-9-II-Ko water-cooled inline engine and armament consisted of two 7,7-mm synchronised machine guns. Two prototypes of the Ki-28 were completed in November and December 1936, and were subsequently evaluated in competition with the Mitsubishi Ki-33 and Nakajima Ki-27. The Ki-28 was marginally faster than the other contenders and offered better climb, acceleration and altitude performance.

The Ki-28 (above and below) was bested by the Nakajima Ki-27, which had superior manoeuvrability.

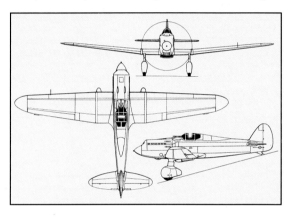

These advantages were offset by poorer manoeuvrability, however, and, in particular, a larger turning radius. Thus, the Ki-28 was rejected by the Army in favour of the Ki-27. No further development of the Ki-28 was undertaken, but this fighter provided Kawasaki with invaluable experience in developing the Ki-60 and Ki-61. *Max speed, 301 mph (485 km/h) at 11,480 ft (3 500 m). Time to 16,405 ft (5 000 m), 5.16 min. Range, 620 mls (1 000 km). Empty weight, 3,130 lb (1 420 kg). Loaded weight, 3,880 lb (1 760 kg). Span, 39 ft 4⅜ in (12,00 m). Length, 25 ft 11 in (7,90 m). Height, 8 ft 6⅓ in (2,60 m). Wing area, 204.52 sq ft (19,00 m²).*

KAWASAKI Kɪ-45   Japan

In December 1937, Kawasaki was ordered to begin work on a twin-engined two-seat fighter which was assigned the *Kitai* designation Ki-45. Stemming from an earlier design study (the Ki-38), the Ki-45 was of all-metal construction with a stressed-skin semi-monocoque fuselage, semi-elliptical wings and a manually retractable undercarriage. It was powered by two Nakajima Ha-20-Otsu nine-cylinder radial engines rated at 820 hp at 11,480 ft (3 500 m). Designed by Takeo Doi, the Ki-45 was armed with a 20-mm cannon and two 7,7-mm machine guns firing forward and a flexibly-mounted 7,7-mm weapon for aft defence. The first of three prototypes was flown in January 1939. Numerous problems were encountered, one of the most serious being excessive engine nacelle drag. In an attempt to reduce this, the third prototype, completed in May 1939, featured close-cowled engines with ducted spinners. This aircraft also featured an electrically-operated undercarriage. Serious engine nacelle stall and disappointing performance led to curtailment

The first prototype Ki-45 (above), and (below) the Ki-45 in the pre-"Phase I Improvement" form.

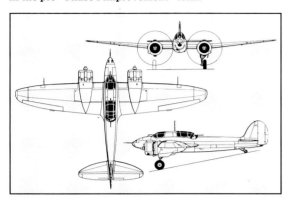

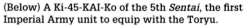

(Above top) Ki-45-KAI-Hei Toryus of 1st *Chutai* and (immediately above) *Shinten* unit of the 53rd *Sentai*.

(Below) A Ki-45-KAI-Ko of the 5th *Sentai*, the first Imperial Army unit to equip with the Toryu.

of work on pre-series aircraft until April 1940. At this time work was resumed and eight further aircraft were built under the so-called "Phase I Performance Improvement" programme. These aircraft were powered by Nakajima Ha-25 14-cylinder radials each offering 1,050 hp and housed by redesigned nacelles, flight testing commencing in July 1940. In the meantime, on his own initiative, Takeo Doi began an aerodynamic reappraisal and a complete structural redesign of the fighter which was to result in an essentially new design. The following data relate to the Ki-45 "Phase I Performance Improvement" aircraft. *Max speed, 323 mph (520 km/h) at 11,485 ft (3 500 m). Empty weight, 6,945 lb (3 150 kg). Loaded weight, 9,700 lb (4 400 kg). Span, 47 ft 6⅞ in (14,50 m). Length, 33 ft 7⅞ in (10,26 m). Height, 11 ft 8½ in (3,57 m). Wing area, 312.16 sq ft (29,00 m²).*

KAWASAKI Kɪ-45-KAI TORYU   Japan

Although possessing little more in common with the original Ki-45 than a similar configuration, Takeo Doi's redesigned fighter retained the original *Kitai* designation with the added suffix KAI (indicating *Kaizo*, or Modified). By comparison with the earlier fighter, the Ki-45-KAI had a reprofiled fuselage of reduced cross section, entirely new tail surfaces, a straight-tapered wing in place of the semi-elliptical planform, increased fuel capacity and heavier armament. The Ha-25 engines were initially retained and the first Ki-45-KAI prototype was completed in May 1941. Two further prototypes and 12 pre-series aircraft followed, all of which were delivered by the end of the year. Satisfactory flight testing led to adoption of the fighter as the Type 2 Two-seat Fighter Model Ko (Ki-45-KAI-Ko), the name

Toryu (Dragon Slayer) later being applied. The initial model carried a fixed forward-firing armament of one 20-mm cannon and two 12,7-mm machine guns, a 7,92-mm gun being provided for rear defence. A variant optimised for ground and anti-shipping attack, the Ki-45-KAI-Otsu, featured revised forward-firing armament which comprised one 20-mm cannon and a hand-loaded 37-mm cannon. Later production of this version switched to the Mitsubishi Ha-102 rated at 1,080 hp for take-off. This engine was standardised by the next

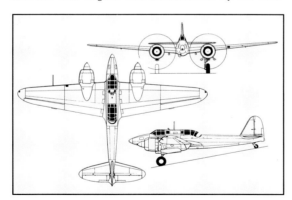

(Above and below) The Ki-45-KAI-Hei, those depicted by the photograph belonging to the 3rd *Chutai* of the 53rd *Sentai* operating from Matsudo, 1945.

model, the Ki-45-KAI-Hei, intended primarily for the nocturnal intercept rôle. This had armament of one forward-firing semi-automatic 37-mm cannon, two 20-mm cannon mounted to fire upward at an oblique angle and a 7,92-mm gun for rear defence. An anti-shipping version, the Ki-45-KAI-Tei, supplemented the forward-firing 37-mm cannon with two 20-mm cannon and also carried two 551-lb (250-kg) bombs. A half-dozen Toryus were each fitted with a hand-loaded 75-mm cannon for the dual bomber intercept/shipping attack rôle. The last Toryu (a Ki-45-KAI-Hei) was completed in July 1945, bringing total production to 1,691 aircraft, excluding prototypes. A proposed further development, the Ki-45-II, evolved into the single-seat Ki-96 (which see). The following data relate to the Ha-102-engined Ki-45-KAI-Hei. *Max speed, 340 mph (547 km/h) at 19,685 ft (6 000 m). Max range, 1,243 mls (2 000 km). Time to 16,405 ft (5 000 m), 6.12 min. Empty weight, 8,146 lb (3 695 kg). Loaded weight, 11,631 lb (5 276 kg). Span, 49 ft 3¼ in (15,00 m). Length, 36 ft 1 in (11,00 m). Height, 12 ft 1¾ in (3,70 m). Wing area, 344.46 sq ft (32,00 m²).*

KAWASAKI Kɪ-60   Japan

To meet a requirement for a heavily-loaded, cannon-armed specialised interceptor fighter, Takeo Doi, assisted by Shin Owada, designed the Ki-60 around the Daimler-Benz DB 601 12-cylinder inline engine. Representing a complete reversal of previous Japanese single-seat fighter design practice in that emphasis was placed on speed rather than manoeuvrability, the

(Below) The experimental Ki-60 interceptor fighter.

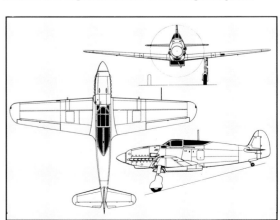

The first Ki-60 prototype (above) which began its flight test programme in March 1941.

Ki-60 was a compact all-metal stressed-skin monoplane with a 1,175 hp DB 601A engine and an armament of two 20-mm cannon and two 12,7-mm machine guns. The first of three prototypes was completed in March 1941, but during test was found to be laterally unstable and to possess dangerous spinning characteristics. Furthermore, its stalling speed was extremely high and its controls excessively heavy. In an attempt to mitigate the more undesirable of these characteristics, the second and third prototypes received a small increase in wing area of 10.55 sq ft (0,98 m²), some minor aerodynamic improvements and a small reduction in normal loaded weight (by replacing the wing-mounted cannon with 12,7-mm machine guns). Only minor improvements resulted and further development of the Ki-60 was abandoned. *Max speed, 348 mph (560 km/h) at 14,765 ft (4 500 m). Time to 16,405 ft (5 000 m), 6.0 min. Empty weight, 4,740 lb (2 150 kg). Loaded weight, 6,063 lb (2 750 kg). Span, 34 ft 5½ in (10,50 m). Length, 27 ft 9½ in (8,47 m). Wing area, 174.38 sq ft (16,20 m²).*

KAWASAKI Kı-61 HIEN   Japan

(Above) A Ki-61-I-Otsu of the 37th *Sentai* at Taipei, Taiwan, early 1945, and (below) a general arangement drawing of the Ki-61-I-KAI-Hei.

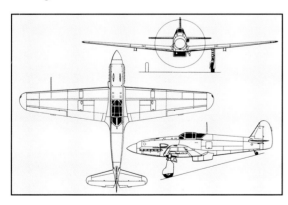

Developed in parallel with the Ki-60 as a somewhat lighter general-purpose fighter, the Ki-61 was similarly conceived by Takeo Doi and Shin Owada. Also designed around the DB 601A engine, which was adopted for licence manufacture by Kawasaki as the Ha-40, the Ki-61 was flown for the first time in December 1941. A total of 12 prototypes was built, series production being initiated as the Type 3 Fighter Model 1, the Model 1-Ko (Ki-61-I-Ko) having an armament of two 12,7-mm and two 7,7-mm guns, and the Model 1-Otsu (Ki-61-I-Otsu) having a quartet of 12,7-mm weapons. Later to be named Hien (Swallow), the Ki-61-I was powered by an Ha-40 engine rated at 1,175 hp for take-off. Three hundred and eighty-eight were either converted in the field or on the assembly line to take 20-mm MG 151 cannon in place of the wing-mounted machine

Key to Kawasaki Ki-61-KAI-Hei

1. Starboard navigation light
2. Wing rib bracing
3. Wing spar
4. Starboard aileron
5. Aileron tab
6. Starboard flap
7. Wing gun access panel
8. Gun port
9. Three-blade constant-speed Sumitomo Hamilton propeller
10. Auxiliary drop tank (43.9 Imp gal/200 l capacity)
11. Propeller boss
12. Propeller reduction gear housing
13. Auxiliary intake
14. Starboard mainwheel
15. Lower cowling quick-release catches
16. Ejector exhaust stubs
17. Anti-vibration mounting pad
18. Engine bearer
19. Upper cowling quick-release catches
20. Kawasaki Ha-40 (Army Type-2) engine
21. Engine accessories
22. Gun port
23. Cannon barrels
24. Firewall
25. Cowling panel line
26. Supercharger
27. Supercharger intake
28. Ammunition tanks
29. Ammunition feed chute
30. Two 20-mm Ho-5 cannon
31. Sloping windscreen
32. Gunsight
33. Control column
34. Pilot's seat (armoured)
35. Fuselage frame
36. Rearward-sliding cockpit canopy
37. Pilot's headrest
38. Rear-vision cut-out
39. Aft glazing
40. Canopy track
41. Spring-loaded handhold
42. Fuselage fuel tank (36.2 Imp gal/165 l capacity)
43. Fuselage equipment access door (upward hinged)
44. Type 99 Hi-3 radio pack
45. Aerial mast
46. Aerial lead-in
47. Aerial
48. Elevator control cables
49. Upper longeron
50. Rudder cable
51. Fuselage join
52. Starboard tailplane
53. Starboard elevator
54. Tailfin root fairing
55. Tailfin structure
56. Rear navigation light (port and starboard)
57. Aerial stub mast
58. Rudder balance
59. Rudder fixed trim tab
60. Rudder post
61. Rudder framework
62. Elevator tab
63. Elevator fixed trim tab
64. Port elevator
65. Elevator control cable
66. Rudder hinge
67. Rear fuselage frame/tailplane attachment
68. Tailwheel retraction jack (later deleted)
69. Tailwheel doors (later deleted)
70. Retractable tailwheel (later replaced by fixed unit)
71. Tailwheel shock absorber oleo
72. Lower longeron
73. Radiator bath air outlet
74. Adjustable gill
75. Radiator
76. Radiator intake ducting
77. Radiator air intake
78. Main spar/fuselage attachment point
79. Inboard mainwheel doors
80. Mainwheel well
81. Landing light
82. Mainwheel pivot point
83. Mainwheel leg
84. Oleo shock absorber section (leather-sleeved)
85. Mainwheel single fork
86. Port mainwheel
87. Mainwheel door
88. Separate mainwheel fairing
89. Gun port
90. Machine gun barrel
91. Wing-mounted 12,7-mm Ho-103 machine gun
92. Gun access panel
93. Bomb/tank shackle
94. Port flap
95. Main spar
96. Wing ribs
97. Auxiliary drop tank (43.9 Imp gal/200 l)
98. Pitot head
99. Metal wing skin
100. Aileron tab
101. Port aileron
102. Wingtip structure
103. Port navigation light

(Above top) A Ki-61-I-Otsu of 3rd *Chutai*, 59th *Sentai*, at Ashiya, northern Kyushu, August 1945.

(Immediately above) A Ki-61-I-KAI-Hei of the 23rd Independent *Chutai*, Yontan, Okinawa, April 1945.

guns. The -Ko and -Otsu models were supplanted in production by the Ki-61-I-KAI-Hei with twin fuselage-mounted 20-mm cannon, strengthened wings and modified rear fuselage. A further development of the basic design, the Ki-61-II, featured an Ha-140 engine rated at 1,500 hp for take-off. Flown in prototype form in December 1943, the Ki-61-II employed a new wing of increased (10 per cent) area and some structural revision. Eight prototypes were followed by the Ki-61-II-KAI which reverted to the standard wing and entered production in both -Ko (12,7-mm wing guns) and -Otsu

(20-mm wing cannon) versions. Production being inhibited by shortages of Ha-140s, only 129 Ki-61-II-KAI fighters (including prototypes) were delivered, following 1,380 Ki-61-Is and 1,274 Ki-61-I-KAIs. The following data relate to the Ki-61-I-KAI-Hei. *Max speed, 360 mph (580 km/h) at 16,405 ft (5 000 m). Time to 16,405 ft (5 000 m), 7,0 min. Normal range, 360 mls (580 km). Empty weight, 5,798 lb (2 630 kg). Loaded weight, 7,650 lb (3 470 kg). Span, 39 ft 4½ in (12,00 m). Length, 29 ft 2¾ in (8,94 m). Height, 12 ft 1¾ in (3,70 m). Wing area, 215.28 sq ft (20,00 m²).*

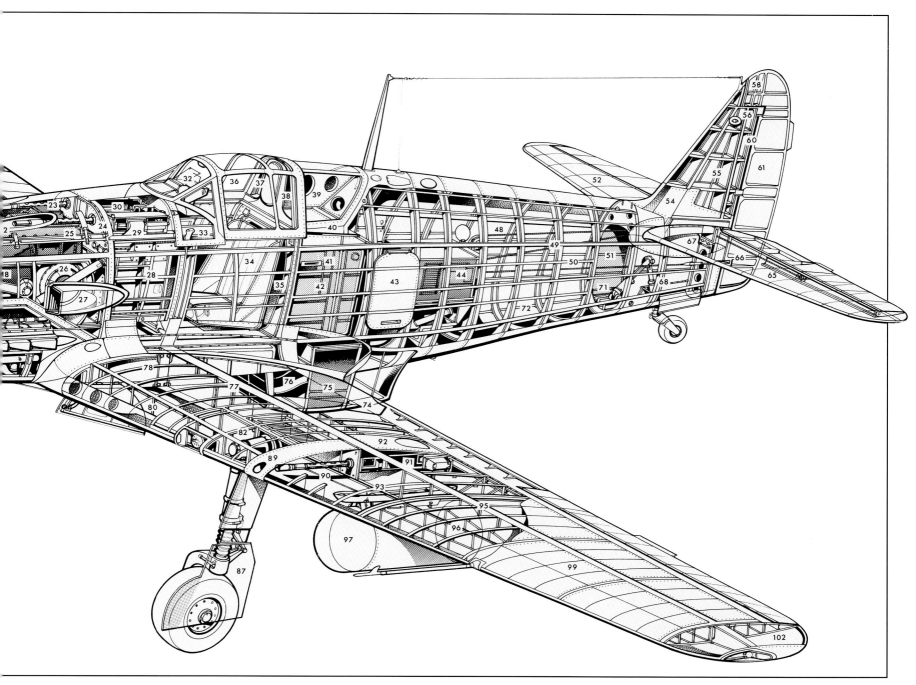

A Ki-61-I-Otsu (above) flown by Maj Kobayashi, CO of the 244th *Sentai* during the winter of 1944-45.

(Below) The sole prototype of the Ki-64 seen here during its initial take-off in December 1943.

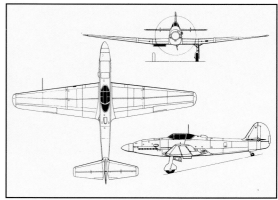

(Above) The Ki-64 centreline-thrust fighter.

KAWASAKI Kɪ-64   Japan

Unorthodox in that it was of centreline thrust concept – with two engines both delivering their thrust along the centreline of the aircraft – the Ki-64 was powered by a Kawasaki Ha-201 power plant comprising tandem-mounted Ha-40 engines. These offered a combined take-off rating of 2,350 hp and drove contra-rotating propellers. This unusual arrangement was combined with a steam vapour cooling system, the cooling sur-

faces occupying three-sevenths of the gross wing area. A single-seat all-metal semi-monocoque monoplane

with a proposed armament of four 20-mm cannon, or two cannon and two 12,7-mm machine guns, the proto-type Ki-64 was completed in November 1943. During the fifth flight, a fire developed in the rear engine bay, necessitating an emergency landing, and the damage was still unrepaired when, in mid-1944, it was decided to suspend further work on the Ki-64. The following performance data are manufacturer's estimates. *Max speed, 435 mph (700 km/h) at 13,125 ft (4 000 m). Time to 16,405 ft (5 000 m), 5.5 min. Range, 310 mls (500 km). Empty weight, 8,929 lb (4 050 kg). Loaded weight, 11,244 lb (5 100 kg). Span, 44 ft 3½ in (13,50 m). Length,*

The Ki-64 (above) featured tandem engines, surface evaporation cooling and contraprops.

36 ft 2¼ in (11,03 m). Height, 13 ft 11¼ in (4,25 m). Wing area, 301.39 sq ft (28,00 m²).

KAWASAKI Kɪ-96   Japan

Initiated as the Ki-45-II and intended as a successor to the two-seat *Toryu*, the Ki-96 was to emerge as a *single*-seat heavy fighter. Three prototypes of the Ki-45-II had been under construction when, in December 1942, requirements were revised, the second crew member no longer being wanted and the designation being changed to Ki-96. Whereas the first prototype, completed in September 1943, merely had the second cockpit faired over, two further prototypes were completed as single-seaters from the outset. In the event, the Imperial Army lost interest in single-seat twin-engined fighters, but authorisation was given to continue development of the basic design as a two-seater and this was eventually to result in the Ki-102. The Ki-96 was powered by two Mitsubishi Ha-112-II radials rated at 1,500 hp for take-off and carried an armament of one 37-mm and two 20-mm cannon. *Max speed, 391 mph (630 km/h) at 31,170 ft (9 500 m). Time to 16,405 ft (5 000 m), 6.0 min. Max range, 373 mls (600 km). Empty weight, 10,031 lb (4 550 kg). Loaded weight, 13,228 lb (6 000 kg). Span, 51 ft 1 in (15,57 m). Length, 37 ft 6¾ in (11,45 m). Height, 12 ft 1⅝ in (3,70 m). Wing area, 365.98 sq ft (34,00 m²).*

The general arrangement drawing (below) represents the second and the photo (above) the third Ki-96.

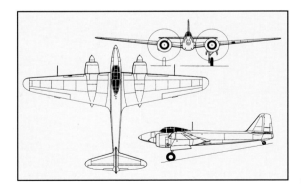

KAWASAKI Kɪ-100   Japan

Kawasaki's design team headed by Takeo Doi had evolved an excellent high-altitude interceptor fighter as the Ki-61-II-KAI, but, by the late autumn of 1944, a shortage of the Ha-140 liquid-cooled inline engine was resulting in substantial numbers of engineless airframes being held in storage. The airframe was, therefore, mated with the Mitsubishi Ha-112-II air-cooled radial affording 1,500 hp for take-off, and the first of three prototype conversions was flown on 1 February 1945 under the designation Ki-100. Authorisation was promptly given to complete all existing engineless

(Above) Ki-100-I-Ko fighters of the 59th *Sentai* at Omura airfield, Kyushu, in the summer of 1945.

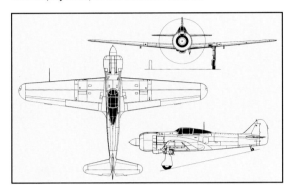

(Above and below) The Ki-100-I-Otsu, that shown by the photo belonging to the 5th *Sentai* in May 1945.

Ki-61-II-KAI airframes with this power plant as the Type 5 Fighter Model 1-Ko (Ki-100-I-Ko). Armament remained unchanged and comprised two 20-mm cannon and two 12,7-mm machine guns. With the termination of Ki-61-II-KAI production, a new-build version of the Type 5 replaced it on the line. This, the Ki-100-I-Otsu, differed from the -Ko conversion in having a cut-down rear fuselage with all-round vision cockpit canopy. A development, the Ki-100-II fitted with an Ru-102 turbo-supercharger, was flown as a prototype in May 1945, two further prototypes of this version being completed and tested. Production of the Ki-100 totalled 389 aircraft – 271 of the -Ko version and 118 of the -Otsu model. Pre-

parations for series production of the Ki-100-II were in hand when hostilities ceased. The following data relate to the Ki-100-I-Otsu. *Max speed, 360 mph (580 km/h) at 19,685 ft (6 000 m). Time to 16,405 ft (5 000 m), 6.0 min. Range (internal fuel), 870 mls (1 400 km). Empty weight, 5,567 lb (2 525 kg). Loaded weight, 7,705 lb (3 495 kg). Span, 39 ft 4½ in (12,00 m). Length, 29 ft 3⅛ in (8,92 m). Height, 12 ft 3⅝ in (3,75 m). Wing area, 215.28 sq ft (20,00 m²).*

KAWASAKI Kɪ-102   Japan

Retaining the basic structure and engines of the Ki-96, but reverting to a cockpit arrangement similar to that originally proposed for the Ki-45-II, the Ki-102 was offered in two versions. These were the Ki-102-Ko high-

A Ki-102-Otsu (below) with the 3rd Operational Test and Training *Chutai* at Fussa early in 1945.

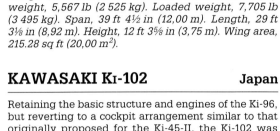

altitude interceptor with Ru-102 turbo-superchargers and an armament of one 37-mm and two 20-mm cannon, and the Ki-102-Otsu ground attack fighter without turbo-superchargers and with a 57-mm cannon replacing the 37-mm weapon. The first Ki-102 prototype was completed and flown in March 1944, powered by two 1,500 hp Mitsubishi Ha-112-II radials. This aircraft, like the two additional prototypes and 20 pre-series aircraft, was intended for the Ki-102-Otsu development programme, but, in the event, priorities were changed and six of the pre-series airframes were allocated as prototypes for the Ki-102-Ko, the first of these being flown in June 1944. Production deliveries of

(Immediately below) A Ki-100-I-Ko of the 3rd *Chutai*, 59th *Sentai* at Ashiya, Kyushu, and (bottom) a Ki-100-I-Otsu of the 5th *Sentai*, Kiyosu, Nagoya.

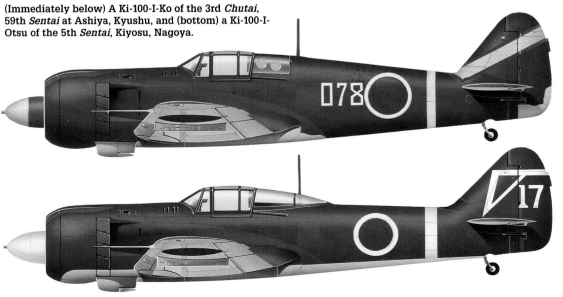

(Above) The Ki-102-Otsu ground attack fighter, and (below) the Ki-102-Ko high-altitude interceptor.

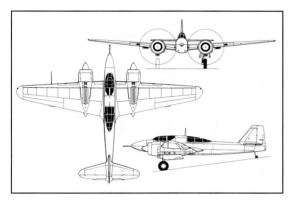

the Ki-102-Otsu began in October 1944 as the Type 4 Assault Aircraft, but because of difficulties with the Ru-102 turbo-superchargers, series production of the Ki-102-Ko was delayed and only six pre-series Ki-102-Ko fighters were completed, with a further 20 being modified to -Ko standards from Ki-102-Otsu airframes. Two other -Otsu aircraft were modified as prototypes of the Ki-102-Hei which had similar Ha-112-II-Ru engines to the -Ko, but featured a longer-span wing, a lengthened fuselage, redesigned tail surfaces, a relocated second cockpit and a pair of 30-mm cannon. However, the Ki-102-Hei did not achieve flight test status before hostilities came to an end in 1945. A total of 215 of the Ki-102-Otsu model was completed. The following data relate to the Ki-102-Ko. *Max speed, 360 mph (580 km/h) at 19,685 ft (6 000 m). Time to 16,405 ft (5 000 m), 8.7 min. Range (internal fuel), 994 mls (1 600 km). Empty weight, 11,354 lb (5 150 kg). Loaded weight, 15,763 lb (7 150 kg). Span, 51 ft 1 in (15,57 m). Length, 37 ft 6⅞ in (11,45 m). Height, 12 ft 1 in (3,70 m). Wing area, 430.57 sq ft (40,00 m²).*

KAWASAKI Kɪ-108   Japan

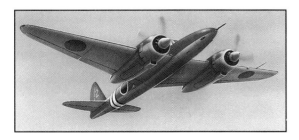

An artist's impression (above) of the definitive Ki-108 prototype, which is also illustrated below.

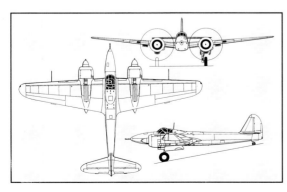

Intended to meet a requirement for a specialised heavy interceptor fighter capable of operating at extreme altitudes, the Ki-108 was a derivative of the two-seat Ki-102, the seventh and eighth pre-series Ki-102 airframes being employed as prototypes. Apart from the structure surrounding a single-seat pressure cabin, the airframe of the Ki-108 was fundamentally similar to that of the Ki-102, as was also the armament of one 37-mm and two 20-mm cannon. Power was provided by two turbo-supercharged Mitsubishi Ha-112-II-Ru radial engines of 1,500 hp. Flight testing of the Ki-108 commenced in July 1944 without the turbo-superchargers fitted. By late 1944, changes being introduced on the Ki-102-Hei (eg, longer-span wing, lengthened aft fuselage) were also being applied to the Ki-108, and two further prototypes were built, these being designated Ki-108-KAI. The first of these was completed in March 1945, but flight testing was incomplete when the Pacific War ended. *Max speed, 385 mph (620 km/h) at 32,800 ft (10 000 m). Time to 16,405 ft (5 000 m), 9.0 min. Range, 994 mls (1 600 km). Empty weight, 11,685 lb (5 300 kg). Loaded weight, 15,873 lb (7 200 kg). Span, 51 ft 4⅞ in (15,67 m). Length, 38 ft 5 in (11,71 m). Height, 12 ft 1 in (3,70 m). Wing area, 365.98 sq ft (34,00 m²).*

KAZYANENKO No 5   Russia

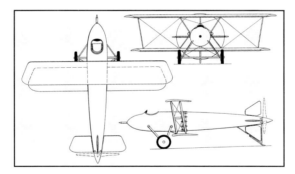

(Above) The highly original Kazyanenko No 5.

A highly original single-seat fighter was designed at the Kiev Polytechnic Institute in 1917 by three brothers, Yevgeny, Ivan and Andrei Kazyanenko. Built in the Institute workshops and referred to as the No 5, the fighter was a single-bay biplane and the angle of the mainplanes was adjustable relative to the centre struts. The 100 hp Gnome Monosoupape rotary engine was mounted over the cg in the plywood monocoque fuselage, driving a three-bladed pusher propeller mounted behind a cruciform tail. The pilot was seated in the nose of the aircraft and was provided with a single machine gun. Flight testing was initiated at the end of June 1917, but, on 1 July, the tailskid broke during landing, resulting in serious damage to the propeller, the tail assembly and the extension shaft. It would seem that further development was abandoned. *Span, 23 ft 9½ in (7,25 m). Length, 22 ft 10 in (6,96 m).*

KJELLER FF 6 (T.2)   Norway

Acquisition from Spain of five 150 hp Hispano-Suiza eight-cylinder Vee-type engines prompted the Norwegian Army Flying-Service (*Haerens Flyvevaesen*) to order the design of a single-seat fighter around this power plant. Design was begun by Ing Hellesen at the Kjeller Flyfabrikk in the autumn of 1919, by which time the requirement had changed to that of a two-seat

fighter-reconnaissance aircraft. Of wooden construction with a plywood monocoque fuselage and designated FF 6 by the factory and T.2 by the Army, the prototype was flown in 1921. It immediately displayed unacceptable characteristics which were exacerbated by the fact that the Hispano-Suiza engine was found to develop only 103 hp. A max speed of only 62 mph (100 km/h) was attained compared with an anticipated maximum of 82 mph (132 km/h). Further development was therefore abandoned after the first test flight. *Span, 38 ft 6⅔ in (11,75 m). Length, 23 ft 9½ in (7,25 m). Height, 11 ft 8½ in (3,57 m).*

The FF 6 (below) was conceived as a single-seater, but redesigned as a two-seat reconnaissance fighter.

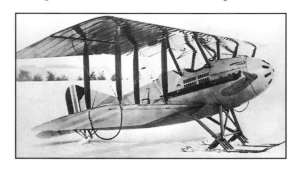

KNOLLER 70.01   Austria-Hungary

The K.u.k.Fliegerarsenal Fischamend began construction during 1917 of two single-seat fighter prototypes, the 70.01 and 70.02, to the designs of Prof Richard Knoller. A single-bay unstaggered biplane of wooden construction powered by a 230 hp Hiero water-cooled six-cylinder inline engine, the Knoller fighter featured a flexible wing section intended to reduce drag by flattening with increased speed. Intended armament comprised two synchronised 8-mm Schwarzlose machine guns. Initially fitted with wing warping, the 70.01 flew for the first time on 23 November 1917, but suffered damage during a ground manoeuvre within a few days. During repairs at the Fliegerarsenal, the prototype was fitted with ailerons on the upper wing. From March until 20 June 1918, when it was damaged in a landing accident, it underwent official testing at Aspern. Having higher priority activities, the Fliegerarsenal transferred the tasks of repairing the 70.01 and completing the 70.02 to the Flugzeug Reparatur und Bau Anstalt (Fruba) in Vienna. The 70.01 was subjected to load testing in August 1918, and the 70.02, completed in

The Knoller 70.01 (above and below) as originally flown in November 1917 with wing warping control.

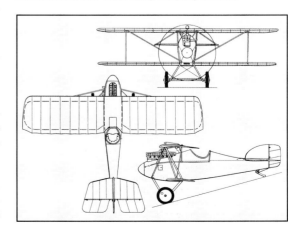

September, was intended to continue the flight test programme, which, if successful, was to have resulted in an order (to be fulfilled by Fruba) for 10 pre-series aircraft. The end of hostilities was accompanied by discontinuation of the fighter development programme. *Max speed (estimated), 149 mph (240 km/h). Span, 26 ft 3 in (8,00 m). Length, 20 ft 10 in (6,35 m). Height, 9 ft 4⅕ in (2,85 m).*

KOCHERIGIN DI-6 — USSR

Designed at the TsKB (*Tsentralny Konstruktorskoye Byuro*) by Sergei A Kocherigin and Vladimir P Yatsenko, the DI-6 two-seat fighter commenced flight trials early in 1935 as the TsKB-11. Of mixed construction with an all-metal fuselage and wooden wings, all but the forward fuselage being fabric covered, the DI-6 was an unequal-span single-bay staggered biplane with manually-retractable main undercarriage members.

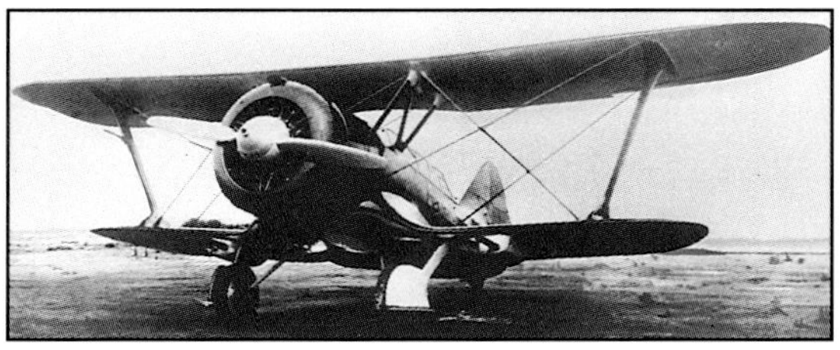

(Above) Second prototype DI-6 with low tailplane, and (below) the DI-6 in production configuration.

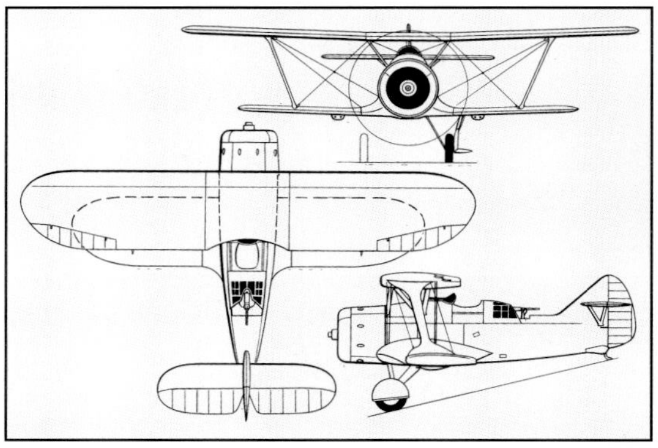

Armament comprised two fixed forward-firing 7,62-mm machine guns and a similar weapon on a flexible mounting for the gunner. The two prototypes were powered by the 710 hp Wright Cyclone SR-1820-F-3 radial. After the successful completion of State Acceptance Trials between 27 May and 21 November 1935, the fighter was ordered into production with the 700 hp M-25 engine, a licence-built version of the Cyclone. Deliveries to the V-VS commenced in the late spring of 1937. Only one regiment was issued with the DI-6 for use in the fighter rôle, this seeing action in the summer of 1939 against the Japanese on the Manchukuoan-Mongolian border. The aircraft had meanwhile been relegated to the assault, or *shturmovik*, rôle, limited production for this task being undertaken as the DI-6Sh. *Max speed, 231 mph (372 km/h) at 9,840 ft (3 000 m). Time to 16,405 ft (5 000 m), 10.0 min. Range, 342 mls (550 km). Empty weight, 3,102 lb (1 407 kg). Loaded weight, 4,380 lb (1 987 kg). Span, 32 ft 9½ in (10,00 m). Length, 22 ft 11½ in (7,00 m). Height (tail up), 10 ft 6 in (3,20 m). Wing area, 270.72 sq ft (25,15 m^2).*

KONDOR DREIDECKER — Germany

In the summer of 1917, the Kondor Flugzeugwerke of Essen was joined by Walter Rethel and Paul G Ehrhardt, formerly with LVG, to initiate a series of original designs. The company had previously been concerned primarily with licence manufacture of the Albatros B II and B IIa. The first original design produced by Rethel and Ehrhardt was a single-seat fighter triplane (*dreidecker*) which entered flight test in October 1917. Initial trials with an unrecorded engine type evidently revealed performance shortcomings as an *Idflieg* report of the same month refers to the aircraft being re-engined by Kondor with a geared six-cylinder water-cooled Mercedes D III of 160 hp. Testing of the triplane fighter was terminated as a result of severe vibration problems, the fuselage, lower wing assembly and tail subsequently being utilised by the D 7 biplane. No illustrations or data relating to the Kondor triplane have survived.

KONDOR D 1 — Germany

Designed by Rethel and Ehrhardt in parallel with the triplane,the D 1 single-seat fighter was an unequal-span single-bay staggered biplane powered by a 100 hp Gnome-Monosoupape rotary engine. Following Albatros practice in having a single-spar lower wing with V-type interplane strutting, the D 1 was dubbed unofficially and somewhat scathingly as the *Kondorlaus* and was extensively test flown by Ehrhardt. Intended armament comprised two synchronised LMG 08/15 machine guns with 500 rounds. Flight testing was initiated in the late autumn of 1917, but performance proved disappointing, this possibly being the cause of the prototype's unofficial appellation. In the spring of 1918, when Ehrhardt left the Kondor Flugzeugwerke for health reasons, redesign of the aircraft was undertaken by Walter Rethel as the D 2. *Empty weight, 855 lb (388 kg). Loaded weight, 1,252 lb (568 kg). Span, 24 ft 11¼ in (7,60 m). Length, 15 ft 10⅞ in (4,85 m). Height, 7 ft 10½ in (2,40 m). Wing area, 143.7 sq ft (13,35 m^2).*

The Kondor D 1 (below), which, flown late autumn 1917, was unofficially known as the *Kondorlaus*.

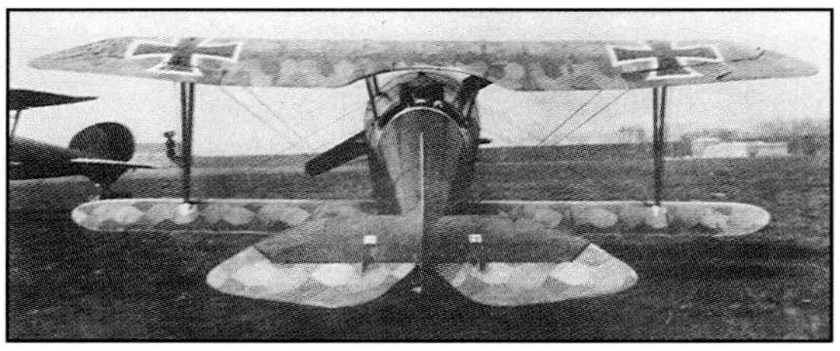

KONDOR D 2 — Germany

The D 2 single-seat fighter was essentially similar to the D 1, but changes included a two-spar lower wing with parallel interplane bracing struts. Power was provided by a 110 hp Oberursel Ur II rotary engine and armament comprised two synchronised LMG 08/15 machine guns. The D 2 was first flown in May 1918, and two examples participated in the second D-type contest held at Adlershof in June 1918. These were temporarily referred to for convenience as the D I (w/n 200) and D II (w/n 201), one having ailerons on all four wings and one apparently having ailerons on the upper wings only. Oblt Herman Göring, in his report on the potential of these Kondor fighters, gave his opinion that they were "very fine in regard to flight characteristics, but not worthy of further consideration owing to their poor performance". No further development of the D 2 was undertaken. *Max speed, 109 mph (175 km/h). Time to 9,840 ft (3 000 m), 10.4 min. Endurance, 1.5 hrs. Empty weight, 838 lb (380 kg). Loaded weight, 1,235 lb (560 kg). Span, 24 ft 10⅘ in (7,59 m). Length, 15 ft 11¾ in (4,87 m). Height, 7 ft 10$\frac{9}{10}$ in (2,41 m). Wing area, 143.59 sq ft (13,34 m^2).*

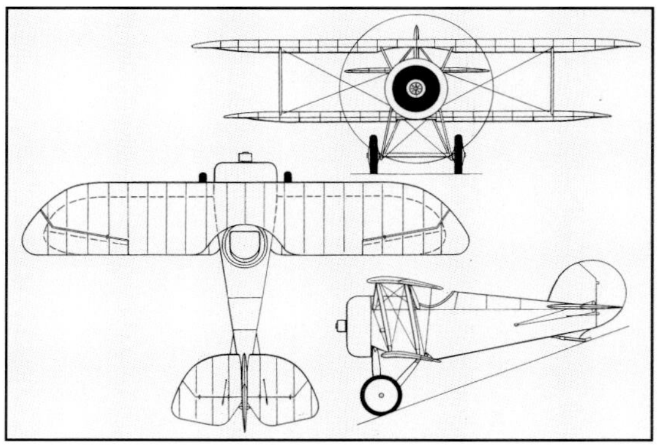

The Kondor D 2 (above and below) participated in the second D-type contest at Adlershof in June 1918.

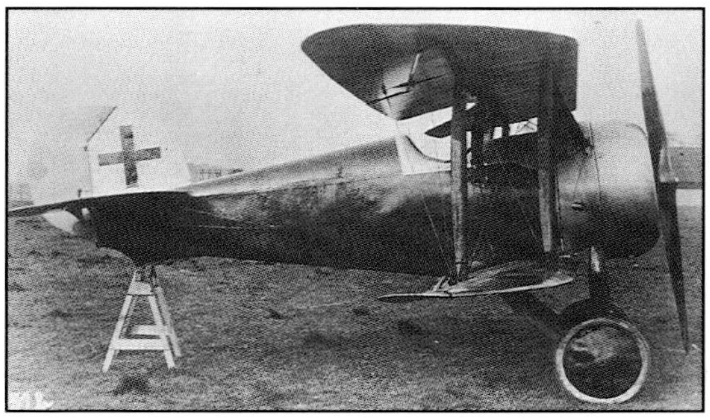

KONDOR D 6 — Germany

Developed by Walter Rethel in the summer of 1918, and powered by a 145 hp Oberursel Ur III rotary engine, the D 6 represented an attempt to provide maximum forward and upward visibility for the pilot. Like preceding Kondor fighters, the D 6 had a steel-tube fuselage, but this was fabric- rather than plywood-covered. The normal upper wing centre section was completely deleted, a tripod of struts, each strut of differing length, bracing

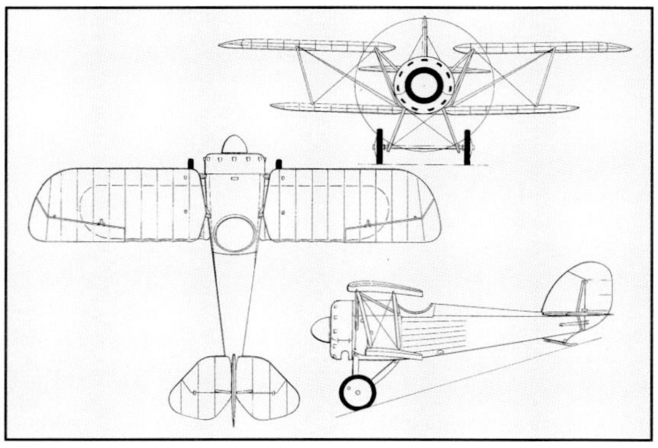

The D 6 (above and below) was innovative in its approach to improving forward and upward visibility.

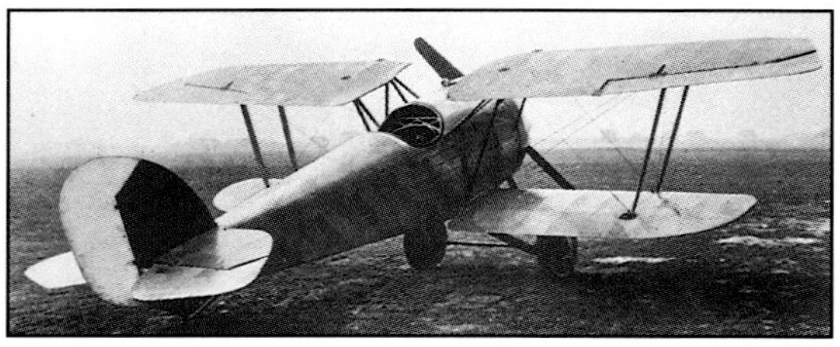

the upper wing halves to the fuselage. Armament consisted of the usual pair of synchronised LMG 08/15 machine guns of 7,9-mm calibre. Although some flight testing was conducted during the summer of 1918, the curious upper wing arrangement had its shortcomings, including dubious structural integrity. The induced tip drag was twice that of a normal wing, and the D 6 never appeared in the monthly *Idflieg* reports, development apparently being discontinued at an early stage. *Max speed, 106 mph (170 km/h). Endurance, 1.5 hrs. Empty weight, 926 lb (420 kg). Loaded weight, 1,422 lb (645 kg). Span, 27 ft 0⅘ in (8,25 m). Length, 19 ft 0⅓ in (5,80 m). Height, 8 ft 3½ in (2,53 m). Wing area, 148.54 sq ft (13,80 m^2).*

KONDOR D 7 — Germany

The D 7 single-seat fighter was essentially a re-work of the original Kondor triplane fighter as a biplane, retaining the plywood-covered steel tube fuselage, tail and lower wing. The bracing of the wing cellule was novel, the interplane struts taking the form of inverted tripods, and the fuselage was mounted *between* the wings, the lower wing being braced to the robust undercarriage rather than directly to the fuselage. The initial flight tests of the D 7 are unrecorded, but an *Idflieg* report stated that the D 7 had *now* been fitted with a standard 160 hp Mercedes D III engine with which it was expected to resume flight testing in early

The D 7 (above) was a biplane rework of the earlier Kondor fighting triplane flown in October 1917.

May 1918. The D 7 did not make an appearance at the second D-type contest in June 1918, development having apparently been discontinued meanwhile. *Max speed, 112 mph (180 km/h). Endurance, 1.45 hrs. Empty weight, 1,300 lb (590 kg). Loaded weight, 1,731 lb (785 kg). Span, 27 ft 10⅔ in (8,50 m). Length, 20 ft 4 in (6,20 m). Height, 7 ft 6½ in (2,30 m). Wing area, 169 sq ft (15,70 m²).*

KONDOR E 3 (D I)   Germany

In July 1918, Walter Rethel initiated design of a single-seat parasol-wing fighter monoplane patterned on the Fokker E V (D VIII) and designated E 3 by the Kondor Flugzeugwerke. A unique cantilever wing construction was devised for the new fighter and patented by Kondor. This consisted of thin veneer sheets laid chordwise across the wing between protruding ribs to which the veneer was attached with opposing L-shaped strips. This wing structure was exceptionally robust and, according to Kondor, the protruding ribs resulted in improved aerodynamic characteristics. Powered by a 160 hp Oberursel Ur III rotary, the E 3 was sent to Adlershof for type test in September 1918, and participated in the Third D-type contest held in the following month. The E 3 was reported as having excellent flying characteristics only marginally inferior to those of the Siemens-Schuckert D IV, and its wing did not oscillate at high speeds as did that of the Fokker D VIII. Hptm Eduard Ritter von Schleich, CO of *Jagdgeschwader* 4, regarded the E 3 as the best fighter of the competition. A second E 3 (referred to by Kondor as the E 3a) was built with a new 160 hp Goebel Goe III rotary engine, this having a full cowling rather than the cutaway

(Above) The Goe III-powered E 3a and (below) the fundamentally similar Ur III-powered E 3.

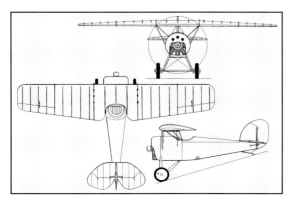

horseshoe-type cowling partly enclosing the Ur III rotary. This version had a max speed of 124 mph (200 km/h) and attained an altitude of 16,405 ft (5 000 m) in 11 min. The Kondor parasol was assigned the official designation of D I, but it is not known with certainty how many were built, although it is believed that 100 fighters of this type were ordered and some 8-10 completed. After World War I, a single E 3a was acquired by the Swiss Comte, Mittelholzer concern for aerobatic displays, two others being procured by the Dutch NAVO firm early in 1920. *Max speed, 118 mph (190 km/h). Time to 16,405 ft (5 000 m), 16.0 min. Ceiling, 20,275 ft (6 180 m). Empty weight, 1,014 lb (460 kg). Loaded weight, 1,411 lb (640 kg). Span, 29 ft 6⅓ in (9,00 m). Length, 18 ft 0½ in (5,50 m). Height, 9 ft 0¼ in (2,75 m). Wing area, 137.24 sq ft (12,75 m²).*

KOOLHOVEN F.K.52   Netherlands

(Above) Second prototype F.K.52 in service with the Finnish LeLv 6, and (below) series production model.

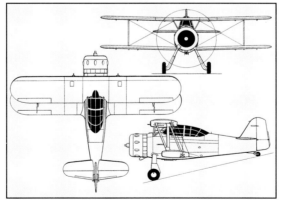

Built by N.V. Koolhoven Vliegtuigen (formed after the failure of the NVI, or Nationale Vliegtuig Industrie), the F.K.52 was designed as both a two-seat escort fighter and as a general-purpose successor to the Fokker C VD. An equi-span single-bay biplane with plywood-covered wooden wings and a fabric-covered steel-tube fuselage, the F.K.52 was first flown on 9 February 1937, crashing six months later, on 11 August. A second prototype, representative of the intended production standard, flew on 6 May 1938, this being powered by a Bristol Mercury VIII affording 840 hp at 14,000 ft (4 265 m). It had provision for two drum-fed 20-mm cannon in the upper wing and a single machine gun on a flexible mounting in the rear cockpit. Four series air-

craft were built, and, although the *Luchtvaart Afdeling* was initially disinclined to accept the F.K.52, interest revived towards the end of 1939, and 36 aircraft were ordered, these incorporating various modifications. Production had just started when the Netherlands were occupied in 1940. The second prototype and one of the four series F.K.52s had meanwhile been purchased by Count C G von Rosen and presented to the Finnish Air Force. The remaining three aircraft were destroyed in crates during the German attack on the Koolhoven factory. *Max speed, 236 mph (380 km/h) at 15,600 ft (4 750 m). Cruising speed, 204 mph (328 km/h). Initial climb, 1,970 ft/min (10 m/sec). Range, 702 mls (1 130 km). Empty weight, 3,638 lb (1 650 kg). Loaded weight, 5,511 lb (2 500 kg). Span, 32 ft 1 in (9,80 m). Length, 24 ft 3 in (8,30 m). Height, 10 ft 10 in (3,30 m). Wing area, 305.7 sq ft (28,40 m²).*

KOOLHOVEN F.K.55   Netherlands

The F.K.55 (above) with fixed undercarriage as flown, and (below) with planned retractable gear.

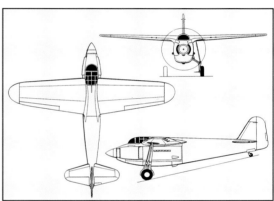

The F.K.55 single-seat fighter was of radical design in that its Lorraine Pétrel 12Hars 12-cylinder Vee liquid-cooled engine was installed immediately behind the pilot over the cg and drove contra-rotating two-bladed propellers via an extension shaft and Duplex reduction gear. Initially, it was proposed to dispense with conventional ailerons in favour of "slot-spoilers" for lateral control, but, in the event, conventional ailerons were adopted for the prototype. The F.K.55 was of mixed construction, the forward and centre fuselage sections being of welded steel tube and the aft section of wood, and the wings were of wooden construction. The Pétrel engine afforded 860 hp for take-off. It was proposed to install a supercharged Lorraine Sterna engine offering 1,200 hp for take-off in the production version. The initial flight took place on 30 June 1938, the aircraft remaining airborne for two minutes and no further flight testing being attempted. The F.K.55 was intended to carry an armament of one 20-mm cannon firing through the propeller and four wing-mounted 7,7-mm machine guns. The following performance data are those estimated by the manufacturer. *Max speed, 317 mph (510 km/h) at 11,810 ft (3 600 m). Cruising speed, 280 mph (450 km/h). Initial climb, 2,580 ft/min (13,1 m/sec). Range, 528 mls (850 km). Empty weight, 3,527 lb (1 600 kg). Loaded weight, 5,026 lb (2 280 kg). Span, 31 ft 6 in (9,60 m). Length, 30 ft 4 in (9,25 m). Height, 8 ft 6 in (2,60 m). Wing area, 172.23 sq ft (16,00 m²).*

KOOLHOVEN F.K.58   Netherlands

Evolved specifically to meet a French requirement, the F.K.58 single-seat fighter, designed by Dr Erich Schatzki, was created within barely three months and flew for the first time on 17 July 1938. A second proto-

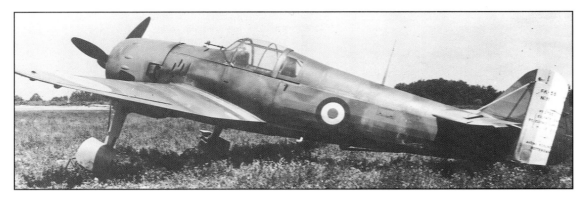

(Above) This F.K.58, newly delivered to the *Armée de l'Air*, was the eleventh production example.

type followed, and production was launched before, in January 1939, an order was placed by France for 50 F.K.58 fighters powered by the Gnome-Rhône 14N-39 engine rated at 1,036 hp at 16,405 ft (5 000 m) and armed with four 7,5-mm FN-Browning Mle 38 machine guns. Both the second prototype and the first *production* fighter were completed on 27 January 1939. These and the next three production examples were fitted with the Hispano-Suiza 14AA engine, all subsequent aircraft having the Gnome-Rhône. The F.K.58 was of standard Koolhoven construction, with plywood-covered wooden wings and a welded steel tube fuselage with duralumin and fabric covering. Interest in the F.K.58 was meanwhile being shown by the *Luchtvaart Afdeling*, and Koolhoven arranged with the Belgian SABCA concern to sub-contract some of the future F.K.58 production, commencing with 10 of the French contract aircraft. In the event, the French government was unable to furnish SABCA with the necessary engines, and the Belgian-built airframes were scrapped after the occupation of the country by the *Wehrmacht*. On 22 July 1939, an order was placed by the *Luchtvaart Afdeling* for 36 F.K.58s powered by the 1,080 hp Bristol Taurus III engine, the first Gnome-Rhône-engined production aircraft having meanwhile flown on 26 June. Thirteen were delivered to France before the start of World War II, prior to which the remaining 23 aircraft also being built by the parent company against the French contract and in various stages of assembly were shipped to Le Havre. From there they were transported to Nevers where it was proposed that they be completed. Only one F.K.58 was in fact finished at Nevers, and those under construction for the *Luchtvaart Afdeling* were destroyed by bombing before completion at the Koolhoven factory. *Max speed, 295 mph (475 km/h) at 16,405 ft (5 000 m). Initial climb, 2,756 ft/min (14 m/sec). Loaded weight, 6,063 lb (2 750 kg). Span, 35 ft 11⅞ in (10,97 m). Length, 28 ft 5¾ in (8,68 m). Wing area, 186.22 sq ft (17,30 m²).*

(Above) The first GR-powered F.K.58, and (below) the production F.K.58 with definitive engine cowl.

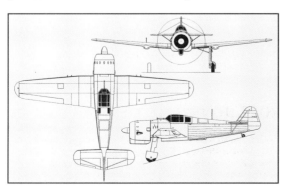

KORVIN MK-1 RYBKA   USSR

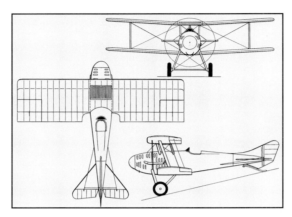

The MK-1 Rybka is illustrated (above) with wheel undercarriage and (below) in floatplane form.

The MK-1 Rybka (Little Fish) single-seat single-bay fighter biplane was built by V L Korvin at the Taganrog aircraft factory to meet a specification drawn up by the *Upravlyeniye VVS* (Air Force Command) in the autumn of 1920. This called for a fighter floatplane powered by a 200 hp Hispano-Suiza water-cooled engine. The design of the MK-1 was undertaken by N G Mikhelson, work being initiated on 1 May 1921. Construction was eventually transferred to the *Krassny Lyotchik* (Red Airman) factory at Petrograd where the prototype was completed in the spring of 1923. During initial hydrodynamic trials the twin floats were found to be too small and had to be lengthened before testing could continue. In the event, the MK-1 was not flown off water, Mikhelson modifying the aircraft to take either

Fitted with skis, the MK-1 Rybka (below) was flown successfully, but no series production ensued.

skis or wheels. It was initially test flown with the former in the winter of 1923-24. The MK-1 was of all-wood construction, interesting features being the monocoque fuselage of birch strips glued together and the location of the radiator in the upper wing centre section. Although flight testing of the MK-1 was successful, the UVVS concluded that fighters with a 200 hp engine were *passé* and no production orders were placed. *Max speed, 118 mph (190 km/h) at sea level, 106 mph (171 km/h) at 3,280 ft (1 000 m). Span, 23 ft 7½ in (7,20 m). Length, 21 ft 7⅘ in (6,59 m). Height (with floats), 9 ft 10 in (3,00 m). Wing area, 231.43 sq ft (21.50 m²).*

KYUSHU J7W1 SHINDEN   Japan

One of the few types of piston-engined single-seat fighters of canard configuration to be built and flown (others being the SAI Ambrosini S.S.4 and the Curtiss XP-55 Ascender), and the only one to be ordered into series production (albeit before the initiation of flight test), the J7W1 Shinden (Magnificent Lightning) was designed by a team led by Capt Masaoki Tsuruno. An

The J7W1 Shinden (above and below) was the only piston-engined canard fighter ordered in series.

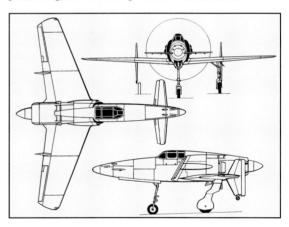

all-metal interceptor, the J7W1 was powered by a 2,130 hp Mitsubishi MK9D 18-cylinder radial installed as a pusher and driving a six-bladed propeller via an extension shaft. Intended for operation from shore-based naval squadrons and carrying an armament of four 30-mm cannon, the Shinden was ordered into production before the first of two prototypes was completed and flown. Difficulties delayed this event until 3 August 1945, but only some 45 min of testing in three flights had been completed before hostilities terminated. *Max speed (estimated), 466 mph (750 km/h) at 28,545 ft*

The canard pusher configuration of the J7W1 (above) was to remain unproven in combat.

(8 700 m). Range, 528 mls (850 km). Time to 26,245 ft (8 000 m), 10.66 min. Empty weight, 7,639 lb (3 465 kg). Max loaded weight, 11,526 lb (5 228 kg). Span, 36 ft 5½ in (11,11 m). Length, 31 ft 8¼ in (9,66 m). Height, 12 ft 10⅓ in (3,92 m). Wing area, 220.67 sq ft (20,50 m²).

LANZIUS L II   USA

The L II was derived from the tandem two-seat L I developed by the Lanzius Aircraft Company of New York in 1917 under US Army Signal Corps contract (and referred to by the manufacturer as the "Lanzius Variable Speed Aeroplane"). The L II single-seat fighting scout of *circa* 1919 was novel in featuring wings possessing both variable camber and variable incidence. A two-bay equi-span biplane powered by a 350 hp Packard 1A-1237 six-cylinder vertical inline water-cooled engine, the L II utilised a system of cables and pulleys to change camber and incidence, the latter varying from 0 deg to 15 deg. Flight testing is believed to have been conducted at McCook Field, only one prototype being completed. *Loaded weight, 1,200 lb (544 kg). Span, 38 ft 0 in (11,58 m). Length, 25 ft 0 in (7,62 m).*

Wings of variable camber and incidence were a feature of the Lanzius L II illustrated below.

LAVILLE DI-4   USSR

Developed in competition with the Grigorovich DI-3 two-seat fighter biplane, the DI-4 was designed by André Laville (who had formerly worked with Nieuport-Delage), with the assistance of Semyon A Lavochkin, at the *Buro Novyikh Konstruktsii* (Bureau of New Constructions) in Moscow. Powered by a 600 hp Curtiss Conqueror 12-cylinder water-cooled engine and flown for the first time on 4 January 1932, the DI-4 was

(Below) The Conqueror-powered DI-4 of André Laville.

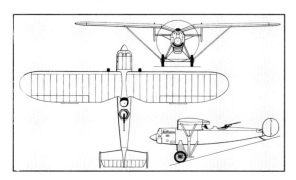

of all-duralumin construction with duralumin skin. It carried an armament of two synchronised 7,62-mm PV-1 machine guns and either one or two similar weapons on a ring mounting in the rear cockpit. Although flight testing of the DI-4 was generally successful and performance notably superior to that of the competitive DI-3, the braced and gulled high wing was viewed with some suspicion and the Conqueror engine around which the DI-4 was designed was in short supply. As a consequence, no series production was undertaken. *Max speed, 199 mph (320 km/h) at sea level. Ceiling, 26,900 ft (8 200 m). Empty weight, 2,271 lb (1 030 kg). Loaded weight, 3,527 lb (1 600 kg). Span (approx), 39 ft 4½ in (12,00 m). Length (approx), 25 ft 7 in (7,80 m). Wing area (approx), 258.34 sq ft (24,00 m²).*

The Curtiss engine and gulled wing of the DI-4 (below) militated against series production.

LAVOCHKIN LaGG-1   USSR

Semyon A Lavochkin, together with V P Gorbunov and M I Gudkov, established a new design bureau in September 1938, and began work on a single-seat tactical fighter. Initially designated I-22, the fighter was novel in that plastic-impregnated wood known as *delta drevesina* was used extensively in its construction, with stressed bakelite plywood skinning. Power was provided by a 1,100 hp Klimov M-105P engine with a 23-mm VYa-23V cannon mounted between the cylinder banks, the remaining armament comprising two 12,7-mm UB machine guns in the forward upper decking. Work began simultaneously on seven prototypes, and a pre-series of 100 fighters was laid down. The first prototype was flown on 30 March 1940, the designation having meanwhile been changed to LaGG-1. It demonstrated inadequate range, ceiling and manoeuvrability, and potentially dangerous handling characteristics. The exigencies of the times did not permit fundamental redesign of the fighter, and the Lavochkin team therefore initiated a programme aimed at alleviating the more serious of the fighter's defects. Improvements were progressively introduced, while the design was subjected to a thoroughgoing weight analysis. The large-calibre machine guns were replaced by 7,62-mm ShKAS guns, and the 23-mm cannon gave place to one of 20-mm. Various palliatives for the handling shortcomings were applied, and the first LaGG-1 prototype to introduce these changes was referred to as the I-301 (from the numerical designation of the factory — GAZ-301). This also featured redesigned outer wing panels incorporating additional fuel tanks. The I-301 entered flight test on 14 June 1940, the modified aircraft being assigned the designation LaGG-3 (which see) and most pre-series examples of the LaGG-1 being completed to the later standard. *Max speed, 311 mph (500 km/h) at sea level, 373 mph (600 km/h) at 16,405 ft (5 000 m). Range, 410 mls (660 km). Climb to 16,405 ft (5 000 m), 6.2 min. Empty weight, 6,543 lb (2 968 kg). Loaded weight, 7,451 lb (3 380 kg). Span, 32 ft 1⅞ in (9,80 m). Length, 28 ft 11 in (8,81 m). Height, 14 ft 5¼ in (4,40 m). Wing area, 188.37 sq ft (17,50 m²).*

LAVOCHKIN LaGG-3   USSR

Captured on 14 September 1942 at Ala-Sedoksa, the LaGG-3 illustrated above was successively operated by LeLv 32 and HLeLv 11 of the Finnish air arm.

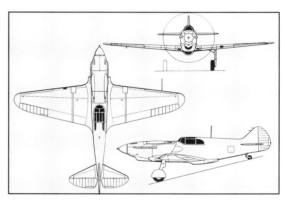

(Above) Late series LaGG-3 and (below) a LaGG-3 of the 3 Guards IAP, Ladoga area, winter 1943.

The LaGG-3 was essentially the series production version of the LaGG-1 with a revised outer wing incorporating fuel tanks, and an armament of one 20-mm and two 7,62-mm weapons. Fixed wing slats – later replaced by automatic slats – were introduced and balance weights were added on the elevators and rudder, but were later discarded in favour of statically and dynamically balanced surfaces. Weight was reduced as a result of a structural analysis. LaGG-3 deliveries com-

(Immediately below) LaGG-3 serving with the 6th Fighter Aviation Division, Moscow PVO, 1942-43, and (bottom) with 9 IAP of Black Sea Fleet AF, 1944.

Flown to Manchuria by a Soviet defector in 1942, this LaGG-3 (left) was tested by the Japanese Army.

cases, and a pair of 12,7-mm underwing guns was sometimes fitted. Three aircraft were each fitted with a 37-mm cannon and referred to as LaGG-3K-37s, and one example was fitted with the 1,650 hp Klimov M-107A engine. Production of the LaGG-3 was completed in the late summer of 1942 with a total of 6,528 built. *Max speed, 307 mph (495 km/h) at sea level, 354 mph (570 km/h) at 13,125 ft (4 000 m). Range, 498 mls (800 km). Climb to 16,405 ft (5 000 m), 5.6 min. Empty weight, 5,776 lb (2 620 kg). Loaded weight, 6,944 lb (3 150 kg). Dimensions as for LaGG-1.*

LAVOCHKIN La-5   USSR

Adaptation of the basic LaGG-3 airframe for a 14-cylinder two-row radial Shvetsov M-82 engine without major redesign of fundamental components resulted in the La-5 (examples converted from existing LaGG-3 air-

menced in the spring of 1941, initially with the M-105P engine, but, from late in the year, with the M-105PF affording 1,260 hp at 2,625 ft (800 m). Provision was

later made to replace one or both machine guns by weapons of 12,7-mm calibre, the 20-mm hub-mounted cannon being replaced by one of 23-mm calibre in some

(Left) An La-5FN presentation aircraft from the Mongolian People's Republic, and (lower left) an La-5FN flown by V I Ivanovich (15th Soviet ace).

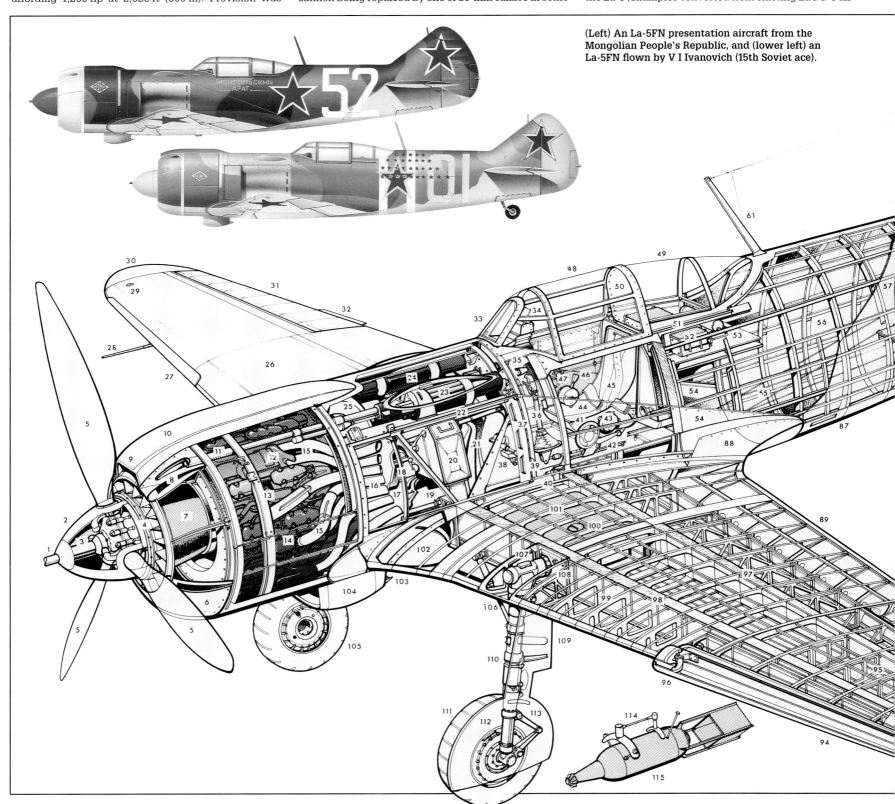

Early series La-5F (right) distinguished by short supercharger air intake trunk fairing over cowling.

frames on the production line sometimes being referred to as LaG-5s). The prototype conversion was first flown in March 1942 with an M-82 rated at 1,700 hp for take-off, and the La-5 was cleared for service testing in the following September with an armament of two 20-mm cannon. With completion of the conversion of existing LaGG-3 airframes, minor changes were introduced in new production aircraft, the principal of these being the cutting down of the aft fuselage decking and the introduction of a 360-deg-vision canopy. Late in 1942, the improved M-82F engine became available, producing 1,650 hp at 5,415 ft (1 650 m), aircraft fitted with this engine being designated La-5F, and, from early 1943, fuel tankage was revised. From late March 1943, the fuel injection M-82FN engine offering 1,850 hp for take-off replaced the carburettor-equipped M-82F, and with this power plant the fighter became the La-5FN. When the La-5 was withdrawn from production late in 1944, a total of 9,920 aircraft of this type (in-

cluding La-5UTI two-seat trainers) had been built. The following data relate to the La-5FN. *Max speed, 342 mph (550 km/h) at sea level, 403 mph (648 km/h) at*

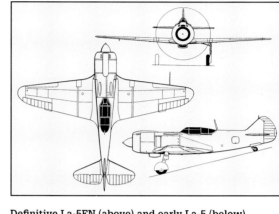

Definitive La-5FN (above) and early La-5 (below) serving with 159 IAP in Karelia during 1944.

20,670 ft (6 300 m). Max range, 475 mls (765 km). Time to 16,405 ft (5 000 m), 4.7 min. Empty weight, 6,173 lb (2 800 kg). Loaded weight, 7,407 lb (3 360 kg). Span, 32 ft 1⅔ in (9,80 m). Length, 28 ft 2½ in (8,60 m). Height, 8 ft 4 in (2,54 m). Wing area, 188.37 sq ft (17,50 m²).

LAVOCHKIN La-7   USSR

The ultimate refinement of the basic La-5 rather than a new design, the La-7 was developed from the autumn of 1943 under the bureau designation of La-120. This embodied the results of a TsAGI wind tunnel programme aimed at defining areas in which the basic La-5FN could be aerodynamically improved. Incorporating the modified wing structure (metal spars replacing the wooden box spars) intended for application to the definitive La-5FN (but not to be introduced on that fighter until the late spring of 1944), a revised inboard wing leading edge and an entirely new cowling

(Below) Three-cannon-armed Yaroslavl-built La-7.

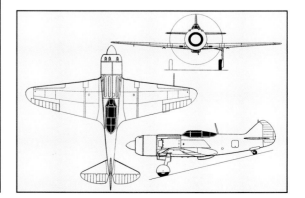

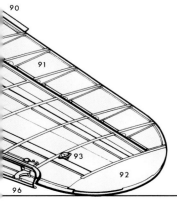

Key to Lavochkin La-5FN

1 Hucks-type starter dog
2 Spinner
3 Propeller balance
4 Controllable frontal intake louvres
5 VISh-105V metal controllable-pitch three-bladed propeller
6 Nose ring profile
7 Intake centrebody
8 ShVAK cannon port
9 Supercharger air intake
10 Supercharger intake trunk fairing
11 Blast tube
12 Shvetsov M-82FN 14-cylinder two-row radial
13 Cowling ring
14 Cowling panel hinge-line
15 Exhaust pipes
16 Exhaust cluster (seven per side)
17 Outlet cover panel
18 Engine accessories
19 Mainspar/fuselage attachment
20 Ammunition tanks (200 rpg)
21 Link and cartridge ejection chutes
22 Engine bearer upper support bracket
23 Cannon breech fairing
24 Paired 20-mm ShVAK cannon
25 Supercharger intake trunking
26 Stressed plywood skinning
27 Automatic leading-edge slat
28 Pitot head
29 Starboard navigation light
30 Wingtip
31 Metal-framed fabric-covered aileron
32 Aileron trim tab
33 Armourglass (55-mm) windscreen
34 PBP-1a reflector gunsight
35 Cockpit air
36 Control column
37 Outlet louvres
38 Rudder pedal assembly
39 Underfloor control linkage
40 Rear spar/fuselage attachment
41 Rudder and elevator trim handwheels
42 Seat height adjustment
43 Boost controls
44 Seat harness
45 Pilot's seat
46 Throttle quadrant
47 Hydraulics main valve
48 Aft-sliding cockpit canopy
49 Fixed aft transparent cockpit fairing
50 Armourglass panel
51 Canopy track
52 RSI-4 HF R/T installation
53 Radio equipment shelf
54 Dural fuselage side panels
55 Control cables
56 Plywood-sheathed birch frames with triangular-section wooden stringers
57 Stressed plywood skinning
58 Accumulator
59 Accumulator access panel
60 Talfin front spar attachment
61 Aerial mast
62 Radio aerials
63 Starboard tailplane
64 Elevator hinge
65 Metal-framed fabric-covered elevator
66 Tailfin leading edge
67 Tailfin wooden structure (plywood skinning)
68 Aerial stub
69 Rudder balance
70 Rudder upper hinge
71 Metal-framed fabric-covered rudder
72 Rudder trim tab
73 Rear navigation light
74 Rudder centre hinge
75 Elevator control lever
76 Tailplane/fuselage attachment
77 Rudder control lever
78 Elevator trim tab
79 Metal-framed fabric-covered elevator
80 Wooden two-spar tailplane structure (plywood skinning)
81 Tailwheel doors
82 Rearward-retracting tailwheel (usually locked down)
83 Tailwheel leg
84 Tailwheel shock strut
85 Retraction mechanism
86 Stressed plywood skinning
87 Retractable entry step
88 Wing root fillet
89 Dural-skinned flap construction
90 Aileron tab
91 Metal-framed fabric-covered aileron
92 Wingtip
93 Port navigation light
94 Leading-edge slat
95 Outboard ribs
96 Automatic slat actuating mechanism
97 Rear boxspar
98 Front boxspar
99 Leading edge ribs
100 Fuel filler cap
101 Port fuel tank of three-tank set (105.6 Imp gal/480 l total capacity)
102 Mainwheel well
103 Oil cooler outlet flap
104 Engine oil cooler intake
105 Starboard mainwheel
106 Undercarriage hydraulic jack and ram
107 Undercarriage knuckle joint
108 Undercarriage/front spar attachment
109 Mainwheel leg fairing plate
110 Mainwheel oleo leg
111 Port mainwheel
112 Mainwheel fairing plate
113 Torque links
114 Underwing stores shackles
115 110-lb (50-kg) bomb

(Above) This La-7 is believed to have been the personal aircaft of the CO of 163 GvIAP, and (below) an La-7 on the Central Sector, 1944-45.

for the Shvetsov M-82FN engine, the La-120 was first flown in November 1943. In the following spring it entered production as the La-7. The intended armament comprised three 20-mm Berezina B-20 cannon, but while this armament *was* installed in aircraft built at Yaroslavl, those built at Moscow reverted to the twin ShVAK cannon of the La-5FN. Variants included the tandem two-seat La-7UTI trainer, the La-7TK with a pair of TK-3 turbo-superchargers, and the rocket-boosted La-7R. The La-7TK was test flown in July-August 1944, but was destroyed when a turbo-supercharger exploded. Another example was fitted with the 2,000 hp ASh-71TK, trials soon being discontinued owing to the erratic behaviour of this engine's turbo-superchargers. The La-7R, of which two prototypes were tested, was fitted in the rear fuselage with an RD-1KhZ liquid rocket motor of 660 lb (300 kg) thrust, the first prototype being destroyed during the initial take-off run in October 1944. Flight testing of the second prototype continued until February 1945, and a further example – a conversion of one of the original prototype airframes and therefore referred to as the La-120R – entered test in January 1945, this having an improved rocket motor and local airframe structural changes. Testing of the La-120R continued until late 1946. A total of 5,753 La-7s had been manufactured when production ended in 1946. *Max speed, 423 mph (680 km/h) at 19,030 ft (5 800 m). Time to 16,405 ft (5 000 m), 4.52 min. Range, 615 mls (990 km). Empty weight, 5,842 lb (2 620 kg). Loaded weight, 7,496 lb (3 400 kg). Span, 32 ft 1¾ in (9,80 m). Length, 28 ft 2½ in (8,60 m). Height, 8 ft 6¼ in (2,60 m). Wing area, 189.34 sq ft (17,59 m²).*

The La-7R (above) was one of two rocket-boosted prototypes, and (below) a Moscow-built twin-gun La-7 with the 1st Czech Fighter Regt, April 1945.

LAVOCHKIN La-126　　　USSR

By the end of 1944, the Lavochkin bureau had abandoned further development of the mixed-construction La-7 in favour of an entirely new all-metal design bearing only a configurational similarity to its predecessor, and, early in 1945, work began on this as the La-126.

Despite its design bureau designation, which suggested that it was a development of the La-120 (La-7), the La-126 possessed no commonality with the Lavochkin bureau's previous fighter, apart from an M-82FN (ASh-82FN) engine. It featured an all-metal monocoque fuselage and a TsAGI laminar-section wing. Armament was restricted to two 20-mm ShVAK cannon and prototype flight testing was completed at the factory on 10 January 1945, but no production was undertaken, the La-126 serving as a basis for the La-130 (see La-9 entry). The prototype was subsequently fitted with two Bondaryuk VRD-430 ramjets as the La-126PVRD, and these, it was claimed, increased maximum speed in level flight by 62 mph (100 km/h). The La-126PVRD was tested between June and September 1946, attaining a max speed of 497 mph (800 km/h) at 26,245 ft (8 000 m).

The La-126 (below) after attachment of VRD-430 ramjets underwing for performance boosting trials.

LAVOCHKIN La-9　　　USSR

Closely related to the La-126, the La-130 – first flown on 16 June 1946 – embodied a number of refinements, both aerodynamic and structural, and featured a revised fuel system of increased capacity. It retained the ASh-82FN radial of the preceding fighters, but provision was made for a quartet of 23-mm NS-23 cannon. Series production was authorised in November 1946 as the La-9,

The La-9, the second prototype of which is shown below, began to enter service from mid-1947.

deliveries to the VVS commencing February 1947 from GAZ 21 at Gor'kiy. A tandem two-seat training version, the La-9UTI, was flown in July 1947, and series production continued for three years, 1,630 single-seaters and 265 two-seaters being built. One example, designated La-138, was fitted with two PVRD-430 ramjets of 660 lb (300 kg) underwing, factory testing being performed during March and April 1947, and increases in level speed of 66 to 70 mph (107 to 112 km/h) were recorded in level flight. A small batch of aircraft was completed

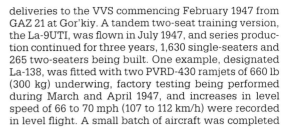

(Above) An experimental version of the La-9, the ramjet-equipped La-138, and (below) one of a number of La-9RDs fitted with RD-13 pulse-jets.

with underwing provision for RD-13 pulsating athodyds, or pulse-jets, as La-9RDs. These boosters were found to have a deleterious effect on handling characteristics. *Max speed, 429 mph (690 km/h) at 20,500 ft (6 250 m). Time to 16,405 ft (5 000 m), 4.7 min. Max range, 1,078 mls (1 735 km). Empty weight, 5,864 lb (2 660 kg). Max loaded weight, 8,104 lb (3 676 kg). Span, 32 ft 1⅔ in (9,80 m). Length, 28 ft 3⅓ in (8,62 m). Wing area, 190.63 sq ft (17,72 m²).*

(Below) The standard series production La-9.

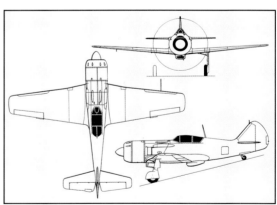

LAVOCHKIN La-11 — USSR

Evolved from the La-9 to meet a requirement for a fighter with sufficient range to fulfil the escort rôle, the La-11 was destined to be the last piston-engine fighter from the Lavochkin bureau. It had a wing fundamentally similar to that of the La-9 and retained the ASh-82FN engine, but provision was made to attach auxiliary fuel tanks at the wingtips, the ventral oil cooler was incorporated in the engine cowling and armament was reduced to three 23-mm NS-23 cannon. The first prototype was flown in June 1947 under the design bureau designation La-134, and production (1947-51) at Gor'kiy was to total 1,182 aircraft. The La-11 was supplied in some numbers to both the Chinese and the North Korean air forces, and saw operational use during the Korean conflict. It was finally phased out of first line VVS service in the early 'fifties. *Max speed, 419 mph (674 km/h) at 20,340 ft (6 200 m). Time to 16,405 ft (5 000 m), 6.6 min. Max range, 1,584 mls (2 550 km). Empty weight, 6,107 lb (2 770 kg). Max loaded weight, 8,810 lb (3 996 kg). Dimensions as for La-9.*

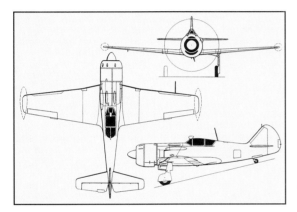

Last of the Lavochkin piston-engined fighters, the La-11 (above and below) had provision for wingtip tanks.

LAVOCHKIN La-150 — USSR

The Lavochkin bureau's response to Yosif Stalin's order of February 1945 to design and build a single-seat jet fighter around a Junkers Jumo 004B turbojet, the La-150 was of distinctive pod-and-boom layout with a shoulder-mounted wing. Like the competitive designs from the Mikoyan-Gurevich and Yakovlev bureaux, the La-150 was awarded a prototype/pre-series aircraft order, the first of the prototypes flying in September 1946 powered by the Soviet derivative of the Jumo engine, the RD-10 rated at 1,984 lb st (900 kgp). Unique among first-generation Soviet jet fighters in having a fuselage-mounted undercarriage, the La-150 featured a somewhat complex, overly robust and heavy structure and was, in consequence, underpowered. Excessive dihedral effect resulting from the wing positioning was rectified on the second prototype by drooping the wingtips, but excessive oscillation of the tail surfaces at high speeds resulting from inadequate stiffness of the tail-boom could not be overcome. In the event, only five airframes were completed. Armament comprised two

An La-11 (above) serving with an IAP attached to the Group of Soviet Forces in Germany, *circa* 1949.

23-mm NS-23 cannon. *Max speed, 500 mph (805 km/h) at 16,405 ft (5 000 km). Time to 16,405 ft (5 000 m), 7.2 min. Range, 311 mls (500 km) at 373 mph (600 km/h). Empty weight, 4,539 lb (2 059 kg). Max weight, 6,528 lb (2 961 kg). Span, 26 ft 10¾ in (8,20 m). Length, 30 ft 10¾ in (9,42 m). Wing area, 130.78 sq ft (12,15 m²).*

The first prototype La-150 (above and below) which entered flight test in September 1946.

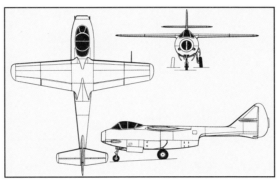

Downturned wingtips characterised the second prototype Lavochkin La-150 illustrated below.

LAVOCHKIN La-152 — USSR

Despite its designation, the La-152 bore little more relation to the La-150 than its common design bureau origin. The wing, although similar in planform to that of the earlier fighter, employed a new profile of only 9.1 per cent – the thinnest section adopted up to that time

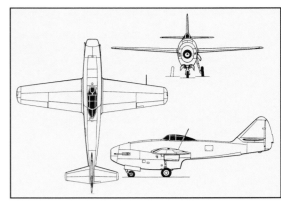

The La-152 (above and below) was dissimilar to but developed in parallel with the La-150.

in the Soviet Union – and was lowered to mid position. The RD-10 turbojet was retained, but to avoid the duct losses suffered by the La-150, the power plant was installed in the extreme nose, exhausting beneath a sturdier rear fuselage. The cg position was restored by moving the cockpit aft, and armament comprised three 23-mm NS-23 cannon. Work on the La-152 was, in fact, initiated by the Lavochkin bureau within two months of a start being made on the La-150, possibly as a result of latent doubts concerning the efficacy of the configuration of the earlier fighter. Thus, factory flight testing began in October 1946, only a few weeks after the La-150 had entered flight test. Three prototypes were built in parallel, all similarly armed and differing primarily in power plant, the second and third aircraft being designated La-154 and La-156 respectively. The La-154 was to have been fitted with a Lyulka TR-1 turbojet of 2,976 lb st (1 350 kgp), but was never flown owing to difficulties with this engine. After initial trials with a standard RD-10, the La-156, which had increased tankage and had initially flown in February 1947, was fitted with an RD-10F engine equipped with an afterburner extension boosting thrust by 30 per cent. The RD-10F-equipped La-156 was flown for the first time in September 1947 – the first Soviet aircraft to fly with an afterburning engine – and attained a max speed of 562 mph (905 km/h) at 6,560 ft (2 000 m). The flight test programme continued until the end of January 1948. The following data relate to the La-152. *Max speed, 483 mph (778 km/h) at 16,405 ft (5 000 m). Time to 16,405 ft (5 000 m), 6.5 min. Range, 306 mls (492 km) at 340 mph (547 km/h). Empty weight, 5,093 lb (2 310 kg). Loaded weight, 7,140 lb (3 239 kg). Span, 26 ft 10¾ in (8,20 m). Length, 29 ft 11 in (9,12 m). Wing area, 130.78 sq ft (12,15 m²).*

The La-156 (below) became in 1947 the first Soviet jet fighter to be flown with an afterburner.

LAVOCHKIN Lᴀ-160 USSR

The first Soviet fighter to utilise wing sweepback, and consequently known unofficially as the *Strelka* (Dart), the La-160 featured 35 deg of leading-edge sweep on a wing of 9.5 per cent thickness. When initially flown on 24 June 1947, the La-160 was fitted with an RD-10 turbojet rated at 1,984 lb st (900 kgp), with which it could not get airborne fully laden. After initial handling trials, the La-160 was fitted with an RD-10F which provided an afterburning thrust of 2,580 lb (1 170 kg) and with which, after diving and then levelling off, a speed of 659 mph (1 060 km/h) was allegedly attained at 18,700 ft (5 700 m), this being equivalent to Mach=0.92. The La-160 carried an armament of two 37-mm NS-37 cannon, but was utilised primarily as a research vehicle in the development of more advanced fighters. *Max speed, 559 mph (900 km/h) at sea level. Empty weight, 6,036 lb (2 738 kg). Loaded weight, 8,951 lb (4 060 kg). Span, 29 ft 4⅓ in (8,95 m). Length, 33 ft 0 in (10,07 m). Wing area, 171.15 sq ft (15,90 m²).*

(Above and below) Dubbed *Strelka*, the La-160 was the first Soviet fighter to feature wing sweepback.

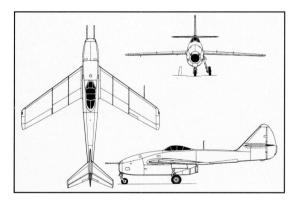

LAVOCHKIN Lᴀ-168 USSR

In March 1946, Yosif Stalin assigned the task of developing advanced single-seat fighters around the newly-acquired Rolls-Royce Nene turbojet to the design bureaux of Semyon A Lavochkin, Artem Mikoyan and Mikhail Gurevich, and Aleksandr Yakovlev on a competitive basis. The Lavochkin contender, the La-168, featured a shoulder-mounted wing sweptback 37 deg 20 min at the leading edge and fitted with Fowler flaps. An armament of two 23-mm NS-23KM cannon and one 37-mm N-37 cannon was fitted and power was provided by a 5,000 lb st (2 268 kgp) Nene R.N.2 turbojet. The La-168 was first flown on 22 April 1948, subsequently attaining 674 mph (1 084 km/h) at 9,020 ft (2 750 m), representing Mach=0.914. During the test programme, the cockpit canopy collapsed when all three guns were fired simultaneously at 49,215 ft (15 000 m), but the pilot succeeded in landing the aircraft. The La-168 test programme continued until 19 February 1949, but the Mikoyan-Gurevich bureau's

The La-168 (below) competed unsuccessfully with the MiG-15, remaining a single prototype.

competitive I-310 (Type S) had meanwhile been selected for large-scale production. *Max speed, 674 mph (1 084 km/h) at 9,020 ft (2 750 m). Time to 16,405 ft (5 000 m), 2.0 min. Range, 792 mls (1 275 km). Empty weight, 6,554 lb (2 973 kg). Loaded weight, 9,727 lb (4 412 kg). Span, 31 ft 2 in (9,50 m). Length, 34 ft 7¾ in (10,56 m). Wing area, 194.62 sq ft (18,08 m²).*

The La-168 (below) with large ventral fuel tank.

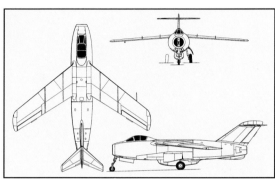

LAVOCHKIN Lᴀ-172 USSR

In parallel with the specification to which the La-168 was to be developed, a requirement was formulated for a lighter "frontal fighter" powered by the Rolls-Royce Derwent turbojet. To meet the latter demand, the Lavochkin bureau evolved two designs, the La-172 and the La-174TK. The former was effectively a scaled-down version of the La-168 tailored for the lower-powered, smaller engine and the latter featured exceptionally thin, unswept wings and a configuration generally similar to that of the earlier La-152 series of fighters. The La-172 was powered by an NII-1 turbojet (as the pre-series Soviet version of the Derwent was designated) rated at 3,527 lb st (1 600 kgp), and entered flight test early in 1948, with armament comprising three 23-mm NS-23 cannon. Early in the test programme, while being flown by I Ye Fedorov, the La-172 suffered uncontrollable flutter at 26,250 ft (8 000 m) and entered a flat spin. Recovery was effected at 9,840 ft (3 000 m), but the prototype was heavily damaged in a subsequent crash landing. Nevertheless, development was continued via the La-174D to result in the La-15. *Max speed, 646 mph (1 040 km/h) at 9,840 ft (3 000 m). Time to 16,405 ft (5 000 m), 3.0 min. Range, 808 mls (1 300 km). Empty weight, 5,364 lb (2 433 kg). Loaded weight, 8,175 lb (3 708 kg). Span, 28 ft 11⅔ in (8,83 m). Length, 31 ft 4⅓ in (9,56 m). Wing area, 173.95 sq ft (16,16 m²).*

Powered by a Soviet version of the Derwent, the La-172 (below) was a predecessor of the La-15.

Bearing no design relationship to the La-174D, the La-174TK (above) used a wing of low thickness ratio.

LAVOCHKIN Lᴀ-174TK USSR

Whereas sweptback surfaces had been adopted for both the La-168 and La-172, the La-174TK, designed to meet the demands of the same specification as the latter, featured unswept surfaces. The wing possessed a thickness ratio of only six per cent (the "TK" suffix indicating *Tonkoye Krylo*, or Thin Wing) which the Lavochkin bureau believed might offer most of the advantages of a thicker sweptback wing while avoiding some of its disadvantages. The basic configuration of the La-174TK reverted to that of the earlier La-152 series fighters, although the relationship was confined to a common design origin, with the single 3,505 lb st (1 590 kgp) NII-1 (RD-500) turbojet exhausting under the rear fuselage. Armament comprised three 23-mm NS-23 cannon and flight testing commenced early 1948. Although lighter than the La-172, the La-174TK demonstrated inferior handling and performance characteristics, further development being discontinued. The design bureau designation was reassigned to the replacement prototype for the La-172 which became the La-174D. *Max speed, 603 mph (970 km/h) at sea level, 600 mph (965 km/h) at 16,405 ft (5 000 m). Time to 16,405 ft (5 000 m), 2.5 min. Range, 597 mls (960 km). Empty weight, 5,093 lb (2 310 kg). Loaded weight, 7,308 lb (3 315 kg). Span, 28 ft 4¼ in (8,64 m). Length, 30 ft 10½ in (9,41 m). Wing area, 145.53 sq ft (13,52 m²).*

(Below) The La-174TK with a Soviet Derwent engine.

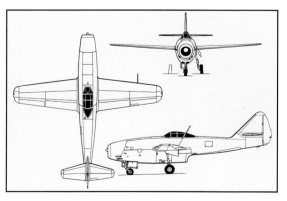

LAVOCHKIN Lᴀ-15 USSR

A replacement prototype for the La-172 was designated La-174D (the suffix signifying *dubler*, literally "replacement"), and entered flight test in August 1948. This differed in only minor respects from the preceding prototype, and series production was ordered during the same month as the La-15, armament being reduced from three to two 23-mm NS-23 cannon, and 6 deg of wing anhedral being added. The La-15 was powered by the RD-500 turbojet, the Soviet series version of the Derwent, deliveries to the VVS commencing in the late autumn of 1949. Production plans for the La-15 were, in the event, scaled down because of difficulties experienced in manufacturing in sufficient quantity the numerous milled parts employed in the structure, but several hundred were produced, these remaining in VVS service until 1954. A tandem two-seat conversion trainer version was evolved as the La-180, but only two examples of this variant were built. *Max speed, 638 mph (1 026 km/h) at 9,840 ft (3 000 m). Time to 16,405 ft (5 000 m), 3.1 min. Range, 727 mls (1 170 km). Empty weight, 5,677 lb (2 575 kg). Loaded weight, 8,488 lb (3 850 kg). Span, 28 ft 11⅔ in (8,83 m). Length, 31 ft 4⅓ in (9,56 m). Wing area, 173.95 sq ft (16,16 m²).*

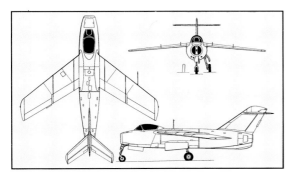

First deployed by the VVS late 1949, the La-15 (above) remained in the inventory until 1954.

The La-15 (above and below) was the only Lavochkin jet fighter to achieve series production.

LAVOCHKIN Lᴀ-176   USSR

Combining a fuselage essentially similar to that of the Lavochkin La-168 with wings sweptback 45 deg at quarter-chord, the La-176 was flown in September 1948 with a 5,005 lb st (2 270 kgp) RD-45F turbojet, and armament comprising one 37-mm N-37 and two 23-mm NS-23 cannon. Re-engined with a Klimov VK-1 turbojet of 5,952 lb (2 700 kgp), the La-176 was claimed to have exceeded Mach=1.0 in a dive from 29,690 ft (9 050 m) to 19,685 ft (6 000 m) on 26 December 1948. It was initially believed that an ASI error had been involved, but the process was repeated six times during January 1949, 687 mph (1 105 km/h) being recorded at 24,605 ft (7 500 m), this being equivalent to Mach=1.02. The La-176 thus became the first Soviet aircraft to achieve supersonic flight. Further development was abandoned shortly afterwards when the canopy locks failed at high speed, resulting in test pilot O V Sokolovsky losing his life. *Max speed, 648 mph (1 043 km/h) at sea level, 627 mph (1 010 km/h) at 36,090 ft (11 000 m). Time*

(Below) The La-176 first flew in September 1948.

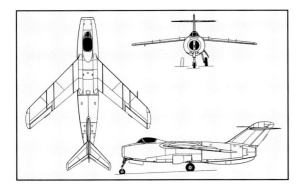

The La-176 (above) was the first Soviet aircraft to achieve supersonic speed, albeit in a dive.

to 16,405 ft (5 000 m), 1.8 min. Range, 620 mls (1 000 km). Empty weight, 6,858 lb (3 111 kg). Loaded weight, 10,209 lb (4 631 kg). Span, 28 ft 2¼ in (8,59 m). Length, 35 ft 11⅞ in (10,97 m). Wing area, 196.45 sq ft (18,25 m²).

LAVOCHKIN Lᴀ-190   USSR

Owing little or nothing to earlier fighters from the Lavochkin design bureau, the La-190 was conceived to meet the demand of Yosif Stalin for the "fastest fighter in the world". Other contenders were the I-350, progenitor of the MiG-19, and the Yak-1000, which, in the event, was to be abandoned before flight testing. The requirement called for use of the new Lyulka AL-5 turbojet which had an initial rating of 10,140 lb st (4 600 kgp). The La-190 featured a tapered wing sweptback 55 deg at the leading edge, bicycle-type main undercarriage members with wingtip outrigger stabilising wheels, and an armament of two 37-mm N-37 cannon. Innovations insofar as Soviet design was concerned included integral fuel tankage occupying virtually the entire interspar box of the 6.1 per cent thickness wing which featured machined upper and lower skins. All control surfaces were powered by irreversible actuators. The sole prototype La-190 was completed in February 1951. The AL-5 engine offered less thrust than predicted and its unreliability led to cancellation of the development programme after only eight flights. However, a speed of 739 mph (1 190 km/h) at 16,405 ft (5 000 m), or Mach=1.03, was attained in level flight during one test in March 1951. *Max speed, 739 mph (1 190 km/h) at 16,405 ft (5 000 m). Time to 16,405 ft (5 000 m), 1.5 min. Normal range, 715 mls (1 150 km). Empty weight, 16,127 lb (7 315 kg). Loaded weight, 20,408 lb (9 257 kg). Span, 32 ft 5¾ in (9,90 m). Length, 53 ft 7¾ in (16,35 m). Wing area, 419.05 sq ft (38,93 m²).*

The La-190 (above and below) was conceived to meet a demand for the "fastest fighter in the world".

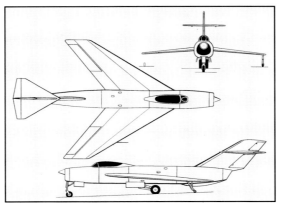

LAVOCHKIN Lᴀ-200   USSR

Designed to meet a requirement formulated in 1948 for a two-seat twin-engined all-weather interceptor, the La-200 was flown for the first time on 9 September 1949.

Two prototypes were built, each powered by two 5,952 lb st (2 700 kgp) Klimov VK-1 turbojets mounted in tandem with the exhaust of the foremost engine ducted beneath the fuselage. The prototypes differed one from the other primarily in the location of the *Torii* (Thorium) AI radar, the first prototype having a conical intake centrebody and the second prototype having a radome underslung on the upper intake lip. Armament consisted of three 37-mm N-37 cannon, one to port and two to starboard. The wing, sweptback 40 deg at the leading edge, was largely occupied by integral tankage and two large underwing slipper-type auxiliary tanks could boost maximum range from 724 to 1,243 mls (1 165 to 2 000 km). The first prototype was flown on 9 September 1949, and the first and second flight test phases were completed by February and October 1950 respectively, Mach=0.946 being attained in level flight and Mach=1.01 in a dive. The second prototype joined the flight programme early 1951, the repositioned radar being of the improved *Torii-A* type, ammunition capacity being increased, a ventral keel being introduced and normal loaded weight rising to 23,325 lb (10 580 kg). With the final NII VVS test phase completed in April 1951, a recommendation was made that series production of the La-200 should be initiated. This was thwarted, however, by the issue of a replacement specification in November 1951 calling for a substantial increase in range to permit all-weather standing patrols, and for the provision of heavier, longer-ranging radar.

The first (above) and second (below) prototypes of the La-200 differed essentially in radar location.

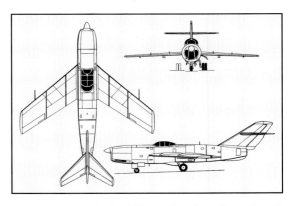

Further work on the La-200 was therefore discontinued in favour of the revised La-200B. The following data relate to the first prototype. *Max speed, 677 mph (1 090 km/h) at 11,485 ft (3 500 m). Time to 16,405 ft (5 000 m), 2.6 min. Normal range, 724 mls (1 165 km). Empty weight, 15,630 lb (7 090 kg). Normal loaded weight, 22,873 lb (10 375 kg). Span, 42 ft 4⅔ in (12,92 m). Length, 54 ft 5¼ in (16,59 m). Wing area, 432.5 sq ft (40,18 m²).*

LAVOCHKIN Lᴀ-200B   USSR

The issue in November 1951 of a specification for an all-weather fighter capable of mounting standing patrols led the Lavochkin bureau to undertake some redesign of the La-200. The side-by-side seating for the two crew members was retained, and the centre and aft fuselage were comparatively unchanged, but the forward fuselage was entirely redesigned. The extreme nose was formed by a large dielectric radome of more than 3.28 ft (1,0-m) diameter. The early single-antenna *Torii-A* radar was replaced by a large RP-6 *Sokol* (Falcon) radar with three different scan modes, and twin ventral strakes supplanted the single strake of the second La-200. The additional fuel required to achieve the specified endurance was provided by increasing the capacity of each underwing tank from 246 Imp gal (1 120 l) to 583 Imp gal (2 650 l). Two 6,834 lb st (3 100 kgp) Klimov VK-1 turbojets were installed, the

The La-200B (above) was developed to compete with the Yak-120 and to carry the large RP-6 *Sokol* radar.

A feature of the La-200B all-weather fighter (below) was its large-capacity underwing tanks.

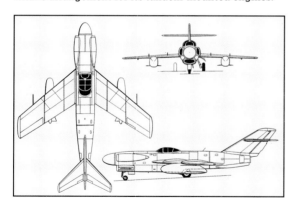

forward engine's air being supplied through a chin intake and that for the aft engine being provided by "elephant ear" type intakes on the sides of the extended nose. Armament remained three 37-mm cannon and the first flight test was made on 3 July 1952, a mock-up of the *Sokol* radar initially being fitted, tests with the radar installed commencing on 10 September. An extensive test programme was conducted, but, in the event, the competitive Yak-120 was selected to fulfil the requirement. *Max speed, 640 mph (1 030 km/h) at 16,405 ft (5 000 m). Time to 16,405 ft (5 000 m), 2.8 min. Max range, 1,740 mls (2 800 km). Empty weight, 19,422 lb (8 810 kg). Normal loaded weight, 28,000 lb (12 700 kg). Span, 42 ft 6¼ in (12,96 m). Length, 56 ft 10 in (17,32 m). Wing area, 430.57 sq ft (40,00 m²).*

The La-200B (above and below) had an unusual air intake arrangement for its tandem-mounted engines.

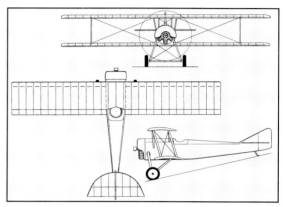

LAVOCHKIN La-250   USSR

Destined to be the last aircraft produced by the Lavochkin design bureau, the La-250, known unofficially as the *Anaconda*, was designed to meet a very demanding 1954 requirement for an ultra long-range, high-altitude single-seat super interceptor armed exclusively with missiles. Featuring a 57-deg delta wing and an enormous fuselage of near-constant cross section, the La-250 was powered by two Lyulka AL-7F turbojets each rated at 14,330 lb st (6 500 kgp) which were later to be fitted with afterburners boosting thrust to 19,840 lb (9 000 kg). All control surfaces were fully powered with duplex systems and without manual reversion. Intended to carry the 18.6-mile (30-km) acquisition-range *Uragan* (Hurricane) radar, the La-250 had a planned armament of two large K-15 beam-riding missiles. Although the La-250 was intended as a single-seater in operational form, prototypes were completed

as two-seaters to provide accommodation for a test observer, and the first of three flying examples was completed in July 1956. The first flight was attempted on 16 July, but the test pilot, A G Kochetkov, encountered an unexpectedly rapid roll moment and lost control. Extensive testing of a systems rig followed before acceptable characteristics were attained and flight testing could be resumed. The second aircraft was lost in a landing accident on 28 November 1957, and the third aircraft also suffered a landing accident on 8 September 1958. The flight test programme suffered continual delays as a result of poor engine reliability and the full testing had not been completed when the programme was cancelled. *Max speed, 1,243 mph (2 000 km/h) or Mach=1.88. Approx empty weight, 33,070 lb (15 000 kg). Approx loaded weight, 66,135 lb (30 000 kg). Span, 45 ft 7¼ in (13,90 m). Length, 83 ft 11¾ in (25,60 m). Wing area, 861.14 sq ft (80,00 m²).*

(Above and below) The fourth La-250 prototype was the third flying example, but was never fully tested.

(Below) The La-250 in two-seat form as flown.

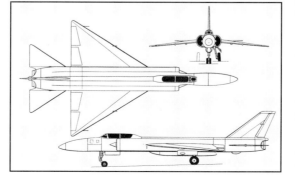

LEBED' X   Russia

In 1916, the Aktionernoe Obitsestvo Vozdukhoplavaniya V A Lebedev, a company established in St Petersburg in 1912 by Vladimir A Lebedev and Prof A A Lebedev, developed an equi-span biplane of original design as the Lebed' X. Owing much to experience gained with the Lebed' VII, an unarmed copy of the Sopwith Tabloid, the Lebed' X was built in two versions: a single-bay biplane intended as a single-seat fighter and a two-bay biplane intended for the reconnaissance rôle. Both were powered by the 80 hp Le Rhône rotary and were armed with a single synchronised machine gun, but proved underpowered. Neither fighter nor reconnaissance model progressed further than prototype test. *Max speed, 84 mph (135 km/h). Empty weight, 915 lb (415 kg). Span, 34 ft 5⅓ in (10,50 m). Length, 22 ft 11½ in (7,00 m). Wing area, 312.16 sq ft (29,00 m²).*

The Lebed' X experimental fighter (below) of 1916.

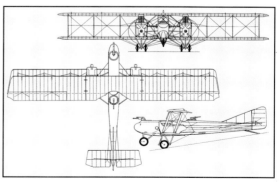

LETORD 6   France

Derived from the Letord 3 Bn3 three-seat night bomber for use in the escort fighter rôle, the Letord 6 Ca3 prototype was completed late in 1917 and entered flight test in January 1918. Like its bomber counterpart, the Letord 6 was a four-bay equi-span biplane with negative wing stagger. Powered by two 220 hp Hispano-Suiza 8Be eight-cylinder water-cooled engines, it carried a pilot and two gunners, the nose gunner being provided with a 37-mm Hotchkiss cannon and the dorsal gunner having a single 7,7-mm Lewis gun. The Letord 6 was undoubtedly obsolescent in concept by the time that it entered test, and development appears to have been discontinued at an early stage. *Max speed, (approx) 93 mph (150 km/h). Span, 58 ft 10⅔ in (17,95 m). Length, 36 ft 3 in (11,05 m). Height, 11 ft 5¾ in (3,50 m). Wing area, 742.73 sq ft (69,00 m²).*

The Letord 6 (below) derivative of the Letord 3.

LETORD-BECHEREAU 2   France

Designed by Louis Béchereau and built by the Société d'Aviation Letord to participate in the 1921 C1 (single-seat fighter) programme, the innovative LB2 was effectively a shoulder-wing monoplane in that the rear spar mated with the fuselage frames, although the forward spar was raised slightly above the forward decking by a shallow cabane. A substantial auxiliary planing surface enclosed the mainwheel axle, this being attached to inclined aerofoil surfaces and serving to brace the anhe-

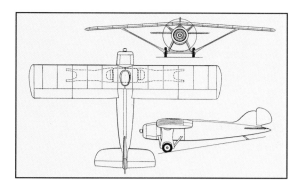

The LB2 (above) was innovative but unsuccessful.

dralled wing at mid span. The LB2 was of wooden construction and was powered by a 500 hp Salmson 18Z 18-cylinder radial engine installed close to the aircraft CG and driving the propeller via an extension shaft. The LB2 was displayed at the Paris *Salon de l'Aéronautique* in December 1922. This fighter was not selected for production, but Louis Béchereau persisted with development, a revised prototype being built by Buscaylet Pére et Fils-Bobin (as the Buscaylet-Béchereau C1 – which see) and entered in the 1923 C1 programme. *Max speed, 155 mph (250 km/h). Range, 373 mls (600 km). Loaded weight, 3,880 lb (1 760 kg). Span, 45 ft 11⅓ in (14,00 m). Length, 32 ft 9¾ in (10,00 m). Height, 9 ft 10 in (3,00 m). Wing area, 376.75 sq ft (35,00 m²).*

LETOV Š 3   Czechoslovakia

The first original fighter design produced by the *Vojenská továrna na letadla* (Military Aircraft Works) "*Letov*", the Š 3 was created by Ing Alois Šmolik, who had formerly worked for the Austro-Hungarian government. Initially designated as Š B.1, the original prototype was destroyed in a fire at the Prague-Letnany factory on 5 November 1921, but a second prototype entered flight test early in 1922. A single-seat parasol monoplane powered by a 185 hp BMW IIIa six-cylinder in-line engine and carrying an armament of two 7,7-mm Vickers machine guns, the Š 3 was of mixed construction with a wooden wing and metal fuselage and tail.

The second Š 3 with (above) Lamblin radiators and (below) with "cheek"-type radiators.

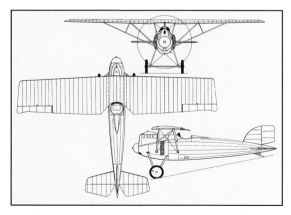

The Š 3 participated in the International Meeting at Zürich in 1922, taking third place in the precision take-off and landing contest and seventh place in the aerobatic contest. Further development was discontinued in favour of the Š 4. *Max speed, 140 mph (225 km/h). Time to 9,840 ft (3 000 m), 5.9 min. Range, 293 mls (472 km). Empty weight, 1,459 lb (662 kg). Loaded weight, 2,046 lb (928 kg). Span, 33 ft 2⅔ in (10,13 m). Length, 23 ft 2¾ in (7,08 m). Height, 9 ft 8⅛ in (3,04 m). Wing area, 189.45 sq ft (17,60 m²).*

LETOV Š 4   Czechoslovakia

Intended as a successor to the SPAD S.VII and XIII in service with the newly-created Czechoslovak Air Force, and selected in preference to the Š 3 parasol monoplane, the Š 4 was initially designated Š HS.1. It was a neat single-bay unstaggered biplane of mixed construction, with fabric-covered wooden wings, and metal fuselage and tail. Flown in 1922, the Š 4 was powered by a 220 hp Hispano-Suiza 8Ba engine and carried an armament of two synchronised 7,7-mm Vickers machine guns. A series of 20 Š 4 fighters was ordered, but several of these were completed with the 180 hp HS 8Aa engine as Š 4a aerobatic trainers. As a result of low manufacturing standards, a number of difficulties were experienced with the Š 4s, which were grounded in 1927, surviving aircraft being rebuilt in 1928 to Š 4a trainer standard. *Max speed, 144 mph (232 km/h). Time to 9,840 ft (3 000 m), 9.3 min. Range, 310 mls (500 km). Empty weight, 1,484 lb (673 kg). Loaded weight, 2,160 lb (980 kg). Span, 26 ft 2⅞ in (8,00 m). Length, 21 ft 7 in (6,58 m). Height, 8 ft 7⅛ in (2,62 m). Wing area, 176.86 sq ft (16,43 m²).*

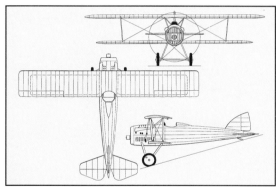

Structural weakness dogged the career of the Š 4 (above and below) which was grounded in 1927.

LETOV Š 7   Czechoslovakia

The Š 7 was designed by Alois Šmolik and built in 1923 to participate in an official competition for single-seat fighters powered by the 300 hp Škoda-manufactured Hispano-Suiza 8Fb engine. Of similar construction to preceding Šmolik-designed fighters, the Š 7 was an equi-span single-bay staggered biplane with twin 7,7-mm gun armament. The Š 7 was initially flown with a ring-type frontal radiator, but cooling problems dictated modification of the radiator system, and the prototype was fitted with a redesigned engine cowling and a ventral radiator as the Š 7a. This type failed to attract a production order and further development was discontinued. *Max speed, 158 mph (255 km/h). Time to 3,280 ft (1 000 m), 1.5 min. Empty weight,*

The Š 7a (below) adopted a redesigned engine cowling and a ventral radiator.

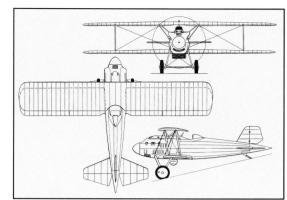

(Above) The Letov Š 7a in its definitive form.

1,682 lb (763 kg). Loaded weight, 2,315 lb (1 050 kg). Span, 30 ft 6½ in (9,30 m). Length, 22 ft 10⅜ in (6,97 m). Height, 8 ft 8⅓ in (2,65 m). Wing area, 238.43 sq ft (22,15 m²).

LETOV Š 13   Czechoslovakia

The Š 13 was built in 1924 as an equi-span biplane with cantilever wings utilising a thick Zhukovsky section. During the initial flight test programme, test pilots were nervous of the cantilever wing arrangement and, in consequence, N-type (later replaced by Vee-type) steel-tube interplane struts were added. The Š 13 was fitted with a Škoda HS 8 water-cooled engine of 300 hp and was originally intended to have a ring-type frontal radiator, but, as a result of difficulties experienced with this cooling arrangement on other fighters, it was fitted with a ventral radiator. Although the Š 13 demonstrated good flying characteristics, some problems were experienced with stability and development was abandoned. *Max speed, 143 mph (230 km/h). Time to 16,405 ft (5 000 m), 18.15 min. Range, 342 mls (550 km). Empty weight, 1,742 lb (790 kg). Loaded weight, 2,570 lb (1 166 kg). Span, 26 ft 2⅞ in (8,00 m). Length, 22 ft 10⅜ in (6,97 m). Height, 9 ft 4½ in (2,86 m). Wing area, 215.29 sq ft (20,00 m²).*

Interplane struts were added (above and below) to the original cantilever wings of the Š 13.

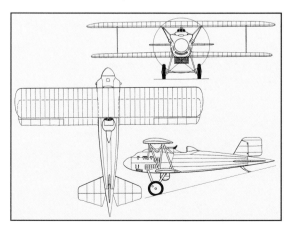

LETOV Š 14   Czechoslovakia

Built in parallel with the Š 13 and powered by a similar Škoda HS 8Fb engine, the Š 14 single-seat single-bay biplane fighter employed a more conventional wing profile. Of mixed construction, with wooden wings and metal fuselage, the Š 14 was discontinued in favour of the Š 20. The prototype was rebuilt as a cantilever

Discarded as a fighter, the Š 14 (above) was rebuilt as a monoplane for speed contests.

monoplane to participate in the 3rd Speed Contest of 1924, and during which it recorded a speed of 153.13 mph (246,44 km/h). The following data relate to the Š 14 in its original fighter form. *Max speed, 148 mph (238 km/h). Time to 16,405 ft (5 000 m), 18.5 min. Range, 308 mls (495 km). Empty weight, 1,464 lb (664 kg). Loaded weight, 1,975 lb (896 kg). Span, 26 ft 6⅞ in (8,10 m). Length, 21 ft 1⅛ in (6,43 m).*

LETOV Š 20   Czechoslovakia

Flown in 1925, the Š 20 was a rotund unequal-span single-bay biplane of mixed construction, with a 300 hp Škoda HS 8Fb water-cooled engine and Lamblin strut-type radiators on the front undercarriage legs. Armament comprised two synchronised 7,7-mm Vickers machine guns. Whereas the upper wing of the first prototype was mounted with no gap above the fuselage, the series model introduced a narrow gap and an inverted-Vee cabane, the upper fuselage decking being recontoured to improve view from the cockpit. In 1926, the Š 20 was the winner in a contest for a new fighter for the Czechoslovak Air Force, and a total of 105 was built for that service. The Š 20 took fourth place at the International Air Meeting in Zürich in 1927, the type serving with all three air regiments of the CzAF. Ten examples were exported to the Latvian Air Force (as the Š 20L), one experimental model was completed with a slimmer fuselage (as the Š 20R) and another was fitted with a Walter-built Bristol Jupiter air-cooled radial of 480 hp

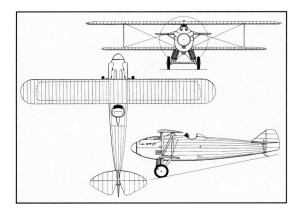

The Š 20 (above and below) is shown by the photo in service with the 5th Air Regiment at Brno.

(as the Š 20J). This last-mentioned model attained an altitude of 28,543 ft (8 700 m). *Max speed, 160 mph (257 km/h). Time to 3,280 ft (1 000 m), 1.33 min. Range, 328 mls (528 km). Empty weight, 1,631 lb (740 kg). Loaded weight, 2,315 lb (1 050 kg). Span, 31 ft 6 in (9,60 m). Length, 24 ft 4⅞ in (7,44 m). Height, 8 ft 4¾ in (2,56 m). Wing area, 198.06 sq ft (18,40 m²).*

With a Jupiter radial engine, the Š 20J (below) was effectively progenitor of the series Š 31.

LETOV Š 22   Czechoslovakia

Inspired by the success of the Dewoitine monoplanes, the Š 22 all-metal single-seat parasol monoplane fighter was completed by Alois Šmolík in 1926. It was powered by a three-row W-type Škoda L engine of 450 hp. Intended armament comprised two synchronised 7,7-mm Vickers machine guns. Flight testing was conducted during March and April 1926, but results proved unsatisfactory and development was discontinued. *Empty weight, 2,059 lb (934 kg). Loaded weight, 2,833 lb (1 285 kg). Span, 33 ft 4¾ in (10,18 m). Length, 25 ft 1⅛ in (7,65 m). Wing area, 167.81 sq ft (15,59 m²).*

Dewoitine influence was obvious in the design of the Š 22 parasol monoplane (below) of 1926.

LETOV Š 31   Czechoslovakia

Derived from the Š 20J, the Š 31 was a competitor of the Avia BH-33L and was an unequal-span single-bay unstaggered biplane with a 480 hp Walter-built Bristol Jupiter VI or VII radial engine. Of all-metal construction with fabric skinning and carrying an armament of two 7,7-mm synchronised Vickers guns, the Š 31 was the unsuccessful contender for series production orders after comparative trials with the BH-33L in 1929-30. However, a production series of 32 Š 31 fighters was ordered to assure employment at the State-owned Letov factory, these being built during 1931-32. Various engine cowlings were tested, but unsuccessful results with these resulted in the Š 31 having an uncowled

engine in service. Considered already obsolescent by the time that it was delivered, the Letov fighter was largely relegated to the training rôle. The Š 31a featured modified tail surfaces and undercarriage struts. *Max speed, 158 mph (254 km/h) at 6,560 ft (2 000 m). Time to 3,280 ft (1 000 m), 1.5 min. Range, 199 mls (320 km). Empty weight, 1,830 lb (830 kg). Loaded weight, 2,765 lb (1 254 kg). Span, 32 ft 1¾ in (9,80 m). Length, 23 ft 5½ in (7,15 m). Height, 9 ft 8⅛ in (2,95 m). Wing area, 234.66 sq ft (21,80 m²).*

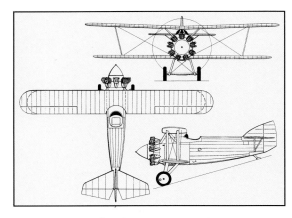

Production of the Š 31 (above and below) was ordered to provide work for the Letov factory.

LETOV Š 131   Czechoslovakia

One Š 31 was completed in 1929 with a 525 hp BMW-built Pratt & Whitney Hornet nine-cylinder radial engine as the Š 131. This prototype was entered in the 1929 *Petite Entente* contest, which it won with an average speed of 155.76 mph (250,66 km/h), attaining 186 mph (299,4 km/h) on the Prague-Brno leg of the competition, the highest speed attained during the entire contest. Two further Š 131 prototypes were built,

The Š 131 (below) won the 1929 *Petite Entente* contest, but failed to gain a production contract.

the aircraft being offered with optional Jupiter VI or VII engines. These were demonstrated in the Balkan states and in China, but failed to gain a production contract. The Š 131 was of similar all-metal construction to the Š 31 and carried an armament of two synchronised 7,7-mm machine guns. *Max speed, 171 mph (275 km/h) at sea level. Time to 3,280 ft (1 000 m). 0.98 min. Range, 280 mls (450 km). Empty weight, 2,072 lb (940 kg). Loaded weight, 3,069 lb (1 392 kg). Dimensions as for Š 31.*

LETOV Š 231   Czechoslovakia

An extensively revised derivative of the Š 131, the Š 231 was an all-metal unequal-span single-bay staggered biplane flown for the first time in 1933. Powered by a 560 hp Gnome-Rhône Mercury 9brs nine-cylinder air-cooled radial enclosed by a Townend ring, the Š 231 car-

Built in small numbers for the national air arm, the Š 231 (above and below) was readily released for sale to the Spanish Republican government.

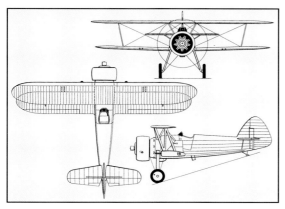

ried an armament of four 7,92-mm MG vz.38 machine guns. These weapons were installed in the upper wing of the first prototype and lower wing of the second prototype. A total of 26 Š 231 fighters was completed, including prototypes, the production series being delivered to the Czechoslovak Air Force in 1936. Inferior to the Avia B 534, the production Š 231 was powered by a Walter-built Mercury VS2 engine and its service with the CzAF proved to be singularly brief. The aircraft were relinquished within a few months and passed on to the Spanish Republican government via an Estonian agent. The first eight reached Santander on 17 March 1937, these being transferred to the Bilbao sector where two were promptly damaged during test flights, two were damaged and two shot down in combat, one was written off in an accident, and, in October 1937, the eighth was captured by the Nationalists. Nine more Š 231s arrived in Barcelona in May-June 1938, and were assigned to coastal patrol and city defence tasks, three surviving the Civil War. As delivered to Spain, the Š 231s were armed with only two Vickers machine guns in the lower wing, some later being fitted with a synchronised third weapon. *Max speed, 216 mph (348 km/h) at 16,405 ft (5 000 m). Time to 16,405 ft (5 000 m), 8.2 min. Range, 280 mls (450 km). Empty weight, 2,822 lb (1 280 kg). Loaded weight, 3,902 lb (1 770 kg). Span, 33 ft 0 in (10,06 m). Length, 25 ft 7 in (7,80 m). Height, 9 ft 10 in (3,00 m). Wing area, 231.43 sq ft (21,50 m²).*

LETOV Š 331   Czechoslovakia

As a further extrapolation of the basic Š 131, the Š 331 retained the airframe of the Š 231, mated with a 900 hp Walter-built Gnome-Rhône K14 two-row radial engine driving a three-bladed metal propeller. In May 1935, shortly after entering flight test, the Š 331 established a new Czechoslovak altitude record by attaining 34,941 ft (10 650 m). The sole prototype was demonstrated in

Turkey, where a speed of 416 mph (670 km/h) was allegedly attained in a dive, the fuselage suffering some damage during the pull-out. After repairs, the prototype Š 331 was sold to representatives of the Spanish Republican government, its ultimate fate being unrecorded. *Max speed, 252 mph (405 km/h). Time to 16,405 ft (5 000 m), 6.7 min. Range, 225 mls (410 km). Empty weight, 3,197 lb (1 450 kg). Loaded weight, 4,299 lb (1 950 kg). Span, 33 ft 0 in (10,06 m). Length, 25 ft 11 in (7,90 m). Wing area, 231.43 sq ft (21,50 m²).*

Eventually sold to the Spanish Republicans, the Š 331 (below) progressed no further than prototype.

LETOV Š 431   Czechoslovakia

The final development of Alois Šmolik's line of single-seat fighters stemming from the Š 31, the Š 431 was essentially similar to its immediate predecessor, but was powered by a 680 hp Armstrong Siddeley Tiger 14-cylinder two-row radial driving a fixed-pitch two-bladed wooden propeller. Flown for the first time in 1936, the sole Š 431 prototype was handed over to the Czechoslovak Air Force, but crashed and was destroyed during flight trials, no further development being undertaken. *Max speed, 230 mph (370 km/h). Time to 16,405 ft (5 000 m), 7.0 min. Range, 280 mls (450 km). Empty weight, 2,888 lb (1 310 kg). Loaded weight, 3,979 lb (1 805 kg). Dimensions as for Š 331.*

Final development of the Šmolik fighter line, the Š 431 (below) failed to survive its flight trials.

LEVASSEUR P.L.5   France

Designed by Jean Biche to meet a Navy requirement for a shipboard two-seat fighter for operation from the carrier *Béarn*, the P.L.5 C2b was a single-bay sesquiplane. Of wooden construction, the fuselage was watertight, the undercarriage being jettisonable and flush-fitting stabilising floats being provided to allow the aircraft to alight on water in an emergency. Four prototypes were built in 1924, the first, second and fourth having a 450 hp Hispano-Suiza 12Ha and the third having a 480 hp Renault 12Kd engine. After successful trials at Saint-Raphaël, a series of 20 aircraft was ordered, these being delivered between July and December 1926. The series version of the P.L.5 carried an armament of two forward-firing 7,7-mm Vickers machine guns and twin Lewis guns of similar calibre on a ring mounting in the rear cockpit. Power was provided by a 450 hp Lorraine-Dietrich water-cooled engine. *Max speed, 140 mph (225 km/h) at sea level, 134 mph (215 km/h) at 16,405 ft (5 000 m). Time to 16,405 ft (5 000 m), 22 min. Range, 497 mls (800 km). Empty weight, 2,535 lb (1 150 kg). Loaded weight, 3,968 lb (1 800 kg). Span, 40 ft 8¼ in (12,40 m). Length, 28 ft 10½ in (8,80 m). Height, 10 ft 2 in (3,10 m). Wing area, 398.28 sq ft (37,00 m²).*

The P.L.5 shipboard fighter (above and below) was operated from the carrier *Béarn* in the mid '20s.

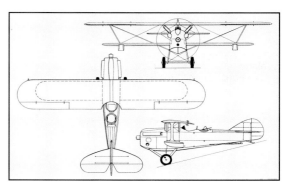

LEVASSEUR P.L.6   France

The single prototype P.L.6 (above) was intended to meet a 1925 *Armée de l'Air* fighter requirement.

Conceived to meet the requirements of the 1925 C2 programme calling for a diurnal two-seat fighter and reconnaissance aircraft, the P.L.6 C2 was a single-bay biplane powered by a 500 hp Hispano-Suiza 12Hb twelve-cylinder Vee-type water-cooled engine. It carried an armament of two fixed forward-firing Vickers guns and two Lewis guns on a ring mounting in the rear cockpit. Having no relationship to the shipboard P.L.5, the P.L.6 prototype entered flight test in 1926 and was displayed at the *Salon de l'Aéronautique* of that year in Paris. The P.L.6 was in competition with the Avimeta 88, the Mureaux 3 and 4, the Blériot-SPAD 60, the Villiers 24 and the Wibault 12. In the event, the C2 programme was abandoned in 1928, and further development of the P.L.6 was discontinued. *Max speed, 134 mph (215 km/h) at 16,405 ft (5 000 m). Range, 435 mls (700 km). Empty weight, 2,976 lb (1 350 kg). Loaded weight, 4,795 lb (2 175 kg). Span, 40 ft 0 in (12,20 m). Length, 28 ft 8½ in (8,75 m). Height, 10 ft 2 in (3.10 m). Wing area, 430.57 sq ft (40,00 m²).*

LEVY-BICHE LB 2   France

Designed by Jean Biche and built by Constructions Aéronautiques J Levy, the LB 2 was a single-bay sesquiplane single-seat shipboard fighter featuring a boat-type watertight fuselage divided into a number of compartments. A jettisonable undercarriage was fitted and small stabilising floats provided for use when alighting on water in an emergency. Powered by a 330 hp Hispano-Suiza 8Se water-cooled engine and carrying an armament of two 7,7-mm Vickers machine guns, the LB 2 was of wooden construction and was intended to operate from the carrier *Béarn*. The LB 2 was flown for the first time in 1927, and, in October of that year, with a twin-float undercarriage from Saint-Raphaël. With the failure of the J Levy company, the rights in the LB 2 design were transferred to the Etablissements P. Levasseur, which manufactured a series of 20 aircraft, designated LB 2 AMC1, during 1928-29. These saw limited service aboard the *Béarn* and from shore bases. *Max speed, 136 mph (219 km/h). Time to 16,405 ft (5 000 m), 25 min. Empty weight, 2,028 lb (920 kg). Loaded weight, 2,976 lb (1 350 kg). Span, 34 ft 1½ in (10,40 m). Length, 24 ft 8¼ in (7,52 m). Height, 11 ft 5⅓ in (3,49 m). Wing area, 258.34 sq ft (24,00 m²).*

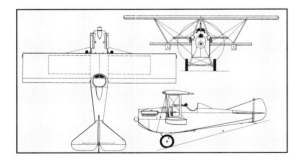

A limited service career was achieved by the LB 2 (above and below), which was built by Levasseur.

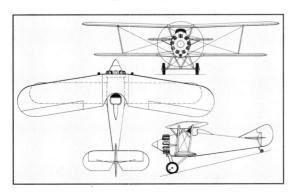

LEVY-BICHE LB 6   France

The LB 6 single-seat single-bay biplane fighter, designed by Jean Biche, was intended for shipboard operation, and was, like the LB 2, transferred to the Etablissements P Levasseur with the failure of the J Levy company. Characterised by sweptback upper wing surfaces and powered by a 420 hp Gnome-Rhône Jupiter nine-cylinder radial engine, the LB 6 had interchangeable wheel and float undercarriages. Five examples of the LB 6 were built by Levasseur in the late 'twenties, most of these being fitted with a single-float undercarriage, but no further details of this type are available.

(Below) The LB 6 shipboard single-seat fighter.

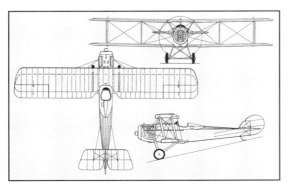

LEWIS & VOUGHT VE-7   USA

Designed specifically as a tandem two-seat advanced trainer for the US Army, the VE-7 was the first product of the Lewis & Vought Corp. Founded on 18 June 1917 by Birdseye B Lewis and Chance M Vought, this was predecessor of the Chance Vought Corp (established in May 1922). A wooden two-bay equi-span biplane powered by a 150 hp Hispano-Suiza Model A engine, the VE-7 was completed in February 1918. It was adopted by the US Navy in October 1919, with the 180 hp Wright Hispano E-2 engine. A total of 129 was to be completed (69 by the Naval Aircraft Factory) and of these a substantial proportion emerged as VE-7G two-seat and VE-7S single-seat fighters. The former was a modification of the VE-7H unarmed single-float observation seaplane with controls transferred from rear to forward cockpit. A single fixed forward-firing synchronised 0.3-in (7,62-mm) Vickers gun was provided, together with a Lewis gun of similar calibre in the rear cockpit, and a wheel undercarriage was fitted. When provided with emergency flotation gear and hydrovanes, this type was designated VE-7GF. The single-seat fighter model was introduced in 1921. Forty were produced by Lewis & Vought and a further 24 by the Naval Aircraft Factory. These had the forward cockpit deleted and an armament of one synchronised 0.3-in (7,62-mm) Vickers gun. With wheel undercarriage, flotation gear and hydrovanes, it was designated VE-7SF, and with single main float and outrigger stabilising

The two-seat VE-7G (above) and single-seat VE-7S (below) were fighter variants of a trainer design.

A single-seat VE-7S built by Lewis & Vought (above) and an NAF-built two-seat VE-7GF (below) showing flotation gear and hydrovanes.

floats it was known as the VE-7SH. The VE-7S equipped the US Navy's first shipboard fighter squadron, VF-2, aboard the USS *Langley*. The following data relate to the VE-7SF. *Max speed, 117 mph (188 km/h) at sea level. Time to 5,000 ft (1 525 m), 5.5 min. Range, 290 mls (467 km). Empty weight, 1,505 lb (683 kg). Loaded weight, 2,100 lb (953 kg). Span, 34 ft 1⅜ in (10,40 m). Length, 24 ft 5⅛ in (7,44 m). Height, 8 ft 7 in (2,62 m). Wing area, 284.5 sq ft (26,43 m²).*

LEWIS & VOUGHT VE-8   USA

The VE-8 (above and below) proved unsuccessful when tested at McCook Field in 1920.

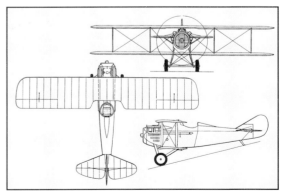

Based on the VE-7, but with a 300 hp Hispano-Suiza Model H engine, reduced overall dimensions, increased wing area, a shorter, faired cabane and paired 0.3-in (7,62-mm) synchronised Vickers guns, the VE-8 single-seat fighter was completed in July 1919. Four were ordered by the US Army, but, in the event, only two were completed and one of these was assigned to static tests. The VE-8 was flight tested at McCook Field in 1920, but the results were highly unfavourable. The aircraft proved overweight, with heavy controls, in-adequate stability and sluggish performance. *Max speed, 140 mph (225 km/h) at sea level. Time to 5,000 ft (1 525 m), 4.25 min. Loaded weight, 2,435 lb (1 105 kg). Span, 31 ft 0 in (9,45 m). Length, 21 ft 4 in (6,50 m). Height, 8 ft 7⅞ in (2,64 m). Wing area 307 sq ft (28,52 m²).*

LEWIS & VOUGHT VE-9   USA

Essentially an improved VE-7, the VE-9 embodied com-paratively minor changes, and these were mostly con-fined to the fuel system, a pair of interconnected tanks replacing the single tank of the earlier model. The VE-9 was powered by a 180 hp Wright Hispano E-3, and 21 were ordered by the US Navy in two versions; the single-seat VE-9 fighter with wheel undercarriage for shipboard use and the two-seat VE-9H unarmed obser-vation float seaplane for catapult use from battleships and cruisers. The latter had modified vertical tail sur-faces for improved water and catapult stability. The first VE-9 was delivered to the US Navy on 24 June 1922, the fighter version serving alongside the VE-7S aboard the USS *Langley*. Data for the VE-9 are as for the VE-7S.

The VE-9 was, like the VE-7, built in single- (below) and two-seat fighter versions.

LFG ROLAND D I   Germany

Shortly before World War I, the Luft-Fahrzeug Gesell-schaft (LFG) adopted the corporate tradename "Roland" to avoid confusion with the Luft-Verkehrs-Gesellschaft (LVG). In 1916, the company initiated the design of a single-seat fighter under the direction of Dipl-Ing Tantzen. It was proposed that the new fighter should embody the innovative structural techniques adopted for the highly successful C II *Walfisch* (Whale) which utilised the so-called *Wickelrumpf*, or "wrapped fuselage", a moulded two-piece shell composed of thin bands of spruce veneer reinforced with fabric. Three prototypes of the new D I fighter were ordered in April

Small-scale production of the Roland D I (above and below) was achieved during the course of 1916.

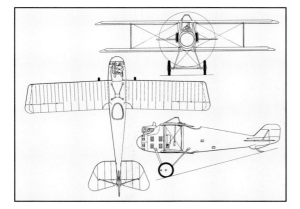

1916, and with the completion of *Idflieg* (*Inspektion der Fliegertruppen*) testing in August, LFG was awarded a contract for 60 aircraft. Concurrently, the Pfalz Flug-zeugwerke received a contract for a further 20 aircraft. The D I was powered by a 160 hp Mercedes D III water-cooled engine and carried an armament of two syn-chronised LMG 08/15 machine guns. Although the D I made its appearance at the Front in October 1916, a severe fire at the LFG factory in the previous month had reduced deliveries to little more than a token quantity. The D I inventory at the Front attained a peak of 12 air-craft in February 1917, and the type had disappeared from front-line units in the following June, a few con-tinuing to serve as fighter trainers through 1918. The D I was unofficially known as the *Haifisch* (Shark). *Max speed, 112 mph (180 km/h) at sea level. Time to 3,280 ft (1 000 m), 7 min. Empty weight, 1,541 lb (699 kg). Loaded weight, 2,055 lb (932 kg). Span, 29 ft 2⅓ in (8,90 m). Length, 22 ft 3⅔ in (6,80 m). Height, 9 ft 6 in (2,90 m). Wing area, 247.58 sq ft (23,00 m²).*

LFG ROLAND D II   Germany

Improved forward and downward view from the cockpit was offered by the Roland D II (above).

While the pilot of the D I enjoyed an excellent upward view, the view downwards, impeded by the somewhat rotund fuselage and twin ear radiators, left much to be desired and was the subject of much criticism. Dipl-Ing Tantzen and his team therefore undertook some rede-sign, which resulted in the D II. Whereas the upper decking of the D I fuselage was faired into the upper wing, that of the D II was cut down and a narrow pylon faired into the wing, the lateral radiators being dis-carded in favour of a radiator in the upper wing. The D II proved more difficult to fly and somewhat less manoeuvrable than the Albatros D I, and had a ten-dency to enter a spin from a steep bank. Nonetheless, in October 1916, LFG received a contract for 30 D II fighters powered by the 160 hp Mercedes D III and armed with two 7,9-mm LMG 08/15 guns. A contract for an additional 100 aircraft was awarded to the Pfalz Flugzeugwerke in the following month. With the avail-ability of the new 180 hp Argus As III water-cooled engine, this power plant was mated with the D II air-

frame and production continued as the D IIa, of which 40 were ordered in November 1916, 100 in January 1917 and a final 50 in the following March. Performances of the D II and IIa were essentially similar, but the Argus engine of the latter unexpectedly demonstrated a severe power loss at higher altitudes, seriously restrict-ing the fighter's usefulness. The D II reached the Front in February 1917, strength peaking at 97 aircraft in April and tapering off until the type disappeared from the first line inventory in October. The D IIa reached the Front in June 1917, in which month the inventory reached 128 aircraft, and it was withdrawn from first line service in December 1917. Data relate to the D II. *Max speed, 103 mph (165 km/h). Time to 16,405 ft (5 000 m), 23 min. Empty weight, 1,400 lb (635 kg). Loaded weight, 1,797 lb (815 kg). Span, 29 ft 3⅞ in (8,94 m). Length, 22 ft 8¾ in (6,93 m). Height, 10 ft 2½ in (3,11 m). Wing area, 245.21 sq ft (22,78 m²).*

LFG ROLAND D III   Germany

In a further attempt to improve visibility for the pilot, LFG evolved the D III. Using a fuselage essentially simi-lar to that of the D II, this introduced staggered, un-equal-span and unequal-chord wings, and a cabane of broad aerofoil-section struts. Retaining the 180 hp Argus As III engine of the D IIa and the paired 7,9-mm LMG 08/15 armament, the D III received type test approval in May 1917. LFG and Pfalz respectively re-ceived contracts for 150 and 200 aircraft. In the event, Pfalz did not build the LFG fighter, switching instead to the Pfalz D III, and as the former was powered by the marginally-performing Argus engine, very few Roland D IIIs were assigned to the Front, a maximum of nine being with first line units in February 1918 and the last being withdrawn in the following April. *Max speed, 109 mph (175 km/h) at sea level. Empty weight, 1,581 lb (717 kg). Loaded weight, 2,119 lb (961 kg). Wing area, 213.45 sq ft (19,83 m²).*

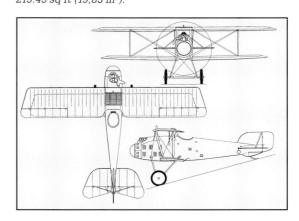

A raised top wing and a conventional cabane distinguished the Roland D III (above and below) from the earlier Roland fighter biplanes.

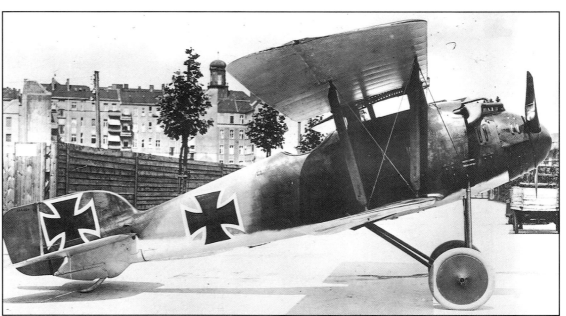

LFG ROLAND D IV (Dr I) Germany

The D IV single-seat fighter triplane of mid-1917 marked a noteworthy departure from previous LFG structural methods in that the *Wickelrumpf* that had characterised all previous aircraft gave place to the so-called *Klinkerrumpf* – clinker-built or lapstrake construction utilising the planking methods commonly employed in the construction of small boat hulls. Strips of spruce overlapped one another by some two-thirds over a light framework of stringers and formers. This method of construction was less time-consuming than the *Wickelrumpf* and comparably robust. The D IV – later to be redesignated Dr I when the "Dr" prefix was adopted for triplanes – was powered by a 160 hp Mercedes D III water-cooled engine and carried the usual armament of twin synchronised 7,9-mm LMG 08/15 machine guns. A single prototype was ordered by the *Idflieg* for evaluation, but this crashed at the end of September 1917. It was promptly rebuilt utilising a D VI fuselage, but subsequent testing revealed no particularly outstanding characteristics and further development was discontinued. *Max speed, 96 mph (155 km/h). Service ceiling, 19,685 ft (6 000 m). Empty weight, 2,050 lb (930 kg). Loaded weight, 2,665 lb (1 208 kg). Span, 31 ft 0 in (9,45 m). Length, 24 ft 0 in (7,32 m).*

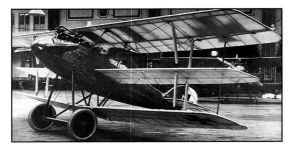

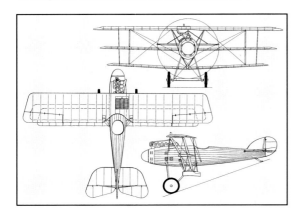

The D IV (above and below) was the first Roland fighter to adopt the *Klinkerrumpf* construction method.

LFG ROLAND W Germany

The Roland W twin-float fighter seaplane was an adaptation of the D I. Flown for the first time on 29 June 1917, and powered by a 160 hp Mercedes D III engine, it arrived for evaluation at the base of the *Seeflugzeug-Versuchs-Kommando* (SVK) at Warnemünde in the following month. It was promptly returned to LFG for modifications aimed at improving the flying characteristics and the view from the cockpit. It was returned to the SVK in September 1917, modified once more and then flight tested, but the poor visibility it offered the

The Roland W (below) was a twin-float seaplane adaptation of the D I, remaining a prototype.

pilot led to its prompt rejection. The sole prototype, after further modification to the fuselage, was assigned to the marine single-seat fighter school in November 1917. *Time to 3,280 ft (1 000 m), 5.4 min. Empty weight, 2,531 lb (1 148 kg). Span, 33 ft 1⅔ in (10,10 m). Length, 29 ft 4⅓ in (8,95 m). Height, 10 ft 5⅞ in (3,20 m).*

LFG ROLAND D V Germany

The D V (above and below) was derived from the D III, the shortcomings of which were not overcome.

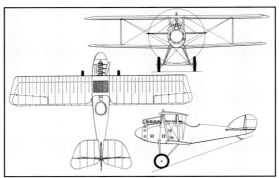

During the autumn of 1917, three prototypes of the D V were built in an attempt to eradicate the shortcomings revealed by the D III. Retaining the moulded two-piece shell-type fuselage construction of the earlier fighter, and being, in fact, the last LFG type to utilise this so-called *Wickelrumpf*, the D V employed the complete wing cellule of the D III. The fuselage cross section was reduced and the decking lowered to improve vision from the cockpit. Armament remained two 7,9-mm LMG 08/15 machine guns, and while one prototype retained the 180 hp Argus As III engine of the earlier D II and D III, the other two were powered by the 160 hp Mercedes D III. Testing revealed little advance over the D III and development was discontinued in favour of the D VI. No data relating to the D V are available.

LFG ROLAND D VI Germany

On 17 October 1917, the first of three prototypes of the D VI fighter was rolled out as the 1,000th aircraft manufactured by LFG. Whereas the D V had been essentially an attempt to enhance the capabilities of the D III design, the D VI was an entirely new design. Utilising the *Klinkerrumpf* fuselage constructional method first employed by the abortive D IV (Dr I), the D VI entered flight test in November 1917, initially with a 160 hp Mercedes D III engine. As supplies of this engine were restricted, the 185 hp Benz Bz IIIa was installed in at least one of the three prototypes. Testing continued through January 1918, being hampered by inclement weather and difficulties in achieving a suitable propeller match with the engine-airframe combination. After participating in the 1st D-type contest at Adlershof, the D VI passed its type test on 9 February 1918, an initial order being placed for 50 aircraft. By the time World War I came to an end, orders had been placed for 350 D VIa (Mercedes D IIIa) and D VIb (Benz Bz IIIa) fighters. Both the D VIa and D VIb began to reach combat units in May-June 1918, 58 of the former and 12 of the latter being included in the frontline inventory of 31 August. Pilots did not consider the D VI to be anything more

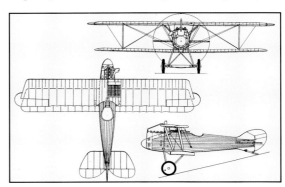

The Mercedes-engined D VIa (above) was, in other respects, similar to the Benz-engined D VIb (below).

than a marginal improvement over the Albatros D Va and Pfalz D IIIa that it was intended to replace – it was slightly faster and more manoeuvrable, but had a lower climb rate – yet it remained in limited production until the end of the conflict. Of the 350 built, 200 were of the D VIb version to which the following data relate. *Max speed, 124 mph (199 km/h). Time to 16,405 ft (5 000 m), 19 min. Endurance, 2 hrs. Empty weight, 1,446 lb (656 kg). Loaded weight, 1,865 lb (846 kg). Span, 30 ft 10⅞ in (9,42 m). Length, 20 ft 8⅞ in (6,32 m). Height, 9 ft 2¼ in (2,80 m). Wing area, 238.1 sq ft (22,12 m²).*

The Roland D VIb fighter (below) began to reach combat units at the Front in mid-1918.

LFG ROLAND D VII Germany

Evolved in parallel with the D VI and also participating in the 1st D-type contest at Adlershof, the D VII was of similar construction and carried an identical armament of two 7,9-mm LMG 08/15 machine guns. It was powered, however, by the still-experimental 185 hp Benz Bz IIIbo eight-cylinder direct-drive engine. Although pilots considered forward view from the cockpit to be outstanding, thanks to the Vee-type arrangement of the engine, the Bz IIIbo was still suffering teething troubles. In the course of further development, the ailerons were revised and D VI-type vertical tail surfaces introduced. The aircraft again participated

Revised ailerons and tail unit were applied to the D VII (below) before it was finally abandoned.

in a D-type contest, the 2nd, in May 1918. The engine was still insufficiently developed, however, and its recurrent problems dictated termination of the D VII test programme. *Max speed, 118 mph (190 km/h). Time to 16,405 ft (5 000 m), 16.2 min. Endurance, 1.5 hrs. Empty weight, 1,468 lb (666 kg). Loaded weight, 1,892 lb (858 kg). Span, 29 ft 0 in (8,84 m). Length, 20 ft 0 in (6,10 m). Height, 9 ft 2¼ in (2,80 m). Wing area, 224.22 sq ft (20,83 m²).*

LFG ROLAND D VIII   Germany

Built by LFG concurrently with the D VII, the D VIII differed essentially in having a geared Benz Bz IIIbm eight-cylinder Vee-type engine of 185 hp in place of the direct-drive Bz IIIbo. According to *Idflieg* reports, the D VIII was scheduled to make its appearance on 5 May 1918, in time to participate in the 2nd D-type contest. Although records concerning the D VIII are sparse, the debriefing minutes of the contest stated that "due to the results obtained during the trials, the Roland D VIII cannot be considered for series production". It is known that the reduction gearing of the Bz IIIbm engine suffered severe vibration and recurrent mechanical faults, and it may be assumed that further development was discontinued after the Competition. No data or illustrations of the D VIII are available.

LFG ROLAND D IX   Germany

The second D IX (above) with overhung ailerons, and (below) with enlarged, horn-balanced rudder.

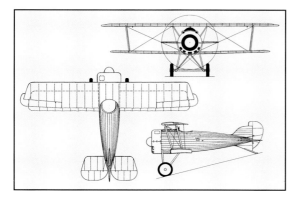

With the advent of more powerful rotary engines in the spring of 1918, *Idflieg* supported the development of compatible fighters, one such being the D IX powered by the new 160 hp Siemens-Halske Sh III rotary. The first D IX prototype demonstrated excellent performance at the 1st D-type contest in January 1918, before being destroyed as a result of a freak accident. While the D IX was in flight, the pilot's seat collapsed, its occupant inadvertently pulling the aircraft into a tight loop in which the resultant *g* forces propelled him through the bottom of the fuselage before the aircraft broke up. At the time, two more prototypes were in assembly, the first of these being successfully load-tested in April prior to resumption of flight testing. The second D IX differed in having enlarged tail surfaces and unbalanced ailerons. Armament comprised twin synchronised 7,9-mm LMG 08/15 machine guns. It appeared in the 2nd D-type contest in May, but, according to the debriefing minutes, was considered unsuited for series production. The third D IX had been completed meanwhile with overhung, unbalanced ailerons and a larger horn-balanced rudder. *Max speed, 115 mph (185 km/h). Time to 16,405 ft (5 000 m), 16.4 min. En-*

durance, 1.5 hrs. Empty weight, 1,177 lb (534 kg). Loaded weight, 1,596 lb (724 kg). Span, 29 ft 3¼ in (8,92 m). Length, 19 ft 4¼ in (5,90 m). Height, 9 ft 0 in (2,75 m). Wing area, 198.92 sq ft (18,48 m²).

LFG ROLAND D XIII   Germany

Based on the D VII, the single D XIII (above) had the experimental Körting Vee-type engine.

In March 1918, after the experimental 195 hp Körting Kg III eight-cylinder water-cooled Vee-type engine had completed a 24-hour duration test, an example of this power plant fitted with reduction gear was delivered to the Luft-Fahrzeug Gesellschaft for installation in the prototype of a new single-seat fighter, the D XIII. Based on the D VII and ordered in April 1918, the D XIII entered flight test in May 1918, but crankshaft cooling proved inadequate and difficulties were experienced with the oil system. In July, the Kg III engine was removed from the prototype and returned to the manufacturer for modification. It was destined not to be re-installed, however, as the D XIII was one of 10 prototypes destroyed in a hangar fire on 25 July 1918. The D XIII was fitted with two synchronised LMG 08/15 machine guns. No performance data were recorded. *Span, 29 ft 6⅓ in (9,00 m). Wing area, 247.58 sq ft (23,00 m²).*

LFG ROLAND D XIV   Germany

Essentially similar to the D XIII, the D XIV was ordered by *Idflieg* in April 1918 to evaluate the new Goebel Goe III 11-cylinder rotary engine of 160 hp. Fitted with the standard twin 7,9-mm LMG 08/15 gun armament, the prototype D XIV was completed in time to participate in the 2nd D-type contest in May 1918. Flying was strictly limited by the recalcitrant engine, and this, in accordance with competition protocol, eliminated the D XIV from further consideration as a production type. No data relating to the D XIV are available.

Basically similar to the D XIII, the D XIV (below) was powered by the unsatisfactory Goebel rotary.

LFG ROLAND D XV   Germany

Three prototypes of the D XV were ordered in April 1918, the original intention being to fit each aircraft with a different engine for comparison purposes. The D XV perpetuated the use of the *Klinkerrumpf* (clinker-built) fuselage first used on the D IV. The wing cellule was of the "wireless" type, having no bracing cables, and featured appreciably more stagger than that of any preceding LFG fighter. The first D XV was powered by a 160 hp Mercedes D IIIa engine and was completed before the end of April, but flight testing was interrupted in May by the decision to return the prototype to the factory for modifications. A second, similarly-powered, D XV appeared in June 1918, the principal changes being replacement of the paired interplane struts by single I-type struts and the introduction of overhanging ailerons on the upper wing. This proto-

type was flight tested with both the Mercedes engine and a 185 hp BMW IIIa, demonstrating a good turn of speed, but proving deficient in climb rate. In September 1918, *Idflieg* demanded further modifications in the light of the trials conducted with the first two prototypes. Instead, the LFG designed a completely *new* fighter which retained the D XV designation. The following data relate to the initial version of the D XV with the Mercedes D IIIa engine. *Empty weight, 1,609 lb (730 kg). Loaded weight, 2,006 lb (910 kg). Span, 28 ft 4⅛ in (8,64 m). Wing area, 256.19 sq ft (23,80 m²).*

In its initial form, the D XV prototype (below) had paired interplane struts and Mercedes engine.

LFG ROLAND D XV (II)   Germany

Rather than introduce the modifications in the D XV demanded by *Idflieg*, LFG produced an entirely *new* fighter bearing no relationship to its predecessor, but, nevertheless, retaining the D XV designation. Bearing a strong similarity to the Fokker D VII and claimed by some to be no more than an unauthorised copy of that fighter, the new D XV was of different construction. The clinker-built fuselage gave place to one of rectangular cross section with plywood skinning, tubular steel N-type interplane bracing struts were employed and two prototypes were built. The first of these appeared late in October 1918 with a 185 hp BMW IIIa engine, and the second was rolled out shortly afterwards with a 200 hp Benz Bz IIIa. Neither prototype participated in the 3rd D-type contest, and further development was halted by the Armistice. No data relating to the second D XV design are available.

Retaining the D XV designation, a wholly new design (below) was produced late in 1918.

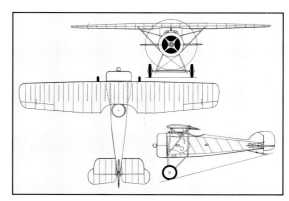

LFG ROLAND D XVI   Germany

Two versions of the D XVI parasol monoplane fighter – initially designated E I – were completed in September-October 1918, one powered by a 160 hp Goebel Goe III rotary and the other by a similarly-rated Siemens-

(Below) Second prototype of the D XVI fighter.

A Siemens-Halske Sh III engine distinguished the second of the two D XVI fighter prototypes (above).

Halske Sh III rotary. The D XVI had a fully-cantilevered fabric-covered parasol wing and a slab-sided plywood-covered fuselage, armament comprising twin synchronised 7,9-mm LMG 08/15 machine guns. Although the 3rd D-type contest was officially restricted to types powered by the BMW engine, *Idflieg* permitted participation of the Sh III-engined D XVI as it was considered "an interesting type". The D XVI proved faster than the Siemens-Schuckert D IV and Fokker D VII up to an altitude of 13,125 ft (4 000 m), but was slower above that height. *Span 31 ft 0½ in (9,46 m). Length, 19 ft 4 in (5,90 m).*

LFG ROLAND D XVII Germany

The last single-seat fighter to be developed by LFG was the D XVII parasol monoplane powered by a 185 hp BMW IIIa engine. Rolled out on 18 October 1918, the D XVII was in time to be included in the 3rd D-type contest held at Adlershof that month, but was considered markedly inferior to the similarly-powered Fokker V 29 parasol monoplane. During turns the wing of the D XVII oscillated alarmingly and landing was difficult because of a tendency to stall suddenly during the approach if speed was not maintained. No further details are available.

Last of the Roland single-seat fighters, the D XVII (below) was flown just before the end of World War I.

LIORE et OLIVIER LeO 8 France

In April 1919, the *Direction de l'Aéronautique* established a new programme for the development of successors for the World War I aircraft types then equipping the *Aéronautique Militaire*. Among several categories of fighter included in this programme was a two-seat night fighter and reconnaissance aircraft (CAN 2), the specification for which demanded a max speed of at least 124 mph (200 km/h) at 9,840 ft (3 000 m). To meet this requirement, the Lioré et Olivier concern developed a large, angular parasol monoplane powered by a 300 hp Renault 12F 12-cylinder water-cooled engine and designated LeO 8 CAN 2. Of metal construction and with provision for two forward-firing Vickers guns and two Lewis guns in the rear cockpit, the LeO 8 was flown for the first time at Villacoublay in April 1923. Although no production order was placed,

the prototype was prepared for an attempt on the world altitude record with a 1,102-lb (500-kg) payload. This attempt, which took place in 1925, ended in a tragedy with the death of the pilot. *Max speed, 134 mph (215 km/h) at sea level, 121 mph (195 km/h) at 9,840 ft (3 000 m). Ceiling, 20,670 ft (6 300 m). Empty weight, 2,809 lb (1 274 kg). Loaded weight, 4,138 lb (1 877 kg). Span, 50 ft 10¼ in (15,50 m). Length, 28 ft 6½ in (8,70 m). Height, 9 ft 10⅛ in (3,00 m). Wing area, 344.46 sq ft (32,00 m²).*

As a two-seat night fighter, the LeO 8 (above and below) entered flight test at Villacoublay in 1923.

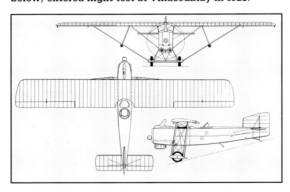

LIORE et OLIVIER LeO 9 France

Derived from a 1917 project designated LeO 3, the LeO 9 single-seat cantilever monoplane fighter was of metal construction and of advanced aerodynamic concept. Powered by a 300 hp Hispano-Suiza 8Fb eight-cylinder water-cooled engine, the LeO 9 was exhibited, prior to first flight at the Paris *Salon* in 1921. Flight testing was initiated in the following year, but, on 24 September 1923, the wing folded during a very sharp turn and the aircraft crashed at Villacoublay with the death of the pilot, Gaston Martin. Further development of the LeO 9

The LeO 9 is seen here displayed at the 1921 Paris *Salon* prior to the commencement of flight testing.

was then discontinued. *Estimated max speed, 186 mph (300 km/h). Estimated ceiling, 16,405 ft (5 000 m). Empty weight, 2,590 lb (1 175 kg). Span, 35 ft 10⅔ in (10,94 m). Length, 21 ft 7½ in (6,59 m). Height, 7 ft 1⅘ in (2,18 m). Wing area, 185.15 sq ft (17,20 m²).*

LIUCHOW KWANGSI Type 3 China

Under the direction of Chee Wing Jeang, the Liuchow Mechanical and Aircraft Factory in the Chinese province of Kwangsi – which had achieved a measure of autonomy in 1937 – completed prototypes of two aircraft, the Kwangsi Types 2 and 3. Both were unequal-span biplanes with spruce and plywood wings, and fabric-covered welded steel-tube fuselages, and were respectively a tandem two-seat trainer and a single-seat lightweight fighter. The latter, the Type 3, was powered by an Armstrong Siddeley Cheetah IIA seven-cylinder radial rated at 260 hp at 2,500 ft (760 m) and carried an armament of a single 7,7-mm machine gun synchronised to fire through the propeller. The Type 3 was flown in July 1937, but performance proved insufficient to justify further development. *Max speed, 176 mph (283 km/h). Time to 5,200 ft (1 585 m), 5 min. Endurance, 3 hrs. Empty weight, 1,675 lb (760 kg). Loaded weight, 2,300 lb (1 043 kg). Span, 26 ft 3 in (8,00 m). Length, 20 ft 6 in (6,25 m). Height, 8 ft 3 in (2,50 m).*

Flown in 1937, the lightweight Kwangsi Type 3 (above) was one of China's first indigenous types.

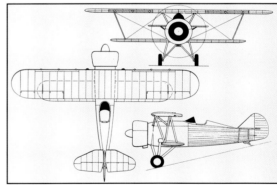

The Kwangsi Type 3 (above and below) in its definitive form with fully-cowled engine.

LLOYD 40.15 Austria-Hungary

In the late summer of 1917, the Magyar "Lloyd" Repülögép és Motogyár (Ungarische Flugzeug-und Motorenfabrik "Lloyd") initiated design of a single-seat fighter triplane. The centre and lower wings of this fighter were fully cantilevered, the upper wing being supported by Vee-type struts. Another unusual feature was the adoption of rotating ailerons on the centre wing. The Lloyd 40.15, as the fighter was designated, was powered by a 185 hp Daimler (MAG) six-cylinder water-cooled engine. It reportedly made its début in December 1917 (although, according to a report dated

1 March 1918, the prototype was in process of assembly at that time). No information regarding subsequent flight testing has survived. *Loaded weight, 1,984 lb (900 kg). Span, 24 ft 11¼ in (7,60 m). Length, 23 ft 3½ in (7,10 m). Height, 9 ft 3 in (2,82 m). Wing area, 238.96 sq ft (22,20 m²).*

(Below) The Lloyd 40.15 fighter triplane.

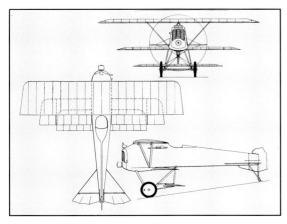

LLOYD 40.16   Austria-Hungary

Evolved in parallel with the Lloyd 40.15 and designed by Ing Hanns Wizina and Ing von Melczer, the Lloyd 40.16 single-seat fighter biplane was completed in December 1917. It offered an unconventional solution to the problem of providing the pilot with the best possible forward and downward view. The wings were given extreme stagger and were mounted independently, the upper wing being supported by a massive aerofoil-section strut which contributed some lift, a smaller triangular strut supporting the semi-canti-levered lower wing. The Lloyd 40.16 was originally intended to be powered by a 200 hp Benz (Mar) engine and to have rotating wingtip ailerons. In the event, the 220 hp engine was supplanted by a 185 hp Daimler (MAG) engine for demonstration during the fighter evaluation of July 1918, and conventional ailerons were fitted to the upper wing. No record of the results of flight testing has survived. *Loaded weight, 2,216 lb (1 005 kg). Span, 28 ft 1⅞ in (8,58 m). Length, 22 ft 8⅖ in (6,92 m). Height, 8 ft 5½ in (2,58 m). Wing area, 264.05 sq ft (24,53 m²).*

(Below) The unconventional Lloyd 40.16 biplane.

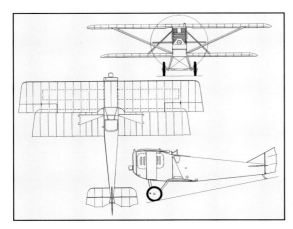

LOCKHEED YP-24 (XP-900)   USA

A two-seat fighter based broadly on the Lockheed 8D Altair monoplane by Robert J Wood, the XP-900 (Wright Field project number) was the first military aircraft produced by the Lockheed Aircraft Corporation, at that time a division of the Detroit Aircraft Corporation. Of mixed construction, combining metal fuselage and tail surfaces with wooden wings, and powered by a 600 hp Curtiss Conqueror V-1570C engine, the XP-900 was delivered to Wright Field on 29 September 1931. It was then purchased by the Army Air Corps and redesignated YP-24. Carrying an armament of two synchronised machine guns (one 0.3-in/7,62-mm and one 0.5-

in/12,7-mm) and one 0.3-in (7,62-mm) gun on a flexible mount, the YP-24 was lost on 19 October 1931, but prior to this event a contract had been placed for five Y1P-24 two-seat fighters and four examples of the Y1A-9 attack version. The bankruptcy of the company led to the shelving of the contract until Robert Woods joined the Consolidated Aircraft Corporation whereupon the YP-24 was developed into the all-metal Consolidated Y1P-25 (which see). *Max speed, 235 mph (378 km/h). Initial climb, 1,820 ft/min (9,24 m/sec). Range, 556 mls (895 km). Empty weight, 3,010 lb (1 365 kg). Loaded weight, 4,360 lb (1 978 kg). Span, 42 ft 9½ in (13,04 m). Length, 28 ft 9 in (8,76 m). Height, 8 ft 6 in (2,59 m). Wing area, 292 sq ft (27,13 m²).*

Development of the YP-24 (below) was passed to Consolidated after Lockheed's collapse in 1931.

LOCKHEED XP-38 TO P-38G LIGHTNING   USA

Of radical configuration for its day in featuring twin tail-booms, the Lightning was conceived as a turbo-super-charged, twin-engined, high-altitude interceptor, the prototype, designated XP-38, flying on 27 January 1939. A service test batch of 13 aircraft designated YP-38 followed, the first of these flying on 16 September 1940 with two 1,150 hp Allison V-1710-27/29 (F2) engines. The YP-38 had an armament of one 37-mm cannon and a pair each of 0.3-in (7,62-mm) and 0.5-in (12,7-mm) machine guns. USAAC production contracts were preceded by orders from France and the UK for a total of 667 aircraft, the latter country taking over the contracts of the former with the fall of France. The RAF rejected the Lightning after receipt of only three aircraft, 140 built against these contracts being absorbed by the USAAC as operational trainers. The initial USAAC production model, the P-38, differed from the YP-38s primarily in replacing the 0.3-in (7,62-mm) guns with weapons of 0.5-in (12,7-mm) calibre. One of 30 P-38s built was completed as the XP-38A with a pressure cabin. The P-38s were followed by 36 P-38Ds differing

(Above, top) P-38H-5 flown by CO of 55th FG at Nuthampstead, 1943, and (immediately above) a P-38F-5 of the 347th FG, Guadalcanal, 1943.

essentially in having protected fuel tanks of reduced capacity. The first major production version was the P-38E which had the 37-mm cannon replaced with a 20-mm weapon, 210 being built prior to delivery of the first combat-ready version. This, the P-38F, was powered by 1,325 hp V-1710-49/53 engines and 527 were built before production began of the P-38G. The latter had similarly rated V-1710-51/55 engines, various improvements being introduced progressively in successive production batches, and 1,082 being produced with deliveries completed in March 1943. The following data relate to the P-38G. *Max speed, 345 mph (555 km/h) at 5,000 ft (1 525 m), 400 mph (644 km/h) at 25,000 ft (7 620 m). Max range, 1,670 mls (2 688 km) at 211 mph (340 km/h). Empty weight, 12,200 lb (5 534 kg). Max loaded weight, 19,800 lb (8 981 kg). Span, 52 ft 0 in (15,85 m). Length, 37 ft 10 in (11,53 m). Height, 9 ft 10 in (3,00 m). Wing area, 327.5 sq ft (30,42 m²).*

(Above) The P-38F, G and H models of the Lightning were externally identical.

(Above) A Model 322 Lightning I in the UK, and (below) the XP-38, first flown in January 1939.

LOCKHEED P-38H TO P-38L LIGHTNING   USA

With the availability of the F15 version of the Allison engine, a new sub-type of the Lightning appeared, the P-38H with 1,425 hp V-1710-89/91s. The first pre-production P-38H was tested in September 1942, and, apart from power plant, was similar to the P-38G in all major respects. However, inadequate cooling restricted available power, and after production of 601 P-38Hs (128 of which were completed as F-5C photo aircraft), a new beard radiator was introduced to improve cooling. Production thus continued with the P-38J from August 1943, this proving to be the fastest of all Lightning variants. In the course of P-38J production, in-

(Left) A P-38J-10 of the 55th Fighter Sqn, 20th Fighter Group with the 8th AF in the UK, 1944.

Key to Lockheed P-38J Lightning

1 Starboard navigation light
2 Wingtip trailing-edge strake
3 Landing light (underwing) location
4 Starboard aileron
5 Aileron control rod/quadrant
6 Wing outer spar
7 Aileron tab drum
8 Aileron tab control pulleys
9 Aileron tab control rod
10 Aileron trim tab
11 Fixed tab
12 Tab cable access
13 Flap extension/retraction cables
14 Control pulleys
15 Flap outer carriage
16 Fowler-type flap (extended)
17 Control access panel
18 Wing spar transition
19 Outer section leading-edge fuel tanks (P-38J-5 and subsequent), capacity 46 Imp gal (208 l) each
20 Engine bearer/bulkhead upper attachment
21 Firewall
22 Triangular tubular engine bearer supports
23 Polished mirror surface panel (undercarriage visual check)
24 Cantilever engine bearer
25 Intake fairing
26 Accessories cooling intake
27 Oil radiator (outer sections) and intercooler (centre section) triple intake
28 Spinner
29 Curtiss-Electric three-blade (left) handed propeller
30 Four machine gun barrels
31 Cannon barrel
32 Camera-gun aperture
33 Nose panel
34 Bulkhead
35 Machine gun blast tubes
36 Four 0.5-in (12,7-mm) machine guns
37 Cannon flexible hose hydraulic charger
38 Chatellerault-feed cannon magazine (150 rounds)
39 Machine gun firing solenoid
40 Cannon ammunition feed chute
41 Nose armament cowling clips
42 Case ejection chute (port lower machine gun)
43 Ammunition box and feed chute (port lower machine gun)
44 Case ejection chute (port upper machine gun)
45 Ammunition box and feed chute (port upper machine gun)
46 Radio antenna
47 Ejection chute exit (shrouded when item 52 attached)
48 Nosewheel door
49 Nosewheel shimmy damper assembly and reservoir
50 Torque links
51 Towing eye
52 Type M10 triple-tube 4.5-in (11,4-cm) rocket-launcher
53 Rearward-retracting nosewheel
54 Alloy spokes cover plate
55 Fork
56 Rocket-launcher forward attachment (to 63)
57 Nosewheel lower drag struts
58 Nosewheel oleo leg
59 Nosewheel pin access
60 Side struts and fulcrum
61 Actuating cylinder
62 Upper drag strut

63 Rocket-launcher forward attachment bracket
64 Rudder pedal assembly
65 Engine controls quadrant
66 Instrument panel
67 "Spectacle grip" cantilevered control wheel
68 Non-reflective shroud

69 Lynn-3 reflector sight mounting
70 Optically-flat bullet-proof windscreen (P-38J-10 and later)
71 External rear-view mirror
72 Armoured headrest
73 Rearward-hinged canopy
74 Pilot's armoured seat back
75 Canopy bracing
76 Downward-winding side windows
77 Wing root fillets
78 Nosewheel well
79 Port reserve fuel tank, capacity 50 Imp gal (227 l)
80 Fuel filler cap
81 Main (double I-beam) spar

82 Fuel filler cap
83 Flap inner carriage
84 Port main fuel tank, capacity 75 Imp gal (341 l)
85 Flap control access
86 Flap structure
87 Entry ladder release
88 Flap drive motor
89 Fuel surge tank and main hydraulic reservoir in aft nacelle
90 Radio equipment compartment
91 Turnover support pylon
92 Flap control access
93 Aerial attachment
94 Starboard inner flap

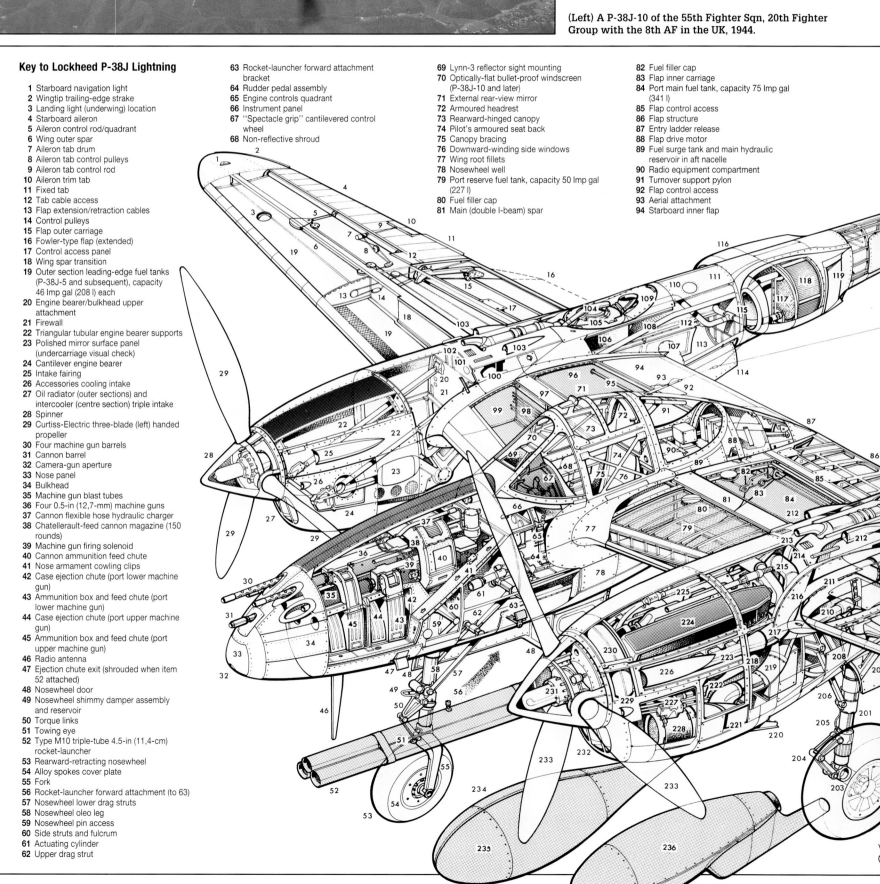

ternal fuel capacity was increased, an electrically-operated dive flap was fitted and power-boosted ailerons were provided. A total of 2,970 J-model Lightnings was built, one being completed as the sole XP-38K with V-1710-75/77 engines and larger propellers, and 205 as F-5E photo aircraft. The final production Lightning was the P-38L, which began to appear in June 1944 and had V-1710-111/113 engines offering a war emergency rating of 1,600 hp at 26,500 ft (8 075 m). A total of 3,923 P-38Ls was delivered, of which 500 were completed as F-5F photo aircraft. The following data relate to the P-38J. *Max speed, 360 mph (579 km/h) at 5,000 ft (1 525 m), 414 mph (666 km/h) at 25,000 ft (7 620 m). Max range, 2,260 mls (3 637 km) at 186 mph (299 km/h). Empty weight, 12,780 lb (5 797 kg). Max loaded weight, 21,600 lb (9 798 kg). Dimensions as for P-38G.*

P-38J-10 (right) showing larger tailboom intakes.

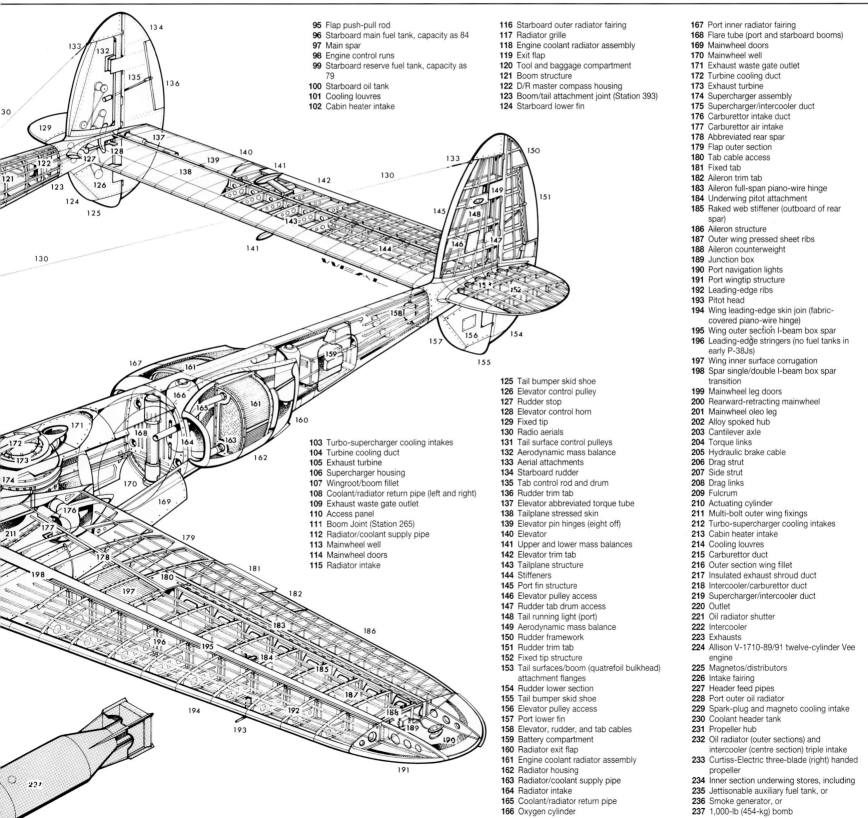

95 Flap push-pull rod
96 Starboard main fuel tank, capacity as 84
97 Main spar
98 Engine control runs
99 Starboard reserve fuel tank, capacity as 79
100 Starboard oil tank
101 Cooling louvres
102 Cabin heater intake

103 Turbo-supercharger cooling intakes
104 Turbine cooling duct
105 Exhaust turbine
106 Supercharger housing
107 Wingroot/boom fillet
108 Coolant/radiator return pipe (left and right)
109 Exhaust waste gate outlet
110 Access panel
111 Boom Joint (Station 265)
112 Radiator/coolant supply pipe
113 Mainwheel well
114 Mainwheel doors
115 Radiator intake

116 Starboard outer radiator fairing
117 Radiator grille
118 Engine coolant radiator assembly
119 Exit flap
120 Tool and baggage compartment
121 Boom structure
122 D/R master compass housing
123 Boom/tail attachment joint (Station 393)
124 Starboard lower fin

125 Tail bumper skid shoe
126 Elevator control pulley
127 Rudder stop
128 Elevator control horn
129 Fixed tip
130 Radio aerials
131 Tail surface control pulleys
132 Aerodynamic mass balance
133 Aerial attachments
134 Starboard rudder
135 Tab control rod and drum
136 Rudder trim tab
137 Elevator abbreviated torque tube
138 Tailplane stressed skin
139 Elevator pin hinges (eight off)
140 Elevator
141 Upper and lower mass balances
142 Elevator trim tab
143 Tailplane structure
144 Stiffeners
145 Port fin structure
146 Elevator pulley access
147 Rudder tab drum access
148 Tail running light (port)
149 Aerodynamic mass balance
150 Rudder framework
151 Rudder trim tab
152 Fixed tip structure
153 Tail surfaces/boom (quatrefoil bulkhead) attachment flanges
154 Rudder lower section
155 Tail bumper skid shoe
156 Elevator pulley access
157 Port lower fin
158 Elevator, rudder, and tab cables
159 Battery compartment
160 Radiator exit flap
161 Engine coolant radiator assembly
162 Radiator housing
163 Radiator/coolant supply pipe
164 Radiator intake
165 Coolant/radiator return pipe
166 Oxygen cylinder

167 Port inner radiator fairing
168 Flare tube (port and starboard booms)
169 Mainwheel doors
170 Mainwheel well
171 Exhaust waste gate outlet
172 Turbine cooling duct
173 Exhaust turbine
174 Supercharger assembly
175 Supercharger/intercooler duct
176 Carburettor intake duct
177 Carburettor air intake
178 Abbreviated rear spar
179 Flap outer section
180 Tab cable access
181 Fixed tab
182 Aileron trim tab
183 Aileron full-span piano-wire hinge
184 Underwing pitot attachment
185 Raked web stiffener (outboard of rear spar)
186 Aileron structure
187 Outer wing pressed sheet ribs
188 Aileron counterweight
189 Junction box
190 Port navigation lights
191 Port wingtip structure
192 Leading-edge ribs
193 Pitot head
194 Wing leading-edge skin join (fabric-covered piano-wire hinge)
195 Wing outer section I-beam box spar
196 Leading-edge stringers (no fuel tanks in early P-38Js)
197 Wing inner surface corrugation
198 Spar single/double I-beam box spar transition
199 Mainwheel leg doors
200 Rearward-retracting mainwheel
201 Mainwheel oleo leg
202 Alloy spoked hub
203 Cantilever axle
204 Torque links
205 Hydraulic brake cable
206 Drag strut
207 Side strut
208 Drag links
209 Fulcrum
210 Actuating cylinder
211 Multi-bolt outer wing fixings
212 Turbo-supercharger cooling intakes
213 Cabin heater intake
214 Cooling louvres
215 Carburettor duct
216 Outer section wing fillet
217 Insulated exhaust shroud duct
218 Intercooler/carburettor duct
219 Supercharger/intercooler duct
220 Outlet
221 Oil radiator shutter
222 Intercooler
223 Exhausts
224 Allison V-1710-89/91 twelve-cylinder Vee engine
225 Magnetos/distributors
226 Intake fairing
227 Header feed pipes
228 Port outer oil radiator
229 Spark-plug and magneto cooling intake
230 Coolant header tank
231 Propeller hub
232 Oil radiator (outer sections) and intercooler (centre section) triple intake
233 Curtiss-Electric three-blade (right) handed propeller
234 Inner section underwing stores, including
235 Jettisonable auxiliary fuel tank, or
236 Smoke generator, or
237 1,000-lb (454-kg) bomb

LOCKHEED P-38M LIGHTNING USA

In order to provide the USAAF with an interim radar-equipped two-seat night fighter, in 1944 Lockheed undertook the conversion of a P-38L as a prototype P-38M with AN/APS-4 radar in an external radome and a second cockpit for the radar operator aft of the pilot. The success of trials, beginning on 5 February 1944, resulted in the conversion of 75 additional P-38Ls to P-38M configuration. These were just entering service when World War II came to an end, a few seeing service in Japan in 1945/46. Despite its increased weight and drag, the P-38M suffered little performance penalty over the single-seater. The armament of one 20-mm cannon and four 0.5-in machine guns was retained, and launching racks for HVAR rockets were provided beneath the wings. *Max speed, 361 mph (581 km/h) at 5,000 ft (1 525 m), 406 mph (635 km/h) at 15,000 ft (4 570 m). Dimensions as P-38L.*

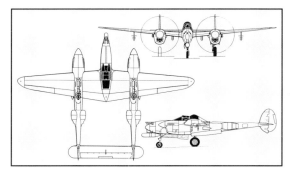

A radome beneath the nose and a second crew member distinguished the P-38M (above and below).

LOCKHEED XP-49 USA

To meet the requirements of a Circular Proposal issued on 11 March 1939 by the US Materiel Division and calling for a more advanced interceptor fighter, Lockheed offered a pressurised version of the P-38 powered by two 24-cylinder Pratt & Whitney X-1800-SA2-G engines. Gaining first place in the ensuing evaluation of proposals, the Lockheed project was allocated the designation XP-49, and a contract for one prototype was placed on 30 November 1939. In March 1940, the

The XP-49 (above and below) retained two-thirds airframe commonality with the production P-38.

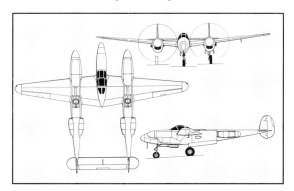

decision was taken to substitute 1,540 hp Continental XIV-1430-9/11 12-cylinder liquid-cooled engines for the Pratt & Whitneys and the prototype was flown with these on 11 November 1943. The airframe of the XP-49 possessed approximately two-thirds commonality with that of the production P-38, but at an early flight test stage it was concluded that performance was insufficient to warrant further development. Furthermore, the future of the Continental engine was questionable, and the sole XP-49 was therefore fitted with a two-seat cockpit and relegated to the rôle of trials aircraft. *Max speed, 406 mph (653 km/h) at 15,000 ft (4 575 m). Initial climb, 3,300 ft/min (16,76 m/sec). Normal range, 680 mls (1 095 km). Empty weight, 15,410 lb (6 990 kg). Loaded weight, 18,750 lb (8 505 kg). Span, 52 ft 0 in (15,85 m). Length, 40 ft 1 in (12,22 m). Height, 9 ft 9½ in (2,98 m). Wing area, 327.5 sq ft (30,42 m²).*

LOCKHEED XP-58 USA

Under an agreement of 12 April 1940 between the US Army Air Corps and Lockheed whereby the P-38 was released for sale to Britain and France, the manufacturer was to develop an improved version of the fighter at its own cost. A P-38 derivative powered by Continental IV-1430 engines was offered in both single- and two-seat versions, and the latter was selected for development as a long-range escort fighter under the designation XP-58. It was subsequently decided to fit the aircraft with 1,800 hp Pratt & Whitney XH-2600-9/11 engines, but, in the event, the XP-58 was powered by two Allison V-3420-11/13 turbo-supercharged 24-cylinder liquid-cooled engines rated at 3,000 hp at 28,000 ft (8 535 m). The proposed armament comprised four fixed 37-mm cannon and four 0.5-in (12,7-mm) machine guns, the latter in remotely-controlled dorsal and ventral barbettes. An alternative nose-mounted armament comprised a single 75-mm cannon and two 0.5-in (12,7-mm) machine guns, the large-calibre

Lockheed's final extrapolation of the twin-boom theme was the big, heavily-armed XP-58 (above and below), only one prototype of which was completed.

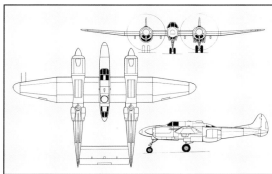

(Immediately below) P-80A-1 of 62nd FS, 56th FG, Germany, July 1948, and (bottom) P-80B-5, 94th FS, Ladd Field, Fairbanks, Alaska, 1947.

The sole XP-58 (above) suffered protracted development and made relatively few flights.

weapon being intended for use in breaking up bomber formations. The first of two XP-58s finally flew on 6 June 1944, more than four years after design initiation. No cabin pressurisation equipment was installed, and the gun barbettes and related fire control system were omitted. Some 25 flights were made by the manufacturer, considerable difficulties arising from torching from the turbo-superchargers. USAAF acceptance testing was not undertaken because of maintenance difficulties, and the second prototype was cancelled. *Max speed, 436 mph (702 km/h) at 25,000 ft (7 620 m). Initial climb, 2,660 ft/min (13,51 m/sec). Normal range, 1,250 mls (2 012 km). Empty weight, 31,624 lb (14 344 kg). Loaded weight, 39,192 lb (17 777 kg). Span, 70 ft 0 in (21,34 m). Length, 49 ft 4 in (15,04 m). Height, 16 ft 0 in (4,88 m). Wing area, 600 sq ft (55,74 m²).*

LOCKHEED P-80 SHOOTING STAR USA

Destined to be the USAAF's first operational jet fighter, the Shooting Star was evolved from the XP-80, which had been designed around the 2,460 lb st (1 116 kgp) de Havilland H-1B turbojet. Work on the XP-80 began on 23 June 1943, and the first flight was effected on 8 January 1944. The aircraft attained 502 mph (808 km/h) at 20,480 ft (6 240 m) during flight test, but non-availabil-

Flown in January 1944, the XP-80 (above) bore little more than a conceptual resemblance to the series P-80A (below) which was larger and heavier.

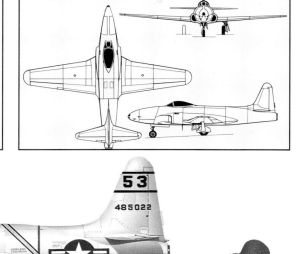

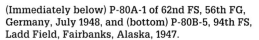

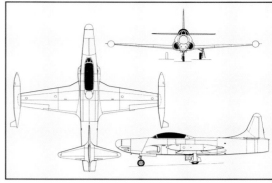

(Above) The F-94B, with centreline wingtip tanks.

The XP-80A (below) introduced rounded wingtips and tail similar to those of the series P-80A (above).

ity of the H-1B engine necessitated extensive redesign to accommodate the 3,850 lb st (1 746 kgp) General Electric I-40 turbojet. Overall dimensions were increased and maximum weight was raised from 8,916 lb (4 044 kg) to 13,780 lb (6 250 kg). Two additional prototypes were built as XP-80As, these flying on 10 June and 1 August 1944, and being followed by 13 similar service test YP-80As. The initial production version was ordered on 4 April 1944 as the P-80A, a letter contract covering 1,000 aircraft. This was supplemented by orders for a further 2,500 in the following year. Following V-J Day, the supplementary contract was cancelled and the initial contract reduced to 917 aircraft. The first 345 P-80As were powered by the 3,850 lb st (1 746 kgp) General Electric J33-GE-11 and carried an armament of six 0.5-in (12,7-mm) guns. The next 218 aircraft differed in having the 4,000 lb st (1 814 kgp) J33-A-17. The first P-80A was accepted by the USAAF in February 1945, the last being delivered in the following December. The next 240 aircraft were delivered as P-80Bs, these differing in having armament, equipment and engine upgrades. The final production model was the P-80C, the first 238 of which (including 50 delivered to the USMC as TO-1s) were powered by the 4,600 lb st (2 086 kgp) J33-A-23 and the remaining 561 by the 5,400 lb st (2 450 kgp) J33-A-35. The Shooting Star, meanwhile redesignated F-80, was phased out of the active inventory shortly after the end of the Korean conflict, but remained with the Air National Guard until March 1961. After withdrawal from USAF service, F-80Cs were supplied to the air arms of a number of

A P-80B (below) of the 56th FG which took its fighters to Germany during the 1948 Berlin crisis.

Latin American countries, these (with the quantities delivered indicated in parentheses) comprising Brazil (33), Chile (18), Colombia (16), Ecuador (16), Peru (16) and Uruguay (14). The following data relate to the P-80A. *Max speed, 558 mph (898 km/h) at sea level. Time to 20,000 ft (6 100 m), 5.5 min. Range (internal fuel), 780 mls (1 255 km). Empty weight, 7,920 lb (3 593 kg). Normal loaded weight, 11,700 lb (5 307 kg). Span, 38 ft 10½ in (11,85 m). Length, 34 ft 6 in (10,52 m). Wing area, 237.6 sq ft (22,07 m²).*

LOCKHEED F-94A & F-94B STARFIRE   USA

Large underwing tip tanks were carried by the F-94A version (above) of the Starfire fighter.

Evolved from the TF-80C (T-33A) trainer derivative of the P-80C clear-weather fighter as an interim two-seat all-weather fighter, the F-94 was developed under a contract awarded in January 1949. To provide the additional power needed to cater for the weight of electronic equipment and armament, an afterburning General Electric J33-A-33 turbojet was introduced to provide a maximum of 6,000 lb st (2 722 kgp). The forward fuselage was lengthened to house APG-32 radar and four 0.5-in (12,7-mm) guns. Two TF-80Cs were modified to serve as YF-94 prototypes, flight testing commencing on 16 April 1949. The initial production

(Immediately below) An F-94B-1 with stylish "shark's mouth" decoration, and (bottom) an F-94B of the 319th FIS serving in Korea in 1952.

contract called for 109 F-94As, essentially similar to the YF-94s apart from operational equipment. The 19th F-94A airframe was completed as the YF-94B with upgraded equipment and a further 355 aircraft were completed as F-94Bs. The F-94A entered operational service in May 1950, with the F-94B following in April 1951. These initial Starfire models had been phased out of the USAF's first-line inventory by mid-1954. The following data relate to the F-94B. *Max speed, 606 mph (975 km/h) at sea level. Initial climb, 6,850 ft/min (34,8 m/sec). Normal range, 665 mls (1 070 km). Empty weight, 10,064 lb (4 565 kg). Max loaded weight, 16,844 lb (7 640 kg). Span, 37 ft 6 in (11,43 m). Length, 40 ft 1 in (12,22 m). Height, 12 ft 8 in (3,86 m). Wing area, 234.8 sq ft (21,81 m²).*

LOCKHEED F-94C STARFIRE   USA

The F-94A and B versions of the Starfire were of limited effectiveness, being deficient in climb rate, range and firepower. In an attempt to improve these characteristics, a thoroughgoing redesign was undertaken which resulted in virtually a new type. This was initially ordered under the designation F-97, work on the radically modified fighter actually predating the

In its final configuration, the F-94C (above) had wing-mounted rocket pods and reinforced canopy.

F-94B. The latter was introduced only as a result of delays in the development of the more advanced type, which was redesignated F-94C before its service introduction. The F-94C had a thinner wing with increased dihedral, a sweptback horizontal tail, a new and larger engine – the Pratt & Whitney J48-P-5 with a military thrust of 6,350 lb (2 880 kg) and an afterburning thrust of 8,750 lb (3 969 kg) – and an all-rocket

armament with a new E-5 fire control system. Flight testing commenced on 19 January 1950, two YF-97As (later redesignated YF-94Cs) being based on F-94B airframes. A total of 387 F-94Cs was built, these being accepted between July 1951 and May 1954, the type entering service in June 1953. Armament initially comprised 24 2.75-in (70-mm) unguided rockets in the nose, these later being augmented by two wing leading-edge pods each containing 12 additional rockets. The F-94C was finally phased out of the active USAF inventory in February 1959, and from the Air National Guard during the following summer. *Max speed, 640 mph (1 030 km/h) at sea level. Initial climb, 7,980 ft/ min (40,54 m/sec). Normal range, 805 mls (1 295 km). Empty weight, 12,708 lb (5 764 kg). Loaded weight, 18,300 lb (8 301 kg). Span, 37 ft 4 in (11,38 m). Length, 44 ft 6 in (13,56 m). Height, 14 ft 11 in (4,55 m). Wing area, 232.8 sq ft (21,63 m²).*

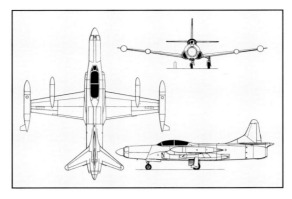

The F-94C (above) represented a thoroughgoing redesign of the Starfire, first known as the F-97.

LOCKHEED XFV-1   USA

The XFV-1 was designed under the leadership of Art Flock as part of a US Navy programme (which included the Convair XFY-1) to investigate the feasibility of operating tail-sitting vertical-take-off-and-landing fighters from small platforms as a means of protecting convoys beyond the range of shore-based air cover. Featuring equi-span cruciform tail surfaces on which the aircraft was intended to stand, with the tips of the tail surfaces embodying fully-castoring wheels, the XFV-1 was powered by a 5,850 shp Allison XT40-A-6 turboprop driving Curtiss Electric contraprops. It was proposed that this would eventually be replaced by an XT40-A-16 rated at 6,825 shp for take-off and having a military rating of 6,955 shp with which a power-to-weight ratio of 1.2:1.0 was anticipated. The XT40-A-6 was not capable of sustained operation in the vertical mode and

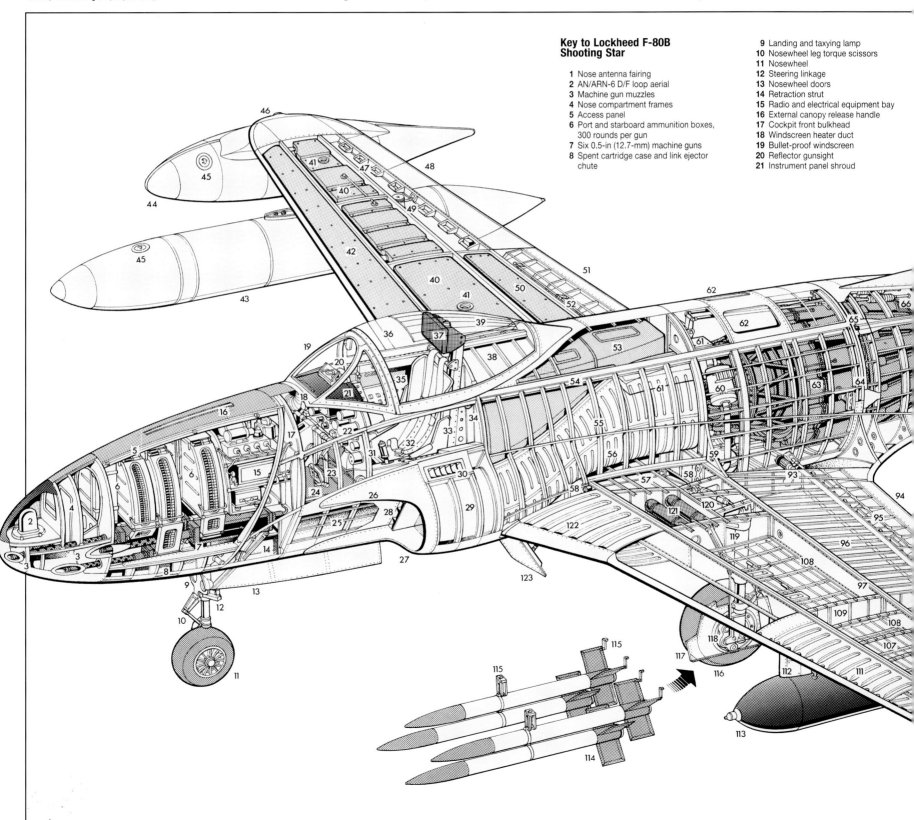

Key to Lockheed F-80B Shooting Star

1 Nose antenna fairing
2 AN/ARN-6 D/F loop aerial
3 Machine gun muzzles
4 Nose compartment frames
5 Access panel
6 Port and starboard ammunition boxes, 300 rounds per gun
7 Six 0.5-in (12.7-mm) machine guns
8 Spent cartridge case and link ejector chute
9 Landing and taxying lamp
10 Nosewheel leg torque scissors
11 Nosewheel
12 Steering linkage
13 Nosewheel doors
14 Retraction strut
15 Radio and electrical equipment bay
16 External canopy release handle
17 Cockpit front bulkhead
18 Windscreen heater duct
19 Bullet-proof windscreen
20 Reflector gunsight
21 Instrument panel shroud

provided inadequate power for VTOL operation. The XFV-1 was therefore fitted with a temporary non-re-tractable undercarriage to permit flight testing in the conventional (horizontal) mode. The aircraft was briefly airborne on 23 December 1953, the first genuine test flight taking place on 16 June 1954. A further 26 flights were made during which the XFV-1 transitioned from conventional to vertical flight mode and back, being held briefly in hover at altitude. Armament of the FV-1 was planned to comprise four 20-mm cannon or 48 2.75-in (70-mm) rockets in wingtip pods. The XT40-A-16 engine never became available, and, although Lockheed proposed an FV-2 version powered by the more powerful T54-A-16 engine, control difficulties and inadequate anticipated performance prompted cancel-lation of the programme in June 1955. The following data are applicable to the planned XT40-A-16-powered aircraft. *Max speed, 580 mph (934 km/h) at 15,000 ft*

Little success attended the XFV-1 (above) which was to have operated from small ship platforms.

(4 575 m). Initial climb, 10,820 ft/min (54,96 m/sec). En-durance, 1.17 hrs at 35,000 ft (10 670 m). Empty weight, 11,599 lb (5 261 kg). Max loaded weight, 16,221 lb (7 358 kg). Span, 27 ft 5 in (8,36 m). Length, 36 ft 10¼ in (11,23 m). Wing area, 246 sq ft (22,85 m²).

Resulting from a US Navy programme, the single XFV-1 (above and below) flew in 1954-55 and successfully demonstrated transition from conventional to vertical flight.

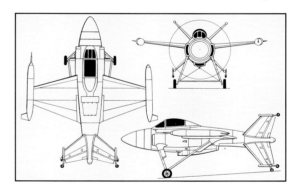

55 Centre fuselage frames
56 Intake trunking
57 Main undercarriage wheel well
58 Wing spar attachment joints
59 Pneumatic reservoir
60 Hydraulic accumulator
61 Port and starboard water injection tanks
62 Spring loaded intake pressure relief doors
63 Allison J33-A-21 centrifugal flow turbojet engine
64 Main engine mounting
65 Rear fuselage attachment bolts (three)
66 Elevator control rods
67 Jet pipe bracing cables
68 Fin root fillet
69 Elevator control link
70 Starboard tailplane
71 Starboard elevator
72 AN/ARA-8 radio homing aerial
73 AN/ARA-8 communications aerial
74 Pitot tube
75 AN/ARC-3 radio "pick-axe" antenna
76 Rudder construction
77 Fixed tab
78 Elevator and rudder hinge controls
79 Tail navigation light
80 Jet pipe nozzle
81 Elevator tabs
82 Port elevator construction
83 Elevator mass balance
84 Tailplane construction
85 Fin/tailplane attachment joints
86 Tailplane fillet fairing
87 Jet pipe mounting rail
88 Gyrosyn radio compass flux valve
89 Rear fuselage frame and stringer construction
90 Fuselage skin plating
91 Jet pipe support frame
92 Trailing-edge wing root fillet
93 Flap drive motor
94 Port split trailing-edge flap
95 Flap shroud ribs
96 Trailing-edge fuel tank bay
97 Rear spar
98 Trailing-edge ribs
99 Port aileron tab
100 Aileron hinge control
101 Upper skin panel aileron hinge line
102 Aileron construction
103 Wing tip fairing construction
104 Tip tank
105 Port navigation light
106 Tip tank mounting and jettison control
107 Detachable lower wing skin/fuel tank bay panels
108 Port wing fuel tank bays
109 Inter tank bay ribs
110 Front spar
111 Corrugated leading edge inner skin
112 Port stores pylon
113 1,000-lb (454-kg) HE bomb
114 5-in (12,7-cm) HVAR ground attack rockets (10 rockets maximum load)
115 HVAR rocket mountings
116 Port mainwheel
117 Mainwheel doors
118 Wheel brake pad
119 Main undercarriage leg strut
120 Retraction jack
121 Oxygen tanks
122 Wing root leading edge extension
123 Port ventral airbrake

22 Instrument panel
23 Rudder pedals
24 Cockpit floor level
25 Nosewheel bay
26 Intake lip fairing
27 Port air intake
28 Boundary layer bleed air duct
29 Intake ducting
30 Boundary layer air exit louvres
31 Engine throttle lever
32 Safety harness
33 Pilot's ejection seat
34 Cockpit rear bulkhead
35 Starboard side console panel
36 Sliding cockpit canopy cover
37 Ejection seat headrest
38 Canopy aft decking
39 D/F sense antenna
40 Starboard wing fuel tanks
41 Fuel filler caps
42 Leading-edge tank
43 Fletcher-type tip-tank, capacity 166.5 Imp gal (757 l)
44 Tip tank, capacity 137.5 Imp gal (625 l)
45 Tip tank filler cap
46 Starboard navigation light
47 Aileron balance weights
48 Starboard aileron
49 Aileron hinge control
50 Trailing-edge fuel tank
51 Starboard split trailing-edge flap
52 Flap control links
53 Fuselage fuel tank, total internal capacity 354 Imp gal (1 609 l)
54 Fuselage main longeron

LOCKHEED XF-90   USA

Shortly after World War II, the USAF conceived a re-quirement for a turbojet-powered long-range penetra-tion fighter suitable for both bomber escort and tactical support duties. Project design began in July 1945 under the leadership of Clarence L "Kelly" Johnson. Lock-heed's contender received a contract for two proto-types, these eventually being assigned the designation XF-90. The first was flown on 3 June 1949, power being provided by two 3,000 lb st (1 361 kgp) Westinghouse XJ34-WE-11 turbojets, proposed armament being six 20-mm cannon. The second prototype was fitted with XJ34-WE-15 turbojets offering a military power of 3,600 lb st (1 633 kgp) boosted to 4,200 lb (1 905 kg)

Designed as a long-range fighter, the XF-90 (below) lost out to the competitive McDonnell XF-88.

with afterburning. The XF-90 attained Mach=1.12 in a dive on 17 May 1950, but performance in level flight was considered inadequate. In June 1950, the McDonnell XF-88 was selected as winning contender and further development of the XF-90 was discontinued. The following performance data relate to the XJ34-WE-15-powered XF-90. *Max speed, 665 mph (1 070 km/h) at 1,000 ft (330 m). Time to 25,000 ft (7 620 m), 4.5 min. Normal range, 1,050 mls (1 690 km). Empty weight, 18,520 lb (8 401 kg). Loaded weight, 27,200 lb (12 338 kg). Span, 40 ft 0 in (12,19 m). Length, 56 ft 2 in (17,17 m). Height, 15 ft 9 in (4,80 m). Wing area, 345 sq ft (32,05 m²).*

The XF-90 (below) exceeded Mach unity during 1950.

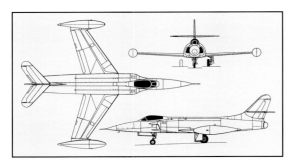

LOCKHEED F-104A & F-104C STARFIGHTER   USA

The first fighter capable of sustained speeds in excess of M=2.0, and the first aircraft ever to hold world speed and altitude records simultaneously, the Starfighter was conceived by a team led by C L "Kelly" Johnson as a single-seat lightweight air superiority fighter. Two prototypes were ordered for the USAF as XF-104s on 12 March 1953, the first of these performing its initial full test flight on 4 March 1954 (a short, straight hop having been effected on 28 February). Powered by a Wright XJ65-W-6 with afterburning thrust of 10,200 lb (4 627 kg), the XF-104 attained M=1.79 on 25 March 1955. Seventeen YF-104A service trials aircraft followed from 17 February 1956, these featuring 5.5 ft (1,68 m) fuselage lengthening and a General Electric J79-GE-3 engine. The initial production model, the F-104A, was accepted by the USAF in December 1958 with a J79-GE-3B engine with dry and afterburning ratings of 9,600 lb st (4 355 kgp) and 14,800 lb st (6 713 kgp). Some aircraft were later retrofitted with the J79-GE-19 with afterburning thrust boosted to 17,900 lb (8 119 kg). Armament comprised one 20-mm M-61 rotary cannon and two AIM-9B Sidewinder AAMs. A total of 153 F-104As was built, of which 10 were later supplied to Pakistan and 24 to Taiwan (22 of the latter being transferred to Jordan from mid-1969). The F-104A was succeeded in production by the single-seat tactical strike F-104C with a detachable flight refuelling probe, provision for bombs or missiles on wing and fuselage stations and a J79-GE-7 engine with dry and afterburning ratings of 10,000 lb st (4 536 kgp) and 15,800 lb st (7 167 kgp). Seventy-seven F-104Cs were delivered to the USAF between September 1958 and June 1959. The F-104As were deactivated by the USAF

Wingtip tanks, seen (above) on the XF-104, could be replaced by Sidewinder AAMs, as tested (below) by the ARDC on an F-104A Starfighter.

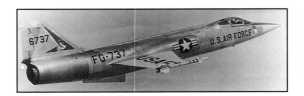

Key to Lockheed F-104G Starfighter

1 One-piece all-moving tailplane
2 Tailplane rib construction
3 Tailplane spar
4 Rocking control arm
5 Tailplane pivot fixing
6 Fin trailing-edge ribs
7 Rudder
8 Rudder rib construction
9 Power control actuators
10 Power actuator servo valves
11 Variable-area afterburner nozzle
12 Nozzle control flaps
13 Afterburner duct
14 Fin attachment fuselage main frames
15 Tailfin construction
16 Tailplane control rods
17 All-moving tailplane dual hydraulic actuators
18 Power control unit servo valves
19 Port airbrake (open)
20 Hydraulic connectors (3,000-psi/211 kg/cm² system)
21 Tailplane control push rod linkage
22 Rear fuselage break point (engine removal)
23 Upper rear navigation light (red)
24 Afterburner nozzle control jacks
25 Brake parachute housing (open)
26 Lower rear navigation light (white)
27 Jet pipe thrust mounting
28 Runway emergency arrester hook (lowered)
29 Starboard airbrake (open)
30 Airbrake hinge linkage
31 Airbrake housing

41 Engine oil tank
42 Compressor section variable stators
43 Engine withdrawal rail
44 Bleed air supply duct
45 Anti-collision light
46 Port "blown" flap (down position)
47 Power control servo units
48 Aileron hydraulic actuator
49 Port aileron
50 Tip tank attachment joint
51 Port wing tip fuel tank (capacity 283 imp gal/1 287 l)
52 Fuel filler caps
53 Tip tank vane
54 Port leading-edge flap (lowered)
55 Wing pylon hardpoint
56 Port wing panel multi-spar construction
57 Dorsal spine air duct fairing
58 Fuselage rear main fuel tank; total internal fuel capacity, 746 Imp gal (3 391 l)
59 Upper main longeron
60 Intake duct spill flaps (engine bay ventilation)
61 Engine starter
62 Wing attachment fuselage main frames
63 Hydraulic reservoir
64 Aileron control cable quadrant

74 Flap rib construction
75 Starboard "blown" flap (down position)
76 Auxiliary fuel tank tail fins
77 Starboard navigation light
78 Wing tip fuel tank
79 Starboard aileron
80 Aileron ten-cylinder hydraulic actuator
81 Tip tank fuel connectors
82 Jettisonable tip tank attachment joint
83 Fuel filler caps
84 Front spar
85 Starboard leading-edge flap (lowered)
86 Underwing fuel tank, capacity 283 Imp gal (1 287 l)
87 Starboard wing pylon
88 Pylon attachment hard point
89 Starboard wing panel multi-spar construction
90 Leading-edge flap lock actuator and linkage
91 Wing root rib
92 Forged wing root attachment fittings

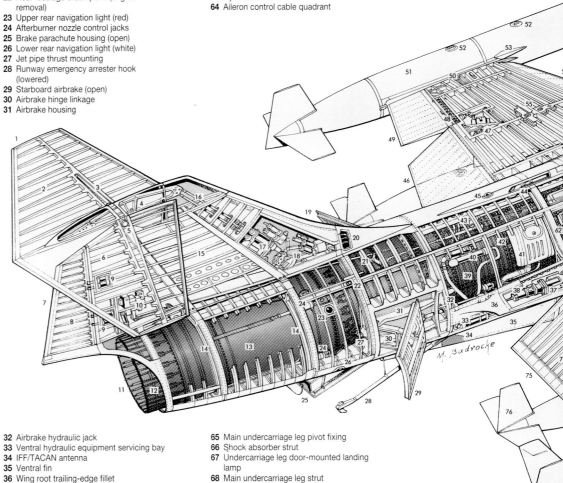

32 Airbrake hydraulic jack
33 Ventral hydraulic equipment servicing bay
34 IFF/TACAN antenna
35 Ventral fin
36 Wing root trailing-edge fillet
37 Flap actuator
38 Electric drive motor
39 General Electric J79-GE-11 afterburning turbojet
40 Oil coolers

65 Main undercarriage leg pivot fixing
66 Shock absorber strut
67 Undercarriage leg door-mounted landing lamp
68 Main undercarriage leg strut
69 Swivelling axle control rods
70 Starboard mainwheel
71 Aileron servo control valves
72 Rear spar
73 Flap blowing air duct

in December 1969, and the F-104Cs remained in service (with the Air National Guard) until July 1975. The following data relate to the F-104C. *Max speed, 1,150 mph (1 850 km/h) at 50,000 ft (15 250 m). Max climb, 54,000 ft/min (274 m/sec). Normal range, 850 mls (1 370 km). Empty weight, 12,760 lb (5 788 kg). Max loaded weight, 27,853 lb (12 634 kg). Span, 21 ft 9 in (6,63 m). Length, 54 ft 8 in (16,66 m). Height, 13 ft 5 in (4,09 m). Wing area, 196.1 sq ft (18,22 m²).*

LOCKHEED F-104G & F-104S STARFIGHTER   USA

Based on the F-104C, the F-104G was evolved by Lockheed as a multi-rôle all-weather fighter to meet a *Luftwaffe* requirement (the "G" suffix indicating Germany).

Retaining the external dimensions of the earlier model, the F-104G featured a strengthened structure, enlarged tail surfaces and fully-powered rudder, combat manoeuvering flaps, increased fuel tankage, greatly enhanced electronics and provision for up to 4,000 lb (1 814 kg) of external stores on five stations. Power was provided by a J79-GE-11A engine with dry and afterburning ratings of 10,000 lb st (4 536 kgp) and 15,600 lb st (7 076 kgp). The first F-104G (built against an initial contract for 66 from the *Luftwaffe*) was flown on 7 June 1960. Lockheed built 139 (for Federal Germany, Greece, Norway and Turkey), Canadair built 140 (for Denmark, Greece, Norway, Spain, Taiwan and Turkey) in addition to 200 essentially similar CF-104s for the RCAF, and 843 were built in Europe by four groups (for Belgium, Federal Germany, Italy and the Netherlands). Lockheed built 40 examples of a tactical

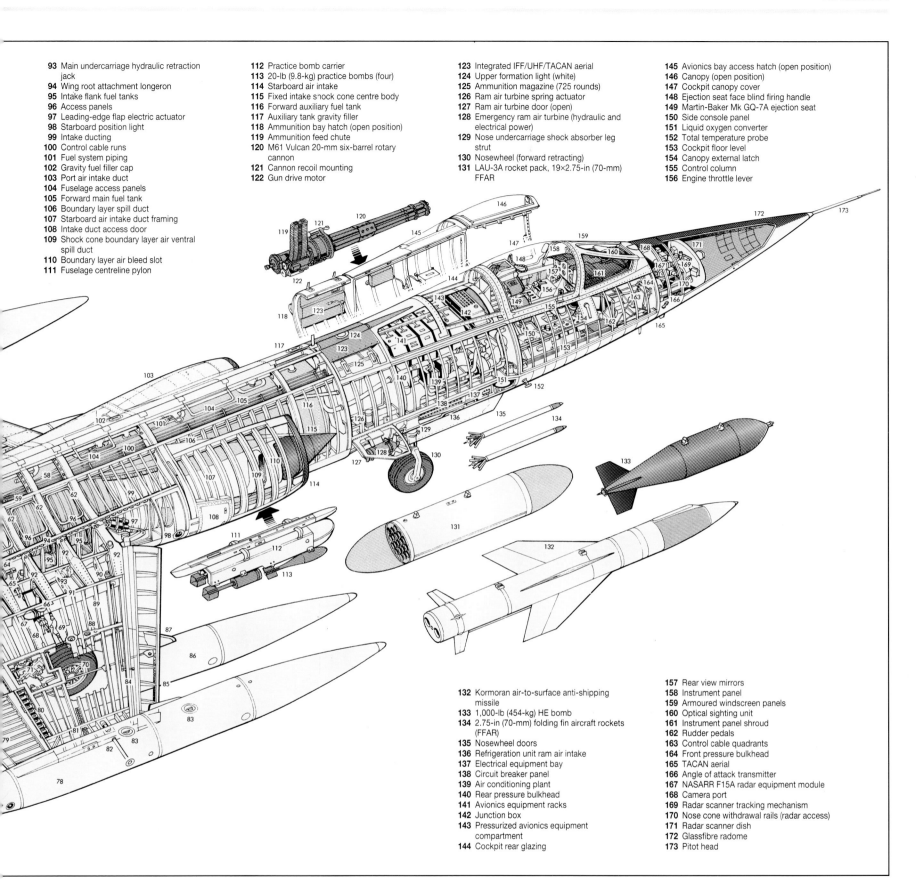

93 Main undercarriage hydraulic retraction jack
94 Wing root attachment longeron
95 Intake flank fuel tanks
96 Access panels
97 Leading-edge flap electric actuator
98 Starboard position light
99 Intake ducting
100 Control cable runs
101 Fuel system piping
102 Gravity fuel filler cap
103 Port air intake duct
104 Fuselage access panels
105 Forward main fuel tank
106 Boundary layer spill duct
107 Starboard air intake duct framing
108 Intake duct access door
109 Shock cone boundary layer air ventral spill duct
110 Boundary layer air bleed slot
111 Fuselage centreline pylon

112 Practice bomb carrier
113 20-lb (9.8-kg) practice bombs (four)
114 Starboard air intake
115 Fixed intake shock cone centre body
116 Forward auxiliary fuel tank
117 Auxiliary tank gravity filler
118 Ammunition bay hatch (open position)
119 Ammunition feed chute
120 M61 Vulcan 20-mm six-barrel rotary cannon
121 Cannon recoil mounting
122 Gun drive motor

123 Integrated IFF/UHF/TACAN aerial
124 Upper formation light (white)
125 Ammunition magazine (725 rounds)
126 Ram air turbine spring actuator
127 Ram air turbine door (open)
128 Emergency ram air turbine (hydraulic and electrical power)
129 Nose undercarriage shock absorber leg strut
130 Nosewheel (forward retracting)
131 LAU-3A rocket pack, 19×2.75-in (70-mm) FFAR

145 Avionics bay access hatch (open position)
146 Canopy (open position)
147 Cockpit canopy cover
148 Ejection seat face blind firing handle
149 Martin-Baker Mk GQ-7A ejection seat
150 Side console panel
151 Liquid oxygen converter
152 Total temperature probe
153 Cockpit floor level
154 Canopy external latch
155 Control column
156 Engine throttle lever

132 Kormoran air-to-surface anti-shipping missile
133 1,000-lb (454-kg) HE bomb
134 2.75-in (70-mm) folding fin aircraft rockets (FFAR)
135 Nosewheel doors
136 Refrigeration unit ram air intake
137 Electrical equipment bay
138 Circuit breaker panel
139 Air conditioning plant
140 Rear pressure bulkhead
141 Avionics equipment racks
142 Junction box
143 Pressurized avionics equipment compartment
144 Cockpit rear glazing

157 Rear view mirrors
158 Instrument panel
159 Armoured windscreen panels
160 Optical sighting unit
161 Instrument panel shroud
162 Rudder pedals
163 Control cable quadrants
164 Front pressure bulkhead
165 TACAN aerial
166 Angle of attack transmitter
167 NASARR F15A radar equipment module
168 Camera port
169 Radar scanner tracking mechanism
170 Nose cone withdrawal rails (radar access)
171 Radar scanner dish
172 Glassfibre radome
173 Pitot head

The F-104S version of the Starfighter (below) was evolved to meet specific Italian needs and was produced by Aeritalia in Turin.

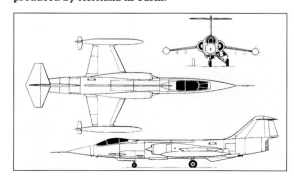

(Above top) F-104G of 30th TFW, Republic of China AF, Taiwan, and (immediately above) an ex-Canadian CF-104G in service with the Danish Air Force.

reconnaissance version, the RF-104G, a further 154 being built in Europe, and 178 of the structurally similar F-104J optimised for all-weather intercept were built by Mitsubishi (following three built by Lockheed and 29 assembled from component kits). A development with improved capability both as an interceptor and as a fighter-bomber, the F-104S, was evolved specifically for Italy, a Lockheed-produced prototype flying in December 1966. Capable of carrying paired AIM-7 Sparrow II and AIM-9 Sidewider AAMs, or up to 7,500 lb (3 402 kg) of ordnance on nine external stations, the F-104S was powered by the J79-GE-19 rated at 11,870 lb (5 384 kgp) dry and 17,900 lb st (8 119 kgp) with afterburning. A total of 245 F-104S Starfighters was built in Italy (including 40 for Turkey). The following data relate to the F-104G. *Max speed, 1,146 mph (1 844 km/h) at 50,000 ft (15 250 m). Max climb, 48,000 ft/min (243,8 m/sec). Normal range, 1,080 mls (1 740 km). Empty weight, 13,996 lb (6 348kg). Max loaded weight, 29,038 lb (13 171 kg). Dimensions as for F-104C.*

LOCKHEED YF-12A   USA

The YF-12A was an interceptor derivative of the A-12, the world's first Mach=3.0 cruise-capable aircraft which had first flown on 26 April 1962. Three of a total of 18 A-12 strategic reconnaissance aircraft – predecessors of the larger and heavier SR-71 – were completed as dedicated single-seat interceptor fighters (the 11th, 12th and 13th airframes) under the designation YF-12A, the first of these flying on 7 August 1963. Powered by two Pratt & Whitney JT11D-20B (J58) turbo-ramjets each having an afterburning thrust rating of 32,500 lb (14 742 kg), the YF-12A was of unique blended-body design and largely constructed of titanium alloy. The YF-12A had a Hughes AN/ASG-18 pulse doppler fire control system and provision for four Hughes AIM-47A (GAR-9) AAMs in each of two bays in the fuselage chines. The YF-12A established a series of absolute world speed and altitude records in May 1965, but was not the recipient of production contracts and was relegated to the rôle of research aircraft in a programme commencing in December 1969 and continuing into 1979. *Max speed, 2,275 mph (3 661 km/h) at 80,000 ft (24 385m) or Mach=3.0. Max range, 2,500 mls (4 023 km) at Mach=3.0. Loaded weight, 140,000 lb (63 504 kg). Span, 55 ft 7 in (16,94 m). Length, 101 ft 8 in (30,99 m). Height, 18 ft 3 in (5,56m). Wing area, 1,795 sq ft (166,75 m²).*

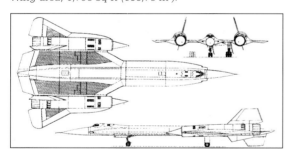

(Above) The Lockheed YF-12A Mach=3.35 interceptor.

LOCKHEED F-22A RAPTOR   USA

In September 1985, the USAF issued a Request for Proposals for an Advanced Tactical Fighter (ATF) able to achieve air superiority over hostile territory. The initial requirements were stringent. Max speed was to be Mach 2.5; supercruise (supersonic flight using military power only) was mandatory; an operational radius of at least 700 nm (1 297 km); an operational ceiling of 70,000 ft (21 335 m), which would require the pilot to wear a full pressure suit, and the ability to operate from a 2,000 ft (610 m) runway. All-up weight was set at 50,000 lb (22 680 kg). It had also to be stealthy, which ruled out external carriage of weapons and drop tanks. A new engine in the 35,000 lb (15 876 kgp) class was needed, either the Pratt & Whitney YF119 or the General Electric YF120. Lockheed (now Lockheed Martin), teamed with Boeing and General Dynamics and responded with the YF-22, which first flew on 29 September 1990,

A three-month flight evaluation programme with two YF-22s (above and right) resulted in a production go-ahead for the ATF during 1991.

piloted by Dave Ferguson. Meanwhile, when it became clear that the Soviet threat was defunct, the requirements were relaxed. Supercruise was retained, but the need for Mach 2.5 was dropped. This was a tremendous advantage in terms of stealth, as it meant that variable inlets were no longer required. The operational altitude was also relaxed in favour of a sustained turn of 2g at 50,000 ft (15 239 m), which eliminated the full pressure suit. The short field requirement was also abandoned, while the upper weight limit proved impossible to meet. Given the operational radius, and the fact that all fuel and weaponry must be carried internally, the YF-22 could hardly be other than big. Overall, it resembled an F-15 Eagle extensively modified for stealth, but with thrust vectoring nozzles. After an exhaustive flyoff against the futuristic rival Northrop F-23 (which see), an Engineering/Manufacturing Development (EMD) contract was awarded to the YF-22 powered by the YF119 engine in August 1991. Various changes were introduced, and only in March 1992 was the design finally frozen. Even then problems persisted. On 25 April a software anomaly in the quadruplex digital FBW system caused test pilot Tom Morgenfeld to belly in at Edwards. Fortuitously, more than 90 per cent of the test programme was complete, and equally fortuitously he survived. Unofficially the type was at first named Lightning II, after the Second World War fighter, but common sense later prevailed, and on 9 April 1997, it became the Raptor. Air-to-air weaponry consists of a 20-mm M61A2 Vulcan cannon, a single AIM-9 Sidewinder in each of the two side weapons bays, and up to six "cropped" AIM-120C Amraam in the central bay. Radar is the APG-77, a fixed active array low probability of intercept type, while the EW suite, which includes an IR missile launch detector, is the ALR-94. If the Raptor has one fault, it is that it lacks an IRST. It has a "glass cockpit", a sidestick controller covered in buttons, as are the throttles, covering more than 60 time-critical functions. It also has Pilot's Associate, which gives aural warnings of the tactical situation while speech recognition reduces the manual workload. Four wings of Raptors are planned, the first to enter service in 2005. As at late winter 2001, low-rate production has yet to be authorised. *Max speed hi, Mach 2 plus. Max speed lo, Mach 1.2. Supercruise, Mach 1.58 plus. Empty weight, 31,670 lb (14 365 kg). Max takeoff weight, 55,000 lb (24 948 kg). Span, 44 ft 6 in (13,56 m). Length, 62 ft 1 in (18,92 m). Height, 16 ft 8 in (5,08 m). Wing area 840 sq ft (78,04 m²). Internal fuel 25,000 lb (11 340 kg).*

LOCKHEED MARTIN X-35 JSF   USA

The Lockheed Martin X-35 is in direct competition with the Boeing X-32 (which see) to supply the Joint Strike Fighter for the USAF, USN, USMC and RN. Unsurprisingly, it resembles the much larger F-22A in many ways, due largely to the fact that many of the

(Below) YF-22 Advanced Tactical Fighter.

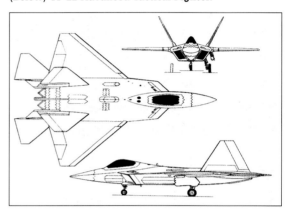

same stealth features have been adopted. The main point of external variance is that it has cheek intakes, raked inwards like those of the 1950s vintage F-105 Thunderchief. From these, steeply raked root extensions lead back to the wing. The X-35 is powered by a single Pratt & Whitney F119-611 afterburning turbofan, modified from the F-22 engine. For conventional or short takeoff, this will have a low-observable axi-symmetric vectoring nozzle. For vertical flight, mainly the landing, the engine is coupled to a shaft-driven lift fan just aft of the cockpit, engaged and disengaged via a multi-layer clutch and gearing system. The tailpipe is a three-bearing lobsterback, similar to that used by the Russian Yak-141, which can vector through 108 degrees. Lateral control is via two ducts leading to roll posts in the wings. For vertical flight, the lift fan is expected to generate about 18,000 lb (8 165 kgp) of thrust, and the main engine a similar amount. Add the roll posts to this, and the total available thrust for engine-borne flight is expected to be about 37,000 lb (16 783 kgp). For conventional flight, the lift fan must be covered in top and bottom, and getting the perfect fit demanded by stealth is a major precision engineering job. Like its Boeing rival, the X-35 is dimensionally small, but very chunky. High lift devices occupy both leading and trailing edges of the wings. An internal gun will be carried on USAF and USN aircraft. The size and weight of the 20-mm M61A is against it; the answer may well be the 27-mm Mauser BK27 revolver cannon. It seems probable that the USMC and RN will

One of the three airframes, ordered as A-12 recce aircraft, completed as YF-12A (below) interceptors.

Full-scale mock-up of Lockheed Martin X-35 JSF.

settle for a podded cannon, as on the Harrier. Other air-to-air weaponry is to be two AIM-120C Amraam carried internally. The first X-35A took to the air on 24 October 2000, piloted by Tom Morgenfeld, while the carrier-compatible X-35C flew on 16 December 2000, with Joe Sweeney at the controls. The ASTOVL X-35B was expected to fly in 2001. But with no serious threat on the horizon, it cannot be certain that JSF will ever enter service. Just one extraneous fact enters the equation: if JSF is cancelled, or if the award is made to Lockheed Martin, the USA will have only one major fighter manufacturer. Data all provisional. *Max speed, Mach 1.7. Supercruise, Mach 1.4. Operational radius, 600 nm (1 112 km). Empty weight, X-35A 21,600 lb (9798 kg), X-35C 23,000 lb (10 433 kg), X-35B similar. Max takeoff weight, 50,000 lb (22 680 kg). Span, 32 ft 10 in (10 m). Length, 50 ft 10 in (15,50 m). Wing area, X-35C 540 sq ft (50,2 m²), X-35A and B 450 sq ft (41,81 m²).*

LOENING M-8   USA

The Armistice of 1918 ended plans for large-scale production of the M-8 (above and below).

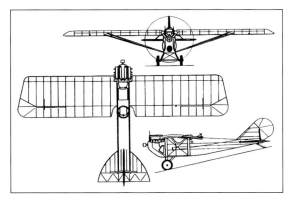

Daringly innovative for its day, the M-8 two-seat fighter, flown for the first time in August 1918, was the first product of the Loening Engineering Corp formed earlier that year by Grover C Loening. Despite some prejudice against the monoplane configuration, the M-8, designed around the new 300 hp Wright (Hispano-Suiza) Model H engine, was a braced shoulder-wing monoplane. Possessing an exceptionally low structural weight, the M-8 carried an armament of two 0.3-in (7,62-mm) Lewis guns in the rear cockpit, the gunner having an excellent field of fire. The M-8 was of wooden construction and two prototypes were completed. These demonstrated such outstanding performance that a contract was placed for 5,000 aircraft before the Armistice terminated plans for large-scale production. Although only the prototypes went to the Army, the Navy ordered a single example as the M-8-0, following this with orders for a further 54 aircraft (of which 36 were built by the Naval Aircraft Factory). Forty-six of these were of the M-8-0 and M-8-1 types, which, although designed as fighters, were used for observation purposes, the remaining six being completed as twin-float seaplanes under the Navy designation LS-1. *Max speed, 144 mph (232 km/h) at sea level. Time to 6,500 ft (1 980 m), 5.2 min. Empty weight, 1,663 lb (754 kg). Loaded weight, 2,368 lb (1 074 kg). Span, 32 ft 9 in (9,98 m). Length, 24 ft 0 in (7,31 m). Height, 6 ft 7 in (2,00 m). Wing area, 238.9 sq ft (22,19 m²).*

LOENING PW-2   USA

Embodying the design concept of the M-8, the PW-2 single-seat fighter monoplane was designed around the same 300 hp Wright (Hispano-Suiza) H water-cooled engine. Three examples were ordered by the US Army in 1920, of which one was for static testing. As originally delivered, the second flight test PW-2 had twin fins and rudders, but this arrangement soon gave place to the single fin-and-rudder as fitted to the first aircraft. Flight testing commenced in September 1921, and two improved versions were ordered as PW-2As, these featuring a more conventional rudder post and a balanced rudder without vertical fin. In the event, the second was completed with a 350 hp Packard 1A-1237 water-cooled engine with which it was designated PW-2B. This last aircraft also featured a smaller wing with an area of 225 sq ft (20,90 m²) and a span of 34 ft 1¼ in (10,39 m), and achieved a maximum speed of 140 mph (225 km/h). A further eight PW-2As were ordered, but structural and aerodynamic inadequacies became apparent, the fighter proving susceptible to wing flutter, and, on 20 October 1922, a PW-2A lost a wing and its pilot took to his parachute – the first Army pilot

As originally delivered, the PW-2 (above) had twin fins and rudders close-set on the fuselage.

so to do. In consequence, the last six PW-2As were cancelled and further development was discontinued. The following data relate to the PW-2A. *Max speed, 136 mph (219 km/h) at sea level. Time to 10,000 ft (3 050 m), 9. 8 min. Endurance, 2.5 hrs. Empty weight, 1,876 lb (851 kg). Loaded weight, 2,799 lb (1 270 kg). Span, 39 ft 9 in (12,11 m). Length, 26 ft 0½ in (7,94 m). Height, 8 ft 1 in (2,46 m). Wing area, 299 sq ft (27,78 m²).*

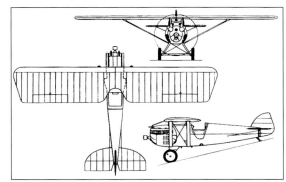

The standard PW-2A (above) and the sole PW-2B (below) with an engine change and smaller wing.

LOENING PA-1   USA

Continuing prejudice against the monoplane configuration and the disappointing results achieved with the PW-2 led the Loening Engineering Corporation to develop a single-seat fighter *biplane* in the hope of attracting an order from the US Army Air Service. The PA-1 was a single-bay equi-span staggered biplane, the wings employing an unusually thick aerofoil and the centre section of the upper wing being thickened to accommodate the fuel tank. Armament comprised two 0.3-in (7,62-mm) Vickers machine guns and power was provided by a Wright R-1 (R-1454) nine-cylinder radial rated at 350 hp. A contract was placed for two prototype PA-1s, these entering flight test in 1922, but the results of testing did not warrant a production order and the Loening concern left the fighter business. *Max speed, 130 mph (209 km/h) at sea level. Time to 6,500 ft (1 980 m), 7.0 min. Empty weight, 1,536 lb (697 kg). Loaded weight, 2,463 lb (1 117 kg). Span, 28ft 0 in (8,53 m). Length, 19 ft 9 in (6,02 m). Height, 8 ft 8 in (2,64 m). Wing area, 283 sq ft (26,29 m²).*

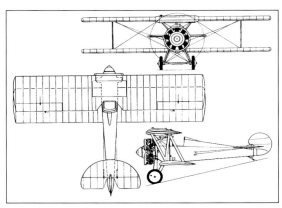

Only two prototypes of the PA-1 (above and below) were built for testing by the US Army.

LOHNER Typ AA (10.20A)   Austria-Hungary

During 1916, the Lohnerwerke of Vienna received a contract from the *K.u.K.Luftfahrttruppen* (Imperial and Royal Air Service of the Austro-Hungarian Army) for four single-seat fighter prototypes powered by the 185 hp Austro-Daimler six-cylinder inline engine. The first of these, the Lohner 10.20, or Typ AA, appeared at Aspern on 5 September 1916. A single-bay biplane with an armament of twin synchronised Schwarzlöse machine guns, the Lohner 10.20 was characterised by a singularly abbreviated and deep, slab-sided fuselage. This was suspended between the wings by a short, inverted-Vee cabane and the faired struts supported the undercarriage. The wing cellule had broad, aerofoil-section I-type struts, and the vertical tail possessed no fixed surface. Taxying trials revealed insufficient control. The rudder area was increased several times and the fuselage lengthened before the aircraft flew on 29 December 1916. The fighter demonstrated poor stability, and, after suffering severe damage in

The original Typ AA (below) featured a very deep, but short, slab-sided fuselage.

Extensive revision of the Lohner 10.20 resulted in a single 10.20A prototype (above and below).

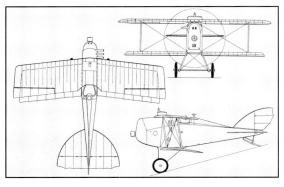

February 1917, was returned to the Lohnerwerke for repair and extensive modification. The aircraft re-emerged in the following month as the Lohner 10.20A, the lower wing having been raised to the base of the fuselage, the cabane being eliminated, a twin-strutted wing cellule being adopted, the fuselage being lengthened and the redesigned tail surfaces embodying a fixed fin. The Lohner 10.20A was destroyed in a crash on 6 June 1917, and no data relating to this type are recorded.

LOHNER Typ AA (10.20B)   Austria-Hungary

The second fighter prototype from the Lohnerwerke, the 10.20B (later redesignated 111.02), possessed essentially similar wing and tail surfaces to those of the 10.20A. It had a ''wireless'' wing cabane, however, which reverted to aerofoil-section I-struts supplemented by inclined Vee-struts. It also introduced a deep dorsal fin. Powered by a similar 185 hp Austro-Daimler engine to that of its predecessor and carrying a twin-Schwarzlöse gun armament, the Lohner 10.20B made its initial flight at Aspern on 2 June 1917. The prototype was taken over by the *K.u.K.Luftfahrt-*

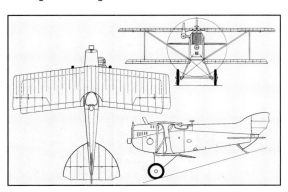

The Lohner 10.20B (above and below) combined a new fuselage with wings and tail of the 10.20A.

truppen in August 1917, and official trials continued through October when further development was halted. No data relating to this type are available.

LOHNER Typ AA (111.03)   Austria-Hungary

The third Typ AA series prototype produced by the Lohnerwerke, the 111.03 differed from its immediate predecessor, the 10.20B alias 111.02, in having a conventional wire-braced wing cellule, a redesigned rudder and unfaired undercarriage strutting. Retaining the 185 hp Austro-Daimler engine, the Lohner 111.03 was flown for the first time on 28 June 1917, and flight testing continued through October. At this stage, the Lohnerwerke was assigned a manufacturing licence for the Aviatik D I, and further development of the Typ AA series was ended. *Max speed, 120 mph (193 km/h). Time to 3,280 ft (1 000 m), 2.66 min. Range, 240 mls (386 km). Empty weight, 1,373 lb (623 kg). Loaded weight, 2,085 lb (946 kg). Span, 24 ft 11¼ in (7,60 m). Length, 20 ft 10 in (6,35 m). Height, 9 ft 10⅛ in (3,00 m). Wing area, 215.28 sq ft (20,00 m²).*

The third Typ AA series fighter, the Lohner 111.03 (below) was abandoned in favour of the Aviatik D I.

LOHNER Typ A (111.04)   Austria-Hungary

Possessing fundamentally similar fuselage and tail surfaces to the final Typ AA biplane, the Typ A (111.04) triplane was completed on 23 June 1917. Similarly powered and armed to the preceding Lohner fighters, the Typ A had comparatively high aspect ratio wings braced by a unique canted strut arrangement. Official trials were conducted on 7 July 1917 with mediocre results, and the prototype was returned to the Lohnerwerke for modification. It reappeared in September 1917, and subsequent performance trials proved satisfactory, but the handling characteristics were poor and view from the cockpit was deemed inadequate, with the result that the programme was terminated. *Max speed, 111 mph (178 km/h). Time to 3,280 ft (1 000 m), 2.8 min. Range, 221 mls (356 km). Empty weight,*

Tested in 1917, the Typ A triplane (below) was destined to be the last of the Lohner fighters.

1,527 lb (692,5 kg). Loaded weight, 2,041 lb (926 kg). Span, 28 ft 10½ in (8,80 m). Length, 20 ft 10 in (6,35 m). Height, 9 ft 10⅛ in (3,00 m). Wing area, 226.05 sq ft (21,00 m²).

(Below) The Lohner Typ A (111.04) fighter triplane.

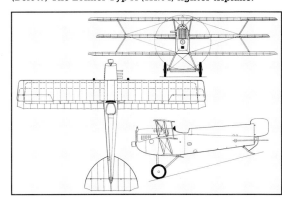

LOIRE 43   France

In 1927, the shipbuilding concern Ateliers et Chantiers de la Loire established an aircraft division and, in 1929, initiated design of a lightweight fighter for which alternative engines were proposed. These were the 300 hp Gnome-Rhône Titan II (Loire 40), the 500 hp Hispano-Suiza 12Mc (Loire 41) and the 420 hp Gnome-Rhône 9Asb Jupiter VII (Loire 42). When, in 1930, the lightweight fighter concept was discarded by the *Service Technique de l'Aéronautique* (STAé), a new C1 (single-seat fighter) programme was initiated for which there

Flown in 1933, the Loire 43 (above and below) was destroyed before it could be fully evaluated.

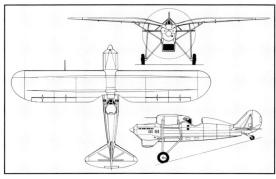

were 10 official contenders. All of these were powered by the supercharged Hispano-Suiza 12Xbrs 12-cylinder liquid-cooled engine. As one of these contenders, the Loire 43 was a further development of the Loire 40 series of fighter projects. It was a gull-winged, braced monoplane of all-metal stressed-skin construction with an armament of two synchronised 7,7-mm MAC-built Vickers guns. The Loire 43 was flown on 17 October 1932, but 13 weeks later, on 14 January 1933, and before it could undergo official evaluation, its pilot apparently lost consciousness after climbing to 29,530 ft (9 000 m) and the aircraft spun into the ground. *Max speed, 224 mph (360 km/h) at 11,485 ft (3 500 m), 195 mph (314 km/h) at sea level. Time to 21,325 ft (6 500 m), 10 min. Range, 373 mls (600 km). Empty weight, 2,745 lb (1 245 kg). Loaded weight, 3,803 lb (1 725 kg). Span, 39 ft 4½ in (12,00 m). Length, 26 ft 0¼ in (7,93 m). Wing area, 221.74 sq ft (20,60 m²).*

LOIRE 45   France

Built as a replacement for the Loire 43, the Loire 45 employed a fundamentally similar airframe, but was fitted with an 800 hp Gnome-Rhône 14Kds 14-cylinder radial air-cooled engine and had more robust wing bracing struts. Flown for the first time on 20 February 1933, the prototype was transferred to Villacoublay in June for official testing. During the course of trials several modifications were made to the wing roots in attempts to improve visibility from the cockpit, an 880 hp Gnome-Rhône 14Kcs was installed in August 1934, and, in the following October, the vertical tail surfaces were enlarged. Armament comprised two 20-mm cannon in underwing gondolas, but visibility for the pilot was deemed unacceptable and, after re-engining with a 900 hp Gnome-Rhône 14Kfs, the sole prototype was relegated to the rôle of parachute testing as the Loire 45 LP1. It flew in this form for the first time in July 1935. The following data relate to the Loire 45 with the G-R 14Kcs engine. *Max speed, 230 mph (370 km/h) at 13,615 ft (4 150 m). Time to 21,325 ft (6 500 m), 8.15 min. Empty weight, 2,954 lb (1 340 kg). Loaded weight, 3,935 lb (1 785 kg). Span, 39 ft 2⅞ in (11,96 m). Length, 24 ft 6¾ in (7,48 m). Wing area, 221.74 sq ft (20,60 m²).*

The Loire 45 (below) was the immediate predecessor of the Loire 46 which was only conceptually similar.

LOIRE 46   France

In order to rectify the inadequate visibility from the cockpit suffered by the Loire 45, a major redesign was undertaken and yet another prototype was built as the Loire 46. This retained little more than a conceptual similarity to its predecessor. The wing centre section was more deeply "gulled", and the untapered wing leading and trailing edges gave place to tapered outboard leading edges and semi-elliptical trailing edges. The engine thrust line was lowered, the cockpit was

The prototype Loire 46 (below), as originally fitted with a pair of drum-fed 20-mm wing cannon.

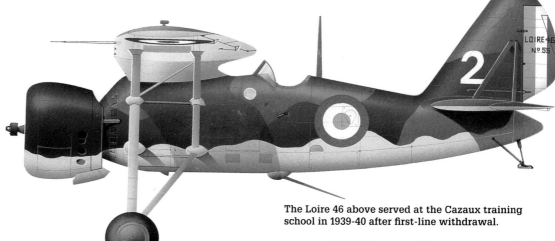

The Loire 46 above served at the Cazaux training school in 1939-40 after first-line withdrawal.

The Loire 46 (above and below) saw only brief French service just prior to World War II.

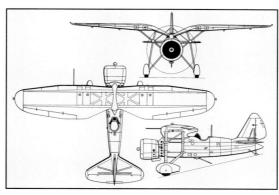

moved farther aft, the rear fuselage was deepened and all tail surfaces were enlarged. Powered by an 880 hp Gnome-Rhône 14Kcs engine, the Loire 46 flew on 1 September 1934. Re-engined with a 930 hp Gnome-Rhône 14Kfs in February 1935, the Loire 46 demonstrated excellent handling characteristics, and a contract for five pre-series aircraft was followed by orders for 60 production aircraft. Armament comprised a quartet of wing-mounted 7,5-mm MAC 1934 guns. The first production Loire 46 C1 was flown in February 1936, deliveries commencing in the following August to the 6ᵉ *Escadre* of the *Armée de l'Air*. The five pre-production examples were relinquished by the French Service and supplied to the Spanish Republican government between 5 and 7 September 1936. The last Loire 46 was delivered in July 1937, by which time its gull-winged configuration was manifestly obsolescent. Only three remained on the effective first line strength of the *Armée de l'Air* at the beginning of World War II. *Max speed, 230 mph (370 km/h) at 13,125 ft (4 000 m). Time to 9,840 ft (3 000 m), 3.3 min. Range, 466 mls (750 km) at 200 mph (322 km/h). Empty weight, 3,197 lb (1 450 kg). Max loaded weight, 4,630 lb (2 100 kg). Span, 38 ft 9¾ in (11,83 m). Length, 25 ft 10¼ in (7,88 m). Height, 13 ft 6⅝ in (4,13 m). Wing area, 209.9 sq ft (19,50 m²).*

LOIRE 210   France

In 1933, the *Marine Nationale* formulated and issued a requirement for a modern float-equipped fighter that could be launched from the rotatable catapults of such cruisers as the *Foch* and the *Richelieu*. Contenders were built by Loire, Bernard (H.52), Potez (452) and

Romano (R-90). The Loire 210, first flown on 21 March 1935, was of all-metal construction with metal skinning apart from the outboard sections of the wings which were fabric covered. It employed a fuselage essentially similar to that of the Loire 46. Powered by a 720 hp Hispano-Suiza 9Vbs nine-cylinder radial, the Loire 210 began official trials in June 1936. A production order, which called for 20 aircraft, was not placed until 19 March 1937, the first series aircraft flying on 18 November 1938. The production model carried an armament of four wing-mounted 7,5-mm Darne machine guns, two *escadrilles* forming with this fighter in August 1939.

The prototype Loire 210 (above) employed a very similar fuselage to that of the land-based Loire 46.

However, after several accidents resulting from wing structural failures, the remaining aircraft were withdrawn from service and their units disbanded. *Max speed, 186 mph (299 km/h) at 9,840 ft (3 000 m). Time to 9,840 ft (3 000 m), 5.35 min. Range, 466 mls (750 km). Empty weight, 3,175 lb (1 440 kg). Loaded weight, 4,806 lb (2 180 kg). Span, 38 ft 8⅛ in (11,79 m). Length, 31 ft 2¾ in (9,51 m). Height, 12 ft 5¼ in (3,80 m). Wing area, 218.5 sq ft (20,30 m²).*

The Loire 210 (above and below) enjoyed only a short career owing to structural weaknesses.

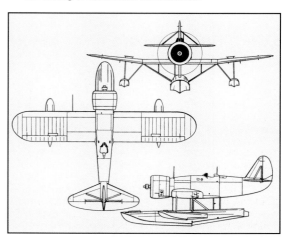

LOIRE 250   France

In 1934, the *Service Technique* issued an outline speci-fication for a new single-seat fighter, all the contenders but one having all-metal stressed-skin monocoque structures with enclosed cockpits and retractable undercarriages. The structural exception was the MS 405. The Loire 250 was powered by a 1,000 hp Hispano-Suiza 14Ha-79 two-row radial and was first flown on 27 September 1935 temporarily with a fixed-pitch two-bladed wooden propeller. Intended armament com-prised two synchronised 20-mm cannon and two 7,5-mm machine guns, but trials with the Loire 250 proved disappointing from the outset, the prototype suffering serious drag problems. Various palliatives were applied to reduce drag, the vertical tail was rede-signed to rectify a stability problem and a three-bladed variable-pitch propeller was fitted. Nonetheless the fighter proved incapable of attaining the max speed of "at least 485 km/h (301 mph)" called for by the speci-fication, and thus the Loire 250 was eliminated from the contest at an early stage. *Max speed, 298 mph (480 km/h) at 14,765 ft (4 500 m). Time to 14,765 ft (4 500 m), 5.5 min. Range, 544 mls (875 km) at 217 mph (350 km/h). Empty weight, 3,307 lb (1 500 kg). Loaded weight, 4,850 lb (2 200 kg). Span, 35 ft 5⅛ in (10,80 m). Length, 25 ft 7¾ in (7,81 m). Height, 12 ft 2½ in (3,72 m). Wing area, 175.45 sq ft (16,30 m²).*

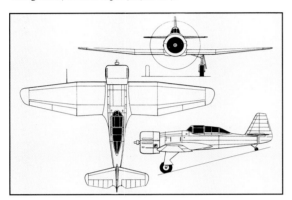

The Loire 250 (above and below) in its definitive form with redesigned tail and variable-pitch propeller.

LOIRE-GOURDOU-LESEURRE   France

From late 1925 until 1928, the Gourdou-Leseurre con-cern operated as a subsidiary of the Ateliers et Chan-tiers de la Loire. During the three years of this association, the aircraft designed and built by Gour-dou-Leseurre received the LGL prefix in their designa-tion. For ease of reference, Loire-Gourdou-Leseurre types are listed under Gourdou-Leseurre.

LOIRE-NIEUPORT 161   France

During 1934, the Ateliers et Chantiers de la Loire amal-gamated with the Société Nieuport-Astra to result in the Groupement Aviation Loire-Nieuport. The two con-cerns maintained separate design offices which, at times, were to find themselves in competition, a case in point being the LN 161. This, like the Loire 250, was in-tended to meet the requirements of the 1934 *Service Technique* specification for a new single-seat fighter. Designed by engineers Mary and Dieudonné, it was of advanced structural concept with an all-metal mono-coque fuselage and a metal stressed-skin wing. Arma-ment comprised a 20-mm engine-mounted cannon and two wing-mounted 7,5-mm machine guns. Although designed for the 860 hp Hispano-Suiza 12Ycrs engine,

(Above) The third Loire-Nieuport 161 prototype which entered flight testing in March 1938.

the non-availability of this power plant dictated in-stallation of a 690 hp HS 12Xcrs engine driving a two-bladed fixed-pitch propeller. The prototype flew as the Nieuport 160 on 5 October 1935. In the following November, it was returned to the factory for various modifications and installation of the definitive engine, resuming flight test at the end of March 1936 as the Nieuport 161 fitted with a three-bladed two-pitch pro-peller. The prototype showed considerable promise and was the favoured contender for *Armée de l'Air* orders, three additional prototypes being contracted. The first prototype crashed on 22 September 1936, and the second prototype, temporarily designated SNCAO 161 (Loire-Nieuport having meanwhile been absorbed by the Société Nationale de Constructions Aéronau-tiques de l'Ouest), did not enter flight test until 15 October 1937. The third prototype, bearing the defin-itive designation of Loire-Nieuport 161, followed in March 1938. During the next month, the second proto-type was written off in a landing accident, but the re-sults of testing were by then of purely academic in-terest as the Morane-Saulnier contender had been ordered into production. Consequently, the fourth pro-totype was not completed. *Max speed, 297 mph (478 km/h) at 13,125 ft (4 000 m). Time to 13,125 ft (4 000 m), 4.96 min. Empty weight, 3,854 lb (1 748 kg). Loaded weight, 5,022 lb (2 278 kg). Span, 36 ft 1 in (11,00 m). Length, 31 ft 4⅜ in (9,56 m). Height, 9 ft 8⅛ in (2,95 m). Wing area, 161.46 sq ft (15,00 m²).*

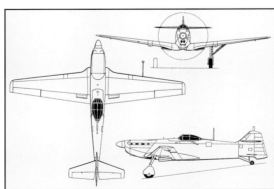

(Above and below) The Loire-Nieuport 161, the photo depicting the first prototype of this fighter.

LORING C.I   Spain

During the mid-'twenties, Spain's *Aviación Militar* established a requirement for a new single-seat fighter. In an attempt to fulfil this requirement, the Jorge Loring concern of Carabanchel Alto, Madrid, built a single-seat sesquiplane designed by Eduardo Barrón, who, in

(Below) The Loring C.I, which, designed by Eduardo Barrón, was bested by the Nieuport-Delage 42.

1919, had designed a single-seat fighter for La Hispano Aviación. The Loring C.I was powered by a 500 hp His-pano-Suiza 12Hb 12-cylinder water-cooled engine and was flown late in 1927. Designed, built and tested within two-and-a-half months, the C.I competed for *Aviación Militar* orders against the Fiat CR.20, the Dewoitine D.21 and the Nieuport-Delage NiD 42. The last-mentioned type was pronounced winning con-tender with the Loring fighter taking second place. No specification for the Loring C.I is available.

LTG FD 1   Germany

The Luft Torpedo Gesellschaft (LTG) was established in March 1915, primarily for the development of an aerial torpedo. It expanded into aircraft sub-contract, and, on 8 February 1917, received a contract for three prototypes of an original single-seat twin-float fighter, the FD 1. A single-bay staggered equi-span biplane, the FD 1 was powered by a 150 hp Benz Bz III driving the propeller via a Loeb reduction gearbox. The first FD 1 was delivered in May 1917, in which month a further contract was placed for three additional prototypes em-bodying improvements. The three FD 1s ordered under the initial contract were tested through September 1917, after overcoming engine and gearbox mounting

The LTG FD-1 floatplane fighter is seen above and below in its definitive form with extended fins.

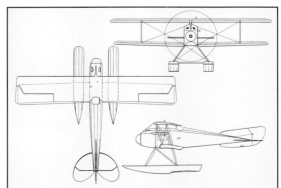

deficiencies, but demonstrated poor manoeuvrability. The aircraft built against the second contract differed primarily in having extended dorsal and ventral fins, the first of these being delivered in late October 1917. The FD 1 was finally approved for service in March 1918, five aircraft being added to the *Marine* seaplane inventory, the first prototype having been destroyed during static load testing. The FD 1s were not flown in combat, being placed in storage at Hage where they were discovered by the Allies in December 1918. One example of a landplane version of the FD 1 was flight tested at Johannisthal during 1917. *Max speed, 90 mph (145 km/h). Time to 3,280 ft (1 000 m), 4.5 min. Empty weight, 1,973 lb (895 kg). Loaded weight, 2,568 lb (1 165 kg). Span, 32 ft 9¾ in (10,00 m). Length, 29 ft 6⅓ in (9,00 m). Height, 11 ft 7¾ in (3,55 m).*

LVG E I   Germany

The first fighter of original design produced by the Luft-Verkehrs-Gesellschaft (LVG) of Berlin-Johannisthal was a two-seat monoplane designed by Franz Schneider. This, the E I powered by a 120 hp Mercedes D II engine and flown in 1915, was fitted with both a synchronised machine gun for the pilot and a machine gun on a ring mounting for the second crew member. The LVG E I was unusual in that, unlike most contemporaries, it featured ailerons, most monoplanes at the time employing wing warping for control. Although a promising design, the sole prototype was lost while being ferried to the Front for operational evaluation. It was subsequently ascertained that the screws of the wing bracing struts had worked loose with the result that the wings had collapsed. No data relating to the LVG E I are available.

(Below) The LVG E I two-seat fighter monoplane, the company's first fighter of original design.

LVG D 10   Germany

The Luft-Verkehrs-Gesellschaft (LVG), which had initiated licence manufacture of 75 Albatros D II fighters in August 1916, began work during the course of that

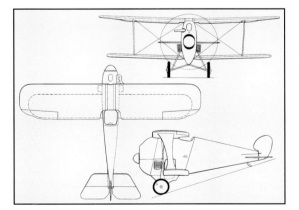

The D 10 (above and below) possessed an unusually deep fuselage which filled the entire wing gap.

year on an original single-seat, single-bay fighter biplane. Of unusual appearance to the designs of engineers Ehrhardt and Rethel, it was designated D 10. Powered by a 120 hp Mercedes D II engine, the LVG fighter was noteworthy for its extraordinarily deep fuselage which completely filled the wide wing gap. This *Walfisch*-type fuselage was of wrapped plywood strip semi-monocoque form, and the wing cellule featured exceptionally broad aerofoil-section interplane struts. The D 10 is known to have demonstrated unsatisfactory characteristics in flight, but no data are available.

LVG D 12 (D II)   Germany

At the end of 1916, the LVG produced the prototype of an elegant and more orthodox single-seat fighter biplane, the D 12, also known as the D II (the LVG D I being the licence-built Albatros D II). An unequal-span single-bay biplane with an Albatros-style wooden semi-monocoque fuselage which filled the gap between the wings, the D 12 was powered by a 160 hp Mercedes D III engine and allegedly attained 124 mph (200 km/h) during the course of prototype trials. After suffering accidental damage the type was not further developed. No data relating to the D 12 are available.

The D 12 (below) appeared in late 1916, and was abandoned after damage during prototype trials.

LVG D III   Germany

Retaining the plywood-covering and semi-monocoque type construction of the D 10 and D 12, the LVG D III made its appearance in the summer of 1917. It was a competitor of the very successful Albatros D III and differed in virtually every respect from its predecessors. The gap-filling fuselage configuration was discarded and an attempt was made to utilise semi-rigid bracing in that the landing wires were replaced by struts, although flying wires were retained. The D III was powered by a 185 hp NAG C III six-cylinder inline engine and carried an armament of two LMG 08/15 machine guns. Official type testing was completed on 2 June 1917, but the D III was adjudged too heavy and too large, and was therefore discounted as a potential production aircraft. *Max speed, 109 mph (175 km/h). Time*

The D III (above) was considered too large and heavy by the *Idflieg* to warrant production.

to 3,280 ft (1 000 m), 3.0 min. Empty weight, 1,704 lb (773 kg). Loaded weight 2,266 lb (1 028 kg). Span, 32 ft 9¾ in (10,00 m). Length, 24 ft 8½ in (7,53 m). Height, 9 ft 7 in (2,92 m). Wing area, 282.02 sq ft (26,20 m²).

LVG D IV   Germany

Retaining the aerodynamically clean, plywood-covered semi-monocoque fuselage style of the D III and a generally similar wing cellule, with single-spar lower wing and Vee-type interplane struts, the LVG D IV was in the final stages of assembly in September 1917, according to an *Idflieg* report. Serving as a test-bed for the new 185 hp Benz Bz IIIbo eight-cylinder Vee-type direct-drive engine, the D IV was flight tested intermittently until, on 5 January 1918, the crankshaft broke in flight. The aircraft caught fire and was destroyed. A second D IV prototype was completed in late January, but suffered recurrent engine problems. Nevertheless, it was entered in the 1st D-type contest at Adlershof, but on 29 January, the first day of the competition, the engine caught fire and the aircraft was destroyed, further development being discontinued. *Time to 16,405 ft (5 000 m), 28 min. Empty weight, 1,499 lb*

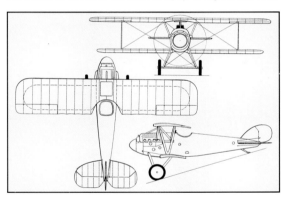

The D IV (above and below) had the misfortune to suffer recurrent engine problems which resulted in the destruction of both prototypes of this fighter.

(680 kg). Loaded weight, 2,061 lb (935 kg). Span, 27 ft 10⅔ in (8,50 m). Length, 20 ft 7¼ in (6,28 m). Height, 8 ft 10¼ in (2,70 m). Wing area, 194.4 sq ft (18,06 m²).

LVG D V   Germany

Designed by Paul Ehrhardt and flown for the first time in June 1918, the LVG D V was unusual in that the lower wing was of much broader chord than the upper. The narrow-chord upper wing panels outboard of the centre section pivoted differentially to act as "ailerons" for lateral manoeuvres. The fuselage was slab-sided and plywood covered, armament comprised two 7,9-mm LMG 08/15 machine guns and power was provided by a geared Vee-eight Benz Bz IIIbm engine affording 185 hp. The D V proved fast, but it was unstable at full speed and its controllability was poor. During a test flight with Ehrhardt at the controls in July 1918, the sole D V prototype made a crash landing and turned turtle, further development being halted. No data are available on this type.

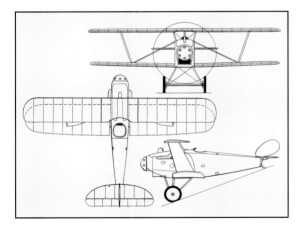

Differentially pivoting upper wing tips were an unusual feature of the D V (above and below).

LVG D VI   Germany

The last single-seat fighter to emerge from LVG, the D VI single-bay biplane was in final assembly in September 1918, flight testing being initiated shortly before hostilities terminated. Like the preceding D V, it featured a slab-sided plywood-covered fuselage, a twin-LMG 08/15 gun armament and a 185 hp Benz Bz IIIbm geared Vee-eight engine with a chin-type air intake. However, the wing configuration was totally dif-

Last of the LVG fighters, the D VI (below) was not tested until the last week of World War I.

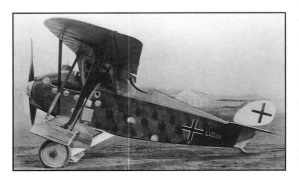

ferent, the lower wing being sweptback and the I-type interplane struts being supplemented by metal strap cross bracing. No data relating to the D VI are available.

L.W.F. MODEL G-2   USA

The L.W.F. Engineering Company, established in December 1915 by Edward Lowe, Charles Willard and Robert Fowler, developed the Model G in late 1917 as a two-seat reconnaissance aircraft. The Model G was destroyed in a crash on 16 January 1918, but a more powerful version, the G-2, was completed and flown in the spring of 1918, this being intended as a two-seat heavy fighter and reconnaissance-bomber. Powered by a 435 hp Liberty 12 water-cooled engine, the G-2 carried an unprecedented armament of seven 0.3-in (7,62-mm) machine guns, four of these being grouped around the engine and synchronised to fire through the propeller disc, two being Scarff-mounted in the rear cockpit and the remaining gun firing through a ventral aperture. Although flight testing was considered successful, the sole G-2 crashed and was destroyed in fog on 18 November 1918. A third example was subsequently completed as a mailplane, but further development as a combat aircraft was abandoned. *Max speed, 138 mph (222 km/h) at sea level. Time to 10,000 ft (3 050 m), 9.3 min. Endurance, 4 hrs. Empty weight, 2,675 lb (1 213 kg). Loaded weight, 4,023 lb (1 825 kg). Span, 41 ft 7½ in (12,69 m). Length, 29 ft 1¾ in (8,88 m). Height, 9 ft 4¾ in (2,86 m). Wing area, 516 sq ft (47,94 m²).*

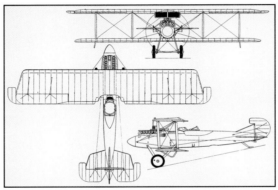

Flight testing during 1918 of the L.W.F. G-2 (above and below) was dogged by misfortune.

M

MACCHI M.5 (Tɪᴘᴏ M)   Italy

The Società Anonima Nieuport-Macchi (predecessor of Aeronautica Macchi) gained experience in flying boat design by producing improved copies of the Austro-Hungarian Lohner 'boat. Early in 1917, engineers Buzio and Calzavara developed a single-seat fighter for the *Regia Marina* based on the L.3 (M.3) two-seat bomber-reconnaissance flying boat. Initially known as the *Tipo* (Type) M, the fighter was of wooden construction with fabric and plywood skinning, and was powered by a six-cylinder Isotta-Fraschini V.4B engine strut-mounted above the hull and driving a pusher propeller, maximum output being 187 bhp. The pilot sat beneath the radiator and was provided with a single 7,7-mm Vickers machine gun. Intended for use in the Adriatic,

The M.5 (above) was the first of a series of fighter flying boats developed by Macchi.

the *Tipo* M was fully aerobatic, further prototypes being produced as *Tipo* Ma and, with control refinements, as *Tipo* M *bis* and Ma *bis*, the last-mentioned entering production and the designation M.5 subsequently being adopted. The M.5 entered service with the *Regia Marina* in November 1917, frequently escorting bombers attacking Austro-Hungarian naval bases in the Adriatic and proving faster than opposing Phönix land-based fighters. The single Vickers gun was replaced by a twin-gun arrangement in some aircraft, and a total of 244 was built (44 of these by the Società Aeronautica Italiana) of which 68 were completed in 1917, and production giving place to the M.5 mod during 1918. *Max speed, 117 mph (189 km/h). Time to 3,280 ft (1 000 m), 3.5 min. Endurance, 3.66 hrs. Empty weight, 1,587 lb (720 kg). Loaded weight, 2,183 lb (990 kg). Span, 39 ft 0½ in (11,90 m). Length, 26 ft 6⅛ in (8,08 m). Height, 9 ft 4¼ in (2,85 m). Wing area, 301.4 sq ft (28,00 m²).*

(Below) The Macchi M.5, which appeared in 1917.

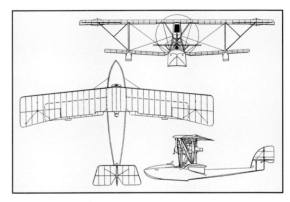

MACCHI M.5 Mᴏᴅ   Italy

Early in 1918, Nieuport-Macchi developed a more powerful version of the M.5 single-seat fighter flying boat as an interim measure pending availability of the higher-performance M.7. The latter was being developed to the designs of Alessandro Tonini to counter the increased efficacy of Austro-Hungarian fighters being encountered over the Adriatic. Designated M.5 mod, the interim fighter achieved enhanced performance by using a 247 bhp Isotta-Fraschini V.6 engine, its installation being accompanied by a 7-ft 2⅝-in (2,20-m) reduction in the span of the upper wing. A twin 7,7-mm Vickers gun armament was standardised. One hundred M.5 mod fighters were built, these progressively replacing the M.5s in *Regia Marina* service, and 66 of them were still on strength when the *Regia Aeronautica* was formed in 1923. These subsequently gave place to the M.7ter in the mid-'twenties. *Max speed, 127 mph (205 km/h). Time to 3,280 ft (1 000 m), 3.5 min. Endurance, 3.66 hrs. Empty weight, 1,664 lb (755 kg). Loaded weight, 2,381 lb (1 080 kg). Span, 31 ft 9⅞ in (9,70 m). Length, 26 ft 6⅞ in (8,10 m). Height, 9 ft 4¼ in (2,85 m). Wing area, 279.87 sq ft (26,00 m²).*

MACCHI M.6   Italy

Completed in 1917 for comparison with the M.5, the M.6 single-seat fighter differed essentially in having a modified wing cellule. The Vee-type interplane bracing struts and sloping auxiliary Vee struts supporting the overhanging portion of the upper wing gave place to parallel struts positioned farther outboard, additional parallel steel tube struts being introduced farther inboard. The M.6 was similarly powered to the M.5 (Isotta-Fraschini V.4B) and carried a single 7,7-mm Vickers gun. Comparative trials revealed no advantages over the standard M.5 and further development of the M.6 was discontinued. *Max speed, 117 mph (189 km/h). Time to 13,125 ft (4 000 m), 20 min. Endurance, 3.0 hrs. Empty weight, 1,675 lb (760 kg). Loaded weight, 2,271 lb (1 030 kg). Wing area, 312.16 sq ft (29,00 m²).*

The single M.6 (below) was built for comparison with the M.5, differing in wing cellule design.

MACCHI M.7   Italy

The M.7 was essentially a progressive development of the M.5 and entered flight testing early in 1918. Powered by a 247 bhp Isotta-Fraschini V.6 engine, the M.7 was of wooden construction similar to that of its predecessors and carried an armament of twin 7,7-mm Vickers guns. It featured a simplified wing cellule, with paired, splayed interplane struts. Series production was initiated, but orders were curtailed with the end of hostilities, 11 being completed of which three were delivered before the end of World War I. Two each were purchased by Argentina and Sweden in 1919, and three were procured by Brazil in 1921. Despite the cancellation of orders for the *Regia Marina*, development of the basic design continued, one example being fitted with a hull of increased fineness ratio, and two were modified to M.7*bis* standard for participation in the 1921 Schneider Trophy contest. The M.7*bis* had wing span and area reduced to 25 ft 5 in (7,75 m) and 256.19 sq ft (23,80 m²) respectively, and captured the Trophy in August 1921 with an average speed of 117.75 mph (189,50 km/h) in a contest in which the Macchi 'boat was, in fact, the only participant. *Max speed, 130 mph (210 km/h). Time to 16,405 ft (5 000 m), 23 min. Endurance, 3.66 hrs. Empty weight, 1,708 lb (775 kg). Loaded weight, 2,381 lb (1 080 kg). Span, 32 ft 7¾ in (9,95 m). Length, 26 ft 6⁹⁄₁₀ in (8,10 m). Height, 9 ft 8⅛ in (2,95 m). Wing area, 286.33 sq ft (26,60 m²).*

A further development of the M.5, the M.7 (below) continued the Macchi fighter flying boat formula.

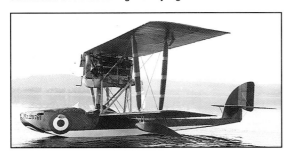

MACCHI M.7TER   Italy

Only nominally a development of the wartime M.7 fighter, the M.7*ter*, flown as a prototype in October 1923, was virtually a new design, with a redesigned hull, a revised and lighter structure and wings of revised planform and reduced area. Primarily of wooden construction, with a 247 bhp Isotta-Fraschini V.6 engine and twin-Vickers gun armament, the M.7*ter* was ordered into series production to re-equip the *Squadriglie Caccia Marittima* as the M.7*ter*A, the

M.7*ter*AR having folding wings for operation from the seaplane carrier *Miraglia*. The M.7*ter*B was powered by a 480 hp Lorraine 12Db engine, and, in 1927, the Società Aeronautica Italiana re-engined 14 M.7*ter*A 'boats with the 250 hp Isotta-Fraschini Semi-Asso engine. Total production of the M.7*ter* exceeded 100 machines and these equipped all six *Squadriglie Caccia Marittima* by 1925 at the principal Italian naval bases, these eventually forming the 80° *Gruppo*. Eighty-three were in service in 1927, including 29 of the folding-wing AR version, the last being withdrawn from first line service in 1930. *Max speed, 129 mph (208 km/h). Time to 3,280 ft (1 000 m), 2.75 min. Endurance, 3 hrs. Empty weight, 1,775 lb (805 kg). Loaded weight, 2,381 lb (1 080 kg). Span, 32 ft 7¾ in (9,95 m). Length, 29 ft 0⅓ in (8,85 m). Height, 9 ft 8⁹⁄₁₀ in (2,97 m). Wing area, 252.96 sq ft (23,50 m²).*

Remaining in service until 1930, the M.7ter (above and below) was almost wholly a new design.

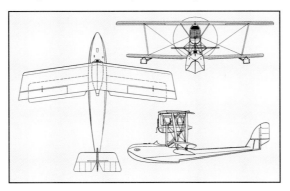

MACCHI M.14   Italy

Owing little to the Hanriot HD.1 that was licence-built by Nieuport-Macchi, the M.14 single-seat sesquiplane fighter was designed by Alessandro Tonini. Of wooden construction and featuring Warren truss style interplane bracing, the M.14 was powered by a 110 hp Le Rhône 9J nine-cylinder rotary engine and had provision for an armament of twin synchronised 7,7-mm Vickers guns. Flight testing commenced in the spring of 1918, but the prototype was destroyed in June of that year. Nevertheless, a series of 10 M.14 fighters was built, official evaluation trials being conducted at Montecelio during 1919. However, no additional orders were placed for the type and those M.14s completed were

Macchi's first landplane fighter, the M.14 (above and below) served primarily in the training rôle.

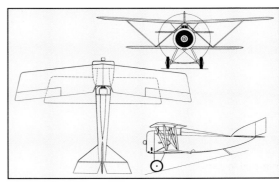

employed as advanced trainers, at least one receiving a civil registration (I-BADG). *Max speed, 113 mph (182 km/h) at sea level. Time to 3,280 ft (1 000 m), 3.5 min. Endurance, 2 hrs. Empty weight, 970 lb (440 kg). Loaded weight, 1,411 lb (640 kg). Span, 26 ft 10⅘ in (8,20 m). Length, 18 ft 6½ in (5,65 m). Height, 8 ft 7⅛ in (2,62 m). Wing area, 178.69 sq ft (16,60 m²).*

MACCHI M.26   Italy

Designed by Mario Castoldi as a potential successor to the M.7*ter*, the M.26 single-seat fighter flying boat was completed and tested in 1924. Powered by a 296 bhp Hispano-Suiza 42 eight-cylinder Vee-type engine strut-braced above the hull and driving a pusher propeller,

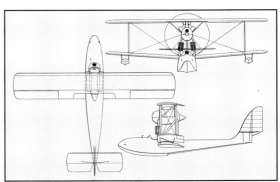

Despite an excellent performance, the M.26 (above and below) was not ordered into production.

the M.26 was of wooden construction and of extremely clean aerodynamic design. Armament consisted of two 7,7-mm Vickers guns. Although the M.26 demonstrated an extremely good performance, no production order was forthcoming from the *Regia Aeronautica*, only two prototypes being completed. *Max speed, 152 mph (244 km/h). Time to 13,125 ft (4 000 m), 12.3 min. Endurance, 2.5 hrs. Empty weight, 1,907 lb (865 kg). Loaded weight, 2,634 lb (1 195 kg). Span, 30 ft 2¼ in (9,20 m). Length, 26 ft 8⅞ in (8,15 m). Height, 9 ft 10 in (3,00 m). Wing area, 279.87 sq ft (26,00 m²).*

MACCHI M.41BIS   Italy

Two squadrons of the 88° *Gruppo, Regia Aeronautica*, flew the M.41*bis* (above and below) from 1930 to 1938.

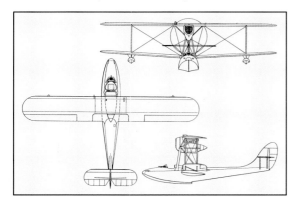

Carrying the single-seat biplane fighter flying boat to the apex of its development and owing much to the earlier and abortive M.26, with which it shared a similar equi-span single-bay unstaggered wing configuration and wooden construction with plywood and fabric skinning, the M.41 commenced tests in 1927. Powered by a 420 hp Fiat A 20 pusher engine and carrying a twin 7,7-mm gun armament, the first prototype was followed two years later by a second aircraft, the M.41*bis*, and this modified version (which differed primarily in having a vertical rather than oblique frontal radiator) was ordered into production, 41 being built. These equipped the two *squadriglie* of the 88° *Gruppo Autonomo Caccia Marittima* when this was formed on 10 May 1930 at Vigna di Valle, and remained in the first line inventory until supplanted by the I.M.A.M. Ro 44 float fighter in 1938. *Max speed, 163 mph (262 km/h). Time to 3,280 ft (1 000 m), 2.0 min. Endurance, 3.5 hrs. Empty weight, 2,579 lb (1 170 kg). Loaded weight, 3,527 lb (1 600 kg). Span, 36 ft 5¾ in (11,12 m). Length, 28 ft 4⅞ in (8,66 m). Height, 10 ft 2⅖ in (3,12 m). Wing area, 343.38 sq ft (31,90 m²).*

MACCHI M.71   Italy

During the course of 1930, Aeronautica Macchi completed a version of the M.41*bis* specifically for catapult launching from warships of the Italian Navy. A new and more robust wing cellule was introduced which could be dismantled rapidly for shipboard stowage, the bracing wires between the vertical interplane struts, the hull and the upper wing centre section being replaced by pairs of inclined steel tube struts. Apart from this change and the provision of catapult pick-up points and related equipment, the M.71 was similar to the M.41*bis*, and a small series was built (believed to be no more than a dozen), these seeing brief service aboard Italian naval vessels, including the cruiser *Di Giussano*, before being replaced by the I.M.A.M. Ro 43 and Ro 44. *Max speed, 161 mph (259 km/h). Empty weight, 2,778 lb (1 260 kg). Loaded weight, 3,726 lb (1 690 kg). Dimensions as for M.41bis.*

Last of the Macchi flying boat fighters, the M.71 (below) saw brief service on Italian naval vessels.

MACCHI C.200 SAETTA   Italy

Design of the C.200 Saetta (Lightning) was initiated by Ing Mario Castoldi in 1935 as a short-range, lightly-armed interceptor, two prototypes being ordered of which the first was flown on 24 December 1937. Powered by the 870 hp Fiat A.74 R.C.38 14-cylinder radial and carrying twin 12,7-mm Breda-SAFAT

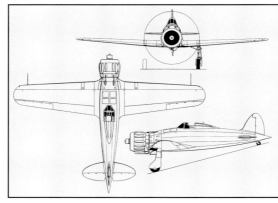

(Above) The definitive Macchi C.200. (Immediately below) C.200 of the 373ª *Squadriglia*, 153° *Gruppo*, serving in Cirenaica, 1941. (Bottom) C.200 of 86ª *Squadriglia*, 7° *Gruppo*, Palermo, early 1942.

A VII *serie* production C.200 (above) with the semi-enclosed cockpit introduced with the VI *serie*.

Key to Macchi C.200 (Serie XIX) Saetta

1 Propeller hub
2 Variable-pitch Piaggio P.1001 propeller
3 Hub plate
4 Casing
5 Pitch control mechanism
6 Oil radiator
7 Cowling ring
8 Fiat A.74 R.C.38 14-cylinder radial air-cooled engine
9 Cowling rocker arm fairings
10 Carburettor intake
11 Intake housing
12 Starboard mainwheel
13 Intake filter
14 Exhaust outlet
15 Engine mounting ring
16 Exhaust collector ring
17 Adjustable cowling gills
18 Zenith compressor
19 Engine ring bearer frames
20 Oil filler access
21 Undercarriage retraction jack attachment

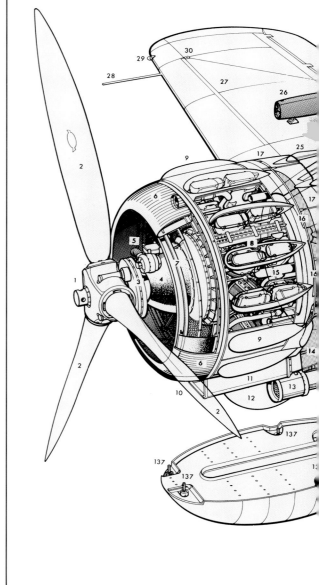

machine guns, the first production C.200s were completed in July 1939, 156 having been officially taken on strength by the *Regia Aeronautica* when Italy entered World War II on 10 June 1940. The first 240 aircraft were delivered with fully enclosed cockpits, but subsequent C.200s had partially or completely open cockpits. The C.200 A.S. (*Africa Settentrionale*) was equipped with dust filters and hard points were introduced in the wing as a field modification, these permitting two bombs of up to 352 lb (160 kg) to be carried. Late production examples had wings identical to those introduced with the *VII serie* C.202, these adding two

C.200s (right) from the 371ª *Squadriglia*, based at Ciampino in 1940 for the defence of Rome.

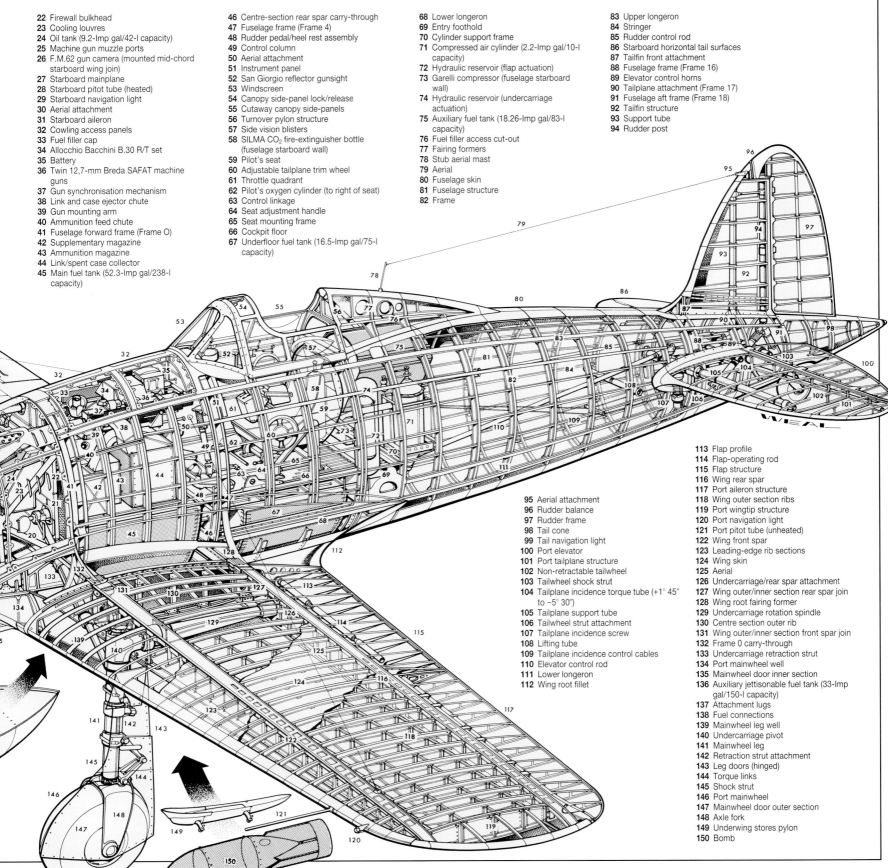

22 Firewall bulkhead
23 Cooling louvres
24 Oil tank (9.2-Imp gal/42-l capacity)
25 Machine gun muzzle ports
26 F.M.62 gun camera (mounted mid-chord starboard wing join)
27 Starboard mainplane
28 Starboard pitot tube (heated)
29 Starboard navigation light
30 Aerial attachment
31 Starboard aileron
32 Cowling access panels
33 Fuel filler cap
34 Allocchio Bacchini B.30 R/T set
35 Battery
36 Twin 12,7-mm Breda SAFAT machine guns
37 Gun synchronisation mechanism
38 Link and case ejector chute
39 Gun mounting arm
40 Ammunition feed chute
41 Fuselage forward frame (Frame O)
42 Supplementary magazine
43 Ammunition magazine
44 Link/spent case collector
45 Main fuel tank (52.3-Imp gal/238-l capacity)
46 Centre-section rear spar carry-through
47 Fuselage frame (Frame 4)
48 Rudder pedal/heel rest assembly
49 Control column
50 Aerial attachment
51 Instrument panel
52 San Giorgio reflector gunsight
53 Windscreen
54 Canopy side-panel lock/release
55 Cutaway canopy side-panels
56 Turnover pylon structure
57 Side vision blisters
58 SILMA CO$_2$ fire-extinguisher bottle (fuselage starboard wall)
59 Pilot's seat
60 Adjustable tailplane trim wheel
61 Throttle quadrant
62 Pilot's oxygen cylinder (to right of seat)
63 Control linkage
64 Seat adjustment handle
65 Seat mounting frame
66 Cockpit floor
67 Underfloor fuel tank (16.5-Imp gal/75-l capacity)
68 Lower longeron
69 Entry foothold
70 Cylinder support frame
71 Compressed air cylinder (2.2-Imp gal/10-l capacity)
72 Hydraulic reservoir (flap actuation)
73 Garelli compressor (fuselage starboard wall)
74 Hydraulic reservoir (undercarriage actuation)
75 Auxiliary fuel tank (18.26-Imp gal/83-l capacity)
76 Fuel filler access cut-out
77 Fairing formers
78 Stub aerial mast
79 Aerial
80 Fuselage skin
81 Fuselage structure
82 Frame
83 Upper longeron
84 Stringer
85 Rudder control rod
86 Starboard horizontal tail surfaces
87 Tailfin front attachment
88 Fuselage frame (Frame 16)
89 Elevator control horns
90 Tailplane attachment (Frame 17)
91 Fuselage aft frame (Frame 18)
92 Tailfin structure
93 Support tube
94 Rudder post
95 Aerial attachment
96 Rudder balance
97 Rudder frame
98 Tail cone
99 Tail navigation light
100 Port elevator
101 Port tailplane structure
102 Non-retractable tailwheel
103 Tailwheel shock strut
104 Tailplane incidence torque tube (+1° 45″ to −5° 30″)
105 Tailplane support tube
106 Tailwheel strut attachment
107 Tailplane incidence screw
108 Lifting tube
109 Tailplane incidence control cables
110 Elevator control rod
111 Lower longeron
112 Wing root fillet
113 Flap profile
114 Flap-operating rod
115 Flap structure
116 Wing rear spar
117 Port aileron structure
118 Wing outer section ribs
119 Port wingtip structure
120 Port navigation light
121 Port pitot tube (unheated)
122 Wing front spar
123 Leading-edge rib sections
124 Wing skin
125 Aerial
126 Undercarriage/rear spar attachment
127 Wing outer/inner section rear spar join
128 Wing root fairing former
129 Undercarriage rotation spindle
130 Centre section outer rib
131 Wing outer/inner section front spar join
132 Frame 0 carry-through
133 Undercarriage retraction strut
134 Port mainwheel well
135 Mainwheel door inner section
136 Auxiliary jettisonable fuel tank (33-Imp gal/150-l capacity)
137 Attachment lugs
138 Fuel connections
139 Mainwheel leg well
140 Undercarriage pivot
141 Mainwheel leg
142 Retraction strut attachment
143 Leg doors (hinged)
144 Torque links
145 Shock strut
146 Port mainwheel
147 Mainwheel door outer section
148 Axle fork
149 Underwing stores pylon
150 Bomb

7,7-mm guns to the armament. A total of 1,153 C.200 fighters was produced by Aeronautica Macchi, Breda and SAI-Ambrosini, a few surviving the war to serve in the training rôle at Lecce until 1947. *Max speed, 312 mph (503 km/h) at 14,765 ft (4 500 m). Time to 9,840 ft (3 000 m), 3.4 min. Normal range, 354 mls (570 km). Empty equipped weight, 4,451 lb (2 019 kg). Normal loaded weight, 5,597 lb (2 339 kg). Span, 34 ft 8½ in (10,58 m). Length, 26 ft 10⅖ in (8,19 m). Height, 11 ft 5¾ in (3,51 m). Wing area, 180.84 sq ft (16,80 m²).*

MACCHI C.200BIS — Italy

In 1942, the Breda concern, which was to be responsible for the manufacture of 800 C.200 fighters, attempted to improve the performance of the basic fighter by installing a Piaggio P.XIX R.C.45 radial engine rated at 1,180 hp at 14,765 ft (4 500 m). Development was under the leadership of Dr Ing Mario Pittoni and the re-engined fighter was designated C.200*bis*. The standard twin 12,7-mm gun armament was retained and the prototype – a conversion of a VII production batch aircraft – was first flown on 11 April 1942 with a standard Fiat A.74 propeller at an all-up weight of 6,173 lb (2 800 kg). Disappointing performance led to revision of the engine cowling and the introduction of a new, larger-diameter propeller with which the C.200*bis* first flew on 7 May 1942. After the completion of manufacturer's testing at Bresso, the prototype was ferried to Guidonia on 18 May, but the results of official trials were by now considered academic owing to the appearance of superior types and development was discontinued. The following data relate to the final tests conducted on 15 May. *Max speed, 332 mph (535 km/h) at 20,670 ft (6 300 m). Time to 9,840 ft (3 000 m), 3.33 min. Service ceiling, 33,795 ft (10 300 m). Empty weight, 3,975 lb (1 803 kg). Max loaded weight, 6,305 lb (2 860 kg). Dimensions as for C.200.*

The sole C.200*bis* (below) was developed by the Breda company during 1942, with a Piaggio engine.

MACCHI C.201 — Italy

In an attempt to meet a requirement formulated by the *Ministero dell' Aeronautica* late in 1938 for a more advanced fighter than the C.200 which had just entered production, Ing Mario Castoldi evolved the C.201. This mated the wings, undercarriage and tail assembly of the C.200 with the more powerful Fiat A.76 R.C. 40 engine rated at 1,000 hp at 13,125 ft (4 000 m) and a new, slimmer fuselage. This eliminated the humped contour of the earlier fighter that had resulted from emphasis placed on field of view from the cockpit. The standard twin 12,7-mm gun armament was retained. The A.76 engine proved to suffer from insoluble teething troubles and no specimen was cleared for flight testing. In consequence, the prototype was fitted with an A.74 for initial testing which commenced in August

The C.201 prototype (below) combined a new, slimmer fuselage with C.200 wings and tail.

1940, but it proved seriously underpowered, and, as its intended engine was abandoned, no further development of the C.201 was undertaken. The following data are manufacturer's estimates for the fighter powered by the intended A.76 engine. *Max speed, 342 mph (550 km/h) at 14,765 ft (4 500 m). Normal cruising speed, 286 mph (460 km/h). Range, 373 mls (600 km). Service ceiling, 29,530 ft (9 000 m). Empty weight, 4,206 lb (1 949 kg). Loaded weight, 5,258 lb (2 385 kg). Dimensions as for C.200.*

MACCHI C.202 FOLGORE — Italy

Mating a Daimler-Benz engine with the airframe of the C.200 produced the C.202 (above and below).

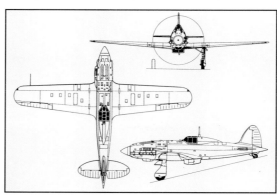

The importation by Italy of an example of the Daimler-Benz DB 601Aa liquid-cooled engine and simultaneous redesign of the basic C.200 to accept this German power plant resulted in commencement of testing on 10 August 1940 of the C.202. This was to be subsequently christened Folgore, which, like Saetta, meant Lightning. The excellent results achieved with the prototype led to a licence for the Daimler-Benz engine being acquired by Alfa Romeo. The importation of 400 examples of this power plant expedited production of the C.202 which was ordered from Breda and SAI-Ambrosini as well as from the parent company. Deliveries of the C.202 to the *Regia Aeronautica* began within 11 months of the commencement of prototype trials. Powered by the Alfa Romeo-built DB 601A, the R.A.1000 R.C.41-I° Monsoni (Monsoon), rated at 1,075 hp for take-off, the C.202 was initially fitted with two 12,7-mm guns, but after completion of more than 500 fighters provision was made for the installation in the wings of two 7,7-mm guns, although these were rarely fitted. One C.202 was experimentally fitted with twin gondola-mounted 20-mm cannon, late series air-

A factory-fresh C.202 (above), some 1,200 examples of which were delivered to the *Regia Aeronautica*.

craft could carry two drop tanks or two bombs (C.202 C.B.) under the wings, and one was fitted with a chin-type radiator bath as the C.202D. Production contracts were placed for 1,300 C.202s, but it is unlikely that more than 1,200 were actually delivered. *Max speed, 372 mph (599 km/h) at 18,370 ft (5 600 m). Time to 9,840 ft (3 000 m), 2.47 min. Range, 475 mls (765 km) at 267 mph (430 km/h). Empty equipped weight, 5,545 lb (2 515 kg). Max loaded weight, 6,766 lb (3 069 kg). Span, 34 ft 8½ in (10,58 m). Length, 29 ft 0½ in (8,85 m). Height, 9 ft 11½ in (3,04 m). Wing area, 180.84 sq ft (16,80 m²).*

MACCHI C.205V VELTRO — Italy

A logical development of the C.202 Folgore and initially known as the C.202*bis*, the C.205V Veltro (Greyhound) was tendered as an interim solution to the so-called *caccia della serie* 5 requirement of the *Regia Aeronautica* for more advanced fighters powered by the Daimler-Benz DB 605 engine. A manufacturing licence for this power plant had been acquired and it was to be built as the Fiat R.A.1050 R.C.58 Tifone (Typhoon) and rated at 1,475 hp for take-off. Fundamentally an adaptation of the C.202 airframe to take the more powerful engine, the first prototype C.205V was flown on 19 April 1942, and the first series aircraft followed five months later. The first 100 C.205Vs carried an armament of two 12,7-mm and two 7,7-mm guns, the latter being replaced in subsequent aircraft by two 20-mm MG 151 cannon. Although production of 700 C.205Vs was authorised, only 177 were delivered prior to the armistice of 8 September 1943. With the formation of the *Aviazione della Repubblica Sociale Italiana*, production of the C.205V was reinstated by Aeronautica Macchi, 112 being delivered before manufacture was finally halted by air attack in May 1944. Earlier, 18 aircraft were modified for the escort rôle (C.205S) by removal of the paired 12,7-mm guns and their replacement with a 44 Imp gal (200 l) fuel tank in the forward fuselage.

A C.205V Serie III (above) of the 1ª *Squadriglia*, 1° *Gruppo Caccia*, ARSI, and (below) a restored C.205V in 1983, earlier modified from a C.202 for Egypt.

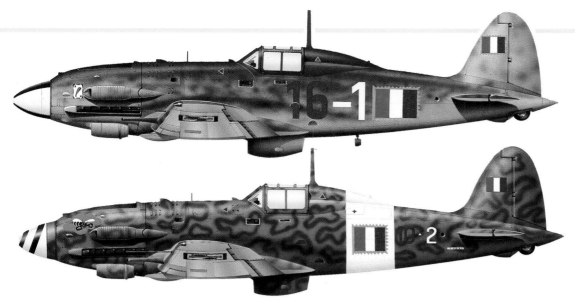

(Top) A C.205V Serie III of 1ª *Squadriglia*, 1º *Gruppo*, ARSI at Reggio Emilia, 1944. (Immediately above) C.205V of 2ª *Squadriglia*, Campoformido, 1944.

During 1948-49, contracts were placed by Egypt for 62 refurbished C.205Vs (41 of these being conversions of C.202 airframes) of which 42 were delivered, the first batch of 15 seeing combat with the Israeli air arm prior to the truce of 13 January 1949. *Max speed, 399 mph (642 km/h) at 23,620 ft (7 200 m). Max cruising speed, 310 mph (400 km/h). Time to 9,840 ft (3 000 m), 2.66 min. Normal range, 590 mls (950 km). Empty equipped weight, 5,690 lb (2 581 kg). Normal loaded weight, 7,513 lb (3 408 kg). Span, 34 ft 8½ in (10,58 m). Length, 29 ft 0½ in (8,85 m). Height, 9 ft 11½ in (3,04 m). Wing area, 180.84 sq ft (16,80 m²).*

MACCHI C.205N ORIONE   Italy

During 1941, Ing Mario Castoldi drew up a proposal for a new fighter based on use of the DB 605A engine to a *Ministero dell' Aeronautica* requirement. Fiat and Reggiane also tendered proposals for what was subsequently to be referred to as a *caccia della serie 5*. Castoldi's proposal mated a new wing of increased span, area and aspect ratio, and a new forward fuselage, with the centre and aft fuselage and tail assembly of the C.202. With the decision to proceed with the interim C.205V, this more innovative fighter became the C.205N (*Nuovo*, or New) and was dubbed Orione (Orion). The first prototype, the C.205N/1, was flown on 1 November 1942, and possessed an armament of four fuselage-mounted 12,7-mm machine guns and an engine-mounted 20-mm cannon. Production orders were placed for 1,200 aircraft, of which 600 were to be licence-built by Breda. A second prototype, the C.205N/2 flown on 19 May 1943, featured a revised

armament arrangement, two of the 12,7-mm guns being deleted and two 20-mm cannon being introduced in the wings. Progress of the war rendered it apparent that large-scale production of the Orione was no longer practical, production orders being cancelled in consequence. The following data relate to the second prototype. *Max speed, 390 mph (628 km/h) at 22,965 ft (7 000 m). Time to 9,840 ft (3 000 m), 2.4 min. Service ceiling, 36,910 ft (11 250 m). Empty equipped weight, 5,941 lb (2 695 kg). Normal loaded weight, 7,983 lb (3 621 kg). Span, 36 ft 10⅞ in (11,25 m). Length, 31 ft 4 in (9,33 m). Height, 10 ft 8 in (3,25 m). Wing area, 204.52 sq ft (19,00 m²).*

Second of the Orione prototypes, the C.205N/2 (below) introduced additional cannon armament.

MANN EGERTON TYPE H   UK

The first original design produced by Mann Egerton and Company, which had previously manufactured various aircraft types under licence, the Type H single-seat shipboard fighter was designed by J W Carr to Specification N.1a. Powered by a 200 hp Hispano-Suiza 8Bd eight-cylinder water-cooled engine, the Type H was an equi-span unstaggered two-bay biplane armed with a single fixed 0.303-in (7,7-mm) Vickers gun mounted to port on the fuselage and a Lewis gun of

similar calibre mounted above the wing centre section. The wings could be folded manually and the first prototype had a large, flush-fitting float attached to the underside of the fuselage. In addition, flotation chambers were included in the fuselage, and the undercarriage, which was attached to the underside of the float, could be jettisoned in the event that the aircraft was forced to alight on water. Flight testing of the first prototype commenced in the autumn of 1917, but the aircraft failed flotation testing and was therefore considered unacceptable. The second prototype differed in having inflatable flotation bags in place of the fixed float, a more conventional undercarriage and a horn-balanced rudder. This aircraft underwent official testing during December 1917, but the Type H was not accepted for service use and further development was discontinued. The following data relate specifically to the second prototype. *Max speed, 113 mph (182 km/h) at 6,500 ft (1 980 m). Time to 6,500 ft (1 980 m), 6.45 min. Endurance, 3.25 hrs. Empty weight, 1,760 lb (798 kg). Loaded weight, 2,326 lb (1 055 kg). Span, 30 ft 9 in (9,37 m). Length, 21 ft 11 in (6,68 m). Height, 8 ft 11½ in (2,73 m). Wing area, 310 sq ft (28,80 m²).*

Tested at the end of 1917, the Type H (second prototype below) found no official acceptance.

MANN & GRIMMER M.1   UK

Designed by R F Mann and R P Grimmer, the M.1 two-seat fighter represented an attempt to combine the superior performance offered by a tractor configuration with the clear forward field of fire provided by a pusher arrangement. The conventionally-mounted Anzani 10-cylinder air-cooled radial engine drove two pusher propellers by means of an extended shaft via a gearbox and chains. The gunner was seated immediately aft of the engine, the pilot's cockpit being just behind the plane of the propellers. The M.1 was first flown on 19 February 1915, but difficulties were experienced with the chain transmission and with handling. Various modifications were made and the 100 hp Anzani engine was replaced by one rated at 125 hp, but after some 18

(Above and below) The C.205N/1, the first prototype of this *caccia della serie 5* fighter flown in 1942.

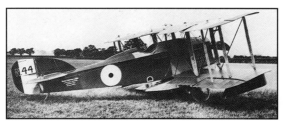

Flush-fitting floats on the first Type H (above) were discarded for the second aircraft (below).

In its definitive form, the M.1 (above and below) flew for fewer than 20 hrs before it crashed.

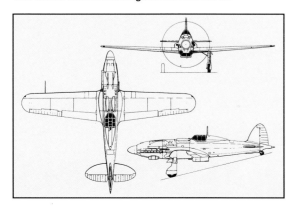

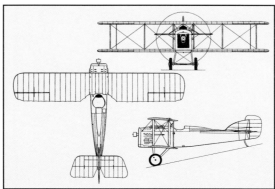

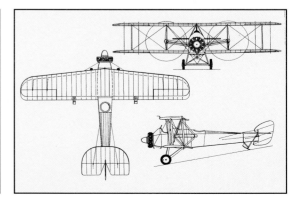

hours of flight testing, the M.1 was wrecked on 16 November 1915 before it could be evaluated by the RFC, and although work on the prototype of an improved version, the M.2, was begun, no further aircraft was completed. *Max speed, 85 mph (137 km/h). Time to 3,000 ft (915 m), 8 min. Endurance, 4.5 hrs. Approx empty weight, 2,100 lb (953 kg). Approx loaded weight, 2,800 lb (1 270 kg). Span, 34 ft 9 in (10,59 m). Length, 26 ft 5 in (8.05 m). Wing area, 322 sq ft (29,91 m²).*

MARCHETTI MVT (S.50) Italy

Designed by Alessandro Marchetti and built by the Vickers-Terni industrial organisation at La Spezia, the MVT single-seat fighter biplane was flown in 1919. Of all-metal construction, the MVT was powered by a 220 hp SPA 6a water-cooled engine and carried an armament of two synchronised Vickers machine guns.

As the S.50 (above and below), the Marchetti MVT was entered in the Italian fighter contest of 1923.

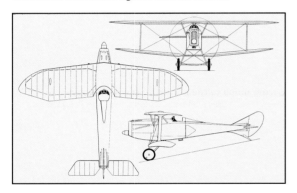

The fuselage, which was suspended between the upper and lower mainplanes, was flattened aft to emulate an aerofoil surface, and the semi-elliptical wings were of extremely thin section, lateral control being provided by wing warping. On 9 December 1919, the MVT recorded a speed of 155 mph (250 km/h) – absence of FAI officials preventing this being certified as a world speed record – and demonstrated the ability to climb to 16,405 ft (5 000 m) in 11 min. In 1920, the MVT was fitted with longer-span wings, splayed interplane bracing struts, a revised cabane and a redesigned horizontal tail. A 285 hp SPA 62a engine was fitted with which 171 mph (275 km/h) was attained under test at Montecelio. When Marchetti was appointed chief designer to SIAI, the MVT was redesignated S.50 and was entered in the official fighter contest of 1923. Three were supplied to the newly-created *Regia Aeronautica* for evaluation, but a plan to procure a batch of 12 failed to materialise. One S.50 was modified as a twin-float seaplane. The following data relate to the SPA 62a-powered MVT. *Max speed, 155 mph (250 km/h). Time to 3,280 ft (1 000 m), 2.0 min. Endurance, 2.1 hrs. Empty weight, 1,647 lb (747 kg). Loaded weight, 2,176 lb (987 kg). Span, 28 ft 6½ in (8,70 m). Length, 25 ft 5⅛ in (7,75 m). Height, 8 ft 6⅓ in (2,60 m). Wing area, 231.43 sq ft (21,50 m²).*

MARK D I Germany

The Märkische Flugzeugwerke of Golm in der Mark was established in 1916 for aircraft repair, the training of military pilots and the eventual licence manufacture of training biplanes. In 1918, Ing Wilhelm Hillman left the Schütte-Lanz organisation to join the Märkische Flugzeugwerke, for which he designed a single-seat fighter, the Mark D I, powered by a 195 hp Benz Bz IIIb water-cooled eight-cylinder Vee engine. The D I was scheduled to participate in the second fighter com-

The sole Mark D I (above) was destroyed before it could take part in evaluation at Adlershof.

petition at Adlershof in May 1918, but the first prototype was destroyed in a crash prior to the contest. A second prototype, on which the warping of the lower wing surfaces was allegedly to have been replaced by conventional ailerons, was under construction in September 1918, but work was apparently terminated with the end of hostilities. No data are available apart from a time of 14 min to climb to 16,405 ft (5 000 m).

MARTIN-BAKER M.B.2 UK

Designed by James Martin with the collaboration of Capt Valentine H Baker, the M.B.2 was built to conform to the requirements of Specification F.5/34, but funded as a private venture. Conceived for manufacture in large numbers by semi-skilled workers at low cost, the M.B.2 employed a steel-tube structure with fabric skinning, was powered by a Napier Dagger III 24-cylinder H-type engine with a rated output of 798 hp at 5,500 ft (1 675 m), and carried an armament of eight 0.303-in (7,7-mm) Browning guns in the wings. The depth of the fuselage was virtually constant from nose to tail and vertical tail surfaces were eliminated, the rudder being hinged to the sternpost behind the elevators. First flown on 3 August 1938, the M.B.2 demonstrated serious directional instability and a rudimentary fixed tailfin was immediately introduced. A level speed of 320 mph (515 km/h) was recorded with full armament, but official reports of trials at Martlesham Heath, while enthusiastic concerning its engineering design, pronounced the M.B.2 unstable about all axes and generally unpleasant to fly. More orthodox vertical tail surfaces were fitted early in 1939, these markedly improving handling, but the RAF evinced no interest in the fighter, development being discontinued. *Max*

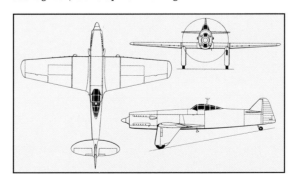

In its definitive form, the Martin-Baker M.B.2 (above and below) had orthodox tail surfaces.

speed, 320 mph (515 km/h). Loaded weight, 5,537 lb (2 512 kg). Span, 34 ft 0 in (10,36 m). Length, 34 ft 6 in (10,51 m). Height, 9 ft 9 in (2,97 m). Wing area, 213 sq ft (19,79 m²).

MARTIN-BAKER M.B.3 UK

During 1939, Martin-Baker Aircraft designed a new fighter around which was drawn up Specification F.18/39. As with its predecessor the precepts of structural simplicity and sturdiness dominated the design. The fuselage still made use of a patented system of steel tubes, but the skin was stressed light alloy and the wing had a more conventional torsion box structure. Three prototypes were ordered and, designated M.B.3, the first of these was flown on 31 August 1942 with a 2,020 hp Napier Sabre II 24-cylinder horizontal-H type engine. Armament comprised six 20-mm cannon. Only limited handling and performance data had been obtained when, on 12 September 1942, the M.B.3 was destroyed in an accident. Extensive redesign was introduced prior to the completion of the second prototype, which emerged as the M.B.5 (which see). *Max speed, 415 mph (668 km/h) at 20,000 ft (6 100 m). Initial climb, 4,350 ft/min (22,09 m/sec). Loaded weight, 11,497 lb (5 215 kg). Span, 35 ft 0 in (10,67 m). Length, 35 ft 4 in (10,77 m). Height, 15 ft 6¾ in (4,74 m). Wing area, 262.64 sq ft (24,40 m²).*

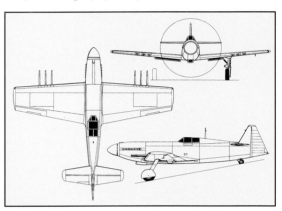

The single M.B.3 (above and below) was destroyed two weeks after making its first flight.

MARTIN-BAKER M.B.5 UK

Retaining the wings, undercarriage and fuselage primary structure of the M.B.3, the M.B.5, first flown on 23 May 1944, was considered by many to represent the peak of single-seat piston-engined fighter develop-

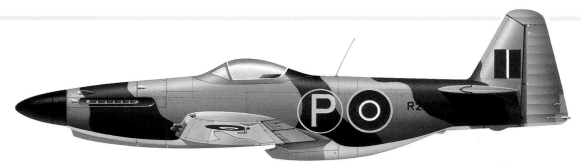

Extensive redesign of the M.B.3 resulted in the second prototype emerging as the M.B.5 (above).

Too late for wartime service, the M.B.5 (below) had a high performance and outstanding manoeuvrability.

ment. Powered by a Rolls-Royce Griffon 83 affording 1,900 hp for take-off and driving a six-bladed counter-rotating propeller, the M.B.5 carried an armament of four 20-mm Hispano cannon. Lack of directional stability resulted in the introduction of taller vertical tail surfaces at an early flight development stage, but despite superlative qualities subsequently demonstrated, the M.B.5 proved of no more than academic interest to the RAF in view of the availability of jet fighters. Flight testing continued into 1947, the sole prototype being scrapped thereafter. *Max speed, 460 mph (740 km/h) at 20,000 ft (6 100 m). Initial climb, 3,800 ft/min (19,3 m/sec). Range, 1,100 mls (1 770 km) at 250 mph (402 km/h). Empty weight, 9,233 lb (4 192 kg). Normal loaded weight, 11,010 lb (4 994 kg). Span, 35 ft 0 in (10,67 m). Length, 37 ft 0¾ in (11,30 m). Height, 14 ft 4 in (4,37 m). Wing area, 262.64 sq ft (24,40 m²).*

(Below) The M.B.5, powered by a R-R Griffon 83.

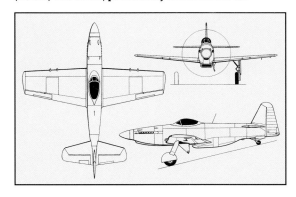

MARTINSYDE ELEPHANT   UK

An unusually large aircraft by contemporary standards for a single-seater, the Elephant two-bay equi-span staggered biplane was designed by A A Fletcher of the

The Martinsyde Elephant (below) in its initial G.100 production form with 120 hp Beardmore.

Martinsyde Company, a prototype powered by a 120 hp Austro-Daimler engine entering test in the autumn of 1915. The initial production version, the G.100, was powered by a 120 hp six-cylinder Beardmore engine and was armed with a single 0.303-in (7,7-mm) Lewis gun mounted above the centre section (this later being augmented by a similar weapon bracket-mounted to port behind the cockpit), deliveries to the RFC commencing in 1916. The G.100 was succeeded by the G.102 version which differed in having a 160 hp Beardmore engine and replaced the lower-powered model progressively. The G.100 and G.102 Elephants were used in France and the Middle East, although only one RFC squadron was completely equipped with this type, a total of 270 being manufactured. While not particularly successful as a fighter owing to its poor agility by comparison with its smaller contemporaries, the Elephant performed a useful service as a bomber, carrying up to 230 lb (104 kg). The following data relate to the G.102. *Max speed, 103 mph (166 km/h) at sea level. Time to 3,000 ft (915 m), 3.5 min. Endurance, 4.5 hrs. Empty weight, 1,793 lb (813 kg). Loaded weight, 2,458 lb (1 115 kg). Span, 38 ft 0 in (11,58 m). Length, 26 ft 6½ in (8,08 m). Height, 9 ft 8 in (2,95 m). Wing area, 410 sq ft (38,09 m²).*

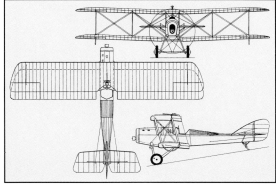

In its G.102 form (above) the Elephant had a more powerful engine than was used in the G.100 (below).

MARTINSYDE R.G.   UK

Derived from the Elephant via a single-bay experimental variant of the earlier design by A A Fletcher, the R.G. bore a close resemblance to its predecessor and was initially flown late in 1916 with a 190 hp Rolls-Royce Falcon I 12-cylinder water-cooled engine. Armament comprised a fixed 0.303-in (7,7-mm) Vickers gun on the port upper longeron, outside the cabane struts, and a Lewis gun on the starboard side of the cockpit. After official trials in February 1917, the R.G. was revised in a number of respects. The cockpit was moved aft and the centre section cut-out was enlarged. The span of the lower wing was reduced and the rear top decking was raised. Armament was changed and consisted of two 0.303-in (7,7-mm) Vickers guns immediately in front of the cockpit, and a 275 hp Falcon III engine was fitted. In this form, the R.G. had, according to the official report, a "performance . . . far and away better than any other machine manufactured". However, development was discontinued in favour of the superior F.3. The following data relate to the definitive R.G. *Max speed, 132 mph (212 km/h) at 6,500 ft (1 980 m). Time to 10,000 ft (3 050 m), 7.33 min. Endurance, 2 hrs. Empty weight, 1,740 lb (789 kg). Loaded weight, 2,261 lb (1 026 kg). Span, 32 ft 0 in (9,75 m). Length, 25 ft 10 in (7,87 m). Height, 9 ft 10 in (2,30 m). Wing area, 310 sq ft (28,80 m²).*

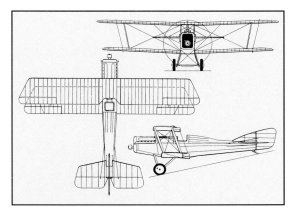

Owing much to the Elephant, the R.G. (above and below) was discontinued in favour of the Buzzard.

MARTINSYDE F.1   UK

The F.1 two-seat fighter was conceived late in 1915 as a tractor biplane in which the gunner occupied the forward cockpit and stood upright to fire a 0.303-in (7,7-mm) Lewis gun on a mount built into the upper wing centre section. Powered by a 250 hp Rolls-Royce Mk III engine (later to become known as the Eagle III), the F.1 suffered a somewhat protracted development and, by the time that it was officially tested in July 1917, was already obsolete. Obviously not acceptable for operational use, the F.1 was not further developed. *Max speed, 109 mph (175 km/h) at 6,500 ft (1 980 m). Time to 10,000 ft (3 050 m), 13.66 min. Endurance, 3.75 hrs.*

The sole prototype of the F.1 two-seat fighter (below) was tested with little success in 1917.

Empty weight, 2,198 lb (997 kg). Loaded weight, 3,260 lb (1 479 kg). Span, 44 ft 6 in (13,56 m). Length, 29 ft 1 in (8,86 m). Height, 8 ft 6 in (2,59 m). Wing area, 467 sq ft (43,38 m²).

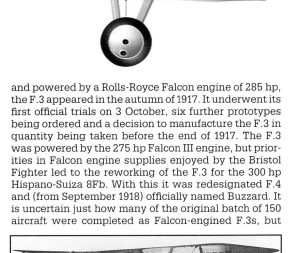

(Above) F.4 Buzzard of *Esquadrilha Independente de Aviaçao de Caça*, Tancos, Portugal, 1923.

MARTINSYDE F.2   UK

Of more modern concept that the F.1, the F.2 two-seat fighter was, like its predecessors, of wooden construction with fabric skinning, apart from the sides and top decking of the fuselage which were plywood covered.

Evolved in parallel with the F.1, the Martinsyde F.2 (above) was no more successful.

Designed and built while the F.1 was under construction, the F.2 underwent official testing two months *prior* to its predecessor, in May 1917. The F.2 was powered by a 200 hp Hispano-Suiza 8Bd eight-cylinder water-cooled engine and carried an armament of one fixed and synchronised 0.303-in (7,7-mm) Vickers gun and one Lewis gun on a Scarff ring. Shortcomings revealed during official trials ruled out a production order, and the prototype was utilised as a test-bed for the then-new Sunbeam Arab engine. *Max speed, 120 mph (193 km/h) at sea level. Time to 10,000 ft (3 050 m), 13.5 min. Endurance, 2.5 hrs. Empty weight, 1,547 lb (702 kg). Loaded weight, 2,355 lb (1 068 kg). Span, 32 ft 0 in (9,75 m). Length, 25 ft 0 in (7,62 m). Height, 8 ft 2 in (2,49 m). Wing area, 334 sq ft (31,03 m²).*

MARTINSYDE BUZZARD   UK

Widely considered to have been one of the best single-seat fighters to emerge during World War I, the Buzzard began life as a private venture design by G H Handasyde designated F.3. A single-bay staggered biplane of conventional wooden construction with fabric skinning

The F.3 version of the Buzzard (above) used the Falcon engine, whereas the HS 8Fb was used in the definitive F.4 version (below) seen in Portuguese service.

and powered by a Rolls-Royce Falcon engine of 285 hp, the F.3 appeared in the autumn of 1917. It underwent its first official trials on 3 October, six further prototypes being ordered and a decision to manufacture the F.3 in quantity being taken before the end of 1917. The F.3 was powered by the 275 hp Falcon III engine, but priorities in Falcon engine supplies enjoyed by the Bristol Fighter led to the reworking of the F.3 for the 300 hp Hispano-Suiza 8Fb. With this it was redesignated F.4 and (from September 1918) officially named Buzzard. It is uncertain just how many of the original batch of 150 aircraft were completed as Falcon-engined F.3s, but

The two-bay two-seat version of the Buzzard (above) supplied to Spain and (below) the standard F.4.

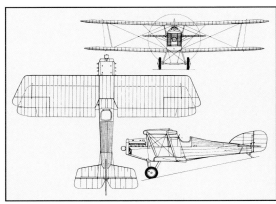

most were certainly finished as HS 8Fb-engined F.4s, the first of the latter being tested at Martlesham Heath in June 1918. Additional contracts for the F.4 were placed with the parent company (300), Boulton & Paul (500), Hooper (200) and Standard Motor (300). Armed with two synchronised 0.303-in (7,7-mm) Vickers guns, the F.4 differed from the F.3, apart from power plant, in having revised fuselage decking contours and more extensive plywood skinning. Belated engine deliveries

and other factors delayed production, only seven having been handed over by November 1918, and, in the event, no RAF squadron was to be equipped with the type. Production of the F.4 by the parent company continued for a time after the Armistice (no other contractor apparently producing any complete Buzzards) and more than 370 airframes were built, some being fitted with Falcon engines. A number of F.4 Buzzards was sold abroad by the Aircraft Disposal Company, the principal recipients being Finland (15), Portugal (4), Spain (20) and the USSR, the last-mentioned procuring 100 aircraft of this type. A two-seat variant, the F.4A, was produced in 1920, a much-modified derivative with two-bay wings of increased span appearing in the following year. This had a Lewis gun in the rear cockpit and several were supplied to Spain in June 1921, both single- and two-seat Buzzards being referred to as F.4As in Spanish service. The following data relate to the standard F.4 Buzzard. *Max speed, 132 mph (212 km/h) at 15,000 ft (4 570 m). Time to 10,000 ft (3 050 m), 7.9 min. Empty weight, 1,811 lb (821 kg). Loaded weight, 2,398 lb (1 088 kg). Span, 32 ft 9½ in (9,99 m). Length, 25 ft 5½ in (7,76 m). Height, 8 ft 10 in (2,69 m). Wing area, 320 sq ft (29,73 m²).*

MARTINSYDE A.D.C.1   UK

With the liquidation of the Martinsyde Company in February 1924, and the acquisition of its stores, stocks and goodwill by the Aircraft Disposal Company (A.D.C.), the latter continued development of the Buzzard under the design leadership of John Kenworthy.

Jaguar-engined A.D.C.1 derivatives of the Buzzard (above) were supplied to Latvia in 1926.

This resulted in the A.D.C.1, which was fundamentally an F.4 Buzzard airframe mated with a 380 hp Armstrong Siddeley Jaguar radial engine. The prototype A.D.C.1 was first flown on 11 October 1924, this subsequently participating in the 1925 and 1926 King's Cup races, and considerable foreign interest was displayed in the type. In the event, only one order for the A.D.C.1 materialised, this being from Latvia for eight aircraft which were delivered in 1926, at least two of these surviving until 1938. The armament of the A.D.C.1 comprised two synchronised 0.303-in (7,7-mm) Vickers guns. *Max speed, 163 mph (262 km/h) at sea level. Time to 5,000 ft (1 525 m), 2.42 min. Empty weight, 1,865 lb (846 kg). Loaded weight, 2,650 lb (1 202 kg). Span, 32 ft 9 in (9,98 m). Length, 25 ft 0 in (7,62 m). Wing area, 320 sq ft (29,73 m²).*

MARTINSYDE A.D.C. NIMBUS   UK

In 1926, John Kenworthy developed a further single-seat fighter based on the F.4 Buzzard, but utilising a 330 hp A.D.C. Nimbus six-in-line water-cooled engine. Usually referred to as the "Nimbus-Martinsyde", it utilised an essentially similar airframe to that of the Buzzard, but featured modified vertical tail surfaces with a

The Nimbus-engined A.D.C. version of the Buzzard (above) did not proceed beyond prototypes.

horn-balanced rudder and revised aft upper fuselage decking. Its intended armament comprised two synchronised 0.303-in (7,7-mm) Vickers machine guns, but these were never installed. Two prototypes were completed and flown, both participating in the King's Cup Air Race of 9-10 July 1926, and, in 1927, the first prototype was modified with faired undercarriage legs and cylinder head fairings. No orders were placed for the Nimbus-powered aircraft and both prototypes were scrapped. *Max speed, 150 mph (241 km/h) at sea level. Time to 10,000 ft (3 050 m), 7.5 min. Endurance, 2.5 hrs. Empty weight, 2,014 lb (913 kg). Loaded weight, 2,665 lb (1 209 kg). Span, 32 ft 9 in (9,98 m). Length, 26 ft 10 in (8,18 m). Height, 9 ft 6 in (2,89 m). Wing area, 320 sq ft (29,73 m²).*

MAVAG HÉJJA II   Hungary

When, on 27 December 1939, Hungary contracted to purchase 70 Reggiane Re 2000 fighters for the Hungarian Royal Air Force, or *Magyar Király Légierö*, a manufacturing licence was also procured. The version to be built by the MAVAG (*Magyar Allami Vaggon Es Gepgyar*, or Hungarian State Waggon and Engineering Factory) was to differ in a number of respects from the Reggiane-built fighter. Dubbed *Héjja* (Raptor) II, the MAVAG-built fighter was powered by a Manfréd Weiss-built Gnome-Rhône 14Kfs Mistral-Major 14-cylinder radial designated WMK-14B and rated at 930 hp at 14,860 ft (4 530 m). Lighter and of smaller diameter than the engine it replaced, the WMK-14B necessitated a 1 ft 3¾ in (40 cm) lengthening of the engine mounts for cg reasons. Armament comprised two 12,7-mm Danuvia/Gebauer GKM machine guns and the first *Héjja* II flew on 30 October 1942. One hundred and thirty were delivered during 1943, a further 73 following in 1944, with the last being completed on 1 August. Most *Héjja* IIs were delivered to fighter training units, but one Independent Fighter Group equipped with this type and saw combat during the final weeks before Hungary's capitulation. *Max speed, 332 mph (535 km/h) at 19,685 ft (6 000 m), 301 mph (485 km/h) at 10,500 ft (3 200 m). Time to 19,685-ft (6 000 m), 6.0 min. Endurance, 2.5 hrs. Empty weight, 4,563 lb (2 070 kg). Loaded weight, 5,555 lb (2 520 kg). Span, 36 ft 1 in (11,00 m). Length, 27 ft 6¼ in (8,39 m). Height, 10 ft 2 in (3,10 m). Wing area, 219.58 sq ft (20,40 m²).*

Brief combat use was made by the MKL of the Héjja II Hungarian version of the Re 2000 (below).

McDONNELL XP-67   USA

On 29 July 1941, the McDonnell Aircraft Corporation, formed on 6 July 1939, received a contract for two prototypes of its Model 23 long-range single-seat fighter, designated XP-67 by the USAAC. The design embodied several innovatory features. Not least of these was an

attempt to maintain true aerofoil sections throughout the entire fighter, the centre fuselage and the rear portions of the engine nacelles merging to give the aircraft a unique appearance. The two 1,350 hp Continental XI-1430 12-cylinder inverted-Vee engines were fitted with General Electric D-23 turbo-superchargers and featured exhaust thrust augmentation. The cabin was designed to be pressurised and proposed armament comprised six 37-mm M-4 cannon. The first XP-67, unpressurised and unarmed, was flown on 6 January 1944, and flight trials continued until 6 September 1944, when the prototype suffered irreparable fire damage.

Flown in 1944, the XP-67 (above) was an early attempt to achieve a blended wing/fuselage design.

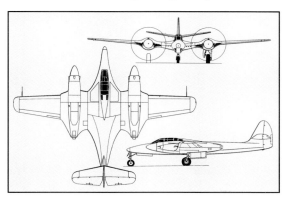

Only a single prototype of the XP-67 (above and below) was completed, achieving little success.

This accident and the unsatisfactory nature of certain aspects of the fighter's performance led to the decision to abandon the second prototype and terminate the development contract. *Max speed, 405 mph (652 km/h) at 25,000 ft (7 620 m). Max climb, 2,600 ft/min (13,20 m/sec). Max range, 2,385 mls (3 838 km). Empty weight, 17,745 lb (8 049 kg). Normal loaded weight, 22,114 lb (10 031 kg). Span, 55 ft 0 in (16,76 m). Length, 44 ft 9¼ in (13,65 m). Height, 15 ft 9 in (4,80 m). Wing area, 414 sq ft (38,46 m²).*

McDONNELL FH-1 PHANTOM   USA

The first pure jet aircraft designed from the outset for shipboard operation, the Phantom was initiated on 7 January 1943, when a Letter of Intent was issued by the

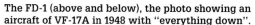

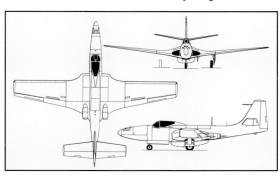

The FD-1 (above and below), the photo showing an aircraft of VF-17A in 1948 with "everything down".

Bureau of Aeronautics for two prototypes under the designation XFD-1. The basic configuration of the fighter was not finalised until early 1944, however, and although intended to be powered by two 1,600 lb st (726 kgp) Westinghouse WE-19XB-2B turbojets, only one engine was available for installation at the beginning of 1945. The first brief hop being effected on 2 January with the single turbojet installed, followed on 26 January by the first full flights (two) with both engines fitted. The first tests aboard a carrier, the USS *Franklin D Roosevelt*, were performed on 19 July 1946, and prior to this event, on 7 March 1945, production of 100 FD-1s was ordered. This contract was subsequently reduced to 60 aircraft, which were delivered under the revised designation FH-1. These were powered by two 1,600 lb st (726 kgp) Westinghouse J30-WE-20 turbojets and carried an armament of four 0.5-in (12,7-mm) machine guns. The first FH-1 was flown on 28 October 1946, and this type subsequently equipped one US Navy squadron and two USMC squadrons, being finally withdrawn in 1950. *Max speed, 479 mph (771 km/h) at sea level. Initial climb, 4,230 ft/min (21,48 m/sec). Normal range, 695 mls (1 115 km). Empty weight, 6,683 lb (3 031 kg). Loaded weight, 10,035 lb (4 552 kg). Span, 40 ft 9 in (12,42 m). Length, 37 ft 3 in (11,35 m). Height, 14 ft 2 in (4,32 m). Wing area, 276 sq ft (25,64 m²).*

McDONNELL F2H BANSHEE   USA

Designed by a team headed by Herman D Barkley and of configuration essentially similar to that of the FH-1, the Banshee was basically an enlarged Phantom. Three

A pair of F2H-1s from Atlantic Fleet's VF-171 (below) fly formation in June 1949.

The F2H-2 version of Banshee (above) introduced wing-tip tanks and a slightly longer fuselage.

prototypes were ordered as XF2D-1s on 22 March 1945, the first of these flying on 11 January 1947. Fifty-six of the initial production version, redesignated as the F2H-1 with paired 3,000 lb st (1 361 kgp) Westinghouse J34-WE-22 turbojets, were ordered with deliveries commencing in August 1948. Armament comprised four 20-mm cannon, and this initial model was characterised by a slightly longer fuselage than the prototypes. It was followed by the F2H-2 powered by 3,250 lb st (1 474 kgp) J34-WE-34 engines (306 built), sub-types being the F2H-2B (27 built) with wing rack for the carriage of a single nuclear bomb, the F2H-2N (14 built) with AI radar housed in a slightly longer nose, and the F2H-2P (89 built) reconnaissance model with lengthened nose housing six cameras. The F2H-3 (250 built) was 8 ft 1½ in (2,48 m) longer than the -2 with more than double the internal fuel capacity and APQ-41 radar in the nose to provide adverse weather capability. The F2H-3 featured redesigned vertical tail surfaces, and, from November 1955, 39 were transferred to serve with the Royal Canadian Navy. The F2H-4 (150 built) was an improved adverse weather version with APG-37 radar and the J34-WE-34 engines replaced by -38s of 3,600 lb st (1 633 kgp). The last was delivered on 31 October 1953. The Banshee was finally phased out of first-line US Navy use on 30 September 1959, but remained with reserve units until the mid-'sixties, by which time the F2H-3 and -4 had been redesignated F-2C and -2D. The last RCN F2H-3s were struck off strength on 12 September 1962. The following data relate to the F2H-3. *Max speed, 580 mph (933 km/h) at sea level. Initial climb, 6,000 ft/min (30,48 m/sec). Normal range, 1,170 mls (1 885 km). Empty weight, 13,183 lb (5 980 kg). Normal loaded weight, 21,013 lb (9 531 kg). Span, 41 ft 9 in (12,73 m). Length, 48 ft 2 in (14,68 m). Height, 14 ft 6 in (4,42 m). Wing area, 294 sq ft (27,31 m²).*

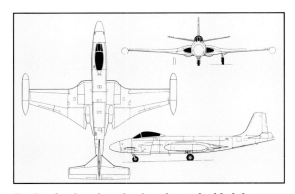

Further fuselage lengthening almost doubled the range of the F2H-3 variant (above and below).

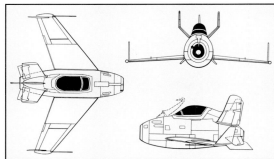

McDONNELL XF-85 GOBLIN   USA

The XF-85 Goblin resurrected the concept of a parasite fighter – an aircraft carried by and launched from a bomber for which it was intended to provide defence. Designed as the Model 27 under the leadership of Herman D Barkley, the XF-85 was intended to be carried by the Convair B-36 bomber and was the subject of a Letter of Intent for two prototypes on 9 October 1945. A small, egg-shaped aircraft with vertically-folding wings and triple vertical tail surfaces, the fighter was intended to be launched from and recovered by a retractable trapeze. This was to be extended beneath the parent bomber, no undercarriage being fitted to the fighter. Flight trials were initiated by the second prototype which was powered by a 3,000 lb st (1 361 kgp) Westinghouse J34-WE-37 turbojet. After five captive flights on the trapeze of a specially modified Superfortress (EB-29B), the XF-85 was launched at 20,000 ft (6 100 m) on 23 August 1948, this first free flight terminating in an emergency landing. Three flights with successful recoveries followed, but the test programme was a dismal failure and the programme was terminated after 2 hr 19 min of test flying, including a single flight by the first prototype on 8 April 1949. *Max speed (calculated), 664 mph (1 068 km/h). Combat endurance, 30 min. Empty weight, 3,740 lb (1 696 kg). Loaded weight, 4,550 lb (2 064 kg). Span, 21 ft 1½ in (6,44 m). Length, 14 ft 10½ in (4,53 m). Height, 8 ft 3¼ in (2,56 m). Wing area, 90 sq ft (8,36 m²).*

Unique among US fighters, the XF-85 (above and below) was designed as a bomber parasite.

McDONNELL XF-88   USA

Designed to meet a requirement for a single-seat long-range escort fighter, the XF-88 (Model 36) was recipient of a contract for two prototypes (initially XP-88s) on 14 February 1947. Powered by two 3,000 lb st (1 361 kgp) Westinghouse XJ34-WE-13 turbojets, the first XF-88 was flown on 20 October 1948, but proved seriously underpowered. The second XF-88 was therefore fitted with two XJ34-WE-15 engines with short afterburners which boosted maximum thrust from 3,600 lb (1 633 kg) to 4,825 lb (2 190 kg), a change in designation to

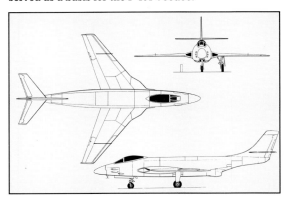

The XF-88 (above and below) long-range escort fighter served as a basis for the F-101 Voodoo.

XF-88A accompanying this modification. Performance was still insufficient, but the XF-88 was considered by the USAF to possess development potential and a Letter of Intent was issued covering further evolution of the basic design into what was eventually to become the F-101 Voodoo (which see). Subsequently, the XF-88 was fitted with an Allison XT38-A-5 turboprop in the nose and used as a test-bed for transonic and supersonic propellers as the XF-88B. The following data relate to the XF-88. *Max speed, 641 mph (1 034 km/h) at sea level. Time to 35,000 ft (10 670 m), 14.5 min. Range, 1,737 mls (2 795 km). Empty weight, 12,140 lb (5 507 kg). Normal loaded weight, 18,500 lb (8 391 kg). Span, 39 ft 8 in (12,09 m). Length, 54 ft 1½ in (16,50 m). Height, 17 ft 3 in (5,26 m). Wing area, 350 sq ft (32,52 m²).*

McDONNELL F3H DEMON   USA

The first swept-wing single-seat fighter to fly designed from the outset for shipboard operation, the Demon (Model 58) was conceived as a day fighter, two prototypes being ordered under the designation XF3H-1 on 30 September 1949. Designed under the leadership of Richard Deagen, the first of these flew on 7 August 1951 with a Westinghouse XJ40-WE-6 engine rated at 6,500 lb st (2 948 kgp) dry and 9,200 lb st (4 173 kgp) with afterburning. In the meantime, the requirement had been revised to call for limited all-weather capability, production being initiated as the F3H-1N before commencement of prototype trials. The first F3H-1N was flown on 24 December 1953 with a J40-WE-8 engine rated at 7,500 lb st (3 402 kgp) dry and

The unsuccessful F3H-1N (above) was superseded by the F3H-2 (below), optimised as a strike fighter.

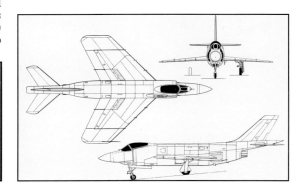

(Above) An F3H-2N of VF-131 serving aboard the USS *Constellation* in the late 'fifties.

10,500 lb st (4 763 kgp) with afterburning, and carrying an armament of four 20-mm cannon. Production was terminated after completion of 58 aircraft, the F3H-1N never entering US Navy service. The 32nd and 34th airframes were completed with the Allison J71-A-2 turbojet as F3H-2Ns, this power plant being rated at 9,500 lb st (4 308 kgp) dry and 14,250 lb st (6 462 kgp) with afterburning. The first of these flew on 23 April 1955, 140 series aircraft subsequently being built and armament being augmented by four short-range AIM-9 Sidewinder AAMs. Eighty F3H-2Ms were produced in parallel, these having provision for four medium-range AAM-N-2 Sparrow I AAMs. These models were to be redesignated as F-3C and MF-3B respectively in September 1962. They were followed by 239 F3H-2s (F-3Bs) optimised as strike fighters and capable of carrying up to 6,000 lb (2 722 kg) of ordnance externally, including the Sparrow III and Sidewinder IA AAMs. The Demon was phased out of US Navy first-line service in September 1964. The following data relate to the F3H-2 (subsequently F-3B). *Max speed (clean), 625 mph (1 006 km/h) at 35,000 ft (10 670 m), or Mach=0.94, 693 mph (1 116 km/h) at sea level, or Mach=0.91. Initial climb, 12,410 ft/min (63 m/sec). Combat range (with external fuel), 1,470 mls (2 366 km). Empty weight, 21,287 lb (9 656 kg). Max loaded weight, 39,000 lb (17 690 kg). Span, 35 ft 4 in (10,77 m). Length, 58 ft 11½ in (17,97 m). Height, 14 ft 7 in (4,45 m). Wing area, 519 sq ft (48,21 m²).*

F3H-2M version of the Demon (below) was specially fitted to carry four AIM-7 Sparrow Is.

McDONNELL F-101A & F-101C VOODOO   USA

Evolved from the XF-88 by a team led by E M Flesh as a deep penetration escort fighter, the Voodoo was the subject of an initial production contract on 28 May 1953, 29 aircraft being ordered as F-101As. The first of these flew on 29 September 1954. The F-101A was powered by two Pratt & Whitney J57-P-13 turbojets of 10,200 lb st (4 627 kgp) dry and 15,000 lb st (6 804 kgp) with afterburning, and carried a gun armament of four 20-mm cannon. The 16th and 17th F-101A airframes

First version of the Voodoo, the F-101A (below) entered USAF service at Bergstrom AFB, Texas, in 1957.

were completed as YRF-101A reconnaissance aircraft, 35 series RF-101As following. A total of 77 F-101As was completed, the single-seat Voodoo being restressed for low-altitude tactical operations owing to changing requirements. Production continued as the F-101C, the first example of this version flying on 21 August 1957, three months prior to delivery of the last F-101A. Only 47 F-101Cs were completed, the last of these being delivered on 27 June 1958, but 166 tactical reconnaissance RF-101Cs were delivered, these being similar to the RF-101A, but having the strengthened wing structure of the F-101C. In addition, 61 F-101As and Cs were later modified to RF-101G and H tactical recce aircraft. The

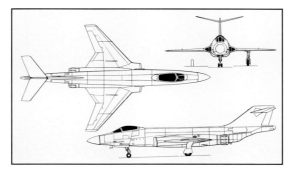

(Above) F-101A Voodoo penetration escort fighter.

following data relate to the F-101C. *Max speed, 1,005 mph (1 618 km/h) at 35,000 ft (10 670 m), or Mach=1.51. Initial climb, 33,750 ft/min (171,5 m/sec). Normal range, 1,315 mls (2 116 km). Empty weight, 26,277 lb (11 919 kg). Loaded weight, 48,908 lb (22 185 kg). Span, 39 ft 8 in (12,09 m). Length, 67 ft 5 in (20,55 m). Height, 18 ft 0 in (5,49 m). Wing area, 368 sq ft (34,19 m²).*

McDONNELL F-101B & F-101F VOODOO   USA

Development of a two-seat all-weather interceptor version of the Voodoo was officially initiated in August 1955 as the F-101B, the first test example flying on 27 March 1957. The F-101B mated a new tandem two-seat forward fuselage with the centre and rear fuselage sections, wings and tail assembly of the F-101A. It was fitted with two Pratt & Whitney J57-P-55 turbojets each rated at 10,700 lb st (4 854 kgp) dry and 16,900 lb st (7 666 kgp) with afterburning. A Hughes MG-13 fire-control system was installed and armament initially comprised four AIM-4 Falcon missiles, two internally and two externally on the rotary weapons bay door. Later, the Falcons were supplemented by two nuclear-tipped AIR-2A Genie missiles. Two-seat Voodoo production comprised 401 F-101Bs and 79 F-101Fs, the latter having dual controls and combat capability. Some F-101Bs modified to have dual controls, but with less combat capability, were designated TF-101Bs. Fifty-six

(Immediately below) F-101A of 81st Tactical Fighter Wing at RAF Bentwaters, 1964. (Bottom) CF-101B of 409 Sqn, Canadian Armed Forces, Comox, 1975.

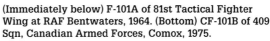

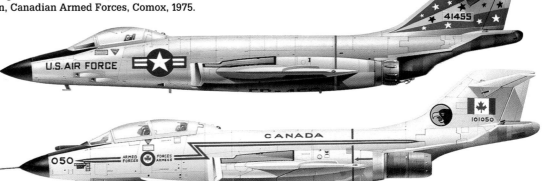

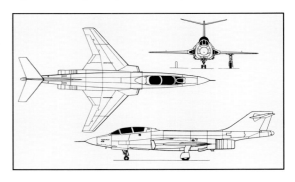

An F-101B (above) serving in the summer of 1960 with the USAF's 29th Fighter Interceptor Squadron.

of the F-101Bs were delivered to the RCAF between July 1961 and May 1962 as CF-101Bs. A total of 153 F-101Bs was fitted with an improved fire-control system and an IR detection system in place of provision for flight refuelling as F-101Fs. Ten F-101Fs delivered to the RCAF received the designation CF-101F, and, in 1970-71, the remaining nine of these, and the 47 surviving CF-101Bs, were exchanged for 56 lower-timed and upgraded ex-USAF F-101Bs and another 10 F-101Fs. Twenty-two of the ex-RCAF CF-101Bs were then modified for the reconnaissance rôle and employed by the Nevada Air National Guard as RF-101Bs. USAF operation of the two-seat Voodoo in first-line service terminated in the spring of 1971, after which it remained with Air National Guard units until 1983, and Canadian first-line use of the type ended at the beginning of 1985. *Max speed, 1,094 mph (1 760 km/h) at 35,000 ft (10 670 m), or Mach=1.63. Normal range 1,520 mls (2 446 km). Initial climb, 36,500 ft/min (185 m/sec). Empty weight, 28,492 lb (12 924 kg). Loaded weight, 52,400 lb (23 769 kg). Span, 39 ft 8 in (12,09 m). Length, 67 ft 5 in (20,55 m). Height, 18 ft 0 in (5,49 m). Wing area, 368 sq ft (34,19 m²).*

(Above) CF-101B of Canada's No 416 "Black Lynx" squadron and (below) the basically similar F-101B.

McDONNELL DOUGLAS F-4 PHANTOM II (US NAVY)   USA

Unquestionably the most significant and successful Western fighter of the 'sixties, the Phantom II was able to claim uniquity in that it was conceived solely as a shipboard warplane yet was to see far wider usage as a

non-naval shore-based multi-rôle fighter. Intended specifically for carrier-based operation by the US Navy, the Phantom II (Model 98) was designed by a team led by Herman D Barkley, two prototypes being ordered (as XF4H-1s) together with five pre-production aircraft on 25 July 1955. The first XF4H-1 was flown on 27 May 1958, by which time a follow-on order for 16 F4H-1s had been placed, and successive production contracts followed its selection in preference to the Vought F8U-3 Crusader III by the end of that year. A large tandem two-seat aircraft with all-missile armament, the F4H-1 was intended to receive paired General Electric J47-

An F-4N Phantom (left) flown by Marine Reserve Sqn VMFA-321 from NAF Andrews, Washington, DC.

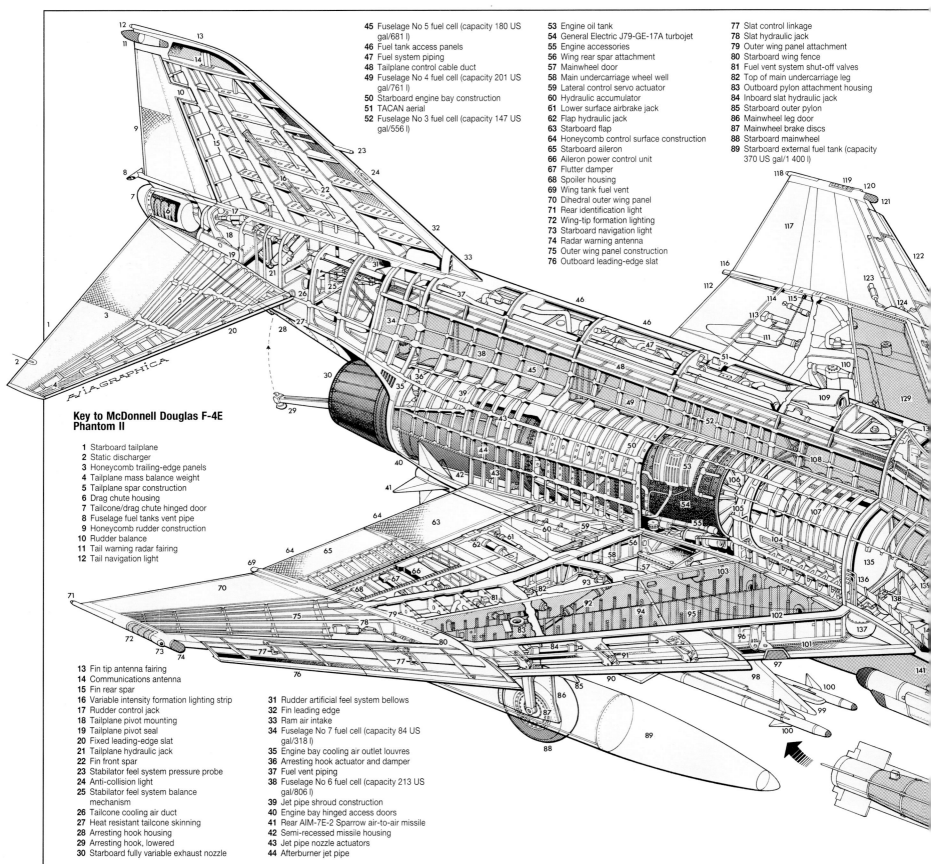

Key to McDonnell Douglas F-4E Phantom II

1 Starboard tailplane
2 Static discharger
3 Honeycomb trailing-edge panels
4 Tailplane mass balance weight
5 Tailplane spar construction
6 Drag chute housing
7 Tailcone/drag chute hinged door
8 Fuselage fuel tanks vent pipe
9 Honeycomb rudder construction
10 Rudder balance
11 Tail warning radar fairing
12 Tail navigation light
13 Fin tip antenna fairing
14 Communications antenna
15 Fin rear spar
16 Variable intensity formation lighting strip
17 Rudder control jack
18 Tailplane pivot mounting
19 Tailplane pivot seal
20 Fixed leading-edge slat
21 Tailplane hydraulic jack
22 Fin front spar
23 Stabilator feel system pressure probe
24 Anti-collision light
25 Stabilator feel system balance mechanism
26 Tailcone cooling air duct
27 Heat resistant tailcone skinning
28 Arresting hook housing
29 Arresting hook, lowered
30 Starboard fully variable exhaust nozzle

31 Rudder artificial feel system bellows
32 Fin leading edge
33 Ram air intake
34 Fuselage No 7 fuel cell (capacity 84 US gal/318 l)
35 Engine bay cooling air outlet louvres
36 Arresting hook actuator and damper
37 Fuel vent piping
38 Fuselage No 6 fuel cell (capacity 213 US gal/806 l)
39 Jet pipe shroud construction
40 Engine bay hinged access doors
41 Rear AIM-7E-2 Sparrow air-to-air missile
42 Semi-recessed missile housing
43 Jet pipe nozzle actuators
44 Afterburner jet pipe

45 Fuselage No 5 fuel cell (capacity 180 US gal/681 l)
46 Fuel tank access panels
47 Fuel system piping
48 Tailplane control cable duct
49 Fuselage No 4 fuel cell (capacity 201 US gal/761 l)
50 Starboard engine bay construction
51 TACAN aerial
52 Fuselage No 3 fuel cell (capacity 147 US gal/556 l)

53 Engine oil tank
54 General Electric J79-GE-17A turbojet
55 Engine accessories
56 Wing rear spar attachment
57 Mainwheel door
58 Main undercarriage wheel well
59 Lateral control servo actuator
60 Hydraulic accumulator
61 Lower surface airbrake jack
62 Flap hydraulic jack
63 Starboard flap
64 Honeycomb control surface construction
65 Starboard aileron
66 Aileron power control unit
67 Flutter damper
68 Spoiler housing
69 Wing tank fuel vent
70 Dihedral outer wing panel
71 Rear identification light
72 Wing-tip formation lighting
73 Starboard navigation light
74 Radar warning antenna
75 Outer wing panel construction
76 Outboard leading-edge slat

77 Slat control linkage
78 Slat hydraulic jack
79 Outer wing panel attachment
80 Starboard wing fence
81 Fuel vent system shut-off valves
82 Top of main undercarriage leg
83 Outboard pylon attachment housing
84 Inboard slat hydraulic jack
85 Starboard outer pylon
86 Mainwheel leg door
87 Mainwheel brake discs
88 Starboard mainwheel
89 Starboard external fuel tank (capacity 370 US gal/1 400 l)

GE-8 turbojets each rated at 10,900 lb st (4 944 kgp) dry and 17,000 lb st (7 711 kgp) with afterburning. Non-availability of this engine dictated installation of the lower-rated J79-GE-2 or -2A in the first 45 aircraft which were designated F4F-1Fs. These became F-4As in September 1962, when the final production standard F4H-1 with J47-GE-8 engines became the F-4B. Six hundred and forty-nine F-4Bs were to be built between June 1961 and March 1967 for the US Navy and Marine Corps. These had APQ-72 fire-control radar and an armament of four or six AIM-9 Sidewinders. Twelve

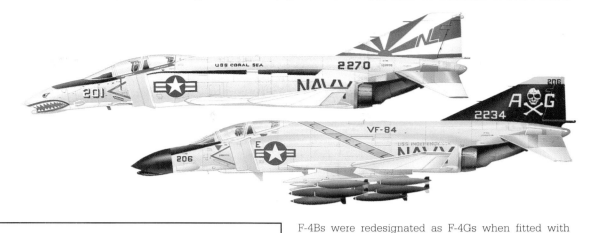

(Right top) F-4N of VF-111 "Sundowners" serving aboard USS *Coral Sea*. **(Immediately right)** F-4D of VF-84 "Jolly Rogers" on USS *Independence* in 1965.

90 Inboard leading-edge slat (open)
91 Slat hinge linkages
92 Main undercarriage retraction jack
93 Undercarriage uplock
94 Starboard wing fuel tank (capacity 315 US gal/1 192 l)
95 Integral fuel tank construction
96 Inboard pylon fixing
97 Leading-edge ranging antenna
98 Starboard inboard pylon
99 Twin missile launcher
100 AIM-9 Sidewinder air-to-air missiles
101 Hinged leading-edge access panel
102 Wing front spar
103 Hydraulic reservoir
104 Centre fuselage formation lighting
105 Fuselage main frame
106 Engine intake compressor face
107 Intake duct construction
108 Fuselage No 2 fuel cell (capacity 185 US gal/700 l)
109 Air-to-air refuelling receptacle (open)
110 Port main undercarriage leg
111 Aileron power control unit
112 Port aileron
113 Aileron flutter damper
114 Port spoiler
115 Spoiler hydraulic jack
116 Wing fuel tank vent pipe
117 Port outer wing panel
118 Rearward identification light
119 Wing tip formation lighting
120 Port navigation light
121 Radar warning antenna
122 Port outboard leading-edge slat
123 Slat hydraulic jack
124 Wing fence
125 Leading-edge dog tooth
126 Inboard leading-edge slat, open
127 Port external fuel tank (capacity 370 US gal/1400 l)
128 Inboard slat hydraulic jack
129 Port wing fuel tank (capacity 315 US gal/1192 l)
130 Upper fuselage light
131 IFF antenna
132 Avionics equipment bay
133 Gyro stabiliser platform
134 Fuselage No 1 fuel cell (capacity 215 US gal/814 l)
135 Intake duct
136 Hydraulic connections
137 Starter cartridge container
138 Pneumatic system air bottle
139 Engine bleed air supply pipe
140 Forward AIM-7 missile housing
141 Ventral fuel tank (capacity 600 US gal/2 271 l)
142 Bleed air louvre assembly (lower)
143 Avionics equipment bay
144 Variable intake ramp jack
145 Bleed air louvre assembly (upper)
146 Radar operator's Martin-Baker ejection seat
147 Safety harness
148 Face blind seat firing handle
149 Rear cockpit canopy cover
150 Front canopy hinges
151 Inter-canopy bridge section glazing
152 Radar operator's instrument console
153 Canopy jack
154 Port intake
155 Pilot's Martin-Baker ejection seat
156 Intake front ramp
157 Starboard intake
158 Bleed air holes
159 Boundary layer splitter plate
160 ALQ-72 electronic countermeasures pod (replaces forward Sparrow missile)
161 HOBOS 2000-lb (908-kg) guided bomb
162 Nosewheel door
163 AIM-7E-2 Sparrow missile semi-recessed housing
164 Forward formation lighting
165 Air conditioning plant
166 Battery
167 Pilot's starboard side console
168 Ejection seat safety harness
169 Engine throttles
170 Port intake front ramp
171 Forward cockpit canopy cover
172 Port inboard wing pylon
173 Pylon attachments
174 Triple ejector release unit
175 Mk 84 low-profile 500-lb (227-kg) bombs
176 Extended bomb fuses
177 Windscreen panels
178 Pilot's lead computing sight and head-up-display
179 Instrument panel shroud
180 Control column
181 Rudder pedals
182 Cockpit front pressure bulkhead
183 Refrigeration plant
184 Communications antenna
185 Nosewheel jack
186 Nose undercarriage leg strut
187 Twin nosewheels
188 Nosewheel torque links
189 Landing and taxiing lamps
190 Air conditioning ram air intake
191 Angle of attack probe
192 Ammunition drum (639 rounds)
193 Rain dispersal duct nozzle
194 ADF antenna
195 Gun bay frame construction
196 M61A-1 20-mm rotary barrel cannon
197 Cannon fairing
198 AN/APQ-120 fire control radar
199 Radar antenna mounting
200 Gun muzzle fairing
201 Radar scanner
202 Radome
203 Pitot tube

F-4Bs were redesignated as F-4Gs when fitted with AN/ASW-21 two-way data link and an automatic carrier landing system for service in the Vietnam area, 1965-66. Forty-six examples of a reconnaissance version of the F-4B were delivered to the USMC as RF-4Bs from May 1965. Three F-4Bs were modified as YF-4Js with drooping ailerons, slotted tailplanes, AWG-10 fire-control radar, an AJB-7 bombing system and J79-GE-10 engines rated at 17,900 lb st (8 119 kgp) with afterburning. These modifications were adopted for the next production model for the US Navy and Marine Corps, a total of 522 F-4Js being built. In the mid-'seventies, 228 F-4Bs were structurally strengthened and fitted with upgraded avionics as F-4Ns, and the similar structural strengthening of 265 F-4Js, the application of leading-edge slats, the upgrading of the avionics and the installation of modified J79-GE-10B engines from 1978 resulted in the F-4S. The following data relate to the F-4B. *Max speed, 1,499 mph (2 413 km/h) at 45,000 ft (13 715 m), or Mach=2.27. Initial climb, 40,800 ft/min (207,26 m/sec). Combat range (four Sparrow IIIs and one 500-Imp-gal/2 270-l drop tank), 1,800 mls (2 896 km). Empty weight, 27,897 lb (12 654 kg). Max loaded weight, 54,800 lb (24 857 kg). Span, 38 ft 4³/4 in (11,71 m). Length, 58 ft 3³/4 in (17,77 m). Height, 16 ft 3 in (4,95 m). Wing area, 530 sq ft (49,24 m²).*

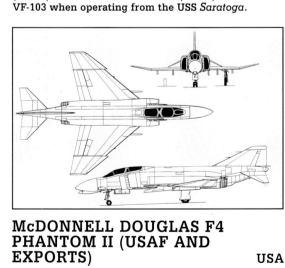

(Below) The F-4B Phantom II and **(above)** an F-4J with VF-103 when operating from the USS *Saratoga*.

McDONNELL DOUGLAS F4 PHANTOM II (USAF AND EXPORTS) USA

Although the Phantom II was designed specifically for shipboard operation, it was announced in March 1962 that this type was to be adopted by the USAF as its standard tactical fighter. Twenty-nine F-4Bs were loaned to the USAF, and the first version embodying changes specified by that service, the F-4C (initially F-110A) was flown on 27 May 1963. This differed from the US Navy's F-4B in having dual controls, a boom-type flight-refuelling system, low-pressure tyres and substantially different electronic equipment to suit it for both air superiority and ground attack rôles. Engines were J79-GE-15s rated at 10,900 lb st (4 944 kgp) dry and 17,000 lb st (7 711 kgp) with after-

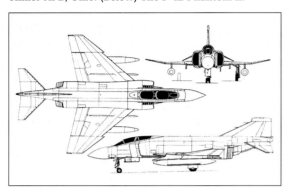

(Above) An F-4D flown by the 465th TFS, AFRES, from Tinker AFB, Ohio. (Below) The F-4E Phantom II.

burning, armament for the air-air rôle being basically four AIM-7 Sparrow III missiles. A total of 583 F-4Cs was built of which 40 were transferred to Spain. A further 503 were produced for the tactical reconnaissance mission as the RF-4C of which 27 transferred in batches to South Korea, and 12 to Spain. The F-4D, first flown on 7 December 1965, featured significant changes in internal systems to enhance air-to-ground capability. Deliveries commenced in March 1966, and 825 were built, including 32 for Iran and 66 transferred by the USAF to South Korea between 1969 and 1988. Also, 24 were used (on loan) by the RAAF, 1970-1973. The F-4E introduced a 20-mm rotary cannon, a different radar and an additional fuel tank, late production aircraft being fitted with wing leading-edge manoeuvre slats. A total of 1,387 was built. J79-GE-17 engines with a 17,900 lb st (8 119 kgp) max afterburning rating were fitted and 993 F-4Es were supplied to the USAF, 86 to Israel (plus 188 ex-USAF), 72 to Turkey (plus 30 ex-USAF), 177 to Iran and 56 to Greece. Ninety-five F-4Es were supplied to South Korea (including 37 as new) and 35 to Egypt, ex-USAF, and 132 examples of a tactical reconnaissance version, the RF-4E, were built for export of which 14 were supplied to Japan (as RF-4EJs), eight to Greece, eight to Turkey, 16 to Iran, 12 to Israel and 88 to Federal Germany. In addition, Mitsubishi delivered 138 (including 11 assembled from knockdown kits) to the JASDF as F-4EJs following supply of two aircraft by the parent company. One hundred and seventy-five were supplied to Federal Germany under the designation F-4F, these being optimised for the air superiority rôle. The F-4G was an electronic warfare adaptation of the F-4E which entered USAF service late 1978, 116 conversions being made. A total of 5,068 was built by the parent company and 127 in Japan. Of these, USAF Phantoms are long gone; the last variant to leave the service was the F-4G Wild Weasel, which was phased out in 1996. Israel experimentally re-engined a Phantom with two PW1120 turbojets rated at 20,620 lb (9 353 kgp) max and 13,550 lb (6 146 kgp) military thrust. Called the Super Phantom, this first flew on 24 April 1987 and showed marked performance improvements at subsonic speeds, but no further progress was made. The other Israeli programme was the Phantom 2000, essentially a structural and avionics upgrade, the most important features of which were the LMAS APG-76 multi-mode radar, multi-function liquid crystal displays, HOTAS, and an improved ECM system. First flown on 11 August 1987, the Phantom 2000 entered Israeli service on 5 February 1991. As at the beginning of 2001, Egypt still operated 30 F-4Es; the Luftwaffe had 145 F-4Fs, including 110 modified to ICE standards with the APG-65 radar and compatible with AIM-120 Amraam; Greece had 62 F-4Es and RF-4Es; Iran is believed to have had about 40

F-4D/Es; Israel operated about 40 F-4Es and 53 Phantom 2000s; Japan had some 109 F-4EJs, 90 of which are fitted with the APG-66 radar; South Korea retained about 60 F-4Ds and 70 F-4Es, plus 18 RF-4Es; the Spanish F-4Cs were long gone, and only 14 RF-4Cs remained in service; Turkey had 163 F-4Es, of which 54 are modified to Phantom 2000 standards, plus 44 RF-4Es. This is less than half of the 2,000 Phantoms which were confidently predicted to remain in service in 2000, but for a fighter approaching its half-century, it is still remarkable. It must also be remembered that more than 300 Phantoms have been modified in the USA to become QF-4 drone targets. The following data relate to the F-4E. *Max speed, 1,472 mph (2 369 km/h) at 40,000 ft (12 190 m), or Mach=2.23. Initial climb, 41,300 ft/min (209,8 m/sec). Combat range (one 500 Imp-gal/12 270-l and two 308-Imp-gall/400-l tanks), 1,613 mls (2 596 km). Empty weight, 30,328 lb (13 757kg). Max loaded weight, 61,795 lb (28 030 kg). Span, 38 ft 4¹/₂ in (11, 70 m). Length, 63 ft 0 in (19,20 m). Height, 16 ft 6 in (5,03 m). Wing area, 530 sq ft (49,24 m²).*

McDONNELL DOUGLAS
F4 PHANTOM II (UK)   USA

In the mid-'sixties, the UK government elected to adopt the Phantom II for both RAF land-based and Royal Navy shipboard use, but insisted that the power plant and many of the sub-systems be of British origin and manufacture. The Rolls-Royce RB.168-25R Spey 201 turbofan was substituted for

(Above and below) The Phantom FGR Mk 2, the photograph showing an aircraft of No 56 Sqn, RAF.

the J79, this engine, which was rated at 12,250 lb st (5 557 kgp) dry and 20,515 lb st (9 305 kgp) with afterburning, demanding a. 20 per cent increase in air intake area and some aft fuselage redesign. Various other changes were introduced and the first of two YF-4K prototypes for the Royal Navy version was flown on 27 June 1966, followed on 17 February 1967 by the first of two YF-4M prototypes for the RAF version. Similarly rated Spey 202 and 203 engines were introduced later. The mating of Spey engine and Phantom II airframe was not entirely satisfactory, performance of the Spey-Phantom being significantly inferior in speed, range and ceiling to that of its J79-powered counterpart. Nevertheless, 50 F-4Ks were ordered for the RN as Phantom FG Mk 1s and 116 F-4Ms for the RAF as Phantom FGR Mk 2s, deliveries commencing in April and July 1968 respectively. Basic armament of four AIM-7 Sparrow III missiles was retained. In 1977, the remaining FG Mk 1s were phased out of Royal Navy service and transferred to the RAF, continuing in service until 1990. The Spey-Phantoms were augmented in RAF service in 1984 by 15 ex-US Navy F-4Js (upgraded almost to FAS standard), these being operated under the designation F-4J(UK) until 1990. All the service's Phantoms were capable of being armed with a mix of AIM-9L Sidewinder and Sparrow III or Sky Flash missiles and the SUU-23A gun pod. *Max speed, 1,452 mph (2 337 km/h) at 36,090 ft (11 000 m), or Mach=2.2.*

(Immediately below) F-4E of 32nd TFS, 36th TFW at Soesterberg in 1970. (Second below) F-4EJ of 301 *Hikotai*, 7th *Kokudan*, JASDF, Hyakuri, 1980.

(Immediately below) Phantom FGR Mk 2 of No 23 Sqn, RAF Wattisham, 1980. (Bottom) Phantom FG Mk 1, No 43(F) Sqn, RAF Leuchars, 1980.

Max initial climb, 45,600 ft/min (231,65 m/sec). Combat range (one 500-Imp gal/2 270-l and two 308-Imp gal/1 400-l tanks), 2,047 mls (3 295 km). Empty weight, 30,918 lb (14 024 kg). Max loaded weight, 58,000 lb (26,309 kg). Span, 38 ft 4⁹/₁₀ in (11,71 m). Length, 57 ft 7¹/₈ in (17,55 m). Height, 16 ft 1 in (4,90 m). Wing area, 530 sq ft (49,24 m²).

McDONNELL DOUGLAS
F-15A & F-15C EAGLE   USA

Uncompromisingly designed for the air superiority mission, the F-15 resulted from a USAF-sponsored study initiated in 1965. McDonnell Douglas was named winning contender on 23 December 1969, and the first of 20 R&D aircraft (18 single-seaters and two two-seaters) then ordered flew on 27 July 1972. First entering USAF service in November 1974, the F-15A and its two-seat combat-capable equivalent, the F-15B, were powered by two Pratt & Whitney F100-PW-100 turbofans of 14,870 lb st (6 745 kgp) dry and 23,830 lb st (10 809 kgp) with maximum afterburning, and armament included a built-in 20-mm M61A1 six-barrel rotary cannon. Provision was made for up to four AIM-9L/M Sidewinder and four AIM-7F/M Sparrow AAMs. Manufacture of the initial production versions of the Eagle (including FSD aircraft) totalled 365 F-15As and 59 F-15Bs for the USAF, and 19 F-15As and two F-15Bs for Israel. Israel currently operates 38 F-15As and six F-15Bs. The F-15C, with upgraded avionics and the ability to carry Fuel And Sensor Tactical (FAST)

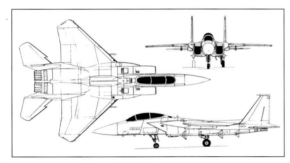

(Above) McDonnell Douglas F-15C Eagle.

packs, later renamed Conformal Fuel Tanks (CFTs), first flew on 26 February 1979, followed by the two-seat F-15D on 19 June of that year. In June 1979, production of the F-15C/D began. From 1984, this model was powered by the F100-PW-220 turbofan, rated at 23,770 lb (10 782 kgp) max and 14,590 lb (6 618 kgp) military thrust. While at first sight this appeared to be a retrograde step, the -220 was a more reliable engine. The USAF received 470 F-15C/Ds, while Israel currently operates 27. Saudi Arabia was the next export customer, and as at early 2001 had 109 C/Ds in service. Meanwhile Mitsubishi in Japan undertook licence manufacture of the C/D from 1980 as the F-15J. Currently Japan has 153 F-15Js and 38 DJs in the inventory. The first Mitsubishi aircraft flew on 26 August 1981, and production was complete by 1992. Also in the 1990s, the AIM-7 Sparrow had

(Immediately below) An F-15C of 32nd TFS at Soesterberg, 1986. (Bottom) F-15A of 5th FIS based at Minot AFB, North Dakota, in 1986.

Early production F-15A Eagles (above) flying with the 48th FIS in the US First Air Force.

largely been supplanted by AIM-120 Amraam, although the older missile still found a role over the Balkans, mainly because against multiple targets, when Amraam goes active, doubt exists as to which one it will go for, whereas SARH concentrates on the target locked up. In the USA from 1989, F-15 Eagle production concentrated on the dual role F-15E, which see. The following data relate to the F-15C. *Max speed hi, Mach 2.50. Max speed lo, Mach 1.20. Min flying speed, 100 kt (185 km/h). Operational ceiling, 65,000 ft (19 811 m). Rate of climb, 50,000 ft/min (254 m/sec). Empty weight, 28,600 lb (12 973 kg). Normal takeoff weight, 44,500 lb (20 185 kg). Span, 42 ft 9¹/₂ in (13.05 m). Length 63 ft 9 in (19,43 m). Height, 18 ft 5¹/₂ in (5,63 m). Wing area 608 sq ft (56,50,m²).*

McDONNELL DOUGLAS
F-15E EAGLE   USA

Derived from the basic F-15 as a two-seat dual-rôle (air-air and air-ground) fighter, the F-15E was selected by the USAF in preference to the General Dynamics F-16XL, the choice being announced by the US Department of Defense on 24 February 1984. Featuring 60 per cent structural redesign, the F-15E was developed to perform high-ordnance-payload, long-range, deep interdiction air-ground missions by day or night, in addition to an air superiority rôle, maximum weapons load being 24,500 lb (11 113 kg) on centreline and two wing stations plus four tangential carriers on conformal fuel tanks. Built-in armament of one 20-mm M61A1 six-barrel rotary cannon in the starboard wing root was augmented in the air-air mission by up to four each AIM-7 and AIM-9 AAMs or up to eight AIM-120 AAMs. After evaluation of an FSD TF-15A modified to YF-15B Strike Eagle configuration as a demonstrator, the first production F-15E was flown on 11 December 1986, power being provided by two 14,370 lb st (6 518

kgp) Pratt & Whitney F100-PW-220 turbofans each boosted to 23,450 lb st (10 637 kgp) with afterburning. Production aircraft subsequent to August 1991 were powered by -229 engines affording an afterburning thrust of 29,000 lb (13 154 kg), the first F-15E equipped with these uprated engines having flown on 2 May 1990. F-15E derivatives were ordered by Israel (30 F-15I) and Saudi Arabia (72 F-15S). *Max speed (short endurance dash), 1,676 mph (2 698 km/h) at 40,000 ft (12 190 m), or Mach=2.54, (sustained), 1,518 mph (2 443 km/h), or Mach=2.3. Combat radius, 790 mls (1 270 km). Range (max external fuel), 2,765 mls (4 450 km). Operational empty weight, 31,700 lb (14 379 kg). Max loaded weight, 81,000 lb (36 741 kg). Dimensions as for F-15C.*

(Above and below) The F-15E Strike Eagle, the photo depicting the first series aircraft.

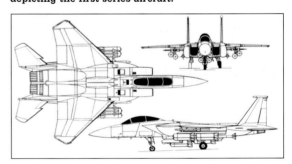

McDONNELL DOUGLAS
F/A-18A & C HORNET   USA

In January 1975, the General Dynamics YF-16 was declared the winner of the USAF Lightweight Fighter competition. The margins over the opposing Northrop YF-17 had been small, but conclusive. Even as the USAF had found F-15s to be unaffordable in sufficient quantities, so the USN was in the same position with

A pair of F/A-18A Hornets serving in 1988 with US Navy VFA-86 "Sidewinders" squadron.

the F-14. The Navy and Marines needed to replace no fewer than 54 squadrons of Phantoms and Corsairs in the near and medium term future. Rather than start from scratch, they decided to explore the potential of the contenders in the USAF competition. As neither company had any experience of carrier aircraft, General Dynamics was teamed with Ling Temco Vought, and Northrop with McDonnell Douglas. The evaluation showed that the Northrop YF-17 had more growth potential to meet the dual needs of the fighter and attack missions. In part, this was due to the fact that the YF-17 was twin-engined which, in the days when engine reliability was not all it later became, was a strong influence as a safety factor on long over-water flights. McDonnell Douglas basically scaled up the YF-17 into a much larger aircraft. At the same time, General Electric developed the YF101 turbofan into the

A Marine Corps F/A-18A from VMFA-531 sets off on a Red Flag "aggressor" mission.

much more powerful F-404. The result was the F/A-18. There were however three important innovations. The FBW system, which in the YF-17 had been analogue, became digital, a world first on a production aircraft, although mechanical backup to the stabilators gave a "get you home" facility at need. Radar was the Hughes

APG-65, the first multi-mode production radar ever to have a programmable signal processor, which allowed modes to be modified via software, rather than hard wiring. Then came the world's first "glass cockpit", in which virtually all conventional dials and instruments were replaced by three colour multi-function displays on which all necessary flight data could be called up at the touch of a button. HOTAS was of course obligatory. Initially the Hornet was to be in two variants, the dedicated fighter F-18A, and the attack A-18A. However, it was soon found that a single aircraft could be made to perform both functions with small changes of kit, and the dual role designation F/A-18 was adopted. The initial order was for 11 Full Scale Development aircraft, two of which were to be two-seater conversion trainers. These last were fully combat capable, but carried about 600 lb (272 kg) less fuel. First flight took place on

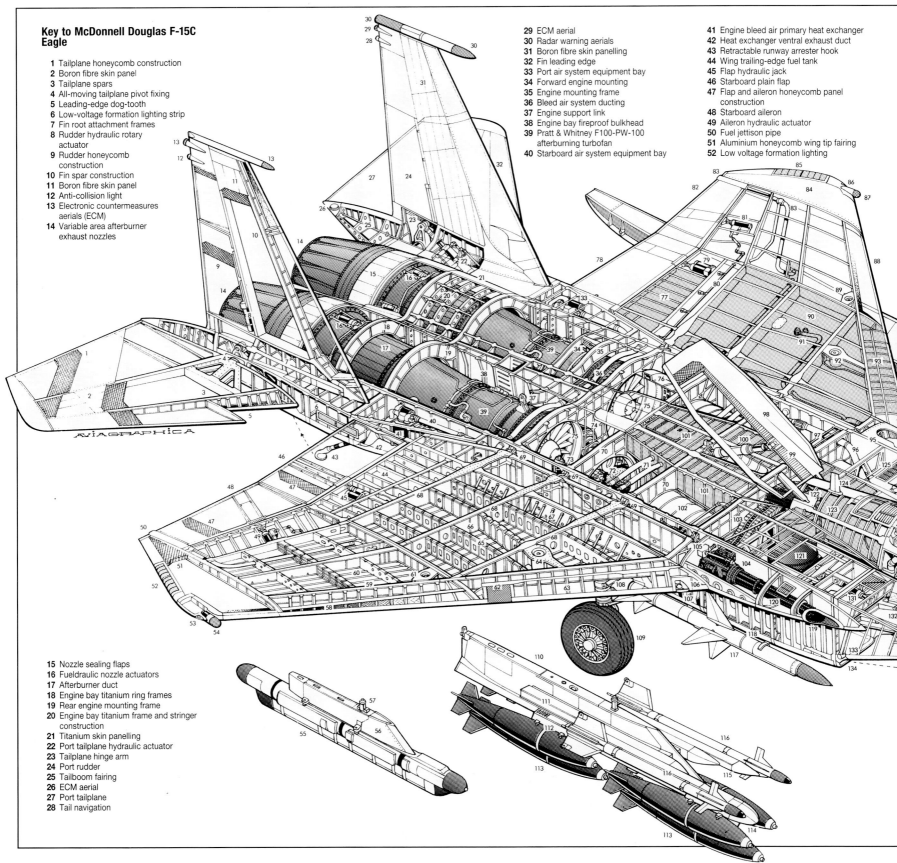

Key to McDonnell Douglas F-15C Eagle

1 Tailplane honeycomb construction
2 Boron fibre skin panel
3 Tailplane spars
4 All-moving tailplane pivot fixing
5 Leading-edge dog-tooth
6 Low-voltage formation lighting strip
7 Fin root attachment frames
8 Rudder hydraulic rotary actuator
9 Rudder honeycomb construction
10 Fin spar construction
11 Boron fibre skin panel
12 Anti-collision light
13 Electronic countermeasures aerials (ECM)
14 Variable area afterburner exhaust nozzles

29 ECM aerial
30 Radar warning aerials
31 Boron fibre skin panelling
32 Fin leading edge
33 Port air system equipment bay
34 Forward engine mounting
35 Engine mounting frame
36 Bleed air system ducting
37 Engine support link
38 Engine bay fireproof bulkhead
39 Pratt & Whitney F100-PW-100 afterburning turbofan
40 Starboard air system equipment bay

41 Engine bleed air primary heat exchanger
42 Heat exchanger ventral exhaust duct
43 Retractable runway arrester hook
44 Wing trailing-edge fuel tank
45 Flap hydraulic jack
46 Starboard plain flap
47 Flap and aileron honeycomb panel construction
48 Starboard aileron
49 Aileron hydraulic actuator
50 Fuel jettison pipe
51 Aluminium honeycomb wing tip fairing
52 Low voltage formation lighting

15 Nozzle sealing flaps
16 Fueldraulic nozzle actuators
17 Afterburner duct
18 Engine bay titanium ring frames
19 Rear engine mounting frame
20 Engine bay titanium frame and stringer construction
21 Titanium skin panelling
22 Port tailplane hydraulic actuator
23 Tailplane hinge arm
24 Port rudder
25 Tailboom fairing
26 ECM aerial
27 Port tailplane
28 Tail navigation

AVIAGRAPHICA

AIM-7 Sparrow and AIM Sidewinder AAMs are carried by both the CF-18A (immediately above) and the two-seat F/A-18B (directly below).

18 November 1978, at St. Louis. The moderately swept wing featured automatic camber, but its most noticeable features were huge, carefully contoured leading edge root extensions (LERX), and twin vertical tail surfaces canted outwards and set well forward on the fuselage. The LERX were designed both to shed vortices over the wings to inhibit spanwise airflow, and to act as compression wedges for the engine inlets. This however caused problems with siting the M61A Vulcan cannon. Whereas both the F-15 and F-16 had it buried in a wing root, this was impossible for the Hornet. Finally it was located in the nose, with the vibration damped so as not to interfere with the radar. Flight trials were not without problems, but these were overcome. The great success story was the General Electric F404-400 turbofan, rated at 16,000 lb (7 258 kgp) max and 10,860 lb (4 925 kgp) military thrust. Unlike the early F100 used by the F-15 and F-16, the F404 proved well able to stand up to rough handling. The first service Hornets reached the Fleet Replacement Air Group VFA-125 Rough Raiders in February 1981, and the first operational squadron was VMFA-314 Black Knights, from January 1983. Standard armament for air-to-air consisted of two AIM-7 Sparrows and two AIM-9 Sidewinders. In service, the main problem was that while the Hornet was fully dual-role capable, pilots were often not. The answer to this was to assign some squadrons to air combat, the others as ground-attack. In the export market, the Hornet was a success, even though it was usually pitted against the F-16. Australia currently operates 71 F/A-18A/Bs and Canada 80, while Spain has 81. Like most modern fighters, the Hornet has been continually upgraded, although so good was APG-65 that apart from software it remained unchanged for a decade. The main changes concerned the avionics: mission computers with greater capacity; improved ECM systems; provision for first six, then 10 AIM-120 Amraam while retaining two Sidewinders on wingtip rails; ACES ejection seats, and many other things. This resulted in the F/A-18C/D, the first production example of which was rolled out in September 1987. This also has done well in the export market; Finland operates 64 C/Ds, Kuwait 40, Switzerland 33, Spain has 24 Cs, and Malaysia 8 Ds. Also in service with the USMC are dedicated two-seater F/A-18D night attack Hornets, fitted with the Hughes AAR-50 Thermal Imaging Navigation Set and the Loral AAS-38 FLIR targeting pod. Whereas most two-seater Hornets have dual controls, the Marine F/A-18D has an optimised cockpit for the back seater to handle the systems. The F/A-18C/D has had two major upgrades. Creeping weight growth demanded more power, and this was provided by the F404-402, first flown in 1991 and rated at 17,700 lb (8 029 kgp) max and 10,860 lb (4 925 kgp) military thrust. Then, from 1994, the APG-65 began to be supplanted by the APG-73, which has tripled memory capacity and processing speed. It is planned to increase the service life of about one quarter of the F/A-18C/D fleet until 2019. The following data relate to the -402 powered F/A-18C. *Max speed hi, Mach 1.7. Max speed lo, Mach 1.01. Operational ceiling, 50,000 ft (15 239 m). Rate of climb, 50,000 ft/min (254 m/sec). Range varies with payload, atmospheric conditions, and flight profile. Empty weight, 23,000 lb (10 433 kg). Normal takeoff weight, 36,970 lb (16 769 kg). Span, 37 ft 6 in (11,43 m). Length 56 ft 0 in (11,43 m). Height 15 ft 3¹/₂ in (4.66 m). Wing area, 400 sq ft (37,16 m²).*

(Below) McDonnell Douglas F/A-18C Hornet.

53 Starboard navigation light
54 ECM aerial
55 Westinghouse ECM equipment pod
56 Outboard wing stores pylon
57 Pylon attachment spigot
58 Cambered leading-edge ribs
59 Front spar
60 Machined wing skin/stringer panels
61 Outboard pylon fixing
62 HF flush aerial
63 Leading-edge fuel tank
64 Inboard pylon fixing
65 Wing rib construction
66 Starboard wing integral fuel tank, total internal fuel load 13,455 lb (6 103 kg)
67 Wing root rib support struts
68 Titanium wing spars
69 Wing spar/fuselage attachment pin joints
70 Machined fuselage main bulkheads
71 Wing/fuselage fuel tank interconnections
72 Airframe mounted engine accessory gearbox
73 Standby hydraulic generator
74 Jet fuel starter (JFS)/auxiliary power unit (APU)
75 Engine intake compressor face
76 Cooling system intake bleed air spill duct
77 Port wing trailing-edge fuel tank
78 Port plain flap
79 Flap hydraulic jack
80 Aileron control rod
81 Aileron hydraulic actuator
82 Port aileron
83 Fuel jettison pipe
84 Wing tip fairing
85 Low-voltage formation lighting
86 Port navigation light
87 ECM aerial
88 Cambered leading edge
89 Outboard pylon fixing
90 Port wing internal fuel tank
91 Fuel system piping
92 Inboard pylon fixing
93 Leading-edge fuel tank
94 Anti-collision light
95 Boom-type air refuelling receptacle
96 Bleed air duct to air conditioning plant
97 Control rod runs
98 Dorsal airbrake (open)
99 Airbrake glass-fibre honeycomb construction
100 Airbrake hydraulic jack
101 Centre fuselage fuel tanks
102 Intake ducting
103 Ammunition feed chute
104 M61A-1 Vulcan 20-mm cannon
105 Hydraulic rotary cannon drive unit
106 Starboard anti-collision light
107 Ventral main undercarriage wheel bay
108 Main undercarriage leg strut
109 Starboard mainwheel
110 Inboard stores pylon
111 Air-to-air missile adaptor
112 Bomb rack
113 Mk 82 500-lb (227-kg) low drag HE bombs
114 Bomb triple ejector rack
115 Missile launch rail
116 AIM-9L Sidewinder air-to-air missile
117 AIM-7F Sparrow air-to-air missile
118 Sparrow missile launcher unit
119 Cannon muzzle aperture
120 Cannon barrels
121 Central ammunition drum (940 rounds)
122 Airbrake hinges
123 Forward fuselage fuel tanks
124 UHF aerial
125 Intake duct bleed air louvres
126 Intake by-pass air spill duct
127 Variable area intake ramp hydraulic actuator
128 Air conditioning system cooling air exhaust duct
129 Canopy hinge point
130 Air conditioning plant
131 Intake incidence control jack
132 Intake duct variable area ramp doors
133 Intake pivot fixing
134 Starboard engine air intake
135 Nosewheel leg door
136 Nose undercarriage leg strut
137 Nosewheel
138 Landing/taxiing lamps
139 Nosewheel retraction strut
140 Rear underfloor equipment bay
141 Tactical electronic warfare system (TEWS) racks
142 Cockpit coaming
143 Rear pressure bulkhead
144 Canopy jack
145 Cockpit pressurization valves
146 Structural space provision for second crew member (F-15D)
147 Cockpit aft decking
148 Canopy arch
149 Port intake external compression lip
150 Fuel and sensor tactical (FAST) pack (conformal fuel pallet, capacity 5,000 lb/2 268 kg)
151 600-US gal/(2 271-l) external fuel tank
152 Cockpit canopy cover
153 Ejection seat headrest
154 Seat safety handle/arming lever
155 Canopy emergency jettison linkage
156 Ejection seat launch rails
157 Safety harness
158 McDonnell Douglas ACES II "zero-zero" ejection seat
159 Cockpit sloping bulkhead
160 Pilot's side console panel
161 Air conditioning ducting
162 Forward underfloor equipment bay – built-in test equipment (BITE) and liquid oxygen converter
163 Low-voltage formation lighting strip
164 Port side retractable boarding ladder
165 TACAN aerial
166 Angle of attack probe
167 Rudder pedals
168 Control column
169 Pilot's head-up display (HUD)
170 Instrument panel shroud
171 Frameless windscreen panel
172 ADF sense aerial
173 Radio and electronics equipment bay (port and starboard)
174 Cockpit front pressure bulkhead
175 Pitot tube
176 UHF aerial
177 Radar mounting bulkhead
178 Radome hinge mounting
179 ILS aerial
180 Radar scanner mounting and tracking mechanism
181 Hughes APG-63 pulse doppler radar scanner
182 Scanner-mounted IFF aerial array
183 Glass-fibre radome

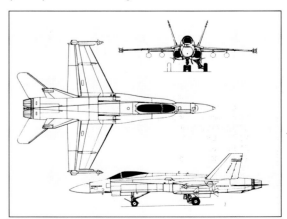

McDONNELL DOUGLAS (NOW BOEING) F/A-18E/F SUPER HORNET   USA

The Hornet was scheduled to be replaced in the attack role by the A-12, a stealthy triangular-shaped aircraft with no vertical surfaces. Due to excessive cost overruns, this was cancelled in 1991. Its replacement is the F/A-18E/F Super Hornet. While this looks like a Hornet, it is considerably larger and heavier. Wing area is 25 per cent larger, and varies by having a dogtooth on the leading edge to increase aileron authority. The LERX are larger to allow the angle of attack to be increased to 40deg or more. The tail surfaces have been increased in size; internal fuel has been increased by 3,100 lb (1 406 kg), and the thrust/weight ratio has been maintained by two F414-GE-400 turbofans, rated at 22,000 lb (9 979 kgp) max and 14,400 lb (6 532 kgp) military thrust. They have trapezoidal stealthy intakes, and other low observable features are incorporated, including a projected active array, low probability of intercept radar. Problems were encountered during flight testing, including severe wing drop, but this has now been overcome. The Super Hornet entered service with VFA-122 in November 1999, and operational deployment is scheduled for 2002. An active aero-elastic wing was scheduled for testing in mid-2001, giving greater manoeuvrability, and one of the displays is touch-sensitive liquid crystal. The Super Hornet has no speedbrake; slowing is accomplished by deflecting control surfaces. For the future, the F/A-18G Growler, fitted with four ALQ-99 jamming pods, is expected to replace the ancient EA-6B Prowler in the EW role. One problem has been encountered with the ALE-50 towed radar decoy. When using afterburner, the cable is easily burnt through. This will probably be resolved in the near future. The following data apply to the F/A-18E. *Max speed hi, Mach 1.8 plus. Max speed lo, Mach 1.01. Operational ceiling, 50,000 ft (15 239 m). Rate of climb n/a. Range "much better than F/A-18C". Span 44 ft 8½ in (13,63 m). Length, 60 ft 1½ in (18,32 m). Height, 16 ft 0 in (4,88 m). Wing area 500 sq ft (46,45 m²). Empty weight, 29,574 lb (13 415 kg). Normal takeoff weight, 46,200 lb (20 956 kg).*

McDONNELL DOUGLAS AV-8B HARRIER II PLUS   USA

The *raison d'être* of the US Marine Corps is to carry out amphibious operations, secure a beachhead, then fight their way inland. Obviously, air power is necessary, and it is part of the USMC charter that they should have their own organic air support rather than have to rely on another service, however capable and willing this might be. Be that as it may, for many years the Marines flew the same aircraft types as the Navy, often from Navy carriers. Only when the troops were ashore, and had captured a reasonably secure landing strip, could USMC squadrons join them. It is therefore little wonder that Marine flyers saw the Harrier, back in 1968, as being uniquely suited to their needs. Its STOVL qualities allowed it to operate from small helicopter carriers relatively close inshore, as opposed to the huge fleet carriers, which generally lay well back over the horizon. The name of the game was rapid reaction. If close air support could not be provided to the troops on the ground within 10 minutes of a call for help, it was often too late. Armed Harriers on standby

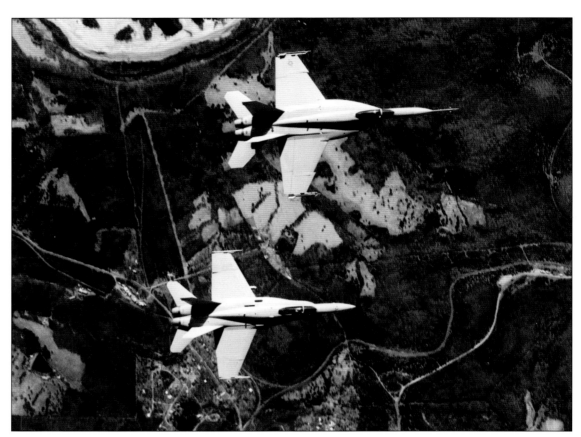

An F/A-18E Super Hornet (above) displays its larger size yet similar profile as it leads an F/A-18C Hornet on a training flight.

could be up and away in about 90 seconds, providing the rapid reaction that was needed. Once inshore, the Harrier did not need miles of concrete from which to take off and land. Any area larger than a tennis court would suffice, provided only that it could be kept supplied with fuel and weapons. Licence production by McDonnell Douglas supplied the Marines with Harriers as the AV-8A. The first Harriers were notably short on payload/range, and in the mid-1970s this problem was addressed jointly by British Aerospace and McDonnell Douglas. They concluded that payload/range could be doubled: either twice the weight of ordnance, or the same weight twice as far. The first of two YAV-8B aerodynamic prototypes took to the air on 9 October 1978. Full Scale Development aircraft were then funded, the first of which flew on 5 November 1981. Progress was swift; the first production AV-8B left the ground on 29 August 1983, and the type entered USMC service in the following January. It was powered by a single non-afterburning F402-RR-408 turbofan, rated at 23,850 lb (10 818 kgp), exhausting through zero-scarf rotating nozzles in front and standard swivelling nozzles further aft. To improve thrust-borne flight, lift-improvement devices (LIDS) were fitted. The greatest difference between the AV-8B and its predecessor was the wing. Of greater span and area, and a much deeper cross-section, its primary structure was all of carbon-fibre composite, and it

(Below) Harrier II Plus of the US Marine Corps.

could hold almost 75 per cent more fuel – 4,950 lb (2 245 kg) against 2,834 lb (1 285 kg). Leading edge sweep was reduced from 40deg to 36deg, and the outrigger landing gears were moved inboard, between the ailerons and enormous double-slotted flaps. The cockpit canopy, formerly flush with the top of the fuselage, was raised to give a better view astern. The tail surfaces were modified and constructed of composites, as was the forward fuselage and the panels on its top midsection. It could carry two Sidewinders, and a double gun pod was fitted ventrally. One pod held the 25-mm five barrel GAU-12 cannon, while the other contained 300 rounds of ammunition, fed across to the other pod. But the armaments described were largely to give a credible self-defence capability; the AV-8B was a close air support machine, and despite the improvements it was marginally slower than the AV-8A. The Marines were still dependent on the Navy for air superiority over the battle zone, and this did not suit them. The obvious answer was to produce a fighter variant, as the British had done with the multi-role Sea Harrier. Nothing could be done about performance; the AV-8B would always be firmly subsonic. But as in the Marine scenario most fighting would be defensive in nature, supersonic performance was of less importance than might otherwise have been the case. What was needed was a weapons system: radar and missiles. Thus was born the AV-8B Harrier II Plus, which first flew on 22 September 1992. The radar selected was the APG-65 as used by the Hornet, but with the antenna slightly reduced in diameter, housed in a bulged radome. Typical air-to-air armament consisted of up to six AIM-120 Amraam, or two Amraam and four Sidewinders. The Harrier II Plus can also double in the air-to-ground role. As at the end of 2000, three Marine squadrons had the Harrier II Plus on strength, while it also serves with the Italian and Spanish navies as a fleet air defence fighter. The following data relate to the Harrier II Plus. *Max speed hi, Mach 0.91. Max speed lo, Mach 0.86. Operational ceiling, c45,000 ft (13 715 m). Rate of climb, c50,000 ft/min (254 m/sec). Empty weight, 14,867 lb (6 744 kg). Takeoff weight, c23,650 lb (10 728 kg). Span, 30 ft 4 in (9,25 m). Length, 47 ft 9 in (14,55 m). Height, 11 ft 8 in (3,56 m). Wing area, 230 sq ft (21,37 m²).*

MEMEL A.F.G.1   Lithuania

The A.F.G.1 was the Albatros L 65 (which see) built in Memel by the Allgemeine Flug-Gesellschaft (A.F.G.) to evade Allied Control Commission restrictions.

The Kestrel-engined Bf 109 V1 (above) was radical in concept when it entered flight test in May 1935.

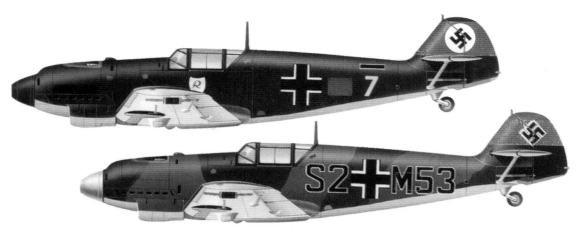

MESSERSCHMITT
Bf 109B to D   Germany

Designed under the leadership of Dipl-Ing Willy Messerschmitt, the Bf 109 was the first all-metal stressed-skin monocoque single-seat fighter monoplane with enclosed cockpit and retractable undercarriage to attain service. Powered by a 695 hp Rolls-Royce Kestrel, the first of three prototypes, the Bf 109 V1, was flown on 28 May 1935. The second and third prototypes, the Bf 109 V2 and V3, powered by the 680 hp Junkers Jumo 210A, flew in January and June 1936 respectively. A pre-series of 10 aircraft was ordered as Bf 109B-0s, these subsequently being

(Above and below) The Bf 109B, that illustrated by the photo serving with 3./JG 334 at Wiesbaden, 1938.

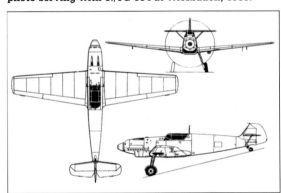

(Above) The first Bf 109D delivered to the Swiss *Fliegertruppe*, and (below) one of the five Bf 109Ds delivered to 3./J 88 of the *Legion Condor* in Spain.

Bf 109Bs (above, top) of 6./JG 132 *Richthofen* at Jüterbog-Damm, 1937, and (immediately above) at the *Luftwaffe Schule (Luftkreiskommando II*, Berlin) 1939.

assigned *Versuchs* numbers (V4 *et seq*) – the V4 and V5, along with the V3, were sent to Spain for operational evaluation in December 1936 – and the first series Bf 109B was completed in February 1937, this having a 720 hp Jumo 210Da and an armament of two 7,9-mm machine guns. Sixteen Bf 109Bs reached Spain for use by the *Legion Condor* in March 1937. These were to be followed by a further 29 of this model. The next series model, the Bf 109C-1, was delivered from the spring of 1938, powered by the Jumo 210Ga engine rated at 730 hp at 3,280 ft (1 000 m) and carrying an armament of four 7,9-mm guns, five being sent to Spain. Produced in parallel, the Bf 109D reverted from the direct fuel injection Jumo 210Ga engine to the carburettor-equipped Jurno 210Da, but possessed a similar four-gun armament. Ten Bf 109Ds were supplied to Switzerland from late 1938, three were delivered to Hungary and 35 reached Spain. The following data relate to the Bf 109C-1. Max speed, 292 mph (470 km/h) at 14,765 ft (4 500 m). Time to 16,405 ft (5 000 m), 8.75 min. Range, 405 mls (625 km). Empty weight, 3,522 lb (1 597 kg). Loaded weight, 5,062 lb (2 296 kg). Span, 32 ft 4½ in (9,87 m). Length, 28 ft 0²⁄₃ in (8,55 m). Height, 8 ft 0½ in (2,45 m). Wing area, 174.05 sq ft (16,17 m²).

MESSERSCHMITT
Bf 109E   Germany

From the outset of Bf 109 design, provision had been

(Below) The Bf 109E-3, the first cannon-armed model.

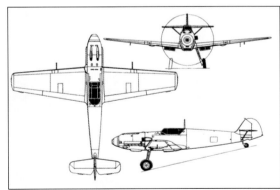

made for introduction of the Daimler-Benz DB 600 series of engines, the first such installation being made in the Bf 109 V10 which flew with a DB 600Aa engine in June 1937. This was, to all intents and purposes, the first prototype of the Bf 109E. Several other *Versuchs* airframes were fitted with the carburettor-equipped DB 600Aa, but the Bf 109 V15 and subsequent aircraft received the direct-fuel-injection DB 601A rated at 1,175 hp. The initial series models, the Bf 109E-1 and E-3, differed in armament, the former having four 7,9-mm machine guns and the latter mating two of these guns with two 20-mm MG FF cannon. The first series Bf 109Es were completed late in 1938, a total of 1,540 being delivered during the course of the following year, with 45 reaching Spain by the end of February 1939. The Bf 109E-3 was succeeded in production by the E-4 with improved MG FF cannon, the E-4/B being a fighter-bomber version (one 551-lb/250-kg or four 110 lb/50-kg bombs) and the E-4/N replacing the DB 601Aa engine with a 601N affording 1,200 hp. The Bf 109E-5 and E-6 were recce fighters differing in camera equipment, with the former having the cannon removed. Production of the E-4/N gave place to the similarly-powered Bf 109E-7, which had provision for a 66-Imp gal (300-l) drop tank, the E7/Trop being a tropicalised version, the E-7/U2 having additional armour and the E-7/Z having a nitrous oxide (GM 1) power boost system. The Bf 109E-8 had a 1,350 hp DB 601E engine and improved pilot armour, the E-9 being a photo-recce equivalent. The last E-series fighters were completed early in 1942, exports of the E model including 80 to Switzerland, 73 to Yugoslavia and three to the Soviet Union. Japan received three, 69 went to Romania, 19 to Bulgaria, 14 to Slovakia and others to Croatia. Twenty Bf 109Es were transferred from the *Legion Condor* to Spain's *Ejército del Aire*. The following data apply to the Bf 109E-3. *Max speed, 348 mph (560 km/h) at*

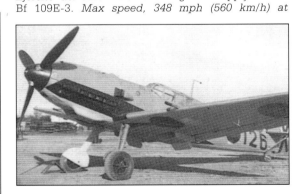

A Bf 109E-3 (above) serving with the 25 *Grupo* of the 23 *Regimiento* of Spain's *Ejército del Aire*, 1952.

A Bf 109E-7 of *Jagdgeschwader 5* (above) flying over the Northern Sector of the Eastern Front during 1942.

One of eight Bf 109E-3s assembled from spares by Doflug at Altenrhein for the Swiss *Fliegertruppe*, 1946.

14,560 ft (4 440 m). Initial climb, 3,510 ft/min (17,83 m/sec). Max range, 410 mls (660 km). Empty weight, 4,189 lb (1 900 kg). Loaded weight, 5,875 lb (2 665 kg). Span, 32 ft 4½ in (9,87 m). Length, 28 ft 4½ in (8,64 m). Height, 8 ft 2⅓ in (2,50 m). Wing area, 174.05 sq ft (16,17 m²).

MESSERSCHMITT Bf 109T Germany

The Bf 109T-2 (above) was a shore-based adaptation of the T-1 and was operated by I/JG 77 from Stavanger.

To meet a requirement for a shipboard fighter for operation from the carriers *Graf Zeppelin* and *Peter Strasser*, a dedicated version of the Bf 109E was developed as the Bf 109T (the suffix indicating *Träger* or Carrier). The wing span was extended, together with the leading-edge slats and ailerons, flap travel was increased, break points were incorporated in the main-spar for manual wing folding, and the structure adjacent to the seventh mainframe was strengthened to absorb the stresses of an arrester hook. The Fieseler Werke was assigned responsibility for development, converting 10 Bf 109E-1s to Bf 109T-0 configuration, trials being conducted during the winter of 1939-40. Retractable spoilers were introduced in the upper wing surfaces and strengthened undercarriage oleo legs were fitted. Sixty series aircraft were ordered as Bf 109T-1s, these differing from the T-0 in having the DB 601A engine supplanted by the DB 601N. With the decision to remove all carrier-associated equipment and operate the fighters from short strips as land-based aircraft these were redesignated as Bf 109T-2s. The first

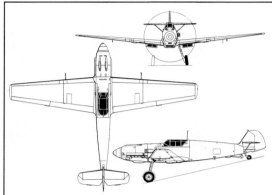

(Above) The Bf 109T-1, a shipboard Bf 109E version.

was completed in the early spring of 1941, and the Bf 109T-2 equipped I/JG 77 operating from Stavanger-Sola, some remaining in service (with IV/JG 5) until the end of 1944. Max speed, 357 mph (575 km/h) at 19,685 ft (6 000 m). Initial climb, 3,346 ft/min (17,00 m/sec). Max range (with auxiliary tank), 568 mls (915 km). Empty weight, 4,409 lb (2 000 kg). Max loaded weight, 6,768 lb (3 078 kg). Span, 36 ft 4¼ in (11,08 m). Length, 28 ft 9 in (8,76 m). Height, 8 ft 6½ in (2,60 m). Wing area, 188.37 sq ft (17,50 m²).

MESSERSCHMITT Bf 109F Germany

A programme of aerodynamic refinement of the basic Bf 109 design, initiated early in 1940 to take full advantage of DB 601 engine power increases, resulted in the Bf 109F. Substantial changes were made to the geometry of the high-lift devices and the radiators. A deeper, more symmetrical engine cowling was adopted, this being mated with an enlarged propeller spinner. Rudder area was reduced, the tailplane bracing struts eliminated and numerous other modifications applied. The first of four F-series prototypes was the Bf 109 V21 (the

(Immediately below) A Bf 109F-4/Trop of II/JG 27 at Sanyet, September 1942, and (bottom) an F-2/Trop of I/JG 77 at Comiso, Sicily, during summer 1942.

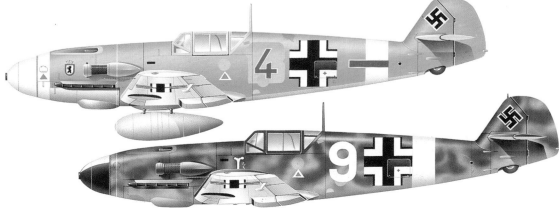

others being the V22, V23 and V24) and the intention was to standardise on the 1,350 hp DB 601E engine with a 20-mm MG 151 cannon firing through the propeller shaft, the wing-mounted MG FF cannon being discarded. Neither engine nor cannon was available for pre-series Bf 109F-0 fighters delivered in the autumn of 1940, these having the 1,200 hp DB 601N and an engine-mounted MG FF/M cannon coupled with two 7,9-mm machine guns. The series Bf 109F-1, which appeared in November 1940, had a similar engine and armament, the Bf 109F-2 differing in having a 15-mm MG 151 in place of the MG FF/M. The availability of the DB 601E engine at the beginning of 1942 resulted in the Bf 109F-3, quickly followed by the F-4 in which the calibre of the MG 151 was increased from 15-mm to 20-mm. Variants were the tropicalised F-4/Trop and fighter-bomber F-4/B, while the F-4/R1 introduced a pair of 20-mm MG 151s in underwing gondolas. The Bf 109F-4/Z featured nitrous oxide (GM 1) boost, and the Bf 109F-5 and F-6 were tactical reconnaissance models, the former having the engine-mounted cannon removed. Production of the F-series was already phasing out by the end of 1941, but was to continue until mid-1942, substantially more than 2,000 having been manufactured. From 1942, ex-*Luftwaffe* BF 109F-4s were flown by the air forces of Spain, Italy and Hungary. The following data relate to the Bf 109F-4. Max speed, 388 mph (624 km/h) at 21,325 ft (6 500 m). Initial climb, 4,350 ft/min (22,1 m/sec). Range (with auxiliary tank), 528 mls (850 km). Empty equipped weight, 5,269 lb (2 590 kg). Max loaded weight, 6,872 lb (3 117 kg). Span, 32 ft 6½ in (9,92 m). Length, 29 ft 2⅓ in (8,90 m). Height, 8 ft 6⅓ in (2,60 m). Wing area, 173.30 sq ft (16,10 m²).

A Bf 109F-4/R1 (above) landing in Tunisia in 1943, and (below) a three-view drawing of the basic Bf 109F.

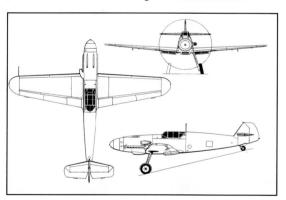

MESSERSCHMITT Bf 109G Germany

Destined to become numerically the most important of all models of the Bf 109 fighter, the Bf 109G was evolved to use the more powerful and heavier DB 605 engine and to make provision for cockpit pressurisation. A pre-series batch of Bf 109G-0 fighters was begun in the late summer of 1941, the first example being completed in October and the series Bf 109G-1 appearing during the following spring. The Bf 109G-1 and G-2 (the latter lacking cabin pressurisation) were produced in parallel, were powered by the 1,475 hp DB 605A-1 engine with GM 1 boost and carried an armament of one 20-mm MG 151 cannon and two 7,9-mm machine guns. The G-3 and G-4 differed in having wider mainwheel tyres and later radio, the G-4 being a photo-recce variant. The G-1/Trop had 13-mm guns in place of the 7,9-mm weapons, all subsequent variants standardising on the larger-calibre guns. These commenced with the Bf 109G-5 delivered with both the DB 605A and GM 1 combination,

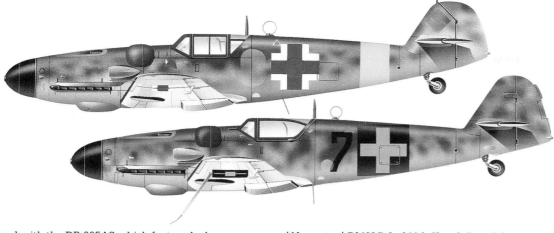

and with the DB 605AS which featured a larger super-charger. The G-5/U2 differed in having a wooden tail-plane. From the late autumn of 1942, the Bf 109G-6 reached the assembly lines, this being the first ''standard'' model capable of accepting various *Rüst-sätze* (Field Conversion Sets) and usually powered by the DB 605AM with MW 50 (methanol-water) boost, the engine-mounted cannon being either a 20-mm MG 151 or a 30-mm MK 108. Fitted with a *Rüstsätz* for a 551-lb (250-kg) bomb, the fighter was designated Bf 109G-6/R1; with two 21-cm mortars it became the G-6/R2; with two additional 30-mm MK 108 cannon underwing it was the G-6/R4 and with these replaced by 20-mm MG 151s it was the G-6/R6. The Bf 109G-6/N was a specially-equipped version for nocturnal operations and the Bf 109G-8 was a recce version of the G-6, the G-8/U2 and U3 having GM 1 and MW 50 boost respectively. By 1944, two new models were being developed, the Bf 109G-10 and G-14, the latter preceding the former into service. The G-10 was powered by the new DB 605D engine, while the G-14 represented an attempt to standardise all the progressive refinements that had been applied to DB 605A- and AM-engined models. The DB 605D engine of the Bf 109G-10 provided 1,850 hp, the basic armament of this sub-type of the fighter being twin 13-mm guns and a single 20-mm or 30-mm cannon, and, in clean condition, max speed was 426 mph (685 km/h) at 24,280 ft (7 400 m). In excess of 30,000 G-series Bf 109 fighters were produced, including licence manufacture in Hungary and Romania. Bf 109Gs were used by most of the air arms flying alongside the *Luftwaffe*. In addition, 160 were supplied to

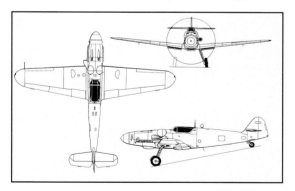

The Bf 109G-14 (above) and an HA-1112-M1L (below) flown April 1982 with DB 605 to represent the Bf 109G.

(Above, top) Bf 109G-6 of 14th Slovak Sqn, Crimea, spring 1943, and (immediately above) G-14/U2 of the Hungarian 101 Fighter Group, Germany, April 1945.

Finland and 12 to Switzerland. The following data relate to the Bf 109G-6. *Max speed, 386 mph (621 km/h) at 22,640 ft (6 900 m). Initial climb, 3,346 ft/min (17,00 m/sec). Range (with auxiliary tank), 620 mls (998 km). Empty equipped weight, 5,893 lb (2 673 kg). Max loaded weight, 7,496 lb (3 400 kg). Span, 32 ft 6½ in (9,92 m). Length, 29 ft 7½ in (9,03 m). Height, 8 ft 2½ in (2,50 m). Wing area, 173.30 sq ft (16,10 m²).*

A Bf 109G-5 of 7./JG 27 (above) flying over Eastern Mediterranean, late 1943, and (below) a G-6/R6 with *II Gruppe* of JG 26 operating in France, autumn 1942.

MESSERSCHMITT Bf 109H Germany

At the beginning of 1943, work was proceeding on the development of a dedicated high-altitude fighter based on the Bf 109F. Designated Bf 109H, this was essentially a Bf 109F airframe with a higher-rated DB 601 engine and a parallel-chord centre section inserted in the wing, increasing overall span to 39 ft 1¼ in (11,92 m). A

demand for improved service ceiling resulted in the decision to adopt the DB 628A engine, which, with an induction cooler and two-stage mechanical super-charger, promised 1,580 hp at 6,560 ft (2 000 m). This engine was mated with a broad-bladed propeller and a ducted spinner, the forward fuselage being lengthened by 2 ft 6¾ in (78 cm) and the cg being restored by moving forward the wing attachment points and enlarging the tail. These modifications were applied to a Bf 109G-5 airframe which entered flight test in June 1943 as the Bf 109H V54. Work had meanwhile been proceeding on the adaptation of a number of Bf 109F-4 airframes for flight development purposes as Bf 109H-0s. Apart from the addition of the parallel-chord wing centre section and an extended, strut-braced tailplane, the Bf 109H-0 was similar to the Bf 109F-4/Z, retaining the DB 601E-1 engine with GM 1 boost and the armament of one 20-mm cannon and two 7,9-mm machine guns. The generally similar Bf 109H-1s that followed were based on the Bf 109G-5 airframe and DB 605A engine with GM 1 boost, armament being identical to that of the H-0.

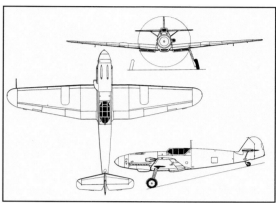

(Above) The Bf 109H-1 high-altitude fighter.

Several Bf 109H-1s were delivered to a service evaluation unit early in 1944. Development of the Bf 109H was discontinued in favour of the Ta 152H, but, in the meantime, one further prototype had been completed as the Bf 109H V55, which first flown on 22 December 1943, had a DB 605B engine with the larger DB 603 supercharger. The following data relate to this last-mentioned aircraft. *Max speed, 427 mph (687 km/h). Service ceiling, 44,290 ft (13 500 m). Empty equipped weight, 6,338 lb (2 875 kg). Loaded weight, 7,804 lb (3 540 kg). Span, 43 ft 6 in (13,26 m). Length, 33 ft 7½ in (10,55 m). Height, 10 ft 7½ in (3,24 m). Wing area, 235.73 sq ft (21,90 m²).*

MESSERSCHMITT Bf 109K Germany

The final production version of the Bf 109 represented an attempt to reduce the number of sub-types and modifications, and standardise on a basic model to which all facilities devoted to the production of this fighter would convert. Designated Bf 109K, it was based on the Bf 109G-10 airframe, but embodied as standard certain of the progressive changes introduced as *Umrüst-Bausätze* (Factory Conversion Sets) as well as some minor aerodynamic refinements. The pre-series Bf 109K-0 appeared in September 1944, powered by the DB 605DB engine, but the only sub-type to attain series production was the Bf 109K-4 powered by the 1,800 hp DB 605DCM and deliveries of which began in October 1944. Standard armament consisted of an engine-mounted 30-mm MK 108 cannon and two fuse-lage-mounted 13-mm MG 131 machine guns, and this could be augmented by a pair of 20-mm MG 151 cannon

A Bf 109K-4 (below) seen in May 1945 and believed to have been on the strength of *I Gruppe* of JG 51.

Bf 109K-4s (above, top) of *I Gruppe* of JG 27 at Rheine and (immediately above) *II Gruppe* of JG 77 at Bönninghardt, both during December 1944.

underwing (Bf 109K-4/R4). Late production Bf 109K-4s replaced the MK 108 cannon with an MK 103 of similar calibre, this being standardised by the Bf 109K-6 which also carried a pair of MK 108s mounted internally in the wings. Only a handful of BF 109K-6s reached the *Luftwaffe*, but some 700 examples of the K-4 had been completed when production of the Bf 109 came to an end with the collapse of Germany in 1945. These data apply to the Bf 109K-4. *Max speed, 452 mph (727 km/h) at 19,685 ft (6 000 m). Initial climb rate, 4 820 ft/min (24,5 m/sec). Range, 356 mls (573 km). Empty equipped weight, 6,070 lb (2 753 kg). Loaded weight, 7,410 lb (3 361 kg). Span, 32 ft 6½ in (9,92 m). Length, 29 ft 7½ in (9,03 m). Height, 8 ft 2½ in (2,50 m). Wing area, 173.30 sq ft (16,10 m²).*

(Below) The Bf 109K-4, delivered from October 1944.

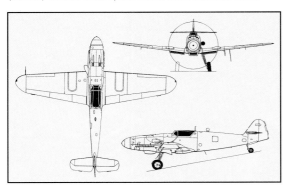

MESSERSCHMITT
Bf 110A & Bf 110B   Germany

The Bf 110 was designed as a three-seat strategic fighter, or *Zerstörer*: a warplane possessing sufficient performance and armament for deep-penetration offensive sorties, bomber escort missions and the mounting of long-distance standing patrols. Conceived around the Daimler-Benz DB 600, the first of three prototypes, the Bf 110 V1, was flown with two of these engines on 12 May 1936. The decision to replace the carburettor-equipped DB 600 with the direct-fuel-injection DB 601, and the delays in Daimler-Benz engine availability in consequence, dictated installation of the 680 hp Junkers Jumo 210Da in the four examples of the pre-series Bf 110A-0. All of these were assigned *Versuchs* numbers and featured revised nose contours, the first, the Bf 110 V4, flying on 21 January 1938. Ten additional pre-series aircraft were powered by Jumo 210Ga

The Bf 110 V3 (below) introduced three-bladed propellers and abbreviated engine nacelle tails.

engines of 730 hp at 3,280 ft (1 000 m) as Bf 110B-0s. The first of the similarly-powered production Bf 110B-1s followed in July 1938. The armament of the Bf 110B-1 comprised two 20-mm MG FF cannon and four 7,9-mm machine guns in the nose, and a single 7,9-mm gun in the rear cockpit. The Jumo-engined B-series were considered as interim aircraft pending availability of the DB 601-engined C-series, and only some 45 were completed. Of these, several were delivered as Bf 110B-2s with cannon removed and camera installed, and most were later modified as Bf 110B-3 trainers. *Max speed, 283 mph (455 km/h) at 13,125 ft (4 000 m). Max range, 1,070 mls (1 720 km). Max loaded weight, 12,562 lb (5 700 kg). Span, 55 ft 5⅓ in (16,90 m). Length, 41 ft 4 in (12,60 m). Height, 11 ft 4⅔ in (3,47 m). Wing area, 418.72 sq ft (38,90 m²).*

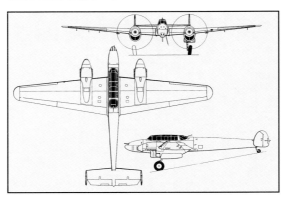

(Above) The Bf 110B and (below) the Bf 110B-01 delivered without armament in the spring of 1938.

MESSERSCHMITT
Bf 110C to Bf 110F   Germany

With the clearance of the DB 601A-1 engine for service, production of the Bf 110B gave place to the Bf 110C, which, apart from power plant, differed from its predecessor in only minor respects. A pre-series of 10 Bf 110C-0 fighters was delivered in early January 1939, the initial production version, the Bf 110C-1, following before the month's end. Armed with two 20-mm MG FF cannon and four 7,9-mm machine guns in the nose, plus an additional 7,9-mm weapon on a flexible mount, the Bf 110C-1 was powered by two DB 601A-1 engines each rated at 1,050 hp for take-off. The Bf 110C-2 differed from the C-1 in radio equipment; the C-3 had improved MG FF cannon and the C-4 introduced armour for pilot and gunner. With the provision of bomb racks and substitution of 1,200 hp DB 601N engines, the last-mentioned sub-type became the Bf 110C-4/B, a parallel development being the C-5 dedicated reconnaissance model with DB 601A-1s and C-5/N with DB 601Ns.

The 25th Bf 110C-1 built under sub-contract by Focke-Wulf (above), and a Bf 110C-3 (below) of *II Gruppe* of ZG 76, the so-called *Haifischgruppe*.

Several Bf 110C-3s were fitted with flush-fitting ventral fuel tanks as Bf 110D-0s, the series version being the D-1/R1, the D-1/R2 replacing the ventral tank with two jettisonable wing tanks. The D-1/U1 was a night fighting version with infra-red sensor. The Bf 110C-6 replaced the twin 20-mm cannon with a single 30-mm weapon, and the C-7 was a fighter-bomber version with DB 601N engines, while the D-2 differed from the D-1/R2 in having bomb racks. The D-3 had increased external fuel capacity for the shipping escort rôle. Introduced during the spring of 1941, the Bf 110E featured four bomb racks under the outer wing panels, the E-0 and early E-1 retaining DB 601A engines, but the DB 601N soon being standardised. Versions were the E-1/U1 night fighter, the E-1/U2 with crew increased

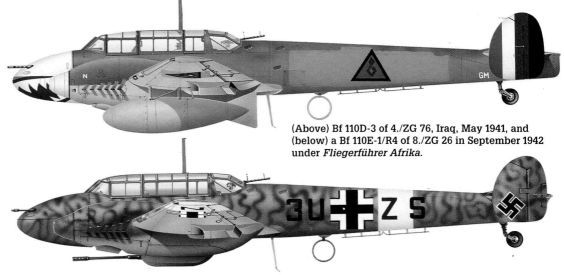

(Above) Bf 110D-3 of 4./ZG 76, Iraq, May 1941, and (below) a Bf 110E-1/R4 of 8./ZG 26 in September 1942 under *Fliegerführer Afrika*.

from two to three members, the E-2 having a dinghy housing in the tail and the E-3 being a recce model with cannon and bomb racks deleted. The Bf 110F was a derivative with 1,350 hp DB 601F engines. The F-1 had increased armour protection for the crew; the F-2 had the bomb racks removed; the F-3 was a recce equivalent and the F-4 was a night fighter with the standard armament supplemented by twin 30-mm cannon in a ventral tray. The Bf 110F-4/U1 had the ventral tray replaced by a pair of upward-firing 30-mm cannon in a so-called "*schräge Musik*" installation, and the F-4a replaced the forward-firing 20-mm MG FF cannon with MG 151 cannon of similar calibre and carried FuG 202 intercept radar. The following data relate to the DB 601F-powered Bf 110F-2. *Max speed, 352 mph (566 km/h) at 17,700 ft (5 395 m). Time to 19,685 ft (6 000 m), 9.2 min. Max range (internal fuel), 745 mls (1 200 km). Empty equipped weight, 12,346 lb (5 600 kg). Normal loaded weight, 15,873 lb (7 200 kg). Span, 53 ft 3¾ in (16,25 m). Length, 39 ft 7¼ in (12,07 m). Height, 13 ft 6½ in (4,13 m). Wing area, 413.33 sq ft (38,40 m²).*

MESSERSCHMITT Bf 110G Germany

A Bf 110G-4b/R3 (above) serving as test-bed for revised SN-2 radar array of the G-4d/R3.

Reinstatement of the Bf 110 in full-scale production in 1942 resulted in impetus being placed behind a more powerful and more versatile version of the fighter, the Bf 110G. Work on this had begun in the summer of 1941. The 1,475 hp DB 605B-1 engine was standardised, the first series model being the Bf 110G-2 dual-rôle (destroyer or heavy fighter-bomber) version, of which deliveries began in May 1942. Basic forward-firing armament remained a pair of 20-mm cannon and a quartet of 7,9-mm guns, but a twin 7,9-mm MG 81Z installation was provided in the rear cockpit, and two bomb racks beneath the fuselage were interchangeable with a tray containing two additional forward-firing 20-mm cannon. Gun armament was varied by application of *Rüstsätze* (Field Conversion Sets), the standard 20-mm weapons being removed and a single 37-mm cannon being mounted beneath the fuselage (Bf 110G-2/R1), the four 7,9-mm guns being removed and replaced by twin 30-mm cannon (Bf 110G-2/R3), or both *Rüstsätze* being applied (Bf 110G-2/R5). Evolved in parallel were the Bf 110G-3 long-range reconnaissance fighter and

(Below) The Bf 110G-4c/R3 and (above) a G-4d/R3 preserved in the RAF's "Battle of Britain" Museum.

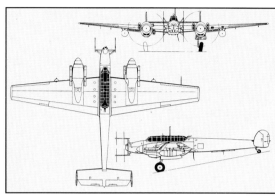

the Bf 110G-4 night fighter. The former had forward-firing armament restricted to the 7,9-mm weapons (except when *Rüstsätz* 3 was applied), but the rear-firing MG 81Z was augmented by a fixed 20-mm cannon. The Bf 110G-4 carried standard fixed forward-firing armament in its basic form, the intercept radar being installed as *Umrüst-Bausätze* (Factory Conversion Sets), the Bf 110G-4/U5 having FuG 212 *Lichtenstein* C-1 and the Bf 110G-4/U6 having FuG 221a *Rosendaal-Halbe*. When, in the autumn of 1943, the *Lichtenstein* C-1 was standardised on the assembly line, the basic night fighter became the Bf 110G-4a, and with introduction of *Lichtenstein* SN-2 this became the Bf 110G-4b, various *Rüstsätze* being added (eg, Bf 110G-4b/R1, R3, etc). With the *Lichtenstein* C-1 discarded and only the SN-2 fitted, the fighter became the Bf 110G-4c, production terminating with the Bf 110G-4d/R3 which differed from the -4c/R3 in having a reduced-drag aerial array. The last Bf 110G was completed in March 1945, bringing total production of this fighter (all versions) to approximately 6,050 aircraft. The following data relate to the Bf 110G-4c/R3. *Max speed, 342 mph (550 km/h) at 22,900 ft (6 980 m). Max climb, 2,170 ft/min (11,0 m/sec). Max range (internal fuel), 560 mls (900 km). Empty equipped weight, 11,230 lb (5 094 kg). Max loaded weight, 21,799 lb (9 888 kg). Span, 53 ft 3¼ in (16,25 m). Length (including antennae), 42 ft 9¾ in (13,05 m). Height, 13 ft 8½ in (4,18 m). Wing area, 413.33 sq ft (38,40 m²).*

MESSERSCHMITT Me 209 Germany

A single-seat fighter derivative of an aircraft designed solely for an attempt on the world absolute speed record, the Me 209 V4, first flown on 12 May 1939, possessed little commonality with its progenitor other than the fuselage. The Me 209 V1, which had first flown on 1 August 1938, and had succeeded in raising the record to 469.22 mph (755,11 km/h) on 26 April 1939, was powered by a special Daimler-Benz DB 601ARJ with a max output of 1,550 hp boosted for one minute to 2,300 hp by the use of methyl alcohol as an additive. The Me 209 V4 was (initially) fitted with a standard DB 601A engine, featured an entirely new, longer-span wing, enlarged vertical tail surfaces and a shorter undercarriage. It had provision for an armament of one 20-mm MG FF/M cannon and two 7,9-mm MG 17 machine guns. Surface evaporation cooling gave place to orthodox radiators after the eighth test flight; the wing leading-edge slots were replaced by cambered surfaces; the tail was further enlarged and the wing span was progressively increased. During the summer of 1940, a 1,200 hp DB 601N engine was installed. Poor handling characteristics, persistent engine overheating and inadequate performance eventually led to the abandonment of further development in favour of an entirely new design, the Me 209 II (which see). *Loaded weight (initial), 4,806 lb (2 180 kg), (definitive), 6,173 lb (2 800 kg). Span (initial), 30 ft 5¾ in (9,29 m), (definitive), 32 ft 11½ in (10,04 m). Wing area (initial), 119.16 sq ft (11,07 m²).*

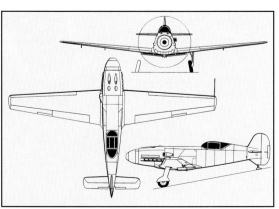

(Above and below) The Me 209 V4 demonstrated poor handling characteristics and inadequate performance.

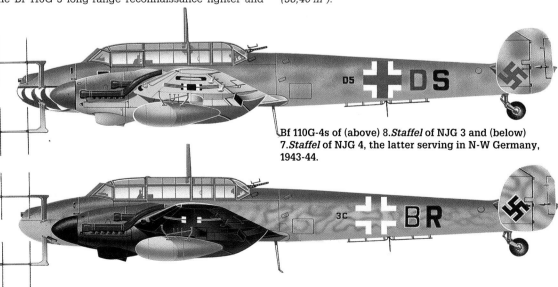

Bf 110G-4s of (above) 8.*Staffel* of NJG 3 and (below) 7.*Staffel* of NJG 4, the latter serving in N-W Germany, 1943-44.

MESSERSCHMITT Me 210A Germany

Conceived as a successor to the Bf 110 in the *Zerstörer* rôle, the Me 210 was first projected in 1937, when the earlier aircraft was still in prototype status. The first

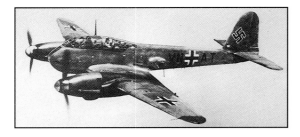

One of the last Me 210A-1s completed (above) under test with new rear fuselage in the summer of 1942.

prototype, the Me 210 V1, was flown on 5 September 1939. From the outset, the new aircraft displayed unsatisfactory handling characteristics, and successive prototypes were to be subjected to continuous modification which failed to eradicate entirely the undesirable features of the new *Zerstörer*. Nevertheless, deliveries of a large pre-series – which, in the event, was to embrace no fewer than 94 aircraft – began in April 1941. These Me 210A-0s were primarily two-seat fighters with secondary dive-bombing capability, and work began on two series production versions, the Me 210A-1 *Zerstörer* with secondary fighter-bomber capabilities and the Me 210A-2 dive bomber with secondary *Zerstörer* potential. These were powered by the

1,350 hp DB 601F engine and carried an armament of two 20-mm MG 151 cannon and two 7,9-mm MG 17 machine guns firing forward, and two 13-mm MG 131 machine guns in remotely-controlled lateral barbettes firing aft. Production was halted at the end of January 1942, after completion of 90 Me 210A-1s, a further 370 being in various stages of construction at that time. Despite the decision to stop production, development of the Me 210A continued and stability problems were resolved by lengthening the rear fuselage and markedly increasing its depth from a point immediately aft of the cockpit. Together with automatic wing slots, this modification was first flown on the Me 210 V17 on 14 March 1942. Further revision was to result in the more powerful Me 410, but, pending availability of this type, existing Me 210As and those that had attained an advanced stage in assembly when production was halted were fitted with a new rear fuselage, wing slots and parallel-bar-type wing air brakes, and placed in service, mostly with *Zerstörergruppen*. The following data relate to the definitive Me 210A-1. *Max speed, 350 mph (563 km/h) at 17,820 ft (5 430 m). Time to 13,125 ft (4 000 m), 7.5 min. Max range, 1,130 mls (1 820 km). Empty equipped weight, 15,586 lb (7 070 kg). Max loaded weight, 21,397 lb (9 705 kg). Span, 53 ft 7⅓ in (16,34 m). Length, 39 ft 9¼ in (12,12 m). Height, 14 ft 0½ in (4,28 m). Wing area, 389.66 sq ft (36,20 m²).*

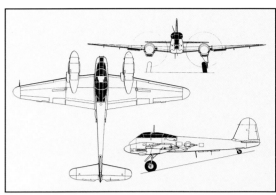

The Me 210A-1 (above and below), that depicted by the photo belonging to *Gruppenstab* of III/ZG 1.

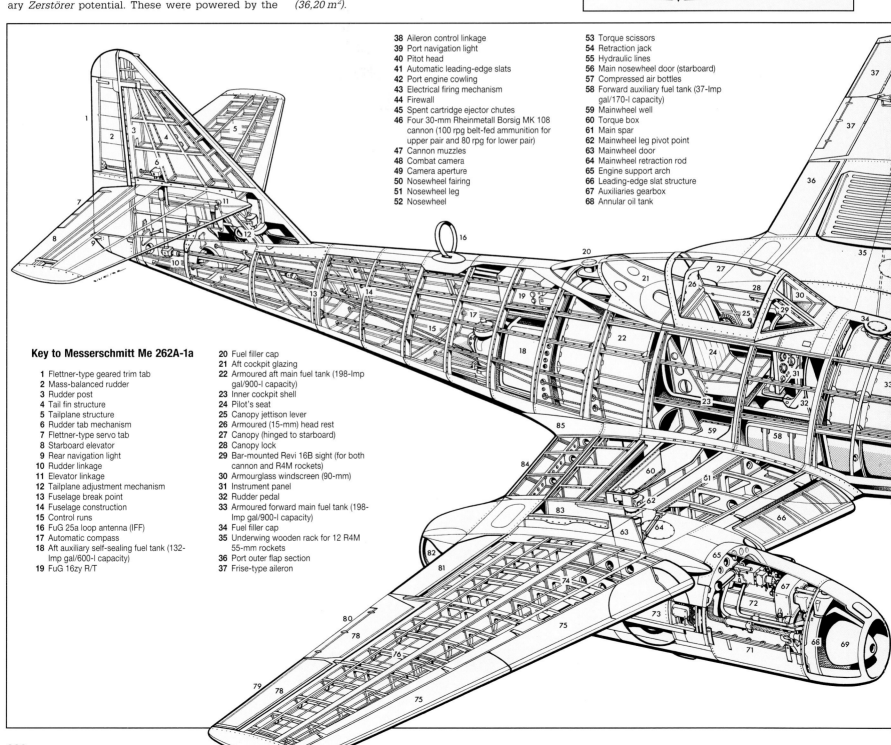

38 Aileron control linkage
39 Port navigation light
40 Pitot head
41 Automatic leading-edge slats
42 Port engine cowling
43 Electrical firing mechanism
44 Firewall
45 Spent cartridge ejector chutes
46 Four 30-mm Rheinmetall Borsig MK 108 cannon (100 rpg belt-fed ammunition for upper pair and 80 rpg for lower pair)
47 Cannon muzzles
48 Combat camera
49 Camera aperture
50 Nosewheel fairing
51 Nosewheel leg
52 Nosewheel

53 Torque scissors
54 Retraction jack
55 Hydraulic lines
56 Main nosewheel door (starboard)
57 Compressed air bottles
58 Forward auxiliary fuel tank (37-Imp gal/170-l capacity)
59 Mainwheel well
60 Torque box
61 Main spar
62 Mainwheel leg pivot point
63 Mainwheel door
64 Mainwheel retraction rod
65 Engine support arch
66 Leading-edge slat structure
67 Auxiliaries gearbox
68 Annular oil tank

Key to Messerschmitt Me 262A-1a

1 Flettner-type geared trim tab
2 Mass-balanced rudder
3 Rudder post
4 Tail fin structure
5 Tailplane structure
6 Rudder tab mechanism
7 Flettner-type servo tab
8 Starboard elevator
9 Rear navigation light
10 Rudder linkage
11 Elevator linkage
12 Tailplane adjustment mechanism
13 Fuselage break point
14 Fuselage construction
15 Control runs
16 FuG 25a loop antenna (IFF)
17 Automatic compass
18 Aft auxiliary self-sealing fuel tank (132-Imp gal/600-l capacity)
19 FuG 16zy R/T

20 Fuel filler cap
21 Aft cockpit glazing
22 Armoured aft main fuel tank (198-Imp gal/900-l capacity)
23 Inner cockpit shell
24 Pilot's seat
25 Canopy jettison lever
26 Armoured (15-mm) head rest
27 Canopy (hinged to starboard)
28 Canopy lock
29 Bar-mounted Revi 16B sight (for both cannon and R4M rockets)
30 Armourglass windscreen (90-mm)
31 Instrument panel
32 Rudder pedal
33 Armoured forward main fuel tank (198-Imp gal/900-l capacity)
34 Fuel filler cap
35 Underwing wooden rack for 12 R4M 55-mm rockets
36 Port outer flap section
37 Frise-type aileron

MESSERSCHMITT
Me 210C   Germany

Under the German-Hungarian Mutual Armament Programme, a factory was established at Horthyliget specifically for manufacture of the Me 210 for the *Magyar Királyi Légierö* (Royal Hungarian Air Force) or MKL. An advanced stage in production preparations had been reached when Me 210 production was halted in Germany. Rather than accept the delays that would have resulted from retooling for another type, the Hungarians elected to produce a more powerful version of the Me 210 embodying the improvements incorporated in the Me 210 V17. Designated Me 210C by the parent company, this was powered by two 1,475 hp DB 605B engines and two production versions were proposed, the Me 210Ca-1 combining the tasks of *Zerstörer* and dive bomber, and the Me 210C-1 long-range reconnaissance aircraft with secondary *Zerstörer* capability. The Me 210C possessed a similar armament to that of the Me 210A, and deliveries from the Duna Repülögépgyár commenced at the beginning of 1943, the intention being to supply two-thirds to the *Luftwaffe* and one-third to the MKL. When Hungarian production of the Me 210C was halted in March 1944, a total of 267 had been completed of which 108 had been transferred to the *Luftwaffe* with which they enjoyed a relatively brief operational career before being supplanted by Me 410s.

The Me 210Ca-1 (above and below) built by the Duna Repülögépgyár and seen here in service with Hungary was also supplied to the *Luftwaffe*.

Max speed, 359 mph (578 km/h) at 21,400 ft (6 520 m). Max range, 1,075 mls (1 730 km). Empty equipped weight, 16,055 lb (7 283 kg). Loaded weight, 21,482 lb (9 744 kg). Dimensions as for Me 210A.

MESSERSCHMITT
Me 262A   Germany

Although pre-empted by the Heinkel He 280 as the world's first turbojet-powered fighter to fly, the Me 262 was destined to become the first such fighter to attain service status. The first of five prototypes, the Me 262 V1, was flown on 18 April 1941, albeit with a Jumo 210G piston engine in lieu of its intended power plant owing to a delay in the availability of flight-cleared turbojets. An example was eventually to fly purely on turbojet power on 18 July 1942, when the third prototype, the Me 262 V3, flew with two Junkers Jumo 004A turbojets. Thirty pre-series Me 262A-0 airframes were laid down, most of these being assigned *Versuchs* numbers commencing with the Me 262 V6 flown on 17 October 1943. All but one (the V3) of the first eight *Versuchs* aircraft were lost during the flight test programme, these subsequently being replaced by additional test aircraft as the Me 262 V1 Ers (indicating *Ersatz* or Substitute) *et seq*. The first series production model, the Me 262A-1a single-seat interceptor, known semi-officially as the

Schwalbe (Swallow), was powered by two 1,980 lb st (900 kgp) Jumo 004B-1 (-2 or -3) turbojets. It carried an armament of four 30-mm MK 108 cannon, later augmented with 12 55-mm R4M rocket missiles on racks beneath each wing. The application of certain *Umrüst-Bausätze* (Factory Conversion Sets) resulted in the Me 262A-1a/U1 (revised armament comprising two MK 103s replacing two of the MK 108s and the addition of two 20-mm MG 151s), U2 (addition of FuG 125 *Hermine*) and U3 (armament replaced by two Rb 50/30 cameras). Adapted to carry one 1,102-lb (500-kg) or two 551-lb (250-kg) bombs for the fighter-bomber rôle as the Me 262A-2a, it was known as the *Sturmvogel* (Stormbird). The Me 262A-2a/U1 had gun armament restricted to two 30-mm MK 108s to provide accommodation for a TSA dive-bombing aid, and the U2 had provision for a second crew member to operate a gyro-stabilised Lotfe 7H bomb sight. The Me 262A-1b exchanged the standard Revi 16B reflector sight for an EZ 42 gyroscopic sight. The *Luftwaffe* accepted its first 28 production Me 262As in June 1944, the EKdo 262 trials unit flying its first intercept missions with the jet fighter

(Above and below) The Me 262A-1a, the first series model, known semi-officially as the *Schwalbe*.

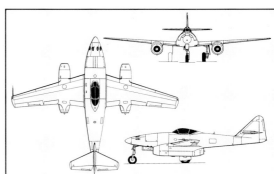

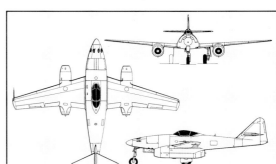

(Above, top) Me 262A-2a of KG 51, and (above) Me 262A-2a/U1 of *Erprobungskommando Schenck*.

(Below) An Me 262A-1a preserved in the "Planes of Fame" collection at the Air Museum, Chino, California.

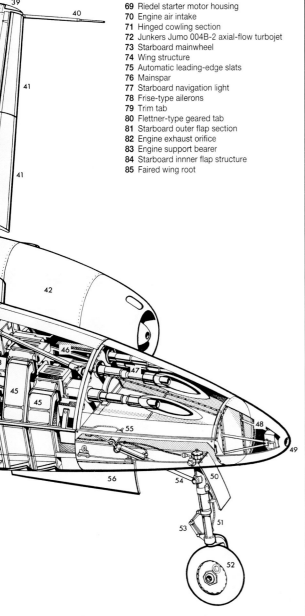

69 Riedel starter motor housing
70 Engine air intake
71 Hinged cowling section
72 Junkers Jumo 004B-2 axial-flow turbojet
73 Starboard mainwheel
74 Wing structure
75 Automatic leading-edge slats
76 Mainspar
77 Starboard navigation light
78 Frise-type ailerons
79 Trim tab
80 Flettner-type geared tab
81 Starboard outer flap section
82 Engine exhaust orifice
83 Engine support bearer
84 Starboard innner flap structure
85 Faired wing root

during the course of that month, and 315 aircraft had been accepted by the beginning of November, with a further 1,065 being delivered by the end of April 1945. The following data relate to the Me 262A-1a. *Max speed, 540 mph (870 km/h) at 19,685 ft (6 000 m). Initial climb, 3,937 ft/min (20 m/sec). Range (normal internal fuel), 652 mls (1 050 km) at 29,530 ft (9 000 m). Empty equipped weight, 9,742 lb (4 420 kg). Normal loaded weight, 14,101 lb (6 396 kg). Span, 41 ft 0½ in (12,51 m). Length, 34 ft 9½ in (10,60 m). Height, 11 ft 6¾ in (3,83 m). Wing area, 233.58 sq ft (21,70 m²).*

MESSERSCHMITT ME 262B Germany

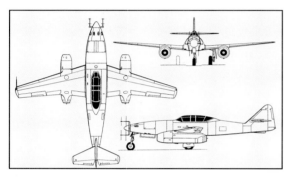

An Me 262B-1a/U1 (above) and the Me 262B-2a (below) of which only one prototype was allegedly flown.

Adaptation of the Me 262 for the nocturnal intercept rôle was initiated in the autumn of 1944, when the Me 262B-2 was proposed as a derivative of the Me 262B-1a tandem two-seat conversion trainer. This trainer, first flown in prototype form as the Me 262 S5 in April 1944, differed fundamentally from the Me 262A in omitting the rear main fuselage fuel tank in favour of a second cockpit for the instructor, all but 53 Imp gal (240 l) of the fuel loss being restored by suspending two tanks from the so-called *Wikingerschiff* pylons beneath the forward fuselage. It was intended that the Me 262B-2 fighter would differ from the B-1a trainer in having additional fuselage sections inserted fore and aft of the cockpits, increasing overall length by 3 ft 11¼ in (1,20 m) and permitting reinstatement of the rear main fuselage tank. On 5 October 1944, however, it was proposed that, as an interim measure, the Me 262B-1a trainer, itself, be utilised for the night fighting mission. This was to be effected by installing FuG 218 *Neptun V* intercept radar with its associated *Hirschgeweih* aerial array and FuG 350 *Naxos Z* for homing onto H2S emissions, the standard quartet of 30-mm MK 108 cannon being retained. The adaptation of trainers to Me 262B-1a/U1 night fighter configuration was undertaken by the DLH workshops at Berlin-Staaken, but there are records of only seven actually attaining service status (with 10./NJG 11). The definitive night fighting Me 262B-2a was proposed in two forms, one possessing similar radar to that of the B-1a/U1 and the other having centimetric FuG 240/1 *Berlin* N-1a. Armament was to be augmented by two additional 30-mm MK 108 cannon in a "*schräge Musik*" arrangement. The first FuG 218-equipped Me 262B-2a allegedly flew in late March 1945, but the FuG 240-equipped second aircraft was still in assembly at the time of Germany's collapse. The follow-

ing data relate to the Me 262B-2. *Max speed, 522 mph (840 km/h) at 19,685 ft (6 000 m). Empty equipped weight, 10,502 lb (4 764 kg). Normal loaded weight, 15,652 lb (7 100 kg). Span, 41 ft 0½ in (12,51 m). Length, 38 ft 6⅔ in (11,75 m). Height, 11 ft 6¾ in (3,83 m). Wing area, 233.58 sq ft (21,70 m²).*

MESSERSCHMITT ME 262C Germany

In the summer of 1944, considerable importance was assigned to rocket-boosted versions of the Me 262 under the *Heimatschützer* (Home Protector) programme, itself an outgrowth of the *Interzeptor* programme for fast-climbing mixed-power versions of the Messerschmitt fighter dating back to mid-1943. The initial version, the Me 262C-1a *Heimatschützer I*, was an adaptation of the Me 262A with a Walter R II-211/3 (HWK 509) bi-fuel rocket motor mounted in the rear fuselage, the forward and aft fuselage fuel tanks accommodating the *T-Stoff* and *C-Stoff* respectively.

(Below) The Me 262 V6 Ers which served as a prototype for the rocket-boosted Me 262C-1a.

The lower portion of the rudder was cut away to avoid damage from the rocket blast, a fuel jettison pipe was introduced under the rear fuselage and a pair of auxiliary mainwheels was added, these being jettisoned after take-off. A prototype of the Me 262C-1a, the Me 262 V6 Ers, was flown on 16 October 1944, but the rocket motor was not fired until 27 February 1945, and only three further flight tests were performed with the rocket motor operating. The Me 262C-2b *Heimatschützer II* differed essentially in having two BMW 003R units each consisting of a 1,760 lb st (800 kgp) BMW 003A turbojet and a 2,700 lb st (1 225 kgp) BMW 718 bi-fuel rocket motor. The prototype of this version, the Me 262 V12 Ers, was flown on 8 January 1945 on turbojet power alone, its sole test flight on rocket power taking place on the following 26 March. A third version, the Me 262C-3 *Heimatschützer IV* with a ventrally-mounted jettisonable R II-211 rocket motor and externally-mounted *T-Stoff* tanks, was abandoned before completion. The following data apply to the Me 262C-1a which it was proposed to equip with six 30-mm MK 108 cannon. *Max speed, 577 mph (928 km/h) at 19,685 ft (6 000 m). Time to 38,400 ft (11 705 m) from standing start, 4.5 min. Empty equipped weight, 12,522 lb (5 680 kg). Loaded weight, 18,210 lb (8 260 kg). Dimensions as for Me 262A.*

MESSERSCHMITT ME 410 Germany

Evolved from the Me 210, production of which had been ignominiously cancelled in January 1942, and barely distinguishable externally from its predecessor, the Me 410, known unofficially as the *Hornisse* (Hornet), was intended as a multi-rôle aircraft. Embodying the lengthened and deepened rear fuselage, and automatic wing slots finally applied to the Me 210 to resolve its

An Me 410A-2 (below) of 9.*Staffel* of ZG 76 operating in northern Italy during 1944.

stability problems and coupling these changes with sweptback outboard wing panels and revised camber-changing flaps, radiator flaps and ailerons, the Me 410 V1 was flown in the autumn of 1942. The DB 601F engines were supplanted by DB 603A engines rated at 1,750 hp for take-off, and the first production aircraft were accepted by the *Luftwaffe* in January 1943. These were of the Me 410A-1 *Schnellbomber* and Me 410A-2 *Zerstörer* sub-types, which, fundamentally similar, carried a fixed forward-firing armament of two 20-mm MG 151 cannon and two 7,9-mm MG 17 machine guns, plus two barbette-mounted remotely-controlled aft-firing 13-mm MG 131 machine guns. Each featured an internal weapons bay, that of the A-1 being supplemented by tandem bomb carriers beneath each wing root. Despite its intended *Schnellbomber* rôle, the A-1 was fitted with a *Waffenbehälter* (Weapon Container) in the weapons bay containing two 20-mm MG 151 cannon, with which it served in the *Zerstörer* rôle as the Me 410A-1/U2. Specifically intended for use against USAAF day bomber formations, the Me 410A-2/U4 was fitted with a 50-mm BK 5 cannon. From April 1944, the A-series gave place to the Me 410B on the assembly lines, this having DB 603G engines each rated at 1,900 hp for take-off. The Me 410B-1 and B-2 were respectively similar in other respects to the A-1 and A-2. The Me 410B-2/U4 with the BK 5 cannon had a pair of 30-mm MK 103 cannon, however, in place of the standard forward-firing combination of cannon and machine guns. Various changes in armament resulted from application of *Rüstsätze* (Field Conversions Sets) such as (R2) two 30-mm MK 103 or (R5) four 20-mm MG 151 cannon which could replace the *Waffenbehälter*, or (R4) which could supplement it and consisted of two 20-mm MG 151s in a *Waffentropfen* (Weapon Drop). On 8 May 1944, an order was issued that all Me 410 bombers were to be converted to A-1/U2 and B-1/U2 standards for the *Zerstörer* multi-rôle mission. Production of the Me 410 totalled 1,160 aircraft (all versions) when finally phased out in September 1944. The following data relate to the Me 410B-2 *Zerstörer. Max speed, 391 mph (630 km/h) at 26,575 ft (8 100 m). Endurance, 2.4 hrs. Empty equipped weight, 17,598 lb (7 982 kg). Normal loaded weight, 24,772 lb (11 236 kg). Span, 53 ft 7¾ in (16,35 m). Length, 40 ft 11½ in (12,48 m). Height, 14 ft 0½ in (4,28 m). Wing area, 389.69 sq ft (36,20 m²).*

(Above and below) The Me 410B-2/U2/R4 with paired 20-mm cannon in a so-called *Waffentropfen*.

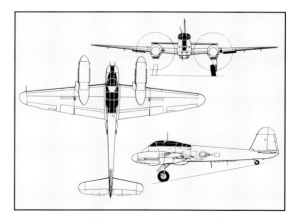

MESSERSCHMITT ME 309 Germany

During the latter part of 1940, Messerschmitt initiated work on what was then seen as an advance-of-the-art single-seat fighter, the Me 309. This embodied such in-

(Above) The Me 309 V1, which entered flight test in July 1942 as a potential successor to the Bf 109.

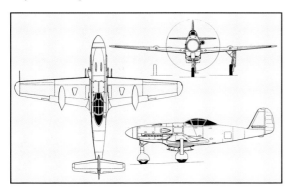

An artist's impression of the Me 309 V3 (below) and general arrangement drawing (above) of the Me 309 V4.

novations as cabin pressurisation, a tricycle undercarriage and variable radiator geometry. Relatively low priority was attached to the project as the *Oberbefehlshaber der Luftwaffe* did not consider a successor to the Bf 109 to be an urgent requirement. Various Bf 109F test-bed airframes were assigned to the evaluation of features of the proposed fighter, detail design of which was completed at the end of 1941. The first prototype, the Me 309 V1, was flown on 18 July 1942, and during the following November, the vertical tail surfaces were twice redesigned and enlarged. The Me 309 V2 was flown on 29 November 1942, but the nosewheel leg collapsed during the landing and the aircraft was written off. Whereas the V1 was powered by a DB 603A-1 engine, the V2 had a 1,475 hp DB 605B, as did the Me 309 V3 flown in March 1943. By this time, the RLM had elected to restrict the programme to four *Versuchs* aircraft, the last of which, the Me 309 V4 flown in July 1943, carried the armament proposed for the *schwerer Jäger* version. This consisted of two 30-mm MK 108 and two 20-mm MG 151 cannon, and four MG 131 13-mm machine guns, the MK 108s being partly enclosed by streamlined bodies on the upper wing surfaces extending aft of the trailing edges. The following data relate to the Me 309 V4. *Max speed, 360 mph (580 km/h) at 7,220 ft (2 200 m). Time to 13,125 ft (4 000 m), 5.2 min. Range, 683 mls (1 100 km). Max loaded weight, 10,736 lb (4 870 kg). Span, 36 ft 1 in (11,00 m). Length, 32 ft 7 in (9,93 m). Height, 11 ft 3 in (3,43 m). Wing area, 177.39 sq ft (16,50 m²).*

MESSERSCHMITT
ME 163B   Germany

Evolved from the Me 163A rocket-propulsion research aircraft designed by Dr Alexander M Lippisch, the Me 163B, which retained no more than the basic config-

uration of its predecessor, was conceived as a single-seat target defence fighter. Of radical design, the Me 163B featured a constant 22.3 deg of wing sweepback at quarter chord, lacked horizontal tail surfaces and utilised a jettisonable twin-wheel dolly for take-off and a retractable skid for landing. Six prototypes and 70 pre-series aircraft were ordered all being assigned *Versuchs* numbers. The first prototype, the Me 163B V1, was completed in April 1942, but the first Walter HWK R II-211 rocket motor intended to power the fighter was delayed, the first powered flight (Me 163B V2) taking place on 23 June 1943. The bi-fuel rocket motor (which became the HWK 509A-1 in production form) possessed a max thrust of 3,750 lb (1 700 kg) delivered for 7.5 min.

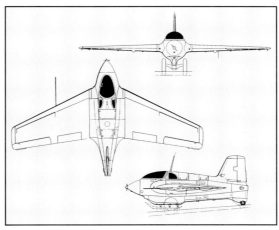

The Me 163B-1a (above and below), that illustrated by the photo belonging to 2./JG 400 at Brandis.

The pre-series aircraft, the Me 163Ba-1, carried an armament of two 20-mm MG 151 cannon whereas the series Me 163B-1a had two 30-mm MK 108 cannon. The first production aircraft, which had been unofficially named *Komet*, was accepted by the *Luftwaffe* in May 1944, and a total of 279 was delivered. The service record of the Me 163B was to prove dismal, 80 per cent of attrition resulting from take-off or landing accidents and 15 per cent being attributable to fire in the air or loss of control in a dive. A proposed development of the basic design was the Me 163C. This was to have dif-

fered from the Me 163B primarily in having an HWK 509C rocket motor with an auxiliary cruise chamber with which powered endurance was to have been increased to 19 min. Armament was two MK 103 and two MK 108 cannon, the fuselage was lengthened by 35.4 in (90 cm) and an all-round vision canopy was provided. Construction of four Me 163C prototypes began in January 1943, with partial testing scheduled to commence April 1944, full-scale testing in August 1944, and completion of testing by February 1945. In the event, no example of the Me 163C was completed and flown. The following data relate to the Me 163B-1a. *Max speed, 593 mph (955 km/h) between 9,850 and 29,500 ft (3 000 and 9 000 m). Initial climb, 15,950 ft/min (81 m/sec). Normal radius of action, 22 mls (35,5 km). Empty equipped weight, 4,206 lb (1 908 kg). Loaded weight, 9,502 lb (4 310 kg). Span, 30 ft 7⅓ in (9,33 m). Length, 19 ft 2⅓ in (5,85 m). Height (on dolly), 9 ft 0⅔ in (2,76 m). Wing area, 199.13 sq ft (18,50 m²).*

A standard Me 163B-1a (below) at Bad Zwischenahn with *Erprobungskommando* 16 in the autumn of 1944.

MESSERSCHMITT ME 263   Germany

In the late summer of 1944, the Junkers-Werke was requested to develop a successor to the Me 163B under the cover name *Flunder* (Flounder) and to which the designation Ju 248 was assigned. While configurationally similar to the Me 163B in having a modestly swept-back wing and lacking horizontal tail surfaces, the Junkers fighter was fundamentally a new design. The combination of jettisonable take-off dolly and landing skid featured by the Me 163B was discarded in favour of a conventional retractable tricycle undercarriage (which was tested by the Me 163B V18), fuel capacity was increased and an HWK 509C rocket motor (similar to that proposed for the Me 163C) was adopted. This bi-fuel power plant comprised a main chamber with a thrust of 4,410 lb (2 000 kg) and an auxiliary chamber providing a further 882 lb (400 kg). The wooden wings were essentially similar to those of the Me 163B and the

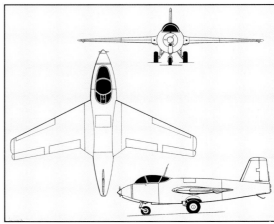

(Above and below) The Me 263 V1, which was first flown in March 1945 with ballast in place of engine.

dural fuselage incorporated a pressure cabin, armament comprising two 30-mm MK 108 cannon. The Waggonfabrik Dessau built the jigs, mock-up inspection took place on 15 December 1944 at Raguhn and in that month the designation of the fighter was changed by the RLM from Ju 248 to Me 263 despite the fact that all design and production responsibility remained invested in the Junkers organisation. Meanwhile work began on three prototypes which, to accelerate the programme, had Me 163B wings modified and rebuilt by Fa Puklitsch at Zeitz, and similar controls and instrumentation. The *Oberkommando der Luftwaffe* (OKL) vacillated in its attitude towards the Me 263 *née* Ju 248. On 13 January 1945, the OKL report pressed strongly for the large-scale production of the new fighter, and, of two OKL reports dated 29 January, one demanded termination of Me 263 development and the other replacement of the Me 163B by the Me 263 in service with *Jagdgeschwader* 400 as rapidly as possible. The attachment points of the HWK 509C rocket motors did not match the drawings, necessitating lengthening of the fuselages of the first two prototypes, the Me 263 V1 and V2, after construction. Initial flight testing began in March 1945, the power plant of the V1 being replaced by ballast, the undercarriage being fixed in extended configuration and the aircraft being towed into the air for gliding trials. The V2 and V3 were also apparently tested in gliding flight, but there is no evidence of the HWK 509C having been lit in flight. One prototype was acquired by the Soviet Union and played a rôle in the development of the MiG I-270 (which see). The following data are manufacturer's estimates. *Max speed, 547 mph (880 km/h) at 10,000-36,090 ft (3 050-11 000 m). Max climb, 14,765 ft/min (75 m/sec). Endurance (powered), 14.75 min at 36,090 ft (11 000 m). Empty weight, 4,233 lb (1 920 kg). Loaded weight, 11,684 lb (5 300 kg). Span, 31 ft 2 in (9,50 m). Length, 25 ft 8¼ in (7,83 m). Height, 10 ft 4¾ in (3,17 m). Wing area, 191.6 sq ft (17,80 m²).*

MESSERSCHMITT
Me 209 II   Germany

Despite its designation, the Me 209 II bore no relationship to the original Me 209 (which see) other than a common design source. Like its similarly-designated predecessor, the Me 209 II was promoted as a production successor to the Bf 109, and it was originally envisaged that there would be some 65 per cent airframe commonality between the new fighter and the Bf 109G. In the event, when the first prototype, the Me 209 V5, was flown on 3 November 1943, it was to possess little commonality with the earlier fighter. Powered initially by a Daimler-Benz DB 603A engine, it was re-engined at an early flight test stage with a DB 603G rated at 1,900 hp for take-off and with which it resumed flight test on 12 November 1943. At the request of the *Technische Amt*, a second prototype, the Me 209 V6, was completed with a 1,750 hp Junkers Jumo 213E engine, and this, flown in April 1944, carried full armament comprising one engine-mounted 30-mm cannon and two 20-mm cannon. Two production versions were pro-

The Me 209 V5 (below) bore no relationship to the original Me 209 despite its designation.

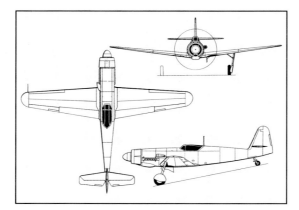

A general arrangement drawing of the Me 209A-1.

posed, the DB 603-engined Me 209A-1 and the Jumo 213E-engined Me 209A-2. Further development included the Me 209H high-altitude fighter with an enlarged wing of 235.73 sq ft (21,90 m²), and a DB 603G-engined prototype of this version, the Me 209H V1, was eventually completed in June 1944, by which time the entire Me 209 programme had been *officially* abandoned. The following data relate to the Me 209 V5. *Max speed, 416 mph (670 km/h) at 19,685 ft (6 000 m), 463 mph (745 km/h) at 24,200 ft (7 375 m). Empty equipped weight, 7,360 lb (3 338 kg). Loaded weight, 9,006 lb (4 085 kg). Span, 35 ft 11 in (10,95 m). Length, 31 ft 11½ in (9,74 m). Height, 13 ft 1½ in (4,00 m). Wing area, 184.6 sq ft (17,15 m²).*

M.F.9   Norway

The last M.F.9 built was fitted with redesigned tail surfaces and ventral fin as the M.F.9C (above).

Known unofficially as the *Høverjager*, the M.F.9 single-seat float seaplane fighter was designed by Johan Høver and built by the *Marinens Flyvebåtfabrikk* (Navy Flying Boat Factory) at Horten. The prototype M.F.9 was first flown on 4 June 1925, and was an unequal-span unstaggered single-bay biplane of wooden construction powered by a 300 hp Hispano-Suiza Type 42 eight-cylinder water-cooled engine with strut-mounted Lamblin radiators. Armament comprised one synchronised 7,62-mm Colt machine gun. Three additional M.F.9s were built for evaluation by *Marinens Flyvevæsen* and flown in May 1926, by which time the prototype had established a new European altitude record of 28,215 ft (8 600 m). To correct the prototype's unacceptable spinning characteristics, these and the next

Key to Messerschmitt Me 163B-1a

1 Generator drive propeller
2 Generator
3 Compressed air bottle
4 Battery and electronics packs
5 Cockpit ventilation intake
6 Solid armour (15-mm) nose cone

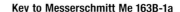

four M.F.9s, completed during July and August 1928, were fitted with a larger rudder, being designated M.F.9B in modified form. As the original prototype was lost in an accident, a replacement was built and flown in June 1930, six further M.F.9s being built during the spring and summer of 1932 (two of these also being replacements for aircraft lost as a result of accidents). The last production aircraft was fitted with redesigned tail surfaces, the tailplane being raised and strut-braced and a ventral fin being added. One of the aircraft of the final batch was experimentally fitted with a licence-built 575 hp Armstrong Siddeley Panther II air-cooled radial. The extreme control sensitivity of the M.F.9 and its spinning proclivity rendered this fighter unpopular, but it remained in service until 1936. *Max speed,*

(Below) The M.F.9 single-seat fighter floatplane.

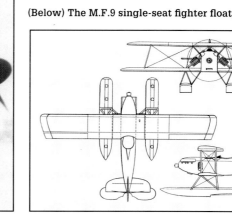

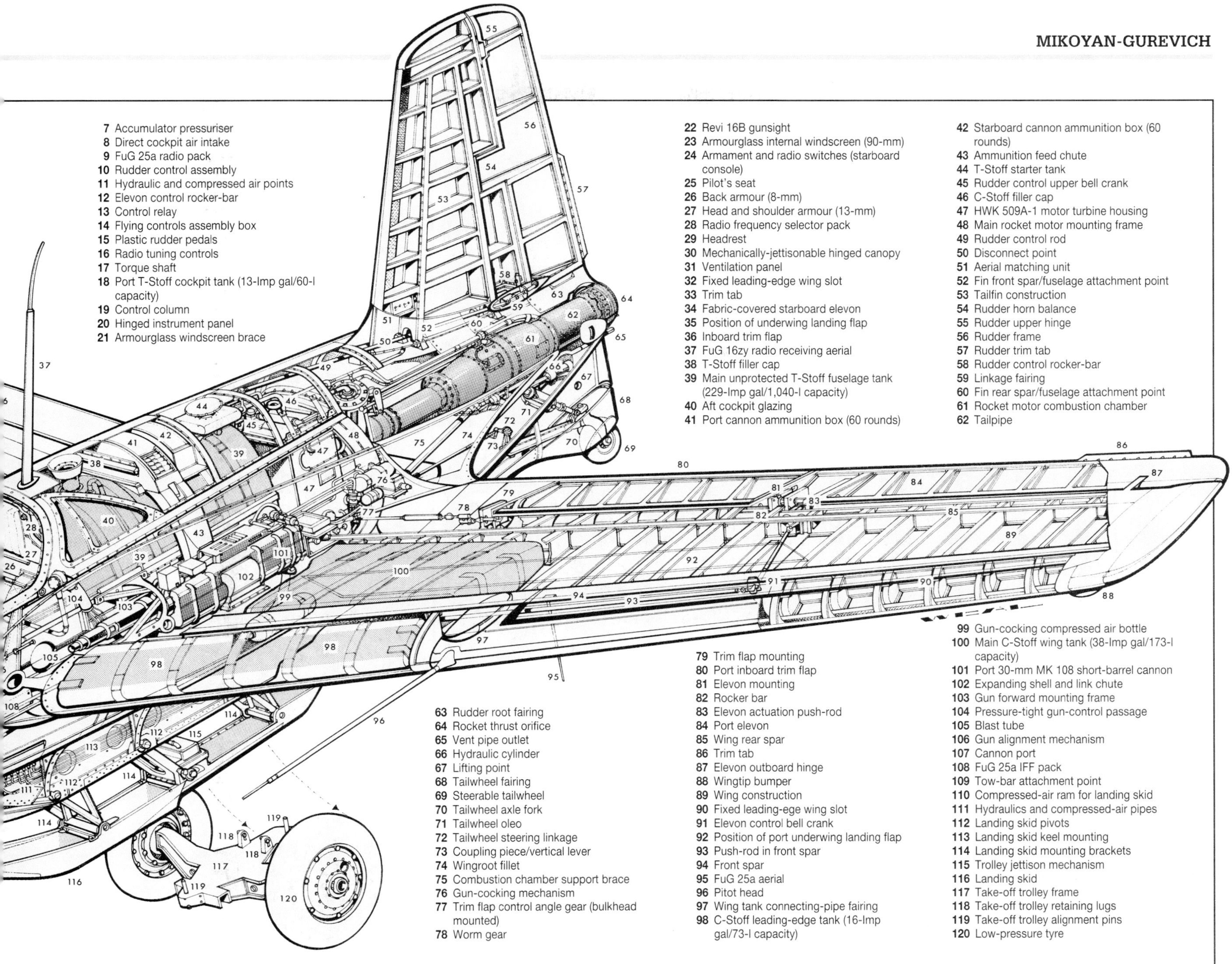

7 Accumulator pressuriser
8 Direct cockpit air intake
9 FuG 25a radio pack
10 Rudder control assembly
11 Hydraulic and compressed air points
12 Elevon control rocker-bar
13 Control relay
14 Flying controls assembly box
15 Plastic rudder pedals
16 Radio tuning controls
17 Torque shaft
18 Port T-Stoff cockpit tank (13-Imp gal/60-l capacity)
19 Control column
20 Hinged instrument panel
21 Armourglass windscreen brace
22 Revi 16B gunsight
23 Armourglass internal windscreen (90-mm)
24 Armament and radio switches (starboard console)
25 Pilot's seat
26 Back armour (8-mm)
27 Head and shoulder armour (13-mm)
28 Radio frequency selector pack
29 Headrest
30 Mechanically-jettisonable hinged canopy
31 Ventilation panel
32 Fixed leading-edge wing slot
33 Trim tab
34 Fabric-covered starboard elevon
35 Position of underwing landing flap
36 Inboard trim flap
37 FuG 16zy radio receiving aerial
38 T-Stoff filler cap
39 Main unprotected T-Stoff fuselage tank (229-Imp gal/1,040-l capacity)
40 Aft cockpit glazing
41 Port cannon ammunition box (60 rounds)
42 Starboard cannon ammunition box (60 rounds)
43 Ammunition feed chute
44 T-Stoff starter tank
45 Rudder control upper bell crank
46 C-Stoff filler cap
47 HWK 509A-1 motor turbine housing
48 Main rocket motor mounting frame
49 Rudder control rod
50 Disconnect point
51 Aerial matching unit
52 Fin front spar/fuselage attachment point
53 Tailfin construction
54 Rudder horn balance
55 Rudder upper hinge
56 Rudder frame
57 Rudder trim tab
58 Rudder control rocker-bar
59 Linkage fairing
60 Fin rear spar/fuselage attachment point
61 Rocket motor combustion chamber
62 Tailpipe
63 Rudder root fairing
64 Rocket thrust orifice
65 Vent pipe outlet
66 Hydraulic cylinder
67 Lifting point
68 Tailwheel fairing
69 Steerable tailwheel
70 Tailwheel axle fork
71 Tailwheel oleo
72 Tailwheel steering linkage
73 Coupling piece/vertical lever
74 Wingroot fillet
75 Combustion chamber support brace
76 Gun-cocking mechanism
77 Trim flap control angle gear (bulkhead mounted)
78 Worm gear
79 Trim flap mounting
80 Port inboard trim flap
81 Elevon mounting
82 Rocker bar
83 Elevon actuation push-rod
84 Port elevon
85 Wing rear spar
86 Trim tab
87 Elevon outboard hinge
88 Wingtip bumper
89 Wing construction
90 Fixed leading-ege wing slot
91 Elevon control bell crank
92 Position of port underwing landing flap
93 Push-rod in front spar
94 Front spar
95 FuG 25a aerial
96 Pitot head
97 Wing tank connecting-pipe fairing
98 C-Stoff leading-edge tank (16-Imp gal/73-l capacity)
99 Gun-cocking compressed air bottle
100 Main C-Stoff wing tank (38-Imp gal/173-l capacity)
101 Port 30-mm MK 108 short-barrel cannon
102 Expanding shell and link chute
103 Gun forward mounting frame
104 Pressure-tight gun-control passage
105 Blast tube
106 Gun alignment mechanism
107 Cannon port
108 FuG 25a IFF pack
109 Tow-bar attachment point
110 Compressed-air ram for landing skid
111 Hydraulics and compressed-air pipes
112 Landing skid pivots
113 Landing skid keel mounting
114 Landing skid mounting brackets
115 Trolley jettison mechanism
116 Landing skid
117 Take-off trolley frame
118 Take-off trolley retaining lugs
119 Take-off trolley alignment pins
120 Low-pressure tyre

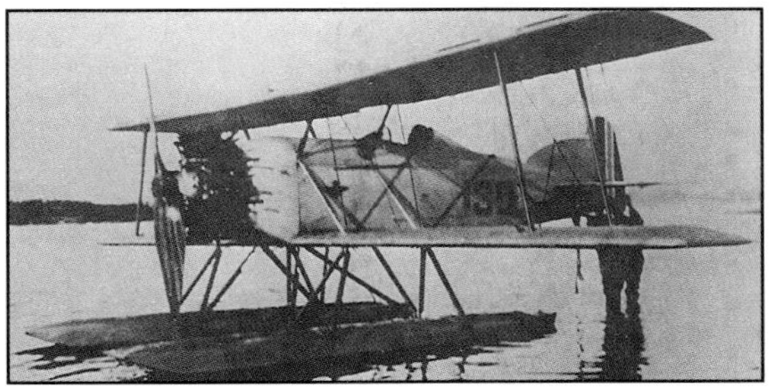

One of the final batch of M.F.9s was fitted with a Panther II air-cooled radial as seen above.

130 mph (210 km/h). Time to 13,125 ft (4 000 m), 17 min. Range, 311 mls (500 km). Empty weight, 1,896 lb (860 kg). Loaded weight, 2,712 lb (1 230 kg). Span, 34 ft 3⅖ in (10,45 m). Length, 25 ft 5⁹⁄₁₀ in (7,77 m). Height, 10 ft 2⅞ in (3,12 m). Wing area, 301.4 sq ft (28,00 m²).

MIKOYAN-GUREVICH MIG-1 USSR

The first design to achieve production status of an OKB (Experimental Construction Bureau) headed by Artem I Mikoyan and Mikhail Y Gurevich (the acronym "MiG" being derived from the two names), the MiG-1 was conceived as a high-altitude interceptor under the OKB's *Izdeliya* (Product) designation Kh. Also assigned the initial military designation I-200, the first of three prototypes was flown on 5 April 1940, attaining 403 mph (648,5 km/h) at 22,640 ft (6 900 m) on the following 24 May. Second and third prototypes flew on 9 May and 6 June 1940 respectively, factory and state testing being performed in parallel, with the former completed on 25 August and the latter on 12 September 1940. The MiG-1 was powered by a 1,350 hp Mikulin AM-35A and carried an armament of one 12,7-mm UBS and two 7,62-mm ShKAS guns. Manoeuvrability and handling were considered inadequate, longitudinal stability and control responses were poor, and a programme of peripheral redesign paralleled manufacture of an initial batch of 100 aircraft, the last of which was completed in December 1940. The first eight MiG-1s had non-jettisonable side-hinged cockpit canopies, the remainder having jettisonable aft-sliding canopies. The first MiG-1 was delivered to a VVS regiment in April 1941, by which time this fighter had been supplanted in production by the MiG-3. *Max speed, 302 mph (486 km/h) at sea level, 390 mph (628 km/h) at 23,620 ft (7 200 m). Time to 16,405 ft (5 000 m), 5.9 min. Range (10% reserve), 360 mls (580 km) at 342 mph (550 km/h). Empty weight, 5,736 lb (2 602 kg). Loaded weight, 6,832 lb (3 099 kg), Span, 33 ft 5½ in (10,20 m). Length, 26 ft 9¼ in (8,16 m). Height, 8 ft 7⅛ in (2,62 m). Wing area, 187.73 sq ft (17,44 m²).*

The first prototype of the MiG-1 (below) which entered flight test in April 1940 without armament.

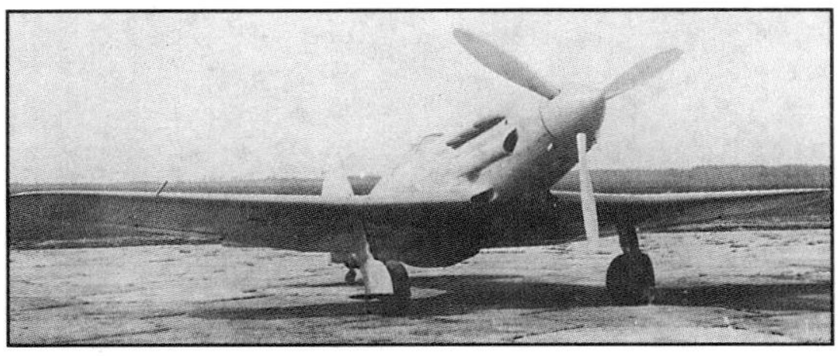

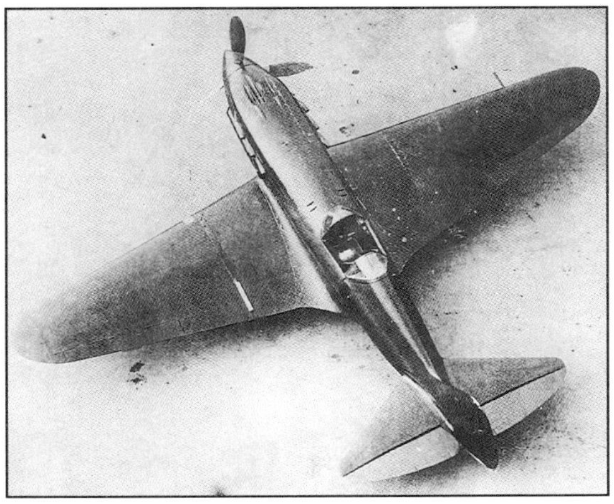

One of the first eight series MiG-1s (above) with side-hinged cockpit canopy discarded.

MIKOYAN-GUREVICH MIG-3 USSR

Exigencies of the times precluding fundamental redesign of the MiG-1 to eradicate the fighter's less acceptable characteristics, a series of what were, in effect,

MiG-3 of (above, top) 16 GvIAP flown by Aleksandr Pokryshkin, 1942, and (immediately above) of 6 IAK, Moscow Air Defence Zone, flown by A V Shlopov, 1942.

palliatives were applied to the basic design to result in the MiG-3. Power plant and (initially) armament remained unchanged, but some structural simplification and strengthening was introduced. The engine was moved forward 4 in (10 cm); dihedral of the outer wing panels was increased by one degree; a 55-Imp gal (250-1) supplementary fuel tank was introduced beneath the pilot's seat; the aft fuselage decking was cut down; the radiator bath fairing was enlarged and extended forward; the supercharger intakes were revised; 9-mm seat armour was provided, together with radio, and four wing points were introduced for a maximum external load of 485 lb (220 kg). The first MiG-3 left the factory in December 1940, 11 being completed by the end of the month; 140 were produced in January 1941, and, by June, production had peaked at 25 aircraft

A MiG-3 (above) of the 7 IAP on the Leningrad Front, July 1941, with canopy and radio mast discarded.

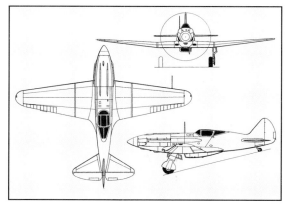

(Above and below) The standard series MiG-3, that shown by the photo being on the Leningrad Front, 1941.

every 24 hours. The first MiG-3 was delivered to a VVS regiment in April 1941 – simultaneously with the MiG-1 – and production continued until 23 December 1941 with approximately 3,120 built, but 50 more were completed from component stocks in the early summer of 1942. Some MiG-3s had a supplementary pair of 12,7-mm BK machine guns under the wings – raising take-off weight to 7,738 lb (3 510 kg) – and others were fitted with two UBK guns of similar calibre *in* the wings. Tests were also performed with two fuselage-mounted 20-mm ShVAK cannon. *Max speed, 314 mph (505 km/h) at sea level, 398 mph (640 km/h) at 25,590 ft (7 800 m). Range, 510 mls (820 km) at 342 mph (550 km/h). Empty weight, 5,950 lb (2 699 kg). Loaded weight, 7,385 lb (3 350 kg). Span, 33 ft 5½ in (10,20 m). Length, 27 ft 0⅞ in (8,25 m). Height, 8 ft 8⅓ in (2,65 m). Wing area, 187.73 sq ft (17,44 m²).*

MIKOYAN-GUREVICH DIS USSR

Assigned the *Izdeliya* (Product) designation T, the design of a DIS (*Dalniy istrebitel soprovozhdenya*), or long-range escort fighter, began in 1940, competing proposals being the Grushin Gr-1, Polikarpov TIS and Tairov Ta-3. The MiG DIS-200 was designed initially for Charomskii M-30 or M-40 engines, but the non-availability of these led to installation of two 1,400 hp Mikulin AM-37 12-cylinder Vee-type engines in the first prototype, which had an armament of two 12,7-mm BS and four 7,62-mm ShKAS machine guns, plus one 23-mm VYa cannon in a detachable ventral pod which could be replaced by a single 2,205-lb (1 000-kg) bomb or a torpedo. Ground tests began on 15 May 1941, and the first flight took place before the end of the month. Series production of the DIS (as the MiG-5) was ordered, but cancelled shortly afterwards owing to lack of manufacturing capacity. Nonetheless, a second prototype, also referred to as the DIS-200, but assigned the *Izdeliya* designation IT, was flown in January 1942 with 1,700 hp Shvetsov M-82F 14-cylinder radials. This had an armament of four 7,62-mm ShKAS and two 12,7-mm BS machine guns and two 23-mm VYa cannon, a maximum

(Above) The AM-37-powered first prototype DIS-200 single-seat long-range escort fighter.

speed of 375 mph (604 km/h) at 16,405 ft (5 000 m), attaining that altitude within 6.3 min and having a range of 1,553 miles (2 500 km). The primary VVS requirement at this stage of the conflict was short-range tactical aircraft, and further DIS development was discontinued. The following data relate to the first prototype. *Max speed, 379 mph (610 km/h) at 22,310 ft (6 800 m). Time to 16,405 ft (5 000 m), 5.5 min. Range, 1,417 mls (2 280 km). Empty weight, 13,536 lb (6 140 kg). Loaded weight, 17,769 lb (8 060 kg). Span, 49 ft 6½ in (15,10 m). Length, 35 ft 8 in (10,87 m). Height (tail up), 11 ft 1⅞ in (3,40 m). Wing area, 418.73 sq ft (38,90 m²).*

The M-82F-powered second prototype DIS-200 (above) and the AM-37-powered first prototype (below).

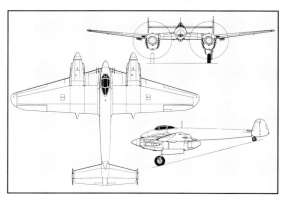

MIKOYAN-GUREVICH I-210 (IKH) USSR

Late in 1941, as series production of the MiG-3 phased out following the decision to discontinue manufacture of its AM-35A engine (priority having been assigned to the AM-38 for the Il-2 *shturmovik*), an attempt was made to adapt the basic airframe to take the 1,700 hp Shvetsov M-82A 14-cylinder air-cooled radial. Assigned the *Izdeliya* designation IKh by the OKB and the provisional official designation I-210, and also referred to unofficially as the MiG-3M-82, the first of five airframes adapted to take the new engine was flown in December 1941. The M-82A weighed only 44 lb (20 kg) more than the AM-35A that it supplanted, but was 15 in (38 cm) wider, a new forward fuselage being necessary to cater for the cross section translation from the circular cowling to the oval centre fuselage. The armament consisted of three 12,7-mm guns. Plans were prepared to initiate IKh production as the MiG-9, but flight test revealed a serious drag problem, severe tail vibration and poor control characteristics. Despite the disappointing results of factory testing, the first aircraft was fitted with yet two more 7,62-mm guns and sent to the Kalinin Front. The TsAGI, meanwhile, conducted full-scale wind tunnel testing with one of the IKh aircraft, re-

(Below) The I-210 M-82A-engined MiG-3 derivative.

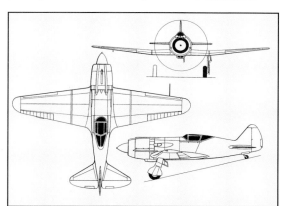

Although confined to five examples, the I-210 (above) was evaluated on the Kalinin Front.

sulting in development of the I-211 (which see). *Max speed, 295 mph (475 km/h) at sea level, 351 mph (565 km/h) at 20,175 ft (6 150 m). Time to 16,405 ft (5 000 m), 6.7 min. Range, 665 mls (1 070 km). Empty weight, 5,996 lb (2 720 kg). Loaded weight, 7,456 lb (3 382 kg). Span, 33 ft 5½ in (10,20 m). Length, 26 ft 6 in (8,08 m). Wing area, 187.73 sq ft (17,44 m²).*

MIKOYAN-GUREVICH I-211(YE)   USSR

After completion by the TsAGI of full-scale wind tunnel testing of the I-210 alias IKh, the OKB redesigned the junction between the engine cowling and the fuselage. It moved the pilot's cockpit aft, enlarged the vertical tail surfaces, redesigned the engine cowling and repositioned the oil cooler intakes in the wing roots. The undercarriage was redesigned, power was provided by a Shvetsov M-82F radial engine of 1,700 hp and armament was restricted to a pair of wing-mounted 20-mm ShVAK cannon. Only the outer wing panels of the MiG-3 remained and slots were applied to these. This thoroughgoing redesign of the I-210 was referred to as the I-211, or Ye, a pre-series batch of 10 aircraft being laid down of which the first flew in August 1942. Factory testing was completed within one month, the results being highly successful, but no manufacturing capacity was available for production, and all aerodynamic data and information on the slots were passed to the Lavochkin OKB as a result of a ministerial request. *Max speed, 416 mph (670 km/h) at 22,965 ft (7 000 m). Time to 16,405 ft (5 000 m), 4.0 min. Range, 708 mls (1 140 km). Empty weight, 5,573 lb (2 528 kg). Loaded weight, 6,834 lb (3 100 kg). Span, 33 ft 5½ in (10,20 m). Length, 26 ft 1 in (7,95 m). Height (tail up), 11 ft 10⅞ in (3,63 m). Wing area, 187.73 sq ft. (17,44 m²).*

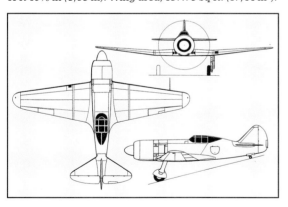

(Above and below) The I-211 resulted from TsAGI wind tunnel testing of the unsuccessful I-210.

MIKOYAN-GUREVICH I-230 (MIG-3U)   USSR

With the primary objective of improving the aerodynamics of the basic MiG-3 design, the OKB began work late in 1941 on an enhanced version of the fighter

The second prototype I-230 (above) which had a larger wing than the initial prototype.

to which it gave the *Izdeliya* designation of D. Known officially as the I-230, and later as the MiG-3U – the suffix letter signifying *ulushchenyi* (improved) – the new fighter was first flown in August 1942. Whereas the fuselage of the MiG-3 was primarily of steel tube with duralumin skinning, that of the I-230 was almost entirely of wood owing to the contemporary metal shortages. By comparison with the MiG-3, the fuselage was lengthened by 14.57 in (37 cm), but the Mikulin AM-35A engine was retained and the wing of the first prototype was unchanged, armament consisting of two 20-mm SP-20 (ShVAK) cannon mounted above the engine. The second prototype differed in having a larger wing of 193.76 sq ft (18,00 m²) area and spanning 36 ft 1 in (11,00 m). Performance proved good during factory and state trials, but it was not possible to reinstate production of the AM-35A and production of the I-230 was therefore restricted to a pre-series of five aircraft which were assigned to a Guards Regiment (1 GvIAP) on the Kalinin front for service evaluation. *Max speed, 348 mph (560 km/h) at sea level, 410 mph (660 km/h) at 19,685 ft (6 000 m). Time to 16,405 ft (5 000 m), 6.2 min. Range, 839 mls (1 350 km). Empty weight, 5,758 lb (2 612 kg). Loaded weight, 7,242 lb (3 285 kg). Span, 33 ft 5½ in (10,20 m). Length, 28 ft 3⅓ in (8,62 m). Wing area, 187.73 sq ft (17,44 m²).*

The first prototype of the I-230 (below) was an aerodynamically improved derivative of the MiG-3.

MIKOYAN-GUREVICH I-231   USSR

A third I-230 airframe was completed early in 1943 with a 1,800 hp Mikulin AM-39 12-cylinder Vee-type engine and the *Izdeliya* designation 2D. Apart from the tailplane which was set 7.87 in (20 cm) lower, this aircraft

(Below) The AM-39-powered I-231 flown early 1943.

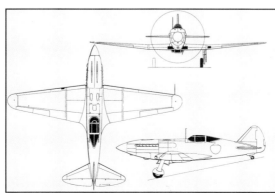

The I-231 (below) was written off soon after the factory tests, development then being abandoned.

was basically similar to the first I-230 and retained the same armament of twin synchronised cannon. Assigned the official designation of I-231, the prototype was written off in a landing accident shortly after the completion of factory testing and development was discontinued. *Max speed, 439 mph (707 km/h) at 23,295 ft (7 100 m). Time to 16,405 ft (5 000 m), 4.5 min. Max range, 839 mls (1 350 km). Empty weight, 5,694 lb (2 583 kg). Loaded weight, 7,246 lb (3 287 kg). Dimensions as for the first I-230 prototype.*

MIKOYAN-GUREVICH I-220   USSR

Late in 1942, work was well advanced at the MiG bureau on several aircraft in parallel and referred to as Series "A" prototypes, with which the OKB hoped to fulfil a VP (*vosotny perekhvatchik*, or high-altitude interceptor) requirement raised earlier in the year. The first of these, the I-220, owed little or nothing to earlier MiG fighters and was of mixed construction, the fuselage being of metal forward of the cockpit and a wooden monocoque aft, and the wings making use of steel main and auxiliary spars with spruce outer panel ribs. The first prototype, which was rolled out of the factory in June 1943 and was first flown during the following month, was initially powered with a low-altitude Mikulin AM-38F engine of 1,700 hp. Armed with two synchronised 20-mm ShVAK cannon, the AM-38F-powered I-220 achieved speeds of 355 mph (572 km/h) at sea level and 391 mph (630 km/h) at 22,965 ft (7 000 m), practical ceiling being 31,170 ft (9 500 m). The prototype was then re-engined with a medium-altitude AM-39 affording 1,800 hp for take-off and flown in January 1944, flight testing continuing until the following August. A second prototype also powered by the AM-39 flew in September 1944, but differed in armament, being the first Soviet fighter to carry four 20-mm ShVAK cannon. The following data relate to the second prototype. *Max speed, 355 mph (571 km/h) at sea level, 433 mph (697 km/h) at 22,965 ft (7 000 m).*

The first prototype I-220 (below) in its original AM-38F-engined form as flown in July 1943.

Time to 19,685 ft (6 000 m), 4.5 min. Ceiling, 36,090 ft (11 000 m). Range, 391 mls (630 km). Empty weight, 6,836 lb (3 101 kg). Loaded weight, 8,040 lb (3 647 kg). Span, 36 ft 10⅔ in (11,00 m). Length, 31 ft 6 in (9,60 m). Height (tail up), 10 ft 4⅜ in (3,16 m). Wing area, 219.37 sq ft (20,38 m²).

The AM-39-powered second prototype I-220 (above and below), the first Soviet fighter with four cannon.

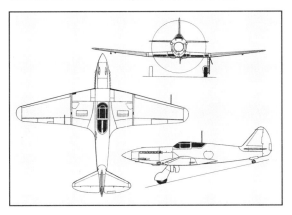

MIKOYAN-GUREVICH I-221   USSR

The second Series "A" high-altitude fighter (see I-220) and referred to as the 2A, the I-221 was the first of the OKB's fighter prototypes to be fitted with turbo-superchargers. The I-221 was fitted with an AM-39A engine rated at 1,700 hp for take-off and equipped with a centrifugal compressor and paired TsIAM-developed TK-2B turbo-superchargers which, it was anticipated, would permit maximum power to be maintained to an altitude of 42,650 ft (13 000 m). Although adhering closely in most other respects to the preceding I-220, the I-221 had a rear fuselage of dural construction rather than a wooden monocoque, and the outer wing panels were extended, increasing span by a total of 6 ft 6¾ in (2,00 m). Armament consisted of two synchronised 20-mm cannon. The initial flight test took place on 2 December 1943, but the programme came to an abrupt end when, during one of the prototype's early trials, a piston rod fractured, the engine seized and the aircraft crashed. The following performance data are based on OKB estimates. *Max speed, 428 mph (689 km/h) at 22,965 ft (7 000 m). Time to 16,405 ft (5 000 m), 4.6 min. Ceiling, 47,570 ft (14 500 m). Empty weight, 7,008 lb (3 179 kg). Loaded weight, 8,571 lb (3 888 kg). Span, 42 ft 7¾ in (13,00 m). Length, 31 ft 4 in (9,55 m). Wing area, 241.55 sq ft (22,44 m²).*

MIKOYAN-GUREVICH I-222   USSR

The turbo-supercharged and pressurised I-222 (below).

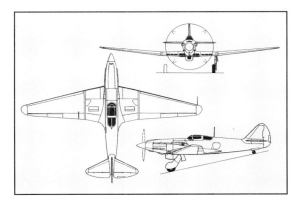

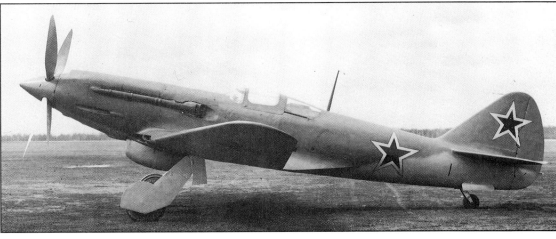

The first prototype I-222 (above) after introduction of a four-bladed AV-9L-26 high-altitude propeller.

The first of the "A" high-altitude fighter series to mate turbo-supercharger and cabin pressurisation, the I-222, or 3A, was powered by a Mikulin AM-39B-1 engine which afforded 1,750 hp for take-off and had a TK-300B turbo-supercharger on its port side. Armament consisted of two synchronised 20-mm ShVAK cannon. Reverting to the wooden monocoque rear fuselage of the I-220, the I-222 employed a Shchyerbakov-designed pressure cabin of welded dural sheet with inflatable rubber seals and pressurized by air tapped from the compressor. The cockpit was air conditioned for the first time in a Soviet fighter. The flight test programme began on 7 May 1944, but although plans had been formulated to produce the "A" series altitude fighters in quantity, the course of the war had meanwhile virtually eliminated the threat of high-altitude *Luftwaffe* attack.

The first prototype I-222 (above) with TK-300B turbo-supercharger as first flown in May 1944.

Priorities were therefore changed and although the development programme was continued all proposals for series production were discarded. *Max speed, 424 mph (682 km/h) at 21,980 ft (6 700 m), 429 mph (691 km/h) at 41,010 ft (12 500 m). Time to 16,405 ft (5 000 m), 6.0 min. Ceiling, 47,570 ft (14 500 m). Range, 620 mls (1 000 km). Empty weight, 6,982 lb (3 167 kg). Normal loaded weight, 8,355 lb (3 790 kg). Span, 42 ft 7¾ in (13,00 m). Length, 31 ft 6 in (9,60 m). Wing area, 241.55 sq ft (22,44 m²).*

MIKOYAN-GUREVICH I-225   USSR

Although, by early 1944, the VP programme was of little more than academic interest, work continued on two further "A" series prototypes, the I-224 and I-225, which had been assigned the *Izdeliya* designations 4A and 5A respectively. The I-225 was destined to enter flight test three months before the I-224, the first of two prototypes flying on 21 July 1944. This was powered by

The first prototype of the I-225 (below), which, flown in July 1944, preceded the I-224 into the air.

a Mikulin AM-42B 12-cylinder liquid-cooled Vee engine equipped with a TK-300B turbo-supercharger on its starboard side and affording 2,000 hp for take-off and 1,750 hp at 24,605 ft (7 500 m). Featuring a much improved Shchyerbakov pressure cabin, a 2½-in (64-mm) armourglass windscreen, 8-mm seat armour and an armament of four synchronised 20-mm ShVAK cannon, the I-225 was of all-metal construction and was flown for the first time on 21 July 1944. On 2 August, the I-225 attained 439 mph (707 km/h) at 27,885 ft (8 500 m), but, two days later, during its fifteenth flight, the engine of the I-225 seized at an altitude of 50 ft (15 m) and the aircraft crashed and proved irreparable. The second prototype was not flown until 14 March 1945 as the OKB was devoting priority to the I-250. During subsequent testing, the I-225-02, which was powered by an AM-42FB engine with similar ratings to the AM-42B, attained 451 mph (726 km/h) which, at the time, was believed to be the highest speed attained by a Soviet piston-engined fighter. This distinction had been gained, however, by the M-108-powered Yak-3M. *Max speed, 383 mph (617 km/h) at sea level, 451 mph (726 km/h) at 27,885 ft (8 500 m). Time to 16,405 ft (5 000 m), 4.5 min. Ceiling, 41,340 ft (12 600 m). Range, 808 mls (1 300 km). Empty weight, 6,636 lb (3 010 kg). Normal loaded weight, 8,598 lb (3 900 kg). Span, 36 ft 10⅔ in (11,00 m). Length, 31 ft 5⅞ in (9,60 m). Height (tail up), 12 ft 1⅔ in (3,70 m). Wing area, 219.38 sq ft (20,38 m²).*

The I-225 (below) had a starboard turbo-supercharger.

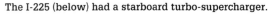

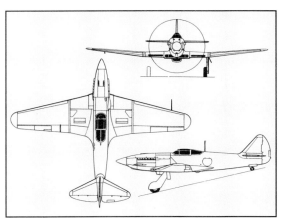

MIKOYAN-GUREVICH I-224   USSR

The last of the "A" series high-altitude fighter prototypes to enter flight test, the I-224 was flown for the first time on 20 October 1944. Powered by a Mikulin AM-39B engine rated at 1,750 hp for take-off, driving an 11 ft 5¾-in (3,50-m) diameter propeller with 15¾-in (40-cm) chord "paddle" blades, and equipped with a single TK-300B turbo-supercharger on the starboard side, the I-224 carried an armament of two synchronised 20-mm ShVAK cannon. An unusual feature of the I-224 was its exhaust system which included four fixed aft-facing ejection "chimneys". The I-224 achieved an altitude of 46,260 ft (14 100 m) during its brief flight test programme which reportedly terminated when a malfunctioning supercharger resulted in an uncontrollable

A starboard side view of the first I-224 (above) showing the turbo-supercharger exhaust duct.

engine fire. *Max speed, 373 mph (601 km/h) at sea level, 431 mph (693 km/h) at 42,980 ft (13 200 m). Time to 16,405 ft (5 000 m), 4.8 min. Ceiling, 46,260 ft (14 100 m). Range, 621 mls (1 000 km). Empty weight, 6,845 lb (3 105 kg). Max loaded weight, 8,644 lb (3 921 kg). Span, 42 ft 7¾ in (13,00 m). Length, 31 ft 2 in (9,51 m). Height (tail up), 11 ft 9¾ in (3,60 m). Wing area, 241.55 sq ft (22,44 m²).*

A port side view of the first I-224 (below), which underwent comparatively brief flight testing.

MIKOYAN-GUREVICH
MiG-13 (I-250)   USSR

In February 1944, the MiG OKB initiated the design of a mixed-power single-seat fighter with the *Izdeliya* designation N. Conceived to use the so-called "accelerator", or VRDK (*Vozdushno-reaktivny dvigatyel kompressorny*, or Air-reaction engine compressor), which had been developed at the TsIAM under the leadership of K V Kholshchevnikov, the N preliminary design was finished on 28 March 1944. Drawings were completed

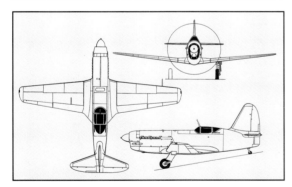

The pre-series MiG-13 (above and below) which served briefly with the Baltic Fleet Air Force.

by 30 November 1944, by which time the official designation I-250 had been applied to the project, and three months later, on 26 February 1945, the first of two prototypes, the N-1, left the factory. Primary power was provided by a Klimov M-107A (VK-107A) 12-cylinder Vee-type engine rated at 1,650 hp for take-off and armament consisted of three 20-mm G-20 cannon, one between the engine cylinder banks and the others flanking the engine. The first flight took place on 3 March 1945, and the VRDK was fired for the first time during the third test flight. The VRDK consisted of an engine-driven compressor which fed compressed air via a water radiator to a mixing chamber in which fuel was introduced under pressure, the mixture being ignited in a double-walled combustion chamber and then ejected through a variable orifice. This provided 660 lb (300 kg) of thrust for up to 10 minutes, boosting speed by 62 mph (100 km/h). N-1 crashed during mid-May when the permissible load factor was exceeded and the horizontal tail collapsed at low altitude, but a second prototype, the N-2, was rolled out on 26 May 1945. This lacked armament and the vertical tail was enlarged to rectify some longitudinal instability, but this prototype, too, was destroyed in an accident. In July 1945, the OKB received instructions to supervise the construction of 10 I-250 aircraft to participate in the Air Parade that was planned for 7 November 1945, barely four months later.

The first prototype I-250 (below) after provision of a larger vertical tail and other modifications.

Nine I-250s were ready on time, but inclement weather resulted in cancellation of the Parade. These aircraft, together with a further seven, were subsequently delivered to the Navy as MiG-13s, equipping an evaluation unit based at Skultye airfield, near Riga. Several of the pre-series MiG-13s were experimentally fitted with sabre-shaped propeller blades, and official NII VVS trials were conducted between 9 October 1947 and 8 April 1948. Production of the I-250 alias MiG-13 had totalled 16 pre-series aircraft, and although the fighter was essentially successful, it had been overtaken by pure jet fighters and surviving examples were retired by the Navy in May 1948. The following performance data relate to the N-1, weights and dimensions being applicable to the MiG-13. *Max speed (combined power), 385 mph (620 km/h) at sea level, 513 mph (825 km/h) at 22,965 ft (7 000 m). Time to 16,405 ft (5 000 m) with VRDK, 3.9 min. Ceiling with VRDK, 39,240 ft (11 960 m). Range, 857 mls (1 380 km). Empty weight, 6,675 lb (3 028 kg). Loaded weight, 8,666 lb (3 931 kg). Span, 31 ft 2 in (9,50 m). Length, 26 ft 10¼ in (8,18 m). Wing area, 161.4 sq ft (15,00 m²).*

MIKOYAN-GUREVICH
MiG-9 (I-300)   USSR

Assigned the *Izdeliya* designation F by the OKB and the initial military designation I-300, the first Soviet turbojet-powered fighter of indigenous design was singularly noteworthy for the brevity of its development programme – 14 months between inception and test. The primary design responsibility of Aleksei T Karyev, the I-300 was powered by paired 1,760 lb st (800 kgp) BMW 003A turbojets, and the first prototype performed a 13-ft (4,00-m) "hop" on 19 April 1946, and its first true test flight on the following 24 April. It crashed during its 19th flight, after logging 6 hrs 23 min, when a wing root fairing detached and destroyed the horizontal tail.

The I-302 (below) was an attempt to resolve gun gas ingestion problems by moving the 37-mm cannon.

Second and third prototypes were flown on 11 and 9 August 1946 respectively, and on the 20th of that month a directive was issued by the NKAP (People's Commissariat for the Aircraft Industry) that 10 more aircraft be built by hand and completed by 22 October. Considered as pre-series aircraft, these were designated FS by the OKB and I-301 officially. With the decision to manufacture the fighter in series the appellation MiG-9 was also assigned – this being curiously non-sequential and previously tentatively issued to the I-210. The first pre-series aircraft was completed on 13 October 1946 – 54 days after issue of the directive – and flown on 26 October, subsequent production aircraft being externally similar. These were powered by paired RD-20 turbojets – reverse-engineered BMW 003As – and armament consisted of one 37-mm and two 23-mm cannon. Two tandem two-seat prototypes were also built, the first of these, the FT-1 (I-301T), retaining the standard armament and flying for the first time in July 1947. The FT-2, which followed on 25 August 1947, had a redesigned cockpit canopy, air brakes and provision for drop tanks. This aircraft was later fitted with the first Soviet production ejection seats. The I-301 version of the MiG-9 suffered from engine stoppages above 24,605 ft (7 500 m) as a result of gun gas ingestion.

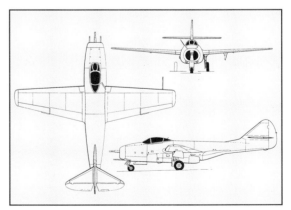

The series MiG-9 (above) and with experimental 51.7-Imp gal/235-l tanks under the wingtips (below).

Among attempts to eradicate this problem was the FP (I-302) which simply displaced the 37-mm cannon from intake splitter to upper fuselage portside. Rearranged armament was also featured by the more extensively revised FR (I-308), the 37-mm weapon being transferred to the starboard side of an entirely redesigned

The first pre-series MiG-9 alias I-301 (above), as now preserved in the VVS Museum at Monino.

forward fuselage with the 23-mm cannon being relocated to port. The forward fuselage embodied a forward-positioned, pressurised cockpit, air brakes and afterburning derivatives of the RD-20 turbojet developed by Koliesov. These engines, designated RD-21 (initially RD-20F) each developed 2,205 lb st (1 000 kgp). Flown in July 1947, the FP was the first MiG-9 to attain Mach=0.8 under test, and an altitude of 16,405 ft (5 000 m) was reached in 2.7 min. Like the FP, the FR did not progress beyond prototype status, but, similarly powered to the latter, the FF (I-307) was built as a small pre-series. Flown in September 1947, the FF (externally similar to the FS) had improved pilot protection (12-mm front and back armour, and a 44-mm windscreen). This model attained 590 mph (950 km/h) at sea level and reached 16,405 ft (5 000 m) in 2.9 min, empty and loaded weights being 7,652 lb (3 471 kg) and 11,281 lb (5 117 kg) respectively. The following data relate to the FS version which preponderated among the 604 MiG-9s built. *Max speed, 537 mph (864 km/h) at sea level, 566 mph (911 km/h) at 14,765 ft (4 500 m). Time to 16,405 ft (5 000 m), 4.3 min. Range (with external fuel), 497 mls (800 km). Empty weight, 7,540 lb (3 420 kg). Loaded weight, 10,941 lb (4 963 kg). Span, 32 ft 9¾ in (10,00 m). Length, 32 ft 3 in (9,83 m). Height, 10 ft 6⅞ in (3,22 m). Wing area, 195.9 sq ft (18,20 m²).*

The MiG-9M alias I-308 (below) had a pressurised cockpit and afterburning RD-21 turbojets.

MIKOYAN-GUREVICH I-270 USSR

Created by the OKB as the Zh to meet a 1945 requirement for a rocket-propelled target defence fighter, the I-270 was based broadly on the Messerschmitt Me 263 (which see), but was of a less radical configuration, featuring a straight wing and conventional horizontal tail. Adopting an ejection seat for the first time in a Soviet fighter and having a wing of near-laminar flow profile, the first of two prototypes was towed into the air behind a Tu-2 – with ballast replacing the rocket motor – in December 1946. Only the second prototype was to be fitted with the rocket motor. This, the RD-2M-3V developed by L Dushkin and V Glushko, was a bi-propellant dual-chamber unit affording a total thrust of 3,197 lb (1 450 kg) of which the cruise chamber contributed 882 lb (400 kg). The cabin was pressurised and proposed armament comprised two 23-mm cannon and eight RS-82 rockets. The second prototype flew under power early in 1947, but was written off as a result of a landing crash while being flown by an NII VVS pilot.

(Below) The I-270 rocket-propelled interceptor.

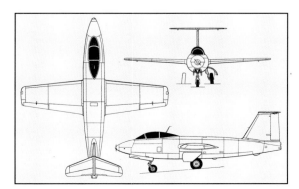

Shortly afterwards, the first prototype was damaged in a belly landing and was not repaired. *Max speed, 621 mph (1 000 km/h) at sea level, 582 mph (936 km/h) at 49,215 ft (15 000 m). Time to 32,810 ft (10 000 m), 2.37 min. Endurance (both chambers), 4.25 min, (cruise chamber only), 9.05 min. Empty weight, 3,408 lb (1 546 kg). Loaded weight, 9,083 lb (4 120 kg). Span, 29 ft 5 in (7,75 m). Length, 29 ft 3 in (8,91 m). Height, 10 ft 1¼ in (3,08 m). Wing area, 129.17 sq ft (12,00 m²).*

The first prototype I-270 (below) which was flown with rocket motor replaced by ballast.

MIKOYAN-GUREVICH MIG-15 (I-310) USSR

Conceived to meet a March 1946 requirement for a high-altitude day interceptor designed around the British Rolls-Royce Nene turbojet – acquisition of which was then being negotiated by the Soviet government – the *Izdeliya* S, alias I-310, was evolved in parallel with the reverse engineering of the British engine by Vladimir Klimov's bureau as the RD-45. This designation signified *Reaktivny dvigatel*, or reaction engine, and *Zavod*, or Factory, 45 in which it was placed in production. The first of three prototypes, S-01 with a Nene 1 engine, flew on 30 December 1947, the second, S-02 with a Nene 2, following on 27 May 1948, and the essentially similar pre-production prototype, the S-03, flying on 17 June and being assigned to the NII VVS on 1 November 1948. Full-scale production as the MiG-15 was meanwhile launched, the series version having the OKB de-

The first of three MiG-15 prototypes, the S-01 (below), which flew with a Nene in December 1947.

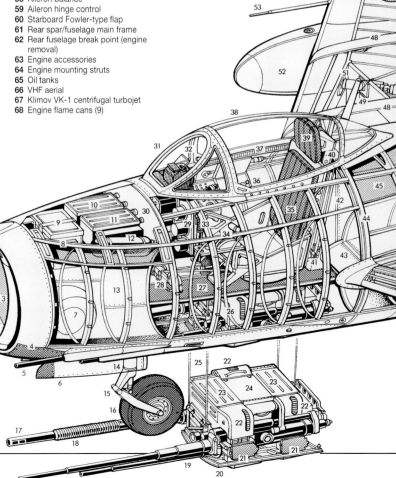

Key to MiG-15bis (SD)

1 Engine air intake
2 S-13 gun camera aperture
3 Intake centre divider
4 Cannon blast shield
5 Cannon muzzles
6 Nosewheel doors
7 Nosewheel well between intake ducts
8 Forward fuselage equipment bay
9 Battery
10 RSIU-3M VHF transmitter
11 VHF radio receiver
12 Oxygen bottle
13 Bifurcated intake ducting
14 Nosewheel leg strut
15 Pivoted axle beam
16 Nosewheel
17 Starboard 37-mm N-37 cannon
18 Recoil spring
19 Port twin NR-23 KM 23-mm cannon
20 Gun pack ventral door
21 Cartridge case ejection chutes
22 Ammunition feed chutes
23 23-mm ammunition boxes (80 rounds per gun)
24 37-mm ammunition box, 40 rounds
25 Gun pack winching cables
26 Ventral gun pack in position beneath cockpit floor
27 Cockpit floor level
28 Rudder pedals
29 Instrument panel
30 Cockpit front pressure bulkhead
31 Bullet proof windscreen
32 ASP-3N reflector-type gunsight
33 Control column
34 Engine throttle
35 Pilot's ejection seat
36 Canopy handles
37 Sliding canopy rail
38 Cockpit canopy cover
39 Ejection seat headrest
40 Seat guide rails
41 Control rod runs

42 Cockpit pressure bulkhead
43 Wing centre-section carry through
44 Front spar/fuselage main frame
45 Main fuel tank (total internal fuel capacity 310 Imp gal/1 410 l)
46 Fuselage upper longeron
47 Fuel filler cap access panel
48 Starboard wing fences
49 Radio aerial mast
50 Starboard flap jack
51 Main undercarriage pivot fixing
52 Slipper-type drop tank (57-Imp gal/260-l capacity)
53 Pitot tube
54 Remote compass transmitter
55 Anti-flutter weight
56 Starboard navigation light
57 Starboard aileron
58 Aileron balance
59 Aileron hinge control
60 Starboard Fowler-type flap
61 Rear spar/fuselage main frame
62 Rear fuselage break point (engine removal)
63 Engine accessories
64 Engine mounting struts
65 Oil tanks
66 VHF aerial
67 Klimov VK-1 centrifugal turbojet
68 Engine flame cans (9)

69 Rear engine mounting bulkhead
70 Rear fuselage fuel tank filler cap access
71 Fin mounting main frames
72 Heat shrouded jet pipe
73 Sloping fin spar bulkhead
74 Fin attachment joints
75 Tail control rods
76 Fin construction
77 Tailplane attachment joint
78 HF aerial cable
79 Starboard tailplane
80 Fin tip fairing
81 Rudder anti-flutter weight
82 Upper rudder segment

one, referred to by the OKB as the SU, which was particularly interesting in having two 23-mm Sh-3 cannon pod-mounted under the fuselage nose, and pivoted to allow vertical movement from −7 to +11 deg. The first flight test of the SU was made on 30 June 1951, but it was soon ascertained that between 15 and 20 flights were necessary to train pilots in the correct use of the movable weapons in aerial combat, a disadvantage considered to outweigh the possible advantages of the system. The following data relate to the standard SV production model. *Max speed, 652 mph (1 050 km/h) at sea level, 641 mph (1 031 km/h) at 16,405 ft (5 000 m). Time to 16,405 ft (5 000 m), 2.5 min. Range (internal fuel), 730 mls (1 175 kg) at 32,810 ft (10 000 m). Empty weight, 7,767 lb (3 523 kg). Loaded weight (clean), 10,941 lb (4 963 kg). Span, 33 ft 1 in (10,08 m). Length, 32 ft 11¼ in (10,04 m). Height, 12 ft 1⅔ in (3,70 m). Wing area, 221.75 sq ft (20,60 m²).*

The first series production MiG-15 (above) which flew in December 1948, a year after the prototype.

signation of SV and the first example flying on 30 December 1948, exactly one year after the first prototype's initial flight. The MiG-15 (SV) was powered by the 5,005 lb st (2 270 kgp) RD-45F engine and armament comprised one 37-mm N-37 and two 23-mm NS-23 cannon. The initial series MiG-15 remained in production for less than a year before giving place to the improved MiG-15bis. Licence manufacture of the MiG-15

was initiated in Poland and Czechoslovakia *after* its withdrawal from Soviet production in favour of the MiG-15bis, however. Two hundred and twenty-seven were built in Poland with the designation Lim-1 between January 1953 and September 1954 after assembly of six from kits, the MiG-15 then giving place to the MiG-15bis as the Lim-2. Eight hundred and fifteen MiG-15s were built simultaneously in Czechoslovakia as S.102s, these, too, giving place in production in 1954 to the MiG-15bis as the S.103. Among experimental variants of the basic MiG-15 was

The SU version of the MiG-15 (below) with two 23-mm cannon that could be tilted vertically through 18 deg.

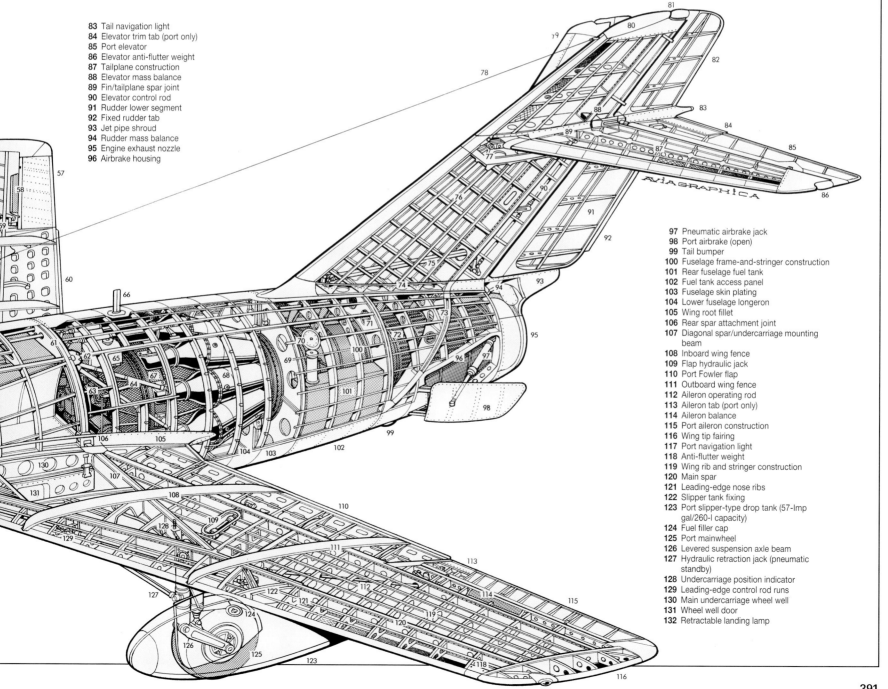

83 Tail navigation light
84 Elevator trim tab (port only)
85 Port elevator
86 Elevator anti-flutter weight
87 Tailplane construction
88 Elevator mass balance
89 Fin/tailplane spar joint
90 Elevator control rod
91 Rudder lower segment
92 Fixed rudder tab
93 Jet pipe shroud
94 Rudder mass balance
95 Engine exhaust nozzle
96 Airbrake housing
97 Pneumatic airbrake jack
98 Port airbrake (open)
99 Tail bumper
100 Fuselage frame-and-stringer construction
101 Rear fuselage fuel tank
102 Fuel tank access panel
103 Fuselage skin plating
104 Lower fuselage longeron
105 Wing root fillet
106 Rear spar attachment joint
107 Diagonal spar/undercarriage mounting beam
108 Inboard wing fence
109 Flap hydraulic jack
110 Port Fowler flap
111 Outboard wing fence
112 Aileron operating rod
113 Aileron tab (port only)
114 Aileron balance
115 Port aileron construction
116 Wing tip fairing
117 Port navigation light
118 Anti-flutter weight
119 Wing rib and stringer construction
120 Main spar
121 Leading-edge nose ribs
122 Slipper tank fixing
123 Port slipper-type drop tank (57-Imp gal/260-l capacity)
124 Fuel filler cap
125 Port mainwheel
126 Levered suspension axle beam
127 Hydraulic retraction jack (pneumatic standby)
128 Undercarriage position indicator
129 Leading-edge control rod runs
130 Main undercarriage wheel well
131 Wheel well door
132 Retractable landing lamp

MIKOYAN-GUREVICH
MiG-15BIS   USSR

Early service use of the MiG-15 having revealed various deficiencies, the OKB proposed a number of modifications and changes, to be combined with introduction of the VK-1 engine in the *Izdeliya* SD. Submitted to state trials in November 1948, the VK-1 was an improved RD-45F developed by Vladimir Klimov's bureau and affording 5,952 lb st (2 700 kgp). The changes introduced in the SD version included a strengthened wing box, servo aileron control, increased elevator balance, redesigned air brakes and modifications to the leading edge of the vertical fin. The SD was ordered into production as the MiG-15bis, the first example flying in September 1949. Armament consisted of one 37-mm N-37 and two 23-mm NS-23KM cannon, and provision was made for two 110- or 220-lb (50- or 100-kg) bombs and two 55-Imp gal (250-l) fuel tanks to be carried. Two versions were built, one with and one without ILS

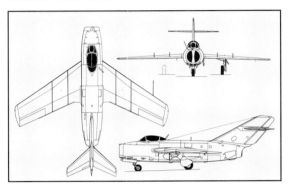

(Above) The series production MiG-15bis.

(OSP-48) equipment, and licence manufacture was undertaken in Poland and Czechoslovakia as the Lim-2 and S.103 respectively from the autumn of 1954 until late 1956. Some 500 Lim-2s had been built in Poland when production terminated on 23 November 1956, and the total of S.103s built in Czechoslovakia by Aero at Vodochody was 620, these contributing to an overall production total of MiG-15s of all versions (including the tandem two-seat tuitional MiG-15UTI) of some 12,000 aircraft, serving with almost 40 air forces. Variants that failed to achieve quantity production included the MiG-15Sbis (SD-UPB) and MiG-15Rbis (SR), respectively escort fighter and tactical reconnaissance versions capable of carrying twin 132-Imp-gal (600-l) auxiliary tanks, and the radar-equipped MiG-15Pbis which was tested in two versions. The first of these, the SP-1, carried a *Torii* (Thorium) fixed-scan AI radar in a bulbous nose radome and flew in December 1949, NII VVS trials being performed between 31 January and 20 May 1950. The second version, the SP-5, five examples of which were tested during 1951, differed in having RP-1M *Izumrud* (Emerald) radar with the ranging scanner accommodated in an intake lip extension and an intake splitter housing for the scan dish. The following data relate to the standard production MiG-15bis. *Max*

The first radar-equipped MiG-15Pbis, the SP-1 (above) with a *Torii* radar, and the second version, the SP-5 (below) with an *Izumrud* radar.

(Top) MiG-15bis of *Magyar Légierö*, Pécs District, *circa* 1960, and (immediately above) a MiG-15bis of Chinese People's Liberation Army, Korean War, 1952.

speed, 667 mph (1 076 km/h) at sea level, 688 mph (1 107 km/h) at 9,840 ft (3 000 m). Time to 16,405 ft (5 000 m), 1.95 min. Range (internal fuel), 826 mls (1 330 km). Empty weight, 8,115 lb (3 681 kg). Loaded weight (clean), 11,861 lb (5 380 kg). Span, 33 ft 1 in (10,08 m). Length, 35 ft 7½ in (10,86 m). Height, 12 ft 1⅔ in (3,70 m). Wing area, 221.75 sq ft (20,60 m²).

MIKOYAN-GUREVICH I-320   USSR

(Above) The first and (below) second prototype of the I-320 tandem-engined all-weather fighter.

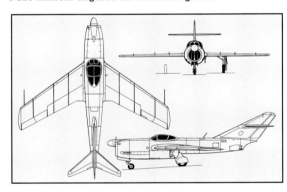

To meet a requirement for a twin-engined all-weather fighter formulated in January 1948, the MiG OKB proffered the *Izdeliya* R, a side-by-side two-seat sweptwing fighter with the engines disposed in tandem. Competing with proposals from the Lavochkin and Yakovlev bureaux – all three contenders being awarded three-prototype contracts – the MiG fighter was assigned the official designation I-320. The nose intake fed a plenum chamber around the forward engine compressor, this engine exhausting below the fuselage and a duct leading back to the rear engine which exhausted via an orifice in the extreme tail. Armament comprised two 37-mm N-37 cannon, and the first prototype, the R-1 flown on 16 April 1949, was powered by two 5,005 lb st (2 270 kgp) RD-45F engines,

The second prototype I-320 (below) introduced more powerful engines and initially had *Torii-A* radar.

whereas the R-2 and R-3 were each powered by paired 5,952 lb st (2 700 kgp) VK-1s. The VK-1-powered prototypes could take-off and cruise on the power of either engine, and the I-320 was initially tested with *Torii-A* (Thorium-A) radar. This single-antenna radar which demanded manual tracking was succeeded by the basically similar but improved *Korshun* (Kite) radar with which the I-320 was tested during July-August 1951. Development of the I-320 was discontinued when the requirement to which it had been designed was overtaken by a more advanced one. The following data relate specifically to the R-2. *Max speed, 677 mph (1 090 km/h) at 3,280 ft (1 000 m). Time to 32,810 ft (10 000 m), 5.25 min. Range (internal fuel), 749 mls (1 205 km) at 32,810 ft (10 000 m). Normal loaded weight, 23,644 lb (10 725 kg). Max loaded weight, 26,664 lb (12 095 kg). Span, 46 ft 7 in (14,20 m). Length, 51 ft 8⅞ in (15,77 m). Wing area, 443.49 sq ft (41,20 m²).*

MIKOYAN-GUREVICH
MiG-17 (I-330)   USSR

In parallel with work on the SD (MiG-15bis), the MiG OKB launched, early in 1949, a further refinement of the basic *Izdeliya* S concept as the SI, to be assigned the official designation of I-330. The SI was intended to have improved transonic behaviour by adding the existing fuselage (forward of the rear frame of the engine plenum chamber) to a lengthened rear section to improve fineness ratio, and mating the result to an entirely new wing possessing better compressibility characteristics. This new wing – unofficially referred to as the "sickle" wing – featured 45 deg quarter-chord sweepback inboard reducing to 42 deg outboard. The Klimov VK-1 engine of the SD was retained, and the first prototype to fly, the SI-2, achieved 692 mph (1 114 km/h) at 7,220 ft (2 200 m), or Mach=0.95, on 1 February 1950 after a few flights. This aircraft was lost on 20 March and replaced by the SI-02, and, in September 1951, the SI was ordered into production at six factories as the MiG-17, first achieving operational capability with the VVS in October 1952. Armament remained, as in the MiG-15bis, one 37-mm N-37D and paired 23-mm NR-23 cannon, and the VK-1 engine quickly gave place to the similarly rated but improved VK-1A. Production of the

(Below) The SI-2, the first prototype of the MiG-17 to fly, and (above) the SI-01, the fourth MiG-17 prototype built and the third to enter flight test.

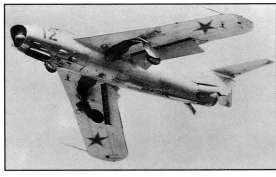

The cannon-armed MiG-17PF (above) and the K-5 AAM-armed MiG-17PFU limited all-weather fighter (below).

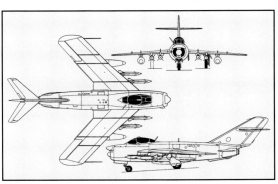

basic clear-weather MiG-17 gave place to the MiG-17F (which see) from the end of 1952. *Max speed, 665 mph (1 070 km/h) at 16,405 ft (5 000 m). Time to 16,405 ft (5 000 m), 3.0 min. Range, 628 mls (1 010 km) at 16,405 ft (5 000 m). Empty weight, 8,373 lb (3 798 kg). Loaded weight (clean), 11,468 lb (5 202 kg). Span, 31 ft 7⅛ in (9,63 m). Length, 36 ft 11⅓ in (11,26 m). Height, 12 ft 5⅝ in (3,80 m). Wing area, 243.27 sq ft (22,60 m²).*

MIKOYAN-GUREVICH
MⅰG-17F   USSR

With the successful development in 1951 of the VK-1F afterburning version of the VK-1 engine, this was fitted to an SI airframe and flown on 29 September 1951 as the SF. Series production of this version of the fighter was launched at the end of 1952 as the MiG-17F, the suffix letter signifying *Forsirovannyi* (literally, "boosted"). The VK-1F engine offered an afterburning thrust of 7,452 lb (3 380 kg) for three minutes up to 22,965 ft (7 000 m) and 10 minutes above that altitude, and apart from a cut-back rear fuselage exposing the variable nozzle, the MiG-17F had shorter and deeper air brakes. Armament remained one N-37D and two NR-23 cannon, and this could be augmented by four 190-mm TRS-190 or two 212-mm ARS-212 rockets. The MiG-17F achieved service status with the VVS in 1953, and was eventually to be employed by more than 30 air forces. Production of the MiG-17F terminated in the Soviet Union in 1958, but continued under licence in Poland and China. A total of 477 MiG-17F fighters was built in Poland as Lim-5s between November 1956 and June 1960, followed between November 1960 and May 1961 by 60 examples of the Lim-5M, an indigenously-developed dedicated ground attack and battlefield support aircraft. The Lim-5M introduced thickened and extended wing roots and twin-wheel main undercarriage members. After receiving two pattern aircraft, 15

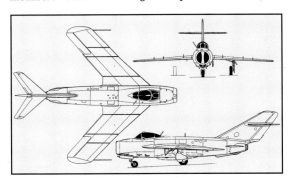

The 850th MiG-17 was the first to receive the VK-1F engine as the MiG-17F (above and below).

An Egyptian-supplied MiG-17F (above) of the Nigerian Air Force in use against Biafra at Enugu, mid-1969.

knocked-down kits and forgings, and materials for a further 10 aircraft, China began licence manufacture of the MiG-17F as the J-5. The first J-5 produced entirely from Chinese parts was completed at Shenyang in the summer of 1956, and 767 had been delivered by the end of 1959 when production was continuing. An exclusively Chinese tandem two-seat training version, the JJ-5, was developed and flown on 8 May 1966, a total of 1,061 having been built when production terminated at the end of 1986. Slightly more than 8,000 MiG-17s (all versions) were built in the Soviet Union and Poland. *Max speed, 711 mph (1 145 km/h) at 9,840 ft (3 000 m). Initial climb, 12,795 ft/min (65 m/sec). Range (max external fuel), 913 mls (1 470 km). Empty weight, 8,664 lb (3 930 kg). Loaded weight (clean), 11,773 lb (5 340 kg). Span, 31 ft 7⅛ in (9,63 m). Length, 36 ft 4⅝ in (11,09 m). Height, 12 ft 5⅝ in (3,80 m). Wing area, 243.27 sq ft (22,60 m²).*

MIKOYAN-GUREVICH
MⅰG-17P   USSR

The SP-2 (above), a version of the MiG-17F equipped with a single-antenna *Korshun* AI radar set.

The first radar-equipped interceptor built in series for the VVS, the MiG-17P – the suffix letter signifying *Poiskovyi*, or search – was evolved from a modified version of the MiG-15bis, which, fitted with the dual-antenna RP-1M *Izumrud* (Emerald) as the SP-5, first introduced the combined upper intake lip and intake splitter housings. The nose section of the SP-5 was grafted onto a VK-1A-powered MiG-17 airframe as the SP-7, the

Mig-17Fs of (immediately below) Egyptian Air Force and Air Defence Command at Bilbeis, 1981, and (bottom) of Democratic Republic of Vietnam, 1971.

37-mm N-37 cannon giving place to a third 23-mm NR-23 for cG reasons, and comparative trials being conducted with a MiG-17 fitted with a single-antenna *Korshun* (Kite) radar as the SP-2. Tests were concluded in the summer of 1952, the *Izumrud* radar being adopted in preference to the *Korshun* and production of the SP-7 being undertaken as the MiG-17P limited all-weather fighter for both the PVO and Navy. The MiG-17P entered production simultaneously with the MiG-17F, and comparatively few of the former had been produced before the afterburning VK-1F was standardised to result in the MiG-17PF, this having been preceded by the SP-7F flown in October 1952. Powered by a VK-1F rated at 5,842 lb st (2 650 kgp) boosted to 7,451 lb st (3 380 kgp) with afterburning, and armed with three 23-mm cannon, the MiG-17PF was fitted with progressively improved versions of the *Izumrud*, culminating with the RP-5 model. In 1953, progress with the beam-riding K-5 (RS-2US) AAM permitted the cannon armament of a MiG-17 to be replaced by a quartet of these missiles on underwing pylons. Successful trials with this, the SP-6, led, in 1955, to the majority of MiG-17PFs being similarly modified as MiG-17PFUs, combining the RP-5 *Izumrud* with four K-5 AAMs. Licence production of the RP-5-equipped MiG-17PF was undertaken in Poland as the Lim-5P, the first being delivered on 18 January 1959 and the 129th and last being rolled out on 29 December 1960. As late as 1961, China acquired a licence to produce the MiG-17PF, manufacture being undertaken by the Chengdu Aircraft Factory as the J-5A. Owing to non-delivery by the Soviet Union of some equipment and drawings, construction of a prototype J-5A took three-and-a-quarter years, the first flight taking place on 11 November 1964, and initial deliveries to the Air Force of the Chinese People's Republic began

The MiG-17PFU (above) with RP-5 *Izumrud* and launch rails for a quartet of K-5 alias RS-2US missiles.

in May 1966. The following data relate to the MiG-17P. *Max speed, 659 mph (1 060 km/h) at sea level, 693 mls (1 115 km/h) at 9,840 ft (3 000 m). Initial climb, 7,283 ft/ min (37 m/sec). Range (clean), 801 mls (1 290 km) at 39,370 ft (12 000 m). Empty weight, 9,158 lb (4 154 kg). Max loaded weight, 13,845 lb (6 280 kg). Span, 31 ft 7⅛ in (9,63 m). Length, 38 ft 3⅞ in (11,68 m). Height, 12 ft 1 in (3,68 m). Wing area, 243.27 sq ft (22,60 m²).*

MIKOYAN-GUREVICH I-350   USSR

Characterised by what was at the time extreme wing sweepback – 60 deg at the leading edge – and the first MiG fighter designed for sustained supersonic flight, the OKB's *Izdeliya* M was initiated to accept the new Lyulka TR-3A single-shaft turbojet which was to be committed to production as the AL-5. Assigned the official designation I-350, one prototype was built, the M-1 with RP-1 *Izumrud* AI radar, a second, the M-2 with *Korshun* AI radar, being abandoned before completion. Armament comprised one 37-mm N-37 and two 23-mm NR-23 cannon. The M-1 was flown for the first time on 16 June 1951, but the TR-3A turbojet, which was rated at 10,140 lb st (4 600 kgp), failed shortly after take-off. The hydraulic system also failed, but the pilot nonetheless effected a successful landing. Four further flight tests were performed, but engine difficulties persisted, and, as it was obvious that the Lyulka turbojet demanded considerable further development, the I-350 programme was terminated in August 1951. The following performance data are OKB estimates. *Max speed, 770 mph (1 240 km/h) at sea level, or Mach=1.01, 787 mph (1 266 km/h) at 32,810 ft (10 000 m), or Mach=1.175. Time to 16,405 ft (5 000 m), 1.1 min. Range (internal fuel), 696 mls (1 120 km). Empty weight, 13,503 lb (6 125 kg). Max loaded weight, 19,202 lb (8 710 kg). Span, 31 ft 11 in (9,73 m). Length, 54 ft 7½ in (16,65 m). Wing area, 387.51 sq ft (36,00 m²).*

The I-350 (above and below) was the first MiG fighter designed for sustained supersonic flight, but suffered persistent engine difficulties.

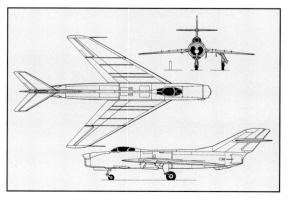

MIKOYAN-GUREVICH I-360   USSR

At the end of 1951, the MiG OKB had completed an adaptation of the MiG-17 airframe for a pair of 5,732 lb st (2 600 kgp) Mikulin AM-5 turbojets as the *Izdeliya* SM-1, or I-340. Purely an engine test bed, the SM-1 had demonstrated the efficacy of the side-by-side installation of the small-diameter turbojets, achieving speeds of 741 mph (1 193 km/h) at 3,280 ft (1 000 m) and 717 mph (1 154 km/h) at 16,405 ft (5 000 m), an altitude attained in 0.94 min. The success achieved with the

(Above and below) The first I-360, alias SM-2, the first MiG fighter to use side-by-side turbojets.

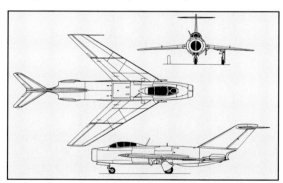

SM-1 determined choice of engine and power plant arrangement for the SM-2 single-seat fighter proposal embodying an essentially similar wing to that of the I-350 with 55 deg sweepback at quarter chord (60 deg at leading edge). Powered by two AM-5F turbojets each with an afterburning rating of 5,952 lb st (2 700 kgp) and having an armament of two 37-mm N-37D cannon in the wing roots, the first SM-2 – by now assigned the official designation of I-360 – was flown on 24 May 1952. This was unique in having a T-type horizontal tail, and, on 25 June, it attained Mach=1.04 in level flight. Subsequent testing revealed that the wing tended to blanket the tailplane at high angles of attack, and, to rectify this deficiency, the tailplane was lowered to a mid point on the fin. Flight test (as the SM-2A) revealed little improvement and the surface was then further lowered to the base of the fin (as the SM-2B), this being accompanied by some increase in

The second I-360 (below) with horizontal tail lowered to the base of an enlarged vertical tail.

the vertical tail surface area, and satisfactory handling characteristics resulting. Nonetheless, the prototype was lost on its 132nd flight as a result of tail flutter. It was calculated that the maximum attainable Mach number of the fighter was 1.19, but no details of performance are available. *Loaded weight, 15,035 lb (6 820 kg). Span, 29 ft 7⅞ in (9,04 m). Length, 45 ft 7¼ in (13,90 m). Height, 12 ft 11½ in (3,95 m).*

MIKOYAN-GUREVICH SN   USSR

Despite termination of trials in 1951 with the SU derivative of the MiG-15 featuring paired 23-mm cannon on articulated mountings, the basic concept of gun armament capable of elevation and depression for air-air use was persisted with by the MiG OKB. In 1953, flight testing of a more sophisticated development of the concept began as *Izdeliya* SN. A variation of the MiG-17, the SN was the first fighter of MiG design to feature lateral air intakes, the 5,952 lb st (2 900 kgp) VK-1A turbojet being fed via circular orifices against concave fuselage sides forward of the wing roots. This arrangement permitted installation of the so-called SV-25 armament system consisting of a trio of 23-mm TKB-495 cannon mounted asymmetrically (one to port and two to starboard) on an articulated mounting in the nose section. Operated electrically, the cannon could be elevated to 27 deg 26 min and depressed to 9 deg 48 min, the complete SV-25 system weighing 1,034 lb (469 kg). Trials with the SN were discontinued owing to aiming complexities combined with advances in air-to-air missiles.

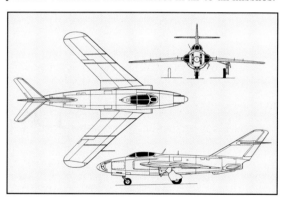

The SN (above and below) was the MiG OKB's second attempt to use vertically-controllable gun armament.

Derived from the MiG-17, the SN (below) was the first of the OKB's fighters to have lateral intakes.

Max speed, 650 mph (1 047 km/h) at 6,560 ft (2 000 m), 657 mph (1 058 km/h) at 16,405 ft (5 000 m). Time to 16,405 ft (5 000 m), 2.54 min. Ceiling, 47,570 ft (14 500 m). Empty weight, 9,153 lb (4 152 kg). Normal loaded weight, 12,390 lb (5 620 kg). Span, 31 ft 7 in (9,63 m). Length, 40 ft 5⅜ in (12,33 m). Height, 12 ft 5⅔ in (3,80 m). Wing area, 243.27 sq ft (22,60 m²).

MIKOYAN-GUREVICH MiG-19S   USSR

The first Soviet production fighter capable of exceeding Mach=1.0 in level flight, the MiG-19 was derived from the SM-9, which, in turn, evolved from the SM-2 (I-360).

The MiG-19SU, or SM-50, quick-reaction interceptor (above) with an RU-013 rocket boost system.

(Above, top) A MiG-19S (F-6) of No 11 Sqn, Pakistan Air Force, Sargodha, 1979, and (immediately above) a J-6 (MiG-19S) of People's Republic of China AF.

Development of the SM-9 as a single-seat clear-weather day fighter armed with three 23-mm cannon and powered by two AM-9B turbojets was launched on 15 August 1953. The first prototype, the SM-9/1, was flown on 5 January 1954 powered by two AM-9Bs – derived from the AM-5F by Sergei K Tumansky and later to be redesignated RD-9B – each of 5,732 lb st (2 600 kgp) boosted by afterburning to 7,165 lb st (3 250 kgp). On 17 February, six weeks after its initial flight, the SM-9 entered production, on the recommendation of Marshal Zigarev, as the MiG-19 at both Gor'kiy and Novosibirsk, although state trials did not commence until 30 September. The second prototype, the SM-9/2, flew on 16 September 1954 with the specified armament of three 23-mm NR-23 cannon, the first production MiG-19s being delivered in March 1955. These latter revealed several significant problems, the most serious being inadequate control effectiveness at

supersonic speeds. This problem was resolved primarily by application of a slab-type, all-flying horizontal tail. This was standardised for the production fighter, together with a spoiler system interlinked with the ailerons and an armament of three 30-mm NR-30 cannon as first flown on the third prototype, the SM-9/3, on 27 November 1955. With these changes, the fighter was designated MiG-19S – the suffix letter signifying *stabilizator*, or stabilator – and achieved VVS service from mid 1956. Production versions of the fighter manufactured in comparatively limited numbers included the MiG-19SV high-altitude interceptor, which, with a reduced armament of two NR-30 cannon, 21.53 sq ft (2,00 m²) more wing area and two AM-9BF2 turbojets with afterburning thrust of 7,275 lb (3 300 kg), reached an altitude of 68,045 ft (20 740 m) on 6 December 1956.

(Above) The SM-9/3, third MiG-19 prototype, and (below) the SM-30 ramp-launched target defence interceptor version of the MiG-19S.

Slightly more than 2,000 MiG-19s (all versions) had been built in the Soviet Union when production phased out in 1958, and, in the same year, licence manufacture began in Czechoslovakia as the S.105, 103 being built when the programme ended in 1963. The MiG-19S was also built under licence in China as the J-6, the first being flown on 30 September 1959. The J-6 was built in very large numbers at Shenyang, both for the Air Force and Navy of the Chinese People's Republic, and for export (Albania, Bangladesh, Egypt, Iraq, Kampuchea, North Korea, Pakistan, Somalia, Sudan, Tanzania, Vietnam and Zambia), production including the improved J-6 III (F-6C) – see next entry – and allegedly involving more than 4,000 aircraft when completed in the mid 'eighties. Experimental versions of the MiG-19S included the SM-10 with flight refuelling probe (mid 1955), the SM-30 ramp-launched target defence inter-

ceptor (1957), and the SM-50 quick-reaction interceptor with RU-013 rocket boost system. Data relate to the standard MiG-19S. *Max speed, 902 mph (1 452 km/h) at 32,810 ft (10 000 m), or Mach=1.34. Initial climb, 22,640 ft/min (115 m/sec). Range (internal fuel), 863 mls (1 390 km). Empty weight, 11,399 lb (5 172 kg). Max loaded weight, 19,470 lb (8 832 kg). Span, 29 ft 6⅓ in (9,00 m). Length, 41 ft 4 in (12,60 m). Height, 12 ft 9½ in (3,90 m). Wing area, 269.1 sq ft (25,00 m²).*

MIKOYAN-GUREVICH MiG-19P USSR

Whereas the MiG-19 had been conceived as a simple, clear-weather fighter, with gyro gunsight and no radar ranging, some limited all-weather capability was introduced at an early stage in the fighter's development life with what the OKB designated SM-7. Equipped with an RP-1 *Izumrud* AI radar in a revised, extended nose, the SM-7/1, flown for the first time on 28 August 1954, was in other respects similar to the SM-9/1. Transferred to the NII VVS on 15 December 1954, it entered production for both the PVO and the Navy as the MiG-19P (*Poiskovyi*, or Search), the second prototype, the SM-7/2, having aerodynamic modifications similar to those adopted for the MiG-19S and these being standardised. Powered by two AM-9B (RD-9B) engines, the MiG-19P was armed with two 30-mm NR-30 cannon and entered service during 1956. In the meantime, a modified prototype, the SM-7/M, had entered flight test in January of that year. Equipped with *Izumrud*-2 radar, the SM-7/M discarded the wing root-mounted cannon and introduced four wing pylons for beam-riding K-5M missiles. As the MiG-19PM, this version supplanted the MiG-19P in production. Licence manufacture of the MiG-19P was undertaken in China, the first Chinese-assembled example – presumably from a Soviet-supplied kit – flying on 17 December 1958. The MiG-19P did not achieve production in China until 1963, being initially built at Shenyang and subsequently at Nanchang as the J-6 I, and joined in production at Nanchang by the MiG-19PM as the J-6 II, with the K-5M missile also being licence-built as the PL-1. Further

(Above) The first prototype MiG-19, the SM-9/1, and (below) the series production MiG-19S day fighter.

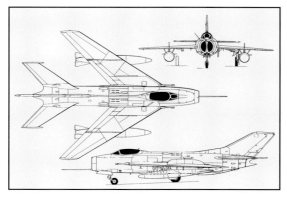

(Below) A Chinese-built MiG-19S (F-6) of No 19 Sqn, PAF, at Marsoor, with 165-Imp gal/750-l belly tank.

(Above) One of the SM-7 prototypes of the MiG-19P, and, (below) the MiG-19PM which discarded cannon armament in favour of a quartet of K-5M missiles.

Chinese developments included the J-6Xin, which replaced the *Izumrud* with a Chinese-developed AI radar accommodated in a needle-shaped radome mounted centrally on the intake splitter, and the J-6 III, which, with a similar radar to the J-6Xin, had a reduced wing span and wingtip-mounted AAMs. The following data relate to the MiG-19PM. *Max speed, 777 mph (1250km/h) at 32,810 ft (10 000 m), or Mach=1.15,702 mph (1130 km/h) at 49,210 ft (15 000 m), or Mach=1.06. Time to 49,210 ft (15 000 m), 4.8 min. Range (internal fuel), 621 mls (l 000 km) at 32,810ft (10 000 m). Loaded weight (clean), 17,041 lb (7 730 kg), (with two 88-Imp-gal/400-l tanks), 18,660 lb (8 464 kg). Dimensions as for MiG-19S apart from a length of 43 ft 5¹/₂ in (13,25 m).*

MIKOYAN-GUREVICH I-370 USSR

During 1953, the MiG OKB launched the design of a single-engined tactical fighter which was to utilise a wing fundamentally similar to that of the twin-engined SM-9, forerunner of the MiG-19, work on which was proceeding in parallel. Officially designated I-370 and assigned the OKB appellation of I-1, the new fighter received a Klimov VK-7 turbojet rated at 7,771 lb st (3 525 kgp) and boosted to 11,541 lb st (5 235 kgp) with afterburning. The prototype was flown for the first time on 16 February 1955, but high speed performance proved disappointing. It was therefore returned to the factory where an uprated VK-7 engine was installed, this having normal maximum and afterburning thrust ratings of 8,675 lb (3 935 kg) and 13,823 lb (6 270 kg) respectively. With a new wing, the quarter-chord sweepback of which was increased from 55 to 57 deg, the prototype was redesignated I-2 by the OKB. Limited testing of the I-2 was undertaken during which design maximum speed proved unobtainable. A further development of the basic design, the I-3 (I-380), remained unflown owing to the non-delivery of its more powerful VK-3 engine. *Max speed, 902 mph (1 452 km/h) at 35,435 ft (10 800 m), or Mach=1.37. Time to 16,405 ft (5 000 m), 1.15 min. Ceiling, 55,775 ft (17 000 m). Range (max external fuel), 1,553 mls (2 500 km). Empty weight, 11,212 lb (5 086 kg). Max loaded weight, 18,298 lb (8 300 kg). Span, 29 ft 6¹/₃ in (9,00 m). Length, 41 ft 8 in (12,70 m). Wing area, 269.1 sq ft (25, 00 m²).*

The I-370 (below) was flown under OKB designations I1 and I-2, but failed to meet performance demands.

MIKOYAN-GUREVICH YE-2 USSR

By early 1954, the MiG OKB was involved in a design programme with the objective of developing a comparatively lightweight interceptor fighter capable of attaining Mach=2.0 and altitudes of the order of 65,600 ft (20 000 m). At this time, the respective advantages of two favoured configurations - the thin, highly sweptback wing and the pure delta wing, both mated with slab-type horizontal tail surfaces - had still to be resolved. The OKB elected, therefore, to build aerodynamic test vehicles in parallel utilizing both configurations, the first to fly being that with the sweptback wing. Referred to as the Ye-1, this aircraft was originally to have been powered by an AM-5A turbojet. With

(Below) The Ye-2 and (above) the Ye-2A underwent comparison trials with parallel delta-winged types.

The Ye-2A (below) was built in pre-series quantity.

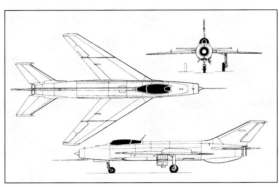

the availability of the AM-9B engine of 5,732 lb st (2 600 kgp) and 7,165 lb st (3 250 kgp) with afterburning, the airframe was modified to take the more powerful unit, and, armed with two 30-mm NR-30 cannon, was flown as the Ye-2 on 14 February 1955. As no clear advantage between the Ye-2 and the delta-winged Ye-4 was immediately obvious, an additional prototype of each configuration, the Ye-2A and Ye-5, was ordered, these having the Tumansky-developed AM-11 (R-11) engine of 8,377 lb st (3 800 kgp) and 11,243 lb st (5 100 kgp) with afterburning. The swept-back Ye-2A flew for the first time on 22 March 1956, and a pre-series of five more aircraft was built - these being provisionally assigned the designation MiG-23 - for evaluation purposes, but, in the event, the delta-winged Ye-5 was deemed to offer marginally superior characteristics and was chosen for large-scale production. *Max speed, 1,181 mph (1900 km/h). Time to 32,810 ft (10 000 m), 7.3 min. Ceiling, 59,055 ft (18 000 m). Max range, 1,243 mls (2 000 km). Empty weight, 9,568 lb (4 340 kg). Normal loaded weight, 13,779 lb (6 250 kg). Span, 26 ft 7¹/₄ in (8, 11 m). Length, 43 ft 4⁷/₈ in (13,23 m). Wing area, 226.05 sq ft (21, 00 m²).*

MIKOYAN-GUREVICH MIG-21F USSR

The MiG-21, NATO reporting name Fishbed, has many claims to fame. Not counting the Chinese J-7/F-7 but including two-seat trainers, more than 10,000 were produced, far exceeding that of any other supersonic fighter. In all, a record 30 variants were produced, of which no fewer than 15 were primary, while "specials" set a total of 17 world records. It served with 49 nations in all, and took part in more wars than any other fighter. Its greatest weaknesses were short endurance, and a rear view from the cockpit that varied from appalling to non-existent! At the beginning of 2001, almost 2,000 were still in service with 29 air forces. The requirement which led to the MiG-21 was issued in 1953. It called for a point defence bomber interceptor with a high rate of climb, a maximum dash speed of Mach 2, a service ceiling of 65,620 ft (20 000 m), a range-only radar, compatibility with air-to-air missiles, and two large cannon. It had to be affordable in quan-

tity, and maintainable, manoeuvrable, easy to fly, and be able to operate from semi-prepared fields. In 1953 this was a tall order. The sciences of aerodynamics, systems, and propulsion were all breaking new ground. For sheer performance, the optimum was the smallest possible airframe wrapped around the largest possible engine. For handling and manoeuvrability, a tailed delta configuration was chosen. The delta Ye-4 was

The Ye-4 (above) was the true progenitor of the MiG-21, becoming the Ye-4/2 with airflow fences (below).

The Ye-5 (below) was essentially similar to the Ye-4/2 apart from the more powerful AM-11 engine.

The definitive prototypes of the MiG-21 were designated Ye-6, the second, the Ye-6/2, being seen (below) with K-13 (R3S) IR missiles at the wingtips.

General arrangement drawing (below) of MiG-21F-13 seen (above) with Finnish *Ilmavoimien*, August 1985.

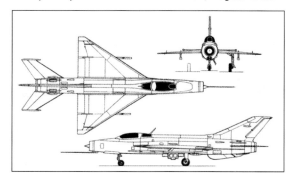

powered by the same AM-9B turbojet as the Ye-2, and had an identical fuselage and empennage. It first flew on 16 June 1955, piloted by A. Sedov. This and the similar Ye-4/2 were followed on 9 January 1956 by the Ye-5, flown by V. A. Nefyedov. This had wing fences and the AM-11 turbojet, later redesignated R-11, rated at 11,243 lb (5 100 kgp) max and 8,377 lb (3 800 kgp) military thrust. The next stage was to build three Ye-6 prototypes, which were effectively MiG-21 prototypes. Powered by the Tumansky R-11F-300, rated at 12,654 lb (5 740 kgp) max and 8,554 lb (3 880 kgp) military thrust, they differed from the Ye-5 mainly in having the horizontal tail surfaces set lower, a single rather than a double ventral fin, and a slimmed-down fuselage. Ye-6/1 attained a speed of Mach 2.05, but on 28 May 1958, suffered an engine failure. It crashed on landing, and Nefyedov was killed. Ye-6/2 was mainly notable for having wingtip launch rails for missiles, while the Ye-6/3, which first flew in December 1958, set two new world speed records. Stripped and tuned, it became the Ye-66. On 31 October 1959, it clocked 1,289.52 kt (2 388 km/h) over a 15-25 km course. Then on 16 September 1960 it recorded 1,349.46 kt (2 499 km/h) over a 100 km closed circuit. On 28 April 1961, extensively modified as the Ye-66A, with the R-37F-TRD turbojet and a rocket motor, it set a new absolute altitude record of 113,862 ft (34 714 m). The first production model was the Ye-6T, later MiG-21F. An SRD-5 ranging radar was accommodated in the three-position shock cone in the pitot-style intake. Air-to-air armament consisted of two 30-mm NR-30 cannon each with 60 rounds, and two rocket pods each containing 16 57-mm S-5M unguided rockets. Only 40 were built before it was replaced on the production lines in 1960 by the MiG-21F-13. This model carried the SRD-5M Kvant ranging radar. Other differences were a broader fin, and a fully variable afterburner. Two K-13 heat homing AAMs could be carried on underwing pylons. The -13 was produced in the USSR until 1965, and in Czechoslovakia until 1972. It also formed the basis of the Chinese Chengdu J-7/F-7 (which see). The MiG-21F and -21F-13 were clear air day fighters. The obvious next step was to introduce a limited night and all-weather capability. This emerged as the Ye-7, later the MiG-21P. To hold the TsD-30T radar, an enlarged fixed inlet centrebody was used, while to preserve the same mass flow to the R-11F-300 engine, the nose was lengthened and widened. Other avionics improvements included guidance and navigation systems. The 30-mm cannon were omitted; the sole air-to-air armament consisted of two K-13 AAMs. Other changes were a new fuel tank behind the cockpit, an enlarged dorsal spine, and larger wheels for use on semi-prepared strips. The Ye-7/1 first flew on 10 August 1958, and production of the MiG-21P commenced in June 1960. Next came the MiG-21PF, powered by the R-11F-300, rated at 13,492 lb (6 120 kgp) max and 8,708 lb (3 950 kgp) military thrust. The shock

cone, which on the PF was translating, housed the RP-21 Sapfir radar. A larger dorsal fairing made space for more fuel, something of which all MiGs were notoriously short, and the rear cockpit transparencies were eliminated, reducing even further the poor view astern. Provision was made for a GP-9 gun pack holding a 23-mm GSh-23 twin barrel cannon. The MiG-21PF was produced in the USSR between 1962 and 64, and an export "monkey" version, the MiG-21FL with the inferior R-2L radar and the same engine as the MiG-21F, from 1965 until 1968. This last was also licence-built by HAL in India over the same period. The MiG-21PF was replaced on the production lines by the MiG-21PFM, which had a larger fin, a tail parachute as standard, and blown flaps. The engine was the R-11F2S-300, giving a maximum thrust of 13,613 lb (6 175 kgp). On previous models, the canopy and windshield opened forward, to give some protection to the pilot during ejection. On the PFM, the windshield was fixed, and the canopy opened to starboard. The radar was the RP-21M, and this was linked to the carriage of two K-5M beam-riding missiles. The MiG-21 PFM was produced in the USSR in 1964-65 and its "monkey" version, the MiG-21PFS, from 1966 until 1968. Next came the MiG-21S, which was built between 1965 and 1968. An interceptor with the R-11F2S-300 turbojet, flap blowing, a three-axis autopilot and the improved Lazur-M guidance system, this carried the RP-22S radar. It was followed by the MiG-21SM, powered by the Tumansky R-

The Ye-7/1 (above), first prototype of the MiG-21P, production of which gave place in 1962 to the MiG-21PF (below) with uprated engine and new radar.

13-300, rated at 14,308 lb (6 360 kgp) max and 8,973 lb (4 070 kgp) military thrust. In a reversal of previous trends, the SM had an integral cannon; the 23-mm GSh-23, with a gunsight designed to cope with high-g manoeuvres. Radar was the RP-22 Saphir 21, and missile armament consisted of two K-13T or K-13Rs. Production lasted from 1968 to 1974. The export version was the MiG-21M, with the R-11F2S-300 turbojet, and the RP-21MA radar. HAL licence-built the type for India until 1981. The MiG-21MF was an upgraded -21M, powered by the R-13-300 turbojet and carrying the Sapfir-21 radar. At low level this was much faster than its predecessors, which surprised American flyers over North Vietnam. It was armed with a built-in 23-mm GSh-23L cannon with 200 rounds, and could carry four AAMs, typically two K-13S and two K-13T, although later a mix of radar and heat homing K-60s was used. Production in the USSR continued until 1975. Also developed from the MiG-21M was the MiG-21MT. A transitional aircraft, it was marked by an

(Above) MiG-21MF of 1 SLP (Fighter Regiment), Czechoslovak *Letectvo*, at Budejovice, 1978.

increase in fuel of more than 20 per cent, most of the extra housed in an enlarged dorsal spine. Only 15 were built, in 1971. This led on to the MiG-21SMT, a hybrid with the airframe and weaponry of the M, and the engine and fuel capacity of the MT. However, the huge dorsal tank caused stability problems, and its capacity had to be reduced by one third. It was built in the USSR in 1971/2. The final major and most potent variant was the MiG-21bis. To improve low level performance, it was re-engined with the R-25-300. This had two afterburning ratings: 21,826 lb (9 900 kgp), which could only be used when supersonic and below 13,124 ft (4 000 m), for a maximum of three minutes. In all other flight regimes, maximum thrust was 16,653 lb (7 100 kgp). Military thrust was an unexceptional 9,039 lb (4 100 kgp). Internal fuel tankage was increased, and new avionics enabled the pilot to navigate in poor conditions. The 23-mm GSh-23 cannon was retained, and the AAM load was a mix of K-60M, and K-13M, the latter with twice the range and less stringent launch parameters than early K-13s. USSR production was from 1972 to 75, while HAL continued until 1987. During the 1990s, upgrades have proliferated. Sokol is converting the MiG-21bis to the MiG-21-93 for India, given it a "glass cockpit" with HOTAS and a wrap-around windshield, modern avionics with the Kopyo multi-mode radar and an IRST. It carries up to six R-60MKs or four R-73Es. The first -93 is believed to have flown on 25 May 1995, and final delivery should be complete by 2004. Sokol also has a contract to refurbish Vietnam's MiG-21bis fleet, but precise details are lacking. The other Sokol proposal, to upgrade MiG-21Ms and MFs as

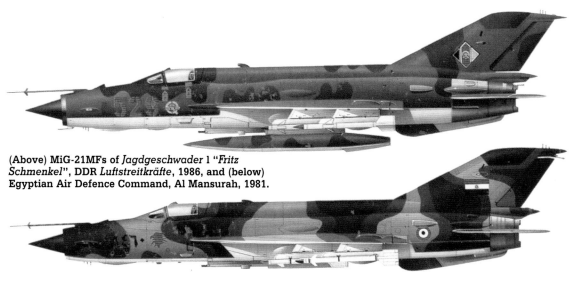

(Above) MiG-21MFs of *Jagdgeschwader* 1 "*Fritz Schmenkel*", DDR *Luftstreitkräfte*, 1986, and (below) Egyptian Air Defence Command, Al Mansurah, 1981.

Type	MiG-21F	MiG-21F-13	MiG-21PF	MiG-21FL
NB. All variants- span 23.47 ft (7,15 m), length 44.16 ft (13,46 m), wing area 248 sq ft (23,00 m²).				
Height (ft/m)	13.46/4,10	13.46/4,10	13.46/4,10	13.46/4,10
Norm takeoff weight (lb/kg)	15,102/6 850	16,248/7 370	17,086/7 750	17,262/7 830
Loadfactor (g)	7	7	8	8
Max speed hi (kt/kmh)	1,174/2 175	1,174/2 175	1,174/2 175	1,174/2 175
Max speed lo (kt/kmh)	594/1 100	621/1 150	702/1 300	610/1 130
Ceiling (ft/m)	62,339/19 000	62,339/19 000	62,339/19 000	62,339/19 000
Range (nm/km)	820/1 520	702/1 300	755/1 440	782/1 450

Type	MiG-21PFM/PFS	MiG-21SM	MiG-21MF	MiG-21bis
NB. All variants- span 23.47 ft (7,15 m), length 44.16 ft (13,46 m), wing area 248 sq ft (23,00 m²).				
Height (ft/m)	13.53/4,125	13.53/4,125	13.53/4,125	13.53/4,125
Norm takeoff weight (lb/kg)	17,240/7 870	18,078/8 200	18,078/8 200	19,235/8 725
Loadfactor (g)	8.5	8.5	8.5	8.5
Max speed hi (kt/kmh)	1,203/2 230	1,203/2 230	1,203/2 230	1,174/2 175
Max speed lo (kt/kmh)	702/1 300	702/1 300	702/1 300	702/1 300
Ceiling (ft/m)	62,339/19 000	56,761/17 300	59,714/18 200	57,418/17 500
Range (nm/km)	702/1 300	567/1 030	567/1 030	604/1 120

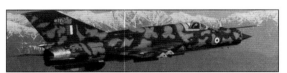

A general arrangement drawing of the MiG-21bis (below) and an Indian Air Force MiG-21bis (above).

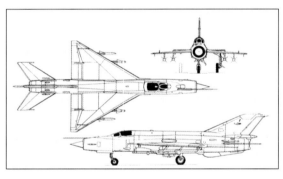

the MiG-21-98, aimed at older variants, with a smaller radar and a "glass cockpit", has yet to find a customer. Israel's IAI has produced the MiG-21-2000, based on the MiG-21bis. This includes a service life extension and a "glass cockpit" with HOTAS, and state of the art avionics, including the Elta EL/M 2032 multi-mode radar. Four Python 3s is the standard AAM fit. A simpler version of the -2000 is also on offer; takers to date include Cambodia, Ethiopia, and Uganda. A major programme to upgrade Romania's MiG-21MFs is underway with Elbit of Israel and Aerostar. The airframes are zero-lifed to allow them to continue in service until 2010. Named Lancer, it has a "glass cockpit" with HOTAS, and a mainly new avionics suite, including the Elta EL/M 2032 multi-mode radar, although some original equipment is retained. The maiden flight of the Lancer took place on 23 August 1995. Only 25 Lancers are being modified for air defence; the remainder are for ground attack.

MIKOYAN-GUREVICH YE-50   USSR

In 1954, the MiG OKB began to investigate the potential of a mixed-power, short-range point defence interceptor as a variation of the Ye-2, the result being designated Ye-50. Designed around a Tumansky AM-9Ye (RD-9Ye) turbojet with an afterburning thrust of 8,377 lb (3 800 kg) and a Duslikin S-155 bi-fuel rocket motor of 2,866 lb st (1 300 kgp), the first of three prototypes, the Ye-50/1, flew on 9 January 1956. It began trials with the rocket motor on 8 June 1956. A year later, on 17 June 1957, the sec-

The third prototype Ye-50 mixed-power point defence interceptor (below) featured a lengthened nose.

ond prototype, the Ye-50/2, attained a speed of Mach=2.33 and an altitude of 83,990 ft (25 600 m). The Ye-50/2 introduced some modifications to the rear fuselage and vertical tail, and the Ye-50/3 featured a lengthened fuselage nose and increased internal fuel. This last prototype was lost during flight test when its vertical tail detached. The Gor'kiy factory was ordered to build a batch of 20 aircraft, which, powered by the AM-11 engine and S-155 rocket, were to be designated Ye-50A. These were intended for operational evaluation, but none of them was built owing to a lack of rocket motors, the Duslikin OKB having meanwhile closed down. *Max speed, 1,529 mph (2 460 km/h) at 42,650ft (13 000 m), or Mach =2.3. Time to 32,810 ft (10 000 m), 6.7 min. Ceiling, 75,460 ft (23 000 m). Range, 280 mls (450 km). Loaded weight, 18,739 lb (8 500 kg). Span, 26 ft 7¹/₄ in (8,11 m). Length (Ye-50/1), 44 ft 8¹/₃in (13,62 m), (Ye-50/3), 48 ft 8²/₃ in (14,85 m). Wing area, 226.05 sq ft (21,00 M²).*

MIKOYAN-GUREVICH SM-12   USSR

In its definitive form the ultimate extrapolation of the basic MiG-19 design, the SM-12 evolved, by a process of incremental modification, as a mixed-power point defence interceptor. As the MiG-19S was phased into service with the VVS mid-1956, the MiG OKB was continuing the refinement of the *Izdeliya* SM twin-engined fighter initiated in 1951 with the SM-1 (I-340). The SM-12 first saw life as an exercise in drag reduction by

(Below) The second SM-12 prototype derived from the MiG-19S with an extended, straight-tapered nose.

(Above) The SM-12/3, which was the first prototype to be powered by the Sorokin-developed R3-26.

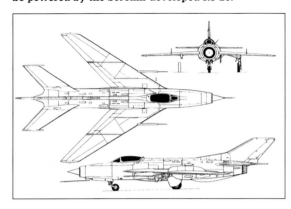

(Above) The SM-12PM and (below) the SM-12PMU with a permanent U-19D ventral rocket pack.

means of new air intake configurations, and the first of three prototypes, the SM-12/1, was essentially a MiG-19S with an extended and straight-tapered nose with sharp-lipped orifice and a pointed, two-position shock cone on the intake splitter. The third prototype, the SM-12/3, differed from its two predecessors primarily in discarding the paired AM-9B (RD-9B) engines for two R3-26 turbojets developed from the earlier power plant by V N Sorokin. These each offered an afterburning thrust of 7,936 lb (3 600 kg), enabling the SM-12/3 to attain speeds ranging between 888 mph (1430 km/h) at sea level, or Mach=1.16, and 1,199 mph (1930 km/h) at 39,370 ft (12 000 m), or Mach=1.8, and an altitude of between 57,415 and 59,055 ft (17 500 and 18 000 m) during its test programme. This outstanding performance prompted further development with a view to production as a point defence interceptor. Similarly powered by R3-26 engines and embodying major nose redesign with a larger orifice permitting introduction of a substantial two-position conical centrebody for a TsD-30 radar, a further prototype was completed as the SM-12PM. Discarding the wing root NR-30 cannon of preceding prototypes, the SM-12PM was armed with two K-5M (RS-2U) beam-riding missiles and entered flight test in 1957. This was joined at the end of 1958 by yet another prototype, the SM-12PMU. This had R3M-26 turbojets uprated to 8,377 lb st (3 800 kgp) with afterburning and augmented by a U-19D accelerator which took the form of a permanent ventral pack containing an RU-013 rocket motor and its propellant tanks. Developed by D D Sevruk, the RU-013 delivered 6,614 lb (3 000 kg) of thrust. With the aid of this rocket motor, the SM-12PMU attained an altitude of 78,740 ft (24 000 m) and a speed of Mach=1.69, but the decision had been taken meanwhile to manufacture the Ye-7 in series as the MiG-21P and further development of the SM-12 series was therefore discontinued. The following data relate to the SM12PM. *Max speed, 1, 069 mph (1720 km/h) at 32,810 ft (10 000 m), or Mach =1.59. Time to 32, 810 ft (10 000 m), 4. 0 min. Service ceiling, 57,085 ft (17 400 m). Range (internal fuel), 1,056 mls (1 700 km).*

(Below) The SM-12PM, seen here with RS-2U AAMs, introduced a two-position conical intake centrebody.

MIKOYAN-GUREVICH I-7U   USSR

Prior to abandonment of the I-3 (I-380) without flight test owing to the Klimov bureau's inability to develop the intended VK-3 engine to an acceptable standard for installation, a further prototype had been completed as the I-3U (I-410). Similarly intended for the VK-3 engine and also destined, therefore, to remain unflown, the I-3U (also known as the I-5) was intended to be part of the so-called *Uragan* (Hurricane) automated air interception system. When, in the summer of 1956, it became evident to the MiG OKB that the Klimov engine would not be forthcoming, work began on the redesign of the aircraft to take a Lyulka AL-7F turbojet of 13,757 lb st (6 240 kgp) and 20,326 lb st (9 220 kgp) with afterburning. In this form, the aircraft became the I-7U which flew for the first time on 22 April 1957. With quarter-chord sweepback reduced from the 57 deg of the I-3U to 55 deg, the I-7U carried a pair of 30-mm NR-30 cannon in the wing roots and had four wing stores stations each capable of carrying a rocket pod containing 16 57-mm ARS-57Ms. On 21 June 1957, the sole prototype I-7U suffered damage as a result of the starboard undercarriage leg failing when the aircraft landed following its 13th flight. After repair, the test programme was resumed but involved only six more flights, the last of these taking place on 24 January 1958. The I-7U was then re-engined with an AL-7F-1 to become the I-75. *Max speed, 1,031 mph (1 660 km/h) at 16,405 ft (5 000 m), or Mach=1.44, 1,429 mph (2 300 km/h) at 36,090 ft (11 000 m), or Mach=2.16. Time to 16,405 ft (5 000 m), 0.6 min, to 32,810 ft (10 000 m), 1.18 min. Range, 935 mls (1 505 km). Empty weight, 17,531 lb (7 952 kg). Loaded weight, 25,441 lb (11 540 kg). Span, 32 ft 8¾ in (9,98 m). Length, 55 ft 6⅓ in (16,92 m). Wing area, 343.38 sq ft (31,90 m²).*

The I-7U (below) was flown only 19 times before extensive modifications and testing as the I-75.

MIKOYAN-GUREVICH I-75   USSR

Retaining the wing of the I-7U and designed around the 18.6-mile (30-km) acquisition-range *Uragan* 5 radar and a pair of heavy, long-range K-8 beam-riding AAMs, the I-75 was flown for the first time on 28 April 1958. Powered by a Lyulka AL-7F-1 turbojet offering 13,757 lb st (6 240 kgp) and 20,315 lb st (9 215 kgp) with afterburning, the I-75 flew five times before being grounded on 15 May for installation of the *Uragan* 5B. Testing was resumed on 25 December 1958. Although

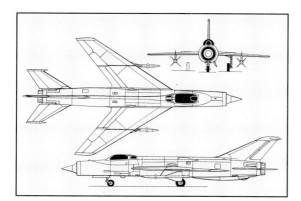

(Above and below) The I-75 with *Uragan* 5B radar and long-range K-8 beam-riding missiles.

the I-75 demonstrated exceptional performance, the prototype was flown only 18 times after the resumption of the test programme, which was terminated on 11 May 1959 with the decision to adopt the competitive Sukhoi T-431 for series production (as the Su-9). *Max speed, 1,274 mph (2 050 km/h) at 37,400 ft (11 400 m), or Mach=1.93, 1,162 mph (1 870 km/h) at 42,325 ft (12 900 m), or Mach=1.76. Time to 19,685 ft (6 000 m), 0.93 min, to 36,090 ft (11 000 m), 3.05 min. Range, 913 mls (1 470 km) at 39,370 ft (12 000 m). Empty weight, 18,241 lb (8 274 kg). Normal loaded weight, 24,140 lb (10 950 kg). Span, 32 ft 8¾ in (9,98 m). Length, 59 ft 11½ in (18,27 m). Wing area, 343.38 sq ft (31,90 m²).*

MIKOYAN-GUREVICH YE-152A   USSR

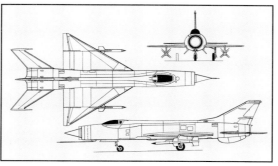

(Above) The Ye-152A twin-engined interceptor fighter.

For high speed development purposes and as a test bed for a 15-*tonne* engine that was being developed by the Tumansky bureau with a view to powering a proposed Mach=3.0 high-altitude interceptor (which was to materialise as the MiG-25), the MiG OKB developed what was ostensibly a pure research aircraft, the Ye-150. Powered by a Tumansky R-15-300 engine of 15,080 lb st (6 840 kgp) boosted to 22,376 lb st (10 150 kgp) with afterburning, the Ye-150 flew for the first time on 8 July 1960, and was subsequently to attain a speed of Mach=2.65 or 1,750 mph (2 816 km/h) and a ceiling of 73,820 ft (22 500 m). Design of an all-weather high-altitude interceptor based on the research aircraft had paralleled work on the Ye-150. As the Ye-152A, this had been adapted to take two thoroughly proven R-11F-300 engines owing to development problems with the large R-15 engine which were resulting in serious delays. In consequence, the Ye-152A interceptor fighter was ready to fly *before* the Ye-150 research aircraft upon which it was based, this event taking place on 10 July 1959. Powered by two R-11F-300 engines each rated at 8,598 lb st (3 900 kgp) and 12,654 lb st (5 740 kgp) with afterburning, the Ye-152A was intended to carry the *Uragan* 5B radar accommodated in a large, fixed intake centrebody and a pair of MiG-developed K-9 (K-155) long-range beam-riding missiles. While the intake centrebody of the Ye-152A was non-translatable, the ex-

The Ye-152A (above) was evolved from the Ye-150 high-speed research aircraft and was the first to fly.

treme forward fuselage with intake orifice was hydraulically movable, thus achieving the same effect as a fully-variable shock cone. The Ye-152A was overtaken by the R-15-powered Ye-152 (which see), and its flight test programme was terminated after 55 flights of which only two were made carrying K-9 AAMs. *Max speed, 1,327 mph (2 135 km/h) at 44,945 ft (13 700 m), or Mach=2.0, 1,553 mph (2 500 km/h) at 65,615 ft (20 000 m), or Mach=2.35. Time to 32,810 ft (10 000 m), 1.48 min. Ceiling, 64,960 ft (19 800 m). Normal loaded weight, 27,557 lb (12 500 kg). Max loaded weight, 30,776 lb (13 960 kg). Span, 27 ft 10⅛ in (8,49 m). Length, 62 ft 4 in (19,00 m). Wing area, 366.2 sq ft (34,02 m²).*

MIKOYAN-GUREVICH YE-152(P)   USSR

With the availability of the R-15-300 engine in acceptable form for fighter installation, the MiG OKB built two further prototypes of the Ye-152 with a single turbojet of this type supplanting the paired R-11F-300s of the Ye-152A. Retaining the systems of the Ye-152A, the Ye-152/1 and /2 were powered by the R-15-300 rated at 15,190 lb st (6 890 kgp) and boosted to 22,510 lb st (10 210 kgp) with afterburning. A larger delta wing swept back to 53 deg 47 min on the leading edge was

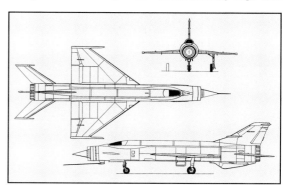

(Above) The Ye-152P and (below) the first R-15-300-engined heavy interceptor prototype, the Ye-152/1.

fitted, and the tips terminated in launchers for two K-9 AAMs. Equipped with *Uragan* 5B, the Ye-152/1 flew for the first time on 16 May 1961, and in the course of the following flight test programme, the Ye-152/2 attained 1,703 mph (2 740 km/h) and an altitude of 73,820 ft (22 500 m), Mach=2.28 being recorded at 59,055 ft (18 000 m) with two K-9 missiles *in situ*. Continuing development of the basic design resulted in the construction of two more prototypes, the first of these joining the test programme early in 1961 as the Ye-152P. Fitted with more sophisticated intercept and navigation equipment, the Ye-152P had a deeper and broader dorsal fairing substantially increasing internal fuel capacity and was intended to be fitted with an 11 ft 5¾-in (3,50-m) canard surface which was to be free-floating at subsonic speeds and locked at supersonic speeds. In the event, this canard was not fitted. Development of the Ye-152 series of interceptors was stopped as a result of the OKB's preoccupation with the Ye-155P (MiG-25P), but the remaining prototype was completed for high-speed research as the Ye-152M with an R-15B-300 engine providing an afterburning thrust of 22,510 lb (10 210 kg). This aircraft established (as the Ye-166) an absolute speed record over a 100-km (62-mile) closed-circuit of 1,616 mph (2 601 km/h) on 7 October 1961, and an absolute speed record of 1,666 mph (2 681 km/h) on 7 July 1962. The following data relate to the Ye-152/2. *Max speed, 1,560 mph (2 510 km/h) at 32,810 ft (10 000 m), or Mach=2.33. Time to 32,810 ft (10 000 m), 3.67 min. Ceiling, 74,375 ft (22 670 m). Range (with 330 Imp gal/1 500 l of external fuel), 913 mls (1 470 km). Empty weight, 24,030 lb (10 900 kg). Loaded weight, 31,636 lb (14 350 kg). Span, 28 ft 10⅛ in (8,79 m). Length, 64 ft 5⅞ in (19,66 m). Wing area, 452.31 sq ft (42,02 m²).*

The Ye-152P (below) is seen with wingtip-mounted dummies of an AAM subsequently discontinued.

MIKOYAN-GUREVICH YE-8   USSR

During 1961, the MiG OKB initiated work on an upgraded fighter based on the basic MiG-21PF airframe and referred to contemporaneously as the MiG-23. Assigned the OKB designation Ye-8, it featured a bifurcated ventral air intake for the R-21F engine, which, developed by N Metskhvarishvili, was rated at 9,920 lb st

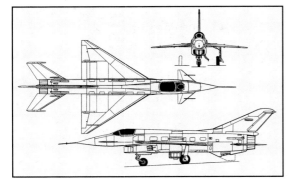

A general arrangement drawing of the Ye-8 (above) and (below) a photograph of the first prototype.

The second Ye-8 (above), the testing of which was discontinued after loss of the first aircraft.

(4 500 kgp) and 15,432 lb st (7 000 kgp) with afterburning. A variable-incidence canard spanning 8 ft 6⅓in (2,60 m) was fitted – this having been earlier tested by a Ye-6T – and it was proposed to install *Sapfir* 21 radar to accompany an armament of two K-13 AAMs. The first of two prototypes, the Ye-8/1, was flown on 17 April 1962, followed on 29 June by the Ye-8/2. On 11 September, the R-21F engine of the Ye-8/1 exploded at Mach=1.7 at 32,810 ft (10 000 m). It was subsequently ascertained that the sixth compressor stage fan had penetrated the engine casing and had then continued on to destroy the starboard aileron. At this time, the Ye-8/2 had effected 13 flights, but the programme was abandoned. *Max speed, 1,386 mph (2 230 km/h) at 36,090 ft (11 000 m), or Mach=2.1. Ceiling, 65,615 ft (20 000 m). Max loaded weight, 18,078 lb (8 200 kg). Span, 23 ft 5½ in (7,15 m). Length, 48 ft 10⅔ in (14,90 m). Wing area, 248.98 sq ft (23,13 m²).*

MIKOYAN-GUREVICH MiG-25   USSR

During 1964, the MiG OKB was devoting its primary effort to a high-altitude interceptor capable of speeds approaching Mach=3.0 as a counter to the Lockheed A-12 which was being developed in the USA as a long-range strategic reconnaissance aircraft – and *not* as an antidote to the North American B-70 Valkyrie bomber, as was subsequently to be alleged in the West. Ordered in February 1962, this aircraft was foreseen as having two Tumansky R-15B-300 turbojets with maximum dry and afterburning ratings of 16,534 lb st (7 500 kgp) and 22,509 lb st (10 210 kgp), a *Smerch* (Whirlwind) A radar with a 31-mile (50-km) acquisition range and an automatic pursuit mode, and a mix of radar-guided and IR-homing AAMs. The first prototype of the interceptor, the Ye-155P-1, flew on 9 September 1964 – five months after a strategic reconnaissance prototype, the Ye-155R, which had flown on 6 March – and series production as the MiG-25P began in 1969, with the first delivery to the VVS following on 13 April 1972 as the fastest and highest flying combat aircraft to that time. Prior to and subsequent to the service introduction of the MiG-25P, pre-series aircraft established (as the Ye-266) a number of international speed and altitude records. The MiG-25P equipped with the RP-25 *Smerch* radar carried a complement of two radar-guided R-40R and two IR-homing R-40T AAMs, this version giving place in production in 1978 to the upgraded MiG-25PD. This featured an improved RP-25 radar with lookdown/shoot-down capability, an armament of two R-40Rs and four R-60 IR-homing AAMs, and two R-15BD-300 turbojets of 19,400 lb st (8 800 kgp) and 24,690 lb st (11 200 kgp) with afterburning. From 1979, all MiG-25Ps were converted to MiG-25PD standard under the designation MiG-25PDS. Manufacture of the MiG-25PD continued at Gor'kiy until 1982, more than 1,200 MiG-25 aircraft of all versions having been

(Below) The MiG-25PD interceptor with two radar-guided R-40R and four IR-homing R-60 AAMs.

---

built of which in excess of 900 were interceptors. Foreign recipients of the interceptor comprised Iraq, Syria and Libya, all three having originally obtained the MiG-25P model, but those of the Libyan air arm subsequently being brought up to MiG-25PDS standard. The following data relate to the MiG-25P. *Max speed, 746 mph (1 200 km/h) at sea level, or Mach=0.98, 1,864 mph (3 000 km/h) at 42,650 ft (13 000 m), or Mach=2.83. Time to 65,615 ft (20 000 m), 8.9 min. Service ceiling, 67,915 ft (20 700 m). Range (internal fuel), 1,075 mls (1 730 km). Normal loaded weight (four R-40 AAMs), 80,952 lb (36 720 kg). Span, 45 ft 11¾ in (14,01 m). Length, 64 ft 9½ in (19,75 m). Wing area, 660.93 sq ft (61,40 m²).*

(Above) The Ye-155P prototype and (below) a general arrangement drawing of the MiG-25P.

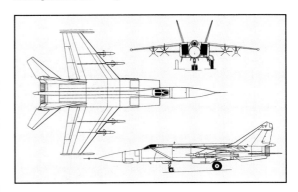

MIKOYAN-GUREVICH MiG-23PD (23-01)   USSR

One of two parallel studies to meet a VVS requirement for a new frontal fighter capable of operating from small, austerely-equipped forward bases, the MiG-23PD – *Pod'yomnye dvigateli*, or, literally, "lifting engines" – or 23-01 was first flown on 3 April 1967. Featuring a 57-deg delta wing planform fundamentally similar to that of the MiG-21 but scaled up 73.6 per cent, the MiG-23PD alias 23-01 featured auxiliary lift engines close to the CG. Two 5,180 lb st (2 350 kgp) Koliesov RD-36-35 engines were accommodated by a bay inserted in the centre fuselage and provided with a rear-hinged and louvred dorsal trap-type intake box and a ventral grid of transverse louvres deflecting the jet thrust during accelerating transition. A similar arrangement had been tested by the OKB in the previous year with the MiG-21PD test bed, which, with a 35.4-in (90-cm) fuselage lengthening aft of the cockpit and two RD-36-35 lift engines, had entered flight test on 16 June 1966. The primary power plant of the MiG-23PD was a Khachaturov R-27-300 of 11,464 lb st (5 200 kgp) and 17,196 lb st (7 800 kgp) with afterburning, and air was bled from the last compressor stage for flap blowing, the combination of lift engines and blown flaps reducing take-off distance to 590-650 ft (180-200 m). Armament consisted of one 23-mm GSh-23 cannon and two AAMs – one radar-guided K-23R and one IR-homing K-23T. Flight test continued until the

(Above) A MiG-23M and (below) a MiG-23ML both with an R-23 missile on the fixed wing glove pylon and a quartet of IR-homing R-60 AAMs on fuselage pylons.

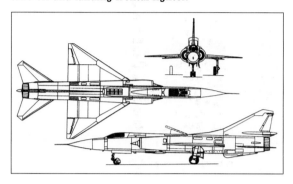

(Above and below) The MiG-23PD tailed-delta short-take-off-and-landing frontal fighter.

(Below) The prototype 23-11/1 with a K-23 AAM on the fixed wing glove pylon and wings fully swept back.

MIKOYAN MiG-31   USSR

Although Mikhail I Gurevich retired in 1964, the Experimental Construction Bureau was not formally redesignated as the A I Mikoyan OKB until 1971, the acronym "MiG" being retained. At this time, the OKB was engaged in a study of the upgrading potential of the basic MiG-25 as a tandem two-seat all-weather interceptor with emphasis on range capability. The first prototype, the Ye-155MP, flew for the first time on 16 September 1975, series production being launched at Gor'kiy in 1979. Powered by two Soloviev D-30F-6 turbofans each having an afterburning thrust of 34,170 lb (15 500 kg), the production development, the MiG-31, introduced the 124-mile (200-km) range SBI-16 Zaslon phased-array pulse-Doppler radar with lookdown/shoot-down and multiple-target engagement capabilities. This was mated with new semi-active radar-homing long-range R-33 AAMs – four in tandem pairs on fuselage centreline and two medium-range IR-homing R-40T AAMs on each of two wing stations, or a mix of these and R-60 close-combat IR-homing AAMs – the missiles being supplemented by a 23-mm multibarrel GSh-6-23 cannon. The MiG-31 achieved initial operational capability in 1983, and as at 2001 about 300 are believed to be in the inventory. However, following high accident and unserviceability rates, whether any are still operational is open to question. The prototype MiG-31M first flew in 1986. A bulged radome housed the improved Zaslon-M radar, stated to double existing detection ranges. The cockpit canopy was remodelled, multi-function displays were added, and a digital FCS replaced the hydraulic system. The dorsal spine was enlarged to increase internal fuel capacity to a massive 39,683 lb (18 000 kg); fin height and rudder area were increased slightly, and small pods appeared on the wingtips, presumably for ECM and other kit. The AAM fit was to be a combination of the R-37 and R-77. The MiG-31M proved unaffordable, and failed to enter

The MiG-31 (above and below) in standard form.

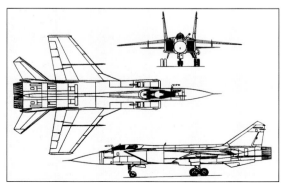

autumn of 1967 when further development was discontinued in favour of the parallel MiG-23-11. *Normal loaded weight, 35,273 lb (16 000 kg). Max loaded weight, 40,785 lb (18 500 kg). Span, 25ft 3⁷/₈in (7,72 m). Length, 55 ft 1³/₈ in (16,80 m). Height, 16ft 10³/₄ in (5,15 m). Wing area, 430.57 sq ft (40,00 m²).*

MIKOYAN-GUREVICH MiG-23S   USSR

Developed and built in parallel with the previously described MiG-23PD, the variable-geometry MiG-23-11 was flown for the first time on 10 June 1967, and its first 13 flights were devoted to preparation for the air parade over Domodyedovo a month later, on 9 July (where the prototype appeared on its 14th flight). Three prototypes, the 11/1, 11/2 and 11/3, were built, these being powered by the Khachaturov R-27F-300, and the hydraulically-operated wing having three angles of sweepback: 16 deg, 45 deg and 72 deg. Armament comprised four K-23 AAMs, and the three prototypes had logged 97 flights by July 1968 when the decision was taken to initiate series production as the MiG-23S, the aircraft being re-engined with the R-27F2M-300 of 15,212 lb st (6 900 kgp) and 22,046 lb st (10 000 kgp) with afterburning. It had been intended to instal *Sapfir* 23 radar, but as this was not ready, the shorter search

(Above) The prototype 23-11/1 and (below) a general arrangement drawing of the initial series MiG-23S.

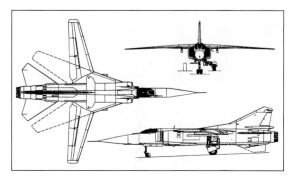

and track range *Sapfir* 21 had to be fitted, which necessitated an armament of four R-3 AAMs. The first MiG-23S was flown on 28 May 1969, but this was considered an interim version of the fighter, only 50 being built and production giving place to the extensively modified MiG-23M at the end of 1970. The following data relate to the MiG-23S. *Max speed (72 deg sweep), 795 mph (1 280 km/h) at 41,995 ft (12 800 m), or Mach=1.2, (with four R-3S AAMs), 733 mph (1 180 km/h), or Mach = 1. 11. Range (16 deg sweep and four R-3S AAMs), 1,118 mls (1 800 km). Span (16 deg), 45 ft 9⁷/₈ in (13,96 m), (72 deg), 25 ft 6¹/₄ in (7,78 m). Length, 54 ft 9¹/₂ in (16,70 m). Wing area (16 deg), 345.53 sq ft (32,10 m²), (72 deg), 321.74 sq ft (29,89 m²).*

MIKOYAN-GUREVICH MiG-23M   USSR

The first model of the variable-geometry MiG-23 to be built on a large scale, the MiG-23M differed extensively from the MiG-23S. The overall dimensions remained unchanged, but the wings were moved forward by some 2 ft (60 cm), increasing the gap between the wing and tail surfaces, and new broader-chord wing outer panels were introduced, increasing wing area by 45.96-56.51 sq ft (4,27-5,25 m²). An ogival dielectric radome was adopted for the new *Sapfir* 23D-Sh radar in place of the conical radome of the MiG-23S, and a TP-23 IR search/track pod was introduced under the cockpit. The new Khachaturov R-29-300 engine was introduced with maximum dry and afterburning thrusts of 18,298 lb (8 300 kg) and 26,896 lb (12 200 kg) respectively, internal fuel capacity was raised, provision was made for three 174-Imp gal (790-1) external tanks, and armament comprised a twin-barrel 23-mm GSh-23L cannon and four radar-guided R-23R and IR-homing R-23T AAMs. The MiG-23M was built from the end of 1970 until 1976 when this model was phased out in favour of the MiG-23ML with the Khachaturov R-35-300 of 18,850 lb st (8 550 kgp) and 28,660 lb st (13 000 kgp) and the upgraded *Sapfir* 23ML radar, and four hard points on the fuselage and two on the wing glove. A version fitted with special avionics for the PVO was assigned the designation MiG-23P, while the MiG-23MLD was a retrofit with upgraded equipment and SOS-3-4 controlled wing leading-edge slots for use at an intermediate 33-deg sweepback angle. The MiG-23MLD also introduced a dog-tooth notch at the junction of the wing glove leading edge and the intake trunk on each side. Production of the MiG-23ML terminated in 1981, and of more than 5,800 MiG-23s of all versions (including ground attack and two-seat combat training models) built, approximately two-thirds were air-air fighters which were exported to 18 countries. The following data relate to the MiG-23ML. *Max speed (72 deg sweep), 839 mph (1 350 km/h) at sea level, or Mach=1.1, 1,553 mph (2 500 km/h) at altitude, or Mach=2.35. Ceiling, 60,695 ft (18 500 m). Range (internal fuel), 1,212 mls (1 950 km). Loaded weight, 32,407 lb (14 700 kg). Max loaded weight, 39,242 lb (17 800 kg). Dimensions as for MiG-23S apart from length of 51 ft 04¹/₈ in (15,65 m) and wing areas of (16 deg sweep) 402 sq ft (37,35 m²) and (72 deg sweep) 367.7 sq ft (34,16m²).*

A MiG-31 long-range all-weather interceptor of which production was continuing in Russia in 1993.

service. The following data apply to the MiG-31. *Max speed hi, Mach 2.83. Max speed lo, Mach 1.23. Operational ceiling, 67,589 ft (20 600 m). Time to 32,810 ft (10 000 m), 7.9 min. Max range, 1,781 nm (3 300 km). Empty weight, 48,104 lb (21 820 kg). Normal takeoff, 90,389 lb (41 000 kg). Span, 44 ft 2 in (13,46 m). Length, 74 ft 5 in (22,69 m). Height, 20 ft 2 in (6,15 m). Wing area, 663 sq ft (61,60m²).*

MiG-31 with Phazotron S-800 Zaslon radar.

MIKOYAN MiG-29   USSR

Conceived primarily as a highly agile counterair fighter, but possessing secondary attack capability, the MiG-29 was developed to an LFI *Logkii frontovoi istrebityel,* or light frontline fighter requirement, formulated at the beginning of the '70s. The first of 19 prototypes was flown on 6 October 1977. Development of the engines was not without problems; both the second and fourth prototypes crashed, although both pilots, Valeriy Menitsky and Alexsandr Fedotov, ejected safely. Not until June 1983 did the MiG-29 start to reach the operational units. A twin-engined single-seater, it had a moderately swept wing with large leading edge extensions; twin outwardly canted fins, and the stabilators were carried on booms outside the engine nacelles. The FCS was hydraulic, and the cockpit displays old-fashioned "steam-gauge". One definite advance was the view from the cockpit, which was far better than any previous Mikoyan fighter. However, the MiG-29 had several unusual features. The Klimov RD-33 augmented turbofans, each rated at 18,298 lb (8 300 kgp) max and 11,110 lb (5 040 kgp) military thrust, were widely spaced and underslung. Variable geometry inlets, necessary for Mach 2 plus, had top-hinged perforated blanks which closed when the aircraft was on the ground; air was drawn through overwing louvred vents. This measure had been adopted to prevent the ingestion of ice or stones when operating from semi-prepared runways, but it later transpired that the doors could be closed in flight at speeds up to 432 kt (800 kmh). Another unusual feature was the KOLS-29 IRST, which featured a laser ranger. This provided exceptionally accurate tracking for the 30-mm GSh-30-1 cannon. The IRST was also linked to the Phazotron N O19 multi-mode radar, and if contact by one was lost, the other cut in automatically. The original air-to-air armament consisted of six R-60s, or two medium range R-27Rs and four R-60s. Later the R-60s were supplanted by the extremely agile R-73, aided by a helmet-mounted sight. The conversion trainer was the MiG-29UB. Usual Soviet practice was to extend the cockpit aft, at the expense of fuel. With the short-legged MiG-29, this was not a viable option, and on the UB, the cockpit was extended forward, displacing the radar, although the optronics were retained. In consequence the MiG-29UB had only marginal combat capability. The first upgrade was the MiG-29S/SE, which first flew on 23 December 1980. This had an enlarged dorsal spine to hold more fuel and extra avionics, while five-segment computer-controlled flaps on the wing leading edge replaced the four of the earlier model. Two hardpoints were plumbed for external tanks, and the N-019M radar allowed simultaneous engagement of two targets and was compatible with the new R-77 Amraamski missile. The MiG-29SE was an export

Key to MiG-23ML (23-12)

1 Pitot tube
2 Radome
3 Flat dish radar scanner
4 Scanner tracking mechanism
5 Sapfir (Sapphire) 23ML J-band pulse-Doppler (34-mile/55-km range) radar module
6 RSBN-6S ILS aerial
7 Radar mounting bulkhead
8 Cooling air scoop
9 Ventral Doppler navigation aerial
10 Weapons system avionics equipment
11 Nose compartment access doors
12 Yaw vane
13 Dynamic pressure probe (q-feel)
14 SRO-2 IFF antenna
15 Temperature probe
16 Cockpit front pressure bulkhead
17 TP-23M IR search/track pod
18 Nosewheel steering control
19 Torque scissor links
20 Pivoted axle beam
21 Twin aft-retracting nosewheels
22 Nosewheel spray/debris guards
23 Shock absorber strut
24 Nosewheel doors
25 Hydraulic retraction jack
26 Angle of attack transmitter
27 Rudder pedals
28 Control column
29 Three-position SPK-1 wing sweep control lever
30 Engine throttle lever
31 Cockpit section framing
32 KM-1 ejection seat firing handles
33 Radar "head-down" display
34 Instrument panel
35 Instrument panel shroud
36 Weapons sighting unit "head-up" display
37 Armoured glass windscreen panel
38 R-3S infra-red homing air-to-air missile
39 Missile launch rail
40 R-3R radar homing air-to-air missile
41 Wing glove pylon
42 Cockpit canopy cover, upward hingeing
43 Electrically heated rear view mirror
44 KM-1 "zero-zero" ejection seat
45 Ejection seat headrest/drogue parachute container
46 Canopy hinge point
47 Canopy hydraulic jack
48 Boundary layer splitter plate
49 Boundary layer ramp bleed air holes

50 Port engine air intake
51 Adjustable intake ramp screw jack control
52 Intake internal flow fences
53 Retractable landing/taxiing lamp (port and starboard)
54 Pressure sensor, automatic intake control system
55 Variable area intake ramp doors

56 Intake duct framing
57 Ventral cannon ammunition magazine
58 Control rod linkages
59 Intake ramp bleed air ejector
60 Boundary layer spill duct
61 Avionics equipment
62 ADF sense aerial
63 Tailplane control rods
64 Forward fuselage fuel tanks
65 Wing glove fairing
66 Intake duct suction relief doors
67 Ground power and intercom sockets
68 Twin missile carrier/launch unit
69 Port fuselage stores pylon
70 Weapons system electronic control units
71 Electronic countermeasures equipment
72 Wing glove pylon attachment fitting
73 SO-69 radar warning and suppression aerials
74 Wing sweep control horn
75 Screw jack wing sweep rotary actuator
76 Twin hydraulic motors
77 Central combining gearbox
78 Wing pivot box carry-through unit (welded steel construction)
79 Pivot box integral fuel tank (total internal fuel capacity: 1,034 Imp gal/4 700 l)
80 VHF aerial
81 Wing pivot bearing
82 Starboard SO-69 radar warning and suppression aerials

83 Extended-chord saw-tooth leading edge
84 Fixed portion of leading edge
85 Non-swivelling, jettisonable wing pylon (wing restricted to forward swept position)
86 Jettisonable fuel tank (174-Imp gal/790-l capacity)
87 Nose section of MiG-23UB tandem seat combat trainer
88 Student pilot's cockpit
89 Folding blind-flying hood
90 Rear seat periscope, extended
91 Instructor's cockpit
92 MiG-23BN dedicated ground attack variant
93 Radar ranging antenna
94 Laser ranging nose fairing
95 Raised cockpit canopy
96 Armoured fuselage side panels
97 Starboard wing leading-edge flap (lowered)
98 Leading-edge flap hydraulic actuator
99 Starboard wing integral fuel tank

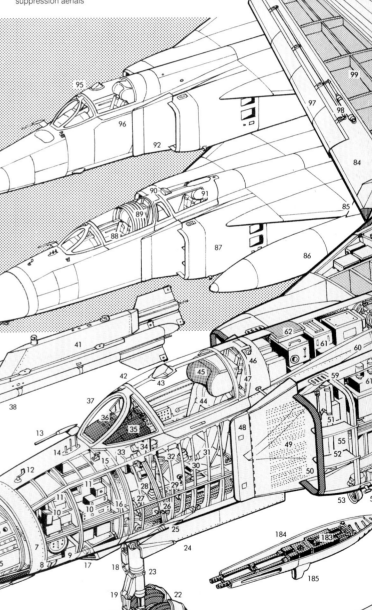

100 Starboard navigation light
101 Wing fully forward (16-deg sweep) position
102 Static discharger
103 Full-span three-segment plain flap (lowered)
104 Starboard wing intermediate (45-deg sweep) position
105 Starboard wing full (72-deg sweep) position
106 Two-segment spoilers/lift dumpers (open)
107 Spoiler hydraulic actuators
108 Flap hydraulic jack
109 Wing glove flexible seal
110 Flap mechanical interconnection and disengage mechanism
111 Wing root housing
112 Dorsal spine fairing
113 Engine intake compressor face
114 Wing root housing sealing plate
115 Rear fuselage fuel tanks
116 Tailplane control linkages
117 Fin root fillet
118 Afterburner duct cooling air scoop
119 Artificial feel control units
120 Control system hydraulic accumulator
121 Artificial feel and autopilot controls
122 Tailplane trim controls
123 Starboard all-moving tailplane
124 Fin leading edge
125 Tailfin construction
126 Short wave ground control communications aerial
127 Fin-tip UHF aerial fairing
128 ILS aerial
129 ECM aerial
130 SO-69 tail warning radar
131 Tail navigation light
132 Static discharger
133 Rudder
134 Honeycomb core construction
135 Rudder hydraulic actuators, port and starboard
136 Parachute release links
137 Brake parachute housing
138 Split conic fairing parachute doors
139 Variable-area afterburner nozzle
140 Fixed tailplane tab
141 Honeycomb core trailing-edge panel
142 Static discharger
143 Port all-moving tailplane construction
144 Afterburner nozzle control jacks (6)
145 Tailplane pivot bearing
146 Tailplane actuator
147 Airbrakes (4) upper and lower surfaces
148 Airbrake hydraulic jacks
149 Afterburner duct heat shroud
150 Ventral fin, folded (undercarriage down) position
151 Ventral fin down position
152 Screw jack fin actuator
153 Fin attachment fuselage main frame
154 Khachaturov R-35-300 afterburning turbojet engine
155 Lower UHF aerial
156 Engine accessory equipment compartment
157 Air conditioning system equipment
158 Port plain flap
159 Spoiler actuators
160 Port spoilers/lift dumpers
161 Flap guide rails
162 Fixed spoiler strips
163 Static discharger
164 Wing tip fairing
165 Port navigation light
166 Port leading-edge flap
167 Leading-edge flap control linkage
168 Front spar
169 Wing rib construction
170 Rear spar
171 Auxiliaries centre spar
172 Wing skin support struts
173 Port wing integral fuel tank
174 Wing pylon attachment fitting
175 Leading-edge rib construction
176 Port mainwheel
177 Mainwheel door/debris guard
178 Shock absorber strut
179 Pivoted axle beam
180 Articulated mainwheel leg strut
181 Mainwheel leg doors
182 R-60 short range air-to-air missile
183 GSh-23L twin-barrel 23-mm cannon
184 Ventral cannon pack
185 Gun gas venting air scoop
186 Fuselage centreline pylon
187 Ventral fuel tank (174-Imp gal/790-l capacity)
188 R-23 missile launch rail
189 Launch rail attachment hardpoints
190 R-23R long-range radar-guided air-to-air missile

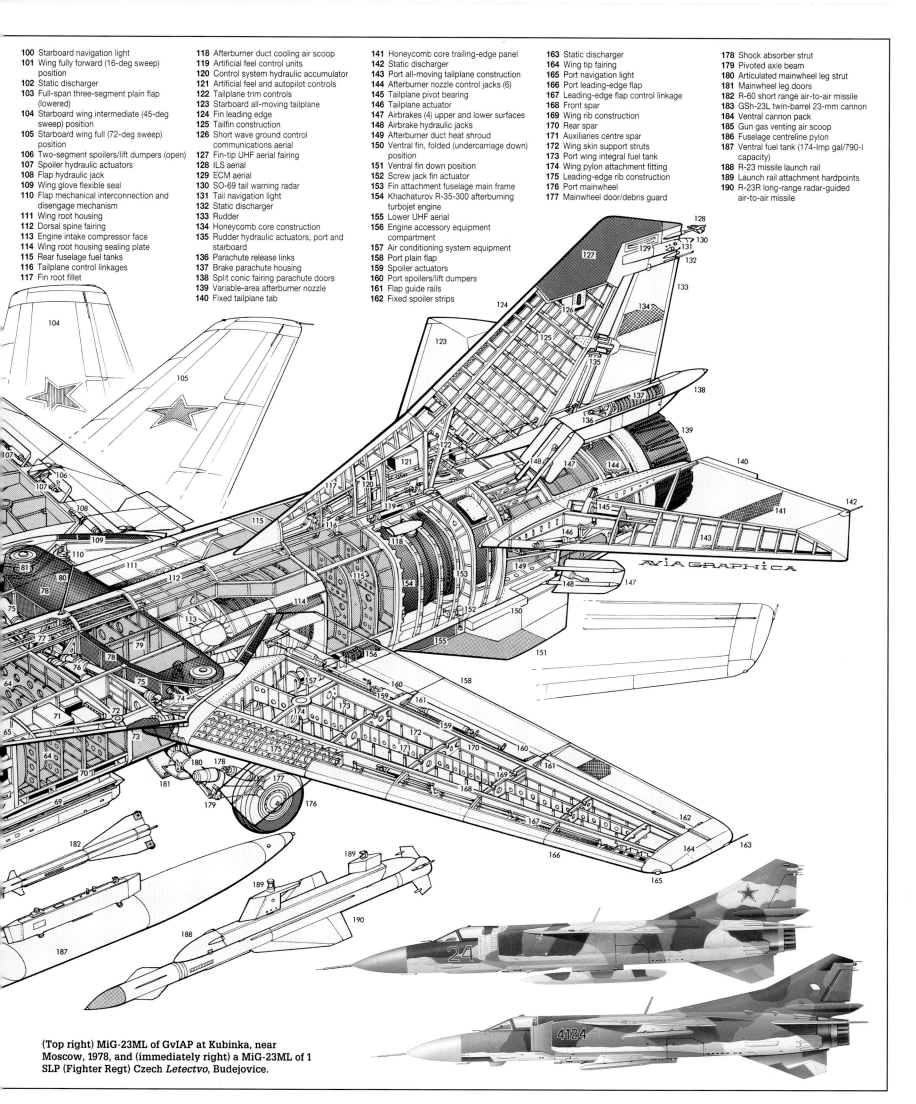

(Top right) MiG-23ML of GvIAP at Kubinka, near Moscow, 1978, and (immediately right) a MiG-23ML of 1 SLP (Fighter Regt) Czech *Letectvo*, Budejovice.

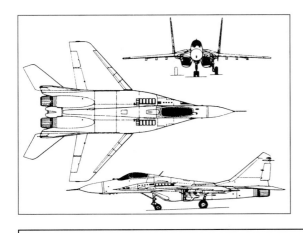

(Below) The first prototype MiG-29, and (left) a general arrangement drawing of initial series model.

version with downgraded avionics. The MiG-29M, first flown on 25 April 1986, was a second generation aircraft. Extensively redesigned under the skin, this had analogue FBW and even greater fuel capacity. The

The Mikoyan 1.44, formerly known by the factory code name 1.42.

intake blanks were replaced by mesh guards and the

Key to MiG-29

1 Pitot head
2 Vortex generator
3 Glass-fibre radome
4 Flat plate radar antenna
5 Scanner tracking mechanism
6 NO-19 "look-down/shoot down" coherent pulse-Doppler radar equipment module
7 Radar mounting bulkhead
8 ILS aerial
9 Lower SRO-2 IFF aerial
10 Angle-of-attack transmitter
11 UHF aerial
12 No 1 bay avionics equipment racks
13 Upper SRO-2 IFF aerial
14 KOLS infra-red search and track sensor and laser ranger
15 Dynamic pressure probe
16 One-piece frameless windscreen panel
17 Instrument panel shroud
18 Temperature probe
19 Cockpit front pressure bulkhead
20 Underfloor control linkages
21 Rudder pedals
22 Control column
23 Pilot's head-up display
24 Canopy arch
25 Rear view mirrors
26 Cockpit canopy cover, upward hingeing
27 Ejection seat headrest
28 Pilot's "zero-zero" K-36DM ejection seat
29 Canopy latch
30 External canopy control handle
31 Engine throttle levers
32 Side console panel
33 Cockpit floor level
34 Cannon muzzle aperture
35 Blast suppression air ducts
36 Forward fuselage chine fairing
37 Cannon barrel
38 Nose undercarriage hydraulic retraction jack
39 Torque scissor links
40 Levered suspension axle beam
41 Twin nosewheels (aft retracting)
42 Articulated "floating" mudguard
43 Hydraulic nosewheel steering control
44 ECM aerial panels
45 Ventral intake lip
46 GSh-301 30-mm cannon
47 Cannon bay venting air louvres
48 Cockpit rear pressure bulkhead
49 No 2 bay avionics equipment racks
50 Canopy jack
51 Canopy hinge point
52 HF aerial
53 No 3 bay avionics equipment
54 Control system linkages
55 Upper surface (ground running) air intake louvres/suction relief doors
56 Variable-area intake ramp doors
57 Door hydraulic actuators
58 Radar warning antenna
59 Port engine air intake
60 Forward intake ramp (closed ground running position)

61 Intake duct framing
62 Weapons interlock access
63 Forward fuselage integral fuel tank
64 Intake spill air louvres
65 Hydraulic reservoir
66 Control linkage and cable runs
67 Air system ducting
68 Fuselage main upper longeron
69 Centre-section fuel tankage
70 ADF aerial
71 Starboard mainwheel (stowed position)
72 Forward fuselage wing root fuel tank
73 Starboard wing root extension/chine member
74 R-27R1 air-to-air missile
75 MiG-29UB two-seat trainer nose profile
76 Student pilot's cockpit enclosure
77 Periscope fairing
78 Instructor's cockpit enclosure
79 R-73E air-to-air missile
80 R-60T air-to-air missile
81 Starboard wing missile pylons
82 Two-segment leading-edge flap (lowered)
83 Leading-edge flap hydraulic actuators
84 Cambered wing-tip fairing
85 Downward identification lights
86 Starboard navigation light
87 Radar warning antenna
88 Static dischargers
89 Starboard aileron
90 Aileron hydraulic actuator
91 Starboard plain flap (down position)
92 Flap hydraulic jack
93 Starboard wing integral fuel tank
94 Fin root extension chaff/flare launcher
95 Centre fuselage fuel tankage of 561-Imp gal (2 550-l) capacity (part of 960-Imp gal/4 365-l total internal capacity)
96 Dorsal spine fairing
97 Engine intake compressor face
98 Machined wing attachment main fuselage bulkheads (3)
99 Forward engine mounting (inboard and outboard)
100 Engine oil tanks
101 Power take-off shaft
102 Engine fuel control equipment
103 Airframe-mounted auxiliary equipment gearbox
104 Cooling air intake
105 Klimov RD-33 afterburning augmented bypass turbojet engine
106 Starboard engine bay

107 Rear fuselage integral fuel tank
108 Engine bay/tailplane spar attachment machined "spectacle" bulkheads
109 Afterburner ducting
110 Rear engine mounting
111 Fuselage side-body extension fairing
112 Starboard tailplane pivot fixing
113 Fin root structure integral with side-body fairing
114 Starboard tailfin
115 Carbon-fibre skin panelling
116 Fin-tip VHF aerial fairing
117 Tail radar warning antenna
118 ILS aerial
119 Static discharger
120 Starboard rudder
121 Rudder hydraulic actuator
122 Tailplane hydraulic actuator
123 Starboard all-moving tailplane
124 Fuselage side-body and fairing
125 Nozzle-sealing flaps

126 Upper airbrake panel (open position)
127 Airbrake hydraulic jack
128 Airbrake hinge linkage
129 Afterburner nozzle control jacks
130 Brake parachute housing
131 Parachute door fairing
132 Airbrakes, upper and lower surfaces (closed position)
133 Afterburner nozzle outer fairing flaps
134 Variable-area afterburner nozzle
135 Fin leading edge
136 Port fin construction
137 Fin-tip VHF aerial fairing
138 Tail navigation light
139 ECM aerial fairing
140 Port rudder
141 Rudder carbon-fibre skin panelling
142 Honeycomb core construction
143 Port engine afterburner nozzle
144 Port all-moving tailplane
145 Honeycomb core construction

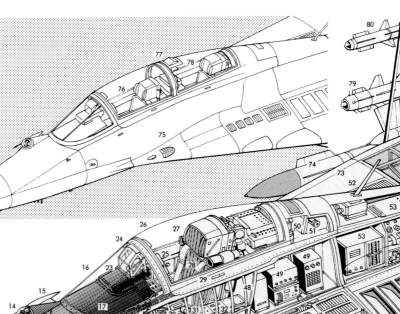

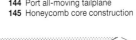

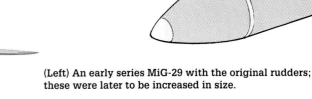

(Left) An early series MiG-29 with the original rudders; these were later to be increased in size.

The MiG-29K (above) landing on the *Kuznetsov* (ex-*Tbilisi*) during initial deck trials late 1989.

dozen countries by 1990, when several single-seat variants were under development. These included the MiG-29K shipboard fighter (the suffix letter signifying *Korabelnyi*, or shipborne) which performed its first deck trials aboard the carrier *Kuznetsov* (formerly *Tbi-*

lisi) late in 1989, and the advanced MiG-29M which was first flown in April 1985. The navalised MiG-29K introduced increased wing area (484.39 sq ft/45,00m²), upward-folding outer wing panels, discarded the intake foreign-object-damage doors and accompanying overwing louvre intakes, and featured increased internal fuel capacity, strengthened undercarriage and arrester hook, and RD-33K engines of 19,400 lb st (8 800 kgp). The MiG-29M embodied advanced features, including fly-by-wire controls accompanied by a change in the CG, an NO-10 *Zhuk* multi-mode radar, CRT displays supplanting conventional instruments and RD-33K engines. A 1990 modification, the MiG-29S, involved raising the dorsal fairing to house equipment transferred from the lower fuselage. Production of the basic MiG-29 was to end in 1994 with some 2,000 built. *Max speed, 805 mph (1 300 km/h) at sea level, or*

Mach=1.06, 1,518 mph (2 445 km/h) at 39,370 ft (12 000 m) or Mach=2.3. Max initial climb, 64,960 ft/min (330 m/sec). Range (internal fuel), 932 mls (1 500 km), (with max external fuel), 1,802 mls (2 900 km). Loaded weight, 33,598 lb (15 240 kg). Max loaded weight, 40,785 lb (18 500 kg). Span, 37 ft 3¼ in (11,36 m). Length (including probe), 56 ft 9⅞ in (17,32 m). Height, 15 ft 6¼ in (4,73 m). Wing area, 409.04 sq ft (38,00 m²).

MILES M.24 MASTER FIGHTER UK

The possibility that the RAF would run short of fighters during the Battle of Britain prompted adaptation of the 750 hp Rolls-Royce Kestrel 30-engined M.9 tandem two-seat advanced trainer as an emergency single-seat

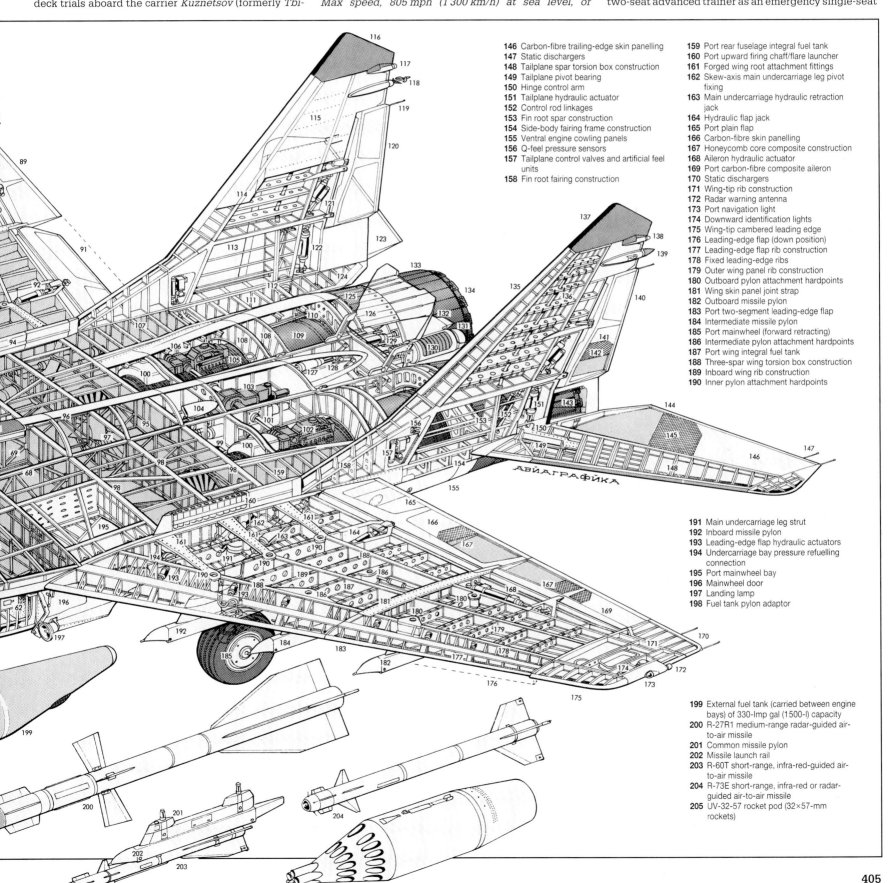

146 Carbon-fibre trailing-edge skin panelling
147 Static dischargers
148 Tailplane spar torsion box construction
149 Tailplane pivot bearing
150 Hinge control arm
151 Tailplane hydraulic actuator
152 Control rod linkages
153 Fin root spar construction
154 Side-body fairing frame construction
155 Ventral engine cowling panels
156 Q-feel pressure sensors
157 Tailplane control valves and artificial feel units
158 Fin root fairing construction
159 Port rear fuselage integral fuel tank
160 Port upward firing chaff/flare launcher
161 Forged wing root attachment fittings
162 Skew-axis main undercarriage leg pivot fixing
163 Main undercarriage hydraulic retraction jack
164 Hydraulic flap jack
165 Port plain flap
166 Carbon-fibre skin panelling
167 Honeycomb core composite construction
168 Aileron hydraulic actuator
169 Port carbon-fibre composite aileron
170 Static dischargers
171 Wing-tip rib construction
172 Radar warning antenna
173 Port navigation light
174 Downward identification lights
175 Wing-tip cambered leading edge
176 Leading-edge flap (down position)
177 Leading-edge flap rib construction
178 Fixed leading-edge ribs
179 Outer wing panel rib construction
180 Outboard pylon attachment hardpoints
181 Wing skin panel joint strap
182 Outboard missile pylon
183 Port two-segment leading-edge flap
184 Intermediate missile pylon
185 Port mainwheel (forward retracting)
186 Intermediate pylon attachment hardpoints
187 Port wing integral fuel tank
188 Three-spar wing torsion box construction
189 Inboard wing rib construction
190 Inner pylon attachment hardpoints

191 Main undercarriage leg strut
192 Inboard missile pylon
193 Leading-edge flap hydraulic actuators
194 Undercarriage bay pressure refuelling connection
195 Port mainwheel bay
196 Mainwheel door
197 Landing lamp
198 Fuel tank pylon adaptor

199 External fuel tank (carried between engine bays) of 330-Imp gal (1500-l) capacity
200 R-27R1 medium-range radar-guided air-to-air missile
201 Common missile pylon
202 Missile launch rail
203 R-60T short-range, infra-red-guided air-to-air missile
204 R-73E short-range, infra-red or radar-guided air-to-air missile
205 UV-32-57 rocket pod (32×57-mm rockets)

been widely publicised, even though a selection had not been made at that time. Initial proposals approved, Mikoyan began work in 1989 on what was given the factory code name of 1.42. Early in 1994, the first, and believed to be the only, prototype of what was now known as the 1.44MFI (*multifunktsionalny istrebitel*), or multi-function fighter, was delivered to the LII Gromov Flight Research Institute airfield at Zhukovsky. High speed taxi trials were carried out in December of that year, and the first flight seemed imminent. However, lack of funding halted progress. Then, in January 1999, years of speculation were ended when 1.44 was first revealed to the world. It was a huge canard delta. The canards, with notched leading edges, were carried on fixed stubs aft of the cockpit, while the mid-mounted wings do not have root extensions. Twin fins and rudders, carried on booms outside the engine nacelles, are canted outwards, and below them are large ventral fins which, unusually, have moveable control surfaces. Power consists of two AL-41F turbofans each rated at 40,565 lb (18 400 kgp) max thrust, the vectoring nozzles of which have a heat-resisting ceramic coating. The engines are fed by two square-section, raked-back variable inlets in the chin position. The inlet ducts are serpentine to conceal the compressor face from hostile radar emissions, and are lined with radar-absorbent coatings. This apart, there seems little enough attempt at stealth; the finish is the usual Russian "good-enough", although composites are widely used. The radar is stated to be a "fifth generation" multi-mode type, with a fixed phased array scanner, able to control six simultaneous missile attacks, while tracking 20 or more targets. It is also stated that a new generation of AAMs has been developed specifically for the aircraft. Some will be carried in one or more internal bays, but the 1.44 also has underwing hardpoints. An internal 30-mm cannon is also carried, probably a GSh-30. It has also been rumoured that the 1.44 will use plasma shielding, surrounding itself with a cloud of ionised gas to prevent radar detection, but whether this will ever become a reality is open to question. It finally flew on 29 February 2000, with chief test pilot Vladimir Gorbunov at the controls. While scheduled to enter service in 2010, little apparent progress has been made. *Max speed hi, Mach 2.5. Supercruise capability. Normal takeoff weight, c66,138 lb (30 000 kg). Max takeoff weight, c77,161 lb (35 000 kg). Span, 55 ft 10¹/₂ in (17,03 m). Length, 74 ft 10³/₄ in (22,83 m). Height, 18 ft 9 in (5,72 m). Wing area, 974 sq ft (90,50 m²).*

MILES M.24 MASTER FIGHTER UK

Never used operationally, the Master Fighter (above) was developed as a "panic measure" in 1940.

The possibility that the RAF would run short of fighters during the Battle of Britain prompted adaptation of the 750 hp Rolls-Royce Kestrel 30-engined M.9 tandem two-seat advanced trainer as an emergency single-seat fighter. The rear seat was removed, together with part of the rear cockpit glazing, a gunsight was installed and six 0.303-in (7,7-mm) machine guns were mounted in the wings. Assigned the designation M.24 retrospectively, a total of 23 fighter conversions was produced, but, in the event, no need arose for their operational use. *Max speed, 195 mph (314 km/h) at sea level, 229 mph (369 km/h) at 14,500 ft (4 420 m). Initial climb, 2,250 ft/min (11,43 m/sec). Empty weight, 4,722 lb (2 142 kg). Loaded weight, 5,650 lb (2 563 kg). Span, 39 ft 0 in (11,89 m). Length, 30 ft 5in (9,27 m). Height, 10 ft 0 in (3,05 m). Wing area, 325 sq ft (30,19 m²).*

MILES M.20 UK

Conceived as an emergency fighter for production in the event that the RAF began to run short of more orthodox fighting aircraft, the M.20 was designed by Walter Capley to Specification F.19/40. Of wooden construction with all emphasis placed on rapidity of manufacture, the M.20 dispensed with a retractable undercarriage, thereby eliminating the need for hydraulics, utilised a one-piece wing, adopted a standard Rolls-Royce Merlin XX installation interchangeable with that of the Beaufighter II and employed standard Master cockpit equipment. The first prototype was designed, built and flown in the remarkably short time of 65 days. Powered by a 1,300 hp Merlin XX engine and fitted with eight 0.303-in (7,7-mm) machine guns (but having provision for up to 12 guns), the M.20 was first flown on 15 September 1940. In the event, the Battle of Britain terminated before the RAF exhausted its available supplies of Hurricanes and Spitfires, and the M.20 was not, therefore, placed in production. However, Specification

(Below) The navalised M.20.

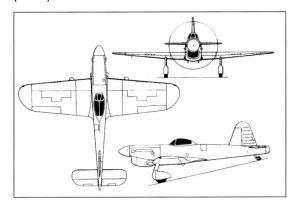

Small differences in the undercarriage design distinguished the rebuilt M.20 (above).

N.1/41 for a single-seat shipboard fighter covered reconstruction of the prototype with a jettisonable undercarriage, suiting it for use from catapults on the CAM-ships. It was tested in 1941-42 but no further development was undertaken. *Max speed, 333 mph (536 km/h) at 20,600 ft (6 280 m). Initial climb, 3,200 ft/min (16,25 m/sec). Normal range, 550 mls (885 km). Empty weight, 5,870 lb (2 663 kg). Loaded weight, 7,758 lb (3 519 kg). Span, 34 ft 7 in (10,54 m). Length, 30 ft 1 in (9,17 m). Height, 12 ft 6 in (3,81 m). Wing area, 234 sq ft (21,74 m²).*

MITSUBISHI Type 10 (1MF1 TO 1MF5) Japan

At the beginning of 1921, Mitsubishi invited a team of eight former Sopwith engineers led by Herbert Smith to establish a design office with the aim of creating a series of Type 10 (10th year of the Taisho regime) shipboard aircraft for the Imperial Navy. Work was initiated on four categories of aircraft, including a single-seat fighter referred to as the 1MF1 (Single-seat Mitsubishi Fighter First Model). Of wooden construction with fabric skinning and powered by a 300 hp Hispano-Suiza eight-cylinder Vee water-cooled engine, the 1MF1 prototype was completed in October 1921, and accepted by the Navy in the following month as the first fighter of indigenous design. The second prototype, the 1MF1A, embodied a 13-sq-ft (1,21-m²) increase in wing area, the 1MF2 introduced enlarged horizontal tail surfaces and the 1MF3 discarded the frontal radiator in favour of Lamblin-type radiators beneath the centre fuselage. The last-mentioned version entered series production for the Imperial Navy as the Type 10, arma-

First indigenous Japanese fighter built in quantity was the 1MF3, or Type 10 (above and below).

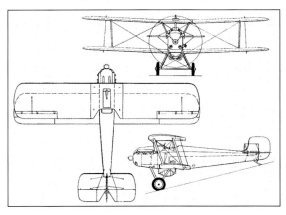

ment comprising two 7,7-mm guns, and the fighter alighted on the deck of Japan's first carrier, the *Hosho*, for the first time in February 1923. The 1MF4 differed from the 1MF3 in having the cockpit moved forward, stagger reduced by forward shift of the lower wing and redesign of the vertical tail surfaces. The 1MF5 introduced more minor changes (the 1MF5A being a fighter trainer with increased wing span) and production continued until December 1929, a total of 128 aircraft being built (including prototypes). The following data relate to the final production version of the Type 10, the 1MF5. *Max speed, 132 mph (213 km/h). Time to 9,840 ft (3 000 m), 10.32 min. Endurance, 2.6 hrs. Empty weight, 2,063 lb (936 kg). Loaded weight, 2,820 lb (1 279 kg). Span, 28 ft 11⁷/₈ in (8,84 m). Length, 22 ft 9 in (6,93 m). Height, 10 ft 3¹/₃ in (3,13 m).*

MITSUBISHI 1MF9 TAKA Japan

Seeking a second-generation fighter as a successor to the Type 10, in April 1926, the Imperial Navy solicited proposals from Aichi, Mitsubishi and Nakajima for an aircraft embodying a watertight fuselage, watertight wing leading edge and jettisonable undercarriage for emergency alighting on water. To meet the requirement, a team led by Joji Hattori developed the 1MF9 Taka (Hawk) equi-span biplane of wooden construction which featured a Vee-shaped fuselage planing bottom. Powered by a 600 hp 12-cylinder water-cooled Hispano-Suiza engine and carrying an armament of two 7,7-mm guns, with provision for two 66-lb (30-kg) bombs, the first prototype Taka was delivered in July 1927, and was the first aircraft of Japanese design to feature wing flaps, these being discarded by the second prototype delivered in the following September. The water-proofing demanded by the Imperial Navy resulted in some weight penalty, and the competition

(Below) The second Mitsubishi 1MF9 Taka.

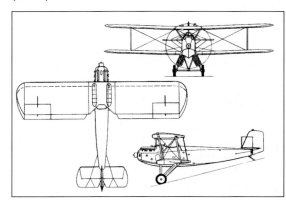

Wing flaps were a feature of the first of the two prototypes (above) of the Mitsubishi 1MF9.

was won by the Nakajima-submitted Gloster Gambet (see Nakajima A1N1), the 1MF9 Taka being abandoned. *Max speed, 152 mph (245 km/h). Time to 9,840 ft (3 000 m), 6.17 min. Endurance, 3.5 hrs. Empty weight, 2,804 lb (1 272 kg). Loaded weight, 4,089 lb (1 855 kg). Span, 35 ft 5¼ in (10,80 m). Length, 27 ft 8⅜ in (8,44 m). Height, 11 ft 1⅞ in (3,40 m). Wing area, 446.71 sq ft (41,50 m²).*

MITSUBISHI 1MF2 HAYABUSA   Japan

In March 1927, the Imperial Army ordered Kawasaki, Nakajima and Mitsubishi to investigate design of a fighter on a competitive basis to replace the ageing Ko-4 (Nieuport-Delage NiD 29). Designed by Nobushiro Nakata assisted by Jiro Horikoshi and Jiro Tanaka, the Mitsubishi contender in the contest, the 1MF2 Hayabusa (Peregrine Falcon), was of advanced concept, being a parasol monoplane without wire bracing, emphasis being placed on ease of assembly and disassembly. Powered by a 600 hp Mitsubishi Hispano-Suiza water-cooled V-12 engine, the first prototype Hayabusa was completed in May 1928. After manufacturer's flight testing at Kagamigahara, both first and second prototypes were transferred to the Tokorozawa Army test centre where the Hayabusa recorded a maximum speed of 168 mph (270 km/h) at 9,840 ft (3 000 m), but during a diving test the Mitsubishi fighter broke up in the air after exceeding 248 mph (400 km/h). The Army suspended evaluation of the contending types, cancelling the programme and testing the other prototypes to destruction. The Hayabusa was of mixed construction with wooden wing and metal fuselage, its armament being two 7,7-mm guns. *Max speed, 168 mph (270 km/h) at 9,840 ft (3 000 m). Time to 16,405 ft (5 000 m), 11.3 min. Empty weight, 2,789 lb (1 265 kg).*

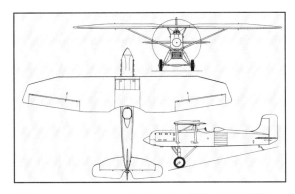

Only one prototype was built of the Mitsubishi 1MF2 parasol monoplane fighter (above and below).

Loaded weight, 3,968 lb (1 800 kg). Span, 41 ft 4⅞ in (12,62 m). Length, 26 ft 10⅞ in (8,20 m). Height, 10 ft 11⅞ in (3,35 m). Wing area, 247.58 sq ft (23,00 m²).

MITSUBISHI 1MF10   Japan

To meet a 7-*Shi* (1932) requirement for an advanced single-seat shipboard fighter to succeed the Nakajima A1N (Type 90), a Mitsubishi design team led by Jiro Horikoshi and assisted by Eitaro Sano, Takanosuke Nakamura and Tomio Kubo initiated work on the first cantilever low-wing monoplane to be designed in Japan, the 1MF10. Featuring a duralumin monocoque fuselage and a fabric-skinned duralumin wing, the 1MF10 was powered by a 710 hp Mitsubishi A-4 14-cylinder two-row radial and carried an armament of two 7,7-mm machine guns. The first of two prototypes was flown in March 1933, but was lost during the following July when the vertical tail surfaces disintegrated in a dive. The second prototype, which was completed shortly afterwards, differed essentially in having a new undercarriage, the three struts of each unit being replaced by single legs enclosed by trouser-type fairings. The 1MF10's max speed at 9,840 ft (3 000 m) proved to be 30 mph (48 km/h) less than that required by the Imperial Navy and climbing performance was considered inadequate. The fighter was rejected for series production, the second prototype being lost after its pilot failed to extricate it from a flat spin in June 1934. *Max speed, 199 mph (320 km/h) at 9,840 ft (3 000 m). Time to 10,000 ft (3 050 m), 4.2 min. Endurance, 3.0 hrs. Empty weight, 2,700 lb (1 225 kg). Loaded weight, 3,479 lb (1 578 kg). Span, 32 ft 9⅔ in (10,00 m). Length, 22 ft 8⅔ in (6,92 m). Height, 10 ft 10⅓ in (3,31 m). Wing area, 190.53 sq ft (17,70 m²).*

Boeing influence could be seen in the 1MF10 second prototype (above and below) of 1933.

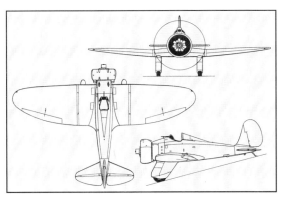

MITSUBISHI KA-8   Japan

In 1933, the Imperial Navy, influenced by trends in Western Europe and the USA, issued both Mitsubishi and Nakajima with a request for proposals for a two-seat shipboard fighter. The Mitsubishi contender, the

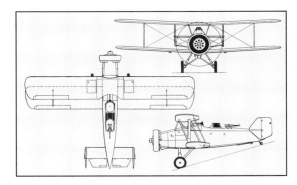

Development of the Ka-8 (above and below) ended after a prototype suffered structural failure.

Ka-8 designed by Joji Hattori who was assisted by Eitaro Sano and Takanosuke Nakamura, was a single-bay equi-span staggered biplane of mixed construction, the fabric-covered wings having duralumin spars and wooden ribs, and the similarly-covered fuselage being of steel tube. An unusual feature of the design was its use of twin endplate fins and rudders. Powered by a 580 hp Nakajima Jupiter II nine-cylinder radial, the Ka-8 carried an armament of two fixed forward-firing 7,7-mm guns and a similar weapon on a rotating mount in the rear cockpit. The first of two prototypes was completed in January 1934, both being delivered to the Navy during the early summer. However, the second prototype broke up in the air when pulling out of a dive over Yokosuka airfield on 16 September, resulting in the suspension of the test programme and the subsequent abandonment of further development. *Max speed, 178 mph (286 km/h) at 9,840 ft (3 000 m). Empty weight, 2,542 lb (1 153 kg). Loaded weight, 3,748 lb (1 700 kg). Span, 32 ft 9⅔ in (10,00 m). Length, 24 ft 3 in (7,39 m). Height, 11 ft 0 in (3,35 m). Wing area, 279.87 sq ft (26,00 m²).*

MITSUBISHI KA-14   Japan

Among several 9-*Shi* requirements, in February 1934, the Imperial Navy issued an outline specification for a single-seat fighter. Carrier compatibility was not demanded. It was assumed that accommodating the dictates of deck use from the outset would inhibit the design team in achieving an advance in the state of the fighter design art. It was, of course, self-evident that the service would have no use for a fighter incapable of shipboard operation. In view of his experience with the earlier 7-*Shi* fighter, design responsibility was assigned by Mitsubishi to Jiro Horikoshi who created an all-metal semi-monocoque stressed-skin monoplane of inverted gull form designated Ka-14. Powered by a 600 hp Nakajima Kotobuki (Congratulation) 5 nine-cylinder radial and carrying two 7,7-mm guns, the first

(Below) The Ka-14 with close-fitting engine cowling.

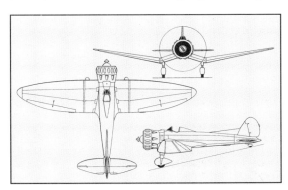

The first Ka-14 was originally flown with the short-chord cowling seen in the photograph above.

Ka-14 was flown on 4 February 1935. Latent doubts concerning the wing "gulling" had, meanwhile, led to elimination of this feature from the wing of the second prototype Ka-14, which also embodied split flaps and switched to a 715 hp Kotobuki 3 engine. This prototype was to provide the basis for the series production A5M1 (Type 96) fighter (which see), the first Ka-14 being fitted with a close-fitting, long-chord cowling as part of a drag reduction programme. The following data relate to the first Ka-14. *Max speed, 276 mph (444 km/h) at 10,500 ft (3 200 m). Time to 16,405 ft (5 000 m), 5.9 min. Loaded weight, 3,027 lb (1 373 kg). Span, 36 ft 1¼ in (11,00 m). Length, 25 ft 1⅞ in (7,67 m). Height, 10 ft 8½ in (3,26 m). Wing area, 172.23 sq ft (16,00 m²).*

MITSUBISHI KI-18   Japan

The sole Ki-18 prototype (above) was developed for the Imperial Army from the Navy's Ka-14.

As soon as the Imperial Navy had expressed its satisfaction with the performance of the Ka-14, the Imperial Army placed a contract with Mitsubishi for a modified example, fundamentally similar to the second prototype, for evaluation as the Ki-18. Powered by a Kotobuki 5, like the first Ka-14, the Ki-18 introduced a longer-chord engine cowling, an enlarged rudder and larger mainwheels and spats. Tested throughout the autumn and winter of 1935, the Ki-18 carried the standard twin 7,7-mm gun armament, but was considered insufficiently agile by conservative Army test pilots, and failed to gain favour. Nevertheless, the Ki-18 encouraged the Army to accept the coming demise of the biplane as a fighter configuration, resulting in the framing of a requirement for what was termed an "advanced fighter". *Max speed, 276 mph (445 km/h) at 10,000 ft (3 050 m). Time to 16,405 ft (5 000 m), 6.43 min. Empty weight, 2,447 lb (1 110 kg). Loaded weight, 3,135 lb (1 422 kg). Span, 36 ft 1¼ in (11,00 m). Length, 25 ft 1⅛ in (7,65 m). Height, 10 ft 4 in (3,15 m). Wing area, 191.6 sq ft (17,80 m²).*

MITSUBISHI KI-33   Japan

The acceptance of the Ka-14 9-*Shi* fighter by the Imperial Navy and evaluation of a modified prototype of this aircraft as the Ki-18 by the Imperial Army encouraged the formulation by the latter service during 1935 of a requirement for what was termed an "advanced fighter". Kawasaki, Mitsubishi and Nakajima were each asked to produce prototypes of a fighter surpassing the performance of the Ki-18. Whereas both Kawasaki and Nakajima produced fighters of entirely new design to meet the requirement (as the Ki-28 and Ki-27 respectively), Mitsubishi, preoccupied with refining the Ka-14 for series production for the Navy, lacked sufficient design capacity to develop yet a further fighter. The Ki-18, with comparatively minor changes, was

therefore resubmitted. As the Ki-33, the modified fighter was powered by a Nakajima Ha-1-Ko engine rated at 745 hp at 12,140 ft (3 700 m) and enclosed by a broader-chord cowling. An aft-sliding part-canopy was added, the aft fuselage decking was raised and the vertical tail surfaces were modified. Completed during the early summer of 1936, the Ki-33 was submitted to comparative trials with the Ki-27 and Ki-28 from November 1936 until the spring of 1937. It was found to offer marginally superior max speeds between 8,200 ft (2 500 m) and 11,480 ft (3 500 m) over the 357-lb (167-kg) lighter Ki-27, but the Ki-33 revealed an inferior turn rate and climb to those of the Nakajima contender which was selected for series production. *Max speed, 294 mph (474 km/h) at 9,840 ft (3 000 m). Time to 9,840 ft (3 000 m), 3.37 min. Empty weight, 2,496 lb (1 132 kg). Loaded weight, 3,223 lb (1 462 kg). Span, 36 ft 1¼ in (11,00 m). Length, 24 ft 9 in (7,54 m). Height, 10 ft 5⅝ in (3,19 m). Wing area, 191.6 sq ft (17,80 m²).*

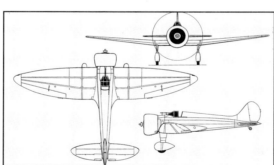

A progressive development of the Ki-18 for the Army, the Ki-33 (above and below) was flown in 1936.

MITSUBISHI A5M1 TO A5M3   Japan

In the autumn of 1936, the Ka-14 finally passed all service trials and was officially accepted by the Imperial Navy for production as the A5M1, or Type 96 Carrier Fighter Model 1. Fundamentally similar to the second Ka-14, the A5M1 was powered by the Nakajima Kotobuki 2 KAI-ko engine rated at 630 hp at 4,920 ft (1 500 m) and carried an armament of two 7,7-mm guns. It possessed the distinction of being the world's first service shipboard single-seat cantilever monoplane fighter. Seventy-five A5M1s were delivered before in-

(Above) An A5M1 and (below) A5M2-ko, both serving with the 12th *Kokutai*, second shore-based unit of the Imperial Navy to fly the type over China.

Kotobuki 3-powered A5M2-otsu (below), of 12th *Kokutai*, Hankow, 1938, showing aft-sliding canopy.

troduction of the Kotobuki 2 KAI 3-ko engine offering 690 hp at 12,795 ft (3 900 m) and more minor changes resulted in the A5M2-ko from late spring of 1937. Further refinement produced the A5M2-otsu (Model 2-2) which reverted to the Kotobuki 3 engine (of the second Ka-14) in a narrower-chord NACA cowling and adopted an aft-sliding cockpit canopy, 124 being manufactured before the latter feature was discarded. Two examples of the experimental A5M3-ko were built, these having the 12-cylinder liquid-cooled Hispano-Suiza 12Xcrs engine rated at 690 hp at 12,795 ft (3 900 m) and a 20-mm cannon between the cylinder banks. The following data are applicable to the A5M2-otsu. *Max speed, 262 mph (422 km/h) at 11,190 ft (3 410 m). Range (clean), 657 mls (1 058 km). Time to 9,840 ft (3 000 m), 3.85 min. Empty weight, 2,654 lb (1 204 kg). Loaded weight, 3,657 lb (1 659 kg). Span, 36 ft 1⅛ in (11,00 m). Length, 24 ft 9⅞ in (7,56 m). Height, 10 ft 8¾ in (3,27 m). Wing area, 191.6 sq ft (17,80 m²).*

MITSUBISHI A5M4   Japan

Developed hurriedly in an attempt to counter the initial withdrawal of Chinese aircraft beyond the effective range of the A5M2, the A5M4 (Model 2-4) shipboard fighter, which entered service early 1938, was externally virtually identical to the late-production A5M2-otsu, apart from raised aft decking, and revised windscreen and quarter lights. It was powered, however, by a Kotobuki 41 engine offering 785 hp at 9,845 ft (3 000 m) and had provision for a 35.2-Imp-gal (160-l) drop tank (later a 46-Imp gal/210-l tank). Production was phased out by Mitsubishi early in 1940 after com-

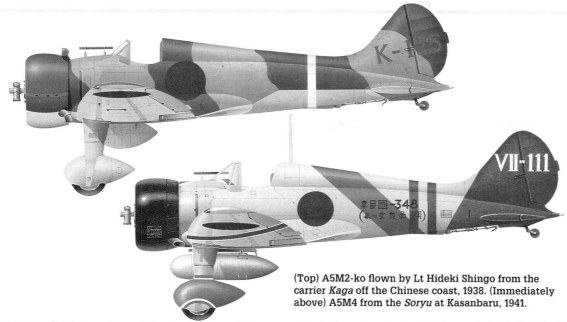

with long-barrelled cannon, as the Model 22-ko, a further 560 being built between autumn 1942 and summer 1943. The following data relate to the Model 21. *Max speed, 331 mph (533 km/h) at 14,930 ft (4 550 m). Initial climb, 3,100 ft/min (15,75 m/sec). Max range, 1,930 mls (3 105 km). Empty weight, 3,704 lb (1 680 kg). Loaded weight, 5,313 lb (2 410 kg). Span, 39 ft 4½ in (12,00 m). Length, 29 ft 8¾ in (9,06 m). Height, 10 ft 0⅛ in (3,05 m). Wing area, 241.55 sq ft (22,44 m²).*

MITSUBISHI A6M5 TO A6M8   Japan

Delays in the achievement of service status by fighters intended to succeed the *Rei-sen* dictated an attempt to upgrade the Type 0 in 1943. This was represented by the A6M5, or Type 0 Carrier Fighter Model 52, which flew in the summer of 1943. Based essentially on the A6M3 with a similar Sakae 21 engine, the A6M5 differed primarily in having thrust-augmentation exhaust stacks and a revised wing with heavier-gauge skin and new, non-folding, tips. The A6M5-ko, deliveries of which began in March 1944, featured belt- rather than drum-fed cannon and still heavier gauge wing skinning. Built in parallel was the A6M5-otsu with armour-glass, automatic fire extinguishers and a 13,2-mm gun in place of one of the two 7,7-mm weapons. The A6M5-hei omitted the remaining 7,7-mm gun, but had two additional 13,2-mm weapons mounted in the wings (in-

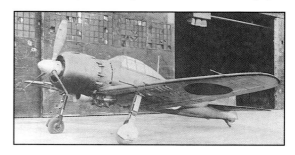

Final production version of the *Rei-sen*, the A6M7 (above) was optimised as a fighter-bomber.

creasing total armament to three 13,2-mm and two 20-mm guns), armour protection for the pilot and an additional self-sealing tank behind the pilot. The A6M5-hei flew in November 1944, but only 93 were built. One example was built with a Sakae 31-ko engine with water-methanol injection and self-sealing wing tanks as the A6M6-hei, and the final production model of the *Rei-sen* was the A6M7, or Model 63. This also employed the Sakae 31 with water-methanol injection, the five-gun armament of the A6M5-hei and some structural strengthening in order to carry a 551-lb (250-kg) bomb. The A6M7 flew in May 1945, series production commencing the same month. Possessing a similar airframe to the A6M7, the A6M8 featured a revised forward fuselage for a Kinsei 62 engine rated at 1,560 hp for take-off, this dictating discarding of the fuselage-

A preserved A6M5 (below) in markings of 261 *Kokutai* at Chino's "Planes of Fame" Museum, California.

pletion of 782 series Type 96 Carrier Fighters of all versions (A5M1 to -4), a further 39 being built by Watanabe and 161 by the 21st Naval Air Arsenal which delivered the last early in 1941. The A5M4 was withdrawn from operations mid-1942. *Max speed, 270 mph (435 km/h) at 9,845 ft (3 000 m). Range (external fuel), 746 mls (1 200 km). Time to 9,840 ft (3 000 m), 3.58 min. Empty weight, 2,784 lb (1 263 kg). Max loaded weight, 4,017 lb (1 822 kg). Dimensions as for A5M2-otsu.*

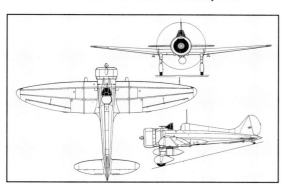

(Top) A5M2-ko flown by Lt Hideki Shingo from the carrier *Kaga* off the Chinese coast, 1938. (Immediately above) A5M4 from the *Soryu* at Kasanbaru, 1941.

Zuisei 13 engine rated at 875 hp at 11,810 ft (3 600 m). On 14 September, the 12-*Shi* aircraft was accepted as the Type 0 Carrier Fighter, or *Rei shiki Kanjo sentoki*, a contraction of this formal designation, *Rei-sen*, becoming the unofficial popular appellation of the fighter. The less formal official designation was A6M, the first two prototypes being A6M1s, and the third prototype, flown on 18 January 1940 with a Nakajima Sakae 12 engine rated at 950 hp at 13,780 ft (4 200 m), being the A6M2. The Sakae-engined model was adopted for series production, an additional prototype, 15 similar pre-series examples (committed to combat in China from July 1940) and 48 series aircraft being delivered as the Type 0 Carrier Fighter Model 11. With the 68th *Rei-sen*, manually-folded wingtips were introduced, 740 with this feature being built as Model 21s, the two sub-types being similar in other respects and carrying an armament of two 20-mm and two 7,7-mm guns. A further development, the A6M3 flown in June 1941, discarded the folding wingtips, thus reducing wing span by 3 ft 3⅓ in (1,00 m), and adopted the Sakae 21 engine providing 1,130 hp for take-off. A total of 343 was built as Model 32s before the folding wingtips were reinstated, production continuing as the Model 22, and,

(Above and below) The A5M4, the photo showing a 14th *Kokutai* aircraft over China in January 1940.

(Below) Mitsubishi A6M2, the so-called *Rei-sen*.

MITSUBISHI A6M1 TO A6M3   Japan

An outline specification for a 12-*Shi* successor for the A5M shipboard fighter was issued by the Imperial Navy Staff on 19 May 1937, the design of Mitsubishi's contender being assigned to a team led by Jiro Horikoshi. The first prototype, flown on 1 April 1939, was powered, like the second prototype, by a Mitsubishi

The A6M2 (below) was the initial version of the Mitsubishi Type 0 Carrier Fighter.

mounted gun. Although allocated production priority as the Model 64, the A6M8 failed to progress further than prototype status. Production of the *Rei-sen* totalled approximately 10,500 aircraft of which in excess of 6,000 were Model 52s. The following data relate to the A6M5-ko. *Max speed, 351 mph (565 km/h) at 19,685 ft (6 000 m). Max range, 1,194 mls (1 920 km). Time to 19,685 ft (6 000 m), 7.05 min. Empty weight, 4,136 lb (1 876 kg). Loaded weight, 6,025 lb (2 733 kg). Span, 36 ft 1¼ in (11,00 m). Length, 29 ft 11⅛ in (9,12 m). Height, 11 ft 6⅛ in (3,51 m). Wing area, 229.28 sq ft (21,30 m²).*

This J2M3 Raiden (above) served with the 302 *Kokutai* based at Atsugi, Japan, in 1944.

MITSUBISHI J2M1 Japan

Signifying a radical departure from previous Japanese Navy fighter design practice in being optimised for speed and climb rather than agility, the J2M1 was conceived to meet an Imperial Navy requirement for a shore-based *Kyokuchi Sentoki*, or Local [defence] Interceptor, usually abbreviated to *Kyokusen*. Although a 14-*Shi* (1939) requirement, the definitive specification for the *Kyokusen* was not formulated until April 1940, design being undertaken by Jiro Horikoshi assisted by Yoshitoshi Sone and Kiro Takahashi. Of all metal construction with a low aspect ratio laminar-flow wing, the J2M1 was powered by a 14-cylinder Mitsubishi MK4C Kasei 13 radial rated at 1,430 hp for take-off. In order to reduce aerodynamic drag, this drove the propeller via an extension shaft, a fan drawing cooling air through a narrow annular intake. Armament comprised two 7,7-mm and two 20-mm guns. The first of three J2M1 prototypes flew on 20 March 1942, but the test programme was plagued with technical difficulties and service test pilots were critical of some of the prototype's characteristics. Consequently, Mitsubishi was instructed to introduce numerous changes for the *Kyokusen-KAI*, or J2M2, these being added on the fourth of 14 experimental airframes that had been laid down. *Max speed, 359 mph (577 km/h) at 19,685 ft (6 000 m). Empty weight, 4,830 lb (2 191 kg). Normal loaded weight, 6,307 lb (2 861 kg). Span, 35 ft 5¼ in (10,80 m). Length, 32 ft 5¾ in (9,90 m). Height, 12 ft 6⅜ in (3,82 m). Wing area, 215.82 sq ft (20,05 m²).*

The J2M1 (below) was designed as a shore-based interceptor for the Imperial Navy.

MITSUBISHI J2M2 TO J2M6 RAIDEN Japan

On 13 October 1942, the fourth *Kyokusen* prototype was flown as the J2M2, this embodying numerous changes. The most noticeable external change was the replacement of the extremely shallow, curved windscreen by one of deeper, more conventional form, with a suitably

(Below) The Mitsubishi J2M3 Raiden interceptor.

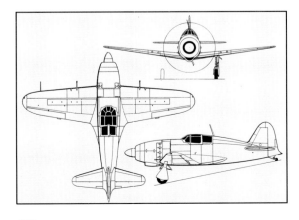

Key to Mitsubishi A6M2 "Rei-sen"

1 Tail navigation light
2 Tail cone
3 Tailfin fixed section
4 Rudder lower brace
5 Rudder tab (ground adjustable)
6 Fabric-covered rudder
7 Rudder hinge
8 Rudder post
9 Rudder upper hinge
10 Rudder control horn (welded to torque tube)
11 Aerial attachment
12 Tailfin leading-edge
13 Forward spar
14 Tailfin structure
15 Tailfin nose ribs
16 Port elevator
17 Port tailplane
18 Piano-hinge join
19 Fuselage dorsal skinning
20 Control turnbuckles
21 Arrester hook release/retract steel cable runs
22 Fuselage frame/tailplane centre-brace
23 Tailplane attachments
24 Elevator cables
25 Elevator control horns/torque tube
26 Rudder control horns
27 Tailwheel combined retraction/shock strut
28 Elevator trim tab
29 Tailwheel leg fairing
30 Castored tailwheel
31 Elevator frame (fabric covered)
32 Elevator outer hinge
33 Tailplane structure
34 Forward spar
35 Elevator trim tab control rod (chain driven)
36 Fuselage flotation bag rear wall
37 Arrester hook (extended)
38 Arrester hook pivot mounting
39 Elevator trim tab cable guide
40 Fuselage skinning
41 Fuselage frame stations
42 Arrester hook position indicator cable (duralumin tube)
43 Rudder cables
44 Elevator cables
45 Trim tab cable runs
46 Arrester hook pulley guide
47 Fuselage stringers
48 Fuselage flotation bag front wall
49 Fuselage construction join
50 Wingroot fillet formers
51 Compressed air cylinder (wing gun charging)
52 Transformer
53 "Ku"-type radio receiver
54 Oxygen cylinder (starboard); CO₂ fire-extinguisher cylinder (port)
55 Battery
56 Radio tray support
57 Radio transmitter
58 Canopy/fuselage fairing
59 Aerial mast support/lead-in
60 Aerial
61 Aerial mast (forward raked)
62 Canopy aft fixed section
63 Aluminium and plywood canopy frame
64 Crash bulkhead/headrest support
65 "Ku"-type D/F frame antenna mounting (late models)
66 Canopy track
67 Turnover truss
68 Pilot's seat support frame
69 Starboard elevator control bell-crank
70 Aileron control push-pull rod
71 Wing rear spar/fuselage attachment
72 Fuselage aft main double frame
73 Aileron linkage

74 Landing-gear selector lever
75 Flap selector lever
76 Seat adjustment lever
77 Pilot's seat
78 Cockpit canopy rail
79 Seat support rail
80 Elevator tab trim handwheel
81 Fuel gauge controls
82 Throttle quadrant
83 Reflector gunsight mounting (offset to starboard)
84 Sliding canopy
85 Plexiglass panels
86 Canopy lock/release
87 Windscreen
88 Fuselage starboard 0.303-in (7.7-mm) machine gun
89 Control column
90 Radio control box
91 Radio tuner
92 Elevator control linkage
93 Rudder pedal bar assembly
94 Cockpit underfloor fuel
95 Wing front spar/fuselage attachment

96 Fuselage forward main double frame
97 Ammunition magazine
98 Ammunition feed
99 Blast tube
100 Cooling louvres
101 Fuselage fuel tank (capacity 34 Imp gal/155 l)
102 Firewall bulkhead
103 Engine bearer lower attachment
104 Engine bearer upper attachment
105 Oil tank (capacity 12.7 Imp gal/58 l)
106 Bearer support struts
107 Cowling gill adjustment control
108 Machine gun muzzle trough
109 Barrel fairing
110 Oil filler cap
111 Fuselage fuel tank filler cap
112 Port flap profile
113 Port fuselage machine gun
114 Port wing gun access panels
115 Port inner wing identification light
116 Port wing flotation bag inner wall
117 Wing spar joins
118 Aileron control rods
119 Port aileron (fabric covered)
120 Aileron tab (ground adjustable)
121 Aileron external counter-balance
122 Control linkage
123 Wing skinning
124 Port outer wing identification light
125 Port navigation light lead conduit
126 Wingtip hinge
127 Wing end rib
128 Port wing flotation bag outer wall
129 Wingtip structure
130 Port wingtip (folded)
131 Port navigation light
132 Port wingtip hinge release catch
133 Pitot head
134 Wing leading-edge skinning
135 Wing front spar
136 Port wing gun muzzle
137 Port undercarriage visual indicator
138 Undercarriage hydraulics access
139 Nacelle gun troughs
140 Cowling gills
141 Fuselage gun synchronization cable

142 Bearer support strut assembly
143 Carburettor
144 Exhaust manifold
145 Cowling panel fastener clips
146 Nakajima Sakae 12 radial engine
147 Cowling inner ring profile
148 Cowling nose ring
149 Three-bladed propeller
150 Spinner
151 Propeller gears
152 Hub
153 Carburettor intake
154 Port mainwheel
155 Oil cooler intake
156 Exhaust outlet
157 Starboard mainwheel inner door fairing
158 Engine bearer support brace
159 Oil cooler
160 Wingroot fasteners

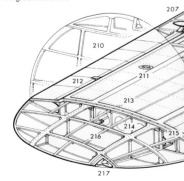

161 Starboard mainwheel well
162 Front auxiliary spar cut-outs
163 Auxiliary fuel tank (capacity 74 Imp gal/337 l)
164 Cockpit air intake
165 Intake trunking
166 Front main spar
167 Starboard wing fuel tank (capacity 43 Imp gal/195 l)
168 Fuel filler cap

enlarged canopy and raised aft fuselage decking. The MK4R-A Kasei 23 Ko engine drove a four- rather than three-bladed propeller via a shorter extension shaft, the power plant benefiting from water-methanol injection and affording 1,800 hp for take-off. Individual exhaust stacks were introduced, fuel tankage was rearranged, and the pilot's seat was moved both forward (2.75 in/70 mm) and upward (3.15 in/80 mm). In this form, the *Kyokusen*, or J2M2, was adopted as the Navy Interceptor Fighter Raiden (Thunderbolt) Model 11, armament remaining as for the J2M1. In the event, only eight J2M2 (Model 11) Raidens were built as this version was overtaken by the J2M3 (Model 21) charac-

The J2M3 (above), with four-cannon armament, was the first service version of the Raiden.

terised by an armament of four wing-mounted 20-mm cannon. The J2M3 thus became the first service Raiden, the J2M3-Ko (Model 21Ko) differing in the type of cannon installed. The J2M5 (Model 33) and J2M6 (Model 31) were developed in parallel, entering flight test in May and June 1944 respectively, and both were committed to production. The J2M6 differed from the J2M3 essentially in having a wider and taller windscreen, the basic model reverting to J2M2 armament and the J2M6-Ko (Model 31Ko) having four wing cannon. The J2M5 had a Kasei 26Ko engine equipped with a mechanically-driven three-stage supercharger, and was ordered into production by the Takaza Arsenal

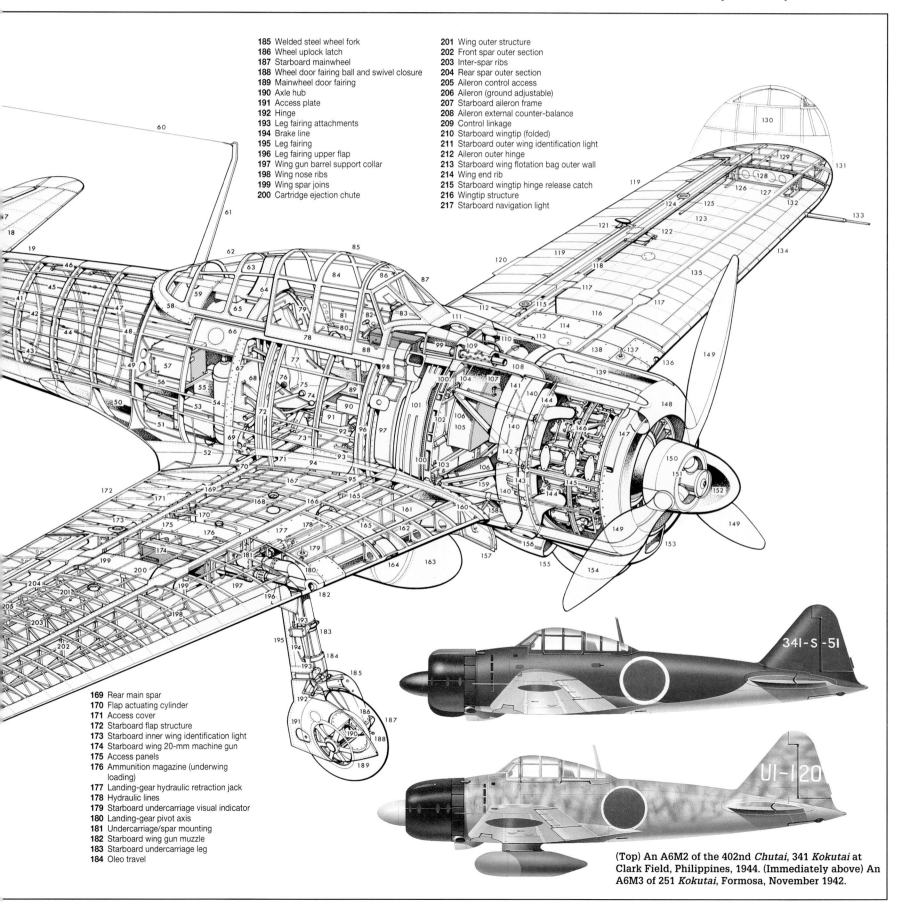

185 Welded steel wheel fork
186 Wheel uplock latch
187 Starboard mainwheel
188 Wheel door fairing ball and swivel closure
189 Mainwheel door fairing
190 Axle hub
191 Access plate
192 Hinge
193 Leg fairing attachments
194 Brake line
195 Leg fairing
196 Leg fairing upper flap
197 Wing gun barrel support collar
198 Wing nose ribs
199 Wing spar joins
200 Cartridge ejection chute

201 Wing outer structure
202 Front spar outer section
203 Inter-spar ribs
204 Rear spar outer section
205 Aileron control access
206 Aileron (ground adjustable)
207 Starboard aileron frame
208 Aileron external counter-balance
209 Control linkage
210 Starboard wingtip (folded)
211 Starboard outer wing identification light
212 Aileron outer hinge
213 Starboard wing flotation bag outer wall
214 Wing end rib
215 Starboard wingtip hinge release catch
216 Wingtip structure
217 Starboard navigation light

169 Rear main spar
170 Flap actuating cylinder
171 Access cover
172 Starboard flap structure
173 Starboard inner wing identification light
174 Starboard wing 20-mm machine gun
175 Access panels
176 Ammunition magazine (underwing loading)
177 Landing-gear hydraulic retraction jack
178 Hydraulic lines
179 Starboard undercarriage visual indicator
180 Landing-gear pivot axis
181 Undercarriage/spar mounting
182 Starboard wing gun muzzle
183 Starboard undercarriage leg
184 Oleo travel

(Top) An A6M2 of the 402nd *Chutai*, 341 *Kokutai* at Clark Field, Philippines, 1944. (Immediately above) An A6M3 of 251 *Kokutai*, Formosa, November 1942.

and Nihon Kentetsu, as well as Mitsubishi. The J2M5 was the most efficacious version of the Raiden, attaining 382 mph (615 km/h) at 22,310 ft (6 800 m), but only some 40 were delivered by the time hostilities ended. The J2M4, which had been under development meanwhile, had a Kasei 23 Hei engine with a turbo-supercharger and two of the wing cannon transferred to the fuselage to fire at an oblique angle. The first of three prototypes of the J2M4 flew on 24 September 1944, but persistent difficulties with its turbo-supercharger led to its discontinuation. Mitsubishi production of the Raiden (excluding prototypes) totalled 470 aircraft. The following data relate to the J2M3. *Max speed, 363 mph (584 km/h) at 17, 880 ft (5 450 m). Initial climb, 3,838 ft/min (19,50 m/sec). Normal range, 655 mls (1 055 km). Empty weight, 5,489 lb (2 490 kg). Loaded weight, 7,584 lb (3 440 kg). Span, 35 ft 5¼ in (10,80 m). Length, 32 ft 7½ in (9,94 m). Height, 12 ft 11¼ in (3,94 m). Wing area, 215.82 sq ft (20,05 m²).*

MITSUBISHI A7M1 & 2 REPPU   Japan

The Reppu (Hurricane) was designed to the requirements of a 17-*Shi* specification as an A6M successor, and, again, was the responsibility of Jiro Horikoshi. A large aircraft with hydraulically-operated folding outer wing panels, the first of two A7M1 prototypes of the Reppu was flown on 6 May 1944 with a Nakajima NK9K Homare 22 engine rated at 2,000 hp for take-off. The A7M1 proved underpowered and the third prototype was fitted, as the A7M2, with a Mitsubishi MK9A engine affording 2,200 hp for take-off, this flying on 13 October 1944. Plans for large-scale production were immediately initiated, and it was proposed that series aircraft would have either four 20-mm cannon or two cannon and two 13,2-mm machine guns. A further six A7M2 prototypes and one production aircraft had been completed by the time hostilities terminated, at which time work was proceeding on the extensively modified A7M3-J which was to have been powered by a turbo-supercharged version of the MK9A engine and carry an armament of four wing-mounted and two oblique-firing fuselage-mounted 30-mm cannon. The following data relate to the A7M2. *Max speed, 390 mph (628 km/h) at 21,655 ft (6 600 m). Time to 19,685 ft (6 000 m), 6.15 min. Range (internal fuel), 570 mls (917 km). Empty weight, 7,112 lb (3 226 kg). Loaded weight, 10,406 lb (4 720 kg). Span, 45 ft 11¼ in (14, 00 m). Length, 36 ft 1¼ in (11, 00 m). Height, 14 ft 0½ in (4,28 m). Wing area, 332. 18 sq ft (30,86 m²).*

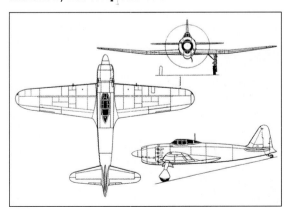

Only a single production example of the A7M2 (above and below) was completed before hostilities ended.

MITSUBISHI Ki-109   Japan

Derived from the Ki-67 Hiryu bomber as a heavy interceptor, the Ki-109 was originally conceived in two versions: the Ki-109-ko mounting two obliquely-firing 37-

The Ki-109 (above and below) was evolved from the Ki-67 Hiryu as a heavy interceptor.

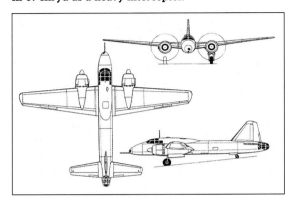

mm cannon and the Ki-109-otsu equipped with radar and a 15.75-in (40-cm) searchlight. The intention was that the two versions of the aircraft would work as a team. Soon thereafter the Ki-109 project was redefined as a bomber interceptor mounting a 75-mm Type 88 cannon with which it could attack its quarry while remaining beyond the range of opposing defensive armament. Converted from a Ki-67 airframe and retaining the dorsal, lateral and tail gun positions of the bomber, and the Mitsubishi Ha104 engines each rated at 1,900 hp for take-off, the first Ki-109 prototype was completed in August 1944. The second prototype was powered by Ha-104ru engines with Ru-3 turbo-superchargers, and it was intended that these would be installed in the final 22 aircraft of an initial batch of 42 Ki-109s. The first series Ki-109 dispensed with the dorsal and lateral gun positions, retaining only the tail position which mounted a single 12,7-mm machine gun. Primary armament was the single 75-mm cannon with 15 shells individually loaded by the co-pilot. In the event, production difficulties with the Ru-3 turbo-supercharger prevented its application to any series Ki-109s, and only 20 production aircraft were completed, these having standard Ha-104 engines. *Max speed, 342 mph (550 km/h) at 19,980 ft (6 090 m). Range, 1,367 mls (2 200 km). Empty weight, 16,367 lb (7 424 kg). Loaded weight, 23, 810 lb (10 800 kg). Span, 73 ft 9⅞ in (22,50 m). Length, 58 ft 10¾ in (17,95 m). Height, 19 ft 1 in (5, 80 m). Wing area, 708. 8 sq ft (65,85 m²).*

MITSUBISHI Ki-46-KAI   Japan

In June 1943, the Rikugun Kokugijutsu Kenkyujo, or Army Aerotechnical Research Institute, began to study the adaptation of the Ki-46-III reconnaissance aircraft for the high-altitude interceptor fighter rôle. Development was actively pursued from May 1944 as the Ki-46-III KAI, or Army Type 100 Air Defence Fighter, and the Army Air Arsenal at Tachikawa instituted a conversion programme. The nose was redesigned to accommodate two 20-mm cannon and the top centre fuselage fuel tank was removed to provide space for a 37-mm cannon firing forward and upward at an angle of 30 deg. The two Mitsubishi Ha-112-II engines rated at 1,500 hp for take-off were retained, and the first Ki-46-III KAI two-seat interceptor

A dedicated fighter derivative of the Ki-46-III, the Ki-46-III KAI (above) was developed by Tachikawa.

tor was completed and flown in October 1944, deliveries to operational units commencing during November. Operational results were disappointing owing to the poor climb rate of this type, but the conversion programme was continued at Tachikawa until March 1945, a substantial number being delivered., *Max speed, 391 mph (630 km/h) at 19,685 ft (6 000 m). Range, 1,243 mls (2 000 km) plus one hour combat. Time to 26,250 ft (8 000 m), 19, min. Empty weight, 8,446 lb (3 831 kg). Loaded weight, 13,730 lb (6 228 kg). Span, 48 ft 2¾ in (14,70 m). Length, 37 ft 8¼ in (11,48 m). Height, 12 ft 8¾ in (3,88 m). Wing area, 344.46 sq ft (32, 00 m²).*

(Below) The Mitsubishi Ki-46-III KAI interceptor.

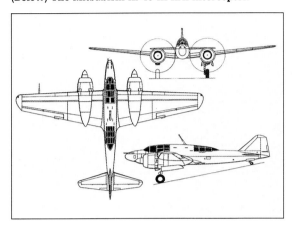

MITSUBISHI Ki-83   Japan

Development of the Ki-83 (above) was curtailed by the ending of hostilities in 1945.

Intended to meet a requirement formulated in 1943 for an advanced two-seat long-range escort fighter, the Ki-83 was designed by a team headed by Tomio Kubo, who had previously been responsible for the Ki-46. Aerodynamically exceptionally clean and powered by two turbo-supercharged Mitsubishi Ha-211ru 18-cylinder radials, the Ki-83 possessed an armament of two 20-mm and two 30-mm cannon. The first of four prototypes was flown on 18 November 1944, demonstrating spectacular performance and remarkable manoeuvrability for its size – a 2,200-ft (670-m) diameter loop being executed at 403 mph (648 km/h) at 9,500 ft (2 900 m) within 31 sec. However, definitive plans for series manufacture of the Ki-83 were still being finalised when hostilities terminated. *Max speed, 438 mph (704 km/h) at 32,810 ft (10 000 m). Normal range, 1, 213 mls (1 953 km). Time to 32,810 ft (10 000 m), 10. 5 min. Empty weight, 13,184 lb (5 980 kg). Normal loaded weight, 19,390 lb (8 795 kg). Span, 50 ft 10¼ in (15,50 m). Length, 41 ft 0⅛ in (12,50 m). Height, 15 ft 1¼ in (4,60 m). Wing area, 360.8 sq.ft (33,52 m²).*

(Below) Mitsubishi Ki-83 long-range escort fighter.

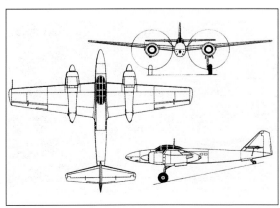

MITSUBISHI J8M1 SHUSUI — Japan

In July 1944, the Imperial Navy issued a 19-*Shi* specification for a rocket-propelled target defence interceptor to be based on the Messerschmitt Me 163B. The task of developing this aircraft was assigned to Mitsubishi under the Navy designation J8M1, but as it was a joint Navy-Army venture it received the designation Ki-200 from the latter service and the name Shusui (Sword Stroke) was also adopted. While work on the Walter HWK 109-509 rocket motor (as the Toku Ro.2) was largely confined to its adaptation for Japanese manufacturing techniques, inadequate German data on the airframe dictated considerable original structural design work. For the training of pilots, a full-scale wooden version, the MXY8 Akikusa (Autumn Grass), was designed and built by the Navy Air Technical Arsenal at Yokosuka, and the first Shusui made an unpowered test flight on 8 January 1945. The first powered flight test took place six months later, on 7 July, but the aircraft was destroyed and no further flight testing was undertaken before the termination of hostilities. Four more Shusui interceptors had been completed by that time, and six more were virtually complete. Powered by a 3,307 lb (1 500 kg) thrust Toku Ro.2 bi-fuel rocket, the Shusui was armed with two 30-mm cannon and the following data are manufacturer's estimates. *Max speed, 559 mph (900 km/h) at 32, 810 ft (10 000 m). Time to 19,685 ft (6 000 m), 2.26 min. Service ceiling, 39,370 ft (12 000 m). Empty weight, 3,318 lb (1 505 kg). Loaded weight, 8,565 lb (3 885 kg). Span, 31 ft 2 in (9,50 m). Length, 19 ft 10¹/₄ in (6,05 m). Height (on dolly), 8 ft 10¹/₄ in (2,70 m). Wing area, 190.85 sq ft (17,73 m²).*

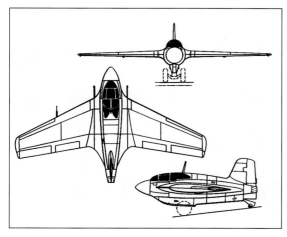

Based on the Me 163B rocket interceptor, the J8M1 (above and below) did not become operational.

MITSUBISHI F-1 — Japan

Japan's first indigenous combat aircraft to be produced after the end of World War II, the F-1 originated from a 1972 decision to develop a single-seat close air support fighter with secondary air-air capability from the Mitsubishi T-2 supersonic trainer. The overall performance of the latter was such that virtually no aerodynamic modifications had to be made, the principal change from the T-2 to the F1 being the fairing over of the rear cockpit without changing the contours. The two prototypes of the F-1, both of which flew for the first time in June 1975, were modified T2s with weapons systems equipment and test instrumentation in the rear cockpits. Powered by two 7,070 lb st (3 207 kgp) with afterburning Ishikawajima-Harima TF40-IHI-801A (licence-built Rolls-Royce/Turboméca Adour) turbofans, the F-1 was armed with a single 20-mm JM61 multi-barrel cannon in the lower front fuselage and had provision for up to 6,000 lb (2 721 kg) of bombs

Two squadrons of the 3rd *Kokudan* at Misawa flew the F-1 (above) in the 1990s, with one in the 8th *Kokudan*.

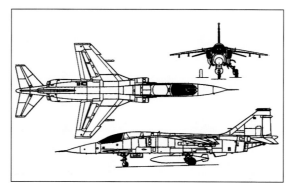

The Mitsubishi F-1 close support fighter (above and below) was derived from the T-2 trainer.

or rockets on the fuselage centreline and four wing hardpoints. Normal armament comprised two ASM-1 air-to-surface missiles and two or four AIM-9 Sidewinder AAMs. The Air Self-Defence Force purchased 77 F-1s 70 of these were upgraded in 1991-93 with an advanced fire control system and a stronger cockpit canopy. At the end of 2000, the 61 remaining were being phased out in favour of the F-2. *Max speed, 1,056 mph (1 700 km/h) at 40,000 ft (12 190 m), or Mach=1.6. Initial climb, 35, 000 ft/min (177,8 m/sec). Combat radius, 346 mls (556 km) with ASM-1s. Empty weight, 14,017 lb (6 358 kg). Max loaded weight, 30,146 lb (13 674 kg). Span, 25 ft 10¹/₄ in (7,88 m). Length, 58 ft 7in (17,66 m). Height, 14 ft 4³/₄ in (4,39 m). Wing area, 228 sq ft (21,18 m²).*

MITSUBISHI F-2 — Japan

In the mid-1980s, Japan started to look for a replacement for the only marginally adequate F-1. After examining several contenders, the FS-X, an indigenous fighter based on the F-16C but using advanced technology, was selected. Agreement was reached in 1987, but it was 1990 before work really started. Mitsubishi became prime contractor, working closely with General Dynamics. The rear fuselage was stretched, and the radome made slightly larger. The horizontal tail surfaces were enlarged, and the trailing edges cropped outboard. But the biggest change was the wing. This was based on GD's Agile Falcon proposal of some years earlier, with greater span and area, and the LERX were increased to match. The spars, major ribs and lower skin were a single piece of carbon composite, produced by co-curing; a Japanese process. Unlike the F-16, titanium and composites were extensively used. With the accent on attacking surface targets, decoupled flight modes as pioneered by the F-16CCV were adopted, allowing sideforce control and direct lift control, although the ventral control surfaces of the F-16CCV were not used. Nor was the one-piece canopy, which was replaced by a strong two-piece windshield to meet Japanese birdstrike requirements. The engine selected was the F110-GE-129. Radar was the Melco phased array multi-mode type, while a 20-mm M61A Vulcan cannon supplements Japanese Amraam and Sidewinder equivalents. The F-2 has 13 hardpoints for weaponry. First flight

The F-2 developed by Mitsubishi and General Dynamics (now Lockheed Martin)

took place from Nagoya on 7 October 1995, with Yoshiyuki Watanabe at the controls. Although problems with cracking in the wings have been encountered, the first of 130 production F-2s were delivered late in 2000. *Max speed, Mach 2. Empty weight, 26,455 lb (12 000 kg). Max takeoff weight, 48,722 lb (22 100 kg). Span, 36 ft 6 in (11,13 m). Length, 50 ft 11 in (15,52 m). Height, 16 ft 3¹/₂ in (4,96 m). Wing area, 357 sq ft (33,17 m²).*

MORANE-SAULNIER TYPE L — France

The most famous parasol monoplane of its period, the Type L two-seater, which appeared in 1913, saw service as a fighter as a result of fortune rather than original intent. Derived from the Type G-19 – the first aircraft of Léon Morane and Raymond Saulnier to feature a parasol wing configuration – the Type L emulated previous Morane-Saulnier types in its use of wing warping for lateral control. At the start of World War I, 50 examples ordered by Turkey were immediately sequestered for use by France's *Aviation Militaire*, and, in October 1914, chosen by *Commandant* Barés, the *Chef du Service Aéronautique aux Armées*, for *fighting* duties. Powered by either the seven-cylinder Gnome or nine-cylinder Le Rhône 9C rotary, both rated at 80 hp, the Type L was described as a *Morane de chasse*, and, at times, was armed with an 8-mm Hotchkiss or 7,7-mm Lewis machine gun fired from the rear cockpit. Sometimes flown as a single-seater in the fighting rôle, the Type L gained the distinction of carrying into combat the first fixed forward-firing machine gun to be used operationally by a tractor aircraft. Just over 50 Type L aircraft were delivered to the Royal Flying Corps, with which they performed unspectacular service throughout 1915 in the reconnaissance rôle, and others were supplied to the Russian Military Air Fleet. The following data relate to the standard two-seat Type L. *Max speed, 71 mph (115 km/h) at 6,560 ft (2 000 m). Time to 3,280 ft (1 000 m), 5.75 min. Endurance, 2.5 hrs. Empty weight, 849 lb (385 kg). Loaded weight, 1,444 lb (655 kg). Span, 36 ft 9 in (11,20 m). Length, 22 ft 6³/₄ in (6, 88 m). Height, 12 ft 10³/₄ in (3,93 m). Wing area, 196.9 sq ft (18, 30 m²).*

The two-seat Type L was also used in single-seat form, such as this one (below) in Russian service.

MORANE-SAULNIER TYPE N — France

Effectively the earliest operational single-seat fighters were the Morane-Saulnier Type N and its German contemporary, the Fokker E I, although the former had not been conceived with a military application in mind. Both types were flown in May 1914, the latter as the M 5, and the Type N was demonstrated in the following month at Aspern, Vienna. Retaining the wing warping lateral control of earlier Morane-Saulnier shoulder-wing monoplanes, but embodying noteworthy aerodynamic refinements, the Type N was powered by an 80 hp Le Rhône 9C rotary engine, and its operational use was pioneered by Eugène Gilbert who flew an early example fitted with a forward-firing 8-mm Hotchkiss machine gun with propeller-mounted steel bullet deflectors and dubbed *Le Vengeur*. This armament was similar to that of the Type L flown by Roland Garros. The performance of *Le Vengeur* prompted an official order for a small series of aircraft for use by the *Aviation Militaire* and these entered service in the summer of 1915. In January 1916, 24 Type N aircraft were ordered for the Royal Flying Corps, these being delivered between March and June 1916, and becoming known unofficially to the service as "Morane Bullets". A few were delivered to the Russian Military Air Fleet, but most had been withdrawn from French operational service before the end of 1915, and those delivered to the RFC were phased out in the following summer. As supplied to the RFC, the Type N was fitted with either the Lewis or Vickers machine gun, both of 7,7-mm calibre. *Max speed, 89 mph (144 km/h) at sea level. Time to 3,280 ft (1 000 m), 4.0 min. Endurance, 1.5 hrs. Loaded weight, 976 lb (443 kg). Span, 26 ft 8⅝ in (8,15 m). Length, 19 ft 1½ in (5,83 m). Height, 7 ft 4½ in (2,25 m). Wing area, 118.4 sq ft (11,00 m².)*

The Type N (above and below) had propeller-mounted bullet deflectors for its single machine gun.

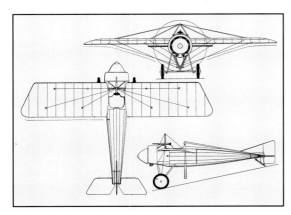

MORANE-SAULNIER TYPE G France

The appellation Type G was something of a generic designation in that several very different Morane-Saulnier designs were known as such, the last of these being a single-seat fighter designed in the summer of 1915 and built after the initial production batch of Type N aircraft for the *Aviation Militaire*. A refined development of the basic Type G of 1912, but featuring a fully-faired fuselage and powered by an 80 hp Le Rhône 9C, the Type G fighter had a centrally-mounted 8-mm Hotchkiss machine gun with standard bullet deflectors on the propeller. Possessing a general resemblance to the Type N, the Type G fighter's *raison d'être* has gone

No production took place of the fighter version (below) of the Morane-Saulnier Type G.

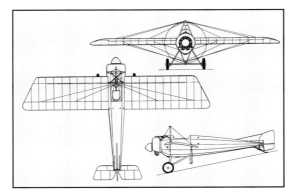

(Above) A single gun armed the Type G fighter.

unrecorded, but it is improbable that more than one or two examples were built as no production contract was placed on behalf of the *Aviation Militaire*. No data other than the overall dimensions have survived. *Span, 29 ft 11 in (9,12 m). Length, 21 ft 8⅔ in (6,62 m). Height, 8 ft 4 in (2,54 m).*

MORANE-SAULNIER TYPE I France

The Type I single-seat fighter was fundamentally a Type N re-engined with a 110 hp Le Rhône 9J nine-cylinder rotary and stemmed from interest evinced by Maj-Gen Trenchard in a more powerful version of the basic aircraft. An order was placed in January 1916 on behalf of the RFC for one aircraft. Twelve more were ordered during the following March when the first example was flown for the first time. The Type I was intended to have a single 7,7-mm Lewis gun with French Alkan synchronising mechanism, but the four examples supplied to the RFC mid-July 1916 were fitted with a centrally-mounted Vickers gun. No additional Type I fighters were delivered to the British service as this aircraft had meanwhile been overtaken by the similarly-powered, but extensively redesigned, Type V which afforded greater endurance. The Type I was not adopted by the *Aviation Militaire*. *Max speed, 104 mph (168 km/h) at sea level. Time to 6,560 ft (2 000 m), 6.75 min. Endurance, 1.33 hrs. Empty weight, 736 lb (334 kg). Loaded weight, 1,124 lb (510 kg). Span, 27 ft 0½ in (8,24 m). Length, 19 ft 1 in (5,81 m). Height, 8 ft 2½ in (2,50 m). Wing area, 118.4 sq ft (11,00 m².)*

Essentially a Type N variant, the Type I (below) had a more powerful Le Rhône engine.

MORANE-SAULNIER TYPE V France

Developed in parallel with the Type I, the Type V single-seat fighter was a larger aircraft with a three-hour endurance. First flown in April 1916, and powered

(Below) The Morane-Saulnier Type V.

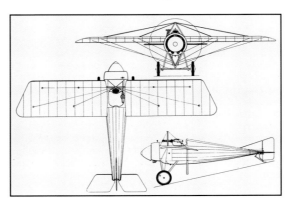

by a 110 hp Le Rhône 9J engine, it differed from the Type I in having larger wings and deepened ventral contours to accommodate increased fuel tankage. Armed with a single 7,7-mm Vickers gun mounted centrally ahead of the cockpit, the Type V was intended primarily to meet an RFC requirement formulated at the beginning of 1916, and the first of 12 aircraft for that service was officially accepted on 13 May 1916. The Type V proved singularly unpopular, as did also the Type I, and the operational career of the 110 hp Morane-Saulnier fighters with the RAF proved to be brief, terminating on 19 October 1916. A number of 110 hp aircraft, probably Type Vs but possibly Type Is, was supplied to Russia, 18 of these being in service on 1 April 1917, and several reportedly survived the revolution of that year to see operational use with the Red Air Fleet. *Max speed, 102 mph (165 km/h) at sea level. Time to 3,280 ft (1 000 m), 3.35 min. Span, 28 ft 7½ in (8,75 m). Length, 19 ft 1 in (5,81 m).*

Little success attended the Type V (below), a dozen examples of which saw brief service with the RFC.

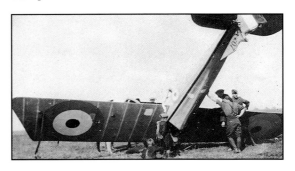

MORANE-SAULNIER TYPE P (MoS 21) France

During the summer of 1916, Morane-Saulnier produced two different single-seat fighter versions of the Type P reconnaissance two-seat parasol monoplane. Both were powered by the 110 hp Le Rhône 9J nine-cylinder rotary, but whereas the first single-seater was a simple conversion retaining the forward cockpit of the two-seater and carrying a single synchronised 7,7-mm Vickers gun, the second version featured a lower-mounted wing, an armament of twin synchronised 7,7-mm guns and an aft-positioned cockpit. Allegedly the first Allied twin-gun fighter, the latter was 183 lb (83 kg) heavier than the former in loaded condition and 5.6 mph (9 km/h) slower at sea level, recorded performance figures proving inferior to those of the *two*-seat Type P. Two prototypes of the initial version and at least one prototype of the two-gun version were evaluated by the *Aviation Militaire*, but neither was adopted for

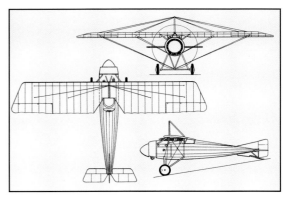

The second fighter version of the Type P (above and below) introduced twin-gun armament.

series production and the single-seat Type P was offi-cially abandoned in December 1916. The following data relate to the two-gun version. *Max speed, 97 mph (156 km/h) at sea level. Time to 6,560 ft (2 000 m), 8.67 min. Endurance, 2.5 hrs. Empty weight, 955 lb (433 kg). Loaded weight, 1,528 lb (693 kg). Span, 36 ft 9 in (11,20 m). Length, 23 ft 7½ in (7,20 m). Height, 10 ft 8¾ in (3,27 m).*

MORANE-SAULNIER TYPE AC (MoS 23)   France

Differing from earlier single-seat Morane-Saulnier shoulder-wing monoplanes essentially in having ailerons for lateral control rather than utilising wing warping and in employing rigid wing bracing, the Type AC appeared in the autumn of 1916. Powered by either the 110 hp Le Rhône 9J or 120 hp Le Rhône 9JB nine-cylinder rotary engine and carrying a single synchro-nised 7,7-mm gun, the Type AC was aerodynamically clean by contemporary standards, its fuselage being faired to a circular cross section. Thirty production air-craft were ordered for the *Aviation Militaire*, deliveries commencing late 1916. Although of advanced design and possessing a good performance, the Type AC was considered inferior to the SPAD S.VII, and, in conse-quence, was not adopted in quantity. Two examples were supplied to the UK for RFC evaluation. *Max speed, 111 mph (178 km/h) at sea level. Time to 6,560 ft (2 000 m), 5.92 min. Endurance, 2.5 hrs. Empty weight, 959 lb (435 kg). Loaded weight, 1,451 lb (658 kg). Span, 32 ft 1⅘ in (9,80 m). Length, 23 ft 1½ in (7,05 m). Height, 8 ft 11½ in (2,73 m). Wing area, 161.46 sq ft (15,00 m²).*

(Below) The Morane-Saulnier Type AC fighter.

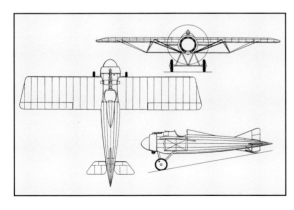

MORANE-SAULNIER TYPE AI (MoS 27)   France

In the summer of 1917, Morane-Saulnier produced two new fighters in parallel, the Type AI (MoS 27) parasol monoplane and the Type AF (MoS 28) single-bay biplane. Powered by a 150 hp Gnome Monosoupape 9Nb nine-cylinder rotary, the Type AI was primarily of wooden construction and carried a single synchronised 7,7-mm Vickers gun. The prototype was officially tested in early August 1917 at Villacoublay, demon-strating an exceptional performance. In the following month, a Type AI was tested with a twin-gun installa-tion, this aircraft having slightly enlarged tail surfaces and revealing only a modest reduction in climbing per-formance. Accordingly, the Type AI was ordered into production both in its single-gun version as the MoS 27

Ailerons replaced wing warping on the Type AC (above), which also featured rigid wing bracing.

and with twin guns as the MoS 29. Considerably in ex-cess of 1,000 examples of the two versions were sub-sequently built, deliveries commencing early in 1918. However, the Type AI had been withdrawn from *Aviation Militaire* service in May 1918 – as a result, said some sources, of structural deficiencies. Others blamed the temperamental nature of the Monosoupape engine.

Both single-gun MoS 27 (above) and twin-gun MoS 29 (below) versions of the Type AI were produced.

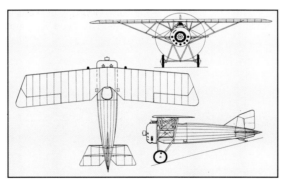

Following withdrawal, most Type AIs were re-engined with the 120 hp Le Rhône 9JB or 135 hp 9Jby and employed as fighter trainers under the designation MoS 30. Two examples of the Type AI were completed with a full wooden monocoque fuselage, one having the Monosoupape engine and the other a 170 hp Le Rhône 9R, but further development was not pursued. The following data relate to the twin-gun MoS 29 ver-sion. *Max speed, 137 mph (221 km/h) at sea level. Time to 6,560 ft (2 000 m), 5.25 min. Empty weight, 912 lb (414 kg). Loaded weight, 1,486 lb (674 kg). Span, 27 ft 11 in (8,51 m). Length, 18 ft 6⅖ in (5,65 m). Height, 7 ft 10½ in (2,40 m). Wing area, 144.13 sq ft (13,39 m²).*

MORANE-SAULNIER TYPE AF (MoS 28)   France

Although possessing a fuselage closely resembling that of the Type AI monoplane developed in parallel, the Type AF was not merely a biplane version of its con-temporary, the two aircraft differing dimensionally. The first single-seat fighter of biplane configuration to be developed by Morane-Saulnier, the Type AF was fit-ted with a 150 hp Gnome Monosoupape 9Nb rotary and a single 7,7-mm Vickers gun. First flown on 23 June 1917, the Type AF demonstrated excellent handling qualities and good performance, but it offered little im-provement on the SPAD S.XIII which was already in quantity production. The Morane-Saulnier biplane,

therefore, was not ordered for the *Aviation Militaire*. However, in November 1917, a derivative designated Type AFH was readied for testing, this being intended for launching from a ship's deck. The Type AFH had a single central pontoon-type float with a beam of 8 ft 10⅓ in (2,70 m) and a length of 4 ft 8⅔ in (1,44 m), and a small tail float, allowing the fighter to alight on water and take-off on wheels incorporated in the central float. Some flight testing of the Type AFH was conducted, but this shipboard fighter version was not adopted. The following data relate to the Type AF. *Max speed, 129 mph (207 km/h) at 3,280 ft (1 000 m). Time to 6,560 ft (2 000 m), 4.83 min. Empty weight, 928 lb (421 kg). Loaded weight, 1,431 lb (649 kg). Span, 24 ft 6 in (7,47 m). Length, 16 ft 10¾ in (5,15 m). Height, 7 ft 8½ in (2,35 m). Wing area, 164.8 sq ft (15,31 m²).*

The first Morane-Saulnier biplane fighter, the Type AF (above and below), did not achieve production.

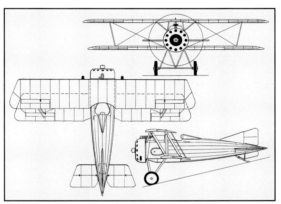

MORANE-SAULNIER TYPE AN (MoS 31 TO MoS 34)   France

Designed to use a 450 hp Bugatti 16-cylinder water-cooled engine, the Type AN two-seat fighter completed in the summer of 1918 was a large, two-bay equi-span

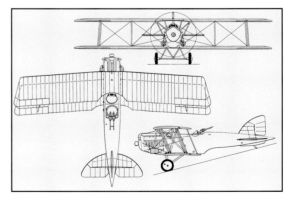

Type AN-derived, the Renault-powered ANR (above) was similar to the Salmson-engined ANS (below).

With a Liberty engine, the ANL (above) was a further prototype derived from the sole Type AN.

staggered biplane with a monocoque fuselage. Officially tested at Villacoublay on 27 October 1918, the Type AN produced disappointing results and alternatives to the unorthodox Bugatti engine were investigated. The 400 hp Liberty 12 was installed in the Type ANL and the 450 hp Renault 12Kb in the Type ANR, both being tested in 1919. The armament of the AN series aircraft consisted of a forward-firing 7,7-mm Vickers gun and twin 7,7-mm Lewis guns on a flexible mount in the rear cockpit. The final variant of the basic design, the Type ANS, was fitted with a 530 hp Salmson 18Z 18-cylinder water-cooled two-row radial. Development continued through 1919, the Type ANL becoming the MoS 32, the ANR becoming the MoS 33 and the ANS becoming the MoS 34, but, although some promising results were obtained, further development was discontinued. The following data relate to the Bugatti-engined prototype. *Max speed, 140 mph (225 km/h) at sea level. Time to 6,560 ft (2 000 m), 6.66 min. Loaded weight, 3,902 lb (1 770 kg). Span, 38 ft 5⅘ in (11,73 m). Length, 27 ft 4½ in (8,34 m). Height, 9 ft 1 in (2,77 m). Wing area, 441.33 sq ft (41,00 m²).*

MORANE-SAULNIER
MoS (MS) 121   France

As a direct result of concern over the escalating costs of fighter manufacture, a programme for the development of so-called *chasseurs légers*, or light fighters, for France's *Aviation Militaire* was promoted in 1926. To become known unofficially as the *Jockey* programme, this envisaged the use of moderate power, minimal equipment and a pair of 7,7-mm Vickers guns with only 300 rounds each. Emphasis was to be placed on climb rate, an endurance of one-and-a-half hours at full throttle was called for and a ceiling of 26,245 ft (8 000 m) was specified. To meet this requirement, Morane-Saulnier designed and built its first post-World War I fighter, the MoS 121, the prefix being changed to "MS" shortly after the appearance of the prototype in 1927. Possessing lower wing and power loadings than other contending designs (with the exception of the MS 221 developed in

The lightweight MS 121 (above and below) was the first post-war Morane-Saulnier fighter design.

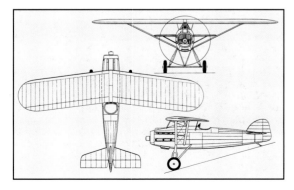

parallel), the MS 121 was a single-seat parasol monoplane of mixed construction and powered by a 465 hp Hispano-Suiza 12Jb 12-cylinder water-cooled engine. It proved underpowered and incapable of attaining specified climb rates, and was, in consequence, discarded in favour of the more powerful MS 221. *Max speed, 160 mph (257 km/h) at 4,920 ft (1 500 m). Time to 4,920 ft (1 500 m), 3.37 min. Empty weight, 2,229 lb (1 011 kg). Loaded weight, 2,813 lb (1 276 kg). Span, 32 ft 1⅘ in (9,80 m). Length, 22 ft 0½ in (6,72 m). Height, 9 ft 5⅔ in (2,88 m). Wing area, 172.23 sq ft (16,00 m²).*

MORANE-SAULNIER
MS 221 TO MS 223   France

The MS 221 (above and below) was an unsuccessful derivative of the MS 121 for the "Jockey" programme.

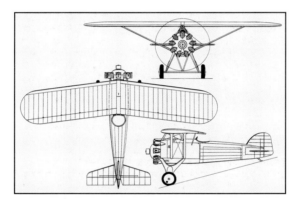

Modified from the second MS 221, the sole MS 222 (below) had a turbo-supercharged engine.

Retaining the basic airframe of the MS 121, the MS 221, which appeared in 1928 as a replacement contender in the *Jockey* programme, carried a similar twin-7,7-mm gun armament, but was powered by the Gnome-Rhône 9Ae Jupiter nine-cylinder radial rated at 600 hp, and weighed 101 lb (46 kg) less. Both lighter and more powerful than competing *Jockey* entries, the MS 221 was nevertheless at a disadvantage in level speed, which proved appreciably lower than those of other contenders. One of the two prototypes of the MS 221 was accordingly fitted with a turbo-supercharged G-R 9As Jupiter developing its full 600 hp at 12,465 ft (3 800 m). At the same time, an attempt was made to reduce aerodynamic drag by redesigning the wing bracing. Redesignated MS 222, this prototype was 55 lb (25 kg) heavier, but climbed to 22,965 ft (7 000 m) in 12 min. The maximum speed of 166 mph (267 km/h) at 11,975 ft (3 650 m) remained inadequate, however, and in a further attempt to reduce drag, the cross-axle type undercarriage was replaced by one of split-axle type, the modified aircraft flying in 1930 as the MS 223. In the meantime, Morane-Saulnier had initiated a more fundamental redesign of the fighter as the MS 224, and, in consequence, further development of the MS 223

was discontinued. The following data relate to the MS 221. *Max speed, 166 mph (268 km/h) at sea level. Time to 16,405 ft (5 000 m), 8.75 min. Empty weight, 2,017 lb (915 kg). Loaded weight, 2,712 lb (1 230 kg). Span, 32 ft 1⅘ in (9,80 m). Length 21 ft 3¾ in (6,50 m). Height, 9 ft 9⅓ in (2,98 m). Wing area, 172.22 sq ft (16,00 m²).*

MORANE-SAULNIER
MS 224 & MS 225   France

Shortly after the initiation of MS 223 flight testing, the entire *Jockey* fighter concept was adjudged a failure and, with the inhibitions imposed by the *chasseur léger* programme removed, Morane-Saulnier developed a larger and heavier fighter, the MS 224, which entered flight test in 1931. Based on experience with the preceding prototypes, the MS 224 retained the mixed structure (dural spars and wooden ribs) of the earlier aircraft for the wing, mating this with a metal-and-fabric covered dural fuselage, the ovoid cross section of which was widened to the near-circular. Wing area was increased by 10.76 sq ft (1,00 m²) to 182.99 sq ft (17,00 m²), and loaded weight was raised to 3,086 lb (1 400 kg). Powered by a Gnome-Rhône 9Asb, the MS 224 attained 188 mph (303 km/h) during trials. A modified version, the MS 225, was adopted by the *Aviation Militaire* (to become the *Armée de l'Air* in 1934) as an interim fighter pending availability of more advanced aircraft meanwhile called for by the 1931 C1 programme. The MS 225 differed from the MS 224 primarily in having a fully-cowled Gnome-Rhône 9Kdrs engine of 500 hp. Armed with two 7,7-mm guns, 74 MS 225s were delivered during 1933-34. Of these, 55 were supplied to the *Aviation Militaire* (one being fitted with a 690 hp Hispano-Suiza 12Xcrs engine with a 20-mm cannon mounted between the cylinder banks and flown as a test-bed under the designation MS 227), 16 to the

Transferred to the 8ème Escadre, this MS 225 (above) retained the markings of Aéronavale's 3C1.

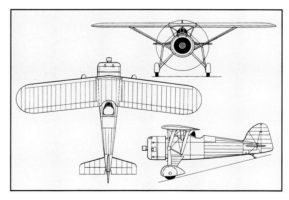

Limited service use with the Aviation Militaire was achieved by the MS 225 (above and below).

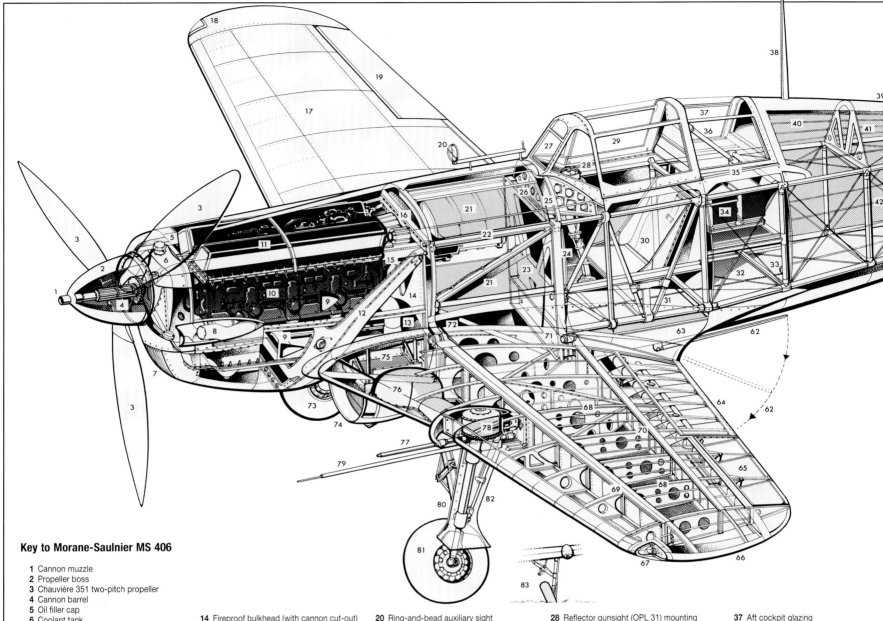

Marine Nationale and three were exported to China. The last MS 225 fighters were phased out of first-line service during 1938. The following data apply to the MS 225. *Max speed, 207 mph (334 km/h) at 12,630 ft (3 850 m). Time to 9,840 ft (3 000 m), 5.7 min. Range, 435 mls (700 km). Empty weight, 2,544 lb (1 154 kg). Loaded weight, 3,505 lb (1 590 kg). Span, 34 ft 7⅔ in (10,56 m). Length, 23 ft 9½ in (7,25 m). Height, 10 ft 8½ in (3,26 m). Wing area, 185.14 sq ft (17,20 m²).*

MORANE-SAULNIER MS 226 France

In 1932, Morane-Saulnier initiated study of a dedicated shipboard version of the MS 225 fighter. Designated MS 226 and powered by a similar Gnome-Rhône 9Kdrs to that of the shore-based fighter, the shipboard aircraft differed initially in having some structural strengthening, an arrester hook and naval equipment. Three prototypes were ordered in 1933, the first two being completed as MS 226s and the third as the MS 226bis which differed in having aft-folding wings. No series production of the MS 226 was undertaken as the *Marine Nationale* considered the type to be conceptually obsolescent. *Max speed, 172 mph (277 km/h) at 1,640 ft (500 m). Ceiling, 24,605 ft (7 500 m). Loaded weight, 3,615 lb (1 640 kg). Dimensions as for MS 225.*

In *Aéronavale* markings for evaluation (below), the MS 226 was soon found to be obsolescent.

MORANE-SAULNIER MS 275 France

The C1 (*monoplace de chasse*) requirement first issued by the *Service Technique Aéronautique* in 1930 – when it was finally conceded that the *Jockey* programme had failed – and upgraded on 26 January 1931, resulted in no

Of typically M-S parasol monoplane configuration, the MS 275 was a completely new design.

The MS 225 No 41 (above) served with the 1*er escadrille*, 7*ème Escadre* in 1935.

fewer than 10 designs being awarded prototype contracts. These included two Morane-Saulnier proposals. The first, the MS 275, retained the classic parasol monoplane configuration of preceding Morane-Saulnier fighters and was flown in 1934. Powered by a Gnome-Rhône 9Krse nine-cylinder radial rated at 600 hp at 13,125 ft (4 000 m) and armed with two synchronised 7,7-mm guns, the MS 275 proved exceptionally manoeuvrable and offered a very respectable performance. It found little favour, however, owing to its dated concept, development being discontinued, together with that of the more innovative MS 325, in

(Above) Morane-Saulnier MS 275, flown in 1934.

favour of the more promising MS 405 then in preliminary design. *Max speed, 225 mph (363 km/h) at 16,405 ft (5 000 m). Time to 13,125 ft (4 000 m), 6.6 min. Service ceiling, 35,105 ft (10 700 m). Range, 715 mls (1 150 km). Empty weight, 3,000 lb (1 361 kg). Loaded weight, 3,801 lb (1 724 kg). Span, 36 ft 7⅔ in (10,56 m). Length, 23 ft 9 in (7,24 m). Height, 10 ft 9¾ in (3,29 m). Wing area, 185.14 sq ft (17,20 m²).*

MORANE-SAULNIER MS 325 France

To meet the same C1 requirement for which the MS 275 was proffered, Morane-Saulnier developed in parallel the MS 325. This, for the first time since the company resumed single-seat fighter development in 1926, discarded the classic parasol wing configuration in favour of a low-mounted wing. Flown for the first time early in 1933, the prototype MS 325 was powered by an Hispano-Suiza 12Xbrs engine rated at 690 hp and was an all-metal dural-skinned braced low-wing monoplane with an armament of two wing-mounted 7,7-mm guns. Initial flight testing dictated lowering of the tailplane

(Below) Morane-Saulnier MS 325, a 1933 prototype.

and introduction of wing root fairings in an attempt to eradicate a serious buffet problem. Trials continued to suffer aerodynamic difficulties, and, in 1934, further development was discontinued. Full performance trials were never concluded, and the following figures are manufacturer's estimates. *Max speed, 227 mph (365 km/h) at 14,765 ft (4 500 m). Service ceiling, 39,370 ft (12 000 m). Empty weight, 2,985 lb (1 354 kg). Loaded weight, 3,944 lb (1 789 kg). Span, 38 ft 8½ in (11,80 m). Length, 27 ft 0¾ in (8,25 m). Height, 12 ft 1⅔ in (3,70 m). Wing area, 212.38 sq ft (19,73 m²).*

The single prototype of the MS 325 (below) suffered aerodynamic problems resulting in its abandonment.

MORANE-SAULNIER MS 405 France

Designed in response to a C1 requirement initially issued in September 1934, the MS 405 was of classic tubular metal construction, but unusual in that, other than the fabric-covered rear fuselage, it had *Plymax* – okoumé plywood bonded to aluminium – stressed skinning. Powered by an 860 hp Hispano-Suiza 12Ygrs engine, the first prototype flew on 8 August 1935, and the second, with a 900 hp HS 12Ycrs, 17 months later, on 20 January 1937. A pre-series of 16 aircraft was ordered on 1 March 1937, the first flying on 3 February 1938 with an HS 12Ygrs engine and an armament of one 20-mm and two 7,5-mm guns. Various changes had been proposed meanwhile for the series model to which the designation MS 406 (which see) was assigned, the new features being progressively introduced on successive MS 405s (eg, the second featured an enlarged fuel tank, the fourth was fitted with the HS 12Y31 engine and the 12th had a simplified and lightened wing structure).

The MS 405 (above) served as the pre-production form of the MS 406, and two examples went to Switzerland as MS 406H (below) pattern aircraft.

The HS 12Y31-engined 13th and 15th aircraft were delivered to Switzerland (as MS 406Hs) in September 1938 and April 1939 as pattern aircraft for a licence-built version (see D-3800). The 12th was subsequently re-engined with a 910 hp HS 12Y45 and fitted with a fixed rather than semi-retractable radiator as the MS 411 to provide a basis for the HS 12Y51-engined MS 412 (which see) built in Switzerland as the D-3801. The final MS 405 was flown on 21 June 1938 as a pattern aircraft for the series MS 406. The following data apply to the HS 12Ycrs-powered MS 405. *Max speed, 275 mph (443 km/h) at 13,125 ft (4 000 m). Time to 13,125 ft (4 000 m), 6.78 min. Range, 620 mls (1 000 km). Loaded weight, 5,379 lb (2 440 kg). Span, 34 ft 9⅝ in (10,62 m). Length, 26 ft 9⅓ in (8,17 m). Height, 8 ft 10¾ in (2,71 m). Wing area, 184.07 sq ft (17,10 m²).*

Key to Morane-Saulnier MS 406

1 Cannon muzzle
2 Propeller boss
3 Chauvière 351 two-pitch propeller
4 Cannon barrel
5 Oil filler cap
6 Coolant tank
7 Oil cooler
8 Coolant intake
9 Louvres
10 Exhaust ports
11 Hispano-Suiza 12Y31 12-cylinder Vee engine
12 Main engine support bearer
13 Supercharger

14 Fireproof bulkhead (with cannon cut-out)
15 Hispano-Suiza S7 cannon of 20-mm calibre
16 Cannon ammunition drum (60 rounds capacity)
17 Plymax (okoumé plywood bonded to aluminium) stressed wing skinning
18 Starboard navigation light
19 Starboard aileron

20 Ring-and-bead auxiliary sight
21 Fuselage fuel tank (90-Imp gal/410-l capacity)
22 Main upper longeron
23 Fuselage frame
24 Control column
25 Part instrument console
26 Main instrument console
27 Unarmoured windscreen

28 Reflector gunsight (OPL 31) mounting
29 Sliding cockpit canopy
30 Pilot's seat
31 Seat support frame
32 Provision for oxygen stowage
33 Control runs
34 Transmitter/receiver (Radio-Industrie 537)
35 Canopy track
36 Crash support bar

37 Aft cockpit glazing
38 Aerial mast
39 Plymax decking
40 Alloy skin (over wooden stringers)
41 Elektron formers
42 Main aft fuselage framework (Dural tubing)
43 Cross bracing
44 Fuselage/fin attachment frame

MORANE-SAULNIER MS 406 France

Numerically the most important *Armée de l'Air* fighter at the commencement of World War II, the MS 406 combined the structural design and equipment changes applied to individual MS 405s. Deliveries of the MS 406 commenced late in 1938, a production tempo of six daily being attained by April 1939, and 11 daily four months later. Possessing an armament of one engine-mounted 20-mm cannon and two 7,5-mm machine guns, the MS 406 had an 860 hp Hispano-Suiza 12Y31 engine with which it was markedly underpowered. Production terminated in March 1940, at which time the *Armée de l'Air* had taken on charge 1,064 MS 406s, of which 30 had been supplied to Finland during December 1939-January 1940, and 30 had gone to Turkey during February-March 1940. Subsequent purchases from the German authorities between late 1940 and late 1942 brought total procurement of the Morane-Saulnier fighter by Finland to 87 aircraft (including a number of MS 410s – which see). With the occupation of Vichy France in November 1942, German forces acquired a further 46 MS 406s which (apart from two delivered to Finland) were supplied to the Croat Air Force. The Italians obtained 52 MS 406s of which the 25 airworthy

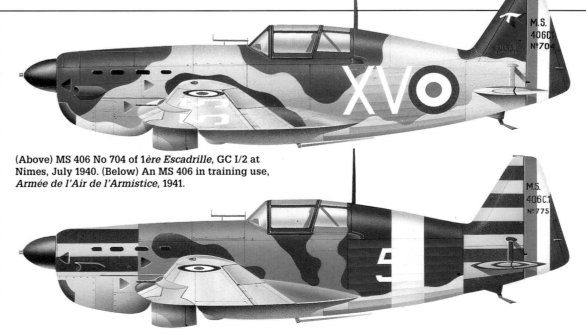

(Above) MS 406 No 704 of 1ère *Escadrille*, GC I/2 at Nimes, July 1940. **(Below)** An MS 406 in training use, *Armée de l'Air de l'Armistice*, 1941.

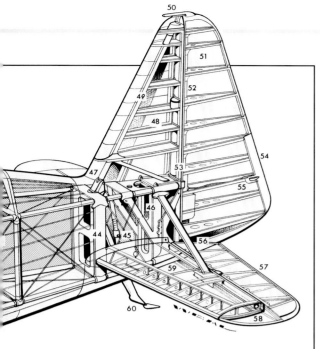

45 Tailskid bracing
46 Rear fuselage frame
47 Fin attachment point
48 Fin construction
49 Fin spar (Duralumin)
50 Balance
51 Rudder framework
52 Rudder post
53 Rudder hinge
54 Rudder tab
55 Tab cable
56 Tailplane strut
57 Elevator construction
58 Elevator balance
59 Tailplane structure
60 Tail skid
61 Ventral fabric
62 Hinged ventral aerial
63 Wing root fairing
64 Flap construction
65 Port aileron
66 Wingtip construction
67 Port navigation light
68 Wing ribs
69 Forward (main) wing spar
70 Aft wing spar
71 Rear spar/fuselage attachment point
72 Front spar/fuselage attachment points (two)
73 Starboard mainwheel
74 Retractable radiator
75 Radiator retraction links
76 Undercarriage well inner shell
77 Port 7.5-mm MAC 1934 machine gun
78 Pitot tube
79 Mainwheel leg
80 Port mainwheel (low-pressure tyre shown at ground angle)
81 Mainwheel leg fairing
82 Head-on view of canted mainwheel when under load

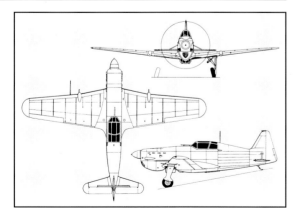

The standard production MS 406 (above).

examples were delivered to the *Regia Aeronautica*. *Max speed, 302 mph (486 km/h) at 16,405 ft (5 000 m). Initial climb, 2,559 ft/min (13 m/sec). Max range, 621 mls (1 000 km). Empty weight, 4,173 lb (1 893 kg). Normal loaded weight, 5,348 lb (2 426 kg). Dimensions as for MS 405.*

MORANE-SAULNIER
MS 406H (D-3800)   Switzerland

Two MS 406H fighters were supplied to Switzerland in September 1938 and April 1939 to serve as pattern aircraft for a licence-manufactured version. These were, in fact, hybrids, mating the MS 405 airframe with the HS 12Y31 engine of the MS 406 and Swiss-specified instrumentation, armament and radio. Production was initiated by the Eidgenössisches Konstruktions-Werkstätte as the D-3800, the Hispano-Suiza 12Y31 engine being manufactured by Adolph Saurer AG. The drum-fed 7,5-mm wing guns were replaced by belt-fed weapons, the two-pitch Chauvière propeller was supplanted by an Escher-Wyss EW-V3 controllable-pitch unit, and the original MS 405 wing structure was retained (rather than the simplified and lighter wing of the MS 406). A pre-series of eight D-3800s was built in 1939, and the first series aircraft was delivered in January 1940. Seventy-four series D-3800s were built, the last of these being delivered on 29 August 1940, and later, in 1942, two further aircraft were assembled from spares. During 1943, all D-3800s underwent modification of cooling and hydraulic systems to standardise with the D-3801, and were fitted with similar ejector exhausts. Employed for advanced training after withdrawal from first-line service, the last D-3800s were scrapped in 1954. *Max speed, 295 mph (475 km/h). Initial climb, 2,683 ft/min (13,4 m/sec). Endurance, 1.75 hrs. Empty weight, 3,968 lb (1 800 kg). Max loaded weight, 5,467 lb (2 480 kg). Dimensions as for MS 405.*

As the D-3800 (below), an MS 405 derivative was built by EKW in Switzerland in 1940.

MORANE-SAULNIER MS 410 France

During the winter of 1939-40, development of an upgraded version of the MS 406 was begun as the MS 410. The programme was based on the use of existing MS 406 airframes which were to be fitted with a fixed radiator bath to overcome problems presented by the standard semi-retractable radiator and a revised wing permitting installation of two belt-fed 7,5-mm guns rather than one drum-fed weapon. It was also proposed to fit ejector exhausts. The radiator bath and modified wing were flight tested during January and February 1940, 500 pairs of two-gun wings being ordered, and the ejector exhausts were tested in April 1940, these boosting max speed to 316 mph (509 km/h) at 13,125 ft (4 000 m). The events of May 1940 interrupted the programme when only five MS 410s had been completed. At the time, a further dozen conversions were virtually complete and some 150 sets of modified wings had been produced. After the Armistice, a modification centre was established under the auspices of the Ger-

man authorities, repairable MS 406s being sent to this centre for conversion to MS 410 standard. In the event, 74 aircraft were fitted with the new wings, but some were completed as hybrids in that they retained the semi-retractable radiator, and none was fitted with the ejector exhausts. Eleven MS 410s were delivered to Finland and others were included among the Morane-Saulnier fighters supplied to the Croat Air Force. *Max speed, 292 mph (470 km/h) at 13,125 ft (4 000 m). Empty weight, 4,239 lb (1 923 kg). Loaded weight, 5,690 lb (2 581 kg). Dimensions as for MS 405.*

With radiator fully extended, this MS 406 (above) also displays the characteristic in-tilted wheels.

Via Germany, Finland received 11 MS 410s (below) in 1941, used by HLeLv 28 alongside MS 406s.

MORANE-SAULNIER
MS 412 (D-3801)   Switzerland

Prior to the Franco-German Armistice, the MS 412, an improved version of the MS 406, was under development primarily to fulfil a Swiss requirement. As an interim development aircraft, the twelfth pre-series MS 405 had been fitted with the more powerful Hispano-

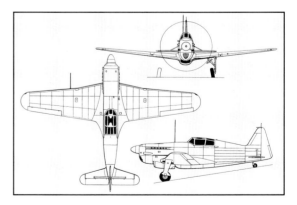

Swiss-built D-3801 (above and below), the photo showing an aircraft of *Fliegerkompagnie* 21, 1944.

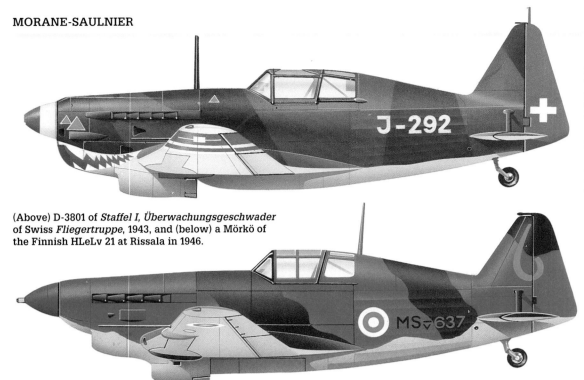

(Above) D-3801 of *Staffel I, Überwachungsgeschwader* of Swiss *Fliegertruppe*, 1943, and (below) a Mörkö of the Finnish HLeLv 21 at Rissala in 1946.

Suiza 12Y45 engine and flown as the MS 411, but a prototype of the MS 412 with the still more powerful HS 12Y51 engine was not completed in France, the programme continuing in Switzerland as the D-3801. Flown for the first time in October 1940, the D-3801 had an HS 12Y51 rated at 1,050 hp for take-off, a fixed radiator bath similar to that developed for the MS 410 and the same armament as that of the D-3800. Although protracted teething troubles were suffered by the Saurer-built HS 12Y51 engine, series production of the D-3801 was undertaken by the Eidgenössisches Flugzeugwerke, the Dornier-Werke AG (Doflug) and SWS, deliveries commencing in 1941 and continuing until 1945, and a total of 207 being manufactured. These were augmented by a further 17 built in 1947-48 from spare assemblies remaining from the main production run. After withdrawal from first-line service, some D-3801s remained in use as advanced trainers and target-tugs until 1959. *Max speed, 332 mph (535 km/h) at 13,780 ft (4 200 m). Initial climb, 3,287 ft/min (16,7 m/sec). Range, 746 mls (1 200 kg), Empty weight, 4,682 lb (2 124 kg). Loaded weight, 5,996 lb (2 720 kg). Dimensions as for MS 405 apart from height, 10 ft 10¾ in (3,32 m).*

MORANE-SAULNIER MÖRKÖ — Finland

The increasing obsolescence of the MS 406 led the Finnish Air Force to order, on 22 October 1942, the installation of a Klimov M-105P in an MS 406 airframe. The M-105P engine, derived from the HS 12Y, afforded 1,100 hp for take-off, and a substantial quantity of this power plant, together with suitable VISh-61P propellers, had been captured by the *Wehrmacht* and was available to the Finns. A 20-mm MG 151 cannon was mounted between the cylinder banks, a Bf 109G oil cooler was adopted, an aerodynamically-improved engine cowling was introduced, and, with some local structural strengthening, the prototype conversion was flown on 4 February 1943 as the Mörkö (Ghost) or Mörkö-Moraani. Successful trials resulted in the decision to bring all surviving MS 406 and MS 410 fighters to Mörkö standard, but only two more were completed before termination of the Finnish-Soviet conflict.

(Below) The so-called Mörkö (Ghost) derivative of the MS 406/410 placed in service by *Ilmavoimat*.

Nevertheless, the conversion programme continued, and by 21 November 1945, the remaining Morane-Saulnier fighters had been modified, bringing the total number of Mörkös delivered into the Finnish inventory to 41 aircraft. These retained the two or (in the case of the MS 410 conversion) four wing-mounted 7,5-mm machine guns, but shortages of the MG 151 cannon necessitated this engine-mounted weapon being replaced by a 12,7-mm Berezina UB machine gun in some aircraft. The Mörkö remained in service until 11 September 1948, when the survivors were placed in storage, being scrapped four years later. *Max speed, 326 mph (525 km/h) at 13,125 ft (4 000 m). Initial climb, 4,921 ft/min (25 m/sec). Empty weight, 4,643 lb (2 106 kg). Loaded weight, 6,280 lb (2 849 kg). Dimensions as for MS 405 apart from length, 27 ft 6 in (8,38 m).*

(Below) The Finnish Mörkö MS 406/410 derivative.

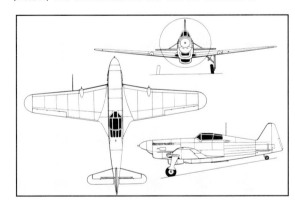

MORANE-SAULNIER MS 450 — France

On 27 February 1937, a new C1 requirement was issued by the *Service Technique Aéronautique* and one of the fighters designed to conform with its requirements was the MS 450. Featuring a dural monocoque fuselage and *Plymax*-skinned metal wings, the MS 450 was powered by an Hispano-Suiza 12Y51 engine affording 1,050 hp for take-off and carried an armament of one 20-mm engine-mounted cannon and two wing-

The first of three MS 450 prototypes (below) flown in April 1939 as a potential MS 406 successor.

mounted 7,5-mm machine guns. The first of three prototypes of the MS 450 was flown on 14 April 1939, but, a month earlier, an initial production order had been placed for the competitive Dewoitine D 520. Although the MS 450 test programme was continued – the second prototype being completed in November 1939 – its failure to display any marked advantage over the D 520 prevented the placing of a production order for the *Armée de l'Air*. Development of the basic design was continued, however, culminating in the MS 540 which was built in Switzerland by the Dornier-Werke AG (Doflug) as the D-3802 (which see). *Max speed, 348 mph (560 km/h) at 16,405 ft (5 000 m). Time to 16,405 ft (5 000 m), 6.8 min. Range, 466 mls (750 km). Loaded weight, 5,813 lb (2 637 kg). Span, 34 ft 9⅝ in (10,62 m). Length, 28 ft 11¼ in (8,82 m). Height, 9 ft 0¼ in (2,75 m). Wing area, 184.07 sq ft (17,10 m²).*

(Below) The Morane-Saulnier MS 450 fighter.

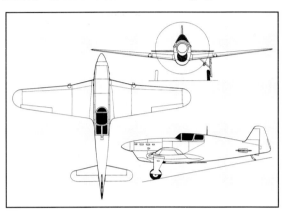

MOSCA-B BIS — Russia

The Mosca-B bis fighter (above) was built in series with both Le Rhône and Clerget rotary engines.

During 1916, the MB Mosca-Bystritsky (Moskva-MB) developed a single-seat fighter derivative of its two-seat reconnaissance monoplane. Appreciably smaller and more powerful than the two-seater, the Mosca-B bis fighter retained such features as wing warping for lateral control and detachable flying surfaces permitting the aircraft to be towed along roads. Powered by either an 80 hp Le Rhône or Clerget rotary engine, the Mosca-B bis was delivered with either a 7,7-mm unsynchronised forward-firing machine gun with propeller-mounted steel bullet deflectors or, alternatively, with a similar weapon mounted above the cockpit and firing clear of the propeller disc. A total of 50 Mosca-B bis fighters had been built up to 1918, and a few additional aircraft of this type were reportedly built after the Revolution. *Max speed, 81 mph (130 km/h). Time to 3,280 ft (1 000 m), 3.5 min. Empty weight, 710 lb (322 kg). Loaded weight, 1,074 lb (487 kg). Span, 25 ft 11 in (7,90 m). Length, 20 ft 0⅛ in (6,10 m). Wing area, 129.17 sq ft (12,00 m²).*

MOSKALEV SAM-7 SIGMA — USSR

One of the most innovative fighter designs of the mid-thirties was the SAM-7 Sigma produced by Aleksandr A Moskalev. Of all-metal stressed-skin construction, the SAM-7 was of tailless configuration, the low-set, two-spar trapezoidal wing carrying endplate vertical surfaces. Powered by a 750 hp M-34 12-cylinder water-cooled engine utilising a combination of retractable and surface-evaporation radiators, the SAM-7 was a two-seater. The second crew member occupied an en-

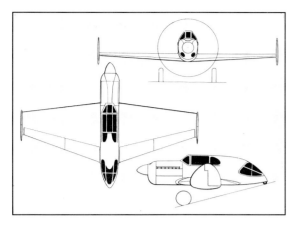

(Above) The highly innovative SAM-7 Sigma fighter.

tirely separate compartment and operated twin aft-firing 7,62-mm machine guns, the remaining armament comprising twin forward-firing sychronised guns of similar calibre. The main undercarriage members were manually retractable. The SAM-7 was completed and flown in the spring of 1936, but although it proved stable in the air, it was considered too radical and factory trials were terminated. The following data include design bureau estimated performance figures. *Max speed, 302 mph (486 km/h) at 16,405 ft (5 000 m). Range, 485 mls (780 km). Empty weight, 2,072 lb (940 kg). Loaded weight, 3,263 lb (1 480 kg). Span, 31 ft 6 in (9,60 m). Wing area, 215.28 sq ft (20,00 m²).*

MOSKALEV SAM-13   USSR

There can be little doubt that the inspiration for the SAM-13 was provided by the Fokker D XXIII, but the two twin-engined single-seat fighters shared no more than *conceptual* similarity, the Soviet fighter being lower-powered and appreciably smaller and lighter. Of wooden construction with two 236 hp Renault MV-6 six-cylinder inverted air-cooled engines disposed in fore and aft arrangement, the SAM-13 was fitted with a retractable tricycle undercarriage, the armament comprising two synchronised 7,62-mm guns in the forward fuselage and a similar weapon in the forward end of each tailboom. Flight testing was initiated late in 1940, but the development programme was halted when Germany invaded the Soviet Union, the sole prototype being destroyed when the design bureau was evacuated. No reliable performance data are available. *Maximum speed (reported to be) 323 mph (520 km/h) at 11,485 ft (3 500 m). Span, 23 ft 11½ in (7,30 m). Length, 25 ft 2⅔ in (7,68 m). Wing area, 96.88 sq ft (9,00 m²).*

(Below) The lightweight SAM-13 twin-boom fighter.

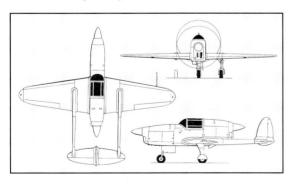

MUREAUX A.M.1 EXPRESS-MARIN   France

The first original design to be produced by the Ateliers des Mureaux, the A.M.1, referred to as the Express-Marin, was produced in 1924 as a single-seat shipboard fighter developed to meet a *Marine Nationale* requirement. Powered by a 300 hp Hispano-Suiza 8F eight-cylinder water-cooled Vee-type engine and carrying an armament of two synchronised 7,7-mm Vickers machine guns, the A.M.1, in its Marin II form, performed manufacturer's flight tests at Villacoublay in November 1924, before transferring to St Raphaël for

The A.M.1 Express-Marin, seen (above and below) in its Marin II form, featured a small foreplane.

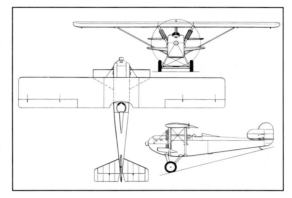

official trials. Basically a parasol monoplane, the A.M.1 incorporated a jettisonable undercarriage and a flotation bag to enable the aircraft to remain afloat pending retrieval in the event that it was forced to alight on water, a foreplane and drogue preventing nosing over. Only one prototype of the A.M.1 was completed and tested. *Max speed, 124 mph (200 km/h) at sea level. Empty weight, 1,984 lb (900 kg). Loaded weight, 3,130 lb (1 420 kg). Span, 39 ft 4⅓ in (12,00 m). Length, 24 ft 3⅓ in (7,40 m). Height, 10 ft 6 in (3,20 m). Wing area, 361.68 sq ft (33,60 m²).*

MUREAUX (BRUNET) 3   France

Built by the Ateliers des Mureaux and designed by André Brunet, the Mureaux 3 C2 (originally also known as the Brunet 3 C2) was an all-metal two-seat fighter monoplane powered by a 500 hp Hispano-Suiza 12Hb 12-cylinder liquid-cooled engine. Flown for the first time in June 1927, the Mureaux 3 C2 carried an armament of two fixed forward-firing 7,7-mm machine guns and two Lewis guns of similar calibre on a rear-cockpit ring mounting. Unfortunately, a month after its initial flight the Mureaux 3 C2 was destroyed as a result of the pilot being incapacitated when his oxygen mask malfunctioned at 22,970 ft (7 000 m), and further development concentrated on the Mureaux 4 C2. *Max speed, 152 mph (245 km/h) at sea level, 143 mph (231 km/h) at 16,405 ft (5 000 m). Time to 19,685 ft (6 000 m), 25.25 min. Empty weight, 2,557 lb (1 160 kg). Loaded weight, 4,387 lb (1 990 kg). Span, 49 ft 2½ in (15.00 m). Length, 27 ft 8¾ in (8,45 m). Height, 10 ft 2 in (3,10 m). Wing area, 349.84 sq ft (32,50 m²).*

The Brunet-designed Mureaux 3 (below) was tested for only one month before being destroyed in an accident.

MUREAUX (BRUNET) 4   France

Essentially similar to the 3 C2, the Mureaux 4C2 tandem two-seat parasol fighter monoplane differed pri

marily in having a 500 hp Salmson CM 18 air-cooled 18-cylinder radial engine and was flown for the first time in 1928. Armament was similar to that of its predecessor, but the Mureaux 4 C2 failed to obtain a production order and the basic design was subsequently adapted for the tactical reconnaissance (*Corps d'Armée* A2) rôle as the Mureaux 130. *Max speed, 145 mph (233 km/h) at sea level. Empty weight, 2,906 lb (1 318 kg). Loaded weight, 4,671 lb (2 119 kg). Span, 49 ft 2½ in (15,00 m). Length, 27 ft 2¾ in (8,30 m). Height, 10 ft 2 in (3,10 m). Wing area, 349.84 sq ft (32,50 m²).*

Essentially similar to its predecessor apart from engine, the Mureaux 4 was adapted for reconnaissance.

MUREAUX   France

See ANF-Mureaux for details of the Mureaux 114, 170, 180 and 190, the Ateliers des Mureaux having amalgamated in 1930 with the Ateliers de Construction du Nord de la France (ANF).

N

NAGLO D II   Germany

The only Naglo fighter to be flown, the D II (above) appears to have had an Albatros D V-type fuselage.

The D II quadruplane built by the Naglo Werft of Pichelsdorf, near Berlin, was designed by Ing Gnädig, who was, at the time, still in the employ of the Albatros Werke. It participated in the second D-type contest at Adlershof in the summer of 1918, the debriefing minutes of which indicated that it was to appear for further testing after modification. Powered by a 160 hp Mercedes six-cylinder water-cooled engine and intended to carry an armament of two LMG 08/15 machine guns, the Naglo D II appears to have been based on an Albatros D V-type fuselage. The bottom wing, completely independent of the three main lifting surfaces, was attached to an extruded keel and braced with splayed struts. Official type testing was undertaken on 24 May 1918, and during the D-type contest evaluation pilots praised the excellence of the con-

NAGLO

struction and workmanship of the D II while calling for an improvement in the flight characteristics. No details of the performance of this quadruplane fighter have survived. *Empty weight, 1,596 lb (724 kg). Loaded weight, 2,015 lb (914 kg). Span, 29 ft 6⅓ in (9,00 m). Wing area, 241.12 sq ft (22,40 m²).*

NAKAJIMA A1N1 & A1N2 (Type 3) (UK) Japan

The A1N1 (above) was the initial Japanese production version of the Gloster Gambet shipboard fighter.

The Gloster Gambet (which see) was submitted by Nakajima in the competition announced in April 1926 by the Imperial Navy for a new single-seat shipboard fighter. The Gambet was officially accepted in April 1929 as the Type 3 Carrier Fighter, or A1N1. About 50 Gambets were built by Nakajima with the 420 hp Nakajima Jupiter VI engine, these being followed by approximately 100 of the improved A1N2 version with the 450 hp Nakajima Kotobuki 2 engine. Production was completed in 1932. The A1N2 was the first Japanese fighter to engage in combat during the "Shanghai Incident" of February 1932. Data similar to Gambet.

NAKAJIMA NC Japan

The NC, the third prototype of which is illustrated (above and below), served as a basis for the Type 91.

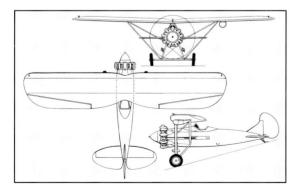

Designed by Shigejiro Owada and Yasushi Koyama, working under the supervision of two engineers seconded from the Dewoitine concern (André Marie and Maxime Robin), the NC was Nakajima's contender in the competition organised by the Imperial Army in March 1927 with the aim of providing a successor for the Ko-4 (Nieuport-Delage Ni-D 29). Featuring an all-metal monocoque fuselage and fabric-covered metal wings, the NC was powered by a 450 hp Bristol Jupiter

VI nine-cylinder radial and carried an armament of two 7,7-mm machine guns. Two prototypes were completed in May and June 1928 respectively, but structural testing led to rejection by the Army. The contest was, in the event, cancelled, but Nakajima persisted with the NC as a company-funded venture, building five more prototypes between 1929 and 1931. The final two of these prototypes were, in fact, of an essentially new design, retaining no more than the rear fuselage of the preceding prototypes. These were to serve as a basis for the series Type 91 fighter (which see). No data relating to the original NC prototype series are available.

NAKAJIMA Type 91 Japan

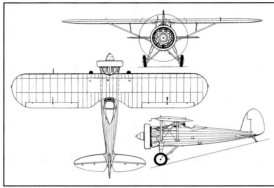

(Above) The Type 91-1 manufactured during 1931-1934.

Retaining the company appellation NC, the sixth prototype so designated was of fundamentally different design and powered by a supercharged 520 hp Bristol Jupiter VII radial. New wings of smaller area incorporated an internal (jettisonable) fuel tank to port, replacing the podded tank of preceding prototypes; the engine was enclosed by a Townend ring; the diameter of the forward fuselage was increased; both fore and aft main bracing struts were attached to the fuselage and the tail surfaces were redesigned. In addition, the cross-axle gave place to one of split type and the guns were repositioned. This prototype was ordered into production by the Army as the Type 91, deliveries commencing late-1931, but service introduction was delayed by CG and directional stability problems. A total of 320 fighters of this type was built by the parent company during 1931-34 (and 100 more by Ishikawajima), the initial version subsequently becoming the Type 91-1 with the appearance of a version powered by a Jupiter derivative, the Nakajima Kotobuki 2 of 580 hp. A prototype of this variant, the Type 91-2, was completed in July 1934, this being followed by 22 series aircraft, production terminating in September 1934. One experimental example was fitted with a Kotobuki 5 engine. The Type 91 remained in service until succeeded by the Kawasaki Type 95 in 1936-37. The follow-

The Type 91-1 (above) was the first Japanese Army fighter of indigenous design to be built in quantity.

ing data relate to the Type 91-1. *Max speed, 186 mph (300 km/h). Time to 9,845 ft (3 000 m), 4.0 min. Endurance, 2 hrs. Empty weight, 2,370 lb (1 075 kg). Loaded weight, 3,373 lb (1 530 kg). Span, 36 ft 1 in (11,00 m). Length, 23 ft 9¾ in (7,26 m). Height, 9 ft 1⅘ in (2,79 m). Wing area, 215.28 sq ft (20,00 m²).*

NAKAJIMA A2N1 to A2N3 (TYPE 90) Japan

After importation in 1928 of a Boeing 69-B (F2B-1) by the Imperial Navy, and, in the following year, the fourth Boeing 100 (essentially similar to the F4B-1), the two aircraft were shown to industry as examples of the then-current US shipboard fighter technology. Nakajima, which had previously built the Gloster Gambet (A1N1-2) for the Imperial Navy, initiated development of a carrier fighter based broadly on the Boeing design as a private venture. Responsibility for the fighter was assigned to Takao Yoshida and two prototypes powered by the Jupiter VI engine were completed in December 1929. Evaluated by the Navy in the following year, these prototypes were rejected as they were considered to offer an insufficient improvement over the A1N1. Some redesign was undertaken by Jingo Kurihara, and, with a 580 hp Kotobuki 2 engine, a further

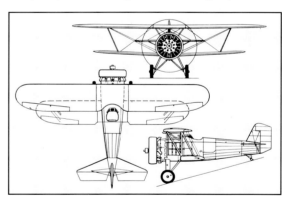

The A2N2 (above and below) was the principal version of Nakajima's first original shipboard fighter.

422

prototype was completed in May 1931. Another prototype followed later in 1931, the type then being adopted by the Navy in April 1932 as the A2N1 (Type 90). With a fabric-covered metal fuselage and a similarly skinned wing of mixed construction, the A2N1 carried an armament of two 7,7-mm machine guns. The principal production version was the A2N2 (Type 90-II) with re-arranged fuel tankage and armament, the A2N3 (Type 90-III) differing in having five deg of dihedral on the upper wing main panels. Series production was undertaken from 1932 until 1936 by both the parent company and Sasebo, about 100 Type 90 fighters being manufactured. The A3N1 was a two-seat training derivative of which 66 were produced between 1936 and 1939. The following data relate to the A2N1. *Max speed, 182 mph (293 km/h) at 9,845 ft (3 000 m). Time to 9,845 ft (3 000 m), 5.75 min. Endurance 3 hrs. Empty weight, 2,304 lb (1 045 kg). Loaded weight, 3,417 lb (1 550 kg). Span, 30 ft 8 9/10 (9,37 m). Length, 20 ft 3 3/5 in (6,18 m). Height, 9 ft 11 in (3,02 m). Wing area, 212.49 sq ft (19,74 m^2).*

NAKAJIMA NAF-1 — Japan

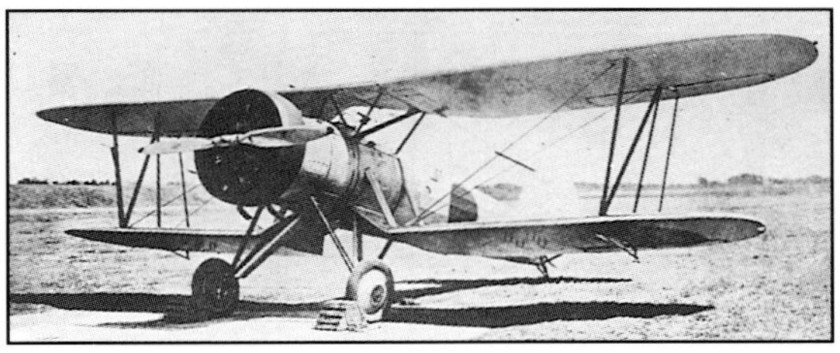

The sole prototype of the NAF-1 (above and below) was lost during official acceptance testing.

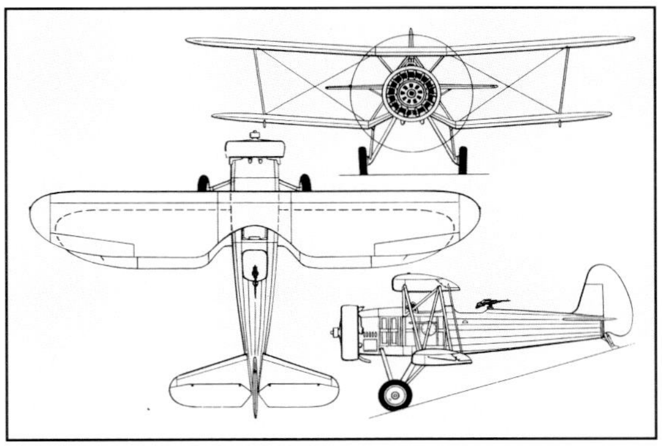

In 1931, the Imperial Navy instructed Nakajima to design and build, as part of a 6-*Shi* programme, a two-seat shipboard fighter with secondary dive-bombing capability and provision for an auxiliary fuel tank to suit the aircraft for long-range reconnaissance missions. Of all-metal construction with fabric skinning and designed by Kiyoshi Akegawa, the fighter received the company designation NAF-1, signifying Nakajima Akegawa Fighter No 1. The wings could be folded aft, provision was made for an external 61.6-Imp gal (280-l) auxiliary fuel tank and power was provided by a 530 hp Nakajima Kotobuki 2 engine. Armament comprised two fixed forward-firing 7,7-mm guns and a weapon of similar calibre on a flexible mount. The sole prototype was completed in the summer of 1932, but delivery to the Navy did not take place until the following year, the NAF-1 being destroyed in a forced landing terminating an official acceptance flight on 8 April 1933, and the programme was cancelled. *Max speed, 173 mph (278 km/h). Time to 9,845 ft (3 000 m), 7.5 min. Endurance (without external tank), 4 hrs. Empty weight, 2,800 lb (1 270 kg). Loaded weight, 4,065 lb (1 844 kg). Span, 35 ft 2 1/4 in (10,72 m). Length, 23 ft 7 in (7,19 m). Height, 9 ft 3 in (2,82 m). Wing area, 316.36 sq ft (29,39 m^2).*

NAKAJIMA 7-SHI FIGHTER — Japan

To meet a 7-*Shi* (1932) requirement for an advanced single-seat shipboard fighter with which the Imperial Navy hoped to replace the A2N1 that had just been

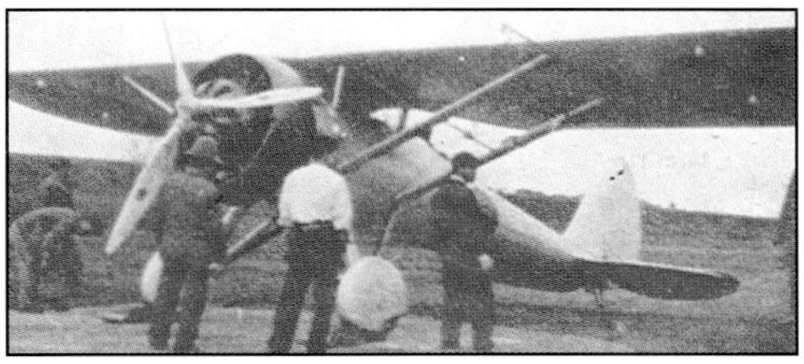

The 7-*Shi* shipboard fighter (above) was essentially a navalised version of the Imperial Army's Type 91.

adopted, Nakajima was instructed in April 1932 to develop a suitable aircraft in competition with Mitsubishi. Whereas the latter elected to adopt a cantilever low-wing monoplane configuration (1MF10), Nakajima chose to base its contender on the Army's Type 91 parasol monoplane then entering service. A single prototype of a navalised Type 91 was completed in the autumn of 1932, this differing from the Army fighter essentially in having a 560 hp Nakajima Kotobuki 5 engine driving a three-bladed propeller, wheel spats and an arrester hook. Armament remained the standard two 7,7-mm guns. The 7-*Shi* fighter was considered to offer an insufficient advance to warrant further development. *Max speed, 184 mph (296 km/h). Empty weight, 2,425 lb (1 100 kg). Loaded weight, 3,527 lb (1 600 kg). Span, 36 ft 1 in (11,00 m). Length, 23 ft 7 1/2 in (7,20 m). Height, 10 ft 6 in (3,20 m). Wing area, 215.28 sq ft (20,00 m^2).*

NAKAJIMA NAF-2 — Japan

With the destruction of the NAF-1 shipboard two-seat fighter prototype in April 1933, Kiyoshi Akegawa began design of a further two-seater to meet an 8-*Shi* requirement, the NAF-2. Of all metal construction with fabric skinning, the NAF-2 was powered by a 580 hp Nakajima Kotobuki 2 nine-cylinder radial and was a single-bay staggered biplane with pronounced sweepback on the upper wing. Armament comprised three 7,7-mm guns, two fixed and one on a flexible mount, and the first of two prototypes was completed in March 1934, these differing in that the first had N-type interplane struts and the second had aerofoil-section I-type struts. Although the NAF-2 met Imperial Navy requirements, a change in policy led to the abandonment of the two-seat fighter concept, and both prototypes were sold to the Asahi Press. *Max speed, 186 mph (300 km/h). Time to 9,845 ft (3 000 m), 9.66 min. Endurance, 4.5 hrs. Empty weight, 2,718 lb (1 233 kg). Loaded weight, 3,770 lb (1 710 kg). Span, 33 ft 9 1/2 in (10,30 m). Length, 23 ft 9 4/5 in (7,26 m). Height, 9 ft 4 1/5 in (2,85 m). Wing area, 283.64 sq ft (26,35 m^2).*

The NAF-2 (below) represented a second attempt by Nakajima to provide the Navy with a two-seat fighter.

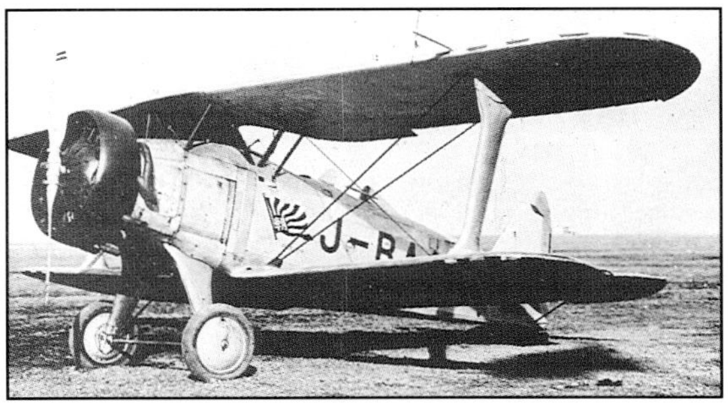

NAKAJIMA KI-8 — Japan

Although the Imperial Navy had discarded the two-seat fighter requirement that had resulted in the NAF-1 and -2, western developments in this category of aircraft stimulated some interest on the part of the Army to which, in 1933, Nakajima offered an advanced company-funded two-seat fighter project. Designed by Shigejiro Owada and Toshio Matsuda, and assigned the designation Ki-8 by the Army, the aircraft was an all-metal low-wing cantilever monoplane with a monocoque fuselage and spatted cantilever fixed undercarriage. Powered by a Nakajima Kotobuki 3 engine rated at 710 hp for take-off and carrying an armament of two fixed forward-firing 7,7-mm guns and one 7,7-mm gun on a flexible mount, the Ki-8 was conceptually advanced and five prototypes were built between March 1934 and May 1935. Army evaluation revealed stability and other problems, and although these were subsequently rectified, doubts concerning the practicability of the two-seat fighter concept led to the discontinuation of further development. *Max speed, 204 mph (328 km/h) at 13,125 ft (4 000 m). Time to 9,845 ft (3 000 m), 5.65 min. Empty weight, 3,362 lb (1 525 kg). Loaded weight, 4,654 lb (2 111 kg). Span, 42 ft 3 in (12,88 m). Length, 26 ft 9 1/4 in (8,17 m). Height, 11 ft 8 1/4 in (3,57 m). Wing area, 306.78 sq ft (28,50 m^2).*

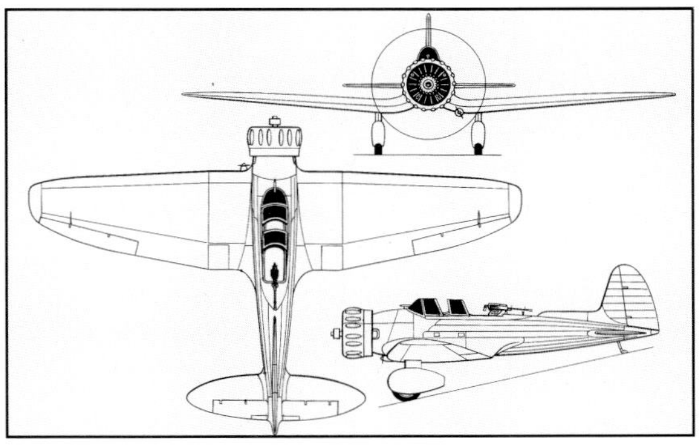

The Ki-8 (above and below) was, both structurally and aerodynamically, advanced for its time.

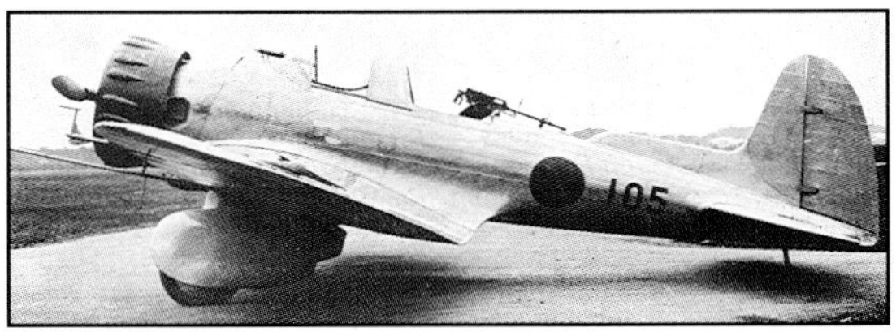

NAKAJIMA A4N1 (TYPE 95) — Japan

With the rejection of the 7-*Shi* (1932) single-seat shipboard fighter contenders, Nakajima began, at the behest of the Imperial Navy, to upgrade the Type 90 as an interim measure pending the results of a 9-*Shi* requirement issued in February 1934. Externally, the upgraded fighter bore a close resemblance to its progenitor, but virtually the entire structure was redesigned. It was larger overall and it was powered by a Nakajima Hikari 1 rated at 730 hp for take-off, armament remaining unchanged at two 7,7-mm synchronised weapons. Designated A4N1, a prototype was completed in the autumn of 1934, but official adoption was delayed until January 1936 when it became the Type 95. The last Imperial Navy fighter of biplane configuration, the A4N1 appeared in service only 10 months before the 9-*Shi* Mitsubishi A5M1 monoplane, and, in consequence, was soon relegated to the fighter training rôle. Nevertheless, some A4N1s saw service in China where they were employed for air base defence, tactical reconnaissance and close support with two 132-lb (60-kg) bombs. Production continued until 1940, by which time a total of 221 had been built. *Max speed, 219 mph*

(Below) The A4N1: last Imperial Navy fighter biplane.

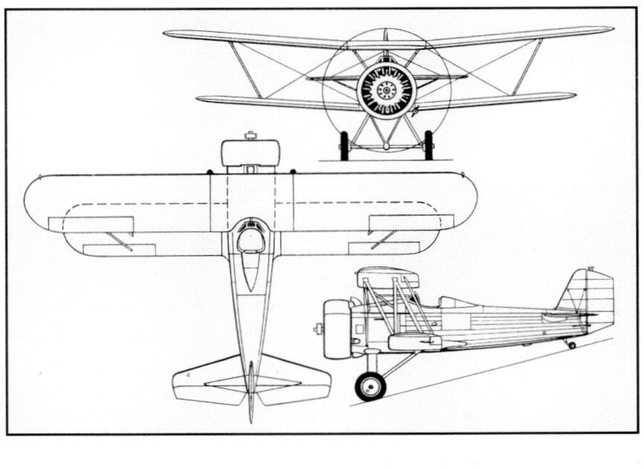

The A4N1 (above) was adopted in 1936 and remained in production for the Imperial Navy as late as 1940.

(352 km/h) at 10,500 ft (3 200 m). Time to 9,845 ft (3 000 m), 3.5 min. Range, 457 mls (735 km). Empty weight, 2,813 lb (1 276 kg). Loaded weight, 3,880 lb (1 760 kg). Span, 32 ft 9⁷⁄₁₀ in (10,00 m). Length, 21 ft 9½ in (6,64 m). Height, 10 ft 0⁴⁄₅ in (3,07 m). Wing area, 246.39 sq ft (22,89 m²).

NAKAJIMA KI-11   Japan

The failure of the gull-winged Kawasaki Ki-5 led the Imperial Army in 1934 to hold a further contest in the search for a replacement for the Nakajima Type 91. Only Kawasaki and Nakajima were contenders in this new contest, the latter submitting the Ki-11 obviously inspired by the Boeing P-26. Designed by Yasushi Koyama and Shinroku Inoue, the Ki-11 was powered by a Nakajima Kotobuki 3 nine-cylinder radial providing 710 hp for take-off. It possessed a metal monocoque fuselage and a wing of mixed construction covered by plywood and fabric, and wire-braced to the fuselage and undercarriage fairings. Considerable effort was expended in reducing aerodynamic drag, and four Ki-11s were built between April and December 1935, the last of these having an enclosed cockpit and spats rather than trousers enclosing the main undercarriage members. The Ki-11 lacked the agility of the competing Kawasaki Ki-10 biplane which was favoured by the more conservative elements of the Army and therefore ordered as the Type 95. Thus, it was to be said, Japanese fighter evolution was seriously delayed. One navalised prototype powered by a 560 hp Kotobuki 5

The third prototype Ki-11 (above) and the fourth prototype (below) with enclosed cockpit.

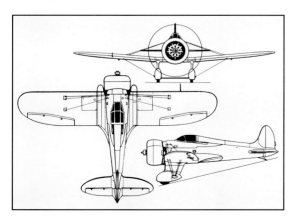

The fourth prototype Ki-11 (below) after sale to the Asahi newspaper concern as the AN-1.

engine was built during 1935 for Imperial Navy evaluation as a 9-*Shi* (1934) shipboard fighter, but the Mitsubishi Ka-14 was selected in preference (providing the basis for the A5M1). The last of the Ki-11 prototypes was sold to the Asahi newspaper concern (as the AN-1), establishing several national records. *Max speed, 261 mph (420 km/h) at 14,110 ft (4 300 m). Time to 16,405 ft (5 000 m), 6.15 min. Empty weight, 2,798 lb (1 269 kg). Max loaded weight, 3,748 lb (1 700 kg). Span, 35 ft 5⅛ in (10,80 m). Length, 24 ft 5⅓ in (7,45 m). Height, 11 ft 0⅔ in (3,37 m). Wing area, 193.76 sq ft (18,00 m²).*

NAKAJIMA KI-12   Japan

Early in 1935, the Nakajima company launched as a private venture a fighter intended to incorporate the latest Western innovations. Designed by Shigenobu Mori under the overall supervision of two Dewoitine engineers (Roger Robert and Jean Beziaud), the new fighter, the Ki-12, was powered by a 670 hp Hispano-Suiza 12Xcrs water-cooled V-12 engine. It was of all-metal construction with a monocoque fuselage, and featured split flaps and an hydraulically-retractable undercarriage. Armament consisted of a 20-mm engine-mounted cannon and two 7,7-mm wing guns. A prototype of this sophisticated fighter was completed in October 1936. Despite its high performance, the Ki-12 lacked the agility still sought by Imperial Army fighter pilots, and appreciating the fact that this fighter might be *too* advanced for the Army, Nakajima had already launched, again as a private venture, a less sophisticated fighter, the PE. In the event, the PE was to pro-

(Below) The private-venture Ki-12 fighter of 1936.

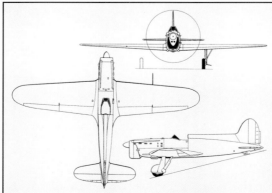

Key to Nakajima Ki-27-Otsu

1 Starboard navigation light
2 Wing skinning
3 Aileron
4 Aileron control rod inspection/access panel
5 Aileron fixed tab
6 Aileron nose balance weight
7 Flare igniter wire and release/drop cables
8 Magnesium flare illuminator tubes
9 Flap profile
10 Aerial mast
11 Access panels
12 Engine circumferential ring
13 Exhaust collector ring
14 650 hp Type 97 (Ha-1 otsu) radial engine
15 Carburettor air intakes
16 Support struts
17 Oil cooler assembly
18 Two-bladed propeller
19 Starter dog
20 Auxiliary drop tank (attached starboard inner wing section)
21 Fuel pipe join
22 Aft attachment
23 Anti-swing fittings
24 Forward attachment
25 Fuel filler
26 Air vent
27 Mainwheel leg fairing
28 Starboard mainwheel spat
29 Axle fork
30 Starboard mainwheel
31 Nose ring
32 Exhaust
33 7,7-mm Type 89 machine gun
34 Engine bearers
35 Ammunition magazine
36 Cartridge ejector chute
37 Wing spar/fuselage forward attachment
38 Engine bearer mounting
39 Cooling gills
40 Fuselage main frame/engine bearer upper mounting
41 Control column
42 Gun loading/inspection panels
43 Seat support
44 Canted frame
45 Canopy track stop
46 Instrument panel
47 Fuel filler
48 Telescopic sight
49 Windshield
50 Rear-view mirror (internal)
51 Aerial
52 Rearward-sliding canopy hood
53 Turnover/crash pylon
54 Cockpit sill
55 Pilot's seat

vide the basis for the highly successful Ki-27, and the elegant Ki-12 came to be looked upon more as a design exercise than as a serious contender for Army orders. The full performance envelope was not explored and the following data include manufacturer's estimates. *Max speed, 298 mph (480 km/h). Time to 16,405 ft (5 000 m), 6.5 min. Range, 497 mls (800 km). Empty weight, 3,086 lb (1 400 kg). Loaded weight, 4,189 lb (1 900 kg). Span, 36 ft 0⁹⁄₁₀ in (11,00 m). Length, 27 ft 2¾ in (8,30 m). Wing area, 182.99 sq ft (17,00 m²).*

Design of the comparatively advanced Ki-12 (below) was supervised by two engineers from Dewoitine.

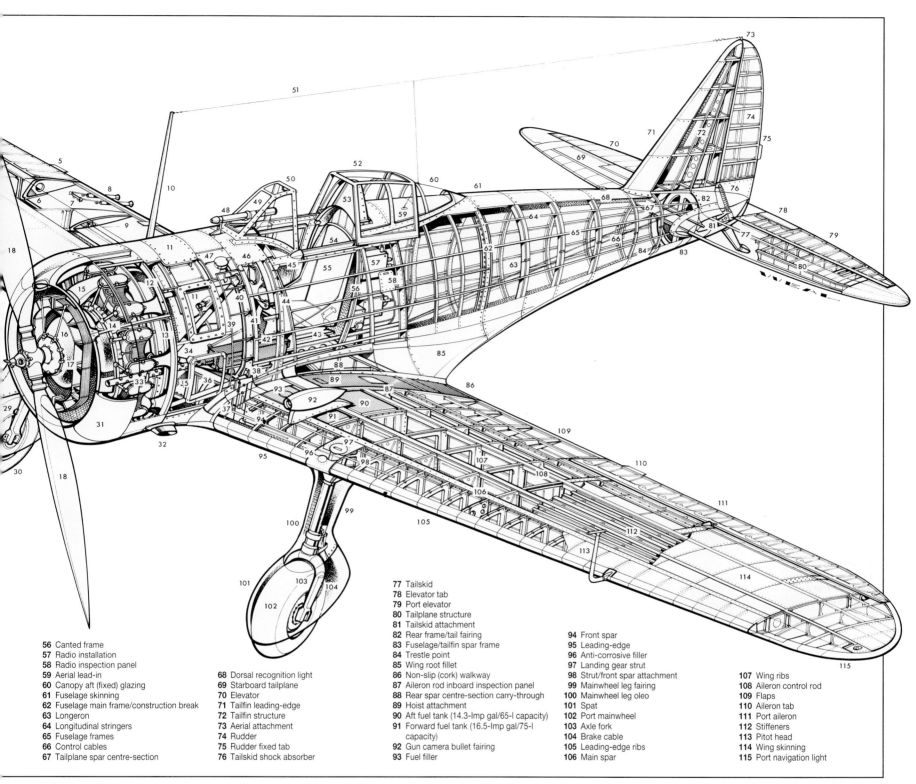

56 Canted frame
57 Radio installation
58 Radio inspection panel
59 Aerial lead-in
60 Canopy aft (fixed) glazing
61 Fuselage skinning
62 Fuselage main frame/construction break
63 Longeron
64 Longitudinal stringers
65 Fuselage frames
66 Control cables
67 Tailplane spar centre-section

68 Dorsal recognition light
69 Starboard tailplane
70 Elevator
71 Tailfin leading-edge
72 Tailfin structure
73 Aerial attachment
74 Rudder
75 Rudder fixed tab
76 Tailskid shock absorber

77 Tailskid
78 Elevator tab
79 Port elevator
80 Tailplane structure
81 Tailskid attachment
82 Rear frame/tail fairing
83 Fuselage/tailfin spar frame
84 Trestle point
85 Wing root fillet
86 Non-slip (cork) walkway
87 Aileron rod inboard inspection panel
88 Rear spar centre-section carry-through
89 Hoist attachment
90 Aft fuel tank (14.3-Imp gal/65-l capacity)
91 Forward fuel tank (16.5-Imp gal/75-l capacity)
92 Gun camera bullet fairing
93 Fuel filler

94 Front spar
95 Leading-edge
96 Anti-corrosive filler
97 Landing gear strut
98 Strut/front spar attachment
99 Mainwheel leg fairing
100 Mainwheel leg oleo
101 Spat
102 Port mainwheel
103 Axle fork
104 Brake cable
105 Leading-edge ribs
106 Main spar

107 Wing ribs
108 Aileron control rod
109 Flaps
110 Aileron tab
111 Port aileron
112 Stiffeners
113 Pitot head
114 Wing skinning
115 Port navigation light

NAKAJIMA Kɪ-27 (Tʏᴘᴇ 97) Japan

In June 1935, the *Koku Hombu* – Air Headquarters of the Imperial Army – framed a requirement for what it termed an advanced fighter, bringing competing designs from Kawasaki, Mitsubishi and Nakajima. The Nakajima team, led by Yasushi Koyama, designed, as a company-funded project, the PE. An all-metal stressed-skin cantilever monoplane, the PE was completed in July 1936, two essentially similar prototypes being produced as Ki-27s for the official competition, the first of these flying on 15 October 1936. Comparative trials with the other contenders resulted in an order for 10 pre-series Ki-27s for service evaluation. Series production was ordered on 28 December 1937 as the Type 97 Fighter Model Ko (Ki-27-Ko) with a Nakajima Kotobuki Ha-1-Otsu engine rated at 780 hp at 9,515 ft (2 900 m). Armament comprised two 7,7-mm machine guns. Production of the Ki-27-Ko gave place to the Ki-27-Otsu embodying minor changes. Two were experimentally fitted with an additional fuselage fuel tank under the designation Ki-27-KAI, but flush-fitting external wing tanks were subsequently standardised. By December

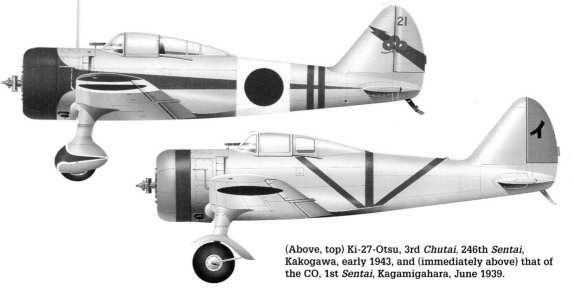

(Above, top) Ki-27-Otsu, 3rd *Chutai*, 246th *Sentai*, Kakogawa, early 1943, and (immediately above) that of the CO, 1st *Sentai*, Kagamigahara, June 1939.

rated at 1,150 hp for take-off and designated Ki-43-II. The first of five prototypes was flown in February 1942, three pre-series examples being built for service trials. The wing was strengthened, attachment points being introduced for two 551-lb (250-kg) bombs or two 44-Imp gal (200-l) drop tanks, and span and area being reduced by 23.6 in (60 cm) and 6.46 sq ft (0,60 m²) respectively. Rudimentary fuel tank protection was provided, together with head and back armour for the pilot, but the twin 12,7-mm gun armament of the Ki-43-I-Hei was retained. In November 1942, production was authorised as the Ki-43-II-Ko (Type 1 Fighter Model 2-Ko) and the 1st Army Air Arsenal at Tachikawa was ordered to establish a supplementary production line (in the event to be phased out of the programme in November 1943 after delivering only 49 aircraft). Entering service from early 1943, the Ki-43-II-Ko quickly gave place to the II-Otsu (initially featuring only carburettor intake and oil cooler changes). Progressive modifications made on the assembly line were incorporated in the Ki-43-II-KAI, three prototypes of which were flown between June and August 1943. The Tachikawa Hikoki KK had meanwhile joined the programme and, when the parent company phased out of the Hayabusa programme in October 1944, having built 2,492 of the series Model 2, this company continued manufacture. Tachikawa built 2,629 (including a small number of the later Model 3) by the time production terminated in August 1945. The following data relate to the Ki-43-II-Otsu. *Max speed, 329 mph (530 km/h) at 13,125 ft (4 000 m). Time to 16,405 ft (5 000 m), 5.82 min. Range, 1,006 mls (1 620 km). Empty weight, 3,812 lb (1 729 kg). Max loaded weight, 5,320 lb (2 413 kg). Span, 35 ft 6¾ in (10,84 m). Length, 29 ft 3¼ in (8,92 m). Height, 10 ft 2 in (3,10 m). Wing area, 230.36 sq ft (21,40 m²).*

A Ki-43-II-Otsu (below) of the 2nd *Chutai* leader, 25th *Sentai*, deployed in China during 1943.

NAKAJIMA Kɪ-43-III (Tʏᴘᴇ 1 Mᴏᴅᴇʟ 3) HAYABUSA　　Japan

As late as May 1944, work began on yet another version of the Hayabusa as the Ki-43-III-Ko (Type 1 Fighter Model 3-Ko), with an Ha-115-II engine providing 1,230 hp at 9,185 ft (2 800 m). Ten prototypes were built by the parent company and production was assigned to Tachikawa. This company also produced two prototypes of a dedicated interceptor version, the Ki-43-III-Otsu, powered by a 1,300 hp Mitsubishi Ha-112 engine and carrying an armament of two 20-mm cannon. This model was still under test when the Pacific War terminated. Numerically, the Hayabusa was the most important aircraft of the Imperial Army, serving on every front to which that service was committed. *Max speed,*

(Immediately below) Ki-43-II-Ko, Manchukuo Army, Mukden (Shenyang), 1944, and (bottom) Ki-43-II-Otsu of HQ *Chutai*, 77th *Sentai*, deployed in Burma, 1943.

The Ki-27-Otsu (above and below), the photo showing an aircraft of the 1st *Chutai*, 64th *Sentai*, in 1939.

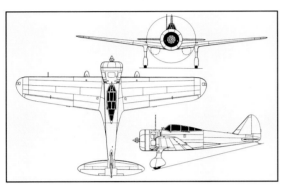

1940, production of the Ki-27 had been transferred from the parent company to Mansyu in Manchuria where production continued until July 1942. When production ended, 3,396 had been delivered, 2,017 of these having been built by Nakajima. At the commencement of the Pacific War, the Ki-27 equipped all but two first-line fighter *Sentais* of the Imperial Army, and it remained in service with the Manchukuo (Manchuria) Air Force until the end of the conflict. *Max speed, 292 mph (470 km/h) at 11,480 ft (3 500 m). Time to 6,560 ft (2 000 m), 2.1 min. Normal range, 390 mls (630 km). Empty weight, 2,447 lb (1 110 kg). Max loaded weight, 3,946 lb (1 790 kg). Span, 37 ft 1¼ in (11,31 m). Length, 24 ft 8½ in (7,53 m). Height, 10 ft 8 in (3,28 m). Wing area, 199.78 sq ft (18,56 m²).*

The PE (below) was a company-funded prototype which led to the Ki-27, the "advanced fighter".

NAKAJIMA Kɪ-43-I (Tʏᴘᴇ 1 Mᴏᴅᴇʟ 1) HAYABUSA　　Japan

When, in December 1937, the Ki-27 was officially accepted by the Imperial Army, Nakajima was ordered to start work on a potential successor. Designated Ki-43 and designed by a team headed by Hideo Itokawa and Yasushi Koyama, the first of three prototypes of the new fighter was completed on 12 December 1938, and was powered by a Nakajima Ha-25 14-cylinder radial offering 990 hp for take-off. Ten pre-series aircraft followed, and, on 9 January 1941, official approval was given for series production as the Type 1 Fighter Model 1-Ko (Ki-43-I-Ko) and the name Hayabusa (Peregrine Falcon) was assigned. Armament comprised two 7,7-mm guns or (Ki-43-I-Otsu) one 7,7-mm and one 12,7-mm weapon. Acceptances of the Ki-43 began during June 1941, two *Sentais* being equipped with this type when the Pacific War commenced. Armament was

(Below) One of the 10 pre-series Ki-43 fighters which were similar to the production Ki-43-I-Ko.

changed to two 12,7-mm guns (Ki-43-I-Hei) at an early production stage, and a total of 716 series Model 1 Hayabusas had been completed in February 1943 when production gave place to the Model 2. The following data relate to the Ki-43-I-Hei. *Max speed, 306 mph (492 km/h) at 16,405 ft (5 000 m). Time to 16,405 ft (5 000 m), 5.5 min. Range (max external fuel), 808 mls (1 300 km). Empty weight, 3,505 lb (1 590 kg). Max loaded weight, 5,694 lb (2 583 kg). Span, 37 ft 6 in (11,44 m). Length, 28 ft 11⁷⁄₁₀ in (8,83 m). Height, 10 ft 8¾ in (3,27 m). Wing area, 236.81 sq ft (22,00 m²).*

(Below) The first series Hayabusa, the Ki-43-I-Ko.

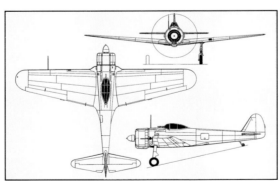

NAKAJIMA Kɪ-43-II (Tʏᴘᴇ 1 Mᴏᴅᴇʟ 2) HAYABUSA　　Japan

Before the Hayabusa joined combat, work had begun on an enhanced version with a Nakajima Ha-115 engine

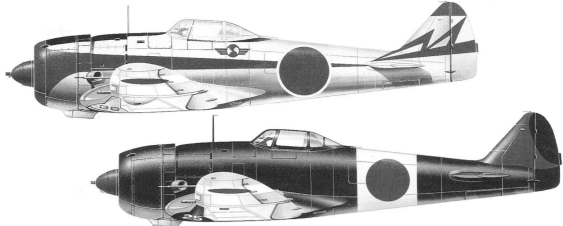

A Ki-43-III-Ko (above) built by Tachikawa and in the insignia of the 48th *Sentai* in China, early 1945.

358 mph (576 km/h) at 21,920 ft (6 680 m). Time to 16,405 ft (5 000 m), 5.32 min. Range, 1,320 mls (2 120 km). Empty weight, 4,233 lb (1 920 kg). Max loaded weight, 6,746 lb (3 060 kg). Dimensions as for Ki-43-II.

NAKAJIMA Ki-44 (Type 2) SHOKI — Japan

Denoting radical rethinking on the part of the Imperial Army in being a dedicated interceptor with the emphasis on speed at some expense to manoeuvrability, the Ki-44 Shoki (Devil-Queller) was first flown in August 1940. Three prototypes were built with Nakajima Ha-42 engines rated at 1,250 hp at 13,125 ft (4 000 m) and each armed with two 7,7-mm and two 12,7-mm guns. Seven pre-series aircraft followed and these, together with two of the prototypes, underwent operational trials in China from late 1941. A further pre-series batch comprising 40 aircraft was built, these being designated Ki-44-Is (the -I-Ko having an armament of four 12,7-mm guns and the -I-Hei having a relocated oil cooler and mainwheel fairing doors). In September 1942, the Ki-44 was officially adopted, by which time five prototypes and three pre-series examples of an improved version, the Ki-44-II, were under construction. These were powered by the two-stage supercharged Nakajima Ha-109 engine providing 1,520 hp for take-off, and featured pilot armour and fuel tank protection. The initial series Shokis were designated Ki-44-II-Ko and carried two fuselage-mounted 7,7-mm and four wing-mounted 12,7-mm guns. These were delivered late in 1942, but an armament of twin fuselage-mounted and twin wing-mounted 12,7-mm weapons was subsequently standardised for the Ki-44-II-Otsu, while the

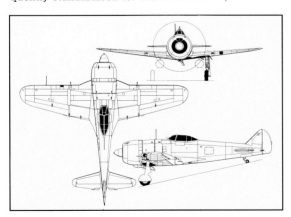

(Above) The Ki-44-II-Otsu and (below) a Ki-44-II-Ko of the Instructors' *Chutai*, Akeno school, 1944.

(Above, top) A Ki-44-II-Otsu of *Shinten* unit, 47th *Sentai*, Narimasu, Tokyo, 1944, and (immediately above) of 2nd *Chutai*, 87th *Sentai*, early 1945.

Ki-44-II-Hei replaced the wing-mounted machine guns with 20-mm cannon. The principal production version was the -II-Otsu and manufacture was phased out late in 1944 after delivery of 1,167 Ki-44-IIs, a final variant, the Ki-44-III, having proved unacceptable. This, powered by a Nakajima Ha-145 engine rated at 2,000 hp for take-off, had a 26.6 per cent increase in wing area to 204.52 sq ft (19,00 m²) and a larger tail. The first prototype was completed in June 1943, and evaluation examples with differing armament arrangements were built, comprising four 20-mm cannon or (Ki-44-III-Ko) two 20-mm and two 37-mm cannon. The following data relate to the Ki-44-II-Otsu. *Max speed, 376 mph (605 km/h) at 17,060 ft (5 200 m). Time to 16,405 ft (5 000 m), 4.43 min. Max range (with external fuel), 1,050 mls (1 690 km). Empty weight, 4,643 lb (2 106 kg). Max loaded weight, 6,598 lb (2 993 kg). Span, 31 ft 0⅛ in (9,45 m). Length, 29 ft 0 in (8,84 m). Height, 10 ft 8 in (3,25 m). Wing area, 161.46 sq ft (15,00 m²).*

NAKAJIMA J1N1 GEKKO — Japan

A J1N1-C-KAI (above), a night fighting adaptation of a J1N1-C recce aircraft deployed to Rabaul, 1943.

To meet a 13-*Shi* (1938) Imperial Navy requirement for a three-seat, twin-engined, long-range fighter, Katsuji Nakamura designed an aerodynamically clean all-metal monoplane powered by two 1,130 hp Nakajima NK1F Sakae 14-cylinder radials. Forward-firing armament comprised one 20-mm and two 7,7-mm guns, and an innovatory feature was provided by tandem, vertically-staggered barbettes each mounting twin aft-firing 7,7-mm guns. Designated J1N1, the first of two prototypes flew in May 1941, but the type was not accepted for its intended rôle, being reworked as the J1N1-C reconnaissance aircraft. In the spring of 1943, a

few aircraft of this type were deployed to Rabaul as J1N1-C-KAI night fighters, one crew station being removed and armament comprising four 20-mm cannon, two firing obliquely upward and two others firing obliquely downward. The success of this conversion led to series production of a dedicated two-seat night fighter version as the J1N1-S Gekko (Moonlight) from

The J1N1-Sa Gekko (above and below) which was a redesign of the J1N1-C for the night fighter rôle.

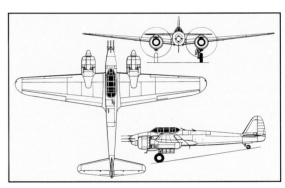

August 1943. This retained the armament of the J1N1-C-KAI, but the J1N1-Sa had the downward-firing guns deleted, with an additional upward-firing gun installed plus either a single forward-firing 20-mm cannon or a small searchlight in the nose. Later, both versions were fitted with nose-mounted AI radar. A total of 470 J1N1 aircraft was built (excluding prototypes) of which at least two-thirds were Gekko night fighters. The following data relate to the J1N1-S. *Max speed, 315 mph (507 km/h) at 19,160 ft (5 840 m). Time to 16,405 ft (5 000 m), 9.58 min. Max range, 2,348 mls (3 780 km). Empty weight, 10,670 lb (4 840 kg). Max loaded weight, 18,042 lb (8 184 kg). Span, 55 ft 8½ in (16,98 m). Length, 41 ft 10¾ in (12,77 m). Height, 14 ft 11⅔ in (4,56 m). Wing area, 430.57 sq ft (40,00 m²).*

NAKAJIMA A6M2-N — Japan

Developed by Nakajima as an interim single-seat fighter floatplane pending availability of the 15-*Shi* (1940) fighter designed from the outset for waterborne

The A6M2-N (below) was an interim float-equipped fighter variant of the Mitsubishi A6M2 Rei-sen.

operation, the A6M2-N was an adaptation of the Mitsubishi A6M2 shipboard fighter. Retaining the 950 hp Nakajima NK1C Sakae 14-cylinder radial engine, the armament (two 20-mm cannon and two 7,7-mm machine guns) and airframe of the A6M2, the A6M2-N replaced the retractable wheel undercarriage with a fixed central float and two wing-mounted stabilising floats. The vertical tail surfaces were enlarged and a small ventral fin added. First flown on 7 December 1941, the A6M2-N entered production as the Type 2 Floatplane Fighter Model 11, manufacture being continued until September 1943, by which time 327 aircraft of this type had been built. *Max speed, 271 mph (435 km/h) at 16,405 ft (5 000 m). Time to 16,405 ft (5 000 m), 6.72 min. Max range, 1,107 mls (1 780 km). Empty weight, 4,235 lb (1 912 kg). Loaded weight, 5,423 lb (2 460 kg). Span, 39 ft 4⅓ in (12,00 m). Length, 33 ft 1½ in (10,10 m). Height, 14 ft 1¼ in (4,30 m). Wing area, 241.55 sq ft (22,44 m²).*

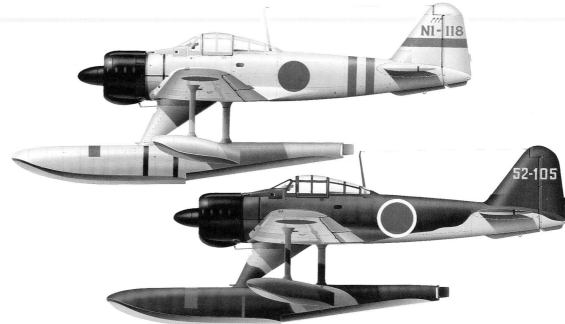

(Below) The Nakajima-developed A6M2-N float fighter.

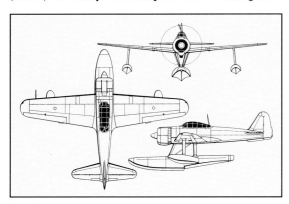

A6M2-N fighters of (above, top) the 802nd *Kokutai*, Shortland Island, January 1943, and (immediately above) the 452nd *Kokutai*, Shumushu, summer 1943.

NAKAJIMA Kı-84 HAYATE   Japan

Intended as a replacement for the Ki-43 Hayabusa and designed by a team led by Yasushi Koyama to a specification issued by the Imperial Army a few weeks after the Pearl Harbor attack, the Ki-84 Hayate (Gale) represented a major advance in Japanese fighter design.

The Ki-84-I-Ko (above and below), the photo showing an aircraft of the 1st *Chutai* of the 73rd *Sentai*.

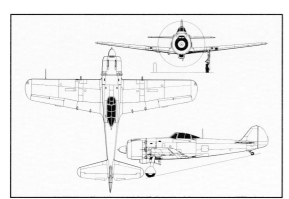

Powered by a 2,000 hp Nakajima Ha-45 (Type 4) 18-cylinder radial and carrying an armament of two 20-mm cannon and two 12,7-mm machine guns, the first of two prototypes flew in March 1943. Production was launched with 83 service trials and 42 pre-series aircraft, deliveries of series aircraft commencing in April 1944 as the Type 4 Fighter Model 1-Ko. A total of 1,670 pre-series and series Hayates was delivered to the Imperial Army by the end of 1944, the Ki-84-I-Ko being followed by the -I-Otsu which differed in having an addi-

tional pair of 20-mm cannon. The Ki-84-I-Hei with 30-mm cannon replacing the 20-mm wing-mounted weapons was a specialised bomber interceptor built in small numbers, and the Ki-84-II Hayate-KAI differed from previous models in having a wooden rear fuselage and wooden wing tips. An *all*-wood version was built by Tachikawa as the Ki-106 (which see). Apart from prototypes, service trials and pre-series aircraft, production of the Hayate totalled 3,382 aircraft, of which 94 were built by Mansyu. *Max speed, 388 mph (624 km/h) at 21,325 ft (6 500 m). Initial climb, 3,790 ft/min (19,25 m/sec). Range (internal fuel), 1,025 mls (1 650 km). Empty weight, 5,864 lb (2 660 kg). Normal loaded weight, 8,192 lb (3 716 kg). Span, 36 ft 2 in (11,24 m). Length, 32 ft 6½ in (9,92 m). Height, 11 ft 1 in (3,38 m). Wing area, 226.04 sq ft (21,00 m²).*

NAKAJIMA Kı-87   Japan

Formulation of a requirement for a dedicated high-altitude fighter with exhaust-driven turbo-supercharger and pressurised cockpit began early in 1942 within the Technical Division of the Imperial Army Headquarters. This type was assigned the *Kitai* designation Ki-87 and a contract was placed with Nakajima for three prototypes. Design was undertaken by a team led by Kunihiro Aoki, but owing to delays with the turbo-supercharger, the first prototype was not rolled out until February 1945, flight test commencing during the following April. The first prototype Ki-87 was powered by a 2,400 hp Nakajima Ha-44-12 18-cylinder radial which was cooled by a 16-blade fan, the turbo-supercharger being mounted on the starboard side of the forward fuselage. A 20-mm cannon was mounted in each wing root and a 30-mm cannon in the root of each outer wing panel, and the pressurised cockpit was of "cold wall" type. In the event, only five brief test flights were made, with the undercarriage remaining extended on each occasion. It was intended to power the succeeding prototypes with the 2,450 hp Ha-44-21 (Ha-219-Ru) engine, and the following data, based on manufacturer's esti-

Ki-84-I-Ko Hayates of (immediately below) the HQ *Chutai*, 29th *Sentai*, Formosa, 1945, and (bottom) the 58th *Shimbu-tai*, home defence, August 1945.

mates, assume the use of this power plant. *Max speed, 439 mph (706 km/h) at 36,090 ft (11 000 m). Time to 19,685 ft (6 000 m), 7.7 min. Normal endurance, 2.0 hrs. Empty weight, 9,672 lb (4 387 kg). Normal loaded weight, 12,416 lb (5 632 kg). Span, 44 ft 0½ in (13,42 m). Length, 38 ft 9⅓ in (11,82 m). Wing area, 279.86 sq ft (26,00 m²).*

The Ki-87 (above and below) featured a pressurised cockpit and exhaust-driven turbo-supercharger.

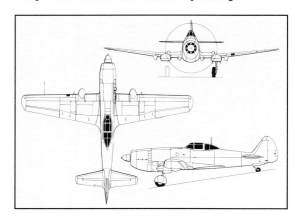

NAKAJIMA J5N1 TENRAI   Japan

Designed by Katsuji Nakamura and Kazuo Ohno to meet an 18-*Shi* Navy requirement for a single-seat, shore-based, twin-engined interceptor, the J4N1 Tenrai (Heavenly Thunder) bore no more than a configurational resemblance to the preceding J1N1. Powered by two 1,990 hp Nakajima NK9H Homare 21 18-cylinder radials and armed with two 20-mm and two 30-mm

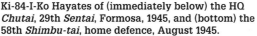

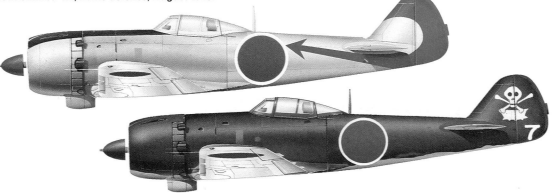

The J5N1 Tenrai (above and below) was intended to fulfil an Imperial Navy interceptor requirement.

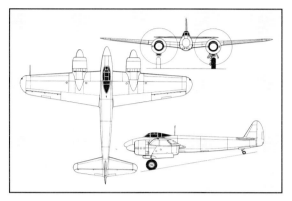

cannon, the J5N1 was first flown in July 1944, but both performance and handling qualities proved disappointing. A total of six prototypes was built, the last two of these being adapted as two-seaters, but development was cancelled when it became obvious that the shortcomings of the Tenrai could not be rectified without major redesign. *Max speed, 371 mph (597 km/h) at 19,685 ft (6 000 m). Time to 19,685 ft (6 000 m), 8.0 min. Normal range, 400 mls (644 km). Empty weight, 11,883 lb (5 390 kg). Loaded weight, 16,093 lb (7 300 kg). Span, 47 ft 2⁹⁄₁₀ in (14,40 m). Length, 37 ft 7¼ in (11,46 m). Height, 11 ft 7¾ in (3,55 m). Wing area, 344.46 sq ft (32,00 m²).*

NAMC J-12   China

In the late 'sixties, a team under the leadership of Lu Xiao-Pcheng initiated design of a lightweight single-seat air superiority fighter at the NAMC (Nanchang Aircraft Manufacturing Company) under the designation J-12 (Jianjiji-12). Powered by a single WP-6 (Chinese-

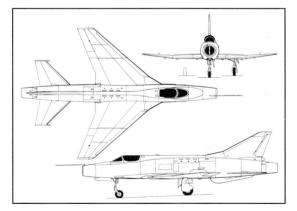

(Above and below) The definitive version of the J-12 lightweight air superiority fighter.

built Tumansky RD-9BF-811) with a maximum rating of 7,165 lb st (3 454 kgp), the first of three prototypes was flown on 26 December 1970. Owing to the indifferent results achieved during flight testing, the J-12 was subjected to considerable redesign. The structure was simplified and lightened, area ruling was applied to the fuselage, the air intake was redesigned, the gun armament was moved aft and simple split flaps supplanted an arrangement of slats and triple-slotted flaps. The extensively revised J-12 flew as a prototype in July 1975, and six pre-series aircraft were built, these each carrying an armament of one 23-mm and one 30-mm cannon. A total of 61 hrs 12 min of flight testing had been accumulated in 135 test flights by January 1977, when further development was discontinued owing to the superior characteristics of the J-7 (licence-built MiG-21F-13) already with the People's Republic of China Air Force. The following data relate to the definitive version. *Max speed, 808 mph (1 300 km/h) at 36,090 ft (11 000 m), or Mach=1.22. Max initial climb, 35,433 ft/min (180 m/sec). Ceiling, 55,675 ft (16 970 m). Range (internal fuel), 427 mls (688 km). Empty weight, 6,993 lb (3 172 kg). Normal loaded weight, 9,987 lb (4 530 kg). Span, 23 ft 7½ in (7,20 m). Length, 33 ft 9½ in (10,30 m). Height, 12 ft 2⅞ in (3,73 m).*

NAVAL AIRCRAFT FACTORY TF   USA

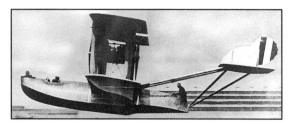

The TF escort and patrol fighter is illustrated (above) with the definitive vertical tail surfaces.

Designed and built by the US Naval Aircraft Factory in Philadelphia as a four-seat escort and patrol fighter flying boat, the TF (Tandem Fighter) was first flown in October 1920. Powered by two Wright-built 300 hp Hispano-Suiza H eight-cylinder water-cooled engines mounted in tandem between upper wing and hull, the TF was a two-bay biplane with tail surfaces carried on tubular booms projecting aft. Armament comprised three 0.3-in (7,62-mm) Lewis guns mounted in open turrets in the bow and the stern of the hull. Four TF flying boats were procured, the final three differing from the initial aircraft in having redesigned vertical tail surfaces. *Max speed, 107 mph (172 km/h). Loaded weight, 8,846 lb (4 012 kg). Span, 60 ft 0 in (18,29 m). Length, 44 ft 5 in (13,54 m). Wing area, 930 sq ft (86,40 m²).*

NAVAL AIRCRAFT FACTORY TS-1   USA

With establishment of the US Navy's Bureau of Aeronautics on 10 August 1921, one of the responsibilities of the Naval Aircraft Factory became manufacture of token quantities of aircraft of which principal production was to be contracted out to industry. This practice was followed with the TS-1, the first purpose-designed US shipboard single-seat fighter. Powered by a 200 hp

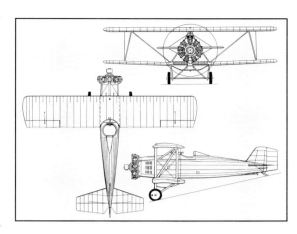

The first US purpose-built shipboard fighter, the TS-1 (above and below) later became the F4C-1.

Lawrance J-1 nine-cylinder radial (later to become the Wright J-4 Whirlwind) and of wooden construction, the TS-1 was an equispan unstaggered biplane, the fuselage being raised above the lower wing which incorporated a jettisonable fuel tank in its centre section. It was intended to operate with either a normal wheel chassis or twin floats, and armament comprised one 0.30-in (7,62-mm) Browning gun. The TS-1 appeared in June 1922, five being built by the Naval Aircraft Factory and contracts for 34 being placed with Curtiss. The first Curtiss-built TS-1s reached the USS *Langley* in December 1922, and float-equipped TS-1s were crane-operated from battleships during 1925-26. Four additional airframes produced by the Naval Aircraft Factory were purely experimental aircraft for comparative trials with water-cooled engines, two being equipped with the 240 hp Aeromarine as TS-2s and two with the 180 hp Wright-Hispano E as TS-3s. Also for comparative purposes, two all-metal TS-1s (later redesignated F4C-1s) were built by Curtiss, these embodying considerable redesign. The following data relate to the Wright J-4-powered TS-1 with a wheel undercarriage. *Max speed, 123 mph (200 km/h) at sea level. Time to 5,000 ft (1 525 m), 5.5 min. Range, 482 mls (776 km). Empty weight, 1,240 lb (562 kg). Loaded weight, 1,920 lb (871 kg). Span, 25 ft 0 in (7,62 m). Length, 22 ft 1 in (6,73 m). Height, 9 ft 7 in (2,92 m). Wing area, 228 sq ft (21,18 m²).*

NESTLER SCOUT   UK

In 1916, F C Nestler Limited established it own design office under E Boudot and embarked on the design of a single-seat fighting scout as a private venture. Of conventional wire-braced, fabric-covered wooden construction, this was a single-bay staggered biplane powered by a 100 hp Gnome Monosoupape nine-

(Below) The single Nestler Scout was built as a private-venture prototype during 1916.

cylinder rotary engine. Of compact design, the Nestler fighting scout proved very manoeuvrable, but crashed on 26 March 1917, the damage being too extensive for the aircraft to be rebuilt. No data concerning this aircraft have apparently survived and the intended armament is unknown.

NFW E I   Germany

In the spring of 1916, the National-Flugzeug-Werke built at Johannisthal a single-seat monoplane to the designs of Dipl Ing Hergt. Referred to as the E I (although this is unlikely to have been an official designation) and apparently intended for the fighting rôle, it was a shoulder wing monoplane of wooden construction. It had a plywood-covered, single-piece, two-spar wing, and the pilot's cockpit was situated between the spars. The E I was powered by an 80 hp Oberursel U 0 (Gnome) seven-cylinder rotary engine, but no details of its flight testing have survived, development apparently being discontinued in favour of a larger and more powerful monoplane (E II). *Max speed, 97 mph (156 km/h). Time to 4,265 ft (1 300 m), 6.0 min. Empty weight, 944 lb (428 kg). Loaded weight, 1,367 lb (620 kg). Span, 32 ft 9⁷⁄₁₀ in (10,00 m). Length, 21 ft 3⁹⁄₁₀ in (6,50 m). Wing area, 169.21 sq ft (15,72 m²).*

The NFW E I (below) was apparently discontinued in favour of the larger and more powerful E II of 1917.

NFW E II   Germany

Although the National-Flugzeug-Werke was largely preoccupied with aircraft repair and flying school operation, in 1917 this concern again built an original single-seat monoplane. To the designs of Dipl Ing Heinrich and completed at Leipzig, this aircraft was of wooden construction and was powered by a 160 hp Daimler D IIIa six-cylinder water-cooled engine. Referred to as the E II, although, again, this is unlikely to have been an official designation, this aircraft progressed no further than a single prototype. *Max speed, 116 mph (186 km/h). Time to 9,515 ft (2 900 m), 6.3 min. Empty weight, 1,230 lb (558 kg). Loaded weight, 1,693 lb (768 kg). Span, 39 ft 4½ in (12,00 m). Wing area, 182.99 sq ft (17,00 m²).*

The last original fighter built by the NFW, the E II (below) progressed no further than a prototype.

NIELSEN & WINTHER TYPE Aᴀ   Denmark

Designed and built by Nielsen & Winther A/S, a Copenhagen machine tool manufacturer, possibly with some assistance from the Swedish Thulin concern, the Type Aa single-seat fighter was first flown on 21 January 1917. Of wooden construction, the Type Aa was powered by a 90 hp Thulin rotary engine (a copy of the Le Rhône) and was armed with a single 8-mm Madsen machine gun mounted on the upper wing and firing above the propeller disc. Ground tests with synchronising equipment took place in 1918, reportedly using a Type Aa with the gun mounted on the side of the fuselage, but there is no evidence that air firing tests took place. Six Type Aa fighters were delivered to the

The Type Aa (above and below) was delivered to the Danish Army in 1917, but was withdrawn in 1919.

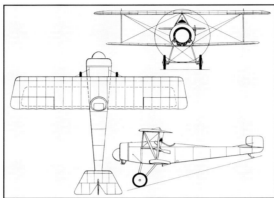

Danish Army during 1917, but these were withdrawn from service in 1919 owing to the unreliability of their engines. Prototypes were completed of a two-seat reconnaissance version, the Type Ab, and a float-equipped version of the single-seater, the Type Ac. *Max speed, 93 mph (150 km/h). Time to 9,840 ft (3 000 m), 15 min. Empty weight, 772 lb (350 kg). Loaded weight, 1,212 lb (550 kg). Span, 25 ft 3⅛ in (7,70 m). Length, 21 ft 7⁷⁄₁₀ in (6,60 m). Height, 9 ft 2¼ in (2,8 m).*

NIEUPORT 10   France

Founded in 1910 by Edouard Nieuport, the Etablissements Nieuport became responsible for a series of fighting aircraft to the designs of Gustave Delage that was to extend over a quarter-century. The first of this distinguished line, the Nie 10, was allegedly derived from a racing biplane intended for the Gordon-Bennett contest and appeared before the end of 1914 as a military two-seater. At first, the French authorities evinced

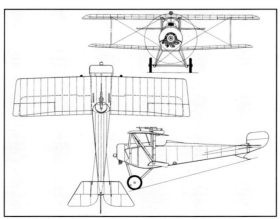

The definitive single-seat (above) and early two-seat (below) versions of the Nie 10 sesquiplane.

little interest, but subsequent to the British Royal Naval Air Service ordering 24, the Nie 10 was purchased in quantity. Initially, there were two versions: the Nie 10 AV (*avant*) in which the observer occupied the front seat and the Nie 10 AR (*arrière*) in which he occupied the rear seat. These were mostly converted to single-seat configuration for the fighting rôle, with a single machine gun mounted above the upper wing. Of orthodox wood-and-fabric construction, the Nie 10 was of sesquiplane configuration, the narrow-chord lower wing having less than half the area of the upper wing, and was powered by an 80 hp Gnome or Le Rhône rotary engine. It entered service with both France's *Aviation Militaire* and the Royal Naval Air Service in May 1915, and was licence-built by Nieuport-Macchi in Italy, and by Dux and Lebedev in Russia, where production continued until 1920. Some Russian-built single-seaters were powered by the 100 hp Monosoupape or 110 hp and 120 hp Le Rhône engines, and were referred to as the Nie 10bis. The following data relate to the 80 hp single-seat version. *Max speed, 91 mph (146 km/h) at sea level. Time to 6,560 ft (2 000 m), 16.5 min. Empty weight, 904 lb (410 kg). Loaded weight, 1,455 lb (660 kg). Span, 25 ft 11 in (7,90 m). Length, 22 ft 11½ in (7,00 m). Height, 8 ft 10¼ in (2,70 m). Wing area, 193.76 sq ft (18,00 m²).*

The single-seat Nie 10 (below) was widely used and was licence-built by Italian and Russian companies.

NIEUPORT 11   France

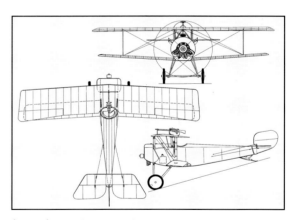

(Above) The Nie 11, popularly known as the *Bébé*.

One of the outstanding landmarks in the history of fighter evolution, the Nie 11, promptly christened the *Bébé* by its pilots, was a scaled-down refinement of the Nie 10. The first operational Nie 11 was delivered to the *Aviation Militaire* on 5 January 1916, and within a month there were 90 at the Front. Relatively fast and highly manoeuvrable, the Nie 11 soon outfought and contained the Fokker monoplanes. Armed with an overwing Hotchkiss or Lewis machine gun and powered by an 80 hp Le Rhône rotary, it was supplied to the Royal Naval Air Service in some numbers and was licence-built by Dux in Russia and by Nieuport-Macchi and Elettro-Ferroviarie in Italy. The former Italian company built 450 and the latter 93. Twenty were also built in the Netherlands. In addition to the gun, some Nie 11s carried eight Le Prieur rockets attached to the interplane struts. Although the Nie 11 was referred to as a sesquiplane, its lower wing had exactly half the area of the upper wing. Its main weakness was in the lower wing, which tended to twist and break under stress. *Max speed, 104 mph (167 km/h) at sea level. Time to 9,840 ft (3 000 m), 15 min. Empty weight, 705 lb (320 kg). Loaded weight, 1,058 lb*

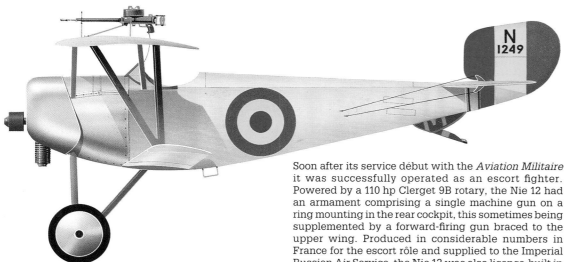

(Above) An Nie 11 of the Romanian Army's 3rd Fighter Sqn, September 1917, and (below) an Nie 11 licence-built by Nieuport-Macchi in Italy.

(480 kg). Span, 24 ft 8 in (7,52 m). Length, 18 ft 6 in (5,64 m). Height, 7 ft 10½ in (2,40 m). Wing area, 143.16 sq ft (13,30 m²).

NIEUPORT 12   France

A larger, more powerful derivative of the Nie 10, the Nie 12 was conceived as a two-seat reconnaissance fighter.

The Nie 12bis (above) was an improved Nie 12 which appeared in 1916 with an uprated Clerget engine.

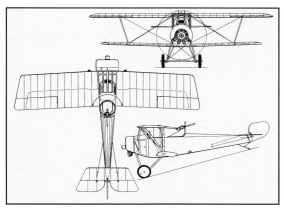

The Nie 12 (above and below) was fundamentally a larger and more powerful derivative of the Nie 10.

Soon after its service début with the *Aviation Militaire* it was successfully operated as an escort fighter. Powered by a 110 hp Clerget 9B rotary, the Nie 12 had an armament comprising a single machine gun on a ring mounting in the rear cockpit, this sometimes being supplemented by a forward-firing gun braced to the upper wing. Produced in considerable numbers in France for the escort rôle and supplied to the Imperial Russian Air Service, the Nie 12 was also licence-built in the UK by William Beardmore for the RNAS. The Beardmore-built Nie 12s featured an extended lower wing, some having full engine cowlings and fixed fin and plain rudder replacing the Nieuport balanced rudder. Forty Nie 12s were transferred to the Royal Flying Corps. In 1916, an improved two-seat fighter version, the Nie 12bis with a 130 hp Clerget 9, was introduced by the *Aviation Militaire*. The following data relate to the 110 hp model. *Max speed, 91 mph (146 km/h) at 6,560 ft (2 000 m). Time to 6,560 ft (2 000 m), 14.25 min. Empty weight, 1,213 lb (550 kg). Loaded weight, 1,874 lb (850 kg). Span, 29 ft 6 in (9,00 m). Length, 22 ft 11½ in (7,00 m). Height, 8 ft 10¼ in (2,70 m). Wing area, 236.81 sq ft (22,00 m²).*

NIEUPORT 16   France

Fundamentally the Nie 11 adapted to take the more powerful Le Rhône 9J rotary engine of 110 hp, the Nie 16 was faster, but, retaining the wing area of its predecessor, its higher wing loading adversely affected its handling characteristics and it was nose heavy. The standard overwing Lewis gun remained the normal armament, but some Nie 16s had the gun mounted on the forward decking and synchronised by the Alkan mechanism to fire through the propeller. Additionally, eight Le Prieur rockets could be carried on the interplane struts. The Nie 16 began to appear in the early spring of 1916, supplementing and then replacing the Nie 10s and 11s. It was ordered by the RNAS, which transferred 17 of the Nie 16s to the RFC from 18 March 1916, the latter subsequently ordering more and taking at least 28 into its inventory. Small numbers were delivered to Belgium and it was licence-built by Dux in Russia. Its service life was comparatively brief as it was soon succeeded by the superior Nie 17. *Max speed, 103 mph (165 km/h) at sea level. Time to 9,840 ft (3 000 m), 10.16 min. Empty weight, 827 lb (375 kg). Loaded weight, 1,213 lb (550 kg). Span, 24 ft 8 in (7,52 m). Length, 18 ft 6 in (5,64 m). Height, 7 ft 10½ in (2,40 m). Wing area, 143.16 sq ft (13,30 m²).*

(Below) An Nie 16 with eight Le Prieur rocket missiles attached to the wing interplane struts.

NIEUPORT 17   France

An Nie 17 (above) of the RFC, this particular example serving in Palestine with No 111 Squadron.

Appearing mid-1916, the Nie 17 rapidly established itself as an outstanding fighter. Although it retained the basic geometry and proportions of the Nie 11 and 16, it was a new, somewhat larger and more refined aircraft. Most Nie 17s were powered by either the Le Rhône 9Ja of 110 hp or 9Jb of 120 hp, but a few of the earliest had the 110 hp or 130 hp Clerget. At some time in 1916, the Nie 17 equipped *every* fighter *escadrille* of the *Aviation Militaire*, and at least one naval unit. Many of those in French service had a synchronised Vickers gun, while the substantial number supplied to the RFC were armed with a Lewis gun on a Foster overwing mounting. One hundred and fifty were built in Italy by Nieuport-Macchi, and the Nie 17 was supplied to Belgium and Russia. Twenty were also supplied to the Netherlands and two to Finland, and, in September 1917, the American Expeditionary Force received 75 fighters of this type. A classic design, the Nie 17 was to serve as a basis for a number of later types. *Max speed, 103 mph (165 km/h) at sea level. Time to 9,840 ft (3 000 m), 11.5 min. Range, 155 mls (250 km). Empty weight, 827 lb (375 kg). Loaded weight, 1,235 lb (560 kg). Span, 26 ft 9 in (8,16 m). Length, 19 ft 0 in (5,80 m). Height, 7 ft 10 in (2,40 m). Wing area, 158.8 sq ft (14,75 m²).*

NIEUPORT 17BIS   France

Despite a preference for the Le Rhône engine to the Clerget on the part of Gustave Delage, a modified Nie 17 appeared late in 1916 with a 130 hp Clerget and full-

(Above) The Nie 17bis saw only limited French service, but was used in some numbers by the RNAS.

length fuselage side fairings as the Nie 17bis. Seeing only limited French service, the Nie 17bis was ordered by the RNAS, both from the parent company and from British Nieuport & General Aircraft, some 80 eventually being delivered to the British service. Most RNAS Nie 17bis fighters mounted both a synchronised Vickers gun and an overwing Lewis gun, but the type failed to attain expectations, and later British Nieuport contracts for 100 aircraft were cancelled. Replaced in first line use by the Camel from June 1917, the Nie 17bis was relegated to the training rôle. *Max speed, 118 mph (190 km/h) at sea level. Loaded weight, 1,263 lb (573 kg). Span, 26 ft 9 in (8,16 m). Length, 19 ft 0 in (5,80 m). Height, 7 ft 10 in (2,40 m). Wing area, 158.8 sq ft (14,75 m²).*

(Below) The Nie 17bis which appeared late in 1916.

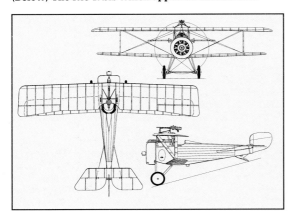

NIEUPORT Triplane — France

During 1915, Gustave Delage had fitted a Nieuport 10 fuselage with triplane wings of unusual fore-and-aft geometry for experimental purposes, the arrangement being patented on 10 January 1916. Progressive development led, later in 1916, to an even more unorthodox triplane arrangement in which the middle wing, attached to the forward ends of the upper fuselage longerons, was foremost and the upper wing rearmost. Utilising a Nie 17 fuselage, powered by a 110 hp Le Rhône engine and armed with a single synchronised Lewis gun, this triplane was officially tested late in 1916, but was not ordered for the *Aviation Militaire*, and, in consequence, received no official SFA type designation. One example armed with a Vickers gun was acquired for evaluation by the RFC on 26 January 1917, but its flying characteristics were found to be unacceptable. The RNAS also acquired one example in March 1917, this differing in having a Nie 17bis fuselage and a

The first of the extraordinary Nieuport triplanes (above and below) with centre wing foremost.

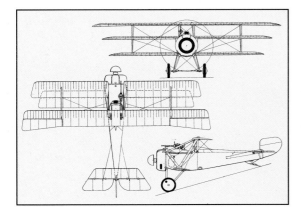

The second Nieuport triplane (above), the unusual configuration proving to offer poor handling.

130 hp Clerget engine. Although allotted to No 11 (Naval) Sqn, it had been discarded by 27 June 1917. The following data relate to the 110 hp version. *Max speed, 110 mph (176 km/h) at 3,000 ft (915 m). Time to 10,000 ft (3 050 m), 13.6 min. Empty weight, 919 lb (417 kg). Loaded weight, 1,386 lb (629 kg). Span, 26 ft 3½ in (8,01 m). Length, 19 ft 2½ in (5,85 m). Height, 7 ft 5 in (2,26 m). Wing area, 143.16 sq ft (13,30 m²).*

NIEUPORT 18 — France

Despite being assigned an official SFA designation, the Nie 18 single-seat fighter sesquiplane powered by an 80 hp Le Rhône 9C rotary apparently failed to attain service status and little is recorded of this type. Its external appearance suggested that it was a derivative of the Nie 11, the fuselage and tail assembly of the earlier type being mated with a wider-track undercarriage and a wing cellule with revised bracing geometry, the V-type interplane struts having a pronounced outward rake. A contemporary manual quoted the wing area of the Nie 18 as 13,00 m² (139.9 sq ft) which was possibly a rounded figure.

The Nie 18 (below) was an Nie 11 derivative, but failed to attain production status.

NIEUPORT 20 — France

By mid-1916, the RFC in France possessed a small number of Nieuport two-seaters in which the 110 hp Le Rhône engine had replaced the 110 hp Clerget of the standard Nie 12. This version of the two-seat fighter was apparently built in small numbers only for the RFC with the SFA designation Nie 20. By early August 1916, 30 had been allotted to the RFC by the French authorities, the first two production aircraft being delivered on 15 September 1916. Anxiety to secure as many Nieuport single-seaters as possible led to a reduction in Nie 20 deliveries, only 21 being supplied to the RFC, with which the type saw limited operational use. *Max speed, 98 mph (157 km/h) at sea level. Time to 6,560 ft (2 000 m), 12.05 min. Empty weight, 999 lb (453 kg). Loaded weight, 1,658 lb (752 kg). Span, 29 ft 6 in (9,00 m). Length, 22 ft 11½ in (7,00 m). Height, 8 ft 10¼ in (2,70 m). Wing area, 236.8 sq ft (22,00 m²).*

The Nie 20 (below) was a two-seater manufactured in comparatively small numbers for the RFC.

NIEUPORT 21 — France

Although apparently intended as a fighter *trainer*, the single-seat Nie 21 was flown operationally as a fighter in French *escadrilles*. Fundamentally a variant of the Nie 17 in which the 110 hp Le Rhône 9J gave place to the 80 hp Le Rhône 9C, the Nie 21 was built in considerable numbers, and, because many were fitted with a horseshoe-form engine cowling, it was frequently mistaken for the Nie 11. It had the larger wings and bracing geometry of the Nie 17, however, and in RNAS service (at least five being acquired) it was known confusingly as the Nie 17B. The Nie 21 was supplied to Russia, and, from September 1917, 181 were acquired by the US Air Service for training duties. At least one was tested with the 90 hp Le Rhône 9Ga engine. *Max speed, 94 mph (150 km/h) at sea level. Time to 9,840 ft (3 000 m), 15.7 min. Empty weight, 705 lb (320 kg). Loaded weight, 1,091 lb (495 kg). Span, 26 ft 9 in (8,16 m). Length, 19 ft 8¼ in (6,00 m). Height, 7 ft 10 in (2,40 m). Wing area, 158.77 sq ft (14,75 m²).*

The Nie 21, that below being a replica with some genuine components in Brazil's *Museu Aeroespacial*.

NIEUPORT 23 — France

The Nie 23 (above) served side-by-side in French *escadrilles* with the fundamentally similar Nie 17.

The Nie 23 differed from the Nie 17 in comparatively minor respects. A new form of interrupter gear for the Vickers gun led to the weapon's installation slightly to starboard of the centreline and dictated some internal structural changes. There were minor modifications to the upper wing and the 120 hp Le Rhône 9Jb rotary was adopted as standard. The Nie 23 was used side by side with the Nie 17 in French *escadrilles* and was licence-built by Dux in Russia where it became the most numerous Nieuport serving with the Imperial Russian Air Service. It was supplied to Belgium and at least 80 were delivered to the RFC with which it entered service mid-March 1917. In British squadrons, replacement of the Vickers by a Foster-mounted Lewis gun rendered distinguishing Nie 23 from Nie 17 almost impossible. *Max speed, 103 mph (165 km/h) at sea level. Time to 9,840 ft (3 000 m), 11.5 min. Empty weight, 827 lb (375 kg). Loaded weight, 1,235 lb (560 kg). Span, 26 ft 9 in (8,16 m). Length, 19 ft 0¼ in (5,80 m). Height, 7 ft 10 in (2,40 m). Wing area, 158.77 sq ft (14,75 m²).*

NIEUPORT 17BIS (DERIVATIVE I)   France

Nieuport single-seat fighter prototypes were numerous, but apparently undesignated – no record of their chronology having apparently survived. One that appears to have been related to the Nie 17bis and which has been described incorrectly as the Nie 25 was a Clerget-powered fighter with a faired fuselage like that of the Nie 17bis. This was mated to an upper wing lacking sweepback and a wooden fin and plain rudder rather than the characteristic Nieuport steel-tube balanced rudder. Setting this prototype apart from other Nieuports was its immense *cône de pénétration* mounted as a stationary fairing ahead of the propeller. It may conceivably have had a 150 hp Clerget 9Bd rotary engine, but this is uncertain.

An Nie 17bis derivative (below) featuring an enormous stationary "*cône de pénétration*".

NIEUPORT 17BIS (DERIVATIVE II)   France

By early November 1916, Nieuport had built and flown a single-seat fighter prototype reported to be "practically the same as" the Nie 17bis, but powered by a 150 hp Le Rhône engine. It is assumed – though without *positive* evidence – that this was the prototype featuring a Le Rhône engine enclosed by an unusually long-chord cowling. Having an Nie 17bis-type faired fuselage, it possessed vertical tail surfaces of generally similar profile to those of the Clerget-engined Nie 17bis derivative (see previous entry) with the *cône de pénétration*, but with a horn-balanced rudder and a new tailplane and elevator assembly. The upper wing was mounted on two inverted Vee-type cabane struts and the Vickers gun was mounted on the port upper longeron. It would seem likely that this aircraft was an early prototype for the Nie 24.

(Below) A further prototype evolved from the Nie 17bis featuring a long-chord engine cowling.

NIEUPORT (HISPANO-SUIZA)   France

Construction began early in November 1916 of a new single-seat Nieuport fighter "designed to compete with the SPAD" and powered by a 150 hp Hispano-Suiza water-cooled engine with a circular frontal radiator. A contemporary report stated that "the empennage, rudder and elevators are all covered with three-ply wood and fabric", and indicated that "M Delage expects great things of this machine". The Hispano-Suiza powered prototype was a clean and elegant aircraft, with a faired fuselage and close coamings around the cockpit. The lower wing was broader in chord than that of preceding Nieuport fighters, but the fact that this prototype was not developed beyond the flight test stage suggests that its performance offered an insuffi-

cient improvement on that of the similarly-powered SPAD S.VII.

An Hispano-Suiza-engined Nieuport prototype (below) was "designed to compete with the SPAD".

NIEUPORT 24   France

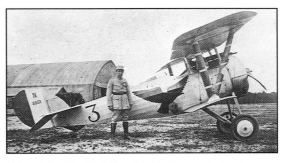

(Above) An Nie 24 of *Escadrille* N.91, and (below) a preserved example with Nungesser emblem in USA.

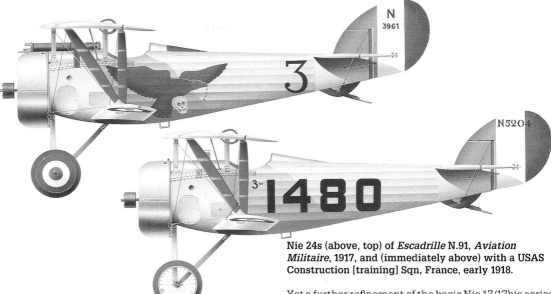

Nie 24s (above, top) of *Escadrille* N.91, *Aviation Militaire*, 1917, and (immediately above) with a USAS Construction [training] Sqn, France, early 1918.

Yet a further refinement of the basic Nie 17/17bis series, the Nie 24 employed a new aerofoil section, was fitted with a wooden tail unit and was powered by a 130 hp Le Rhône 9Jb rotary. Official trials in February and March 1917 of an aircraft designated Nie 24 produced results not significantly better than those of the Nie 17 and 23. Nevertheless, the Nie 24 was ordered in quantity and was in service with French *escadrilles* in June 1917. The fact that the Nie 24 was, in the event, preceded operationally by the Nie 24bis suggests that some problems delayed the service début of the earlier model. A few Nie 24s were supplied to the RFC in the summer of 1917, others were supplied to Russia, a total of 121 was acquired by the USA in November 1917, and production of 77 was undertaken by Nakajima in Japan from 1921/22 as the Ko-3 fighter-trainer with the 80 hp Le Rhône engine. *Max speed, 109 mph (176 km/h) at sea level. Time to 9,840 ft (3 000 m), 9.4 min. Empty weight, 783 lb (355 kg). Loaded weight, 1,206 lb (547 kg). Span, 26 ft 11 in (8,21 m). Length, 19 ft 3 in (5,87 m). Height, 7 ft 10 in (2,40 m). Wing area, 158.77 sq ft (14,75 m²).*

NIEUPORT 24BIS   France

Precisely why the Nie 24bis preceded the Nie 24 in operational service has never been satisfactorily explained. However, the Nie 24bis had something of the appearance of a stop-gap hybrid in that the elegant vertical tail, comprising fixed fin and horn-balanced rudder, adopted for the Nie 24 was discarded in favour of the balanced rudder of such types as the Nie 17bis. It seems likely that problems had been encountered with the manufacture or strength of the new vertical tail, and the earlier form had been retained while these were being resolved. With its fully-faired fuselage, the Nie 24bis therefore resembled the Nie 17bis with a

The Nie 24bis (above) actually preceded the Nie 24 into service and closely resembled the Nie 17bis.

130 hp Le Rhône 9Jb in place of the similarly rated Clerget. It is also assumed that the Nie 24bis had the new aerofoil section adopted for the Nie 24. Normal armament comprised a single synchronised Vickers gun, while those delivered to the RFC – which service received at least five – conservatively retained the unsynchronised overwing Lewis gun. The American Expeditionary Force received 140 Nie 24bis fighters and the type was manufactured in Russia by Duks from 1917 until 1920. In service with France's *Aviation Militaire*, the Nie 24bis was rapidly superseded by the Nie 24. *Max speed, 106 mph (170 km/h) at sea level. Time to 9,840 ft (3 000 m), 9.66 min. Loaded weight, 1,225 lb (556 kg). Dimensions as for Nie 24.*

NIEUPORT 25   France

The Nie 25 was essentially a re-engined Nie 24, that illustrated being flown by Charles Nungesser.

Gustave Delage retained an affection for the Vee-strutted sesquiplane that exceeded the basic design's realisable potential, and the Nie 25 apparently represented the ultimate variant, at least in respect of engine power. The Nie 25 was essentially a Nie 24 airframe adapted to take a 200 hp Clerget 11E 11-cylinder rotary. Armament consisted of a single synchronised Vickers gun. This type is believed to have first flown in July 1917, possibly initially with a 150 hp Clerget 9Bd engine, and the fact that it had an SFA type number suggests that series production was contemplated. However, the Clerget 11E was beset with difficulties and it was presumably for this reason that the Nie 25 was not built in quantity. One example was flown by Charles Nungesser and bore his colourful personal markings. *Time to 9,840 ft (3 000 m), 8.0 min. No other data available for publication.*

NIEUPORT 27   France

Despite receiving a new SFA designation, the Nie 27 differed from the Nie 24 only in having an articulated two-part undercarriage axle and simplified tailskid similar to those of the Nie 25. The standard engine remained the Le Rhône 9Jb or 9Jby of 120 hp and 130 hp respectively, and the single synchronised Vickers gun

The Nie 27 (below) was the last Vee-strutted Nieuport sesquiplane to achieve operational status.

Key to Nieuport 27

1 Two-bladed Lang wooden propeller
2 Propeller hub
3 Propeller fixing bolts
4 Aluminium engine cowling
5 Cowling strengthening ribs
6 130 hp Clerget 9b rotary engine
7 Cowling ventilation cut-outs
8 Oil tank
9 Heavy gauge steel engine bearer plate
10 Vickers 0.303-in (7,7-mm) machine gun
11 Fuel filler cap
12 Fuel tank
13 Centre-section vertical front struts
14 Fabric-taped upper longeron
15 Fuselge bearer plate
16 Carburettor air intake
17 Inspection panel
18 Lower longeron/undercarriage front strut attachment
19 Fabric-taped lower longeron
20 Rudder pedals
21 Foot boards
22 Diagonal wooden frame
23 Ammunition tank
24 Control column
25 Cartridge case ejector chute
26 Gun mounting framework
27 Aileron push-pull rod
28 Lewis gun front support bracket
29 Plywood covered leading edge
30 Starboard lower mainplane fabric
31 Outboard interplane Vee-strut
32 Pressure head for ASI
33 Wing rib construction
34 Starboard aileron
35 Aileron torque shaft
36 Aileron vertical/horizontal rod-link quadrant
37 Lewis gun Foster-mounting
38 Centre-section steel tube inverted Vee rear struts
39 Windscreen frame
40 Airspeed indicator
41 Fuselage upper cross member
42 Throttle and ignition controls
43 Pilot's seat
44 Seat support frame
45 Plywood cockpit decking
46 Headrest
47 Headrest fairing
48 Fuselage side fairing stringers
49 Dorsal fairing stringer construction
50 Rear fuselage upper longeron
51 Vertical frame members
52 Horizontal spacers
53 Diagonal wire bracing
54 Elevator control cables
55 Rudder control cables
56 Tailskid elastic cord shock-absorber
57 Tailplane attachment
58 Starboard tailplane fabric covering
59 Starboard elevator
60 Tailplane bracing wire
61 Rudder construction
62 Elevator hinge control
63 Rudder post
64 Rudder framework construction
65 Fabric covered rudder surface
66 Rudder hinge control
67 Port elevator construction
68 Tailplane framework construction
69 Tailplane lower bracing wire

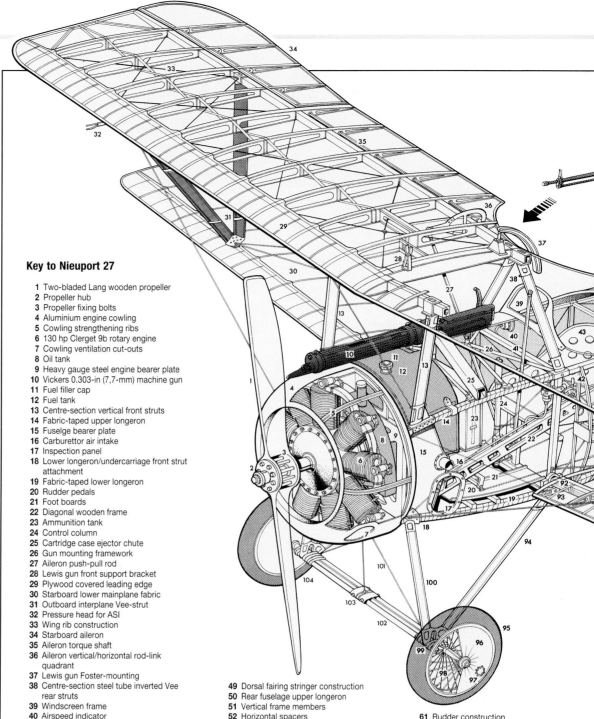

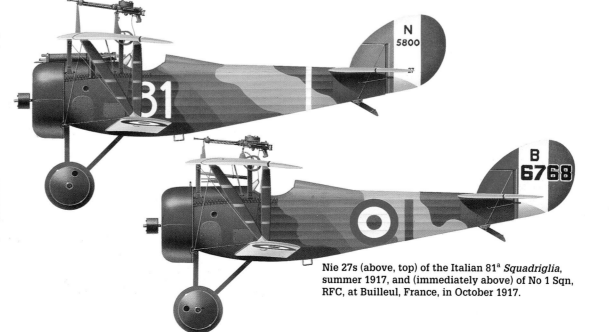

Nie 27s (above, top) of the Italian 81ª *Squadriglia*, summer 1917, and (immediately above) of No 1 Sqn, RFC, at Builleul, France, in October 1917.

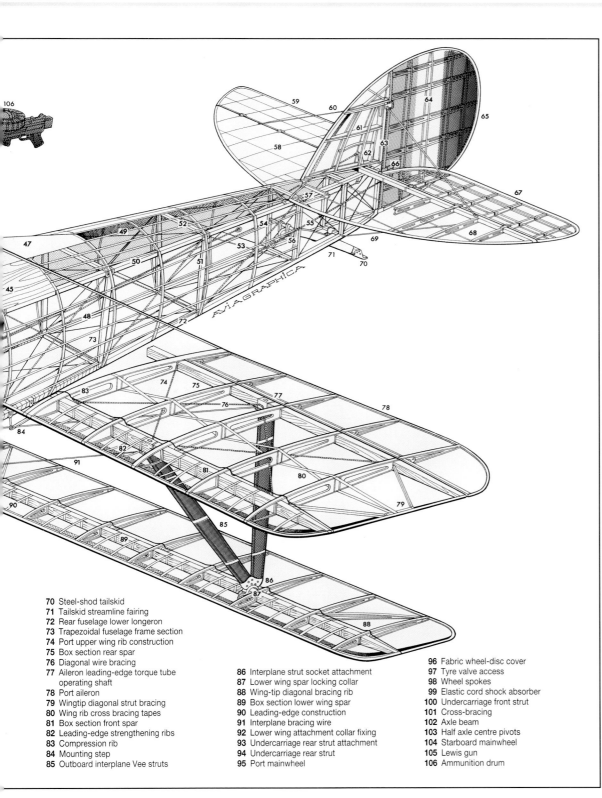

70 Steel-shod tailskid
71 Tailskid streamline fairing
72 Rear fuselage lower longeron
73 Trapezoidal fuselage frame section
74 Port upper wing rib construction
75 Box section rear spar
76 Diagonal wire bracing
77 Aileron leading-edge torque tube operating shaft
78 Port aileron
79 Wingtip diagonal strut bracing
80 Wing rib cross bracing tapes
81 Box section front spar
82 Leading-edge strengthening ribs
83 Compression rib
84 Mounting step
85 Outboard interplane Vee struts

86 Interplane strut socket attachment
87 Lower wing spar locking collar
88 Wing-tip diagonal bracing rib
89 Box section lower wing spar
90 Leading-edge construction
91 Interplane bracing wire
92 Lower wing attachment collar fixing
93 Undercarriage rear strut attachment
94 Undercarriage rear strut
95 Port mainwheel

96 Fabric wheel-disc cover
97 Tyre valve access
98 Wheel spokes
99 Elastic cord shock absorber
100 Undercarriage front strut
101 Cross-bracing
102 Axle beam
103 Half axle centre pivots
104 Starboard mainwheel
105 Lewis gun
106 Ammunition drum

(Above) The Nie 27 derivative prototype which used a biplane rather than sesquiplane configuration.

rotary engine and Vee-type interplane strut. Retaining the Nie 27 fuselage, tail surfaces, undercarriage and, apparently, the 130 hp Le Rhône 9Jby engine, this prototype in fact departed from the sesquiplane arrangement in adopting a two-spar lower wing of broader chord. The Vee-type struts featured broad apices to provide appropriate pick-up points. Armament consisted of paired synchronised 7,7-mm guns.

NIEUPORT 28   France

Marking the final abandonment by Gustave Delage of the Vee-strutted sesquiplane configuration, the Nie 28 was an elegant fighter of conventional biplane configuration with parallel interplane struts. Powered by a 150 hp Gnome Monosoupape 9N rotary, the Nie 28 was initially fitted with a single 7,7-mm Vickers gun. A prototype was flying in June 1917 with pronounced dihedral on the upper wing, an abbreviated cabane and no dihedral on the lower wing. At least one other aircraft was flown with this configuration. The upper wing arrangement proved unsuccessful, and, in mid-October, the aircraft was tested with a raised upper wing from which dihedral was eliminated. This

The "*dièdre total*" prototype of the Nie 28 (above) with pronounced dihedral and abbreviated cabane.

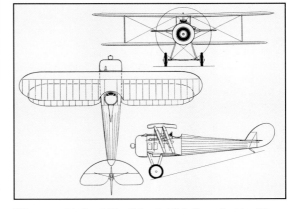

(Above and below) The "*demi-dièdre*" production Nie 28 with 1.5-deg dihedral and deeper cabane.

was retained. The last Vee-strutted Nieuport sesquiplane to see operational service, the Nie 27 attained use with French *escadrilles* during the summer of 1917, but was rapidly outmoded. At least 87 were supplied to the RFC, which was not to withdraw this type finally until 20 April 1918, long after the Nie 27 was outclassed on

(Below) The Nie 27 was a further Nie 24 derivative.

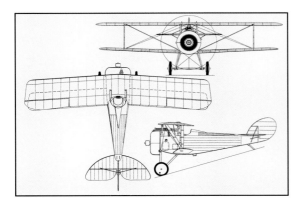

the Western Front. It was used in quantity by Italy, and, in November 1917, a total of 287 Nie 27s was acquired by the US Air Service for the fighter training rôle. In Japan, Nakajima built 25 Nie 27s in 1923, and these served in the Imperial Army as fighters with the same Ko 3 designation as the Nie 24s. *Max speed, 107 mph (172 km/h) at sea level. Time to 9,840 ft (3 000 m), 9.42 min. Loaded weight, 1,179 lb (535 kg). Span, 26 ft 11 in (8,21 m). Length, 19 ft 3 in (5,87 m). Height, 7 ft 10 in (2,40 m). Wing area, 158.77 sq ft (14,75 m²).*

NIEUPORT 27 (DERIVATIVE)   France

On 22 October 1917, Gustave Delage's Vee-strutted sesquiplane fighter was described in the following terms by *Général* Pétain: "The Nieuport is inferior to all enemy aircraft. It is essential that it be withdrawn very soon from all the *escadrilles* at the Front." Whether a prototype apparently derived from the Nie 27 and intended to overcome that fighter's shortcomings made its début before or after Pétain's condemnation is not recorded, but it would seem to have represented Delage's very last attempt to keep alive the combination of

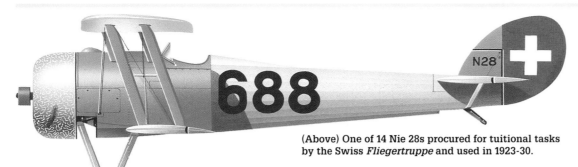

(Above) One of 14 Nie 28s procured for tuitional tasks by the Swiss *Fliegertruppe* and used in 1923-30.

arrangement was, in turn, superseded a month later by a compromise which retained the wing position but adopted 1.5 deg dihedral for the upper wing, and this was standardised for production. The single-gun armament was deemed inadequate and a second Vickers gun was attached to the fuselage portside. The Nie 28 was not adopted by France's *Aviation Militaire*, but it was acquired for the American Expeditionary Force, which received 297 from March 1918. Unpopular for its tendency to shed its wing fabric at high speeds or during high-*g* manoeuvres, the Nie 28 was found to be no match for the Fokker D VII and was withdrawn after four months of unsatisfactory service. Twelve were acquired by the US Navy, 15 by Switzerland and a few by Greece. *Max speed, 123 mph (198 km/h) at 6,560 ft (2 000 m). Time to 6,560 ft (2 000 m), 5.5 min. Range, 248 mls (400 km). Empty weight, 961 lb (436 kg). Loaded weight, 1,539 lb (698 kg). Span, 26 ft 9¼ in (8,16 m). Length, 21 ft 0 in (6,40 m). Height, 8 ft 2½ in (2,50 m). Wing area, 172.23 sq ft (16,00 m²).*

NIEUPORT (CLERGET 11E) France

The Clerget 11E-powered Nieuport fighter (above) that was under test in France late in 1917.

By 1 December 1917, Nieuport was flying the prototype of an enlarged development of the Nie 28 powered by a 200 hp Clerget 11E 11-cylinder rotary and carrying an armament of twin 7,7-mm Vickers guns. Compared with the Nie 28, this prototype had larger dimensions overall – the wing area being increased by 53.82 sq ft (5,00 m²) – wings rigged with appreciable dihedral and a cut-back wing centre section to improve the pilot's upward view. To what extent the development problems suffered by the Clerget 11E engine affected this prototype is not known, but the aircraft had been abandoned by 1 May 1918. *Max speed, 124 mph (200 km/h) at 13,125 ft (4 000 m). Time to 13,125 ft (4 000 m), 12 min. Endurance, 2.5 hrs. Empty weight, 1,168 lb (530 kg). Loaded weight, 1,874 lb (850 kg). Wing area, 226.05 sq ft (21,00 m²).*

NIEUPORT MONOCOQUE France

In parallel with the Clerget 11E-engined prototype, Nieuport produced the company's first monocoque fighter, this being reported to be ready for testing on 1 December 1917. With an appearance suggesting a close relationship with the Nie 28, this prototype was powered by a 165 hp Gnome Monosoupape 9N rotary engine enclosed by a bulbous cowling and carried an armament of a single 7,7-mm Vickers gun to port of the tandem faired centreline struts forming the cabane. The wooden monocoque fuselage was characterised by extremely clean lines and the tail surfaces were of

The Nieuport monocoque fighter (above) was tested early in 1918, but had been abandoned by April.

basically similar geometry to that adopted for the later Nie 29. The monocoque prototype had apparently been abandoned by April 1918, by which time a second aircraft had been tested with a 170 hp Le Rhône 9R. Performance was only marginally better than that of the Nie 28 and neither Monosoupape 9N or Le Rhône 9R was satisfactory. It is probably for these reasons that further development of the first Nieuport monocoque fighter was not pursued. *Max speed (Le Rhône), 123 mph (198 km/h) at 6,560 ft (2 000 m). Time to 9,840 ft (3 000 m), 7.33 min. Endurance, 2.25 hrs. Loaded weight (Monosoupape), 1,411 lb (640 kg).*

NIEUPORT MONOPLANE France

In October 1917, Nieuport had a prototype fighter monoplane under construction with the aim of combining the structural simplicity and reduced drag of this configuration with a reasonable downward view for the pilot. The shoulder-mounted wing was braced by substantial lift struts attached to a rigid undercarriage structure incorporating a substantial spanwise surface of broad chord and streamline section. Glazed cut-outs in the wing roots gave the pilot some downward view and the wings and faired fuselage were fabric-covered. Powered by a 150 hp Gnome Monosoupape 9N rotary, the monoplane is presumed to have flown at the end of 1917 or beginning of 1918, at which time a second prototype with a 180 hp Le Rhône 9R was scheduled to fly about the end of January. The latter embodied some revision of the wings, which introduced inverse taper on

The Nieuport monoplane of 1917 in initial form (above) and in its second form (below).

the inboard trailing edges, and an extended fin. As of 1 May 1918, the Monosoupape-powered prototype was still under test, while the prototype with the Le Rhône had been abandoned. Armament comprised two synchronised 7,7-mm Vickers guns. Although the monoplane was not officially accepted, it represented the first Nieuport application of the configuration that was later to be greatly refined as the Nie 31. The following data is based on manufacturer's estimates. *Max speed, 137 mph (220 km/h) at 13,125 ft (4 000 m). Time to 13,125 ft (4 000 m), 13 min. Endurance, 2.0 hrs. Empty weight, 955 lb (433 kg). Loaded weight, 1,565 lb (703 kg). Wing area, 188.37 sq ft (17,50 m²).*

NIEUPORT (LORRAINE-DIETRICH) France

The rotary engine having reached its development limit by late 1917, Gustave Delage turned his attention to stationary engines, and, on 23 October 1917, it was reported that a Nieuport fighter with a Lorraine-Dietrich water-cooled eight-cylinder Vee engine was under test. Fitted with either a 240 hp Lorraine-Dietrich 8Bb or 275 hp 8Bd, this was a somewhat ungainly aircraft, with a large gap and an aft-positioned cockpit. Forward view was impaired by large fairings over the engine cylinder blocks with the radiator mounted between them. Although this prototype was undergoing what were described as ''acceptance tests'' at Villacoublay, it was evidently discarded in favour of a similarly-powered, but more refined, prototype which, according to one report, was to be ready at the end of

(Above) The first and (below) the second of the Lorraine-Dietrich-engined Nieuport prototypes.

January 1918. This differed markedly from its predecessor, having equi-span sweptback wings of increased area, horn-balanced ailerons on both upper and lower mainplanes, a larger vertical tail and the radiator repositioned in the wing centre section. It is reasonably certain that the engine was the 275 hp 8Bd and flight testing was reported to be continuing late in April 1918. Previously, in February, time to 6,560 ft (2 000 m) had been recorded as 5.66 min and to 13,125 ft (4 000 m) as 16.5 min. An early estimate of maximum speed with a Lorraine-Dietrich engine of 220 hp was 137 mph (220 km/h) at 13,125 ft (4 000 m). The following data for weights are estimated. *Empty weight, 1,179 lb (535 kg). Loaded weight, 1,874 lb (850 kg). Wing area, 226.05 sq ft (21,00 m²).*

NIEUPORT
(HISPANO-SUIZA)　France

Produced in parallel with the second Lorraine-Dietrich-engined prototype, a virtually identical airframe was fitted with one of the first 300 hp Hispano-Suiza eight-cylinder water-cooled engines and was reported to be in course of testing on 1 May 1918. As the prototype was fitted with two 7,7-mm Vickers machine guns it was obviously not merely a test vehicle for the HS 8Fb engine which it was intended to install in the Nie 29 and the prototype of which was nearing completion. Much was expected of the Nie 29 at that time, and it would have been logical for the Nieuport company to have abandoned its first 300 hp Hispano-Suiza-engined fighter in order to concentrate on the more advanced and refined monocoque-type fighter. That is as may be, but development of the former would seem to have been discontinued by the time that the Nie 29 entered flight test. The following data are based on manufacturer's estimates. *Max speed, 143 mph (230 km/h) at 13,125 ft (4 000 m). Time to 13,125 ft (4 000 m), 10 min. Endurance, 2.5 hrs. Empty weight, 1,323 lb (600 kg). Loaded weight, 2,094 lb (950 kg). Wing area, 226.05 sq ft (21,00 m²).*

Under test in May 1918, the Hispano-Suiza-engined prototype (below) was overtaken by the Nie 29.

NIEUPORT 29　France

Flown for the first time early in June 1918, the Nie 29 combined several features previously tested by Gustave Delage on earlier prototype fighters. A nominally staggered two-bay equi-span biplane powered by a 300 hp Hispano-Suiza 8Fb eight-cylinder water-cooled engine and carrying an armament of two 7,7-mm Vickers guns, the Nie 29 featured a wooden monocoque fuselage (thin tulip wood strips glued in spirals in alternating directions) and fabric-covered wings. An initial series order on behalf of the *Aviation Militaire* was placed in 1920, the first being delivered on 11 February 1921. A variant referred to as the "Nie 29 Type 22 m²" with wing area reduced by 53.82 sq ft (5,00 m²) was displayed at the *Salon de l'Aéronautique* in December 1922, but did not attract a production contract. Another variant, with a Gnome 9N rotary engine, was identified as the Nieuport 29G. With the death of Louis Nieuport, the Etablissements Nieuport amalgamated with the Astra concern in 1921 to become Nieuport-Astra, and subsequent to the commencement of production deliveries of the Nie 29, Nieuport aircraft were restyled Nieuport-Delage, the new fighter thus becoming the Ni-D 29. The *Aviation Militaire* strength peaked at 25 *escadrilles* equipped with this type in 1925. In excess of 250 were built by Nieuport-Astra, Schreck, Levasseur, Potez, Blériot, Letord, Farman and Buscaylet, the excellent manoeuvrability and sturdiness of the Ni-D 29

(Above and below) The Nie (later Ni-D) 29 was built in substantial numbers in five countries.

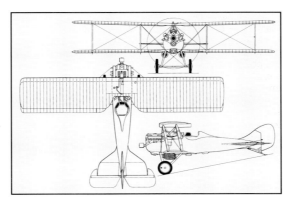

attracting considerable foreign attention. Several were exported to Argentina, 21 were supplied to Belgium (where 87 more were built by SABCA), six were delivered as pattern aircraft to Italy (where 80 were built by Caproni and 95 by Macchi) and one as a pattern aircraft to Japan. In this last-mentioned country, no fewer than 608 were built by Nakajima with the designation Ko-4 for the Imperial Army between 1923 and 1932, these remaining in service until 1933, and seeing extensive use during the Manchurian and Shanghai conflicts. Twenty were sold to Spain (where 10 more were licence-built) and nine went to Sweden. *Max speed, 147 mph (236 km/h) at sea level. Time to 16,405 ft (5 000 m), 14 min. Endurance, 2.5 hrs. Empty weight, 1,874 lb (850 kg). Loaded weight, 2,623 lb (1 190 kg). Span, 31 ft 2 in (9,50 m). Length, 21 ft 1½ in (6,44 m). Height, 8 ft 8¾ in (2,66 m). Wing area, 290.63 sq ft (27,00 m²).*

NIEUPORT 31　France

Developed in 1918 to a slightly later timescale than the Nie 29, the Nie 31 was a refined derivative of the earlier monoplane prototypes from which, configurationally, it differed primarily in having an enlarged spanwise auxiliary aerofoil surface. Technically a sesquiplane, but effectively a shoulder-wing monoplane, the Nie 31 (also

referred to as the Nie 31 Rh indicating the engine type) was powered by a 180 hp Le Rhône 9R nine-cylinder rotary and was tested during the course of 1919. The wing, which was of exceptionally broad chord, incorporated substantial cut-outs at the trailing-edge roots to provide the pilot with a measure of downward view. The auxiliary surface braced beneath the fuselage provided attachment points for the inclined aerofoil-section wing bracing struts. It also enclosed the undercarriage axle and the upper portions of the wheels. The wooden monocoque fuselage was essentially similar to that of the Nie 29, and the intended armament consisted of two 7,7-mm Vickers guns. Development was abandoned despite excellent performance achieved on comparatively low power, possibly as a result of the rotary engine being by consensus *passé* by this time. *Max speed, 143 mph (230 km/h). Endurance, 2.0 hrs. Empty weight, 1,102 lb (500 kg). Loaded weight, 1,720 lb (780 kg). Span, 28 ft 2½ in (8,60 m). Length, 21 ft 7⅘ in (6,60 m). Height, 7 ft 10½ in (2,40 m). Wing area, 193.76 sq ft (18,00 m²).*

The Nie 31 (above and below), technically a sesquiplane, entered flight test during 1919.

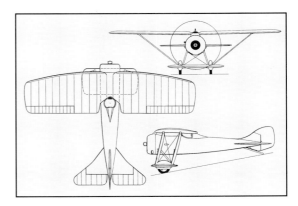

NIEUPORT 32 (RH)　France

Intended for shipboard operation, the Nie 32Rh was a derivative of the Nieuport 29G which was, itself, a variant of the Hispano-engined fighter powered by a Gnome 9N rotary engine. The Nieuport 32, which appeared in 1920 – at which time the French naval staff was planning construction of its first aircraft carrier – was allegedly the second Nieuport 29G airframe powered by a 180 hp Le Rhône 9R rotary engine. The wooden monocoque fuselage was similar to that of the Nieuport 29, and while the two-bay wings were essen-

An Ni-D 29 of the *Escadrille Lafayette*, part of the 35e *Régiment d'Aviation Mixte*.

The Nie 32 (above) was essentially a shipboard derivative of the Nie 29, but was not ordered.

tially similar, long-span overhanging ailerons were adopted. No production order followed flight trials. *Max speed, 120 mph (194 km/h). Endurance, 4.0 hrs. Empty weight, 1,329 lb (603 kg). Loaded weight, 1,889 lb (857 kg). Span (excluding aileron overhang), 31 ft 9 9/10 in (9,70 m). Length, 21 ft 11 3/4 in (6,70 m). Height, 8 ft 1 2/3 in (2,48 m). Wing area, 322.93 sq ft (30,00 m²).*

NIEUPORT-DELAGE 37   France

Flown for the first time in April 1923, but previously displayed statically during the *Salon de l'Aéronautique* of December 1922, the Ni-D 37 single-seat fighter designed by E Dieudonné utilised a modification of the innovative design concept of the Nieuport 31. It was fundamentally a shoulder-wing monoplane with a small foreplane braced beneath the forward fuselage and enclosing the mainwheel axle and shock absorbers. Entirely of wooden construction with a monocoque fuselage, the Ni-D 37 was powered by a 300 hp Hispano-Suiza 8Fb with a Rateau turbo-supercharger. For

A general arrangement drawing (below) of the Ni-D 37 exhibited (above) at the 1922 Paris *Salon*.

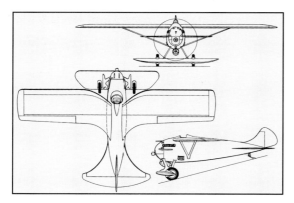

optimum view from the cockpit, the pilot was situated immediately aft of and above the engine on which the rudder pedals were placed, and the leading-edge wing roots were cut back to provide a measure of downward vision aft of the foreplane. Armament comprised two 7,7-mm Vickers guns. Estimated performance included a maximum speed of 155 mph (250 km/h) at 22,965 ft (7 000 m), but this was never attained during flight trials, the Ni-D 37 proving too heavy by comparison with more orthodox competitors. Furthermore, lack of the necessary heat-resistant alloys resulted in problems with the turbo-supercharger and further development of both aircraft and turbo-supercharger was discontinued. *Empty weight, 2,160 lb (980 kg). Loaded weight, 3,153 lb (1 420 kg). Span, 38 ft 8 1/2 in (11,80 m). Length, 23 ft 5 9/10 in (7,16 m). Height, 9 ft 9 in (2,97 m). Wing area, 288.48 sq ft (26,80 m²) of which 54 sq ft (5,02 m²) provided by foreplane.*

NIEUPORT-DELAGE 42   France

Early in 1923, a requirement was issued for a new single-seat fighter to meet which Gustave Delage and Robert Duhamel of Nieuport-Astra produced a design based on the Ni-D 42 racing monoplane (which was to win the *Coupe Beaumont* on 23 June 1924). Utilising the same monocoque fuselage as the racing aircraft – two tulip wood half-shells joined horizontally – mated with a wing of parasol rather than shoulder-mounted configuration and of increased area, an enlarged vertical tail and a new tailplane, the fighter retained the Ni-D 42 designation, being distinguished by the suffix C1 (*avion monoplace de chasse*). The wing was of mixed construction with two duralumin spars, plywood ribs and fabric skinning, the engine was a 12-cylinder Vee water-cooled Hispano-Suiza 12Ha of 450 hp and armament comprised two 7,7-mm Vickers guns in the fuselage with provision for two wing-mounted 7,7-mm Darne guns. An extremely elegant aircraft, the Ni-D 42 C1 was rolled out in the spring of 1924. Built in parallel, the second prototype was completed as a two-seat fighter, the Ni-D 42 C2. Apart from the second cockpit, this differed from the single-seater in being of sesquiplane configuration, a short-span wing of 45.75-sq ft (4,25-m²) area being added to the base of the fuselage. The Ni-D 42 C2 was displayed statically at the 1924 *Salon de l'Aéronautique*, but was apparently not flight tested before conversion to single-seat configuration. The additional wing was subsequently applied to the first prototype, the wheel track was increased, and the aircraft participated in the contest between the contending prototypes which had formally commenced on 15 July 1924. The contest extended over a year and the Ni-D 42 was declared the winner, official contracts for two and 25 aircraft being signed on 4 December 1925 and 29 January 1927 respectively. Several were built and flown in advance of the main contract (one participating in a Turkish Air Force contest between 3 June and 19 July 1926). The third and fourth airframes were powered by the 450 hp Lorraine-Dietrich 12Eb and 500 hp Hispano-Suiza 12Gb W-type engines as the Ni-D 44 and 46 respectively, these being placed tenth and fifth among the competition finalists. Although pro-

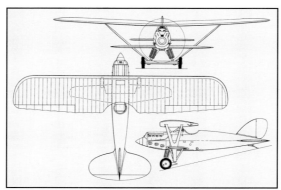

The Ni-D 42 (above and below) was advanced for its time and progenitor of a long series of fighters.

duced only in small quantity, the Ni-D 42 was the progenitor of a series of derivative fighters. *Max speed, 165 mph (266 km/h) at 13,125 ft (4 000 m). Time to 16,405 ft (5 000 m), 13.05 min. Range, 248 mls (400 km). Empty weight, 3,040 lb (1 379 kg). Loaded weight, 3,986 lb (1 808 kg). Span, 39 ft 4 1/2 in (12,00 m). Length, 24 ft 7 1/4 in (7,50 m). Height, 9 ft 10 1/8 in (3,00 m). Wing area, 317.54 sq ft (29,50 m²).*

NIEUPORT-DELAGE 43   France

The Ni-D 43 (above) was developed to meet a two-seat shipboard fighter requirement and flew in 1924.

Conceived by Robert Duhamel in collaboration with MM Albert Mary and Bonnemaison, the Ni-D 43 was submitted to Nieuport-Astra as the company's contender for a two-seat shipboard fighter requirement, entering flight test in 1924. A two-bay biplane with ailerons on the lower wing only, the Ni-D 43 AMC2 (*Avion Marin Biplace de Chasse*) featured two abbreviated, stepless floats which, attached by N-type struts, projected ahead of the fuselage and housed the mainwheels. The aft fuselage bottom was watertight so that, after alighting on water (an option intended for emergency use only), the aircraft adopted a ''three-point'' attitude, keeping the propeller clear of the water and permitting taxying until retrieval. The Ni-D 43 was powered by a 500 hp Hispano-Suiza 12Hb 12-cylinder water-cooled engine and carried an armament of twin synchronised 7,7-mm Vickers guns and twin Lewis guns of the same calibre on a ring mounting. The sole prototype underwent competitive evaluation at Saint Raphaël in 1925, but the Levasseur P.L.5 was selected to meet the requirement and further development of the Ni-D 43 was discontinued. *Max speed, 124 mph (200 km/h) at sea level. Time to 19,685 ft (6 000 m), 40 min. Endurance, 2.5 hrs. Empty weight, 3,704 lb (1 680 kg). Loaded weight, 5,115 lb (2 320 kg). Span, 41 ft 11 9/10 in (12,80 m). Length, 32 ft 9 2/3 in (10,00 m). Height, 12 ft 7 1/2 in (3,85 m). Wing area, 476.86 sq ft (44,30 m²).*

NIEUPORT-DELAGE 44   France

Alternative contenders to the Ni-D 42 submitted by Nieuport-Astra for participation in the 1923 *programme chasseur monoplace* were the Ni-D 44 and Ni-D 46, all three fighters possessing similar airframes, fuel capacity and armament. The Ni-D 44 differed from the Ni-D

The Ni-D 44 (above) was an alternative contender to the Ni-D 42 in the 1923 fighter programme.

42 essentially in having a 450 hp Lorraine-Dietrich 12Eb 12-cylinder W-type water-cooled engine with a frontal-type honeycomb radiator. The Ni-D 44 was lighter than the Ni-D 42 from which it was derived, but offered inferior level speed and climb performance, and was, in consequence, rejected in favour of the latter. *Max speed, 150 mph (241 km/h) at sea level. Time to 16,405 ft (5 000 m), 15.23 min. Endurance, 2.0 hrs. Empty weight, 2,575 lb (1 168 kg). Loaded weight, 3,796 lb (1 722 kg). Dimensions as for Ni-D 42 apart from overall length of 23 ft 7½ in (7,20 m).*

NIEUPORT-DELAGE 46   France

Like the previously described Ni-D 44, the Ni-D 46 differed from the Ni-D 42 essentially in the type of engine installed, this being a 500 hp Hispano-Suiza 12Gb 12-cylinder W-type water-cooled unit with a similar honeycomb-type frontal radiator to that of the Ni-D 44.

One of a trio of fundamentally similar fighters, the Ni-D 46 (above) was another 1923 programme contender.

Carrying the same armament, it was lighter than the Ni-D 42, as was also the Ni-D 44, but, again, level speed and climb performance were inferior to those of its progenitor which was adjudged the winning contender in the contest. The sole Ni-D 46 prototype was, in fact, the fourth airframe of the series of 25 Ni-D 42s, manufacture of which predated the official contract. *Max speed, 157 mph (252 km/h) at 3,280 ft (1 000 m). Time to 16,405 ft (5 000 m), 15.25 min. Endurance, 2.0 hrs. Empty weight, 2,632 lb (1 194 kg). Loaded weight, 3,955 lb (1 794 kg). Dimensions as for Ni-D 42 apart from overall length of 23 ft 11⅘ in (7,30 m).*

NIEUPORT-DELAGE 48   France

Conceptually similar to the Ni-D 42 apart from being of parasol monoplane rather than sesquiplane configuration and intended as a competitor in the 1926 *programme de chasseurs légers*, known unofficially as the "Jockey" programme, the Ni-D 48 was first flown early in November 1926. Designed around a 400 hp Hispano-Suiza 12Jb 12-cylinder Vee-type liquid-cooled engine and carrying an armament of two 7,7-mm (0.303-in) synchronised machine guns, the Ni-D 48 was effectively a scaled-down and refined Ni-D 42 with full-span ailerons and a circular-section fuselage, there being no commonality between the types. Three Ni-D 48 airframes were built, the first of these being used for static load testing in October 1926, and the first flying prototype, the Ni-D 48 No 1, underwent official trials during May-August 1927. The second flying prototype, designated Ni-D 48bis No 1, appeared in September 1927 with a 500 hp Hispano-Suiza 12Hb engine, but official trials in March 1928 revealed little performance improvement – apart from climb – over the Ni-D 62, which,

The Ni-D 48 (above and below) was a lightweight fighter participant in the 1926 "Jockey" programme.

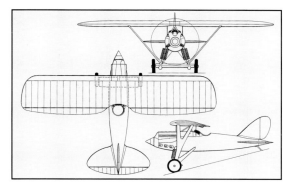

by that time, was already in production. On 3 July 1929, the Ni-D 48 prototype was flown to Etampes for use as a trainer, and, in the summer of 1930, the Ni-D 48bis prototype was re-engined (as the Ni-D 481) with a 240 hp Lorraine Algol Junior nine-cylinder radial as a civil aerobatic aircraft. The following data relate to the HS 12Jb-powered Ni-D 48 No 1. *Max speed, 171 mph (276 km/h) at sea level. Time to 16,405 ft (5 000 m), 16.26 min. Endurance, 1.5 hrs. Empty weight, 2,275 lb (1 032 kg). Loaded weight, 2,844 lb (1 290 kg). Span, 32 ft 9⅔ in (10.00 m). Length, 20 ft 11⅞ in (6,40 m). Wing area, 197.85 sq ft (18,38 m²).*

NIEUPORT-DELAGE 52   France

Evolved in parallel with the Ni-D 62 (which see) as a progressive development of the Ni-D 42, the Ni-D 52 was rolled out in prototype form during the closing weeks of 1927. Some pitch-up with consequent inadvertent stalls and spins experienced with the Ni-D 42 had led to the introduction of a number of changes which were applied to both the Ni-D 52 and Ni-D 62. The chord of the main wing was adjusted to reduce area by 4.3 sq ft (0,4 m²) and the tailplane was enlarged. In the case of the Ni-D 52, a further change was a reduction of 14.53 sq ft (1,35 m²) in the area of the auxiliary wing. Apart from this last-mentioned modification, the Ni-D 52 differed from the Ni-D 42 and the Ni-D 62 in using light alloy tubing, rather than wood, for the wing ribs, and metal in place of tulip wood for the fuselage monocoque. The Ni-D 52 was thus, effectively, a metallised Ni-D 62, and retained the same 500 hp Hispano-Suiza 12Hb 12-cylinder Vee-type engine. The Ni-D 52 was not ordered by the French government, which elected to procure the Ni-D 62 owing to its closer com-

monality with the Ni-D 42 and consequent lower cost. However, earlier in 1927, the Ni-D 42 had been pronounced winning contender in a *Concurso de Aviones* held to select a new fighter for Spain's *Aviación Militar*, and the Spanish government procured a manufacturing licence for its Ni-D 52 derivative. The production programme was undertaken by the Guadalajara facility of La Hispano (later La Hispano-Suiza) which was awarded an order for 125 Ni-D 52s – subsequently known as "Hispano-Nieuports" – of which the first 34 were assembled from component kits supplied by the parent company, deliveries to the *Aviación Militar* commencing in 1929. The Hispano-built Ni-D 52 differed from the prototype in replacing the Lamblin radiators with a single external Corominas chin-type radiator, and its armament comprised two 7,7-mm machine guns. Ninety-one were entirely manufactured in Spain and at least 10 more were later assembled from 20 complete sets of spares also produced. When hostilities commenced in Spain in July 1936, 48 remained in government hands and eight were acquired by the Nationalists (to which three were later added when a government *patrulla* inadvertently landed at a Nationalist-held airfield), but most had been with-

(Above) The prototype and (below) the series Ni-D 52 which was manufactured under licence in Spain.

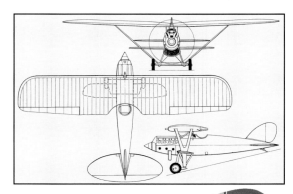

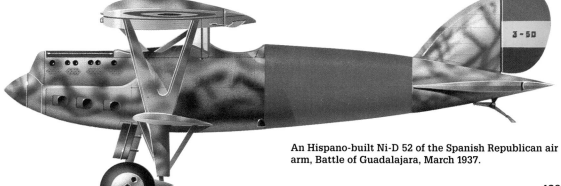

An Hispano-built Ni-D 52 of the Spanish Republican air arm, Battle of Guadalajara, March 1937.

439

This Ni-D 52 (above), relegated to training, winter 1936-37, was restored to operational use in March 1937.

drawn from operational use and relegated to the instructional rôle by the year's end. *Max speed, 162 mph(260 km/h) at 5,905 ft (1 800 m). Time to 16,405 ft (5 000 m), 13.5 min. Empty weight, 2,998 lb (1 360 kg). Loaded weight, 3,968 lb (1 800 kg). Span, 39 ft 4½ in (12,00 m). Length, 25 ft 0¾ in (7,64 m). Height, 9 ft 10⅛ in (3,00 m). Wing area, 298.71 sq ft (27,75 m²).*

NIEUPORT-DELAGE 62 — France

Essentially a refinement of the Ni-D 42 developed in parallel with the metallised Ni-D 52 and sharing the changes to wing and horizontal tail (with the exception of the reduction in area of the auxiliary wing), the Ni-D 62 was flown in January 1928. The first aircraft, Ni-D 62 No 26, followed on the Nieuport-Astra line from the last Ni-D 42 (ie, No 25). Apart from the previously-mentioned wing and tail changes, the Ni-D 62 was fundamentally similar to the Ni-D 42, retaining the twin-gun armament and 500 hp Hispano-Suiza 12Hb engine. The remaining Ni-D 42s were brought up to Ni-D 62 standard during the first months of 1928, and the last of an initial batch of 25 new-build aircraft, Ni-D 62 No 50, was experimentally fitted with a 600 hp HS 12Lb engine. Contracts were placed for a further 295 aircraft (including 50 for the *Aéronautique Maritime*), the last,

An Ni-D 62 (above) of the *7ème Escadrille* of the *34ème Regiment Mixte* at Le Bourget during 1930.

Ni-D 62 No 345, being completed in 1930. By comparison with the Ni-D 42, the Ni-D 62 offered improved longitudinal stability, but demonstrated a predilection to enter a flat spin owing to the position of the CG. This was to lead to some wing redesign (see Ni-D 622). Two Ni-D 62s were supplied to Turkey and three to Romania for evaluation, and three were adapted in 1930 as Ni-D 621 twin-float trainers for pilots selected to participate in the Schneider Trophy contest, these subsequently being reconverted to standard Ni-D 62 configuration. *Max speed, 168 mph (270 km/h) at sea level. Time to 16,405 ft (5 000 m), 13.3 min. Max range, 559 mls (900 km). Empty weight, 2,906 lb (1 318 kg). Loaded weight, 4,017 lb (1 822 kg). Span, 39 ft 4½ in (12,00 m). Length, 25 ft 0⅓ in (7,63 m). Height (tail up), 9 ft 10⅛ in (3,00 m). Wing area, 313.24 sq ft (29,10 m²).*

NIEUPORT-DELAGE 622 TO 626 — France

The tendency of the Ni-D 62 to enter a flat spin resulted, in 1930, in redesign of the wing around the existing spars to move the centre of lift aft, the result being the Ni-D 622. Retaining the original span, the new wing was of reduced chord ahead of the front spar, with a recontoured trailing edge and new ailerons of almost constant chord extending from wing tip to centre section

Key to Nieuport-Delage 62

1 Starboard mainplane panel
2 Two-bladed fixed-pitch wooden propeller
3 Spinner
4 Propeller hub fixing
5 Propeller shaft
6 Engine bay cooling air scoop
7 Cylinder head cowlings
8 Coolant pipe
9 Crankcase extension
10 Forward engine mounting ring frame

11 Ventral oil tank
12 Starboard lower auxiliary wing panel
13 Starboard Y-strut lower segment
14 Forward fuselage light alloy frame construction
15 Carburettor air intakes
16 Engine mounting deck
17 Hispano-Suiza 12Hb 12-cylinder Vee-type engine
18 Carburettors
19 Exhaust stubs
20 Port cylinder head/rocker cover

21 Starboard wing fuel tank
22 Centre section cabane struts
23 Wing panel centreline joint/strut fixing
24 Coolant system header tank
25 Wing panel fabric covering
26 Machine gun barrels
27 Cabane strut attachment joint
28 Fuselage double main frame
29 Engine magnetos
30 Fuel pump
31 Auxiliary wing spar attachment joint
32 Fuel collector tank

cut-out, and area being reduced by 18.19 sq ft (1,69 m²). In all other respects the Ni-D 622 remained similar to the preceding Ni-D 62. Despite approaching obsolescence of the basic design, an order for 180 Ni-D 622s was placed in September 1930, the first series aircraft being Ni-D 622 No 346, and *Forces Aériennes de Terre* and *Forces Aériennes de Mer* Ni-D 62s were re-winged as Ni-D 622s when returned to the manufacturer for major overhaul. A further 68 new-build Ni-D 622s were subsequently built for the former service together with 62 for the latter. One Ni-D 622 (No 280, a former Ni-D 62) was tested from December 1931 until June 1932 with a mechanically-driven Farman-Waseige two-stage supercharger. Another (former Ni-D 62 No 61) was fitted with a non-supercharged 600 hp Lorraine 12Fa Courlis W-type engine with frontal radiator in 1931 as the Ni-D 623, the auxiliary wing being removed and increased taper being applied to the outer main wing panels. Two others were re-engined with the unsupercharged Hispano-Suiza 12M as Ni-D 624s, these also having the auxiliary wing removed, as did the sole example of the Ni-D 625 for parachute trials which appeared mid-1929. The Ni-D 626 was an export model developed for the Peruvian government. Sometimes referred to as the Ni-D 62 *Péruvien*, this was powered by an unsupercharged 500 hp Lorraine 12Hdr Pétrel engine and had the Ni-D

The Ni-D 622 (above and below) differed from the Ni-D 62 primarily in having a smaller, revised wing.

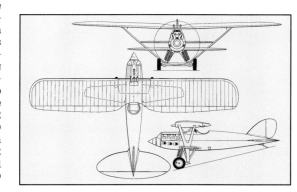

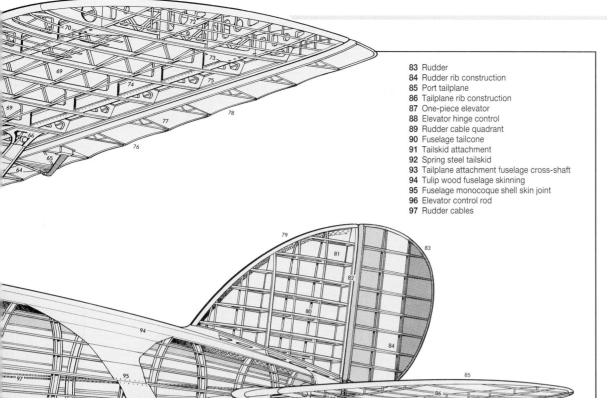

83	Rudder
84	Rudder rib construction
85	Port tailplane
86	Tailplane rib construction
87	One-piece elevator
88	Elevator hinge control
89	Rudder cable quadrant
90	Fuselage tailcone
91	Tailskid attachment
92	Spring steel tailskid
93	Tailplane attachment fuselage cross-shaft
94	Tulip wood fuselage skinning
95	Fuselage monocoque shell skin joint
96	Elevator control rod
97	Rudder cables

33	Rudder pedals
34	Central cartridge case collector box
35	Ammunition magazines (port and starboard)
36	Fire extinguisher fluid tank
37	Machine gun mounting deck
38	Adjustable gun mountings
39	Vickers 7,7-mm machine guns (2)
40	Ammunition feed chute
41	Rear spar attachment fuselage double frame
42	Compass
43	Control column
44	Control column handgrip and trigger
45	Instrument panel (port and starboard)
46	Pilot's seat
47	Throttle lever
48	Safety harness
49	Seat back parachute pack
50	Cockpit coaming
51	Interplane Y-struts
52	Gun cocking lever
53	Windscreen panel
54	OPL gunsight
55	Aileron control rod
56	Trailing edge cut-out
57	Rear view mirror
58	Rear spar/cabane strut joint
59	Wing internal diagonal bracing
60	Plywood leading-edge skinning
61	Port wing fuel tank
62	Aileron torque shaft
63	Fixed portion of trailing edge
64	Aileron operating rod
65	Control horn
66	Interplane strut attachment joints
67	Leading-edge nose ribs
68	Box-section light alloy main spar
69	All-wood wing lattice rib construction
70	Inter-rib stiffeners
71	Curved spruce leading-edge member
72	Wing tip fairing construction
73	Spar box joint plate
74	Box-section light alloy rear spar
75	Aileron hinge rib
76	Port aileron
77	Fabric covered aileron rib construction
78	Steel wire trailing edge
79	Tailfin
80	Fin rib construction
81	Stressed plywood skin panelling
82	Sternpost
98	Rear fuselage frame and stringer construction
99	Stowage locker
100	Moulded plywood auxiliary wing tip fairing
101	Oxygen bottle
102	Fuselage light alloy keel member
103	Boarding step
104	Control rod linkage
105	Wing strut attachment joint
106	Ventral flare launcher
107	Y-strut lower segment
108	Lower auxiliary wing panel rib construction
109	Cartridge case collector access panel
110	Undercarriage strut attachment joint
111	Main undercarriage N-struts
112	Diagonal wire bracing
113	Port mainwheel
114	Mainwheel disc fabric covering
115	Tyre inflation valve
116	Wheel spokes
117	Pivoted stub axle
118	Elastic cord shock absorber
119	Coolant radiators, port and starboard
120	Axle box fairing construction
121	Starboard mainwheel

622 main wing, but dispensed with the auxiliary wing. Twelve were ordered, the first of these flying in the summer of 1932, and deliveries continuing into late 1933. The following data relate to the standard Ni-D 622. *Max speed, 168 mph (270 km/h) at sea level. Time to 16,405 ft (5 000 m), 13.6 min. Max range, 559 mls (900 km). Empty weight, 3,038 lb (1 378 kg). Loaded weight, 4,050 lb (1 837 kg). Span, 39 ft 4½ in (12,00 m). Length, 25 ft 0⅓ in (7,63 m). Height (tail up), 9 ft 10⅛ in (3,00 m). Wing area, 295.05 sq ft (27,41 m².*

The Ni-D 623 (below) was a one-off aircraft with a Courlis engine and the auxiliary wing removed.

NIEUPORT-DELAGE
628 & 629   France

During 1931, two Ni-D 622s were fitted with the 500 hp Hispano-Suiza 12Md Vee-type 12-cylinder water-cooled engine in place of the standard HS 12Hb, one having a Farman-Waseige mechanically-driven supercharger and the other a supercharger of Szydlowski-Planiol type. These were respectively designated Ni-D 628 and Ni-D 629, and performed comparative trials which resulted in selection of the Szydlowski-Planiol supercharger, the engine so fitted being designated HS 12Mdsh. Another Ni-D 622 was converted as a second prototype Ni-D 629, and the last 50 aircraft ordered against Ni-D 622 contracts were completed as Ni-D 629s. The first of these (Ni-D 629 No 670) commenced acceptance trials late in 1933, but final acceptances were not completed until May 1935. At the beginning of World War II, 153 Ni-D 62 series fighters (including 18 Ni-D 629s) were still on *Armée de l'Air* charge, 39 of these in North Africa. One hundred and nine were with the *Escadrilles Régionale de Chasse* or with the *Centres d'Instruction de Chasse* and the remainder in storage. *Max speed, 173 mph (279 km/h) at 13,125 ft (4 000 m). Time to 13,125 ft (4 000 m), 7.73 min. Range, 373 mls (600 km). Empty weight, 3,053 lb (1 385 kg).*

Loaded weight, 4,145 lb (1 880 kg). Span, 39 ft 4½ in (12,00 m). Length, 25 ft 0⅓ in (7,63 m). Height (tail up), 9 ft 10⅛ in (3,00 m). Wing area, 295.05 sq ft (27,41 m²).

NIEUPORT-DELAGE 72   France

First flown in January 1928, almost simultaneously with the Ni-D 52, the Ni-D 72 was a further "metallised" version of the basic single-seat fighter sesquiplane design. It differed from the Ni-D 52 in several respects. A narrower main wing chord reduced the area of that surface from 267.49 sq ft (24,85 m²) to 251.88 sq ft (23,40 m²). The same 31.22 sq ft (2,90 m²) auxiliary wing was retained, but the areas of both tailplane and elevator were reduced. The essential difference between the two types, however, was the replacement of fabric by light metal alloy for the skinning of the main wing. Weighing 441 lb (200 kg) less than the Ni-D 52, the prototype was referred to as the Ni-D 72 *Léger* and retained the standard 500 hp Hispano-Suiza 12Hb engine and twin 7,7-mm gun armament. The radiators were transferred from the foremost undercarriage bracing struts to the undersides of the auxiliary wings.

(Above) An Ni-D 72 supplied to Brazil in 1931.

Three were ordered by Belgium, the production Ni-D 72 having similar extended ailerons to those adopted for the Ni-D 622. The first Belgian aircraft was flown on 24 October 1929 from Villacoublay to Diest in 1.05 hrs to establish a speed record for the Paris-Brussels route. Four Ni-D 72s were also ordered for Brazil's *Aviação Militar*, entering service in 1931, and participating in the aerial warfare that accompanied the revolution of the following year, one of the Ni-D 72s serving with the revolutionaries and the others with the government forces. *Max speed,166 mph (268 km/h) at 13,125 ft (4 000 m). Max climb, 1,873 ft/min (9,5 m/sec). Range, 373 mls (600 km). Empty weight, 2,667 lb (1 210 kg). Loaded weight, 3,527 lb (1 600 kg). Span, 39 ft 4½ in (12,00 m). Length, 24 ft 7¼ in (7,50 m). Height (tail up), 9 ft 10⅛ in (3,00 m). Wing area, 283.1 sq ft (26,30 m²).*

NIEUPORT-DELAGE 82   France

Displayed, prior to completion, at the Paris *Salon de l'Aéronautique* during November-December 1930, and flown for the first time in October 1931, the Ni-D 82 resembled preceding Nieuport-Delage fighters configurationally, but differed in virtually all other respects.

The Ni-D 82 (above) was only configurationally similar to preceding Nieuport-Astra-built fighters.

Between its appearance at the Paris *Salon* and the initiation of flight testing, the sesquiplane configuration was discarded in favour of that of parasol monoplane, and the height of the cabane was increased. Of all-metal construction, the Ni-D 82 featured an entirely new wing of rectangular planform, a semi-monocoque metal fuselage of revised form (by comparison with that of the Ni-D 52), new, more angular tail surfaces and a 500 hp Lorraine 12Ha Pétrel 12-cylinder Vee-type water-cooled engine. Intended armament remained

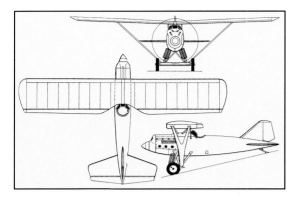

(Above) The Ni-D 82 which was flown in 1931.

two 7,7-mm synchronised machine guns. By the time that the Ni-D 82 prototype commenced flight test, the Ni-D 120 series of fighters was already on the drawing boards, and, considered conceptually *passé*, the Ni-D 82 was discontinued. *Max speed, 175 mph (281 km/h) at sea level. Time to 16,405 ft (5 000 m), 10.33 min. Range, 323 mls (520 km). Empty weight, 2,853 lb (1 294 kg). Loaded weight, 3,527 lb (1 600 kg). Span, 39 ft 4½ in (12,00 m). Length, 24 ft 11⅛ in (7,60 m). Wing area, 282.56 sq ft (26,25 m²).*

NIEUPORT-DELAGE 121   France

A new single-seat fighter requirement framed by the *Service Technique* in 1930 (and amended in 1931) resulted in no fewer than 27 submissions, from which 11 basic designs were eventually selected for development to prototype stage. To this requirement, Nieuport-Astra evolved its Ni-D 120 series fighters under a design team led by Albert Mary. Of all-metal construction, the Ni-D 120 series was of parasol monoplane configuration with a singularly abbreviated cabane, the rear wing spar actually being attached to the fuselage decking aft of the cockpit, with the wing centre section being of tapered thickness and cut out above the cockpit so that the pilot's eye level was fractionally above the wing when his seat was raised. The first prototype in the series, although the second to enter flight test, was the Ni-D 121 which was unique among contenders in having a Lorraine 12H Pétrel 12-cylinder Vee-type engine. The cooling liquid was led through pipes in the wing leading edge where they were bathed in air sucked in through a series of 11 slots on each side and then ejected over the trailing edges. The proposed armament comprised two 7,5-mm MAC 1934 machine guns. The Ni-D 121 was first flown on 25 November 1932, being re-engined with a geared and supercharged Lorraine 12Hars engine rated at 710 hp at 9,020 ft (2 750 m) before evaluation at the official test centre commencing 1 May 1934. By this time, the Dewoitine D.500 had been pronounced winning contender and committed to production. The level speed and climb rates of the Ni-D 121 were commended, but landing speed was considered excessive, the undercarriage weak and the large wing surface radiator area vulnerable. *Max speed, 228 mph (367 km/h) at 16,405 ft*

The Ni-D 121 (below) was one of 27 submissions to the fighter requirement framed by STAé in 1930.

(5 000 m). Time to 16,405 ft (5 000 m), 7.1 min. Range, 497 mls (800 km). Empty weight, 3,159 lb (1 433 kg). Loaded weight, 4,114 lb (1 866 kg). Span, 42 ft 7⅘ in (13,00 m). Length, 23 ft 6⅔ in (7,18 m). Height, 9 ft 11 in (3,02 m). Wing area, 236.81 sq ft (22,00 m²).

NIEUPORT-DELAGE 122   France

First flown on 23 July 1932, four months before the Ni-D 121, the Ni-D 122 differed essentially in having a 690 hp Hispano-Suiza 12Xbrs engine (similar to that powering all other contenders for the requirement other than the Ni-D 121 and Wibault-Penhoët 313). The first of two prototypes commenced official flight evaluation on 28 September, but, on 13 April 1933, was lost when, during a demonstration flight before parliamentary representatives, violent wing flutter was experienced and an aileron became detached. As a result, mass balances were applied to the ailerons of the second prototype, which first flew on 13 July 1933. Official testing of the second machine commenced in January 1934, but was of no more than academic interest in view of the prior selection of the Dewoitine D.500. *Max speed, 226 mph (363 km/h) at 16,405 ft (5 000 m). Time to 16,405 ft (5 000 m), 6.08 min. Range, 497 mls (800 km). Empty weight, 2,859 lb (1 297 kg). Loaded weight, 3,814 lb (1 730 kg). Span, 42 ft 7⅘ in (13,00 m). Length, 23 ft 4½ in (7,12 m). Height, 9 ft 9⅛ in (2,97 m). Wing area, 236.81 sq ft (22,00 m²).*

The HS 12Xbrs-powered Ni-D 122 (above and below) featured, like the Ni-D 121, unorthodox cooling.

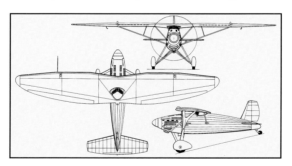

NIEUPORT-DELAGE 123   France

In September 1933, shortly after the conclusion of the war between Peru and Colombia, a Peruvian delegation evaluated the Ni-D 121 at Villacoublay, placing an order with Nieuport-Astra for six of a modified version for the *Cuerpo de Aeronáutica*. As the *Cuerpo* was anxious to procure a fighter with interchangeable wheel and float undercarriages, the Ni-D 121 was strengthened to accept pick-up points for the bracing members of a twin-float undercarriage, and enlarged

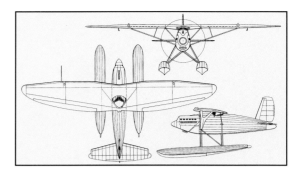

The Ni-D 123 (above) in float seaplane form.

vertical tail surfaces were introduced to compensate for the floats. Initially referred to as the Ni-D 121 *Péruvien*, but subsequently redesignated Ni-D 123, a prototype was flown with a wheel undercarriage on 18 July 1934, the aircraft later being tested from the Seine with floats, and in February 1935, the six series Ni-D 123s, together with six pairs of metal floats, were shipped to Peru. These were powered by the supercharged Lorraine 12Hdrs engine rated at 720 hp and had provision for two machine guns. The following data relate to the float-equipped Ni-D 123. *Max speed, 199 mph (320 km/h). Range, 373 mls (600 km). Empty weight, 2,943 lb (1 335 kg). Loaded weight, 3,942 lb (1 788 kg). Span, 42 ft 7⅘ in (13,00 m). Length, 25 ft 4 in (7,72 m). Height, 12 ft 1⅔ in (3,70 m). Wing area, 236.81 sq ft (22,00 m²).*

NIEUPORT-DELAGE 125   France

Considerable confusion has existed between the Ni-D 125 and the Ni-D 225 (see next entry), as the latter actually preceded the former into the air by some two months. The Ni-D 125 was powered by the 860 hp Hispano-Suiza 12Ycrs engine with provision for a 20-mm *moteur-canon*, and differed in several other respects from preceding Ni-D 120 series fighters. The wing leading-edge coolant pipe system was discarded in favour of surface radiators comprising three panels of small-bore pipes attached on each side of the fuselage beneath the wing centre section; several degrees of dihedral were applied from the wing centreline; the wing cabane was marginally deepened and the cut-out above the cockpit was enlarged. The sole prototype of the Ni-D 125 entered flight test in June 1934, and, on 16 July, commenced official trials at the *Centre d'Essais du Matériel Aérien*. There, on 9 August, it suffered minor damage during minimum approach speed trials. Testing was resumed later in the month, but despite what was by consensus an excellent performance, no further development was undertaken as the similarly-powered Dewoitine D.510 had entered flight test and offered the advantages of a high degree of commonality with the D.500 already in production. Furthermore, work had already begun on the very much more advanced Ni 160

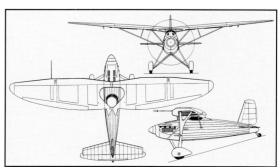

The Ni-D 125 (above and below) used panels of small-bore pipes under the wing for engine cooling.

cantilever low-wing monoplane fighter. *Max speed, 248 mph (400 km/h) at 14,765 ft (4 500 m). Time to 16,405 ft (5 000 m), 6.0 min. Empty weight, 3,221 lb (1 461 kg). Loaded weight, 4,343 lb (1 970 kg). Span, 42 ft 7⅘ in (13,00 m). Length, 23 ft 10⅔ in (7,28 m). Height, 11 ft 1 in (3,38 m). Wing area, 236.81 sq ft (22,00 m²).*

NIEUPORT-DELAGE 225   France

Developed in parallel with the Ni-D 125, the similarly-powered Ni-D 225 flew for the first time on 12 April 1934. Unlike its predecessors, the Ni-D 225 was not a parasol wing monoplane, both wing spars being attached to the fuselage to produce a shoulder-wing arrangement. To overcome the reduced downward visibility from the cockpit, the adjacent portions of the wing root featured Perspex skinning. On 26 April, two weeks after initiation of flight testing, a runaway propeller followed by an engine fire necessitated evacuation of the aircraft by the test pilot. A second Ni-D 225 prototype was flown on 13 July 1934, and, in the following February, a variable-pitch (in flight) propeller was fitted. In October, further development of this fighter, by now considered configurationally obsolescent, was officially abandoned to permit concentration on the Ni 160. No illustrations of the Ni-D 225 nor data appear to have survived.

NIEUPORT 140   France

The Ni 140 (above and below) was primarily a two-seat fighter, the first prototype being illustrated.

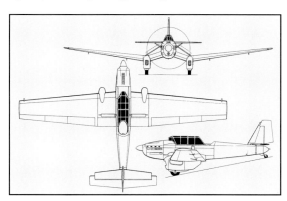

Conceived as a two-seat shipboard fighter and dive bomber, the Ni 140 was designed in 1932 – the omission of the "D" from the designation signifying the prior departure from the Nieuport-Astra company of Gustave Delage – and was of fabric-covered metal construction. Of inverted gull wing configuration, the Ni 140 featured unusual dive brakes comprising narrow aerofoil surfaces above the wing centre section, which, attached to the rear spar and the top of a fuselage frame, were pivoted pneumatically. A 690 hp Hispano-Suiza 12Xcrs engine with provision for a 20-mm *moteur-canon* was fitted, the radiators being incorporated in the trouser-type main undercarriage fairings. The Ni 140 was intended to operate as a two-seat fighter with a flexibly-mounted 7,5-mm machine gun in the rear cockpit and as a single-seat dive bomber with a 441-lb (200-kg) bomb hung from a cradle beneath the fuselage. The first prototype was flown in March 1935, but, on 8 July, the aircraft was lost after the engine failed in a dive. The second prototype was flown in November 1935, this introducing bracing for the tailplane and shorter-chord undercarriage fairings. On 15 May 1936, this aircraft began to break up during a dive and crashed into the sea. Nieuport-Astra had by this time been acquired

by Ateliers et Chantiers de la Loire, further development of the Ni 140 being discontinued in favour of a dedicated shipboard dive bomber, the Loire-Nieuport LN 40, which, although similarly powered to the Ni 140 and not dissimilar configurationally, was an entirely new design, the French Navy's two-seat fighter requirement having meanwhile been abandoned. *Max speed, 205 mph (330 km/h) at 11,485 ft (3 500 m). Loaded weight, 5,458 lb (2 476 kg). Span, 45 ft 11⅛ in (14,00 m). Length, 31 ft 4¾ in (9,57 m). Wing area, 288.7 sq ft (26,82 m²).*

NIEUPORT 160   France

See Loire-Nieuport 161, produced by the Groupement Aviation Loire-Nieuport.

NIEUPORT (& GENERAL) B.N.1   UK

The Nieuport & General Aircraft Company was established in November 1916 for the purpose of manufacturing Nieuport designs in the UK. When H P Folland joined the company following dispersal of the Royal Aircraft Factory design office, work began on an original single-seat fighter. Designated B.N.1 (the initials signifying "British Nieuport"), the new fighter was not related to any French Nieuport design and was an equi-span, two-bay, unstaggered biplane powered by a Bentley B.R.2 nine-cylinder rotary engine. Of fabric-covered wooden construction, the B.N.1 carried an armament of two synchronised 0.303-in (7,7-mm) guns and a gun of similar calibre above the wing centre section. Three prototypes were ordered and the first of these was flown early in March 1918. After destruction of the prototype in a crash on the 10th of that month, development was discontinued and the remaining two prototypes were scrapped before completion. *Max speed, 127 mph (204 km/h) at 15,000 ft (4 570 m). Time to 15,000 ft (4 570 m), 16 min. Endurance, 3.0 hrs. Loaded weight, 2,030 lb (921 kg). Span, 28 ft 0 in (8,53 m). Length, 18 ft 6 in (5,64 m). Height, 9 ft 0 in (2,74 m). Wing area, 260 sq ft (24,15 m²).*

The B.N.1 (above and below) bore no relationship to any French Nieuport, being designed by H P Folland.

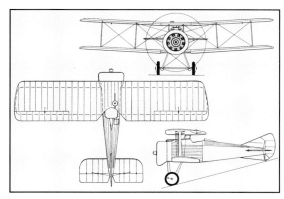

NIEUPORT (& GENERAL) NIGHTHAWK   UK

Work on the Nighthawk single-seat fighter was initiated by H P Folland in May 1918, the aircraft being designed to accept the new A.B.C. Dragonfly nine-cylinder radial engine. Three prototypes were ordered and the decision to proceed with quantity production was taken by the Air Ministry before the first of these had flown. Orders were placed with both the parent company and Gloucestershire Aircraft, but defects

The Nighthawk, the third prototype of which is illustrated (above), evolved into the Sparrowhawk.

with the Dragonfly engine created delays in the programme and a prototype was not flown until after the Armistice. Production Nighthawks from both contractors appeared late in 1919, these being powered by the 320 hp Dragonfly, but none saw service with the RAF. When, in August 1920, Nieuport & General closed down, the rights to the Nighthawk, together with the services of its designer, were acquired by Gloucestershire Aircraft which continued development (see Gloster Sparrowhawk I). *Max speed, 151 mph (243 km/h) at sea level. Time to 10,000 ft (3 050 m), 7.16 min. Endurance, 3.0 hrs. Empty weight, 1,500 lb (680 kg). Loaded weight, 2,218 lb (1 006 kg). Span, 28 ft 0 in (8,53 m). Length, 18 ft 6 in (5,64 m). Height, 9 ft 6 in (2,90 m). Wing area, 276 sq ft (25,64 m²).*

NIKITIN-SHEVCHENKO IS-1   USSR

Perhaps the most innovatory single-seat fighter to undergo flight testing in the late 'thirties was the IS-1. Polymorphic in concept in that it could translate from biplane to monoplane configuration and back again in the air, the IS-1 (*Istrebitel' skladny* or folding fighter) was conceived by Vladimir V Shevchenko and designed in collaboration with Vasili V Nikitin. The IS-1 was intended to take-off as an unequal-span biplane, subsequently retracting its mainwheels pneumatically into the lower wing and then folding this wing (again pneumatically), the centre section into recesses in the fuselage sides and the outer panels into shallow depressions in the upper wing. Theoretically, the lower wing could be extended during combat to increase manoeuvrability. The IS-1 was powered by a 1,100 hp Shvetsov M-63 nine-cylinder radial and carried an armament of four 7,62-mm ShKAS machine guns. Construction was all metal and the prototype was flown for the first time on 6 November 1940, the lower wing being successfully retracted and extended within 7-10 seconds during subsequent trials. Refinement of the basic design for series production had meanwhile re-

The IS-1 (above and below) was the world's first variable-geometry fighter to achieve flight status.

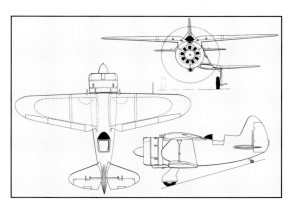

sulted in the IS-2 (which see), only one prototype of the IS-1 being completed. *Max speed, 281 mph (453 km/h) at 16,075 ft (4 900 m). Time to 16,405 ft (5 000 m), 8.2 min. Range, 373 mls (600 km). Empty weight, 3,086 lb (1 400 kg). Loaded weight, 5,070 lb (2 300 kg). Span, 28 ft 2⅜ in (8,60 m). Length, 22 ft 3⅓ in (6,79 m). Wing area (biplane), 224.22 sq ft (20,83 m²), (monoplane), 139.93 sq ft (13,00 m²).*

NIKITIN-SHEVCHENKO IS-2   USSR

Intended as the series version of the IS-1 polymorphic single-seat fighter, the IS-2 embodied some aerodynamic refinement, but, flown early in 1941, did not incorporate the results of the flight testing of its predecessor. The principal changes introduced by the IS-2 were replacement of the M-63 engine by a similarly-rated, but smaller-diameter, Tumansky M-88 14-cylinder radial; replacement of two of the four 7,62-mm guns by 12,7-mm weapons and re-design of the tail surfaces, including introduction of a cantilever tailplane. Realisation that the variable-geometry arrangement would be difficult to maintain under wartime conditions and the fact that battle damage to the actuating mechanism would inevitably prove disastrous, coupled with the comparatively low level speed performance attainable, led to the discontinuation of development of the *Istrebitel' skladny* upon the commencement of the German assault on the Soviet Union. A more advanced model, the IS-4, was abandoned without flight testing. *Estimated max speed, 315 mph (507 km/h). Dimensions as for IS-1 apart from a length of 23 ft 3½ in (7,10 m).*

A refined derivative of the IS-1, the IS-2 (above and below) was discontinued with the German assault.

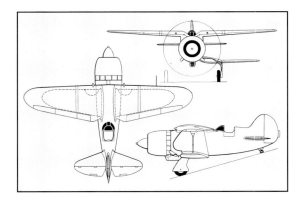

NORD 2200   France

In June 1946, the *Service Technique Aéronautique* issued a preliminary requirement for a shipboard fighter armed with three 20-mm or 30-mm cannon and capable of carrying two 1,102-lb (500-kg) bombs or eight 90-mm rockets. Responding to this requirement, the SNCA du Nord tendered the Nord 2200, designed by a team led by Messrs Coroller, Dupin and Buret, in competition with the Aérocentre NC 1080 and the Arsenal VG 90. Powered by a 5,000 lb st (2 268 kgp) Hispano-Suiza Nene 102 turbojet and featuring a 24-deg swept-back laminar-flow wing with large Fowler-type flaps, the Nord 2200 was first flown on 16 December 1949, and was fitted with neither wing folding nor armament. On 24 June 1950, the sole prototype was damaged and the opportunity was taken to fit a servo control system, introduce redesigned and larger vertical tail surfaces, and make provision for an AI radar scanner over the engine air intake. Flight testing was resumed on 24 May 1951, but in 1952 the decision was taken by the *Aéronavale* to adopt the de Havilland Sea Venom to meet its shipboard fighter requirement. Nevertheless,

(Above and below) The Nord 2200 is illustrated in its definitive form with redesigned intake and tail.

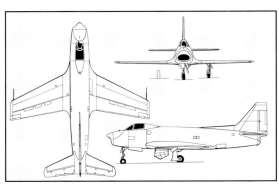

flight testing of the Nord 2200 continued until June 1954. *Max speed, 582 mph (936 km/h) at 16,405 ft (5 000 m). Initial climb, 4,527 ft/min (23 m/sec). Empty weight, 10,648 lb (4 830 kg). Loaded weight, 17,394 lb (7 890 kg). Span, 39 ft 4½ in (12,00 m). Length, 45 ft 7¼ in (13,90 m). Height, 15 ft 9 in (4,80 m). Wing area, 340.15 sq ft (31,60 m²).*

NORTH AMERICAN NA-50   USA

Conceived as a low-cost fighter for use by smaller nations demanding comparatively simple warplanes, yet embodying such modern features as an enclosed cockpit and a retractable undercarriage, the NA-50 was a single-seat derivative of the NA-16 tandem two-seat basic trainer. Of all-metal construction with semi-monocoque fuselage, the NA-50 was powered by an 870 hp Wright R-1820-77 Cyclone radial and carried an armament of two 0.3-in (7,62-mm) machine guns. In January 1938, a contract was placed on behalf of the *Cuerpo de Aeronáutica del Peru* for seven NA-50s, de-

The NA-50 (above and below) saw active service with the Peruvian *Cuerpo de Aeronáutica* during 1941.

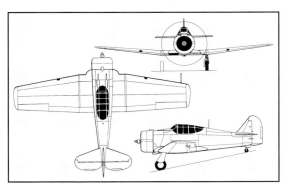

livery being completed in May 1939. In Peruvian service, the NA-50s were equipped with racks for up to 550 lb (249 kg) of bombs, and the type saw active service in 1941 during a conflict with Ecuador. The last Peruvian NA-50 was withdrawn in 1961. *Max speed, 295 mph (475 km/h) at 9,500 ft (2 895 m). Range, 645 mls (1 038 km). Time to 10,000 ft (3 050 m), 3.0 min. Empty weight, 4,470 lb (2 028 kg). Loaded weight, 5,700 lb (2 585 kg). Span, 37 ft 3 in (11,35 m). Length, 26 ft 11⅛ in (8,21 m). Height, 8 ft 9 in (2,67 m). Wing area, 236.09 sq ft (21,93 m²).*

NORTH AMERICAN NA-68 (P-64)   USA

Fundamentally similar to the NA-50, the NA-68 single-seat fighter differed principally in having a longer-chord cowling for its 870 hp Wright R-1820-77 Cyclone engine, redesigned wingtips and tail surfaces similar to those adopted for later production models of the NA-16 two-seat trainer, larger undercarriage fairing doors and heavier armament. Two 20-mm cannon were mounted in underwing fairings and two 0.3-in (7,62-mm) machine guns in the wings. Six NA-68s were ordered for use by the Royal Thai Air Force in November 1939, but these were aboard ship in Hawaii en route to Thailand when the Japanese invaded that country. The NA-68s were promptly sequestered by the US government and returned to the USA. With their cannon armament removed, they were then assigned the advanced fighter training rôle as P-64s. *Max speed, 270 mph (434 km/h) at 8,700 ft (2 650 m). Range, 630 mls (1 014 km). Empty weight, 4,660 lb (2 114 kg). Loaded weight, 5,990 lb (2 717 kg). Span, 37 ft 3 in (11,35 m). Length, 27 ft 0 in (8,23 m). Height, 9 ft 0 in (2,74 m). Wing area, 227.5 sq ft (21,13 m²).*

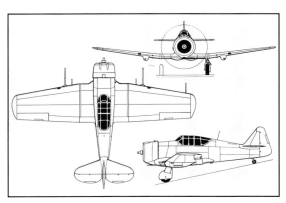

Ordered for the Royal Thai Air Force, the NA-68 (above and below) was sequestered by the USA.

NORTH AMERICAN XP-51 TO P-51A MUSTANG   USA

Design of a single-seat fighter to meet British needs was started by North American Aviation early in 1940, leading to the emergence of one of the most successful and widely produced fighters of World War II. As the NA-73X, a prototype was completed with a 1,150 hp Allison V-1710-F3R engine and first flew on 26 October 1940. Provision was made for an armament of two 0.50-in (12,7-mm) machine guns in the lower front fuselage and one such gun plus two of 0.30-in (7,62-mm) calibre in each wing. As the Mustang I, the UK ordered 620 similar aircraft, the first of these entering service in February 1942. A further 150, supplied under Lend-Lease, had four wing-mounted 20-mm cannon in lieu of machine guns and were designated Mustang IA. The USAAF evaluated two XP-51s, identical with the Mustang I, and then ordered 500 P-51s for use as support dive bombers, these having six 0.50-in (12,7-mm) guns and provision for two 500-lb (227-kg) bombs on the wings. They were redesignated as A-36As before delivery. In addition, the USAAF requisitioned 57 British Mustang IAs, fitted them with cameras in the rear fuselage and used them as F-6As (sometimes referred to as P-51-1s) for tactical reconnaissance. With uprated 1,200 hp Allison V-1710-81 engine, four 0.50-in (12,7-mm) guns in the wings and racks for bombs or long-range tanks, the P-51A followed the A-36A into USAAF

(Above) The NA-73X, the first Mustang prototype, and (immediately below) a P-51A-5 prior to delivery.

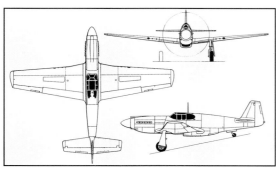

The P-51A (above) for the USAAF was preceded by the A-36A (below) originally ordered as the P-51.

(Above, top to bottom) A P-51A-10 of the CO of the 1st Air Commando Group, Hailakandi, India, March 1944; Mustang I of No 613 Sqn, Ringway, Manchester, 1942;

service, 310 being built, including 50 for the RAF as Mustang IIs. With rear fuselage cameras, some P-51As become F-6Bs. The following data relate to the P-51A. *Max speed, 390 mph (628 km/h) at 20,000 ft (6 100 m); 340 mph (547 km/h) at 5,000 ft (1 525 m). Max range, 1,250 mls (2 011 km) with two drop tanks. Max loaded weight, 10,600 lb (4 812 kg). Span, 37 ft 0 in (11,28 m). Length, 32 ft 3 in (9,83 m). Height, 12 ft 2 in (3,71 m). Wing area, 233 sq ft (21,65 m²).*

NORTH AMERICAN P-51B & P-51C MUSTANG   USA

A version of the P-51 Mustang fitted with a Rolls-Royce Merlin 61-series engine evolved during 1942 through the initiative of the Rolls-Royce company. Five Mustang Is were fitted with Merlins by Rolls-Royce – the first of these (known as Mustang Mk X) flying with a 1,705 hp Merlin 65 and four-bladed propeller on 13 October 1942 – and two P-51s were modified by North

P-51B-5 flown by Don Gentile, 336th FS, 4th FG, Debden, March 1944, and Mustang IIIB of No 316 (Polish) Sqn, Coltishall, June 1944.

American to have 1,298 hp Packard-built Merlin V-1650-3 engines. Initially designated XP-78s, the American prototypes became XP-51Bs, and the first was flown on 30 November 1942. Successful testing led to the adoption of the Packard Merlin for all subsequent Mustang production, with the P-51B as the first variant.

The first Merlin-engined Mustang (above), known as the Mustang Mk X, and (below) the first of two Merlin-engined XP-51B Mustang prototypes.

Generally similar to the P-51A, the P-51B could carry a 1,000-lb (454-kg) bomb on each wing and had increased fuel capacity. Starting in 1943, North American delivered 1,988 P-51Bs from its Inglewood, Los Angeles, factory and 1,750 similar P-51Cs from a factory at Dallas, Texas. Of the total, 274 P-51Bs and 636 P-51Cs went to the RAF as Mustang IIIs, and 91 others became F-6Cs when fitted with oblique cameras behind the cockpit.

The following data relate to the P-51B with V-1650-3 engine (later aircraft having the V-1650-7). *Max speed, 440 mph (708 km/h) at 30,000 ft (9 145 m), 424 mph (682 km/h) at 15,000 ft (4 572m). Max range, 1,600 mls (2 575 km) with two drop tanks. Empty weight, 7,450 lb (3 380 kg). Max loaded weight, 11,200 lb (5 080 kg). Span, 37 ft 0 in (11,28 m). Length, 32 ft 3 in (9,83 m). Height, 13 ft 8 in (4,16 m). Wing area, 233 sq ft (21,65 m²).*

(Right) A P-51C-1 built at the Dallas factory.

NORTH AMERICAN P-51D & P-51K MUSTANG
USA

To improve the pilot's view downwards and to the rear, many P-51Bs and Cs (see previous entry) were fitted with bulged cockpit hoods developed in Britain. North American adopted a more radical means to achieve a similar result by cutting-down the rear fuselage and fitting a 360-deg vision tear-drop canopy on the next major production version, the P-51D. Armament remained unchanged, with six 0.50-in (12,7-mm) guns in

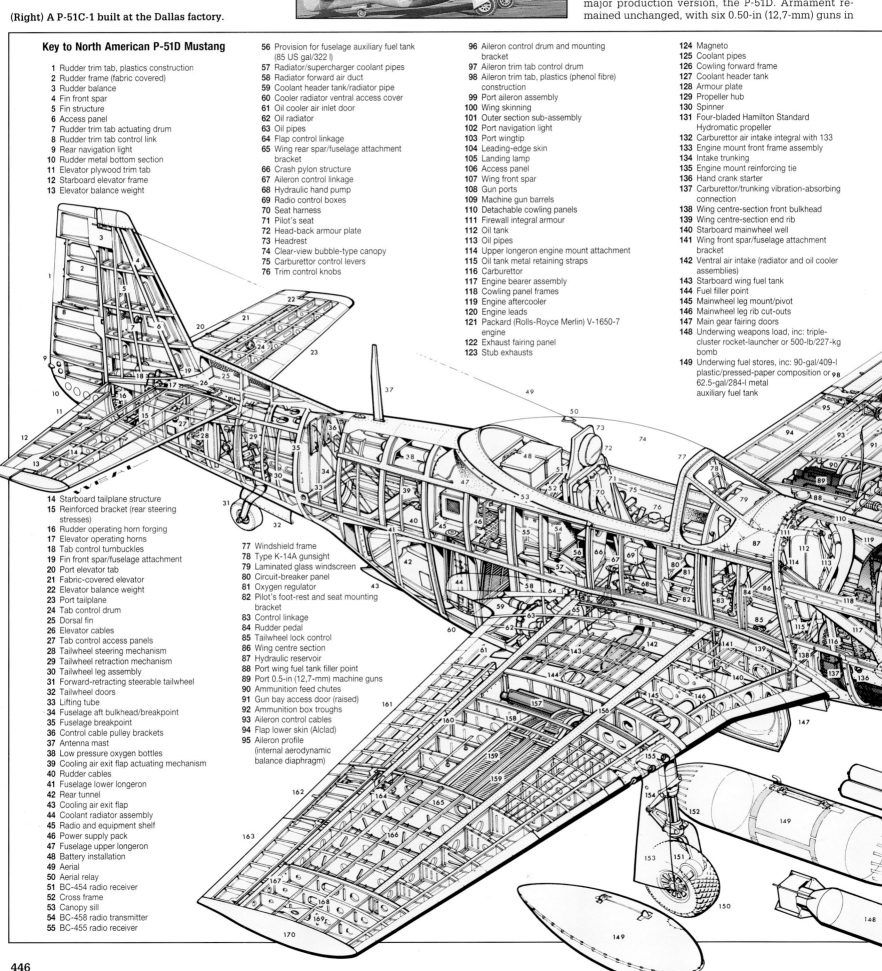

Key to North American P-51D Mustang

1 Rudder trim tab, plastics construction
2 Rudder frame (fabric covered)
3 Rudder balance
4 Fin front spar
5 Fin structure
6 Access panel
7 Rudder trim tab actuating drum
8 Rudder trim tab control link
9 Rear navigation light
10 Rudder metal bottom section
11 Elevator plywood trim tab
12 Starboard elevator frame
13 Elevator balance weight
14 Starboard tailplane structure
15 Reinforced bracket (rear steering stresses)
16 Rudder operating horn forging
17 Elevator operating horns
18 Tab control turnbuckles
19 Fin front spar/fuselage attachment
20 Port elevator tab
21 Fabric-covered elevator
22 Elevator balance weight
23 Port tailplane
24 Tab control drum
25 Dorsal fin
26 Elevator cables
27 Tab control access panels
28 Tailwheel steering mechanism
29 Tailwheel retraction mechanism
30 Tailwheel leg assembly
31 Forward-retracting steerable tailwheel
32 Tailwheel doors
33 Lifting tube
34 Fuselage aft bulkhead/breakpoint
35 Fuselage breakpoint
36 Control cable pulley brackets
37 Antenna mast
38 Low pressure oxygen bottles
39 Cooling air exit flap actuating mechanism
40 Rudder cables
41 Fuselage lower longeron
42 Rear tunnel
43 Cooling air exit flap
44 Coolant radiator assembly
45 Radio and equipment shelf
46 Power supply pack
47 Fuselage upper longeron
48 Battery installation
49 Aerial
50 Aerial relay
51 BC-454 radio receiver
52 Cross frame
53 Canopy sill
54 BC-458 radio transmitter
55 BC-455 radio receiver

56 Provision for fuselage auxiliary fuel tank (85 US gal/322 l)
57 Radiator/supercharger coolant pipes
58 Radiator forward air duct
59 Coolant header tank/radiator pipe
60 Cooler radiator ventral access cover
61 Oil cooler air inlet door
62 Oil radiator
63 Oil pipes
64 Flap control linkage
65 Wing rear spar/fuselage attachment bracket
66 Crash pylon structure
67 Aileron control linkage
68 Hydraulic hand pump
69 Radio control boxes
70 Seat harness
71 Pilot's seat
72 Head-back armour plate
73 Headrest
74 Clear-view bubble-type canopy
75 Carburettor control levers
76 Trim control knobs
77 Windshield frame
78 Type K-14A gunsight
79 Laminated glass windscreen
80 Circuit-breaker panel
81 Oxygen regulator
82 Pilot's foot-rest and seat mounting bracket
83 Control linkage
84 Rudder pedal
85 Tailwheel lock control
86 Wing centre section
87 Hydraulic reservoir
88 Port wing fuel tank filler point
89 Port 0.5-in (12,7-mm) machine guns
90 Ammunition feed chutes
91 Gun bay access door (raised)
92 Ammunition box troughs
93 Aileron control cables
94 Flap lower skin (Alclad)
95 Aileron profile (internal aerodynamic balance diaphragm)

96 Aileron control drum and mounting bracket
97 Aileron trim tab control drum
98 Aileron trim tab, plastics (phenol fibre) construction
99 Port aileron assembly
100 Wing skinning
101 Outer section sub-assembly
102 Port navigation light
103 Port wingtip
104 Leading-edge skin
105 Landing lamp
106 Access panel
107 Wing front spar
108 Gun ports
109 Machine gun barrels
110 Detachable cowling panels
111 Firewall integral armour
112 Oil tank
113 Oil pipes
114 Upper longeron engine mount attachment
115 Oil tank metal retaining straps
116 Carburettor
117 Engine bearer assembly
118 Cowling panel frames
119 Engine aftercooler
120 Engine leads
121 Packard (Rolls-Royce Merlin) V-1650-7 engine
122 Exhaust fairing panel
123 Stub exhausts

124 Magneto
125 Coolant pipes
126 Cowling forward frame
127 Coolant header tank
128 Armour plate
129 Propeller hub
130 Spinner
131 Four-bladed Hamilton Standard Hydromatic propeller
132 Carburettor air intake integral with 133
133 Engine mount front frame assembly
134 Intake trunking
135 Engine mount reinforcing tie
136 Hand crank starter
137 Carburettor/trunking vibration-absorbing connection
138 Wing centre-section front bulkhead
139 Wing centre-section end rib
140 Starboard mainwheel well
141 Wing front spar/fuselage attachment bracket
142 Ventral air intake (radiator and oil cooler assemblies)
143 Starboard wing fuel tank
144 Fuel filler point
145 Mainwheel leg mount/pivot
146 Mainwheel leg rib cut-outs
147 Main gear fairing doors
148 Underwing weapons load, inc: triple-cluster rocket-launcher or 500-lb/227-kg bomb
149 Underwing fuel stores, inc: 90-gal/409-l plastic/pressed-paper composition or 62.5-gal/284-l metal auxiliary fuel tank

(Above) A P-51D-25 of South Korean 10th Fighter Wing at Seoul, Korea, *circa* 1954.

(Above) A Guatemalan P-51D (F-51D), *circa* 1960, and (below) a P-51K-5 built at NA's Dallas facility.

150 27-in (68,6-cm) smooth-contour
    mainwheel
151 Axle fork
152 Towing lugs
153 Landing gear fairing
154 Main gear shock strut
155 Blast tubes
156 Wing front spar
157 Gun bay
158 Ammunition feed chutes
159 Ammunition boxes
160 Wing rear spar
161 Flap structure
162 Starboard aileron tab
163 Starboard aileron
164 Starboard aileron tab adjustment
    mechanism (ground setting)
165 Wing rib strengthening
166 Outboard section structure
167 Outer section single spar
168 Wingtip sub-assembly
169 Starboard navigation light
170 Detachable wingtip

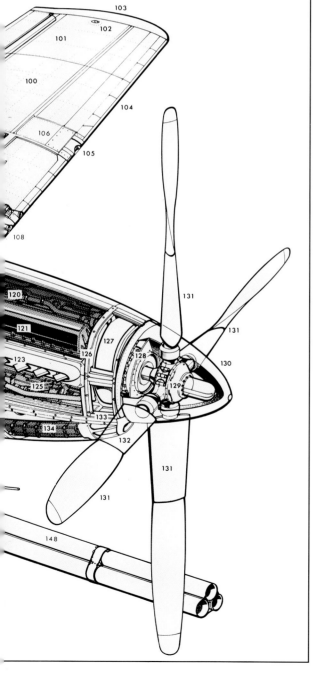

the wings, and like late-production P-51B/Cs, the P-51D used a 1,450 hp V-1650-7 Merlin with a Hamilton Standard four-bladed propeller. The XP-51D prototype, a modified P-51B, made its first flight on 17 November 1943. Production of the P-51D totalled 6,502 at Inglewood and 1,454 at Dallas, where a further 1,337 similar aircraft with Aeroproducts propellers were built as P-51Ks. For the RAAF, Commonwealth Aircraft Corporation in Australia produced P-51Ds under licence, comprising 80 CA-17 Mustang Mk 20s (from imported sets of components) with V-1650-3 engines, 26 CA-18 Mustang 21s with V-1650-7s, 28 Mustang 22s with fuselage-mounted oblique cameras and 66 Mustang 23s with British-built Merlin 70 engines. The RAAF also received 299 P-51Ds and Ks from US production. The following data relate to the P-51D. *Max speed, 437 mph (703 km/h) at 25,000 ft (7 625 m) and 395 mph (636 km/h) at 5,000 ft (1 525 m). Max range, 1,650 mls (2 655 km) with two drop tanks. Empty weight, 7,635 lb (3 466 kg). Max loaded weight, 12,100 lb (5 493 kg). Span, 37 ft 0 in (11,28 m). Length, 32 ft 3 in (9,83 m). Height, 13 ft 8 in (4,16 m). Wing area, 233 sq ft (21,65 m²).*

A Mustang 21 (above) built in Australia under licence by Commonwealth Aircraft Corporation.

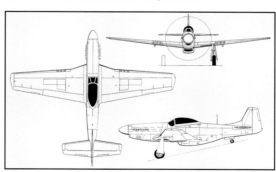

A general arrangement drawing of the P-51D (above) and (below) a P-51D-5 of 374th FS, 361st FG, 1944.

NORTH AMERICAN XP-51F, XP-51G & XP-51J MUSTANG   USA

(Above) The XP-51F and (below) the XP-51G were similar Merlin-engined lightweight developments of the P-51D Mustang that were both flown during 1944.

The XP-51F was developed as a lightweight version of the P-51D to gain improved performance with the same V-1650-7 engine. Changes included the use of some plastics, removal of some items of equipment, smaller wheel wells in the wing (and smaller wheels), reduced fuel capacity and reduced armament of four 0.50-in (12,7-mm) guns. Three XP-51Fs were built (first flight 14 February 1944) and two similar XP-51Gs (first flight 10 August 1944) had Merlin 145 engines and Rotol five-bladed propellers. Two XP-51Js (first flight 23 April 1945) were also similar to the XP-51F, but powered by the 1,500 hp Allison V-1710-119 engine and with the carburettor air intake moved to the ventral radiator to elim-

447

inate the P-51's usual "lip" beneath the spinner. The following data relate to the XP-51F. *Max speed, 466 mph (750 km/h) at 29,000 ft (8 840 m). Range, 650 mls (1 046 km) without drop tanks. Empty weight, 5,635 lb (2 556 kg). Max take-off weight, 9,060 lb (4 110 kg). Dimensions, as P-51D.*

(Above) The Merlin-engined XP-51G, and (below) the V-1710-powered but otherwise similar XP-51J.

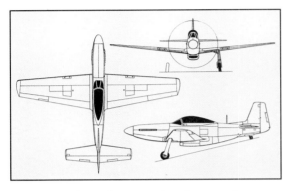

Two XP-51Js (below) were produced as part of a programme aimed at evolving a lightweight Mustang.

NORTH AMERICAN
P-51H & P-51M MUSTANG   USA

The P-51H was the final series production version of the Mustang, a P-51H-5 being illustrated above.

Based on testing of the XP-51F (see previous entry), the P-51H was put into production at North American's Inglewood factory in 1944, and 555 were built, the first flight being made on 3 February 1945. The engine was the 2,218 hp (war emergency rating) Packard V-1650-9 with an Aeroproducts propeller, and armament was four or six 0.50-in (12,7-mm) guns plus underwing bombs or rockets. A taller fin and rudder distinguished the P-51H externally. The P-51M, built at Dallas, was a variant similar to the P-51H and fitted with a V-1650-9A Merlin engine, but only one was delivered before cancellation of contracts at the end of the war. The P-51L was to have been the P-51H fitted with the V-1610-11 engine with direct fuel injection, but was cancelled before any had been built. The following data relate to the P-51H. *Max speed, 487 mph (783 km/h) at 25,000 ft (7 620 m), 463 mph (745 km/h) at 15,000 ft (4 572 m). Range, 1,160 mls (1 866 km) with two drop tanks. Empty weight, 7,040 lb (3 193 kg). Max take-off weight, 11,500 lb (5 221 kg) with two 1,000 lb (454 kg) bombs.*

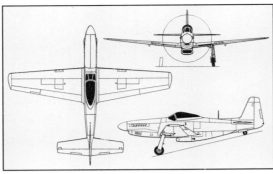

The P-51H (above and below) embodied experience gained with its lightweight predecessors.

Span, 37 ft 0 in (11,28 m). Length, 33 ft 4 in (10,16 m). Height, 11 ft 1 in (3,37 m). Wing area, 235 sq ft (21,83 m²).

NORTH AMERICAN F-82E
TWIN MUSTANG   USA

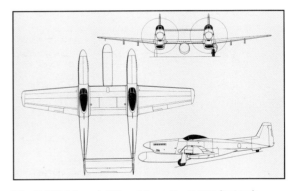

The twin fuselages of the XP-82 (above) were basically similar to that of the P-51H Mustang.

Despite its name, the Twin Mustang was far from being just two Mustangs joined by a new centre wing. North American did save time and money, however, with the concept of using P-51 power plant and other components to produce a two-seat twin-engined escort fighter. Such an aircraft was needed by the USAAF to accompany B-29s on late-World War II missions against Japan, and three prototypes of the NA-120 design were ordered: two as XP-82s with Packard Merlin V-1650-23/25 engines and one as an XP-82A with Allison V-1710-119s. All three flew in 1945, the first on 6 July, but a contract for 500 P-82Bs was cancelled after 20 had been built, these being delivered early in 1946. In October 1946, the USAF reinstated a contract for 100 of the fighters as F-82Es – similar to the P-82B – to serve in Strategic Air Command as escort fighters for B-50s. Delivered in 1948, they were the last piston-engined day fighters to enter USAF service, but were phased out in

(Above) The second of two Merlin-engined XP-82s which entered flight test in the second half of 1945.

1950. Powered by 1,600 hp V-1710-143/145 engines, the F-82E was armed with six 0.50-in (12,7-mm) Browning machine guns and could carry 4,000 lb (1 814 kg) of bombs externally. *Max speed, 460 mph (740 km/h) at 20,000 ft (6 100 m). Rate of climb, 4,020 ft/min (20,4 m/sec). Service ceiling, 29,800 ft (9 083 m). Combat radius, 1,125 mls (1 810 km) at sea level. Empty weight, 14,914 lb (6 765 kg). Normal loaded weight, 24,864 lb (11 278 kg). Span, 51 ft 3 in (15,62 m). Length, 39 ft 1½ in (11,92 m). Height, 13 ft 10 in (4,22 m). Wing area, 408 sq ft (37,90 m²).*

NORTH AMERICAN F-82F
& F-82G TWIN MUSTANG   USA

To fill a gap between the Northrop P-61 and forthcoming jet night fighters, USAF instructed North American in 1946 to adapt the Twin Mustang for the night/all-weather rôle. In this guise, the aircraft carried air intercept radar in a pod under the centre section and a radar operator in place of the second pilot. Two P-82Bs were modified in 1946 to P-82C and P-82D, respectively with SCR-720 and APS-4 radar, to serve as prototypes, and North American then built 100 F-82Fs with AN/APG-28 and 50 F-82Gs with SCR-720C. Both models were powered by 1,600 hp V-1710-143/145 engines and carried an armament of six Browning guns. Night fighter

The F-82G (above) differed from the F-82F (below) solely in the type of radar installed in the pod.

The F-82F (above and below) was the principal night fighter version of the Twin Mustang.

(Above) An F-82G of the 4th Fighter Sqn, 347th FG (All-Weather) at Naha AB, Okinawa, 1949.

Twin Mustangs equipped nine All-Weather Squadrons in the USAF's Air Defence Command, and saw some combat in Korea. Fourteen F-82Hs were winterised F and G models for operation in Alaska. The following data relate to the F-82G. *Max speed, 456 mph (734 km/h) at 21,000 ft (6 400 m). Rate of climb, 3,770 ft/min (19,15 m/sec). Service ceiling, 28,300 ft (8 626 m). Combat radius, 1,015 mls (1 634 km) at sea level. Empty weight, 15,997 lb (7 256 kg). Normal loaded weight, 25,891 lb (11 744 kg). Span, 51 ft 7 in (15,73 m). Length, 42 ft 2½ in (12,86 m). Height, 13 ft 10 in (4,22 m). Wing area, 408 sq ft (37,90 m²).*

NORTH AMERICAN FJ-1 FURY USA

Against a US Navy contract issued on 1 January 1945, North American Aviation built three prototypes of its NA-134 design for a straight-wing fighter, the company's first to use gas turbine propulsion, as the XFJ-1.

The FJ-1 (above and below), the first production aircraft being illustrated by the photograph.

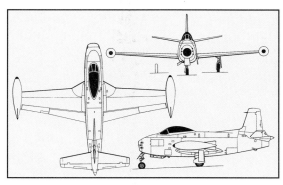

Powered by a 3,820 lb st (1 733 kgp) General Electric J35-GE-2, the first XFJ-1 flew on 27 November 1946. A Navy contract for 100 was cut back to 30, production FJ-1s being named Fury and powered by the 4,000 lb st (1 814 kgp) Allison J35-A-2. Navy Fighter Squadron VF-5A (later VF-51) equipped on the FJ-1 as the first jet fighter unit to go to sea under operational conditions, making the first carrier landings on 10 March 1948, but the type remained in the frontline inventory for only 14 months. The armament of the FJ-1 comprised six 0.50-in (12,7-mm) machine guns in the wings. *Max speed, 547 mph (880 km/h) at 9,000 ft (2 743 m). Rate of*

An FJ-1 (below) flown by VF-51 (previously VF-5A) from NAS San Diego in 1949.

climb, 3,300 ft/min (16,8 m/sec). Service ceiling, 32,000 ft (9 754 m). Range, 1,500 mls (2 414 km). Empty weight, 8,843 lb (4 100 kg). Loaded weight, 15,600 lb (7 076 kg). Span, 38 ft 2 in (11,63 m). Length, 34 ft 5 in (10,48 m). Height, 14 ft 10 in (4,52m). Wing area, 221 sq ft (20,53 m²).

A US Naval Air Reserve FJ-1 (below) based at NAS Oakland, California, for training tasks in 1951.

NORTH AMERICAN F-86A SABRE USA

First flown on 1 October 1947, the North American XP-86 (NA-140) was the prototype of the first swept-wing jet fighter to enter production and service with the USAF. Powered by a 3,750 lb st (1 700 kgp) Allison J35-C-3 turbojet, the XP-86 had a pressurised cockpit

The F-86A (above and below) was the first swept-wing jet fighter to achieve service with the USAF.

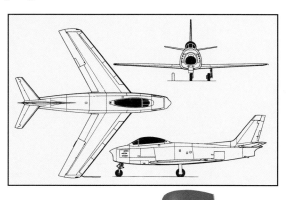

and wing sweepback of 35 deg, its design benefitting from information on German research during World War II. To be named Sabre when put into production against an initial USAF contract for 221 F-86As, the aircraft was designed to carry six 0.50-in (12,7-mm) machine guns in the nose, with rockets or bombs on the wings. Production aircraft, the first of which flew on 18 May 1948, were powered by 5,200 lb st (2 359 kgp) J47-GE-3, -7, -9 or -13 engines and entered service in 1949. Production of the F-86A totalled 554 aircraft. *Max speed, 601 mph (967 km/h) at 35,000 ft (10 670 m). Rate of climb, 7,470 ft/min (37,9 m/sec). Service ceiling, 48,000 ft (14 630 m). Combat radius, 330 mls (531 km). Empty weight, 10,536 lb (4 780 kg). Loaded weight, 16,223 lb (7 359 kg). Span, 37 ft 1½ in (11,31 m). Length, 37 ft 6 in (11,43 m). Height, 14 ft 9 in (4,50 m). Wing area, 287.9 sq ft (26,75 m²).*

NORTH AMERICAN F-86D SABRE USA

Conceived as an all-weather derivative of the F-86A day fighter, the F-86D retained, in the event, barely 25 per cent commonality and was briefly redesignated F-95A. Conceptually sophisticated in that all previous all-weather fighters had carried two crew members and in relinquishing the classic gun armament in favour of rockets, the first of two YF-86D prototypes flew on 22 December 1949. The first production F-86D was accepted by the USAF in March 1951, but development problems delayed service introduction until 1953.

The F-86D (above and below), the photo depicting an F-86D-45 of the 406th FIW at RAF Manston, 1957.

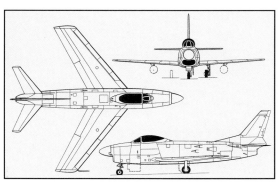

Armament comprised 24 2.75-in (70-mm) rockets in a retractable missile tray (later to be augmented by two AIM-9 Sidewinder AAMs) and power was initially provided by a General Electric J47-GE-17 turbojet rated at 5,000 lb st (2 268 kgp) boosted to 6,650 lb st (3 026 kgp) with afterburning. This engine gave place successively (in the D-40 block) to the -17B of 5,425 lb st (2 460 kgp) and 7,500 lb st (3 402 kgp), and (late in the D-45 block) to the J47-GE-33 of 5,550 lb st (2 517 kgp) and 7,650 lb st (3 470 kgp). Production was completed in September 1955, a total of 2,504 having been built. The

Converted from an F-86D, the aircraft below is an F-86L-55 of No 12 Sqn, 1 Wing, Royal Thai Air Force.

NORTH AMERICAN YF-93A   USA

Initially designated F-86C, the YF-93A was intended as a deep penetration escort fighter derivative of the F-86A to meet the same requirement as that to which the Lockheed XF-90 and McDonnell XF-88 were developed. Only the wings of the F-86A were retained by

The YF-93A (below) was a deep penetration escort fighter retaining the wings of the F-86 Sabre.

transfer of ex-USAF aircraft to foreign nations began in 1958, recipients being Denmark (56), Japan (114), Greece (50), Philippines (18), Yugoslavia (130), South Korea and Nationalist China, the last F-86D being withdrawn from service (by Yugoslavia) in 1974. The following data relate to the F-86D-45. *Max speed, 693 mph (1 115 km/h) at sea level, 616 mph (991 km/h) at 40,000 ft (12 190 m). Initial climb, 12,000 ft/min (60,96 m/sec).*

An F-86D-35 of the *Eskadrille* 726 of the Royal Danish Air Force at Aalborg during 1959-65 (above).

Range (internal fuel), 554 mls (890 km). Empty weight, 13,498 lb (6 123 kg). Normal loaded weight, 18,160 lb (8 237 kg). Span, 37 ft 1½ in (11,31 m). Length, 40 ft 3¼ in (12,27 m). Height, 15 ft 0 in (4,57 m). Wing area, 287.9 sq ft (26,75 m²).

Key to North American F-86E Sabre

1 Radome
2 Radar antenna
3 Engine air intake
4 Gun camera
5 Nosewheel leg doors
6 Nose undercarriage leg strut
7 Nosewheel
8 Torque scissor links
9 Steering control valve
10 Nose undercarriage pivot fixing
11 Sight amplifier
12 Radio and electronics equipment bay
13 Electronics bay access panel
14 Battery
15 Gun muzzle blast troughs
16 Oxygen bottles
17 Nosewheel bay door
18 Oxygen servicing point
19 Canopy switches
20 Machine gun barrel mountings
21 Hydraulic system test connections
22 Radio transmitter
23 Cockpit armoured bulkhead
24 Windscreen panels
25 A-1CM radar gunsight
26 Instrument panel shroud
27 Instrument panel
28 Control column
29 Kick-in boarding step
30 Used cartridge case collector box
31 Ammunition boxes (267 rounds per gun)
32 Ammunition feed chutes
33 0.5-in (12,7-mm) Colt-Browning machine guns
34 Engine throttle
35 Starboard side console panel
36 North American ejection seat
37 Rear view mirror
38 Sliding cockpit canopy cover
39 Ejection seat headrest
40 ADF sense aerials
41 Pilot's back armour
42 Ejection seat guide rails
43 Canopy handle

44 Cockpit pressure valves
45 Armoured side panels
46 Tailplane trim actuator
47 Fuselage/front spar main frame
48 Forward fuselage fuel tank (total internal fuel capacity 362 Imp gal/1 644 l)
49 Fuselage lower longeron
50 Intake trunking
51 Rear radio and electronics bay
52 Canopy emergency release handle
53 ADF loop aerial
54 Cockpit pressure relief valve
55 Starboard wing fuel tank
56 Leading edge slat guide rails
57 Starboard automatic leading edge slat, open
58 Cable drive to aileron actuator
59 Pitot tube

60 Starboard navigation light
61 Wing tip fairing
62 Starboard aileron
63 Aileron hydraulic control unit
64 Aileron balance
65 Starboard slotted flap, down position
66 Flap guide rail
67 Upward identification light
68 Air conditioning plant
69 Intake fairing starter/generator
70 Fuselage/rear spar main frame
71 Hydraulic system reservoirs
72 Longeron/main frame joint
73 Fuel filler de-icing fluid tank

74 Cooling air outlet
75 Engine equipment access panel
76 Heat exchanger exhaust duct
77 Engine suspension links
78 Fuselage skin plating
79 Engine withdrawal rail
80 Starboard side oil tank (4.75 Imp gal/21,6 l)
81 General Electric J47-GE-13 turbojet
82 Bleed air system primary heat exchanger
83 Ground power connections
84 Fuel filler cap
85 Fuselage break point sloping frame (engine removal)
86 Upper longeron joint
87 Engine bay cooling air duct
88 Cooling air outlet
89 Engine firewall bulkhead
90 Engine flame cans
91 Rear fuselage framing
92 Fuel jettison pipe
93 Fuselage top longeron
94 Fin/tailplane root fillet fairing
95 Control cable duct
96 Fin spar attachment joint
97 Tailplane/rudder control cables
98 All-moving tailplane hydraulic jack
99 Tailfin construction
100 Flush HF aerial panel

101 Starboard tailplane
102 Fin tip di-electric aerial fairing
103 VHF aerial
104 Rudder construction
105 Rudder trim tab
106 Tail navigation light
107 Port elevator/tailplane flap
108 All-moving tailplane construction
109 Engine exhaust nozzle
110 Fuel jettison
111 Heat shrouded jet pipe
112 Power control compensator
113 Emergency hydraulic valves
114 Airbrake housing
115 Airbrake hydraulic jack
116 Port airbrake, open
117 Hydraulic system emergency pump
118 Cooling air intake
119 Lower longeron joint
120 Trailing-edge root fillet
121 Aft main fuel tank
122 Main undercarriage wheel bay
123 Hydraulic retraction jack

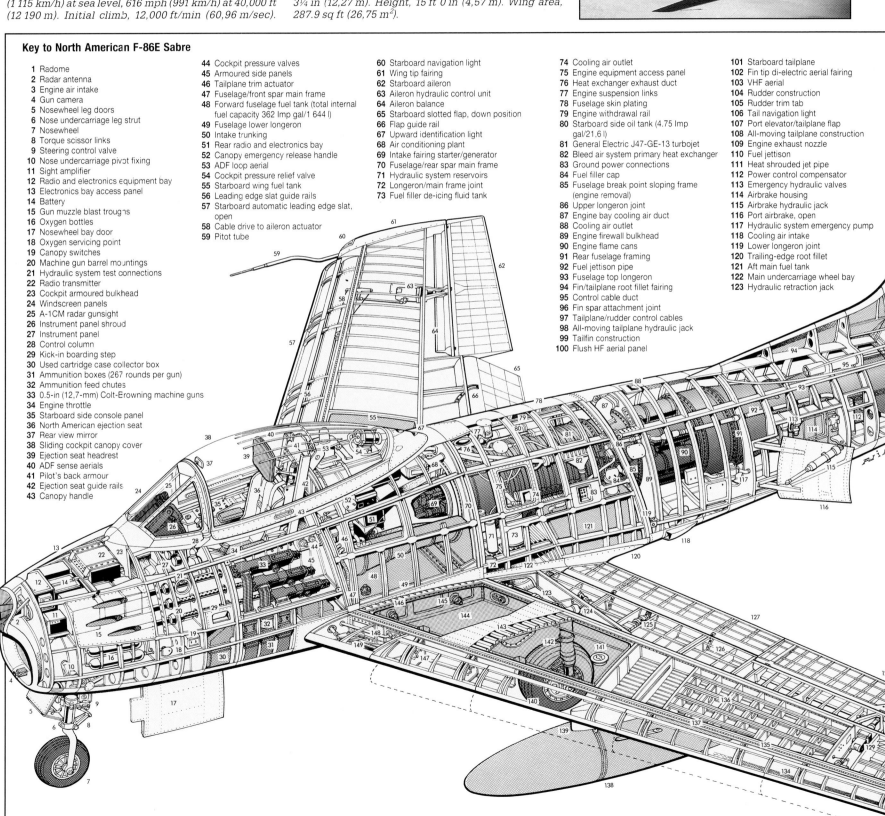

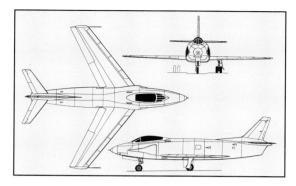

(Above) The YF-93A deep penetration fighter.

the YF-93A, these being mated with an entirely new and enlarged fuselage accommodating additional fuel,

124 Main undercarriage pivot fixing
125 Hydraulic flap jack
126 Flap shroud ribs
127 Port slotted flap
128 Port aileron construction
129 Aileron hydraulic power control unit
130 Gyrosyn compass remote transmitter
131 Wing tip fairing
132 Port navigation light
133 Port automatic leading-edge slat open position
134 Leading-edge slat rib construction
135 Front spar
136 Wing rib and stringer construction
137 Wing skin/leading-edge piano hinge attachment joint
138 100-Imp gal (454-l) drop tank
139 Drop tank pylon
140 Port mainwheel
141 Fuel filler cap
142 Main undercarriage leg strut
143 Fuel tank bay corrugated double skin
144 Port wing fuel tank
145 Tank interconnectors
146 Skin panel attachment joint strap
147 Slat guide rails
148 Fuel feed pipe
149 Aileron cable drive

a Pratt & Whitney J48-P-1 turbojet of 6,000 lb st (2 722 kgp) and 8,000 lb st (3 629 kgp) with afterburning, and an armament of six 20-mm cannon. One hundred and eight F-93As were ordered in June 1948, but cancelled six months later, and the first of two YF-93As was flown on 25 January 1950. Both prototypes were eventually transferred to the NACA for comparison tests between the original flush air intakes and enlarged scoop-type air intakes. *Max speed, 708 mph (1 139 km/h) at sea level, 622 mph (1 000 km/h) at 35,000 ft (10 670 m). Initial climb, 11,960 ft/min (60,75 m/sec). Range, 1,967 mls (3 165 km). Empty weight, 14,035 lb (6 366 kg). Normal loaded weight, 21,610 lb (9 802 kg). Span, 38 ft 11 in (11,86 m). Length, 44 ft 1 in (13,43 m). Height, 15 ft 8 in (4,77 m). Wing area, 306 sq ft (28,43 m²).*

NORTH AMERICAN
F-86E SABRE
USA

A Canadair-built CL-13 Sabre 2 (above) of No 441 Sqn, No 1 Wing, RCAF, North Luffenham, 1952.

By the time that the last F-86A was completed in December 1950, production of the Sabre day fighter had given place to the F-86E, the first example of which had flown on 23 September 1950. In most respects identical to the late production F-86A and retaining the J47-GE-13 engine of 5,200 lb st (2 359 kgp), the F-86E differed essentially in having an all-flying tail. A total of 336 F-86E Sabres was built by the parent company, the prime production source being Canadair. The Canadian company applied the designation CL-13 Sabre 2 to the licence-built F-86E-6 (the Sabre 1 being a single F-86A-5 assembled by Canadair), the first being flown on 31 January 1951. One example was completed as a Sabre 3 with a 6,000 lb st (2 722 kgp) Avro Orenda 3, this being the 100th Canadian-built aircraft – see Canadair CL-13 Sabre. A total of 350 Sabre 2s was followed by 438 Sabre 4s, the first of these being flown on 28 August 1952 and differing from preceding aircraft solely in having improved air conditioning. The Sabre 2 entered RCAF service in the spring of 1951, all but 60 diverted to the USAF being assigned to that air arm. In 1954-55 most of the RCAF Sabre 2s were transferred under MDAP to the Greek and Turkish air arms which received 104 and 105 respectively. Meanwhile, during 1952-53, 431 Sabre 4s were delivered to the RAF under MDAP, these serving until 1955-56 when the surviving aircraft were reassigned to Italy (180) and Yugoslavia (121) as F-86E(M) Sabres. *Max speed, 679 mph*

(Immediately below) F-86F-35 of Norwegian *Skvadron* 336, Gardermoen, 1959, and (bottom) F-86E(M) of Italian 4° *Stormo*, Pratica di Mare, late 'fifties.

(1 093 km/h) at sea level, 601 mph (967 km/h) at 35,000 ft (10 670 m). Initial climb, 7,250 ft/min (36,83 m/sec). Empty weight, 10,845 lb (4 919 kg). Loaded weight, 17,806 lb (8 077 kg). Dimensions as for F-86A.

NORTH AMERICAN
FJ-2 FURY
USA

Despite its designation and retention of the name Fury, the FJ-2 bore no design relationship to the earlier FJ-1, being essentially a navalised F-86 Sabre. The first of three prototypes converted from F-86E airframes was flown on 27 December 1951 as the XFJ-2B, this having an armament of four 20-mm cannon, an A-frame arrester hook and catapult spools. The second (without armament) and third (with six 0.5-in/12,7-mm guns) prototypes featured a lengthened nosewheel leg and were designated as XFJ-2s, and 300 FJ-2s were ordered (this subsequently being cut back to 200) with acceptances commencing in November 1952. The FJ-2 was powered by a 6,000 lb st (2 722 kgp) General Electric J47-GE-2 engine, carried an armament of four 20-mm cannon and featured folding wings, a modified undercarriage, catapult and arrester gear. Production was completed in September 1954, and all were delivered to the USMC for operation from shore bases. At a later stage, the gun armament was augmented by a pair of AIM-9 Sidewinder AAMs. *Max speed, 676 mph (1 088 km/h) at sea level, 602 mph (969 km/h) at 35,000 ft (10 670 m). Initial climb, 7,230 ft/min (36,73 m/sec). Range (two 200-US gal/757-l drop tanks), 990 mls*

(Above) The first XFJ-2 leaving the carrier *Coral Sea* in November 1952, and (below) the 19th series FJ-2 prior to delivery from NA's Columbus plant.

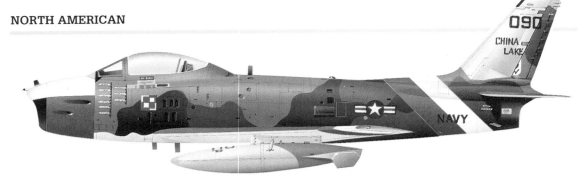

Adapted from an F-86H-5, this QF-86H target drone (above) served at the US Naval Weapon Center.

(1 593 km). Empty weight, 11,802 lb (5 353 kg). Loaded weight (with drop tanks), 18,791 lb (8 524 kg). Span, 37 ft 1½ in (11,31 m). Length, 37 ft 7 in (11,45 m). Height, 13 ft 7 in (4,14 m). Wing area, 287.9 sq ft (26,75 m²).

NORTH AMERICAN
F-86F SABRE USA

Flown for the first time on 19 March 1952, and destined to be numerically the most important of the Sabre day fighters, the F-86F differed fundamentally from the preceding F-86E in having a 5,910 lb st (2 681 kgp) J47-GE-27 engine, progressive changes being introduced during the production run which terminated (insofar as the parent company was concerned) on 28 December 1956. The principal of these changes were the introduction of 200-US gal (757-l) drop tanks (from F-86F-20), a dual-store wing (from F-86F-30) with additional hardpoints enabling two drop tanks or other stores to be carried beneath each wing, and a new non-slatted wing leading edge (introduced with the 171st F-25 and 200th F-30). Deletion of the slats and extension of the leading edge, increasing wing area by 14.4 sq ft (1,34 m²), improved both high-altitude manoeuvrability and Mach numbers at some cost to low-speed characteristics.

An F-86F-30 (above) of the 334th FIS, the F-series being numerically the most important of the Sabres.

Production terminated in 1954, but was reinstated in the following year to fulfil additional MDAP Sabre commitments with the F-86F-40, this reverting to wing slats which were added to the extended wing leading edge and combined with 1-ft (0,30-m) wing-tip extensions. These changes were applied retrospectively to

An F-86F-35 of the USAF's *Skyblazers* aerobatic team (below) over France in October 1955.

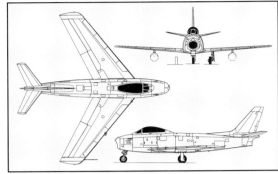

(Above) F-86F-40, the definitive F-series model.

all F-86F-25s and -30s. Production by the parent company totalled 1,539 aircraft, a further 300 (F-86F-40s) being assembled in Japan by Mitsubishi from component sets, the first of these flying on 9 August 1956. From 1954, the delivery of ex-USAF F-86Fs began under the MDAP, one of the first recipients being Nationalist China which received 320 plus seven converted for reconnaissance as RF-86Fs. Other nations to receive the F-86F included Argentina (28), Iraq (5), Japan (180 of which 45 returned to the USAF), Norway (90), Pakistan (120), Peru (14), Philippines (40), Portugal (50), South Korea (112 plus 10 RF-86Fs), Spain (244), Thailand (47), Turkey (12) and Venezuela (22). A derivative of the F-86F with Rolls-Royce Avon engine was built in Australia by CAC (which see). The following data relate to the definitive F-86F-40. *Max speed, 678 mph (1 091 km/h) at sea level, 599 mph (964 km/h) at 35,000 ft (10 670 m). Initial climb, 8,100 ft/min (41,15 m/sec). Range (two 200-US gal/757-l drop tanks), 926 mls (1 490 km). Empty weight, 11,125 lb (5 046 kg). Loaded weight (clean), 15,198 lb (6 894 kg). Span, 39 ft 1½ in (11,92 m). Length, 37 ft 6½ in (11,44 m). Height, 14 ft 8⁹⁄₁₀ in (4,49 m). Wing area, 313.37 sq ft (29,11 m²).*

NORTH AMERICAN
F-86H SABRE USA

Destined to be the final production version of the Sabre for the USAF, the F-86H featured a deeper fuselage to accommodate the larger air intake required for an 8,920 lb st (4 046 kgp) General Electric J73-GE-3 engine and to provide a substantial increase in internal fuel capacity. The first F-86H was flown on 30 April

1953, this retaining the slatted wing of the F-86E, but subsequent aircraft omitted the slats and adopted the extended wing leading edge introduced during F-86F production – the final 10 aircraft having both slats *and* extended wing. Intended for the fighter rôle, the F-86H had four underwing stores stations, and could carry a pair of 1,000-lb (454-kg) GP bombs or 750-lb (340-kg) napalm bombs in addition to drop tanks, or a 1,200-kg (544-kg) 100-kT nuclear store under the port wing. Deliveries to the USAF commenced in January 1954, the first 113 having an armament of six 0.5-in (12,7-mm) machine guns which gave place to four 20-mm cannon in subsequent aircraft, and a total of 473 (plus two pre-series) F-86H Sabres was built with the last being accepted on 11 April 1956. *Max speed, 692 mph (1 114 km/h) at sea level, 617 mph (993 km/h) at 35,000 ft (10 670 m). Initial climb, 12,900 ft/min (65,53 m/sec). Range (two 200-US gal/757-l drop tanks), 1,040 mls (1 674 km). Empty weight, 13,836 lb (6 276 kg). Loaded weight (with two drop tanks), 21,852 lb (9 912 kg). Span, 39 ft 1½ in (11,92 m). Length, 38 ft 10 in (11,84 m). Wing area, 313.37 sq ft (29,11 m²).*

(Above) An early cannon-armed F-86H-10 in 1954, and (below) an F-86H-10 serving with the 136th TFS, 102nd TFW, New York Air National Guard, early 1963.

(Below) The F-86H with extended wing leading-edge.

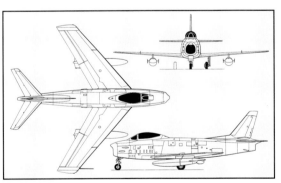

NORTH AMERICAN
FJ-3 FURY USA

On 3 March 1952, the design of a new Fury shipboard fighter began around the newly-available Sapphire engine built by Wright under licence from Armstrong

The FJ-3 Fury (below) differed from the FJ-2 primarily in having a totally redesigned fuselage.

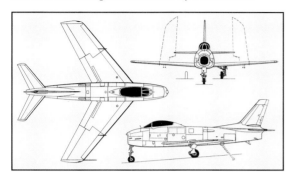

(Above) An FJ-3M of VF-142 aboard the USS *Hornet* in 1957, and (below) a general arrangement drawing of the FJ-3 with wing fold indicated by dotted lines.

Siddeley. Assigned the designation FJ-3, the new fighter differed from the FJ-2 primarily in having a redesigned fuselage with a deeper air intake to accommodate the Wright J65 engine, as the US-built version of the Sapphire was known. The fifth FJ-2 was adapted to take the new engine as the XFJ-3 and flew on 3 July 1953, and the first production FJ-3, powered by a J65-W-4 engine rated at 7,650 lb st (3 470 kgp) and carrying an armament of four 20-mm cannon, followed on 11 December 1953. Deliveries to the US Navy began in September 1954, and, in the following year, the wing slats were discarded in favour of extended leading edges, while, with the 345th aircraft, additional wing stores stations were introduced for 500- or 1,000-lb (227- or 454-kg) bombs or rocket packs. In August 1956, as the 538th and last FJ-3 was delivered, a new weapon capability was introduced in the form of the Sidewinder AAM, 80 aircraft subsequently being modified as FJ-3Ms which had the cannon armament augmented with a pair of the AAMs. In 1962, under the tri-service designation system, the FJ-3 became the F-1C, the FJ-3M becoming the MF-1C. *Max speed, 681 mph (1 096 km/h) at sea level, 623 mph (1 002 km/h) at 35,000 ft (10 670 m). Initial climb, 8,450 ft/min (42,93 m/sec). Range (clean), 990 mls (1 593 km). Empty weight, 12,205 lb (5 536 kg). Loaded weight (clean), 17,189 lb (7 797 kg). Span, 37 ft 1½ in (11,31 m). Length, 37 ft 7 in (11,45 m). Height, 13 ft 8 in (4,16 m). Wing area, 302.3 sq ft (28,08 m²).*

NORTH AMERICAN
F-86K SABRE   USA

Evolved from the F-86D specifically for supply to NATO forces under the MDAP, the F-86K differed from its predecessor primarily in having a simpler fire control system and cannon armament which could be supplemented by a pair of AIM-9B Sidewinder AAMs. Development began on 14 May 1953, two F-86D-40s being modified as YF-86K prototypes and the first of these flying on 15 July 1954. These were subsequently sent to Italy to serve as pattern aircraft for similar aircraft assembled under licence by Fiat. The parent company built 120 F-86Ks, deliveries commencing in May 1955, these being powered by the J47-GE-17B engine rated

A Fiat-built F-86K (below) of *Jagdgeschwader* 74, this aircraft later being transferred to Venezuela.

at 5,425 lb st (2 460 kgp) and boosted to 7,500 lb st (3 402 kgp) with afterburning. Built-in armament comprised four 20-mm cannon. Of the NAA-built F-86Ks, 60 were supplied to Norway and 59 to the Netherlands. The first Fiat-assembled F-86K was flown on 23 May 1955, a total of 221 being delivered of which 63 were supplied to the Italian air arm, 60 to France, 88 to Germany, six to the Netherlands and four to Norway. The last 45 Fiat-assembled aircraft had the extended wing of the F-86F-40, others being retroactively modified. The Dutch F-86Ks were passed on to Turkey in 1963-64, and, in 1967-68, 47 ex-German aircraft were passed to Venezuela, four of the latter being sold to Honduras in 1969. *Max speed, 692 mph (1 114 km/h) at sea level, 612 mph (985 km/h) at 40,000 ft (12 190 m). Initial climb, 12,000 ft/min (60,96 m/sec). Range (with two 120-US gal/454-l drop tanks), 744 mls (1 197km). Empty weight, 13,367 lb (6 063 kg). Loaded weight (clean), 18,379 lb (8 337 kg). Span, 37 ft 1½ in (11,31 m). Length, 40 ft 11⅛ in (12,47 m). Height, 15 ft 0 in (4,57 m), Wing area, 287.9 sq ft (26,75 m²).*

The F-86K served with JG 74 of the *Luftwaffe* (below) from 1961 to 1965, operating from Neuburg.

NORTH AMERICAN
FJ-4 FURY   USA

Designation notwithstanding, the FJ-4 effectively represented, by comparison with previous Furies, a complete structural redesign to produce a wholly new aircraft. The wing was totally new, the fuselage was new with greater depth and the tail surfaces were larger

(Below) The FJ-4, last of the North American Furies.

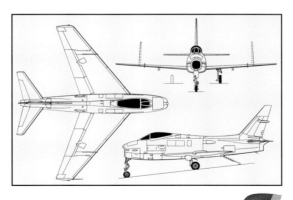

An FJ-4B (above) of VX-4 at the Point Mugu Naval Air Missile Test Center with Bullpup ASMs in 1958.

and thinner, internal fuel capacity being 50 per cent greater than that of the FJ-3. Power was provided by a 7,700 lb st (3 493 kgp) Wright J65-W-16A turbojet, four wing stations were provided for external stores and all stations were capable of carrying the Sidewinder AAM to supplement the four-cannon built-in armament. The first of two FJ-4 prototypes flew on 28 October 1954, these being followed by 150 series aircraft, all being accepted by the US Navy by March 1957. Previously, on 4 December 1956, an attack fighter version, the FJ-4B, had flown, this having a stiffer wing with six stores stations and the ability to carry the Bullpup air-to-surface missile (five plus guidance pod). The 222nd and last FJ-4B was delivered in May 1958. Two FJ-4s (2nd and 4th series aircraft) were fitted experimentally with both monopropellant and bipropellant auxiliary rocket motors as FJ-4Fs. The following data relate to the FJ-4. *Max speed, 680 mph (1 094 km/h) at sea level, 631 mph (1 015 km/h) at 35,000 ft (10 670 m). Initial climb, 7,660 ft/min (38,91 m/sec). Range (clean), 1,485 mls (2 390 km). Empty weight, 13,210 lb (5 992 kg). Loaded weight (clean), 20,130 lb (9 131 kg). Span, 39 ft 1 in (11,91 m). Length, 36 ft 4 in (11,07 m). Height, 13 ft 11 in (4,24 m). Wing area, 338.66 sq ft (31,46 m²).*

NORTH AMERICAN
F-86L SABRE   USA

First flown in October 1956, the F-86L all-weather fighter was an upgraded F-86D introducing the longer-span wing with extended and slatted leading edge first adopted by the F-86F-40, and modernised avionics including a data link installation. The J47-GE-33 engine and rocket armament of the F-86D were retained.

The F-86L (above and below) was an upgraded F-86D with modified wing and modernised avionics that remained with the Air National Guard until 1965.

Under a programme known as *Project Follow-On*, 981 F-86D aircraft were modified to F-86L standards between 1956 and 1958. The F-86L remained in service with the Air National Guard until 1965, and 17 were transferred to Thailand. *Max speed, 693 mph (1 115 km/h) at sea level, 616 mph (991 km/h) at 40,000 ft (12 190 m). Initial climb, 12,200 ft/min (61,98 m/sec). Range (with two 120-US gal/454-l drop tanks), 750 mls (1 207 km). Empty weight, 13,822 lb (6 270 kg). Loaded weight (clean), 18,484 lb (8 384 kg). Span, 39 ft 1½ in (11,92 m). Length, 40 ft 3¼ in (12,27 m). Height, 15 ft 0 in (4,57 m). Wing area, 313.37 sq ft (29,11 m²).*

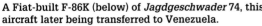

An F-100D-10 (above) of *Escadron 1/11 Roussilon, Armée de l'Air*, Toul 1972, and (below) an F-100D-6 of 308th TF Sqn, 31st TFW, Tuy Hoa, Vietnam, 1970.

NORTH AMERICAN F-100A & F-100C SUPER SABRE USA

First of the USAF's "Century-series" fighters and one of the first fighters capable of level-flight supersonic performance, the Super Sabre was first flown on 25 May 1953. Two YF-100A prototypes were followed by the first series F-100A on 29 October 1953, initial operational capability being achieved by the USAF two years later. The F-100A was powered by a Pratt & Whitney J57-P-7 rated at 9,700 lb st (4 400 kgp) boosted to 14,800 lb st (6 713 kgp) with afterburning. This was supplanted by the J57-P-39 with similar ratings in the last 36 of the 203 of this initial model built. Armament comprised four 20-mm cannon. Six were later adapted as RF-100As with armament removed and five reconnaissance cameras installed in a "canoe" fairing beneath the cockpit. From mid-1959, 118 ex-USAF F-100As (upgraded in some respects to F-100D standards and designated F-100A Rehab) and four RF-100As were supplied to Nationalist China. The F-100A had been optimised for the air superiority rôle, but its production successor, the F-100C was a fighter-bomber with substantially increased internal fuel capacity resulting from introduction of a "wet" wing, an enlarged vertical tail and a J57-P-21 engine rated at 10,200 lb st (4 627 kgp) dry and 16,000 lb st (7 258 kgp) with afterburning. The first series F-100C flew on 17 January 1955, and a total of 476 was built, the last being delivered in July 1956. The four 20-mm cannon armament was retained and six wing stores stations were provided for external loads of bombs and rocket pods.

An F-100C-20 (below) of the 36th Fighter Day Wing operating from Bitburg, Germany, during 1956.

From 1972, Turkey received 92 ex-USAF F-100Cs to supplement its fleet of F-100Ds and Fs. The following data relate to the F-100C. *Max speed, 914 mph (1 471 km/h) at 35,000 ft (10 670 m). Initial climb, 19,000 ft/min (96,52 m/sec). Range (clean), 572 mls (920 km). Empty weight, 19,270 lb (8 741 kg). Normal loaded weight, 27,587 lb (12 513 kg). Span, 38 ft 9⅓ in (11,82 m). Length, 47 ft 0¾ in (14,34 m). Height, 15 ft 4 in (4,67 m). Wing area, 385 sq ft (35,77 m²).*

NORTH AMERICAN F-100D & F-100F SUPER SABRE USA

Whereas the F-100C was theoretically a dual-rôle version of the Super Sabre, capable of both air superiority and fighter-bomber missions, its successor, the F-100D, was a dedicated fighter-bomber. Possessing the same wing stores stations (but with ejectable pylons) and four-cannon built-in armament as those of the F-100C, and retaining the J57-P-21 (or -21A) engine, the F-100D

The F-100D-70 (below) was from a late Super Sabre production batch and was a dedicated fighter-bomber.

had increased wing and tail surface area, in-flight refuelling capability, inboard landing flaps and improved avionics. The first F-100D was flown on 24 January 1956, this being followed 13 months later, on 7 March 1957, by a tandem two-seat version, the F-100F, intended to combine the fighter-bomber task with that of combat proficiency training, these two versions of the Super Sabre subsequently being built in parallel. The series two-seater had been preceded by the single TF-100C prototype which had flown on 3 August 1956.

An F-100D-10 (above) of *Escadron 2/11 Vosges* of the *Armée de l'Air*, and (below) a general arrangement drawing of the F-100D Super Sabre.

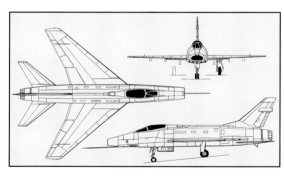

A total of 1,274 F-100Ds was built, together with 339 F-100Fs, and, of these, 85 Ds and 15 Fs were assigned to France, 48 Ds and 10 Fs (later supplemented by 14 TF-100Fs) to Denmark, and 131 Ds and 50 Fs to Turkey under the Military Assistance Program. The following data relate to the F-100D. *Max speed, 891 mph (1 434 km/h) at 35,000 ft (10 670 m). Initial climb, 18,000 ft/min (91,95 m/sec). Normal range (clean), 534 mls (859 km). Empty weight, 21,000 lb (9 526 kg). Normal loaded weight, 2,847 lb (13 085 kg). Span, 38 ft 9⅓ in (11,82 m). Length, 47 ft 4⅔ in (14,44 m). Height, 16 ft 2⅔ in (4,94 m). Wing area, 400 sq ft (37,16 m²).*

NORTH AMERICAN YF-107A USA

Initiated as an advanced derivative of the Super Sabre and originally designated F-100B, the F-107A evolved as an entirely new dual-rôle (all-weather interceptor and fighter-bomber) aircraft, and the first of three YF-107A prototypes was flown on 10 September 1956. Featuring innovative engine air intake positioning (above and behind the pilot's cockpit), the YF-107A was powered by a Pratt & Whitney J75-P-9 rated at 17,200 lb st (7 802 kgp) and 24,500 lb st (11 113 kgp) with afterburning, and intended built-in armament was four 20-mm cannon. The F-107A was in competition with the Republic F-105, and, when the latter was selected, further development of the former was discontinued and two of the YF-107As were passed to the NACA. *Max speed, 890 mph (1 432 km/h) at sea level, 1,295 mph (2 084 km/h) at 36,000 ft (10 975 m). Time to 39,900 ft (12 160 m), 1.0 min. Normal range, 788 mls (1 268 km). Empty weight, 22,696 lb (10 295 lb). Normal loaded weight, 39,755 lb (18 033 kg). Span, 36 ft 7 in (11,15 m). Length, 61 ft 10 in (18,84 m). Height, 19 ft 8 in (5,99 m). Wing area, 376 sq ft (34,93 m²).*

The first YF-107A (above) lacked the so-called "Variable Inlet Duct" applied to the third aircraft.

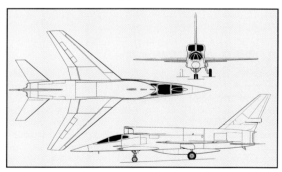

(Above and below) The YF-107A, the photo showing the first prototype landing in October 1956.

NORTHROP XFT-1 & 2 USA

Despite some scepticism concerning the practicability of the monoplane configuration for the shipboard fighter, the US Navy's BuAer issued a second require-

(Above) The XFT-1 returned to Northrop after brief evaluation for reworking as the XFT-2 (below).

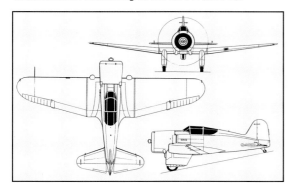

The Northrop 3A (above and below) was briefly flown at Wright Field and then returned to Northrop.

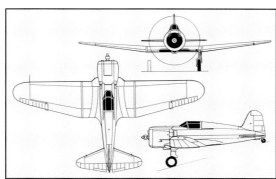

ment for such a warplane on 24 January 1933, the first having been issued seven weeks earlier and for which the Boeing Model 273 was designed and built (as the XF7B-1). To meet the later but essentially similar requirement, a contract was let to Northrop for a prototype assigned the designation XFT-1. A single-seat all-metal cantilever monoplane with split flaps, spatted main undercarriage members and an enclosed cockpit, the XFT-1 was designed by a team led by Ed Heinemann. Powered by a Wright R-1510-26 14-cylinder radial rated at 600 hp at sea level and 625 hp at 6,000 ft (1 830 m), and carrying two 0.30-in (7,62-mm) cowl guns, the XFT-1 first flew on 16 January 1934. The US Navy was critical of its manoeuvrability, its tendency to spin out of certain manoeuvres, its low speed characteristics and its landing speed. During the course of initial tests, an XR-1510-8 engine affording 650 hp at 8,500 ft (2 590 m) was substituted for the -26, and, in April 1936, the XFT-1 was returned to the manufacturer for more extensive modification. A Pratt & Whitney R-1535-72 Twin Wasp Jnr 14-cylinder radial rated at 700 hp for take-off and 650 hp at 7,500 ft (2 285 m) was installed, this having a long-chord cowling; the vertical tail surfaces were enlarged, and the mainwheel spats were revised. Redesignated XFT-2, the fighter was now 261 lb (118 kg) heavier in empty condition, speed and climb performance were marginally improved, but manoeuvrability and low speed characteristics were worse. It was pronounced unairworthy by the US Navy and crashed on 21 July 1936 while being returned to its manufacturer. The following data relate to the XFT-1 with the -26 engine. *Max speed, 235 mph (378 km/h) at 6,000 ft (1 830 m). Time to 6,000 ft (1 830 m), 2.6 min. Max range, 976 mls (1 570 km). Empty weight, 2,469 lb (1 120 kg). Loaded weight, 3,756 lb (1 704 kg). Span, 32 ft 9 in (9,75 m). Length, 21 ft 1 in (6,43 m). Height, 9 ft 5 in (2,87 m). Wing area, 177 sq ft (16,44 m².)*

The XFT-2 (below) was rejected by the US Navy owing to poor low-speed handling and poor manoeuvrability.

NORTHROP 3A (XP-948)   USA

Based on the design of the XFT, the Model 3A was developed as a contender in the US Army's Matériel Division competition for a successor to the P-26 in service with the USAAC. A low-wing all-metal semi-monocoque monoplane with fully-retractable main undercarriage members and an enclosed cockpit, the Model 3A was powered by a Pratt & Whitney SR-1535-6 Twin Wasp Junior 14-cylinder radial engine rated at 700 hp

for take-off. It had provision for one 0.30-in (7,62-mm) and one 0.50-in (12,7-mm) gun in the fuselage. Completed in July 1935, it was briefly tested at Wright Field where it was found to be somewhat unstable and prone to spinning. Returned to the manufacturer for modification, the Model 3A was under test over the Pacific on 30 July, but failed to return, no trace of the aircraft nor its pilot ever being found. The design of the Model 3A was subsequently sold to Chance Vought Aircraft which further developed it as the V-141. The following data are based on manufacturer's estimates. *Max speed, 270 mph (434 km/h) at sea level, 258 mph (415 km/h) at 10,000 ft (3 050 m). Time to 10,000 ft (3 050 m), 3.3 min. Endurance, 3.1 hrs. Loaded weight, 3,900 lb (1 769 kg). Span, 33 ft 6 in (10,21 m). Length, 22 ft 3 in (6,78 m). Height, 9 ft 1 in (2,77 m). Wing area, 187 sq ft (17,37 m².)*

NORTHROP XP-56   USA

One of the most radical of US experimental fighters of World War II, the XP-56 was conceived as a result of an informal competition initiated late in 1939 for innovative fighter designs, the winning contractors being Vultee (XP-54), Curtiss (XP-55) and Northrop (XP-56). The XP-56 was a tailless pusher of all-magnesium, all-

The first (above) and second (below) prototypes of the highly innovative Northrop XP-56 fighter.

welded construction, two prototypes being ordered on 26 September 1940 and 13 February 1942 respectively. Power was provided by a 2,000 hp Pratt & Whitney R-2800-29 Double Wasp 18-cylinder radial engine buried in the rear fuselage and driving contra-rotating pusher propellers. Proposed armament comprised two 20-mm cannon and four 0.50-in (12,7-mm) machine guns. The first two flights were conducted on 6 September 1943, dorsal fin area subsequently being increased and flight test being resumed on 8 October, the aircraft being written-off as a result of a landing accident on the second flight of that day. The second prototype, which differed in having bellows-type, split-flap wingtip "rudders" and a further increase in dorsal fin area, flew on 23 March 1944. Lateral instability and control reversal were experienced at low speeds, and high speeds were not attainable owing to inability to obtain full power. After the 10th flight of this XP-56, the USAAF concluded that further flight testing was "too hazardous" and development was discontinued. The following data are based on manufacturer's estimates. *Max speed, 417 mph (671 km/h) at sea level, 465 mph (748 km/h) at 25,000 ft (7 620 m). Time to 20,000 ft (6 100 m), 7.2 min. Range, 660 mls (1 062 km). Empty weight, 8,700 lb (3 946 kg). Design loaded weight, 11,350 lb (5 148 kg). Span, 42 ft 6 in (12,98 m). Length, 27 ft 6 in (8,38 m). Height, 9 ft 8 in (2,94 m). Wing area, 307 sq ft (28,52 m².)*

(Below) The second prototype of the Northrop XP-56.

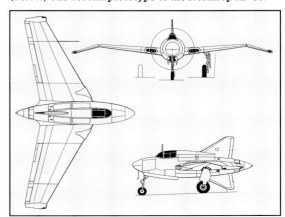

NORTHROP P-61A & P-61B BLACK WIDOW   USA

The first warplane evolved from the outset for the nocturnal intercept rôle to achieve service status, the Black Widow was designed to meet the requirements of an outline specification issued on 2 October 1940. The XP-61 was a radar-equipped, heavily-armed three-seater of twin-engined, twin-boom configuration, two prototypes being ordered on 11 January 1941, and the first of these flying 15 months later, on 21 May 1942. By this time, 13 pre-series YP-61s and 560 series aircraft had been ordered, the first 45 of the latter (P-61A-1s) having similar Pratt & Whitney R-2800-10 Double Wasp 18-cylinder radials each rated at 2,000 hp. Subsequent aircraft received the R-2800-65, with a war emergency

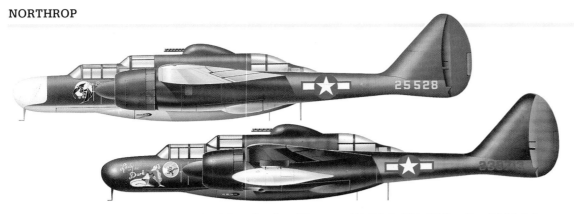

rating of 2,250 hp. Armament comprised four fixed 20-mm cannon, and the 13 YP-61s and first 37 P-61As also had a remotely-controlled dorsal barbette mounting four 0.50-in (12,7-mm) machine guns. This barbette resulted in tail buffet problems, and the remaining 163 P-61As were completed as two-seaters with the turret omitted. Deliveries of the P-61A commenced in October 1943, giving place to the P-61B in July 1944, 450 of this sub-type being built. The P-61B featured an 8-in (20,3-cm) nose cone extension, but was otherwise essentially similar to the P-61A, and with the 201st B-series aircraft the four-gun dorsal barbette was reinstated.

The sixteenth production P-61A-1 (above), which was one of 37 A-series aircraft with the gun barbette.

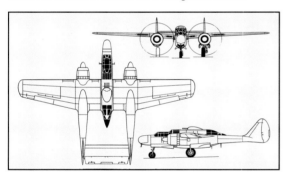

The P-61B-15 (below) and B-20 (above) Black Widow batches had the dorsal gun barbette reinstated.

(Below) A P-61A-10 of the 425th NF Sqn, US 9th Air Force, operating from Etain, France, January 1945.

(Above, top) P-61A-1 of 6th NF Sqn, East Field, Saipan, summer 1944, and (immediately above) a P-61B-15 of 548th NF Sqn, Ie Shima, August 1945.

The following data relate to the P-61B-20. *Max speed, 330 mph (531 km/h) at sea level, 362 mph (582 km/h) at 15,000 ft (4 570 m). Initial climb, 2,550 ft/min (12,9 m/sec). Range (internal fuel), 940 mls (1 513 km). Empty weight, 21,282 lb (9 654 kg). Normal loaded weight, 29,700 lb (13 471 kg). Span, 66 ft 0¾ in (20,14 m). Length, 49 ft 7 in (15,11 m). Height, 14 ft 8 in (4,47 m). Wing area, 662.36 sq ft (61,53 m²).*

NORTHROP P-61C & P-61D BLACK WIDOW USA

Reports from combat zones having indicated that improvement in the Black Widow's speed and altitude performance was desirable, Northrop evolved the P-61C with R-2800-73 engines equipped with CH-5

(Above) A P-61C-1 of the final Black Widow series batch, of which only 41 were completed.

turbo-superchargers and having a war emergency rating of 2,800 hp. To provide more control latitude, interconnected air brakes were fitted above and below the wing. Max take-off weight rose to 40,300 lb (18 280 kg), and when flight test of the P-61C commenced in July 1945, it was found that at weights above 35,000 lb (15 876 kg), the aircraft became sluggish, difficult to handle and tended to "wallow" in flight. Furthermore, excessive ground roll was necessary for take-off – it was recommended that, at 40,000 lb (18 144 kg) a take-off should not be attempted without at least three miles (4,82 km) of unobstructed run. Series manufacture of the P-61C had already commenced, however, 41 being completed before VJ Day, when a further 476 were cancelled. Earlier, two P-61A airframes had undergone adaptation as XP-61Ds with R-2800-14 engines with CH-5 turbo-superchargers, flight test having commenced in November 1944. Tests were plagued with repeated engine failures, however, preventing exploration of the full performance envelope, and as the P-61C had been completed in the meantime, further development of the P-61D was abandoned. The following data relate to the P-61C. *Max speed, 430 mph (692 km/h) at 30,000 ft (9 150 m). Time to 30,000 ft*

(9 150 m), 14.6 min. Range (internal fuel), 1,000 mls (1 609 km). Empty weight, 24,000 lb (10 866 kg). Normal loaded weight, 30,600 lb (13 880 kg). Dimensions as for P-61B.

NORTHROP XP-61E USA

In an effort to evolve a high-performance, long-range escort fighter, two P-61B airframes were selected for modification as XP-61Es. Retaining the R-2800-65 engines of the earlier sub-type, the XP-61E two-seat day fighter had the decking of the fuselage nacelle cut down flush with the wing, and the tandem cockpits enclosed by a hinged single-piece blown canopy (the second prototype having a similar but aft-sliding canopy). The centre and aft sections of the fuselage nacelle accommodated additional fuel tankage and the nose-mounted AI radar was supplanted by four 0.50-in (12,7-mm) guns, the ventral battery of four 20-mm cannon being retained. With the end of World War II, the requirement for the two-seat day fighter XP-61E was cancelled, the second aircraft having been written off in a take-off accident on 11 April 1945, and the first prototype was subsequently converted to the XF-15 photo-reconnaissance aircraft. *Max speed, 376 mph (605 km/h) at 17,000 ft (5 180 m). Time to 20,000 ft (6 100 m), 13.0 min. Normal range, 2,550 mls (4 104 km). Empty weight, 21,350 lb (9 684 kg). Normal loaded weight, 31,425 lb (14 254 kg). Span, 66 ft 0¾ in (20,14 m). Length, 49 ft 7 in (15,11 m). Height, 14 ft 8 in (4,47 m). Wing area, 662.36 sq ft (61,53 m²).*

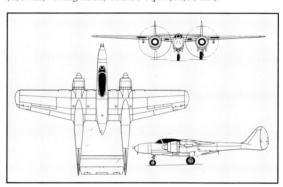

The XP-61E (above and below) was a long-range escort fighter developed from the P-61B.

NORTHROP XP-79B USA

In January 1943, Northrop was awarded a USAAF contract for the design and construction of three prototypes of a highly original rocket-propelled interceptor fighter of all-wing configuration and designated XP-79. To be powered by a single 2,000 lb (907 kg) Aerojet rocket motor, the XP-79 was to have accommodated its pilot in the prone position, but, in the event, development problems with the rocket led to cancellation of the project. However, a contract was placed for the redesign of the fighter for turbojet power, one prototype being ordered as the XP-79B. Manufactured of Heliarc-welded heavy-gauge magnesium plate, the XP-79B featured reinforced wing leading edges which were intended to enable it to withstand ramming attacks on the tail surfaces of enemy bombers. Provision was also made for an armament of four 0.50-in (12,7-mm) machine guns. The wing was fitted with elevons and bellows-type rudders, and power was provided by two 1,365 lb st (619 kgp) Westinghouse 19B turbojets. The

The XP-79B (above and below) was lost in an accident that ended its first and only flight.

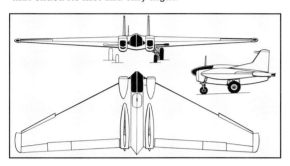

XP-79B was flown for the first time on 12 September 1945, but in a climbing turn during its second pass over Muroc Dry Lake, an inadvertent roll was followed by a stall and then a spin from which the pilot was unable to recover, and following this accident the programme was cancelled. The following data are based on manufacturer's estimates. *Max speed, 547 mph (880 km/h) at sea level, 508 mph (817 km/h) at 25,000 ft (7 620 m). Time to 25,000 ft (7 620 m), 4.3 min. Range, 995 mls (1 600 km). Empty weight, 5,840 lb (2 649 kg). Loaded weight, 8,669 lb (3 932 kg). Span, 38 ft 0 in (11,58 m). Length, 14 ft 0 in (4,27 m). Height, 7 ft 0 in (2,13 m). Wing area, 278 sq ft (25,83 m²).*

NORTHROP F-89A TO F-89C SCORPION   USA

The second F-89A (above) with 5-in (12,7-cm) HVARs underwing, and (below) an F-89B of the Wisconsin Air National Guard, *circa* 1955.

Representative of the first generation of turbojet-powered fighters designed from the outset for the all-weather intercept rôle, the Scorpion stemmed from a letter contract for two XP-89 prototypes received by Northrop on 13 June 1946. The first of these, redesignated XF-89 and powered by two 4,000 lb st (1 814 kgp) Allison J35-A-9 turbojets, was flown on 16 August 1948, a contract being placed in May 1949 for the second prototype to be modified to YF-89A standards and for 48 series F-89As. The YF-89A and F-89A received J35-A-21 engines each rated at 5,000 lb st (2 268 kgp) boosted to 6,800 lb st (3 084 kgp) with afterburning, the latter flying for the first time on 28 September 1950, and built-in armament comprising six 20-mm cannon. In the event, only 18 F-89As were completed, the remaining

30 of the initial order being built to F-89B standard, this differing only in avionics. Subsequent Scorpion orders called for the F-89C first flown on 25 October 1951 and distinguished externally from preceding sub-types in replacing the interim external elevator balances with internal mass balances. There were also various internal changes, and, with the 35th aircraft, the J35-A-21A engine was installed, this (retrofitted to all earlier aircraft) having a dry rating of 5,100 lb st (2 313 kgp). With the 65th aircraft the engine was again changed, to the 5,400 lb st (2 450 kgp) J35-A-33 boosted to 7,400 lb st (3 357 kgp) with afterburning. Production of the F-89C totalled 164 aircraft. During 1952, six Scorpions – mostly F-89Cs – disintegrated in mid-air, necessitating grounding of the entire fleet. The failures were attributed to wing aero-elasticity, necessitating some major wing structural redesign, and all Scorpions were rotated through a modification programme. The F-89C left the active USAF inventory in 1954, by which time all aircraft had been re-engined with the J35-A-47. One F-89A was experimentally fitted with a rotating turret in the nose mounting four 20-mm cannon, two F-89Cs were fitted with an armament of four 30-mm cannon and another tested a pair of rocket guns firing 2.75-in (70-mm) rockets from rifled barrels. The following data relate to the J35-A-33-powered F-89C. *Max speed, 650 mph (1 046 km/h) at sea level, 562 mph (904 km/h) at 40,000 ft (12 190 m). Initial climb, 12,300 ft/min (62,48 m/sec). Max range, 905 mls (1 456 km). Empty weight, 24,570 lb (11 145 kg). Normal loaded weight, 37,348 lb (16 941 kg). Span (over tip tanks), 56 ft 0 in (17,06 m). Length, 53 ft 5 in (16,28 m). Height, 17 ft 6 in (5,33 m). Wing area, 606 sq ft (56,30 m²).*

NORTHROP F-89D TO F-89J SCORPION   USA

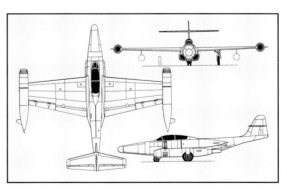

(Above) The F-89D, which lacked the cannon.

With the D-series of the F-89, a fundamental change in armament took place, the sextet of 20-mm cannon carried by all earlier sub-types of the Scorpion giving place to 2.75-in (70-mm) folding-fin unguided rockets accom-

(Below) An F-89D-25 of the 64th FIS, Elmendorf AFB, Alaska, October 1954.

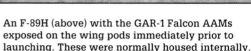

An F-89H (above) with the GAR-1 Falcon AAMs exposed on the wing pods immediately prior to launching. These were normally housed internally.

(Above) An F-89D-5, armed entirely with unguided folding-fin rockets accommodated in wing-tip pods.

(Above and below) The F-89J was an adaptation of the F-89D to carry nuclear-tipped AIR-2A Genie AAMs.

modated in wing-tip pods. One F-89B was modified to test this armament as the YF-89D, flying in this form for the first time on 23 October 1951, and the first series F-89D followed on 10 January 1952. The F-89D, which was the most-produced Scorpion sub-type with 862 being built, carried 52 of the rockets in each wing-tip pod, together with 308 US gal (1 166 l) of fuel, the space occupied by the cannon in earlier versions also being occupied by fuel, and J35-A-35 or -35A engines were standardised. Deliveries to the USAF commenced in June 1952, and production continued until 1955 before switching to the final production model, the F-89H, of which 156 were built with the last being delivered in October 1956. The prototype of the H-series, the YF-89H, was an F-89D flown in modified form on 21 October 1953. Retaining the engines of the F-89D, the F-89H differed essentially from the earlier model in armament, extensively revised wing-tip pods each accommodating three GAR-1 Falcon guided missiles

and 21 2.75-in (70-mm) unguided rockets. Deliveries of the F-89H commenced in September 1955. Subsequently, 350 F-89Ds were modified to carry the nuclear-tipped AIR-2A Genie guided missile as the F-89J. One Genie was carried beneath each wing, together with two Falcons, and either a 600-US gal (2 271-l) fuel tank or, when first delivered, the F-89D-style pod of unguided rockets and fuel at the wing tip. With this last item, gross weight rose to a possible 47,720 lb (21 646 kg) with a full load of Genies and Falcons. The F-89J was first flown on 15 March 1956, and deliveries to the USAF commenced in the following November, the modification of F-89Ds to F-89Js being completed on 21 February 1958. The last Scorpions left the active USAF inventory in 1960, but were not finally withdrawn from the Air National Guard until 1969. The following data relate to the F-89D. *Max speed, 636 mph (1 024 km/h) at 10, 600 ft (3 230 m), 523 mph (842 km/h) at 46,500 ft (14 175 m). Initial climb, 7,440 ft/min (37, 80 m/sec). Max range (with drop tanks), 1, 367 mls (2 200 km). Span (over tip tanks), 59 ft 8¹/₂ in (18,20 m). Length, 53 ft 9¹/₂ in (16,40 m). Height, 17ft 6 in (5,33 m). Wing area, 606 sq ft (56,30 m²).*

NORTHROP F-5A & F-5C   USA

In an attempt to reverse the upward size-weight-complexity-cost spiral in single-seat fighter design, Northrop began in 1954 private-venture design of a lightweight multi-rôle fighter as the N-156F. Evolved by a team led by Welko Gasich, the N-156F was the subject of a three-prototype US DoD contract in May 1958, the first prototype flying on 30 July 1959. Three years later, in April 1962, the N-156F was chosen for MAP supply to nations allied to the USA, and assigned the designation F-5A, a two-seat training equivalent being the F-5B. Powered by two General Electric J85-

The F-5A (above and below) represented an attempt to reverse the fighter size-weight-complexity spiral.

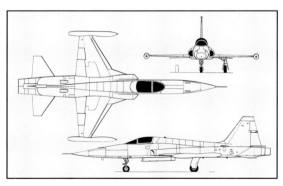

GE-13 engines rated at 2,720 lb st (1 234 kgp) boosted with afterburning to 4,080 lb st (1 851 kgp), the F-5A had a built-in armament of two 20-mm cannon and provision for two wingtip-mounted AIM-9 Sidewinder AAMs. A maximum military load of 6,200 lb (2 812 kg) could be carried for short-range missions and (in the RF-5A) the standard cannon nose could be replaced by a camera nose. The first F-5A flew in October 1963, and the type was subsequently supplied to MAP recipient and direct-purchase countries, a total of 799 having been built (plus 107 RF-5As and 293 two-seat F-5Bs) when production of the initial F-5 series was completed in June 1972. Of these, 164 were built by Canadair for the Canadian Armed Forces (89 CF-5As) and Netherlands Air Force (75 NF-5As), together with 76 two-seaters (46 CF-5Ds and 30 NF-5Bs), while CASA assembled 36 in Spain as SF-5As SF-5Bs). In all, the F-5A and its two-seater conversion trainer the F-5B, given the uninspiring name "Freedom Fighter", served with 20 air forces. Apart from those already mentioned these are: Brazil, Ethiopia, Greece, Iran, Jordan, Libya, Malaysia, Morocco, Norway, the

A dozen F-5As were used by the USAF as F-5Cs (above) for combat evaluation in Vietnam in 1965.

Phillippines, Saudi Arabia, South Korea, Taiwan, Thailand, Turkey, and Venezuela. Of these only seven (Greece, Morocco, the Phillippines, South Korea, Thailand, Turkey and Venezuela) still operate the type, although they were joined in 1996 by Botswana. Turkey has the majority of the 210 F-5As and 56 F-5Bs still operational, with 110 and 30. There was also the F-5C, which had flight refuelling and other modifications. A dozen were used by the USAF in South Vietnam for the 1965 Skoshi Tiger evaluation. These aircraft were later donated to the South Vietnamese Air Force. *Max speed, 925 mph (1 490 km/h) at 36,090 ft (11 000 m), 731 mph (1,176 km/h) at sea level. Max initial climb, 29,800 ft/min (151,38 m/sec). Range (clean), 558 mls (898 km). Empty weight, 8,085 lb (3 667 kg). Loaded weight (clean), 13,663 lb (6 197 kg). Span, 25 ft 3 in (7,70 m). Length, 47 ft 2 in (14,38 m). Height, 13 ft 2 in (4,01 m). Wing area, 170 sq ft (15,79 m²).*

Key to Northrop F-5E Tiger II

1 Pitot head
2 Radome
3 Radar scanner dish
4 AN/APQ-159 X-band miniature radar
5 Scanner tracking mechanism
6 Radar mounting bulkhead
7 TACAN aerial
8 UHF/IFF combined aerial
9 Radar warning antenna, optional AN/ALQ-46 system
10 Radar transmitter/receiver
11 Fuselage nose frame construction
12 Retractable gun blast deflector doors
13 Deflector actuating jack
14 Cannon barrels
15 Central air data computer
16 TACAN transceiver
17 Coaxial switching unit
18 Radar and electronics cooling air duct
19 Starboard gun bay hinged access doors
20 Nose undercarriage wheel bay
21 Nose compartment central keel construction
22 Cannon recoil mounting
23 Gun gas venting air ducts
24 M-39A2 revolver-type 20-mm cannon
25 Ammunition loading door
26 Ammunition tank (280 rounds per gun)
27 Temperature probe
28 Nose undercarriage retraction/breaker strut
29 Torque scissor links
30 Forward retracting nosewheel
31 Nosewheel forks
32 Shock absorber leg strut
33 Steering linkages
34 Nosewheel leg door
35 Ammunition feed chute
36 Cartridge case ejector chute
37 Cannon rear mounting
38 Cockpit front pressure bulkhead
39 Windscreen rain dispersal air duct (optional)
40 Non-retracting detachable in-flight refuelling probe (optional)
41 One-piece frameless windscreen panel
42 Instrument panel shroud
43 Cockpit coaming/instrument panel access door
44 Position of angle-of-attack transmitter on starboard side
45 Canopy emergency release
46 Static ports
47 Rudder pedals
48 Cockpit pressure floor
49 Cockpit section framing
50 Engine throttle levers
51 Control column
52 Instrument panel
53 AN/ASG-31 lead-computing optical sight
54 Stand-by compass
55 Canopy arch
56 Rear view mirror
57 Cockpit canopy cover (upward hingeing)
58 AGM-65A Maverick air-to-surface missile
59 Ejection seat headrest
60 Canopy breaker strut
61 Ejection seat guide rails
62 Pilot's lightweight rocket-powered ejection seat
63 Safety harness
64 Portside console panel
65 Pull-out boarding step
66 Canopy external handle
67 Cockpit rear pressure bulkhead
68 Liquid oxygen converter
69 Boundary layer splitter plate
70 Port engine air intake
71 Perforated bleed air louvres
72 Air conditioning system ram air intake
73 Cockpit and avionics air conditioning plant
74 Avionics equipment racks (port and starboard)
75 Electro-luminescent formation lighting strip
76 Canopy counterbalanced hinge mechanism
77 Additional avionics equipment stowage
78 Engine bleed air duct to air conditioning plant
79 Sloping canopy bulkhead
80 "Sky-Spot" aerial
81 Fuselage longerons
82 Fuselage frame construction
83 Boundary layer spill duct
84 Intake duct framing
85 Ventral pressure refuelling connection
86 Port navigation light
87 Retractable landing/taxiing lamp (port and starboard)
88 Fixed leading-edge root extension
89 Leading-edge flap drive motor
90 Wing spar/fuselage frame attachment joint
91 Ventral airbrake (2)
92 Airbrake hydraulic jack
93 Port engine intake ducting
94 Front spar attachment main frame
95 Forward fuselage bag-type fuel tanks (total internal fuel capacity 766 US gal/2 536 l)
96 Fuel filler caps
97 VHF aerial (optional VHF communications system)
98 Starboard wing panel
99 Aileron tandem hydraulic jacks
100 Aileron control linkage
101 Starboard wing stores pylons
102 Leading-edge manoeuvre flap (down position)
103 Missile launch rail
104 AIM-9P Sidewinder air-to-air missile
105 Starboard position light
106 Fixed portion of trailing edge
107 Starboard inset aileron
108 Starboard plain flap (down position)
109 Engine bleed air ducting
110 Fuel system piping
111 Rear fuselage bag-type fuel tank
112 Dorsal access panels
113 Starboard engine bay
114 Fin root fillet
115 Fin spar root attachment joint
116 Torsion box fin spar construction
117 Fin rib construction
118 Fuel vent system piping
119 Starboard all-moving tailplane
120 Bonded honeycomb fin leading edge
121 Anti-collision light
122 Tail position light
123 Fin tip aerial fairing
124 UHF aerial
125 Trailing-edge communications aerials
126 Fixed portion of trailing edge
127 Fuel vent
128 Rudder
129 Rudder honeycomb construction
130 Parachute release linkage
131 Brake parachute housing
132 Engine exhaust nozzles
133 Tailpipe augmentor shroud
134 Variable area afterburner nozzle
135 Nozzle control jack
136 Afterburner duct
137 Port all-moving tailplane
138 Tailplane honeycomb construction
139 Tailplane spar
140 Pivot fixing

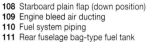

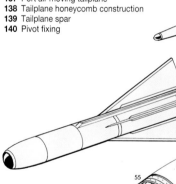

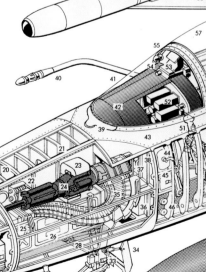

NORTHROP F-5E TIGER II   USA

In 1968, the US began to consider a successor to the F-5A optimised for the air superiority rôle under a continuation of the Military Assistance Program. Eight companies were invited to submit proposals based on existing fighters as the IIFA (Improved International Fighter Aircraft), and, on 20 November 1970, the Northrop submission was announced winning contender. This, the F-5E Tiger II (initially known as the F-5-21) was flown on 11 August 1972. It differed from the F-5A primarily in having J85-GE-21 engines each having military and afterburning thrusts of 3,500 lb st (1 588 kgp) and 5,000 lb st (2 268 kgp) respectively. It featured additional fuselage fuel, new air intake ducts, a wider reprofiled fuselage, a larger wing with leading-

(Above, top) A Canadair-built CF-5A of No 434 Sqn, Canadian Armed Forces, Chatham CFB, Canada, 1980.

(Immediately above) An F-5A-40 of the 341 *Mira*, 111ª *Pterix Mahis*, Hellenic Military Aviation, 1971.

141 Tailplane hydraulic actuator
142 Rear fuselage break point sloping frame (engine removal)
143 Rudder hydraulic actuator
144 Main engine mounting
145 Fin spar sloping bulkhead
146 General Electric J85-GE-21 engine
147 Engine accessory equipment gearbox
148 Compressor intake
149 Generator
150 Runway emergency arrester hook (lowered)
151 Engine auxiliary air intake doors (open)
152 Port hydraulic reservoir
153 Flap drive motor
154 Rear spar attachment main frame
155 Main undercarriage wheel bay
156 Flap shroud structure
157 Flap rib construction

158 Port plain flap
159 Trailing-edge honeycomb panels
160 Aileron rib construction
161 Aileron tandem hydraulic jacks
162 Control cable linkages
163 Port aileron
164 Fixed portion of trailing edge
165 Port position light
166 AIM-9P Sidewinder air-to-air missile
167 Missile launch rail
168 Port outboard stores pylon
169 Pylon attachment hardpoints
170 Outer wing panel spars
171 Main undercarriage leg door
172 Port mainwheel
173 Inboard stores pylon
174 Main undercarriage leg strut
175 Hydraulic retraction jack
176 Undercarriage leg pivot fixing
177 Side-locking breaker strut
178 Main undercarriage mounting rib
179 Wing panel multi-spar construction
180 Leading-edge flap rib construction
181 Port leading-edge manoeuvre flap
182 2,000-lb (907-kg) low-drag HE bomb
183 Fuselage centreline pylon (3,000-lb/1 360 kg capacity)

184 Centreline external fuel tank (275 US gal/1 041 l)
185 Wing pylon tank (150 US gal/568 l)
186 LAU-31A rocket pack (19 x 2.75-in ground attack rockets)
187 2.75-in (68-mm) folding fin aircraft rocket (FFAR)
188 1,000-lb (454-kg) Mk 83 HE bomb
189 CBU 24 or 49 cluster bomb
190 Snakeye retarded bomb

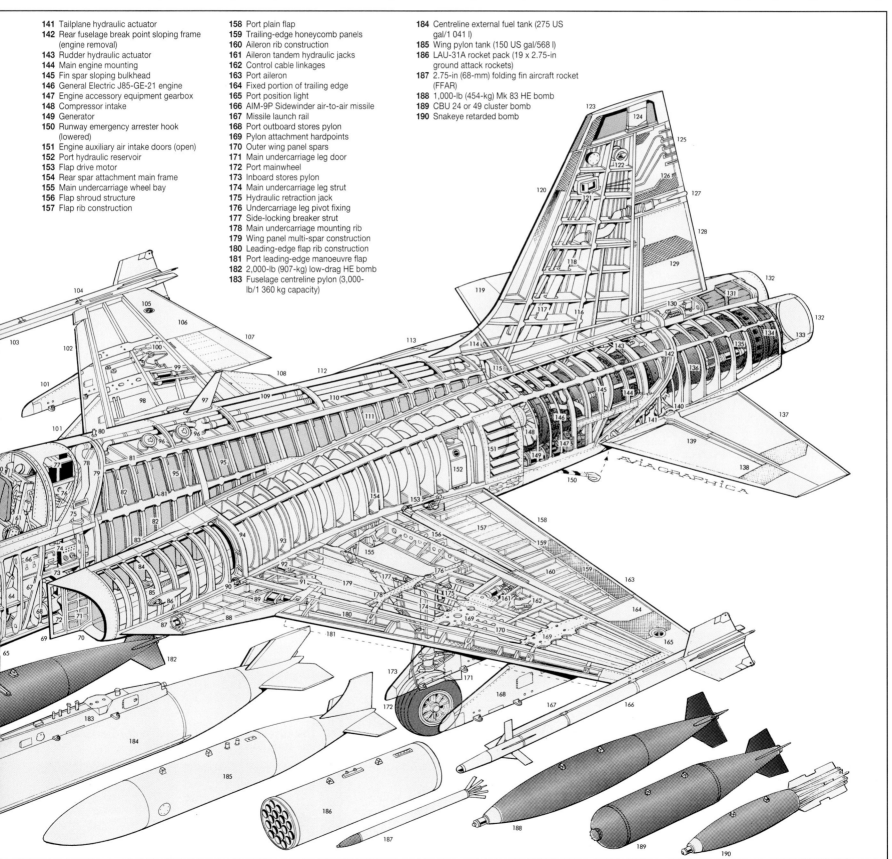

edge root extensions, multi-mode manoeuvring flaps (as earlier applied to the Dutch NF-5A and B), X-band radar, a central air data computer and provision for up to 7,000 lb (3 175 kg) of underwing stores. Built-in armament remained two 20-mm cannon and provision was made for two wingtip-mounted AIM-9 Sidewinder AAMs. First deliveries were made to the USAF in the spring of 1973, with deliveries to foreign air forces commencing early 1974. A combat-capable two-seat training equivalent, the F-5F with a built-in armament of one 20-mm cannon, flew on 25 September 1974, with the initial production F-5F following in April 1976. Production totalled 1,171 F-5Es, 244 F-5Fs, and 12 RF-5Es, although a considerable number of F-5Es were later converted to RF-5Es, and more than 800 remain in service, making it a prime candidate for upgrading. In all, some 26 nations have operated the Tiger II, of which 20 (Bahrain, Brazil, Chile, Honduras,

The F-5E (above and below) was winning contender in the Improved International Fighter competition.

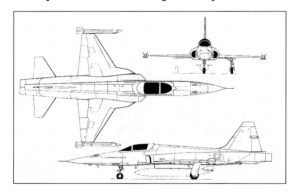

Indonesia, Iran, Jordan, Kenya, Malaysia, Mexico, Morocco, Paraguay, Saudi Arabia, Singapore, South Korea, Spain, Switzerland, Taiwan, Tunisia and Yemen) continue to do so, although in a few cases serviceability must be questionable. The Tiger II is probably best known for its adversary role with the USAF and USN, in which it acted as a MiG-21 simulator, for which its small size, agility, and poor rearward view uniquely suited it. Over the past decade, upgrades have proliferated, with everything from new radars and a "glass cockpit", to an avionics refit. Botswanan CF-5A/Bs (ex-Canadian Defence Force) had had an avionics upgrade by Bristol Aerospace prior to delivery, while 48 Brazilian F-5E/Fs began an extensive avionics upgrade by Elbit, including the FIAR Grifo multi-mode radar, from October 1998. Chilean F-5E/Fs received a new multi-mode radar and a "glass cockpit" from Elbit, while Indonesian aircraft had their radar upgraded by SABCA in 1995. Singaporean F-5E/Fs were locally upgraded from 1997 as the F-5S/T, with the Grifo radar, a new HUD, and MFDs. Spanish SF-5s were first upgraded by Bristol Aerospace, then in mid-2000 IAI was contracted to provide a "glass cockpit" and advanced training systems to 22 SF-5Bs. In May 2000, Elbit

(Below) One of the F-5Es of the Moroccan Royal Air Force delivered between June 1981 and January 1983.

(Above, top) An F-5E "Chung Cheng", 1st TFW, Republic of China AF, Tainan, 1982, and (immediately above) F-5E of Moroccan RAF, Kénitra, 1982-83.

received a contract from Thailand for a new EW suite, RWR and IFF for 31 Tiger IIs, while Turkey placed an order with IAI/Elbit/Singapore Aerospace for a new cockpit and avionics suite for 48 A/Bs. Finally, Venezuela has booked Singapore Aerospace to fit new avionics kit. To date, the one company that has missed out on the update market is Northrop Grumman, despite having a graduated programme called Tiger IV. *Max speed, 1, 082 mph (1 741 km/h) at 36,090 ft (11 000 m), 753 mph (1 212 km/h) at sea level. Max initial climb, 34,500 ft/min (175,25 m/sec). Range (clean), 553 mls (890 km). Empty weight, 9,723 lb (4 410 kg). Loaded weight (clean), 15,745 lb (7 142 kg). Span, 26ft 8 in (8,13 m). Length, 48 ft 2¼ in (14,68 m). Height, 13 ft 4½ in (4,08 m). Wing area, 186 sq ft (17,28 m²).*

NORTHROP YF-17   USA

Based on the company-funded P530 Cobra project, the YF-17 was developed to meet a USAF Request for Proposals for a lightweight day air superiority fighter. Of the companies making submissions for the RFP, Northrop and General Dynamics were each awarded contracts on 13 April 1972 for their contenders as the YF-17 and YF-16 respectively. The two YF-17 prototypes were flown on 9 June and 21 August 1974, these each being powered by two General Electric YJ101-GE-100 engines rated at 14,400 lb st (6 532 kgp) with afterburning. Proposed armament comprised one 20-mm rotary cannon and two AIM-9 Sidewinder AAMs, provision being made for one centreline and four wing stores stations to give the YF-17 multi-mission capability. In 1974, the YF-16 was selected by the USAF, the YF-17 providing the basis for a shipboard tactical fighter for the US Navy, being further developed in collaboration with McDonnell Douglas as the F/A-18 Hornet (which see). *Max speed, 1,287 mph (2 071 km/h) at 36,090 ft (11 000 m). Range (max external fuel), 2,800 mls (4 506 km). Empty equipped weight, 21,000 lb (9 526 kg). Max loaded weight, 30,630 lb (13 894 kg). Span, 35 ft 0 in (10, 66 m). Length, 55 ft 6 in (16,92 m). Height, 14 ft 6 in (4,42 m). Wing area, 350 sq ft (32,51 m²).*

The YF-17 (above and below) was to be developed in collaboration with McDonnell Douglas as the F/A-18.

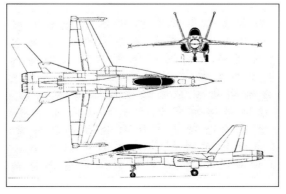

NORTHROP F-20 TIGERSHARK   USA

The F-20 (above and below), the photo depicting the second and third prototypes of this fighter.

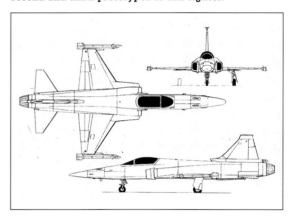

Initially known as the F-5G and officially redesignated F-20 in November 1982, the Tigershark single-seat tactical fighter was evolved as a company-funded development of the basic F-5E, having an 80 per cent increase in engine thrust and only 21 per cent increase in empty weight. Powered by a single General Electric F404-GE-100 turbofan rated at 17,000 lb st (7 711 kgp) with afterburning, the F-20 had an armament of two 20-mm cannon and could carry up to 7,000 lb (3 175 kg) of ordnance on five stations. Three prototypes of the F-20, each embodying progressive improvements, were flown, these entering flight test on 30 August 1982, 26 August 1983 and 12 May 1984. A fourth prototype in the proposed fully-operational configuration was under construction when, following the October 1986 decision that an upgraded F-16A was to succeed F-4s and F-106s as the USAF's air defence fighter, Northrop terminated further development of the F-20 and thereafter ceased marketing efforts. *Max speed, 800 mph (1 288 km/h) at sea level and 1,320 mph (2 124 km/h) above 36,000 ft (10 975 m). Max initial climb (at combat weight), 52, 800 ft/min (268,3 m/sec). Range (ferry with max external fuel), 1,842 mls (2 965 km). Empty weight, 11,220 lb (5 089 kg). Max loaded weight, 27,502 lb (12 475 kg). Span, 26 ft 8 in (8,13 m). Length, 46 ft 6 in (14,17 m). Height, 13ft 10in (4,22 m). Wing area, 186 sq ft (17,28 m²).*

The first prototype F-20 (below) as demonstrated at the Paris *Salon*, Le Bourget, 1983.

NORTHROP/McDONNELL DOUGLAS YF-23 USA

To meet the USAF's ATF (Advanced Tactical Fighter) requirement, the Northrop Corporation entered partnership with the McDonnell Douglas Corporation, receiving an order in October 1986 for two prototypes which were assigned the designation YF-23. These were respectively powered by paired Pratt & Whitney YF119-PW-100 and General Electric YF120-GE-100 turbofans each in the 32,000-35,000 lb st (14 515-15 875 kgp) category. The YF119-engined YF-23 flew on 27 August 1990 followed on 26 October by that with YF120s. Technically innovative with low observable characteristics and the ability to achieve high angles of attack (up to 60 deg) without thrust vectoring, the YF-23 featured a trapezoidal wing with 40 deg of taper on leading and trailing edges and Vee-type tail surfaces. The engines exhausted through narrow slots above the flattened rear fuselage to reduce IR signature and primary armament was disposed in tandem weapons bays. Two short-range AIM-9 AAMs were accommodated in the forward bay and four medium-range AIM-120s were housed in vertically and horizontally staggered pairs in the larger rear bay. In addition, provision was made for a single 20-mm M61A1 six-barrel rotary cannon. The competing Lockheed YF-22 was announced winning ATF contender on 23 April 1991 following a three-month comparative test programme. During this the two YF-23s flew 50 sorties over 104 days, accumulated 7.2 hours of supersonic cruise time (Mach=1.4 to 1.6) and demonstrated an 18-

The YF-23 (above and below), the photo depicting the YF119-engined first prototype aircraft.

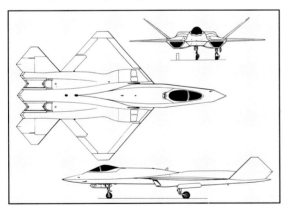

(Below) The second YF-23 in the foreground with the first YF-23 peeling off in the background.

min combat turnaround (including refuelling and simulated rearming) and combat surge capability by flying six missions during a 10-hour daylight period. The following data are estimated. *Max speed, 915 mph (1 470 km/h) at low altitude, or Mach=1.2, 1,190 mph (1 915 km/h) above 36,000 ft (10 975 m), or Mach=1.8. Max sustained cruise, 925-990 mph (1 490-1 595 km/h) above 36,000 ft (10 975 m), or Mach=1.4 – 1.6. Combat radius (internal fuel and full AAM armament), 800-900 mls (1 290-1 450 km). Empty weight, 33,000 lb (14 970 kg). Normal loaded weight, 55,000 lb (24 950 kg). Span, 43 ft 7¼ in (13,29 m). Length, 67 ft 4¾ in (20,54 m). Height, 13 ft 10¾ in (4,24 m).*

NVI F.K.31 Netherlands

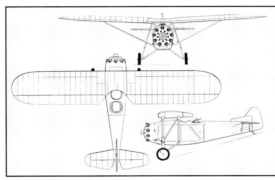

The F.K.31 (above and below) was built in small series for the East Indies and for Finland.

The F.K.31 two-seat parasol monoplane reconnaissance fighter was designed by Frits Koolhoven for the Nationale Vliegtuig Industrie, the first prototype being flown in June 1923. Initial trials dictated some fuselage lengthening, an increase in rudder area and the application of dihedral to the wings, these changes being made on the second prototype flown in the following autumn. Four series F.K.31s were ordered by the *Luchtvaart Afdeling* for use in the East Indies, and, embodying further modifications, were completed in the autumn of 1925. These saw only limited service and were withdrawn in 1930. A manufacturing licence for the F.K.31 was acquired by the Etablissements Louis de Monge, the French concern building one example as the M.101 C2 (which see). A manufacturing licence was also acquired by the Finnish government, eight F.K.31s being purchased from the parent company and being delivered to Finland during July-September 1926. A further four were built in Finland by the State Aircraft Factory in 1929-30, these featuring revised vertical tail

surfaces, but they were rejected by the air arm. The F.K.31 proved to possess extremely poor flying characteristics, the eight Koolhoven-built aircraft being scrapped by the Finns in September 1931, and those built by the State Aircraft Factory in February 1932. The F.K.31 was powered by a 420 hp Bristol Jupiter IV nine-cylinder radial engine and was of mixed construction, the wings being of wood with fabric skinning and the fuselage being of steel tube with metal skinning forward and fabric aft. Armament comprised either one or two forward-firing synchronised machine guns and a further weapon on a flexible mounting in the rear cockpit. *Max speed, 158 mph (255 km/h) at 13,125 ft (4 000 m). Max endurance, 6.0 hrs. Empty weight, 2,293 lb (1 040 kg). Loaded weight, 3,968 lb (1 800 kg). Span, 44 ft 11⅓ in (13,70 m). Length, 25 ft 7 in (7,80 m). Height, 11 ft 1⅘ in (3,40 m). Wing area, 292.79 sq ft (27,20 m²).*

O

OEFFAG TYPE CF (50.14) Austria-Hungary

Late in 1917, the Oesterreichische Flugzeugfabrik (Oeffag) of Wiener Neustadt initiated the design of its first and, in the event, only single-seat fighter, the Type CF.

The Type CF (above and below) appeared in the July 1918 Fighter Evaluation held at Aspern.

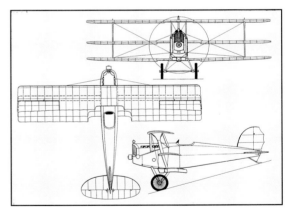

An equi-span triplane of wooden construction with I-type interplane struts, the Type CF was powered by a 225 hp Austro-Daimler six-cylinder water-cooled engine, intended armament comprising two synchronised 8-mm Schwarzlose machine guns. Flight testing began in May 1918, but the triplane was already outmoded by contemporary biplane development, the Type CF being viewed by the *K.u.K.Luftfahrttruppen* as retrogressive. Nevertheless, the prototype appeared in the Fighter Evaluation held at Aspern in July 1918. In the meantime, the two-piece upper wing had given place to a one-piece wing with ailerons of increased area, a 200 hp Austro-Daimler engine having supplanted the more powerful unit. Too heavy and unwieldy, the Type CF aroused no enthusiasm, having neither performance nor manoeuvrability to commend it, and further development was abandoned. *Loaded weight, 2,138 lb (970 kg). Span, 27 ft 6⅔ in (8,40 m). Length, 20 ft 11⁹/₁₀ in (6,40 m). Height, 9 ft 9⅓ in (2,98 m). Wing area, 256.19 sq ft (23,80 m²).*

OL'KHOVSKY TORPEDO   Russia

Capt Vladimir M Ol'khovsky, Commanding Officer of the 5th Air Park at Bryansk, undertook the design and construction of a two-seat fighter-reconnaissance aircraft which, dubbed the Torpedo – an allusion to the shape of its fuselage – featured the first wooden monocoque fuselage to be built in Russia. A parasol monoplane utilising wing warping for control and entirely of wooden construction, the Torpedo was completed in Odessa in February 1917 with an 80 hp Le Rhône 9C rotary engine. This was replaced by a 110 hp Le Rhône 9J prior to the flight test programme, which was conducted between 6 and 20 March 1917. The flying characteristics of the Torpedo were considered good, and, after completion of tests, the aircraft was handed over to the Odessa part-unit of the Gatchina school, no further examples being built. *Time to 3,280 ft (1 000 m), 4.0 min. Service ceiling, 16,405 ft (5 000 m). No further details available.*

The so-called Torpedo fighter-reconnaissance aircraft (below) designed by Vladimir Ol'khovsky.

ORDNANCE ENGINEERING TYPE B   USA

In 1917, Etienne Dormoy, formerly a designer with the Société Pour Aviation et ses Dérivés (SPAD) and a member of the French Aeronautical Mission to the USA, designed a single-seat fighter for the Ordnance Engineering Corporation founded in the previous year. This concern (which was to use the acronym Orenco from early 1919) completed a prototype known as the Type B (the Type A having been a two-seat training biplane) which was flown early in 1918. A two-bay staggered biplane of wooden construction, the Type B was powered by a 160 hp Gnome Monosoupape nine-

The Type B (above and below), the first example of this fighter being illustrated by the photograph.

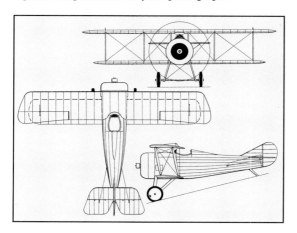

cylinder rotary engine and was intended to carry an armament of three 0.3-in (7,62-mm) Marlin machine guns – one beneath the upper wing and two beneath the lower wing. Four examples were ordered by the Aviation Section of the Signal Corps (together with five examples of the Type C trainer derivative), but the US government had meanwhile elected to manufacture proven European fighters, and no series production of the Type B was therefore undertaken. *Max speed, 135 mph (217 km/h) at sea level. Time to 5,000 ft (1 525 m), 3.3 min. Range, 200 mls (322 km). Empty weight, 935 lb (424 kg). Loaded weight, 1,295 lb (587 kg). Span, 26 ft 0 in (7,92 m). Length, 18 ft 10 in (5,74 m). Height, 7 ft 4 in (2,23 m). Wing area, 180 sq ft (16,72 m²).*

ORDNANCE ENGINEERING (ORENCO) TYPE D   USA

Towards the end of 1918, the Ordnance Engineering Corporation offered a new single-seat fighter designed around the 300 hp Hispano-Suiza H eight-cylinder water-cooled engine, the Type D, receiving an order for four aircraft. A two-bay equi-span staggered biplane of wooden construction with an armament of two 0.3-in (7,62-mm) guns, the first Type D was completed in January 1919 (and shortly thereafter the company adopted the acronym Orenco). Tested by what had by then become known as the Air Service, the Type D received a glowing commendation, but Curtiss submitted the winning bid for the production of a series of 50 aircraft, for which various modifications were introduced (see Curtiss-Orenco D). The parent company further developed the design as the Type D2 with un-equal-span wings of single-bay configuration, three being ordered by the Air Service as PW-3s. Demonstrating structural weaknesses during ground trials, these were declared unsafe and were not flown. The following data relate to the Orenco-built Type D prototypes. *Max speed, 147 mph (237 km/h) at sea level. Time to 5,000 ft (1 525 m), 4.3 min. Range, 275 mls (442 km). Empty weight, 1,666 lb (756 kg). Loaded weight, 2,432 lb (1 103 kg). Span, 30 ft 0 in (9,14 m). Length, 21 ft 6 in (6,55 m). Height, 8 ft 3 in (2,52 m). Wing area, 261 sq ft (24,25 m²).*

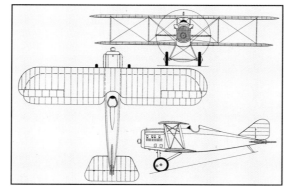

Although developed by Ordnance Engineering, the Type D fighter (above and below) was destined to be built in series by the Curtiss company.

PACKARD LUSAC-11   USA

Designed at the behest of the US Army Engineering Division by Georges Lepère, a member of the French Aeronautical Mission to the USA, the LUSAC (an acronym for Lepère US Army Combat) was a two-seat two-bay staggered biplane of wooden construction powered by a 425 hp Liberty 12 water-cooled engine.

The LUSAC-11 (above and below) was ordered into production, but failed to achieve service status.

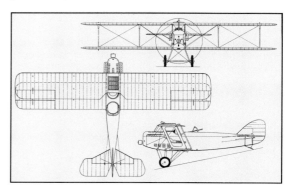

Intended armament comprised two fixed forward-firing 0.3-in (7,62-mm) guns with a third on a flexible mounting in the rear cockpit. Flown for the first time in August 1918, the Lepère two-seat fighter was placed in production as the LUSAC-11 by the Packard Motor Company, but although large-scale manufacture was envisaged, only 30 had been completed when contracts were terminated with the end of World War I. The LUSAC-11 never entered service with the Air Service, but established several world altitude records in the early 'twenties. *Max speed, 133 mph (214 km/h) at sea level. Time to 6,500 ft (1 980 m), 6.0 min. Range, 320 mls (515 km). Empty weight, 2,561 lb (1 162 kg). Loaded weight, 3,746 lb (1 699 kg). Span, 41 ft 7 in (12,67 m). Length, 25 ft 3 in (7,69 m). Height, 10 ft 7 in (3,22 m). Wing area, 415.6 sq ft (38,60 m²).*

PANAVIA TORNADO ADV   UK

The Tornado ADV (Air Defence Version) was a British-developed dedicated fighter derivative of the multi-national (UK, Federal Germany and Italy) Tornado IDS (Interdictor Strike) aircraft with which it possessed

One of eight dual-control Tornado F Mk 2Ts (above) of No 229 OCU at RAF Coningsby late in 1985.

some 80 per cent commonality. Developed specifically to meet an RAF requirement, but manufactured by the Panavia consortium in similar fashion to the IDS, the ADV first flew on 27 October 1979. Three development aircraft were followed on 5 March 1984 by the first of 18 examples of the initial service version, the Tornado F Mk 2 with two Turbo-Union RB199-34R Mk 103 turbofans of 9,656 lb st (4 380 kgp) and 16,920 lb st (7 675 kgp) with max afterburning. Production continued with the F Mk 3, first flown 20 November 1985, with Mk 104 engines (affording higher afterburning ratings), RAF orders for the ADV totalling 165 aircraft, and a further 24 being ordered by Saudi Arabia. Armament comprised one 27-mm cannon and Sky Flash (4) and AIM-9L (4) AAMs. *Max speed, 920 mph (1 480 km/h) at sea level, or Mach=1.2, 1,450 mph (2 333 km/h) at 40,000 ft (12 190 m), or Mach=2.2. Empty weight, 31,970 lb (14 500 kg). Max loaded weight, 61,700 lb (27 986 kg). Span (25-deg sweep), 45ft 7¹/₄ in (13,90 m), (68-deg sweep), 28 ft 2¹/₂ in (8,59 m). Length, 59 ft 3⁷/₈ in (18,08 m). Height, 18 ft 8¹/₂ in (5,70 m). Wing area, 322.9 sq ft (30, 00 m²).*

The Tornado F Mk 3 (above and below), the photograph illustrating aircraft from the Coningsby-based No 29 Sqn with full complement of air-to-air missiles.

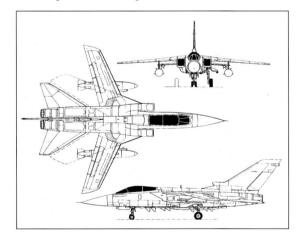

PARNALL SCOUT　　　　UK

Parnall and Sons of Bristol initiated work on the company's first original aircraft, a single-seat anti-airship fighter to the designs of A Camden Pratt, in 1916. Intended to meet a requirement formulated by the Admiralty, this aircraft, unofficially known as the Zeppelin Chaser, was a large, two-bay staggered biplane of wooden construction. It was powered by a 260 hp Sunbeam Maori 12-cylinder water-cooled engine and armed with a single 0.303-in (7,7mm) gun offset to starboard and firing upward at an angle of 45 deg. Two prototypes were ordered, but the first of these proved appreciably overweight. Although the Scout

reportedly flew twice, it was considered to possess unacceptably low safety factors and was returned to the manufacturer, development being abandoned. The following data are manufacturer's estimates. *Max speed, 113 mph (182 km/h) at sea level. Span, 44 ft 0 in (13,41 m). Wing area, 516 sq ft (47,94 m²).*

Known unofficially as the Zeppelin Chaser, the Parnall Scout (below) reportedly flew only twice.

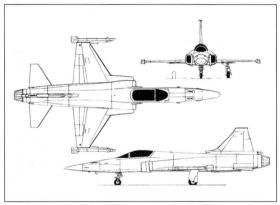

(Below) The Parnall Scout airship interceptor.

PARNALL PLOVER　　　　UK

Designed by Harold Bolas to meet a specification (6/22) for a single-seat shipboard fighter to succeed the Gloster Mars X Nightjar, the Plover appeared in 1922, three prototypes being built. Of wood and fabric construction, and designed around a 436 hp Bristol Jupiter IV nine-cylinder radial, the Plover could be fitted with either a normal wheel undercarriage or with twin floats

from which wheels projected to provide amphibious capability. Armed with two synchronised 0.303-in (7,7mm) guns, the Plover was ordered into small-scale production, ten being built of which at least six served briefly with Fleet Fighter Flights, being superseded by the superior Fairey Flycatcher. *Max speed, 142 mph (228 km/h). Time to 20,000 ft (6 100 m), 25.2 min. Empty weight, 2,035 lb (923 kg). Loaded weight, 2,984 lb (1 354 kg). Span, 29 ft 0 in (8,84 m). Length, 23 ft 0 in (7, 00 m). Height, 12 ft 0 in (3,65 m). Wing area, 306 sq ft (28,43 m²).*

A Plover fitted with amphibious floats (above) and in standard form with wheel undercarriage (below).

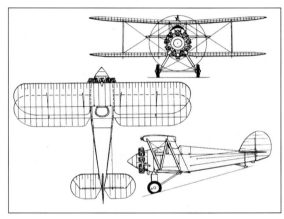

PARNALL PIPIT　　　　UK

A fabric-covered all-metal single-seat shipboard fighter designed by Harold Bolas to Specification 21/26, the Pipit equi-span single-bay staggered biplane was powered by a 495 hp Rolls-Royce FM 12-cylinder water-cooled engine and could be fitted with either wheels or floats. The first of two prototypes was flown in 1928, but crashed when a tailplane spar failed as a result of flutter. The second prototype, with a 520 hp FXIIS engine and many other changes, was also lost as a result of violent flutter which fractured the sternpost whereupon the vertical tail surfaces were carried away. Further development of the Pipit was then abandoned. *Max speed, 173 mph (278 km/h) at 3,000ft*

(Below) The first of the two prototypes of the Pipit.

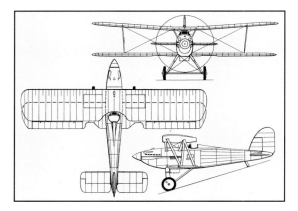

(Above) The Pipit single-seat shipboard fighter.

(915 m). Initial climb, 1,600 ft/min (8,13 m/sec). Loaded weight, 3,980 lb (1 805 kg). Span, 35 ft 0 in (10,67 m). Length, 26 ft 0 in (7,92 m). Height, 10 ft 5⅓ in (3,18 m).

PASHININ I-21 USSR

Early in 1939, Mikhail M Pashinin, a former deputy of N N Polikarpov, designed a single-seat fighter reflecting Spanish and Japanese (Nomonhan Incident) experience as part of the high priority programme to produce a successor to the I-16. Assigned the designation I-21 (despite its earlier use for the Ilyushin-designed TsKB-32), the fighter was of mixed construction, with a plywood-covered metal wing, a welded steel tube forward fuselage and a wooden monocoque rear fuselage.

The second prototype Pashinin I-21 (above) with revised outer wing panels.

Intended to take the Klimov-developed M-107 engine, the prototypes were fitted with the Klimov M-105P of 1,050 hp because of the non-availability of the more powerful unit. Armament comprised an engine-mounted 23-mm cannon and two wing-mounted 7,62-mm machine guns. The first prototype was flown on 18 May 1940, State Trials, which commenced on 6 June, revealing poor stability. The second prototype was therefore fitted with revised outer wing panels with tapered leading and trailing edges. This prototype attained speeds of 303 mph (488 km/h) at sea level and 356 mph (573 km/h) at 16,405 ft (5 000 m). As handling qualities still left much to be desired, a third prototype, flown in January 1941, embodied considerable wing redesign. The outer panels were sweptback and clipped, reducing span by 5 ft 1⅘ in (1,57 m), and the tailplane was modified. Landing characteristics remained poor, the I-21 demanding an unacceptably long runway, and a pre-series of five aircraft was discontinued. The fol-

(Below) The third prototype of the Pashinin I-21.

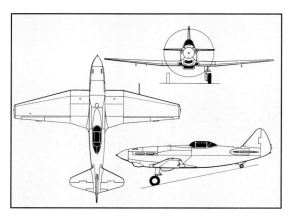

lowing data relate to the third prototype. Max speed, 360 mph (580 km/h) at 15,585 ft (4 750 m). Endurance, 2 hrs. Span, 30 ft 11¼ in (9,43 m). Length, 28 ft 7¾ in (8,73 m).

PEMBERTON-BILLING P.B.23E UK

Designed in 1915 by Noel Pemberton-Billing, and built by the company bearing his name, the P.B.23E single-seat pusher fighting scout biplane was of wooden construction, but the nacelle mounted between the wings and accommodating the pilot was unusual for its time in being covered with light alloy sheet metal. Armament consisted of a single 0.303-in (7,7-mm) machine gun mounted in the nose of the nacelle and power was provided by an 80 hp Le Rhône rotary. The P.B.23E was first flown in September 1915, but was not adopted in its original form, being further developed as the P.B.25. No data relating to the P.B.23 appear to have survived.

The P.B.23E (below) was unusual for its time in having a light alloy sheet-covered fuselage nacelle.

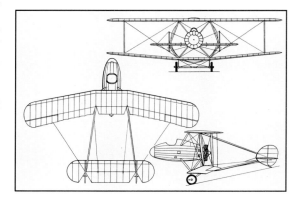

PEMBERTON-BILLING P.B.25 SCOUT UK

Known officially as the Scout, the P.B.25 was a development of the P.B.23. The most obvious differences were in the design of the nacelle, which was fabric covered, and in the wing cellule, the mainplanes featuring 11 deg of sweepback and inversely-tapered ailerons. Twenty P.B.25s were ordered by the Admiralty, all but one of these being powered by the 100 hp Gnome Monosoupape, the exception having a 110 hp Clerget rotary. Armament comprised a single 0.303-in (7,7-mm) machine gun mounted on the nacelle.

The P.B.25 (above and below) was ordered for the RNAS, but proved to be unsuited for operational use.

The last P.B.25 was delivered to the RNAS in February 1917, by which time this type had acquired an unenviable reputation, the take-off and landing characteristics being particularly hazardous. Apart from poor flying qualities, its performance was inadequate and,

being viewed as something of an anachronism, the Scout was quickly discarded. Max speed, 89 mph (143 km/h) at sea level. Time to 6,000 ft (1 830 m), 11 min. Endurance, 2.5 hrs. Empty weight, 1,080 lb (490 kg). Loaded weight, 1,541 lb (699 kg). Span, 32 ft 11½ in (10,04 m). Length, 24 ft 1 in (7,34 m). Height, 10 ft 5 in (3,17 m). Wing area, 277 sq ft (25,73 m²).

PEMBERTON-BILLING P.B.29E UK

One of the most extraordinary interceptor fighters flown during World War I, the P.B.29E twin-engined quadruplane was conceived as an anti-airship aircraft. Intended to be capable of prolonged cruise at low speeds during the nocturnal hours, the P.B.29E featured high aspect ratio wings with a pair of 90 hp Austro-Daimler six-cylinder water-cooled engines underslung from the second mainplane and driving pusher propellers. The entire wing cellule was braced as a two-bay structure, the fuselage being attached to the second wing and accommodating two crew members, and a gunner with a single 0.303-in (7,7-mm) machine gun occupying a nacelle that filled the gap between the centre sections of the upper mainplanes. The P.B.29E was flown in the winter of 1915-16, and was destroyed comparatively early in its flight test programme, but aroused sufficient interest to warrant development of the P.B.31E of similar concept. No data relating to the P.B.29E are available.

The extraordinary P.B.29E anti-airship quadruplane (below) intended for prolonged nocturnal cruise.

PEMBERTON-BILLING (SUPERMARINE) P.B.31E UK

When Pemberton-Billing Ltd changed its name to Supermarine Aviation in December 1916, work on a further airship fighter, the P.B.31E, had reached an advanced stage and the first prototype of this quadruplane was to fly shortly afterwards, in February 1917. Fundamentally an extrapolation of the P.B.29E, and unofficially known as Night Hawk, the P.B.31E was designed to have a maximum endurance in excess of 18 hours to enable it to lie in wait for intruding airships. The entire concept was fallacious as, in the unlikely event that the P.B.31E found itself fortuitously in the same area of sky as its prey, it would have been totally incapable of pursuing the airship which could have risen out of range before any guns could have been brought to bear. A three-bay quadruplane powered by two 100 hp Anzani nine-cylinder radials, the P.B.31E carried a searchlight in the extreme nose. The intended armament comprised a one-and-a-half pounder Davis

(Below) The P.B.31E anti-airship fighter quadruplane.

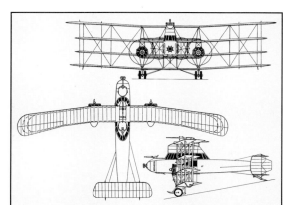

The P.B.31E (above) was flown only briefly before the inadequacy of its concept was accepted.

gun on a traversing mounting in a forward position level with the top wing, a 0.303-in (7,7-mm) machine gun being located in a second position immediately aft and a similar weapon occupying a forward fuselage position. Shortly after the start of flight trials, the short-comings of the concept were finally appreciated, and, on 23 July 1917, the first prototype was scrapped and the second incomplete prototype abandoned. *Max speed, 75 mph (121 km/h). Time to 10,000 ft (3 050 m), 1 hr. Normal endurance, 9 hrs. Empty weight, 3,677 lb (1 668 kg). Loaded weight, 6,146 lb (2 788 kg). Span, 60 ft 0 in (18,29 m). Length, 36 ft 10½ in (11,24 m). Height, 17 ft 8½ in (5,40 m). Wing area, 962 sq ft (89,37 m².)*

PETLYAKOV VI-100   USSR

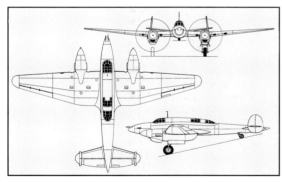

The extremely advanced VI-100 (above and below) which was reworked to fulfil the rôle of dive bomber.

Singularly advanced in concept in being an aero-dynamically clean, all-metal monoplane equipped with turbo-superchargers and pressurised accommodation for its two crew members, the VI-100 (the prefix letters indicating *vysotny istrebitel* – high-altitude interceptor) was conceived in 1938 by a team led by Vladimir M Petlyakov. Because of delays in the development of the proposed pressure cabin, the first prototype VI-100 was completed without this feature, and the turbo-superchargers, too, were omitted when flight testing began on 22 December 1939. Powered by two 1,050 hp Klimov M-105 engines, the VI-100 carried an armament of four 20-mm cannon in the nose and a single 7,62-mm gun on a flexible mounting in the rear cockpit. Speeds of 273 mph (440 km/h) at sea level and 320 mph (530 km/h) at 16,405 ft (5 000 m) were attained during trials, and it was calculated that with TK-3 turbo-superchargers a speed of 385 mph (620 km/h) would be achieved at 32,810 ft (10 000 m). Priority attached to the development of a dedicated high-altitude interceptor had meanwhile been withdrawn, however, and the design was reworked to fulfil the rôle of dive bomber as the PB-100, this subsequently entering production as the Pe-2. The following data are estimated and relate to

the proposed series version of the VI-100. *Max speed, 385 mph (620 km/h) at 32,810 ft (10 000 m). Time to 16,405 ft (5 000 m), 6.0 min. Range, 932 mls (1 500 km). Loaded weight, 16,005 lb (7 260 kg). Span, 56 ft 3⅔ in (17,16 m). Length, 41 ft 4 in (12,60 m). Wing area, 430.57 sq ft (40,00 m²).*

PETLYAKOV Pe-3   USSR

One early production example of the Pe-2 dive bomber was completed as a prototype for the Pe-3 multi-rôle fighter and was flown in the spring of 1941. Although the basic airframe was unchanged, the Pe-3 was a two-seater with pilot and observer/gunner seated back-to-back. The ventral gunner's station was deleted, the air brakes were discarded, controllable slats were introduced on the wing leading edges and additional fuel capacity was provided in place of the main bomb-bay and the bomb-bays in the tails of the engine nacelles.

The Pe-3 multi-rôle fighter (above) was built in small numbers prior to the *Wehrmacht* invasion.

Powered by two 1,100 hp Klimov M-105 engines – to which it was proposed to apply TK-2 turbo-superchargers, although, in the event these were never fitted – the Pe-3 carried an armament of two 20-mm cannon, two 12,7-mm machine guns, and a 12,7-mm gun for the observer in an MV-3 dorsal turret. In the event, only 23 Pe-3 fighters were built prior to the German invasion of the Soviet Union, when further manufacture of this model was discontinued. *Max speed, 325 mph (523 km/h) at 16,405 ft (5 000 m). Time to 16,405 ft (5 000 m), 8.5 min. Range, 932 mls (1 500 km). Empty weight, 12,941 lb (5 870 kg). Loaded weight, 17,372 lb (7 880 kg). Span, 56 ft 3⅔ in (17,16 m). Length, 41 ft 11 in (12,78 m). Height, 11 ft 2⅔ in (3,42 m). Wing area, 435.95 sq ft (40,50 m²).*

PETLYAKOV Pe-3BIS   USSR

The Pe-3bis was essentially an interim fighter resulting from the exigencies of the times, every second aircraft on the Pe-2 assembly line at GAZ 22 being completed in fighter configuration under this designation from the early summer of 1941. Possessing closer affinity with the basic dive bomber than had the Pe-3, the Pe-3bis dispensed with the air brakes and introduced wing leading-edge slats, and carried twin 20-mm cannon in the bomb-bay. Some aircraft had the twin nose-mounted 7,62-mm guns replaced by 12,7-mm weapons. The MV-3 dorsal turret housing a single 12,7-mm gun was retained. Powered by two 1,100 hp Klimov M-105RA engines, the Pe-3bis was delivered to first-line regiments from August 1941, some being assigned the nocturnal intercept rôle for which special instrumentation was provided. Some were assigned to Naval Aviation for the anti-shipping mission and others were fitted with vertical and oblique cameras for use as re-

(Above and below) The Pe-3bis, the photo depicting an example serving with the Finnish 1/LeLv 48, 1943.

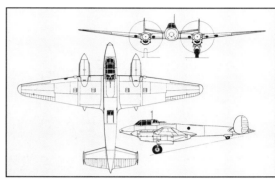

connaissance-fighters (Pe-2R). Deliveries of the interim Pe-3bis were halted after the completion of some 300 aircraft. One Pe-3bis was captured by Finnish forces and used in concert with Pe-2 bombers by LeLv 48 from February 1943 until June 1944. *Max speed, 329 mph (530 km/h) at 17,390 ft (5 300 m). Time to 16,405 ft (5 000 m), 10.2 min. Max range, 1,056 mls (1 700 km). Empty weight, 12,941 lb (5 870 kg). Loaded weight, 17,725 lb (8 040 kg). Span, 56 ft 3⅔ in (17,16 m). Length, 41 ft 4½ in (12,60 m). Height, 11 ft 2⅔ in (3,42 m). Wing area, 435.95 sq ft (40,50 m²).*

PFALZ E I   Germany

Early in 1914, the Pfalz Flugzeug-Werke, which had been established in the previous year specifically to manufacture aircraft for the Bavarian Flying Service, acquired a licence to manufacture the Morane-Saulnier Types H and L. In 1915, Pfalz produced its first aircraft to carry a machine gun, this, the E I, being broadly based on the Type H and powered by an 80 hp Oberursel U 0 (Gnome) rotary engine. This shoulder-wing monoplane

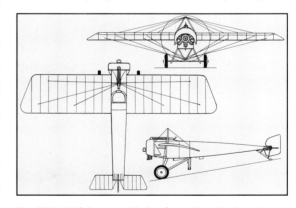

The Pfalz E I (above and below) was broadly based on the Morane-Saulnier Type H and began to arrive at the Front from late October 1915.

of wooden construction passed its *Typen-Prüfung* in September 1915. Two were at the Front by the end of the following month and the number of E Is at the Front peaked at 27 aircraft by the end of April 1916. Their principal rôle was as armed escorts for observation flights, armament comprising a single synchronised LMG 08/15 machine gun. Some E Is saw action in Palestine during the 1916 Sinai desert campaign, and others were flown by Bavarian units as unarmed high-speed reconnaissance aircraft. *Max speed, 87 mph (140 km/h). Time to 2,625 ft (800 m), 3.0 min. Endurance, 1.5 hrs. Empty weight, 760 lb (345 kg). Loaded weight, 1,179 lb (535 kg). Span, 30 ft 4½ in (9,26 m). Length, 20 ft 8 in (6,30 m). Height, 8 ft 4⅖ in (2,55 m). Wing area, 150.7 sq ft (14,00 m²).*

PFALZ E II   Germany

Fundamentally an improved E I, the E II completed its *Typen-Prüfung* in July 1916, but by that time 30 were already at the Front with various Bavarian squadrons. Following manufacture of some 60 E Is, Pfalz introduced a 100 hp Oberursel U I rotary engine, increased overall span by 3 ft 1 in (94 cm) and continued production as the E II. Armament remained a single synchronised LMG 08/15 machine gun, and the E II served alongside the lower-powered E I in twos and threes with two-seat reconnaissance aircraft units to undertake escort tasks.

The E II (above) was an improved, more powerful development of the E I with longer-span wing.

Like the E I, the E II was entirely of wooden construction and, apart from having a fabric-skinned rear fuselage, was plywood covered. The E II had disappeared from the Western Front by the end of 1916, some having served in Macedonia, Palestine and Syria. *Max speed, 93 mph (150 km/h). Time to 2,625 ft (800 m), 2.75 min. Endurance, 1.5 hrs. Empty weight, 904 lb (410 kg). Loaded weight, 1,261 lb (572 kg). Span, 33 ft 5½ in (10,20 m). Length, 21 ft 1⁹⁄₁₀ in (6,45 m). Height, 8 ft 4⅖ in (2,55 m). Wing area, 172.23 sq ft (16,00 m²).*

PFALZ E III   Germany

The E III (above) was considered an interim type and was evolved from the Morane-Saulnier Type L.

The Morane-Saulnier Type L parasol monoplane two-seater, for which the Pfalz Flugzeug-Werke acquired a manufacturing licence in 1914, was built primarily for the reconnaissance and training rôles as the A I and A II with the 80 hp Oberursel U 0 and 100 hp Oberursel U I rotaries respectively, 60 being delivered during 1914-15. In 1915, the rear seat and gun mounting were removed, a single synchronised LMG 08/15 machine gun was mounted ahead of the cockpit, and, with the 100 hp U I engine, the modified aircraft was produced in small numbers as the E III fighter. Although having a rate of climb superior to that of the E II, the E III was considered as essentially an interim type and the largest number of these fighters at the Front at any one

time was eight (June 1916). *Max speed, 95 mph (153 km/h). Time to 3,280 ft (1 000 m), 3.0 min. Endurance, 2.0 hrs. Empty weight, 981 lb (445 kg). Loaded weight, 1,554 lb (705 kg). Span, 36 ft 9 in (11,20 m). Length, 22 ft 5¾ in (6,85 m). Height, 11 ft 1⅞ in (3,40 m). Wing area, 193.76 sq ft (18,00 m²).*

PFALZ E IV   Germany

Restricted to a small series, the E IV (above) saw little frontline use owing to its shortcomings.

Retaining the ply- and fabric-covered wooden airframe of the E II, the E IV differed primarily in having a two-row Oberursel U III rotary engine of 160 hp and an armament of two synchronised LMG 08/15 machine guns. Type-tested in January 1916, the E IV was found to be a poor gun platform and its U III engine proved unreliable. A series of 24 aircraft was built, but the E IV saw little frontline use owing to its shortcomings, and the maximum number at the Front at any one time was five aircraft (April 1916). *Max speed, 99 mph (160 km/h). Time to 9,840 ft (3 000 m), 10 min. Endurance, 1 hr. Empty weight, 1,038 lb (471 kg). Loaded weight, 1,530 lb (694 kg). Dimensions as for E II apart from length of 21 ft 7⅞ in (6,60 m).*

PFALZ E V & E VI   Germany

The E V (above) was a Daimler-powered derivative of the E IV, but rendered obsolescent by biplanes.

Although, by early 1916, the more rugged and manoeuvrable biplane configuration was demonstrating a clear superiority over the monoplane in the fighting rôle, the Pfalz Flugzeug-Werke persisted with the latter and developed the E V and E VI. The E V, which completed its *Typen-Prüfung* in July 1916, employed an essentially similar airframe to that of the E IV, this being mated with a 105 hp Daimler D I six-cylinder water-cooled engine, armament reverting to a single LMG 08/15 machine gun. Twenty E Vs were built, but the advent of more efficient and more powerful biplanes rendered the E V obsolescent prior to delivery and only three saw frontline service. The E VI differed primarily in having the 100 hp Oberursel U I rotary engine, and some redesign of the vertical tail surface, but this type saw no combat, the 20 built being assigned to the instructional rôle. The following data relate to the E V. *Max speed, 102 mph (165 km/h). Endurance, 2.0 hrs. Empty weight, 1,124 lb (510 kg). Loaded weight, 1,534 lb (696 kg). Dimensions as for E IV.*

Last of the Pfalz monoplanes, the E VI below was similar to the E V apart from its Oberursel engine.

PFALZ D.4   Germany

Designated D.4 by its manufacturer, the Pfalz Flugzeug-Werke's first essay in the single-seat fighting biplane category, flown in the summer of 1916, was powered by a 105 hp Daimler D I six-cylinder water-cooled engine with a car-type radiator. An unequal-span, slightly-staggered single-bay biplane, the D.4 featured an exceptionally deep fuselage eliminating the normal cabane structure and afforded an extremely poor forward view for the pilot who was unable to see the horizon in level flight and was virtually blind for take-off and landing. Flight testing revealed poor handling characteristics, the rudder being blanketed by the deep fuselage and directional stability being totally inadequate. A fixed vertical fin was added at an early stage, but this failed to ameliorate the more serious shortcomings, development being discontinued and Pfalz building the LFG Roland D I (and subsequently the D II). No data relating to the D.4 have survived.

The D.4 (above and below) was the first Pfalz fighter biplane, but offered poor handling.

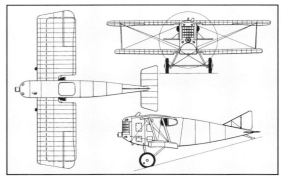

PFALZ D III   Germany

Designed by Ing Geringer assisted by Ing Paulus and Ing Geldmacher, the D III owed much to experience gained in manufacture of the LFG Roland D I and II, and was an unequal-span single-bay biplane of wooden construction with a semi-monocoque fuselage.

(Below) The D III which saw service from autumn 1917.

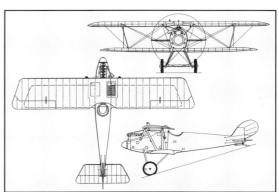

Powered by a 160 hp Daimler D III six-cylinder water-cooled engine and carrying an armament of twin LMG 08/15 machine guns, the D III completed *Typen-Prüfung* at Adlershof in June 1917. By October 1917, 145 D IIIs were already in squadron service, the number at the Front attaining a peak of 276 by the year's end. The D IIIa, which embodied relatively minor changes including a redesigned, longer-span tailplane, repositioned guns and modified lower-wing tips, reached the Front in December 1917. The D IIIa attained its peak ser-

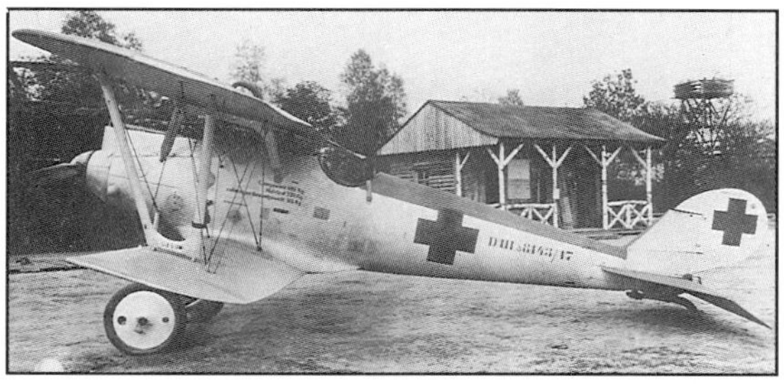

The D IIIa (above) embodied relatively minor changes from the D III and reached the Front in December 1917.

vice usage in April 1918 when 433 were at the Front. Similarly powered and armed to the D III, the D IIIa, which remained in first-line use until the end of hostilities, had a basically similar specification, the following data relating to the earlier model. *Max speed, 102 mph (165 km/h) at 9,840 ft (3 000 m). Time to 4,920 ft (1 500 m), 6.9 min. Endurance, 2.2 hrs. Empty weight, 1,521 lb (690 kg). Loaded weight, 2,039 lb (925 kg). Span, 30 ft 10 in (9,40 m). Length, 22 ft 9⅔ in (6,95 m). Height, 9 ft 9⅛ in (2,67 m). Wing area, 238.32 sq ft (22,14 m^2).*

PFALZ DR-TYP — Germany

In the late autumn of 1917, the Pfalz Flugzeug-Werke completed and flew a triplane derivative of the standard D III biplane. Retaining the 160 hp Daimler D III engine, this experimental model (for which no designation is recorded) featured ailerons on both upper and lower wings. It would seem that manufacturer's trials were unsuccessful, however, as this triplane was never demonstrated to the military authorities at Adlershof.

The Pfalz triplane fighter (below) was based on the standard D III biplane, but was unsuccessful.

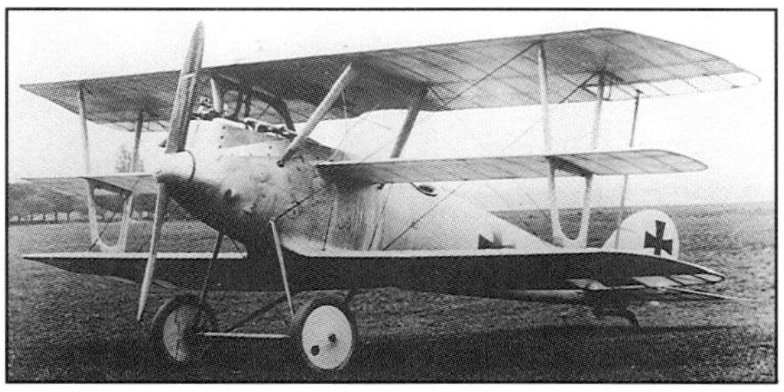

PFALZ D IV — Germany

No details of the D IV single-seat single-bay biplane fighter are available apart from the fact that it was powered by a 110 hp Oberursel U II rotary engine and was built in parallel with the D VI (there being no record of a D V). The D IV is believed to have been flown early in 1917.

PFALZ D VI — Germany

Submitted for inclusion in the first D-type Competition at Adlershof in January 1918 (together with the D VII and D VIII), the D VI was an elegant single-bay biplane in which careful attention had been paid to aerodynamic cleanliness. Flown early in 1917, and employing the semi-monocoque wrapped plywood fuselage construction of the D III, the D VI was powered by a 110 hp Oberursel U II rotary. Armament comprised the standard twin LMG 08/15 arrangement and acceptance testing was completed satisfactorily in September 1917, but a comparatively poor rate of climb seems to have militated against a production order. *Time to 16,405 ft (5 000 m), 24 min. Empty weight, 882 lb (400 kg). Loaded weight, 1,336 lb (606 kg). Span, 23 ft 2¾ in (7,08 m). Wing area, 143.16 sq ft (13,30 m^2).*

The D VI (below) was one of three Pfalz submissions in the first D-type Competition of January 1918.

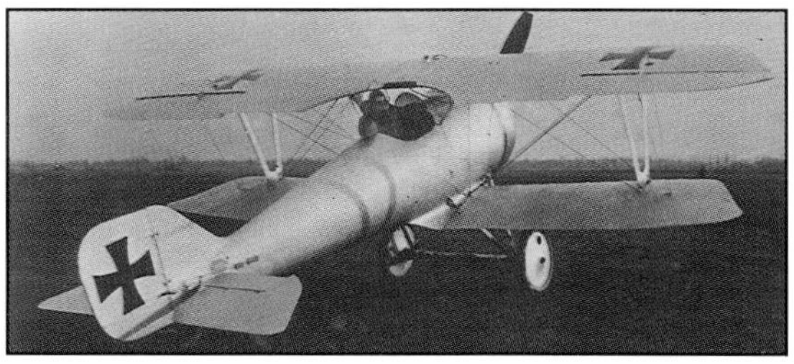

(Below) The D VI which was flown early in 1917.

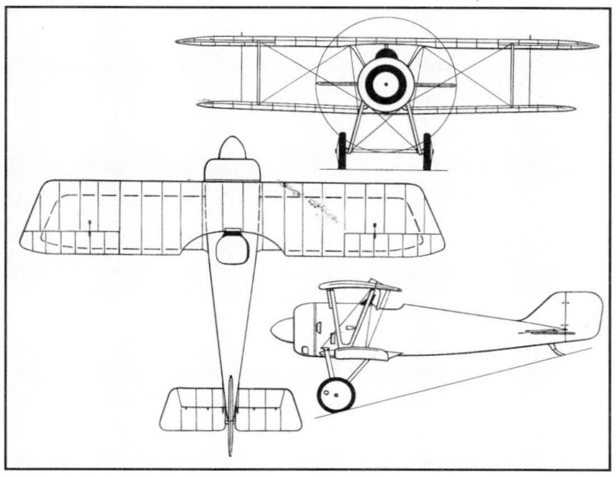

PFALZ DR I — Germany

Official interest in the potential of the triplane configuration for single-seat fighters prompted Pfalz to develop the Dr I. Powered by a 160 hp Siemens Halske Sh III 11-cylinder geared rotary engine, this underwent *Typen-Prüfung* in October 1917. Armed with twin synchronised LMG 08/15 guns, the Dr I was of sufficient promise to warrant a pre-series evaluation batch of 10 aircraft, all of which arrived at the Front by the end of April 1918. Service pilots considered the Dr I too slow and its Sh III engine insufficiently reliable for frontline use, and no further examples were produced. *Max speed, 118 mph (190 km/h) at 13,125 ft (4 000 m). Time to 16,405 ft (5 000 m), 13.5 min. Endurance, 1.5 hrs. Empty weight, 1,124 lb (510 kg). Loaded weight, 1,554 lb (705 kg). Span, 28 ft 0⅔ in (8,55 m). Length, 18 ft 0½ in (5,50 m). Height, 9 ft 0⅔ in (2,76 m). Wing area, 185.14 sq ft (17,20 m^2).*

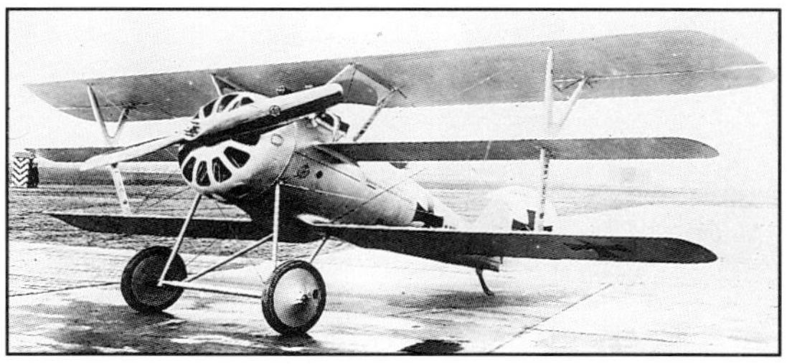

The Dr I (above and below) was tested at the Front in pre-production form during the spring of 1918.

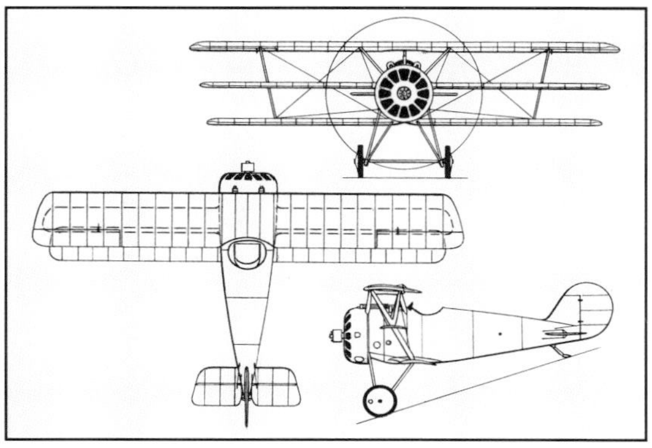

PFALZ D VII — Germany

A further Pfalz contender in the first D-type Competition, the D VII single-bay staggered biplane passed its

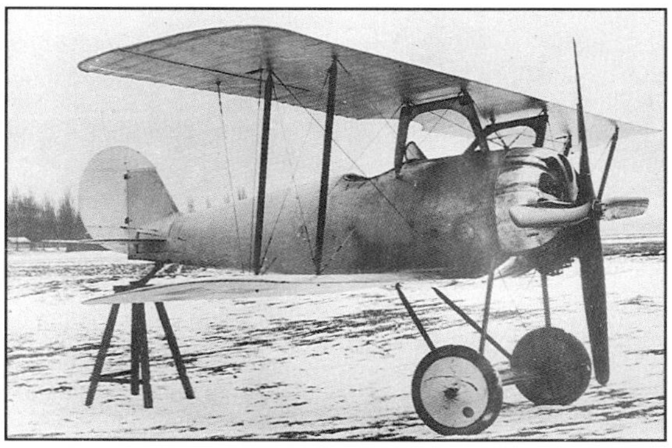

The D VII (above) was another of the Pfalz entries in the January 1918 D-type Competition at Adlershof.

Typen-Prüfung in February 1918, but was not the recipient of a production contract. The D VII was tested with both balanced and unbalanced ailerons, with two-bladed and four-bladed propellers, and with at least three engines: the 160 hp Siemens Halske Sh III, the 160 hp Goebel Goe III and the 145 hp Oberursel U III. Armament consisted of the standard twin LMG 08/15 machine guns. The following data relate to the Sh III-powered model. *Max speed, 118 mph (190 km/h) at 13,125 ft (4 000 m). Time to 19,685 ft (6 000 m), 25.25 min. Endurance, 1.5 hrs. Empty weight, 1,146 lb (520 kg). Loaded weight, 1,576 lb (715 kg). Span, 24 ft 8 in (7,52 m). Length, 18 ft 6½ in (5,65 m). Height, 9 ft 4¼ in (2,85 m). Wing area, 185.14 sq ft (17,20 m^2).*

PFALZ DR II — Germany

Developed in parallel with the Dr I, the Dr II was a smaller and lighter single-seat fighter triplane utilising the well-proven Oberursel Ur II rotary of 110 hp. A second prototype, the Dr IId, differed in having a 110 hp Siemens Halske Sh I rotary, but neither offered sufficient promise to warrant further development. The following data relate to the Ur II-powered aircraft. *Time to 9,840 ft (3 000 m), 10.2 min. Endurance, 1.5 hrs. Empty weight, 882 lb (400 kg). Loaded weight, 1,314 lb (596 kg). Span, 23 ft 7½ in (7,20 m). Length, 19 ft 6¼ in (5,95 m). Height, 9 ft 6⅛ in (2,90 m).*

Actually developed in parallel with the Dr I, the Dr II (below) was both smaller and lighter.

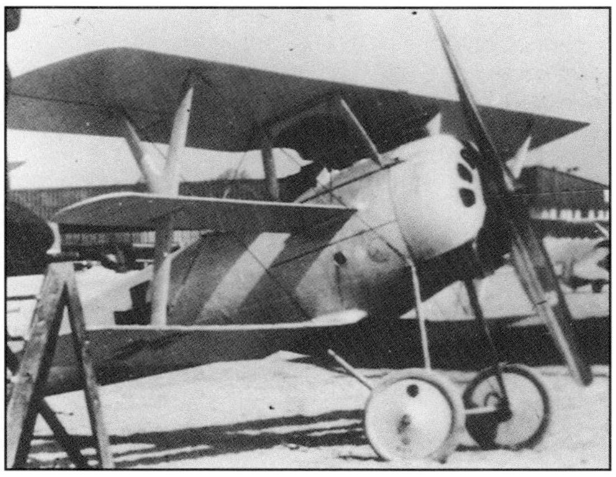

PFALZ D VIII — Germany

A contender in the second D-type Competition at Adlershof in May 1918, the D VIII was in all respects similar to the D VII apart from having two-bay wing bracing. The slightly raked wings were of equal parallel chord with slightly splayed interplane struts, and a standard Pfalz-type wooden structure was employed, with a semi-monocoque fuselage. The *Typen-Prüfung* was performed in January 1918, with a D VIII powered by a 160 hp Siemens Halske Sh III 11-cylinder rotary, but one of two D VIIIs participating in the D-type Competition had N-type interplane struts, horn-balanced ailerons and a 160 hp Goebel Goe III engine. Limited production of the Sh III-powered D VIII was undertaken, this being introduced to squadron service in

June 1918, but by the end of August only 19 fighters of this type were at the Front, a total of 40 having been built. A D VIII was tested with a 145 hp Oberursel U III engine and another with a Rhemag R II driving counter-rotating propellers, but only the Sh III version saw service. Armed with two LMG 08/15 machine guns, the D VIII possessed pleasant handling characteristics and offered a good standard of manoeuvrability and a high climb rate, but it suffered a weak undercarriage. Data relate to the Sh III-powered D VIII. *Max speed, 118 mph (190 km/h). Time to 9,840 ft (3 000 m), 3.1 min. Endurance, 1.5 hrs. Empty weight, 1,197 lb (543 kg). Loaded weight, 1,627 lb (738 kg). Dimensions as for D VII.*

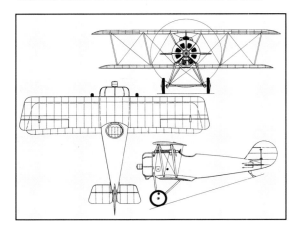

The D VIII (above and below) saw limited production and was tested at the Front in the summer of 1918.

PFALZ D XII   Germany

Participating in the second D-type Competition alongside the D VIII, the D XII was adjudged one of the winning contenders and Pfalz was awarded a contract for 500 aircraft of this type. The four examples participating in the competition each had a different engine, one having a 180 hp Daimler D IIIaü, one having a 185 hp BMW IIIa, one having a 195 hp Benz Bz IIIboü and

The D XII (above and below) began to reach the Front in quantity in August 1918, but proved unpopular.

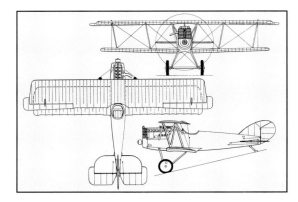

A Pfalz D XII (above) photographed at Riverside, California, in 1959 when owned by Frank Tallman.

another having a 170 hp Daimler D IIIa. The last mentioned six-cylinder water-cooled engine was adopted for the series D XII, *Typen-Prüfung* taking place on 19 June 1918. Armed with twin LMG 08/15 machine guns, the D XII began to reach the Front in quantity in August 1918, but it was reputedly unpopular with its pilots owing to poor control response. By October 1918, 180 D XIIs were at the Front, but although sturdy aircraft, they did not compare favourably with the contemporary Fokker D VII. *Max speed, 106 mph (170 km/h). Time to 3,280 ft (1 000 m), 3.4 min. Endurance, 1.5 hrs. Empty weight, 1,578 lb (716 kg). Loaded weight, 1,977 lb (897 kg). Span, 29 ft 6⅓ in (9,00 m). Length, 20 ft 10 in (6,35 m). Height, 8 ft 10¼ in (2,70 m). Wing area, 233.58 sq ft (21,70 m²).*

PFALZ D XIV   Germany

The D XIV, which underwent *Typen-Prüfung* on 15 May 1918, was very similar to its immediate predecessor, but featured wings of greater span and area, a deeper fuselage, an enlarged vertical fin and a high-compression Benz Bz IVü six-cylinder water-cooled engine.

The D XIV (below) was a participant in the second D-type Competition, but was not ordered in quantity.

Structurally similar to preceding Pfalz fighters and carrying the standard twin-gun armament, the D XIV participated in the second D-type Competition, but did not demonstrate any appreciable advance over the D XII, development being discontinued. *Max speed, 112 mph (180 km/h) at 13,125 ft (4 000 m). Time to 3,280 ft (1 000 m), 3.0 min. Endurance, 1.5 hrs. Empty weight, 1,836 lb (833 kg). Loaded weight, 2,275 lb (1 032 kg). Span, 32 ft 9⅔ in (10,00 m). Length, 20 ft 8⅘ in (6,32 m). Height, 8 ft 10¼ in (2,70 m). Wing area, 273.73 sq ft (25,43 m²).*

PFALZ D XV   Germany

Certainly *one* of the last, if not *the* last, single-seat fighter to be accepted for production in Germany during World War I – having completed its *Typen-Prüfung* on 4 November 1918, a few days before the Armistice – the D XV participated in the third D-type Competition in October 1918. Departing from previous Pfalz practice in having the fuselage suspended between the single-bay wings and all flying and landing

wires deleted, the D XV was developed during the summer of 1918, and flew in D XVf and D XV(*Spezial*) versions in the competition. The former had unbalanced ailerons and the latter had balanced ailerons which were adopted for the series version, both having the 185 hp BMW IIIa engine, although the Daimler D IIIa of 180 hp could also be fitted. The D XV was highly manoeuvrable and possessed a good performance, but was allegedly tail heavy and difficult to land. Too late to see operational service, several series D XVs were completed and Allied inspection teams found 74 finished D XV fuselages at the Pfalz Flugzeug-Werke in September 1919. *Max speed, 126 mph (203 km/h). Time to 3,280 ft (1 000 m), 2.0 min. Endurance, 1.5 hrs. Empty weight, 1,627 lb (738 kg). Loaded weight, 2,024 lb (918 kg). Span, 28 ft 2⅔ in (8,60 m). Length, 21 ft 3⁹⁄₁₀ in (6,50 m). Height, 8 ft 10⅓ in (2,70 m). Wing area, 215.28 sq ft (20,00 m²).*

The D XV (above and below) was the last of the Pfalz single-seat fighters to appear during World War I.

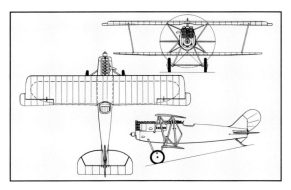

PHÖNIX 20.14   Austria-Hungary

Shortly after commencing licence manufacture of the Brandenburg D I, the Phönix-Flugzeugwerke initiated work on an "improved fighter with a Nieuport [ie, sesquiplane] cellule" under the design leadership of Dipl-Ing Kirste. The prototype, completed early in December 1916, utilised the fuselage of Brandenburg D I 28.48 (48th 28-Series fighter) to which was applied a deepened forward portion eliminating the centre-section cabane of bracing struts. This was mated with an enlarged-area upper wing and shorter-span narrow-chord lower wing to provide the desired sesquiplane cellule. Crashed during flight testing on 16 January 1917, the prototype was rebuilt, redesignated 20.14 (ie, 14th experimental aircraft produced by Phönix), and fitted with modified ailerons and a new, lengthened fuselage. Retaining the 185 hp Austro-Daimler six-cylinder water-cooled engine, the 20.14 entered flight test in June 1917, proving to possess an inferior climb rate to the parallel 20.15. The sole 20.14 was eventually sold to the Navy and flown from Trieste. *Empty weight (approx), 1,466 lb (665 kg). Loaded weight (approx), 2,028 lb (920 kg). Span, 28 ft 2⅜ in (8,60 m). Length, 20 ft 8 in (6,30 m). Height, 8 ft 11½ in (2,73 m). Wing area, 209.9 sq ft (19,50 m²).*

The sole example of the Phönix 20.14 (above and below) which was completed in December 1916.

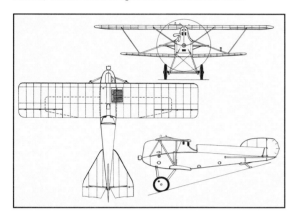

PHÖNIX 20.15   Austria-Hungary

While the 20.14 sesquiplane prototype was being rebuilt from the 28.48, Phönix completed a further fighter prototype, the 20.15, with a Sparmann-designed single-bay biplane wing cellule. The fuselage of Brandenburg D I 28.50 was used and the 185 hp Austro-Daimler engine was retained. Of fabric-covered wooden construction, the 20.15 was first flown in June 1917, and demonstrated handling characteristics far superior to those of the Brandenburg D I, but a barely improved performance. However, the 20.15 was to be considered as a lineal predecessor of the production Phönix D I, and, later assigned the training rôle, this prototype survived World War I, being offered for sale to Czechoslovakia in April 1920. No data are available.

The Phönix 20.15 (below) mated the fuselage of a Brandenburg D I with a new wing cellule.

PHÖNIX 20.16   Austria-Hungary

Destined to be Dipl-Ing Kirste's final attempt to produce a successful single-seat fighter of sesquiplane configuration, the 20.16 mated a Brandenburg D I (ex 28.73) fuselage with a new wing cellule (as did the 20.14). The wings featured rounded tips and the upper wing, which utilised a new high-lift profile, was set lower on the fuselage to improve forward view for the pilot. The

The Phönix 20.16 (above and below) is illustrated here in its original sesquiplane configuration.

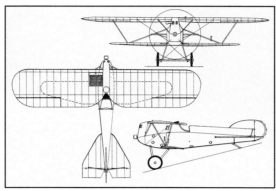

After tests in June 1917, the Phönix 20.16 was rebuilt (below) with an entirely new wing cellule.

20.16 was fitted with a 200 hp Austro-Daimler engine and was flight tested in the late spring of 1917, but, having failed to demonstrate desirable characteristics, by June of that year it was undergoing reconstruction with a Sparmann-designed biplane cellule similar to that of the 20.15. In this form it was to become the true prototype of the Phönix D I. No data are available apart from the wing span of 31 ft 6 in (9,60 m).

PHÖNIX D I
(TYPE 8)   Austria-Hungary

Having proved the superiority of the Sparmann-designed biplane cellule over the sesquiplane cellule, Phönix began in June 1917 to prepare engineering drawings for a series production fighter based on the 20.15 and the rebuilt 20.16 prototypes, and powered by a 200 hp Hiero six-cylinder water-cooled engine. Of wooden construction with plywood and fabric skinning, the new fighter, designated D I, carried an armament of two synchronised Schwarzlose 8-mm machine guns, and the first 11 aircraft were accepted by the *K.u.k.Luftfahrttruppen* in October 1917. Production for this service totalled 120 aircraft, deliveries being completed in the late spring of 1918, and 20 were also supplied to the Austro-Hungarian Navy. The D I remained

(Below) The D I, the first Phönix series fighter.

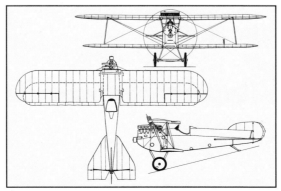

at the Front until the end of hostilities (72 being at the Front on 1 August 1918) and was noteworthy for its sturdiness and excellent handling characteristics, although most pilots considered climb rate and level speed to be inadequate. *Max speed, 111 mph (178 km/h). Time to 3,280 ft (1 000 m), 3.05 min. Empty weight, 1,578 lb (716 kg). Loaded weight, 2,096 lb (951 kg). Span, 32 ft 1⅘ in (9,80 m). Length, 22 ft 1¾ in (6,75 m). Height, 8 ft 8⅓ in (2,65 m). Wing area, 269.1 sq ft (25,00 m²).*

Based on the 20.16 prototype, the Phönix D I (below) was built in series during 1917-18.

PHÖNIX D II
(TYPE 9)   Austria-Hungary

Testing of the D I in October 1917 had elicited such responses from pilots as "superb flight characteristics, but only average performance." Phönix responded rapidly with a new prototype, the 20.18, which weighed some 176 lb (80 kg) less than the D I, flight trials commencing in November 1917. This was ordered into production as the D II. Similarly powered to the D I, the D II had a one-piece upper wing, higher aspect ratio ailerons and dihedral eliminated. Balanced ailerons

(Above) The Phönix 20.18 prototype of the D II and Oblt Linke-Crawford's Phönix D II (below).

(Below) The Phönix D II illustrated by the general arrangement drawing entered service in March 1918.

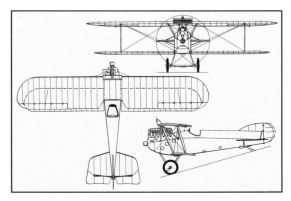

The D IIa (above) was essentially a more powerful version of the basic D II, appearing in May 1918.

A preserved example of the Phönix D III, or Phönix 222, acquired by the Swedish Army in August 1920.

were fitted and tailplane chord was reduced. During trials, the D II attained 16,405 ft (5 000 m) within 20 min as compared with 28 min required by the D I. Acceptances of the first of 48 D II fighters began in March 1918, these being followed by 48 of the D IIa version which differed in having a 230 hp Hiero engine in place of the 200 hp unit, although shortages of the uprated power plant resulted in some 20 per cent of the D IIa fighters being delivered to the *K.u.k.Luftfahrttruppen* with the lower-powered engine. The first D IIa fighters were despatched to the Front in late May 1918. Ten D IIa fighters were transferred to the Austro-Hungarian Navy in August 1918. The following performance data relate specifically to the D IIa. *Max speed, 115 mph (185 km/h). Time to 3,280 ft (1 000 m), 3.0 min. Span, 32 ft 1⅘ in (9,80 m). Length, 22 ft 1¾ in (6,75 m). Height, 8 ft 8⅓ in (2,65 m). Wing area, 269.1 sq ft (25,00 m²).*

PHÖNIX D III Austria-Hungary

Among D II derivatives participating in the July 1918 Fighter Evaluation held at Aspern was one D IIa (422.23) with ailerons on both upper and lower wings.

(Above) A modified D IIa (422.23) with ailerons on both upper and lower wings for D III development.

After flying all participating fighters, Oblt Benno von Fiala and Oblt Frank Linke-Crawford expressed a preference for the four-aileron D IIa derivative on the basis of handling and manoeuvrability. Phönix immediately initiated work on a production version with a new four-aileron wing cellule of improved planform and the aileron interconnecting struts (which tended to vibrate) replaced by cables. Formal permission to proceed with series production of this aircraft (which had been tentatively designated "D II Series 222-*neü*) as the D III was received on 18 September 1918, with delivery of 100 aircraft to the *K.u.k.Luftfahrttruppen* scheduled to start in the following month. A contract had earlier been placed by the Austro-Hungarian Navy for 50 similar fighters powered by the 230 hp Hiero engine, and two or three of these had been accepted by November 1918. However, none was accepted by the *K.u.k.Luftfahrttruppen*, and when hostilities terminated 60 D III airframes were complete but without engines, 14 were 98 per cent complete and the remaining 26 were 75 per cent complete. On 6 July 1919, Dipl-Ing Edmund Sparmann and Max Perini demonstrated one of the naval D IIIs in Stockholm. This was purchased by the Thulin company from which, in April 1920, it was procured by *Flygkompaniet* of the Swedish Army, 20 more D IIIs being purchased via Germany for *Flygkompaniet*. These, referred to as Phönix 222s, were powered by the 200 hp Hiero engine and delivered in August 1920. Subsequently, in 1925, the Army Aircraft Factory at Malmen (CMF) built a further 10 Phönix 222s, these having the 185 hp BMW IIIa engine and additional fuel tanks faired into the upper wing. The first Swedish-built aircraft was delivered on 16 September 1925, and, like the original aircraft built by the parent company, carried two 6.5-mm Schwarzlose M 17 guns. When *Flygvapnet* was established on 1 July 1926, the new service

absorbed 12 ex-Army Phönix 222s (including three of the original fighters) which were assigned the designation J 1, these being relegated to the training rôle from 1928 and the last being withdrawn in 1933. The following data relate to the 230 hp Hiero-powered D III. *Max speed, 117 mph (188 km/h). Time to 3,280 ft (1 000 m), 2.0 min. Range, 217 mls (350 km). Empty weight, 1,510 lb (685 kg). Loaded weight, 2,097 lb (951 kg). Span, 32 ft 1⅘ in (9,80 m). Length, 21 ft 8⅔ in (6,62 m). Height, 9 ft 10½ in (3,01 m). Wing area, 269.1 sq ft (25,00 m²).*

(Above) A Phönix 222 alias D III in Swedish service in 1936 when employed for weather reconnaissance.

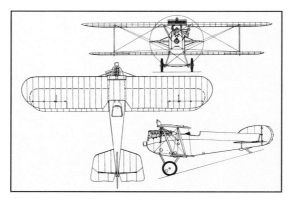

A general arrangement drawing of the D III (above) seen (below) in Austro-Hungarian Navy service.

PHÖNIX 20.22
TO 20.25 Austria-Hungary

During the Fighter Evaluation held at Aspern in July 1918, Phönix submitted (in addition to the previously-

mentioned D IIa 422.23) two modified D IIa fighters, the 230 hp Hiero-powered 20.22 and the 225 hp Austro-Daimler-powered 20.23. These differed from the standard D IIa fundamentally in having ailerons on both upper and lower wings. In addition, the upper wing was marginally raised, that of the 20.22 being increased slightly in area and combined with a reduced-span lower wing. Whereas 20.22 had struts interconnecting the ailerons, 20.23 had aileron cables running through the lower wing. Neither type was pursued further, but two additional Phönix prototypes participated in the evaluation. These, the 20.24 and 20.25, were representative of an entirely new design, whereas the 20.22 and 20.23 had, like all preceding Phönix fighters, stemmed from the Brandenburg D I. The 20.24 and 20.25 differed one from the other in engine type, the former having a 230 hp Hiero and the latter a 225 hp Austro-Daimler. Single-bay staggered biplanes with oval-section plywood-skinned fuselages, they were designed by Dipl-Ing Kirste assisted by Ing Zwerina and were flown only on the last day of the Fighter Evaluation (13 July). Demonstrating outstanding qualities, they were recipients of an order for two pre-series prototypes (20.28 and 20.29) in anticipation of series production as the Phönix D IV. Hostilities terminated, however, before these could be completed. The following data relate to the Hiero-powered 20.24. *Max speed, 115 mph (185 km/h). Time to 3,280 ft (1 000 m), 2.0 min. Empty weight, 1,466 lb (665 kg). Loaded weight, 2,094 lb (950 kg). Span, 27 ft 10⅔ in (8,50 m). Length, 21 ft 7⅘ in (6,60 m). Height, 9 ft 6⅛ in (2,90 m). Wing area, 252.96 sq ft (23,50 m²).*

The Phönix 20.24 (above and below) was ordered in anticipation of series production as the D IV.

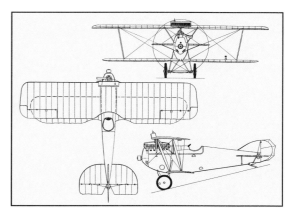

PIAGGIO P.2   Italy

Of exceptionally advanced concept for its time in being a low-wing cantilever monoplane with a monocoque fuselage, the P.2 single-seat fighter was designed by Ing Giovanni Pegna and was under construction in the Pegna-Bonmartini workshops when, in 1923, that company was taken over by the Piaggio concern. Representing the smallest airframe that could be designed around the 300 hp Hispano-Suiza HS 42 eight-cylinder water-cooled engine, the P.2 was of wooden construction with plywood skinning and fabric-covered movable control surfaces. Possessing a high degree of aerodynamic cleanliness, the P.2 carried an armament of two synchronised 12,7-mm machine guns and two prototypes were built. The P.2 was entered in the 1923 official fighter contest, but demonstrated performance fell somewhat short of that promised by Pegna, a fact which, coupled with the prevailing distrust of the monoplane formula, resulted in its rejection. Nevertheless, one prototype was purchased for evaluation by the Air Force and delivered on 23 March 1924. *Max speed, 145 mph (233 km/h) at sea level. Time to 3,280 ft (1 000 m), 3.3 min. Endurance, 2.6 hrs. Empty weight, 1,911 lb (867 kg). Loaded weight, 2,606 lb (1 182 kg). Span, 34 ft 8½ in (10,58 in). Length, 22 ft 11⅔ in (7,00 m). Height, 7 ft 2⅔ in (2,20 m). Wing area, 216.15 sq ft (20,08 m²).*

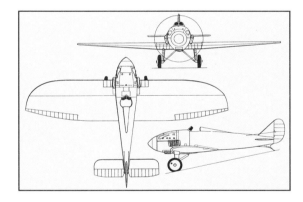

The Piaggio P.2 (above and below) employed advanced aerodynamics by the standards of the early 'twenties.

PIAGGIO P.119   Italy

Unusual in utilising a buried power plant driving a tractor propeller via an extension shaft, and unique among such aircraft in employing an air-cooled radial engine, the P.119 single-seat fighter was conceived in 1938 by Giovanni Casiraghi as a private venture. Official interest was shown in March 1940, at which time it was proposed to power the prototype with a 1,500 hp Piaggio P.XV RC 45 18-cylinder two-row radial, replacing this in the series model with a 1,700 hp P.XV RC 60/2V.

(Below) The P.119 with buried air-cooled radial.

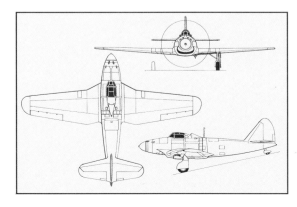

The P.119 (above) failed to undergo evaluation by the *Regia Aeronautica* owing to the 1943 Armistice.

Armament comprised a 20-mm cannon firing through the propeller hub and four 12,7-mm machine guns close-grouped in the fuselage nose. Of all-metal construction with a monocoque fuselage, the P.119 was first flown on 19 December 1942, flight trials continuing up to 2 August 1943, when the prototype was to have been evaluated by the *Regia Aeronautica*, after which it was anticipated that series production would commence. However, the Armistice of 8 September 1943 resulted in the termination of development. *Max speed, 400 mph (644 km/h) at 22,300 ft (6 795 m). Time to 10,000 ft (3 050 m), 3.25 min. Range, 940 mls (1 513 km). Empty weight, 5,374 lb (2 438 kg). Loaded weight, 9,020 lb (4 091 kg). Span, 42 ft 7⅘ in (13,00 m). Length, 31 ft 9⁹⁄₁₀ in (9,70 m). Height, 9 ft 6⅛ in (2,90 m). Wing area, 299.24 sq ft (27,80 m²).*

PIGEON-FRASER PURSUIT   USA

At a time when the biplane configuration had become the norm for single-seat fighting aircraft, George N Albree designed a single-seat shoulder-wing monoplane intended for use as a fighting scout. Two prototypes were delivered to the US Army Signal Corps by the Pigeon Hollow Spar Company in September 1917. The aircraft was of wooden construction and powered by a 100 hp Gnome rotary engine. One of the two prototypes was used for static testing and the second was test flown on behalf of the Signal Corps. The aircraft was intended to be fitted with a single machine gun, but no armament was ever provided and the Signal Corps considered the aircraft both unreliable and too slow. Consequently, no series production was undertaken. *Max speed, 103 mph (166 km/h). Loaded weight, 1,250 lb (567 kg). Span, 37 ft 11 in (11,56 m). Length, 24 ft 0 in (7,31 m).*

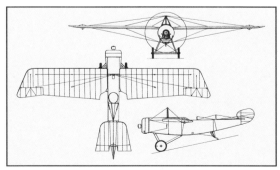

The second of the two prototypes of the Pigeon-Fraser Pursuit (above and below) of 1917.

POLIKARPOV I-1M-5 (IL-400)   USSR

Working at the former Duks factory (GAZ 1) at Khodinka, Moscow, Nikolai N Polikarpov, assisted by I M Kostkin, designed a conceptually advanced single-seat fighter, the IL-400, which flew on 15 August 1923. A cantilever low-wing monoplane of wooden construction powered by a 400 hp Liberty water-cooled engine,

the IL-400 proved longitudinally unstable and crashed shortly after becoming airborne on its first flight. Extensive redesign, both aerodynamic and structural, resulted in the IL-400b (also to be known as the IL-2), which, flown on 18 July 1924, retained a plywood-covered wooden fuselage mated with an entirely new, shorter span, thinner-section wing with dural ribs and corrugated dural skinning. Armament comprised two 7,62-mm machine guns. Following State trials, contracts were placed for eight and then a further 25 of a modified version of the fighter which reverted to all-wood construction. Designated I-1M-5 (and also referred to as the IL-3) and powered by an M-5 engine – the licence-built version of the 400 hp Liberty – this completed State tests on 16 March 1926. The series I-1M-5 suffered from low manufacturing standards, however, was seriously overweight and dangerously unstable. It was not, therefore, delivered to service units. *Max speed, 163 mph (263 km/h) at sea level. Time to 6,560 ft (2 000 m), 4.2 min. Endurance, 2.5 hrs. Empty weight, 2,451 lb (1 112 kg). Loaded weight, 3,373 lb (1 530 kg). Span, 35 ft 5 in (10,8 m). Length, 25 ft 5 in (7,75 m). Wing area, 215.28 sq ft (20,00 m²).*

The IL-400b (above and below), this second example of Polikarpov's fighter employing mixed construction.

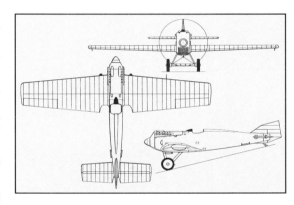

POLIKARPOV 2I-N1 (DI-1)   USSR

The first two-seat fighter of indigenous Soviet design, the 2I-N1 (the designation signifying *Dvukhmyestny istrebitel*, or two-seat fighter, with one Napier engine) was a single-bay unequal-span biplane of wooden construction with a monocoque fuselage and a 450 hp Napier Lion water-cooled engine. The sole prototype of the 2I-N1 (also referred to as the DI-1) was flown on 12 January 1926, and demonstrated a performance higher than that of contemporary *single*-seat fighters. Armament comprised one fixed 7,62-mm gun and a similar calibre weapon on a ring mount in the rear cockpit. On

(Below) The Polikarpov 2I-N1 two-seat fighter.

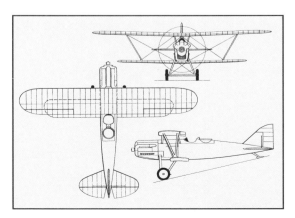

31 March 1926, high speed tests during the ninth flight terminated with the destruction of the aircraft as a result of a structural failure, no further development being undertaken. *Max speed, 166 mph (268 km/h). Time to 3,280 ft (1 000 m), 1.8 min. Endurance, 3 hrs. Empty weight, 2,542 lb (1 153 kg). Loaded weight, 3,748 lb (1 700 kg). Span, 39 ft 4½ in (12,00 m). Length, 31 ft 11⅞ in (9,75 m). Wing area, 292.25 sq ft (27,15 m²).*

The Polikarpov 2I-N1 (below) was the first Soviet two-seat fighter of indigenous design.

POLIKARPOV I-3   USSR

Despite loss of the two-seat 2I-N1 as a result of a structural failure, Polikarpov retained the structural precepts of this aircraft when designing his first single-seat fighter biplane, the I-3. As a result of this accident, however, safety factors were adopted that were afterwards to be considered excessive. An unequal-span, single-bay biplane of wooden construction with a monocoque fuselage, the I-3 was powered by a 750 hp BMW VI 7,3 12-cylinder water-cooled engine (subsequently licence-built as the M-17) and first flew on 4 May 1928. Armament consisted of two 7,62-mm machine guns. Following successful NII VVS testing, series production was ordered, 240 being manufactured during 1929-31, this fighter equipping 15 *eskadrilii* during the peak of its service in 1931-32. *Max speed, 173 mph (278 km/h) at sea level. Time to 3,280 ft (1 000 m), 1.8 min. Range, 264 mls (585 km). Empty weight, 3,086 lb (1 400 kg). Loaded weight, 4,070 lb (1 846 kg). Span, 36 ft 0⅞ in (11,00 m). Length, 26 ft 3⅓ in (8,01 m). Height, 10 ft 11⁹⁄₁₀ in (3,35 m). Wing area, 299.78 sq ft (27,85 m²).*

The Polikarpov I-3 (above and below) was the first single-seat fighter of Soviet origin to be built in quantity, equipping 15 *eskadrilii*.

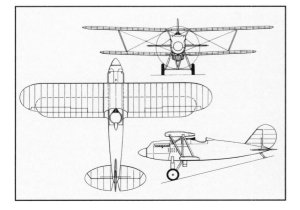

POLIKARPOV DI-2   USSR

Essentially a slightly scaled-up two-seat derivative of the I-3, the DI-2 was powered by a similar 750 hp BMW VI 7,3 engine and possessed a similar structure. Armament consisted of two synchronised 7,62-mm machine guns and two guns of the same calibre on a Scarff ring in the rear cockpit. Flight testing of the DI-2 commenced in 1929, but early in the programme the horizontal tail separated in flight as a result of flutter and further development was discontinued. *Max speed, 159 mph (256 km/h). Time to 3,280 ft (1 000 m), 2.2 min. Range, 317 mls (510 km). Empty weight, 3,433 lb (1 557 kg). Loaded weight, 4,678 lb (2 122 kg). Span, 38 ft 8½ in (11,80 m). Length, 26 ft 10¾ in (8,20 m). Wing area, 342.3 sq ft (31,80 m²).*

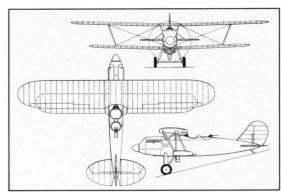

The DI-2 (above and below) was a two-seat fighter development of the basic I-3 single-seater design.

POLIKARPOV I-6   USSR

With acceptance of the I-3 for series production, Polikarpov and his team commenced work on a smaller, lighter fighter, the I-6, powered by a 450 hp Gnome-Rhône Jupiter VI air-cooled radial. A single-bay, unequal-span biplane of wooden construction with fabric-skinned wings and a monocoque fuselage, the I-6 was flown on 30 March 1930, two prototypes appearing in the annual May Day fly-past over Moscow in that year. Prior to the commencement of flight testing, Polikarpov had been arrested (in September 1929), accused of "exercising insufficient energy in bringing assigned work to fruition", and, together with Dmitri P Grigorovich, was already working whilst in detention on a further fighter (see I-5). Comparative trials were subsequently performed between the I-6 and the I-5, the latter being selected for series manufacture after prolonged evaluation. The I-6 was the faster in level flight, but offered

The I-6 (above and below) lost out to the I-5 as a contender for large-scale production contracts.

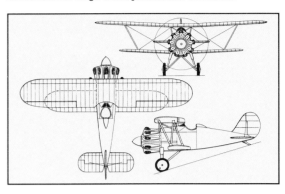

a poorer rate of climb and was less manoeuvrable. Development was therefore discontinued in favour of the I-5. *Max speed, 174 mph (280 km/h). Time to 3,280 ft (1 000 m), 1.57 min. Range, 435 mls (700 km). Empty weight, 1,914 lb (868 kg). Loaded weight, 2,822 lb (1 280 kg). Span, 31 ft 9⅞ in (9,70 m). Length, 22 ft 2⅞ in (6,78 m). Wing area, 220.67 sq ft (20,50 m²).*

POLIKARPOV I-5 (VT-11)   USSR

The first VT-11 (above), which, flown in April 1930, was the initial prototype for the successful I-5.

Despite its earlier designation, the I-5 was chronologically slightly later than the I-6, flying 31 days later, and its design having been initiated more than a year later. Designed within two months by Polikarpov in collaboration with Dmitri Grigorovich during incarceration in a *Vnutrennaya Turma* (Internal Prison), the first of

The second VT-11 (below) featured helmeted cylinder heads which were discarded for the third VT-11.

three prototypes of the I-5 was flown as the VT-11 on 29 April 1930. Of mixed construction, with fabric-covered welded steel-tube and dural fuselage and similarly-covered wooden wings, the VT-11 was an unequal-span single-bay staggered biplane. The first prototype was powered by a 450 hp Gnome-Rhône Jupiter VII, the second by a 525 hp Jupiter VI and the third by a 450 hp licence-built version of the latter engine known as the M-15. Whereas the first and second VT-11s featured helmeted engine cowlings, the third introduced a Townend ring cowl, this being adopted for the series I-5 for which the improved M-22 licence-built version of the Jupiter VI was standardised, this producing 480 hp. Armament consisted of two synchronised 7,62-mm machine guns. Production of the I-5 commenced in 1932 and continued until late 1935, a total of 800 being built and 39 first-line *eskadrilii* being equipped with this type at the peak of its service. *Max speed, 173 mph (278 km/h) at sea level. Time to 9,845 ft (3 000 m), 5.6 min. Range, 410 mls (660 km). Empty weight, 2,079 lb (943 kg). Loaded weight, 2,987 lb (1 355 kg). Span, 33 ft 7⅛ in (10,24 m). Length, 22 ft 2⁹⁄₁₀ in (6,78 m). Height, 9 ft 10 in (3,00 m). Wing area, 228.74 sq ft (21,25 m²).*

The I-5 (above and below) of which some 800 were built in 1932-35, equipping 39 first-line *eskadrilii*.

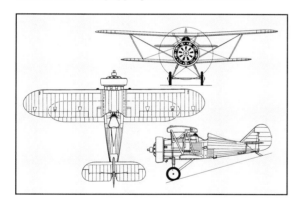

POLIKARPOV I-15 (TsKB-3)   USSR

Rehabilitated in the eyes of the Soviet hierarchy by the success of the I-5, Polikarpov initiated design of a potential successor, which, as the TsKB-3 (this designation indicating *Tsentralnoye konstruktorskoye byuro*, or Central Design Bureau), flew in October 1933. Powered by a Wright SGR-1820-F-3 Cyclone nine-cylinder radial rated at 715 hp at 6,990 ft (2 130 m), it was of mixed construction and embodied such refinements as I-type interplane struts, the upper wing "gulled" into the fuselage and cantilever mainwheel legs. Exceptional handling and manoeuvrability re-

An I-15 (below) serving with an *Escuadrilla de Chatos* of the Spanish Republican air arm in 1939.

I-15s of (above, top) 2ᵃ and (immediately above) 1ᵃ *Escuadrillas de Chatos* of the Spanish Republicans.

sulted in immediate series production as the I-15 with deliveries of the initial model commencing late in 1934. This was powered by a 480 hp M-22 engine and carried an armament of two 7,62-mm guns. A total of 404 M-22-engined I-15s was delivered before, in 1936, the imported Cyclone engine became available, this being installed in 59 aircraft before the licence-built version of the Cyclone, the M-25 rated at 700 hp at 7,545 ft (2 300 m), was delivered for installation in the final 270 I-15s, production being completed in 1937. In the meantime, armament had been doubled to four 7,62-mm guns and an armoured (9-mm) seat fitted. Popularly known as the *Chaika* (Gull), an epithet resulting from its "gulled" upper wing, the I-15 fought in Spain to where 155 were delivered, and was licence-built by the Spanish CASA concern which completed 237 M-25-engined examples, a few of these having the M-25V engine affording 775 hp for take-off. Some 40 late-production I-15s were fitted with twin 12,7-mm guns rather than the quartet of 7,62-mm weapons. The following data relate to the M-25-powered I-15. *Max speed, 228 mph (367 km/h) at 9,840 ft (3 000 m). Time*

(Below) The M-25-engined I-15 single-seat fighter.

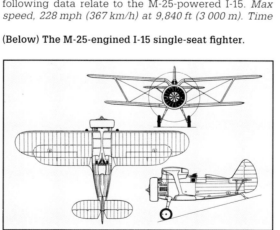

A Spanish Republican I-15 (below) photographed over Spain during an escort mission late in 1938.

to 9,840 ft (3 000 m), 3.3 min. Range, 317 mls (510 km). Empty weight, 2,231 lb (1 012 kg). Max loaded weight, 3,283 lb (1 489 kg). Span, 31 ft 11⅛ in (9,75 m). Length, 20 ft 0 in (6,10 m). Height, 7 ft 2¾ in (2,20 m). Wing area, 235.74 sq ft (21,90 m²).

POLIKARPOV I-16 TIP 1 TO 17 (TsKB-12)   USSR

Destined to become the world's first service single-seat low-wing cantilever monoplane fighter with retractable undercarriage, the I-16 combined a wooden monocoque fuselage with a metal wing. Initially known as the TsKB-12, the first prototype was flown on 30 December 1933 with a 480 hp M-22 engine, a second prototype, the TsKB-12bis, following on 18 February 1934 with a Wright SGR-1820-F-3 Cyclone affording 715 hp at 6,990 ft (2 130 m). A small pre-series designated I-16 *Tip* (Type) 1 was delivered from early 1935 with the M-22 engine, this being retained by the initial series model, the I-16 *Tip* 4, which differed externally in having a longer-chord cowling and of which about 400 were built. With availability of the M-25 (licence-built Cyclone) rated at 700 hp at 7,545 ft (2 300 m), production switched to the I-16 *Tip* 5 which introduced an entirely new tapered and shuttered engine cowling. Like

(Immediately below) An I-16 *Tip* 5 flown at Cuatro Vientos in 1939 by Nationalists, and (bottom) an I-16 *Tip* 10 of the 3ª *Escuadrilla de Moscas*, 1938.

The TsKB-12 (above), the M-22-powered first I-16 prototype, and (below) a modified I-16 *Tip* 5 beneath the wing of a TB-3 during Zveno 6SPB trials.

Loaded weight, 3,781 lb (1 715 kg). Span, 29 ft 6⅓ in (9,00 m). Length, 19 ft 11⅛ in (6,07 m). Height, 8 ft 4¾ in (2,56 m). Wing area, 156.51 sq ft (14,54 m²).

(Above, top) I-16 *Tip* 24 of 4 IAP, Lake Ladoga area, winter 1940-41 and (immediately above) I-16 *Tip* 18 of 72 AP at Keg-Ostrov, Murmansk, during summer 1941.

the preceding series version, the *Tip* 5 carried two 7,62 mm wing guns. It saw combat over Spain in November 1936. From late 1936, the I-16 *Tip* 6 with an M-25A engine rated at 730 hp at 7,545 ft (2 300 m) was produced, this being succeeded in the following year by the *Tip* 10. Following 2,200 twin-gun I-16s (ie, *Tip* 4, 5 and 6), the *Tip* 10 added two fuselage-mounted 7,62-mm guns and finally discarded the forward-sliding canopy of (but frequently removed from) earlier sub-types in favour of a fixed windscreen, and introduced landing flaps. During 1938, the Spanish Hispano-Suiza began licence production of the *Tip* 10, but with US-manufactured R-1820-F54 Cyclone engines, 10 being delivered before the end of hostilities to supplement 278 (*Tip* 5, 6 and 10) delivered by the Soviet Union. The I-16 *Tip* 12, built in small series, had the wing-mounted machine guns replaced with 20-mm cannon, a similar armament being employed from early 1939 by the *Tip* 17 which used the M-25V engine offering 750 hp at 9,515 ft (2 900 m). ShVAK cannon availability limited *Tip* 17 production – only 734 (*Tip* 12 and 17) of the 6,555 single-seat I-16s manufactured to Spring 1940 receiving cannon armament. A total of 142 *Tip* 10 and *Tip* 17 I-16s was supplied to China. The following data relate to the I-16 *Tip* 10. *Max speed, 273 mph (440 km/h) at 9,840 ft (3 000 m). Time to 16,405 ft (5 000 m), 6.9 min. Range, 497 mls (800 km). Empty weight, 2,976 lb (1 350 kg).*

The I-16 *Tip* 5 (above) and a cannon-armed I-16 *Tip* 17 (below) of 4 IAP attached to Baltic Fleet, 1942.

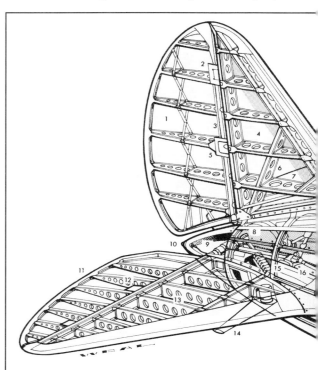

engine and some local structural strengthening, fundamentally similar to the *Tip* 10, armament being four 7,62-mm guns. What was seen as the definitive development, the *Tip* 24, introduced a stiffened wing and a Shvetsov M-63 engine rated at 930 hp. Like the *Tip* 18,

POLIKARPOV I-16 TIP 18 TO 29 USSR

From the service début of the I-16 to the phase-in of the *Tip* 17 version of the fighter early in 1939, normal loaded weight had risen by 41.7 per cent and take-off power by only 5.5 per cent, the effect on virtually every aspect of performance being adverse. Therefore, as a fall-back in case development of its intended successor, the I-180, should prove unsuccessful, adaptation began in 1938 of the I-16 for the two-stage supercharged M-62 and direct-geared M-63 engines. The Shvetsov M-62 rated at 800 hp at 13,780 ft (4 200 m) was adopted for the first stage of what might be referred to as the "second generation" I-16, this being introduced on the assembly lines in the spring of 1939 in the *Tip* 18 version. Essentially an interim model, the I-16 *Tip* 18 was, apart from

(Above) A Spanish Republican I-16 *Tip* 5, and (below) an I-16 *Tip* 6 with definitive cockpit windscreen.

Key to Polikarpov I-16 *Tip* 10

1 Rudder construction
2 Rudder upper hinge
3 Rudder post
4 Fin construction
5 Rudder lower hinge
6 Fin auxiliary spar
7 Port tailplane
8 Rudder actuating mechanism
9 Tail cone
10 Rear navigation light
11 Elevator construction
12 Elevator hinge
13 Tailplane construction
14 Tailskid
15 Tailskid damper
16 Control linkage (elevator and rudder)
17 Tailplane fillet
18 Fuselage half frames
19 Fin root fairing
20 Dorsal decking
21 Fuselage monocoque construction
22 Main upper longeron
23 Rudder control cable
24 Elevator control rigid rod
25 Main lower longeron
26 Control linkage crank
27 Seat support frame
28 Pilot's seat
29 Headrest
30 Cockpit entry flap (port)

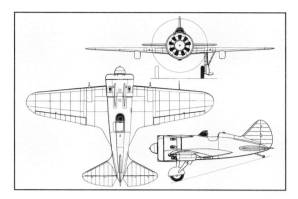

the *Tip* 24 had provision for two flush-fitting 22-Imp-gal (100-l) wing tanks, armament comprising four 7,62-mm guns, while the otherwise-similar *Tip* 27 combined the fuselage-mounted 7,62-mm weapons with two wing-mounted 20-mm cannon, and the *Tip* 29 could supplement a fuselage-mounted armament of one 12,7-mm and two 7,62-mm guns with four or six 82-mm RS-82 rockets which could be carried in addition to the auxiliary tanks, overload weight rising to 4,663 lb (2 115 kg).

(Immediately left) A general arrangement drawing of the I-16 *Tip* 24, (below left) an I-16 *Tip* 18 that was captured by the Finns after forced landing in 1940, and (below) I-16 *Tip* 18 fighters of the 72 AP with the Northern Fleet Air Force near Murmansk.

Phased out in the spring of 1940, production of the I-16 was resumed a year later, a further 450 being built (mostly *Tip* 27 and *Tip* 29) to bring the total of single-seat models built to 7,005 (a further 1,639 having been built as *Tip* 4 UTI-2 and *Tip* 15 UTI-4 two-seat trainers). The I-16 formed marginally more than 65 per cent of the entire Soviet fighter inventory at the time of the German assault. The following data relate to the M-63-engined I-16 *Tip* 24. *Max speed, 304 mph (489 km/h) at 15,750 ft (4 800 m). Time to 16,405 ft (5 000 m), 5.8 min. Normal range, 373 mls (600 km). Empty weight, 3,252 lb (1 475 kg). Loaded weight, 4,215 lb (1 912 kg). Span, 29 ft 1⅗ in (8,88 m). Length, 20 ft 1⅓ in (6,13 m). Height, 7 ft 9¾ in (2,41 m). Wing area, 160.06 sq ft (14,87 m²).*

31 Open cockpit
32 Rear-view mirror (optional)
33 Curved one-piece windshield
34 Tubular gunsight (PBP-1 reflector sight optional)
35 Instrument panel
36 Undercarriage retraction handcrank
37 Control column
38 Rudder pedal
39 Fuselage fuel tank, capacity 56 Imp gal (255 l)
40 Fuel filler caps
41 Ammunition magazines
42 Machine gun fairing
43 Split-type aileron (landing flap)
44 Aileron hinge fairing
45 Fabric wing covering
46 Port navigation light
47 Aluminium alloy leading-edge skin
48 Two-bladed propeller
49 Conical spinner
50 Hucks-type starter dog
51 Hinged mainwheel cover
52 Port mainwheel
53 Lip intake
54 Adjustable (shuttered) cooling apertures
55 Propeller shaft support frame
56 Machine gun muzzles
57 750 hp M-25V radial engine
58 Oil tank
59 Starboard synchronized 7,62-mm ShKAS machine gun
60 Exhaust exit ports
61 Engine bearers
62 Firewall/bulkhead
63 Centre-section trussed-type spar carry-through
64 Wheel well
65 Fuselage/front spar attachment point
66 Retraction linkage
67 Fuselage/rear spar attachment point
68 Wingroot frames
69 Wingroot fillet
70 Aileron construction
71 Ammunition access panel
72 Starboard wing 7,62-mm ShKAS machine gun
73 Undercarriage pivot point
74 Machine gun muzzle

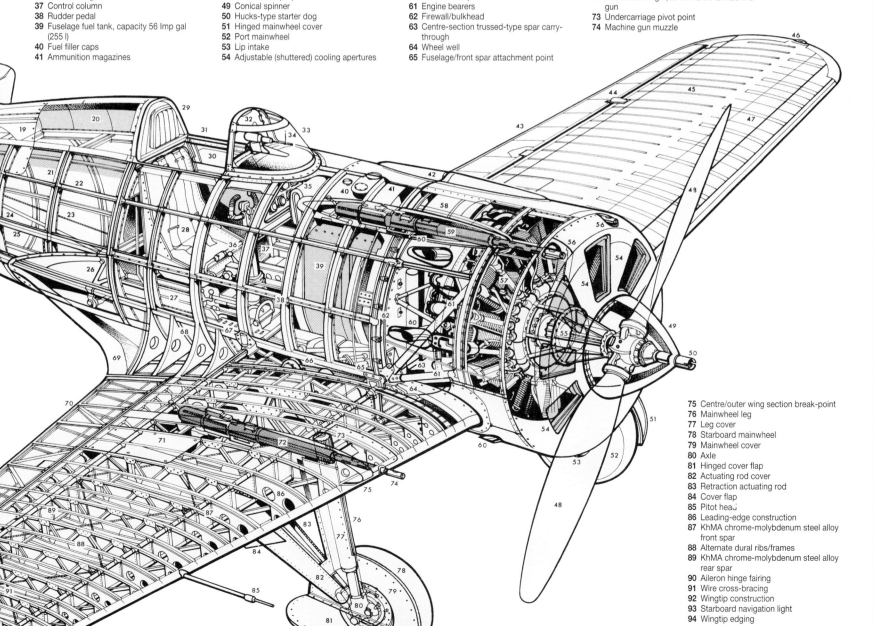

75 Centre/outer wing section break-point
76 Mainwheel leg
77 Leg cover
78 Starboard mainwheel
79 Mainwheel cover
80 Axle
81 Hinged cover flap
82 Actuating rod cover
83 Retraction actuating rod
84 Cover flap
85 Pitot head
86 Leading-edge construction
87 KhMA chrome-molybdenum steel alloy front spar
88 Alternate dural ribs/frames
89 KhMA chrome-molybdenum steel alloy rear spar
90 Aileron hinge fairing
91 Wire cross-bracing
92 Wingtip construction
93 Starboard navigation light
94 Wingtip edging

POLIKARPOV I-17 USSR

During 1934, the Polikarpov team began work on an advanced single-seat fighter with a water-cooled engine for comparison with the I-16. The first prototype was flown in 1 September 1934 as the TsKB-15 with a 760 hp Hispano-Suiza 12Ybrs 12-cylinder water-cooled engine. A low-wing cantilever monoplane with manually-retractable main undercarriage members and a forward-sliding cockpit canopy, the TsKB-15 was of mixed construction with a wooden monocoque fuselage and metal wing. The radiator bath was manually retractable and armament comprised four wing-mounted 7,62-mm machine guns. With empty and loaded weights of 2,976 lb (1 350 kg) and 3,649 lb (1 655 kg) respectively, the TsKB-15 attained 283 mph (455 km/h) in level flight and climbed to 16,405 ft (5 000 m) in 6.5 min, this being considered sufficiently promising for the allocation of the designation I-17 and construction of a modified second prototype, the TsKB-19. Flown in 1935, the TsKB-19 differed in having a wider-track inward-retracting undercarriage in place of the narrow-track outward-retracting gear, an M-100 engine (a licence-built version of the HS 12Y) rated at 750 hp and twin radiators on semi-retractable pylons under the wing roots. Armament remained unchanged.

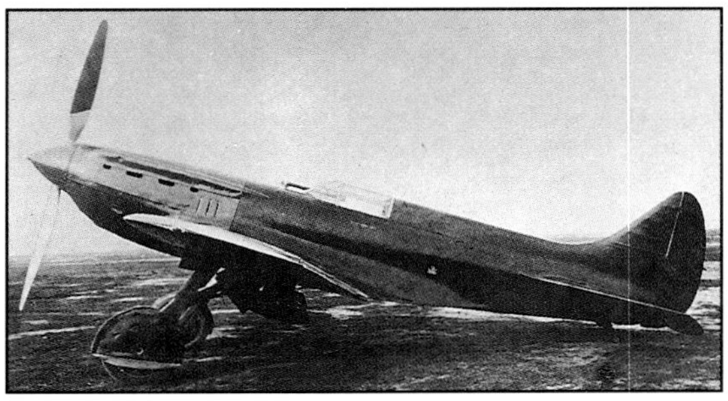

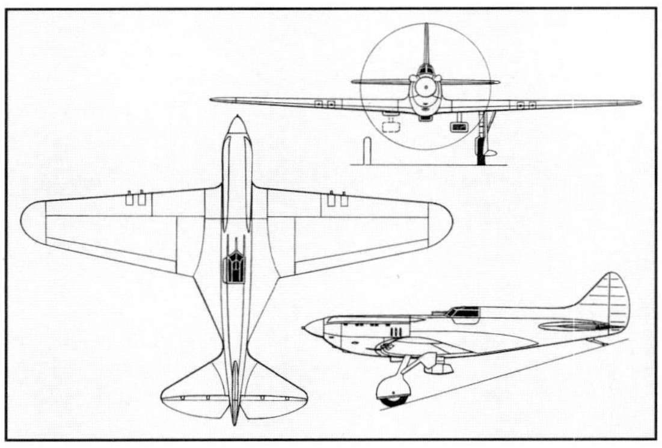

The second prototype I-17, the TsKB-19 (above and below), which entered flight test during 1935.

The TsKB-19 demonstrated improved level speed, but an inferior performance in most other respects. Work began on a third prototype, the TsKB-33, featuring surface-evaporation steam cooling, but development was discontinued when it was concluded that the developed I-16 was adequate for the time being. The following data relate to the TsKB-19. *Max speed, 311 mph (500 km/h). Time to 16,405 ft (5 000 m), 7.2 min. Range, 497 mls (800 km). Empty weight, 3,439 lb (1 560 kg). Loaded weight, 4,299 lb (1 950 kg). Span, 32 ft 9⅔ in (10,00 m). Length, 24 ft 9⅗ in (7,56 m). Height, 8 ft 4⅓ in (2,55 m). Wing area, 192.68 sq ft (17,90 m^2).*

POLIKARPOV I-152 (I-15BIS) USSR

Criticism of the "gulled" upper wing centre section of the I-15, which restricted the pilot's view for take-off and landing, led indirectly to major redesign of the fighter as the I-152 (I-15bis). The structure was restressed and extensively revised, a new Clark YH aerofoil was adopted, the span and area of the upper wing were increased, the wing centre section was carried above the fuselage by a cabane of splayed N-struts, and the 775 hp M-25V engine was enclosed by a long-chord cowling. Fuel capacity was increased, but armament remained four 7,62-mm guns. The I-152 was first flown early in 1937, production deliveries commencing mid-year. One of the first recipients of the I-152 was the Chinese Central Government, which was assigned 186 from late 1937 through early 1938 (an additional 86 being supplied later), and 31 reached Spain in January 1939 (a further 62 being held at the French frontier, of which 20 were subsequently released to the new Nationalist government). One example was fitted with two TK-3 turbo-superchargers as the I-152TK, one was equipped with a pressure cabin (*Germeticheskaya kabina*) as the I-152GK, and another was tested with DM-2 ramjets as the I-152DM. Production of the I-152 was phased out early in 1939, having totalled 2,408 examples, 60 *eskadrilii* being equipped with this type during 1939. *Max speed, 226 mph (364 km/h) at 9,840 ft (3 000 m). Time to 16,405 ft (5 000 m), 6.7 min. Normal range, 280 mls (450 km). Empty weight, 2,888 lb (1 310 kg). Max loaded weight, 4,044 lb (1 834 kg). Span, 33 ft 5½ in (10,20 m). Length, 20 ft 7 in (6,27 m). Wing area, 242.19 sq ft (22,50 m^2).*

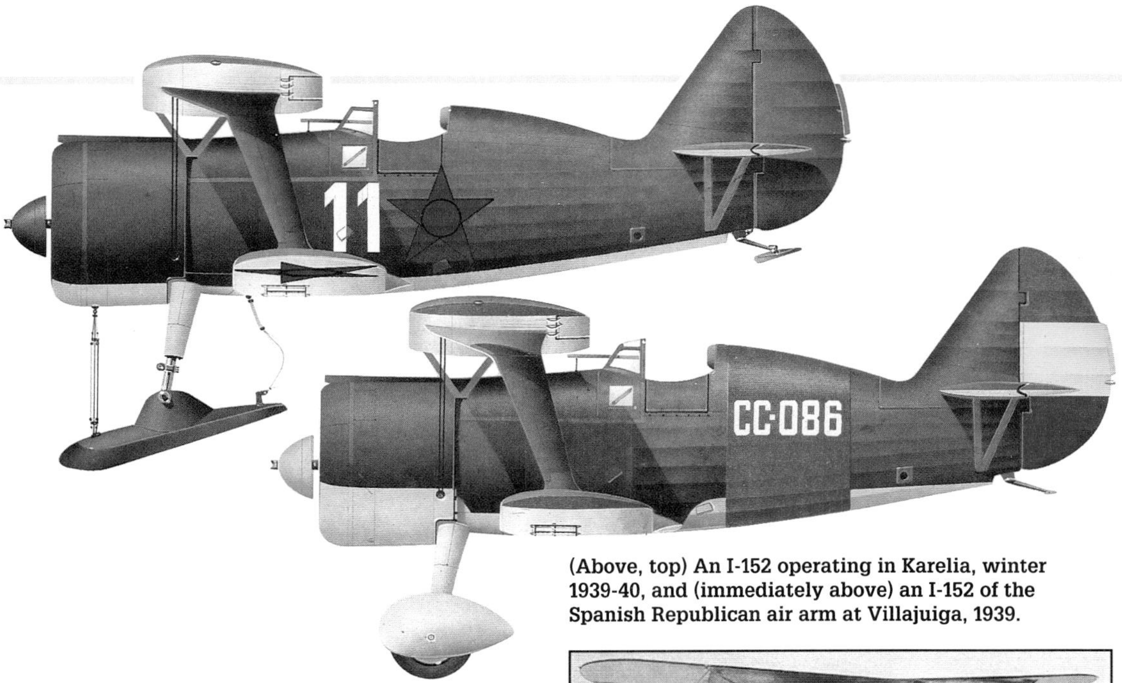

(Above, top) An I-152 operating in Karelia, winter 1939-40, and (immediately above) an I-152 of the Spanish Republican air arm at Villajuiga, 1939.

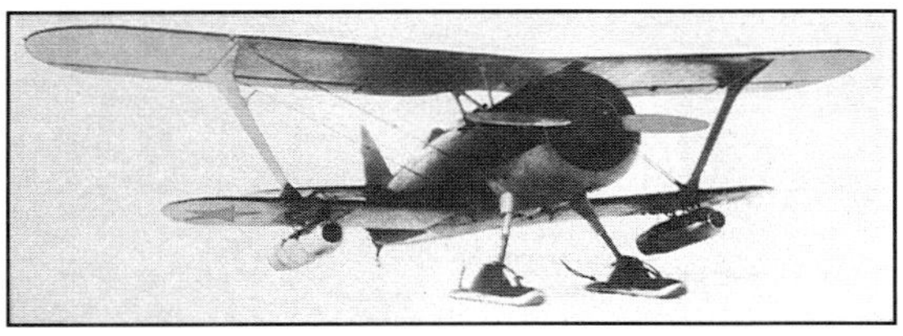

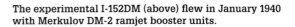

The experimental I-152DM (above) flew in January 1940 with Merkulov DM-2 ramjet booster units.

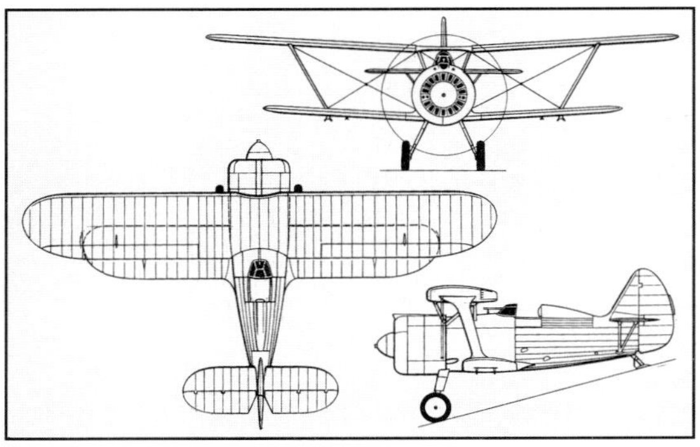

The I-152 alias I-15bis (above and below) equipped 60 *eskadrilii* in 1939 despite its obsolescence.

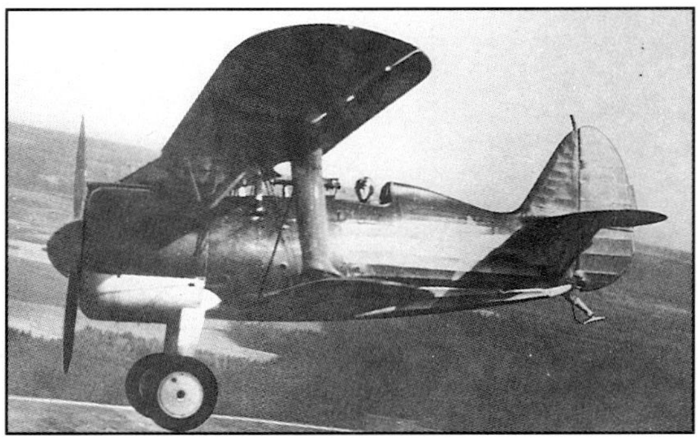

(Below) One of five captured I-152 fighters in service with the Finnish 2/T-LLv 35 in 1942.

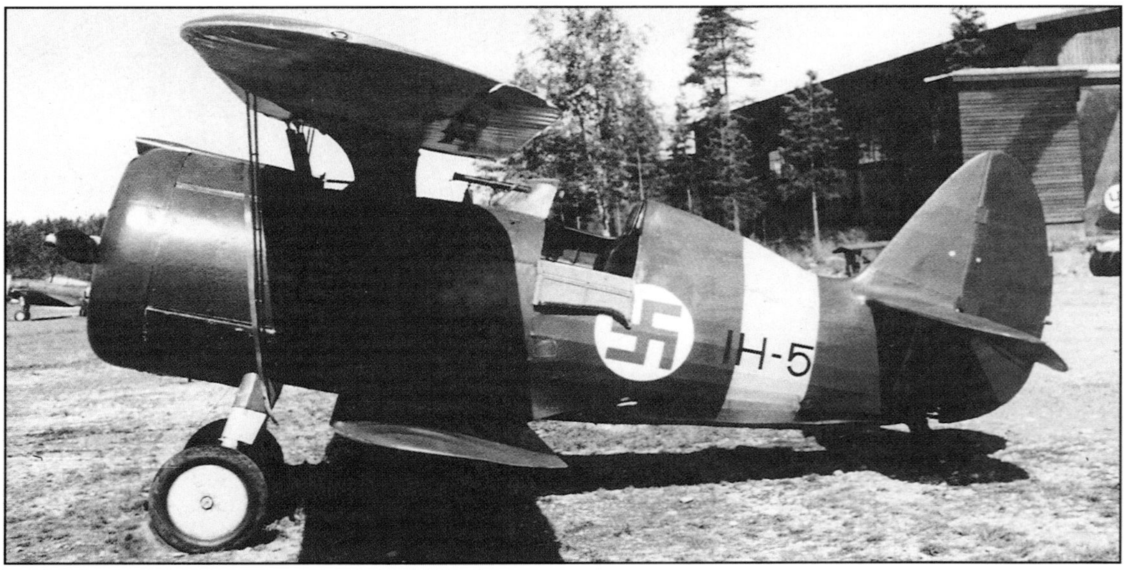

POLIKARPOV I-153 (I-15TER) USSR

Despite an international trend away from the biplane configuration for fighters by the mid 'thirties, the Soviet Air Force vigorously demanded continuation of such warplanes, and, in 1937, one of Polikarpov's principal team leaders, Aleksei Ya Shcherbakov, was assigned the task of developing a more potent fighter biplane. Assisted by Mikhail Gurevich, Shcherbakov created the I-153 (I-15ter), prototype trials commencing in summer 1938. The basic structure of the I-152 was extensively restressed, the Clark YH wing profile was retained, but configuration reverted to the "gulled" upper

The I-180.3 (above) introduced a cockpit canopy, an M-88R engine and a redesigned wing structure, but was lost during acceptance trials.

In the meantime, a pre-series of 10 aircraft based on the I-180.2 had been under construction as the I-180S (*Seriyny* or Series), the first three of these having been completed in December 1939. The I-180S was powered by the M-88R and carried an armament of two 12,7-mm and two 7,62-mm fuselage-mounted guns, and, like the I-180.3, featured an enclosed cockpit. The I-180S was cleared for service trials, but the results of these were somewhat academic as this fighter had been overtaken by the more advanced I-185. As a part of the I-185 development programme, one pre-series I-180S fighter had the dated triangulated pattern mainwheel legs replaced with legs of cantilever type, this aircraft being referred to as the I-180Sh, the suffix indicating *Shassi* (chassis). In the event, it was not completed and flown, the entire I-180 programme having meanwhile been abandoned. *Max speed, 363 mph (585 km/h) at 23,460 ft (7 150 m). Time to 16,405 ft (5 000 m), 5.0 min. Empty weight, 4,510 lb (2 046 kg). Loaded weight, 5,414 lb (2 456 kg). Span, 33 ft 1¼ in (10,09 m). Length, 22 ft 6⅞ in (6,88 m). Wing area, 173.41 sq ft (16,11 m²).*

POLIKARPOV I-190　　　　USSR

Stemming from operational experience in Spain and on the Khalkhin Gol, the I-190 single-seat fighter was intended to maximise manoeuvrability by use of the biplane configuration and to operate in concert with high-speed monoplanes. Flown on 30 December 1939 as a derivative of the I-153, the I-190 differed in having a Tumansky M-88 14-cylinder two-row radial engine with a ducted propeller spinner and some structural revision. Proposed armament comprised four synchronised 7,62-mm or two synchronised 20-mm weapons, and the first prototype was progressively fitted with M-88, M-88R and M-88A engines of 900 to 1,100 hp. This aircraft was destroyed on 13 February 1941, and further work on the I-190 was discontinued, a second prototype with a turbo-supercharger and a flexible rubber-sealed pressure cabin being abandoned prior to completion. A proposed development, the I-195, was to have had a 1,500 hp Shvetsov M-90 18-cylinder radial engine, cantilever wings and an increase of 63 sq ft (5,86 m²) in wing area. The following data relate to the I-190 with the 1,100 hp M-88A engine. *Max speed, 280 mph (450 km/h) at 23,130 ft (7 050 m). Time to 16,405 ft (5 000 m), 5.9 min. Empty weight, 3,882 lb (1 761 kg). Loaded weight, 4,656 lb (2 112 kg). Dimensions as for I-153 except overall length of 21 ft 3⅛ in (6,48 m).*

POLIKARPOV I-185　　　　USSR

The M-71-powered I-185 *Etalon* which was intended as the forerunner of the projected series I-186 fighter.

Acceptance that the concept of the I-180 was outmoded coupled with the prospect of the availability of power-

---

(Above, top) An I-153 captured by the *Wehrmacht* in the winter of 1941-42, and (immediately above) an I-153 of the 71 IAP, Baltic Fleet, Suomenlahti, 1942.

wing – resulting in the sobriquet of *Chaika* being resurrected – and, as a concession to modernity, manually-retractable main undercarriage members were introduced. Initially, the 775 hp M-25V engine was retained, armament remaining four 7,62-mm guns, but comparatively early in the production run the 1,000 hp Shvetsov M-62 engine was standardised, boosting max speed from 258 mph (415 km/h) at 9,840 ft (3 000 m) to 280 mph (444 km/h) at 15,090 ft (4 600 m). Some aircraft were fitted with a quartet of 12,7-mm guns (I-153BS) and one, experimentally, with twin synchronised 20-mm cannon (I-153P). Production deliveries began during the early spring of 1939, and continued until late 1940, 3,437 examples being produced. Ninety-three were supplied to the Chinese Central Government early in 1940, and the I-153 remained in first-line service until well into 1943. *Max speed, 280 mph (444 km/h) at 15,090 ft (4 600 m). Time to 9,840 ft (3 000 m), 3.0 min. Normal range, 292 mls*

(Above) An I-153 of Nationalist Chinese Air Force, *circa* 1941, and (below) the M-62-powered I-153.

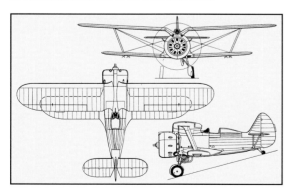

(Below) RS-82 missile-equipped I-153s of the 71 IAP assigned to the Soviet Baltic Fleet, August 1942.

(470 km). Empty weight, 3,201 lb (1 452 kg). Max loaded weight, 4,652 lb (2 110 kg). Span, 32 ft 9½ in (10,00 m). Length, 19 ft 3 in (6,17 m). Height, 9 ft 2¼ in (2,80 m). Wing area, 238.31 sq ft (22,14 m²).

A prototype I-153 (below) fitted with retractable skis and photographed during the winter of 1938-39.

POLIKARPOV I-180　　　　USSR

Developed from mid 1938 by Dmitrii L Tomashevich (one of Polikarpov's deputies), the I-180 was originally conceived with an all-metal structure. Limited all-metal construction experience, however, led the Polikarpov OKB to adopt an essentially similar structure to that of the earlier I-16, with a wooden monocoque fuselage and a fabric-skinned metal wing. The first prototype, the I-180.1, was powered by a 1,100 hp Tumansky M-88 14-cylinder two-row radial, intended armament being four 7,62-mm guns. This aircraft was lost as a result of engine failure during its first flight on 15 December 1938. The second prototype, the I-180.2, differed primarily in having a 1,000 hp Tumansky M-87A (later M-87B) 14-cylinder two-row radial and lengthened wing outer panels. These increased wing span from 29 ft 6⅓ in (9,00 m) to 32 ft 11⅔ in (10,05 m) and area from 158 sq ft (14,68 m²) to 173.41 sq ft (16,11 m²). First flown on 19 April 1939, the I-180.2 was lost on its 53rd flight. A third prototype, the I-180.3 flown on 10 February 1940, featured a redesigned and more advanced wing structure, a 1,100 hp M-88R engine, a cockpit canopy and an armament of two 12,7-mm and two 7,62-mm guns concentrated in the fuselage. Flown with both wheel and ski undercarriages, the I-180.3 was lost in an accident during State Acceptance Trials.

(Below) The I-180.3 which began tests February 1940.

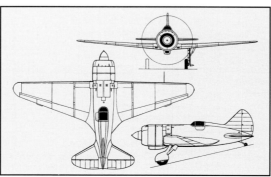

ful 18-cylinder radial engines led the Polikarpov OKB to design the I-185 within an extraordinarily short period of time (25 January to 10 March 1940). Intended for the 1,750 hp Shvetsov M-90 engine, the I-185 was of mixed construction, having a wooden monocoque fuselage mated with metal wings featuring automatic leading-edge slats *à la* Bf 109. Armament consisted of twin 12,7-mm and twin 7,62-mm guns, all fuselage-mounted. Development delays with the M-90 – which, by December 1940, was cleared only for restricted flight testing – resulted in dismantling of the first prototype unflown, this having been known as *Samolet* (Aircraft) *R*. A second prototype, *Samolet RM*, was completed with a Shvetsov M-81 18-cylinder two-row radial and a ducted propeller spinner. This was flown on 11 January 1941, but the M-81 was found to develop insufficient power and was replaced by the Shvetsov M-71 of 1,900 hp in May 1941. A third prototype, *Samolet I*, was completed with a 14-cylinder Shvetsov M-82 engine rated at 1,330 hp (later 1,400 hp), the fuselage being lengthened for CG reasons from 25 ft 2⅓ in (7,68 m) to 26 ft 6⅞ in (8,10 m), and fuselage-mounted armament being changed to three 20-mm cannon. State Acceptance Tests were conducted successfully between 13 April and 5 July 1942. A fourth prototype reverted to the M-71 engine and this underwent operational evaluation on the Kalinin Front alongside *Samolet I*. A redesigned wing (of single- in place of two-spar construction) was featured by this aircraft, which was tested with both the four-machine gun and three-cannon armament arrangements. A pre-production prototype, the so-called I-185 *Etalon* (Standard), was flown on 10 June 1942. Regarded as the forerunner of the intended production derivative, the I-186, this standardised on the M-71 engine and three-cannon armament, and had a similarly lengthened fuselage to that of *Samolet I*. State Acceptance Testing was conducted between November 1942 and January 1943, the NII VVS evaluation reports describing the I-185 *Etalon* as "superior to all contemporary fighters." In the event, it was found impracticable to manufacture the M-71 in large numbers and airframe production capacity was unavailable. *Max speed, 422 mph (680 km/h) at 20,015 ft (6 100 m). Time to 16,405 ft (5 000 m), 4.7 min. Empty weight, 6,900 lb (3 130 kg). Loaded weight, 8,234 lb (3 735 kg). Span, 32 ft 1⅞ in (9,80 m). Length, 26 ft 4⅞ in (8,05 m). Wing area, 167.17 sq ft (15,53 m²).*

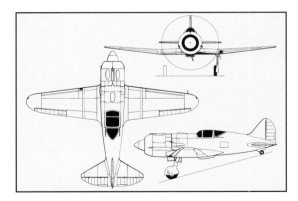

(Above and below) **The I-185M-82, the third prototype or** *Samolet I*, **which was tested on the Kalinin Front.**

POLIKARPOV TIS   USSR

To meet a requirement for a heavy escort fighter, or TIS (*Tyazhely istrebitel soprovozhdeniya*), formulated in the autumn of 1938, the Polikarpov OKB designed a low-wing monoplane of all-metal construction powered by two 1,400 hp Mikulin AM-37 engines. Fixed forward-firing armament comprised four 7,62-mm and two 20-mm guns, rear protection being

(Above) **The second prototype Polikarpov TIS, or** *Samolet MA*, **entered flight test in June 1944.**

provided by single flexible 7,62-mm guns fired from dorsal and ventral positions by the second crew member. The first prototype, *Samolet A*, was flown in September 1941, but evacuation of the Polikarpov facilities to Novosibirsk delayed the programme, and an improved second prototype, *Samolet MA*, was not flown until 13 June 1944. The *MA* was intended to be powered by 1,700 hp Mikulin AM-39 engines, but their non-availability dictated installation of 1,665 hp AM-38 engines. Fixed forward-firing armament was changed to two 37-mm cannon and two 12,7-mm machine guns. The flight testing of the *MA* was in its early stages when, on 30 July 1944, Polikarpov died and his OKB was almost immediately disbanded, the TIS programme being abandoned. The following data relate to the first prototype. *Max speed, 345 mph (555 km/h) at 19,030 ft (5 800 m). Time to 16,405 ft (5 000 m), 7.35 min. Normal range, 665 mls (1 070 km). Empty weight, 12,787 lb (5 800 kg). Loaded weight, 17,284 lb (7 840 kg). Span, 50 ft 10¼ in (15,50 m). Length, 38 ft 5 in (11,70 m). Height, 14 ft 3¼ in (4,35 m). Wing area, 375.12 sq ft (34,85 m²).*

(Above) **The** *Samolet A* **and (below)** *MA*, **the two prototypes of Polikarpov's heavy escort fighter.**

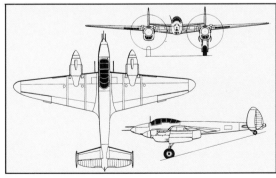

POLIKARPOV ITP   USSR

In 1941, the Polikarpov OKB began work on an *istrebitel'tyazhely pushechny* – heavy cannon [-armed] fighter – which was to mount a 37-mm cannon between the cylinder banks of a 1,650 hp Klimov M-107P 12-cylinder liquid-cooled Vee engine, and also carry two synchronised 20-mm cannon. The aircraft was of mixed construction, the fuselage being a wooden monocoque and the wing of steel and dural. The first prototype, referred to as the M-1, was completed in October 1941, but difficulties with the engine delayed the initiation of flight testing until 23 February 1942. An M-107A replaced the M-107P late in 1942, but engine difficulties were still experienced, and a second prototype, the

(Below) **The second prototype of the Polikarpov ITP, the M-2, differed from the first primarily in engine.**

M-2, was completed with an AM-37 engine of 1,400 hp with which it flew on 23 November 1943. The M-2 had an armament of three 20-mm cannon and eight RS-82 unguided rocket projectiles, the engine eventually being replaced by an AM-39 of 1,700 hp. Factory flight testing continued until June 1944 when the programme was abandoned. The following data relate to the M-1. *Max speed, 407 mph (655 km/h) at 20,670 ft (6 300 m). Time to 16,405 ft (5 000 m), 5.9 min. Range, 795 mls (1 280 km). Empty weight, 6,426 lb (2 960 kg). Loaded weight, 7,870 lb (3 570 kg). Span, 32 ft 9¾ in (10,00 m). Length, 29 ft 4⅓ in (8,95 m). Wing area, 177.07sq ft (16,45 m²).*

(Below) **The M-1, first prototype of the ITP.**

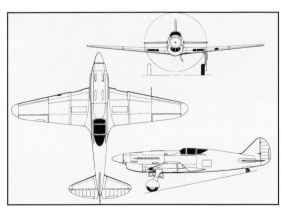

POMILIO GAMMA   Italy

Early in 1918, the Pomilio concern of Turin completed the prototype of a single-seat fighter designated Gamma (the third letter of the Greek alphabet). Powered by a 200 hp SPA 6A water-cooled engine, the Gamma was a single-bay, unequal-span biplane of wooden construction. Demonstrated for an official commission, the Gamma proved both fast and manoeuvrable, but was considered to possess an inadequate climb rate. The second prototype was therefore fitted with a 250 hp Isotta-Fraschini V6 engine as the Gamma IF. The official commission disagreed on the merits of the fighter and it was not until the closing weeks of World War I that a small batch of Gamma IF fighters was ordered, but these did not enter service with the *Aviazione Militare*. Ottorino Pomilio and his brother settled in the USA in 1918, establishing the Pomilio Brothers Corp. The following data relate to the Gamma

The Pomilio Gamma, first (above) and second (below) prototypes being illustrated, was not adopted.

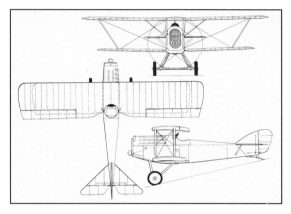

IF. *Max speed, 140 mph (225 km/h). Time to 9,840 ft (3 000 m), 7.5 min. Endurance, 3.0 hrs. Empty weight, 1,499 lb (680 kg). Loaded weight, 2,094 lb (950 kg). Span, 26 ft 2½ in (7,99 m). Length, 20 ft 8 in (6,30 m). Wing area, 235.74 sq ft (21,90 m²).*

POMILIO FVL-8 · USA

See Engineering Division FVL-8.

PONNIER M.1 · France

In 1915, Avions Ponnier produced the M.1 single-seat fighter, allegedly to the designs of Emile Eugène Dupont, who was subsequently to be responsible for the Hanriot HD-1. An unequal span single-bay nominally staggered biplane of wooden construction with fabric skinning and powered by an 80 hp Le Rhône 9C rotary engine, the M.1 had a single 7,7-mm Lewis gun on an overwing mounting. Featuring an inordinately large propeller spinner and extremely small tail surfaces, an early example of the M.1 (possibly the prototype) crashed on 29 January 1916 while being evaluated at Avord by Charles Nungesser. Nonetheless, production was undertaken by La Société Anonyme Française de Constructions Aéronautiques, which, early in 1916, succeeded Avions Ponnier, but was still controlled by Louis Alfred Ponnier. Most M.1s were procured by the *Aviation Militaire Belge*, which apparently received at least 18, and one or two went to French units. Some Belgian M.1s were flown without the spinner and they were later fitted with fixed fins of low aspect ratio, and enlarged tailplanes and elevators. According to the Bel-

The Ponnier M.1 (below) is illustrated here in its initial production form without fixed tail fin.

gian ace Willy Coppens, the M.1 was found to be unusable and soon disappeared. It never equipped a French unit and was declared obsolete in November 1916. A similar, but slightly larger, Ponnier two-seater was designed as the M.2 and offered to the RFC in January 1916. There is no evidence that it was built, however. *Max speed, 104 mph (167 km/h) at sea level. Time to 3,280 ft (1 000 m), 4.67 min. Empty weight, 671 lb (304 kg). Loaded weight, 1,023 lb (464 kg). Span, 20 ft 3⅓ in (6,18 m). Length, 18 ft 10⅕ in (5,75 m). Height, 7 ft 6½ in (2,30 m). Wing area, 145.3 sq ft (13,50 m²).*

The definitive M.1 (above and below) with fixed fin and enlarged tailplane and elevators.

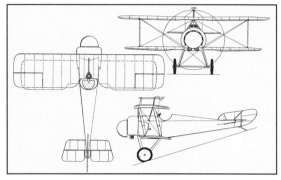

PORT VICTORIA P.V.2. · UK

The P.V.2 (above and below) anti-Zeppelin aircraft which was intended to carry a two-pounder Davis gun.

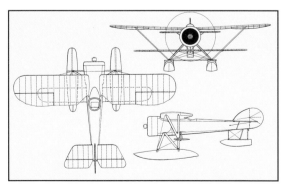

The Royal Naval Aeroplane Repair Depot was commissioned at the Isle of Grain early in 1915, and to distinguish it from the seaplane station already established there it was named Port Victoria. Ultimately it became known as the Marine Experimental Aircraft Depot and undertook original design work. Its first entirely original design was the P.V.2 single-seat anti-Zeppelin seaplane. Of wooden construction and powered by a 100 hp Gnome Monosoupape rotary, the P.V.2 was an exceptionally clean sesquiplane, the wing cellule being almost devoid of bracing wires with the

upper wing attached to the upper fuselage longerons and the lower wing passing beneath the fuselage. The intended armament was a two-pounder Davis gun, although this was never fitted. The P.V.2 was first flown in June 1916 with floats of the pontoon type, these later being replaced by Linton Hope floats. Trials showed considerable promise and it was decided to develop the design further as the P.V.2bis (which see). *Max speed, 95 mph (153 km/h) at sea level. Time to 3,000 ft (915 m), 5.0 min. Empty weight, 1,087 lb (493 kg). Loaded weight, 1,590 lb (721 kg). Span, 27 ft 0 in (8,23 m). Length, 22 ft 0 in (6,70 m). Height, 8 ft 4 in (2,54 m). Wing area, 168 sq ft (15,60 m²).*

PORT VICTORIA P.V.2BIS · UK

The decision to develop the P.V.2 as the P.V.2bis single-seat fighter seaplane resulted in major changes to the original prototype, the most significant being the raising of the upper wing by 1 ft (30 cm) to improve the pilot's view for alighting and the insertion of centre-section struts. The span and area of the upper wing were increased by introduction of a 2-ft (61-cm) centre section, and the planned armament was two 0.303-in (7,7-mm) machine guns to fire forward and upward above the propeller, although, in the event, only one such gun was apparently fitted. The P.V.2bis was flown early in 1917, providing data for later Port Victoria types. *Max speed, 93 mph (150 km/h) at sea level. Time to 3,000 ft (915 m), 6.0 min. Empty weight, 1,211 lb (549 kg). Loaded weight, 1,702 lb (772 kg). Span, 29 ft 0 in (8,84 m). Length, 22 ft 0 in (6,70 m). Height, 9 ft 4 in (2,84 m). Wing area, 180 sq ft (16,72 m²).*

The P.V.2bis (below) introduced significant design changes compared with the original P.V.2.

PORT VICTORIA P.V.4 · UK

Early in 1916, the Marine Experimental Aircraft Depot initiated the design of a land-based two-seat fighter, the P.V.3. Although this was never built, the Depot was officially requested to develop a float seaplane version carrying radio equipment and a single 0.303-in (7,7-mm) machine gun. This, the P.V.4, was a small and compact sesquiplane with a central nacelle for the two crew members and a pusher engine, and the tail assembly carried by four slim booms. The gunner occupied the forward cockpit, which was equipped with a Scarff ring for the gun. The intention was to fit the P.V.4 with a 150 hp Smith "Static" radial engine but, as this was unavailable, a 110 hp Clerget rotary was installed for flight testing in mid-1917. This created CG problems, resolution of which would have involved considerable redesign, and, as the P.V.4 was considered to possess insufficient promise to warrant this work, development was discontinued. *Max speed, 81 mph (130 km/h). Loaded weight 2,400 lb (1 089 kg). Span, 32 ft 0 in (9,75 m). Wing area, 220 sq ft (20,44 m²).*

The two-seat P.V.4 sesquiplane float fighter (below) lacked the promise to warrant further development.

PORT VICTORIA P.V.5   UK

Shortly after the Depot initiated work on the P.V.4, it was asked to develop a single-seat fighter seaplane also capable of performing light bombing tasks with two internally-stowed 65-lb (29,5-kg) bombs. To meet this requirement, two different aircraft were designed and built, the P.V.5 and the P.V.5a. The former was developed from the P.V.2bis and employed a similar sesquiplane wing cellule devoid of flying wires and braced by struts to the float undercarriage. The wings employed a high-lift aerofoil section, the armament comprised a single synchronised 0.303-in (7,7-mm) machine gun plus the two 65-lb (29,5-kg) bombs specified and power was provided by a 150 hp Hispano-Suiza engine. Fitted with pontoon-type floats rather than the Linton Hope floats for which it had been designed, the P.V.5 was flight tested in mid-1917 with promising results, but the original requirement had been overtaken and development was discontinued. *Max speed, 94 mph (151 km/h) at 2,000 ft (610 m). Time to 2,000 ft (610 m), 4.83 min. Empty weight, 1,788 lb (811 kg). Loaded weight, 2,456 lb (1 114 kg). Span, 32 ft 0 in (9,75 m). Length, 25 ft 6 in (7,77 m). Height, 9 ft 9 in (2,97 m). Wing area, 245 sq ft (22,76 m²).*

The P.V.5 (above and below) was fitted with pontoon-type floats and was flight tested in mid-1917.

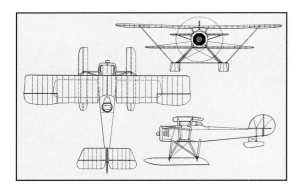

PORT VICTORIA P.V.5A   UK

Designed along more conventional lines than the P.V.5, the P.V.5a was an equi-span single-bay biplane with cable bracing, sharing with the former type only the fuselage, tail surfaces and armament. The pontoon-type floats were supplanted by Linton Hope floats, the internal accommodation for a bomb load was eliminated and a 200 hp Hispano-Suiza engine was fitted. Work on the P.V.5 and 5a was initiated in parallel, but work on the latter was discontinued early in 1917, and only reinstated after the P.V.5 had flown, the P.V.5a commencing flight test in the spring of 1918. It proved inferior to the P.V.5 in terms of manoeuvrability and pilot's view, but was satisfactory in most other respects. Development was discontinued after completion of flight testing as no service requirement for this category of aircraft existed. *Max speed, 102 mph*

The P.V.5a (below) discarded the sesquiplane form of the P.V.5 in favour of that of equi-span biplane.

PORT VICTORIA P.V.7 (GRAIN KITTEN)   UK

To meet a requirement for a diminutive lightweight single-seat airship interceptor suitable for operation from platforms on relatively small seagoing vessels, the Depot produced the P.V.7 to the designs of W H Sayers. To become known as the Grain Kitten to distinguish it from a competitive design created by the RNAS Experimental Flight at Eastchurch (which accordingly became known as the Eastchurch Kitten), the P.V.7 was an extremely small sesquiplane intended to be powered by a 45 hp geared ABC Gnat two-cylinder air-cooled engine. Armament consisted of a single 0.303-in (7,7-mm) machine gun mounted above the wing centre section. Unavailability of the geared Gnat engine led to installation of a 35 hp direct-drive Gnat with which the P.V.7 was completed in the summer of 1917. Difficulties were experienced with the engine from the start of flight testing in June, the aircraft being tail-heavy and performance disappointing. A series of modifications was introduced, but the P.V.7 was not flown subsequently. *Max speed, 89 mph (143 km/h) at 2,000 ft (610 m). Time to 6,500 ft (1 980 m), 10.8 min. Empty weight, 272 lb (123 kg). Loaded weight, 491 lb (223 kg). Span, 18 ft 0 in (5,49 m). Length, 14 ft 11 in (4,55 m). Height, 5 ft 3 in (1,60 m). Wing area, 85 sq ft (7,90 m²).*

The P.V.7 single-seat lightweight anti-Zeppelin fighter (above and below) flew in June 1917.

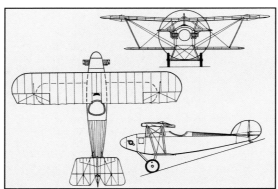

PORT VICTORIA P.V.8 (EASTCHURCH KITTEN)   UK

Although designed by Lt G H Millar of the RNAS Experimental Flight at Eastchurch and partly built by that establishment, this competitor for the P.V.7 as a lightweight single-seat interceptor was completed in the workshops at Port Victoria and assigned the designation P.V.8. Becoming known as the Eastchurch Kitten, the P.V.8 was an angular single-bay staggered biplane intended, like the P.V.7, to be powered by the geared ABC Gnat engine, but of necessity fitted with the 35 hp ungeared version of this two-cylinder power plant. When initially flown on 1 September 1917, the P.V.8 possessed no fixed tailplane, but the horizontal tail surfaces were redesigned to incorporate a small tailplane prior to the second flight. Proving itself superior to the P.V.7 in every way, the P.V.8 suffered similar problems with its engine. On 13 March 1918, the Eastchurch Kitten was packed for despatch to the USA, where it was to be evaluated, but there is no record that it ever

(164 km/h) at 2,000 ft (610 m). Time to 2,000 ft (610 m), 2.33 min. Endurance, 2.5 hrs. Empty weight, 1,972 lb (894 kg). Loaded weight, 2,518 lb (1 142 kg). Span, 33 ft 1 in (10,08 m). Length, 26 ft 9 in (8,15 m). Height, 13 ft 1 in (3,99 m). Wing area, 309 sq ft (28,71 m²).

Intended to compete with the P.V.7, the P.V.8 (above and below) was dubbed Eastchurch Kitten.

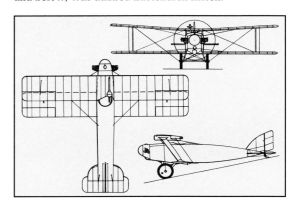

reached its destination. *Max speed, 94 mph (151 km/h) at 2,000 ft (610 m). Time to 6,500 ft (1 980 m), 11.0 min. Empty weight, 340 lb (154 kg). Loaded weight, 586 lb (266 kg). Span, 18 ft 11½ in (5,78 m). Length, 15 ft 7½ in (4,76 m). Height, 5 ft 2 in (1,57 m). Wing area, 106 sq ft (9,85 m²).*

PORT VICTORIA P.V.9   UK

Owing much to the P.V.2, the P.V.9 single-seat fighter seaplane, first flown in December 1917, was a sesquiplane braced entirely by faired steel tubes. With a fuselage mounted between the wings, an armament of one synchronised 0.303-in (7,7-mm) machine gun and a similar-calibre weapon mounted on top of the fuselage, the P.V.9 had single-step pontoon-type floats and a 150 hp Bentley B.R.1 rotary engine. Protracted engine problems delayed the initiation of full-scale trials until May 1918, at which time it was alleged to be the best float-equipped single-seat fighter extant. However, lack of a suitable propeller prevented full exploitation of its performance potential and, no longer fulfilling a service requirement, its development was discontinued. *Max speed, 110 mph (177 km/h) at 2,000 ft (610 m). Time to 6,500 ft (1 980 m), 13.33 min. Endurance, 2.5 hrs.*

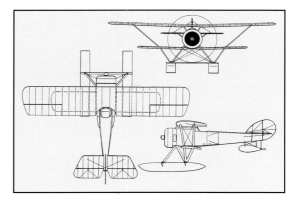

Delayed by engine difficulties, the P.V.9 (above and below) was discontinued in the summer of 1918.

Empty weight, 1,404 lb (637 kg). Loaded weight, 1,965 lb (891 kg). Span, 30 ft 11 in (9,42 m). Length, 25 ft 2 in (7,67 m). Height, 9 ft 0 in (2,75 m). Wing area, 227 sq ft (21,09 m²).

POTEZ XI   France

Designed to meet the demands of a CAP (*Chasse Armée Protection*) 2 requirement formulated in 1919 by the newly-appointed *Directeur de l'Aéronautique*, *Général* Duval, the Potez XI was a two-seater intended to fulfil bomber intercept and tactical reconnaissance at Army Corps level, and escort fighter tasks. The specification called for the use of a turbo-supercharged engine, and the Potez XI, which appeared in 1922, was powered by a 370 hp Lorraine-Dietrich 12D water-cooled 12-cylinder engine equipped with a Rateau turbo-supercharger. Competing with the Hanriot HD.15, the Potez XI had a fabric-covered light alloy structure and was an equi-span two-bay biplane with over-hung ailerons on the lower wing. Armament comprised two fixed forward-firing 7,7-mm machine guns and two similar weapons on a swivelling mount in the rear cockpit. The inadequacies of then-current steels to withstand prolonged operation of exhaust-driven turbo-superchargers led to cancellation of the CAP2 programme and development of the Potez XI was discontinued. *Max speed, 137 mph (220 km/h) at 13,125 ft (4 000 m). Service ceiling, 26,245 ft (8 000 m). Empty weight, 2,976 lb (1 350 kg). Loaded weight, 4,409 lb (2 000 kg). Span, 41 ft 8 in (12,70 m). Length, 29 ft 9½ in (9,08 m). Wing area, 497.3 sq ft (46,20 m²).*

The Potez XI two-seater (below) was intended for both bomber intercept and reconnaissance missions.

POTEZ 23   France

During 1923, the design team led by Louis Coroller initiated work on two fundamentally similar aircraft in parallel, the Potez 23 single-seat fighter and the Potez 24 two-seat army co-operation aircraft. Differing primarily dimensionally, these were fabric-covered unequal-span, single-bay biplanes of wooden construction, with provision for interchangeable Lorraine-Dietrich and Hispano-Suiza engines. Powered by a 400 hp Lorraine-Dietrich 12Db water-cooled 12-cylinder engine, the Potez 23 carried an armament of two fixed forward-firing 7,7-mm machine guns and was flown early in 1924. Whereas the Potez 24 provided a basis for the highly successful Potez 25, development of the Potez 23 was discontinued, only a single prototype being tested. *Max speed, 140 mph (225 km/h) at 13,125 ft (4 000 m). Time to 13,125 ft (4 000 m), 18 min. Empty weight, 2,458 lb (1 115 kg). Loaded weight,*

The Potez 23 (below) was designed in 1923, together with a two-seat army co-operation version.

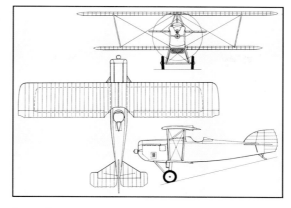

(Above) The Potez 23 single-seat fighter of 1924.

3,395 lb (1 540 kg). Span, 34 ft 5⅓ in (10,50 m). Length, 24 ft 11¼ in (7,60 m). Height, 10 ft 2⅞ in (3,12 m). Wing area, 344.46 sq ft (32,00 m²).

POTEZ 26   France

The Potez 26 (above and below) was essentially a single-seat version of the army co-op Potez 25

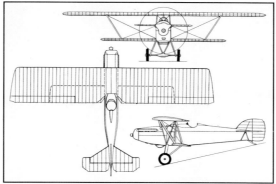

Essentially a single-seat fighter version of the Potez 25 two-seat army co-operation aircraft, the Potez 26 was, in fact, the first to fly, commencing its test programme in August 1924. A single-bay, staggered sesquiplane with a narrow-chord lower wing and inclined N-type interplane struts, the Potez 26 was of wooden construction with fabric covering, and was designed to accept either Lorraine-Dietrich or Hispano-Suiza engines. The sole prototype was powered by a 450 hp Hispano-Suiza 12Ha water-cooled 12-cylinder engine and its armament consisted of two synchronised 7,7-mm machine guns. No series production was

undertaken. *Max speed, 155 mph (250 km/h) at 16,405 ft (5 000 m). Time to 16,405 ft (5 000 m), 20 min. Ceiling, 27,885 ft (8 500 m). Empty weight, 2,425 lb (1 100 kg). Loaded weight, 3,417 lb (1 550 kg). Span, 39 ft 4½ in (12,00 m). Length, 26 ft 2⅞ in (8,00 m). Height, 10 ft 4 in (3,15 m). Wing area, 344.46 sq ft (32,00 m²).*

POTEZ 31   France

(Above) The Potez 31 two-seat night fighter and diurnal reconnaissance-fighter of 1929.

The Potez 31 was designed to meet the requirements of the 1925 C2 programme calling for a two-seat night fighter and diurnal reconnaissance-fighter. Not flown until 1929, and closely resembling the Potez 25M monoplane variant of the Potez 25 army co-operation biplane, the Potez 31 was a parasol monoplane of wooden construction with fabric covering. Embodying the facility developed for preceding types of accepting either Hispano-Suiza or Lorraine-Dietrich W-type water-cooled engines, the Potez 31 was tested with both the 500 hp HS 12Mb and the 450 hp L-D 12Eb. Armament consisted of two fixed forward-firing 7,7-mm guns, two similar weapons on a flexible mount in the rear cockpit and a fifth gun firing through a hatch in the rear cockpit floor. Development of the Potez 31 was terminated with the discontinuation of the C2 programme. The following data relate to the aircraft powered by the HS 12Mb engine. *Max speed, 150 mph (242 km/h) at 16,405 ft (5 000 m). Empty weight, 2,800 lb (1 270 kg). Loaded weight, 4,696 lb (2 130 kg). Span, 46 ft 11 in (14,30 m). Length, 31 ft 2 in (9,50 m). Height, 11 ft 1⅞ in (3,40 m). Wing area, 430.57 sq ft (40,00 m²).*

(Below) The Potez 31 night fighter and recce type.

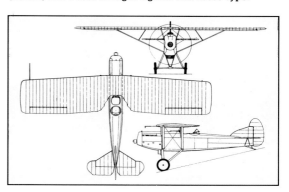

POTEZ 453   France

A contender to fulfil the 1933 *Marine Nationale* requirement for a single-seat float fighter suitable for catapult operation from 10,000-ton cruisers, the Potez 453 was based broadly on the design of the two-seat Potez 452 light observation flying boat. Competing with floatplanes tendered by Bernard (H.52), Loire (210) and Romano (R-90), the Potez 453 flying boat first flew on 24 September 1935. Of mixed construction, it was powered by an 800 hp Hispano-Suiza 14Hbs radial engine and was intended to carry an armament of two 7,5-mm machine guns. The engine was carried on bracing struts ahead of the wing, the thrust axis passing high above the cg of the flying boat with the result that, in view of the small dimensions of the aircraft, a considerable diving moment was induced at full throttle which could not be easily counteracted. Take-off was, in consequence, difficult and could be effected only by reducing engine power. Further development of the Potez 453 was therefore abandoned. *Max speed, 198 mph (318 km/h) at 9,840 ft (3 000 m). Time to*

The Potez 453 (above and below) single-seat catapult fighter flying boat based on an observation type.

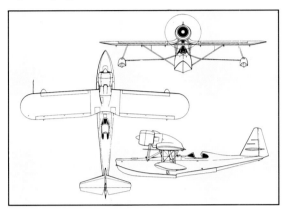

9,840 ft (3 000 m), 3.83 min. Range, 335 mls (540 km). Empty weight, 3,382 lb (1 534 kg). Loaded weight, 4,270 lb (1 937 kg). Span, 36 ft 8⁹⁄₁₀ in (11,20 m). Length, 33 ft 5½ in (10,20 m). Height, 11 ft 3⅞ in (3,45 m). Wing area, 204.51 sq ft (19,00 m²).

POTEZ 630 — France

Created to meet the requirements of the October 1934 specification for a three-seat fighter suitable for bomber interception, escort and (single-seat) fighter director rôles, the Potez 630 was first flown on 25 April 1936. Aerodynamically an exceptionally clean all-metal cantilever monoplane, the Potez 630 demonstrated outstanding capabilities, and a contract for four pre-series aircraft was followed by one for 80 production aircraft powered by two 670 hp Hispano-Suiza 14AB 10/11 radial engines. The first of these was flown in February 1938, armament comprising two fixed 20-mm cannon and one flexibly-mounted 7,5-mm machine gun. The Potez 630 entered service in two-seat night fighter (CN2) form, but unsatisfactory features of its Hispano-Suiza engines resulted in the re-equipment of the two Potez 630 *Groupes de Chasse* with the Potez 631 (which see) prior to the commencement of World War II. The HS-engined aircraft was reallocated to diurnal *Escadres de Chasse*, 65 being on the first-line strength when hostilities commenced. By early 1940, the few remaining Potez 630s in the operational inventory were in process of withdrawal with the intention of converting them as dual-control instructional aircraft. Two Potez 630s were supplied to Switzerland as three-seat reconnaissance-bombers with provision for a ventral

One of two Potez 630s (above) bought by Switzerland.

twin 20-mm cannon pack. *Max speed, 278 mph (448 km/h) at 13,125 ft (4 000 m). Time to 13,125 ft (4 000 m), 7.05 min. Range, 808 mls (1 300 km). Empty weight, 6,193 lb (2 808 kg). Loaded weight, 8,487 lb (3 850 kg). Span, 52 ft 6 in (16,00 m). Length, 36 ft 3⅞ in (11,07 m). Height, 9 ft 11⅔ in (3,04 m). Wing area, 351.99 sq ft (32,70 m²).*

POTEZ 631 — France

The second prototype of the Potez 63 series differed from the first prototype (Potez 630) principally in having the smaller-diameter Gnome-Rhône 14M Mars radial engine in place of the Hispano-Suiza 14AB. Designated Potez 631, this first flew in March 1937, a pre-series of three being followed by orders for 10 Potez 631-INST two-seat instructional aircraft and 30 Potez 631 C3 three-seat day fighters. Additional orders placed during the course of 1938 raised the total number of Potez 631s under contract for the *Armée de l'Air* to 207 aircraft. These were to be delivered both as Potez 631 CN2 two-seat night fighters (supplanting the Potez 630 CN2s) and as Potez 631 C3 day fighters. Powered by two 660 hp Gnome-Rhône 14M6/7 radial engines, the Potez 631 was intended to be fitted with two forward-firing 20-mm cannon (although one of the cannon was replaced by a 7,5-mm machine gun in a number of aircraft) and a 7,5-mm gun on a flexible dorsal mounting.

(Above) The second Potez 63 series prototype, the 631.01, and (below) the series production Potez 631.

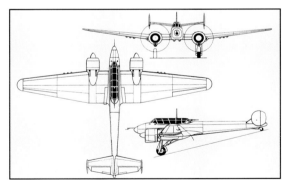

Two hundred and six Potez 631s were on *Armée d l'Air* charge at the commencement of World War II, of which 117 were included in the first-line inventory. Inadequate firepower led to a decision to fit all aircraft with four 7,5-mm guns underwing, although only a small number of Potez 631s were in the event so modified. One hundred and twelve of these aircraft survived the Battle of France, most subsequently serving with

(Above) A Potez 631 of *Escadrille de Chasse de Nuit* (ECN) 4/13 at Etampes during winter of 1939-40.

the *Armée de l'Air de l'Armistice*, which had 82 Potez 631s on strength on 1 November 1941. This number had dwindled to 64 by the time Vichy France was occupied, these aircraft being seized and mostly refurbished for supply to Romania as trainers and target-tugs. One Potez 631 (No 40) was re-engined with Pratt & Whitney Twin Wasp Juniors and flown on 29 December 1938 as the Potez 63.12 C3. *Max speed, 275 mph (442 km/h) at 14,765 ft (4 500 m). Time to 13,125 ft (4 000 m), 5.93 min. Range, 758 mls (1 200 km). Empty weight, 6,256 lb (2 838 kg). Loaded weight, 8,289 lb (3 760 kg). Dimensions as for Potez 630.*

POTEZ 670 & 671 — France

Designed to meet a requirement for a three-seat fighter with an endurance of three hours at 90 per cent max speed, the Potez 670 was configurationally similar to the Potez 630 and 631. Flown for the first time on 30 March 1939, the Potez 670 had meanwhile been modified as a two-seat long-range escort fighter and bomber destroyer. Initially powered by two 700 hp Gnome-Rhône 14M radials, it was re-engined after initial flight trials with two 800 hp Hispano-Suiza 14AB 12/13 radials, with which it resumed flight tests in July 1939 as the Potez 671. Several production variants were proposed, but flight trials were incomplete at the time of the French collapse and the sole prototype was destroyed during the German onslaught. At the time, work had begun on an initial batch of 40 Potez 671 C2 fighters. The following data relate to the HS-powered model. *Max speed, 311 mph (500 km/h) at 19,685 ft (6 000 m). Time to 9,840 ft (3 000 m), 1.58 min. Range, 1,243 mls (2 000 km). Empty weight, 7,023 lb (3 186 kg). Loaded weight, 10,419 lb (4 726 kg). Span, 49 ft 5½ in (15,10 m). Length, 35 ft 5⅛ in (10,80 m). Height, 10 ft 8¾ in (3,27 m). Wing area, 349.83 sq ft (32,50 m²).*

The Potez 670 (above and below) was being built in two-seat night fighter form when France collapsed.

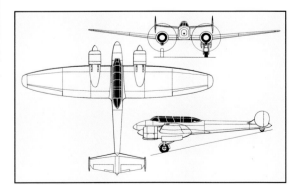

POTEZ 230 — France

With the absorption of ANF-Mureaux in 1937 as a component of the SNCA du Nord (which also included Potez and retained the appellation for its products), André Brunet and his co-designers Lemaitre and Hubert continued the line of lightweight fighter development commenced with the ANF-Mureaux 190. In the autumn of

An ex-*Armée de l'Air de l'Armistice* Potez 631 with the Romanian *Fortelor Aeriene Regal*, summer 1944.

The Potez 230 (above and below) was a lightweight fighter evolved from the ANF-Mureaux 190 of 1936.

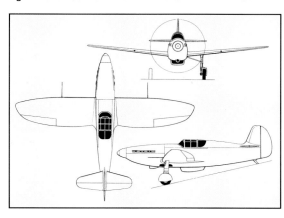

1938, work on a progressive development, the Potez 230, was begun. While possessing a number of features in common with the earlier fighter (eg, elliptical wings), the new aircraft was of more advanced design. Powered by a 670 hp Hispano-Suiza 12Xcrs 12-cylinder liquid-cooled engine and having a proposed armament of one engine-mounted 20-mm cannon and four wing-mounted 7,5-mm machine guns, the Potez 230 was flown on 30 March 1940. When German forces occupied Villacoublay, the sole prototype of the Potez 230 was seized and transported to Germany for examination of the wing torsion box, which, of integral construction, was the first of its type to have been flown. *Max speed, 348 mph (560 km/h) at 16,405 ft (5 000 m). Endurance, 1.5 hrs. Loaded weight, 3,986 lb (1 800 kg). Span, 28 ft 8 in (8,74 m). Length, 24 ft 10 in (7,57 m). Height, 7 ft 1¾ in (2,18 m). Wing area, 118.08 sq ft (10,97 m²).*

PRAGA BH-44 (E-44)   Czechoslovakia

In 1932, shortly after the Praga engine concern opened an aircraft department, the company participated in a design contest for a new single-seat fighter organised by the Czechoslovak Defence Ministry. Designed by Pavel Beneš and Miroslav Hajn, the ČKD-Praga contender, the BH-44, was an exceptionally clean single-bay staggered biplane with wooden wings and a fabric-covered, welded steel-tube fuselage. The first BH-44 prototype was powered by a 750 Praga ESV 12-cylinder water-cooled engine and was flown on 19 July 1932. Although the ESV engine was supposed to afford 750 hp, it proved to give only some 500 hp. The second prototype flew from April 1934 with an ESVK engine, which, fitted with a compressor, was rated at 650 hp (this aircraft sometimes being referred to as the BH-144), but results remained unsatisfactory. Proposals were made to fit the fighter with either the Gnome-Rhône Mistral 14K (BH-244) or Hispano-Suiza 12Ybrs (BH-344), but, in the event, the first prototype was re-engined with a 650 hp Rolls-Royce Kestrel VII with which it flew on 30 October 1934. The Kestrel performed poorly on the special fuel mix (BiBoLi) used by the Air Force (to which the BH-44 was known as the

E-44) and the Avia B-34 was chosen as winning contender. The following performance data are manufacturer's estimates based on the fully-rated ESV engine. *Max speed, 205 mph (330 km/h). Time to 9,840 ft (3 000 m), 5.2 min. Endurance, 1.8 hrs. Empty weight, 3,223 lb (1 462 kg). Loaded weight, 4,050 lb (1 837 kg). Span, 30 ft 4¼ in (9,25 m). Length, 25 ft 0 in (7,62 m). Wing area, 249.08 sq ft (23,14 m²).*

The Praga BH-44 (above and below) was a contender in a Czech Defence Ministry competition of 1932.

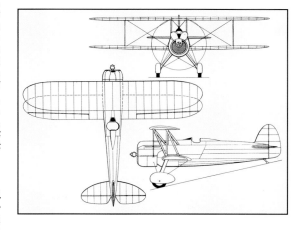

PRAGA E-45   Czechoslovakia

Designed by Jaroslav Šlechta to the same specification as that which was to produce the Avia B-534, the E-45 single-seat fighter was flown for the first time on 8

Possessing exceptionally clean contours, the Praga E-45 (below) was bested by the Avia B-534 fighter.

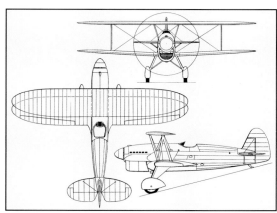

(Above) The Praga E-45 single-seat fighter of 1934.

October 1934 with a 710 hp Rolls-Royce Kestrel VI engine (rather than the preferred Hispano-Suiza 12Ydrs). Of similar construction to the earlier BH-44, the E-45 was an equi-span single-bay staggered biplane with an armament of two 7,92-mm Mk 30 machine guns. The E-45 proved extremely manoeuvrable and an excellent gun platform, but the more powerful B-534 offered superior performance and was selected for series production, development of the E-45 being discontinued. *Max speed, 231 mph (372 km/h). Initial climb, 3,070 ft/min (15,6 m/sec). Range, 396 mls (640 km). Empty weight, 2,970 lb (1 347 kg). Loaded weight, 3,728 lb (1 691 kg). Span, 27 ft 10⅔ in (8,50 m). Length, 24 ft 5½ in (7,45 m). Wing area, 217.98 sq ft (20,25 m²).*

P.W.S.1   Poland

The P.W.S.1 (above and below) was flown in April 1927 as a two-seat reconnaissance fighter.

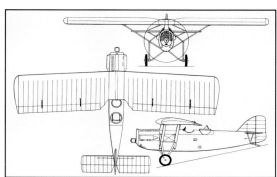

Evolved by the Podlaska Wytwórnia Samolotów (Podlasian Aeroplane Plant), or P.W.S., to meet an official requirement for a fast two-seat reconnaissance fighter, the P.W.S.1 parasol monoplane was designed by a team led by Stanislaw Cywiński and first flown on 25 April 1927. Of wooden construction apart from a steel-tube forward fuselage, the P.W.S.1 was powered by a 450 hp Lorraine-Dietrich LD 12Eb 12-cylinder water-cooled engine and carried an armament of two fixed synchronised 7,7-mm guns and two similar-calibre weapons on a Scarff mount in the rear cockpit. In the latter half of 1927, the aircraft was extensively re-designed and re-built as the P.W.S.1bis, flight testing being resumed early in 1928. The P.W.S.1bis featured an entirely new wing and new vertical tail surfaces, empty weight being reduced marginally but performance remaining virtually unchanged. As the aircraft held little promise

P.W.S.

of any major improvement over existing *Lotnictwo Woj-skowe* equipment, further development was discontinued. The following data relate to the P.W.S.1bis. *Max speed, 144 mph (232 km/h). Initial climb, 1,063 ft/min (5,4 m/sec). Range, 466 mls (750 km). Empty weight, 3,031 lb (1 375 kg). Loaded weight, 4,299 lb (1 950 kg). Span, 44 ft 11⅓ in (13,70 m). Length, 28 ft 6½ in (8,70 m). Height, 10 ft 10 in (3,30 m). Wing area, 322.93 sq ft (30,00 m²).*

P.W.S.10 — Poland

Designed by Aleksander Grzedzielski and Augustyn Bobek-Zdaniewski, the P.W.S.10 single-seat parasol monoplane fighter was the recipient of an order for two prototypes in 1929, the first of these flying in May 1930. Powered by a Škoda-built Lorraine-Dietrich LD 12Eb engine of 450 hp, the P.W.S.10 was of mixed construction with a wooden wing and steel tube fuselage.

The P.W.S.10 (above and below) saw comparatively brief Polish service and 20 drawn from Polish Air Force stocks were shipped to Spain during 1936-37.

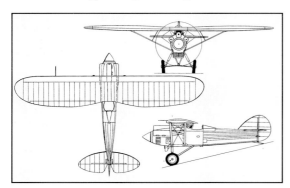

Armament consisted of two 7,7-mm Vickers guns. A contract was placed for 80 aircraft with deliveries commencing in the second half of 1931. Rather difficult to fly and never popular with its pilots, the P.W.S.10 was progressively withdrawn from 1933, but 20 reconditioned examples were sold to the Spanish Nationalist forces in 1936. Because of their inadequate performance they were restricted to the training rôle. *Max speed, 160 mph (258 km/h). Initial climb, 1,142 ft/min (5,8 m/sec). Range, 186 mls (300 km). Empty weight, 2,458 lb (1 115 kg). Loaded weight, 3,306 lb (1 500 kg). Span, 36 ft 1¼ in (11,00 m). Length, 24 ft 7½ in (7,50 m). Wing area, 193.76 sq ft (18,00 m²).*

P.W.S.15 — Poland

The shortcomings in handling qualities and manoeuvrability demonstrated by the P.W.S.10 prototypes led its designers, Grzedzielski and Bobek-Zdaniewski, in 1930 to develop a biplane version, the P.W.S.15, as a private venture for comparative testing. One of the two P.W.S.10 prototypes was fitted with a modestly staggered unequal-span single-bay biplane cellule with N-type interplane struts. Retaining the engine and armament of the P.W.S.10, the P.W.S.15 lacked the shortcomings of the parasol monoplane, possessing a superior climb rate and an essentially similar maximum speed. However, while the P.W.S.15 was under test, the company received a production contract for the P.W.S.10, and, rather than risk its cancellation in favour of the biplane with consequent production disruption, dismantled the prototype biplane without submitting it to official flight test. *Max speed, 155 mph (250 km/h) at sea level. Empty weight, 2,315 lb (1 050 kg). Loaded weight, 3,130 lb (1 420 kg). Span, 32 ft 9¾ in (10,00 m). Length, 24 ft 7½ in (7,50 m). Height, 10 ft 8¼ in (2,70 m). Wing area, 247.58 sq ft (23,00 m²).*

P.Z.L. P.1 — Poland

The first fighter of indigenous Polish design, the P.1 produced by the Państwowe Zaklady Lotnicze (P.Z.L.), or National Aviation Establishment, embodied several technical innovations. Designed by Zygmunt Pulawski, the P.1 was of all-metal construction, its most novel feature being the "gulling" into the fuselage of the centre section of the high wing, thus eliminating the normal cabane. This both reduced drag and improved the forward view for the pilot. Powered by a 12-cylinder water-cooled Hispano-Suiza 12 Lb Vee-type engine affording 630 hp for take-off, the first prototype, the P.1/I, was flown on 25 September 1929. Armament comprised two 7,7-mm Vickers machine guns. The second prototype, the P.1/II, featured a repositioned radiator bath and redesigned vertical tail surfaces, and joined the test programme in March 1930. Further development was discontinued in favour of radial-engined variants, as the Polish air arm, the *Lotnictwo Woj-skowe*, was biased against liquid-cooled engines. The following data relate to the second prototype. *Max speed, 188 mph (302 km/h) at sea level. Time to 6,560 ft (2 000 m), 2.66 min. Range, 373 mls (600 km) at 155 mph (250 km/h). Empty weight, 2,465 lb (1 118 kg). Loaded weight, 3,482 lb (1 580 kg). Span, 35 ft 7⅛ in (10,85 m). Length, 22 ft 10¾ in (6,98 m). Height, 9 ft 8½ in (2,96 m). Wing area, 209.9 sq ft (19,50 m²).*

The P.Z.L. P.1/I (below) and the P.1/II (above) were the first Pulawski fighter prototypes.

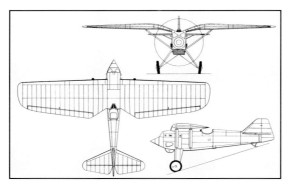

P.Z.L. P.6 — Poland

Evolved from the P.1 by Zygmunt Pulawski and developed in parallel with the P.7, the P.6 was powered by a low-altitude Gnome-Rhône Jupiter 9Ac (VI.FH) nine-

The P.6/I (above) fighter prototype participated in the 1931 Cleveland National Air Races.

cylinder radial rated at 450 hp. The principal change from the P.1, apart from the power plant, was to be found in the fuselage structure and fuel disposition, the rear fuselage being a semi-monocoque and the wing tanks of the earlier fighter giving place to a jettisonable fuselage tank. Armament remained two Vickers "E" machine guns (rebored to 7,92-mm calibre). The first of two P.6 prototypes was flown in August 1930, and, in the following year, participated in the National Air Races at Cleveland, Ohio. The second prototype, the P.6/II, differed primarily in having a Townend ring cowling in place of the narrow ring of the P.6/I. The *Lotnictwo Wojskowe* elected to order the contemporary P.7 for series production and no further development of the P.6 was undertaken. *Max speed,181 mph (292 km/h) at sea level. Time to 6,560 ft (2 000 m), 2.83 min. Range, 373 mls (600 km). Empty weight, 2,002 lb (908 kg). Loaded weight, 2,988 lb (1,355 kg). Span, 33 ft 9½ in (10,30 m). Length, 23 ft 5¾ in (7,16 m). Height, 9 ft 0¼ in (2,75 m). Wing area, 186.22 sq ft (17,30 m²).*

P.Z.L. P.7 — Poland

A parallel development to the P.6, from which it differed essentially in having a higher-altitude engine and some steel elements in the otherwise all-duralumin fuselage structure, the P.7 was powered by a supercharged Bristol Jupiter VII.F radial affording 520 hp at 10,000 ft (3 050 m). The first of two prototypes, the P.7/I, was flown in October 1930, and featured a close-fitting,

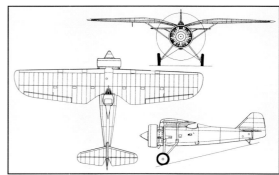

The P.7a (above and below) was Pulawski's first service fighter, the photo showing the 27th example.

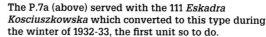

The P.7a (above) served with the 111 *Eskadra Kosciuszkowska* which converted to this type during the winter of 1932-33, the first unit so to do.

A Romanian licence-built P.11f (above) and the P.11c (below) which provided almost the entire Polish first-line fighter strength at the start of World War II.

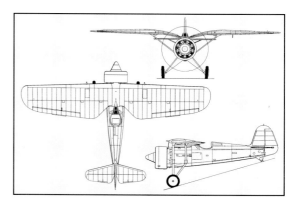

helmeted engine cowling, which gave place to a Townend ring on the P.7/II. Work on a pre-series batch of 10 of the P.7a fighters began in June 1931 for the *Lotnictwo Wojskowe*, a further 139 being subsequently ordered. The P.7a carried two 7,92-mm Vickers "E" machine guns and differed from the prototypes in having a P.Z.L.-developed ring cowling, a revised cockpit, shorter ailerons and modified tail surfaces. The P.7a entered service in the winter of 1932-33, and three first line squadrons were still equipped with this type when the *Wehrmacht* assault on Poland was launched on 1 September 1939. *Max speed, 203 mph (327 km/h) at 13,125 ft (4 000 m). Initial climb, 2,047 ft/min (10,40 m/sec). Range, 373 mls (600 km). Empty weight, 2,403 lb (1 090 kg). Loaded weight, 3,254 lb (1 476 kg). Span, 34 ft 8⅛ in (10,57 m). Length, 22 ft 10¾ in (6,98 m). Height, 8 ft 9¾in (2,69 m). Wing area, 192.68 sq ft (17,90 m²).*

(Below) Photographed at Deblin in 1942, this was one of several P.7a fighters captured by the Wehrmacht.

P.Z.L. P.8 — Poland

The P.8 represented an attempt on the part of Zygmunt Pulawski and his assistant, Wsiewolod Jakimiuk, to establish new standards in aerodynamic cleanliness and fighter performance. It combined a wing that was fundamentally similar to that of the P.6 and P.7 with a liquid-cooled engine and a new fuselage of improved fineness ratio covered by smooth duralumin skinning.

The P.8/II (above) seen here in its original form with flush-fitting engine water-cooling panels.

The first of two prototypes, the P.8/I, was flown in August 1931 with an Hispano-Suiza 12Mc 12-cylinder water-cooled engine providing a maximum output of 640 hp. The second prototype, the P.8/II, embodied some structural simplification, the ventral radiator bath being discarded in favour of flush-fitting lateral panels, and was powered by a Lorraine 12H Petrel water-cooled engine providing 675 hp at 11,485 ft (3 500 m).

Armament comprised the standard twin 7,92-mm machine guns. The first prototype was destroyed in an accident in July 1932 at Innsbruck, and the P.8/II was displayed some months afterwards at the 1932 Paris *Salon*, but development had already been discontinued in favour of the radial-engined P.11. The following data relate to the P.8/II. *Max speed, 217 mph (350 km/h) at sea level. Time to 16,405 ft (5 000 m), 7.5 min. Range, 310 mls (500 km). Empty weight, 2,429 lb (1 102 kg). Max loaded weight, 3,468 lb (1 573 kg). Span, 34 ft 5⅓ in (10,50 m). Length, 24 ft 9½ in (7,56 m). Height, 9 ft 0¼ in (2,75 m). Wing area, 193.76 sq ft (18,00 m²).*

(Below) A general arrangement drawing of the P.8/I.

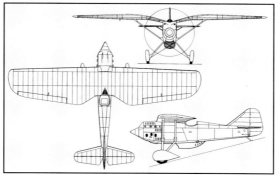

P.Z.L. P.11 — Poland

A progressive development of the P.7 stressed to accept more powerful radial engines, the P.11 stemmed from a decision to adapt the basic fighter for the Bristol Mercury engine. The first of three prototypes, the P.11/I,

(Above) The P.11/III prototype, and (below) P.11c fighters of the 112 *Eskadra* photographed in May 1936 during a courtesy visit to Sweden.

was fitted with a Jupiter 9Aab because of non-availability of the Mercury and flew in August 1931, the P.11/II and /III following with the Mercury IV engine. Thirty P.11a fighters powered by the Mercury IV.S2 with a maximum output of 575 hp were purchased for the *Lotnictwo Wojskowe*, and 50 similar aircraft powered by the 670 hp Gnome-Rhône 9Krsd Mistral were purchased by Romania as P.11bs. The P.11c, first flown late in 1933, featured a lower engine thrust line, a modified wing centre section and re-positioned pilot's cockpit. The first 50 or so for the *Lotnictwo Wojskowe* had the Mercury V.S2 rated at 600 hp at 14,765 ft (4 500 m), and a further 125 had the Mercury VI.S2 producing 645 hp at 15,500 ft (4 725 m). Armament comprised two 7,92-mm machine guns, but provision was made for the installation of two similar guns in the wings. A Romanian licence-built version of the P.11c with an IAR-K9 engine of 640 hp at 13,125 ft (4 000 m) and four 7,92-mm FN-Browning guns was designated P.11f, 70 being built by Industria Aeronautica Româna (IAR) during 1936-37. A decision to reinstate the P.11 in production was taken in the spring of 1939, in a version known as the P.11g Kobuz (a small species of falcon) with a P.Z.L.-built Mercury VIII engine rated at 840 hp at 14,000 ft (4 265 m). A prototype was produced by modifying a P.11c and this was flown on 15 August 1939, but series production had not begun when Poland was overrun by the *Wehrmacht*. The following data relate to the Mercury VI.S2-powered P.11c. *Max speed, 242 mph (390 km/h) at 18,045 ft (5 500 m). Initial climb, 2,440 ft/min (12,40 m/sec). Range, 435 mls (700 km). Empty weight, 2,529 lb (1 147 kg). Max loaded weight, 3,968 lb (1 800 kg). Span, 35 ft 2 in (10,72 m). Length, 24 ft 9¼ in (7,55 m). Height, 9 ft 4¼ in (2,85 m). Wing area, 192.68 sq ft (17,90 m²).*

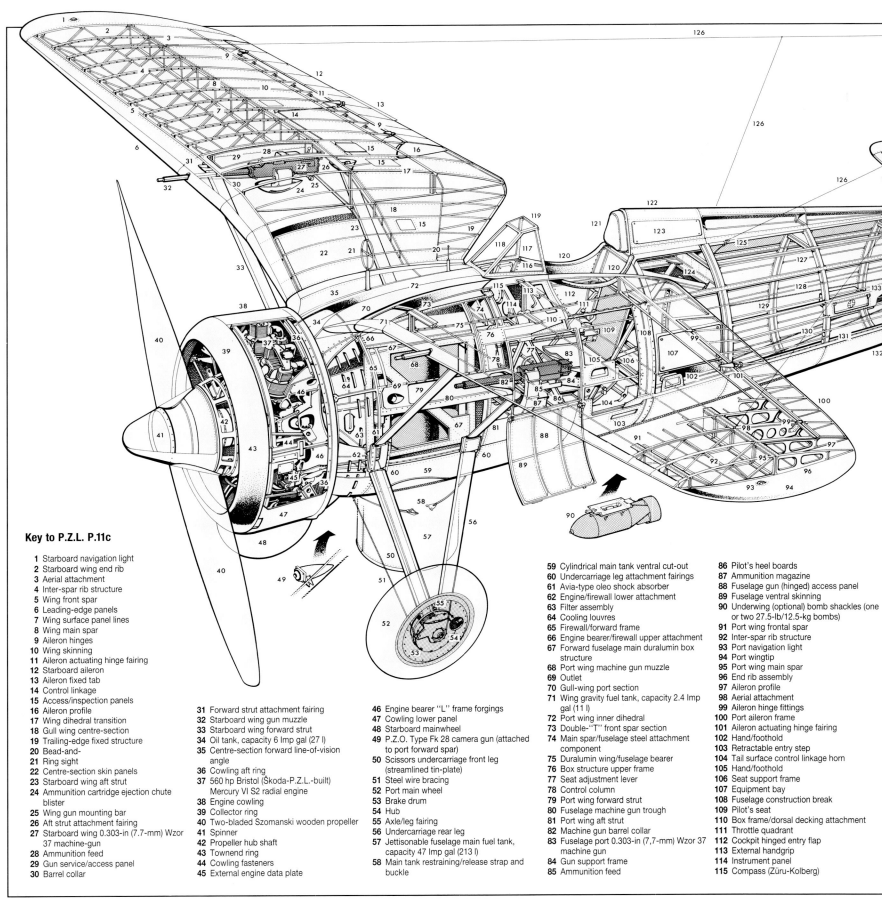

Key to P.Z.L. P.11c

1 Starboard navigation light
2 Starboard wing end rib
3 Aerial attachment
4 Inter-spar rib structure
5 Wing front spar
6 Leading-edge panels
7 Wing surface panel lines
8 Wing main spar
9 Aileron hinges
10 Wing skinning
11 Aileron actuating hinge fairing
12 Starboard aileron
13 Aileron fixed tab
14 Control linkage
15 Access/inspection panels
16 Aileron profile
17 Wing dihedral transition
18 Gull wing centre-section
19 Trailing-edge fixed structure
20 Bead-and-
21 Ring sight
22 Centre-section skin panels
23 Starboard wing aft strut
24 Ammunition cartridge ejection chute blister
25 Wing gun mounting bar
26 Aft strut attachment fairing
27 Starboard wing 0.303-in (7.7-mm) Wzor 37 machine-gun
28 Ammunition feed
29 Gun service/access panel
30 Barrel collar

31 Forward strut attachment fairing
32 Starboard wing gun muzzle
33 Starboard wing forward strut
34 Oil tank, capacity 6 Imp gal (27 l)
35 Centre-section forward line-of-vision angle
36 Cowling aft ring
37 560 hp Bristol (Škoda-P.Z.L.-built) Mercury VI S2 radial engine
38 Engine cowling
39 Collector ring
40 Two-bladed Szomanski wooden propeller
41 Spinner
42 Propeller hub shaft
43 Townend ring
44 Cowling fasteners
45 External engine data plate

46 Engine bearer "L" frame forgings
47 Cowling lower panel
48 Starboard mainwheel
49 P.Z.O. Type Fk 28 camera gun (attached to port forward spar)
50 Scissors undercarriage front leg (streamlined tin-plate)
51 Steel wire bracing
52 Port main wheel
53 Brake drum
54 Hub
55 Axle/leg fairing
56 Undercarriage rear leg
57 Jettisonable fuselage main fuel tank, capacity 47 Imp gal (213 l)
58 Main tank restraining/release strap and buckle

59 Cylindrical main tank ventral cut-out
60 Undercarriage leg attachment fairings
61 Avia-type oleo shock absorber
62 Engine/firewall lower attachment
63 Filter assembly
64 Cooling louvres
65 Firewall/forward frame
66 Engine bearer/firewall upper attachment
67 Forward fuselage main duralumin box structure
68 Port wing machine gun muzzle
69 Outlet
70 Gull-wing port section
71 Wing gravity fuel tank, capacity 2.4 Imp gal (11 l)
72 Port wing inner dihedral
73 Double-"T" front spar section
74 Main spar/fuselage steel attachment component
75 Duralumin wing/fuselage bearer
76 Box structure upper frame
77 Seat adjustment lever
78 Control column
79 Port wing forward strut
80 Fuselage machine gun trough
81 Port wing aft strut
82 Machine gun barrel collar
83 Fuselage port 0.303-in (7,7-mm) Wzor 37 machine gun
84 Gun support frame
85 Ammunition feed

86 Pilot's heel boards
87 Ammunition magazine
88 Fuselage gun (hinged) access panel
89 Fuselage ventral skinning
90 Underwing (optional) bomb shackles (one or two 27.5-lb/12.5-kg bombs)
91 Port wing frontal spar
92 Inter-spar rib structure
93 Port navigation light
94 Port wingtip
95 Port wing main spar
96 End rib assembly
97 Aileron profile
98 Aerial attachment
99 Aileron hinge fittings
100 Port aileron frame
101 Aileron actuating hinge fairing
102 Hand/foothold
103 Retractable entry step
104 Tail surface control linkage horn
105 Hand/foothold
106 Seat support frame
107 Equipment bay
108 Fuselage construction break
109 Pilot's seat
110 Box frame/dorsal decking attachment
111 Throttle quadrant
112 Cockpit hinged entry flap
113 External handgrip
114 Instrument panel
115 Compass (Züru-Kolberg)

P.Z.L. P.24   Poland

Essentially a refinement of the P.11c capable of accepting the most powerful radial engines available, the P.24 was intended primarily for export. The first of three prototypes, the P.24/I, flew in May 1933 with a Gnome-Rhône 14Kds engine with a max output of 760 hp at 12,140 ft (3 700 m). The P.24/III had a G-R 14Kfs engine with a max output of 930 hp at 14,860 ft (4 530 m), production models being the P.24A with two 20-mm Oerlikon cannon and two 7,92-mm machine guns, and the P.24B with four of the latter weapons. Sixty P.24s were ordered by Turkey, of which 20 were supplied by P.Z.L. as kits for indigenous assembly and 40 in flyaway con-

The P.24/IV (above) served as a production prototype for the P.24B and was shown at the 1936 Paris *Salon*.

dition. Fourteen of the latter were to P.24A standard and 26 were P.24Cs, these being similar to the P.24B

but embodying minor aerodynamic changes. The availability of the G-R 14N 07, which provided 970 hp at 15,090 ft (4 600 m), resulted in its installation in the P.24A to produce the P.24F, and in the P.24B producing the P.24G. Of the 20 aircraft assembled in Turkey, six were completed as P.24Fs and 14 as P.24Gs. Greece ordered 30 P.24As and six P.24Bs, but the contract was changed to cover 25 P.24Fs and six Gs after delivery of five P.24As. A Bulgarian contract for 14 P.24Bs was followed by a contract for 12 P.24Fs, four of the latter, in the event, not being delivered. Romania ordered a version similar to the P.24A, but powered by the IAR-K 14-II C32 engine providing 900 hp for take-off, this being designated P.24E. Six were supplied to Romania

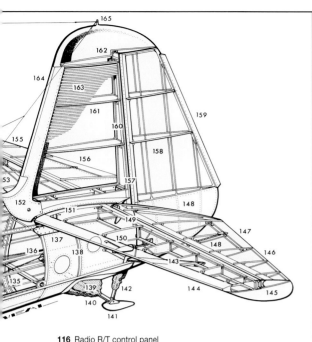

116 Radio R/T control panel
117 Quarterlights
118 Plexiglas windscreen
119 Windscreen frame
120 Cockpit padded coaming
121 Pilot's headrest
122 Dorsal decking
123 Upper spine equipment bay
124 Radio support tray (Type N2L/M R/T optional)
125 Aerial lead-in
126 Aerial array
127 Fuselage frame
128 Upper longeron
129 Rudder control cables
130 Elevator control cables
131 Lower longeron
132 Fuselage lower skinning
133 First-aid kit stowage
134 Stringers
135 Lift/hoist tube
136 Fuselage aft frame
137 Tailplane attachment external plate
138 Access panels (tailskid shock/control linkage)
139 Leather cuffs
140 Tailskid oleo strut
141 Tailskid
142 Tailskid attachment strut
143 Port tailplane brace strut
144 Port tailplane structure
145 End rib
146 Port elevator
147 Elevator tab
148 Tab hinge linkage
149 Elevator control linkage
150 Rudder actuating hinge fairing
151 Tailplane attachments
152 Tailfin root fairing
153 Starboard tailplane brace strut
154 Starboard tailplane
155 Starboard elevator
156 Elevator tab
157 Rudder centre hinge
158 Rudder
159 Rudder fixed tab
160 Rudder post
161 Tailfin
162 Rudder upper hinge
163 Tailfin corrugated skin
164 Tailfin leading-edge panels
165 Aerial attachment stub

(Below) A Kayseri-assembled P.24F in service in 1939 with the Turkish 4th Air Regiment at Kütahya.

(Above, top) A P.11c of the Polish 121 *Eskadra*, 1939, and (immediately above) an IAR-manufactured P.11f in service with the Romanian *Fortelor Aeriene Regal*.

(Above, top) A P.24F of the Greek 22 *Mira Dioxeos*, spring 1941, and (immediately above) a P.24B of the Bulgarian 2nd *Istrebitelen Orliak*, Karlovo, 1939.

by P.Z.L. and a further 44 were licence-built by IAR, the last being delivered in the late autumn of 1939. The following data relate to the cannon-armed P.24F. *Max speed,267 mph (430 km/h) at 13,945 ft (4 250 m). Initial climb, 2,264 ft/min (11,5 m/sec). Range, 342 mls (550 km). Empty weight, 2,936 lb (1 332 kg). Max loaded weight, 4,409 lb (2 000 kg). Span, 35 ft 0¾ in (10,68 m). Length, 24 ft 11½ in (7,60 m). Height, 8 ft 10¼ in (2,69 m). Wing area, 192.68 sq ft (17,90 m²).*

(Above) P.24F fighters of the Greek 22 *Mira Dioxeos*, October 1940, and (below) the P.24G with 7,9-mm guns.

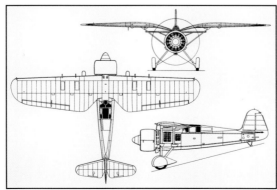

P.Z.L. P.38 WILK   Poland

Conceived as a multi-rôle fighter and designed by a team led by Franciszek Misztal, the Wilk (Wolf) was intended primarily as an attack fighter with secondary

escort and intercept tasks. Of all-metal construction, the Wilk was projected with the indigenous P.Z.L.Foka (Seal) eight-cylinder inverted-Vee air-cooled engine, the proposed armament consisting of two 20-mm Wz 38 cannon and twin 7,92-mm Wz 36 machine guns in the nose, and twin 7,92-mm guns on a flexible mounting for the second crew member. Difficulties in development of the Foka engine led to the second prototype, the P.38/II, being fitted with two 450 hp Ranger SGV-770B 12-cylinder engines. This aircraft flew in May 1938, the first prototype with 620 hp Foka II engines not flying until January 1939. In the meantime, a more refined development of the basic design, the P.48 Lampart (Leopard) powered by 700 hp Gnome-Rhône 14M Mars radials, had succeeded the Wilk in future planning, but prototypes had yet to be completed at the time of the German invasion of Poland. The following data relate to the Foka II-powered Wilk prototype. *Max speed, 289 mph (465 km/h) at 13,125 ft (4 000 m). Range,*

The Foka-powered P.38/I Wilk (above and below) which flew after the Ranger-engined P.38/II.

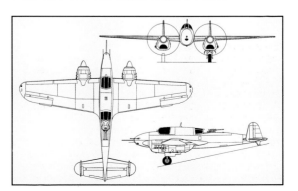

777 mls (1 250 km). Empty weight, 3,781 lb (1 715 kg). Loaded weight, 6,107 lb (2 770 kg). Span, 36 ft 3 in (11,05 m). Length, 27 ft 4¾ in (8,35 m). Height, 8 ft 2½ in (2,50 m). Wing area, 204.52 sq ft (19,00 m²).

P.Z.L. P.50 JASTRZAB   Poland

Intended as a successor in *Lotnictwo Wojskowe* service to the P.11, the P.50 Jastrzab (Hawk) was designed under the leadership of Wsiewolod Jakimiuk. The first of two prototypes, the P.50/I, was flown in February 1939 with an 840 hp Bristol Mercury VIII nine-cylinder radial. Of all-metal stressed-skin monocoque construction, the P.50 was armed with four wing-mounted 7,92-mm Wz 36 machine guns. The Mercury-engined model was referred to as the Jastrzab A, an initial batch of 30 of this version being under construction at the time of the German invasion. The second prototype, the P.50/II, was intended to serve as a development aircraft for the more advanced Jastrzab II. This featured a revised rear fuselage, armament augmented by two 20-mm cannon and pilot armour, the engine being a 1,375 hp Bristol Hercules to be replaced in the series model by the 1,200 hp P.Z.L. Waran radial. The P.50/II was still awaiting its power plant at the time of the German assault. The first pre-series Jastrzab A was to be fitted with an 870 hp Gnome-Rhône 14Kirs as a development aircraft for the Jastrzab B, and this was almost ready for flight test in September 1939. The following data relate to the Mercury VIII-powered Jastrzab A. *Max speed, 311 mph (500 km/h) at 14,110 ft (4 300 m). Range, 466 mls (750 km). Empty weight, 3,748 lb (1 700 kg). Loaded weight, 5,511 lb (2 500 kg). Span, 31 ft 9⅞ in (9,70 m). Length, 25 ft 3⅛ in (7,70 m). Height, 8 ft 10¼ in (2,70 m). Wing area, 208.83 sq ft (19,40 m²).*

An artist's impression (above) and a general arrangement drawing (below) of the P.50 Jastrzab A.

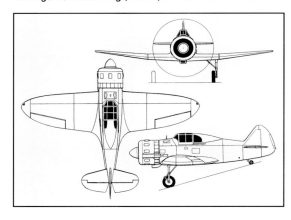

R

RBVZ S-XVI   Russia

Conceived in response to a demand for an escort fighter for the *Ilya Muromets* bombers and similarly built by the RBZV (*Russko-Baltiiskii Vagonnyi Zavod* – Russo-Baltic Wagon Works), the S-XVI was an equi-span single-bay two-seat biplane designed by Igor I Sikorsky. Of wooden construction, the S-XVI accommodated its two crew members in slightly staggered side-

The RBVZ S-XVI (above and below), the first fighter to be designed by Igor I Sikorsky.

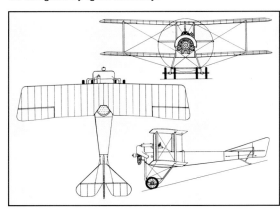

by-side seats and was noteworthy in utilising the Lavrov-developed synchronisation gear for its single 7,7-mm gun. It was, in fact, one of the world's first fighters to possess gun-synchronising equipment. Intended to be powered by a 100 hp Le Rhône rotary, the first S-XVI was completed on 6 February 1915 with an 80 hp Gnome rotary because of the non-availability of the more powerful engine. Two more S-XVIs were delivered in the following month and a contract for 18 was placed with the RBVZ on 17 December 1915, these being delivered between January and March 1916. Although highly manoeuvrable, the S-XVI possessed a comparatively poor performance because of insufficient power. A further small batch of S-XVIs was completed in 1917, some being used during the Revolution and examples remaining in service until 1923. One S-XVI was fitted with a 60 hp Kalep rotary engine, had an enlarged upper wing (by 21.53 sq ft/2,0 m²) and lacked the lower-wing ailerons of the standard model. Another was unsuccessfully tested with floats and others were operated with ski undercarriages. Several were fitted with a 7,7-mm gun above the upper wing to supplement the synchronised weapon. *Max speed, 75 mph (120 km/h). Time to 3,280 ft (1 000 m), 8.0 min. Empty weight, 897 lb (407 kg). Loaded weight, 1,490 lb (676 kg). Span, 27 ft 6¾ in (8,40 m). Length, 20 ft 4 in (6,20 m). Height, 9 ft 1½ in (2,78 m). Wing area, 272.98 sq ft (25,36 m²).*

RBVZ S-XX   Russia

Displaying some Nieuport influence, the S-XX single-seat fighter designed by Igor Sikorsky was a single-bay unequal-span unstaggered biplane of wooden construction with fabric skinning. Armament comprised a single synchronised 7,7-mm machine gun, and five S-XXs were built in September 1916. The first of these

was powered by a 100 hp Gnome rotary, but the second and, presumably, the remaining three S-XXs received the 120 hp Le Rhône engine with which they were allegedly faster than the Nieuport 17. However, the S-XX was considered inferior to the newer enemy aircraft that had begun to appear at the Front, and, therefore, no series production was undertaken. The following data relate to the S-XX with the Le Rhône engine. *Max speed, 118 mph (190 km/h). Time to 6,560 ft (2 000 m), 6.33 min. Empty weight, 871 lb (395 kg). Loaded weight, 1,257 lb (570 kg). Span, 28 ft 2½ in (8,60 m). Length, 21 ft 3⅞ in (6,50 m). Wing area, 182.99 sq ft (17,00 m²).*

The S-XX (above and below) failed to achieve series production, being inferior to newer enemy aircraft.

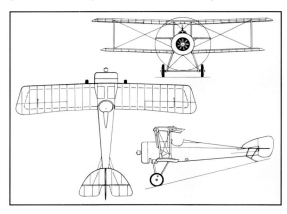

REGGIANE Re 2000   Italy

Developed by Officine Meccaniche Italiane "Reggiane" to the designs of Roberto G Longhi, the Re 2000 was of all-metal construction and innovatory by Italian standards in having a five-spar wing embodying integral fuel tankage. First flown on 24 May 1939, the Re 2000 was the recipient of orders from Hungary and Sweden, these countries purchasing 70 and 60 examples respectively, the former acquiring a manufacturing licence (see MAVAG *Héjja II*). Powered by a

The prototype Re 2000 (above) photographed on 12 July 1939, and (below) Re 2000s of 1./I *Vadàsz Szazad* of the Hungarian *Királyi Légierö* at Snolnok.

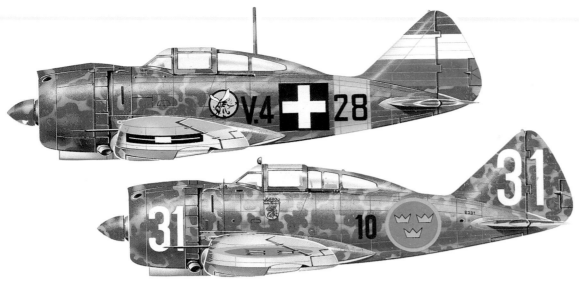

An Re 2001 C.N. (above) of 82ª *Squadriglia*, and (below) the sole example of the Re 2001 Delta.

Re 2000s of (above, top) the Hungarian 1./I *Vadàsz Szazad*, early 1942, and (immediately above) 3rd Division of the Swedish *Flottilj* 10 during 1943.

Piaggio P.XI RC 40D 14-cylinder radial rated at 1,040 hp at 13,125 ft (4 000 m), the Re 2000 was armed with two 12,7-mm SAFAT machine guns. A total of 25 Re 2000s was supplied to the *Regia Aeronautica* (17) and the *Aviazione Ausiliaria per la Regia Marina* (eight). Sixteen of the *Regia Aeronautica* aircraft were fitted with additional fuel tankage in the fuselage with which they were designated Re 2000 GA (*Grande Autonomia*, or Long Range), while those for the *Regia Marina* were provided with catapult pick-up points. *Max speed, 329 mph (530 km/h) at 16,405 ft (5 000 m). Time to 13,125 ft (4 000 m), 4.7 min. Range, 870 mls (1 400 km) at 289 mph (466 km/h). Empty weight, 4,563 lb (2 070 kg). Loaded weight, 6,349 lb (2 880 kg). Span, 36 ft 1 in (11,00 m). Length, 26 ft 2½ in (7,99 m). Height, 10 ft 5⅞ in (3,20 m). Wing area, 219.59 sq ft (20,40 m²).*

(Above) An Re 2000 of *Flottilj* 10 at Ängelholm, July 1942, and (below) with definitive canopy fairing.

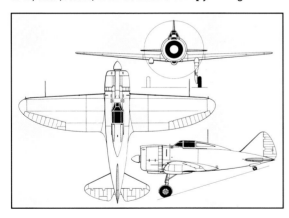

12,7-mm SAFAT machine guns and two wing-mounted 7,7-mm SAFAT guns. Variants included the Re 2001 C.N. (*Caccia Notturno*), with 20-mm MG 151 cannon replacing the wing-mounted 7,7-mm weapons, and the Re 2001 C.B. (*Caccia Bombardiere*) with provision for a single 551-lb (250-kg) bomb. Known as the Re 2001 Delta, one example was fitted with a 12-cylinder inverted-Vee air-cooled Isotta-Fraschini Delta RC 16/48 engine rated at 840 hp at 17,390 ft (5 300 m). *Max speed, 339 mph (545 km/h) at 17,945 ft (5 470 m). Time to 16,405 ft (5 000 m), 6.33 min. Range, 684 mls (1 100 km). Empty weight, 5,423 lb (2 460 kg). Loaded weight, 7,231 lb (3 280 kg). Span, 36 ft 1 in (11,00 m). Length, 27 ft 5 in (8,36 m). Height, 10 ft 4 in (3,15 m). Wing area, 219.59 sq ft (20,40 m²).*

A *Serie II* Re 2001 C.N. (above) and a general arrangement drawing (below) of the *Serie I* Re 2001.

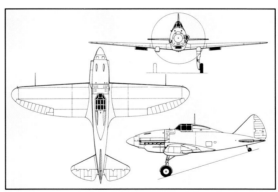

Re 2001s of (immediately below) 82ª *Sqd*, 21º *Gruppo*, Italian Co-Belligerent Air Force, Puglia, 1943, and (bottom) 150ª *Sqd*, 2º *Gruppo*, Pantelleria, mid 1942.

REGGIANE Re 2001 ARIETE I   Italy

Basically an adaptation of the Re 2000 to take a liquid-cooled inverted-Vee Daimler-Benz DB 601A engine, the Re 2001 featured a redesigned wing structure, the five-spar arrangement giving place to three-spar construction and the integral fuel tankage feature being eliminated. The Re 2001 was first flown on 14 July 1940, and 237 fighters of this type were eventually delivered to the *Regia Aeronautica* as the Ariete (Ram), these being powered for the most part by a licence-built version of the DB 601A, the Alfa Romeo RA 1000 RC 41-1a Monsonie (Monsoon) rated at 1,175 hp for take-off. Armament of the initial version comprised two fuselage-mounted

REGGIANE Re 2002 ARIETE II   Italy

Based on the Re 2000 but having the five-spar wing and integral tankage replaced by a three-spar wing housing conventional fuel tanks, the Re 2002 Ariete II single-seat ground attack fighter was developed in parallel with the Re 2001 and was powered by a 14-cylinder radial Piaggio P.XIX RC 45 Turbine-B rated at 1,175 hp at 14,765 ft (4 500 m). Flown as a prototype for the first time in October 1940, the Re 2002 was ordered into production on 10 September 1941 with 100 each Iª and IIª

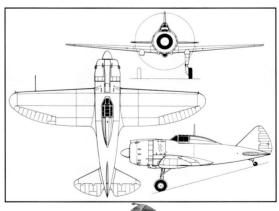

(Above and below) The Re 2002, the photo depicting an example with 239ª *Sqd*, Co-Belligerent Air Force.

(Above, top) An Re 2002 of the Co-Belligerent 102° *Gruppo*'s 239ª *Sqd*, Lecce, 1944, and (immediately above) an Re 2002 of a *Luftwaffe Schlachtgruppe*.

Serie aircraft, 147 of which had been delivered to the *Regia Aeronautica* by the time of the Armistice. Production was subsequently continued on behalf of the *Luftwaffe*, 76 being completed but only 35 entering German service, the others being destroyed by the Germans themselves in April 1945. The Re 2002 had an armament of two 12,7-mm and two 7,7-mm SAFAT machine guns, plus one bomb of up to 1,389 lb (630 kg) weight on a centreline rack and two 353-lb (160-kg) or 220-lb (100-kg) bombs on wing racks. One example of the Re 2002bis was tested, this utilising an Re 2005 wing complete with outward-retracting undercarriage. *Max speed, 334 mph (537 km/h) at 20,015 ft (6 100 m). Range, 683 mls (1 100 km) at 259 mph (417 km/h). Empty weight, 5,269 lb (2 390 kg). Loaded weight, 7,143 lb (3 240 kg). Span, 36 ft 1 in (11,00 m). Length, 26 ft 9½ in (8,16 m). Height, 10 ft 4 in (3,15 m). Wing area, 219.59 sq ft (20,40 m²).*

An Re 2002 (below) seen at Taliedo early 1945 prior to delivery to a *Schlachtgruppe* of the *Luftwaffe*.

REGGIANE Re 2005 SAGITTARIO   Italy

Development of the Re 2005 Sagittario (Archer) was initiated in 1941 by Roberto Longhi to take advantage of the Daimler-Benz DB 605A engine, and a prototype was flown for the first time on 10 May 1942. The decision to start production was not taken until February 1943, when orders were placed for 34 pre-series and 750 production aircraft to be powered by the Italian-manufactured version of the DB 605A, the Fiat RA 1050 RC 58 Tifone (Typhoon) rated at 1,475 hp for take-off. Armament of the Re 2005 comprised three 20-mm MG 151 cannon and two 12,7-mm SAFAT machine guns. In the event, only the pre-series aircraft were completed, 11 of these plus the second prototype being requisitioned by the *Luftwaffe* after the Armistice and 20 of the others

The second prototype Re 2005 (below) which had a VDM rather than the normal Piaggio propeller.

seeing brief operational service with the *Regia Aeronautica*. *Max speed, 421 mph (678 km/h) at 22,965 ft (7 000 m). Range, 776 mls (1 250 km) at 320 mph (515 km/h). Empty weight, 5,732 lb (2 600 kg). Loaded weight, 7,959 lb (3 610 kg). Span, 36 ft 1 in (11,00 m). Length, 28 ft 7¾ in (8,73 m). Height, 10 ft 4 in (3,15 m). Wing area, 219.59 sq ft (20,40 m²).*

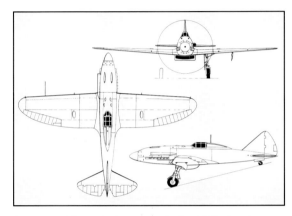

(Above and below) The pre-series Re 2005, the photo depicting the tenth immediately prior to Armistice.

RENARD EPERVIER   Belgium

Designed by Georges and Alfred Renard to compete in a government-sponsored design contest, the Epervier (Sparrowhawk) single-seat all-metal fighter monoplane was intended for a 12-cylinder liquid-cooled Hispano-Suiza 12J Vee-type engine. Unavailability of this power plant led to installation of a 480 hp Gnome-Rhône Jupiter VI nine-cylinder radial in the first prototype, which was built by Stampe et Vertongen as the Epervier Type 2 and flown in 1928. The Epervier Type 2 car-

(Below) The Stampe et Vertongen-built Epervier 2bis.

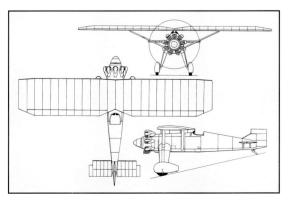

ried an armament of two synchronised 7,7-mm guns and was lost in October 1928 after failing to recover from a flat spin. A second prototype, the Epervier Type 2bis, introduced revised streamlined fairings for the cantilever mainwheel legs, mainwheel spats and cylinder aft-fairings, and was built by SABCA (Société Anonyme Belge de Constructions Aéronautiques). Demonstrated early in 1930 in competition with various foreign types for an *Aviation Militaire* order, the Epervier Type 2bis was rejected in favour of the Fairey Firefly. A further development of the basic design, the Epervier Type 3 powered by a 480 hp Rolls-Royce "F" engine and utilising mixed construction and a redesigned wing, was studied under government contract, but was not built. The following data relate to the Type 2bis. *Max speed, 170 mph (273 km/h) at sea level. Time to 13,125 ft (4 000 m), 8.5 min. Empty weight, 1,750 lb (794 kg). Loaded weight, 2,866 lb (1 300 kg). Span, 33 ft 5⅔ in (10,20 m). Length, 22 ft 11⅔ in (7,00 m). Height, 9 ft 0⅔ in (2,76 m). Wing area, 215.28 sq ft (20,00 m²).*

RENARD R-36   Belgium

The R-36 (above and below) was designed to succeed the Firefly with the Belgian *Aviation Militaire*.

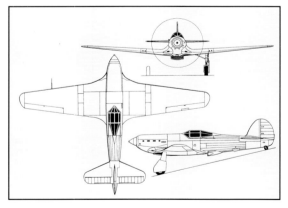

Designed by Alfred Renard as a replacement for the Fairey Firefly in service with the *Aviation Militaire*, the R-36 was flown for the first time on 5 November 1937. Of all-metal construction and carrying an armament of one engine-mounted 20-mm cannon and four wing-mounted 7,7-mm machine guns, the R-36 was powered by a 910 hp Hispano-Suiza 12Ycrs 12-cylinder Vee-type liquid-cooled engine. Various modifications were introduced during the test programme – notably the relocation of the radiator bath and the enlargement of the rudder – and, late in 1938, the government took an option on a batch of 40 aircraft. The loss of the prototype on 17 January 1939 resulted in the programme being placed in abeyance and then dropped when the decision was taken to procure Hawker Hurricanes. *Max speed, 314 mph (505 km/h) at 13,125 ft (4 000 m). Time to 13,125 ft (4 000 m), 4.93 min. Range, 620 mls (1 000 km). Empty weight, 3,902 lb (1 770 kg). Loaded*

weight, 5,445 lb (2 470 kg). Span, 38 ft 2¼ in (11,64 m). Length, 28 ft 10½ in (8,80 m). Height, 9 ft 6⅛ in (2,90 m). Wing area, 215.28 sq ft (20,00 m²).

RENARD R-37   Belgium

The R-37 (above) was first flown by a *Luftwaffe* pilot possibly unaware that it had not been tested.

With an airframe fundamentally similar to that of the R-36, the R-37 differed primarily in having a close-cowled 1,100 hp Gnome-Rhône 14N-21 14-cylinder radial engine. Cooling air reached the engine via a narrow annulus, was mixed with exhaust gases and ejected through two groups of nozzles to provide some thrust augmentation. The proposed armament consisted of four 7,7-mm or two 13,2-mm machine guns mounted in the wings. Although the R-37 was displayed statically at the *Salon de Bruxelles* in July 1939, no attempt had been made to fly this prototype before the German occupation of Belgium in May 1940. The R-37 was discovered at Evere by the occupation forces and a *Luftwaffe* pilot – possibly unaware that the aircraft had not previously been flown – flew the aircraft to Beauvechain. There is no record of any subsequent flight testing, although it is known that the R-37 was taken to Germany. Prior to the German occupation, Alfred Renard had prepared a project for a two-seat version, the R-37B, for use as a ground attack aircraft. *Estimated max speed, 317 mph (510 km/h) at 16,405 ft (5 000 m). Empty weight, 3,987 lb (1 810 kg). Loaded weight, 5,418 lb (2 460 kg). Dimensions as for R-36 except length, 27 ft 6½ in (8,40 m).*

(Above and below) The R-37 employed an essentially similar airframe to that of the HS 12Y-powered R-36.

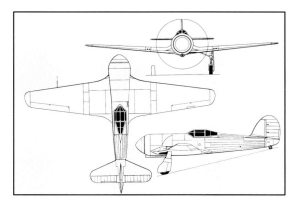

RENARD R-38   Belgium

Developed in parallel with the R-37, the R-38 was essentially similar to the R-36 apart from having a 1,030 hp Rolls-Royce Merlin II engine. It was originally proposed with wings of two different sizes, but the sole prototype retained a similar wing to that of the R-36 and R-37. Armament comprised four wing-mounted 7,7-mm or 13,2-mm machine guns. The R-38 flew for the first time on 4 August 1939, and gave excellent results during its test programme, which was still in process

Flown a month before commencement of World War II, the R-38 (above and below) was still under flight test at the time that Belgium was occupied.

when German forces occupied Belgium. The sole prototype was flown to Bordeaux when the final collapse of Belgian resistance became inevitable, but was scrapped after capture in France by German forces. *Max speed, 339 mph (545 km/h) at 16,405 ft (5 000 m). Time to 16,405 ft (5 000 m), 5.37 min. Max range, 840 mls (1 350 km). Empty weight, 4,295 lb (1 950 kg). Loaded weight, 5,727 lb (2 600 kg). Dimensions as for R-36.*

R.E.P. C1   France

Confined through most of World War I to manufacture of aircraft under licence (eg, Voisin biplanes, Sopwith 1½-Strutters, Caproni trimotors), the R.E.P. (Robert Esnault-Pelterie) concern completed a single-seat fighter of original design early in 1918. This, the R.E.P. C1, was a rather angular single-bay biplane of steel-tube construction with fabric skinning. Powered by a 250 hp Salmson (Canton-Unné) CU9Za engine, it placed emphasis on upward and forward view for the pilot,

(Above and below) The sole fighter of original design built by Robert Esnault-Pelterie (R.E.P.)

having an abbreviated cabane with the centre section cut away above the cockpit. Armament consisted of two asymmetrically-mounted, synchronised Vickers guns in the fuselage. Performance tests were flown at Villacoublay on 27 March and 11 April 1918, and, although the recorded figures were good for the power available, the design did not find favour. *Max speed, 135 mph (217 km/h) at 3,280 ft (1 000 m), 122 mph (196 km/h) at 16,405 ft (5 000 m). Time to 9,840 ft (3 000 m), 8.52 min. Endurance, 1.5 hrs. Empty weight, 1,451 lb (658 kg). Loaded weight, 2,134 lb (968 kg). Span, 27 ft 6 in (8,38 m). Length, 20 ft 10 in (6,35 m). Height, 8 ft 3½ in (2,53 m). Wing area, 220.34 sq ft (20,47 m²).*

REPUBLIC EP-1 (P-35A)   USA

Late in 1938, the Seversky Aircraft Corporation completed a company demonstrator single-seat fighter, the EP-1 (Export Pursuit No 1) -68. Powered by a 1,050 hp Pratt & Whitney R-1830-S1C1-G Twin Wasp 14-cylinder radial engine, the EP-1-68 was similar in most other respects to the P-35 (see under Seversky) for the US Army Air Corps, but used the lengthened rear fuselage introduced with the Seversky AP-4. The EP-1 was demonstrated in Sweden in April 1939, and, on 29 June, the Swedish government signed a contract for 15 EP-1-106s with the S3C1-G engine. A follow-up contract for a further 45 was signed on 11 October, by which time the Seversky company had changed its name to Republic Aviation Corporation, Alexander Kartveli remaining chief engineer. The EP-1-68 demonstrator was later sold, in what was to be described as a "highly irregular transaction", to Ecuador's *Fuerza Aérea*, together with the Seversky AP-7 and AP-9. The initial batch of 18 EP-1-106s was completed on 18 January 1940: two weeks earlier, on 5 January, Sweden had placed yet another contract, for an additional 60 fighters of this type. The 60 EP-1-106s ordered under the first and second contracts had all reached Sweden by the end of July 1940, and, with an armament of two 7,9-mm KSP M/22 cowl guns and two 13,2-mm AKAN M/39 wing guns, these entered Swedish service as the J 9. The aircraft on the third contract, the last of which was completed

Republic EP-1-106s (below) of the Swedish *Flygflottilj* 3 serving in the recce rôle shortly after World War II.

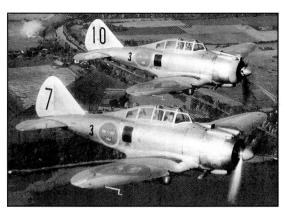

on 7 February 1941, were requisitioned by the US government on 24 October 1940. The EP-1-106s thus acquired by the USAAC received the designation P-35A, 48 being shipped to the Philippines, where they flew operationally (8 December 1941 – 3 January 1942) but were outclassed by opposing fighters. Those P-35As retained in the USA served as instructional aircraft and the EP-1s remained in Swedish service throughout World War II. *Max speed, 316 mph (508 km/h) at 15,950 ft (4 860 m). Initial climb, 1,920 ft/min (9,75 m/sec). Range, 950 mls (1 530 km). Empty weight, 4,575 lb (2 075 kg). Normal loaded weight, 6,118 lb (2 775 kg). Span, 36 ft 0 in (10,97 m). Length, 26 ft 10 in (8,20 m). Height, 9 ft 9 in (2,97 m). Wing area, 220 sq ft (20,44 m²).*

A P-35A (below) photographed in July 1943 when serving in the fighter training rôle with the USAAF.

REPUBLIC AP-9   USA

The AP-9 single-seat fighter was completed in 1939, shortly after the reorganisation of the Seversky Aircraft Corporation as Republic Aviation. Closely related to the rebuilt Seversky AP-7 (which see), with a similar wing profile and inward retracting undercarriage, the AP-9 was powered by a 1,050 hp Pratt & Whitney R-1830-SC3-G Twin Wasp 14-cylinder radial and carried the standard cowl armament of one 0.3-in (7,62-mm) and one 0.5-in (12,7-mm) machine gun. The USAAC, by this time, favoured the turbo-supercharged AP-4 and consequently evinced no interest in the AP-9. Thus, on 6 April 1940, the aviatrix Jacqueline Cochran used the prototype to establish a new woman's record by averaging 332 mph (534 km/h) over a 1,243-mile (2 000-km) flight from California to New Mexico and return. The AP-9 was subsequently sold to Ecuador. No specification is available.

The Republic AP-9 (below) which was flown to New Mexico from California and back in record time.

REPUBLIC P-43 LANCER   USA

After the USAAC had placed a contract with the Seversky Aircraft Corporation, on 12 May 1939, for 13 service evaluation AP-4s under the designation YP-43, some redesign was undertaken by what now became Republic Aviation. A Pratt & Whitney R-1830-35 turbo-supercharged engine of 1,200 hp was adopted; armament was increased to two 0.5-in (12,7-mm) cowl and two 0.3-in (7,62-mm) wing guns; the turbo-supercharger intake was transferred from the port wing root to beneath the engine and, as part of a drag reduction programme, the rear decking raised and the transparent area aft of the pilot's seat reduced. The first YP-43 was delivered in September 1940, and the last in April 1941. The intention was to follow these with 80 examples of a more powerful version, the P-44 with a 1,400 hp Pratt & Whitney R-2180-1 engine. In the event, the P-44 was overtaken by an entirely new design, the P-47B, and, as it became necessary to keep the factory occupied pending introduction of the more advanced fighter, the order

(Above, top) A P-35A of the CO, 17th Pursuit Sqn, USAAC, Philippines, 1941, and (immediately above) an EP-1-106 of *Flygflottilj* 8, Barkarby, Sweden, 1942.

for P-44s was cancelled and an order for 54 P-43s substituted. Further delays in the P-47B led to this order being followed by a contract for 80 P-43As powered by the R-1830-49 engine with similar ratings to the -35. The first P-43 Lancer was delivered on 16 May 1941.

A P-43 (above) of the 55th Pursuit Group, USAAF, 1941, and (below) the P-43A-1, which was intended specifically for use by Nationalist China.

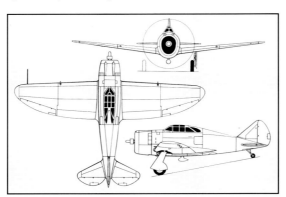

In the following month, delays with the P-47B having arisen, 125 P-43A-1s were ordered, using Lend-Lease funds, for China, although only 51 were eventually delivered to that country. The P-43A-1 (R-1830-57 engine) introduced self-sealing fuel tanks and all four guns were of 0.5-in (12,7-mm) calibre. Deliveries of the P-43A-1 were completed in March 1942, by which time most aircraft, other than those shipped to China, were being converted for the tactical reconnaissance mission as P-43Bs (150), P-43Cs (two), P-43Ds and P-43Es according to the camera installation. Four P-43A-1s and four P-43Ds were supplied to the RAAF to serve on PR duties. In China, the P-43A-1 – several of which were flown by the American Volunteer Group – saw only re-

The P-43A-1 (below) was intended for Lend-Lease delivery to China which received only 51 examples.

stricted operational use because of its unreliable self-sealing fuel tanks and difficulties with the turbo-supercharger. The following data relate to the P-43A-1. *Max speed, 356 mph (573 km/h) at 20,000 ft (6 100 m). Initial climb, 2,850 ft/min (14,48 m/sec). Normal range, 800 mls (1 287 km). Empty weight, 5,996 lb (2 720 kg). Normal loaded weight, 7,435 lb (3 372 kg). Span, 36 ft 0 in (10,97 m). Length, 28 ft 6 in (8,68 m). Height, 14 ft 0 in (4,27 m). Wing area, 223 sq ft (20,72 m²).*

REPUBLIC P-47B & C THUNDERBOLT   USA

One of the largest and heaviest single-seat, single piston-engined fighters ever to attain production, the Thunderbolt was, like previous fighters built by Republic and its predecessor, Seversky Aircraft, designed by Alexander Kartveli. Offered to the USAAC on 12 June 1940 and owing much to a study of combat reports from Europe, this fighter was ordered on 6 September as a prototype under the designation XP-47B. This had no relationship – other than a common drawing board – with the previously-contracted XP-47 and XP-47A (AP-10), which were then cancelled. The XP-47B was designed around a Pratt & Whitney R-2800 Double Wasp 18-cylinder radial engine, an immense turbo-supercharger and its ducting, and an armament of eight 0.50-in (12,7-mm) guns. When flown for the first time on 6 May 1941, the XP-47B dwarfed most previous fighters. Contracts were placed for 171 P-47Bs and 602 P-47Cs, the latter having an 8-in (20-cm) fuselage extension at the firewall, a new engine mount, a redesigned rudder and elevator balance system, and a ventral wet point for a 200-US gal (757-l) drop tank. The first production P-47B was completed in March 1942 with a 2,000 hp R-2800-21 engine, and this sub-type of the Thunderbolt, as the P-47 was named, joined combat (with the 78th Fighter Group of the 8th AF) on 13 April 1943. The 171st and last P-47B was completed with a pressurised cockpit (as the XP-47E) and another P-47B

The XP-47B (above) and P-47Bs (below) of the 61st Fighter Sqn, 56th Fighter Group, USAAF, in 1942, the foremost aircraft being flown by the Group CO.

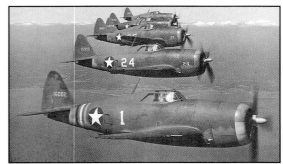

The P-47C-1 (below) and C-2 (above), the latter with the 495th Fighter Training Group, UK, 1943.

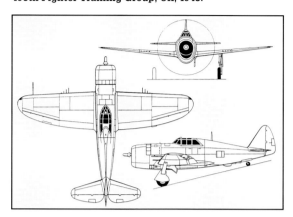

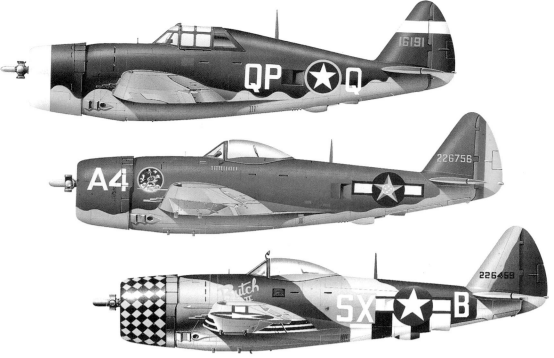

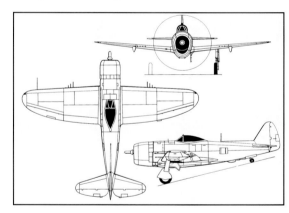

airframe was utilised to test laminar-flow wings (as the XP-47F). The first P-47C was completed in September 1942. The initial batch (P-47C-1-RE) retained the -21 engine of the P-47B, but this gave place (P-47C-5-RE) to the water-injection -59 engine with a war emergency rating of 2,300 hp. The P-47C was followed in production by the P-47D early 1943. The following data relate to the P-47C-5-RE. *Max speed, 433 mph (697 km/h) at 30,000 ft (9 150 m), 353 mph (568 km/h) at 5,000 ft (1 525 m). Max initial climb, 2,780 ft/min (14,12 m/sec). Range, (with external tank), 1,250 mls (2 011 km) at 10,000 ft (3 050 m) at 231 mph (372 km/h). Empty weight, 9,900 lb (4 491 kg). Max loaded weight, 14,925 lb (6 770 kg). Span, 40 ft 9¾ in (12,44 m). Length, 36 ft 1¾ in (11,02 m). Height, 14 ft 1¾ in (4,31 m). Wing area, 300 sq ft (27,87 m²).*

(Below) The XP-47E with pressurised cockpit that was originally the 171st and last production P-47B.

REPUBLIC P-47D & G THUNDERBOLT USA

First ordered on 13 October 1941, the P-47D, with which Thunderbolt production really got into its stride, differed from the P-47C-5 in only minor respects. These changes were confined to the turbo-supercharger exhaust system, engine accessory vents and the provision of additional pilot armour. P-47Ds began to leave two Republic assembly lines early in 1943, Curtiss-Wright commencing deliveries of an identical type as the P-47G in December 1942. The latter company went on to manufacture a total of 354 P-47Gs with deliveries continuing until March 1944. The P-47D-6-RE to -11-RE and P-47G-10-CU to -15-CU production batches had a ventral shackle that could lift either a drop tank or a 500-lb (227-kg) bomb, subsequent batches having suitably stiffened wings for underwing pylons and being able to carry two 1,000-lb (454-kg) bombs. Either six or eight 0.50-in (12,7-mm) guns were fitted and ammunition capacity was increased. Totals of 3,962 P-47D-1-RE to -22-RE Thunderbolts were manufactured at Farmingdale and 1,461 -2-RAs to -23-RAs at Evansville, and these, together with the Curtiss-Wright-built P-47Gs, all featured the original framed sliding cockpit canopy introduced on the initial production B-model. Two P-47D-15-RE airframes were adapted as test-beds for the 16-cylinder inverted-Vee Chrysler XIV-2220-1 engine, the first of these flying on 26 July 1945 (as the

(Above, top) P-47C-2 of 334th FS, Debden, Essex, 1943-44, (above, centre) a P-47D-25 of the Brazilian 1º *Gruppo de Caça*, Tarquinia, Italy, November 1944, and (immediately above) a P-47D-25 of 352nd FS, Raydon, Suffolk, July 1944.

XP-47H). One P-47D (redesignated XP-47K) had a cut-down rear fuselage and an all-round vision canopy from a Hawker Typhoon. Tested in July 1943, these changes were introduced on the P-47D assembly lines with Farmingdale's P-47D-25-RE and Evansville's P-47D-26-RA. Internal fuel was simultaneously increased, the modified D-series airframe that had tested this change having been designated XP-47L. With water-injection R-2800-59 or -63 engines with a war emergency rating of 2,535 hp, these batches employed the so-called "universal" wing (introduced on the P-47D-20-RE) which could carry a variety of drop tanks or bombs. Paddle-bladed, larger-diameter propellers were fitted and stronger ventral shackles were adopted, and from the -27-RE batch a dorsal fin was added. Subsequent to the introduction of the all-round vision canopy, Farmingdale built a total of 2,547 P-47Ds and Evansville built 4,632. The Soviet Union was allocated 203 P-47Ds of

(Above) A P-47D-11 of the 379th FS, 362nd FG, 9th Air Force, and (below) a P-47C-3 of the 61st FS, 56th FG, Horsham St Faith, in the summer of 1943.

which 196 reached their destination; 88 were supplied to Brazil and 25 were delivered to Mexico. A further 825 were allocated to the RAF, the first 240 of these having the original framed cockpit canopy and entering service as Thunderbolt Is, and the remainder, with all-round vision canopies, being known as Thunderbolt IIs.

A P-47D-25 (above) of the 82nd Fighter Squadron, 78th Fighter Group, Spring 1944, and (below) a general arrangement drawing of the P-47D-30.

Four hundred and forty-six P-47Ds were also supplied to the Free French forces, and, after the end of World War II, surplus USAF P-47Ds were supplied to Bolivia.

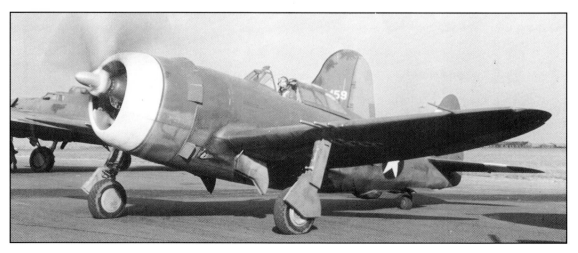

Key to Republic P-47D-10 Thunderbolt

1 Rudder upper hinge
2 Aerial attachment
3 Fin flanged ribs
4 Rudder post/fin aft spar
5 Fin front spar
6 Rudder trim tab worm-and-screw actuating mechanism chain driven
7 Rudder centre hinge
8 Rudder trim tab
9 Rudder structure
10 Tail navigation light
11 Elevator fixed tab
12 Elevator trim tab
13 Starboard elevator structure
14 Elevator outboard hinge
15 Elevator torque tube
16 Elevator trim tab worm-and-screw actuating mechanism
17 Chain drive
18 Starboard tailplane
19 Tail jacking point
20 Elevator control cables
21 Elevator control rod and linkage
22 Fin spar/fuselage attachment points
23 Port elevator
24 Aerial
25 Port tailplane structure (two spars and flanged ribs)
26 Tailwheel retraction worm gear
27 Tailwheel anti-shimmy damper
28 Tailwheel oleo
29 Tailwheel doors
30 Retractable and steerable tailwheel
31 Tailwheel fork
32 Tailwheel mount and pivot
33 Rudder cables
34 Rudder and elevator trim control cables
35 Lifting tube
36 Elevator rod linkage
37 Semi-monocoque all-metal fuselage construction
38 Fuselage dorsal "razorback" profile
39 Aerial lead-in
40 Fuselage stringers
41 Supercharger air filter
42 Supercharger
43 Turbine casing
44 Turbo-supercharger compartment air vent
45 Turbo-supercharger exhaust hood fairing (stainless steel)
46 Outlet louvres
47 Intercooler exhaust doors (port and starboard)
48 Exhaust pipes
49 Cooling air ducts

50 Intercooler unit (cooling and supercharged air)
51 Radio transmitter and receiver packs (Detrola)
52 Canopy track
53 Elevator rod linkage
54 Aerial mast
55 Formation light
56 Rearward-vision frame cut-out and glazing
57 Oxygen bottles
58 Supercharged and cooling air pipe (supercharger to carburettor) port
59 Elevator linkage
60 Supercharged and cooling air pipe (supercharger to carburettor) starboard
61 Central duct (to intercooler unit)
62 Wing root air louvres
63 Wing root fillet
64 Auxiliary fuel tank (capacity 83 Imp gal/379 l)
65 Auxiliary fuel filler point
66 Rudder cable turnbuckle
67 Cockpit floor support
68 Seat adjustment lever
69 Pilot's seat
70 Canopy emergency release (port and starboard)
71 Trim tab controls
72 Back and head armour
73 Headrest
74 Rearward-sliding canopy
75 Rearview mirror fairing
76 "Vee" windshields with central pillar
77 Internal bulletproof glass screen
78 Gunsight
79 Engine control quadrant (cockpit port wall)
80 Control column
81 Rudder pedals
82 Oxygen regulator
83 Underfloor elevator control quadrant
84 Rudder cable linkage
85 Wing rear spar/fuselage attachment (tapered bolts/bushings)
86 Wing supporting lower bulkhead section
87 Main fuel tank (capacity 170 Imp gal/776 l)
88 Fuselage forward structure
89 Stainless steel/Alclad firewall bulkhead
90 Cowl flap valve
91 Main fuel filler point
92 Anti-freeze fluid tank
93 Hydraulic reservoir
94 Aileron control rod
95 Aileron trim tab control cables

96 Aileron hinge access panels
97 Aileron and tab control linkage
98 Aileron trim tab (port wing only)
99 Frise-type aileron
100 Wing rear (No 2) spar
101 Port navigation light
102 Pitot head
103 Wing front (No 1) spar
104 Wing stressed skin
105 Four-gun ammunition troughs (individual bays)
106 Staggered gun barrels
107 Removable panel
108 Inter-spar gun bay access panel
109 Forward gunsight bead
110 Oil feed pipes
111 Oil tank (capacity 24 Imp gal/108 l)
112 Hydraulic pressure line
113 Engine upper bearers
114 Engine control correlating cam
115 Eclipse pump (anti-icing)
116 Fuel level transmitter
117 Generator
118 Battery junction box
119 Storage battery
120 Exhaust collector ring
121 Cowl fuel actuating cylinder
122 Exhaust outlets to collector ring
123 Cowl flaps
124 Supercharged and cooling air ducts to carburettor (port and starboard)
125 Exhaust upper outlets
126 Cowling frame
127 Pratt & Whitney R-2800-59 eighteen-cylinder twin-row engine
128 Cowling nose panel
129 Magnetos
130 Propeller governor
131 Propeller hub
132 Reduction gear casing
133 Spinner
134 Propeller cuffs
135 Four-blade Curtiss constant-speed electric propeller
136 Oil cooler intakes (port and starboard)
137 Supercharger intercooler (central) air intake
138 Ducting
139 Oil cooler feed pipes
140 Starboard oil cooler
141 Engine lower bearers
142 Oil cooler exhaust variable shutter
143 Fixed deflector
144 Excess exhaust gas gate
145 Belly stores/weapons shackles

146 Metal auxiliary drop tank (capacity 62.5 Imp gal/284 l)
147 Inboard mainwheel well door
148 Mainwheel well door actuating cylinder
149 Camera gun port
150 Cabin air-conditioning intake (starboard wing only)
151 Wing root fairing
152 Wing front spar/fuselage attachment (tapered bolts/bushings)
153 Wing inboard rib mainwheel well recess
154 Wing front (No 1) spar
155 Undercarriage pivot point
156 Hydraulic retraction cylinder
157 Auxiliary (undercarriage mounting) wing spar
158 Gun bay warm air flexible duct
159 Wing rear (No 2) spar
160 Landing flap inboard hinge
161 Auxiliary (No 3) wing spar inboard section (flap mounting)
162 NACA slotted trailing-edge landing flaps
163 Landing flap centre hinge
164 Landing flap hydraulic cylinder
165 Four 0.5-in (12,7-mm) Browning machine guns
166 Inter-spar gun bay inboard rib
167 Ammunition feed chutes
168 Individual ammunition troughs
169 Underwing stores/weapons pylon
170 Landing flap outboard hinge
171 Flap door
172 Landing flap profile
173 Aileron fixed tab (starboard wing only)
174 Frise-type aileron structure

175 Aileron hinge/steel forging spar attachments
176 Auxiliary (No 3) wing spar outboard section (aileron mounting)
177 Multi-cellular construction
178 Wing outboard ribs
179 Wingtip structure
180 Starboard navigation light
181 Leading-edge rib sections
182 Bomb shackles
183 500-lb (227-kg) M-43 demolition bomb
184 Undercarriage leg fairing (overlapping upper section)
185 Mainwheel fairing (lower section)
186 Wheel fork
187 Starboard mainwheel
188 Brake lines
189 Landing gear air-oil shock strut
190 Machine gun barrel blast tubes
191 Staggered gun barrels
192 Rocket-launcher slide bar
193 Centre strap
194 Front mounted (attached below front spar between inboard pair of guns):-
195 Deflector arms
196 Triple-tube 4.5-in (11,5-cm) rocket-launcher (Type M10)
197 Front retaining band
198 4.5-in (11,5-cm) M8 rocket projectile

The XP-47K (below) was a modified P-47D with a cut-down fuselage and a canopy from a Typhoon.

The sole example of the XP-47J (above) which was to achieve 505 mph (813 km/h) in August 1944.

Chile, Nationalist China, Columbia, Dominican Republic, Ecuador, Honduras, Iran, Italy, Nicaragua, Peru, Portugal, Turkey, Venezuela and Yugoslavia. The following data relate to the P-47D-35-RA, but are generally applicable to all D-series sub-types. *Max speed, 363 mph (584 km/h) at 5,000 ft (1 525 m), 426 mph (686 km/h) at 30,000 ft (9 150 m). Max initial climb, 3,120 ft/min (15,85 m/sec). Range (with max external fuel), 1,800 mls (2 897 km) at 195 mph (314 km/h) at 10,000 ft (3 050 m). Empty weight, 10,000 lb (4 536 kg). Max loaded weight, 17,500 lb (7 938 kg). Dimensions as for P-47B.*

REPUBLIC XP-47J THUNDERBOLT   USA

At a Wright Field conference held on 22 November 1942, Alexander Kartveli proposed development for the USAAF of a refined version of the basic P-47. This was to combine an improved engine featuring water injection and fan cooling with a lower airframe weight achieved by means of reductions in armament, fuel and radio provisions, and a lighter wing structure. Assigned the designation P-47J, the new model called for changes in some 70 per cent of production tooling. A formal contract for two prototypes was issued on 18 June 1943, but less than two months later, on 31 July, Republic recommended concentration on the more advanced P-72, which was expected to offer a higher performance than the P-47J. Accordingly, the P-47J programme was restricted to a single prototype, which was flown on 26 November 1943. This was powered by a close-cowled Pratt & Whitney R-2800-57(C) 18-cylinder engine with a War Emergency rating of 2,800 hp, and carried an armament of six 0.5-in (12,7-mm) machine guns. Plans to fit contra-rotating propellers and an R-2800-61 engine were discarded in March 1944, but a level speed of 493 mph (793 km/h) was achieved at 33,350 ft (10 165 m) on 11 July 1944. During the following month, on 5 August, after being fitted with a new propeller and a General Electric CH-5 turbo-

supercharger, the XP-47J achieved 505 mph (813 km/h) at 34,450 ft (10 500 m), claimed to be the highest speed attained in level flight by any piston-engined fighter during World War II. This speed was already being exceeded by turbojet-powered fighters, however, and further development of this Thunderbolt derivative was therefore discontinued. *Max speed, 507 mph (816 km/h) at 34,300 ft (10 455 m). Initial climb, 4,900 ft/min (24,9 m/sec). Max range, 1,070 mls (1 722 km). Empty weight, 9,663 lb (4 383 kg). Normal loaded weight, 12,400 lb (5 625 kg). Span, 40 ft 11 in (12,47 m). Length, 33 ft 3 in (10,13 m). Height, 14 ft 2 in (4,31 m). Wing area, 300 sq ft (27,87 m²).*

REPUBLIC P-47M THUNDERBOLT   USA

With the advent in *Luftwaffe* service of the Fieseler Fi 103 (V-1) missile and rocket- and turbojet-powered fighters, a "sprint" version of the P-47 was hurriedly

(Below) The second YP-47M, one of three prototypes of the so-called "sprint" model of the Thunderbolt.

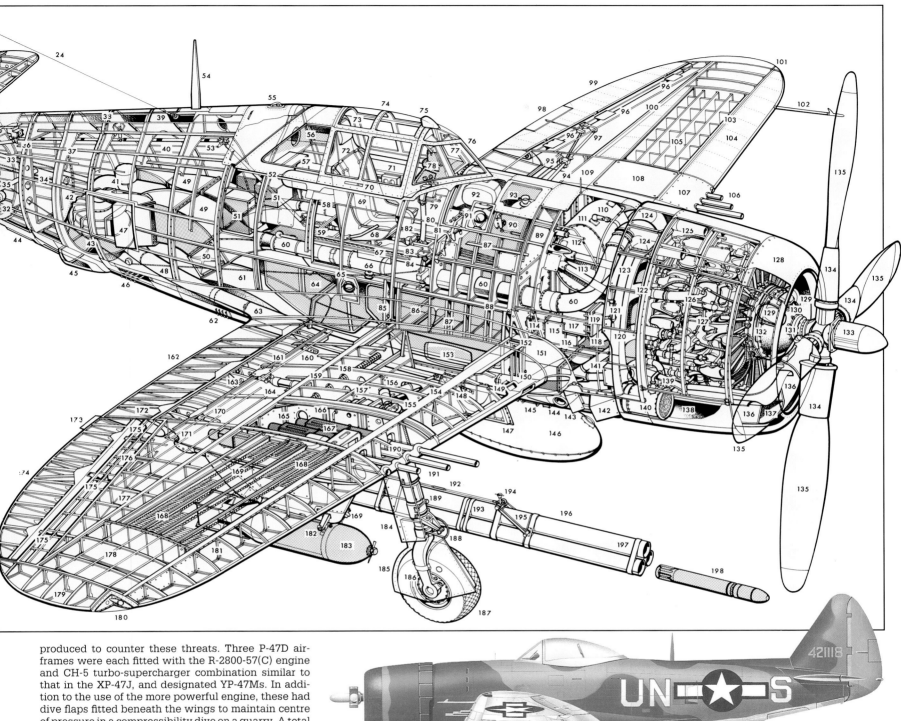

produced to counter these threats. Three P-47D airframes were each fitted with the R-2800-57(C) engine
and CH-5 turbo-supercharger combination similar to
that in the XP-47J, and designated YP-47Ms. In addition to the use of the more powerful engine, these had
dive flaps fitted beneath the wings to maintain centre
of pressure in a compressibility dive on a quarry. A total
of 130 series P-47Ms was subsequently built, with deliveries commencing in December 1944. *Max speed,
453 mph (729 km/h) at 25,000 ft (7 620 m), 470 mph
(756 km/h) at 30,000 ft (9 145 m). Initial climb, 3,500 ft/
min (17,8 m/sec). Range (internal fuel), 560 mls
(900 km). Empty weight, 10,423 lb (4 728 kg). Normal
loaded weight, 13,275 lb (6 022 kg). Span, 40 ft 9¾ in
(12,44 m). Length, 36 ft 4 in (11,07 m). Height, 14 ft 9 in
(4,49 m). Wing area, 308 sq ft (28,61 m²).*

REPUBLIC P-47N
THUNDERBOLT   USA

As part of a programme to develop a version of the
Thunderbolt specifically for operations in the Pacific
Theatre, where the principal requirement was range,
the second YP-47M was fitted with a modified, strengthened and slightly enlarged wing, with which it flew
in September 1944 as the XP-47N. The R-2800-57(C)
engine and CH-5 turbo-supercharger combination was
retained, the new wing embodied internal tankage for
the first time, and a strengthened undercarriage was
provided to cater for a substantial increase in maximum
gross weight which was to result in the P-47N being
the heaviest production model of the Thunderbolt. The
P-47N standardised on the battery of eight 0.5-in (12,7-

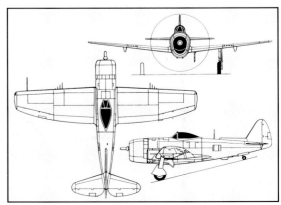

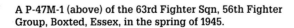
A P-47M-1 (above) of the 63rd Fighter Sqn, 56th Fighter
Group, Boxted, Essex, in the spring of 1945.

mm) machine guns, and the P-47N-5-RE and subsequent production batches had zero-length rocket
launchers added, the R-2800-77 engine supplanting the
-57 in late production examples. The P-47N saw extensive service in the Pacific, frequently escorting B-29
Superfortresses and having the ability to fly with the
bombers all the way from Saipan to Japan. The final
production version of the Thunderbolt, the P-47N was

The P-47N introduced so-called "stub-wings", one of
the P-47N-5 batch being illustrated below.

manufactured between December 1944 and December
1945, a total of 1,667 being produced at Farmingdale
and a further 149 at Evansville. *Max speed, 397 mph
(639 km/h) at 10,000 ft (3 050 m), 467 mph (752 km/h) at*

General arrangement drawing (below) of the P-47N,
designed to fight in the Pacific Theatre.

(789 km/h) at 25,000 ft (7 620 m). Initial climb, 5,280 ft/min (26,82 m/sec). Range (with max external fuel), 1,530 mls (2 462 km). Empty weight, 11,475 lb (5 205 kg). Max loaded weight, 17,492 lb (7 934 kg). Span, 40 ft 11 in (12,47 m). Length, 36 ft 7 in (11,15 m). Height, 16 ft 0 in (4,87 m). Wing area, 300 sq ft (27,87 m²).

REPUBLIC F-84B TO F-84D THUNDERJET   USA

Conceived during 1944 as the AP-23 and the first turbojet-powered fighter offering a radius of action permitting penetration missions, the Thunderjet was distinctive at the time of its debut in utilising the straight-through airflow concept. A simple pitot-type engine air intake combined maximum flow efficiency

(Above) A P-47N-25 with one 500-lb (227-kg) bomb and four 5-in (12,7-cm) rockets under each wing.

(Below) The second XP-72 introduced a six-bladed contra-rotating propeller and flew in June 1944.

The first of three XP-84s (below) taking-off on its initial flight test from Muroc Dry Lake (Edwards).

32,500 ft (9 905 m). Initial climb, 2,770 ft/min (14,1 m/sec). Max range (max external fuel), 2,350 mls (3 782 km). Empty weight, 11,170 lb (5 067 kg). Max loaded weight, 20,700 lb (9 390 kg). Span, 42 ft 7 in (12,97 m). Length, 36 ft 1 in (11,00 m). Height, 14 ft 8 in (4,47 m). Wing area, 322 sq ft (29,91 m²).

REPUBLIC XP-72   USA

Within two months of the first flight of the XP-47B Thunderbolt, Alexander Kartveli and his team had begun the design of a more advanced fighter around the 28-cylinder Pratt & Whitney R-4360 Wasp Major radial engine, and this was eventually to emerge as the XP-72. Incorporating many features of the Thunderbolt, the XP-72 , for which a contract for two prototypes was placed on 18 June 1943, had a close-cowled, fan-cooled R-4360-13 engine rated at 3,450 hp. The engine supercharger was placed aft of the cockpit, compressibility recovery flaps were fitted and built-in armament consisted of six 0.5-in (12,7-mm) machine guns. The USAAF placed an order with Republic for 100 P-72 fighters, which were to be similar to the XP-72 apart from having the R-4360-19 engine and an armament of four 37-mm cannon. The first XP-72 was flown on 2 February 1944, and the second aircraft, which was completed on the following 26 June, differed in having a six-bladed contra-rotating propeller in place of the four-bladed propeller of the initial aircraft. Despite an impressive performance, this fighter had been overtaken by the advent of turbojet-powered aircraft, and, in consequence, the production contract was cancelled and further development abandoned. *Max speed, 490 mph*

Key to Republic F-84G Thunderjet

The XP-72 (above and below), the first example of which is illustrated by the photograph.

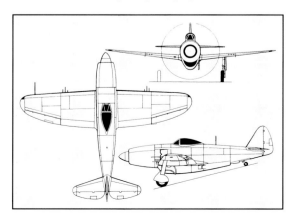

1 Engine air intake
2 Gun laying radar seeker
3 Machine gun muzzles
4 Pitot tube
5 Main undercarriage leg strut
6 Steering control
7 Nosewheel
8 Shimmy damper
9 Taxying lamp
10 Nosewheel retraction strut
11 Nosewheel doors
12 Bifurcated intake ducting
13 Nosewheel hydraulic retraction jack
14 Machine gun barrels
15 Gyro compass unit
16 Ballast weights
17 Ammunition tanks (300 rounds per gun)
18 M-3, 0.5-in (12,7-mm) machine guns
19 Spent cartridge case collector chute
20 Nosewheel bay between intake ducts
21 Battery
22 Servicing access panels
23 Gun bay access panel latch
24 Oxygen converter
25 Hydraulic system header tank
26 Gun bay access panel
27 Armoured bulkhead
28 Cockpit front pressure bulkhead
29 Rudder pedals
30 Instrument panel
31 Control column
32 Instrument panel shroud
33 Sperry radar gunsight
34 Bullet proof windscreen
35 Cockpit canopy cover
36 Canopy framing
37 Starboard side console panel
38 Pilot's ejection seat
39 Engine throttle control
40 Cockpit floor level
41 Intake suction relief door
42 Intake trunking
43 Port side console panel
44 Cockpit rear pressure bulkhead
45 Canopy external latch
46 Ejection seat headrest
47 Pilot's back and head armour
48 Cockpit air system
49 Starboard wing fuel tank bays. Total internal fuel system capacity 376 Imp gal (1 709 l)
50 Fuel tank interconnecting piping
51 Starboard navigation light
52 Fixed tip tank (capacity 191.5 Imp gal/870 l)
53 Tip tank stabilising fin
54 Rear identification light
55 Starboard aileron
56 Aileron aerodynamic seal

57 Fixed tab
58 Aileron hinge control
59 Starboard lower flap
60 Hydraulic flap jack
61 Starboard main undercarriage pivot fixing
62 D/F loop aerial
63 Cockpit air system vent
64 Sliding canopy cover electric motor and rail
65 Fuselage top longeron
66 Main fuselage fuel tank
67 Intake centre fairing accessory compartment
68 Fuselage/main spar attachment frame
69 Wing root machine gun ammunition tank (300 rounds)
70 Ammunition feed chute
71 Allison J35-A-29 axial-flow turbojet
72 Fuselage/rear spar attachment main frame
73 Rear fuselage break point (engine removal)
74 Engine flame cans
75 Cooling air vent
76 Radio and electronics equipment bay
77 VHF radio transmitter and receiver
78 Jet pipe cooling air intake
79 Jet pipe heat shroud
80 Control cable runs
81 Fin root fillet
82 Fin/tailplane attachment joints
83 Starboard tailplane
84 Starboard elevator
85 Tailfin construction
86 Fin tip VHF aerial fairing
87 Rudder hinge post
88 Rudder construction
89 Fixed rudder tab
90 Tail navigation light
91 Elevator trim tab
92 Jet exhaust nozzle
93 Port elevator
94 Tailplane construction
95 Elevator hinge control
96 Fin/tailplane fixing main frames
97 Ventral fin/tail bumper
98 Fuel system vent
99 Jet pipe
100 Fuselage skin plating
101 Rear fuselage framing
102 Wing root trailing-edge fillet
103 Wing walkway
104 Spar attachment joint
105 Rear spar
106 Flap shroud ribs
107 Main undercarriage hydraulic retraction jack
108 Undercarriage leg pivot fixing
109 Flap hydraulic jack

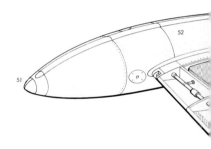

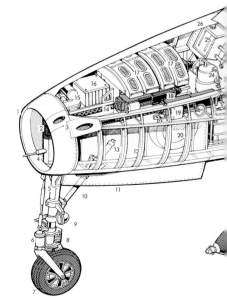

The fourth YP-84A (above) accepted by the USAF in February 1947, and later redesignated as YF-84A.

The F-84D, the 39th example being illustrated above, was considered an interim model of the Thunderjet.

with the highest possible critical Mach number, but penalised internal fuel capacity. This dictated mating the comparatively high fineness ratio fuselage with a thick (12 per cent) constant-section aerofoil in order to provide the desired tankage space in the wing. Designed around the General Electric TG-180 (J35) turbojet, the Thunderjet – an appellation formally adopted late 1946 – was the subject of a USAAF Materiel Division contract on 11 November 1944 covering three prototypes designated as XP-84s. Two months later, on 4 January 1945, a further contract was let for 25 preseries and 75 series aircraft, later to be revised to 15 of the former and 85 of the latter. The first XP-84 flew on 28 February 1946 with a 3,750 lb st (1 701 kgp) J35-GE-7 turbojet. The second, similarly-powered, followed in August, and, on 7 September, established a US national speed record of 611 mph (983 km/h). The third prototype was fitted with a similarly-rated Allison J35-A-15 as the XP-84A, this turbojet also powering the 15 pre-

series YP-84As (redesignated YF-84As from mid-1948) accepted by the USAF in February 1947. The YP-84As each mounted six 0.5-in (12,7-mm) M2 guns and had provision for wingtip auxiliary tanks. The initial series model, the P-84B (later F-84B) differed solely in having higher-fire-rate M3 guns, deliveries starting in August 1947 and terminating in February 1948 with 226 built, of which the final 141 each had eight retractable rocket launchers beneath their wings. One hundred and ninety-one F-84Cs followed from May 1948, these having the similarly-rated J35-A-13C engine and a new electrical system. Both F-84B and C displayed reliability and durability deficiencies – these sub-types were to be retired by the end of 1952 and played no part in the Korean War. Several palliatives were introduced on the F-84D, which was considered as an interim model pending availability of a major rework of the basic design which Republic had proposed early in 1948 and eventually emerged as the F-84E. The F-84D intro-

duced thicker wing and aileron skins, a winterised fuel system, lightweight fuel cells and mechanical rather than hydraulic undercarriage compression linkages. At the same time, jettisonable rather than retractable ordnance racks were adopted. The F-84Ds were delivered between November 1948 and April 1949, a total of 154 being manufactured, and Thunderjets of this model (together with F-84Es) of the 27th Fighter Escort Group of the USAF began flying combat missions in Korea on 6 December 1950. In 1952, a further 102 F-84Ds were sent to Korea to replenish depleted F-84E-equipped units. The F-84Ds were later flown by units of the Air National Guard, and were eventually retired mid-1957. The following data relate to the F-84D. *Max speed, 587 mph (945 km/h) at 4,000 ft (1 220 m). Initial climb, 4,060 ft/min (20,62 m/sec). Range (with two 230-US gal/870-l tip tanks), 1,198 mls (1 928 km). Empty weight, 9,860 lb (4 472 kg). Max loaded weight, 20,076 lb (9 106 kg). Span, 36 ft 5 in (11,09 m). Length, 37 ft 5 in (11,40 m). Height. 12 ft 10 in (3,91 m). Wing area, 260 sq ft (24,15 m²).*

REPUBLIC F-84E & F-84G THUNDERJET USA

The Thunderjet lacked the agility for effectiveness in fighter-versus-fighter combat – although it was to serve in the escort rôle during early operational service in Korea – and development emphasis was accordingly

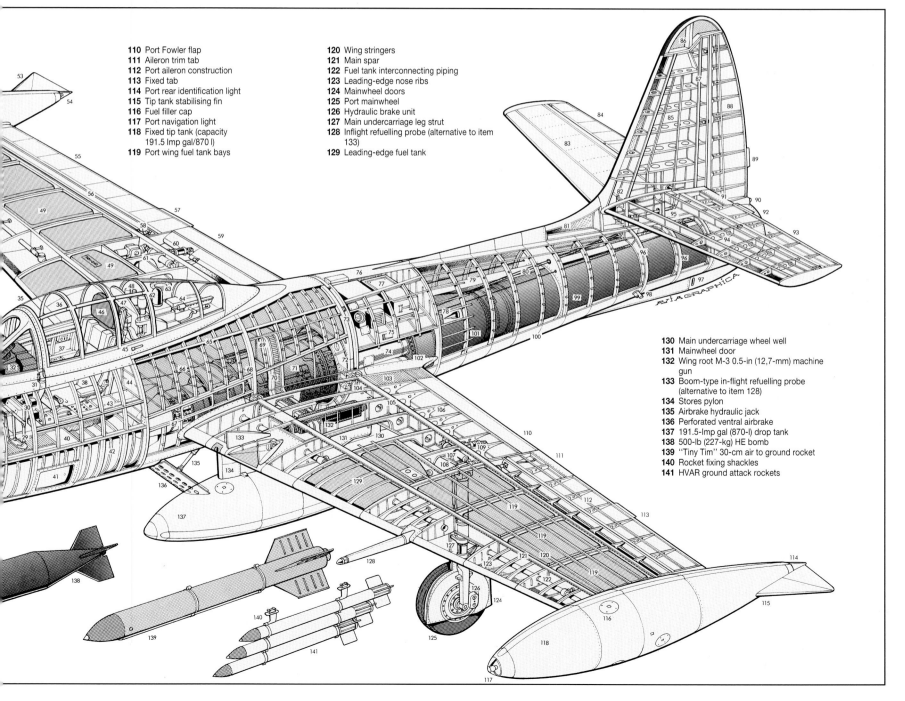

110 Port Fowler flap
111 Aileron trim tab
112 Port aileron construction
113 Fixed tab
114 Port rear identification light
115 Tip tank stabilising fin
116 Fuel filler cap
117 Port navigation light
118 Fixed tip tank (capacity 191.5 Imp gal/870 l)
119 Port wing fuel tank bays

120 Wing stringers
121 Main spar
122 Fuel tank interconnecting piping
123 Leading-edge nose ribs
124 Mainwheel doors
125 Port mainwheel
126 Hydraulic brake unit
127 Main undercarriage leg strut
128 Inflight refuelling probe (alternative to item 133)
129 Leading-edge fuel tank

130 Main undercarriage wheel well
131 Mainwheel door
132 Wing root M-3 0.5-in (12,7-mm) machine gun
133 Boom-type in-flight refuelling probe (alternative to item 128)
134 Stores pylon
135 Airbrake hydraulic jack
136 Perforated ventral airbrake
137 191.5-Imp gal (870-l) drop tank
138 500-lb (227-kg) HE bomb
139 "Tiny Tim" 30-cm air to ground rocket
140 Rocket fixing shackles
141 HVAR ground attack rockets

(Above, top) An F-84G-16 of 182 *Filo*, *Türk Hava Kuvvetleri*, Diyarbakir, 1954, and (immediately above) an F-84E-30 of the 49th FBG, Taegu, 1953.

placed on the enhancement of its fighter-bomber capabilities. The interim F-84D was succeeded by the F-84E, which, first flown on 18 May 1949, embodied major changes, including a stronger wing structure and a 12-in (30,5-cm) fuselage stretch. The J35-A-17 engine was rated at 4,900 lb st (2 223 kgp), and provision made for attachment of JATO (Jet Assisted Take-Off) rockets permitted an increase in take-off weight. Internal fuel capacity was increased and two 230-US gal (870-l) drop tanks could be carried on the bomb shackles underwing. Built-in armament remained six 0.5-in (12,7-mm) guns and up to 4,500 lb (2 041 kg) of external ordnance could be carried. The last of 843 F-84Es was completed in July 1951, 100 of these being assigned to NATO air forces – mostly France's *Armée de l'Air* – and the last were phased out (from the Air National Guard) mid-1959. Meantime, delays in resolving problems posed by the swept-wing F-84F had dictated retention of the Thunderjet in production, and a further sub-type had been developed as the F-84G, which incorporated in-flight refuelling capability – being the first production fighter to be built with this feature – and provision for carrying a tactical nuclear store. With deliveries to the USAF commencing in August 1951, the F-84G also differed from the F-84E in having a 5,600 lb st (2 540 kgp) Allison J35-A-29 turbojet. The USAF took delivery of 789 F-84Gs, 2,236 more being delivered

(Above) An F-84E-15 and (below) an F-84G-6 of No 12 Sqn, Royal Thai Air Force, Don Muang, 1956.

(Below) A general arrangement drawing of the F-84G, the Thunderjet sub-type built in largest numbers.

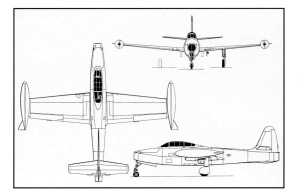

to foreign nations, 1,936 of these under the MDAP (Mutual Defense Assistance Program) with deliveries terminating in July 1953. Recipients comprised Belgium, Denmark, France, Iran, Italy, Netherlands, Norway, Portugal, Taiwan, Thailand, Turkey and Yugoslavia, with the *Força Aérea Portuguesa* becoming the final operator of the F-84G, phasing out its last fighters of this type during the course of 1976. *Max speed, 622 mph (1 001 km/h) at sea level, 575 mph (925 km/h) at 20,000 ft (6 100 m). Time to 35,000 ft (10 670 m), 7.9 min. Range (internal fuel), 670 mls (1 078 km), (max external fuel), 2,000 mls (3 217 km). Empty weight, 11,095 lb (5 033 kg). Max loaded weight, 23,525 lb (10 670 kg). Dimensions as for F-84D apart from length of 38 ft 1 in (11,60 m).*

An F-84G (below) of the Portuguese *Esquadra* 21 of the *Grupo Operacional de Aviação de Caça*, Ota, 1954.

REPUBLIC F-84F THUNDERSTREAK   USA

One of only two US swept-wing fighters derived directly from existing straight-wing aircraft to achieve production status (the other being the Grumman F9F Cougar), the Thunderstreak was conceived during a period of acute governmental parsimony towards new warplane development. Stemming from a late-1949 proposal (AP-23M) to mate the fuselage of the F-84E with sweptback surfaces and utilise up to 55 per cent of existing tooling, the project underwent incremental re-design that produced a fundamentally new fighter-bomber retaining no commonality with its precursor. A standard F-84E fuselage fitted with a new wing sweptback 40 deg at quarter-chord and sweptback tail surfaces flew on 3 June 1950 as the YF-96A powered by a 5,300 lb st (2 404 kgp) Allison J35-A-25. This designation was changed to YF-84F on the following 8 September, at which time the name Thunderstreak was adopted. The first of two further YF-84Fs with the J35-A-25 supplanted by the imported Armstrong Siddeley Sapphire engine flew on 14 February 1951, this having a deeper nose air intake and fuselage to accommodate

An F-84F-25 (below) of 315 Squadron of the Dutch *Koninklijke Luchtmacht* based at Eindhoven in 1968.

the larger turbojet. The third YF-84F which followed had extended wing roots embodying engine air intakes, but these lateral orifices caused substantial thrust losses and were consequently rejected for the series fighter, although subsequently adopted for the tactical reconnaissance RF-84F Thunderflash. As the Wright J65, the Sapphire was licence-manufactured for the series F-84F, the first example of which flew on 22 November 1952 with a YJ65-W-1 engine of 7,220 lb st (3 275 kgp). The -1 power plant equipped the first 275 Thunderstreaks, and a further 100 or so had the

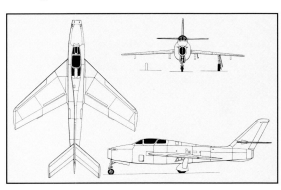

(Above) The first YF-84F, and (below) a three-view drawing of the basic F-84F Thunderstreak.

improved -1A. These engines then gave place (F-84F-5) to the similarly-rated, but more reliable, J65-W-3 (or Buick-built J65-B-3). The USAF accepted its first F-84Fs on 3 December 1952, these presenting numerous problems, not least of which was inadequate high-speed longitudinal and lateral control. In consequence, initial operational deployment (506th SFW) was delayed until January 1954, but the F-84F remained of limited use as a result of its unsatisfactory engine and other deficiencies. Some of the less pleasant handling characteristics of the Thunderstreak were alleviated by introduction of an all-flying tail (F-84F-25) in 1954, and NATO began to receive this fighter-bomber early in 1955. The F-84F carried a built-in armament of six 0.5-in (12,7-mm) M3 guns and was capable of lifting 6,000 lb (2 722 kg) of ordnance externally. Late production aircraft (F-84F-50) received the J65-W-7 (or J65-B-7) engine of 7,800 lb st (3 538 kgp), and the last of 2,348 Thunderstreaks (of which 237 were built by General Motors) was delivered in August 1957. Eight hundred

(Above) The third YF-84F with nose cone and extended wing roots embodying engine air intakes

REPUBLIC XF-91   USA

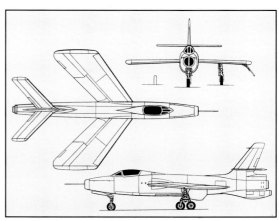

The XF-91 (above and below) in its original form, the photo depicting the first example of this type.

(Above, top) An F-84F-25 of *Jagdbombergeschwader* 36 at Rhein-Hopsten, 1963, and (immediately above) an F-84F of the French EC 3/3 "Ardennes", Reims, 1956.

and fifty-two of these were allocated to NATO air forces, which also received a further 449 built against USAF contracts, these being assigned as follows: Belgium (197), France (328), Germany (450), Italy (150) and Netherlands (180). Subsequently, Germany transferred 106 F-84Fs to Turkey and 63 to Greece, the Netherlands also transferred 19 to the former and 18 to the latter nation. The USAF Tactical Air Command transferred its last F-84F to the Air National Guard in July 1964, and the type remained in the active inventory of the Guard until November 1971. Two F-84F airframes were adapted to take General Electric XJ73-GE-5 or -7 engines of 8,750 lb st (3 969 kgp) and 8,920 lb st (4 046 kgp) respectively, and the first of these flew as the YF-84J on 7 May 1954, attaining Mach=1.09 during a 52-min flight, but the second XJ73-engined aircraft remained unflown. The following data relate to the J65-W-7-powered F-84F-50. *Max speed, 658 mph (1 059 km/h) at sea level, or Mach=0.86, 612 mph (985 km/h) at 35,000 ft (10 670 m), or Mach=0.92. Initial climb, 7,400 ft/min (38 m/sec). Range (internal fuel), 860 mls (1 384 km), (max external fuel), 2,343 mls (3 770 km). Empty weight, 13,645 lb (6 789 kg). Max loaded weight, 27,000 lb (12 247 kg). Span, 33 ft 7¼ in (10,24 m). Length, 43 ft 4¾ in (13,23 m). Height, 15 ft 0 in (4,57 m). Wing area, 325 sq ft (30,19 m²).*

An F-84F-25 (below) of the Hellenic Air Force's 115[a] *Pterix Mahis* operating from Soúda Bay, 1975.

REPUBLIC XF-84H   USA

In the early '50s, both the USAF and the US Navy evinced interest in a high-performance turboprop-powered fighter-bomber. The former service saw such an aircraft as offering the ability to lift greater ordnance loads from shorter runways and over greater ranges than pure jet fighter-bombers; the US Navy appreciated this potential which it coupled with greater compatibility with its existing carriers than was being offered by the first generation of shipboard jet aircraft. In response to a joint USAF/US Navy request, Republic tendered its AP-46 proposal developed under project engineer Joseph Freeman, a contract being placed for three aircraft. Foreseen as carrying a 4,000-lb (1 814-kg) external ordnance load coupled with a gun armament

The first of two XF-84H fighter-bombers (below) which entered flight test in July 1955.

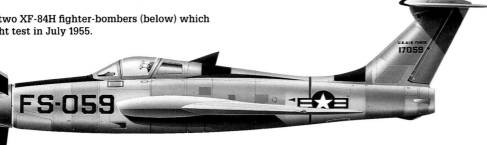

of either one or three 16-mm cannon, the new aircraft was initially assigned the designation XF-106, but was subsequently redesignated XF-84H. The US Navy lost interest in the programme at an early stage, and the aircraft that was to have been built at that service's expense was cancelled, but the USAF continued to support the XF-84H, funding of two prototypes being maintained. The XF-84H was powered by an Allison XT40-A-1, consisting of two T38 power sections joined to one remote gearbox and driving a 12-ft (3,66-m) three-bladed Aeroproducts propeller, and generating 5,332 hp plus 1,296 lb (588 kg) residual thrust. Derived

The XF-84H (above and below) was conceived to meet both USAF and US Navy requirements, but problems presented during testing proved insoluble.

from the F-84F Thunderstreak and utilising a fundamentally similar wing with modified roots accommodating intake ducting, the XF-84H featured a T-type "all-flying" horizontal tail and an anti-torque fin mounted immediately aft of the pilot's cockpit. The first aircraft was flown on 22 July 1955, but the test programme was constantly interrupted by gearbox malfunctions and other problems, and the noise emitted by the supersonic propeller produced nausea in personnel within several hundred yards of the aircraft during ground running. The second prototype was flown briefly, but the full flight envelope was not explored as a result of the USAF decision to discontinue the programme. The following performance data are based on manufacturer's estimates. *Max speed, 670 mph (1 078 km/h) at 10,000 ft (3 050 m), or Mach=0.92. Time to 35,000 ft (10 670 m), 12.0 min. Range (internal fuel), 1,027 mls (1 653 km), (max external fuel), 2,356 mls (3 792 km). Empty weight, 17,389 lb (7 888 kg). Normal loaded weight, 23,000 lb (10 433 kg). Span, 33 ft 6 in (10,21 m). Length, 51 ft 6 in (15,69 m). Height, 15 ft 4¾ in (4,69 m). Wing area, 331 sq ft (30,75 m²).*

Conceptually highly innovative, the XF-91 was developed under a March 1946 two-aircraft contract initially as a penetration fighter and subsequently as an interim high-altitude interceptor intended to receive supplementary rocket power. The wing, sweptback 35 deg at quarter chord, embodied variable incidence, permitting the most effective angle to be adopted for varying flight conditions, and was of inverse taper configuration, having substantially greater chord at the tip than at the root. The main undercarriage members each consisted of paired, tandem-mounted, small-diameter narrow-tyred wheels which retracted outwards into wingtip bays. Another radical feature proposed from the outset was a V-type or "butterfly" tail, although, in the event, both XF-91s were initially flown with conventional tail surfaces. Unofficially known as the "Thunderceptor", the first XF-91 flew on 9 May 1949 with a 5,200 lb st (2 359 kgp) General Electric J47-GE-3 turbojet. Provision was made for an afterburner, which, boosting power by 30 per cent, was installed and flown during October 1949. A quartet of 1,500 lb st (680 kgp) Reaction Motors XLR11-RM-9 rockets was then fitted, these being paired in fairings above and below the turbojet exhaust orifice. Provision was made for the installation of four 20-mm cannon, but this armament had

The second XF-91 (above) after the application of a V-type or "butterfly" tail assembly.

not been installed when, in October 1951, the USAF decided to accelerate the Convair MX-1554 interceptor programme (which was to produce the F-102) and dispense with an interim type. Thus, production planning for the F-91A was terminated and the two XF-91s were modified to serve as high-speed test vehicles. In December 1952, the first XF-91, utilising combined turbojet and rocket power, became the first US fighter to exceed Mach unity, attaining Mach=1.12, or 740 mph (1 191 km/h) at 50,000 ft (15 240 m). Earlier, in late 1951, a fire had destroyed the aft section of the second XF-91, and this was then rebuilt with the "butterfly" tail originally intended for the fighter, resuming flight testing late in 1952. The first XF-91, meanwhile, was fitted with a recontoured nose to accommodate AI radar above a chin-type air intake resembling that of the F-86D Sabre. *Max speed, 984 mph (1 584 km/h) at*

The first XF-91 (above) after application of a recontoured nose embodying chin-type air intake.

47,500 ft (14 480 m), or Mach=1.49. Time to 50,000 ft (15 240 m), 5.5 min. Range (with external fuel), 1,171 mls (1 885 km). Empty weight, 15,853 lb (7 191 kg). Max loaded weight, 28,516 lb (12 935 kg). Span, 31 ft 3 in (9,52 m). Length, 43 ft 3 in (13,18 m). Height, 18 ft 1 in (5,51 m). Wing area, 320 sq ft (29,73 m²).

REPUBLIC F-105B THUNDERCHIEF   USA

In developing as a private venture a Mach=1.5 successor to the F-84F Thunderstreak – then at an early flight test stage – Alexander Kartveli studied a variety of potential configurations under the generic designation of AP-63. The definitive study (AP-63-31) which was to meet with USAF approval envisaged an exceptionally large single-seat all-weather aircraft optimised for the delivery of an internally-housed nuclear store in a HI-LO-LO-HI penetration sortie, but possessing secondary air-air capability. Assigned the designation F-105, the projected fighter-bomber was the subject of a September 1952 contract covering pre-production engineering and material procurement for 199 aircraft. The programme was progressively reduced, eventually to 15 F-105s, after cancellation, in July 1956, of a proposed RF-105 tactical recce version. Non-availability of the specified Pratt & Whitney J75 engine necessitated installation of the J57-P-25 in the first two aircraft, which flew as YF-105As on 22 October 1955 and 28 January 1956, this engine being rated at 10,200 lb st (4 627 kg) and 15,000 lb st (6 804 kgp) with afterburning. Sixty-five F-105Bs (and 17 RF-105s, later cancelled) were ordered in March 1956, these, like the remaining pre-series aircraft, embodying significant changes, the principal of which was the installation of the J75 engine accompanied by unique swept-forward variable-area air intakes and the application of area-ruling to the fuselage. Incorporating these modifications, the first of four F-105B-1s flew on 26 May 1956, powered by a YJ75-P-3 rated at 16,000 lb st (7 258 kgp) and 23,500 lb st (10 659 kgp) with afterburning. The 15th and last pre-series aircraft (F-105B-6) became, on 26 May 1958, the first Thunderchief to be delivered to an operational squadron (the 335th TFS), but this unit was not to be fully equipped until mid-1959. The first 27 production aircraft (F-105B-10 and -15) were fitted with the J75-P-5 engine with similar ratings to the -3, and the remaining

The second YF-105A (below) at Edwards AFB in May 1956, the air intakes subsequently being redesigned.

38 production aircraft (F-105B-20), the first of which flew in June 1959, were powered by the J75-P-19 of 16,100 lb st (7 303 kgp) and 24,500 lb st (11 113 kgp) with afterburning. The wing of the F-105B was swept-back 45 deg at quarter-chord and was fitted with low-speed ailerons and high-speed spoilers for lateral control, and full-span leading-edge flaps. Large air brakes were arranged as four segments around the jetpipe fairing, the flight controls were hydraulically power-operated and irreversible, an integrated automatic flight control system being fitted and provision being made for probe-and-drogue in-flight refuelling. Built-in armament consisted of a single 20-mm M61A-1 rotary cannon, and although the weapons bay had been intended to accommodate a single Mk 28 or Mk 43 nuclear store, transfer of emphasis to conventional strike missions led to this bay normally being occupied by a 390-US gal (1 476-l) fuel tank. Up to 12,000 lb (5 443 kg) of ordnance could be carried on a fuselage centreline and four wing stations. The F-105B version of the Thunderchief equipped only two squadrons of

F-105B-15s (above) of the USAF's 335th Tactical Fighter Sqn, 4th Tactical Fighter Wing, 1960.

the 4th TFW, which, in 1964, after re-equipment with the F-105D (which see), passed them to the Air National Guard. The following data relate to the F-105B-20. *Max speed, 1,386 mph (2 230 km/h) at 36,000 ft (10 975 m), or Mach=2.1. Initial climb, 35,000 ft/min (177,8 m/sec). Max range, 2,228 mls (3 586 km). Empty weight, 25,855 lb (11 728 kg). Max loaded weight, 52,000 lb (23 587 kg). Span, 34 ft 11 in (10,64 m). Length, 63 ft 1 in (19,22 m). Height, 19 ft 8 in (5,99 m). Wing area, 385 sq ft (35,76 m²).*

REPUBLIC F-105D & F-105F THUNDERCHIEF   USA

Following the F-105B in production, the F-105D was the definitive single-seat service version of the Thunderchief. The F-105D differed from the preceding model in many respects. The principal changes were introduction of a J75-P-19W engine affording 26,500 lb st (12 020 kgp) with water injection, modifications to the intake ducting and structure, provision of a stronger undercarriage and improved all-weather capability derived from installation of a General Electric FC-5 fully integrated automatic flight and fire control system. Externally, the most noticeable difference displayed by the newer model was the longer nose housing the R-14A search and ranging radar. The first of three F-105D-1s flew on 9 June 1959, problems similar to those that had plagued the F-105B being encountered during initial testing. Formal acceptance by the USAF

of its first F-105D took place on 28 September 1960, but the aircraft did not enter operational service (with the 4th TFW) until the summer of the following year. Progressive equipment upgrading and other changes were introduced by successive production batches, which totalled a further 353 aircraft before phase-in of the F-105D-25 which was the first version to embody *all* the changes. Eighty -25 Thunderchiefs were delivered and all earlier aircraft were brought up to the same standard under Project *Look Alike*. Remaining production of the single-seat fighter-bomber consisted of 39 F-105D-30s with instrumentation changes followed by 135 F-105D-31s introducing dual in-flight refuelling systems (both flying boom and hose-and-drogue). These brought total D model deliveries to 610 aircraft.

The F-105D (above and below), the photo depicting a -31 aircraft of the 466th TFS, 419th TFW, in 1982.

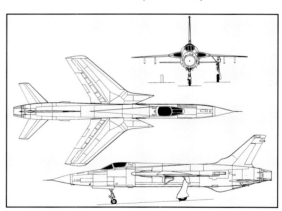

Orders for a further 143 F-105Ds were transferred to the two-seat F-105F which first flew on 11 July 1963. Earlier, a dedicated two-seat tuitional version of the F-105B had been offered to the USAF as the F-105C, but this, like the subsequent two-seat F-105E fighter-bomber, had

An F-105D-5 (below) trials aircraft toting sixteen 500-lb (227-kg) bombs and photographed in August 1962.

The sole prototype of the Ki-93 to be completed (above) performed only one flight test.

An F-105D-31 (above, top) in Vietnam, June 1965, and (immediately above) an F-105D-15 at McConnell AFB in 1972, both belonging to the 563rd TFS, 23rd TFW.

been rejected owing to budgetary limitations. The F-105F had a 31-in (79-cm) fuselage stretch, the dual in-flight refuelling capability of the D-31 and a larger vertical tail, and had the full operational capability of the D model which it was intended to combine with an instructional rôle. In the event, F-105Fs served purely for combat missions alongside the D model, delivery of the last F-105F in January 1965 bringing Thunderchief production to an end. Shortly afterwards, on 14 April, the Thunderchief flew its first operational sorties over Vietnam. These were to continue until 6 October 1970. Eighty-six F-105Fs were assigned to the *Wild Weasel* programme, being adapted to locate, classify and attack radar sites. In the early '70s, *Wild Weasel III* equipment was combined with provision for launching the AGM-78B anti-radiation missile in the F-105F to result in the F-105G, this programme covering 56 conversions. Transfer of the surviving D and F model Thunderchiefs to the Air National Guard and Air Force Reserve began in January 1971, the last F-105Gs in the USAF's active inventory being relinquished to the former in July 1980. The Reserve flew the F-105D for the last time on 25 February 1984, and, by early in the following year, the Guard had also retired its last Thunderchiefs. The following data relate to the F-105D-31. *Max speed, 1,372 mph (2 208 km/h) at 36,090 ft (11 000 m), or Mach=2.08, 836 mph (1 345 km/h) at sea level, or Mach=1.1. Initial climb, 38,500 ft/min (195,6 m/sec). Max range, 2,207 mls (3 552 km). Empty weight, 26,855 lb (12 181 kg). Max loaded weight, 52,838 lb (23 967 kg). Dimensions as for F-105B apart from overall length of 64 ft 4¾ in (19,63 m).*

(Below) An F-105F-1 of the 562nd TFS, 35th TFW, at George Air Force Base, California, in 1972.

REX D 6   Germany

Early in 1916, the Flugmaschine Rex Gesellschaft of Köln-Bickendorf produced its first single-seat fighter to the designs of Dipl-Ing Friedrich Hansen, the D 6, which allegedly owed its inspiration to the Bristol Scout. A thoroughly conventional equi-span single-bay

The first prototype of the Rex D 6 (below) featured a nose-over structure ahead of the undercarriage.

biplane, the D 6 was of wooden construction with fabric skinning and was powered by an 80 hp Oberursel (Gnome) U 0 seven-cylinder rotary engine. The first prototype D 6 crashed on its first flight while being flown by its designer from Cologne airfield, but a second example was built, this differing in only minor respects, such as omission of the nose-over structure projecting ahead of the undercarriage. No further details of the D 6 have been recorded, but it may be assumed that performance was insufficient to justify an *Idflieg* contract.

(Below) The second prototype of the Rex D 6 which allegedly owed its inspiration to the Bristol Scout.

REX D 7   Germany

Designed by Dipl-Ing Friedrich Hansen and built as a private venture in the summer of 1917, allegedly to the specific requirements of Lt Werner Voss, the D 7 was a small sesquiplane of wooden construction and powered by a 100 hp Hansen seven-cylinder single-valve rotary engine. Featuring a slab-sided, plywood-skinned fuselage with fabric-covered wings and horizontal tail surfaces, the D 7 was novel in that the lower wing halves pivoted about the bases of the V-type interplane struts, either collectively or differentially, thus serving as flaps or ailerons, a scheme that was the subject of a patent. No record of the flight testing of the D 7 has survived, but the arrangement would seem to have been of dubious practicality as the prototype appears to have been abandoned after the death of Voss, on 23 September 1917.

The Rex D 7 (below) was supposedly sponsored by the German fighter "ace", *Leutnant* Werner Voss.

RIKUGUN (GIKEN) Kɪ-93   Japan

Derived from a strategic fighter project drafted by the *Koku Hombu*, or Air Headquarters of the Imperial Army, shortly before the outbreak of the Pacific War, the Ki-93 was designed by the *Rikugun Koku Gijutso Kenkyujo* (Army Aerotechnical Research Institute, usually known by the abbreviation *Giken*. Evolving as a multi-rôle heavy fighter, the aircraft suffered rather protracted design gestation, and it was not until 22 February 1943 that authorization was given for the con-

struction of two flying prototypes and a static test airframe, and the *Kitai* (Experimental Airframe) designation Ki-93 assigned. A true multi-rôle aircraft for low- and medium-altitude operation, with a mission potential including anti-armour and anti-shipping tasks, the Ki-93 had a two-spar laminar-flow wing with full-span slotted flaps and an oval-section monocoque fuselage, construction being all metal. Two crew members were seated back to back in a heavily-armoured cockpit, power was provided by two 18-cylinder two-row radial Mitsubishi Ha-214 engines each rated at 1,970 hp for take-off, and armament comprised a 57-mm Ho-401 cannon with a 20-round rotating magazine in a ventral gondola, two 20-mm Ho-5 cannon in the wing roots and an aft-firing, flexibly-mounted 12,7-mm Ho-103 machine gun. The first Ki-93 was completed in March 1945 by the 1st Army Air Arsenal (Dai-Ichi Rikugun Kokusho) at Tachikawa and flown on 8 April. Through pilot error, the aircraft suffered damage during the landing, repairs taking four weeks to complete, and the night before the flight test programme was scheduled to be resumed, the Ki-93 was destroyed in a USAF attack on Tachikawa airfield. Equipment installation in the second prototype was still incomplete when hostilities terminated. The following performance data is based on manufacturer's estimates. *Max speed, 388 mph (624 km/h) at 27,230 ft (8 300 m), 310 mph (500 km/h) at 3,280 ft (1 000 m). Time to 19,685 ft (6 000 m), 9.05 min. Range, 1,243 mls (2 000 km) plus one hour cruise reserve. Max loaded weight, 25,132 lb (11 440 kg). Span, 62 ft 4 in (19,00 m). Length, 46 ft 7⅞ in (14,21 m). Height, 15 ft 10⅞ in (4,85 m). Wing area, 589.34 sq ft (54,75 m²).*

(Below) The Ki-93 multi-rôle two-seat fighter.

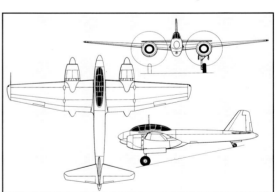

ROBEY PETERS R.R.F.25   UK

Tests conducted in the USA led the British Admiralty to adopt the Davis recoilless gun for the RNAS, several types of aircraft being designed around this immense weapon, essentially for the anti-Zeppelin rôle. Among these was the Robey Peters R.R.F.25, designed by J A Peters for Robey & Company. Powered by a 250 hp Rolls-Royce 12-cylinder Vee-type water-cooled engine (later to be named Eagle), the R.R.F.25 was an unequal-span two-bay biplane with a crew of three comprising a pilot and two gunners. The pilot was accommodated far aft, immediately ahead of the vertical tail, and the gunners occupied nacelles suspended beneath the upper wing. The port nacelle accommodated a 0.303-in (7,7-mm) Lewis gun and the starboard nacelle housed a two-pounder version of the Davis gun which exceeded 7 ft (2,13 m) in length. Eight shells for the gun were fitted into the nacelle and two more in the adjacent wing. Two prototypes were ordered, the first of these flying in September 1916. It suffered minor damage as a result of turning over during the take-off run for what was to

The first prototype R.R.F.25 anti-Zeppelin aircraft with two-pounder Davis gun in the port nacelle.

have been its second flight, and when it did succeed in getting airborne once more a fire at low altitude resulted in a crash in which it was destroyed. The second prototype, referred to as the Mk II, featured a new equi-span three-bay wing cellule, introduced a fixed tail fin, and side windows were added for the pilot. Overall span was reduced by 2 ft (61 cm) and wing area was increased by 63.5 sq ft (5,89 m²). It was intended that a Davis gun be carried in each nacelle. This aircraft was, in fact, cancelled by the Admiralty, but was completed nonetheless in January 1917 and flown during the course of the month. It stalled on take-off, however, and crashed, further work on the aircraft being finally abandoned. The following data relate to the first prototype. *Loaded weight, 3,700 lb (1 678 kg). Span, 54 ft 6 in (16,61 m). Length, 29 ft 4½ in (8,95 m). Wing area, 483.5 sq ft (44,92 m²).*

The unequal-span first prototype (above) and equal-span second prototype (below) of the R.R.F.25.

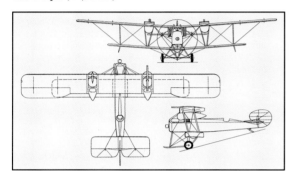

ROGOŽARSKI IK-3 (IK-Z) Yugoslavia

During 1935, Ljubomir Ilić and Kosta Sivčev, responsible for the design of the Ikarus-built IK-2 (which see), were joined by Slobodan Zrnić in the design of a private-venture single-seat fighter for the Rogožarski AD. This aircraft was designated IKZ or IK-Z, but the similarity between the cyrillic ''Z'' and the arabic ''3'' led to confusion, and, as a result of common usage, the fighter became known widely as the IK-3. Rogožarski received a contract for a single prototype late in March 1937, and this was flown towards the end of May 1938. Powered by an Hispano-Suiza 12Y29 engine rated at 920 hp at 11,810 ft (3 600 m), the IK-3 carried an armament of one 20-mm engine-mounted HS 404 cannon and two 7,92-mm machine guns, and was of mixed construction, with plywood-covered wooden wings and a steel-tube fuselage with wooden stringers, metal skinning forward and fabric aft. An initial contract for 12 series IK-3 fighters was signed in November 1938, but, on 19 January 1939, the prototype was destroyed after a failure in the starboard wing when recovering from a terminal velocity dive. The series IK-3 featured a modified wing structure, a new cockpit canopy and revised undercarriage fairings, and the French HS 404 cannon gave place to a Swiss Oerlikon FF of similar calibre, while the HS 12Y29 engine was replaced by an Avia-built Hispano-Suiza 12Ycrs rated at 860 hp at 13,125 ft (4 000 m). The first six series IK-3s were delivered by

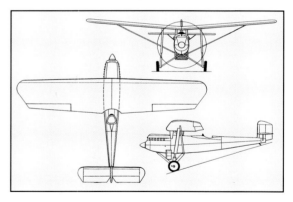

A series IK-3 (above), with damaged undercarriage, in service with the Yugoslav 51 *Grupa*, Zemun, in 1940.

late March 1940 and the remaining six built against the initial order were completed by the following July, by which time a further series of 25 IK-3s was in course of construction by Rogožarski. One IK-3 airframe was fitted with a Daimler-Benz DB 601A engine, but this had not been completed before the *Wehrmacht* onslaught. On 6 April 1941, at the time of the German invasion of Yugoslavia, only six IK-3s were serviceable (with the 51st Independent Sqn), but these were claimed to have accounted for at least 10 *Luftwaffe* aircraft before, during the night of 11-12 April, the survivors were burned on Veliki Radinci airstrip. *Max speed, 327 mph (527 km/h) at 17,715 ft (5 400 m), 261 mph (420 km/h) at sea level. Time to 16,405 ft (5 000 m), 6.9 min. Range, 488 mls (785 km). Empty weight, 4,560 lb (2 068 kg). Loaded weight, 5,799 lb (2 630 kg). Span, 33 ft 9¾ in (10,30 m). Length, 26 ft 3 in (8,00 m). Height, 10 ft 8 in (3,25 m). Wing area, 177.6 sq ft (16,50 m²).*

(Below) The standard series version of the IK-3.

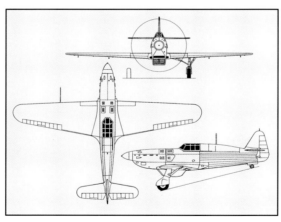

ROHRBACH Ro IX ROFIX   Germany

In December 1925, the Turkish government invited the Rohrbach Metall Flugzeugbau of Berlin to tender for a requirement for 50 single-seat fighters. To meet this requirement, an all-metal parasol monoplane was designed under the leadership of Kurt Tank. Embodying

The first prototype Ro IX Rofix (below) photographed at Kastrup, Copenhagen, in November 1926.

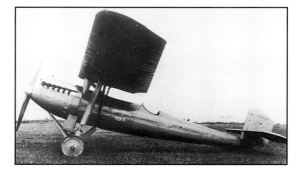

the advanced structural precepts established earlier by Rohrbach, which included stressed skinning and wings set at a coarse dihedral angle, the fighter, designated Ro IX Rofix, was powered by a 600 hp BMW VI 5,5 water-cooled 12-cylinder engine. Armament comprised two synchronised rifle-calibre machine guns in the fuselage, provision being made for two more guns in the wings. Construction of two prototypes commenced in April 1926 at the Rohrbach Metall Aeroplan A/S at Kastrup, Copenhagen, a subsidiary earlier established in Denmark to evade restrictions imposed by the Allied Control Commission. Flight testing of the Rofix commenced late in 1926, but the first prototype was destroyed in a crash on 27 January 1927. The second prototype was presented to a Turkish technical mission in July 1927, but this, too, crashed on the 15th of that month with a consequent loss of Turkish interest and termination of further work. *Max speed, 162 mph (260 km/h). Time to 9,840 ft (3 000 m), 7.0 min. Range, 478 mls (770 km). Empty weight, 2,910 lb (1 320 kg). Loaded weight, 4,299 lb (1 950 kg). Span, 45 ft 11⅛ in (14,00 m). Length, 31 ft 2 in (9,50 m). Height, 12 ft 1⅔ in (3,70 m). Wing area, 301.39 sq ft (28,00 m²).*

(Below) Kurt Tank's first fighter, the Ro IX Rofix.

ROLAND   Germany

Shortly before World War I, the Luft-Fahrzeug Gesellschaft, or LFG, adopted the corporate tradename ''Roland'' to avoid confusion with the Luft-Verkehrs-Gesellschaft (LVG). All aircraft progeny of this company were thus designated as LFG Roland types (which see), but were frequently referred to simply as Rolands.

ROMANO R-90   France

Dated in concept by comparison with other contenders designed to meet the 1933 *Marine Nationale* requirement for a single-seat float fighter, the R-90 proffered by the Chantiers Aéronavale Etienne Romano was a twin-float single-bay equi-span staggered biplane of mixed construction, the fuselage being of welded steel-tube and the wings of wood. Powered by a 720 hp Hispano-Suiza 9Vbrs nine-cylinder radial, the R-90 was flown in August 1935, attaining a speed of 219 mph (352 km/h) at 11,480 ft (3 500 m). During the following October, it was re-engined with a smaller-diameter 14-

cylinder HS 14Hbrs two-row radial enclosed by a long-chord NACA cowling. At the same time, the volume of the floats was increased and more substantial float-bracing struts were provided. At the request of the *Services Techniques*, the prototype was again re-engined, this time with a liquid-cooled 12-cylinder HS 12Ycrs-1 rated at 900 hp at 6,235 ft (1 900 m). A 20-mm cannon was mounted between the cylinder banks, and, in this form, the R-90 could exceed 248 mph (400 km/h) in level flight. It flew with the HS 12Y engine in October 1937, but in the previous March, the *Marine Nationale* had selected the Loire 210 to meet its requirement, and subsequent testing of the R-90 was related to the clandestine development of a shore-based version specifically for the Spanish Republican government. The following data relate to the R-90 powered by the HS 14Hbrs engine. *Max speed, 229 mph (368 km/h) at 11,485 ft (3 500 m). Range, 404 mls (650 km). Empty weight, 3,620 lb (1 642 kg). Loaded weight, 4,387 lb (1 990 kg). Span, 29 ft 1½ in (8,88 m). Length, 28 ft 5¼ in (8,67 m). Height, 12 ft 10¾ in (3,93 m). Wing area, 226.05 sq ft (21,00 m²).*

The R-90 with its original nine-cylinder HS 9Vbrs engine with Townend ring (above) and with HS 14Hbrs engine and long-chord cowling (below).

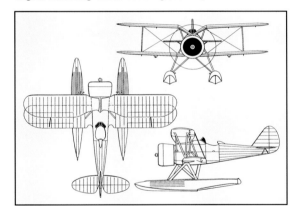

ROMANO R-83   France

One of several contracts, most of which were clandestine, negotiated with representatives of Etienne Romano by a purchasing commission of the Spanish Republican government early in 1937, involved 24 land-based derivatives of the R-90 single-seat float fighter. To support the subterfuge that Spain had actually ordered a re-engined version of the entirely different tandem two-seat R-82 trainer, the land-based fighter was allocated the non-sequential designation R-83, part manufacture and final assembly being undertaken

An R-83 fighter (below) undergoing final assembly by the LACEBA concern in Belgium early 1938.

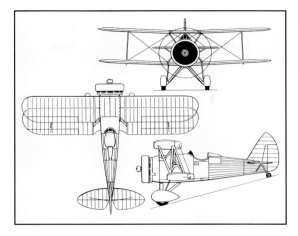

(Above) The Romano-designed R-83 fighter for Spain.

clandestinely in Belgium by LACEBA (Les Ateliers de Construction et d'Exploitation de Brevets Aéronautiques). The R-83 was fundamentally similar to the R-90 apart from having a 450 hp Pratt & Whitney R-985 Wasp Junior engine, a cabane replacing the gulled upper wing centre section and a spatted wheel undercarriage. In order to further the pretence that the R-83 was purely a tuitional aircraft, a 280 hp Salmson 9Aba radial engine was fitted in Belgium for flight testing and delivery to Spain where it was intended that the Wasp Junior engine be installed. The first of an initial batch of six R-83s reached Spain on 20 April 1938, and the last on the following 5 July, these allegedly being re-engined as planned after arriving in Barcelona. The ultimate fate of these aircraft is unknown. The wings and fuselages of the remaining 18 were completed, but the aircraft had still to be assembled when the Spanish conflict terminated. No data relating to the R-83 have apparently survived.

ROMANO R-92   France

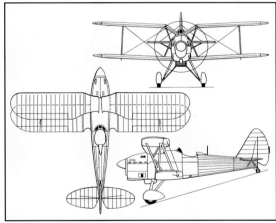

(Above) The sole example of the Romano R-92 fighter.

Apart from their contract for the R-83, the Spanish Republicans financed development as the R-92 of a version of the same design powered by an Hispano-Suiza 12Ycrs-1 liquid-cooled 12-cylinder Vee engine rated at 900 hp at 6,235 ft (1 900 m). Similar to the R-83 apart from engine installation, an increase in vertical tail area, some local structural strengthening and the addition of a 20-mm engine-mounted cannon to the armament, and in reverting to the gull configuration of the R-90, the R-92 prototype was apparently transported to a Sabena hangar at Evere, Brussels, for final assembly. Euphemistically referred to as a *"sportive plane"* and assigned a Belgian civil registration, the R-92 was flight tested under the utmost secrecy by Jacques Lecarme of the French *Centre d'Essais du Matériel Aérien* (CEMA) before delivery to Barcelona in the summer of 1938. The subsequent fate of the sole example of the R-92 is unrecorded and no data are available apart from dimensions which were similar to those of the R-90 other than a length of 25 ft 0½ in (7,63 m) and a height of 10 ft 2 in (3,10 m).

ROMANO R-110   France

Intended to fulfil the demands of an October 1934 specification calling for a three-seat fighter to serve as an aerial command post for single-seat fighters – a rôle to which were subsequently added those of bomber interception and escort – the R-110 was flown for the first time on 30 March 1938. Of mixed construction, with plywood-covered wooden wings and a welded steel-tube fuselage, the R-110 was powered by two 450 hp Renault 12 Ro 2/3 12-cylinder air-cooled engines and carried an armament of two fixed 20-mm cannon and a single 7,5-mm machine gun on a flexible mount in the aft cockpit. The R-110 was unusual in that the pilot and aircraft commander were seated behind separate vertically-staggered stepped windscreens. The competing Potez 630 had appeared in production form before the R-110 prototype entered flight test and further development of the latter was discontinued. *Max speed, 292 mph (470 km/h). Range, 795 mls (1 280 km). Empty weight, 4,773 lb (2 165 kg). Loaded weight, 7,275 lb (3 300 kg). Span, 41 ft 11⅞ in (12,80 m). Length, 31 ft 8⅓ in (9,66 m). Height, 11 ft 0⅔ in (3,37 m). Wing area, 258.34 sq ft (24,00 m²).*

The Romano R-110 three-seat fighter (above and below) was intended to compete with the Potez 630.

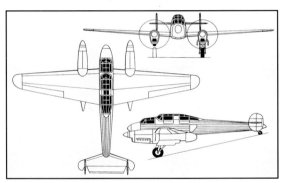

ROUSSEL 30   France

Conceived as a private-venture single-seat lightweight fighter, the Roussel 30 was flown for the first time in April 1939, and featured a duralumin monocoque fuselage and all-metal wing with fabric-covered movable surfaces. Powered by a 690 hp Gnome-Rhône 14M7 14-cylinder radial, the Roussel 30 had provision for an armament of two wing-mounted 20-mm cannon and a centreline fuselage rack for a single 551-lb (250-kg) bomb. Official trials were conducted from August 1939, and the prototype was in process of being re-engined with an 800 hp version of the G-R 14M when the *Wehrmacht* approached Paris. The aircraft was dismantled and trucked to Bordeaux, but was subsequently des-

(Below) The Roussel 30 private-venture fighter.

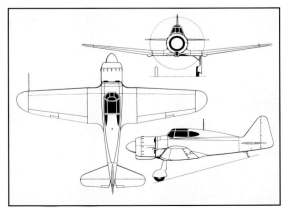

The single prototype of the Roussel 30 (above) was flown only for a few months during 1939.

troyed when the building in which it was stored caught fire. *Max speed, 323 mph (520 km/h) at 19,030 ft (5 800 m). Initial climb, 3,740 ft/min (19,0 m/sec). Endurance, 2.0 hrs. Empty weight, 2,270 lb (1 030 kg). Loaded weight, 3,891 lb (1 765 kg). Span, 25 ft 5⅛ in (7,75 m). Wing area, 107.64 sq ft (10,00 m²).*

ROYAL AIRCRAFT FACTORY
F.E.3   UK

Located at Farnborough and engaged primarily in aeronautical research, the Royal Aircraft Factory (so named in April 1912) was responsible for the design and development of a number of warplanes during World War I. In accordance with the factory's purpose they received designations combining a prefix letter (at first indicating the general configuration, but later the rôle) with E for experimental (although several, such as the B.E.2, F.E.2, R.E.8 and S.E.5, were to be built in large numbers). Built in 1913, the F.E.3 was thus the third design in the "Farman Experimental" series of pusher biplanes, and was designed to carry a COW one-pounder quick-firing gun. Alternatively known as the A.E.1 ("Armoured Experimental"), the two-seat F.E.3 was a two-bay biplane with overhanging upper wing, and a four-bladed pusher propeller driven by a shaft and chain from the 100 hp Chenu eight-cylinder water-cooled inline engine mounted in the front of the fuselage. The large cruciform tail unit was carried on a single central boom secured through the hollow propeller shaft and braced by wires to the upper wing and the undercarriage. Flight tests showed that the tail attachment was not sufficiently rigid and the gun, fitted in front of the fuselage, was fired only in static tests at Farnborough after flight testing was abandoned.

Designed to carry a COW gun, the sole F.E.3 (above) was of unusual "pod-and-boom" configuration.

The F.E.3 used fabric-covered wooden construction for the wings and tail unit, but the fuselage nacelle was of steel tube construction with aluminium and plywood skinning. A large central orifice in the nose took in air for the engine radiators, which were inside the nacelle. *Max speed, 75 mph (121 km/h) at sea level. Initial climb, 350 ft/min (1,78 m/sec). Service ceiling, 5,000 ft (1 525 m). Empty weight, 1,400 lb (635 kg). Loaded weight, 2,080 lb (943 kg). Span, 40 ft 0 in (12,19 m). Length, 29 ft 3 in (8,91 m). Height, 11 ft 3 in (3,43 m). Wing area, 436.5 sq ft (40,55 m²).*

ROYAL AIRCRAFT FACTORY
S.E.2   UK

The S.E.2 was a rebuild of the unarmed B.S.1, which was designed at Farnborough by Geoffrey de Havilland assisted by H P Folland and S J Waters, and flown in

early 1913. Designated as a "Bleriot Scout", the B.S.1 was an attractive single-bay equi-span biplane with a circular-section fuselage which was of monocoque construction aft of the single-seat cockpit. Power was provided by a partially-cowled 100 hp Gnome rotary engine. The B.S.1 achieved 92 mph (148 km/h) and a climb rate of 900 ft/min (4,6 m/sec) in early tests, but was badly damaged on 27 March 1913. It was then rebuilt with a redesigned tail unit that included a semi-circular tailplane with a lifting profile, divided elevators, a small fin and large rudder. With a fully-cowled 80 hp Gnome nine-cylinder rotary engine, the aircraft flew again in October 1913, being redesignated S.E.2 as a Scouting Experimental (although the S.E. series had earlier been intended for "Santos Experimental", of canard configuration). RFC handling trials took place (with No 5 Squadron) early in 1914, after which the S.E.2 was again rebuilt, with a more conventional rear fuselage of wooden construction and fabric covering, larger fin and rudder, constant-chord tailplane and other smaller changes. Taken to France (by No 3 Squadron) later in 1914, the S.E.2 was fitted with two Army rifles firing at outward angles to clear the propeller, and other (revolver) armament was also tried during the several months it remained with the squadron. *Max speed, 85 mph (137 km/h) at sea level. Empty weight, 720 lb (327 kg). Loaded weight, 1,132 lb (513 kg). Span, 27 ft 6 in (8,38 m). Length, 20 ft 5 in (6,22 m). Height, 9 ft 3½ in (2,83 m). Wing area, 188 sq ft (17,47 m²).*

In its reconstructed form (below), the sole S.E.2 was used briefly in France with make-shift armament.

ROYAL AIRCRAFT FACTORY
F.E.6   UK

Of similar construction to the F.E.3, the F.E.6 was built in 1914 and was powered by a 120 hp Austro-Daimler six-cylinder water-cooled engine. Standard R.E.5 components were used for the wings, which were of equi-span, and the tail unit was carried on a cantilever boom, without bracing wires. The F.E.6 was flown at Farnborough on 14 November 1914 but this may have been its only flight, and, if fitted, the COW gun that it was designed to carry was not fired. *Empty weight, 2,000 lb (907 kg). Loaded weight, 2,630 lb (1 193 kg). Span, 49 ft 4 in (15,03 m). Length, 29 ft 6 in (8,99 m). Height, 15 ft 0 in (4,57 m). Wing area, 542 sq ft (50,35 m²).*

The F.E.6 (below) was a derivative of the F.E.3.

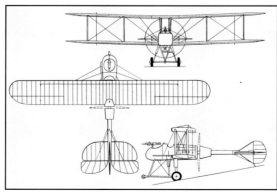

ROYAL AIRCRAFT FACTORY
B.E.2c   UK

Second of the Farnborough designs to bear a "Bleriot Experimental" designation as a general-purpose tractor biplane, the B.E.2 appeared in 1912 and provided the basis for a family of variants produced in large quantity for use by the RFC, principally as an unarmed two-seat

A B.E.2c in single-seat configuration (above) with single gun, Vee-type undercarriage and original fin.

scout. With modifications to enhance the inherent stability of the basic design, the B.E.2c was developed in 1914 and many of the 1,216 of this variant built were to serve with various *ad hoc* armament installations. The B.E.2c was a two-bay biplane with unstaggered equi-span wings, a conventional tail unit with separate fin, rudder, tailplane and elevators, and an undercarriage incorporating skids to help prevent nose-overs. The 70 hp Renault eight-cylinder Vee-type engine powered early production aircraft, but the 90 hp RAF 1a eight-cylinder Vee-type engine soon became standard. Construction of the B.E.2c was of wood throughout, with fabric covering. A variety of mounts was evolved for a single 0.303-in (7,7-mm) Lewis machine gun in the observer's (front) cockpit, primarily for self-defence. More specifically to serve as a fighter with Home Defence squadrons of the RFC and the RNAS, numerous B.E.2c's were modified as single-seaters, armament comprising a single Lewis gun mounted to fire upwards behind the wing centre section or, in some cases, on the side of the fuselage alongside the cockpit, angled outwards to clear the propeller disc. Flying by night, despite a lack of nocturnal flight aids, B.E.2c's shot down five raiding Zeppelins over the UK during 1916. B.E.2c's were also used for a number of armament experiments. The following data are for the B.E.2c with RAF 1a engine. *Max speed, 72 mph (116 km/h) at 6,500 ft (1 980 m). Time to 6,500 ft (1 980 m), 20 min. Service ceiling, 10,000 ft (3 050 m). Endurance, 3.25 hrs. Empty weight, 1,370 lb (621 kg). Loaded weight, 2,142 lb (972 kg). Span, 36 ft 10 in (11,23 m). Length, 27 ft 3 in (8,30 m). Height, 11 ft 4 in (3,45 m). Wing area, 396 sq ft (36,79 m²).*

The B.E.2c (below) in its early standard form.

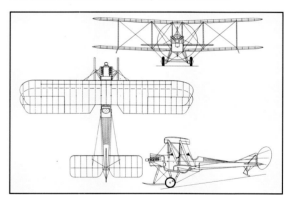

ROYAL AIRCRAFT FACTORY
B.E.2e   UK

First flown in February 1916 and destined to be built in larger numbers than the B.E.2c, the B.E.2e differed from the former in having single bay wings of unequal span and a new tailplane. Provision was made for extra fuel in a tank under the port upper wing or for dual controls, but the former was seldom fitted. The large upper wing overhang was braced from inverted-Vee kingposts above the interplane struts, and the standard engine remained the 90 hp RAF 1a, as the 105 hp RAF 1b that was intended to be used in the B.E.2e did not reach production. From production totalling 1,320 aircraft (plus some B.E.2c and 2d conversions), B.E.2e's were issued to 11 Home Defence squadrons of the RFC (as well as many units on the Western Front and elsewhere). Like the B.E.2c, the 2e often carried a single Lewis gun in the front cockpit, for which assorted mountings were available. An alternative

A two-seat B.E.2e (above) armed with four Le Prieur rockets on the interplane struts.

A "presentation" aircraft from the Gold Coast, this F.E.2b (above) served with No 25 Sqn, RFC.

armament tried by some of the Home Defence aircraft for anti-Zeppelin patrols comprised a quartet of Le Prieur rockets, the launching rails for which were attached to the interplane struts, two each side and angled upwards. Little success was achieved by the B.E.2e as a fighter, its performance being inadequate for aerial combat by 1916, and heavy losses were suffered by the RFC squadrons flying the type in France. Retroactively, the designations B.E.2f and B.E.2g were applied to distinguish, respectively, between those B.E.2e's converted from 2c's and those built as 2e's or converted from 2d's, as their fuel systems and capacities were significantly different. *Max speed, 90 mph (145 km/h) at sea level, 75 mph (121 km/h) at 10,000 ft (3 050 m). Time to 10,000 ft (3 050 m), 53 min. Service ceiling, 9,000 ft (2 743 m). Endurance, 4 hrs. Empty weight, 1,431 lb (649 kg). Loaded weight, 2,100 lb (953 kg). Span, 40 ft 9 in (12,42 m). Length, 27 ft 3 in (8,31 m). Height, 12 ft 0 in (3,66 m). Wing area, 360 sq ft (33,44 m²).*

ROYAL AIRCRAFT FACTORY
F.E.2A & F.E.2B — UK

Sharing little more than its configuration with the F.E.2 flown at Farnborough in 1913, the F.E.2a appeared early in 1915 and was designed to provide the RFC with an armed reconnaissance aircraft. It was a large three-bay biplane, using a flat centre section and outer panels that were identical with those of the B.E.2c (which see), and incorporating dihedral. A short nacelle carried the observer/gunner in the nose ahead of the pilot, and the pusher engine. The tail unit was carried by four booms extending aft from the wings and comprised a large tailplane with elevators, a kidney-shaped rudder and small triangular fin above the tailplane. A small nose-wheel was provided ahead of the oleo-strutted main wheels to help prevent nosing over, and the whole of the upper wing centre section trailing-edge aft of the rear spar was hinged for use as a flap-cum-airbrake. Armament normally comprised a 0.303-in (7,7-mm) Lewis machine gun in the front cockpit on one of several alternative mounts. The first F.E.2a flew on 26 January 1915 with a 100 hp Green six-cylinder inline water-cooled engine but proved underpowered and

the 120 hp Austro-Daimler built under licence by Beardmore became the standard for 11 more F.E.2a's and early production examples of the F.E.2b. The latter was the "productionised" version with the Beardmore engine, trailing-edge flap deleted, simplified fuel system and other changes to facilitate large-scale production by inexperienced companies. These comprised, apart from the RAF itself (which built only 47 F.E.2b's): Boulton & Paul (250); Barclay Curle (100); Garrett & Sons (60); Ransome, Sims & Jefferies (350); Alex Stephen and Sons (150) and G & J Weir (600). A 160 hp Beardmore engine was adopted later, and the oleo u/c with nosewheel gave way to a simplified form without the nosewheel or, later, a non-oleo V-strut

A Green-engined F.E.2a (above) and the more numerous Beardmore-engined F.E.2b (below).

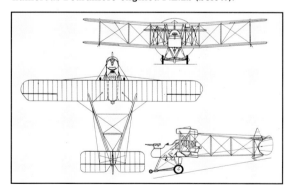

arrangement. All 12 F.E.2a's and almost a thousand F.E.2b's went to RFC squadrons in France, where they engaged in offensive patrols over the enemy lines in the rôle of fighter escort for unarmed reconnaissance

aircraft. Over 200 were issued to Home Defence units, some of these flying as single-seaters, and service use of the F.E.2b continued until the Armistice in November 1918. The following data are for the version with 160 hp Beardmore engine. *Max speed, 91.5 mph (147 km/h) at sea level, 76 mph (122 km/h) at 10,000 ft (3 050 m). Time to 4,000 ft (1 220 m), 9.85 min. Service ceiling, 11,000 ft (3 353 m). Empty weight, 2,061 lb (935 kg). Loaded weight, 3,037 lb (1 378 kg). Span, 47 ft 9 in (14,56 m). Length, 32 ft 3 in (9,83 m). Height, 12 ft 7½ in (3,84 m). Wing area, 494 sq ft (45,89 m²).*

ROYAL AIRCRAFT FACTORY
F.E.2c — UK

Among the 12 F.E.2a's sent to France in 1915, where they were flown by No 6 Squadron RFC and sometimes known by the alternative official designation of Fighter Mark I, one had its seating arrangement reversed. Thus, the pilot occupied the front cockpit – located a little farther aft than in the F.E.2a and 2b – and the gunner was in an elevated aft position. An additional Lewis gun was fitted in the nose, remotely controlled by the pilot. In this form, the aircraft was designated F.E.2c. Conversion of a small number of F.E.2b's to 2c configuration was put in hand at the RAF, Farnborough, but only two are thought to have been completed as the F.E.2c was found to offer no advantage over the F.E.2b.

In the few F.E.2c's built (below), the positions of the pilot and gunner were reversed.

Six more 2b's were converted to 2c's in late 1917, however, to serve as night bombers with No 100 Squadron, for which rôle the improved view for the pilot outweighed the difficulties posed for the gunner. Data for the F.E.2c were as for the F.E.2b.

ROYAL AIRCRAFT FACTORY
F.E.2D — UK

On 7 April 1916, a version of the F.E.2b was flown at the RAF Farnborough, fitted with a 250 hp Rolls-Royce Mk I (later, Eagle I) 12-cylinder water-cooled V-type engine, becoming thus the prototype F.E.2d. Compared with the 160 hp F.E.2b, the Rolls-Royce-engined version had better rate of climb and ceiling and slightly improved speed performance, and although the heavier engine adversely affected manoeuvrability and field performance, the F.E.2d was ordered into production as an interim supplement for the F.E.2b. Eighty-five were built at Farnborough and 270 by Boulton & Paul, although many of these were completed, in the event, with Beardmore engines as F.E.2b's. In those F.E.2d's completed, several versions of the Rolls-Royce engine were fitted; as well as the Mk I these comprised the 250 hp Marks III and IV (later, 284 hp Eagle III and IV) and the 275 hp Marks I and II (later, 322 hp Eagle V and VI). The first few F.E.2d's had the oleo undercarriage with nosewheel extension, but the modified oleo type

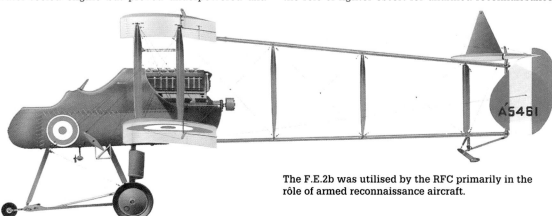

The F.E.2b was utilised by the RFC primarily in the rôle of armed reconnaissance aircraft.

An early series F.E.2d (above) built at Farnborough, showing the low-sided pilot's cockpit.

without the nosewheel was soon adopted. The F.E.2d was in service in France by July 1916, and the type also served with Home Defence units, although its low speed performance made it an ineffective Zeppelin-chaser. Most F.E.2d's were armed with two Lewis guns, one on a flexible mounting in the nose and another fixed forward-firing for the pilot; in some cases a third gun, on a telescopic pillar mounting, was also provided between the two cockpits. The following data apply to the F.E.2d with 250 hp Rolls-Royce Mark I engine. *Max speed, 94 mph (151 km/h) at 5,000 ft (1 525 m), 88 mph (142 km/h) at 10,000 ft (3 050 m). Time to 5,000 ft (1 525 m), 7.15 min. Service ceiling, 17,500 ft (5 334 m). Endurance, 3.5 hrs. Empty weight, 2,509 lb (1 138 kg). Loaded weight, 3,470 lb (1 574 kg). Span, 47 ft 9 in (14,55 m). Length, 32 ft 3 in (10,13 m). Height, 12 ft 7½ in (3,85 m). Wing area, 494 sq ft (45,89 m²).*

ROYAL AIRCRAFT FACTORY
S.E.4A   UK

Designed at Farnborough by H P Folland at the end of 1914, the S.E.4a was one of a series of "Scouting Experimentals" used to study the interplay of stability and manoeuvrability. Unrelated, except in configuration and design authorship, to the high performance S.E.4 of mid-1914, the S.E.4a was a sturdy little single-bay biplane with equi-span wings incorporating 3.5 deg of dihedral and having no centre section. The square-section fuselage was of conventional spruce construction with steel tubes to accept the loads from the lower wings, and, like the wooden wings and tail unit, was fabric-covered. Full-span ailerons were fitted to both sets of wings, and power was provided by an 80 hp Gnome seven-cylinder rotary in a fully circular short-chord cowling. The first of four S.E.4a's built at the RAF flew there on 25 June 1915, and differed from its successors in having faired fuselage sides and an outsize spinner. The fourth and last S.E.4a flew on 13 August that year. The third, flown on 27 July, was at first fitted with an 80 hp Le Rhône engine, the Gnome being substi-

The first of the three "productionised" S.E.4a's, (below) showing the flat-sided fuselage.

tuted later, and in October 1916 this same S.E.4a was provided with an 80 hp Clerget. In the hands of the RFC, at least one of the S.E.4a's was armed with a 0.303-in (7,7-mm) Lewis gun mounted on the centre line above the upper wing to clear the propeller disc. *Span, 27 ft 6 in (8,38 m). Length, 20 ft 10½ in (6,37 m). Height, 9 ft 5 in (2,87 m).*

The S.E.4a (below) with Le Rhône engine.

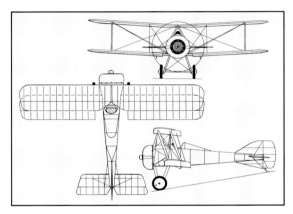

ROYAL AIRCRAFT FACTORY
B.E.12   UK

Evolved at Farnborough during 1915 as a marriage of the B.E.2c airframe with the then-new R.A.F.4 air-cooled 12-cylinder Vee-type engine of 140 hp, the B.E.12 prototype began test flying at the end of July that year. Although flown from the start as a single-seater, it was at first unarmed and was intended for such rôles as bombing and photography rather than as a fighter. The prototype was tested in France in September 1915 and its generally satisfactory performance encouraged the War Office to order production of the B.E.12 in that same month. Delivered from March 1916 onwards, production aircraft had the R.A.F.4a engine (with increased stroke), twin upright exhaust stacks, an auxiliary gravity fuel tank under the port upper wing and, after the first few, an enlarged rudder with curved leading edge. At first serving with RFC squadrons in France for general duties, the B.E.12 was fitted with a 0.303-in (7,7-mm) Lewis machine gun on an oblique mounting on the fuselage side, or over the wing centre section, but several other experimental installations were tried at Farnborough before the decision to adopt the newly-available Vickers-Challenger interrupter gear, using a Vickers gun firing through the propeller disc. Difficulties with the gear, combined with the excessive stability of the B.E.12 (to overcome which the B.E.2e-type tailplane and elevators were used on some B.E.12s), made the type ineffectual as a fighter, however, and it was soon withdrawn from France, having served with only two squadrons. B.E.12s remained in service with Home Defence squadrons through 1917, many alternative armament installations being tried, including a quartet of Lewis guns, and sets of Le Prieur rockets on the interplane struts. One Zeppelin was shot

A production B.E.12 (above) with enlarged fuel tank between the centre-section struts, and rounded fin.

down by a B.E.12, in June 1917. At Farnborough, one was tested with a Davis six-pounder recoilless gun, firing upwards at 45 deg for anti-Zeppelin use, but this was not adopted for production. Contracts were placed with two companies for B.E.12 production, Daimler building 200 and Standard Motor Co, 50, against the original orders placed in 1915, and Daimler receiving a contract for 200 more in August 1917. Many of the latter, however, were completed as B.E.12b's (which see). *Max speed, 102 mph (164 km/h) at sea level, 91 mph (146 km/h) at 10,000 ft (3 050 m). Time to 10,000 ft (3 050 m), 33 min. Service ceiling, 12,500 ft (3 810 m). Endurance, 3 hrs. Empty weight, 1,635 lb (742 kg). Loaded weight, 2,352 lb (1 067 kg). Span, 37 ft 0 in (11,3 m). Length, 27 ft 3 in (8,31 m). Height, 11 ft 1½ in (3,39 m). Wing area, 371 sq ft (34,47 m²).*

ROYAL AIRCRAFT FACTORY
B.E.12A   UK

With the B.E.12 established in production in 1916, based on the B.E.2c airframe with its equi-span two-bay wing and massive horizontal tail surfaces, a further marriage was arranged to combine the R.A.F.4a engine with the newer B.E.2e airframe. This introduced the single-bay cellule with overhanging upper wing and a smaller tailplane/elevator combination, together with the larger, rounded fin of the B.E.12. Designated B.E.12a in this form, the type was ordered from Coventry Ordnance Works and Daimler, each of which received contracts for 50 during 1916 (some of the Daimler batch being completed as B.E.12s). The B.E.12a's served briefly with Home Defence units and more extensively in Palestine, with the Australian-manned No 67 Squadron. *Max speed, 105 mph (169 km/h) at sea level, 80.5 mph (129.5 km/h) at 10,000 ft (3 050 m). Time to 10,000 ft (3 050 m), 24.25 min. Empty weight, 1,610 lb (730 kg). Loaded weight, 2,327 lb (1 056 kg). Span, 40 ft 0 in (12,19 m). Length, 27 ft 3 in (8,30 m). Height, 12 ft 0 in (3,66 m). Wing area, 360 sq ft (33,44 m²).*

A Daimler-built B.E.12a (above) and a drawing (below) of the standard aircraft, without armament.

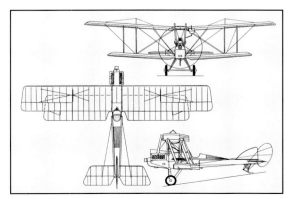

ROYAL AIRCRAFT FACTORY
B.E.12B UK

In an attempt to improve the performance of the B.E.12, primarily for the benefit of Home Defence squadrons, a 200 hp Hispano-Suiza water-cooled eight-cylinder Vee-type engine was substituted for the 150 hp R.A.F.4a. The first such installation was completed in September 1917 by the Southern Aircraft Repair Depot at Farnborough and demonstrated a dramatic improvement in speed and climb performance. Consequently, it was decided that 150 of the 200 B.E.12s ordered from Daimler in August 1917 should be completed with the Hispano engines as B.E.12b's. Airframes built by Daimler were fitted with these engines at the Northern Aircraft Repair Depot at Aston, near Sheffield, and deliveries began late in 1917. As Zeppelin raids on the UK had by this time virtually come to an end, many B.E.12b's went straight into store, their urgently-needed engines being removed for use in other aircraft types, such as the S.E.5a. It is believed that production of B.E.12b's ended some 12-20 short of the intended total. The standard armament of the B.E.12b comprised a 0.303-in (7,7-mm) Lewis gun above the centre section, firing over the propeller disc. Performance and weight data for the B.E.12b are not recorded. Dimensions similar to those of the B.E.12.

The standard B.E.12b (below), as used by several RFC Home Defence squadrons in 1917/18.

ROYAL AIRCRAFT FACTORY
F.E.8 UK

Designed under the direction of John Kenworthy, the F.E.8 was the first single-seat fighter evolved as such at Farnborough, where the first of two prototypes was flown on 15 October 1915. Of pusher configuration to allow an uninterrupted forward field of fire for the 0.303-in (7,7-mm) Lewis gun, the F.E.8 was a two-bay equi-span biplane with a short fuselage nacelle to accommodate the gun, the pilot and a 100 hp Gnome Monosoupape nine-cylinder rotary engine, and four slender booms to carry the cruciform tail unit. Construction of the nacelle was of welded steel-tube with aluminium sheet covering; the wings and tail unit used conventional wooden spars and ribs with fabric covering. Trials with the second prototype in France in late 1915 led to a change in the gun installation, which was mounted within the nacelle nose and could be moved through a limited range by means of a control in the cockpit. Production F.E.8s, which began to appear in May and June 1916 from the factories of Darracq Motor Engineering at Fulham and Vickers at Weybridge, had a more practical gun mounting on the nose immediately

(Below) The F.E.8 with Gnome Monosoupape engine.

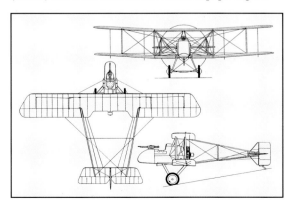

Somewhere "over the front" in 1916, an F.E.8 (above) flies in the markings of No 41 Sqn, RFC.

ahead of the cockpit. Production totalled 220 by Darracq and 50 by Vickers. Service use by RFC squadrons in France began in August 1916, and, although soon obsolescent, the F.E.8 remained in service for a year, becoming the last single-seater of pusher configuration in general use. Trial installations of the 110 hp Le Rhône and 110 hp Clerget engines were made, but the Monosoupape remained the standard fit and the following data apply to this version. *Max speed, 94 mph (151 km/h) at sea level, 70 mph (113 km/h) at 10,000 ft (3 050 m). Service ceiling, 15,210 ft (4 636 m). Endurance, 2.5 hrs. Empty weight, 895 lb (406 kg). Loaded weight, 1,346 lb (611 kg). Span, 31 ft 6 in (9,60 m). Length, 23 ft 8 in (7,21 m). Height, 9 ft 2 in (2,79 m). Wing area, 218 sq ft (20,25 m²).*

ROYAL AIRCRAFT FACTORY
S.E.5 UK

Second only to the Sopwith Camel in reputation as the RFC's outstanding fighter of World War I, the S.E.5 was designed under the direction of H.P. Folland. Of classic tractor biplane configuration, the S.E.5 was initiated to take advantage of the new Hispano-Suiza engine that began test-running in Spain in February 1915 and was in production in France a few weeks later. Two versions of the engine became available during 1916, the basic direct-drive 150 hp unit and a geared version producing 200 hp. Examples of both were included in the British orders placed in France and, subsequently, with Wolseley for licence-built examples (as the 150 hp Python and 200 hp Adder respectively). The S.E.5 was intended, from the outset, to be powered by the 200 hp geared engine and to be armed with a 0.303-in (7,7-

mm) Lewis machine gun firing through a hollow propeller shaft, but, in the event, early aircraft had to use the 150 hp Hispano 8Aa, and had an armament of one Vickers gun in the front fuselage, offset to port, with interrupter gear, and a Lewis on a Foster mount above the centre section. Unarmed, the first of three prototypes of the S.E.5 flew on 22 November 1916. It was a compact single-bay biplane with equi-span wings featuring raked tips, a similarly-raked tailplane, triangular fin and almost rectangular rudder, with a small ventral fin and a V-strut undercarriage. A large windscreen was provided over the front of the cockpit. All major components were of conventional wood construction, with fabric covering. Of two further prototypes, one was similarly powered and first flew on 4 December 1916, whereas the other introduced the 200 hp engine and became, effectively, the prototype for the S.E.5a (which see). Production of the S.E.5 was ordered "off the drawing board" with a first batch of 24 built by the RAF at Farnborough, where the first was completed in March 1917. A second batch of 50 followed on, but at least 15 of these were to emerge as S.E.5a's, and some S.E.5s in service were also modified to have 200 hp engines. In service with the RFC in France by early 1917, production S.E.5s were modified in various ways, particularly by removal of the windscreen. Other changes tried out on S.E.5s to improve the lateral control were consolidated in the S.E.5a. *Max speed, 122 mph (196 km/h) at 3,000 ft (915 m), 98 mph (158 km/h) at 15,000 ft (4 570 m). Time to 6,500 ft (1 980 m), 8 min. Service ceiling, 19,000 ft (5 790 m). Endurance, 2.5 hrs. Empty weight, 1,399 lb (635 kg). Loaded weight, 1,935 lb (878 kg). Span, 27 ft 11 in (8,51 m). Length, 20 ft 11 in (6,38 m). Height, 9 ft 5 in (2,87 m). Wing area, 249.8 sq ft (23,20 m²).*

A Farnborough-built, early-production S.E.5 (below) for service with No 56 Sqn in 1917.

ROYAL AIRCRAFT FACTORY
S.E.5A UK

The third prototype of the S.E.5 flew at Farnborough on 12 January 1917 powered by a 200 hp geared Hispano-Suiza 8B water-cooled eight-cylinder V-type engine, but otherwise similar to the 150 hp-engined earlier prototypes. While production deliveries of the 200 hp engine were awaited, airframe modifications were introduced in the light of early experience with the first production batch of S.E.5s. In particular, the wing rear spars were shortened at the tips to provide greater

Built by Wolseley, this S.E.5a (below) once used for "skywriting" was restored at the RAE in 1972.

(Above, top) S.E.5a, No 74 Sqn, RAF, at Teteghem, France, April 1919, as flown by "Mick" Mannock. (Immediately above) S.E.5a in Polish service.

strength, this serving to blunt the previously raked tips and reduce overall span by 15½ in (39,4 cm). At the same time, lateral control was improved by shortening the levers on the ailerons. With a small Avro-type windscreen in place of the S.E.5's voluminous structure, a small fabric-covered head fairing behind the cockpit, the blunt wings and the standard Vickers + Lewis gun armament, the version with 200 hp engine became the subject of large-scale production as the S.E.5a, starting with part of the second batch S.E.5s already ordered from the RAF. Two hundred more were built at Farnborough itself and, in addition, by the time the war came to an end in November 1918, some 5,125 S.E.5a's had been built by five companies in less than 18 months: Austin (1,550), Bleriot & Spad (560), Martinsyde (400), Vickers (2,215) and Wolseley (400). Production of the 200 hp Hispano (in several sub-variants, and including licence-production by Wolseley as the W.4B Adder I, II and III) failed to keep pace with this prodigious output, and numerous operational difficulties with the engine enhanced the problem. Consequently, many S.E.5a's were fitted (without change of designation) with the 200 hp direct-drive Wolseley W.4A Viper, a derivative of the French engine. At least six S.E.5a's were flown with the 200 hp Sunbeam Arab I (geared) or Arab II (direct drive) water-cooled eight-cylinder engine in trials at Farnborough, and some production aircraft received high-compression versions of the French-built Hispano-Suiza engine, increasing maximum output to 220 hp. Twenty-two squadrons of the RFC and the US

A "presentation" S.E.5a (above) from Addis Ababa and a drawing (below), both showing the fighter's standard armament.

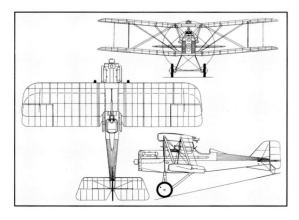

Air Service were flying the S.E.5a by the time of the Armistice, but this brought an end to planned large-scale production by Curtiss in the US when only one of 1,000 on order had been completed (in addition to 56 assembled from British components). Service use con-

One of 50 S.E.5a's (above), rebuilt in the US by Eberhart as S.E.5E's with Wright-Hispano E engines.

tinued on a small scale for only a short time after the end of the war, in Australia, Canada and South Africa as well as with the RAF. The following data refer to the S.E.5a with the 200 hp Hispano-Suiza engine. *Max speed, 126 mph (203 km/h) at 10,000 ft (3 050 m), 116 mph (187 km/h) at 15,000 ft (4 570 m). Time to 10,000 ft (3 050 m), 13.25 min. Service ceiling, 17,000 ft (5 180 m). Endurance, 2.25 hrs. Empty weight, 1,531 lb (694 kg). Loaded weight, 2,048 lb (929 kg). Span, 26 ft 7½ in (8,11 m). Length, 20 ft 11 in (6,37 m). Height, 9 ft 6 in (2,89 m). Wing area, 245.8 sq ft (22,83 m²).*

ROYAL AIRCRAFT FACTORY
S.E.5B UK

The final aircraft built at Farnborough against contracts for 74 S.E.5s placed in 1917 was used early the following year for an experimental programme aimed at improving the performance and fighting ability of the type. Fitted with a 200 hp Hispano-Suiza 8B engine and armed with the Lewis and Vickers gun combination of the standard S.E.5a, it had new single-bay wings of unequal span and chord. In addition, a retractable radiator was provided in the forward fuselage, and a large, shallow, propeller spinner was fitted, to combine with a re-

The sole example of the S.E.5b (below), photographed at Farnborough in April 1918, was fitted with a standard S.E.5a wing cellule in 1919.

profiled cowling and give better streamlining of the fuselage. The head-fairing behind the cockpit was also improved. Tests in 1918 revealed little performance gain or handling benefit, with the extra drag of the big upper wing offsetting gains from the more streamlined fuselage. Standard S.E.5a wings were fitted to the S.E.5b in 1919, as well as a modified horizontal tail, for comparative testing at Martlesham Heath, and this aircraft made an appearance at the RAF Pageant at Hendon in 1920. *Loaded weight, 1,950 lb (885 kg). Span, 30 ft 7 in (9,32 m). Length, 20 ft 10 in (6,35 m). Height, 9 ft 6 in (2,89 m). Wing area, 278 sq ft (25,83 m²).*

ROYAL AIRCRAFT FACTORY
F.E.9 UK

Conceived as a replacement for the F.E.2b in the fighter-reconnaissance rôle, the F.E.9 was of similar pusher configuration and therefore already obsolescent by the time it appeared in 1917. Emphasis was placed in the design upon providing the gunner with a good field of fire and the pilot a good all-round view. To this end, the nacelle was located close beneath the upper wing and was carried on struts above the shorter-span lower wing. The large overhang of the upper wing brought the F.E.9 almost into the sesquiplane category, and called for bracing wires from triangular kingposts above the interplane struts of the single-bay cellule. A cruciform tail unit was carried on four slender booms, as on the F.E.2, and the Vee-strutted undercarriage incorporated oleo legs. Construction was largely of wood, but pairs of steel tube N-struts linked the nacelle to the upper and lower wings. Power was provided by a 200 hp Hispano-Suiza eight-cylinder V-type water-cooled engine and the planned armament comprised two 0.303-in (7,7-mm) Lewis guns on pillar mounts, ahead of and behind the front cockpit, and both fired by the observer – the latter rearwards over the pilot's head and the top wing. Installation of a third gun, on the side of the fuselage for use by the pilot, was planned. Authority was given by the War Office for construction of three prototypes and a production batch of 24 in October 1916, and testing began in April 1917.

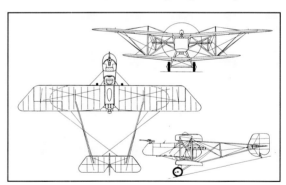

The F.E.9 (above and below) is seen with the original single-bay wings, the photograph illustrating the first of the three aircraft built.

Handling and performance of the prototypes were disappointing, however, and production was cancelled, to allow the Hispano engines to be used in more worthwhile types. Testing of the prototypes continued, in the course of which two-bay wings were tried on the second aircraft, which was also flown for a time by No 78 Home Defence Squadron, RFC. *Max speed, 105 mph (169 km/h) at 10,000 ft (3 050 m), 88 mph (142 km/h) at 15,000 ft (4 570 m). Time to 10,000 ft (3 050 m), 21.35 min. Service ceiling, 15,500 ft (4 725 m). Loaded weight, 2,480 lb (1 125 kg). Span, 40 ft 1 in (12,22 m). Length, 28 ft 3 in (8,61 m). Height, 9 ft 9 in (2,97 m). Wing area, 365 sq ft (33,91 m²).*

ROYAL AIRCRAFT FACTORY N.E.1 — UK

As a derivative of the F.E.9 (which see), the RAF planned to develop a dedicated night fighter as the F.E.12. This was to have used the same 200 hp Hispano-Suiza eight-cylinder Vee-type water-cooled engine, the same undercarriage, tailbooms, tail unit and wing centre section as the F.E.9, and basically the same nacelle, but with the crew positions reversed.

Designed for night fighting, the N.E.1 (above) was derived from the F.E.9, with three-bay wing cellule.

New equi-span, three-bay wings were planned, with plain unbalanced ailerons. The pilot, in the front cockpit for the best possible view during unaided nocturnal operations, was to have a forward-firing 0.303-in (7,7-mm) Lewis gun, whereas the observer was to be armed with a Vickers rocket gun for which two mounts were to be provided for firing forwards or aft. Provision was to be made for a searchlight in the nose, and another on the forward mount for the rocket gun, with a wind-driven generator under the nacelle. Six prototypes were planned, but before construction began the designation was changed to N.E.1 (for "Night-flying Experimental") and some changes were made. These eliminated the second searchlight, increased the span of the wing centre section, changed the tail unit design, moved the boom attachment points on the tailplane outwards, and introduced a wide-track undercarriage with a divided axle arrangement. Flown early in September 1917, the first N.E.1 was almost immediately damaged and was then modified, before resuming flying on 4 October, to accommodate the observer in the front cockpit with the rocket gun and the pilot behind with a fixed Lewis gun. In this form, the N.E.1 was submitted to official trials at Martlesham Heath in November 1917, but was not thought to have adequate performance to serve as a night fighter. The other five prototypes were all completed by January 1918, but one was used only for static testing, another probably remained unflown and only one was issued to an RFC squadron for home defence. *Max speed, 95 mph (153 km/h) at 10,000 ft (3 050 m), 85 mph (137 km/h) at 16,500 ft (5 030 m). Time to 1,000 ft (305 m), 1.6 min. Service ceiling, 17,500 ft (5 335 m). Endurance, 2.75 hrs. Empty weight, 2,071 lb (939 kg). Loaded weight, 2,946 lb (1 336 kg). Span, 47 ft 10 in (14,57 m). Length, 30 ft 2 in (9,19 m). Height, 9 ft 8 in (2,94 m). Wing area, 555.1 sq ft (51,57 m²).*

ROYAL AIRCRAFT FACTORY A.E.3 RAM — UK

The last aircraft type to emerge from the Royal Aircraft Factory at Farnborough, before its change of name in June 1918 to Royal Aircraft Establishment, the A.E.3 was itself an extrapolation from the N.E.1 (which see). Designated as an "Armoured Experimental" type, the A.E.1 was intended as a specialised ground-attack

Conceived as a ground-attack fighter, the A.E.3 Ram (below) was the only Farnborough design to be named.

fighter, for which purpose it was to mount a pair of 0.303-in (7,7-mm) Lewis guns in the nose, with a limited degree of movement in azimuth and depression. A third Lewis was to be pillar-mounted in the front, observer's, cockpit for self-defence. Like the N.E.1, the A.E.3 was a large three-bay equi-span biplane, differing principally in the construction and shape of the nacelle, which was armoured with steel plate and provided stowage for 32 ammunition drums. Intended to be powered by the 200 hp Hispano engine as used in the N.E.1, the A.E.3 prototype emerged at the end of March 1918 with a 200 hp Sunbeam Arab, whilst the second, eight weeks later, had a 230 hp Bentley B.R.2 rotary. Flight testing of the latter began on 4 June, and larger ailerons and rudders were fitted before this A.E.3 went to France for service trials, which aroused little enthusiasm. The third aircraft, also completed in June 1918, had an Arab engine like the first and in this form the A.E.3 was named the Ram I, whilst the B.R.2 version became the Ram II. A proposed derivative, the Ram III, was not built and no production ensued, other, better, types having become available. The following speed is estimated with a 200 hp Hispano engine. *Max speed, 95 mph (153 km/h). Span, 47 ft 10½ in (14,59 m). Length, 27 ft 8½ in (8,44 m). Height, 10 ft 0 in (3,05 m). Wing area, 560 sq ft (52,02 m²).*

(Below) The A.E.3 Ram II with B.R.2 engine.

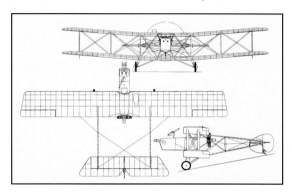

RUMPLER 6A 2 — Germany

In May 1916, the Rumpler Flugzeug-Werke initiated flight test of a tandem two-seat reconnaissance fighter referred to by the company designation 6A 2 (the first digit indicating the year, the letter indicating the aircraft category and the second digit signifying the design sequence in that category and year). Whereas all preceding Rumpler biplanes had featured two-bay wing cellules, the 6A 2 broke new ground in being of single-bay configuration with Y-type interplane struts. Of mixed construction with plywood and fabric skinning, it was initially powered by a 160 hp Mercedes D III six-cylinder water-cooled engine with *Stirnkühler* radiator beneath the wing centre section and a "rhino horn" exhaust pipe. Proposed armament comprised a synchronised 7,9-mm LMG 08/15 machine gun and a swivelling Parabellum in the rear cockpit. At an early phase in flight development some strengthening of the wings was undertaken and more orthodox paired struts substituted, and, subsequently, the 6A 2 was fit-

Rumpler's first fighter was the 6A 2 (below), which was tested with little success in 1916.

ted with a geared eight-cylinder Mercedes D IV engine of 220 hp. Excessive vibration led to discontinuation of the flight test programme, the type being overtaken by the more innovative 7C 1. *Loaded weight, 2,778 lb (1 260 kg). Span, 33 ft 5½ in (10,20 m).*

RUMPLER 6B 1 — Germany

The first essay in the single-seat fighter category by Rumpler was a twin-float seaplane intended for both offensive patrol and seaplane station defence. Assigned the company designation 6B 1, the fighter was a derivative of the highly successful 5A 2 (C I) two-seat general-purpose biplane, possessing a fundamentally similar structure and retaining the 160 hp Mercedes D III engine. The two-bay wing cellule was also retained, but a modest stagger was applied, the rear cockpit was discarded and armament comprised a single synchronised 7,9-mm LMG 08/15 machine gun.

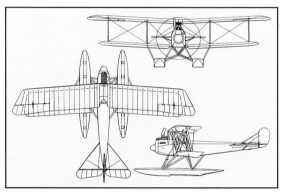

The Rumpler 6B 1 (above and below) and similar 6B 2 were ordered in quantity after prototype test.

The largest of five single-seat float fighter prototypes ordered in June 1916 for evaluation by the *Marine-Flieger*, the 6B 1 entered production after acceptance of three prototypes during July-August 1916. Forty series aircraft followed between November and May 1917, production continuing with the 6B 2 of which 50 had been delivered when the programme terminated in January 1918. The 6B 2 differed in comparatively minor respects, the most visible modification being use of the tailplane of "wing-nut" form of the C IV. The following data relate to the 6B 1 in standard form. *Max speed, 84 mph (135 km/h) at sea level. Time to 9,840 ft (3 000 m), 25 min. Range, 342 mls (550 km). Empty weight, 1,742 lb (790 kg). Loaded weight, 2,513 lb (1 140 kg). Span, 39 ft 10⅓ in (12,15 m). Length, 29 ft 8⅓ in (9,05 m). Height, 11 ft 5¾ in (3,50 m). Wing area, 384.28 sq ft (35,70 m²).*

RUMPLER 7C 1   Germany

Late in 1916, the Rumpler team headed by Edmund Rumpler initiated design of both a two-seat and a single-seat fighter embodying a novel, if complex, method of fuselage construction. This, protected by a patent filed early in 1915, sought to combine minimum weight with maximum strength. The fuselage was built up from plywood frames with numerous thin stringers, the whole being covered by two layers of doped fabric strips applied diagonally in opposite directions and intended to provide the necessary torsional stiffness. A close-cowled 160 hp Mercedes D III engine was attached to a fuselage extrusion supporting the upper wing, which embodied an offset flush radiator. The upper wing was of parallel chord, the lower wing being of so-called *Libelle* (Dragonfly) form featuring a curved trailing edge, the wing cellule being braced by single broad-chord I-section struts with cables running to two fuselage points. This formula, which resulted in what was, aerodynamically, an outstandingly clean aeroplane, was applied to the 7C 1 two-seat fighter and the 7D 1 single-seat fighter. The 7C 1 entered flight test in the spring of 1917, initially with vertical tail surfaces confined to a pivoting rudder. The tail was subsequently redesigned to embody a fixed fin, but development was discontinued at a comparatively early stage, presumably as a result of difficulties similar to those experienced with the parallel single-seat 7D 1. No specification for the 7C 1 appears to have survived.

The Rumpler 7C 1, seen (below) with original and (above) definitive vertical tails, featured the so-called *Libelle* (Dragonfly) form lower wing.

RUMPLER 7D 1   Germany

Evolved in parallel with the two-seat 7C 1 and embodying similar aerodynamic and structural features, the 7D 1 single-seat fighter was the recipient of an *Idflieg* (Inspectorate of Flying Troops) contract for three prototypes, flight testing commencing in the spring of 1917. The *Idflieg* requirement called for a speed of 103 mph (165 km/h) at 16,405 ft (5 000 m), that altitude

(Below) The Rumpler 7D 1 single-seat fighter.

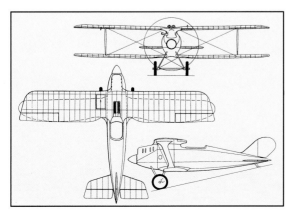

The Rumpler 7D 1 (above) utilised novel fuselage construction and was aerodynamically advanced.

being attained in 31.5 minutes, and an endurance of 1.5 hrs. An armament of two synchronised 7,9-mm LMG 08/15 machine guns was specified and provision for oxygen breathing apparatus requested. A second identical prototype was designated 7D 2. Flight testing revealed that the pilot's field of vision was seriously impaired by the broad-chord interplane struts and there were aerodynamic problems associated with the upper wing/fuselage junction. Furthermore, there were servicing difficulties related to the engine installation. In consequence, the 7D 1 and 2 were abandoned in favour of a more conventional fighter, the 7D 3. *Max speed, 109 mph (175 km/h). Service ceiling, 22,965 ft (7 000 m). Span, 26 ft 10¾ in (8,20 m). Length, 19 ft 4¼ in (5,90 m). Height, 8 ft 6⅓ in (2,60 m).*

RUMPLER 7D 3   Germany

The shortcomings displayed by the 7D 1 and 2 led the Rumpler team to evolve a more conventional derivative fighter retaining the same structural precepts. This, the 7D 3, retained the Mercedes D III engine, but a more orthodox installation was adopted, the flush radiator being centrally mounted in the wing centre section which was raised above the forward fuselage decking by means of a cabane structure. The broad-chord I-type interplane struts were discarded in favour of more conventional twin struts. The 7D 3 was tested during the summer of 1917, but it may be presumed that results were not entirely satisfactory, as, by the late autumn, work had begun on an entirely new aircraft, the 7D 4, intended to participate in the first D-type contest that was to take place at Adlershof early in the following year. No further details of the 7D 3 are available.

Seen (below) being exhibited at Breslau in December 1918, the Rumpler 7D 3 flew in the summer of 1917.

RUMPLER 7D 4   Germany

To compete in the first D-type contest (20 January-12 February 1918), intended to select single-seat fighters for service introduction in mid-1918, Rumpler built two prototypes of the 7D 4. One prototype was completed with a conventional twin-strut cellule and the other with a cellule employing "reverse-C" interplane struts braced by fabric-wrapped triple cables. The fuselage structure remained unchanged, but in an attempt to eradicate some torsional problems experienced earlier with this type of construction, a thin plywood veneer skinning was applied to the nose and tail sections to increase rigidity. Again, the Mercedes D III engine was retained and specified armament was two 7,9-mm LMG 08/15 synchronised guns. Flight testing of the 7D 4 had commenced by October 1917, and during the D-type contest the example fitted with "reverse-C" interplane struts attained an altitude of 16,405 ft

The Rumpler 7D 4 (above) in its original form with a cellule employing "reverse-C" interplane struts.

(5 000 m) within 23.8 min. This prototype was considered to afford excellent visibility from the cockpit, but was, by consensus, somewhat temperamental in handling and difficult to land. Nevertheless, it appeared to possess sufficient promise to warrant an order for a pre-series of 50 examples of a developed version (7D 7) for further investigation and possible operational evaluation. Another prototype was completed as the 7D 5, this differing essentially in having an automobile-style frontal radiator. No specification for the 7D 4 is available.

(Above and below) The Rumpler 7D 4 with a twin-strut cellule which entered flight test in October 1917.

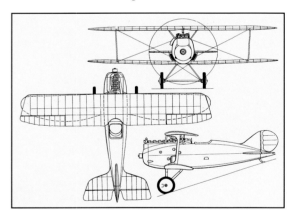

RUMPLER 7D 7   Germany

Too late to participate officially in the first D-type contest, the 7D 7 was an improved derivative of the 7D 4 with the "reverse-C" type interplane struts. A new Göttingen aerofoil was employed for the wing, which had control surfaces of marginally reduced area, the cockpit was smaller and was moved forward 13⅘ in (35 cm), and the buried wing radiator gave place to ear-type

(Below) The Rumpler 7D 7 with new Göttingen aerofoil.

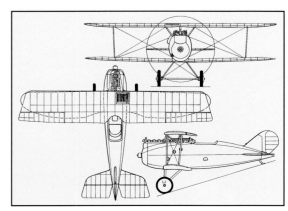

radiators mounted immediately above the lower wing roots. Flight testing proved the 7D 7 faster than the 7D 4, and an unofficial climb to 16,405 ft (5 000 m) within 18 min was reported. The 7D 7 was powered by the 160 hp Mercedes D III engine and possessed an armament of two synchronised 7,9-mm LMG 08/15 machine guns, static load testing and flight evaluation occupying the period 22 February to 1 May 1918. Some disconcerting twisting of the tail was encountered during certain manoeuvres, calling for structural reinforcement, the *Idflieg* reporting in May 1918 that the 7D 7 was "unacceptable for the Front and would be rebuilt."

An improved derivative of the 7D 4, the Rumpler 7D 7 (below) was found "unacceptable for the Front".

RUMPLER 8D 1 (D I)   Germany

To overcome the lack of rear fuselage rigidity experienced during testing of the 7D 7, the fabric-wrapped, multi-stringered fuselage structure first featured by the 7C 1 and 7D 1 was finally and reluctantly abandoned in favour of a stronger, more conventional semi-monocoque of diagonally-wrapped strips of glued plywood. The wing cellule was reinforced, balanced ailerons were fitted, and the fin and rudder were redesigned and enlarged. Designated 8D 1, this revised fighter provided the standard for the 50 pre-series aircraft previously ordered from Rumpler as D Is. Three pre-series D Is powered by the 160 hp Mercedes D IIIa engine and one powered by the 180 hp D IIIaü high-compression engine participated in the second D-type contest (27 May – 28 June 1918), the last-mentioned attaining an altitude of 16,405 ft (5 000 m) in 18.7 min

The pre-series D I (above and below), the Rumpler 8D 1, which participated in two D-type contests.

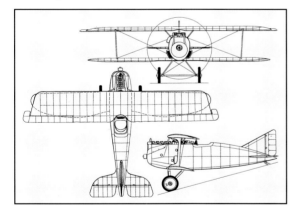

compared with 27 min required by the D IIIa-engined D I. Excellent climb and altitude capabilities notwithstanding, the evaluation pilots' consensus of the D I was unfavourable, particularly criticised being aileron response – which was considered slow and erratic – the gliding and landing characteristics, and the level of vibration. One D I powered by a 185 hp BMW IIIa engine participated in the third D-type contest (10-22 October 1918), being the only contender to attain an altitude of 26,900 ft (8 200 m), but the fighter was deemed of

"limited usefulness" in close-in combat. Military acceptance testing of the Rumpler fighter had still to be completed at the time the conflict terminated when 22 had been built. Another 27 were completed after the Armistice. The following data relate to the standard D I. *Max speed, 112 mph (180 km/h) at 16,405 ft (5 000 m). Time to 16,405 ft (5 000 m), 23.75 min. Endurance, 1.5 hrs. Empty weight, 1,356 lb (615 kg). Loaded weight, 1,775 lb (805 kg). Span, 27 ft 7½ in (8,42 m). Length, 18 ft 10⅖ in (5,75 m). Height, 8 ft 4¾ in (2,56 m). Wing area, 179.33 sq ft (16,66 m²).*

RYAN STA-SPECIAL   USA

In the mid 'thirties, Ryan offered a single-seat armed version of its tandem two-seat STM primary trainer, which, in turn, had been derived from the S-T initially flown on 8 June 1934. Dubbed STA-Special, the single-seater was powered by a 150 hp Menasco C4S air-cooled engine, and a second batch of six ordered in December 1938 for the Guatemalan *Cuerpo de Aviación Militar* were each fitted with two 0.7-mm wing-mounted guns and referred to as light fighters.

The STA-Special (below) with faired guns over the wings as supplied to Guatemala and referred to euphemistically as a fighter.

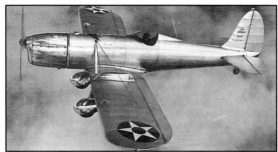

RYAN FR-1 FIREBALL   USA

In December 1942, nine US aircraft manufacturers received a Request for Proposals from the Bureau of Aeronautics for a single-seat shipboard fighter combining piston engine and turbojet, the former to be the main power source and the latter to provide boost in climb and combat. The Ryan Model 28, designed by Benjamin T Salmon and William T Immenschuh, was selected as winning contender by the Bureau and three prototypes were ordered on 11 February 1943 as XFR-1s. A low-

The first XFR-1 (below) with the tail configuration with which it entered flight test in June 1944.

(Above and below) The FR-1, the photo depicting an aircraft cruising on the jet engine power alone.

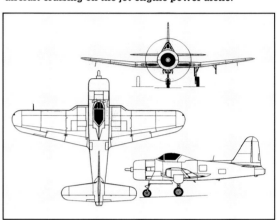

wing, cantilever monoplane of classic design, the XFR-1 was the first carrier aircraft designed from the outset to use a laminar-flow aerofoil and the first US Navy aircraft to have an entirely flush-riveted exterior and metal-skinned movable control surfaces. Power was provided by a 1,350 hp Wright R-1820-72W Cyclone nine-cylinder air-cooled radial and, in the rear fuselage, a 1,600 lb st (726 kgp) General Electric I-16 (later redesignated J31) turbojet. Proposed armament consisted of four 0.5-in (12,7-mm) machine guns with provision for a 1,000-lb (454-kg) bomb under port inboard wing panel. Other features were hydraulically-folding outer wings and a tricycle undercarriage. A contract for 100 production FR-1s was placed on 2 December 1943, the first XFR-1 flying seven months later, on 25 June 1944, with only the piston engine installed. The turbojet was added a few days later. Initial flight tests led to the major redesign and enlargement of the vertical tail and lowering of the horizontal tail. On 31 January 1945, by which time a number of series FR-1s had been completed and were under test, a contract was placed for 600 FR-2s which were to differ in having the R-1820-74W engine of 1,500 hp with water injection. In the event, neither the FR-2 nor the XFR-3 was to be built, the latter being intended to mate the 2,000 lb st (907 kgp) General Electric I-20 turbojet with the -74W piston engine. The XFR-4, on the other hand, entered flight test in November 1944. Utilising the 19th FR-1 production airframe, this replaced the J31-GE-3 turbojet with a 3,400 lb st (1 542 kgp) Westinghouse J34-WE-22, discarded the wing root intakes of the FR-1 in favour of flush inlets in the sides of the forward fuselage, and had the aft fuselage extended by 8 in (20 cm). It was found, however, that the thrust of the J34 was too great to permit efficient use of both engines and the XFR-4 programme was discontinued accordingly. Deliveries of the FR-1 to the US Navy began in March 1945, the Fireballs equipping one squadron (VF-66) and completing carrier qualification in May (aboard the USS *Ranger*). After VJ-Day, the 34 FR-1s remaining to be delivered were cancelled, together with all 600 FR-2s. On 18 October 1945, VF-66 was de-commissioned and its FR-1s transferred to VF-41 (redesignated VF-1E on 15 November 1946) which continued to fly them until mid-July 1947. Only 17 of the 66 FR-1s built saw squadron usage, the remainder being assigned for various test

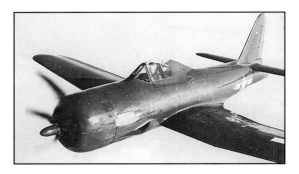

The XFR-4 (above) with flush turbojet air intakes and modified wing roots, and (below) an FR-1 of VF-41 flying with propeller feathered.

programmes. *Max speed (both engines), 399 mph (642 km/h) at sea level, 426 mph (686 km/h) at 18,100 ft (5 515 m), (Cyclone only), 320 mph (515 km/h). Initial climb (both engines), 4,800 ft/min (24,4 m/sec). Time to 20,000 ft (6 095 m), 5.6 min. Range (internal fuel), 1,030 mls (1 658 km). Empty weight, 7,689 lb (3 488 kg). Max loaded weight, 11,652 lb (5 285 kg). Span, 40 ft 0 in (12,19 m). Length, 32 ft 4 in (9,85 m). Height, 13 ft 11 in (4,24 m). Wing area, 275 sq ft (25,54 m²).*

RYAN XF2R-1   USA

The XF2R-1 (above and below) utilised the 15th FR-1 airframe and differed essentially in having the Cyclone piston engine replaced by a turboprop.

A major modification of the FR-1 Fireball, the Model 29 resulted from a Bureau of Aeronautics requirement for a single-seat fighter combining a turboprop with a turbojet. Assigned the designation XF2R-1 and later to become known unofficially as the "Dark Shark", the single prototype utilised the fifteenth FR-1 production airframe and retained that fighter's J31-GE-3 turbojet, mated with a General Electric XT31-GE-2 turboprop developing 1,700 hp plus 500 lb (227 kg) of residual thrust. Although lacking the wing folding and the catapult and arrester gear standard on the FR-1, the XF2R-1 weighed 1,042 lb (473 kg) more than its predecessor when it flew for the first time in November 1946. The XT31 drove a propeller with four square-tipped hollow-steel blades which could be fully feathered or reversed to zero blade angle extremely rapidly, the drag of the flatter blade angle serving as an effective air brake for landing. By comparison with the FR-1, the vertical tail surfaces of the XF2R-1 were enlarged to compensate for the lengthening forward to accommodate the turboprop,

but the airframe of the later fighter was similar in most other respects. The XF2R-1 underwent extensive testing at Muroc Dry Lake, but no further development was undertaken. *Max speed, 497 mph (800 km/h) at sea level. Initial climb rate, 4,850 ft/min (24,64 m/sec). Service ceiling, 39,100 ft (11 920 m). Loaded weight, 11,000 lb (4 990 kg). Span, 42 ft 0 in (12,80 m). Length, 36 ft 0 in (10,97 m). Height, 14 ft 0 in (4,27 m). Wing area, 305 sq ft (28,33 m²).*

S

SAAB 21A   Sweden

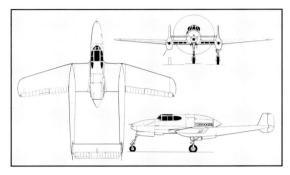

(Above) The J 21A twin-boom, pusher fighter.

Conceptually highly innovative, the Saab 21 single-seat fighter was designed by a team led by Frid Wänström at the Svenska Aeroplan AB. Powered by an aft-mounted 1,475 hp Daimler-Benz DB 605B 12-cylinder inverted-Vee engine driving a pusher propeller between twin tailbooms, the first of three prototypes flew on 30 July 1943. The initial production version was designated J 21A-1 by *Flygvapnet* and armament comprised one 20-mm cannon and four 13,2-mm machine guns. Production deliveries of the J 21A-1 commenced in July 1945, 54 being built. This model was followed by the J 21A-2 featuring internal changes, 124 being manufactured. The J 21A suffered heavy control forces and was prone to engine overheating which adversely affected climb and top speed. Considered obsolescent in the fighter rôle, it was adapted for the attack mission, a further 119 being delivered between May 1947 and January 1949 as A 21A-3s with provision for various external ordnance loads. The Saab 21 was the world's second fighter equipped with an ejection seat to attain operational service (the first being the He 219) and was

(Above) A J 21A-1 of *Flottilj* 9 which operated from Säve, Gothenburg, and (below) a preserved example in the markings of *Flottilj* 12 at Linköping.

configurationally unique among piston-engined production fighters. *Max speed 398 mph (640 km/h). Initial climb, 2,955 ft/min (15 m/sec). Max range, 932 mls (1 500 km). Empty weight, 7,165 lb (3 250 kg). Max loaded weight, 9,730 lb (4 413 kg). Span, 38 ft 1 in (11,61 m). Length, 34 ft 3 in (10,44 m). Height, 13 ft 1½ in (4,00 m). Wing area, 238.97 sq ft (22.20 m²).*

SAAB 21R   Sweden

(Above) A J 21R after reassignment to the Såtenäs-based *Flottilj* 7 for the attack task as the A 21R.

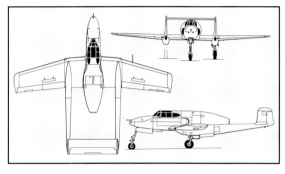

The J 21R (above and below), the photo depicting an aircraft of *Flottilj* 10 at Ängelholm in 1950.

The annals of aviation record only two fighter designs that achieved production and service with a piston engine and a turbojet successively, one of these being the Saab 21. In late 1945, a team led by Ragnar Härdmark began studying adaptation of the Saab 21 for the de Havilland Goblin turbojet. Four J 21A-1 airframes were assigned to the programme for conversion, these being designated J 21Rs, the first of these flying on 10 March 1947, and some 50 per cent of the original airframe being retained. The J 21R proved something less than a success, its critical Mach number and maximum speed virtually coinciding, and roll rate being low whilst its fuel capacity limited it to 40 min flying time. Procurement was consequently reduced from the planned 120 to 60 aircraft, 30 of these being J 21RAs powered by the 3,000 lb st (1 360 kgp) British-built Goblin II and the remaining 30 being J 21RBs with the SFA-built Goblin III of 3,305 lb st (1 500 kgp). Armament consisted of one 20-mm cannon and four 13,2-mm machine guns, with provision for an external pack of eight 8-mm machine guns or eight 14,5-cm rockets. The

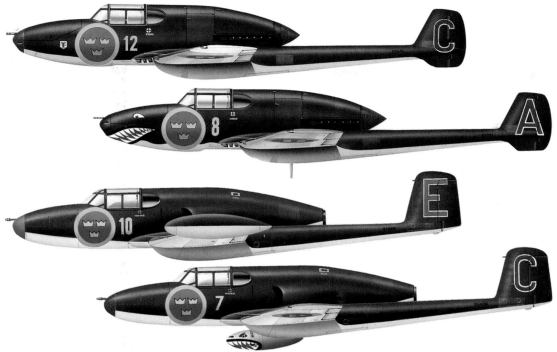

(Above, top) A J 21A-2 serving with *Flottilj* 12 at Kalmar, 1947, and (second from top) the second of the J 21A prototypes while being evaluated by *Flottilj* 8.

J 21R entered service at the beginning of 1950, but within a year the fighter was being relegated to the attack rôle as the A 21R and was finally withdrawn from service mid-1954. Data relate to the J 21RB. *Max speed, 497 mph (800 km/h). Initial climb, 3,346 ft/min (17 m/ sec). Empty weight, 6,861 lb (3 112 kg). Loaded weight, 11,096 lb (5 033 kg). Span, 37 ft 3¾ in (11,37 m). Length, 34 ft 7¾ in (10,56 m). Height, 9 ft 6¼ in (2,90 m). Wing area, 240.04 sq ft (22,30 m²).*

SAAB 29   Sweden

Europe's first swept-wing jet fighter to attain service, the Saab 29 was designed under the leadership of Lars Brising and the first of three prototypes was flown on 1 September 1948. Deliveries of the initial production version to *Flygvapnet* as the J 29A commenced on 10 May 1951, power being provided by an SFA-built de Havilland Ghost 50 (RM 2) turbojet of 5,005 lb st (2 270 kgp) and armament comprising four 20-mm cannon. A total of 224 of this version was built before production switched, in 1954, to the J 29B with drop tanks and external ordnance, 360 of these being built. In December 1953, one J 29A was flown with "dog-tooth" wing extensions, and, in March 1954, another was flown with an afterburner (as the Saab 29D). Twenty-nine aircraft were then retroactively fitted with the wing modification as J 29Es, and both afterburner and

J 29F fighters (below) of *Flottilj* 3 from Malmslätt in 1963 equipped with Rb 24 Sidewinder AAMs.

(Above, third from top) A J 21R in service with *Flottilj* 10 at Ängelholm, 1950, and (immediately above) an A 21R conversion of *Flottilj* 7 at Såtenäs.

(Above) A J 29A of *Flottilj* 13 at Norrköping in 1952, and (below) the definitive production series J 29F.

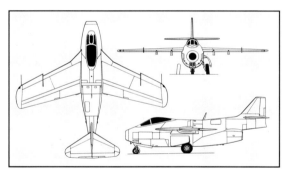

modified wing were fitted to the definitive version, the J 29F. The latter was powered by the RM 2B version of the Ghost rated at 6,173 lb st (2 800 kgp) with afterburning, and 308 J 29Fs were produced by conversion of J 29Bs and J 29Es. Production of the Saab 29 was

completed in March 1956, and the type was finally retired by *Flygvapen* on 29 August 1976. Thirty ex-*Flygvapen* J 29Fs were supplied to Austria 1961-64, serving until 1970-72. The following data relate to the J 29F. *Max speed, 659 mph (1 060 km/h). Time to 32,810 ft (10 000 m), 5.2 min. Range, 680 mls (1 100 km). Empty weight, 10,681 lb (4 845 kg). Max loaded weight, 18,463 lb (8 375 kg). Span, 36 ft 10¼ in (11,00 m). Length, 33 ft 6¾ in (10,23 m). Height, 12 ft 3⅔ in (3,75 m). Wing area, 259.96 sq ft (24,15 m²).*

A J 29F (below) of 1 *Staffel* of the Hörsching-based *Jagdbombergeschwader*, Austrian *Luftstreitkräfte*, 1961

SAAB 32B LANSEN   Sweden

Evolved from the Saab 32A Lansen (Lance) attack aircraft, the Saab 32B two-seat night and all-weather fighter embodied considerable internal structural redesign, new avionics, a more powerful engine and heavier cannon armament. The first of two prototypes was flown on 7 January 1957, and 118 were delivered to *Flygvapnet* as the J 32B between July 1958 and April 1960. The Saab 32B was powered by an SFA-built RM 6A (RB 90 Avon Mk 47A) engine of 10,560 lb st (4 790 kgp) boosted to 14,683 lb st (6 660 kgp) with afterburning. Armament comprised four 30-mm cannon with provision for four Rb 24 (Sidewinder) AAMs, and the Saab 32B was retired from operational service in 1973. *Max speed, 614 mph (988 km/h) at 36,000 ft (10 975 m), or Mach=0.93. Max climb, 19,685 ft/min (100 m/sec). Max range, 1,240 mls (2 000 km). Empty weight, 16,535 lb (7 500 kg). Max loaded weight, 29,762 lb (13 500 kg). Span, 42 ft 7¾ in (13,00 m). Length, 49 ft 0¼ in (14,94 m). Height, 15 ft 3 in (4,65 m). Wing area, 402.58 sq ft (37,40 m²).*

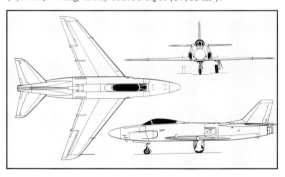

(Above and below) The J 32B Lansen, that illustrated by the photo belonging to *Flottilj* 12 based at Kalmar.

SAAB 35 DRAKEN   Sweden

Characterised by outstanding aerodynamic individuality, its double-delta wing geometry being unique, the Saab 35 Draken (Dragon) single-seat interceptor fighter was designed under the leadership of Erik Bratt. The first of three prototypes was flown on 25 October 1955, and the initial series model, designated J 35A by *Flygvapnet*, began to enter service in March 1960, 90 being built of which 25 were later converted to SK 35C trainers Equipped for conventional lead pursuit attack, this

A J 35A (above) with *Flottilj* 13 at Norrköping in 1963, in which it was succeeded by the J 35D (below) which featured an uprated engine.

Provision for radar- and IR-guided Falcon AAMs distinguished the J 35F seen (above) with *Flottilj* 13.

model was powered by the SFA-built RM 6B (RA.24 Avon Mk 48A) engine of 10,780 lb st (4 890 kgp) and 14,407 lb st (6 535 kgp) with afterburning, and was armed with two 30-mm cannon. The next model, the J 35B (72 built), was equipped for collision course attack with two 30-mm cannon and four Rb 24 (Sidewinder) AAMs, six being leased (and subsequently sold) to Finland in May 1972. The J 35D (120 built), which entered service from 1962, differed essentially in having an RM 6C (RB.146 Avon Mk 60) engine of 12,710 lb st (5 765 kgp) and 17,635 lb st (8 000 kgp) with afterburning, max speed being boosted from Mach=1.65 to Mach=2.0. Twenty-eight were converted for tactical recce as S 35Es and 24 were delivered to Austria (as Saab 35Ös) 1987-88. The definitive production model, the J 35F (230 built) delivered from 1965, featured upgraded avionics and provision for Falcon AAMs comprising two radar-guided Rb 27s and two IR-guided Rb 28s, with cannon armament reduced to a single weapon. Six ex-*Flygvapen* J 35Fs were sold to Finland to supplement 12 essentially similar Saab 35S Drakens assembled by Valmet in-country. Fifty-four J 35Fs were upgraded in 1988 to J 35J standard with avionics modifications and provision for additional external stores, all being redelivered by the end of 1989. A multi-rôle ex-

port version, the Saab 35X based on the Saab 35F airframe, was supplied to Denmark from 1970. Two singleseat versions were delivered, 20 as A 35XDs (F 35s) for both attack and intercept tasks, and 20 as S 35XDs (RF 35s) for tactical reconnaissance. The following data relate to the Saab 35F. *Max speed, 1,320 mph (2 124 km/h) at 36,090 ft (11 000 m), or Mach=2.0. Max climb, 34,450 ft/min (175 m/sec). Max range (with max external fuel), 2,020 mls (3 250 km). Empty weight, 17,339 lb (7 865 kg). Max loaded weight, 35,273 lb (16 000 kg). Span, 30 ft 10 in (9,42 m). Length, 50 ft 4 in (15,34 m). Height, 12 ft 9 in (3,89 m). Wing area, 529.82 sq ft (49,22 m²).*

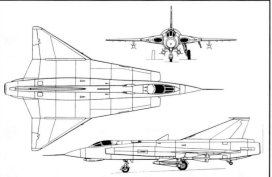

The J 35F (above) seen serving with *Flottilj* 13, introduced the Ericsson-built Hughes IR seeker.

The J 35F (below) and a Saab 35Ö (above) serving with 2. *Staffel* of the Austrian *Überwachungsgeschwader.*

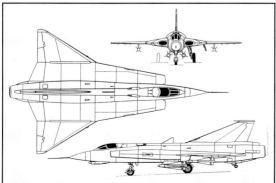

Key to Saab JA 37 Viggen

1 Dielectric nose cone
2 Radar scanner
3 PS-46/A radar pack
4 Avionics equipment
5 Forward pressure bulkhead
6 Avionics/electronics bay
7 Screen forward fairing
8 Canopy frame windscreen de-icing
9 One-piece windscreen assembly
10 Weapons sight
11 Fixed frame
12 Pilot's control column
13 Rudder pedal assembly
14 Control linkage
15 Fuselage skin panels
16 Nosewheel bay door
17 Twin nosewheels (forward retracting)
18 Nosewheel leg assembly
19 Nosewheel retraction strut linkage
20 Nosewheel bay
21 Nosewheel leg pivot
22 Control links/pulleys
23 Pilot's seat frame support
24 Pilot's ejection seat
25 Starboard intake lip
26 Hinged canopy
27 Headrest
28 Ejection seat guide rails/mechanism
29 Cockpit canopy hinges
30 Main fuselage fuel tank bay
31 Fuselage frame structures
32 Intake separator
33 Forward wing root fairing
34 Port intake
35 Intake duct frames
36 Low-vision light panels
37 Forward wing structure
38 Forward wing main spar
39 Fuselage/forward wing main attachment point
40 Engine oil coolers
41 Air conditioning bay
42 Radio equipment
43 Starboard forward wing
44 Flap hinge fairing
45 Honeycomb flap structure
46 Dorsal identification/recognition light
47 Cooling equipment bay
48 Cabin air outlet scoop
49 Cooling pipes
50 Coolers/blowers
51 Fuselage saddle fuel tanks
52 Forward wing aft attachment
53 Avionics bay
54 Ram-air turbine
55 Forward wing flap hinge fairing
56 Honeycomb flap structure
57 Hydraulic pump
58 Low-vision light panels (2)
59 Engine intake face
60 Fuselage upper main longeron
61 Fabricated fuselage frames
62 Volvo Flygmotor RM 8B turbofan
63 Skin panels
64 Dorsal auxiliary intake/outlet panel
65 Forged/machined main fuselage/wing frame member
66 Starboard wing skinning
67 Starboard wing fuel bay
68 Starboard ECM bullet
69 Leading-edge extension
70 Starboard outer elevon hinge
71 Starboard elevon
72 Pitot tube
73 Fin leading-edge extension
74 Tailfin structure
75 Tailfin forward spar
76 Fin spar/fuselage pick-up
77 Fuel lines
78 Gearbox pre-cooler installation
79 Wing root fairing
80 Wing main spar/fuselage attachment
81 Airbrake actuating ram
82 Fuselage port airbrake
83 Engine pipe
84 Afterburner assembly
85 Thrust-reverser aperture
86 Reverser lids
87 Lid actuating ram
88 Aft fuselage frame
89 Linkage
90 Tailfin aft attachment
91 Rudder operating ram
92 Rudder post
93 Tailfin leading edge
94 Tip extension
95 VHF antenna
96 Honeycomb rudder structure
97 Rudder
98 Rudder operating ram fairing
99 Blade antenna
100 Tail fairing
101 Tail fairing formers
102 Tail navigation light
103 Fuselage aft fairing
104 Tailplane exhaust
105 Inner elevon actuator fairings
106 Honeycomb elevon (inner)
107 Elevon outer fairing
108 Honeycomb elevon (outer)
109 Inner structure
110 Outboard leading-edge extension
111 Port outer weapons pylon
112 Port ECM bullet
113 Wing structure
114 Outer actuator ram
115 Inner actuator ram

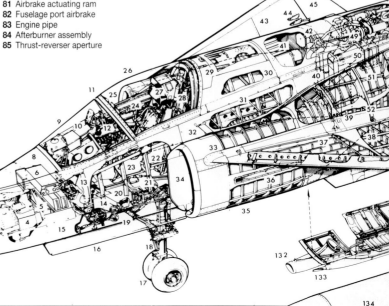

SAAB 37 VIGGEN Sweden

Of unusual close-coupled canard delta configuration, the Saab 37 Viggen (Thunderbolt) was designed to conform with the "standard platform" concept: a basic airframe suited for a number of rôles, each version being mission-optimised. The initial model, assigned the *Flygvapen* designation AJ 37, was essentially a single-seat attack aircraft, the extensively re-engineered "second generation" JA 37 being optimised for the interceptor fighter task and featuring a more powerful engine and new systems and weaponry. The first series JA 37 was flown on 4 November 1977, following six R&D Viggens each testing various features of the fighter variant. One hundred and forty-nine JA 37s were ordered, deliveries commencing in 1979 with final

(Below) The JA 37 optimised fighter Viggen variant.

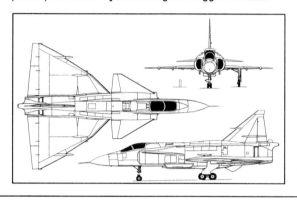

delivery June 1990. They were used to equip eight squadrons in the F4, F13, F16, F17 and F21 *flottiljer* (wings). The JA 37 was powered by a Volvo RM 8B turbofan affording 16,200 lb st (7 350 kgp) boosted to 28,110 lb st (12 750 kgp) with maximum afterburning. Armament comprised one 30-mm cannon and two Rb 71 (Sky Flash) and two or four Rb 24 (Sidewinder) AAMs. *Max speed, 1,365 mph (2 195 km/h) at 36,090 ft (11 000 m), or Mach=2.1. Time to 32,810 ft (10 000 m), 1.4 min. Normal loaded weight, 37,040 lb (16 800 kg). Span, 341t 9¼ in (10,60 m). Length, 53ft 9¾ in (16,40 m). Height, 19 ft 4¼ in (5,90 m). Wing area (including foreplane) 561.89 sq ft (52,20 m²).*

In "air superiority grey", a JA 37 from *Flottilj* 13 at Norrköping (above) displays primary AAM armament. (Below) A JA 37 Viggen from *Flottilj* 17 from Ronneby.

116 Port wing integral fuel bay
117 Wing ribs
118 Wing skin panels
119 Inner honeycomb panels
120 Undercarriage support rib member
121 Machined wing main spar
122 Wheel well diagonal member
123 Mainwheel leg pivot
124 Mainwheel retraction strut
125 Port wheel well
126 Inboard leading-edge structure
127 Undercarriage inner door
128 Oerlikon 30-mm KCA revolver gun ventral pack
129 Ammunition feed
130 Gun support frame
131 Access panels
132 Cooling air
133 Muzzle fairing
134 Ventral auxiliary drop tank
135 Tandem mainwheels
136 Axle fork assembly
137 Torque links
138 Mainwheel oleo leg
139 Leg door (outer)
140 Wing inner weapons pylon
141 BAe Sky Flash air-to-air missile
142 AIM-9L Sidewinder air-to-air missile

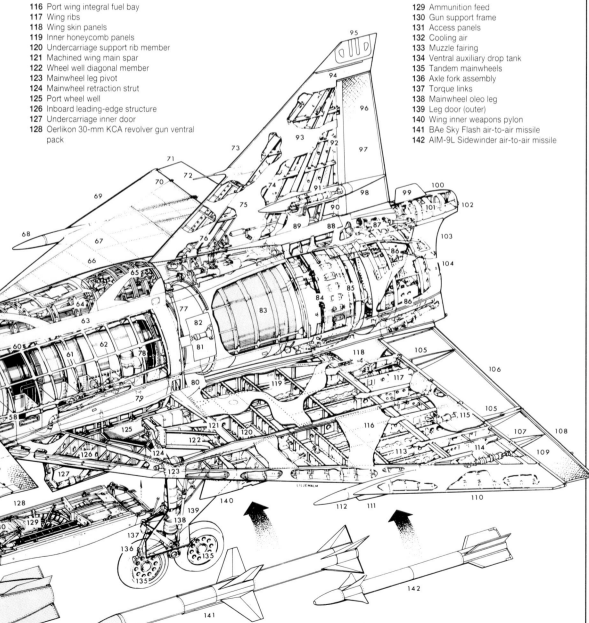

SAAB IG JAS 39 GRIPEN Sweden

In 1980, *Industri Gruppen JAS* was formed to develop Gripen, a multirole fighter, hence JAS *(Jakt/Attack/Spåning)* fighter/attack /reconnaissance to replace Viggen while combining affordability with capability. A small close-coupled canard delta, it is powered by a single Volvo Flygmotor RM 12, developed from the F404-GE-400, rated at 18,105 lb (8 212 kgp) max and 12,141 lb (5 507 kgp) military thrust. Its small size demanded compromises; these took the form of fixed side intakes rather than a chin inlet, and a mid-position wing to allow clearance for stores. The wing is almost entirely of composite construction, and a leading edge dogtooth protects against spanwise flow. Composites are widely used elsewhere in the structure. The obligatory short landing run is achieved with a combination of efficient brakes, speed brakes on the aft fuselage, and deflection of the canards. "Glass cockpit" displays with HOTAS are used, and radar is the Ericsson PS-05/A multi-mode. Stig Holmstrom took Gripen aloft for the first time on 9 December 1988. Problems were encountered with the triplex digital

The JAS 39 Gripen (above and below), the photo showing the first series aircraft, flown 10 September 1992.

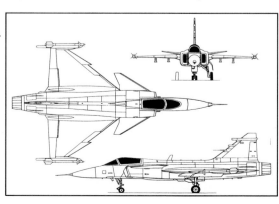

First flown in March 1991, the JAS 39 Gripen No 3 (above) was the first complete systems prototype.

FBW system, resulting in two crashes, and this was not rectified until 1995. Initial operational capability was achieved late in 1997, and by the end of 2000 about 100 Gripens had entered service. Sweden has ordered 176 single-seater JAS 39As and 28 two-seater Bs. Weaponry consists of a 27-mm Mauser BK 27 cannon, two Skyflash or Amraam, and four Sidewinders. An upgraded version, the JAS 39C/D with a more powerful engine and a flight refuelling probe, is expected to enter service between 2003 and 2006. South Africa, with an order for 28 aircraft, is the first export customer. *Max speed hi, Mach 1.8. Max speed lo, "supersonic". Operational ceiling, 50,000 ft (15 239 m). Rate of climb, c50,000 ft/min (254 m/sec). Empty weight, c12,346 lb (15 600 kg). Normal takeoff weight, c19,224 lb (8 720 kg). Span, 27 ft 7in (8.40 m). Length 46 ft 3 in (14,10 m). Height, 14 ft 9 in (4,50 m). Wing area, c275 sq ft (25,54 m²).*

SAB 1   France

After resigning as a director of SPAD (Société Pour Aviation et ses Dérivés), Louis Béchereau established SAB (Société et Ateliers Béchereau) and was joined in designing a single-seat fighter by Bernard, Blériot and Birkigt. This, the SAB 1, was built by Avions Pierre Levasseur, and was a somewhat corpulent two-bay biplane powered by a 300 hp Hispano-Suiza 8Fb watercooled eight-cylinder engine. Flight testing was initiated during 1918 in competition with the Nieuport 29, five examples being built. Selection of the Nieuport fighter by the *Aviation Militaire* resulted in discontinuation of further development of the SAB fighter. *Max speed, 130 mph (210 km/h). Time to 6,560 ft (2 000 m), 5.78 min. Empty weight, 1,726 lb (783 kg). Loaded weight, 2,474 lb (1 122 kg). Span, 30 ft 6¹/₈ in (9,30 m). Length, 22 ft 7⁵/₈ in (6,90 m). Height, 8ft 4¹/₃ in (2,55 m). Wing area, 311.09 sq ft (28,90 m²).*

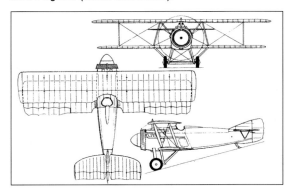

Five examples were built for testing in 1918 of the SAB 1 fighter (above and below).

SABLATNIG SF 3   Germany

Designed by the Sablatnig-Flugzeugbau of Berlin to meet a requirement for a two-seat fighter for escort and

offensive patrols, the SF 3 was a large twin-float, two-bay biplane, a single prototype of which was flown in 1916. Powered by a 200 hp Benz Bz IV six-cylinder water-cooled engine with a "rhino horn" type exhaust pipe and lateral ear-type radiators, the SF 3 had a ply-covered fuselage and an armament of one fixed forward-firing 7,9-mm LMG 08/15 machine gun and a swivelling Parabellum in the rear cockpit. The SF 3 displayed unsatisfactory characteristics and development was discontinued. No further details are recorded.

The sole prototype of the SF 3 escort fighter (below) proved to possess unsatisfactory characteristics.

SABLATNIG SF 4   Germany

A *Marineflieger* demand for a single-seat waterborne fighter for offensive patrol and seaplane station defence resulted in the design of the SF 4, one of five such types ordered for prototype evaluation in June 1916. The SF 4, of which two examples were ordered, was powered by a 150 hp Benz Bz III six-cylinder water-cooled engine. The first prototype, delivered on 17 February 1917, was an unequal-span staggered single-bay biplane with twin floats. The X-type interplane struts and the small inverted V-type struts (the latter

Only one prototype of the SF 4 was completed in biplane configuration (above and below).

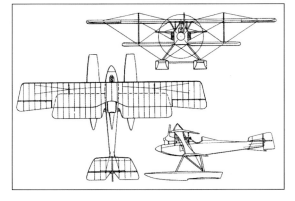

Elegant appearance belied the poor manoeuvrability displayed by the SF 4 biplane.

providing anchorage points above the upper wing for bracing) were faired by fabric. The first prototype proved to possess poor manoeuvrability and the Sablatnig-Flugzeugbau elected to undertake major redesign and to complete the second SF 4 as a triplane (which see). The SF 4 had an armament of one synchronised 7,9-mm LMG 08/15 machine gun. *Max speed, 98 mph (158 km/h) at sea level. Time to 3,280 ft (1,000 m), 5.5 min. Empty weight, 1,742 lb (790 kg). Loaded weight, 2,359 lb (1 070 kg). Span, 39 ft 4³/₈ in (12,00 m). Length, 27 ft 4 in (8,33 m). Height, 12 ft 2⁷/₈ in (3,73 m). Wing area, 304.2 sq ft (28,26 m²).*

SABLATNIG SF 4Dʀ   Germany

The poor manoeuvrability demonstrated by the first prototype of the SF 4 biplane led to major redesign, the second prototype being completed as an equi-span triplane. This, the SF 4Dr, retained the Bz III engine and single-gun armament of the first prototype, together with the fuselage structure and floats. The interplane and cabane struts were of broad-chord I-type and the tail surfaces were entirely redesigned. No details of the results achieved during flight testing of the SF 4Dr have survived and no further examples were built. *Span, 30 ft 4¹/₈ in (9,25 m). Length, 27 ft 4 in (8,33 m). Wing area, 305.49 sq ft (28,38 m²).*

The second example of the SF 4 was completed as a triplane (below), but showed little improvement.

SABLATNIG SF 7   Germany

When the *Marineflieger* formulated a requirement for a longer-range two-seat waterborne fighter, the Sablatnig-Flugzeugbau developed the SF 7 in competition with the Friedrichshafen FF 48 and the Brandenburg W 19, three prototypes of each being ordered in April 1917. The SF 7 was a two-bay twin-float biplane with I-type interplane struts and rigid diagonal struts bracing the inboard wire-less bay. Power was provided by a six-cylinder water-cooled Maybach Mb IV engine of 240 hp and armament consisted of a single fixed 7,9-mm LMG 08/15 machine gun and a Parabellum on a flexible

Three examples of the SF 7 (below) built in 1917 were accepted by the *Marineflieger* for evaluation.

mounting in the rear cockpit. The SF 7s were accepted by the Navy in September 1917, but comparative trials with the W 19 proved the superiority of the Brandenburg design, which was selected to fulfil the requirement. *Max speed, 101 mph (164 km/h) at sea level. Ceiling, 14,765 ft (4 500 m). Range, 466 mls (750 km). Empty weight, 3,433 lb (1 557 kg). Loaded weight, 4,665 lb (2 116 kg). Span, 51 ft 0½ in (15,58 m). Length, 30 ft 2¼ in (9,20 m). Height, 12 ft 1⅔ in (3,70 m). Wing area, 571.9 sq ft (53,13 m²).*

SAGE TYPE 2 UK

Designed by Clifford W Tinson for Frederick Sage & Company, the Type 2 two-seat fighting scout was of original concept. Considerable care was taken to reduce aerodynamic drag, the 100 hp Gnome Monosoupape nine-cylinder rotary engine being fully cowled, a large propeller spinner being provided and the crew being accommodated in a fully-glazed cabin. Of conventional wire-braced wooden construction, the Type 2 was a single-bay biplane with considerable gap, the upper wing being supported by the cabin structure and having an aperture above the observer's seat. When standing to fire his 0.303-in (7,7-mm) machine gun, the observer had a wide and clear field of fire. Remarkably small, the Type 2 had rod-activated ailerons in the upper wing only. First flown on 10 August 1916, it proved to possess a very good performance, but gun synchronization had meanwhile become available, and after the sole prototype had been wrecked in a forced landing on 20 September 1916, no attempt was made to rebuild the aircraft or develop it. *Max speed, 112 mph (180 km/h) at sea level. Time to 10,000 ft (3 050 m), 14.75 min. Endurance, 2.5 hrs. Empty weight, 890 lb (404 kg). Loaded weight, 1,546 lb (701 kg). Span, 22 ft 2½ in (6,77 m). Length, 21 ft 1⅝ in (6,45 m). Height, 9 ft 6 in (2,89 m). Wing area, 168 sq ft (15,61 m²).*

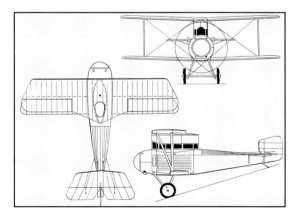

Very short wings and fully enclosed cockpits were featured by the two-seat Sage 2 (above and below).

S.A.I. (AMBROSINI) S.S.4 Italy

The first fighter monoplane of canard or tail-first configuration and one of the first with a retractable nosewheel undercarriage, the single-seat S.S.4 designed by Ing Sergio Stefanutti and built by the Società Aeronautica Italiana Ing A Ambrosini was among the most innovative warplanes of its time. Of all-metal construction and powered by a 960 hp liquid-cooled 12-cylinder Isotta-Fraschini Asso XI R.C.40 engine driving a three-bladed variable-pitch pusher propeller, the S.S.4 had a proposed armament of one 30-mm and twin 20-mm cannon. The sole prototype was flown for the first time

The canard layout of the single-seat S.S.4, (above and below), with a pusher propeller, rendered it highly unusual among piston-engined fighters.

on 7 March 1939, but was destroyed during its second flight on the following day, when, after the starboard aileron separated, the wing developed a high amplitude oscillation and the aircraft entered a dive and crashed. No further development was undertaken. The following data are based on manufacturer's estimates. *Max speed, 335 mph (540 km/h) at 16,405 ft (5 000 m). Empty weight, 3,968 lb (1 800 kg). Loaded weight, 5,392 lb (2 446 kg). Span, 40 ft 5 in (12,32 m). Length, 22 ft 1½ in (6,74 m). Height, 8 ft 1¾ in (2,48 m). Wing area, 188.37 sq ft (17,50 m²).*

The S.A.I. Ambrosini S.S.4 (below) flew only twice.

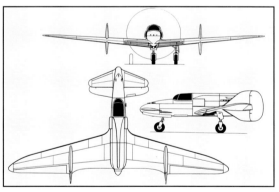

S.A.I. (AMBROSINI) S.107 Italy

The potentialities of the wooden lightweight single-seat fighter were under investigation in several countries during the late 1930s, an Italian proponent of the concept being Ing Sergio Stefanutti. Working at the Società Aeronautica Italiana of Ing Angelo Ambrosini, Stefanutti developed the S.107 lightweight fighter from the S.7 tandem two-seat aerobatic trainer and competition aircraft. This was flown for the first time early

An outgrowth of the S.7 trainer, the S.107 is shown (below) in original form with elongated windscreen.

in 1940, and was powered by a 515 hp Isotta-Fraschini Gamma R.C.35-I 12-cylinder inverted-Vee air-cooled engine. It carried an armament of one 7,7-mm machine gun. As initially flown, the S.107 was fitted with a long, faired windscreen extending over the engine in an attempt to reduce aerodynamic drag. As this elongated transparency was found to impair vision from the cockpit it was replaced by an orthodox stepped windscreen. Outstanding performance was demonstrated at Guidonia, and progressive development of the basic design led to the S.207, the sole example of the S.107 being lost meantime in an accident on 18 July 1941. *Max speed, 311 mph (500 km/h) at 15,750 ft (4 800 m). Time to 19,685 ft (6 000 m), 8.0 min. Range, 497 mls (800 km). Empty weight, 2,822 lb (1 280 kg). Loaded weight, 3,527 lb (1 600 kg). Span, 29 ft 3⅓ in (9,00 m). Length, 26 ft 3 in (8,00 m). Height, 7 ft 10½ in (2,40 m). Wing area, 141 sq ft (13,10 m²).*

Good results were obtained with the S.107 (below) after it had received a conventional windscreen.

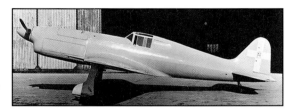

S.A.I. (AMBROSINI) S.207 Italy

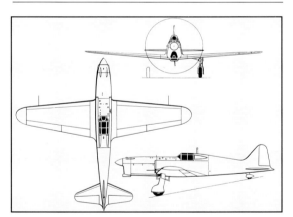

The S.207 (above) evolved from the S.107 in 1940.

Evolved from the S.107 lightweight single-seat fighter and featuring a similar wooden structure with monocoque fuselage, the S.207 was essentially a more powerful, productionised version of the basic design. The first of two prototypes of the S.207 was flown in the autumn of 1940, and was powered by an Isotta-Fraschini Delta R.C.35 12-cylinder inverted-Vee air-cooled engine rated at 705 hp, this giving place in the second prototype to the R.C.40 version of the engine rated at 750 hp at 13,125 ft (4 000 m). Armament comprised two synchronised 12,7-mm machine guns, and a pre-series of 12 S.207s was built during March-July 1943, several of these being assigned to the 83ª *Squadriglia* (18° *Gruppo*, 3° *Stormo*) for evaluation, and six being assigned in August 1943 to the 162ª and 163ª *squadriglie* (161° *Gruppo*). These demonstrated excellent handling characteristics and outstanding manoeuvrability, prompting the *Ministero dell'Aeronautica* to order 2,000 S.207s. In the event, this contract was to be

Planned large scale production of the S.207 (above) was overtaken by development of the S.403.

overtaken by an order for a progressive development of the fighter, the S.403 Dardo. One pre-series S.207 was fitted with an armament of two 20-mm cannon. The following data relate to the pre-series S.207. *Max speed, 388 mph (625 km/h) at 16,405 ft (5 000 m). Time to 6,560 ft (2 000 m), 2.1 min. Range, 528 mls (850 km). Empty weight, 3,858 lb (1 750 kg). Max loaded weight, 5,324 lb (2 415 kg). Span, 29 ft 6⅓ in (9,00 m). Length, 26 ft 3¾ in (8,02 m). Height, 7 ft 10½ in (2,40 m). Wing area, 149.62 sq ft (13,90 m²).*

S.A.I. (AMBROSINI) S.403 DARDO   Italy

The ultimate development of the Stefanutti-designed wooden lightweight fighter, the S.403 Dardo (Dart), which flew for the first time in January 1943, differed from the S.207 in having a new wing profile, redesigned tail surfaces – the incidence of the tailplane being variable in flight – a redesigned rear fuselage, a fully-retractable tailwheel, provision for wing guns and a more robust structure. The S.403 was powered by an Isotta-Fraschini R.C.21/60 engine of 750 hp, and three series production versions were proposed: a light point defence interceptor with armament restricted to a pair of 12,7-mm machine guns; a general-purpose fighter with the machine guns complemented by a pair of wing-mounted 20-mm cannon, and a long-range version with provision for two external tanks to extend its range to 1,384 mls (2 227 km). Orders were placed for 3,000 examples of the S.403 (an earlier order for 2,000

The sole example of the S.403 (above and below), production being thwarted by the 1943 Armistice.

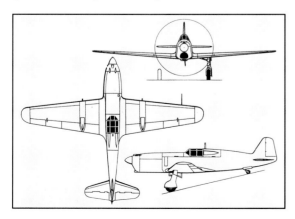

S.207s being cancelled as a consequence) of which 800 were to be built by the parent company, the Società Aeronautica Italiana (S.A.I.), 1,000 by Caproni and 1,200 by SIAI-Marchetti. This programme was thwarted by the Armistice, and, apart from the prototype, no S.403s were completed. The following data relate to the prototype. *Max speed, 403 mph (648 km/h) at 23,620 ft (7 200 m). Time to 19,685 ft (6 000 m), 6.66 min. Range, 582 mls (937 km). Empty weight, 4,372 lb (1 983 kg). Loaded weight, 5,820 lb (2 640 kg). Span, 32 ft 1¾ in (9,80 m). Length, 26 ft 10¾ in (8,20 m). Height, 9 ft 6 in (2,90 m). Wing area, 155.65 sq ft (14,46 m²).*

SALMSON 3   France

Engine-maker Salmson designed the Sal 3 fighter (above and below) to make use of the company's unusual Salmson 9Z water-cooled radial engine.

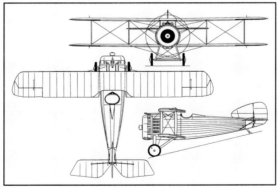

In the autumn of 1917, Société des Moteurs Salmson designed a single-seat fighter powered by the unusual Salmson 9Z nine-cylinder water-cooled radial engine successfully employed for the Sal 2 A2 two-seat reconnaissance aircraft. This, the Sal 3, was undergoing testing, according to an official report, on 1 December 1917, which commented "Visibility bad in all directions and fatiguing to fly." A two-bay equi-span biplane, the Sal 3 fighter was at Villacoublay in January 1918 with a 230 hp Salmson 9Za engine "having its radiator fitted", suggesting that modifications had been made to the design. Despite the initially unfavourable official opinion of this type, the makers persevered, and although the Sal 3 was not accepted for series production, it was listed in an October 1918 data chart of "New experimental aeroplanes", this indicating that the Sal 3

then had a 260 hp Salmson 9Zm engine. Armament comprised two 7,7-mm Vickers guns. No subsequent development was undertaken. The following data relate to the fighter with the higher-powered engine. *Max speed, 134 mph (215 km/h) at 6,560 ft (2 000 m). Time to 6,560 ft (2 000 m), 5.73 min. Empty weight, 1,537 lb (697 kg). Loaded weight, 2,264 lb (1 027 kg). Span, 32 ft 3⅘ in (9,85 m). Length, 21 ft 0 in (6,40 m). Height, 8 ft 1⅔ in (2,48 m). Wing area, 257.69 sq ft (23,94 m²).*

SALMSON-BECHEREAU 5   France

With the appointment of Louis Béchereau as chief designer, the Salmson company resumed aircraft construction in 1925 with a prototype for participation in the C2 two-seat fighter programme of that year. This, the Salmson-Béchereau 5, or SB5, adhered closely to the concept of the single-seat Buscaylet-Béchereau 2 single-seat fighter, being a heavily-braced, shoulder-wing monoplane of wooden construction powered by a 520 hp Salmson 18Cmb water-cooled 18-cylinder radial engine which drove the propeller via a 3 ft 3⅓ in (1,00 m) extension shaft. The wing featured three degrees of anhedral, and an additional aerofoil of 48.44 sq ft (4,50 m²) area enclosing the undercarriage axle contributed substantially to total lift. Provision was made for an armament of two fixed forward-firing 7,7-mm machine guns and two similar weapons on a flexible mount in the rear cockpit. Unsatisfactory handling characteristics resulted in a number of modifications, the prototype re-appearing in the summer of 1926 as the SB6. *Max speed, 138 mph (223 km/h) at 9,840 ft (3 000 m). Range, 373 mls (600 km). Empty weight, 3,053 lb (1 385 kg). Loaded weight, 4,828 lb (2 190 kg). Span, 45 ft 11⅓ in (14,00 m). Length, 32 ft 9⁷⁄₁₀ in (10,00 m). Height, 9 ft 10 in (3,00 m). Wing area, 430.57 sq ft (40,00 m²).*

SALMSON-BECHEREAU 6 (S.R.A.P. 2)   France

The designation SB6 was assigned to the modified SB5 prototype when it resumed flight test in the summer of 1926. Apart from modifications to the wing, which included extension of the ailerons along the entire wing trailing edge and a reduction in the size of the trailing edge cutout above the forward cockpit, the SB6 had a shorter extension shaft from the Salmson 18Cmb engine. During trials at Villacoublay, the SB6 took 43 min to attain an altitude of 22,965 ft (7 000 m), and this, coupled with a sea level max speed of 132 mph (212 km/h), was adjudged insufficient to meet the requirements of the programme which was, itself, to be abandoned subsequently. A naval version, the SB7,

The Béchereau-designed SB6 (above) was a modification of the SB5, later becoming the S.R.A.P.2.

was projected, featuring two abbreviated stepless floats outboard of the mainwheels and projecting ahead of the fuselage, but construction of a prototype was discontinued with the departure from Salmson of Louis Béchereau who then formed the S.R.A.P. (Société pour la Réalisation d'Avions Prototypes). This organisation exhibited the SB6 in December 1926 at the Paris *Salon de l'Aéronautique* under the designation S.R.A.P.2, but further development was discontinued with the termination of the C2 programme in which it had been designed to participate. *Max speed, 137 mph (220 km/h) at 9,840 ft (3 000 m). Time to 9,840 ft (3 000 m), 9.0 min. Empty weight, 3,435 lb (1 558 kg). Loaded weight, 5,203 lb (2 360 kg). Span, 47 ft 10⅘ in (14,60 m). Length, 31 ft 9⅞ in (9,70 m). Height, 9 ft 10 in (3,00 m). Wing area, 376.75 sq ft (35,00 m²).*

SAUNDERS A.10   UK

Having specialised in flying boats for a decade, in 1926 S E Saunders Limited began the design of a land-based single-seat all-metal fighter sesquiplane. This, the A.10 proposal, featured what was, for its time, the unusually heavy armament of four 0.303-in (7,7-mm) machine guns, power being provided by a 480 hp Rolls-Royce F.XI 12-cylinder Vee-type engine. After revising the design in 1927 to comply with Specification F.20/27, Saunders built a prototype which flew on 27 January 1929. Possessing an all-metal structure with fabric covering and all four guns located in the fuselage, the A.10 suffered handling and performance shortcomings which led to numerous modifications, including fuselage lengthening. It was assessed at the A&AEE against other F.20/27 contenders and also for F.10/27 (which called for six-gun armament), but it aroused little enthusiasm and was struck off Air Ministry charge in November 1933 – by which time its manufacturer had become Saunders-Roe Limited. *Max speed, 200 mph (322 km/h) at 18,500 ft (5 640 m). Ceiling, 29,000 ft (8 840 m). Empty weight, 2,674 lb (1 213 kg). Loaded weight, 3,600 lb (1 633 kg). Span, 32 ft 0 in (9,75 m). Length, 24 ft 5 in (7,44 m). Height, 9 ft 9 in (2,97 m). Wing area, 273 sq ft (25,36 m²).*

Little success attended the first venture into fighter design by Saunders, the A.10 (above and below).

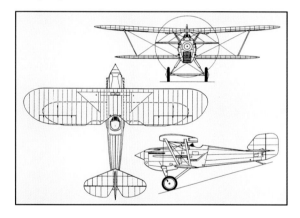

SAUNDERS-ROE SR.A/1   UK

Conceived as a means of applying the promised advantages of jet propulsion to a single-seat fighter flying boat for use in the Pacific, the SR.44 was proposed by Saunders-Roe (Saro) during 1943. This proposal led to a contract for three prototypes being placed in May 1944 to Specification E.6/44. To be designated SR.A/1 before first flight, the fighter was of light alloy construction throughout, power being provided by two Metropolitan Vickers F2/4 Beryl turbojets and provision being made for an armament of four 20-mm cannon grouped in the forward hull above the air intake. The first SR.A/1 did not fly until 16 July 1947, its Beryl turbojets each

Three prototypes were built of the Saro SR.A/1 (below), a single-seat fighter flying boat.

The first SR.A1 (above) and a drawing (below) showing the later modification to reinforce the cockpit canopy.

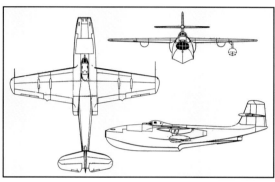

being rated at 3,230 lb st (1 465 kgp). The second flew on 30 April 1948 with 3,500 lb st (1 587 kgp) Beryls and the third followed on 17 August of that year with fully-rated Beryls of 3,850 lb st (1 746 kgp). As no operational requirement remained for a fighter flying boat, official interest waned, and, after a brief revival of interest during the Korean War, the last surviving SR.A/1 was retired in June 1951. *Max speed, 512 mph (824 km/h). Max initial climb, 5,800 ft/min (29,5 m/sec). Max endurance, 2.4 hrs. Empty weight, 11,262 lb (5 108 kg). Max loaded weight, 19,033 lb (8 633 kg). Span, 46 ft 0 in (14,02 m). Length, 50 ft 0 in (15,24 m). Height, 16 ft 9 in (5,11 m). Wing area, 415 sq ft (38,60 m²).*

SAUNDERS-ROE SR.53   UK

In the forefront of British rocket propulsion studies by 1952, Saunders-Roe produced a design, the SR.53, for a single-seat target defence interceptor combining a liquid-fuel rocket motor with an auxiliary turbojet. Submitted to meet the requirements of Specification F.124T, the SR.53 was recipient of a three-prototype contract in October 1952. Of clipped delta wing configuration with a specified armament of two wingtip-mounted Blue Jay (de Havilland Firestreak) AAMs, the SR.53 was powered by an 8,000 lb st (3 629 kgp) de Havilland Spectre HTP rocket and a 1,640 lb st (744 kgp) Armstrong Siddeley Viper turbojet superimposed one above the other in the rear fuselage. In the event, only two of the SR.53s were to be completed, these making their initial flights on 16 May and 8

Carrying Firestreak AAMs at the wingtips, the Saro SR.53 (below) used a clipped delta layout.

December 1957, prior to which, in April 1957, all rocket-powered fighter development in the UK had been cancelled. Nonetheless, the two SR.53s performed 42 test flights before, on 15 June 1958, the second aircraft crashed, the surviving aircraft then being permanently grounded. *Max speed, 1,320 mph (2 135 km/h) above 36,000 ft (10 975 m), or Mach=2.0. Time to 50,000 ft (15 240 m), 2.2 min. Empty weight, 7,400 lb (3 357 kg). Max loaded weight, 19,000 lb (8 618 kg). Span, 25 ft 1¼ in (7,65 m). Length, 45 ft 0 in (13,72 m). Height, 10 ft 10 in (3,29 m). Wing area, 274 sq ft (25,45 m²).*

The SR.53 (above and below) was the result of brief British interest in the potential of rocket propulsion.

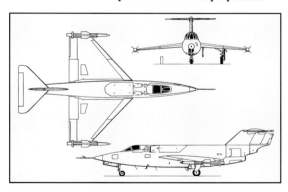

SCHNEIDER D-Typ   Germany

The Franz Schneider Flugmaschinen-Werke was established in January 1917 by Franz Schneider for aircraft repair and servicing. Schneider had been associated with Edouard Nieuport prior to World War I and was subsequently responsible for the design of a num-

Few records have survived of the diminutive Schneider fighter (below), tested in 1918.

ber of LVG types. In 1918, Schneider designed and built a single-seat fighter powered by a 200 hp Goebel Goe III nine-cylinder rotary engine and carrying an armament of two 7,9-mm LMG 08/15 machine guns. Of conventional appearance, this fighter was unusual in having a patented arrangement of variable-incidence wings. A single-bay equi-span biplane with ailerons on the lower wings, the Schneider fighter allegedly demonstrated good climb and manoeuvrability, and was reportedly to have been fitted with an innovative arrangement whereby the engine could be tilted several degrees in flight, although there is no record of such an installation having been made. No specification for the Schneider fighter has survived.

Variable wing incidence was an innovative feature of the single Schneider fighter (below).

SCHÜTTE-LANZ D I   Germany

The Luftfahrzeugbau Schütte-Lanz produced, in 1915, what was subsequently claimed to be the first German single-seat *biplane* fighter. Designed by Dipl-Ing W Hillmann and Walter Stein, this, the D I, was a lightweight single-bay staggered biplane which had apparently found its inspiration in the Sopwith Tabloid. Of wooden construction throughout with fabric skinning, it was powered by an 80 hp Oberursel (Gnome) seven-cylinder rotary engine, but was rejected by the *Idflieg* on the grounds that the biplane afforded inferior pilot vision to the monoplane and was therefore unsuited for the single-seat fighter rôle. Hillmann and Stein introduced some redesign and installed a 100 hp Mercedes six-cylinder water-cooled engine to result in the D II, which, in the event, was never flown. *Max speed, 84 mph (135 km/h) at sea level. Span, 24 ft 7¼ in (7,50 m). Length, 17 ft 8⅔ in (5,40 m).*

Built in 1915, the Schütte-Lanz D I (below) was the first fighter biplane tested in Germany.

SCHÜTTE-LANZ D III   Germany

Designed to participate in the first D-type contest organised by the *Idflieg* at Adlershof, which took place between 20 January and 12 February 1918, the D III was a conventional single-bay staggered biplane with N-type interplane struts. Armament comprised two 7,9-mm LMG 08/15 machine guns and power was provided by a 160 hp Mercedes D III six-cylinder inline water-cooled engine, an unusual feature being the use of an individual exhaust pipe for each cylinder, an aerofoil-shaped radiator being offset to port in the upper wing centre section. Of wooden construction with fabric skinning, the D III revealed an unspectacular performance, and, during the D-type contest, on 25 January, recorded climbing times of 3.0 min to 3,280 ft (1 000 m) and 31.9 min to 16,405 ft (5 000 m). *Max speed,*

Thoroughly conventional, the D III (above and below) proved unspectacular when tested in 1918.

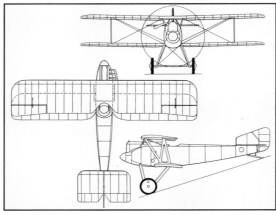

121 mph (195 km/h). Loaded weight, 1,896 lb (860 kg). Span, 26 ft 3 in (8,00 m). Length, 21 ft 3⁹⁄₁₀ in (6,50 m).

SCHÜTTE-LANZ D IV   Germany

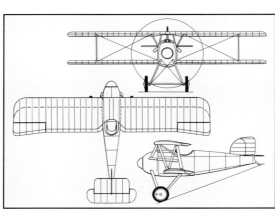

(Above) The D IV with Benz Bz IIIbo engine.

Built in parallel with the D III, but possessing no commonality, the D IV was powered by a 220 hp Benz Bz IIIbo eight-cylinder Vee-type water-cooled engine and carried an armament of two 7,9-mm LMG 08/15 machine guns. Of wooden construction, it was a single-bay staggered biplane with N-type interplane struts and ailerons on both upper and lower mainplanes. Flown late in 1917, the D IV was found to posses a performance inferior to that of the D III and was therefore withdrawn as a contender in the D-type contest. A second prototype, the D IVa, differed in having a frontal radiator for the Benz engine, shallower underside fuselage contours which did not project below the lower wing, a redesigned undercarriage and revised cabane struts. A further development of the basic design, the D V, was intended to be powered by the 160 hp Mercedes D III engine fitted with a Brown Boveri compressor. Difficulties with this compressor resulted in work on the

D V being discontinued by May 1918. *Time to 16,405 ft (5 000 m), 14.0 min. Empty weight, 1,532 lb (695 kg). Loaded weight, 1,951 lb (885 kg). Span, 29 ft 6⅓ in (9,00 m). Length, 19 ft 0¼ in (5,80 m). Wing area, 247.15 sq ft (22,96 m²).*

The D IV (below) awaiting installation of its Bz IIIbo engine in March 1918.

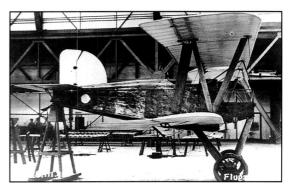

SCHÜTTE-LANZ Dr I   Germany

The operational début of the Sopwith triplane on the Western Front in the spring of 1917 aroused considerable interest in this configuration within the *Idflieg* which immediately encouraged the development of conceptually similar fighters by the German industry. Among single-seat fighter triplanes submitted as a re-

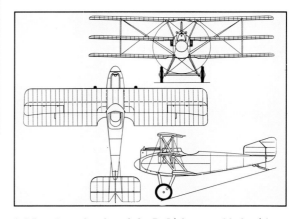

Schütte-Lanz developed the Dr I (above and below) in 1918 after studying the Sopwith Triplane.

sult was the Dr I proffered by the Luftfahrzeugbau Schütte-Lanz. Powered by a 160 hp Mercedes D III six-cylinder inline water-cooled engine and carrying the then standard armament of twin 7,9-mm LMG 08/15 machine guns, the Dr I mated the fuselage and vertical tail surfaces of the D III biplane with a triplane wing cellule. The arrangement of the wings was unusual in that forward stagger was applied to the centre plane, presumably in an attempt to improve view. The Dr I participated in the second D-type contest (27 May–28 June 1918). *Loaded weight, 1,984 lb (900 kg). Span, 26 ft 3 in (8,00 m). Length, 20 ft 6½ in (6,26 m).*

SCHÜTTE-LANZ D VI   Germany

A unique single-seat fighter created by the Luftfahrzeugbau Schütte-Lanz in the spring of 1918 was the D VI, which was fundamentally a parasol monoplane, but featured additional lifting surface in the form of an aerofoil-section fairing between the parallel struts bracing the outer wing panels to the base of the fuselage. Powered by a 160 hp Mercedes D III engine, the D VI was flown for the first time on 29 May 1918, but crashed and was not rebuilt. *Span, 35 ft 5⅛ in (10,80 m). Length, 21 ft 4⅓ in (6,51 m).*

The D VI (above and below) crashed on its first flight in May 1918, and was not rebuilt.

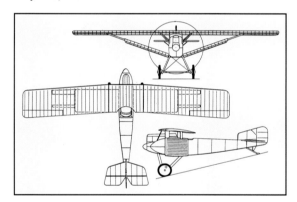

SCHÜTTE-LANZ D VII   Germany

A progressive development of the basic D III design, the D VII was completed in time to compete in the second D-type contest (27 May – 28 June 1918). Powered by a Mercedes D IIIavü six-cylinder water-cooled engine of 180 hp with a frontal, automobile-type radiator, the D VII was of wooden construction with a plywood-covered fuselage, the wing cellule being essentially similar to that of the earlier fighter, but having ailerons also on the lower wing for improved lat-

The Schütte-Lanz D VII (below) of mid 1918.

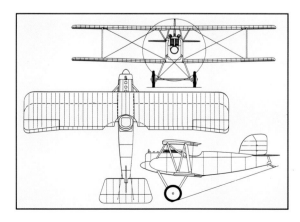

Derived from the D III, the Schütte-Lanz D VII (above) was a conventional, but uninspiring, biplane.

eral control. Armament comprised twin 7,9-mm LMG 08/15 machine guns. Three prototypes of the D VII were ordered, the first of these entering flight test in May 1918. This type did not display a particularly outstanding performance during the D-type contest, but flight testing was continuing at the time of the Armistice. *Max speed, 112 mph (180 km/h). Time to 3,280 ft (1 000 m), 2.4 min, to 16,405 ft (5 000 m), 31.6 min. Endurance, 1.5 hrs. Empty weight, 1,631 lb (740 kg). Loaded weight, 2,028 lb (920 kg). Span, 29 ft 6⅓ in (9,00 m). Length, 19 ft 8¼ in (6,00 m).*

SCHWADE
KAMPFEINSITZER NR 1   Germany

In 1914, the Otto Schwade concern of Erfurt initiated the flight test of a small single-seater powered by an 80 hp Schwade Stahlherz seven-cylinder rotary engine installed as a pusher behind an abbreviated circular section nacelle. A single-bay biplane with tubular outriggers supporting the tail surfaces, the Schwade single-seater, known as the Nr 1, was fitted with a Bergmann LMG 15 7,9-mm machine gun on a flexible mounting during the course of flight trials, but no details of these are recorded and development is believed to have been abandoned at an early stage in favour of a more advanced design, the Nr 2.

Built in 1914, the Schwade Nr 1 pusher (below) used triangulated strutting to carry the tail unit.

SCHWADE
KAMPFEINSITZER NR 2   Germany

Late in 1915, Otto Schwade produced a single-seat two-bay biplane twin-boom pusher fighter, the Nr 2, which appears to have been developed in the light of experience gained with the company's first *Kampfeinsitzer*. A somewhat ungainly aircraft with the pilot accommodated in a circular-section nacelle suspended

Retaining the twin-boom pusher layout of the Nr 1, the Nr 2 (below) was better streamlined.

between the wings by a profusion of struts, and twin vertical tail surfaces carried by ply-covered booms of narrow oval section, this aircraft was powered by a Schwade Stahlherz seven-cylinder rotary engine of 80 hp. No further details of this aircraft have been recorded.

A Schwade Stahlherz engine was used to power the same company's Nr 2 fighter (below).

S.E.A.4   France

Orders were placed for 1,000 S.E.A.4s (above), but the Armistice cut production to only 145.

The *Société d'Etudes Aeronautiques* (S.E.A.) was formed in 1916 by Henry Potez and Marcel Bloch. Together with Louis Coroller, they designed in 1917 a two-seat fighter-reconnaissance aircraft, the S.E.A.4, which was powered by the new 370 hp Lorraine-Dietrich 12Da 12-cylinder water-cooled engine. An equi-span two-bay biplane, the prototype flew in April 1918, and underwent official testing at Villacoublay on the 28th of that month. As a result of this and subsequent operational evaluation at Le Plessis-Belleville and Perthe, 1,000 examples of the S.E.A.4 C2 were ordered. Potez, Bloch and an industrialist, Bessonneau, established the Société Anjou Aéronautique to fulfil part of this order, the remainder being contracted to SFCA (Société Anonyme Française de Constructions Aéronautiques), the Ateliers d'Aviation L Janoir and SAIB (Société Anonyme d'Applications Industrielles du Bois). The first series S.E.A.4 C2 was completed on Armistice Day, 11 November 1918, Anjou Aéronautique finishing 30 before going into liquidation. A new company was then set up at Aubervilliers, Aéroplanes Henry Potez, with the initial task of completing unfinished S.E.A.4 C2s, a total of 115 reportedly being finished, and another 25 adapted as passenger transports being built as Potez

The S.E.A.4 C2 (below) two-seat recce-fighter.

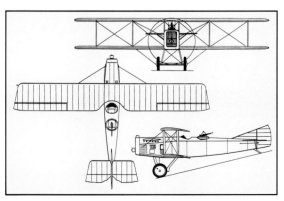

S.E.A.

VIIs. *Max speed, 128 mph (206 km/h) at 6,560 ft (2 000 m). Time to 6,560 ft (2 000 m), 6.3 min. Endurance, 2.25 hrs. Empty weight, 2,210 lb (1 002 kg). Loaded weight, 3,401 lb (1 543 kg). Span, 39 ft 4½ in (12,00 m). Length, 27 ft 10½ in (8,50 m). Height, 10 ft 2 in (3,10 m). Wing area, 403.66 sq ft (37,50 m².)*

S.E.T. XV — Romania

In an attempt to meet a requirement formulated by the *Aeronautica Militara* for a single-seat fighter to succeed the I.A.R.-built Dewoitine D.27, in 1934 the Fabrica de Avione of the S.E.T. (*Societatea pentru exploatâri technice*, or Technical Development Society) in Bucharest built the S.E.T. XV to the designs of Ing Grigore C Zamfirescu. One static test specimen and one flying prototype were completed, the latter commencing flight evaluation in 1934. The S.E.T. XV was a sesquiplane of all-metal construction with fabric skinning.

The good-looking S.E.T. XV biplane (above and below) failed to impress Romania's *Aeronautica Militara*.

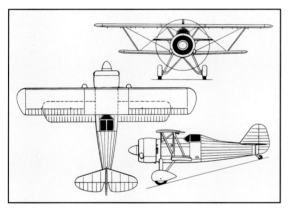

Powered by a 500 hp Gnome-Rhône 9Krsd nine-cylinder radial, it carried an armament of two 7,62-mm machine guns. The S.E.T. XV competed with the I.A.R.15 for an order from the *Aeronautica Militara*, but its sesquiplane configuration was considered *passé* by the service, which opted for the Polish P.Z.L. P.11b. The prototype of the S.E.T. XV was flown for several months by an experimental squadron at Pipera before being scrapped. *Max speed, 211 mph (340 km/h) at 13,125 ft (4 000 m). Time to 16,405 ft (5 000 m), 8.42 min. Empty weight, 2,535 ft (1 150 kg). Loaded weight, 3,417 lb (1 550 kg). Span, 30 ft 10 in (9,40 m). Length, 22 ft 11⅔ in (7,00 m). Height, 10 ft 11⅞ in (3,35 m). Wing area, 200.75 sq ft (18,65 m²).*

SEVERSKY SEV-2XP — USA

The SEV-2XP (the designation indicating 2-seat eXperimental Pursuit) designed by Alexander Kartveli was a derivative of the first product of the Seversky Aircraft Corporation, the commercial SEV-3 three-seat monoplane. An all-metal semi-monocoque aircraft with a fixed spatted undercarriage, the SEV-2XP was flown in the spring of 1935 with the unsatisfactory Wright R-1670 14-cylinder radial offering 735 hp for take-off, provision being made for an armament of two synchronised machine guns, one of 0.3-in (7,62-mm) and the other of 0.5-in (12,7-mm) calibre, and one 0.3-in gun on a flexible mount in the rear cockpit. In May 1935, the USAAC Matériel Division initiated a contest for a new single-seat fighter. Maj Alexander P de Seversky, believing the SEV-2XP capable of out-performing any *single*-seat fighter, entered this aircraft as a contender.

The first of numerous fighter designs by A Kartveli for Seversky (later, Republic) was the SEV-2XP (above).

In the event, the SEV-2XP was damaged in an accident on 18 June while en route to the contest. It was therefore returned to the manufacturer and reworked as the single-seat SEV-1XP. *Max speed, 274 mph (441 km/h) at 11,000 ft (3 350 m). Initial climb, 2,050 ft/min (10,41 m/sec). Max range, 950 mls (1 529 km). Empty weight, 3,600 lb (1 633 kg). Loaded weight, 5,300 lb (2 404 kg). Span, 36 ft 0 in (10,97 m). Length, 24 ft 6¾ in (7,49 m). Height, 8 ft 7 in (2,62 m). Wing area, 220 sq ft (20,44 m²).*

SEVERSKY SEV-1XP — USA

The SEV-1XP single-seat adaptation of the SEV-2XP initially retained the R-1670 engine. By now featuring a semi-retractable undercarriage, the prototype was re-engined with an ungeared nine-cylinder Wright R-1820 Cyclone. This engine failed to produce its rated power, however, the predicted 300 mph (483 km/h) maximum speed proving unobtainable in consequence. The USAAC Matériel Division's decision to defer fighter choice pending further evaluation to be held in March 1936 enabled the SEV-1XP to be re-engined once more, this time with an 850 hp 14-cylinder Pratt & Whitney R-1830-9 Twin Wasp. This was succeeded, in turn, by a geared R-1820-G5 offering 950 hp for take-off, but the Twin Wasp was subsequently re-installed. With this last engine and an armament of one 0.3-in (7,62-mm) and one 0.5-in (12,7-mm) gun, the SEV-1XP was selected on 16 June 1936, approval being given for production of 77 fighters against a contract confirmed early in 1937, with the designation P-35. The following data relate to the geared Cyclone-engined SEV-1XP. *Max speed, 289 mph (465 km/h) at 10,000 ft (3 050 m). Time to 10,000 ft (3 050 m), 4.8 min. Max range, 1,192 mls (1 918 km). Empty weight, 3,706 lb (1 681 kg). Loaded weight, 5,014 lb (2 274 kg). Span, 36 ft 0 in (10,97 m). Length, 24 ft 2 in (7,59 m). Height, 8 ft 10 in (2,69 m). Wing area, 220 sq ft (20,44 m²).*

When the two-seat SEV-2XP was rebuilt as a single-seater (below) the designation changed to SEV-1XP.

SEVERSKY (AP-1) P-35 — USA

Introducing the US Army Air Corps fighter fraternity to such refinements as enclosed cockpit, constant-speed propeller and retractable undercarriage, the P-35 entered service in 1937. The first series aircraft, later to be assigned the company designation AP-1 (Army Pur-

suit No 1), embodied all the modifications and changes stipulated by the USAAC when selecting the SEV-1XP as winner of the 1936 contest, but was nonetheless rejected by the Matériel Division after delivery to Wright Field in May 1937. The full mainwheel fairings were discarded in favour of partial fairings, a redesigned windscreen introduced and some dangerous characteristics

Key to Seversky P-35

1 Aerial attachment
2 Aerials
3 Tailfin leading-edge
4 Tail navigation lights
5 Tailfin structure
6 Rudder upper hinge
7 Rudder structure
8 Rudder centre hinge fairing
9 Rudder tab
10 Rudder lower section
11 Elevator tab
12 Starboard elevator
13 Starboard tailplane
14 Elevator hinge
15 Tailplane attachment
16 Tailwheel folding door
17 Retractable tailwheel
18 Axle fork
19 Lifting point
20 Fuselage frame
21 Tailwheel shock absorber
22 Control rods
23 Elevator control linkage
24 Fuselage longerons
25 Skinning

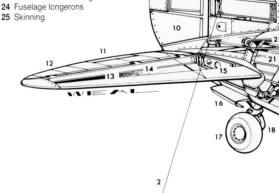
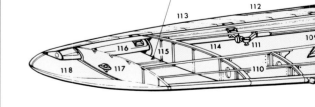

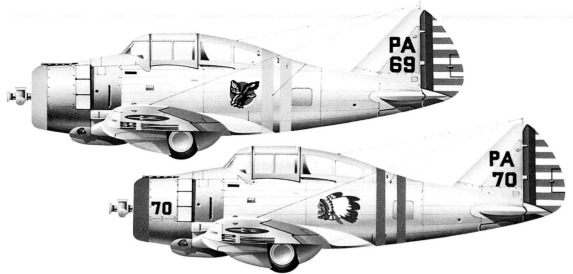

The first series P-35 (above) was returned to Seversky for development purposes, becoming the AP-1. A large spinner was fitted (below) for later tests.

displayed during aerobatics dictated application of seven degrees of dihedral to the outer wing panels. The P-35 was powered by a Pratt & Whitney R-1830-9 Twin Wasp rated at 950 hp for take-off and 850 hp at 8,000 ft (2 440 m), armament comprising one 0.3-in (7,62-mm) and one 0.5-in (12,7-mm) machine gun. The P-35 was a robust aircraft, but was too stable and lacked perform-

Seversky P-35s flown by the commanding officers of (top) the 27th and (immediately above) 94th Pursuit Sqns, 1st PG, Selfridge Field, Michigan, in 1938.

ance, and by the time that the 76th and last aircraft (the 77th on contract being completed as the XP-41) had been delivered in August 1938, it was considered obso-

26 Radio equipment	36 Canopy track	53 Instrument panel	73 Aileron hinge	91 Engine bearer lower attachment
27 Aerial lead-in	37 Canopy fixed aft glazing	54 Two 0.3-in (7,62-mm) Browning machine guns	74 Aerial lead-in attachment	92 Wing spar/fuselage attachment
28 Radio support tray	38 Dorsal spine fairing		75 Port navigation light	93 Wing root walkway
29 Fuselage frame	39 Aerial lead-in	55 Instrument panel shroud	76 Port wingtip	94 Centre-section fuel tanks
30 Wing root/fuselage fairing fillet	40 Headrest/turnover structure	56 Windscreen side panels	77 Wing leading-edge	95 Starboard mainwheel well
31 Door catches	41 Sliding cockpit canopy	57 Gunsight mounting	78 Wing spar	96 Mainwheel leg pivot (front spar)
32 Baggage floor	42 Pilot's seat and harness	58 Narrow-width windscreen	79 Nose cowling ring	97 Leading-edge aerodynamic fairing
33 Baggage door	43 Oxygen cylinder (behind seat)	59 Fuselage panels	80 Three-blade propeller	98 Mainwheel leg box
34 Large capacity baggage compartment (design provision additional crew/ equipment)	44 Seat support strut	60 Oil tank	81 Casing	99 Mainwheel leg
	45 Attachment bracket	61 Engine bearer upper attachment	82 Propeller hub	100 Axle fork
	46 Aileron/elevator control linkage	62 Starboard ammunition magazine	83 Mainwheel fairing	101 Starboard mainwheel
35 Main fuselage bulkhead frame	47 Control rod	63 Cooling louvre	84 Port mainwheel	102 Hub cover plate
	48 Wing root fairing	64 Magazine removal clip	85 Undercarriage leg box	103 Retraction strut (worm shaft)
	49 Rudder pedal assembly	65 Engine controls	86 Air intake	104 Wheel/fairing retracted position
	50 Engine firewall/bulkhead	66 Cowling gills	87 Pratt & Whitney R-1830-9 Twin Wasp radial	105 Flap actuating rod
	51 Control column	67 Exhaust collector		106 Trailing-edge aerodynamic fairing
	52 Case ejection chute	68 Cowling frame	88 Fairing	107 Pitot head
		69 Machine gun blast tubes	89 Exhaust stub	108 Multi(5)-spar wing structure
		70 Machine gun ports	90 Leading-edge intake	109 Flap profile
		71 Port aileron		110 Wing ribs
		72 Aileron control rod		111 Aileron control linkage
				112 Aileron tab
				113 Starboard aileron
				114 Aileron balance
				115 Aerial lead-in attachment
				116 Aileron outer hinge
				117 Starboard navigation light
				118 Starboard wingtip

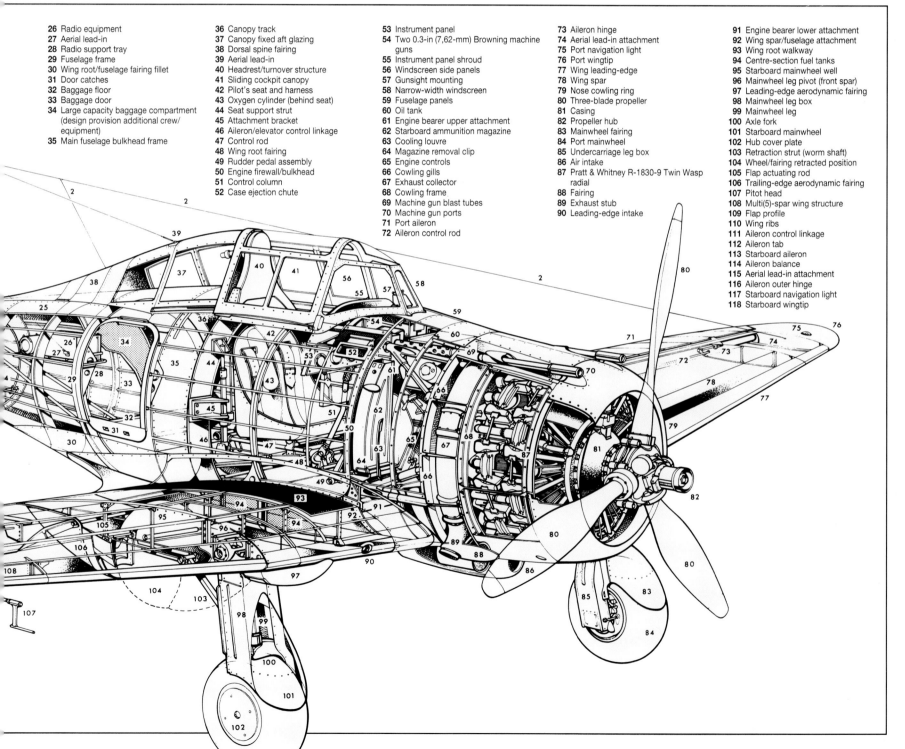

Japan acquired 20 Seversky 2PA-B3s (above) but found performance disappointing. (Below) The 2PA-L.

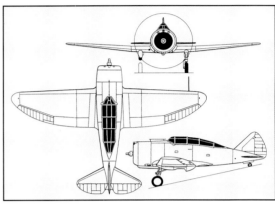

The P-35 (above), seen here with the 27th Pursuit Sqn, served in USAAC squadrons from 1938 to 1941.

lescent. The P-35 was finally withdrawn from first-line service in 1941, but it was survived by an export derivative (see Republic EP-1), sequestered examples of which were to serve with the USAAF as the P-35A. *Max speed, 282 mph (454 km/h) at 10,000 ft (3 050 m). Initial climb, 2,440 ft/min (12,39 m/sec). Range, 1,150 mls (1 850 km). Empty weight, 4,315 lb (1 957 kg). Normal loaded weight, 5,599 lb (2 540 kg). Span, 36 ft 0 in (10,97 m). Length, 25 ft 2 in (7,67 m). Height, 9 ft 1 in (2,77 m). Wing area, 220 sq ft (20,44 m²).*

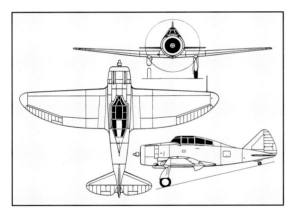

Extensive cockpit glazing gave the P-35 (above and below) the appearance of a two-seater.

SEVERSKY 2PA   USA

Evolved in parallel with the P-35, the 2PA was a two-seat fighter and fighter-bomber with a fundamentally similar airframe and offered with either a similar undercarriage to that of the single-seater as the 2PA-L (Land) or with an amphibious float undercarriage as the 2PA-A (Amphibian). Dubbed "Convoy Fighter" by the manufacturer, the 2PA was powered by a Wright R-1820-G2 or G3 Cyclone nine-cylinder radial engine, the former rated at 1,000 hp for take-off and the latter at 875 hp. Armament comprised two wing-mounted 0.3-in (7,62-mm) or 0.5-in (12,7-mm) Browning guns, one 0.3-in Browning on a flexible mount in the rear cockpit, plus two forward-firing fuselage-mounted 0.3-in or 0.5-in Browning guns. Provision was made for a bomb load of up to 500 lb (227 kg) on internal wing racks. Early in 1939, Major Seversky embarked upon a European

The two-seat 2PA was made available in land form (2PA-L, below) or with amphibious floats.

sales tour in a 2PA-202 or 2PA-BX which was fitted with a 1,100 hp Pratt & Whitney R-1830-S3C Twin Wasp. This aircraft was tested at the A&AEE Martlesham Heath, in March 1939, at the instigation of the Air Ministry. One 2PA-A and one 2PA-L were procured by the Soviet Union in March 1938, together with a manufacturing licence, which, in the event, was not to be utilised. Twenty R-1820-G2-powered examples were ordered clandestinely by the Japanese Imperial Navy for use over China as long-range escort fighters.

Large amphibious floats were an obvious feature of the 2PA-A (above and below), which was otherwise identical with the 2PA-L.

Designated 2PA-B3, these received an armament of two fuselage-mounted 0.3-in machine guns and a similar weapon in the rear cockpit. Assigned the Japanese designation A8V1, the 2PAs were found to possess unacceptable levels of manoeuvrability and climb rate for the escort fighter rôle and were therefore relegated to reconnaissance missions in Central China, two later being passed to the *Asahi Shimbun* newspaper group. Fifty-two 2PA-BXs were ordered by Sweden as dive-bombers (the Seversky company having meanwhile become the Republic Aviation Corporation), but only two of these were delivered to Sweden, the remainder being taken over by the USAAC as AT-12 Guardsman advanced trainers. The following data are for the SEV-2PA with R-1830 engine. *Max speed, 316 mph (508 km/h) at 15,000 ft (4 570 m). Initial climb, 2,690 ft/*

min (13,67 m/sec). Max range, 1,950 mls (3 138 km). Empty weight, 4,581 lb (2 078 kg). Normal loaded weight, 7,658 lb (3 474 kg). Span, 36 ft 0 in (10,97 m). Length, 26 ft 11 in (8,20 m). Height, 9 ft 9½ in (2,99 m). Wing area, 220 sq ft (20,44 m²).

The Asahi Shimbun newspaper group received two 2PA-B3s (below) from the Japanese Navy.

SEVERSKY NF-1 (XFN-1)   USA

As a contender in the 1937 US Navy shipboard single-seat fighter competition, the Seversky-designated NF-1 (Naval Fighter No 1) was derived from the basic P-35 design and flown for the first time in June 1937. Powered by a Wright R-1820-22 Cyclone nine-cylinder radial rated at 950 hp for take-off and having provision for one 0.3-in (7,62-mm) and one 0.5-in (12,7-mm) gun in the forward fuselage, the NF-1 was delivered to Anacostia NAS for evaluation under the US Navy designation XFN-1 on 24 September 1937. This designation was actually applied for "book-keeping purposes", no Navy contract being issued. The NF-1 had initially flown with a vertical windscreen similar to that first fitted to the AP-1, but this had been replaced by a more conventional windscreen prior to delivery to Anacostia, and at an early phase in the evaluation the fairings

The NF-1 (below) in June 1937, before removal of the main oleo leg fairings.

Derived from the P-35, the NF-1 (above) was found unsuitable for aircraft carrier operations.

attached to the main oleo legs, which fully enclosed the undercarriage when retracted, were removed. By consensus, the XFN-1 lacked the low-speed handling characteristics demanded for shipboard operation and the fighter was rejected by the Navy, further development being discontinued. *Max speed, 267 mph (430 km/h) at 15,000 ft (4 570 m). Initial climb, 2,600 ft/ min (13,2 m/sec). Normal range, 975 mls (1 570 km). Empty weight, 4,020 lb (1 823 kg). Loaded weight, 5,231 lb (2 373 kg). Dimensions as for P-35 apart from a length of 24 ft 5 in (7,44 m).*

SEVERSKY AP-2 USA

A progressive development of the basic P-35, the AP-2 (Army Pursuit No 2) differed essentially in having a modified centre wing structure incorporating wells for an entirely new flush-housed inward-retracting undercarriage. Together with a shallower cockpit canopy, these refinements were expected to raise maximum speed above the 300 mph (483 km/h) mark. The AP-2 was powered by a 1,050 hp Pratt & Whitney R-1830-9 Twin Wasp engine and armament was proposed to comprise the standard combination of one 0.3-in (7,62-mm) and one 0.5-in (12,7-mm) machine gun. It was ascertained that the flush-retracting undercarriage did not result in as much drag reduction as anticipated, but performance was still markedly superior to that of the P-35. Seversky's bid price was considered too high, however, and the AP-2 was rejected by the USAAC. It had been entered in the September 1937 Bendix Trophy contest, but prior to this event suffered an undercarriage failure while landing at Floyd Bennett Field. Much of the airframe was re-used for the AP-7. No specification is available.

SEVERSKY AP-7 USA

Developed as an improved P-35, the AP-7 (above) set new speed records, but gained no orders.

Representing an attempt to obtain maximum performance from the basic P-35 design without introducing radical changes, the AP-7 employed much of the airframe of the earlier AP-2 but was powered by a 1,200 hp Pratt & Whitney R-1830 Twin Wasp engine. As first completed early in 1938, the AP-7 reverted to the semi-retractable mainwheel arrangement of the P-35, and in this form was used by the celebrated aviatrix Jacqueline Cochran to capture the 1938 Bendix Trophy, having been used by Maj Alexander P de Seversky two days prior to this event to establish a new US transcontinental record with an elapsed time of 10 hr 3 min 7 sec. The

In 1939, the AP-7 was fitted with a new wing and an inwards-retracting undercarriage (below).

AP-7 was subsequently fitted with a new wing, with an improved leading-edge profile, and an inward-retracting undercarriage similar to that of the AP-2. It was intended that the modified AP-7 should participate in the 1939 Bendix Trophy contest, but was withdrawn after two aborted take-offs and later sold in a somewhat irregular transaction to Ecuador's *Fuerza Aérea*. No specification is available.

SEVERSKY AP-4 USA

Tested early-1939, the private venture AP-4 (above) led to a production order for the (Republic) P-43.

Preceded by the AP-7, the AP-4 possessed a superficial resemblance to the AP-2 and was intended as a high-altitude interceptor. The first Seversky fighter to feature flush-riveted skinning, the AP-4 was powered by a 1,200 hp Pratt & Whitney R-1830-SC2G equipped with a belly-mounted turbo-supercharger. As a company-funded development, the AP-4 was intended to participate in a USAAC competition scheduled for 25 January 1939 and was expected to demonstrate the superior medium- and high-altitude performance obtainable with a turbo-supercharged R-1830. The same engine, fitted with a mechanical supercharger, had been specified by the USAAC for the XP-41. The

For a drag investigation programme, the AP-4 (below) was fitted with large spinner and close cowling.

AP-4 was evaluated at Wright Field during February-March 1939, demonstrating exceptional climb and altitude performance. Early 1939, it was fitted with a close-fitting, high-inlet-velocity engine cowling matched with an oversize propeller spinner as a continuation of a drag reduction programme supervised by the NACA and initiated earlier with the AP-1. The AP-4 was subsequently fitted with a modified engine cowling, without the spinner, but, on 22 March 1939, caught fire in the air, the pilot bailing out. On 12 May 1939, a contract was awarded for 13 service evaluation models under the designation YP-43 (see Republic P-43 Lancer). *Max speed, 332 mph (534 km/h) at 20,000 ft (6 095 m). Initial climb, 3,200 ft/min (16,26 m/sec). Normal range, 780 mls (1 255 km). Empty weight, 5,427 lb (2 462 kg). Loaded weight, 6,780 lb (3 075 kg). Span, 36 ft 0 in (10,97 m). Length, 27 ft 0 in (8,23 m). Height, 12 ft 6 in (3,81 m). Wing area, 220 sq ft (20,44 m²).*

SEVERSKY XP-41 USA

When, in 1936, the USAAC Matériel Division placed an order for the SEV-1XP as the P-35, it had stipulated that the 77th and last series aircraft be fitted with a more powerful supercharged engine. The chosen engine was the Pratt & Whitney R-1830-19 of 1,200 hp, fitted with an integral medium-altitude two-stage mechanical supercharger. A contractual modification enabled Seversky to complete the airframe to a standard similar to that of the private-venture AP-4. The AP-9 (see Republic) was, in fact, used for competitive evaluation at Dayton in lieu of the XP-41 until the latter became available. Power plant apart, the aircraft was in virtually all respects similar to the AP-4. The XP-41 was delivered to Wright Field for USAAC evaluation in February 1939, but the Air Corps preferred the turbo-supercharged AP-4 and further development of the XP-41 was discontinued, although trials continued at Langley. This was the last of the Kartveli-designed fighters to bear the Seversky appellation, as the company thereafter became the Republic Aviation Corporation. *Max speed, 323 mph (520 km/h) at 15,000 ft (4 570 m). Normal range, 730 mls (1 175 kg). Empty weight, 5,390 lb (2 445 kg). Normal loaded weight, 6,600 lb (2 994 kg). Span, 36 ft 0 in (10,97 m). Length, 27 ft 0 in (8,23 m). Height, 12 ft 6 in (3,81 m). Wing area, 220 sq ft (20,44 m²).*

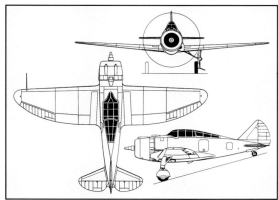

The last production P-35, fitted with an uprated engine, was tested as the XP-41 (above and below).

SHCHETININ Sнсн-I Russia

The M-11 single-seat fighter flying boat designed in 1916 by Dmitri P Grigorovich for the Imperial Russian Navy was built in the Shchetinin factory in Petrograd and was sometimes referred to as the Shch-I (see Grigorovich M-11).

SHENYANG (SAC) J-8 China

The second indigenous jet fighter to be built and flown in China, the Jian (Fighter) -8, or J-8, was developed by the Shenyang Aircraft Design Institute, initially under the leadership of Huang Zhiqian, from October 1964. Its specification called for Mach=2.2 speed, a 39,370 ft/min (200 m/sec) climb rate and a range of 932 mls (1 500 km) on internal fuel. Featuring a thin-section 60deg delta wing and employing much MiG technology, the J-8 was powered by two Chengdu WP-7A turbojets (Tumansky R-11s) of 11,243 lb st (5 100 kgp) with afterburning. Following the May 1965 death of Huang Zhiqian, design leadership passed to Wang Nanshou.

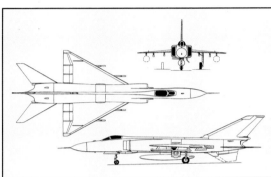

Lateral intakes, in place of the MiG-style pitot-type, distinguished the J-8 II (above and below).

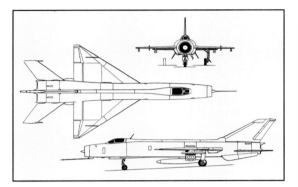

Based on MiG technology, the J-8 I (above and below) achieved limited production in the 'eighties.

Work on two prototypes began early in 1967 at the Shenyang Aircraft Factory (later Shenyang Aircraft Company, or SAC), the first of these flying on 5 July 1969. Development was suspended as a result of the "cultural revolution" and not resumed until 1977, Gu Songfen becoming chief designer in September 1978, and small-scale production being authorised in the following year. Lack of a suitable radar initially restricted the J-8 to a purely diurnal intercept rôle, armament comprising a twin-barrel 23-mm cannon and four Pili (Thunderbolt) PL-2B AAMs. An improved version, the J-8 I, was meanwhile developed, the first of three prototypes being lost on 25 June 1980 prior to flight test. The second prototype flew on 24 April 1981 and the third followed in October. The J-8 I was equipped with Sichuan SR-4 fire control radar, which was also retroactively applied to the J-8 from 1984, and embodied a number of systems changes, small-scale production being authorised on 27 July 1985. Some 70-80 (including J-8s) were expected to have been completed when production terminated in 1988. *Max speed, 1,386 mph (2 230 km/h) at 36,090 ft (11 000 m). Max combat range, 1,243 mls (2 000 km). Normal loaded weight (approx), 28,000 lb (12 700 kg). Span, 30 ft 7⅛ in (9,34 m). Length (including probe), 67 ft 3 in (20,50 m). Height, 16 ft 6 in (5,06 m). Wing area, 454.25 sq ft (42,20 m²).*

SHENYANG (SAC) J-8 IIM China

In April 1981, a conceptual study for an all-weather dual-rôle development of the J-8 I was begun, under the leadership of Gu Songfen, as the J-8 II. The most

The SAC J-8 (below) served in small numbers with the air force of the Chinese People's Republic.

dramatic change was the discarding of the pitot-type nose intake in favour of twin lateral air intakes to provide both increased airflow for more powerful engines and accommodation for a larger fire control radar. A major redesign of the J-8 I, the J-8 II was powered by two Liyang WP-13A afterburning turbojets. The first of six prototypes was flown on 12 June 1984, and pre-series aircraft were delivered in 1988. Armament was a 23-mm twin-barrel cannon with 200 rounds, and up to four PL-2A or PL-4 AAMs. In 1989, two aircraft were delivered to Grumman for installation of American avionics, but the contract was cancelled in 1990. The J-8 II was replaced by the J-8 IIM, with Chinese avionics and the Russian Phazotron Zhuk-8 radar, while the "steam-gauge" cockpit instruments have been supplemented with two MFDs. Power is two Liyang WP-13B afterburning turbojets, each rated at 15,432 lb (7 000 kgp) max and 10,597 lb (4 807 kgp) military thrust. The J-8 IIM carries two PL-2B IR homers, and up to four PL-7A SARH homers. *Max speed hi, Mach 2.20. Max speed lo, Mach 1.06. Operational ceiling, 59,058 ft (18 000 m). Rate of climb, 44,097 ft/min (224 m/sec). Empty weight, 22,864 lb (10 371 kg). Normal takeoff weight, 33,704 lb (15 288 kg). Span, 30 ft 8 in (9,344 m). Length 70 ft 2 in (21,39 m). Height, 17 ft 9 in (5,41 m). Wing area, 454 sq ft (42.20 m²).*

A contract to adapt the J-8 II (below) with US avionics was cancelled in 1990.

SHORT S.10 GURNARD UK

A contender to Specification 0.22/26 calling for a high-speed shipboard reconnaissance-fighter capable of being flown with either wheel or float undercarriage

and suitable for catapult operation from cruisers and larger warships, the S.10 Gurnard was awarded a two-prototype contract. One of the prototypes, the Gurnard I, was to be powered by a 525 hp Bristol Jupiter X nine-cylinder air-cooled radial engine, and the other, the Gurnard II, was to have a 525 hp Rolls-Royce Kestrel IIS water-cooled 12-cylinder Vee-type engine. A single-bay biplane of metal construction with fabric skinning, the Gurnard had an armament of one fixed forward-firing 0.303-in M7-mm) machine gun and a similar calibre weapon on a Scarff ring for the second crew member. The Gurnard II was the first to fly, on 16 April 1929, as a floatplane, the Gurnard I following in landplane form three weeks later, on 8 May. Both prototypes were tested at the A&AEE, but the Hawker Osprey was selected in preference and no production of the Gurnard was ordered. The Gurnard II was flown – commencing on 15 June 1931 – as an amphibian with a single main float. The following data relate to the Gurnard II. *Max speed, 160 mph (258 km/h). Endurance 3.5 hrs. Empty weight, 3,660 lb (1 662 kg). Loaded weight, 5,194 lb (2 360 kg). Span, 37 ft 0 in (11,27 m). Length, 31 ft 6 in (9,60 m). Wing area, 429 sq ft (39,85 m²).*

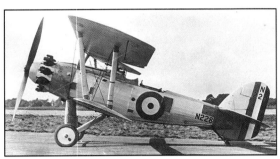

The first (of two) Gurnard prototypes (above) was fitted with a Jupiter radial engine.

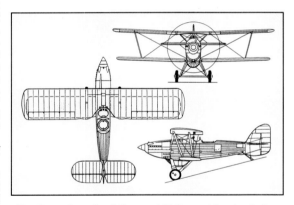

The Kestrel-engined Gurnard II flew with wheeled (above) and float (below) alighting gear.

SIAI S.50 Italy

When Alessandro Marchetti was appointed chief designer of the SIAI (Società Idrovolanti Alta Italia), his MVT (which see) was redesignated S. 50 and entered in the official fighter contest of 1923.

SIAI S.52 Italy

Although the S.50 was proposed as a contender in the official single-seat fighter contest of 1923, it did not entirely meet the specification with which entrants were

A derivative of the S.50, the S.52 (above) was completed too late for the 1923 fighter contest.

supposed to conform. This called for a 300 hp Hispano-Suiza HS 42 eight-cylinder water-cooled engine whereas the S.50 was powered by a 285 hp SPA 62a six-cylinder unit. Alessandro Marchetti therefore evolved an HS 42-powered derivative of the S.50, although this, the S.52, was too late to participate in the contest, entering flight test in 1924. Apart from its engine, the S.52 differed from its predecessor in a number of respects. The configuration remained basically unchanged, but the wings were of increased area, conventional ailerons replaced wing warping for lateral control and more conventional horizontal tail surfaces replaced the all-moving tailplane. Two prototypes of the S.52 were built, one of these being demonstrated in Latin America where it was still flying in 1927, being used in that year for a flight from Argentina to Paraguay. Previously, in 1925, it was proposed to fit the other prototype with a 410 hp Fiat A 20 engine with which a maximum speed of 177 mph (285 km/h) was anticipated. *Max speed, 168 mph (270 km/h). Time to 3,280 ft (1 000 m), 1.5 min. Endurance, 2.5 hrs. Empty weight, 1,764 lb (800 kg). Loaded weight, 2,425 lb (1 100 kg). Span, 35 ft 1¼ in (10,70 m). Length, 23 ft 6⅔ in (7,18 m). Wing area, 258.34 sq ft (24,00 m²).*

The S.52 (below) had an unusual wing planform.

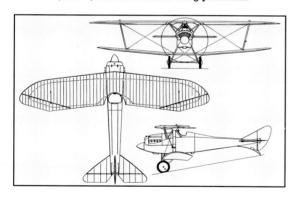

SIAI S.58   Italy

Designed in competition with the Macchi M.26 as a potential successor to the M.7*ter* in service with the *Squadriglie Caccia Marittima* of Italy's *Aviazione per la Marina*, the S.58 single-seat fighter flying boat flew in the early summer of 1924. On 25 August that year, the first prototype established an international record for waterborne aircraft in its category by attaining an altitude of 19,130 ft (5 831 m) with a 551-lb (250-kg) payload. A single-bay biplane of wooden construction with a planing bottom based on that developed for the S.51 racing flying boat, the S.58 was powered by a 296 bhp Hispano-Suiza 42 eight-cylinder Vee-type engine strut-braced above the hull and driving a pusher propeller. The intended armament comprised two 7,7-mm Vickers guns mounted in the forward hull and flanking the cockpit. In the event, for reasons of economy, the *Aviazione per la Marina* elected to retain the M.7*ter* in ser-

The S.58 (below) competed for production orders but lost out three times to Macchi alternatives.

vice and no production contract was placed for the S.58, of which three prototypes had been built. At least one more S.58 was built, however, and this was used as a trainer at the *Scuola di Alta Velocità* (High Speed School) at Desenzano. In 1927, a new contest to replace the M.7*ter* was organised and the S.58 was again submitted. The first prototype had meanwhile been re-engined with the 420 hp Fiat A 20 12-cylinder Vee-type engine and had been redesignated S.58*bis*. This flying boat won the contest and the *Aviazione per la Marina* prepared plans to procure 97 S.58*bis* fighters for the *Squadriglie Caccia*. However, the decision was taken again to extend the service life of the M.7*ter* by re-engining the ageing flying boat with an Isotta Fraschini Semiasso and no contract was placed for the SIAI aircraft. The contest was resurrected yet again in 1929, and the SIAI entered a slightly modified version of its fighter flying boat, the S.58*ter*, which had begun flight test in the autumn of the previous year. Retaining the A 20 engine, the S.58*ter* came second in the competition to the Macchi M.41*bis*. The following data relate to the S.58*bis*. *Max speed, 166 mph (267 km/h). Time to 9,840 ft (3 000 m), 7.66 min. Empty weight, 2,462 lb (1 117 kg). Loaded weight, 3,256 lb (1 477 kg). Span, 36 ft 10⅘ in (11,25 m). Length, 29 ft 10¼ in (9,10 m). Height, 9 ft 0¼ in (2,75 m). Wing area, 313.24 sq ft (29,10 m²).*

SIAI S.67   Italy

First flown on 28 January 1930, the S.67 single-seat monoplane fighter flying boat prototype was built under an official contract placed in the previous year. Of

(Below) The Fiat-engined S.67 fighter flying-boat.

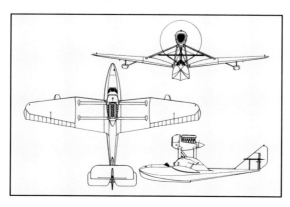

Limited service use was achieved with two examples of the S.67 (above) in the mid 'thirties.

wooden construction and powered by a 420 hp Fiat A 20 liquid-cooled engine strut-braced above the hull, the S.67 had an armament of two 7,7-mm Vickers guns in the upper section of the bow. The wing spars were hinged to the fuselage and the steel-tube bracing struts were each attached to the engine mount by a single pin. The S.67 was intended for catapult-launch from *Condottieri* class cruisers, and the aircraft could be erected for launching within five minutes by a team of six men. Testing at the *II Centro Sperimentale* began at the beginning of March 1930, but the prototype crashed on 3 April. Nonetheless, a contract was placed for three more S.67s, of which two were built and taken on charge by the 162ᵃ *Squadriglia* of the 88° *Gruppo Caccia Marittima* and used until 1935. One S.67 was tested with a concave hull. *Max speed, 160 mph (258 km/h). Time to 9,840 ft (3 000 m), 9.78 min. Endurance, 3.7 hrs. Empty weight, 2,665 lb (1 209 kg). Loaded weight, 3,613 lb (1 639 kg). Span, 42 ft 11¾ in (13,10 m). Length, 29 ft 5⅛ in (8,97 m). Height, 9 ft 6⅛ in (2,90 m). Wing area, 292.79 sq ft (27,20 m²).*

SIAI-MARCHETTI S.M.91   Italy

In 1941, the *Ministero dell' Aeronautica* framed a requirement for a two-seat multi-rôle combat aircraft to fulfil the tasks of long-range escort fighter, interceptor, reconnaissance-fighter and fighter-bomber. The SIAI-Marchetti concern proffered two contenders, the S.M.91 and S.M.92. The former, a prototype of which was flown on 10 March 1943, was an all-metal, twin-boom, tandem two-seat monoplane powered by two 1,290 hp Daimler-Benz DB 605A-1 inverted-Vee 12-cylinder liquid-cooled engines. Armament consisted of three 20-mm cannon in the nose of the fuselage nacelle plus two similar weapons in the wing roots, and provision was made for external carriage of one 1,102-lb

Daimler-Benz engines were adopted to power the single prototype of the S.M.91 (above and below).

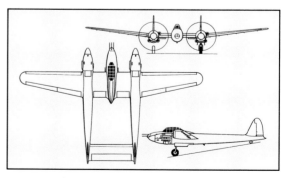

The S.M.91 (below) was of "conventional" twin-boom layout, by comparison with the parallel S.M.92.

(500 kg) bomb, or four 220-lb (100-kg) or 353-lb (160-kg) bombs. Only limited flight testing of the S.M.91 had been conducted prior to the German evacuation of Northern Italy, and subsequent proposals for a version powered by 1,300 hp Rolls-Royce Merlin 620s did not see fruition. *Max speed, 363 mph (585 km/h) at 22,965 ft (7 000 m). Continuous cruise, 320 mph (515 km/h) at 20,340 ft (6 200 m). Time to 19,685 ft (6 000 m), 8.5 min. Empty weight, 14,109 lb (6 400 kg). Loaded weight, 19,599 lb (8 890 kg). Span, 64 ft 7½ in (19,70 m). Length, 43 ft 5¾ in (13,25 m). Height, 12 ft 7½ in (3,85 m). Wing area, 449.51 sq ft (41,76 m²).*

SIAI-MARCHETTI S.M.92 Italy

The S.M.92 (above and below) was unusual in having an asymmetric arrangement for the crew.

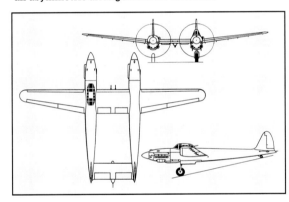

Evolved in parallel with the S.M.91 to meet the 1941 requirement for a two-seat multi-rôle fighter, the S.M.92 retained the basic wing and tail surfaces, and a similar starboard tailboom, and was also powered by two 1,290 hp Daimler-Benz DB 605A-1 engines. By comparison with the S.M.91, however, the central fuselage nacelle was eliminated and tandem accommodation for the crew members provided in the port boom. The proposed armament of the S.M. 92 consisted of two 20-mm cannon in the wing centre section, a similar weapon mounted in the starboard engine, two 12,7-mm

The sole S.M.92 prototype (above) underwent limited flight testing under German auspices in late 1943.

machine guns beneath each engine and one 12,7-mm gun firing aft from a remotely-controlled barbette beneath the tailplane. The sole prototype of the S.M.92 was flown under German auspices on 12 November 1943, and although it was anticipated that the substantial reduction in drag resulting from the elimination of the central fuselage nacelle would result in an exceptional performance, little flight testing was undertaken and the following data are manufacturer's estimates. *Max speed, 382 mph (615 km/h) at 24,935 ft (7 600 m). Max continuous cruise, 335 mph (540 km/h) at 22,965 ft (7 000 m). Time to 19,685 ft (6 000 m), 7.15 min. Empty weight, 13,779 lb (6 250 kg). Loaded weight, 19,290 lb (8 750 kg). Span, 60 ft 10⅓ in (18,55 m). Length, 44 ft 11⅓ in (13,70 m). Height, 13 ft 7⅓ in (4,15 m). Wing area, 414.64 sq ft (38,52 m²).*

SIDDELEY S.R.2. SISKIN UK

When, in January 1917, Capt F M Green became chief aeronautical engineer of the Siddeley-Deasy Motor Car Company, he began the design of a single-seat fighter, the S.R.2. A compact single-bay sesquiplane predominantly of wooden construction with fabric skinning, the S.R.2 was powered by a 320 hp A.B.C. Dragonfly nine-cylinder radial engine. Armament comprised two synchronised 0.303-in (7,7-mm) machine guns. A contract for six prototypes was reduced to three in mid 1918, the first of these flying in April 1919, by which time the fighter had been officially named Siskin. The first proto-

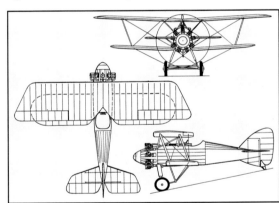

The Siddeley Siskin (above and below) in its initial form with the A.B.C. Dragonfly engine.

type Siskin was subsequently re-engined with an Armstrong Siddeley Jaguar, development in this form continuing after Siddeley Deasy acquired in 1921 the name and goodwill of Sir W G Armstrong Whitworth & Co Ltd, and the Armstrong Whitworth Siskin II (which see) emerging in 1922. *Max speed, 145 mph (233 km/h) at 6,500 ft (1 980 m). Time to 6,500 ft (1 980 m), 4.5 min. Service ceiling, 23,800 ft (7 255 m). Empty weight, 1,463 lb (664 kg). Loaded weight, 2,181 lb (989 kg). Span, 27 ft 6 in (8,38 m). Length, 21 ft 3 in (6,48 m). Height, 9 ft 9 in (2,97 m). Wing area, 247 sq ft (22,95 m²).*

SIEMENS-SCHUCKERT (SSW) E I Germany

The E I (above and below) which achieved operational service in small numbers in the summer of 1916.

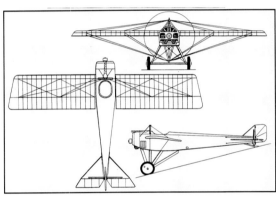

The first single-seat fighter to be produced by the Siemens-Schuckert-Werke (SSW), the E I monoplane was designed by Franz Steffen and completed in October 1915. Of conventional shoulder-wing arrangement with warp control rather than ailerons, the E I had steel-tube wing spars, fabric-covered wings and plywood-covered fuselage, power being provided by a Siemens-Halske Sh I nine-cylinder rotary engine of 100 hp and armament comprising a single synchronised 7,9-mm LMG 08/15 machine gun. After completion of flight testing on 17 March 1916, the E I was recommended for service, and the *Idflieg* placed a contract for 20 aircraft with the SSW Nürnberg facility. Only five E Is were listed as being at the Front on 31 October 1916, by which time the type had been rendered obsolescent by the appearance during the Battle of the Somme of the Nieuport 11. *Max speed, 87 mph (140 km/h) at sea level. Range, 130 mls (210 km). Empty weight, 1,043 lb (473 kg). Loaded weight, 1,484 lb (673 kg). Span, 32 ft 9⅔ in (10,00 m). Length, 23 ft 3½ in (7,10 m). Height, 9 ft 2¼ in (2,80 m). Wing area, 172.23 sq ft (16,00 m²).*

SIEMENS-SCHUCKERT (SSW) E II Germany

Completed early in 1916, the E II was essentially similar to the E I apart from its power plant, the Sh I rotary being replaced by a six-cylinder inline Argus As II engine rated at 120 hp. Armament remained a single

The E II (below) failed to progress further than a single prototype which was destroyed in June 1916.

7,9-mm LMG 08/15 machine gun. The sole prototype of the E II was destroyed on 26 June 1916 during a demonstration at Döberitz, its designer, Franz Steffen, who was flying the aircraft, losing his life. No details of the E II are available.

SIEMENS-SCHUCKERT (SSW) E III   Germany

Following the small production batch of E I monoplanes, the Siemens-Schuckert-Werke received an *Idflieg* contract for six additional aircraft designated E III. These differed from the E I only in power plant type. Powered by a 100 hp Oberursel U I nine-cylinder rotary engine, the E III retained the airframe and armament of the E I, a proposed development, the E IV, being similar apart from a circular-section fuselage. The dimensions and performance of the E III were similar to those of the E I. *Empty weight, 1,054 lb (478 kg). Loaded weight, 1,495 lb (678 kg).*

SIEMENS-SCHUCKERT (SSW) DD 5   Germany

The first single-seat fighter biplane to be designed by Franz Steffen (who was subsequently to lose his life while demonstrating the E II monoplane), the DD 5 featured sharply tapered wings built up around steel tube spars, steel I-type interplane struts and a similar fuselage and tail to those of the E I monoplane. Powered by a 100 hp Siemens-Halske Sh I nine-cylinder rotary engine, the DD 5 was tested by the *Idflieg* in August 1916, but was rejected owing to its poor aerodynamic qualities and the restricted field of view provided by the cockpit. Armament comprised a single 7,9-mm LMG 08/15 machine gun. Only one prototype of the DD 5 was built and tested, development being discontinued in favour of an almost identical copy of the Nieuport 11 that was being developed (as the D I) in parallel. No specification for the DD 5 is available.

The single prototype of the DD 5 (below) was rejected owing to poor aerodynamic qualities.

SIEMENS-SCHUCKERT (SSW) D I   Germany

The début of the Nieuport 11 on the Western Front came as a serious blow to Germany, and, with no immediate prospect of a superior fighter forthcoming from the German aircraft industry, the *Idflieg* requested Albatros, Euler and SSW to produce improved copies of the Nie 11 with the utmost urgency. The SSW version, designed by Franz Steffen shortly before his death in the E II, was powered by a 110 hp Siemens-Halske Sh I rotary and armed with a single synchronised 7,9-mm LMG 08/15 machine gun, but was in most other respects virtually identical to the French fighter. In October 1916, Bruno Steffen, brother of the designer, made a noteworthy climb to 16,405 ft (5 000 m) in 45 min in the prototype of the SSW version of the Nie 11, and, on 25 November, a contract was placed for 150 aircraft under the designation D I. In the event, production tempo was slowed by delays in deliveries of the geared rotary engine, and as, by mid 1917, the SSW D I had been overtaken in performance by other types, only 95 were completed (the remaining 55 airframes being delivered uncovered to Adlershof). An order for a further 100 placed on 21 March 1917 had meanwhile been cancelled. Only small numbers of SSW D Is appeared on the Western Front, most being assigned to flying schools. Attempts to improve the basic fighter resulted in a single D Ia and two D Ib aircraft. The D Ia featured a twin-gun armament

The D I (above and below) was, in most respects, a very close copy of the Nieuport 11 fighter.

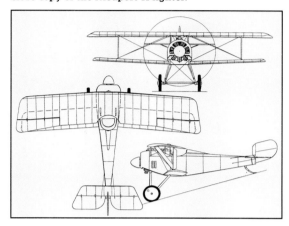

Representing an attempt to improve the basic D I design, the D Ia (below) featured an increase in wing area and a twin-gun armament.

and a 14-sq ft (1,30-m²) increase in wing area, and the D Ib's had one-piece upper wings, one having a further increase in wing area to 174.38 sq ft (16,20 m²) and the other having a high-compression version of the Sh I engine affording 140 hp and enabling the fighter to attain 16,405 ft (5 000 m) in 20.5 min. *Max speed, 96 mph (155 km/h). Time to 3,280 ft (1 000 m), 3.5 min. Endurance, 2.3 hrs. Empty weight, 979 lb (444 kg). Loaded weight, 1,442 lb (654 kg). Span, 24 ft 7¼ in (7,50 m). Length, 19 ft 8¼ in (6,00 m). Height, 8 ft 5⅞ in (2,59 m). Wing area, 155 sq ft (14,40 m²).*

SIEMENS-SCHUCKERT (SSW) D II   Germany

Late in 1916, at the suggestion of the *Idflieg*, SSW began work on a new single-seat fighter designed by Dipl Ing Harald Wolff around the new 11-cylinder Siemens-Halske Sh III geared rotary engine rated at 160 hp. The result, the D II, was a rotund single-bay biplane primarily of wooden construction, the wings featuring

The D IIc *lang* (long) prototype which featured increased wing span and reduced upper wing chord.

two hollow box spars and the fuselage being a circular-section semi-monocoque of three-ply, intended armament being two 7,9-mm LMG 08/15 machine guns. Three prototypes were initially built, the D II, the D IIa and the D IIb. Although completed early 1917, delays in availability of the Sh III engine prevented flight test of the prototypes, the first of these flying in June. Erratic engine behaviour notwithstanding, the D IIs demonstrated excellent climb performance – the D IIb attaining 16,405 ft (5 000 m) in 15.5 min during August – and three more development aircraft were ordered. Two of these, designated D IIc *kurz* (short) and D IIc *lang* (long), differed in wing span and area. The D IIc *kurz* had a span of 27 ft 10⅔ in (8,50 m) and a wing area of 208.8 sq ft (19,40 m²) whereas the D IIc *lang* had a span and area of 29 ft 6⅓ in (9,00 m) and 193.97 sq ft (18,02 m²) respectively, and reduced chord on the upper wing. The third aircraft, the D IIe, had dural wing spars, broad-chord I-type interplane struts and unbraced wings. The D IIc *kurz* entered flight test on 22 October 1917, the D IIc *lang* following on 15 November, and an initial order for 20 series aircraft, designated D III and based on the D IIc *kurz* was placed in December. The D IIc wing cellule was found to lack rigidity in flight, dictating introduction of interplane bracing cables which negated the original purpose of the dural spars, this aircraft later being rebuilt to D IV standards.

SIEMENS-SCHUCKERT (SSW) Dr I   Germany

In parallel with development of the D II, the SSW evolved a single-seat triplane fighter, the Dr I. First flown in July 1917, the Dr I was powered by a 110 hp Siemens-Halske Sh I nine-cylinder rotary engine and employed a D I fuselage. In the course of flight testing, the Dr I crashed and was seriously damaged. During reconstruction the wing area was increased by 31.22 sq ft (2,90 m²), and in this rebuilt form the fighter climbed to an altitude of 15,420 ft (4 700 m) in 20.6 min. A development of the design, the Dr II with a 160 hp Sh III engine, was discontinued at an advanced stage in construction. The following data relate to the Dr I prior to reconstruction. *Empty weight, 1,124 lb (510 kg). Loaded weight, 1,532 lb (695 kg). Span, 28 ft 2⅝ in (8,60 m). Length, 17 ft 4⅔ in (5,30 m). Wing area, 194.83 sq ft (18,10 m²).*

SIEMENS-SCHUCKERT (SSW) DDr I   Germany

Embodying the centreline thrust concept with fore and aft mounted engines, the DDr I (above and below) proved to possess inadequate stability.

Dubbed unofficially the "Flying Egg", the DDr I represented one of the earliest examples of the twin-engined centreline thrust concept, 120 hp Sh Ia rotary engines being mounted fore and aft of the pilot in an abbreviated nacelle, with the tractor engine driving a two-bladed propeller and the pusher engine driving a fourblader. An equi-span staggered triplane with the rudders and elevator carried by tubular steel outriggers, the DDr I carried an armament of two synchronised 7,9-mm LMG 08/15 machine guns. The design found favour with the *Idflieg*, to which it was presented in June 1917, the prototype flying for the first time in November, but crashing on its maiden flight. Engine control problems and inadequate stability revealed during the brief flight of the DDr I led to cancellation of a more powerful version of the basic design, the DDr II with Sh III engines. *Empty weight, 1,499 lb (680 kg). Loaded weight, 2,006 lb (910 kg). Span, 35 ft 9⅛ in (10,90 m). Length, 19 ft 0¼ in (5,80 m). Wing area, 322.93 sq ft (30,00 m²).*

(Below) The extraordinary twin-engined DDr I.

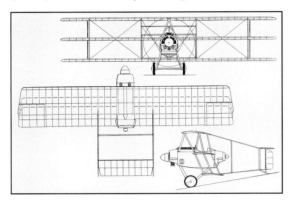

SIEMENS-SCHUCKERT (SSW) D III — Germany

With the choice of the D IIc *kurz* (short) as the basis for the initial production Sh III-powered SSW fighter biplane to which the designation D III was assigned, an order for 20 aircraft was placed in December 1917, this being augmented by an order for a further 30 in February 1918. The first two series D IIIs initially had a two-bladed propeller similar to that of the D II, but this was replaced by a smaller-diameter four-bladed propeller which permitted a reduction in the height of the undercarriage chassis. The Siemens-Halske Sh III 11-cylinder rotary engine had a nominal rating of 160 hp, but its maximum output was 210 hp at sea level. The standard armament of twin 7,9-mm LMG 08/15 synchronised machine guns was fitted. The first D IIIs came off the line in January 1918, and, between March and May, a total of 41 was sent to the Front where they demonstrated good handling qualities and outstanding climb capabilities. The Sh III engine proved troublesome, however, having been placed in service pre-

The D III (above and below), the photo depicting a first series aircraft in February 1918.

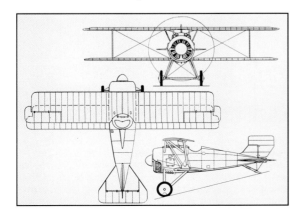

A D III of the first production series (above), flown in service by Lt V Ziegesar.

maturely, and all D IIIs were returned to SSW for modification. This involved introduction of the improved Sh IIIa engine and the cutting away of the lower portion of the engine cowling to improve cooling. In addition, some revision was made to the rudder contours. These modifications were also incorporated in a further 30 D IIIs ordered in the interim, to bring total production to 80 aircraft. A modified version, the D IIIa with ailerons on the upper wing only, participated in the second D-type contest (17 May – 28 June 1918), but was not found to offer worthwhile advantages over the standard model. *Max speed, 110 mph (177 km/h) at sea level. Time to 3,280 ft (1 000 m), 1.75 min. Range, 224 mls (360 km). Empty weight, 1,153 lb (523 kg). Loaded weight, 1,598 lb (725 kg). Span, 27 ft 7⅞ in (8,43 m). Length, 18 ft 8½ in (5,70 m). Height, 9 ft 2¼ in (2,80 m). Wing area, 202.8 sq ft (18,84 m²).*

SIEMENS-SCHUCKERT (SSW) D IV — Germany

By the end of 1917, the *Idflieg* regarded the D III as an interim development and was pressing for acceleration of work on the D IV. Retaining the Sh IIIa engine and twin LMG 08/15 gun armament, the D IV differed from its predecessor fundamentally in having a revised wing configuration developed by Heinrich Kann, the basic structure remaining unchanged. The D IV utilised an improved wing profile, the chord of the upper wing being reduced to that of the lower wing, resulting in a reduction of 40 sq ft (3,72 m²) in gross area. Rate of climb remained virtually unchanged from that of the D III, but most other aspects of the performance were improved. No fewer than 280 D IVs were ordered in March 1918, although the type did not attain operational use until August, and no more than 50-60 were to achieve active service. Production did not cease with the Armistice, continuing through January 1919, a total of 119 having been completed prior to the end of World War I. A number of D IVs (and D IIIs) continued to be operated by the *Reichswehr* and by the *Grenzschutz Ost* (Border Protection East) force, flown by volunteers to protect the German population against the Red Army in the Baltic states and Germany's eastern borders. *Max speed, 114 mph (184 km/h). Time to 3,280 ft (1 000 m), 1.9 min. Range, 239 mls (385 km). Empty weight, 1,190 lb (540 kg). Loaded weight, 1,627 lb (738 kg). Span, 27 ft 4¾ in (8,35 m). Length, 18 ft 8½ in (5,70 m). Wing area, 162.75 sq ft (15,12 m²).*

The D IV (below) attained operational service in small quantities from August 1918.

SIEMENS-SCHUCKERT (SSW) D V — Germany

Developed in parallel with the D IV, the D V was an essentially similar Sh IIIa-powered fighter differing only in having a two-bay wing cellule. Three prototypes of the D V were ordered, the first of these participating in the second D-type contest at Adlershof in May-June 1918, and the third being completed in August. By consensus the D V held less promise than the D IV, two of the prototypes being rebuilt to D IV configuration and one being lost during flight test. *Time to 3,280 ft (1 000 m), 1.8 min. Empty weight, 1,133 lb (514 kg). Loaded weight, 1,618 lb (734 kg). Span, 29 ft 0¾ in (8,86 m). Length, 18 ft 8½ in (5,70 m).*

SIEMENS-SCHUCKERT (SSW) D VI — Germany

The SSW was awarded a contract by the *Idflieg* in April 1918 for the development of a single-seat parasol monoplane fighter powered by the Sh IIIa rotary engine, three prototypes being ordered under the designation E IV, but this being changed to D VI in the following September. A unique feature of the D VI was the provision of a jettisonable main fuel tank beneath the fuselage. No prototype was completed prior to the Armistice, but two emerged in 1919, flight trials being carried out between February and May of that year. During these one of the prototypes was destroyed and the other was allegedly sabotaged by SSW workers to prevent it falling into the hands of the Allied Control Commission. *Max speed, 137 mph (220 km/h). Time to 19,685 ft (6 000 m), 16 min. Range, 217 mls (350 km). Empty weight, 1,190 lb (540 kg). Loaded weight, 1,565 lb (710 kg). Span, 30 ft 8⅞ in (9,37 m). Length, 21 ft 3⅞ in (6,50 m). Height, 8 ft 11 in (2,72 m). Wing area, 134.12 sq ft (12,46 m²).*

Flight trials with the D VI (above and below) were carried out in 1919, after the Armistice.

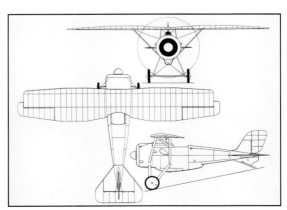

SILVANSKY IS   USSR

In 1938, A V Silvansky, assisted by Yu B Sturtsel and V D Yarovitsky, established an OKB (Experimental Construction Bureau) with the express purpose of designing and building a single-seat frontal fighter to a requirement formulated by the UV-VS (Administration of the Air Forces). Referred to as the IS (*Istrebitel Silvansky*), the fighter was a low-wing cantilever monoplane of mixed construction powered by a Tumansky M-88 14-cylinder two-row radial engine with a two-speed

Only one attempt was made to fly the prototype Silvansky fighter (below) which was then scrapped.

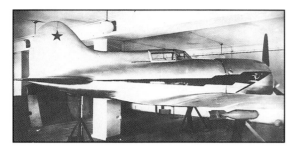

supercharger and rated at 1,100 hp. Owing to a "miscalculation", the inward-retracting mainwheel legs were of longer stroke than could be accommodated by the bays into which they were intended to retract. Once shortened, the legs provided insufficient ground clearance for the propeller, and, as a temporary expedient and in order not to delay flight testing, this was allegedly cropped by four inches (10 cm). The prototype SI was transferred to the LII (Flight Research Institute) at Moscow in the summer of 1939. There it was found that, with its cropped propeller, the aircraft required an inordinately long take-off run. Nonetheless, one attempt was apparently made to fly the aircraft, the test pilot succeeding in attaining an altitude of some 1,000 ft (300 m) at which the aircraft proved virtually unmanageable. He managed to effect a landing, pronounced that the IS was unflyable, and the prototype was scrapped, Silvansky's team being dispersed. No data relating to the IS seem to have survived.

S.I.M.B.(BERNARD) 10   France

In 1922, the Etablissements Adolphe Bernard was reorganised as the Société Industrielle des Métaux et du Bois (S.I.M.B.), this concern being joined by Jean Hubert as chief designer. Hubert was primarily responsible for the creation of a single-seat fighter of extremely advanced concept, an all-metal cantilever monoplane which was to be exhibited at the *Salon de l'Aéronautique* in Paris in 1922. Initially designated AdBE C1 (signifying *Adolphe Bernard Chasse monoplace*), the fighter was powered by a 300 hp Hispano-Suiza 8Fb eight-cylinder water-cooled engine and was

Although advanced in concept, the S.I.M.B.10 (below) suffered from poor performance and handling.

claimed at the *Salon* to be capable of 196 mph (315 km/h). Unusual features of the AdBE C1 included a ventral pylon at the base of which was an auxiliary aerofoil to which were attached the undercarriage mainwheels, a Lamblin radiator being mounted on the pylon. First flown some 18 months after its appearance at the *Salon*, the AdBE C1 was found to require major modification, the primary change being a 31½-in (80-cm) lengthening of the wing, which increased gross area to 206.67 sq ft (19,20 m²) from 182.99 sq ft (17,00 m²). Flight testing was resumed in August 1924 as the S.I.M.B.10 (or Bernard 10) at Etampes, but neither

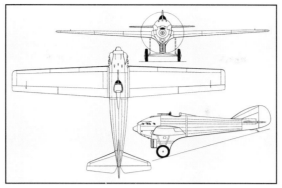

(Above) The Bernard-designed S.I.M.B.10 monoplane.

handling qualities nor performance warranted continued development. The following data relate to the fighter in its definitive form. *Max speed, 154 mph (248 km/h) at 3,280 ft (1 000 m). Empty weight, 2,094 lb (950 kg). Loaded weight, 2,976 lb (1 350 kg). Span, 36 ft 1 in (11,00 m). Length, 22 ft 11½ in (7,00 m). Height, 9 ft 0¼ in (2,75 m). Wing area, 206.67 sq ft (19,20 m²).*

S.I.M.B.(BERNARD) 12   France

Owing much to the S.I.M.B.(Bernard) 10 and employing similar constructional methods, but featuring a more conventional undercarriage arrangement, the S.I.M.B.(Bernard) 12 was a single-seat low-wing cantilever monoplane. It was powered by a 420 hp Gnome-Rhône Jupiter 9Ab nine-cylinder radial air-cooled engine and featured what was, for the mid 'twenties, the unusually heavy armament of four 7,7-mm machine guns, two in the wings and two in the fuselage. It was flown for the first time in May 1926, at which time it was proposed that the production model should have an Hispano-Suiza or Lorraine water-cooled engine of 500 hp. However, the monoplane configuration had few adherents in French military aviation circles at the time, consensus favouring the biplane and sesquiplane configurations. As a consequence further development of the fighter was discontinued. *Max speed, 165 mph (265 km/h). Ceiling, 26,247 ft (8 000 m). Empty weight, 2,006 lb (910 kg). Loaded weight, 3,395 lb (1 540 kg). Span, 39 ft 4½ in (12,00 m). Length, 23 ft 7½ in (7,20 m). Height, 8 ft 10⅓ in (2,70 m). Wing area, 226.05 sq ft (21,00 m²).*

The S.I.M.B. 14 (above and below) owed much to the experience gained with the much earlier S.I.M.B.10.

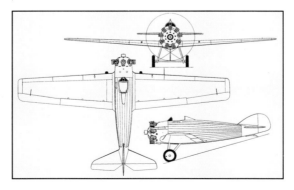

S.I.M.B.(BERNARD) 14   France

Developed in parallel with the S.I.M.B.(Bernard) 12, but owing nothing to this or previous fighters developed by the company, the S.I.M.B.(Bernard) 14, designed under the leadership of Jean Hubert, was a single-seat ses-

quiplane of wooden construction, powered by a 500 hp Hispano-Suiza 12Hb 12-cylinder water-cooled engine. Armament comprised four 7,7-mm machine guns, of which two were mounted in the wing above the fuselage and two were mounted in the fuselage nose. Flown for the first time at the end of 1925, it was destroyed at Villacoublay on 22 February 1926 as a result of a structural failure in the upper wing. Further development was discontinued after this accident. *Max speed, 165 mph (265 km/h). Time to 16,405 ft (5 000 m), 12 min. Empty weight, 2,756 lb (1 250 kg). Loaded weight, 3,968 lb (1 800 kg). Span, 41 ft 0⅛ in (12,50 m). Length, 24 ft 3⅓ in (7,40 m). Height, 10 ft 2 in (3,10 m). Wing area, 290.63 sq ft (27,00 m²).*

The sole prototype S.I.M.B. 14 (above and below) was destroyed as a result of structural failure.

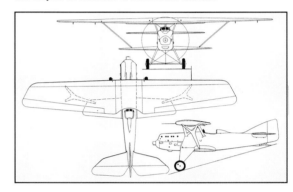

S.I.M.B.(BERNARD) 15   France

The last fighter developed by the Société Industrielle des Métaux et du Bois (S.I.M.B.) before the company terminated its activities at the end of 1926, the S.I.M.B.(Bernard) 15 was of similar sesquiplane configuration to its immediate predecessor, had the same armament, was also of wooden construction and had a 500 hp Hispano-Suiza 12Hb 12-cylinder water-cooled engine. It differed from the S.I.M.B.(Bernard) 14 principally in having a redesigned and smaller wing, and was flown during the course of 1926. Only one prototype was completed and no further development was undertaken. *Max speed, 168 mph (270 km/h). Time to 13,125 ft (4 000 m), 15 min. Loaded weight, 3,946 lb (1 790 kg). Span, 37 ft 4¾ in (11,40 m). Length, 24 ft 7¼ in (7,50 m). Height, 10 ft 2 in (3,10 m). Wing area, 258.34 sq ft (24,00 m²).*

(Below) The S.I.M.B. 15 fighter sesquiplane of 1926.

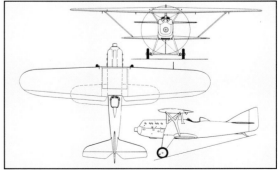

SLYUSARENKO   Russia

In the second half of 1917, the factory of V V Slyusarenko in St Petersburg, which had previously licence-built Farman, Morane and Lebed' types, built an original single-seat fighter to the designs of G P Adler. A mid-wing monoplane of wooden construction, it had a circular-section plywood monocoque fuselage and a fabric-covered wing, the power plant being either a 130 hp Clerget or 120 hp Le Rhône nine-cylinder rotary engine. Material shortages and labour difficulties which were to lead to the closure of the V V Slyusarenko factory early in 1918 prevented completion of the flight testing of the fighter, which was claimed to have attained a speed of 101 mph (163 km/h) during initial trials. No illustrations of the Slyusarenko fighter nor data relating to this type are available.

SÖDERTELGE SW 15   Sweden

Designed by V Forssman and owing much to the Siemens-Schuckert D Ia – the drawings of which had been supplied by the German company to Baron Carl Cederström, the first Swedish aviator and manager of the Södertelge Verkstäder – the SW 15 was built in 1917. A single-seat fighting scout powered by a Vabis-built Benz Bz II six-cylinder water-cooled engine rated at 110 hp, the SW 15 was primarily of wooden construction with steel-tube wing spars and fabric skinning. An unequal-span single-bay staggered biplane, the prototype crashed on 17 June 1917, ground looping and killing its pilot, Bertil de Maré. The SW 15 was repaired and fitted with two 8-mm Schwarzlose m/14 machine guns with synchronization gear developed by Capt G von Porat and Ing Kolthoff. As a result of further flight testing, two more SW 15s were built for *Flygväsendet*, but these enjoyed strictly limited success, one flying 19 times and the other four times, both being finally grounded in December 1921. *Max speed, 78 mph (125 km/h) at sea level. Span, 27 ft 1¼ in (8,26 m). Length, 19 ft 4¼ in (5,90 m). Height, 8 ft 2⅓ in (2,50 m).*

The SW 15 (above and below) enjoyed strictly limited success and only three examples were built.

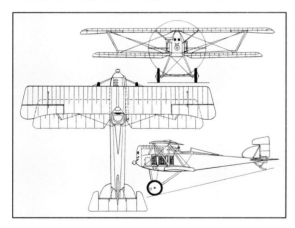

SOKO J-22 ORAO   Yugoslavia

The J-22 Orao (Eagle) single-seat transonic battlefield support fighter with secondary air defence capability was designed by the Yugoslav Air Force's Technical Institute, the *Vazduhoplovno Technicki Institut*, in col-

The second prototype of the Orao 2 version of a joint Yugoslav-Romanian design (below).

The Orao 2 (above and below) for the Yugoslav Air Force introduced afterburning engines.

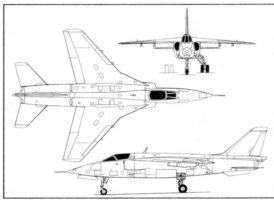

laboration with Romania's aeronautical research institute, the *Institutul de Aviatie – INCREST* under the YuRom programme. The aircraft was manufactured in both Yugoslavia and Romania, being designated I.A.R.93 (which see) in the latter country.

SOPWITH GUN BUS   UK

The Gun Bus was essentially a landplane derivative of the S.P.Gn (Sopwith Pusher, gun), a gun-carrying two-seat pusher biplane with twin floats. Six of these float-planes were ordered from the recently-founded Sopwith Aviation Company by the Greek government in March 1914, but immediately commandeered by the Admiralty when war was declared in August that year, subsequently serving with the RNAS. The Gun Bus, intended for the fighting rôle, carried a 0.303-in (7,7-mm) machine gun on a flexible mount in the forward cockpit

The Sunbeam-powered Gun Bus (above and below) which was developed specifically for the RNAS.

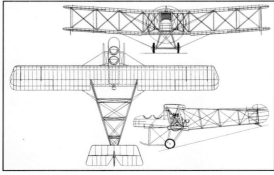

and was powered by a 100 hp Gnome Monosoupape rotary engine. A more powerful version, with a 150 hp Sunbeam eight-cylinder water-cooled engine, was developed specifically for the RNAS, this having a redesigned nacelle and a revised undercarriage. Six of the Sunbeam-powered Gun Buses were built for the RNAS by Sopwith, a further 30 being ordered for the service from Robey & Company, these last being intended for bombing (and possibly anti-submarine) duties as distinct from fighting. The pilot was moved forward to the front cockpit, a bombing panel being let into the floor and four bomb carriers being fitted beneath the lower wing. The following data relate to the Sunbeam-powered two-seat fighter Gun Bus. *Max speed, 80 mph (129 km/h). Span, 50 ft 0 in (15,24 m). Length, 32 ft 6 in (9,90 m). Height, 11 ft 4 in (3,45 m). Wing area, 474 sq ft (44,03 m²).*

SOPWITH SCHNEIDER   UK

Derived from the Tabloid float seaplane which won the Schneider Trophy contest in April 1914, and named, appropriately enough, the Schneider, the single-seat twin-float seaplane ordered into production in November 1914 for the RNAS resembled closely the aircraft that had gained the Trophy at Monaco. Retaining the same 100 hp Gnome Monosoupape nine-cylinder rotary – the upper half of which was enclosed by a ''bull-nose'' cowling – and wing-warping lateral control, the Schneider had a larger fin and rudder, reinforced float bracing and an aperture in the centre section for an upward-angled 0.303-in (7,7-mm) machine gun. Used for patrol duties against enemy airships from seaplane stations around the British coast, the Schneiders were provided with incendiary ammunition and operated against Zeppelins from early 1915. Schneiders were also carried aboard light cruisers of the North Sea Patrol for anti-Zeppelin operations, and served in the Dardanelles, in the Aegean and in the Eastern Mediterranean. Two Schneiders operated from the carrier *Ark Royal* in April 1915 at Mudros, and the type was still serving in the Aegean as late as November 1916, one shooting down an enemy aircraft which had attacked the airship shed at Mudros on the 21st of that month. A total of 136 Schneiders is believed to have been built, progressive development resulting in the Baby. *Max speed, 89 mph (143 km/h) at sea level. Time to 8,500 ft (2 500 m), 33.8 min. Endurance, 2.5 hrs. Loaded weight, 1,530 lb (694 kg). Span, 25 ft 8 in (7,82 m). Length, 22 ft 8 in (6,90 m). Height, 9 ft 9 in (2,97 m). Wing area, 240 sq ft (22,30 m²).*

A series example of the Sopwith Schneider (below) serving with the RNAS in 1915.

By 1920, Norway's *Marinens Flyvevæsen* had received 17 ex-RNAS Baby floatplanes (above).

Baby was widely used by the RNAS to provide fighter aircraft for use with patrol ships, as escorts for two-seaters and for operation from early aircraft carriers. A total of 286 Babies was built of which 195 were produced by Blackburn – and sometimes known as Blackburn Babies – 105 of the latter being fitted with the 130 hp Clerget engine, and, of these, 40 were fitted (initially) to carry the Ranken dart and no gun armament. A more extensive modification of the Sopwith float fighter was the Fairey Hamble Baby (which see). The following data relate to the 130 hp Blackburn-built Baby. *Max speed, 100 mph (161 km/h) at sea level. Time to 10,000 ft (3 050 m), 35 min. Endurance, 2.25 hrs. Empty weight, 1,226 lb (556 kg). Loaded weight, 1,715 lb (778 kg). Span, 25 ft 8 in (6,90 m). Length, 23 ft 0 in (7,01 m). Height, 10 ft 0 in (3,05 m). Wing area, 240 sq ft (22,30 m²).*

SOPWITH BABY UK

Derived from the Schneider single-seat fighter seaplane, the Baby first appeared in September 1915, and differed from its predecessor primarily in having a 110 hp Clerget nine-cylinder rotary in place of the Monosoupape, this being accommodated by a horseshoe-shaped open-fronted cowling. As on late production Schneiders, ailerons replaced wing warping for lateral control, and armament usually consisted of a single 0.303-in (7,7-mm) machine gun synchronised to fire through the propeller, although a few Babies retained the arrangement of the Schneider with the gun attached to the centre section and firing upward to clear the propeller. Several Babies were fitted with two 0.303-in (7,7-mm) guns side by side over the wing; one batch of Blackburn-built Babies was fitted with Ranken explosive darts as anti-airship weapons, and at least one was fitted with Le Prieur rockets, 10 of these devices being attached to the interplane bracing struts. Two 65-lb (29,5-kg) bombs could also be carried. The

A Blackburn-built Baby (above) with overwing guns and (below) a three-view drawing of the Baby.

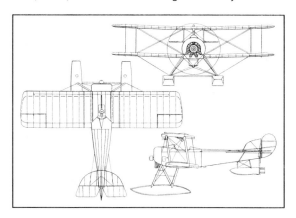

Ten Le Prieur rockets were fitted to a Baby (below) for use in the anti-Zeppelin rôle.

SOPWITH 1½-STRUTTER UK

Deriving its extraordinary appellation from a characteristic arrangement of cabane struts – a name that was initially unofficial, but came to be accepted as a result of common usage – the 1½-Strutter was both the first British aircraft to be built with a synchronised gun as standard equipment and the first true two-seat fighter to see RFC service. Designed and built for the Admiralty, the unarmed prototype was completed in December 1915, and series deliveries to the RNAS followed from February 1916. A single-bay biplane of wooden construction with fabric skinning, the 1½-Strutter featured air brakes in the lower wing and an adjustable-incidence tailplane. At an early production stage, armament was standardised on a synchronised 0.303-in (7,7-mm) gun with a second weapon of similar calibre on a Scarff ring mounting in the rear cockpit. The 1½-Strutter was used by the RNAS in both escort and (without observer) bombing rôles, and 77 of the first 150 aircraft ordered by the Admiralty were transferred to the RFC owing to the exigencies of the times. A single-seat bomber version of the 1½-Strutter was built in parallel, some examples of this variant being converted as two-seat fighters. Initial production aircraft were powered by the 110 hp Clerget 9Z nine-cylinder rotary engine, but, in the autumn of 1916, this gave place to a 130 hp Clerget 9B. At least 1,513 1½-Strutters were built in the UK (by the parent company, Fairey Aviation, Hooper & Co, Mann, Egerton & Co, Ruston, Proctor & Co, Vickers Ltd, Wells Aviation and Westland Aircraft). The 1½-Strutter was licence-built in France as a single- and two-seat bomber (SOP 1B1 and 1B2) and two-seat reconnaissance aircraft (SOP 1A2), primarily with the 110 hp and 135 hp Le Rhône 9J and 9Jby nine-cylinder rotaries, 4,500 allegedly being produced by Lioré et Olivier, Hanriot, Amiot, Besso-

Sopwith 1½-Strutter (below) in service in France late 1916 with No 70 Sqn, RFC.

neau, Darracq, REP and Sarazin Frères. The US government procured 514 from France, and others were supplied to Belgium and Imperial Russia. The following data apply to the 130 hp Clerget-engined model. *Max speed, 100 mph (161 km/h) at 6,500 ft (1 980 m). Time to 6,500 ft (1 980 m), 9.15 min. Endurance, 3.75 hrs. Empty weight, 1,305 lb (592 kg). Loaded weight, 2,150 lb (975 kg). Span, 33 ft 6 in (10,21 m). Length, 25 ft 3 in (7,69 m). Height, 10 ft 3 in (3,12 m). Wing area, 346 sq ft (32,14 m²).*

A Sopwith 1½-Strutter in RNAS service (above), and (below) a three-view drawing of the 1½-Strutter.

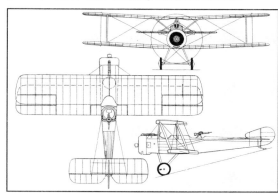

SOPWITH PUP UK

Possessing an obvious resemblance to the 1½-Strutter, the Pup – again an unofficial appellation which was to become inseparable from the aircraft to which it was affectionately applied – flew in the early spring of 1916 as the Sopwith Scout. A conventional single-bay equi-span staggered biplane primarily of wooden construction with fabric skinning, the Pup had a single 0.303-in (7,7-mm) synchronised machine gun, and all six prototypes and the initial 11 Beardmore-built aircraft had the 80 hp Clerget nine-cylinder rotary engine. Subsequently, the 80 hp Le Rhône rotary was standardised. The Pup was ordered by the Admiralty from Sopwith and Beardmore, and by the War Office from Standard

A Sopwith-built Pup (above) ready for delivery to the Royal Naval Air Service.

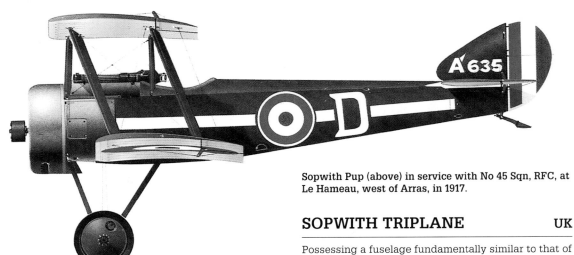

Sopwith Pup (above) in service with No 45 Sqn, RFC, at Le Hameau, west of Arras, in 1917.

for all the Triplanes then on order for the RFC. As a result, contracts were reduced and only some 150 were completed, the Triplane's operational career being brief, and its replacement by the Camel in Naval squadrons commencing as early as July 1917. The following data relate to the 130 hp Clerget-engined Triplane. *Max speed, 116 mph (187 km/h) at 6,000 ft (1 830 m). Time to 6,500 ft (1 980 m), 6.33 min. Endurance, 2.75 hrs. Empty weight, 993 lb (450 kg). Loaded weight, 1,415 lb (642 kg). Span, 26 ft 6 in (8,08 m). Length, 19 ft 6 in (5,94 m). Height, 10 ft 6 in (3,20 m). Wing area, 231 sq ft (21,46 m²).*

(Below) Three-view drawing of the Sopwith Triplane.

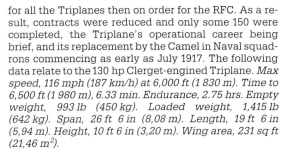

Motor and Whitehead Aircraft, the first production examples appearing in September 1916. Obsolescent as a frontline fighter by the late summer of 1917 – although production continued in 1918, 733 being delivered in that year to bring the grand total to 1,770 – the Pup was assigned to Home Defence units. To improve combat capability against the Gotha bombers then attacking the UK, the Pup was fitted with a 100 hp Gnome Monosoupape, the installation being characterised by a horseshoe-shaped cowling. Many RNAS Pups were armed with a 0.303-in (7,7-mm) gun on a tripod mount in front of the cockpit and some 20 were equipped to carry eight Le Prieur rockets, four each on the interplane struts. Early in 1917, the Pup came into use as a shipboard fighter and was used on the carriers *Campania, Furious* and *Manxman*. The following data relate to the standard Le Rhône 9C-powered Pup. *Max speed, 111 mph (179 km/h) at sea level. Time to 5,000 ft (1 525 m), 5.33 min. Endurance, 3.0 hrs. Empty weight, 787 lb (357 kg). Loaded weight, 1,225 lb (556 kg). Span, 26 ft 6 in (8,08 m). Length, 19 ft 3¾ in (5,89 m). Height, 9 ft 5 in (2,87 m). Wing area, 254 sq ft (23,60 m²).*

The Sopwith Pup (above and below), the photo showing an example built by Standard Motors Co.

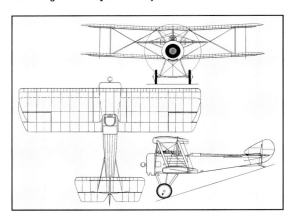

A Beardmore-built RNAS Pup (below) with Le Prieur rockets on the interplane struts.

SOPWITH TRIPLANE   UK

Possessing a fuselage fundamentally similar to that of the Pup, although the disposition of spacers, formers and stringers differed, Sopwith's next single-seat fighter – designed, like the Pup, by Herbert Smith – initiated a vogue: that of the fighting triplane. The first prototype of what was to be referred to simply as the Triplane was completed in May 1916, its radical wing arrangement of triple narrow-chord mainplanes, with ailerons on all three wings and single broad-chord interplane and centre section struts, resulted in exemplary manoeuvrability and, for its day, a phenomenal climb rate. A measure of the success of the Sopwith Triplane after making its combat début with the RNAS was provided by the extraordinary variety of single-seat fighters of similar configuration hurriedly developed by German and Austro-Hungarian companies. Initially powered by the 110 hp Clerget 9Z nine-cylinder rotary, but more usually being fitted with the 130 hp Clerget 9B, the Triplane began to appear in production form late in 1916, joining combat in the following

A Sopwith-built Triplane (above) for the RNAS, with standard armament of a single Vickers gun.

February. Armament normally comprised one synchronised 0.303-in (7,7-mm) gun, but a few were fitted with twin weapons of this calibre. At least one aircraft was tested with a 110 hp Le Rhône engine. Although the Triplane was ordered for both the RNAS and RFC, it was, in fact, used operationally by the former service only, an agreement having been reached in February 1917 under which the RNAS exchanged all its SPAD S.VIIs

SOPWITH Hispano-Suiza TRIPLANE   UK

Although Sopwith's Hispano-Suiza-engined triplane fighter was almost contemporary with the Clerget-engined Triplane, it was a completely different aeroplane, common design features being confined to the wing configuration and the style of interplane struts. Designed around the new Hispano-Suiza eight-cylinder water-cooled engine, two prototypes were completed, one with the 150 hp direct-drive version of the engine and the other with a 200 hp geared version.

The first of two prototypes of the Hispano-Suiza Triplane (above) at Brooklands.

The Hispano-Suiza Triplane featured a circular nose radiator and was generally larger than the Clerget-engined aircraft, all mainplane dimensions being greater and the fuselage apparently owing more to that of the 1½-Strutter than to the Pup. Armament was again one synchronised 0.303-in (7,7-mm) machine gun.

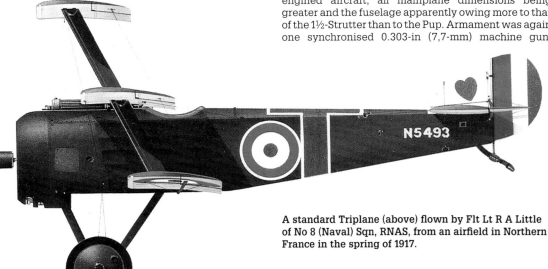

A standard Triplane (above) flown by Flt Lt R A Little of No 8 (Naval) Sqn, RNAS, from an airfield in Northern France in the spring of 1917.

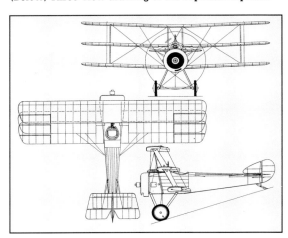

SOPWITH

534

Engine availability delayed the completion of the two prototypes until the late autumn of 1916. The 200 hp second prototype was lost on 20 October 1916 as the result of a flutter-induced tail failure, and the 150 hp first prototype continued flying until the autumn of 1917, during which it flew several home defence sorties from Manston. No further development was undertaken. The following data relate to the second prototype. *Max speed, 120 mph (193 km/h). Time to 10,000 ft (3 050 m), 9.0 min. Span, 28 ft 6 in (8,69 m). Length, 23 ft 2 in (7,06 m). Wing area, 340 sq ft (31,59 m²).*

SOPWITH L.R.T.Tr.   UK

The L.R.T.Tr., presumably signifying Long-Range Tractor Triplane, was designed to meet an RFC requirement for a combined escort fighter and airship interceptor. Other contenders were the Armstrong Whitworth F.K.6, also of triplane arrangement, and the Vickers F.B.11, which was of more conventional biplane layout.

Sopwith's long-range tractor triplane (above and below) was a contemporary of the Clerget and Hispano-Suiza triplanes, but was not a success.

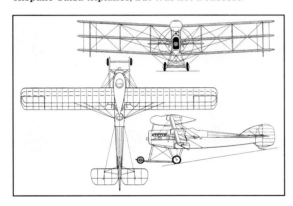

Of bizarre appearance, the L.R.T.Tr. was a three-bay triplane with narrow-chord wings, all of which were fitted with ailerons. Power was provided by a 250 hp Rolls-Royce Mk I (Eagle I) 12-cylinder water-cooled engine, and the crew comprised a pilot and two gunners. One gunner occupied the rear cockpit and the other a streamlined nacelle built around the upper wing centre section, both having a single 0.303-in (7,7-mm) machine gun. By the time flight test commenced in 1916, it was appreciated that the concept of the L.R.T.Tr. had been rendered outdated by the advent of practical gun synchronisation equipment and the success against airships enjoyed by more conventional aircraft. This clumsy aeroplane, meanwhile assigned the epithet of *Egg Box*, was duly abandoned. *Span, 52 ft 9 in (16,08 m). Length, 35 ft 3 in (10,74 m).*

SOPWITH F.1 CAMEL   UK

Evolved from the Pup, to which it bore a close family resemblance, the F.1 design – rapidly nicknamed Camel because of its hump-backed appearance, an epithet eventually to be recognised officially – was passed by the Sopwith experimental department on 22 December 1916. Possessing conventionally wire-braced and fabric-covered wooden wings, and a wire-braced wooden box girder fuselage covered by light alloy panels forward, plywood to aft of the cockpit and fabric, the Camel had an armament of twin synchronised 0.303-in (7,7-mm) guns. It was produced in series powered with the 130 hp Clerget 9B, the 150 hp Bentley

One of the few surviving Camels, this 2F.1 (above) is now preserved in the US Marine Corps Museum.

B.R.1 or the 110 hp Le Rhône nine-cylinder rotaries. The Camel (F.1 and 2F.1, the latter listed separately) was to be ordered in large numbers from various contractors (Boulton & Paul, British Caudron, Clayton & Shuttleworth, Hooper, March, Jones & Cribb, Nieuport & General, Portholme Aerodrome and Ruston, Proctor) for both the RFC and RNAS, deliveries commencing in May 1917. A total of 5,597 (F.1 and 2F.1) was ordered, of which 5,490 were apparently delivered. The F.1 Camel was adapted for the nocturnal intercept rôle as a replacement for the 1½-Strutter on Home Defence duties.

A two-gun Camel F.1 (above) in RFC service, with bombs under the fuselage and (below) a three-view drawing of the standard Camel fighter.

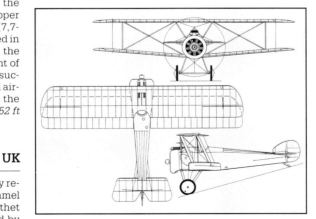

Mostly Le Rhône-powered, Camel night fighters were armed with twin 0.303-in (7,7-mm) guns above the wing centre section and firing upwards at an angle of 45 deg, the cockpit being moved one bay farther aft and the centre section cut-out being enlarged. A total of 2,519 F.1 Camels (plus 129 2F.1 Camels) was on RAF charge on 31 October 1918, but these did not survive long after the Armistice, giving place to the Sopwith

Snipe. The following data relate to the 130 hp Clerget 9B-powered F.1 Camel. *Max speed, 115 mph (185 km/h) at 6,500 ft (1 980 m). Time to 6,500 ft (1 980 m), 6.0 min. Endurance, 2.5 hrs. Empty weight, 929 lb (421 kg). Loaded weight, 1,453 lb (659 kg). Span, 28 ft 0 in (8,53 m). Length, 18 ft 9 in (5,71 m). Height, 8 ft 6 in (2,59 m). Wing area, 231 sq ft (21,46 m²).*

SOPWITH 2F.1 CAMEL   UK

A shipboard version of the F.1 Camel single-seat fighter, the 2F.1 differed essentially in having an abbreviated upper wing centre section and correspondingly shorter lower wing; narrower, steel-tube cabane struts; external elevator cables, and a detachable rear fuselage to facilitate stowage aboard ship. The standard engine was the 150 hp Bentley B.R.1, but the 130 hp Clerget 9B was regarded as an alternative, and armament comprised one synchronised 0.303-in (7,7-mm) machine gun and a second weapon of similar calibre above the wing centre section. Deliveries of the 2F.1 to the RNAS began in the autumn of 1917 against an initial order for 50 fighters placed with the parent company. William Beardmore & Co subsequently became the major contractor for this version of the Camel, building a further 150 of which the first flew on 20 February 1918. The 2F.1 Camels were employed by the RNAS and (after the amalgamation of that service with the RFC on 1 April 1918) RAF from shore bases, towed lighters, battle cruisers, large light cruisers and from the carriers *Argus, Furious, Pegasus* and *Eagle.* On 31 October 1918, 129 were on charge with the RAF, of which 112 were with units of the Grand Fleet. The 2F.1 Camel remained in service as a carrier-borne fighter for some years after World War I, a number was supplied to Latvia and Estonia, and others supplied to Canada continued in use until the late 'twenties. The following data relate to the B.R.1-powered 2F.1 Camel. *Max speed, 122 mph (196 km/h) at 10,000 ft (3 050 m). Time to 10,000 ft (3 050 m), 11.5 min. Empty weight, 1,036 lb (470 kg). Loaded weight, 1,530 lb (694 kg). Span, 26 ft 11 in (8.20 m). Length, 18 ft 8 in (5,69 m). Height, 9 ft 1 in (2,77 m). Wing area, 221 sq ft (20,53 m²).*

A pair of the 2F.1 shipboard versions of the Camel (below) serving at Turnhouse in 1918.

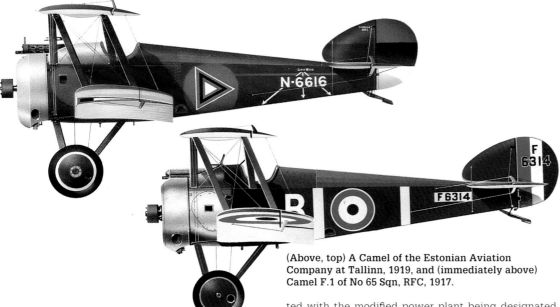

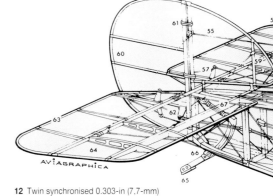

(Above, top) A Camel of the Estonian Aviation Company at Tallinn, 1919, and (immediately above) Camel F.1 of No 65 Sqn, RFC, 1917.

SOPWITH 5F.1 DOLPHIN   UK

Designed to provide the pilot with the best possible view in tactically important directions, the 5F.1 Dolphin was unusual in being a two-bay equi-span biplane with negative stagger. The pilot was seated with his head in the open framework connecting the upper mainplanes.

The Sopwith Dolphin with two guns (below) and a service example (above) showing upward-firing guns.

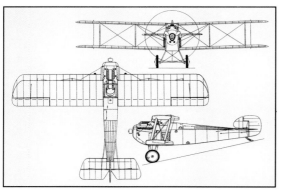

Primarily of fabric-covered wire-braced wooden construction with an upper centre section of steel tube, the Dolphin was powered by a 200 hp Hispano-Suiza geared eight-cylinder water-cooled engine in its initial production form. Armament consisted of two fixed and synchronised 0.303-in (7,7-mm) guns and either one or two guns of similar calibre mounted over the wing centre section and movable, but usually firing forwards and upwards. The prototype was flown in late May 1917, the first production contract was placed in the following month, on 29 June, and quantity deliveries to the RFC began late in the year. The first Dolphin squadron was deployed to France in February 1918, and the decision was taken to licence-build a version for the US Air Service in France. This, the Dolphin Mk II powered by a 300 hp Hispano-Suiza engine, was to be manufactured by the SACA (Société Anonyme des Constructions Aéronautiques) and the Air Service anticipated taking delivery of 2,194 by mid 1919. In the event, only a few Dolphin Mk IIs were completed before the Armistice prompted cancellation of all contracts. Difficulties with the reduction gear of the original 200 hp engine led to the conversion of many to direct drive, aircraft fit-

ted with the modified power plant being designated Dolphin Mk III and some engines having their compression ratio raised to boost output to 220 hp. Production of the Dolphin totalled 1,532 aircraft, of which all but 121 were built during 1918. Both Dolphin Mks I and III were finally withdrawn from RAF service mid 1919. The following data relate to the Dolphin Mk III. *Max speed, 128 mph (206 km/h) at 6,500 ft (1 980 m). Time to 6,500 ft (1 980 m), 6.33 min. Empty weight, 1,466 lb (665 kg). Loaded weight, 2,000 lb (907 kg). Span, 32 ft 6 in (9,90 m). Length, 22 ft 3 in (6,78 m). Height, 8 ft 6 in (2,59 m). Wing area, 263.25 sq ft (24,46 m²).*

SOPWITH 7F.1 SNIPE   UK

Conceived in the summer of 1917 as a successor to the Camel, the Sopwith 7F.1 single-seat fighter, later to be named the Snipe, was intended to utilise the new and more powerful Bentley B.R.2 nine-cylinder rotary engine (which was to commence bench running in October 1917) rated at 234 hp, and to afford a superior view for the pilot. Six prototypes were ordered, and, being adjudged superior to its competitors, (the Boulton & Paul Bobolink and the Nieuport B.N.1), the Snipe was ordered into large-scale production. The first prototype (with a B.R.1 engine) entered flight test in the early autumn of 1917, and production Snipes began to appear in the summer of 1918, contracts having been placed with the parent company, Boulton & Paul, the Coventry Ordnance Works, Napier, Nieuport & General, Portholme Aerodrome and Ruston, Proctor. Armament consisted of the standard pair of synchronised 0.303-in (7,7-mm) machine guns, and the Snipe was employed operationally for the first time on 23 September 1918. For long-range escort duties, the 7F.1a Snipe Mk Ia was developed, increased fuel tankage extending endurance to 4.5 hours, and deliveries of this version commenced early in 1919. The last prototype, referred to as the Snipe Mk II, was fitted with the 320 hp A.B.C. Dragonfly nine-cylinder radial engine, this being

(Below) A Sopwith-built Snipe flown by No 208 Sqn RAF, which re-equipped on this type at Maretz, SE of Cambrai, France, in November 1918.

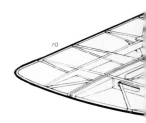

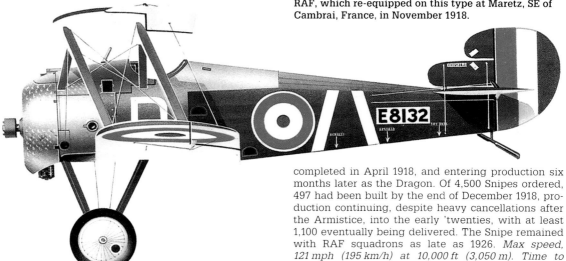

completed in April 1918, and entering production six months later as the Dragon. Of 4,500 Snipes ordered, 497 had been built by the end of December 1918, production continuing, despite heavy cancellations after the Armistice, into the early 'twenties, with at least 1,100 eventually being delivered. The Snipe remained with RAF squadrons as late as 1926. *Max speed, 121 mph (195 km/h) at 10,000 ft (3,050 m). Time to 6,500 ft (1 980 m), 5.15 min. Endurance. 3.0 hrs. Empty*

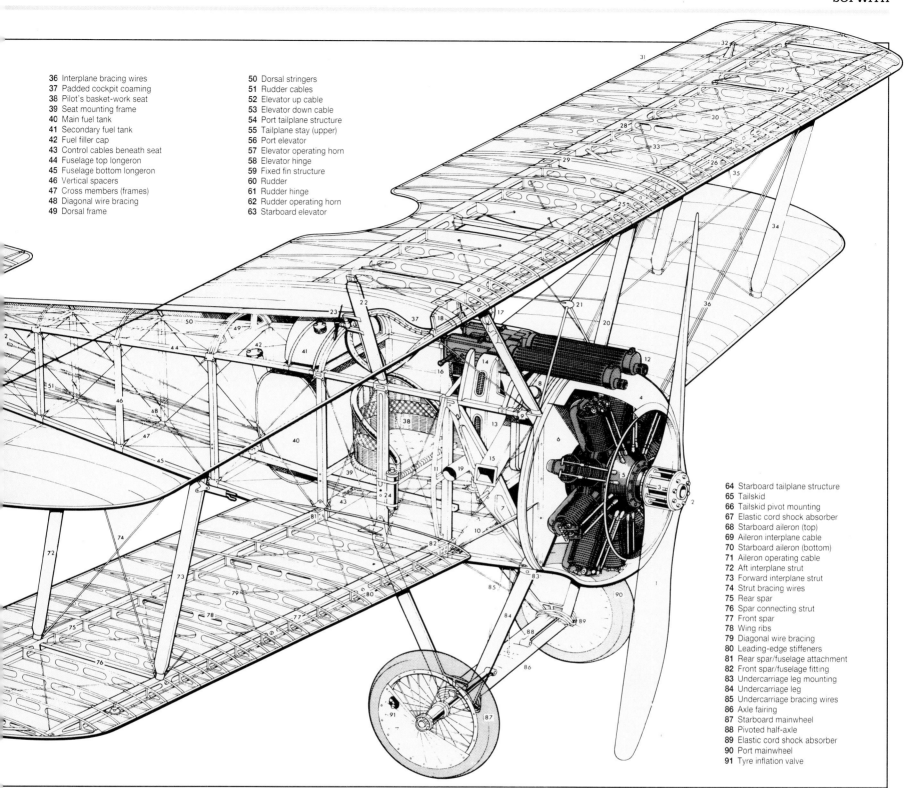

36 Interplane bracing wires	50 Dorsal stringers
37 Padded cockpit coaming	51 Rudder cables
38 Pilot's basket-work seat	52 Elevator up cable
39 Seat mounting frame	53 Elevator down cable
40 Main fuel tank	54 Port tailplane structure
41 Secondary fuel tank	55 Tailplane stay (upper)
42 Fuel filler cap	56 Port elevator
43 Control cables beneath seat	57 Elevator operating horn
44 Fuselage top longeron	58 Elevator hinge
45 Fuselage bottom longeron	59 Fixed fin structure
46 Vertical spacers	60 Rudder
47 Cross members (frames)	61 Rudder hinge
48 Diagonal wire bracing	62 Rudder operating horn
49 Dorsal frame	63 Starboard elevator

64 Starboard tailplane structure
65 Tailskid
66 Tailskid pivot mounting
67 Elastic cord shock absorber
68 Starboard aileron (top)
69 Aileron interplane cable
70 Starboard aileron (bottom)
71 Aileron operating cable
72 Aft interplane strut
73 Forward interplane strut
74 Strut bracing wires
75 Rear spar
76 Spar connecting strut
77 Front spar
78 Wing ribs
79 Diagonal wire bracing
80 Leading-edge stiffeners
81 Rear spar/fuselage attachment
82 Front spar/fuselage fitting
83 Undercarriage leg mounting
84 Undercarriage leg
85 Undercarriage bracing wires
86 Axle fairing
87 Starboard mainwheel
88 Pivoted half-axle
89 Elastic cord shock absorber
90 Port mainwheel
91 Tyre inflation valve

weight, 1,312 lb (595 kg). Loaded weight, 2,020 lb (916 kg). Span, 31 ft 1 in (9,47 m). Length, 19 ft 10 in (6,04 m). Height, 8 ft 3 in (2,51 m). Wing area, 271 sq ft (25,17 m²).

Snipe three-view drawing (below) and (right) a series aircraft with No 5 FTS, Sealand, early 1920.

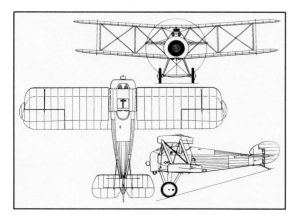

SOPWITH 3F.2 HIPPO UK

Built as a private venture, the Hippo two-seat fighter featured negative wing stagger, the gap between the wings being completely filled by the deep fuselage, and the first of two prototypes was flown on 13 September 1917. A two-seat biplane powered by a 200 hp Clerget 11Eb 11-cylinder rotary, the Hippo had an armament of two fixed synchronised 0.303-in (7,7-mm) and (initially) two free-mounted guns of similar calibre, or (later) one 0.303-in (7,7-mm) gun on a Scarff mount in the rear cockpit. Official trials were performed at Martlesham Heath in January 1918, these having been delayed by engine problems. The performance of the Hippo was considered inferior to that of the Bristol F.2B and lateral control was criticised, and, on 2 February 1918, the aircraft was returned to Sopwith. Despite official rejection, the manufacturer fitted new wings, plain ailerons and an enlarged fin. Wing dihedral was increased and stagger was reduced, and with these modifications the Hippo re-emerged in April 1918, with a second prototype following in June. By that time, the F.2B was giving satisfaction in service and it became apparent to Sopwith that the Hippo was too late, further development being discontinued. The following data relate to the Hippo in its original form. *Max speed, 115 mph (185 km/h) at 10,000 ft (3 050 m). Time to 10,000 ft (3 050 m), 13.25 min. Empty weight, 1,481 lb (672 kg). Loaded weight, 2,590 lb (1 175 kg). Span, 38 ft 9 in (11,81 m). Length, 24 ft 6 in (7,47 m). Height, 9 ft 4 in (2,84 m). Wing area, 340 sq ft (31,59 m²).*

The first Hippo (above) in its original form and (below) as later flown with dorsal gun fitted, added fin area and increased dihedral.

SOPWITH 2FR.2 BULLDOG UK

A fighter-reconnaissance two-seater, the Bulldog was a compact aircraft which, in its initial form as first flown late 1917, was a single-bay staggered biplane with a 200 hp Clerget 11Eb 11-cylinder rotary engine and an armament of two synchronised and two pillar-mounted 0.303-in (7,7-mm) machine guns. The Bulldog proved heavier than projected and difficult to control, and in an attempt to improve handling qualities it was fitted with two-bay wings with balanced ailerons, flight test being resumed in March 1918. With the balanced ailerons replaced by plain surfaces, the Bulldog was submitted to Martlesham Heath for official trials on 22 April 1918. There it was found to handle well, but to possess disappointing performance. It was eventually to be re-engined with a Bentley B.R.2. The second prototype was completed with an A.B.C. Dragonfly nine-cylinder

The first Bulldog (below) showing the single-bay wings and Clerget engine installation.

With an A.B.C. Dragonfly engine, the second of the two Bulldogs (above) had two-bay wings.

radial of 320 hp, being delivered to the RAE at Farnborough on 25 June 1918 as the Bulldog Mk II and serving as an engine test bed. Work began on a third prototype, but the Bulldog's failure to win official approval led to discontinuation of the programme before this aircraft could be completed. The following data relate to the Clerget-engined Bulldog with two-bay wings and plain ailerons. *Max speed, 109 mph (175 km/h) at 10,000 ft (3 050 m). Time to 8,000 ft (2 440 m), 8.4 min. Endurance, 2.0 hrs. Empty weight, 1,441 lb (654 kg). Loaded weight, 2,495 lb (1 132 kg). Span, 33 ft 9 in (10,29 m). Length, 23 ft 0 in (7,00 m). Height, 8 ft 9 in (2,67 m). Wing area, 335 sq ft (31,12 m²).*

SOPWITH 8F.1 SNAIL UK

Only one of the two Sopwith Snails with monocoque plywood fuselages was completed (above).

In October 1917, the A.B.C. Wasp seven-cylinder radial air-cooled engine was considered to offer much promise, and on the 31st of that month Sopwith was invited by the Air Board to tender designs for a single-seat fighter utilising that power plant. Four prototypes were ordered, these being of conventional construction, and, on 23 November, the company was asked to build two additional prototypes with plywood monocoque fuselages. In view of its intended function adoption of the name Snail for the new single-seater was bizarre, this being approved on 16 February 1918. Powered by a 170 hp Wasp I, the first prototype Snail was completed in April 1918, this having negative wing stagger and fabric skinning for its circular-section fuselage. Intended armament comprised two synchronised 0.303-in (7,7-mm) machine guns, a third weapon of similar calibre being mounted above the wing centre section, to starboard of the cut-out. The remaining three prototypes of conventional construction were not

completed, the next Snail to fly being the first of the two with plywood monocoque fuselages and positive wing stagger. On 9 May, the monocoque Snail was sent to Martlesham Heath for official trials, the reports being less than complimentary about its manoeuvrability and low-speed control. When, in October 1918, it was decided to abandon the Wasp engine, further work on the Snail was terminated, the second monocoque prototype being discontinued before completion. The following data relate to the monocoque Snail. *Max speed, 115 mph (185 km/h) at sea level. Time to 6,000 ft (1 830 m), 6.25 min. Empty weight, 1,390 lb (630 kg). Loaded weight, 1,920 lb (871 kg). Span, 25 ft 4 in (7,72 m). Length, 19 ft 0 in (5,79 m). Height, 7 ft 10 in (2,39 m). Wing area, 228.6 sq ft (21,24 m²).*

(Below) The 8F.1 Snail with monocoque fuselage.

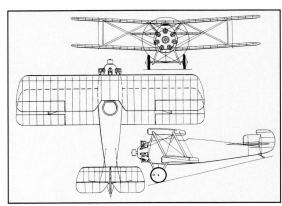

SOPWITH T.F.2 SALAMANDER UK

A requirement for an armoured single-seat ground attack fighter was issued to the Sopwith company in January 1918, a standard F.1 Camel being rapidly fitted with armour protection and triple-gun armament, and flying as the T.F.1 in the following month (T.F. indicating Trench Fighter). The T.F.1 was a stop-gap type that could be made available rapidly by modifying existing aircraft, but the requirement had specified the use of a 230 hp Bentley B.R.2 nine-cylinder rotary engine and Sopwith discarded the T.F.1 in favour of a modified Snipe design as the T.F.2 Salamander. Despite many similarities to the Snipe, the Salamander differed extensively and there was little or no interchangeability between the two aircraft. The forward portion of the fuselage was a simple armoured box, the bottom being 11-mm plate, the sides 6-mm plate, the front – the engine backplate – 8-mm plate and the rear 10-mm plate with a second 6-mm plate separated by 3.75 in (9,50 cm). Armament comprised two synchronised 0.303-in (7,7-mm) guns with provision for four 25-lb (11,34-kg) bombs. The first of three prototypes was flown on 27 April 1918, and the Salamander was ordered in large numbers (contracts were placed with the parent company, Air Navigation Co, Glendower

One of the prototype Salamanders (below) at Brooklands, with staggered gun installation.

Aircraft, National Aircraft, Palladium Autocars and Wolseley Motors), 37 being on RAF charge by 31 October. When hostilities ceased, production of the Salamander continued with a view to its use by the postwar RAF, and by mid 1919, when manufacture eventually terminated, Sopwith had delivered 334 and other contractors had contributed a further 85. However, no squadron was ever equipped with this type which was abandoned in favour of the Snipe. *Max speed, 125 mph (201 km/h) at 3,000 ft (915 m). Time to 5,000 ft (1 525 m), 6.5 min. Endurance, 1.5 hrs. Empty weight, 1,844 lb (836 kg). Loaded weight, 2,512 lb (1 139 kg). Span (balanced upper ailerons), 31 ft 2⅝ in (9,52 m). Length, 19 ft 6 in (5,94 m). Height, 9 ft 4 in (2,84 m). Wing area, 272 sq ft (25,27 m²).*

SOPWITH DRAGON UK

The sixth and last prototype of the Snipe was fitted with the 320 hp A.B.C. Dragonfly nine-cylinder radial engine as the Snipe Mk II. Despite the shortcomings of this engine, it endowed the Snipe with an outstanding performance when it could be persuaded to function efficiently, and, with the Dragonfly's faults still to be recognised as incurable, 30 Snipes were ordered with the A.B.C. engine on 3 May 1918. Assigned the name Dragon, these were delivered in June and July 1919, the production prototype having appeared in the previous January. The Dragonfly-engined Snipes were produced in parallel with aircraft built from the ground up as Dragons, these having horn-balanced upper ailerons and the 360 hp Dragonfly Ia engine, armament comprising the standard pair of synchronised 0.303-in (7,7-mm) guns. About 200 of a 300-aircraft contract were completed and efforts to cure the engine's troubles continued until the autumn of 1921, the Dragon, officially adopted at that time as a standard RAF single-seat fighter, never being issued to a squadron and being officially declared obsolete in April 1923. *Max speed, 105 mph (241 km/h). Time to 10,000 ft (3 050 m), 7.5 min. Loaded weight, 2,132 lb (967 kg). Span, 31 ft 1 in (9,47 m). Length, 21 ft 9 in (6,63 m). Height, 9 ft 6 in (2,90 m). Wing area, 271 sq ft (25,18 m²).*

The first Dragon (above) completed from a Snipe airframe and (below) Dragon three-view drawing.

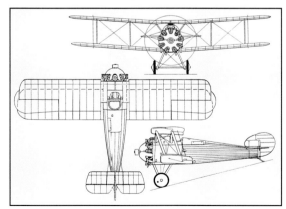

SOPWITH SWALLOW UK

Utilising an F.1 Camel fuselage mated with a parasol wing, the Swallow single-seat fighter monoplane was powered by a 110 hp Le Rhône 9J nine-cylinder rotary engine and carried the standard armament of twin synchronised 0.303-in (7,7-mm) machine guns. Flown for the first time in September 1918, the Swallow was delivered to Martlesham Heath for official trials on 29 October 1918, remaining there until May 1919, the trials

The sole Swallow (above) used the fuselage of a series Camel, with a new monoplane wing.

having been delayed by fuel system problems. The performance of the Swallow as revealed at Martlesham did not warrant further development, and the prototype was scrapped. *Max speed, 113 mph (182 km/h) at 10,000 ft (3 050 m). Time to 6,500 ft (1 980 m), 5.6 min. Empty weight, 889 lb (403 kg). Loaded weight, 1,420 lb (644 kg). Span, 28 ft 10 in (8,79 m). Length, 18 ft 9 in (5,72 m). Height, 10 ft 2 in (3,10 m). Wing area, 160 sq ft (14,86 m²).*

SOPWITH SNARK UK

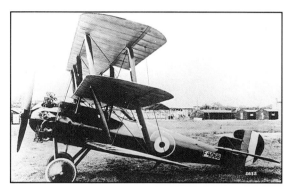

Too late for wartime service, the Snark (above) was the last of the Sopwith triplane fighter designs.

Despite the fact that, by 1918, the triplane configuration was widely considered as *passé* for the fighter, on 14 May of that year, Sopwith was awarded a contract for three prototypes of a new single-seat fighting triplane, conforming to the RAF Type I specification and named the Snark. Powered by a 320 hp A.B.C. Dragonfly I nine-cylinder radial and featuring a plywood monocoque fuselage, the Snark was an equi-span staggered triplane and its designed armament was somewhat radical in the weight of fire that it offered, consisting of two synchronised 0.303-in (7,7-mm) guns on the fuselage and four weapons of similar calibre mounted two per side under the bottom wing. The first Snark was passed for flight test in September 1918, but unavailability of a Dragonfly engine and the decision to make various minor modifications delayed manufacturer's trials until September of the following year, the aircraft arriving at Martlesham Heath for official trials on 12 November 1919. The second prototype reached Martlesham on 17 March 1920, and the third prototype, with a 360 hp Dragonfly Ia engine, late in the year. Apart from engine problems, the Snark triplanes suffered fuselage deterioration and all three were written off in 1921. *Max speed, 130 mph (209 km/h) at 3,000 ft (915 m). Loaded weight, 2,283 lb (1 036 kg). Span, 26 ft 6 in (8,08 m). Length, 20 ft 6 in (6,25 m). Height, 10 ft 10 in (3,30 m). Wing area, 322 sq ft (29,91 m²).*

SOPWITH SNAPPER UK

Designed in parallel with the Snark triplane and similarly intended to meet the requirements of the RAF's Type I specification, the Snapper single-bay staggered equi-span biplane was destined to be the last fighter to bear the Sopwith name before the company went into liquidation in September 1920. Three prototypes of the Snapper were ordered on 6 June 1918, and, although originally designed with a plywood monocoque fuselage, all three aircraft were completed with conventional fabric-covered fuselages. Powered by a 320 hp A.B.C. Dragonfly I nine-cylinder radial engine and

carrying the standard pair of synchronised 0.303-in (7,7-mm) machine guns, the first Snapper performed manufacturer's trials in the second half of July 1919, being delivered to Martlesham Heath for official trials on 1 August. Flight test was somewhat spasmodic owing to recurring difficulties with the engine, but all three Snappers were at the RAE, Farnborough, in mid-1920. It is presumed that trials continued until the decision was taken to discontinue further attempts to rectify the engine's problems. *Max speed, 140 mph (225 km/h) at 3,000 ft (915 m). Time to 3,000 ft (915 m), 1.93 min. Empty weight, 1,462 lb (663 kg). Loaded weight, 2,190 lb (993 kg). Span, 28 ft 0 in (8,53 m). Length, 20 ft 7 in (6,27 m). Height, 10 ft 0 in (3,05 m). Wing area, 292 sq ft (27,13 m²).*

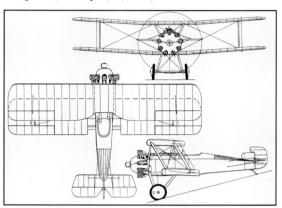

Designed in parallel with the Snark, the Snapper (above and below) appeared in April 1919.

SPAD SA.1 France

The acronym SPAD originally signified the Société Provisoire des Aéroplanes Deperdussin. In 1913, following Armand Deperdussin's involvement in a major financial scandal, the company went into liquidation. Its assets, including the services of its chief designer, Louis Béchereau, were acquired in August 1914 by a syndicate headed by aviation pioneer Louis Blériot. This retained the SPAD acronym which now stood for Société Pour Aviation et ses Dérivés. The first fighter designed by Béchereau for the new SPAD organisation, the SA.1 was of somewhat bizarre concept, attempting to offer effective forward-firing armament while retaining a tractor engine arrangement. Powered by an 80 hp Le Rhône rotary engine and first flown on 21 May 1915, the SA.1 was of so-called "pulpit" type in that the

The unusual SA.1 (below) was the first of many SPAD fighter designs by Louis Béchereau.

observer/gunner occupied a small plywood nacelle *ahead* of the propeller. A two-seat unstaggered equi-span single-bay biplane, with auxiliary intermediate struts stiffening the points of intersection of the flying and landing cables and giving the superficial impression of a two-bay arrangement, the SA.1 was of fabric-covered wood and wire construction. The armament consisted of a single 7,7-mm Lewis gun with limited traverse and elevation mounted in the forward nacelle, which was supported by two V-struts pivoted to the undercarriage struts and secured to the propeller hub by an extension of the propeller shaft revolving in a ball-race attached to the rear of the nacelle. The entire nacelle had to be swung downwards to provide access to the engine. Very limited production (possibly fewer than a half-dozen) of the SA.1 was undertaken for the *Aviation Militaire* before, by November 1915, it gave place to the SA.2. Neither SA.1 nor its successor proved popular with the aircrews, the observer/gunner inevitably being crushed by the engine in the event of the aircraft nosing over. *Max speed, 84 mph (135 km/h) at sea level. Endurance, 2.75 hrs. Empty weight, 928 lb (421 kg). Loaded weight, 1,562 lb (708 kg). Span, 31 ft 4 in (9,55 m). Length, 23 ft 11 in (7,29 m). Height, 8 ft 6½ in (2,60 m). Wing area, 273 sq ft (25,36 m²).*

SPAD SA.2   France

Evolved from the SA.1, from which it differed essentially in having a 110 hp Le Rhône 9J engine, modified nacelle attachments and gun mount, and a revised horizontal tail with parallel leading and trailing edges, the SA.2 was introduced in November 1915. The 7,7-mm Lewis gun was provided with an unusual mounting, being suspended between two curved vertical steel tubes hinged at their top to a vertical pylon and rotating at their base through some 180 deg, thus providing both elevation and traverse. SPAD apparently received contracts for 100 SA.2 two-seat fighters, of which 57 were supplied to the Russian Imperial Air Service and at least one was completed as an SA.3. The remainder were supplied to the *Aviation Militaire*, but these saw relatively limited use at the Front, where, on 1 February

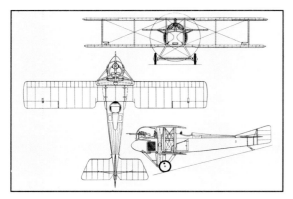

The SA.2 (above and below) saw service with both the *Aviation Militaire* and the Russian Imperial air arm.

1916, only four SA.2s were with operational units, a further five being recorded with (presumably) training elements. *Max speed, 87 mph (140 km/h) at sea level. Time to 3,280 ft (1 000 m), 6.5 min. Endurance, 3.0 hrs. Empty weight, 913 lb (414 kg). Loaded weight, 1,485 lb (674 kg). Dimensions as for SA.1 apart from a length of 25 ft 9 in (7,85 m).*

SPAD SA.3   France

While based fundamentally on the SA.2 two-seat fighter, the SA.3 was of highly innovatory concept in that it featured fore- and aft-mounted 7,7-mm Lewis guns and it was intended that either occupant could control the aircraft while the other operated his gun. No record has apparently survived of the geometry of the dual control arrangement, which must have been exceptionally complex, but the difficulty of adequate communication between the two widely-spaced cockpits – with the 110 hp Le Rhône 9J rotary engine and its propeller between – must have proved insurmountable. The SA.3 may have inspired the SPAD Type C, a "pulpit" type three-seater (presumably for a pilot plus front and rear gunners), although it is doubtful that this type was built. It may be presumed that data for the SA.3 were generally similar to those for the SA.2.

The SA.3 (below) featured dual controls and fore- and aft-mounted machine guns.

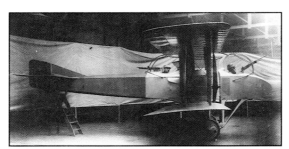

SPAD SA.4   France

Despite the patent obsolescence of concept of the basic Type A design, it was surprisingly taken a stage further as late as February 1916 when the SA.4 made its début. This reverted to the 80 hp Le Rhône 9C rotary – possibly owing to cooling problems with the 110 hp 9J – and was apparently intended solely for the Russian Imperial Air Service, which had received more than half of the total production of the SA.2. In the event, only 10 SA.4s were built by SPAD for Russia, the first example flying on 22 February 1916. One example was supplied to the *Aviation Militaire*. Armament was similar to that of the SA.2 and at least some of the Russian SA.4s had a revised upper wing in which outboard panels were attached to a centre section (earlier models had had two wing panels meeting on the centreline). The SA.4 had ailerons on the upper wing only, the chord of this wing being increased over that of the lower. *Max speed, 96 mph (154 km/h) at sea level. Time to 3,280 ft*

An SA.4 (above) serving with the Russian Imperial Air Service which received 10 examples of this type.

(1 000 m), 5.0 min, to 9,840 ft (3 000 m), 23.5 min. Endurance, 2.5 hrs. Span, 31 ft 4 in (9,55 m). Length, 25 ft 9 in (7,85 m). Height, 8 ft 6½ in (2,60 m).

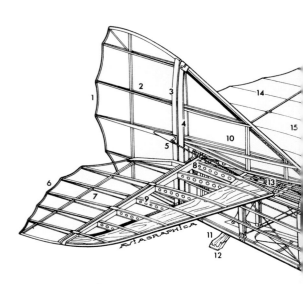

Key to SPAD S.VII

1 Steel wire trailing edge
2 Rudder construction
3 Rudder post
4 Sternpost
5 Rudder hinge control
6 Starboard elevator
7 Elevator construction
8 Elevator hinge control
9 Tailplane construction
10 Fin construction
11 Tailskid
12 Steel shoe
13 Elastic cord shock absorber
14 Port elevator
15 Port tailplane
16 Fin attachment
17 Fuselage fabric covering
18 Dorsal construction
19 Dorsal stringers
20 Top longeron
21 Tailplane control cables
22 Vertical spacers
23 Bottom longeron
24 Fuselage stringers
25 Diagonal wire bracing
26 Headrest fairing
27 Plywood decking
28 Headrest
29 Padded cockpit coaming
30 Fuel filler cap
31 Used cartridge belt storage drum
32 Exhaust pipe tail fairing
33 Control cable pulleys
34 Pilot's seat
35 Safety harness
36 Underfloor fuel tank
37 Starboard upper wing panel construction
38 Upper wing spars
39 Compression rib
40 Internal wire bracing
41 Aileron horn control
42 Starboard aileron
43 Leading-edge carry-round
44 Leading-edge stiffeners
45 Interplane strut
46 Aileron control rod

SPAD SG.1   France

Louis Béchereau's first attempt to produce a single-seat fighter was apparently the Type G which had the gunner's nacelle ahead of the propeller of the SA series replaced by a similarly-shaped nacelle containing remotely-controlled armament. A concept prototype was provided by modifying the original SA.1 prototype with a revised forward nacelle from which four *dummy* machine gun barrels protruded. It is not known whether this aircraft was ever fully armed and flown – if so it would have a strong claim to having been the world's first multi-gun fighter with fixed weapons. The SG.1 – a designation which has still to be authenticated – was a single-seat fighter presumably based on the modified SA.1 prototype, but with a single fixed heavy machine gun in the forward nacelle and which, according to French sources, emerged in April 1916 with a 110 hp Le Rhône rotary engine. What must have been

The concept prototype of the SG.1 (above) was apparently Louis Béchereau's first attempt to produce a single-seat fighter for the SPAD concern.

the SG.1 was mentioned in a Royal Flying Corps report on French aircraft of April 1916, which stated that the fighter was armed with a "heavy Hotchkiss *mitrailleuse d'infanterie* with a belt of 1,000 rounds carried in a streamlined basket in front of the propeller". The following data were provided by the report, the wing area quoted suggesting that the SG.1 was somewhat smaller than the SA types. No photograph of the SG.1 has apparently survived. *Max speed, 100 mph (161 km/h) at 6,560 ft (2 000 m), 96 mph (154 km/h) at 9,840 ft (3 000 m). Time to 6,560 ft (2 000 m), 7.25 min, to 9,840 ft (3 000 m), 11.5 min. Wing area, 200 sq ft (18,58 m²).*

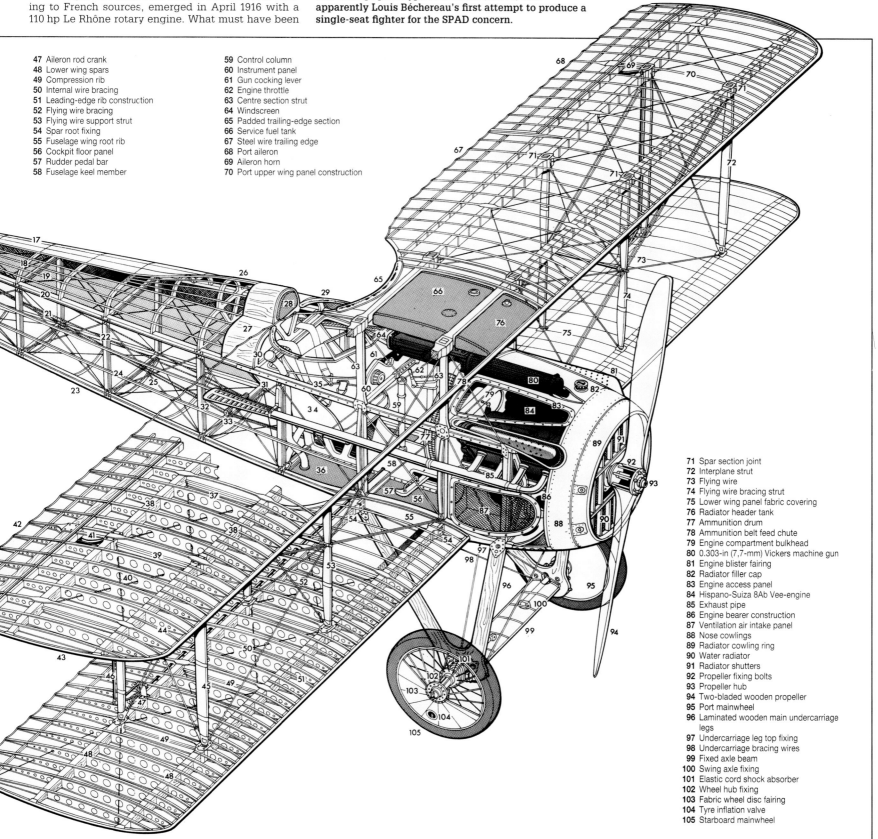

47 Aileron rod crank
48 Lower wing spars
49 Compression rib
50 Internal wire bracing
51 Leading-edge rib construction
52 Flying wire bracing
53 Flying wire support strut
54 Spar root fixing
55 Fuselage wing root rib
56 Cockpit floor panel
57 Rudder pedal bar
58 Fuselage keel member
59 Control column
60 Instrument panel
61 Gun cocking lever
62 Engine throttle
63 Centre section strut
64 Windscreen
65 Padded trailing-edge section
66 Service fuel tank
67 Steel wire trailing edge
68 Port aileron
69 Aileron horn
70 Port upper wing panel construction
71 Spar section joint
72 Interplane strut
73 Flying wire
74 Flying wire bracing strut
75 Lower wing panel fabric covering
76 Radiator header tank
77 Ammunition drum
78 Ammunition belt feed chute
79 Engine compartment bulkhead
80 0.303-in (7,7-mm) Vickers machine gun
81 Engine blister fairing
82 Radiator filler cap
83 Engine access panel
84 Hispano-Suiza 8Ab Vee-engine
85 Exhaust pipe
86 Engine bearer construction
87 Ventilation air intake panel
88 Nose cowlings
89 Radiator cowling ring
90 Water radiator
91 Radiator shutters
92 Propeller fixing bolts
93 Propeller hub
94 Two-bladed wooden propeller
95 Port mainwheel
96 Laminated wooden main undercarriage legs
97 Undercarriage leg top fixing
98 Undercarriage bracing wires
99 Fixed axle beam
100 Swing axle fixing
101 Elastic cord shock absorber
102 Wheel hub fixing
103 Fabric wheel disc fairing
104 Tyre inflation valve
105 Starboard mainwheel

SPAD

An S.VII of (above, top) the French *Escadrille* SPA 81 and (immediately above) of No 23 Sqn of the RFC at La Lovie in France, July 1917.

SPAD S.VII   France

Evolved by Louis Béchereau virtually in parallel with the unorthodox Type G (SG.1) was the relatively conventional Type H which retained the characteristic interplane bracing of preceding SPAD fighters and was of similar construction. Powered by the new 150 hp water-cooled Hispano-Suiza 8Aa eight-cylinder Vee-type engine, the prototype, referred to contemporaneously as the SH.1, was flown in April 1916. Trials indicated that the SH.1 offered a pronounced advance on existing fighter equipment and SPAD received a contract on 10 May for 268 aircraft under the official designation Spa.VII C1 (*monoplace de chasse*). The derivation of this designation is obscure, but SPAD's series of letter designations in alphabetical sequence appears to have been discarded in favour of a system more or less conforming with the designation assigned by the SFA (*Service des Fabrications de l'Aviation*). Consequently, the production version of the Type H was given the *company* designation S.VII. A sturdy aircraft possessing great structural strength and fine handling qualities, the S.VII closely resembled the SH.1. It retained the circular frontal radiator, but dispensed with the large spinner with frontal opening, and wing area was increased by 19.90 sq ft (1,85 m²). Armament com-

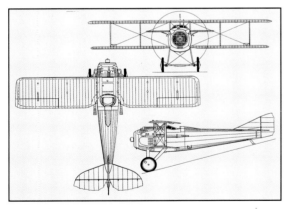

The S.VII (above and below), that illustrated by the photo being a Mann Egerton-built example.

A Czechoslovak Army S.VII (above) photographed at Cheb in Western Bohemia during 1920-21.

prised a single 7,7-mm Vickers gun with Birkigt synchronisation mechanism. Initial delivery tempo was slow; by 25 February 1917, only 268 S.VIIs had been delivered to the *Aviation Militaire* plus 39 to the Royal Flying Corps. The S.VII was initially referred to as the *mitrailleuse volante* of Georges Guynemer (France's leading ace), but by December 1916, he had told Béchereau that "the 150 hp SPAD is no match for the Halberstadt ... it [the Halberstadt] climbs better and, consequently, has an overall advantage". One consequence was the introduction of the 180 hp HS 8Ab engine in S.VIIs from the spring of 1917. Apart from production by the parent company, the S.VII was to be built in France by the Société SPAD et Janoir, Blériot Aéronautique, Kellner, Regy, Gremont, S.E.A. and De Marçay, some 5,500 being produced. In addition, 120 were built in the UK by Mann Egerton and 100 by L Blériot (Aeronautics) for the RFC, and in Russia slightly more than 100 had been built by Dux when lack of engines terminated production. Most French *escadrilles de chasse* flew the S.VII at one time or another, and, in addition to its use in the UK and Russia, it was operated by Belgium, Italy and the USA. After World War I, S.VIIs served with Brazil, Czechoslovakia, Estonia, Finland, Greece, Peru, Poland, Portugal, Romania, Siam and Yugoslavia. The following data relate to the 180 hp S.VII. *Max speed, 132 mph (212 km/h) at 6,560 ft (2 000 m). Time to 6,560 ft (2 000 m), 4.67 min. Endurance, 1.5 hrs. Empty weight, 1,102 lb (500 kg). Loaded weight, 1,552 lb (704 kg). Span, 25 ft 8 in (7,82 m). Length, 19 ft 11⅜ in (6,08 m). Height, 7 ft 2⅝ in (2,20 m). Wing area, 192.14 sq ft (17,85 m²).*

SPAD S.XI   France

The basic SPAD S.XI was intended by Louis Béchereau as a two-seat fighter. When the prototype appeared in September 1916, it was clearly descended from the S.VII, but it had conventional two-bay interplane bracing for its longer wings, which were staggered and featured sweepback. Powered by a 220 hp Hispano-Suiza 8Bc eight-cylinder water-cooled Vee-type engine, the S.XI was found to possess extremely sensitive handling qualities and was deemed unsuited for the fighter rôle. It was adopted as a *Corps d'Armée* reconnaissance aircraft, however, entering production as the S.XI A2. It proved a dismal failure in service, largely for reasons unassociated with the basic design, yet 1,000 examples were produced. In an attempt to create a two-seat night fighter, one of these was experimentally fitted with a frontal searchlight as the S.XI Cn2. The mounting of the searchlight *ahead* of the propeller clearly drew on SPAD's earlier experience in mounting the forward nacelle of the Type A series. It may be assumed that the S.XI Cn2 proved unsuccessful under test as only one example was completed. The following data are for the S.XI A2, but those for the Cn2 version can be assumed to have been similar. *Max speed, 112 mph (180 km/h). Time to 9,845 ft (3 000 m), 12.6 min. Endurance, 2.25 hrs. Empty weight, 1,497 lb (679 kg). Loaded weight, 2,282 lb (1 035 kg). Span, 36 ft 9⅓ in (11,21 m). Length, 25 ft 8⅔ in (7,84 m). Height, 9 ft 2¼ in (2,80 m). Wing area, 322.93 sq ft (30,00 m²).*

The sole two-seat night fighter version of the S.XI (below) with a searchlight in front of the propeller.

SPAD S.XII   France

Late in 1916, France's leading fighter ace, Georges Guynemer, asked Louis Béchereau to design for him a fighter capable of mounting a 37-mm shell-firing gun. Béchereau developed from the S.VII a generally similar aircraft powered by a 200 hp Hispano-Suiza 8C engine and incorporating a 37-mm Puteaux cannon firing through a hollow propeller shaft, an arrangement made possible by the engine's spur reduction gear. A supplementary 7,7-mm Vickers gun was fitted, and the mainplanes, unlike those of the S.VII, had modest stagger. The SFA designation of the aircraft was Spa.XII Ca1. Series aircraft were powered by the 220 hp Hispano-Suiza 8Cb engine, and, although 300 of the cannon-armed S.XII fighters were ordered, their operational use proved to be very limited. They could be flown with any hope of success only by pilots of considerable skill and experience. The cannon was a single-shot weapon, fumes filled the cockpit when it was fired and reloading in combat was tricky. Owing to the bulk of the gun, the S.XII used (at Guynemer's suggestion) Deperdussin-type flying controls (ie, a wheel on a rocking arch). No

(Below) The S.XII which mounted a 37-mm cannon.

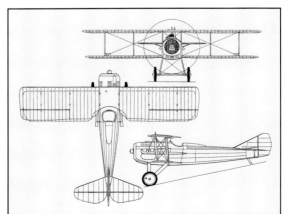

The cannon-armed S.XII (above) never equipped a complete *escadrille* of the *Aviation Militaire*.

escadrille was ever completely equipped with this fighter, which was allotted in small numbers and only to selected pilots. Guynemer made his first operational sortie on the S.XII on 5 July 1917, and 15 months later, on 1 October 1918, there were only eight S.XIIs with operational *escadrilles*. *Max speed, 126 mph (203 km/h) at 6,560 ft (2 000 m). Time to 6,560 ft (2 000 m), 6.05 min. Endurance, 1.75 hrs. Empty weight, 1,295 lb (587 kg). Loaded weight, 1,947 lb (883 kg). Span, 26 ft 3 in (8,00 m). Length, 21 ft 0 in (6,40 m). Height, 8 ft 4½ in (2,55 m). Wing area, 217.44 sq ft (20,20 m²).*

SPAD S.XIII   France

The S.XIII (above and below), the photo depicting an aircraft of the 22nd Aero Sqn of US Air Service, 1919.

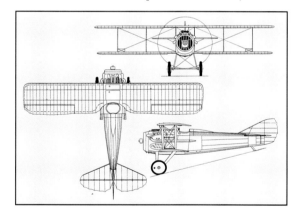

The combat inadequacies of the S.VII led to substantial revision of the basic design to accept the 200 hp Hispano-Suiza 8B engine and paired synchronised 7,7 mm Vickers machine guns. Designated S.XIII (Spa.XIII C1), the new fighter embodied many features of the S.VII, notably the single-bay interplane bracing with intermediate struts, rod-and-crank aileron actuation and circular radiator cowling. It bore a close family resemblance to the S.XII, but was, in fact, a completely separate and structurally different aircraft. All major dimensions were larger than those of the S.VII, and an initial batch of 20 S.XIIIs was under construction in

An S.XIII (above) flown by Capt Eddie Rickenbacker (seen in front of aircraft) of the 94th Aero Sqn.

February 1917. The *Aviation Militaire* had 372 S.XIIIs on strength by 1 April 1918. Orders placed with the parent company and eight other contractors (ACM de Colombes, Bernard, Blériot, Borel, Kellner, Levasseur, Nieuport and S.C.A.) were eventually to exceed 8,470 aircraft, but it seems unlikely that more than 7,300 were completed. In service, the S.XIII was handicapped by the several shortcomings of the geared engine, but saw widespread service. As at 1 October 1918, 764 S.XIIIs were with operational units of the *Aviation Militaire*, and the RFC received 61 Kellner-built examples between November 1917 and April 1918. Others went to Italian, Belgian and US fighter units, and later production aircraft had modified wings with blunt tips and the 220 hp Hispano-Suiza 8Bc, 8Bd or 8Be. The S.XIII remained in French service until 1923. The following data relate to the 220 hp S.XIII. *Max speed, 135 mph (218 km/h) at 6,560 ft (2 000 m). Time to 6,560 ft (2 000 m), 4.67 min. Endurance, 1.67 hrs. Empty weight, 1,326 lb (601 kg). Loaded weight, 1,888 lb (856 kg). Span, 27 ft 1 in (8,25 m) and later 26 ft 6 in (8,08 m). Length, 20 ft 6 in (6,25 m). Height, 8 ft 6½ in (2,60 m). Wing area, 227.23 sq ft (21,11 m²) and later 217.44 sq ft (20,20 m²).*

SPAD S.XIV   France

The cannon-armed S.XIV (above) which was built in small numbers for France's *Aviation Maritime*.

Based on the fuselage and engine/armament combination of the S.XII, with the 37-mm Puteaux cannon firing through the hollow propeller shaft, the S.XIV was a single-seat twin-float fighter designed by André Herbemont, Béchereau's assistant. Powered by the 220 hp Hispano-Suiza 8Bc engine and armed with a single

7,7-mm Vickers machine gun in addition to the cannon, the S.XIV had long-span wings with true two-bay bracing, and the prototype was flown for the first time on 15 November 1917. SPAD built a further 39 S.XIVs for the *Aviation Maritime*, their floats being manufactured by Levasseur. The recorded maximum level speed of this fighter was claimed as a record for float-equipped aircraft at that time. *Max speed, 127 mph (205 km/h) at sea level. Time to 6,560 ft (2 000 m), 7.3 min. Empty weight, 1,696 lb (770 kg). Loaded weight, 2,337 lb (1 060 kg). Span, 32 ft 2 in (9,80 m). Length, 24 ft 3 in (7,40 m). Height, 13 ft 1½ in (4,00 m). Wing area, 282 sq ft (26,20 m²).*

(Below) The S.XIV floatplane fighter of 1917.

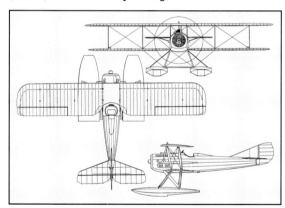

SPAD S.XV   France

After Louis Béchereau left SPAD in the spring of 1917, responsibility for subsequent aircraft design devolved upon André Herbemont, and the first fighter entirely of his creation was the S.XV, a small single-seater with twin synchronised 7,7-mm Vickers guns, and, initially, a 160 hp Gnome Monosoupape rotary engine. The S.XV had a clean, wooden monocoque fuselage, single-bay wings and a large spinner-like fairing ahead of the propeller (probably similar to the Nieuport *cône de pénétration*). The S.XV first flew on 31 July 1917, and a

(Below) The S.XV/2 with extended wing and new tail.

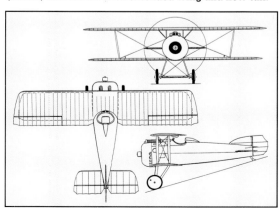

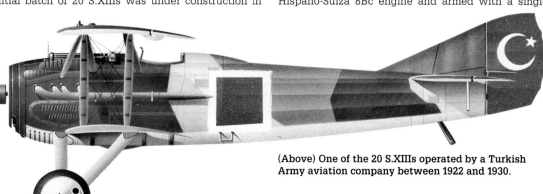

(Above) One of the 20 S.XIIIs operated by a Turkish Army aviation company between 1922 and 1930.

The first S.XV (above) in its initial form with a large spinner-like fairing ahead of the propeller.

second version, the S.XV/2 with extended wings, a redesigned tail and a simplified engine installation, followed in August. Neither was a success and some redesign was undertaken, the S.XV/3 with a lengthened fuselage having reportedly flown in January 1918. A fourth version, the S.XV/4, was to have had a 170 hp Le Rhône engine, but appears to have been abandoned by 1 May 1918, the date of an official listing. Two much-modified examples of the S.XV were built after the end of the War with the 80 hp Le Rhône engine as sporting single-seaters. The following data relate to the S.XV/2. *Max speed, 124 mph (199 km/h) at 6,560 ft (2 000 m). Time to 6,560 ft (2 000 m), 5.67 min. Endurance, 2.5 hrs. Empty weight, 811 lb (368 kg). Loaded weight, 1,378 lb (625 kg). Span, 23 ft 3½ in (7,10 m). Length (S.XV), 17 ft 6⅝ in (5,35 m). Height, 7 ft 6½ in (2,30 m). Wing area, 188.4 sq ft (17,50 m²).*

The S.XV/2 (below) which featured extended wings, redesigned tail and modified engine installation.

SPAD S.XVII — France

Essentially a strengthened S.XIII airframe with a 300 hp Hispano-Suiza 8Fb engine, the S.XVII had the same overall dimensions as the earlier fighter, but the fuselage was bulkier and fully faired throughout its length, the stringers being set closer together. The wing structure was substantially strengthened, a visible reinforcement being the auxiliary flying wires under the lower wings. Late in 1917, the 300 hp engine had been installed in an S.XIII airframe, presumably as a prototype for the S.XVII, but this had crashed early in its test programme. Subsequent production apparently did not extend beyond the 20 aircraft of what may be assumed to have been an initial development batch. Operational trials with the S.XVII were performed in June 1918, and examples were flown by pilots of *Les Cicognes. Max speed, 135 mph (217 km/h) at 6,560 ft (2 000 m). Time to 6,560 ft (2 000 m), 5.4 min. Endurance, 1.25 hrs. Empty weight, 1,411 lb (640 kg). Loaded weight, 1,984 lb (900 kg). Span, 26 ft 6 in (8,08 m). Length, 20 ft 6 in (6,25 m). Height, 8 ft 6½ in (2,60 m). Wing area, 215.28 sq ft (20,00 m²).*

The S.XVII (below) was fundamentally an S.XIII airframe with a 300 hp Hispano-Suiza 8Fb engine.

SPAD S.XX — France

Late in 1917, Herbemont designed a new fighter with a monocoque fuselage and a 37-mm Puteaux cannon mounted in the Vee of a 300 hp Hispano-Suiza 8G engine and firing through the propeller shaft, as on the S.XII. This, the S.XVIII (the SFA designation being Spa.XVIII Ca1-2), was under construction in April 1918, and was described as a *monoplace protégé*, being intended to be flown as a single-seater in combat, but having provision for a second crew member. Both wings were two-spar structures, the upper having pronounced sweepback, and the single interplane struts were of broad-chord I-type. Development problems with the 300 hp engine-cannon combination led to revision of the design to take a standard 300 hp direct-drive HS 8Fb engine and an armament of twin 7,7-mm Vickers guns, the designation being changed to S.XX and the prototype appearing in August 1918. Official

The prototype S.XX (above), which appeared in August 1918, and (below) the series S.XX which differed primarily in having an enlarged vertical tail.

(Below) The series production SPAD S.XX fighter.

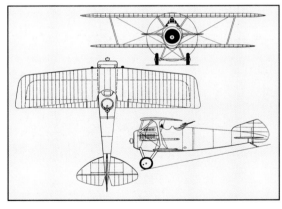

trials were conducted in the following month and the S.XX was ordered into production with a planned output of 200 aircraft monthly. Initially a Lewis gun was provided for the second occupant, whose function was now to fend off stern attacks by enemy fighters, and later twin Lewis guns on a T.O.3 mounting were provided. Production was scaled down with the Armistice, and only 95 S.XXs were built, these remaining in

French service until 1923. One example was purchased by Japan in October 1921, being designated Hei 2. *Max speed, 142 mph (229 km/h) at 6,560 ft (2 000 m). Time to 6,560 ft (2 000 m), 4.6 min. Loaded weight, 2,438 lb (1 106 kg). Span, 32 ft 2½ in (9,80 m). Length, 23 ft 11½ in (7,34 m). Height, 9 ft 5 in (2,87 m). Wing area, 312 sq ft (29,00 m²).*

SPAD S.XXI — France

The S.XXI (above) was basically similar to the S.XVII, but had ailerons on both upper and lower wings.

Virtually contemporary with and very similar to the S.XVII, the S.XXI single-seat fighter was powered by the 300 hp Hispano-Suiza 8Fb engine and carried an armament of twin 7,7-mm Vickers guns. The fuselage and tail unit of the S.XXI were fundamentally similar to those of the S.XVII, but whereas the latter had ailerons on the upper wing only, the S.XXI had ailerons on both upper and lower surfaces of slightly extended, equi-span wings. Test flying of the S.XXI had been concluded by October 1918, and the type was abandoned for operational purposes in the following month. Two S.XXIs were briefly retained for experimental purposes after World War I terminated. *Max speed, 137 mph (221 km/h) at 6,560 ft (2 000 m). Time to 6,560 ft (2 000 m), 5.67 min. Endurance, 1.67 hrs. Span, 27 ft 7¼ in (8,44 m). Length, 21 ft 0 in (6,40 m). Height, 7 ft 11 in (2,42 m). Wing area, 253 sq ft (23,50 m²).*

SPAD S.XXII — France

The S.XXII (above) was unusual in having an aft-mounted, inverse-taper, forward-swept lower wing.

The pilot's view from the cockpit of the S.VII and all its Béchereau-designed successors had been adversely criticised from 1916 onwards. In an attempt to remedy this defect, the S.XXII was evolved just as hostilities were drawing to a close. The design development was undertaken by Louis Béchereau, presumably by special arrangement or contract as he had left SPAD in the spring of 1917. The result was a single-seat fighter of highly unusual appearance. To improve downward view, the lower wing was attached well aft and given pronounced forward sweep and inverse taper towards the root. The three-spar upper wing had equally

(Above) An S.XX of the 6e *Escadrille* of the 2e *Régiment d'Aviation de Chasse, circa* 1922.

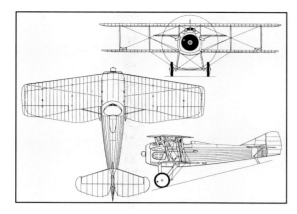

(Above) The SPAD S.XXII fighter flown in 1919.

marked sweepback. Like preceding Béchereau single-seat fighters, the S.XXII had single-bay interplane bracing with intermediate struts. Power was provided by the 300 hp Hispano-Suiza 8Fb and armament consisted of twin 7,7-mm Vickers guns. As late as 29 November 1918, the prototype S.XXII had still to be assembled at Buc. This aircraft was completed in 1919 and flown, but the extent of flight testing has gone unrecorded and the design was taken no further in the post-Armistice period. Neither weights nor performance data are available. *Span, 26 ft 6⅛ in (8,08 m). Length, 20 ft 6 in (6,25 m). Wing area, 217.44 sq ft (20,20 m²).*

SPAD S.XXIV — France

Last in the line of wartime SPAD single-seat fighters of Béchereau origin, the S.XXIV was developed as a carrier-based fighter for France's *Aviation Maritime.*

The S.XXIV (above) was the last in the line of Béchereau-designed fighters of World War One.

Flown for the first time on 5 November 1918, the S.XXIV was a wheel undercarriage-equipped version of the S.XIV twin-float fighter seaplane that had flown almost a year earlier. The tardiness in developing the S.XXIV apparently resulted in the discontinuation of further development at an early stage in flight testing. Like the S.XIV, the S.XXIV was powered by a 220 hp Hispano-Suiza 8Bc engine and was intended to be fitted with a similar armament. No performance data are available. *Empty weight, 1,433 lb (650 kg). Span, 32 ft 2 in (9,80 m). Length, 21 ft 3⅛ in (6,48 m). Height, 8 ft 4⅘ in (2,56 m). Wing area, 282 sq ft (26,20 m²).*

SPYKER-TROMPENBURG V.3 — Netherlands

The N V Nederlandsche Automobiel- en Vliegtuigenfabriek Trompenburg, manufacturer of the Spyker automobile, developed the Spyker-Trompenburg V.3

The Spyker-Trompenburg V.3 (below) was cancelled by the *Luchtvaartafdeling* with the Armistice of 1918.

single-seat fighting scout in 1918, specifically to meet a requirement of the Army's Aviation Division, the LVA (*Luchtvaartafdeling*). Contracts were placed for 72 V.3 fighters on behalf of the LVA, a further 20 for the naval air component, the MLD (*Marineluchtvaartdienst*), and six for the LVA of the Royal Netherlands Indies Army. The V.3 was a single-bay unstaggered biplane of wooden construction with fabric covering and powered by a 130 hp Clerget rotary engine. Proposed armament comprised twin synchronised 7,92-mm machine guns. In the event, the prototype V.3 was not flown until July 1919, by which time, as a result of the Armistice, the LVA had cancelled its contract, and development of the V.3 was discontinued. *Max speed, 112 mph (180 km/h). Time to 3,280 ft (1 000 m), 3.0 min. Span, 26 ft 10⅓ in (8,19 m), Length, 20 ft 0⅛ in (6,30 m). Height, 8 ft 6⅓ in (2,60 m).*

(Below) The Spyker-Trompenburg V.3, flown mid-1919.

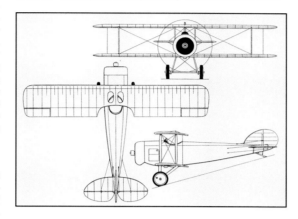

STANDARD M-DEFENSE — USA

During 1917, the Aviation Section of the US Army Signal Corps placed an order with the Standard Aircraft Corporation for six examples of a single-seat fighter designed by Charles H Day. Intended specifically as a lightweight target defence interceptor, the Standard fighter was dubbed the M-Defense and was a two-bay staggered biplane of wooden construction with fabric skinning, power being supplied by an 80 hp Le Rhône nine-cylinder rotary engine. The first two M-Defense fighters were delivered in January 1918, but although manoeuvrability and handling qualities were commended, performance was considered to be inadequate for the combat rôle. The remaining four M-Defense fighters were therefore cancelled, but production was ordered of a modified version, the E-1, for the advanced training task, a total of 168 being built. *Max speed, 97 mph (156 km/h) at sea level, 82 mph (132 km/h) at 10,000 ft (3 050 m). Time to 6,000 ft (1 830 m), 10.6 min. Endurance, 1.8 hrs. Loaded weight, 1,150 lb (522 kg). Span, 24 ft 0 in (7,31 m). Length 18 ft 10 in (5,74 m). Height, 8 ft 1 in (2,46 m). Wing area, 152.5 sq ft (14,17 m²).*

The first example of the M-Defense (below) which was delivered to the Signal Corps in January 1918.

STURTEVANT B — USA

One of the most unusual single-seat pursuit aircraft designed and built in the USA during World War I was the Sturtevant B, created by Grover C Loening of the Sturtevant Aeroplane Company of Boston, Mass. Embodying a number of advanced features, such as a welded steel tube structure, the Sturtevant B was a sesquiplane of

The sole Sturtevant B to be completed (above), which was destined to effect only one test flight.

unique configuration in that the lower plane was a narrow-chord surface with the primary purpose of providing anchorage for the apices of the quadrupod bracing struts. The mainplane was faired into the forward fuselage decking. Power was provided by a 140 hp Sturtevant A5 eight-cylinder water-cooled engine with radiators mounted beneath the mainplane centre section leading edge on each side of the fuselage. Four examples of the Sturtevant B were ordered by the US Army Signal Corps in 1916, the first of these flying on 20 March 1917. Malfunction of the tail control surfaces led the test pilot to decide to terminate the flight and the virtually unmanageable aircraft struck a tree during the landing approach and was wrecked. This accident led to the US Army cancelling the remaining three aircraft. No specification for the Sturtevant B is available.

The Sturtevant B (below) employed a sesquiplane configuration of extremely unusual form.

SUD-EST SE 100 — France

With the issue of a specification for a successor to the Potez 631 twin-engined fighter in service with the *Armee de l'Air*, P-E Mercier and Jacques Lecarme of the Société Nationale de Constructions Aéronautiques de Sud-Est (SNCASE) tendered the design of a highly innovative aircraft, the SE 100. Of mixed construction with a wooden wing and a duralumin-covered welded steel-tube fuselage, the SE 100 featured a retractable tricycle undercarriage with a steerable nosewheel and small outrigger wheels retracting into the bases of the endplate vertical tail surfaces. Powered by two 1,030 hp Gnome-Rhône 14N 14-cylinder radial engines, the first prototype SE 100 was flown on 29 March 1939. Various modifications, including provision of a retrac-

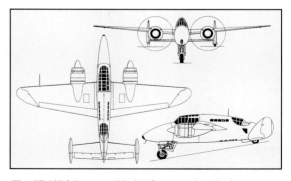

The SE 100 (above and below) was a singularly innovative two/three-seat day and night fighter.

table ventral fin, were introduced as a result of initial flight test, maximum speed being raised from 348 mph (560 km/h) to 360 mph (580 km/h) as a result. The proposed armament comprised a nose-mounted battery of four 20-mm cannon and a single aft-firing cannon on an electro-pneumatic mount. It was proposed that the crew would comprise two members for diurnal operations and three members for nocturnal missions, and a crawl tunnel was provided between the cockpits. On 5 April 1940, during a landing approach, the pitch mechanism of the starboard propeller malfunctioned and the aircraft was destroyed. At this time, assembly of a second prototype had begun, this possessing slightly larger overall dimensions, dispensing with the crawl tunnel to increase fuselage fuel capacity and having an all-metal one-piece wing. Armament was also revised, the forward-firing battery being increased to six 20-mm cannon, paired weapons of the same calibre being mounted in a dorsal turret and an additional 20-mm cannon being mounted to fire through a

The sole prototype of the SE 100 to be completed (above) was lost in an accident during April 1940.

ventral hatch. The Citroën factory in the suburbs of Paris began tooling-up to assemble 300 SE 100s for deliveries to commence at the end of 1940, but the German occupation of Paris prevented final assembly of the second prototype. Proposed variants included the SE 101 and 102 with 1,200 hp Pratt & Whitney Twin Wasp and 1,050 hp G-R 14N-2/3 engines respectively. The following data relate to the first prototype. *Max speed, 360 mph (580 km/h) at 21,325 ft (6 500 m). Cruise, 310 mph (500 km/h) at 16,405 ft (5 000 m). Range, 808 mls (1 300 km). Empty weight, 12,169 lb (5 520 kg). Max loaded weight, 16,534 lb (7 500 kg). Span, 51 ft 6 in (15,70 m). Length, 38 ft 8½ in (11,80 m). Height, 14 ft 0½ in (4,28 m). Wing area, 355.87 sq ft (33,06 m²).*

SUD-EST SE 530 MISTRAL   France

After assembling 67 Vampire FB Mk 5 single-seat fighters from British-supplied components and licence-building a further 120 aircraft in their entirety, the Société Nationale de Constructions Aéronautiques de Sud-Est (SNCASE) began production of a more powerful version of the basic aircraft. Assigned the designation Vampire Mk 53 by the parent company and given the appellation of SE 530 by Sud-Est, this was developed at the behest of the *Armée de l'Air*. It utilised the basic Mk 5 airframe mated with the 5,005 lb st

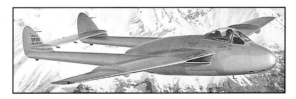

The fourth pre-series Mistral (above) and a general arrangement drawing of the series Mistral (below).

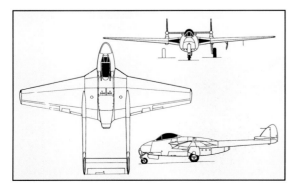

(2 270 kgp) Hispano-built Nene 102, the wing root intakes being enlarged and the split-trunk intake of the Hawker P.1040 being adapted to provide the extra air demanded for the rear face of the Nene's double-sided impeller. Fuel tankage was increased, cabin pressurisation introduced and the pilot was provided with an SNCASO ejection seat. A pre-series of four aircraft was built, the first of these flying on 1 April 1951. Baptised Mistral, the type entered series production in SE 532 form, the first flying in December 1951 and 97 being built. These were followed by 150 examples of the SE 535, the last of which was delivered on 25 March 1954. The SE 535 was powered by the Nene 104 with similar rating to the Nene 102B of the SE 532, and, in addition to its four 20-mm HS 404 cannon, could carry eight T-10 or HVAR rockets, or two 992-lb (450-kg) bombs. The Mistral entered *Armée d l'Air* service in 1952 and was finally withdrawn in 1961. The following data relate to the SE 535. *Max speed, 575 mph (925 km/h) at sea level, 557 mph (896 km/h) at 19,685 ft (6 000 m). Time to 39,370 ft (12 000 m), 11.35 min. Range (max external fuel), 1,118 mls (1 800 km). Empty equipped weight, 7,672 lb (3 480 kg). Max loaded weight, 13,448 lb (6 100 kg). Span, 38 ft 2⅓ in (11,60 m). Length, 30 ft 9 in (9,37 m). Wing area, 258.66 sq ft (24,03 m²).*

SUD-EST AQUILON 201 TO 204 France

An Aquilon 203 (above) in service aboard the carrier *Clémenceau* during the course of 1961.

Failure of the shipboard fighter requirement issued by the *Service Technique Aéronautique* in June 1946 (and which had resulted in Aérocentre NC 1080, Arsenal VG 90 and Nord 2200 prototypes being built) led to consideration being given to adoption by the *Aéronavale* of the Grumman F9F-5 Panther. In January 1951, however, the *Ministère de la Marine* announced the decision to adopt the de Havilland Sea Venom Mk 20, which was being developed for the Royal Navy as a side-by-side two-seat shipboard all-weather fighter and had yet to enter flight test. Four aircraft were supplied to the SNCASE in knocked down form for assembly as a "pre-series", the first of these flying on 31 October 1952, and the name Aquilon (North Wind) being adopted. A fifth "pre-series" aircraft and 25 production aircraft employ-

(Below) An Aquilon 203 of *Escadrille* 59S, the *Aéronavale* all-weather fighter school at Hyères.

The first of the pre-series Aquilon 20s (above) on test in 1954, before redesignation as Aquilon 201 and (below) the standard Aquilon 203.

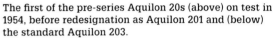

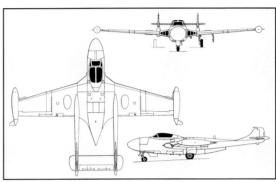

ing sub-assemblies provided by Airspeed were initially known as Aquilon 20s and subsequently as Aquilon 201s, the first of these flying on 24 March 1954. These were powered by the 4,850 lb st (2 200 kgp) Fiat-built de Havilland Ghost 48 Mk 1, armament comprising four 20-mm cannon. Non-availability of the intended Thomson AI radar restricted the Aquilon 201s to diurnal operation, the same restriction being imposed on the next 25 aircraft which, delivered as Aquilon 202s, were entirely manufactured in France and differed in having ejection seats, an aft-sliding rather than aft-hinged cockpit canopy and a strengthened undercarriage. A decision was taken to adopt the Westinghouse APQ 65 AI radar, but, without major redesign of the airframe, it was found impossible to fit this equipment in the ejection seat-equipped two-seater. Production therefore continued with the Aquilon 203 *single*-seater, the last 25 of the 40 production examples of this version being equipped with APQ 65 radar as were the six two-seat Aquilon 204 radar trainers (not fitted with ejection seats) that brought production to an end, the last of these being flown at the beginning of 1958. The Aquilon was flown operationally by *Flottilles* 11F and 16F, eventually serving in the fighter training rôle and being phased out during 1964-65. The following data relate to the Aquilon 203. *Max speed, 581 mph (935 km/h). Time to 39,370 ft (12 000 m), 12.8 min. Range (max external fuel), 967 mls (1 557 km) at 40,000 ft (12 190 m). Normal loaded weight, 12,125 lb (5 500 kg). Span (over tip tanks), 42 ft 10⅔in (13,07 m). Length, 36 ft 7½ in (11,17 m). Height, 8 ft 6⅓ in (2,60 m). Wing area, 279.87 sq ft (26,00 m²).*

SUD-EST SE 5000 AND SE 5003 BAROUDEUR   France

A private-venture single-seat tactical support fighter, the SE 5000 Baroudeur – a name derived from the Arabic word *baroud* for battle, and, in French Foreign Legion parlance, describing a pugnacious fighter – was

designed by Wsiewolod J Jakimiuk. Of all-metal construction with a wing sweptback 36 deg at quarter-chord, the Baroudeur represented an attempt to achieve a measure of independence from permanent runways. In place of a conventional undercarriage, it was provided with a combination of jettisonable take-off trolley and landing skids *a la* Me 163B Komet. The first prototype was powered by a 5,280 lb st (2 395 kgp) SNECMA Atar 101B turbojet and flew on 12 May 1954. The

The first prototype SE 5000 (above) and a general arrangement drawing (below) of the SE 5003 with flush fuselage-side auxiliary fuel tanks.

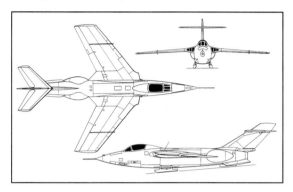

(Below) The second prototype SE 5000 mounted on its jettisonable take-off trolley.

Proposed armament comprised two 30-mm or 37-mm cannon. The Baroudeur was progressively re-engined with the Atar 101C and 101D-1, this last, rated at 5,732 lb st (2 600 kgp), powering a second prototype, which flew on 12 May 1954 and featured a three degree increase in wing anhedral. Two months earlier, an official contract covered both SE 5000 prototypes as well as three SE 5003 pre-series aircraft. The first SE 5003 was flown in September 1955 with an 8,157 lb st (3 700 kgp) Atar 101E-4, the second and third aircraft having a 6,283 lb st (2 850 kgp) Atar 101D-3 and a 7,716 lb st (3 500 kgp) Atar 101E-3 respectively. The Baroudeur eventually demonstrated the ability to take-off without recourse to the jettisonable trolley and the first SE 5003 was flown with flush-fitting auxiliary fuel tanks on the aft fuselage sides. The NATO nations elected to adopt a more conventional aircraft to meet the lightweight tactical fighter requirement and development of the Baroudeur was discontinued. The following data relate to the Atar 101E-4-powered SE 5003. *Max speed, 642 mph (1 033 km/h) at 36,090 ft (11 000 m), or*

Mach=0.973. Max initial climb, 13,975 ft/min (71 m/ sec). Time to 39,370 ft (12 000 m), 6.5 min. Empty weight, 9,965 lb (4 520 kg). Max loaded weight, 15,763 lb (7 150 kg). Span, 32 ft 9⅔ in (10,00 m). Length, 44 ft 9⅞ in (13,66 m). Height, 10 ft 8 in (3,25 m). Wing area, 272.33 sq ft (25,30 m².)

The third prototype Baroudeur, the SE 5003 (below), operating without the take-off trolley.

SUD-EST SE 212 DURANDAL France

From the end of 1951, the *bureau d'études* headed by Pierre Satre at the SNCA du Sud-Est undertook a series of studies of potential lightweight mixed-power interceptor fighters under what was effectively the generic designation SE 212. These studies crystallized in the shape of a small, 60-deg delta powered by a SNECMA Atar 101F with an afterburning thrust of 8,377 lb (3 800 kg) and a 1,653 lb (750 kg) SEPR 75 rocket motor. The primary armament was intended to consist of a single AA 20 or R 052 missile carried externally on the fuselage centreline, alternative armament being two 30-mm DEFA cannon or 24 SNEB rockets of 68-mm calibre. An official contract was placed for two prototypes, the first of which was flown on 20 April 1956 without the rocket motor fitted. The Atar 101F turbojet was subsequently replaced by an Atar 101G with an afterburning thrust of 9,700 lb (4 400 kg), and the first flight during which the rocket motor was lit took place on 19 December 1956. The second prototype SE 212 was flown on 30 March 1957. During flight testing a speed of 898 mph (1 444 km/h), or Mach=1.36, was attained at 40,355 ft (12 300 m) without the rocket motor and 1,036 mph (1 667 km/h), or Mach=1.57, was reached at 38,715 ft (11 800 m) with the rocket motor lit. These speeds were achieved without armament fitted, and the test programme terminated in 1958. *Max speed, 1,036 mph (1 667 km/h) at 38,715 ft (11 800 m), or Mach=1.57. Max initial climb, 39,370 ft/min (200 m/ sec). Empty weight, 10,086 lb (4 575 kg). Loaded*

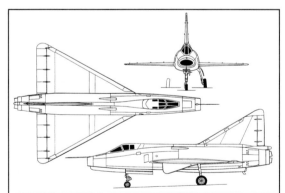

(Above and below) The first prototype Durandal lightweight mixed-power interceptor which entered flight test in April 1956.

The first prototype Durandal (above) which attained Mach = 1.57 during tests with rocket motor lit.

weight, 14,770 lb (6 700 kg). Span, 24 ft 5 in (7,44 m). Length, 39 ft 7¼ in (12,07 m). Wing area, 318.6 sq ft (29,60 m²).

SUD-OUEST SO 6020 AND SO 6025 ESPADON France

The first prototype SO 6020 (above and below) which featured an aft-mounted ventral air intake, this proving unacceptable during a brief test career.

The first turbojet-powered single-seat fighter of French design to be built, the SO 6020 Espadon (Swordfish) interceptor was developed by the Société Nationale de Constructions Aéronautiques de Sud-Ouest (SNCASO) under the design leadership of Lucien Servanty. Conceived to meet the requirements of a programme promulgated on 25 March 1946, and the subject of an order for three prototypes placed two months later, on 28 June, the SO 6020 was powered by a 5,000 lb st (2 268 kgp) Rolls-Royce Nene turbojet with, unusually, an aft-mounted ventral air intake. Proposed armament was initially to have comprised four 30-mm cannon and four 12.7-mm machine guns, this later being changed to six 20-mm or 15-mm weapons. The first prototype flew on 12 November 1948 and the second on 16 September 1949, the latter being modified, after initial test, with NACA-type lateral intakes in place of the ventral intake. It was appreciated at an early stage that the SO 6020 was underpowered and would offer inadequate performance, a major redesign as the SO 6021 therefore paralleling initial flight testing of the SO 6020. The third prototype, intended for tactical reconnaissance, was

The second SO 6020 (above) after modification with NACA-type lateral air intakes, and (below) the third prototype completed as the mixed-power SO 6025.

completed as the SO 6025 with lateral intakes and a ventrally-mounted SEPR 25 auxiliary rocket motor of 3,307 lb (1 500 kg) thrust, this flying on 28 December 1949. The second prototype, with a similar rocket motor installed in the rear fuselage, became the SO 6026, flying in this form for the first time on 28 March 1953. *Max speed, 601 mph (967 km/h) at sea level. Initial climb, 6,102 ft/min (31 m/sec). Endurance, 1.5 hrs. Empty weight, 11,803 lb (5 354 kg). Normal loaded weight, 16,433 lb (7 454 kg). Span, 34 ft 9⅓ in (10,60 m). Length, 49 ft 2½ in (15,00 m). Height, 14 ft 11⅛ in (4,55 m). Wing area, 271.26 sq ft (25,20 m²).*

SUD-OUEST SO 6021 ESPADON   France

The SO 6021 represented an attempt to reduce the weight and alleviate some of the aerodynamic problems that had beset the SO 6020 from the outset of flight test. Retaining the same Nene engine, but having a 14 sq ft (1,30 m²) increase in wing area, an entirely redesigned vertical tail and a 1,331 lb (604 kg) reduction in empty weight, the SO 6021 was equipped with servo controls and flew on 3 September 1950. Armament comprised six 20-mm cannon. In June 1951, a ground attack version of the SO 6021 was offered to the *Armée de l'Air* with an afterburning Rolls-Royce Tay engine and an armament of two 30-mm cannon. However, testing of the SO 6021 indicated that some of the difficulties experienced with the SO 6020, notably the shortcomings of the air intake arrangement, had not been overcome.

The SO 6021 (above and below) was a lighter version of the SO 6020 with a larger wing, a redesigned tail and servo controls.

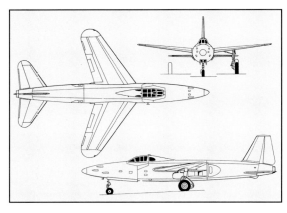

A speed of Mach=0.96 was attained in a shallow dive, but serious buffet occurred at Mach=0.75, and further development was abandoned, the sole SO 6021 serving as a test bed for small wingtip-mounted turbojets associated with the SO 9000 programme, continuing in this rôle until 1956. *Initial climb, 5,315 ft/min (27 m/sec). Endurance, 2.5 hrs. Empty weight, 10,472 lb (4 750 kg). Normal loaded weight, 15,145 lb (6 870 kg). Span, 34 ft*

The SO 6021 (below) did not offer any noteworthy improvement over the SO 6020 and was abandoned.

9⅓ in (10,60 m). Length, 49 ft 2½ in (15,00 m). Height, 15 ft 5⅔ in (4,72 m). Wing area, 285.25 sq ft (26,50 m²).*

SUD-OUEST SO 8000 NARVAL   France

The second prototype SO 8000 (above and below) was found generally unsatisfactory during evaluation.

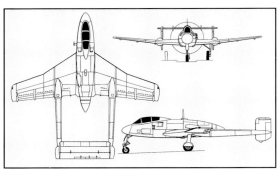

The subject of an order for two prototypes on 31 May 1946, the SO 8000 Narval (Narwhal) was conceived by a team under the leadership of Ing Dupuy at the Société Nationale de Constructions Aéronautiques de Sud-Ouest (SNCASO) as a shipboard fighter and attack aircraft. Of twin-boom configuration with a sweptback wing – 24 deg inboard and 13.5 deg outboard on the leading edge – and a tricycle undercarriage, the Narval was powered by an Arsenal 12 H-02 (Junkers Jumo 213) engine rated at 2,250 hp, installed as a pusher and driving contra-rotating propellers. Proposed armament comprised six 20-mm cannon with provision for up to 2,205 lb (1 000 kg) of external ordnance. Development was somewhat protracted, and the first flight (by the second prototype) did not take place until 1 April 1949, the second following on 30 December. Numerous problems arose during the test programme, dictating changes in the control surfaces, the air intakes and the propellers (Rotol propellers replacing the original Chauvière units); constant troubles were experienced with the engine, and, following the generally unfavourable results of evaluation at the *Centre d'Essais en Vol* in January 1950, development of the Narval was discontinued. The second prototype effected its 43rd and last flight on 8 January 1950, and the first prototype flew

A Vautour IIN (above) of the 30ème *Escadre de Chasse Tous Temps* (ECTT 3/30 *Lorraine*), BA-112 Reims, 1962.

only once. Proposals to adapt the design for a Rolls-Royce Nene turbojet as the SO 8010 were not pursued. The quoted performance was not, in fact, achieved during flight test. *Max speed, 454 mph (730 km/h) at 27,885 ft (8 500 m). Max range, 2,796 mls (4 500 km) at 329 mph (530 km/h). Empty weight, 10,628 lb (4 821 kg). Normal loaded weight, 14,563 lb (6 606 kg). Span, 38 ft 7⅓ in (11,77 m). Length, 38 ft 9¾ in (11,83 m). Height, 10 ft 6 in (3,20 m). Wing area, 283.1 sq ft (26,30 m²).*

SUD-OUEST SO 4050 VAUTOUR IIN   France

Conceived as a multi-rôle aircraft to meet the requirements of a 1951 *Armée de l'Air* Specification, the SO 4050 Vautour (Vulture) was designed by a team led by Jean-Charles Parot and was intended from the outset for production in three versions: Vautour N (*Nuit*) two-seat night and all-weather fighter, Vautour A (*Attaque*) single-seat close support aircraft and Vautour B (*Bombardement*) two-seat bomber. The first prototype was completed in Vautour N configuration and flew on 16 October 1952. This was powered by two 5,290 lb st (2 400 kgp) Atar 101B turbojets. Six pre-production aircraft were delivered in the following year of which three were Vautour Ns, the last of these being powered by 10,000 lb st (4 536 kgp) Rolls-Royce Avon RA 28 engines. Contracts were placed for 140 Vautours, of which 70 were to be fighters, designated Vautour IINs.

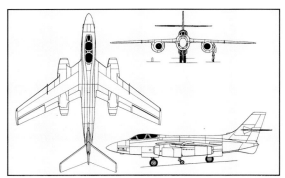

(Above) The Vautour II-1N with all-flying tailplane.

The first of these entered service with the *Armée de l'Air* in 1957. The Vautour IIN was powered by the 7,716 lb st (3 500 kgp) Atar 101E-3, giving place (final 40 aircraft) to the 8,157 lb st (3 700 kgp) Atar 101E-5. The two crew members were seated in tandem and primary armament comprised four 30-mm DEFA 552 cannon in the lower front fuselage, with a missile launcher immediately aft of the gun bay accommodating 104 SNEB 68-mm rockets. The final 25 production aircraft were fitted with an all-flying rather than variable-incidence tailplane, these being identified as Vautour II-1Ns. The phase-out of the Vautour IIN from *Armée de l'Air* service began late in 1973 when the 30ème *Escadre de Chasse* began to relinquish its aircraft, some being transferred to the 92e *Escadre de Bombardement* in the following year. Seven Vautour IINs were supplied to Israel's *Heyl Ha'Avir* in 1958-59 to serve with No 119 Sqn, these being ex-*Armée de l'Air* aircraft. From March 1963, their radar was replaced with ballast and the Vautour IINs were reassigned to No 110 Sqn for the attack rôle alongside Vautour IIAs and IIBs, remaining in service with the *Heyl Ha'Avir* until the early 'seventies. *Max speed, 721 mph (1,160 km/h) at sea level, or Mach=0.95. Max initial climb, 11,810 ft/min (60 m/sec). Normal endurance, 4 hrs. Empty weight, 32,850 lb (14 900 kg). Max loaded weight, 45,635 lb (20 700 kg). Span, 49 ft 6½ in (15,10 m). Length, 56 ft 9 in (17,30 m). Height, 16 ft 8¾ in (5,10 m). Wing area, 484.39 sq ft (45,00 m^2).*

SUD-OUEST SO 9000 TRIDENT — France

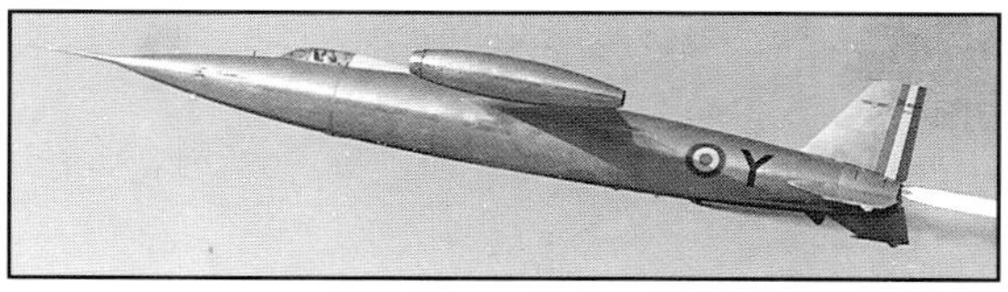

The first prototype SO 9000 seen (above and below) in its original form with wingtip-mounted Marboré turbojets and (upper photo) with rocket lit.

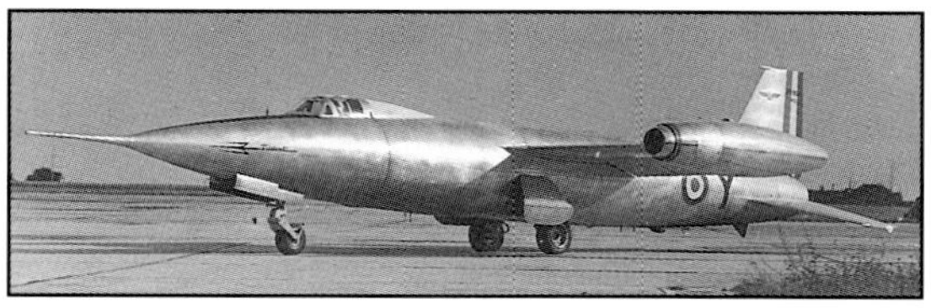

Stemming from the lightweight fighter philosophy that emerged from the Korean conflict, the SO 9000 Trident single-seat interceptor developed by a team led by Lucien Servanty was of unusual concept in employing turbojets for auxiliary power and a rocket motor for primary thrust. Two prototypes of the Trident were ordered on 8 April 1951, the first of these flying on 2 March 1953 solely on the power of two wingtip-mounted Turboméca Marboré II turbojets each rated at 882 lb st (400 kgp). The second prototype was destroyed on its first flight on 1 September 1953, but development continued with the first example, which, on 4 September 1954, flew for the first time with its primary power plant, a triple-barrel SEPR 481 liquid rocket motor providing a total thrust of 9,920 lb (4 500 kg). As the aircraft could not take-off on the power of the Marborés at fully loaded weight, these gave place to Dassault MD 30 (Viper ASV 5) turbojets of 1,642 lb st (745 kgp), with which it flew on 17 March 1955. Although conceived as a combat aircraft, the SO 9000 had meanwhile been overtaken by a more advanced development, the SO 9050, and its test programme was terminated on 10 December 1956, the prototype having achieved a speed of Mach=1.63 – the highest speed attained by any piloted aircraft in Europe at that time – and an altitude of 49,210 ft (15 000 m). *Empty weight, 5,368 lb (2 435 kg). Loaded weight, 11,144 lb (5 055 kg). Span, 24 ft 10 in (7,57 m). Length, 47 ft 1¾ in (14,37 m). Height, 9 ft 3⅘ in (2,84 m). Wing area, 178.47 sq ft (16,58 m^2).*

SUD-OUEST SO 9050 TRIDENT II — France

Embodying experience gained with the SO 9000, the SO 9050 – two prototypes of which were ordered in 1954 – embodied considerable redesign. A smaller wing of reduced thickness/chord ratio was adopted, the cockpit was enlarged, air brakes were transferred from the wing to the rear fuselage, a taller undercarriage was provided and a two-barrel SEPR 631 rocket

The first prototype of the SO 9050 (below) on an early test flight without use of the rocket engine.

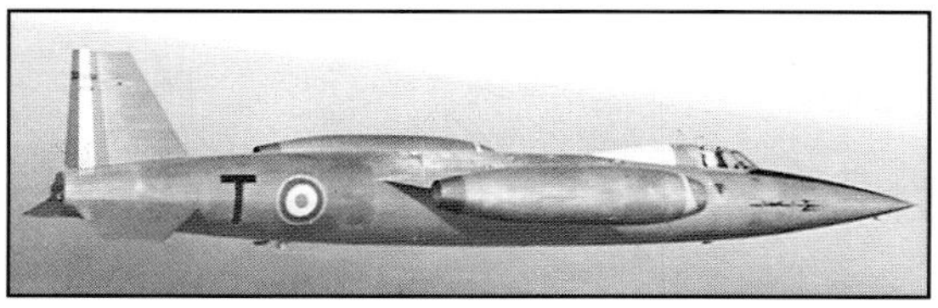

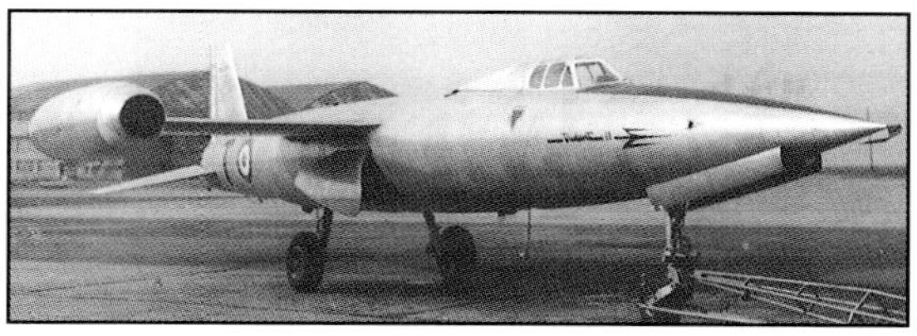

(Above) The first prototype of the SO 9050 Trident II mixed-power interceptor fighter.

motor of 6,614 lb (3 000 kg) was adopted. The first prototype SO 9050 was flown on 19 July 1955, its first flight on rocket power taking place on the following 21 December, and the second prototype flew on 4 January 1956, but was destroyed during its second flight. A third prototype had meanwhile been ordered, this flying on 30 March 1956, and some 10 weeks later, on 11 June, a contract was placed for six pre-series aircraft, a supplementary contract for a further four following (although the latter was to be cancelled on 24 October 1957 as an economy measure). The pre-series SO 9050 differed from the prototypes primarily in having 2,425 lb st (1 100 kgp) Turboméca Gabizo turbojets in place of the Vipers at the wingtips and provision for nose-mounted AI radar and a single ventrally-mounted Matra R 511 air-air missile. The first pre-series aircraft was flown on 3 May 1957 and the third on 30 January 1958, but three months later, on 26 April, the programme was cancelled. During tests, Mach=1.9 was achieved at 63,975 ft (19 500 m) and an altitude of 85,300 ft (26 000 m) exceeded. *Empty weight, 6,415 lb (2 910 kg). Loaded weight, 13,007 lb (5 900 kg). Span, 22 ft 9⅔ in (6,95 m). Length, 43 ft 6 in (13,26 m). Height, 10 ft 6 in (3,20 m). Wing area, 156.08 sq ft (14,50 m^2).*

(Below) The pre-series SO 9050 Trident II fighter.

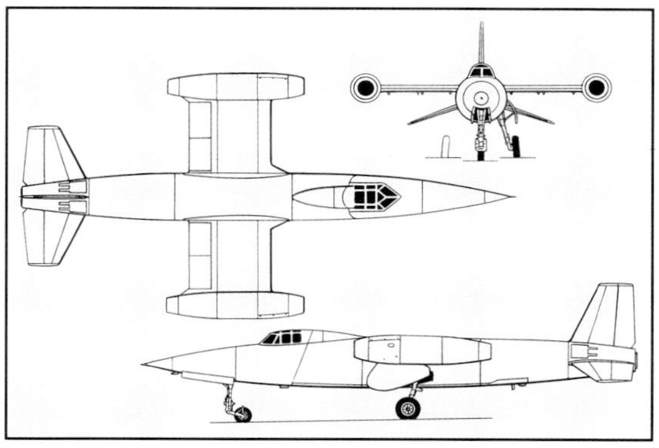

SUKHOI Su-1 (I-330) — USSR

Pavel O Sukhoi established his own OKB, or Experimental Design Bureau, in December 1938, and, early in the following year, was assigned the task of designing an advanced single-seat high-altitude fighter. Initially designated I-330, the fighter was of mixed construction, with a single-spar all-metal wing of comparatively high aspect ratio with flush-riveted light alloy skinning, and a wooden semi-monocoque fuselage with *shpon*, or bakelite-ply, skinning. Power was provided by a Klimov M-105P 12-cylinder liquid-cooled Vee-type engine rated at 1,100 hp for take-off and fitted with a pair of TsIAM-developed TK-2 exhaust-driven turbo-superchargers, the radiator being accommodated in the fuselage aft of the cockpit and exhausting over the rear decking. Armament consisted of one 20-mm cannon and two 7,62-mm machine guns. Factory testing commenced late 1940, by which time the designation Su-1 had been adopted, State testing being performed in the

The first Sukhoi fighter (below), the Su-1 which embodied a number of advanced features for its time.

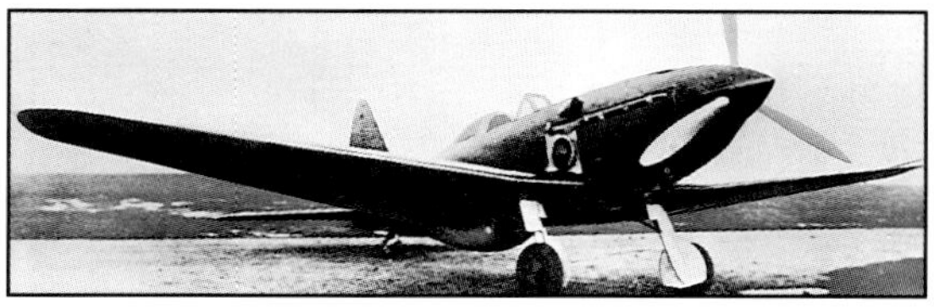

following summer. The turbo-superchargers proved capricious and the Su-1 was flown on several occasions with the TK-2s removed. Although the fighter met its specified performance with the turbo-superchargers functioning, their failure frequency was unacceptable and the TsIAM had failed to improve reliability by October 1941, when the OKB was evacuated from Moscow to Novosibirsk, the Su-1 being damaged in the process. This prototype was not rebuilt, development continuing with the Su-3. *Max speed, 398 mph (641 km/h) at 32,810 ft (10 000 m), 317 mph (510 km/h) at sea level. Time to 32,810 ft (10 000 m), 10.33 min. Range, 447 mls (720 km). Empty weight, 5,500 lb (2 495 kg). Loaded weight, 6,338 lb (2 875 kg). Span, 37 ft 8¾ in (11,50 m). Length, 27 ft 7½ in (8,42 m). Height, 8 ft 10⅔ in (2,71 m). Wing area, 204.52 sq ft (19,00 m^2).*

(Below) The Su-1 turbo-supercharged fighter.

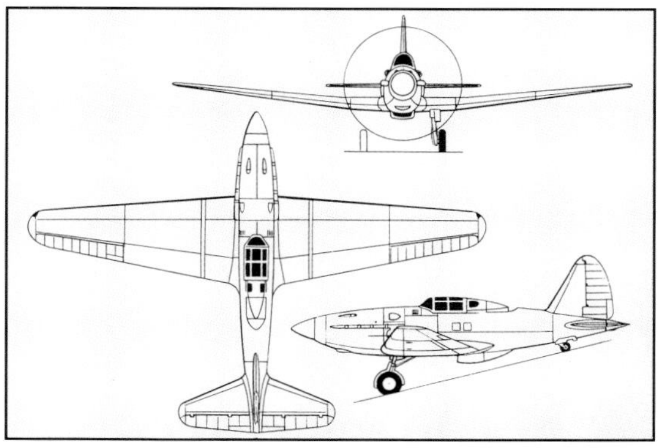

SUKHOI Su-3 (I-360) — USSR

At the time of the evacuation of the Sukhoi OKB to Novosibirsk, the prototype of a developed version of the Su-1, the Su-3, was under construction. Initiated under the designation I-360, the Su-3 mated the Su-1 fuselage and tail surfaces with an entirely new wing of revised profile with shorter-span outer panels resulting in a 21.53 sq ft (2,00 m^2) reduction in wing area. The radiator bath was enlarged, but in all other major respects the Su-3 was similar to the Su-1. Retaining the M-105P engine and the same armament, the Su-3 was completed at Novosibirsk and entered flight test in the late summer of 1942. Although the TsIAM had meanwhile undertaken much development work on the TK-2 turbo-supercharger, the principal defects were found to remain, and, as a consequence, development of the Su-3 was discontinued towards the end of 1942. *Max speed, 396 mph (638 km/h) at 32,810 ft (10 000 m), 310 mph (500 km/h) at sea level. Time to 16,405 ft (5 000 m), 5.5 min. Range, 435 mls (700 km). Empty weight, 5,489 lb (2 490 kg). Loaded weight, 6,305 lb (2 860 kg). Span, 33 ft 1⅔ in (10,10 m). Length, 27 ft 7½ in (8,42 m). Height, 8 ft 10⅔ in (2,71 m). Wing area, 183 sq ft (17,00 m^2).*

The Su-3 (below) was essentially a refined version of the Su-1, but was discontinued late in 1942.

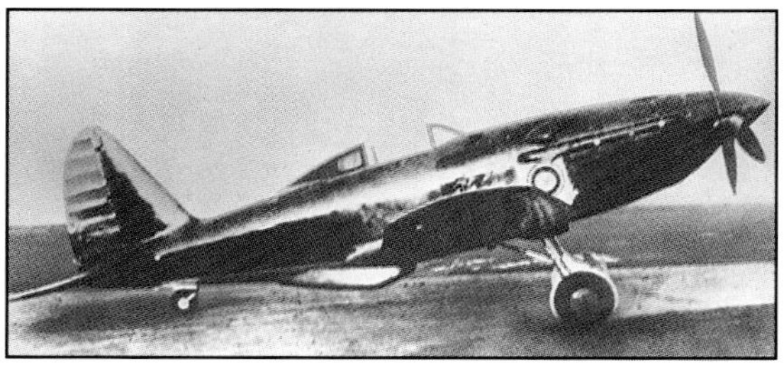

SUKHOI Su-7 (I) — USSR

Chronologically, the Su-7 mixed-power high-altitude interceptor preceded the Su-5, being based broadly on the single-seat Su-6(A) assault aircraft. Intended to fulfil a 1943 requirement, the Su-7 retained the single-spar metal wing of the experimental *shturmovik*, mated to a new all-metal semi-monocoque fuselage. It was proposed that the fighter be powered by the 2,200 hp Shvetsov M-71 18-cylinder two-row radial engine with

The Su-7 mixed-power fighter (above and below) which was based broadly on the Su-6 assault type.

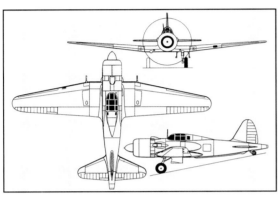

paired TK-3 turbo-superchargers, but non-availability of this power plant led to the decision to install a 14-cylinder two-row Shvetsov M-82FN radial engine rated at 1,850 hp and supplemented by a Korol'ev-Glushko RD-1KhZ bi-fuel rocket motor developing 661 lb (300 kg) thrust with a burn time of four minutes. Flight testing of the Su-7 with the rocket motor commenced in the late summer of 1944. Although the unstable nature of the rocket power plant motivated against adoption of the Su-7, flight testing revealed that it boosted maximum speed by 51 mph (83 km/h) at 24,605 ft (7 500 m) and by 121 mph (195 km/h) at 42,650 ft (13 000 m). Armament comprised two wing-mounted 20-mm cannon, and the sole rocket-powered Su-7 prototype was being prepared for the first post-World War II air display over Moscow in 1945 when the rocket motor exploded, killing the pilot and destroying the aircraft. *Max speed, 371 mph (597 km/h) or (with RD-1KhZ operating) 423 mph (680 km/h) at 24,605 ft (7 500 m). Approx range, 770 mls (1 240 km). Loaded weight, 9,568 lb (4 340 kg). Span, 44 ft 3½ in (13,50 m). Length, 31 ft 6 in (9,60 m). Wing area, 279.87 sq ft (26,00 m²).*

SUKHOI Su-5 (I-107) USSR

The development at the TsIAM (Central Aero Engine Institute) by K V Kholshchevnikov of the so-called "accelerator", or VRDK (*Vozdushno-reaktivny dvigatyel kompressorny*, or Air-reaction engine compressor), prompted the development of mixed-power single-seat fighters as an interim means of meeting the potential threat of German turbojet-powered fighters. Both Mikoyan-Gurevich and Sukhoi bureaux were assigned the task of creating such fighters, the former developing the MiG-13 alias I-250(N) and the latter the Su-5 alias I-107. The VRDK (see MiG-13) provided 660 lb (300 kg) thrust for up to 10 min at high altitude to boost the power available from the Klimov M-107A (VK-107A)

The Su-5 (below) had piston engine power augmented with Kholshchevnikov's so-called "accelerator".

12-cylinder Vee-type liquid-cooled engine which delivered 1,650 hp for take-off. An all-metal stressed-skin single-seat monoplane with a monocoque fuselage, the Su-5 had an armament of one 23-mm engine-mounted cannon and two 12,7-mm machine guns. First flown in April 1945, the prototype was soon thereafter fitted with a new wing of laminar-flow type developed by the TsAGI, and during one subsequent flight test a speed of 493 mph (793 km/h) was attained at 14,270 ft (4 350 m), this being 15 mph (25 km/h) faster than had been calculated for that altitude. The effect of the VRDK was a gain of 56 mph (90 km/h) at low altitude rising to 68 mph (110 km/h) at 25,590 ft (7 800 m), at which it was anticipated that maximum speed would be 503 mph (810 km/h). Early in July 1945, before this speed could be attained, the M-107A engine suffered some damage in flight and when it was found to be irreparable, the Su-5 flight test programme was abandoned. *Max speed (estimated), 503 mph (810 km/h) at 25,590 ft (7 800 m). Time to 16,405 ft (5 000 m), 7.0 min. Max range, 373 mls (600 km). Empty weight, 6,512 lb (2 954 kg). Loaded weight, 8,387 lb (3 804 kg). Span, 34 ft 7¾ in (10,56 m). Length, 27 ft 11 in (8,51 m). Height, 11 ft 7 in (3,53 m). Wing area, 182.99 sq ft (17,00 m²).*

(Below) The Su-5 mixed-power single-seat fighter.

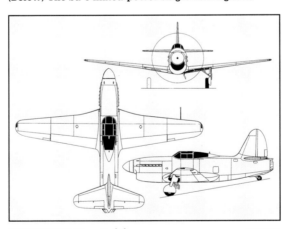

SUKHOI Su-9 (I) USSR

Displaying a close conceptual similarity to the Messerschmitt Me 262, the Su-9 single-seat fighter, also known as *Samolet* (Aircraft) *K*, entered flight test in the autumn of 1946. Of all-metal construction with a semi-monocoque, oval-section fuselage and single-spar wings, the Su-9 had an armament of one 37-mm and two 23-mm cannon, and was powered by two 1,984 lb st (900 kgp) Junkers Jumo 004B turbojets (which had been copied for manufacture in the Soviet Union as the RD-10). The Su-9 embodied a number of innovatory features insofar as Soviet technology was

The Su-9 (below) was conceptually similar to the Me 262 and was, in consequence, rejected by Stalin.

concerned, these including hydraulically-boosted control surfaces, a cordite-fired ejection seat, a variable-incidence tailplane, provision for assisted take-off rockets and a braking parachute. Racks under the centre fuselage permitted carriage of one 1,102-lb (500 kg) or two 551-lb (250-kg) bombs. The Su-9 was shown publicly over Tushino on 3 August 1947, and with completion of State testing in the following December, series production was recommended. However, although possessing no more than a superficial resemblance to the Me 262, its configurational similarity to the German fighter was a stigma which led Yosif Stalin to reject the Su-9 out of hand. *Max speed, 526 mph (847 km/h) at sea level, 559 mph (900 km/h) at 19,685 ft (6 000 m). Time to 16,405 ft (5 000 m), 4.2 min. Range, 708 mls (1 140 km). Empty weight, 8,951 lb (4 060 kg). Max loaded weight, 14,065 lb (6 380 kg). Span, 36 ft 9 in (11,21 m). Length, 34 ft 7⅓ in (10,57 m). Height, 12 ft 2½ in (3,72 m). Wing area, 217.87 sq ft (20,24 m²).*

When state tests of the Su-9 (above and below) were completed, series production was recommended.

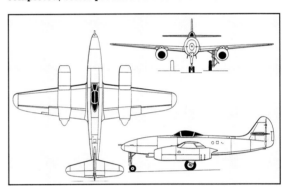

SUKHOI Su-11 (I) USSR

In late May 1947, flight testing commenced of a development of the Su-9, the Su-11 or *Samolet LK*, which was destined to be the first Soviet jet fighter powered by a turbojet of indigenous design. The fuselage of the Su-11 was fundamentally similar to that of the Su-9, apart from some structural revision, but because of the appreciably larger engines, the wing structure was extensively modified. The Su-11 was powered by two Lyulka TR-1 turbojets each developing 2,866 lb st

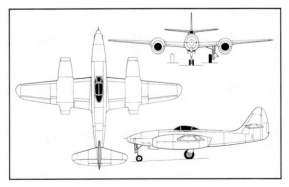

The Su-11 (above and below) was handicapped, like its predecessor, by a similarity to the Me 262.

(1 300 kgp), these being mounted ahead of the mainspar. Armament was the same as that of the Su-9. Factory trials were completed in April 1948, but the TR-1 turbojet was inadequately developed and, like its predecessor, the Su-11 was handicapped by the suggestion that it copied German technology,. Aleksandr Yakovlev telling Yosif Stalin that it was no more than a ''warmed over Me 262''. *Max speed, 584 mph (940 km/h) at sea level, 565 mph (910 km/h) at 19,685 ft (6 000 m). Time to 16,405 ft (5 000 m), 3.2 min. Range, 565 mls (910 km). Empty weight, 9,910 lb (4 495 kg). Loaded weight, 13,999 lb (6 350 kg). Span, 38 ft 8½ in (11,80 m). Length, 34 ft 7⅓ in (10,57 m). Height, 12 ft 2½ in (3,72 m). Wing area, 230.35 sq ft (21,40 m²).*

SUKHOI Su-15 (I)   USSR

Rolled out at Novosibirsk on 25 October 1948 and first flown in January 1949, the Su-15, or *Samolet P*, was a single-seat all-weather interceptor. It was powered by two 5,005 lb st (2 270 kgp) RD-45F turbojets mounted in tandem, the forward engine exhausting beneath the centre fuselage and the aft engine exhausting via an orifice in the extreme tail. The pilot's pressurised cockpit was offset to port, a tunnel feeding air to the rearmost turbojet passing to starboard. The air intake was surmounted by a radome intended to accommodate *Izumrud* (Emerald) AI radar, the single-spar wings were sweptback 35 deg at quarter chord and armament comprised two 37-mm cannon. During its 39th flight, on 3 June 1949, the Su-15 developed uncontrollable flutter, its pilot ejecting. At that time a second prototype was still incomplete and the development programme was abandoned. *Max speed, 641 mph (1 032 km/h) at 14,930 ft (4 550 m), or Mach=0.89, 612 mph (985 km/h) at 35,925 ft (10 950 m), or Mach=0.926. Time to 16,405 ft (5 000 m), 2.5 min. Range, 994 mls (1 600 km). Empty weight, 16,334 lb (7 409 kg). Loaded weight, 23,009 lb (10 437 kg). Span, 42 ft 2⅔ in (12,87 m). Length, 50 ft 7⅞ in (15,44 m). Wing area, 387.51 sq ft (36,00 m²).*

The Su-15 (above and below) embodied several odd features, including tandem-mounted turbojets.

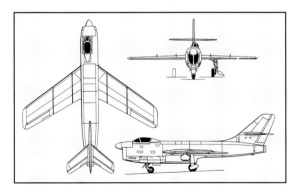

The cockpit of the Su-15 (below) was unusual in being offset to port.

SUKHOI Su-7(II)   USSR

During reorganisation of the Soviet aircraft industry in November 1949, Pavel O Sukhoi's OKB was disbanded, being resurrected three-and-a-half years later, in May 1953, to pursue development of two fighter projects.

The Sukhoi S-1 (above) photographed during its public début over Tushino in June 1956.

These were referred to as the S-1 and T-3 respectively, the prefix letters signifying *strelovidnyi* (arrowhead) and *treugolnyi* (triangular) in reference to the wing configuration (ie, sweptback and delta). Both aircraft were designed around the large, new Lyulka AL-7 (TRD-31) turbojet, but enjoyed only limited design commonality.

The S-2 (above) was the second prototype of what was to enter series production as the Su-7.

The S-1 was conceived as a so-called ''frontal'' fighter – a tactical air superiority warplane intended to operate in the vicinity of the battlefront – and was the first Soviet aircraft to feature a slab-type tail and a translating nose cone. Flown on 8 September 1955, the S-1 was initially fitted with an unaugmented AL-7 rated at 14,330 lb st (6 500 kgp). This was replaced by an afterburning AL-7F of 20,944 lb st (9 500 kgp) with which the S-1 established a national speed record of 1,348 mph (2 170 km/h), or Mach=2.04, in April 1956. Featuring 60 deg of sweepback, the S-1 had an armament of three 30-mm cannon and provision for a retractable ventral tray for 32 spin-stabilised 57-mm rockets. Demonstrated over Tushino on 24 June 1956, this prototype crashed on 21 November that year. A second prototype, the S-2, embodying some aerodynamic refinements, had joined the test programme in the meantime and – although this was not to complete State testing until the autumn of 1957 – manufacture of a pre-series went ahead simultaneously. Built in sufficient quantity to equip a regiment for evaluation purposes, these fighters, which possessed a primary air-to-air rôle and entered service in the Soviet Far East in early 1959, were assigned the designation Su-7. This repeated the appellation of the mixed-power experimental fighter tested in 1944. A requirement change led to the further development of the basic design as a dedicated ground attack fighter under the designation Su-7B (S-22). The following data relate to the pre-series Su-7. *Max speed, 1,135 mph (1 827 km/h) at 39,370 ft (12 000 m), or Mach=1.72, 720 mph (1 160 km/h) at sea level, or Mach=0.945. Normal loaded weight, 20,774 lb (9 423 kg). Span, 30 ft 0 in (9,15 m). Length (excluding probe), 54 ft 10¼ in (16,72 m).*

SUKHOI T-3   USSR

Unofficially dubbed *Balalaika* thanks to its resemblance in shape to the sound box of that musical instrument, the T-3 initiated the series of missile-armed single-seat tailed-delta interceptor fighters developed by Pavel Sukhoi's OKB. Evolved in parallel with the S-1 ''frontal'' fighter and first flown on 26 May 1956, the T-3 pos-

sessed 57 deg of wing leading-edge sweepback, was intended to be armed with two K-8 or K-9 missiles and was to have had an *Almaz* (Diamond) search-and-track radar. The elements of the *Almaz* were to have been housed within a broad elliptical radome above, and a circular housing on, the intake splitter plate. Powered initially by an unaugmented Lyulka AL-7 turbojet – which was to give place to an AL-7F rated at 14,330 lb st (6 500 kgp) boosted to 19,974 lb st (9 060 kgp) with afterburning – the T-3 was demonstrated over Tushino on 24 June 1956. TsAGI wind tunnel testing of the efficiency of air intake/radar housing combinations being inconclusive, two further prototypes, the PT-7 and PT-8, were completed with different arrangements. The former, flown in September 1956, retained the chin intake position and superimposed elliptical radome, but with a variable-angle lower wedge to produce a two-dimensional intake. The PT-8, which joined the test programme two months later, featured a lengthened – by approximately 4.1 ft (1,25 m) – nose with circular air intake and conical translating centrebody. The T-3 and its PT variations provided the basis for the further T-4 series from which the first production Sukhoi tailed-delta fighters were to be derived. The following data relate to the AL-7F-powered T-3. *Max speed, 1,305 mph (2 100 km/h), or Mach=1.98. Ceiling, 59,055 ft (18 000 m). Max range, 1,143 mls (1 840 km). Span, 27 ft 7⅞ in (8,43 m). Length, 54 ft 11½ in (16,75 m). Wing area, 260.49 sq ft (24,20 m²).*

The T-3 (above and below) was the first of a series of tailed-delta fighters developed by the Sukhoi OKB.

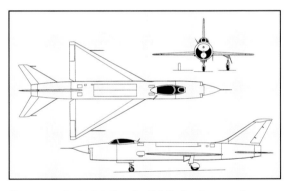

Known as the *Balalaika*, the T-3 (below) was to have had an *Almaz* radar and paired K-8 or K-9 missiles.

SUKHOI Su-9 (II)   USSR

Within an unusually short timescale, the Pavel Sukhoi OKB succeeded in developing a successful limited all-weather single-seat interceptor fighter from the T-3 and its immediate derivatives. Assigned the designation Su-9, this interceptor was available to enter IA-PVO *Strany* service from 1961. The Su-9 was directly evolved from the T-4 series of prototypes, which, sharing the 57-deg delta wing and Lyulka AL-7F turbojet with the preceding prototypes, differed from one

The T-49 (above) featured box-type intakes flanking an ogival nose radome.

another in detail design, systems and equipment. With a single exception, the T-4 prototypes featured a circular ncse intake with a translating centrebody to accommodate the S-band R1L search-and-track radar. The exception, the T-49, had a unique arrangement of box-type intakes flanking a slim, ogival nose radome. The first T-4 series prototype, apparently designated T-401, entered flight test during 1957, and, in May 1960, an essentially similar aircraft, the T-405, established a new 100-km closed-circuit record of 1,300 mph (2 092 km/h). The definitive fighter development, the T-43, was first flown in 1958 as the T-431, and established a zoom climb altitude record of 94,652 ft (28,850 m) on 14 July 1959. Three years later, the T-431 set both a sustained altitude record of 69,455 ft (21 170 m) and a 500-km closed-circuit record of 1,452 mph (2 337 km/h). Series production of the T-43

(Above and below) The early-production Su-9 which entered service at the beginning of the 'sixties.

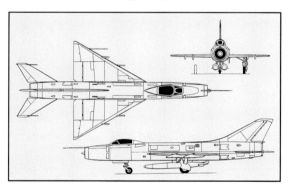

An early series Su-9 (below) with paired fuel tanks on side-by-side fuselage stores stations.

as the Su-9 was launched in 1959, standard armament comprising four beam-riding K-5 AAMs on underwing pylons. Production of the Su-9 is believed to have exceeded 1,000 aircraft, and this type remained in Soviet service until the beginning of the 'eighties. *Estimated max speed, 720 mph (1 160 km/h) at sea level, or Mach=0.945, 1,190 mph (1 915 km/h) at 39,370 ft (12 000 m), or Mach=1.8. Estimated empty weight, 19,290 lb (8 750 kg). Estimated loaded weight, 26,455 lb (12 000 kg). Span, 27 ft 7⅞ in (8,43 m). Approx length (excluding probe), 54 ft 9½ in (16,70 m). Wing area, 282.56 sq ft (26,25 m²).*

SUKHOI P-1   USSR

The P-1 (above and below) was discontinued at a relatively early flight test stage owing to poor engine reliability and radar development delays.

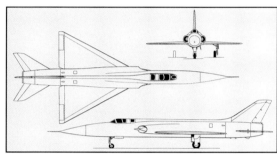

During 1957, the Sukhoi OKB began construction of the prototype of a new tailed-delta interceptor, the two-seat P-1 (the prefix letter indicating *Perekhvatchik*, or interceptor) intended to meet a requirement for a fighter equipped with collision-course radar and carrying a mixed armament of guided and unguided missiles plus cannon. Flown in 1958, the P-1 had a 57-deg delta wing with dog-tooth leading edges and lateral air intakes with translating centrebodies. Power was provided by an unspecified turbojet with a maximum afterburning thrust of 23,370 lb (10 600 kg) and armament included a battery of 50 unguided spin-stabilised 57-mm rocket missiles, provision being made for a single 37-mm cannon and guided missiles on underwing pylons. Poor engine reliability and serious delay in development of the intended X-band radar led to discontinuation of development of the P-1 at a comparatively early stage in flight test. The following data are based on manufacturer's estimates. *Max speed, 1,274 mph (2 050 km/h), or Mach=1.93. Ceiling, 63,975 ft (19 500 m). Range, 1,243 mls (2 000 km). Loaded weight, 37,500 lb (17 010 kg). Estimated span, 31 ft 2 in (9,50 m). Estimated length, 70 ft 0 in (21,30 m).*

SUKHOI Su-7B (S-22)   USSR

The second S-22 prototype (above) with 28 S-3K rockets suspended from wing and fuselage stations.

With the change in the VVS FA heavy fighter requirement from a primary air-to-air rôle to that of ground attack, the Sukhoi OKB undertook revision of the basic S-2 "frontal" fighter as the S-22. Embodying some structural changes to cater for the primarily low-level mission, together with equipment and armament changes, the S-22 retained the highly sweptback (60 deg at quarter chord) wing, circular-section fuselage and Lyulka AL-7F turbojet of the S-2 (Su-7). The first prototype of the ground attack fighter flew in April 1959. Preparations for series production of the S-22 as the Su-7B (the suffix letter signifying *Bombardirovshchik*) at Novosibirsk had begun prior to the prototype testing, thus allowing this ground attack fighter to enter the VVS FA inventory early in 1960. The Su-7B possessed a gun armament of twin 30-mm cannon, and four external stores stations (two fuselage and two wing) had a theoretical maximum ordnance load of four *tonnes*. The Su-7B was succeeded in 1961 by the Su-7BM (*Modifikatsirovanny*) with an AL-7F-1 turbojet, this engine, standardised for all subsequent versions, being rated at 15,432 lb st (7 000 kgp) boosted to 22,288 lb st (10 110 kgp) with afterburning. The Su-7BM (S-22M) also introduced a revised fuel system with prominent external piping ducts along the upper rear fuselage. To improve rough field capability in a version designated Su-7BKL (S-22KL) the flaps were redesigned, provision made for ATO rockets and twin braking chutes, and a unique wheel-skid (*kolyosnolyzhnyi*) undercarriage introduced. The main undercarriage members embodied small, extensible steel skids for use on soft ground and were accommodated, when retracted, in bulged bays. The definitive series model introduced in the mid 'sixties and remaining in production into the early 'seventies was the Su-7BMK – the suffix letters signifying *modifikatsirovanny kolyosno* – with new mainwheel members (from which the skids

An early series Su-7B (above) and a Czechoslovak Su-7BM (below) which introduced prominent external piping ducts along the upper rear fuselage.

had been eliminated) retracting into flush wheel wells. This modification was accompanied by upgrading of the avionics fit, provision of zero-zero ejection seat and standardisation on a further pair of wing stores pylons as introduced by late Su-7BKLs. Finally withdrawn from VVS-FA first-line service in 1986, the Su-7B was supplied to Afghanistan, Algeria, Czechoslovakia, Egypt, Hungary, India, Iraq, North Korea, Poland, Romania, Syria, Vietnam and South Yemen. The following data relate to the Su-7BM. *Max speed, 715 mph*

(Above) An export Su-7BMK and (below) the Su-7BKL which introduced a wheel-skid undercarriage.

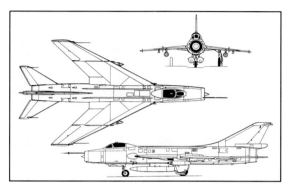

(1 150 km/h) at sea level, or Mach=0.94, 1,055 mph (1 700 km/h) at 39,370 ft (12 000 m), or Mach=1.6. Max climb, 29,525 ft/min (150 m/sec). Max range, 900 mls (1 450 km). Operational empty weight, 18,360 lb (8 328 kg). Max loaded weight, 29,630 lb (13 440 kg). Span, 29 ft 3½ in (8,93 m). Length (excluding probe), 54 ft 5½ in (16,60 m). Height, 15 ft 5 in (4,70 m). Wing area, 322.93 sq ft (30,00 m²).

An Su-7BKL (above) and an Su-7BM (below) of the CO of No 32 "Thunderbirds" Sqn, the last but one Indian unit to relinquish the Sukhoi fighter.

(Immediately below) An Su-7BMK of the Czech Air Force in 1980 and (bottom) an Su-7BM of the Algerian Air Force in 1977.

SUKHOI Su-11 (II)   USSR

The availability of a more powerful radar, the *Uragan* (Hurricane) 5B, matched with new medium-range AAMs available in alternative semi-active radar guidance and infra-red homing versions in the mid 'sixties, led to upgrading of the basic T-43 (Su-9). The

The Su-11 (above and below) was fundamentally a progressive development of the Su-9 with new radar and a new missile armament.

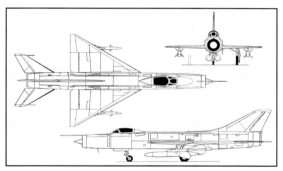

larger-diameter dish of the *Uragan* I-band radar necessitated an intake centrebody of almost twice the cross-section area of that of the series Su-9. This, in turn, required increasing the intake lip diameter to allow for the same airflow, which, the AL-7F engine being retained, remained essentially unchanged. External piping ducts along the upper rear fuselage, similar to those of the Su-7BM, signified a revised fuel system, and armament comprised two medium-range missiles (one radar-guided and the other IR-homing). With the AL-7F-1 turbojet providing an afterburning thrust of

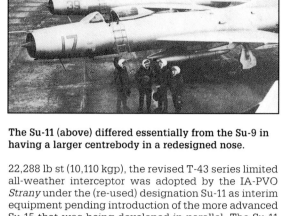

The Su-11 (above) differed essentially from the Su-9 in having a larger centrebody in a redesigned nose.

22,288 lb st (10,110 kgp), the revised T-43 series limited all-weather interceptor was adopted by the IA-PVO *Strany* under the (re-used) designation Su-11 as interim equipment pending introduction of the more advanced Su-15 that was being developed in parallel. The Su-11 supplemented and partly replaced the Su-9 until similarly withdrawn in the early 'eighties. The following data are estimated. *Max speed, 720 mph (1 160 km/h) at sea level, or Mach=0.95, 1,190 mph (1 915 km/h) at 39,370 ft (12 000 m), or Mach=1.8. Normal loaded weight, 27,000 lb (12 247 kg). Span, 27 ft 7⅞ in (8,43 m). Length (excluding probe), 57 ft 0 in (17,37 m).*

SUKHOI Su-15 (II)   USSR

Development of a single-seat interceptor fighter providing better supersonic performance while (initially) preserving a fundamentally similar wing was begun as the T-5 in the late 'fifties. This was a larger aircraft than the preceding T-43 and was powered by paired Tumansky R-11 turbojets with lateral air intakes. Retaining the tailed-delta configuration and 57-deg sweepback at wing quarter chord, the interceptor was built as the

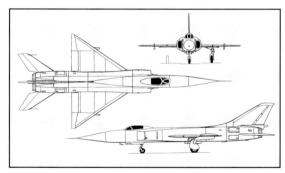

The pre-series Su-15 (above and below) retained the delta wing planform of earlier Sukhoi fighters.

T-58 prototype and flown on 30 May 1962, and, as the Su-15, 10 examples participated in the July 1967 air display at Domodedovo. The initial version, effectively confined to a large pre-series for service evaluation, possessed a wing similar to that of the Su-9 and Su-11, with some 12 in (30 cm) removed adjacent to the fuselage each side. The *Oriol-D* AI radar and two R-8 AAMs were fitted, and power was provided by two R-11F2S-300 turbojets each rated at 8,598 lb st (3 900 kgp) and 13,668 lb st (6 200 kgp) with max afterburning. The virtually pure delta wing gave place on the next version, the Su-15T (the suffix signifying introduction of *Taifun* radar), to a cranked leading edge with outboard sweepback reduced to 47 deg, overall span remaining unchanged. Su-15T production was limited to 10 aircraft delivered during 1969. A V/STOL technology demonstrator derivative, the Su-15VD (*vertikal'nye dvigateli*, or vertical engines), was demonstrated at Domodedovo in July 1967, this having a trio of 5,180 lb st (2 350 kgp) Koliesov RD-36-35 lift engines mounted vertically in the centre of the fuselage. The

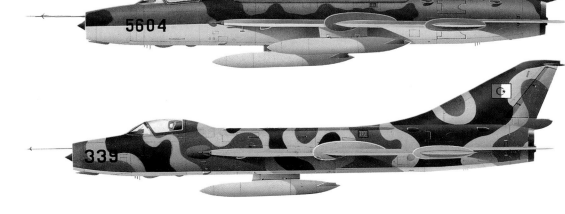

The Su-15VD technology demonstrator (above) and the definitive Su-15TM (right) with the ogival radome.

definitive wing appeared on the Su-15TM (*Taifun modifikatsiya*) which became the major production version in 1972 and achieved operational status in the second half of 1973. This introduced a further variation of the

cranked planform with a span extension of 23.5 in (60 cm), the improved *Taifun-M* radar, and Gavrilov-developed R-13F-300 turbojets rated at 9,340 lb st (4 237 kgp) and 14,550 lb st (6 600 kgp) with afterburn-

ing. Armament, too, was upgraded, two additional wing pylons being introduced inboard and a pair of IR-homing R-23TE and two radar-guided R-23RE AAMs normally being carried. Twin pods each containing a

Key to Sukhoi Su-17M-4

1 Instrumentation data probe
2 Yaw and pitch vanes
3 Fire control system computer transducers
4 Pitot head
5 Conical intake centre-body shock cone/radome
6 Engine air intake
7 SRD-5M I-band ranging radar
8 Laser marked target designator
9 Radar altimeter
10 Ventral antennae
11 Doppler navigation aerial
12 Angle of attack transmitter
13 Radar equipment module
14 Bifurcated intake ducting
15 Spring-loaded intake suction relief doors, open
16 Temperature probe
17 Nose avionics equipment compartment, ASP-5ND fire control system
18 Su-17UM two-seat tandem trainer variant (nose profile)
19 Boarding ladder
20 Student pilot's cockpit
21 Retractable forward vision periscope
22 Instructor's cockpit
23 Rear cockpit access ramp
24 Armoured glass windscreen panels
25 Pilot's head-up display and attack sight
26 Instrument panel shroud
27 Control column
28 Rudder pedals
29 Nose undercarriage wheel bay
30 Retractable landing/taxiing lamp, port and starboard
31 Nosewheel doors
32 Nosewheel forks
33 Steerable nosewheel, forward retracting
34 Nosewheel leg-mounted taxiing lamp
35 SRO-2M IFF aerials
36 Nosewheel leg pivot fixing
37 Hydraulic retraction jack
38 Cockpit floor level
39 Close-pitched fuselage frames in pressurised section
40 Port side console
41 Engine throttle lever
42 Canopy latch
43 Rear view mirrors
44 Pilot's K-36 ejection seat
45 Ejection seat headrest
46 Mirror fairing
47 Cockpit canopy cover, upward-hinging
48 Canopy jack
49 Cockpit pressurisation valve
50 Rear pressure bulkhead
51 Air conditioning plant
52 Intake duct framing
53 Ground power and intercom sockets
54 Cannon muzzle blast shield/skin doubler
55 Avionics equipment racks
56 Dorsal fairing additional avionics equipment
57 Fuel system access panel
58 Intake trunking
59 Main fuel pumps
60 Inverted flight accumulator
61 Front wing spar attachment main frame
62 Centre fuselage frame-and-stringer construction
63 Fuselage fuel tanks
64 Fuel piping
65 Ammunition feed chute

66 Ammunition magazine (70 rounds per gun, port and starboard)
67 ADF aerial
68 Dorsal fuel tanks
69 Starboard wing fixed root segment
70 Strike camera
71 Wing pivot bearing
72 Outboard wing fence
73 Fuselage centreline tactical reconnaissance pod
74 GSh-23L cannon pod
75 Leading-edge slats, down position
76 Slat hydraulic jack
77 Starboard wing integral fuel tank
78 Aileron hydraulic actuator
79 Slat guide rails
80 RPK-100, 220-lb (100-kg) bombs
81 Multiple ejector rack (wing glove and inboard pylons)
82 Starboard navigation light
83 Wing tip fairing
84 Static discharger
85 Starboard aileron
86 Starboard wing fully-swept position
87 Outboard single-slotted flap (down position)
88 Wing glove section
89 Dorsal spine aft fairing
90 Forward chaff/flare dispensers (port and starboard)
91 Wing main spar attachment double main frame
92 Engine compressor intake
93 Oil tank
94 (Saturn) Lyulka AL-21F-3 afterburning engine
95 Rear fuselage break point (engine removal)
96 Access panels
97 Engine bay cooling air ram air intakes
98 Engine turbine section
99 Heat exchanger ram air intake
100 Primary heat exchanger
101 Starboard upper airbrake, open
102 Cooling air spill duct
103 Rear chaff/flare dispensers, port and starboard
104 Autopilot controller
105 HF aerial
106 Starboard tailplane anti-flutter weight
107 Rudder control linkages
108 Rudder hydraulic actuator
109 Tailfin construction
110 RSIU, very short wave fighter control aerial
111 Fin tip UHF aerial fairing
112 Rear radar warning receiver
113 Tail navigation light
114 Rudder
115 Rudder rib construction
116 ECM aerial
117 Parachute release link
118 Brake parachute housing
119 Conical fairing parachute doors, open
120 Transponder aerial
121 Engine exhaust nozzle
122 Port all-moving tailplane
123 Static discharger
124 Tailplane tip anti-flutter weight
125 Tailplane rib construction
126 Tailplane spar
127 Pivot mounting
128 Tailplane limit stops

129 Faired control linkages
130 Variable area afterburner nozzle
131 Nozzle control jacks
132 Fin and tailplane attachment fuselage double frame
133 Afterburner ducting
134 Tailplane hydraulic actuator
135 SRO-2M IFF aerial
136 Airbrake housing
137 Airbrake hydraulic jack
138 Rear fuselage frame and stringer construction
139 Ventral fin (detachable)
140 Port lower airbrake (open)
141 Engine accessory equipment access panel
142 Accessory equipment gearbox compartment
143 Port inboard single-slotted flap
144 Flap actuator
145 Auxiliary rear spar
146 Wing sweep control hydraulic jack
147 Rear spar guide rails
148 Wing glove section external stiffeners
149 Outboard wing fence
150 Outboard single-slotted flap
151 Flap rib construction
152 Flap actuator
153 Aileron rib construction
154 Port wing fully-swept (62-degree) position
155 Port aileron
156 Aileron hinge control linkage
157 Static discharger
158 Wing tip fairing
159 Port wing fully-forward (28-degree) position
160 Port navigation light

161 Three-segment leading-edge slats, down position
162 BETA B-250 550-lb (250-kg) retarded concrete-piercing bomb
163 240-mm S-24 aircraft rocket
164 R-3S air-to-air self-defence missile
165 Missile launch rail
166 Leading-edge slat rib construction
167 Aileron hydraulic actuator
168 Port wing integral fuel tank
169 Wing rib construction
170 Leading-edge slat hydraulic jack
171 Outer wing panel main spar
172 Wing pivot bearing
173 Mainwheel doors

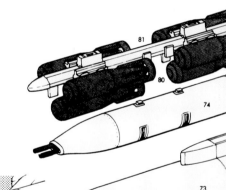

twin-barrel 23-mm cannon could be carried side-by-side on fuselage pylons. From 1975, the conical radome was replaced by one of ogival shape, production of the Su-15TM ending in the late 'seventies after manufac-

(Below) The definitive series Su-15TM interceptor.

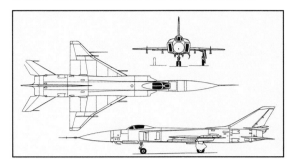

ture of some 1,500 interceptors of this type. The following data are estimated. *Max speed (with external ordnance), 1,386 mph (2 230 km/h) at 39,370 ft (12 000 m), or Mach=2.1. Max climb, 35,000 ft/min (178 m/sec). Combat radius (with external fuel), 620 mls (1 000 km). Empty weight, 24,250 lb (11 000 kg). Max loaded weight, 39,680 lb (18 000 kg). Span, 30 ft 0 in (9,15 m). Length (excluding probe), 65 ft 0 in (19,80 m). Height, 16 ft 6 in (5,00 m). Wing area, 385 sq ft (35,77 m²).*

The Su-15TM (below) with the original conical radome which was replaced by one of ogival shape in the '70s.

SUKHOI Su-17 (II)   USSR

The Su-17 (S-32) single-seat ground attack fighter was the product of an extraordinary process of incremental redesign of the Su-7B (S-22). Under the leadership of Nikolai Zyrin, the Sukhoi OKB adapted an Su-7BMK as a low risk, low cost variable wing geometry demonstrator. Mid-span pivot points were introduced so that the outer wing panels could be sweptback from 28-deg to 45-deg and 62-deg positions. As the Su-7IG (*Izmenyaemaya Geometriya*, or variable geometry), or S-22I, the demonstrator flew on 8 August 1966, proving the efficacy of the variable-geometry arrangement and providing the basis for a production aircraft, the Su-17. This entered the VVS-FA inventory in 1970. The Su-17 was powered by the Lyulka AL-21F-3 turbojet with a military power of 17,196 lb st (7 800 kgp) and 24,690 lb st (11 200 kgp) with afterburning. Maximum external stores load was 8,820 lb (4 000 kg) distributed between

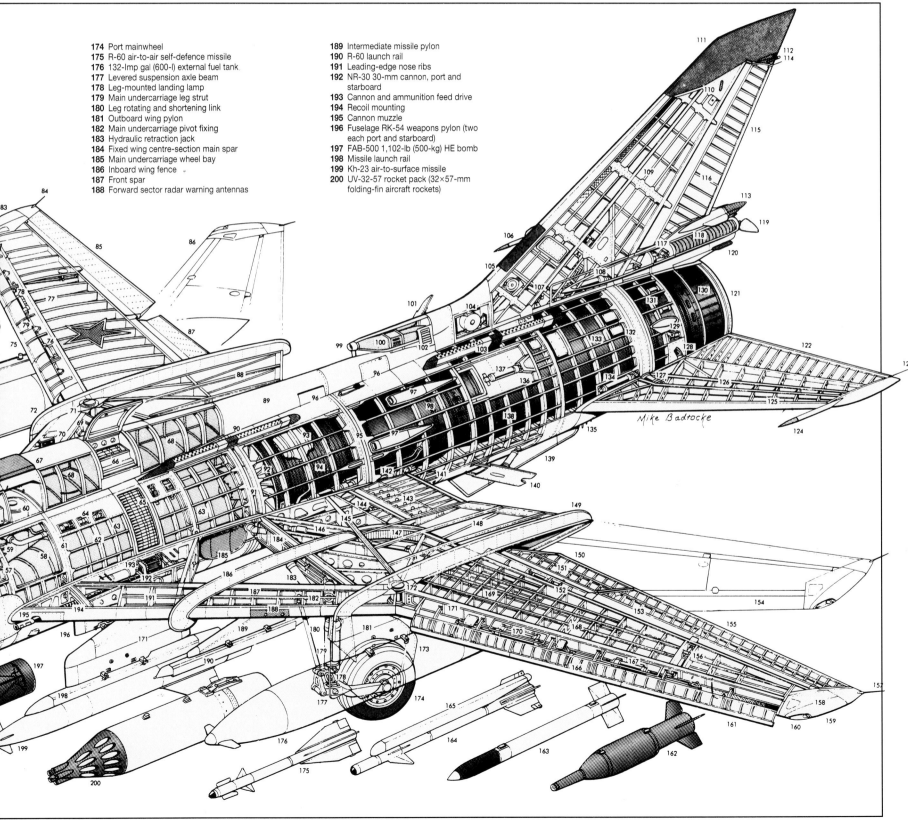

174 Port mainwheel
175 R-60 air-to-air self-defence missile
176 132-Imp gal (600-l) external fuel tank
177 Levered suspension axle beam
178 Leg-mounted landing lamp
179 Main undercarriage leg strut
180 Leg rotating and shortening link
181 Outboard wing pylon
182 Main undercarriage pivot fixing
183 Hydraulic retraction jack
184 Fixed wing centre-section main spar
185 Main undercarriage wheel bay
186 Inboard wing fence
187 Front spar
188 Forward sector radar warning antennas

189 Intermediate missile pylon
190 R-60 launch rail
191 Leading-edge nose ribs
192 NR-30 30-mm cannon, port and starboard
193 Cannon and ammunition feed drive
194 Recoil mounting
195 Cannon muzzle
196 Fuselage RK-54 weapons pylon (two each port and starboard)
197 FAB-500 1,102-lb (500-kg) HE bomb
198 Missile launch rail
199 Kh-23 air-to-surface missile
200 UV-32-57 rocket pack (32×57-mm folding-fin aircraft rockets)

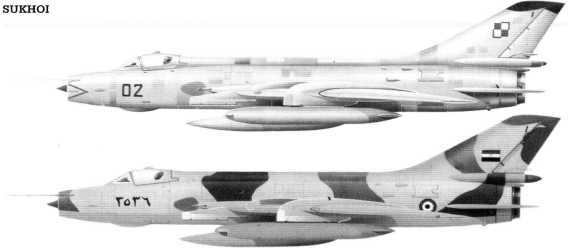

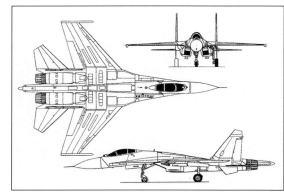

(Immediately left) An Su-20 of the 7 BLB-R, Polish Air Force and Air Defence Force at Powidz, 1974, and (below left) an Su-20 of 35 Sqn, Egyptian Air Force, Katamia AB, in 1981.

(Below) The standard production single-seat Su-27.

nine external stations, and built-in armament comprised two 30-mm cannon. An upgraded version, the Su-17M (S-32M), entered production in 1974, this having a drooped and lengthened – by 15 in (38 cm) – fuselage nose with ventral Doppler navaid pod. This, like the preceding Su-17, was exported as the Su-20 (S-32MK), recipients including Algeria, Egypt, Iraq, North Korea, Vietnam and Poland. A further export derivative using the basic Su-17M airframe, but re-engined with a Tumansky R-29BS-300 augmented turbojet with a max thrust of 25,350 lb st (11 500 kgp), received the designation Su-22 and was supplied to Angola, Libya and Peru. Featuring a deeper forward fuselage and

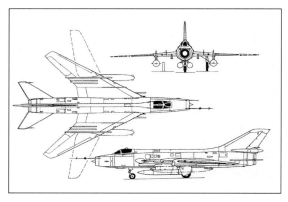

(Above) The Su-17 which entered VVS-FA service from the early 'seventies, and (below) an Su-22 of the Libyan Arab Air Force photographed in 1986.

(Below) The Su-17M-4 which entered service mid '80s.

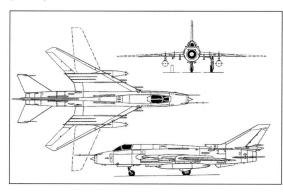

enlarged spine, and a redesigned tail to restore yawing stability, yet a further single-seat version, the Su-17M-1, appeared in mid-1979. The Su-17M-2, which appeared almost simultaneously, differed in equipment fit, with the export version, the Su-22M-2, supplied to both Libya and Peru, having the Tumansky engine. The definitive single-seat production versions were the Su-

17M-3 and M-4, the former supplied to Hungary as the Su-22M-3 and the latter to Afghanistan, Czechoslovakia, East Germany and Poland as the Su-

An Su-17M-2 (below), which, together with the M-1, introduced a deeper forward fuselage in 1979-80.

(Above) A Libyan Su-22M-2 over the Mediterranean in August 1981, and (below) an Su-22M-4 of JGB 77, *Gebhard von Blucher, Luftstreitkräfte*, Germany, 1990.

22MA. These AL-25-powered models embodied much improved avionics and introduced extra stations for R-60 or R-73 close range AAMs. With more than 3,000 built, including two-seat training variants, production of the Su-17 terminated in 1984. The following data relate to the Su-17MA. *Max speed, 870 mph (1 400 km/h) at sea level, or Mach=1.14, 1,380 mph (2 220 km/h) at 39,370 ft (12 000 m), or Mach=2.09. Max range, 1,430 mls (2 300 km). Max loaded weight, 42,990 lb (19 500 kg). Span (max), 44 ft 9⁴/₅ in (13,66 m), (min), 32 ft 11¹/₄ in (10,04 m). Length (including probes), 62 ft 8 in (19, 10 m). Height, 15 ft 11¹/₃ in (4,86 m).*

SUKHOI Su-27   USSR

The Sukhoi T-10 project was selected in 1971 for development to meet a Soviet need for a future tactical fighter. On 20 May 1977 the T-10-1 finally took to the air, piloted by Vladimir Ilyushin. It was very large, powered by two Ly'ulka AL-21F3 turbojets. It had a moderately swept wing with LERX and curved tips; low-set horizontal tails, and twin fins set forward atop widely spaced engine nacelles. Triplex analogue FBW with mechanical backup was used, but with neutral rather than relaxed stability. From the outset the T-10 had handling problems; drag was higher than predicted, as was the specific fuel consumption of the AL-21F3s. As computer studies showed it to be much inferior to the F-15, it was almost totally redesigned. The new aircraft, the T-10-7, took to the skies on 20 April 1981, once again piloted by Vladimir

Ilyushin. Problems remained, but these were eventually overcome, and project T-10 entered production as the Su-27 in 1983, though full operational capability was not attained until 1986. The Ly'ulka AL-31F turbofans, each rated at 27,558 lb (12 500 kgp) max and 16,755 lb (7 600 kgp) military thrust, retained the original wide spacing, but the original "beaver tail" between them was replaced by a long "sting". Wing area was increased, and the formerly rounded tips squared off and given missile rails. The fins were made larger, and moved to booms outboard of the engine nacelles. The cockpit displays were analogue, but the control column and throttle levers were festooned with switches in the first Russian attempt at HOTAS. More importantly, the pilot, seated high under a two-piece bubble canopy, had a magnificent all-round view. Two more major innovations were a quadruplex analogue FBW system and internal fuel tankage which, although holding a normal load of 13,228 lb (6 000 kg), could allow a total of 20,723 lb (9 400 kg) to be carried in an overload condition. The advantages of this were that external tanks were not needed to extend range, while it left all 10 (later 12) hardpoints free for ordnance. For air combat, this was initially four R-27ER/ET and six R-27R/T AAMs. For close combat, a 30-mm GSh-301 cannon with 150 rounds was located in the starboard wing root. Radar is the NIIP N-001 multi-mode coupled, like the MiG-29, with an IRST and laser ranger. In all, between 400-500 Su-27s are believed to have been delivered to the Russian Air Forces, of which only about 200 were serviceable at the end of 2000. The Su-27, NATO reporting name Flanker B, has spawned many variants. The first was the fully combat-capable conversion trainer, the Su-27UB Flanker C. Then came the Su-27SK export version, with down-graded avionics. The most important was the Su-27K (OKB designation Su-33) Flanker D carrier fighter. First flown by Viktor Pugachev on 17 August 1987, this combined a ski-jump takeoff with an arrested landing, and entered Navy service in October 1994. It differed from the baseline aircraft in having wing folding and full-span trailing edge flaps and ailerons; tailplane folding, moveable canards and a much shorter "sting"; a

(Above) An Su-27M development aircraft for the Su-35, but lacking the thrust vectoring intended for the definitive fighter. Apart from canards, the Su-35 is fundamentally externally similar to the Su-27 (below).

tailhook and a flight refuelling probe. 24 Su-27Ks are currently based on the carrier *Admiral Kuznetsov*. As is standard Russian practice, fighters carry odd numbers, while interdiction/attack aircraft have even numbers. The Su-30 two-seater multi-role, Su-32FN and Su-34 are therefore largely outside of the scope of this work, although they have fighter capability, and in fact the midlife update of Russian Su-27s is to Su-30MK standard, while the AAM fit now consists of R-73s and R-77s. As at the end of 2000, nine air forces outside Russia operated, or have ordered Flankers. They are Belarus (25); China (76) plus 200-plus to be licence-built as the J-11 and 28 Su-30MKK; Ethiopia (10); India (50) plus 140 Su-30MKIs with canards and thrust-vectoring to be licence-built; Kazakhstan (20); Syria (14 on order); Ukraine (70); Uzbekistan (31) and Vietnam (11). The following data apply to the Su-27. *Max speed hi, Mach 2.35. Max speed lo, Mach 1.14. Ceiling, 59,058 ft (18 000 m). Rate of climb, 60,000 ft/min (305 m/sec). Range (normal fuel), 1,512 nm (2 800 km). Empty weight, 36,112 lb (16 380 kg). Normal takeoff weight, 51,015 lb (23 140 kg). Span, 48 ft 3 in (14,70 m). Length, 71 ft 11 in (21,94 m). Height, 19 ft 6 in (5,93 m). Wing area, 668 sq ft (62,04 m²).*

The Su-27K-1 prototype (above) for the shipboard derivative of the Su-27, the Su-33 (below).

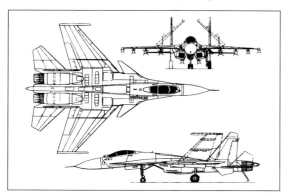

SUKHOI Su-35 AND Su-37   USSR

First flown on 28 June 1988 as the T-10M-1, the Su-35 (Russian Air Force designation Su-27M) is widely known as the Super Flanker. Designed for increased manoeuvrability, the Su-35 has much greater static instability, and uses a quadruplex digital FBW system, coupled with moving canard surfaces, which caused the brochure to describe it as a "triplane". Other external differences are square-topped fins, and wingtip pods which house EW kit. Power is the Ly'ulka AL-35F, rated at 30,865 lb (14 000 kgp) max and 17,637 lb (8 000 kgp) military thrust. The long-awaited "glass cockpit" finally emerged on the Su-35, and the production aircraft is expected to feature a sidestick controller. Two radars are reported to be in contention – the NIIP N-011 and the Phazotron Zhuk-PH – both with phased array antennas. These will both give a maximum search range of 216 nm (400 km), track up to 20 targets, and engage six simultaneously. The number of hardpoints has been increased to 14, giving outstanding combat persistence. Super Flanker was followed by the Su-37, first flown by Eugeny Frolov on 2 April 1996. This is essentially a Super Flanker powered by two thrust-vectoring Ly'ulka AL-37FU turbofans, rated at 32,000 lb (14 515 kgp) max and 18,740 lb (8 500 kgp) military thrust. Thrust vectoring allows "impossible" manoeuvres to be carried out, as first demonstrated in public

by Eugeny Frolov at Farnborough Air Show 1996. Thrust vectoring has of course been adopted for Indian and Chinese Flankers, but primarily as an aid to short-field performance. Whether either the Su-35 or Su-37 will enter service remains to be seen. The following data apply to the Su-35. *Performance all as Su-27 except range, 2,160 nm (4 000 km). Empty weight, 40,565 lb (18 400 kg). Normal takeoff weight, 56,659 lb (25 700 kg). Span, 48 ft 3 in (14,70 m). Length, 72 ft 10 in (22,20 m). Height, 21 ft (6,40 m). Wing area, 668 sq ft (62,04 m²).*

SUKHOI S-37 BERKUT   USS

First flown on 25 September 1997 by Igor Votintsev, the S-37 is a fighter demonstrator with a forward-swept wing, with canard foreplanes and twin outward-canted fins. Forward sweep is a method of enhancing manoeuvrability, although why Sukhoi would bother when they are so far advanced with thrust-vectóring is a mystery, apart from the fact that it offers considerable weight saving. Other puzzles abound. The engines were stated to be Perm D-34F6 turbofans as used by the MiG-31M Foxhound, but the thrust figures stated equate far more closely to Ly'ulka AL-31Fs as fitted to the Su-27. Or is the S-37 a red herring, designed to offer at least token opposition to Mikoyan's 1.44, trading super-manoeuvrability against sheer brute force performance, in an attempt to leave the field clear for Super Flanker? One thing is certain: the S-37 flight test programme has been far from intensive and, so far as is known, thrust vectoring has not been installed. The following data are from a highly placed Sukhoi source. *Max speed hi, Mach 1.6 (although Mach 2 has been claimed). Takeoff weight, 52,910 lb (24 000 kg). Span, 54 ft 9¹/2in (16,70 m). Length, 74 ft 2 in (22,60 m).*

(Below) The Sukhoi S-37 Berkut technology demonstrator.

The Supermarine F.7/30 (below) owed much to the float seaplanes designed for the Schneider Trophy contests.

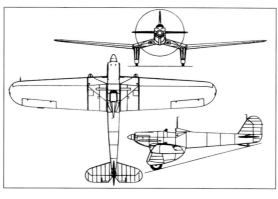

SUPERMARINE TYPE 224   UK

Issue of Specification F7/30 in 1930 for a single-seat fighter led Supermarine to build its first aircraft intended for this rôle. Designed under the direction of Reginald J Mitchell as Type (or Drawing) 224, Supermarine's proposal was one of three to gain Air Ministry backing for prototype construction (along with Westland and Blackburn), an order for one aircraft being placed in 1932. Based on experience gained with the Supermarine float seaplanes designed for participation in the Schneider Trophy contests, the Type 224 was of all-metal construction with fabric covering of the wing aft of the mainspar and of the tail surfaces. Its 600 hp Rolls-Royce Goshawk II engine had an evaporative cooling system, which was to prove to be a major reason for the eventual failure of the Type 224 to gain acceptance. Armament comprised two 0.303-in (7,7mm) guns in the fuselage and one in each mainwheel fairing. First flown on 19 February 1934, the Type 224 failed to achieve its performance estimates, and, after a prolonged sojourn at the RAE Farnborough, went to the A&AEE and eventually ended its days as a gunnery target. *Max speed, 228 mph (367 km/h) at 15,000 ft (4 570 m). Time to 15,000 ft (4 570 m), 9.5 min. Ceiling, 38,800 ft (11 825 m). Empty weight, 3,422 lb (1 552 kg). Loaded weight, 4,743 lb (2 151 kg). Span, 45 ft 10in (13,97 m). Length, 29ft 5¹/4m (8,97 m). Height (tail up), 11 ft 11 in (3,63 m). Wing area, 295 sq ft (27,40 m²).*

SUPERMARINE SPITFIRE I, II & III   UK

In succession to the Type 224, Reginald Mitchell and his team developed the single-seat fighter theme during 1934 as the elegant Type 300. An all-metal cantilever monoplane with a retractable, narrow-track undercarriage and enclosed cockpit, the Type 300 was ordered as a single prototype by the end of the year. Power was provided by a Rolls-Royce PV12 ethylene glycol-cooled engine (which was to enter production as the Merlin), and, during 1935, an armament of eight 0.303-in (7,7-mm) machine guns was adopted. The Type 300 flew on 5 March 1936, by which time the name Spitfire had been chosen. Production commenced as the Spitfire I three months later, this being powered by a 1,000 hp Merlin II or III 12-cylinder Vee-type engine

The Spitfire prototype in August 1936 (below) after being fitted with a modified rudder.

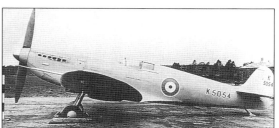

(Immediately below) Ex-RAF Spitfire IA for Portugal's *Esquadrilha XZ*, Tancos, 1943.
(Bottom) Spitfire IIA of No 41 Sqn, RAF Hornchurch, December 1940.

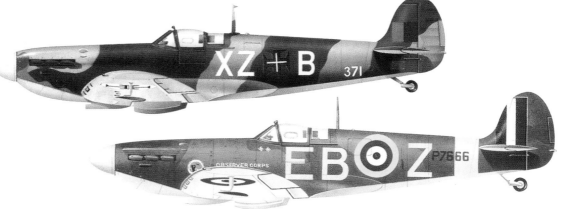

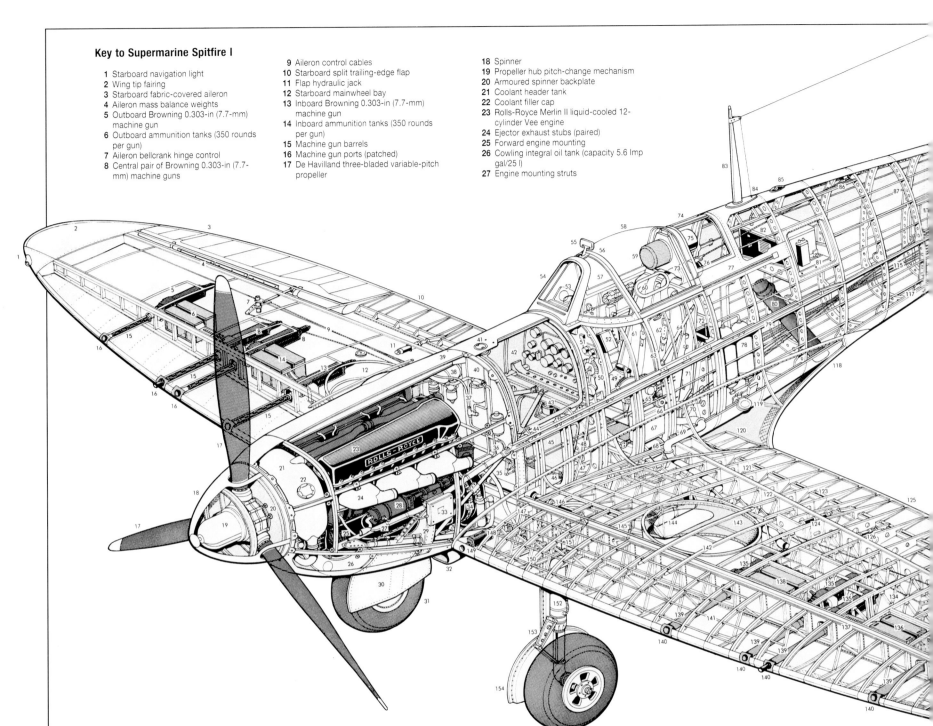

Key to Supermarine Spitfire I

1 Starboard navigation light
2 Wing tip fairing
3 Starboard fabric-covered aileron
4 Aileron mass balance weights
5 Outboard Browning 0.303-in (7.7-mm) machine gun
6 Outboard ammunition tanks (350 rounds per gun)
7 Aileron bellcrank hinge control
8 Central pair of Browning 0.303-in (7.7-mm) machine guns

9 Aileron control cables
10 Starboard split trailing-edge flap
11 Flap hydraulic jack
12 Starboard mainwheel bay
13 Inboard Browning 0.303-in (7.7-mm) machine gun
14 Inboard ammunition tanks (350 rounds per gun)
15 Machine gun barrels
16 Machine gun ports (patched)
17 De Havilland three-bladed variable-pitch propeller

18 Spinner
19 Propeller hub pitch-change mechanism
20 Armoured spinner backplate
21 Coolant header tank
22 Coolant filler cap
23 Rolls-Royce Merlin II liquid-cooled 12-cylinder Vee engine
24 Ejector exhaust stubs (paired)
25 Forward engine mounting
26 Cowling integral oil tank (capacity 5.6 Imp gal/25 l)
27 Engine mounting struts

Spitfire Is of No 65 Sqn (above), up from RAF Hornchurch shortly before World War II.

A Spitfire I of No 19 Squadron (above) displays colours and markings typical of the Battle of Britain.

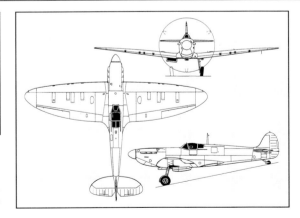

(Above) The Spitfire IA in its standard series form.

and the first series aircraft flying on 14 May 1938. Service use began in August of that year and production of the Spitfire I totalled 1,567, of which 30 were fitted with twin 20-mm cannon in place of four of the machine guns during 1940. With cannon, these became known as Mk IBs, the eight-gun version then becoming the Mk IA.

With a 1,175 hp Merlin XII engine and various minor improvements, the Spitfire II followed the Mk I from June 1940, production totalling 751 Mk IIAs and 170 Mk IIBs. A more comprehensive improvement of the basic airframe emerged in March 1940 as the prototype Mk III, this having a reduced wing span, a Merlin XX engine and a retractable tailwheel. Plans to produce 1,000 Spitfire IIIs were superseded when the Mk V was introduced, one Mk V being converted as a second Mk III prototype with a four-cannon armament. The following data relate to the Spitfire IA. *Max speed, 346 mph*

(557 km/h) at 15,000 ft (4 570 m). Time to 15,000 ft (4 570 m), 6.85 min. Ceiling, 30,500 ft (9 295 m). Range, 630 mls (1 014 km). Empty weight, 4,517 lb (2 049 kg). Loaded weight, 5,844 lb (2 651 kg). Span, 36 ft 10 in (11,23 m). Length, 29 ft 11 in (9,12 m). Height, 12 ft 7¾ in (3,86 m). Wing area, 242 sq ft (22,48 m²).

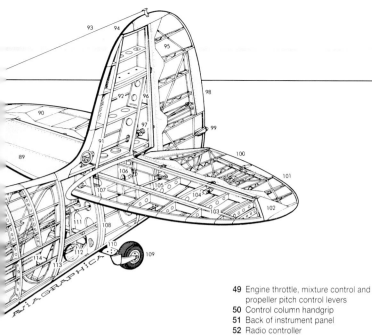

97 Trim control jack
98 Rudder trim tab
99 Tail navigation light
100 Elevator tab
101 Port elevator rib construction
102 Elevator mass balance
103 Tailplane rib construction
104 Elevator trim control jack
105 Rudder control rod
106 Elevator hinge control
107 Tailplane spar/fuselage frame attachment joint
108 Fuselage double frame
109 Non-retracting castoring tailwheel
110 Tailwheel strut
111 Tailplane control cable quadrants
112 Control access panel
113 Sloping tail assembly attachment main frame
114 Tailwheel shock absorber strut
115 Tailplane control cables
116 Rear fuselage starboard side access hatch
117 Fuselage bottom longeron
118 Wing root trailing-edge fillet
119 Radio and electrical systems ground socket
120 Inboard auxiliary flap segment
121 Trailing-edge flap shroud ribs
122 Wing rear spar
123 Flap torque shaft
124 Flap hydraulic jack
125 Port split trailing-edge flap
126 Flap synchronising jack
127 Aileron control bellcrank
128 Aileron hinge control rod
129 Port fabric covered aileron
130 Aileron rib construction
131 Wing tip construction
132 Port navigation light
133 Ventral pitot tube
134 Wing lattice rib construction
135 Browning 0.303-in (7.7-mm) machine guns
136 Outboard ammunition tanks (350 rounds per gun)
137 Front spar
138 Inboard ammunition tanks (350 rounds per gun)
139 Machine gun muzzle blast tubes
140 Machine gun ports (patched)
141 Leading-edge rib construction
142 Wheel bay external skin stiffeners
143 Port main undercarriage wheel bay
144 Ventral oil cooler (coolant radiator on starboard side)
145 Undercarriage position indicator
146 Hydraulic retraction jack
147 Wing spar/fuselage attachment joint
148 Gun camera
149 Camera port
150 Inboard leading-edge lattice ribs
151 Main undercarriage pivot fixing
152 Mainwheel leg shock absorber strut
153 Torque scissor links
154 Mainwheel fairing door
155 Port mainwheel

49 Engine throttle, mixture control and propeller pitch control levers
50 Control column handgrip
51 Back of instrument panel
52 Radio controller
53 Reflector gunsight
54 Externally armoured windscreen panel
55 Pilot's rear view mirror
56 Canopy framing
57 Windscreen side panels
58 Sliding cockpit canopy cover
59 Headrest
60 Canopy direct vision panel
61 Pilot's seat
62 Safety harness
63 Folding side entry hatch
64 Crowbar stowage
65 Elevator trim handwheel
66 Rudder trim handwheel
67 Chart case
68 Windscreen de-icing fluid reservoir
69 Gun heater air ducting
70 Adjustable seat mounting
71 Pilot's back armour
72 Battery
73 Pilot's head armour
74 Canopy aft glazing
75 Voltage regulator
76 Starboard side oxygen bottle
77 Sliding canopy rail
78 Pneumatic system air bottles
79 Fuselage main longeron
80 Flare launch tube
81 Radio compartment access hatch
82 HF radio transmitter/receiver
83 Aerial mast
84 Aerial lead-in
85 Upper identification light
86 Harness cable anchorage and release unit
87 Rear fuselage frame and stringer construction
88 Fuselage skin panelling
89 Starboard tailplane
90 Starboard fabric-covered elevator
91 Fin front spar (fuselage frame extension)
92 Fin rib construction
93 HF aerial cable
94 Rudder horn balance
95 Fabric-covered rudder construction
96 Sternpost

28 Generator
29 Main engine mounting sub-frame
30 Starboard wheel fairing door
31 Starboard mainwheel
32 Carburettor air intake
33 Suppressor
34 Single-stage supercharger
35 Engine control linkages
36 Main engine-bearer attachment joint
37 Engine accessory equipment
38 Hydraulic reservoir
39 Detachable engine cowling panels
40 Engine bay firewall/fuel tank bay bulkhead
41 Fuel filler cap
42 Upper main fuel tank (capacity 48 Imp gal/218 l)
43 Compass mounting
44 Fuel tank/longeron attachments
45 Lower fuel tank (capacity 37 Imp gal/168 l)
46 Rudder pedal bar
47 Sloping fuel tank bay bulkhead
48 Rudder pedals

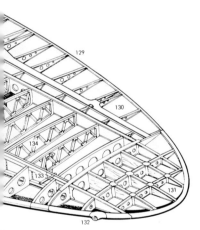

A Spitfire IIA of No 65 Sqn (above) at RAF Kirton-in-Lindsey in July 1941, this being one of three designated as "East India" squadrons. (Below) The Spitfire III in its original form, March 1940.

SUPERMARINE SPITFIRE V & VI   UK

Installation in a Mk I airframe of a 1,185 hp Merlin 45 engine with a combat rating of 1,470 hp at 9,250 ft (2 820 m) resulted in the Spitfire V, a prototype being flown in December 1940. Production of this version of

A clipped-wing Spitfire VB (above) from the Air Fighting Development Unit, RAF Duxford.

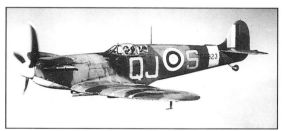

(Above) The standard Spitfire VC and (below) a Mk VB in service with No 92 Sqn at RAF Biggin Hill, 1941.

the Spitfire was to total 6,487, in addition to about 150 Mk I and II conversions. Of the total, 94 were Mk VAs with eight-gun armament, 3,911 were Mk VBs with two 20-mm cannon and four 0.303-in (7,7-mm) machine guns, and, apart from 15 reconnaissance examples, the remaining 2,467 were Mk VCs with four-cannon armament. Service use of the Mk VB began in March 1941, many later having their wings "clipped" to improve low-altitude handling, span being reduced to 32 ft 2 in (9,80 m). To optimise the Mk V for low-altitude operations, Merlin 45M, 50M and 55M engines were progressively introduced, aircraft so powered becoming LF Mk VBs, while the medium-altitude F Mks VA, VB and VC could use the Merlin 45, 46, 50, 50A, 55 or 56. Another change in wing span, increasing to 40 ft 2 in (12,24 m), was associated with introduction of the Spitfire VI which had a 1,415 hp Merlin 47 engine and an early type of pressure cabin. In other respects, the Spitfire VI (sometimes HF Mk VI) used the Mk VB airframe. Deliveries of the Mk VI began early in 1942, and 100 of this

(Immediately below) A Spitfire VB with No 133 "Eagle" Sqn, RAF Biggin Hill, 1942, and (bottom) a Mk VC of 107th Sqn, 67th Recce Group, USAAF, Membury, 1943.

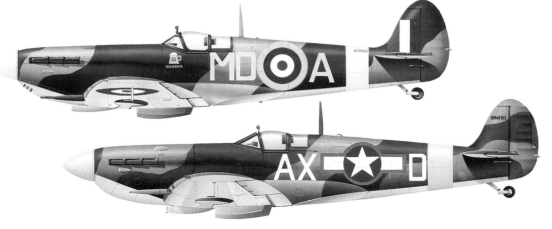

The Spitfire VI prototype (above) featured long-span wings, a pressure cabin and Merlin 46 engine.

version were built. The following data relate to the Spitfire VC. *Max speed, 374 mph (602 km/h) at 13,000 ft (3 960 m). Time to 20,000 ft (6 100 m), 7.5 min. Ceiling, 37,000 ft (11 280 m). Range, 470 mls (756 km). Empty weight, 5,100 lb (2 313 kg). Loaded weight, 6,785 lb (3 078 kg). Span, 36 ft 10 in (11,23 m). Length, 29 ft 11 in (9,12 m). Height, 12 ft 7¾ in (3,86 m).*

SUPERMARINE
SEAFIRE I, II & III UK

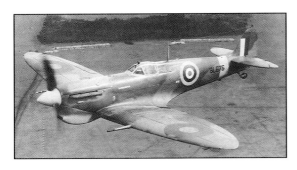

A Hooked Spitfire VB (above) with A-frame hook, used for first trials aboard HMS *Illustrious*, January 1942.

In response to the Admiralty interest in a ''Sea Spitfire'', Supermarine prepared designs in January 1940 for an adaptation of the Spitfire I with an arrester hook (and a folding wing option) for shipboard operation. RAF needs for the Spitfire took precedence and, in consequence, the first ''Hooked Spitfire'', a modified Mk VB, did not fly until 7 January 1942. A second conversion introduced catapult spools and strengthened undercarriage, in addition to the A-frame arrester hook, and these prototype conversions were retrospectively designated Seafire I and II. From early 1942, the Royal Navy took delivery of 166 Seafire IB conversions of Spitfire VBs, modifications being limited to arrester hook and local rear-fuselage strengthening. Commencing in

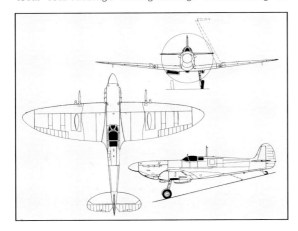

The Seafire III (above, with wing-fold dotted) and a Seafire IIC of No 801 Sqn from HMS *Furious*, 1942.

June 1942, the Royal Navy then received 372 Seafire IICs (later F Mk IICs), which, diverted from Spitfire VC contracts, had catapult spools, a strengthened undercarriage and a Merlin 45 or 46 engine. Low altitude performance was improved by substituting the 1,645 hp Merlin 32 with four-bladed propeller, the accompanying designation being changed to L Mk IIC. Post-production modifications in 1943 introduced one vertical and one oblique camera to produce the PR L Mk II, later designations being FR Mk IIC and LR Mk IIC for these camera-equipped versions according to engine. In November 1942, a Seafire IIC was fitted with folding wings as a prototype for the Mk III which differed in having the 1,470 hp Merlin 55. The folding-wing Seafire III began to reach the Royal Navy in June 1943, production (by Westland and Cunliffe-Owen) totalling 1,263 (including 1,031 LF Mk IIIs with 1,585 hp Merlin 55Ms and 129 two-camera FR Mk IIIs). The following data apply to the LF Mk III. *Max speed, 348 mph (560 km/h) at 6,000 ft (1 830 m). Time to 5,000 ft (1 525 m), 1.9 min. Ceiling, 24,000 ft (7 315 m). Range (with external tank), 513 mls (825 km). Empty weight, 6,204 lb (2 814 kg). Loaded weight, 7,640 lb (3 465 kg). Span, 36 ft 10 in (11,23 m). Length, 30 ft 2½ in (9,21 m). Height, 11 ft 5½ in (3,49 m). Wing area, 242 sq ft (22,48 m²).*

SUPERMARINE
SPITFIRE IX & XVI UK

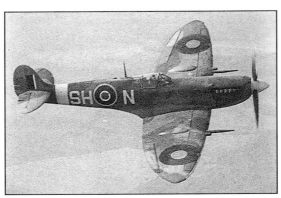

A standard production Spitfire IX (above) serving in 1943 with No 64 Sqn from RAF Fairlop.

While Supermarine was engaged in evolving the Spitfires VII and VIII to use the new two-stage, two-speed supercharged Merlin 60 series engine, advantage was taken of this improved power plant to mate it with a Mk VC airframe and thus introduce an enhanced-performance Spitfire in a shorter timescale. The result was the interim Spitfire IX, two Merlin 61-powered Mk VC airframes serving as prototypes early in 1942, and demonstrating a 10,000-ft (3 050-m) gain in fighting altitude and a 70 mph (113 km/h) increase in maximum speed. Production of the Mk IX totalled 5,656 aircraft (plus 282 Mk V conversions), service introduction commencing in July 1942. Differing altitude ratings distinguished the Merlin variants used in the LF Mk IX (Merlin 66), F

A Spitfire LF Mk IX (above) restored in Italian air force markings of 1946. (Below) A clipped-wing Spitfire F Mk XVIE of the Central Gunnery School.

Mk IX (Merlin 61 or 63) and HF Mk IX (Merlin 70). Some Mk IXs were flown with clipped wings and later modifications introduced (not simultaneously) a broad-chord rudder with pointed tip, a cut-down rear fuselage with all-round vision canopy, extra fuel, bomb racks and a tropical carburettor filter. Similar to the Spitfire IX, the LF Mk XVI was powered by a US-built Packard Merlin 266, and 1,054 were delivered from October 1944, most having the clipped wings. Like the Mk IXs, later Spitfire LF Mk XVIs had the new rudder, cut-down rear fuselage, and, in 1945, an ''E'' wing armament of two 20-mm cannon in the outer bays and two 0.5-in (12,7-mm) machine guns in the inner bays. The following data refer to the F Mk IX. *Max speed, 408 mph (657 km/h) at 25,000 ft (7 620 m). Time to 20,000 ft (6 100 m), 5.7 min. Ceiling, 43,000 ft (13 105 m). Max range (external fuel), 980 mls (1 577 km). Empty weight, 5,634 lb (2 556 kg). Loaded weight, 9,500 lb (4 309 kg). Span, 36 ft 10 in (11,23 m). Length, 31 ft 1 in (9,47 m). Height, 12 ft 7¾ in (3,86 m). Wing area, 242 sq ft (22,48 m²).*

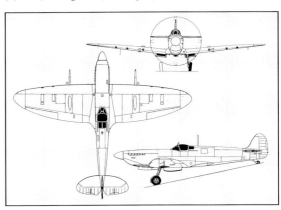

Spitfire IXC (above) and a restored Mk XVI (below) as displayed on the Spitfire's 40th anniversary.

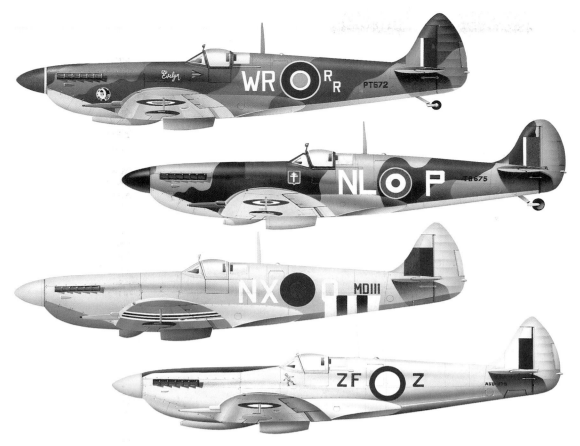

A Spitfire VIII prototype (above) displays the first tear-drop canopy applied to a Spitfire.

(657 km/h) at 25,000 ft (7 620 m). Time to 20,000 ft (6 100 m), 7.0 min. Ceiling, 43,000 ft (13 105 m). Max range (external fuel), 1,180 mls (1 900 km). Empty weight, 5,800 lb (2 630 kg). Max loaded weight, 7,767 lb (2 523 kg). Span, 36 ft 10 in (11,23 m). Length, 31 ft 3½ in (9,54 m). Height, 12 ft 7¾ in (3,86 m). Wing area, 242 sq ft (22,48 m²).

SUPERMARINE SPITFIRE
FLOATPLANE
UK

The third of the Spitfire VB floatplanes (above) while in the Middle East in early 1944.

The idea of adapting the Spitfire to operate as a float seaplane arose in 1940, at the time of the German invasion of Norway, and a trial installation was made by Supermarine of a Spitfire I on floats from a Blackburn Roc. This was not flown, but, during 1941, Folland Aircraft built a pair of floats to Supermarine design and fitted them to a Spitfire VB which used a four-bladed propeller for flight testing. This aircraft and two other similar conversions were based on the Great Bitter Lake, Egypt, for a short period in late 1943, after the abandonment of plans to base them on an island in the Dodecanese chain to attack enemy transport aircraft supplying Greek garrisons, but no operational sorties

SUPERMARINE
SPITFIRE VII & VIII
UK

Converted from a Mk V airframe, the Spitfire VII prototype (above) featured a retractable tailwheel.

More extensively modified versions of the basic Spitfire airframe intended specifically for the two-stage Merlin 60 series engine were being developed while the Mk IX was committed to production with this power plant as an interim model. This development led to the Spitfire VII high-altitude fighter and the Spitfire VIII general-purpose fighter, which shared features other than the former's pressure cabin. Extended wingtips were standard on the 140 Mk VIIs, but were an option on the Mk VIII, later examples of the latter adopting such "Mk IX" features as the broad-chord rudder, cut-down rear fuselage, bomb racks and "E" wing armament. The

Splendidly restored in Italy in 1982, this Spitfire VIII flew in Burma with No 17 Sqn in 1944-45.

(Above, top) Spitfire IXC as preserved by SAAF Museum in 40 Sqn markings. (Second top) Mk IXC of No 341 (Free French) Sqn. (Second above) Spitfire HF Mk VII of No 131 Sqn, 1943. (Immediately above) An F Mk VIII of No 549 Sqn, RAF, at Darwin in 1944.

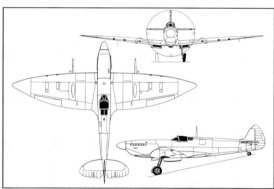

The pressurised Spitfire HF Mk VII (above).

Spitfire VII entered service in September 1942 with a 1,710 hp Merlin 64, or (HF Mk VII) 1,475 hp Merlin 71. Spitfire VIII production totalled 1,658 aircraft and included the F Mk VIII (1,565 hp Merlin 61 or 1,710 hp Merlin 63), LF Mk VIII (1,705 hp Merlin 66) and HF Mk VIII (1,655 hp Merlin 70). The Spitfire VIII was first introduced in mid-1943 in the Middle East. The following data refer to the F Mk VIII. *Max speed, 408 mph*

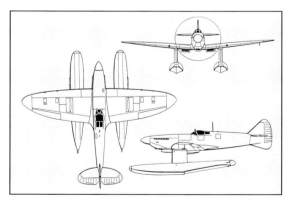

The sole Spitfire IX floatplane (above and below) as tested at Beaumaris in mid-1944.

were flown. Folland also modified one Spitfire IX as a floatplane before the programme ended in 1944. The following data refer to the Spitfire VB floatplane. *Max speed, 324 mph (521 km/h) at 19,500 ft (5 945 m). Time to 25,000 ft (7 625 m), 12.3 min. Ceiling, 33,400 ft (10 180 m). Empty weight, 6,014 lb (2 728 kg). Loaded weight, 7,580 lb (3 440 kg). Span, 36 ft 10 in (11,23 m). Length, 35 ft 4 in (10,76 m). Height, 13 ft 10 in (4,22 m). Wing area, 242 sq ft (22,48 m²).*

SUPERMARINE SPITFIRE XII   UK

Early in 1940, two prototype Spitfire airframes were ordered to be powered by the new 1,735 hp Rolls-Royce Griffon IIB engine, the designation Mk IV being initially applied and an order for 750 having been placed by the time the first of the prototypes flew on 27 November 1941. Early in the following year, the designation was changed to Mk XX to avoid confusion with the PR Mk IV designation that had meanwhile been applied to the Spitfire I Type D photo-reconnaissance aircraft. After testing a six-cannon mock-up installation, the Mk XX became the prototype Spitfire XII in which guise it first flew on 24 August 1942. Features of the Mk XII included the low-altitude Griffon III or IV engine with the same rating as the Griffon IIB in the prototype, a four-bladed propeller, "C"-type wing armament, broad-chord rudder, and, after the first few, retractable tailwheel and clipped wings. The Spitfire XII entered service in 1943, but only 100 were built and these used airframes that had been initiated in production as Mk VCs. *Max speed, 393 mph (632 km/h). Time to 20,000 ft (6 100 m), 6.7 min. Range (with external tank), 493 mls (793 km). Empty weight, 5,600 lb (2 540 kg). Max loaded weight, 7,400 lb (3 357 kg). Span, 32 ft 7 in (9,94 m). Length, 31 ft 10 in (9,70 m). Height, 11 ft 0 in (3,35 m). Wing area, 231 sq ft (21,46 m²).*

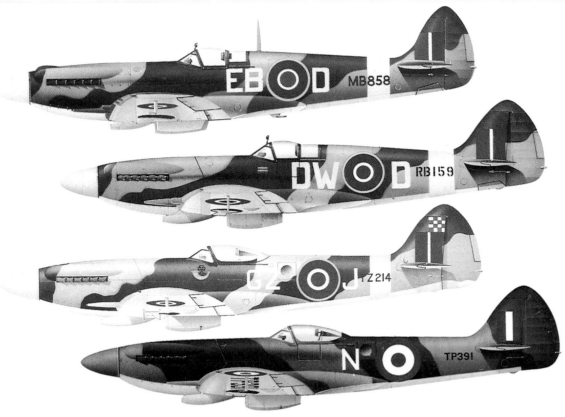

(Above, top) Spitfire XII with Griffon IV engine serving with No 41 Sqn, 1944. (Second top) A Mk XIV flown by CO of No 610 Sqn on "anti-Diver" patrols from Lympne, 1944. (Second above) An FR Mk XVIII, No 32 Sqn, in the Suez Canal Zone, 1947-48. (Immediately above) An FR Mk XVIII with No 208 Sqn, 1950.

The original Griffon-engined Spitfire IV (above) in Mk XII form and (below) a series Mk XII with bomb.

SUPERMARINE SPITFIRE XIV & XVIII   UK

Like the Mk XII that preceded it, the Spitfire XIV was essentially an interim stage in the development of the Griffon-engined fighter. While the definitive refinement of the Spitfire with this engine was eventually to emerge as the Mk 21, the Mk XIV, which entered service in January 1944, was based on the Mk VIII airframe, six of which, fitted with the two-stage, two-

A Spitfire XIVE trials aircraft (below) with tear-drop canopy and cut-down rear fuselage.

speed supercharged Griffon 60 series engine, served to test various features (some of which, including a contra-prop, were not adopted for service use). In production form, the Spitfire XIV emerged with a 2,035 hp Griffon 65 engine, a five-bladed propeller, a lengthened nose and larger radiators and vertical tail. Early aircraft

A series production Spitfire XIVC (above) while on test at the A&AEE Boscombe Down, July 1944.

had two 20-mm cannon and four 0.303-in (7.7-mm) machine guns, but the "E"-wing armament, substituting a pair of 0.5-in (12,7-mm) guns for the quartet of smaller-calibre weapons, was later standardised. The cut-down rear fuselage also became standard and many Mk XIVs were eventually flown with clipped wings for low altitude operations. A total of 957 Spitfire XIVs was built (these including a number of FR Mk XIVs for the fighter reconnaissance rôle). Production gave way in 1944 to the Spitfire F Mk XVIII (200 built) and FR Mk XVIII (100 built). These differed from the Mk XIV in having the enlarged vertical tail (adopted with the FR Mk XIV), a lengthened fuselage, strengthened wing and undercarriage, and increased fuel capacity. Deliveries began mid-1945, and the Spitfire XVIIIs served postwar in the Middle and Far East. The following data relate to the F Mk XIV. *Max speed, 448 mph (721 km/h) at 26,000 ft (7 925 m). Time to 20,000 ft (6 100 m), 7.0 min. Range (with external fuel), 850 mls (1 368 km). Empty weight, 6,600 lb (2 994 kg). Max*

Spitfire FR Mk XVIII (below) showing the rear-fuselage camera installation of this variant.

loaded weight, 8,500 lb (3 856 kg). Span, 36 ft 10 in (11,23 m). Length, 32 ft 8 in (9,96 m). Height, 12 ft 7¾ in (3,86 m). Wing area, 242 sq ft (22,48 m²).

The original Spitfire F Mk XIVE (below).

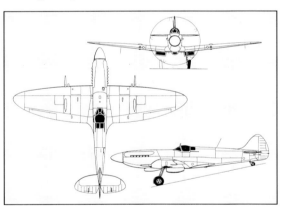

SUPERMARINE SEAFIRE XV & XVII   UK

The development of versions of the Spitfire with Griffon engines and, eventually, modified wings, was paralleled by the introduction of Seafire variants to succeed the Merlin-engined Mks I, II and III. To avoid confusion, the Griffon-engined Seafires used mark numbers that did not duplicate those of Spitfires. Powered by a 1,750 hp Griffon VI, the Seafire XV was based on the Seafire III airframe with features of the Spitfire XII

First prototype of the Seafire F Mk XV (below) soon after completion at the end of 1943.

Seafire F Mk XVII (above) from No 899 Sqn on HMS *Hunter*, showing tear-drop hood and "sting" hook.

engine installation. Delivery of 384 Seafire F Mk XVs began in September 1944, the majority having "sting"-type arrester hooks at the base of the (enlarged) rudder. Production then switched to the F Mk XVII which, like the last few F Mk XVs, featured a cut-down rear fuselage. It also had a curved windscreen, provision for wing ordnance and a longer-stroke undercarriage. Production totalled 232, some having a two-camera installation in the rear fuselage. The following data relate to the Seafire XV. *Max speed, 383 mph (616 km/h) at 13,500 ft (4 115 m). Time to 20,000 ft (6 100 m), 7.0 min. Ceiling, 35,500 ft (4 115 m). Range (internal fuel), 430 mls (692 km). Empty weight, 6,200 lb (2 812 kg). Loaded weight, 8,000 lb (3 629 kg). Span, 36 ft 10 in (11,23 m). Length, 32 ft 3 in (9,90 m). Height, 10 ft 8½ in (3,25 m). Wing area, 242 sq ft (22,48 m²).*

SUPERMARINE
SPITFIRE 21, 22 & 24   UK

The first and (illustrated above) second prototypes of the Spitfire 21 retained the original wing.

The definitive Griffon-engined Spitfire emerged in late 1942 as the prototype Mk 21 which had originally been ordered as the second prototype Mk IV. Featuring a new wing with enlarged ailerons, revised tip shape and increased area, the Spitfire 21 (for which the name Victor was used for a time) was powered by a 2,035 hp Griffon 61 (later supplanted by the 2,375 hp Griffon 64) driving a five-bladed propeller, possessed enlarged fuel capacity, featured increased undercarriage track

(Immediately below) Spitfire F Mk 22 of No 91 Sqn, RAF Manston, 1945. (Second below) Spitfire F Mk 24 serving in Hong Kong in 1950 with No 80 Sqn. (Bottom) A Seafire FR Mk 47 of 800 Sqn aboard HMS *Triumph* during the Korean War.

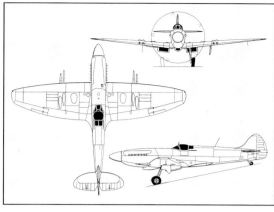

Spitfire F Mk 21 three-view drawing (above) with the definitive wing and four-cannon armament.

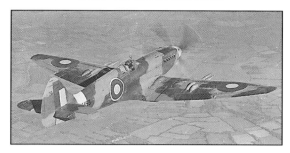

A series Spitfire F Mk 21 (above) compared with the F Mk 22 (below) with a tear-drop hood.

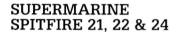

and carried an armament of four 20-mm cannon. The prototype Mk 21 flown on 4 October 1942, and a second flown on 24 July 1943, initially had the standard Spitfire wing with extended ("high altitude") tips. Production was to total 120 aircraft, service use commencing in April 1945, but early handling problems prevented rapid deployment. Production continued with the Spitfire F Mk 22, which had the cut-down rear fuselage and rearview hood, and a revised electrical system. Production of the F Mk 22 totalled 287 aircraft. The F Mk 23 was intended to have a wing of improved laminar flow, development being discontinued, and the ultimate

A Spitfire F Mk 24 (above) after transfer from No 80 Sqn RAF to the Hong Kong Aux AF in 1955.

Spitfire emerged as the F Mk 24. This differed from the F Mk 22 in having two auxiliary fuel tanks in the rear fuselage and – like final production F Mk 22s – an enlarged tail unit similar to that of the Spiteful. Fifty-four F Mk 24s were built, and, together with 27 converted F Mk 22s, were delivered between April 1946 and March 1948. The following data relate to the F Mk 21. *Max speed, 454 mph (731 km/h) at 26,000 ft (7 925 m). Time to 20,000 ft (6 100 m), 8.0 min. Ceiling, 43,500 ft (12 260 m). Empty weight, 6,900 lb (3 130 kg). Max loaded weight, 9,200 lb (4 173 kg). Span, 36 ft 11 in (11,25 m). Length, 32 ft 8 in (9,96 m). Height, 13 ft 6 in (4,11 m). Wing area, 244 sq ft (22,67 m²).*

SUPERMARINE
SEAFIRE 45, 46 & 47   UK

Effectively a navalised Spitfire F Mk 21, the Seafire F Mk 45 appeared in 1945 and was similarly powered by the Rolls-Royce Griffon 61. The F Mk 45 had the "sting"-type arrester hook of the Seafire XV and, lacking any form of wing folding, was used primarily from shore bases for training. Of 51 built, at least three were flown with contraprops (on Griffon 85 engines) to overcome a tendency to swing on take-off, and this type of propeller was standardised on the F Mk 46, which had larger tail surfaces (similar to those of the Spitfire 22 and 24) and cut-down fuselage with all-round vision canopy. The engine was the Griffon 87 or (in one example) 88, and 24 F Mk 46s were built during 1945-46. Finally, a new type of wing fold was developed for this Seafire series, with the outer panels (only) hinged upwards outboard of the four 20-mm cannon armament, and, eventually, hydraulic power folding. Designated Seafire F Mk 47, this variant also featured increased fuel, and production totalled 90 during 1946-47. The F Mk 47 was similarly powered to the preceding F Mk 46, some examples of both marks having cameras in the rear fuselage as FR Mks 46 and 47. Service use of the Seafire 47 ended in 1952, after operations in the Korean conflict. The following data refer to the F Mk 47. *Max speed, 452 mph (727 km/h) at 20,500 ft (6 250 m). Time to 20,000 ft*

The fifth production example of the Seafire F Mk 45 (above) and a drawing of the FR Mk 47 (below).

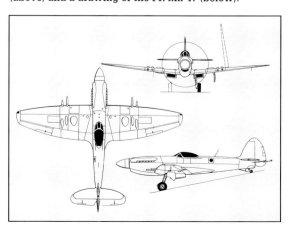

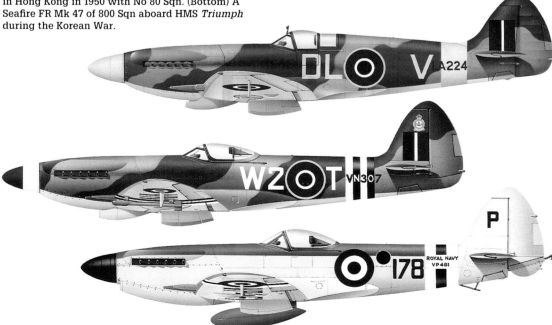

The second series Seafire F Mk 46 (above), production
of which totalled only 24, and an FR Mk 47 (below) of
No 1833 Sqn, RNVR, Bramcote, in 1954.

The first series Spiteful F Mk XIV (above), of which
variant only 19 examples were built.

The Seafang F Mk 32 (second prototype, below) was
the ultimate development of the Spitfire design.

*(6 100 m), 4.9 min. Ceiling, 43,100 ft (13 135 m). Max
range (with external fuel), 940 mls (1 513 km). Empty
weight, 8,680 lb (3 937 kg). Max loaded weight,
12,530 lb (5 684 kg). Span, 36 ft 11 in (11,25 m). Length,
34 ft 4 in (10,46 m). Height, 12 ft 9 in (3,88 m). Wing
area, 243.6 sq ft (22,63 m²).*

SUPERMARINE SPITEFUL   UK

A new laminar-flow wing mated to a Spitfire XIV
fuselage produced the prototype Spiteful (above).

Conceived as a successor to the Spitfire, the Type 371
was projected from November 1942, initially mating a
laminar flow wing with a Griffon-engined Spitfire XIV
and progressively embracing a new fuselage. Three
prototypes were ordered to Specification F.1/43, which
was written around the project, and the first of these
flew on 30 June 1944. This prototype comprised a Spitfire XIV fuselage with the new wing, a 2,035 hp Rolls-
Royce Griffon 61 engine and an armament of four

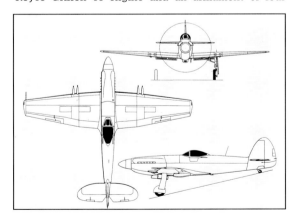

The series Spiteful F Mk XIV (above) and the third
prototype Spiteful in definitive form (below).

20-mm cannon. Named Spiteful, the second prototype
flew on 8 January 1945 with the new fuselage, an all-
round vision cockpit canopy and a 2,375 hp Griffon 69
driving a five-bladed propeller. Production orders were
placed for 188 Spitefuls, but only 16 were flown of 19
built or partially-completed (from April 1945) as the end
of World War II and the advent of the jet fighter terminated plans for RAF use of the Spiteful. The designation
F Mk 14 was applied to the Griffon 69-powered Spiteful;
the proposed F Mk 15 had either the Griffon 89 or 90
with a six-bladed contraprop, and a single F Mk 16 had
a Griffon 101 with a three-speed supercharger and five-
bladed propeller. The following data apply to the Spiteful F Mk 14. *Max speed, 483 mph (777 km/h) at 26,000 ft
(7 925 m). Time to 20,000 ft (6 100 m), 4.9 min. Ceiling,
42,000 ft (12 800 m). Range (clean), 564 mls (908 km).
Empty weight, 7,350 lb (3 334 kg). Loaded weight,
9,950 lb (4,513 kg). Span, 35 ft 0 in (10,67 m). Length,
32 ft 11 in (10,03 m). Height, 13 ft 5 in (4,08 m). Wing
area, 210 sq ft (19,51 m²).*

SUPERMARINE SEAFANG   UK

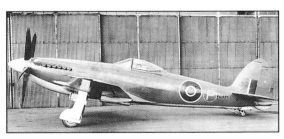

Completed late in 1945, the first Seafang F Mk 31
(above) had non-folding wings.

Development of a navalised Spiteful was pursued
during 1945 to Specification N.5/45, and a contract was
placed for two prototypes and 150 series aircraft, the
name Seafang being assigned. A Spiteful F Mk 15 with a
"sting"-type arrester hook was tested early in 1945, and
the Seafang prototypes flew in the following year. One
of these represented the production Seafang F Mk 31
with Griffon 61 engine and a long-stroke undercarriage,
but non-folding wings. The other represented the Seafang F Mk 32 with a Griffon 89 engine with contraprop,
and upward-folding wings. Armament comprised four
20-mm cannon and provision was made for carrying a
pair of 1,000-lb (454-kg) bombs or six 300-lb (136-kg)
rockets. After completion during 1946-47 of 10 Mk 31s
and six Mk 32s (some of which were never flown) production was cancelled. The following data refer to the F
Mk 32. *Max speed, 475 mph (764 km/h) at 21,000 ft
(6 400 m). Max climb, 4,630 ft/min (23,5 m/sec). Ceiling,
41,000 ft (12 500 m). Range, 393 mls (632 km). Empty
weight, 8,000 lb (3 629 kg). Loaded weight, 10,450 lb*

*(4 740 kg). Span, 35 ft 0 in (10,67 m). Length, 34 ft 1 in
(10,39 m). Height, 12 ft 6½ in (3,82 m). Wing area,
210 sq ft (19,51 m²).*

SUPERMARINE ATTACKER   UK

Conceived in the same month that the Spiteful entered
flight test and mating that fighter's laminar flow wing
(with radiators removed) with a new fuselage and tail,
the Type 392 was powered by the new Rolls-Royce
RB.41 turbojet which was to enter production as the
Nene. Three prototypes were ordered in August 1944 of
which two were to be navalised. The first prototype
was covered by Specification E.10/44 and the navalised
examples by E.1/45. The first prototype flew on 27 July
1946 with a 4,300 lb st (1 950 kgp) Nene, but a 5,100 lb st
(2 313 kgp) Nene 3 (or Mk 101) was later standardised
for the E.1/45 prototypes – the first of which was flown
on 17 June 1947 – and for subsequent production aircraft which were designated Attacker F Mk 1. The
naval prototypes were fitted with A-frame arrester

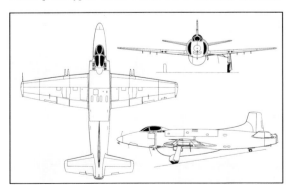

A drawing of the Attacker F Mk 2 (above) and the first
prototype (below), evolved as a "Jet Spiteful".

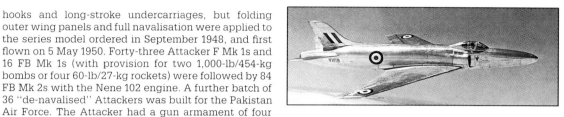

One of the 36 "de-navalised" Attackers (above) supplied to the Pakistan Air Force.

The first Swift F Mk 1 prototype (above) and a trials F Mk 4 (below) which introduced an all-flying tailplane and "eye-lid" tailpipe.

hooks and long-stroke undercarriages, but folding outer wing panels and full navalisation were applied to the series model ordered in September 1948, and first flown on 5 May 1950. Forty-three Attacker F Mk 1s and 16 FB Mk 1s (with provision for two 1,000-lb/454-kg bombs or four 60-lb/27-kg rockets) were followed by 84 FB Mk 2s with the Nene 102 engine. A further batch of 36 "de-navalised" Attackers was built for the Pakistan Air Force. The Attacker had a gun armament of four 20-mm cannon and entered Royal Navy service in August 1951, being retained until 1954 and then flown for two more years by the Volunteer Reserve. The following data relate to the FB Mk 2. *Max speed, 590 mph (949 km/h) at sea level and 538 mph (866 km/h) at 30,000 ft (9 150 m). Time to 30,000 ft (9 150 m), 6.66 min. Ceiling, 45,000 ft (13 715 m). Range (with overload tank), 1,190 mls (1 915 km). Empty weight, 9,910 lb (4 495 kg). Max overload weight, 17,350 lb (7 870 kg). Span, 36 ft 11 in (11,25 m). Length, 37 ft 6 in (11,43 m). Height, 9 ft 11 in (3,02 m). Wing area, 226.4 sq ft (21,03 m²).*

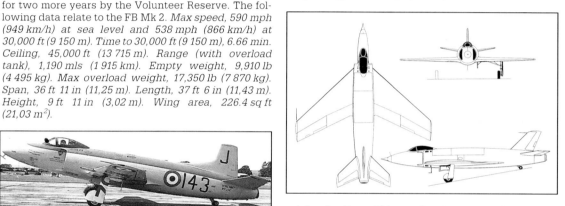

The Type 535 (above) was an extrapolation from the original Type 510 design (below).

two 30-mm cannon in the lower front fuselage. The pre-production aircraft flew on 1 August 1951 and 18 July 1952, and the first production Swift F Mk 1 followed on 25 August 1952. This entered RAF service on 13 February 1954 with a 7,500 lb st (3 402 kgp) Avon 105.

An Attacker FB Mk 2 (above) of No 803 Sqn, HMS *Eagle* in 1953, and a bomb- and rocket-armed FB Mk 2 (below) carrying a belly fuel tank.

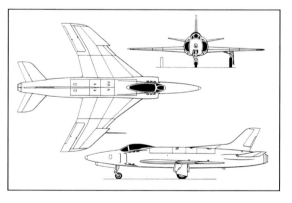

The Swift FR Mk 5 (below), and a preserved example (above) in the markings of No 79 Sqn, RAF.

SUPERMARINE Types 510 & 535 UK

During 1946, in response to a contract to build two prototypes of a single-seat high-speed fighter to Specification E.41/46, Supermarine combined sweptback wing and tail surfaces with what was essentially an Attacker fuselage to create the Type 510. This retained the Rolls-Royce Nene 2 engine and tailwheel undercarriage of the Attacker, and the first prototype was flown on 29 December 1948. No armament was fitted, but provision was made for four wing-mounted 20-mm cannon. The second prototype, designated Type 528, flew in similar configuration on 27 March 1950, and, on 8 November of that year, the Type 510, fitted with an Attacker-style A-frame arrester hook, made a series of landings and take-offs from the carrier HMS *Illustrious*. Later, the first aircraft (now redesignated Type 517) was fitted with a movable rear fuselage permitting the incidence of the integral tailplane to be varied. Mean-

Supermarine's first swept-wing jet prototype (below), the Type 510 was based on the Attacker.

while, the Type 528 was fitted with an afterburning version of the Nene, a lengthened nose and a tricycle undercarriage as the Type 535, flying in this form for the first time on 23 August 1950, and providing the basis for the development of the Swift. The following data relate to the Type 510. *Max speed, 610 mph (982 km/h) at 36,000 ft (10 975 m), or Mach=0.924, 630 mph (1 014 km/h) at 10,000 ft (3 050 m), or Mach=0.86. Loaded weight, 12,200 lb (5 534 kg). Span, 31 ft 8½ in (9,66 m). Length, 38 ft 1 in (11,61 m). Height, 8 ft 9¾ in (2,68 m). Wing area, 273 sq ft (25,36 m²).*

SUPERMARINE SWIFT UK

Second prototype of the Swift F Mk 1 fighter (above), which introduced the Avon engine.

Evolved from the Types 510 and 535 as a fully operational fighter, the Type 541 closely resembled the latter, and two pre-production examples were ordered on 9 November 1950, with an initial production contract for 100 aircraft following a few weeks later. To be named Swift, the new fighter substituted a 7,000 lb st (3 175 kgp) Rolls-Royce Avon RA7 axial-flow turbojet for the centrifugal-flow Nene 2, armament consisting of

After 18 F Mk 1s, production switched to the F Mk 2 with increased wing chord and four 30-mm cannon, 17 Swifts being built to this standard. Numerous handling problems were encountered with these early Swifts, resulting in a series of modifications and curtailed production. This included 25 F Mk 3s with 9,500 lb st (4 310 kgp) afterburning RA7R Avon 108s, 94 FR Mk 5s with cameras in a lengthened nose, dog-tooth wing leading edges and other improvements, and 12 F Mk 7s with AI radar and four Blue Sky (Fireflash) AAMs. Pro-

Swift FR Mk 5 (below) in service 1956 with No 2 Sqn at Geilenkirchen in RAF Germany.

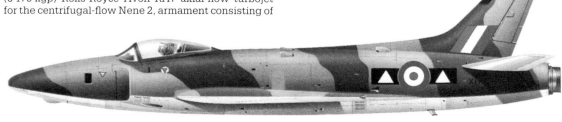

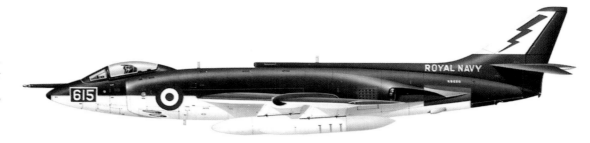

duction of the Swift ended in July 1957, service use (of the FR Mk 5) continuing until 1960. The following data refer to the Swift FR Mk 5. *Max speed, 713 mph (1 148 km/h) at sea level, or Mach=0.935. Time to 40,000 ft (12 200 m), 4.7 min. Ceiling, 45,800 ft (13 960 m). Range, 630 mls (1 014 km). Empty weight, 13,435 lb (6 094 kg). Loaded weight, 21,673 lb (9 831 kg). Span, 32 ft 4 in (9,85 m). Length, 42 ft 3 in (12,88 m). Height, 13 ft 2½ in (4,02 m). Wing area, 327.7 sq ft (30,44 m²).*

A Swift F Mk 7 (below) carrying a pair of Fairey Fireflash beam-riding air-to-air guided missiles.

SUPERMARINE
TYPES 508 & 529   UK

Responding to Admiralty interest in "undercarriage-less" aircraft suitable for operation from flexible decks on aircraft carriers, Supermarine designed the Type 505 single-seat fighter in 1945. Two Rolls-Royce AJ65 (later to be named Avon) turbojets were located side-by-side in a broad centre fuselage to provide a stable base for alighting on the "carpet" and a Vee configuration kept the tail surfaces clear of the jet efflux. An armament of twin 20-mm cannon was planned and provision was made to provide for a fixed tricycle undercarriage for flight development and operation from shore bases. It was thus relatively simple to incorporate a retractable undercarriage in the design when Admiralty interest in the flexible deck concept waned in late 1947 and the fighter was modified as the more conventional Type 508. Three aircraft were ordered to Specification N.9/47 for a naval fighter, and, configurationally similar to the Type 505 apart from the undercarriage, the first of these flew on 31 August 1951.

The Supermarine Type 508 (above and below) was distinctive by virtue of its "butterfly" tail.

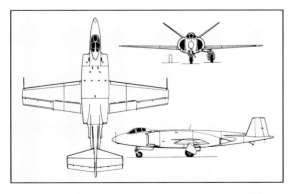

The second (as the essentially similar Type 529) followed a year later, on 29 August 1952. Prior to these events, in February 1950, the contract covering the third prototype was amended to introduce sweptback wings, and this, as the Type 525, became, in effect, the prototype of the Scimitar (which see). The Types 508 and 529 were each powered by a pair of 6,500 lb st (2 948 kgp) Avon RA3 engines and had provision for an armament of four 20-mm cannon. The following data relate specifically to the Type 529. *Max speed, 607 mph*

(977 km/h) at 36,000 ft (10 975 m), or Mach=0.92. Empty weight, 18,460 lb (8 373 kg). Loaded weight, 22,584 lb (10 244 kg). Span, 41 ft 0 in (12,50 m). Length, 50 ft 0 in (15,24 m). Height, 11 ft 7½ in (3,54 m). Wing area, 340 sq ft (31,59 m²).

SUPERMARINE SCIMITAR   UK

Proposed in June 1949 as an extrapolation of the straight-winged Type 508 naval fighter, the Type 525 had a wing with 45 deg of sweepback at quarter chord and a more conventional cruciform tail. The Type 525 was flown on 27 April 1954, by which time three pre-production examples (Type 544) had been ordered to

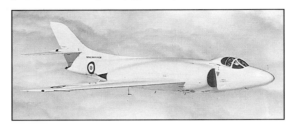

The Type 525 (above) was, in effect, the prototype for the Scimitar, a production F Mk 1 being seen (below) arriving on the deck of HMS *Centaur*, 1961.

Specification N.113D and series production aircraft to N.113P. Compared with the Type 525, the Type 544 featured a longer nose, area-ruled fuselage, a dorsal spine, dog-tooth wing leading edges and an all-moving tailplane. Named Scimitar F Mk 1, the series version had paired Rolls-Royce Avon RA28 Mk 202 turbojets each rated at 11,250 lb st (5 100 kgp) and an armament of four 20-mm cannon, provision being made for external ordnance loads. The first of the pre-production aircraft was flown on 19 January 1956, the first series

With wings folded, a Scimitar F Mk 1 from No 803 Sqn serving on HMS *Ark Royal* in 1964.

(Above) Scimitar F Mk 1 of No 736 Sqn at Lossiemouth in 1960 for advanced pilot training.

aircraft following on 11 January 1957. A total of 75 Scimitar F Mk 1s was built for the Royal Navy, and service use extended from 1958 to 1969. *Max speed, 737 mph (1 186 km/h) at sea level, or Mach=0.967, 676 mph (1 088 km/h) at 30,000 ft (9 150 m), or Mach=0.98. Time to 45,000 ft (13 715 m), 6.65 min. Ceiling, 46,000 ft (14 020 m). Range, 1,422 mls (2 288 km). Span, 37 ft 2 in (11,33 m). Length, 55 ft 3 in (16,84 m). Height, 17 ft 4 in (5,28 m). Wing area, 484.9 sq ft (45,05 m²).*

(Below) Scimitar F Mk 1 single-seat naval fighter.

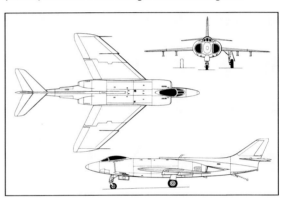

SVENSKA AERO
S.A.14 JAKTFALK   Sweden

In March 1929, the Svenska Aero AB of Lidingö initiated the development of a single-seat fighter as a private venture. Dubbed Jaktfalk (Gyrfalcon), this, the S.A.14, was flown in October, and was a single-bay biplane with a welded steel tube fuselage and wooden wings, and powered by a 14-cylinder two-row Armstrong Siddeley Jaguar geared engine with a maximum output of 510 hp at sea level. Demonstrated to *Flygvapnet* on 11 November 1929, the prototype was purchased by that service during January 1930 as the J 5. On the following 28 March, two examples powered by the 450 hp nine-cylinder Bristol Jupiter VI engine were ordered as the J 6, a contract for a further five following on 5 June. Armament consisted of twin synchronised 8-mm machine guns. Some revision of the fighter was undertaken as the J 6A, a Jupiter VIIF supercharged engine rated at 520 hp at 10,000 ft (3 050 m) being installed, rectangular steel tube wing spars supplanting the wooden spars of the J 6 and the aft fuselage being lengthened by 15¾ in (40 cm). Three were ordered by *Flygvapnet* and an essentially similar aircraft powered by a 530 hp Armstrong Siddeley Panther IIIA 14-

The first of the J 6s (above) compared with the single Panther-engined example supplied to Norway for evaluation in 1932 (below).

cylinder two-row radial enclosed by a Townend ring and featuring spatted main undercarriage members was supplied in September 1932 to Norway for comparative evaluation with the Curtiss Hawk. With completion of delivery of the J 6A Jaktfalkar in late 1932, Svenska Aero AB terminated its activities owing to financial difficulties, and further development of the fighter was taken over by the AB Svenska Järnvägsverkstäderna (ASJA) as the Jaktfalk II. The Jaktfalkar served with *Flygflottilj* 1 at Västeras, and, in December 1939, one J 6A (together with two ASJA-built J 6Bs) was donated to Finland. The following data relate to the J 5, those for the J 6A being essentially similar to the ASJA-built J 6B (which see). *Max speed, 186 mph (300 km/h). Cruising speed, 154 mph (248 km/h). Time to 16,405 ft (5 000 m), 12.6 min. Empty weight, 2,149 lb (975 kg). Loaded weight, 3,252 lb (1 475 kg). Span, 29 ft 6⅓ in (9,00 m). Length, 23 ft 3½ in (7,10 m). Height, 11 ft 4¼ in (3,46 m). Wing area, 236.81 sq ft (22,00 m²).*

T

TACHIKAWA Kɪ-106   Japan

On 8 September 1943, instructions were issued to redesign the Nakajima Ki-84 Hayate all-metal single-seat fighter (which see) for wooden construction because of the increasingly critical light alloy supply situation. The task of redesigning the airframe was assigned to the Tachikawa Hikoki which was to collaborate with the Army Aerotechnical Research Institute at Tachikawa. Assigned the designation Ki-106, the wooden fighter was intended to utilise a high proportion of semi-skilled labour in its construction and to be broken down into components to be built by small wood-working shops grouped around designated assembly points. Prototype construction was sub-contracted to Ohjo Koku, but the first of three prototypes was not flown until July

The Tachikawa Ki-106 (below) did not progress beyond completion of two prototypes.

1945. The external characteristics of the Ki-84 were faithfully retained by the Ki-106, apart from some minor revision of the vertical tail, the first prototype being powered by the 2,000 hp Nakajima Ha-45-21 engine and carrying an armament of four 20-mm cannon. Appreciably heavier than the standard Ki-84, the Ki-106 was subjected to various weight saving measures, one of these being a reduction in the armament to two 20-mm cannon, and the second prototype flew with this armament during the last week of the war. *Max speed, 385 mph (620 km/h) at 21,325 ft (6 500 m). Time to 16,405 ft (5 000 m), 7.85 min. Normal range, 497 mls (800 km) plus 1.5 hrs. Empty weight, 6,499 lb (2 948 kg). Loaded weight, 8,598 lb (3 900 kg). Dimensions as for Ki-84 apart from height of 11 ft 9¼ in (3,59 m).*

TAIROV Tᴀ-1 (OKO-6)   USSR

In the mid 'thirties, Vsevolod K Tairov assisted in forming in Kiev an OKO (*Opytny konstruktorsky otdel*, or experimental design section) which, in 1938, was assigned the task of developing a twin-engined escort fighter. This, the OKO-6, was of mixed construction and powered by two 1,000 hp Tumansky M-88 14-cylinder two-row radial engines. Armament comprised four 20-mm cannon in the underside of the forward fuselage and two 12,7-mm machine guns in the upper portion of the nose. The OKO-6 was assigned the service designation TA-1 and was flown on 31 December 1939. Satisfactory performance was demonstrated, this including a maximum speed of 303 mph (488 km/h) at sea level and 352 mph (567 km/h) at 24,770 ft (7 550 m), and the ability to climb to 16,405 ft (5 000 m) within 5.5 min, but the fighter possessed unacceptable directional stability. The second prototype (OKO-6bis) was therefore completed with twin endplate fins and rudders in place of the single vertical tail surfaces, the fuselage was lengthened and 1,100 hp M-88R engines with reduction gear and improved propellers were fitted. A single-seater like its predecessor, the second prototype replaced the latter's 12,7-mm guns with weapons of 7,62-mm calibre and entered flight test in October 1940.

Second prototype Tairov TA-1 (above and below) showing the endplate fins and rudders.

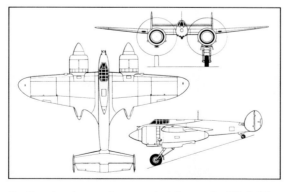

Further development was undertaken as the TA-3. *Max speed, 296 mph (477 km/h) at sea level, 370 mph (595 km/h) at 23,620 ft (7 200 m). Time to 16,405 ft (5 000 m), 6.3 min. Range, 659 mls (1 060 km). Loaded weight, 13,227 lb (6 000 kg). Span, 41 ft 6⅓ in (12,66 m). Length, 32 ft 3 in (9,83 m). Height, 12 ft 4 in (3,76 m).*

TAIROV Tᴀ-3 (OKO-7)   USSR

To meet a 1940 requirement calling for a fighter attack aircraft with heavy cannon armament, Vsevolod Tairov and his team working at the Kiev OKO developed the TA-3. The design was based broadly on that of the

TA-1, the single-seat fuselage being essentially similar to that of the second prototype of the earlier fighter, but armament was changed to one 37-mm and two 20-mm cannon, and the wing was of increased span and area, and embodied some redesign. Power was provided by two 1,150 hp 14-cylinder M-89 air-cooled radials and flight testing commenced in May 1941. The characteristics of the TA-3 were well regarded by its test pilots and it was recommended that series production be initiated of a version powered by 1,330 hp Shvetsov M-82s. Tairov lost his life in an accident in December 1941, but the OKO continued work on the TA-3, which, in 1942, was fitted with a larger wing and increased fuel tankage, range being increased by 662 mls (1 065 km) and loaded weight by 1,380 lb (626 kg). However, the situation in the Soviet aircraft industry in 1942 militated against series production, and development ended late in that year. *Max speed, 286 mph (460 km/h) at sea level, 360 mph (580 km/h) at 23,295 ft (7 100 m). Range, 1,283 mls (2 065 km). Time to 9,840 ft (3 000 m), 5.0 min. Empty weight, 9,921 lb (4 500 kg). Loaded weight, 14,608 lb (6 626 kg). Span, 45 ft 11⅛ in (14,00 m). Length, 40 ft 0 in (12,20 m). Height, 12 ft 4 in (3,76 m). Wing area, 360.6 sq ft (33,50 m²).*

TEBALDI-ZARI (BREDA)   Italy

Built in Milan in 1919, the sole Tebaldi-designed fighter (above) was of distinctive appearance and is seen with lower outer wing panels attached.

In 1919, the Zari brothers' factory in Bovisio Mombello, Milan, completed the prototype of a single-seat fighter sesquiplane to the designs of one Ing Tebaldi. Of wooden construction and of unequal-span, heavily-staggered sesquiplane configuration, it was powered by a 190 hp Isotta-Fraschini V6 six-cylinder water-cooled engine and was unusual in that it had oversize mainwheels on an undercarriage of exceptionally wide track, the axle for which was incorporated in the lower wing. The design rights and prototype were purchased by Breda, and, re-engined with a 300 hp Hispano-Suiza HS 42 eight-cylinder water-cooled power plant, the Tebaldi fighter became the subject in 1922 of a draft agreement between Breda and the *Commissariato d'Aeronautica* for three aircraft. No contract followed, but the original prototype was modified for participation in the 1923 fighter contest of the newly-created *Regia Aeronautica*. Carrying an armament of two 7,7-mm guns, the Tebaldi fighter was given redesigned wings, with the upper wing of longer span and narrower chord, stagger was reduced, and the gap between the fuselage and the lower wing increased. The incline of the outer struts was also increased to attach at the undercarriage axle, so that the outer panels of the

(Below) The final form of the Tebaldi-Zari fighter with detachable lower outer wing panels shown dotted.

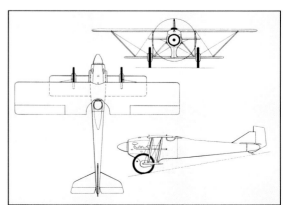

lower wing could be removed for comparative flight testing of the aircraft as a sesquiplane. Further redesign was then undertaken, the chord of the upper wing being increased, ailerons enlarged and the outer panels of the lower wing eventually being discarded permanently. The fighter did not find favour with the *Regia Aeronautica* and Breda abandoned further development. The following data relate to the final HS 42-powered sesquiplane configuration. *Max speed, 158 mph (255 km/h) at 6,560 ft (2 000 m). Time to 16,405 ft (5 000 m), 16 min. Endurance, 3.0 hrs. Empty weight, 1,819 lb (825 kg). Loaded weight, 2,425 lb (1 100 kg). Span, 29 ft 6⅓ in (9,00 m). Length, 25 ft 7 in (7,80 m). Height, 6 ft 6¾ in (2,00 m). Wing area, 236.81 sq ft (22,00 m²).*

TERESHCHENKO No 7   Russia

Built in the workshops of the Kiev Polytechnic Institute under the direction of engineer Vladimir P Grigoriev, a side-by-side two-seat reconnaissance-fighter, referred to as No 7 and designed by F Tereshchenko, was completed on 28 August 1916. A single-bay biplane of wooden construction with fabric covering and a 100 hp Gnome Monosoupape nine-cylinder rotary engine, the Tereshchenko No 7 featured 10 deg of sweepback on the wings, the angle of attack of which could be adjusted in flight. Flight testing was initiated in Moscow in September 1916, and was continued until January 1917, when the prototype was returned to Kiev for modifications. Flight testing was resumed on 29 June 1917, but the ultimate fate of the prototype is unknown. *Max speed, 87 mph (140 km/h). Empty weight, 1,102 lb (500 kg). Loaded weight, 1,896 lb (860 kg). Span, 26 ft 3 in (8,00 m). Length, 19 ft 8¼ in (6,00 m). Wing area, 236.81 sq ft (22,00 m²).*

A Gnome Monosoupape engine powered the Tereshchenko No 7 prototype (below).

THOMAS-MORSE MB-1   USA

The Thomas-Morse Aircraft Corporation, formed in January 1917 by a merger of the Thomas Brothers Aeroplane Company with the Morse Chain Works, established itself with the S-4, the first aircraft specifically designed for fighter pilot training. Late in 1917, the designer of the S-4, B Douglas Thomas (unrelated to the founding brothers), initiated design of a two-seat fighter, the MB-1. A parasol monoplane primarily of wooden construction and powered by a 400 hp Liberty

First of the Thomas-Morse fighters, the MB-1 (below) made only a single test flight.

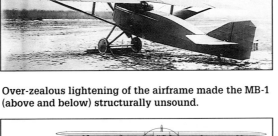

Over-zealous lightening of the airframe made the MB-1 (above and below) structurally unsound.

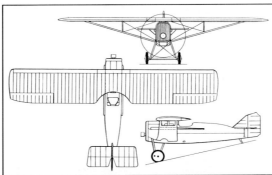

12 water-cooled 12-cylinder Vee-type engine, the MB-1 represented an exercise in achieving minimum structural weight in order to enhance performance. All metal parts were provided with lightening holes – even the control column being perforated – and plywood bulkheads featured large cut-outs, the result being inadequate strength. The undercarriage of the first of two MB-1s collapsed during the first attempted take-off early in 1918, and although it has been alleged that the MB-1 was never flown, repairs were performed on the first prototype and the aircraft *was* flown once, crashing following take-off. The two airframes were delivered to McCook Field, but all further testing was prudently abandoned in favour of the more orthodox MB-2. *Loaded weight, 2,375 lb (1 077 kg). Span, 37 ft 0 in (11,28 m). Length, 22 ft 0 in (6,70 m).*

THOMAS-MORSE MB-2   USA

First built in single-bay form, the MB-2 (above) was soon modified to have this two-bay configuration.

Designed after the crash of the MB-1, the MB-2 was a two-seat fighter of unstaggered, equi-span biplane configuration intended to use a geared Liberty 12 engine. Of fabric-covered wooden construction, the upper wing was a two-spar structure and the lower wing a three-spar structure. Intended armament comprised two synchronised machine guns (one 0.3-in/7,62-mm and the other 0.5-in/12,7-mm) in the for-

ward fuselage and one 0.3-in weapon on a ring mount in the rear cockpit. The flight test MB-2 was delivered in November 1918, two prototypes having been ordered by the Signal Corps, and the first of these being completed in single-bay configuration. Structural testing indicated that the wing cellule possessed insufficient strength and the aircraft was modified as a conventional-structure two-bay biplane. The US Army did not consider the potential performance of the MB-2 to warrant series production and development was discontinued. No performance details of the MB-2 are recorded. *Empty weight, 2,047 lb (929 kg). Loaded weight, 2,773 lb (1 258 kg). Span, 31 ft 0 in (9,45 m). Length, 24 ft 0 in (7,31 m). Height, 8 ft 0 in (2,43 m). Wing area, 323 sq ft (30,00 m²).*

THOMAS-MORSE MB-3   USA

Ordered by the US Army on the basis of a promised 150 mph (241 km/h) maximum speed and a 1,500 ft/min (7,62 m/sec) initial climb, the MB-3 designed by B Douglas Thomas was a single-seat unstaggered single-bay biplane of wooden construction with fabric covering. It featured intermediate interplane struts through which the flying and landing wires passed. Powered by a 300 hp Hispano-Suiza H eight-cylinder water-cooled Vee-type engine, the MB-3 carried an armament of two 0.3-in (7,62-mm) guns, the first of four prototypes entering flight test on 21 February 1919, and subsequently becoming the structural test article at McCook Field.

The second prototype MB-3 (above) with original tail, and (below) the basic series form of the MB-3A

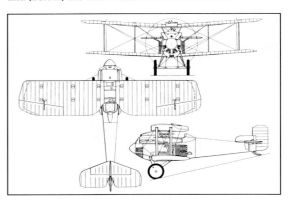

Handling and manoeuvrability were adjudged excellent, but the small size of the cockpit and the poor view for the pilot that it offered were criticised, as was also the fuel system, the main tank developing leaks and tending to break through the fuselage after a few hours flying owing to inadequate structural support. The engine cooling system was inefficient and modifications – at some cost in performance – were necessary before, in June 1920, Thomas-Morse received a contract for 50 MB-3s powered by the licence-built Wright-Hispano H. An Army requirement for a further 200 aircraft was to be fulfilled (after competitive bidding) by Boeing, these aircraft being of the improved MB-3A model (radiators transferred from upper wing to fuselage sides, additional fuel and a 320 hp Wright-Hispano H-3 engine) and delivered between 29 July and 27 December 1922. These, like the production MB-3s, carried an armament of one 0.5-in (12,7-mm) and one 0.3-in (7,62-mm) gun rather than the twin guns of the smaller calibre mounted by the prototypes. The last 50 MB-3As were fitted with an entirely new tail unit (not retrofitted to earlier aircraft). Eleven MB-3s (not MB-3As) were ordered from Thomas-Morse by the US Navy for use by the Marine Corps, this contract being completed in February 1922. In November of the following year, the

The TM-23 was totally rebuilt (above) before being submitted for Air Service testing, without success.

sidered excessive and the TM-23 was rejected. *Max speed, 167 mph (269 km/h) at sea level, 150 mph (241 km/h) at 15,000 ft (4 570 m). Time to 10,000 ft (3 050 m), 7.3 min. Endurance, 2.15 hrs. Empty weight, 1,919 lb (870 kg). Loaded weight, 2,706 lb (1 227 kg). Span, 26 ft 8 in (8,12 m). Length, 21 ft 8 in (6,60 m). Wing area, 264 sq ft (24,52 m².)*

A Boeing-built MB-3A in USAAS service (above), showing the modified, enlarged fin finally adopted.

10 surviving Marine MB-3s, having been in storage from July 1922, were "sold" to the Army and several were flown at Langley Field. The following data relate to the late-production MB-3A. *Max speed, 140 mph (225 km/h) at sea level, 138 mph (222 km/h) at 6,500 ft (1 980 m). Initial climb, 1,235 ft/min (6,27 m/sec). Endurance, 2.25 hrs. Empty weight, 1,716 lb (778 kg). Loaded weight, 2,539 lb (1 152 kg). Span, 26 ft 0 in (7,92 m). Length, 20 ft 0 in (6,10 m). Height, 8 ft 6 in (2,59 m). Wing area, 228.55 sq ft (21,23 m²).*

THOMAS-MORSE MB-9 USA

During the winter of 1919-20, B Douglas Thomas initiated the design of two parasol monoplanes of all-metal construction with corrugated metal skinning, the MB-9 single-seat fighter and the MB-10 tandem two-seat trainer. The latter was the first to fly, entering flight test late in 1921 and suffering its demise during preliminary trials. The MB-9 was powered by a 320 hp Wright-Hispano H-3 eight-cylinder water-cooled engine, the proposed armament consisting of one 0.3-in (7,62-mm) and one 0.5-in (12,7-mm) machine gun. Flown early in 1922, the fighter was found to suffer poor flight characteristics and excessive vibration, undergoing a number of modifications which failed to resolve the problem. This led to the discontinuation of MB-9 development without submission to the Air Service for evaluation. *Max speed, 170 mph (274 km/h). Span, 29 ft 0 in (8,84 m). Length, 19 ft 0 in (5,79 m).*

Little success was achieved with the MB-9 (above and below) which was tested by Thomas-Morse in 1922, but was abandoned before Air Service evaluation.

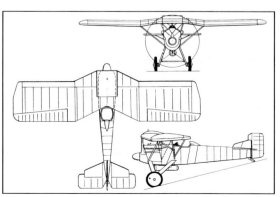

THOMAS-MORSE TM-23 USA

A second attempt on the part of B Douglas Thomas to create a successful all-metal single-seat fighter was represented by the TM-23, which, referred to as an "Alert Pursuit", was effectively the smallest biplane practical with a 440 hp Curtiss D-12 water-cooled 12-cylinder Vee-type engine. Conceived as a cantilever biplane, but with I-type interplane struts being introduced as an afterthought prior to the initiation of testing in 1924, the TM-23 possessed an overall wing span of 19 ft 6 in (5,94 m), the overall length being only 16 ft 7¾ in (5,07 m). Apart from the smooth alloy sheet-covered forward fuselage, the entire aircraft had corrugated light metal skinning. It was proposed that the standard Army armament of twin synchronised guns (one 0.5 in/12,7 mm and the other 0.3 in/7,62 mm) would be carried. The TM-23 proved nose heavy and difficult to control, turning over on its back during its

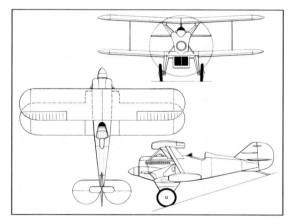

Using all-metal construction like the MB-9, the TM-23 was tested in 1924 in the form shown (above and below), but was then rebuilt.

first landing. The upper wing was moved forward for further testing, but overall characteristics remained unsatisfactory. It was then totally rebuilt, with wing stagger reduced, span and area increased, ailerons transferred from the upper to the lower wing, the cabane simplified to improve forward view, the fuselage lengthened and the tail surfaces redesigned and enlarged. With these changes, the TM-23 was shipped to McCook Field for Air Service evaluation. The handling qualities were criticised, landing speed was con-

THOMAS-MORSE XP-13 VIPER USA

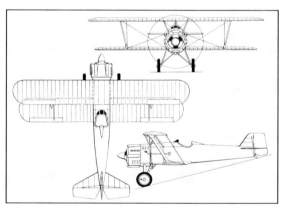

The final Thomas-Morse effort to produce a fighter for the Army Air Service was the XP-13 (above and below).

Destined to be the last fighter designed and built by Thomas-Morse before the company was sold, on 5 August 1929, to Consolidated Aircraft, the XP-13, dubbed Viper by its manufacturer, was built as a private venture. Mating a metal-framed, corrugated alloy-covered fuselage with fabric-covered metal wings, the XP-13 was effectively designed around the new 600 hp Curtiss H-1640-1 Chieftain 12-cylinder two-row radial engine. This engine proved to possess insurmountable cooling problems, and the prototype, which was delivered to the Army in June 1929 – the service purchasing it shortly afterwards – was re-engined in September 1930 as the XP-13A with a 525 hp Pratt & Whitney SR-1340-C Wasp nine-cylinder radial. The characteristics and performance of the Viper were considered satisfactory. However, following loss of the XP-13A as a result of an in-flight fire, no consideration

With a Wasp engine and enlarged tail surfaces, the XP-13A (below) suffered an ignominious end.

was given to series production. The following data relate to the XP-13 with the Chieftain engine, performance being improved by some 10 per cent with the Wasp engine. *Max speed, 172 mph (277 km/h) at sea level, 170 mph (273 km/h) at 5,000 ft (1 525 m). Time to 5,000 ft (1 525 m), 3.0 min. Empty weight, 2,262 lb (1 026 kg). Loaded weight, 3,256 lb (1 477 kg). Span, 28 ft 0 in (8,53 m). Length, 23 ft 6 in (7,16 m). Height, 8 ft 5 in (2,56 m). Wing area, 189 sq ft (17,56 m².*

THULIN K   Sweden

In 1917, Dr Enoch Thulin of the AETA (AB Enoch Thulins Aeroplanfabrik) produced his first single-seat fighter, the Thulin K. A shoulder-wing monoplane of wooden construction employing the wing warping principle for lateral control, the fighter was powered by a 90 hp Thulin A (licence-built Gnome) rotary engine and was intended to carry a single machine gun. Two Thulin K fighters had been ordered on 19 December 1916 for *Flygkompaniet*, these being financed by collections made by women in Southern Sweden. The first was delivered in March 1917, the second being delivered later in the year and neither being fitted with

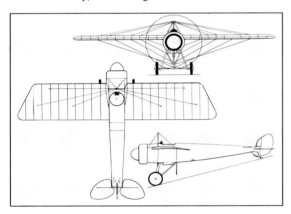

The Thulin K (above and below) was used primarily by the Dutch Navy, some being tested with a cannon.

armament. Earlier, in January, the Dutch Navy had placed an order for five Thulin Ks, one of which was to be completed as a two-seater. This order was increased to 10 single-seaters and three two-seaters in May 1917, a supplementary order for two more single-seaters being placed in 1919. All the Thulin K fighters were delivered to the Netherlands without armament, but the Dutch Navy fitted them with a synchronised machine gun and several were tested with a 20-mm Madsen cannon. *Max speed, 93 mph (150 km/h) at sea level. Service ceiling, 18,000 ft (5 485 m). Loaded weight, 1,146 lb (520 kg). Span, 29 ft 10¼ in (9,10 m). Length, 21 ft 3⁹⁄₁₀ in (6,50 m). Height, 8 ft 4²⁄₅ in (2,55 m). Wing area, 150.7 sq ft (14,00 m²).*

TNCA Serie C
MICROPLANO   Mexico

In February 1918, the Talleres Nacionales de Construcciones Aeronáuticas (TNCA), or National Aircraft Manufacturing Workshops, at Balbuena Airfield, Mexico City, completed the prototype of a single-seat fighting scout to the designs of Francisco Santarini and Capt Guillermo Villasana. A single-bay unstaggered biplane known as the Microplano, the aircraft was powered by a 180 hp Hispano-Suiza eight-cylinder Vee-type water-cooled engine driving a Mexican Anahuac

The Microplano (above and below) failed to achieve production owing to the overthrow of its sponsors.

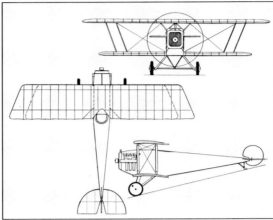

propeller, and was of metal construction. The intended armament was either one or two synchronised machine guns. Although flight trials of the Microplano were allegedly satisfactory, no series production was undertaken owing to the overthrow of the Carranza régime and the ensuing civil war. *Max speed, 137 mph (220 km/h). Empty weight, 1,014 lb (460 kg). Loaded weight, 1,433 lb (650 kg). Span, 26 ft 2⅞ in (8,00 m). Length, 21 ft 7⅘ in (6,60 m). Height, 8 ft 4²⁄₅ in (2,55 m). Wing area, 193.76 sq ft (18,00 m²).*

TNCA 3-E-130 TOLOLOCHE   Mexico

Following the appointment of Ing Angel Lascurain y Osio as director of the TNCA in 1920, several original designs were developed by this organisation, including, in 1924, a single-seat fighter for the air component of the Mexican Army. Known as the 3-E-130 Tololoche (a colloquial name for a type of guitar) and designed by

The Tololoche (above and below) was built in small numbers for the Mexican Army in the mid 'twenties.

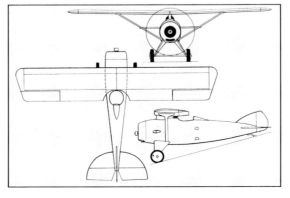

Antonio Zea, this was a parasol monoplane of wooden monocoque construction powered by a 160 hp Le Rhône rotary air-cooled engine. Apart from the engine, all elements of the Tololoche were of Mexican origin, the structure being primarily of spruce with three-ply veneer skinning. A batch of four fighters of this type was built. *Max speed, 140 mph (225 km/h). Time to 3,280 ft (1 000 m), 2.6 min. Endurance, 1.5 hrs. Empty weight, 1,477 lb (670 kg). Loaded weight, 1,896 lb (860 kg). Wing area, 172.23 sq ft (16,00 m²).*

All elements of the Tololoche (below) were of Mexican origin apart from the engine.

TOKOROZAWA KOSHIKI-2   Japan

The Imperial Army's Department of Research at the Tokorozawa Aviation School initiated work in 1921 on the first Japanese single-seat fighter of indigenous design. Designated Koshiki-2 (School-2), indicating the origin rather than the rôle of the aircraft, the fighter embodied features from the SPAD S.XIII and Salmson 2 A2, and was designed by a team led by Maj (Eng) Akira Matsui. A single-bay biplane with I-type interplane struts, the Koshiki-2 was of wooden construction with fabric covering, and was powered by the water-cooled Salmson 9Z nine-cylinder radial of 260 hp, armament comprising two synchronised 7,7-mm machine guns.

The Koshiki-2 (above) appeared to owe much to the SPAD S.XIII and the Salmson 2 A2 fighters.

The prototype was flown in 1922, but demonstrated some low-speed instability and was destroyed in a crash which ensued when its pilot attempted to land after the fighter's fourth flight. A second prototype was completed during 1923, but still displayed a measure of instability and no further development was undertaken. *Max speed, 128 mph (206 km/h) at 9,840 ft (3 000 m). Time to 6,560 ft (2 000 m), 9.0 min. Endurance, 2.0 hrs. Empty weight, 1,433 lb (650 kg). Loaded weight, 2,094 lb (950 kg). Span, 32 ft 9²⁄₃ in (10,00 m). Length, 21 ft 7⅘ in (6,60 m). Height, 7 ft 10½ in (2,40 m). Wing area, 215.28 sq ft (20,00 m²).*

TOMASHEVICH 110   USSR

Dmitrii L Tomashevich was a deputy of Nikolai Polikarpov and responsible for the I-180, the failure of which led to his imprisonment. Transferred from Special Prison KB-29 to Kulomzino, a suburb of Omsk, in October 1941, Tomashevich established his own project bureau and developed a single-seat fighter referred to simply as *Samolet* (Aircraft) 110. Placing emphasis on suitability for dispersed manufacture, largely by semi-skilled and unskilled labour, and ease of repair and maintenance under primitive field conditions, the 110 was of mixed construction, with a two-spar wooden wing and welded steel-tube fuselage. The wings, fixed tail surfaces and aft fuselage had Bakelite ply, or *shpon*, skinning, the remainder of the fuselage being covered by light alloy. The engine was a Klimov M-107P 12-cylinder Vee-type rated at 1,400 hp and armament comprised one 20-mm cannon and two 12,7-mm machine guns. The first prototype was flown in December 1942, but the 110 proved substantially overweight and the

The Tomashevich 110 (above and below) emphasized ease of manufacture and of maintenance in the field.

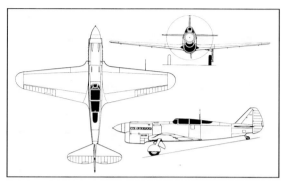

insufficiently-developed Klimov engine proved unreliable. Furthermore, series production of another fighter at that stage in the conflict was impracticable, and, in consequence, development was discontinued. *Max speed, 316 mph (508 km/h) at sea level, 379 mph (610 km/h) at 20,500 ft (6 250 m). Time to 16,405 ft (5 000 m), 7.03 min. Max range, 652 mls (1 050 km). Empty weight, 7,242 lb (3 285 kg). Normal loaded weight, 8,774 lb (3 980 kg). Span, 33 ft 5½ in (10,20 m). Length, 32 ft 6⅛ in (9,91 m). Wing area, 201.61 sq ft (18,73 m²).*

TUPOLEV ANT-5 (I-4)   USSR

The first prototype of the ANT-5 (above), with large-diameter spinner, which entered flight test in 1927.

Designed by Pavel O Sukhoi when a brigade leader of Andrei N Tupolev's AGOS (*Aviatsiya, Gidroaviatsiya i Opytniye Stroityelstvo* – Aviation, Hydro-aviation and Experimental Construction) collective within the TsAGI (*Tsentralnyi Aero-gidrodinamicheskii Institut* – Central Aero and Hydro-dynamic Institute), the ANT-5 was the first Soviet all-metal fighter. A single-seat sesquiplane powered by a nine-cylinder Gnome-Rhône Jupiter radial of 420 hp, the first prototype performed factory testing between 10 August and 25 September 1927. A second prototype, or *dubler*, with a 480 hp Gnome-Rhône Jupiter 9ASB, was flown in July 1928, and underwent state testing between 1 December 1928

(Below) The standard series I-4 with helmeted cowl.

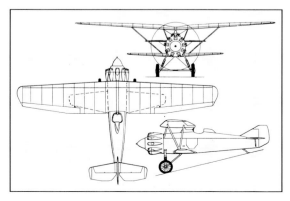

and 4 April 1929, series production of the type having meanwhile been initiated as the I-4. The first series I-4 underwent state testing between 15 October and 26 November 1929, subsequent aircraft having the 480 hp M-22 engine, a licence-built version of the G-R Jupiter 9ASB, and an armament of twin 7,62-mm guns. Second series aircraft had the 43 sq ft (4,00 m²) lower wing removed, controllable slats occupying 44.5 per cent of the remaining wing's leading edge, and a Townend ring-type engine cowling incorporating cylinder helmets. Designated I-4bis in this form, the prototype was tested by the NII VVS, the Air Force's Scientific Research Institute, between 11 and 23 September 1931. No further development of the I-4bis was undertaken. Three I-4s

The I-4bis (above) dispensed with the lower wing and had controllable wing leading-edge slats.

were fitted with very much smaller lower wings for aerial launch and retrieval trials from 31 December 1931 by Vladimir S Vakhmistrov utilising a TB-1 bomber as an *Aviamatka*, or "mother aircraft". Also in December 1931, one I-4 was tested with a 76-mm Kurchevski recoilless cannon mounted beneath each upper wing half. A total of 369 I-4s was built to January 1934, these equipping 18 *eskadrii* at their service peak; the type remaining in first-line service through 1933 and for tuitional tasks until 1937. *Max speed, 137 mph (220 km/h) at sea level, 144 mph (231 km/h) at 9,840 ft (3 000 m). Time to 16,405 ft (5 000 m), 14.3 min. Range, 522 mls (840 km). Empty weight, 2,156 lb (978 kg). Loaded weight, 3,152 lb (1 430 kg). Span, 37 ft 4¾ in (11,40 m). Length, 23 ft 10⅔ in (7,28 m). Wing area, 256.19 sq ft (23,80 m²).*

TUPOLEV ANT-13 (I-8)   USSR

The ANT-13 (above) was completed only as a result of the workers donating their time to the project.

Conceived to make use of new high-strength steels obtainable from Germany in the late 'twenties, the ANT-13 was a small unequal-span staggered biplane single-seat fighter. Utilising steel for the wing spars and the welded truss fuselage – the remainder of the structure being dural – the ANT-13 was fabric covered and powered by a 600 hp Curtiss V-1570 Conqueror 12-cylinder water-cooled engine. Armament consisted of twin 7,62-mm synchronised guns. Construction of the prototype, designated I-8, was threatened with cancellation in 1929 through the pressures of higher priority projects at the AGOS, but each worker donated 70 hours to completing the I-8, which was flown on 28 October 1930. Dubbed unofficially the *Zhokei* (Jockey), the fighter was the first aircraft to exceed 300 km/h (186.4 mph) in the Soviet Union, but the decision not to licence manufacture the Conqueror engine militated against series production of the ANT-13. *Max speed, 188 mph (303 km/h) at sea level, 194 mph (313 km/h) at 11,810 ft (3 600 m). Time to 16,405 ft (5 000 m), 6.7 min.*

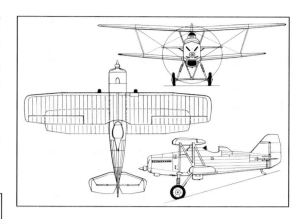

(Above) The Conqueror-powered ANT-13 alias I-8.

Range, 273 mls (440 km). Empty weight, 2,116 lb (960 kg). Loaded weight, 3,139 lb (1 424 kg). Span, 29 ft 6⅓ in (9,00 m).

TUPOLEV ANT-21 (MI-3)   USSR

The ANT-21 (above) was very much state-of-the-art by international standards when flown in August 1933.

Designed at the KOSOS (*Konstruktorski otdel opytnovo samolyetostroeniya*, or Design Department for Experimental Aircraft Construction) within TsAGI by a brigade headed by Aleksandr A Arkhangel'sky, the ANT-21 MI (*mnogomestnyi istrebitel* – multi-seat fighter) was, by international standards of its day, very much state-of-the-art. Featuring all-metal stressed-skin semi-monocoque construction with partial flush-riveting and a retractable main undercarriage, the ANT-21, which was assigned the service designation MI-3, was powered by two M-17B (BMW VI) 12-cylinder water-cooled engines of 680 hp. Proposed armament consisted of one 12,7-mm machine gun or 20-mm cannon on a pivoted nose mounting, two 7,62-mm guns firing from a dorsal position and a single 7,62-mm gun firing from a ventral tunnel. Three crew members were carried. Work on the ANT-21 began on 18 January 1932, first flight taking place in August 1933. On 14 September, the starboard rudder suffered damage and separated as a result of violent flutter in a shallow dive. Arkhangel'sky elected to undertake major redesign as the ANT-21bis. *Max speed, 215 mph (346 km/h) at sea level, 223 mph (359 km/h) at 9,840 ft (3 000 m). Range, 696 mls (1,120 km). Empty weight, 8,091 lb (3 670 kg). Loaded weight, 12,125 lb (5 500 kg). Span, 68 ft 1⅓ in (20,76 m). Length, 38 ft 4⅔ in (11,70 m). Wing area, 593.1 sq ft (55,10 m²).*

Seen below "tufted" to study airflow characteristics, the ANT-21 was forerunner of a series of fighters.

TUPOLEV ANT-21BIS (MI-3D)   USSR

Retaining the wings, engines and undercarriage of the ANT-21, the ANT-21bis alias MI-3D (the suffix letter indicating *dubler*, or, literally, "understudy") mated these elements with an entirely new fuselage, which provided enclosed cockpits for all crew members, and a single fin-and-rudder. Completed in April 1934, the ANT-21bis had provision for the same armament as that of the ANT-21, but the ventral tunnel was omitted, the gun being fired instead through a trap. During initial flight trials some tail oscillation at certain power settings led to the introduction of tailplane bracing struts. State acceptance trials were conducted between July and December 1934, but the results were somewhat academic as there was little official interest in an M-17B-powered aircraft which had, in any case, been largely overtaken by the ANT-29. Consequently, further work on the ANT-21bis was discontinued. *Max speed, 218 mph (351 km/h) at sea level, 221 mph (356 km/h) at 9,840 ft (3 000 m). Empty weight, 8,377 lb (3 800 kg). Loaded weight, 11,596 lb (5 260 kg). Span, 68 ft 1⅓ in (20,76 m). Length, 40 ft 4¼ in (12,30 m). Wing area, 593.1 sq ft (55,10 m²).*

Derived from the ANT-21, the ANT-21bis (above) introduced a new fuselage and redesigned tail.

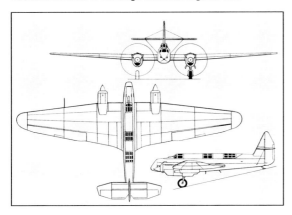

Unlike its predecessor, the ANT-21bis (above and below) provided enclosed accommodation for the crew.

TUPOLEV ANT-23 (I-12)   USSR

Of unconventional design in employing a tandem fore-and-aft engine arrangement and twin tailbooms embodying recoilless gun tubes as integral, but non-load-carrying, structural components, the ANT-23 single-seat fighter was conceived at the AGOS TsAGI by Viktor N Chernyshov, one of Tupolev's brigade leaders. Of all-metal construction with smooth stressed skinning for the fuselage and wing – the latter and the tail surfaces being strengthened by externally-attached inverted "U" strips – and tail covering, the fighter was powered by two 525 hp Gnome-Rhône 9AK nine-cylinder air-cooled radial engines. Armament consisted of two 76-mm Kurchevski APK-4 recoilless weapons which were embodied in the tailbooms, the gun gases

The tailbooms of the ANT-23 (below) served as the housings for the barrels of recoilless APK-4 guns.

being discharged from their tails. Known unofficially as the *Baumanskii Komsomolyets* – in memory of the pre-revolutionary Communist after whom the district in which the TsAGI was situated was named – and officially as the I-12, the ANT-23 was first flown in late December 1931. Flight testing continued through early 1932, but, on 19 May, the port gun exploded, the tail-boom collapsing on touchdown. The aircraft was overweight and suffered substantially higher drag than had been calculated. Chernyshov and his team were developing a means of jettisoning the aft propeller to afford safe escape for the pilot in an emergency, but, at the beginning of 1933, the ANT-23 was abandoned. *Max speed, 186 mph (300 km/h) at sea level, 174 mph (280 km/h) at 16,405 ft (5 000 m). Loaded weight, 5,291 lb (2 400 kg). Span, 51 ft 2⅛ in (15,60 m). Length, 31 ft 2 in (9,50 m). Wing area, 322.93 sq ft (30,00 m²).*

(Below) The recoilless-gun-toting ANT-23 fighter.

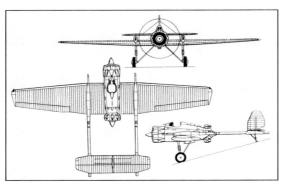

TUPOLEV ANT-29 (DIP)   USSR

A progressive development of the basic ANT-21bis design, the ANT-29 was a DIP (*Dvukhmotorny istrebitel pushechny*, or twin-engined cannon fighter) designed by Aleksandr Arkhangel'sky's brigade. Of flush-riveted all-metal construction and powered by two 760 hp Hispano-Suiza 12Ybrs 12-cylinder liquid-cooled engines, the ANT-29 carried a 102-mm Kurchevski DRP, a recoilless gun of 13 ft 1½-in (4,00-m) length, the exhaust gases of which were discharged through a steel tube projecting from the rear of the fuselage. This weapon was hand-loaded by the second crew member. In addition, one 20-mm cannon was mounted in each wing root and provision was made for a dorsally-mounted 7,62-mm machine gun. Priority assigned to other programmes delayed completion, and flight testing of the ANT-29 did not begin until the end of 1935, although

(Below) The ANT-29 twin-engined cannon fighter.

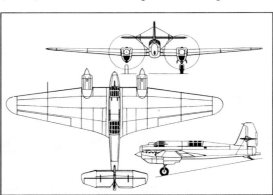

The ANT-29 (above and below) carried a 102-mm gun of recoilless type, the exhaust gases from which were discharged beneath the tail assembly.

the prototype had been rolled out in the previous February. State acceptance testing was scheduled for the first half of 1936, but, in the event, never took place as numerous problems were revealed by factory testing, including serious longitudinal instability. The project was abandoned after a loss of interest in Kurchevski's recoilless guns for which the ANT-29 had been designed. These had suffered repeated failures leading to Kurchevski's arrest and subsequent disappearance. *Max speed, 199 mph (320 km/h) at sea level, 219 mph (352 km/h) at 13,125 ft (4 000 m). Empty weight, 8,598 lb (3 900 kg). Loaded weight, 11,684 lb (5 300 kg). Span, 62 ft 11½ in (19,19 m). Length, 38 ft 2⅔ in (11,65 m).*

TUPOLEV ANT-31 (I-14)   USSR

Possessing the distinction of being the world's first all-metal single-seat cantilever monoplane fighter to be graced with a retractable main undercarriage and an enclosed cockpit, the ANT-31 was designed at the KOSOS TsAGI by Pavel O Sukhoi's brigade. Featuring a smooth, stressed-skin fuselage with corrugated skinning for the wing, tailplane and rudder, the first prototype was powered by a 580 hp nine-cylinder Bristol Mercury VIS2 radial, and had a manually-operated inwards-retracting undercarriage and an aft-hinging cockpit canopy incorporating the windscreen. This aircraft entered flight test with a fixed-ski undercarriage early in May 1933, by which time major redesign was being undertaken and work had begun on a *dubler* prototype, the ANT-31bis. Fitted with a 712 hp Wright Cyclone SGR-1820-F2, the ANT-31bis featured a new,

The Mercury-engined first prototype ANT-31 (above) and the Cyclone-engined second prototype (below), both seen during tests with ski undercarriages.

The first production I-14bis (above) without wing cannon and (below) in definitive series form.

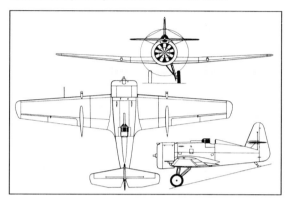

narrow-track undercarriage retracting outwards and a narrower canopy which, sliding fore and aft on runners, still incorporated the windscreen. This aircraft, too, was initially flown with fixed skis, in March 1934, and, equipped with an armament of two 37-mm Kurchevski APK-11 recoilless guns installed immediately outboard of the wing centre section and one fuselage-mounted 7,62-mm machine gun, then underwent State testing from the following October. The decision was taken to initiate series production of the ANT-31bis as the I-14bis, with smooth metal skinning overall, an open cockpit with fixed windscreen, the 700 hp M-25 licence-built version of the Cyclone and armament of two 20-mm cannon and two 7,62-mm machine guns. Orders were placed for 55 I-14bis fighters, the intention being to install the 730 hp M-25A engine at an early stage. The spin recovery characteristics of the I-14bis were not entirely satisfactory and difficulties were experienced with the narrow-track undercarriage. In consequence, the similarly-powered I-16 *Tip* 4 having meanwhile demonstrated generally superior characteristics, production was terminated in December 1936 with the 18th aircraft, the remaining 37 fighters of this type then under construction being scrapped. *Max speed, 233 mph (375 km/h) at sea level, 279 mph (440 km/h) at 11,155 ft (3 400 m). Time to 16,405 ft (5 000 m), 6.5 min. Empty weight, 2,579 lb (1 170 kg). Loaded weight, 3,395 lb (1 540 kg). Span, 36 ft 9 in (11,20 m). Length, 20 ft 0 in (6,10 m). Wing area, 181.92 sq ft (16,90 m²).*

TUPOLEV ANT-46 (DI-8) USSR

The ANT-46 (above) with 100-mm APK-100 recoilless guns carried outboard of the engine nacelles.

Ordered in December 1934 as a single prototype under the designation DI-8, the ANT-46 was a two-seat fighter (*Dvukhmestny istrebitel*) derivative of Aleksandr Arkhangel'sky's SB high-speed bomber (ANT-40). Featuring a lightened structure and powered by two 800 hp Gnome-Rhône 14Krsd 14-cylinder air-cooled radial engines, the ANT-46 was intended to carry two 100-mm Kurchevski APK-100 recoilless guns as its primary armament, these weapons

being buried in the outer wings between the ailerons and the flaps, and projecting fore and aft. In addition, it was intended to mount a battery of four 7,62-mm guns in the extreme nose, but these were not carried by the prototype, which featured a glazed nose generally similar to that of the SB. First flown on 9 August 1935, the ANT-46 was actually flown *before* the ANT-29, the factory flight test programme being completed successfully in June 1936, but state acceptance testing was not undertaken as official interest in the recoilless gun – for which the ANT-46 had been specifically developed – had terminated with the arrest, in February 1936, of Leonid Kurchevski. *Max speed, 214 mph (344 km/h) at sea level, 241 mph (388 km/h) at 13,945 ft (4 250 m). Time to 9,840 ft (3 000 m), 6.8 min. Range, 1,106 mls (1 780 kg). Empty weight, 7,687 lb (3 487 kg). Loaded weight, 12,242 lb (5 553 kg). Span, 66 ft 7¼ in (20,30 m). Length, 40 ft 1⅞ in (12,24 m). Wing area, 599.57 sq ft (55,70 m²).*

(Below) The ANT-46 fighter derivative of the SB.

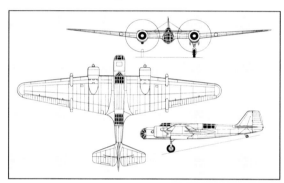

TUPOLEV ANT-63P (Tu-1) USSR

An attempt to produce a radar-equipped three-seat long-range night and all-weather fighter also suited for the escort mission, the ANT-63P, alias Tu-1, was one of a number of progressive developments of the ANT-61

The ANT-63P (above and below) was a radar-equipped fighter evolved from the ANT-61 attack bomber.

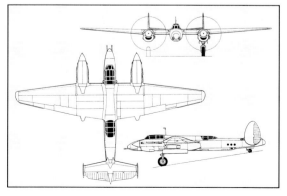

(Tu-2S) bomber. Initially powered by two 1,900 hp Mikulin AM-39F 12-cylinder liquid-cooled engines, the ANT-63P (the suffix letter indicating *Perekhvatchik*, or "Interceptor") carried a fixed forward-firing armament of four 23-mm cannon, two in the wing roots and two in the lower forward fuselage. The nose was intended to accommodate a PNB-1 *Gneiss*-7 airborne intercept radar based on the German FuG 220. First flown on 30 December 1946, the ANT-63P attained 422 mph (680 km/h) and demonstrated a range of 1,553 miles (2 500 km). Official interest in piston-engined fighters was waning by this time, and although the ANT-63P was re-engined with 1,950 hp Mikulin AM-43V engines driving four-bladed propellers, being tested in this form in December 1947, no production was undertaken. The following data relate to the ANT-63P with AM-43V engines. *Max speed, 298 mph (479 km/h) at sea level, 398 mph (641 km/h) at 28,215 ft (8 600 m). Time to 16,405 ft (5 000 m), 11.6 min. Range, 1,398 mls (2 250 km). Max loaded weight, 31,878 lb (14 460 kg). Span, 61 ft 10½ in (18,86 m). Length, 44 ft 7⅖ in (13,60 m). Wing area, 525.3 sq ft (48,80 m²).*

TUPOLEV Tu-128 USSR

A prototype of the Tu-128 (above), the Tu-28-80, with ventral housing, and (below) the series Tu-128.

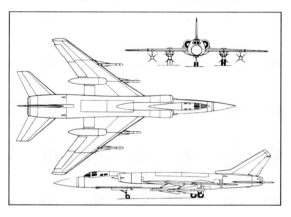

The largest and heaviest interceptor fighter ever to have achieved service status, the Tu-128 was developed by a team led by I. Nezval'. A dedicated interceptor fighter intended for the high-altitude patrol of sections of the Soviet periphery unprotected by surface-to-air missile screens, the Tu-128 was flown as a prototype (Tu-28-80) on 18 March 1961 powered by two TRD-31 (Lyulka AL-7) turbojets. Production deliveries to the *Voyska PVO* began in late 1966, the Tu-128 having a crew of two and paired AL-7F-2 turbojets each rated at 16,370 lb st (7 425 kgp) unaugmented and 22,046 lb st (10 000 kgp) with afterburning. Equipped with a large I-band radar, the Tu-128 had a primary armament of two radar-homing and two infra-red homing Bisnovat R-4 missiles. Progressively withdrawn from the *Voyska PVO* home defence fighter force through the 'eighties, the Tu-128 was finally succeeded by the MiG-31 in late 1990. *Max speed (with four R-4 AAMs), 1,036 mph*

The Tu-128 (below) was the largest and heaviest interceptor fighter to have achieved service status.

Tupolev Tu-128 heavy interceptors (above) in service with the *Voyska PVO* in the late 'sixties.

(1 667 km/h) at 39,370 ft (12 000 m), or Mach=1.57. Range, 1,594 mls (2 565 km). Empty equipped weight, 57,230 lb (25 960 kg). Normal loaded weight, 94,797 lb (43 000 kg). Span, 57 ft 5 in (17,50 m). Length, 98 ft 5 in (30,00m).

VEF I-16   Latvia

Owing much to a line of light cabin monoplanes and advanced trainers, the I-16, designed by Karlis Irbitis and built as a single prototype by the Valsts Elektrotechniska Fabrika (State Electro-Technical Factory) at Riga, was a single-seat lightweight fighter. Of wooden construction with plywood skinning and a fixed, faired undercarriage, the I-16 was powered by a 454 hp Walter Sagitta I-SR 12-cylinder inverted-Vee engine. It carried an armament of two 7,9-mm fuselage-mounted machine guns which could be augmented by two wing-mounted 20-mm cannon. The success of initial flight testing of the I-16 in 1939 prompted the Latvian authorities to order prototypes of the heavier and more powerful I-19 air superiority fighter, but this was still on the drawing boards when Latvia was occupied by Soviet forces on 17 June 1940. The sole prototype of the I-16 was subsequently flown in Soviet markings which gave place to *Luftwaffe* markings when the *Wehrmacht* advanced into Latvia during the following year. *Max speed, 300 mph (483 km/h) at 25,920 ft*

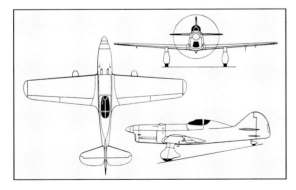

The sole prototype of the I-16 (above) ended its days in the hands of the *Luftwaffe* (below).

(7 900 m). Range, 500 mls (805 km) at 248 mph (400 km/h). Empty weight, 2,425 lb (1 100 kg). Loaded weight, 3,395 lb (1 540 kg). Span, 27 ft 0 in (8,23 m). Length, 24 ft 0 in (7.30 m). Wing area, 123 sq ft (11,43 m²).

VICKERS E.F.B.1   UK

On 19 November 1912, Vickers received a contract from the Admiralty for an experimental fighting biplane armed with a machine gun. Various configurations were investigated before the desirability of placing the gunner in the extreme nose of the aircraft, in order to achieve a clear field of fire, led to choice of a fuselage nacelle carrying at its rear an engine driving a pusher propeller. This nacelle was mated with an unequal-span heavily-staggered biplane configuration, the tail surfaces being carried by paired and vertically disposed booms attaching to the upper and lower rear wing spars on each side of the engine. Designated E.F.B. (Experimental Fighting Biplane) 1 and dubbed "Destroyer", the Vickers aircraft was, if not the very first, then one of the earliest dedicated fighter aircraft, and was armed with a single 0.303-in (7,7-mm) Maxim machine gun on a mount affording 60 deg elevation and traverse. The airframe of the E.F.B.1 was primarily of metal construction, the nacelle accommodating the pilot and gunner, and carrying an 80 hp Wolseley eight-cylinder Vee-type engine, being of steel tube with duralumin skinning. Wing warping was employed for lateral control. Prior to its first flight, the E.F.B.1 was displayed at the Aero Show held at Olympia, London, in February 1913. The gun was fitted for the first flight test, made at Joyce Green, but this rendered the aircraft so nose-heavy that it briefly left the ground, then nosed down, struck the ground and turned over. The following performance data are estimated. *Max speed, 70 mph (113 km/h) at sea level. Initial climb, 450 ft/min (2,3 m/sec). Endurance, 4.5 hrs. Empty weight, 1,760 lb (798 kg). Loaded weight, 2,660 lb (1 207 kg). Span, 40 ft 0 in (12,19 m). Length, 27 ft 6 in (8,38 m). Height, 11 ft 11 in (3,63 m). Wing area, 385 sq ft (35,77 m²)*

(Below) Vickers' E.F.B.1, one of the earliest dedicated fighter aircraft.

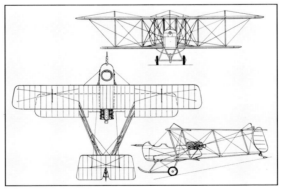

VICKERS E.F.B.2   UK

Following the loss of the E.F.B.1, Vickers undertook major redesign of its gun carrier while retaining the basic configuration to result in the E.F.B.2, again against an Admiralty contract. The E.F.B.2 eliminated the wing stagger of the previous aircraft and increased the span of the lower wing while retaining warping for

lateral control. The fuselage nacelle was redesigned and large celluloid windows were inserted in its sides; the angular horizontal tail surfaces gave place to surfaces of elliptical form and a 100 hp Gnome Monosoupape nine-cylinder rotary engine was fitted. The 0.303-in (7,7-mm) machine gun on a ball-and-socket mounting in the forward cockpit was retained, and the E.F.B.2 entered flight test at Bognor in the autumn of 1913, but crashed there during the course of October.

The short-lived E.F.B.2 (above and below) was a revision of the original E.F.B.1 design.

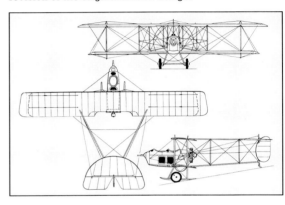

Max speed, 60 mph (97 km/h) at sea level. Initial climb, 200 ft/min (1,02 m/sec). Range, 150 mls (241 km). Empty weight, 1,050 lb (476 kg). Loaded weight, 1,760 lb (798 kg). Span, 38 ft 7 in (11,76 m). Length, 29 ft 2 in (8,89 m). Height, 9 ft 7 in (2,92 m). Wing area, 380 sq ft (35,30 m²).

VICKERS E.F.B.3   UK

Appearing in 1914, the E.F.B.3 (above) was the first Vickers warplane to achieve production.

In December 1913, a third Vickers Experimental Fighting Biplane, the E.F.B.3, made its début. The slight overhang of the top wing was eliminated to result in an equi-span biplane, the fuselage nacelle underwent further redesign, the celluloid windows being eliminated, and, most important, ailerons on both upper and lower wings supplanted the wing-warping control of its predecessors. The 100 hp Gnome Monosoupape rotary was retained as was also the 0.303-in (7,7-mm) Vickers gun. Displayed at the Aero Show held at Olympia in 1914, the E.F.B.3. was the subject of an order from the Admiralty for six aircraft placed in December 1913. This contract was subsequently taken over by the War Office, the six aircraft embodying a number of modifications – at least one was fitted with an eight-cylinder Vee-type 80 hp Wolseley engine – and being referred to as the Vickers No (or Type) 30. These were to lead in turn to the E.F.B.5 and F.B.5 Gunbus. The following data relate to the early E.F.B.3 with Gnome engine. *Max speed, 60 mph (97 km/h) at sea level. Initial climb, 300 ft/min (1,52 m/sec). Range, 300 mls (483 km). Empty weight, 1,050 lb (476 kg). Loaded weight, 1,680 lb (762 kg). Span, 37 ft 4 in (11,38 m). Length, 27 ft 6 in (8,38 m). Height, 9 ft 9 in (2,97 m). Wing area, 385 sq ft (35,77 m²).*

VICKERS F.B.5 GUNBUS   UK

Progressive changes introduced by successive E.F.B.3s led to the E.F.B.5 – the E.F.B.4 being a project with a more streamlined nacelle centred between the wings and only two tailbooms – which was flown from Joyce Green to Brooklands on 17 July 1914. In parallel, Vickers developed the E.F.B.6, which, basically similar to the E.F.B.5, had longer-span upper wings. It lacked top decking between the two crew seats and had ailerons in the upper wings only. At Brooklands on 14 July 1914, the E.F.B.6 was taken on strength by the Royal Flying Corps when World War I began, but was not developed. The E.F.B.5, on the contrary, was ordered into production for both the RFC and the RNAS on 14 August 1914, the first series aircraft being completed in the following October. At this time, the aircraft became simply F.B. (Fighting Biplane) 5 and was dubbed Gunbus. The E.F.B.5 had retained the semi-circular tailplane of the E.F.B.2 and early E.F.B.3, but the series F.B.5 had an enlarged tailplane of rectangular planform and a larger rudder. A Lewis gun on a more practical mount supplanted the similar-calibre Vickers in the nose and the standard power plant was the 100 hp Gnome Monosoupape nine-cylinder rotary. The first F.B.5 reached the Western Front early February 1915, and, on the following 25 July, the first squadron of any air service formed specifically for fighting duties and equipped throughout with a single aircraft type arrived in France, this being the RFC's No 11 Sqn with F.B.5s.

The F.B.5 (above and below) in its series form with enlarged rudder and tailplane.

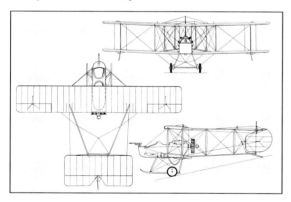

A dozen examples of the Vickers F.B.5 were built in Denmark; illustrated (below) is No 7.

The RNAS made little use of the F.B.5, and, after the delivery of four to that service, the large majority of subsequent deliveries went to the RFC, although the RNAS did receive two further F.B.5s which, ordered in May 1915, were fitted with the 150 hp Smith Static radial engine, its large diameter propeller necessitating the raising of the fuselage nacelle several inches above the lower wing. Two hundred and forty-one F.B.5s were delivered to the RFC, of which 109 were sent to the British Expeditionary Force in France (60 in 1915 and 49 in 1916). Licence production of the F.B.5 was undertaken in France by the Société Anonym Darracq (which built a total of 99 of these and the later F.B.9) between May 1915 and June 1916. Twelve were also built under licence in Denmark in 1917-18 by the *Tojhusværksted*. At least four F.B.5As were built with armour-plated fuselage nacelles and these were powered by 110 hp Clerget 9Z nine-cylinder rotary engines and had oleo undercarriages. Suffering an unreliable engine and a marginal performance throughout its operational career, the F.B.5 was finally withdrawn from the Western Front in the autumn of 1916, being subsequently confined to RFC instructional units. *Max speed, 70 mph (113 km/h) at 5,000 ft (1 525 m). Time to 5,000 ft (1 525 m), 16.0 min. Service ceiling, 9,000 ft (2 745 m). Endurance, 4.5 hrs. Empty weight, 1,220 lb (553 kg). Loaded weight, 2,050 lb (930 kg). Span, 36 ft 6 in (11,13 m). Length, 27 ft 2 in (8,28 m). Height, 11 ft 1 in (3,38 m). Wing area, 382 sq ft (35,49 m²).*

VICKERS F.B.7   UK

On the outbreak of World War I, Vickers engaged R L Howard-Flanders to design a twin-engined fighting aeroplane capable of carrying a Vickers one-pounder quick-firing gun with armour protection for the gunner. Powered by two 100 hp Gnome Monosoupape nine-cylinder rotaries mounted overhung between the mainplanes and suspended on simple steel-tube open framework, the prototype was designated E.F.B.7 and was flown for the first time in August 1915. An ungainly unequal-span biplane with two bays of struts, the E.F.B.7 accommodated the pilot aft of the mainplanes, several feet from the gunner in the extreme nose. The substantial gun mount was bolted to the centre of the forward cockpit floor, the gunner's seat being attached to the mount with which it traversed – sufficient room

The E.F.B.7 in its original form (above) and with engine cowlings removed (below).

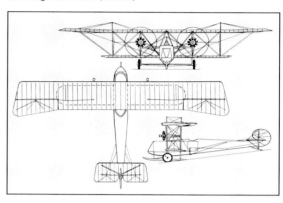

was provided in the cockpit to permit gun and gunner to turn through a full 360 deg. The E.F.B.7 was one of the first twin-engined military aircraft to fly successfully, and an order for 12 production F.B.7s was placed on 20 August 1915, immediately after the initial flight tests of the E.F.B.7, but, in the event, the series model was to differ in a number of major respects. The distance separating the two-man crew was found unacceptable and the pilot was brought forward of the wings in sensible proximity to the gunner, the structure of the upper wing was completely redesigned and the fuselage was revised in cross section, becoming rectangular throughout rather than having an inverted triangular cross section aft. Owing to a shortage of Gnome rotaries, the first production aircraft was fitted with 80 hp Renault eight-cylinder air-cooled engines as the F.B.7A, the engine change resulting in a major loss of performance. As the F.B.7A obviously possessed no operational usefulness, Vickers persuaded the War Office to cancel the contract for the remaining aircraft (which were being built by A Darracq & Company at Fulham under subcontract). The following data relate to the Gnome-engined E.F.B.7. *Max speed, 75 mph (121 km/h) at 5,000 ft (1 525 m). Time to 5,000 ft (1 525 m), 18.0 min. Ceiling, 9,000 ft (2 745 m). Endurance, 2.5 hrs. Empty weight, 2,136 lb (969 kg). Loaded weight, 3,196 lb (1 450 kg). Span, 59 ft 6 in (18,17 m). Length, 36 ft 0 in (10,97 m). Wing area, 640 sq ft (59,46 m²).*

VICKERS E.S.1   UK

Early in 1915, Rex K Pierson was tasked with the redesign of the so-called Barnwell Bullet, an unarmed single-seat biplane designed as a private venture by Vickers' then chief test pilot, Harold Barnwell.

Based on a design by Frank Barnwell, the unarmed E.S.1 (below) led to development of the F.B.19.

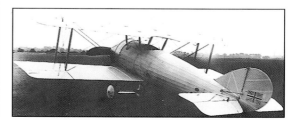

Two examples of the E.S.1 Mk II were built (above and below) and, also known as E.S.2s, were briefly tested by the RFC.

Assigned the designation E.S. (Experimental Scout) 1 and completed in August 1915, the redesigned aircraft was powered by a 100 hp Gnome Monosoupape rotary and carried no armament. An equi-span single-bay un-staggered biplane, the E.S.1 was aerodynamically clean and possessed an excellent performance, but view for the pilot was extremely poor. An improved version was then developed, powered by the 110 hp Clerget nine-cylinder rotary engine. This was assigned the official designation E.S.1 Mk II, although it was known to Vickers as the E.S.2. Two E.S.1 Mk IIs were built, one of these being fitted with a 0.303-in (7,7-mm) Vickers machine gun with Vickers-Challenger synchronising gear and sent to France in the summer of 1916 for operational trials with No 11 Sqn, RFC. The other E.S.1 Mk II was eventually similarly armed and tested with a 110 hp Le Rhône rotary, while the original E.S.1, too, was fitted with the gun and synchronization gear, and was at one time included on the strength of an RFC Home Defence squadron (No 50). The official evaluation of the E.S.1 in both versions pronounced the aircraft tiring to fly and difficult to land, and no production was ordered. The E.S.1 did, however, serve as a basis for the design of the later F.B.19. The following data relate to the Clerget-engined E.S.1 Mk II. *Max speed, 112 mph (180 km/h) at sea level, 106 mph (170 km/h) at 8,000 ft (2 440 m). Time to 8,000 ft (2 440 m), 12.65 min. Endurance, 2.0 hrs. Empty weight, 981 lb (445 kg). Loaded weight, 1,502 lb (681 kg). Span, 24 ft 4½ in (7,43 m). Length, 20 ft 3 in (6,17 m). Height, 7 ft 8 in (2,34 m). Wing area, 215 sq ft (19,97 m²).*

VICKERS F.B.8   UK

Only a single example was built of the F.B.8 (above and below), developed from the F.B.7.

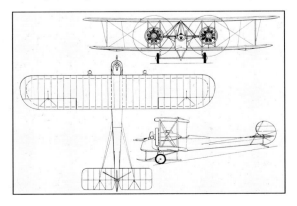

Although possessing a superficial resemblance to the F.B.7, the F.B.8, designed in the autumn of 1915 by Rex K Pierson, was a very much smaller, lightly-armed two-seat fighter carrying only a single 0.303-in (7,7-mm) Lewis gun as armament. Powered by two 100 hp Gnome Monosoupape rotaries, the F.B.8 began flight testing in November 1915, and performance proved to be good. The gunner was accommodated in the extreme nose and the pilot was seated beneath the trailing edge of the upper wing. From the outset, it was obvious that the armament carried by the F.B.8 could equally well be accommodated by a smaller, single-engined aircraft, but it had been hoped that an appreciably higher performance could be obtained by doubling the power available. Insufficient attention had been paid to the drag of such an aircraft, however, and performance proved lower than had been anticipated. Furthermore, the aircraft was insufficiently manoeuvrable for fighting duties and was discontinued. *Max speed, 98 mph (158 km/h) at 5,000 ft (1 525 m). Time to 5,000 ft (1 525 m), 10 min. Service ceiling, 14,000 ft (4 270 m). Endurance, 3.0 hrs. Empty weight, 1,840 lb (835 kg). Loaded weight, 2,700 lb (1 225 kg). Span, 38 ft 4 in (11,68 m). Length, 28 ft 2 in (8,58 m). Height, 9 ft 10 in (3,00 m). Wing area, 468 sq ft (43,48 m²).*

VICKERS F.B.9   UK

Dubbed unofficially the *Streamline Gunbus*, the F.B.9, which emerged towards the end of 1915, introduced numerous refinements over its predecessor, the F.B.5.

A derivative of the F.B.5, the F.B.9 (above and below) saw service in the Battle of the Somme.

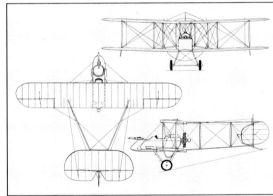

The fuselage nacelle was of improved aerodynamic form; the wings and tailplane sported rounded tips; streamlined Rafwires replaced stranded steel cables and turnbuckles for interplane bracing, and a plain, Vee-type undercarriage supplanted the twin skids previously used. The standard power plant remained the 100 hp Gnome Monosoupape rotary. Vickers built a

One of 95 examples of the F.B.9 (above) built by Vickers. Others were licence-built in France.

total of 95 F.B.9s, and a further 20-30 were built by Darracq in France, some of which were issued to the RFC (No 11 Sqn) and were used during the Battle of the Somme which began on 1 July 1916. The manufacture of the F.B.9 in Italy by Vickers-Terni fell through owing to political reasons. A version designated F.B.10 powered by an Isotta-Fraschini engine was proposed but not built. Outclassed by more advanced fighting aeroplanes, the F.B.9s saw only brief first-line service, the great majority being assigned tuitional tasks on delivery to the RFC, for which some were retrofitted with dual controls. For gunnery training, some F.B.9s were fitted with a Scarff ring on the front cockpit, but none remained on charge at the time of the Armistice. *Max speed, 83 mph (134 km/h) at sea level, 75 mph (121 km/h) at 6,500 ft (1 980 m). Time to 6,500 ft (1 980 m), 19 min. Service ceiling, 11,000 ft (3 355 m). Endurance, 4.5 hrs. Empty weight, 1,029 lb (467 kg). Loaded weight, 1,892 lb (858 kg). Span, 33 ft 9 in (10,29 m). Length, 28 ft 5½ in (8,67 m). Height, 11 ft 6 in (3,50 m). Wing area, 340 sq ft (31,59 m²).*

VICKERS F.B.12   UK

A compact two-bay biplane of pusher type, the F.B.12 was designed for the 150 hp Hart static radial engine, in the development of which the Hart Engine Company was being assisted by Vickers. With a single-seat nacelle faired out to a circular cross section and mounted in mid wing-gap, and tailbooms converging in side elevation to meet at the rear spar of the tailplane, the F.B.12 had a basic structure primarily of steel tube. Unavailability of an airworthy Hart engine led to the first F.B.12 being fitted with an 80 hp Le Rhône rotary, with which it flew in June 1916. Although underpowered, it demonstrated a creditable performance when tested at the Central Flying School in the following August. The Le Rhône was then replaced by a 100 hp Gnome Monosoupape, and, subsequently, new wings of greater span were fitted – overall span being extended by 3 ft 7 in (1,09 m) – with straight raked rather than elliptical tips. Redesignated F.B.12A, this aircraft was sent to France for operational evaluation in December 1916. A further aircraft was built – by Wells Aviation of Chelsea – with the Hart engine as the F.B.12B. This was flown early in 1917, but promptly crashed, helping to seal the fate of the Hart radial. A contract for 50 aircraft powered by the Hart had, on 10 November 1916, been awarded Vickers, the intention being to fit the series aircraft with a new, wooden

Elliptical wing-tips distinguished the first F.B.12 (below), here with Gnome Monosoupape engine.

The F.B.12 (above) achieved little success and was never fitted with the intended Hart engine.

nacelle and enlarged vertical tail surfaces as the F.B.12C. Production of the F.B.12C was sub-contracted to Wells Aviation, but with the loss of the F.B.12B, the Hart engine was abandoned. In the event, only 18 F.B.12C airframes were completed and these were fitted with a variety of engines, including the 110 hp Le Rhône nine-cylinder rotary and the 100 hp Anzani 10-cylinder radial. Testing at Martlesham Heath in May 1917 revealed insufficient elevator control at low speeds, heavy lateral control and other problems. Furthermore, the gun (a 0.303-in/7,7-mm Lewis) was considered to be badly positioned for changing ammunition drums. By this time, tractor fighters of superior performance were in RFC service and further development of the F.B.12 was therefore discontinued. The following data relate to the Le Rhône-powered F.B.12C. *Max speed, 87 mph (140 km/h) at 6,500 ft (1 980 m), 81 mph (130 km/h) at 10,000 ft (3 050 m). Time to 6,500 ft (1 980 m), 9.7 min. Service ceiling, 14,500 ft (4 420 m). Endurance, 3.25 hrs. Empty weight, 927 lb (420 kg). Loaded weight, 1,447 lb (656 kg). Span, 29 ft 7 in (9,02 m). Length, 21 ft 10 in (6,65 m). Height, 8 ft 7 in (2,62 m). Wing area, 237 sq ft (22,02 m²).*

VICKERS F.B.16   UK

Conceived, like the F.B.12, to utilise the 150 hp Hart engine, the F.B.16 was designed by Rex K Pierson. Completed and flown in the summer of 1916, it was a single-bay staggered biplane with a fuselage faired out fully to an elliptical cross section, the Hart engine being partly cowled, and armament consisting of a single centrally-mounted synchronised 0.303-in (7,7-mm) Vickers gun. During the course of testing, the part-cowling was removed from the engine to improve cooling, the decking aft of the cockpit was cut down and new vertical tail surfaces were fitted. With the ending of Hart engine development, the basic F.B.16 underwent very considerable redesign, reappearing as the F.B.16A with a 150 hp Hispano-Suiza water-cooled Vee-eight engine. This aircraft was destroyed in a crash on 20 December 1916, but a second identical aircraft was completed in the following month. The F.B.16A had flat fuselage sides and the single synchronised Vickers gun was supplemented by a Lewis mounted above the centre section. After receiving favourable reports during Martlesham Heath trials, it was re-engined with a 200 hp Hispano-Suiza engine as the F.B.16D, a wider-chord wing being fitted, with both gap and stagger increased, and a larger vertical tail fitted. The synchronised Vickers gun was replaced by a Lewis firing through the hollow propeller shaft. Because large contracts had been placed for the contemporary S.E.5a, particularly with Vickers, and because Martlesham Heath evaluation contained numerous design criticisms of which rectification would have been time consuming, the F.B.16D was not ordered into production. Nonetheless, work on a further development, the

The F.B.16A (below) was the rebuilt prototype with an Hispano-Suiza replacing the Hart engine.

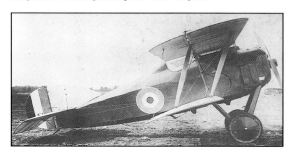

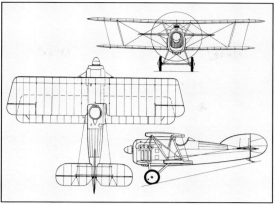

Increased wing chord and more vertical tail area distinguished the F.B.16D (above and below).

F.B.16E, continued, this having a 275 hp Lorraine-Dietrich 8Bd eight-cylinder Vee-type water-cooled engine and two 0.303-in (7,7-mm) synchronised Vickers guns totally enclosed in elongated blisters between the cylinder block fairings. The F.B.16E was tested at Villacoublay by the French authorities, encouraged by the manufacturer's performance claims, including a speed of 137 mph (220 km/h) at 10,000 ft (3 050 m) and the ability to climb to that altitude within 7.85 min. During Villacoublay trials, the F.B.16E allegedly returned performance figures unsurpassed by any of its contemporaries, but no production order was placed, and on 29 July 1918, the prototype crashed after its propeller disintegrated. The following data relate to the F.B.16D. *Max speed, 135 mph (217 km/h) at 10,000 ft (3 050 m), 126 mph (203 km/h) at 15,000 ft (4 570 m). Time to 10,000 ft (3 050 m), 10.45 min. Service ceiling, 18,500 ft (5 640 m). Endurance, 2.25 hrs. Empty weight, 1,376 lb (624 kg). Loaded weight, 1,875 lb (850 kg). Span, 25 ft 0 in (7,62 m). Length, 19 ft 6 in (5,94 m). Height, 8 ft 9 in (2,67 m). Wing area, 207 sq ft (19,23 m²).*

With a Lorraine-Dietrich engine, the F.B.16E (above) was tested in France, crashing there in July 1918.

VICKERS F.B.19   UK

Designed in 1916 by G H Challenger and flown for the first time in August of that year, the F.B.19 was a single-bay unstaggered equi-span biplane with a single 0.303-in (7,7-mm) Vickers gun mounted on the port side of the fuselage and a 100 hp Gnome Monosoupape engine. Ordered by the War Office for the RFC, the series version was powered by either the Gnome or the 110 hp Le Rhône. Some 50 F.B.19s were built, and, late in 1916, a batch of six was sent to France where, after operational evaluation, the fighter was deemed unsuited for the fighting conditions then evolving. At this time, some of the F.B.19s were delivered to the Russian government following demonstrations in Petrograd, Moscow, Kiev and Tiflis, but several were still in their crates on the docks at Archangel at the commencement of the Bolshevik revolution. These aircraft were destroyed by the Royal Navy, but a few others assembled prior to the Navy's action were flown in Bolshevik service. A modified version, the F.B.19 Mk II, was developed with wing stagger and either the Le Rhône or Cler-

Descended from the E.S.1, the Vickers F.B.19 (above) in its Mk I form had no wing stagger.

get 110 hp rotary. Only 12 Mk IIs were built and several of these were included in a batch of 12 F.B.19s sent to the Middle Eastern theatres of war. These were flown in Palestine and Macedonia from June 1917, but no squadron used the type exclusively and it was not well liked. The following data relate to the Le Rhône-powered F.B.19. *Max speed, 98 mph (158 km/h) at 10,000 ft (3 050 m) 90 mph (145 km/h) at 15,000 ft (4 570 m). Time to 5,000 ft (1 525 m), 5.6 min. Ceiling, 17,000 ft (5 180 m). Endurance, 3.25 hrs. Empty weight, 892 lb (405 kg). Loaded weight, 1,478 lb (670 kg). Span, 24 ft 0 in (7,31 m). Length, 18 ft 2 in (5,54 m). Height, 8 ft 3 in (2,51 m). Wing area, 215 sq ft (19,97 m²).*

In its Mk II form, the F.B.19 (above and below) was produced in small numbers for RFC service.

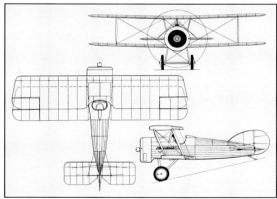

VICKERS F.B.11   UK

Designed by Howard Flanders as an airship destroyer, for which purpose it had an elevated gunner's station, or ''fighting top'', mounted on the centre section of the upper wing, the F.B.11 flew in late November 1916. Carrying a crew of three, including two gunners each provided with a 0.303-in (7,7-mm) Lewis gun, the F.B.11 was powered by a 250 hp Rolls-Royce Mk III 12-cylinder water-cooled engine – later to be named Eagle. The F.B.11 proved to be deficient in lateral control and the

A ''fighting top'' was an unusual feature of the F.B.11 (below), designed to combat airships.

first prototype eventually crashed and was written off, a second example never being completed as, in the meantime, it had been realised that the entire concept of the large airship destroyer was fundamentally unsound. *Max speed, 96 mph (154 km/h) at 5,000 ft (1 525 m), 81 mph (130 km/h) at 10,000 ft (3 050 m). Time to 5,000 ft (1 525 m), 16.5 min. Ceiling, 11,000 ft (3 355 m). Endurance, 7.5 hrs. Empty weight, 3,340 lb (1 515 kg). Loaded weight, 4,934 lb (2 238 kg). Span, 51 ft 0 in (15,54 m). Length, 43 ft 0 in (13,10 m). Height, 13 ft 8 in (4,16 m). Wing area, 845 sq ft (78,50 m²).*

VICKERS F.B.24   UK

A two-seat fighter-reconnaissance aircraft, the F.B.24 was yet another Vickers aircraft originally designed for the ill-fated and Vickers-sponsored Hart radial engine.

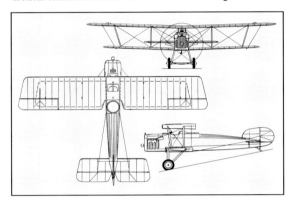

The F.B.24C (above and below) in its version with a frontal radiator for the Lorraine-Dietrich engine.

The prototype was completed in December 1916, but unavailability of the Hart engine resulted in its modification to accept the 150 hp Hispano-Suiza water-cooled engine as the F.B.24A, and the second airframe, the F.B.24B, being similarly powered. An unequal-span two-bay biplane, the F.B.24 had an armament of one fixed synchronised Vickers gun and one Lewis on a Scarff ring mounting. Both F.B.24A and 24B were re-engined with the 200 hp Hispano-Suiza with which they were redesignated as F.B.24Ds. Similar in general configuration was the F.B.24C, which was powered by a 275 hp Lorraine-Dietrich 8Bd water-cooled eight-cylinder Vee-type engine and armed with two synchronised Vickers guns, provision being made for emergency dual control in the gunner's cockpit. The F.B.24C and D both possessed good performance, but the limited view offered from the pilot's cockpit was considered unacceptable. Consequently, the Vickers team revised the basic design by lowering the upper wing so that it was attached directly to the upper longerons, the front cockpit being situated between the wing spars. With this change, the aircraft was de-

signated F.B.24E and power was provided by a 200 hp Hispano-Suiza. This same configuration was adopted for yet a further version of the design, the F.B.24G, which was a larger aircraft than its predecessors, with two-bay wings of equal span and chord and a 375 hp Lorraine-Dietrich 12-cylinder Vee-type engine. The F.B.24G was built in France by the Darracq concern, but it did not fly until 26 May 1919, and its performance and fate have gone unrecorded. The following data relate to the F.B.24D. *Max speed, 118 mph (190 km/h) at 10,000 ft (3 050 m). Time to 10,000 ft (3 050 m), 15 min. Endurance, 3.0 hrs. Empty weight, 1,630 lb (739 kg). Loaded weight, 2,610 lb (1 184 kg). Span, 35 ft 6 in (10,82 m). Length, 26 ft 0 in (7,92 m). Wing area, 340 sq ft (31,59 m²).*

VICKERS F.B.25   UK

Derived from the abortive F.B.23 design intended as a successor to the F.B.9, the F.B.25 two-seat night fighter was conceived to fulfil the same requirement as the Royal Aircraft Factory's N.E.1. Completed in the early spring of 1917, the F.B.25 carried its two crew members in staggered side-by-side seats, the gunner being positioned ahead and to starboard. Like the N.E.1, the F.B.25 was intended to carry the Vickers-built Crayford rocket gun with which it was supposed to attack hostile airships, and a small searchlight was originally to have been mounted in the extreme nose of the nacelle. The intention was to power the F.B.25 with the 200 hp Hispano-Suiza eight-cylinder water-cooled engine, and in order to minimise the risk of the aircraft turning over during a nocturnal landing, it was proposed to provide a nosewheel. In the event, non-availability of a 200 hp unit dictated installation of a 150 hp Hispano-Suiza, and neither searchlight nor nosewheel was fitted. A two-bay unstaggered equi-span biplane with tailbooms converging in elevation to meet at the rear spar of the tailplane, the F.B.25 carried its unusually wide nacelle at mid wing-gap. As well as the Crayford rocket gun, an interesting feature was the oleo-pneumatic undercarriage. Flight testing revealed poor characteristics, and when sent to Martlesham Heath in May 1917 (where it was eventually to crash), the official reports were sin-

With nose-mounted searchlight removed, the F.B.25 (below) is here seen carrying a Crayford rocket gun.

gularly unflattering, dismissing the F.B.25 as wholly unsuited for night fighting. The following performance data were established at Martlesham Heath. *Max speed, 86 mph (138 km/h) at 5,000 ft (1 525 m), 77 mph (124 km/h) at 10,000 ft (3,050 m). Time to 6,000 ft (1 830 m), 11.9 min. Service ceiling, 11,000 ft (3 355 m).*

Alone among Vickers' World War I fighters, the F.B.26 (below) received a name, being dubbed Vampire.

Endurance, 4.5 hrs. Empty weight, 1,608 lb (729 kg). Loaded weight, 2,454 lb (1 113 kg). Span, 41 ft 6 in (12,65 m). Length, 28 ft 1 in (8,56 m). Height, 10 ft 10 in (3,30 m). Wing area, 500 sq ft (46,45 m²).

VICKERS F.B.26 VAMPIRE   UK

Curiously retrogressive in design when built in May 1917, the pusher fighter with boom-carried empennage being decidedly *passé* at that stage in World War I, the F.B.26 single-seat fighter had its nacelle attached directly to the upper wing. The original concept provided for a single 0.303-in (7,7-mm) Lewis gun, but an additional Lewis had been introduced by the time that the F.B.26 reached Martlesham Heath for official testing in July 1917. Power was provided by a 200 hp Hispano-Suiza engine, but inadequate cooling led to the original single flat radiator being replaced by two separate radiator blocks. On 25 August 1917, the prototype was spun into the ground by Vickers' test pilot Harold Barnwell. Nonetheless, a month later, on 19 September, a contract was placed for six examples of a modified version of the F.B.26. The wing structure was

The F.B.26 (above and below) fitted with Eeman triple-gun mounting in the nose and the definitive wings.

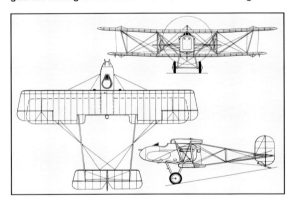

completely revised, radiator blocks were attached to the nacelle sides and a larger vertical tail was introduced. Interest in the F.B.26 centred on its potential as a Home Defence fighter, and it was proposed that armament would consist of two Lewis guns coupled with an Aldis sight and capable of several degrees of elevation and depression. However, in order to obtain greater firepower, the nacelle of the F.B.26 was modified to permit installation of an Eeman three-gun universal mounting. The first two F.B.26s had the trio of Lewis guns fixed to fire horizontally, but it was intended that the next aircraft would have a modified Eeman mounting capable of 45 deg of elevation. The first of the modified F.B.26s was flown in December 1917 with a 200 hp Hispano-Suiza engine. After testing at Martlesham Heath, this aircraft was assigned to No 141 Sqn in February 1918 for service evaluation. It was concluded that the F.B.26 was unsuited for Home Defence duties and work on the incomplete machines was halted, although the second and third examples had been completed and flown meanwhile. As the basic design was considered to possess potential in the close air support rôle, the second of the modified F.B.26s was fitted with a redesigned nacelle incorporating armour protection for the pilot and a 230 hp Bentley B.R.2 nine-cylinder rotary. This armoured "trench-strafer" was assigned the designation F.B.26A, and, under the official nomenclature scheme introduced in the spring of 1918, became the Vampire II, the F.B.26 being the Vampire I. In the event, the Vampire II had still to be completed by the end of June 1918, and thus came too late on the wartime scene. The following data are applicable to the Hispano-Suiza-engined modified F.B.26. *Max speed, 121 mph (195 km/h) at 5,000 ft (1 525 m),*

117 mph (188 km/h) at 10,000 ft (3 050 m). Time to 5,000 ft (1 525 m), 4.33 min. Service ceiling, 22,500 ft (6 860 m). Endurance, 3,0 hrs. Empty weight, 1,470 lb (667 kg). Loaded weight, 2,030 lb (921 kg). Span, 31 ft 6 in (9,63 m). Length, 23 ft 5 in (7,14 m). Height, 9 ft 5 in (2,87 m). Wing area, 267 sq ft (24,80 m²).

VICKERS 121 WIBAULT SCOUT   UK

Following the establishment in the UK on 8 June 1925 of Wibault Patents Limited as a subsidiary of Vickers and controlling Michel Wibault's light alloy aircraft manufacturing patents, Vickers began, in November 1925, to manufacture a series of WIB fighters (which see) against a contract obtained from Chile. The Vickers-built WIB 7 all-metal single-seat fighter, assigned the designation Type 121 and referred to as the Wibault Scout, differed from the standard French model in a number of respects. As a prototype of the Type 121, Wibault re-engined a standard aircraft with a 455 hp Bristol Jupiter VI nine-cylinder radial and fitted a Vickers oleo-pneumatic undercarriage, this aircraft being ferried to the UK in February 1926. Further modifications were introduced by Vickers, including the provision of stronger wing bracing struts, and the first Vickers-built Wibault Scout was flown at the end of June 1926, this being provided with an armament of two synchronised 0.303-in (7,7-mm) Vickers machine guns.

Vickers Type 121 (below) was the Wibault WIB 7 built under licence in the UK for the Chilean Army.

This, the first fighter to be built against a Chilean contract for 26 aircraft, was lost when its pilot was unable to extricate it from a spin, a replacement subsequently being produced. Deliveries to the air component of the Chilean Army began in November 1926, Wibault Scouts equipping *escuadrillas* within the *Grupo Mixto de Aviación* 1 at El Bosque. The fighters were freighted to Valparaiso in small batches as and when Chilean payments were forthcoming, the last of the batch being dispatched in October 1927. The Wibault Scouts proved somewhat unsatisfactory in Chilean service, several being lost in accidents – one, at least, as a result of shedding a wing in the air – but the type remained at least nominally in service with the *Fuerza Aérea de Chile* from that service's establishment in March 1930 until late-1934. The original Jupiter-engined WIB 7 was returned to its manufacturer in France for use as a demonstrator and no further examples were built by Vickers. *Max speed, 144 mph (232 km/h) at 15,700 ft (4 785 m). Time to 17,000 ft (5 180 m), 12 min. Service ceiling, 23,000 ft (7 010 m). Range, 300 mls (483 km). Empty weight, 1,920 lb (871 kg). Loaded weight, 2,970 lb (1 347 kg). Span, 36 ft 1 in (11,00 m). Length, 23 ft 8 in (7,21 m). Height, 11 ft 6 in (3,50 m). Wing area, 237 sq ft (22,00 m²).*

VICKERS 123   UK

Believing, at the end of 1925, that the time was right for the development of a new British fighter with a liquid-cooled engine and Rolls-Royce having a potentially suitable power plant under development, Vickers began work on the Type 123. Pending the availability of the Rolls-Royce engine, an Hispano-Suiza 12Jb 12-cylinder Vee-type engine of 465 hp was acquired from France and installed in the private-venture fighter which first flew on 9 November 1926. Of all-metal construction with fabric skinning, the Type 123 had the standard armament of twin synchronised 0.303-in (7,7-mm) Vickers machine guns and was a heavily-stag-

The Type 123 Hispano Scout (above and below) was designed to make use of the Rolls-Royce F.XI.

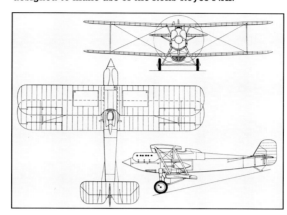

gered equi-span biplane with the fuselage carried within the gap, but with an abbreviated cabane. A semi-circular radiator was carried beneath the centre section of the lower wing. The availability in May 1927 of the Rolls-Royce F.XI engine made possible the original intention of the design team to be revived insofar as power plant was concerned, and the prototype was then rebuilt as the Type 141 (which see). *Max speed, 149 mph (240 km/h) at 10,000 ft (3 050 m). Time to 10,000 ft (3 050 m), 6.6 min. Empty weight, 2,278 lb (1 033 kg). Loaded weight, 3,300 lb (1 497 kg). Span, 34 ft 0 in (10,36 m). Length, 28 ft 6 in (8,69 m). Height, 9 ft 4 in (2,84 m). Wing area, 378 sq ft (35,12 m²).*

VICKERS 141   UK

After re-engining of the Type 123 with the 510 hp Rolls-Royce F.XI 12-cylinder Vee-type water-cooled engine as the Type 141, this fighter became a contender in January 1928 in a competition held at Martlesham Heath to select for the RAF a single-seat fighter meeting the requirements of Specification F.9/26. The Type 141 carried single 0.303-in (7,7-mm) machine guns in bulged housings on each side of the fuselage beneath the cockpit, and, apart from its engine, it differed from the Type 123 in having a retractable radiator in the forward fuselage in place of the fixed radiator beneath the wing centre section. Although possessing light and responsive controls, and a good performance, the Type

Rebuilt with an F.XI engine, the Type 123 became the Type 141 (above), being tested at Martlesham Heath before the civil markings were restored (below).

141 was bested by the Bristol Type 105 Bulldog and the Hawker Hawfinch. After its return from Martlesham Heath, the Type 141 was fitted with a revised vertical tail, a chin radiator and shortened rear undercarriage legs (enabling them to be anchored to the front wing spar), and was submitted for deck trials as a shipboard fighter to Specification 21/26. Other modifications included provision of an arrester hook, wheel brakes, interconnected elevators, detachable wing spar joints and hoist attachments. After initial trials, the dihedral of the lower wings was increased from three to five deg in an attempt to improve lateral stability. Sea trials took place aboard HMS *Furious* in June 1929, but these were not entirely satisfactory, and, after its return to Vickers, the Type 141 was flown in the 1929 King's Cup Air Race (5-6 July), but was forced to retire, the aircraft subsequently being scrapped. *Max speed, 177 mph (285 km/h). Empty weight, 2,650 lb (1 202 kg). Loaded weight, 3,700 lb (1 678 kg). Span, 34 ft 0 in (10,36 m). Length, 27 ft 0 in (8,23 m). Height, 8 ft 11 in (2,72 m). Wing area, 378 sq ft (35,12 m²).*

VICKERS 125 VIREO   UK

The Wibault system of construction was used by Vickers for the single Vireo (above and below).

Only one Vireo (below) was built. At one stage it was fitted with floats, but never flew in seaplane form.

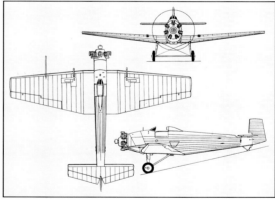

The Wibault system of metal airframe construction, with which Vickers had gained experience in building the Type 121 Wibault Scout, was utilised for a low-powered shipboard fighter to Specification 17/25. Submitted to the Air Ministry on 15 December 1925, this type, to be named Vireo, was awarded a one-aircraft contract. Intended to use either wheel or float undercarriage, and suitable for launching from a catapult, the Vireo was powered by a 230 hp supercharged Armstrong Siddeley Lynx IV seven-cylinder radial air-cooled engine and had provision for two wing-mounted 0.303-in (7,7-mm) machine guns firing outside the propeller disc. The structural design of the Vireo followed closely that of the Type 121, with the airframe virtually entirely covered by corrugated metal skinning. Flown early in March 1928 – flight testing having been delayed by extensive aerodynamic and structural tests undertaken at the Royal Aircraft Establishment – the Vireo was evaluated at Martlesham Heath in April and deck trials then took place aboard HMS *Furious* on 12 July. The Vireo was fitted with a twin-float undercarriage, but, in the event, seaplane trials that were to have taken place at the MAEE, Felixstowe, were not proceeded with. The speed performance of the Vireo was inevitably poor owing to the combination of low engine power and high drag resulting from the corrugated surfaces, and it suffered extremely unpleasant stalling characteristics. In consequence, development was terminated. *Max speed, 120 mph (193 km/h). Service ceiling, 14,750 ft (4 495 m). Empty weight, 1,951 lb (885 kg). Loaded weight, 2,550 lb (1 157 kg). Span, 35 ft 0 in (10,67 m). Length, 27 ft 8 in (8,43 m). Height, 11 ft 5 in (3,48 m). Wing area, 214 sq ft (19,88 m²).*

VICKERS 143   UK

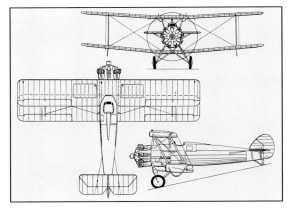

(Above) The Type 143 Bolivian Scout based on Type 141.

Evolved from the Type 141 to meet a Bolivian requirement which was to result, in 1929, in an order for six aircraft, the Type 143 was flown for the first time on 11 June of that year. The Type 143, known unofficially as the Bolivian Scout, differed from the Type 141 in having squared-off wingtips, longer-span, narrow-chord ailerons, a larger cut-out above the pilot's cockpit, a split-axle undercarriage, hoop-skids under the interplane struts and a modified fuselage faired to a broader oval section to mate with a 450 hp Bristol Jupiter VIA nine-cylinder air-cooled radial engine. As with the Type 141, the upper wing centre section was carried above the fuselage on splayed, cross-braced struts, the fuselage being supported above the lower wing by N-type struts. Construction was all metal and armament comprised two 0.303-in (7,7-mm) Vickers guns firing through troughs in the fuselage sides. The first of the six Type 143 fighters for Bolivia's *Cuerpo de Aviación* reached El Alto, La Paz, in January 1930, the sixth having been fitted with a Jupiter VII for Air Ministry trials at Martlesham Heath before being re-engined with a Jupiter VIA for shipment to Bolivia. By the time sporadic border disputes between Bolivia and Paraguay in the Chaco Boreal escalated, in June 1932, into full-scale warfare, the *Cuerpo de Aviación* of the former nation had already written off three of its Type 143s. On 30 September, one of the surviving Type 143s was effectively responsible for the first Paraguayan loss as a result of air-to-air combat – probably the first loss of an aircraft in such circumstances in the history of Latin-American military aviation – when a Wibault 73 received damage that, indirectly, was to lead to its destruction. *Max speed, 150 mph (241 km/h) at 11,500 ft*

Four of the six Vickers Type 143 Bolivian Scouts (above) at El Alto, La Paz, in 1931.

(3 505 m). Time to 13,100 ft (3 990 m), 10 min. Service ceiling, 20,000 ft (6 100 m). Empty weight, 2,246 lb (1 019 kg). Loaded weight, 3,120 lb (1 415 kg). Span, 34 ft 0 in (10,36 m). Length, 27 ft 10½ in (8,50 m). Height, 11 ft 3 in (3,43 m). Wing area, 336 sq ft (31,21 m²).

VICKERS 177   UK

Effectively the seventh Type 143 airframe, the Type 177 was intended as a single-seat shipboard fighter to Specification 21/26 – for which the Type 141 was also a contender – and flew for the first time on 26 November 1929. Powered by a 540 hp Bristol Jupiter XFS nine-cylinder radial air-cooled engine, the Type 177 was purely a private venture and was the final development in the line of Vickers single-seat tractor-engined fighter biplanes. Armament comprised the standard pair of synchronised 0.303-in (7,7-mm) Vickers machine guns. On 20 May 1930, the Type 177 demonstrated a terminal velocity dive from 20,000 ft (6 100 m) in which it attained a speed of 300 mph (483 km/h), and, in the following month, deck landing trials were performed aboard HMS *Furious*. Unaccustomed to steerable hydraulic brakes – an innovation featured by the Type 177 – one pilot applied the brakes too harshly and put the aircraft on its nose, after which these trials were discontinued. The Type 177 proved unacceptable for shipboard use and development was discontinued. *Max speed, 190 mph (306 km/h) at 13,120 ft (4 000 m). Time to 13,120 ft (4 000 m), 9.5 min. Range, 470 mls (756 km) at 175 mph (282 km/h) at 15,000 ft (4 570 m). Empty weight, 2,835 lb (1 286 kg). Loaded weight, 4,050 lb (1 837 kg). Span, 34 ft 3 in (10,44 m). Length, 27 ft 6 in (8,38 m). Height, 11 ft 3 in (3,43 m). Wing area, 336 sq ft (31,21 m²).*

The Vickers 177 shipboard fighter (below) was built as a private venture for official trials.

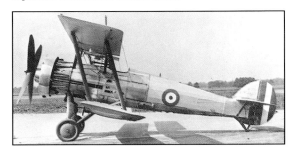

VICKERS 151 JOCKEY   UK

During the mid 'twenties, the Air Ministry accepted the philosophy that the primary concern of the RAF's fighter element should be interception of intruding enemy bombers. Accordingly, a specification was drawn up for a single-seat day interceptor capable of

overtaking an enemy aircraft flying at 150 mph (241 km/h) at 20,000 ft (6 100 m). This specification, F.20/27, resulted in contending monoplanes being ordered from de Havilland, Vickers and Westland. The Vickers design, the Type 151, was constructed on Wibault principles, but the rear portion of the fuselage was fabric covered. Power was provided by a nine-cylinder Bristol Mercury IIA radial engine rated at 480 hp at 13,000 ft (3 960 m), provision was made for an armament of twin 0.303-in (7,7-mm) Vickers guns, and the manufacturer assigned the appellation of Jockey to the fighter. Among novel features embodied by the Type 151 was a sideways-hinging engine mounting to ease accessibility for maintenance, all controls, wiring and piping, and even the Constantinesco gun synchronisation equipment hinging without disconnection.

The Vickers Type 151 (above) in its original form, with an uncowled Mercury engine.

Designed by Rex Pierson and J Bewsher, the Type 151 was flown in April 1930, but oscillation and inadequate torsional rigidity in the rear fuselage were encountered. Various palliatives were applied, such as wing root leading-edge slots to rectify the buffeting that was believed to create the problems, but these proved ineffectual, and in January 1932, when the Mercury IIA gave place to a 530 hp Jupiter VIIF, structural redesign of the rear fuselage was undertaken. It was intended to re-engine the Type 151 once more, this time with a Mercury IVS2 supercharged power plant, but, in June 1932, before this change could be made, the fighter failed to recover from a flat spin while undergoing trials at Martlesham Heath. Progressive redesign of the Type 151 was subsequently undertaken as the Jockey II, which, in its definitive form, was submitted to meet Specification F.5/34 as the Venom (which see). *Max speed, 218 mph (351 km/h) at 10,000 ft (3 050 m). Initial climb, 1,850 ft/min (9,40 m/sec). Time to 10,000 ft (3 050 m),*

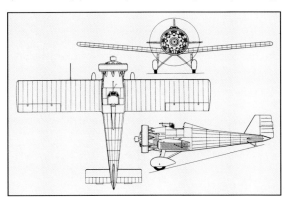

With a Jupiter engine and new rear fuselage, the Type 151 (above and below) also featured wheel spats.

(Above) A Type 143 Bolivian Scout of the *Cuerpo de Aviación*, as used in the conflict with Paraguay.

4.8 min. Empty weight, 2,260 lb (1 025 kg). Loaded weight, 3,161 lb (1 434 kg). Span, 32 ft 6 in (9,90 m). Length, 23 ft 0 in (7,01 m), Height, 8 ft 3 in (2,51 m). Wing area, 150 sq ft (13,93 m²).

VICKERS 161   UK

In the mid 'twenties, the British Air Ministry found attractive the possibility of the 37-mm COW (Coventry Ordnance Works) gun for use against bombers. Accordingly, Specification F.29/27 was issued calling for a single-seat dedicated bomber-interceptor armed with this large and heavy weapon. The specification called for the gun to be mounted in a fixed position to fire forward and upward at an oblique angle of at least 45 deg.

As first flown, the Type 161 (above) did not carry the COW gun for which it was designed.

Provision was to be made for oversize and automatically-fed ammunition clips totalling 50 shells, the entire COW gun mechanism had to be easily accessible to the pilot and steadiness as a gun platform was a prime requisite. Vickers submission to this Specification, the Type 161, was extraordinary in that it reverted to the long-abandoned pusher biplane formula with tail surfaces carried by booms. Despite its archaic configuration, however, the Type 161 embodied some advanced features and became the subject of a single-aircraft Air Ministry contract. An unequal-span two-bay biplane with comparatively high aspect ratio wings with duralumin plate and tube structure, it had a metal monocoque nacelle, accommodating the pilot to port and the COW gun to starboard, which was faired into the upper wing and raised above the lower wing by splayed N-type struts. The 530 hp Bristol Jupiter VIIF nine-cylinder radial carried at the rear of the nacelle drove a four-bladed propeller, aft of which was a curious, long tapered cone which, intended to promote directional stability, was supported by struts from the tubular tail-booms and the tailplane. The Type 161 was flown for the first time on 21 January 1931, and after provision of a broader-chord rudder, it flew extremely well, arriving at Martlesham Heath in September 1931 for official evaluation. Development was discontinued when official interest in promoting the quick-firing COW gun lapsed. Max speed, 185 mph (298 km/h) at 10,000 ft (3 050 m). Time to 10,000 ft (3 050 m), 5.8 min. Empty weight, 2,381 lb (1 080 kg). Loaded weight, 3,350 lb (1 520 kg). Span, 32 ft 0 in (9,75 m). Length, 23 ft 6 in (7,16 m). Height, 12 ft 4 in (3,76 m). Wing area, 270 sq ft (25,08 m²).

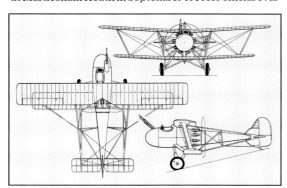

Modified for its Service trials, the Type 161 (above and below) had additional fin area.

VICKERS 279 VENOM   UK

The Venom (above), based on the Type 151 design, was Vickers' first retractable-undercarriage fighter.

Fundamentally a redesigned and improved Type 151 Jockey and, indeed, initially known as the Jockey II, the Type 279, for which Vickers adopted the name Venom, was intended to meet the requirements of Specification F.5/34. Powered by a 625 hp Bristol Aquila AE.3S nine-cylinder sleeve-valve radial engine enclosed by a long-chord NACA cowling, the Venom was a highly sophisticated aircraft, with a metal monocoque fuselage, its stressed skin being affixed by countersunk rivets. It was unique at the time it entered flight test, on 17 June 1936, in having 90-deg-deflection flaps. The Venom retained the sideways-hinging engine feature of the Type 151, and a battery of eight 0.303-in (7,7-mm) machine guns was mounted in the wings from the start of test flying. The Venom proved exceptionally manoeuvrable, with outstanding roll rate and turning radius, but it lacked the power to compete seriously with its Rolls-Royce liquid-cooled Vee-type-engined contemporaries, and, as no sufficiently compact British air-cooled radial of adequate power was available for installation, it was scrapped in 1939. Max speed, 312 mph (502 km/h) at 16,250 ft (4 955 m). Initial climb, 3,000 ft/min (15,25 m/sec). Service ceiling, 32,000 ft (9 755 m). Loaded weight, 4,156 lb (1 885 kg). Span, 32 ft 9 in (9,98 m). Length, 24 ft 2 in (7,36 m). Height, 10 ft 9 in (3,27 m). Wing area, 146 sq ft (13,56 m²).

By the time the Venom (above and below) was on test, the F.5/34 Specification had already been overtaken by later requirements.

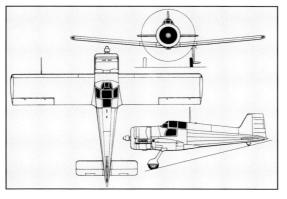

VICKERS 432   UK

The final attempt by Vickers to develop a fighter for the RAF began in 1939 with a design for a twin-engined

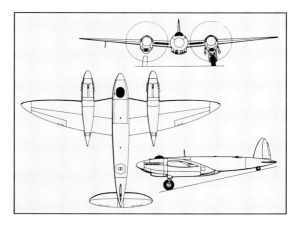

A pressure cabin and a six-cannon armament were features of the Vickers 432 (above and below).

heavy fighter featuring an armament of a 40-mm Vickers cannon in a dorsal turret. As the Type 414, this corresponded with the requirements of Specification F.22/39 and gained a two-aircraft contract in 1939. Turret development began in a Wellington test-bed but, in the course of 1940, the requirement was changed via Specification F.16/40, to emphasise high-altitude performance, as there were growing fears that the Luftwaffe would be able to launch operations over Britain at altitudes beyond the capabilities of existing RAF fighters. A more conventional armament of 20-mm cannon was adopted in the revised Vickers 420 design to the new specification, but further changes were called for in Specification F.7/41, including a pressure cabin. The Vickers response to this final requirement was Type 432, completely re-stressed and with an armament of six 20-mm cannon in a ventral blister. The original contract for the Type 414/420s was cancelled in 1941 and a new one substituted for two Type 432s. As finally built, the Type 432 was the first Vickers aircraft of wholly stressed-skin construction, and it made use of a so-called "lobster-claw" design for the wing torsion box, in which heavy-gauge skin had a thickened section to house the spanwise spar booms, giving a profile shaped like a lobster claw. The fuselage was a streamlined tube and the coolant radiators for the engines were buried within the wing. The pilot was accommodated in a relatively small, self-contained pressure cabin, his head being enclosed by a small, double-glazed dome, or "bubble", which hinged to one side for access and egress. Powered by two Rolls-Royce Merlin 61 12-cylinder Vee-type engines rated at 1,520 hp, the first prototype Type 432 was flown on 24 December 1942, initial trials revealing serious handling difficulties on the ground, the aircraft snaking while taxying and necessitating aft movement of the mainwheels to correct the bad tracking. The impossibility of making a three-point landing was only rectified by replacement

Of two prototypes ordered, only one Vickers 432 was completed (below), and tested in 1943-44.

of the Irving-type ailerons with surfaces of Westland type and alteration of tail settings. The competitive Westland Welkin was ordered into production and the second prototype of the Vickers fighter, the Type 446, was cancelled on 1 May 1943 before completion, although the first prototype was retained by Vickers for test purposes until the end of 1944. The estimated maximum speed of 435 mph (700 km/h) at 28,000 ft (8 535 m) was never attained as the Merlin 61 engines did not run satisfactorily above 23,000 ft (7 010 m). *Max speed (achieved), 380 mph (611 km/h) at 20,000 ft (6 100 m). Initial climb, 2,750 ft/min (13,97 m/sec). Time to 15,000 ft (4 570 m), 5.4 min. Estimated service ceiling, 37,000 ft (11 280 m). Range, 1,500 mls (2 414 km) at 30,000 ft (9 145 m). Empty weight, 16,373 lb (7 427 kg). Loaded weight, 20,168 lb (9 148 kg). Span, 56 ft 10½ in (17,34 m). Length, 40 ft 7½ in (12,38 m). Height, 13 ft 9 in (4,19 m). Wing area, 441 sq ft (40,97 m²).*

VILLIERS II (2AMC2) France

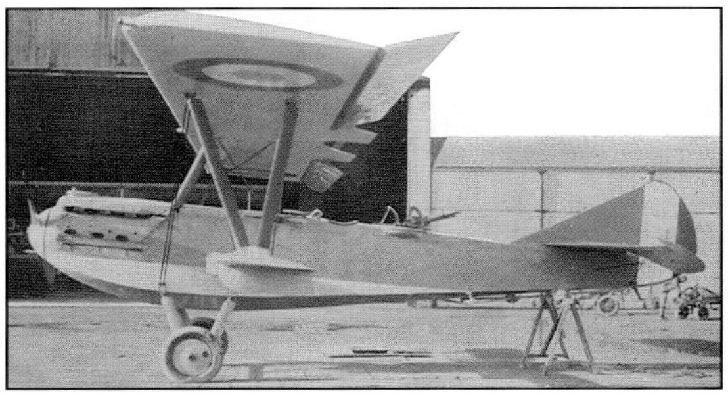

A watertight hull-type fuselage allowed the Villiers II (above and below) to alight on water in emergency.

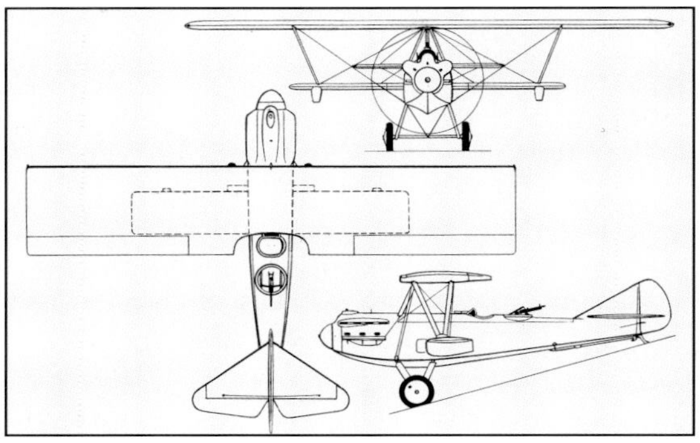

In 1924, the Ateliers d'Aviation François Villiers at Meudon, near Paris, designed a two-seat shipboard fighter to meet an official requirement. Assigned the company designation Type II, the fighter was a single-bay sesquiplane of mixed wood and steel construction with a jettisonable undercarriage and a watertight, boat-type fuselage planing bottom to permit alighting on water in an emergency. Armament consisted of two synchronised 7,7-mm Vickers guns and two Lewis guns of the same calibre on a flexible mounting in the rear cockpit. Two prototypes were ordered under the service designation Vil 2AMC2 (*Avion Marin Chasse biplace*), one powered by a 450 hp Hispano-Suiza 12HA 12-cylinder Vee-type engine and the other by a similarly-rated Lorraine-Dietrich 12Eb 12-cylinder W-type engine, the former undergoing comparative trials conducted by the *Aéronautique maritime* at Saint-Raphaël which ended in May 1925. Of the four contending types, two, the Vil 2AMC2 and the Levasseur P.L.5C2B, were selected for production, 30 of the former and 20 of the latter being ordered. The order for the Vil 2AMC2 placed on 19 December 1925 specified the Lorraine-Dietrich 12Eb engine, and at least one aircraft made simulated deck landings at Saint-Raphaël, but there is no record of any landing aboard the solitary French carrier *Béarn*. In May 1927, a number of Vil 2AMC2 fighters joined P.L.5C2BS in the land-based *Escadrille* 5C1 (redesignated *Escadrille* 3C1 on 1 February 1928) at Hyères. Both of these two-seat types were to give place to non-navalised single-seat Loire-Gourdou-Leseurre LGL 32s from *Aviation militaire* stocks in September 1928. *Max speed, 135 mph (217 km/h) at sea level, 122 mph (197 km/h) at 19,685 ft (6 000 m). Time to 19,685 ft (6 000 m), 28 min. Endurance, 3.0 hrs. Empty weight, 2,778 lb (1 260 kg). Loaded weight, 4,189 lb (1 900 kg). Span, 42 ft 7⅘ in (13,00 m). Length, 31 ft 2 in (9,50 m). Height, 12 ft 11⅞ in (3,96 m). Wing area, 430.57 sq ft (40,00 m²).*

VILLIERS V (5CN2) France

The Type V appeared in 1926 to meet an *Aviation militaire* requirement for a new two-seat night fighter. Powered by a 450 hp Lorraine-Dietrich 12Eb water-cooled 12-cylinder W-type engine, it was an unequal-span single-bay staggered biplane of wooden construction, the fuselage being a plywood monocoque and the wings being fabric covered. Armament consisted of the standard paired, synchronised 7,7-mm Vickers guns and twin Lewis guns on a flexible mounting in the rear cockpit. Provision was made for jettisoning the 105.6-Imp gal (480-l) fuel tank, and equipment included two landing beacons, flares and R/T. Evaluated as the Vil 5CN2, it was not considered by the *Aviation militaire* to offer an adequate advance in performance over the existing equipment of the *Escadrilles de Chasse de Nuit* to warrant a production order. *Max speed, 139 mph (224 km/h) at sea level, 130 mph (210 km/h) at 13,125 ft (4 000 m). Time to 21,325 ft (6 500 m), 43 min. Service ceiling, 22,965 ft (7 000 m). Empty weight, 2,809 lb (1 274 kg). Loaded weight, 4,641 lb (2 105 kg). Span, 39 ft 4⅓ in (12,00 m). Length, 28 ft 8½ in (8,75 m). Height, 10 ft 9⅞ in (3,30 m). Wing area, 430.57 sq ft (40,00 m²).*

The Villiers V (below) as tested in 1926.

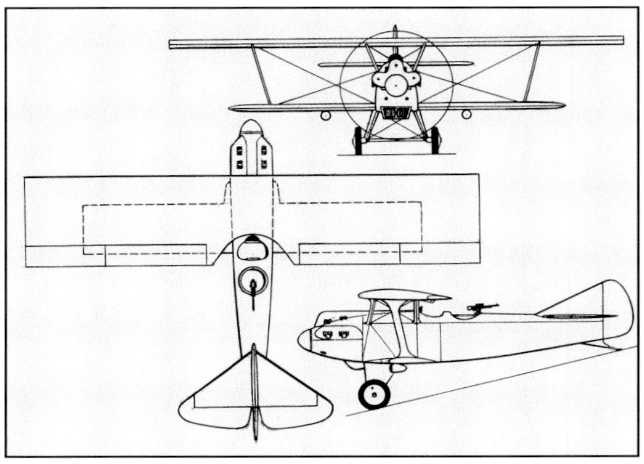

VILLIERS VIII (8AMC1) France

Undergoing operational trials at Saint-Raphaël during the closing weeks of 1926, the Type VIII was built in competition with the Levy-Biche LB 2AMC1 as a single-seat shipboard fighter with the ability to alight on water in an emergency. A parasol monoplane of wooden construction with a plywood-covered fuselage and fabric-covered wings, it featured a fuselage divided into watertight compartments and incorporated a boat-type planing bottom. The undercarriage was jettisonable and stabilising floats were attached to the steel-tube wing bracing struts. Powered by a 300 hp Hispano-Suiza 8Fb eight-cylinder Vee-type water-cooled engine and having an armament of twin synchronised 7,7-mm machine guns, the Type VIII underwent competitive tests as the Vil 8AMC1, but the LB 2AMC1 was selected to equip an *Escadrille* aboard the carrier *Béarn* and no further development was undertaken. *Max speed, 130 mph (210 km/h) at sea level, 114 mph (184 km/h) at 14,765 ft (4 500 m). Time to 19,685 ft (6 000 m), 49 min. Empty weight, 2,458 lb (1 115 kg). Loaded weight, 3,417 lb (1 550 kg). Span, 38 ft 5⅜ in (11,72 m). Length, 27 ft 6⅓ in (8,39 m). Height, 9 ft 1½ in (2,78 m). Wing area, 299.25 sq ft (27,80 m²).*

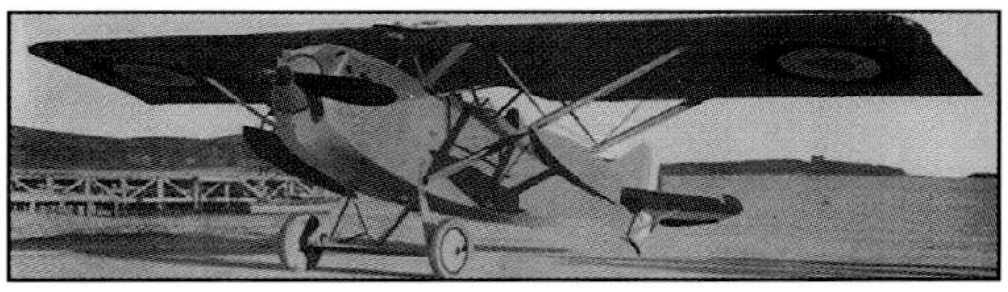

Continuing the theme of the Villiers II, the Type VIII (above and below) failed to obtain official approval.

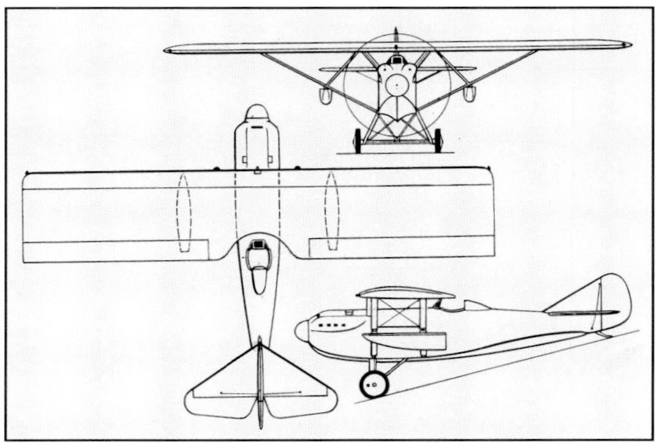

VILLIERS XXIV (24 CAN2) France

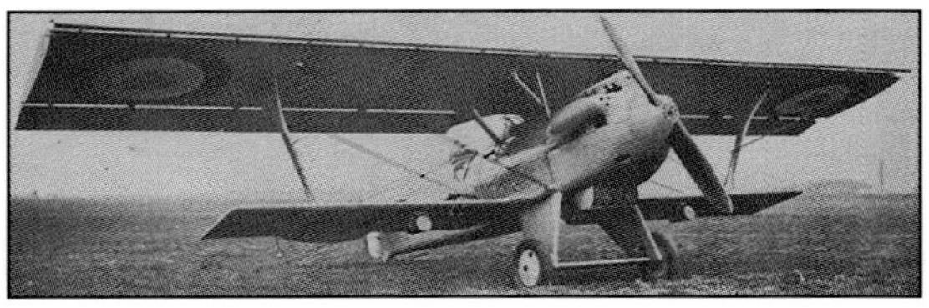

The Villiers XXIV (above) was based on the Type V with longer-span main wing, HP slots and flaps.

The first military aircraft built in France to embody Handley Page slots and flaps – the former occupying the entire leading edge of the upper wing and the latter extending from the wingtip to the cut-out over the pilot's seat, with the outer sections acting as ailerons – the Type XXIV was flown in March 1928. The manually-operated high-lift devices – comparatively rare at the time – were intended to reduce take-off and landing speeds for nocturnal operations, the aircraft being intended to meet a CAN2 (*Chasse, Armée, Nuit, biplace*) requirement. Powered by a 450 hp Lorraine-Dietrich 12Eb W-type water-cooled engine with a retractable ventral radiator bath, the Type XXIV, alias Vil 24 CAN2, had an armament of two fixed, synchronised 7,7-mm guns and paired guns on a Scarff ring in the rear cockpit. Construction was mixed, the upper wing being of spruce and the lower wing having duralumin spars and spruce ribs, both being fabric covered, and the plywood-covered fuselage was built up on laminated formers. The high-lift devices were subjected to prolonged trials, and, with a wing loading of 10.8 lb/sq ft (52,8 kg/m²), the Type XXIV had a minimum flying speed of 63 mph (101 km/h) with slots closed and 43 mph (70 km/h) with slots open. In the event, the *Aviation militaire* discontinued its CAN2 programme and further development of the Villiers contender stopped. *Max speed, 132 mph (212 km/h) at sea level, 124 mph (200 km/h) at 16,405 ft (5 000 m). Time to 19,685 ft (6 000 m), 50 min. Endurance, 3.0 hrs. Empty weight, 3,239 lb (1 469 kg). Loaded weight, 4,892 lb (2 219 kg). Span, 42 ft 7⅘ in (13,00 m). Length, 28 ft 8½ in (8,75 m). Height, 10 ft 9⅞ in (3,30 m). Wing area, 452.09 sq ft (42,00 m²).*

VL (FOKKER) D XXI (Netherlands) Finland

In 1940, the Finnish government reinstated production of the D XXI fighter at the VL (Valtion Lentokonetehdas, or State Aircraft Factory), Fokker having previously undertaken the design work necessary to adapt the basic airframe to take the Pratt & Whitney R-1535-SB4-C and -G Twin Wasp Junior engine of 825 hp. Eighty examples of this engine were procured from the USA (priority in the supply of Tampella-built Mercury engines having been earlier assigned to the Blenheim). Changes, other than the new engine, included the installation of all four 7,7-mm guns in the wings, the enlarging of the vertical tail surfaces and the revision of the cockpit canopy, the transparent areas being extended aft. The first R-1535-engined aircraft was flown in January 1941, and, although slower and less manoeuvrable than the Mercury-engined model, a total

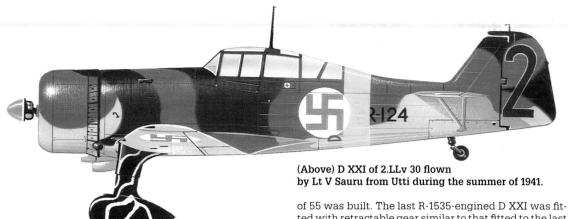

Finnish-built, Wasp-engined Fokker D XXIs (above and below) served with *Ilmavoimat* for 10 years, these being flown by 2.LLv 30 in the "Continuation War".

The last of 55 VL-built D XXIs (below) was completed with a retractable undercarriage.

(Above) D XXI of 2.LLv 30 flown by Lt V Sauru from Utti during the summer of 1941.

of 55 was built. The last R-1535-engined D XXI was fitted with retractable gear similar to that fitted to the last Finnish-built Mercury-engined D XXI. Flown on 2 March 1942, the example with the new gear demonstrated a 9 mph (14,5 km/h) increase in max speed, but reduced climb rate and manoeuvrability. After an accident suffered by this aircraft on 22 May 1944, the standard fixed undercarriage was fitted. The last R-1535-engined D XXIs were withdrawn from Finnish service in 1951. *Max speed, 272 mph (434 km/h) at 9,000 ft (2 745 m). Time to 3,280 ft (1 000 m), 1.4 min. Empty weight, 3,380 lb (1 533 kg). Loaded weight, 4,820 lb (2 186 kg). Span, 36 ft 1 in (11,00 m). Length, 27 ft 9 in (8,46 m). Height, 9 ft 8 in (2,95 m). Wing area, 174.38 sq ft (16,20 m^2).*

VL MYRSKY   Finland

On 8 June 1939, the VL (Valtion Lentokonetehdas) received a contract from the Ministry of Defence to design a new single-seat fighter. Chief designer was Dipl Ing A Ylinen, who was assisted by T Verkkola and M Vainio, and, within nine months of receiving the definitive prototype contract on 20 December 1940, the prototype of the Myrsky (Storm) was in final assembly. A conventional low-wing cantilever monoplane, the Myrsky had a plywood-skinned two-spar wooden wing and a welded steel-tube fuselage covered by dural panels forward and fabric aft. Power was provided by a Pratt & Whitney R-1830-SC3-G Twin Wasp 14-cylinder radial rated at 1,115 hp for take-off. The prototype was flown on 23 December 1941, but immediately encountered the first of what were to be many teething troubles. On 30 May 1942, the VL received a contract for three development aircraft which were to embody numerous detail structural and other changes, these including an increase in wing area of 14 sq ft (1,3 m^2) and a change in armament from two 12,7-mm and four 7,7-mm guns to three (in first and second) or four (in third aircraft) of the larger-calibre weapons. The first of these was completed on 30 April 1943, but crashed a week later, and the second suffered a wheels-up landing three months later, and broke up in the air shortly after resuming flight test. The third was evaluated in service, and, on 17 March 1944, lost both wings in a dive. In the meantime, VL had initiated production of the first series model which was referred to as the Myrsky II Series. All

(Immediately below) The 18th production Myrsky Srs II as flown by HLeLv 26, Kemi, Oct 1944, and (bottom) the penultimate series aircraft in post-war markings.

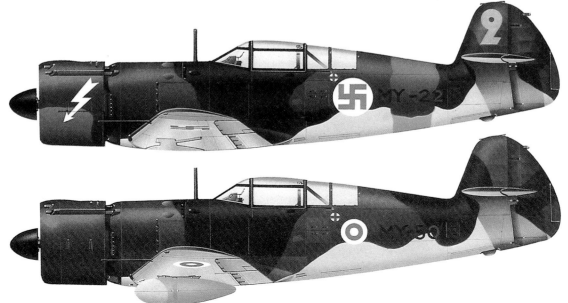

The first production VL Myrsky II (above), which flew at Tampere in December 1943.

the progressive changes that had been introduced in the pre-series aircraft were incorporated, armament was standardised on four 12,7-mm LKK/42 guns, and by the end of July 1944 the VL had completed 14 of the II Series aircraft, a further 16 having been delivered by the truce of 4 September. Production continued after the truce and the last five of the 47 built were delivered straight to the Air Force Depot on 30 December 1944 without flight testing. The Myrsky II series was assigned to a tactical reconnaissance squadron (TLeLv 12) which received its first aircraft on 23 July 1944, 20 being delivered to the squadron before the Armistice, and a second squadron (TLeLv 16) initiating conversion to the Myrsky meanwhile. The Myrsky was flown operationally over Lapland against the *Wehrmacht* under the terms of the Finnish-Soviet agreement, but *Ilmavoimat* flew this fighter only to a limited extent, and the service's doubts as to its durability and sturdiness, despite continuous reinforcement of various components, finally came to a head on 9 May 1947 when a Myrsky broke up in a dive, all aircraft of this type then being grounded. *Max speed, 292 mph (470 km/h) at sea level, 333 mph (535 km/h) at 11,155 ft (3 400 m). Time to 9,840 ft (3 000 m), 3.5 min. Range (internal fuel), 310 mls (500 km). Empty weight, 5,152 lb (2 337 kg). Max loaded weight, 7,083 lb (3 213 kg). Span, 36 ft 1 in (11,00 m). Length, 27 ft 5¾ in (8,35 m). Height, 9 ft 10 in (3,00 m). Wing area, 193.76 sq ft (18,00 m^2).*

Service use of the Myrsky II (above and below) by *Ilmavoimat* began with TLeLv 12 in mid-1944.

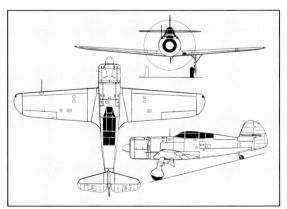

VL HUMU   Finland

One of the most extraordinary fighters built and flown during World War II was the Humu – literally "Reckless" – produced by Valtion Lentokonetehdas. It was not that the Humu was unconventional in any respect.

It was a *copy* of a seven-year-old American design adapted to make use of locally-available materials and captured equipment, and built without benefit of licence or assistance from the parent manufacturer. The Finnish air arm, *Ilmavoimat*, had acquired 43 Brewster B-239 shipboard fighters (which see) that had been declared surplus to US Navy requirements. These had proved singularly successful in *Ilmavoimien* service, and, in 1942, it was proposed that an attempt be made by the VL to remedy a shortfall of fighters of this type by producing a copy. Because of shortages of metal, this was to make as much use as possible of wood and to embody so-called "war booty" instrumentation and power plant – equipment captured from the Soviet forces by the Finns themselves and similar equipment captured by the *Wehrmacht* and sold to the Finns. The task of designing an entirely new wooden wing was assigned to M T Vainio, who was also responsible for the overall project, and, in October 1942, an order was placed with the VL for four prototypes, the intention at that time being to build a series of 90 aircraft. The chosen engine was the 930 hp Shvetsov M-63, which was flown on 5 June 1943 in a B-239. Static testing of the wooden wing was not entirely satisfactory. Nevertheless, in September 1943, orders were confirmed for five prototypes of the Humu and 55 production aircraft. The wooden wing was found to add 551 lb (250 kg) to airframe weight, however, and the transfer of the fuel tanks from the wing to the fuselage shifted the cg aft, adversely affecting manoeuvrability. Initiation of series production was, therefore, delayed pending results of prototype tests, and in the summer of 1944 the programme was terminated as it was concluded that the Humu would have inadequate combat capability by the time it achieved service. Only one prototype Humu was completed and, this, having an armament of three 12,7-mm guns and a mix of Finnish and Soviet instrumentation, flew on 8 August 1944. The M-63 engine failed to give its full power during subsequent flight testing, but 19 hrs 50 min were flown before, in 1945, the sole example of this remarkable aircraft was placed in storage. *Max speed, 267 mph (430 km/h) at 15,090 ft (4 600 m). Time to 13,125 ft (4 000 m), 5.0 min. Empty weight, 4,519 lb (2 050 kg). Loaded weight, 6,382 lb (2 895 kg). Dimensions as for B-239 apart from length of 26 ft 4⅛ in (8,03 m).*

Although five prototypes had been ordered, only one example of the VL Humu (below) was completed.

VL PYÖRREMYRSKY   Finland

Conceived to make maximum use of indigenous materials with emphasis on suitability for operation from small Finnish frontline airfields under the most severe climatic conditions, the Pyörremyrsky (Whirlwind) was designed by Dipl-Ing Torsti R Verkkola. Powered by a 12-cylinder inverted-Vee Daimler-Benz DB 605AC engine rated at 1,475 hp, the Pyörremyrsky had a single-spar wooden wing with plywood skinning and a fuselage of steel-tube construction with detachable metal panels forward and a wooden ply-covered monocoque aft. Armament comprised one engine-mounted 20-mm MG 151 cannon and two 12,7-mm LKK/42 machine guns, provision being made for two 441-lb (200-kg) bombs underwing. Prototype construction was slowed by the preoccupation of the VL with higher priority programmes, and work on the Pyörremyrsky, which had languished for several months, came to a halt with the Finnish-Soviet Armistice of 4 September 1944. Somewhat surprisingly, construction of the fighter was resumed later, in January 1945. A DB 605AC engine was removed from a Bf 109G and installed in the prototype, which flew for the first time on

Operational experience with the Messerschmitt Bf 109G influenced design of the Pyörremyrsky (above and below), only one prototype of which was built.

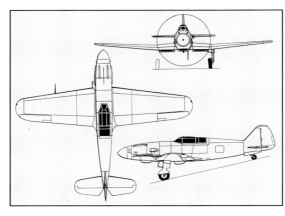

21 November 1945. The Pyörremyrsky could outclimb the Bf 109G-6 and was more manoeuvrable, but, as no funds were available for the purchase of new aircraft for *Ilmavoimat* and sufficient Bf 109Gs remained to equip the *Ilmavoimien* fighter force that was permitted under the Armistice terms, the prototype was grounded after 30 hours flying and the programme terminated. *Max speed, 324 mph (522 km/h) at sea level, 385 mph (620 km/h) at 21,000 ft (6 400 m). Time to 16,405 ft (5 000 m), 4.5 min. Endurance (internal fuel), 1.5 hrs. Empty weight, 5,774 lb (2 619 kg). Loaded weight, 7,297 lb (3 310 kg). Span, 34 ft 0⅔ in (10,38 m). Length, 32 ft 3¾ in (9,85 m). Height, 12 ft 9¼ in (3,89 m). Wing area, 204.52 sq ft (19,00 m²).*

VOUGHT FU-1   USA

In May 1922, the former Lewis and Vought Corporation was reorganised as the Chance Vought Corporation and the first product of the company under its new appellation was the UO-1 catapult-launched two-seat observation floatplane. In 1926, two promising catapult fighter designs were being developed by Boeing (XF3B-1) and Curtiss (XF7C-1), but, as production deliveries of these were some distance in the future, in June 1926, the US Naval Bureau of Aeronautics (BuAer) ordered for interim use aboard the catapults of US Navy capital vessels a single-seat fighter variant of the two-

Usually flown as a floatplane, the Vought FU-1 (below) served ashore briefly with wheeled undercarriage.

seater as the UO-3. In October 1926, the designation of this interim fighter, of which 20 had been ordered, was changed to FU-1, and by April 1927 all had been delivered. The FU-1 was a fabric-covered two-bay biplane of wood and steel-tube construction powered by a Wright J-5 (R-790) Whirlwind radial with an integral supercharger and rated at 220 hp. By comparison with the UO-1, structural strength was increased to permit unlimited aerobatics and diving speeds of up to 200 mph (322 km/h), and standard fighter armament of two 0.3-in (7,62-mm) cowl guns was fitted. Provision was made for interchangeable wheel and float undercarriages. From October 1927 to June 1928, 12 of the FU-1s were embarked aboard the battleships of the Battle Fleet. They were subsequently fitted with wheel undercarriages and were shore-based for three months until replaced by Boeing F3B-1s, all 20 having been converted to two-seat deck-landing trainers by the end of 1928 under the designation FU-2. The following data relate to the FU-1 in float fighter form. *Max speed, 144 mph (232 km/h) at 13,000 ft (3 960 m). Time to 5,000 ft (1 525 m), 5.0 min. Range, 410 mls (660 km). Empty weight, 2,074 lb (941 kg). Loaded weight, 2,774 lb (1 258 kg). Span, 34 ft 4 in (10,46 m). Length, 28 ft 4½ in (8,65 m). Height, 10 ft 2 in (3,10 m). Wing area, 290 sq ft (26,94 m²).*

A Vought FU-1 (above) serving with VF-2B from USS *Langley*, and (below) a three-view drawing of the FU-1.

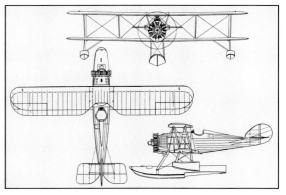

VOUGHT XF2U-1   USA

Early in 1927, the US Navy BuAer conceived a requirement for a two-seat fighter for fleet defence and contracts were signed on 30 June for the XF2U-1 and the Curtiss XF8C-2. As it was found that the fighter

The F2U-1 (above and below) was completed too late to compete effectively for a US Navy order.

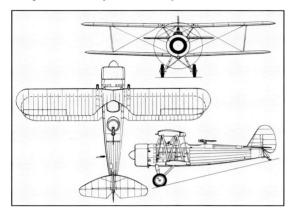

could not be based, as at first hoped, on the O2U observation aircraft, considerable delay resulted in completing the Vought prototype, which was not flown until 21 June 1929. The XF2U-1 had a steel-tube fuselage, wooden wings and fabric skinning, power being supplied by a 450 hp Pratt & Whitney R-1340C Wasp engine and armament comprising two 0.3-in (7,62-mm) machine guns in the upper wing centre section and a similar calibre weapon on a flexible mount in the rear cockpit. By the time that the XF2U-1 reached Anacostia for official evaluation, the BuAer had already placed a contract for further development of the competitive Curtiss fighter (XF8C-4), and although the Vought aircraft met all contractual guarantees it was rejected. Assigned to the Naval Aircraft Factory in February 1930 as a utility aircraft, it was damaged beyond repair on 6 March 1931. *Max speed, 146 mph (235 km/h) at sea level. Time to 9,100 ft (2 775 m), 10 min. Max range, 495 mls (797 km). Empty weight, 2,532 lb (1 148 kg). Loaded weight, 3,886 lb (1 763 kg). Span, 36 ft 0 in (10,97 m). Length, 27 ft 0 in (8,23 m). Height, 10 ft 0 in (3 05 m). Wing area, 318.5 sq ft (29,59 m²).*

VOUGHT V-80   USA

Based on the two-seat Corsair reconnaissance biplane, this V-80-F (above) was built for Argentina in 1934.

In 1932, the Vought company, believing an export market to exist for a single-seat fighter among its existing customers for the two-seat Corsair observation aircraft and reconnaissance-bomber (eg, V-65 and V-66), developed the V-80. Designed to adhere structurally as closely as possible to the two-seater to simplify spares supply and maintenance, a V-80 demonstrator was flown early in 1933. Powered by a Pratt & Whitney R-1340-SD Hornet engine rated at 675 hp at 6,000 ft (1 830 m), the V-80 had provision for an armament of four 0.3-in (7,62-mm) guns, two in the upper wing centre section and two firing through the engine cowling, and could carry a 500-lb (227-kg) bomb load. The standard wheel undercarriage was interchangeable with a single central float with outrigger stabilising floats. Three examples (V-80P) were ordered by Peru, these having the 700 hp R-1690-T1D1 Hornet and the first example flew on 19 May 1933. These were supplied with the interchangeable float undercarriages. One

further example was built, the V-80F with a similarly-rated R-1690-SD engine, this being flown on 10 April 1934 and sold to Argentina. The original V-80 demonstrator, with armament removed, was sold as the V-135 to the Connecticut State Department of Aeronautics, and, in 1935, was utilised by Pratt & Whitney as an engine test bed. The following data relate to the V-80P with wheel undercarriage. *Max speed, 189 mph (304 km/h) at 6,000 ft (1 830 m). Time to 15,400 ft (4 695 m), 10 min. Range, 760 mls (1 233 km). Empty weight, 3,546 lb (1 608 kg). Loaded weight, 4,856 lb (2 203 kg). Span, 36 ft 0 in (10,97 m). Length, 30 ft 11¾ in (9,44 m). Height, 10 ft 5½ in (3,19 m). Wing area, 337 sq ft (31,31 m²).*

VOUGHT XF3U-1   USA

By the spring of 1931, several months of operation of the Curtiss F8C-4 aboard the USS *Saratoga* had proved conclusively that this type was unsatisfactory in the fleet fighter rôle. As a consequence, the US Navy's BuAer reformulated its two-seat fighter requirement, and, from seven proposals received in April 1932, those of Vought and Douglas were selected, contracts being signed on 30 June 1932 for one prototype of each as the XF3U-1 and XFD-1 respectively. The XF3U-1 was flown on 9 May 1933, and was of all-metal construction with fabric skinning apart from the metal-covered fixed tail surfaces. Powered by a 14-cylinder Pratt & Whitney R-1535-64 Twin Wasp Junior geared and supercharged engine rated at 700 hp at 8,900 ft (2 715 m), the XF3U-1 had an armament of two 0.3-in (7,62-mm) cowl guns and a third gun of similar calibre on a flexible mounting in the rear cockpit. It demonstrated a marginal performance superiority over the competitive XFD-1, but the BuAer had meanwhile lost interest in the two-seat fighter category, and, in November 1933, it was decided to adapt the XF3U-1 for the scout-dive bomber rôle as the XSBU-1. *Max speed, 210 mph (338 km/h) at 8,900 ft (2 710 m). Range, 570 mls (917 km). Empty weight, 3,435 lb (1 558 kg). Loaded weight, 5,100 lb (2 313 kg). Span, 31 ft 6 in (9,60 m). Length, 26 ft 6½ in (8,09 m). Height, 10 ft 11 in (3,33 m). Wing area, 294.6 sq ft (27,37 m²).*

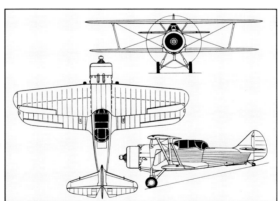

The XF3U-1 (above and below) was built to a US Navy requirement that failed to lead to production.

VOUGHT V-141   USA

When, on 30 July 1935, the experimental Northrop 3A single-seat fighter (which see) was lost over the Pacific, the Northrop Corporation elected to discontinue development of this type. Anxious to participate in the USAAC single-seat pursuit contest for which it had been designed, Chance Vought Aircraft acquired the

Built rapidly in 1936, the V-141 (above) was a slightly modified version of the Northrop 3A.

rights to the Northrop 3A early in 1936, and, on 29 March, 43 days after the decision to build the aircraft had been taken, a modified prototype was flown as the V-141. The Vought aircraft adhered closely to the Northrop design, apart from having a new undercarriage and a shorter-chord engine cowling housing a marginally more powerful Pratt & Whitney R-1535-A5G Twin Wasp Junior 14-cylinder radial rated at 750 hp. The V-141 displayed poor directional control and spinning characteristics and was rejected by the USAAC. In an attempt to improve the handling characteristics of the V-141, the rudder was substantially enlarged and the tailplane redesigned, the fighter being redesignated V-143 (which see). *Max speed, 274 mph (441 km/h) at 10,000 ft (3 050 m). Time to 10,000 ft (3 050 m), 3.9 min. Range, 704 mls (1 133 km). Empty weight, 3,515 lb (1 594 kg). Loaded weight, 4,430 lb (2 009 kg). Span, 33 ft 6 in (10,21 m). Length, 22 ft 10 in (6,95 m). Height, 9 ft 8 in (2,94 m). Wing area, 187 sq ft (17,37 m²).*

Illustrated below with enlarged tail, the V-141 failed to arouse the interest of the USAAC.

VOUGHT V-143   USA

The V-141 having acquired a somewhat alarming reputation, the aircraft was redesignated V-143 and, with modifications to the tail unit, entered in an Argentine fighter contest. As the spinning characteristics of the fighter were still unsatisfactory, the prototype was fitted with an anti-spin chute before demonstration, a fact of which a competing manufacturer made capital. In May 1937, in an attempt to improve the marketing prospects of the V-143, a number of engineering changes were introduced. The rear fuselage was lengthened considerably and an SB2U-1-style tail assembly was fitted in an attempt to eradicate the handling shortcomings of the fighter. At the same time, a Pratt & Whitney R-1535-SB4G engine of 825 hp was installed. The USAAC evaluated the modified prototype on 18 June 1937, but again rejected the aircraft. As no export orders for the fighter – which was also offered with a 525 hp Wasp Junior engine as the V-150 – materialised, the sole V-143 prototype was sold to the Japanese Imperial Navy, which assigned it the designation AXV1. Although it was later to be widely alleged that the Mitsubishi A6M Zero-Sen was based on the V-143, there was no truth in such allegations, although Vought's method of undercarriage retraction provided the

Built as the V-141, the slightly modified prototype was offered to Argentina as the V-143 (below).

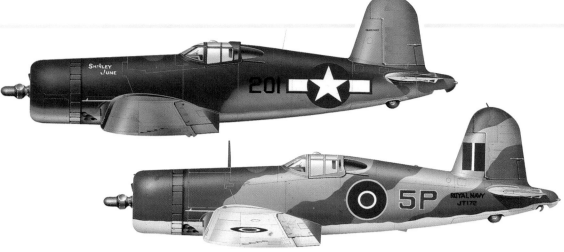

With lengthened rear fuselage and new tail, the V-143 (above and below) was sold to Japan.

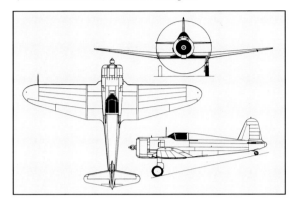

inspiration for that of the Japanese fighter. The following data relate to the V-143 in its definitive form. *Max speed, 292 mph (470 km/h) at 11,485 ft (3 500 m). Time to 10,000 ft (3 050 m), 3.1 min. Range, 808 mls (1 300 km). Empty weight, 3,490 lb (1 583 kg). Loaded weight, 4,370 lb (1 982 kg). Span, 33 ft 6 in (10,21 m). Length, 26 ft 0 in (7,92 m). Height, 9 ft 4 in (2,84 m). Wing area, 187 sq ft (17,37 m²).*

VOUGHT F4U-1 & F4U-2 CORSAIR   USA

An October 1940 photograph (above) of the XF4U-1, which, in that month, surpassed 400 mph (644 km/h).

Following receipt on 1 February 1938 of a US Navy BuAer request for single-seat shipboard fighter proposals, a Vought team led by Rex B Beisel effectively designed the smallest practical airframe that could be built around the largest and most powerful air-cooled radial engine then under development. Assigned the company designation V-166B, the fighter employed an inverted gull wing in order to provide the necessary ground clearance for the immense propeller demanded by the big engine while keeping undercarriage length and ground angle to a minimum. A prototype was ordered on 30 June 1938 as the XF4U-1, this flying for the first time two years later, on 29 May 1940, powered by a Pratt & Whitney XR-2800-4 Double Wasp 18-cylinder radial of 1,850 hp for take-off. Armament comprised a 0.5-in (12,7-mm) gun in each wing and one similar weapon plus a 0.3-in (7,62-mm) gun in the forward fuselage. On 1 October 1940, the XF4U-1 became the first US aircraft of any type to exceed 400 mph (644 km/h) in level flight, attaining 404 mph (650 km/h) during a flight between Stratford and Hartford. In the light of European combat reports, modifications were requested by the US Navy to improve the operational capability of the series F4U-1, for which an initial contract calling for 584 aircraft was placed on 30 June 1941. Retaining the name Corsair, which had previously been a company appellation for several Vought aeroplanes, the F4U-1 had six 0.5-in (12,7-mm) Browning MG 53-2 guns in the wings, the fuselage-mounted weapons being discarded. The fuel system was revised, necessitating repositioning of the pilot's cockpit 3 ft (91.4 cm) aft to restore the CG position, and a

2,000 hp R-2800-8 engine was installed, the first series aircraft flying on 25 June 1942. Sufficient F4U-1s had been delivered by the following September to permit a US Marine Corps squadron (VMF-124) to equip with the type, this being declared combat ready on 28 December and arriving on Guadalcanal on 12 February 1943. The US Navy considered the Corsair unsuitable for deck operation, and, in the event, was not to clear it for shipboard use until April 1944 – some nine months after the Royal Navy commenced carrier operations with the type. The raising of the cockpit by 7 in (18 cm) and introduction of a frameless, clear-view-type canopy resulted in the F4U-1A, this standard being introduced with the 689th production aircraft. The 862nd and subsequent F4U-1As were fitted with the water injection-equipped R-2800-8W engine providing 2,250 hp. By the end of 1943, Vought had delivered 1,958 Corsairs. To these were added 377 Goodyear-built aircraft (as FG-1s) and Brewster had delivered a further 136 (as F3A-1s). Under Lend-Lease, the UK took delivery of 95 F4U-1s (as Corsair Is) and 510 F4U-1As (as Corsair IIs), with deliveries commencing 1 June 1943. British Corsairs had some 16 in (41 cm) clipped from their wingtips to permit below-deck stowage on the smaller British carriers. With four 20-mm M2 cannon mounted in the wings in place of the 0.5-in (12,7-mm) weapons, 200 aircraft were delivered as F4U-1Cs, and the next version, the F4U-1D, reverted to the smaller-calibre guns, but had twin pylons beneath the centre section for drop tanks or a pair of 1,000-lb (454-kg) bombs. The F4U-1D entered production in April 1944, being built by Brewster as the F3A-1D and by Goodyear as the FG-1D. Vought-built Lend-Lease Corsairs for the UK were designated F4U-1B by the US Navy; 430 Brewster-built F3A-1Ds supplied to the UK became Corsair IIIs and 977 Goodyear-built FG-1Ds became Corsair IVs, the UK thus receiving 2,012 Corsairs (which equipped 19 squadrons). A further 370 F4U-1Ds were delivered to New Zealand. Vought built a total of 4,102 F4U-1s, Brewster completed 735 F3A-1s before this production line was terminated in July 1944, and Goodyear manufactured 3,808 FG-1s. In December 1941, Vought had been asked to design a night fighting version of the Corsair as the XF4U-2. Other priorities led to this model being dropped, but modifications were made to 12 F4U-1s by the Naval Aircraft Factory at Philadelphia to

Carefully restored, this surviving F4U-1D Corsair (below) is seen in 1944 US Navy markings.

(Top) An F4U-2 night fighter of USMC Sqn VMF(N)532, Kwajalein, 1944. (Immediately above) Corsair I of No 1835 Sqn at Brunswick, NS, late 1943.

suit them for nocturnal operations. Two guns were deleted and a radome containing early AI radar was fitted on the starboard wingtip. Also fitted with an autopilot, this adaptation was designated F4U-2, six being sent to Munda, New Georgia, to equip a specialist night fighting unit (VFN-75), and the other six equipping a unit (VFN-101) aboard the USS *Essex*. The data relate to the F4U-1D. *Max speed, 320 mph (515 km/h) at sea level, 392 mph (631 km/h) at 24,000 ft (7 315 m). Time to 10,000 ft (3 050 m), 5.1 min. Max range (internal fuel),*

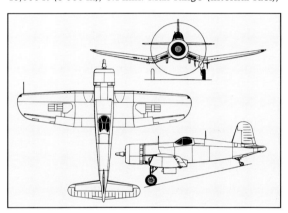

(Above) The initial series Vought F4U-1.

Flown by Lt (jg) Ira C Kepford, USN, this F4U-1A of VF-5B (above) displays the pilot's 16 victories.

1,562 mls (2 514 km). Empty weight, 8,873 lb (4 025 kg). Max loaded weight, 13,846 lb (6 280 kg). Span, 40 ft 11¾ in (12,49 m). Length, 32 ft 9½ in (9,99 m). Height, 15 ft 0¼ in (4,58 m). Wing area, 314 sq ft (29.17 m²).

VOUGHT XF4U-3 (FG-3) CORSAIR   USA

As early as 14 June 1941, the US Navy requested a design study for a high-altitude Corsair with a turbo-supercharged engine, three prototypes being ordered in March 1942 under the designation XF4U-3. These were to be powered by the Pratt & Whitney XR-2800-16(C) engine, which, with a 1009A turbo-supercharger, maintained 2,000 hp up to 40,000 ft (12 190 m), and were to be conversions of series (F4U-1 and -1A) airframes. Twenty-seven similar Goodyear-built FG-3s were ordered, although, owing to the relatively low priority enjoyed by the programme, this quantity was reduced to 13. The first XF4U-3 flew on 22 April 1944, and only one FG-3 was completed, and this as a conversion from an FG-1A, before the entire programme was cancelled. Max speed, 314 mph (505 km/h) at sea level,

The XF4U-3B (above), third of the -3 Corsair prototypes, featured revised armament.

412 mph (663 km/h) at 30,000 ft (9 145 m). Initial climb, 2,990 ft/min (15,20 m/sec). Range (max external fuel), 1,430 mls (2 300 km). Empty weight, 9,039 lb (4 100 kg). Max loaded weight, 13,143 lb (5 962 kg). Dimensions as for F4U-1D apart from overall length of 33 ft 4 in (10,16 m).

VOUGHT F4U-4 & F4U-5 CORSAIR   USA

The final series version of the Corsair manufactured during World War II was the F4U-4, first projected mid 1943. The first prototype, a modified F4U-1 redesignated F4U-4XA, was flown on 19 April 1944, followed on 12 July by a second prototype, the F4U-4XB. The first series F4U-4 flew on 20 September 1944, and the initial aircraft of this sub-type was accepted by the US Navy five weeks later, on 31 October, with 500 being delivered by the following April. The principal changes between the F4U-4 and the preceding series model were provision of an R-2800-18W (R-2800-42W in later series aircraft) with water injection boosting the normal maximum rating of 2,100 hp to 2,450 hp, and a rede-

Air-to-ground rockets became an armament option for the F4U-4B Corsair (above). Uruguay was one of several Corsair users post-World War II (below).

To provide a nocturnal fighting capability, the F4U-5N (above) carried radar in a wing pod.

signed cockpit. The engine drove a new four-bladed, 13 ft 2 in (4,01 m) diameter propeller and was fitted with a down-draught carburettor, the intake ducts for which were moved from the wing leading edges to a position beneath the engine cowling. The standard sextet of 0.5-in (12,7-mm) guns was retained for the principal production series, but 297 were completed as F4U-4Bs with an armament of four 20-mm cannon. Goodyear was to have produced the F4U-4 as the FG-4, but orders for 2,371 FG-4s were cancelled following V-J Day and before completion of any examples of this model. Production of the F4U-4 by Vought continued, however, a total of 2,357 being delivered – including one F4U-4N night fighter and nine F4U-4P reconnaissance aircraft – with the final example being completed in August 1947.

The F4U-7 (above) was produced in 1952 for France, with which it served with four Aéronavale squadrons, including Flotille 12F (below).

A new Corsair variant had meanwhile been developed by fitting an R-2800-32W engine and four 20-mm cannon to the F4U-4, and the first of two prototypes of this version flew as the XF4U-5 on 4 April 1946. The -32W engine had twin auxiliary blowers which demanded twin cheek inlets – the only external change from the F4U-4 – and offered a maximum output of 2,675 hp at sea level. The outer wing panels were metal covered (all preceding Corsairs having fabric-covered outer panels) and provision was made for an external bomb load of up to 5,200 lb (2 359 kg) for field operation. The US Navy purchased 223 F4U-5 fighter-bombers, 315 F4U-5N and -5NL night fighters and 30 F4U-5P reconnaissance-fighters, the last of these (an F4U-5N) being delivered on 22 October 1951. One F4U-5NL was adapted as the XF4U-6 dedicated close-air support aircraft with a single-stage R-2800-83W, 111 similar aircraft being built under the designation AU-1 for the US Marine Corps and delivered between 7 February and 10 October 1952. The Corsair line ended with the MDAP (Military Defense Assistance Program) – funded F4U-7 specifically for use by France's Aéronavale. Provided for use in Indochina, the F4U-7 was similar to the AU-1, but powered by an R-2800-18W engine, and 94 were supplied, these being completed between 2 July 1952

and 31 January 1953, the last being the 12,571st and final Corsair to come off the line. The following data are applicable to the F4U-5. Max speed, 403 mph (649 km/h) at sea level, 470 mph (756 km/h) at 26,800 ft (8 170 m). Initial climb, 3,780 ft/min (19,20 m/sec). Normal range, 1,120 mls (1 802 km). Empty weight, 9,683 lb (4 392 kg). Max loaded weight, 14,610 lb (6 627 kg). Dimensions as for F4U-1A apart from length of 34 ft 6½ in (10,53 m) and height of 14 ft 9 in (4,49 m).

VOUGHT F6U-1 PIRATE   USA

Vought's first jet fighter, the XF6U-1 (above) was flown in 1946, and attracted a production contract.

On 5 September 1944, the US Navy's BuAer distributed a proposal request for a single-seat shipboard fighter powered by the Navy-sponsored Westinghouse 24C (J34) turbojet. Vought proffered the V-340 and this, assigned the designation XF6U-1, was awarded a three-prototype contract. Powered by a 3,000 lb st (1 361 kgp) J34-WE-22 turbojet, the first XF6U-1 flew on 2 October 1946. A low mid-wing monoplane with an all-metal structure and an armament of four 20-mm M3 cannon, the XF6U-1 was largely covered by Vought-developed Metalite skinning, this comprising two thin sheets of aluminium sandwiching a balsa wood core, and used Fabrilite, a glassfibre and balsa sandwich, for the vertical tail and intake ducts. Dubbed Pirate by the manufacturer, the XF6U-1 displayed a number of unsatisfactory characteristics from the outset, the vertical tail undergoing several redesigns and numerous other modifications being introduced to improve handling. The XF6U-1 was also underpowered, and to rectify this particular shortcoming, the third XF6U-1, which had entered flight test on 10 November 1947, was fitted with a Solar A-103A afterburner with which it resumed flight test in May 1948, becoming the first US Navy fighter with this form of power boost. In the meantime, on 5 February 1947, a production order for 30 F6U-1s had been placed and these were to be powered by the J34-WE-30A engine with a military thrust of 3,150 lb (1 429 kg) boosted by afterburning to 4,100 lb (1 860 kg).

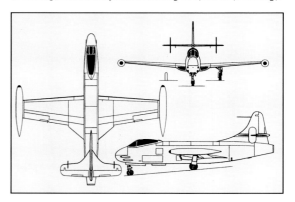

The production F6U-1 Pirate (above and below) featured an afterburner and auxiliary fin surfaces.

(Above) A series Vought F6U-1 serving at the Naval Air Test Center, Patuxent River, Md, in July 1950.

The first F6U-1 was flown on 5 March 1949, 20 being assigned to a development squadron (VX-3), but the type was considered thoroughly unsatisfactory, and, on 30 October 1950, Vought was informed by the BuAer: "The F6U-1 had proven so sub-marginal in performance that combat utilization is not feasible." Consequently, the 30 176U-1s – which had averaged only 31.5 flying hours per aircraft – were consigned to arrester gear and barrier development, damage trials and technical training. *Max speed, 596 mph (959 km/h) at sea level, 550 mph (885 km/h) at 31,000 ft (9 450 m). Initial climb, 8,060 ft/min (40,95 m/sec). Time to 30,000 ft (9 145m), 5.4 min. Range (two 140-US gal/530-1 wingtip tanks), 1,170 mls (1 880 km) at 432 mph (695 km/h). Empty weight, 7,320 lb (3 320 kg). Max loaded weight, 12,900 lb (5 851 kg). Span, 32 ft 10 in (10,00 m). Length, 37 ft 8 in (11,48 m). Height, 12 ft 11 in (3,93 m). Wing area, 203.5 sq ft (18,90 m²).*

VOUGHT F7U-1 CUTLASS USA

Winning submission in a US Navy competition launched on 1 June 1945 for a single-seat shipboard fighter capable of achieving 600 mph (966 km/h) at 40,000 ft (12 190 m), the Vought V-346 was highly unconventional. Subject of an order for three prototypes on 25 June 1946 as XF7U-1s, it dispensed with orthodox horizontal tail surfaces and featured a very low aspect ratio wing sweptback 38 deg on the leading edge. The entire wing leading edge was occupied by slats, elevons performed the functions of both ailerons and elevators, and the vertical tail surfaces were mounted at the extremities of the wing centre section. The cockpit was pressurised and all controls were hydraulically operated. Powered by two Westinghouse J34-WE-22 engines each rated at 3,000 lb st (1 361 kgp) and 4,250 lb st (1 928 kgp) with afterburning, the first XF7U-1 flew on 29 September 1948, but crashed a few weeks later after all control was lost. The second XF7U-1 crashed shortly afterwards, while the third was lost on 7 July 1950. A contract for 14 pre-series F7U-1s had been placed on 28 July 1948, and the first of these flew on 1 March 1950. The F7U-1 had an armament of four 20-mm cannon and was powered by two J34 WE-32 engines, these having military and afterburning thrusts of 3,600 lb (1 633 kg) and 4,250 lb (1 928 kg) respectively. Meanwhile, major changes had been introduced into the design and 88 had been ordered as

A Vought F7U-1 at the NATC (above) and a similar aircraft (below) awaiting delivery to the US Navy, which did not put this model into service.

the F7U-2 with J34-WE-42 engines. These were cancelled owing to continuing difficulties with the J34 engine, contracts being transferred to the more extensively redesigned F7U-3 (which see). The F7U-1s were assigned to the Advanced Training Command, several being lost in accidents and the Cutlass acquiring an alarming reputation. *Max speed, 693 mph (1 115 km/h) at sea level, or Mach=0.91, 672 mph at 20,000 ft (6 100 m), or Mach=0.96. Initial climb, 15,100 ft/min (76,70 m/sec). Range (internal fuel), 1,123 mls (1 807 km) at 460 mph (740 km/h). Empty weight, 12,837 lb (5 823 kg). Max loaded weight, 24,000 lb (10 886 kg). Span, 38 ft 8 in (11,78 m). Length, 39 ft 7 in (12,06 m). Height, 11 ft 10 in (3,61 m). Wing area, 496 sq ft (46,08 m²).*

VOUGHT F7U-3 CUTLASS USA

In the hands of Navy experimental squadron VX-4, this F7U-3M (above) carries four Sparrow I AAMs.

Simultaneously with submission on 1 November 1948 of proposals for the F7U-2, Vought tendered a more radical proposal, the V-366, envisaging extensive redesign of the highly unorthodox Cutlass shipboard fighter. This was awarded an initial production contract (28 aircraft) as the F7U-3 on 21 August 1950. Virtually the only commonality remaining between F7U-1 and -3 was the wing and this only in planform. Thus, the F7U-3 was effectively a new design only conceptually similar to its predecessor. The F7U-1 was not considered structurally strong enough for shipboard operation, and the -3 was therefore restressed throughout; the overall dimensions were enlarged; J46 engines were specified in place of the J34s; to improve serviceability and maintenance, over 100 more access doors and panels were introduced, and an appreciably deeper fuselage was provided. This last enabled the pilot to be seated higher over the nose to improve visibility during approach and landing. Because of engine development problems, the first 16 F7U-3s were powered by non-afterburning Allison J35-A-29 turbojets, the first of these flying on 20 December 1951. These aircraft had reached too advanced a stage in construction to be modified by the time that F7U-1 carrier suitability trials revealed that the F7U-3 still made inadequate provision for cockpit visibility. The nose was therefore redesigned once more, the pilot being seated still higher, under an entirely new and much enlarged canopy, and, at the same time, the nosewheel oleo leg was lengthened and strengthened, and fitted with twin wheels rather than a single wheel. These changes and the provision of Westinghouse J46-WE-8 engines each rated at 4,600 lb st (2 086 kgp) and 6,100 lb st (2 767 kgp) with afterburning, brought the 17th F7U-3 to the definitive Cutlass configuration. The four 20-mm cannon of the F7U-3 could be augmented by up to 2,0001b (907 kg) of external ordnance, and the first fighters of this type

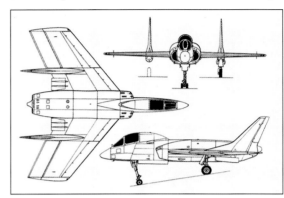

The F7U3 (above and below) was one of the most unusual fighters to achieve service with the US Navy.

were delivered (to VF-124 and V17-81) in 1954. Two additional US Navy squadrons (VF-83 and VF-122) were equipped with the F7U-3, production of this version of the Cutlass totalling 180 aircraft. These were followed by 98 F7U-3Ms which had provision for a quartet of beam-riding Sparrow AAMs on wing pylons, the first production example flying on 12 July 1954. Twelve examples of an unarmed, camera-equipped reconnaissance version, the F7U-3P, were also built. The last Cutlass to be manufactured (an F7U-3M) was delivered on 12 August 1955. Progressively withdrawn from service during 1956-57 – although the last F7U-3P was not retired until 2 March 1959 – the Cutlass had established an unenviable record, more than 25 per cent of the 290 F7U-3s built having been lost in accidents. *Max speed, 696 mph (1 120 km/h) at sea level, or Mach=0.91, 680 mph (1 094 km/h) at l0,000 ft (3 050 m), or Mach=0.93. Initial climb, 11,150 ft/min (56,64 m/sec). Range (internal fuel), 696 mls (1 120 km). Empty weight, 18,262 lb (8 284 kg). Max loaded weight, 31,642 lb (14 353 kg). Span, 39 ft 8 in (12,09 m). Length, 43 ft 1 in (13,13 m). Height, 14 ft 4 in (4,36 m). Wing area, 496 sq ft (46,08 m²).*

VOUGHT F-8A TO F-8L CRUSADER USA

In September 1952, the US Navy announced a requirement for a supersonic shipboard day fighter, and, in May 1953, the Vought V-383 proposal was selected for further development, two prototypes being ordered as XF8U-1s. (Under the combined service designation system adopted in September 1962, these prototypes were redesignated as XF-8As). The XF8U-1 was designed around the Pratt & Whitney J57 engine and was unusual in having a variable-incidence shoulder-mounted wing, the first example flying on 25 March and the second on 30 September 1955, these having the J57-P-11 of 10,000 lb st (4 536 kgp) and 14,500 lb st (6 577 kgp) with afterburning. The first production F8U-1 (F-8A) was flown on the same day as the second prototype, was powered by a J57-P-12 with ratings

(Below) One of two of the pre-production F7U-1s that were used by the US Navy's Panther-equipped Blue Angels Precision Aerobatic Team to give solo performances.

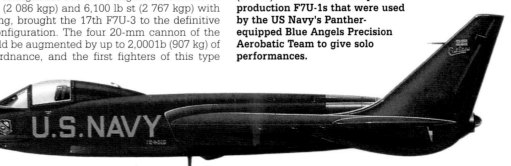

similar to those of the -11, and had a built-in armament of four 20-mm cannon and 32 folding-fin 2.75-in (70mm) rockets in a retractable pack. The 31st F8U-1 switched from the -12 engine to the J57-P-4A rated at 10,900 lb st (4 944 kgp) and 16,600 lb st (7 530 kgp) with afterburning. The cannon armament was supplemented by two IR-homing Sidewinder AAMs mounted on the fuselage sides, the rocket pack being retained, but unused and normally sealed shut. F8U-1 deliveries (to VF-32) began in March 1957, production of this model totalling 318 aircraft. These were followed by 130 F8U-1Es (F-8Bs) with AN/APS-67 radar and limited all-weather intercept capability, a related variant being the unarmed photo-recce F8U-1P (RF-8A), 144 examples of which were built. Succeeding the F8U-1 in production for the air superiority role was the F8U-2 (F-8C) with the J57-P-16 engine with a 16,900 lb (7 666 kg) afterburning thrust, production of 187 examples of which took place between January 1959 and September 1960. To resolve a high-altitude yawing problem, ventral fins were applied beneath the rear fuselage, and two Y-type racks enabled a pair of Sidewinder AAMs to be carried on each side of the

A pair of F8U-1s of VF-211 (above) and a three-view (below) of the F-8J, a re-work of the F-8E.

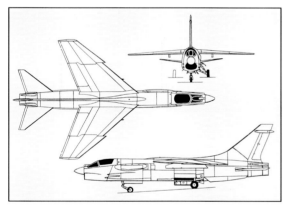

fuselage. A limited all-weather version, the F8U-2N (F-8D) first flown on 16 February 1960, finally discarded the internal fuselage rocket pack, the space that this occupied being used to increase internal fuel capacity. It also introduced the J57-P-20 engine with the enhanced afterburning rating of 18,000 lb st (8 165 kgp). One hundred and fifty-two F8U-2Ns were delivered to the US Navy between June 1960 and January 1962. Production of the fighter for this service ended with the F8U-2NE (F-8E), which, with a J57-P-20A engine, had an enlarged nose cone to accommodate the larger dish scanner of an AN/APQ-94 radar, and a dorsal avionics hump associated with provision for Bullpup ASMs, external ordnance capacity being increased (on all but the first few aircraft) to 5,000 lb (2 268 kg). The first F8U-2NE flew on 30 June 1961, carrier trials being completed early in 1962, and, in

An F8U-2 in service with US Navy squadron VF-142 (below) operating from Atsugi, Japan.

An F-8H rebuild of an F-8D (above) on a pre-delivery flight in 1966.

September of that year, it was redesignated F-8E. The final production model was the F-8E(FN) developed specifically for France's *Aéronavale* as a dedicated air superiority fighter. To meet the requirements of the smaller French carriers, the F8E(FN) introduced a Boundary Layer Control (BLC) system with full-span, double-droop wing leading edges, ailerons and flaps capable of 40-deg extension, and twice the amount of wing control. In addition, the tailplane was enlarged. Forty-two F-8E(FN) Crusaders were supplied to the *Aéronavale*, the last of these rolling from the line in January 1965. During 1966, a remanufacturing programme was initiated which eventually covered 448 aircraft. Eighty-nine F-8Ds were rebuilt as F-8Hs, 136 F-8Es became F-8Js, 87 F-8Cs were restored to US Navy service as F-8Ks, while 61 F-8Bs emerged from the programme as F-8Ls. Modifications included strengthened wings and main undercarriage, and lengthened nose-wheel strut. BLC and double droop wing leading edges – similar to those of the F-8E(FN) – were installed on the F-8J. The US Navy and Marine Corps began to phase out the Crusader from 1972 onwards, and 25 ex-US Navy F-8Hs were delivered to the Philippine Air Force after re-furbishment. These aircraft served as

Serving with France's *Aéronavale*, the F-8E(FN) (above) was armed with the Matra R.530 ASM.

F-8Ps from 1978 until withdrawal late in 1986. The F-8E(FN) Crusaders of the *Aéronavale* were armed with two Matra R.530 and up to four R.550 Magic or AIM-9 Sidewinder AAMs, and 17 were committed to a limited life extension programme in 1991. These were finally retired in mid-2000, leaving the *L'Aeronavale* carrier *Charles de Gaulle* without air defence until the first Rafale M unit forms in 2001.The following data relate to the F-8D (F8U-2N). Max speed, 762 mph (1 226 km/h) at sea level, or Mach=1.0, 1,228 mph (1 976 km/h) at 36,000 ft (10 975 m), or Mach=1.86. Initial

(Immediately below) An F8U-1 in the markings of VF-211, USS *Hancock*, 1960. (Bottom) An F-8P with 7 TFS, 5 Fighter Wing of the Philippine Air Force.

An F-8P (below) – ex-US Navy F-8H – serving with 7 TFS, 5 Fighter Wing, of the Philippine AF.

climb, 31,950 ft/min (162,30 m/sec). Range (max external fuel), 1,737 mls
(2 795 km). Empty weight, 17,541 lb (7 957 kg). Max loaded weight, 29,000 lb (13 154 kg). Span, 35ft 8 in (10,87 m). Length, 54 ft 3 in (16,53 m). Height, 15 ft 9 in (4, 80 m). Wing area, 375 sq ft (34,84 m²).

VOUGHT F8U-3   USA

Despite its designation of F8U-3, the V-401, first flown on 2 June 1958, was a totally new fighter developed in competition with the McDonnell F4H-1 Phantom II. Vought received contracts for 18 F8U-3s, although, in the event, only five were actually built and two of these remained unflown when cancellation of contracts terminated further work. Known to the manufacturer as the Crusader III, the F8U-3 retained some of the features of the original F8U, such as the variable wing incidence, but was a substantially larger, heavier and more powerful single-seat fighter. The F8U-3 was powered by a Pratt & Whitney J75-P-5A engine affording 16,500 lb st (7 484 kgp) boosted to 29,500 lb st (13 381 kgp) with afterburning. Provision was made for a 6,000 lb st (2 722 kgp) Rocketdyne auxiliary rocket motor in the rear fuselage, and the all-missile armament consisted of three beam-riding Sparrow III AAMs. The F8U-3 had a forward-raked, variable-position, chintype air intake, and a pair of large ventral fins was linked to the undercarriage retraction mechanism, being raised to the horizontal position when the wheels were extended and adopting a near-vertical attitude when the wheels were retracted. The F8U-3 attained 1,760 mph (2 832 km/h), or Mach=2.6, during flight test, but Vought believed that it was capable of Mach=2.9. With selection of the F4H-1 as the US Navy's next generation shipboard fighter, the F8U-3 was cancelled, the three examples flown having accumulated a

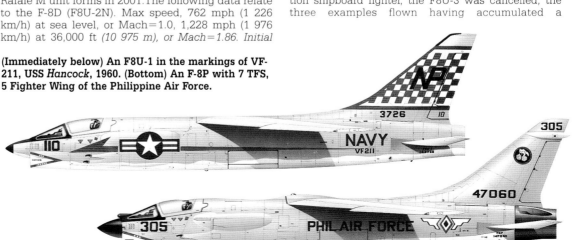

An unusual feature of the F8U-3 (above and below) was the pair of large ventral fins, which had to be folded sideways for take-off and landing.

total of 190 flight tests. *Max speed, 800 mph (1 287 km/h) at sea level, or Mach=1.05, 1,457 mph (2 345 km/h) at 50,000 ft (15 240 m), or Mach=2.2. Initial climb, 32,500 ft/min (165 m/sec). Range (with max external fuel), 2,044 mls (3 289 km). Empty weight, 21,862 lb (9 917 kg). Max loaded weight, 38,772 lb (17 587 kg). Span, 39 ft 11 in (12,16 m). Length, 58 ft 8 in (17,88 m). Height, 16 ft 4 in (4,98 m). Wing area, 450 sq ft (41,80 m²).*

(Below) The Vought F8U-3, of which three were built.

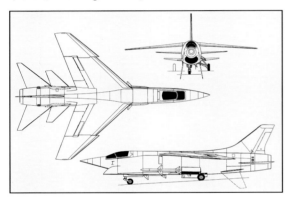

VULTEE 48 VANGUARD (P-66) USA

In 1938, Richard Palmer of Vultee Aircraft initiated the design of four aircraft all possessing a high degree of structural commonality, one of these being the Model 48 single-seat fighter. An all-metal aircraft with a semi-monocoque fuselage and fabric-covered control surfaces, the Model 48 was powered by a close-cowled 1,200 hp Pratt & Whitney R-1830-S4C4-G 14-cylinder radial air-cooled engine which drove the propeller via an extension shaft, cooling being effected by means of a variable air intake beneath the nose. First flown on 9 September 1939, the Model 48 was assigned the name Vanguard by the company. From the outset, engine overheating and poor stability were experienced, necessitating revision of the vertical tail and modifications to the air intakes. The second prototype, the Model 48X flown on 11 February 1940, featured an orthodox radial cowling, compound wing dihedral and

As first flown (below), the Vultee 48 featured a closely-cowled radial engine – which overheated.

provision for twin 0.5-in (12,7-mm) cowl guns and two 0.3-in (7,62-mm) wing guns. After an accident on 9 May 1940, the first prototype was rebuilt with a similar radial engine cowling. On 6 February 1940, the Swedish government placed an order with Vultee for 144 aircraft, the series model being designated Model 48C and a production prototype flying on 6 September 1940. This was essentially similar to the Model 48X with the redesigned and enlarged vertical and horizontal tail surfaces applied to that aircraft at an early flight test stage. With an R-1830-S3C4-G engine which possessed a similar take-off rating but superior altitude ratings to the S4C4-G and two additional 0.3-in (7,62-mm) wing guns, the first production Model 48C was flown in September 1941, by which time export of the fighter to Sweden had been embargoed by the US government.

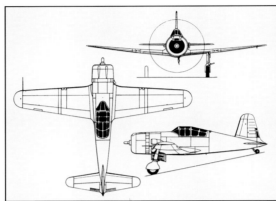

Ordered by Sweden, the Vultee 48C (above and below) eventually served only in China and the US.

The contract for the Model 48C was accordingly taken over by the British government, but subsequently relinquished in favour of China which was selected to receive the fighters under Lend-Lease arrangements, the USAAF designation P-66 being applied for this purpose. The Model 48C fighters were shipped to China, via India, during the second half of 1942, production by Vultee having been completed in April of that year, but only 79 were, in fact, received by the Chinese Air Force, these being used comparatively briefly by the 3rd and 11th Pursuit Groups. Some Model 48Cs retained in the USA were assigned to pursuit training bases on the US West Coast as P-66s. *Max speed, 340 mph (547 km/h) at 15,100 ft (4 600 m). Initial climb, 2,520 ft/min (12,8 m/sec). Normal range, 850 mls (1 368 km). Empty weight, 5,235 lb (2 374 kg). Normal loaded weight, 7,100 lb (3 220 kg). Span, 36 ft 0 in (10,97 m). Length, 28 ft 5 in (8,66 m). Height, 9 ft 5 in (2,87 m). Wing area, 197 sq ft (18,30 m²).*

Shown here in RAF markings (below), the Vanguard was rejected for service with the RAF.

VULTEE XP-54 USA

On 22 June 1940, Vultee Aircraft received a USAAC contract for a prototype of its Model 84 as part of a programme to investigate unconventional fighter configurations. By the time the prototype was completed, as

the XP-54, Vultee had merged with Consolidated and this aircraft is therefore described under the Consolidated-Vultee heading.

W

WACO CSO-A (240A) USA

In late 1931, the Waco Aircraft Company adapted an example of its CSO tandem two-seat sports and training biplane as a single-seat lightweight fighter. The CSO had proved popular with several Latin American governments and it was believed that they would provide a market for an armed single-seat version. The CSO was a single-bay staggered biplane with a welded steel-tube fuselage and wooden wings, powered by a 250 hp Wright R-760E Whirlwind seven-cylinder radial engine. For the fighter rôle the forward cockpit was faired in and a pair of synchronised 0.3-in (7,62-mm) machine guns was mounted above the forward fuselage decking. Shackles for light bombs were fitted beneath the fuselage. Brazil's *Aviação Militar* had procured five CSO two-seaters as trainers, and when, on 9 July 1932, revolution broke out, the singe-seat demonstrator was in Brazil. Designated CSO-A – and also referred to as the "240A", although this was, in fact, its Approved Type Certificate number – the aircraft was promptly purchased for the *Aviação Militar*. At the same time an order was placed for 36 similar fighters, but with 7-mm machine guns. Only 10 of these reached Brazil and were assembled in time to participate in the fighting, but they proved useless in their intended fighter task as the indigenously-manufactured 7-mm ammunition jammed their guns. With the termination of hostilities all these aircraft, including the original demonstrator, reverted to two-seat configuration and the remaining aircraft on order were delivered as two-seaters. *Max speed, 130 mph (209 km/h). Initial climb, 1,200 ft/min (6,1 m/sec). Range, 539 mls (868 km). Empty weight, 1,627 lb (738 kg). Loaded weight, 2,599 lb (1 179 kg). Span, 30 ft 6⅞ in (9,32 m). Length, 22 ft 5⅔ in (6,85 m). Height, 9 ft 2 in (2,79 m). Wing area, 287.94 sq ft (26,75 m²).*

The Waco CSO-A (below) was a light-fighter modification of a two-seat trainer.

WACO CTO-A USA

Developed in parallel with the CSO from the Model 10, the CTO, known as the Taperwing, differed in having tapered wings of smaller area. In all other respects the CSO and CTO were similar. As the CTO was more manoeuvrable and marginally faster than the CSO, it was considered by Waco to be more suitable for adaptation as a lightweight fighter. Accordingly, one example of the CTO was modified in the summer of 1932 in similar fashion to the CSO-A, the forward cockpit being faired over and twin synchronised 0.3-in (7,62-mm) machine guns being provided. The demonstrator was flown in Brazilian national insignia, but there is no record of it actually being flown to Brazil, although the *Aviação Militar* did acquire 22 examples of the standard two-seat CTO – which were dubbed *Waco Eliptico* in Brazil – in 1933 for advanced and instrument training. The ultimate fate of the CTO-A demonstrator is not known with certainty, but it is believed to have been reconverted to standard two-seat form. *Max speed, 140 mph (222 km/h). Initial*

Derived from the CTO Taperwing, the Waco CTO-A light fighter (above) failed to find a customer.

climb, 1,100 ft/min (5,58 m/sec). Endurance, 5.66 hrs. Empty weight, 1,678 lb (761 kg). Loaded weight, 2,599 lb (1 179 kg). Span, 30 ft 5 in (9,27 m). Length, 22 ft 5⅔ in (6,85 m). Height, 9 ft 0 in (2,74 m). Wing area, 226.91 sq ft (21,08 m²).

WEISS [MANFRÉD] WM-23 EZÜSTNYIL   Hungary

Following the termination of plans for the aircraft division of the Weiss Manfréd concern to build the Heinkel He 112 single-seat fighter under licence, the division's chief designer, Béla Samu, initiated work on an indigenous fighter. Designated WM-23 and named Ezüstnyil (Silver Arrow), the fighter's design was launched in July 1940, and owed much to the He 112. The wing section and planform of the He 112 were retained, together with the camber-changing Fowler flaps and Heinkel's use of anhedral to reduce undercarriage height, but metal gave place to wooden construction. The plywood-covered wooden wings were mated with a welded steel-tube fuselage, also primarily plywood covered, and a WM-K-14B (licence-built Gnome-Rhône 14Kfrs Mistral Major) 14-cylinder radial engine of 1,000 hp. The proposed armament comprised two 7,62-mm Gebaur machine guns in the wings and two synchronised 20-mm MG 151 cannon in the fuselage.

Flown in 1941, the WM-23 Ezüstnyil (above and below) owed much to the design of the He 112.

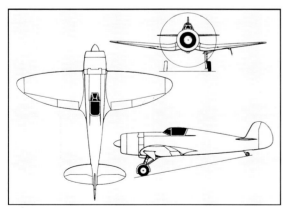

The prototype WM-23 was flown for the first time in September 1941, and demonstrated good flying characteristics, but suffered intermittent aileron oscillation, and, in the late spring of 1942, the starboard aileron detached in a climb, forcing the pilot to abandon the aircraft. Plans had meanwhile reached an advanced stage for the all-metal Ezüstnyil II with a monocoque fuselage and a DB 605 engine. However, this programme was eventually discontinued with the decision that Weiss Manfréd would build the Messerschmitt Bf 109G under licence. *Max speed, 329 mph (530 km/h) at 16,405 ft (5 000 m). Time to 19,685 ft (6 000 m), 6.0 min. Endurance, 1.75 hrs. Loaded weight, 7,253 lb (3 290 kg). Span, 34 ft 9⅓ in (10,60 m). Length,*

35 ft 5 in (10,80 m). Height, 11 ft 7¾ in (3,55 m). Wing area, 252.96 sq ft (23,50 m²).

WESTLAND N.1B   UK

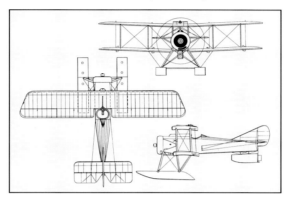

The Westland N16 (above and below), as originally flown, with short floats of Sopwith design.

Westland Aircraft began design of its first aircraft in 1917, in response to an Admiralty requirement for a single-seat fighting scout seaplane. In the Admiralty's N.1B category, the aircraft was designed by Robert Bruce and Arthur Davenport, and was a compact two-bay equi-span biplane of conventional wooden structure and fabric covering. First flown in August 1917, it was powered by a 150 hp Bentley BR 1 rotary engine. Inboard of the ailerons, on both upper and lower wings, the trailing-edge camber could be varied to obtain the effect of plain flaps. The wings could be folded backwards for shipboard stowage. Armament comprised one synchronised 0.303-in (7,7-mm) Vickers gun and a flexibly-mounted Lewis of the same calibre above the upper wing centre section. Two prototypes were built and sometimes referred to as the Westland N16 and N17 from their RNAS serial numbers. The first was flown with short Sopwith floats and a large strut-mounted tailfloat whereas the second was used to evaluate long Westland floats that eliminated the need for a tail float. This second aircraft, which lacked the camber-changing mechanism on the wings, also flew with the Sopwith floats and a tail float directly attached to the underside of the rear fuselage. By the time the N.1Bs were on test at the Isle of Grain, the RNAS was experimenting successfully with the shipboard operation of wheeled aircraft and the requirement for a floatplane fighting scout faded away. The following data refer to the second prototype with Sopwith floats. *Max speed, 108 mph (175 km/h) at 3,750 ft (1 145 m). Time to 2,000 ft (610 m), 3.8 min, to 10,000 ft (3 050 m), 28.65 min. Service ceiling, 12,700 ft (3 870 m). Endurance, 2.75 hrs. Empty weight, 1,504 lb (682 kg). Loaded weight,*

Second of the Westland N.1B scouts, N17 (below) was flown with long floats designed by Westland.

1,978 lb (897 kg). Span, 31 ft 3½ in (9,53 m). Length, 25 ft 5½ in (7,76 m). Height, 11 ft 2 in (3,40 m). Wing area, 278 sq ft (25,83 m²).

WESTLAND WAGTAIL   UK

A contemporary of the Sopwith Snail and the BAT Bantam, the Wagtail was similarly designed to comply with the A.1(a) Specification drawn up by the Air Board in 1917 to define its requirements for a single-seat fighter. Emphasis was to be placed upon manoeuvrability and climb, with the ability to achieve 135 mph (217 km/h) at 15,000 ft (4 570 m) when carrying oxygen equipment and three machine guns. Like its competitors, the Wagtail was powered by the 170 hp ABC Wasp I seven-cylinder radial, an engine that eventually thwarted further development of all three A.1(a) types. A well-proportioned, diminutive single-bay biplane, the Wagtail gained a contract for three prototypes late in 1917, and the first was flown in April 1918. Construction was of fabric-covered wood, with metal-framed rudder and elevators, and two synchronised 0.303-in (7,7-mm) Vickers guns were fitted. An overwing Lewis gun was planned, but not fitted to the prototypes. Whereas the first Wagtail to fly had equal dihedral (2 deg 30 min) on upper and lower wings, the second and third were completed (and the first later modified) to have a larger cut-out in the upper wing centre section with 5 deg of dihedral on the outer panels of the upper wing and a flat lower wing. Destroyed in a fire at Yeovil soon after its first flight on 29 April 1918, the second Wagtail had to be replaced later that year; the third went to Martlesham Heath on 8 May, but problems with the Wasp limited flying. In October 1918, the engine was officially abandoned, and with it any plans to produce Wasp-engined aircraft. Two more Wagtails were ordered from Westland in 1919, to serve as test-beds for the 160 hp Armstrong-Siddeley Lynx seven-cylinder radial engine. Unarmed, these two aircraft were delivered to the RAE in September/October 1921. The following data for the Wasp-engined Wagtail include performance estimates.

Thanks to the unreliability of its ABC Wasp engine, the Wagtail (above) achieved little success.

Max speed, 125 mph (201 km/h) at 10,000 ft (3 050 m). Time to 5,000 ft (1 525 m), 3.5 min. Endurance, 2.5 hrs. Empty weight, 746 lb (338 kg). Loaded weight, 1,330 lb (603 kg). Span, 23 ft 2 in (7,06 m). Length, 18 ft 11 in (5,77 m). Height, 8 ft 0 in (2,44 m). Wing area, 190 sq ft (17,65 m²).

WESTLAND WEASEL   UK

In April 1918, Westland gained a three-prototype contract for a two-seat fighter-reconnaissance aircraft that was designed to provide a successor to the Bristol F. 2b fighter. In configuration, the new fighter, to which the name Weasel was given, closely resembled a scaled-up Wagtail. The pilot was located beneath the trailing edge of the upper wing, with the observer/gunner close behind, with a single 0.303-in (7,7-mm) Lewis gun on a Scarff ring. Two fixed and synchronised forward-firing Vickers guns of the same calibre were provided for the pilot. The Weasel had a two-spar wooden wing and a wire-braced wooden fuselage, with fabric covering for all but the ply-covered front fuselage. In common with the competing Austin Greyhound and Bristol Badger, the Weasel was powered by the 320 hp ABC Dragonfly nine-cylinder air-cooled radial engine, which (like the ABC Wasp in the Wagtail) proved so unsatisfactory as to rule out any possibility of production, even if the ending of World War I had not

Designed to succeed the Bristol F.2B, the Weasel (above and below) failed to attain production.

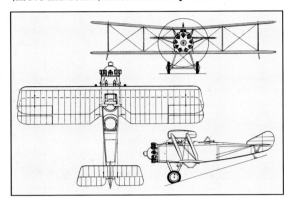

removed the urgency from the requirement. Flight testing did not begin until November 1918 and a Weasel went to Martlesham Heath in April the following year, followed by the third prototype in November. Subsequently, two of the Weasels were used for engine development at the RAE Farnborough, one being re-engined with a 385 hp Cosmos Jupiter II nine-cylinder radial and the other with a 350 hp Armstrong Siddeley Jaguar II 14-cylinder radial. A Jupiter II was also used to power a fourth Weasel, which was ordered in August 1919 and delivered in 1920 with full armament, although also used primarily for engine development. The following data refer to the Dragonfly-powered Weasel. *Max speed, 130 mph (210 km/h) at 6,500 ft (1 980 m). Time to 10,000 ft (3 050 m), 10 min. Service ceiling, 20,700 ft (6 310 m). Empty weight, 1,867 lb (847 kg). Loaded weight, 3,071 lb (1 393 kg). Span, 35 ft 6 in (10,82 m). Length, 24 ft 10 in (7,56 m). Height, 10 ft 1 in (3,07 m). Wing area, 368 sq ft (34,19 m²).*

WESTLAND WESTBURY　　　UK

In its final modified state, the first of the two Westbury heavy fighters (above) tested in 1927.

Specification 4/24 issued by the Air Ministry during 1924 called for the design of a heavily armed, twin-engined, night defence fighter, although the precise nature of the planned armament was not made known to the two companies that successfully tendered for prototype contracts, Westland and Bristol (with the Bagshot). Two prototypes of the Westland submission were ordered in 1925, and only late in that year was the armament specified as two 37-mm Coventry Ordnance Works (COW) cannon, to be disposed in front and dorsal positions, plus a 0.303-in (7,7-mm) Lewis gun firing through a ventral hatch in the rear fuselage. Powered by a pair of uncowled 450 hp Bristol Jupiter VI nine-cylinder radial engines, the Westbury – as the Westland fighter was duly named – was a three-bay biplane of mixed construction, combining a wooden wing with a fuselage of composite steel and wood, duralumin wing spars being introduced in the second prototype. Open cockpits were provided for the two gunners and the pilot, who was located ahead of the upper wing,

which attached directly to the deep fuselage. The nose COW gun was on a rotating mounting, and that in the aft cockpit fired forwards and upwards (aimed by the pilot). A second cockpit, to the rear, carried a 0.303-in (7,7-mm) Lewis gun on a Scarff ring, and the rear gunner also had the use of a second Lewis gun fired downwards through the entrance hatch. Flight testing of the Westbury began in September 1926, and the COW gun was successfully fired from both cockpits during later trials with the second aircraft, but no requirement was found for production of this category of fighter. The second prototype, as the Westbury II, was fitted with 480 hp Jupiter VIII engines and had a rounded, rather than blunt, nose profile and aft-extended nacelle tails, features that were also introduced later on the first aircraft. *Max speed, 125 mph (201 km/h) at 5,000 ft (1 525 m). Service ceiling, 21,000 ft (6 400 m). Empty weight, 4,845 lb (2 198 kg). Loaded weight, 7,877 lb (3 573 kg). Span, 68 ft 0 in (20,73 m). Length, 43 ft 5 in (13,23 m). Height, 13 ft 9 in (4,19 m). Wing area, 860 sq ft (79,89 m²).*

WESTLAND WIZARD　　　UK

As first submitted for Air Ministry testing, the Wizard (above) offered poor forward visibility.

The first attempt by Westland to develop a monoplane fighter evolved from a private venture prototype designed – by the company's draughtsmen in their spare time – during 1926 with high speed performance the primary objective. Known simply as the *Racer*, this unarmed parasol monoplane of mixed construction was powered by a 275 hp Rolls Royce Falcon III inline engine and flew in November 1926. Badly damaged in a forced landing in 1927, the *Racer* was rebuilt in much modified form as the Wizard fighter. In this form, it was primarily of metal construction and the 490 hp unsupercharged Rolls-Royce F.XI 12-cylinder Vee-type water-cooled engine in a more streamlined nose cowling, with a retractable radiator in the underside of the fuselage. The Wizard – which was flying by late 1927 – used a similar parasol wing to that of the *Racer*, this being mounted close to the fuselage on tandem pylons on the fuselage centreline. Two 0.303-in (7,7-mm) Vickers guns were mounted semi-externally in the fuselage sides. The Wizard's performance, and particularly its rate of climb, attracted a modicum of Air Ministry interest and a contract to cover testing at Martlesham Heath. There, the pilot's forward view was found un-

A new cabane and raised wing were adopted for the Wizard (below), seen with radiator extended.

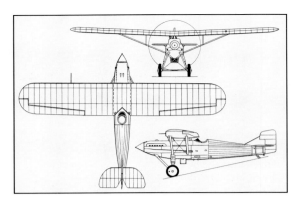

(Above) The Westland Wizard in its original form.

satisfactory, leading Westland to design and fit a new wing with changed planform outboard, new inset ailerons and a thinner centre section, mounted on more conventional cabane strutting. A supercharged 500 hp Kestrel II (F.XIS) was fitted, but in this final form, the Wizard II, as it was sometimes known, demonstrated a reduced performance and failed to persuade the Air Ministry to change its policy towards monoplane fighters. The following data refer to the Wizard with F.XI engine. *Max speed, 188 mph (303 km/h) at 10,000 ft (3 050 m). Rate of climb, 2,000 ft/min (10,2 m/sec) at 10,000 ft (3 050 m). Empty weight, 2,352 lb (1 067 kg). Loaded weight, 3,275 lb (1 486 kg). Span, 39 ft 6 in (12,04 m). Length, 26 ft 10 in (8,18 m). Height, 9 ft 4 in (2,84 m). Wing area, 238 sq ft (22,11 m²).*

WESTLAND F.20/27 INTERCEPTOR　　　UK

Despite the known antipathy of the Air Ministry towards the monoplane as a fighter configuration, and its lack of success with the Wizard, Westland chose a low-wing monoplane design for its response to Specification F.20/27. An air-cooled radial engine and twin-gun armament were specified. From numerous proposals, the Air Ministry chose to order prototypes of two biplanes and two monoplanes, including that offered by Westland. First flown in August 1928 and known as the Interceptor, this was of metal construction and fabric covering except the forward fuselage, which had detachable metal panels. Two 0.303-in (7,7-mm) Vickers guns were installed low in the open cockpit and

The single F.20/27 (above) twin-gun fighter, showing the original small fin and rudder.

(Above) A Whirlwind I in service with No 263 Sqn, RAF, which operated this fighter from bases in south and south-west England from 1940 to 1943.

were totally enclosed behind a series of louvres along the line of the blast tubes. As first flown, the F.20/27 was powered by an uncowled 440 hp Bristol Mercury IIA nine-cylinder air-cooled radial, but this was soon replaced by a 480 hp Mercury IIIA and, eventually, a 420 hp Bristol Jupiter VII, to which a Townend ring was later added. To overcome handling problems, successive modifications were introduced, including automatic wing slots on the wing roots, redesigned wing fillets and a modified, taller fin and rudder. Performance remained mediocre, however, and the Hawker biplane design to F.20/27 was chosen instead, evolving into the Fury. *Max speed, 192 mph (309 km/h) at 10,000 ft (3 050 m). Empty weight, 2,350 lb (1 066 kg). Loaded weight, 3,325 lb (1 508 kg). Span, 38 ft 0 in (11,58 m). Length, 25 ft 4¼ in (7,73 m). Height, 9 ft 8 in (2,95 m). Wing area, 204 sq ft (18,95 m²).*

(Below) The F.20/27 with enlarged vertical tail.

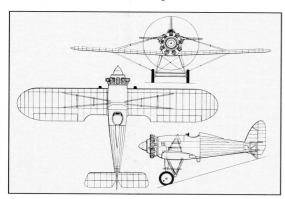

WESTLAND F.29/27   UK

Similar to the F.20/27, the F.29/27 (above) was built to carry an upward-firing COW gun, as shown.

Usually known as the COW-Gun Fighter, this prototype monoplane was one of two ordered by the Air Ministry (with the unorthodox Vickers Type 161) in fulfilment of Specification F.29/27. This called for an aircraft armed with the 37-mm Coventry Ordnance Works (COW) cannon that had been evolved during World War I and was thought to have potential as an anti-bomber weapon. The COW gun was to be mounted at an upward angle of at least 45 deg from the horizontal, with the idea that the fighter would approach enemy bombers from below and astern. The Westland prototype was, in effect, an enlargement of the F.20/27 prototype, and had the COW gun mounted to fire upwards at 55 deg, with the breech casing in the starboard side of the open cockpit. Aiming was by means of a periscopic sight, and a special "ammunition dispenser" carried 39 rounds. The fighter was of similar all-metal construction to the F.20/27 and, like the latter, was first flown with a small fin and rudder which later had to be considerably enlarged to obtain satisfactory spinning characteristics. Powered by a 485 hp Bristol Mercury IIIA nine-cylinder air-cooled radial, the F.29/27 first

flew in December 1930, but the RAF quickly lost interest in the COW gun. With a Mercury IVA, the COW-Gun Fighter remained at the A & AEE until July 1934. *Max speed, 184 mph (296 km/h). Time to 10,000 ft (3 050 m), 6.1 min. Service ceiling, 29,200 ft (8 900 m). Empty weight, 2,615 lb (1 186 kg). Loaded weight, 3,885 lb (1 762 kg). Span, 40 ft 10 in (12,45 m). Length, 29 ft 10 in (9,09 m). Height, 10 ft 6¾ in (3,22 m). Wing area, 222 sq ft (20,62 m²).*

WESTLAND F.7/30   UK

To meet the requirements of Specification F.7/30 for a four-gun day and night fighter powered by the Rolls-Royce Goshawk engine using evaporative cooling, Westland schemed a parasol monoplane in continuation of the Wizard concept, but found it impossible to combine the required slow landing speed with the 250 mph (402 km/h) maximum. An alternative biplane, the P.4, was successfully tendered, however, one prototype being ordered in 1931. With a 600 hp Goshawk VIII buried in the fuselage behind the pilot, driving the propeller via a long extension shaft, this single-bay biplane featured a gulled upper wing with short inboard struts in place of the usual cabane, and a staggered lower wing of slightly shorter span. When first flown on 23 March 1934, the F.7/30 had an open cockpit, but a full canopy was soon added. Armament of four 0.303-in (7,7-mm) Vickers guns was concentrated in the nose. Construction was of metal throughout, with metal skins for the forward fuselage and engine bay, and fabric elsewhere. Ailerons were fitted to the upper wing only, this also having Handley Page slots.

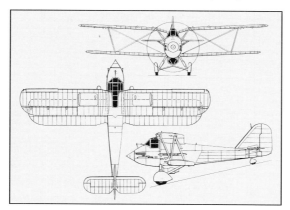

Although first flown with an open cockpit – and a smaller fin – the Westland F.7/30 soon took on the form depicted here (above and below).

Although it handled well, the F.7/30 was found deficient in performance when tested at Martlesham Heath, and no further development occurred. *Max speed, 185 mph (298 km/h) at 15 000 ft (4 575 m). Initial climb, 1,455 ft/min (7,4 m/sec). Empty weight, 3,687 lb (1 672 kg). Loaded weight, 5,200 lb (2 359 kg). Span, 38 ft 6 in (11,73 m). Length, 29 ft 6 in (8,99 m). Height, 10 ft 9 in (3,28 m). Wing area, 370 sq ft (34,37 m²).*

WESTLAND WHIRLWIND   UK

The only Westland fighter to achieve operational status with the RAF, the Whirlwind was designed in response to Specification F.37/35 for a "cannon fighter" armed with four 20-mm guns. As the P.9, the Westland design emerged as a low-wing monoplane with two Rolls-Royce Peregrine I 12-cylinder liquid-cooled Vee engines, each rated at 885 hp at 15,000 ft (4 575 m). The four Hispano Mk I guns were grouped in the nose, the pilot enjoyed a good all-round view from a fully-enclosed cockpit in line with the wing trailing edge, and radiators were buried in the wing leading edges inboard of the nacelles. Construction was of metal throughout, with flush-riveted stressed skins, a novelty being the use of magnesium rather than aluminium sheet to cover the monocoque fuselage aft of the cockpit. Two prototypes were ordered by the Air Ministry in February 1937, and the first of these flew on 11 October 1938. Despite delays in development and production of the Peregrine engine, two contracts were placed in 1939, each for 200 fighters as Whirlwind Is, and the first series aircraft flew in June 1940. In the event, production ended with 114 aircraft built, these serving with only two RAF squadrons (Nos 263 and 137). Armament problems and changing operational needs curtailed the usefulness of the Whirlwind, which was enhanced in late 1942 by the addition of a pair of wing racks to carry two 250-lb (113-kg) or 500-lb (227-kg) bombs. Operational use of the Westland fighter came to an end in November 1943. *Max speed, 360 mph (579 km/h) at 15,000 ft (4 575 m). Initial climb, 1,300 ft/min (6,6 m/sec). Time to 20,000 ft (6 100 m), 8.6 min. Service ceiling, 30,000 ft (9 150 m). Endurance, approx 1.25 hrs. Empty weight, 8,310 lb (3 770 kg). Loaded weight (with bombs), 11,388 lb (5 165 kg). Span, 45 ft 0 in (13,72 m). Length, 32 ft 3 in (9,83 m). Height, 10 ft 6 in (3,20 m). Wing area, 250 sq ft (23,22 m²).*

The Whirlwind I (above and below) was the only Westland fighter to achieve RAF service use.

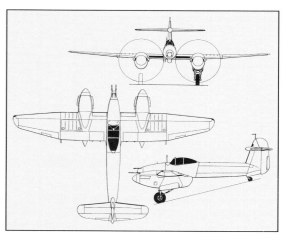

WESTLAND WELKIN I   UK

On 9 January 1941, Westland was authorised by the Ministry of Aircraft Production to proceed with two prototypes of its P.14 design for a twin-engined high-altitude fighter, in compliance with Specification F.4/40. Conceived as a two-seater with six 20-mm cannon armament, the P.14 went ahead as a four-cannon single-seater with a pressurized cockpit. Revised to conform to F.7/41, and thus competing with the Vickers Type 432, the P.14, to be named the Welkin, first flew on 1 November 1942. The wing was located in the mid position, and power was provided by two Rolls-Royce Merlin Mk 61s of 1,565 hp, these being succeeded by 1,650 hp Merlin 72/73 or Merlin 76/77 in the production

Designed to fight at high altitudes, the Welkin (above and below) was not in the event required.

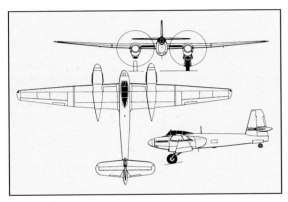

Welkin I. Pressurization of the cockpit was achieved by means of a Rotol blower on the starboard engine. Production of the Welkin I was initiated in 1941, contracts for 100 and then 200 being placed, and the first series aircraft was under test at Boscombe Down by mid-September 1943. However, handling problems combined with reduced operational interest in high-altitude fighters led to cancellation of production after the completion of 75, plus 26 airframes without engines. The Welkin I saw no service use. *Max speed, 387 mph (623 km/h) at 26,000 ft (7 925 m). Initial climb, 3,850 ft/min (19,6 m/sec). Time to 40,000 ft (12 200 m), 20 min. Service ceiling, 44,000 ft (13 410 m). Range, approx 1,500 mls (2 414 km). Empty weight, 14,375 lb (6 520 kg). Max loaded weight, 19,775 lb (8 970 kg). Span, 70 ft 0 in (21,34 m). Length, 41 ft 6 in (12,65 m). Height, 15 ft 3 in (4,65 m). Wing area, 460 sq ft (42,73 m²).*

WESTLAND WELKIN NF Mk II UK

During 1943, Westland studied a number of possible derivatives of the Welkin I in order to take advantage of the design work already completed. Of these possibilities, one for a two-seat night fighter variant received a go-ahead on 4 February 1943, subsequent development of this as the Welkin NF Mk II being in accordance with Specification F.9/43. Two prototypes were ordered, as conversions of Mk I airframes during production, and

The single example of the Welkin NF Mk II (below) carried nose-mounted radar for the nocturnal rôle.

orders were given for 60 of the final production batch of Mk Is to be to this standard. As flown on 23 October 1944, the prototype Welkin NF Mk II introduced AI Mk VIII radar in a lengthened bulbous nose and a new one-piece canopy over a two-seat cockpit in which the observer faced aft behind the pilot. Production plans for the Welkin NF Mk II were cancelled during 1945, along with those for the F Mk I, and the second prototype was not completed. *Max speed, 360 mph (579 km/h) at 30,000 ft (9 150 m). Time to 10,000 ft (3 050 m), 3.7 min. Service ceiling, 41,000 ft (12 500 m). Empty weight, 15,635 lb (7 092 kg). Loaded weight, 21,892 lb (9 930 kg). Span, 70 ft 0 in (21,34 m). Length, 44 ft 1 in (13,44 m). Height, 15 ft 9 in (4,80 m). Wing area, 460 sq ft (42,73 m²).*

WESTLAND WYVERN TF Mk 1 UK

Powered by an Eagle piston engine, the Wyvern I (above) was overtaken by the advent of the turboprop.

Under the project designation P.10, Westland began to study early in 1944 a long-range shipboard day fighter for Naval use, with the added capability of carrying a torpedo, rockets or bombs for anti-shipping strikes. Around this proposal, Specification N.11/44 was written, and, in November 1944, a contract was confirmed for six prototypes (including two in land-based RAF configuration to Spec F.13/44). Redesignated W.34, and subsequently named the Wyvern TF Mk 1, the Westland aircraft was a low-wing monoplane of relatively conventional layout, but larger and heavier than any previous British single-seat Naval fighter. It had upward-folding outer wing panels with hinged tips, and a 3,500 hp Rolls-Royce Eagle 24-cylinder liquid-cooled H-type engine driving eight-blade contraprops. Provision was made in the design for the later introduction of a turboprop engine, such as the Rolls-Royce Clyde. Basic armament comprised four 20-mm Hispano Mk V cannon in the wings, with the possibility of carrying an 18-in (46-cm) Mk VIII torpedo under the fuselage three 1,000-lb (464-kg) bombs or eight 60-lb (27-kg) rocket projectiles. In August 1946, an order for 20 pre-series Wyverns with Eagle engines was confirmed, but a planned batch of 10 for the RAF was dropped, together with the F.13/44 prototypes. Subsequently, the pre-production batch was halved. The first of six prototypes flew on 16 December 1946. However, a turboprop version with the Armstrong Siddeley Python had meanwhile been given the go-ahead and the Wyvern TF Mk 1s were assigned to various development tasks, never

becoming operational. All six prototypes were flown, as were six pre-series TF Mk 1s, but the final four of the latter, although built, remained unflown as all development effort switched to the TF Mk 2 (which see). The following performance data are manufacturer's estimates for the production TF Mk 1. *Max speed, 456 mph (734 km/h) at 23,000 ft (7 010 m). Service ceiling, 32,100 ft (9 785 m). Range (with external fuel), 1,186 mls (1 908 km). Empty weight, 15,443 lb (7 005 kg). Max loaded weight (with torpedo), 21,879 lb (9 924 kg). Span, 44 ft 0 in (13,42 m). Length, 39 ft 3 in (11,96 m). Height, 15 ft 6 in (4,72 m). Wing area, 355 sq ft (32,98 m²).*

(Below) The Wyvern TF Mk 1 in its final form.

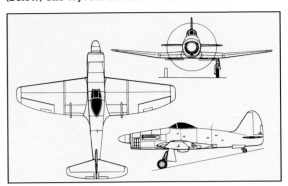

WESTLAND WYVERN TF Mk 2 to S Mk 4 UK

Almost a year before the first flight of the Wyvern TF Mk 1, the Naval Air Staff had decided to sponsor development of Britain's first turboprop-powered shipboard fighter by ordering three prototypes of the (W.35) Wyvern TF Mk 2, to Specification N.12/45. Two were to be powered by the Armstrong Siddeley Python and the third by a 4,500 hp Rolls-Royce Clyde. In the event, the former engine was to be preferred for production aircraft. In overall configuration and armament the Wyvern TF Mk 2 closely resembled the Mk 1, although there were differences in detail, and the first flight of the Clyde-engined prototype was made on 18 January 1949, followed by the first with a Python on 22 March 1949. Flight testing soon showed the need for modifications, noticeably to the tail unit with the progressive introduction of a larger tailplane, more fin area, dihedral on the tailplane and, eventually, finlets. Prolonged testing and development also proved necessary to achieve a satisfactory engine/propeller/throttle response system for the special demands of carrier landings, involving the two Python prototypes and most of 20 pre-series TF Mk 2s ordered in 1948 (together with a single W.38 Wyvern T Mk 3 two-seat training version). The first pre-series TF Mk 2, with a Python 2, flew on 16 February 1950, and, in June that year, became the first British turboprop aircraft to engage in carrier deck landings, aboard HMS *Illustrious*. The final seven pre-series aircraft were completed as Wyvern S Mk 4s, this being the designation of the definitive variant with all

A pre-production Wyvern TF Mk 2 (above) carrying torpedo and rockets and (below) an S Mk 4 in final configuration, serving in No 813 Sqn in 1953.

(Above) Wyvern S Mk 4 of No 830 Sqn, marked for service in Suez campaign, from HMS *Eagle,* 1956.

the handling and engine modifications, and the primary mission changed to strike. The S Mk 4 was powered by a Python 3 rated at 3,670 shp plus 1,180 lb (535 kg) residual thrust. Production of 87 Wyvern S Mk 4s ensued, and deliveries to the first FAA squadron (No 813) began during 1953. Three other squadrons subsequently flew the Wyvern S Mk 4, front-line service continuing until March 1958. Operational use of the Wyvern during the Suez campaign in 1956 marked the only occasion on which British turboprop-powered aircraft saw combat use. The following data refer to the definitive S Mk 4. *Max speed, 383 mph (613 km/h) at sea level. Initial climb, 2,350 ft/min (11,9 m/sec). Service ceiling, 28,000 ft (8 535 m). Range (with external fuel), 910 mls (1 464 km). Empty weight, 15,600 lb (7 076 kg). Max loaded weight, 24,500 lb (11 113 kg). Span, 44 ft 0¼ in (13,42 m). Length, 42 ft 0 in (12,80 m). Height, 15 ft 0 in (4,57 m). Wing area, 355 sq ft (32,98 m²).*

(Below) The definitive Wyvern S Mk 4.

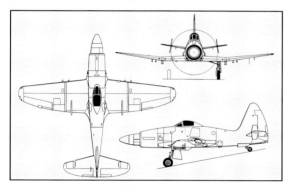

WEYMANN W-1 France

An extraordinarily innovative single-seat fighter completed at Villacoublay by the Société de St Chamond in the autumn of 1915 to the designs of Charles Terrès-Weymann was the W-1, with an extension shaft-driven stern-mounted pusher propeller reminiscent of that used by the 1911 Tatin-Paulhan Torpille. An all-metal, single-bay unstaggered equi-span biplane with ailerons in both upper and lower wings, the W-1 had a slab-sided fuselage occupying the entire wing gap and a cruciform tail with rudders above and below. The pilot was seated immediately ahead of the wings with two fixed machine guns, and an 80 hp Clerget seven-cylinder rotary engine was mounted behind the cockpit at the CG. Entirely enclosed, this engine, which drove a two-bladed propeller aft of the cruciform tail via an extension shaft, drew cooling air from an intake immediately below the pilot's seat, exhaust gases being ducted to an efflux above and behind. The W-1, which

(Below) The Weymann W-1 with Clerget engine.

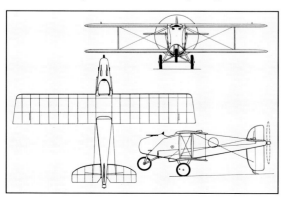

had a tricycle undercarriage and a skid under the ventral fin, offered its pilot excellent visibility from the cockpit. However, engine cooling presented insurmountable problems and testing of the aircraft was abandoned in December 1915 after only two short flights. No data relating to the W-1 appear to have survived other than wing area of 247.58 sq ft (23,00 m²).

The design of the Weymann W-1 (below), built at Villacoublay in 1915, defied convention.

WHITEHEAD COMET UK

At the end of 1916, the Whitehead Aircraft Company completed, at its Richmond, Surrey, works, a small single-seat fighting scout. Not unlike the Camel in general appearance – and perhaps inspired by the Sopwith type, for the production of which Whitehead was a major contractor – the aircraft was a compact single-bay biplane, with ailerons on all four wings. The fuselage was faired to a near-circular cross section and the engine was an 80 hp Le Rhône nine-cylinder rotary. The name Comet was bestowed upon the fighter by its manufacturer, although it was also known within the works as the Boyle Scout, in an allusion to its principal designer, Edwin Boyle. No details of the planned armament appear to have survived, nor of any flight testing, although the Comet was reported to have flown. No data are available.

Probably inspired by Sopwith practice, the Whitehead Comet (below) was designed by Edwin Boyle.

WIBAULT WIB 1 France

Initially known simply as the WIB C1 (*Avion monoplace de chasse*) and later as the WIB 1 C1, the first design of Michel Wibault was a single-bay slightly staggered biplane built by Niepce et Fetterer at Boulogne-Billancourt. Of all-metal construction with fabric-covered wings and a fuselage covered by detachable light alloy panels forward and fabric aft, the Wibault fighter was powered by a 220 hp Hispano-Suiza 8B eight-cylinder water-cooled engine and armed with twin synchronised 7,7-mm Vickers machine guns. By contemporary standards, the engine installation of the WIB 1 was aerodynamically very clean, with the cowling fairing neatly into a large propeller spinner and shallow radiators mounted on each side beneath the lower wing. Short, broad-chord ailerons were carried by the lower wing only. The prototype was completed at the

Tested in 1919, the Wibault WIB 1 (above and below) was bested by the Nieuport 29 in official trials.

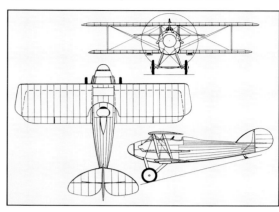

end of October 1918, and was flown for the first time shortly afterwards at Villacoublay. The combination of modest weight and aerodynamic cleanliness resulted in very good performance despite a relatively low powered engine during its official evaluation on 12 February 1919. The WIB 1 proved slightly faster than the more powerful Nieuport 29 with which it was in competition for an *Aviation Militaire* contract. In the event, however, the Nieuport was selected for production because of its faster climb and lighter controls, and further work on the Wibault fighter was discontinued. *Max speed, 147 mph (237 km/h) at sea level, 128 mph (206 km/h) at 16,405 ft (5 000 m). Service ceiling, 22,965 ft (7 000 m). Loaded weight, 1,975 lb (896 kg). Span, 25 ft 7 in (7,80 m). Length, 20 ft 8 in (6,30 m). Height, 7 ft 10½ in (2,40 m). Wing area, 235.2 sq ft (21,85 m²).*

WIBAULT WIB 3 France

In 1921, the *Service Technique de l'Aéronautique* (STAé) issued a requirement for a turbo-supercharger-equipped single-seat high-altitude fighter capable of attaining 149 mph (240 km/h) at 22,965 ft (7 000 m) and having a service ceiling of 27,885 ft (8 500 m). To meet this demand, Michel Wibault produced an all-metal parasol monoplane constructed primarily of duralumin as the WIB 3 C1 – major components being displayed in the Société du Duralumin exhibit at the 1922 Paris *Salon de l'Aéronautique.* The wing was of constant chord and utilised a Wibault-patented section which tapered only outboard of the bracing strut attachment points. The fighter had fabric skinning and its undercarriage cross axle was enclosed by a fairing which contributed 16 sq ft (1,50 m²) of lifting surface. Power was provided by a 300 hp Hispano-Suiza 8Fb eight-cylinder Vee-type water-cooled engine and armament consisted of the standard pair of synchronised 7,7-mm Vickers guns. The WIB 3 flew at Villacoublay during the first quarter

(Below) The Wibault WIB 3 as flown in 1923.

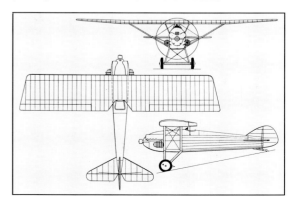

of 1923 without the intended exhaust-driven Rateau turbo-supercharger being fitted. Owing to the lack of heat-resistant alloys, the turbo-supercharger had meanwhile suffered repeated failures, and as its problems appeared insurmountable further development was terminated by the STAé. Flight testing of the WIB 3 continued until the autumn of 1923, when the *Aviation Militaire* elected to procure small quantities of the Blériot SPAD 81 and Dewoitine D 1 to fulfil its requirement, and further work on the Wibault fighter was discontinued. *Max speed, 150 mph (241 km/h) at sea level, 140 mph (225 km/h) at 16,730 ft (5 100 m). Service ceiling, 22,965 ft (7 000 m). Endurance, 3.0 hrs. Empty weight, 2,191 lb (994 kg). Loaded weight, 3,130 lb (1 420 kg). Span, 38 ft 5⅜ in (11,72 m). Length, 26 ft 10⅘ in (8,20 m). Height, 9 ft 11⅔ in (3,04 m). Wing area, 269.11 sq ft (25,00 m²).*

The WIB 3 (below) was designed to use a turbo-supercharger, development of which failed.

WIBAULT WIB 7 SRS — France

To meet the requirements of the 1923 C1 (*Avion monoplace de chasse*) specification issued by the STAé, Avions Michel Wibault tendered the WIB 7 C1 as one of 12 competing fighters submitted by six manufacturers. Like the preceding WIB 3, the WIB 7 employed the Wibault-patented system of light alloy construction and was powered by a 480 hp Gnome-Rhône 9Ad Jupiter nine-cylinder air-cooled radial engine, armament consisting of two synchronised 7,7-mm Vickers machine guns. Designed by M Martinet, the WIB 7 was first flown in 1924, and was joined in the following year by a second, modified prototype which was to undergo performance trials at Villacoublay during August 1925. Powered by a 420 hp Gnome-Rhône 9Ac engine, the second prototype featured a redesigned undercarriage, reinforced wing bracing, a redesigned vertical tail and replacement of the smooth fuselage dural panelling by corrugated sheet. The two synchronised fuselage-mounted guns were augmented by two wing-mounted 7,7-mm Darne 1919 guns, and this prototype demonstrated 145 mph (234 km/h) at 13,125 ft (4 000 m) during Villacoublay trials. The Nieuport-Delage 42 and the Gourdou-Leseurre 32 were respectively adjudged first and second among the dozen contenders, each being awarded a 25-aircraft contract. Surprisingly, the

The second of three WIB 7 prototypes (above), as tested at Villacoublay in 1925. (Below) The series aircraft.

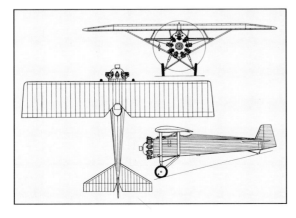

WIB 7, which took eleventh place in the contest, was recipient of a similar contract which was placed in January 1927. A third WIB 7 prototype had meanwhile been completed, and the 25 pre-series differed from the second and third prototypes primarily in discarding the wing-mounted guns, deliveries commencing in 1928 to the two *escadrilles de chasse* of the 32ᵉ *Régiment d'Aviation Mixte*. Earlier, in November 1925, one WIB 7 powered by a 455 hp Bristol Jupiter VI had been despatched to the UK as a prototype of the Vickers Type 121 (which see). One airframe fitted in 1926 with a 400 hp Hispano-Suiza 12Jb 12-cylinder Vee-type engine for comparison purposes as the WIB 71 was redesignated WIB 9 before completion. A follow-on order for the *Aviation Militaire* involved 60 WIB 72s which differed from the WIB 7 solely in having some strengthening of the wing structure. The WIB 72s were delivered to the 32ᵉ *Régiment*, which, on 1 October 1932, became the 7ᵉ *Escadre de Chasse* with a complement of four *escadrilles* and 45 WIB 72s. Following demonstration in Poland of the third pre-series WIB 7 in 1925, a licence was obtained for the manufacture of 30 aircraft by P.Z.L., 26 of these being completed as WIB 72s and four

The navalised WIB 74 (above) was operated by *Escadrille* 7C1 from the aircraft carrier *Béarn*.

as WIB 73s. The latter differed in having the 450 hp Lorraine-Dietrich 12EB 12-cylinder "broad-arrow" type water-cooled engine. Seven WIB 73s were supplied in 1929 to Paraguay's *Fuerzas Aéreas Nacionales*, equipping the 1er *Escuadrón de Caza*, but proved troublesome, only three remaining when full-scale warfare between Paraguay and Bolivia began in June 1932. In April 1929, one WIB 7 was flown experimentally aboard the carrier *Béarn* by *Escadrille* 7C1, leading to an order for 18 aircraft for the *Aviation maritime*. Designated WIB 74, the navalised model was fitted with an arrester hook and the wing was moved marginally aft to adjust the CG. The WIB 74s were delivered in March 1932 to *Escadrille* 7C1 which retained them until 1938. The following data relate to the WIB 7 C1. *Max speed, 141 mph (227 km/h) at 16,405 ft (5 000 m). Time to 16,405 ft (5 000 m), 15.3 min. Service ceiling, 27,885 ft (8 500 m). Empty weight, 1,823 lb (827 kg). Loaded weight, 3,183 lb (1 444 kg). Span, 36 ft 1⅛ in (11,00 m). Length, 24 ft 5⅓ in (7,45 m). Height, 9 ft 6⅛ in (2,90 m). Wing area, 236.81 sq ft (22,00 m²).*

WIBAULT WIB 8 SIMOUN — France

Designed to the requirements of a 1925 specification for a two-seat fighter, the WIB 8 Simoun tandem two-seat parasol monoplane employed a light alloy structure similar to that of preceding Wibault fighters and was powered by a 500 hp Hispano-Suiza 12Hb 12-cylinder Vee-type engine. The WIB 8 featured a retractable radiator, auxiliary controls in the gunner's cockpit and an armament of two 7,7-mm synchronised Vickers guns in the fuselage, two Darne machine guns of similar calibre in the wings and a pair of 7,7-mm Lewis guns on a Scarff ring in the rear cockpit. The WIB 8 prototype was flown for the first time in May 1926, but none of the contenders attempting to fulfil the STAé specification was considered to offer an adequate performance, and

(Above) Wibault 72 C1 of the 5ᵉ *Escadrille*, 32ᵉ *Régiment d'Aviation d'Observation*, 1928.

the two-seat fighter requirement was cancelled. *Max speed, 147 mph (236 km/h) at 6,560 ft (2 000 m), 137 mph (220 km/h) at 13,125 ft (4 000 m). Time to 16,405 ft (5 000 m), 18.8 min. Empty weight, 2,718 lb (1 233 kg). Loaded weight, 4,550 lb (2 064 kg). Span, 41 ft 5¼ in (12,63 m). Length, 29 ft 4⅓ in (8,95 m). Height, 10 ft 6 in (3,20 m). Wing area, 318.62 sq ft (29,60 m²).*

Named Simoun, the WIB 8 (below) was built to an official specification which was later abandoned.

WIBAULT WIB 9 — France

During the course of the official trials which took place at Villacoublay between mid 1925 and mid 1926 of the contenders in the 1923 C1 single-seat fighter contest, Avions Michel Wibault elected to build a version of the WIB 7 with a 400 hp Hispano-Suiza 12Jb 12-cylinder Vee-type engine as the WIB 71. Too late to participate in the contest, the HS-engined prototype was redesignated WIB 9 C1 before completion. Armament was similar to that of the second prototype WIB 7, consisting of two fuselage-mounted synchronised and two wing-mounted unsynchronised 7,7-mm guns. Faster than the Gnome-Rhône-engined WIB 7, the WIB 9 had reduced fuel capacity – from 79 Imp gal (360 l) to 66 Imp gal (300 l) – to compensate for the heavier engine and reduce loaded weight to a figure approximating to that of the radial fighter. The WIB 9 failed to attract a contract and development was discontinued after limited flight test. *Max speed, 151 mph (243 km/h). Service ceiling, 23,295 ft (7 100 m). Empty weight, 2,022 lb (917 kg). Loaded weight, 3,265 lb (1 481 kg). Dimensions as for WIB 7 apart from length of 20 ft 10⅘ in (8,20 m).*

Essentially a re-engined version of the WIB 7, the WIB 9 (below) was tested late in 1926.

WIBAULT WIB 12 SIROCCO SERIES — France

Possessing a close external similarity to the WIB 8 C2, the WIB 12 Sirocco two-seat fighter was, structurally, a largely new design and was, effectively, the result of a thoroughgoing reappraisal of the earlier aircraft undertaken by Avions Marcel Wibault while the Simoun was still under construction. Indeed, the WIB 12 flew for the first time barely a month after the maiden flight of the WIB 8. The STAé notified Wibault of an order for two WIB 12s on 11 February 1926, and the first of these prototypes entered flight test late in the following May. The WIB 12 possessed a stronger and lighter (by 12 per cent) airframe than the WIB 8, box spars being replaced by I-type spars in the wings, and many other changes being introduced. Like the earlier two-seat fighter, the WIB 12 was powered by a 500 hp Hispano-Suiza 12Hb 12-cylinder Vee-type engine, but the wing-mounted

Darne guns of the WIB 8 were omitted, armament being confined to a pair of Lewis guns on a Scarff ring and twin synchronised Vickers guns. The second prototype was completed as a WIB 121 fighter-reconnaissance aircraft with wing guns reinstated and provision for an F 50 camera, this entering flight test in the spring of 1926.

The prototype WIB 12 (above and below) shared many features of the WIB 8, although a new design.

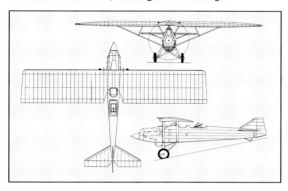

A further example of the two-seat fighter was built as the WIB 122 to a British Air Ministry contract in 1928. With the Hispano-Suiza engine replaced by a 550 hp Napier Lion XI 12-cylinder "broad arrow" type engine and the synchronised Vickers guns lowered from their position in front of the forward cockpit to the fuselage flanks, the WIB 122 – also referred to as the Vickers-Wibault Type 122 – was assembled by Vickers, but was dogged by engine cooling problems during trials at Martlesham Heath. The discontinuation of the two-seat fighter programme by the STAé caused by the inadequate performance of the contenders led Avions Marcel Wibault to concentrate, albeit without success, on the development of the basic design for the army co-operation task as the WIB 124 A2 and 125 A2. The WIB 121 was demonstrated in Turkey in 1928, but did not attract an order. The following data relate to the WIB 121 C2. *Max speed, 150 mph (242 km/h) at 9,840 ft (3 000 m), 143 mph (230 km/h) at 13,125 ft (4 000 m). Time to 13,125 ft (4 000 m), 14.15 min. Service ceiling, 20,340 ft (6 200 m). Empty weight, 2,672 lb (1 212 kg). Loaded weight, 4,519 lb (2 050 kg). Span, 41 ft 6⅔ in (12,66 m). Length. 30 ft 11⅔ in (9,44 m). Height, 10 ft 4 in (3,15 m). Wing area, 318.94 sq ft (29,63 m²).*

WIBAULT WIB 13 (130) TROMBE — France

In response to the STAé attempt, in 1926, to arrest the escalating spiral of fighter weights and costs by calling for lightweight fighters, or *chasseurs légers*, under the so-called *Jockey* programme, Avions Marcel Wibault proffered the WIB 13 C1. Of light alloy construction throughout, with the usual Wibault corrugated sheet skinning, the WIB 13 was dubbed Trombe (Whirlwind) and was powered by a 400 hp Hispano-Suiza 12Jb 12-cylinder water-cooled Vee-type engine. Initially fitted with a cantilever tailplane, which was lowered and braced early in the flight test programme, the Trombe carried an armament of two synchronised 7,7-mm Vick-

In response to the call for a lightweight fighter in 1926, Wibault offered the WIB 13 (below).

ers machine guns. Redesignated WIB 130 by the time that it entered flight test at Villacoublay in 1928, the Trombe was an extremely robust aircraft and possessed excellent agility, but was adjudged to possess insufficient power, leading to further development as the WIB 170 Tornade (which see). *Max speed, 150 mph (242 km/h) at sea level, 157 mph (253 km/h) at 9,840 ft (3 000 m). Time to 9,840 ft (3 000 m), 5.95 min. Endurance, 3.0 hrs. Empty weight, 1,971 lb (894 kg). Loaded weight, 2,725 lb (1 236 kg). Span, 29 ft 9 in (9,07 m). Length, 22 ft 4¾ in (6,82 m). Height, 9 ft 1 in (2,77 m). Wing area, 182.99 sq ft (17,00 m²).*

WIBAULT WIB 170 TORNADE — France

After proposing a more powerful WIB 130 as the WIB 160 Trombe II, Avions Marcel Wibault produced a further *chasseur léger* to participate in the so-called *Jockey* programme, the WIB 170 Tornade (Tornado). The Tornade was fundamentally similar to the earlier Trombe, but was powered by an Hispano-Suiza 12Hb engine rated at 500 hp and fuel capacity was increased from 48 to 66 Imp gal (220 to 300 l). Armament remained a pair of synchronised 7,7-mm guns, and the wing and tail surfaces were common to Trombe and Tornade. The first of two prototypes of the WIB 170 Tornade was displayed statically at the 1928 *Salon de l'Aéronautique* in Paris, and entered flight test early 1929. Although it overcame the climb and speed shortcomings of the WIB 130, and demonstrated an excellent performance during Villacoublay trials, the entire *Jockey* programme had meanwhile been pronounced a failure. *Max speed, 169 mph (272 km/h) at sea level, 171 mph (275 km/h) at 16,405 ft (5 000 m). Time to 16,405 ft (5 000 m), 9.15 min. Ceiling, 31,495 ft (9 600 m). Empty weight, 2,127 lb (965 kg). Loaded weight, 2,976 ft (1 350 kg). Dimensions as for WIB 130 apart from length of 23 ft 5½ in (7,15 m).*

A second attempt by Wibault to produce a light fighter, the WIB 170 (above and below) was tested in 1928.

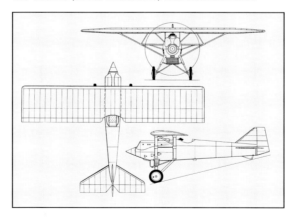

WIBAULT WIB 210 — France

Designed to meet the requirements of a 1928 C1 programme, the WIB 210 discarded Marcel Wibault's previously preferred parasol wing configuration in favour of that of cantilever low-wing, but adhered to the *chasseur léger* concept. The STAé awarded a contract for two prototypes of the WIB 210 powered by the 500 hp Hispano-Suiza 12Hb Vee-type engine and carrying an armament of two synchronised 7,7-mm machine guns. Of typical Wibault light alloy construction, the WIB 210 was flown for the first time at Villacoublay during the second half of April 1929, encountering severe oscillation in the rear fuselage and tail assembly. After modifi-

Breaking with its high wing tradition, Wibault produced the WIB 210 (above and below) in 1929.

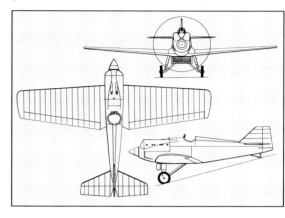

cation, flight test was resumed at the end of May, but it was ascertained that, at speeds in excess of 217 mph (350 km/h) which could be achieved easily in a shallow dive, the aircraft vibrated excessively, flight test reports being unfavourable in general and development being abandoned. *Max speed, 186 mph (300 km/h) at sea level, 183 mph (295 km/h) at 9,840 ft (3 000 m). Time to 9,840 ft (3 000 m), 7.7 min. Ceiling, 26,245 ft (8 000 m). Empty weight, 2,240 lb (1 016 kg). Loaded weight, 2,910 lb (1 320 kg). Span, 30 ft 10 in (9,40 m). Length, 22 ft 6½ in (6,87 m). Height, 7 ft 6½ in (2,30 m). Wing area, 172.23 sq ft (16,00 m²).*

WIBAULT-PENHOËT WIB 313 — France

The 1930 C1 programme resulted in a large number of contending single-seat fighters, all of these being powered by the 12-cylinder Vee-type Hispano-Suiza 12Xbrs liquid-cooled engine – favoured by the *Direction Générale Technique* – with but one exception, the WIB 313. A low-wing cantilever monoplane, the WIB 313 eschewed the angular contours that had characterised all earlier Wibault fighter monoplanes, having a deep, oval-section fuselage and tapered wings with rounded tips. Retaining the high aspect ratio ailerons favoured by Wibault, the WIB 313 had spatted main undercarriage members and was powered by a 520 hp Gnome-Rhône 9Kbrs nine-cylinder air-cooled radial engine

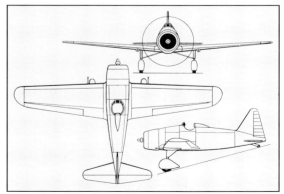

Last of the Wibault fighters, the WIB 313 (above and below) demonstrated a good performance in 1933.

driving a variable-pitch propeller, this last an innovation at the time of the Wibault fighter's début. Construction was all metal and intended armament comprised one 7,7-mm unsynchronised Darne machine gun housed in a shallow fairing immediately outboard of each mainwheel leg fairing. In 1931, while the Wib 313 was under construction, Avions Marcel Wibault merged with the Chantiers de Saint-Nazaire to form a new company, the Chantiers Aéronautiques Wibault-Penhoët. The prototype was transported to Villacoublay in November 1932 and flown for the first time during the last week of that month. During the course of subsequent testing, the Wib 313 attained an altitude of 36,910 ft (11 250 m) in 50 min and exceeded 230 mph (370 km/h) at 16,405 ft (5 000 m). On 3 September 1933, the prototype was returned to the manufacturer for further modification, reappearing at Villacoublay at the end of the year, but, by that time, the Dewoitine D 500 had been selected to fulfil the requirement, and, in January 1934, testing of the Wib 313 was discontinued. The STAé report on the Wib 313 stated that it possessed an insufficient rate of climb and afforded the pilot inadequate view from the cockpit. Shortly afterwards, the Wibault-Penhoët concern was taken over by Louis Breguet. *Max speed, 231 mph (372 km/h) at 16,405 ft (5 000 m). Range, 497 mls (800 km). Empty weight, 2,542 lb (1 153 kg). Loaded weight, 3,430 lb (1 556 kg). Span, 37 ft 2⅘ in (11,35 m). Length, 22 ft 11⅗ in (7,00 m). Height, 11 ft 3⅘ in (3,45 m). Wing area, 178.26 sq ft (16,56 m²).*

WIGHT QUADRUPLANE — UK

Confusingly, aircraft of original design produced by the J S White company bore the appellation Wight, to link them with the location of the works at Cowes on the Isle of Wight. The last of some eight types developed under the direction of Howard T Wright as chief designer was the only Wight aircraft in the fighter category. This was a quadruplane of most unusual layout, in which the fuselage filled the gap between the two middle wings, with the upper and lower mainplanes carried above and below it on struts. At first, single wide-chord struts were used for the cabane and for the single wing bays between the upper, mid-upper and mid-lower wings, all of which had ailerons. The bottom wing, of shorter span, was carried on pairs of struts under the fuselage, and from the mid lower wing. The main wheels were carried on single struts each side and were notched into the bottom wing, with which the axle was in line. Construction was of wood, with mixed fabric and plywood covering. The engine was a 110 hp Clerget 9Z nine-cylinder rotary, but there is no record of the planned armament. Early flight testing, in mid-1916, led to a complete redesign and rebuild, by Howard T Wright and his team, with a fuselage of increased cross-section area and changed profile in side elevation, an enlarged tail unit and a new set of wings of varying chord. The original broad-chord struts gave way to pairs of narrow struts throughout and the undercarriage was lengthened. Possibly first tested at Martlesham Heath in February 1917, the Quadruplane acquired a third set of wings, with span progressively decreasing from top to bottom and ailerons on the two upper sets only. Further tests in July 1917 were unsatisfactory and the Quadruplane was written off in February 1918. No data have survived other than the dimensions. *Span 19 ft 0 in (5,79 m). Length (final form), 20 ft 6 in (6,25 m). Height, 10 ft 6 in (3,20 m).*

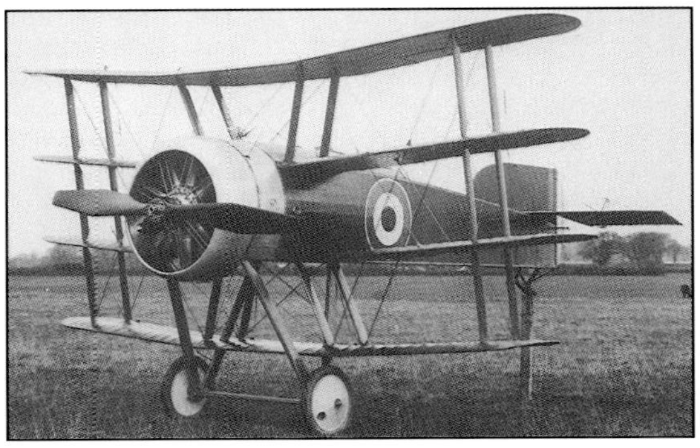

The extraordinary short-span Wight Quadruplane (above and below) was tested at Martlesham in 1917.

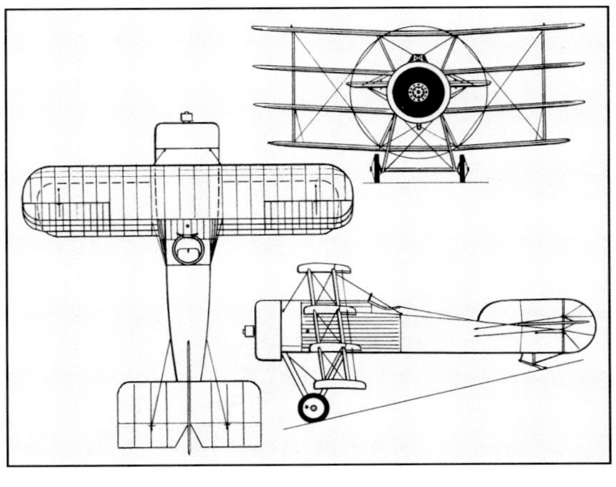

W.K.F. 80.05 — Austria-Hungary

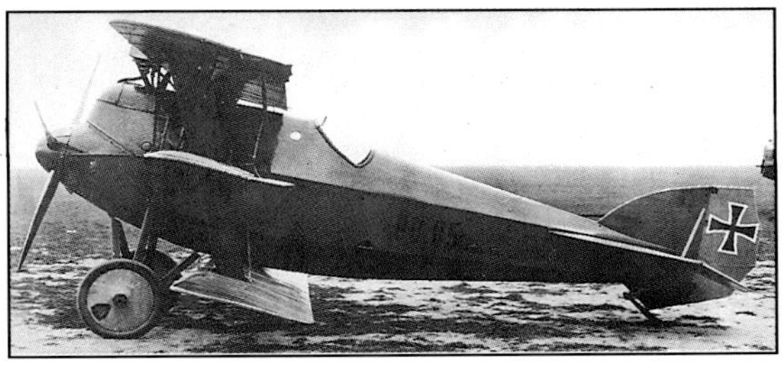

The W.K.F. 80.05 (above and below) saw only limited testing owing to restricted view from its cockpit.

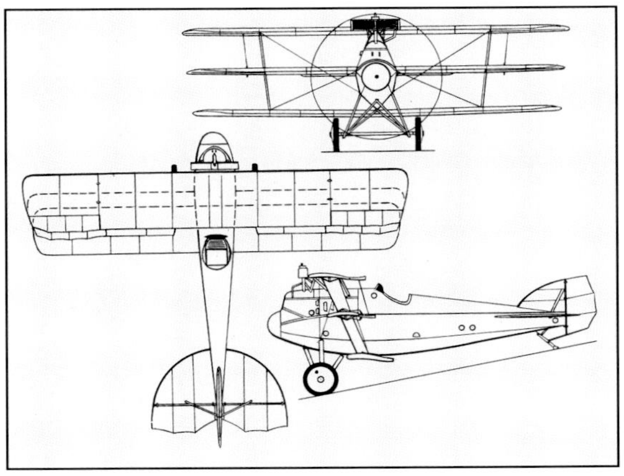

The first fighter of original design to be produced by W.K.F. (Wiener Karosserie- und Flugzeugfabrik Dr W v Gutmann), the W.K.F. 80.05 single-bay staggered triplane designed by Ing Alfred Gassner was completed in November 1917. Of wooden construction, it utilised a so-called *Fischrumpf*, or "Fish[-shaped] Fuselage", of hexagonal cross section with plywood skinning, and the wings, which had I-type, aerofoil-section interplane struts, had ailerons on the upper and centre planes only. The W.K.F. 80.05 was powered by a 200 hp Austro-Daimler six-cylinder inline water-cooled engine and provision was made for an armament of twin synchronised Schwarzlöse machine guns. Forward view from the cockpit was extremely limited by the very shallow cabane and the radiator bracing, and only limited flight testing of the sole W.K.F. 80.05 prototype was undertaken. *Max speed, 124 mph (200 km/h). Endurance, 1.5 hrs. Max range, 155 mls (250 km). Empty weight, 1,477 lb (670 kg). Loaded weight, 2,061 lb (935 kg). Span, 26 ft 2⅞ in (8,00 m). Length, 19 ft 9 in (6,02 m). Height, 9 ft 8⅛ in (2,95 m). Wing area, 242.09 sq ft (22,49 m²).*

W.K.F. 80.06 — Austria-Hungary

A single-bay staggered biplane following closely on the W.K.F. 80.05 triplane and possessing a number of common features, such as the *Fischrumpf*, the W.K.F. 80.06 was similarly powered with a 200 hp Austro-Daimler engine and was also of wooden construction with ply-

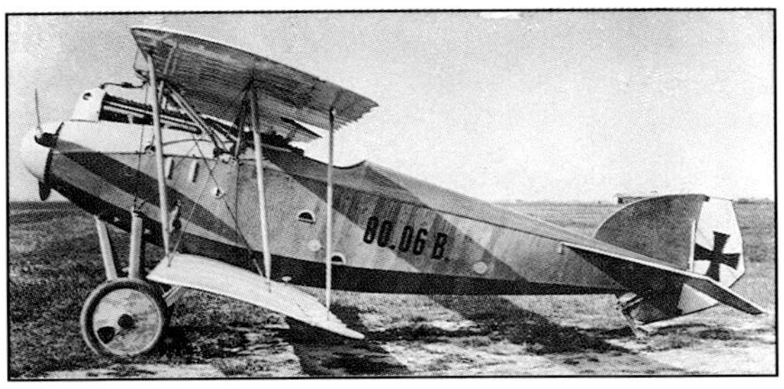

The W.K.F. 80.06 (above) was officially tested at Aspern, but crashed and was written off.

wood skinning. First flown early in 1918, the W.K.F. 80.06 was fitted with its twin synchronised Schwarzlöse gun armament during February, and, in March, it demonstrated the ability to attain an altitude of 16,405 ft (5 000 m) within 22 min, matching the climb of such fighters as the Albatros D III (Oef) and Phönix D II. Re-engined with a 230 hp Hiero, the prototype arrived at Aspern for official testing on 30 April 1918, but was written off as a result of a crash. A second, modified prototype, the W.K.F. 80.06B powered by a 225 hp Austro-Daimler engine, was delivered to Aspern. Ing Alfred Gassner had elected to reduce the wing gap and fit ailerons to both wings of the 80.06B, and, as a weight-saving measure, had replaced the plywood skinning of the wings with fabric. The prototype was flown at Aspern in July 1918 during the Fighter Evaluation along side two fundamentally similar prototypes, the W.K.F. 80.10 and 80.12, these differing from the 80.06B essentially in having the 230 hp Hiero engine. As a result of the excellent performance demonstrated by these prototypes, W.K.F. was awarded a production contract for the fighter as the D I, flight testing of the W.K.F. 80.06B continuing through August 1918. The end of hostilities terminated the W.K.F. D I programme. The 230 hp Hiero-engined fighter achieved an altitude of 16,405 ft (5 000 m) within 18 min and a maximum speed of 121 mph (195 km/h), no further data being available.

WRIGHT WP-1 — USA

The US Navy designation WP-1 (for Wright Pursuit) was given to a single example of the Dornier Do H Falke (which see) that was imported to the USA in 1923. It was entered in a Navy fighter competition by the Wright Aeronautical Corp, but its monoplane configuration and all-metal construction proved too advanced to win US Navy support.

WRIGHT XF3W-1 APACHE — USA

Despite its designation, the XF3W-1 was the first (and only) fighter designed and built by the aircraft division of the Wright Aeronautical Corp (preceding designations in the US Navy series having been applied to Wright racing seaplanes). Under US Navy contract, the single prototype – named Apache by Wright – was designed to operate from battleships as a seaplane, or from the decks of aircraft carriers with a wheel undercarriage. A single-bay equi-span biplane of mixed construction, the F3W-1, as the prototype was at first known, had a steel-tube fuselage and tail unit, and wooden wings, all fabric covered. As a seaplane for catapult launching, it had a large single float and stabilising floats under the wing tips. When first flown, the F3W-1 was powered by the experimental 325 hp

The XF3W-1 Apache (below) in landplane form and with the original Wright R-1300 Simoon engine.

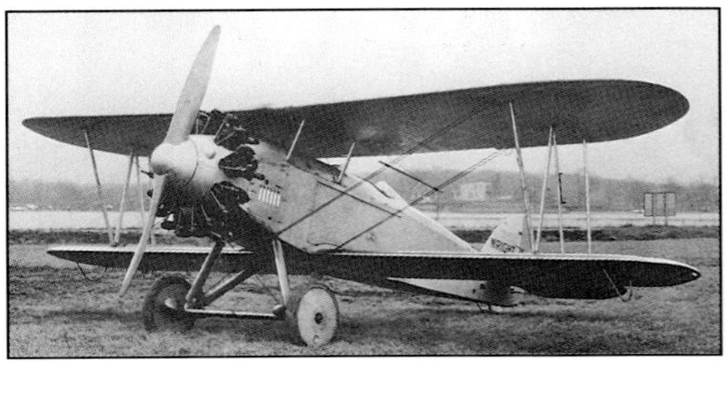

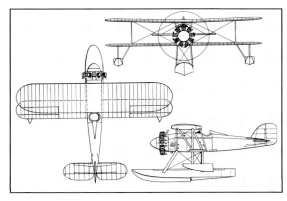

The XF3W-1 (above and below) as tested by the US Navy with central main float and outrigger floats.

Wright R-1300 Simoon nine-row air-cooled radial engine, but persistent difficulties led to early substitution of a 450 hp Pratt & Whitney R-1340B with which flight testing resumed on 5 May 1926. The Apache was tested by the Navy in both wheel and float configuration, but there is no record of the planned armament ever being fitted, and – redesignated as the XF3W-1 – the aircraft was used until 1930 as an engine test-bed. In both configurations, a series of altitude records was set by the XF3W-1, which, aided by a supercharger on the Wasp engine, eventually reached 38,560 ft (11 753 m) as a seaplane and 43,166 ft (13 157 m) as a landplane. For the later altitude flights, the span of the upper wing was increased. The following data apply to the F3W-1 with R-1340B engine and equi-span wings. *Max speed, 161 mph (260 km/h) at sea level. Service ceiling, 33,400 ft (10 180 m). Empty weight, 1,414 lb (641 kg). Loaded weight, 2,180 lb (989 kg). Span, 27 ft 4 in (8,33 m). Length, 22 ft 1 in (6,73 m). Height, 8 ft 6 in (2,59 m).*

X Y Z

XAC JH-7   China

The JH-7 – *Jianhongzhaji* (Fighter-bomber) 7 – was, at the time of its début, the most ambitious Chinese combat aircraft of indigenous design. A tandem two-seater intended to combine counterair fighter tasks with deep penetration interdiction and maritime strike in dedicated versions, the JH-7 was intended to enter the inventories of both the Air Force and the Navy during the mid 'nineties. Appearing in August 1988, when the XAC (Xian Aircraft Company) rolled out the first of three prototypes, the JH-7 was intended to carry up to 15,430 lb (7 000 kg) of ordnance distributed between six underwing stores stations, other armament including a single 23-mm cannon and wingtip close-range AAMs. The prototypes of the JH-7 were allegedly each

A model (below) of the JH-7 fighter-bomber of which three prototypes were completed during 1988-90.

powered by paired LMC WP13A II turbojets rated at 9,590 lb st (4 350 kgp) and 14,815 lb st (6 720 kgp) with afterburning, but it was anticipated that the series JH-7 would have the LM WS6A augmented turbofan with a maximum afterburning thrust of 31,085 lb (14 100 kg). *Max speed, 1,120 mph (1 800 km/h) above 36,090 ft (11 000 m), or Mach = 1.7. Service ceiling, 52,495 ft (16 000 m). Approx max loaded weight, 60,626 lb (27 500 kg). Span, 41 ft 11⅞ in (12,80 m). Length (including probe), 68 ft 10¾ in (21,00 m). Height, 20 ft 4¾ in (6,22 m). Wing area, 562.97 sq ft (52,30 m²).*

YAKOVLEV I-29 (YA-22)   USSR

The I-29 prototype (above and below) was one of three versions of the Ya-22 multi-rôle design.

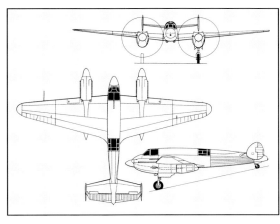

In 1938, the UV-VS (*Upravlenie Voenno-vozdushnikh Sily* – Administration of the Air Force) formulated a requirement for a two-seat multi-rôle high-speed combat aircraft. To meet this demand, the OKB (Experimental Construction Bureau) headed by Aleksandr S Yakovlev evolved the Ya-22, or *Samolet 22*. An aerodynamically clean, low-wing cantilever monoplane of mixed construction and powered by two 960 hp M-103A (V Ya Klimov-developed two-speed supercharged derivative of the Hispano-Suiza 12Y) 12-cylinder Vee-type engines, the Ya-22 was proposed in three dedicated versions: long-range escort fighter, short-range bomber and tactical reconnaissance aircraft. Prototypes of all three variants were built simultaneously, the first to fly being the fighter, which, assigned the NKAP (State Commissariat for Aviation Industry) designation I-29, entered flight test in February 1939. This was closely followed by the BB-22 bomber and R-12 reconnaissance prototypes. These differed from the I-29 primarily in that the

Yak-1s flown by (immediately below) Lt Col A E Golubov, 18 IAP, spring 1943, and (bottom) woman pilot Lilya Litvak of the 73 IAP.

fuel tank immediately aft of the cockpit was supplanted by a bay accommodating either eight 110-lb (50-kg) bombs in the BB-22 or photo-flashes (for use in conjunction with a single AFA-13 camera) in the R-12. The I-29 had twin 20-mm ShVAK cannon in fairings beneath the forward fuselage and a single 7,62-mm ShKAS for the aft-positioned observer/navigator, deployment of this gun being permitted by lowering of the aft-fuselage top decking. On 15 March 1939, shortly after commencement of flight testing, Yosif Stalin personally decided to order production of the bomber variant (as the M-105-powered Yak-2) to the exclusion of both fighter and reconnaissance versions. *Max speed, 352 mph (567 km/h) at 16,405 ft (5 000 m). Time to 16,405 ft (5 000 m), 5.75 min. Range, 652 mls (1 050 km). Empty weight, 8,369 lb (3 796 kg). Loaded weight, 11,074 lb (5 023 kg). Span, 45 ft 11⅛ in (14,00 m). Length, 33 ft 4¾ in (10,18 m). Height, 10 ft 9⅞ in (3,30 m). Wing area, 316.47 sq ft (29,40 m²).*

YAKOVLEV YAK-1 (I-26)   USSR

The second prototype Yak-1 (above) photographed in the OKB's overall red test finish with tail striping.

In parallel with the two-seat twin-engined combat aircraft requirement to which Aleksandr Yakovlev's OKB tendered the Ya-22, the UV-VS called for single-seat "frontal" and high-altitude fighters. The former was intended to be a general-purpose tactical fighter with best combat capability between 9,840 and 13,125 ft (3 000 and 4 000 m), and the latter was foreseen as a dedicated interceptor for use between 27,885 and 39,370 ft (8 500 and 12 000 m). Yakovlev tendered the Ya-26 and Ya-28 proposals to meet these requirements, these subsequently being assigned the NKAP designations I-26 and I-28 respectively. The "frontal" I-26 was intended to utilise the 1,350 hp M-106-I engine evolved by Vladimir Ya Klimov's bureau, but non-availability of this power plant led to installation of the M-105P 12-cylinder Vee-type liquid-cooled engine affording 1,100 hp for take-off. Flown on 13 January 1940, the I-26 was of mixed construction, with a plywood-covered, wooden wing and a steel-tube fuselage, with dural panelling forward and fabric-covered plywood skinning aft. Planned armament consisted of one engine-mounted 20-mm ShVAK cannon and two synchronised 7,62-mm ShKAS machine guns. The first prototype was destroyed on 27 April 1940, but a second prototype was by that time available and production preparations had begun at GAZ 115. Sixty-four pre-series and production aircraft had been completed by the end of December 1940, at which time the designation of the fighter was

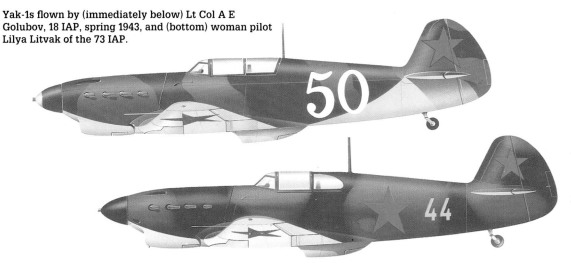

(Above, top) A Yak-1M used by the 1st "Warszawa" Fighter Regiment, late 1944, and (immediately above) Yak-1M flown by B N Yevemen, Stalingrad.

changed to Yak-1. Both overweight and underpowered, the Yak-1 was subjected to a weight reduction programme under the direction of Konstantin V Sinelshchikov. Re-engined with a higher-boosted M-105PF engine giving 1,210 hp for take-off and 1,260 hp at 2,625 ft (800 m), the prototype of a so-called *oblechenny*, or "lightweight", Yak-1 flew on 25 June 1941. Production deliveries of the Yak-1 continued with both the M-105PF and (from October 1941) the M-105PA which was rated at 1,100 hp, the paired 7,62-mm guns frequently being discarded in favour of a single 12,7-mm UBS offset to port, six 82-mm RS-82 rockets often being mounted underwing for close support missions. Progressive changes were introduced, the leg fairing plates being redesigned, the wing root carburettor air intakes being revised and some Yak-1s receiving a wing similar to that adopted for the Yak-7 (which see), this featuring more pointed tips that increased overall span by 9⅘ in (25 cm). The most obvious external change, however, resulted from cutting down the rear fuselage decking and adopting a three-piece all-round-vision cockpit canopy, which, standardised from January 1943, resulted in the Yak-1M (*Modifikatsirovanny*, or "modified"). The definitive Yak-1M also introduced revised exhaust stubs, redesigned oil cooler intake and radiator bath, and a retractable tailwheel. Among the first units to receive the Yak-1M were the French *Normandie-Niémen* regiment, the Polish 1 *Pulku Lotnictwa Mysliwskiego Warszawa*, and three Yugoslav regiments, the 111th, the 112th and the 113th. Production of the Yak-1 was phased out in the early summer of 1943, 8,721 aircraft having been delivered. The following data relate to the M-105PF-1-powered Yak-1. *Max speed, 314 mph (505 km/h) at sea level, 364 mph (585 km/h) at 12,465 ft (3 800 m). Max range,*

A Yak-1M (above) serving in October 1943 with the French *Normandie-Niémen* regiment at Monastirchina.

528 mls (850 km). Time to 16,405 ft (5 000 m), 5.4 min. Empty weight, 5,313 lb (2 410 kg). Loaded weight, 6,382 lb (2 895 kg). Span, 32 ft 9¾ in (10,00 m). Length, 27 ft 9½ in (8,47 m). Height, 5 ft 6⅞ in (1,70 m). Wing area, 184.6 sq ft (17,15 m²).

YAKOVLEV Yak-3 (I-30)   USSR

In the early summer of 1940, with the I-26 established in production in the GAZ 115, Aleksandr Yakovlev's OKB initiated the redesign of the fighter for all-metal construction as the I-30 (Ya-30), and the first of two prototypes entered flight test in the spring of 1941 as the Yak-3. Powered by a Klimov M-105P 12-cylinder liquid-cooled Vee-type engine rated at 1,100 hp for take-off and fitted with a Ye-100 mechanically-driven supercharger developed by V A Dollezhal, the Yak-3 had a three-piece wing with dihedral on the outer panels only and possessed an exceptionally heavy armament by contemporary standards. The single engine-mounted 20-mm ShVAK cannon and twin synchronised 7,62-mm ShKAS machine guns of the Yak-1 were augmented by two wing-mounted ShVAK cannon. The initial flight

test programme suffered constant difficulties with the supercharger, the engine being replaced three times in seven weeks with the result that the Dollezhal supercharger was discarded from the second prototype Yak-3 (I-30-II) which was flown in the summer of 1941 with a standard M-105P engine. The second prototype differed in having the radiator bath moved farther aft, the oil cooler air intake transferred from beneath the nose of the wing root leading edge and an additional pair of synchronised ShKAS machine guns mounted above the engine. With such exceptionally heavy armament and the increased fuel resulting from the larger-capacity tanks rendered possible by the metal wing, the Yak-3 was underpowered by the M-105P. In addition, the prevailing shortage of dural militated against continued development at that stage in the conflict with Germany, the Yak-3 programme being discontinued in the late autumn of 1941, and the designation subsequently being reassigned to an unrelated design. The following data relate to the first prototype. *Max speed, 304 mph (490 km/h) at sea level, 363 mph (584 km/h) at 15,585 ft (4 750 m). Max range, 559 mls (900 km). Empty weight, 5,622 lb (2 550 kg). Loaded weight, 6,900 lb (3 130 kg). Span, 31 ft 11½ in (9,74 m). Length, 27 ft 10⅔ in (8,50 m). Height (tail up), 9 ft 10 in (3,00 m). Wing area, 184.6 sq ft (17,15 m²).*

YAKOVLEV Yak-5 (I-28)   USSR

Originally proposed in parallel with the Ya-26 (I-26), the Ya-28 (I-28) was a dedicated high-altitude interceptor fighter developed in competition with the Mikoyan-Gurevich OKB's Kh (I-200). Flown in the late spring of 1941 – shortly *after* the I-30 alias Yak-3 – the high-altitude fighter had meanwhile been redesignated Yak-5 and its test programme had been delayed by development problems with its mechanically-driven two-stage Dollezhal supercharger. Possessing a fundamentally similar mixed structure to that of the Yak-1, but featuring a modified wing structure with automatic outboard leading-edge slats, the Yak-5 was powered by a Klimov M-105PD – the M-105P with the Dollezhal supercharger – rated at 1,220 hp for take-off and 1,150 hp at 8,860 ft (2 700 m). Armament was similar to that of the Yak-1. To improve all-round vision for the pilot, the cockpit canopy was extended aft. Two further prototypes of the Yak-5 were built, but the two-stage supercharger proved troublesome, and this problem, coupled with the higher priority assigned to the "frontal" Yak-1, led to rejection of the Yak-5 as a production type. Nonetheless, flight testing continued and it was alleged that a speed of 404 mph (650 km/h) was attained at 27,885 ft (8 500 m), and that, during June 1942, an altitude of 42,290 ft (12 890 m) was reached by one of the Yak-5 prototypes. *Max range, 286 mls (460 km). Service ceiling, 39,370 ft (12 000 m). Loaded weight, 6,592 lb (2 990 kg). Dimensions as for Yak-3.*

Early production standard Yak-1 (above and below) which achieved service status late in 1940.

The first of two I-30 all-metal fighter prototypes (above and below) which flew in 1941 as the Yak-3.

The I-28 (above and below) was an experimental high-altitude interceptor flown in the spring of 1941.

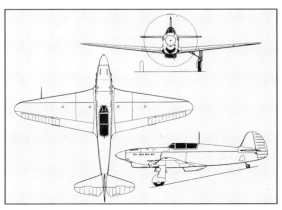

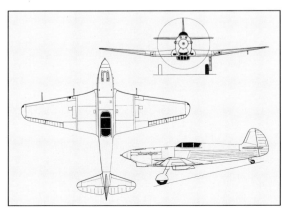

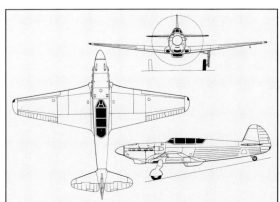

YAKOVLEV YAK-7   USSR

Newly-manufactured Yak-7s (above) prior to collection for the VVS at GAZ 292 at Saratov in mid-1942 when production was switching to the Yak-7B.

Late in 1939, the Yakovlev OKB initiated development of the Ya-27, a tandem two-seat version of the Ya-26 (I-26) single-seat fighter. Assigned the NKAP designation of UTI-26 (the prefix letters signifying *Uchebno-trenirovochny istrebitel*, or, literally, "instructional training fighter"), the Ya-27 featured dual control, but was intended for several tasks, including liaison and priority transport missions. The prototype UTI-26, flown on 4 July 1940, was, in fact, an adaptation of the fifth pre-series I-26, a second cockpit being inserted in the space previously occupied by the radio bay, and, for CG reasons, the ventral radiator bath being moved forward. Under test, the UTI-26 displayed handling characteristics superior to those of the I-26, but while the V-VS accepted the usefulness of the two-seater, it was clear that the changes from the single-seater made its production on the same line impracticable. The Yakovlev OKB therefore proposed an analogous single-seater utilising the space occupied by the second cockpit for a 22-Imp gal (100-l) fuel tank which was to be readily removable, its bay – covered by a hinged plywood panel – then being available for urgent freight or transportation of a ground-crew member. Armament was to comprise paired 12,7-mm UB machine guns and an engine-mounted 20-mm ShVAK cannon. The aircraft was redesignated Yak-7 – the two-seater becoming the Yak-7V, the suffix letter indicating *vyvoznoi*, or, literally, "familiarisation" – work on a small pre-series being undertaken by GAZ 115 and quantity production being assigned to GAZ 292 at Saratov, with 166 delivered by the end of 1941, two-seat Yak-7Vs preponderating. The Yak-7 was powered by the M-105P engine of 1,100 hp, but this gave place to higher-boosted M-105PF in the Yak-7B from mid 1942, this providing 1,210 hp for take-off. The Yak-7B, which appeared at the beginning of 1942, introduced improved equipment, a jettisonable cockpit canopy, an entirely new undercarriage, a retractable tailwheel and increased ammunition capacity. The more pointed tips that had given the Yak-7 a wingspan of 33 ft 7½ in (10,25 m) gave place to tips similar to those of the original Yak-1, and provision was made for an external load of two 220-lb (100-kg) bombs or six RS-82 rockets. Early production Yak-7Bs were powered, like the original Yak-7, by the M-105P. Test versions of the Yak-7B included one fitted with a pressure cabin designed by A Ya Scherbakov and two fitted with the engine-mounted 37-mm Shpital'ny-Komaritsky cannon. Several were fitted with more comprehensive instrumentation for use by IA-PVO regiments as Yak-7MPVOs, and, with increased availability of steel alloys, the wing structure of the Yak-7B was partly redesigned with steel-alloy H-spars supplanting the wooden box-spars to permit an 8.5 per cent increase in wing tank capacity. This wing modification was adopted on the GAZ 292 assembly line, and, at the same time, the rear-fuselage decking was cut down

(Below) A Yak-7 of an unidentified IAP presented to the VVS by the Bashkirian Republic (summer 1942).

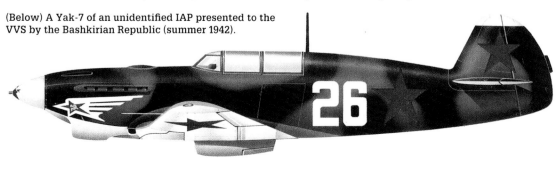

and a three-piece all-round-vision cockpit canopy was introduced, with these changes the fighter being designated Yak-7DI – *dal'ny istrebitel*, or, literally "long [distance] fighter". With completion of a pre-series batch of Yak-7DI fighters during the autumn of 1942, full-scale production of this type, embodying a number of refinements and redesignated Yak-9 (which see), was undertaken at GAZ 115 and GAZ 153. By the time that the last Yak-7 left the GAZ 115 assembly line early 1943, a total of 6,399 single- and two-seat aircraft of this type had been delivered, in excess of 5,000 of these being Yak-7Bs to which version the following data are applicable. *Max speed, 336 mph (542 km/h) at sea level, 382 mph (615 km/h) at 10,170 ft (3 100 m). Time to 16,405 ft (5 000 m), 5.7 min. Max range, 509 mls (820 km). Empty weight, 5,467 lb (2 480 kg). Loaded weight, 6,680 lb (3 030 kg). Span, 32 ft 9¾ in (10,00 m). Length, 27 ft 9½ in (8,47 m,). Height, 9 ft 0¼ in (2,75 m). Wing area, 184.6 sq ft (17,15 m²).*

The Yak-7B (above and below), the photo depicting an aircraft of the 18 (Guards) IAP, Khationki, 1943.

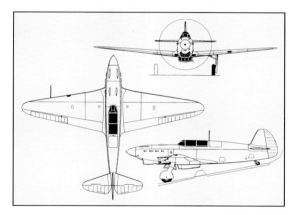

YAKOVLEV YAK-7M-82   USSR

An official directive issued in the summer of 1941 dictated adaptation of all existing production inline-engined single-seat fighter airframes to take an air-cooled radial engine to safeguard against any shortfall in deliveries of inline units (see Mikoyan-Gurevich I-210 and Lavochkin La-5). The Yakovlev OKB's response to this directive was ostensibly an adaptation of the Yak-7 for the Shvetsov M-82 14-cylinder radial air-cooled engine. Referred to as the Yak-7M-82, it was, designation notwithstanding, virtually a new fighter. Weighing more than the M-105P engine that it replaced, possessing a different thrust line and having a substantially greater width than the Yak-7 cross section, the M-82 demanded an entirely new fuselage, which was mated with a structurally extensively modified Yak-7 wing. The M-82 engine with two-speed supercharger was rated at 1,700 hp for take-off and was enclosed by an extremely close fitting, tapered cowling incorporating a single 12,7-mm UBS machine gun in its portside. By comparison with the wing of the standard Yak-7, the wing of the Yak-7M-82 incorporated automatic leading-edge slats and larger flaps, and a 20-mm ShVAK cannon

The Yak-7M-82 (above and below) featured an entirely new fuselage and an extensively revised wing.

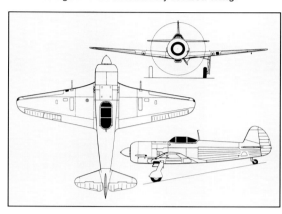

was installed immediately outboard of each main undercarriage attachment point. The sole prototype Yak-7M-82 was first flown on 28 February 1942, an innovation being a three-piece all-round vision cockpit canopy similar to that subsequently standardised for the Yak-1M and Yak-7DI. The flight test programme was reportedly successful, but the Lavochkin OKB's M-82 conversion of a LaGG-3 airframe, which had entered flight test some two weeks after the Yak-7M-82, appeared more promising and further development of the Yakovlev fighter was discontinued, although experience gained with this type was to be utilised in development of the Yak-3U (which see) three years later. *Max speed, 320 mph (515 km/h) at sea level, 355 mph (571 km/h) at 8,695 ft (2 650 m). Time to 16,405 ft (5 000 m), 5.5 min. Range, 547 mls (880 km). Span, 31 ft 11½ in (9,74 m). Length, 26 ft 9⅝ in (8,17 m). Height, 9 ft 0¼ in (2,75 m). Wing area, 184.6 sq ft (17,15 m²).*

YAKOVLEV YAK-9   USSR

Yak-9s of a Guards Regiment (above) flying over Sevastopol, Crimea, in early summer of 1944.

First appearing operationally in small numbers during the Soviet counter-attacks of November 1942, the Yak-9, in its original production form, was lighter than the pre-series Yak-7DI from which it had been derived. Initially, it differed from its immediate predecessor only in detail – deeper radiator bath, refined oil cooler intake, modified rudder and (standardised) external tabs on control surfaces. Power was provided by an M-105PF-1 engine rated at 1,210 hp for take-off and 1,260 hp at 2,625 ft (800 m), and armament comprised a 20-mm engine-mounted ShVAK, cannon and one 12,7-mm machine gun. Progressive changes included increased-area wing flaps accompanied by more angular wingtips (signifying introduction of metal in place of wooden ribs), and, in the case of the Yak-9D – *dal'ny*, or "long" [distance] – two additional fuel tanks in the outer wing panels and an optional tank under the cockpit. The Yak-9D made its debut in May 1943, and was

(Above, top) Yak-9 used by CO of 4° *Esc, Normandie-Niémen* IAP, Dubrovka, 1944. (Immediately above) Yak-9P of Korean People's Armed Forces Air Force, 1950.

followed by an even longer-ranging version, the Yak-9DD – *dal'noye deistviye*, or, literally, "ultra long range" – with virtually double the tankage of the original Yak-9 and a range of up to 1,367 mls (2 200 km). Whereas the Yak-9DD had an all-up weight of 7,222 lb (3 276 kg), the Yak-9B fighter-bomber, intended for pinpoint attacks on heavily-defended targets, weighed 7,628 lb (3 460 kg) all-up. This variant housed four 220-lb (100-kg) bombs nose-up in tubes immediately aft of the pilot's cockpit, and inclined forwards 80 deg. The Yak-9B equipped a full V-VS division operating on the 3rd Bielo-Russian Front. Other sub-types included the Yak-9MPVO, which featured night flying equipment and served with the IA-PVO, and the "stripped" Yak-9PD which was effectively a resurrection of the Yak-5 programme (which see). A high-altitude interceptor of which only five examples were built, the Yak-9PD had an M-105PD engine with a Dollezhal mechanically-driven two-stage supercharger, and succeeded in attaining an altitude of 45,930 ft (14 000 m). Large-calibre gun close-support fighter versions, the Yak-9T and -9K (which see) involved more extensive modification to the basic design. By mid-1944, the Yak-9 outnumbered all other V-VS fighters combined on the major war fronts, and a second generation of fighters in this series (see Yak-9U and -9P) had achieved production status. The following data are applicable to the Yak-9D with the M-105PF-3 engine rated at 1,360 hp at 2,625 ft (800 m). *Max speed, 332 mph (535 km/h) at sea level, 374 mph (602 km/h) at 10,170 ft (3 100 m). Time to 16,405 ft (5 000 m), 6.0 min. Max range, 870 mls (1 400 km). Empty weight, 6,107 lb (2 770 kg). Max loaded weight, 6,790 lb (3 080 kg). Span, 31 ft 11½ in (9,74 m). Length, 28 ft 0¾ in (8,55 m). Height (tail up), 9 ft 10 in (3,00 m). Wing area, 184.6 sq ft (17,15 m²).*

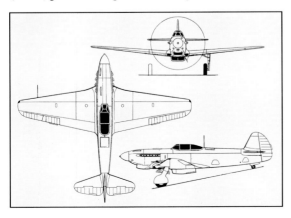

Yak-9s (above) of the 18 (Guards) IAP, Summer 1943, and (below) general arrangement drawing of the Yak-9D.

YAKOVLEV Yak-9T & Yak-9K USSR

The Yak-9T-37 (above) which entered service with the V-VS in the early summer of 1943.

Adaptation of the basic Yak-9 design to accept very large calibre guns for use in the anti-armour, anti-shipping and anti-bomber rôles began in 1942, and involved quite extensive modification. The principal change was a bodily aft shift of the pilot's cockpit by 15.75 in (40 cm) to accommodate the breech of the gun and to preserve the CG. It was necessary to reduce internal fuel tankage by 79 Imp gal (360 l) and a single 12,7-mm UBS was provided for aiming purposes. Designated Yak-9T – *tyazhely*, or "heavy" [cannon] – the first large-calibre gun version entered flight test in December 1942 with a 37-mm NS-11-P-37 cannon (later redesignated NS-37). Sometimes referred to as the Yak-9T-37, this version of the fighter entered V-VS service in the early summer of 1943, and, by the autumn, was operating in the anti-shipping rôle in the Black Sea. Most were fitted with wing racks for boxes of PTAB-2,5 bomblets, and cannon availability necessitated some aircraft being delivered with a 23-mm VYa (MP-23-VV) cannon in place of the 37-mm weapon. A further large-calibre gun version was the Yak-9K – *krupnyi kalibr*, or "heavy calibre" [cannon] – with a 45-mm NS-P-45 weapon which was intended primarily for use against *Panther* and *Tiger* tanks. Proposals to install a 57-mm cannon did not see fruition. The following data relate to the Yak-9T-37 with the M-105PF-3 engine. *Max speed, 330 mph (532 km/h) at sea level, 371 mph (597 km/h) at 9,840 ft (3 000 m). Time to 16,405 ft (5 000 m), 5.5 min. Max range, 516 mls (830 km). Empty weight, 6,063 lb (2 750 kg). Max loaded weight, 6,746 lb (3 060 kg). Dimensions as for basic Yak-9D apart from length of 28 ft 5 in (8,66 m).*

YAKOVLEV Yak-9U & Yak-9P USSR

Development of what would come to be considered as a second-generation Yak-9 effectively began in late December 1942 with flight test of a Yak-9 airframe adapted to take the new and appreciably more powerful Klimov M-107 12-cylinder Vee-type engine. This aircraft was destroyed as a result of engine failure on 25 February 1943, during the final manufacturer's flight test prior to initiation of State Acceptance trials. This accident, coupled with teething troubles, delayed clearance of the M-107A, and, in consequence, deliveries of the definitive Yak-9U (*Uluchshennyi*, or "improved") for which it was primarily intended. Embodying considerable aerodynamic refinement, the first genuine prototype of the Yak-9U flew in December 1943, but with an M-105PF-2 engine, this power plant also being installed in the initial production batches of

Yak-9Us delivered in the late summer and early autumn of 1944. The M-107A (later VK-107A) was phased in on the assembly line in the late autumn, a number of changes being made after further flight testing had seen instances of separation of the plywood skinning of the fighter, and engine overheating leading to unacceptable cockpit temperatures. The oil cooler intake was transferred from beneath the nose to the port wing root, an enlarged radiator bath was moved farther aft, the supercharger intake was centred on the top decking of the engine cowling and multiple ejector exhausts were introduced. The wing was moved forward 3.9 in (10 cm), the thickness of the ply skinning was increased and fuel capacity was boosted by 12.7 per cent. Increased availability of metal alloys soon made it possible to discard plywood skinning in favour of light alloy stressed skinning for the entire aircraft. The Yak-9U, with an M-107A (VK-107A) engine rated at 1,650 hp for take-off, an output maintained up to 5,905 ft (1 800 m), normally had a hub-mounted 20-mm MP-20 cannon and two 12,7-mm UBS machine guns. The cannon could be replaced by a 23-mm VYa-23. During the closing months of the conflict in Europe, the first regiments of the V-VS to equip with the M-107-powered Yak-9U received their aircraft, and with the end of hostilities, the Yakovlev OKB was engaged in development of an enhanced version that was to appear in 1946. This, designated Yak-9P – the suffix indicating *pushka*, or "cannon" [armed] – replaced the 12,7-mm weapons with synchronised 20-mm ShVAK cannon and had upgraded communications and navigational equipment. In the immediate postwar years, the Soviet Union exported substantial numbers of Yak-9Us and -9Ps.

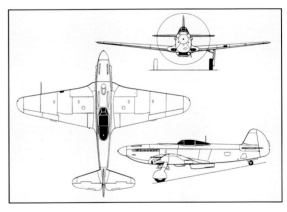

The Yak-9U in standard form (below) and with non-standard windscreen and short rear canopy (above).

Forty of the latter were delivered to Yugoslavia, where their troublesome VK-107A (M-107A) engines were replaced by refurbished M-105PFs with which they were to serve until the early '50s. A mix of some 60 Yak-9Us and -9Ps was supplied to Poland, 53 surviving examples being relegated to the advanced training rôle in 1950. China, too, was recipient of a number of Yak-9Ps, transferring some to North Korea which employed them during the initial stages of the Korean conflict that began in June 1950. Bulgaria received a modified version designated Yak-9P(Bulg) which omitted the outboard wing tanks and augmented the standard armament with a pair of wing-mounted 12,7-mm UBS guns, and, from September 1949, Hungary took delivery of about 120 Yak-9Ps, which, dubbed *Vércse* (Falcon), remained in service until the mid '50s. Production of the "second generation" Yak-9 was finally phased out during 1947, by which time a total of 16,769 Yak-9 fighters of all types – including 3,900 Yak-9U and -9P variants – had been manufactured. The following data relate to the Yak-9P. *Max speed, 367 mph (590 km/h) at sea level, 418 mph (673 km/h) at 18,700 ft (5 700 m). Initial climb, 4,528 ft/min (23,0 m/*

sec). Max range, 746 mls (1 200 km). Empty weight, 5,988 lb (2 716 kg). Normal loaded weight, 7,485 lb (3 395 kg). Span, 32 ft 0½ in (9,77 m). Length, 28 ft 0½ in (8,55 m). Height (tail up), 9 ft 8½ in (2,96 m). Wing area, 185.68 sq ft (17,25 m²).

YAKOVLEV Yak-3 (II)   USSR

Early in 1941, the Yak-3 was conceived to meet a specific V-VS requirement for an exceptionally agile single-seat fighter capable of maximum performance at low altitude and suitable for maintenance of aerial superiority in the immediate vicinity of the battlefield. The Yak-3 appeared in V-VS service in the summer of 1944 as the smallest and lightest warplane in its category to see large-scale operational service during World War II. Originally intended to use the M-107 engine, the Yak-3 – the designation being re-assigned from the defunct I-30 programme (which see) – was developed via a modified Yak-1M which, fitted with a smaller wing, was flown late in 1942. Further refinement of the aircraft undertaken by Konstantin V Sinelshchikov led to the oil cooler air intake sharing wing root positioning with those for the carburettor and supercharger. Non-availability of the M-107A engine led to adoption of the M-105PF-2, which, operating at higher revs than the PF-1 version in the Yak-1M, afforded 1,300 hp at 2,625 ft (800 m). Armament consisted of one engine-mounted 20-mm ShVAK cannon and two 12,7-mm UBS machine guns. The development programme was delayed when the prototype Yak-3 suffered a structural failure, full State Acceptance trials not being completed until October 1943, by which time a small pre-series was under construction at GAZ 286 at Kamensk Ural'ski. These were immediately assigned on completion to an operational regiment for service trials, and, in the event, saw combat during the Soviet counter-offensive to Operation *Zitadelle*. Despite the success of these combat trials, the Yak-3 was not *officially* cleared by the NII V-VS for production until June 1944, but the 91 IAP had re-equipped with this type by July, and, on the 16th of that month, was able to claim destruction of 24 Bf 109Gs and Fw 190s in one low-altitude mêlée involving 18 of the IAP's Yak-3s. Virtually simultaneously, the French *Normandie-Niémen* regiment began re-equipping with the Yak-3. The basic Yak-3 was the subject of considerable experimentation, test variants including the Yak-3RD fitted with a so-called "auxiliary accelerator" in the form of a Glushko RD-1 (KhZ) bi-fuel (nitric acid and kerosene) rocket motor in the tail. A speed of 498 mph (801 km/h) was attained with the aid of this rocket while in a shallow climb, but on 16 August 1944, the Yak-3RD was lost when the rocket exploded. Second-generation Yak-3s were evolved with M-107 and M-108 engines (which see), but these were not to achieve large-scale production, contributing comparatively few to the total of 4,848 of this fighter that had been delivered when pro-

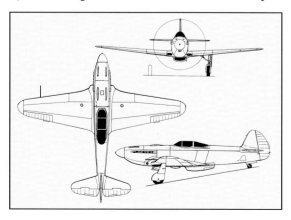

The Yak-3 (above and below), the photo depicting a *Normandie-Niémen* aircraft flown by René Challe.

duction ended at the beginning of 1946. *Max speed, 367 mph (590 km/h) at sea level, 407 mph (655 km/h) at 10,170 ft (3 100 m). Initial climb, 3,800 ft/min (19,30 m/sec). Max range, 560 mls (900 km). Empty weight, 4,641 lb (2 105 kg). Loaded weight, 5,622 lb (2 550 kg). Span, 30 ft 2¼ in (9,20 m). Length, 27 ft 10¼ in (8,49 m). Height, 7 ft 11¼ in (2,42 m). Wing area, 159.63 sq ft (14,83 m²).*

YAKOVLEV Yak-3M-107   USSR

The Yak-3M-107 (above) afforded a spectacular performance, but was too late to be built in quantity.

In parallel with second-generation Yak-9 development using the M-107 engine, the Yakovlev OKB undertook similar development of the basic Yak-3. The first M-107A-powered Yak-3 – referred to simply as the Yak-3M-107 – was flown in the late autumn of 1943, the fighter having been intended for this engine from the outset. At this time, work was proceeding on the redesign of the airframe for light alloy stressed-skin construction, and the all-metal Yak-3 with the M-107A engine was to undergo State Acceptance tests between February and May 1945, demonstrating a spectacular performance. The nose was marginally lengthened, the cockpit was repositioned 12.6 in (32 cm) aft for CG reasons and a deeper radiator bath was adopted. The M-107A engine was rated at 1,650 hp for take-off and armament remained similar to that of the first-generation Yak-3, comprising two synchronised 12,7-mm UBS machine guns and one 20-mm engine-mounted ShVAK cannon. The official report following completion of State Acceptance tests stated: "The experimental Yak-3 powered by the M-107A . . . ..appears to offer the best performance of all indigenous and known foreign fighters." Nonetheless, the Yak-3M-107 was too late for large scale production, only a limited series being built, including a number with revised armament under the designation Yak-3P – *pushka*, or "cannon" [armed]. This comprised two synchronised 20-mm B-20 cannon and a third firing through the propeller hub. An anti-armour version, the Yak-3T – *tyazhely*, or "heavy" [cannon] – was similar but had the engine-mounted B-20 replaced with a 37-mm NS-37, and one example (flown only once) was fitted with a 57-mm engine-mounted OKB-16-57 cannon. Known unofficially to the few V-VS regiments that equipped with the Yak-3M-107 during 1945-46 as the *Ubiytsa* (Killer) – an appellation reflecting its predatory capabilities rather than any malicious intent towards its pilot – it was alleged to have been the fastest piston-engined fighter to have attained service status. *Max speed, 386 mph (622 km/h) at 1,640 ft (500 m), 477 mph (720 km/h) at 18,045 ft (5 500 m). Time to 16,405 ft (5 000 m), 3.9 min. Loaded weight, 6,578 lb (2 984 kg). Dimensions as for standard Yak-3 apart from overall length of 29 ft 1¼ in (8,87 m).*

YAKOVLEV Yak-3M-108   USSR

Destined to be the fastest of all piston-engined Yakovlev fighters, the Yak-3M-108 possessed a similar all-metal airframe to the definitive Yak-3M-107 from which it differed only in engine and armament. With the availability of the Klimov M-108 12-cylinder Vee-type engine rated at 1,850 hp, the Yakovlev OKB initiated adaptation of an airframe to take this power plant in August 1944. The aircraft was rolled out on 7 October that year, and the first two flights were effected on 19 December. Armament consisted of a single engine-mounted 23-mm NS-23 cannon, and, on 21 December, this

The Yak-3M-108 (above) recorded the highest speed attained by any Soviet piston-engined fighter.

Yak-3M-108 recorded a speed of 463 mph (745 km/h) at 19,685 ft (6 000 m) and climbed to 16,405 ft (5 000 m) in 5 min. Yakovlev subsequently claimed the speed attained on that occasion to be the highest ever achieved in level flight by a Soviet piston-engined aircraft. The M-108 engine presented numerous development problems, inhibiting the flight test programme until, in January 1945, further work on the power plant and prototype was cancelled. *Max speed, 388 mph (625 km/h) at sea level, 463 mph (745 km/h) at 19,685 ft (6 000 m). Loaded weight, 6,239 lb (2 830 kg). Dimensions as for Yak-3M-107.*

YAKOVLEV Yak-3U   USSR

The last piston-engined fighter to be produced by the Yakovlev OKB, the Yak-3U – *Uluchshennyi*, or "improved" – bore no relationship to the bureau's earlier radial-engined single-seater, the Yak-7M-82, other than its common design origin. Retaining the light alloy stressed-skin metal wing and tail surfaces of the second-generation M-107A-engined Yak-3, it mated these elements with an entirely new fuselage and an M-82FN (ASh-82FN) 14-cylinder two-row radial rated at 1,850 hp. The engine was extremely close cowled, careful attention was given to the hermetic sealing of the fuselage and power loading was reduced to 3.35 lb/hp (1.5 kg/cv) from the 4.02 lb/hp (1.8 kg/cv) of the M-107A-engined fighter. Armament consisted of twin synchronised 20-mm B-20 cannon, but these were interchangeable with paired 23-mm NS-23 guns. The Yak-3U was developed under a comparatively low-priority programme and was not flown until 12 May 1945. During its test programme it proved outstandingly manoeuvrable – it was claimed by the test team to be more agile than any known fighter – but, being considered conceptually obsolescent, the Yak-3U was not subjected to State Acceptance testing, and only the one prototype was completed. *Max speed, 385 mph (620 km/h) at sea level, 441 mph (710 km/h) at 20,015 ft (6 100 m). Time to 16,405 ft (5 000 m), 3.8 min. Range, 441 mls (710 km).*

Derived from the Yak-3M-107, the Yak-3U (above and below) was the OKB's last piston-engined fighter.

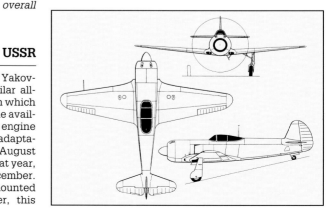

603

Loaded weight, 6,151 lb (2 790 kg). Span, 30 ft 10 in (9,40 m). Length, 27 ft 5⅛ in (8,36 m).

YAKOVLEV YAK-15   USSR

A prototype Yak-15 (above) taking-off for the first flight of the type on 24 April 1946.

The series production Yak-15 (above and below) which was manufactured by GAZ 153 until late in 1947.

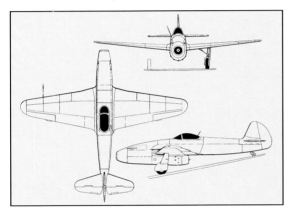

Flown for the first time on 24 April 1946, just three hours after the Mikoyan-Gurevich OKB's I-300 (MiG-9), the Yak-15 was to achieve the distinction of being one of only two *service* jet fighters in aviation's annals to have been derived from a piston-engined *service* fighter (the other being the Swedish Saab 21R). Primarily the responsibility of Yevgenii Adler and Leon Shekhter, development of the Yak-15 began in May 1945, the all-metal second-generation Yak-3 airframe being used as a basis and enabling the first of three prototypes to be completed in the following October. Taxying trials and short "hops" were performed, but flight testing was delayed while the possibility of the jet efflux attaching to the fuselage at high incidences was explored in the TsAGI T-101 full-scale wind tunnel. The Yak-15 retained most of the wing, rear fuselage, tail and undercarriage of the Yak-3, a new fuselage nose housing a Junkers Jumo 004B turbojet being introduced, and the main-spar being arched over the jetpipe. The Yak-15 was demonstrated over Tushino during Aviation Day on 18 August 1946, and two days later, on 20 August, the NKAP (People's Commissariat for the Aircraft Industry) issued a directive that 12 additional aircraft be built to participate in the October Revolution Parade to be held on the following 7 November, 80 days later. Produced by hand, the first of these flew on 5 October and the last in time to participate in the Parade, which, in the event, was cancelled because of inclement weather. State Acceptance testing was completed in May 1947, and, despite being structurally limited to Mach=0.68 below 10,500 ft (3 200 m), the Yak-15 was ordered into production at GAZ 153 as an *interim* type. One of the pre-series Yak-15s had meanwhile been adapted as a tandem two-seat conversion trainer under the designation Yak-21. The series Yak-15 carried an armament of two 23-mm NS-23 cannon and was powered by a Jumo 004B turbojet which had been adapted by I F Koliesov of the Lyulka bureau for manufacture at Kazan as the RD-10

with a rating of 1,967 lb st (892 kgp). Production gave place late in 1947 to the Yak-17 after completion of 280 Yak-15s. *Max speed, 435 mph (700 km/h) at 8,200 ft (2 500 m), 500 mph (805 km/h) at 16,405 ft (5 000 m). Time to 16,405 ft (5 000 m), 4.8 min. Max range, 317 mls (510 km). Empty weight, 5,181 lb (2 350 kg). Loaded weight, 6,029 lb (2 735 kg). Span, 30 ft 2¼ in (9,20 m). Length, 28 ft 6½ in (8,70 m). Height, 7 ft 5⅓ in (2,27 m). Wing area, 159.85 (14,85 m²).*

YAKOVLEV YAK-17   USSR

During the autumn of 1946, the Yakovlev OKB initiated a relatively modest redesign of the Yak-15 which was initially referred to as the Yak-15U – *Uluchshennyi* (improved). The prototype, flown early in 1947, differed from its progenitor essentially in having a nosewheel rather than tailwheel undercarriage. Owing to the position of the engine, it was physically impossible to retract the nosewheel completely, and this was therefore partly enclosed by a fixed fairing. Introduction of a nosewheel demanded transfer of the main undercarriage members from the forward to the rear wing spar and dictated considerable structural redesign and a reduction in wing tankage. To compensate for the latter, a jettisonable 66-Imp gal (300-l) tank was added beneath each wing tip. Redesignated Yak-17, this fighter was restressed throughout and, in series form, was fitted with a redesigned vertical tail and an RD-10A engine rated at 2,205 lb st (1 000 kgp). Armament remained two 23-mm NS-23 cannon. Production of the Yak-17 followed on from the Yak-15 in late 1947, and continued for a year, a total of 430 being built, including a proportion of tandem two-seat Yak-17UTI conversion trainers. The Yak-17UTI entered flight test in April 1948, and about 150 were eventually built, 20 of these being exported to Poland and several to China. One Yak-17 fighter was delivered to Czechoslovakia for evaluation, where it received the designation S 100, and three were supplied to Poland. The latter country acquired manufacturing licences in 1950 for both the Yak-17 and its RD-10A turbojet, which were to be built at Mielec and Rzeszow respectively. The Polish programme was terminated in the winter of 1950-51 before any aircraft had been built as the Yak-17 had been overtaken by more efficacious fighters, but 30 RD-10A engines were completed at Rzeszow. The Yak-17 and Yak-17UTI were phased out by the V-VS in 1951 and 1953 respectively, and the latter from the Polish air arm by 1955. *Max speed, 447 mph (720 km/h) at 7,875 ft (2 400 m), 466 mph (750 km/h) at 19,685 ft (6 000 m). Time to 16,405 ft (5 000 m), 5.8 min. Range, 446 mls (717 km). Empty weight, 5,357 lb (2 430 kg). Max loaded weight, 7,326 lb (3 323 kg). Span, 30 ft 2¼ in (9,20 m). Length, 28 ft 9⅔ in (8,78 m). Wing area, 159.85 sq ft (14,85 m²).*

The Yak-17 (above and below) represented a modest redesign of the Yak-15 and featured a nosewheel.

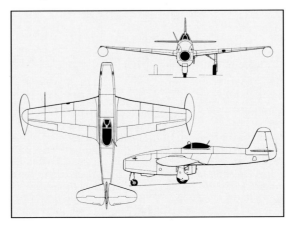

YAKOVLEV YAK-19   USSR

Virtually simultaneously with redesign of the Yak-15 to produce the Yak-17, the Yakovlev OKB embarked upon the design of a markedly more advanced single-seat fighter, the Yak-19. Conceptually not dissimilar to the Republic XP-84 – flown six months earlier – in utilising the straight-through airflow arrangement, the Yak-19, like its US counterpart, employed a 12 per cent thickness straight wing. In all other respects, however, the two aircraft differed. The Yak-19 was appreciably smaller than the American fighter and accommodated all fuel within the fuselage. Of all-metal stressed-skin construction with a semi-monocoque fuselage, the Yak-19 had a laminar-flow wing of TsAGI S-1-12 section, and armament of two 23-mm cannon. Equipped with an ejection seat, it was the first Soviet fighter to be fitted with an afterburner, this boosting the thrust of its RD-10F turbojet to 2,425 lb (1 100 kg). Two prototypes were built, the first of these entering flight test in January 1947. The second prototype differed in having revised vertical tail surfaces, several degrees of anhedral applied to the horizontal tail and provision for a 44-Imp gal (200-l) drop tank beneath each wingtip. Difficulties were experienced with the afterburner, and as more powerful turbojets (eg, the RD-500) were by now available, the Yak-19 test programme was terminated on 21 August 1947. *Max speed (with afterburning), 544 mph (875 km/h) at sea level, 564 mph (907 km/h) at 17,225 ft (5 250 m), (without afterburning), 472 mph (760 km/h) at sea level, 508 mph (818 km/h) at 17,225 ft (5 250 m). Time to 16,405 ft (5 000 m), 4.0 min. Range (internal fuel), 342 mls (550 km). Empty weight, 4,832 lb (2 192 kg). Normal loaded weight, 6,724 lb (3 050 kg). Span, 28 ft 6½ in (8,70 m). Length, 27 ft 5⅛ in (8,36 m). Wing area, 145.32 sq ft (13,50 m²).*

The first (above) and second (below) prototypes of the Yak-19, development of which ended in mid-1947.

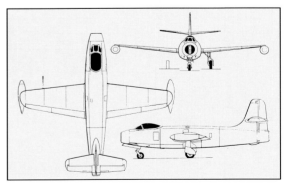

YAKOVLEV YAK-23   USSR

Reverting to the so-called *redan* (stepped) configuration of the first Yakovlev jet fighters, the Yak-23 possessed wing and horizontal tail surfaces similar to those of the Yak-19, and was intended to fulfil a requirement for a lightweight day interceptor capable of operating from existing fields. The first of three prototypes of the Yak-23, which were of all-metal stressed-skin construction and powered by imported Rolls-Royce Derwent turbojets, was flown on 17 June 1947. Seen as something of a back-up for the very much more advanced Nene-engined fighters with wing sweep-back then under development, the Yak-23 proved itself an outstandingly agile warplane. Manufacturer's trials were completed on 12 September 1947. State Acceptance testing had been successfully completed before the year's end and series production began in the late spring of 1948. The series Yak-23 was powered by a Soviet copy of the Derwent known as the RD-500 – a designation derived from GAZ-500, the factory in which the engine was produced – and rated at 3,505 lb st (1 590 kgp). Its armament consisted of two 23-mm NS-23 (later NR-23) cannon. Deliveries to the V-VS began early in 1949, by which time the first production examples of the MiG-15 had already flown. In consequence, only two V-VS regiments reportedly re-equipped (from the Yak-17) with the Yak-23, which was quickly released for export. Twelve were delivered to Czechoslovakia during 1950 (and there assigned the designation S 101) and the supply of some 95 to Poland began late that year, while, in 1951, 12 each were delivered to Romania and Bulgaria. Both Czechoslovakia and Poland were to have licence-built the Yak-23 but, in the event, manufactured the MiG-15, and Soviet production of the Yakovlev type terminated in 1950 with 310 built. One example was converted by the OKB as a tandem two-seat conversion trainer (Yak-23UTI), this first being flown in the spring of 1949. One Yak-23 was rebuilt as a tandem two-seater in Romania, but the type had given place to the MiG-15 in all Warsaw Pact air forces by the mid '50s. *Max speed, 575 mph (925 km/h) at sea level, 544 mph (875 km/h) at 16,405 ft (5 000 m). Initial climb, 6,693 ft/min (34 m/sec). Max range (external tanks), 746 mls (1 200 km). Empty weight, 4,365 lb (1 980 kg). Max loaded weight, 7,460 lb (3 384 kg). Span, 28 ft 7¾ in (8,73 m). Length, 26 ft 8 in (8,13 m). Height, 10 ft 10⅓ in (3,31 m). Wing area, 145.32 sq ft (13,50 m²).*

The third prototype (above) and series Yak-23 (below), an outstandingly agile fighter.

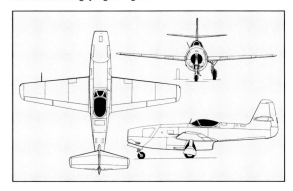

YAKOVLEV YAK-25 (I)   USSR

Developed in parallel with the Yak-23, the similarly-powered Yak-25 was conceptually more advanced and derived from the Yak-19. By comparison with the earlier fighter, the Yak-25 employed the higher-speed TsAGI S-9S-9 laminar section at the wing root translating to a KV-4-9 section at the tip with a constant thickness of 9 per cent throughout. Despite the greater diameter of the 3,580 lb st (1 625 kgp) Rolls-Royce Derwent – similar to that installed in the Yak-23 prototypes – than the RD-10F of the Yak-19, the diameter of the fuselage of the Yak-25 was unchanged. Sweptback horizontal tail surfaces were adopted, provision was made for two 44-Imp gal (200-l) drop tanks under the wing tips and armament comprised three 23-mm NR-23 cannon. The first of two prototypes was flown on 31 October 1947, but, although the subsequent flight test programme was allegedly successful, no production contract was issued for the Yak-25. One of the prototypes was util-

The second prototype Yak-25 (above) developed in parallel with the less advanced but preferred Yak-23.

ised during 1948 for (fixed) tandem-wheel undercarriage trials as part of the Yak-50 development programme. *Max speed, 590 mph (950 km/h) at sea level, 604 mph (972 km/h) at 9,840 ft (3 000 m). Time to 16,405 ft (5 000 m), 2.6 min. Max range, 898 mls (1 445 km). Empty weight, 5,037 lb (2 285 kg). Normal loaded weight, 7,132 lb (3 235 kg). Span, 29 ft 1⅔ in (8,88 m). Length, 28 ft 4½ in (8,65 m). Wing area, 150.7 sq ft (14,00 m²).*

(Below) The Yak-25 with a TsAGI laminar flow wing.

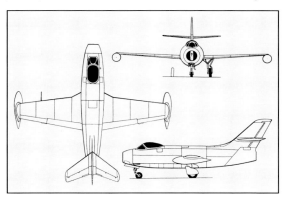

YAKOVLEV YAK-30   USSR

The Yakovlev OKB's response to the March 1946 requirement for a Rolls-Royce Derwent-powered Mach=0.9 "frontal" or general-purpose tactical fighter suitable for use from existing unpaved airfields was the Yak-30. Derived from the Yak-25 from which it differed primarily in having wings sweptback 35 deg at quarter chord, the Yak-30 retained the fuselage, tail surfaces and undercarriage of the earlier fighter fundamentally unchanged, together with the three-NR-23 cannon armament. Powered by a 3,505 lb st (1 590 kgp) RD-500 turbojet, the first of two Yak-30 prototypes was flown on 4 September 1948. The second prototype, the Yak-30D, which joined the flight test programme early in 1949, had a 15-in (38-cm) section inserted in the aft fuselage, revised mainwheel doors forming a large section of the fuselage skinning, Fowler-type flaps in place of split flaps, increased fuel and ammunition capacity, and changes to the oxygen system and radio equipment. The Yak-30D was also fitted with air brakes on the aft fuselage. Normal loaded weight (without external fuel) was increased by 242 lb (110 kg). Although the modifications introduced by the Yak-30D eradicated several shortcomings displayed by the first prototype, the first production deliveries of the superior MiG-15 were already taking place by the time that the improved version of the Yakovlev fighter entered flight test, and the results of NII V-VS trials were, therefore, little more than academic. The following data relate to the first prototype. *Max speed, 628 mph (1 010 km/h) at 18,045 ft (5 500 m), 597 mph (960 km/h) at 32,810 ft (10 000 m). Time to 16,405 ft (5 000 m), 2.2 min. Range (with external fuel), 1,069 mls (1 720 km). Empty*

The first prototype Yak-30 (below) which was intended to compete with the MiG-15 as a "frontal" fighter.

weight, 5,324 lb (2 415 kg). Normal loaded weight, 7,341 lb (3 330 kg). Span, 28 ft 4½ in (8,65 m). Length, 28 ft 1⅘ in (8,58 m). Wing area, 162.54 sq ft (15,10 m²).

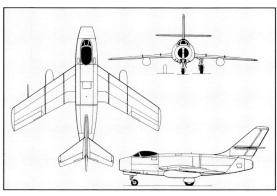

The Yak-30D (above and below) had a lengthened aft fuselage, Fowler flaps and many other changes.

YAKOVLEV YAK-50   USSR

With V-VS formulation of a requirement for a single-seat limited all-weather fighter, the Yakovlev OKB developed the Yak-50 in competition with the MiG-15Pbis. The wing, mounted in full mid position, was a two-spar structure of constant 12 per cent thickness sweptback 45 deg at quarter chord. The OKB used magnesium alloys in the structure for the first time to any great extent as a contribution to weight reduction, a further weight-saving measure being the adoption of a *velosipedno tipa*, or "bicycle type" undercarriage. This zero-track arrangement, earlier tested by the Yak-25, comprised a single nosewheel member and a twin-wheel main unit, the latter taking 85 per cent of the total aircraft weight; in addition, small outrigger stabilising wheels retracted into wingtip fairings. Power was provided by a single 5,952 lb st (2 700 kgp) Klimov VK-1 turbojet, armament consisted of two 23-mm NR-23 cannon and provision was made for the installation of a single-antenna, fixed-scan, manually-tracked *Korshun* (Kite) AI radar in a housing above the nose air intake splitter. The first of three Yak-50 prototypes was flown on 15 July 1949, several months before the first radar-equipped MiG-15Pbis (SP-1), and demonstrated an outstanding speed performance, exceeding Mach=1.01 in a shallow dive on several occasions during manufacturer's trials and Mach=1.048 during State Acceptance testing. It could take-off within 1,895 ft (578 m) and land within 3,165 ft (965 m), but in more than a 10-kt (18,5-km/h) crosswind, the Yak-50 tended to swerve from the runway, and it was barely controllable on a wet surface. In level flight at speeds between Mach=0.92 and 0.97, the Yak-50 suffered lateral oscillation preventing gun aiming. These shortcomings, coupled with the fact that the Mikoyan-Gurevich OKB was offering the potentially superior *Izumrud* radar-equipped MiG-17P, led to termination

The second prototype (below) of the Yak-50 limited all-weather fighter, which lost out to the MiG-17P.

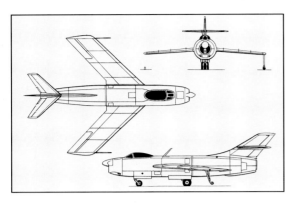

(Above) The Yak-50 limited all-weather fighter.

on 30 May 1950. *Max speed, 727 mph (1 170 km/h) at sea level, or Mach=0.954, 699 mph (1 125 km/h) at 16,405 ft (5 000 m), or Mach 0.99. Time to 32,810 ft (10 000 m), 3.5 min. Range, 684 mls (1 100 km). Empty weight, 6,889 lb (3 125 kg). Loaded weight, 9,160 lb (4 155 kg). Span, 26 ft 2⅛ in (7,98 m). Length, 36 ft 8⅞ in (11,20 m). Wing area, 172.23 sq ft (16,00 m².)*

YAKOVLEV Yak-25 (II)   USSR

In the summer of 1951, the NKAP issued a requirement for an all-weather interceptor fighter possessing sufficient internal fuel capacity to mount standing patrols of up to 2.5 hours duration and capable of accommodating a large, new radar. This supplanted an earlier requirement to which the Mikoyan-Gurevich I-320 and Lavochkin La-200 had been evolved. The new radar, known as the *Sokol* (Falcon), had a 31½-in (80-cm) diameter dish, three different scan modes and an installed mass weight of almost 1,100 lb (500 kg). To meet this new requirement, the Lavochkin and Yakovlev OKBs respectively developed the La-200B and Yak-120. The latter, an all-metal stressed-skin tandem two-seater, was powered by a pair of small-diameter Mikulin AM-5A turbojets each rated at 4,850 lb st (2 200 kgp) and hung beneath a wing swept back 45 deg at quarter chord and mounted in full-mid position. The undercarriage was of zero-track type, with wingtip-housed outrigger stabilisers, and armament comprised two 37-mm N-37L cannon with their barrels accommodated in external fairings beneath the fuselage. The first of three Yak-120 prototypes was flown on 19 June 1952, State acceptance testing paralleling construction of a pre-series of 20 aircraft for avionics development and, commencing late 1953, service evaluation. With ballast equivalent in weight to the *Sokol* radar – which did not attain service status until late 1955 – the Yak-120 had a loaded weight of 20,326 lb (9 220 kg), series production commencing late 1953 as the Yak-25 with RD-9 turbojets each rated at 5,798 lb st (2 630 kgp). Confusing repetition of the "Yak-25" designation resulted from its initial use as an *OKB* appellation and subsequent use by the NKAP as an *official* and sequential designation, the previous Yakovlev service fighter having been the Yak-23. The Yak-25 was assigned primarily to defence sectors in the Far North of the USSR, production being completed in 1958 after the delivery of 480 aircraft and service phase-out taking place in the mid 'sixties. A tactical reconnaissance derivative with the navigator accommodated in a glazed nose was built in 1953 as the Yak-125, but was not produced in series owing to prior adoption of the Il-28R. Other derivatives of the basic design were the Yak-25L ejection-seat test bed with individual cockpits, and the Yak-25RV long-range high-altitude strategic reconnaissance aircraft. *Max speed, 677 mph (1 090 km/h) at 16,405 ft (5 000 m), or Mach = 0.95.*

(Below) A pre-series Yak-120 that served in the avionics development role in the early 'fifties.

Cruise, 509 mph (820 km/h) at 29,530 ft (9 000 m). Ceiling, 45,605 ft (13 900 m). Max range, 1,696 mls (2 730 km). Loaded weight, 24,030 lb (10 900 kg). Span, 36 ft 1 in (11,00 m). Length, 51 ft 4⅞ in (15,67 m). Height, 14 ft 2 in (4,32 m). Wing area, 311.51 sq ft (28,94 m²).

The Yak-25 (above and below) was assigned primarily to defence sectors in the Far North of the USSR.

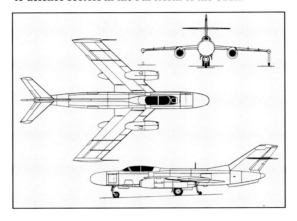

YAKOVLEV Yak-27   USSR

In 1955, the Yakovlev OKB flew the prototype of a light tactical bomber, the Yak-26, which, evolved from the Yak-25, embodied aerodynamic refinement and was powered by two Tumansky RD-9AK turbojets each rated at 7,165 lb st (3 250 kgp) with afterburning.

The Yak-27 (below) failed to attain production as a fighter because of its major instability problems.

During test, the Yak-26 achieved 767 mph (1 235 km/h) at 9,840 ft (3 000 m), or Mach = 1.05, but suffered from serious instability at high attack angles, development consequently being discontinued in favour of a tandem two-seat all-weather fighter, the Yak-27, as a potential successor to the Yak-25. Similarly powered to the Yak-26 and flown in 1956, the Yak-27 featured extended wing root leading edges increasing sweepback inboard of the engine nacelles to 62 deg, and a sharply pointed nose radome to reduce drag and lessen rain erosion. Armament remained paired 37-mm N-37L cannon, but provision was made to supplement this with two RS-2U beam-riding AAMs. Parallel development was undertaken of a tactical reconnaissance aircraft, the Yak-27R, which accommodated the navigator in a pointed, glazed nose. Recurrence of the instability problems that had afflicted the Yak-26 led to major redesign of the wing, broader-chord outer panels being introduced and the tips were extended beyond the outriggers which were enclosed by streamlined underwing blisters. Series production of the Yak-27 fighter was not undertaken – although 180 examples of the Yak-27R were built – but a single-seat mixed-power development, the Yak-27V, underwent extensive evaluation. Intended as a high-altitude interceptor and first flown in May 1957, the Yak-27V was powered by two RD-9Ye turbojets with an afterburning thrust of 8,377 lb (3 800 kg) each and a tail-mounted Dushkin S-155 bi-fuel rocket motor of 2,866 lb st (1 300 kgp). Basic armament remained two 37-mm cannon. The

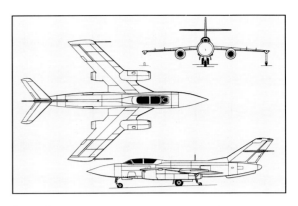

(Above) The Yak-27 two-seat all-weather fighter.

Yak-27V attained zoom altitudes of up to 82,000 ft (25 000 m) during a test programme that continued for two years, but the disbandment of the Dushkin OKB and a loss of interest in rocket propulsion resulted in termination of the programme. The following data relate to the basic Yak-27. *Max speed, 715 mph (1 150 km/h) at 36,090 ft (11 000 m), or Mach = 1.08. Initial climb, 18,700 ft/min (95 m/sec). Ceiling, 50,030 ft (15 250 m). Range, 1,864 mls (3 000 km). Normal loaded weight (approx), 25,000 lb (11 340 kg). Span, 39 ft 0½ in (11,90 m). Length, 54 ft 11⅞ in (16,76 m). Height, 13 ft 3½ in (4,05 m).*

YAKOVLEV Yak-28P   USSR

Possessing no more than a configurational similarity to preceding twin-engined Yakovlev combat aircraft, the Yak-129 multi-rôle aircraft was first flown on 5 March 1958 in tactical attack bomber form. Powered by two Tumansky R-11AF-300 turbojets each rated at 12,676 lb st (5 750 kgp) with afterburning and 8,554 lb st (3 880 kgp) maximum military power, the Yak-129 had a shoulder-mounted wing swept back 63 deg inboard of the engine nacelles and 44 deg outboard. Although of zero-track arrangement as on the Yak-25 and -27, the undercarriage of the Yak-129 consisted of long-base twin-wheel units sharing aircraft weight almost equally. Assigned the service designation Yak-28, the first series version of the aircraft was the Yak-28B with an RBR-3 radar bombing system. This was followed by the Yak-28I and -28L tactical attack aircraft, differing in avionic equipment, which were joined under test during 1960 by the Yak-28P dedicated all-weather interceptor fighter. This featured tandem cockpits for the two crew members and was intended for low- and medium-altitude operation with an *Orel-D* radar and one beam-riding and one radar-homing R-30 (K-8M) AAM. The Yak-28P entered IA-PVO service during the winter of 1961-62. Progressive upgrading resulted in R-11AF-2-300 engines uprated to 8,708 lb st (3 950 kgp) and 13,492 lb st (6 120 kgp) with afterburning, and enclosed by forward-lengthened nacelles, a longer, sharply-pointed radome housing an upgraded radar and affording lower supersonic drag and reduced erosion, and an additional stores station beneath each wing permitting two short-range dogfight IR missiles to be carried. With all these changes incorporated the designation was changed to Yak-28PM. With further upgrading, the fighter was evaluated as the Yak-28PD, but this suffered high-speed aileron reversal during trials, and by the time that this problem had been overcome production of the Yak-28P was phasing out, terminating in 1967 with limited production of the Yak-28PP electronic warfare version. Production of the fighter totalled 437 aircraft. The following data relate to

The initial series Yak-28P (below) with ogival radome, short engine nacelles and twin wing AAM pylons.

The Yak-28PM (above and below) with forward-lengthened nacelles and longer *Orel-DM* radome.

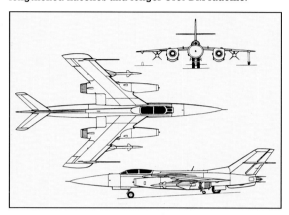

(Above) The Yak-38M, the definitive development of the Yakovlev shipboard fighter, seen with vertical-lift turbojets operating. Production, totalling 231, had been completed by 1987.

(1 000 kg) more engine thrust, a steerable nosewheel and provision for paired 132-Imp gal (600-l) underwing auxiliary tanks, entered production in succession to the Yak-38. The Yak-38M had a 15,300 lb st (6 940 kgp) R-27V-300 thrust-vectoring turbojet and two vertical-lift RD-38 turbojets each rated at 7,165 lb st (3 250 kgp).

(Below) The Yak-38M shipboard V/STOL fighter which embodied uprated engines and other upgrading.

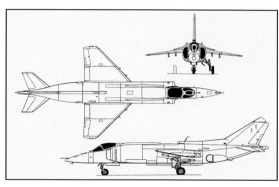

Two wing stations immediately inboard of vertically-folding panels provided for two gun pods each containing a twin-barrel 23-mm GSh-23 cannon, rocket packs or bombs weighing up to 1,100 lb (500 kg) each, two R-60 IR-homing AAMs or short-range ASMs. The tuitional version, the Yak-38UM, had vertically-staggered tandem seats, a plug being inserted in the aft fuselage to compensate for a lengthened nose. Each of the four Soviet Navy *Kiev*-class carrier cruisers received a 14-aircraft squadron of Yak-38s or -38Ms (each including two two-seaters), and production was completed by 1987 with a total of 231 Yak-38s (all versions) built. Data are estimated for the Yak-38M. *Max speed, 608 mph (978 km/h) at sea level, or Mach = 0.8, 628 mph (1 010 km/h) at 36,090 ft (11 000 m), or Mach = 0.94. Max initial climb, 14,760 ft/min (75 m/sec). Max loaded weight, 25,795 lb (11 700 kg). Span, 24 ft 0 in (7,32 m). Length, 50 ft 10 in (15,50 m). Height, 14 ft 4 in (4,37 m). Wing area, 199 sq ft (18,50 m²).*

the Yak-28PM. *Max speed (clean), 1,174 mph (1 890 km/h) at 39,370-42,650 ft (12 000-13 000 m), or Mach 1.78, (with four AAMs), 976 mph (1 570 km/h), or Mach 1.48. Range (two AAMs and two 198-Imp gal/900-l slipper tanks), 1,634 mls (2 630 km). Service ceiling, 52,495 ft (16 000 m). Normal loaded weight, 34,612 lb (15 700 kg). Span, 38 ft 2¼ in (11,64 m). Length, 67 ft 9 in (20,65 m).*

YAKOVLEV Yak-36 & Yak-38 USSR

The first combat aircraft of Soviet design conceived specifically for shipboard operation to achieve series production, the Yak-38 single-seat carrier-borne air defence and strike fighter was evolved from the Yak-36M. Flown in prototype form in 1971, the Yak-36M was developed under the design leadership of S Mordovin for the primary tasks of fleet air defence against shadowing maritime surveillance aircraft, reconnaissance and anti-ship strike. Power plant combined a Yu Gusev-developed Tumansky R-27V thrust-vectoring turbojet with two Rybinsk (Koliesov) RD-36-35 vertical-lift turbojets designed by a team led by A Dynkin. Hydraulic drives synchronised by a transverse shaft rotated the thrust-vectoring nozzles aft of the wing, their output in vertical take-off and landing operations being balanced during hover and transition by the paired lift engines mounted in tandem immediately aft of the cockpit and inclined forward 13 deg from the vertical. Shipboard trials with the Yak-36M began aboard the *Moskva* half-deck anti-submarine cruiser in 1972, and, in the following year, the decision was taken to build a pre-series of Yak-36M fighters for service evaluation, the first two of these landing aboard the carrier-cruiser *Kiev* in 1975. An evaluation squadron comprising 12 single-seat Yak-36Ms and two two-seat Yak-36Us embarked aboard the *Kiev* in the summer of 1976, the aircraft being confined to vertical take-off with conversion following at 15-20 ft (5,0-6,0 m) above the deck. During 1976, production was initiated of a much improved version of the basic design as the Yak-38. Externally similar to the Yak-36M, apart from substantial strakes either side of the intake for the lift engines, the Yak-38 possessed a full weapons system and an automatic control system permitting a short roll leading into vertical take-off as distinct from an orthodox short take-off benefiting from wing-induced lift. The Yak-38 entered service with the Soviet Navy in 1978, and, during 1980, was evaluated under operational conditions in Afghanistan. Progressive development resulted in the Yak-38M, which, with 2,205 lb

YAKOVLEV Yak-141 USSR

Designed to meet the requirements of a 1975 specification for an advanced successor to the Yak-38 – which, at the time, was just entering production – the Yak-141 was to become the world's second V/STOL combat aircraft possessing supersonic capability, the first being the Dassault Mirage IIIV. Employing a fundamentally similar engine arrangement to that of the Yak-38, the Yak-141 was optimised for air defence missions, but embodied secondary attack capability. The first of two

flying prototypes was flown in March 1989 powered by a Khachaturov/Koptchyenko R-79 vectored-thrust augmented turbofan with a level flight afterburning thrust of 34,170 lb (15 500 kg), reducing to 27,336 lb st (12 400 kgp) in the hover mode in which it was balanced by two 9,390 lb st (4 260 kgp) Rybinsk RD-41 lift engines mounted in tandem immediately aft of the cockpit. Unusual in having twin cantilever booms extending aft to carry the horizontal and vertical tail surfaces, the Yak-141 embodied a digital fly-by-wire system, and its structure making extensive use of aluminium-lithium alloy, with 26 per cent of the airframe by weight being of composite construction. With an OI-93 *Zhuk* coherent pulse-Doppler engagement radar, the Yak-141 was provided with a 30-mm GSh-301 cannon, external ordnance loads of up to 5,732 lb (2 600 kg) being possible for short take-off operation, and a mix of R-60 or R-73 IR-homing and R-27 radar-guided AAMs being intended for the air defence mission. The Yak-141 encountered problems with hot gas ingestion in the vertical take-off mode and the effects of afterburning impingement on concrete, and the development programme was reported to be shelved in 1992. The Yak-141 established a dozen new FAI-recognised class records for V/STOL aircraft early 1991, comprising altitudes and times to altitudes with loads. *Max speed, 1,118 mph (1 800 km/h) above 36,090 ft (11 000 m), or Mach=1.69. Range (VTO), 870 mls (1 400 km), (STO with external fuel), 1,305 mls (2 100 km). Max loaded weight (STO), 42,989 lb (19 500 kg). Span, 33 ft 1⅔ in (10,10 m). Length (including probe), 60 ft 0 in (18,30 m).*

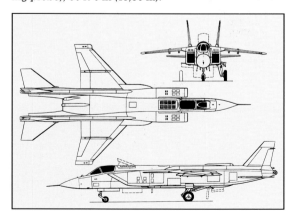

The Yak-141 (above and below) was, at its début, the world's only shipboard supersonic V/STOL fighter.

YATSENKO I-28   USSR

Establishing an OKB (Experimental Construction Bureau) in the autumn of 1938, Vladimir P Yatsenko was ordered to build two prototypes of a single-seat fighter which he had designed while supervising production of the Kocherigin DI-6. Assigned the designation I-28 by the NKAP (State Commissariat for Aviation Industry), the fighter was a low-wing cantilever monoplane of mixed construction, with a two-spar wooden wing, a steel-tube forward fuselage and a wooden semi-monocoque aft fuselage, the whole being covered by birch *shpon* – impregnated birch strips glued across the grain. The wing was of shallow inverted-gull form and armament consisted of two 20-mm ShVAK cannon and two 7,62-mm ShKAS machine guns, all synchronised and firing through the engine cowling lip. The I-28 was to have been powered by a 1,500 hp Shvetsov M-90 18-cylinder radial engine, but the non-availability of this power plant led to adoption of the 14-cylinder Tumansky M-87 affording only 930 hp. Completed on 30 April 1939, and flown shortly afterwards, the first prototype was submitted to the NII V-VS for State Acceptance testing in June, but broke up in a terminal velocity dive. The second prototype, completed in August 1939, differed in having a marginally more powerful M-87B engine and an armament of one ShVAK cannon and two 12,7-mm UBS guns. This prototype lacked the aft-sliding cockpit canopy of the first aircraft. Production of a pre-series of I-28 fighters powered by the 1,100 hp Tumansky M-88B engine had meanwhile commenced, but only five had been completed by February 1940, when the programme was terminated and Yatsenko's GAZ transferred to the Yakovlev OKB, the I-28 designation being re-used by the NKAP for a Yakovlev fighter. The following data relate to the second prototype. *Max speed, 262 mph (421 km/h) at sea level, 358 mph (576 km/h) at 19,685 ft (6 000 m). Time to 16,405 ft (5 000 m), 6.1 min. Range, 497 mls (800 km). Empty weight, 4,976 lb (2 257 kg). Loaded weight, 5,996 lb (2 720 kg). Span, 34 ft 1⅜ in (10,40 m). Length, 28 ft 0 in (8,54 m). Wing area, 177.61 sq ft (16,50 m²).*

The first prototype I-28 (above) and the series model (below), of which only five were completed.

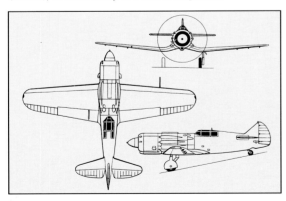

YOKOSUKA P1Y2-S KYOKKO   Japan

The excellent performance demonstrated by the P1Y1 Ginga (Milky Way) medium bomber resulted in Imperial Navy interest in its potential as a night fighter. The P1Y1 had been designed by the Dai-Ichi Kaigun Koku Gijitsucho (1st Naval Air Technical Arsenal) at Yokosuka, production responsibility having been assigned to Nakajima. The decision to adapt the aircraft for nocturnal interception tasks led to a production contract for such a variant being awarded to Kawanishi. Assigned the designation P1Y2-S and named Kyokko (Aurora), the night fighter was fitted with two

The first prototype P1Y2-S (above) at Kobe on 3 May 1944, and (below) the series version of the P1Y2.

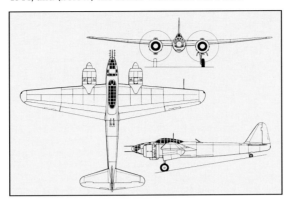

1,850 hp Mitsubishi Kasei 25 14-cylinder radial engines in place of the Nakajima NK9B Homare 11 18-cylinder engines of the bomber. The ventral bomb-bay was retained to facilitate use of the aircraft as a nocturnal intruder. The flexibly-mounted aft-firing cannon of the bomber was retained, this being augmented by a pair of fixed 20-mm cannon obliquely mounted in the fuselage to fire upwards and forwards. The first night fighter prototype was flown in June 1944, and the P1Y2-S entered series production as the Navy Night Fighter Kyokko with AI radar, the external antennae of which were attached to the nose of the aircraft. The performance of the Kyokko at altitude proved disappointing, and, found unsuited for the interception of B-29 Superfortresses, the majority of the 96 P1Y2-S fighters built by Kawanishi had their angled guns and AI radar removed and served as bombers. A night fighting adaptation of the Nakajima-built P1Y1 was also evolved as the P1Y1-S, or Navy Night Fighter Byakko (White Light). Powered by two 1,825 hp NK9C Homare 12 engines, the P1Y1-S had two pairs of obliquely-mounted 20-mm cannon, one pair forward and the other aft of the cockpit. A limited number of Byakko conversions was undertaken, but these proved no more efficacious than the P1Y2-S. The following data relate to the P1Y2-S. *Max speed, 325 mph (523 km/h) at 17,715 ft (5 400 m). Cruise, 230 mph (371 km/h) at 13,125 ft (4 000 m). Time to 16,405 ft (5 000 m), 9.4 min. Max range, 2,476 mls (3 985 km). Empty weight, 17,196 lb (7 800 kg). Max loaded weight, 29,762 lb (13 500 kg). Span, 65 ft 7⅓ in (20,00 m). Length (excluding AI antennae), 49 ft 2½ in (15,00 m). Height, 14 ft 1¼ in (4,30 m). Wing area, 592.03 sq ft (55,00 m²).*

ZEPPELIN-LINDAU V1   Germany

The V1 was a single-seat all-metal fighter designed by Dipl-Ing Claudius Dornier and built in the summer of 1916 by the Abteilung "Dornier" of the Zeppelin-Werke Lindau GmbH at Lindau-Reutin. Featuring a fuselage of pod type, a 160 hp Maybach Mb III engine mounted as a pusher with the propeller revolving within the wire-braced steel-tube framework carrying the tail assembly, the V1 employed newly-developed metal-working techniques, but proved seriously overweight. A series of ground hops was performed by Bruno E

The Dornier-designed V1 (below) which crashed immediately after taking-off on its first flight.

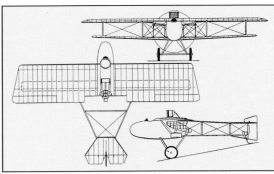

(Above) The Zeppelin-Lindau V1 single-seat fighter.

Schröter during September 1916, but this pilot refused to fly the prototype owing to its extreme tail-heaviness. On 13 November 1916, an initial flight test was performed by Oblt Haller von Hallerstein, but the V1 performed a loop immediately after take-off, crashing and killing the pilot. *Span, 34 ft 7⅜ in (10,55 m). Length, 23 ft 3⅝ in (7,10 m). Height, 8 ft 8¼ in (2,65 m). Wing area, 264.8 sq ft (24,60 m²).*

ZEPPELIN-LINDAU D I   Germany

The D I single-seat fighter biplane created by the Abteilung "Dornier" in 1918 at the Lindau-Reutin plant was of all-metal construction with stressed fuselage skinning and cantilever wings of torsion-box construction, and carried a jettisonable fuel tank beneath the fuselage – features well ahead of the contemporary state of the art. Powered by a 160 hp Mercedes D IIIa engine, the first prototype flew on 4 June 1918, but shed the upper wing during flight testing in the following month, apparently justifying the caution with which the innovatory Dornier fighter was viewed by the *Inspektion der Fliegertruppen (Idflieg)*. Nevertheless, two further prototypes powered by the 185 hp BMW IIIa engine were completed, with strengthened wing bracing and attachments. One of these participated in the third D-Type contest, but displayed a disappointing performance. The D I carried twin synchronised 7,92-mm machine guns. Although no production was ordered, three additional examples were completed (two with the Mercedes and one with the BMW engine), two of these being taken to the USA for evaluation after the Armistice. The data relate to the BMW IIIa-engined model. *Max speed, 124 mph (200 km/h) at sea level. Time to 3,280 ft (1 000 m), 2.6 min. Range, 168 mls (270 km). Empty weight, 1,598 lb (725 kg). Loaded weight, 1,947 lb (883 kg). Span, 25 ft 7 in (7,80 m). Length, 20 ft 11⁹⁄₁₀ in (6,40 m). Height, 8 ft 6⅓ in (2,60 m). Wing area, 200.86 sq ft (18,66 m²).*

Two of the four examples of the D I (above and below) were taken to the USA for evaluation.

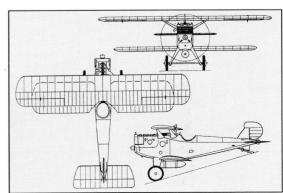